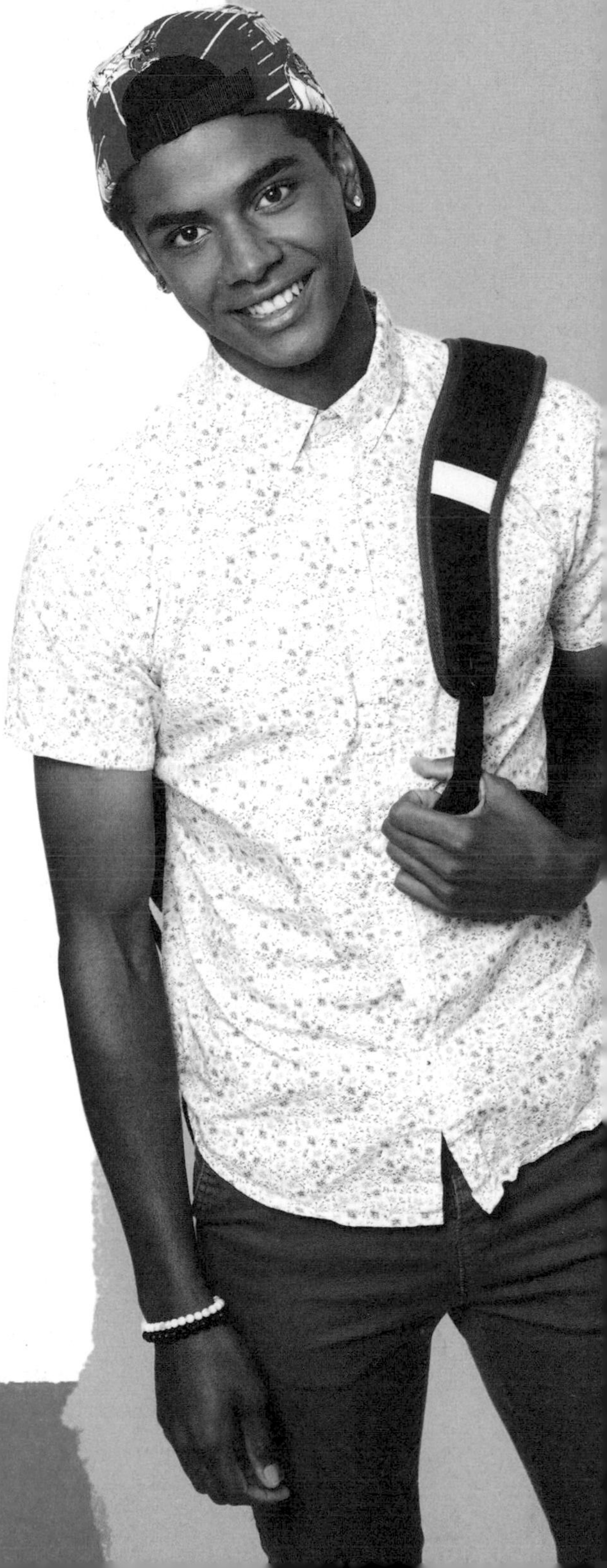

8th EDITION

STANDARD EDITION

BUSINESS LAW

AND THE LEGAL ENVIRONMENT

Jeffrey F. Beatty
Boston University

Susan S. Samuelson
Boston University

Patricia Sánchez Abril
University of Miami

Australia • Brazil • Mexico • Singapore • United Kingdom • United States

***Business Law and the Legal Environment—Standard Edition,* 8th Edition**
Jeffrey F. Beatty, Susan S. Samuelson, and Patricia Sánchez Abril

Senior Vice President/General Manager Social Sciences, Business, & Humanities: Erin Joyner

Executive Product Director Business & Economics: Mike Schenk

Product Director: Bryan Gambrel

Senior Product Manager: Vicky True-Baker

Senior Content Developer: Kristen Meere

Product Assistant: Christian Wood

Marketing Manager: Katie Jergens

Senior Content Project Manager: Kim Kusnerak

Production Service/Composition: SPi Global

Senior Art Director: Bethany Bourgeois

Cover/Internal Design: Mike Stratton/Stratton Design

Intellectual Property

Analyst: Jennifer Bowes

Project Manager: Reba Frederics

For product information and technology assistance, contact us at
Cengage Customer & Sales Support, 1-800-354-9706

For permission to use material from this text or product, submit all requests online at **www.cengage.com/permissions**
Further permissions questions can be emailed to
permissionrequest@cengage.com

Library of Congress Control Number: 2017948377

Student Edition:
ISBN: 978-1-337-40453-2

Loose-leaf Edition:
ISBN: 978-1-337-40466-2

Cengage
20 Channel Center Street
Boston, MA 02210
USA

Cengage is a leading provider of customized learning solutions with employees residing in nearly 40 different countries and sales in more than 125 countries around the world. Find your local representative at **www.cengage.com.**

Cengage products are represented in Canada by Nelson Education, Ltd.

To learn more about Cengage platforms and services, visit **www.cengage.com**

To register or access your online learning solution or purchase materials for your course, visit **www.cengagebrain.com**

Printed in the United States of America
Print Number: 03 Print Year: 2018

CONTENTS: OVERVIEW

CONTENTS

UNIT 9
Property 1057

NOTE FROM THE AUTHORS

Enhanced Digital Content—*MindTap*™

Our goal—and yours—is for the students to learn the material. With that singular goal in mind, Cengage has created an extremely useful tool for both instructors and students. *MindTap*™ is a fully online, highly personalized learning experience combining readings, multimedia, activities, and assessments into a singular Learning Path. It integrates seamlessly with Learning Management Systems. *MindTap* guides students through their course with ease and engagement. Instructors can personalize the Learning Path by customizing Cengage resources and adding their own content via apps that integrate with *MindTap*.

Our students who use *MindTap* are better prepared for, and earn better grades on, our exams. We recognize that the online experience is as important to the students—and you—as the book itself. Thus, unlike other texts, we (the authors) have reviewed every question in the *MindTap* product to ensure that it meets the high standards of our book.

We have heard that business law instructors want to help students **Prepare** for class, **Engage** with the course concepts to reinforce learning, **Apply** these concepts in real-world scenarios, use legal reasoning and critical thinking to **Analyze** business law content, and **Evaluate** real business scenarios and their legal implications.

Accordingly, our *MindTap* product provides a five-step Learning Path designed to meet these critical needs while also allowing instructors to measure skills and outcomes with ease.

- **Prepare**—Interactive worksheets are designed to prepare students for classroom discussion by ensuring that they have read and understood the reading.
- **Engage**—Real-world videos with related questions help engage students by displaying the relevance of business law in everyday life.
- **Apply**—Brief hypothetical case scenarios help students practice spotting issues and applying the law in the context of short factual scenarios.
- **Analyze**—Case-problem analysis promotes deeper critical thinking and legal reasoning by building on acquired knowledge. These exercises guide students step by step through a case problem and then add in a critical thinking section based on "What If the Facts Were Different?" In a **new third section**, a writing component requires students to demonstrate their ability to forecast the legal implications of real-world business scenarios.
- **Evaluate**—New **business case** activities develop students' *skills* to apply critical thinking and legal reasoning through relevant real-world business scenarios. These exercises give students the opportunity to advocate, evaluate, and make a decision through a variety of flexible assessment options including Discussion Questions, Multiple-Choice Questions, Short-Answer Essays, Group Work, and Ethical Dilemmas. Whether you have a large class, small class, teach online or in a traditional classroom setting, promote group work, or individual assignments, the *MindTap* Business Cases offer a variety of activity types to complement and enhance how YOU teach.

Each and every item in the Learning Path is assignable and gradable. Thus instructors have up-to-the-minute information on the class' general understanding of concepts as well as data on the performance of each individual student. Students also know where they stand—both individually and compared to the highest performers in the class. Thus, both faculty and students are less likely to face unpleasant surprises on exams.

MindTap also includes:

- **Case Collection** where instructors can find over 1,600 additional cases that were included in several previous editions of all of the Cengage Business Law or Legal Environment texts. These cases are searchable by name, year, state, and subject matter.
- **Adaptive Test Prep** for students, where they can generate their own practice quizzes with questions similar to those found on most exams.

To view a demo video and learn more about *MindTap*, please visit **www.cengage.com/mindtap**.

The Beatty/Samuelson/Abril Difference

Our goal in writing this book was to capture the passion and excitement, the sheer enjoyment, of the law. Business law is notoriously complex, and, as authors, we are obsessed with accuracy. Yet this intriguing subject also abounds with human conflict and hard-earned wisdom, forces that we wanted to use to make this book sparkle. Look, for example, at Chapter 33 on corporations. A robust discussion of the nitty gritty of corporate governance is enlivened by court cases featuring intense personal conflict.

Once we have the students' attention, our goal is to provide the information they will need as business people and as informed citizens. Of course, we present the *theory* of how laws work, but we also explain when *reality* is different. To take some examples, traditionally business law textbooks have simply taught students that shareholders elect the directors of public companies. Even Executive MBA students rarely understand the reality of corporate elections. But our book explains the complexity of corporate power. The practical contracts chapter focuses not on the theory of contract law but on the real-life issues involved in making an agreement: Do I need a lawyer? Should the contract be in writing? What happens if the contract has an unclear provision or an important typo? What does all that boilerplate mean anyway?

Nobel Laureate Paul Samuelson famously said, "Let those who will write the nation's laws, if I can write its textbooks." As authors, we never forget the privilege—and responsibility—of educating a generation of business law students. Our goal is to write a business law text like no other—a book that is authoritative, realistic, and yet a pleasure to read.

Strong Narrative. The law is full of great stories, and we use them. It is easier to teach students when they come to class curious and excited. Every chapter begins with a story that is based in fact, to illustrate important issues. We also include stories in the body of the chapters. Look at Chapter 3 on dispute resolution. No tedious list of next steps in litigation, this chapter teaches the subject by tracking a double-indemnity lawsuit. An executive is dead. Did he drown accidentally, obligating the insurance company to pay? Or did the businessman commit suicide, voiding the policy? Students follow the action from the discovery of the body, through each step of the lawsuit, to the final appeal.

Context. Most of our students were not yet born when Bill Clinton was elected president. They come to college with varying levels of preparation; many arrive from other countries. We have found that to teach business law most effectively we must provide its context. In the chapter on employment discrimination, we provide a historical perspective to help students understand how the laws developed. In the chapter on securities laws, we discuss the impact of the depression on the major statutes. Only with this background do students grasp the importance and impact of our laws.

Student Reaction. Students have responded enthusiastically to our approach. One professor asked a student to compare our book with the one that the class was then using. This was the student's reaction: "I really enjoy reading the [Beatty] textbook, and I have decided that I will give you this memo ASAP, but I am keeping the book until Wednesday so that I may continue reading. Thanks! :-)"

This text has been used in courses for undergraduates, MBAs, and Executive MBAs, with students ranging in age from 18 to 65. This book works, as some unsolicited comments indicate:

From verified purchasers on Amazon:

- "If you have this textbook for your business law class, then you are in luck! This is one of the best and most helpful textbooks that I have ever had the pleasure of using. (I mostly just use my textbooks as a pillow.) I actually did enjoy reading this and learning the material. The author breaks down the concepts so they are easy to understand. Even if you hate law, if you put forth the effort to learn this, you should have no trouble at all learning and understanding the concepts."
- "I enjoyed this book so much that I will not be selling it back to the bookstore (or anyone) because I know that I will use the book for years."

From undergraduates:

- "This is the best textbook I have had in college, on any subject."
- "The textbook is awesome. A lot of the time I read more than what is assigned—I just don't want to stop."
- "I had no idea business law could be so interesting."

From MBA students:

- "Actually enjoyed reading the textbook, which is a rarity for me."
- "The law textbook was excellent through and through."

From a Fortune 500 vice president, enrolled in an Executive MBA program:

- "I really liked the chapters. They were crisp, organized, and current. The information was easy to understand and enjoyable."

From business law professors:

- "The clarity of presentation is superlative. I have never seen the complexity of contract law made this readable."
- "Until I read your book I never really understood UCC 2-207."
- "With your book, we have great class discussions."

From a state supreme court justice:

- "This book is a valuable blend of rich scholarship and easy readability. Students and professors should rejoice with this publication."

Current. This 8th edition contains more than 40 new cases. Most were reported within the last two or three years, and many within the last 12 months. The law evolves continually, and our willingness to toss out old cases and add important new ones ensures that this book—and its readers—remain on the frontier of legal developments.

Authoritative. We insist, as you do, on a law book that is indisputably accurate. To highlight the most important rules, we use bold print, and then follow with vivid examples written in clear, forceful English. We cheerfully venture into contentious areas, relying on very recent decisions. Can a Delaware court order the sale of a successful business? Is discrimination based on attractiveness or sexual orientation legal? Is the list of names in a LinkedIn group a trade secret? What are the limits to free speech on social media? Where there is doubt about the current (or future) status of a doctrine, we say so. In areas of particularly heated debate, we footnote our work. We want you to have absolute trust in this book.

Humor. Throughout the text we use humor—judiciously—to lighten and enlighten. We revere the law for its ancient traditions, its dazzling intricacy, and its relentless, though imperfect, attempt to give order and decency to our world. But because we are confident of our respect for the law, we are not afraid to employ some levity, for the simple reason that humor helps retention. Research shows that the funnier or more original the example, the longer students will remember it. They are more likely to recall an intellectual property rule involving the copyrightability of yoga than a plain-vanilla example about a common widget.

Features

Each feature in this book is designed to meet an essential pedagogical goal. Here are some of those goals and the matching feature.

Exam Strategy

GOAL: To help students learn more effectively and to prepare for exams. In developing this feature, we asked ourselves: *What do students want?* The short answer is—a good grade in the course. How many times a semester does a student ask you, "What can I do to study for the exam?" We are happy to help them study and earn a good grade because that means that they will also be learning.

About six times per chapter, we stop the action and give students a two-minute quiz. In the body of the text, again in the end-of-chapter review, and also in the Instructor's Manual, we present a typical exam question. Here lies the innovation: We guide the student in analyzing the issue. We teach the reader—over and over—how to approach a question: to start with the overarching principle, examine the fine point raised in the question, apply the analysis that courts use, and deduce the right answer. This skill is second nature to lawyers and teachers, but not to students. Without practice, too many students panic, jumping at a convenient answer, and leaving aside the tools they have spent the course acquiring. Let's change that. Students love the Exam Strategy feature.

You Be the Judge Cases

GOAL: Get them thinking independently. When reading case opinions, students tend to accept the court's "answer." But we strive to challenge them beyond that. We want students to think through problems and reach their own answers guided by sound logic and legal knowledge. The You Be the Judge features are cases that provide the facts of the case and conflicting appellate arguments. But the court's decision appears only in the Instructor's Manual. Because students do not know the result, class discussions are more complex and lively.

Ethics

GOAL: Make ethics real. We include the latest research on ethical decision-making, such as ethics traps (why people make decisions they know to be wrong). We have also introduced the Giving Voice to Values curriculum, which focuses on the effective implementation of an ethics decision.

End-of-Chapter Exam Review and Questions

GOAL: Encourage students to practice! At the end of the chapters, we provide a list of review points and several additional Exam Strategy exercises. We also challenge the students with 15 or more problems—Multiple-Choice Questions, Case Questions, and Discussion Questions. The questions include the following:

- *You Be the Judge Writing Problem.* Students are given appellate arguments on both sides of the question and then must prepare a written opinion.
- *Ethics.* This question highlights the ethics issues of a dispute and calls upon the student to formulate a specific, reasoned response.
- *CPA Questions.* For topics covered by the CPA exam, administered by the American Institute of Certified Public Accountants, the Exam Review includes questions from previous CPA exams.

Answers to the odd-numbered Multiple-Choice Questions and Case Questions are available in Appendix C of the book.

Cases

GOAL: Let the judges speak. Each case begins with a summary of the facts and a statement of the issue. Next comes a tightly edited version of the decision, in the court's own language, so that students "hear" the law developing in the voices of our judges. In the principal cases in each chapter, we provide the state or federal citation, unless it is not available, in which case we use the LEXIS and Westlaw citations. We also give students a brief description of the court.

TEACHING MATERIALS

For more information about any of these ancillaries, contact your Cengage Consultant, or visit the Beatty Samuelson Abril Business Law website at **www.cengagebrain.com**.

MindTap. *MindTap* is a fully online, highly personalized learning experience combining readings, multimedia, activities, and assessments into a singular Learning Path. Instructors can personalize the Learning Path by customizing Cengage resources and adding their own content via apps that integrate into the *MindTap* framework seamlessly with Learning Management Systems. To view a demo video and learn more about *MindTap*, please visit **www.cengage.com/mindtap**.

Instructor's Manual. The Instructor's Manual, available on the Instructor's Support Site at **www.cengagebrain.com**, includes special features to enhance class discussion and student progress:

- Answers to You Be the Judge cases from the main part of the chapter and to the Exam Review questions found at the end of each chapter.
- Current Focus. This feature offers updates of text material.
- Additional cases and examples.

- Exam Strategy Problems. If your students would like more of these problems, there is an additional section of Exam Strategy problems in the Instructor's Manual.
- Dialogues. These are a series of questions-and-answers on pivotal cases and topics. The questions provide enough material to teach a full session. In a pinch, you could walk into class with nothing but the manual and use the Dialogues to conduct an effective class.
- Action learning ideas. Interviews, quick research projects, drafting exercises, classroom activities, and other suggested assignments get students out of their chairs and into the diverse settings of business law.

Cengage Testing Powered by Cognero. Cognero is a flexible online system that allows you to author, edit, and manage test bank content from multiple Cengage solutions; create multiple test versions in an instant; and deliver tests from your LMS, your classroom, or wherever you want.

PowerPoint Lecture Review Slides. PowerPoint slides are available for use by instructors for enhancing their lectures and to aid students in note taking. Download these slides at **www.cengagebrain.com.**

Interaction with the Authors. This is our standard: Every professor who adopts this book must have a superior experience. We are available to help in any way we can. Adopters of this text often call or email us to ask questions, offer suggestions, share pedagogical concerns, or inquire about ancillaries. One of the pleasures of writing this book has been this link to so many colleagues around the country. We value those connections, are eager to respond, and would be happy to hear from you.

Jeffrey F. Beatty

Susan S. Samuelson
Phone: (617) 353-2033
Email: ssamuels@bu.edu

Patricia Sánchez Abril
Phone: (305) 284-6999
Email: pabril@miami.edu

ACKNOWLEDGMENTS

The list of people who have contributed helpful comments and suggestions for this book is long. We are grateful to all of the reviewers and instructors from around the country who have helped us refine this book through all of its editions.

ABOUT THE AUTHORS

Jeffrey F. Beatty (1948–2009) was an Associate Professor of Business Law at the Boston University Questrom School of Business. After receiving his B.A. from Sarah Lawrence and his J.D. from Boston University, he practiced with the Greater Boston Legal Services representing indigent clients. At Boston University, he won the Metcalf Cup and Prize, the university's highest teaching award. Professor Beatty also wrote plays and television scripts that were performed in Boston, London, and Amsterdam.

Susan S. Samuelson is a Professor of Business Law at the Boston University Questrom School of Business. After earning her A.B. at Harvard University and her J.D. at Harvard Law School, Professor Samuelson practiced with the firm of Choate, Hall and Stewart. She has written many articles on legal issues for scholarly and popular journals, including the *American Business Law Journal, Ohio State Law Journal, Boston University Law Review, Harvard Journal on Legislation, National Law Journal, Sloan Management Review, Inc. Magazine*, and *Boston Magazine*. At Boston University she won the Broderick Prize for excellence in teaching.

Patricia Sánchez Abril is a Professor of Business Law and Vice Dean for Graduate Business Programs and Executive Education at the University of Miami School of Business Administration. Professor Abril's research has appeared in the *American Business Law Journal, Harvard Journal of Law & Technology, Florida Law Review, Houston Law Review, Wake Forest Law Review*, and *Columbia Business Law Journal*, among other journals. In 2011, the American Business Law Journal honored her with its Distinguished Junior Faculty Award, in recognition of exceptional early career achievement. Her research has won the Outstanding Proceedings competition at the annual conference of the Academy of Legal Studies in Business and has twice earned the Hoeber Memorial Award for Excellence in Research. Professor Abril has won awards for her teaching in both the undergraduate and graduate programs at the University of Miami.

To w.f.s., *"the fountain from the which my current runs"*
s.s.s.

To a.f.a., *with gratitude and love*
p.s.a.

The Legal Environment

UNIT

1

CHAPTER 1

INTRODUCTION TO LAW

The Pagans were a motorcycle gang with a reputation for violence. Two of its rougher members, Rhino and Backdraft, entered a tavern called the Pub Zone, shoving their way past the bouncer. The pair wore gang insignia, in violation of the bar's rules. For a while, all was quiet, as the two sipped drinks at the bar. Then they followed an innocent patron toward the men's room, and things happened fast.

"Wait a moment," you may be thinking. "Are we reading a chapter on business law or one about biker crimes in a roadside tavern?" Both.

Law is powerful, essential, and fascinating. We hope this book will persuade you of all three ideas. Law can also be surprising. Later in the chapter, we will return to the Pub Zone (with armed guards) and follow Rhino and Backdraft to the back of the pub. Yes, the pair engaged in street crime, which is hardly a focus of this text. However, their criminal acts will enable us to explore one of the law's basic principles—negligence. Should a pub owner pay money damages to the victim of gang violence? The owner herself did nothing aggressive. Should she have prevented the harm? Does her failure to stop the assault make her liable?

Should a pub owner pay money damages to the victim of gang violence?

We place great demands on our courts, asking them to make our large, complex, and sometimes violent society into a safer, fairer, more orderly place. The *Pub Zone* case is a good example of how judges reason their way through the convoluted issues involved. What began as a gang incident ends up as a matter of commercial liability. We will traipse after Rhino and Backdraft because they have a lesson to teach anyone who enters the world of business.

1-1 EXPLORING THE LAW

1-1a The Role of Law in Society

The strong reach of the law touches nearly everything we do, especially at work. Consider a mid-level manager at Sublime Corp., which manufactures and distributes video games.

During the course of a day's work, she might negotiate a deal with a game developer (contract law). Before signing any deals, she might research whether similar games already exist, which might diminish her ability to market the proposed new game (intellectual property law). One of her subordinates might complain about being harassed by a coworker (employment law). Another worker may complain about being required to work long hours (administrative law). And she may consider investing her own money in her company's stock, but she may wonder whether she will get into trouble if she invests based on inside information (securities law).

It is not only as a corporate manager that you will confront the law. As a voter, investor, juror, entrepreneur, and community member, you will influence and be affected by the law. Whenever you take a stance about a legal issue, whether in the corporate office, in the voting booth, or as part of local community groups, you help to create the fabric of our nation. Your views are vital. This book will offer you knowledge and ideas from which to form and continually reassess your legal opinions and values.

Law is also essential. *Every* society of which we have any historical record has had some system of laws. For example, consider the Visigoths, a nomadic European people who overran much of present-day France and Spain during the fifth and sixth centuries A.D. Their code admirably required judges to be "quick of perception, clear in judgment, and lenient in the infliction of penalties." It detailed dozens of crimes.

Our legal system is largely based upon the English model, but many societies contributed ideas. The Iroquois Native Americans, for example, played a role in the creation of our own government. Five major nations made up the Iroquois group: the Mohawk, Cayuga, Oneida, Onondaga, and Seneca. Each nation governed its own domestic issues. But each nation also elected "sachems" to a League of the Iroquois. The league had authority over any matters that were common to all, such as relations with outsiders. Thus, by the fifteenth century, the Iroquois had solved the problem of *federalism:* how to have two levels of government, each with specified powers. Their system impressed Benjamin Franklin and others and influenced the drafting of our Constitution, with its powers divided between state and federal governments.[1]

In 1835, the young French aristocrat Alexis de Tocqueville traveled through the United States, observing the newly democratic people and the qualities that made them unique. One of the things that struck de Tocqueville most forcefully was the American tendency to file suit: "Scarcely any political question arises in the United States that is not resolved, sooner or later, into a judicial question."[2] De Tocqueville got it right: For better or worse, we do expect courts to resolve many problems.

Not only do Americans litigate—they watch each other do it. Every television season offers at least one new courtroom drama to a national audience breathless for more cross-examination. Almost all of the states permit live television coverage of real trials. The most heavily viewed event in the history of television was the O. J. Simpson murder trial, in which

[1]Jack Weatherford, *Indian Givers* (New York: Fawcett Columbine, 1988), pp. 133–150.

[2]Alexis de Tocqueville, *Democracy in America* (1835), Vol. 1, Ch. 16.

a famous football star was accused of killing his wife. In most nations, coverage of judicial proceedings is not allowed.[3]

The law is a big part of our lives, and it is wise to know something about it. Within a few weeks, you will probably find yourself following legal events in the news with keener interest and deeper understanding. In this chapter, we develop the background for our study. We look at where law comes from: its history and its present-day institutions. In the section on jurisprudence, we examine different theories about what "law" really means. And finally we see how courts—and students—analyze a case.

1-1b Origins of Our Law

It would be nice if we could look up "the law" in one book, memorize it, and then apply it. But the law is not that simple, and *cannot* be that simple, because it reflects the complexity of contemporary life. In truth, there is no such thing as "the law." Principles and rules of law actually come from *many different* sources. This is so, in part, because we inherited a complex structure of laws from England.

Additionally, ours is a nation born in revolution, and created, in large part, to protect the rights of its people from the government. The Founding Fathers created a national government but insisted that the individual states maintain control in many areas. As a result, each state has its own government with exclusive power over many important areas of our lives. To top it off, the Founders guaranteed many rights to the people alone, ordering national *and* state governments to keep clear. This has worked, but it has caused a multilayered system, with 50 state governments and one federal government all creating and enforcing law.

English Roots

England in the tenth century was a rustic agricultural community with a tiny population and very little law or order. Vikings invaded repeatedly, terrorizing the Anglo-Saxon peoples. Criminals were hard to catch in the heavily forested, sparsely settled nation. The king used a primitive legal system to maintain a tenuous control over his people.

England was divided into shires, and daily administration was carried out by a "shire reeve," later called a sheriff. The shire reeve collected taxes and did what he could to keep peace, apprehending criminals and acting as mediator between feuding families. Two or three times a year, a shire court met; lower courts met more frequently. Today, this method of resolving disputes lives on as mediation, which we will discuss in Chapter 3.

Because there were so few officers to keep the peace, Anglo-Saxon society created an interesting method of ensuring public order. Every freeman belonged to a group of 10 freemen known as a "tithing," headed by a "tithingman." If anyone injured a person outside his tithing or interfered with the king's property, all ten men of the tithing could be forced to pay. Today, we still use this idea of collective responsibility in business partnerships. All partners are personally responsible for the debts of the partnership. They could potentially lose their homes and all assets because of the irresponsible conduct of one partner. That liability has helped create new forms of business organization, including limited liability companies.

When cases did come before an Anglo-Saxon court, the parties would often be represented by a clergyman, by a nobleman, or by themselves. There were few professional lawyers. Each party produced "oath helpers," usually 12 men, who would swear that one version of events was correct. The Anglo-Saxon oath helpers were forerunners of our modern jury of 12 persons.

In 1066, the Normans conquered England. William the Conqueror made a claim never before made in England: that he owned all of the land. The king then granted sections of his lands to his

---

[3]Regardless of whether we allow cameras, it is an undeniable benefit of the electronic age that we can obtain information quickly. From time to time, we will mention websites of interest. Some of these are for nonprofit groups, while others are commercial sites. We do not endorse or advocate on behalf of any group or company; we simply wish to alert you to what is available.

favorite noblemen, as his tenants in chief, creating the system of feudalism. These tenants in chief then granted parts of their land to *tenants in demesne*, who actually occupied a particular estate. Each tenant in demesne owed fidelity to his lord (hence, "landlord"). So what? Just this: Land became the most valuable commodity in all of England, and our law still reflects that. One thousand years later, American law still regards land as special. The Statute of Frauds, which we study in the section on contracts, demands that contracts for the sale or lease of property be in writing. And landlord–tenant law, vital to students and many others, still reflects its ancient roots. Some of a landlord's rights are based on the 1,000-year-old tradition that land is uniquely valuable.

North Wind / North Wind Picture Archives

Medieval tenants in demesne harrowing, plowing, and seeding a field.

In 1250, Henry de Bracton (d. 1268) wrote a legal treatise that still influences us. *De Legibus et Consuetudinibus Angliae* (*On the Laws and Customs of England*), written in Latin, summarized many of the legal rulings in cases since the Norman Conquest. De Bracton was teaching judges to rule based on previous cases. He was helping to establish the idea of **precedent**. **The doctrine of precedent, which developed gradually over centuries, requires that judges decide current cases based on previous rulings.** This vital principle is the heart of American common law. Precedent ensures predictability. Suppose a 17-year-old student promises to lease an apartment from a landlord, but then changes her mind. The landlord sues to enforce the lease. The student claims that she cannot be held to the agreement because she is a minor. The judge will look for precedent, that is, older cases dealing with the same issue, and he will find many holding that a contract generally may not be enforced against a minor. That precedent is binding on this case, and the student wins. **The accumulation of precedent, based on case after case, makes up the common law.**

Precedent
The tendency to decide current cases based on previous rulings

Common law
Judge-made law

Today's society is dramatically different from that of medieval English society. But interestingly, legal disputes from hundreds of years ago are often quite recognizable today. Some things have changed but others never do.

Here is an actual case from more than six centuries ago, in the court's own language. The plaintiff claims that he asked the defendant to heal his eye with "herbs and other medicines." He says the defendant did it so badly that he blinded the plaintiff in that eye.

The Oculist's Case (1329)

LI MS. Hale 137 (1), fo. 150, Nottingham[4]

Attorney Launde [for defendant]: Sir, you plainly see how [the plaintiff claims] that he had submitted himself to [the defendant's] medicines and his care; and after that he can assign no trespass in his person, inasmuch as he submitted himself to his care: But this action, if he has any, sounds naturally in breach of covenant. We demand [that the case be dismissed].

Excerpts from Judge Denum's Decision: I saw a Newcastle man arraigned before my fellow justice and me for the death of a man. I asked the reason for the indictment, and it was said that he had slain a man under his care, who died within four days afterwards. And because I saw that he was a [doctor] and that he had not done the thing feloniously but [accidentally] I ordered him to be discharged. And suppose a blacksmith, who is a man of skill, injures your horse with a nail, whereby you lose your horse: You shall never have recovery against him. No more shall you here.

Afterwards the plaintiff did not wish to pursue his case any more.

[4] J. Baker and S. Milsom, *Sources of English Legal History* (London: Butterworth & Co., 1986).

This case from 1329 is an ancient medical malpractice action. Attorney Launde does not deny that his client blinded the plaintiff. He claims that the plaintiff has brought the wrong kind of lawsuit. Launde argues that the plaintiff should have brought a case of "covenant"; that is, a lawsuit about a contract.

Judge Denum decides the case on a different principle. He gives judgment to the defendant because the plaintiff voluntarily sought medical care. He implies that the defendant would lose only if he had attacked the plaintiff. As we will see when we study negligence law, this case might have a different outcome today. Note also the informality of the judge's ruling. He rather casually mentions that he came across a related case once before and that he would stand by that outcome. The idea of precedent is just beginning to take hold.

Law in the United States

The colonists brought with them a basic knowledge of English law, some of which they were content to adopt as their own. Other parts, such as religious restrictions, were abhorrent to them. Many had made the dangerous trip to America precisely to escape persecution, and they were not interested in recreating their difficulties in a new land. Finally, some laws were simply irrelevant or unworkable in a world that was socially and geographically so different. American law ever since has been a blend of the ancient principles of English common law and a zeal and determination for change.

During the nineteenth century, the United States changed from a weak, rural nation into one of vast size and potential power. Cities grew, factories appeared, and sweeping movements of social migration changed the population. Changing conditions raised new legal questions. Did workers have a right to form industrial unions? To what extent should a manufacturer be liable if its product injured someone? Could a state government invalidate an employment contract that required 16-hour workdays? Should one company be permitted to dominate an entire industry?

In the twentieth century, the rate of social and technological change increased, creating new legal puzzles. Were some products, such as automobiles, so inherently dangerous that the seller should be responsible for injuries even if no mistakes were made in manufacturing? Who should clean up toxic waste if the company that had caused the pollution no longer existed? If a consumer signed a contract with a billion-dollar corporation, should the agreement be enforced even if the consumer never understood it? New and startling questions arise with great regularity. Before we can begin to examine the answers, we need to understand the sources of contemporary law.

1-2 SOURCES OF CONTEMPORARY LAW

Throughout the text, we will examine countless legal ideas. But binding rules come from many different places. This section describes the significant categories of laws in the United States.

1-2a United States Constitution

America's greatest legal achievement was the writing of the United States Constitution in 1787. It is the supreme law of the land.[5] Any law that conflicts with it is void. This federal Constitution does three basic things. First, it establishes the national government

---

[5]The Constitution took effect in 1788, when 9 of 13 colonies ratified it. Two more colonies ratified it that year, and the last of the 13 did so in 1789, after the government was already in operation. The complete text of the Constitution appears in Appendix A.

of the United States, with its three branches. Second, it creates a system of checks and balances among the branches. And third, the Constitution guarantees many basic rights to the American people.

Branches of Government

The Founding Fathers sought a division of government power. They did not want all power centralized in a king or in anyone else. And so, the Constitution divides legal authority into three pieces: legislative, executive, and judicial power.

Legislative power gives the ability to create new laws. In Article I, the Constitution gives this power to the Congress, which is comprised of two chambers—a Senate and a House of Representatives. Voters in all 50 states elect representatives who go to Washington, D.C., to serve in the Congress and debate new legal ideas.

The House of Representatives has 435 voting members. A state's voting power is based on its population. States with large populations (Texas, California, Florida) send dozens of representatives to the House, while sparsely populated states (Wyoming, North Dakota, Delaware) send only one. The Senate has 100 voting members—two from each state.

Executive power is the authority to enforce laws. Article II of the Constitution establishes the president as commander in chief of the armed forces and the head of the executive branch of the federal government.

Judicial power gives the right to interpret laws and determine their validity. Article III places the Supreme Court at the head of the judicial branch of the federal government. Interpretive power is often underrated, but it is often every bit as important as the ability to create laws in the first place. For instance, in *Roe v. Wade*, the Supreme Court ruled that privacy provisions of the Constitution protect a woman's right to abortion, although neither the word "privacy" nor "abortion" appears in the text of the Constitution.[6]

At times, courts void laws altogether. For example, in 2016, the Supreme Court struck down a Texas law regulating abortion clinics and the doctors who worked in them. The Court found that those rules created an undue burden for Texas women by causing many clinics to close and making abortions unreasonably difficult to obtain.[7]

Checks and Balances

The authors of the Constitution were not content merely to divide government power three ways. They also wanted to give each part of the government some power over the other two branches. Many people complain about "gridlock" in Washington, but the government is slow and sluggish by design. The Founding Fathers wanted to create a system that, without broad agreement, would tend towards inaction.

The president can veto Congressional legislation. Congress can impeach the president. The Supreme Court can void laws passed by Congress. The president appoints judges to the federal courts, including the Supreme Court, but these nominees do not serve unless approved by the Senate. Congress (with help from the 50 states) can override the Supreme Court by amending the Constitution. The president and the Congress influence the Supreme Court by controlling who is placed on the court in the first place.

Many of these checks and balances will be examined in more detail later in this book, starting in Chapter 4.

---

[6]Roe v. Wade, 410 U.S. 113 (1973).

[7]Whole Woman's Health v. Hellerstedt, 136 S. Ct. 2292 (2016).

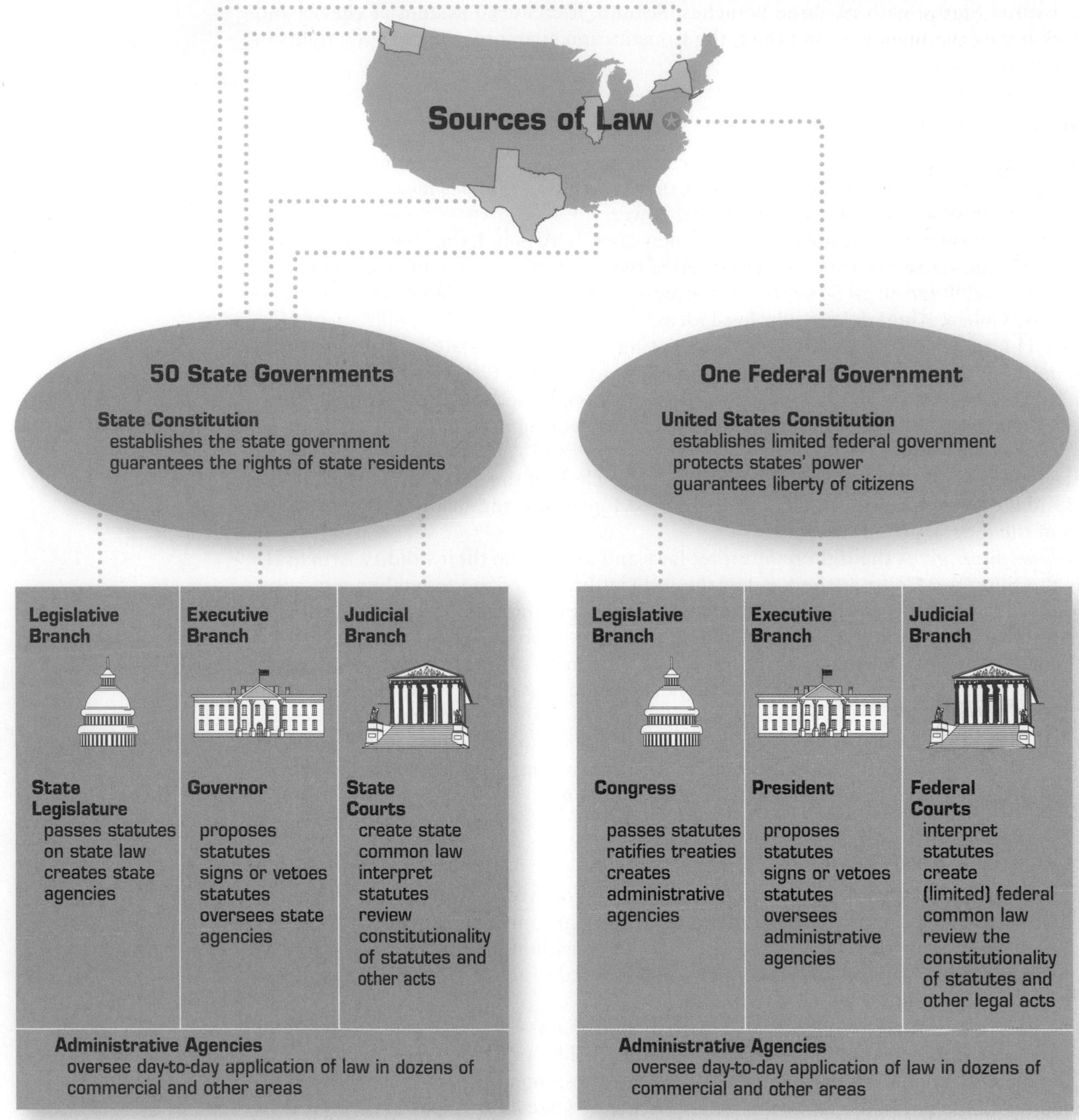

Federal Form of Government. Principles and rules of law come from many sources. The government in Washington creates and enforces law throughout the nation. But 50 state governments exercise great power in local affairs. And citizens enjoy constitutional protection from both state and federal government. The Founding Fathers wanted this balance of power and rights, but the overlapping authority creates legal complexity.

Fundamental Rights

The Constitution also grants many of our most basic liberties. For the most part, those liberties are found in the amendments to the Constitution. The First Amendment guarantees the rights of free speech, free press, and the free exercise of religion. The Fourth, Fifth, and

Sixth Amendments protect the rights of any person accused of a crime. Other amendments ensure that the government treats all people equally and that it pays for any property it takes from a citizen.

By creating a limited government of three branches, and guaranteeing basic liberties to all citizens, the Constitution became one of the most important documents ever written.

1-2b Statutes

The second important source of law is statutory law. The Constitution gave to the U.S. Congress the power to pass laws on various subjects. These laws are called **statutes**, and they can cover absolutely any topic, so long as they do not violate the Constitution.

Statute
A law created by a legislature

Almost all statutes are created by the same method. An idea for a new law—on taxes, health care, texting while driving, or any other topic, big or small—is first proposed in the Congress. This idea is called a *bill*. The House and Senate then independently vote on the bill. To pass Congress, the bill must win a simple majority vote in each of these chambers.

If Congress passes a bill, it goes to the White House for the president's approval. If the president signs it, a new statute is created. It is no longer a mere idea; it is the law of the land. If the president refuses to approve, or *vetoes*, a bill, it does not become a statute unless Congress overrides the veto. To do that, both the House and the Senate must approve the bill by a two-thirds majority. If this happens, it becomes a statute without the president's signature.

1-2c Common Law

Binding legal ideas often come from the courts. Judges generally follow *precedent*. When courts decide a case, they tend to apply the legal rules that other courts have used in similar cases.

The principle that precedent is binding on later cases is called *stare decisis*, which means "let the decision stand." *Stare decisis* makes the law predictable and this, in turn, enables businesses and private citizens to plan intelligently.

It is important to note that precedent is binding only on *lower* courts. For example, if the Supreme Court decided a case in one way in 1965, it is under no obligation to follow precedent if the same issue arises in 2020.

Sometimes, this is quite beneficial. In 1896, the Supreme Court decided (unbelievably) that segregation—separating people by race in schools, hotels, public transportation, and other public services—was legal under certain conditions.[8] In 1954, on the exact same issue, the court changed its mind.[9]

In other circumstances, it is more difficult to see the value in breaking with an established rule.

1-2d Court Orders

Judges have the authority to issue court orders that place binding obligations on specific people or businesses. A court can both compel a party to and prohibit it from doing something. An injunction is an example of a court order. Injunctions can require people to do things, like perform on a contract or remove a nuisance. A judge might also issue an injunction to stop a salesperson from using his former company's client list or prevent a counterfeiter from selling fake goods. Courts have the authority to imprison or fine those who violate their orders.

---

[8]Plessy v. Ferguson, 163 U.S. 537 (1896).

[9]Brown v. Board of Education of Topeka, 347 U.S. 483 (1954).

1-2e Administrative Law

In a society as large and diverse as ours, the executive and legislative branches of government cannot oversee all aspects of commerce. Congress passes statutes about air safety, but U.S. senators do not stand around air traffic towers, serving coffee to keep everyone awake. The executive branch establishes rules concerning how foreign nationals enter the United States, but presidents are reluctant to sit on the dock of the bay, watching the ships come in. Administrative agencies do this day-to-day work.

> U.S. senators do not stand around air traffic towers, serving coffee to keep everyone awake.

Most government agencies are created by Congress. Familiar examples are the Environmental Protection Agency (EPA), the Securities and Exchange Commission (SEC), and the Internal Revenue Service (IRS), whose feelings are hurt if it does not hear from you every April 15. Agencies have the power to create laws called *regulations.*

1-2f Treaties

A treaty is an agreement between two or more sovereign countries. Treaties range in topics from human rights and peace, to commerce and intellectual property. The Constitution authorizes the president to make treaties, but these pacts must also be approved by the U.S. Senate by a two-thirds vote. Once ratified, treaties are binding and have the force of federal law. In 1994, the Senate ratified the North American Free Trade Agreement (NAFTA), which aimed to reduce trade barriers between the United States, Mexico, and Canada. NAFTA was controversial then and remains so today—but it is the law of the land.

1-3 CLASSIFICATIONS

We have seen where law originated. Now we need to classify the various types of laws. First, we will distinguish between criminal and civil law. Then, we will take a look at the intersection between law and morality.

1-3a Criminal and Civil Law

Criminal law
Criminal law prohibits certain behavior for the benefit of society.

It is a crime to embezzle money from a bank, to steal a car, and to sell cocaine. **Criminal law concerns behavior so threatening that society outlaws it altogether.** Most criminal laws are statutes, passed by Congress or a state legislature. The government itself prosecutes the wrongdoer, regardless of what the bank president or car owner wants. A district attorney, paid by the government, brings the case to court. The victim is not in charge of the case, although she may appear as a witness. The government will seek to punish the defendant with a prison sentence, a fine, or both. If there is a fine, the money goes to the state, not to the injured party.

Civil law
Civil law regulates the rights and duties between parties.

Civil law is different, and most of this book is about civil law. **The civil law regulates the rights and duties between parties.** Tracy agrees in writing to lease you a 30,000-square-foot store in her shopping mall. She now has a *legal duty* to make the space available. But then another tenant offers her more money, and she refuses to let you move in. Tracy has violated her duty, but she has not committed a crime. The government will not prosecute the case. It is up to you to file a civil lawsuit. Your case will be based on the common law of contract. You will also seek equitable relief, namely, an injunction ordering Tracy not to lease to anyone else. You should win the suit, and you will get your injunction and some monetary damages. But Tracy will not go to jail.

Some conduct involves both civil and criminal law. Suppose Tracy is so upset over losing the court case that she becomes drunk and causes a serious car accident. She has committed the crime of driving while intoxicated, and the state will prosecute. Tracy may be fined or imprisoned. She has also committed negligence, and the injured party will file a lawsuit against her, seeking money. We will see civil and criminal law joined together again in the *Pub Zone* case, later in the chapter.

1-3b Law and Morality

Law is different from morality, yet the two are obviously linked. There are many instances when the law duplicates what all of us would regard as a moral position. It is negligent to text while driving, and few would dispute the moral value of seeking to limit harm to others. And the same holds with contract law: If the owner of land agrees in writing to sell property to a buyer at a stated price, both the buyer and the seller must go through with the deal, and the legal outcome matches our moral expectations.

On the other hand, we have had laws that we now clearly regard as immoral. At the turn of the century, a factory owner could typically fire a worker for any reason at all—including, for example, his religious or political views. It is immoral to fire a worker because she is Jewish—and today the law prohibits it.

Finally, there are legal issues where the morality is less clear. You are walking down a country lane and notice a three-year-old child playing with matches near a barn filled with hay. Are you obligated to intervene? No, says the law, though many think that is preposterous. (See Chapter 4, on common law, for more about this topic.) A company buys property and then discovers, buried under the ground, toxic waste that will cost $300,000 to clean up. The original owner has gone bankrupt. Should the new owner be forced to pay for the cleanup? If the new owner fails to pay for the job, who will? (See Chapter 40, on environmental law, for more discussion on this issue.)

Chapter 2 will further examine the bond between law and morality, but our ethics discussion does not end there. Throughout the text, you will find ethics questions and features, like the one that follows, which ask you to grapple with the moral dimensions of legal questions.

Guillermo LEGARIA/AFP/Getty Images

Would you break the law to help an employee?

Ethics

The season between Valentine's Day and Mother's Day is big business for the Colombian flower industry. The country supplies 75 percent of all cut flowers sold in the United States during these months.

Leo owns a flower production facility near Bogotá, Colombia, where he employs hundreds of workers. He pays his workers less than $1 per hour, a rate consistent with Colombian minimum wage laws. Colombian law does not allow employees to work more than 56 hours per week, with various daily breaks. Employers must give minimum wage employees one rest day per week or face penalties.

Leo's employees anxiously await the high season's production increase and the chance for overtime pay, which is 25 percent over the base rate. Many count on this extra money for survival. Iris is one of Leo's most loyal and efficient employees. This year, Iris has a serious problem: Her daughter needs a complicated surgery that will cost more than $300, which is more than Iris's monthly salary. If she does not pay for the surgery in advance, the girl will likely die. To raise this large amount of money, Iris asks that Leo allow her to work 140 hours a week during high season—that is, 20-hour days, 7 days a week. She is willing to work through her breaks and give up her rest day, working through her exhaustion.

What are Leo's legal and moral obligations? What would you do?

1-4 JURISPRUDENCE

Jurisprudence
The philosophy of law

We have had a glimpse of legal history and a summary of the present-day sources of American law. But what *is* law? That question is the basis of a field known as **jurisprudence**. What is the real nature of law? Can there be such a thing as an "illegal" law?

1-4a Legal Positivism

Sovereign
The recognized political power, whom citizens obey

This philosophy can be simply stated: Law is what the sovereign says it is. The **sovereign** is the recognized political power whom citizens obey, so in the United States, both state and federal governments are sovereign. A legal positivist holds that whatever the sovereign declares to be the law *is* the law, whether it is right or wrong.

The primary criticism of legal positivism is that it seems to leave no room for questions of morality. A law permitting a factory owner to fire a worker because she is Catholic is surely different from a law prohibiting arson. Do citizens in a democracy have a duty to consider such differences? Consider the following example.

Most states allow citizens to pass laws directly at the ballot box, a process called voter referendum. California voters often do this, and during the 1990s, they passed one of the state's most controversial laws. Proposition 187 was designed to curb illegal immigration into the state by eliminating social spending for undocumented aliens. Citizens debated the measure fiercely but passed it by a large margin. One section of the new law forbade public schools from educating illegal immigrants. The law obligated a principal to inquire into the immigration status of all children enrolled in the school and to report undocumented students to immigration authorities. Several San Diego school principals rejected the new rules, stating that they would neither inquire into immigration status nor report undocumented aliens. Their statements produced a heated response. Some San Diego residents castigated the school officials as lawbreakers, claiming that:

- A school officer who knowingly disobeyed a law was setting a terrible example for students, who would assume they were free to do the same;
- The principals were advocating permanent residence and a free education for anyone able to evade our immigration laws; and
- The officials were scorning grass-roots democracy by disregarding a law passed by popular referendum.

Others applauded the principals' position, asserting that:

- The referendum's rules would transform school officials from educators into border police, forcing them to cross-examine young children and their parents;

- The new law was foolish because it punished innocent children for violations committed by their parents; and
- Our nation has long respected civil disobedience based on humanitarian ideals, and these officials were providing moral leadership to the whole community.

Ultimately, no one had to decide whether to obey Proposition 187. A federal court ruled that only Congress had the power to regulate immigration and that California's attempt was unconstitutional and void. The debate over immigration reform—and ethics—did not end, however. It continues to be a thorny issue.

1-4b Natural Law

St. Thomas Aquinas (1225–74) answered the legal positivists even before they had spoken. In his *Summa Theologica*, he argued that an unjust law is no law at all and need not be obeyed. It is not enough that a sovereign makes a command. The law must have a moral basis.

Where do we find the moral basis that would justify a law? Aquinas says that "good is that which all things seek after." Therefore, the fundamental rule of all laws is that "good is to be done and promoted, and evil is to be avoided." This sounds appealing, but also vague. Exactly which laws promote good and which do not? Is it better to have a huge corporation dominate a market or many smaller companies competing? Did the huge company get that way by being better than its competitors? If Walmart moves into a rural area, establishes a mammoth store, and sells inexpensive products, is that "good"? Yes, if you are a consumer who cares only about prices. No, if you are the owner of a Main Street store driven into bankruptcy. Maybe, if you are a resident who values small-town life but wants lower prices.

1-4c Legal Realism

Legal realists take a very different tack. They claim it does not matter what is written as law. What counts is who enforces that law and by what process it is enforced. All of us are biased by issues such as income, education, family background, race, religion, and many other factors. These personal characteristics, they say, determine which contracts will be enforced and which ignored, why some criminals receive harsh sentences while others get off lightly, and so on.

Judge Jones hears a multimillion dollar lawsuit involving an airplane crash. Was the airline negligent? The law is the same everywhere, but legal realists say that Jones's background will determine the outcome. If she spent 20 years representing insurance companies, she will tend to favor the airline. If her law practice consisted of helping the "little guy," she will favor the plaintiff.

Other legal realists argue, more aggressively, that those in power use the machinery of the law to perpetuate their control. The outcome of a given case will be determined by the needs of those with money and political clout. A court puts "window dressing" on a decision, they say, so that society thinks there are principles behind the law. A problem with legal realism, however, is its denial that any lawmaker can overcome personal bias. Yet clearly some do act unselfishly.

Summary of Jurisprudence

Legal Positivism	Law is what the sovereign says.
Natural Law	An unjust law is no law at all.
Legal Realism	Who enforces the law counts more than what is in writing.

No one school of jurisprudence is likely to seem perfect. We urge you to keep the different theories in mind as you read cases in this book. Ask yourself which school of thought is the best fit for you.

1-5 WORKING WITH THE BOOK'S FEATURES

In this section, we introduce a few of the book's features and discuss how you can use them effectively. We will start with *cases*.

1-5a Analyzing a Case

A law case is the decision a court has made in a civil lawsuit or criminal prosecution. Cases are the heart of the law and an important part of this book. Reading them effectively takes practice. This chapter's opening scenario is fictional, but the following real case involves a similar situation. Who can be held liable for the assault? Let's see.

Kuehn v. Pub Zone

364 N. J. Super. 301
Superior Court of New Jersey, 2003

Facts: Maria Kerkoulas owned the Pub Zone bar. She knew that several motorcycle gangs frequented the tavern. From her own experience tending bar and conversations with city police, she knew that some of the gangs, including the Pagans, were dangerous and prone to attack customers for no reason. Kerkoulas posted a sign prohibiting any motorcycle gangs from entering the bar while wearing "colors"; that is, insignia of their gangs. She believed that gangs without their colors were less prone to violence, and experience proved her right.

Rhino, Backdraft, and several other Pagans, all wearing colors, pushed their way past the tavern's bouncer and approached the bar. Although Kerkoulas saw their colors, she allowed them to stay for one drink. They later moved towards the back of the pub, and Kerkoulas believed they were departing. In fact, they followed a customer named Karl Kuehn to the men's room, where, without any provocation, they savagely beat him. Kuehn was knocked unconscious and suffered brain hemorrhaging, disc herniation, and numerous fractures of facial bones. He was forced to undergo various surgeries, including eye reconstruction.

Although the government prosecuted Rhino and Backdraft for their vicious assault, our case does not concern that prosecution. Kuehn sued the Pub Zone, and that is the case we will read. The jury awarded him $300,000 in damages. However, the trial court judge overruled the jury's verdict. He granted a judgment for the Pub Zone, meaning that the tavern owed nothing. The judge ruled that the pub's owner could not have foreseen the attack on Kuehn, and had no duty to protect him from an outlaw motorcycle gang. Kuehn appealed, and the appeals court's decision follows:

Issue: ***Did the Pub Zone have a duty to protect Kuehn from the Pagans' attack?***

Excerpts from Judge Payne's Decision: Whether a duty exists depends upon an evaluation of a number of factors including the nature of the underlying risk of harm, that is, its foreseeability and severity, the opportunity and ability to exercise care to prevent the harm, the comparative interests of and the relationships between or among the parties, and, ultimately, based on considerations of public policy and fairness, the societal interest in the proposed solution.

Since the possessor [of a business] is not an insurer of the visitor's safety, he is ordinarily under no duty to exercise any care until he knows or has reason to know that the acts of the third person are occurring, or are about to occur. He may, however, know or have reason to know, from past experience, that there is a likelihood of conduct on the part of third persons in general which is likely to endanger the safety of the visitor, even though he has no reason to expect it on the part of any particular individual.

We find the totality of the circumstances presented in this case give rise to a duty on the part of the Pub Zone to have taken reasonable precautions against the danger posed by the Pagans as a group. In this case, there was no reason to suspect any particular Pagan of violent conduct. However, the gang was collectively known to Kerkoulas to engage in random violence. Thus, Kerkoulas had knowledge as the result of past experience and from other sources that there was a likelihood of conduct on the part of third persons in general that was likely to endanger the safety of a patron at some unspecified future time. A duty to take precautions against the endangering conduct thus arose.

We do not regard our recognition of a duty in this case to give rise to either strict or absolute liability on the part of the Pub Zone. To fulfill its duty in this context, the Pub Zone was merely required to employ "reasonable" safety precautions. It already had in place a prohibition against bikers who were wearing their colors, and that prohibition, together with the practice of calling the police when a breach occurred, had been effective in greatly diminishing the occurrence of biker incidents on the premises. The evidence establishes that the prohibition was not enforced on the night at issue, that three Pagans were permitted entry while wearing their colors, and the police were not called. Once entry was achieved, the Pub Zone remained under a duty to exercise reasonable precautions against an attack.

The jury's verdict must therefore be reinstated.

Analysis

Let's take it from the top. The case is called *Kuehn v. Pub Zone*. Karl Kuehn is the **plaintiff**, the person who is suing. The Pub Zone is being sued, and is called the **defendant**. In this example, the plaintiff's name happens to appear first, but that is not always true. When a defendant loses a trial and files an appeal, *some* courts reverse the names of the parties. *Del Lago Partners v. Smith*, a case discussed later in this chapter, is an example of this reversal. In that case, the injured plaintiff Smith won at the lower court and the defendant Del Lago appealed. Read the case closely to understand who is suing whom.

Plaintiff
The party who is suing

Defendant
The party being sued

The next line gives the legal citation, which indicates where to find the case in a law library. We explain in the footnote how to locate a book if you plan to do research.[10]

The *Facts* section provides a background to the lawsuit, written by the authors of this text. The court's own explanation of the facts is often many pages long, and may involve complex matters irrelevant to the subject covered in this book, so we relate only what is necessary. This section will usually include some mention of what happened at the trial court. Lawsuits always begin in a trial court. The losing party often appeals to a court of appeals, and it is usually an appeals court decision that we are reading. The trial judge ruled in favor of Pub Zone, but later, in the decision we are reading, Kuehn wins.

The *Issue* section is very important. It tells you what the court had to decide—and also why you are reading the case. In giving its decision, a court may digress. If you keep in mind the issue and relate the court's discussion to it, you will not get lost.

---

[10]If you want to do legal research, you need to know where to find particular legal decisions. A citation is the case's "address," which guides you to the official book in which it is published. Look, for example, at *Kuehn v. Pub Zone*, which has this citation: 364 N. J. Super. 301, Superior Court of New Jersey, 2003. The string of numbers identifies the volume and page of the official court reporter for the state of New Jersey (N. J. Super) in which you can find the full text of this decision. New Jersey, like most states, reports its law cases in a series of numbered volumes. This case appears in volume 364 of the New Jersey Superior Court reporters. If you go to a law library and find that book, you can then turn to page 301 and—*voila*!—you have the case. Because some of the cases in this text are so new, the official books that will eventually contain them have not yet been published, so their citations will be incomplete. In this event, we will also give you an alternate "address" where you can find the full case. Most cases are now available online. Your professor or librarian can show you how to find them electronically.

Excerpts from Judge Payne's Decision begins the court's discussion. This is called the *holding*, meaning a statement of who wins and who loses. The holding also includes the court's *rationale*, which is the reasoning behind the decision.

The holding that we provide is an edited version of the court's own language. Some judges write clear, forceful prose; others do not. Either way, their words give you an authentic feel for how judges think and rule, so we bring it to you in the original. Occasionally we use brackets [ ] to substitute our language for that of the court, either to condense or to clarify. Notice the brackets in the second paragraph of the *Pub Zone* decision. Judge Payne explains the point at much greater length, so we have condensed some of his writing into the phrase "of a business."

We omit a great deal. A court's opinion may be 3 pages long, or it may be 75. We do not use ellipses (…) to indicate these deletions because there is more taken out than kept in, and we want the text to be clean. When a court quotes an earlier decision verbatim but clearly adopts those words as its own, we generally delete the quotation marks, as well as the citation to the earlier case. If you are curious about the full holding, you can always look it up.

Let us look at a few of Judge Payne's points. The holding begins with a discussion of *duty*. The court explains that whether one person (or bar) owes a duty to protect another depends upon several factors, including whether the harm could be foreseen, how serious the injury could be, and whether there was an opportunity to prevent it.

Judge Payne then points out that the owner of a business is not an insurer of a visitor's safety. Typically, the owner has a duty to a visitor *only* if he has a reason to know that some harm is likely to occur. How would a merchant know that? Based on the character of the business, suggests the judge, or the owner's experience with particular people.

The judge then applies this general rule to the facts of this case. He concludes that the Pub Zone did, in fact, have a duty to protect Kuehn from the Pagans' attack. Based on Kerkoulas's experience, and warnings received from the police, she knew that the gang was dangerous and should have foreseen that admitting them in their "colors" greatly increased the chance of an attack.

Next, the court points out that it is not requiring the Pub Zone to *guarantee* everyone's safety. The bar was merely obligated to do a *reasonable* job. The prohibition on colors was a good idea, and calling the police had also proven effective. The problem, of course, was that in this case Kerkoulas ignored her own rule about gang insignia and failed to call the police.

Based on all the evidence, the jury's finding of liability was reasonable, and its verdict must be reinstated. In other words, Kuehn, who lost at the trial, wins on appeal. What the court has done is to *reverse* the lower court's decision, meaning to turn the loser into the winner. In other cases, we will see an appellate court *remand* the case, meaning it sends the case back down to the lower court for additional steps. Or the appellate court could *affirm* the lower court's decision, meaning it leaves the case unchanged.

1-5b Exam Strategy

This feature gives you practice analyzing cases the way lawyers do—and the way *you* must on tests. Law exams are different from most others because you must determine the issue from the facts provided. Too frequently, students faced with a law exam forget that the questions relate to the issues in the text and those discussed in class. Understandably, students new to law may focus on the wrong information in the problem or rely on material learned elsewhere. Exam Strategy features teach you to figure out exactly what issue is at stake, and then guide your analysis in a logical, consistent manner. Here is an example relating to the element of "duty," which the court discussed in the *Pub Zone* case.

EXAMStrategy

Question: The Big Red Traveling (BRT) Carnival is in town. Tony arrives at 8:00 p.m., parks in the lot—and is robbed at gunpoint by a man who beats him and escapes with his money. There are several police officers on the carnival grounds, but no officer is in the parking lot at the time of the robbery. Tony sues, claiming that brighter lighting and more police in the lot would have prevented the robbery. There has never before been any violent crime—robbery, beating, or otherwise—at any BRT Carnival. BRT claims it had no duty to protect Tony from this harm. Who is likely to win?

Strategy: Begin by isolating the legal issue. What are the parties disputing? They are debating whether BRT had a duty to protect Tony from an armed robbery committed by a stranger. Now ask yourself: How do courts decide whether a business has a duty to prevent this kind of harm? The *Pub Zone* case provides our answer. A business owner is not an ensurer of the visitor's safety. The owner generally has no duty to protect a customer from the criminal act of a third party unless the owner knows the harm is occurring or could foresee it is about to happen. (In *Pub Zone*, the business owner knew of the gang's violent history, and could have foreseen the assault.) Now apply that rule to the facts of this case.

Result: There has never been a violent attack of any kind at a BRT Carnival. BRT cannot foresee this robbery, and has no duty to protect against it. The carnival wins.

1-5c You Be the Judge

Many cases involve difficult decisions for juries and judges. Often both parties have legitimate, opposing arguments. Most chapters in this book will have a feature called "You Be the Judge," in which we present the facts of a case but not the court's holding.

We offer you two opposing arguments based on the kinds of claims the lawyers made in court. We leave it up to you to debate and decide which position is stronger or to add your own arguments to those given.

The following case is another negligence lawsuit, with issues that overlap those of the *Pub Zone* case. This time the court confronts a fight in a hotel bar that caused a young man permanent brain damage. The victim sued the owner of the hotel, claiming that its employees were partly responsible for the injuries—even though they did not participate in the brawl. Could the hotel be held legally responsible? You be the judge.

You Be the Judge

Del Lago Partners, Inc. v. Smith

307 S.W. 3D 762
Supreme Court of Texas, 2010

Facts: It was late night at the Del Lago hotel bar. Bradley Smith and 40 of his closest fraternity brothers had been partying there for hours. Around midnight, guests from a wedding party made a rowdy entrance. One of Smith's friends brashly hit on a young woman in the wedding party, infuriating her date. Verbal confrontations ensued. For the next 90 minutes, the fraternity members and the wedding party exchanged escalating curses and threats, while the bartender looked on and served drinks. Until … the inevitable occurred. Punches were thrown. Before Smith knew it, someone placed him in a headlock and threw him against a wall.

As dozens fought, the bar manager fumbled to call hotel security, but realized he did not even have the phone number. When security eventually arrived, the free-for-all had ended … and Smith had suffered a fractured skull, among other serious injuries.

Smith sued Del Lago for negligence. He argued that the hotel was liable because it knew that the brawl was imminent and could have easily prevented it by calling security or ejecting the angry drunks. The lower court agreed. The hotel appealed.

You Be the Judge: *Did the hotel have a duty to protect Smith from imminent assault?*

Argument for the Plaintiff-Appellant (Hotel): Your honors, my client did nothing wrong. The Del Lago staff did not create the danger. Smith was a grown man who drank voluntarily and joined the fight knowing that he was at risk for injury. The hotel did not owe a duty to someone who engages in such reckless behavior. And let's face it: Accidents happen, especially at a bar late at night. Moreover, a bar owner cannot possibly monitor the words exchanged between patrons that may lead to a fight.

The law has developed sensibly. People are left to decide for themselves whether to jump into a dangerous situation. Smith made his decision, and Del Lago should not be held accountable for his poor choices.

Argument for the Defendant-Appellee (Smith): Your honors, Del Lago had a moral and legal duty to protect its guests from this obvious and imminent assault. When a business has knowledge of something that poses an unreasonable risk of harm to its patrons, it has a duty to take reasonable action to reduce or eliminate that risk. The hotel knew that a fight was going to break out, and should have taken the proper precautions to protect guests from that foreseeable danger.

During the 90 minutes of escalating tensions, the bar staff continued to serve alcohol, ignored the blatant risks, and did not even call security. When the bar staff finally decided to call for help, they did not even have the number. It was too little, too late. The establishment had already breached its duty of care to protect its guests from foreseeable harm.

CHAPTER CONCLUSION

We depend upon the law to give us a stable nation and economy, a fair society, a safe place to live and work. These worthy goals have occupied ancient kings and twenty-first-century lawmakers alike. But while law is a vital tool for crafting the society we want, there are no easy answers about how to create it. In a democracy, we all participate in the crafting. Legal rules control us, yet *we* create *them*. A working knowledge of the law can help build a successful career—and a solid democracy.

EXAM REVIEW

1. **THE FEDERAL SYSTEM** Our federal system of government means that law comes from a national government in Washington, D.C., and from 50 state governments.

2. **LEGAL HISTORY** The history of law foreshadows many current legal issues, including mediation, partnership liability, the jury system, the role of witnesses, the special value placed on land, and the idea of precedent.

3. PRIMARY SOURCES OF LAW The primary sources of contemporary law are:

- United States Constitution and state constitutions;
- Statutes, which are drafted by legislatures;
- Common law, which is the body of cases decided by judges as they follow earlier cases, known as precedent;
- Court orders, which place obligations on specific people or companies;
- Administrative law, which are the rules and decisions made by federal and state administrative agencies; and
- Treaties and agreements between the United States and foreign nations.

EXAMStrategy

Question: The stock market crash of 1929 and the Great Depression that followed were caused, in part, because so many investors blindly put their money into stocks they knew nothing about. During the 1920s, it was often impossible for an investor to find out what a corporation was planning to do with its money, who was running the corporation, and many other vital things. Congress responded by passing the Securities Act of 1933, which required a corporation to divulge more information about itself before it could seek money for a new stock issue. What kind of law did Congress create?

Strategy: What is the question seeking? The question asks you which *type* of law Congress created when it passed the 1933 Securities Act. What are the primary kinds of law? Administrative law consists of rules passed by agencies. Congress is not a federal agency. Common law is the body of cases decided by judges. Congress is not a judge. Statutes are laws passed by legislatures. Congress is a legislature. (See the "Result"at the end of this Exam Review section.)

4. CRIMINAL AND CIVIL LAW Criminal law concerns behavior so threatening to society that it is outlawed altogether. Civil law deals with duties and disputes between parties, not with outlawed behavior.

EXAMStrategy

Question: Bill and Diane are hiking in the woods. Diane walks down a hill to fetch fresh water. Bill meets a stranger who introduces herself as Katrina. Bill sells a kilo of cocaine to Katrina who then flashes a badge and mentions how much she enjoys her job at the Drug Enforcement Agency. Diane, heading back to camp with the water, meets Freddy, a motorist whose car has overheated. Freddy is late for a meeting where he expects to make a $30 million profit; he's desperate for water for his car. He promises to pay Diane $500 tomorrow if she will give him the pail of water, which she does. The next day, Bill is in jail and Freddy refuses to pay for Diane's water. Explain the criminal law/civil law distinction and what it means to Bill and Diane. Who will do what to whom, with what results?

Strategy: You are asked to distinguish between criminal and civil law. What is the difference? The criminal law concerns behavior that threatens society and is therefore outlawed. The government prosecutes the defendant. Civil law deals with the rights and duties between parties. One party files a suit against the other. Apply those different standards to these facts. (See the "Result" at the end of this Exam Review section.)

5. **JURISPRUDENCE** Jurisprudence is concerned with the basic nature of law. Three theories of jurisprudence are:

- Legal positivism: The law is what the sovereign says it is.
- Natural law: An unjust law is no law at all.
- Legal realism: Who enforces the law is more important than what the law says.

RESULTS

3. Result: The Securities Act of 1933 is a statute.

4. Result: The government will prosecute Bill for dealing in drugs. If convicted, he will go to prison. The government will take no interest in Diane's dispute. However, if she chooses, she may sue Freddy for $500, the amount he promised her for the water. In that civil lawsuit, a court will decide whether Freddy must pay what he promised; however, even if Freddy loses, he will not go to jail.

MULTIPLE-CHOICE QUESTIONS

1. The United States Constitution is among the finest legal accomplishments in the history of the world. Which of the following influenced Ben Franklin, Thomas Jefferson, and the rest of the Founding Fathers?
   (a) English common-law principles
   (b) The Iroquois's system of federalism
   (c) Both A and B
   (d) None of the above
2. Which of the following parts of the modern legal system are "borrowed" from medieval England?
   (a) Jury trials
   (b) Special rules for selling land
   (c) Following precedent
   (d) All of these
3. Union organizers at a hospital wanted to distribute leaflets to potential union members, but hospital rules prohibited leafleting in areas of patient care, hallways, cafeterias, and any areas open to the public. The National Labor Relations Board (NLRB), a government agency, ruled that these restrictions violated the law and ordered the hospital to permit the activities in the cafeteria and coffee shop. What kind of law was NLRB creating?
   (a) A statute
   (b) Common law
   (c) A constitutional amendment
   (d) Administrative regulation
4. If Congress creates a new statute with the president's support, it must pass the idea by a ______________ majority vote in the House and the Senate. If the president

vetoes a proposed statute and the Congress wishes to pass it without his support, the idea must pass by a ____________ majority vote in the House and Senate.

(a) simple; simple
(b) simple; two-thirds
(c) simple; three-fourths
(d) two-thirds; three-fourths

5. Dr. Martin Luther King, Jr., wrote "An unjust law is no law at all." As such, "One has … a moral responsibility to disobey unjust laws." Dr. King's view is an example of:

(a) legal realism.
(b) jurisprudence.
(c) legal positivism.
(d) natural law.

CASE QUESTIONS

1. Lance a hacker, stole 15,000 credit card numbers and sold them on the black market, making millions. Police caught Lance, and two legal actions followed, one civil and one criminal. Who will be responsible for bringing the civil case? What will be the outcome if the jury believes that Lance was responsible for identity thefts? Who will be responsible for bringing the criminal case? What will be the outcome if the jury believes that Lance stole the numbers?

2. As *The Oculist's Case* indicates, the medical profession has faced a large number of lawsuits for centuries. In Texas, a law provides that, so long as a doctor was not reckless and did not intentionally harm a patient, recovery for "pain and suffering" is limited to $750,000. In many other states, no such limit exists. If a patient will suffer a lifetime of pain after a botched operation, for example, he might recover millions in compensation. Which rule seems more sensible to you—the "Texas" rule or the alternative?

3. ***YOU BE THE JUDGE*** **WRITING PROBLEM** Should trials be televised? Here are a few arguments on both sides of the issue. You be the judge. **Arguments against live television coverage:** We have tried this experiment and it has failed. Trials fall into two categories: those that create great public interest and those that do not. No one watches dull trials, so we do not need to broadcast them. The few trials that are interesting have all become circuses. Judges and lawyers have shown that they cannot resist the temptation to play to the camera. Trials are supposed to be about justice, not entertainment. If a citizen seriously wants to follow a case, she can do it by reading the daily newspaper. **Arguments for live television coverage:** It is true that some televised trials have been unseemly affairs, but that is the fault of the presiding judges, not the media. Indeed, one of the virtues of television coverage is that millions of people now understand that we have a lot of incompetent people running our courtrooms. The proper response is to train judges to run a tight trial by prohibiting grandstanding by lawyers. Access to accurate information is the foundation on which a democracy is built, and we must not eliminate a source of valuable data just because some judges are ill-trained or otherwise incompetent.

4. Leslie Bergh and his two brothers, Milton and Raymond, formed a partnership to help build a fancy saloon and dance hall in Evanston, Wyoming. Later, Leslie met with his friend and drinking buddy, John Mills, and tricked Mills into investing in the saloon. Leslie did not tell Mills that no one else was investing cash or that the entire enterprise was already bankrupt. Mills mortgaged his home, invested \$150,000 in the saloon—and lost every penny of it. Mills sued all three partners for fraud. Milton and Raymond defended on the grounds that they did not commit the fraud; only Leslie did. The defendants lost. Was that fair? By holding them liable, what general idea did the court rely on? What Anglo-Saxon legal custom did the ruling resemble?

5. The father of an American woman killed in the Paris terrorist attacks sued Twitter, Facebook, and YouTube, alleging the sites knowingly allowed ISIS terrorists to recruit members, raise money, and spread extremist propaganda. The sites defended themselves by saying that their policies prohibit terrorist recruitment and that, when alerted to it, they quickly remove offending videos. What type of lawsuit is this—criminal or civil? What responsibilities, if any, should social media sites have for the spread of terrorism?

DISCUSSION QUESTIONS

1. In the 1980s, the Supreme Court ruled that it is legal for protesters to burn the American flag. This activity counts as free speech under the Constitution. If the Court hears a new flag-burning case in this decade, should it consider changing its ruling or should it follow precedent? Is following past precedent something that seems sensible to you: always, usually, sometimes, rarely, or never?

2. When should a business be held legally responsible for customer safety? Consider the following statements, and consider the degree to which you agree or disagree.
   - A business should keep customers safe from its own employees.
   - A business should keep customers safe from other customers.
   - A business should keep customers safe from themselves. (Example: an intoxicated customer who can no longer walk straight.)
   - A business should keep people outside its own establishment safe if it is reasonable to do so.

3. In his most famous novel, *The Red and the Black*, the French author Stendhal (1783–1842) wrote: "There is no such thing as 'natural law': This expression is nothing but old nonsense. Prior to laws, what is natural is only the strength of the lion, or the need of the creature suffering from hunger or cold, in short, need." What do you think? Does legal positivism or legal realism seem more sensible to you?

4. Before becoming a Supreme Court justice, Sonia Sotomayor stated in a speech to students: "I would hope that a wise Latina woman with the richness of her experiences would more often than not reach a better conclusion than a white male who hasn't lived that life." During her Senate confirmation proceedings, this statement was heavily probed and criticized. One senator said that the focus of the hearings

was to determine whether Judge Sotomayor would "decide cases based only on the law as made by the people and their elected representatives, not on personal feelings or politics." (Sotomayor convinced many of her critics because the Senate confirmed her by a vote of 68–31.) Should judges ignore their life experiences and feelings when making judicial decisions?

5. The late Supreme Court Justice Antonin Scalia argued that because courts are not elected representative bodies, they have no business determining certain critical social issues. He wrote:

> Judges are selected precisely for their skill as lawyers; whether they reflect the policy views of a particular constituency is not (or should not be) relevant. Not surprisingly then, the Federal Judiciary is hardly a cross-section of America. Take, for example, this Court, which consists of only nine men and women, all of them successful lawyers who studied at Harvard or Yale Law School. Four of the nine are natives of New York City. Eight of them grew up in east- and west-coast States. Only one hails from the vast expanse in-between. Not a single Southwesterner or even, to tell the truth, a genuine Westerner (California does not count). Not a single evangelical Christian (a group that comprises about one quarter of Americans), or even a Protestant of any denomination. To allow [an important social issue] to be considered and resolved by a select, patrician, highly unrepresentative panel of nine is to violate a principle even more fundamental than no taxation without representation: no social transformation without representation.

Do you agree?

2 CHAPTER

ETHICS AND CORPORATE SOCIAL RESPONSIBILITY

Eating is one of life's most fundamental needs and greatest pleasures. Yet all around the world many people go to bed hungry. Food companies have played an important role in reducing hunger by producing vast quantities of food cheaply. So much food, so cheaply that, in America, one in three adults and one in five children are obese. Some critics argue that food companies bear responsibility for this overeating because they make their products *too* alluring. Many processed food products are harmful calorie bombs of fat, sugar, and salt which, in excess, are linked to heart disease, diabetes, and cancer. What obligation do food producers and restaurants have to their customers? After all, no one is forcing anyone to eat. Do any of the following examples cross the line into unethical behavior?

Many processed food products are harmful calorie bombs.

1. **Increasing addiction.** Food with high levels of fat, sugar, and salt not only taste better, but they are also more addictive.[1] Food producers hire neuroscientists who perform MRIs on consumers to gauge the precise level of these ingredients that will create the most powerful cravings, the so-called "bliss point." For example, in some Prego tomato sauces, sugar is the second most important ingredient after tomatoes, with two heaping teaspoons of sugar in a small serving?[2]

2. **Increasing quantity.** Food companies also work hard to create new categories of products that increase the number of times a day that people eat and the amount of calories in each session. For example, they have created a new category of food that is meant to be more than a snack but less than a meal, such as Hot Pockets.

---

[1]Researchers report that rats find Oreo cookies as addictive as cocaine. And they like the creamy middle best too. Valerie Strauss, "Rats find Oreos as addictive as cocaine," *The Washington Post*, October 18, 2013.

[2]To find nutritional information on this or other products, search the internet for the name of the product with the word "nutrition."

But some versions of this product have more than 700 calories, which would be a lot for lunch, never mind for just a snack. And candy companies carefully package their products to encourage consumers to nibble all day. When Hershey's learned that the wrappers on a Reese's Peanut Butter Cup deter nonstop eating (because, after all, it takes time to open each wrapper), the company created Reese's minis, which are unwrapped candies in a resealable bag. Food executives argue that they are just providing what consumers want.

3. **Increasing calories.** Uno Chicago Grill serves a macaroni and cheese dish that, by itself, provides more than two-thirds of the calories that a moderately active man should eat in one day and almost three times the amount of saturated fat. But this dish is at least *food.* Dunkin' Donuts offers a Frozen Caramel Coffee Coolatta with more than one-third the calories that an adult male should have in a day and 50 percent more saturated fat. Of course, these items are even worse choices for women and children. Should restaurants serve items such as these? If they do, what disclosure should they make?
4. **Targeting children.** Kraft Food developed Lunchables, packaged food designed for children to take to school. The first version contained bologna, cheese, crackers, and candy—all of which delivered unhealthy levels of fat, sugar, or salt. The company lured children by advertising during children's television shows.
5. **Targeting poorer countries.** Because of health concerns, consumption of sweetened soft drinks in the United States is declining. In response, soda companies have dramatically increased their marketing budgets in lower income countries, such as Brazil and China. Much of this marketing focuses on children.[3] These countries struggle to provide health care to their populations even without the additional burden that soft drinks create.
6. **Funding dubious science.** Both the soft drink and sugar industries generously fund scientific research. Is that good news? Studies they have financed are much more likely to find that there is no connection between sodas and weight gain.[4] Similarly, a nonprofit founded

---

[3]Allyn L. Taylor, and Michael F. Jacobson, "Carbonating the World," Center for Science in the Public Interest, 2016.

[4]Maira Bes-Rastrollo, Matthias B. Schulze, Miguel Ruiz-Canela, and Miguel A. Martinez-Gonzalez, "Financial Conflicts of Interest and Reporting Bias Regarding the Association between Sugar-Sweetened Beverages and Weight Gain: A Systematic Review of Systematic Reviews," *PLOS Medicine*, December 31, 2013, http://dx.doi.org/10.1371/journal.pmed.1001578.

and funded by Coca-Cola supports scientists who argue that exercise is more important than calorie-cutting in losing weight. They make this argument despite evidence that eating less is much more effective in weight loss than exercising more. On average, Americans exercise only 17 minutes a day. How likely is it that everyone who drinks a Coke will go out and walk the three miles it would take to burn off those calories?[5]

2-1 WHY STUDY ETHICS?

Ethics
How people should behave

Ethics decision
Any choice about how a person should behave that is based on a sense of right and wrong

This text, for the most part, covers legal ideas. The law dictates how a person *must* behave. This chapter examines **ethics**, or how people *should* behave. Any choice about how a person should behave that is based on a sense of right and wrong is an **ethics decision**. This chapter will explore ethics dilemmas that commonly arise in workplaces and present tools for making decisions when the law does not require or prohibit any particular choice.

If a person is intent on lying, cheating, and stealing his way through a career, then he is unlikely to be dissuaded by anything in this or any other course. But for the majority of people who want to do the right thing, it is useful to study new ways of recognizing and dealing with difficult problems.

Laws represent society's view of basic ethics rules. And most people agree that certain activities such as murder, assault, and fraud are wrong. **However, laws may permit behavior that some feel is wrong, and it may criminalize acts that some feel are right**. For example, assisted suicide is legal in a few states. Some people believe it is wrong under all circumstances, while others think it is the right thing to do for someone suffering horribly from a terminal illness. Likewise, many people feel it is ethical to hire illegal immigrants, even when doing so is a violation of federal law.

In this chapter, the usual legal cases are replaced by ethics cases with discussion questions. In some of these cases, reasonable people may disagree about the right thing to do. In others, the right answer is obvious, but actually doing it is difficult. These cases give you the opportunity to practice applying your values to the types of ethics issues you will face in your life. It is also important during class discussions for you to hear different points of view. In your career, you will work with and manage a variety of people, so it is useful to have insight into different perspectives on ethics.

Life Principles
The rules by which you live your life

We also hope that hearing these various points of view will help you develop your own **Life Principles**. These principles are the rules by which you live your life. As we will see, **research shows that people who think about the right rules for living are less likely to do wrong**. Developing your own Life Principles, based on your values, may be the most important outcome of reading this chapter and studying ethics.

How do you go about preparing a list of Life Principles? Think first of important categories. A list of Life Principles should include your rules on:

- Lying
- Stealing
- Cheating

[5]Anahad O'Connor, "Coca-Cola Funds Scientists Who Shift Blame for Obesity Away from Bad Diets," *The New York Times*, August 9, 2015.

- Applying the same or different standards at home and at work
- Your responsibility as a bystander when you see other people doing wrong or being harmed

Specific is better than general. Many people say, for example, that they will maintain a healthy work/life balance, but such a vow is not as effective as promising to set aside certain specific times each week for family activities. Many religions honor the Sabbath for this reason. Another common Life Principle is: "I will always put my family first." But what does that mean? You are willing to engage in unethical behavior to keep your job? Increase your income by cheating everyone you can? Or live your life so that you serve as a good example?

Some Life Principles focus not so much on right versus wrong but, rather, serve as a general guide for living a happier, more engaged life: I will keep promises, forgive those who harm me, say I'm sorry, appreciate my blessings every day, understand the other person's point of view, try to say "yes" when asked for a favor.

Remember that, no matter what you *say*, every ethics decision you make illustrates your *actual* Life Principles. One MBA student told the story of how his boss had ordered him to cheat on his expense report. The company did not require any receipts for meals that cost less than $25. He and his fellow salespeople habitually ate at fast-food restaurants where it was almost impossible to spend $25. Everyone else was reporting a lot of $24 meals while he was submitting bills for $12. His boss told him he was making everyone else look bad, and he needed to increase the amounts he claimed. What is your Life Principle in this case? Understand that if you fudge the expense report, your Life Principle is effectively: I am willing to cheat if I am unlikely to get caught or if my boss orders it. An alternative would be: I will not cheat even if my boss tells me to—I'll look for another job instead.

It is important to think through your Life Principles now, so that you will be prepared when facing ethics dilemmas in the future.

In this chapter, we will discuss: (1) the benefits of being ethical, (2) a process for making ethics decisions, (3) the traps that prevent us from doing what we know to be right, (4) implementation tools, and (5) corporate social responsibility.

2-1a Ethics in Business

Nobel Prize–winning economist Milton Friedman (1912–2006) famously argued that a corporate manager's primary responsibility is to the owners of the organization, that is, to shareholders. Unless the owners explicitly provide otherwise, managers should make the company as profitable as possible while also complying with the law.[6]

Others have argued that corporations should instead consider all company stakeholders, not just shareholders. Stakeholders include employees, customers, and the communities and countries in which a company operates. This choice can create an obligation to such broad categories as "society" or "the environment." After 20 first-graders and 6 educators were shot to death at the Sandy Hook Elementary School in Newtown, Connecticut, General Electric Co. (GE) stopped lending funds to shops that sell guns. GE headquarters were near Newtown, many of its employees lived in the area, and some had children in the Sandy Hook School. GE was putting its employees ahead of its investors.

If treating employees well or making charitable donations improves the company's image enough to increase profits, that is not an ethics dilemma. In a true dilemma, a company considers an action that would not increase shareholder returns in any certain or measurable way, but would benefit other stakeholders.

---

[6]He also mentions that managers should comply with "ethical custom," but never explains what that means. Milton Friedman, *The New York Times Magazine*, September 13, 1970.

As we will see in this chapter, managers face many choices in which the most profitable option is not the most ethical choice. For example, Michael Mudd, a former top executive at Kraft Foods, had this to say about his fellow executives:

> In so many other ways, these are good people. But, little by little, they strayed from the honorable business of feeding people appropriately to the deplorable mission of "increasing shareholder value" by enticing people to consume more and more high-margin, low-nutrition branded products.[7]

When profitability increases and, with it, a company's stock price, managers benefit because their compensation is often tied to corporate results, either explicitly or through ownership of stock and options. Thus, managers who say that they are just acting in the best interest of shareholders are also conveniently benefiting themselves. That connection creates an incentive to ignore other stakeholders.

Conversely, doing the right thing will sometimes lead to a loss of profits or even one's job. Hugh Aaron worked for a company that sold plastic materials.[8] One of the firm's major clients hired a new purchasing agent who refused to buy any product unless he was provided with gifts, vacations, and prostitutes. When Aaron refused to comply with these requests, the man bought from someone else. And that was that—the two companies never did business again. Aaron did not regret his choice. He believed that his and his employees' self-respect was as important as profits. But if your *only* concern is maximizing your company's profitability in the short run, you will find yourself in a position of making unethical choices.

2-1b Why Be Ethical?

Ethical conduct may not always be the most profitable, but it does generate a range of benefits for employees, companies, and society.

Society as a Whole Benefits from Ethical Behavior

John Akers, the former chairman of IBM, argued that without ethical behavior a society could not be economically competitive:

> No society anywhere will compete very long or successfully with people stabbing each other in the back; with people trying to steal from each other; with everything requiring notarized confirmation because you can't trust the other fellow; with every little squabble ending in litigation; and with government writing reams of regulatory legislation, tying business hand and foot to keep it honest. That is a recipe not only for headaches in running a company, but for a nation to become wasteful, inefficient, and noncompetitive. There is no escaping this fact: The greater the measure of mutual trust and confidence in the ethics of a society, the greater its economic strength.[9]

In short, ethical behavior builds trust, which is important in all of our relationships. It is the ingredient that allows us to live and work together well.

On this metric, business is not doing well. A recent Gallup poll found that only 21 percent of Americans have "a great deal" or "quite a lot" of confidence in big business. By contrast, more Americans have confidence in the police (52%) and organized labor (24%). The only institution *less* trusted than big business? Congress at 17 percent.[10]

---

[7]Michael Mudd, "How to Force Ethics on the Food Industry," *The New York Times*, March 16, 2013.

[8]Virtually all of the examples in this chapter are true events involving real people. Only their first names are used unless the individual has agreed to be identified or the events are a matter of public record.

[9]David Grier, "Confronting Ethical Dilemmas," unpublished manuscript of remarks at the Royal Bank of Canada, September 19, 1989.

[10]www.gallup.com/poll/1597/confidence-institutions.aspx.

Ethical Behavior Makes People Happier

What makes people happy? Being rich and famous? Or having good friends? In 1938, researchers in Boston set out to answer these questions by studying the lives of a large group of people over 75 years. **This study revealed that the secret to long-term happiness is having good relationships with a spouse, family, and friends.** These connected people suffered fewer mental and physical illnesses and less memory loss as they aged.[11] Other research has confirmed that people who focus on good relationships are happier than those who rely on external goals, such as money or fame, for satisfaction.[12]

It is difficult to maintain good relationships while behaving unethically. Every businessperson has many opportunities to be dishonest. But each of us must ask ourselves: What kind of person do we want to be? What kind of relationships do we want to have? In what kind of world do we want to live?

Managers want to feel good about themselves and the decisions they have made; they want to sleep well at night. Their decisions—to lay off employees, recall defective products, burn a cleaner fuel—affect people's lives. Bad decisions are painful to remember.

An executive, whom we will call Hank, told a story that still haunts him. His boss had refused to pay his tuition for an MBA program, so Hank went over his head and asked Sam, an executive several levels higher. Sam interceded immediately and personally approved the tuition reimbursement. He then took Hank under his wing, checking with him regularly to find out how the program and his work were going. Naturally, Hank felt grateful and indebted. Then one day, some other higher-ups told him that they were planning a coup against Sam. They were trying to get him fired in a complete blindside. They offered Hank a big promotion in return for his help. All went according to plan and Sam was fired. When Sam found out about Hank's betrayal, he called to tell the younger man exactly what he thought of his character. Hank said that he will carry that phone call and his guilt forever. And because he was so untrustworthy, he finds it hard to trust others.

Ethical Behavior Provides Financial Benefits

A company with a good reputation can pay employees less and charge consumers more.[13] Indeed, consumers even believe that food made by a trustworthy company has fewer calories than the same product made by a disreputable competitor.[14]

Conversely, unethical behavior causes financial harm: Companies that are caught engaging in socially irresponsible or illegal activities typically suffer a significant decline in stock price. Unethical behavior can also cause other, subtler damage. In one survey, a majority of those questioned said that they had witnessed unethical behavior in their workplace and that this behavior had reduced productivity, job stability, and profits. Questionable behavior in an organization creates a cynical, resentful, and unproductive workforce.

Although there is no *guarantee* that ethical behavior pays in the short or long run, there is evidence that the ethical company is more *likely* to win financially. Ethical companies tend to have more creative employees and higher returns than those that engage in wrongdoing.[15]

Once we decide that we want to behave ethically, how do we know what ethical behavior is?

---

11 www.adultdevelopmentstudy.org.

12 Christopher P. Niemiec, Richard M. Ryan, and Edward L. Deci. "The Path Taken: Consequences of Attaining Intrinsic and Extrinsic Aspirations in Post College Life." *Journal of Research in Personality*, June 2009, vol. 43, issue 3: 291–306.

13 Remi Trudel, and June Cotte, "Does It Pay to Be Good?" *Sloan Management Review*, January 8, 2009.

14 John Peloza, Christine Ye, and William J. Montford, "When Companies Do Good, Are Their Products Good for You? How Corporate Social Responsibility Creates a Health Halo," *Journal of Public Policy & Marketing*, Spring 2015, vol. 34, no. 1: 19–31. See also ethicalsystems.org for a review of research on this topic: www.ethicalsystems.org/content/ethics-pays.

15 For sources, see "Ethics: A Basic Framework," Harvard Business School case 9-307-059.

2-2 THEORIES OF ETHICS

When making ethics decisions, people sometimes focus on the *reason* for the decision—they want to do what is right. Thus, if they think it is wrong to lie, then they will tell the truth no matter what the consequence. In other cases, people think about the *outcome* of their actions. They will do whatever it takes to achieve the right result. This choice—between doing right and getting the right result—has been the subject of much philosophical debate.

2-2a Utilitarian Ethics

In 1863, Englishman John Stuart Mill (1806–73) wrote *Utilitarianism*. **To Mill, a correct decision is one that maximizes overall happiness and minimizes overall pain, thereby producing the greatest net benefit**. As he put it, his goal was to produce the greatest good for the greatest number of people. Risk management and cost–benefit analysis are examples of utilitarian business practices.

Suppose that an automobile manufacturer could add a device to its cars that would reduce air pollution. As a result, the incidence of strokes and cancer would decline dramatically, saving society hundreds of millions of dollars and years of suffering. But by charging a higher price to cover the cost of the device, the company would sell fewer cars and shareholders would earn lower returns. A utilitarian would argue that, despite the decline in profits, the company should install the device.

Consider this example that a student told us:

> During college, I used drugs—some cocaine, but mostly prescription painkillers. Things got pretty bad. At one point, I would wait outside emergency rooms hoping to buy drugs from people who were leaving. But that was three years ago. I went into rehab and have been clean ever since. I don't even drink. I've applied for a job, but the application asks if I have ever used drugs illegally. I am afraid that if I tell the truth, I will never get a job. What should I say on the application?

A utilitarian would ask: What harm will be caused if she tells the truth? She will be less likely to get that job, or maybe any job—a large and immediate harm. What if she lies? She might argue that no harm would result because she is now clean, and her past drug addiction will not have an adverse impact on her new employer.

Critics of utilitarianism argue that it is very difficult to *measure* utility accurately, at least in the way that one would measure distance or the passage of time. The car company does not really know how many lives will be saved or how much its profits will decline if the air-pollution device is installed. It is also difficult to *predict* benefit and harm accurately. The recovered drug addict may relapse, or her employer may find out about her lie. And, let's face it, **not all lives are of equal value to us**. If forced to make a choice, a parent might decide to sacrifice ten strangers in exchange for his own child's life.

Furthermore, a focus on outcome can justify some really terrible behavior. Among other things, it can be used to legitimize torture. After the 9/11 terrorist attacks, Americans debated the acceptability of torture. Is it ethical to torture a terrorist with the hope of obtaining the details of an upcoming attack?

Or suppose that wealthy old Ebenezer has several chronic illnesses that cause him great suffering and prevent him from doing any of the activities that once gave meaning to his life. Also, he is such a nasty piece of work that everyone hates him. If he were to die, all of his heirs would benefit tremendously from his money, including a disabled grandchild who could then afford care that would improve his life dramatically. Would it be ethical to kill Ebenezer?

2-2b Deontological Ethics

The word **deontological** comes from the Greek word for *obligation*. **Proponents of deontological ethics believe that utilitarians have it all wrong and that the *results* of a decision are not as important as the *reason* for making it.** To a deontological thinker, the ends do not justify the means. Rather, it is important to do the right thing, no matter the result.

Deontological
From the Greek word for *obligation*; the duty to do the right thing, regardless of the result

The best-known proponent of the deontological model is the eighteenth-century German philosopher Immanuel Kant (1724–1804). He believed in what he called the **categorical imperative**. He argued that you should not do something unless you would be willing to have everyone else do it too. Applying this idea, he concluded that one should always tell the truth because, if *everyone* lied, the world would be awful. Thus, Kant would say that the drug user should tell the truth on job applications, even if that meant she would never get hired. The truth should be told, no matter the outcome.

Kant's categorical imperative
An act is only ethical if it would be acceptable for everyone to do the same thing.

Kant also believed that human beings possess a unique dignity, and it is wrong to treat them as commodities, even if such a decision maximizes overall happiness. Thus, Kant would argue against killing Ebenezer, no matter how beneficial the result.

The problem with Kant's theory is that the ends *do* matter. Yes, it is wrong to kill, but a country might not survive unless it is willing to fight wars. Although many people disagree with some of Kant's specific ideas, most people acknowledge that a utilitarian approach is incomplete and that winning in the end does not automatically make a decision right.

2-2c Rawlsian Justice

How did you manage to get into college or graduate school? Presumably, some combination of talent, hard work, and support from family and friends was critical. Imagine that you had been born into different circumstances—say, in a country where the literacy rate is only 25 percent and almost all of the population lives in desperate poverty. Would you be reading this book now? Most likely not. People are born with wildly different talents into very different circumstances, all of which dramatically affect their outcomes. Even for people born poor in the United States, circumstances matter hugely. For example, poor children in San Francisco are almost three times more likely to prosper as adults than are poor children from Atlanta.[16]

Life prospects
The circumstances into which we are born

Veil of ignorance
The rules for society that we would propose if we did not know how lucky we would be in life's lottery

John Rawls was an American philosopher who referred to the circumstances into which we are born as **life prospects**. In his view, hard work certainly matters, but so does luck. Rawls argued that we should think about what rules for society we would propose if we faced a **veil of ignorance**. In other words, suppose that there is going to be a lottery tomorrow that would determine all our attributes. We could be a winner, ending up a hugely talented, healthy person in a loving family, or we could be poor and ill in a broken, abusive family in a violent neighborhood with deplorable schools and social services.

Andy Dean Photography/Shutterstock.com

Healthy, talented children born into a loving family are lucky to have such good life prospects.

What type of society would we establish now if we did not know our life prospects after tomorrow's

16David Leonhardt, "In Climbing Income Ladder, Location Matters," *The New York Times*, July 22, 2013.

lottery? First, we would design some form of democratic system that provided equal liberty to all and important rights such as freedom of speech and religion. Second, we would apply the **difference principle**. Under this principle, we would *not* plan a system in which everyone received an equal income because society is better off if people have an incentive to work hard. But we would reward the type of work that provides the most benefit to the community as a whole. We might decide, for example, to pay doctors more than baseball players. But maybe we wouldn't pay *all* doctors equally well—perhaps just the ones who research cancer cures or provide care for the ill, not cosmetic surgeons operating on the vain.

Difference principle
Rawls' suggestion that society should reward behavior that provides the most benefit to the community as a whole

Rawls argues that everyone should have the opportunity to earn great wealth so long as the tax system provides enough revenue to provide decent health care, education, and welfare for all. **In thinking about ethics decisions, it is worth remembering that many of us have been winners in life's lottery and that the unlucky also deserve opportunities.**

2-2d Front Page Test

When faced with a difficult decision, think about how you would feel if your actions went viral—on YouTube, Facebook, or on the front page of national newspapers. Would that help you decide what to do? Would such exposure have caused Hank to tell Sam about the planned coup?

The Front Page test is not foolproof—there are times you might have legitimate reasons to do something private. If you had helped a terminally ill person die, you might not want everyone to know that you had done so, especially if you lived in a state where assisted suicide is illegal.

2-2e Moral Universalism and Relativism

For many ethics dilemmas, reasonable people may well disagree about what is right. As we have seen, a Kantian approach may lead to a different decision than a utilitarian view. However, many people believe that some types of behavior are always right or always wrong, regardless of what others may think. This approach is called **moral universalism**. Alternatively, others believe that it is right to be tolerant of different views and customs. And, indeed, a decision may be acceptable even if it is not in keeping with one's own ethics standards. This approach is referred to as **moral relativism**. Pope Benedict XVI wrote that homosexuality is "a strong tendency ordered toward an intrinsic moral evil," while his successor, Pope Francis, took a different approach, saying, "If someone is gay and he searches for the Lord and has good will, who am *I* to judge?"[17] Pope Benedict's view reflects a moral universalism—he believes that homosexuality is always wrong—while Pope Francis is taking a more relativistic approach—under certain circumstances, he will not judge.

Moral universalism
A belief that some acts are always right or always wrong

Moral relativism
A belief that a decision may be right even if it is not in keeping with one's own ethics standards

There are at least two types of moral relativism: cultural and individual. To cultural relativists, what is right or wrong depends on the norms and practices in each society. Some societies permit men to have more than one wife, while others find that practice abhorrent. A cultural relativist would say that polygamy is an ethical choice in societies where such practice is long-standing and culturally significant. And, as outsiders to that society, who are we to judge? In short, culture defines what is right and wrong.

To individual relativists, people must develop their own ethics rules. And what is right for *me* might not be good for *you*. Thus, I might believe that being faithful to one partner is the cornerstone of an ethical life. But you might believe that, because monogamy goes against human nature, it is right to have relationships with many partners. The danger of individual relativism is obvious: It can justify just about anything.

---

[17]Rachel Donadio, "On Gay Priests, Pope Francis Asks, 'Who Am I to Judge?'" *The New York Times*, July 30, 2013.

Like so much in ethics, none of these approaches will always be right or wrong. It is, however, ethically lazy simply to default to moral relativism as an excuse for condoning any behavior.

2-2f Ethics Case: Up in Smoke

James is on the management team of a health insurance company called HIC. At a team meeting, the CEO announces that, from now on, HIC will not hire smokers, and all employees will be regularly tested for nicotine. This policy would reduce the company's expenses (an estimated $4,000 per smoker each year) while increasing its productivity (no smoking breaks, fewer sick days). In addition, the policy will encourage healthy choices by employees and the community as a whole—people will quit smoking to work at HIC. The CEO is convinced that society will benefit if smoking is "de-normalized." He also believes that this policy will enhance HIC's position as a progressive enterprise, setting a good example for other businesses. Already, many companies in the medical industry are instituting such policies.

Although James does not smoke, he is troubled by this new policy. HIC is located in a city with high rates of unemployment and poverty as well as a large minority population. He is familiar with the following data:[18]

Group	Percent of Adults Who Smoke	Group	Percent of Adults Who Smoke
Native Americans	42	Asian women	8
People living *below* poverty level	36	People living *above* poverty level	22.5
People with less than a high school education	32	College graduates	13
Unemployed	45	Full-time employed	28

James fears that the policy will prevent HIC from hiring the very people who need jobs the most. Also, he knows that nicotine is highly addictive and that many people who want to stop smoking struggle to do so.

Lifestyle choices affect a whole range of illnesses, including diabetes, cancer, heart disease, and sexually transmitted diseases. Is it fair to single out smokers for punishment? While only one-tenth of the company's workers smoke, two-thirds are overweight or obese, which also increases health costs. Even some *healthy* activities may increase costs—the CEO had been injured in a bike accident. Should the company refuse to hire overweight and cyclist groups as well?

To complicate James's decision, the CEO tends to resent employees who disagree with him. If James speaks out against the nonsmoking policy, his job prospects could be damaged.

Questions

1. What would Mill, Kant, and Rawls have said about the CEO's plans? About what James should do?
2. What would have been the result if James had applied the Front Page test?

[18]Harald Schmidt, Kristin Voigt, and Ezekiel J. Emanuel, "The Ethics of Not Hiring Smokers," *New England Journal of Medicine*, April 11, 2013, 368:1369–1371.

2-3 ETHICS TRAPS

Very few people wake up one morning and think, "Today I'll do something unethical." Then why do we make unethical decisions? Because we are very good at allowing our brains to trick us into believing wrong is right. It is important to understand the ethics traps that create great temptation to do what we know to be wrong or fail to do what we know to be right.

2-3a Money

Money is a powerful lure because most people believe that they would be happier if they had more. As we have seen, that is not necessarily true. Good health, companionship, and enjoyable leisure activities all contribute more to happiness than money does. And, regardless of income, 85 percent of Americans feel happy on a day-to-day basis anyway.

Money *can*, of course, provide some protection against the inevitable bumps in the road of life. Being hungry is no fun. If you lose your winter coat, you will be happier if you can replace it. It is easier to maintain friendships if you can afford to go out together occasionally. So money can contribute to happiness, but research indicates that this impact disappears when yearly household income exceeds $75,000. Above that level, income seems to have no impact on day-to-day happiness, possibly because higher income often means more stressful time spent working. Also, there is some evidence that higher income levels actually *reduce* the ability to appreciate small pleasures. Interestingly, too, people who come into a windfall are happier if they spend it on others or save it, rather than blowing it in a spree.[19]

Money is also a way of keeping score. If I earn more than you, that must mean I am better than you. So, although an increase in income above $75,000 does not affect *day-to-day* happiness, higher pay can make people feel more satisfied with their lives. They consider themselves more successful and feel that their life is going better.

In short, the relationship between money and happiness is complicated. Above a certain level, more money does not make for more day-to-day happiness. Higher pay can increase general satisfaction with life, but when people work so hard or so dishonestly that their health, friendships, and leisure activities suffer, it has the reverse effect.

2-3b Competition

Humans are social animals who cannot help but compare themselves with other people. Deep down, most of us want to be better than the other guy. In one telling experiment, young children elected to get *fewer* prizes for themselves, as long as they still got more than other participants: They chose to get one prize for themselves and zero for the other child, rather than two for themselves and two for the other participant. For an adult example, consider Rajat Gupta, who was worth $100 million when he retired as CEO of the consulting firm McKinsey. As CEO, he had been top dog. But in retirement, he began spending time with far wealthier businesspeople, such as Bill Gates, who were *giving away* hundreds of millions of dollars. To "keep up with the Gateses," Gupta began illegal insider trading. He was ultimately sentenced to two years in prison.

Humans are social animals who cannot help but compare themselves with other people.

[19]Elizabeth Dunn, and Michael Norton, "Don't Indulge, Be Happy," *The New York Times*, July 8, 2012; and Daniel Kahneman, and Angus Deaton, "High Income Improves Evaluation of Life but Not Emotional Well-Being," *Proceedings of the National Academy of Sciences of the United States of America*, August 4, 2010.

In a related phenomenon, researchers have found that **the mere process of negotiating the price of a product reduces a person's sense of morality**. Participants in an experiment were offered a payment of €10, but, in return, a young, healthy mouse would be euthanized. If they rejected the payment, the mouse would continue to live in a happy mouse environment to the end of its natural life, which was about two years. In a different version of the experiment, two participants—a buyer and a seller—negotiated the payment for euthanizing the mouse. And in a third version, larger groups of buyers and sellers negotiated against each other. People in the multi-party negotiations were more likely to kill the mouse than were the pairs of two people, and those pairs were much more likely to choose the mouse's death than individuals acting on their own. In short, being involved in a market reduced the players' sense of morality, at least when mice were involved.[20]

2-3c Rationalization

A recent study found that more creative people tend to be less ethical. The reason? They are better at rationalizing their bad behavior. Virtually any foul deed can be rationalized. Some common rationalizations include:

- If I don't do it, someone else will.
- I deserve this because ...
- They had it coming.
- I am not harming a *person*—it is just a big company.
- This is someone else's responsibility.

The Fudge Factor

The fudge factor is an important type of rationalization. Duke professor Dan Ariely found in his groundbreaking research that almost everyone is willing to cheat, at least on a small scale. We all want to think of ourselves as honest, but we would also like to benefit from dishonesty, whether it be by speeding, cheating on our taxes, or using an old photo on our online dating profile. If we cheat—just a little—then we can tell ourselves it does not really count.

Ariely conducted an experiment in which he paid people for solving math problems. When a neutral person graded the tests, participants averaged four correct answers. But when people were allowed to grade their own tests without anyone checking the results, all of a sudden they began averaging six correct answers.[21] You can imagine how they might have rationalized that behavior—"I was close on this one. I normally would have gotten that one right. Today was an off day for me."

Of the 40,000 people who participated in this experiment, 70 percent fudged a little, but only 20 cheated big. Surprisingly, when the participants were paid *more* for each correct answer ($10 as opposed to $0.50), they cheated *less*. Presumably, they would have felt worse about themselves if they stole a lot of money rather than a little.

To present a real example, mostly elderly volunteers ran the gift shop at the Kennedy Center for the Performing Arts in Washington, D.C. The shop had revenues of $400,000 a year, but someone was stealing $150,000 of that. An investigation revealed that there was not one thief but, rather, dozens of volunteers were each stealing a little, which added up. These people felt good about themselves for being volunteers so they thought that stealing a little was fine.[22]

---

20 Armin Falk, and Nora Szech, "Morals and Markets," *Science*, 340:707 (2013).

21 Dan Ariely, "Why We Lie," *The Wall Street Journal*, May 26, 2012.

22 David Brooks, "The Moral Diet," *The New York Times*, June 7, 2012.

I Did It for Someone Else

When explaining why they have behaved unethically, people often rationalize it by saying that they did it for their family. In his research, Ariely found that if someone else benefits when participants cheat on a math test, the amount of cheating increases.

The Slippery Slope

So many truly awful outcomes begin with that first step down the slippery slope. How easy to rationalize, "Just this once."

Many publicly traded companies feel pressure to meet earnings expectations. As an accountant at a life insurance company, Brian was responsible for calculating sales. Each day during the last week of the quarter, higher-ups called him to ask anxiously, "Will we make our number?" That answer depended on how Brian evaluated certain policies that had not actually been signed but were close . . . or maybe not so close. The first quarter Brian did stretch metrics to make the number, on the theory that, next quarter, the sales department would fill in the hole. When, instead, the hole simply got bigger, he faced increased pressure to stretch the metrics even more. Next thing he knew, his division was just making up policies. And that is fraud.

Part of the problem with the slippery slope is that, once we lie, it becomes easier to lie again. The part of our brain that is stimulated by lying gets less and less stimulation each time we lie. Have you had the experience of telling a lie often enough that it becomes easy? Or lying to the point where you believe the lie is true?

2-3d We Cannot Be Objective about Ourselves

Are your leadership skills above average? Of course! What about your driving? Definitely! **People are not objective when comparing themselves to others**. We all tend to think of ourselves as better than the other fellow. As a result, we evaluate other people's behavior more harshly. It is not a big deal if we cheat on our expense account because we are basically honest and deserve that extra income. But if Rachelle down the hall cheats, she is just corrupt.[23]

Similarly, we all tend to believe that we have done more than our fair share of work at home, on our team, in our study group. Many studies looking at groups as varied as married couples, athletes, MBA students, and organizational behavior professors have found a tendency for people to overestimate their own contribution to a group effort.[24]

Participants in a study had to decide whether they or someone else got an easy assignment. When asked in the abstract what would be a fair method for assigning tasks, everyone said that the computer should make the assignments randomly. But when another group of people was actually given the authority to decide, three-quarters ignored the computer option and just assigned themselves the easy jobs. And then they rated themselves high on a fairness scale.[25] **In making a decision that affects you, it is important to remember that you are unlikely to be objective.**

---

23 Jared Harris, Morela Hernandez, and Cristiano Guarana, "Ethics Beneath the Surface," Case Study, *Harvard Business Review* (2015).

24 MBA students were asked what percentage of the work each had done in their study groups. The total credit claimed per group averaged 139 percent. Organizational behavior professors overestimated their own contribution by a similar amount. Mahzarin R. Banaji, Max H. Bazerman, and Dolly Chugh, "How (Un)Ethical Are You?" *Harvard Business Review*, December 2003.

25 John Tierney, "Deep Down, We Can't Fool Even Ourselves," *The New York Times*, July 1, 2008.

2-3e Moral Licensing

After doing something ethical, many people then have a tendency to act unethically. We refer to this tendency as **moral licensing**. It is as if people keep a running total in their heads about how ethical they are, and, if they do one ethical act in the morning, they are then entitled to act unethically in the afternoon. For example, researchers found that people who buy an environmentally friendly product are more likely to cheat and steal afterwards than are those who have chosen the less socially conscious item.[26]

Moral licensing
After doing something ethical, many people then have a tendency to act unethically.

2-3f Conflicts of Interest

In another Ariely experiment, participants were paid more if the right rectangle had a larger number of dots than the left. Their tendency was to say the right rectangle had more even when the left one clearly did.

Do you care if your doctor uses a pen given to her by a pharmaceutical company? You should. The evidence is that doctors are influenced by even small gifts. One study found that doctors who were treated to inexpensive lunches by a pharmaceutical company were much more likely to prescribe that company's medication over cheaper alternatives.[27] Small gifts are surprisingly influential because the recipients do not make a conscious effort to overcome any bias these tokens create. And it is not just doctors who are affected. The bias created by a conflict of interest causes unconscious self-serving behavior. **In short, if ethical decisions are your goal, it is better to avoid all conflicts of interest—both large and small.** No one—including you—is good at overcoming the biases that these conflicts create.

2-3g Conformity

Famed investor Warren Buffett has been quoted as saying, "The five most dangerous words in business may be: 'Everybody else is doing it.'" Because humans are social animals, they are often willing to follow the leader, even to a place where they do not really want to go. Researchers have found that if one company misstates its earnings, others in the industry are likely to fudge the exact same accounts—unless the original offender suffers some penalty (such as SEC punishment or a class action suit).[28] **Evidently many people believe that if everybody else is doing it, then it must be okay.**

Conformity can also work to the good. People are more likely to pay their taxes on time if they are told that everyone else does.

2-3h Ethics Case: Diamonds in the Rough

Orlanda was a software engineer who had just started a new job. The company was in shambles, but, after months of killer hours, she managed to initiate huge improvements. One of her biggest accomplishments was to help a major supplier solve its technical problems so that its product would work reliably. On her birthday, her contact at the supplier (who was a friend of her boss) gave her a diamond watch. Her company had no policy on accepting gifts, so she kept it. Afterward, she realized that she was spending even more time working on this supplier's issues. But, she said to herself, this was good for her company too. Also, no one at her company had high ethics standards anyway.

---

[26] Nina Mazar, and Chen-Bo Zhong, "Do Green Products Make Us Better People?" *Psychological Science*, April 2010, vol. 21, no. 4: 494–498.

[27] Nicholas Bakalar, "Drug Company Lunches Have Big Payoffs," *The New York Times*, June 20, 2016.

[28] Simi Kedia, Kevin Koh, and Shivaram Rajgopal, "Evidence on Contagion in Earnings Management," *The Accounting Review*, November 2015, vol. 90, no. 6: 2337–2373.

Some months later, the same supplier offered to buy her a diamond necklace if she would make his company a preferred supplier. He said the necklace would look just like the one he had given her boss.

Questions

1. What ethics traps is Orlanda facing?
2. Is there anything wrong with accepting these gifts?

2-3i Following Orders

When someone in authority issues orders, even to do something clearly wrong, it is very tempting to comply. Fear of punishment, the belief in authority figures, and the ability to rationalize, all play a role. Amanda worked at a private school that was struggling to pay its bills. As a result, school administrators kept the lights turned off in the hallways. On a particularly cloudy day, a visitor tripped and fell in one of these darkened passages. When the visitor sued, the principal told Amanda to lie on the witness stand and say that the lights had been on. The school's lawyer reinforced this instruction. Amanda did as she was told. When asked why, she said, "I figured it must be the right thing to do if the lawyer said so. Also, if I hadn't lied, the principal would have fired me, and I might not have been able to get another job in teaching."

In your life, you are likely to face the dilemma of a boss who orders you to do something wrong. Executives have told us that they have been ordered to:

- Misrepresent data in a presentation to the board (so it would approve a project that the boss wanted to do but which did not meet profitability requirements).
- Avoid hiring certain ethnic groups or pregnant women.
- "Smooth" numbers, that is, report sales that had not actually taken place.

When you are a boss, be aware that setting goals for your subordinates carries risks, especially if the goals are too narrowly focused. A law firm partner once said, "If we tell associates they have to bill 2,000 hours a year, they will bill 2,000 hours. Whether they will *work* 2,000 hours is another matter." Research supports this view. Participants in an experiment were more likely to cheat if they had been assigned specific goals, whether or not they were actually being paid for meeting the targets.[29]

As you might expect, employees who work for firms with a culture of blind obedience are twice as likely to report having seen unethical behavior as are workers at companies with a more collaborative environment.[30]

2-3j Euphemisms and Reframing

The term "friendly fire" has a cheerful ring to it, much better than "killing your own troops," which is what it really means. "Enhanced interrogation techniques" seem like a great idea, until you learn that it means "torture." In a business setting, to "smooth earnings" sounds a lot better than "cook the books" or "commit fraud." And "right-sizing" is more palatable than "firing a whole bunch of people." In making ethics decisions, it is important to use accurate terminology. Anything else is just a variation on rationalization.

---

[29] Alina Tugend, "Experts' Advice to the Goal-Oriented: Don't Overdo It," *The New York Times*, October, 5, 2012.

[30] "The View from the Top and Bottom," *The Economist*, September 24, 2011.

Aerospace engineer Roger Boisjoly (pronounced "Boh-zho-lay") tried to convince his superiors at Morton-Thiokol, Inc., to postpone the launch of the space shuttle *Challenger*. His superiors were engineers too, so they were qualified to evaluate Boisjoly's concerns. But during the discussion, one of the bosses said, "We have to make a management decision." Once the issue was reframed as "management," not "engineering," their primary concern was to please their customer, NASA. The flight had already been postponed twice and, as managers, they had to be convinced that it was *not* safe to fly. With clear evidence lacking, these men approved the launch, which ended catastrophically when the space shuttle exploded 73 seconds after liftoff, killing all seven astronauts onboard. If they had asked an engineering question—"Is the space shuttle definitely safe?"—they would have made a different decision. In asking or answering a question, it is always a good idea to consider whether the frame is correct.

Similarly, people's behavior changes if an event is framed as a loss rather than a gain. Our tendency is to feel any harm twice as strongly as we do a benefit. If salespeople are told that an event creates a 75 percent probability of *losing* their commission, they are more likely to engage in unethical behavior than if they are told that an event creates a 25 percent probability that they will *earn* their commission.[31] Although the information is the same, the way it is presented affects behavior.

2-3k Lost in a Crowd

After being struck by a car, a two-year-old child lies at the side of the road as people walk and ride by. No one stops to help, and the child dies. On a busy street, a man picks up a seven-year-old girl and carries her away while she screams, "You're not my dad—someone help me!" No one responds. The first incident was real; the second one was a test staged by a news station. It took hours and many repetitions before anyone tried to prevent the abduction.

When in a group, people are less likely to take responsibility because they assume (hope?) that someone else will. They tend to check the reactions of others and, if everyone else seems calm, they assume that all is right. Bystanders are much more likely to react if they are alone and have to form an independent judgment.

Thus, in a business, if everyone is lying to customers, smoothing earnings, or sexually harassing the staff, it is tempting to go with the flow rather than protest the wrongdoing. In the example about food companies that began this chapter, one former executive says that producers shrug off responsibility for obesity in America by pointing to all the "other causes": a car culture, too much screen time, less outdoor play, fewer women at home to cook. The companies rationalize that they are not responsible and there is nothing they can do.

2-3l Ethics Case: Man Down

Wesley Autrey was standing on a train platform with his two young daughters and a man he did not know. Suddenly, the man had a seizure, causing him to fall on the tracks. Autrey could hear a train approaching, so he knew he had only seconds to act. Leaping onto the track, he pulled the man between the rails and lay on top of him to protect him from the train. The train engineer tried to stop, but five cars passed over the two men. Both were unharmed.

Some years later in New York City, a homeless man pushed Ki-Suck Han onto subway tracks while many people watched. No one reacted, except a photographer who took photos as Han was killed by a train.

---

31 Jared Harris, Morela Hernandez, and Cristiano Guarana, "Ethics Beneath the Surface," Case Study, *Harvard Business Review* (2015).

Questions

1. Why was Autrey more likely to act than the crowds watching Han?
2. Do you have an ethical obligation to act when someone needs help? Or when you observe wrongdoing?
3. Imagine that, at your work, you know that someone is:
   - Lying on an expense account
   - Wrongly booking sales that have not yet occurred
   - Sexually harassing staff members

   What is your ethical obligation? What would you do, under what circumstances?

2-3m Short-Term Perspective

Many times, people make unethical decisions because they are thinking short term. Engineers at General Motors discovered that the ignition switch on some of its cars was faulty, causing the engine to shut off and, with it, the steering and airbags—clearly a life-threatening situation. Rather than fix the problem, which would have required an immediate and expensive recall, engineers hid the fault, preferring their own short-term objective of profits and job security over the long-term health and safety of drivers. After all, maybe the engineers would no longer be working at the company by the time the problem was discovered. This short-term perspective not only led to over 100 deaths, it was hugely damaging to the company's finances and reputation.

Optimism bias
A belief that the outcome of an event will be more positive than the evidence warrants

Dmitry Kalinovsky/Shutterstock.com

In ignoring an ignition problem, engineers at General Motors took a short-term perspective. As a result, more than 100 people died.

Part of the problem is that many of us have an **optimism bias**: We are overly confident in predicting our own success. In another Ariely experiment, participants took math tests in two rounds. In the first round, the tests had the answers at the bottom of the page. Although they were told not to look, the participants (not surprisingly) did better than average. For the second round of the experiment, participants were promised money if they accurately predicted how many problems they would get right, but the tests did not include an answer key. In an example of optimism bias, the participants predicted they would do as well without the answer key as they had with it, even though this optimism cost them money.

2-3n Ethics Case: Wobbly Platform

An IT professional describes how short-term thinking threatened him and his company:

> The CIO of my company was the kind of boss who expected people to do as they were told. Everyone in the company kowtowed to him, even his peers. Years before, he had introduced a new IT platform to the company. Although the platform was now out of date and unstable, he recommended that the company continue to use it in the United States, even adding a new product suite to it. I knew this decision was a huge technical mistake, full of risks and hidden costs. After a sleepless night, I went to talk with the CIO, presenting all of the facts rationally and completely. He ordered me to implement his decision anyway. So I did.

Fast-forward four years. Our work on this flawed platform is still not complete. We have spent millions of dollars and customers are very unhappy. Yet, the CIO is now recommending that we expand the use of this same platform throughout the entire company—overseas as well as in the United States.

I was so wrong. I had a short-term perspective—focused on keeping my job. I ignored my integrity, my responsibility to the company, and, if I had to do it all over again, I would have voiced my concerns to the business leaders or I would have left.

Questions

1. Besides a short-term perspective, what other ethics traps did this employee face?
2. Over the long term, did this problem get better or worse? Who was harmed by his decision?
3. What else could the employee have done?

2-3o Blind Spots

As Bob Dylan memorably sang, "How many times can a man turn his head and pretend that he just doesn't see?" The answer is: a whole lot. **We all have a tendency to ignore blatant evidence that we would rather not know.**

Bernard Madoff alleged he was a money manager who earned consistent high returns year in and year out, even when the market was down. His explanation for these results was implausible—no one else was able to replicate them using his purported methods. Yet, many financial advisors recommended Madoff funds to their clients. In fact, Madoff was running a Ponzi scheme—a fraud in which he would not invest at all, but rather use the money from new investors to give the old ones quick returns. In the end, his thefts totaled $65 billion.

2-3p Avoiding Ethics Traps

Ethics traps represent potential dangers for us all. But they are not, by any means, inevitable. **Three practices will help us avoid these traps:**

1. **Slow down.** We all make worse decisions when in a hurry. In one experiment, a group of students at Princeton Theological Seminary (that is, people in training to be ministers) were told to go to a location across campus to give a talk. On their walk over, they encountered a man lying in distress in a doorway. Only one-tenth of those participants who had been told they were late for their talk stopped to help the ill man, while almost two-thirds of those who thought they had plenty of time did stop.[32]
2. **Do not trust your first instinct.** You make many decisions without thinking. When sitting down for dinner, you do not ask yourself, "Which hand should I use to pick up the fork? How will I cut up my food?" You use System 1 thinking—an automatic, instinctual, sometimes emotional process. This approach is efficient but can also lead to more selfish and unethical decisions. When taking an exam, System 1 thinking would not get you far. For that, you need System 2 thoughts—those that are conscious and logical.

   Being in a hurry, or in a crowd, rationalizing, using euphemisms, doing what every else does, receiving an order, being dazzled by money, these can all lead you to make a quick and wrong System 1 decision. Before making an important choice, bring in System 2 thinking.

32John M. Darley, and Daniel C. Batson, "From Jerusalem to Jericho: A Study of Situational and Dispositional Variables in Helping Behavior," *Journal of Personality and Social Psychology*, July 1973, vol. 27(1): 100–108.

3. **Remember your Life Principles**. In his research, Ariely found that participants were less likely to cheat if they were reminded of their school honor code or the Ten Commandments. This result was true even if their school did not have an honor code, the participants were atheists, or they did not actually remember all of the Ten Commandments. (No one remembered all ten.) Also, in the case of the seminary students, the topic of the talk mattered. Those who were speaking on the Parable of the Good Samaritan (in which a man offers aid to an injured person from a different clan) were twice as likely to help the ill man than those who were giving a talk on careers for seminarians. It is a good practice to remind yourself of your values.

2-3q Lying: A Special Case

Lying is the act of intentionally misrepresenting the truth, by word, deed, or omission. We are taught from an early age that this is wrong. Yet research shows that we tell between one and two lies a day.[33]

Is honesty the best policy? The consequences of lying can be severe: Students are suspended, employees are fired, and witnesses are convicted of perjury. Sometimes the impact is subtler but still significant: a loss of trust or of opportunities. In addition, research has shown that liars get sick more (suffering from more headaches, nausea, and sore throats), experience more mental health issues, and have worse relationships.

When is lying acceptable? If poker players bluff their way through lousy hands, we consider them skilled because that is an accepted part of the game. What about white lies to make others feel better: I love your lasagna. You're not going bald. No, that sweater doesn't make you look fat. When Victoria McGrath suffered a terrible wound to her leg in the Boston Marathon bombing, Tyler Dodd comforted her at the scene by telling her that he had recovered from a shrapnel wound in Afghanistan. His story was not true—he had never been in combat or Afghanistan. McGrath was grateful to him for his lie because it gave her strength and hope. Was he right or wrong? What are your Life Principles about lying?

Kant felt that any lie violated his principle of the categorical imperative. Because the world would be intolerable if everyone lied all the time, no one should lie ever. He gave the example of the murderer who knocks on your door and asks, "Where's Lukas?" You know Lukas is cowering just inside, but you might be tempted to lie and send the murderer off in the opposite direction. Kant preferred that you tell what is now called a **Kantian Evasion** or a **palter**. That is, you make a truthful statement that is nonetheless misleading. So, you might say, truthfully, "I saw Lukas in the park just an hour ago." And off the murderer would go.

Kantian Evasion or palter
A truthful statement that is nonetheless misleading

Is a Kantian Evasion really more ethical than a lie? For example, when Bill Clinton was a candidate for the presidency, he was asked if he had ever smoked marijuana. He answered that he "never broke the laws of my state or of the United States." Later, it was revealed that he had used marijuana while a student in England. So, although technically correct, his statement was misleading. Was that really better than lying about marijuana use?

One could argue that Clinton was at least honoring the importance of truth-telling. He went to some effort *not* to lie. However, some commentators argue that paltering is actually worse than lying. Although the harm to the victim is the same, palterers are less likely to be caught and are, therefore, more likely to palter again.

What are your Life Principles on this issue? There may indeed be good reasons to lie but what are they? Would it be right to say that you would only lie to benefit other people? Hiding Lukas from the murderer? Deceiving children who believe in Santa Claus? It is useful to analyze this issue now rather than to rationalize later.

---

[33]Bella M. DePaulo, Deborah A. Kashy, Susan E. Kirkendol, and Melissa M. Wyer, "Lying in Everyday Life," *Journal of Personality and Social Psychology*, 1996, vol. 70, no. 5: 979–995.

What about in business? Does the presence of *competition* make a difference? When do the ends justify the means?

2-3r Ethics Case: Truth (?) in Borrowing

Rob is in the business of buying dental practices. He finds solo practitioners, buys their assets, signs them to a long-term contract, and then improves their management and billing processes so effectively that both he and the dentists are better off.

Rob has just found a great opportunity with a lot of potential profit. There is only *one* problem. The bank will not give him a loan to buy the practice without checking the dentist's financial record. Her credit rating is fine, but she filed for bankruptcy 20 years ago. That event no longer appears on her credit record, but the bank form asks about *all* bankruptcies. Although she is perfectly willing to lie on the form, Rob insists that she be honest. But when the bank learns about the bankruptcy, it denies his loan even though *her* bankruptcy in no way affects *his* ability to pay the loan. And the incident is ancient history—the dentist's current finances are strong. Subsequently four other banks also refuse to make the loan.

Rob is feeling pretty frustrated. He figures the return on this deal would be 20 percent. Everyone would benefit—the dentist would earn more, her patients would have better technology, he could afford a house in a better school district, and the bank would make a profit. There is one more bank he could try.

Questions

1. Should Rob file loan documents with the bank knowing the dentist has lied?
2. Who would be harmed by this lie?
3. What rationalizations might Rob use?
4. What if Rob pays back the loan without incident? Was the lie still wrong? Do the ends justify the means?
5. What is your Life Principle about telling lies? When is making a misrepresentation acceptable? To protect someone's life or physical safety? To protect a job? To protect another person's feelings? To gain an advantage? When others are doing the same? When it makes sense from a cost–benefit perspective?
6. Do you have the same rule when lying to protect yourself, as opposed to benefiting others?

2-4 REACTING TO UNETHICAL BEHAVIOR

When faced with unethical behavior in your organization, you have three choices.

2-4a Loyalty

It is always important to pick one's battles. For example, a firm's accounting department must make many decisions about which reasonable people could disagree. Just because someone's judgment is different from yours does not mean that they are behaving unethically. Being a team player means allowing other people to make their own choices sometimes. However, the difference between being a team player and starting down the slippery slope can be very small. If you are carrying out a decision or simply observing one that makes you uncomfortable, then it is time to consult your Life Principles and review the section on ethics traps.

2-4b Exit

When faced with the unacceptable, one option is to walk out the door quietly. You resign "to spend more time with your family," "to explore other opportunities," or "to accept an offer that is too good to refuse." This approach may be the safest for you because you are not ruffling any feathers or making any enemies. It is a small world, and you never know when someone you have offended will be in a position to do you harm. But a quiet exit leaves the bad guys in position to continue the unsavory behavior. As the saying goes, "The only thing necessary for the triumph of evil is that good men do nothing." For example, when the CEO sexually harassed Laura, she left quietly for fear that if she reported him, he would harm her career. No one likes to hire a troublemaker. So the CEO proceeded to attack other women at the company until finally a senior executive found out and confronted the chief. The braver and better option may be to exit loudly—reporting the wrongdoing on the way out the door.

2-4c Voice

As we saw in our discussion of conformity, wrongdoing often occurs because everyone just goes along to get along. One valiant soul with the courage to say "This is wrong" can be a powerful force for the good. But confrontation may not be the only, or even the best, use of your voice. Learning to persuade, cajole, or provide better options are all important leadership skills. Keith felt that the CEO of his company was about to make a bad decision, but he was unable to persuade the man to choose a different alternative. When Keith turned out to be correct, the CEO gave him no credit, saying, "You are equally responsible because your arguments weren't compelling enough." Keith thought the man had a point.

How can you learn to implement ethical decisions in the most effective and painless way? University of Virginia professor Mary Gentile has developed a curriculum to teach these crucial implementation skills, which she calls "Giving Voice to Values" or "GVV."[34] She proposes that, **when implementing a difficult ethical decision, you ask the following four questions:**

1. What are the main arguments you are trying to counter? That is, what are the reasons and rationalizations you need to address?
2. What is at stake for the key parties, including those with whom you disagree?
3. What levers can you use to influence those with whom you disagree?
4. What is your most powerful and persuasive response to the reasons and rationalizations you need to address?

2-4d Ethics Case: Truth or Consequences

A former colleague recruited Luke to join his new company as a director, leading a team of about 30 people. Luke was replacing Jill, who had been fired for failing to deliver on an important project. The team he was to lead suffered from low morale and a poor reputation in the company. Luke's job was to rebuild both.

He quickly found that, although most of the team members were able and hard-working, Jill had never allowed them to be honest about their workload or deadlines. She agreed to any and all requests from other managers, even if there was no hope of meeting the deadline, and then let her team figure out how to muddle through. No wonder the team was demoralized and had a reputation for being unreliable.

---

[34] The Aspen Institute was Founding Partner, along with the Yale School of Management, and incubator for Giving Voice to Values. GVV is now based and supported at the University of Virginia. For more information on GVV, see www.GivingVoicetoValues.org and www.MaryGentile.com.

Luke immediately explained to his team that they were to be open and honest both inside and outside the team. Though this approach sounds simple, it was a completely foreign concept to them. Some of them told him bluntly that he was sure to be fired within a few months.

His new approach was soon put to the test. A vice president from the customer service team told him that the company's largest customer was going to be conducting an on-site audit. In Luke's area, the customer would be particularly interested in seeing the dedicated computing equipment that was a key part of its contract with the company. As it turns out, there was no dedicated computing equipment. Nor were there any funds in the budget to buy the equipment.

At first, the VP did not believe Luke because Jill had lied to him many times, promising that the equipment was there. To survive the audit from this important customer, the VP asked Luke to lie just this once and also to put fake labels on some of the machines to show the customer. But to do so would have violated Luke's values and diminished his standing with his team.

Questions with Suggested Answers

1. What are the main arguments Luke is trying to counter? That is, what are the reasons and rationalizations he needs to address?
   a. There is no money in the budget this year to buy the necessary equipment.
   b. If the customer is told there is no equipment, it will most likely fire the company.
   c. The customer is unlikely to find out the truth unless it is told.
   d. It is okay to lie just this once, for a short time. Next year, the team could budget for the new equipment.
   e. This problem is not the team's fault—it is Jill's.
2. What is at stake for the key parties, including those with whom Luke disagrees?
   a. If the customer leaves the company, performance reviews—and bonuses—for Luke, his boss, and his team would be adversely affected. Luke's job, and possibly the boss's, might also be at risk.
   b. Lying to a customer harms employee morale and respect both for the boss and for the company.
   c. If the customer finds out that the company has violated its contract, it will certainly fire the company. It may even sue.
   d. A "just this once" attitude could lead to other unethical acts. After all, employees model the behavior they see in their bosses.
3. What levers can Luke use to influence those with whom he disagrees?
   a. It is important to think about the long-term success of the company. Over the long run, customers will be best served and happiest if the company abides by its contracts with them and if they are treated with respect and honesty.
   b. This is an opportunity to show the team that this company has integrity.
   c. Given the choice between lying to a customer and going over budget, it is better for the company, and for the customer, to spend the money to buy the necessary equipment.
4. What is Luke's most powerful and persuasive response to the reasons and rationalizations he needs to address?
   a. In the end, Luke used all of these arguments and also said, flatly, that he was not going to lie to the customer. He persuaded the CFO to allocate additional funds to buy and install the necessary equipment before the customer audit. The result: The customer was satisfied, the boss was pleased, and both the team's morale and its reputation in the company improved. This experience was a turning point for everyone.

Here is how Luke concluded his story:

> This was not the last challenge of this sort that I faced with the company, and in each situation I used the same approach—to always be open, transparent, and honest about issues and problems. In my opinion, the minute that you take that approach you begin to lay a foundation that makes all of the coming decisions that much easier, and over time you are able to build a strong ethical base on which to work and live. I think you also build a reputation as being open and honest, which influences people around you.

2-5 APPLYING THE PRINCIPLES

Having thought about ethics principles, traps, and implementation, it is time to practice applying what you have learned to situations that are similar to those you are likely to face in your life.

Be aware that some of these ethics dilemmas illustrate the trade-off between shareholders and stakeholders. It is important to recognize explicitly the forces that push or pull you when making a decision. Unless you are aware of these factors, you cannot make a truly informed decision.

2-5a Personal Ethics in the Workplace

Should you behave in the workplace the way you do at home, or do you have a separate set of ethics for each part of your life? What if your employees behave badly outside of work—should that affect their employment?

2-5b Ethics Case: Weird Wierdsma

Beatrix Szeremi immigrated to the United States from Hungary, but her American dream turned into a nightmare when she married Charles Wierdsma. He repeatedly beat her and threatened to suffocate and drown her. Ultimately, he pleaded guilty to one felony count and went to jail. Despite his son's guilt, Thomas Wierdsma pressured his daughter-in-law to drop the charges and delete photos of her injuries from her Facebook page. When she refused, he threatened her and her lawyer that he would report her to immigration officials (although she was in the country legally with a green card). Father and son discussed how they could wrongfully get her deported. Thomas also testified in a deposition that it was not bad to lie to a federal agency. "It happens all the time," he said.[35] Thomas Wierdsma is the senior vice president at The GEO Group, Inc.

Research indicates that CEOs who break the law outside the office are more likely to engage in workplace fraud. Although their legal infractions—driving under the influence, using illegal drugs, domestic violence, even speeding tickets—were unrelated to their work, these violations seemed to indicate a disrespect for the rule of law and a lack of self-control.[36]

Questions

1. What would Kant and Mill say is the right thing to do in this case? What is the result under the Front Page test?
2. What ethics traps might Wierdsma's boss face in this situation?

---

[35] Nancy Lofholm, "GEO Investigated in Son's Domestic Violence Case," *The Denver Post*, April 8, 2013.
[36] Robert Davidson, Aiyesha Dey, and Abbie Smith, "Executives' 'Off-the-Job' Behavior, Corporate Culture, and Financial Reporting Risk," 2013. Available at SSRN: https://ssrn.com/abstract=2096226.

3. What is your Life Principle? What behavior are you willing to tolerate in the interest of profitability?
4. If you were the CEO of Thomas Wierdsma's company, would you fire him? Impose some other sanction?
5. Which is worse—Wierdsma's threatening his daughter-in-law or stating that it is acceptable to lie to a federal agency?
6. Would you fire a warehouse worker who behaved this way? How high in the hierarchy does an employee have to be for this behavior to be forgiven?
7. GEO runs prisons and immigration facilities for the government. Does that fact change any of your answers?
8. Wierdsma's woes were reported in major newspapers, and his statement about lying to a federal agency was on YouTube. Do these facts change any of your answers?
9. What would you say to someone who argues that the goal at work is to make as much money as possible, but at home it is to be a kind and honorable human being?

2-5c The Organization's Responsibility to Society

Many products can potentially cause harm to customers or employees. Does it matter if they willingly accept exposure to these products? What constitutes informed consent? What is the company's responsibility to those who are *unwittingly* harmed by its products?

2-5d Ethics Case: Breathing the Fumes

Every other year, the National Institutes of Health publish the "Report on Carcinogens," which lists products that cause cancer. Among those in the most recent report was formaldehyde, found in furniture, cosmetics, building products, carpets, and fabric softeners. Unless we take heroic efforts to avoid this chemical, we are all exposed to it on a daily basis. Indeed, almost all homes have formaldehyde levels that exceed government safety rules. In an effort to shoot the messenger, the American Chemistry Council, which is an industry trade group, lobbied Congress to cut off funding for the "Report on Carcinogens"—not improve it, but defund it.

Questions

1. If you were one of the many companies selling products that contain formaldehyde, what would you do? What would you be willing to pay to provide a safer product?
2. What would Mill and Kant recommend?
3. What ethics traps would you face in making a decision?
4. What Life Principle would you apply?
5. If you were an executive at Exxon, Dow, or DuPont, all members of the American Chemistry Council, how would you react to this effort to hide the facts on formaldehyde?
6. How would you convince the CEO of your company to take the steps you think best? What arguments would you have to counter? What reasons and rationalizations would you have to address?
7. What is at stake for the key parties, including those with whom you disagree?
8. What levers can you use to influence those with whom you disagree?
9. What is your most powerful and persuasive response to the reasons and rationalizations you need to address?

2-5e The Organization's Responsibility to Its Employees

Organizations cannot be successful without good workers. In many circumstances, the shareholder and stakeholder models agree that employees should be treated well. Disgruntled workers are likely to be unmotivated and unproductive. But sometimes doing what is best for employees may not lead to higher profits. In these cases, does an organization have a duty to take care of its workers? The shareholder model says no; the stakeholder model takes the opposite view.

Corporate leaders are often faced with difficult decisions when the issue of layoffs arises. These choices can be particularly difficult when outsourcing is an option, that is, cutting jobs at home and relocating operations to another country.

2-5f Ethics Case: The Storm after the Storm

Yanni is the CEO of Butterfly, Inc., which manufactures tractors. A tornado recently destroyed one of the company's plants which was near Farmfield, Arkansas, a town with a population of roughly 5,000 people. Farmfield is a two-hour drive from the nearest city, Little Rock.

Here is the good news: The insurance payout will cover the full cost of rebuilding. The bad news? Manufacturing plants are much more expensive to build and operate in the United States than overseas. Yanni has asked Adam and Zoe to present the pros and cons of relocating to someplace cheaper.

Adam says, "If we rebuild overseas, our employees will never find equivalent jobs. We pay $20 an hour, and the other jobs in town are mostly minimum wage. And remember how some of the guys worked right through Christmas to set up for that new model? They have been loyal to us—we owe them something in return. Going overseas is not just bad for Farmfield or Arkansas; it's bad for the country. We can't continue to ship jobs overseas."

Zoe responds, "That is the government's problem, not ours. We'll pay to retrain the workers, which, frankly, is a generous offer. Our investors get a return of 4 percent; the industry average is closer to 8 percent. If we act like a charity to support Farmfield, we could all lose our jobs. It is our obligation to do what's best for our shareholders—which, in this case, happens to be what's right for us, too."

Questions

1. What ethics traps does Yanni face in this situation?
2. Do you agree with Zoe's argument that it is the government's responsibility to create and protect American jobs and that it is a CEO's job to increase shareholder wealth?
3. Imagine that you personally own shares in Butterfly, Inc. Would you be upset with a decision to rebuild the manufacturing plant in the United States?
4. If you were in Yanni's position, would you rebuild the plant in Arkansas or relocate overseas?
5. If Butterfly, Inc. decides to rebuild in Arkansas, should it pay the workers while the center is being rebuilt? If yes, should it pay all workers or just the high-level ones who might leave if they were not paid?
6. What is your Life Principle on this issue? Would you be willing to risk your job to protect your employees?

2-5g The Organization's Responsibility to Its Customers

Customers are another group of essential stakeholders. A corporation must gain and retain loyal buyers if it is to stay in business for long. But when, if ever, does an organization go too far? Is a leader acting appropriately when she puts customers first in a way that significantly diminishes the bottom line? The shareholder model says no. What do you say?

2-5h Ethics Case: Mickey Weighs In

As we have seen, some food companies manipulate products to maximize their appeal, without regard to the health of their customers. Disney took a different approach, deciding that only healthful foods could be advertised on its children's television channels, radio stations, and websites. Candy, fast food, and sugared cereals were banned from its parks.

Its characters could no longer associate with unhealthy foods. No more Mickey Pop-Tarts or Buzz Lightyear Happy Meals. Said Disney chairman, Robert Iger, "Companies in a position to help with solutions to childhood obesity should do just that."[37]

Disney lost advertising, but would not say how much. Food sales at its theme parks could decline if children found the options unappealing. Its licensing revenues were also affected by its decision to remove Disney characters from the likes of Pop-Tarts and Happy Meals.

On the other hand, this healthy initiative enhanced its reputation, at least with parents, who increasingly sought healthy food options for their children. Disney also profited from license fees it received for the use of a Mickey Check logo on healthy food in grocery aisles and restaurants. This food initiative might also help forestall more onerous government regulation.

In contrast, the Nickelodeon television channel, home to SpongeBob SquarePants and Dora the Explorer, decided to continue allowing ads for such nutritional failures as Trix and Cocoa Puffs cereals. It said that its goal was "to make the highest quality entertainment content in the world for kids … [while leaving] the science of nutrition to the experts." Food ads were the third highest source of advertising revenues for Nickelodeon. Also, it did not have as many other revenue streams as Disney does—no theme parks, for example.

Questions

1. What obligation did Disney and Nickelodeon have to their young customers? Did they owe anything other than entertainment?
2. What would Mill or Kant have said? What is the result under the Front Page test?
3. What ethics traps do Disney and Nickelodeon face?
4. How much advertising and licensing revenue would you be willing to give up to protect children from ads for unhealthy foods? Does your answer depend on how profitable the division is?
5. Does this information make you more likely to buy Disney products or allow your children to watch Disney TV? Less likely to watch Nickelodeon?
6. What is your Life Principle? How much profitability (or income) would you be willing to give up to protect children you do not know?

---

[37] Brooks Barnes, "Promoting Nutrition, Disney to Restrict Junk-Food Ads," *The New York Times*, June 5, 2012.

2-5i The Organization's Responsibility to Overseas Workers

What ethical duties does an American manager have overseas to stakeholders in countries where the culture and economic circumstances are very different? Should American companies (and consumers) buy goods that are produced in sweatshop factories?

Industrialization has always been the first stepping-stone out of dire poverty.

Industrialization has always been the first stepping-stone out of dire poverty—it was in England in centuries past, and it is now in the developing world. Eventually, higher productivity leads to higher wages. The results in China have been nothing short of remarkable. During the Industrial Revolution in England, per capita output doubled in 58 years; in China, it took only ten years.

During the past 50 years, Taiwan and South Korea welcomed sweatshops. During the same period, India resisted what it perceived to be foreign exploitation. Although all three countries started at the same economic level, Taiwan and South Korea today have much lower levels of infant mortality and much higher levels of education than India.[38]

In theory, then, sweatshops might not be all bad. But are there limits?

2-5j Ethics Case: A Worm in the Apple

"Riots, Suicides, and More," blares an internet headline about a FoxConn factory where iPhones and other Apple products are assembled. Apple is not alone in facing supplier scandals. So have Nike, Coca-Cola, and Gap, among many others. Do companies have an obligation to the employees of their suppliers? If so, how can they, or anyone, be sure what is really going on in a factory on the other side of the world? Professor Richard Locke of MIT has studied supply chain issues.[39] His conclusions:

- The first step that many companies took to improve working conditions overseas was to establish a code of conduct and then conduct audits. Professor Locke found that these coercive practices do not work and that compliance is sporadic, at best. For example, despite Hewlett-Packard's best efforts, only a handful of its 276 overseas factories consistently met its standards.
- A more collaborative approach worked better—when the auditors saw their role as less of a police officer and more as a partner, committed to problem solving and sharing of best practices.
- It can be hard to improve conditions without also changing a company's business model. One of the reasons that Apple uses Chinese manufacturers such as FoxConn is that its workers have fewer overtime restrictions. Just before the first iPhone was released, Steve Jobs decided that the screens had to be unscratchable glass instead of plastic. One Chinese company supplied a team of engineers that was housed in a dormitory and willing to work around the clock to design the right glass. When the glass arrived at FoxConn in the middle of the night, thousands of assemblers were put to work immediately.

What would you do if you were a manager in the following circumstances?

- In clothing factories, workers often remove the protective guards from their sewing machines because the guards slow the flow of work. As a result, many workers suffer

38The data in this and the preceding paragraph are from Nicholas D. Kristof and Sheryl Wu Dunn, "Two Cheers for Sweatshops," *The New York Times Magazine*, September 24, 2000, p. 70.

39"When the Jobs Inspector Calls," *The Economist*, March 31, 2012.

needle punctures. Factories resist the cost of buying new guards because the workers just take them off again. Is there a solution?

- In a factory in Central America, powerful chemicals were used to remove stains from clothing. The fumes from these chemicals were a health hazard, but ventilation systems were too expensive. What could be done?
- Timberland, Nike, and Hewlett-Packard have recognized that selling large numbers of new products creates great variation in demand and therefore pressure on factory workers to work overtime. What can a company do to reduce this pressure? [40]

2-5k Corporate Social Responsibility (CSR)

So far, we have largely been talking about a company's duty not to cause harm. But do companies have a **corporate social responsibility**—that is, an obligation to contribute positively to the world around them? Do businesses have an affirmative duty to do good?

Corporate social responsibility
An organization's obligation to contribute positively to the world around it

You remember Milton Friedman's view that a manager's obligation is to make the company as profitable as possible while also complying with the law. Harvard professor Michael Porter has written that CSR often benefits a company. For example, improving economic and social conditions overseas can create new customers with money to spend. Educational programs may provide a better workforce. One study found that MBA students are willing to accept lower pay to work at a company with a good reputation for ethics and CSR. And employees feel more loyalty to companies that treat their workers and the community right.

In Porter's view, a company should only undertake a CSR project if it is profitable for the company in its own right, regardless of any secondary benefits the company may receive from, say, an improved reputation.[41] Yoplait has periodically run a "Save Lids to Save Lives" campaign. For every Yoplait lid mailed in, the company makes a donation to a breast cancer charity. During these campaigns, Yoplait profits by gaining market share.

But should companies be willing to improve the world even if their efforts *reduce* profitability?

2-5l Ethics Case: The Beauty of a Well-Fed Child

Cosmetic companies often use gift-with-purchase offers to promote their products. For example, with any $35 Estée Lauder purchase at Nordstrom's, you can choose a free gift of creams and makeup valued at $135, plus a designer cosmetics bag.

Because so many cosmetic companies provide gift-with-purchase offers, it is difficult for any single business to stand out from the crowd. But Clarins put a new spin on these offers with what it calls "gift with *purpose*." Spend $75 on Clarins items at Macy's and you receive free products *and* the companies will provide school meals to children in need.

Clarins and Macy's hope that cosmetics buyers (many of whom are women with children) will find this opportunity to feed children particularly compelling. Said the Macy's vice president for national media relations and cause marketing, "With no energy or lift on the customers' part, they get this really feel-good element with the shopping experience."[42]

40These examples are from Richard Locke, Matthew Amengual, and Akshay Mangla, "Virtue out of Necessity? Compliance, Commitment, and the Improvement of Labor Conditions in Global Supply Chains," *Politics & Society*, September 2009, 37: 319–351.

41Michael E. Porter, and Mark R. Kramer, "The Competitive Advantage of Corporate Philanthropy," *Harvard Business Review*, December 2002.

42Adam Andrew Newman, "A Cosmetic Freebie with a Cause," *The New York Times*, April 7, 2013.

Questions

1. If you were an executive at Clarins or Macy's, what would you want to know before approving this promotion?
2. How important is it to improve the image of these two companies? Would this promotion do so?
3. Would you approve this promotion if it were not profitable on its own account? How much of a subsidy would you be willing to grant?

CHAPTER CONCLUSION

Many times in your life, you will be tempted to do something that you know in your heart of hearts is wrong. Referring to your own Life Principles, being aware of potential traps, and knowing how to voice your values will help you make and implement the right decisions. But it is also important that you be able to afford to do the right thing. Having a reserve fund to cover six months' living expenses makes it easier for you to leave a job that violates your personal ethics. Too many times, people make the wrong, and sometimes the illegal, decision for financial reasons.

Managers wonder what they can do to create an ethical environment in their companies. In the end, the surest way to infuse ethics throughout an organization is for top executives to behave ethically themselves. Few will bother to do the right thing unless they observe that their bosses value and support such behavior. Even employees who are ethical in their personal lives may find it difficult to uphold their standards at work if those around them behave differently. To ensure a more ethical world, managers must be an example for others, both within and outside their organizations.

EXAM REVIEW

1. **ETHICS** The law dictates how a person *must* behave. Ethics governs how people *should* behave.

2. **LIFE PRINCIPLES** Life Principles are the rules by which you live your life. If you develop these Life Principles now, you will be prepared when facing ethics dilemmas in the future.

3. **ETHICS IN BUSINESS** There is an ongoing debate about whether managers should focus only on what is best for shareholders or whether they should consider the interests of other stakeholders as well.

4. **WHY BE ETHICAL?**
   - Society as a whole benefits from ethical behavior.
   - Ethical behavior makes people happier.
   - Ethical behavior provides financial benefits.

5. THEORIES OF ETHICS

- Utilitarian thinkers such as John Stuart Mill believe that the right decision maximizes overall happiness and minimizes overall pain.
- Deontological thinkers such as Immanuel Kant believe that the ends do not justify the means. Rather, it is important to do the right thing, no matter the result.
- With his categorical imperative, Kant argued that you should not do something unless you would be willing to have everyone else do it too.
- John Rawls asked us to consider what rules we would propose for society if we did not know how lucky we would be in life's lottery. He called this situation "the veil of ignorance."
- Under the Front Page test, you ask yourself what you would do if your actions were going to be reported publicly.
- Moral universalism is the belief that some types of behavior are always right or always wrong, regardless of what others may think.
- Moral relativism is the belief that it is right to be tolerant of different views and customs. A decision may be acceptable even if it is not in keeping with one's own ethics standards.

6. ETHICS TRAPS

- Money
- Competition
- Rationalization
    - The fudge factor
    - I did it for someone else
    - The slippery slope
- Inability to be objective about ourselves
- Moral licensing
- Conflicts of interest
- Conformity
- Following orders
- Euphemisms and reframing
- Lost in a crowd
- Short-term perspective
    - Optimism bias
- Blind spots

7. TO AVOID ETHICS TRAPS:

- Slow down.
- Do not trust your first instinct.
- Remember your Life Principles.

8. **KANTIAN EVASION OR PALTER** A truthful statement that is nonetheless misleading.

9. **REACTING TO UNETHICAL BEHAVIOR** When faced with unethical behavior in your organization, you have three choices:
   - Loyalty
   - Exit (either quiet or noisy)
   - Voice

10. **GIVING VOICE TO VALUES (GVV)** To implement an ethics decision, use the information you derive from answering the following questions:
    - What are the main arguments you are trying to counter? What are the reasons and rationalizations you need to address?
    - What is at stake for the key parties, including those with whom you disagree?
    - What levers can you use to influence those with whom you disagree?
    - What is your most powerful and persuasive response to the reasons and rationalizations you need to address?

11. **CORPORATE SOCIAL RESPONSIBILITY** An organization's obligation to contribute positively to the world around it.

MULTIPLE-CHOICE QUESTIONS

1. Milton Friedman was a strong believer in the ______________ model. He ______________ argue that a corporate leader's sole obligation is to make money for the company's owners.
   (a) shareholder; did
   (b) shareholder; did not
   (c) stakeholder; did
   (d) stakeholder; did not

2. Which of the following wrote the book *Utilitarianism* and believed that ethical actions should "generate the greatest good for the greatest number"?
   (a) Milton Friedman
   (b) John Stuart Mill
   (c) Immanuel Kant
   (d) John Rawls

3. Which of the following believed that the dignity of human beings must be respected and that the most ethical decisions are made out of a sense of obligation?
   (a) Milton Friedman
   (b) John Stuart Mill
   (c) Immanuel Kant
   (d) John Rawls

4. Kant believed that:
   (a) it is ethical to tell a lie if necessary to protect an innocent person from great harm.
   (b) it is ethical to tell a lie if the benefit of the lie outweighs the cost.
   (c) it is ethical to make a true, but misleading, statement.
   (d) it is wrong to tell an outright lie or to mislead.
5. The following statement is true:
   (a) Most people are honest the vast majority of the time.
   (b) Even people who do not believe in God are more likely to behave honestly after reading the Ten Commandments.
   (c) Most people are accurate when comparing themselves to others.
   (d) People make their best ethical decisions when in a hurry.

CASE QUESTIONS

1. Senate investigators found that executives at JPMorgan Chase lied to investors and the public. Also, traders, acting with the knowledge of top management, changed risk limits to facilitate more trading and then violated even these higher limits. Executives revalued the bank's investment portfolio to reduce apparent losses. The bank's internal investigation failed to find this wrongdoing. Into what ethics traps did these JPMorgan employees fall? What options did the executives and traders have for dealing with this wrongdoing?

2. Located in Bath, Maine, Bath Iron Works builds high-tech warships for the Navy. Winning Navy contracts is crucial to the company's success—it means jobs for the community and profits for the shareholders. Navy officials held a meeting at Bath's offices with its executives and those of a competitor to review the specs for an upcoming bid. Both companies desperately wanted to win the contract. After the meeting, a Bath worker realized that one of the Navy officials had left a folder labeled "Business Sensitive" on a chair. It contained information about the competitor's bid that would be a huge advantage to Bath. William Haggett, the Bath CEO, was notified about the file just as he was walking out the door to give a luncheon speech. What ethics traps did he face? How could he avoid these traps? What would result if he considered Mill, Kant, or the Front Page test? What should he do? How would you give voice to your values in this situation?

3. A group of medical schools conducted a study on very premature babies—those born between 24 and 27 weeks of gestation (instead of the normal 40 weeks). These children face a high risk of blindness and death. The goal of the study was to determine which level of oxygen in a baby's incubator produced the best results. Researchers did not tell the families that being in the study could *increase* their child's risk of blindness or death. The study made some important discoveries about the best oxygen level. These results will benefit many children. What would Mill and Kant say about this decision *not* to tell the families?

4. Each year, the sale of Girl Scout cookies is the major fund-raiser for local troops. But because the organization was criticized for promoting such unhealthy food, it introduced a new cookie, Mango Cremes with Nutrifusion. It promoted this cookie as a vitamin-laden, natural whole food: "A delicious way to get your vitamins." But

these vitamins were a minuscule part of the cookie. The rest had more unhealthy fat than an Oreo. The Girl Scouts do much good for many girls. And to do this good, they need to raise money. What would Kant and Mill say about Mango Cremes? What about the Front Page test? What do you say?

5. The CEO of Volkswagen set an ambitious goal: to triple sales in the United States and become the largest car manufacturer in the world. Employees listened carefully because the CEO had a reputation for punishing those who did not make their goals. Then the VW engineers realized that the emissions equipment on the company's cars could not meet tough U.S. standards. Fixing the equipment would take time, raise costs, and reduce sales. The engineers believed that other car companies had the same problem. Instead of fixing the equipment, an engineer figured out how to install software that would cheat on the emissions tests. Engineers predicted that the chance of being discovered was low, and executives thought the cost of being caught would be manageable. (Indeed, the company continued on its cheating ways, even after it knew that regulators were investigating.) VW produced 11 million cars with this deceptive software. After the company was caught, it spent $18 billion on fines, legal costs, and car repairs. Its sales and stock price plummeted, and it faced criminal investigations.[43] Into what traps did these VW employees fall?

DISCUSSION QUESTIONS

1. Darby has been working for 14 months at Holden Associates, a large management consulting firm. She is earning $95,000 a year, which *sounds* good but does not go very far in New York City. It turns out that her peers at competing firms are typically paid 20 percent more and receive larger annual bonuses. Darby works about 60 hours a week—more if she is traveling. A number of times, she has had to reschedule her vacation or cancel personal plans to meet client deadlines.

   Holden has a policy that permits any employee who works as late as 8:00 p.m. to eat dinner at the company's expense. The employee can also take Uber home. Darby is in the habit of staying until 8:00 p.m. every night, whether or not her workload requires it. She then orders enough food for dinner, with leftovers for lunch the next day. She has managed to cut her grocery bill to virtually nothing. Sometimes she invites her boyfriend to join her for dinner. As a student, he is always hungry and broke. Darby often uses the Holden Uber account to charge a ride back to his apartment, although the cost is twice as high as to her own place.

   Darby has also been known to return online purchases through the Holden mailroom on the company dime. Many employees do that, and the mailroom workers do not seem to mind.

   Is Darby doing anything wrong? What ethics traps is she facing? What would your Life Principle be in this situation?

[43] Jack Ewing, "VW Presentation in '06 Showed How to Foil Emissions Tests," *The New York Times*, April 26, 2016.

2. Steve supervises a team of account managers. One night at a company outing, Lawrence, a visiting account manager, made some wildly inappropriate sexual remarks to Maddie, who is on Steve's team. When she told Steve, he was uncertain what to do, so he asked his boss. She was concerned that if Steve took the matter further, and Lawrence was fired or even disciplined, her whole area would suffer. Lawrence was one of the best account managers in the region, and everyone was overworked as it was. She told Steve to get Maddie to drop the matter. Just tell her that these things happen, and Lawrence did not mean anything by it.

   What should Steve do? What ethics traps does he face? What would be your Life Principle in this situation? What should Maddie do?

3. Many people enjoy rap music, at least in part, because of its edgy, troublemaking vibe. The problem is that some of this music could cause real trouble. Thus, Ice-T's song "Cop Killer" generated significant controversy when it was released. Among other things, its lyrics celebrated the idea of slitting a police officer's throat. Rick Ross rapped about drugging and raping a woman. Time Warner Inc. did not withdraw Ice-T's song, but Reebok fired Ross over his lyrics. One difference: Time Warner was struggling with a $15 billion debt and a depressed stock price. Reebok, at first, refused to take action, but then singing group UltraViolet began circulating an online petition against the song and staged a protest at the main Reebok store in New York.

   What obligation do companies have to their customers? What factors matter when making a decision about the content of entertainment?

4. You are negotiating a new labor contract with union officials. The contract covers a plant that has experienced operating losses over the past several years. You want to negotiate concessions from labor to reduce the losses. However, labor is refusing any compromises. You could tell them that, without concessions, the plant will be closed, although that is not true.

   Is bluffing ethical? Under what circumstances? What would Kant and Mill say? What is the result under the Front Page test? What is your Life Principle?

5. Craig Newmark founded craigslist, the most popular website in the country for classified ads. Rather than maximizing its profits, craigslist instead focused on developing a community among its users. It was a place to find an apartment, a pet, a job, a couch, a date, a babysitter, and, it turned out, a prostitute. Most of the ads on craigslist were free, but blatant ads for sex were not.

   Much of the company's revenue was from these illegal services. Many of the prostitutes available on craigslist were not independent entrepreneurs; they were women and girls bought and sold against their will. To fight sex trafficking, craigs-list required credit cards and phone numbers, and it reported any suspicious ads. Law enforcement officials pressured craigslist to close the sex section of its website.

   Some people argued that blocking these ads was a violation of free speech and would just drive this business more underground where law enforcement officials were less likely to be able to find it. Others said that banning these ads made the business model of selling children for sex less profitable. Does it seem that trafficking women and children was in keeping with the founder's Life Principles? What were his options? Could he have had any real impact on this thriving industry? What traps did he face?

6. Many socially responsible funds are now available to investors who factor their values into their investment choices. For example, the Appleseed Fund avoids tobacco products, alcoholic beverages, gambling, weapons systems, and pornography. The TIAA-CREF Social Choice Equity Premier Fund invests in companies that are "strong stewards of the environment," devoted to serving local communities, and committed to high labor standards. Are socially responsible funds attractive to you? Would it matter if they were less profitable than other alternatives? How much less profitable? Do you now, or will you in the future, use them in saving for your own retirement?

7. What percentage of your income should you donate to charities? Which charities are most worthwhile? Peter Singer, a Princeton professor, argues that people should give away one-third of their income to worthy charities. But, when entertainment mogul David Geffen donated $100 million to renovate a New York concert hall, Singer said that he could not understand "how anyone could think that giving to the renovation of a concert hall that could impact the lives of generally well-off people living in Manhattan and well-off tourists that come to New York could be the best thing that you could do with $100 million."[44] He added that a donation of less than $100 could restore sight to someone who is blind. To what theory of ethics is Professor Singer subscribing? Do you agree with him? What obligation do you have to help others? What is the best way to help others?

8. I was working on a trading desk. One year, my team did not make its number, which meant no bonuses and maybe even some of us would be fired. My boss was a good friend of the head of our division so the head agreed to "reallocate" some of the profit from other teams to ours. So my team got a bonus. When I asked my boss about the ethics of this action, she was annoyed that I was not just grateful. What ethics traps did I face? What should I have done? What is the best way to implement my decision?

9. I was a plant manager at a factory that used a lot of steel equipment. When a piece of equipment failed and was not worth repairing, it was sold for scrap. Plant managers usually kept the scrap money for themselves without telling headquarters. That money was considered an unofficial bonus. (After all, the equipment was no longer functional, and plant managers are underpaid.) I felt a little uncomfortable taking the money, but my boss warned me that, if I didn't, I would make the other plant managers look bad. I could have paid off my credit card debt with that money but, instead, I hosted an employee BBQ and bought work boots for the low-wage workers. Did I do the right thing? What traps did I face?

44Alexandra Wolfe, "Peter Singer on the Ethics of Philanthropy," *The Wall Street Journal*, April 3, 2015.

CHAPTER 3

INTERNATIONAL LAW

During periods of war and insecurity, international laws are hotly contested. The following is an excerpt of an unsigned letter published in the *London Times* during an uncertain time—the American Civil War. It puts great pressure on the authors of this book—and on any student of international law.

They affect the misery or the happiness of whole generations of mankind.

> The text-writer on international law assumes a noble task, but he at the same time accepts a grave responsibility. His speculations, if unsound, must too often be refuted by the sword. They deal out the lots of peace and of war; they affect the destinies of nations and determine the misery or the happiness of whole generations of mankind.
>
> Nevertheless, on most questions of international law, the student has to make for himself his own textbook; to extract from scattered documents the records of historical precedents; to deduce from judicial decisions the principles of established law.
>
> It is from these difficulties that ill-informed and shallow reasoners have question[ed] the existence of international law. Yet this idea is about as reasonable as if a man who had neither the instruments nor the knowledge requisite to take an observation, should dispute the possibility of a science of astronomy.[1]

[1] Excerpts from the Preamble to *Letters by Historicus on Some Questions of International Law* (London: Macmillan & Co. 1863), v–viii.

Many people throughout the ages have asked this basic question: What is international law? In Chapter 1, we learned that the law is a system of rules that predictably regulates our behavior. It secures our rights and balances government power. For any legal system to thrive, it must have clear rules, shared values, and a system of enforcement that its subjects acknowledge and respect.

International law is different. It has no single source of law or enforcement mechanism. It is a hodgepodge of different actors, legal systems, and cultures. For this reason, as the mysterious letter writer noted, some people have wondered whether international law exists at all. But it *does* exist, and is important to study, because our globalized world is more and more dependent on it each day. And luckily, you do not have to make your own textbook.

3-1 INTERNATIONAL LAW: PUBLIC AND PRIVATE

International law covers a wide array of topics relevant to, well, everything and everyone in the world. **It consists of rules and principles that apply to the conduct of states,[2] international organizations, businesses, and individuals across borders.** It is important to distinguish between two branches of international law: public and private.

Public international law
Rules and norms governing relationships among states and international organizations

Public international law is the law governing relations among governments and international organizations. It includes the law of war (yes, we have to fight fair), the acquisition of territory, and the settlement of disputes among nations. Public international law also has rules governing the globe's shared resources and common elements: the sea, outer space, trade, and communications. Finally, it addresses people: Public international law sets out the basic rules of human rights and laws defining the treatment of refugees, prisoners of war, and international criminals.

Private international law
International rules and standards applying to cross-border commerce

Private international law applies to private parties (such as businesses and individuals) in international commercial and legal transactions. It deals with two fundamental issues: Which law applies to a private agreement? How will people from one country settle their private disputes with parties on foreign soil?

Private international law is highly influenced by treaties and other sources of public international law. Because this is a business law text, we will focus on private international law and those areas of public international law that affect business.

3-2 ACTORS IN INTERNATIONAL LAW

Because international law must balance the interests and roles of many different people, organizations, and states, there are many significant actors. The United Nations is one of the most important.

3-2a The United Nations

After World Wars I and II, people and governments around the world were intent on preventing future conflict. They sought the creation of a supranational organization that could ensure international peace and security, encourage economic and social cooperation, and protect human rights. So, in 1945, 50 nations signed the Charter of the United Nations,

[2] Throughout the chapter, the authors use "state" to have the same meaning as "country" and "nation."

binding themselves to its terms and obligations. Today, 193 countries are members of the United Nations (UN).

The UN Charter sets out the organization's governance:

- The **Secretariat**, headed by the Secretary General, administers the day-to-day operations of the UN.
- The **General Assembly** is the UN's lawmaking body. It is composed of all of its member nations, which propose and vote on resolutions.
- The **Security Council** is charged with maintaining international peace. It has 15 member nations. Ten are elected by the General Assembly; five are permanent members: China, France, Russia, the United Kingdom, and the United States. The five permanent members were the primary victors in World War II. They have the right to veto any Security Council resolution.

Much of the UN's work is done through its Specialized Agencies and related organizations, including influential agencies like the International Labor Organization (ILO), the World Health Organization (WHO), and the UN Educational, Scientific, and Cultural Organization (UNESCO).

The following agencies, which operate under the UN's umbrella, have great impact on world business:

- The **World Bank's** mandate is to end poverty by encouraging development. Among other activities, it loans money to the poorest countries on favorable terms.
- The **International Monetary Fund** (IMF) aims to foster worldwide economic growth and financial stability.
- The **World Intellectual Property Organization** (WIPO) was established to promote the protection of intellectual property: patents, copyrights, trademarks, and industrial design. The organization also has a system for domain name dispute resolution, to which private parties often resort when challenging the illicit international use of domain names.
- The **UN Commission on International Trade Law** (UNCITRAL) aims to harmonize international business law by proposing model legislation on such topics as international payments and e-commerce. This agency was responsible for putting forth the UN Convention for the International Sale of Goods (CISG) and the Convention on the Recognition and Enforcement of Foreign Arbitral Awards (New York Convention), both significant business-related treaties discussed later in this chapter.

International Court of Justice (ICJ)
The judicial branch of the United Nations

3-2b The International Court of Justice

In 1946, the UN opened the doors of the **International Court of Justice (ICJ)**. Also known as the World Court, the ICJ settles international legal disputes and gives advisory opinions to the UN and its agencies. It is comprised of 15 elected judges from 15 countries representing the world's principal legal systems.

Rob Keeris/AFP/Getty Images

The World Court Sits in the Hague, Netherlands.

EXHIBIT 3.1

The Basic Structure of the UN

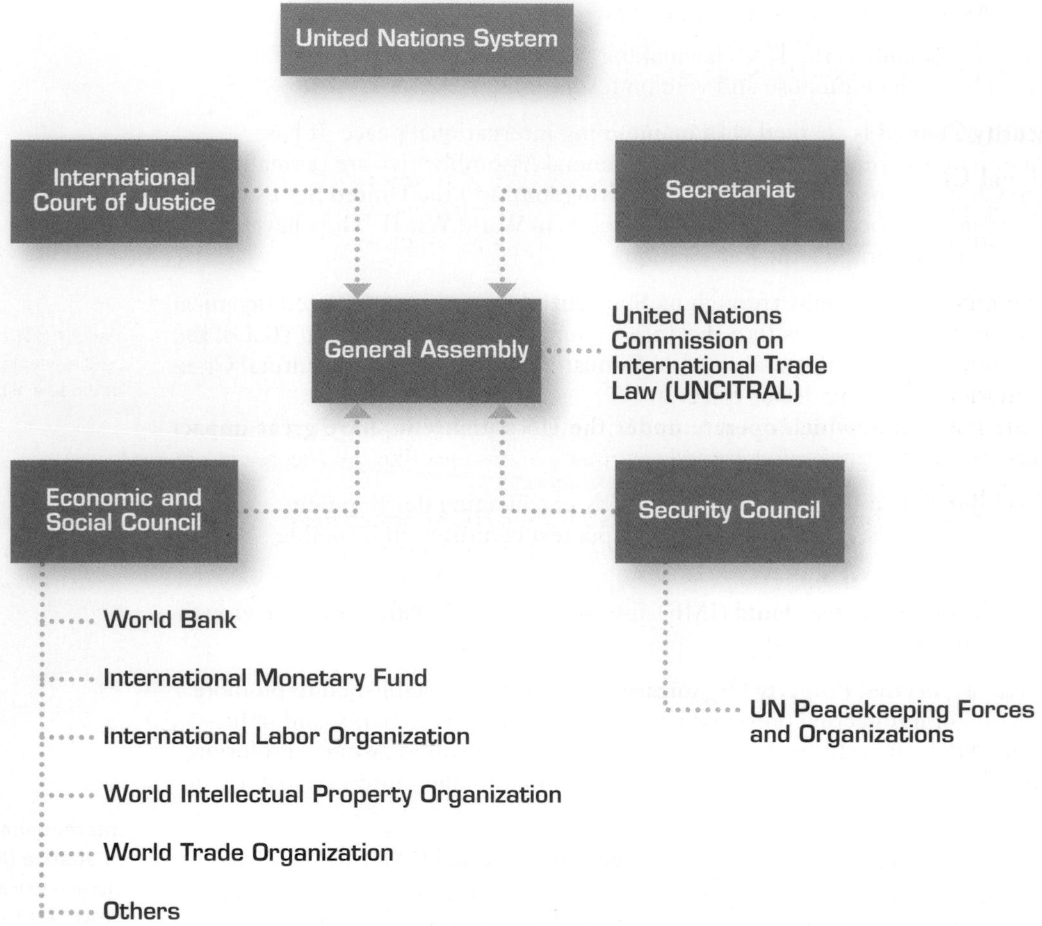

In its seven-decade history, the court has heard fewer than 200 cases. The ICJ has not been an important force in resolving international business disputes for several reasons:

- **Only states can be a party to litigation before the ICJ.** To have their day in court, individuals and businesses must persuade their country to initiate a case on their behalf. Most states are reluctant to bring business associated with cases on behalf of their citizens because of the political and financial costs that may result from suing another country.
- **The ICJ only has jurisdiction over states that have agreed to be bound by its decisions.** The United States had accepted the ICJ's authority—until it lost a case. When the ICJ determined that the United States violated international law by secretly supporting Nicaraguan rebels, it simply withdrew from ICJ jurisdiction.[3] Today the United States agrees to ICJ jurisdiction on a case-by-case basis.

[3]Case Concerning Military and Paramilitary Activities in and Against Nicaragua (Nicaragua v. United States of America), 1986 I.C.J. 14 (June 27).

- **The court has no enforcement power.** Mexico accused the United States of breaching its treaty obligations by failing to notify its consulate when American police arrested Mexican citizens on U.S. soil. Fifty-four Mexican nationals on death row in the United States had been denied their right to consult with the local Mexican consulate. The ICJ agreed with Mexico and ordered the United States to reconsider the death sentences in these cases.[4] But the U.S. Supreme Court held that in this situation domestic law trumped treaty obligations—and that the United States was free to disobey the ICJ.[5]

3-2c International Chamber of Commerce

The International Chamber of Commerce (ICC) is the world's largest global business organization. Its purpose is to facilitate international business. To that end, the ICC advocates on matters of international business policy and develops uniform rules to aid cross-border transactions.

In 1936, the organization first proposed the **Incoterms rules**, which define a series of three-letter codes commonly used in international contracts for the sale of goods. No matter what language contracting parties speak, it is known that Incoterm "FOB" means the buyer pays for transportation of the purchased goods. ("FOB" stands for "free on board.")

Incoterms rules
A series of three-letter codes used in international contracts for the sale of goods

Note that the ICC does not make law. Instead, it proposes rules whose adoption is voluntary. However, its influence is so widespread that many of its rules like the Incoterms are now accepted as the global standard in international business.

The ICC also runs the **International Court of Arbitration (ICA)**, which hears over half of the world's private commercial disputes. Contracting parties seeking a politically neutral forum for arbitration agree to submit their claims to the ICA, usually when they sign their contracts. The ICA's decision, also called an award, can be enforced by domestic courts in more than 145 countries around world, including the United States.

International Court of Arbitration (ICA)
A forum for international dispute resolution, run by the ICC

3-2d Sovereign Nations

Last but certainly not least, we cannot discount the role that countries themselves play in international law. They are its most important and influential actors.

In ancient times, when kings were seen as gods, it was well-established that no "god" could interfere in the internal affairs of another. Out of this idea grew the fundamental principle of international law: **sovereignty**, which means that each government has the absolute authority to rule its people and its territory. Under this principle, states are prohibited from interfering in each other's legislative, administrative, or judicial activities.

Sovereign Immunity

Sovereign immunity holds that the courts of one nation lack the jurisdiction (power) to hear suits against foreign governments. Most nations respect this principle. In the United States, the **Foreign Sovereign Immunities Act (FSIA)** provides that American courts generally cannot hear suits against foreign governments. This is a difficult hurdle to overcome, but there are three possible exceptions.

Foreign Sovereign Immunities Act (FSIA)
A U.S. statute that provides that American courts generally cannot entertain suits against foreign governments

Waiver. A lawsuit is permitted against a foreign country that waives its immunity, that is, voluntarily gives up this protection. Suppose the Czech government wishes to buy fighter planes from an American manufacturer. If the manufacturer insists on a waiver in the sales contract, the Czech Republic might be willing to grant one to get the weapons it desires. If the planes land safely but the checks bounce, the manufacturer has the right to sue.

Commercial Activity. A plaintiff in the United States can sue a foreign country engaged in commercial, but not political, activity. If a business can engage in the activity, it is considered

---

[4]Avena and Other Mexican Nationals (Mexico v. United States of America), 2004 I.C.J. 12 (Mar. 31).
[5]Medellin v. Texas, 552 U.S. 491 (2008).

to be commercial. If, however, the foreign government is doing something that only a government has the power to do (e.g., printing money, making laws), it is a state activity and the country is immune from litigation.

Suppose the government of Iceland hires an American consulting firm to help its fishermen replenish depleted fishing grounds. Because fishing is a for-profit activity, the contract is commercial, and if Iceland refuses to pay, the company may sue in American courts.

Violation of International Law. **A plaintiff in this country may sue a foreign government that has confiscated property in violation of international law**, provided that the property either ends up in the United States or is involved in commercial activity that affects someone in the United States. Suppose a foreign government, acting in violation of international law, confiscates a visiting American ship, and begins to use it for shipping goods for profit. Later, the ship carries some American produce. The taking was illegal, and it now affects American commerce. The original owner may sue.

EXAMStrategy

Question: Fabric World, a U.S. company, owns and operates a textile factory in the country of Parador. After a political revolution, the new government seizes the factory and refuses to pay for it. It also sells bonds to investors in the United States to raise money to fund government operations and then defaults on their payment. Both Fabric World and the bond investors sue Parador in New York, where it has some large bank accounts. Parador denies liability in both lawsuits, claiming "sovereign immunity." Will this argument succeed in either case?

Strategy: Examine the nature of the government's activities: Did it waive sovereign immunity? Are its activities commercial?

Result: Parador has never waived sovereign immunity. In the *Fabric World* case, the government enacted new laws that expropriated private property. This is an act of state—not something a business or private citizen could ever do—and so Parador retains immunity. In the case of the bonds, the investors win because the country is engaged in a commercial activity.

3-3 THE WORLD'S LEGAL SYSTEMS

In Chapter 1, we began to explore the origins of our Anglo-American legal tradition. But it is important for every international businessperson to recognize that the great majority—roughly 84 percent—of the world is governed by legal systems that take a very different approach from our own.

3-3a Common Law

As discussed in Chapter 1, we inherited our legal system from England. The United States shares this legacy with most former British colonies, including Australia, Canada, and India.

The hallmarks of common law are:

- The use of an adversarial process of dispute resolution presided over by an impartial judge. After the Norman conquest of England, William the Conqueror introduced trial by combat to settle disputes: The winner of the battle was right.
- This practice formed the basis of the common law's assumption that the role of lawyers is to battle on behalf of the client by making the most persuasive arguments.

- The doctrine of ***stare decisis***, which requires judges to base their decisions on prior cases.[6]
- The use of a jury to determine questions of fact.

Stare decisis
The principle that legal conclusions must be reached after an analysis of past judgments

3-3b Civil Law

More than 70 percent of the world's population is subject to civil law, including most European countries, Russia, Central and South America, China, large swaths of Asia, and parts of Africa.[7] Exhibit 3.2 shows the legal systems used throughout the world. You may be asking: How did Mexico end up with the same legal methodology as Germany?

EXHIBIT 3.2

Legal Systems throughout the World

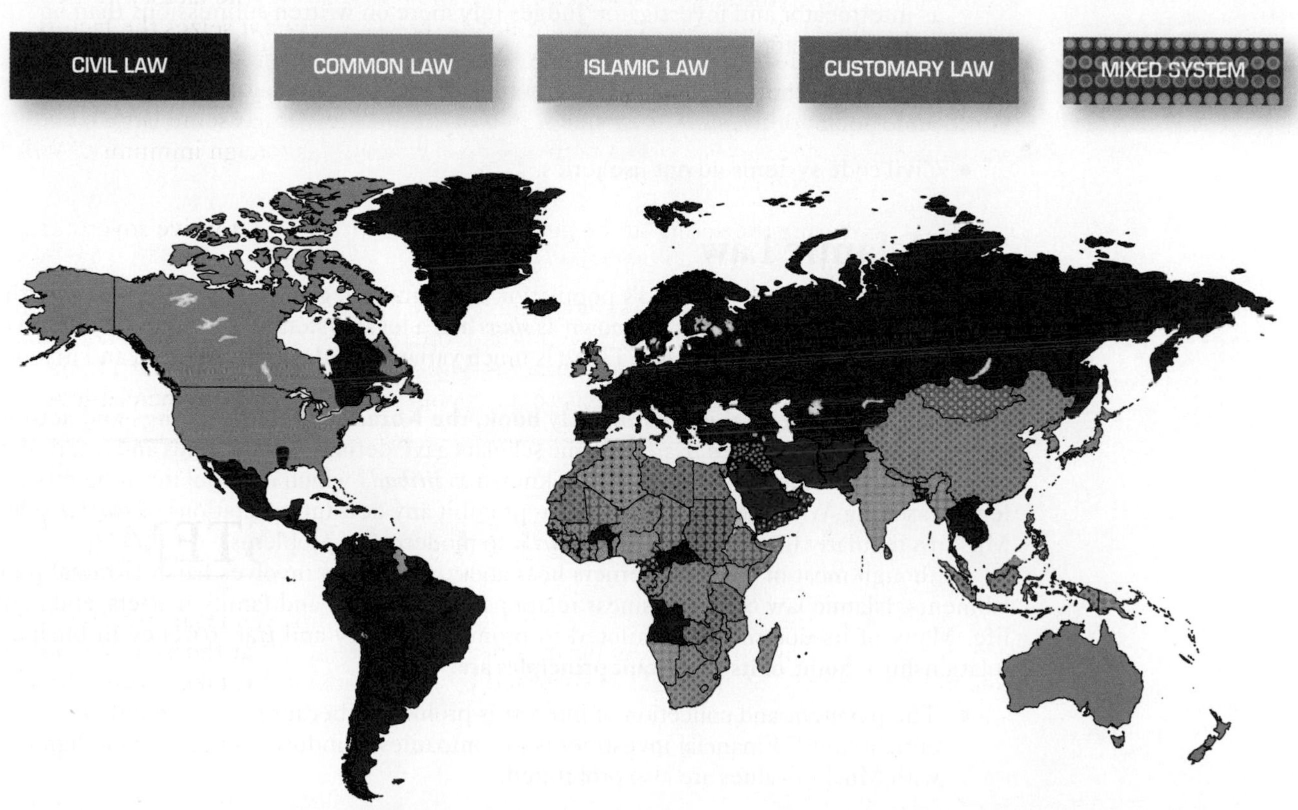

Source: http://www.juriglobe.ca/eng/; http://outsourceportfolio.com/mexicos-potential-nearshore-servicesoutsourcing-leader/; and http://chartsbin.com/view/aq2

[6] *Stare decisis* is Latin for "to let the decision stand."

[7] Note that "civil law," as referred to in this chapter, is a legal system based on codes (i.e., civil law versus common law systems). In common law systems, such as ours, the same term is also used to describe contract, tort, and other areas of private law (i.e., civil law versus criminal law).

The civil code tradition grew out of Roman Emperor Justinian's *Corpus Juris Civilis* in the sixth century. To solidify his power, Justinian set out to organize and record Roman laws. A widespread empire demanded uniform laws—and their uniform application—so **the main principle of civil law is that the law is found primarily in the statute books, or codes**.

Centuries later, European legal scholars unearthed Justinian's code and spread its methodology to continental Europe—Germany, Italy, France, Spain, and Portugal. Under the Emperor Napoleon, the French adopted the code system, but infused it with its own ideals and values, resulting in the Napoleonic Code. Other countries similarly developed their own versions of the code before exporting them to most of the world through conquest (including Louisiana, where the Napoleonic Code is still the basis for that state's laws).

Statute-based systems also have a clear appeal to countries whose political systems demand strong central authority rather than a focus on individual rights. China and Russia both have code-based systems overlaid with socialist law.

The main characteristics of the civil code tradition are:

- The use of an inquisitorial process of dispute resolution, in which the judge acts as interrogator and investigator. Judges rely more on written submissions than on lawyers' oral arguments.
- Courts base their judgments on the code, and statutes, and on the writings of law professors.
- Civil code systems do not use juries.

3-3c Islamic Law

More than one-fifth of the world's population lives under legal systems influenced by the religion of Islam. Islamic law, also known as ***shari'a***, is a legal system most commonly found in Africa, Asia, and the Middle East.[8] There is much variation in the interpretation and practice of both Islam and Islamic law.

Shari'a* is based on the Muslim holy book, the Koran, and the teachings and actions of the Prophet Muhammed.** Early Islamic scholars gave definitive guidelines and interpretations on *shari'a* using a reasoning process known as ***ijtihad,[9] which incorporates religious and legal reasoning. While some Islamic groups prohibit any new interpretations of *shari'a*, other Muslims regularly use *ijtihad* to adapt *shari'a* to modern-day problems.

Although most of what Westerners hear about *shari'a* law involves harsh criminal punishments, Islamic law covers business relationships, personal and family matters, and daily life. Many of its doctrines are tailored to promote honesty and transparency in business relationships. **Some of its important principles are:**

- The payment and collection of interest is prohibited because it causes unfair enrichment.[10] Financial investments in companies or industries that do not align with Muslim values are also prohibited.
- The concept of ***gharar***[11] prohibits any contract gain that is not clearly outlined at the time of contract, especially when it involves risk and deception.

Gharar
The Islamic prohibition on risk and deception

8 *Shari'a* means "path" in Arabic.

9 *Ijtihad* is Arabic for "independent reasoning" or "effort."

10 McKesson Corp. v. Islamic Republic of Iran, 672 F.3d 1066 (2012).

11 *Gharar* is Arabic for "deceptive uncertainty" and is the basis for other prohibitions in Islamic finance, such as risky deals whose outcome is unknown.

The following case may come as a surprise because most people do not realize that U.S. courts can apply foreign law to resolve disputes. The parties filed suit in a U.S. court, even though the dispute was governed by *shari'a* law.

Saudi Basic Industries Corporation v. Mobil Yanbu Petrochemical Company, Inc. and Exxon Chemical Arabia, Inc.

A.2d 1
Delaware Supreme Court, 2005

Facts: Saudi Basic Industries Corporation (SABIC) was a Saudi Arabian corporation owned by the Saudi government. In the 1970s, it entered into joint ventures with Mobil and Exxon, under contracts governed by Saudi law. The agreements forbade the participants from charging a "mark-up" on any products purchased for the joint venture, but SABIC violated this provision for two decades.

ExxonMobil and SABIC sued each other in federal court in Delaware for breach of contract and tort.[12] Because the Delaware court was required to apply Saudi law, the judge brought in notable experts in *shari'a* law for instruction.

The jury found SABIC liable for Saudi tort of usurpation (*ghasb*) and awarded ExxonMobil $416 million. SABIC appealed to the Delaware Supreme Court for a new trial, arguing that that the trial court's application of Saudi law was flawed.

Issue: ***Did the U.S. court err in its application of shari'a law?***

Excerpts from Justice Jacobs's Decision: In Saudi Arabia, Islamic law (*shari'a*), which is a fundamentally religious law based on both the Q'uran and the model behavior of the Prophet Muhammed, is the law of the land. Although early Islamic law scholars eventually coalesced into various guilds or schools, only four of those guilds have survived in modern times: the *Hanbali*, the *Hanafi*, the *Shafi'i* and the *Maliki*. In Saudi Arabia, the judges are instructed to rule exclusively in accordance with the teachings of the *Hanbali* guild.

The Saudi law system differs in critically important respects from the system of legal thought employed by the common law countries, including the United States. Perhaps most significant is that Islamic law does not embrace the common-law system of binding precedent and *stare decisis*. Indeed, in Saudi Arabia, judicial decisions are not in themselves a source of law, and with minor exceptions, court decisions in Saudi Arabia are not published or even open to public inspection. The trial judge was keenly mindful of this distinctive characteristic of Saudi law.

Instead of relying upon statutes or decisional precedent to discern the law applicable to a particular case, judges in Saudi Arabia must "first and last navigate within the boundaries" of the Hanbali school's authoritative works, which are the scholarly treatises. Using these writings as guides, Saudi judges identify a spectrum of possibilities on any given question, rather than a single 'correct' answer.

Thus, in this highly different legal environment, the predominate factor in determining the Saudi law on a given issue is the study and analysis, or *ijtihad*, that a judge brings to bear in each particular case. To state it in different terms, the critical inquiry is whether the proper analytical procedures are followed in reaching the results.

The judge made exceptional efforts to ensure that she was fully informed of the Hanbali teachings. Before trial, the parties presented [her] with seven reports from four Saudi law experts. [She also] retained an independent expert, who conduct[ed] additional research in Saudi Arabia. After reviewing a total of nine reports and over one thousand pages of testimony, the judge then held a day-long pretrial hearing, to [hear] live testimony from [the experts]. Only after this extensive process did the trial court undertake to determine the disputed elements of *ghasb*.

It is remarkable that SABIC, having [purposefully] selected this forum instead of a Saudi Court, knowing the United States legal system is dramatically different than the Saudi legal system, comes forward after a verdict against it to claim that no American judge is qualified to interpret and apply Saudi law. This is particularly incredible in light of SABIC's vehement argument that this case should be tried by a U.S. judge.

For the foregoing reasons, the judgment of the Superior Court awarding damages to ExxonMobil is affirmed.

[12] Exxon and Mobil entered into separate contracts with SABIC, but by the time of this lawsuit had merged to form one company named ExxonMobil.

As we see from this case, the world—and the law—is increasingly internationalized. Greater interaction among societies has led to convergence among some legal traditions. In particular, common law and civil law systems have borrowed significant concepts from each other:

- Common law countries exhibit a trend toward codification. In the United States, many laws, notably in intellectual property, bankruptcy, banking, securities, and tax, are statute-based. The Uniform Commercial Code (UCC) now applies to contracts for the sale of goods in the United States, an area of law previously governed only by common law.
- Civil law countries have begun to take precedents into account. One study found that German courts followed precedent in all but 12 out of 4,000 decisions.[13] Spain has enacted laws making the rulings of higher courts binding on lower courts.[14]

3-4 SOURCES AND APPLICABILITY OF INTERNATIONAL LAW

3-4a Sources of International Law

This section outlines the three major sources of international law: treaties, custom, and general principles of law.

Treaties

Treaty
An agreement between two or more states that is governed by international law

Recall from Chapter 1 that the president makes treaties with foreign nations. According to the Vienna Convention on the Law of Treaties, a **treaty** is an international agreement governed by international law. Since treaties have their own treaty, they also have their own vocabulary:

- A **bilateral treaty** is between two countries—similar to a contract between states. The United States and the Bahamas have a bilateral **extradition** treaty, outlining the process that each country must follow when returning a fugitive to another country's legal system. A **multilateral treaty** involves three or more countries.
- A **convention** is a treaty on a specific issue that affects all the participants, like the UN Convention on Contracts for the International Sale of Goods or the Vienna Convention on the Law of Treaties.
- A **protocol** is an amendment to a treaty. In 1891, a group of countries signed the Madrid Agreement, a treaty creating a registration system for trademarks. Almost 100 years later, the Madrid Protocol updated and strengthened the original treaty to create a uniform process for registering trademarks worldwide.
- A treaty is said to be **adopted** when those who have drafted it agree that it is in final form.
- A treaty is **ratified** when a nation indicates its intent to be bound by it. **To take effect in the United States, treaties must be approved by at least two-thirds of the Senate.**
- A treaty **enters into force** when it becomes legally binding on its signatories. This date may be specified in the treaty or it may be the date on which the treaty receives a certain number of ratifications.

This section examines treaties that are critical to international business.

---

13 T. Lundmark, '*Stare decisis in der Rechtssprechung des Bundesverfassungsgerichts*.' Rechtstheorie (1999).
14 Ley Orgánica 6/1985, de 1 de julio, del Poder Judicial §5.1.

GATT. GATT is the General Agreement on Tariffs and Trade. Any discussion of international trade issues must begin with free trade, which has been a contentious issue since David Ricardo first advocated it in the early nineteenth century. He, and economists since, have argued that citizens of the world will benefit overall if each country produces whatever goods it can make most efficiently and then trades them for goods that other countries make more efficiently. Thus, a developing country with unskilled labor should produce clothing and then trade it to the United States for commercial aircraft and semiconductors (two major categories of U.S. exports).

Such a plan makes great economic sense, unless you happen to work in the clothing industry in the United States (or one of the other manufacturing industries adversely affected by free trade). While, in theory, American workers should be retrained to work in more highly-skilled fields, in reality, repurposing human beings (who all have different preferences and abilities) has proven to be easier said than done. Many workers whose jobs have been outsourced to low-wage countries feel abandoned and discouraged.

Thus, countries are often tempted to impose protectionist tariffs and quotas on imports to shield local industries and workers. When David Ricardo was writing, England had recently passed the Corn Laws, which restricted the importation of wheat. These laws caused higher food prices in England, but helped maintain the value of farmland and the wages of farmworkers.

Ethics

In Ricardo's time, the Corn Laws protected the wealth of the British aristocracy, who owned most of the land in England. Today, in the United States, workers without a college degree are the people most harmed by free trade. In deciding whether to adopt protectionist policies, does it matter who benefits? Should a decision be based on a cost benefit analysis for society as a whole or for particular groups within society?

A reduction in free trade will lead to higher consumer prices. How much more would you be willing to pay for cars or clothes made in the United States, employing American workers? What is your limit?

GATT is a massive international treaty that has been negotiated on and off since the 1940s as nations have sought to eliminate trade barriers and bolster commerce. To strengthen this treaty, GATT signatories created the **World Trade Organization (WTO)** in 1995. Its mandate is to stimulate international commerce and resolve trade disputes.

World Trade Organization (WTO)
An international organization whose mandate is to lower trade barriers

GATT and the WTO are founded on the following principles:

- **Free Trade.** The major focus of this treaty is to reduce trade barriers.
- **Most Favored Nation.** Although it sounds like a requirement to give someone special treatment, "**most favored nation**" means that countries must treat every other country equally. If Brazil grants Australia a special discount on customs duties for certain products, that treatment must be extended to all other WTO members.
- **National Treatment.** After imported products have entered the country, they must be treated the same as locally produced goods. In other words, countries may not discriminate against foreign goods by imposing additional sales taxes, requirements, or standards that do not apply to domestic goods. Japan taxed imported vodka seven times higher than its own domestic version, *shochu*, even though both were distilled similarly. Because this tax violated national treatment provisions, the WTO required that Japan revise its laws.

Most favored nation
WTO/GATT requires that favors offered to one country must be given to all member nations.

National treatment
The principle of nondiscrimination between foreigners and locals

John S Lander/Getty Images

The WTO found that shochu was like vodka and had to be taxed similarly.

The WTO tries to promote free trade by limiting countries' efforts to unfairly protect their domestic industries. **Among the techniques that countries use (and the WTO tries to limit) are:**

- **Customs duties:** taxes imposed on goods when they enter a country
- **Excise taxes:** taxes levied on a particular activity, such as the purchase of wine or cigarettes
- **Nontariff barriers:** such as quotas on the amount of a particular good that can be imported

The WTO is empowered to settle trade disputes between its member states. It may order compliance and impose penalties in the form of trade sanctions. Suppose that the United States believes that Brazil is unfairly restricting trade. Via the WTO, the United States can request a consultation with Brazil's trade representative. In the majority of cases, these discussions lead to a satisfactory settlement. If the consultation does not resolve the problem, the United States asks the WTO's Dispute Settlement Body (DSB) to form a panel, which consists of three nations uninvolved in the dispute. After the panel hears testimony and arguments from both countries, it prepares a report. The DSB generally approves this report, unless either nation appeals. If there is an appeal, the WTO Appellate Body hears the dispute and generally makes the final decision, subject to approval by the entire WTO. No single nation has the power to block final decisions.

If a country refuses to comply with the WTO's ruling, affected nations may retaliate by imposing punitive tariffs or other measures. The United States and four Central American countries filed a complaint with the WTO alleging that the European Union (EU) had placed unfair restrictions on the importation of bananas. The WTO agreed, and then granted the United States and Ecuador the right to impose sanctions on EU imports into their countries.

GATT has had a considerable impact. In 1947, the worldwide average tariff on industrial goods was about 40 percent. Now it is about 3 percent. Over the past six decades, the world's economy has grown explosively. Leading supporters of WTO/GATT suggest that lower tariffs have vastly increased world trade. The United States is one of the biggest beneficiaries because, for decades, this country has imposed lower duties than most other nations. A typical American family's annual income has increased due to the more vigorous domestic economy, and, at the same time, many goods are less expensive because they enter with low duties.

But opponents claim that the United States now competes against nations with unlimited pools of exploited labor. These countries dominate labor-intensive industries such as textiles, clothing, and manufacturing, and are steadily taking jobs from millions of American workers. Because domestic job losses come in low-end employment, those put out of work are precisely those least able to find a new job.

Ethics

Child labor is a wrenching issue. The practice exists to some degree in all countries and is common throughout the developing world. The International Labor Organization estimates that more than 144 million children under the age of 14 work—many of them in hazardous and otherwise deplorable conditions, in households, fields, mines, and factories.[15]

[15] Yacouba Diallo, Alex Etienne, and Farhad Mehran, *Global child labour trends 2008–2012*, International Programme on the Elimination of Child Labour, International Labour Office (2013).

Child labor raises compelling moral questions, but the solution is not always obvious. Historically, poor children have worked. Indeed, for many people and for many centuries, the point of having children was to create a supply of free labor to help support the family. In England in 1860, almost 40 percent of 14-year-old boys worked, and that was not just a few hours at Burger Box, but more likely 60 hours a week. That percentage is higher than in Africa or India today. Children in desperately poor families work because, for them, the choice is not work or school, it is work, starvation, or prostitution.

Congress passed a statute prohibiting the importation of goods created by forced or indentured child labor. Is this law an example of humane legislation or cultural imperialism dressed as a nontariff barrier? Should the voters of this country or the WTO decide the issue?

Regional Trade Agreements. **Regional trade agreements (RTAs)** reduce trade restrictions and promote common trade policies among member nations, who are located near each other. Today, RTAs cover more than half of international trade.

Regional trade agreements (RTAs)
Treaties that reduce trade restrictions and promote common policies among member nations

NAFTA. The **North American Free Trade Agreement (NAFTA)** is an RTA that has had a large impact on the United States. Signed by the United States, Canada, and Mexico in 1993, its principal goal was to eliminate almost all trade barriers among the three nations. This treaty has been controversial, for all the usual reasons.

North American Free Trade Agreement (NAFTA)
A treaty that reduced trade barriers among Canada, the United States, and Mexico

Trade between the three nations has increased enormously. Mexico now exports more goods to the United States than do Germany, Britain, and Korea combined. Opponents of the treaty argue that NAFTA costs the United States jobs and lowers the living standards of American workers by forcing them to compete with low-paid labor. Swingline Staplers closed a factory in Queens, New York, after 75 years of operation and moved to Mexico. Instead of the $11.58 per hour that its American employees earned, Swingline can now pay Mexican workers 50 cents an hour to do the same job.

Proponents contend that although some jobs are lost, many others are gained, especially in fields with a promising future, such as high technology. They claim that, as new jobs invigorate the Mexican economy, consumers there will be able to afford certain categories of American goods for the first time, providing an enormous new market. Also, NAFTA provides American consumers with more, and cheaper, products.

GATS and TRIPS. The **General Agreement on Trade in Services**, or **GATS**, extends the WTO/GATT principles to transnational services. The **Agreement on Trade Related Aspects of Intellectual Property (TRIPS)** covers intellectual property (IP).[16] The WTO administers both treaties.

General Agreement on Trade in Services (GATS)
A treaty on transnational services

Agreement on Trade Related Aspects of Intellectual Property (TRIPS)
A treaty on intellectual property

Before TRIPS, many countries had dissimilar and confusing IP rules covering copyright, trademark, and patents: One country might grant a patent for 20 years, while another offered only 10. TRIPS has succeeded in harmonizing the international practice.

The following case is about a tiny country with big dreams of becoming a gambling giant. Without access to the U.S. market, it was just a pipe dream. But would the United States obey the WTO's ruling? Don't bet on it.

This issue has been in dispute for over a decade. In retaliation for U.S. noncompliance, the WTO authorized Antigua to sell up to $21 million worth of U.S. intellectual property without paying royalties.

16Annex 1C to the WTO Agreement.

United States—Measures Affecting the Cross-Border Supply of Gambling and Betting Services

WT/DS285/ARB
WTO Arbitral Body, 2007

Facts: Antigua is a small Caribbean nation. When it began hosting gambling websites, its economy thrived, boosted by U.S. gamblers. But when the United States started criminally prosecuting internet gambling, Antigua's profits plummeted. The United States had the right to take this step, but it had to do so consistently—treating foreign and domestic sites the same. The problem was that it allowed internet betting on horseracing within its borders.

Antigua challenged U.S. gambling laws in the WTO, arguing that they discriminated against foreign betting services. Both the United States and Antigua were members of GATS, under which each agree to free trade (including nondiscrimination and national treatment) in online services.

A WTO panel ruled that the United States' inconsistent gambling laws violated GATS and ordered that it bring them into compliance. Two years passed and the U.S. government did not act.

Frustrated, Antigua requested permission from the WTO to suspend its obligations to the United States under TRIPS. This suspension would mean that Antigua could freely use, reproduce, and distribute any U.S.-copyrighted, trademarked, or patented works—a real blow to the U.S. entertainment, pharmaceutical, and technology industries. The United States objected and submitted the matter to a panel of WTO experts.

Issue: ***When one WTO Member refuses to comply with a WTO ruling, can the injured Member retaliate by suspending its duties under another treaty?***

Excerpts from the WTO Arbitrator's Decision: Antigua considers it unconscionable for the United States to have done nothing to come into compliance in the time that it should have, and now requests to be authorized to suspend [its] obligations under the TRIPS Agreement.

Antigua, a developing country, is by far the smallest WTO Member to have made a request for the suspension of concessions and realizes the difficulty of providing effective countermeasures against the world's dominant economy.

When a complaining party wishes to seek suspension in another agreement than that in which a violation was found, it must prove that (1) it is not effective for it to suspend the same agreement and (2) that the circumstances are serious enough to suspend obligations under another agreement.

Antigua considers that suspension of obligations in [GATS] would most likely impair the already limited options available to Antiguan citizens while having virtually no impact on the United States at all. The trade disparity [between the countries] is so great that United States service providers would suffer little harm at all, if any, while Antiguan consumers would be forced to scramble for replacement services at uncertain cost. The volume of its imports from the United States in services is nowhere near sufficient to absorb the level of suspension of concessions that it is entitled to.

In order to demonstrate the seriousness of the circumstances, Antigua first presents some basic figures comparing the population, size, GDP, exports and imports of the United States and Antigua, which illustrate a considerable disparity in all of these areas.

Antigua also highlights that it has extremely limited natural resources and very limited arable land, such that it cannot produce sufficient agricultural products to satisfy domestic needs, let alone for export. Antigua further notes that its economy has become highly dependent on tourism and associated services. Third, Antigua highlights the need to diversify its economy, and that in order to do this it has tried to develop trade in services, including trade in remote gambling.

In our view, the various considerations highlighted by Antigua are such as to exacerbate the difficulties in finding a way to suspend obligations in an effective manner under the GATS.

Accordingly, we find that Antigua may seek to suspend obligations under the TRIPS Agreement.

EXAMStrategy

Question: To limit the number of cars on city streets, Shanghai, China, set up a system under which drivers could only acquire automobile license plates through a monthly auction. But Shanghai ran two different auctions: One for foreign-made cars, in which the government limited the number of license plates to 30 a month and set a high minimum bid, and another auction for Chinese cars, in which 3,000 license plates a month were available with no minimum bid. The United States complained that Shanghai's system had a direct effect on its imports. Is China in violation of WTO principles?

Strategy: As a signatory to the WTO, China committed to treating imported cars the same as its own domestic products. Does China have the right to impose these restrictions? Is traffic regulation a valid excuse?

Result: National treatment means that a WTO country cannot give special treatment or benefits to its own goods. Even though Shanghai may not have intended its rules to disrupt international trade, it did because the license auctions had a direct effect on the price of imported cars. Shanghai's rules violated WTO principles.

CISG. The **United Nations Convention on Contracts for the International Sale of Goods (CISG)** aims to make sales law more uniform and predictable—and to make international contracting easier. To that end, the treaty relaxes some of the formal rules found in contract law throughout the world, making it simpler for parties to form contracts and live by them. The United States and most of its principal trading partners (except for the United Kingdom) have adopted this important treaty, which governs over two-thirds of the world's trade.

The most important provisions are:

- **The CISG applies to contracts for the sale of commercial goods,** but not to consumer goods bought for personal use.
- **The CISG applies automatically when contracts are formed between two parties located in different signatory countries.** Note that the treaty's application does not depend on nationality, rather on location. Starbucks is a U.S. company with coffee shops in 62 countries. If the Starbucks store in Colombia contracts with a seller in Brazil, the CISG automatically applies because both Brazil and Colombia are members of the CISG. But if a Starbucks in England buys goods from a French seller, the CISG does not apply because, although France is a signatory, the United Kingdom is not.
- **Contracting parties can opt out.** If the parties want to be governed by other law, their contract must state very clearly that they exclude the CISG and elect, for example, French, Israeli, or any other country's law.
- **International sales contracts do not need to be in writing.** Unlike many nations' contract laws, the CISG does not require a writing to prove the existence of a contract. Parties can prove the terms of contracts by any means, including witnesses and their course of dealing.
- **Contracting parties must be flexible and fair.** The CISG requires parties to negotiate in good faith and modify the contract in case of unforeseen circumstances.
- **A buyer can avoid payment under a contract only after giving the seller notice and an opportunity to remedy.** As we will see in Unit 4 on sales, U.S. contract law excuses buyers from paying if the seller's performance is not absolutely perfect. The CISG is much less strict on sellers.

- **Countries may use their own national laws to (1) replace some CISG provisions or (2) fill in the blanks on issues that the CISG does not cover at all.** For example, the CISG does not provide rules for determining whether a contract is fraudulent: This substantive rule is left to the discretion of each country.

In the following case, each country had different contract rules and divergent interpretations of the CISG. The result? A huge mess, in any language. Which law applies?

Forestal Guarani S.A. v. Daros International, Inc.

613 F.3d 395
United States Court of Appeals for the Third Circuit, 2010

Facts: Forestal Guarani S.A., in Argentina, entered into an oral agreement to sell wooden finger joints to Daros International, Inc., in New Jersey.[17] Forestal sent Daros the products, but Daros declined to pay the full amount.

When Forestal sued Daros in the United States for breach of contract, Daros denied owing anything because, under New Jersey sales law, the contract would have had to be in writing to be enforceable. Further, it claimed, Argentina had not accepted the CISG's elimination of the writing requirement when it ratified the CISG. Since the contract was not in writing, it was also possible that Argentine law applied.

The district court dismissed Forestal's claim because the parties' agreement was not in writing. Forestal appealed.

Issue: ***Which law applied to this contract—the CISG, Argentine law, or New Jersey law?***

Excerpts from Judge Fisher's Decision: The CISG applies to contracts of sale of goods between parties whose places of business are in different States when the States are Contracting States. Because both the United States, where Daros is based, and Argentina, where Forestal is based, are signatories to the CISG and the alleged contract at issue involves the sale of goods, the CISG governs Forestal's claim.

The CISG dispenses with certain formalities associated with proving the existence of a contract. Specifically, a contract of sale need not be evidenced by writing and it may be proved by any means, including witnesses. [But the] elimination of formal writing requirements does not apply in all instances in which the CISG governs. A Contracting State whose legislation requires contracts of sale to be evidenced by writing may at any time make a declaration that [that rule] does not apply where any party has his place of business in that State. The United States has not made [such a] declaration. Argentina, however, has opted out of [this CISG rule].

There is no dispute here that Forestal's contract with Daros was verbal at best, so we could feasibly apply both New Jersey and Argentine law. In the end, we think it unwise to engage in a largely speculative exercise about the viability of Forestal's claim under either jurisdiction's law. Because these issues deserve a full airing, we conclude that remand is a better course of action.

Customary international law
International rules that have become binding through a pattern of consistent, long-standing behavior

Custom and General Principles of Law

For hundreds of years, until treaties became common, custom was the main way international law was created. A custom is a widely accepted way of doing something. Over time, patterns of states' behavior, action, and inaction crystallized into the compulsory rules of **customary international law**.

17A finger joint is a method of attaching two pieces of wood. Rectangular cut-outs are made in the end of each piece. Then the pieces are joined together so that the cut-outs on one piece fit the projections on the other. It is as if you bent your fingers at the knuckle and then slid your hands together.

Today, courts recognize a custom as binding international law if:

- It is widespread and widely accepted,
- It is longstanding, and
- Nations follow it out of a sense of obligation to each other.

Customary international law governed behavior on the battlefield and the treatment of prisoners of war until the creation of the Geneva Conventions, which codified these customary practices.

In addition, there is the concept of ***jus cogens***, which means a fundamental principle that must be followed.[18] It is different from customary international law because it cannot be altered by custom or practice. Slavery, genocide, piracy, and torture are examples of *jus cogens*. Although these practices still exist in the modern world, no civilized state would say they are acceptable.

Jus cogens
When rule of customary international law becomes a fundamental legal principle across all nations, it cannot be changed by custom or practice.

Ethics

Is torture always wrong? That issue has been deeply and bitterly debated in the United States ever since the terrorist attacks of 9/11. On one side of this debate are those who believe that torture should be used if necessary to obtain information that might help prevent other acts of terrorism. They believe that the harsh treatment of suspected terrorists has been successful in keeping America safe. On the other side are those who say that torture is less effective at eliciting useful information than other interrogation methods. The United States' use of brutality, these critics claim, undermines our legal and moral standing worldwide and gives other countries a license to torture our citizens.

Under what circumstances, if any, should torture be permitted? What would Kant and Mill say?

3-4b Interaction of Foreign and Domestic Laws

You might be wondering how the laws and rulings of sovereign nations interact with one another. Do the laws of one nation have force in another? Can one country's court judgments be enforced in another? Predictably, these questions are not easy. Read on to decipher some of these sticky situations, with which international businesses and multinationals must contend on a daily basis.

Application of U.S. Law Abroad

When developing their own laws, countries sometimes look to other nations for models. The U.S. Constitution has served as a model for constitutions around the world. European nations have borrowed U.S. legal concepts, especially in the areas of contract and product liability laws. Australian antitrust law is based on American statutes. But it is one thing for a country to voluntarily adopt a U.S. law; it is quite another for the United States to impose its own laws in other countries.

Extraterritoriality is the power of one nation to impose its laws in other countries.[19] Many U.S. statutes regulate conduct outside the country. Title VII of the 1964 Civil Rights Act and the Americans with Disabilities Act expressly protect U.S. citizens working for U.S.

Extraterritoriality
The power of one country's laws to reach activities outside of its borders

18 *Jus cogens* means "compelling law" in Latin.

19 Extraterritoriality can also refer to exemption from local laws. For example, ambassadors are generally exempt from the law of the nation in which they serve.

employers from discrimination—even when they live and work abroad. The Foreign Corrupt Practices Act, discussed in Chapter 7 on crime, prohibits bribery on foreign soil. Price-fixing conducted abroad is a violation of the Sherman Antitrust Act if it has an impact on the United States. **But, as a general rule, U.S. statutes do not apply abroad, unless the laws themselves explicitly say so.**

In the following case, victims of *jus cogens* violations in Nigeria sought remedies in American law. No one disputed that what happened to them was horrific—and illegal. But could a U.S. statute grant them relief?

Kiobel v. Royal Dutch Petroleum Co.

133 S. Ct. 1659
United States Supreme Court, 2013

Facts: Throughout the early 1990s, Royal Dutch Petroleum, a Dutch company, and Shell, a British company, were engaged in oil exploration and production in Nigeria. When local residents protested the oil companies' practices, the firms allegedly paid the Nigerian government to suppress the protests by beating, raping, killing, and arresting locals.

A group of Nigerian victims of these attacks sued the oil companies in U.S. federal court for violations of customary international law under the Alien Tort Statute (ATS), a statute passed by the first Congress in 1789. The ATS allows U.S. district courts to hear certain lawsuits brought by non-U.S. citizens for violations of international law occurring in the United States or on the high seas, outside the sovereignty of any country. According to the plaintiffs, the oil companies violated customary international law and *jus cogens* by helping the Nigerian government commit many crimes against humanity.

The appeals court dismissed the case. The Supreme Court granted *certiorari* on the question of whether the ATS permitted U.S. courts to hear a suit for violations of customary international law that occurred outside the United States.

Issue: ***Does U.S. law extend to violations of customary international law occurring entirely outside the United States?***

Excerpts from Chief Justice Roberts's Decision:[20] The question here is whether a claim under the ATS may reach conduct occurring in the territory of a foreign sovereign. The oil companies contend the [it does] not. They rely primarily on the presumption of extraterritoriality [whose premise is] that United States law governs domestically but does not rule the world. This presumption serves to protect against unintended clashes between our laws and those of other nations which could result in international discord.

We typically apply the presumption of extraterritoriality to discern whether an Act of Congress regulating conduct applies abroad. The ATS allows federal courts to recognize certain causes of action based on sufficiently definite norms of international law. But we think the principles of interpretation constrain courts considering causes of action that may be brought under the ATS.

Since many attempts by federal courts to craft remedies for the violation of new norms of international law would raise risks of adverse foreign policy consequences, they should be undertaken, if at all, with great caution. These concerns are all the more pressing when the question is whether a cause of action reaches conduct within the territory of another sovereign.

There is no indication that the ATS was passed to make the United States a uniquely hospitable forum for the enforcement of international norms. As Justice Story put it, "No nation has ever yet pretended to be the *custos morum*[21] of the whole world ...." It is implausible to suppose that the First Congress wanted their fledgling Republic—struggling to receive international recognition—to be the first. Indeed, the parties offer no evidence that any nation, meek or mighty, presumed to do such a thing.

U.S. law governs domestically but does not rule the world.

[20]For ease of reading, "respondents" has been replaced with "oil companies" and "petitioners" with "Kiobel."

[21]In Latin, *custos morum* means "guardian of manners or morals."

Moreover, accepting Kiobel's view would imply that other nations could hale our citizens into their courts for alleged violations of the law of nations occurring in the United States, or anywhere else in the world. The presumption against extraterritoriality guards against our courts triggering such serious foreign policy consequences.

We therefore conclude that the presumption against extraterritoriality applies to claims under the ATS. Kiobel's case seeking relief for violations of the law of nations occurring outside the United States is barred. If Congress were to determine otherwise, a statute more specific than the ATS would be required.

The judgment of the Court of Appeals is affirmed.

In our modern world, sometimes borders are irrelevant. Or are they? What should happen when the government wants access to information on a foreign server? You make the call.

You Be the Judge

Microsoft Corp. v. United States

829 F.3d 197
United States Court of Appeals for the Second Circuit, 2016

Facts: The Stored Communications Act (SCA) protects the privacy of electronic communications stored by service providers (that is, by companies offering an internet connection). This statute prohibits the government from accessing a user's electronic files without a warrant supported by probable cause. But because Congress passed the statute in 1986—before the use of the internet was so widespread—it did not specifically state whether or not the statute applied overseas.

Microsoft, a U.S. corporation, operates Outlook.com, a free web-based email service. When Microsoft customers send and receive Outlook emails, the company stores the emails on a network of servers housed in datacenters spread over 40 countries. Microsoft's system automatically determines which datacenter will store emails based on the user's self-reported country code. Once the data transfer is complete, Microsoft deletes all information associated with the account from its U.S.-based servers.

A federal judge issued an SCA warrant ordering Microsoft to disclose the contents of a particular user's email account. Because those emails were located in its Dublin datacenter, Microsoft refused to comply, arguing that the SCA did not apply to data housed abroad. The lower court disagreed and ordered Microsoft to comply with the warrant. The company appealed.

You Be the Judge: *Does the SCA authorize the U.S. government to obtain emails stored exclusively on foreign servers?*

Argument for Microsoft: Your honors, Congress clearly did not intend the SCA's warrant provisions to apply extraterritorially. If it did, it would have said so. The presumption *against* extraterritorial application of U.S. statutes is strong and binding: Courts must presume that Congress meant to legislate domestically unless the statute specifically mentions its extraterritorial application.

The information sought in this case is stored in Dublin. No court should allow a fishing expedition into data stored beyond American borders. To enforce the warrant as the government proposes would be an unlawful extraterritorial application of the SCA and an intrusion on the privacy of Microsoft's customer.

Argument for the Government: In today's globally-connected internet, information travels freely across borders. The fact that the data are stored abroad is irrelevant. Microsoft is a U.S. company and can obtain the requested information on its domestic computers without having to travel to Ireland or enter the premises there. The warrant only imposes obligations in the United States, where the government would review the digital content.

Nothing in the SCA's text, structure, purpose, or history indicates that Congress wanted to limit where electronic records could be seized. Preventing SCA warrants from reaching foreign servers would seriously impede U.S. law enforcement efforts. A wrongdoer could easily shield illegal content from the police just by reporting a different country code—a result that the SCA could not have intended.

EXAMStrategy

Question: U.S. citizens Alberto Vilar and Gary Tanaka managed $9 billion in investments through their companies, some of which were located in Panama. The two were arrested in the United States for a massive securities fraud: They had lied to their clients about investments—and used some of the money entrusted to them to repair their homes and buy horses. Vilar and Tanaka claimed that U.S. securities laws did not apply to sales that occurred outside the country. These laws were silent as to their application abroad. Do Vilar and Tanaka have a valid argument?

Strategy: Review the *Kiobel* court's discussion of the presumption of extraterritoriality.

Result: The court agreed with the defendants: When laws do not explicitly state that they cover conduct abroad, judges cannot interpret them to do so.[22] (Unfortunately for the defendants, they still went to jail on other charges.)

Foreign Laws and Rulings in the United States

One of the major legal debates of our time involves the blurring line between sovereignty and international law. While Americans are proud to say that our Constitution has influenced the laws of other countries, the debate becomes considerably more heated when it involves the influence of foreign or international law on the United States.

What is the proper role of foreign and international law within our own borders? Questions abound. Supreme Court Justice Ruth Bader Ginsburg has cited foreign court rulings and *jus cogens* to argue against the constitutionality of the death penalty. Should the decisions of foreign courts and international law inform our interpretation of our own Constitution?

Should the United States be bound by the rulings of international tribunals like the WTO and the ICJ? This chapter posed three examples of cases in which the United States refused to comply: the cases of gambling in Antigua (WTO), rebels in Nicaragua (ICJ), and imprisoned citizens of Mexico (ICJ). On one hand, sovereignty demands that others do not meddle in domestic affairs, especially laws. On the other hand, the United States was a founding member of both the WTO and the ICJ. If it ignores their rulings, what is the use of these international bodies?

Application of Foreign Law in U.S. Courts. Recall the *SABIC* case, in which a U.S. court applied the law of Saudi Arabia. Clearly, U.S. judges are not experts in the laws of every country, yet federal courts commonly apply the laws of other countries to resolve disputes. Judges may consult experts, request briefs from the parties, listen to testimony, and conduct their own extensive research on the foreign law. While this process may seem inefficient, some foreign litigants are willing to incur the expense for the benefits of the American judicial system, which is internationally regarded as fair and relatively free from political influence.

Recognition and Enforcement of Foreign Judgments. Imagine that you obtain a court judgment for a million dollars against a foreign seller who sent you defective goods. Great news, right? Well, you may not want to celebrate too soon. If the seller has no assets in the country where you won in court, your award may be worthless.

22 United States v. Vilar, 729 F.3d 62 (2d Cir. 2013).

To address this common situation, most major trading nations have rules for recognizing and enforcing foreign judgments within their borders. **Foreign recognition** means that a decision by a court outside a country is legally valid inside. **Foreign enforcement** means that a judgment rendered outside a country can be collected inside, just as an internal judgment can be.

Foreign recognition
Means that a foreign judgment has legal validity in another country

Foreign enforcement
Means that the court system of a country will assist in enforcing or collecting on the verdict awarded by a foreign court

In the United States, most states have adopted the **Uniform Foreign Money Judgments Recognition Act. This act provides that U.S. courts will recognize foreign judgments if:**

- The award was based on a full and fair trial by an impartial tribunal with proper jurisdiction;
- The defendant was given notice and an opportunity to appear;
- The judgment was not fraudulent or against public policy; and
- The foreign court was the proper forum to hear the case.

The Ecuadorian Supreme Court awarded $9.5 billion to the Ecuadorian victims of a massive, decades-long environmental contamination of an area known as Lago Agrio by oil company Texaco (now Chevron). Because Chevron did not have sufficient assets in Ecuador for the victims to collect, the plaintiffs sought to enforce the judgment in the United States. In a 500-page decision, a federal court in New York refused to recognize the award. The court found that the Ecuadorian judges were paid off, the decision was ghost written, and the investigation was replete with corruption and fraud.[23] The court concluded:

> Justice is not served by inflicting injustice. The ends do not justify the means. There is no "Robin Hood" defense to illegal and wrongful conduct. And the defendants' "this-is-the-way-it-is-done-in-Ecuador" excuses—actually a remarkable insult to the people of Ecuador—do not help them. The[se] wrongful actions would be offensive to the laws of any nation that aspires to the rule of law, including Ecuador.[24]

Arbitration. Parties who prefer to avoid courts altogether generally opt for arbitration. **Arbitration** is a binding process in which the parties submit their dispute to a neutral private body for resolution. It is especially advantageous when the disputing parties are from different countries because it is generally faster, more private, less expensive, and less political than litigating in foreign courts. International arbitral bodies, such as the ICC, issue arbitral awards, but enforcement depends upon the laws of the individual countries where the parties operate.

Arbitration
A binding process of resolving legal disputes by submitting them to a neutral third party

The Convention on the Recognition and Enforcement of Foreign Arbitral Awards (also known as the **New York Convention**) is an international treaty with 149 signatories that provides common rules for recognizing arbitration agreements. But each country has its own specific requirements. **In the United States, an arbitral award will generally be enforced if:**

New York Convention
Widely accepted treaty on the court enforcement of arbitral awards

- It is enforceable under the local law of the country where the award was granted;
- The arbitral tribunal had proper jurisdiction;
- The defendant was given notice of the arbitration and an opportunity to be heard; and
- Enforcement of the award is not fraudulent or contrary to public policy.

---

23 This legal saga was the subject of a 2009 documentary, *Crude*—which was made by the allegedly corrupt plaintiffs' legal team.

24 Chevron Corp. v. Donzinger, 974 F. Supp. 2d 362 (S.D.N.Y. 2014).

3-4c Choosing the Applicable Law and Jurisdiction

International business brings great reward, but also carries significant risks. Distance, language, politics, culture, and different legal systems all pose potential hurdles to successful transactions.

However, some of these risks can be controlled by carefully thinking about contract terms beforehand. In this chapter, we witnessed what happened to Forestal, an Argentine company that made an oral agreement with a New Jersey buyer. First it was not paid—perhaps due to a miscommunication or cultural difference. Then, it was dragged into a common law court system in a foreign country more than 5,000 miles away, only to spend thousands of American dollars on pricey U.S. lawyers to figure out *which law* applied to its deal. Unfortunately, these outcomes are not uncommon in international business.

To ensure that you do not end up in a similar predicament, be sure to consider the following when you negotiate international deals:

- **Choice of Law: Which Law Governs?** As we have seen, there are a variety of legal systems and each country has a different way of applying whatever legal system it uses. Therefore, when making an agreement, it is *essential* to negotiate which country's law will control. Each side will prefer the law it is most familiar with.

  How to compromise? Perhaps by using a neutral law. But before reaching any agreement, be sure to seek the advice of an attorney who specializes in the law of that country. It is a good idea to have a trusted legal advisor in any foreign country where you do business.
- **Choice of Forum: Where Will the Case Be Heard?** The parties must decide not only what law governs, but also where disagreements will be resolved. This can be a significant part of a contract, because legal and court systems are dramatically different in terms of speed, cost, transparency, and trustworthiness.
- **Choice of Language and Currency.** The parties must select a language for the contract and a currency for payment. Language counts because legal terms seldom translate literally. Currency is vital because the exchange rate may alter between the signing and payment.

CHAPTER CONCLUSION

International law is increasingly relevant to our globalized business world. While it was once the domain of nations, today it affects individuals, businesses, and groups all over the world. As the world gets smaller, these issues will become more and more pressing.

EXAM REVIEW

1. **PUBLIC INTERNATIONAL LAW** The law governing relations among governments and international organizations.

2. **PRIVATE INTERNATIONAL LAW** The law governing private parties in international commercial and legal transactions.

3. **INTERNATIONAL COURT OF JUSTICE (ICJ)** The World Court settles international legal disputes among states.

4. **THE INTERNATIONAL CHAMBER OF COMMERCE (ICC)** The world's largest global business organization.

5. **SOVEREIGN IMMUNITY** Sovereign immunity holds that the courts of one nation lack the jurisdiction (power) to hear suits against foreign governments, unless the foreign nation has waived immunity, is engaging in commercial activity, or has violated international law.

6. **COMMON LAW** The legal system based on precedent and adversarial process that was inherited by most British colonies, including the United States and Australia.

7. **CIVIL LAW** The most widespread legal system in the world, whose main principle is that law is found primarily in statutes rather than in judicial decisions.

8. **ISLAMIC LAW** Based on the Koran and the action and teachings of Muhammad.

EXAMStrategy

Question: No matter where you are in the world, the relationship between landlords and tenants can be a tense one. How would judges in common law, civil law, and Islamic law jurisdictions approach a landlord/tenant controversy?

Strategy: Review the process that judges use to examine and apply the laws in each of these legal systems. (See the "Result" at the end of this Exam Review section.)

9. **GATT, GATS, AND TRIPS** The goal of the General Agreement on Tariffs and Trade (GATT) is to lower trade barriers worldwide. The General Agreement on Trade in Services (GATS) and the Trade Related Aspects of Intellectual Property (TRIPS) extend GATT principles to services and intellectual property, respectively.

10. **WTO** GATT created the WTO, which resolves disputes between signatories to the treaty.

EXAMStrategy

Question: When fishermen trawled for shrimp, they often caught sea turtles as well. The U.S. Environmental Protection Agency (EPA) sought to protect the endangered sea turtles by requiring that fisherman use costly technology called a Turtle Excluder Device (TED). The United States prohibited the importation of shrimp caught without TEDs. Several developing nations claimed that American laws on shrimp fishing were unfair and illegal. Who won and why? The case demonstrated a conflict between two important values. What were the values? In your view, which is more important?

Strategy: Apply the GATT principles to determine the outcome. (See the "Result" at the end of this Exam Review section.)

11. **REGIONAL TRADE AGREEMENTS** Trade agreements promoting common policies among member states.

12. **CISG** The goal of CISG is to make sales law more uniform and predictable—and to make international contracting easier. A sales agreement between an American company and a foreign company may be governed by American law, by the law of the foreign country, or by the CISG.

EXAMStrategy

Question: Paula, a U.S. citizen, purchased a lamp for her home from Interieures, a lighting website based in Paris. The company's website stated that the governing law would be the law of France and only French courts could hear claims. When the company breached its contract, Paula sought to sue in the United States under the CISG. Does the CISG apply to Paula's claim?

Strategy: Review the scope and applicability of the CISG and the section on "Essential Clauses in International Contracts." (See the "Result" at the end of this Exam Review section.)

13. **CUSTOMARY INTERNATIONAL LAW** Courts recognize custom as binding international law if it is (1) widespread and widely accepted, (2) longstanding, and (3) nations obey it out of a sense of obligation to each other.

14. ***JUS COGENS*** A fundamental principle of law that must be followed. It cannot be altered by custom or practice.

15. **EXTRATERRITORIALITY** The power of one nation to impose its laws in other countries. In the United States, courts presume that U.S. laws do not apply to conduct abroad unless the statute explicitly says so.

16. **UNIFORM FOREIGN MONEY JUDGMENTS RECOGNITION ACT** A U.S. act requiring states to recognize foreign judgments under certain conditions.

17. **NEW YORK CONVENTION** An international treaty that provides rules for the recognition and enforcement of foreign arbitral awards.

RESULTS

8. Result: The common law judge would hear the arguments of lawyers, who formulate their argument based on prior courts' rulings. The civil law judge would consult the applicable code that deals with landlord and tenant disputes. The Islamic law judge would engage in a process of *ijtihad*, which incorporates legal knowledge with religious reasoning based on the Koran and teachings and actions of Mohammad.

10. Result: Small nations sued, claiming that American regulations made it difficult or impossible for them to fish, devastating their economic growth. The United States argued that vital environmental concerns mandated such rules. The WTO found in favor of the small nations, ruling that before the United States imposed its environmental standards on other countries, it must engage in multinational negotiations, seeking an acceptable compromise. Environmentalists argued that the decision was short-sighted, and contributed to the destruction of an endangered species. Supporters of the decision responded that long-term environmental concerns sound patronizing and hollow to people with empty stomachs.

12. Result: Paula is out of luck. First, the CISG only applies to commercial sales contracts, not personal ones. Even if it applied, Interieures has conspicuously opted out of it. As the section on choice of law clauses discusses, these clauses are widely acceptable internationally. The only way U.S. law would have applied is if the two parties had agreed to such a provision.

MULTIPLE-CHOICE QUESTIONS

1. For which of the following activities can a foreign sovereign be sued?
(a) Operating a factory dangerously
(b) Issuing a law that discriminates against a certain group
(c) Suspending the civil rights of its people
(d) None of the above

2. Outdoor Technologies (an Australian company) obtained a judgment for $500,000 against Silver Star (a Chinese company) in a court in Australia. Silver Star owned property in Iowa, so Outdoor filed suit in Iowa to collect the judgment. Which of the following statements is true?
(a) Outdoor cannot collect a judgment in the United States that was issued by an Australian court.
(b) Outdoor cannot collect in the United States because Silver Star is not an American company.
(c) Outdoor can collect in the United States if the Australian court was fair and proper.
(d) Outdoor can collect in the United States because both the United States and Australia have common law systems.

3. The president negotiates a defense agreement with a foreign government. To take effect, the agreement must be ratified by which of the following?
(a) Two-thirds of the House of Representatives
(b) Two-thirds of the Senate
(c) The Supreme Court
(d) A and B
(e) A, B, and C

4. Lynn is an author living in Nevada. She contracted with a company in China, which promised to print her custom children's books. After receiving Lynn's payment, the company disappeared without performing. Lynn wants to sue for fraud, but the contract does not say anything about which country's law will be used to resolve disputes. Both China and the United States are signatories of the CISG. Will the CISG apply in this case?
(a) Yes, because both countries are signatories.
(b) Yes, because the parties did not opt out of the CISG.
(c) No, because the contract does not involve goods.
(d) No, because the CISG does not establish rules for fraud.

5. Austria, Indonesia, and Colombia are all members of the WTO. If Austria imposes a tariff on imports of coffee beans from Colombia, but not from Indonesia, is it in violation of WTO principles?
   (a) Yes, the WTO prohibits tariffs.
   (b) Yes, the WTO prohibits excise taxes.
   (c) Yes, Austria is violating the WTO's most favored nation rules.
   (d) No, the WTO's most favored nation rules permit Austria to do this.

CASE QUESTIONS

1. A Saudi Arabian government-run hospital hired American Scott Nelson to be an engineer. The parties signed the employment agreement in the United States. On the job, Nelson reported that the hospital had significant safety defects. For this, he was arrested, jailed, and tortured for 39 days. Upon his release to the United States, Nelson sued the Saudi government for personal injury. Can Nelson sue Saudi Arabia?

2. The Instituto de Auxilios y Viviendas is a government agency of the Dominican Republic. Dr. Marion Fernandez, the general administrator of the Instituto and Secretary of the Republic, sought a loan for the Instituto. She requested that Charles Meadows, an American citizen, secure the Instituto a bank loan of $12 million. If he obtained a loan on favorable terms, he would receive a fee of $240,000. Meadows did secure a loan, which the Instituto accepted. He then sought his fee, but the Instituto and the Dominican government refused to pay. He sued the government in United States federal court. The Dominican government claimed immunity. Comment.

3. Many European nations fear the effects of genetically modified foods, so they choose to restrict their importation. The EU banned the entry of these foods and subjected them to strict labeling requirements. Does this policy contravene the principles of WTO/GATT?

4. Boston Scientific (BSC), an American multinational, hired Carnero to work in its Argentine subsidiary. Carnero was paid in pesos, and his contract was governed by Argentine law. After BSC fired Carnero, he sued in the United States, claiming that the company terminated him for blowing the whistle on its accounting fraud. If this allegation was true, BSC would be in violation of an American statute, the Sarbanes-Oxley Act (SOX). BSC argued that, because SOX made no mention of extraterritorial application, it did not apply to overseas employees. Should SOX apply to an employee of a U.S. subsidiary working abroad?

5. Chateau, a Canadian winery, contracted over the phone to buy 1.2 million wine corks from Sabate USA, the U.S. subsidiary of Sabate France. The parent company shipped the corks from France to Canada, along with a pre-printed invoice. The invoice contained a forum selection clause providing that any dispute would be heard in a French court. When Chateau realized that the corks altered the taste of its wine, it sued Sabate in California for breach of contract. Chateau argued that the forum selection clause was not part of the original deal. Furthermore, it had an enforceable oral agreement with Sabate USA, which was governed by the CISG because both Canada and the United States were signatories. Did the CISG govern the dealings between Chateau and Sabate USA? If so, did the contract between Chateau and Sabate USA have to be in writing? Was the forum selection clause enforceable against Chateau?

DISCUSSION QUESTIONS

1. After reading this chapter, do you believe that international law exists? Has your concept of law and legal rules changed?

2. After the 9/11 terrorist attacks, the U.S. government imprisoned suspected terrorists in Guantanamo Bay, Cuba. Officials argued that these detainees did not enjoy constitutional rights because they were not on U.S. soil, even though they were held by Americans. Are the freedoms guaranteed by the U.S. Constitution reserved for U.S. citizens on U.S. soil or do they apply more broadly?

3. The United Kingdom has not signed the CISG. Until recently, major world traders like Japan and Brazil had refused to sign. Imagine that you are a legislator from one of these countries. What might your objections be to ratifying a treaty on sales law?

4. Generally speaking, should the United States pass laws that seek to control behavior outside its borders? Or, when in Rome, should our companies and subsidiaries be allowed to do as the Romans do?

5. What responsibility, if any, does the United States have to obey international law? Is it any different from other countries' responsibility to uphold international law? Why or why not?

CHAPTER 4

COMMON LAW, STATUTORY LAW, AND ADMINISTRATIVE LAW

The finale of the *Seinfeld* TV series illustrated an important legal issue. After striking a deal with NBC to produce their pilot television show, New Yorkers Jerry, George, Elaine, and Kramer decided to celebrate by going to Paris on NBC's private jet. In-flight hijinks ensued, causing the plane to nosedive and make an emergency landing in Latham, Massachusetts.

While the four friends awaited repairs to their jet, they took a walk around the small town. There, they witnessed a crime in progress—a gunman carjacking a helpless man in a red subcompact car. Unmoved and unaffected, the bunch stood by—cracking insensitive jokes about the victim's weight, and laughing smugly.

The bunch stood by—cracking insensitive jokes about the victim's weight, and laughing smugly.

As the gunman jerked the man out of the driver's seat, Jerry quipped, "There goes the money for the lipo." Elaine observed that a large victim is easier to outrun. George supposed the thief was actually doing the victim a favor because "it's less money for him to buy food." As the thief drove away with the stolen car, Kramer proudly captured the crime on his video camera and bragged about selling the footage to a major television network.

4-1 COMMON LAW

Jerry, George, Elaine, and Kramer represent more than a classic television show. Their story also presents a classic legal puzzle: What, if anything, must a bystander do when he sees someone in danger? We will examine this issue to see how the common law works.

The **common law** is judge-made law. It is the sum total of all the cases decided by appellate courts. The common law of Pennsylvania consists of all cases decided by appellate courts in that state. The Illinois common law is made up of all of the cases decided by Illinois appellate courts. Two hundred years ago, almost all of the law was common law. Today, common law still predominates in tort, contract, and agency law, and it is very important in property, employment, and some other areas.

Common law
Judge-made law

4-1a Stare Decisis

Nothing perks up a course like Latin. ***Stare decisis*** means "let the decision stand." It is the essence of the common law. Once a court has decided a particular issue, it will generally apply the same rule in similar cases in the future. Suppose the highest court of Arizona must decide whether a contract signed by a 16-year-old can be enforced against him. The court will look to see if there is **precedent**; that is, whether the high court of Arizona has already decided a similar case. The Arizona court looks and finds several earlier cases, all holding that such contracts may *not* be enforced against a minor. The court will probably apply that precedent and refuse to enforce the contract in this case. Courts do not always follow precedent, but they generally do: *stare decisis*.

Stare decisis
"Let the decision stand," that is, the ruling from a previous case

Precedent
An earlier case that decided the issue

A desire for predictability created the doctrine of *stare decisis*. The value of predictability is apparent: People must know what the law is. If contract law changed daily, an entrepreneur who leased factory space and then started buying machinery would be uncertain if the factory would actually be available when she was ready to move in. Will the landlord slip out of the lease? Will the machinery be ready on time? The law must be knowable. Yet there must also be flexibility in the law—some means to respond to new problems and a changing social climate. Sometimes, we are better off if we are not encumbered by ironclad rules established before electricity was discovered. These two ideas are in conflict: The more flexibility we permit, the less predictability we enjoy. We will watch the conflict play out in the bystander cases.

4-1b Bystander Cases

This country inherited from England a simple rule about a **bystander's obligations: You have no duty to assist someone in peril unless you created the danger.** In *Union Pacific Railway Co. v. Cappier*,[1] through no fault of the railroad, a train struck a man. Railroad employees saw the incident happen but did nothing to assist him. By the time help arrived, the victim had died. The court held that the railroad had no duty to help the injured man:

> With the humane side of the question courts are not concerned. It is the omission or negligent discharge of legal duties only which come within the sphere of judicial cognizance. For withholding relief from the suffering, for failure to respond to the calls of worthy charity, or for faltering in the bestowment of brotherly love on the unfortunate, penalties are found not in the laws of men but in [the laws of God].

As harsh as this judgment might seem, it was an accurate statement of the law at that time in both England and the United States: Bystanders need do nothing. Contemporary writers found the rule inhumane and cruel, and even judges criticized it. But—*stare decisis*—they followed it. With a rule this old and well established, no court was willing to scuttle it. What courts did do was seek openings for small changes.

---

[1] 66 Kan. 649 (1903).

Eighteen years after the Kansas case of *Cappier*, a court in nearby Iowa found the basis for one exception. Ed Carey was a farm laborer working for Frank Davis. While in the fields, Carey fainted from sunstroke and remained unconscious. Davis simply hauled him to a nearby wagon and left him in the sun for an additional four hours, causing serious permanent injury. The court's response:

> It is unquestionably the well-settled rule that the master is under no legal duty to care for a sick or injured servant for whose illness or injury he is not at fault. Though not unjust in principle, this rule, if carried unflinchingly and without exception to its logical extreme, is sometimes productive of shocking results. To avoid this criticism [we hold that where] a servant suffers serious injury, or is suddenly stricken down in a manner indicating the immediate and emergent need of aid to save him from death or serious harm, the master, if present is in duty bound to take such reasonable measures as may be practicable to relieve him, even though such master be not chargeable with fault in bringing about the emergency.[2]

And this is how the common law often changes: bit by tiny bit. In Iowa, a bystander could now be liable *if* he was the employer and *if* the worker was suddenly stricken and *if* it was an emergency and *if* the employer was present. That is a small change but an important one.

For the next 50 years, changes in bystander law came very slowly. Consider *Osterlind v. Hill*, a case from 1928.[3] Osterlind rented a canoe from Hill's boatyard, paddled into the lake, and promptly fell into the water. For *30 minutes*, he clung to the side of the canoe and shouted for help. Hill heard the cries but did nothing; Osterlind drowned. Was Hill liable? No, said the court: A bystander has no liability. Not until half a century later did the same court reverse its position and begin to require assistance in extreme cases. Fifty years is a long time for the unfortunate Osterlind to hold on.[4]

In the 1970s, changes came more quickly.

Tarasoff v. Regents of the University of California

17 Cal. 3d 425
Supreme Court of California, 1976

Facts: On October 27, 1969, Prosenjit Poddar killed Tatiana Tarasoff. Tatiana's parents claimed that two months earlier Poddar had confided his intention to kill Tatiana to Dr. Lawrence Moore, a psychologist employed by the University of California at Berkeley. They sued the university, claiming that Dr. Moore should have warned Tatiana and/or should have arranged for Poddar's confinement.

Issue: ***Did Dr. Moore have a duty to Tatiana Tarasoff, and did he breach that duty?***

Excerpts from Justice Tobriner's Decision: Although under the common law, as a general rule, one person owed no duty to control the conduct of another, nor to warn those endangered by such conduct, the courts have carved out an exception to this rule in cases in which the defendant stands in some special relationship to either the person whose conduct needs to be controlled or in a relationship to the foreseeable victim of that conduct. Applying this exception to the present case, we note that a relationship of defendant therapists to either Tatiana or Poddar will suffice to establish a duty of care.

We recognize the difficulty that a therapist encounters in attempting to forecast whether a patient presents a serious danger of violence. Obviously we do not require that the therapist, in making that determination, render a perfect performance; the therapist need only exercise that reasonable degree of skill,

---

2Carey v. Davis, 190 Iowa 720 (1921).
3263 Mass. 73 (1928).
4Pridgen v. Boston Housing Authority, 364 Mass. 696 (1974).

knowledge, and care ordinarily possessed and exercised by members of [the field] under similar circumstances.

In the instant case, however, the pleadings do not raise any question as to failure of defendant therapists to predict that Poddar presented a serious danger of violence. On the contrary, the present complaints allege that defendant therapists did in fact predict that Poddar would kill, but were negligent in failing to warn.

In our view, once a therapist does in fact determine, or under applicable professional standards reasonably should have determined, that a patient poses a serious danger of violence to others, he bears a duty to exercise reasonable care to protect the foreseeable victim of that danger.

[The Tarasoffs have stated a legitimate claim against Dr. Moore.]

The *Tarasoff* exception applies when there is some special relationship, such as therapist–patient. In *Carey v. Davis*, another exception applied if the bystander was an employer. If there is no such relationship, the law does not require a total stranger to put himself in harm's way for another.

Let's apply them to the opening scenario. If the carjacking victim sues Jerry and his friends, will he be successful? Probably not. Jerry and his friends did not employ the victim, nor did they have any special relationship. The New Yorkers did not stand in the way of someone else trying to call the police. They may be morally culpable for refusing to help and making cruel jokes, but they will not be liable in a civil case unless the common law changes entirely.

The bystander rule, that hardy oak, is alive and well. Various initials have been carved into its bark—the exceptions we have seen and a variety of others—but the trunk is strong and the leaves green. Perhaps someday the proliferating exceptions will topple it, but the process of the common law is slow and that day is nowhere in sight.

EXAMStrategy

Question: When Rachel is walking her dog, Bozo, she watches a skydiver float to earth. He lands in an enormous tree, suspended 45 feet above ground. "Help!" the man shouts. Rachel hurries to the tree and sees the skydiver bleeding profusely. She takes out her cell phone to call 911 for help, but just then Bozo runs away. Rachel darts after the dog, afraid that he will jump in a nearby pond and emerge smelling of mud. She forgets about the skydiver and takes Bozo home. Three hours later, the skydiver expires.

The victim's family sues Rachel. She defends by saying she feared that Bozo would have an allergic reaction to mud, and that, in any case, she could not have climbed 45 feet up a tree to save the man. The family argues that the dog is not allergic to mud; that even if he is, a pet's inconvenience pales compared to human life; and that Rachel could have phoned for emergency help without climbing an inch. Please rule.

Strategy: The family's arguments might seem compelling, but are they relevant? Rachel is a bystander, someone who perceives another in danger. What is the rule concerning a bystander's obligation to act? Apply the rule to the facts of this case.

Result: A bystander has no duty to assist someone in peril unless she created the danger. Rachel did not create the skydiver's predicament. She had no obligation to do anything. Rachel wins.

4-2 STATUTORY LAW

If you are a *Seinfeld* fan, you may remember what happened to Jerry and his friends in the episode recounted in the introduction to this chapter. When the victim reported that Jerry's group did nothing to help him, the police officer promptly arrested them for failing to act.

Arrested? Why, you might wonder. The Latham officer informed them that a recently enacted state *criminal statute* required bystanders to help anyone in danger. Jerry, George, Elaine, and Kramer were mercilessly thrown in jail for violating this criminal Good Samaritan statute. At trial, the four were found guilty and sentenced to one year in prison.

Although this was a fictional "made-for-TV" law, Massachusetts and nine other states *do* have versions of a "Duty to Rescue" statute based on the Good Samaritan common law principles discussed earlier.[5] These criminal statutes require witnesses of certain violent crimes to *report* the crime as soon as they can, if they can do so without endangering themselves or others. (There is no obligation to try to *prevent* the crime or *go to the aid* of the victim.) These laws differ from the common law because they are enacted by a legislature, criminalize certain actions, and spell out their penalties. (In Massachusetts, the penalty is a fine ranging from $500 to $2,500, not a jail sentence.)

How are statutes different from common law? In fact, more law is created by statute than by the courts. Statutes affect each of us every day, in our business, professional, and personal lives. When the system works correctly, this is the one part of the law over which "we the people" have control. We elect the legislators who pass state statutes; we vote for the senators and representatives who create federal statutes.

Every other November, voters in all 50 states cast ballots for members of Congress. The winners of Congressional elections convene in Washington, D.C., and create statutes. In this section, we look at how Congress does its work creating statutes.[6] Using the Civil Rights Act as a backdrop, we will follow a bill as it makes its way through Congress and beyond.

4-2a Bills

Bill
A proposed statute submitted to Congress or a state legislature

Veto
The power of the president to reject legislation passed by Congress

Congress is organized into two houses, the House of Representatives and the Senate. Either house may originate a proposed statute, which is called a **bill**. **To become law, the bill must be voted on and approved by both houses.** Once both houses pass it, they will send it to the president. If the president signs the bill, it becomes law and is then a statute. If the president opposes the bill, he will **veto** it, in which case, it is not law.[7]

If you visit either house of Congress, you will probably find half a dozen legislators on the floor, with one person talking and no one listening. This is because most of the work is done in committees. Both houses are organized into dozens of committees, each with special functions. The House currently has about 20 committees (further divided into about 100 subcommittees), and the Senate has approximately 17 committees (with about 70 subcommittees). For example, the armed services committee of each house oversees the huge defense budget and the workings of the armed forces. Labor committees handle legislation concerning organized labor and working conditions. Banking committees develop expertise on financial institutions. Judiciary committees review nominees to the federal courts. There are dozens of other committees, some very powerful because they control vast amounts of money, and some relatively weak. Few of us ever think about the House Agricultural Subcommittee on Specialty Crops. But if we owned a family peanut farm, we would pay close attention to the subcommittee's agenda because those members of Congress would pay close attention to us.

When a bill is proposed in either house, it is referred to the committee that specializes in that subject. Why are bills proposed in the first place? For any of several reasons:

- **New issue, new worry.** If society begins to focus on a new issue, Congress may respond with legislation. We consider in following sections, for example, the Congressional response in the 1960s to employment discrimination.

---

[5]In addition to Massachusetts, California, Florida, Hawaii, Minnesota, Ohio, Rhode Island, Vermont, Washington, and Wisconsin have Good Samaritan statutes.

[6]State legislatures operate similarly in creating state laws.

[7]Congress may, however, attempt to override the veto as we will learn in the next section.

- **Unpopular judicial ruling.** If Congress disagrees with a judicial interpretation of a statute, the legislators may pass a new statute to modify or "undo" the court decision. For example, if the Supreme Court misinterprets a statute about musical copyrights, Congress may pass a new law correcting the Court's error. However, the legislators have no such power to modify a court decision based on the Constitution. When the Supreme Court ruled that lawyers had a right *under the First Amendment* to advertise their services, Congress lacked the power to change the decision.
- **Criminal law.** Statutory law, unlike common law, is prospective. Legislators are hoping to control the future. And that is why almost all criminal law is statutory. A court cannot retroactively announce that it *has been* a crime for a retailer to accept kickbacks from a wholesaler. Everyone must know the rules in advance because the consequences—prison, a felony record—are so harsh.

4-2b Discrimination: Congress and the Courts

The civil rights movement of the 1950s and 1960s convinced most citizens that African-Americans suffered significant and unacceptable discrimination in jobs, housing, voting, schools, and other basic areas of life. Demonstrations and boycotts, marches and counter-marches, church bombings and killings persuaded the nation that the problem was vast and urgent.

In 1963, President Kennedy proposed legislation to guarantee equal rights in these areas. The bill went to the House Judiciary Committee, which heard testimony for weeks. Witnesses testified that blacks were often unable to vote because of their race, that landlords and home sellers adamantly refused to sell or rent to African-Americans, that education was grossly unequal, and that blacks were routinely denied good jobs in many industries. Eventually, the Judiciary Committee approved the bill and sent it to the full House.

The bill was dozens of pages long and divided into "titles," with each title covering a major issue. Title VII concerned employment. We will consider the progress of Title VII in Congress and in the courts. Here is one section of Title VII, as reported to the House floor:[8]

> Sec. 703(a). It shall be an unlawful employment practice for an employer—
>
> (1) to fail or refuse to hire or to discharge any individual, or otherwise to discriminate against any individual with respect to his compensation, terms, conditions, or privileges of employment, because of such individual's race, color, religion, or national origin; or
>
> (2) to limit, segregate, or classify his employees in any way which would deprive or tend to deprive any individual of employment opportunities or otherwise adversely affect his status as an employee, because of such individual's race, color, religion, or national origin.

AP Images/Bill Hudson

A civil rights demonstrator being arrested by the police.

[8]The section number in the House bill was actually 704(a). We use 703 here because that is the number of the section when the bill became law and the number to which the Supreme Court refers in later litigation.

4-2c Debate

The proposed bill was intensely controversial and sparked argument throughout Congress. Here are some excerpts from one day's debate on the House floor, on February 8, 1964:[9]

> MR. WAGGONNER. I speak to you in all sincerity and ask for the right to discriminate if I so choose because I think it is my right. I think it is my right to choose my social companions. I think it is my right if I am a businessman to run it as I please, to do with my own as I will. I think that is a right the Constitution gives to every man. I want the continued right to discriminate and I want the other man to have the right to continue to discriminate against me, because I am discriminated against every day. I do not feel inferior about it.
>
> I ask you to forget about politics, forget about everything except the integrity of the individual, leaving to the people of this country the right to live their lives in the manner they choose to live. Do not destroy this democracy for a Socialist government. A vote for this bill is no less.
>
> MR. CONTE. If the serious cleavage which pitted brother against brother and citizen against citizen during the tragedy of the Civil War is ever to be justified, it can be justified in this House and then in the other body with the passage of this legislation which can and must reaffirm the rights to all individuals which are inherent in our Constitution.
>
> The distinguished poet Mark Van Doren has said that "equality is absolute or no, nothing between can stand," and nothing should now stand between us and the passage of strong and effective civil rights legislation. It is to this that we are united in a strong bipartisan coalition today, and when the laws of the land proclaim that the 88th Congress acted effectively, judiciously, and wisely, we can take pride in our accomplishments as free men.

Other debate was less rhetorical and aimed more at getting information. The following exchange anticipates a 30-year controversy on quotas:

> MR. JOHANSEN. I have asked for this time to raise a question and I would ask particularly for the attention of the gentleman from New York [Mr. Goodell] because of a remark he made—and I am not quarreling with it. I understood him to say there is no plan for balanced employment or for quotas in this legislation. . . . I am raising a question as to whether in the effort to eliminate discrimination—and incidentally that is an undefined term in the bill—we may get to a situation in which employers, and conceivably union leaders, will insist on legislation providing for a quota system as a matter of self-protection.
>
> Now let us suppose this hypothetical situation exists with 100 jobs to be filled. Let us say 150 persons apply and suppose 75 of them are Negro and 75 of them are white. Supposing the employer . . . hires 75 white men. [Does anyone] have a right to claim they have been discriminated against on the basis of color?
>
> MR. GOODELL. It is the intention of the legislation that if applicants are equal in all other respects there will be no restriction. One may choose from among equals. So long as there is no distinction on the basis of race, creed, or color it will not violate the act.

The debate on racial issues carried on. Later in the day, Congressman Smith of Virginia offered an amendment that could scarcely have been smaller—or more important:

> Amendment offered by Mr. Smith of Virginia: On page 68, line 23, after the word "religion," insert the word "sex."

---

[9] The order of speakers is rearranged, and the remarks are edited.

In other words, Smith was asking that discrimination on the basis of sex also be outlawed, along with the existing grounds of race, color, national origin, and religion. Congressman Smith's proposal produced the following comments:

> MR. CELLER. You know, the French have a phrase for it when they speak of women and men. They say "vive la difference." I think the French are right. Imagine the upheaval that would result from adoption of blanket language requiring total equality. Would male citizens be justified in insisting that women share with them the burdens of compulsory military service? What would become of traditional family relationships? What about alimony? What would become of the crimes of rape and statutory rape? I think the amendment seems illogical, ill timed, ill placed, and improper.
>
> MRS. ST. GEORGE. Mr. Chairman, I was somewhat amazed when I came on the floor this afternoon to hear the very distinguished chairman of the Committee on the Judiciary [Mr. Celler] make the remark that he considered the amendment at this point illogical. I can think of nothing more logical than this amendment at this point.
>
> There are still many States where women cannot serve on juries. There are still many States where women do not have equal educational opportunities. In most States and, in fact, I figure it would be safe to say, in all States—women do not get equal pay for equal work. That is a very well-known fact. And to say that this is illogical. What is illogical about it? All you are doing is simply correcting something that goes back, frankly to the Dark Ages.

The debate continued. Some supported the "sex" amendment because they were determined to end sexual bias. But politics are complex. Some *opponents* of civil rights supported the amendment because they believed that it would make the legislation less popular and cause Congress to defeat the entire Civil Rights bill.

That strategy did not work. The amendment passed, and sex was added as a protected trait. And, after more debate and several votes, the entire bill passed the House. It went to the Senate, where it followed a similar route from Judiciary Committee to full Senate. Much of the Senate debate was similar to what we have seen. But some senators raised a new issue, concerning §703(2), which prohibited *segregating or classifying* employees based on any of the protected categories (race, color, national origin, religion, or sex). Senator Tower was concerned that §703(2) meant that an employee in a protected category could never be given any sort of job test. So the Senate amended §703 to include a new subsection:

> Sec. 703(h). Notwithstanding any other provision of this title, it shall not be an unlawful employment practice for an employer . . . to give and to act upon the results of any professionally developed ability test provided that such test . . . is not designed, intended or used to discriminate because of race, color, religion, sex or national origin.

With that amendment, and many others, the bill passed the Senate.

4-2d Conference Committee

Civil rights legislation had now passed both houses, but the bills were no longer the same due to the many amendments. This is true with most legislation. The next step is for the two houses to send representatives to a House–Senate Conference Committee. This committee examines all of the differences between the two bills and tries to reach a compromise. With the Civil Rights bill, Senator Tower's amendment was left in; other Senate amendments were taken out. When the Conference Committee had settled every difference between the two versions, the new, modified bill was sent back to each house for a new vote.

The House of Representatives and the Senate again angrily debated the compromise language reported from the Conference Committee. Finally, after years of violent public demonstrations and months of debate, each house passed the same bill. President Johnson promptly signed it. The Civil Rights Act of 1964 was law. See Exhibit 4.1.

EXHIBIT 4.1

The two houses of Congress are organized into dozens of committees, a few of which are shown here. The path of the 1964 Civil Rights Act (somewhat simplified) was as follows: (1) The House Judiciary Committee approved the bill and sent it to the full House; (2) the full House passed the bill and sent it to the Senate, where it was assigned to the Senate Judiciary Committee; (3) the Senate Judiciary Committee passed an amended version of the bill and sent it to the full Senate; (4) the full Senate passed the bill with additional amendments. Since the Senate version was now different from the bill the House passed, the bill went to a Conference Committee. The Conference Committee (5) reached a compromise and sent the new version of the bill back to both houses. Each house (6 and 7) passed the compromise bill and sent it to the president (8), who signed it into law.

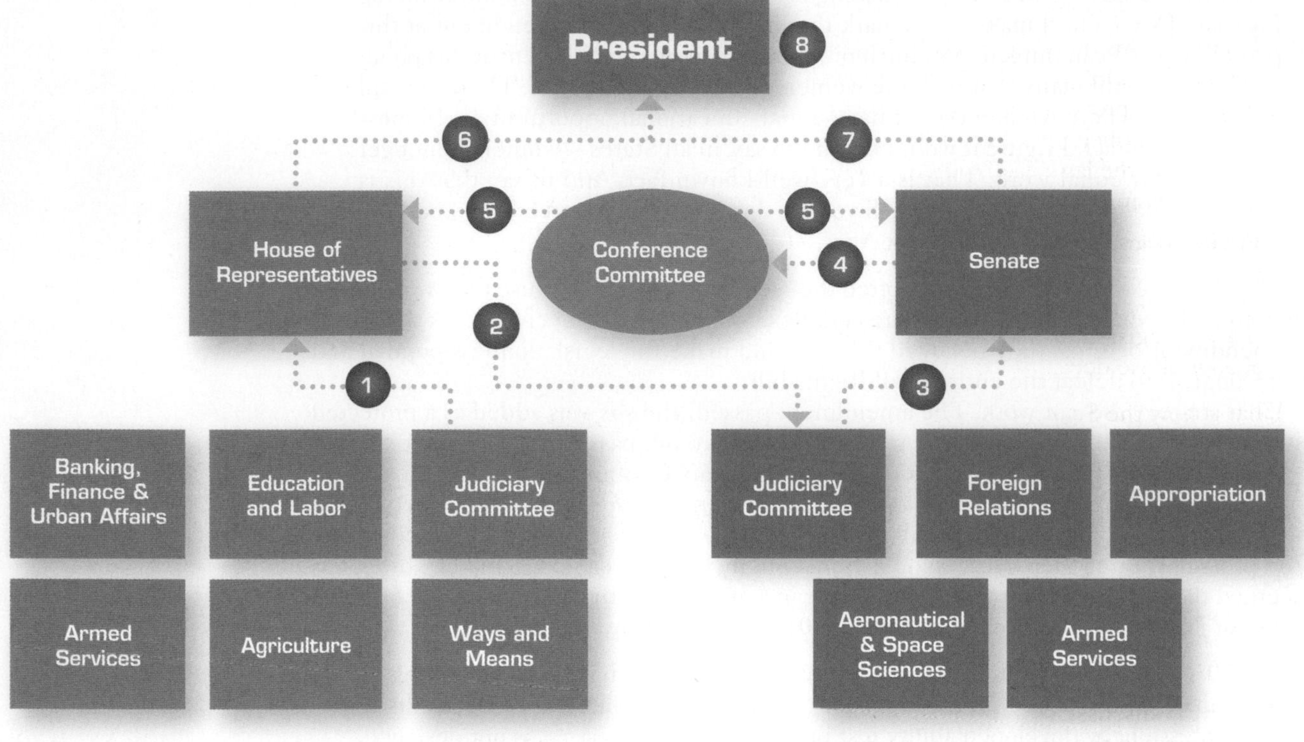

But the passing of a statute is not always the end of the story. Sometimes courts must interpret Congressional language and intent.

4-2e Statutory Interpretation

Title VII of the Civil Rights Act obviously prohibited an employer from saying to a job applicant, "We don't hire minorities." In some parts of the country, that had been common practice; after the Civil Rights Act passed, it became rare. Employers who routinely hired whites only, or promoted only whites, found themselves losing lawsuits. A new group of cases arose, those in which some job standard was set that appeared to be racially neutral, yet had a discriminatory effect. In North Carolina, the Duke Power Co. required that applicants for higher paying, promotional positions meet two requirements: They must have a high school diploma, and they must pass a standardized written test. There was no evidence that either requirement related to successful job performance. Blacks met the requirements in lower percentages than whites, and consequently whites obtained a disproportionate share of the good jobs.

Title VII did not precisely address this kind of case. It clearly outlawed overt discrimination. Was Duke Power's policy overt discrimination, or was it protected by Senator Tower's amendment, §703(h)? The case went all the way to the Supreme Court, where the Court had to interpret the new law.

Courts are often called upon to interpret a statute, that is, to explain precisely what the language means and how it applies in a given case. There are three primary steps in a court's statutory interpretation:

- **Plain meaning rule.** When a statute's words have ordinary, everyday significance, the court will simply apply those words. Section 703(a)(1) of the Civil Rights Act prohibits firing someone because of her religion. Could an employer who had fired a Catholic because of her religion argue that Catholicism is not really a religion, but more of a social group? No. The word "religion" has a plain meaning and courts apply its commonsense definition.
- **Legislative history and intent.** If the language is unclear, the court must look deeper. Section 703(a)(2) prohibits classifying employees in ways that are discriminatory. Does that section prevent an employer from requiring high school diplomas, as Duke Power did? The explicit language of the statute does not answer the question. The court will look at the law's history to determine the intent of the legislature. The court will examine committee hearings, reports, and the floor debates that we have seen.
- **Public policy.** If the legislative history is unclear, courts will rely on general public policies, such as reducing crime, creating equal opportunity, and so forth. They may include in this examination some of their own prior decisions. Courts assume that the legislature is aware of prior judicial decisions, and, if the legislature did not change those decisions, the statute will be interpreted to incorporate them.

Here is how the Supreme Court interpreted the 1964 Civil Rights Act.

Landmark Case

Griggs v. Duke Power Co.

401 U.S. 424
United States Supreme Court, 1971

Facts: See the discussion of the Duke Power Company's job requirements in the "Statutory Interpretation" section.

Issue: ***Did Title VII of the 1964 Civil Rights Act require that employment tests be job-related?***

Excerpts from Chief Justice Burger's Decision: The objective of Congress in the enactment of Title VII is plain from the language of the statute. It was to achieve equality of employment opportunities and remove barriers that have operated in the past to favor an identifiable group of white employees over other employees. Under the Act, practices, procedures, or tests neutral on their face, and even neutral in terms of intent, cannot be maintained if they operate to "freeze" the status quo of prior discriminatory employment practices.

The Act proscribes not only overt discrimination but also practices that are fair in form, but discriminatory in operation. The touchstone is business necessity. If an employment practice which operates to exclude Negroes cannot be shown to be related to job performance, the practice is prohibited.

On the record before us, neither the high school completion requirement nor the general intelligence test is shown to bear a demonstrable relationship to successful performance of the jobs for which it was used.

Senator Tower offered an amendment which was adopted verbatim and is now the testing provision of section 703(h). Speaking for the supporters of Title VII, Senator Humphrey endorsed the amendment, stating: "Senators on both sides of the aisle who were deeply interested in Title VII have examined the text of this amendment and have found it to be in accord with the intent and purpose of that title." The amendment was then adopted. From the sum of the legislative history relevant in this case, the conclusion is inescapable that the requirement that employment tests be job related comports with congressional intent.

And so the highest Court ruled that if a job requirement had a discriminatory impact, the employer could use that requirement only if it was related to job performance. Many more cases arose. For almost two decades courts held that, once workers showed that a job requirement had a discriminatory effect, the employer had the burden to prove that the requirement was necessary for the business. The requirement had to be essential to achieve an important goal. If there was any way to achieve that goal without discriminatory impact, the employer had to use it.

4-2f Changing Times

But things changed. In 1989, a more conservative Supreme Court decided *Wards Cove Packing Co. v. Atonio.*[10] The plaintiffs were nonwhite workers in salmon canneries in Alaska. The canneries had two types of jobs, skilled and unskilled. Nonwhites (Filipinos and native Alaskans) invariably worked as low-paid, unskilled workers, canning the fish. The higher paid, skilled positions were filled almost entirely with white workers, who were hired during the off-season in Washington and Oregon.

There was no overt discrimination. But plaintiffs claimed that various practices led to the racial imbalances. The practices included failing to promote from within the company, hiring through separate channels (cannery jobs were done through a union hall; skilled positions were filled out of state), nepotism, and an English language requirement. Once again the case reached the Supreme Court, where Justice White wrote the Court's opinion.

If the plaintiffs succeeded in showing that the job requirements led to racial imbalance, said the Court, the employer now only had to demonstrate that the requirement or practice "serves, in a significant way, the legitimate employment goals of the employer . . . . [T]here is no requirement that the challenged practice be 'essential' or 'indispensable' to the employer's business." In other words, the Court removed the "business necessity" requirement of *Griggs* and replaced it with "legitimate employment goals."

4-2g Voters' Role

The response to *Wards Cove* was quick. Liberals decried it; conservatives hailed it. Everyone agreed that it was a major change that would make it substantially harder for plaintiffs to bring successful discrimination cases. Democrats introduced bills to reverse the interpretation of *Wards Cove.* President George H. W. Bush strongly opposed any new bill. He said it would lead to "quotas," that is, that employers would feel obligated to hire a certain percentage of workers from all racial categories to protect themselves from suits. This was the issue that Congressman Johansen had raised in the original House debate in 1964.

Both houses passed bills restoring the "business necessity" holding of *Griggs.* Again there were differences, and a Conference Committee resolved them. After acrimonious debate, both houses passed the compromise bill in October 1990. Was it therefore law? No. President Bush immediately vetoed the bill. He said it would compel employers to adopt quotas.

4-2h Congressional Override

When the president vetoes a bill, Congress has one last chance to make it law: an override. If both houses repass the bill, each by a two-thirds margin, it becomes law over the president's veto. Congress attempted to pass the 1990 Civil Rights bill over the Bush veto, but it fell short in the Senate by one vote.

Civil rights advocates tried again, in January 1991, introducing a new bill to reverse the *Wards Cove* rule. Again both houses debated and bargained. The new bill stated that, once an employee proves that a particular employment practice causes a discriminatory impact,

---

[10] 490 U.S. 642 (1989).

the employer must "demonstrate that the challenged practice is job related for the position in question and consistent with business necessity."

Now the two sides fought over the exact meanings of two terms: "job related" and "business necessity." Each side offered definitions, but they could not reach agreement. It appeared that the entire bill would founder over those terms. So Congress did what it often does when faced with a problem of definition: It dropped the issue. Liberals and conservatives agreed not to define the troublesome terms. They would leave that task to courts to perform through statutory interpretation.

With the definitions left out, the new bill passed both houses. In November 1991, President Bush signed the bill into law. The president stated that the new bill had been improved and no longer threatened to create racial quotas. His opponents charged he had reversed course for political reasons, anticipating the 1992 presidential election.

And so, the Congress restored the "business necessity" interpretation to its own 1964 Civil Rights Act. No one would say, however, that it had been a simple process.

EXAMStrategy

Question: Kelly Hackworth took a leave of absence from her job at Progressive Insurance to care for her ailing mother. When she offered to return, Progressive refused to give her the same job or one like it. She sued based on the Family Medical Leave Act, a federal statute that requires firms to give workers returning from family leave their original job or an equivalent one. However, the statute excludes from its coverage workers whose company employs "fewer than 50 people within 75 miles" of the worker's jobsite. Between Ms. Hackworth's jobsite in Norman, Oklahoma, and the company's Oklahoma City workplace (less than 75 miles away), Progressive employed 47 people. At its Lawton, Oklahoma, facility, Progressive employed three more people—but Lawton was 75.6 miles (wouldn't you know it) away from Norman. Progressive argued that the job was not covered by the statute. Hackworth claimed that this distance should be considered "within 75 miles," thereby rendering her eligible for FMLA leave. Even if it were not, she urged, it would be absurd to disqualify her from important rights based on a disparity of six-tenths of a mile. Please rule.

Strategy: The question asks you to interpret a statute. How do courts do that? There are three steps: the plain meaning rule; legislative history; and public policy. Apply those steps to these facts.

Result: In this real case, the court ruled that the plain meaning of "within 75 miles" was *75 miles or less*. Lawton was not 75 miles or less from Norman. The statute did not apply and Ms. Hackworth lost.[11]

4-3 ADMINISTRATIVE LAW

Before beginning this section, please return your seat to its upright position. Stow the tray firmly in the seatback in front of you. Turn off any laptops, cell phones, or other electronic devices. Sound familiar? Administrative agencies affect each of us every day in hundreds of ways. They have become the fourth branch of government. Supporters believe that they provide unique expertise in complex areas; detractors regard them as unelected government run amok.

---

[11] Hackworth v. Progressive Casualty Ins. Co., 468 F.3d 722 (10th Cir. 2006).

Before beginning this section, please return your seat to its upright position. Stow the tray firmly in the seatback in front of you.

Many administrative agencies are familiar. The Federal Aviation Administration, which requires all airlines to ensure that your seats are upright before takeoff and landing, is an administrative agency. The Internal Revenue Service expects to hear from us every April 15. The Environmental Protection Agency regulates the water quality of the river in your town. The Federal Trade Commission oversees the commercials that shout at you from your television set.

Other agencies are less familiar. You may never have heard of the Bureau of Land Management, but if you go into the oil and gas industry, you will learn that this powerful agency has more control over your land than you do. If you develop real estate in Palos Hills, Illinois, you will tremble every time the Appearance Commission of the City of Palos Hills speaks, since you cannot construct a new building without its approval. If your software corporation wants to hire an Argentine expert on databases, you will get to know the complex workings of Immigration and Customs Enforcement: No one lawfully enters this country without its nod of approval.

4-3a Creation of Agencies

By the 1880s, trains crisscrossed America. But this technological miracle became an economic headache. Congress worried that the railroads' economic muscle enabled a few powerful corporations to reap unfair profits. The railroad industry needed closer regulation. Who would do it? **Courts decide individual cases; they do not regulate industries.** Congress itself passes statutes, but it has no personnel to oversee the day-to-day working of a huge industry. For example, Congress lacks the expertise to establish rates for freight passing from Kansas City to Chicago, and it has no personnel to enforce rates once they are set.

A new entity was needed. Congress passed the Interstate Commerce Act, creating the Interstate Commerce Commission (ICC), the first administrative agency. The ICC began regulating freight and passenger transportation over the growing rail system and continued to do so for more than 100 years. Congress gave the ICC power to regulate rates and investigate harmful practices, to hold hearings, issue orders, and punish railroads that did not comply.

The ICC was able to hire and develop a staff that was expert in the issues that Congress wanted controlled. The agency had enough flexibility to deal with the problems in a variety of ways: by regulating, investigating, and punishing. And that is what has made administrative agencies an attractive solution for Congress: One entity, focusing on one industry, can combine expertise and flexibility. However, the ICC also developed great power, which voters could not reach, and thereby started the great and lasting conflict over the role of agencies.

During the Great Depression of the 1930s, the Roosevelt administration and Congress created dozens of new agencies. Many were based on social demands, such as the need of the elderly population for a secure income. Political and social conditions dominated again in the 1960s, as Congress created agencies, such as the Equal Employment Opportunity Commission, to combat discrimination.

Then during the 1980s, the Reagan administration made an effort to decrease the number and strength of the agencies. For several years some agencies declined in influence, though others did not. Today, there is still controversy about how much power agencies should have.

Classification of Agencies

Agencies exist at the federal, state, and local level. We will focus on federal agencies because they have national impact and great power. Most of the principles discussed apply to state and local agencies as well. Virtually any business or profession you choose to work in will be regulated by at least one administrative agency, and it may be regulated by several.

Types of Agencies: Executive and Independent. Some federal agencies are part of the executive branch, while others are independent agencies. This is a major distinction. The president has much greater control of executive agencies for the simple reason that he can fire the agency head at any time. An executive agency will seldom diverge far from the president's preferred policies. Some familiar executive agencies are the Internal Revenue Service (part of the Treasury Department), the Federal Bureau of Investigation (Department of Justice), the Food and Drug Administration (Department of Health and Human Services), and the Nuclear Regulatory Commission (Department of Energy).

The president has no such removal power over independent agencies. The Federal Communications Commission (FCC) is an independent agency. For many corporations involved in broadcasting, the FCC has more day-to-day influence on their business than Congress, the courts, and the president combined. Other powerful independent agencies are the Federal Trade Commission, the Securities and Exchange Commission, the National Labor Relations Board, and the Environmental Protection Agency.

Enabling Legislation. Congress creates a federal agency by passing **enabling legislation**. The Interstate Commerce Act was the enabling legislation that established the ICC. Typically, the enabling legislation describes the problems that Congress believes need regulation, establishes an agency to do it, and defines the agency's powers.

Critics argue that Congress is delegating to another body powers that only the legislature or courts are supposed to exercise. This puts administrative agencies above the voters. But legal attacks on administrative agencies have consistently failed for several decades. Courts acknowledge that agencies have become an integral part of a complex economy, and so long as there are some limits on an agency's discretion, courts will generally uphold its powers.

4-3b Power of Agencies

Administrative agencies use three kinds of power to do the work assigned to them: They make rules, they investigate, and they adjudicate.

Rulemaking

One of the most important functions of an administrative agency is to make rules. In doing this, the agency attempts, prospectively, to establish fair and uniform behavior for all businesses in the affected area. **To create a new rule is to promulgate it.** Agencies promulgate two types of rules: legislative and interpretive.

Types of Rules: Legislative and Interpretive. Legislative rules are the most important agency rules, and they are much like statutes. Here, an agency creates law by requiring businesses or private citizens to act in a certain way. Suppose you operate a website for young shoppers, ages 10 to 18. Like most online merchants, you consider yourself free to collect as much data as possible about consumers. Wrong. The Federal Trade Commission, a federal agency, has promulgated detailed rules governing any site directed to young children. Before obtaining private data from these immature consumers, you must let them know exactly who you are, how to contact site operators, precisely what you are seeking, and how it will be used. You must also obtain verifiable parental consent before collecting, using, or disclosing any personal information. Failure to follow the rules can result in a substantial civil penalty. This modest legislative rule, in short, will be more important to your business than most statutes passed by Congress.

Interpretive rules do not change the law. They are the agency's interpretation of what the law already requires. But they can still affect all of us. For example, in 1977, Congress amended the Clean Air Act in an attempt to reduce pollution from factories. The act required the Environmental Protection Agency (EPA) to impose emission standards on "stationary sources" of pollution. But what did "stationary source" mean? It was the EPA's job to define that term. Obscure work, to be sure, yet the results could be seen and even smelled, because the EPA's definition would determine the quality of air entering our lungs every time we breathe. Environmentalists wanted the term defined to include every smokestack in a factory so that the EPA could regulate each one. The EPA, however, developed the "bubble concept," ruling that "stationary source" meant an entire factory, but not the individual smokestacks. As a result, polluters could shift emission among smokestacks in a single factory to avoid EPA regulation. Environmentalists howled that this gutted the purpose of the statute, but to no avail. The agency had spoken, merely by interpreting a statute.[12]

How Rules Are Made. Corporations fight many a court battle over whether an agency has the right to issue a particular rule and whether it was promulgated properly. The critical issue is this: How much participation is the public entitled to before an agency issues a rule? There are two basic methods of rulemaking.[13]

Informal Rulemaking. On many issues, agencies may use a simple "notice and comment" method of rulemaking. The agency must publish a proposed rule in advance and permit the public a comment period. During this period, the public may submit any objections and arguments, with supporting data. The agency will make its decision and publish the final rule.

For example, the Department of Transportation may use the informal rulemaking procedure to require safety features for all new automobiles. The agency must listen to objections from interested parties, notably car manufacturers, and it must give a written response to the objections. The agency is required to have rational reasons for the final choices it makes. However, it is not obligated to satisfy all parties or do their bidding.

Formal Rulemaking. In the enabling legislation, Congress may require that an agency hold a hearing before promulgating rules. Congress does this to make the agency more accountable to the public. After the agency publishes its proposed rule, it must hold a public hearing. Opponents of the rule, typically affected businesses, may cross-examine the agency experts about the need for the rule and may testify against it. When the agency makes its final decision about the rule, it must prepare a formal, written response to everything that occurred at the hearing.

When used responsibly, these hearings give the public access to the agency and can help formulate sound policy. When used irresponsibly, hearings can be manipulated to stymie needed regulation. The most famous example concerns peanut butter. The Food and Drug Administration (FDA) began investigating peanut butter content in 1958. It found, for example, that Jif peanut butter, made by Procter & Gamble, had only 75 percent peanuts and 20 percent vegetable oil shortening. P&G fought the investigation, and any changes, for years. Finally, in 1965, the FDA proposed a minimum of 90 percent peanuts in peanut butter; P&G wanted 87 percent. The FDA wanted no more than 3 percent hydrogenated vegetable oil; P&G wanted no limit.

The hearings dragged on for months. One day, the P&G lawyer objected to the hearing going forward because he needed to vote that day. Another time, when an FDA official testified that consumer letters indicated the public wanted to know what was really in peanut butter, the P&G attorney demanded that the official bring in and identify the letters—all 20,000 of them. Finally, in 1968, a decade after beginning its investigation, the FDA promulgated final rules requiring 90 percent peanuts but eliminating the 3 percent cap on vegetable oil.[14] But delay does not end when the FDA issues final rules because they can still be challenged in court.

---

12 An agency's interpretation can be challenged in court, and this one was.

13 Certain rules may be made with no public participation at all. For example, an agency's internal business affairs and procedures can be regulated without public comment, as can its general policy statements. None of these directly affect the public, and the public has no right to participate.

14 For an excellent account of this high-fat hearing, see Mark J. Green, *The Other Government* (New York: W. W. Norton & Co., 1978), 136–150.

Investigation

Agencies do a wide variety of work, but they all need broad factual knowledge of the field they govern. Some companies cooperate with an agency, furnishing information and even voluntarily accepting agency recommendations. For example, the U.S. Consumer Product Safety Commission investigates hundreds of consumer products every year and frequently urges companies to recall goods that the agency considers defective. Many firms comply.

Other companies, however, jealously guard information, often because corporate officers believe that disclosure would lead to adverse rules. To force disclosure, agencies use *subpoenas* and *searches*.

Subpoenas. A **subpoena** is an order to appear at a particular time and place to provide evidence. A **subpoena *duces tecum*** requires the person to appear and bring specified documents. Businesses and other organizations intensely dislike subpoenas and resent government agents plowing through records and questioning employees. What are the limits on an agency's investigation? The information sought:

Subpoena
An order to appear at a particular place and time. A subpoena *duces tecum* requires the person to produce certain documents or things.

- Must be *relevant* to a lawful agency investigation. The FCC is clearly empowered to investigate the safety of broadcasting towers, and any documents about tower construction are obviously relevant. Documents about employee racial statistics might indicate discrimination, but the FCC lacks jurisdiction on that issue and thus may not demand such documents.
- Must not be *unreasonably burdensome*. A court will compare the agency's need for the information with the intrusion on the corporation.
- Must not be *privileged*. The Fifth Amendment privilege against self-incrimination means that a corporate officer accused of criminal securities violations may not be compelled to testify about his behavior.

Search and Seizure. At times an agency will want to conduct a surprise **search** of an enterprise and **seize** any evidence of wrongdoing. May an agency do that? Yes, although there are limitations. When a particular industry is *comprehensively regulated*, courts will assume that companies know they are subject to periodic, unannounced inspections. In those industries, an administrative agency may conduct a search without a warrant and seize evidence of violations. For example, the mining industry is minutely regulated, with strict rules covering equipment, mining depths, and air quality. Mining executives understand that they are closely watched. Accordingly, the Bureau of Mines may make unannounced, warrantless searches to ensure safety.[15]

The following Landmark Case established many of the principles just described.

Landmark Case

United States v. Biswell

406 U.S. 311
United States Supreme Court, 1972

Facts: Biswell operated a pawnshop and had a license to sell "sporting weapons." Treasury agents demanded to inspect Biswell's locked storeroom. The officials claimed that the Gun Control Act of 1968 gave them the right to search without a warrant.

That law says, in part, "the Secretary [of the Treasury] may enter during business hours the premises of any firearms dealer for the purpose of inspecting or examining (1) any records or documents required to be kept by such dealer, and (2) any firearms or ammunition kept or stored by such dealer."

15 Donovan v. Dewey, 452 U.S. 594 (1981).

Biswell voluntarily opened the storeroom, and the agent found two sawed-off rifles inside. The guns did not remotely meet the definition of "sporting weapons," and Biswell was convicted on firearms charges.

The appellate court found that because the search violated the Fourth Amendment, the rifles could not be admitted as evidence. It reversed the conviction, and the government appealed to the Supreme Court.

Issue: *Did the agent's warrantless search violate the Constitution?*

Excerpts from Justice White's Decision: When the officers asked to inspect respondent's locked storeroom, they were merely asserting their statutory right, and respondent was on notice as to their identity and the legal basis for their action. Respondent's submission to lawful authority and his decision to step aside and permit the inspection rather than face a criminal prosecution is analogous to a householder's acquiescence in a search pursuant to a warrant when the alternative is a possible criminal prosecution for refusing entry or a forcible entry. In neither case does the lawfulness of the search depend on consent; in both, there is lawful authority independent of the will of the householder who might, other things being equal, prefer no search at all.

In the context of a regulatory inspection system of business premises that is carefully limited in time, place, and scope, the legality of the search depends not on consent but on the authority of a valid statute.

Federal regulation of the interstate traffic in firearms is undeniably of central importance to federal efforts to prevent violent crime. Large interests are at stake, and inspection is a crucial part of the regulatory scheme.

Here, if inspection is to be effective and serve as a credible deterrent, unannounced, even frequent, inspections are essential. In this context, the prerequisite of a warrant could easily frustrate inspection; and if the necessary flexibility as to time, scope, and frequency is to be preserved, the protections afforded by a warrant would be negligible.

It is also plain that inspections for compliance with the Gun Control Act pose only limited threats to the dealer's justifiable expectations of privacy. When a dealer chooses to engage in this pervasively regulated business and to accept a federal license, he does so with the knowledge that his business records, firearms, and ammunition will be subject to effective inspection. Each licensee is annually furnished with a revised compilation of ordinances that describe his obligations. The dealer is not left to wonder about the purposes of the inspector or the limits of his task.

We have little difficulty in concluding that where, as here, regulatory inspections further urgent federal interest, and the possibilities of abuse and the threat to privacy are not of impressive dimensions, the inspection may proceed without a warrant where specifically authorized by statute. The seizure of respondent's sawed-off rifles was not unreasonable under the *Fourth Amendment*, the judgment of the Court of Appeals is reversed, and the case is remanded to that court.

Adjudicate
To hold a formal hearing about an issue and then decide it

Administrative law judge (ALJ)
An agency employee who acts as an impartial decision maker

Adjudication. To **adjudicate** a case is to hold a hearing about an issue and then decide it. Agencies adjudicate countless cases. The FCC adjudicates which applicant for a new television license is best qualified. The Occupational Safety and Health Administration (OSHA) holds adversarial hearings to determine whether a manufacturing plant is dangerous.

Most adjudications begin with a hearing before an **administrative law judge (ALJ)**. There is no jury. An ALJ is an employee of the agency but is expected to be impartial in her rulings. All parties are represented by counsel. The rules of evidence are informal, and an ALJ may receive any testimony or documents that will help resolve the dispute.

After all evidence is taken, the ALJ makes a decision. The losing party has a right to appeal to an appellate board within the agency. The appellate board may ignore the ALJ's decision. If it does not, an unhappy party may appeal to federal court.

4-3c Limits on Agency Power

There are four primary methods of reining in these powerful creatures: statutory, political, judicial, and informational.

Statutory Control

As discussed, the enabling legislation of an agency provides some limits. It may require that the agency use formal rulemaking or investigate only certain issues. The Administrative Procedure Act imposes additional controls by requiring basic fairness in areas not regulated by the enabling legislation.

Political Control

The president's influence is greatest with executive agencies. Congress, though, "controls the purse." No agency, executive or independent, can spend money it does not have. An agency that angers Congress risks having a particular program defunded or its entire budget cut. Further, Congress may decide to defund an agency as a cost-cutting measure. In its effort to balance the budget, Congress abolished the Interstate Commerce Commission, transferring its functions to the Transportation Department.

Congress has additional control because it must approve presidential nominees to head agencies. Before approving a nominee, Congress will attempt to determine her intentions. And, finally, Congress may amend an agency's enabling legislation, limiting its power.

Judicial Review

An individual or corporation directly harmed by an administrative rule, investigation, or adjudication may generally have that action reviewed in federal court.[16] The party seeking review, for example, a corporation, must have suffered direct harm; the courts will not listen to theoretical complaints about an agency action.[17] And that party must first have taken all possible appeals within the agency itself.[18]

Standard on Review. Suppose OSHA promulgates a new rule limiting the noise level within steel mills. Certain mill operators are furious because they will have to retool their mills in order to comply. After exhausting their administrative appeals, they file suit seeking to force OSHA to withdraw the new rule. How does a court decide the case? Or, in legal terms, what standard does a court use in reviewing the case? Does it simply substitute its own opinion for that of the agency? No, it does not. The standard a court uses must take into account:

Facts. Courts generally defer to an agency's fact finding. If OSHA finds that human hearing starts to suffer when decibels reach a particular level, a court will probably accept that as final. The agency is presumed to have expertise on such subjects. As long as there is *substantial evidence* to support the fact decision, it will be respected.

Law. Courts often—but not always—defer to an agency's interpretation of the law. This is due in part to the enormous range of subjects that administrative agencies monitor. Consider the following example. "Chicken catchers" work in large poultry operations, entering coops, manually capturing broilers, loading them into cages, and driving them to a processing plant where they . . . well, never mind. On one farm, the catchers wanted to organize a union, but the company objected, pointing out that *agricultural* workers had no right to do so. Were chicken catchers agricultural workers? The National Labor Relations Board, an administrative agency, declared that chicken catchers were in fact *ordinary* workers, entitled to organize. The Supreme Court ruled that courts were obligated to give deference to the agency's decision about chicken catchers. If the agency's interpretation was *reasonable*, it was binding,

---

[16]In two narrow groups of cases, a court may not review an agency action. In a few cases, courts hold that a decision is "committed to agency discretion," a formal way of saying courts will keep hands off. This happens only with politically sensitive issues, such as international air routes. In some cases, the enabling legislation makes it absolutely clear that Congress wanted no court to review certain decisions. Courts will honor that.

[17]The law describes this requirement by saying a party must have standing to bring a case. A college student who has a theoretical belief that the EPA should not interfere with the timber industry has no standing to challenge an EPA rule that prohibits logging in a national forest. A lumber company that was ready to log that area has suffered a direct economic injury: It has standing to sue.

[18]This is the doctrine of exhaustion of remedies. A lumber company may not go into court the day after the EPA publishes a proposed ban on logging. It must first exhaust its administrative remedies by participating in the administrative hearing and then pursuing appeals within the agency before venturing into court.

even if the court itself might not have made the same analysis. The workers were permitted to form a union—though the chickens were not.

In the following case, however, the Supreme Court disagreed with the FCC's standards about profanity on TV. The high court ruled that these standards were too vague to be enforceable. The case contains vulgar language, so *please do not read it.*

Federal Communications Commission v. Fox Television Stations, Inc.

132 S. Ct. 2307
United States Supreme Court, 2012

Facts: U.S. law provides that "[w]hoever utters any obscene, indecent, or profane language by means of radio communication shall be fined . . . or imprisoned not more than two years, or both." The Federal Communications Commission has been instructed by Congress to enforce this law between the hours of 6 a.m. and 10 p.m.

In the 2002, Billboard Music Awards, broadcast by Fox, the singer Cher exclaimed: "I've also had my critics for the last 40 years saying that I was on my way out every year. Right. So f*** 'em." [During Fox's] Billboard Music Awards in 2003, Nicole Richie made the following unscripted remark while presenting an award: "Have you ever tried to get cow s*** out of a Prada purse? It's not so f***ing simple." During [NBC's] 2003 Golden Globe Awards, the singer Bono exclaimed: "This is really, really, f***ing brilliant. Really, really great," upon winning the award for Best Original Song.

The Commission had long held that fleeting, or single and unscripted, expletives were not indecent. But after the first two incidents, involving Cher and Richie, the Commission changed its policy, holding that even one-time use could be a violation. It then punished NBC for Bono's use of the F-word. Even though the Cher and Nicole Richie incidents took place before this policy change, the Commission retroactively applied its new policy to them and found Fox to be in violation of it.

Fox challenged the Commission's indecency regulations, claiming it did not have fair notice of what was forbidden. The Second Circuit found the policy was vague and, as a result, unconstitutional because it failed to give broadcasters sufficient notice of what would be considered indecent and because the Commission acted inconsistently. The Commission had on occasion found the fleeting use of the F-word and the S-word not indecent provided they occurred during a news interview or were "essential to an artistic or educational work." This standard left broadcasters guessing and led to a chill on protected speech. The FCC appealed and the Supreme Court granted *certiorari.*

Issue: ***Did the Commission give broadcasters fair notice of its policies?***

Excerpts from Justice Kennedy's Opinion: A fundamental principle in our legal system is that laws which regulate persons or entities must give fair notice of conduct that is forbidden or required. This requirement of clarity in regulation is essential to the protections provided by the Due Process Clause of the Fifth Amendment. It requires the invalidation of laws that are impermissibly vague.

Even when speech is not at issue, the regulated parties should know what is required of them so they may act accordingly. Precision and guidance are necessary so that those enforcing the law do not act in an arbitrary or discriminatory way.

In 2001, the Commission stated that for material to be indecent it must depict sexual or excretory organs or activities and be patently offensive as measured by contemporary community standards. A key consideration was "whether the material dwell[ed] on or repeat[ed] at length." In 2004, the Commission changed course and held that fleeting expletives could be a statutory violation. Now the Commission determined fleeting expletives were actionably indecent.

This history makes it apparent that the Commission policy in place at the time of the broadcasts gave no notice to Fox that a fleeting expletive could be actionably indecent; yet Fox [was] found to be in violation. The Commission's standards were vague. The lack of notice and vague standards render the Commission's policy unconstitutional. The Commission's orders must be set aside.

Informational Control and the Public

We started this section describing the pervasiveness of administrative agencies. We should end it by noting one way in which all of us have some direct control over these ubiquitous authorities: information.

> A popular government, without popular information, or the means of acquiring it, is but a Prologue to a Farce or a Tragedy—or perhaps both. Knowledge will forever govern ignorance, and a people who mean to be their own Governors must arm themselves with the power which knowledge gives.
>
> James Madison, President, 1809–17

Two federal statutes arm us with the power of knowledge.

Freedom of Information Act. Congress passed the landmark Freedom of Information Act (known as "FOIA") in 1966. It is designed to give all of us, citizens, businesses, and organizations alike, access to the information that federal agencies are using. The idea is to avoid government by secrecy.

Any citizen may make a "FOIA request" (pronounced "foy yah") to any federal government agency. It is simply a written request that the agency furnish whatever information it has on the subject specified. Two types of data are available under FOIA. Anyone is entitled to information about how the agency operates, how it spends its money, and what statistics and other information it has collected on a given subject. People routinely obtain records about agency policies, environmental hazards, consumer product safety, taxes and spending, purchasing decisions, and agency forays into foreign affairs. A corporation that believes that OSHA is making more inspections of its textile mills than it makes of the competition could demand all relevant information, including OSHA's documents on the mill itself, comparative statistics on different inspections, OSHA's policies on choosing inspection sites, and so forth.

Second, all citizens are entitled to any records the government has *about them*. You are entitled to information that the Internal Revenue Service, or the Federal Bureau of Investigation, has collected about you.

FOIA does not apply to Congress, the federal courts, or the executive staff at the White House. Note also that, since FOIA applies to federal government agencies, you may not use it to obtain information from state or local governments or private businesses.

Exemptions. An agency officially has ten days to respond to the request. In reality, most agencies are unable to meet the deadline but are obligated to make good faith efforts. FOIA exempts altogether nine categories from disclosure. The most important exemptions permit an agency to keep confidential information that relates to criminal investigations, internal agency matters such as personnel or policy discussions, trade secrets or financial institutions, an individual's private life, or national security.

In the following case, the American Civil Liberties Union (ACLU) demanded to know more about the government's use of unmanned aerial vehicles (drones) to kill humans. But how far would the court go in balancing national security with freedom of information. How far would you go?

Privacy Act. This 1974 statute prohibits federal agencies from giving information about an individual to other agencies or organizations without written consent. There are exceptions, but overall this act has reduced the government's exchange of information about us "behind our back." For more on privacy law, see Chapter 7 on privacy and internet law.

You Be the Judge

American Civil Liberties Union v. United States Department of Justice

2016 U.S. App. LEXIS 7308, 2016 WL 1657953
United States Court of Appeals, District of Columbia Circuit, 2016

Facts: Alarmed at the reported use of drones to kill human targets, the American Civil Liberties Union (ACLU) submitted a broad request under the Freedom of Information Act (FOIA) to the Central Intelligence Agency (CIA). The request sought information on drone strikes, including selection of targets, number of strikes, and number and identity of civilians killed.

The CIA denied the FOIA request. After years of litigation, it released only one heavily-edited document. The agency argued that FOIA exempted it from disclosure for two reasons. First, the CIA contended that the requested information related to intelligence activity, the integral legal mission of the CIA. Second, FOIA exempts classified information in the interest of national security. The CIA argued that the disclosure of drone strike records would imperil defense and foreign policy.

The ACLU did not agree. It maintained that the requested information was not secret because government officials had discussed drone strikes publicly. In fact, both President Obama and his CIA Director Leon Panetta had talked about the use of drone strikes in the fight against al-Qaeda.

The district court granted summary judgment in favor of the CIA. The ACLU appealed.

You Be the Judge: *Does FOIA require the disclosure of CIA records on drone strikes?*

Argument for the ACLU: Your honors, the CIA is improperly withholding information to which the American public is entitled. First, it is hiding behind the FOIA exemption that protects the disclosure of information about its functioning. The CIA's principal mission is foreign intelligence. A targeted-killing program is not an intelligence program; drone strikes are not a primary function of the CIA.

Under the CIA's interpretation of the national security exemption, it could refuse to provide any information about anything it does because everything in some way relates to foreign activities or national security. Is that the blanket license we want to give the CIA? We only request facts and figures, not anything that would reveal an intelligence operation.

Finally, a FOIA exemption can serve no purpose if the protected information is already public. The president and the director of the CIA had already acknowledged that the United States engages in drone strikes. All we respectfully request is the ability to keep the American public informed.

Argument for the CIA: The law gives the CIA broad power to protect the secrecy and integrity of the intelligence process. Responding to the ACLU's FOIA request would reveal sensitive information about the CIA's capabilities, limitations, priorities, and resources. There is no doubt that this kind of detail would reveal intelligence activities and is properly protected under FOIA exemptions. The law protects this information from disclosure for good reason, as its revelation would unnecessarily compromise the Agency's efforts and endanger Americans. As for President Obama's disclosures, acknowledging that drone strikes exist has very different implications from disclosing all of the details surrounding their use. The latter goes too far in the name of freedom of information—and compromises other freedoms in the process.

Ethan Miller/Getty Images News/Getty Images

CHAPTER CONCLUSION

"Why can't they just fix the law?" They can, and sometimes they do—but it is a difficult and complex task. "They" includes a great many people and forces, from common law courts to members of Congress to campaign donors to administrative agencies. The courts have made the bystander rule slightly more humane, but it has been a long and bumpy road. Congress managed to restore the legal interpretation of its own 1964 Civil Rights Act, but it took months of debating and compromising. The FDA squeezed more peanuts into a jar of Jif, but it took nearly a decade to get the lid on.

A study of law is certain to create some frustrations. This chapter cannot prevent them all. However, an understanding of how law is made is the first step toward controlling that law.

EXAM REVIEW

1. **COMMON LAW** The common law evolves in awkward fits and starts because courts attempt to achieve two contradictory purposes: predictability and flexibility.

2. **STARE DECISIS** *Stare decisis* means "let the decision stand" and indicates that once a court has decided a particular issue, it will generally apply the same rule in future cases.

3. **BYSTANDER RULE** The common law bystander rule holds that, generally, no one has a duty to assist someone in peril unless the bystander himself created the danger. Courts have carved some exceptions during the last 100 years, but the basic rule still stands.

4. **LEGISLATION** Bills originate in Congressional committees and go from there to the full House of Representatives or Senate. If both houses pass the bill, the legislation normally must go to a Conference Committee to resolve differences between the two versions. The compromise version then goes from the Conference Committee back to both houses, and if passed by both, to the president. If the president signs the bill, it becomes a statute; if he vetoes it, Congress can pass it over his veto with a two-thirds majority in each house.

5. **STATUTORY INTERPRETATION** Courts interpret a statute by using the plain meaning rule; then, if necessary, legislative history and intent; and finally, if necessary, public policy.

EXAMStrategy

Question: Whitfield, who was black, worked for Ohio Edison. Edison fired him, but then later offered to rehire him. Another employee argued that Edison's original termination of Whitfield had been race discrimination. Edison rescinded its offer to rehire Whitfield. Whitfield sued Edison, claiming that the company was retaliating for the other employee's opposition to discrimination. Edison pointed out that Title VII of the 1964 Civil Rights Act did not explicitly apply in such cases. Among other things, Title VII prohibits an employer from retaliating against *an employee* who has opposed illegal discrimination. But it does not say anything about retaliation based on *another employee's* opposition to discrimination. Edison argued that the statute did not protect Whitfield.

Strategy: What three steps does a court use to interpret a statute? First, the plain meaning rule. Does that rule help us here? The statute neither allows nor prohibits Edison's conduct. The law does not mention this situation, and the plain meaning rule is of no help. Second step: legislative history and intent. What did Congress intend with Title VII generally? With the provision that bars retaliation against a protesting employee? Resolving those issues should give you the answer to this question. (See the "Result" at the end of this Exam Review section.)

6. **ADMINISTRATIVE AGENCIES** Congress creates federal administrative agencies with enabling legislation. The Administrative Procedure Act controls how agencies do their work.

7. **RULEMAKING** Agencies may promulgate legislative rules, which generally have the effect of statutes, or interpretive rules, which merely interpret existing statutes.

8. **INVESTIGATION** Agencies have broad investigatory powers and may use subpoenas and, in some cases, warrantless searches to obtain information.

EXAMStrategy

Question: When Hiller Systems, Inc., was performing a safety inspection on board the M/V *Cape Diamond*, an ocean-going vessel, an accident killed two men. The Occupational Safety and Health Administration (OSHA), a federal agency, attempted to investigate, but Hiller refused to permit any of its employees to speak to OSHA investigators. What could OSHA do to pursue the investigation? What limits would there have been on OSHA's actions?

Strategy: Agencies make rules, investigate, and adjudicate. Which is involved here? Investigation. During an investigation, what power has an agency to force a company to produce data? What are the limits on that power? (See the "Result" at the end of this Exam Review section.)

9. **ADJUDICATION** Agencies adjudicate cases, meaning that they hold hearings and decide issues. Adjudication generally begins with a hearing before an administrative law judge and may involve an appeal to the full agency or ultimately to federal court.

10. **AGENCY LIMITATIONS** The four most important limitations on the power of federal agencies are statutory control in the enabling legislation and the Administrative Procedure Act, political control by Congress and the president, judicial review, and the informational control created by the FOIA and the Privacy Act.

RESULTS

5. Result: Congress passed Title VII as a bold, aggressive move to end race discrimination in employment. Further, by specifically prohibiting retaliation against an employee, Congress indicated it was aware that companies might punish those who spoke in favor of the very goals of Title VII. Protecting an employee from anti-discrimination statements made by a *coworker* is a very slight step beyond that, and appears consistent with the goals of Title VII and the anti-retaliation provision. Whitfield should win, and in the real case, he did.[19]

8. Result: OSHA can issue a subpoena *duces tecum*, demanding that those on board the ship, and their supervisors, appear for questioning, and bring with them all relevant documents. OSHA may ask for anything that is (1) relevant to the investigation, (2) not unduly burdensome, and (3) not privileged. Conversations between one of the ship inspectors and his supervisor are clearly relevant; a discussion between the supervisor and the company's lawyer is privileged.

MULTIPLE-CHOICE QUESTIONS

1. A bill is vetoed by ____________.

(a) the speaker of the House
(b) a majority of the voting members of the Senate
(c) the president
(d) the Supreme Court

2. If a bill is vetoed, it may still become law if it is approved by ____________.

(a) two-thirds of the Supreme Court
(b) two-thirds of registered voters
(c) two-thirds of the Congress
(d) the president
(e) an independent government agency

3. When courts interpret statutes, they ask ____________.

(a) what the words in the statute ordinarily mean
(b) which political parties endorsed the law
(c) what Congress intended the law to do
(d) whether or not the law supports good public policy
(e) all of these except (b)

4. Under FOIA, any citizen may demand information about ____________.

(a) how an agency operates
(b) how an agency spends its money
(c) files that an agency has collected on the citizen herself
(d) all of these

5. If information requested under FOIA is not exempt, an agency has ____________ to comply with the request.

(a) 10 days
(b) 30 days
(c) 3 months
(d) 6 months

[19]EEOC v. Ohio Edison, 7 F.3d 541 (6th Cir. 1993).

CASE QUESTIONS

1. In 1988, terrorists bombed Pan Am Flight 103 over Lockerbie, Scotland, killing all passengers on board. Congress sought to remedy security shortcomings by passing the Aviation Security Improvement Act of 1990, which, among other things, ordered the Federal Aviation Authority (FAA) to prescribe minimum training requirements and staffing levels for airport security. The FAA promulgated rules according to the informal rulemaking process. However, the FAA refused to disclose certain rules concerning training at specific airports. A public interest group called Public Citizen, Inc., along with family members of those who had died at Lockerbie, wanted to know the details of airport security. What steps should they take to obtain the information? Are they entitled to obtain it?

2. The Aviation Security Improvement Act (ASIA) states that the FAA can refuse to divulge information about airport security. The FAA interprets this to mean that it can withhold data in spite of the FOIA. Public Citizen and the Lockerbie family members interpret FOIA as being the controlling statute, requiring disclosure. Is the FAA interpretation binding?

3. Federal antitrust statutes are complex, but the basic goal is straightforward: to prevent a major industry from being so dominated by a small group of corporations that they destroy competition and injure consumers. Does Major League Baseball violate the antitrust laws? Many observers say that it does. A small group of owners not only dominate the industry, but actually own it, controlling the entry of new owners into the game. This issue went to the United States Supreme Court in 1922. Justice Holmes ruled, perhaps surprisingly, that baseball is exempt from the antitrust laws, holding that baseball is not "trade or commerce." Suppose that members of Congress dislike this ruling and the current condition of baseball. What can they do?

4. Iseberg, Slavin, and Gross were business partners. After Iseberg forced Slavin out of the business, Slavin told Gross he wanted to shoot Iseberg. Two years later, Slavin did just that, rendering Iseberg a paraplegic. Iseberg sued Gross, arguing he had a duty to warn his former partner of the danger. Who wins and why?

5. The FDA issued regulations requiring tobacco companies to put graphic warning images on their packages. The mandatory images included a corpse after an autopsy, a smoker's damaged lung, and a man exhaling smoke out of a hole in his neck, among others. What recourse do tobacco companies have if they want to challenge the FDA's rule?

DISCUSSION QUESTIONS

1. Courts generally follow precedent, but in *Tarasoff*, it did not. Consider the opening scenario based on the *Seinfeld* season finale. *Should* Jerry and his friends bear any civil *legal* responsibility for the carjacking or should a court follow precedent and hold the smug bunch blameless?

2. Revisit the *Fox* case. Do you agree with the opinion? What would a sensible broadcast obscenity policy contain? When (if ever) should a network face fines for airing bad language?

3. This chapter presents various examples where the law intersects with ethics. Jerry and his friends were rude and refused to help. Artists Cher and Nicole Richie uttered profanity on live national television at a time when children were watching. What are your Life Principles on these issues?

4. During live national coverage of a Super Bowl half-time show, Justin Timberlake tore off part of Janet Jackson's shirt, exposing her breast for nine-sixteenths of a second. Television network CBS called it a "wardrobe malfunction," but the "malfunction" coincidentally occurred just as Timberlake was singing the lyrics, "Gonna have you naked by the end of this song." The FCC fined CBS $550,000, but the network challenged the fine in court. The appeals court held CBS did not have to pay because the FCC did not have a clear policy on momentary displays of nudity. Do you agree with this conclusion? Do you think the incident was intentional or truly accidental? If it was intentional, should CBS have known better, regardless of FCC policies? If it was accidental, should CBS still be held accountable? Should it matter if it was intentional or accidental?

5. Should the law require restaurant employees to know and employ the Heimlich maneuver to assist a choking victim? If they do a bad job, they could cause additional injury. Should it permit them to do nothing at all? Is there a compromise position? What social policies are most important?

5

CHAPTER

CONSTITUTIONAL LAW

TO MAJOR JOHN CARTWRIGHT. MONTICELLO, June 5, 1824.
DEAR AND VENERABLE SIR,

I am much indebted for your kind letter . . .

Our Revolution presented us an album on which we were free to write what we pleased. We had no occasion to search into musty records, to hunt up royal parchments, or to investigate the laws and institutions of a semi-barbarous ancestry. We appealed to those of nature, and found them engraved on our hearts.

We had never been permitted to exercise self-government. When forced to assume it, we were novices in its science. Its principles and forms had entered little into our former education. We established, however, some, although not all, its important principles.

The wit of man cannot devise a more solid basis for a free, durable and well-administered republic.

The constitutions of most of our States assert that all power is inherent in the people; that they may exercise it by themselves, or they may act by representatives, freely and equally chosen; that it is their right and duty to be at all times armed; that they are entitled to freedom of person, freedom of religion, freedom of property, and freedom of the press.

In the structure of our legislatures, we think experience has proved the benefit of subjecting questions to two separate bodies of deliberants. The wit of man cannot devise a more solid basis for a free, durable and well-administered republic.

[O]ur State and federal governments are coordinate departments of one simple and integral whole. To the State governments are reserved all legislation and administration, in affairs which concern their own citizens only, and to the federal government is given whatever concerns foreigners, or the citizens of other States.

You will perceive that we have not so far [made] our constitutions unchangeable. [W]e consider them not otherwise changeable than by the authority of the people.

Can one generation bind another, and all others, in succession forever? I think not. A generation may bind itself as long as its majority continues in life; when that has disappeared, another majority is in place, holds all the rights and powers their predecessors once held, and may change their laws and institutions to suit themselves. Nothing is unchangeable but the inherent and unalienable rights of man.

Your age of eighty-four and mine of eighty-one years, insure us a speedy meeting. In the meantime, I pray you to accept assurances of my high veneration and esteem for your person and character.

Yours truly,
Thomas Jefferson

5-1 WHO WILL HAVE POWER?

5-1a Overview

The Constitution of the United States is the greatest legal document ever written. No other written constitution has lasted so long, governed so many, or withstood such challenge. This amazing work was drafted in 1787, when two weeks were needed to make the horseback ride from Boston to Philadelphia, a pair of young cities in a weak and disorganized nation.

Yet today, when that trip requires less than two hours by jet, the same Constitution successfully governs the most powerful country on Earth. This longevity is a tribute to the wisdom and idealism of the Founding Fathers. The Constitution is not perfect, but, overall, it has worked astonishingly well and has become the model for many constitutions around the world.

The Constitution is short and relatively easy to read. Because the language is general, it is open to interpretation. Its brevity is potent. And so is its reach: The Constitution sits above everything else in our legal system. No law can conflict with it. As Thomas Jefferson recounts in the introduction to this chapter, the Founding Fathers, or **Framers**, wanted it to last for centuries, and they understood that would happen only if the document was not "unchangeable." Indeed, the Constitution has been amended 27 times. Also, the interpretation of its provisions has changed over the years. As a result, the Constitution has stayed relevant in the face of changing social mores, times, and technology. The Constitution's versatility is striking.

This chapter discusses (1) the creation of the Constitution, (2) its division of power among the three branches of government, and (3) the individual rights that it guarantees to citizens.

5-1b Creating the Constitution: Important Principles

Thirteen American colonies declared independence from Great Britain in 1776, and gained it in 1783. The new status was exhilarating. Ours was the first nation in modern history founded on the idea that the people could govern themselves, democratically. The idea was daring, brilliant, and fraught with difficulties. The states were governing themselves under the Articles of Confederation, but these articles gave the central government no real power. The government could not tax any state or its citizens and had no way to raise money.

The national government also lacked the power to regulate commerce between the states or between foreign nations and any state. This was disastrous. States began to impose taxes on goods entering from other states. The young "nation" was a collection of poor relations, threatening to squabble themselves to death.

In 1787, the states sent a group of 55 delegates to Philadelphia. Rather than amend the old articles, the Framers set out to draft a new document and to create a government from scratch. In Jefferson's words, it was "an album on which we were free to write what we pleased." It was hard going. What structure should the government have? How much power? Representatives like Alexander Hamilton, a *federalist*, urged a strong central government. The new government must be able to tax and spend, regulate commerce, control the borders, and do all things that national governments routinely do. But Patrick Henry and other *antifederalists* feared a powerful central government. They had fought a bitter war precisely to get rid of autocratic rulers; they had seen the evil that a distant government could inflict. The antifederalists insisted that the states retain maximum authority, keeping political control closer to home.

The debate continues to this day, and periodically it plays a key role in elections. The "tea party" movement, for example, is a modern group of antifederalists.

Another critical question was how much power the *people* should have. Many of the delegates had little love for the common people and feared that extending this idea of democracy too far would lead to mob rule. Antifederalists again disagreed. The British had been thrown out, they insisted, to guarantee individual liberty and a chance to participate in the government. Power corrupted. It must be dispersed among the people to avoid its abuse.

How to settle these basic differences? By compromise, of course. **The Constitution is a series of compromises about power.** We will see many provisions granting power to one branch of the government while at the same time restraining the authority given.

Separation of Powers

The Framers did not want to place too much power in any single place. One method of limiting power was to create a national government divided into three branches, each independent and equal. Each branch would act as a check on the power of the other two. Article I of the Constitution created a Congress, which was to have legislative, or lawmaking, power. Article II created the office of president, defining the scope of executive, or enforcement, power. Article III established judicial, or interpretive, power by creating the Supreme Court and permitting additional federal courts.

Consider how the three separate powers balance one another: Congress was given the power to pass statutes, a major grant of power. But the president was permitted to veto, or block, proposed statutes, a nearly equal grant. Congress, in turn, had the right to override the veto, ensuring that the president would not become a dictator. The president was allowed to appoint federal judges and members of his cabinet, but only with a consenting vote from the Senate.

Individual Rights

The original Constitution was silent about the rights of citizens. This alarmed many who feared that the new federal government would have unlimited power over their lives. So in 1791, the first ten amendments, known as the **Bill of Rights**, were added to the Constitution, guaranteeing many liberties directly to individual citizens.

In the next two sections, we look in more detail at the two sides of the great series of compromises: power granted and rights protected.

5-1c Powers Granted

Congressional Power

To recap two key ideas from Chapter 1:

1. Voters in all 50 states elect representatives who go to Washington, D.C., to serve in Congress.
2. The Congress is comprised of the House of Representatives and the Senate. The House has 435 voting members, and states with large populations send more representatives. The Senate has 100 members—two from each state.

Congress wields tremendous power. Its members create statutes that influence our jobs, money, health care, military, communications, and virtually everything else. But can Congress create *any* kind of law it wishes? No.

Article I, section 8 is a critically important part of the Constitution. It lists the 18 types of statutes that Congress is allowed to pass, such as imposing taxes, declaring war, and coining money. Thus, only the national government may create currency. The state of Texas cannot print $20 bills with George W. Bush's profile.

States, like Texas, *are* supposed to create all other kinds of laws for themselves because the Tenth Amendment says, "All powers not delegated to the United States by the Constitution . . . are reserved to the States."

The **Commerce Clause** is the specific item in Article I, section 8, most important to your future as a businessperson. It calls upon Congress "to regulate commerce . . . among the several States," and its impact is described in the next section.

Commerce Clause
The part of Article I, section 8, that gives Congress the power to regulate commerce with foreign nations and among states

Interstate Commerce. With the Commerce Clause, the Framers sought to accomplish several things in response to the commercial chaos that existed under the Articles of Confederation. They wanted the federal government to speak with one voice when regulating commercial relations with foreign governments. The Framers also wanted to give Congress the power to bring coordination and fairness to trade among the states, and to stop the states from imposing the taxes and regulations that were wrecking the nation's domestic trade.

Virtually all of the numerous statutes that affect businesses are passed under the Commerce Clause. But what does it mean to regulate interstate commerce? Are all business transactions "interstate commerce," or are there exceptions? In the end, the courts must interpret what the Constitution means.

An important test of the Commerce Clause came in the Depression years of the 1930s, in *Wickard v. Filburn*.[1] The price of wheat and other grains had fluctuated wildly, severely harming farmers and the national food market. Congress sought to stabilize prices by limiting the bushels per acre that a farmer could grow. Filburn grew more wheat than federal law allowed and was fined. In defense, he claimed that Congress had no right to regulate him because none of his wheat went into *interstate* commerce. He sold some locally and used the rest on his own farm as food for livestock and as seed. The Commerce Clause, Filburn claimed, gave Congress no authority to limit what he could do.

The Supreme Court disagreed and held that **Congress may regulate any activity that has a substantial economic effect on interstate commerce**. Filburn's wheat *affected* interstate commerce because the more he grew for use on his own farm, the less he would need to buy in the open market of interstate commerce. In the end, "interstate commerce" does not require that things travel from one state to another.

In *United States v. Lopez*,[2] however, the Supreme Court ruled that Congress *had* exceeded its power under the Commerce Clause. Congress had passed a criminal statute called the "Gun-Free School Zones Act," which forbade any individual from possessing a firearm in a school zone. The goal of the statute was obvious: to keep schools safe. Lopez was convicted of violating the act and appealed his conviction all the way to the high Court, claiming that Congress had no power to pass such a law. The government argued that the Commerce Clause gave it the power to pass the law, but the Supreme Court was unpersuaded:

> The possession of a gun in a local school zone is in no sense an economic activity that might, through repetition elsewhere, substantially affect any sort of interstate commerce. [Lopez] was a local student at a local school; there is no indication that he had recently moved in interstate commerce, and there is no requirement that his possession of the firearm have any concrete tie to interstate commerce. To uphold the Government's contentions here, we would have to pile inference upon inference in a manner that would bid fair to convert Congressional authority under the Commerce Clause to a general police power of the sort retained by the States. [The statute was unconstitutional and void.]

[1] 317 U.S. 111 (1942).
[2] 514 U.S. 549 (1995).

In the following case, the Supreme Court was faced with a decision that would profoundly affect the health care and pocketbook of every American: Does the Commerce Clause allow Congress to *compel* people to enter into commerce?

National Federation of Independent Business v. Sebelius

132 S. Ct. 2566
United States Supreme Court, 2012

Facts: In 2010, Congress enacted the Patient Protection and Affordable Care Act (the Act), which aimed to increase the number of Americans covered by health insurance and decrease the cost of health care. The Act required most Americans either to maintain health insurance coverage or pay a "penalty" to the IRS. This provision was commonly referred to as the "individual mandate." The logic was that, if everyone—even healthy young people—had health insurance, health care costs would go down for all.

On the day President Barack Obama signed the Act into law, 13 states challenged it, alleging that neither the Constitution's Commerce provision nor its Taxing Clause gave Congress the authority to enact the individual mandate. Both the federal district court and the appeals court agreed. The Supreme Court granted *certiorari.*

Issue: ***Did Congress have the power to make every American purchase health insurance?***

Excerpts from Chief Justice Roberts's Decision: In our federal system, the National Government possesses only limited powers; the States and the people retain the remainder. In this case we must determine whether the Constitution grants Congress power to enact the individual mandate under the Commerce Clause or as an exercise of its power to tax.

The Constitution authorizes Congress to regulate interstate commerce and activities that substantially affect interstate commerce. [The Government argues] Congress may order individuals to buy health insurance because the failure to do so affects interstate commerce.

[But] the individual mandate does not regulate existing commercial activity. It instead compels individuals to become active in commerce by purchasing a product, on the ground that their failure to do so affects interstate commerce.

Every day individuals do not do an infinite number of things. Allowing Congress to justify federal regulation by pointing to the effect of inaction on commerce would bring countless decisions within the scope of federal regulation, and empower Congress to make those decisions.

[This] logic would justify a mandatory purchase to solve almost any problem. Many Americans do not eat a balanced diet. The failure of that group to have a healthy diet increases health care costs to a greater extent than the failure of the uninsured to purchase insurance. Under the Government's theory, Congress could address the diet problem by ordering everyone to buy vegetables.

The Commerce Clause is not a general license to regulate an individual from cradle to grave, simply because he will predictably engage in particular transactions. Any police power to regulate individuals as such, as opposed to their activities, remains vested in the States.

The individual mandate forces individuals into commerce precisely because they elected to refrain from commercial activity. Such a law cannot be sustained under a clause authorizing Congress to "regulate Commerce."

Congress also has the power to "lay and collect Taxes." Even if Congress lacks the power to direct individuals to buy insurance, the only effect of the individual mandate is to raise taxes on those who do not do so, and thus the law may be upheld as a tax.

Under the mandate, if an individual does not maintain health insurance, the only consequence is that he must pay the IRS. The mandate is not a legal command to buy insurance. Rather, it makes going without insurance just another thing the Government taxes, like buying gasoline or earning income. And if the mandate is in effect just a tax hike on certain taxpayers who do not have health insurance, it [is] within Congress's constitutional power to tax.

The [Act's penalty] looks like a tax in many respects, regardless of labels. It is paid into the Treasury by taxpayers when they file their tax returns. The IRS must assess and collect it in the same manner as taxes. This process yields the essential feature of any tax: It produces at least some revenue for the Government.

The Federal Government does not have the power to order people to buy health insurance. The Federal Government does have the power to impose a tax on those without health insurance. [The individual mandate] is therefore constitutional, because it can reasonably be read as a tax. Because the Constitution permits such a tax, it is not our role to forbid it, or to pass upon its wisdom or fairness.

The judgment of the Eleventh Circuit is *affirmed* in part and *reversed* in part.

State Legislative Power. The "dormant" or "negative" aspect of the Commerce Clause governs state efforts to regulate interstate commerce. **The dormant aspect holds that a state statute discriminating against interstate commerce is almost always unconstitutional**. Here is an example. Michigan and New York permitted in-state wineries to sell directly to consumers. They both denied this privilege to out-of-state producers, who were forced to sell to wholesalers, who offered the wine to retailers, who sold to consumers. This created an impossible barrier for many small vineyards, which did not produce enough wine to attract wholesalers. Even if they did, the multiple resales drove their prices prohibitively high.

Local residents and out-of-state wineries sued, claiming that the state regulations violated the dormant Commerce Clause. The Supreme Court ruled that these statutes obviously discriminated against out-of-state vineyards; the schemes were illegal unless Michigan and New York could demonstrate an important goal that could not be met any other way. The states' alleged motive was to prevent minors from purchasing wine over the internet. However, Michigan and New York offered no evidence that such purchases were really a problem. The Court said that minors seldom drink wine and, when they do, they seek instant gratification, not a package in the mail. States that allowed direct shipment to consumers reported no increase in purchases by minors. This discrimination against interstate commerce, like most, was unconstitutional.[3]

Supremacy Clause. What happens when both the federal and state governments pass regulations that are permissible, but conflicting? For example, Congress passed the federal Occupational Safety and Health Act (OSHA) establishing many job safety standards, including those for training workers who handle hazardous waste. Congress had the power to do so under the Commerce Clause. Later, Illinois passed its own hazardous waste statutes, seeking to protect both the general public and workers. The state statute did not violate the Commerce Clause because it imposed no restriction on interstate commerce.

Each statute specified worker training and employer licensing. But the requirements differed. Which statute did Illinois corporations have to obey? Article VI of the Constitution contains the answer. **The Supremacy Clause** states that the Constitution, and federal statutes and treaties, shall be the supreme law of the land.

The Supremacy Clause
Makes the Constitution, and federal statutes and treaties, the supreme law of the land

- If there is a conflict between federal and state statutes, the federal law **preempts** the field, meaning it controls the issue. The state law is void.
- Even in cases where there is no conflict, if Congress demonstrates that it intends to exercise exclusive control over an issue, federal law preempts.

Thus state law controls only when there is no conflicting federal law *and* Congress has not intended to dominate the issue. In the Illinois case, the Supreme Court concluded that Congress intended to regulate the issue exclusively. Federal law therefore preempted the field, and local employers were obligated to obey only the federal regulations.

EXAMStrategy

Question: Dairy farming was more expensive in Massachusetts than in other states. To help its farmers, Massachusetts taxed all milk sales, regardless of where the milk was produced. The revenues went into a fund that was then distributed to in-state dairy farmers. Discuss.

Strategy: By giving a subsidy to local farmers, the state is treating them differently than out-of-state dairies. This raises Commerce Clause issues. The dormant aspect applies. What does it state? Apply that standard to these facts.

Result: The dormant aspect holds that a state statute that discriminates against interstate commerce is almost always invalid. Massachusetts was subsidizing its farmers at the expense of those from other states. The tax violates the Commerce Clause and is void.

---

[3]Granholm v. Heald, 544 U.S. 460 (2005).

Executive Power

Article II of the Constitution defines executive power. The president's most basic job function is to enforce the nation's laws. Three of his key powers concern appointment, legislation, and foreign policy.

Appointment? Administrative agencies play a powerful role in business regulation, and the president nominates the heads of most of them. These choices dramatically influence what issues the agencies choose to pursue and how aggressively they do it. For example, a president who seeks to expand the scope of regulations on air quality may appoint a forceful environmentalist to run the Environmental Protection Agency (EPA), whereas a president who dislikes federal regulations will choose a more passive agency head.[4]

Legislation. The president and his advisers propose bills to Congress. During the past 50 years, a vast number of newly proposed bills have come from the executive branch. Some argue that *too many* proposals come from the president and that Congress has become overly passive. When a president proposes controversial legislation on a major issue, such as Social Security reform, the bill can dominate the news—and Congress—for months or even years. The president, of course, also has the power to veto bills.[5]

Foreign Policy. The president conducts the nation's foreign affairs, coordinating international efforts, negotiating treaties, and so forth. The president is also the commander in chief of the armed forces, meaning that he heads the military. But Article II does not give him the right to declare war—only the Senate may do that. A continuing tension between the president and Congress has resulted from the president's use of troops overseas *without* a formal declaration of war.

Judicial Power

Article III of the Constitution creates the Supreme Court and permits Congress to establish lower courts within the federal court system.[6] Federal courts have two key functions: adjudication and judicial review.

Adjudicating Cases. The federal court system hears criminal and civil cases. Generally, prosecutions of federal crimes begin in United States District Court. That same court has limited jurisdiction to hear civil lawsuits, a subject discussed in Chapter 3, on dispute resolution.

Judicial Review. One of the greatest "constitutional" powers appears nowhere in the Constitution. In 1803, the Supreme Court decided *Marbury v. Madison.*[7] Congress had passed a relatively minor statute that gave certain powers to the Supreme Court, and Marbury wanted the Court to use those powers. The Court refused. In an opinion written by Chief Justice John Marshall, the Court held that the statute violated the Constitution because Article III of the Constitution did not grant the Court those powers. The details of the case were insignificant, but the ruling was profound: Because the statute violated the Constitution, said the Court, it was void. **Judicial review refers to the power of federal courts to declare a statute or governmental action unconstitutional and void.**

This formidable grab of power has produced two centuries of controversy. The Court was declaring that it alone had the right to evaluate acts of the other two branches of

---

[4]For a discussion of administrative agency power, see Chapter 4 on administrative law.

[5]For a discussion of the president's veto power and Congress's power to override a veto, see Chapter 4 on statutory law.

[6]For a discussion of the federal court system, see Chapter 3 on dispute resolution.

[7]5 U.S. 137(1803).

government—the legislative and the executive—and to decide which were valid and which void. The Constitution nowhere grants this power. Undaunted, Marshall declared that "[I]t is emphatically the province and duty of the judicial department to say what the law is." In later cases, the Supreme Court expanded on the idea, holding that it could also nullify state statutes, rulings by state courts, and actions by federal and state officials. In this chapter, we have already encountered an example of judicial review in the *Lopez* case, where the justices declared that Congress lacked the power to pass local gun regulations.

Is judicial review good for the nation? Those who oppose it argue that federal court judges are all appointed, not elected, and that we should not permit judges to nullify a statute passed by elected officials because that diminishes the people's role in their government. Those who favor judicial review insist that there must be one cohesive interpretation of the Constitution, and the judicial branch is the logical one to provide it.

The following example of judicial review shows how immediate and emotional the issue can be. This is a criminal prosecution for a brutal crime. Cases like this force us to examine two questions about judicial review. What is the proper punishment for such a horrible crime? Just as important, *who should make that decision*—appointed judges or elected legislators?

North Wind Picture Archives/Alamy Stock Photo

Chief Justice John Marshall

Kennedy v. Louisiana

554 U.S. 407
United States Supreme Court, 2008

Facts: Patrick Kennedy raped his eight-year-old stepdaughter. Her injuries were the most severe that the forensic expert had ever seen. Kennedy was convicted of aggravated rape because the victim was under 12 years of age.

The jury voted to sentence Kennedy to death, which was permitted by the Louisiana statute. The state supreme court *affirmed* the death sentence, and Kennedy appealed to the United States Supreme Court. He argued that the Louisiana statute was unconstitutional. The Eighth Amendment prohibits cruel and unusual punishment, which includes penalties that are out of proportion to the crime. Kennedy claimed that capital punishment was out of proportion to rape and violated the Eighth Amendment.

Issues: ***Did the Louisiana statute violate the Constitution by permitting the death penalty in a case of child rape? Is it proper for the Supreme Court to decide this issue?***

Excerpts from Justice Kennedy's Decision: The constitutional prohibition against excessive or cruel and unusual punishments mandates that the State's power to punish be exercised within the limits of civilized standards. Evolving standards of decency that mark the progress of a maturing society counsel us to be most hesitant before interpreting the Eighth Amendment to allow the extension of the death penalty, a hesitation that has special force where no life was taken in the commission of the crime.

Consistent with evolving standards of decency and the teachings of our precedents we conclude that, in determining whether the death penalty is excessive, there is a distinction between intentional first-degree murder on the one hand and nonhomicide crimes against individual persons, even including child rape, on the other. The latter crimes may be devastating in their harm, as here, but in terms of moral depravity and of the injury to the person and to the public, they cannot be compared to murder in their severity and irrevocability.

Louisiana reintroduced the death penalty for rape of a child in 1995. Five States have since followed Louisiana's lead: Georgia, Montana, Oklahoma, South Carolina, and Texas. By contrast, 44 states have not made child rape a capital offense. As for federal law, Congress in the Federal Death Penalty Act of 1994 expanded the number of federal crimes for which the death penalty is a permissible sentence, including certain nonhomicide offenses; but it did not do the same for child rape or abuse. [The court concludes that there is a national consensus against imposing the death penalty for rape, and strikes down the Louisiana statute.]

Justice Alito, dissenting: If anything can be inferred from state legislative developments, the message is very different from the one that the Court perceives. In just the past few years, five States have enacted targeted capital child-rape laws. Such a development would not be out of step with changes in our society's thinking. During that time, reported instances of child abuse have increased dramatically; and there are many indications of growing alarm about the sexual abuse of children.

Judicial Activism/Judicial Restraint. The power of judicial review is potentially dictatorial. The Supreme Court nullifies statutes passed by Congress (*Marbury v. Madison, United States v. Lopez*) and executive actions. May it strike down any law it dislikes? In theory, no—the Court should nullify only laws that violate the Constitution. But in practice, yes—the Constitution means whatever the majority of the current justices says it means, because it is the Court that tells us which laws are violative.

Judicial activism
A court's willingness to decide issues on constitutional grounds

Judicial restraint
A court's attitude that it should leave lawmaking to legislators

Judicial activism refers to a court's willingness, or even eagerness, to become involved in major issues and to decide cases on constitutional grounds. Activists are sometimes willing to "stretch" laws beyond their most obvious meaning. **Judicial restraint** is the opposite, an attitude that courts should leave lawmaking to legislators and nullify a law only when it unquestionably violates the Constitution. Some justices believe that the Founding Fathers never intended the judicial branch to take a prominent role in sculpting the nation's laws and its social vision. In certain high-profile political cases, the Court has reminded us of its role. Notice the last sentence in the earlier *Sebelius* case: "Because the Constitution permits [the law], it is not our role to forbid it, or to pass upon its wisdom or fairness."

From the 1950s through the 1970s, the Supreme Court took an activist role, deciding many major social issues on constitutional grounds. The landmark 1954 decision in *Brown v. Board of Education* ordered an end to racial segregation in public schools, not only changing the nation's educational systems, but also forever altering its expectations about race.[8] The Court also struck down many state laws that denied minorities the right to vote. Beginning with *Miranda v. Arizona*, the Court began a sweeping reappraisal of the police power of the state and the rights of criminal suspects during searches, interrogations, trials, and appeals.[9] And in *Roe v. Wade*, the Supreme Court established certain rights to abortion, most of which remain after nearly 40 years of continuous litigation.[10]

Beginning in the late 1970s, and lasting to the present, the Court has pulled back from its social activism. Exhibit 5.1 illustrates the balance among Congress, the president, and the Court.

5-2 PROTECTED RIGHTS

The amendments to the Constitution protect the people of this nation from the power of state and federal governments. The First Amendment guarantees rights of free speech, free press, and religion; the Fourth Amendment protects against illegal searches; the Fifth

[8] 347 U.S. 483 (1954).
[9] 384 U.S. 436 (1966).
[10] 410 U.S. 113 (1973).

Amendment ensures due process; the Sixth Amendment demands fair treatment for defendants in criminal prosecutions; and the Fourteenth Amendment guarantees equal protection of the law. We consider the First, Fifth, and Fourteenth Amendments in this chapter and the Fourth, Fifth, and Sixth Amendments in Chapter 7 on crime.

The "people" who are protected include citizens and, for most purposes, corporations. Corporations are considered persons and receive most of the same protections. The great majority of these rights also extend to citizens of other countries who are in the United States.

Constitutional rights generally protect only against governmental acts. The Constitution generally does not protect us from the conduct of private parties, such as corporations or other citizens.

5-2a Incorporation

A series of Supreme Court cases has extended virtually all of the important constitutional protections to *all levels* of national, state, and local government. This process is called **incorporation** because rights explicitly guaranteed at one level are incorporated into rights that apply at other levels.

EXHIBIT 5.1

The Constitution established a federal government of checks and balances. Congress may propose statutes; the president may veto them; and Congress may override the veto. The president nominates cabinet officers, administrative heads, and Supreme Court justices, but the Senate must confirm his nominees. Finally, the Supreme Court (and lower federal courts) exercises judicial review over statutes and executive actions. Unlike the other checks and balances, judicial review is not provided for in the Constitution, but is a creation of the Court itself in *Marbury v. Madison*.

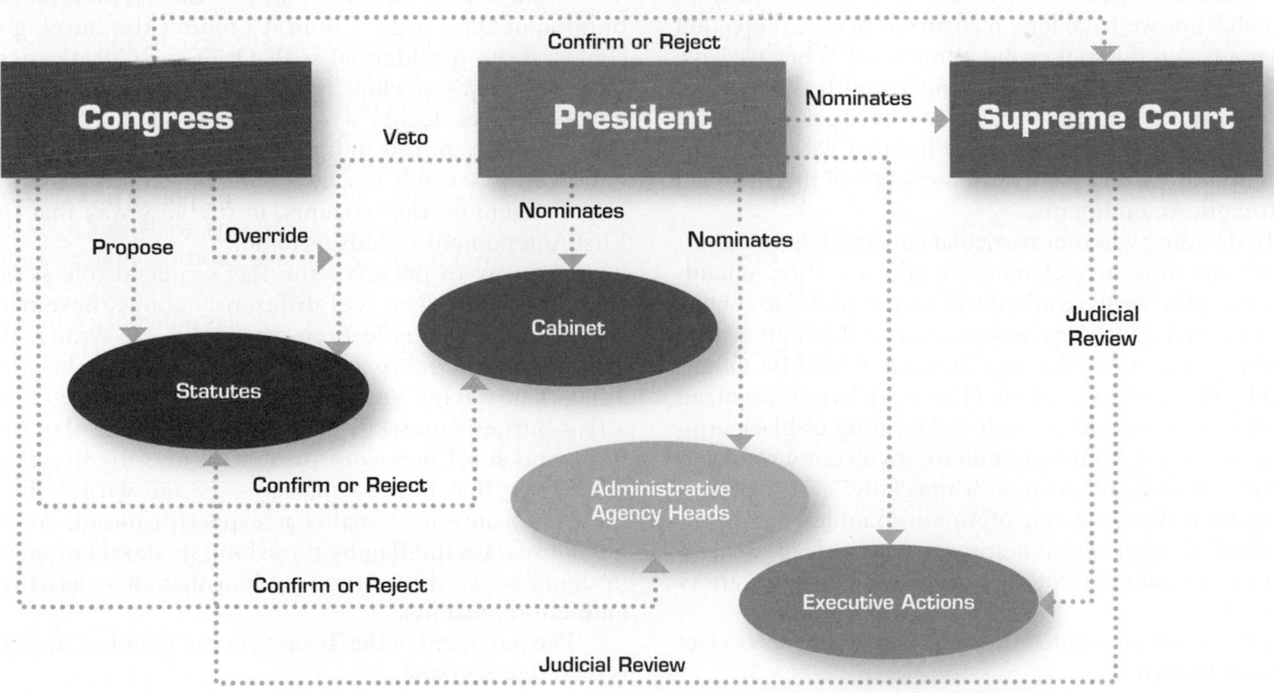

5-2b First Amendment: Free Speech

The First Amendment states that "Congress shall make no law . . . abridging the freedom of speech. . . ." In general, we expect our government to let people speak and hear whatever they choose. The Founding Fathers believed democracy would work only if the members of the electorate were free to talk, argue, listen, and exchange viewpoints in any way they wanted. The people could only cast informed ballots if they were informed. "Speech" also includes symbolic conduct, as the following case flamingly illustrates.

Texas v. Johnson

491 U.S. 397
United States Supreme Court, 1989

Facts: Outside the Republican National Convention in Dallas, Gregory Johnson participated in a protest against policies of the Reagan administration. Participants gave speeches and handed out leaflets. Johnson burned an American flag. He was arrested and convicted under a Texas statute that prohibited desecrating the flag, but the Texas Court of Criminal Appeals *reversed* on the grounds that the conviction violated the First Amendment. Texas appealed to the United States Supreme Court.

Issue: ***Does the First Amendment protect flag burning?***

Excerpts from Justice Brennan's Decision: The First Amendment literally forbids the abridgment only of "speech," but we have long recognized that its protection does not end at the spoken or written word. While we have rejected the view that an apparently limitless variety of conduct can be labeled "speech," we have acknowledged that conduct may be sufficiently imbued with elements of communication to fall within the scope of the First and Fourteenth Amendments.

In deciding whether particular conduct possesses sufficient communicative elements to bring the First Amendment into play, we have asked whether an intent to convey a particularized message was present, and [whether] the likelihood was great that the message would be understood by those who viewed it. Hence, we have recognized the expressive nature of students' wearing of black armbands to protest American military involvement in Vietnam; of a sit-in by blacks in a "whites only" area to protest segregation; of the wearing of American military uniforms in a dramatic presentation criticizing American involvement in Vietnam; and of picketing about a wide variety of causes.

[The Court concluded that burning the flag was in fact symbolic speech.]

It remains to consider whether the State's interest in reserving the flag as a symbol of nationhood and national unity justifies Johnson's conviction. Johnson was prosecuted because he knew that his politically charged expression would cause "serious offense."

If there is a bedrock principle underlying the First Amendment, it is that the Government may not prohibit the expression of an idea simply because society finds the idea itself offensive or disagreeable. Nothing in our precedents suggests that a State may foster its own view of the flag by prohibiting expressive conduct relating to it.

Could the Government, on this theory, prohibit the burning of state flags? Could it prohibit the burning of copies of the presidential seal? Or of the Constitution? In evaluating these choices under the First Amendment, how would we decide which symbols were sufficiently special to warrant this unique status? To do so, we would be forced to consult our own political preferences, and impose them on the citizenry, in the very way that the First Amendment forbids us to do.

The way to preserve the flag's special role is not to punish those who feel differently about these matters. It is to persuade them that they are wrong. We can imagine no more appropriate response to burning a flag than waving one's own, no better way to counter a flag-burner's message than by saluting the flag that burns, no surer means of preserving the dignity even of the flag that burned than by—as one witness here did—according its remains a respectful burial. We do not consecrate the flag by punishing its desecration, for in doing so we dilute the freedom that this cherished emblem represents.

The judgment of the Texas Court of Criminal Appeals is therefore *affirmed*.

Political Speech

Gordon Galbraith/Shutterstock.com

Protected speech?

Because the Framers were primarily concerned with enabling democracy to function, political speech has been given an especially high degree of protection. Such speech may not be barred even when it is offensive or outrageous. A speaker, for example, could accuse a U.S. senator of being insane and could use crude, violent language to describe him. The speech is still protected. **Political speech is protected unless it is intended and likely to create imminent lawless action.**[11] For example, suppose the speaker said, "The senator is inside that restaurant. Let's get some matches and burn the place down." Speech of this sort is not protected. The speaker could be arrested for attempted arson or attempted murder.

Time, Place, and Manner

Even when speech is protected, the government may regulate the *time*, *place*, and *manner* of such speech. A town may require a group to apply for a permit before using a public park for a political demonstration. The town may insist that the demonstration take place during daylight hours and that there be adequate police supervision and sanitation provided. However, the town may not prohibit such demonstrations outright.

Many public universities have designated "free speech zones" located in high-traffic areas of campus that are not immediately adjacent to a large number of classrooms. The zones allow for debates to proceed and reach many students, but they minimize the chances that noisy demonstrations will interfere with lectures.

Morality and Obscenity

The regulation of morality and obscenity presents additional problems. Obscenity has never received constitutional protection. The Supreme Court has consistently held that obscenity does not play a valued role in our society and has refused to give protection to obscene works. That is well and good, but it merely forces the question: What is obscene?

In *Jacobellis v. Ohio*, the Supreme Court held that the First Amendment protected a cinema manager who had been convicted of showing a racy French film.[12] But having ruled that that particular movie was not obscene, the Court did not go the next step and define what obscenity is. In his concurrence, Justice Potter Stewart famously described his own test for obscenity as "I know it when I see it." In 1973, in *Miller v. California*, the Court created a three-part test to determine if a creative work is obscene.[13] The basic guidelines for the fact finder are:

- Whether the average person, applying contemporary community standards, would find that the work, taken as a whole, appeals to the prurient interest;
- Whether the work depicts or describes, in a patently offensive way, sexual conduct specifically defined by the applicable state law; and
- Whether the work, taken as a whole, lacks serious literary, artistic, political, or scientific value.

---

11 Brandenburg v. Ohio, 395 U.S. 444 (1969).
12 378 U.S. 184 (1964).
13 413 U.S. 15 (1973).

If the trial court finds that the answer to all three of those questions is "yes," it may judge the material obscene; the state may then prohibit the work. If the state fails to prove any one of the three criteria, though, the work is not obscene. While *Miller* clarified the obscenity test, many questions remain, as these cases can be quite subjective. One court held that 2 Live Crew's 1989 rap album *As Nasty As They Wanna Be* was not obscene because it had artistic merit.[14] Another appeals court held that Japanese anime cartoons depicting sexual acts with minors were obscene, even though they did not show real people.[15]

Commercial Speech

Speech does not lose its First Amendment protection because someone paid for it. **Commercial speech is that which proposes a commercial transaction.** Most advertisements are **commercial speech**. This sort of speech is protected by the First Amendment, but the government is permitted to regulate it more closely than other forms of speech. Commercial speech that concerns an illegal activity or misleads consumers may be outlawed altogether. The Federal Trade Commission legitimately forced Listerine to stop running ads that falsely claimed its mouthwash helped prevent colds.[16]

Commercial speech
Communication, such as advertisements, that has the dominant theme of proposing a business transaction

When commercial speech is not illegal or misleading, the government may regulate it if:

1. It has a substantial interest in regulating the speech;
2. The speech restriction directly advances this interest; and
3. The regulation restricts no more speech than necessary.

In other words, the government may regulate commercial speech provided that the rules are reasonable and directly advance a legitimate government goal. The Food and Drug Administration passed a labeling law requiring tobacco companies to place large graphic images on every cigarette package as a warning to consumers. One of the photographs showed a corpse; another depicted black, smoke-filled lungs. Tobacco companies sued, arguing that the new rules violated the First Amendment because they were compelling the company to speak against their will. A federal appeals court struck down the law because, even though the government had a legitimate interest in communicating the ill-effects of smoking, it could not prove that the strong images would best achieve that goal.[17] A later case overruled that decision, reasoning that the state can mandate speech where it has an interest in correcting past deception. Since tobacco companies had a history of downplaying the negative effects of cigarettes and the cigarette labels were meant to correct that previous deception, the government's interest was justified and the graphic warnings passed First Amendment muster.[18]

EXAMStrategy

Question: Maria owns a lot next to a freeway that passes through Tidyville. She has rented a billboard to Huge Mart, a nearby retailer, and a second billboard to Green, a political party. However, Tidyville prohibits off-premises signs (those not on the advertiser's property) that are visible from the freeway. Tidyville's rule is designed to make the city more attractive, to increase property values, and to eliminate distractions that may cause freeway accidents. Huge Mart and Green sue claiming that Tidyville's law violates their First Amendment rights.

---

14 Luke Records, Inc. v. Navarro, 960 F. 2d 134 (11th Cir. 1992).

15 U.S. v. Whorely, 550 F.3d 326 (4th Cir. 2008).

16 Warner-Lambert Co. v. Federal Trade Commission, 562 F.2d 749 (D.C. Cir. 1977).

17 R. J. Reynolds Tobacco v. FDA, 696 F.3d 1205 (D.C. Cir. 2012).

18 American Meat Institute v. U.S. Department of Agriculture, 760 F.3d 18 (2014).

A. Huge Mart is likely to win; Green is likely to lose.

B. Green is likely to win; Huge Mart is likely to lose.

C. Huge Mart and Green are both likely to win.

D. Huge Mart and Green are both likely to lose.

Strategy: What is the difference between the two cases? Huge Mart wants the billboard for commercial speech; Green wants it for a political message. What are the legal standards for commercial and political free speech? Apply those standards.

Result: The government may regulate commercial speech, provided that the rules are reasonable and directed to a legitimate goal. Political speech is given much stronger protection, and can be prohibited only if it is intended and likely to create imminent lawless action. The regulation outlawing *advertising* will be upheld, but Tidyville will not be allowed to block political messages.

5-2c Fifth Amendment: Due Process and the Takings Clause

You are a senior at a major state university. You feel great about a difficult exam you took in Professor Watson's class. The Dean's Office sends for you, and you enter curiously, wondering if your exam was so good that the dean is awarding you a prize. Not quite. The exam proctor has accused you of cheating. Based on the accusation, Watson has flunked you. Four years of work and your entire career is suddenly on the line. You protest that you are innocent and demand to know the accusation. The dean says that you will learn the details at a hearing, if you wish to have one. She reminds you that if you lose the hearing, you will be expelled from the university.

Four years of work and your entire career is suddenly on the line.

The hearing is run by Professor Holmes, who will make the final decision. Holmes is a junior faculty member in Watson's department. (Next year, Watson will decide Holmes's tenure application.) At the hearing, the proctor accuses you of copying from a student sitting in front of you. Both Watson and Holmes have already compared the two papers and concluded that they are strongly similar. Holmes tells you that you must convince him the charge is wrong. You examine the papers, acknowledge that there are similarities, but plead as best you can that you never copied. Holmes doesn't buy it. The university expels you, placing on your transcript a notation of cheating.

Have you received fair treatment? To answer that, we must look to the Fifth Amendment, which provides several vital protections. We will consider two related provisions, the Due Process Clause and the Takings Clause. Together, they state: "No person shall be . . . deprived of life, liberty, or property without due process of law; nor shall private property be taken for public use, without just compensation." These clauses prevent the government from arbitrarily taking the most valuable possessions of a citizen or corporation. The government has the right to take a person's liberty or property. But there are three important limitations:

- **Procedural Due Process**. Before depriving anyone of liberty or property, the government must go through certain steps, or procedures, to ensure that the result is fair.
- **The Takings Clause**. When the government takes property for public use, such as to build a new highway, it has to pay a fair price.

Takings Clause
A clause in the Fifth Amendment that ensures that when any governmental unit takes private property for public use, it must compensate the owner

- **Substantive Due Process.** Some rights are so fundamental that the government may not take them from us at all. The substance of any law or government action may be challenged on fundamental fairness grounds.

Procedural Due Process

The government deprives citizens or corporations of their property in a variety of ways. The Internal Revenue Service may fine a corporation for late payment of taxes. The Customs Service may seize goods at the border. As to liberty, the government may take it by confining someone in a mental institution or by taking a child out of the home because of parental neglect. The purpose of **procedural due process** is to ensure that before the government takes liberty or property, the affected person has a fair chance to oppose the action. There are two steps in analyzing a procedural due process case:

Procedural due process The doctrine that ensures that before the government takes liberty or property, the affected person has a fair chance to oppose the action

- Is the government attempting to take liberty or property?
- If so, how much process is due? (If the government is *not* attempting to take liberty or property, there is no due process issue.)

Is the Government Attempting to Take Liberty or Property? Liberty interests are generally easy to spot: Confining someone in a mental institution and taking a child from her home are both deprivations of liberty. A property interest may be obvious. Suppose that, during a civil lawsuit, the court **attaches** a defendant's house, meaning it bars the defendant from selling the property at least until the case is decided. This way, if the plaintiff wins, the defendant will have assets to pay the judgment. The court has clearly deprived the defendant of an important interest in his house, and the defendant is entitled to due process. However, a property interest may be subtler than that. A woman holding a job with a government agency has a "property interest" in that job because her employer has agreed not to fire her without cause, and she can rely on it for income. If the government does fire her, it is taking away that property interest, and she is entitled to due process. A student attending any public school has a property interest in her education. If a public university suspends a student as described earlier, it is taking her property, and she, too, should receive due process.

How Much Process Is Due? Assuming that a liberty or property interest is affected, a court must decide how much process is due. Does the person get a formal trial, or an informal hearing, or merely a chance to reply in writing to the charges against her? If she gets a hearing, must it be held before the government deprives her of her property, or is it enough that she can be heard shortly thereafter? **What sort of hearing the government must offer depends upon how important the property or liberty interest is and on whether the government has a competing need for efficiency**. The more important the interest, the more formal the procedures must be.

Neutral Fact Finder. Regardless of how formal the hearing, one requirement is constant: The fact finder must be neutral. Whether it is a superior court judge deciding a multimillion-dollar contract suit or an employment supervisor deciding the fate of a government employee, the fact finder must have no personal interest in the outcome. In *Ward v. Monroeville*, the plaintiff was a motorist who had been stopped for traffic offenses in a small town.[19] He protested his innocence and received a judicial hearing. But the "judge" at the hearing was the town mayor. Traffic fines were a significant part of the town's budget. The motorist argued that the town was depriving him of procedural due process because the mayor had a financial interest in the outcome of the case. The United States Supreme Court agreed and *reversed* his conviction.

[19] 409 U.S. 57 (1972).

Attachment of Property. As described earlier, a plaintiff in a civil lawsuit often seeks to *attach* the defendant's property. This protects the plaintiff, but it may also harm the defendant if, for example, he is about to close a profitable real estate deal. Attachments used to be routine. In *Connecticut v. Doehr*, the Supreme Court required more caution.[20] Based on *Doehr*, when a plaintiff seeks to attach at the beginning of the trial, a court must look at the plaintiff's likelihood of winning. Generally, the court must grant the defendant a hearing *before* attaching the property. The defendant, represented by a lawyer, may offer evidence as to how attachment would harm him and why it should be denied.

Government Employment. A government employee must receive due process before being fired. Generally, this means some kind of hearing, but not necessarily a formal court hearing. The employee is entitled to know the charges against him, to hear the employer's evidence, and to have an opportunity to tell his side of the story. He is not entitled to have a lawyer present. The hearing "officer" need only be a neutral employee. Further, in an emergency where the employee is a danger to the public or the organization, the government may suspend with pay, before holding a hearing. It then must provide a hearing before the decision becomes final.

Academic Suspension. There is still a property interest here, but it is the least important of those discussed. When a public school concludes that a student has failed to meet its normal academic standards, such as by failing too many courses, it may dismiss him without a hearing. Due process is served if the student receives notice of the reason and has some opportunity to respond, such as by writing a letter contradicting the school's claims.

In cases of disciplinary suspension or expulsion, courts generally require schools to provide a higher level of due process. In the hypothetical at the beginning of this section, the university has failed to provide adequate due process. [21] The school has accused the student of a serious infraction. The school must promptly provide details of the charge and cannot wait until the hearing to do so. The student should see the two papers and have a chance to rebut the charge. Moreover, Professor Holmes has demonstrated bias. He appears to have made up his mind in advance. He has placed the burden on the student to disprove the charges. And he probably feels obligated to support Watson's original conclusion because Watson will be deciding his tenure case next year.

The Takings Clause

Florence Dolan ran a plumbing store in Tigard, Oregon. She and her husband wanted to enlarge it on land they already owned. But the city government said that they could expand only if they dedicated some of their own land for use as a public bicycle path and for other public use. Does the city have the right to make them do that? For an answer, we must look to a different part of the Fifth Amendment.

The Takings Clause prohibits a state from taking private property for public use without just compensation. A town wishing to build a new football field may boot you out of your house. But the town must compensate you. The government takes your land through the power of **eminent domain**. Officials must notify you of their intentions and give you an opportunity to oppose the project and to challenge the amount the town offers to pay. But when the hearings are done, the town may write you a check and level your house, whether you like it or not.

Eminent domain
The power of the government to take private property for public use

More controversial issues arise when a local government does not physically take the property but passes regulations that restrict its use. Tigard is a city of 30,000 in Oregon. The city developed a comprehensive land use plan for its downtown area in order to preserve

20 501 U.S. 1 (1991).

21 See, for example, University of Texas Medical School at Houston v. Than, 901 S.W.2d 926 (1995).

green space, to encourage transportation other than autos, and to reduce its flooding problems. Under the plan, when a property owner sought permission to build in the downtown section, the city could require some of her land to be used for public purposes. This has become a standard method of land use planning throughout the nation. States have used it to preserve coastline, urban green belts, and many environmental features.

When Florence Dolan applied for permission to expand, the city required that she dedicate a 15-foot strip of her property to the city as a bicycle pathway and that she preserve, as greenway, a portion of her land within a floodplain. She sued, and though she lost in the Oregon courts, she won in the United States Supreme Court. The Court held that Tigard City's method of routinely forcing all owners to dedicate land to public use violated the Takings Clause. The city was taking the land, even though title never changed hands.[22]

The Court did not outlaw all such requirements. What it required was that, **before a government may require an owner to dedicate land to a public use, it must show that this owner's proposed building requires this dedication of land.** In other words, it is not enough for Tigard to have a general plan, such as a bicycle pathway, and to make all owners participate in it. Tigard must show that it needs *Dolan's* land *specifically for a bike path and greenway*. This will be much harder for local governments to demonstrate than merely showing a citywide plan.

A related issue arose in the following controversial case. A city used eminent domain to take property on behalf of *private developers*. Was this a valid public use?

Kelo v. City of New London, Connecticut

545 U.S. 469
United States Supreme Court, 2005

Facts: New London, Connecticut, was declining economically. The city's unemployment rate was double that of the state generally, and the population was at its lowest point in 75 years. In response, state and local officials targeted a section of the city, called Fort Trumbull, for revitalization. Located on the Thames River, Fort Trumbull comprised 115 privately owned properties and 32 additional acres of an abandoned naval facility. The development plan included one section for a waterfront conference hotel and stores, a second one for 80 private residences, and one for research facilities.

The state bought most of the properties from willing sellers. However, nine owners of 15 properties refused to sell, and filed suit. The owners claimed that the city was trying to take land for *private* use, not public, in violation of the Takings Clause. The case reached the United States Supreme Court.

Issue: ***Did the city's plan violate the Takings Clause?***

Excerpts from Justice Stevens's Decision: It has long been accepted that the sovereign may not take the property of A for the sole purpose of transferring it to another private party B, even though *A* is paid just compensation. On the other hand, it is equally clear that a State may transfer property from one private party to another if future "use by the public" is the purpose of the taking; the condemnation of land for a railroad with common-carrier duties is a familiar example.

This is not a case in which the City is planning to open the condemned land—at least not in its entirety—to use by the general public. Nor will the private lessees of the land in any sense be required to operate like common carriers, making their services available to all comers. But this Court long ago rejected any literal requirement that condemned property be put into use for the general public, [embracing] the broader and more natural interpretation of public use as "public purpose." Thus, in a case upholding a mining company's use of an aerial bucket line to transport ore over property it did not own, Justice Holmes' opinion for the Court stressed "the inadequacy of use by the general public as a universal test."

The City has carefully formulated an economic development plan that it believes will provide appreciable benefits to the community, including—but by no means limited to—new jobs and increased tax revenue. As with

[22]Dolan v. City of Tigard, 512 U.S. 374 (1994).

other exercises in urban planning and development, the City is endeavoring to coordinate a variety of commercial, residential, and recreational uses of land, with the hope that they will form a whole greater than the sum of its parts. Because that plan unquestionably serves a public purpose, the takings challenged here satisfy the public use requirement of the Fifth Amendment.

To avoid this result, petitioners urge us to adopt a new bright-line rule that economic development does not qualify as a public use. [However, promoting] economic development is a traditional and long-accepted function of government. There is, moreover, no principled way of distinguishing economic development from the other public purposes that we have recognized. In our cases upholding takings that facilitated agriculture and mining, for example, we emphasized the importance of those industries to the welfare of the States in question. Clearly, there is no basis for exempting economic development from our traditionally broad understanding of public purpose.

The judgment of the Supreme Court of Connecticut is *affirmed*.

Justice O'Connor, dissenting: The Court today significantly expands the meaning of public use. It holds that the sovereign may take private property currently put to ordinary private use, and give it over for new, ordinary private use, so long as the new use is predicted to generate some secondary benefit for the public—such as increased tax revenue, more jobs, maybe even aesthetic pleasure. But nearly any lawful use of real private property can be said to generate some incidental benefit to the public. Thus, if predicted (or even guaranteed) positive side effects are enough to render transfer from one private party to another constitutional, then the words "for public use" do not realistically exclude *any* takings, and thus do not exert any constraint on the eminent domain power.

Any property may now be taken for the benefit of another private party, but the fallout from this decision will not be random. The beneficiaries are likely to be those citizens with disproportionate influence and power in the political process, including large corporations and development firms. As for the victims, the government now has license to transfer property from those with fewer resources to those with more.

In a sad twist, the proposed redevelopment never came to pass. Over a decade later, the New London properties remain empty, a victim of the subsequent economic downturn.

The *Kelo* decision sparked significant backlash. Some property rights activists were so upset that they proposed using the *Kelo* process to condemn Supreme Court Justice David Souter's own property in New Hampshire. In response to the public outcry, most states passed laws prohibiting eminent domain abuse. Justice Stevens later acknowledged that *Kelo* was the most unpopular opinion he ever wrote.[23]

Substantive Due Process

This doctrine is part of the Due Process Clause, but it is entirely different from procedural due process and from government taking. During the first third of the twentieth century, the Supreme Court frequently nullified state and federal laws, asserting that they interfered with basic rights. For example, in a famous 1905 case, *Lochner v. New York*, the Supreme Court invalidated a New York statute that had limited the number of hours that bakers could work in a week.[24] New York had passed the law to protect employee health. But the Court declared that private parties had a basic constitutional right to contract. In this case, the statute interfered with the rights of the employer and the baker to make any bargain they wished. Over the next three decades, the Court struck down dozens of state and federal laws that were aimed at working conditions, union rights, and social welfare generally. This was called **substantive due process** because the Court was looking at the underlying rights being affected, such as the right to contract, not at any procedures.[25]

Substantive due process
A form of due process that holds that certain rights are so fundamental that the government may not eliminate them

[23]Jess Bravin, "Justice Stevens on His 'Most Unpopular Opinion'," *Wall Street Journal*, Nov. 11, 2011.
[24]198 U.S. 45 (1905).
[25]The accent goes on the first syllable: <u>sub</u>stantive.

Critics complained that the Court was interfering with the desires of the voting public by nullifying laws that the justices personally disliked (judicial activism). During the Great Depression, however, things changed. Beginning in 1934, the Court completely *reversed* itself and began to uphold the types of laws it had struck down earlier.

The Supreme Court made an important substantive due process ruling in the case of *BMW v. Gore*.[26] A BMW dealership sold Gore a car that had sustained water damage. Instead of telling him of the damage, they simply repainted the car and sold it as new.

In Chapter 6, we will examine two different types of cash awards that juries may make in tort cases. For now, let's call them "ordinary" and "punitive" damages. When plaintiffs win tort cases, juries may always award ordinary damages to offset real, measureable losses. In addition, juries are sometimes allowed to add to an award to further punish a defendant for bad behavior.

In the *BMW* case, the jury awarded Gore $4,000 in ordinary damages as the difference in value between a flawless new car and a water-damaged car. The jury then awarded a delighted Gore $4 *million* in punitive damages. In the end, the Supreme Court decided that the punitive award was so disproportionate to the harm actually caused that it violated substantive due process rights.

5-2d Fourteenth Amendment: Equal Protection Clause

Shannon Faulkner wanted to attend The Citadel, a state-supported military college in South Carolina. She was a fine student who met every admission requirement that The Citadel set except one: She was not a man. The Citadel argued that its long and distinguished history demanded that it remain all male. Faulkner responded that she was a citizen of the state and ought to receive the benefits that others got, including the right to a military education. Could the school exclude her on the basis of gender?

Equal Protection Clause
A clause in the Fourteenth Amendment that generally requires the government to treat people equally

The Fourteenth Amendment provides that "No State shall . . . deny to any person within its jurisdiction the equal protection of the laws." This is the **Equal Protection Clause**, and it means that, generally speaking, **governments must treat people equally.** Unfair classifications among people or corporations will not be permitted. A notorious example of unfair classification would be race discrimination: Permitting only white children to attend a public school violates the Equal Protection Clause.

Yet clearly, governments do make classifications every day. People with high incomes pay a higher tax rate than those with low incomes; some corporations are permitted to deal in securities, while others are not. To determine which classifications are constitutionally permissible, we need to know what is being classified. There are three major groups of classifications. The outcome of a case can generally be predicted by knowing which group it is in.

- **Minimal Scrutiny: Economic and Social Relations.** Government actions that classify people or corporations on these bases are almost always upheld.
- **Intermediate Scrutiny: Gender.** Government classifications are sometimes upheld.
- **Strict Scrutiny: Race, Ethnicity, and Fundamental Rights.** Classifications based on any of these are almost never upheld.

Minimal Scrutiny: Economic and Social Regulation

Just as with the Due Process Clause, laws that regulate economic or social issues are presumed valid. They will be upheld if they are *rationally related to a legitimate goal.* This means a statute may classify corporations and/or people, and the classifications will be upheld if they make any sense at all. The New York City Transit Authority excluded all methadone users

[26] 517 U.S. 559 (1996).

from any employment. A federal district court concluded that this practice violated the Equal Protection Clause by unfairly excluding all those who were on methadone. The court noted that even those who tested free of any illegal drugs and were seeking non-safety-sensitive jobs, such as clerks, were turned away. That, said the district court, was irrational.

Not so, said the United States Supreme Court. The Court admitted that the policy might not be the wisest. It would probably make more sense to test individually for illegal drugs rather than automatically exclude methadone users. But, said the Court, it was not up to the justices to choose the best policy. They were only to decide if the policy was rational. Excluding methadone users related rationally to the safety of public transport and therefore did not violate the Equal Protection Clause.[27]

Intermediate Scrutiny: Gender

Classifications based on sex must meet a tougher test than those resulting from economic or social regulation. Such laws must *substantially relate to important government objectives*. Courts have increasingly nullified government sex classifications as societal concern with gender equality has grown.

At about the same time Shannon Faulkner began her campaign to enter The Citadel, another woman sought admission to the Virginia Military Institute (VMI), an all-male state school. The Supreme Court held that Virginia had violated the Equal Protection Clause by excluding women from VMI. The Court ruled that gender-based government discrimination requires an "exceedingly persuasive justification," and that Virginia had failed that standard of proof. The Citadel promptly opened its doors to women as well.[28]

Strict Scrutiny: Race, Ethnicity, and Fundamental Rights

Any government action that intentionally discriminates against racial or ethnic minorities, or interferes with a fundamental right, is presumed invalid. In such cases, courts will look at the statute or policy with *strict scrutiny*; that is, courts will examine it very closely to determine whether there is compelling justification for it. The law will be upheld only if it is *necessary to promote a compelling state interest*. Very few meet that test.

- **Racial and Ethnic Minorities.** Any government action that intentionally discriminates on the basis of race, or ethnicity, is presumed invalid. For example, in *Palmore v. Sidoti*, the state had refused to give child custody to a mother because her new spouse was racially different from the child.[29] The practice was declared unconstitutional. The state had made a racial classification, it was presumed invalid, and the government had no *compelling need* to make such a ruling.

- **Fundamental Rights**. A government action interfering with a fundamental right also receives strict scrutiny and will likely be declared void. For example, New York State gave an employment preference to any veteran who had been a state resident when he entered the military. Newcomers who were veterans were less likely to get jobs, and therefore this statute interfered with the right to travel, a fundamental right. The Supreme Court declared the law invalid.[30]

Fundamental rights
Rights so basic that any governmental interference with them is suspect and likely to be unconstitutional

Both parts of the Fourteenth Amendment have traditionally protected the right to marry: The Due Process Clause guarantees it as a fundamental liberty and the Equal Protection Clause ensures that the law treats all married people equally. But would these time-worn principles apply to same-sex marriages? The following landmark decision had the last word.

27 New York City Transit Authority v. Beazer, 440 U.S. 568 (1979).

28 United States v. Virginia, 518 U.S. 515 (1996).

29 466 U.S. 429 (1984).

30 Attorney General of New York v. Soto-Lopez, 476 U.S. 898 (1986).

Obergefell v. Hodges

134 S. Ct. 2584
United States Supreme Court, 2015

Facts: For two decades, James Obergefell and John Arthur were in a committed same-sex relationship in Ohio. Arthur got very sick, and the couple was eager to marry before he died. Since same-sex marriage was illegal in Ohio and Arthur could not easily move, the couple wed inside a medical transport plane parked on the tarmac in Maryland, which allowed same-sex marriage. Three months later, Arthur died. Ohio refused to list Obergefell on Arthur's death certificate.

Many other states besides Ohio, including Michigan, Kentucky, and Tennessee, also defined marriage as a union between one man and one woman. These states not only prohibited same-sex marriage they also refused to recognize unions performed in states where it was legal. Many other same-sex couples from those states had suffered similar experiences to Obergefell's. They were denied adoption and parental rights, hospital access, and basic inheritance and tax benefits, among other important privileges.

Obergefell and over two dozen others claimed these laws violated the Fourteenth Amendment. The appellate court held that the Constitution did not require the states to license same-sex marriages or to recognize those performed out of state. The petitioners appealed to the Supreme Court.

Issue: ***Does the Fourteenth Amendment require states to legally recognize a marriage between two people of the same sex?***

Excerpts from Justice Kennedy's Decision: The Constitution promises liberty to all within its reach, a liberty that includes certain specific rights that allow persons, within a lawful realm, to define and express their identity. The petitioners in these cases seek to find that liberty by marrying someone of the same sex and having their marriages deemed lawful on the same terms and conditions as marriages between persons of the opposite sex.

Under the Due Process Clause of the Fourteenth Amendment, no State shall "deprive any person of life, liberty, or property, without due process of law." The fundamental liberties protected by this Clause extend to certain personal choices central to individual dignity and autonomy, including intimate choices that define personal identity and beliefs.

The nature of injustice is that we may not always see it in our own times. The generations that wrote and ratified the Bill of Rights and the Fourteenth Amendment did not presume to know the extent of freedom in all of its dimensions, and so they entrusted to future generations a charter protecting the right of all persons to enjoy liberty as we learn its meaning. When new insight reveals discord between the Constitution's central protections and a received legal stricture, a claim to liberty must be addressed.

The nature of injustice is that we may not always see it in our own times.

First, marriage is inherent in the concept of individual autonomy. Choices about marriage shape an individual's destiny. The nature of marriage is that, through its enduring bond, two persons together can find other freedoms, such as expression, intimacy, and spirituality.

A second principle is that the right to marry is fundamental because it supports a two-person union unlike any other in its importance to the committed individuals. Same-sex couples have the same right as opposite-sex couples to enjoy intimate association.

A third basis for protecting the right to marry is that it safeguards children and families. Without the recognition, stability, and predictability marriage offers, children suffer the stigma of knowing their families are somehow lesser. The marriage laws at issue here thus harm and humiliate the children of same-sex couples.

Fourth and finally, this Court's cases and the Nation's traditions make clear that marriage is a keystone of our social order. Just as a couple vows to support each other, so does society pledge to support the couple, offering symbolic recognition and material benefits to protect and nourish the union. States have made marriage the basis for an expanding list of governmental rights, benefits, and responsibilities, including: taxation; inheritance and property rights; spousal privilege in the law of evidence; hospital access; medical decision making authority; adoption rights; workers' compensation benefits; health insurance; and child custody, support, and visitation rules. As the State itself makes marriage all the more precious by the significance it attaches to it, exclusion from that status has the effect of teaching that gays and lesbians are unequal in important respects.

No union is more profound than marriage, for it embodies the highest ideals of love, fidelity, devotion, sacrifice, and family. In forming a marital union, two people become something greater than once they were. As some of the petitioners in these cases demonstrate, marriage embodies a love that may endure even past death. It would misunderstand these men and women to say they disrespect the idea of marriage. Their plea is that they do respect it, respect it so deeply that they seek to find its fulfillment for themselves. Their hope is not to be condemned to live in loneliness, excluded from one of civilization's oldest institutions.

They ask for equal dignity in the eyes of the law. The Constitution grants them that right.

EXAMStrategy

Question: Megan is a freshman at her local public high school; her older sister Jenna attends a nearby private high school. Both girls are angry because their schools prohibit them from joining their respective wrestling teams, where only boys are allowed. The two girls sue based on the U.S. Constitution. Discuss the relevant law and predict the outcomes.

Strategy: One girl goes to private school and one to public school. Why does that matter? Now ask what provision of the Constitution is involved, and what legal standard it establishes.

Result: The Constitution offers protection from the *government*. A private high school is not part of the government, and Jenna has no constitutional case. Megan's suit is based on the Equal Protection Clause. This is gender discrimination, meaning that Megan's school must convince the court that keeping girls off the team *substantially relates to an important government objective*. The school will probably argue that wrestling with stronger boys will be dangerous for girls. However, courts are increasingly suspicious of any gender discrimination and are unlikely to find the school's argument persuasive.

CHAPTER CONCLUSION

The legal battle over power never stops. The obligation of a state to provide equal educational opportunity for both genders relates to whether Tigard, Oregon, may demand some of Dolan's store lot for public use. Both issues are governed by one amazing document. The same Constitution determines what tax preferences are permissible and even whether a state may require you to wear clothing. As social mores change in step with broad cultural developments, as the membership of the Supreme Court changes, the balance of power between federal government, state government, and citizens will continue to evolve. There are no easy answers to these constitutional questions because there has never been a democracy so large, so diverse, or so powerful.

EXAM REVIEW

1. **CONSTITUTION** The Constitution is a series of compromises about power.
2. **ARTICLES I, II, AND III** Article I of the Constitution creates the Congress and grants all legislative power to it. Article II establishes the office of president and defines executive powers. Article III creates the Supreme Court and permits lower federal courts; the article also outlines the powers of the federal judiciary.

3. **COMMERCE CLAUSE** Under the Commerce Clause, Congress may regulate any activity that has a substantial effect on interstate commerce.

4. **INTERSTATE COMMERCE** A state may not regulate commerce in any way that will interfere with interstate commerce.

EXAMStrategy

Question: Maine exempted many charitable institutions from real estate taxes but denied this benefit to a charity that primarily benefited out-of-state residents. Camp Newfound was a Christian Science organization, and 95 percent of its summer campers came from other states. Camp Newfound sued Maine. Discuss.

Strategy: The state was treating organizations differently depending on what states their campers came from. This raised Commerce Clause issues. Did the positive aspect or dormant aspect of that clause apply? The dormant aspect applied. What does it state? Apply that standard to these facts. (See the "Result" at the end of this Exam Review section.)

5. **SUPREMACY CLAUSE** Under the Supremacy Clause, if there is a conflict between federal and state statutes, the federal law preempts the field. Even without a conflict, federal law preempts if Congress intended to exercise exclusive control.

6. **PRESIDENTIAL POWERS** The president's key powers include making agency appointments, proposing legislation, conducting foreign policy, and acting as commander in chief of the armed forces.

7. **FEDERAL COURTS** The federal courts adjudicate cases and also exercise judicial review, which is the right to declare a statute or governmental action unconstitutional and void.

8. **FREEDOM OF SPEECH** Freedom of speech includes symbolic acts. Political speech by both people and organizations is protected unless it is intended and likely to create imminent lawless action.

9. **REGULATION OF SPEECH** The government may regulate the time, place, and manner of speech.

10. **COMMERCIAL SPEECH** Commercial speech that is false or misleading may be outlawed; otherwise, regulations on this speech must be reasonable and directed to a legitimate goal.

EXAMStrategy

Question: A federal statute prohibits the broadcasting of lottery advertisements, except by stations that broadcast in states permitting lotteries. The purpose of the statute is to support efforts of states that outlaw lotteries. Truth Broadcasting operates a radio station in State A (a nonlottery state) but broadcasts primarily in State B (a lottery state). Truth wants to advertise State B's lottery but is barred by the statute. Does the federal statute violate Truth's constitutional rights?

Strategy: This case involves a particular kind of speech. What kind? What is the rule about that kind of speech? (See the "Result" at the end of this Exam Review section.)

11. **PROCEDURAL DUE PROCESS** Procedural due process is required whenever the government attempts to take liberty or property. The amount of process that is due depends upon the importance of the liberty or property threatened.

EXAMStrategy

Question: Fox's Fine Furs claims that Ermine owes $68,000 for a mink coat on which she has stopped making payments. Fox files a complaint and also asks the court clerk to *garnish* Ermine's wages. A garnishment is a court order to an employer to withhold an employee's wages, or a portion of them, and pay the money into court so that there will be money for the plaintiff, if it wins. What constitutional issue does Fox's request for garnishment raise?

Strategy: Ermine is in danger of losing part of her income, which is property. The Due Process Clause prohibits the government (the court) from taking life, liberty, or property without due process. What process is Ermine entitled to? (See the "Result" at the end of this Exam Review section.)

12. **TAKINGS CLAUSE** The Takings Clause prohibits a state from taking private property for public use without just compensation.

13. **SUBSTANTIVE DUE PROCESS** A substantive due process analysis presumes that any economic or social regulation is valid, and presumes invalid any law that infringes upon a fundamental right.

14. **EQUAL PROTECTION CLAUSE** The Equal Protection Clause generally requires the government to treat people equally. Courts apply strict scrutiny in any equal protection case involving race, ethnicity, or fundamental rights; intermediate scrutiny to any case involving gender; and minimal scrutiny to an economic or social regulation.

RESULTS

4. Result: The dormant aspect holds that a state statute that discriminates against interstate commerce is almost always invalid. Maine was subsidizing charities that served in-state residents and penalizing those that attracted campers from elsewhere. The tax rule violated the Commerce Clause and was void.[31]

10. Result: An advertisement is commercial speech. The government may regulate this speech so long as the rules are reasonable and directed to a legitimate goal. The goal of supporting nonlottery states is reasonable, and there is no violation of Truth's free speech rights.[32]

11. Result: Ermine is entitled to notice of Fox's claim and to a hearing before the court garnishes her wages.[33]

[31]Camps Newfound/Owatonna, Inc. v. Town of Harrison, Maine, 520 U.S. 564 (1997).
[32]United States v. Edge Broadcasting, 509 U.S. 418 (1993).
[33]Sniadach v. Family Finance Corp., 395 U.S. 337 (1969).

MULTIPLE-CHOICE QUESTIONS

1. Greenville College, a public community college, has a policy of admitting only male students. If the policy is challenged under the Fourteenth Amendment, ______________ scrutiny will be applied.
   (a) strict
   (b) intermediate
   (c) rational
   (d) none of these

2. You begin work at Everhappy Corp. at the beginning of November. On your second day at work, you wear a political button on your overcoat, supporting your choice for governor in the upcoming election. Your boss glances at it and says, "Get that stupid thing out of this office or you're history, chump." Your boss ______________ violated your First Amendment rights. After work, you put the button back on and start walking home. You pass a police officer who blocks your path and says, "Take off that stupid button or you're going to jail, chump." The officer ______________ violated your First Amendment rights.
   (a) has; has
   (b) has; has not
   (c) has not; has
   (d) has not; has not

3. Which of the following statements accurately describes statutes that Congress and the president may create?
   (a) Statutes must be related to a power listed in Article I, section 8, of the Constitution.
   (b) Statutes must not infringe on the liberties in the Bill of Rights.
   (c) Both A and B
   (d) None of these

4. Which of the following is true of the origin of judicial review?
   (a) It was created by Article II of the Constitution.
   (b) It was created by Article III of the Constitution.
   (c) It was created in the *Marbury v. Madison* case.
   (d) It was created by the Fifth Amendment.
   (e) It was created by the Fourteenth Amendment.

5. Consider *Kelo v. City of New London*, in which a city with a revitalization plan squared off against property owners who did not wish to sell their property. The key constitutional provision was the Takings Clause in the ______________ Amendment. The Supreme Court decided the city ______________ use eminent domain and take the property from the landowners.
   (a) Fifth; could
   (b) Fifth; could not
   (c) Fourteenth; could
   (d) Fourteenth; could not

CASE QUESTIONS

1. In the landmark 1965 case of *Griswold v. Connecticut*, the Supreme Court examined a Connecticut statute that made it a crime for any person to use contraception. The majority declared the law an unconstitutional violation of the right of privacy. Justice Black dissented, saying, "I do not to any extent whatever base my view that this Connecticut law is constitutional on a belief that the law is wise or that its policy is a good one. [It] is every bit as offensive to me as it is to the majority. [There is no criticism by the majority of this law] to which I cannot subscribe—except their conclusion that the evil qualities they see in the law make it unconstitutional." What legal doctrines are involved here? Why did Justice Black distinguish between his personal views on the statute and the power of the Court to overturn it?

2. Carter was an employee of the Sheriff's office in Hampton, Virginia. When his boss, Sheriff Roberts, was up for reelection against Adams, Carter "liked" the Adams campaign's Facebook page. Upon winning reelection, Sheriff Roberts fired Carter, who then sued on free speech grounds. Is a Facebook "like" protected under the First Amendment?

3. A state statute prohibits advertising by any sexually oriented business within 1 mile of the state highways. The state argues that the law protects minors and reduces prostitution. The businesses object, claiming that it is an impermissible restriction on commercial speech. Who should prevail?

4. The year is 1964. Ollie's BBQ is a family-owned restaurant located on a state highway in Georgia, 11 blocks from an interstate highway. The restaurant does not allow African-Americans to eat inside; they must get takeout. More than half of the food served in the restaurant had passed through interstate commerce. According to Title II of the Civil Rights Act of 1964, the federal government has the right to prohibit racial discrimination in hotels, restaurants, and other public facilities because local activities have a substantial effect on interstate commerce. The owner of Ollie's BBQ argues that his business is local and has no impact on interstate commerce. Whose argument will win?

5. Edward Salib owned a donut shop. To attract customers, he displayed large signs in his store window. The city ordered him to remove the signs because they violated its Sign Code, which prohibited covering more than 30 percent of a store's windows with signs. Salib sued, claiming that the Sign Code violated his First Amendment free speech rights. What result?

DISCUSSION QUESTIONS

1. What is the proper role of a judge in interpreting the Constitution? Do you believe in judicial activism or judicial restraint?

2. **ETHICS** The Supreme Court has stated that "although one may find sexually explicit material tasteless and even immoral, it is constitutionally protected so

long as it is not obscene."[34] This chapter discusses the guidelines that determine if speech is obscene for purposes of the First Amendment. Should obscenity ever be protected under the First Amendment? Where you do draw the line?

3. Do you believe that the federal government should be able to create whatever laws it deems to be in the country's best interests, or do you believe that individual states should have more control over the laws within their own borders?

4. This chapter is filled with examples of statutes that have been struck down by the courts. Do you like the fact that courts can void laws which they determine to be in violation of the Constitution? Or is it wrong for appointed judges to overrule "the will of the majority," as expressed by elected members of Congress and state legislatures?

5. Gender discrimination currently receives "intermediate" Fourteenth Amendment scrutiny. Is this right? Should gender receive "strict" scrutiny as does race? Why or why not?

[34] U.S. v. Playboy Entm't Group, Inc., 529 U.S. 803, 811 (2000).

CHAPTER 6

DISPUTE RESOLUTION

Tony Caruso had not returned for dinner, and his wife, Karen, was nervous. She put on some sandals and hurried across the dunes, a half mile to the ocean shore. She soon came upon Tony's dog, Blue, tied to an old picket fence. Tony's shoes and clothing were piled neatly nearby. Karen and friends searched frantically throughout the evening.

A little past midnight, Tony's body washed ashore, his lungs filled with water. A local doctor concluded he had accidentally drowned.

Karen and her friends were not the only ones who were distraught. Tony had been partners with Beth Smiles in an environmental consulting business, Enviro-Vision. They were good friends, and Beth was emotionally devastated. When she was able to focus on business issues, Beth filed an insurance claim with the Coastal Insurance Group. Beth hated to think about Tony's death in financial terms, but she was relieved that the struggling business would receive $2 million on the life insurance policy.

A little past midnight, Tony's body washed ashore, his lungs filled with water.

Several months after filing the claim, Beth received this reply from Coastal: "Under the policy issued to Enviro-Vision, we are conditionally liable in the amount of $1 million in the event of Mr. Caruso's death. If his death is accidental, we are conditionally liable to pay double indemnity of $2 million. But pursuant to section H(5), death by suicide is not covered.

"After a thorough investigation, we have concluded that Anthony Caruso's death was an act of suicide, as defined in section B(11) of the policy. Your claim is denied in its entirety." Beth was furious. She was convinced Tony was incapable of suicide. And her company could not afford the $2 million loss. She decided to consult her lawyer, Chris Pruitt.

This case is a fictionalized version of several real cases based on double indemnity insurance policies. In this chapter, we follow Beth's dispute with Coastal from initial interview through appeal, using it to examine three fundamental areas of law: the structure of our court systems, civil lawsuits, and alternative dispute resolution.

When Beth Smiles meets with her lawyer, Chris Pruitt brings a second attorney from his firm, Janet Booker, who is an experienced **litigator**; that is, a lawyer who handles court cases. If they file a lawsuit, Janet will be in charge, so Chris wants her there for the first meeting. Janet probes about Tony's home life, the status of the business, his personal finances, everything. Beth becomes upset that Janet doesn't seem sympathetic, but Chris explains that Janet is doing her job: She needs all the information, good and bad.

Litigation
The process of filing claims in court and ultimately going to trial

Alternative dispute resolution
Any other formal or informal process used to settle disputes without resorting to a trial

Janet starts thinking about the two methods of dispute resolution: litigation and alternative dispute resolution. **Litigation** refers to lawsuits, the process of filing claims in court, and ultimately going to trial. **Alternative dispute resolution** is any other formal or informal process used to settle disputes without resorting to a trial. It is increasingly popular with corporations and individuals alike because it is generally cheaper and faster than litigation, and we will focus on this topic in the last part of this chapter.

6-1 COURT SYSTEMS

The United States has more than 50 *systems* of courts. One nationwide system of *federal* courts serves the entire country. In addition, each individual state has its court system. The state and federal courts are in different buildings, have different judges, and hear different kinds of cases. Each has special powers and certain limitations.

6-1a State Courts

The typical state court system forms a pyramid, as Exhibit 6.1 shows. Some states have minor variations on the exhibit. For example, Texas has two top courts: a Supreme Court for civil cases and a Court of Criminal Appeals for criminal cases.

Trial Courts

Trial courts
Determine the facts of a particular dispute and apply to those facts the law given by earlier appellate court decisions

Almost all cases start in trial courts, which are endlessly portrayed on television and in film. There is one judge, and there will often (but not always) be a jury. This is the only court to hear testimony from witnesses and receive evidence. **Trial courts** determine the facts of a particular dispute and apply to those facts the law given by earlier appellate court decisions.

In the Enviro-Vision dispute, the trial court will decide all important facts that are in dispute. How did Tony Caruso die? Did he drown? Assuming he drowned, was his death accidental or suicide? Once the jury has decided the facts, it will apply the law to those facts. If Tony Caruso died accidentally, contract law provides that Beth Smiles is entitled to double indemnity benefits. If the jury decides he killed himself, Beth gets nothing.

Facts are critical. That may sound obvious, but in a course devoted to legal principles, it is easy to lose track of the key role that factual determinations play in the resolution of any dispute. In the Enviro-Vision case, we will see that one bit of factual evidence goes undetected, with costly consequences.

Jurisdiction
A court's power to hear a case

Jurisdiction refers to a court's power to hear a case. In state or federal court, a plaintiff may start a lawsuit only in a court that has jurisdiction over that kind of case. Some courts have very limited jurisdiction, while others have the power to hear almost any case.

EXHIBIT 6.1

A trial court determines facts, while an appeals court ensures that the lower court correctly applied the law to those facts.

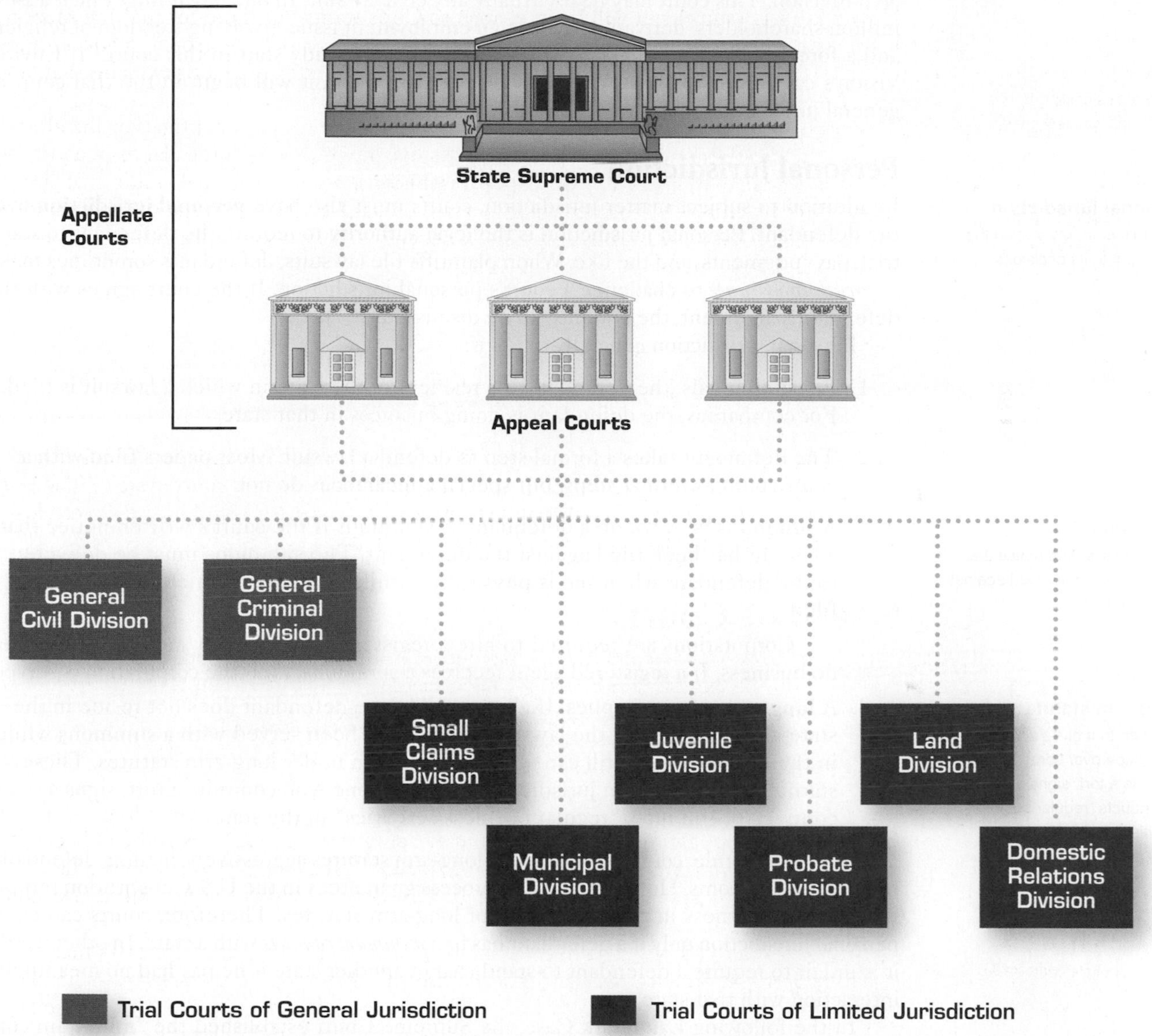

Subject Matter Jurisdiction

Subject matter jurisdiction means that a court has the authority to hear a particular type of case.

Subject matter jurisdiction
A court's authority to hear a particular type of case

Trial Courts of Limited Jurisdiction. These courts may hear only certain types of cases. Small claims court has jurisdiction only over civil lawsuits involving a maximum of, say,

$5,000 (the amount varies from state to state). A juvenile court hears only cases involving minors. Probate court is devoted to settling the estates of deceased persons, though in some states it will hear certain other cases as well.

Trial Courts of General Jurisdiction. Trial courts of general jurisdiction, however, can hear a very broad range of cases. The most important court, for our purposes, is the general civil division. This court may hear virtually any civil lawsuit. In one day it might hear a $450 million shareholders' derivative lawsuit, an employment issue involving freedom of religion, and a foreclosure on a mortgage. Most of the cases we study start in this court.[1] If Enviro-Vision's case against Coastal goes to trial in a state court, it will begin in the trial court of general jurisdiction.

Personal Jurisdiction

Personal jurisdiction
A court's authority to bind the defendant to its decisions

In addition to subject matter jurisdiction, courts must also have **personal jurisdiction** over the defendant. Personal jurisdiction is the legal authority to require the defendant to stand trial, pay judgments, and the like. When plaintiffs file lawsuits, defendants sometimes make a *special appearance* to challenge a court's personal jurisdiction. If the court agrees with the defendant's argument, the lawsuit will be dismissed.

Personal jurisdiction generally exists if:

1. For individuals, the defendant is a resident of the state in which a lawsuit is filed. For companies, the defendant is doing business in that state.
2. The defendant takes a formal step to defend a lawsuit. Most papers filed with a court count as formal steps, but special appearances do not.
3. A **summons** is *served* on a defendant. A summons is the court's written notice that a lawsuit has been filed against the defendant. The summons must be delivered to the defendant when she is physically within the state in which the lawsuit is filed.

   Corporations are required to hire a registered agent in any state in which they do business. If a registered agent receives a summons, then the corporation is served.
4. A **long-arm statute** applies. If all else fails—the defendant does not reside in the state, does not defend the lawsuit, and has not been served with a summons while in the state—a court still can obtain jurisdiction under long-arm statutes. These statutes typically claim jurisdiction over someone who commits a tort, signs a contract, or conducts "regular business activities" in the state.

Summons
The court's written notice that a lawsuit has been filed against the defendant

Long-arm statute
A statute that gives a court jurisdiction over someone who commits a tort, signs a contract, or conducts "regular business activities" in the state

As a general rule, courts tend to apply long-arm statutes aggressively, hauling defendants into their courtrooms. However, the due process guarantees in the U.S. Constitution require fundamental fairness in the application of long-arm statutes. Therefore, courts can claim personal jurisdiction only if a defendant has had *minimum contacts* with a state. In other words, it is unfair to require a defendant to stand trial in another state if he has had no meaningful interaction with that state.

In the following Landmark Case, the Supreme Court established the "minimum contacts" rule.

[1]Note that the actual name of the court of general jurisdiction will vary from state to state. In many states, it is called *superior court* because it has power superior to the courts of limited jurisdiction. In New York, it is called *supreme court* (anything to confuse the layperson); in some states, it is called *court of common pleas*; in Oregon and other states, it is a *circuit court*. Within this branch, some states are beginning to establish specialized business and high-tech courts to hear complex commercial disputes.

Landmark Case

International Shoe Co. v. State of Washington

326 U.S. 310
United States Supreme Court, 1945

Facts: Although International Shoe manufactured footwear only in St. Louis, Missouri, it sold its products nationwide. It did not have offices or warehouses in Washington State, but it did send about a dozen salespeople there. The salespeople rented space in hotels and businesses, displayed sample products, and took orders. They were not authorized to collect payments from customers.

When Washington State sought contributions to the state's unemployment fund, International Shoe refused to pay. Washington sued. The company argued that it was not engaged in business in the state, and, therefore, that Washington courts had no jurisdiction over it.

The Supreme Court of Washington ruled that International Shoe did have sufficient contacts with the state to justify a lawsuit there. International Shoe appealed to the U.S. Supreme Court.

Issue: ***Did International Shoe have sufficient minimum contacts in Washington State to permit jurisdiction there?***

Excerpts from Chief Justice Stone's Decision: Appellant insists that its activities within the state were not sufficient to manifest its "presence" there and that, in its absence, the state courts were without jurisdiction, that, consequently, it was a denial of due process for the state to subject appellant to suit. Appellant [International Shoe] refers to those cases in which it was said that the mere solicitation of orders for the purchase of goods within a state, to be accepted without the state and filled by shipment of the purchased goods interstate, does not render the corporation seller amenable to suit within the state.

Historically the jurisdiction of courts to render judgment is grounded on their power over the defendant's person. Hence his presence within the territorial jurisdiction of a court was prerequisite to a judgment personally binding him. But now due process requires that [a defendant] have certain minimum contacts with it such that the maintenance of the suit does not offend "traditional notions of fair play and substantial justice."

Since the corporate personality is a fiction, its "presence" can be manifested only by those activities of the corporation's agent within the state which courts will deem to be sufficient to satisfy the demands of due process.

"Presence" in the state in this sense has never been doubted when the activities of the corporation there have not only been continuous and systematic, but also give rise to the liabilities sued on, even though no consent to be sued or authorization to an agent to accept service of process has been given. Conversely, it has been generally recognized that the casual presence of the corporate agent or even his conduct of single or isolated items of activities in a state in the corporation's behalf are not enough to subject it to suit on causes of action unconnected with the activities there. To require the corporation in such circumstances to defend the suit away from its home or other jurisdiction where it carries on more substantial activities has been thought to lay too great and unreasonable a burden on the corporation to comport with due process.

But to the extent that a corporation exercises the privilege of conducting activities within a state, it enjoys the benefits and protection of the laws of that state. The exercise of that privilege may give rise to obligations.

Applying these standards, the activities carried on in behalf of appellant in the State of Washington were neither irregular nor casual. They were systematic and continuous throughout the years in question. They resulted in a large volume of interstate business, in the course of which appellant received the benefits and protection of the laws of the state, including the right to resort to the courts for the enforcement of its rights. The obligation which is here sued upon arose out of those very activities. It is evident that these operations establish sufficient contacts or ties with the state of the forum to make it reasonable and just, according to our traditional conception of fair play and substantial justice, to permit the state to enforce the obligations which appellant has incurred there.

The state may maintain the present suit to collect the tax.

Affirmed.

Appellate Courts

Appellate courts are entirely different from trial courts. Three or more judges hear the case. There are no juries, ever. These courts do not hear witnesses or take new evidence. They hear appeals of cases already tried below. **Appeals courts** generally accept the facts given to them by trial courts and review the trial record to see if the court made errors of law.

Appeals courts
Higher courts that review the trial record to see if the court made errors of law

Higher courts generally defer to lower courts on factual findings. Juries and trial court judges see all evidence as it is presented, and they are in the best position to evaluate it. An appeals court will accept a factual finding unless there was *no evidence at all* to support it. If the jury decides that Tony Caruso committed suicide, the appeals court will normally accept that fact, even if the appeals judges consider the jury's conclusion dubious. On the other hand, if a jury concluded that Tony had been murdered, an appeals court would overturn that finding if neither side had introduced any evidence of murder during the trial.

An appeals court reviews the trial record to make sure that the lower court correctly applied the law to the facts. If the trial court made an **error of law**, the appeals court may require a new trial. Suppose the jury concludes that Tony Caruso committed suicide but votes to award Enviro-Vision $1 million because it feels sorry for Beth Smiles. That is an error of law: If Tony committed suicide, Beth is entitled to nothing. An appellate court will reverse the decision. Or suppose that the trial judge permitted a friend of Tony's to state that he was certain Tony would never commit suicide. Normally, such opinions are not permissible in trial, and it was a legal error for the judge to allow the jury to hear it.

Error of law
Because of this, the appeals court may require a new trial.

Court of Appeals. The party that loses at the trial court may appeal to the intermediate court of appeals. The party filing the appeal is the **appellant**. The party opposing the appeal (because it won at trial) is the **appellee**.

Appellant
The party filing the appeal

Appellee
The party opposing the appeal

This court allows both sides to submit written arguments on the case, called **briefs**. Each side then appears for oral argument, usually before a panel of three judges. The appellant's lawyer has about 15 minutes to convince the judges that the trial court made serious errors of law and that the decision should be **reversed**; that is, nullified. The appellee's lawyer has the same time to persuade the court that the trial court acted correctly and that the result should be **affirmed**; that is, permitted to stand.

Briefs
Written arguments on the case

Reversed
Nullified

Affirmed
Permitted to stand

State Supreme Court. This is the highest court in the state, and it accepts some appeals from the court of appeals. In most states, there is no absolute right to appeal to the Supreme Court. If the high court regards a legal issue as important, it accepts the case. It then takes briefs and hears oral argument just as the appeals court did. If it considers the matter unimportant, it refuses to hear the case, meaning that the court of appeals' ruling is the final word on the case.[2]

In most states, seven judges, often called *justices*, sit on the Supreme Court. They have the final word on state law.

6-1b Federal Courts

As discussed in Chapter 1, federal courts are established by the U.S. Constitution, which limits what kinds of cases can be brought in any federal court. See Exhibit 6.2. For our purposes, two kinds of civil lawsuits are permitted in federal court: federal question cases and diversity cases.

---

[2]In some states with smaller populations, there is no intermediate appeals court. All appeals from trial courts go directly to the state supreme court.

EXHIBIT 6.2

Shows the basic structure of the court system in the United States

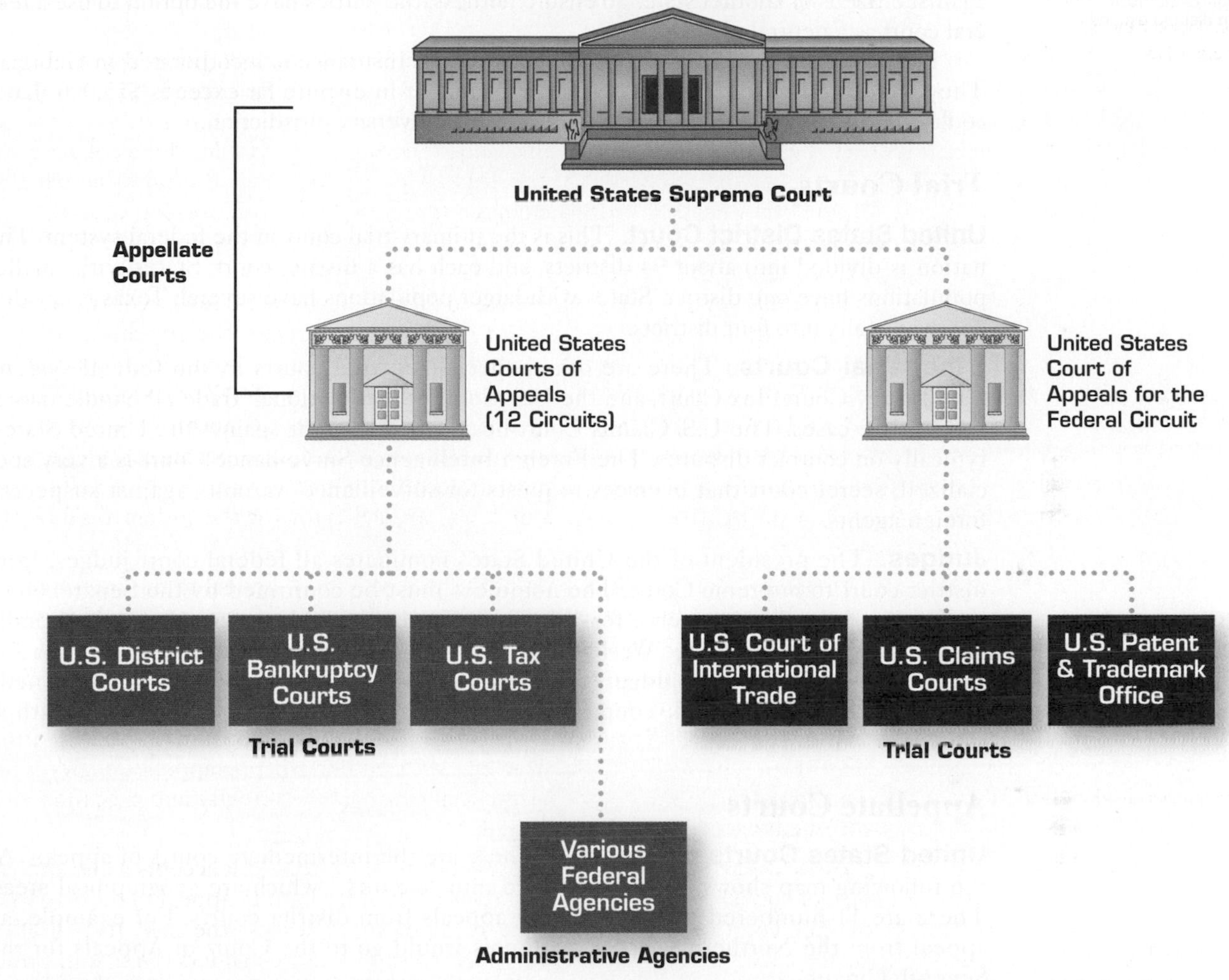

Federal Question Cases

A claim based on the U.S. Constitution, a federal statute, or a federal treaty is called a **federal question** case.[3] Federal courts have jurisdiction over these cases. If the Environmental Protection Agency (EPA), a part of the federal government, orders Logging Company not to cut in a particular forest, and Logging Company claims that the agency has wrongly deprived it of its property, that suit is based on a federal statute and is thus a federal question. If Little Retailer sues Mega Retailer, claiming that Mega has established a monopoly, that claim is also based on a statute—the Sherman Antitrust Act—and creates federal question jurisdiction. Enviro-Vision's potential suit merely concerns an insurance contract. The federal district court has no federal question jurisdiction over the case.

Federal question
A case in which the claim is based on the U.S. Constitution, a federal statute, or a federal treaty

[3] 28 U.S.C. §1331 governs federal question jurisdiction, and 28 U.S.C. §1332 covers diversity jurisdiction.

Diversity Cases

Diversity jurisdiction
Applies when (1) the plaintiff and defendant are citizens of different states and (2) the amount in dispute exceeds $75,000

Even if no federal law is at issue, federal courts have **diversity jurisdiction** when (1) the plaintiff and defendant are citizens of different states *and* (2) the amount in dispute exceeds $75,000. The theory behind diversity jurisdiction is that courts of one state might be biased against citizens of another state. To ensure fairness, the parties have the option to use a federal court as a neutral playing field.

Enviro-Vision is located in Oregon and Coastal Insurance is incorporated in Georgia.[4] They are citizens of different states and the amount in dispute far exceeds $75,000. Janet could file this case in U.S. District Court based on diversity jurisdiction.

Trial Courts

United States District Court. This is the primary trial court in the federal system. The nation is divided into about 94 districts, and each has a district court. States with smaller populations have one district. States with larger populations have several; Texas is divided geographically into four districts.

Other Trial Courts. There are other, specialized trial courts in the federal system. Bankruptcy Court, Tax Court, and the U.S. Court of International Trade all handle name-appropriate cases. The U.S. Claims Court hears cases brought against the United States, typically on contract disputes. The Foreign Intelligence Surveillance Court is a very specialized, secret court that oversees requests for surveillance warrants against suspected foreign agents.

Judges. The president of the United States nominates all federal court judges, from district court to Supreme Court. The nominees must be confirmed by the Senate. Once confirmed, federal judges serve for "life in good behavior." Many federal judges literally stay on the job for life. Judge Wesley Brown of Kansas holds the records as the oldest and the longest-serving federal judge. Appointed to the federal bench by President Kennedy at age 55, Brown had heard federal cases for almost 50 years at the time of his death at age 104.

Appellate Courts

United States Courts of Appeals. These are the intermediate courts of appeals. As the following map shows, they are divided into "circuits," which are geographical areas. There are 11 numbered circuits, hearing appeals from district courts. For example, an appeal from the Northern District of Illinois would go to the Court of Appeals for the Seventh Circuit.

A twelfth court, the Court of Appeals for the District of Columbia, hears appeals only from the district court of Washington, D.C. This court is particularly powerful because so many suits about federal statutes begin in the district court for the District of Columbia. Also in Washington is the Thirteenth Court of Appeals, known as the Federal Circuit. It hears appeals from specialized trial courts, as shown in Exhibit 6.2.

Within one circuit there are many circuit judges, up to about 50 judges in the largest circuit, the Ninth. When a case is appealed, three judges hear the appeal, taking briefs and hearing oral arguments.

---

[4]For diversity purposes, a corporation is a citizen of the state in which it is incorporated and the state in which it has its principal place of business.

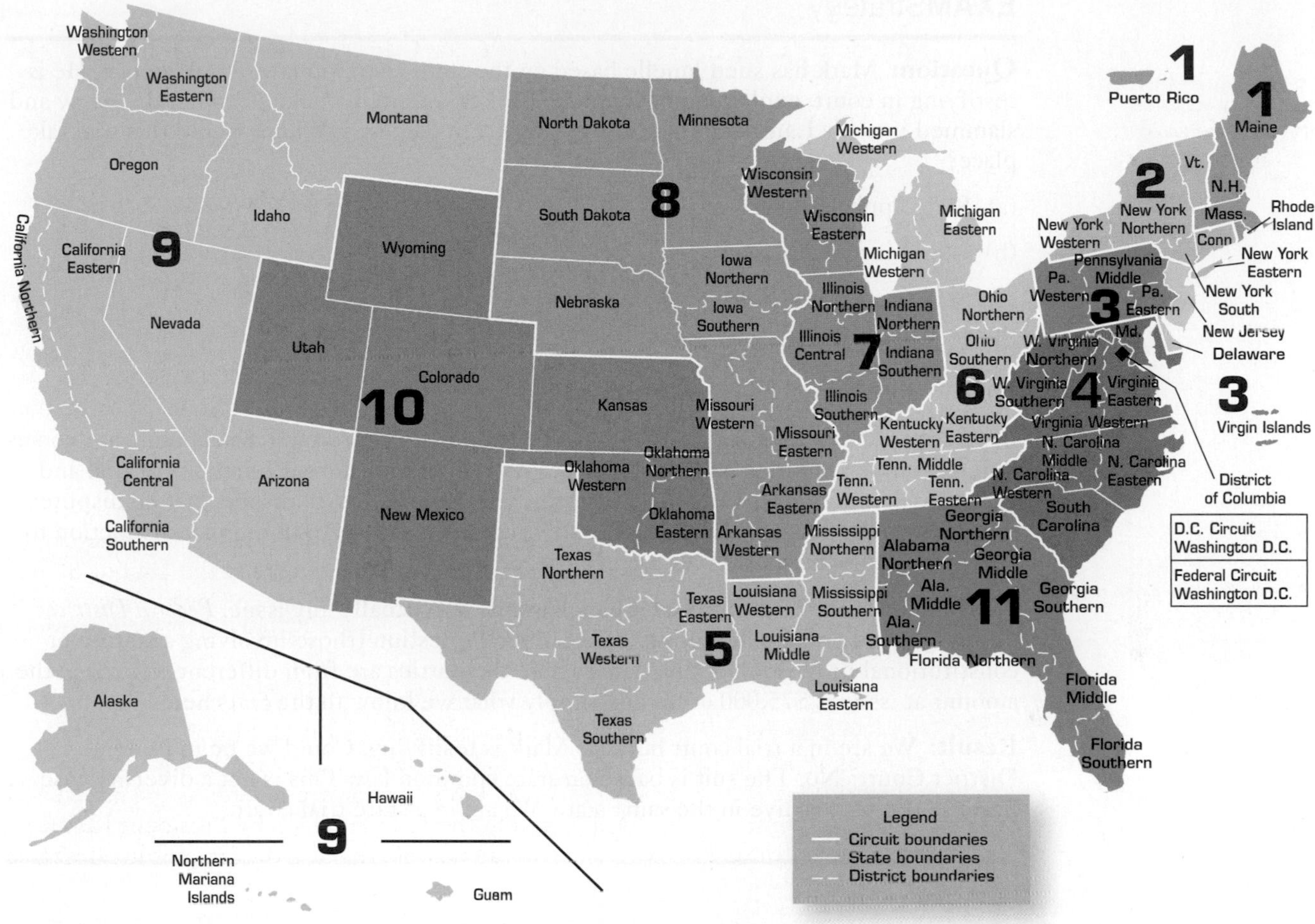

United States Supreme Court. This is the highest court in the country. There are nine justices on the Court. One justice is the chief justice and the other eight are associate justices. When they decide a case, each justice casts an equal vote. The chief justice's special power comes from his authority to assign opinions to a given justice. The justice assigned to write an opinion has an opportunity to control the precise language and thus to influence the voting by other justices.

The Supreme Court has the power to hear appeals in any federal case, and in certain cases that began in state courts. Generally, it is up to the Court whether or not it will accept a case. A party that wants the Supreme Court to review a lower court ruling must file a petition for a **writ of *certiorari***, asking the Court to hear the case. Four of the nine justices must vote in favor of hearing a case before a writ will be granted. The Court receives several thousand requests every year but usually accepts fewer than 100. Most cases accepted involve either an important issue of constitutional law or an interpretation of a major federal statute.

Writ of *certiorari*
A petition asking the Supreme Court to hear a case

EXAMStrategy

Question: Mark has sued Janelle based on the state common law of negligence. He is testifying in court, explaining how Janelle backed a rented truck out of her driveway and slammed into his Lamborghini, causing $82,000 in damages. Where would this trial take place?

(a) State appeals court

(b) U.S. Court of Appeals

(c) State trial court

(d) Federal district court

(e) Either state trial court or federal district court

Strategy: The question asks about trial and appellate courts, and also about state versus federal courts. One issue at a time, please. What are the different functions of trial and appellate courts? *Trial* courts use witnesses, and often juries, to resolve factual disputes. *Appellate* courts never hear witnesses and never have juries. Applying that distinction to these facts tells us whether we are in a trial or appeals court.

Next Issue: *State* trial courts may hear lawsuits on virtually any issue. *Federal District Courts* may only hear two kinds of cases: federal question (those involving a statute or constitutional provision), or diversity (where the parties are from different states *and* the amount at issue is $75,000 or higher). Apply what we know to the facts here.

Result: We are in a trial court because Mark is testifying. Could we be in Federal District Court? No. The suit is based on state common law. This is not a diversity case because the parties live in the same state. We are in a state trial court.

6-2 BEFORE TRIAL

Janet Booker decides to file the Enviro-Vision suit in the Oregon trial court. She thinks that a state court judge may take the issue more seriously than a federal district court judge.

6-2a Pleadings

Pleadings
The documents that begin a lawsuit, consisting of the complaint, the answer, and sometimes a reply

The documents that begin a lawsuit are called the **pleadings**. These consist of the complaint, the answer, and sometimes a reply.

Complaint

Complaint
A short, plain statement of the facts alleged and the legal claims made

The plaintiff files in court a **complaint**, which is a short, plain statement of the facts she is alleging and the legal claims she is making. The purpose of the complaint is to inform the defendant of the general nature of the claims and the need to come into court and protect his interests.

Janet Booker files the complaint, as shown below. Since Enviro-Vision is a partnership, she files the suit on behalf of Beth personally.

STATE OF OREGON
CIRCUIT COURT

Multnomah County Civil Action No. ________

Elizabeth Smiles,
Plaintiff

JURY TRIAL DEMANDED

v.
Coastal Insurance Company, Inc.,
Defendant

COMPLAINT

Plaintiff Elizabeth Smiles states that:

1. She is a citizen of Multnomah County, Oregon.
2. Defendant Coastal Insurance Company, Inc., is incorporated under the laws of Georgia and has as its usual place of business 148 Thrift Street, Savannah, Georgia.
3. On or about July 5, 2018, plaintiff Smiles ("Smiles"), Defendant Coastal Insurance Co, Inc. ("Coastal") and Anthony Caruso entered into an insurance contract ("the contract"), a copy of which is annexed hereto as Exhibit "A." This contract was signed by all parties or their authorized agents, in Multnomah County, Oregon.
4. The contract obligates Coastal to pay to Smiles the sum of two million dollars ($2 million) if Anthony Caruso should die accidentally.
5. On or about September 20, 2018, Anthony Caruso accidentally drowned and died while swimming.
6. Coastal has refused to pay any sum pursuant to the contract.
7. Coastal has knowingly, willingly and unreasonably refused to honor its obligations under the contract.

WHEREFORE, plaintiff Elizabeth Smiles demands judgment against defendant Coastal for all monies due under the contract; demands triple damages for Coastal's knowing, willing, and unreasonable refusal to honor its obligations; and demands all costs and attorney's fees, with interest.
ELIZABETH SMILES,
By her attorney,
[Signed]
Janet Booker
Pruitt, Booker & Bother
983 Joy Avenue
Portland, OR
October 18, 2018

Service

When she files the complaint in court, Janet gets a summons, which is a paper ordering the defendant to answer the complaint within 20 days. A sheriff or constable then *serves* the two papers by delivering them to the defendant. Coastal's headquarters are in Georgia, so the state of Oregon has required Coastal to specify someone as its agent for receipt of service in Oregon.

Answer

Once the complaint and summons are served, Coastal has 20 days in which to file an answer. Coastal's answer, shown below, is a brief reply to each of the allegations in the complaint. The answer tells the court and the plaintiff exactly what issues are in dispute. Because Coastal admits that the parties entered into the contract that Beth claims they did, there is no need for her to prove that in court. The court can focus its attention on the disputed issue: whether Tony Caruso died accidentally.

STATE OF OREGON
CIRCUIT COURT

Multnomah County — Civil Action No. 09-5626

Elizabeth Smiles,
Plaintiff
v.
Coastal Insurance Company, Inc.,
Defendant

ANSWER

Defendant Coastal Insurance Company, Inc., answers the complaint as follows:

1. Admit.
2. Admit.
3. Admit.
4. Admit.
5. Deny.
6. Admit.
7. Deny.

COASTAL INSURANCE COMPANY, INC.,
By its attorney,
[Signed]
Richard B. Stewart
Kiley, Robbins, Stewart & Glote
333 Victory Boulevard
Portland, OR
October 30, 2018

Default judgment
A decision that the plaintiff wins without trial because the defendant failed to answer in time

If the defendant fails to answer in time, the plaintiff will ask for a **default judgment**. In granting a default judgment, the judge accepts every allegation in the complaint as true and renders a decision that the plaintiff wins without a trial.

Two men sued PepsiCo, claiming that the company stole the idea for Aquafina water from them. They argued that they should receive a portion of the profits for every bottle of Aquafina ever sold.

PepsiCo failed to file a timely answer, and the judge entered a default judgment in the amount of $1.26 billion. On appeal, the default judgment was overturned and PepsiCo was able to escape paying the massive sum, but other defendants are sometimes not so lucky. It is important to respond to courts on time.

Counterclaim

Counterclaim
A second lawsuit by the defendant against the plaintiff

Sometimes a defendant does more than merely answer a complaint and files a **counterclaim**, meaning a second lawsuit by the defendant against the plaintiff. Suppose that after her complaint was filed in court, Beth had written a letter to the newspaper, calling Coastal a bunch of "thieves and scoundrels who spend their days mired in fraud and larceny." Coastal would not have found that amusing. The company's answer would have included a counterclaim against Beth for libel, claiming that she falsely accused the insurer of serious criminal acts. Coastal would have demanded money damages.

Reply
An answer to a counterclaim

If Coastal counterclaimed, Beth would have to file a **reply**, which is simply an answer to a counterclaim. Beth's reply would be similar to Coastal's answer, admitting or denying the various allegations.

Class Actions

Suppose Janet uncovers evidence that Coastal denies 80 percent of all life insurance claims, calling them suicide. She could ask the court to permit a **class action**. If the court granted her request, she would represent the entire group of plaintiffs, including those who are unaware of the lawsuit or even unaware they were harmed. Class actions can give the plaintiffs much greater leverage because the defendant's potential liability is vastly increased. In the back of her mind, Janet has thoughts of a class action, *if* she can uncover evidence that Coastal has used a claim of suicide to deny coverage to a large number of claimants.

Class action
One plaintiff represents the entire group of plaintiffs, including those who are unaware of the lawsuit or even unaware they were harmed

Notice how potent a class action can be. From his small town in Maine, Ernie decides to get rich quickly. On the internet, he advertises "Energy Breakthrough! Cut your heating costs 15 percent for only $25." In response, 100,000 people send him their money, and they receive a photocopied graph, illustrating that if you wear two sweaters instead of one, you will feel 15 percent warmer. Ernie has deceitfully earned $2,500,000 in pure profit. What can the angry homeowners do? Under the laws of fraud and consumer protection, they have a legitimate claim to their $25, and perhaps even to treble damages ($75). But few will sue because the time and effort required would be greater than the money recovered.

Economists analyze such legal issues in terms of *efficiency*. The laws against Ernie's fraud are clear and well-intended, but they will not help in this case because it is too expensive for 100,000 people to litigate such a small claim. The effort would be hugely *inefficient*, both for the homeowners and for society generally. The economic reality may permit Ernie to evade the law's grasp.

That is one reason we have class actions. A dozen or so "heating plan" buyers can all hire the same lawyer. This attorney will file court papers in Maine on behalf of *everyone*, nationwide, who has been swindled by Ernie—including the 99,988 people who have yet to be notified that they are part of the case. Now the con artist, instead of facing a few harmless suits for $25, must respond to a multimillion-dollar claim being handled by an experienced lawyer. Treble damages become menacing: Three times $25 times 100,000 is no joke, even to a cynic like Ernie. He may also be forced to pay for the plaintiffs' attorney as well as all costs of notifying class members and disbursing money to them. With one lawyer representing an entire class, the legal system has become fiercely efficient.

Judgment on the Pleadings

A party can ask the court for a judgment based simply on the pleadings themselves, by filing a motion to dismiss. A **motion** is a formal request to the court that it take some step or issue some order. During a lawsuit, the parties file many motions. A **motion to dismiss** is a request that the court terminate a case without permitting it to go further. It asks the court to decide, assuming the facts in the complaint are true, if the law offers a legal remedy for the plaintiff's problem. Suppose that a state law requires claims on life insurance contracts to be filed within three years, and Beth files her claim four years after Tony's death. Coastal would move to dismiss based on this late filing. The court might well agree, and Beth would never get into court.

Motion
A formal request to the court that it take some step or issue some order

Motion to dismiss
A request that the court terminate a case because the law does not offer a legal remedy for the plaintiff's problem

The pleadings are the key to the litigation process. But not every complaint allows a plaintiff to enter and rummage through the defendant's life. The motion to dismiss process sifts out cases that are meritless and not based on sufficient facts. If courts allowed access to the legal system to everyone who filed a complaint, the entire court system would crash.

The following Supreme Court case clarified how much information a plaintiff had to present to survive a motion to dismiss in federal court.

Ashcroft v. Iqbal

556 U.S. 662
United States Supreme Court, 2009

Facts: In the wake of the 9/11 attacks, the FBI questioned more than 1,000 people with suspected terrorist links. It then detained those it deemed to be "of high interest," most of whom were Arab Muslim men.

Javaid Iqbal, a Pakistani Muslim, was arrested and charged with fraud in the use of identification documents. While awaiting trial, Iqbal was confined to his cell 23 hours a day. He alleged that blinding light shone on him around the clock, air conditioning blasted in the summer and heat in the winter. Guards kicked him and refused to let him pray, as required by his religion.

Iqbal ultimately pleaded guilty to the fraud charge, served a prison term and was sent back to Pakistan. He then filed a discrimination lawsuit against John Ashcroft, the former Attorney General who was in charge of the anti-terrorism investigation. Iqbal's complaint contained the following information: (1) Most of the 9/11 detainees were Arab Muslim men; (2) detainees of high interest suffered harsh treatment in prison; and (3) Ashcroft approved the detainment policy. Because these facts were all true, Iqbal argued, Ashcroft must have illegally discriminated against the detainees on the basis of race, religion, and national origin.

Ashcroft moved to dismiss the suit, contending the complaint did not contain enough information to suggest that discrimination was a plausible reason for the detainment. The district court disagreed with Ashcroft and the appeals court affirmed. The case was referred to the Supreme Court.

Issue: ***Did Iqbal's pleadings contain enough information to survive a motion to dismiss?***

Excerpts from Justice Kennedy's Decision: A pleading must contain a short and plain statement of the claim showing that the pleader is entitled to relief. The pleading standard does not require detailed factual allegations, but it demands more than an unadorned, the-defendant-unlawfully-harmed-me accusation.

To survive a motion to dismiss, a complaint must contain sufficient factual matter, accepted as true, to state a claim to relief that is plausible. A claim has plausibility when the plaintiff pleads factual content that allows the court to draw the reasonable inference that the defendant is liable for the misconduct alleged. The plausibility standard is not akin to a probability requirement, but it asks for more than a sheer possibility that a defendant has acted unlawfully. Determining whether a complaint states a plausible claim for relief will be a context-specific task that requires the reviewing court to draw on its judicial experience and common sense.

The complaint must contain facts plausibly showing that [Ashcroft] purposefully adopted a policy of classifying post-September-11 detainees as "of high interest" because of their race, religion, or national origin. This the complaint fails to do. His only factual allegation against [Ashcroft] accuses [him] of adopting a policy approving restrictive conditions of confinement for post-September-11 detainees. The complaint does not show, or even intimate, that [Ashcroft] purposefully housed detainees due to their race, religion, or national origin. All it plausibly suggests is that the Nation's top law enforcement officers, in the aftermath of a devastating terrorist attack, sought to keep suspected terrorists in the most secure conditions available until the suspects could be cleared of terrorist activity. [Iqbal] would need to allege more by way of factual content to nudge his claim of purposeful discrimination across the line from conceivable to plausible.

We hold that respondent's complaint fails to plead sufficient facts to state a claim for purposeful and unlawful discrimination against petitioners.

Iqbal tells us that a valid complaint must show the court that the plaintiff's claims are *plausible*, not just *possible*. Critics argue that this rule may deny the right to sue to plaintiffs with good claims, who could discover more evidence if allowed to conduct the pre-trial process of discovery. Others applaud the stringent standard because it reduces the number of frivolous cases filed.

6-2b Discovery

Relatively few cases are dismissed on the pleadings. Most proceed quickly to the next step.

The theory behind civil litigation is that the best outcome is a negotiated settlement and that parties will move toward agreement if they understand the opponent's case. That is likeliest to occur if both sides have an opportunity to examine most of the evidence the other side will bring to trial. Further, if a case does go all the way to trial, efficient and fair litigation cannot take place in a courtroom filled with surprises. On television dramas, witnesses say astonishing things that amaze the courtroom (and keep viewers hooked through the next commercial). In real trials, the lawyers know in advance the answers to practically all questions asked because discovery has allowed them to see the opponent's documents and question its witnesses. The following are the most important forms of discovery.

Interrogatories

These are written questions that the opposing party must answer, in writing, under oath.

Depositions

These provide a chance for one party's lawyer to question the other party, or a potential witness, under oath. The person being questioned is the **deponent**. Lawyers for both parties are present. During depositions, and in trial, good lawyers choose words carefully and ask questions calculated to advance their cause. A fine line separates ethical, probing questions from those that are tricky, and a similar line divides answers that are merely unhelpful from perjury.

Deponent
The person being questioned in a deposition

Production of Documents and Materials

Each side may ask the other side to produce relevant documents for inspection and copying; to produce physical objects, such as part of a car alleged to be defective; and for permission to enter on land to make an inspection, for example, at the scene of an accident.

Physical and Mental Examination

A party may ask the court to order an examination of the other party, if his physical or mental condition is relevant, for example, in a case of medical malpractice.

Janet Booker begins her discovery with interrogatories. Her goal is to learn Coastal's basic position and factual evidence and then follow up with more detailed questioning during depositions. Her interrogatories ask for every fact Coastal relied on in denying the claim. She asks for the names of all witnesses, the identity of all documents, including electronic records, and the description of all things or objects that they considered. She requests the names of all corporate officers who played any role in the decision and of any expert witnesses Coastal plans to call. Interrogatory No. 18 demands extensive information on all *other* claims in the past three years that Coastal has denied based on alleged suicide. Janet is looking for evidence that would support a class action.

Beth remarks on how thorough the interrogatories are. "This will tell us what their case is." Janet frowns and looks less optimistic: She has done this before.

Coastal has 30 days to answer Janet's interrogatories. Before it responds, Coastal mails to Janet a notice of deposition, stating its intention to depose Beth Smiles. Beth and Janet will go to the office of Coastal's lawyer, and Beth will answer questions under oath. But at the same time Coastal sends the first deposition notice, it also sends *25 other notices of deposition*. The company will depose Karen Caruso as soon as Beth's deposition is over. Coastal also plans to depose all seven employees of Enviro-Vision; three neighbors who lived near Tony and Karen's beach house; two policemen who participated in the search; the doctor and two nurses involved in the case; Tony's physician; Jerry Johnson, Tony's tennis partner; Craig

Bergson, a college roommate; a couple who had dinner with Tony and Karen a week before his death; and several other people.

Beth is appalled. Janet explains that some of these people might have relevant information. But there may be another reason that Coastal is doing this: The company wants to make this litigation hurt. Janet will have to attend every one of these depositions. Costs will skyrocket.

> **But there may be another reason that Coastal is doing this: The company wants to make this litigation hurt.**

Janet files a **motion for a protective order**. This is a request that the court limit Coastal's discovery by decreasing the number of depositions. Janet also calls Rich Stewart and suggests that they discuss what depositions are really necessary. Rich insists that all of the depositions are important. This is a $2 million case, and Coastal is entitled to protect itself. As both lawyers know, **the parties are entitled to discover anything that could reasonably lead to valid evidence.**

Motion for a protective order
Request that the court limit discovery

Before Beth's deposition date arrives, Rich sends Coastal's answers to Enviro-Vision's interrogatories. The answers contain no useful information whatsoever. For example, Interrogatory No. 10 asked, "If you claim that Anthony Caruso committed suicide, describe every fact upon which you rely in reaching that conclusion." Coastal's answer simply says, "His state of mind, his poor business affairs, and the circumstances of his death all indicate suicide."

Janet calls Rich and complains that the interrogatory answers are a bad joke. Rich disagrees, saying that it is the best information they have so early in the case. After they debate it for 20 minutes, Rich offers to settle the case for $100,000. Janet refuses and makes no counteroffer.

Janet files a **motion to compel answers to interrogatories**, in other words, a formal request that the court order Coastal to supply more complete answers. Janet submits a **memorandum** with the motion, which is a supporting argument. Although it is only a few pages long, the memorandum takes several hours of online research and writing to prepare—more costs. Janet also informs Rich Stewart that Beth will not appear for the deposition because Coastal's interrogatory answers are inadequate.

Rich now files *his* motion to compel, asking the court to order Beth Smiles to appear for her deposition. The court hears all of the motions together. Janet argues that Coastal's interrogatory answers are hopelessly uninformative and defeat the whole purpose of discovery. She claims that Coastal's large number of depositions creates a huge and unfair expense for a small firm.

Rich claims that the interrogatory answers are the best that Coastal can do thus far and that Coastal will supplement the answers when more information becomes available. He argues against Interrogatory No. 18, the one in which Janet asked for the names of other policyholders whom Coastal considered suicides. He claims that Janet is engaging in a fishing expedition that would violate the privacy of Coastal's insurance customers and provide no information relevant to this case. He demands that Janet make Beth available for a deposition.

These discovery rulings are critical because they will color the entire lawsuit. A trial judge has to make many discovery decisions before a case reaches trial. At times, the judge must weigh the need of one party to see documents against the other side's need for privacy. One device a judge can use in reaching a discovery ruling is an **in camera inspection**, meaning that the judge views the requested documents alone, with no lawyers present, and decides whether the other side is entitled to view them.

E-Discovery

The internet age changed discovery. Companies send hundreds, or thousands, or millions of emails—every day. Businesses large and small have vast amounts of data stored electronically. And many people post volumes of personal information on social media sites. All of this information is potentially subject to discovery.

Photononstop/SuperStock

It is enormously time-consuming and expensive for companies to locate all of the relevant material, separate it from irrelevant or confidential matter, and furnish it. A firm may be obligated to furnish *millions* of emails to the opposing party. In one case, a defendant had to pay 31 lawyers full time, for six months, just to wade through the e-ocean of documents and figure out which had to be supplied and how to produce them. Not surprisingly, this data eruption has created a new industry: high-tech companies that assist law firms in finding, sorting, and delivering electronic data.

Who is to say what must be supplied? What if an email string contains individual emails that are clearly privileged (meaning a party need not divulge them), but others that are not privileged? May a company refuse to furnish the entire string? Many will try. However, some courts have ruled that companies seeking to protect email strings must create a log describing every individual email and allow the court to determine which ones are privileged.[5]

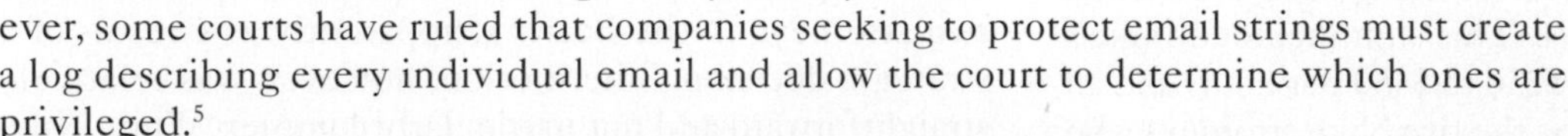

Social media further complicates discovery. When a Facebook profile or Twitter account is public, opposing parties are free to rummage through the treasure trove of personal information. One recent study found that the word "Facebook" occurred in one-third of all U.S. divorce filings and more than 80 percent of divorce lawyers have used social media evidence in court. Likewise, many plaintiffs have lost their tort cases because of incriminating online photos of them engaged in activities that undermine their claims. (What, you claim you can never work at a desk again, but you can still waterski?)

The word "Facebook" occurred in one-third of all U.S. divorce filings.

But what about access to a *private* social media profile? To protect people's privacy, courts require parties to show that the discovery request is reasonably calculated to lead to relevant and admissible evidence. For example, one court denied a company's request that an employee supply a list of all of his time-stamped social media postings during a four-year period because the request was unreasonably burdensome and unlikely to show whether the worker had taken lunch breaks.[6]

Another court found that limited discovery of a plaintiff's Twitter and Facebook accounts was proper because her online activity would likely reveal information about whether or not she was experiencing the emotional distress her lawsuit claimed.[7]

Both sides in litigation sometimes use gamesmanship during discovery. For example, if an individual sues a large corporation, the company may deliberately make discovery so expensive that the plaintiff cannot afford the legal fees. And if a plaintiff has a bad case, he might intentionally try to make the discovery process more expensive for the defendant than his settlement offer.

In the following case, it was not just legends that were forever—discovery was, too. Was the plaintiff's failure to cooperate part of a calculated plan to tire Nike into settling or just a costly decision?

5 Universal Service Fund Telephone Billing Practices Litigation, 232 F.R.D. 669 (D. Kan. 2005).

6 Jewell v. Aaron's Inc., 2013 WL 3770837 (N.D. Ga. 2013).

7 Kear v. Kohl's Department Stores, Inc., 2013 WL 3088922 (D. Kan. 2013).

Legends Are Forever, Inc. v. Nike, Inc.

2013 WL 6086461, 2013 U.S. Dist. LEXIS 164091
U.S. District Court, Northern District, New York, 2013

Facts: Legends Are Forever, Inc. (Legends) trademarked the slogan "Legends Are Forever." When Nike used the slogan in an ad campaign featuring basketball player Kobe Bryant, Legends sued Nike.

But, during discovery, Legends repeatedly failed to comply with Nike's reasonable requests. Ultimately, Nike was forced to file a motion to compel Legends to produce the requested documents and witnesses. So, Nike requested more than just discovery: It also asked the court for recovery of all of the costs and fees it incurred in litigating the motion to compel, totaling $25,186.91. This sum included Nike's attorney's fees (ranging from $250 to $450 per hour) and all the travel expenses incurred by the two Nike attorneys who attended the hearing on the motion to compel.

The court agreed with Nike, granting it both discovery and its fees. Legends challenged the order, arguing that a small company should not have to pay for Nike's high-priced attorneys.

Issue: ***What is a reasonable penalty for unacceptable behavior during discovery?***

Excerpts from Magistrate Judge Peebles's Decision: Discovery in this case has proceeded at an unacceptably slow pace, and Nike has experienced considerable difficulties in obtaining compliance by plaintiff with legitimate discovery demands. An award of costs and attorney's fees is warranted.

Now the task of the court shifts to determining the appropriate amount to award. Fee awards are awarded by determining a reasonable fee, reached by multiplying a reasonable hourly rate by the number of reasonably expended hours.

When establishing a reasonable rate, courts consider the time and labor required, the novelty of the questions, and the level of skill required to perform the legal service properly [among other factors]. Attorney's fees awarded as sanctions are not intended only as compensation of reimbursement for legal services, but also serve to deter abusive litigation practices and, as such, district courts have discretion in determining the amount of an attorney's fee awarded as sanctions. I conclude that the court should apply the following rates: $350 to $250 per hour.

I have reduced the number of hours upon which fees will be awarded for two reasons. First, it appears that several of the entries are excessive, given the description of the work performed. As one example, Nike chose to send two attorneys to the hearing, apparently as a result of a strategic decision. The motion, however, was relatively straightforward and not particularly complex. While Nike certainly retains the prerogative to send multiple attorneys to such a hearing, I decline to award costs and attorney's fees based upon that duplication of effort. Based upon the foregoing, I am awarding attorney's fees in the amount of $11,146.25.

In addition to attorney's fees, Nike has also sought recovery of costs representing travel expenses incurred for the hearing. It is appropriate to award the expense associated with [only one of Nike's attorneys] travel to the hearing, in the amount of $1,186.57.

Plaintiff Legends now complains that, as a small corporation, it would be economically disadvantaged by the award. Nike, however, despite its size and prominence, having been sued, is entitled to the same discovery as any other litigant. When discovery is sought but not provided, it is fair and appropriate to award costs and attorney's fees, notwithstanding the disparity in size of the two parties involved.

Nike, Inc., is hereby awarded the sum of $12,332.82, representing reasonable costs and attorney's fees associated with having to bring and argue the recent motion to compel discovery.

In the Enviro-Vision case, the judge rules that Coastal must furnish more complete answers to the interrogatories, especially as to why the company denied the claim. However, he rules against Interrogatory No. 18, the one concerning other claims Coastal has denied. This simple ruling kills Janet's hope of making a class action of the case. He orders Beth to appear for the deposition. As to future depositions, Coastal may take any ten but then may take additional depositions only by demonstrating to the court that the deponents have useful information.

Rich proceeds to take Beth's deposition. It takes two full days. He asks about Enviro-Vision's past and present. He learns that Tony appeared to have won their biggest contract ever from Rapid City, Oregon, but that he then lost it when he had a fight with Rapid City's mayor. He enquires into Tony's mood, learns that he was depressed, and probes in every direction he can to find evidence of suicidal motivation. Janet and Rich argue frequently over questions and whether Beth should have to answer them. At times, Janet is persuaded and permits Beth to answer; other times, she instructs Beth not to answer. For example, toward the end of the second day, Rich asks Beth whether she and Tony had been sexually involved. Janet instructs Beth not to answer. This fight necessitates another trip into court to determine whether Beth must answer. The judge rules that Beth must discuss Tony's romantic life only if Coastal has some evidence that he was involved with someone outside his marriage. The company lacks any such evidence.

Now limited to ten depositions, Rich selects his nine other deponents carefully. For example, he decides to depose only one of the two nurses; he chooses to question Jerry Johnson, the tennis partner, but not Craig Bergson, the former roommate; and so forth. When we look at the many legal issues this case raises, his choices seem minor. In fact, unbeknownst to Rich or anyone else, his choices may determine the outcome of the case. As we will see later, Craig Bergson has evidence that is possibly crucial to the lawsuit. If Rich decides not to depose him, neither side will ever learn the evidence and the jury will never hear it. A jury can decide a case only based on the evidence presented to it. *Facts are elusive—and often controlling.*

In each deposition, Rich carefully probes with his questions, sometimes trying to learn what he actually does not know, sometimes trying to pin down the witness to a specific version of facts so that Rich knows how the witness will testify at trial. Neighbors at the beach testify that Tony seemed tense; one testifies about seeing Tony, unhappy, on the beach with his dog. Another testifies he had never before seen Blue tied up on the beach. Karen Caruso admits that Tony had been somewhat tense and unhappy the last couple of months. She reluctantly discusses their marriage, admitting there were problems.

Other Discovery

Rich sends Requests to Produce Documents, seeking medical records about Tony. Once again, the parties fight over which records are relevant, but Rich gets most of what he wants. Janet does less discovery than Rich because most of the witnesses she will call are friendly witnesses. She can interview them privately without giving any information to Coastal. With the help of Beth and Karen, Janet builds her case just as carefully as Rich, choosing the witnesses who will bolster the view that Tony was in good spirits and died accidentally.

She deposes all the officers of Coastal who participated in the decision to deny insurance coverage. She is particularly aggressive in pinning them down as to the limited information they had when they denied Beth's claim.

6-2c Summary Judgment

When discovery is completed, both sides may consider seeking summary judgment. **Summary judgment** is a ruling by the court that no trial is necessary on a particular issue because the essential facts are not in dispute. The purpose of a trial is to determine the facts of the case; that is, to decide who did what to whom, why, when, and with what consequences. If there are no relevant facts in dispute, then there is no need for a trial.

Summary judgment
A ruling by the court that no trial is necessary because there are no essential facts in dispute

In the following case, the defendant won summary judgment, meaning that the case never went to trial. That was good news for the defendant, who happened to be the president of the United States at the time.

Jones v. Clinton

990 F. Supp. 657
United States District Court for the Eastern District of Arkansas, 1998

Facts: In 1991, Bill Clinton was governor of Arkansas. Paula Jones worked for a state agency, the Arkansas Industrial Development Commission (AIDC). When Clinton became president, Jones sued him, claiming that he had sexually harassed her. She alleged that, in May 1991, the governor arranged for her to meet him in a hotel room in Little Rock, Arkansas. When they were alone, he put his hand on her leg and slid it toward her pelvis. She escaped from his grasp, exclaimed, "What are you doing?" and said she was "not that kind of girl." She was upset and confused, and sat on a sofa near the door. She claimed that Clinton approached her, "lowered his trousers and underwear, exposed his penis, and told her to kiss it."

Jones was horrified, jumped up, and said she had to leave. Clinton responded by saying, "Well, I don't want to make you do anything you don't want to do," and pulled his pants up. He added that if she got in trouble for leaving work, Jones should "have Dave call me immediately and I'll take care of it." He also said, "You are smart. Let's keep this between ourselves." Jones remained at AIDC until February 1993, when she moved to California because of her husband's job transfer.

President Clinton denied all of the allegations. He also filed for summary judgment, claiming that Jones had not alleged facts that justified a trial. Jones opposed the motion for summary judgment.

Issue: ***Was Clinton entitled to summary judgment, or was Jones entitled to a trial?***

Excerpts from Judge Wright's Decision: [To establish this type of a sexual harassment case, a plaintiff must show that her refusal to submit to unwelcome sexual advances resulted in a tangible job detriment, meaning that she suffered a specific loss. Jones claims that she was denied promotions, given a job with fewer responsibilities, isolated physically, required to sit at a workstation with no work to do, and singled out as the only female employee not to be given flowers on Secretary's Day.]

There is no record of plaintiff ever applying for another job within AIDC, however, and the record shows that not only was plaintiff never downgraded, her position was reclassified upward from a Grade 9 classification to a Grade 11 classification, thereby increasing her annual salary. Indeed, it is undisputed that plaintiff received every merit increase and cost-of-living allowance for which she was eligible during her nearly two-year tenure with the AIDC and consistently received satisfactory job evaluations.

Although plaintiff states that her job title upon returning from maternity leave was no longer that of purchasing assistant, her job duties prior to taking maternity leave and her job duties upon returning to work both involved data input. That being so, plaintiff cannot establish a tangible job detriment. A transfer that does not involve a demotion in form or substance and involves only minor changes in working conditions, with no reduction in pay or benefits, will not constitute an adverse employment action, otherwise every trivial personnel action that an irritable employee did not like would form the basis of a discrimination suit.

Finally, the Court rejects plaintiff's claim that she was subjected to hostile treatment having tangible effects when she was isolated physically, made to sit in a location from which she was constantly watched, made to sit at her workstation with no work to do, and singled out as the only female employee not to be given flowers on Secretary's Day. Plaintiff may well have perceived hostility and animus on the part of her supervisors, but these perceptions are merely conclusory in nature and do not, without more, constitute a tangible job detriment. Although it is not clear why plaintiff failed to receive flowers on Secretary's Day in 1992, such an omission does not give rise to a federal cause of action.

In sum, the Court finds that a showing of a tangible job detriment or adverse employment action is an essential element of plaintiff's sexual harassment claim and that plaintiff has not demonstrated any tangible job detriment or adverse employment action for her refusal to submit to the Governor's alleged advances. The President is therefore entitled to summary judgment [on this claim].

In other words, the court acknowledged that there were factual disputes, but concluded that, even if Jones proved each of her allegations, she would *still* lose the case because her allegations fell short of a legitimate case of sexual harassment. Jones appealed the case. Later the same year, as the appeal was pending and the House of Representatives was considering whether to impeach President Clinton, the parties settled the dispute. Clinton, without acknowledging any of the allegations, agreed to pay Jones $850,000 to drop the suit.

Janet and Rich each consider moving for summary judgment, but both correctly decide that they would lose. There is one major fact in dispute: Did Tony Caruso commit suicide? Only a jury may decide that issue. As long as there is *some evidence* supporting each side of a key factual dispute, the court may not grant summary judgment.

EXAMStrategy

Question: You are a judge. Mel has sued Kevin claiming that, while Kevin was drunk, he negligently drove his car down Mel's street and destroyed rare trees on a lot that Mel owns, next to his house. Mel's complaint stated that three witnesses at a bar saw Kevin take at least eight drinks less than an hour before the damage was done. In Kevin's answer, he denied causing the damage and denied being in the bar that night.

Kevin's lawyer has moved for summary judgment. He proves that three weeks before the alleged accident, Mel sold the lot to Tatiana.

Mel's lawyer opposes summary judgment. He produces a security camera tape proving that Kevin was in the bar, drinking beer, 34 minutes before the damage was done. He produces a signed statement from Sandy, a landscape gardener who lives across the street from the scene. Sandy states that she heard a crash, hurried to the windows, and saw Kevin's car weaving away from the damaged trees. She estimates the tree damage at $30,000 to $40,000. How should you rule on the motion?

Strategy: Do not be fooled by red herrings about Kevin's drinking or the value of the trees. Stick to the question: Should you grant summary judgment? Trials are necessary to resolve disputes about essential factual issues. Summary judgment is appropriate when there are no essential facts in dispute. Is there an essential fact not in dispute? Find it. Apply the rule. Being a judge is easy!

Result: It makes no difference whether Kevin was drunk or sober, whether he caused the harm or was at home in bed. Because Mel does not own the property, he cannot recover for the damage to it. He cannot win. You should grant Kevin's summary judgment motion.

6-2d Final Preparation

More than 90 percent of all lawsuits are settled before trial. But the parties in the Enviro-Vision dispute are unable to compromise, so each side gears up for trial. The attorneys make lists of all witnesses they will call. They then prepare each witness very carefully, rehearsing the questions they will ask. It is considered ethical and proper to rehearse the questions, provided the answers are honest and come from the witness. It is unethical and illegal for a lawyer to tell a witness what to say. It also makes for a weaker presentation of evidence—witnesses giving scripted answers are often easy to spot. The lawyers also have colleagues cross-examine each witness, so that the witnesses are ready for the questions the other side's lawyer will ask.

This preparation takes hours and hours, for many days. Beth is frustrated that she cannot do the work she needs to for Enviro-Vision because she is spending so much time preparing the case. Other employees have to prepare as well, especially for cross-examination by Rich Stewart, and it is a terrible drain on the small firm. More than a year after Janet filed her complaint, they are ready to begin trial.

6-3 THE ANATOMY OF A TRIAL AND APPEAL

6-3a The Trial

Our system of justice assumes that the best way to bring out the truth is for the two contesting sides to present the strongest case possible to a neutral fact finder. Each side presents its witnesses and then the opponent has a chance to cross-examine. The adversary system presumes that by putting a witness on the stand and letting both lawyers question her, the truth will emerge.

The judge runs the trial. Each lawyer sits at a large table near the front. Beth, looking tense and unhappy, sits with Janet. Rich Stewart sits with a Coastal executive. In the back of the courtroom are benches for the public. On one bench sits Craig Bergson. He will watch the entire proceeding with intense interest and a strange feeling of unease. He is convinced he knows what really happened.

Janet has demanded a jury trial for Beth's case, and Judge Rowland announces that they will now impanel the jury.

Right to Jury Trial

Not all cases are tried to a jury. As a general rule, both plaintiff and defendant have a right to demand a jury trial when the lawsuit is one for money damages. For example, in a typical contract lawsuit, such as Beth's insurance claim, both plaintiff and defendant have a jury trial right whether they are in state or federal court. Even in such a case, though, the parties may *waive* the jury right, meaning they agree to try the case to a judge. Also, if the plaintiff is seeking an equitable remedy such as an injunction, there is no jury right for either party.

Voir Dire

Voir dire
The process of selecting a jury

The process of selecting a jury is called **voir dire**, which means "to speak the truth."[8] The court's goal is to select an impartial jury; the lawyers will each try to get a jury as favorable to their side as possible. A court sends letters to potential jurors who live in its county. Those who do not report for jury duty face significant consequences.

Challenges for cause
A claim that a juror has demonstrated probable bias

Peremptory challenges
The right to excuse a juror for virtually any reason

When voir dire begins, potential jurors are questioned individually, sometimes by the judge and sometimes by the two lawyers, as each side tries to ferret out potential bias. Each lawyer may make any number of **challenges for cause**, claiming that a juror has demonstrated probable bias. For example, if a prospective juror in the Enviro-Vision case works for an insurance company, the judge will excuse her on the assumption that she would be biased in favor of Coastal. If the judge perceives no bias, the lawyer may still make a limited number of **peremptory challenges**, entitling him to excuse that juror for virtually any reason, which need not be stated in court. For example, if Rich Stewart believes that a juror seems hostile to him personally, he will use a peremptory challenge to excuse that juror, even if the judge sensed no animosity. The process continues until 14 jurors are seated. Twelve will comprise the jury; the other two are alternates who hear the case and remain available in the event one of the impaneled jurors becomes ill or otherwise cannot continue.

Although jury selection for a case can sometimes take many days, in the Enviro-Vision case, the first day of the hearing ends with the jury selected. In the hallway outside the court, Rich offers Janet $200,000 to settle. Janet reports the offer to Beth and they agree to reject it. Craig Bergson drives home, emotionally confused. Only three weeks before his death, Tony

[8] Students of French note that *voir* means "to see" and assume that *voir dire* should translate as "to see, to speak." However, the legal term is centuries old and derives not from modern French but from Old French, in which *voir* meant "truth."

had accidentally met his old roommate and they had had several drinks. Craig believes that what Tony told him answers the riddle of this case.

Opening Statements

The next day, each attorney makes an opening statement to the jury, summarizing the proof he or she expects to offer, with the plaintiff going first. Janet focuses on Tony's successful life, his business and strong marriage, and the tragedy of his accidental death.[9]

Rich works hard to establish a friendly rapport with the jury. If members of the jury like him, they will tend to pay more attention to his presentation of evidence. He expresses regret about the death. Nonetheless, suicide is a clear exclusion from the policy. If insurance companies are forced to pay claims never bargained for, everyone's insurance rates will go up.

Burden of Proof

In civil cases, the plaintiff has the burden of proof. That means that the plaintiff must convince the jury that its version of the case is correct; the defendant is not obligated to disprove the allegations.

The plaintiff's burden in a civil lawsuit is to prove its case by a **preponderance of the evidence**. It must convince the jury that its version of the facts is at least *slightly more likely* than the defendant's version. Some courts describe this as a "51–49" persuasion; that is, that plaintiff's proof must "just tip" credibility in its favor. By contrast, in a criminal case, the prosecution must demonstrate **beyond a reasonable doubt** that the defendant is guilty. The burden of proof in a criminal case is much tougher because the likely consequences are too. See Exhibit 6.3.

Preponderance of the evidence
The plaintiff's burden of proof in a civil lawsuit

Beyond a reasonable doubt
The government's burden of proof in a criminal prosecution

Plaintiff's Case

Because the plaintiff has the burden of proof, Janet puts in her case first. She wants to prove two things. First, that Tony died. That is easy because the death certificate clearly demonstrates it and Coastal does not seriously contest it. Second, in order to win double indemnity

EXHIBIT 6.3

Burden of Proof. In a civil lawsuit, a plaintiff wins with a mere preponderance of the evidence. But the prosecution must persuade a jury beyond a reasonable doubt in order to win a criminal conviction.

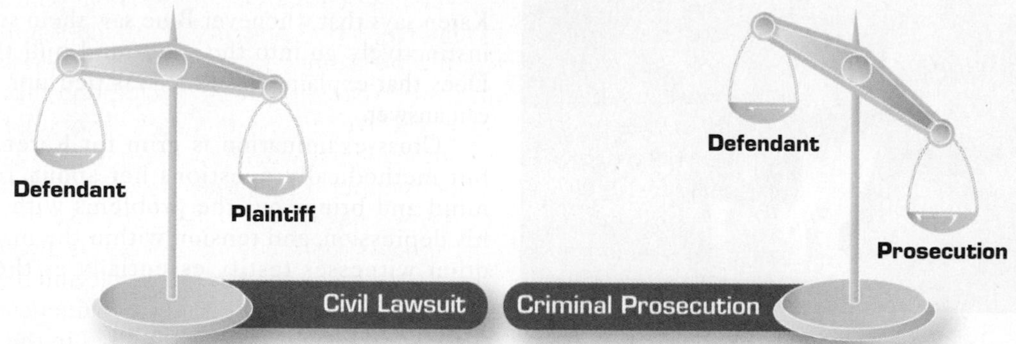

[9] Janet Booker has dropped her claim for triple damages against Coastal. To have any hope of such a verdict, she would have to show that Coastal had no legitimate reason at all for denying the claim. Discovery has convinced her that Coastal will demonstrate some rational reasons for what it did.

damages, she must show that the death was accidental. She will do this with the testimony of the witnesses she calls, one after the other. Her first witness is Beth. When a lawyer asks questions of her own witness, it is **direct examination**. Janet brings out all the evidence she wants the jury to hear: that the business was basically sound, though temporarily troubled, that Tony was a hard worker, why the company took out life insurance policies, and so forth.

Cross-examine
To ask questions of an opposing witness

Then Rich has a chance to **cross-examine** Beth, which means to ask questions of an opposing witness. He will try to create doubt in the jury's mind. He asks Beth only questions for which he is certain of the answers, based on discovery. Rich gets Beth to admit that the firm was not doing well the year of Tony's death; that Tony had lost the best client the firm ever had; that Beth had reduced salaries; and that Tony had been depressed about business.

Rules of Evidence

The lawyers are not free simply to ask any question they want. The law of evidence determines what questions a lawyer may ask and how the questions are to be phrased, what answers a witness may give, and what documents may be introduced. The goal is to get the best evidence possible before the jurors so they can decide what really happened. In general, witnesses may only testify about things they saw or heard.

These rules are complex, and a thorough look at them is beyond the scope of this chapter. However, they can be just as important in resolving a dispute as the underlying substantive law. Suppose that a plaintiff's case depends upon the jury hearing about a certain conversation, but the rules of evidence prevent the lawyer from asking about it. That conversation might just as well never have occurred.

Janet calls an expert witness, a marine geologist, who testifies about the tides and currents in the area where Tony's body was found. The expert testifies that even experienced swimmers can be overwhelmed by a sudden shift in currents. Rich objects strenuously that this is irrelevant, because there is no testimony that there *was* such a current at the time of Tony's death. The judge permits the testimony.

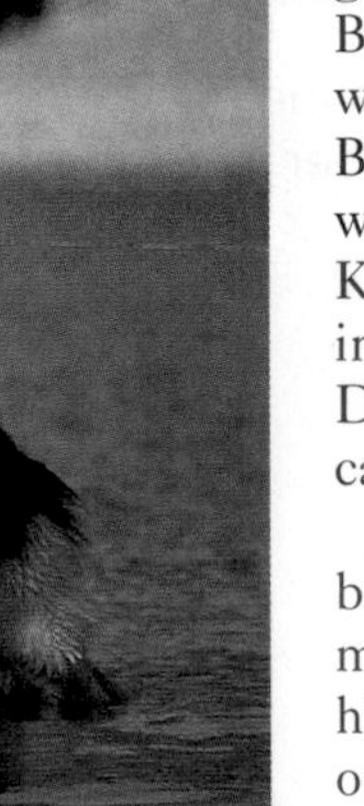
Dave Porter/Alamy Stock Photo

Karen Caruso testifies that Tony was in "reasonably good" spirits the day of his death and that he often took Blue for walks along the beach. Karen testifies that Blue was part Newfoundland. Rich objects that testimony about Blue's pedigree is irrelevant, but Janet insists it will show why Blue was tied up. The judge allows the testimony. Karen says that whenever Blue saw them swim, he would instinctively go into the water and pull them to shore. Does that explain why Blue was tied up? Only the jury can answer.

Cross-examination is grim for Karen. Rich slowly but methodically questions her about Tony's state of mind and brings out the problems with the company, his depression, and tension within the marriage. Janet's other witnesses testify essentially as they did during their depositions.

Motion for Directed Verdict

At the close of the plaintiff's case, Rich moves for a directed verdict; that is, a ruling that the plaintiff has entirely failed to prove some aspect of her case. Rich is seeking to win without even putting in his own case. He argues that it was Beth's burden to prove that Tony died accidentally and that she has entirely failed to do that.

Directed verdict
A ruling that the plaintiff has entirely failed to prove some aspect of her case

A **directed verdict is permissible only if the evidence so clearly favors the defendant that reasonable minds could not disagree on it.** If reasonable minds could disagree, the motion must be denied. Here, Judge Rowland rules that the plaintiff has put in enough evidence of accidental death that a reasonable person could find in Beth's favor. The motion is denied.

There is no downside for Rich to ask for a directed verdict. The trial continues as if he had never made such a motion.

Defendant's Case

Rich now puts in his case, exactly as Janet did, except that he happens to have fewer witnesses. He calls the examining doctor, who admits that Tony could have committed suicide by swimming out too far. On cross-examination, Janet gets the doctor to acknowledge that he has no idea whether Tony intentionally drowned. Rich also questions several neighbors as to how depressed Tony had seemed and how unusual it was that Blue was tied up. Some of the witnesses Rich deposed, such as the tennis partner Jerry Johnson, have nothing that will help Coastal's case, so he does not call them.

Craig Bergson, sitting in the back of the courtroom, thinks how different the trial would have been had he been called as a witness. When he and Tony had the fateful drink, Tony had been distraught: Business was terrible, he was involved in an extramarital affair that he could not end, and he saw no way out of his problems. He had no one to talk to and had been hugely relieved to speak with Craig. Several times Tony had said, "I just can't go on like this. I don't want to, anymore." Craig thought Tony seemed suicidal and urged him to see a therapist Craig knew and trusted. Tony had said that it was good advice, but Craig is unsure whether Tony sought any help.

This evidence would have affected the case. Had Rich Stewart known of the conversation, he would have deposed Craig and the therapist. Coastal's case would have been far stronger, perhaps overwhelming. But Craig's evidence will never be heard. Facts are critical. Rich's decision to depose other witnesses and omit Craig may influence the verdict more than any rule of law.

Closing Arguments

Both lawyers sum up their case to the jury, explaining how they hope the jury will interpret what they have heard. Janet summarizes the plaintiff's version of the facts, claiming that Blue was tied up so that Tony could swim without worrying about him. Rich claims that business and personal pressures had overwhelmed Tony. He tied up his dog, neatly folded his clothes, and took his own life.

Jury Instructions

Judge Rowland instructs the jury as to its duty. He tells them that they are to evaluate the case based only on the evidence they heard at trial, relying on their own experience and common sense.

He explains the law and the burden of proof, telling the jury that it is Beth's obligation to prove that Tony died. If Beth has proven that Tony died, she is entitled to $1 million; if she has proven that his death was accidental, she is entitled to $2 million. However, if Coastal has proven suicide, Beth receives nothing. Finally, the judge states that if they are unable to decide between accidental death and suicide, there is a legal presumption that it was accidental. Rich asks Judge Rowland to rephrase the "legal presumption" part, but the judge declines.

Verdict

The jury deliberates informally, with all jurors entitled to voice their opinion. Some deliberations take two hours; some take two weeks. Many states require a unanimous verdict; others require only, for example, a 10–2 vote in civil cases.

This case presents a close call. No one saw Tony die. Yet even though they cannot know with certainty, the jury's decision will probably be the final word on whether he took his own life. After a day and a half of deliberating, the jury notifies the judge that it has reached a verdict. Rich Stewart quickly makes a new offer: $350,000. (The two sides have the right to settle a case until the moment when the last appeal is decided.) Beth hesitates but turns it down.

The judge summons the lawyers to court, and Beth goes as well. The judge asks the foreman if the jury has reached a decision. He states that it has: The jury finds that Tony Caruso drowned accidentally, and awards Beth Smiles $2 million.

Motions after the Verdict

Judgment *non obstante veredicto* (JNOV)
A judgment notwithstanding the jury's verdict

Rich immediately moves for a **judgment *non obstante veredicto* (JNOV)**, meaning a judgment notwithstanding the jury's verdict. He is asking the judge to overturn the jury's verdict. Rich argues that the jury's decision went against all of the evidence. He also claims that the judge's instructions were wrong and misled the jury.

Judge Rowland denies the JNOV. Rich immediately moves for a new trial, making the same claim, and the judge denies the motion. Beth is elated that the case is finally over—until Janet says she expects an appeal. Craig Bergson, leaving the courtroom, wonders if he did the right thing. He felt sympathy for Beth and none for Coastal. Yet now he is neither happy nor proud.

6-3b Appeals

Two days later, Rich files an appeal to the court of appeals. The same day, he phones Janet and increases his settlement offer to $425,000. Beth is tempted but wants Janet's advice. Janet says the risks of an appeal are that the court will order a new trial, and they would start all over. But to accept this offer is to forfeit over $1.5 million. Beth is unsure what to do. The firm desperately needs cash now, and appeals may take years. Janet suggests they wait until oral argument, another eight months.

Rich files a brief arguing that there were two basic errors at the trial: first, that the jury's verdict is clearly contrary to the evidence; and second, that the judge gave the wrong instructions to the jury. Janet files a reply brief, opposing Rich on both issues. In her brief, Janet cites many cases that she claims are **precedent**: earlier decisions by the state appellate courts on similar or identical issues.

Precedent
Earlier decisions by the state appellate courts on similar or identical issues

Eight months later, the lawyers representing Coastal and Enviro-Vision appear in the court of appeals to argue their case. Rich, the appellant, goes first. The judges frequently interrupt his argument with questions. They show little sympathy for his claim that the verdict was against the facts. They seem more sympathetic with his second point, that the instructions were wrong.

When Janet argues, all of their questions concern the judge's instructions. It appears they believe the instructions were in error. The judges take the case under advisement, meaning they will decide sometime in the future—maybe in two weeks, maybe in five months.

Appeals Court Options

Affirm
To allow the decision to stand

Modify
To affirm the outcome but with changes

Reverse and remand
To nullify the lower decision and return the case for reconsideration or retrial

The court of appeals can **affirm** the trial court, allowing the decision to stand. The court may **modify** the decision, for example, by affirming that the plaintiff wins but decreasing the size of the award. (That is unlikely here; Beth is entitled to $2 million or nothing.) The court might **reverse and remand**, nullifying the lower court's decision and returning the case to the lower court for a new trial. Or it could simply **reverse**, turning the loser (Coastal) into the winner, with no new trial.

What will it do here? On the factual issue, it will probably rule in Beth's favor. There *was* evidence from which a jury could conclude that Tony died accidentally. It is true that there was also considerable evidence to support Coastal's position, but that is probably not enough to overturn the verdict. If reasonable people could disagree on what the evidence proves, an appellate court generally refuses to change the jury's factual findings. The court of appeals is likely to rule that a reasonable jury *could* have found accidental death, even if the appellate judges personally suspect that Tony may have killed himself.

The judge's instructions raise a more difficult problem. Some states would require a more complex statement about "presumptions."[10]

What does a court of appeals do if it decides the trial court's instructions were wrong? If it believes the error rendered the trial and verdict unfair, it will remand the case; that is, send it back to the lower court for a new trial. However, the court may conclude that the mistake was **harmless error**. A trial judge cannot do a perfect job, and not every error is fatal. The court may decide the verdict was fair in spite of the mistake.

Harmless error
A mistake by the trial judge that was too minor to affect the outcome

Janet and Beth talk. Beth is very anxious and wants to settle. She does not want to wait four or five months only to learn that they must start all over. Janet urges that they wait a few weeks to hear from Rich: They don't want to seem too eager.

A week later, Rich telephones and offers $500,000. Janet turns it down, but says she will ask Beth if she wants to make a counteroffer. She and Beth talk. They agree that they will settle for $1 million. Janet then calls Rich and offers to settle for $1.7 million. Rich and Janet debate the merits of the case. Rich later calls back and offers $750,000, saying he doubts that he can go any higher. Janet counters with $1.4 million, saying she doubts she can go any lower. They argue, both predicting that they will win on appeal.

Rich calls, offers $900,000, and says, "That's it. No more." Janet argues for $1.2 million, expecting to nudge Rich up to $1 million. He doesn't nudge, instead saying, "Take it or leave it." Janet and Beth talk it over. Janet telephones Rich and accepts $900,000 to settle the case.

If they had waited for the court of appeals decision, would Beth have won? It is impossible to know. It is certain, though, that whoever lost would have appealed. Months would have passed waiting to learn if the state supreme court would accept the case. If that court had agreed to hear the appeal, Beth would have endured another year of waiting, brief writing, oral argument, and tense hoping. The high court has all of the options discussed: to affirm, modify, reverse and remand, or simply reverse.

6-4 ALTERNATIVE DISPUTE RESOLUTION

As we have seen in the previous section, trials can be trying. Lawsuits can cause prolonged periods of stress, significant legal bills, and general unpleasantness. Many people and companies prefer to settle cases out of court. Alternative dispute resolution (ADR) provides several semiformal methods of resolving conflicts without litigation. We will look at different types of ADR and analyze their strengths and weaknesses.

[10] Judge Rowland probably should have said, "The law presumes that death is accidental, not suicide. So if there were no evidence either way, the plaintiff would win because we presume accident. But if there is competing evidence, the presumption becomes irrelevant. If you think that Coastal Insurance has introduced some evidence of suicide, then forget the legal presumption. You must then decide what happened based on what you have seen and heard in court, and on any inferences you choose to draw." Note that the judge's instructions were different, though similar.

6-4a Negotiation

In most cases, the parties negotiate, either personally or through lawyers. Fortunately, the great majority of disputes are resolved this way. Negotiation often begins as soon as a dispute arises and may last a few days or several years.

6-4b Mediation

Mediation is the fastest-growing method of dispute resolution in the United States. Here, a neutral person, called a *mediator*, attempts to guide the two disputing parties toward a voluntary settlement. (In some cases, there may be two or more mediators, but we will use the singular.) Generally, the two disputants voluntarily enter mediation, although some judges order the parties to try this form of ADR before allowing a case to go to trial.

A mediator does not render a decision in the dispute, but uses a variety of skills to move the parties toward agreement. Often a mediator will shuttle between the antagonists, hearing their arguments, sorting out the serious issues from the less important, prompting the parties and lawyers alike to consider new perspectives, and looking for areas of agreement. Mediators must earn the trust of both parties, listen closely, try to diffuse anger and fear, and build the will to settle. Good mediators do not need a law degree, but they must have a sense of humor and low blood pressure.

Mediation has several major advantages. Because the parties maintain control of the process, the two antagonists can speak freely. They need not fear conceding too much because no settlement takes effect until both parties sign. All discussions are confidential, further encouraging candid talk. This is particularly helpful in cases involving proprietary information that might be revealed during a trial.

Of all forms of dispute resolution, mediation probably offers the strongest "win–win" potential. Because the goal is voluntary settlement, neither party needs to fear that it will end up the loser. This is in sharp contrast to litigation, where one party will lose. Removing the fear of defeat often encourages thinking and talking that are more open and realistic than negotiations held in the midst of a lawsuit. Studies show that more than 75 percent of mediated cases do reach a voluntary settlement. Such an agreement is particularly valuable to parties that wish to preserve a long-term relationship. Consider two companies that have done business successfully for ten years but now are in the midst of a million-dollar trade dispute. A lawsuit could last three or more years and destroy any chance of future trade. However, if the parties mediate the disagreement, they might reach an amicable settlement within a month or two and could quickly resume their mutually profitable business.

6-4c Arbitration

In this form of ADR, the parties agree to bring in a neutral third party, but with a major difference: The arbitrator has the power to impose an award. The arbitrator allows each side equal time to present its case and, after deliberation, issues a binding decision, generally without giving reasons. Unlike mediation, arbitration ensures that there will be a final result, although the parties lose control of the outcome.

Judge Judy and similar TV court shows are examples of arbitration. Before the shows are taped, people involved in a real dispute sign a contract in which they give up the right to go to court over the incident and agree to be bound by Judge Judy's decision.

Parties in arbitration give up many additional rights that litigants retain, including discovery and class action. In arbitration, as already discussed as applied to trials, *discovery* allows the two sides in a lawsuit to obtain documentary and other evidence from the opponent before the dispute is decided. Arbitration permits both sides to keep secret many files that would have to be divulged in a court case, potentially depriving the opposing side of valuable evidence. A party may have a stronger case than it realizes, and the absence of discovery may permanently deny it that knowledge. As discussed earlier in this chapter, a *class action* is a suit in which one injured party represents a large group of people who have suffered similar harm. Arbitration eliminates this possibility because injured employees face the employer one at a time. Finally, the fact that an arbitrator may not provide a written, public decision bars other plaintiffs, and society generally, from learning what happened.

Traditionally, parties sign arbitration agreements *after* some incident took place. A car accident would happen first, and the drivers would agree to arbitration second. But today, many parties agree *in advance* to arbitrate any disputes that may arise in the future. For example, a new employee may sign an agreement requiring arbitration of any future disputes with his employer; a customer opening an account with a stockbroker or bank— or health plan—may sign a similar form, often without realizing it. The good news is fewer lawsuits; the bad news is you might be the person kept out of court.

Assume that you live in Miami. Using the internet, you order a $2,000 ThinkLite laptop computer, which arrives in a carton loaded with six fat instructional manuals and many small leaflets. You read some of the documents and ignore others. For four weeks, you struggle to make your computer work, to no avail. Finally, you call ThinkLite and demand a refund, but the company refuses. You file suit in your local court, at which time the company points out that buried among the hundreds of pages it mailed you was a *mandatory arbitration form*. This document prohibits you from filing suit against the company and states that if you have any complaint with the company, you must fly to Chicago, pay a $2,000 arbitrator's fee, plead your case before an arbitrator selected by the Laptop Trade Association of America, and, should you lose, pay ThinkLite's attorneys' fees, which could be several thousand dollars. Is that mandatory arbitration provision valid?

Courts generally enforce arbitration clauses if they meet two conditions. First, both parties must mutually promise to submit disputes to arbitration. A unilateral arbitration agreement only requiring one party to give up its right to sue is unenforceable. Second, the clause must provide a neutral forum to resolve disputes and adopt sufficient rules to govern a proceeding. One party cannot retain exclusive control over the appointment of arbitrators.

CHAPTER CONCLUSION

No one will ever know for sure whether Tony Caruso took his own life. Craig Bergson's evidence might have tipped the scales in favor of Coastal. But even that is uncertain, since the jury could have found him unpersuasive. After two years, the case ends with a settlement and uncertainty—both typical lawsuit results. The missing witness is less common but not extraordinary. The vaguely unsatisfying feeling about it all is only too common and indicates why most parties settle out of court.

EXAM REVIEW

1. **COURT SYSTEMS** There are many *systems* of courts, one federal and one in each state. A federal court will hear a case only if it involves a federal question or diversity jurisdiction.

2. **TRIAL AND APPELLATE COURTS** Trial courts determine facts and apply the law to the facts; appeals courts generally accept the facts found by the trial court and review the trial record for errors of law.

EXAMStrategy

Question: Jade sued Kim, claiming that Kim promised to hire her as an in-store model for $1,000 per week for eight weeks. Kim denied making the promise, and the jury was persuaded: Kim won. Jade has appealed, and now she offers Steve as a witness. Steve will testify to the appeals court that he saw Kim hire Jade as a model, exactly as Jade claimed. Will Jade win on appeal?

Strategy: Before you answer, make sure you know the difference between trial and appellate courts. What is the difference? Apply that distinction here. (See the "Result" at the end of this Exam Review section.)

3. **PLEADINGS** A complaint and an answer are the two most important pleadings; that is, documents that start a lawsuit.

4. **MOTIONS** A motion is a formal request to the court.

5. **MOTION TO DISMISS** A request that the court terminate a case and not allow it to continue because the law does not offer a legal remedy for the plaintiff's problem.

6. **DISCOVERY** Discovery is the critical pre-trial opportunity for both parties to learn the strengths and weaknesses of the opponent's case. Important forms of discovery include interrogatories, depositions, production of documents and objects, physical and mental examinations, and requests for admission.

7. **SUMMARY JUDGMENT** Summary judgment is a ruling by the court that no trial is necessary because there are no essential facts in dispute.

8. **JURY TRIALS** Generally, both plaintiff and defendant may demand a jury in any lawsuit for money damages.

9. **VOIR DIRE** Voir dire is the process of selecting jurors in order to obtain an impartial panel.

EXAMStrategy

Question: You are a lawyer representing the plaintiff in a case of alleged employment discrimination. The court is selecting a jury. Based on questions you have asked, you believe that juror number 3 is biased against your client. You explain this to the judge, but she disagrees. Is there anything you can do?

Strategy: The question focuses on your rights during voir dire. If you believe that a juror will not be fair, you may make two different types of challenge. What are they? (See the "Result" at the end of this Exam Review section.)

10. **BURDEN OF PROOF** The plaintiff's burden of proof in a civil lawsuit is a preponderance of the evidence, meaning that its version of the facts must be at least slightly more persuasive than the defendant's. In a criminal prosecution, the government must offer proof beyond a reasonable doubt in order to win a conviction.

11. **RULES OF EVIDENCE** The rules of evidence determine what questions may be asked during trial, what testimony may be given, and what documents may be introduced.

12. **VERDICT** The verdict is the jury's decision in a case. The losing party may ask the trial judge to overturn the verdict, seeking a JNOV or a new trial. Judges seldom grant either.

13. **APPEALS** An appeals court has many options. The court may affirm, upholding the lower court's decision; modify, changing the verdict but leaving the same party victorious; reverse, transforming the loser into the winner; and/or remand, sending the case back to the lower court.

14. **ADR** Alternative dispute resolution is any formal or informal process to settle disputes without a trial. Mediation, arbitration, and other forms of ADR have grown in popularity.

RESULTS

2. Result: Trial courts use witnesses to help resolve fact disputes. Appellate courts review the record to see if there have been errors of law. Appellate courts never hear witnesses, and they will not hear Steve. Jade will lose her appeal.

9. Result: You have already made a *challenge for cause*, claiming bias, but the judge has rejected your challenge. If you have not used up all of your *peremptory challenges*, you may use one to excuse this juror, without giving any reason.

MULTIPLE-CHOICE QUESTIONS

1. The burden of proof in a civil trial is to prove a case ________. The burden of proof rests with the ________.
   (a) beyond a reasonable doubt; plaintiff
   (b) by a preponderance of the evidence; plaintiff
   (c) beyond a reasonable doubt; defendant
   (d) by a preponderance of the evidence; defendant

2. Alice is suing Betty. After the discovery process, Alice believes that no relevant facts are in dispute and that there is no need for a trial. She should move for a ________.
   (a) judgment on the pleadings
   (b) directed verdict
   (c) summary judgment
   (d) JNOV

3. Glen lives in Illinois. He applies for a job with a Missouri company, and he is told, amazingly, that the job is open only to white applicants. He will now sue the Missouri company under the Civil Rights Act, a federal statute. Can Glen sue in federal court?
   (a) Yes, absolutely.
   (b) Yes, but only if he seeks damages of at least $75,000. Otherwise, he must sue in a state court.
   (c) Yes, but only if the Missouri company agrees. Otherwise, he must sue in a state court.
   (d) No, absolutely not. He must sue in a state court.

4. A default judgment can be entered if which of the following is true?
   (a) A plaintiff presents her evidence at trial and clearly fails to meet her burden of proof.
   (b) A defendant loses a lawsuit and does not pay a judgment within 180 days.
   (c) A defendant fails to file an answer to a plaintiff's complaint on time.
   (d) A citizen fails to obey an order to appear for jury duty.

5. Barry and Carl are next-door neighbors. Barry's dog digs under Carl's fence and does $500 worth of damage to Carl's garden. Barry refuses to pay for the damage, claiming that Carl's cats "have been digging up my yard for years."

   The two argue repeatedly, and the relationship turns frosty. Of the following choices, which has no outside decision maker and is most likely to allow the neighbors to peacefully coexist after working out the dispute?
   (a) Trial
   (b) Arbitration
   (c) Mediation

CASE QUESTIONS

1. You plan to open a store in Chicago, specializing in rugs imported from Turkey. You will work with a native Turk who will purchase and ship the rugs to your store. You are wise enough to insist on a contract establishing the rights and obligations of both parties and would prefer an ADR clause. But you do not want a clause that will alienate your overseas partner. What kind of ADR clause should you include, and why?

2. Which court(s) have jurisdiction over each of these lawsuits—state or federal? Explain your reasoning for each answer
   - Pat wants to sue his next-door neighbor, Dorothy, claiming that Dorothy promised to sell him the house next door.
   - Paula, who lives in New York City, wants to sue Dizzy Movie Theatres, whose principal place of business is Dallas. She claims that while she was in Texas on holiday, she was injured by their negligent maintenance of a stairway. She claims damages of $30,000.

- Phil lives in Tennessee. He wants to sue Dick, who lives in Ohio. Phil claims that Dick agreed to sell him 3,000 acres of farmland in Ohio, worth more than $2 million.
- Pete, incarcerated in a federal prison in Kansas, wants to sue the U.S. government. He claims that his treatment by prison authorities violates three federal statutes.

3. British discovery practice differs from that in the United States. Most discovery in Britain concerns documents. The lawyers for the two sides, called *solicitors*, must deliver to the opposing side a list of all relevant documents in their possession. Each side may then request to look at and copy those it wishes. Depositions are rare. What advantages and disadvantages are there to the British practice?

4. After Sam got a tattoo, he was fired by his employer, Douglas Corp. Irate, Sam hired an attorney and sued Douglas for discriminating against people with tattoos. His complaint alleged that he was fired days after he showed his supervisor the new tattoo. There is no law prohibiting employment discrimination on this basis. And the Douglas employee handbook clearly stated that employees should have no visible tattoos. What will likely happen in court after Sam's attorney files the complaint?

5. When Giant, Inc., hired Kelly, it gave her an entire binder of papers to sign. Buried in the fine print was a clause requiring any future dispute between the parties to go to arbitration, and the arbitrators would be chosen by Giant. Years later, Kelly filed a sexual harassment suit claiming that her boss fondled her. She demanded her day in court, but Giant's attorneys claim she was barred due to the arbitration clause. Will Kelly prevail?

DISCUSSION QUESTIONS

1. In the Tony Caruso case described throughout this chapter, the defendant offers to settle the case at several stages. Knowing what you do now about litigation, would you have accepted any of the offers? If so, which one(s)? If not, why not?

2. The burden of proof in civil cases is fairly low. A plaintiff wins a lawsuit if he is 51 percent convincing, and then he collects 100 percent of his damages. Is this result reasonable? Should a plaintiff in a civil case be required to prove his case beyond a reasonable doubt? Or, if a plaintiff is only 51 percent convincing, should he get only 51 percent of his damages?

3. The Supreme Court has held that businesses can force consumers to arbitrate rather than bring class actions.[11] But at least one study found that individuals rarely sue on their own because it is too expensive. Various consumer groups have proposed rules to block banks and credit card companies from this practice. Should the law ban consumer arbitration agreements?

[11]AT&T Mobility LLC v. Vincent Concepcion, 563 U.S. 333 (2011).

4. Imagine a state law that allows for residents to sue "spammers"—those who send uninvited commercial messages through email—for $30. One particularly prolific spammer sends messages to hundreds of thousands of people. John Smith, a lawyer, signs up 100,000 people to participate in a class action lawsuit. According to the agreements with his many clients, Smith will keep one-third of any winnings. In the end, Smith wins a $3 million verdict and pockets $1 million. Each individual plaintiff receives a check for $20. Is this lawsuit a reasonable use of the court's resources? Why or why not?

5. Higher courts are reluctant to review a lower court's *factual* findings. Should this be so? Would appeals be fairer if appellate courts reviewed *everything*?

CHAPTER 7
CRIME

Crime can take us by surprise. Stacey tucks her nine-year-old daughter, Beth, into bed. Promising her husband, Mark, that she will be home by 11:00 p.m., she jumps into her car and heads back to Be Patient, Inc. When her iPhone connects to the sound system in her $100,000 sedan, she tries to relax by listening to music. Be Patient is a healthcare organization that owns five geriatric facilities. Most of its patients use Medicare, and Stacey supervises all billing to their largest client, the federal government.

She parks in a well-lighted spot on the street and walks to her building, failing to notice two men, collars turned up, watching from a parked truck. Once in her office, she goes straight to her computer and works on billing issues. Tonight's work goes more quickly than she expected, thanks to new software she helped develop. At 10:30 p.m. she emerges from the building with a quick step and a light heart, walks to her car—and finds it missing.

A major crime has occurred during the 90 minutes Stacey was at her desk, but she will never report it to the police.

A major crime has occurred during the 90 minutes Stacey was at her desk, but she will never report it to the police. It is a crime that costs Americans countless dollars each year, yet Stacey will not even mention it to friends or family. Stacey is the criminal.

When we think of crime, we imagine the drug dealers and bank robbers endlessly portrayed on television. We do not picture corporate executives sitting at polished desks. "Street crimes" are indeed serious threats to our security and happiness. They deservedly receive the attention of the public and the law. But when measured only in dollars, street crime takes second place to white-collar crime, which costs society *tens of billions* of dollars annually.

The hypothetical about Stacey is based on many real cases and is used to illustrate that crime does not always dress the way we expect. Her car was never stolen; it was simply towed. Two parking lot employees, watching from their truck, saw Stacey park illegally and did their job. It is Stacey who committed a crime—Medicare fraud. Every month, she has billed the government for work that her company has not performed. Stacey's scheme was quick and profitable—and a distressingly common crime.

Crime, whether violent or white-collar, is detrimental to all society. It imposes a huge cost on everyone. Just the *fear* of crime is expensive—homeowners buy alarm systems and businesses hire security guards. But the anger and fear that crime engenders sometimes tempt us to forget that not all accused people are **guilty**. Everyone suspected of a crime should have the protections that you would want yourself. As the English jurist William Blackstone said, "Better that ten guilty persons escape than that one innocent suffer."

Guilty
A judge or jury's finding that a defendant has committed a crime

Thus, criminal law is a balancing act—between making society safe and protecting us all from false accusations and unfair punishment.

This chapter has three parts:

- **Criminal procedure**—the *process* by which criminals are investigated, accused, tried, and sentenced;
- Crimes that *harm* businesses; and
- Crimes committed *by* businesses.

Criminal procedure
The process by which criminals are investigated, accused, tried, and sentenced

7-1 CRIMINAL PROCEDURE

Most of this book focuses on civil law, so we begin with a discussion of the differences between a civil and a criminal case.

7-1a A Civil versus a Criminal Case

Civil law involves the rights and liabilities that exist between private parties. As we have seen, if one person claims that another has caused her a civil injury, she bears the burden of filing a lawsuit and convincing a court of her damages.

Criminal law is different. **Conduct is criminal when *society* outlaws it**. When a state legislature or Congress concludes that certain behavior threatens public safety and welfare, it passes a statute forbidding that behavior; in other words, declaring it criminal. Medicare fraud, which Stacey committed, is a crime because Congress has outlawed it. Murder, on the other hand, is generally a state crime, although some particular murders are both state and federal offenses. It is, for example, a violation of a federal statute to murder the president (at any time) or a federal egg inspector (while performing his duties).[1]

Criminal law
Prohibits and punishes conduct that threatens public safety and welfare

The title of a criminal case is usually the government versus someone: *The United States of America v. Simpson or The State of Illinois v. Simpson*, for example. This name illustrates a daunting thought—if you are Simpson, the vast power of the government is against you. Moreover, a criminal defendant often faces an uphill climb because people often assume that anyone accused of a crime must be guilty. Because of these factors, criminal procedure is designed to protect the accused and ensure that criminal trials are fair. Many of the

[1] 18 U.S.C. §1751 and 21 U.S.C. §1041, respectively.

protections for those accused of a crime are found in the first ten amendments to the United States Constitution, known as the Bill of Rights.

Prosecution

Suppose the police arrest Roger and accuse him of breaking into a store and stealing 50 computers. The owner of the store has been harmed, so he has the right to sue the thief in civil court to recover money damages. **But only the government can prosecute a crime and punish Roger by sending him to prison**. The local prosecutor has total discretion in deciding whether to bring Roger to trial on criminal charges.

Burden of Proof

In a civil case, the plaintiff must prove her case only by a preponderance of the evidence.[2] But the penalties for conviction in a criminal case are much more serious, and the stigma of a criminal conviction stays with the guilty person forever, making it more difficult to obtain work and housing. As a result, **the government must prove its case beyond a reasonable doubt**. Therefore, in all criminal cases, if the jury has any significant doubt that Roger stole the computers, it *must* acquit him.

Beyond a reasonable doubt
The very high burden of proof in a criminal trial, demanding much more certainty than required in a civil trial

Right to a Jury

A judge or jury decides the facts of a case. **A criminal defendant has a right to a trial by jury for any charge that could result in a sentence of six months or longer**. The defendant may choose not to have a jury trial, in which case, the judge decides the verdict. When the judge is the fact finder, the proceeding is called a **bench trial**.

Bench trial
There is no jury; the judge reaches a verdict

Felonies and Misdemeanors

A **felony** is a serious crime, for which a defendant can be sentenced to one year or more in prison. Murder, robbery, rape, drug dealing, money laundering, wire fraud, and embezzlement are felonies. A **misdemeanor** is a less serious crime, often punishable by a year or less in a county jail. Public drunkenness, driving without a license, and shoplifting are considered misdemeanors in most states.

Prison time is not the only penalty for a crime. A court can also impose a fine, which the government keeps and does not share with the victim. It can order **restitution**, meaning that the defendant reimburses the victim for harm suffered. The government can also limit the rights of convicted criminals in a surprisingly broad manner. Some states limit the right of felons to vote or the right to apply for a license. For example, someone convicted of a minor drug crime may not be able to obtain a hairdresser's license in some states.[3]

Felony
A serious crime, for which a defendant can be sentenced to one year or more in prison

Misdemeanor
A less serious crime, often punishable by less than a year in a county jail

Restitution
A court order that a guilty defendant reimburse the victim for the harm suffered

7-1b Conduct Outlawed

Crimes are created by statute. To win a conviction, the prosecution must demonstrate to the court that a statute has outlawed the defendant's conduct. The Fifth and Fourteenth Amendments to the Constitution require that **the language of criminal statutes be clear and definite** enough that (1) ordinary people can understand what conduct is prohibited and (2) enforcement cannot be arbitrary and discriminatory. Returning to Roger, the alleged computer thief, the state charged that he stole computer equipment from a store, a crime clearly defined by statute as larceny. On the other hand, the Supreme Court ruled that a statute prohibiting the crime of loitering was unconstitutionally vague because it did not clarify exactly what behavior was prohibited and it tended to be enforced arbitrarily.[4]

---

[2]See the earlier discussion in Chapter 6 on dispute resolution.

[3]To learn more about the consequence of committing a crime, google "aba collateral consequences."

[4]Kolender v. Lawson, 461 U.S. 352 (1983).

The following case does not involve a vagrant wandering the streets but, rather, a high-level corporate executive. Federal prosecutors had charged Jeffrey Skilling with "theft of honest services."[5] You might ask yourself: What does that mean? The fact that you have to ask is one indication that the law may be too vague.

Skilling v. United States

561 U.S. 358
United States Supreme Court, 2010

Facts: Jeffrey Skilling was president and chief operating officer of Enron Corporation, the seventh-largest company in America in terms of revenue. At least, that is what everyone thought. Ten months into Skilling's term of office, Enron filed for bankruptcy protection. Its stock, which had been trading at $90 per share, became virtually worthless. A government investigation discovered that company executives had conducted an elaborate conspiracy to prop up Enron's stock price by overstating the company's finances.

Skilling was charged with the theft of honest services. Traditionally, this federal statute had been used to prosecute public officials who took bribes. But then prosecutors began to charge employees under this statute for having generally breached their duty to their employer—and that is what they decided to do with Skilling. They alleged that his financial shenanigans constituted a theft of honest services. He was convicted, sentenced to more than 24 years in prison, and ordered to pay $45 million in restitution. Skilling appealed, arguing that the honest services statute was unconstitutionally vague. The Fifth Circuit disagreed and affirmed his conviction. The Supreme Court granted *certiorari*.

Issue: ***Was the honest services statute unconstitutionally vague?***

Excerpts from Justice Ginsburg's Decision: To satisfy due process, a penal statute must define the criminal offense [1] with sufficient definiteness that ordinary people can understand what conduct is prohibited and [2] in a manner that does not encourage arbitrary and discriminatory enforcement. According to Skilling, [the honest services statute] meets neither of the two due process essentials. First, the phrase "the right of honest services," he contends, does not adequately define what behavior it bars. Second, he alleges, [the honest services statute's] standardless sweep allows policemen, prosecutors, and juries to pursue their personal predilections, thereby facilitating opportunistic and arbitrary prosecutions.

In the main, prosecutions under this statute involved fraudulent schemes to deprive another of honest services through bribes or kickbacks. Confined to these paramount applications, [the honest services statute] presents no vagueness problem. The Government urges us to go further by locating within [this statute's] compass another category of proscribed conduct: "undisclosed self-dealing by a public official or private employee"—i.e., the taking of official action by the employee that furthers his own undisclosed financial interests while purporting to act in the interests of those to whom he owes a fiduciary duty.

Reading the statute to proscribe a wider range of offensive conduct would raise the due process concerns underlying the vagueness doctrine. To preserve the statute without transgressing constitutional limitations, we now hold that [the honest services statute] criminalizes only the bribe-and-kickback core.

The Government did not, at any time, allege that Skilling solicited or accepted side payments from a third party in exchange for making these misrepresentations. It is, therefore, clear that Skilling did not commit honest-services fraud.[6]

---

[5] 18 U.S.C. §1346.

[6] Skilling had originally been convicted of three crimes: honest services fraud, wire fraud, and securities fraud. When the Supreme Court cleared him of charges under the honest services statute, it remanded the case to the appeals court to determine if the other two convictions were independent enough to stand on their own. If not, he would have had to be retried. Ultimately, Skilling reached a settlement with the government under which he forfeited $42 million to pay back Enron victims and was resentenced to 14 years in prison (a reduction from the original 24).

Although Skilling was not a sympathetic defendant—his misdeeds had cost thousands of people billions of dollars—commentators feared that if the Court upheld the government's broad interpretation of the honest services statute, it could even be used to prosecute a parent who called in sick to attend his child's school play.

Although we sometimes think that the criminal law protections in the Constitution serve only to help the down-and-outs of society, this case demonstrates that these protections are important to all of us, no matter where we reside on the income scale.

7-1c State of Mind

Voluntary Act

A defendant is not guilty of a crime if she was forced to commit it. In other words, she is not guilty if she acted under duress. However, the defendant bears the burden of proving by a *preponderance of the evidence* that she did act under duress. In 1974, a terrorist group kidnapped heiress Patricia Hearst from her apartment near the University of California at Berkeley. After being tortured for two months, she participated in a bank robbery with the group. Despite opportunities to escape, she stayed with the criminals until her capture by the police a year later. The State of California put her on trial for bank robbery. One question for the jury was whether she had voluntarily participated in the crime. This was an issue on which many people had strong opinions. Ultimately, Hearst was convicted, sent to prison, and then later pardoned.

Bettmann/Getty Images

Patty Hearst, before she was kidnapped.

Entrapment

When the government induces the defendant to break the law, the prosecution must prove beyond a reasonable doubt that the defendant was predisposed to commit the crime. The goal is to separate the cases where the defendant was innocent before the government tempted him from those where the defendant was only too eager to break the law.

Kalchinian and Sherman met in the waiting room of a doctor's office where they were both being treated for drug addiction. After several more meetings, Kalchinian told Sherman that the treatment was not working for him and he was desperate to buy drugs. Could Sherman help him? Sherman repeatedly refused, but ultimately agreed to help end Kalchinian's suffering by providing him with drugs. Little did Sherman know that Kalchinian was a police informant. Sherman sold drugs to Kalchinian a number of times. Kalchinian rewarded this act of friendship by getting Sherman hooked again and then turning him in to the police. A jury convicted Sherman of drug dealing, but the Supreme Court overturned the conviction on the grounds that Sherman had been entrapped.[7] The court felt there was no evidence that Sherman was predisposed to commit the crime.

Conspiracy

Jeen and Sunny Han were 22-year-old identical twin sisters. But their relationship was far from sunny; they hated each other. The sisters had a long history of physical and verbal fights. Jeen had even threatened to kill Sunny. One day, Jeen and two teenage boys purchased gloves, twine, tape, Pine Sol, and garbage bags. While Jeen waited outside Sunny's apartment, the boys forced their way in, tied up Sunny and her roommate, and put them in the bathtub. Luckily, Sunny had a chance to dial 911 as she heard the boys breaking in. When

[7]Sherman v. United States, 356 U.S. 369 (1958).

the police arrived, the two boys fled. This case raises several questions: Has Jeen committed a crime? Are the boys guilty of anything more than breaking into Sunny's apartment? How did this family go so terribly wrong? (Because this is a business law text, we can only answer the first two questions.)

If the police discover a plot to commit a crime, they can arrest the defendants before any harm has been done. And if bad guys try to commit a crime, but fail, the police can arrest them without giving them a chance to try again. **It is illegal to *conspire* to commit a crime, even if that crime never actually occurs. A defendant can be convicted of taking part in a conspiracy if:**

- A conspiracy existed,
- The defendants knew about it, and
- Some member of the conspiracy voluntarily took a step toward implementing it.

In the *Han* case, the jury convicted Jeen and the two boys of a conspiracy to murder her sister. As the court asked: What was she planning to do with the Pine Sol and plastic bags, given that she did not have a home?[8] She was sentenced to 26 years to life in prison. The two boys got lesser (but still substantial) sentences because the judge believed Jeen had masterminded the crime.

7-1d Gathering Evidence: The Fourth Amendment

If the police suspect that a crime has been committed, they will need to obtain evidence. **The Fourth Amendment to the Constitution prohibits the government from making illegal searches and seizures.** This amendment applies to individuals, corporations, partnerships, and other organizations. The goal is to protect individuals and businesses from the powerful state.

Warrant

Warrant
Written permission from a neutral officer to conduct a search

Probable cause
It is likely that evidence of a crime will be found in the place to be searched.

As a general rule, the police must obtain a warrant before conducting a search. A **warrant** is written permission from a neutral official, such as a judge or magistrate, to conduct a search.[9] The magistrate will issue a warrant only if there is probable cause. **Probable cause** means that, based on all the information presented, **it is likely that evidence of a crime will be found in the place to be searched.** Often, the police base their applications for a warrant on data provided by an informant. The magistrate will want evidence to support the informant's reliability. If it turns out that this informant has been wrong the last three times he gave evidence to the police, the magistrate will probably refuse the request for a warrant.

If the police search without a warrant, they have, in most cases, violated the Fourth Amendment. But even a search conducted with a warrant violates the Fourth Amendment if:

- There was no probable cause to issue the warrant;
- The warrant does not specify with reasonable precision the place to be searched and the things sought; or
- The search extends beyond what is specified in the warrant.

Thus, if the police say they have reason to believe that they will find bloody clothes in the suspect's car in his garage, they cannot also look through his house and confiscate file folders. In one case, the police had a warrant to search a ground floor apartment for child pornography. But when they arrived at the building, they realized the suspect lived upstairs.

---

[8]The People v. Han, 78 Cal. App. 4th 797 (CA Ct. Appeal 2000).

[9]A magistrate is a judge who tries minor criminal cases or undertakes primarily administrative responsibilities.

The court ruled that the search of the upstairs apartment had violated the Fourth Amendment.[10]

Ryan McGinnis/Alamy Stock Photo

Under what circumstances does the police officer have the right to frisk this man?

Searches without a Warrant

There are seven circumstances under which police may search without a warrant:

Plain View. When Rashad Walker opened his door in response to a police officer's knock, he was holding a marijuana joint in his hand. The court held that the police did not need a warrant to make an arrest because evidence of the crime was in plain view.[11]

Stop and Frisk. None of us wants to live in a world in which police can randomly stop and frisk us on the street anytime they feel like it. **The police do have the right to stop and frisk, but *only if* they have a clear and specific reason to suspect that criminal activity may be afoot and that the person may be armed and dangerous.**[12]

For over a decade, the New York City police had an aggressive stop and frisk policy, halting hundreds of thousands of people on the street each year. More than 80 percent of the stops were of black and Hispanic men, although these two groups made up just slightly more than 50 percent of the population. Once stopped, the suspects were often pushed against the wall and thoroughly searched. Only about 10 percent of the stops yielded evidence of crime. During this time, major crime in New York City fell to historic lows. However, crime also fell in cities that did not have the same stop and frisk policy. To stop this practice in New York, the Center for Constitutional Rights sued the city. At trial, people of color testified about a relentless police presence in their neighborhoods. A judge ultimately ruled this practice unconstitutional and ordered the city to stop.[13] The city appealed this decision but, when a new mayor was elected, the city agreed to halt its aggressive tactics.

What is the appropriate trade-off between a lower crime rate and intrusive police stops? What would you be willing to tolerate personally?

In the *Rodriguez* case on the next page, the court had to decide if the police had the right to search a man's car.

Emergencies. If the police believe that evidence is about to be destroyed, they can search without a warrant. Officers in Lexington, Kentucky, followed a crack dealer into an apartment building. They were not sure if he had entered the apartment on the left or on the right, but they smelled marijuana coming from the one on the right. When they banged on that door and shouted "Police," they heard noises of "things being moved" coming from the apartment. After kicking in the door, they found a man with illegal drugs. They arrested him for drug trafficking. It turned out, however, that the dealer they had been following had gone into the apartment on the left. The Supreme Court held that their search was legal.[14]

---

[10] United States v. Voustianiouk, 685 F.3d 206 (2d Cir. 2012).

[11] State v. Walker, 213 N.J. 281 (N.J. 2013).

[12] Terry v. Ohio, 392 U.S. 1 (1968).

[13] Floyd v. City of New York, 959 F. Supp. 2d 668 (S.D.N.Y. 2013).

[14] Kentucky v. King, 563 U.S. 452 (2011).

Rodriguez v. United States

135 S. Ct. 1609
United States Supreme Court, 2015

Facts: Driving along the Nebraska State Highway just after midnight, Dennys Rodriguez briefly swerved onto the highway shoulder, which is a violation of Nebraska law. At 12:06 a.m., Officer Morgan Struble pulled Rodriguez over for erratic driving. Struble questioned both Rodriguez and his passenger and ran a records check on the car registration and their drivers' licenses. Struble gave Rodriguez a warning ticket.

At 12:27 a.m., Struble finished explaining the warning to Rodriguez and returned the documents to the two men. He then asked permission to walk his police dog around Rodriguez's vehicle, but Rodriguez said no. On the officer's instructions, Rodriguez exited the vehicle. At 12:33 a.m., Struble led the dog twice around the SUV. During the second circuit, the dog signaled the presence of drugs. After searching the car, Struble found methamphetamine, an illegal drug.

At trial, Rodriguez argued that the dog sniff was illegal because Struble had effectively conducted a stop and frisk after the traffic stop was over. But Struble did not have a clear and specific reason to suspect criminal activity for a legal stop and frisk. Both the trial court and the appellate court disagreed with Rodriguez. The Supreme Court granted *certiorari*.

Issues: ***Was the dog sniff legal?***

Excerpts from Justice Ginsburg's Decision: A seizure for a traffic violation justifies a police investigation of that violation. The seizure remains lawful only so long as unrelated inquiries do not measurably extend the duration of the stop. An officer, in other words, may conduct certain unrelated checks during an otherwise lawful traffic stop. But he may not do so in a way that prolongs the stop, absent the reasonable suspicion ordinarily demanded to justify detaining an individual.

Beyond determining whether to issue a traffic ticket, an officer's mission includes ordinary inquiries incident to the traffic stop. Typically such inquiries involve checking the driver's license, determining whether there are outstanding warrants against the driver, and inspecting the automobile's registration and proof of insurance. These checks serve the same objective as enforcement of the traffic code: ensuring that vehicles on the road are operated safely and responsibly. A dog sniff, by contrast, is a measure aimed at detecting evidence of criminal wrongdoing.

Traffic stops are especially fraught with danger to police officers, so an officer may need to take certain negligibly burdensome precautions in order to complete his mission safely [such as asking the driver to exit the car. But] the dog sniff could not be justified on the same basis. Highway and officer safety are interests different in kind from the Government's endeavor to detect crime in general or drug trafficking in particular.

For the reasons stated, the case is remanded for further proceedings consistent with this opinion.

Automobiles. If police have lawfully stopped a car and then observe evidence of other crimes in the car, such as burglary tools, they may search.

Lawful Arrest. Police may always search a suspect they have arrested. The goal is to protect the officers and preserve evidence.

Consent. Anyone lawfully living in a dwelling can allow the police to search it without a warrant. If your roommate gives the police permission to search your house, that search is legal.[15]

No Expectation of Privacy. The police have a right to search any area in which the defendant does not have a reasonable expectation of privacy. For example, Rolando Crowder was staying at his friend Bobo's apartment. Hearing the police in the hallway, he ran down to the basement. The police found Crowder in the basement with drugs nearby. Crowder

[15]United States v. Matlock, 415 U.S. 164 (1974).

argued that the police should have obtained a warrant, but the court ruled that he had no expectation of privacy in Bobo's basement.[16]

Technology and social media have challenged courts to define reasonable expectations of privacy in new settings. For example:

- **DNA tests.** Alonso King was arrested for assault. During the booking process, the police used a cotton swab to take a DNA sample from the inside of his mouth. Because that DNA matched genetic material found on a rape victim in another case, King was convicted of that additional crime. In a 5-4 decision, the Supreme Court held that a cheek swab was not much more intrusive than fingerprinting and, therefore, did not violate King's rights under the Fourth Amendment (provided the swab had been done after an arrest for a "serious" offense).[17] Now, 28 states and the federal government collect DNA after an arrest for such offenses.
- **Blood versus breath tests.** Police can determine if drivers are drunk by testing either their blood or their breath. But the Supreme Court treats these two tests differently—requiring a warrant for blood but not for breath. In the court's view, a blood test is significantly more intrusive than a breath test, which offers a reasonable, less painful, alternative. Also, the police can obtain more information from blood than from breath.[18]
- **Heat-seeking devices.** In another 5-4 decision, the Supreme Court ruled that police officers need a warrant before pointing a heat-seeking device at a house.[19] These devices are used to detect heat lamps used in growing marijuana plants. Some states, however, will not permit police to use these devices even with a warrant.[20]
- **Digital cameras.** After arresting a juvenile, the police searched him and discovered a digital camera. Without obtaining a warrant, they looked at the photos on the camera and found a photo of him with a sawed-off shotgun. The court held that the police officers were not required to obtain a warrant before looking at the pictures.[21]
- **Cell phones.** Police must obtain a warrant before listening in on a telephone conversation or searching the digital contents of a cell phone.[22] However, they do not need a warrant to obtain records from the phone company (such as a phone's location or a list of numbers called).[23]
- **Computers.** People generally have a reasonable expectation of privacy for data stored on their own computer, in their possession. Thus, the police would have to obtain a warrant before searching it.[24] It is not clear whether this protection applies to the same information stored in the cloud. Can your documents, photos, calendars, and financial data stored online be accessed without a warrant? Stay tuned.

---

16 Ohio v. Crowder, 2010 Ohio 3766 (Ohio Ct. Appeals 2010).

17 Maryland v. King, 133 S. Ct. 1958 (2013).

18 Birchfield v. North Dakota, 136 S. Ct. 2160 (2016).

19 Kyllo v. United States, 533 U.S. 27 (2001).

20 Brundige v. State, 291 Ga. 677 (Ga. 2012).

21 In re Alfredo C., 2011 Cal. App. Unpub. LEXIS 7626 (Cal. App. 2d Dist. 2011).

22 Riley v. California, 134 S. Ct. 2473 (2014).

23 United States v. Graham, 2016 U.S. App. LEXIS 9797 (4th Cir., 2016); United States v. Davis, 785 F.3d 498 (11th Cir. 2015).

24 Searching and Seizing Computers and Obtaining Electronic Evidence in Criminal Investigations, Published by Office of Legal Education Executive Office for United States Attorneys, 2009.

- **Global Positioning Systems (GPS).** The Washington, D.C., police suspected that Antoine Jones was a drug dealer. Without a valid search warrant, they attached a GPS tracking device to his car for 28 days. Based on the evidence collected, Jones was convicted of a conspiracy to deal cocaine and was sentenced to life in prison. But the Supreme Court ruled that, without a warrant, the search was illegal.[25]
- **Email.** Police generally do not need a warrant to find out *address information*, such as whom you have emailed. Under the Electronic Communications Privacy Act, police do need a warrant to intercept email in transit, but not to search opened email or messages sent more than six months prior.[26]
- **Websites.** In general, police do not need a warrant to find out what websites you have visited. Google says that it complies with many government requests for account information (and you agreed to those terms if you have a gmail account).
- **Internet messages.** Laurence Bode sent chat messages to other users of a child pornography website. A court upheld the right of Homeland Security agents to access his chats without a warrant.[27]
- **Social media.** Before James Holmes went on a shooting rampage in a movie theater in Aurora, Colorado, he posted, "Will you visit me in prison?" on two of his social media profiles. A judge ruled that Holmes did not have a reasonable expectation of privacy in those posts.[28] Similarly, a court in New York ruled that Twitter users do not have a reasonable expectation of privacy in their tweets.[29] However, the police typically need a warrant to access a private Facebook profile. But if a "friend" of the accountholder allows them access, no warrant is necessary.[30]

Exclusionary Rule

Exclusionary rule
Evidence obtained illegally may not be used at trial.

Under the exclusionary rule, any evidence the government acquires illegally (or any information obtained as a result of this illegal behavior) may not be used at trial. (Information resulting from an illegal search is referred to as "the fruit of the poisonous tree.") Suppose that the police put a GPS on Alice's car, without first obtaining a warrant. From that data, they discover that she has been going to Beau's house. They then see Beau dealing drugs. When they arrest him, he tells them that Caitlyn is his dealer and, indeed, the police find drugs in Caitlyn's apartment. None of this evidence—neither the confession nor the drugs—is admissible in court because it all stemmed from an illegal search of Alice's car.

The Supreme Court created the exclusionary rule to prevent governmental misconduct. The theory is simple: If police and prosecutors know that illegally obtained evidence cannot be used in court, they will not be tempted to make improper searches or engage in other illegal behavior. Is the exclusionary rule a good idea?

---

25 United States v. Jones, 132 S. Ct. 945 (2012).

26 18 U.S.C. §§2510–2522. This statute, which is discussed further in Chapter 10, was passed at a time when email providers strictly limited how much email any one user could store. So recipients would download emails onto their computers and then erase them from the server. Thus, for all practical purposes, once an email was opened, it was not available to the police without a warrant because it only lived on an individual's computer. One of gmail's innovations was to allow users to keep (and search) an unlimited amount of email on its servers.

27 United States v. Bode, 2013 U.S. Dist. LEXIS 118627 (D. Md. 2013).

28 People of the State of Colorado v. James Eagan Holmes, Case Number 12CR1522 (Dt. Ct. Col. 2013).

29 People v. Harris, 36 Misc. 3d 613 (N.Y. City Crim. Ct. 2012).

30 United States v. Meregildo, 883 F. Supp.2d 523 (S.D.N.Y. 2012), aff'd: United States v. Pierce, 785 F.3d 832 (2d Cir. 2015).

Opponents of the rule argue that a guilty person may go free because one police officer bungled. They are outraged by cases like *Coolidge v. New Hampshire*.[31] Pamela Mason, a 14-year-old babysitter, was brutally murdered. Because citizens of New Hampshire were so angry and scared, the state's attorney general personally led the investigation. Police found strong evidence that Edward Coolidge had committed this terrible crime. They took the evidence to the attorney general, who personally issued a search warrant. After a search of Coolidge's car uncovered incriminating evidence, he was found guilty of murder and sentenced to life in prison. But the Supreme Court reversed the conviction. The warrant had not been issued by a neutral magistrate. A law officer may not lead an investigation and simultaneously decide what searches are permissible. Ultimately, Coolidge pleaded guilty to second degree murder and served many years in prison.

There are three exceptions to the exclusionary rule:

- **Inevitable discovery.** A court will admit any evidence that would have been discovered even without the illegal behavior on the part of the police. When the police unlawfully questioned a suspect, he revealed the location of the body of a child he had murdered. His conviction was upheld because, the court ruled, the body would eventually have been discovered in the ditch where he had left it.[32]
- **Independent source.** If the police find the tainted evidence from a different source, then they can use it. The police lied to get a search warrant for Jerome Roberts's cell phone records. They told the magistrate that he was a murder suspect when, in fact, they knew that he had not committed the crime. However, his phone records revealed that he had spoken many times with Andre Bellinger, who turned out to be the real murderer. The police also had arrested someone else who happened to be in possession of the murder weapon. The court ruled that, although the phone records were not admissible, the police would have found Bellinger through the murder weapon. So it refused to overturn the murder conviction.[33]
- **Good faith exception.** Suppose the police use a search warrant believing it to be proper, but it later proves to have been defective. The search is legal so long as the police *reasonably believed* the warrant was valid.[34]

EXAMStrategy

Question: Police bang down the door of Mary Beth's apartment, enter without her permission, and search the apartment. They had no warrant. When the officers discover a meth lab, they arrest her. What motion will the defense lawyer make before trial? Please rule on the defendant's motion. Are there any facts that would make you change your ruling?

Strategy: The defendant's motion is based on the police conduct. What was wrong with that conduct, and what are the consequences?

Result: The defense lawyer will argue that the police violated the Fourth Amendment because they lacked a warrant for the search. He will ask that the court suppress the drug evidence. Ordinarily, the court would grant that motion unless there was other evidence—for example, an informant had just told other officers that Mary Beth was his meth supplier.

---

31 403 U.S. 443 (1971).

32 Nix v. Williams, 467 U.S. 431 (1984).

33 State v. Smith, 212 N.J. 365 (N.J. S. Ct. 2012).

34 Ibid.

7-1e After Arrest

The Fifth Amendment

The Fifth Amendment to the Constitution protects criminal defendants—both the innocent and the guilty—in several ways.

Due process
Requires fundamental fairness at all stages of the case

Due Process. The basic elements of due process are discussed in Chapter 5 on constitutional law. In the context of criminal law, **due process** requires fundamental fairness at all stages of the case. Thus, the prosecution is required to disclose evidence favorable to the defendant. Similarly, if a witness says that a tall white male robbed the liquor store, it would violate due process for the police to place the male suspect in a lineup with four short women of color.

Self-Incrimination. The Fifth Amendment bars the government from forcing any person to provide evidence against himself. In other words, the police may not use mental or physical coercion to force a confession or any other information out of someone. Society does not want a government that engages in torture. Such abuse might occasionally catch a criminal, but it would grievously injure innocent people and make all citizens fearful of the government that is supposed to represent them. Also, coerced confessions are inherently unreliable. The defendant may confess simply to end the torture. (The protection against self-incrimination applies only to people; corporations and other organizations are not protected and may be required to provide incriminating information.)

Miranda Rights. The police cannot legally force a suspect to provide evidence against himself. But sometimes, under forceful interrogation, he might forget his constitutional rights. In the following Landmark Case, the Supreme Court established the requirement that police remind suspects of their rights—with the very same warning that we have all heard so many times on television shows.

Landmark Case

Miranda v. Arizona

384 U.S. 436
United States Supreme Court, 1966

Facts: Ernesto Miranda was a mentally ill, penniless Mexican immigrant. At a Phoenix police station, a rape victim identified him as her assailant. Two police officers took him to an interrogation room but did not tell him that he had a right to have a lawyer present during the questioning. Two hours later, the officers emerged with a written confession signed by Miranda. At the top of the statement was a typed paragraph stating that the confession was made voluntarily "with full knowledge of my legal rights, understanding any statement I make may be used against me."

At Miranda's trial, the judge admitted this written confession into evidence. The officers testified that Miranda had also made an oral confession during the interrogation. The jury found Miranda guilty of kidnapping and rape. He was sentenced to 20 to 30 years imprisonment. On appeal, the Supreme Court of Arizona affirmed the conviction. In reaching its decision, the court relied heavily on the fact that Miranda did not specifically request a lawyer. The Supreme Court of the United States granted *certiorari.*

Issues: ***Was Miranda's confession admissible at trial? Should his conviction be upheld?***

Excerpts from Chief Justice Warren's Decision: Our holding briefly stated is this: the prosecution may not use statements, whether exculpatory or inculpatory, stemming from custodial interrogation of the defendant unless it demonstrates the use of procedural safeguards effective to secure the privilege against self-incrimination. By custodial interrogation, we mean questioning initiated by law enforcement officers after a person has been taken into custody or otherwise deprived of his freedom of action in any significant way.

As for the procedural safeguards to be employed, the following measures are required. Prior to any questioning, the person must be warned that he has a right to remain silent, that any statement he does make may be used as evidence against him, and that he has a right to the presence of an attorney, either retained or appointed.

The defendant may waive these rights, provided the waiver is made voluntarily, knowingly, and intelligently. If, however, he indicates in any manner and at any stage of the process that he wishes to consult with an attorney before speaking, there can be no questioning. Likewise, if the individual is alone and indicates in any manner that he does not wish to be interrogated, the police may not question him. The mere fact that he may have answered some questions or volunteered some statements on his own does not deprive him of the right to refrain from answering any further inquiries until he has consulted with an attorney and thereafter consents to be questioned.

In a series of cases decided by this Court, the police resorted to physical brutality—beating, hanging, whipping—and to sustained and protracted questioning 'incommunicado' in order to extort confessions. Unless a proper limitation upon custodial interrogation is achieved, there can be no assurance that practices of this nature will be eradicated. Not only does the use of the third degree involve a flagrant violation of law by the officers of the law, but it involves also the dangers of false confessions, and it tends to make police and prosecutors less zealous in the search for objective evidence. As [an official] remarked: "If you use your fists, you are not so likely to use your wits."

[C]oercion can be mental as well as physical, and the blood of the accused is not the only hallmark of an unconstitutional inquisition. In a serious case, the interrogation may continue for days, with the required intervals for food and sleep, but with no respite from the atmosphere of domination. It is possible in this way to induce the subject to talk without resorting to duress or coercion.

Even without employing brutality, the very fact of custodial interrogation exacts a heavy toll on individual liberty and trades on the weakness of individuals. In [this case before the Court], the defendant was thrust into an unfamiliar atmosphere and run through menacing police interrogation procedures. It is obvious that such an interrogation environment is created for no purpose other than to subjugate the individual to the will of his examiner. This atmosphere carries its own badge of intimidation. To be sure, this is not physical intimidation, but it is equally destructive of human dignity. The current practice of 'incommunicado' interrogation is at odds with one of our Nation's most cherished principles—that the individual may not be compelled to incriminate himself.

All these policies point to one overriding thought: the constitutional foundation underlying the privilege is the respect a government—state or federal—must accord to the dignity and integrity of its citizens. To maintain a fair state-individual balance, to respect the inviolability of the human personality, our accusatory system of criminal justice demands that the government seeking to punish an individual produce the evidence against him by its own independent labors, rather than by the cruel, simple expedient of compelling it from his own mouth.

Miranda was not in any way apprised of his right to consult with an attorney and to have one present during the interrogation, nor was his right not to be compelled to incriminate himself effectively protected in any other manner. Without these warnings, the statements were inadmissible. The mere fact that he signed a statement which contained a typed-in clause stating that he had "full knowledge" of his "legal rights" does not approach the knowing and intelligent waiver required to relinquish constitutional rights.

Right to a Lawyer

As *Miranda* made clear, a criminal defendant has the right to a lawyer before being interrogated by the police. **The Sixth Amendment guarantees the right to a lawyer at all important stages of the criminal process.** Because of this right, the government must appoint a lawyer to represent, free of charge, any defendant who cannot afford one.

Indictment

Once the police provide the local prosecutor with evidence, he presents this evidence to a **grand jury** and asks its members to indict the defendant. The grand jury is a group of ordinary citizens, like a trial jury, but the grand jury holds hearings for several weeks at a time, on many different cases. At the hearing in front of the grand jury, only the prosecutor presents evidence, not the defense attorney, because it is better for the defendant to save her evidence for the trial jury.

Grand jury
A group of ordinary citizens who decides whether there is probable cause the defendant committed the crime with which she is charged

If the grand jury determines that there is probable cause that the defendant committed the crime with which she is charged, an **indictment** is issued. An indictment is the government's formal charge that the defendant has committed a crime and must stand trial. Because the grand jury never hears the defendant's evidence, it is relatively easy for prosecutors to obtain an indictment. In short, an indictment is not the same thing as a guilty verdict.

Indictment
The government's formal charge that the defendant has committed a crime and must stand trial

Arraignment

At an arraignment, a clerk reads the formal charges of the indictment. The defendant must enter a plea to the charges. At this stage, most defendants plead not guilty.

Plea Bargaining

A **plea bargain** is an agreement between prosecution and defense that the defendant will plead guilty to a reduced charge, and the prosecution will recommend to the judge a relatively lenient sentence. In the federal court system, about 97 percent of all prosecutions end in a plea bargain. Such a high percentage has led to some concern that innocent people may be pleading guilty to avoid the risk of tough mandatory sentences. A judge need not accept the bargain but usually does.

In the federal court system, about 97 percent of all prosecutions end in a plea bargain.

Plea bargain
An agreement in which the defendant pleads guilty to a reduced charge, and the prosecution recommends to the judge a relatively lenient sentence

Discovery

If the defendant does not plead guilty, the prosecution is obligated to hand over any evidence favorable to the defense that the defense attorney requests. The defense has a more limited obligation to inform the prosecution of its evidence. In most states, for example, if the defense will be based on an alibi, counsel must reveal the alibi to the government before trial.

Trial and Appeal

When there is no plea bargain, the case must go to trial. The mechanics of a criminal trial and appeal are similar to those for a civil trial, described in Chapter 6 on dispute resolution.

Double Jeopardy

The prohibition against **double jeopardy** means that a defendant may be prosecuted only once for a particular criminal offense. The purpose is to prevent the government from destroying the lives of innocent citizens with repeated prosecutions.

Double jeopardy
A criminal defendant may be prosecuted only once for a particular criminal offense

Punishment

The Eighth Amendment prohibits cruel and unusual punishment. Courts are generally unsympathetic to claims under this provision. For example, the Supreme Court has ruled that the death penalty is not cruel and unusual as long as it is not imposed in an arbitrary or capricious manner.[35]

Another important case under the Eighth Amendment involved California's "three strikes" law, which dramatically increases sentences for repeat offenders. Gary Ewing, on parole from a nine-year prison term, was prosecuted for stealing three golf clubs worth $399 each. Because he had prior convictions, his crime, normally a misdemeanor, was treated as a felony. Ewing was convicted and sentenced to 25 years to life. The Supreme Court ruled that this sentence was not cruel and unusual and that the three strikes law was a rational response to a legitimate concern about crime.[36]

---

35 Gregg v. Georgia, 428 U.S. 153 (1976).

36 Ewing v. California, 538 U.S. 11 (2003).

The Eighth Amendment also outlaws excessive fines. Forfeiture is the most controversial topic under this clause. **Forfeiture** is a *civil* law proceeding that is permitted by many different *criminal* statutes. Once a court has convicted a defendant under certain criminal statutes—such as a drug law—the government may seek forfeiture of property associated with the criminal act. *How much* property can the government take? To determine if forfeiture is fair, courts generally look at three factors:

- Whether the property was used in committing the crime,
- Whether it was purchased with proceeds from illegal acts, and
- Whether the punishment is disproportionate to the defendant's wrongdoing.

After Neal Brunk pleaded guilty to selling 2.5 ounces of marijuana, the government promptly sought forfeiture of his house on 90 acres, worth about $99,000. The court found that forfeiture was legitimate because Brunk had used drug money to buy the land and then sold narcotics from the property.[37] By contrast, Hosep Bajakajian attempted to leave the United States without reporting to customs officials $375,000 in cash, as the law requires. The government demanded forfeiture of the full sum, but the Supreme Court ruled that seizure of the entire amount was grossly disproportionate to the minor crime of failing to report cash movement.[38]

In a recent case, the Supreme Court ruled that the government could not freeze the assets of an accused criminal, if that action would interfere with the defendant's ability to hire a lawyer.[39]

7-2 CRIMES THAT HARM BUSINESSES (AND THEIR CUSTOMERS)

Businesses must deal with four major crimes: larceny, fraud, arson, and embezzlement.

7-2a Larceny

It is holiday season at the mall, the period of greatest profits—and the most crime. At the Foot Forum, a teenager limps in wearing ragged sneakers and sneaks out wearing Super Sneakers, valued at $145. Sweethearts swipe sweaters; pensioners pocket produce. All are committing larceny.

Larceny is the trespassory taking of personal property with the intent to steal it. "Trespassory taking" means that someone else originally has the property. The Super Sneakers are personal property (not real estate), they were in the possession of the Foot Forum, and the teenager deliberately left without paying, intending never to return the goods. That is larceny. Each year, more than $34 billion in merchandise is stolen from retail stores in the United States.

Larceny
The trespassory taking of personal property with the intent to steal it

7-2b Embezzlement

This crime also involves illegally obtaining property, but with one big difference: The culprit begins with legal possession. **Embezzlement** is the fraudulent conversion of property already in the defendant's possession.

Embezzlement
The fraudulent conversion of property already in the defendant's possession

---

37United States v. Brunk, 11 Fed. Appx. 147 (4th Cir. 2001).

38United States v. Bajakajian, 524 U.S. 321 (1998).

39Luis v. United States, 136 S. Ct. 1083 (2016).

There is no love in this story: For 15 years, Kristy Watts worked part time as a bookkeeper for romance writer Danielle Steele, handling payroll and accounting. During that time, Watts stole $768,000, despite earning a substantial salary. Watts said that she had been motivated by envy and jealousy. She was sentenced to three years in prison and agreed to pay her former boss almost $1 million.

7-2c Fraud

Robert Dorsey owned Bob's Chrysler in Highland, Illinois. When he bought cars, the First National Bank of Highland paid Chrysler, and Dorsey—supposedly—repaid the bank as he sold the autos. Dorsey, though, began to suffer financial problems, and the bank suspected he was selling cars without repaying his loans. A state investigator notified Dorsey that he planned to review all dealership records. One week later, a fire engulfed the dealership. An arson investigator discovered that an electric iron, connected to a timer, had been placed on a pile of financial papers doused with accelerant.

The saddest part of this true story is that it is all too common. Some experts suggest that 1 percent of corporate revenues are wasted on fraud alone. Dorsey was convicted and imprisoned for committing two crimes that cost business billions of dollars annually—fraud (for taking money from the bank even after he knew he could not pay it back) and arson (for burning down the dealership).[40]

Fraud
Deception for the purpose of obtaining money or property

Fraud refers to various crimes, all of which have a common element: **the deception of another person for the purpose of obtaining money or property from him.** Robert Dorsey's precise violation was bank fraud, a federal crime.[41] It is bank fraud to use deceit to obtain money, assets, securities, or other property under the control of any financial institution.

Wire Fraud and Mail Fraud

Wire and mail fraud are additional federal crimes, involving the use of interstate mail, telegram, telephone, radio, or television to obtain property by deceit.[42] For example, if Marsha makes an interstate phone call to sell land that she does not own, that is wire fraud.

Insurance Fraud

Insurance fraud is another common crime. A Ford suddenly swerves in front of a Toyota, causing it to brake hard. A Mercedes, unable to stop, slams into the Toyota, as the Ford races away. Regrettable accident? No: a "swoop and squat" fraud scheme. The Ford and Toyota drivers were working together, hoping to cause an accident with someone else. The "injured" Toyota driver now goes to a third member of the fraud team—a dishonest doctor—who diagnoses serious back and neck injuries and predicts long-term pain and disability. The driver files a claim against the Mercedes's driver, whose insurer may be forced to pay tens or even hundreds of thousands of dollars for an accident that was no accident. Insurance companies investigate countless cases like this each year, trying to distinguish the honest victim from the criminal.

Internet Fraud

The internet's anonymity and speed facilitate fraud. Common scams include advance fee scams,[43] the sale of merchandise that is either defective or nonexistent, the so-called Nigerian

40United States v. Dorsey, 27 F.3d 285 (7th Cir. 1994).

4118 U.S.C. §1344.

4218 U.S.C. §§1341–1346.

43As in, "If you are willing to pay a fee in advance, then you will have access to (pick your choice) favorable financing, lottery winnings from overseas, fabulous investment opportunities."

letter scam,[44] billing for services that are touted as "free," fake scholarship search services, romance fraud (you meet someone online who wants to visit you but needs money for travel expenses), and credit card scams (for a fee, you can get a credit card, even with a poor credit rating). One new scam involves *over*payment. You are renting out a house, selling a pet, or accepting a job, and "by accident," you are sent too much money. You wire the excess back, only to find out that the initial check or funds transfer was no good. Fraud on the internet can be prosecuted under state law, the Computer Fraud and Abuse Act (discussed later in this chapter), and mail and wire fraud statutes.

Other common forms of internet fraud include the following:

Auctions. Internet auctions are the number one source of consumer complaints about online fraud. Wrongdoers either sell goods they do not own, provide defective goods, or offer fakes. In one case that seemed a defeat for consumers, a court held that eBay, the internet auction site, was not liable to Tiffany & Company for the counterfeit Tiffany products sold on the site. The jewelry company had sued after discovering that most items advertised on eBay as Tiffany products were, in fact, fakes. The court held that eBay's only legal obligation was to remove products once told that they were counterfeit.[45]

Shilling is another online auction fraud. **Shilling means that a seller either bids on his own goods or agrees to cross-bid with a group of other sellers**. Shilling is prohibited because the owner drives up the price of his own item by bidding on it. Kenneth Walton, a San Francisco lawyer, auctioned on eBay a painting purportedly by artist Richard Diebenkorn. A bidder offered $135,805 before eBay withdrew the item in response to charges that Walton had placed a bid on the painting himself and had also engaged in cross-bidding with a group of other eBay users. Walton pleaded guilty to charges of federal wire and mail fraud. He was sentenced to almost four years in prison and paid almost $100,000 in restitution to the victims.

Shillers are subject to suit under general anti-fraud statutes. In addition, some states explicitly prohibit shilling.

Identity Theft. Identity theft is one of the scariest crimes against property. Thieves steal the victim's social security number and other personal information such as bank account numbers and mother's maiden name, which they use to obtain loans and credit cards. Victims have the difficult task of proving that they were not responsible for the debts and they may even find themselves unable to obtain a credit card, loan, or job. One victim spent several nights in jail after he was arrested for a crime that his identity thief had committed. Identity theft is broadly defined. For example, a court has ruled that creating a fake Facebook page in someone else's name constituted identity theft.

Although identity fraud existed before computers, the internet has made it much easier. For example, consumer activists were able to purchase the social security numbers of the director of the CIA, the Attorney General of the United States, and other top administration officials. The cost was only $26 each. No surprise then that this crime is so common.

The Identity Theft and Assumption Deterrence Act of 1998 prohibits the use of false identification to commit fraud or other crime and it also permits the victim to seek restitution in court.[46] In addition, the Aggravated Identity Theft statute imposes a mandatory additional

---

[44] Victims receive an email from someone alleging to be a Nigerian government official who has stolen money from the government. He needs some place safe to park the money for a short time. The official promises that, if the victim will permit her account to be used for this purpose, she will be allowed to keep a percentage of the stolen money. Instead, of course, once the "official" has the victim's bank information, he cleans out the account.

[45] Tiffany Inc. v. eBay, Inc., 600 F.3d 93 (2d Cir. 2010) and, *on remand*, 2010 U.S. Dist. LEXIS 96596 (S.D.N.Y. 2010).

[46] 18 U.S.C. §1028.

sentence of two years on anyone who engages in identity theft during the commission of certain crimes.[47] Also, many states have their own identity theft statutes.

Kevin Bollaert was sentenced to eight years in prison for identity theft after a jury found that he had run a "revenge porn" website. He operated a site that invited anonymous users to post nude photographs of their exes, along with their names and addresses. Bollaert then forced the victims to pay hundreds of dollars to have the pictures removed.[48]

Phishing. Have you ever received a message from a Facebook friend saying, "Hey, what's up?" with a link to an IQ test? This message may not be from a friend, but rather from a fraudster hoping to lure you into revealing your personal information. In this case, people who clicked on the link were told that they had to provide their cell phone number to get the test results. Next thing they knew, they had been signed up for some expensive cell phone service. This scam is part of one of the most rapidly growing areas of internet fraud: **phishing. In this crime, a fraudster sends a message directing the recipient to enter personal information on a website that is an illegal imitation of a legitimate site.**

Phishing
A fraudster sends a message directing the recipient to enter personal information on a website that is an illegal imitation of a legitimate site

In a traditional phishing scam, large numbers of generic emails are sprayed over the internet asking millions of people to log on to, say, a fake bank site. **Spear phishing** is something different—it involves personalized messages sent from someone the victim knows. It may appear that your sister is asking for your social security number so she can add you as a beneficiary to her life insurance policy. In reality, this email has come from a fraudster who hacked into her Facebook account to gain access to her lists of friends and family.[49] Even "Like" buttons can be "clickjacked" to take unwary users to bogus sites. Prosecutors can bring criminal charges against phishers for fraud.

Spear phishing
Phishing that involves personalized messages that look as if they have been sent by someone the victim knows

EXAMStrategy

Question: Eric mails glossy brochures to 25,000 people, offering to sell them a one-month time-share in a stylish apartment in Las Vegas. The brochure depicts an imposing building, an opulent apartment, and spectacular pools. To reserve a space, customers need only send in a $2,000 deposit. Three hundred people send in the money. In fact, there is no such building. Eric is planning to flee with the cash. Once arrested, he faces a 20-year sentence. (1) With what crime is he charged? (2) Is this a felony or misdemeanor prosecution? (3) Does Eric have a right to a jury trial? (4) What is the government's burden of proof?

Strategy: (1) Eric is deceiving people, and that should tell you the *type* of crime. (2) The potential 20-year sentence determines whether Eric's crime is a misdemeanor or felony, and whether or not he is entitled to a jury trial. (3) We know that the government has the burden of proof in criminal prosecutions—but *how much* evidence must it offer?

Result: Eric has committed fraud. A felony is one in which the sentence could be a year or more. The potential penalty here is 20 years, so the crime is a felony. Eric has a right to a jury, as does any defendant whose sentence could be six months or longer. The prosecution must prove its case beyond a reasonable doubt, a much higher burden than that in a civil case.

---

47 18 U.S.C. §1028A.

48 People v. Bollaert, 2016 Cal. App. LEXIS 517 (Cal. App., 2016).

49 To prevent your Facebook account from being hacked, be careful when accessing it over a public network (such as in a hotel or airport), where fraudsters might be able to capture your password. If you text "otp" to 32665, you will receive a password that can be used only once (a "one-time password"). Fraudsters thus cannot use this password to access your account.

7-2d Arson

Robert Dorsey, the Chrysler dealer, committed a second serious crime. **Arson is the malicious use of fire or explosives to damage or destroy any real estate or personal property.** It is both a federal and a state crime. Dorsey used arson to conceal his bank fraud. Most arsonists hope to collect on insurance policies. Every year thousands of buildings burn, as owners try to make a quick kill or extricate themselves from financial difficulties. Everyone who purchases insurance ends up paying higher premiums because of this wrongdoing.

Arson
The malicious use of fire or explosives to damage or destroy real estate or personal property

7-2e Hacking

During the 2008 presidential campaign, college student David Kernell guessed vice presidential candidate Sarah Palin's email password, accessed her account, and published the content of some of her emails. To some, his actions seemed like an amusing prank. The joke turned out not to be so funny when Kernell was sentenced to one year in prison.

Gaining unauthorized access to a computer system is called **hacking**. It is a major crime. The FBI ranks cybercrime as its third-highest priority, right behind terrorism and spying. The goal of hackers is varied; some do it for little more than the thrill of the challenge. The objective for other hackers may be industrial espionage, extortion, theft of credit card information, plundering bank accounts, or revenge for perceived slights. Kernell hoped to prevent Palin from being elected vice president. Many governments engage in hacking for national security reasons or to steal intellectual property.

Hacking
Gaining unauthorized access to a computer system

Hacking is a crime under the federal Computer Fraud and Abuse Act of 1986 (CFAA).[50] This statute applies to any computer, cell phone, or other equipment attached to the internet. **The CFAA prohibits:**

- Accessing a computer without authorization and obtaining information from it,
- Computer espionage,
- Theft of financial information,
- Theft of information from the U.S. government,
- Theft from a computer,
- Computer fraud,
- Intentional, reckless, and negligent damage to a computer,
- Trafficking in computer passwords, and
- Computer extortion.

The CFAA also provides for civil remedies so that someone who has been harmed by a hacker can personally recover damages from the wrongdoer.

Courts are now in the process of figuring out how to interpret the CFAA. In the following case, a former employee clearly violated his company's policies, but did he commit a crime? You be the judge.

[50] 18 U.S.C. §1030.

You Be the Judge

United States v. Nosal

676 F.3d 854
United States Court of Appeals for the Ninth Circuit, 2012

Facts: David Nosal worked for an executive search firm, Korn/Ferry (K/F). Shortly after he left the company to start a competing business, he convinced some of his former colleagues to log into the company's confidential database and give him customer names and contact information. K/F had authorized the employees to access the database, but not to disclose confidential client information to outsiders.

The government charged Nosal with aiding and abetting his former colleagues in violating a provision of the CFAA that prohibits employees from exceeding their authorized access to a computer with intent to defraud. The trial court granted Nosal's motion to dismiss. The government appealed.

You Be the Judge: *Did Nosal commit a crime when he aided and abetted others in violating a workplace policy on computer use?*

Argument for the Defendant: This provision of the CFAA can mean one of two things: (1) either it is a crime to access unauthorized data or, (2) in a more expansive view, it can apply to anyone who is legally entitled to access data, but who then uses this data in an unauthorized manner. That is what happened here. The K/F employees were authorized to access the confidential database, but they were not permitted to send it to Nosal.

Congress enacted the CFAA primarily to address the growing problem of computer hacking, i.e., "intentionally trespassing into someone else's computer files." But, under the government's view, everyone who uses a computer in violation of company policy, which may well include everyone who uses an employer's computer, would be a criminal. According to the government, if an employer keeps certain information in a separate database that can be viewed on a computer screen, but not copied or downloaded and an employee copies the information to a thumb drive, he could be charged with a crime.

The computer gives employees new ways to procrastinate: messaging friends, playing games, shopping, or watching sports highlights. Such activities are routinely prohibited by many computer-use policies. Under the broad interpretation of the CFAA, such minor violations would be federal crimes. While it is unlikely that you will be prosecuted for watching cat videos on your work computer, you could be. How will an employee know the difference between a minor personal use and a criminal act?

Employees who call family members from their work phones will become criminals if they send an email instead. They can read the sports section of *USA Today* at work, but they had better not visit ESPN.com. And Sudoku enthusiasts should stick to printed puzzles because visiting www.dailysudoku.com from their work computers might give them more than enough time to hone their Sudoku skills behind bars.

Facebook prohibits its users from sharing login information. Are we going to cart every violator off to prison? The terms of service on dating websites prohibit inaccurate or misleading information. If you describe yourself as "tall, dark, and handsome," when you are actually short and homely, could you end up wearing a handsome orange prison jumpsuit?

Argument for the Government: This statute explicitly requires an intent to commit fraud. Therefore, it has nothing to do with reading ESPN.com, playing Sudoku, checking email, or fibbing on dating sites. Instead, the K/F employees knowingly exceeded their access to a protected company computer, and they did so with intent to defraud.

This distinction is not complicated. A bank teller is entitled to access money for legitimate banking purposes, but not to take the bank's money for himself. A new car buyer may be entitled to take a vehicle around the block on a test drive, but not to drive it to Mexico on a drug run.

7-3 CRIMES COMMITTED BY BUSINESS

Oil company BP pleaded guilty to criminal charges arising out of an oil rig explosion that caused 11 deaths and an enormous oil spill in the Gulf of Mexico. It paid a fine of $4.5 *billion*. SAC Capital paid a fine of $1.2 *billion* for insider trading. But can a company commit a crime? Yes, under federal law. A corporation can be found guilty of a crime based on the conduct of any of its agents, who include anyone undertaking work on behalf of the corporation. An agent can be a corporate officer, an accountant hired to audit financial statements, a sales clerk, or almost any other person performing a job at the company's request. In the case of SAC, a number of its traders were convicted of insider trading. It may be that the firm's impressive investment track record was largely based on a systematic insider trading scheme.

If an agent commits a criminal act within the scope of his employment and with the intent to benefit the corporation, the company is liable.[51] Some critics believe that the criminal law has gone too far. They argue that imposing *criminal* liability on a corporation is unfair to its innocent employees and shareholders, unless high-ranking officers were directly involved in the illegal conduct.

Others argue that making companies criminally liable deters wrongdoing and emphasizes the importance of complying with the law. Indeed, they argue that current fines are too small, that they should be large enough to really hurt the companies and deter future criminal acts.

7-3a Making False Statements

It is illegal to make false statements or engage in a cover-up during any dealings with the U.S. government.[52] Sometimes this provision has been used to convict someone who is suspected of committing a complex crime that may itself be difficult to prove. In the most famous case, the government accused Martha Stewart, the celebrity homemaker and entrepreneur, of engaging in insider trading. At trial, that charge was thrown out but the jury nevertheless convicted her of lying to the officers who had investigated the alleged insider trading. Stewart ultimately served five months in prison. However, the Justice Department recently announced that it would only use this statute against defendants who knew their conduct was illegal.

7-3b Workplace Crimes

The workplace can be dangerous. Working on an assembly line exposes factory employees to fast-moving machinery. For a roofer, the first slip may be the last. The invisible radiation in a nuclear power plant can be deadlier than a bullet. The most important statute regulating the workplace is the federal **Occupational Safety and Health Act of 1970 (OSHA),**[53] which sets safety standards for many industries.[54]

A state government may even go beyond standards set by OSHA and use the criminal law to punish dangerous conditions, In *People v. O'Neill*, the courts of Illinois permitted a *murder prosecution* against corporate executives themselves.[55] Film Recovery Systems was an Illinois corporation in the business of extracting silver from used X-ray film. Workers at the factory soaked the film in large, open vats of sodium cyanide. When one of the workers died of cyanide poisoning caused by inhaling the fumes, Illinois indicted Film Recovery and several of its managers for murder. The indictment charged that the officers had committed murder by not disclosing to the workers that they were using cyanide and by failing to provide them with necessary safety equipment. The officers ultimately pleaded guilty to involuntary manslaughter and received sentences of between four months and three years.

51New York Central & Hudson River R.R. Co. v. United States, 212 U.S. 481 (1909). Note that what counts is the intention to benefit, not actual benefit. A corporation will not escape liability by showing that the scheme failed.

5218 U.S.C.S. §1001.

5329 U.S.C. §§651 *et seq.*

54See Chapter 29 on employment and labor law.

5523194 Ill. App. 3d 79 (Ill. App. Ct. 1990).

7-3c RICO

Racketeer Influenced and Corrupt Organizations Act (RICO)
A powerful federal statute, originally aimed at organized crime, now used against many ordinary businesses

The **Racketeer Influenced and Corrupt Organizations Act (RICO)** is one of the most powerful and controversial statutes ever written.[56] Congress passed the law primarily to prevent gangsters from taking money they earned illegally and investing it in legitimate businesses. But RICO has expanded far beyond the original intentions of Congress and is now used more often against ordinary businesses than against organized criminals. Some regard this wide application as a tremendous advance in law enforcement, but others view it as an oppressive weapon used to club ethical companies into settlements they should never have to make.

RICO prohibits using two or more racketeering acts to accomplish any of these goals: (1) investing in or acquiring legitimate businesses with criminal money, (2) maintaining or acquiring businesses through criminal activity, or (3) operating businesses through criminal activity.

What does that mean in English? It is a two-step process to prove that a person or an organization has violated RICO.

Racketeering acts
Any of a long list of specified crimes, such as embezzlement, arson, mail fraud, wire fraud, and so forth

- The prosecutor must show that the defendant committed two or more **racketeering acts**, which are any of a long list of specified crimes: embezzlement, arson, mail fraud, wire fraud, and so forth. Thus, if a gangster ordered a building torched in January and then burned a second building in October, that would be two racketeering acts. If a stockbroker told two customers that Bronx Gold Mines was a promising stock, when she knew that it was worthless, that would be two racketeering acts.
- The prosecutor must then show that the defendant used these racketeering acts to accomplish one of the three *purposes* listed earlier. If the gangster committed two arsons and then used the insurance payments to buy a dry cleaning business, that would violate RICO. If the stockbroker gave fraudulent advice and used the commissions to buy advertising for her firm, that would also violate RICO.

The government may prosecute both individuals and organizations for violating RICO. It prosecuted financier Michael Milken for manipulating stock prices. It also threatened to prosecute his employer, Drexel Burnham Lambert. If the government proves its case, the defendant can be punished with large fines and a prison sentence of up to 20 years.

RICO also permits the government to seek forfeiture of the defendant's property. A court may order a convicted defendant to hand over any property or money used in the criminal acts or derived from them. Courts often freeze a defendant's assets once charges are brought to ensure that he will not hide the assets. If all his assets are frozen, he will have a hard time paying his defense lawyer, so a freeze often encourages a defendant to plea bargain on a lesser charge. Both Milken and Drexel entered into plea agreements with the government, rather than face a freeze on their assets, and in Milken's case, a long prison sentence.

In addition to criminal penalties, RICO also creates civil law liabilities. The government, organizations, and individuals all have the right to file civil lawsuits, seeking damages and, if necessary, injunctions. A physician sued State Farm Insurance, alleging that the company had hired doctors to produce false medical reports that the company used to cut off claims by injured policy holders. As a result of these fake reports, the company refused to pay the plaintiff for legitimate services he performed on the policy holders. RICO is powerful (and for defendants, frightening) in part because a civil plaintiff can recover treble damages; that is, a judgment for three times the harm actually suffered, as well as attorney's fees.

Money laundering
Using the proceeds of criminal acts either to promote crime or conceal the source of the money

7-3d Money Laundering

Money laundering consists of taking the proceeds of certain criminal acts and either (1) using the money to promote crime or (2) attempting to conceal the source of the money.[57]

---

[56] 18 U.S.C. §§1961–1968.

[57] 18 U.S.C. §§1956 *et seq.*

Money laundering is an important part of major criminal enterprises. Successful criminals earn enormous sums, which they must filter back into the flow of commerce in a way that allows their crimes to go undetected. Laundering is an essential part of the corrosive traffic in drugs. Profits, all in cash, may mount so swiftly that dealers struggle to use the money without attracting the government's attention. Colombian drug cartels set up a sophisticated system in which they shipped money to countries such as Dubai that do not keep records on cash transactions. This money was then transferred to the United States disguised as offshore loans. Prosecution by the U.S. government led to the collapse of some of the banks involved.

But drug money is not the only or even major component of so-called flight capital. Criminals also try to hide the vast sums they earn from arms dealing and tax evasion. Some of this money is used to support terrorist organizations.

7-3e Hiring Illegal Workers

It is illegal to knowingly employ unauthorized workers. Thus, employers are required to verify their workers' eligibility for employment in the United States. Within three days of hiring a worker, the employer must complete an I-9 form, documenting each worker's eligibility. The government has the right to arrest employees working illegally, and to bring charges against the business that hired them.

EXAMStrategy

Question: Mohawk Industries was one of the largest carpet manufacturers in the United States. Some of its workers alleged that the company routinely hired illegal immigrants and, as a result, the pay of legal workers was lower than it otherwise would have been. If these allegations are true, what laws has the company violated?

Strategy: What law prohibits a company from committing two or more illegal acts? What is the illegal act here?

Result: It is illegal to employ unauthorized workers. Repeatedly doing so is a RICO violation.[58]

7-3f Foreign Corrupt Practices Act

The Foreign Corrupt Practices Act (FCPA) prohibits American companies from paying bribes overseas.[59] The FCPA has two principal requirements:

- **Bribes.** The statute makes it illegal for any employee or agent of a U.S. company (and some foreign companies) or any U.S. citizen to bribe foreign officials to influence a governmental decision. The statute prohibits giving anything of value and also bars using third parties as a conduit for such payments. The bribe need not be actually paid. A *promise* to pay bribes violates the FCPA. Also, the bribe need not be successful. If an American company makes an unauthorized payment but never gains any benefit, the company has still violated the law.
- **Recordkeeping.** All publicly traded companies—whether they engage in international trade or not—must keep accurate and detailed records to prevent hiding or disguising bribes. These records must be available for inspection by U.S. officials.

58Williams v. Mohawk Indus., 465 F.3d 1277 (11th Cir. 2006).

5915 U.S.C.S. §78dd-1.

Ethics

In many countries, bribery is common and widely accepted. What is wrong with bribery, anyway? Many businesspeople think it is relatively harmless—just a cost of doing business, like New York City's high taxes or Germany's steep labor costs. But corruption is not a victimless crime. Everyone loses when public officials are on the take; corruption means that good projects are squeezed out by bad ones. Honest officials give up. Bribes grow ever bigger and more ubiquitous. The anticorruption czar in Mexico estimated that bribes reduce Mexico's gross domestic product annually by 9.5 percent, twice the country's education budget. Bribes also distort competition among American companies for foreign contracts, interfere with the free market system, and undermine confidence in business.[60]

Not all payments violate the FCPA. While it is clearly illegal to bribe the high-level decision makers who award contracts in the first place, **a grease or facilitating payment for a routine governmental action is permitted.** Examples of routine governmental action include processing visas or supplying utilities such as phone, power, or water. **To be legal, these payments must simply be hastening an inevitable result that does not involve discretionary action.** Thus, for example, "paying an official a small amount to have the power turned on at a factory might be a facilitating payment; paying an inspector to ignore the fact that the company does not have a valid permit to operate the factory would not be."[61]

A payment does not violate the FCPA if it was legal under the written laws of the country in which it was made. Because few countries establish written codes *permitting* officials to receive bribes, this defense is unlikely to help many Americans who hand out gifts.

Punishments can be severe. A company may face large fines and the loss of profits earned as a result of illegal bribes. In 2016, a Dutch telecommunications company paid $795 million in fines for having paid bribes to Uzbek officials. In addition to financial penalties, individuals who violate the FCPA can face up to five years in prison. However, the Justice Department has been lenient with companies that report their own wrongdoing. Thus, it did not prosecute Ralph Lauren Corporation after the company self-reported that one of its officers had paid bribes to Argentine customs officials.

American executives long complained that the FCPA put their companies at a competitive disadvantage because everyone else was paying bribes. But that is no longer the case. As business has become more globalized, so has the fight against corruption. Members of the OECD (i.e., most developed countries) have agreed to prohibit bribery and the United Nations approved a Convention Against Corruption. In addition, Brazil, Canada, China, and the United Kingdom all now have antibribery laws.

7-3g Other Crimes

Additional crimes that affect business appear elsewhere in the text. An increasing number of federal and state statutes are designed to punish those who harm the environment. (See Chapter 40 on environmental law.) Antitrust violations, in which a corporation fixes prices, can lead to criminal prosecutions. (See Chapter 38 on antitrust law.) Finally, securities fraud is a crime and can lead to severe prison sentences. (See Chapter 37 on securities regulation.)

60Adapted from "Who Will Listen to Mr. Clean?" *The Economist*, August 2, 1997, p. 52.

61U.S. Department of Justice and the U.S. Securities Exchange Commission, "A Resource Guide to the U.S. Foreign Corrupt Practices Act," www.justice.gov/criminal/fraud/fcpa/guide.pdf.

7-3h Punishing a Corporation

Fines

The most common punishment for a corporation is a fine. This makes sense in that a major purpose of a business is to earn a profit, and a fine, theoretically, hurts. But many fines are modest by the standards of corporate wealth. BP was found guilty of two serious legal violations. In Alaska, company pipelines spilled 200,000 gallons of crude oil onto the tundra. In Texas, a catastrophic explosion at a refinery killed 15 people and injured 170 more. The total fine for both criminal violations was $62 million, which sounds like a large number.[62] But it was not enough, evidently, to change BP's practices. As we have seen, the company pleaded guilty to criminal charges in connection with the 2010 oil rig explosion in the Gulf of Mexico, which caused the largest marine oil spill ever. The rig that exploded had many safety violations. Will that $4.5 billion fine change BP's business practices?

Compliance Programs

The **Federal Sentencing Guidelines** are the detailed rules that judges must follow when sentencing defendants convicted of crimes in federal court. The guidelines instruct judges to determine whether, at the time of the crime, the corporation had in place a serious **compliance program**; that is, a plan to prevent and detect criminal conduct at all levels of the company. A company that can point to a detailed, functioning compliance program may benefit from a dramatic reduction in the fine or other punishment meted out. Indeed, a tough compliance program may even convince federal investigators to curtail an investigation and to limit any prosecution to those directly involved, rather than attempting to convict high-ranking officers or the company itself.

Federal Sentencing Guidelines
The detailed rules that judges must follow when sentencing defendants convicted of crimes in federal court

Compliance program
A plan to prevent and detect improper conduct at all levels of the company

For a compliance plan to be deemed effective:

- The program must be reasonably capable of reducing the prospect of criminal conduct.
- Specific, high-level officers must be responsible for overseeing the program.
- The company must not place in charge any officers it knows or should have known, from past experience, are likely to engage in illegal conduct.
- The company must effectively communicate the program to all employees and agents.
- The company must ensure compliance by monitoring employees in a position to break the law and by promptly disciplining any who do.

Punishing corporations involves a complex balancing act. Certainly, companies are capable of bad deeds that can cause enormous harm, but some commentators feel that the criminal law has run amok—more than 300,000 statutes and regulations impose criminal penalties. Large companies often spend more than $40 million a year just to keep up with the records required by these many laws. Compliance programs can also be enormously expensive to run.[63] Is all that money well spent?

---

62 Source: http://epa.gov/.

63 "A Mammoth Guilt Trip," *The Economist*, August 30, 2014.

CHAPTER CONCLUSION

Crime has an enormous impact on society. Companies are victims of crimes, and sometimes they also commit criminal actions. Successful business leaders are ever-vigilant to protect their company from those who wish to harm it, whether from inside or out.

EXAM REVIEW

1. **BURDEN OF PROOF** In all prosecutions, the government must prove its case beyond a reasonable doubt.

EXAMStrategy

Question: A fire breaks out in Arnie's house, destroying the building and causing $150,000 in damage to an adjacent store. The state charges Arnie with arson. Simultaneously, Vickie, the store owner, sues Arnie for the damage to her property. Both cases are tried to juries, and the two juries hear identical evidence of Arnie's actions. But the criminal jury acquits Arnie, while the civil jury awards Vickie $150,000. How did that happen?

Strategy: The opposite outcomes are probably due to the different burdens of proof in a civil and a criminal case. Make sure you know that distinction. (See the "Result" at the end of this Exam Review section.)

2. **RIGHT TO A JURY** A criminal defendant has a right to a trial by jury for any charge that could result in a sentence of six months or longer.

3. **FELONY** A felony is a serious crime for which a defendant can be sentenced to one year or more in prison.

4. **CONDUCT OUTLAWED** The language of criminal statutes must be clear and definite.

5. **VOLUNTARY ACT** A defendant is not guilty of a crime if she committed it under duress. However, the defendant bears the burden of proving by a preponderance of the evidence that she acted under duress.

6. **ENTRAPMENT** When the government induces the defendant to break the law, the prosecution must prove beyond a reasonable doubt that the defendant was predisposed to commit the crime.

7. **CONSPIRACY** It is illegal to conspire to commit a crime, even if that crime never actually occurs.

8. **FOURTH AMENDMENT** The Fourth Amendment to the Constitution prohibits the government from making illegal searches and seizures. This amendment applies to individuals, corporations, partnerships, and other organizations.

9. **WARRANT** As a general rule, the police must obtain a warrant before conducting a search, but there are seven circumstances under which the police may search without a warrant: plain view, stop and frisk, emergencies, automobiles, lawful arrest, consent, and no expectation of privacy.

10. **PROBABLE CAUSE** A magistrate will issue a warrant only if there is probable cause. Probable cause means that it is likely that evidence of a crime will be found in the place to be searched.

11. **THE EXCLUSIONARY RULE** Under the exclusionary rule, any evidence the government acquires illegally (or any information obtained as a result of this illegal behavior) may not be used at trial.

12. **FIFTH AMENDMENT** The Fifth Amendment requires due process in criminal cases and prohibits double jeopardy and self-incrimination.

13. **SIXTH AMENDMENT** The Sixth Amendment guarantees criminal defendants the right to a lawyer at all important stages of the criminal process.

14. **DOUBLE JEOPARDY** A defendant may be prosecuted only once for a particular criminal offense.

15. **EIGHTH AMENDMENT** The Eighth Amendment prohibits excessive fines and cruel and unusual punishments.

16. **LARCENY** Larceny is the trespassory taking of personal property with the intent to steal.

17. **EMBEZZLEMENT** Embezzlement is the fraudulent conversion of property already in the defendant's possession.

18. **FRAUD** Fraud refers to a variety of crimes, all of which involve the deception of another person for the purpose of obtaining money or property.

19. **IDENTITY THEFT** The Identity Theft and Assumption Deterrence Act of 1998 prohibits the use of false identification to commit fraud or other crime, and it also permits the victim to seek restitution in court. The Aggravated Identity Theft statute imposes a mandatory additional sentence of two years on anyone who engages in identity theft during the commission of certain crimes.

20. **ARSON** Arson is the malicious use of fire or explosives to damage or destroy real estate or personal property.

21. **HACKING** The federal Computer Fraud and Abuse Act of 1986 prohibits hacking. It is illegal, among other things, to access a computer without authorization and obtain information from it.

22. **CORPORATE LIABILITY** If a company's agent commits a criminal act within the scope of her employment and with the intent to benefit the corporation, the company is liable.

23. **MAKING FALSE STATEMENTS** It is illegal to make false statements or engage in a cover-up during any dealings with the U.S. government.

24. **RICO** RICO prohibits using two or more racketeering acts to accomplish any of these goals: (1) investing in or acquiring legitimate businesses with criminal money, (2) maintaining or acquiring businesses through criminal activity, or (3) operating businesses through criminal activity.

EXAMStrategy

Question: Cheryl is a bank teller. She figures out a way to steal $99.99 per day in cash without getting caught. She takes the money daily for eight months and invests it in a catering business she is starting with Floyd, another teller. When Floyd learns what she is doing, he tries it, but is caught in his first attempt. He and Cheryl are both prosecuted.

a. Both are guilty only of larceny.

b. Both are guilty of larceny and violating RICO.

c. Both are guilty of embezzlement; Cheryl is also guilty of violating RICO.

d. Both are guilty of embezzlement and violating RICO.

Strategy: You need to know the difference between larceny and embezzlement. What is it? Once you have that figured out, focus on RICO. The government must prove two things: First, that the defendant committed crimes more than once—how many times? Second, that the defendant used the criminal proceeds for a specific purpose—what? (See the "Result" at the end of this Exam Review section.)

25. **MONEY LAUNDERING** Money laundering consists of taking profits from a criminal act and either using them to promote crime or attempting to conceal their source.

26. **IMMIGRATION LAW** It is illegal to knowingly employ unauthorized workers.

27. **FOREIGN CORRUPT PRACTICES ACT** Under the Foreign Corrupt Practices Act, it is illegal for any employee or agent of a U.S. company (and some foreign companies) or any U.S. citizen to give anything of value to any foreign official for purposes of influencing an official decision (unless the payment was merely intended to facilitate a routine governmental action).

EXAMStrategy

Question: Splash is a California corporation that develops resorts. Lawrence, a Splash executive, is hoping to land a $700 million contract with a country in Southeast Asia. He seeks your advice: "I own a fabulous beach house in Australia. What if I allow a government official and his family to stay there for two weeks? That might be enough to close the resort deal. Would that be wrong? Should I do it?" Please advise him.

Strategy: What law governs Lawrence's proposed conduct? Is Lawrence legally safe, given that the land is foreign and the contract will be signed overseas? Are there any circumstances under which this loan of his house would be legal? (See the "Result" at the end of this Exam Review section.)

RESULTS

1. Result: The plaintiff offered enough proof to convince a jury by a preponderance of the evidence that Arnie had committed arson. However that same evidence, offered in a criminal prosecution, was not enough to persuade the jury beyond a reasonable doubt that Arnie had lit the fire.

24. Result: Cheryl and Floyd both committed embezzlement, which refers to fraudulently taking money that was properly in their possession. Floyd did it once, but a RICO conviction requires two or more racketeering acts—Floyd has not violated RICO. Cheryl embezzled dozens of times and invested the money in a legitimate business. She is guilty of embezzlement and RICO; the correct answer is c.

27. Result: If Lawrence gives anything of value (such as rent-free use of his house) to secure a government contract, he has violated the FCPA. It makes no difference where the property is located or the deal signed. He could go to jail, and his company could be harshly penalized. Ethically, his gift would exacerbate corruption in another nation and mean that the agreement was determined by a bribe, not the merits of Splash. Other companies might do a superior job employing local workers, constructing an enduring resort, and protecting the environment, all for less money. The loan of the house would be legal if the official was simply in charge of turning on utilities in the area where the resort would be built.

MULTIPLE-CHOICE QUESTIONS

1. In a criminal case, which statement is true?
   (a) The prosecution must prove the government's case by a preponderance of the evidence.
   (b) The criminal defendant is entitled to a lawyer even if she cannot afford to pay for it herself.
   (c) The police are never allowed to question the accused without a lawyer present.
   (d) All federal crimes are felonies.
2. The police are not required to obtain a warrant before conducting a search if:
   (a) a reliable informant has told them they will find evidence of a crime in a particular location.
   (b) they have a warrant for part of a property and another section of the property is in plain view.
   (c) they see someone on the street who could possibly have committed a criminal act.
   (d) someone living on the property has consented to the search.
3. Under the exclusionary rule, which statement is true?
   (a) Evidence must be excluded from trial if the search warrant is defective, even if the police believed at the time of the search that it was valid.
   (b) The prosecution cannot use any evidence the police found at the site of the illegal search, but it can use any evidence the police discover elsewhere as a result of the illegal search.
   (c) Any statements a defendant makes after arrest are inadmissible if the police do not read him his Miranda rights.
   (d) If a conviction is overturned because of the exclusionary rule, the prosecution is not allowed to retry the defendant.

4. Henry asks his girlfriend, Alina, to drive his car to the repair shop. She drives his car all right—to Las Vegas, where she hits the slots. Alina has committed:
   (a) fraud.
   (b) embezzlement.
   (c) larceny.
   (d) a RICO violation.
5. Which of the following elements is *required* for a RICO conviction?
   (a) Investment in a legitimate business
   (b) Two or more criminal acts
   (c) Maintaining or acquiring businesses through criminal activity
   (d) Operating a business through criminal activity

CASE QUESTIONS

1. ***YOU BE THE JUDGE* WRITING PROBLEM** An undercover drug informant learned from a mutual friend that Philip Friedman "knew where to get marijuana." The informant asked Friedman three times to get him some marijuana, and Friedman agreed after the third request. Shortly thereafter, Friedman sold the informant a small amount of the drug. The informant later offered to sell Friedman three pounds of marijuana. They negotiated the price and then made the sale. Friedman was tried for trafficking in drugs. He argued entrapment. Was Friedman entrapped? **Argument for Friedman:** The undercover agent had to ask three times before Friedman sold him a small amount of drugs. A real drug dealer, predisposed to commit the crime, leaps at an opportunity to sell. If the government spends time and money luring innocent people into the commission of crimes, all of us are the losers. **Argument for the Government:** Government officials suspected Friedman of being a sophisticated drug dealer, and they were right. When he had a chance to buy three pounds, a quantity only a dealer would purchase, he not only did so, but he bargained with skill, showing a working knowledge of the business. Friedman was not entrapped—he was caught.

2. Conley owned video poker machines. Although they are outlawed in Pennsylvania, he placed them in bars and clubs. He used profits from the machines to buy more machines. Is he guilty of a crime? If so, which one?

3. Shawn was caught stealing letters from mailboxes. After pleading guilty, he was sentenced to two months in prison and three years' supervised release. One of the supervised release conditions required him to stand outside a post office for eight hours wearing a signboard stating, "I stole mail. This is my punishment." He appealed this requirement on the grounds that it constituted cruel and unusual punishment. Do you agree?

4. While driving his SUV, George struck and killed a pedestrian. He then fled the scene of the crime. A year later, the police downloaded information from his car's onboard computer which they were able to use to convict him of the crime. Should this information have been admissible at trial?

5. Police arrested Hank on a warrant issued in a neighboring county. When they searched him, the police found drugs and a gun. Only later did the police discover that when they had used the warrant, it was not valid because it had been recalled months earlier. The notice of recall had not been entered into the database. Should the evidence of drugs and a gun be suppressed under the exclusionary rule?

DISCUSSION QUESTIONS

1. Under British law, a police officer must now say the following to a suspect placed under arrest: "You do not have to say anything. But if you do not mention now something which you later use in your defense, the court may decide that your failure to mention it now strengthens the case against you. A record will be made of anything you say and it may be given in evidence if you are brought to trial." What is the goal of this British law? What does a police officer in the United States have to say, and what difference does it make at the time of an arrest? Which approach is better?

2. **ETHICS** You are a prosecutor who thinks it is possible that Nonnie, in her role as CEO of a brokerage firm, has stolen money from her customers. If you charge her and her company with RICO violations, you know that she is likely to plea bargain because otherwise her assets and those of the company may be frozen by the court. As part of the plea bargain, you might be able to get her to disclose evidence about other people who have taken part in this criminal activity. But you do not have any hard evidence at this point. Would such an indictment be ethical? Do the ends justify the means? Is it right to harm Nonnie for the chance of protecting thousands of innocent investors?

3. Officer Trottier stopped Marie for driving 20 miles over the speed limit. He then became suspicious because her son would not make eye contact and she was eating a Powerbar in a "hurried manner." The officer asked for and Marie granted him permission to search her car. During the search, he found a letter, which he read. Has he committed an illegal search?

4. Mickle pleaded guilty to rape. The judge sentenced him to prison for five years and also ordered that he undergo a vasectomy. Was this cruel and unusual punishment?

5. Ramona was indicted on charges of real estate fraud. During a legal search of her home, the police found a computer with encrypted files. Would it be a violation of her Fifth Amendment right against self-incrimination to force her to unencrypt these files?

6. Suppose two people are living together: the suspect and a tenant. If the tenant consents to a police search of the premises, then the police are not required to first obtain a warrant. What if the suspect and the tenant disagree, with the tenant granting permission while the suspect forbids the police to enter? Should the police be required to obtain a warrant before searching? Or what if the suspect denies permission to enter but the police go back later and the tenant consents?

7. Hiring relatives of foreign officials for no-show jobs is a violation of the FCPA. But what about hiring children of government officials into real jobs? Is that also a violation? The U.S. government investigated JPMorgan Chase & Co.'s practice of hiring the children of top Chinese officials in Hong Kong. What are the rules in this situation? What should they be?

8. A police officer in North Carolina stopped Nick's car because it had a broken brake light. Nick allowed the officer to search the car and, during the search, the officer found cocaine. It turns out that the original stop was invalid because drivers in North Carolina are allowed to drive with only one brake light. The cop did not know the law. Does the exclusionary rule prevent the cocaine from being admissible in court?

Torts

UNIT

2

CHAPTER 8

INTENTIONAL TORTS AND BUSINESS TORTS

They say politics can get ugly. *Doubt it*? Just ask John Vogel and Paul Grannis. Both men started off as candidates for public office in California—and then learned about defamation the hard way. They had no defense when mean and nasty statements were posted about them online. Here is their story.

Joseph Felice ran a website that listed "Top Ten Dumb Asses." Vogel and Grannis earned the honor of being number 1 and 2 on the list, respectively. The site also claimed that Vogel was "WANTED as a Dead Beat Dad" because he was behind on his child support payments. When users clicked on Vogel's name, they were led to another website—www.satan.com—that included a picture of him altered to look like a devil.

They had no defense when mean and nasty statements were posted about them online.

Grannis did not fare any better. Felice's site declared him "Bankrupt, Drunk & Chewin' Tobaccy." It stated that Grannis had "bankrupted many businesses throughout California." His name was hyperlinked to a website with the address www.olddrunk.com that accused him of criminal, fraudulent, and immoral conduct.

Understandably offended, Vogel and Grannis sued Felice for libel.[1] But they soon learned that filing such a lawsuit is easier than winning it.

[1] Vogel v. Felice, 127 Cal. App. 4th 1006 (2005).

The odd word *tort* is borrowed from the French, meaning "wrong." And that is what it means in law: a wrong. More precisely, a **tort** is a violation of a duty imposed by the civil law. When a person breaks one of those duties and injures another, it is a tort. The injury could be to a person or her property. Libel, which the politicians in the opening scenario alleged, is one example of a tort. A surgeon who removes the wrong kidney from a patient commits a different kind of tort, called *negligence*. A business executive who deliberately steals a client away from a competitor, interfering with a valid contract, commits a tort called *interference with a contract*. A con artist who tricks you out of your money with a phony offer to sell you a boat commits *fraud*, yet another tort.

Tort
A violation of a duty imposed by the civil law

Because tort law is so broad, it takes a while—and two chapters—to understand its boundaries. To start with, we must distinguish torts from two other areas of law: criminal law and contract law.

It is a *crime* to steal a car, to embezzle money from a bank, and to sell cocaine. As discussed in Chapter 1, society considers such behavior so threatening that the government itself will prosecute the wrongdoer, whether or not the car owner or bank president wants the case to go forward. A district attorney, who is paid by the government, will bring the case to court, seeking to send the defendant to prison, fine him, or both. If there is a fine, the money goes to the state, not to the victim.

In a tort case, it is up to the injured party to seek compensation. She must hire her own lawyer, who will file a lawsuit. Her lawyer must convince the court that the defendant breached some legal duty and ought to pay money damages to the plaintiff. The plaintiff has no power to send the defendant to jail. Bear in mind that a defendant's action might be both a crime and a tort. A man who punches you in the face for no reason commits the tort of battery. You may file a civil suit against him and will collect money damages if you can prove your case. He has also committed a crime, and the state may prosecute, seeking to imprison and fine him.

Differences between Contract, Tort, and Criminal Law

Type of Obligation	Contract	Tort	Criminal Law
How the obligation is created	The parties agree on a contract, which creates duties for both.	The civil law imposes duties of conduct on all persons.	The criminal law prohibits certain conduct.
How the obligation is enforced	Suit by plaintiff	Suit by plaintiff	Prosecution by government
Possible result	Money damages for plaintiff	Money damages for plaintiff	Punishment for defendant, including prison and/or fine
Example	Raul contracts to sell Deirdre 5,000 pairs of sneakers at $50 per pair, but fails to deliver them. Deirdre buys the sneakers elsewhere for $60 per pair and receives $50,000, her extra expense.	A newspaper falsely accuses a private citizen of being an alcoholic. The plaintiff sues and wins money damages to compensate for her injured reputation.	Leo steals Kelly's car. The government prosecutes Leo for grand theft, and the judge sentences him to two years in prison. Kelly gets nothing.

A tort is also different from a contract dispute. A contract case is based on an agreement two people have already made. For example, Deirdre claims that Raul promised to sell her 10,000 pairs of sneakers at a good price but has failed to deliver them.

She files a contract lawsuit. In a tort case, there is usually no "deal" between the parties. John Vogel and Paul Grannis never made any kind of contract with their online critic. The plaintiff in a tort case claims that the law itself creates a duty that the defendant has breached.

Intentional torts
Harm caused by a deliberate action

Tort law is divided into categories. In this chapter, we consider **intentional torts**, that is, harm caused by a deliberate action. When Paula hits Paul, she has committed the intentional tort of battery. In Chapter 9, we examine negligence, strict liability, and product liability, which involve injuries and losses caused by neglect and oversight rather than by deliberate conduct.

A final introductory point: When we speak of intentional torts, we do not necessarily mean that the defendant intended to harm the plaintiff. If the defendant does something deliberately and it ends up injuring somebody, she is probably liable even if she meant no harm. For example, intentionally throwing a snowball at a friend is a deliberate act. If the snowball permanently damages his eye, the *harm* is unintended, but the defendant is liable for the intentional tort of battery because the *act* was intentional.

We look first at the most common intentional torts and then at the most important intentional torts that are related to business.

8-1 INTENTIONAL TORTS

8-1a Defamation

The First Amendment guarantees the right to free speech, a vital freedom that enables us to protect other rights. But that freedom is not absolute.

Libel
Written defamation

Slander
Oral defamation

The law of defamation concerns false statements that harm someone's reputation. Defamatory statements can be written or spoken. Written defamation is called **libel**. Suppose a newspaper accuses a local retail store of programming its cash registers to overcharge customers when the store has never done so. That is libel. Oral defamation is **slander**. If Professor Wisdom, in class, refers to Sally Student as a drug dealer although she has never sold drugs, he has slandered her.

There are four elements to a defamation case. An element is something that a plaintiff must prove to win a lawsuit. The plaintiff in any kind of lawsuit must prove *all* of the elements to prevail. The elements in a defamation case are:

- **Defamatory statement.** This is a factual statement that is likely to harm another person's reputation. Because opinions are not factual, they do not generally count as defamatory statements. In the case from the opening scenario, the judge found that "dumb ass" was not a defamatory statement. The court interpreted that slang phrase as a general expression of contempt, not a fact. On the other hand, the accusations that Vogel owed child support payments and Grannis was bankrupt *were* defamatory statements because they were facts that could be proven true or false.

- **Falsity.** The statement must be false. Felice, the website's author, was ultimately successful in his defense because he proved that Vogel did in fact fail to pay child support and Grannis had filed for bankruptcy. Making a true statement, no matter how mean, is not defamation.

Slander per se
When oral statements relate to criminal or sexual conduct, contagious diseases, or professional abilities, they are assumed to be harmful to the subject's reputation.

- **Communicated.** The statement must be communicated to at least one person *other than the plaintiff*. It stands to reason: If no one else receives the defamatory message, there is no harm done. Defamation protects against injury to reputation, not hurt feelings.

- **Injury.** The plaintiff must show some injury, unless the case involves false statements about sexual behavior, crimes, contagious diseases, and professional abilities. In these cases, the law is willing to *assume* injury without requiring the plaintiff to prove it. Lies in these four categories amount to **slander per se** when they are spoken and **libel per se** when they are published.[2]

Libel per se
When written statements relate to criminal or sexual conduct, contagious diseases, or professional abilities, they are assumed to be harmful to the subject's reputation.

The following case involves libel per se, *The New York Times*, and alleged police brutality. Set in Alabama during the racially charged Sixties, this landmark Supreme Court decision changed the rules of the defamation game for all public personalities.

Landmark Case

New York Times Co. v. Sullivan

376 U.S. 254
United States Supreme Court, 1964

Facts: In 1960, *The New York Times* ran a full-page advertisement paid for by civil rights activists. The ad described an "unprecedented wave of terror" by the police of Montgomery, Alabama, against civil rights protesters. It stated that the police had assaulted nonviolent protesters with shotguns and tear gas and had padlocked a dining hall to starve them into submission. The ad also accused the Montgomery police of bombing the home of Dr. Martin Luther King, Jr., and unjustly arresting him seven times. Most of the ad's statements were true, but a few were not.

L. B. Sullivan was Montgomery's police commissioner. Although the ad did not mention him by name, Sullivan argued that the accusations hurt his reputation because he was head of the police. He sued *The New York Times* under Alabama's law on libel per se.

An Alabama court agreed with Sullivan, awarding him damages of $500,000. The Supreme Court of Alabama affirmed. *The New York Times* appealed to the U.S. Supreme Court, arguing that the ad was protected by the First Amendment and the evidence did not support such an award.

Issue: ***Does the First Amendment protect those who criticize public officials?***

Excerpts from Justice Brennan's Decision: We consider this case against the background of a profound national commitment to the principle that debate on public issues should be uninhibited, robust, and wide-open, and that it may well include vehement, caustic, and sometimes unpleasantly sharp attacks on government and public officials. The present advertisement, as an expression of grievance and protest on one of the major public issues of our time, would seem clearly to qualify for the constitutional protection. The question is whether it forfeits that protection by the falsity of some of its factual statements and by its alleged defamation of respondent.

First Amendment protection does not turn upon the truth, popularity, or social utility of the ideas and beliefs which are offered. Erroneous statement [are] inevitable in free debate, and must be protected. Whatever is added to the field of libel is taken from the field of free debate. Criticism of official conduct does not lose its constitutional protection merely because it diminishes official reputations.

Bettmann/Getty Images

L.B. Sullivan, a public official (pictured second from the right), sued The New York Times *for defamation. Who's protected under the First Amendment?*

[2]The courts consider defamation on radio and television to be libel, not slander, because of their vast audiences. As a result, plaintiffs in broadcasting cases generally do not have to prove damages.

A rule compelling the critic of official conduct to guarantee the truth of all his factual assertions leads to self-censorship. Under such a rule, would-be critics of official conduct may be deterred from voicing their criticism. The rule thus dampens the vigor and limits the variety of public debate. It is inconsistent with the First Amendment.

The constitutional guarantees require a federal rule that prohibits a public official from recovering damages for a defamatory falsehood relating to his official conduct unless he proves that the statement was made with "actual malice"—that is, with knowledge that it was false or with reckless disregard of whether it was false or not.

Applying these standards, we consider that the facts do not support a finding of actual malice as to the *Times*. The *Times* published the advertisement without checking its accuracy. We think the evidence against the *Times* supports at most a finding of negligence in failing to discover the misstatements, and is constitutionally insufficient to show the recklessness that is required for a finding of actual malice.

The judgment of the Supreme Court of Alabama is reversed and the case is remanded.

Now we see another reason why the politicians from our chapter opener lost their defamation case. **The rule from *The New York Times* case is that a public official can win a defamation case only by proving the defendant's actual malice, that is, that the defendant knew the statement was false or acted with reckless disregard of the truth.** As candidates for public office, the politicians had to prove their critic's malice—and they could not do so. The *New York Times* rule has been extended to all public figures, like actors, business leaders, and anyone else who assumes an influential and visible role in society.[3]

EXHIBIT 8.1

Defamation cases show a tension between the public's need for information and a citizen's right to protect his reputation.

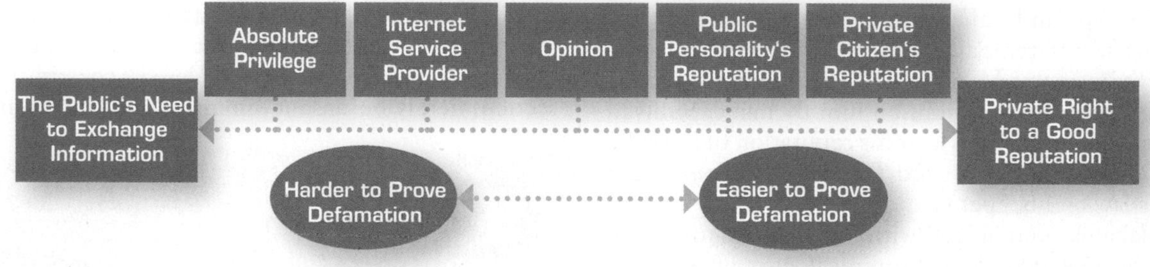

Privilege

Absolute privilege
A witness testifying in a court or legislature may never be sued for defamation.

Defendants receive additional protection from defamation cases when it is important for them to speak freely. **Absolute privilege** exists in courtrooms and legislative hearings. Anyone speaking there, such as a witness in court, can say anything at all and never be sued for defamation. (Deliberately false testimony would be *perjury*, but still not *slander*.)

8-1b False Imprisonment

False imprisonment
The intentional restraint of another person without reasonable cause and without consent

False imprisonment is the intentional restraint of another person without reasonable cause and without consent. Suppose that a bank teller becomes seriously ill and wants to go to the doctor, but the bank will not permit her to leave until she makes a final tally of her accounts. Against

[3]Curtis Publishing Co. v. Butts, 388 U.S. 130 (1967); and Associated Press v. Walker, 388 U.S. 130 (1967).

her wishes, company officials physically bar her from leaving the bank. That is false imprisonment. The restraint was unreasonable because her accounts could have been verified later.[4]

False imprisonment cases most commonly arise in retail stores, which sometimes detain employees or customers for suspected theft. Most states now have statutes governing the detention of suspected shoplifters. **Generally, a store may detain a customer or worker for alleged shoplifting provided there is a reasonable basis for the suspicion and the detention is done reasonably.** To detain a customer in the manager's office for 20 minutes and question him about where he got an item is lawful. To chain that customer to a display counter for three hours and humiliate him in front of other customers is unreasonable and constitutes false imprisonment.

8-1c Intentional Infliction of Emotional Distress

What should happen when a defendant hurts a plaintiff emotionally but not physically? The tort of **intentional infliction of emotional distress** ("IIED") results from extreme and outrageous conduct that causes serious emotional harm. A credit officer was struggling vainly to locate Sheehan, who owed money on his car. The officer phoned Sheehan's mother, falsely identified herself as a hospital employee, and said she needed to find Sheehan because his children had been in a serious auto accident. The mother provided Sheehan's whereabouts, which enabled the company to seize his car. But Sheehan spent seven hours frantically trying to locate his supposedly injured children, who in fact were fine. The credit company was liable for the intentional infliction of emotional distress.[5]

Intentional infliction of emotional distress
An intentional tort in which the harm results from extreme and outrageous conduct that causes serious emotional harm

But tort law cannot possibly address every act that hurts someone's feelings. Not all offensive conduct is "outrageous" enough to be considered IIED. Courts have held that tasteless, rude, inappropriate, or vulgar conduct alone is not enough to establish an IIED claim, even if it really upsets someone. One court found that a particularly brutal employment evaluation was not outrageous enough, even when it caused the employee a mental breakdown.[6]

The following case contains highly offensive language and situations. It presented the authors of this textbook with a dilemma: *Should we risk subjecting our readers to emotional distress to teach them about the tort?* Because it is essential for you to understand the type of behavior considered "outrageous" in IIED cases, we included the disturbing details.

Turley v. ISG Lackawanna, Inc.

774 F.3d 140
United States Court of Appeals for the Second Circuit, 2014

Facts: Elijah Turley was a steelworker at the Lackawanna company's plant near Buffalo, New York. For over a decade, he was the only African-American in his department. For the last three years of his employment, Lackawanna employees tormented and degraded Turley while his supervisors watched, condoned, and even participated.

On a daily basis, Turley's coworkers subjected him to racist epithets and degrading treatment. They referred to him as "boy." One witness estimated that 30 percent of the workers referred to him as "that f****** n*****." Coworkers broadcast monkey sounds over the plant's intercom system. On several occasions, Turley arrived at work to find the initials "KKK"—in reference to the Ku Klux Klan—spray-painted on his workstation. Others vandalized Turley's car.

There were also death threats. Lackawanna employees terrorized Turley anonymously over the intercom, yelling "We[’re] going to f****** kill you, f****** n*****, we're going to kill your f****** Jewish lawyer too." In one incident, a coworker told Turley to check on his car.

[4]Kanner v. First National Bank of South Miami, 287 So.2d 715 (Fla. Dist. Ct. App. 1974).
[5]Ford Motor Credit Co. v. Sheehan, 373 So.2d 956 (Fla. Dist. Ct. App. 1979).
[6]Jarrard v. UPS, 529 S.E.2d 144 (2000).

Turley found, dangling from his side-view mirror, a stuffed toy monkey with a noose around its neck. Another staff member promised Turley that if he ever saw him "on the outside," he would shoot him.

Lackawanna managers knew about the abuse, especially Larry Sampsell, head of security. Management was mostly unresponsive—but sometimes complicit. When a coworker viciously accosted Turley in a meeting, Sampsell just stood by. When Turley reported death threats, Sampsell laughed. In all the years of harassment, the company only disciplined Turley's tormenters twice. Sampsell also denied local police investigators access to company surveillance video. Rather than address Turley's complaints, Sampsell set up a hidden camera that secretly recorded Turley while he worked.

The persecution left Turley a broken man, suffering serious psychiatric problems. Turley sued Lackawanna and his supervisors for intentional infliction of emotional distress ("IIED"), among other claims. Finding Lackawanna and Sampsell liable, a jury awarded Turley $1.3 million in compensatory damages (including $260,000 for IIED) and $5 million in punitive damages, plus attorney's fees and costs.

Lackawanna and Sampsell appealed, arguing that the company and the supervisor's inaction did not meet the standard for IIED.

Issue: ***Did Turley make a valid claim for intentional infliction of emotional distress?***

Excerpts from Judge Sack's Decision: IIED provides a remedy for the damages that arise out of a defendant engaging in extreme and outrageous conduct, which so transcends the bounds of decency as to be regarded as atrocious and intolerable in a civilized society. To prevail on such a claim, a plaintiff must establish that there was extreme and outrageous conduct, that the conduct was undertaken with intent to cause, or disregard of a substantial probability of causing, severe emotional distress and that the conduct did in fact cause severe emotional distress.

The defendants contend that the record contains insufficient evidence to hold Sampsell and Lackawanna liable. Sampsell's acts, the defendants contend, consisted largely of failing to respond appropriately to reports of harassment. General bureaucratic unresponsiveness, lethargy, or a failure to understand the gravity of a situation, although objectionable, is rarely if ever considered so beyond the pale as to reach the extreme threshold necessary for an IIED claim.

Sampsell's behavior cannot be described as a simple failure to take timely action in response to a harassment complaint. Sampsell was a personal witness to the ongoing and severe indignity, humiliation, and torment to which the plaintiff was subjected over a substantial period of time—and he was in a position to do something about it. Instead, he continuously failed to respond for more than three years, blocking others' efforts to investigate serious threats, and, at times, seeming to encourage further harassment. On these facts, we see no error in finding that the defendant's conduct was outrageous, shocking, and beyond the bounds of decency so as to constitute tortious behavior.

8-1d Battery and Assault

Battery
An intentional touching of another person in a way that is harmful or offensive

Assault and battery are related, but not identical. **Battery** is an intentional touching of another person in a way that is harmful or offensive.

If an irate parent throws a chair at a referee during his daughter's basketball game, breaking the man's jaw, he has committed battery. But a parent who cheerfully slaps the winning coach on the back has not committed battery because a reasonable coach would not be offended.

As mentioned earlier, there need be no intention to hurt the plaintiff. If the defendant intended to do the physical act, and a reasonable plaintiff would be offended by it, battery has occurred. An executive who gives an unwanted sexual caress to a secretary also commits this tort, even if he assumed that any normal female would be ecstatic over his attentions. (This is also sexual harassment, discussed in Chapter 29, on employment law.)

Assault
An act that makes a person reasonably fear an imminent battery

Assault occurs when a defendant does some act that makes a plaintiff *fear* an imminent battery. This tort is based on apprehension—it does not matter whether a battery ever occurs. Suppose Ms. Wilson shouts "Think fast!" at her husband and hurls a toaster at him. He turns and sees it flying at him. His fear of being struck is enough to win a case of assault, even if the toaster misses. If the toaster happens to strike him, Ms. Wilson has also committed battery.

Recall the shoplifting problem. Assume that a store guard pulls an unloaded pistol on Sandra Shopper, suspecting her of theft. Sandra faints and strikes her head on a counter. When sued for assault, the store defends by claiming the guard never touched her and the gun was unloaded. Obviously, the store did not have the benefit of this law course. A reasonable shopper would have feared imminent battery, and the store is liable for assault.

EXAMStrategy

Question: Mark is furious because his girlfriend, Denise, just told him she is leaving him. He never saw it coming. On the sidewalk, he picks up a rock and hurls it at Denise's head. She *does* see it coming, and she ducks. The rock misses Denise but hits Terrance (who never saw it coming) in the back of his head. Denise and Terrance both sue Mark for assault and for battery. Outcomes?

Strategy: Separate the two plaintiffs. What injury did Denise suffer? She saw a rock flying at her and thought she would be struck. Now recall the elements of the two torts. Battery is an intentional touching that is offensive. Assault is an act that makes another person *fear* an imminent battery.

Result: Was Denise touched? No. Did she fear an imminent battery? Yes. Denise wins a suit for assault but loses one for battery. Now Terrance: Was he touched? Yes. Did he fear an imminent battery? No. Terrance wins a suit for battery but loses one for assault.

8-1e Trespass, Conversion, and Fraud

Trespass

Trespass is intentionally entering land that belongs to someone else or remaining on the land after being asked to leave. It is also trespass if you have some object, let's say a car, on someone else's property and refuse to remove it. "Intentionally" means that you deliberately walk onto the land. If you walk through a meadow, believing it to be a public park, and it belongs to a private owner, you have trespassed.

Trespass
Intentionally entering land that belongs to someone else or remaining on the land after being asked to leave

Conversion

Conversion is taking or using someone's personal property without consent. Personal property is any possession other than land or structures permanently attached to land, such as houses. Priceless jewels, ratty sneakers, and sailboats are all personal property. If Stormy sails away in Jib's sailboat and keeps it all summer, that is conversion. Stormy owes Jib the full value of the boat. This, of course, is similar to the crime of theft. The tort of conversion enables a plaintiff to pursue the case herself, without awaiting a criminal prosecution, and to obtain compensation.

Conversion
Taking or using someone's personal property without consent

Fraud

Fraud is injuring another person by deliberate deception. Later in this chapter, a plaintiff claims that for many years a cigarette manufacturer fraudulently suggested its product was safe, knowing its assurances were deadly lies. Fraud is a tort, but it typically occurs during the negotiation or performance of a contract, and it is discussed in detail in Unit 3 on contracts.

Fraud
Injuring another person by deliberate deception

8-2 DAMAGES

8-2a Compensatory Damages

Mitchel Bien, who is deaf and mute, enters the George Grubbs Nissan dealership, where folks sell cars aggressively. Very aggressively. Maturelli, a salesman, and Bien communicate by writing messages back and forth. Maturelli takes Bien's own car keys, and the two then test-drive a 300ZX. Bien says he does not want the car, but Maturelli escorts him back inside and fills out a sales sheet. Bien repeatedly asks for his keys, but Maturelli only laughs, pressuring him to buy the new car. Minutes pass. Hours pass. Bien becomes frantic, writing a dozen notes, begging to leave, and threatening to call the police. Maturelli mocks Bien and his physical disabilities. Finally, after four hours, the customer escapes.

Bien becomes frantic, writing a dozen notes, begging to leave, and threatening to call the police.

Bien sues for the intentional infliction of emotional distress. Two former salesmen from Grubbs testify they have witnessed customers cry, yell, and curse as a result of the aggressive tactics. Doctors state that the incident has traumatized Bien, dramatically reducing his confidence and self-esteem and preventing his return to work even three years later.

The jury awards Bien damages. But how does a jury calculate the money? For that matter, why should a jury even try? Money can never erase pain or undo a permanent injury. The answer is simple: Money, however inexact, is often the only thing a court has to give.

Compensatory damages
Money intended to restore a plaintiff to the position he was in before the injury

A successful plaintiff generally receives **compensatory damages**, meaning an amount of money that the court believes will restore him to the position he was in before the defendant's conduct caused injury. Here is how damages are calculated.

Single recovery principle
Requires a court to settle the matter once and for all by awarding a lump sum for past and future expenses

First, a plaintiff receives money for medical expenses that he has proven by producing bills from doctors, hospitals, physical therapists, and psychotherapists. Bien receives all the money he has paid. If a doctor testifies that he needs future treatment, Bien will offer evidence of how much that will cost. The **single recovery principle** requires a court to settle the matter once and for all, by awarding a lump sum for past *and future* expenses, if there will be any. A plaintiff may not return in a year and say, "Oh, by the way, there are some new bills."

Second, the defendants are liable for lost wages. The court takes the number of days or months that Bien missed work and multiplies that number times his salary. If Bien is currently unable to work, a doctor estimates how many more months he will miss work, and the court adds that to his damages.

Third, a plaintiff is paid for pain and suffering. Bien testifies about how traumatic the four hours were and how the experience has affected his life. He may state that he now fears shopping, suffers nightmares, and seldom socializes. To bolster the case, a plaintiff uses expert testimony, such as the psychiatrists who testified for Bien. Awards for pain and suffering vary enormously, from a few dollars to many millions, depending on the injury and depending on the jury. In some lawsuits, physical and psychological pains are momentary and insignificant; in other cases, the pain is the biggest part of the verdict. In this case, the jury awarded Bien $573,815, calculated as in the following table.[7]

[7]The compensatory damages are described in George Grubbs Enterprises v. Bien, 881 S.W.2d 843 (Tex. Ct. App. 1994). In addition to the compensatory damages described, the jury awarded $5 million in punitive damages. The Supreme Court of Texas reversed the award of punitive damages, but not the compensatory. Id., 900 S.W.2d 337 (Tex. 1995). The high court did not dispute the appropriateness of punitive damages, but reversed because the trial court failed to instruct the jury properly as to how it should determine the assets actually under the defendants' control, an issue essential to punitive damages but not compensatory.

Past medical	$ 70.00
Future medical	6,000.00
Past rehabilitation	3,205.00
Past lost earning capacity	112,910.00
Future lost earning capacity	34,650.00
Past physical symptoms and discomfort	50,000.00
Future physical symptoms and discomfort	50,000.00
Past emotional injury and mental anguish	101,980.00
Future emotional injury and mental anguish	200,000.00
Past loss of society and reduced ability to socially interact with family, former fiancée, friends, and hearing (i.e., nondeaf) people in general	10,000.00
Future loss of society and reduced ability to socially interact with family, former fiancée, friends, and hearing people	5,000.00
TOTAL	**$ 573,815.00**

Awards for future harm (such as future pain and suffering) involve the court making its best estimate of the plaintiff's hardship in the years to come. This is not an exact science. If the judgment is reasonable, it will rarely be overturned. Ethel Flanzraich, age 78, fell on stairs that had been badly maintained. In addition to her medical expense, the court awarded her $150,000 for future pain and suffering. The day after the court gave its award, Ms. Flanzraich died of other causes. Did that mean her family must forfeit that money? No. The award was reasonable when made and had to be paid.[8]

8-2b Punitive Damages

Here we look at a different kind of award, one that is more controversial and potentially more powerful: punitive damages. The purpose is not to compensate the plaintiff for harm, because compensatory damages will have done that. **Punitive damages** are intended to punish the defendant for conduct that is extreme and outrageous. Courts award these damages in relatively few cases. The idea behind punitive damages is that certain behavior is so unacceptable that society must make an example of it. A large award of money should deter the defendant from repeating the mistake and others from ever making it. Some believe punitive damages represent the law at its most avaricious, while others attribute to them great social benefit.

Punitive damages
Damages that are intended to punish the defendant for conduct that is extreme and outrageous

Although a jury has wide discretion in awarding punitive damages, the Supreme Court has ruled that a verdict must be reasonable. Ira Gore purchased a new BMW automobile from an Alabama dealer and then discovered that the car had been repainted. He sued. At trial, BMW acknowledged a nationwide policy of not informing customers of predelivery repairs when the cost was less than 3 percent of the retail price. The company had sold about 1,000 repainted cars nationwide. The jury concluded that BMW had engaged in gross, malicious fraud and awarded Gore $4,000 in compensatory damages and $4 million in punitive damages. The Alabama Supreme Court reduced the award to $2 million, but the U.S. Supreme Court ruled that even that amount was grossly excessive. The Court held that in awarding punitive damages, a court must consider three "guideposts":

- The reprehensibility of the defendant's conduct,
- The ratio between the harm suffered and the award, and
- The difference between the punitive award and any civil penalties used in similar cases.

[8] Stinton v. Robin's Wood, 842 N.Y.S.2d 477 (N.Y. App. Div. 2007).

The Court concluded that BMW had shown no evil intent and that Gore's harm had been purely economic (as opposed to physical). Further, the Court found the ratio of 500 to 1, between punitive and compensatory damages, to be excessive, although it offered no definitive rule about a proper ratio. On remand, the Alabama Supreme Court reduced the punitive damages award to $50,000.[9]

The U.S. Supreme Court gave additional guidance on punitive damages in the following landmark case.

Landmark Case

State Farm v. Campbell

538 U.S. 408
United States Supreme Court, 2003

Facts: While attempting to pass several cars on a two-lane road, Campbell drove into oncoming traffic. An innocent driver swerved to avoid Campbell and died in a collision with a third driver. The family of the deceased driver and the surviving third driver both sued Campbell.

As Campbell's insurer, State Farm represented him in the lawsuit. It turned down an offer to settle the case for $50,000, the limit of Campbell's policy. The company had nothing to gain by settling because even if Campbell lost big at trial, State Farm's liability was capped at $50,000.

A jury returned a judgment against Campbell for $185,000. He was responsible for the $135,000 that exceeded his policy limit. He argued with State Farm, claiming that it should have settled the case. Eventually, State Farm paid the entire $185,000, but Campbell still sued the company, alleging fraud and intentional infliction of emotional distress.

His lawyers presented evidence that State Farm had deliberately acted in its own best interests rather than his. The jury was convinced, and in the end, Campbell won an award of $1 million in compensatory damages and $145 million in punitive damages. State Farm appealed.

Issue: ***What is the limit on punitive damages?***

Excerpts from Justice Kennedy's Decision: We address whether an award of $145 million in punitive damages, where full compensatory damages are $1 million, is excessive and in violation of the Due Process Clause. The Utah Supreme Court relied upon testimony indicating that State Farm's actions, because of their clandestine nature, will be punished at most in 1 out of every 50,000 cases as a matter of statistical probability, and concluded that the ratio between punitive and compensatory damages was not unwarranted.

Compensatory damages are intended to redress the concrete loss that the plaintiff has suffered by reason of the defendant's wrongful conduct. By contrast, punitive damages serve a broader function; they are aimed at deterrence and retribution.

The Due Process Clause prohibits the imposition of grossly excessive or arbitrary punishments. The reason is that elementary notions of fairness dictate that a person receive fair notice not only of the conduct that will subject him to punishment, but also of the severity of the penalty that a State may impose. To the extent an award is grossly excessive, it furthers no legitimate purpose and constitutes an arbitrary deprivation of property. A defendant should be punished for the conduct that harmed the plaintiff, not for being an unsavory.

We decline to impose a bright-line ratio which a punitive damages award cannot exceed. Our jurisprudence and the principles it has now established demonstrate, however, that, in practice, few awards exceeding a single-digit ratio between punitive and compensatory damages, to a significant degree, will satisfy due process. Single-digit multipliers are more likely to comport with due process, while still achieving the State's goals of deterrence and retribution, than awards with ratios in the range of 145 to 1.

Nonetheless, because there are no rigid benchmarks that a punitive damages award may not surpass, ratios greater than those we have previously upheld may comport with due process where a particularly egregious act has resulted in only a small amount of economic damages. The precise award in any case must be based upon the

[9]BMW of North America, Inc. v. Gore, 517 U.S. 559 (1996).

facts and circumstances of the defendant's conduct and the harm to the plaintiff.

In sum, courts must ensure that the measure of punishment is both reasonable and proportionate to the amount of harm to the plaintiff and to the general damages recovered. In the context of this case, we have no doubt that there is a presumption against an award that has a 145-to-1 ratio. The compensatory award in this case was substantial; the Campbells were awarded $1 million for a year and a half of emotional distress. This was complete compensation. The harm arose from a transaction in the economic realm, not from some physical assault or trauma; there were no physical injuries; and State Farm paid the excess verdict before the complaint was filed, so Campbell suffered only minor economic injuries.

The judgment of the Utah Supreme Court is reversed, and the case is remanded for proceedings not inconsistent with this opinion.

Dramatic cases may *still* lead to very large awards.

And so, the Supreme Court seeks to limit, but not completely prohibit, enormous punitive damages. A California Court of Appeals decided the following case two years after *State Farm v. Campbell*. How should it implement the Supreme Court's guidelines? You be the judge.

You Be the Judge

Boeken v. Philip Morris, Incorporated

127 Cal. App.4th 1640
California Court of Appeals, 2005

Facts: In the mid-1950s, Richard Boeken began smoking Marlboro cigarettes at the age of 10. Countless advertisements, targeted at boys ages 10 to 18, convinced him and his friends that the "Marlboro man" was powerful, healthy, and manly. Eventually, Richard changed to "Marlboro Lite" cigarettes but continued smoking into the 1990s, when he was diagnosed with lung cancer. He filed suit against Philip Morris, the cigarette manufacturer, for fraud and other torts. He died of cancer before the case was concluded.

Evidence at trial demonstrated that by the mid-1950s, scientists uniformly accepted that cigarette smoking caused lung cancer. However, at about the same time, Philip Morris and other tobacco companies began a decades-long campaign to convince the public that there was substantial doubt about any link between smoking and illness. The plaintiffs also demonstrated that tobacco was physically addictive, and that Philip Morris added ingredients such as urea to its cigarettes to increase their addictive power. Boeken testified that in the late 1960s he saw the Surgeon General warnings about the risk of smoking but trusted the cigarette company's statements that smoking was safe. By the 1970s he tried many times, and many cures, to stop smoking but always failed. He finally quit just before surgery to remove part of his lung but resumed after the operation.

The jury found Philip Morris liable for fraudulently concealing that cigarettes were addictive and carcinogenic. It awarded Boeken $5.5 million in compensatory damages, and also assessed punitive damages—of $3 *billion*. The trial judge reduced the punitive award to $100 million. Philip Morris appealed.

You Be the Judge: *Was the punitive damage award too high, too low, or just right?*

Argument for Philip Morris: The court should substantially reduce the $100 million punitive award because it constitutes an "arbitrary deprivation of property." The Supreme Court has indicated that punitive awards should not exceed compensatory damages by more than a factor of nine. The jury awarded Mr. Boeken $5.5 million in compensatory damages, which means that punitive damages should absolutely not exceed $49.5 million. We argue that they should be even lower.

Cigarettes are a legal product, and our packages have displayed the Surgeon General's health warnings for decades. Mr. Boeken's death is tragic, but his cancer was not necessarily caused by Marlboro cigarettes. And even if cigarettes did contribute to his failing health, Mr. Boeken chose to smoke throughout his life, even after major surgery on one of his lungs.

Argument for Boeken: The Supreme Court says that "few" cases may exceed the 9-to-1 ratio, but that "the precise award in any case must be based upon the facts and circumstances of the defendant's conduct and the harm to the plaintiff." Phillip Morris created ads that targeted children, challenged clear scientific data that its products caused cancer, and added substances to its cigarettes to make them more addictive. Does it get worse than that?

As for harm to the plaintiff, he died a terrible death from cancer. Philip Morris cigarettes kill 200,000 American customers each year. The defendant's conduct could not be more reprehensible. Philip Morris's weekly profit is roughly $100 million. At a minimum, the court should keep the punitive award at that figure. But we ask that the court reinstate the jury's original $3 billion award.

8-2c Tort Reform and the *Exxon Valdez*

Some people believe that jury awards are excessive and need statutory reform, while others argue that the evidence demonstrates excessive awards are rare and modest in size. About one-half of the states have passed limits. The laws vary, but many distinguish between **economic damage** and **noneconomic damages**. In such a state, a jury is permitted to award any amount for economic damages, meaning lost wages, medical expenses, and other measurable losses. However, noneconomic damages—pain and suffering and other losses that are difficult to measure—are capped at some level, such as $500,000. In some states, punitive awards have similar caps. These restrictions can drastically lower the total verdict.

AP Images/Jae C. Hong

Until the 2010 Deepwater Horizon Oil Spill, the Exxon Valdez was the largest ever oil spill in U.S. waters.

In the famous *Exxon Valdez* case, the Supreme Court placed a severe limit on a certain type of punitive award. It is unclear how influential the decision will be because the case arises in the isolated area of maritime law, which governs ships at sea. Nonetheless, the justices wrote at length about punitive awards, and the decision may reverberate in future holdings. This is what happened.

Captain Joseph Hazelwood's negligence caused the *Exxon Valdez* to run aground off the coast of Alaska. The ship dumped 11 million gallons of oil into the sea, damaging 3,000 square miles of vulnerable ecosystem. The oil spill forced fishermen into bankruptcy, disrupted entire communities, and killed hundreds of thousands of birds and marine animals. A decade later, many of the damaged species had not recovered. The jury decided that Exxon had been reckless by allowing Hazelwood to pilot the ship when the company knew he was an alcoholic. The jury awarded compensatory damages to the plaintiffs, and punitive damages of $5 *billion*. Exxon appealed.

Almost two decades after the accident, the Supreme Court ruled. The justices discussed punitive damages in general, noting that much of the criticism of punitive awards appeared overstated. The court declared there had been no major increase in how frequently juries gave punitive damages. In the unusual cases where jurors made such awards, the sums were modest. The problem, declared the justices, was the unpredictability of punitive damages.

The court ruled that *in maritime cases*, the ratio should be no higher than 1:1. The court approved the jury's compensatory award of $507 million, and then reduced the punitive award from $5 billion to $507 million. Supporters of the court's decision stated that it would allow businesses to make plans based on predictable outcomes. Opponents said that the justices ignored the jury's finding of reckless behavior and calamitous environmental harm.[10]

[10] Exxon Shipping Co. v. Baker, 554 U.S. 471 (2008).

EXAMStrategy

Question: Patrick owns a fast-food restaurant which is repeatedly painted with graffiti. He is convinced that 15-year-old John, a frequent customer, is the culprit. The next time John comes to the restaurant, Patrick locks the men's room door while John is inside. Patrick calls the police, but because of a misunderstanding, the police are very slow to arrive. John shouts and cries for help, banging on the door, but Patrick does not release him for two hours. John sues. He claims that he has suffered great psychological harm because of the incident; his psychiatrist asserts that John may have unpredictable suffering in the future. John sues for assault, battery, and false imprisonment. Will he win? May John return to court in the future to seek further damages?

Strategy: The question focuses on two issues: first, the distinction between several intentional torts; second, damages. Analyze one issue at a time. As to the intentional torts, what injury has John suffered? He was locked in the men's room and suffered psychological harm. Recall the elements of the three possible torts. Battery concerns an offensive touching. A defendant commits assault by causing an imminent fear of battery. False imprisonment: A store may detain someone if it does so reasonably. As to damages, review the *single recovery principle*.

Result: Locking John up for two hours, based on an unproven suspicion, was clearly unreasonable. Patrick has committed false imprisonment. The single recovery principle forces John to recover now for all past and future harm. He may not return to court later and seek additional damages.

8-3 BUSINESS TORTS

In this section, we look at several intentional torts that occur almost exclusively in a commercial setting: interference with a contract, interference with a prospective advantage, and Lanham Act violations. Note that several business torts are discussed elsewhere in the book:

- Violations of the rights to privacy and publicity are examined in Chapter 10 on internet law and privacy.
- Patents, copyrights, and trademarks are discussed in Chapter 41 on intellectual property.
- False advertising and other consumer issues are considered more broadly in Chapter 39 on consumer law.

8-3a Tortious Interference with Business Relations

Competition is the essence of business. Successful corporations compete aggressively, and the law permits and expects them to. But there are times when healthy competition becomes illegal interference. This is called *tortious interference with business relations*. It can take one of two closely related forms—interference with a contract or interference with a prospective advantage.

8-3b Tortious Interference with a Contract

Tortious interference with a contract exists if the plaintiff can establish the following four elements:

- There was a contract between the plaintiff and a third party;
- The defendant knew of the contract;

Tortious interference with a contract
An intentional tort in which the defendant improperly induced a third party to breach a contract with the plaintiff

- The defendant improperly *induced* the third party to breach the contract or made performance of the contract impossible; and
- There was injury to the plaintiff.

Because businesses routinely compete for customers, employees, and market share, it is not always easy to identify tortious interference. There is nothing wrong with two companies bidding against each other to buy a parcel of land, and nothing wrong with one corporation doing everything possible to convince the seller to ignore all competitors. But once a company has signed a contract to buy the land, it is improper to induce the seller to break the deal. The most commonly disputed issues in these cases concern elements one and three: Was there a contract between the plaintiff and another party? Did the defendant improperly induce a party to breach it? Defendants will try to show that the plaintiff had no contract.

A defendant may also rely on the defense of **justification**, that is, a claim that special circumstances made its conduct fair. To establish justification, a defendant must show that:

- It was acting to protect an existing economic interest, such as its own contract with the third party;
- It was acting in the public interest, for example, by reporting to a government agency that a corporation was overbilling for government services; or
- The existing contract could be terminated at will by either party, meaning that although the plaintiff had a contract, the plaintiff had no long-term assurances because the other side could end it at any time.

Cases of contract interference can result in enormous verdicts. Pennzoil made an unsolicited bid to buy 20 percent of Getty Oil at $100 per share. This offer was too low to satisfy the Getty board of directors, but it got the parties talking. Negotiations continued, the price moved up to $112.50 a share, and finally the Getty board voted to approve the deal. A press release announced an agreement in principle between Pennzoil and Getty.

Before the ink on the press release was dry, Texaco appeared and offered Getty stockholders $128 per share for the entire company. Getty turned its attention to Texaco, leaving

EXHIBIT 8.2

The $10 *billion* question. Texaco offered to pay $125 per share for Getty stock. The key issue was this: When Texaco made the offer, did a contract exist between Pennzoil and Getty?

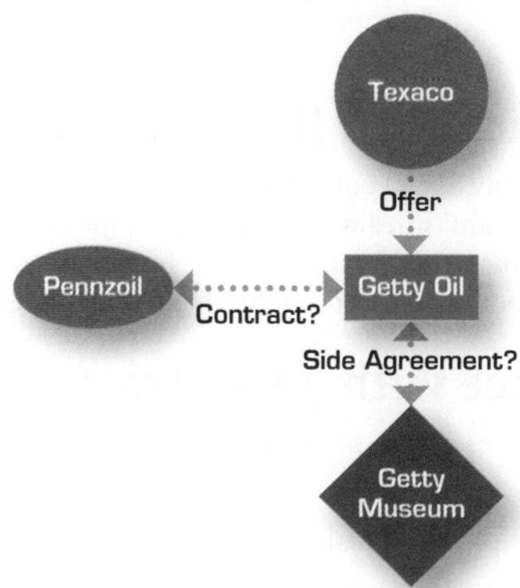

Pennzoil the jilted lover. This lover, though, decided to sue. In Texas state court, Pennzoil claimed that Texaco had maliciously interfered with a Pennzoil–Getty contract, costing Pennzoil vast amounts of money.

Texaco argued that it had acted in good faith, and that there was no binding contract between the other two. But the jury bought Pennzoil's argument, and they bought it big: $7.53 billion in actual damages, plus $3 billion more in punitive damages. After an appeal, the companies settled: Texaco agreed to pay Pennzoil $3 billion—and then filed for bankruptcy.

8-3c Tortious Interference with a Prospective Advantage

Tortious interference with a prospective advantage is an awkward name for a tort that is simply a variation on interference with a contract. The difference is that, for this tort, there need be no contract; the plaintiff is claiming outside interference with an expected economic relationship. Obviously, the plaintiff must show more than just the hope of a profit. **A plaintiff who has a definite and reasonable expectation of obtaining an economic advantage may sue a corporation that maliciously interferes and prevents the relationship from developing.**

Tortious interference with a prospective advantage
Malicious interference with a developing economic relationship

The defense of justification, discussed earlier, applies here as well. A typical example of justification is that the defendant is simply competing for the same business that the plaintiff seeks. There is nothing wrong with that.

To demonstrate interference with a prospective advantage, most courts require a plaintiff to show that the defendant's conduct was independently unlawful. Suppose Pink manufactures valves used in heart surgery. Pink is about to sign a deal for Rabbit to distribute the products. Zebra then says to Pink, "I want that deal. If you sign with Rabbit, I'll spread false rumors that the valves are unreliable." Pink gives in and signs a contract with Zebra. Zebra has committed interference with a prospective advantage because slander is independently illegal.[11]

The ice cream fight that follows demonstrates why plaintiffs often file but seldom win these cases.

Carvel v. Noonan

3 N.Y.3d 182
New York Court of Appeals, 2004

Facts: For decades, Carvel sold its ice cream only through franchised stores. However, a decline in revenues caused the company to begin selling its product in supermarkets. That effort expanded quickly, but many of the franchised stores (franchisees) went out of business. Franchisees filed suit, claiming tortious interference with a prospective advantage. In particular, the plaintiffs argued that Carvel undersold them in supermarkets and issued coupons only redeemable there. The case reached New York's highest court.

Issue: ***Had Carvel committed tortious interference with a prospective advantage?***

Excerpts from Justice Smith's Decision: The franchisees' tort claim is that Carvel unlawfully interfered with the relationships between the franchisees and their customers. The franchisees do not claim that the customers had binding contracts that Carvel induced them to breach; they allege only that, by implementing its supermarket program, Carvel induced the customers not to buy Carvel

[11] For a more detailed explanation, see Wal-Mart Stores, Inc. v. Sturges, 52 S.W.3d 711 (Tex. 2001).

products from the franchisees. The juries have found that Carvel did so induce customers, and the question for us is whether that inducement was tortious interference under New York law.

We have recognized that inducing breach of a binding agreement and interfering with a nonbinding "economic relation" can both be torts, but that the elements of the two torts are not the same. Where there has been no breach of an existing contract, but only interference with prospective contract rights, however, plaintiff must show more culpable conduct on the part of the defendant. The implication is that, as a general rule, the defendant's conduct must amount to a crime or an independent tort.

The franchisees claim that Carvel did use wrongful "economic pressure" but that argument is ill-founded for two independent reasons. First, it is ill-founded because the economic pressure that must be shown is not, as the franchisees assume, pressure on the franchisees, but on the franchisees' customers. Conduct constituting tortious interference with business relations is, by definition, conduct directed not at the plaintiff itself, but at the party with which the plaintiff has or seeks to have a relationship.

Here, all Carvel did to the franchisees' customers was to make Carvel goods available in supermarkets at attractive prices; this was not "pressure" on these third parties but legitimate "persuasion," and thus tortious interference with economic relations was not established.

The franchisees' argument is also ill-founded because the Carvel activities they complain of do not amount to the sort of extreme and unfair "economic pressure" that might be "wrongful." The crux of the franchisees' complaint is that Carvel distributed its products through competitive channels, to an extent and in a way that was inconsistent with the franchisor–franchisee relationship. But the relationship between franchisors and franchisees is a complex one; while cooperative, it does not preclude all competition; and the extent to which competition is allowed should be determined by the contracts between the parties, not by courts or juries seeking after the fact to devise a code of conduct.

Apart from attacking the supermarket program in general as excessively and destructively competitive, the franchisees also attack the coupon-redemption element of that program as excessive "economic pressure." The essence of the coupon program was to give customers who used coupons a better price when they shopped in supermarkets. The mere institution of a coupon program was not "economic pressure" rising to the level of "wrongful" or "culpable" conduct.

Carvel's conduct was not tortious interference with a prospective advantage.

8-3d The Lanham Act

The Lanham Act provides broad protection against false statements intended to hurt another business. In order to win a case, a plaintiff must prove three things:

- That the defendants made false or misleading fact statements about the plaintiff's business. This could be a false comparative ad, showing the plaintiff's product to be worse than it is, or it could be a misleading ad, which, though literally accurate, is misleading about the defendant's own product.
- That the defendants used the statements in commercial advertising or promotion. In order to protect First Amendment rights of free speech, particularly political and social commentary, this act covers only commercial speech. A radio ad for beer could violate the Lanham Act; however, a radio ad urging that smoking be abolished in public places is not a commercial statement and cannot violate the act.
- That statements created the likelihood of harm to the plaintiff.[12]

"Knock It Off brand food supplement will help you lose weight and gain muscle faster than any competing supplement," shrieks the television commercial, offering an independent

[12] 18U.S.C §2511.

study as proof. However, a competitor sues and demonstrates that during the study, users of Knock It Off received free health club memberships and low-fat gourmet meals, distorting the results. Knock It Off has violated the Lanham Act. The court will order the company to knock it off and stop showing the commercial, and also to pay damages to the injured competitor.

CHAPTER CONCLUSION

This chapter has been a potpourri of misdeeds, a bubbling cauldron of conduct best avoided. Although tortious acts and their consequences are diverse, two generalities apply. First, the boundaries of intentional torts are imprecise, the outcome of a particular case depending to a considerable extent upon the fact finder who analyzes it. Second, thoughtful executives and careful citizens, aware of the shifting standards and potentially vast liability, will strive to ensure that their conduct never provides that fact finder an opportunity to give judgment.

EXAM REVIEW

1. **TORT** A tort is a violation of a duty imposed by the civil law.

EXAMStrategy

Question: Keith is driving while intoxicated. He swerves into the wrong lane and causes an accident, seriously injuring Caroline. Which statement is true?

(a) Caroline could sue Keith, who might be found guilty in her suit.

(b) Caroline and the state could start separate criminal cases against Keith.

(c) Caroline could sue Keith, and the state could prosecute Keith for drunk driving.

(d) The state could sue Keith but only with Caroline's consent.

(e) The state could prosecute Keith and sue him at the same time for drunk driving.

Strategy: What party prosecutes a criminal case? The government does, not the injured party. What is the result in a criminal case? Guilt or innocence. What about a tort lawsuit? The injured party brings a tort suit. The defendant may be found liable but never guilty. (See the "Result" at the end of this Exam Review section.)

2. **DEFAMATION** Defamation involves a defamatory statement that is false, uttered to a third person, and causes an injury. Opinion and privilege are valid defenses.

EXAMStrategy

Question: Benzaquin had a radio talk show. On the program, he complained about an incident in which state trooper Fleming had stopped his car, apparently for lack of a proper license plate and safety sticker. Benzaquin explained that the license plate had been stolen and the sticker had fallen onto the dashboard, but Fleming refused to let him drive away. Benzaquin and two young grandsons had to find other transportation. On the show, Benzaquin angrily recounted the incident, and then described Fleming and troopers generally: "we're not paying them to be dictators and Nazis"; "this man is an absolute barbarian, a lunkhead, a meathead." Fleming sued Benzaquin for defamation. Comment.

Strategy: Review the elements of defamation. Can these statements be proven true or false? If not, what is the result? Look at the defenses. Does one apply? (See the "Result" at the end of this Exam Review section.)

3. **MALICE** Public personalities can win a defamation suit only by proving actual malice.

4. **FALSE IMPRISONMENT** False imprisonment is the intentional restraint of another person without reasonable cause and without consent.

5. **EMOTIONAL DISTRESS** The intentional infliction of emotional distress involves extreme and outrageous conduct that causes serious emotional harm.

6. **BATTERY** Battery is an intentional touching of another person in a way that is unwanted or offensive. Assault involves an act that makes the plaintiff fear an imminent battery.

EXAMStrategy

Question: Caudle worked at Betts Lincoln-Mercury dealer. During an office party, many of the employees, including president Betts, were playing with an electric auto condenser, which gave a slight shock when touched. Some employees played catch with it. Betts shocked Caudle on the back of his neck and chased him around. The shock later caused Caudle to suffer headaches, pass out, feel numbness, and eventually to require nerve surgery. He sued Betts for battery. Betts defended by saying that it was all horseplay and that he had intended no harm. Please rule.

Strategy: Betts argues he intended no harm. Is intent to harm an element? (See the "Result" at the end of this Exam Review section.)

7. **DAMAGES** Compensatory damages are the normal remedy in a tort case. In unusual cases, the court may award punitive damages, not to compensate the plaintiff but to punish the defendant.

8. **TORTIOUS INTERFERENCE** Tortious interference with business relations involves the defendant harming an existing contract or a prospective relationship that has a definite expectation of success.

9. **LANHAM ACT** The Lanham Act prohibits false statements in commercial advertising or promotion.

RESULT

1. Result: Choice (a) is wrong because a defendant cannot be found guilty in a civil suit. (b) is wrong because a private party has no power to prosecute a criminal case. (c) is correct. (d) is wrong because the state will prosecute Keith, not sue him. (e) is wrong for the same reason.

2. Result: The court ruled in favor of Benzaquin because a reasonable person would understand the words to be opinion and ridicule. They are not statements of fact because most of them could not be proven true or false. A statement like "dictators and Nazis" is not taken literally by anyone.[13]

6. Result: The court held that it was irrelevant that Betts had shown no malice toward Caudle nor intended to hurt him. Betts *intended the physical contact* with Caudle, and even though he could not foresee everything that would happen, he is liable for all consequences of his intended physical action.[14]

MULTIPLE-CHOICE QUESTIONS

1. Jane writes an article for a newspaper reporting that Ann was arrested for stealing a car. The story is entirely false. Ann is not a public figure. Which of the following torts has Jane committed?
   (a) Ordinary slander
   (b) Slander per se
   (c) Libel
   (d) None of these
2. Refer to question 1. If Ann decides to sue, she ______________ have to show evidence that she suffered an injury. If she ultimately wins her case, a jury ______________ have the option to award punitive damages.
   (a) will; will
   (b) will; will not
   (c) will not; will
   (d) will not; will not
3. Sam sneaks up on Tom, hits him with a baseball bat, and knocks him unconscious. Tom never saw Sam coming. He wakes up with a horrible headache. Which of the following torts has Sam committed?
   (a) Assault
   (b) Battery
   (c) Both A and B
   (d) None of these
4. Imagine a case in which a jury awards compensatory damages of $1 million. In most cases, a jury would rarely be allowed to award more than ______________ in punitive damages.
   (a) $1 million
   (b) $3 million
   (c) $9 million
   (d) $10 million
   (e) $25 million

[13]Fleming v. Benzaquin, 390 Mass. 175, 454 N.E.2d 95 (1983).
[14]Caudle v. Betts, 512 So.2d 389 (La. 1987).

5. Al runs a red light and hits Carol's car. She later sues, claiming the following losses:
   I. $10,000—car repairs
   II. $10,000—medical expenses
   III. $10,000—lost wages (she could not work for two months after the accident)
   IV. $10,000—pain and suffering

   If the jury believes all of Carol's evidence and she wins her case, how much will she receive in *compensatory* damages?
   (a) $40,000
   (b) $30,000
   (c) $20,000
   (d) $10,000
   (e) $0

CASE QUESTIONS

1. You are a vice-president in charge of personnel at a large manufacturing company. In-house detectives inform you that Gates, an employee, was seen stealing valuable computer equipment. Gates denies the theft, but you believe the detectives and fire him. The detectives suggest that you post notices around the company, informing all employees what happened to Gates and why because it will discourage others from stealing. While you are considering that, a phone call from another company's personnel officer asks for a recommendation for Gates. Should you post the notices? What should you say to the other officer?

2. Tata Consultancy of Bombay, India, is an international computer consulting firm. It spends considerable time and effort recruiting the best personnel from India's leading technical schools. Tata employees sign an initial three-year employment commitment, often work overseas, and agree to work for a specified additional time when they return to India. Desai worked for Tata, but then he quit and formed a competing company, which he called Syntel. His new company contacted Tata employees by phone, offering higher salaries, bonuses, and assistance in obtaining permanent resident visas in the United States if they would come work for Syntel. At least 16 former Tata employees left their jobs without completing their contractual obligations and went to work for Syntel. Tata sued. What did it claim, and what should be the result?

3. Pacific Express began operating as an airline in 1982. It had routes connecting western cities with Los Angeles and San Francisco, and, by the summer of 1983, it was beginning to show a profit. In 1983, United Airlines tried to enter into a cooperative arrangement with Pacific in which United would provide Pacific with passengers for some routes so that United could concentrate on its longer routes. Negotiations failed. Later that year, United expanded its routes to include cities that only Pacific had served. United also increased its service to cities in which the two airlines were already competing. By early 1984, Pacific Express was unable to compete and sought protection under bankruptcy laws. It also sued United, claiming interference with a prospective advantage. United moved for summary judgment. Comment.

4. Lindsay had a limp. As she exited a Marshall's store and walked to her car, a store security guard asked her what was wrong. She said had been in a car accident and showed the security guard her handicapped parking permit. The security guard responded, "Hah man, she is all 'f*****-up.'" Lindsay cried all night and suffered damage to her self-esteem. She sued for IIED. What result?

5. Andrew Greene sued Paramount Pictures for defamation arising out of the film "The Wolf of Wall Street." Although the film did not use his name, Greene alleged that the fictitious toupee-wearing character Nicky "Rugrat" Koskoff was based on him. The film portrayed Rugrat as a "criminal, drug user, degenerate, depraved, and devoid of any morality or ethics." What would Greene need to prove to be successful in his claim?

DISCUSSION QUESTIONS

1. The Supreme Court limits punitive damages in most cases to nine times the compensatory damages awarded in the same case. Is this a sensible guideline? If not, should it be higher or lower?

2. You have most likely heard of the *Liebeck v. McDonald's* case. Liebeck spilled hot McDonald's coffee in her lap and suffered third-degree burns. At trial, evidence showed that her cup of coffee was brewed at 190 degrees, and that, more typically, a restaurant's "hot coffee" is in the range of 140 to 160 degrees.

   A jury awarded Liebeck $160,000 in compensatory damages and $2.7 million in punitive damages. The judge reduced the punitive award to $480,000, or three times the compensatory award.

   Comment on the case and whether the result was reasonable.

3. With a national debt in the trillions, people are desensitized to "mere" billions. Stop for a moment and consider $1 billion. If you had that sum, invested it conservatively, and got a 5 percent return, you could spend roughly $1 million *a week* for the rest of your life *without reducing your principal.*

   This chapter described three lawsuits with jackpot punitive damage awards. The jury award was $10 billion in *Texaco v. Pennzoil*, $5 billion in the *Exxon Valdez* case, and $3 billion in *Boeken v. Philip Morris*. Is there any point at which the raw number of dollars awarded is just too large? Was the original jury award excessive in any of these cases? If so, which one(s)?

4. Many retailers have policies that instruct employees *not* to attempt to stop shoplifters. Some store owners fear false imprisonment lawsuits and possible injuries to workers more than losses related to stolen merchandise. Are these "don't be a hero" policies reasonable? Would you put one in place if you owned a retail store?

5. The Supreme Court has defined public figures as those who have "voluntarily exposed themselves to increased risk of injury by assuming an influential role in ordering society." When deciding whether someone is a public figure, courts look at whether this person has received press coverage, sought the public spotlight, and has the opportunity to publicly rebut the accusations. Some have argued that social media makes anyone with a public Facebook profile or a certain number of Twitter followers a public figure. Do you agree? Should the Court revisit the definition of "public figure" in light of social media?

9

CHAPTER

NEGLIGENCE, STRICT LIABILITY, AND PRODUCT LIABILITY

The story you are about to read is true; not even the names have been changed. The participants were the plaintiff and defendant in a tort case. Do not try this at home.

Connie was very depressed. She felt so "overburdened" that she decided to end her life by locking herself inside the trunk of her 1973 Ford LTD.

Fortunately, Connie decided against committing suicide. Unfortunately, her decision occurred after she had already closed the trunk. The LTD did not have an internal release latch or other emergency opening mechanism. And these were the days before cell phones.

Unfortunately, her decision occurred after she had already closed the trunk.

Result? Connie was trapped in her trunk for *nine* days awaiting rescue.

This awful episode caused Connie serious psychological and physical injuries. She sued Ford for damages under negligence and strict liability. According to Connie, Ford was negligent because it had a duty to warn her that there was no latch; and the missing latch was a design defect for which Ford should pay.[1]

But whose fault was it? Was Ford's design defective? Was the car unreasonably dangerous? Or was Connie just unreasonable?

These are all practical questions and moral ones, as well. They are also typical issues in the law of negligence, strict liability, and product liability. In these contentious areas, courts continually face one question: *When someone is injured, who is responsible?*

---

[1]Based on Daniell v. Ford Motor Co., 581 F. Supp. 728 (D. Ct. N.M. 1984).

9-1 NEGLIGENCE

We might call negligence the "unintentional" tort because it concerns harm that arises by accident. Should a court impose liability?

Things go wrong all the time, and people are hurt in large ways and small. Society needs a means of analyzing negligence cases consistently and fairly. We cannot have each court that hears such a lawsuit extend or limit liability based on an emotional response to the facts. One of America's greatest judges, Benjamin Cardozo, offered an analysis more than 85 years ago. In a case called *Palsgraf v. Long Island Railroad*, he made a decision that still influences negligence thinking today.

Landmark Case

Palsgraf v. Long Island Railroad

248 N.Y. 339
Court of Appeals of New York, 1928

Facts: Helen Palsgraf was waiting on a railroad platform. As a train began to leave the station, a man carrying a package ran to catch it. He jumped aboard but looked unsteady, so a guard on the car reached out to help him as another guard, on the platform, pushed from behind. The man dropped the package, which struck the tracks and exploded—because it was packed with fireworks. The shock knocked over some heavy scales at the far end of the platform, and one of them struck Palsgraf, who was injured as a result. She sued the railroad.

Issue: ***Was the railroad liable for Palsgraf's injuries?***

Excerpts from Judge Cardozo's Decision: The conduct of the defendant's guard was not a wrong in its relation to the plaintiff, standing far away. Relatively to her, it was not negligence at all. Nothing in the situation gave notice that the falling package had in it the potency of peril to persons thus removed. Negligence is not actionable unless it involves the invasion of a legally protected interest, the violation of a right. Negligence is the absence of care, according to the circumstances.

If no hazard was apparent to the eye of ordinary vigilance, an act innocent and harmless, at least to outward seeming, with reference to her, did not take to itself the quality of a tort because it happened to be a wrong with reference to someone else. In every instance, before negligence can be predicated of a given act, back of the act must be sought and found a duty to the individual complaining.

What the plaintiff must show is "a wrong" to herself and not merely a wrong to someone else. We are told that one who drives at reckless speed through a crowded city street is guilty of a negligent act because the eye of vigilance perceives the risk of damage. The risk reasonably to be perceived defines the duty to be obeyed.

Here, by concession, there was nothing in the situation to suggest to the most cautious mind that the parcel wrapped in newspaper would spread wreckage through the station.

The law of causation, remote or proximate, is thus foreign to the case before us. If there is no tort to be redressed, there is no occasion to consider what damage might be recovered if there were a finding of a tort. The consequences to be followed must first be rooted in a wrong.

Judge Cardozo ruled that the guard's conduct might have been a wrong as to the passenger, but not as to Ms. Palsgraf, standing far away. Her negligence case failed. "Proof of negligence in the air, so to speak, will not do," declared the judge. Courts are still guided by Judge Cardozo's ruling.

To win a negligence case, a plaintiff must prove five elements. Much of the remainder of the chapter will examine them in detail. They are:

- ***Duty of Due Care.*** The defendant had a legal responsibility *to the plaintiff.* This is the point from the *Palsgraf* case.
- ***Breach.*** The defendant breached her duty of care or failed to meet her legal obligations.
- ***Factual Cause.*** The defendant's conduct actually caused the injury.
- ***Proximate Cause.*** It was *foreseeable* that conduct like the defendant's might cause *this type of harm.*
- ***Damages.*** The plaintiff has actually been hurt or has actually suffered a measureable loss.

To win a case, a plaintiff must prove all the elements listed previously. If a defendant eliminates only one item on the list, there is no liability.

9-1a Duty of Due Care

Each of us has a duty to behave as a reasonable person would under the circumstances. If you are driving a car, you have a duty to all the other people near you to drive like a reasonable person. If you drive while drunk, or send text messages while behind the wheel, then you fail to live up to your duty of care.

But how *far* does your duty extend? Most courts accept Cardozo's viewpoint in the *Palsgraf* case. Judges draw an imaginary line around the defendant and say that she owes a duty to the people within the circle, but not to those outside it. The test is generally "foreseeability." If the defendant could have foreseen injury to a particular person, she has a duty to him. Suppose that one of your friends posts a YouTube video of you texting behind the wheel and her father is so upset from watching it that he falls down the stairs. You would not be liable for the father's fall because it was not foreseeable that he would be harmed by your texting.

Let us apply these principles to a case involving a fraternity party.

Hernandez v. Arizona Board of Regents

177 Ariz. 244
Arizona Supreme Court, 1994

Facts: At the University of Arizona, the Epsilon Epsilon chapter of Delta Tau Delta fraternity gave a welcoming party for new members. The fraternity's officers knew that the majority of its members were under the legal drinking age, but they permitted everyone to consume alcohol. John Rayner, who was under 21 years of age, left the party. He drove negligently and caused a collision with an auto driven by Ruben Hernandez. At the time of the accident, Rayner's blood alcohol level was 0.15, exceeding the legal limit. The crash left Hernandez blind and paralyzed.

Hernandez sued Rayner, who settled the case based on the amount of his insurance coverage. The victim also sued the fraternity, its officers and national organization, all fraternity members who contributed money to buy alcohol, the university, and others. The trial court granted summary judgment for all defendants and the court of appeals affirmed. Hernandez appealed to the Arizona Supreme Court.

Issue: ***Did the fraternity and the other defendants have a duty of due care to Hernandez?***

Excerpts from Justice Feldman's Decision: Before 1983, this court arguably recognized the common-law rule of non-liability for tavern owners and, presumably, for social hosts. Traditional authority held that when "an able-bodied man" caused harm because of his intoxication, the act from which liability arose was the consuming not the furnishing of alcohol.

However, the common law also provides that:

One who supplies [a thing] for the use of another whom the supplier knows or has reason to know to be likely because of his youth, inexperience, or otherwise to use it in a manner involving unreasonable risk of physical harm to himself and others is subject to liability for physical harm resulting to them.

We perceive little difference in principle between liability for giving a car to an intoxicated youth and liability for giving drinks to a youth with a car. A growing number of cases have recognized that one of the very hazards that makes it negligent to furnish liquor to a minor is the foreseeable prospect that the [youthful] patron will become drunk and injure himself or others. Accordingly, modern authority has increasingly recognized that one who furnishes liquor to a minor breaches a common-law duty owed to innocent third parties who may be injured.

Furnishing alcohol to underaged drinkers violates numerous statutes. The conduct in question violates well-established common-law principles that recognize a duty to avoid furnishing dangerous items to those known to have diminished capacity to use them safely. We join the majority of other states and conclude that as to Plaintiffs and the public in general, Defendants had a duty of care to avoid furnishing alcohol to underage consumers.

Arizona courts, therefore, will entertain an action for damages against [one] who negligently furnishes alcohol to those under the legal drinking age when that act is a cause of injury to a third person. [Reversed and remanded.]

In several circumstances, people have special duties to others. Three of them are outlined here.

Special Duty: Landowners

The common law applies special rules to a landowner for injuries occurring on her property. In most states, the owner's duty depends on the type of person injured.

Lowest Liability: Trespassing Adults. A **trespasser** is anyone on the property without consent. A landowner is liable to a trespasser only for intentionally injuring him or for some other gross misconduct. The landowner has no liability to a trespasser for mere negligence. Jake is not liable if a vagrant wanders onto his land and is burned by defective electrical wires.

Trespasser
A person on another's property without consent

Mid-level Liability: Trespassing Children. The law makes exceptions when the trespassers are **children**. If there is some human-made thing on the land *that may be reasonably expected to attract children*, the landowner is probably liable for any harm. Daphne lives next door to a day-care center and builds a treehouse on her property. Unless she has fenced off the dangerous area, she is probably liable if a small child wanders onto her property and injures himself when he falls from the rope ladder to the treehouse.

Higher Liability: Licensee. A **licensee** is anyone on the land for her own purposes but with the owner's permission. A social guest is a typical licensee. A licensee is entitled to a warning of hidden dangers that the owner knows about. If Juliet invites Romeo for a late supper on the balcony and fails to mention that the wooden railing is rotted, she is liable when her hero plunges to the courtyard.

Licensee
A person on another's land for her own purposes but with the owner's permission

But Juliet is liable only for injuries caused by *hidden* dangers—she has no duty to warn guests of obvious dangers. She need not say, "Romeo, oh Romeo, don't place thy hand in the toaster, Romeo."

Highest Liability: Invitee. An **invitee** is someone who has a right to be on the property because it is a public place or a business open to the public. The owner has a duty of reasonable care to an invitee. Perry is an invitee when he goes to the town beach.

Invitee
A person who has a right to enter another's property because it is a public place or a business open to the public

If riptides have existed for years and the town fails to post a warning, it is liable if Perry drowns. Perry is also an invitee when he goes to Dana's coffee shop. Dana is liable if she ignores spilled coffee that causes Perry to slip.

With social guests, you must have *actual knowledge* of some specific hidden danger to be liable. Not so with invitees. You are liable even if you had *no idea* that something on your property posed a hidden danger. Therefore, if you own a business, you must conduct inspections of your property on a regular basis to make sure that nothing is becoming dangerous.

However, you generally do not have an obligation to protect against the wrongdoing of a third person. When a gunman went on a shooting spree at Virginia Tech, students Erin Peterson and Julia Pryde were among the 32 killed. The victims' families sued the university for wrongful death, claiming that it should have warned its students that a killer was on the loose. The Virginia Supreme Court disagreed. It held that the university had no duty to warn its students about this third-party criminal act because it was not reasonably foreseeable that the gunman would continue on and kill others. At the time of the initial shootings, the university believed it was an isolated incident and that gunman had left the university grounds.[2]

Special Duty: Professionals

A person at work has a heightened duty of care. While on the job, she must act as a reasonable person *in her profession*. A taxi driver must drive as a reasonable taxi driver would. A heart surgeon must perform bypass surgery with the care of a trained specialist in that field.

Two medical cases illustrate the reasonable person standard. A doctor prescribes a powerful drug without asking his patient about other medicines she is currently taking. The patient suffers a serious drug reaction from the combined medications. The physician is liable for the harm. A reasonable doctor *always* checks current medicines before prescribing new ones.

On the other hand, assume that a patient dies on the operating table in an emergency room. The physician followed normal medical procedures at every step of the procedure and acted with reasonable speed. In fact, the man had a fatal stroke. The surgeon is not liable. A doctor must do a reasonable professional job, but she cannot guarantee a happy outcome.

9-1b Breach of Duty

The second element of a plaintiff's negligence case is **breach of duty**. If a legal duty of care exists, then a plaintiff must show that the defendant did not meet it. Did the defendant act as a reasonable person, or as a reasonable professional? Did he warn social guests of hidden dangers he knew to exist in her apartment?

Normally, a plaintiff proves this part of a negligence case by convincing a jury that they would not have behaved as the defendant did—indeed, that no reasonable person would.

Negligence Per Se

In certain areas of life, courts are not free to decide what a "reasonable" person would have done because the state legislature has made the decision for them. **When a legislature sets a minimum standard of care for a particular activity, in order to protect a certain group of people, and a violation of the statute injures a member of that group, the defendant has**

[2]Commonwealth of Virginia v. Peterson, 749 S.E.2d 307 (S. Ct. Va. 2013).

committed negligence per se. A plaintiff who can show negligence per se need not prove breach of duty.

In Minnesota, the state legislature became alarmed about children sniffing glue, which they could easily purchase in stores. The legislature passed a statute prohibiting the sale to a minor of any glue containing toluene or benzene. About one month later, 14-year-old Steven Zerby purchased Weldwood Contact Cement from the Coast-to-Coast Store in his hometown. The glue contained toluene. Steven inhaled the glue and died from injury to his central nervous system.

The store clerk had not realized that the glue was dangerous. Irrelevant: He was negligent per se because he violated the statute. Perhaps a reasonable person would have made the same error. Irrelevant. The legislature had passed the statute to protect children, the sale of the glue violated the law, and a child was injured. The store was automatically liable.

9-1c Causation

We have seen that a plaintiff must show that the defendant owed him a duty of care and that the defendant breached the duty. To win, the plaintiff must also show that the defendant's breach of duty *caused* the plaintiff harm. Courts look at two separate causation issues: Was the defendant's behavior the *factual cause* of the harm? Was it the *proximate cause?*

Factual Cause

If the defendant's breach led to the ultimate harm, it is the factual cause. Suppose that Dom's Brake Shop tells a customer his brakes are now working fine, even though Dom knows that is false. The customer drives out of the shop, cannot stop at a red light, and hits a bicyclist crossing the intersection. Dom is liable to the cyclist. Dom's unreasonable behavior was the factual cause of the harm. Think of it as a row of dominoes. The first domino (Dom's behavior) knocked over the next one (failing brakes) which toppled the last one (the cyclist's injury).

Suppose, alternatively, that just as the customer is exiting the repair shop, the cyclist hits a pothole and tumbles off her cycle. Dom has breached his duty to his customer, but he is not liable to the cyclist—she would have been hurt anyway. This is a row of dominoes that veers off to the side, leaving the last domino (the cyclist's injury) untouched. No factual causation.

Proximate Cause

For the defendant to be liable, the *type of harm* must have been reasonably *foreseeable*. In the example just discussed, Dom could easily foresee that bad brakes would cause an automobile accident. He need not have foreseen *exactly* what happened. He did not know there would be a cyclist nearby. What he could foresee was this *general type* of harm involving defective brakes. Because the accident that occurred was of the type he could foresee, he is liable.

By contrast, assume that the collision of car and bicycle produces a loud crash. Two blocks away, a pet pig, asleep on the window ledge of a twelfth-story apartment, is startled by the noise, awakens with a start, and plunges to the sidewalk, killing a veterinarian who was making a house call. If the vet's family sues Dom, should it win? Dom's negligence was the factual cause: It led to the collision, which startled the pig, which flattened the vet. Most courts would rule, though, that Dom is not liable. The type of harm is too bizarre. Dom could not reasonably foresee such an extraordinary chain of events, and it would be unfair to make him pay for it. See Exhibit 9.1. Another way of stating that Dom is not liable to the vet's family is by calling the falling pig a *superseding cause.* When one of the "dominoes" in the row is entirely unforeseeable, courts will call that event a superseding cause, letting the defendant off the hook.

EXHIBIT 9.1

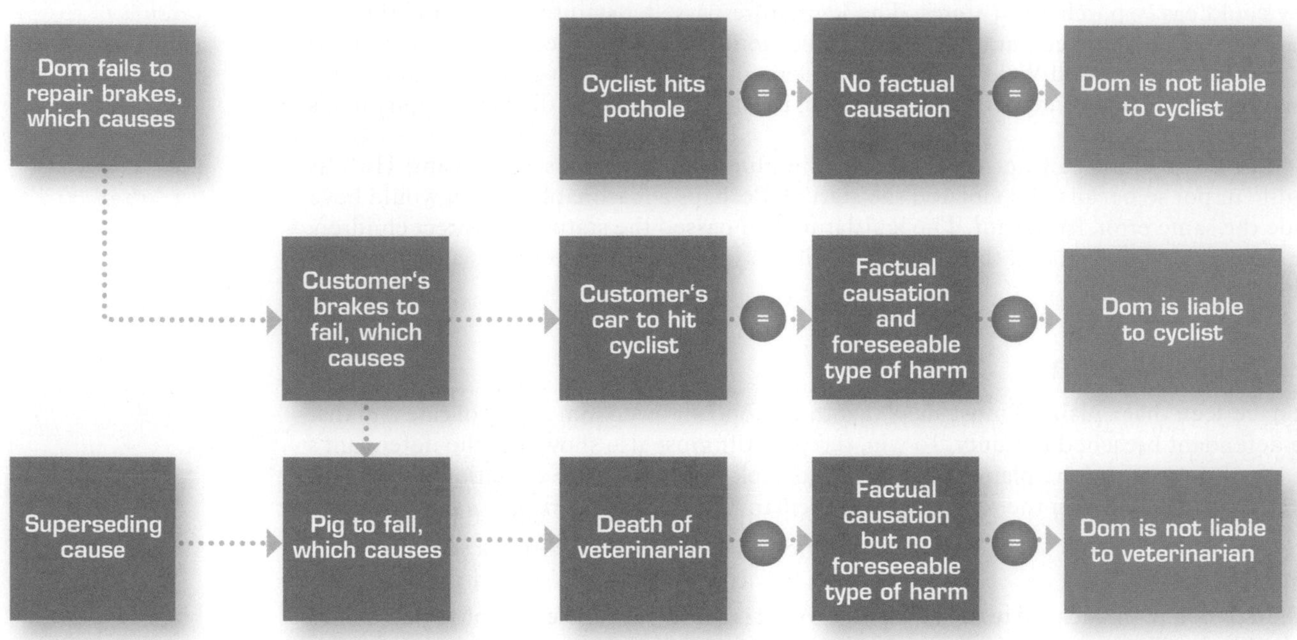

Every minute, about 19 people fall victim to the crime that occurred in the following case. Its perpetrators are hard to find, but its injuries are very real. Whom can we blame for identity theft?

You Be the Judge

Resnick v. AvMed, Inc.

693 F.3d 1317
United States Court of Appeals for the Eleventh Circuit, 2012

Facts: Juana Curry and William Moore, customers of AvMed insurance, took care to protect their private information. They destroyed mail that contained sensitive data and avoided uploading any such information online. Despite their care, they both became victims of identity theft. Unknown identity thieves opened bank accounts in Curry's name and changed her home address with the U.S. Postal Service. Someone opened an E*Trade account in Moore's name.

Curry and Moore blamed AvMed. About a year earlier, two unencrypted laptops containing the health information, Social Security numbers, names, addresses, and phone numbers of 1.2 million AvMed customers had been stolen from the company's offices.

The plaintiffs sued AvMed for negligence, claiming the company breached its duty to keep customer information secure and this breach caused their identity theft. Curry and Moore argued that if it had not been for AvMed's carelessness, they would not have been victims of identity theft. AvMed filed a motion to dismiss, arguing that the plaintiffs could not prove that the breach caused their injuries a year later.

You Be the Judge: *Was AvMed's data breach the proximate cause of the identity theft?*

Argument for Plaintiffs: Your honors, my clients are prudent people who guard their personal information. They are careful when sharing and buying online. Sometimes they even shred their mail. My clients shared their information with AvMed to secure insurance, and lo and behold, someone used that same information to open unauthorized bank accounts. The only way the thieves could have accessed the sensitive data was through AvMed's breach. Had it not been for AvMed's negligence, my clients would not have suffered identity theft.

Argument for AvMed: Your honors, with all due respect, welcome to the twenty-first century. Identity theft is a reality in all of our lives. The Federal Trade Commission estimates that each year this crime affects 9 million people—more than the population of New York City. And we are all at risk: Even the most careful person shares potentially sensitive information every day when she gives her credit card to a waiter, files her taxes online, or registers for a coupon. In this case, the only thing that the plaintiffs can show is that their information was on a stolen laptop and that they were victims of identity theft *a year later*. Was AvMed the only company that had the plaintiff's information? Seems unlikely. There is simply no way to prove a causal connection between the AvMed breach and the subsequent identity thefts.

EXAMStrategy

Question: Jenny asked a neighbor, Tom, to water her flowers while she was on vacation. For three days, Tom did this without incident, but on the fourth day, when he touched the outside faucet, he received a violent electric shock that shot him through the air, melted his sneakers and glasses, set his clothes on fire, and seriously burned him. Tom sued, claiming that Jenny had caused his injuries by negligently repairing a second-floor toilet. Water from the steady leak had flooded through the walls, soaking wires, and eventually causing the faucet to become electrified. You are Jenny's lawyer. Use one (and only one) element of negligence law to move for summary judgment.

Strategy: The four elements of negligence we have examined thus far are duty to this plaintiff, breach, factual cause, and proximate cause. Which element seems to be most helpful to Jenny's defense? Why?

Result: Jenny is entitled to summary judgment because this was not a foreseeable type of injury. Even if she did a bad job of fixing the toilet, she could not reasonably have anticipated that her poor workmanship could cause *electrical* injuries to anyone.[3]

Res Ipsa Loquitur

Normally, a plaintiff must prove factual cause and foreseeable type of harm in order to establish negligence. But in a few cases, a court may be willing to *infer* that the defendant caused the harm under the doctrine of ***res ipsa loquitur*** ("the thing speaks for itself"). Suppose a pedestrian is walking along a sidewalk when an air conditioning unit falls on his head from a third-story window. The defendant, who owns the third-story apartment, denies any wrongdoing, and it may be difficult or impossible for the plaintiff to prove why the air conditioner fell. In such cases, many courts will apply *res ipsa loquitur* and declare that **the facts imply that the defendant's negligence caused the accident**. If a court uses this doctrine, then the defendant must come forward with evidence establishing that it did *not* cause the harm.

Res ipsa loquitur
The facts *imply* that the defendant's negligence caused the accident.

Because *res ipsa loquitur* dramatically shifts the burden of proof from plaintiff to defendant, it applies only when (1) the defendant had exclusive control of the thing that caused the harm, (2) the harm normally would not have occurred without negligence, and (3) the plaintiff had no role in causing the harm. In the air conditioner example, most states would apply the doctrine and force the defendant to prove she did nothing wrong. The following case applies *res ipsa loquitur* to a prickly problem.

3Based on Hebert v. Enos, 60 Mass. App. Ct. 817 (Mass. Ct. App. 2004).

Brumberg v. Cipriani USA, Inc.

2013 NY Slip Op 06759
Supreme Court of New York, 2013

Facts: Cornell professor Joan Jacobs Brumberg attended a university fundraiser catered by Cipriani. During the event, she feasted on fancy appetizers. About 30 minutes later, she felt intense abdominal pain, which did not go away. Weeks later, her doctors removed a 1½-inch piece of wood from her digestive tract. The shard caused internal injuries, which took two surgeries to repair.

Brumberg's physician believed that her injuries were the result of eating wood at Cornell's cocktail party. On that day, she had eaten little else and had experienced no pain until the event, where she ate many appetizers, including shrimp on wood skewers. The doctor supposed that the wood moved through her digestive system for 30 minutes before becoming caught and causing the pain. But when experts compared Brumberg's shard with the wood in Cipriani's toothpicks and skewers, they found that the two were not the same material, eliminating direct evidence of causation.

Brumberg sued Cipriani USA, Inc., for negligence. A lower court dismissed her case on a motion for summary judgment, concluding there was not enough proof that Cipriani caused Brumberg's injury. The professor appealed, relying on the doctrine of *res ipsa loquitur.*

Issue: ***Does* res ipsa loquitur *apply here?***

Excerpts from Judge Lahtinen's Decision: *Res ipsa loquitur* is neither a theory of liability nor a presumption of liability, but instead is simply a permitted inference—that the trier of fact may accept or reject—reflecting a commonsense application of the probative value of circumstantial evidence.

Criteria for *res ipsa loquitur* to apply are that (1) "the event must be of a kind which ordinarily does not occur in the absence of someone's negligence; (2) it must be caused by an agency or instrumentality within the exclusive control of the defendant; and (3) it must not have been due to any voluntary action or contribution on the part of the plaintiff."

The parties dispute the exclusive control element. Here, the event occurred at a banquet hall operated by Cipriani. Cipriani prepared and provided all of the food. Attendees were not permitted to bring food onto the premises. Individuals under Cipriani's control acted as captains, servers, and bartenders. Cipriani thus exclusively prepared, provided, and served the food.

Although the shard possibly could have been present when the ingredients were purchased from suppliers, it was not so small as to have been concealed and not visible upon careful preparation.

Defendants point to the fact that other attendees had access to the hors d'oeuvres as reflecting a lack of exclusive control. Cipriani's personnel were present in the room serving the food both butler style and at stations, thus reducing the likelihood of some third party placing the shard unseen in food. There is sufficient proof under these circumstances to find ample control by defendants for purposes of *res ipsa loquitur.*

Defendants' further contention that *res ipsa loquitur* is foreclosed by their allegation of contributory negligence by plaintiff in not seeing the shard or discerning it while chewing the food in which it was located is without merit.

Plaintiffs' set forth ample proof to avoid summary judgment.

9-1d Damages

Finally, a plaintiff must prove that he has been injured or that he has had some kind of measureable losses. In some cases, injury is obvious. For example, Ruben Hernandez suffered grievous harm when struck by the drunk driver. But in other cases, injury is unclear. **The plaintiff must persuade the court that he has suffered harm that is genuine, not speculative.**

Some cases raise tough questions. Among the most vexing are suits involving *future* harm. Exposure to toxins or trauma may lead to serious medical problems down the road—or it may not. A woman's knee is damaged in an auto accident, causing severe pain for two years. She is clearly entitled to compensation for her suffering. After two years, all pain may cease for a decade—or forever. Yet there is also a chance that in 15 or 20 years, the trauma will lead to painful arthritis. A court must decide today the full extent of present *and future* damages; the single recovery principle, discussed in Chapter 8, prevents a plaintiff from returning to court years later and demanding compensation for newly arisen ailments. The challenge to our courts is to weigh the possibilities and percentages of future suffering and decide whether to compensate a plaintiff for something that might never happen.

9-1e Defenses

Contributory and Comparative Negligence

Sixteen-year-old Michelle Wightman was out driving at night, with her friend Karrie Wieber in the passenger seat. They came to a railroad crossing where the mechanical arm had descended and warning bells were sounding. They had been sounding for a long time. A Conrail train had suffered mechanical problems and was stopped 200 feet from the crossing, where it had stalled for roughly an hour. Michelle and Karrie saw several cars ahead of them go around the barrier and cross the tracks. Michelle had to decide whether she would do the same.

Long before Michelle made her decision, the train's engineer had seen the heavy Saturday night traffic crossing the tracks and realized the danger. The conductor and brakeman also understood the peril, but rather than posting a flagman who could have stopped traffic when a train approached, they walked to the far end of their train to repair the mechanical problem. A police officer had come upon the scene, told his dispatcher to notify the train's parent company Conrail of the danger, and left.

... the mechanical arm had descended and warning bells were sounding. They had been sounding for a long time.

Michelle decided to cross the tracks. She slowly followed the cars ahead of her. Seconds later, both girls were dead. A freight train traveling at 60 miles per hour struck the car broadside, killing both girls instantly.

Michelle's mother sued Conrail for negligence. The company claimed that it was Michelle's foolish risk that led to her death. Who wins when both parties are partly responsible? It depends on whether the state uses a legal theory called contributory negligence. Under contributory negligence, if the plaintiff is even slightly negligent, she recovers nothing. If Michelle's death occurred in a contributory negligence state, and the jury considered her even minimally responsible, her estate would receive no money.

Critics attacked this rule as unreasonable. A plaintiff who was 1 percent negligent could not recover from a defendant who was 99 percent responsible. So most states threw out the contributory negligence rule, replacing it with comparative negligence. In a comparative negligence state, a plaintiff may generally recover even if she is partially responsible. The jury will be asked to assess the relative negligence of the two parties.

Michelle died in Ohio, which is a comparative negligence state. The jury concluded that reasonable compensatory damages were $1 million. It also concluded that Conrail was 60 percent responsible for the tragedy and Michelle 40 percent. See Exhibit 9.2. The girl's mother received $600,000 in compensatory damages.

Today, most, but not all, states have adopted some form of comparative negligence. Critics claim that this principle rewards a careless plaintiff. If Michelle had obeyed the law, she would still be alive. In response to this complaint, many comparative negligence states do *not* permit a plaintiff to recover anything if he was more than 50 percent responsible for his own injury.

In the *Conrail* case, the jury decided that the rail company was extraordinarily negligent. Expert witnesses testified that similar tragedies occurred every year around the nation and the company knew it. Conrail could easily have prevented the loss of life by posting a flagman on the road. The jury awarded the estate $25 million in punitive damages. The trial judge reduced the verdict by 40 percent to $15 million. The state supreme court affirmed the award.[4]

---

[4]Wightman v. Consolidated Rail Corporation, 715 N.E.2d 546 (1999).

EXHIBIT 9.2

Defendant's negligence injures plaintiff, who suffers $1 million in damages.

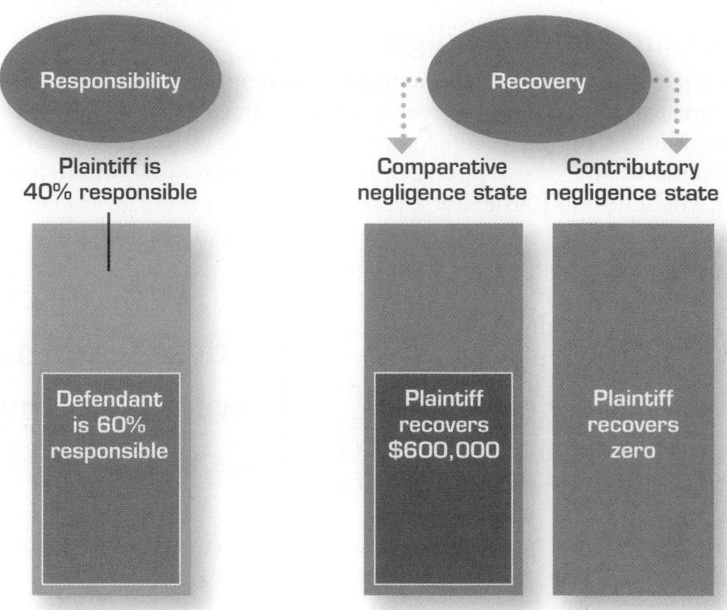

Assumption of Risk

Good Guys, a restaurant, holds an ice fishing contest on a frozen lake to raise money for accident victims. Margie grabs a can full of worms and strolls to the middle of the lake to try her luck, but slips on the ice and suffers a concussion. If she sues Good Guys, how will she fare? She will fall a second time. Wherever there is an obvious hazard, a special rule applies. **Assumption of risk: A person who voluntarily enters a situation that has an obvious danger cannot complain if she is injured.** Ice is slippery and we all know it. If you venture onto a frozen lake, any falls are your own tough luck.

Matt Sullivan/REUTERS

Do NFL players assume the risk of all on-field injuries?

However, the doctrine does not apply if someone is injured in a way that is not an inherent part of the dangerous activity. NFL players assume substantial risks each time they take the field, but some injuries fall outside the rule. In a game between the Jets and the Dolphins, a Jets assistant coach standing on the sideline tripped a Dolphins player during a punt return. The trip was not a "normal" part of a football game, and the "assumption of the risk" doctrine would not prevent the player from recovering damages if injured.

Ethics

Anyone who has watched an NFL game knows that football is a rough sport. But, did the NFL hide some of the sport's risks? In a negligence lawsuit, 4,500 football players with neurological injuries claimed that the NFL had decades of scientific evidence linking blows to the head to long-term brain damage, but it chose to bury these risks to make more money. A rougher sport makes for a better show—and more profit—the players argued. (The NFL makes approximately $10 billion in revenue per year.) Did the NFL owe a legal duty to the players or should the players just know better? What are the NFL's ethical duties to its players, if any?

The following case involves a lake, jet skis, and a great tragedy.

Truong v. Nguyen

67 Cal. Rptr.3d 675
California Court of Appeals, 2007

Facts: On a warm California day, there were about 30 personal watercraft (jet skis) operating on Coyote Lake. The weather was fair and visibility good. Anthony Nguyen and Rachael Truong went for a ride on Anthony's Polaris watercraft. Cu Van Nguyen and Chuong Nguyen (neither of whom were related to Anthony) were both riding a Yamaha Waverunner. Both jet skis permitted a driver and passenger, each seated. The two watercraft collided near the middle of the lake. Rachael was killed, and the others all injured.

Rachael's parents sued Anthony, Cu Van, and Chuong, alleging that negligent operation of their watercraft caused their daughter's death. The defendants moved for summary judgment, claiming that assumption of the risk applies to jet skiing. The parents appealed, arguing that jet skiing was not a sport and Rachael never assumed any risk.

Issue: ***Does assumption of the risk apply to jet skiing?***

Excerpts from Judge McAdams's Decision: In a sports context, [assumption of the risk] bars liability because the plaintiff is said to have assumed the particular risks inherent in a sport by choosing to participate. Thus, a court need not ask what risks a particular plaintiff subjectively knew of and chose to encounter, but instead must evaluate the fundamental nature of the sport and the defendant's role in or relationship to that sport.

In baseball, a batter is not supposed to carelessly throw the bat after getting a hit and starting to run to first base. However, assumption of risk recognizes that vigorous bat deployment is an integral part of the sport and a risk players assume when they choose to participate. A batter does not have a duty to another player to avoid carelessly throwing the bat after getting a hit.

Even when a participant's conduct violates a rule of the game and may subject the violator to internal sanctions prescribed by the sport itself, imposition of legal liability for such conduct might well alter fundamentally the nature of the sport by deterring participants from vigorously engaging in activity. Coparticipants' limited duty of care is to refrain from intentionally injuring one another or engaging in conduct that is so reckless as to be totally outside the range of the ordinary activity involved in the sport.

It appears that an activity falls within the meaning of 'sport' if the activity is done for enjoyment or thrill, requires physical exertion as well as elements of skill, and involves a challenge containing a potential risk of injury.

As a matter of common knowledge, jet skiing is an active sport involving physical skill and challenges that pose a significant risk of injury, particularly when it is done—as it often is—together with other jet skiers in order to add to the exhilaration of the sport by racing, jumping the wakes of the other jet skis or nearby boats, or in other respects making the sporting activity more challenging and entertaining. In response to the plaintiff's complaint that the trial court erroneously assumed that the litigants were contestants in some sort of consensual competition event and/or spectator sport, [we conclude] that the doctrine applies equally to competitive and noncompetitive but active sports.

Plaintiffs urge [that] Rachael was merely a passenger on the Polaris and was not actively involved in the sport. The record supports the conclusion that riding as a passenger on a personal watercraft [is participating in a sport], because it is done for enjoyment or thrill, requires physical exertion as well as elements of skill, and involves a challenge containing a potential risk of injury. The vessel is open to the elements, with no hull or cabin. It is designed for high performance, speed, and quick turning maneuvers. The thrill of riding the vessel is shared by both the operator and the passenger. Obstacles in the environment such as spraying water, wakes to be crossed, and other watercraft are part of the thrill of the sport, both for the operator and the passenger.

The summary judgment is *affirmed*.

9-2 STRICT LIABILITY AND PRODUCT LIABILITY

9-2a Strict Liability

Strict liability
A branch of tort law that imposes a much higher level of liability when harm results from ultrahazardous acts or defective products

Some activities are so naturally dangerous that the law places an especially high burden on anyone who engages in them. A corporation that produces toxic waste can foresee dire consequences from its business that a stationery store cannot. This higher burden is **strict liability**. There are two main areas of business that incur strict liability: *ultrahazardous activity* and *defective products*. Defective products are discussed in the following section on product liability.

Ultrahazardous Activity

Ultrahazardous activities include using harmful chemicals, operating explosives, keeping wild animals, bringing dangerous substances onto property, and a few similar activities where the danger to the general public is especially great. **A defendant engaging in an ultrahazardous activity is almost always liable for any harm that results.** Plaintiffs do not have to prove duty or breach or foreseeable harm. Recall the deliberately bizarre case we posed earlier of the pig falling from a window ledge and killing a veterinarian. Dom, the mechanic whose negligence caused the car crash, could not be liable for the veterinarian's death because the plunging pig was a superseding cause.

But now imagine that the pig is jolted off the window ledge by a company engaged in an ultrahazardous activity. Sam's Blasting Co. sets off a perfectly lawful blast to clear ground for a new building down the street. When the pig is startled and falls, the blasting company is liable. Even if Sam took extraordinary care, it will do him no good at trial. The "reasonable person" rule is irrelevant in a strict liability case.

Because "strict liability" translates into "defendant is liable," parties in tort cases often fight over whether the defendant was engaged in an ultrahazardous activity. If the court rules that the activity was ultrahazardous, the plaintiff is assured of winning. If the court rules that it was not ultrahazardous, the plaintiff must prove all elements of negligence.

The line is often hazy. A lawful fireworks display does not incur strict liability, but crop dusting does. Cutting timber is generally not abnormally dangerous, but hauling logs might be. The enormous diversity of business activities in our nation ensures continual disputes over this important principle.

New Jersey Department of Environmental Protection v. Alden Leeds, Inc.

153 N.J. 272
New Jersey Supreme Court, 1998

Facts: The Alden Leeds Company packages, stores, and ships swimming pool chemicals. The firm does most of its work at its facility in Kearns, New Jersey. At any given time, about 21 different hazardous chemicals are present.

The day before Easter, a fire of unknown origin broke out in "Building One" of the company's site, releasing chlorine gas and other potentially dangerous by-products into the air. There were no guards or other personnel on duty. The fire caused $9 million in damage to company property. Because of the potentially dangerous gas, the Department of Environmental Protection (DEP) closed the New Jersey Turnpike along with half a dozen other major highways, halted all commuter rail and train service in the area, and urged residents to stay indoors with windows closed. An unspecified number of residents went to local hospitals with respiratory problems.

Based on New Jersey's Air Pollution Control Act (APCA), the DEP imposed a civil fine on Alden Leeds for releasing the toxic chemicals. The appellate court reversed, finding that there was no evidence the company had caused the fire or the harm, and the case reached the state's high court.

Issue: ***Did the company cause the harm?***

Excerpts from Justice Coleman's Decision: In 1962, this Court adopted the proposition that "an ultrahazardous activity which introduces an unusual danger into the community should pay its own way in the event it actually causes damage to others." In 1983, the Court expressly recognized "that the law of liability has evolved so that a landowner is strictly liable to others for harm caused by toxic wastes that are stored on his property and flow onto the property of others." The Court explained "that those who use, or permit others to use, land for the conduct of abnormally dangerous activities are strictly liable for resultant damages." The same rationale applies to pollution that is released into the air from chemicals stored at a chemical facility.

An actor who chooses to store dangerous chemicals should be responsible for the release of those chemicals into the air. That Alden Leeds lawfully and properly stored chemicals does not alter that conclusion. The risks attendant to the storage of dangerous substances counsel in favor of precautions to prevent their release. Alden Leeds took no such precautions. On the day of the fire, there was no one stationed at the plant to alert the authorities as soon as a fire or other unforeseen calamity erupted. Nor was there any other early warning system in place. A burglar or smoke alarm sounded, but there was no response to that alarm. The law imposes a duty upon those who store hazardous substances to ensure that the substances on their property do not escape in a manner harmful to the public. Alden Leeds failed to meet that burden.

Although Alden Leeds was not found responsible for the fire, the company's facility caused a release of air pollutants. The required nexus is satisfied by the knowing storage of hazardous chemicals. Regardless of what started the fire, it was the knowing storage of chemicals by Alden Leeds that caused the release of air contaminants once the fire reached the chemicals.

[Affirmed that the APCA is a strict liability statute and that there must be a causal nexus between the defendant and the harm. Reversed that the storing of hazardous chemicals by Alden Leeds does not satisfy that nexus. The DEP does *not* have to prove that the chemical operator started the fire.]

EXAMStrategy

Question: Ahmed plans to transport a 25-foot boa constrictor from one zoo to another. The snake is locked in a special cage, approved by the American Zoo Society, in Ahmed's truck. Experts check the cage to be sure it is locked and entirely secure. Then Ahmed himself checks the cage. During the transport, his engine begins to fail. He pulls into the breakdown lane and sets up four flares, warning motorists of the stalled vehicle. Katy drives off the road and slams into Ahmed's truck. She is badly injured. Somehow the snake escapes and eats a champion show dog, worth $35,000. Katy and the dog's owner both sue Ahmed. What will be the result in each case?

Strategy: Ahmed's behavior seems reasonable throughout this incident. However, the two suits against him are governed by different rules: negligence in one case, strict liability in the other. Apply each rule to the correct case.

Result: The dog was killed by a dangerous snake. Transporting wild animals is an ultrahazardous activity, and Ahmed is strictly liable. His reasonable behavior will not save him. However, when he parked his truck in the breakdown lane, he did a reasonable job. Katy cannot prove that he breached his duty to her, and she loses.

9-2b Product Liability

So far in this chapter, we have discussed how two tort theories—negligence and strict liability—apply when someone's action or inaction harms another. But sometimes products, not people, cause harm. When an exploding cola bottle, a flammable pajama, or a toxic cookie injures, who pays? Someone who is injured by a defective product may have claims in both negligence and strict liability.

Negligence

In negligence cases concerning goods, plaintiffs typically raise one or more of these claims:

- **Negligent design.** The buyer claims that the product injured her because the manufacturer designed it poorly. For example, company engineers placed the Ford Pinto's fuel tank behind the axle, making the car more likely to explode in a rear-end collision. Negligence law requires a manufacturer to design a product free of *unreasonable* risks. The product does not have to be absolutely safe. An automobile that nearly guaranteed a driver's safety could be made, in theory, but it would be prohibitively expensive. Reasonable safety features must be built in, if they can be included at a tolerable cost.
- **Negligent manufacture.** The buyer claims that the design was adequate but the failure to inspect or some other careless conduct caused a dangerous product to leave the plant. Peter Vamos got sick after gulping his Diet Coke—only to discover that there were two AA batteries in the bottle. Because he was able to prove that the batteries were in the bottle when it left the plant, Vamos recovered from the bottler for his injuries.[5]
- **Failure to warn.** A manufacturer is liable for failing to warn the purchaser or users about the dangers of normal use and also foreseeable misuse. However, there is no duty to warn about obvious dangers, a point evidently lost on some manufacturers. A Batman costume came with this statement: "For play only: cape does not enable user to fly."

AP Images

Strict Liability for Defective Products

The other tort claim that an injured person can bring against the manufacturer or seller of a product is strict liability. Like negligence, strict liability is a burden created by the law rather than by the parties. And, as with all torts, strict liability concerns claims of physical harm. But there

[5]Vamos v. The Coca-Cola Bottling Co. of New York, Inc., 627 N.Y.S.2d 265 (1995).

is a key distinction between negligence and strict liability: in a negligence case, the injured buyer must demonstrate that the seller's conduct was unreasonable. Not so in strict liability.

In strict liability, the injured person need not prove that the defendant's conduct was unreasonable. The injured person must show only that the defendant manufactured or sold a product that was defective and that the defect caused harm. Almost all states permit such lawsuits, and most of them have adopted the following model:

1. One who sells any product in a defective condition unreasonably dangerous to the user or consumer or to his property is subject to liability for physical harm thereby caused to the ultimate user or consumer, or to his property, if:
   a. the seller is engaged in the business of selling such a product and
   b. it is expected to and does reach the user or consumer without substantial change in the condition in which it is sold.
2. The rule stated in Part (1) applies although:
   a. the seller has exercised all possible care in the preparation and sale of his product and
   b. the user or consumer has not bought the product from or entered into any contractual relation with the seller.[6]

These are the key terms in Part (1):

- **Defective condition unreasonably dangerous to the user.** The defendant is liable only if the product is defective when it leaves his hands. There must be something wrong with the goods. If they are reasonably safe and the buyer's mishandling of the goods causes the harm, there is no strict liability. If you attempt to open a soda bottle by knocking the cap against a counter and the glass shatters and cuts you, the manufacturer owes nothing. A carving knife can produce a lethal wound, but everyone knows that, and a sharp knife is not unreasonably dangerous. On the other hand, prescription drugs may harm in ways that neither a layperson nor a doctor would anticipate. The manufacturer *must provide adequate warnings* of any dangers that are not apparent.
- **In the business of selling.** The seller is liable only if she normally sells this kind of product. Suppose your roommate makes you a peanut butter sandwich and, while eating it, you cut your mouth on a sliver of glass that was in the jar. The peanut butter manufacturer faces strict liability, as does the grocery store where your roommate bought the goods. But your roommate is not strictly liable because he is not in the food business.
- **Reaches the user without substantial change.** Obviously, if your roommate put the glass in the peanut butter thinking it was funny, neither the manufacturer nor the store is liable.

And here are the important phrases in Part (2):

- **Has exercised all possible care.** This is the heart of strict liability, which makes it a potent claim for consumers. *It is no defense that the seller used reasonable care.* If the product is dangerously defective and injures the user, the seller is liable even if it took every precaution to design and manufacture the product safely. Suppose the peanut butter jar did in fact contain a glass sliver when it left the factory. The manufacturer proves that it uses extraordinary care in keeping foreign particles out of the jars and thoroughly inspects each container before it is shipped. The evidence is irrelevant. The manufacturer has shown that it was not *negligent* in packaging the food, but reasonable care is irrelevant in strict liability cases.

---

[6]Restatement (Second) of Torts §402A.

- **No contractual relation.** When two parties contract, they are in privity. Note that privity only exists between the user and the person from whom she actually bought the goods, but in strict liability cases, *privity is not required.* Suppose the manufacturer that made the peanut butter sold it to a distributor, which sold it to a wholesaler, which sold it to a grocery store, which sold it to your roommate. You may sue the manufacturer, distributor, wholesaler, and store, even though you had no privity with any of them.

As we have seen, an injured plaintiff may sue a manufacturer for both negligence and strict liability. Remember Connie from the chapter opener? Let's see how her story ended.

Daniell v. Ford

581 F. Supp. 728
U.S. District Court, New Mexico 1984

Facts: See the chapter opener. Connie Daniell argued that Ford was both (1) negligent because it did not warn her that there was no opening mechanism in the trunk and (2) strictly liable for this design defect. Ford sought summary judgment.

Issues: ***Was Ford negligent in failing to warn Connie of the missing latch? Was Ford strictly liable for a design defect?***

Excerpts from Judge Baldock's Decision: Under strict products liability or negligence, a manufacturer has a duty to consider only those risks of injury which are foreseeable. A risk is not foreseeable by a manufacturer where a product is used in a manner which could not reasonably be anticipated by the manufacturer and that use is the cause of the plaintiff's injury. The plaintiff's injury would not be foreseeable by the manufacturer.

The purposes of an automobile trunk are to transport, stow, and secure the automobile spare tire, luggage, and other goods and to protect those items from elements of the weather. The design features of an automobile trunk make it well near impossible that an adult intentionally would enter the trunk and close the lid. The dimensions of a trunk, the height of its sill and its load floor are among the design features which encourage closing and latching the trunk lid while standing outside the vehicle. The plaintiff's use of the trunk compartment as a means to attempt suicide was an unforeseeable use. Therefore, the manufacturer had no duty to design an internal release or opening mechanism that might have prevented this occurrence.

Nor did the manufacturer have a duty to warn the plaintiff of the danger of her conduct, given the plaintiff's unforeseeable use of the product. The risk is obvious. There is no duty to warn of known dangers in strict products liability or tort. Moreover, the potential efficacy of any warning, given the plaintiff's use of the automobile trunk compartment for a deliberate suicide attempt, is questionable.

The automobile trunk was not defective under these circumstances. The automobile trunk was not unreasonably dangerous within the contemplation of the ordinary consumer or user of such a trunk when used in the ordinary ways and for the ordinary purposes for which such a trunk is used.

The defendant's Motion for Summary Judgment is granted.

9-2c Contemporary Trends

If the steering wheel on a brand new car falls off, and the driver is injured, that is a clear case of defective manufacturing, and the company will be strictly liable. Those are the easy cases. But defective design cases have been more contentious. Suppose a vaccine that prevents serious childhood illnesses inevitably causes brain damage in a very small number of children because of the nature of the drug. Is the manufacturer liable? What if a racing sailboat, designed only for speed, is dangerously unstable in the hands of a less-experienced sailor? Is the boat's maker responsible for fatalities? Suppose an automobile made of lightweight metal uses less fuel but exposes its occupants to more serious injuries in an accident. How is a court to decide whether the design was defective? Often, these design cases also involve issues of warnings: Did the drug designer diligently detail dangers to doctors? Should a sailboat seller sell speedy sailboats solely to seasoned sailors?

Over the years, most courts have adopted one of two tests for design and warning cases. The first is *consumer expectation*. Here, a court finds the manufacturer liable for defective design if the product is less safe than a reasonable consumer would expect. If a smoke detector has a 3 percent failure rate and the average consumer has no way of anticipating that danger, effective cautions must be included, though the design may be defective anyway.

Many other states use a *risk-utility test*. Here, a court must weigh the benefits for society against the dangers that the product poses. Principal factors in the risk-utility test include:

- The *value* of the product,
- The *gravity*, or seriousness, of the danger,
- The *likelihood* that such danger will occur,
- The mechanical feasibility of a *safer alternative* design, and
- The *adverse consequences* of an alternative design.

Tort Reform

Some people believe that jury awards are excessive and need statutory reform. About two-thirds of the states have passed at least some limits on damages in tort actions. About one-third of states have created new rules for particular kinds of product liability.

Unavoidably unsafe prescription drugs are an example. Vaccines have greatly eliminated many communicable diseases and saved lives. But they, like many other medications, are not foolproof, and can cause serious side effects. The National Childhood Vaccine Injury Act of 1986 eliminates manufacturers' liability for unavoidable, adverse side effects. The goal of the act was to ensure that a flood of lawsuits and large verdicts did not drive vaccine makers out of a business that has great social value. Thus, a court barred Hannah Bruesewitz's parents from suing a vaccine manufacturer when they suspected she was harmed by a diphtheria, tetanus, and pertussis (DTP) vaccine. On appeal, the Supreme Court agreed: Vaccine makers are not liable for vaccine-induced injury as long as the vaccines are accompanied by proper direction and warning.[7]

Opponents consider tort reform dangerous to society. They argue that the real goal of the so-called reform is to free irresponsible corporations from any potential liability, enabling them to save money while injuring innocent people. They insist that giving the 12 average citizens on a jury a say in product safety benefits everyone.

Time Limits: Statutes of Limitations and Statutes of Repose

In tort cases, the passage of time provides a seller with two possible defenses: statutes of limitations and statutes of repose.

The statute of limitations requires that a lawsuit be brought within a specified period. These time limits vary from state to state, ranging from one year to five years, beginning when the defect is discovered or should have been discovered.

A statute of repose places an absolute limit on when a lawsuit may be filed, regardless of when the defect is discovered. Jeffrey Oats was riding in the back seat of a Nissan sports car when it was involved in an accident. Tragically, Oats suffered spinal cord injuries that left him a quadriplegic. Oats sued Nissan, based on defective design, claiming that the rear seat lacked adequate head and leg room and that the car's body panels lacked sufficient strength. He argued that these defects only became apparent in an accident. But the Idaho Supreme Court dismissed his claims because the car was 11 years old at the time of the accident. The Idaho statute of repose prohibits most product liability suits filed more than ten years after the goods were sold, regardless of when the defects were discoverable.[8]

---

[7]Bruesewitz v. Wyeth Laboratories, 131 S. Ct. 1068 (2011).

[8]Oats v. Nissan Motor Corp., 126 Idaho 162 (1994).

EXAMStrategy

Question: Stuart lives in a state that sets a three-year statute of limitations on tort claims. His state also has an eight-year statute of repose. Stuart bought a television on June 1, 2010. On July 1, 2017, a manufacturing defect causes the television to malfunction and cause an electrical fire. Stuart waits for a year and then files a lawsuit on July 1, 2018. Will he win, or will his case be dismissed?

Strategy: Because Stuart is a consumer, the court will not apply either the economic loss doctrine or the UCC's four-year statute of limitations. When does the state's three-year statute of limitations begin to run? What effect will the state's statute of repose have on Stuart's case?

Result: The statute of limitations' three-year period starts to run only when Stuart discovers the defect. Because he filed one year from the fire, the statute of limitations does not bar his recovery. But unfortunately, Stuart's lawsuit will fail because of the statute of repose. That eight-year limit begins to expire when Stuart buys the television, and the lawsuit is not filed for eight years and one month from the time of the sale. Stuart loses.

CHAPTER CONCLUSION

Tort issues necessarily remain in flux, based on changing social values and concerns. There is no final word on what is an ultrahazardous activity, or whether a social host can be liable for the destruction caused by a guest. What is clear is that a working knowledge of these issues and pitfalls can help everyone—business executive and ordinary citizen alike.

EXAM REVIEW

1. **ELEMENTS** The five elements of negligence are duty of due care, breach, factual causation, proximate causation, and damage.

2. **DUTY** If the defendant could foresee that misconduct would injure a particular person, he probably has a duty to her. Special duties exist for people on the job, landowners, and employers.

EXAMStrategy

Question: A supervisor reprimanded an employee for eating in a restaurant when he should have been at work. Later, the employee showed up at the supervisor's office and shot him. Although the employee previously had been violent, management withheld this information from supervisory personnel. Is the company liable for the supervisor's injury?

Strategy: An employer must do a *reasonable* job of hiring and retaining employees. (See the "Result" at the end of this Exam Review section.)

3. **BREACH OF DUTY** A defendant breaches his duty of due care by failing to meet his duty of care.

4. **NEGLIGENCE PER SE** If a legislature sets a minimum standard of care for a particular activity in order to protect a certain group of people, and a violation of the statute injures a member of that group, the defendant has committed negligence per se.

5. **FACTUAL CAUSE** If one event directly led to the ultimate harm, it is the factual cause.

6. **PROXIMATE CAUSE** For the defendant to be liable, the type of harm must have been reasonably foreseeable.

7. **DAMAGE** The plaintiff must persuade the court that he has suffered a harm that is genuine, not speculative. Damages for emotional distress, without a physical injury, are awarded only in select cases.

8. **CONTRIBUTORY AND COMPARATIVE NEGLIGENCE** In a contributory negligence state, a plaintiff who is even slightly responsible for his own injury recovers nothing; in a comparative negligence state, the jury may apportion liability between plaintiff and defendant.

EXAMStrategy

Question: There is a collision between cars driven by Candy and Zeke. The evidence is that Candy is about 25 percent responsible, for failing to stop quickly enough, and Zeke is about 75 percent responsible, for making a dangerous turn. Candy is most likely to win:

(a) a lawsuit for battery.

(b) a lawsuit for negligence in a comparative negligence state.

(c) a lawsuit for negligence in a contributory negligence state.

(d) a lawsuit for strict liability.

(e) a lawsuit for assault.

Strategy: Battery and assault are intentional torts, irrelevant in a typical car accident. Are such collisions strict liability cases? No; therefore, the answer must be either (b) or (c). Apply the distinction between comparative and contributory negligence to the evidence here. (See the "Result" at the end of this Exam Review section.)

9. **STRICT LIABILITY** A defendant is strictly liable for harm caused by an ultrahazardous activity or a defective product. Strict liability means that if the defendant's conduct led to the harm, the defendant is liable, even if she exercises extraordinary care.

EXAMStrategy

Question: Marko owned a cat and allowed it to roam freely outside. In the three years he had owned the pet, the animal had never bitten anyone. The cat entered Romi's garage. When Romi attempted to move it outside, the cat bit her. Romi underwent four surgeries, was fitted with a plastic finger joint, and spent more than $39,000 in medical bills. She sued Marko, claiming both strict liability and ordinary negligence. Assume that state law allows a domestic cat to roam freely. Evaluate both of Romi's claims.

Strategy: Negligence requires proof that the defendant breached a duty to the plaintiff by behaving unreasonably and that the resulting harm was foreseeable. Was it? When would harm by a domestic cat be foreseeable? A defendant can be strictly liable for keeping a wild animal. Apply that rule as well. (See the "Result" at the end of this Exam Review section.)

RESULTS

2. Result: This employer *may* have been liable for negligently hiring a previously violent employee, and it *certainly* did an unreasonable job in retaining him without advising his supervisor of the earlier violence. The assault was easily foreseeable, and the employer is liable.[9]

8. Result. In a contributory negligence state, a plaintiff even 1 percent responsible for the harm loses. Candy was 25 percent responsible. She can win *only* in a comparative negligence state.

9. Result: If Marko's cat had bitten or attacked people in the past, this harm was foreseeable and Marko is liable. If the cat had never done so, and state law allows domestic animals to roam, Romi probably loses her suit for negligence. Her strict liability case definitely fails: a housecat is not a wild animal.

MULTIPLE-CHOICE QUESTIONS

1. Two cars, driven by Fred and Barney, collide. At trial, the jury determines that the accident was 90 percent Fred's fault and 10 percent Barney's fault. Barney's losses total $100,000. If he lives in a state that uses contributory negligence, Barney will recover ______________.
   (a) $0
   (b) $10,000
   (c) $50,000
   (d) $90,000
   (e) $100,000

---

[9]Based on Smith v. National R.R. Passenger Corp., 856 F.2d 467 (2d Cir. 1988).

2. Assume the same facts as in question 1, except now Barney lives in a state that follows comparative negligence. Now Barney will recover ______________.
   (a) $0
   (b) $10,000
   (c) $50,000
   (d) $90,000
   (e) $100,000
3. Zack lives in a state that prohibits factory laborers from working more than 12 hours in any 24-hour period. The state legislature passed the law to cut down on accidents caused by fatigued workers.

   Ignoring the law, Zack makes his factory employees put in 14-hour days. Eventually, a worker at the end of a long shift makes a mistake and severely injures a coworker. The injured worker sues Zack.

   Which of the following terms will be most relevant to the case?
   (a) *Res ipsa loquitur*
   (b) Assumption of the risk
   (c) Negligence per se
   (d) Strict liability
4. Randy works for a vending machine company. One morning, he fills up an empty vending machine that is on the third floor of an office building. Later that day, Mark buys a can of Pepsi from that machine. He takes the full can to a nearby balcony and drops it three floors onto Carl, a coworker who recently started dating Mark's ex-girlfriend. Carl falls unconscious. Which of the following can be considered a factual cause of Carl's injuries?
   (a) Randy
   (b) Mark
   (c) Both Randy and Mark
   (d) None of these
5. For this question, assume the same facts as in question 4. Now determine which of the following can be considered a proximate cause of Carl's injuries.
   (a) Randy
   (b) Mark
   (c) Both Randy and Mark
   (d) None of these
6. **CPA QUESTION** Which of the following factors is least important in determining whether a manufacturer is strictly liable in tort for a defective product?
   (a) The negligence of the manufacturer
   (b) The contributory negligence of the plaintiff
   (c) Modifications to the product by the wholesaler
   (d) Whether the product caused injuries

CASE QUESTIONS

1. Ryder leased a truck to Florida Food Service. Powers, an employee, drove it to make deliveries. He noticed that the strap used to close the rear door was frayed, and he asked Ryder to fix it. Ryder failed to do so in spite of numerous requests. The strap broke, and Powers replaced it with a nylon rope. Later, when Powers was attempting to close the rear door, the nylon rope broke and he fell, sustaining severe injuries to his neck and back. He sued Ryder. The trial court found that Powers's attachment of the replacement rope was a superseding cause, relieving Ryder of any liability, and granted summary judgment for Ryder. Powers appealed. How should the appellate court rule?

2. ***YOU BE THE JUDGE*** **WRITING PROBLEM** When Thomas and Susan Tamplin were shopping at Star Lumber with their six-year-old daughter Ann Marie, a 150-pound roll of vinyl flooring fell on the girl, seriously injuring her head and pituitary gland. Ann was clearly entitled to recover for the physical harm, such as her fractured skull. The plaintiffs also sought recovery for potential future harm. Their medical expert was prepared to testify that, although Ann would probably develop normally, he could not rule out the slight possibility that her pituitary injury might prevent her from sexually maturing. Is Ann entitled to damages for future harm? **Argument for Ann:** This was a major trauma, and it is impossible to know the full extent of the future harm. Sexual maturation is a fundamental part of life; if there is a possibility that Ann will not develop normally, she is entitled to present her case to a jury and receive damages. **Argument for Star Lumber:** A plaintiff may not recover for speculative harm. The "slight possibility" that Ann could fail to develop is not enough for her to take her case to the jury.

3. Texaco, Inc., and other oil companies sold mineral spirits in bulk to distributors, which then resold to retailers. Mineral spirits are used for cleaning. Texaco allegedly knew that the retailers, such as hardware stores, frequently packaged the mineral spirits (illegally) in used half-gallon milk containers and sold them to consumers, often with no warnings on the packages. Mineral spirits are harmful or fatal if swallowed. David Hunnings, aged 21 months, found a milk container in his home, swallowed the mineral spirits, and died. The Hunnings sued Texaco for negligence. The trial court dismissed the complaint, and the Hunnings appealed. What is the legal standard in a negligence case? Have the plaintiffs made a valid case of negligence? Remember that at this stage, a court is not deciding who wins, but what standard a plaintiff must meet in order to take its case to a jury. Assume that Texaco knew about the repackaging and the grave risk but continued to sell in bulk because doing so was profitable. (If the plaintiffs cannot prove those facts, they will lose even if they *do* get to a jury.) Would that make you angry? Does that mean such a case should go to a jury? Or would you conclude that the fault still lies with the retailer, the parents, or both?

4. Boboli Co. wanted to promote its "California-style" pizza, which it sold in supermarkets. The company contracted with Highland Group, Inc., to produce two million recipe brochures, which would be inserted in the carton when the freshly baked pizza was still very hot. Highland contracted with Comark Merchandising to print the brochures. But when Comark asked for details concerning the pizza, the carton, and so forth, Highland refused to supply the information. Comark printed the first

lot of 72,000 brochures, which Highland delivered to Boboli. Unfortunately, the hot bread caused the ink to run, and customers opening the carton often found red or blue splotches on their pizzas. Highland refused to accept additional brochures, and Comark sued for breach of contract. Highland defended by claiming that Comark had breached its warranty of merchantability. Please comment.

5. At the end of a skateboard exhibition, one of the performers tossed a skateboard into the rowdy crowd. David rushed to catch the prize but was injured when his fellow spectators trampled him to snatch it away. What is the likely outcome if David sues the promoter of the skateboarding show for negligence?

DISCUSSION QUESTIONS

1. Self-driving cars are no longer science fiction. These vehicles are programmed to use lasers, sensors, software, and maps to drive themselves. A handful of states have passed laws allowing driverless technology on the road. But what happens when a driverless car harms someone? Who should be at fault? The passenger? The programmer? The manufacturer?

2. Imagine an undefeated high school football team on which the average lineman weighs 300 pounds. Also, imagine a 0–10 team on which the average lineman weighs 170 pounds. The undefeated team sets out to hit as hard as it can on every play and to run up the score as much as possible. Before the game is over, 11 players from the lesser team have been carried off the field with significant injuries. All injuries were the result of "clean hits"—none of the plays resulted in a penalty. Even late in the game, when the score is 70–0, the undefeated team continues to deliver devastating hits that are far beyond what would be required to tackle and block. The assumption of the risk doctrine exempts the undefeated team from liability. Is this reasonable?

3. Recall the Texas case *Del Lago v. Smith* from Chapter 1. In that case, a bartender served drinks when it was obvious that drunken patrons were about to engage in a dangerous bar fight. Smith, who voluntarily participated in the melee, was seriously injured and sued the establishment for negligence. Texas has a comparative negligence system. If you were the judge in that case, how would you assess each party's fault?

4. Are strict liability rules fair? Someone has to dispose of chemicals. Someone has to use dynamite if road projects are to be completed. Is it fair to say to those companies, "You are responsible for all harm caused by your activities, even if you are as careful as you can possibly be"?

5. Congress passed the Protection for Lawful Commerce in Arms Act which provides that gun manufacturers and retailers cannot be sued for injuries arising from the criminal misuse of a weapon. Critics argue that when gun makers market and sell military-style assault rifles to civilians, they should be held liable because these highly dangerous weapons are designed for specially trained soldiers, not the general public. Should makers of assault rifles be liable for these tragedies?

10

CHAPTER

PRIVACY AND INTERNET LAW

Soon after the invention of the telephone, police realized that secretly recording phone calls could help catch criminals. But this innovation created a new legal issue: Did the police need a warrant before installing wiretaps?

In 1928, the Supreme Court answered that question when it ruled that the Fourth Amendment did not require the government to obtain a warrant before listening to, or recording, private telephone conversations.[1] The Court reasoned that wiretaps were not an invasion of privacy because they did not involve *physical* intrusion.

Can it be that the Constitution affords no protection against such invasions of individual security?

Justice Louis Brandeis strongly disagreed. In one of the most important dissents in Supreme Court history, he foresaw the challenges of modern privacy—and argued that any interpretation of the Constitution had to adapt to changing technologies.

He wrote:

> Discovery and invention have made it possible for the Government, by means far more effective than stretching upon the rack, to obtain disclosure of what is whispered in the closet.
>
> In the application of a constitution, our contemplation cannot be only of what has been but of what may be. The progress of science in furnishing the Government with means of espionage is not likely to stop with wire-tapping. Ways may someday be developed by which the Government, without removing papers from secret drawers, can reproduce them in court, and by which it will be enabled to expose to a jury the most intimate occurrences of the home. Advances in the psychic and related sciences may bring means of exploring unexpressed beliefs, thoughts and emotions. Can it be that the Constitution affords no protection against such invasions of individual security? ... [E]very unjustifiable intrusion by the Government upon the privacy of the individual, whatever the means employed, must be deemed a violation of the Fourth Amendment.

[1]The case is Olmstead v. United States, 277 U.S. 438 (1928). The Fourth Amendment to the Constitution protects "the right of the people to be secure in their persons, houses, papers, and effects against unreasonable searches and seizures. . . ."

The internet, social media, big data, the cloud, smart appliances, and artificial intelligence are all components of what we know as the digital world. These massive troves of information and communication shape every aspect of our lives—how we do business, shop, date, apply for jobs, obtain news, campaign for election, make new friends, and even start revolutions. Because the digital world has transformed the way we live, it has forced changes in the law—from criminal law to employment law and constitutional law to contracts. Although this book is filled with examples of technology in diverse areas of law, this chapter focuses on the legal issues that are unique to the digital world—privacy and internet law.

Technology provides a very large window through which the government, employers, businesses, and criminals can find out more than they should about you and your money, activities, location, beliefs, and health—so this chapter begins with privacy and the laws that govern it. We then discuss regulation in the digital world, including net neutrality, online speech, consumer protection, and cybersecurity.

10-1 PRIVACY IN A DIGITAL WORLD

In Justice Brandeis's view, privacy is essential to freedom and democracy. His famous dissent foresaw technological innovations that could uncover an individual's most intimate spaces and private thoughts. Now, as the justice's imagined world has come to reality, the law struggles to keep up with technology's rapid changes.

10-1a How We Lose Our Privacy in the Digital World

Sometimes we voluntarily give up our privacy without considering the consequences; in other cases, it is taken from us without our knowledge.

Data Breaches

Most people store important data about themselves electronically: their photos, emails, music, contacts, documents, and, of course, their passwords. In addition, businesses, employers, and others keep digital records, often including sensitive data such as Social Security numbers and medical or financial records. Thieves eagerly seek access to this treasure trove. Estimates suggest that over 4 million data records are lost or stolen every *day*. In past years, hackers have stolen hundreds of millions of credit card numbers from major retailers. One recent security breach compromised half a billion Yahoo accounts. Individuals, businesses, and governments alike are vulnerable to cyberattacks.

Surveillance and Discrimination

The ability to share our opinions, relationship status, and location on social media sites like Facebook, Twitter, and Instagram has revolutionized the way we communicate and socialize. It has also affected workplace relationships as technology allows employers to monitor what their employees and job applicants do and say on the job and in their spare time.[2]

Employer intrusion into an employee's personal life may lead to discriminatory practices. One study found that 45 percent of employers snooped around in candidates' social media profiles before hiring. More than a third of these employers reported having found content that caused them not to hire the applicants. When this content points to illegality or fraud, employers are within their rights to reject applicants. But what if the employer refuses to hire the candidate because her Facebook page reveals she is religious, married, or planning to have children? In those cases, the illegal discrimination may be damaging, yet virtually impossible to prove.

---

[2]The Supreme Court has recognized that employers have a legitimate interest in monitoring their employees, especially for reasonable work-related reasons. O'Connor v. Ortega, 480 U.S. 709 (1987).

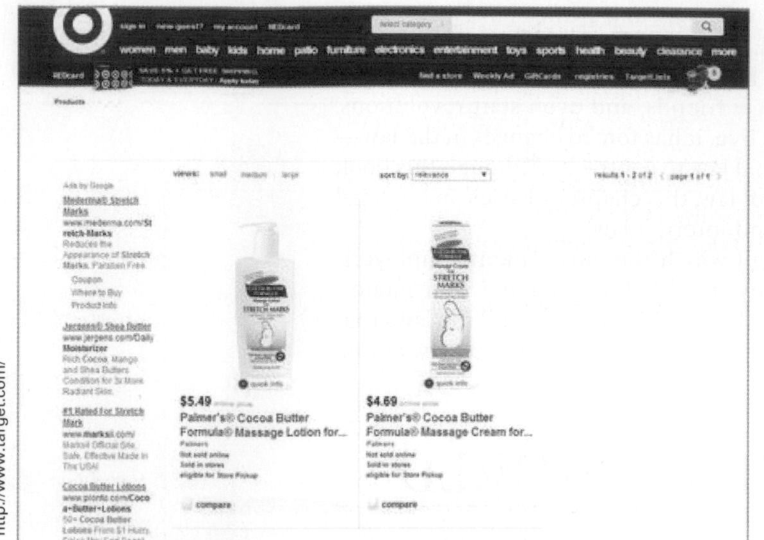

http://www.target.com/

Does buying this lotion suggest that you are pregnant? Target thinks so.

Big Data

Eighty percent of Americans shop online—and most online retailers collect customers' personal data.[3] This information may provide a better shopping experience as websites use information about you to suggest a product you are likely to enjoy or the size that will fit you best.

But merchants have another motive, too: Consumer information is very valuable. U.S. firms spend $2 billion a year on personal data collection.[4] The nation's leading data broker has an estimated 500 million consumer profiles with an average of 1,500 data points per person, mined from 50 trillion data transactions per year.[5] Why is this information so valuable? Because companies can use data-mining tools to find out a lot of information about . . . well . . . you. And data leads to surprising insights: Credit card companies discovered that people who buy anti-scuff pads for their furniture are less likely to default on debts.[6]

Data mining also leads to behavioral marketing, a widespread practice that involves inferring needs and preferences from a consumer's online behavior and then targeting related advertisements to them. Target has found that shoppers who buy cocoa-butter lotion are likely to be pregnant.[7] That information is hugely important because the birth of a baby is one of the few times that consumers change their shopping habits. If Target can lure an expectant mother into one of its stores, it may have a customer for life. But consumers are often unaware of who has access to what personal information, how it is being used, and with what consequences. When Target sent coupons for baby items to one teenager who bought cocoa-butter, it caused family strife by revealing her pregnancy before she told her parents.[8]

In short, internet users are inadvertently providing intensely personal data to unknown people for unknown uses. And the problem is likely to grow with technology. Imagine the price of an airplane ticket increasing *just for you* because airlines know you are flying to your honeymoon—or paying more for your health insurance because an insurer learns that you have purchased a book on diabetes online.

The Internet of Things

Increasingly, the internet is not limited to our computers. Automobiles and household items such as televisions, mattresses, refrigerators, security cameras, and doorbells are network connected in the name of convenience and efficiency. The **internet of things** refers to internet-connected everyday devices, vehicles, and even buildings.

But these gadgets, which gather, send, and receive data, pose new privacy and security challenges. When the police suspected that James Bates had murdered his houseguest, they ordered Amazon to turn over all the records from Bates's Amazon Echo, the voice-activated

---

3Pew Research Center, Report: Online Shopping and E-Commerce, December 19, 2016.

4Stephanie Armour, "Data Brokers Come under Fresh Scrutiny," *The Wall Street Journal*, February 12, 2014.

5Natasha Singer, "Mapping, and Sharing, the Consumer Genome," *The New York Times*, June 16, 2012.

6Jonathan Shaw, "Why 'Big Data' Is a Big Deal," *Harvard Magazine*, March–April 2014.

7Charles Duhigg, "How Companies Learn Your Secrets," *The New Times Magazine*, February 16, 2012.

8Kashmir Hill, "How Target Figured Out a Teen Girl Was Pregnant before Her Father Did," *Forbes*, February 16, 2012.

digital assistant on his kitchen counter. The authorities believed that the device's microphone could offer valuable clues as to what happened in the Bates residence on the night of the murder. Do people give up their privacy when they allow a microphone into their home or share their sleeping habits with their interconnected mattress? Many legal and ethical questions remain unanswered, as the technology moves faster than regulation.

Critics say that privacy is outdated—or even overrated—and argue that, if consumers really cared about it, they would share less information online. One tech CEO commented: "You have zero privacy . . . Get over it."[9] Facebook founder Mark Zuckerberg has said that privacy is an outdated social norm.

But people who care about privacy should be worried. Without updated laws and oversight, it could well be obliterated.

Ethics

Some companies have launched marketplaces for personal data. One firm offers users $8 a month in return for unrestricted access to their social media accounts and credit card transactions. Critics argue that privacy is an important component of human dignity and that it is wrong to cheapen it by turning it into a commodity—like a car or a cheeseburger. They also contend that these companies are exploiting people, who can never really predict how their information may be used against them. Is it ethical to buy people's privacy? Under what conditions? What personal data would you be willing to sell? To whom? For how much?

10-2 THE LAW OF PRIVACY

There is no single source of privacy law. Instead, this area is governed by a patchwork of constitutional law, common law, and federal and state statutes. It is important to remember that the term "privacy" encompasses many topics. Here, we focus on data privacy, or people's right to control information about themselves. We begin with a citizen's constitutional privacy right.

10-2a Constitutional Law: The Fourth Amendment

The Fourth Amendment to the Constitution prohibits unreasonable searches and seizures by the government. As we saw in Chapter 7 on crime, the Fourth Amendment protects the privacy rights of criminal defendants. These same protections also extend to other citizens, such as government workers and public school students.

In enforcing this provision of the Constitution, the courts ask whether a person had a **reasonable expectation of privacy**. The two requirements for establishing a "reasonable expectation of privacy" are:

Reasonable expectation of privacy
The test to analyze whether privacy should be protected

1. **The person had an actual, subjective expectation of privacy.** Most people expect privacy in restrooms, even those at work. Some people might expect that no one will rummage through their desk drawers in their cubicle; others might think that the personal emails they send on the company computers are private. These examples are subjective expectations of privacy.
2. **Society accepts the person's expectation of privacy as reasonable.** Everyone agrees that a bathroom stall is private. (Note to employers: Two-way mirrors in an

[9]Polly Sprenger, "Sun on Privacy: 'Get Over It,'" *Wired.com*, January 26, 1999.

employee bathroom are a bad idea.) However, the privacy of a cubicle or personal emails *depends* on the circumstances. Did the person know the employer might search the area? Did others have access to it? The answers to questions like these help courts determine what people generally would think.

Courts have generally held that employees do not have a reasonable expectation of privacy in the workplace, especially if using hardware provided by the employer,[10] **or if the employee handbook says they may be monitored.**[11] When a police officer persistently exceeded his monthly quota of text messages (SMS), his superior reviewed his texts to determine if they were work related. It turned out that they were mostly sexts (sexual texts) sent to the married officer's mistress. After the officer was disciplined, he filed suit alleging that the department had violated his Fourth Amendment rights. The Supreme Court held that a government employer has the right to review its employee's electronic communications for a work-related purpose, if the search was "justified at its inception" and if "the measures adopted are reasonably related to the objectives of the search and not excessively intrusive in light of the circumstances giving rise to the search."[12]

The Fourth Amendment also protects public school students. In the following case, a bikini-clad teenager claimed she had a reasonable expectation of privacy in her Facebook picture. (Sexts. Bikinis. Who said privacy is boring?)

Chaney v. Fayette County Public School District

2013 U.S. Dist. LEXIS 143030; 2013 WL 5486829
United States District Court for the Northern District of Georgia, 2013

Facts: Chelsea Chaney was a seventeen-year-old high school student in Fayette County, Georgia. At a countywide internet safety seminar, Curtis Cearley, the District's technology director, presented a PowerPoint slideshow to illustrate the permanent and often-embarrassing nature of social media postings.

Cearley's first slide was a cartoon depicting a scene in the future: A curious daughter discovers her mother's old Facebook page, listing her hobbies as "body art, bad boys, and jello shooters." The following slide, entitled "Once It's There—It's There to Stay," featured a picture of Chaney in a bikini posing with a life-size cutout of rapper Snoop Dogg. The slide included Chaney's full name. Cearley distributed copies of the presentation to the hundreds of students and parents in attendance.

Cearley had found Chaney's photo while searching Facebook for materials to use in his presentation. Her page had a semi-private setting that allowed her Facebook "friends" and "friends of friends" to view her page. Neither Chaney nor her parents consented to the use of her picture.

Chaney was embarrassed and humiliated. In her view, Cearley had publicly implied that she was a sexually promiscuous abuser of alcohol who should be more careful about her internet postings. In fact, she contended, the picture was taken on a family vacation that did not involve sex or alcohol.

Chaney sued, claiming that Cearley and the District violated her constitutional right to privacy under the Fourth Amendment. The District filed a motion to dismiss.

Issue: ***Did Chaney have a reasonable expectation of privacy in her bikini Facebook picture?***

Excerpts from Judge Batten's Decision: Chaney argues that she had a reasonable expectation in the privacy of her Facebook picture, and that the District violated this expectation when Cearley used her photo in his presentation.

---

[10]See, for example, Bohach v. City of Reno, 932 F. Supp. 1232 (D. Nev. 1996).

[11]See, for example, Muick v. Glenayre Elec., 280 F.3d 741, 743 (7th Cir. 2002).

[12]City of Ontario v. Quon, 560 U.S. 746 (2010).

In establishing a reasonable expectation of privacy, a person must show that she had a subjective expectation of privacy and must show a willingness of society to recognize that expectation as legitimate. Even if she had a subjective expectation of privacy in her Facebook photos, Chaney cannot show that her expectation is legitimate.

Chaney contends that her privacy-setting choice of "friends and friends of friends" was "semi-private" and that her Facebook page was accessible "only to those people she had specifically approved." However, Chaney fails to acknowledge the lack of privacy afforded her by her selected Facebook setting. While Chaney may select her Facebook friends, she cannot select her Facebook friends' friends. By intentionally selecting the broadest privacy setting available to her at that time, Chaney made her page available to potentially hundreds, if not thousands, of people whom she did not know (i.e., the friends of her Facebook friends).

The Supreme Court consistently has held that a person has no legitimate expectation of privacy in information he voluntarily turns over to third parties. Chaney not only voluntarily turned over the picture to her Facebook friends, but she also chose to share the picture with an additional audience of unknown size, likely comprised of people Chaney did not know, subject to continuous expansion without Chaney's approval.

When an individual shares a photograph with his friends on Facebook, that individual has no justifiable expectation that his "friends" would keep his profile private. Chaney shared her Facebook page, which includes her pictures, not only with her friends but their friends, too. By doing so, Chaney surrendered any reasonable expectation of privacy. Thus, Chaney cannot show that society would be willing to recognize her expectation of privacy as legitimate.

The fact that the photo was of Chaney in a bikini does not require a different result. People have a reasonable expectation not to be unclothed involuntarily and/or not to be observed unclothed. However, this case involves Chaney voluntarily posting a picture of herself in a bikini and sharing that picture on a social media website with the broadest audience possible for a Facebook user her age.

Because Chaney cannot show a violation of her Fourth Amendment rights, the Court will grant Defendants' motion on this claim.

Although the Fourth Amendment does not govern the private sector, the reasonable expectation of privacy analysis is a guide to judges and lawmakers in every area of privacy law, including the privacy torts (which we discuss next) and surveillance laws.

10-2b Common Law: Privacy Torts

Society was more voyeuristic than ever, curious about every detail of other people's lives. Paparazzi were everywhere, using a modern and intrusive technology to pry into the private lives of famous people. Sound familiar? Well, that year was 1890. And even before Louis Brandeis was appointed to the Supreme Court, he was deeply worried about the erosion of privacy. Angered by the nosy press and a new technology called "photography," he wrote a famous article calling for the creation of a new right protecting an individual's personal space.[13] In response, state courts created new torts in common law to protect against violations of privacy: that is, public disclosure of private facts and intrusion.

Public Disclosure of Private Facts

Public disclosure of private facts
A tort providing redress to victims of unauthorized and embarrassing disclosures

The tort of **public disclosure of private facts** prohibits the unjustifiable revelation of truthful, but secret, information. **The public disclosure tort requires the plaintiff to show all of the following:**

- **The defendant made public disclosure.** The defendant must have divulged the secret information to a number of people, not just one other person. Gossip site Gawker posted excerpts of a sex tape featuring the wrestler known as Hulk Hogan. A jury found the site made an unauthorized public disclosure and ordered it to pay $115 million, forcing it into bankruptcy.

[13]Samuel D. Warren and Louis D. Brandeis, "The Right to Privacy," 4 *Harvard Law Review* 193 (1890).

- **The disclosed facts had been private.** The person seeking privacy must prove that she had a reasonable expectation of privacy in the information. But courts have held that people cannot have a reasonable expectation of privacy in information that is generally visible or available. When Ralph Nader, a consumers' rights activist, criticized General Motors publicly, GM sent agents to dig up some dirt on Nader.[14] In an effort to embarrass Nader, GM interviewed his friends (*some* friends) about his racial and religious views, his personal and sexual habits, and his political beliefs. Nader sued GM for public disclosure of private facts, but GM won because the gathered information was not technically secret since Nader had already revealed it to many of his acquaintances.
- **The facts were not of legitimate concern to the public.** The First Amendment protects free speech and, therefore, sometimes undermines privacy rights.

  To protect their privacy, plaintiffs must prove that the revealed secret was not of public concern, that is, that the public was not entitled to know about it.

  A Florida newspaper mistakenly revealed a rape victim's name, which it had obtained from a public police report. The Supreme Court held that it was unconstitutional to prohibit the publication of truthful and legitimately obtained information about an issue of legitimate public interest such as crime.[15]
- **The disclosure is highly offensive to a reasonable person.** Privacy is somewhat subjective. One person's secret is another's reality show. For this reason, defendants must prove that the unauthorized revelation would have offended most reasonable people.

After Calvin Green died of a gunshot wound, his mother, Laura, spoke to him in his hospital room, telling him how much she loved him. Reporters from the *Chicago Tribune* were in the hospital reporting on a story about Chicago's homicide rate. They overheard Laura's words to Calvin, which they then printed in the newspaper. When Laura sued, the court ruled that she had stated a claim under the public disclosure tort because the newspaper had (1) printed the information in the newspaper, (2) Calvin's hospital room had been private, (3) the facts were not of legitimate concern to the public, and (4) the disclosure of information about this extraordinarily painful incident was highly offensive.[16]

EXAMStrategy

Question: A group of college bullies made a flyer with a fellow student's picture, email address, and phone number—all information found on the university's website. The flyer, posted all around campus and online, falsely advertised that he was seeking a male romantic partner. The humiliated victim sued the bullies for public disclosure of private facts—not his sexual orientation but his contact information. What result?

Strategy: Remember that defendants are liable only if they have disclosed secret information.

Result: The bullies committed a horrible act, but they are not liable under the public disclosure tort. The victim's contact information and picture were accessible to all students and faculty via the university's website, so they were not private facts.

---

14 Nader v. Gen. Motors Corp., 255 N.E.2d 765 (N.Y. 1970).

15 The Florida Star v. B.J.F., 491 U.S. 524 (1989).

16 Green v. Chicago Tribune Co., 286 Ill. App. 3d 1 (Ill. App. Ct. 1st Dist. 1996).

Intrusion

The tort of intrusion requires the plaintiff to show that the defendant (1) intentionally intruded, physically or otherwise, (2) upon the solitude or seclusion of another or on his private affairs or concerns, (3) in a manner highly offensive to a reasonable person.[17] Peeping through someone's windows or wiretapping his telephone is an obvious example of intrusion. A court found that a "paparazzo" photographer had invaded Jacqueline Kennedy Onassis's privacy by making a career out of photographing her. He had bribed doormen to gain access to hotels and restaurants she visited, had jumped out of bushes to photograph her young children, and had driven power boats dangerously close to her. The court ordered him to stop. Nine years later the paparazzo was found in contempt of court for again taking photographs too close to Ms. Onassis. He finally agreed to stop—in exchange for a suspended contempt sentence.

Ron Galella/Getty Images

Jacqueline Kennedy Onassis was a frequent target of the paparazzi.

In contrast was a case in which a firm fired two workers who exchanged (they claimed) joking emails threatening violence to sales managers. They sued under the tort of intrusion, but the court ruled for the company on the grounds that a reasonable person would not consider the interception of those emails to have been a highly offensive invasion of privacy.[18] The court reached this decision even though the company had an explicit policy stating that emails were confidential and would not be intercepted or used against an employee.

In the following case, a nurse was offended when her supervisor snooped on her Facebook postings. Was her Facebook wall strong enough to protect her privacy?

Ehling v. Monmouth-Ocean Hosp. Serv. Corp

872 F. Supp. 2d 369
United States District Court for the District of New Jersey, 2012

Facts: Deborah Ehling was a registered nurse and paramedic who worked at the Monmouth-Ocean Hospital Service Corporation (MONOC). The privacy settings on Ehling's Facebook page limited access to just her "friends." Many of her coworkers, but no members of management, were Facebook friends.

A hospital supervisor summoned one of Ehling's coworker Facebook friends into an office where she forced him to access his account so that she could view Ehling's Facebook wall. The supervisor copied Ehling's postings, including the following one, which was reacting to a shooting:

> An 88 yr old sociopath white supremacist opened fire in the Wash D.C. Holocaust Museum this morning and killed an innocent guard (leaving children). Other guards opened fire. The 88 yr old was shot. He survived. I blame the DC paramedics. I want to say 2 things to the DC medics. 1. WHAT WERE YOU THINKING? and 2. This was your opportunity to really make a difference! WTF!!!! And to the other guards go to target practice.

MONOC sent letters with this posting to the boards that regulate nursing and paramedics in New Jersey. MONOC told the boards that it was concerned that this posting showed a disregard for patient safety.

[17] Restatement (Second) of Torts §652B (1977).
[18] Smyth v. Pillsbury Co., 914 F. Supp. 97 (E.D. Pa. 1996).

Ehling alleged that these letters were sent in a malicious attempt to damage her reputation and possibly cause her to lose her license. She filed suit against MONOC, alleging a violation of the tort of intrusion. The hospital filed a motion to dismiss, arguing that she did not have a reasonable expectation of privacy in her Facebook posting.

Issue: *Did Ehling have a reasonable expectation of privacy in her Facebook comment?*

Excerpts from Judge Martini's Decision: Under New Jersey law, to state a claim for intrusion, a plaintiff must allege sufficient facts to demonstrate that (1) her solitude, seclusion, or private affairs were intentionally infringed upon, and that (2) this infringement would highly offend a reasonable person. Expectations of privacy are established by general social norms and must be objectively reasonable—a plaintiff's subjective belief that something is private is irrelevant.

Although most courts hold that a communication is not necessarily public just because it is accessible to a number of people, courts differ dramatically in how far they think this theory extends. [M]ost courts have adopted the concept of "limited privacy," which is the idea that when an individual reveals private information about herself to one or more persons, she may retain a reasonable expectation that the recipients of the information will not disseminate it further. [In one case,] plaintiff's disclosure of facts to sixty people did not render them public, [but in another,] plaintiff's disclosure of facts to two coworkers deprived her of a reasonable expectation of privacy.

What is clear is that privacy determinations are made on a case-by-case basis, in light of all the facts presented. In this case, Plaintiff argues that she had a reasonable expectation of privacy in her Facebook posting because her comment was disclosed to a limited number of people who she had individually invited to view a restricted access webpage. Defendants argue that Plaintiff cannot have a reasonable expectation of privacy because the comment was disclosed to dozens, if not hundreds, of people.

The Court finds that Plaintiff has stated a plausible claim for invasion of privacy, considering that she actively took steps to protect her Facebook page from public viewing. More importantly, however, the question of the reasonableness of the Plaintiffs' expectations of privacy is a question of fact for the jury to decide. Accordingly, the motion to dismiss the Complaint is denied.

10-2c Privacy Statutes

Instead of having a single comprehensive data privacy law, the United States has adopted a collection of federal and state privacy laws that apply to particular types of personal data. Different laws apply to your consumer credit information (discussed in Chapter 39 on consumer protection), your medical data, and even the movies you stream. Some laws also apply to the way information is collected and from whom. We will first focus on federal laws addressing surveillance and spying, then turn to a variety of state laws that broaden privacy rights for their citizens.

Electronic Communications Privacy Act of 1986 (ECPA)
A federal statute prohibiting unauthorized interception of, access to, or disclosure of wire and electronic communications

Wiretap Act
The section of the ECPA that prohibits the interception of face-to-face oral communications and telephone calls

Stored Communications Act
The section of the ECPA that prohibits the unlawful access to stored communications, such as email

Wiretapping and Electronic Surveillance

The **Electronic Communications Privacy Act of 1986 (ECPA)** is a federal statute that prohibits unauthorized interception of, access to, or disclosure of wire and electronic communications. It addresses the real-time interception of conversations in a section known as the **Wiretap Act** and access to communications that have been stored, such as email and voicemail, in the **Stored Communications Act**. We will address each in turn. Violators of the ECPA are subject to both criminal and civil penalties.

Wiretapping. As we saw in the chapter opener, in the early days of the telephone, the Supreme Court held that the police could legally tap into an individual's private telephone lines (or wiretap) without a warrant. Six years later, in 1934, Congress made unauthorized wiretapping illegal for the first time.

Today, the Wiretap Act makes it illegal to intercept or record face-to-face oral communications and telephone calls during their transmission.[19] It also prohibits disclosing the contents of an illegal recording. The statute applies to both law enforcement and private

[19]Title III of the Omnibus Crime Control and Safe Streets Act of 1968, amended by the Electronic Communications Privacy Act, 18 U.S.C. §§2510–2522.

individuals and has both criminal and civil penalties. As a result, police require a valid warrant to listen in or monitor a person's telephone calls.

However, **the Wiretap Act does not protect every conversation.**

- If one party to the conversation consents, secret recording is legal under federal law. However, many states have their own laws requiring the consent of all parties to the conversation for recording to be legal. Thus, when Linda Tripp recorded a conversation with her friend (*some* friend) Monica Lewinsky in which Lewinsky disclosed her sexual relationship with President Clinton, Tripp had not violated federal law, but she was charged under a Maryland statute.[20]
- Businesses may monitor conversations with their customers in the ordinary course of business provided they give notice. This rule explains why we often hear "this call may be monitored for training purposes" when we call companies.
- Finally, wiretap laws only protect speakers with a reasonable expectation of privacy in the conversation. The two-step test for a reasonable expectation is the same as the one for the Fourth Amendment.

Ben Franklin once said, "three may keep a secret, if two of them are dead." In the following case, *one* could not keep a secret—because he had an iPhone in his pocket. Do people have a reasonable expectation of privacy when their smartphones inadvertently place calls? You be the judge.

You Be the Judge

Huff v. Spaw

794 F.3d 543
United States Court of Appeals for the Sixth Circuit, 2015

Facts: James Huff was the chairman of the Kenton County Airport Board, which manages the Cincinnati/Northern Kentucky International Airport (CVG). While at a conference in Italy with his wife Bertha and a colleague named Larry Savage, Huff used his iPhone to call Carol Spaw for help with dinner reservations. Spaw, who was the executive assistant to CVG's CEO, did not answer, so Huff hung up and put his iPhone in his jacket pocket.

Later, Huff and Savage retreated to an outdoor hotel balcony to discuss CVG personnel matters, including the possible firing of the CEO. During this conversation, Huff's iPhone inadvertently placed a call to ("pocket-dialed") Spaw's office phone. When Spaw answered, she quickly realized that the call was unintentional but continued to listen in anyway.

Concerned that the men were plotting against her boss, Spaw put her office phone on speaker mode and used an iPhone to record Huff's call. For one hour and thirty-one minutes, Spaw listened, recorded, and transcribed. Her iPhone first captured Huff's discussion with Savage and, later his personal conversations with Bertha in their hotel room.

Spaw typed up her notes, hired a company to improve the quality of the iPhone recording, and shared the resulting information with other Board members.

Huff sued Spaw under the federal Wiretap Act, alleging that she violated his privacy when she intentionally intercepted and disclosed his confidential communications. The district court entered summary judgment for Shaw, reasoning that Huff did not have a reasonable expectation of privacy in his pocket-dialed call, and therefore the Wiretap Act did not apply. Huff appealed.

You Be the Judge: *Did Huff have a reasonable expectation of privacy in his pocket-dialed conversations?*

Argument for Huff: To demonstrate a reasonable expectation of privacy, Huff must first show that he had an *actual* expectation of privacy and, second, he must prove that his expectation was reasonable. Huff and

[20]Charges were later dropped because of issues about the admissibility of the evidence.

Savage retreated to an outdoor balcony to make sure their conversation was not overheard. Seeing no one within earshot, they had an actual expectation that their conversation was private. The defendant suggests that, because Huff knew his iPhone was capable of pocket-dialing, his expectation was not reasonable. If this view were true, no one in modern society could ever expect privacy.

Argument for Spaw: James Huff's statements do not qualify for Wiretap Act protection because he did not have a reasonable expectation of privacy. The question is not what Huff thought, assumed, or wanted—it is whether it was reasonable for him to believe he was entitled to complete privacy under the circumstances. Huff knew his phone was capable of pocket-dialing and transmitting his conversation, but he took no precautions to safeguard against this foreseeable event. He could have locked his phone or powered it down. His carelessness exposed his conversation to Spaw. If a person inadvertently undresses in front of an uncovered window, he cannot claim that he deserved privacy when a passerby takes his picture. The same concept applies here.

Accessing Email. The Stored Communications Act (Title II of the ECPA) prohibits unauthorized access to or disclosure of stored wire and electronic communications. The definition of electronic communication includes email, voice mail, and social media. An action does not violate the ECPA if it is unintentional or if either party consents.

Under the Stored Communications Act:

- **Any intended recipient of an electronic communication has the right to disclose it.** Thus, if you sound off in an email to a friend about your boss, the (former) friend may legally forward that email to the boss or anyone else.
- **Internet service providers (ISPs) are generally prohibited from disclosing electronic messages to anyone other than the addressee**, unless this disclosure is necessary for the performance of their service or for the protection of their own rights or property.

Internet service providers (ISPs)
Companies that connect users to the internet

The ECPA also applies to employers. An employer has the right to monitor workers' electronic communications if (1) the employee consents; (2) the monitoring occurs in the ordinary course of business; or (3) in the case of email, if the employer provides the computer system.

Thus, an employer has the right to monitor electronic communication even if it does not relate to work activities. This monitoring may include an employee's social media activities.

But one thing employers cannot do to is access an employee's social media profile by trickery or coercion. As we saw earlier in the *Ehling* case, coercion may constitute an invasion of privacy. It may also violate the ECPA. When a restaurant suspected that one of its waiters was disparaging customers on a private social media page, its managers wanted proof. Since the page was private, they convinced another employee to give them her social media login information so they could log in as her. No one won: The restaurant fired the waiter and was later found in violation of the Stored Communications Act. The court concluded that the employer coerced the hostess into disclosing her password.[21]

Foreign Espionage

Former National Security Agency (NSA) contractor Edward Snowden set off an international firestorm when he leaked information revealing the extent of U.S. surveillance on everyone from U.S. citizens to world leaders and international charities. Angela Merkel, Chancellor of Germany and a U.S. ally, was furious to learn that the NSA had been listening in on her cell phone. Snowden reported that, as an NSA agent, he could, sitting at his desk, "wiretap anyone, from you or your accountant, to a federal judge or even the president, if I had a personal email." According to Snowden, the U.S. government was reading emails, mapping cell phone locations, reviewing browser histories, and monitoring just about everything that anyone does online.

---

21 Pietrylo v. Hillstone Rest. Grp., 2009 WL 3128420, 2009 U.S. Dist. LEXIS 88702 (D.N.J.2009).

What is the harm of surveillance? And is there a law against it? If people know that the government could be surveilling them, they self-censor, that is, they proactively limit what they read and communicate. Thus, after Snowden's disclosures, searches on Wikipedia of words relating to terrorism, such as *jihad*, *Hezbollah*, and dirty bomb suddenly declined. It seemed people were scared to create a digital record of such searches, even though there was no evidence that the government was prosecuting people for reading this type of information.[22] If an informed and secure electorate is important in a democracy, self-censorship is dangerous.

The **Foreign Intelligence Surveillance Act (FISA)** sets out the rules that limit the use of electronic surveillance to collect foreign intelligence (otherwise known as spying) within the United States. Congress enacted FISA in 1978 after decades of abuses in the name of national security. However, in the aftermath of the 9/11 terrorist attacks, FISA's protections were weakened. **Now, the FISA provides that:**

Foreign Intelligence Surveillance Act (FISA)
Federal statute governing the government's collection of foreign intelligence in the United States

- To spy on people located in the United States who are communicating abroad, the government does not need a warrant but it must obtain permission from a secret Foreign Intelligence Surveillance Court (FISC). To obtain this permission, the government need only demonstrate that the surveillance (1) targets "persons reasonably believed to be located outside the United States" and (2) seeks "foreign intelligence information." This standard gives the government broad powers to collect emails, phone calls, and other electronic communications between people in the United States and anyone abroad.
- Government agencies must delete irrelevant and personally identifying data before providing it to other agencies.
- The government must notify defendants if the evidence used against them was gathered by FISA surveillance.

In the aftermath of the Snowden leaks, many lawsuits challenged the U.S. government's surveillance practices. Snowden revealed that the FISC ordered Verizon to give the NSA all of its subscribers' communication records, including the numbers called and the time, location, and duration of calls. An appeals court ruled that this massive, bulk collection of phone records was illegal and overbroad. The judge wrote that "such expansive development of government repositories of formerly private records would be an unprecedented contraction of the privacy expectations of all Americans."[23] The balance between privacy and national security will continue to spark heated debates.

State Statutes

An exhaustive list of state privacy laws is beyond the scope of this book, but be aware that many states have passed their own privacy laws—some of which are more protective than their federal counterparts.

Here are some examples:

- **Reader Privacy.** Some states, such as Arizona and Missouri, prohibit libraries from disclosing their patrons' reading habits. California and Delaware prohibit online booksellers from sharing the list of books browsed, read, or purchased by their customers.
- **Online Privacy Policies.** California requires any website that collects personal information from its residents to post a privacy policy conspicuously and then abide by its terms. Companies collecting information from Californians (including by mobile app) must disclose their consumer software tracking policies.

---

22 Jonathan Shaw, "The Watchers," *Harvard Magazine*, January–February 2017, p. 56.

23 American Civil Liberties Union v. Clapper, 785 F.3d 787 (2015).

- **Disclosure of Personally Identifying Information.** Minnesota and Nevada require ISPs to obtain their customers' consent before sharing any of their information, including surfing habits and sites visited.
- **Employee Monitoring.** Delaware and Connecticut require employers to notify their workers before monitoring emails or internet usage.
- **Social Media Passwords.** Over a dozen states now ban employers from requesting job candidates' or employees' social media passwords.[24]

10-2d European Privacy Law

It is important to keep in mind that other countries regulate privacy very differently. Europeans have long considered the privacy of personal information to be a fundamental right. The European Convention on Human Rights declares, "Everyone has the right to respect for his private and family life, his home, and his correspondence."[25] This fundamental right to privacy has been incorporated into the laws of EU member states.

EU General Data Protection Regulation (GDPR)
Sets out the data privacy rights of all Europeans

The EU General Data Protection Regulation (GDPR) protects the data of all Europeans. The GDPR:

- Applies to any business that processes Europeans' data, including companies located outside of Europe.
- Defines "data" as any information that can be used, directly or indirectly, to identify someone, including a name, picture, or geolocation.
- Defines "processing" to mean anything that is done to or with a person's data, including collecting and storing it.
- Allows people to stop companies from processing their personal data.
- Grants individuals broad rights to their data, including the right to know how it is used, the opportunity to edit or delete inaccuracies, and the right to have it erased from the internet if it is no longer relevant or of public concern.
- Requires data processors to notify the authorities and individuals of any data breach.
- Provides significant penalties. Websites that mishandle their customer's information may be fined up to 4 percent of their annual worldwide revenue. Large multinationals like Google could face fines in the billions of euros.

European privacy laws are the strictest in the world, and their effects far-reaching. Because so many companies from outside Europe operate there, these rules affect businesses and employees worldwide.

10-3 REGULATION IN THE DIGITAL WORLD

The "internet," a term derived from "interconnected network," began in the 1960s as a project to link military contractors and universities. Today, it is a giant network that connects smaller groups of linked computer networks. The World Wide Web, a subnetwork of

[24]Oregon, Arkansas, California, Colorado, Illinois, Maryland, Michigan, Nevada, New Jersey, New Mexico, Utah, and Washington are among those states with social media privacy laws.

[25]European Convention on Human Rights, art. 8, November 4, 1950, 213 U.N.T.S. 221.

the internet, is a decentralized collection of documents containing text, pictures, and sound. Users can move from document to document using links that form a "web" of information.

10-3a Net Neutrality

Centuries ago, when travel was limited, businesses that provided travel services, such as inns and stagecoaches, had a virtual monopoly. There might be only one way to get to another town and only one place to stay when there. To protect consumers, the law imposed a set of so-called "common carrier" rules, which required these businesses to serve everyone equally and to charge fair prices.

The same legal principles apply in cyberspace. Internet service providers (ISPs), which are companies like Comcast and Verizon that connect customers to the internet, are today's innkeepers. The Federal Communications Commission (FCC), the federal agency that regulates broadband infrastructure, became concerned that ISPs might disrupt the neutral flow of information on the internet. It worried that an ISP might, for example, limit access to the *USA Today* website if it wanted to spike traffic to its own news website, or it might degrade the quality of the connection to Bing if a competitor like Google paid for prioritized access.

In response to these concerns, the FCC adopted a policy of **net neutrality**: the principle that all information on the internet must receive equal treatment regardless of source. The agency prohibits broadband ISPs from blocking lawful content or giving preferential treatment to some internet content or traffic. Despite many court challenges to net neutrality, judges have consistently held that the policy is constitutional and within the FCC's authority.[26]

Net neutrality
The principle that all information flows on the internet must receive equal treatment

But net neutrality remains highly controversial. Both those in favor and those opposed argue the same thing: that if their side wins, consumers and innovation will benefit. ISPs also argue that they should be able to control internet traffic because some websites, like those that deliver telemedicine or emergency services, deserve priority access.

As of this writing, net neutrality faces many challenges. Its opponents in Congress have threatened to cut FCC funds or write new laws to overturn it. Stay tuned.

10-3b Regulation of User-Generated Content

Sir Tim Berners-Lee, creator of the World Wide Web, described his vision of the Web as "a collaborative medium, a place where we all meet and read and write." Berners-Lee was referring to **user-generated content**—everything from social media posts, blogs, comments, customer reviews, wikis, images, and videos—created by end users and shared publicly through the Web. But Berners-Lee also acknowledged that although the Web does not "inherently make people do good things, or bad things," bad things can happen online. One role of the law is to prevent these bad things.

User-generated content
Any content created and made publicly available by end users

10-3c Online Speech

A recent survey found that 73 percent of adult internet users have witnessed online harassment and 40 percent have personally experienced it. **The First Amendment to the Constitution protects free speech, even when it is dreadful. But there are some exceptions.**

Defamation

How would you like to be called crazy, a cockroach, mega-scumbag, and crook in front of thousands of people? Or be accused of having poor hygiene? Because people are often bolder behind a computer than in person, these posts—and worse—commonly appear online.

[26] United States Telecom Ass'n v. Federal Communications Commission, 825 F.3d 674 (2016).

The law of defamation, discussed in Chapter 8, applies online. As with offline defamation, a plaintiff must prove that the defendant communicated a false statement, which harmed his reputation. The digital world has increased the number of defamation cases, but online defamation lawsuits face some common and unique challenges.

- **Opinions are not defamatory.** Digital lies are particularly harmful because they can spread swiftly and remain a permanent, searchable public record. However, statements that are simply opinions are never defamatory, no matter how harmful or insulting, or offensive. As one court put it, "the fact that society may find speech offensive is not a sufficient reason for suppressing it."[27] Thus, one court ruled that a tweet calling someone "f***ing crazy" was constitutionally protected because it was a statement of opinion. In contrast, a little league dad was found liable for defamation after falsely posting that his son's team encouraged adulterous affairs between the coaches and the players' mothers.[28] Unlike the "crazy" comment, the latter was a fact.
- **Statements must be verifiably false.** When visitors of the Grand Resort Hotel reported the presence of thick dirt and dark hair in the bathtubs, TripAdvisor ranked it one of the "Dirtiest Hotels in America." Grand Resort sued TripAdvisor for defamation, but lost. The appeals court concluded that there was no way to verify whether the hotel was, in fact, the most foul, so the statement was not technically false.
- **Anonymity.** A famous cartoon depicts a dog at a computer. The dog boasts, "on the internet, nobody knows you're a dog." The anonymity afforded by the digital world means that, in many instances, victims of online defamation may not know who posted the harmful comments. **The First Amendment protects anonymous speech, provided it is lawful**.

  When plaintiffs are harmed anonymously, they face the additional burden of persuading a court to force the web host or ISP to unmask the speaker. In making this decision, courts must (1) assess whether there is compelling evidence of wrongful conduct and (2) balance the need for disclosure against First Amendment concerns. Emily Mackie and Mason Awtry had a bad break-up. Around the same time, anonymous, negative reviews of Awtry's company appeared on Glassdoor.com, a website that allows employees to evaluate their workplace. Suspecting that Mackie was the author, Awtry sued Glassdoor to compel disclosure of the poster's identity. A California court denied the motion, reasoning that protecting anonymous speech was more important than saving Awtry's company from minimal reputational harm.[29]

The First Amendment protects anonymous speech, provided it is lawful.

SLAPP

A SLAPP, or strategic lawsuit against public participation, is a defamation lawsuit whose main objective is to silence speech through intimidation, rather than win a defamation case on the merits.

Some powerful plaintiffs abuse the legal system by suing anyone who criticizes them. The goal of a **strategic lawsuit against public participation**, or **SLAPP**, is not to win on the legal merits, but to intimidate and silence critics. Over 30 states have enacted anti-SLAPP laws to curb this practice. These laws typically force plaintiffs to prove upfront that their defamation lawsuit is likely to succeed at trial. Plaintiffs who cannot meet this burden must pay the other side's legal fees.

---

27 Krinsky v. Doe, 6159 Cal. App. 4th 1154 (2008).

28 Bedford v. Dallas Dodgers Baseball, 485 S.W. 3d 641 (Ct. App. Tex., 2016).

29 Awtry v. Glassdoor, Inc., 2016 WL 1275566 (N.D. CA, 2016).

Violence

While the First Amendment may protect offensive or outrageous speech, it does not protect threats of violence against individuals.

In the following case, the Supreme Court addressed the limits of free speech on social media.

Elonis v. United States

135 S.Ct. 2001
United States Supreme Court, 2015

Facts: After his wife left him, Anthony Elonis changed his Facebook name to "Tone Dougie" and began posting self-styled rap lyrics containing violent language and imagery about his friends and family. Elonis always posted disclaimers stating that the lyrics were fictitious, an art form, and even therapeutic. He often made reference to his First Amendment rights. Despite the disclaimers, many who knew him found his posts threatening.

In one instance, Elonis posted a picture of himself holding a toy knife against a co-worker's neck, along with the caption "I wish." His boss fired him and alerted the FBI, who started monitoring Elonis's Facebook activity.

Later, Elonis posted:

> Did you know that it's illegal for me to say I want to kill my wife? . . .
>
> It's one of the only sentences that I'm not allowed to say. . . .
>
> Now it was okay for me to say it right then because I was just telling you that it's illegal for me to say I want to kill my wife. . . .
>
> Um, but what's interesting is that it's very illegal to say I really, really think someone out there should kill my wife . . . But not illegal to say with a mortar launcher.

Accompanying the post was a diagram of his ex-wife's house with instructions on how to make the best getaway. Because of this post, a judge granted Elonis's ex-wife a restraining order against him.

Unhappy about the order, Elonis posted he would make "a name for himself" by initiating "the most heinous school shooting ever imagined." This post prompted two FBI agents to visit Elonis's home. When they left, Elonis immediately took to Facebook, writing that he would "leave [the female FBI agent] bleedin' from her jugular," among other violent acts.

Elonis was arrested for the federal crime of transmitting "any communication containing any threat . . . to injure the person of another" across state lines. The trial judge instructed the jury that the First Amendment does not protect a "true threat." The test of a true threat, according to the judge, was whether a reasonable person would perceive the statement as threatening. Elonis appealed, arguing that the test for a true threat should include the speaker's subjective intent to threaten, not the listener's perception. The appeals court affirmed Elonis's conviction, which was appealed to Supreme Court.

Issue: ***Should a threat be defined by the speaker's intent or by the listener's reasonable perception?***

Excerpts from Justice Roberts's Decision: An individual who "transmits in interstate or foreign commerce any communication containing any threat to kidnap any person or any threat to injure the person of another" is guilty of a felony. This statute does not specify that the defendant must have any mental state with respect to these elements. In particular, it does not indicate whether the defendant must intend that his communication contain a threat.

The fact that the statute does not specify any required mental state does not mean that none exists. A defendant must be blameworthy in mind before he can be found guilty, a concept courts have expressed over time through various terms such as mens rea, scienter, malice aforethought, guilty knowledge, and the like. When interpreting federal criminal statutes that are silent on the required mental state, we read into the statute only that *mens rea* which is necessary to separate wrongful conduct from otherwise innocent conduct.

Elonis's conviction was premised solely on how his posts would be understood by a reasonable person. Such a reasonable person standard is a familiar feature of civil liability in tort law, but is inconsistent with the conventional requirement for criminal conduct—*awareness* of some wrongdoing. Having liability turn on whether a reasonable person regards the communication as a threat—regardless of what the defendant thinks—reduces culpability on the all-important element of the crime to negligence, and we have long been reluctant to infer that a negligence standard was intended in criminal statutes. Under these principles, what Elonis thinks does matter.

In light of the foregoing, Elonis's conviction cannot stand. Federal criminal liability generally does not turn solely on the results of an act without considering the defendant's mental state. That understanding took deep and early root in American soil and Congress left it intact here: wrongdoing must be conscious to be criminal.

Revenge Porn

Revenge porn is the unauthorized posting of sexually explicit photos of someone else, often with the intent to embarrass or shame. Over 35 states now have laws making revenge porn a crime. Although many states already criminalize taking another person's nude picture without consent, these new laws apply to pictures taken consensually, but later posted online for the purpose of intentionally harassing or causing emotional distress.

10-3d Liability of Internet Service Providers

The internet is an enormously powerful tool for disseminating information. But what if some of this information happens to be false or in violation of our privacy rights? Is an ISP or web host liable for transmitting it to the world?

Congress reasoned that if ISPs faced the threat of a lawsuit for every problematic posting, the companies would severely restrict content, and the development of the internet. To prevent his result, Congress passed the **Communications Decency Act of 1996 (CDA)**, which created broad immunity for ISPs and websites.

Communications Decency Act of 1996 (CDA)
Provides ISPs immunity from liability when information was provided by an end user

Under the CDA, end users and anyone who simply provides a neutral forum for information (such as ISPs and website hosts) are not liable for content provided by someone else. Only content providers are liable.[30] But to avoid liability, the ISP or website must not create or otherwise develop the content. When a minor was sexually assaulted by a man she met on social media, her family sued the site, claiming it did not have proper safety measures to prevent the girl from meeting her attacker. The court rejected this claim, reasoning that the site was immune because it had not provided the content.[31]

The following case involves dirty tactics. It illustrates the purpose of the CDA—and its costs.

Jones v. Dirty World Entertainment Recordings LLC

755 F.3d 398
United States Court of Appeals for the Sixth Circuit, 2014

Facts: Sarah Jones, a high school teacher and Cincinnati Bengals cheerleader, was the subject of several posts on TheDirty.com, a gossip website run by Nik Richie. Anonymous submissions accused Jones, among other things, of being promiscuous with many football players and suggested that she had a sexually transmitted disease. Richie then posted some of his own comments to the effect that Jones was a sex addict and unfit to be a teacher.

Jones sent over 27 emails to Richie asking him to remove the posts, but he refused. Jones sued The Dirty for defamation and intentional infliction of emotional distress. A jury awarded her $38,000 in compensatory damages and $300,000 in punitive damages. The Dirty appealed, arguing that the CDA made it immune from liability because it did not create or develop the defamatory content.

Issue: ***Is The Dirty immune from liability under Section 230 of the Communications Decency Act?***

Excerpts from Judge Gibbons's Decision: Section 230 of the CDA immunizes providers of interactive computer services against liability arising from content created by third parties. At its core, Section 230 bars lawsuits seeking to hold a service provider liable for its exercise of a publisher's traditional editorial functions—such as deciding whether to publish, withdraw, postpone or alter content.

Section 230 serves three main purposes. First it maintains the robust nature of Internet communication and keeps government interference to a minimum. Second, the immunity provided protects against the heckler's veto that would chill free speech. Third, section 230 encourages interactive computer service providers to self-regulate.

[30] 47 U.S.C. §230.
[31] Doe v. MySpace, 528 F.3d 413 (5th Cir. 2008).

Section 230's grant of immunity is not without limits however. It applies only to the extent that an interactive computer service provider is not responsible, in whole or in part, for the creation or development of the information.

This case turns on how narrowly or capaciously the statutory term "development" is read. Limited circuit precedent suggests the proper interpretation of "development" means something more involved than merely displaying or allowing access to content created by a third party, otherwise Section 230 would be meaningless. Jones's defamation claims target the statements that were posted by a third party. Because Richie did not materially contribute to the illegality of those statements, the CDA bars Jones's claims. Richie cannot be found to have materially contributed to the defamatory content of the statements simply because those posts were selected for publication. Further, it would break the concepts of responsibility and material contribution to hold Richie responsible for the defamatory content of speech because he later commented on that speech. Although ludicrous, Richie's remarks did not materially contribute to the defamatory content of the posts on the website.

Because (1) the defendants are internet service providers, (2) the statements at issue were provided by another information content provider, and (3) Jones's claim seeks to treat the defendants as a publisher or speaker of those statements, the CDA bars Jones's claims. We vacate the judgment in favor of Jones.

Note that the CDA does not protect web hosts or ISPs that engage in crimes or infringe intellectual property rights. Bright Builders, Inc., hosted Copycatclubs.com, a website that, as you might guess, sold counterfeit golf clubs. The court held that Bright Builders was liable despite the CDA because it participated in the design, building, marketing, and support of Copycatclubs.com. It even helped locate the counterfeit clubs that the website sold.[32] Ultimately, a jury returned a verdict of $770,750 against Bright Builders.

Website operators are also liable for their broken contracts and promises. After Cynthia Barnes broke up with her boyfriend, he created a profile of her on a Yahoo website, where he posted revenge porn, together with her addresses and phone numbers. He also suggested that she was interested in sex with random strangers. Many men were willing to oblige. For months, Yahoo did not even respond to Barnes's request to remove the profile. Not until a television show prepared to run a story about the incident did Yahoo contact Barnes to promise that the profile would be removed immediately. But two months later the company had taken no action, so Barnes sued. The appeals court ruled that Barnes could bring a contract claim against Yahoo under a theory of promissory estoppel—that she had relied on the company's promise.[33]

EXAMStrategy

Question: Someone posted an anonymous review on TripAdvisor.com alleging that the owner of a restaurant had entertained a prostitute there. The allegation was false. TripAdvisor refused to investigate or remove the review. Does the restaurant owner have a valid claim against the website?

Strategy: Remember that web hosts are liable only if they have engaged in wrongdoing.

Result: As a web host, TripAdvisor is not liable for content. It would be liable only if it promised to take down the review and then did not.

---

32 Roger Cleveland Golf Co. v. Price, 2010 U.S. Dist. LEXIS 128044, 2010 WL 5019260 (D.S.C. 2010).

33 Barnes v. Yahoo, Inc., 570 F.3d 1096 (9th Cir. 2008). Promissory estoppel is discussed in Chapter 11.

10-3e Consumer Protection

The Federal Trade Commission Act authorizes the Federal Trade Commission (FTC) to protect consumers and prevent unfair competition. The FTC's regulatory activities are discussed in greater detail in Chapter 38, on antitrust, and Chapter 39, on consumer protection. Here we focus on the FTC's regulation of the internet, including deceptive advertising, spam, and children's privacy.

Unfair or Deceptive Advertising

Section 5 of the FTC Act prohibits unfair and deceptive acts or practices. The FTC applies this statute to online privacy policies. It does not require websites to have a privacy policy, but if they do have one, they must comply with it, and it cannot be deceptive.

The FTC brought action against Twitter after hackers gained access to its users' accounts through its administrative system. Twitter had allowed any employee access to its system, which was protected by an easy-to-guess password (1234, maybe?). The hackers reset passwords and sent fake tweets. For example, an unauthorized person sent a tweet from Barack Obama's Twitter account offering free gasoline to users who answered a survey (which seems benign compared with what the hacker could have done). The FTC found that Twitter had engaged in deceptive acts because its faulty security violated the company's promise to users that it would protect their information from unauthorized access. As part of the settlement, Twitter agreed to strengthen its security practices.

The FTC also regulates truth in advertising and endorsements—and its rules apply equally to bloggers, YouTubers, online reviewers, and others on social media. Under FTC rules, anyone who endorses a product must disclose all compensation (either in cash or free products) they receive for product reviews. Moreover, celebrities must disclose their relationships with advertisers when touting products on social media. On Twitter, these disclosures can be as simple as adding "#ad." The purpose of the rule is to ensure that consumers understand that it is a paid endorsement.

Spam

Spam
Unsolicited commercial email

Spam is officially known as unsolicited commercial email or unsolicited bulk email. Whatever it is called, it is one of the most annoying aspects of email. It has been estimated that 90 percent of email is spam. And roughly half of these messages were fraudulent—either in content (promoting a scam) or in packaging (the headers or return address are false).

The Controlling the Assault of Non-Solicited Pornography and Marketing Act (CAN-SPAM) is a federal statute that regulates spam, but does not prohibit it. This statute applies to virtually all promotional emails, whether or not the sender has a preexisting relationship with the recipient. **Under this statute, commercial email:**

- May not have deceptive headings (From, To, Reply To, Subject),
- Must offer an opt-out system permitting the recipient to unsubscribe (and must honor those requests promptly),
- Must clearly indicate that the email is an advertisement,
- Must provide a valid physical return address (not a post office box), and
- Must clearly indicate the nature of pornographic messages.

A company can avoid these requirements by obtaining advance permission from the recipients.

Children's Online Privacy

The **Children's Online Privacy Protection Act of 1998 (COPPA)** prohibits internet operators from collecting information from children under 13 without parental permission. It also requires sites to disclose how they will use any information they acquire.

Children's Online Privacy Protection Act of 1998 (COPPA)
Federal statute enforced by the FTC regulating children's privacy online

Path Inc. had a mobile app that allowed users to create a daily journal and share it with friends. This app permitted children to register without parental permission. Each time a user posted a "thought" on the app, they were invited to reveal their location through the geo-tracking feature as well as the names of friends who were with them. When challenged by the FTC, Path agreed to stop this practice and pay a fine of $800,000.

Cybersecurity

The internet has ushered in a wave of new crimes, from phishing (attempts to fraudulently acquire personal data from users) to denial-of-service attacks (which paralyze computers and networks). For individuals, these crimes can result in identity theft, financial fraud, and data loss. Hacking can also threaten privacy and health. As more daily devices become interconnected, even household items and medical devices are at risk of breach.

On a larger scale, hacking can affect the operation of basic infrastructure (such as power grids and telecommunications) and can threaten financial, medical, and military operations.

Almost every state now has **data breach laws** that require businesses to notify individuals affected by a security breach. About a dozen states have enacted **data disposal laws**, which mandate that businesses destroy customer data and maintain reasonable security procedures to guard against theft.

Federal agencies have also addressed cybersecurity. The Securities and Exchange Commission (SEC), which regulates the securities industry, requires financial institutions to adopt written policies, procedures, and training programs to safeguard customer records and information.

Fair Information Practices

By now it is clear that we cannot rely on the law or technology alone to safeguard our privacy. But should good privacy practices look like?

The FTC has issued a set of guidelines known as the Fair Information Practices (FIPS). **The core principles of the FIPS are:**

- **Notice/Awareness.** Notice should be given before any personal information is collected.
- **Choice/Consent.** People should be able to control the use and destination of their information.
- **Access/Participation.** People should have the ability to view, correct, or amend any personally identifiable record about them.
- **Integrity/Security.** Information collectors must take reasonable precautions to ensure that the data they collect are accurate and secure.

Although they are not law, the FIPS have guided the creation of many privacy laws and policies. These principles summarize the rights that we as individuals and businesses should demand and protect.

CHAPTER CONCLUSION

The digital world has brought great social benefit and innovation, but also presents challenges. In a race between the law and technology, it is usually technology that wins. Many of the laws that apply to the digital world were written in the time before the internet was part of our daily lives. Courts can apply some of these old laws in new ways, but as legislators and courts learn from experience, new laws and novel problem-solving approaches are required.

EXAM REVIEW

1. **THE FOURTH AMENDMENT** The Fourth Amendment to the Constitution prohibits unreasonable searches and seizures by the government. This provision applies to computers.

2. **REASONABLE EXPECTATION OF PRIVACY** There is a reasonable expectation of privacy if (1) the person had a subjective expectation of privacy and (2) society accepts that expectation as reasonable.

3. **PUBLIC DISCLOSURE OF PRIVATE FACTS** It is a violation of tort law to disclose secret information if disclosure would be highly offensive to a reasonable person and the information is not of legitimate public concern.

4. **INTRUSION** Intrusion into someone's private life is a tort if a reasonable person would find it offensive.

EXAMStrategy

Question: Every time Dave logs on to his company computer, he clicks "I agree" to the firm's computer usage policy, which states that the employer can monitor everything he does online. On his lunch break, Dave logs on to his Facebook account from his company computer to upload some pictures from his weekend's activities. Can Dave's employer snoop?

Strategy: Does Dave have a subjective expectation of privacy? Given the circumstances, is Dave's expectation of privacy accepted by society? (See the "Result" at the end of this Exam Review section.)

5. **THE WIRETAP ACT** This act makes it illegal to intercept or record face-to-face oral communications and telephone calls during their transmission.

6. **THE ELECTRONIC COMMUNICATIONS PRIVACY ACT OF 1986 (ECPA)** The ECPA is a federal statute that prohibits unauthorized interception or disclosure of wire and electronic communications.

EXAMStrategy

Question: Dr. Norman Scott was the head of the orthopedics department at a hospital. His contract with the hospital provided for $14 million in severance pay if the hospital fired him without cause. When the hospital fired him, he filed suit seeking his $14 million. He used the hospital's email system to send emails to his lawyer. The hospital notified him that it had copies of these emails, which it planned to read. He said that the hospital did not have this right because the emails were protected by the attorney-client privilege, which is a legal right to keep communications between a lawyer and a client secret.

Strategy: What does the ECPA provide? Is there an exception for the attorney-client privilege? Should there be? (See the "Result" at the end of this Exam Review section.)

7. **THE FOREIGN INTELLIGENCE SURVEILLANCE ACT (FISA)** The FISA provides the rules for the government's collection of foreign intelligence within the United States.

8. **GENERAL DATA PRIVACY REGULATION** The EU General Data Privacy Regulation gives EU residents broad rights in their personal information, including the right to know how it is used, the opportunity to edit or delete inaccuracies, and the right to have it erased from the internet if it is no longer relevant or of public concern.

9. **NET NEUTRALITY** The principle that all internet content and traffic should receive equal treatment.

10. **THE FIRST AMENDMENT** The First Amendment to the Constitution protects speech on the internet so long as the speech does not violate some other law.

11. **SLAPP** A SLAPP, or strategic lawsuit against public participation, is a defamation lawsuit whose main objective is to silence speech through intimidation, rather than win a defamation case on the merits.

12. **COMMUNICATIONS DECENCY ACT OF 1996 (CDA)** Under the CDA, ISPs and web hosts are not liable for information that is provided by someone else.

EXAMStrategy

Question: Ton Cremers was the director of security at Amsterdam's famous Rijksmuseum and the operator of the Museum Security Network (the Network) website. Robert Smith, a handyman working for Ellen Batzel in North Carolina, sent an email to the Network alleging that Batzel was the granddaughter of Heinrich Himmler (one of Hitler's henchmen) and that she had art that Himmler had stolen. These allegations were completely untrue. Cremers posted Smith's email on the Network's website and sent it to the Network's subscribers. Cremers exercised some editorial discretion in choosing which emails to send to subscribers, generally omitting any that were unrelated to stolen art. Is Cremers liable to Batzel for the harm that this inaccurate information caused?

Strategy: Cremers is liable only if he is a content provider. (See the "Result" at the end of this Exam Review section.)

13. **THE FTC ACT** Section 5 of the FTC Act prohibits unfair and deceptive practices. The FTC does not require websites to have a privacy policy, but if they do have one, it cannot be deceptive and they must comply with it.

14. **THE CONTROLLING THE ASSAULT OF NON-SOLICITED PORNOGRAPHY AND MARKETING ACT (CAN-SPAM)** The CAN-SPAM is a federal statute that does not prohibit spam but instead regulates it. Under this statute, commercial email:
    - May not have deceptive headings (From, To, Reply To, Subject),
    - Must offer an opt-out system permitting the recipient to unsubscribe (and must honor those requests promptly),
    - Must clearly indicate that the email is an advertisement,
    - Must provide a valid physical return address (not a post office box), and
    - Must clearly indicate the nature of pornographic messages.

15. **THE CHILDREN'S ONLINE PRIVACY PROTECTION ACT OF 1998 (COPPA)** The COPPA prohibits internet operators from collecting information from children under 13 without parental permission. It also requires sites to disclose how they will use any information they acquire.

16. **THE FAIR INFORMATION PRACTICES (FIPS)** The FIPS include Notice/Awareness, Choice/Consent, Access/Participation, and Integrity/Security. Although the FIPS are not law, they have had great influence on privacy laws and policy.

RESULTS

4. Result: Dave does not have a reasonable expectation of privacy on his work computer, even if he is on break and on his private Facebook page. He consented to employer surveillance when he logged in.

6. Result: The court ruled that the hospital could read the emails. If the doctor wanted the content of these emails to be protected under the attorney-client privilege, he should not have sent them over the hospital email system.

12. Result: The court found that Cremers was not liable under the CDA.

MULTIPLE-CHOICE QUESTIONS

1. The following agency is charged with the regulation of electronic communications:
   (a) National Security Agency
   (b) Federal Trade Commission
   (c) Federal Communications Commission
   (d) Foreign Intelligence Surveillance Court

2. Because Blaine Blogger reviews movies on his blog, cinemas allow him in for free. Nellie Newspaper Reporter also gets free admission to movies. Blaine ______________ disclose on his blog that he receives free tickets. Nellie ______________ disclose in her articles that she receives free tickets.
   (a) must, must
   (b) need not, need not
   (c) must, need not
   (d) need not, must
3. Which of the following is not protected by the First Amendment?
   (a) True threats
   (b) All threats
   (c) Offensive language
   (d) Insults
4. An employer has the right to monitor workers' electronic communications if:
   (a) the employee consents.
   (b) the monitoring occurs in the ordinary course of business.
   (c) the employer provides the computer system.
   (d) All of these
   (e) None of these
5. Spiro Spammer sends millions of emails a day asking people to donate to his college tuition fund. Oddly enough, many people do. Everything in the emails is accurate (including his 1.9 GPA). Which of the following statements is true?
   (a) Spiro has violated the CAN-SPAM Act because he has sent unsolicited commercial emails.
   (b) Spiro has violated the CAN-SPAM Act if he has not offered recipients an opportunity to unsubscribe.
   (c) Spiro has violated the CAN-SPAM Act because he is asking for money.
   (d) Spiro has violated the CAN-SPAM Act unless the recipients have granted permission to him to send these emails.
6. Sushila suspects that her boyfriend Plum is being unfaithful. While he is asleep, she takes his smart phone out from under his pillow and goes through all his texts. Which law has Sushila violated?
   (a) The First Amendment
   (b) The Communications Decency Act
   (c) The Stored Communications Act
   (d) The Wiretap Act
   (e) None of these

CASE QUESTIONS

1. **ETHICS** Chitika, Inc., provided online tracking tools on websites. When consumers clicked the "opt-out" button, indicating that they did not want to be tracked, they were not—for ten days. After that, the software would resume tracking. Is there a legal problem with Chitika's system? An ethical problem? What Life Principles were operating here?

2. ***YOU BE THE JUDGE* WRITING PROBLEM** Jerome Schneider wrote several books on how to avoid taxes. These books were sold on Amazon.com. Amazon permits visitors to post comments about items for sale. Amazon's policy suggests that these comments should be civil (e.g., no profanity or spiteful remarks). The comments about Schneider's books were not so kind. One person alleged Schneider was a felon. When Schneider complained, an Amazon representative agreed that some of the postings violated its guidelines and promised that they would be removed within one to two business days. Two days later, the posting had not been removed. Schneider filed suit. **Argument for Schneider:** Amazon has editorial discretion over the posted comments. It both establishes guidelines and then monitors the comments to ensure that they comply with the guidelines. These activities make Amazon an information content provider, not protected by the Communications Decency Act. Also, Amazon violated its promise to take down the content. **Argument for Amazon:** The right to edit material is not the same thing as creating the material in the first place.

3. Barrow was a government employee. Because he shared his office computer with another worker, he brought in his personal computer from home to use for office work. No other employee accessed it, but it was connected to the office network. The computer was not password protected, nor was it regularly turned off. When another networked computer was reported to be running slowly, an employee looked at Barrow's machine to see if it was the source of the problem. He found material that led to Barrow's termination. Had Barrow's Fourth Amendment rights been violated?

4. Someone posted a fake profile of actor Christianne Carafano on a dating website, Matchmaker.com. The profile, which included Carafano's photo, telephone number, and home address, invited men with "a strong sexual appetite" to join her in a one-night stand. Carafano received many sexually explicit and threatening messages and was forced to move out of her home. She sued Matchmaker, arguing that the company was liable for invasion of privacy, defamation, and negligence. What result?

5. Suspecting his wife was unfaithful, Simpson attached a recording device to the telephone lines in their home. Through the secret recordings, he was able to prove that she was indeed having an affair. Simpson's wife sued her husband under the Federal Wiretap Act. Who wins and why?

DISCUSSION QUESTIONS

1. Marina Stengart used her company laptop to communicate with her lawyer via her personal, password-protected, web-based email account. The company's policy stated:

   > E-mail and voice mail messages, internet use and communication, and computer files are considered part of the company's business and client records. Such communications are not to be considered private or personal to any individual employee. Occasional personal use is permitted; however, the system should not be used to solicit for outside business ventures, charitable organizations, or for any political or religious purpose, unless authorized by the Director of Human Resources.

   After she filed an employment lawsuit against her employer, the company hired an expert to access her emails that had been automatically stored on the laptop. Are these emails private?

2. Eric Schmidt, former CEO of Google, has written:

   > The communication technologies we use today are invasive by design, collecting our photos, comments, and friends into giant databases that are searchable and, in the absence of outside regulation, fair game for employers, university admissions personnel, and town gossips. We are what we tweet.[34]

   Do you consider this a problem? If so, can the law fix it?

3. Imagine that you are the judge in the *Elonis* case. Would you have excused Elonis's conduct under the First Amendment? When is a threat a true threat and when is it just social media banter?

4. The European Union has created a "right to be forgotten" online. This right allows Europeans to request that websites take down their personal information, as long as it is not in the public interest. For example, a person would be able to request that Facebook delete her unflattering photograph, if it is outdated and is not newsworthy. Is this law a good idea? Would U.S. lawmakers ever consider a law like this? Why or why not?

5. **ETHICS** JuicyCampus.com was a website where college students could anonymously gossip about their schools. To encourage users to "dish dirt," the site promised total anonymity: It did not require a login or username; its slogan was "Always anonymous . . . Always juicy"; and it assured its users that it was impossible "for anyone to find out who you are and where you are located." The site also instructed users on how to download IP-cloaking software to further ensure anonymity. As a result, most of the Juicy Campus posts were more than just juicy: They ranged from shocking accusations to harassment and revenge. These rumors tarnished reputations, hurt feelings, and tore apart college communities. Women, minorities, and gay students were disproportionately affected. Whether or not it is legally liable, does JuicyCampus.com have an ethical duty to its users? What Life Principles are at stake?

---

[34]Eric Schmidt & Jared Cohen, The New Digital Age: Reshaping the Future of People, Nations and Business (2013).

Contracts

UNIT

3

CHAPTER 11

INTRODUCTION TO CONTRACTS

Chris always planned to propose to his girlfriend, Alissa, at Chez Luc, their favorite ritzy restaurant. When he was ready to pop the question, Chris went on Chez Luc's website to reserve a special table. But the website would not grant him a seating time unless he clicked the box that said "No one in my party will use a cell phone at Chez Luc." Chris agreed and was issued a booking at his waterfront table of choice.

After Alissa's exuberant "yes" during the appetizer course, the newly engaged couple could not contain their excitement. First they posted selfies on social media. Then they called their parents to share the good news . . . only to be confronted by the angry maître d', who escorted the couple out of the dining room for breaching their contract with the restaurant.

The angry maître d' escorted the couple out of the dining room.

We make promises and agreements all the time—from the casual "I'll call you later" to more formal business contracts. These agreements may be long or short, written or oral, negotiable or not. But they are not necessarily enforceable through the legal system. One of the aims of contract law is to determine which agreements are "worthy" of legal enforcement. How do we know if an agreement is "worthy"?

Contract law is based on the notion that you are the best judge of your own welfare. By and large, you are free to make whatever agreements you want, subject to whatever rules you choose, and the law will support you. However, this freedom is not limitless: The law does impose seven requirements, which we will analyze in detail in upcoming chapters.

Contract law is a story of freedom and power, rules and relationships—with drama to spare. It is important to study this story to avoid your own contract drama. Let's start with an introduction to contracts.

11-1 CONTRACTS

A contract is a legally enforceable agreement. People regularly make promises, but only some of them are enforceable. For a contract to be enforceable, seven key characteristics *must* be present. We will study this "checklist" at length in the next several chapters.

- **Offer**. All contracts begin when a person or a company proposes a deal. It might involve buying something, selling something, doing a job, or anything else. But only proposals made in certain ways amount to a legally recognized offer.
- **Acceptance**. Once a party receives an offer, he must respond to it in a certain way. We will examine the requirements of both offers and acceptances in Chapter 12.
- **Consideration**. There has to be bargaining that leads to an *exchange* between the parties. Contracts cannot be a one-way street; both sides must receive some measurable benefit.
- **Legality**. The contract must be for a lawful purpose. Courts will not enforce agreements to sell cocaine, for example.
- **Capacity**. The parties must be adults of sound mind.
- **Consent**. Certain kinds of trickery and force can prevent the formation of a contract.
- **Writing**. While verbal agreements are often contracts, some types of contracts must be in writing to be enforceable.

CONTRACTS CHECKLIST

- ☐ Offer
- ☐ Acceptance
- ☐ Consideration
- ☐ Legality
- ☐ Capacity
- ☐ Consent
- ☐ Writing

Once we have examined the essential parts of contracts, the unit will turn to other important issues:

- **Third-Party Interests.** If Jerome and Tara have a contract, and if the deal falls apart, can Kevin sue to enforce the agreement? It depends.
- **Performance and Discharge.** If a party fully accomplishes what the contract requires, his duties are discharged. But what if his obligations are performed poorly, or not at all?
- **Remedies.** A court will award money or other relief to a party injured by a breach of contract.

Let's apply these principles to the opening scenario. Is the "contract" between Chris and Chez Luc legally binding? Can Chez Luc kick out—or even *sue*—Chris for using his phone? In deciding this issue, a judge would consider whether the parties intentionally made an agreement which included:

- **A valid offer and acceptance.** The restaurant's website set forth its terms, which was an offer. Chris accepted when he clicked the box.
- **Consideration.** A judge would then carefully examine whether the parties exchanged something of value that proved that they both meant to be bound by this agreement. And there was. The restaurant gave up a coveted reservation time in exchange for Chris's promise to stay away from his phone.
- **Capacity and Legality.** A judge would also verify that the parties were adults of sound mind and that the subject matter of the contract was legal. It seems that Chris understood what he was doing and was of legal age (we certainly hope so, since he was getting engaged).
- **Consent.** There was no fraud or trickery on the part of the restaurant (the terms were clear, not buried so that Chris was unaware of them).
- **Writing.** The terms were in writing (although they did not have to be).

Therefore, the agreement was valid and enforceable. Whether kicking out a newly engaged couple is good business practice for a restaurant . . . now, that's a different story!

11-1a All Shapes and Sizes

Some contracts—like those in the opener—are small. But contracts can also be large. Lockheed Martin and Boeing spent years of work and millions of dollars competing for a U.S. Defense Department aircraft contract. Why the fierce effort? The deal was potentially good for 25 years and *$200 billion.* Lockheed won. The company earned the right to build the next generation of fighter jets—3,000 planes, with different varieties of the aircraft to be used by each of the American defense services and some allied forces as well.

Many contracts involve public issues. The Lockheed agreement concerns government agencies deciding how to spend taxpayer money for national defense. Other contracts concern intensely private matters. Mary Beth Whitehead signed a contract with William and Elizabeth Stern of New Jersey. For a fee of $10,000, Whitehead agreed to act as a surrogate mother and then deliver the baby to the Sterns for adoption after she carried it to term. But when little Melissa was born, Whitehead changed her mind and fled to Florida with the baby. The Sterns sued for breach of contract. Surrogacy contracts now lead to hundreds of births per year. Are the contracts immoral? Should they be illegal? Are there limits to what one person may pay another to do? The New Jersey Supreme Court, the first to rule on the issue, declared the contract illegal and void. The court nonetheless awarded Melissa to the Sterns, saying that it was in the child's best interest to live with them. Inevitably, legislators disagree about this emotional issue. Some states have passed statutes permitting surrogacy, while others prohibit it.

At times, we even enter contracts without knowing it. We make contracts each time we download an app, purchase software, and order from a restaurant menu. We even form legally enforceable agreements when we buy a bag of chips from a vending machine.

11-1b Contracts Defined

Contract
A legally enforceable agreement

We have seen that a **contract** is a promise that the law will enforce. As we look more closely at the elements of contract law, we will encounter some intricate issues. This is partly because we live in a complex society, which conducts its business in a wide variety of ways.

Remember, though, that we are usually interested in answering three basic questions, all relating to promises:

- Is it certain that the defendant promised to do something?
- If she did promise, is it fair to make her honor her word?
- If she did not promise, are there unusual reasons to hold her liable anyway?

11-1c Development of Contract Law

Courts have not always assumed that promises are legally significant. In the twelfth and thirteenth centuries, promises were not binding unless a person made them *in writing and affixed a seal* to the document. This was seldom done, and therefore most promises were unenforceable.

The common law changed very slowly, but by the fifteenth century, courts began to allow some suits based on a broken promise. There were still major limitations. Suppose a merchant hired a carpenter to build a new shop, and the carpenter failed to start the job on time. Now courts would permit the suit, but only if the merchant had paid some money to the carpenter. If the merchant made a 10 percent down payment, the contract would be enforceable. But if the merchant merely *promised* to pay when the building was done, and the carpenter never began work, the merchant could recover nothing.

In 1602, English courts began to enforce mutual *promises;* that is, deals in which neither party gave anything to the other but both promised to do something in the future. Thus, if a farmer promised to deliver a certain quantity of wheat to a merchant and the merchant agreed on the price, both parties were now bound by their promise, even though there had been no down payment. This was a huge step forward in the development of contract law, but many issues remained. Consider the following employment case from 1792, which raises issues of public policy that still challenge courts today.

Davis v. Mason

Michaelmas Term, 33d George III, p. 118
Court of King's Bench, 1792

Facts: Mason was a surgeon/apothecary in the English town of Thetford. Davis wished to apprentice himself to Mason. The two agreed that Davis would work for Mason and learn his profession. They further agreed that if Davis left Mason's practice, he would not set up a competing establishment within 10 miles of Thetford at any time within 14 years. Davis promised to pay £200 if he violated the agreement not to compete.

Davis began working for Mason in July 1789. In August 1791, Mason dismissed Davis, claiming misconduct, although Davis denied it. Davis then established his own practice within 10 miles of Thetford. Mason sued for the £200.

Davis admitted promising to pay the money. But he claimed that the agreement should be declared illegal and unenforceable. He argued that 14 years was unreasonably long to restrict him from the town of Thetford and that 10 miles was too great a distance. (In those days, 10 miles might take the better part of a day to travel.) He added an additional policy argument, saying that it was harmful to the public health to restrict a doctor from practicing his profession: If the people needed his service, they should have it. Finally, he said that his "consideration" was too great for this deal. In other words, it was unfair that he should pay £200 because he did not receive anything of that value from Mason.

Issue: ***Was the contract too unreasonable to enforce?***

Excerpts from Lord Kenyon's Decision: Here, the plaintiff being established in business as a surgeon at Thetford, the defendant wished to act as his assistant with a view of deriving a degree of credit from that situation; on which the former stipulated that the defendant should not come to live there under his auspices and steal away his patients: this seems to be a fair consideration. Then it was objected that the limits within which the defendant engaged not to practise are unreasonable: but I do not see that they are necessarily unreasonable, nor do I know how to draw the line. Neither are the public likely to be injured by an agreement of this kind, since every other person is at liberty to practise as a surgeon in this town.

Judgment for the Plaintiff.

Noncompetition agreement
A contract in which one party agrees not to compete with another

The contract between Davis and Mason is called a **noncompetition agreement**. Today they are more common than ever, and frequently litigated. The policy issues that Davis raised have never gone away. You may well be asked to sign a noncompetition agreement sometime in your professional life. We look at the issue in detail in Chapter 13 on consideration. That outcome was typical of contract cases for the next 100 years. Courts took a *laissez-faire* approach, declaring that parties had *freedom to contract* and would have to live with the consequences. Lord Kenyon saw Davis and Mason as equals, entering a bargain that made basic sense, and he had no intention of rewriting it. After 500 years of evolution, courts had come to regard promises as almost sacred. The law had gone from ignoring most promises to enforcing nearly all.

By the early twentieth century, bargaining power in business deals had changed dramatically. Farms and small businesses were yielding place to huge corporations in a trend that accelerated throughout the century. In the twenty-first century, multinational corporations span many continents, wielding larger budgets and more power than many of the nations in which they do business. When such a corporation contracts with a small company or an individual consumer, the latter may have little or no leverage. Courts increasingly looked at the basic fairness of contracts. Noncompetition agreements are no longer automatically enforced. Courts may alter them or ignore them entirely because the parties have such unequal power and because the public may have an interest in letting the employee go on to compete. Davis's argument—that the public is entitled to as many doctors as it needs—is frequently more successful in court today than it was in the days of Lord Kenyon.

Legislatures and the courts limit the effect of promises in other ways. Suppose you purchase a lawn mower with an attached tag warning you that the manufacturer is not responsible in the event of any malfunction or injury. You are required to sign a form acknowledging that the manufacturer has no liability of any kind. That agreement is clear enough—but a court will not enforce it. The law holds that the manufacturer *has* warranted the product to be good for normal purposes, regardless of any language included in the sales agreement. If the blade flies off and injures a child, the manufacturer is liable. This is socially responsible, even though it interferes with a private agreement.

The law has not come full circle back to the early days of the common law. Courts still enforce the great majority of contracts. But the possibility that a court will ignore an agreement means that any contract is a little less certain than it would have been a century ago.

11-1d Types of Contracts

Before undertaking a study of contracts, you need to familiarize yourself with some important vocabulary. This section will present five sets of terms.

Bilateral and Unilateral Contracts

Bilateral contract
A promise made in exchange for another promise

In a **bilateral contract**, both parties make a promise. A producer says to Gloria, "I'll pay you $2 million to star in my new romantic comedy, which we are shooting three months from now in Santa Fe." Gloria says, "It's a deal." That is a bilateral contract. Each party has made a promise to do something. The producer is now bound to pay Gloria $2 million, and Gloria is obligated to show up on time and act in the movie. The vast majority of contracts are bilateral contracts. They can be for services, such as this acting contract; they can be for the sale of goods, such as 1,000 tons of steel; or they can be for almost any other purpose. When the bargain is a promise for a promise, it is a bilateral agreement.

In a unilateral contract, one party makes a promise that the other party can accept only by *actually doing* something. These contracts are less common. Suppose the movie producer tacks a sign to a community bulletin board. It has a picture of a dog with a phone number, and it reads, "I'll pay $100 to anyone who returns my lost dog." If Leo sees the sign, finds the producer, and merely promises to find the dog, he has not created a contract.

Because of the terms on the sign, Leo must actually find and return the dog to stake a claim to the $100.

Executory and Executed Contracts

A contract is **executory** when it has been made, but one or more parties has not yet fulfilled its obligations. Recall Gloria, who agrees to act in the producer's film beginning in three months. The moment Gloria and the producer strike their bargain, they have an executory bilateral express contract.

Executory contract
An agreement in which one or more parties has not yet fulfilled its obligations

A contract is **executed** when all parties have fulfilled their obligations. When Gloria finishes acting in the movie and the producer pays her final fee, their contract will be fully executed.

Executed contract
An agreement in which all parties have fulfilled their obligations

EXAMStrategy

Question: Abby has long coveted Nicola's designer handbag because she saw one of them in a movie. Finally, Nicola offers to sell her friend the bag for $350 in cash. "I don't have the money right now," Abby replies, "but I'll have it a week from Friday. Is it a deal?" Nicola agrees to sell the bag. Use two terms to describe the contract.

Strategy: In a bilateral contract, both parties make a promise, but in a unilateral agreement, only one side does so. An executory contract is one with unfulfilled obligations, while an executed agreement is one with nothing left to be done.

Result: Nicola promised to sell the bag for $350 cash, and Abby agreed to pay. Because both parties made a promise, a bilateral agreement resulted. The deal is not yet completed, meaning that they have an executory contract.

Valid, Unenforceable, Voidable, and Void Agreements

A **valid contract** is one that satisfies all of the law's requirements. It has no problems in any of the seven areas listed at the beginning of this chapter, and a court will enforce it. The contract between Gloria and the producer is a valid contract, and if the producer fails to pay Gloria, she will win a lawsuit to collect the unpaid fee.

An **unenforceable agreement** occurs when the parties intend to form a valid bargain, but a court declares that some rule of law prevents enforcing it. Suppose Gloria and the producer orally agree that she will star in his movie, which he will start filming in 18 months. The law, as we will see in Chapter 16, requires that this contract be in writing because it cannot be completed within one year. If the producer signs up another actress two months later, Gloria has no claim against him.

A **voidable contract** occurs when the law permits one party to terminate the agreement. This happens, for example, when an agreement is signed under duress or a party commits fraud. Suppose that, during negotiations, the producer lies to Gloria, telling her that Steven Spielberg has signed on to be the film's director. That is a major reason why she accepts the contract. As we will learn in Chapter 14, this fraudulent agreement is voidable at Gloria's option. If she later decides that another director is acceptable, she may choose to stay in the contract. But if she wants to cancel the agreement and sue, she can do that as well.

Voidable contract
An agreement that may be terminated by one of the parties

A **void agreement** is one that neither party can enforce, usually because the purpose of the deal is illegal or because one of the parties had no legal authority to make a contract.

Void agreement
A contract that neither party can enforce, because the bargain is illegal or one of the parties had no legal authority to make it

Express and Implied Contracts

Express contract
An agreement with all the important terms explicitly stated

In an **express contract**, the two parties explicitly state all the important terms of their agreement. The vast majority of contracts are express contracts. The contract between the producer and Gloria is an express contract because the parties explicitly state what Gloria will do, where and when she will do it, and how much she will be paid. Some express contracts are oral, as that one was, and some are written. They might be bilateral express contracts, as Gloria's was, or unilateral express contracts, as Leo's was. Obviously, it is wise to make express contracts, and to put them in writing. We emphasize, however, that many oral contracts are fully enforceable.

In an implied contract, the words and conduct of the parties indicate that they intended an agreement. Suppose every Friday, for two months, the producer asks Lance to mow his lawn, and loyal Lance does so each weekend. Then, for three more weekends, Lance simply shows up without the producer asking, and the producer continues to pay for the work done. But on the twelfth weekend, when Lance rings the doorbell to collect, the producer suddenly says, "I never asked you to mow it. Scram." The producer is correct that there was no express contract because the parties had not spoken for several weeks. But a court will probably rule that the conduct of the parties has *implied* a contract. Not only did Lance mow the lawn every weekend, but the producer even paid on three weekends when they had not spoken. It was reasonable for Lance to assume that he had a weekly deal to mow and be paid.

Today, the hottest disputes about implied contracts continue to arise in the employment setting. Many corporate employees have at-will relationships with their companies. This means that the employees are free to quit at any time and the company has the right to fire them for virtually any reason. But often a company provides its workers with personnel manuals that lay out certain rights. Does a handbook create a contract guaranteeing those rights? What is your opinion?

You Be the Judge

DeMasse v. ITT Corporation

984 P.2d 1138
Arizona Supreme Court, 1999

Facts: Roger DeMasse and five others were employees-at-will at ITT Corporation, where they started working at various times between 1960 and 1979. Each was paid an hourly wage.

ITT issued an employee handbook, which it revised four times over two decades.

The first four editions of the handbook stated that, within each job classification, any layoffs would be made in reverse order of seniority. The fifth handbook made two important changes. First, the document stated that "nothing contained herein shall be construed as a guarantee of continued employment. ITT does not guarantee continued employment to employees and retains the right to terminate or lay off employees."

Second, the handbook stated that "ITT reserves the right to amend, modify, or cancel this handbook, as well as any or all of the various policies [or rules] outlined in it." Four years later, ITT notified its hourly employees that layoff guidelines for hourly employees would be based not on seniority, but on ability and performance. About ten days later, the six employees were laid off, though less senior employees kept their jobs. The six employees sued.

You Be the Judge: *Did ITT have the right to unilaterally change the layoff policy?*

Argument for the workers: It is true that all of the plaintiffs were originally employees-at-will, subject to termination at the company's whim. However, things changed when the company issued the first handbook. ITT chose to include a promise that layoffs would be based on seniority. Long-term workers and new employees all understood the promise and relied on it. The company put it there to attract and retain good workers. The policy worked. Responsible employees understood that the longer they remained at ITT, the safer their job was. Company and employees worked together for many years with a common understanding, and that is a textbook definition of an implied contract.

Once a contract is formed, whether express or implied, it is binding on both sides. That is the whole point of a contract. If one side could simply change the terms of an agreement on its own, what value would any contract have? The company's legal argument is a perfect symbol of its arrogance: It believes that because these workers are mere hourly workers, they have no rights, even under contract law. The company is mistaken. Implied contracts are binding, and ITT should not make promises it does not intend to keep.

Argument for ITT: Once an at-will employee, always one. ITT had the right to fire any of its employees at any time—just as the workers had the right to quit whenever they wished. That never changed, and, in case any workers forgot it, the company reiterated the point in its most recent handbook. If the plaintiffs thought layoffs would happen in any particular order, that is their error, not ours.

All workers were bound by the terms of whichever handbook was then in place. For many years, the company had made a seniority-[based]-layoff promise. Had we fired a senior worker during that period, he or she would have had a legitimate complaint—and that is why we did not do it. Instead, we gave everyone four years' notice that things would change. Any workers unhappy with the new policies should have left to find more congenial work.

Why should an employee be allowed to say, "I prefer to rely on the old, outdated handbooks, not the new one"? The plaintiffs' position would mean that no company is ever free to change its general work policies and rules. Since when does an at-will employee have the right to dictate company policy? That would be disastrous for the whole economy—but fortunately it is not the law.

11-2 SOURCES OF CONTRACT LAW

11-2a Common Law

We have seen the evolution of contract law from the twelfth century to the present. Express and implied contracts, promissory estoppel, and quasi-contract were all crafted, over centuries, by courts deciding one contract lawsuit at a time. This pattern continues today: Many contract lawsuits continue to be decided using common law principles developed by courts.

11-2b Uniform Commercial Code

Business methods changed quickly during the first half of the last century. Transportation sped up. Corporations routinely conducted business across state borders and around the world. These developments presented a problem. Common law principles, whether related to contracts, torts, or anything else, sometimes vary from one state to another. New York and California courts often reach similar conclusions when presented with similar cases, but they are under no obligation to do so. Businesspeople became frustrated that, to do business across the country, their companies had to deal with many different sets of common law rules.

Executives, lawyers, and judges wanted a body of law for business transactions that reflected modern commercial methods and provided uniformity throughout the United States. It would be much easier, they thought, if some parts of contract law were the same in every state. That desire gave birth to the Uniform Commercial Code (UCC), created in 1952. The drafters intended the UCC to facilitate the easy formation and enforcement of contracts in a fast-paced world.

The Code governs many aspects of commerce, including the sale and leasing of goods, negotiable instruments, bank deposits, letters of credit, investment securities, secured transactions, and other commercial matters. Every state has adopted at least part of the UCC to govern commercial transactions within that state.

For our purposes in studying contracts, the most important part of the Code is Article 2, which governs the sale of goods. **"Goods" means anything movable, except for money, securities, and certain legal rights.** Goods include pencils, commercial aircraft, books, and Christmas trees. Goods do not include land or a house, because neither is movable, nor do they include a stock certificate. A contract for the sale of 10,000 sneakers is governed by the UCC; a contract for the sale of a condominium in Marina del Rey is governed by the California common law. When analyzing any contract problem as a student or businessperson, you must note whether the agreement concerns the sale of goods. For many issues, the common law and the UCC are reasonably similar. But sometimes, the law is quite different under the two sets of rules.

Most of the time, it will be clear whether the UCC or the common law applies. But what if a contract involves both goods and services? When you get your oil changed, you are paying in part for the new oil (goods) and in part for the labor required to do the job (services). In a mixed contract, Article 2 governs only if the *primary purpose* was the sale of goods. In the following case, the court had to decide the primary purpose.

Fallsview Glatt Kosher Caterers, Inc. v. Rosenfeld

794 N.Y.S. 2d 790
Civil Court, City of New York, 2005

Facts: During the Jewish holidays, Fallsview Glatt Kosher Caterers organized programs at Kutcher's Country Club, where it provided all accommodations, food, and entertainment.

Fallsview sued Willie Rosenfeld, alleging that he had requested accommodations for 15 members of his family, agreeing to pay $24,050, and then failed to appear or pay.

Rosenfeld moved to dismiss, claiming that, even if there had been an agreement, it was never put in writing. Under UCC §2-201, any contract for the sale of goods worth $500 or more can be enforced only if it is in writing and signed. Fallsview argued that the agreement was not for the sale of goods, but for services. The company claimed that because the contract was not governed by the UCC it should be enforced even with no writing.

Issue: ***Was the agreement one for the sale of goods, requiring a writing, or for services, enforceable with no writing?***

Excerpts from Judge Battaglia's Decision: Mr. Rosenfeld contends that the "predominant purpose" and "main objective" of the agreement alleged by Fallsview was the "service of Kosher food," while the hotel accommodations and entertainment were merely "incidental or collateral" services.

Defendant's contention that the "predominant purpose" of the alleged agreement is the sale of food is said to be compelled by the very nature of the Passover holiday. [He argues that] "the essential religious obligation during this eight-day period and the principal reason why people attend events similar to the Program sponsored by plaintiff is in order to facilitate their fulfillment of the requirement to eat only food which is prepared in strict accordance with the mandate of Jewish law for Passover, i.e., food which is 'Kosher for Passover.' It is the desire to obtain these 'goods' and not the urge for 'entertainment' or 'accommodations' that motivates customers to subscribe to such 'Programs.'"

[Fallsview submitted] ten sheets, designated "Kutcher's Country Club Daily Activities" for Sunday, April 4, through Tuesday, April 13, 2004. The activities possible include tennis, racquetball, swimming, Swedish massage, "make over face lift show," "trivia time," aerobics, bingo, ice skating, dancing, "showtime," "power walk," arts and crafts, day camp, ping-pong, Yiddish theater, board games, horse racing, horseback riding, wine tasting . . . and that is only through Wednesday. These activities are provided, together with accommodations and food, for an "all inclusive" price that is apparently determined by the size and location of the room(s) and the numbers and ages of the persons in each party.

A review of the characteristics of the "program," which is the subject matter of the alleged agreement, leads the Court to conclude that the "essence" of the family and communal "experience" is defined primarily by "services" and not by "goods."

The intended scope of UCC section 2-201 is also indicated by its provision that "[a]writing is not insufficient because it omits or incorrectly states a term agreed upon but the contract is not enforceable under this paragraph beyond the quantity of goods shown in the writing." For the Code, quantity is even more important than price. A contract of the type involved here would rarely, if ever, specify the "quantity" of the "goods" to be provided.

Nor would, for example, a contract for a week's stay at a weight loss spa, or a zen-vegetarian retreat, or a cruise of the islands.

Plaintiff argues that "Defendant's proposition that a hotel reservation is a sale of goods would render all reservations made via telephone or the internet unenforceable and would leave hotels in a precarious economic position." That may or may not be true, but the argument does highlight the importance of ensuring that a Statute of Frauds structured and outfitted by the Legislature for a particular transactional context not be casually applied to a very different commercial segment and model. The structure and terms of section 2-201 tell us that it was not intended to cover the agreement alleged in this Complaint.

Defendant's motion to dismiss is denied.

EXAM Strategy

Question: Leila agrees to pay Kendrick $35,000 to repair windmills. Confident of this cash, Kendrick contracts to buy Derrick's used Porsche for $33,000. Then Leila informs Kendrick she does not need his help and will not pay him. Kendrick tells Derrick that he no longer wants the Porsche. Derrick sues Kendrick, and Kendrick files suit against Leila. What law or laws govern these lawsuits?

Strategy: Always be conscious of whether a contract is for services or the sale of goods. Different laws govern. To make that distinction, you must understand the term "goods." If you are clear about that, the question is answered easily.

Result: *Goods* means anything movable, and a Porsche is movable—one might say "super-movable." The UCC will control Derrick's suit. Repairing windmills is primarily a service. Kendrick's lawsuit is governed by the common law of contracts.

11-3 ENFORCING NON-CONTRACTS

Now we turn away from "true" contracts and consider two unusual circumstances. Sometimes, courts will enforce agreements even if they fail to meet the usual requirement of a contract. We emphasize that these remedies are uncommon exceptions to the general rules. Most of the agreements that courts enforce are the express contracts that we have already studied. Nonetheless, the next two remedies are still pivotal in some lawsuits. In each case, a sympathetic plaintiff can demonstrate an injury but *there is no contract.* The plaintiff cannot claim that the defendant breached a contract, because none ever existed. The plaintiff must hope for more "creative" relief.

The two remedies can be confusingly similar. The best way to distinguish them is this:

- In promissory estoppel cases, the defendant made a promise that the plaintiff relied on.
- In quasi-contract cases, the defendant received a *benefit* from the plaintiff and retaining that benefit would be unfair.

11-3a Promissory Estoppel

A fierce fire swept through Dana and Derek Andreason's house in Utah, seriously damaging it. The good news was that agents for Aetna Casualty promptly visited the Andreasons and helped them through the crisis. The agents reassured the couple that all of the damage was covered by their insurance, instructed them on which things to throw out and replace, and helped them choose materials for repairing other items. The bad news was that the agents were wrong: The Andreasons' policy had expired six weeks before the fire. When Derek Andreason presented a bill for $41,957 worth of meticulously itemized work that he had done under the agents' supervision, Aetna refused to pay.

Promissory estoppel
A *possible* remedy for an injured plaintiff in a case with no valid contract, when the plaintiff can show a promise, reasonable reliance, and injustice

The Andreasons sued—but not for breach of contract. There *was* no contract—they allowed their policy to expire. They sued Aetna under the legal theory of **promissory estoppel**: even when there is no contract, a plaintiff may use promissory estoppel to enforce the defendant's promise if he can show that:

- The defendant made a promise knowing that the plaintiff would likely rely on it,
- The plaintiff did rely on the promise, and
- The only way to avoid injustice is to enforce the promise.

Aetna made a promise to the Andreasons—namely, its assurance that all of the damage was covered by insurance. The company knew that the Andreasons would rely on that promise, which they did by ripping up a floor that might have been salvaged, throwing out some furniture, and buying materials to repair the house. Is enforcing the promise the only way to avoid injustice? Yes, ruled the Utah Court of Appeals.[1] The Andreasons' conduct was reasonable and based entirely on what the Aetna agents told them. Under promissory estoppel, the Andreasons received virtually the same amount they would have obtained had the insurance contract been valid.

Is enforcing the promise the only way to avoid injustice?

Many promissory estoppel cases involve employment law—bosses make promises that they fail to keep. The following case illustrates what can happen when you bet on the wrong promise.

Harmon v. Delaware Harness Racing Commission

62 A.3d 1198
Delaware Supreme Court, 2013

Facts: The Delaware Harness Racing Commission hired Donald Harmon to be the Presiding Judge of harness racing (charged with enforcing racetrack rules). After years on the job, Harmon was arrested for improperly changing a judging sheet to favor a horse. The Commission suspended him without pay pending the outcome of the criminal case.

John Wayne (yes, his name was John Wayne) was the executive officer of the Commission. During his suspension, Harmon asked Wayne to find out from the Commission whether it would reinstate him if he was acquitted. When Wayne asked the commissioners this question, they looked at each other and then said "Yes." The commissioners told Wayne he could relay that message to Harmon. Based on this promise, Harmon decided not to look for other jobs.

Immediately after his acquittal, Harmon asked for his job back. After some time, the Commission refused to reinstate him as promised. Harmon sued the Commission claiming promissory estoppel. A trial court sided with Harmon and awarded him $102,273, representing the wages he would have earned if the Commission had kept its promise. But the Superior Court reversed the decision, so Harmon appealed to the Supreme Court of Delaware.

Issue: ***Was the commissioners' promise to Harmon enforceable?***

Excerpts from Justice Berger's Decision: To prevail on a promissory estoppel claim, a plaintiff must establish that: (i) a promise was made; (ii) it was the reasonable expectation of the promisor to induce action or forbearance on the part of the promisee; (iii) the promisee reasonably relied on the promise and took action to his detriment; and (iv) such promise is binding because injustice can be avoided only by enforcement of the promise.

---

[1]Andreason v. Aetna Casualty & Surety Co., 1993 Utah App. (1993).

The first element is a promise. The trial court reasoned that [because] no [formal] vote was taken before the members said "Yes," Wayne could not have reasonably believed that the Commission wanted him to commit to reinstate Harmon. But the fact that the Commission members all looked at each other before answering Wayne's question could be construed as a vote, albeit an informal one. Second, the Commission did not address all matters by vote. It was not hiring or reinstating Harmon at the time Wayne conveyed its position to Harmon. The Commission was only promising to take action in the future. In short, there was evidence that the promise was made.

The second element is that the Commission reasonably expected Harmon to rely on Wayne's representations. Wayne had authority to transmit the Commission's decision to Harmon. If Wayne's testimony is credited, there is no real dispute about this point.

The third element is that Harmon reasonably relied on the Commission's promise and took action to his detriment. But for the Commission's promise to reinstate him, [Harmon] would have looked for other work. He was offered several horse training opportunities, but he could not pursue them because, if he did, he would not be allowed to return to his position as a judge. This testimony satisfies Harmon's burden of showing reliance to his detriment.

The final element of a promissory estoppel claim is a finding that the promise must be enforced to avoid injustice. That is another way of saying that it would be unjust not to enforce the Commission's promise because Harmon suffered damages by relying on it. During the time that he was waiting to be reinstated, Harmon could not accept another job, and suffered lost income as a result. That lost income constitutes damages.

Based on the foregoing, the judgment of the Superior Court is reversed.

Jeff Schultes/Shutterstock.com

Promissory estoppel may require compensation even when no contract exists.

Why have we chosen to illustrate an important point of law—promissory estoppel—with a case that fails? Because that is the typical outcome. Plaintiffs allege promissory estoppel very frequently, but seldom succeed. They do occasionally win, as the Andreasons demonstrated earlier, but courts are skeptical of these claims. The lesson is clear: Before you rely on a promise, negotiate a binding contract.

11-3b Quasi-Contract

Don Easterwood leased over 5,000 acres of farmland in Jackson County, Texas, from PIC Realty for one year. The next year, he obtained a second one-year lease. During each year, Easterwood farmed the land, harvested the crops, and prepared the land for the following year's planting. Toward the end of the second lease, after Easterwood had harvested his crop, he and PIC began discussing the terms of another lease. While they negotiated, Easterwood prepared the land for the following year, cutting and plowing the soil. But the negotiations for a new lease failed, and Easterwood moved off the land. He sued PIC Realty for the value of his work preparing the soil.

Easterwood had neither an express nor an implied contract for the value of his work. How could he make any legal claim? By relying on the legal theory of a

Raymond Llewellyn/Shutterstock.com

Easterwood toiled on the land, but did he have a right to it?

Quasi-contract
A *possible* remedy for an injured plaintiff in a case with no valid contract, when the plaintiff can show benefit to the defendant, reasonable expectation of payment, and unjust enrichment

quasi-contract: Even when there is no contract, a court may use **quasi-contract** to compensate a plaintiff who can show that:

- The plaintiff gave some benefit to the defendant,
- The plaintiff reasonably expected to be paid for the benefit and the defendant knew this, and
- The defendant would be unjustly enriched if he did not pay.

Quantum meruit
"As much as he deserves"—the damages awarded in a quasi-contract case

If a court finds all of these elements present, it will generally award the value of the goods or services that the plaintiff has conferred. The damages awarded are called ***quantum meruit***, meaning that the plaintiff gets "as much as he deserves." The court is awarding money that it believes the plaintiff *morally ought to have*, even though there was no valid contract entitling her to it. This again is judicial activism, with the courts inventing a "quasi" contract where no true contract exists. The purpose is justice, the name is contradictory.

Don Easterwood testified that in Jackson County, it was quite common for a tenant farmer to prepare the soil for the following year but then be unable to farm the land. In those cases, he claimed, the landowner compensated the farmer for the work done. Other witnesses agreed that this was the local custom. The court ruled that indeed there was no contract, but that all elements of quasi-contract had been satisfied. Easterwood gave a benefit to PIC because the land was ready for planting. Jackson County custom caused Easterwood to assume he would be paid, and PIC Realty knew it. Finally, said the court, it would be unjust to let PIC benefit without paying anything. The court ordered PIC to pay the fair market value of Easterwood's labors.

The following case poses a question that parents and offspring have debated throughout the ages: How much does a son *deserve*?

Lund v. Lund

848 N.W.2d 266
North Dakota Supreme Court, 2014

Facts: Wendell Lund was a dutiful son to his parents, Orville and Betty. For most of his life, he lived and worked on the family farm. As an adult, he did not pay rent, and his parents provided him meals and general assistance with the work of the farm. Although Wendell's siblings also helped around the house, Wendell claimed that he went above and beyond his duties as a son: He paid half of the real estate taxes and cleared the farm's grassland, which resulted in a 22-acre organic farm.

When Orville and Betty divorced, Orville bought out her half and stayed on the farm; Betty moved to Arizona; and Wendell got nothing. But Wendell thought he deserved more. He sued both his parents under a theory of quasi-contract. He argued that over a 20-year period he expended a significant amount of labor and money on the property, that his parents knew he expected an ownership interest in the farm, and that it would be unfair for them to retain the benefits of his work. Wendell asked the court to order his mother to pay him over $500,000 and his father to give him ownership of the land.

The lower court disagreed and Wendell appealed, but only against his mother.

Issue: ***Was it unfair for Wendell's mother to reap the benefits of her son's work on the family farm?***

Excerpts from Justice McEvers's Decision: A contract implied in law or a claim of unjust enrichment is a fiction of law adopted to achieve justice where no true contract exists. The essential element in recovering under a theory of unjust enrichment is the receipt of a benefit by the defendant from the plaintiff which would be inequitable to retain without paying for its value.

Here, the benefit received by Betty Lund would not be inequitable for her to retain without paying for its value. The benefits provided by Wendell Lund were similar in nature to the benefits provided by his siblings when they returned home. Wendell Lund received reciprocal benefits, including a house, meals, and assistance with work.

On the record in this case, we agree with the district court's determination that any benefits received by Betty Lund would not be inequitable for her to retain without paying for its value. We conclude the court did not err in denying Wendell Lund's claim for unjust enrichment.

The following table sets out the four theories of recovery that contract law provides.

Four Theories of Recovery

Theory	Did the Defendant Make a Promise?	Is There a Contract?	Description
Express contract	Yes	Yes	The parties intend to contract and agree on explicit terms.
Implied contract	Not explicitly	Yes	The parties do not formally agree, but their words and conduct indicate an intention to create a contract.
Promissory estoppel	Yes	No	There is no contract, but the defendant makes a promise that she can foresee will induce reliance, the plaintiff relies on it, and it would be unjust not to enforce the promise.
Quasi-Contract	No	No	There is no intention to contract, but the plaintiff gives some benefit to the defendant, who knows that the plaintiff expects compensation. It would be unjust not to award the plaintiff damages.

EXAMStrategy

Question: The preceding table lists the different theories a plaintiff may use to recover damages in a contract dispute. In the following examples, which one will each plaintiff use in trying to win the case?

1. Company pays all employees 10 percent commission on new business they develop. Company compensates each employee when the new customer pays its first bill. After Leandro obtains three new clients, Company fires him. When the new customers pay their bill, Company refuses to pay Leandro a commission because he is no longer an employee. Leandro sues.
2. Burt agrees in writing to sell Red 100 lobsters for $15 each, payable by credit card, in exactly 30 days. When the lobsters fail to arrive, Red sues.
3. Company handbook, given to all new hires, states that no employee will be fired without a hearing and an appeal. Company fires Delores without a hearing or appeal. She sues.

Strategy: In (1), the Company never promised to pay a commission to nonemployees, so there is no contract. However, the Company *benefited* from Leandro's work. In (2), the parties have *clearly stated all terms* to a simple sales agreement. In (3), the Company and Delores never negotiated termination, but *the handbook suggests* that all employees have certain rights.

Result: (1) is a case of quasi-contract because the company benefited and should reasonably expect to pay. (2) is an express contract because all terms are clearly stated. (3) is an implied contract, similar to the *DeMasse* case, based on the handbook.

CHAPTER CONCLUSION

Contracts govern countless areas of our lives, from intimate family issues to multibillion dollar corporate deals. Understanding contract principles is essential for a successful business or professional career and is invaluable in private life. This knowledge is especially important because courts no longer rubber-stamp any agreement that two parties have made. If we know the issues that courts scrutinize, the agreement we draft is likelier to be enforced. We thus achieve greater control over our affairs—the very purpose of a contract.

EXAM REVIEW

1. **CONTRACTS: DEFINITION AND ELEMENTS** A contract is a legally enforceable promise. Analyzing whether a contract exists involves inquiring into these issues: offer, acceptance, consideration, capacity, legal purpose, consent, and, sometimes, whether the deal is in writing.

2. **DEVELOPMENT** The development of contract law stretches into the distant past. Before the fifteenth century, courts rarely enforced promises at all. By the 1600s, courts enforced many mutual promises, and, by 1900, most promises containing the seven elements of a contract were strictly enforced.

3. **UNILATERAL AND BILATERAL CONTRACTS** In bilateral contracts, the parties exchange promises. In a unilateral contract, only one party makes a promise, and the other must take some action—his return promise is insufficient to form a contract.

4. **EXECUTORY AND EXECUTED CONTRACTS** In an executory contract, one or both of the parties have not yet done everything that they promised to do. In an executed contract, all parties have fully performed.

5. **ENFORCEABILITY**
   - Valid contracts are fully enforceable.
   - An unenforceable agreement is one with a legal defect.
   - A voidable contract occurs when one party has an option to cancel the agreement.
   - A void agreement means that the law will ignore the deal regardless of what the parties want.

EXAMStrategy

Question: Yasmine is negotiating to buy Stewart's house. She asks him what condition the roof is in.

"Excellent," he replies. "It is only 2 years old, and should last 25 more." In fact, Stewart knows that the roof is 26 years old and has had a series of leaks. The parties sign a sales contract for $600,000. A week before Yasmine is to pay for the house and take possession, she discovers the leaks and learns that the mandatory new roof will cost $35,000. At the same time, she learns that the house has increased in value by $60,000 since she signed the agreement. What options does Yasmine have?

Strategy: You know intuitively that Stewart's conduct is as shabby as his roof. What is the legal term for his deception? Fraud. Does fraud make an agreement void or voidable? Does it matter? (See the "Result" at the end of this Exam Review section.)

---

6. **EXPRESS AND IMPLIED CONTRACTS** If the parties formally agreed and stated explicit terms, there is probably an express contract. If the parties did not formally agree but their conduct, words, or past dealings indicate they intended a binding agreement, there may be an implied contract.

7. **UNIFORM COMMERCIAL CODE AND COMMON LAW** If a contract is for the sale of goods, the UCC is the relevant body of law. For anything else, the common law governs. If a contract involves both goods and services, a court will examine the agreement's primary purpose to determine which law applies.

EXAMStrategy

Question: Honeywell, Inc., and Minolta Camera Co. had a contract providing that Honeywell would give Minolta various technical information on the design of a specialized camera lens. Minolta would have the right to use the information in its cameras, provided that Minolta also used certain Honeywell parts in its cameras. Honeywell delivered to Minolta numerous technical documents, computer software, and test equipment, and Honeywell engineers met with Minolta engineers at least 20 times to discuss the equipment. Several years later, Honeywell sued, claiming that Minolta had taken the design information but failed to use Honeywell parts in its cameras. Minolta moved to dismiss, claiming that the UCC required lawsuits concerning the sale of goods to be filed within four years of the breach and that this lawsuit was too late. Honeywell answered that the UCC did not apply, and that, therefore, Minnesota's six-year statute of limitations governed. Who is right?

Strategy: Like many contracts, this one involves both goods, which are governed by the UCC, and services, controlled by the common law. We decide which of those two laws governs by using the predominant purpose test. Was this contract primarily about selling goods or about providing services? (See the "Result" at the end of this Exam Review section.)

---

8. **PROMISSORY ESTOPPEL** A claim of promissory estoppel requires that the defendant made a promise knowing that the plaintiff would likely *rely*, and the plaintiff did so. It would be wrong to deny recovery.

EXAMStrategy

Question: The Hoffmans owned and operated a successful small bakery and grocery store. They spoke with Lukowitz, an agent of Red Owl Stores, who told them that for $18,000 Red Owl would build a store and fully stock it for them. The Hoffmans sold their bakery and grocery store and purchased a lot on which Red Owl was to build the store. Lukowitz then told Hoffman that the price had gone up to $26,000. The Hoffmans borrowed the extra money from relatives, but then Lukowitz informed them that the cost would be $34,000. Negotiations broke off, and the Hoffmans sued. The court determined that there was no contract because too many details had not been worked out—the size of the store, its design, and the cost of constructing it. Can the Hoffmans recover any money?

Strategy: Because there is no contract, the Hoffmans must rely on either promissory estoppel or quasi-contract. Promissory estoppel focuses on the defendant's promise and the plaintiff's reliance. Those suing in quasi-contract must show that the defendant received a benefit for which it should reasonably expect to pay. Does either fit here? (See the "Result" at the end of this Exam Review section.)

---

9. **QUASI-CONTRACT** To enforce a non-contractual promise, quasi-contract requires that the defendant received a benefit knowing that the plaintiff would expect compensation, and it would be unjust not to grant it.

RESULTS

5. Result: Indeed, it does matter. Stewart's fraud makes the contract voidable by Yasmine. She has the right to terminate the agreement and pay nothing. However, she may go through with the contract if she prefers. The choice is hers—but not Stewart's.

7. Result: The primary purpose of this agreement was not the sale of goods but rather the exchange of technical data, ideas, designs, and so forth. The common law governs the contract, and Honeywell's suit may go forward.

8. Result: Red Owl received no benefit from the Hoffmans' sale of their store or purchase of the lot. However, Red Owl did make a promise and expected the Hoffmans to rely on it, which they did. The Hoffmans won their claim of promissory estoppel.

MULTIPLE-CHOICE QUESTIONS

1. An actor, exhausted after his 10-hour workweek, agrees to buy a briefcase full of cocaine from Lewis for $12,000. Lewis and the actor have a(n) ______________ contract.
   (a) valid
   (b) unenforceable
   (c) voidable
   (d) void

2. Carol says, "Pam, you're my best friend in the world. I just inherited a million bucks, and I want you to have some of it. Come with me to the bank tomorrow, and I'll give you $10,000." "Sweet!" Pam replies. Later that day, Carol has a change of heart. She is allowed to do so. Examine the list of the elements of a contract, and cite the correct reason.
   (a) The agreement was not put into writing.
   (b) The agreement lacks a legal purpose.
   (c) Pam did not give consideration.
   (d) Pam does not have the capacity to make a contract.

3. On the first day of the baseball season, Dean orders a new Cardinals hat from Amazon.com. At the moment he submits his order, Dean and Amazon have an ____________ contract. Two days later, Amazon delivers the hat to Dean's house. At this point, Dean and Amazon have an ____________ contract.
   (a) executory; executory
   (b) executory; executed
   (c) executed; executory
   (d) executed; executed

4. Linda goes to an electronics store and buys a Smart television. Lauren hires a company to clean her swimming pool once a week. The ____________ governs Linda's contract with the store, and the ____________ governs Lauren's contract with the pool company.
   (a) common law; common law
   (b) common law; UCC
   (c) UCC; common law
   (d) UCC; UCC

5. Consider the following scenarios:
   I. Madison says to a group of students, "I'll pay $35 to the first one of you who shows up at my house and mows my lawn."
   II. Lea posts a flyer around town that reads, "Reward: $500 for information about the person who keyed my truck last Saturday night in the Wag-a-Bag parking lot. Call Lea at 555-5309."

   Which of these proposes a *unilateral* contract?
   (a) I only
   (b) II only
   (c) Both I and II
   (d) None of these

CASE QUESTIONS

1. Interactive Data Corp. hired Daniel Foley as an assistant product manager at a starting salary of $18,500. Over the next six years, Interactive steadily promoted Foley until he became Los Angeles branch manager at a salary of $56,116. Interactive's officers repeatedly told Foley that he would have his job as long as his performance was adequate. In addition, Interactive distributed an employee handbook that specified "termination guidelines," including a mandatory seven-step pre-termination procedure. Two years later, Foley learned that his recently hired supervisor, Robert Kuhne, was under investigation by the FBI for embezzlement at his previous job. Foley reported this to Interactive officers. Shortly thereafter, Interactive fired Foley. He sued, claiming that Interactive could fire him only for good cause, after the seven-step procedure. What kind of a claim is he making? Should he succeed?

2. **ETHICS** You want to lease your automobile to a friend for the summer but do not want to pay a lawyer to draw up the lease. Joanna, a neighbor, is in law school. She is not licensed to practice law. She offers to draft a lease for you for $100, and you unwisely accept. Later, you refuse to pay her fee, and she sues to collect. Who will win the lawsuit, and why? Apart from the law, was it morally right for the law student to try to help you by drafting the lease? Was she acting helpfully or foolishly or fraudulently? Is it just for you to agree to her fee and then refuse to pay it? What is society's interest in this dispute? Should a court be more concerned with the ethical issue raised by the conduct of the two parties or with the social consequences of this agreement?

3. West purchased a horse from Strauss. When West discovered that the horse had a leg injury, he got a driver to return the horse to Strauss, but Strauss refused to accept delivery. Not knowing what to do with the injured animal, the driver took it to Bailey. Five months later, Bailey sent bills for the horse's care to West, who returned them with a note saying he did not own the horse. Bailey sued West for the expenses incurred in boarding the horse. West argued that, when Bailey accepted the horse, he was aware of the controversy regarding the horse's ownership, so he could not reasonably expect to be compensated. Who wins, and why?

4. ***YOU BE THE JUDGE* WRITING PROBLEM** John Stevens owned a dilapidated apartment that he rented to James and Cora Chesney for a low rent. The Chesneys began to remodel and rehabilitate the unit. Over a four-year period, they installed two new bathrooms, carpeted the floors, installed new septic and heating systems, and rewired, replumbed, and painted the apartment. Stevens periodically stopped by and saw the work in progress. The Chesneys transformed the unit into a respectable apartment. Three years after their work was done, Stevens served the Chesneys with an eviction notice. The Chesneys counterclaimed, seeking the value of the work they had done. Are they entitled to it? **Argument for Stevens:** Mr. Stevens is willing to pay the Chesneys exactly the amount he agreed to pay: nothing. The parties never contracted for the Chesneys to fix up the apartment. In fact, they never even discussed such an agreement. The Chesneys are making the absurd argument that anyone who chooses to perform certain work, without ever discussing it with another party, can finish the job and then charge it to the other person. If the Chesneys expected to get paid, obviously they should have said so. If the court were to allow this claim, it would be inviting other tenants to make improvements and then bill the landlord. The law has never been so foolish. **Argument for the Chesneys:** The law of quasi-contract was crafted for cases exactly like this. The Chesneys have given an enormous benefit to Stevens by transforming the apartment and enabling him to rent it at greater profit for many years to come. Stevens saw the work being done and understood that the Chesneys expected some compensation for these major renovations. If Stevens never intended to pay the fair value of the work, he should have stopped the couple from doing the work or notified them that there would be no compensation. It would be unjust to allow the landlord to seize the value of the work, evict the tenants who did it, and pay nothing.

5. Jennifer worked as a grant writer for Brightway, a Christian nonprofit. When she announced she was moving in with her boyfriend, all of her supervisors, including the company's president, congratulated her and expressed their support. No one told her that her job was in jeopardy. Months later, Brightway fired Jennifer because "living together outside marriage is forbidden by the Scriptures." Suppose Jennifer sues under the theory of promissory estoppel. What is her best argument?

DISCUSSION QUESTIONS

1. Have you ever made an agreement that mattered to you, only to have the other person refuse to follow through on the deal? Looking at the list of elements in the chapter, did your agreement amount to a contract? If not, which element did it lack?

2. Consider promissory estoppel and quasi-contracts. Do you like the fact that these doctrines exist? Should courts have "wiggle room" to enforce deals that fail to meet formal contract requirements? Or, should the rule be "If it's not an actual contract, too bad. No deal."

3. Is it sensible to have two different sets of contract rules—one for sales of goods and another for everything else? Would it be better to have a single set of rules for all contracts?

4. Have you read your apartment lease lately? How about your cellular service agreement? One study found that 67 percent of consumers do not read the contracts they sign. But notice that a contract is still enforceable, whether or not you read it. Which contracts should you read? iTunes terms and conditions? Your mortgage? An employment agreement?

5. Some laws give consumers the right to cancel certain contracts for any reason within a short period of time after entering into them. For example, consumers in the European Union can return anything purchased online for any reason or no reason at all. Consumers in California can get out of gym membership contracts by sending the gym a cancellation notice within five business days of joining. Other state statutes cover insurance, weight loss services, door-to-door sales, and home repair contracts. If these agreements meet all of the requirements for a contract, why would the law allow people to get out of them so easily? Is this good policy? Alternatively, if consumers can cancel these contracts, why not allow everyone to cancel any contract within a few days?

12

CHAPTER

THE AGREEMENT: OFFERS AND ACCEPTANCES

Interior. A glitzy café, New York. Evening. Bob, a famous director, and Katrina, a glamorous actress, sit at a table, near a wall of glass looking onto a New York sidewalk that is filled with life and motion. Bob sips a brandy while carefully eyeing Katrina. Katrina stares at her wineglass.

Bob *(smiling confidently): Body Work* is going to be huge—for the right actress. I know a film that's gonna gross a hundred million when I'm holding one. I'm holding one.

Katrina *(perking up at the mention of money)*: It is quirky. It's fun. And she's very strong, very real.

Bob: She's you. That's why we're sitting here. We start shooting in seven months.

Katrina *(edging away from the table)*: I have a few questions. That nude scene.

I should talk with my agent. I'd need something in writing about the nude scene . . .

Bob: The one on the toboggan run?

Katrina: *That* one was OK. But the one in the poultry factory—very explicit. I don't work nude.

Bob: It's not really nude. Think of all those feathers fluttering around.

Katrina: It's nude.

Bob: We'll work it out. This is a romantic comedy, not tawdry exploitation. Katrina, we're talking $2.5 million. A little accommodation, please. We'll give you $600,000 up front, and the rest deferred, the usual percentages.

Katrina: Bob, my fee is $3 million. As you know. That hasn't changed.

Katrina picks up her drink, doesn't sip it, places it on the coaster, using both hands to center it perfectly. He waits, as she stares silently at her glass.

Bob: We're shooting in Santa Fe, the weather will be perfect. You'll have a suite, plus a private trailer on location.

Katrina: I should talk with my agent. I'd need something in writing about the nude scene, the fee, percentages—all the business stuff. I never sign without talking to her.

BOB: Shrugs and sits back.

KATRINA *(made anxious by the silence)*: I love the character, I really do.

BOB: You and several others love her. *(That jolts her.)* Agents can wait. I have to put this together fast. We can get you the details you want in writing.

Body Work is going to be bigger than *Game of Thrones*.

That one hooks her. She looks at Bob. He nods reassuringly. Bob sticks out his hand, smiling. Katrina hesitates, lets go of her drink, and SHAKES HANDS, looking unsure. Bob signals for the check.

Do Bob and Katrina have a deal? *They* seem to think so. But is her fee $2.5 million or $3 million? What if Katrina demands that all nude scenes be taken out, and Bob refuses? Must she still act in the film? Or suppose her agent convinces her that *Body Work* is no good even with changes. Has Katrina committed herself? What if Bob auditions another actress the next day, likes her, and signs her? Does he owe Katrina her fee? Or suppose Bob learns that the funding has fallen apart and there will be no film. Is Katrina entitled to her money?

Bob and Katrina have acted out a classic problem in *agreement*, one of the basic issues in contract law. Their lack of clarity means that disputes are likely and lawsuits possible. Similar bargaining goes on every day around the country and around the world, and the problems created are too frequently resolved in court. Some negotiating is done in person; more is done over the phone, by text message, by email—or all of them combined. This chapter highlights the most common sources of misunderstanding and litigation so that you can avoid making contracts you never intended—or deals that you cannot enforce.

There almost certainly is no contract between Bob and Katrina. Bob's offer was unclear. Even if it was valid, Katrina counteroffered. When they shook hands, it is impossible to know what terms each had in mind.

CONTRACTS CHECKLIST

- ☑ Offer
- ☑ Acceptance
- ☐ Consideration
- ☐ Legality
- ☐ Capacity
- ☐ Consent
- ☐ Writing

12-1 OFFER

12-1a Meeting of the Minds

Remember from Chapter 11 that contracts have seven key characteristics. Agreements that have a problem in any of the areas do not amount to valid contracts. In this chapter, we examine the first two items on the checklist.

Parties form a contract only if they have a meeting of the minds. For this to happen, one side must make an **offer** and the other must make an **acceptance**. An offer proposes definite terms, and an acceptance unconditionally agrees to them.

Offer
An act or statement that proposes definite terms and permits the other party to create a contract by accepting those terms

Throughout the chapter, keep in mind that courts make *objective* assessments when evaluating offers and acceptances. That is, they do not consider what the parties *meant* to say or do or *thought* they said or did. Instead, courts focus on parties' actual words and conduct, deciding how a reasonable person would interpret them in context.

The following case involves serious drama: a quadruple murder, an eager law student, and a million-dollar challenge. But did it also involve a serious offer?

Kolodziej v. Mason

774 F.3d 736
United States Court of Appeals for the Eleventh Circuit, 2014

Facts: Attorney James Mason represented Nelson Serrano, who was accused of killing four people in Central Florida. But Serrano had an alibi: On the day of the crime, hotel surveillance in Atlanta had captured him on video—both before *and* after the murders. The prosecution did not buy it. It maintained that Serrano had flown back and forth from Atlanta to Florida to commit the murders during a ten-hour span. But in order for this theory to hold, Serrano would have had to land, disembark, and travel back to his distant Atlanta hotel in just 28 minutes. (Quite a feat, as any Atlanta traveler would know.)

Mason argued that his client could not have committed the murders in this tight timeframe—and certainly could not have made it from the gate to the hotel in 28 minutes. Mason appeared on NBC's *Dateline* program, exclaiming: "I challenge anybody to show me—I'll pay them a million dollars if they can do it."

Enter Dustin Kolodziej, a *Dateline*-watching law student. Kolodziej interpreted Mason's words as an offer to form a contract, to make it off a plane in Atlanta and back to Serrano's hotel within 28 minutes in return for one million dollars. Kolodziej did successfully make the journey—and recorded it on his phone. He then demanded payment from Mason. Of course, Mason denied that the televised challenge was an offer, so the law student sued for breach of a unilateral contract. The lower court dismissed the suit, but the determined, budding lawyer appealed.

Sean Pavone/Shutterstock.com

Issue: ***Did Mason make an enforceable offer for a unilateral contract?***

Excerpts from Judge Wilson's Decision: Mutual assent is a prerequisite for the formation of any contract. We evaluate the existence of assent by analyzing the parties' agreement process in terms of offer and acceptance. The determination of whether a party made an offer to enter into a contract requires the court to determine how a reasonable, objective person would have understood the potential offeror's communication.

Mason's purported challenge does not indicate a willingness to enter into a contract. "I challenge anybody to show me—I'll pay them a million dollars if they can do it" appears colloquial. The exaggerated amount of "a million dollars"—the common choice of movie villains and schoolyard wagerers alike—indicates that this was hyperbole.

The law imputes to a person an intention corresponding to the reasonable meaning of his words and acts. Applying the objective standard here leads us to the real million-dollar question: "What did the party say and do?" None of Mason's commentary gave the slightest indication that his statement was anything other than a figure of speech. In the course of representing his client, Mason merely used a rhetorical expression to raise questions as to the prosecution's case. We could just as easily substitute a comparable idiom such as "I'll eat my hat" or "I'll be a monkey's uncle" into Mason's interview in the place of "I'll pay them a million dollars," and the outcome would be the same. We would not be inclined to make him either consume his headwear or assume a simian relationship were he to be proven wrong; nor will we make him pay one million dollars here.

It is basic contract law that one cannot suppose, believe, suspect, imagine or hope that an offer has been made. No reasonable person would think, absent any other indicia of seriousness, that Mason manifested willingness to enter into a contract. With no assent, there is no actionable offer; with no offer, there is no enforceable contract.

Just as people are free to contract, they are also free *from* contract, and we find it neither prudent nor permissible to impose contractual liability for offhand remarks or grandstanding. We affirm the district court's judgment in favor of Mason.

Kolodziej v. Mason teaches us that not everything that sounds like an offer actually creates a contract. In the next section we will explore what makes a valid offer.

The contracting process begins with an offer. The person who makes an offer is the **offeror**. The person to whom he makes that offer is the **offeree**. An offer is a mighty thing: It gives the offeree the power to bind the offeror to a contract.

Offeror
The person who makes an offer

Offeree
The person to whom an offer is made

Two questions determine whether a statement is an offer:

- Do the offeror's words and actions indicate an *intention* to make a bargain?
- Are the terms of the offer reasonably definite?

Zachary says to Sharon, "Come work in my English language center as a teacher. I'll pay you $800 per week for a 35-hour week, for six months starting Monday." This is a valid offer. Zachary's words seem to indicate that he intends to make a bargain and his offer is definite. If Sharon accepts, the parties have a contract that either one can enforce.

In the following section, we present several categories of statements that are generally *not* valid offers.

12-1b Statements That Usually Do Not Amount to Offers

Invitations to Bargain

An invitation to bargain is not an offer. Suppose Martha telephones Joe and leaves a message on his answering machine, asking if Joe would consider selling his vacation condo on Lake Michigan. Joe faxes a signed letter to Martha saying, "There is no way I could sell the condo for less than $150,000." Martha promptly sends Joe a cashier's check for that amount. Does she own the condo? No. Joe's fax was not an offer. It is merely an invitation to negotiate. Joe is indicating that he might well be happy to receive an offer from Martha, but he is not promising to sell the condo for $150,000 or for any amount.

Price Quotes

A price quote is generally not an offer. If Imperial Textile sends a list of fabric prices for the new year to its regular customers, the list is not an offer. Once again, the law regards it merely as a solicitation of offers. Suppose Ralph orders 1,000 yards of fabric, quoted in the list at $40 per yard. *Ralph* is making the offer, and Imperial may decline to sell at $40, or at any price, for that matter.

This can be an expensive point to learn. Leviton Manufacturing makes electrical fixtures and switches. Litton Microwave manufactures ovens. Leviton sent a price list to Litton, stating what it would charge for specially modified switches for use in Litton's microwaves. The price letter included a statement greatly limiting Leviton's liability in the event of any problem with

EXHIBIT 12.1

The *Litton* case demonstrates why it is important to distinguish a valid offer from a mere price quote. Leviton's price list (including a limited warranty) was *not* an offer. When Litton ordered goods (with no limit to the warranty), it was making an offer, which Leviton accepted by delivering the goods. The resulting contract did not contain the limited warranty that Leviton wanted, costing that company a $4 million judgment.

the switches. Litton purchased thousands of the switches and used them in manufacturing its microwaves. But consumers reported fires due to defects in the switches. Leviton claimed that under the contract it had no liability. But the court held that the price letter was not an offer.

It was a request to receive an offer. Thus, the contract ultimately formed did not include Leviton's liability exclusion. Litton won over $4 million.[1] See Exhibit 12.1.

Letters of Intent

Letter of intent
A letter that summarizes negotiating progress

In complex business negotiations, the parties may spend months bargaining over dozens of interrelated issues. Because each party wants to protect itself during the discussions, ensuring that the other side is serious without binding itself to premature commitments, it may be tempting during the negotiations to draft a **letter of intent**. The letter *might* help distinguish a serious party from one with a casual interest, summarize the progress made thus far, and assist the parties in securing necessary financing. Usually, letters of intent do not create any legal obligation. They merely state what the parties are considering, not what they have actually agreed to. But note that it is possible for a letter of intent to bind the parties if its language indicates that the parties *intended* to be bound.

Advertisements

Mary Mesaros received a notice from the U.S. Bureau of the Mint, announcing a new $5 gold coin to commemorate the Statue of Liberty. The notice contained an order form promising that, if her order was received by December 31, she would be entitled to purchase the coins at the discounted price.

Mesaros ordered almost $2,000 worth of the coins. But the Mint was inundated with so many requests for the coin that the supply was soon exhausted. Mesaros and thousands of others never got their coins. This was particularly disappointing because the market value of the coins doubled shortly after their issue. Mesaros sued on behalf of the entire class of disappointed purchasers. Like most who sue based on an advertisement, she lost.[2] **An advertisement**

---

[1] Litton Microwave Cooking Products v. Leviton Manufacturing Co., Inc., 15 F.3d 790 (8th Cir. 1994).
[2] Mesaros v. United States, 845 F.2d 1576 (Fed. Cir. 1988).

is generally not an offer. An advertisement is merely a request for offers. The consumer makes the offer, whether by mail, like Mesaros, or by arriving at a retail store ready to buy. The seller is free to reject the offer. Advertisers should be careful, however, not to be too specific in their ads. Some ads do count as offers, as the following case illustrates.

Landmark Case

Carlill v. Carbolic Smoke Ball Company

1 QB 256
Court of Appeal, 1892

Facts: In the early 1890s, English citizens greatly feared the Russian flu. The Carbolic Smoke Ball Company ran a newspaper ad that contained two key passages:

> "£100 reward will be paid by the Carbolic Smoke Ball Company to any person who contracts the influenza after having used the ball three times daily for two weeks according to the printed directions supplied with each ball.
>
> "£1000 is deposited with the Alliance Bank, shewing our sincerity in the matter."

The product was a ball that contained carbolic acid. Users would inhale vapors from the ball through a long tube.

Carlill purchased a smoke ball and used it as directed for two months. She then caught the flu. She sued, arguing that because her response to the ad had created a contract with the company, she was entitled to £100.

The trial court agreed, awarding Carlill the money. The company appealed.

Issues: ***Did the advertisement amount to an offer? If so, was the offer accepted?***

Excerpts from Lord Justice Lindley's Decision: The first observation I will make is that we are dealing with an express promise to pay £100 in certain events. Read the advertisement how you will, and twist it about as you will, here is a distinct promise expressed in language which is perfectly unmistakable.

We must first consider whether this was intended to be a promise at all. The deposit is called by the advertiser as proof of his sincerity in the matter—that is, the sincerity of his promise to pay this £100 in the event which he has specified. I say there is the promise, as plain as words can make it.

Then it is contended that it is not binding. In the first place, the performance of the conditions is the acceptance of the offer. Unquestionably, as a general proposition, when an offer is made, it is necessary that the acceptance should be notified. But is that so in cases of this kind? I think that in a case of this kind that the person who makes the [offer] shews by his language and from the nature of the transaction that he does not expect and does not require notice of the acceptance apart from notice of the performance.

We, therefore, find here all the elements which are necessary to form a binding contract enforceable in point of law.

It appears to me, therefore, that the defendants must perform their promise, and, if they have been so unwary as to expose themselves to a great many actions, so much the worse for them. Appeal dismissed.

Carlill lived 50 years more, dying at the age of 96—of the flu.

This case serves as a cautionary tale. Running a "normal" ad, which describes a product, its features, and its price, does not amount to an offer. But, if a company proposes to take an action—such as pay $100 to customers who take certain, specific actions—then it may find itself contractually obligated to follow through on its promises. The acceptance of the offer makes a unilateral contract.

Note also that, regardless of whether an ad counts as an offer, consumers have **protection** from deceitful retailers. Almost every state has some form of **consumer protection statute**, which outlaws false advertising. For example, an automobile dealer who advertises a remarkably low price but then has only one automobile at that price has probably violated a

Consumer protection statute
Laws protecting consumers from fraud

AP Images/Seth Wenig

You have the high bid—but you may not win.

consumer protection statute because the ad was published in bad faith, to trick consumers into coming to the dealership. In the *Mesaros* case, the U.S. Mint did not violate any consumer protection statute because it acted in good faith and simply ran out of coins.

Auctions

It is the property you have always dreamed of owning—and it is up for auction! You arrive bright and early, stand in front, bid early, bid often, bid higher, bid highest of all—it's yours! For five seconds. Then, to your horror, the auctioneer announces that none of the bids were juicy enough and he is withdrawing the property. Robbery! Surely he cannot do that? But he can. Auctions are exciting and useful, but you must understand the rules.

Every day, auctions are used to sell exquisite works of art, real estate, and many other things. **Placing an item up for auction is *not* an offer—it is merely a request for an offer.** The *bids* are the offers. If and when the hammer falls, the auctioneer has accepted the offer.

The important thing to know about a particular auction is whether it is conducted with or without reserve. Most auctions are *with reserve*, meaning that the items for sale have a minimum price. The law assumes that an auction is with reserve unless the auctioneer clearly states otherwise. The auctioneer will not sell anything for less than its reserve (minimum price). So when the bidding for your property failed to reach the reserve, the auctioneer was free to withdraw it.

The rules are different in an auction *without reserve*. Here, there is no minimum. Once the first bid is received, the auctioneer *must* sell the merchandise to the highest bidder.

EXAMStrategy

Question: Ahn and Chet are both unhappy. (1) Ahn, an interior designer, is working on a hotel project. In the annual catalog of a furniture wholesaler, she sees that sofa beds cost $3,000. Based on the catalog, she sends an order for 100 sofa beds to the wholesaler. The wholesaler notifies Ahn that the price has gone up to $4,000. (2) At an estate auction, held without reserve, Chet is high bidder on a rare violin. The seller considers Chet's bid too low and refuses to sell. Both Ahn and Chet sue, but only one will win. Which plaintiff will win, and why?

Strategy: (1) A contract requires an offer and an acceptance. When the furniture wholesaler sent out its catalog, did it make an offer that Ahn could accept? (2) Chet was high bidder. At some auctions, the high bidder is merely making an offer, but at others, he wins the item. Which kind of auction was this?

Result: (1) A price quote is generally not an offer. Ahn's order for 100 sofas was the offer, and the company was free to reject it. Ahn loses. (2) Most auctions are with reserve, meaning that the high bidder is merely making an offer. However, this one was without reserve. Chet gets the violin.

12-1c Problems with Definiteness

It is not enough that the offeror indicates that she intends to enter into an agreement. **The terms of the offer must also be definite.** If they are vague, then even if the offeree agrees to the deal, a court does not have enough information to enforce it and there is no contract.

You want a friend to work in your store for the holiday season. This is a definite offer: "I offer you a job as a sales clerk in the store from November 1 through December 29, 40 hours per week at $10 per hour." But suppose, by contrast, you say: "I offer you a job as a sales clerk in the store during the holiday season. We will work out a fair wage once we see how busy things get." Your friend replies, "That's fine with me." This offer is indefinite, and there is no contract. What is a fair wage? $15 per hour? Or $20 per hour? What is the "holiday season"? How will the determinations be made? There is no binding agreement.

The following case, which concerns a famous television series, presents a problem with definiteness.

Baer v. Chase

392 F.3d 609
United States Third Circuit Court of Appeals, 2004

Facts: David Chase was a television writer-producer with many credits, including a detective series called *The Rockford Files*. He became interested in a new program, set in New Jersey, about a "mob boss in therapy," a concept he eventually developed into *The Sopranos*. Robert Baer was a prosecutor in New Jersey who wanted to write for television. He submitted a *Rockford Files* script to Chase, who agreed to meet with Baer.

When they met, Baer pitched a different idea, concerning "a film or television series about the New Jersey Mafia." He did not realize Chase was already working on such an idea. Later that year, Chase visited New Jersey. Baer arranged meetings for Chase with local detectives and prosecutors, who provided the producer with information, material, and personal stories about their experiences with organized crime. Detective Thomas Koczur drove Chase and Baer to various New Jersey locations and introduced Chase to Tony Spirito. Spirito shared stories about loan sharking, power struggles between family members connected with the mob, and two colorful individuals known as Big Pussy and Little Pussy, both of whom later became characters on the show.

Moviestore collection Ltd/Alamy Stock Photo

Back in Los Angeles, Chase wrote and sent to Baer a draft of the first *Sopranos* teleplay. Baer called Chase and commented on the script. The two spoke at least four times that year, and Baer sent Chase a letter about the script.

When *The Sopranos* became a hit television show, Baer sued Chase. He alleged that, on three separate occasions Chase had agreed that, if the program succeeded, Chase would "take care of" Baer, and would "remunerate Baer in a manner commensurate to the true value of his services." This happened twice on the phone, Baer claimed, and once during Chase's visit to New Jersey. The understanding was that if the show failed, Chase would owe nothing. Chase never paid Baer anything.

The district court dismissed the case, holding that the alleged promises were too vague to be enforced. Baer appealed.

Issue: ***Was Chase's promise definite enough to be enforced?***

Excerpts from Judge Greenberg's Decision: A contract arises from offer and acceptance, and must be sufficiently definite so that the performance to be rendered by each party can be ascertained with reasonable certainty. Therefore, parties create an enforceable contract when they agree on its essential terms and manifest an intent that the terms bind them. If parties to an agreement do not agree on one or more essential terms of the purported agreement courts generally hold it to be unenforceable.

New Jersey law deems the price term, that is, the amount of compensation, an essential term of any contract. An agreement lacking definiteness of price, however, is not unenforceable if the parties specify a practicable method by which they can determine the amount. However, in the absence of an agreement as to the manner or method of determining compensation the purported agreement is invalid. Additionally, the duration of the contract is deemed an essential term and therefore any agreement must be sufficiently definitive to allow a court to determine the agreed upon length of the contractual relationship.

Baer premises his argument on his view that New Jersey should disregard the well-established requirement of definiteness in its contract law when the subject matter of the contract is an "idea submission." [However,] New Jersey precedent does not support Baer's attempt to carve out an exception to traditional principles of contract law for submission-of-idea cases. The New Jersey courts have not provided even the slightest indication that they intend to depart from their well-established requirement that enforceability of a contract requires definiteness with respect to the essential terms of that contract.

Nothing in the record indicates that the parties agreed on how, how much, where, or for what period Chase would compensate Baer. The parties did not discuss who would determine the "true value" of Baer's services, when the "true value" would be calculated, or what variables would go into such a calculation. There was no discussion or agreement as to the meaning of "success" of *The Sopranos*. There was no discussion how "profits" were to be defined. There was no contemplation of dates of commencement or termination of the contract. And again, nothing in Baer's or Chase's conduct, or the surrounding circumstances of the relationship, shed light on, or answers, any of these questions.

Affirmed.

"I'll take care of you." You probably have a sense of what this statement meant to Baer when he heard it from Chase: a reliable assurance that he would be paid. However, it was not enough to be a legally enforceable promise. Recall that courts only make *objective* assessments when evaluating offers and acceptances. Judges cannot—and will not—guess what the parties *meant to do* or analyze what was in their heads.

In the following case, the court asked whether a reasonable person would consider a syllabus to be a contract. You be the (objective) judge.

You Be the Judge

Gabriel v. Albany College of Pharmacy and Health Services

No. 2:12-cv 14
United States District Court for the District of Vermont, 2013

Facts: Matthew Gabriel was a student in Professor Pumo's immunology class. Professor Pumo's syllabus outlined course requirements and stated that "plagiarism will not be tolerated." After grading the first assignment, Professor Pumo realized that many papers had sentences copied from other sources without citations. Instead of reporting everyone for plagiarism, Professor Pumo said she would give students a *"free pass"* on one copied sentence. But Gabriel's paper contained many plagiarized sentences, so he received a failing grade for the assignment.

Gabriel sued the professor for breach of contract. He argued that the syllabus was a contract and that the "free pass" policy broke it—because that term was not part of their original agreement. According to Gabriel, since the professor breached the contract, he was no longer obligated to refrain from plagiarizing, and so should not be punished.

You Be the Judge: *Was the professor's syllabus an offer whose acceptance formed an enforceable contract?*

Argument for Gabriel: A syllabus is a contract. On the first day of class, the professor presents the syllabus as an offer and students agree by staying in the course. Who has not chosen a class because of its particular workload or assignments? The terms in the syllabus are promises upon which students rely. Professor Pumo unilaterally changed the written "rules of the game." Once she broke her promise, there was no longer a "deal." Students should not be held to her arbitrary rules.

Argument for Professor: Professors do not intend to make an offer when they hand out a syllabus—much less be legally bound! The syllabus is merely an announcement that provides general information about course requirements, grading policies, and behavior guidelines. Reasonable people do not expect a syllabus to be enforceable in court. It was not a contract—Professor Pumo had the right to change the class rules, make additional assignments, or even kick Gabriel out at any time. Even if the syllabus were a contract, the phrase "plagiarism will not be tolerated" is too indefinite to be a valid offer. Gabriel is not immune from the plagiarism rules.

12-1d The UCC and Open Terms

In Chapter 11, we introduced the Uniform Commercial Code (UCC). Article 2 of the UCC governs contracts when the primary purpose is a sale of goods. Remember that goods are moveable, tangible objects. Usually, UCC provisions are not significantly different from common law rules. But on occasion, the UCC modifies the common law rule in some major way. In such cases, we will present a separate description of the key UCC provision. The UCC as a whole is covered in Unit 3. Depending on the class time available, some instructors prefer to discuss the UCC separately, while others like to include it in the general discussion of contracts. This book is designed to work with either approach.

We have just seen that, under the common law, the terms of an offer must be definite. But under the UCC, many indefinite contracts are allowed to stand. Throughout this unit, we witness how the Uniform Commercial Code makes the law of sales more flexible. There are several areas of contract law where imperfect negotiations may still create a binding agreement under the Code, even though the same negotiations under the common law would have yielded no contract. "Open terms" is one such area.

Yuma County Corp. produced natural gas. Yuma wanted a long-term contract to sell its gas so that it could be certain of recouping the expenses of exploration and drilling. Northwest Central Pipeline, which operated an interstate pipeline, also wanted a deal for ten or more years so it could make its own distribution contracts, knowing it would have a steady supply of natural gas in a competitive market. But neither Yuma nor Northwest wanted to make a long-term *price* commitment because over a period of years the price of natural gas could double—or crash. Each party wanted a binding agreement without a definitive price. If their negotiations had been governed by the common law, they would have run smack into the requirement of definiteness—no price, no contract. But because this was a sale of goods, it was governed by the UCC.

Under UCC §2-204(3), even though one or more terms are left open, a contract does not fail for indefiniteness if the parties have intended to make a contract and there is a reasonably certain basis for giving an appropriate remedy. Thus, a contract for the sale of goods may be enforced when a key term is missing. Business executives may have many reasons to leave open a delivery date, a price, or some other term. But note that the parties must still have *intended* to create a contract. The UCC will not create a contract where the parties never intended one.

In some cases, the contract will state how the missing term is to be determined. Yuma County and Northwest drafted a contract with alternative methods of determining the price. In the event that the price of natural gas was regulated by the Federal Energy Regulatory Commission (FERC), the price would be the highest allowed by the FERC. If the FERC deregulated the price (as it ultimately did), the contract price would be the average of the two highest prices paid by different gas producers in a specified geographic area.

Gap-Filler Provisions

Gap-filler provisions
UCC rules for supplying missing terms

Even if a UCC contract lacks a specific method for determining missing terms, the Code itself contains **gap-filler provisions**, which are rules for *supplying* missing terms. Some of the most important gap-filler provisions of the Code follow.

Open Price. In general, if the parties do not settle on a price, the Code establishes that the goods will be sold for a reasonable price. This will usually be the market value or a price established by a neutral expert or agency.[3]

Output contract
Obligates the seller to sell all of his output to the buyer, who agrees to accept it

Requirements contract
Obligates a buyer to obtain all of his needed goods from the seller

Output and Requirements Provisions. An **output contract** obligates the seller to sell all of his output to the buyer, who agrees to accept it. For example, a cotton grower might agree to sell all of his next crop to a textile firm. A **requirements contract** obligates a buyer to obtain all of his needed goods from the seller. A vineyard might agree to buy all of its wine bottles from one supplier. Output and requirements contracts are by definition incomplete, since the exact quantity of the goods is unspecified. The Code requires that, in carrying out such contracts, both parties act in good faith. Neither party may suddenly demand a quantity of goods (or offer a quantity of goods) that is disproportionate to their past dealings or their reasonable estimates.[4]

12-1e Termination of Offers

Once an offer has been made, it faces only two possible fates—it can be terminated or accepted. If an offer is terminated, it can never be accepted. If it is accepted, and if there are no problems with any of the five remaining elements on the Contracts Checklist, then a valid contract is created. Offers can be terminated in four ways: revocation, rejection, expiration, and by operation of law.

Termination by Revocation

An offer is **revoked** when the offeror "takes it back" before the offeree accepts. In general, the offeror may revoke the offer any time before it has been accepted. Imagine that I call you and say, "I'm going out of town this weekend. I'll sell you my ticket to this weekend's football game for $75." You tell me that you'll think it over and call me back. An hour later, my plans change. I call you a second time and say, "Sorry, but the deal's off—I'm going to the game after all." I have revoked my offer, and you can no longer accept it.

Making Contracts Temporarily Irrevocable

Some offers cannot be revoked, at least for a time. Often, people and businesses need time to evaluate offers. If a car dealer offers you a green sedan for $25,000, you may want to shop around for a few days to try to find a better price. In the meantime, you may want to make sure that the green sedan is still available if you decide to return. Can you legally prevent the car dealer from selling the car to anyone else while you ponder the offer? In some circumstances, yes.

Option Contract (All types of contracts). With an option contract, an interested purchaser *buys* the right to have the offer held open. **The offeror may not revoke an offer during the option period.** Suppose you pay the car dealer $250 to hold open its offer until February 2. Later that day, the dealership notifies you that it is selling to someone else. Result? You can enforce *your* contract. The car dealer had no power to revoke because you purchased an option.

Firm Offers (UCC contracts only). Once again, the UCC has changed the law on the sale of goods. If a promise made in writing is signed by a *merchant*, and if it agrees to hold open an offer for a stated period, then an offer may not be revoked. The open period may

---

[3]UCC §2-305.
[4]UCC §2-306.

not exceed three months. So, if the car dealer gives you a piece of paper that reads, "The offer on the green sedan is open at $25,000 until Friday at noon," he cannot revoke the offer before Friday at noon, even though you have not paid him anything.[5]

Termination by Rejection

If an offeree clearly indicates that he does not want to take the offer, then he has **rejected** it. **If an offeree rejects an offer, the rejection immediately terminates the offer.** Suppose a major accounting firm telephones you and offers a job, starting at $80,000. You respond, "Nah. I'm gonna work on my surfing for a year or two." The next day, you come to your senses and write the firm, accepting its offer. No contract. Your rejection terminated the offer and ended your power to accept it.

Counteroffer. A party makes a **counteroffer** when it responds to an offer with a new and different proposal. Frederick faxes Kim, offering to sell a 50 percent interest in the Fab Hotel in New York for only $135 million. Kim faxes back and says, "That's too much, but I'll pay $115 million." Moments later, Kim's business partner convinces her that Frederick's offer was a bargain, and she faxes an acceptance of his $135 million offer. Does Kim have a binding deal? No. **A counteroffer is a rejection.** When Kim offered $115 million, she rejected Frederick's offer. Her original fax created a new offer, for $115 million, which Frederick never accepted. The parties have no contract at any price.

Counteroffer
A different proposal made in response to an original offer

Termination by Expiration

An offeror may set a time limit. Quentin calls you and offers you a job in his next motion picture. He tells you, "I've got to know by tomorrow night." If you call him in three days to accept, you are out of the picture. **When an offer specifies a time limit for acceptance, that period is binding.**

If the offer specifies no time limit, the offeree has a *reasonable* period in which to accept. A reasonable period varies, depending upon the type of offer, previous dealings between the parties, and any normal trade usage or customary practices in a particular industry.

Termination by Operation of Law

In some circumstances, the law itself terminates an offer. **If an offeror dies or becomes mentally incapacitated, the offer terminates automatically and immediately.** Arnie offers you a job as an assistant in his hot-air balloon business. Before you can even accept, Arnie tumbles out of a balloon at 3,000 feet. The offer terminates along with Arnie.

Destruction of the subject matter terminates the offer. A car dealer offers to sell you a rare 1938 Bugatti for $7,500,000 if you bring cash the next day. You arrive, suitcase stuffed with cash, just in time to see Arnie drop 3,000 feet through the air and crush the Bugatti. The dealer's offer is terminated.

12-2 ACCEPTANCE

As we have seen, when there is a valid offer outstanding, it remains effective until it is terminated or accepted. An offeree accepts by saying or doing something that a reasonable person would understand to mean that he definitely wants to take the offer. Assume that Ellie offers to sell Gene her old iPad for $50. If Gene says, "I accept your offer," then he has indeed accepted, but there is no need to be so formal. He can accept the offer by saying, "It's a deal," or, "I'll take it," or any number of things. He need not even speak. If he hands her a $50 bill, he also accepts the offer.

[5]UCC §2-205.

It is worth noting that **the offeree must say or do *something* to accept**. Marge telephones Vick and leaves a message on his voice mail: "I'll pay $75 for your business law textbook from last semester. I'm desperate to get a copy, so I will assume you agree unless I hear from you by 6:00 tonight." Marge hears nothing by the deadline and assumes she has a deal. She is mistaken. Vick neither said nor did anything to indicate that he accepted.

12-2a Mirror Image Rule

If only he had known! A splendid university, an excellent position as department chair—gone. And all because of the mirror image rule.

Ohio State University wrote to Philip Foster offering him an appointment as a professor and chair of the art history department. His position was to begin July 1, and he had until June 2 to accept the job. On June 2, Foster telephoned the dean and left a message accepting the position, *effective July 15*. Later, Foster thought better of it and wrote the university, accepting the school's starting date of July 1. Too late! Professor Foster never did occupy that chair at Ohio State. The court held that since his acceptance varied the starting date, it was a counteroffer. And a counteroffer, as we know, is a rejection.[6]

Was it sensible to deny the professor a job over a mere 14-day difference? Sensible or not, that is the law.

Mirror image rule
Requires that acceptance be on precisely the same terms as the offer

Was it sensible to deny the professor a job over a mere 14-day difference? Sensible or not, that is the law. The common law **mirror image rule** requires that acceptance be on *precisely* the same terms as the offer. If the acceptance contains terms that add or contradict the offer, even in minor ways, courts generally consider it a counteroffer. The rule worked reasonably well in the nineteenth century, when parties would write an original contract and exchange it, penciling in any changes. But now that businesses use standardized forms to purchase most goods and services, the rule creates enormous difficulties. Sellers use forms they have prepared, with all conditions stated to their advantage, and buyers employ their own forms, with terms they prefer. The forms are exchanged in the mail or electronically, with neither side clearly agreeing to the other party's terms.

The problem is known as the "battle of forms." Once again, the UCC has entered the fray, attempting to provide flexibility and common sense for those contracts involving the sale of goods. But for contracts governed by the common law, such as Professor Foster's, the mirror image rule is still the law.

12-2b UCC and the Battle of Forms

UCC §2-207 dramatically modifies the mirror image rule for the sale of goods. Under this provision, an acceptance that adds additional or different terms often will create a contract.

Additional or Different Terms

One basic principle of the common law of contracts remains unchanged: the key to creation of a contract is a valid offer that the offeree *intends* to accept. If there is no intent to accept, there is no contract. The big change brought about by UCC §2-207 is this: **An offeree who accepts may include in the acceptance terms that are additional to or different from those in the offer**. Thus, even with additional or different terms, the acceptance may well create a contract.

Example A. Wholesaler writes to Manufacturer offering to buy "10,000 wheelbarrows at $50 per unit. Payable on delivery, 30 days from today's date." Manufacturer writes back, "We accept your offer of 10,000 wheelbarrows at $50 per unit, payable on delivery. *Interest at normal trade rates for unpaid balances.*" Manufacturer clearly intends to form a contract. The company has added a new term, but there is still a valid contract.

[6]Foster v. Ohio State University, 41 Ohio App. 3d 86 (1987).

However, if the offeree states that her acceptance is *conditioned on the offeror's assent* to the new terms, there is no contract.

Example B. Same offer as above. Manufacturer adds the interest rate clause and states, "Our acceptance is conditional upon your agreement to this interest rate." Manufacturer has made a counteroffer. There is no contract, yet. If Wholesaler accepts the counteroffer, there is a contract; if Wholesaler does not accept it, there is no contract.

Additional terms are those that bring up *new* issues, such as interest rates, not contained in the original offer. Additional terms in the acceptance are considered proposals to add to the contract. Assuming that both parties are merchants, the additional terms *will generally become part of the contract.* Thus, in Example A, the interest rate will become a part of the binding deal. If Wholesaler is late in paying, it must pay whatever interest rate is current.

In three circumstances, the additional terms in the acceptance *do not* become part of the contract:

- If the original offeror *insisted on its own terms*. In other words, if Wholesaler wrote, "I offer to buy them on the following terms and *no other terms*," then Manufacturer is not free to make additions.
- If the additional terms *materially alter* the original offer. Suppose Manufacturer wrote back, "We accept your offer for 10,000 wheelbarrows. Delivery will be made within 180 days, unless we notify you of late delivery." Manufacturer has changed the time from 30 days to 180 days, with a possible extension beyond that. That is a material alteration, and it will not become part of the contract. By contrast, Manufacturer's new language concerning "interest at normal trade rates" was not a material alteration, and therefore that interest rate becomes part of the contract.
- If the offeror receives the additional terms and *promptly objects* to them.

Different terms are those that contradict terms in the offer. For example, if the seller's form clearly states that no warranty is included, and the buyer's form says the seller warrants all goods for three years, the acceptance contains different terms. An acceptance may contain different terms and still create a contract. But in these cases, courts have struggled to decide what the terms of the contract are. **The majority of states hold that different (contradictory) terms cancel each other out**. Neither term is included in the contract. Instead, the neutral terms from the Code itself are "read into" the contract. These are the gap-filler terms discussed earlier. If, for example, the forms had contradictory warranty clauses (as they almost always do), the different terms would cancel each other out, and the warranty clauses from the UCC would be substituted.[7]

EXAMStrategy

Question: Elaine sends an offer to Raoul. Raoul writes, "I accept. Please note, I will charge 2 percent interest per month for any unpaid money." He signs the document and sends it back to Elaine. Do the two have a binding contract?

Strategy: Slow down, this is trickier than it seems. Raoul has added a term to Elaine's offer. We must take two steps to decide whether there is a contract. In a contract for services, acceptance must mirror the offer, but not so in an agreement for the sale of goods.

Result: If this is an agreement for services, there is no contract. However, if this agreement is for goods, the additional term *may* become part of an enforceable contract.

---

[7]Not all states follow this rule, however. Some courts have held that when the acceptance contains terms that contradict those in the offer, the language in the offer should be final. A few courts have ruled that the terms in the acceptance should control.

Question: Assume that Elaine's offer concerns goods. Is there an agreement?

Strategy: Under UCC §-207, an additional term will become part of a binding agreement for goods except in three instances. What are the three exceptions?

Result: Raoul's extra term will be incorporated in a binding contract unless (1) Elaine's offer made clear she would accept no other terms, (2) Raoul's interest rate is a material alteration of the offer (almost never the case for interest rates), or (3) Elaine promptly rejects the interest rate.

12-2c Clickwrap and Browsewrap Agreements

You want to purchase Attila brand software and download it to your computer. You type in your credit card number and other information, agreeing to pay $99. Attila also requires that you "read and agree to" all of the company's terms. You click "I agree," without having read one word of the terms. Three frustrating weeks later, tired of trying to operate defective Attilaware, you demand a refund and threaten to sue. The company replies that you are barred from suing because the terms you agreed to include an arbitration clause. To resolve any disputes, you must travel to Attila's hometown, halfway across the nation, use an arbitrator that the company chooses, pay one-half the arbitrator's fee, and also pay Attila's legal bills if you should lose. The agreement makes it financially impossible for you to get your money back. Is that contract enforceable?

You have entered into a clickwrap agreement.[8] These contracts require users to accept proposed terms by clicking an "I agree" button. But everyone knows no one reads them, so is *clicking* really acceptance? What if you did not read the contract and it contains unfavorable terms?

Many courts have analyzed clickwrap agreements and concluded that they are indeed binding, even against consumers who choose not to read them. The courts have emphasized that sellers are entitled to offer a product on any terms they wish, and that clickwraps are the most efficient methods of including complicated terms in a small space.[9]

Another type of online contract is a browsewrap. With browsewraps, websites seek to bind users to their terms just by posting them somewhere on their sites or making them accessible through a hyperlink. Unlike clickwraps, browsewraps do not require users to do anything or click anything. Websites often argue that just browsing through the site is enough to constitute acceptance so long as the terms of use are *somewhere in there*. But should this always be true?

Specht v. Netscape Communications Corporation

306 F.3d 17
United States Second Circuit Court of Appeals, 2002

Facts: A group of plaintiffs sued Netscape, claiming that two of the company's products illegally captured private information about files that they downloaded from the internet. The plaintiffs alleged that this was electronic eavesdropping, in violation of two federal statutes.

From Netscape's web page, the plaintiffs had downloaded SmartDownload, a software plug-in that enabled them to download the company's software. The web page advertised the benefits of SmartDownload, and near the bottom of the screen was a button labeled "Download." The plaintiffs clicked to download. If, instead of downloading, they had scrolled further down, they would have seen an invitation to "review and agree to the terms of the Netscape SmartDownload software license agreement."

[8]Clickwraps are also called "clickthrough" agreements.

[9]ProCD, Inc. v. Zeidenberg, 86 F.3d 1447 (7th Cir. 1996).

Among these terms was an agreement to arbitrate any dispute, effectively giving up the right to file suit if anything went wrong. Like most people online, the plaintiffs never read the license terms.

In the district court, Netscape moved to dismiss the case and compel arbitration. It claimed that the plaintiffs had accepted the license agreement. The district court disagreed, ruling that the plaintiffs had not agreed to the terms of the license. Netscape appealed.

Issue: ***Had the plaintiffs agreed to arbitrate their claims?***

Excerpts from Judge Sotomayor's Decision: Defendants argue that plaintiffs must be held to a standard of reasonable prudence and that, because notice of the existence of SmartDownload license terms was on the next scrollable screen, plaintiffs were on "inquiry notice" of those terms. We disagree with the proposition that a reasonably prudent offeree in plaintiffs' position would necessarily have known or learned of the existence of the SmartDownload license agreement prior to acting, so that plaintiffs may be held to have assented to that agreement with constructive notice of its terms.

Receipt of a physical document containing contract terms or notice thereof is frequently deemed, in the world of paper transactions, a sufficient circumstance to place the offeree on inquiry notice of those terms. These principles apply equally to the emergent world of online product delivery, pop-up screens, hyperlinked pages, clickwrap licensing, scrollable documents, and urgent admonitions to "Download Now!" What plaintiffs saw when they were being invited by defendants to download this fast, free plug-in called SmartDownload was a screen containing praise for the product and, at the very bottom of the screen, a "Download" button. Defendants argue that a fair and prudent person using ordinary care would have been on inquiry notice of SmartDownload's license terms.

We are not persuaded that a reasonably prudent offeree in these circumstances would have known of the existence of license terms. Plaintiffs were responding to an offer that did not carry an immediately visible notice of the existence of license terms or require unambiguous manifestation of assent to those terms. Thus, plaintiffs' apparent manifestation of consent was to terms contained in a document whose contractual nature was not obvious. Moreover, the fact that, given the position of the scroll bar on their computer screens, plaintiffs may have been aware that an unexplored portion of the Netscape Web page remained below the download button does not mean that they reasonably should have concluded that this portion contained a notice of license terms.

We conclude that in circumstances such as these, where consumers are urged to download free software at the immediate click of a button, a reference to the existence of license terms on a submerged screen is not sufficient to place consumers on inquiry or constructive notice of those terms. There is no reason to assume that viewers will scroll down to subsequent screens simply because screens are there.

For the foregoing reasons, we affirm the district court's denial of defendants' motion to compel arbitration and to stay court proceedings.

The plaintiffs in *Specht* won because they knew nothing about the hidden arbitration clause. Since *Specht*, courts have generally held browsewrap agreements enforceable when websites give users reasonable notice and access to their terms. One court refused to enforce the Terms of Use of Zappos, an online shoe store. Zappos's browsewrap was not valid because it was inconspicuous and buried among many other links at the bottom of the page. The court found that no reasonable consumer would have found them, and so there could not have been a valid acceptance.[10]

Notice what happens when a user *does* know about terms posted online. Register.com was a registrar of internet domain names, meaning that it issued domain names to people and companies establishing a new website. The company was legally obligated to make available to the public, for free, the names and contact information of its customers. Register was also in the business of assisting owners, for a fee, to develop their websites.

Verio, Inc. competed in the site development business. Verio's automated software program would search Register.com daily, seeking information about new sites. *After* Verio obtained contact information, a notice would appear on the Register site, stating:

> By submitting a query, you agree that under no circumstances will you use this data to support the transmission of mass unsolicited, commercial advertising or solicitation via email.

---

[10] In re Zappos.com, Inc., Customer Data Sec. Breach Litigation, 893 F.Supp.2d 1058 (D. Nevada, 2012).

In fact, though, Verio used the contact information for exactly that purpose, sending mass email blasts to owners of new websites, soliciting their development business. Register sued. Verio defended by stating it was not bound by the notice because the notice did not appear until after it had obtained the information. Verio argued that when it sent the queries, it was unaware of any restrictions on use of the data. The court was unpersuaded and explained its reasoning with a simple but telling metaphor:

> The situation might be compared to one in which plaintiff P maintains a roadside fruit stand displaying bins of apples. A visitor, defendant D, takes an apple and bites into it. As D turns to leave, D sees a sign, visible only as one turns to exit, which says "Apples—50 cents apiece." D does not pay for the apple. D believes he has no obligation to pay because he had no notice when he bit into the apple that 50 cents was expected in return. D's view is that he never agreed to pay for the apple. Thereafter, each day, several times a day, D revisits the stand, takes an apple, and eats it. D never leaves money.
>
> P sues D in contract for the price of the apples taken. D defends on the ground that on no occasion did he see P's price notice until after he had bitten into the apples. D may well prevail as to the first apple taken. D had no reason to understand upon taking it that P was demanding the payment. In our view, however, D cannot continue on a daily basis to take apples for free, knowing full well that P is offering them only in exchange for 50 cents in compensation, merely because the sign demanding payment is so placed that on each occasion D does not see it until he has bitten into the apple.

Register.com won its case. Verio was prohibited from using the contact information for mass emailings because it had actual knowledge of the restrictions placed on its use.[11]

Ethics

Imagine browsing for an airline ticket online, only to discover that the first class fare from New York to India is $1, round trip. Would you rush to purchase it? Airlines regularly make programming mistakes resulting in mispriced online fares. Brian Kelly found a United Airlines first class ticket from New York to Hong Kong—which usually costs about $11,000—for $43 and immediately bought it on the company's online ticketing system.[12] Kelly, who runs a website for frequent flyers, advised his readers to take advantage of the glitch before United discovered it. And many did.

Are these "mistake fares"—which are obviously "too good to be true"—enforceable as contracts? Is there a valid offer and acceptance? Ethically speaking, would you take advantage of this deal? Why or why not?

12-2d Communication of Acceptance

The offeree must communicate his acceptance for it to be effective. The questions that typically arise concern the method, the manner, and the time of acceptance.

Method and Manner of Acceptance

The term *method* refers to whether acceptance is done in person or by mail, telephone, email, or fax. The term *manner* refers to whether the offeree accepts by promising, by making a down payment, by performing, and so forth. **If an offer demands acceptance in a particular method or**

11 Register.Com v. Verio, Inc., 353 F.3d 393 (2d Cir. 2004).

12 Tim Hume, *Too good to be true: New York to Hong Kong for $43*, CNN.com (July 23, 2012).

manner, the offeree must follow those requirements. An offer might specify that it be accepted in writing, or in person, or before midnight on June 23. An offeror can set any requirements she wishes. Omri might say to Oliver, "I'll sell you my bike for $200. You must accept my offer by standing on a chair in the lunchroom tomorrow and reciting a poem about a cow." Oliver can only accept the offer in the exact manner specified if he wants to form a contract.

If the offer does not specify a type of acceptance, the offeree may accept in any reasonable manner and method. An offer generally may be accepted by performance or by a promise, unless it specifies a particular method. The same freedom applies to the method. If Masako faxes Eric an offer to sell 1,000 acres in Montana for $800,000, Eric may accept by mail or fax. Both are routinely used in real estate transactions, and either is reasonable.

Time of Acceptance: The Mailbox Rule

An acceptance is generally effective upon dispatch, meaning the moment it is out of the offeree's control. Terminations, on the other hand, are effective when received. When Masako faxes her offer to sell land to Eric, and he mails his acceptance, the contract is binding the moment he puts the letter into the mail. In most cases, this **mailbox rule** is just a detail. But it becomes important when the offeror revokes her offer at about the same time the offeree accepts. Who wins? Suppose Masako's offer has one twist:

Mailbox rule
Acceptance is generally effective upon dispatch. Terminations are effective when received.

- On Monday morning, Masako faxes her offer to Eric.
- On Monday afternoon, Eric writes, "I accept" on the fax, and Masako mails a revocation of her offer.
- On Tuesday morning, Eric mails his acceptance.
- On Thursday morning, Masako's revocation arrives at Eric's office.
- On Friday morning, Eric's acceptance arrives at Masako's office.

Outcome? Eric has an enforceable contract. Masako's offer was effective when it reached Eric. His acceptance was effective on Tuesday morning, when he mailed it. Nothing that happens later can "undo" the contract.

Even though many of us no longer use mailboxes as our main means of business communication, the mailbox rule remains the default rule for determining the exact time at which an offer becomes a contract. Why is this important? Just ask John Soldau. After he was fired, his employer sent him a letter offering to pay him double severance if he promised not to sue. Although he believed he could sue for discrimination, Soldau signed the waiver and put it in a mailbox outside the post office. *Lo and behold* ... that same day Soldau received a check for double severance. He hustled back to the post office, persuaded a postal worker to open the mailbox, and took back the signed release. Could Soldau still sue? The Ninth Circuit said "no backsies": A contract was formed the instant Soldau placed the letter in the mailbox.[13]

CHAPTER CONCLUSION

The law of offer and acceptance can be complex. Yet for all its faults, the law is not the principal source of dispute between parties unhappy with negotiations. Most litigation concerning offer and acceptance comes from *lack of clarity* on the part of the people negotiating. The many examples discussed are all understandable given the speed and fluidity of the real world of business. But the executive who insists on clarity is likelier in the long run to spend more time doing business and less time in court.

---

[13]Soldau v. Organon, Inc., 860 F.2d 355 (9th Cir., 1988).

EXAM REVIEW

1. **MEETING OF THE MINDS** The parties can form a contract only if they have a meeting of the minds, which requires that they understand each other and show that they intend to reach an agreement.

EXAMStrategy

Question: Norv owned a Ford dealership and wanted to expand by obtaining a BMW outlet. He spoke with Jackson and other BMW executives on several occasions. Norv now claims that those discussions resulted in an oral contract that requires BMW to grant him a franchise, but the company disagrees. Norv's strongest evidence of a contract is the fact that Jackson gave him forms on which to order BMWs. Jackson answered that it was his standard practice to give such forms to prospective dealers, so that if the franchise were approved, car orders could be processed quickly. Norv states that he was "shocked" when BMW refused to go through with the deal. Is there a contract?

Strategy: A court makes an *objective* assessment of what the parties did and said to determine whether they had a meeting of the minds and intended to form a contract. Norv's "shock" is irrelevant. Do the order forms indicate a meeting of the minds? Was there additional evidence that the parties had reached an agreement? (See the "Result" at the end of this Exam Review section.)

2. **OFFER** An offer is an act or statement that proposes definite terms and permits the other party to create a contract by accepting those terms.

3. **OTHER STATEMENTS** Invitations to bargain, price quotes, letters of intent, and advertisements are generally not offers. However, an ad in which a company proposes to take a specific action when a customer takes a specific action can amount to an offer. And letters of intent that indicate the parties intended to be bound can also count as offers.

EXAMStrategy

Question: "Huge selection of Guernsey sweaters," reads a newspaper ad from Stuffed Shirt, a clothing retailer. "Regularly $135, today only $65." Waldo arrives at Stuffed Shirt at 4:00 that afternoon, but the shop clerk says there are no more sweaters. He shows Waldo a newly arrived Shetland sweater that sells for $145. Waldo sues, claiming breach of contract and violation of a consumer protection statute. Who will prevail?

(a) Waldo will win the breach of contract suit and the consumer protection suit.

(b) Waldo will lose the breach of contract suit but might win the consumer protection suit.

(c) Waldo will lose the consumer protection suit but should win the breach of contract suit.

(d) Waldo will win the consumer protection suit only if he wins the contract case.

(e) Waldo will lose both the breach of contract suit and the consumer protection suit.

Strategy: Waldo assumes that he is accepting the store's offer. But did Stuffed Shirt make an offer? If not, there cannot be a contract. Does the consumer protection statute help him? (See the "Result" at the end of this Exam Review section.)

4. **DEFINITENESS** The terms of the offer must be definite, although under the UCC the parties may create a contract that has open terms.

5. **TERMINATION** An offer may be terminated by revocation, rejection, expiration, or operation of law.

EXAMStrategy

Question: Rick is selling his Espresso Coffee Maker. He sends Tamara an email, offering to sell the machine for $350. Tamara promptly emails back, offering to buy the item for $300. She hears nothing from Rick, so an hour later Tamara stops by his apartment, where she learns that he just sold the machine to his roommate for $250. She sues Rick. Outcome?

(a) Tamara will win because her offer was higher than the roommate's.

(b) Tamara will win because Rick never responded to her offer.

(c) Tamara will win because both parties made clear offers, in writing.

(d) Tamara will lose because she rejected Rick's offer.

(e) Tamara will lose because her offer was not definite.

Strategy: A valid contract requires a definite offer and acceptance. Rick made a valid offer. When Tamara said she would buy the machine for a lower amount, was that acceptance? If not, what was it? (See the "Result" at the end of this Exam Review section.)

6. **MIRROR IMAGE RULE AND UCC §2-207** The common law mirror image rule requires acceptance on precisely the same terms as the offer. Under the UCC, an offeree may often create a contract even when the acceptance includes terms that are additional to or different from those in the offer.

7. **CLICKWRAP AND BROWSEWRAP AGREEMENTS** Clickwrap agreements are generally enforceable, but browsewraps are only enforceable when websites provide reasonable notice and access to them.

8. **MANNER OF ACCEPTANCE** If an offer demands acceptance in a particular method or manner, the offeree must follow those requirements. If the offer does not specify a type of acceptance, the offeree may accept in any reasonable manner and medium.

9. **MAILBOX RULE** An acceptance is generally effective upon dispatch, meaning from the moment it is out of the offeree's control. Terminations usually are not effective until received.

RESULTS

1. Result: The order forms are neither an offer nor an acceptance. Norv has offered no evidence that the parties agreed on price, date of performance, or any other key terms. There is no contract. Norv allowed eagerness and optimism to replace common sense.

3. Result: An advertisement is usually not an offer, but merely a solicitation of one. It is Waldo who is making the offer, which the store may reject. Waldo loses his contract case, but he may win under the consumer protection statute. The correct answer is (b). If Stuffed Shirt proclaimed "huge selection" when there were only five sweaters, the store was deliberately misleading consumers, and Waldo wins. However, if there was indeed a large selection, and Waldo arrived too late, he is out of luck.

5. Result: Tamara made a counteroffer of $300. A counteroffer is a rejection. Tamara rejected Rick's offer and simultaneously offered to buy the coffee maker at a lower price. Rick was under no obligation to sell to Tamara at any price. He will win Tamara's suit.

MULTIPLE-CHOICE QUESTIONS

1. Rebecca, in Honolulu, faxes a job offer to Spike, in Pittsburgh, saying, "We can pay you $55,000 per year, starting June 1." Spike faxes a reply, saying, "Thank you! I accept your generous offer, though I will also need $3,000 in relocation money. See you June 1. Can't wait!" On June 1, Spike arrives and finds that his position is filled by Gus. He sues Rebecca.

(a) Spike wins $55,000.
(b) Spike wins $58,000.
(c) Spike wins $3,000.
(d) Spike wins restitution.
(e) Spike wins nothing.

2. Arturo hires Kate to work in his new sporting goods store. "Look," he explains, "I can only pay you $9.00 an hour. But if business is good a year from now, and you're still here, I'm sure I can pay you a healthy bonus." Four months later, Arturo terminates Kate. She sues.

(a) Kate will win her job back, plus the year's pay and the bonus.
(b) Kate will win the year's pay and the bonus.
(c) Kate will win only the bonus.
(d) Kate will win only her job back.
(e) Kate will win nothing.

3. Manny offers to sell Gina his television for $100 on January 1. On January 2, Gina writes out a letter of acceptance. On January 3, Gina drops the letter in a mailbox. On January 4, a postal worker gets the letter out of the mailbox and takes it to the post office. On January 5, the letter arrives in Manny's mailbox. When (if ever) was a contract formed?

(a) January 2
(b) January 3
(c) January 4
(d) January 5
(e) None of these—a contract has not been formed.

4. Frank, an accountant, says to Missy, "I'll sell you my laptop for $100." Missy asks, "Will you give me until tomorrow to make up my mind?" "Sure," Frank replies. Which of the following is true?
   (a) Frank cannot revoke his offer, no matter what.
   (b) Frank cannot revoke his offer, but only if Missy pays him to keep the offer open until tomorrow.
   (c) Frank can revoke his offer no matter what because he is not a merchant.
   (d) Frank can revoke his offer no matter what because he did not promise Missy anything in writing.

5. Which of the following amounts to an offer?
   (a) Ed says to Carmen, "I offer to sell you my pen for $1."
   (b) Ed says to Carmen, "I'll sell you my pen for $1."
   (c) Ed writes, "I'll sell you my pen for $1," and gives the note to Carmen.
   (d) All of these
   (e) A and C only

CASE QUESTIONS

1. The town of Sanford, Maine, decided to auction off a lot it owned. The town advertised that it would accept bids through the mail, up to a specified date. Arthur and Arline Chevalier mailed in a bid that turned out to be the highest. When the town refused to sell them the lot, they sued. Result?

2. The Tufte family leased a 260-acre farm from the Travelers Insurance Co. Toward the end of the lease, Travelers mailed the Tuftes an option to renew the lease. The option arrived at the Tuftes' house on March 30, and gave them until April 14 to accept. On April 13, the Tuftes signed and mailed their acceptance, which Travelers received on April 19. Travelers claimed there was no lease and attempted to evict the Tuftes from the farm. May they stay?

3. When a Tom Cat Bakery delivery van struck Elizabeth Nadel, she suffered significant injuries, Nadel filed suit. Before the trial, Tom Cat's attorney offered a $100,000 settlement, which Nadel refused. While the jury was deliberating, the bakery's lawyer again offered Nadel the $100,000 settlement. She decided to think about it during lunch. Later that day, the jury sent a note to the judge. The bakery owner told her lawyer that if the note indicated the jury had reached a verdict, he should revoke the settlement offer. Back in the courtroom, the bakery's lawyer said, "If the note is a verdict, my client wants to take the verdict." Nadel's lawyer then said, "My client will take the settlement." The trial court judge allowed the forewoman to read the verdict, which awarded Nadel—nothing. Did Nadel's lawyer accept the settlement offer in time?

4. Machado Ford published the following newspaper ad: "Buy a New Ford and Get $3,000 Minimum Trade-In Allowance." Izadi attempted to purchase a new Ford Ranger valued at $6,595 for $3,595 in cash plus his trade-in (assuming the minimum trade-in allowance). Machado refused. The ad's superfine print indicated that the offer was only good toward two other vehicle models and that the trade-in must be worth at least $3,000. Izadi sued, arguing that the ad was misleading. Machado contended that it did not mean for the ad to be interpreted as it was. Who should prevail?

5. Miller listed her home for sale. On August 4th, Norman made an offer, specifying that it must be accepted by 5:00 p.m. on August 5th. Miller received the offer, made several changes, signed it, and returned it to Norman. Norman did not respond. On August 5th at noon, Segal offered to buy Miller's house and Miller accepted. Miller then revoked the counteroffer to Norman. But right before 5:00 p.m., Norman initialed Miller's counteroffer and delivered it with a deposit. To whom, if anyone, did Miller sell her home?

DISCUSSION QUESTIONS

1. Each time employees at BizCorp enter their work computers, the following alert appears: "You are attempting to access the BizCorp network. By logging in, you agree to BizCorp's Computer Usage Policy and certify that your use of this computer is strictly for business purposes. Any activities conducted on this system may be monitored for any reason at the discretion of BizCorp." Once an employee has logged in, have the parties formed a valid contract? Discuss.

2. Case law tells us that a course syllabus is not a binding contract—but how about your school's honor code? Under what conditions could an honor code be a contract?

3. The day after Thanksgiving, known as Black Friday, is the biggest shopping day of the year. One major retailer advertised a "Black Friday only" laptop for $150. On Thanksgiving night, hundreds of people waited for the store to open to take advantage of the laptop deal—only to learn that the store only had two units for sale at the discounted price. Did the retailer breach its contract with the hundreds of consumers who sought the deal? What obligation, if any, does the retailer have to its consumers?

4. Someone offers to sell you a concert ticket for $50, and you reply, "I'll give you $40." The seller refuses to sell at the lower price, and you say, "OK, OK, I'll pay you $50." Clearly, no contract has been formed because you made a counteroffer. If the seller has changed her mind and no longer wants to sell for $50, she doesn't have to. But is this fair? If it is all part of the same conversation, should you be able to accept the $50 offer and get the ticket?

5. If you click an "I agree" box, odds are that its terms are binding on you, even if the box contains dozens or even hundreds of lines of dense text. Is this fair? Should the law change to limit the enforceability of clickwraps?

6. Ryan Leslie, a rapper, was distraught when someone stole his computer and external hard drive because they contained some music he was writing. In an effort to retrieve his items, he created a series of YouTube videos, news articles, and social media postings in which he promised to pay $20,000 to anyone who returned his property. Leslie later increased the reward to $1 million in another YouTube video, which included the following text:

   > In the interest of retrieving the invaluable intellectual property contained on his laptop and hard drive, Mr. Leslie has increased the reward offer from $20,000 to $1,000,000 USD.

   Armin returned the computer and hard drive, but Leslie refused to pay, saying that he could not get his intellectual property from his hard drive. Did Leslie make a valid offer? Did Armin make a valid acceptance?

CHAPTER

13 CONSIDERATION

Have you ever rented a movie that you did not want every one of your friends to know about? Cathryn Harris did. Imagine her shock when she rented a movie online from Blockbuster, only to find out that this news was automatically transmitted to her Facebook page and then broadcast to all her "friends." Just think how bad that could be.

Harris sued Blockbuster for this violation of her privacy, only to find out she had clicked away her right to sue. To rent the movie, she clicked that little box saying she agreed to all the terms and conditions. And one of those terms and conditions was an agreement to arbitrate, not litigate. Can Blockbuster get away with this?

To rent the movie, she had to click that little box saying she agreed to all the terms and conditions.

It turns out that this movie has a happy ending. The court ruled that the contract between Harris and Blockbuster was unenforceable because there was no *consideration*.

CONTRACTS CHECKLIST

- ☐ Offer
- ☐ Acceptance
- ☑ Consideration
- ☐ Legality
- ☐ Capacity
- ☐ Consent
- ☐ Writing

Consideration is our next step on the road to understanding contracts. In Chapter 12, we learned what it takes to create an agreement. But an agreement is not necessarily a legally enforceable contract.

This is the first of four chapters that will examine problems that can prevent an agreement from becoming a contract. A lack of consideration is one of them. Without it, a promise is "just a promise" and nothing more.

13-1 WHAT IS CONSIDERATION?

In early English law, courts would not enforce contracts unless they were under formal seal.[1]

It soon became evident that many other types of mutual promises should be recognized as contracts, regardless of their form. But how would judges know which promises were worth enforcing? How would they distinguish between mere gifts and legally binding commitments?

Consideration
The inducement, price, or promise that causes a person to enter into a contract and forms the basis for the parties' exchange

The answer is **consideration. Consideration is the inducement, price, or promise that causes a person to enter into a contract and forms the basis for the parties' exchange.** The central idea of consideration is simple: Contracts must be a two-way street. If one side gets all the benefit and the other side gets nothing, then an agreement lacks consideration and is not an enforceable contract. Consideration is proof that the parties intended to be bound to their promises.

There are two basic elements of consideration:

1. **Value**. Consideration requires legal benefit to the promisor or legal detriment to the promisee. Legal benefit means receiving something of *measurable value*. That thing can be money, groceries, insurance, a promise not to sue, or anything else of value to the promisee.

2. **Bargained-For Exchange**. According to Supreme Court Justice Oliver Wendell Holmes, Jr., the essence of consideration is that "the promise must induce the detriment and the detriment must induce the promise."[2] Consideration involves reciprocity. The parties must have *bargained for* whatever was exchanged and struck a deal: "If you do this, I'll do that." If you just decide to deliver a cake to your neighbor's house without her knowing, that may be something of value, but since you two did not bargain for it, there is no contract and she does not owe you the price of the cake.

Time Life Pictures/Library Of Congress/The LIFE Picture Collection/Getty Images

For Holmes consideration required a reciprocal bargain

Let's take an example: Sally's Shoe Store and Baker Boots agree that Sally's will pay $20,000 for 100 pairs of boots. As to the $20,000, Sally's is the promisor (because it has committed to paying) and Baker the promisee (because it is the recipient). Regarding the boots, Baker is the promisor, and Sally's the promisee. Both parties get a legal benefit that is of value—Sally gets the boots, Baker gets the money. Also, each incurs a detriment—Sally gives up the money, Baker parts with the boots. Note that a contract

[1] It was once common to authenticate contracts with a seal, an instrument that creates an impression on paper or wax. This practice is rare today.

[2] Wisconsin & Michigan Ry. v. Powers, 191 U.S. 379 (1903).

is formed at the moment when the promises are made because a promise to give something of value counts. The two have bargained for this deal, so there is valid consideration.

Now here's an example where there is no consideration. Marvin works at Sally's. At 9 a.m., he is in a good mood and promises to buy his coworker a Starbucks latte during the lunch hour. The delighted coworker agrees. Later that morning, the coworker is rude to Marvin, who then changes his mind about buying the coffee. He is free to do so. His promise was a one-way street: The coworker stood to receive all the benefit of the agreement, while Marvin got nothing. Because Marvin received no value, there is no contract.

13-1a What Is Value?

As we have seen, an essential part of consideration is that both parties must get something of value. That item of value can be either an "act," a "forbearance," or a promise to do either of these.

Act

A party commits an **act** when she does something she was not legally required to do in the first place. She might do a job, deliver an item, or pay money, for example. An act does not count if the party was simply complying with the law or fulfilling her obligations under an existing contract. Suppose that your professor tells the university that she will not post final grades unless she is paid an extra $5,000. Even if the university agrees to this outrageous demand, that agreement is not a valid contract because the professor is already under an obligation to post final grades.

Act
Any action that a party was not legally required to take in the first place

Forbearance

A **forbearance** is, in essence, the opposite of an act. A person forbears if he agrees *not* to do something he had a legal right to do. An entrepreneur might promise a competitor *not* to open a competing business, or an elderly driver (with a valid driver's license) might promise concerned family members that he will not drive at night.

Forbearance
Refraining from doing something that one has a legal right to do

Promise to Act or Forbear

A promise to do (or not do) something in the future counts as consideration. When evaluating whether consideration exists, the *promise* to mow someone's lawn next week is the equivalent of actually *doing* the yardwork.

Let's apply these ideas to the most famous of all consideration lawsuits. Our story begins in 1869, when a well-meaning uncle made a promise to his nephew. Ever since *Hamer v. Sidway* appeared, generations of U.S. law students have dutifully inhaled the facts and sworn by its wisdom; now you, too, may drink it in.

Landmark Case

Hamer v. Sidway

124 N.Y. 538
New York Court of Appeals, 1891

Facts: This is a story with two Stories. William Story wanted his nephew to grow up healthy and prosperous. In 1869, he promised the 15-year-old boy (who was also named William Story) $5,000 if the lad would refrain from drinking liquor, using tobacco, swearing, and playing cards or billiards for money until his twenty-first birthday. (In that wild era—can you believe it?—the nephew had a legal right to do all those things.) The nephew agreed and, what is more, he kept his word. When he reached his twenty-first birthday, the nephew notified his uncle that he had honored the agreement. The uncle congratulated the young man and promised to give him the money but said he would wait a few more years before handing over the cash, until the nephew was mature enough to handle such a large sum. The uncle died in 1887 without having paid, and his estate refused to honor the promise. Because the nephew had transferred his rights in the money, it was a man named Hamer who eventually sought to collect from the uncle's estate. The estate argued that since the nephew had given no consideration for the uncle's promise, there was no enforceable contract. The trial court found for the plaintiff, and the uncle's estate appealed.

Issue: ***Did the nephew give consideration for the uncle's promise?***

Excerpts from Justice Parker's Decision: The defendant contends that the contract was without consideration to support it, and therefore invalid. He asserts that the promisee, by refraining from the use of liquor and tobacco, was not harmed, but benefited; that that which he did was best for him to do, independently of his uncle's promise, and insists that it follows that, unless the promisor was benefited, the contract was without consideration, a contention which, if well founded, would seem to leave open for controversy in many cases whether that which the promisee did or omitted to do was in fact of such benefit to him as to leave no consideration to support the enforcement of the promisor's agreement. Such a rule could not be tolerated, and is without foundation in the law. Courts will not ask whether the thing which forms the consideration does in fact benefit the promisee or a third party, or is of any substantial value to anyone. It is enough that something is promised, done, forborne, or suffered by the party to whom the promise is made as consideration for the promise made to him.

Now applying this rule to the facts before us, the promisee used tobacco, occasionally drank liquor, and he had a legal right to do so. That right he abandoned for a period of years upon the strength of the promise of the testator [that is, the uncle] that for such forbearance he would give him $5,000. We need not speculate on the effort which may have been required to give up the use of those stimulants. It is sufficient that he restricted his lawful freedom of action within certain prescribed limits upon the faith of his uncle's agreement, and now, having fully performed the conditions imposed, it is of no moment whether such performance actually proved a benefit to the promisor, and the court will not inquire into it.

The issue of value in a contract is an important one, so let's look at another case. In the movies, when a character wants to get serious about keeping a promise—*really* serious—he sometimes signs an agreement in blood. As it turns out, this kind of thing actually happens in real life. In the following case, did the promise of forbearance have value? Did a contract signed in blood count? You be the judge.

You Be the Judge

Kim v. Son

2009 Cal. App. LEXIS 2011, 2009 WL 597232
Court of Appeal of California, 2009

Facts: Stephen Son was a part owner and operator of two corporations. Because the businesses were corporations, Son was not personally liable for the debts of either one.

Jinsoo Kim invested a total of about $170,000 in the companies. Eventually, both of them failed, and Kim lost his investment. Son felt guilty over Kim's losses.

Later, Son and Kim met in a sushi restaurant and drank heroic quantities of alcohol. At one point, Son pricked his finger with a safety pin and wrote the following in his own blood: "Sir, please forgive me. Because of my deeds, you have suffered financially. I will repay you to the best of my ability." In return, Kim agreed not to sue him for the money owed.

Son later refused to honor the bloody document and pay Kim the money. Kim filed suit to enforce their contract.

The judge determined that the promise did not create a contract because there had been no consideration.

You Be the Judge: *Was there consideration?*

Argument for Kim: As a part of the deal made at the sushi restaurant, Kim agreed not to sue Son. What could be more of a forbearance than that? Kim had a right to sue at any time, and he gave the right up. Even if Kim was unlikely to win, Son would still prefer not to be sued.

Besides, the fact that Son signed the agreement in blood indicates how seriously he took the obligation to repay his loyal investor. At a minimum, Son eased his guilty conscience by making the agreement, and surely that is worth something.

Argument for Son: Who among you has not at one point or another become intoxicated, experienced emotions more powerful than usual, and regretted them the next morning? Whether calling an ex-girlfriend and professing endless love or writing out an agreement in your own blood, it is all the same.

A promise not to file a meritless lawsuit has no value at all. It did not matter to Son whether or not Kim filed suit because Kim could not possibly win. If this promise counts as value, then the concept of consideration is meaningless because anyone can promise not to sue anytime. Son had no obligation to pay Kim. And the bloody napkin does not change that fact because it was made without consideration of any kind. It is an ordinary promise, not a contract that creates any legal obligation.

13-1b What Is a Bargained-For Exchange?

The parties must bargain for the consideration. Something is **bargained for** if it is sought by the promisor and given by the promisee in exchange for their respective promises. Eliza hires Joe to be her public relations manager for $15,000 a year. Both Eliza and Joe have made promises to induce the other's action. But what if the going rate for a PR manager with Joe's experience is $65,000?

Bargained for
When something is sought by the promisor and given by the promise in exchange for their promises

Joe made a bad deal, but that does not mean it lacked consideration. **Courts do not analyze the economic terms of an exchange to determine whether consideration was adequate.** For consideration to be adequate in the eyes of the law, it must provide some benefit to the promisor or some detriment to the promisee, but these need not amount to much. Law professors often call this the "peppercorn rule," a reference to a Civil War–era case in which a judge mused, "What is a valuable consideration? A peppercorn."[3] Here, both Eliza and Joe are promisor and promisee; each receives a benefit and incurs a detriment.

Gold can make people crazy. At the turn of the twentieth century, John Tuppela joined the gold rush to Alaska. He bought a mine, but sadly, his prospecting proved futile. In 1914, a court declared him insane and locked him in an institution. Four years later, Tuppela emerged and learned to his ecstasy that gold had been discovered in his mine, now valued at over half a million dollars. Then the bad news hit: A court-appointed guardian had sold the mine for pennies while Tuppela was institutionalized. Destitute and forlorn, Tuppela turned to his lifelong friend, Embola, saying, "If you will give me $50 so I can go to Alaska and get my property back, I will pay you $10,000 when I win my property." After Tuppela won back his mine, his court-appointed guardian refused to pay Embola, arguing that $50 was not enough consideration to support Tuppela's $10,000 promise. The court disagreed. Embola and Tuppela freely bargained for those terms.

Although the difference between Embola's $50 and Tuppela's $10,000 was staggering, it was not for the court to judge whether it was an intelligent bargain. Both parties knew what they were doing, Embola undertook a risk, and his $50 was valid consideration. The question of adequacy is for the parties as they bargain, not for the courts.

EXAMStrategy

Question: 50 Cent has been rapping all day, and he is very thirsty. He pulls his Ferrari into the parking lot of a convenience store. The store turns out to be closed, but luckily for him, a soda machine sits outside. While walking over to it, he realizes that he has left his wallet at home. Frustrated, he whistles to a ten-year-old kid who is walking by. "Hey kid!" he shouts. "I need to borrow fifty cents!" "I know you are!" the kid replies. Fiddy tries again. "No, no, I need to *borrow* fifty cents!" The kid walks over. "Well, I'm

---

[3]Hobbs v. Duff, 23 Cal. 596 (1863).

not going to just give you my last fifty cents. But maybe you can sell me something." 50 Cent cannot believe it, but he really is very thirsty. He takes off a Rolex, which is his least expensive bling. "How about this?" "Deal," the kid says, handing over two quarters. Is the kid entitled to keep the luxury watch?

Strategy: Even in extreme cases, courts rarely take an interest in *how much* consideration is given, or whether everyone got a "good deal." Even though the Rolex is worth thousands of times more than the quarters, the quarters still count under the peppercorn rule.

Result: After this transaction, 50 Cent may have second thoughts, but they will be too late. The kid committed an act by handing over his money—he was under no legal obligation to do so. And 50 Cent received something of small but measurable value. So there is consideration to support this deal, and 50 Cent would not get his watch back.

13-1c What Consideration Is Not

For centuries, scholars and judges have tried unsuccessfully to craft a single, simple rule of consideration but a rigid application of these rules would sometimes interfere with legitimate business goals or, in the worst case, lead to an unfair outcome. As a result, **courts have created three exceptions to the basic rule of consideration: illusory promises, preexisting duties, and past consideration.** Of course, exceptions are the spice of law, and these consideration rules provide us with a rackful. Why, in some cases, we have exceptions to the exception.

Of course, exceptions are the spice of law, and these consideration rules provide us with a rackful.

Illusory Promises

Annabel calls Jim and says, "I'll sell you my bicycle for 325 bucks. Interested?" Jim says, "I'll look at it tonight in the bike rack. If I like what I see, I'll pay you in the morning." At sunrise, Jim shows up with the $325, but Annabel refuses to sell. Can Jim enforce their deal? No. He said he would buy the bicycle *if he liked it,* keeping for himself the power to get out of the agreement for any reason at all. He is not *committing* himself to do anything, and the law considers his promise illusory—that is, not really a promise at all. **An illusory promise is not consideration.** Because he has given no consideration, there is no contract, and *neither party* can enforce the deal.

Let's revisit the Blockbuster case from the opening scenario. Blockbuster's clickwrap box read, in part:

> Blockbuster may at any time, and at its sole discretion, modify these Terms and Conditions of Use, including without limitation the Privacy Policy, with or without notice. Such modifications will be effective immediately upon posting.

Because Blockbuster had the ability to change the rules at any time for any reason, the court determined that the contract was illusory and that Harris was not bound by Blockbuster's arbitration clause.[4]

Requirements contract
Contract in which a buyer agrees to purchase all of her goods from one seller

Output contract
Contract in which the seller guarantees to sell all of its output to one buyer, and the buyer agrees to accept the entire quantity

Exception: Requirements and Output Contracts under the UCC. In a **requirements contract**, the buyer agrees to purchase 100 percent of her goods from one seller. The seller agrees to sell the buyer whatever quantity she reasonably needs. The quantity is not stated in the contract, though it may be estimated based on previous years or best calculations. In an **output contract**, the seller guarantees to sell 100 percent of its output to one

4Harris v. Blockbuster Inc., 622 F. Supp. 2d 396 (N.D. Tex. 2009).

buyer, and the buyer agrees to accept the entire quantity. For example, a vineyard might agree to sell all of its wine to a chain restaurant.

The common law frowned on requirements and output contracts because the promisors are making no real commitment, and hence are giving no consideration. In the view of common law courts, these were illusory contracts.

The problem with the common law rule was that many merchants valued these contracts. Consider the utility of requirements contracts. From the buyer's viewpoint, a requirements contract provides flexibility. The buyer can adjust purchases based on consumer demands. The agreement also guarantees her a source of goods in a competitive market. For a seller, the requirements agreement will ensure him at least this one outlet and will prevent competitors from selling to this buyer. The contract should enable the seller to spend less on marketing and may enable him to predict sales more accurately. Output contracts have similar value.

The UCC responded in a forthright fashion: **Section 2-306 expressly allows output and requirements contracts in the sale of goods.**[5] However, the Code places one limitation on how much the buyer may demand (or the seller may offer):

> A term which measures the quantity by the output of the seller or the requirements of the buyer means such actual output or requirements as may occur *in good faith*, ...

The "good faith" phrase is critical. In requirements contracts, courts have ruled that it is the "good faith" that a buyer brings to the deal that represents her consideration.[6] In other words, by agreeing to act in good faith, she actually is limiting her options. Because she is obligating herself, the deal becomes binding. Beware that this is not just wordplay. A buyer *must make its requirement demands in good faith*, based on the expectations the parties had when they signed the deal.

Suppose that you operate a T-shirt business. You and a wholesaler agree on a two-year requirements contract with a fixed price of $3 per T-shirt and an estimate of 150 T-shirts per week. If business is slow the first two months, you are permitted to purchase only 25 T-shirts per week if that is all you are selling. Should sales suddenly boom and you need 200 per week, you may also require that many. Both of those demands are made in good faith. But suppose the price of cotton skyrockets and the wholesale cost of T-shirts everywhere suddenly doubles. You have a two-year guaranteed price of $3 per T-shirt. Could you demand 2,000 T-shirts per week, knowing that you will be able to resell the shirts to other retailers for a big profit? No. That is not acting in good faith based on the original expectations of the parties. The wholesaler is free to ignore your exorbitant demand. The legal requirement has come full circle: Your good faith is valid consideration and makes the deal enforceable—but it is binding on you too.

EXAMStrategy

Question: Will bought simple wood furniture and custom-painted it for sale to interior designers. He entered into a written agreement to buy all the furniture he needed, for two years, from Wood Knot, Inc. Wood Knot agreed to supply Will with all the furniture he requested. During the second year, Will's business grew, and he requested 28 percent more furniture than in the first year. Wood Knot would not deliver unless Will would pay a higher price per unit, which Will would not. Will sued. What kind of a contract was this? Will Will win? Why or why not?

---

[5]UCC §2-306(2) permits a related type of contract, the exclusive dealing agreement. Here, either a buyer or a seller of goods agrees to deal exclusively with the other party. The results are similar to an output or requirements agreement. Once again, one party is receiving a guarantee in exchange for a promise that the common law would have considered illusory. Under the Code, such a deal is enforceable.

[6]Famous Brands, Inc. v. David Sherman Corp., 814 F.2d 517 (8th Cir. 1987).

Strategy: Because this agreement did not specify the quantity of goods being sold, we know that it was either a requirements contract or an output contract. Review the difference between the two. Which was this agreement? These contracts are now legal, with one major limitation. What is that limitation? Apply it here.

Result: This was a requirements contract because Will agreed to purchase all his furniture from Wood Knot. Under the UCC, requirements contracts are enforceable, provided the buyer makes his demands in good faith. Will's increased order was a result of his booming business. Indeed, he entered into this agreement to protect his ability to grow his company. He made the request in good faith, the contract is enforceable, and yes—Will will win.

Adam Crowley/Getty Images

What if a lifeguard would only protect you if you paid him extra?

Preexisting Duty

Imagine yourself at the beach right now (in our dreams). Into the water you go, where an undertow grabs you and carries you out into deep water. The lifeguard leaps from his chair and runs to the water's edge. But instead of jumping in, he yells to you, "I will save you if you pay me $100." Helplessly, you signal your assent. Once you are safely back on shore, do you owe the lifeguard anything?

You may be relieved to hear that the answer is no. **If someone provides a service that she is already obligated to do, that act does not count as consideration.** A lifeguard who saves people cannot receive additional money for her rescues because, well, that is what lifeguards are supposed to do. A police officer who apprehends a criminal in the line of duty cannot collect the posted reward. A banker cannot get a bonus for upholding the law. In these cases, consideration does not induce their actions, duty does. Since they already have the duty to perform, they suffer no legal detriment when they do their job.

In the following Landmark Case, many fishy things occurred. There was a catch. But was it sufficient consideration?

Landmark Case

Alaska Packers' Ass'n v. Domenico

117 F. 99
United States Court of Appeals for the Ninth Circuit, 1902

Facts: Twenty-one seamen entered into a written contract with the Alaska Packer's Association (APA) to sail from San Francisco to Pyramid Harbor, Alaska, where they would work as fisherman and sailors during the salmon-fishing season. The workers agreed to perform "regular ship's duty, both up and down, discharging and loading; and to do any other work whatsoever when requested to do so by the captain." In return, the APA was to pay each worker $50 for the season, and two cents for each red salmon he caught.

A few days after arriving at Pyramid Harbor, the men collectively stopped working and demanded an additional $50—or else they would return to San Francisco. At that point, it was impossible for the APA to replace them, so after several days of unproductive negotiations, the APA's superintendent in Alaska yielded to their demands—and agreed to double their pay.

When they returned to San Francisco at the close of the fishing season, the seamen demanded their $100, but the APA refused, claiming that the Alaska agreement failed for lack of consideration. The lower court agreed with the seamen, but the APA appealed.

Issue: ***Was there consideration for the promise to pay more money?***

Excerpts from Judge Ross's Decision:[7] The seamen agreed in writing, for certain stated compensation, to render their services to the APA in remote waters where the season for conducting fishing operations is extremely short, and in which enterprise the APA had a large amount of money invested; and, after having entered upon the discharge of their contract, and at a time when it was impossible for APA to secure other men in their places, the seamen, without any valid cause, absolutely refused to continue the services they were under contract to perform unless the APA would consent to pay them more money.

Consent to such a demand, under such circumstances, if given, was, in our opinion, without consideration, for the reason that it was based solely upon the seamen's agreement to render the exact services, and none other, that they were already under contract to render. The case shows that they willfully and arbitrarily broke that obligation.

No astute reasoning can change the plain fact that the party who refuses to perform, and thereby coerces a promise from the other party to the contract to pay him an increased compensation for doing that which he is legally bound to do, takes an unjustifiable advantage of the necessities of the other party. Surely it would be a travesty on justice to hold that the party so making the promise for extra pay was estopped from asserting that the promise was without consideration. A party cannot lay the foundation of an estoppel by his own wrong, where the promise is simply a repetition of a subsisting legal promise.

There can be no consideration for the promise of the other party, and there is no warrant for inferring that the parties have voluntarily rescinded or modified their contract. The promise cannot be legally enforced, although the other party has completed his contract in reliance upon it.

The judgment must be reversed. It is so ordered.

Exception: Additional Work. When a party agrees to do something above and beyond what he is obligated to do, his promise is generally valid consideration. If the seamen had agreed to work overtime or commit to a longer fishing season in exchange for the increased pay, the court would have upheld their second contract. The APA would have been obligated to pay because the seamen's extra work would have been valid consideration.

Exception: Modification. Under the common law, additional consideration is necessary for a modification of contract terms because it is unfair for one party to get something more, while the other does not. As we saw in the *Alaska Packers* case, if one side unfairly coerces the other into the changes, the modification is invalid.

Once again, the UCC has changed the common law, making it easier for merchants to modify agreements for the sale of goods. **UCC §2-209 provides:**

- An agreement modifying a contract within this Article needs no consideration to be binding.
- A signed agreement which excludes modification or rescission except by a signed writing cannot be otherwise modified or rescinded.

Here is how these two provisions work together. Mike's Magic Mania (MMM) agrees to deliver 500 rabbits and 500 top hats to State University for the school's Sleight of Hand 101 course. The goods, including 100 cages and 1,000 pounds of rabbit food, are to arrive no later

---

[7] For readability, the authors have inserted "APA" and "seamen" instead of "appellant" and "libelants."

than September 1, in time for the new semester, with payment on delivery. By September 20, no rabbits have appeared, in or out of hats. The university buys similar products from another supply house at a 25 percent steeper price and sues MMM for the difference. Mike claims that in early September, the dean had orally agreed to permit delivery in October. The dean is on sabbatical in Tahiti and cannot be reached for comment. Is the alleged modification valid?

Under the common law, the modification would have been void because MMM gave no consideration for the extended delivery date. However, this is a sale of goods, and under UCC §2-209, an oral modification may be valid even without consideration. Unfortunately for Mike, though, the original agreement included a clause forbidding oral modification. Any changes had to be in writing, signed by both parties. Mike never obtained such a document. Even if the dean did make the oral agreement, the university wins.

Rescind
To cancel

If both parties agree that a modification is necessary, the surest way to accomplish that result is to rescind the original contract and draft a new one. To **rescind** means to cancel. Thus, if neither party has completed its obligations, the agreement to rescind will terminate each party's rights and obligations under the old contract. This should be done in writing. Then the parties sign the new agreement. Courts will *generally* enforce a rescission and modification provided both parties voluntarily entered into it, in good faith.

EXAMStrategy

Question: Star Struck, a Hollywood talent agency, employs Puneet as one of its young agents and Max as a part-time delivery boy. Puneet's contract is for one year. She earns $5,000 per month, payable on the last day of each month. After she has worked at the firm for four months, a Star Struck executive says to her, "We are having cash flow problems. We cannot pay you this month, and will probably fall about two months behind. However, if you will agree to do Max's job for the next few months, we can pay you on time." Puneet cheerfully agrees to the deal. However, after a few weeks of the extra labor, Puneet confesses that she is overwhelmed and can no longer do Max's job. Star Struck fires her. Puneet sues. Was there a binding agreement for Puneet to do Max's work?

Strategy: Star Struck made an offer to Puneet and she accepted it. But a contract needs more than offer and acceptance. Both parties must give consideration. Had they done more than they were required to do under their preexisting duty?

Result: A promise to do what a party is already obligated to do is not consideration. Star Struck was required to pay Puneet every month, so its "offer" included no consideration. Without consideration, there can be no agreement. Puneet was not obligated to do Max's job, and she will win this lawsuit.

Exception: Unforeseen Circumstances. Hugo has a deal to repair major highways. Hugo hires Hal's Hauling to cart soil and debris. Hal's trucks begin work, but after crossing the work site several times, they sink to their axles in sinister, sucking slime. Hal demands an additional 35 percent payment from Hugo to complete the job, pointing out that the surface was dry and cracked and that neither Hal nor Hugo was aware of the subsurface water. Hal howls that he must use different trucks with different tires and work more slowly to permit the soil to dry. Hugo hems and haws and finally agrees. But when the hauling is finished, Hugo refuses to pay the extra money. Is Hugo liable?

Yes. When unforeseen circumstances cause a party to make a promise regarding an unfinished project, that promise is generally valid consideration. Even though Hal is only promising to finish what he was already obligated to do, his promise is valid consideration because neither party knew of the subsoil mud. Hal was facing a situation quite different from what the parties anticipated. It is almost as though he were undertaking a new project. Hal has given consideration, and Hugo is bound by his promise to pay extra money.

Past Consideration

A completed act cannot be the basis for consideration. When they learn that their son earned an "A" in Advanced Business Law, Pablo's doting parents promise to buy him a car. This star student will surely know that the generous promise is unenforceable in court. It lacks consideration because it is based on something Pablo has already done. However, if early in the semester, Pablo's parents make the same promise, consideration *is* present. Pablo's detriment is his future work, which is induced by the promise of a reward.

In the following case, promises were made and broken. It was the court's job to figure out if the promises were actually contracts.

Lee v. Choi

754 S.E.2d 371
Court of Appeals of Georgia, 2013

Facts: When John Blackwell was seriously injured, he and his wife Ki Tae Lee hired Se Ill Choi to help Lee communicate with her husband's doctors and perform daily chores. Eventually, Choi moved into the Blackwell home and did everything for them from preparing the family's income tax returns to attending parent-teacher conferences for the couple's son. Choi described himself as the Blackwells's "lifeline."

The Blackwells did not pay Choi a salary, but they provided him with room and board, a computer and cell phone, health insurance, and a car. On many occasions, they vowed to support him financially for the rest of his life and promised that he would always "be taken care of."

After 13 years of service, Lee fired Choi suddenly. When Choi demanded immediate payment on the verbal promise of lifetime support, the two drafted and signed the following agreement:

> WHEREAS, BLACKWELL desire to express in writing their agreement [sic] to pay CHOI minimum of $450,000.00 immediatly [sic] for the work CHOI has done for Blackwell. Now with this payment all previous agreements are null and void between two parties. CHOI is willing to provide service in the future if acceptable working condition is provided.

But the relationship between Lee and Choi only got worse. When Choi sued the Blackwells for breach of contract, a jury awarded him $450,000 plus attorney's fees. The Blackwells appealed, arguing that the agreement was void because it lacked consideration.

Issue: ***Was there consideration for Lee and Choi's agreement?***

Excerpts from Judge Boggs's Decision: The trial court ruled: "the fact that Mr. Choi gave up his right to any other lawsuits or any prior action is consideration for which that could be enforceable." But this agreement did not provide that Choi would give up the right to other lawsuits or prior action. Rather, the agreement purported to provide as consideration "the work Choi has done for Blackwell," and merely provided that "all previous agreements and wills are null and void."

With regard to "the work Choi has done for Blackwell," it is well-settled that past consideration will not support a subsequent promise. Therefore, an agreement to pay Choi for work he has already done is unenforceable.

The only possible consideration remaining under the agreement is that "all previous agreements and wills are null and void." Choi argues that this provision includes the oral agreement under which Choi claimed that the Blackwells promised him lifetime support. Any oral agreement to provide Choi "lifetime support" is unenforceable. There is no indication of what was to be encompassed in "lifetime support" and no explanation how it was to be provided. Any such promise without any further particularity fails to support an enforceable contract. Therefore, promise of lifetime support do[es] not provide consideration for the agreement.

Because the agreements Choi relies upon either are unenforceable or cannot provide consideration for the payment of $450,000, the agreement is itself unenforceable as a matter of law and should not have been submitted for the jury's consideration.

Lee v. Choi teaches us various lessons. First, taking a business law course pays: Choi may have known how to prepare income tax returns but drafting a contract on his own cost him a lifetime of support. Second, the court tells us that past actions cannot be consideration—even when it is obvious that the parties intended a valid contract. Does this rule sound too rigid? We now explore its two exceptions.

Exception: Parties Agree in Advance. Moore was psychic. She foresaw that Elmer was going to die before a certain date. In gratitude and amazement, Elmer gave her a signed letter stating that if what she said proved true, he would pay off her mortgage. Apparently, Moore was clairvoyant: Elmer died before her predicted date. What happened next is not difficult to predict. Moore's heirs refused to pay her, claiming his promise lacked consideration.

The court agreed. Although Moore argued that the promise was payment for her services, she had voluntarily offered the information and after that, Elmer gave her the note. Had the parties agreed in advance that he would pay her if her predictions proved true, the court would have foreseen a different outcome: **Past consideration is valid consideration when the parties agree that it will be *in advance*.**

Exception: Promissory Estoppel. As we saw in Chapter 11, promissory estoppel is a theory courts use to enforce promises that are not contracts. It applies when a defendant makes a promise, which the plaintiff reasonably relied on, and enforcing that promise is the only way to avoid injustice.

Courts sometimes use promissory estoppel to validate promises based on past consideration. Feinberg had been a loyal employee for 37 years. She was so beloved that, in gratitude for her service, her employer's board of directors elected to pay her $200 a month for the rest of her life, once she retired. Two years later, she retired in reliance on her monthly pension, which she enjoyed—until new management decided to revoke it. By this time, she was ill, unemployable, and wholly dependent on the pension. The court held for Feinberg, even though the promise was based on past consideration. Because she justifiably relied on the board's offer, Feinberg's pension was upheld under promissory estoppel.

13-2 SPECIAL CONSIDERATION CASES

We have seen what consideration is and what it is not. Now we will look at some special cases that involve two very familiar four-letter words: debt and work.

13-2a Settlement of Debts

You claim that your friend Felicity owes you $90,000, but she refuses to pay. Finally, when you are desperate, Felicity offers you a cashier's check for $60,000—provided you accept it as full settlement. To get your hands on some money, you agree and cash the check. The next day, you sue Felicity for $30,000. Who wins? It will depend principally upon one major issue: Was Felicity's debt liquidated or unliquidated?

Liquidated Debt

Liquidated debt
A debt in which there is no dispute about the amount owed

A **liquidated debt** is one in which there is no dispute about the amount owed. A loan is a typical example. If a bank lends you $10,000, and the note obligates you to repay that amount on June 1 of the following year, you clearly owe that sum. The debt is liquidated. One famous jurist commented that a creditor may accept anything—"a horse, hawk, or robe"—in satisfaction of a liquidated debt.[8]

But the one thing he may not accept? Less than one hundred cents on the dollar. **In cases of liquidated debt, if the creditor agrees to take less than the full amount as full payment, her agreement is not binding.** The debtor has given no consideration to support the creditor's promise to accept a reduced payment, and therefore the creditor is not bound by her word. The reasoning is simply that the debtor is already obligated to pay the full amount, so no bargaining could reasonably cause the creditor to accept less. If Felicity's debt to you is liquidated, your agreement to accept $60,000 is not binding, and you will successfully sue for the balance.

But the one thing he may not accept? Less than one hundred cents on the dollar.

Exception: Different Performance. There is one important exception to this rule. If the debtor offers a *different performance* to settle the liquidated debt, and the creditor agrees to take it as full settlement, the agreement is binding. Suppose that Felicity, instead of paying $60,000, offers you five acres in Alaska, and you accept. When you accept the deed to the land, you have given up your entire claim, regardless of the land's precise value.

Unliquidated Debt: Accord and Satisfaction

A debt is **unliquidated** for either of two reasons: (1) The parties dispute whether any money is owed or (2) the parties agree that some money is owed but dispute how much. When a debt is unliquidated for either reason, the parties may enter into a binding agreement to settle for less than what the creditor demands.

Unliquidated
A debt that is disputed because the parties disagree over its existence or amount

Such a compromise will be enforced if:

- The debt is unliquidated,
- The parties agree that the creditor will accept as full payment a sum less than she has claimed, and
- The debtor pays the amount agreed upon.

This agreement is called an **accord and satisfaction**. The accord is the agreement to settle for less than the creditor claims. The satisfaction is the actual payment of that compromised sum. An accord and satisfaction is valid consideration to support the creditor's agreement to drop all claims. Each party is giving up something: the creditor gives up her full claim, and the debtor gives up his assertion that he owed little or nothing.

Accord and satisfaction
A completed agreement to settle a debt for less than the sum claimed

Accord and Satisfaction by Check. Most accord and satisfaction agreements involve payment by check. UCC §3-311 governs these agreements, using the same common law rules described earlier.[9] The Code specifies that when the debtor writes "full settlement" on the check, a creditor who cashes the check generally has entered into an accord and satisfaction. If Felicity's debt is unliquidated, and she gives you a check with "full payment of all debts" written on the face in bold letters, the moment you deposit the check, you lose any claim to more money. What happens if the debtor makes such a notation but the creditor changes it? A massage therapist learned the answer and felt sore for days.

---

[8]Birdsall v. Saucier, 29 Conn. App. 921 (Conn. App. Ct. 1992).

[9]A check is legally an instrument, which is why this section comes from Article 3 of the Code. For a full discussion of instruments, see Chapters 25 and 26.

Henches v. Taylor

138 Wash. App. 1026
Washington Court of Appeals, 2007

Facts: Jim Henches, a licensed massage therapist, treated Benjamin Taylor after he was injured in a car accident. When all treatments were finished, Henches billed Taylor for more than $7,000. Taylor's insurance company claimed the bill was exorbitant and paid only $2,625, for 24 massage treatments.

Henches continued to send bills to Taylor, not only for the balance due but for additional time spent consulting with Taylor's other healthcare providers, preparing to testify in Taylor's personal injury lawsuit, and attempting to collect his debts. In response to a bill for $11,945.86, Taylor's lawyer, James Harris, sent Henches a letter, stating:

> I have reviewed your billing statements and am having a difficult time understanding a number of charges you included. By my calculations, the amount owed to you is approximately $5,243.45. I have enclosed a check for that amount as payment in full to settle Mr. Taylor's account with you.

The letter was accompanied by a check with "final payment" written on the notation line. Henches filed suit, seeking the full balance. Then he wrote "attorney/fee" on the check, over the word "final," and deposited the check.

The trial court gave summary judgment to Taylor, ruling that deposit of the check constituted accord and satisfaction. Henches appealed.

Issue: ***Was there an accord and satisfaction, discharging the debt?***

Excerpts from Judge Ellington's Decision: A debt is discharged by accord and satisfaction when the debtor and creditor agree to settle a claim by some performance other than that which is claimed due, and the creditor accepts the substituted performance as full satisfaction of the claim. Accord and satisfaction requires a bona fide dispute, an agreement to settle the dispute for a certain sum, and performance of the agreement.

Taylor easily satisfied the first element of accord and satisfaction. The parties' contracts did not establish a liquidated amount for the services provided, and the letter that accompanied Taylor's check to Henches demonstrates a good faith dispute over the amount owed.

As with any contract, an accord and satisfaction cannot be formed without a meeting of the minds. But the required intent is shown when payment is offered in full satisfaction and is accompanied by conduct from which the creditor cannot fail to understand that payment is tendered on condition its acceptance constitutes satisfaction.

Given the undisputed facts here, Henches could not fail to understand that the check was offered on condition of full settlement. Henches' alteration of the "final payment" language is further demonstration that he read and understood the notation. Taylor tendered a check in final payment and Henches deposited the check, thereby accepting that payment.

A creditor can accept payment and avoid formation of an accord only where both parties understand before payment is accepted that the payment will not settle the claim. Henches contends his alteration of the check prevents accord and satisfaction. But a creditor cannot prevent formation of an accord by making a unilateral change to a draft tendered in full payment, even if the creditor endorses the check with the words accepted as partial payment and not as payment in full and not as an accord and satisfaction of the known full amount legally due and owing.

Where the amount due is in dispute, and the debtor sends cash or check for less than the amount claimed, clearly expressing his intention that it is sent as a settlement in full, and not on account or in part payment, the retention and use of the money or the cashing of the check is almost always held to be an acceptance of the offer operating as full satisfaction, even though the creditor may assert or send word to the debtor that the sum is received only in part payment.

Henches' alteration of the check was a unilateral act not communicated to Taylor. Accord and satisfaction discharged Taylor's debts to Henches. We affirm the trial court's summary judgment dismissal of Henches' suit.

UCC Exceptions. The Code creates two exceptions for accord and satisfaction cases involving checks. The first exception concerns "organizations," which typically are businesses. The general rule of §3-311 is potentially calamitous to them because a company that receives thousands of checks every day is unlikely to inspect all notations. A consumer who owes $12,000 on a credit card might write "full settlement" on a $200 check, potentially extinguishing the entire debt through accord and satisfaction. Under the exception, if an organization notifies a debtor that any offers to settle for less than the debt claimed must be made to a particular official, and the check is sent to anyone else in the organization, depositing the check generally does *not* create an accord and satisfaction. Thus, a clerk who deposits 900 checks daily for payment of MasterCard debts will not have inadvertently entered into dozens of accord and satisfaction agreements.

The second exception allows a way out to most creditors who have inadvertently created an accord and satisfaction. If, within 90 days of cashing a "full payment" check, the creditor offers repayment of the same amount to the debtor, there is no accord and satisfaction. Homer claims that Virgil owes him $7 million but foolishly cashes Virgil's check for $3 million, without understanding that "paid in full" means just what it says. Homer has created an accord and satisfaction. But if he promptly sends Virgil a check for $3 million, he has undone the agreement and may sue for the full amount.

13-2b Agreements Not to Compete

In a non-compete agreement, an employee promises not to work for a competitor for some time after leaving the company. It used to be that these covenants were rare and reserved for top officers, but they have now become commonplace throughout many organizations. In many cases, an employer proposes this agreement after the employee is already on board.

We will consider these controversial agreements more in Chapter 14 on legality, but often these covenants also raise an issue of consideration: What consideration does the employee receive for signing a covenant not to compete once she has already started work? After all, the company is already under an obligation to pay the employee for working. What additional value does the employee receive in return for signing the agreement?

Although the law varies by state, the current majority view is that an implied promise to continue employment is enough consideration to validate a non-compete. When James Scott went to work for Snider, he signed a non-compete prohibiting him from working for a competitor for a year after leaving the company. Three years later, he left and immediately went to work for Snider's competitor. He then tried to invalidate the non-compete by arguing it lacked consideration. The court disagreed, reasoning that Snider's continued employment of Scott was sufficient consideration.[10]

13-2c Moral Consideration

Some promises should not be broken. No one wants to live in a society where donors to charity go back on their word or promises to widows and orphans are ignored. These are commitments whose obligation is moral, not necessarily legal, in nature. Under some circumstances, courts will uphold agreements with "moral consideration."

Consider a pledge to charity. If Dave promises to give $25,000 to "Save the Mexican Spotted Owl" and then fails to make the donation, there is no consideration because he has received nothing in return. If the nonprofit sues to enforce the promise, it cannot show that it gave anything up in return for Dave's promise, so there is no consideration.[11]

Nevertheless, some courts will force donors like Dave to make good on their pledges anyway. If, based on Dave's promise, the charity funded a bird-watching program or began construction on a sanctuary, it can prove reliance. As we have seen, judges can use the doctrine of promissory estoppel to enforce promises if there has been reliance and a great injustice would otherwise result.

---

10 Snider Bolt & Screw v. Quality Screw & Nut, 2009 U.S. Dist. LEXIS 50797, 2009 WL 1657549 (U.S. District Court for the Western District of Kentucky, 2009).

11 An exception to this, of course, would be if the charity agreed to give Dave something at the time he made the pledge. As a "fix" for consideration problems, many charities send donors something of trivial value when pledges are made—maybe a water bottle or a tote bag. Under the peppercorn rule, even something of small value counts as a legal act, and it converts a mere promise of a donation into an enforceable contract.

Other courts have dispensed with the reliance requirement, requiring promisors to pay if breaching would simply be unjust. Especially in the case of large donations, courts will often cite the "grave injustices" that can follow from breaking a promise. "If you don't give 'Save the Mexican Spotted Owl' the $25,000 you've pledged, then the bird will become extinct," a judge might say.

It is unwise to make charitable pledges, especially large pledges, if you do not intend to follow through.

Ethics

What is a "moral obligation" and when should it be enforced? Courts are divided on this issue. Two cases illustrate the leading schools of thought:

In an Alabama case, Webb saved McGowin's life by preventing a 75 lb. block of wood from falling on his head. Webb was permanently disabled in the accident and was never able to work again. Later, McGowin promised to give Webb money every two weeks for the rest of his life. McGowin made the payments for a while but then stopped. Webb sued. The court found that "moral consideration" was present because McGowin received a material benefit. Webb was entitled to the payments to prevent substantial injustice.[12]

A famous Massachusetts case reaches the opposite conclusion. Twenty-five-year-old Levi Wyman contracted an illness while at sea. Mills nursed Wyman during his sickness. After Wyman's death, his parents promised to repay Mills for the expenses incurred in caring for their son. Later, Wyman refused to pay, so Mills filed suit. The court sided with Wyman, holding that a moral obligation was not enough to constitute consideration.[13]

Mills v. Wyman is the majority rule; *Webb v. McGowin* is the minority rule. But some commentators have argued that this discrepancy serves another moral purpose: It allows judges the leeway to enforce promises when they feel enforcement is just. Do you agree? How else can these cases be reconciled? Is it possible to formulate a single rule applying to every case of moral obligation?

It is important to note that applications of promissory estoppel and similar doctrines are rare. Ordinarily, if there is no consideration, then there is no contract. However, in extreme cases, it is possible for a court to enforce a deal even without consideration. But this is not something you can count on.

CHAPTER CONCLUSION

This ancient doctrine of consideration is simple to state but subtle to apply. The parties must bargain and enter into an exchange of promises or actions. If they do not, there is no consideration and the courts are unlikely to enforce any promise made. A variety of exceptions modify the law, but a party wishing to render its future more predictable—the purpose of a contract—will rely on a solid bargain and exchange.

EXAM REVIEW

1. **CONSIDERATION** There are two basic rules of consideration:
   - Value: Both parties must get something of *measurable value* from the contract.
   - Bargained for Exchange: The two parties must have *bargained for* whatever was exchanged.

12Webb v. McGowin, 168 So. 196 (Ala. 1935).

13Mills v. Wyman, 20 Mass. (3 Pick.) 207 (Mass. Sup. Jud. Ct. 1825).

2. **ACT, FORBEARANCE, OR PROMISE** The item of value can be either an act or a forbearance.

EXAMStrategy

Question: An aunt saw her eight-year-old nephew enter the room, remarked what a nice boy he was, and said, "I would like to take care of him now." She promptly wrote a note, promising to pay the boy $3,000 upon her death. Her estate refused to pay. Is it obligated to do so?

Strategy: A contract is enforceable only if the parties have given consideration. The consideration might be an act or a forbearance. Did the nephew give consideration? (See the "Result" at the end of this Exam Review section.)

3. **ADEQUACY** The courts examine whether consideration exists, but will seldom inquire if it was enough consideration or a smart financial deal. This is the "peppercorn rule."

4. **ILLUSORY PROMISES** An illusory promise is not consideration.

EXAMStrategy

Question: Eagle ran convenience stores. He entered into an agreement with Commercial Movie in which Commercial would provide Eagle with DVDs for rental. Eagle would pay Commercial 50 percent of the rental revenues. If Eagle stopped using Commercial's service, Eagle could not use a competitor's services for 18 months. The agreement also provided: "Commercial shall not be liable for compensation or damages of any kind, whether on account of the loss by Eagle of profits, sales or expenditures, or on account of any other event or cause whatsoever." Eagle complied with the agreement for two years but then began using a competitor's service, and Commercial sued. Eagle claimed that the agreement was unenforceable for lack of consideration. Please rule.

Strategy: In this case, both parties seem to have given consideration. But there is a flaw in the "promise" that Commercial made. Commercial can never be liable to Eagle—no matter what happens. (See the "Result" at the end of this Exam Review section.)

5. **REQUIREMENTS AND OUTPUT CONTRACTS** Under sales law, requirement and output contracts are valid. Although one side controls the quantity, its agreement to make demands *in good faith* is consideration.

6. **PREEXISTING DUTY** Under the doctrine of preexisting duty, a promise to do something that the party is already legally obligated to perform is generally not consideration.

7. **LIQUIDATED DEBT** A liquidated debt is one in which there is no dispute about the amount owed. For a liquidated debt, a creditor's promise to accept less than the full amount is not binding.

8. **UNLIQUIDATED DEBT** For an unliquidated debt, if the parties agree that the creditor will accept less than the full amount claimed and the debtor performs, there is an accord and satisfaction and the creditor may not claim any balance.

9. **"FULL PAYMENT" NOTATIONS** In most states, payment by a check that has a "full payment" notation will create an accord and satisfaction unless the creditor is an organization that has notified the debtor that full payment offers must go to a certain officer.

EXAMStrategy

Question: When White's wife died, he filed a claim with Boston Mutual for $10,000 death benefits under her insurance policy. The insurer rejected the claim, saying that his wife had misrepresented her medical condition in the application form. The company sent White a check for $478.75, which it said represented "a full refund of all applicable premiums paid" for the coverage. White deposited the check. Had the parties reached an accord and satisfaction?

Strategy: The UCC permits parties to enter into an accord and satisfaction by check. The debtor must make clear that the check is offered in full payment of a disputed debt. Debtors generally do that by writing "Final Settlement," "Accepted as Full Payment of All Debts," or some similar notation on the check. Had the insurance company complied with that requirement? (See the "Result" at the end of this Exam Review section.)

10. **PROMISSORY ESTOPPEL** Sometimes, to prevent injustice, courts will enforce agreements even if no consideration is present. These deals are still not formal contracts, but the courts will enforce a promise nonetheless.

EXAMStrategy

Question: Phil Philanthropist called PBS during a fund drive and pledged to donate $100,000. PBS then planned and began to produce a Fourth of July *Sesame Street* special, counting on the large donation to fund it. Later, Phil changed his mind and said he had decided not to donate the money after all. PBS sued because, without the money, it would not be able to complete the show. Will PBS win the lawsuit?

Strategy: Analyze the promise to donate the $100,000. Does it contain consideration? If not, is there any other legal possibility? (See the "Result" at the end of this Exam Review section.)

RESULTS

2. Result: The nephew gave no consideration. He did not promise to do anything. He committed no act or forbearance. Without consideration, there is no enforceable contract. The estate wins.

4. Result: Commercial's promise was illusory. The company was free to walk away from the deal at any time. Commercial could never be held liable. Commercial gave no consideration, and there was no binding contract for either party to enforce.

9. Result: The insurer merely stated that its check was a refund of premiums. Nowhere did the company indicate that the check was full payment of its disputed obligation. The company should have made it clear that it would not pay any benefits and that this payment was all that it would offer. There was no accord and satisfaction.

10. Result: There is no "regular" consideration here because Phil received no measurable benefit and PBS did not act or forbear. But PBS can likely make a strong case that a great injustice will be done if the money is not paid. A judge might well decide to apply the doctrine of promissory estoppel and require Phil to make the donation.

MULTIPLE-CHOICE QUESTIONS

1. For consideration to exist, there must be:
   (a) a bargained-for exchange.
   (b) a manifestation of mutual assent.
   (c) genuineness of assent.
   (d) substantially equal economic benefits to both parties.

2. Which of the following requires consideration in order to be binding on the parties?
   (a) Modification of a contract involving the sale of real estate
   (b) Modification of a sale of goods contract under the UCC
   (c) Both A and B
   (d) None of these

3. Ted's wallet is as empty as his bank account, and he needs $3,500 immediately. Fortunately, he has three gold coins that he inherited from his grandfather. Each is worth $2,500, but it is Sunday, and the local rare coins store is closed. When approached, Ted's neighbor Andrea agrees to buy the first coin for $2,300. Another neighbor, Cami, agrees to buy the second for $1,100. A final neighbor, Lorne, offers "all the money I have on me"—$100—for the last coin. Desperate, Ted agrees to the proposal. Which of the deals is supported by consideration?
   (a) Ted's agreement with Andrea only
   (b) Ted's agreements with Andrea and Cami only
   (c) All three of the agreements
   (d) None of the agreements

4. In a(n) ______________ contract, the seller guarantees to sell 100 percent of its output to one buyer, and the buyer agrees to accept the entire quantity. This kind of arrangement ______________ acceptable under the UCC.
   (a) output; is
   (b) output; is not
   (c) requirements; is
   (d) requirements; is not

5. Non-compete agreements are common features of employment contracts. Currently, courts ______________ enforce these clauses.
   (a) always
   (b) usually
   (c) rarely
   (d) never

CASE QUESTIONS

1. American Bakeries had a fleet of over 3,000 delivery trucks. Because of the increasing cost of gasoline, the company was interested in converting the trucks to propane fuel. It signed a requirements contract with Empire Gas, in which Empire would convert "approximately 3,000" trucks to propane fuel, as American Bakeries requested, and would then sell all the required propane fuel to run the trucks. But American Bakeries changed its mind and never requested a single conversion. Empire sued for lost profits. Who won?

2. CeCe Hylton and Edward Meztista, partners in a small advertising firm, agreed to terminate the business and split assets evenly. Meztista gave Hylton a two-page document showing assets, liabilities, and a bottom line of $35,235.67, with half due to each partner. Hylton questioned the accounting and asked to see the books. Meztista did not permit Hylton to see any records and refused to answer her phone calls. Instead, he gave her a check in the amount of $17,617.83, on which he wrote "Final payment/payment in full." Hylton cashed the check, but she wrote on it, "Under protest—cashing this check does not constitute my acceptance of this amount as payment in full." Hylton then filed suit, demanding additional monies. Meztista claimed that the parties had made an accord and satisfaction. What is the best argument for each party? Who should win?

3. **ETHICS** Melnick built a house for Gintzler, but the foundation was defective. Gintzler agreed to accept the foundation if Melnick guaranteed to make future repairs caused by the defects. Melnick agreed but later refused to make any repairs. Melnick argued that his promise to make future repairs was unsupported by consideration. Who will win the suit? Is either party acting unethically? Which one, and why?

4. In the bleachers … "You're a prince, George!" Mike exclaimed. "Who else would give me a ticket to the big game?"

   "No one, Mike, no one."

   "Let me offer my thanks. I'll buy you a beer!"

   "Ah," George said. "A large beer would hit the spot right now."

   "Small. Let me buy you a small beer."

   "Ah, well, good enough."

   Mike stood and took his wallet from his pocket. He was distressed to find a very small number of bills inside. "There's bad news, George!" he said.

   "What's that?"

   "I can't buy you the beer, George."

   George considered that for a moment. "I'll tell you what, Mike," he said. "If you march to the concession stand right this minute and get me my beer, I won't punch you in the face."

   "It's a deal!" Mike said.

   Discuss the consideration issues raised by this exchange.

5. Wells Fargo Armored Service offered a $25,000 reward for information leading to the arrest and conviction of the person who shot one of its guards. Slattery worked as an independent contractor conducting lie detector tests in the State Attorney's office. While he was questioning a man about an unrelated event, the fellow confessed to the Wells Fargo crime, and was ultimately convicted. When Slattery sued Wells Fargo for the reward, it refused to pay. Is Slattery entitled to the reward? Why?

DISCUSSION QUESTIONS

Apply the following material to questions 1 and 2 below.

Some view consideration as a technicality that allows people to make promises and then back out of them. Perhaps all promises should be enforced. In Japan, for example, promises to give gifts are enforceable without consideration.[14]

In the United States, if I promise to give you a gift merely because I feel like being nice, I can freely change my mind as far as contract law is concerned. A court will not make me follow through because there is no consideration.

In Japan, I would be obligated to buy the gift if all other elements of a contract were present—an offer, an acceptance, and so forth.

1. When it comes to giving gifts, which is better—the Japanese or American rule?

2. Are there any specific types of agreements (perhaps high-value, long-term, extremely time-consuming ones) that should definitely require consideration?

3. Albert and Luis, lifelong friends, had a tradition. Every Friday, they took turns going to the corner store and buying what they called a "package"—some vodka and a lottery ticket. One lucky Friday, Albert purchased the package, but Luis scratched off the lottery ticket, only to learn that it was a $20,000 winner. Luis refused to share. Albert sued, claiming the former friends had an enforceable contract supported by valid consideration. Rule.

4. The consideration doctrine is controversial. Critics argue that it is a remnant of a bygone era, lacking any reasonable modern purpose and that it undermines the purpose of contract law, which is to enforce the intention of the parties to an agreement. Should consideration be abolished?

5. Amber Williams and Frederick Ormsby were lovers, embroiled in a turbulent romantic relationship. After knowing each other for a short time, Frederick moved into Amber's house and paid off her $310,000 mortgage. She then gave him title to the house. But their happiness was not to last. The couple canceled their plans to marry, and Amber moved out of the house. Two months later, Frederick sought reconciliation. Amber refused to get back together unless Frederick gave her half ownership of the house. Frederick agreed. After the couple split up for the last time, Amber sued for her half of the house. Frederick argued that his promise was not supported by adequate consideration. Was it?

---

[14]See Japan's Civil Code, Article 549.

CHAPTER 14

LEGALITY

Soheil Sadri, a California resident, did some serious gambling at Caesar's Tahoe casino in Nevada. And lost. To keep gambling, he wrote checks to Caesar's and then signed two memoranda pledging to repay all money advanced. After two days, with his losses totaling more than $22,000, he went home. Back in California, Sadri stopped payment on the checks and refused to pay any of the money he owed Caesar's. The casino sued. In defense, Sadri claimed that California law considered his agreements illegal and unenforceable. He was unquestionably correct about one thing: A contract that is illegal is void and unenforceable.

A contract that is illegal is void and unenforceable.

14-1 CONTRACTS THAT VIOLATE A STATUTE

In this chapter, we examine a variety of contracts that may be void, or unenforceable. Illegal agreements fall into two groups: those that violate a statute, and those that violate public policy.

14-1a Wagers

Gambling is big business. Almost all states now permit some form of wagering, from casinos to racetracks to lotteries, and they eagerly collect the billions of dollars in revenue generated. Supporters urge that casinos create jobs and steady income, boost state coffers, and take business away from organized crime. Critics argue that naive citizens inevitably lose money they can ill afford to forfeit, and that addicted gamblers destroy their families and weaken the fabric of communities. With citizens and states divided over the ethics of gambling, it is inevitable that we have conflicts such as the dispute between Sadri and Caesar's. The basic rule, however, is clear: **A gambling contract is illegal unless it is a type of wagering *specifically authorized* by state statute.**

In California, as in many states, gambling on credit is not allowed. In other words, it is illegal to lend money to help someone wager. But in Nevada, gambling on credit is legal, and debt memoranda such as Sadri's are enforceable contracts. Caesar's sued Sadri in California (where he lived). The result? The court admitted that California's attitude toward gambling had changed, and that bingo, poker clubs, and lotteries were common. Nonetheless, the court denied that the new tolerance extended to wagering on credit:

> There is a special reason for treating gambling on credit differently from gambling itself. Having lost his or her cash, the pathological gambler will continue to play on credit, if extended, in an attempt to win back the losses. This is why enforcement of gambling debts has always been against public policy in California and should remain so, regardless of shifting public attitudes about gambling itself. If Californians want to play, so be it. But the law should not invite them to play themselves into debt. The judiciary cannot protect pathological gamblers from themselves, but we can refuse to participate in their financial ruin.[1]

Caesar's lost and Sadri kept his money. However, do not become too excited at the prospect of risk-free wagering. Casinos responded to cases like *Sadri* by changing their practices. Most now extend credit only to a gambler who agrees that disputes about repayment will be settled in *Nevada* courts. Because such contracts are legal in that state, the casino is able to obtain a judgment against a defaulting debtor and—yes—enforce that judgment in the gambler's home state.

Despite these more restrictive casino practices, Sadri's dispute is a useful starting place from which to examine contract legality because it illustrates two important themes.

First, morality is a significant part of contract legality. In refusing to enforce an obligation that Sadri undeniably had made, the California court relied on the human and social consequences of gambling and on the ethics of judicial enforcement of gambling debts. Second, "void" really means just that: A court will not intercede to assist either party to an illegal agreement, even if its refusal leaves one party shortchanged.

[1]Metropolitan Creditors Service of Sacramento v. Sadri, 15 Cal. App. 4th 1821 (1993).

14-1b Insurance

Another market in which "wagering" unexpectedly pops up is that of insurance. You may certainly insure your own life for any sum you choose. But may you insure someone else's life? **Anyone taking out a policy on the life of another must have an insurable interest in that person.** The most common insurable interest is family connection, such as spouses or parents. Other valid interests include creditor-debtor status (the creditor wants payment if the debtor dies) and business association (an executive in the company is so valuable that the firm will need compensation if something happens to him). If there is no insurable interest, there is generally no contract.

EXAMStrategy

Question: Jimenez sold Breton a used motorcycle for $5,500, payable in weekly installments. Jimenez then purchased an insurance policy on Breton's life, worth $320,000 if Breton died in an accident. Breton promptly died in a collision with an automobile. The insurance company offered only $5,500, representing the balance due on the motorcycle. Jimenez sued, demanding $320,000. Make an argument that the insurance company should win.

Strategy: The issue is whether Jimenez had an insurable interest in Breton's life. If he had no interest, he cannot collect on an insurance policy. If he had an interest, what was it? For how much money?

Result: Jimenez had an interest in Breton's life to insure payment of the motorcycle debt—$5,500. Beyond that, this policy represented a wager by Jimenez that Breton was going to die. Contracts for such wagers are unenforceable. Jimenez is entitled only to $5,500.[2]

14-1c Licensing Statutes

You sue your next-door neighbor in small claims court, charging that he keeps a kangaroo in his backyard and that the beast has disrupted your family barbecues by leaping over the fence, demanding salad, and even kicking your cousin in the ear. Your friend Foster, a graduate student from Melbourne, offers to help you prepare the case, and you agree to pay him 10 percent of anything you recover. Foster proves surprisingly adept at organizing documents and arguments. You win $1,200, and Foster demands $120. Must you pay? The answer is determined by the law of licensing.

States require licenses for anyone who practices a profession, such as law or medicine, works as a contractor or plumber, and for many other kinds of work. These licenses are required in order to protect the public. States demand that an electrician be licensed because the work is potentially dangerous to a homeowner: The person doing the work must know an amp from a watt. **When a licensing requirement is designed to protect the public, any contract made by an unlicensed worker is unenforceable.** Your friend Foster is unlicensed to practice law. Even though Foster did a fine job with your small claims case, he cannot enforce his contract for $120.

States use other licenses simply to raise money. For example, most states require a license to open certain kinds of retail stores. This requirement does not protect the public because the state will not investigate the store owner the way it will examine a

[2]Jimenez v. Protective Life Insurance Co., 8 Cal. App. 4th 528 (1992).

prospective lawyer or electrician. The state is simply raising money. **When a licensing requirement is designed merely to raise revenue, a contract made by an unlicensed person is generally enforceable.** Thus, if you open a stationery store and forget to pay the state's licensing fee, you can still enforce a contract to buy 10,000 envelopes from a wholesaler at a bargain price.

Many cases, such as the following one, involve contractors seeking to recover money for work they did without a license.

Authentic Home Improvements v. Mayo

2006 D.C. Super LEXIS 9, 2006 WL 2687533
District of Columbia Superior Court, 2006

Facts: Authentic Home Improvements (Authentic) performed work on Diane Mayo's home, but she sued for return of the money she had paid. In court, Authentic's owner acknowledged that he had no contractor's license when it began the work, but he expected to obtain it soon. The court ordered Authentic to refund Mayo the entire sum she had paid, and the company agreed. Later, however, Authentic returned to court, stating that things had changed. The license had in fact been issued soon after work began. Authentic argued that it should not be obligated to return Mayo's money and was in fact entitled to its full fee for the work accomplished.

Issue: ***Did the new license entitle Authentic to its home improvement fee?***

Excerpts from Judge Goodbread's Decision: This is not a matter of a trial judge doggedly cleaving to his original ruling—one that he frankly wishes he could modify under these circumstances. To use the words of Proteus, "My duty pricks me on to utter that which else no worldly good should draw from me." Shakespeare, "The Two Gentlemen of Verona." Not that it makes any difference to anyone, but the undersigned, a carpenter's son dwelling at this end of the Judicial Food Chain, disagrees with the harsh general rule in these cases and [believes that exceptions to the licensing requirement should be made in deserving cases]. Nevertheless, the undersigned is bound by the repeated rulings of the Court of Appeals.

As early as 1974, our Court of Appeals noted the high incidence of complaints emanating from the home improvement industry, noting that, even then, it was estimated that fraudulent practices in the industry cost consumers from 500 million to 1 billion dollars annually (this would amount to over $4.3 billion in today's dollars). A simple search of the Internet for the term "home improvement fraud" brings up over two million sites.

Not only is it immaterial that the parties may be in equal fault in the home improvement contract matter, but it has also been held that the unlicensed contractor may not recover even in instances wherein the homeowner *already knew* at all times relevant that the contractor was not licensed and impliedly or expressly "waived" that requirement in return for the work being done promptly. Moreover—turning the purpose of the rule inside out—even where it was the contractor who was the "victim" and the home owner herself who knew in advance that the contract would be invalid and unenforceable, yet still benefitted unfairly from the contractor's good work, the homeowner was allowed to prevail, despite what might be termed "malice aforethought."

The unique defense of a "retroactive" license presented in this case does not vitiate the rule. [Authentic's owner argues that he] had every reasonable *expectation* of receiving a license and that, in fact, he *did* receive the license within a reasonable time of beginning work. Yet the requirement to have *already* had issued, and in hand, a license or permit to conduct or perform the act at issue is not a difficult concept to grasp and one need go no further than the common driver's permit or license tags to understand it. No one could legally drive a vehicle in *anticipation* of the license and the plates that had already been approved, on the premise that they would eventually arrive in the mail in due course, and that it would be all right to drive until they do.

The Court's original ruling in this case must stand.

14-1d Usury

It pays to understand usury.

Henry Paper and Anthony Pugliese were real estate developers. They bought property in Florida, intending to erect an office building. Walter Gross, another developer, agreed to lend them $200,000 at 15 percent interest. Gross knew the partners were desperate for the money, so at the loan closing, he demanded 15 percent equity (ownership) in the partnership, in addition to the interest. Paper and Pugliese had no choice but to sign the agreement. The two partners never repaid the loan, and when Gross sued, the court ruled that they need never pay a cent.

Usury laws prohibit charging excess interest on loans. Some states, such as New York, set very strict limits. Others, like Utah, allow for virtually any rate. A lender who charges a usurious rate of interest may forfeit the illegal interest, all interest, or, in some states, the entire loan.

Florida law requires a lender who exceeds 25 percent interest to forfeit the entire debt. Where was the usury in Gross's case? Just here: When Gross insisted on a 15 percent share of the partnership, he was simply extracting additional interest and disguising it as partnership equity. The Paper-Pugliese partnership had equity assets of $600,000. A 15 percent equity, plus interest payments of 15 percent over 18 months, was the equivalent of a per annum interest rate of 45 percent. Gross probably thought that he had made a deal that was too good to be true. And in the state of Florida, it was. He lost the entire debt.[3]

Credit Card Debt

Many consumers are desperate to obtain credit cards on any terms. When First Premier Bank launched a credit card with a 79.9 percent rate of interest, 700,000 people applied for it within the next two years. How can such a rate exist?

Even if a state's usury statute applies to credit cards, savvy lenders can often avoid limits on interest rates. The Supreme Court has ruled that when national banks issue a credit card, they can use the rate of their own state or of that of the consumer's, whichever is higher. Also, many card issuers require borrowers to sign contracts that say the laws of a lender-friendly state will be applied to all future disputes. New York customers might agree to live by Utah laws, for example.

Most courts continue to enforce these contracts that impose high out-of-state rates. But some courts have started to express distaste for this practice. In the following case, a New York court addressed the issue.

American Express Travel Related Services Company, Inc. v. Assih

893 N.Y.S.2d 438
Civil Court of the City of New York, Richmond County, 2009

Facts: American Express Travel Related Services (American Express) alleged that New York resident Titus Assih missed a credit card payment. His interest rate ballooned from 12.24 percent to 21 percent, and eventually to 27.99 percent. Assih made small payments for a time, but soon he stopped paying altogether.

American Express sued Assih. The company sought to enforce this provision of its agreement: "This Agreement is governed by Utah law and applicable federal law." The agreement's only connection to Utah was that American Express assigned its interest to a one-branch bank in Utah.

Assih argued that New York law, which sets strict limits on maximum rates of credit card interest, should apply instead.

Issues: ***Should New York or Utah law apply? Did the increased rates violate usury statutes?***

[3]Jersey Palm-Gross, Inc. v. Paper, 639 So.2d 664 (Fla. Ct. App. 1994).

Excerpts from Judge Straniere's Opinion: Having dealt with thousands of consumer credit cases over the years, the court is sometimes caused to wonder if the regulations governing this industry originated in the Wonderful Land of Oz. For example, the scene where Dorothy and friends approach the gates of the Emerald City and ring the bell seeking entrance seems to present a number of the issues arising in debt collection litigation.

> Guardian: Well, that's more like it! Now state your business!
> Dorothy and Friends: We want to see the Wizard!
> Guardian: The Wizard? But nobody can see the Great Oz! Nobody's ever seen the Great Oz! Even I've never seen him!
> Dorothy: Well, then how do you know there is one?

Like the Land of Oz, run by a Wizard who no one has ever seen, the Land of Credit Cards permits consumers to be bound by agreements they never sign, agreements they may have never received, subject to change without notice and the laws of a state other than those existing where they reside.

The Utah usury statute provides: The parties to a lawful contract may agree upon any rate of interest for the loan that is the subject of their contract.

Is it any wonder that credit card issuers, such as plaintiff, make their agreements subject to Utah law? An interest rate is not usurious so long as the parties "agree upon any rate of interest." If Nathan Detroit had known he could make loans charging 100 percent interest a day by reducing them to writing, signed and subject to Utah law, he would not have had to seek a living running the "oldest, established, permanent floating crap game in New York." Incredibly, courts are expected to enforce these agreements against unsophisticated, unrepresented consumers who reside in states such as New York, which does not have similar statutes, and who have no idea that their agreement is subject to Utah law.

Is New York required to apply the Utah usury statute to credit card interest charges that far exceed the legal rate in New York? New York follows the "substantial relationship" approach, which provides:

> The law of the state chosen by the parties to govern their contractual rights and duties will be applied . . . unless the chosen state has no substantial relationship to the parties.

The corporate plaintiff is incorporated in New York and its principal place of business is in New York. Defendant resides in New York. Most of the transactions charged to the credit card took place in New York. Payments on the credit card are mailed to a New York address. Utah has no substantial relationship to the parties.

Taking all of the above into account, it is clear that New York has the most significant contacts to the parties and New York law will apply to the Agreement.

The legal rate of interest in New York in general obligations [is] sixteen percent. New York still retains a criminal usury statute for interest rates which exceed twenty-five percent. Except for the initial interest rate charged on defendant's account by plaintiff of 12.24%, all other interest charges assessed by plaintiff violated the New York civil usury statutes. The last billings on this account in fact exceeded the criminal usury rate of 25% when they reached 27.99%.

Under New York law, all usurious contracts are void and the lender forfeits both principal and interest.

The Wizard in *The Wizard of Oz* warned Dorothy and friends, "Do not arouse the wrath of the great and powerful Oz." I am sure the court will likewise be arousing the wrath of the plaintiff.

Plaintiff's cause of action is dismissed.

14-2 CONTRACTS THAT VIOLATE PUBLIC POLICY

A judge may declare a contract void even if it does not violate a statute. Contracts that promote immorality or illegality are unenforceable. One court refused to enforce a contract for the sale of a company because its main business was the manufacture of illegal drug paraphernalia.[4] It reasoned that such a contract would have a negative impact on society. This section examines cases in which a *public policy* prohibits certain contracts.

[4]Bovard v. American Horse Enterprises, Inc., 201 Cal. App. 3d 832 (1988).

In the following case, a court faced a tough choice between enforcing a bargain and forcing someone to become a parent. What is the proper role of contract law in determining whether a child is born? You be the judge.

You Be the Judge

A.Z. v. B.Z.[5]

431 Mass. 150
Supreme Judicial Court of Massachusetts, 2000

Facts: A and B, a married couple, were having difficulties conceiving a child. They chose to undergo in vitro fertilization (IVF), which involves removing the woman's eggs and combining them in a petri dish with the man's sperm. A and B's process yielded multiple fertilized eggs (or pre-embryos), which resulted in the birth of their twin daughters. The couple chose to freeze two extra vials of pre-embryos for possible future implantation.

During the fertility process, A and B signed various required, preprinted consent forms agreeing to undergo IVF. The consent form's primary purpose was to explain to the donors the benefits and risks of freezing pre-embryos. At the bottom of one of these forms, the wife wrote in that if they ever separated, she could still use the pre-embryos. The husband duly agreed.

Years later, the marriage was on the rocks. The wife had one of the frozen pre-embryos implanted without informing her husband, who learned of the news from his insurance company. Drama ensued. The husband filed for divorce. The wife got a restraining order. As part of the divorce, the husband asked the court to prohibit his wife from using the remaining pre-embryos. The wife argued that it was a simple matter of contract law. The lower court declared the agreement unenforceable as against public policy. The wife appealed.

You Be the Judge: *Should a court enforce a contract for the use of fertilized eggs against the father's wishes?*

Argument for the Wife: A contract is a contract. Both my client and her husband entered into this agreement freely and with full knowledge of the possible consequences. They each signed multiple consent forms establishing their wishes. Although it is not easy for people to anticipate the future of their relationship when they sign these forms, that has never been a reason to invalidate a perfectly good contract. The possibility of divorce for this (or any) couple was a fact known to the husband when he signed the contracts. The whole point of these contracts was to minimize misunderstanding, ensure the parties' liberty to procreate, and provide needed certainty for the fertility treatments. The court should enforce this contract.

Argument for the Husband: Your honors, those consent forms were not really contracts between the husband and wife, they were merely medical releases required by law. Since the parties signed those consent forms, much has changed. The couple did not anticipate the betrayal, the divorce, the restraining order . . . is that a way to bring a child into the world? This is much more than a simple matter of contract law. Courts have always been hesitant to meddle in intimate family affairs on public policy grounds. No court should force someone to become a parent. It is as simple as that.

14-2a Restraint of Trade: Non-compete Agreements

Recall that a non-compete agreement is a contract in which one party agrees not to compete with another in a stated type of business. For example, an anchorwoman for an NBC news affiliate in Miami might agree that she will not anchor any other Miami station's news for one year after she leaves her present employer. Non-competes are often valid, but the law places some restrictions on them.

[5]To protect the privacy of the litigants, courts sometimes refer to them by their initials, as in this case.

To be valid, an agreement not to compete must be part of a larger agreement. Suppose Cliff sells his gasoline station to Mina, and the two agree that Cliff will not open a competing gas station within 5 miles anytime during the next two years. Cliff's agreement not to compete is ancillary to the sale of his service station. His noncompetition promise is enforceable. But suppose that Cliff and Mina had the only two gas stations within 35 miles. They agree between themselves not to hire each other's workers. Their agreement might be profitable to them because each could now keep wages artificially low. But their deal is not ancillary to a legitimate bargain, and it is therefore void. Mina is free to hire Cliff's mechanic despite her agreement with Cliff.

The two most common settings for legitimate noncompetition agreements are the sale of a business and an employment relationship.

Sale of a Business

Kory has operated a real estate office, Hearth Attack, in a small city for 35 years, building an excellent reputation and many ties with the community. She offers to sell you the business and its goodwill for $300,000. But you need assurance that Kory will not take your money and promptly open a competing office across the street. With her reputation and connections, she would ruin your chances of success. You insist on a non-compete clause in the sale contract. In this clause, Kory promises that for one year, she will not open a new real estate office or go to work for a competing company within a 10-mile radius of Hearth Attack. Suppose, six months after selling you the business, Kory goes to work for a competing real estate agency two blocks away. You seek an injunction to prevent her from working. Who wins?

With her reputation and connections, she would ruin your chances of success.

When a non-compete agreement is ancillary to the sale of a business, it is enforceable if reasonable in time, geographic area, and scope of activity. In other words, a court will not enforce a non-compete agreement that lasts an unreasonably long time, covers an unfairly large area, or prohibits the seller of the business from doing a type of work that she never had done before. Measured by this test, Kory is almost certainly bound by her agreement. One year is a reasonable time to allow you to get your new business started. A 10-mile radius is probably about the area that Hearth Attack covers, and realty is obviously a fair business from which to prohibit Kory. A court will probably grant the injunction, barring Kory from her new job.

If, on the other hand, the noncompetition agreement had prevented Kory from working anywhere within 200 miles of Hearth Attack, and she started working 50 miles away, a court would refuse to enforce the contract. That geographic restriction would be unreasonable since Kory never previously did business 50 miles away, and Hearth Attack is unlikely to be affected if she works there now. An overly broad restriction would make for bad public policy, and it would lack a legal purpose.

Employment

Employers have legitimate worries that workers might go to a competitor and take with them significant business or trade secrets and other proprietary information. Some employers, though, place harsh restrictions on their employees simply to prevent them from leaving. An employee with a burdensome non-compete might be willing to tolerate harsh treatment just to avoid unemployment. A national sandwich chain required its sandwich-makers to sign a non-compete that would ban them from working at just about any other fast-food restaurant. It seems unlikely that headquarters was concerned about the sandwich jockeys taking business or irreplaceable skills with them.

If you have ever been employed, there is more than a one-in-three chance that you had a non-compete. These clauses currently affect nearly 30 million American workers at all salary

Robert W. Ginn/Alamy Stock Photo

Is it fair to bind a sandwich-maker to a non-compete?

levels and across industries.[6] Many employees do not negotiate their non-competes—or even realize they have one until the shocking day when they try to leave their jobs.

Non-competes limit an individual's right to make a living and choose his work. For this reason, a growing number of states have restrictions on the enforceability of employment-related non-competes. Some states have statutes prohibiting non-competes in certain industries: Hawaii has banned them for technology jobs, and New Mexico prohibits them in the healthcare industry. Other states limit their duration: to 18 months in Oregon and one year in Utah.

In the absence of specific state statutes, non-compete agreements are enforceable only if they meet all of the following standards:

- **They are reasonably necessary for the protection of the employer.** Judges usually enforce these agreements to protect trade secrets and confidential information. They may protect customer lists that have been expensive to produce.
- **They provide a reasonable time limit.** A reasonable time for a software engineer might be less than one for a chef because technology changes at a rapid pace.
- **They have a reasonable geographic limit.** Barring an employee from working in tiny Rhode Island is very different from Texas. Courts look closely to make sure that the restrictions are no broader than necessary to meet the employer's objective.
- **They are not harsh or oppressive to the employee.** New York City has over 7,000 fast-food restaurants. Prohibiting a low-wage sandwich-maker with no company secrets from working at any of them is an unfair burden.
- **They are not contrary to public policy.** Employers who hide terms or sneak them into contracts after the employee has accepted the job may be acting unconscionably.

The legality of a non-compete depends on the facts of each case: the type of work, industry, and restrictions imposed. Note, though, that many firms ask employees to sign non-competes that are unenforceable. California prohibits non-competes altogether (except in connection with the sale of a business),[7] but research shows that California businesses require non-competes from their workers more than employers in any other state.[8] For this reason, it is important that every employee know the legal limits of these clauses.

The following chart summarizes the factors that courts look at in all types of noncompetition agreements.

---

[6]Office of Economic Policy U.S. Department of the Treasury, *Non-compete Contracts: Economic Effects and Policy Implications*, March 2016.

[7]Edwards v. Arthur Andersen LLP, 44 Cal., 4th 937 (S. Ct. Cal. 2008).

[8]White House Report, *Non-Compete Agreements: Analysis of the Usage, Potential Issues, and State Responses*, May 2016.

The Legality of Non-Compete Agreements

Type of Noncompetition Agreement	When Enforceable	
Not ancillary to a sale of business or employment	Never	
Ancillary to a sale of business	If reasonable in time, geography, and scope of activity	
Ancillary to employment	Contract is *more* likely to be enforced when it involves:	Contract is *less* likely to be enforced when it involves:
	• Trade secrets or confidential information: these are almost always protected	• Employee who already had the skills when he arrived, or merely developed general skills on the job
	• Customer lists developed over extended period of time and carefully protected	• Customer lists that can be derived from public sources
	• Limited time and geographical scope	• Excessive time or geographical scope
	• Terms essential to protect the employer's business	• Terms that are unduly harsh on the employee or contrary to public interest

Was the non-compete in the following case styled fairly, or was the employee clipped?

King v. Head Start Family Hair Salons, Inc.

886 So.2d 769
Supreme Court of Alabama, 2004

Facts: Kathy King was a single mother supporting a college-age daughter. For 25 years, she had worked as a hair stylist. For the most recent 16 years, she had worked at Head Start, which provided haircuts, coloring, and styling for men and women. King was primarily a stylist, though she had also managed one of the Head Start facilities.

King quit Head Start and began working as manager of a Sport Clips shop, located in the same mall as the store she just left. Sport Clips offered only haircuts and primarily served men and boys. Head Start filed suit, claiming that King was violating the noncompetition agreement that she had signed. The agreement prohibited King from working at a competing business within a 2-mile radius of any Head Start facility for 12 months after leaving the company. The trial court issued an injunction enforcing the non-compete. King appealed.

Issue: ***Was the noncompetition agreement valid?***

Excerpts from Justice Lyons's Decision: King's most persuasive argument is that the geographic restriction contained in the noncompetition agreement imposes an undue hardship on her. King has been in the hair-care industry for 25 years, and it is the only industry in which she is skilled and the only industry in which she can find employment. Head Start has 30 locations throughout the Jefferson County and Shelby County area, making it virtually impossible for her to find employment in the hair-care industry at a facility that does not violate the terms of the noncompetition agreement. According to King, the geographic restriction constitutes a blanket prohibition on practicing her trade.

It cannot reasonably be argued that King, at the age of 40 and having spent more than half of her life as a hair stylist, can learn a new job skill that would allow her to be gainfully employed and meet her needs and the needs of her daughter. Under the circumstances presented here, enforcement of the noncompetition agreement works an undue hardship upon King. The noncompetition agreement cannot so burden King that it would result in her impoverishment.

Head Start is nevertheless entitled to some of the protection it sought in the noncompetition agreement. Head Start has a valid concern that King would be able to attract many of her former Head Start customers if she is allowed to provide hair-care services unencumbered by any limitations. To prevent an undue burden on King and to afford some protection to Head Start, the trial court should enforce a more reasonable geographic restriction—such as one prohibiting King from providing hair-care services within a 2-mile radius of the location of the Head Start facility at which she was formerly employed or imposing some other limitation that does not unreasonably interfere with King's right to gainful employment while, at the same time, protecting Head Start's interest in preventing King from unreasonably competing with it during the one-year period following her resignation.

Reversed and remanded.

EXAMStrategy

Question: Caf-Fiend is an expanding chain of coffeehouses. The company offers to buy Bessie's Coffee Shop, in St. Louis, on these terms: Bessie will manage the store, as Caf-Fiend's employee, for one year after the sale. For four years after the sale, Bessie will not open a competing restaurant anywhere within 12 miles. For the same four years, she will not work anywhere in the United States for a competing coffee retailer. Are the last two terms enforceable against Bessie?

Strategy: This contract includes two non-compete clauses. In the first, Bessie agrees not to open a competing business. Courts generally enforce such clauses if they are reasonable in time, geography, and scope of activity. Is this clause reasonable? The second clause involves employment. Courts take a dimmer view of these agreements. Is this clause essential to protect the company's business? Is it unduly harsh for Bessie?

Result: The first restriction is reasonable. Caf-Fiend is entitled to prevent Bessie from opening her own coffeehouse around the corner and drawing her old customers. The second clause is unfair to Bessie. If she wants to move from St. Louis to San Diego and work as a store manager, she is prohibited. It is impossible to see how such employment would harm Caf-Fiend—but it certainly takes away Bessie's career options. The first restriction is valid, and the second one is unenforceable.

14-2b Exculpatory Clauses

You decide to capitalize on your expert ability as a skier and open a ski and snowboarding school in Colorado, "Pike's Pique." But you realize that skiing and snowboarding sometimes cause injuries, so you require anyone signing up for lessons to sign this form:

> I agree to hold Pike's Pique and its employees entirely harmless in the event that I am injured in any way or for any reason or cause, including but not limited to any acts, whether negligent or otherwise, of Pike's Pique or any employee or agent thereof.

The day your school opens, Sara Beth, an instructor, deliberately pushes Toby over a cliff because Toby criticized her clothes. Eddie, a beginning student, "blows out" his knee attempting an advanced racing turn, and Maureen, another student, reaches the bottom of a steep run and slams into a snowmobile that Sara Beth parked there. Maureen, Eddie, and Toby's families all sue Pike's Pique. You defend based on the form you had them sign. Does it save the day?

The form on which you are relying is an **exculpatory clause**, that is, one that attempts to release you from liability in the event of injury to another party. Exculpatory clauses are common. Ski and snowboarding schools use them, and so do parking lots, landlords, warehouses, sports franchises, fitness centers, and day-care centers. All manner of businesses hope to avoid large tort judgments by requiring their customers to give up any right to recover. Is such a clause valid? Sometimes. Courts frequently—but do not always—ignore exculpatory clauses, finding that one party was forcing the other party to give up legal rights that no one should be forced to surrender.

Exculpatory clause
A contract provision that attempts to release one party from liability in the event the other is injured

An exculpatory clause is generally unenforceable when it attempts to exclude an intentional tort or gross negligence. When Sara Beth pushes Toby over a cliff, that is the intentional tort of battery. A court will not enforce the exculpatory clause. Sara Beth is clearly liable.[9] As to the snowmobile at the bottom of the run, if a court determines that was gross negligence (carelessness far greater than ordinary negligence), then the exculpatory clause will again be ignored. If, however, it was ordinary negligence, then we must continue the analysis.

An exculpatory clause is usually unenforceable when the affected activity is in the public interest, such as medical care, public transportation, or some essential service. Suppose Eddie goes to a doctor for surgery on his damaged knee, and the doctor requires him to sign an exculpatory clause. The doctor negligently performs the surgery, accidentally leaving his cuff links in Eddie's left knee. The exculpatory clause will not protect the doctor. Medical care is an essential service, and the public cannot give up its right to demand reasonable work.

But what about Eddie's suit against Pike's Pique? Eddie claims that he should never have been allowed to attempt an advanced maneuver. His suit is for ordinary negligence, and the exculpatory clause probably *does* bar him from recovery. Skiing and snowboarding are recreational activities. No one is obligated to do them, and there is no strong public interest in ensuring that we have access to ski slopes.

An exculpatory clause is generally unenforceable when the parties have greatly unequal bargaining power. When Maureen flies to Colorado, suppose that the airline requires her to sign a form contract with an exculpatory clause. Because the airline almost certainly has much greater bargaining power, it can afford to offer a "take it or leave it" contract. The bargaining power is so unequal, though, that the clause is probably unenforceable. Does Pike's Pique have a similar advantage? Probably not. Ski and snowboarding schools are not essential and are much smaller enterprises. A dissatisfied customer might refuse to sign such an agreement and take her business elsewhere. A court probably will not see the parties as *grossly* unequal.

An exculpatory clause is generally unenforceable unless the clause is clearly written and readily visible. If Pike's Pique gave all ski and snowboarding students an eight-page contract, and the exculpatory clause was at the bottom of page 7 in small print, the average customer would never notice it. The clause would be void.

CHRISTIAN DE ARAUJO/Shutterstock.com

Exculpatory clauses are important to the operators of businesses that involve some risk, such as ski resorts.

[9]Note that Pike's Pique is probably not liable under agency law principles that preclude an employer's liability for an employee's intentional tort.

Bailment Cases

Bailment
Giving possession and control of personal property to another person

Bailor
One who creates a bailment by delivering goods to another

Bailee
A person who rightfully possesses goods belonging to another

Exculpatory clauses are very common in bailment cases. **Bailment** means giving possession and control of personal property to another person. The person giving up possession is the **bailor**, and the one accepting possession is the **bailee**. When you leave your laptop computer with a dealer to be repaired, you create a bailment. The same is true when you check your coat at a restaurant or lend your Matisse to a museum. Bailees often try to limit their liability for damage to property by using an exculpatory clause.

Judges are slightly more apt to enforce an exculpatory clause in a bailment case because any harm is to *property* and not persons. But courts will still look at many of the same criteria we have just examined to decide whether a bailment contract is enforceable. In particular, when the bailee is engaged in an important public service, a court is once again likely to ignore the exculpatory clause. The following contrasting cases illustrate this.

In *Weiss v. Freeman*,[10] Weiss stored personal goods in Freeman's self-storage facility. Freeman's contract included an exculpatory clause relieving it of any and all liability. Weiss's goods were damaged by mildew, and she sued. The court held the exculpatory clause valid. The court considered self-storage to be a significant business, but not as vital as medical care or housing. It pointed out that a storage facility would not know what each customer stored and therefore could not anticipate the harm that might occur. Freedom of contract should prevail, the clause was enforceable, and Weiss got no money.

But in *Gardner v. Downtown Porsche Audi*,[11] Gardner left his Porsche 911 at Downtown for repairs. He signed an exculpatory clause saying that Downtown was "Not Responsible for Loss or Damage to Cars or Articles Left in Cars in Case of Fire, Theft, or Any Other Cause Beyond Our Control." Due to Downtown's negligence, Gardner's Porsche was stolen. The court held the exculpatory clause void. It ruled that contemporary society is utterly dependent upon automobile transportation and Downtown was therefore in a business of great public importance. No repair shop should be able to contract away liability, and Gardner won. (This case also illustrates that using 17 capitalized words in one sentence does not guarantee legal victory.)

EXAMStrategy

Facts: Shauna flew a World War II fighter aircraft as a member of an exhibition flight team. While the team was performing in a delta formation, another plane collided with Shauna's aircraft, causing her to crash-land and leaving her permanently disabled. Shauna sued the other pilot and the team. The defendants moved to dismiss based on an exculpatory clause that Shauna had signed. The clause was one paragraph long, and it stated that Shauna knew team flying was inherently dangerous and could result in injury or death. She agreed not to hold the team or any members liable in case of an accident. Shauna argued that the clause should not be enforced against her if she could prove the other pilot was negligent. Please rule.

Strategy: The issue is whether the exculpatory clause is valid. Courts are likely to declare such clauses void if they concern vital activities like medical care, exclude an intentional tort or gross negligence, or if the parties had unequal bargaining power.

Result: This is a clear, short clause, between parties with equal bargaining power, and does not exclude an intentional tort or gross negligence. The activity is unimportant to the public welfare. The clause is valid. Even if the other pilot was negligent, Shauna will lose, meaning the court should dismiss her lawsuit.

---

10 1994 Tenn. App. LEXIS 393, 1994 WL 388146 (1994).

11 180 Cal. App. 3d 713 (1986).

14-2c Unconscionable Contracts

An unconscionable contract is one that a court refuses to enforce because of fundamental unfairness. Even if a contract does not violate any specific statute or public policy, it may still be void if it "shocks the conscience" of the court.

Historically, a contract was considered unconscionable if it was "such as no man in his senses and not under delusion would make on the one hand, and as no honest and fair man would accept on the other."[12]

But that standard was unhelpfully vague. Further, anytime a court rejects a contract as unconscionable, it diminishes freedom of contract. If one party can escape a deal based on something as hard to define as unconscionability, then no one can rely as confidently on any agreement. As an English jurist said in 1824, "public policy is a very unruly horse, and when once you get astride it, you never know where it will carry you."[13]

The following historic case provides a classic example of unconscionability.

Landmark Case

Williams v. Walker-Thomas Furniture Co.

350 F.2d 445
United States Court of Appeals for the DC Circuit, 1965

Facts: Walker-Thomas Furniture Company operated a retail furniture store in an economically disadvantaged DC neighborhood. The store's standard boilerplate contract provided, in fine print, that when a purchaser bought more than one item, any payment she made would be applied equally to everything she had purchased. In this way, the purchaser would not actually own any item until she had paid for everything in full. As a result, when customers missed a payment, Walker-Thomas would repossess every item they ever bought.

Ora Williams was a single mother raising seven children on a $218 monthly welfare check. Despite this knowledge, Walker-Thomas sold Williams 14 household items totaling $1,800 from 1957 to 1962. Williams dutifully made her monthly payments. In 1962, Williams bought a stereo valued at $514.95. At the time of this purchase, she still owed $164 from her prior purchases. When Williams defaulted on her payment, Walker-Thomas sought to repossess every item she had ever purchased.

With the help of a legal aid society, Williams and other Walker-Thomas customers sued the company, arguing the contract was void for unconscionability. Lower courts sided with Walker-Thomas, and the customers appealed.

Issue: ***Is an unconscionable contract unenforceable?***

Excerpts from Judge Skelly Wright's Decision: Unconscionability has generally been recognized to include an absence of meaningful choice on the part of one of the parties together with contract terms which are unreasonably favorable to the other party. Whether a meaningful choice is present in a particular case can only be determined by consideration of all the circumstances surrounding the transaction. In many cases the meaningfulness of the choice is negated by a gross inequality of bargaining power.

The manner in which the contract was entered is also relevant to this consideration. Did each party to the contract, considering his obvious education or lack of it, have a reasonable opportunity to understand the terms of the contract, or were the important terms hidden in a maze of fine print and minimized by deceptive sales practices? Ordinarily, one who signs an agreement without full knowledge of its terms might be held to assume the risk that he has entered a one-sided bargain. But when a party of little bargaining power, and hence little real choice, signs a commercially unreasonable contract with little or no knowledge of its terms, it is hardly likely that his consent, or even an objective manifestation of his consent, was ever given to all the terms. In such a case the usual rule that the terms of the agreement are not to be questioned should be abandoned and the court should consider whether the terms of the contract are so unfair that enforcement should be withheld.

The test [of unconscionability] is not simple, nor can it be mechanically applied. The terms are to be considered in the

---

[12]Hume v. United States, 132 U.S. 406 (1889), quoting Earl of Chesterfield v. Janssen, 38 Eng. Rep. 82, 100 (Ch. 1750).

[13]Richardson v. Mellish, 2 Bing. 229 (1824).

light of the general commercial background and the commercial needs of the particular trade or case. The test [is] whether the terms are 'so extreme as to appear unconscionable according to the mores and business practices of the time and place.'

[Now that this court has established the test for determining "unconscionability" the case is remanded to the trial court to decide if this contract meets the test.]

Today, plaintiffs claiming unconscionability must prove two elements: procedural and substantive unconscionability:

Procedural unconscionability
One party uses its superior power to force a contract on the weaker party.

Substantive unconscionability
A contract with extremely one-sided and unfair terms

- **Procedural unconscionability** focuses on oppression or unfair surprise. Oppression exists when the stronger party forces an unfavorable contract on the weaker one, often by taking advantage of their lack of education. Unfair surprise means the weaker part did not fully understand the consequences of the agreement because the terms were hidden in the fine print.
- **Substantive unconscionability** refers to contract terms that are overly harsh or unfairly one-sided.

Paula desperately needed a job. When her prospective employer asked her to sign an employment contract, she did not hesitate. (After all, she thought, it would not bode well for her career if she haggled over the fine print.) The agreement contained an arbitration clause, which provided that Paula would give up her right to litigate in the event of breach. Although such clauses are generally favored as fair and efficient, this one contained a twist: If Paula wanted to arbitrate, she would have to pay $10,000 to bring a claim, a requirement that did not apply to her employer. This sneaky term made it difficult (if not impossible) for an employee to bring a claim, but easy for an employer to do so.[14] Courts have found that disparity in bargaining power, together with fine print and unequal terms, render a contract void for unconscionability.

Adhesion Contracts

Adhesion contracts
Standard form contracts prepared by one party and presented to the other on a "take it or leave it" basis

A related issue concerns **adhesion contracts**, which are standard form contracts prepared by one party and given to the other on a "take it or leave it" basis. We have all encountered them many times when purchasing goods or services. Adhesion contracts are generally enforced, but they are subject to greater scrutiny and unconscionability challenges.

The UCC: Unconscionability and Sales Law

With the creation of the Uniform Commercial Code (UCC), the law of unconscionability got a boost. The Code explicitly adopts unconscionability as a reason to reject a contract.[15] Although the Code directly applies only to the sale of goods, its unconscionability section has proven to be influential in other cases as well, and courts today are more receptive than they were 100 years ago to a contract defense of fundamental unfairness.

The drafters of the UCC reinforced the principle of unconscionability by including it in §2-302:

> If the court as a matter of law finds the contract or any clause of the contract to have been unconscionable at the time it was made the court may refuse to enforce the contract, or it may enforce the remainder of the contract without the unconscionable clause, or it may so limit the application of any unconscionable clause as to avoid any unconscionable result.

[14]See Sonic-Calabasas A Inc. v. Moreno, 57 Cal. 4th 1109 (S. Ct. Cal. 2013).
[15]UCC §2–302.

In Code cases, the issue of unconscionability often arises when a company attempts to limit the normal contract law remedies. Yet the Code itself allows such limitations, provided they are reasonable.

Section 2-719 provides in part:

> [A contract] may provide for remedies in addition to or in substitution for those provided [by the Code itself] *and may limit or alter the measure of damages recoverable* . . . as by limiting the buyer's remedies to return of the goods and repayment of the price. . . .

In other words, the Code includes two potentially competing sections: §2-719 permits a seller to insist that the buyer's only remedy for defective goods is return of the purchase price, but §2-302 says that *any unconscionable* provision is unenforceable. In lawsuits concerning defective goods, the seller often argues that the buyer's only remedies are those stated in the agreement, and the buyer responds that the contract limitation is unconscionable.

Electronic Data Systems (EDS) agreed to create complex software for Chubb Life America at a cost of $21 million. Chubb agreed to make staggered payments over many months as the work proceeded. The contract included a limitation on remedies, stating that if EDS became liable to Chubb, its maximum liability would be equal to two monthly payments.

EDS's work was woefully late and unusable, forcing Chubb to obtain its software elsewhere. Chubb sued, claiming $40 million in damages based on the money paid to EDS and additional funds spent purchasing alternative goods. EDS argued that the contract limited its liability to two monthly payments, a fraction of Chubb's damage. Chubb, of course, responded that the limitation was unconscionable.

The court noted that both parties were large, sophisticated corporations. As they negotiated the agreement, the companies both used experienced attorneys and independent consultants. This was no contract of adhesion presented to a meek consumer, but an allocation of risk resulting from hard bargaining. The court declared that the clause was valid, and EDS owed no more than two monthly payments.[16]

CHAPTER CONCLUSION

It is not enough to bargain effectively and obtain a contract that gives you exactly what you want. You must also be sure that the contract is legal. What appears to be an insurance contract might legally be an invalid wager. Unintentionally forgetting to obtain a state license to perform a certain job could mean you will never be paid for it. Bargaining a contract with a non-compete or exculpatory clause that is too one-sided may lead a court to ignore it. Legality is multifaceted, sometimes nuanced, and always important.

EXAM REVIEW

Illegal contracts are void and unenforceable. Illegality most often arises in these settings:

1. **WAGERING** A purely speculative contract—whether for gambling or insurance—is likely to be unenforceable.

[16]Colonial Life Insurance Co. v. Electronic Data Systems Corp., 817 F. Supp. 235 (D.N.H. 1993).

2. **LICENSING** When the licensing statute is designed to protect the public, a contract by an unlicensed plaintiff is generally unenforceable. When such a statute is designed merely to raise revenue, a contract by an unlicensed plaintiff is generally enforceable.

EXAMStrategy

Question: James Wagner agreed to build a house for Nancy Graham. Wagner was not licensed as a contractor, and Graham knew it. When the house was finished, Graham refused to pay the final $23,000, and Wagner sued. Who will prevail?

Strategy: A licensing statute designed to protect the public is strictly enforced, but that is not true for one intended only to raise revenue. What was the purpose of this statute? (See the "Result" at the end of this Exam Review section.)

3. **USURY** Excessive interest is generally unenforceable and may be fatal to the entire debt. Credit card debt is often exempt from usury laws.

EXAMStrategy

Question: McElroy owned 104 acres worth about $230,000. He got into financial difficulties and approached Grisham, asking to borrow $100,000. Grisham refused, but ultimately the two reached this agreement: McElroy would sell Grisham his property for $80,000, and the contract would include a clause allowing McElroy to repurchase the land within two years for $120,000. McElroy later claimed the contract was void. Is he right?

Strategy: Loans involving usury do not always include a clearly visible interest rate. You may have to do some simple math to see the interest being charged. McElroy wanted to borrow $100,000, but instead sold his property, with the right to repurchase. If he did repurchase, how much interest would he have effectively paid? (See the "Result" at the end of this Exam Review section.)

4. **NON-COMPETE: SALE OF BUSINESS** A non-compete clause in the sale of a business must be limited to a reasonable time, geographic area, and scope of activity.

EXAMStrategy

Question: The purchaser of a business insisted on putting this clause in the sales contract: The seller would not compete, for five years, "anywhere in the United States, the continent of North America, or anywhere else on Earth." What danger does that contract represent *to the purchaser?*

Strategy: This is a non-compete clause based on the sale of a business. Such clauses are valid if reasonable. Is this clause reasonable? If it is unreasonable, what might a court do? (See the "Result" at the end of this Exam Review section.)

5. **NON-COMPETE: EMPLOYMENT** In an employment contract, non-compete agreements are enforceable only if they are reasonably necessary for the protection of the employer, have a reasonable time limit, provide a reasonable geographical limit, are not harsh or oppressive, and are not contrary to public policy.

6. **EXCULPATORY CLAUSES** These clauses are generally void if the activity involved is in the public interest, the parties are greatly unequal in bargaining power, or the clause is unclear. In other cases, they are generally enforced.

7. **PROCEDURAL UNCONSCIONABILITY** Oppression and surprise may create an unconscionable bargain. An adhesion contract is especially suspect when it is imposed by a corporation on a consumer or small company. Under the UCC, a limitation of liability is less likely to be unconscionable when both parties are sophisticated corporations.

8. **SUBSTANTIVE UNCONSIONABILITY** When contract terms are unfairly one-sided at the time of contracting, the contract may be substantively unconscionable.

RESULTS

2. Result: This statute was designed to protect the public. Wagner was unlicensed and cannot enforce the contract. Graham wins.

3. Result: By selling at $80,000 and repurchasing at $120,000, McElroy would be paying $40,000 in interest on an $80,000 loan. The 50 percent rate is usurious. The court prohibited Graham from collecting the interest.

4. Result: "Anywhere else on Earth"? This is almost certainly unreasonable. It is hard to imagine a purchaser who would legitimately need such wide-ranging protection. In some states, a court might rewrite the clause, limiting the effect to the seller's state or some reasonable area. However, in other states, a court finding a clause unreasonable will declare it void in its entirety—enabling the seller to open a competing business next door.

MULTIPLE-CHOICE QUESTIONS

1. At a fraternity party, George mentions that he is going to learn to hang glide during spring break. Vicki, a casual friend, overhears him, and the next day she purchases a $100,000 life insurance policy on George's life. George has a happy week of hang gliding. But on the way home, he is bitten by a parrot and dies of a rare tropical illness. Vicki files a claim for $100,000. The insurance company refuses to pay.
   (a) Vicki will win $100,000, but only if she mentioned animal bites to the insurance agent.
   (b) Vicki will win $100,000 regardless of whether she mentioned animal bites to the insurance agent.
   (c) Vicki will win $50,000.
   (d) Vicki will win nothing.

2. Now assume that Vicki has loaned George $50,000. George again mentions that he is going to learn to hang glide during spring break, so Vicki purchases the $100,000 life insurance policy on George's life. If George dies and the insurance company refuses to pay . . .
   (a) Vicki will win $100,000, but only if she mentioned animal bites to the insurance agent.
   (b) Vicki will win $100,000 regardless of whether she mentioned animal bites to the insurance agent.
   (c) Vicki will win $50,000.
   (d) Vicki will win nothing.

3. KwikFix, a Fortune 500 company, contracts with Allied Rocket, another huge company, to provide the software for Allied's new Jupiter Probe rocket for $14 million. The software is negligently designed, and when the rocket blasts off from Cape Kennedy, it travels only as far as Fort Lauderdale before crashing to Earth. Allied Rocket sues for $200 million and proves that, as a result of the disaster, it lost a huge government contract, worth at least that much, which KwikFix was aware of. KwikFix responds that its contract with Allied included a clause limiting its liability to the value of the contract. Is the contract clause valid?
   (a) The clause is unenforceable because it is unconscionable.
   (b) The clause is unenforceable because it is exculpatory.
   (c) The clause is enforceable because both parties are sophisticated corporations.
   (d) The clause is enforceable because $200 million is an unconscionable claim.

4. Ricki goes to a baseball game. The back of her ticket clearly reads: "Fan agrees to hold team blameless for all injuries—pay attention to the game at all times for your own safety!" In the first inning, a foul ball hits Ricki in the elbow. She _______________ sue the team over the foul ball. Ricki spends the next several innings riding the opposing team's first baseman. The *nicest* thing she says to him is, "You suck, Franklin!" In the eighth inning, Franklin has had enough. He grabs the ballboy's chair and throws it into the stands, injuring Ricki's other elbow. Ricki _______________ sue the team over the thrown chair.
   (a) can; can
   (b) can; cannot
   (c) cannot; can
   (d) cannot; cannot

5. Jim, about to start a pickup soccer game, asks Desiree if she will hold his wallet while he plays. Desiree, a law student, says, "Sure, if you'll sign this exculpatory clause holding me blameless for negligence." Jim is very surprised, but he signs the paper that Desiree holds out for him. A bailment _______________ been created. If Desiree is careless and loses the wallet, she _______________ be liable to Jim.
   (a) has; will
   (b) has; will not
   (c) has not; will
   (d) has not; will not

CASE QUESTIONS

1. Guyan Machinery, a West Virginia manufacturing corporation, hired Albert Voorhees as a salesman and required him to sign a contract stating that if he left Guyan, he would not work for a competing corporation anywhere within 250 miles of West Virginia for a two-year period. Later, Voorhees left Guyan and began working at Polydeck Corp., another West Virginia manufacturer. The only product Polydeck made was urethane screens, which comprised half of 1 percent of Guyan's business. Is Guyan entitled to enforce its non-compete clause?

2. Barbara Richards leased an apartment at a complex owned by Twin Lakes. The lease declared that Twin Lakes would maintain the common areas, but it would not be responsible for any harm, anywhere on the property, even if it was caused by Twin Lakes' negligence. Richards slipped and fell on snow-covered ice in the Twin Lakes parking lot. What result?

3. The Basultos were Cuban immigrants who spoke only Spanish. When they purchased a new minivan from Potamkin Dodge, the dealer had them sign a blank, English-language contract with the promise that he would fill in the agreed-upon numbers later. But then the dealer completed the sales contract with numbers that were higher than those agreed upon. The couple tried to sue, only to realize that they had inadvertently signed away their rights because the contract contained, in tiny print, an arbitration clause. What remedy is available to the Basultos?

4. Cranwell Associates owned a 42-story skyscraper in midtown Manhattan. The building had a central station fire alarm system, which was monitored by Holmes Protection. A fire broke out and Holmes received the signal. But Holmes's inexperienced dispatcher misunderstood the signal and failed to summon the fire department for about nine minutes, permitting tremendous damage. Cranwell sued Holmes, which defended based on an exculpatory clause that relieved Holmes of any liability caused in any way. Holmes's dispatcher was negligent. Does it matter *how* negligent he was?

5. ***YOU BE THE JUDGE* WRITING PROBLEM** Oasis Waterpark, located in Palm Springs, California, sought out Hydrotech Systems, Inc., a New York corporation, to design and construct a surfing pool. Hydrotech replied that it could design the pool and sell all the necessary equipment to Oasis, but it could not build the pool because it was not licensed in California. Oasis insisted that Hydrotech do the construction work because Hydrotech had unique expertise in these pools. Oasis promised to arrange for a licensed California contractor to "work with" Hydrotech on the construction; Oasis also assured Hydrotech that it would pay the full contract price of $850,000, regardless of any licensing issues. Hydrotech designed and installed the pool as ordered. But Oasis failed to make the final payment of $110,000. Hydrotech sued. Can Hydrotech sue for either breach of contract or fraud (trickery)? **Argument for Oasis:** The licensing law protects the public from incompetence and dishonesty. The legislature made

the section strict: no license, no payment. If the court were to start picking and choosing which unlicensed contractors could win a suit, it would be inviting incompetent workers to endanger the public and then come into court and try their luck. That is precisely the danger the legislature seeks to avoid. **Argument for Hydrotech:** This is not the kind of case the legislature was worried about. Hydrotech has never solicited work in California. Hydrotech went out of its way to avoid doing any contracting work, informing Oasis that it was unlicensed in the state. Oasis insisted on bringing Hydrotech into the state to do work. If Oasis has its way, word will go out that any owner can get free work done by hiring an *unlicensed* builder. Make any promises you want, get the work done to your satisfaction, and then stiff the contractor—you'll never have to pay.

DISCUSSION QUESTIONS

1. **ETHICS** Richard and Michelle Kommit traveled to New Jersey to have fun in the casinos. While in Atlantic City, they used their MasterCard to withdraw cash from an ATM conveniently located in the "pit"—the gambling area of a casino. They ran up debts of $5,500 on the credit card and did not pay. The Connecticut National Bank sued for the money. Law aside, who has the moral high ground? Is it acceptable for the casino to offer ATM services in the gambling pit? If a credit card company allows customers to withdraw cash in a casino, is it encouraging them to lose money? Do the Kommits have any ethical right to use the ATM, attempt to win money by gambling, and then seek to avoid liability?

2. The Justice Department shut down three of the most popular online poker websites (Poker Stars, Absolute Poker, and Full Tilt Poker). State agencies take countless actions each year to stop illegal gaming operations. Do you believe that gambling by adults *should* be regulated? If so, which types? Rate the following types of gambling from most acceptable to least acceptable:

   - online poker
   - state lotteries
   - horse racing
   - casino gambling
   - bets on pro sports
   - bets on college sports

3. Van hires Terri to add an electrical outlet to his living room for his new HDTV. Terri does an excellent job, and the new outlet works perfectly. She presents Van with a bill for $200. But Terri is not a licensed electrician. Her state sets licensing standards in the profession to protect the public. And so, Van can refuse to pay Terri's bill. Is this reasonable? *Should* he be able to avoid payment?

4. Imagine that you are starting your own company in your hyper-competitive industry: You are putting your life savings, your professional contacts, and your innovative ideas on the line. As you begin to hire a sales force, you consider binding new employees to non-compete agreements. Outline the ideal terms of your employees' non-competes. What is its duration? What is its geographical radius? Are these terms appropriate for your industry? When you are done, pass your proposed terms to classmates and discuss its enforceability.

5. When Ruth Klopp was injured in a serious accident with an uninsured motorist, she filed a claim under her own policy with Worldwide Insurance. Her policy contained an arbitration provision, stating that if the arbitrators awarded more than $15,000, either side could appeal to the courts, but a low award could not be appealed. The arbitrators awarded Klopp $90,000, and Worldwide demanded a full trial. Klopp claimed that the appeal provision was unconscionable. What was the result?

6. **ETHICS** Some commentators argue that Walker-Thomas Furniture was providing a valuable service to Mrs. Williams and that the litigation ultimately harmed her community. No other business of the time was willing to offer credit to people of such limited means, much less to African-Americans. As a result of that landmark case, Walker-Thomas went out of business and an entire group of people lost access to essential household items. Comment.

15 CHAPTER

VOIDABLE CONTRACTS: CAPACITY AND CONSENT

For 40 years, she lived alone, malnourished, and dehydrated amidst her opulence and her dolls, whom she considered her closest friends.

As the sole heiress to a copper fortune, Mrs. Clark knew unimaginable luxury—a palatial 42-room home on Fifth Avenue and a vast collection of rare art, antiques, and expensive dolls with custom clothes by the House of Dior. But Mrs. Clark was also a recluse: For 40 years, she lived alone, malnourished, and dehydrated amidst her opulence and her dolls, whom she considered her closest friends.

At 85, she was admitted to Beth Israel Medical Center for routine surgery. And there she stayed for 20 years, despite being in reasonably good health. She passed her days watching *The Smurfs* cartoons and tending to her dolls. Finally, she died at the hospital, aged 105.

After her death, peculiar tales surfaced. Over the years, she had given her doctor over $900,000. The hospital aggressively courted her for money. Memos from the hospital's president revealed that he was only too happy to house his wealthy (but healthy) tenant. Ultimately, in addition to the $1,200 per day charged for her stay, Mrs. Clark gave a prized Manet painting and many millions of dollars to Beth Israel.[1]

[1]Bill Dedman, *Empty Mansions* (Ballantine Books, 2013); Anemona Hartocollis, "Hospital Caring for an Heiress Pressed Her to Give Lavishly," *The New York Times*, May 29, 2013.

Clark's estate sued Beth Israel and her doctor, claiming they took advantage of the heiress to extract lavish gifts. Although this case is still pending as of this writing, this true story leads us to examine two issues that interfere with valid contract formation: capacity and consent.

Capacity means the legal ability of a party to enter a contract in the first place. Someone may lack capacity because of youth or mental infirmity. **Consent** refers to whether a contracting party truly understood the terms of the contract and whether she made the agreement voluntarily. Consent issues arise in cases of fraud, mistake, duress, and undue influence.

Problems with capacity and consent make a contract **voidable**. When a contract is voidable, one party has the option either to enforce or terminate the agreement. If her estate can prove that Clark did not understand her promises or was defrauded, mistaken, or coerced, it can terminate the contracts.

Voidable contract
When a contract is voidable, the injured party may choose to terminate it.

15-1 CAPACITY

CONTRACTS CHECKLIST

- ☐ Offer
- ☐ Acceptance
- ☐ Consideration
- ☐ Legality
- ☑ Capacity
- ☐ Consent
- ☐ Writing

Capacity is the legal ability to enter into a contract. An adult of sound mind has capacity. Generally, any deal she enters into will be enforced if all elements on the Contracts Checklist—agreement, consideration, and so forth—are present. But two groups of people usually lack legal capacity: minors and those with a mental impairment.

15-1a Minors

In contract law, a minor is someone under the age of 18. **Because a minor lacks legal capacity, she normally can create only a voidable contract**. A voidable contract may be canceled by the party who lacks capacity. Notice that *only the party lacking capacity* may cancel the agreement. So a minor who enters into a contract generally may choose between enforcing the agreement or negating it. The other party—an adult, or perhaps a store—has no such right. Voidable contracts are very different from those that are void, which we examined in Chapter 14 on legality. A *void* contract is illegal from the beginning and may not be enforced by either party. A *voidable* contract is legal but permits one party to escape, if she so wishes.

Disaffirmance

A minor who wishes to escape from a contract generally may **disaffirm** it; that is, he may notify the other party that he refuses to be bound by the agreement. There are several ways a minor may disaffirm a contract. He may simply tell the other party, orally or in writing, that he will not honor the deal. Or he may disaffirm a contract by refusing to perform his obligations under it. A minor may go further—he can undo a contract that has already been completed by filing a suit to **rescind** the contract; that is, to have a court formally cancel it.

Disaffirm
To give notice of refusal to be bound by an agreement

Rescind
To cancel a contract

Kevin Green was 16 when he signed a contract with Star Chevrolet to buy a used Camaro. Because he was a minor, the deal was voidable. When the Camaro blew a gasket and Kevin informed Star Chevrolet that he wanted his money back, he was disaffirming the contract. He happened to do it because the car suddenly seemed a poor buy, but he could have disaffirmed for any reason at all, such as deciding that he no longer liked Camaros. When Kevin disaffirmed the contract, he was entitled to his money back.

Restitution

A minor who disaffirms a contract must return the consideration he has received, to the extent he is able. Restoring the other party to its original position is called **restitution**. The consideration that Kevin Green received in the contract was, of course, the Camaro.

Restitution
Restoring an injured party to its original position

What happens if the minor is not able to return the consideration because he no longer has it or it has been destroyed? Most states hold that the minor is *still* entitled to his money back. A minority of states follow the status quo rule, which provides that, if a minor cannot return the consideration, the adult or store is only required to return its *profit margin* to the minor.

Assume that Kevin's Camaro was totaled, not just in need of repair. He had originally bought the Camaro for $7,000. Star Chevrolet had paid $5,000 for the used car at auction and then marked it up $2,000.

In most states, Kevin would be entitled to the full $7,000 purchase price, even though the car is now worthless. The dealer would simply have to absorb the loss. But, if Kevin lives in a state with the status quo rule, then the dealer would have to refund only $2,000 to Kevin. It is permitted to keep the other $5,000 so that it breaks even on the transaction, or is "returned to the status quo."

Ethics

The rule permitting a minor to disaffirm a contract is designed to discourage adults from making deals with innocent children, and it is centuries old. Is this rule still workable in our modern consumer society? There are entire industries devoted to (and dependent upon) minors. Think of children's films, breakfast cereal, and gaming apps. Does this rule imperil retailers? Is it *right* to give a 17-year-old high school senior so much power to cancel agreements? Is it *right* for a 17-year-old high school senior to take advantage of this rule?

Timing of Disaffirmance/Ratification

A minor may disaffirm a contract any time before she reaches age 18. She also may disaffirm within a reasonable time *after* turning 18. Suppose that 17-year-old Bret signs a contract to buy a $3,000 3-D television. The following week, he picks up the television and pays for it in full. Four months later, he turns 18, and two months after that—after his Super Bowl party—he disaffirms the contract. His disaffirmance is effective. In most states, he gets 100 percent of his money back. In some cases, minors have been entitled to disaffirm a contract several *years* after turning 18. But the minor's right to disaffirm ends if he ratifies the contract.

Ratification
Words or actions indicating an intention to be bound by a contract

Ratification is made by any words or action indicating an intention to be bound by the contract. Suppose Bret, age 17, buys his television on credit, promising to pay $150 per month. He has made only four payments by the time he turns 18, but after reaching his majority, he continues to pay every month for six more months. He then attempts to disaffirm the contract. Too late. His actions—payment of the monthly bill for six months as an adult—ratified the contract he entered into as a minor. He is now fully obligated to pay the entire $3,000, on the agreed-upon schedule. Hope the party was worth it.

Exception: Necessaries

A necessary is something essential to a minor's life and welfare. Food, clothing, housing, and medical care are necessaries. In some circumstances, courts have considered less essential items, like legal advice, automobiles, and tuition, to be necessaries.

In some circumstances, courts have considered less essential items, like legal advice, automobiles, and tuition, to be necessaries.

On a contract for necessaries, a minor must pay for the value of the benefit received. In other words, the minor may still disaffirm the contract and return whatever is unused. But he is liable to pay for whatever benefit he obtained from the goods while he had them. Thus, the 16-year-old who buys and eats a 99-cent cheeseburger and later disaffirms his contract with Burger Central is only liable for what the burger is *reasonably* worth, which is less than the 99-cent purchase price. (And, no, he does not have to return the burger.)

Exception: Misrepresentation of Age

The rules change somewhat if a minor lies about his age. Sixteen-year-old Dan is delighted to learn from his friend Bret that a minor can buy a fancy television, use it for a year or so, and then get his money back. Dan drops into SoundBlast and asks to buy a $4,000 surround-sound system. The store clerk says that the store no longer sells expensive systems to underage customers. Dan produces a fake driver's license indicating that he is 18, and the gullible clerk sells him the system. A year later, Dan drives up to SoundBlast and unloads the system, now in shambles. He asks for his $4,000 back. Is he still permitted to disaffirm?

States have been troubled by this problem, and there is no clear rule. A few states will still permit Dan to disaffirm the contract entirely. The theory is that a minor must be saved from his own poor judgment, including his foolish lie. Many states, though, will prohibit Dan from disaffirming the contract. They take the reasonable position that the law was intended to protect childhood innocence, not calculated deceit.

15-1b Mentally Impaired Persons

You are a trial court judge. Don wants you to rule that his father, Cedric, is mentally incompetent and, on behalf of Cedric, to terminate a contract he signed. Here is the evidence:

Cedric is a 75-year-old millionaire who keeps $300,000 stuffed in pillow cases in the attic. He lives in a filthy house with a parrot whom he calls the Bishop, an iguana named Orlando, and a tortoise known as Mrs. Sedgely. All of the pets have small beds in Cedric's grungy bedroom, and each one eats at the dining table with its master. Cedric pays college students $50 an hour to read poetry to the animals, but he forbids the reading of sonnets, which he regards as "the devil's handiwork."

Don has been worried about Cedric's bizarre behavior for several years and has urged his father to enter a nursing home. Last week, when Don stopped in to visit, Cedric became angry at him, accusing his son of disrespecting the Bishop and Mrs. Sedgely, who were enjoying a fifteenth-century Castilian poem that Jane, a college student, was reading. Don then blurted out that Cedric was no longer able to take care of himself. Cedric snapped back, "I'll show you how capable I am." On the back of a 40-year-old menu, he scratched out a contract promising to give Jane "$100,000 today and $200,000 one year from today if she agrees to feed, house, and care for the Bishop, Orlando, and Mrs. Sedgely for the rest of their long lives." Jane *quickly* signed the agreement. Don urges that the court, on Cedric's behalf, declare the contract void. How will you rule? Courts often struggle when deciding cases of mental competence.

A person suffers from a mental impairment if, by reason of mental illness or defect, he is unable to understand the nature and consequences of the transaction.[2] The mental impairment can be due to some mental illness, such as schizophrenia, or to mental retardation, brain injury, senility, or any other cause that renders the person unable to understand the nature and consequences of the contract.

A party suffering a mental impairment usually creates only a voidable contract. The impaired person has the right to disaffirm the contract just as a minor does. But again, the contract is voidable, not void. The mentally impaired party generally has the right to full performance if she wishes.

The law creates an exception: If a person has been adjudicated incompetent, then all of his future agreements are void. "Adjudicated incompetent" means that a judge has made a formal finding that a person is mentally incompetent and has assigned the person a guardian by court order.

---

[2]For a similar case, see Harwell v. Garrett, 239 Ark. 551 (1965).

How will a court evaluate Cedric's mental status? Of course, if there had already been a judicial determination that he was insane, any contract he signed would be void. Since no judge has issued such a ruling about Cedric, the court will listen to doctors or therapists who have evaluated him and to anyone else who can testify about Cedric's recent conduct. The court may also choose to look at the contract itself, to see if it is so lopsided that no competent person would agree to it.

How will Don fare in seeking to preserve Cedric's wealth? Poorly. Unless Don has more evidence than we have heard thus far, he is destined to eat canned tuna while Jane and the Bishop dine on caviar. Cedric is decidedly eccentric, and perhaps unwise. But those characteristics do not prove mental impairment. Neither does leaving a fortune to a poetry reader. If Don could produce evidence from a psychiatrist that Cedric, for example, was generally delusional or could not distinguish a parrot from a religious leader, that would persuade a court of mental impairment. But on the evidence presented thus far, Mrs. Sedgely and friends will be living well.[3]

Intoxication

Similar rules apply in cases of drug or alcohol intoxication. **When one party is so intoxicated that he cannot understand the nature and consequences of the transaction, the contract is voidable.**

We wish to stress that courts are *highly* skeptical of intoxication arguments. If you go out drinking and make a foolish agreement, you are probably stuck with it. Even if you are too drunk to drive, you are probably not nearly too drunk to make a contract. If your blood alcohol level is, say, 0.08, your coordination and judgment are poor. Driving in such a condition is dangerous, but you probably have a fairly clear awareness of what is going on around you.

To back out of a contract on the grounds of intoxication, you must be able to provide evidence that you did not understand the "nature of the agreement," or the basic deal that you made.

The following Landmark Case is a rare exception, where the defendant was able to escape the deal.

Landmark Case

Babcock v. Engel

58 Mont. 597
Montana Supreme Court, 1920

Facts: While Charles Engel's wife was out of town, he sat home alone, drinking mightily. During this period, he made an agreement with G. M. Babcock to trade a 320-acre farm and $2,000 worth of personal property for a hotel. Engel's property was worth approximately twice the value of the hotel. Engel later refused to honor the deal on the grounds that he had been intoxicated when he made the agreement. Babcock sued, but the jury sided with Engel and dismissed the complaint. Babcock appealed.

Issue: ***Was Engel so intoxicated that his agreement with Babcock became voidable?***

Excerpts from Justice Holloway's Decision: If, as a matter of fact, Engel was so far under the influence of intoxicating liquor when he signed the contract that he

[3]Barbara's Sales, Inc. v. Intel Corp., 879 N.E.2d 910 (Ill. 2007).

was incapable of giving his assent, it would be voidable at the election of Engel when he became sober.

[T]he jury answered that on November 22, Engel was "so under the influence of intoxicating liquors as to deprive him of his powers of reasoning and render him unable to comprehend the consequences of his act in executing said agreement."

Engel himself testified to the effect that, availing himself of his wife's absence from home, he had been indulging greatly to excess and had been drunk on November 21; that he drank heavily of whisky which he had at his home on the morning of November 22; that immediately upon his arrival in the town, he had four or five drinks of whisky and blackberry before he entered upon the negotiations with Babcock.

Four other witnesses, each apparently disinterested, testified that at the time in question, Engel was intoxicated, could not comprehend the nature of his acts, in other words, that he was not qualified to transact business. The jury determined upon the credibility of the witnesses.

Intoxication is not made a defense by the Codes, and there was a time in the history of our jurisprudence when courts refused to lend their aid to relieve one from the consequences of his own voluntary intemperance, but the doctrine has long since been abandoned. The courts do not now concern themselves so much with the question of intoxication as with the question of contractual capacity, and if in fact either party is not mentally capable of giving his free consent to the terms disclosed by the writing, it is altogether immaterial by what cause his incapacity was produced. The courts have simply recognized the fact that intoxication, among other things, may render a person incapable of making a binding contract.

The test approved by the great majority of the decisions is the same which is applied in other forms of mental derangement, namely, that the deed or contract will be voidable if the person, at the time of its execution, was so far under the influence of intoxicants as to be unable to understand the nature and consequences of his act, and unable to bring to bear upon the business in hand any degree of intelligent choice and purpose.

Affirmed.

Restitution

A mentally infirm party who seeks to void a contract must make restitution. If a party succeeds with a claim of mental impairment, the court will normally void the contract but will require the impaired party to give back whatever she got. Suppose that Danielle buys a Rolls-Royce and promises in writing to pay $5,000 per month for five years. Three weeks later, she seeks to void the contract on the grounds of mental impairment. She must return the Rolls. If the car has depreciated, Danielle normally will have to pay for the decrease in value. What happens if restitution is impossible? Generally, courts require a mentally infirm person to make full restitution if the contract is to be rescinded. If restitution is impossible, the court will not rescind the agreement unless the infirm party can show bad faith by the other party. This is because, unlike minority, which is generally easy to establish, mental competence may not be apparent to the other person negotiating.

15-2 REALITY OF CONSENT

Smiley offers to sell you his house for $300,000, and you agree in writing to buy it. After you move in, you discover that the house is sinking into the earth at the rate of 6 inches per week. In 12 months, your only access to the house may be through the chimney. You sue, seeking to rescind. You argue that when you signed the contract, you did not truly consent because you lacked essential information. In this section, we look at four claims that parties make in an effort to rescind a contract based on lack of valid consent: (1) fraud, (2) mistake, (3) duress, and (4) undue influence.

CONTRACTS CHECKLIST

- ☐ Offer
- ☐ Acceptance
- ☐ Consideration
- ☐ Legality
- ☐ Capacity
- ☑ Consent
- ☐ Writing

15-2a Fraud

Fraud begins when a party to a contract represents something that is factually wrong. "This house has no termites," says a homeowner to a prospective buyer. If the house is swarming with the nasty pests, the statement is a misrepresentation. But does it amount to fraud? An injured person must show the following:

1. The defendant knew that his statement was false, or that he made the statement recklessly and without knowledge of whether it was false;
2. The false statement was material; and
3. The injured party justifiably relied on the statement.

Element One: Intentional or Reckless Misrepresentation of Fact

The injured party must show a false statement of fact. Notice that this does not mean the statement was necessarily a "lie." If a homeowner says that the famous architect Stanford White designed her house, but Bozo Loco actually did the work, it is a false statement.

Now, if the owner knows that Loco designed the house, she has committed the first element of fraud. If she has no idea who designed the house, her assertion that it was "Stanford White" also meets the first element.

But the owner might have a good reason for the error. Perhaps a local history book identifies the house as a Stanford White. If she makes the statement with a reasonable belief that she is telling the truth, she has made an innocent misrepresentation (discussed in the next section) and not fraud.

Opinions and "puffery" do not amount to fraud. An opinion is not a statement of fact. A seller says, "I think land values around here will be going up 20 or 30 percent for the foreseeable future." That statement is pretty enticing to a buyer, but it is not a false statement of fact. The maker is clearly stating her own opinion, and the buyer who relies on it does so at his peril. A close relative of opinion is something called "puffery."

Get ready for one of the most astonishing experiences you've ever had! This section on puffery is going to be the finest section of any textbook you have ever read! You're going to find the issue intriguing, the writing dazzling, and the legal summary unforgettable!

"But what happens," you might wonder, "if this section fails to astonish? What if I find the issue dull, the writing mediocre, and the legal summary incomprehensible? Can I sue for fraud?" No. The promises we made were mere puffery. A statement is puffery when a reasonable person would realize that it is a sales pitch, representing the exaggerated opinion of the seller. Puffery is not a statement of fact. Because puffery is not factual, it is never a basis for rescission.

Consumers filed a class action against Intel Corporation claiming fraud. They asserted that Intel advertised its Pentium 4 computer chip as the "best" in the market when in fact it was no faster than the Pentium III chip. The Illinois Supreme Court dismissed the claims, asserting that no reasonable consumer would make a purchase relying solely on the name Pentium 4. Even if the consumers could show that Intel plotted to persuade the market that the Pentium 4 was the finest processor, they are demonstrating nothing but puffery because "best" could mean the chip is anything from the cheapest to the newest compared to other processors.[4]

Courts have found many similar phrases to be puffery, including "high-quality," "expert workmanship," and "you're in good hands with us."

Element Two: Materiality

The injured party must demonstrate that the statement was material, or important. A minor misstatement does not meet this second element of fraud. Was the misstatement likely to influence the decision of the misled party significantly? If so, it was material.

[4]Laidlaw v. Organ, 15 U.S. 178 (1817).

Imagine a farmer selling a piece of his land. He measures the acres himself and calculates a total of 200 acres. If the actual acreage is 199, he has almost certainly not made a *material* misstatement. But if the actual acreage is 150, he has.

Element Three: Justifiable Reliance

The injured party also must show that she actually did rely on the false statement and that her reliance was reasonable. Suppose the seller of a gas station lies through his teeth about the structural soundness of the building. The buyer believes what he hears but does not much care because he plans to demolish the building and construct a day-care center. There was a material misstatement but no reliance, and the buyer may not rescind.

The reliance must be justifiable—that is, reasonable. If the seller of wilderness land tells Lewis that the area is untouched by pollution, but Lewis can see a large lake on the property covered with 6 inches of oily red scum, Lewis is not justified in relying on the seller's statements. If he goes forward with the purchase, he may not rescind.

No Duty to Investigate. In the previous example, Lewis must act reasonably and keep his eyes open if he walks around the "wilderness" property. But he has no duty to undertake an investigation of what he is told. In other words, if the seller states that the countryside is pure and the lake looks crystal clear, Lewis is not obligated to take water samples and have them tested by a laboratory. A party to a contract has no obligation to investigate the other party's factual statements.

Plaintiff's Remedies for Fraud

In the case of fraud, the injured party generally has a choice of rescinding the contract or suing for damages or, in some cases, doing both. The contract is voidable, which means that injured party is not *forced* to rescind the deal but may if he wants. Fraud *permits* the injured party to cancel. Alternatively, the injured party can sue for damages—the difference between what the contract promised and what it delivered.

Nancy learns that the building she bought has a terrible heating system. A new one will cost $12,000. If the seller told her the system was "like new," Nancy may rescind the deal, but it may be economically harmful for her to do so. She might have sold her old house, hired a mover, taken a new job, and so forth. What are her other remedies? She could move into the new house and sue for the difference between what she got and what was promised, which is $12,000, the cost of replacing the heating system.

In some states, a party injured by fraud may both rescind *and* sue for damages. In these states, Nancy could rescind her contract, get her deposit back, and then sue the seller for any damages she has suffered. Her damages might be, for example, a lost opportunity to buy another house or wasted moving expenses.

In fact, this last option—rescinding and still suing for damages—is available in all states when a contract is for the sale of goods. **UCC §2–721 permits a party to rescind a contract and then sue for damages when fraud is committed.**

Innocent Misrepresentation

If all elements of fraud are present except the misrepresentation of fact was not made intentionally or recklessly, then **innocent misrepresentation** has occurred. So, if a person misstates a material fact and induces reliance, but he had good reason to believe that his statement was true, then he has not committed fraud. Most states allow rescission of a contract, but not damages, in such a case.

Special Problem: Silence

We know that a party negotiating a contract may not misrepresent a material fact. The house seller may not say that "the roof is in great shape" when she sleeps under an umbrella to avoid rain. But what about silence? Suppose that the seller knows the roof is in dreadful condition but the buyer never asks. Does the seller have an affirmative legal obligation to disclose what she knows?

In 1817, the U.S. Supreme Court laid down the general rule that a party had no duty to disclose, even when he knew that the other person was negotiating under a mistake.[5] In other words, the Court was reinforcing the old rule of *caveat emptor,* "let the buyer beware." But social attitudes about fairness have changed. Today, a seller who knows something that the buyer does not know is often required to divulge it.

Nondisclosure of a fact amounts to misrepresentation in these four cases: (1) where disclosure is necessary to *correct a previous assertion*, (2) where disclosure would correct a *basic mistaken assumption* that the other party is relying on, (3) where disclosure would correct the other party's *mistaken understanding about a writing,* or (4) where there is *a relationship of trust* between the two parties.

To Correct a Previous Assertion. During the course of negotiations, one party's perception of the facts may change. When an earlier statement later appears inaccurate, the change generally must be reported.

W. R. Grace & Co. wanted to buy a natural-gas field in Mississippi. An engineer's report indicated the presence of large gas reserves. On the basis of the engineering report, the Continental Illinois National Bank committed to a $75 million nonrecourse production loan. A "nonrecourse loan" meant that Continental would be repaid only with revenues from the gas field. After Continental committed, but before it had closed on the loan, Grace had an exploratory well drilled and struck it rich—with water. The land would never produce any gas. Without informing Continental of the news, Grace closed the $75 million loan. When Grace failed to repay, Continental sued and won. A party who learns new information indicating that a previous statement is inaccurate must disclose the bad news.[6]

Galina Barskaya/Shutterstock.com

What if the defect is . . . a ghost?

To Correct a Basic Mistaken Assumption. When one party knows that the other is negotiating with a mistaken assumption about an important fact, the party who knows of the error must correct it. Jeffrey Stambovsky agreed to buy Helen Ackley's house in Nyack, New York, for $650,000. Stambovsky signed a contract and made a $32,500 down payment. Before completing the deal, he learned that in several newspaper articles, Ackley had publicized the house as being haunted. Ackley had also permitted the house to be featured in a walking tour of the neighborhood as "a riverfront Victorian (*with ghost*)." Stambovsky refused to go through with the deal and sued to rescind. He won. The court ruled that Ackley sold the house knowing Stambovsky was ignorant of the alleged ghosts. She also knew that a reasonable buyer might avoid a haunted house, fearing grisly events—or diminished resale value. Stambovsky could not have discovered the apparitions himself, and Ackley's failure to warn permitted him to rescind the deal.[7]

A seller generally must report any latent defect he knows about that the buyer should not be expected to discover himself. As social awareness of the environment increases, a buyer potentially worries about more and more problems. We now know that underground toxic waste, carelessly dumped in earlier decades, can be dangerous or even lethal. Accordingly, any property seller who realizes that there is toxic waste underground, or any other hidden hazard, must reveal that fact.

---

5 Restatement (Second) of Contracts §161.

6 FDIC v. W. R. Grace & Co., 877 F.2d 614 (7th Cir. 1989).

7 Stambovsky v. Ackley, 169 A.D.2d 254 (N.Y. App. Div. 1991).

To Correct a Mistaken Understanding about a Writing. Suppose the potential buyer of a vacation property has a town map showing that the land he wants to buy has a legal right of way to a beautiful lake. If the seller of the land knows that the town map is out of date and that there is no such right of way, she must disclose her information.

A Relationship of Trust. Maria is planning to sell her restaurant to her brother Ricardo. Maria has a greater duty to reveal problems in the business because Ricardo assumes she will be honest. **When one party naturally expects openness and honesty, based on a close relationship, the other party must act accordingly.** If the building's owner has told Maria he will not renew her lease, she must pass that information on to Ricardo.

What happens if an owner, rather than disclosing hidden defects, sells the property "as is"? The following case provides insight.

Hess v. Chase Manhattan Bank, USA, N.A.

220 S.W.3d 758
Supreme Court of Missouri, 2007

Facts: Billy Stevens owned a paint company. On several occasions, he ordered employees to load a trailer with 55-gallon paint drums and pallets of old paint cans and then dump them on property he owned. This illegal dumping saved Stevens the cost of proper disposal. Later, employees notified the Environmental Protection Agency (EPA) of what Stevens had done, and the EPA began an investigation. (Stevens later served time for environmental crimes.)

Stevens defaulted on his mortgage to the land. While Chase Manhattan Bank was in the process of foreclosing, it learned that the EPA was investigating the property for contamination. Chase foreclosed and put the property up for sale "as is." Several buyers expressed interest. The bank did not inform any of them of the ongoing EPA investigation. Dennis Hess bought the property for $52,000.

After Hess bought the land, he discovered the illegal waste and sued Chase for failing to disclose the EPA's investigation. The jury awarded Hess $52,000 and Chase appealed.

Issue: ***Did Chase have a duty to disclose to Hess the ongoing investigation?***

Excerpts from Judge Stith's Decision: The buyer has a right to rely on the seller to disclose where the undisclosed material information would not be discoverable through ordinary diligence. Chase learned that the EPA was investigating the property before Chase completed its foreclosure of the mortgage. Even with superior knowledge, a duty to disclose will be imposed only if the material facts would not be discovered through the exercise of ordinary diligence. Chase asserts that a reasonable inspection of the property by Hess would have disclosed the presence of the paint cans near the old barn foundation. Chase's argument misapprehends the factual basis of Hess's fraudulent nondisclosure claim. It is the *EPA investigation* into hazardous waste dumping on the property that is the material fact that Hess asserts Chase had a duty to disclose, not the presence (or absence) of paint cans.

Hess presented evidence that two potential buyers who did discover the paint cans each still made an offer to purchase the property. Both testified that the presence of paint cans did not give them notice that the EPA was investigating and that, had they known of its investigation, they would not have made offers for the property. From this evidence, the jury could have found that even had Hess further inspected the property and discovered the paint cans, this would not have put him on notice that the EPA had an ongoing investigation into hazardous waste dumping on the property.

Chase asserts that in spite of the evidence of its knowledge and Hess's inability to discover the EPA investigation, a duty to disclose should not be imposed because the contract specified that Chase was making "no representations, guaranties, or warranties, either written or implied, regarding the property" and that "the property is being sold in AS-IS condition with no express or implied representations or warranties by the seller or its agents." It claims that through these provisions, it bargained for the right to remain silent and no duty to speak ever arose.

What Chase misapprehends is that Hess alleges *fraud in the inducement* to contract, not fraud in the terms of the contract. Missouri law holds that a party may not, by disclaimer or otherwise, contractually exclude liability for fraud in inducing that contract. Each of the individuals who made an offer to purchase this property did so without knowledge that it was under EPA investigation. They all testified that, had they known, they would not have made an offer to purchase this property and would not, therefore, have "bargained for" Chase's silence. Chase's duty to speak arose from its superior knowledge prior to the execution of this contract. The presence of a clause disclaiming warranties in a contract does not negate a pre-contractual duty to speak.

Affirmed.

EXAMStrategy

Question: Mako is selling his country house for $400,000. Guppy, an interested buyer, asks whether there is sufficient water from the property's well. Mako replies, "Are you kidding? Watch this." He turns on the tap, and the water flows bountifully. Mako then shows Guppy the well, which is full. Guppy buys the property, but two weeks later, the well runs dry. In fact, Mako knew the water supply was inadequate, and he had the well filled by a tanker truck while the property was being sold. A hydrologist tells Guppy it will cost $100,000 to dig a better well, with no guarantee of success. Guppy sues Mako. What remedy should Guppy seek? Who will win?

Strategy: Is this a case of innocent misrepresentation or fraud? Fraud. Therefore, Guppy may seek two remedies: damages or rescission. Make sure that you understand the difference. To win, Guppy must show he relied on a fact that was both false and material.

Result: When Mako responded to Guppy's question by demonstrating the apparent abundance of water, he made a false statement. This was fraud (not innocent misrepresentation), because Mako knew the well was inadequate. That was a material fact. Guppy reasonably relied on the demonstration. Guppy will win. He can elect to rescind the contract (return the property to Mako and get his money back) or choose damages (the cost of digging a proper well). Given the uncertain nature of well digging, he would be wise to rescind.

15-2b Mistake

When she heard she was going to lose her job, Laura became very upset, so of course, she went shopping. She bought a pair of $1,345 orange stiletto heels, on final sale for $941.50. The shoes consoled Laura for about two hours, after which she realized she had made a big mistake: She could neither return the impractical shoes nor pay her credit card bill. Despite Laura's retail regret, contract law will not fix her mistake. Nor does it excuse her when she signs a contract without reading it. Generally, contract law forces parties to suffer the consequences of their folly. But in some cases, such as when one party seeks to profit unreasonably from another's error, rescission may be warranted on the grounds of mistake.

Not all mistakes are created equal: Some mistakes lead to voidable contracts; others create enforceable (if unfortunate) deals. How can we know the difference? First, we must ask who was mistaken because different rules apply to unilateral and mutual mistakes. We must also examine the character of the mistake to see if its circumstances warrant rescission.

Unilateral Mistake

Unilateral mistake
Occurs when only one party enters a contract under a mistaken assumption

A **unilateral mistake** occurs when one party enters a contract under a mistaken assumption; the other is not mistaken. It is not easy for the mistaken party to rescind a contract—the more astute party may simply have made a better bargain. So, to rescind a contract, a mistaken party must show something more than just a regrettable deal.

To rescind for unilateral mistake, the mistaken party must demonstrate that he entered the contract because of a basic factual error and that:

- **The nonmistaken party knew or had reason to know of the error, or**
- **The mistake is mathematical or mechanical alone, or**
- **Enforcing the contract would be unconscionable.**

Knowledge of the Error. Every market has information asymmetries. That is, some contracting parties know more than others, which helps them secure favorable deals. The law of unilateral mistake draws the line where one party takes *unfair* advantage of what he knows to be another's error. **If the nonmistaken party knows or has reason to know of the other party's error, courts will not allow him to profit by snapping it up.**

Fernando is an art dealer who specializes in nineteenth-century French painting. At Fiona's flea market stall, he sees a painting that he suspects is by Gustave Courbet. Knowing the painting could be worth millions, Fernando offers Fiona $10 for it. She accepts his offer because she thinks the painting is, at best, by one of Courbet's students. Fernando then does further research, which confirms his guess. He ultimately auctions the masterpiece for $2.4 million. For Fiona to be able to rescind the contract, she must show that Fernando's hunch was much more than a lucky guess, that he had known certainly that the painting was by Courbet. Practically speaking, cases like these are difficult for plaintiffs to win because they must prove that the nonmistaken party knew and that the parties had not assumed the risk of the error.

Mathematical and Mechanical Errors. Two plus two is four; but what happens when it is accidentally forty? Whether the mistake is due to bad math or a typographical error, courts generally allow the nonmistaken party to undo the faulty agreement, if there is clear and convincing evidence that the term was a mistake. A town obtains five bids for construction of a new municipal swimming pool. Four are between $100,000 and $111,000. Fred's bid is for $82,000. His offer includes a figure of $2,000 for excavation work, while all the others have allotted about $20,000 for that work. It is obvious that Fred has inadvertently dropped a zero, resulting in a bid that is $18,000 too low. Town officials are quick to accept Fred's offer. When he sues to rescind, Fred wins. Town officials knew that the work could not be done that cheaply, and it would be unfair to hold Fred to a mathematical error.[8]

Unconscionability. When enforcing the contract would result in exploitation or unfairness, contracts are voidable. St. Mary's School conducts an annual fundraising raffle, whose grand prize is free school tuition for a year. Accidentally, a machine prints multiple raffle tickets with the same number. As a result, ten people hold winning tickets and claim the tuition award. Since enforcing these ten agreements would likely bankrupt the school, a court will look kindly upon St. Mary's (even though the ten winners might not).

In the following case, an automobile dealer made a mistake in the customer's favor—how often does this happen?

AP Images/Art Institute of Chicago

What would you do if you saw this painting in a flea market for $6? (Hint: It is worth a lot more.)

[8]Restatement (Second) of Contracts §153.

Donovan v. RRL Corporation

26 Cal.4th 261
Supreme Court of California, 2001

Facts: Brian Donovan was in the market for a used car. As he scanned the Costa Mesa *Daily Pilot*, he came upon a "Pre-Owned Coup-A-Rama Sale!" at Lexus of Westminster. Of the 16 cars listed in the ad (with vehicle identification numbers), one was a sapphire-blue Jaguar XJ6 Vanden Plas, priced at $25,995.

Brian drove to a Jaguar dealership to do some comparison shopping. Jaguars of the same year and mileage cost about $8,000 to $10,000 more than the auto at the Lexus agency. The next day, Brian and his wife hurried over to the Coup-A-Rama event, spotted the Jaguar and asked a salesperson why it had such a good price. The salesperson responded that, as a Lexus dealership, it could offer better prices than Jaguar and suggested that the Donovans test drive it. Pleased with the ride, Brian said to the salesman, "O.K. We will take it at your price, $26,000." This figure startled the sales representative, who glanced at the newspaper ad Brian showed him, and responded, "That's a mistake."

As indeed it was. The Lexus agency had paid $35,000 for the Jaguar and intended to sell it for about $37,000. Brian was adamant. "No, I want to buy it at your advertised price, and I will write you a check right now." The sales manager was called in, and he refused to sell the car for less than $37,000.

It turned out that the *Daily Pilot*'s typographical and proofreading errors had caused the mistake, although the Lexus dealership had failed to review the proof sheet, which would have revealed the error before the ad went to press.

Brian sued. The trial court found that unilateral mistake prevented enforcement of the contract. The appellate court reversed the decision, and Donovan appealed to the state's highest court.

The state supreme court first ruled that there *was* in fact a contract between the parties. (Generally, a newspaper advertisement is merely a solicitation for an offer, but a California statute generally holds *automobile dealers* to the terms of their offers.) The court then went on to examine the mistake to determine if the contract was enforceable.

Issue: ***Did the Lexus dealer's mistake entitle it to rescind the contract?***

Excerpts from Justice George's Decision: A significant error in the price term of a contract constitutes a mistake regarding a basic assumption upon which the contract is made, and such a mistake ordinarily has a material effect adverse to the mistaken party. The defendant must show that the resulting imbalance in the agreed exchange is so severe that it would be unfair to require the defendant to perform.

Measured against this standard, defendant's mistake in the contract for the sale of the Jaguar automobile constitutes a material mistake regarding a basic assumption upon which it made the contract. Enforcing the contract with the mistaken price of $25,995 would require defendant to sell the vehicle to plaintiff for $12,000 less than the intended advertised price of $37,995—an error amounting to 32 percent of the price defendant intended. The exchange of performances would be substantially less desirable for defendant and more desirable for plaintiff.

The mere fact that a mistaken party could have avoided the mistake by the exercise of reasonable care does not preclude avoidance on the ground of mistake. Indeed, since a party can often avoid a mistake by the exercise of such care, the availability of relief would be severely circumscribed if he were to be barred by his negligence. Nevertheless, in *extreme cases*, the mistaken party's fault is a proper ground for denying him relief for a mistake that he otherwise could have avoided.

If we were to accept plaintiff's position that the dealer always must be held to the strict terms of a contract arising from an advertisement, we would be holding that the dealer intended to assume the risk of all typographical errors in advertisements, no matter how serious the error and regardless of the circumstances in which the error was made. For example, if an automobile dealer proofread an advertisement but, through carelessness, failed to detect a typographical error listing a $75,000 automobile for sale at $75, the defense of mistake would be unavailable to the dealer.

No evidence presented at trial suggested that defendant knew of the mistake before plaintiff attempted to purchase the automobile, that defendant intended to mislead customers, or that it had adopted a practice of deliberate indifference regarding errors in advertisements. The uncontradicted evidence established that the *Daily Pilot* made the proofreading error resulting in defendant's mistake.

We conclude that the municipal court correctly entered judgment in defendant's favor.

Mutual Mistake

A mutual mistake **occurs when both contracting parties share the same mistake. If the contract is based on a fundamental factual error by both parties, the contract is voidable by either one.**

But what types of errors are important enough to warrant rescission? Generally, when the parties are mistaken as to the existence or the identity of the contract's subject matter, the contract is voidable. Believing himself the rightful owner, Arthur contracts to sell a parcel of land to James. When it is later discovered that the land never belonged to Arthur, James can rescind the contract. Both parties were mistaken as to the existence of Arthur's land.

Farnsworth believes he is selling Corbin a topaz, and Corbin thinks he is buying a topaz. In fact, both are wrong: The stone turns out to be a diamond. Since the parties made a material error as to the subject of their contract, there was no valid assent and either one can rescind.

The following case is read by every U.S. law student. It illustrates a basic factual mistake as to the subject matter of a contract. When is a cow more than a cow? Answer: When it is two.

Landmark Case

Sherwood v. Walker

66 Mich. 568
Michigan Supreme Court, 1887

Facts: Rose 2d of Aberlone was a gentle, 1,420 lb. cow that lived in Michigan in 1886. Rose's owner, Hiram Walker & Sons, was a cattle breeder who bought her for $850. After a few years, Walker concluded that Rose could have no calves. As a barren cow, she was worth much less than $850, so Walker agreed to sell her for beef to T. C. Sherwood. Walker told Sherwood that Rose was "probably barren, and would not breed." After some negotiation, Walker agreed to sell Rose for "five and one-half cents per pound, live weight, fifty pounds shrinkage," or $80.

But when Sherwood came to collect Rose, the parties realized that (surprise!) she was pregnant. As a confirmed breeder, Rose was now worth about $1,000. Walker refused to part with the happy mother, and Sherwood sued for breach of contract. Walker defended, claiming that both parties had made a *mistake* and that the contract was voidable. After the lower court ruled the contract was enforceable, Walker appealed.

Issue: ***Does a mutual mistake of fact render a contract voidable?***

Excerpts from Justice Morse's Decision: A party who has given an apparent consent to a contract of sale may refuse to execute it, or he may avoid it after it has been completed, if the assent was founded, or the contract made, upon the mistake of a material fact—such as the subject matter of the sale, the price, or some collateral fact materially inducing the agreement; and this can be done when the mistake is mutual.

If there is a difference as to the substance of the thing bargained for, then there is no contract; but if it be only a difference in some quality or accident, the contract remains binding.

The mistake of the parties went to the whole substance of the agreement. The parties would not have made the contract of sale except upon the understanding and belief that she was incapable of breeding, and of no use as a cow. A barren cow is substantially a different creature than a breeding one. There is as much difference between them for all purposes of use as there is between an ox and a cow that is capable of breeding and giving milk. The mistake affected the character of the animal for all time, and for its present and ultimate use. She was not in fact the animal, or the kind of animal, the defendants intended to sell or the plaintiff to buy.

The mistake affected the substance of the whole consideration, and it must be considered that there was no contract to sell or sale of the cow as she actually was. The thing sold and bought had in fact no existence. Defendants had a right to rescind, and to refuse to deliver, and the verdict should be in their favor.

The defense of mistake is not a cure-all for all bad deals. Courts will not rescind contracts on the basis of a prediction error, a mistaken value, or where the parties assume the risk of error.

Prediction Error. Sherwood and Walker were both wrong about Rose's reproductive ability, and the error was basic enough to cause a tenfold difference in price. Walker, the injured party, was entitled to rescind the contract. Note that the error must be *factual*. Suppose Walker sold Rose thinking that the price of beef was going to drop, when in fact the price rose 60 percent in five months. That would be simply a *prediction* that proved wrong, and Walker would have no right to rescind.

Mistake of Value. Here is one case in which it pays to know less. Suppose that Fiona, the flea market vendor, sold the nineteenth-century masterpiece for $100 to Marguerite, a financial analyst, with no inkling of its real worth. Both Fiona and Marguerite shared the same mistake in their estimate of the painting's market value. Sadly for Fiona, Marguerite will reap the benefit of her bargain, because a mistaken value alone is not enough to take back a deal.

Conscious Uncertainty. No rescission is permitted where one of the parties knows he is taking on a risk; that is, he realizes there is uncertainty about the quality of the thing being exchanged. Rufus offers 10 acres of mountainous land to Priscilla. "I can't promise you anything about this land," he says, "but they've found gold on every adjoining parcel." Priscilla, eager for gold, buys the land, digs long and hard, and discovers—mud. She may not rescind the contract. She understood the risk she was assuming, and there was no mutual mistake.

15-2c Duress

Duress
An improper threat made to force another party to enter into a contract

True consent is also lacking when one party agrees to a contract under **duress**. If kindly Uncle Hugo signs over the deed to the ranch because Niece Nelly is holding a gun to his head, Hugo has not consented in any real sense, and he will have the right to rescind the contract.

If one party makes an improper threat that causes the victim to enter into a contract, and the victim had no reasonable alternative, the contract is voidable.

On a Sunday morning, Bancroft Hall drove to pick up his daughter Sandra, who had slept at a friend's house. The Halls are black and the neighborhood was white. A suspicious neighbor called the police, who arrived, aggressively prevented the Halls from getting into their own car, and arrested the father. The Halls had not violated any law or otherwise done anything wrong. Later an officer told Hall that he could leave immediately if he signed a release relinquishing his right to sue the police, but that if he refused to sign it, he would be detained for a bail hearing. Hall signed the release but later filed suit. The police defended based on the release.

The court held that the release was voidable because Hall had signed it under duress. The threat to detain Hall for a bail hearing was clearly improper because he had committed no crime. He also had no reasonable alternative to signing. A jury awarded the Halls over half a million dollars.[9]

Can "improper threats" take other forms? Does *economic* intimidation count? Many plaintiffs have posed that question over the last half century, and courts have grudgingly yielded.

Today, in most states, economic duress *can* also be used to void a contract. But economic duress sounds perilously close to hard bargaining—in other words, business. The free market system is expected to produce tough competition. A smart, aggressive executive may bargain fiercely. How do we distinguish economic duress from legal, successful business tactics? Courts have created no single rule to answer the question, but they do focus on certain issues.

---

[9]Halls v. Ochs, 817 F.2d 920 (1st Cir. 1987).

In analyzing a claim of economic duress, courts look at these factors:

- Acts that have no legitimate business purpose
- Greatly unequal bargaining power
- An unnaturally large gain for one party
- Financial distress to one party

Is the following case one of duress or hard bargaining?

You Be the Judge

Integra Optics, Inc. v. Messina and OSI Hardware, Inc.

2016 WL 3917764, 2016 N.Y. Misc. LEXIS 2646
Supreme Court, Albany County, New York, 2016

Facts: Jonathan Messina had been a successful sales executive for Integra Optics for over a year when the multinational fiber optics company asked him to sign a non-compete agreement. Integra's proposed agreement prohibited Messina from working for Integra competitors "anywhere in the world" for one year after leaving the company.

On his lawyer's advice, Messina repeatedly refused to sign Integra's non-compete. But the pressure mounted. After a year of refusal, Daniel Maynard, Messina's boss, threatened to withhold Messina's earned commissions and bonuses amounting to over $100,000. Maynard bragged that he had done exactly that to another employee, who had ultimately signed an undesirable non-compete because she could not survive on her base pay alone.

Unwilling to relent, Messina met with the company's top leadership. At the meeting, the chief operating officer reassured Messina: "Jon, this is just a formality. An agreement like this would never be upheld in the courts. We are just trying to get all our ducks in a row as an organization now that we want to grow. We promise we will take care of you, you have nothing to worry about." The COO also said, "things would have to be pretty bad" for Integra to enforce the non-compete. Messina left the meeting feeling that he had no choice but to sign the agreement if he wanted his money.

As you have probably guessed, Messina signed, but then things did get pretty bad. Messina left to work for a competitor, but Integra sought an injunction to prevent him from assuming his new job. Messina and his new employer argued that the non-compete was unenforceable because it was the product of economic duress.

You Be the Judge: *Did Messina suffer from economic duress?*

Argument for the Plaintiff (Integra): Your honors, Messina is a highly compensated, sophisticated businessman who obtained legal advice. He willingly signed the non-compete after an entire year of negotiations. As a successful and marketable salesman, he could have easily left the company instead of signing. But he stayed—and signed—because he wanted to keep earning his hefty salary. Now that he is eager to work for a competitor, he claims that he was threatened into signing. Yes, people posture during negotiations. But that is different from taking advantage of someone or making improper threats. Integra needs to protect itself from competition and did so with a legal, enforceable non-compete.

Argument for the Defendant (Messina): A contract may be voided on the ground of economic duress if one party forces the other side to agree by making wrongful threats that prevent the exercise of his free will. What could be more improper than threatening to withhold substantial compensation that my client had already earned? Integra held Messina's own money hostage. For over a year, the company pressured my client and in the end, these credible threats became increasingly direct. Messina knew the non-compete was an offer he could not refuse. Those threats cannot be the basis of an enforceable contract.

15-2d Undue Influence

Recall the hospital-bound Huguette Clark, who had penchants for the Smurfs and million-dollar gifts. If her estate can prove that Beth Israel and her physician preyed upon her vulnerability to get her money, it can rescind her agreements based on *undue influence*. Where one party has used undue influence, the contract is voidable at the option of the injured party. There are two elements to the plaintiff's case. **To prove undue influence, the injured party must demonstrate:**

- A relationship between the two parties either of trust or of domination and
- Improper persuasion by the stronger party.[10]

Heiresses are not the only victims of undue influence. Eighty-year-old Agnes Seals owned a small building in New York City, but she was homebound and unable to care for herself or the property. A 35-year-old neighbor, David Aviles, seemingly came to her rescue. Promising to take care of her for the rest of her life, he earned her trust by bringing her groceries and ultimately convinced her to sell him her building at a deep discount. At the closing, Mrs. Seals was represented by an attorney of David's choosing whom she had never met. The court ruled that David exploited Mrs. Seals for his own financial gain and that undue influence rendered the transactions voidable.[11]

CHAPTER CONCLUSION

Agreement alone may not be enough to make a contract enforceable. A minor or a mentally impaired person may generally disaffirm contracts. Even if both parties are adults of sound mind, courts will insist that consent be genuine. Misrepresentation, mistake, duress, and undue influence all indicate that at least one party did not truly consent. As the law evolves, it imposes an increasingly greater burden of *good faith negotiating* on the party in the stronger position.

EXAM REVIEW

1. **VOIDABLE CONTRACT** Capacity and consent are different contract issues that can lead to the same result: a voidable contract. A voidable agreement is one that can be canceled by a party who lacks legal capacity or who did not give true consent.

2. **MINORS** A minor (someone under the age of 18) generally may disaffirm any contract while she is still a minor or within a reasonable time after reaching age 18.

10Restatement (Second) of Contracts §177.

11Sepulveda v. Aviles, 762 N.Y.S.2d 358 (NY S. Ct. 2003).

EXAMStrategy

Question: John Marshall and Kirsten Fletcher decided to live together. They leased an apartment, each agreeing to pay one-half of the rent. When he signed the lease, Marshall was 17. Shortly after signing the lease, Marshall turned 18, and two weeks later, he moved into the apartment. He paid his half of the rent for two months and then moved out because he and Fletcher were not getting along. Fletcher sued Marshall for one-half of the monthly rent for the remainder of the lease. Who wins?

Strategy: Marshall was clearly a minor when he signed the lease, and he could have rescinded the agreement at that time. However, after he turned 18, he moved in and began to pay rent. What effect did that have on his contract obligation? (See the "Result" at the end of this Exam Review section.)

3. **MENTAL IMPAIRMENT** A mentally impaired person may generally disaffirm a contract. In such a case, though, he generally must make restitution.

4. **INTOXICATION** A person who is so intoxicated that he fails to understand the nature of an agreement may disaffirm a contract.

5. **FRAUD** Fraud is grounds for rescinding a contract. The injured party must prove all of the following:
   a. A false statement of fact made intentionally or recklessly
   b. Materiality
   c. Justifiable reliance

6. **INNOCENT MISREPRESENTATION** Innocent misrepresentation also allows an injured party to rescind a contract, but it does not allow a plaintiff to sue for damages. It has the same elements as fraud, but it does not require intent or recklessness.

EXAMStrategy

Question: Ron buys 1,000 "Smudgy Dolls" for his toy store. Karen, the seller, tells him the dolls are in perfect condition, even though she knows their heads are defectively attached. Ron sells all of the products, but then he has to face 1,000 angry customers with headless dolls. Ron sues Karen seeking rescission. What is the likely outcome?

(a) This is fraud, and Ron will be able to rescind.

(b) This is an innocent misrepresentation, and Ron will be able to rescind.

(c) This is fraud, but Ron will not be able to rescind.

(d) This is an innocent misrepresentation, but Ron will not be able to rescind.

(e) This is neither fraud nor an innocent misrepresentation.

Strategy: Karen knew her statement was false, so this is a case of fraud if all elements can be met. Ron must prove a false statement of fact, materiality, and reliance. Can he do so? (See the "Result" at the end of this Exam Review section.)

7. **SILENCE** Silence amounts to misrepresentation only in four instances:
   - When disclosure is necessary to correct a previous assertion,
   - When disclosure would correct a basic mistaken assumption on which the other party is relying,
   - When disclosure would correct the other party's mistaken understanding about a writing, or
   - Where there is a relationship of trust between the two parties.

8. **UNILATERAL MISTAKE** In a case of unilateral mistake, the injured party may rescind only upon a showing that the other party knew or had reason to know of the mistake, the mistake was solely mathematical or mechanical, or that enforcement would be unconscionable.

9. **MUTUAL MISTAKE** When both parties to a contract make the same fundamental factual error as to the existence or the identity of the contract's subject matter, either party may rescind.

10. **DURESS** If one party makes an improper threat that causes the victim to enter into a contract, and the victim had no reasonable alternative, the contract is voidable.

EXAMStrategy

Question: Andreini's nerve problem diminished the use of his hands. Dr. Beck operated, but the problem grew worse. A nurse told the patient that Beck might have committed a serious error that exacerbated the problem. Andreini returned for a second operation, which Beck assured him would correct the problem. But after Andreini had been placed in a surgical gown, shaved, and prepared for surgery, the doctor insisted that he sign a release relieving Beck of liability for the first operation. Andreini did not want to sign it, but Beck refused to operate until he did. Later, Andreini sued Beck for malpractice. A trial court dismissed Andreini's suit based on the release. You are on the appeals court. Will you affirm the dismissal or reverse?

Strategy: Andreini is claiming physical duress. Did Beck act *improperly* in demanding a release? Did Andreini have a *realistic alternative?* (See the "Result" at the end of this Exam Review section.)

11. **UNDUE INFLUENCE** Once again the injured party may rescind a contract, but only upon a showing of a special relationship of trust and improper persuasion.

RESULTS

2. Result: A minor can disaffirm a contract. However, if he turns 18 and then ratifies the agreement, he is fully liable. When he paid the rent, Marshall ratified the contract, and thus he is fully liable.

6. Result: Karen made a false statement of fact, knowing it was wrong. It was material, and Ron reasonably relied on her. Karen has committed fraud. Ron is entitled to rescind the agreement. The correct answer is (a).

10. Result: The Utah Supreme Court reversed the trial court, so you probably should as well. Beck forced Andreini to sign under duress. The threat to withhold surgery was improper, and Andreini had no reasonable alternative.

MULTIPLE-CHOICE QUESTIONS

1. Kerry finds a big green ring in the street. She shows it to Leroy, who says, "Wow. That could be valuable." Neither Kerry nor Leroy knows what the ring is made of or whether it is valuable. Kerry sells the ring to Leroy for $100, saying, "Don't come griping if it turns out to be worth two dollars." Leroy takes the ring to a jeweler who tells him it is an unusually perfect emerald, worth at least $75,000. Kerry sues to rescind.

(a) Kerry will win based on fraud.
(b) Kerry will win based on mutual mistake.
(c) Kerry will win based on unilateral mistake.
(d) Kerry will lose.

2. Veronica has a beer and then makes a contract. She continues drinking, and her blood alcohol level eventually rises to 0.09, which is just above her state's threshold for drunk driving. She makes a second contract while in this condition. Veronica's first contract is ________________, and her second contract is ____________.

(a) valid; valid
(b) valid; voidable
(c) voidable; voidable
(d) voidable; void

3. Jerry is so mentally ill that he is unable to understand the nature and consequences of his transactions, but he has not been adjudicated insane. Penny has been adjudicated insane and has a court-appointed guardian. Jerry's contracts are ________________, and Penny's contracts are ____________.

(a) valid; valid
(b) valid; voidable
(c) valid; void
(d) voidable; voidable
(e) voidable; void

4. Angela makes a material misstatement of fact to Lance, which he relies on when he signs Angela's contract. Fraud exists if Angela made the misstatement ____________.

(a) intentionally
(b) recklessly
(c) carelessly
(d) A and B only
(e) A, B, and C

5. Scarborough's Department Store opens for business on a busy shopping day just before Christmas. A hurried clerk places a sign in the middle of a table piled high with red cashmere sweaters. The sign reads, "SALE—100% Cashmere—$0.99 Each." The sign, of course, was supposed to read "$99 each."

   This is a ______________ mistake, and customers ______________ be able to demand that Scarborough's sell the sweaters for 99 cents.

   (a) unilateral; will
   (b) unilateral; will not
   (c) mutual; will
   (d) mutual; will not

CASE QUESTIONS

1. On television and in magazines, Maurine and Mamie Mason saw numerous advertisements for Chrysler Fifth Avenue automobiles. The ads described the car as "luxurious," "quality-engineered," and "reliable." When they went to inspect the car, the salesman told them the warranty was "the best . . . comparable to Cadillacs and Lincolns." After the Masons bought a Fifth Avenue, they began to have many problems with it. Even after numerous repairs, the car was unsatisfactory and required more work. The Masons sued, seeking to rescind the contract based on the ads and the dealer's statement. Will they win?

2. Roy Newburn borrowed money and bought a $49,000 truck from Treadwell Ford. A few months later, the truck developed transmission problems. Newburn learned that the truck had 170,000 more miles on it than the odometer indicated. The company admitted the mileage error and promised to install a new transmission for free. Treadwell did install the new transmission, but when Newburn came to pick up the truck, Treadwell demanded that he sign a general release absolving the dealership of any claims based on the inaccurate mileage. Treadwell refused to turn over the truck until Newburn finally signed. The truck broke down again, and delays cost Newburn so much income that he fell behind on his loan payments and lost the truck. He sued Treadwell, which defended based on the release. Is the release valid?

3. Morell bought a security guard business from Conley, including the property on which the business was located. Neither party knew that underground storage tanks were leaking and contaminating the property. After the sale, Morell discovered the tanks and sought to rescind the contract. Should he be allowed to do so?

4. While on a cruise, DePrince inquired about the price of a 20-carat diamond in the ship's gift shop. After confirming with the cruise line's corporate office, the salesperson told DePrince that the price was $235,000. DePrince's traveling companions, who both happened to be gemologists, told him that the price was too good to be true: A diamond that large should cost at least $2 million. DePrince ignored their advice and purchased the diamond. Soon after the sale was completed, the cruise line realized that the $235,000 price quote was *per carat*, not the *total* price. What kind of mistake did the cruise line make? Can the cruise line void the transaction?

5. Sixteen-year-old Travis Mitchell brought his Pontiac GTO into M&M Precision Body and Paint for body work and a paint job. M&M did the work and charged $1,900, which Travis paid. When Travis later complained about the quality of the work, M&M did some touching up, but Travis was still dissatisfied. He demanded his $1,900 back, but M&M refused to refund it because all of the work was "in" the car and Travis could not return it to the shop. The state of Nebraska, where this occurred, follows the majority rule on this issue. Does Travis get his money?

DISCUSSION QUESTIONS

1. Contract law gives minors substantial legal protection. But does a modern high school student *need* so much protection? Older teens may have been naive in the 1700s, but today, they are quite savvy. Should the law change so that only younger children—perhaps those aged 14 and under—have the ability to undo agreements? Or is the law reasonable the way it currently exists?

2. Ball-Mart, a baseball card store, had a 1968 Nolan Ryan rookie card in almost perfect condition for sale. Any baseball collector would have known that the card was worth at least $1,000; the published monthly price guide listed its market value at $1,200. Bryan was a 12-year-old boy with a collection of over 40,000 baseball cards. When Bryan went to Ball-Mart, Kathleen, who knew nothing about cards, was filling in for the owner. The Ryan card was marked "1200," so Bryan asked Kathleen if this meant twelve dollars. She said yes and sold it to him for that amount. When Ball-Mart's owner realized the mix-up, he sued to rescind the contract. Who wins?

3. Paula was alone, pregnant, and confused. She needed help and support, which she found at Methodist Mission Home of Texas. In the days following her child's birth, representatives of Methodist Mission forcefully told her that she had no moral or legal right to keep her child: She had to place her baby for adoption. Paula signed the adoption papers, but days later, she decided she wanted to keep the baby after all. Was there any ground to rescind?

4. Do you have sympathy for intoxicated people who make agreements? Should the law ever let them back out of deals when they sober up? After all, no one forced them to get drunk. Should the law be more lenient, or is it reasonable as it currently exists?

5. When Steven Simkin and Laura Blank divorced in 2006, they agreed to split their $13.5 million fortune evenly. Two years later, it became evident that Simkin had a problem: His half was invested in Bernard Madoff's giant Ponzi scheme and he lost millions. Simkin asked Blank to revise their deal and she refused, so he sued to rescind their 2006 settlement based on mutual mistake of fact. He argued that the fatal mistake was that neither party knew that his half was invested in a fraud. Should a court invalidate the settlement for this mistake?

16 CHAPTER

WRITTEN CONTRACTS

Lynn and Howard were in love. And when people are in love, they say all kinds of things. In their case, they promised that if either ever won the lottery, they would split the winnings. (You can tell where this is going, right?)

Time passed. Although Howard moved into her house, they never married. Fourteen years later, the relationship was on the brink. One fateful night, on the way home from dinner, they stopped at a convenience store and bought several $20 lottery tickets.

Next thing Howard knew, Lynn was gone—along with the lottery tickets. For over a month, she refused to take his calls. Finally, Lynn returned—with a shiny new car, an eviction notice for Howard, and no intention of sharing a million-dollar lottery prize.

When people are in love, they say all kinds of things.

16-1 THE COMMON LAW STATUTE OF FRAUDS: CONTRACTS THAT MUST BE IN WRITING

The rule we examine in this chapter is not exactly news. Originally passed by the British Parliament in 1677, the Statute of Frauds has changed little over the centuries. The purpose was to prevent lying (fraud) in civil lawsuits. Jury trials of that era invited perjury. Neither the plaintiff nor the defendant was permitted to testify, meaning that the jury never heard from the people who really knew what had happened. Instead, the court heard testimony from people who claimed to have witnessed the contract being created. Knowing that he would never be subjected to aggressive cross-examination, a plaintiff might easily allege that a fake contract was real and then bribe witnesses to support his case. A powerful earl, seeking to acquire 300 acres of valuable land owned by a neighboring commoner, might claim that the neighbor had orally promised to sell his land. Although the claim was utterly false, the earl would win if he could bribe enough "reputable" witnesses to persuade the jury.

To provide juries with more reliable evidence that a contract did or did not exist, Parliament passed the Statute of Frauds. It required that in several types of cases, a contract would be enforced only if it were in writing. Contracts involving interests in land were first on the list.

In the days before the Revolutionary War, when Pennsylvania was still a British possession, the colony's supreme court heard the following case, which centered on the Statute of Frauds. Notice the case citation. This is very nearly the first case reported in U.S. history. Back then, rulings were expressed quite differently (and everything was capitalized), but you will be able to see Judge Coleman's point.

Landmark Case

The Lessee of Richardson v. Campbell

1 U.S. 10
Supreme Court of Pennsylvania, 1764

Facts: A tenant had rented land from Richardson. However, Campbell claimed the leased property was really his. Unless the tenant could prove that Richardson owned the land, he would have no right to stay there.

Richardson's tenant offered a deed (which was then called a *patent*) to support his claim; Campbell provided receipts as evidence that he had bought the property.

To prove that the receipts were for the disputed property, Campbell wanted to introduce statements from an important person—Thomas Penn, whose father, William, had founded the Pennsylvania colony. Obviously, the tenant did not want that evidence admitted in court.

Issue: ***Was oral evidence about the ownership of land admissible in court?***

Excerpts from Justice Coleman's Decision: PLAINTIFF supported his Title by a Patent. The Defendant produced Receipts several Years prior to Plaintiff's Patent; but the Plaintiff contend[ed] that the Receipts were only for Money paid on an adjacent Tract; the Defendant produced a Witness to prove a parol Declaration of Mr. Thomas Penn that the Land in dispute was sold to Defendant.

This piece of Evidence was opposed by the Plaintiff, and refused BY THE COURT.

Almost all states of the United States have passed their own version of the Statute of Frauds. It is important to remember, as we examine the rules and exceptions, that Parliament and the state legislatures all had a commendable, straightforward purpose in passing their respective Statute of Frauds: *to provide a court with the best possible evidence of whether the parties intended to make a contract.* Ironically, the British government has repealed the writing requirement for most contracts. Parliament concluded that the old statute, far from preventing wrongdoing, was helping people commit fraud. A wily negotiator could orally agree to terms and then, if the deal turned unprofitable, walk away from the contract, knowing it was unenforceable without written evidence.

Thus far, no state has entirely repealed its Statute of Frauds. Instead, courts have carved exceptions into the original statute to prevent unfairness. Some scholars have urged state legislatures to go further and repeal the law altogether. Other commentators defend the Statute of Frauds as a valuable tool for justice. They argue that, among other benefits, the requirement of a writing cautions people to be careful before making—or relying on—a promise. For now, the Statute of Frauds is a vital part of law.

The Statute of Frauds requires certain agreements to be in writing to be enforceable. The agreements that must be in writing are those:

- For the transfer of an interest in **land**,
- That **cannot be performed within one year**,
- In which a party promises to pay the **debt of another**,
- Made by an **executor of an estate to pay a debt of the estate**,
- Made **in consideration of marriage**, and
- For the **sale of goods of $500 or more**.

A plaintiff may not enforce any of these six types of agreements unless the agreement, or some memorandum of it, is in writing and signed by the defendant. Suppose that Lynn had also made an oral promise to Howard that he could buy her old car for $5,000. This contract involves the sale of a good worth more than $500 and, therefore, would not be enforceable unless in writing.

Note, however, that even if an agreement is unenforceable, it is not void. Suppose that Lynn did sell her car to Howard but later changed her mind. She then tried to get the car back, claiming that the original contract violated the Statute of Frauds. Lynn loses. **Once a contract is fully executed, it makes no difference that it was unwritten.** The Statute of Frauds prevents the enforcement of an executory contract; that is, one in which the parties have not fulfilled their obligations. But the contract is not *illegal*. Once both parties have fully performed, neither party may demand rescission. The Statute of Frauds allows a party to cancel future obligations but not to undo past actions.

16-1a Agreements for an Interest in Land

A contract for the transfer of any interest in land must be in writing to be enforceable. Notice the phrase "interest in land." This means *any legal right* regarding land. A house on a lot is an interest in land. A mortgage, an easement, and a leased apartment are all interests in land. As a general rule, leases must therefore be in writing, although most states have created an exception for short-term leases. A short-term lease is often one for a year or less, although the length varies from state to state.

Kary Presten and Ken Sailer were roommates in a rental apartment in New Jersey that had a view of the Manhattan skyline. The lease was in Sailer's name, but the two split all expenses. The building became a "cooperative," meaning that each tenant would have the option of buying the apartment.[1] Sailer learned that he could buy his unit for only $55,800 if he promptly paid a $1,000 fee to maintain his rights. He mentioned to Presten that he planned to buy the unit, and Presten asked if he could become half-owner. Sailer agreed and borrowed the $1,000 from Presten to pay his initial fee. But as the time for closing on the purchase came nearer, Sailer realized that he could sell the apartment for a substantial profit. He placed an ad in a paper and promptly received a firm offer for $125,000. Sailer then told Presten that their deal was off, and that he, Sailer, would be buying the unit alone. He did exactly that, and Presten filed suit. Regrettably, the outcome of Presten's suit was only too easy to predict.

A cooperative apartment is an interest in land, said the court. This agreement could be enforced only if put in writing and signed by Sailer. The parties had put nothing in writing, and therefore Presten was out of luck. He was entitled to his $1,000 back but nothing more. The apartment belonged to Sailer, who could live in it or sell it for a large, quick profit.[2]

Suppose that you are interested in buying five expensive acres in a fast-growing rural area. There is no water on the property, and the only way to bring public water to it is through land owned by the neighbor, Joanne, who agrees to sell you an easement through her property. An *easement* is a legal right that an owner gives to another person to make some use of the owner's land. In other words, Joanne will permit you to dig a 200-foot trench through her land and lay a water pipe there in exchange for $15,000. May you now safely purchase the 5 acres? Not until Joanne has signed the written easement. You might ignore this "technicality," since Joanne seems friendly and honest. But you could then spend $300,000 buying your property only to learn that Joanne has changed her mind. She might refuse to go through with the deal unless you pay $150,000 for the easement. Without her permission to lay the pipe, your new land is worthless. Avoid such nightmares: Get it in writing.

Exception: Full Performance by the Seller

If the seller completely performs her side of a contract for an interest in land, a court is likely to enforce the agreement even if it was oral. Adam orally agrees to sell his condominium to Maggie for $150,000. Adam delivers the deed to Maggie and expects his money a week later, but Maggie fails to pay. Most courts will allow Adam to enforce the oral contract and collect the full purchase price from Maggie.

Exception: Part Performance by the Buyer

The buyer of land may be able to enforce an oral contract if she paid part of the purchase price *and either* entered upon the land *or* made improvements to it. Suppose that Eloise sues Grover to enforce an alleged oral contract to sell a lot in Happydale. She claims they struck a bargain in January. Grover defends based on the Statute of Frauds, saying that, even if the two did reach an oral agreement, it is unenforceable. Eloise proves that she paid 10 percent of the purchase price, that she began excavating on the lot in February to build a house, and that Grover knew of the work. Eloise has established part performance and will be allowed to enforce her contract.

This exception makes sense if we recall the purpose of the Statute of Frauds: to provide the best possible evidence of the parties' intentions. The fact that Grover permitted Eloise to enter upon the land and begin building on it is compelling evidence that the two parties had reached an agreement. But be aware that most claims of part performance fail. Merely paying a deposit on a house is not part performance. A plaintiff seeking to rely on part performance must show partial payment *and* either entrance onto the land *or* physical improvements to it.

---

1 Technically, the residents of a "co-op" do not own their apartments. They own a share of the corporation that owns the building. Along with their ownership shares, residents have a right to lease their unit for a modest fee.

2 Presten v. Sailer, 542 A.2d 7 (N.J. Super. Ct. App. Div., 1988).

Exception: Promissory Estoppel

The other exception to the writing requirement is our old friend promissory estoppel. **If a promisor makes an oral promise that should reasonably cause the promisee to rely on it, and the promisee does rely, the promisee may be able to enforce the promise**, despite the Statute of Frauds, if that is the only way to avoid injustice. This exception potentially applies to any contract that must be written, such as those for land, those that cannot be performed within one year, and so forth.

Maureen Sullivan and James Rooney lived together for seven years, although they never married. They decided to buy a house. The two agreed that they would be equal owners, but Rooney told Sullivan that in order to obtain Veterans Administration financing, he would have to be the sole owner on the deed. They each contributed to the purchase and maintenance of the house, and Rooney repeatedly told Sullivan that he would change the deed to joint ownership. He never did. When the couple split up, Sullivan sued, seeking a 50 percent interest in the house. She won. The agreement was for an interest in land and should have been in writing, said the court. But Rooney had clearly promised Sullivan that she would be a half-owner, and she had relied by contributing to the purchase and maintenance. The Statute of Frauds was passed to *prevent* fraud, not to enable one person to mislead another and benefit at her expense.[3]

EXAMStrategy

Question: Aditi and Danielle, MBA students, need an apartment for next September. They find a lovely two-bedroom unit that the owner is rehabbing. The students can see that the owner is honest, his workmanship excellent. The owner agrees to rent them the apartment beginning September 1, for $1,200 per month for one year. "Come back at the end of August. By then, my work will be done and I'll have the papers to sign." Aditi asks, "Should we sign something now, to be sure?" The landlord laughs and replies, "I trust you. You don't trust me?" They both trust him, and they shake hands on the deal. When the students return in August, the landlord has rented it to Danielle's former boyfriend for $1,400 per month. Aditi and Danielle sue. Who wins?

Strategy: Under the Statute of Frauds, a contract for the sale of any interest in land must be in writing to be enforceable. What does "any interest" mean? Does the Statute of Frauds apply to this case?

Result: An "interest" means any legal right. A lease is an interest in land, meaning that the students cannot enforce this agreement unless it is in writing, signed by the owner—and it is not. The students need to look for a different apartment.

16-1b Agreements That Cannot Be Performed within One Year

Contracts that cannot be performed within one year are unenforceable unless they are in writing. This one-year period begins on the date the parties make the agreement. The critical word here is "cannot." If a contract *could possibly* be completed within one year, it need not be in writing. Betty gets a job at Burger Brain, throwing fries in oil. Her boss tells her she can have Fridays off for as long as she works there. That oral contract is enforceable whether

[3]Sullivan v. Rooney, 533 N.E.2d 1372 (1989).

Betty stays one week or 20 years. "As long as she works there" *could* last for less than one year. Betty might quit the job after six months. Therefore, it does not need to be in writing.[4]

If an agreement will *necessarily* take longer than one year to finish, it must be in writing to be enforceable. If Betty is hired for a term of three years as manager of Burger Brain, the agreement is unenforceable unless put in writing. She cannot perform three years of work in one year.

Or, if you hire a band to play at your wedding 15 months from today, the agreement must be in writing. The gig may take only a single day, but that day will definitely not fall in the next 12 months.

The following case picks up the story of Lynn and Howard, the warring couple from the chapter opener. Who wants to be a millionaire? They both do. Who will win? Only one of them.

Browning v. Poirier

165 So.3d 663
Florida Supreme Court, 2015

Facts: As introduced in the chapter opener, Howard Browning and Lynn Poirier were romantic partners. Early on, they promised to share any lottery winnings equally. Fourteen years after that oral promise, Poirier purchased a winning ticket and collected one million dollars. She refused to give Browning half.

Browning sued Poirier for breach of oral contract. Poirier claimed that the oral agreement was unenforceable because the Statute of Frauds requires promises that are not performable within a year to be in writing. The lower court found in her favor and the appeals court affirmed. Browning appealed to the state supreme court.

Issue: ***Is an oral agreement of indefinite duration to share future lottery winnings enforceable?***

Excerpts from Justice Polston's Decision: It is well settled that the oral contracts made unenforceable by the statute because they are not to be performed within a year include only those which *cannot* be performed within that period. A promise which is not likely to be performed within a year, and which in fact is not performed within a year, is not within the statute if at the time the contract is made there is a possibility in law and in fact that full performance such as the parties intended may be completed before the expiration of a year. Stated otherwise, judging from the time the oral contract of indefinite duration is made, if the contract's full performance is possible within one year from the inception of the contract, then it falls outside the statute of frauds.

In this case, the oral agreement between Browning and Poirier is one of indefinite duration because no definite time was fixed by the parties for the performance of their agreement. Additionally, at the time the contract was made there is a possibility in law and in fact that full performance of the agreement between Browning and Poirier could have been completed before the expiration of a year. For example, if Browning or Poirier purchased a winning lottery ticket and they split the proceeds before the expiration of one year, the agreement would have been fully performed before the expiration of one year. Alternatively, either Browning or Poirier could have ended the agreement at any time. Accordingly, judging from the time the oral contract was made, nothing in the terms of their contract demonstrates that it could not be performed within one year.

Because the oral agreement between Browning and Poirier could have possibly been performed within one year, it falls outside the statute of frauds.

---

[4]This is the majority rule. In most states, for example, if a company hires an employee "for life," the contract need not be in writing because the employee could die within one year. "Contracts of uncertain duration are simply excluded [from the Statute of Frauds]; the provision covers only those contracts whose performance cannot possibly be completed within a year." Restatement (Second) of Contracts §130, Comment a, at 328 (1981). However, a few states disagree. The Supreme Court of Illinois ruled that a contract for lifetime employment is enforceable only if written.

Because their oral agreement was outside the Statute of Frauds, it was enforceable and Lynn had to pay Howard. But suppose that Lynn and Howard had agreed their deal would last two years. In that case, the oral promise would not be enforced because a two-year agreement cannot be performed in one year. Lynn would walk away with the million-dollar prize.

Ethics

A promise is a promise … *right*? The purpose of the Statute of Frauds is to give proof of certain promises. Perhaps we need such a rule because people have a tendency to forget, rewrite history, or go back on their word. For example, it is common for family, friends, or coworkers to buy lottery tickets together with the understanding that they will share winnings. But many court cases like *Browning v. Poirier* tell the sad tale of relationships ruined by lottery pools. What result in these cases if you applied the Ethics Theories from Chapter 2? What Ethics Traps might be at play? Even if the law did not require it, what is the right thing for Lynn to do? Would you share your winnings with another? Under what circumstances?

16-1c Promise to Pay the Debt of Another

When one person agrees to pay the debt of another as a favor to that debtor, it is called a collateral promise, and it must be in writing to be enforceable. D. R. Kemp was a young entrepreneur who wanted to build housing in Tuscaloosa, Alabama. He needed $25,000 to complete a project he was working on, so he went to his old college professor, Jim Hanks, for help. The professor said he would see what he could do about getting Kemp a loan. Professor Hanks spoke with his good friend Travis Chandler, telling him that Kemp was highly responsible and would be certain to repay any money loaned. Chandler trusted Professor Hanks but wanted to be sure of his money. Professor Hanks assured Chandler that if for any reason Kemp did not repay the loan, he, Hanks, would pay Chandler in full. With that assurance, Chandler wrote out a check for $25,000, payable to Kemp, never having met the young man.

Kemp, of course, never repaid the loan. (Thank goodness he did not; this textbook has no use for people who do what they are supposed to do.) Kemp exhausted the cash trying to sustain his business, which failed anyway, so he had nothing to give his creditor. Chandler approached Professor Hanks, who refused to pay, and Chandler sued. The outcome was easy to predict. Professor Hanks had agreed to repay Kemp's debt *as a favor to Kemp*, making it a collateral promise. Chandler had nothing in writing, and that is exactly what he got from his lawsuit—nothing.

Exception: The Leading Object Rule

There is one major exception to the collateral promise rule. **When the promisor guarantees to pay the debt of another and *the leading object of the promise is some benefit to the promisor himself*, then the contract will be enforceable even if unwritten.** In other words, if the promisor makes the guarantee not as a favor to the debtor, but primarily out of *self-interest*, the Statute of Frauds does not apply.

Robert Perry was a hog farmer in Ohio. He owed $26,000 to Sunrise Cooperative, a supplier of feed. Because Perry was in debt, Sunrise stopped giving him feed on credit and began selling him feed on a cash-only basis. Perry also owed money to Farm Credit Services, a loan agency. Perry promised Farm Credit he would repay his loans as soon as his hogs were big enough to sell. But Perry couldn't raise hogs without feed, which he lacked the money to purchase. Farm Credit was determined to bring home the bacon, so it asked Sunrise Cooperative to give Perry the feed on credit. Farm Credit orally promised to pay any debt that Perry did not take care of. When Perry defaulted on his payments to Sunrise, the feed supplier sued Farm Credit based on its oral guarantee. Farm Credit claimed the promise was unenforceable, based on the Statute of Frauds. But the court found in favor of Sunrise. The *leading object* of Farm Credit's promise to Sunrise was self-interest, and the oral promise was fully enforceable.[5]

16-1d Promise Made by an Executor of an Estate

This rule is merely a special application of the previous one, concerning the debt of another person. An executor is the person who is in charge of an estate after someone dies. The executor's job is to pay debts of the deceased, obtain money owed to him, and disburse the assets according to the will. In most cases, the executor will use only the estate's assets to pay those debts. The Statute of Frauds comes into play when an executor promises to pay an estate's debts with her own funds. **An executor's promise to use her own funds to pay a debt of the deceased must be in writing to be enforceable.**

Suppose Esmeralda dies penniless, owing Tina $35,000. Esmeralda's daughter, Sapphire, is the executor of her estate. Tina comes to Sapphire and demands her $35,000. Sapphire responds, "There is no money in mamma's estate, but don't worry, I'll make it up to you with my own money." Sapphire's oral promise is unenforceable. Tina should get it in writing while Sapphire is feeling generous.

16-1e Promise Made in Consideration of Marriage

This is not the stuff of fairy tales: Barney is a multimillionaire with the integrity of a gangster and the charm of a tax collector. He proposes to Li-Tsing, who promptly rejects him. Barney then pleads that if Li-Tsing will be his bride, he will give her an island he owns off the coast of California. Li-Tsing begins to see his good qualities and accepts. After they are married, Barney refuses to deliver the deed. Li-Tsing will get nothing from a court either, because **a promise made in consideration of marriage must be in writing to be enforceable.**

16-2 THE COMMON LAW STATUTE OF FRAUDS: WHAT IS A "WRITING"?

Each of the types of contract just described must be in writing in order to be enforceable. What must the writing contain? It may be a carefully typed contract, using precise legal terminology, or an informal memo scrawled on the back of a paper napkin at a business lunch. The writing may consist of more than one document, written at different times, with each document making a piece of the puzzle. But there are some general requirements—the writing must:

- **Be signed by the defendant;** ***and***
- **State with reasonable certainty the name of each party, the subject matter of the agreement, and all of the essential terms and promises.**[6]

16-2a Signature

A state's Statute of Frauds typically requires that the writing be "signed by the party to be charged therewith"; that is, the party who is resisting enforcement of the contract. Throughout this chapter, we refer to that person as the defendant because, when these cases go to court, it is the defendant who is disputing the existence of a contract.

---

[5]Sunrise Cooperative v. Robert Perry, 1992 Ohio App. LEXIS 3913, 1992 WL 179696 (1992).

[6]Restatement (Second) of Contracts §131.

Judges define "signature" very broadly. Using a pen to write one's name certainly counts, but it is not required. A secretary who stamps an executive's signature on a letter fulfills this requirement. In fact, any mark or logo placed on a document to indicate acceptance, even an "X," will generally satisfy the Statute of Frauds. And electronic commerce, as we discuss in the next section, creates new methods of signing.

16-2b Reasonable Certainty

Suppose Garfield and Hayes are having lunch, discussing the sale of Garfield's vacation condominium. They agree on a price and want to make some notation of the agreement even before their lawyers work out a detailed purchase and sales agreement. A perfectly adequate memorandum might say, "Garfield agrees to sell Hayes his condominium at 234 Baron Boulevard, Apartment 18, for $350,000 cash, payable on June 18, 2015, and Hayes promises to pay the sum on that day." They should make two copies of their agreement and sign both. Notice that although Garfield's memo is short, it is *certain* and *complete*. This is critical because problems of vagueness and incompleteness often doom informal memoranda.

16-2c Vagueness

Ella Hayden owned valuable commercial property on a highway called Route 9. She wrote a series of letters to her stepson Mark, promising that several of the children, including Mark, would share the property. One letter said: "We four shall fairly divide on the Route 9 property. [sic]" Other letters said: "When the Route 9 Plaza is sold, you can take a long vacation," and "The property will be sold. You and Dennis shall receive the same amount." Ella Hayden died without leaving Mark anything. He sued, but got nothing. The court ruled:

> The above passages written by Ms. Hayden do not recite the essential elements of the alleged contract with reasonable certainty. The writings do not state unequivocally or with sufficient particularity the subject matter to which the writings relate, nor do they provide the terms and conditions of alleged promises made which constitute a contract. The alleged oral contract between Ms. Hayden and Mr. Hayden cannot be identified from the passages from Ms. Hayden's letters quoted above when applied to existing facts. In sum, Mr. Hayden's cause of action seeking an interest in the Route 9 property is foreclosed by the Statute of Frauds.[7]

16-2d Incompleteness

During Ronald McCoy's second interview with Spelman Memorial Hospital, the board of directors orally offered him a three-year job as assistant hospital administrator. McCoy accepted. Spelman's CEO, Gene Meyer, sent a letter confirming the offer, which said:

> To reconfirm the offer, it is as follows: 1. We will pay for your moving expenses. 2. I would like you to pursue your Master's Degree at an area program. We will pay 100 percent tuition reimbursement. 3. Effective September 26, you will be eligible for all benefits. 4. A starting salary of $48,000 annually with reviews and eligibility for increases at 6 months, 12 months, and annually thereafter. 5. We will pay for the expenses of 3 trips, if necessary, in order for you to find housing. 6. Vacation will be for 3 weeks a year after one year; however, we do allow for this to be taken earlier. [Signed] Gene Meyer.

Spelman Hospital fired McCoy less than a year after he started work, and McCoy sued. The hospital's letter seems clear, and it is signed by an authorized official. The problem is, it is incomplete. Can you spot the fatal omission? The court did.

---

[7]Hayden v. Hayden, Mass. Lawyers Weekly No. 12-299-93 (Middlesex Sup. Ct. 1994).

McCoy wanted to hold the hospital's board to its spoken promise that he would have a job for a term of three years. To be enforceable, a contract for a term of over one year must be in writing under the Statute of Frauds.

To satisfy the Statute of Frauds, an employment contract—[or] its memorandum or note—must contain *all* essential terms, including *duration of the employment relationship.* Without a statement of duration, an employment-at-will arrangement is created, which is terminable at any time by either party with no liability for breach of contract. McCoy's argument that the letter constituted a memorandum of an oral contract fails because the letter does not state an essential element: duration. The letter did not state that Spelman was granting McCoy employment for any term—only that his salary would be reviewed at 6 months, 12 months, and "annually thereafter."[8]

The lawsuits in this section demonstrate the continuing force of the Statute of Frauds. If the promisor had truly wanted to make a binding commitment, he or she could have written the appropriate contract or memorandum in a matter of minutes. Great formality and expense are unnecessary. But the written document *must be clear and complete,* or it will fail.

EXAMStrategy

Question: Major Retailer and Owner negotiated a lease of a strip mall, the tenancy to begin August 1. Retailer's lawyer then drafted a lease accurately reflecting all terms agreed to, including the parties, exact premises, condition of the store, dates of the lease, and monthly rent of $18,000. Retailer signed the lease and delivered it to Owner on July 1. On July 20, Owner leased the same space to a different tenant for $23,000 per month. Retailer sued, claiming that the parties had a binding deal, and the Owner had breached his agreement in order to obtain higher rent. Who will win?

Strategy: To comply with the Statute of Frauds, a writing must state all essential terms. This lease appears to do that. However, the writing must contain one other thing. What is it?

Result: The writing must be *signed* by the party claiming that there is no contract; that is, by the defendant. Owner never signed the lease. This lease does not comply with the Statute of Frauds, and the Retailer will lose his case.

Electronic Contracts and Signatures

Modern life has moved online: We can now buy everything from toothpaste to cars with the click of a mouse. What happens to the writing requirement, though, when there is no paper? The Statute of Frauds requires some sort of "signature" to prove that the defendant committed to the deal. Today, an "electronic signature" could mean a name typed (or automatically included) at the bottom of an email message, a retinal or vocal scan, or a name signed by electronic pen on a writing tablet, among others.

E-signatures are valid in all 50 states. Almost every state has adopted the Uniform Electronic Transactions Act (UETA), which makes *electronic* contracts and signatures as enforceable as those on paper.[9] In other words, the normal rules of contract formation apply, and neither party can avoid a deal merely because it originated electronically. A federal statute, the **Electronic Signatures in Global and National Commerce Act (E-SIGN)** extends UETA's principles to interstate and foreign commerce.

[8]McCoy v. Spelman Memorial Hospital, 845 S.W.2d 727 (Mo. Ct. App. 1993).

[9]Note that while Illinois, New York, and Washington have not adopted UETA, they have adopted their own similar versions of it.

UETA and E-SIGN also require courts, when in doubt, to favor the validity of email contracts. This requirement means that parties must be careful to avoid entering into contracts *unintentionally*. Stevens was renegotiating his employment contract with his boss through several conversational rounds of email. At one point, Stevens wrote "I accept your proposal" on an email with his signature block. Before a formal contract was inked, Stevens changed his mind. But it was too late. A court ruled that the contract was enforceable the moment Stevens pressed "send" with an acceptance and a signature block. Stevens might have considered email to be an informal conversation, but in fact, it created a final, binding contract.[10]

Note that, in many states, certain documents still require a traditional (non-electronic) signature. Wills, adoptions, court orders, and notice of foreclosure are common exceptions. If in doubt, get a hard copy, signed in ink.

16-3 THE UCC'S STATUTE OF FRAUDS

You may have noticed that we have only covered five of the six types of contracts that must be in writing to be enforceable. The sixth category is not governed by the common law, but rather by the Uniform Commercial Code. Remember that UCC rules apply only to contracts involving a sale of goods. This statute has its own writing requirement.

The UCC requires a writing for the sale of goods priced $500 or more. The Code's requirements are easier to meet than those of the common law. Because merchants can make many verbal contracts every day, the drafters of the UCC wanted to make the writing requirement less onerous for the sale of goods. **UCC §2-201,** the Statute of Frauds section, has three important elements:

1. The basic rule
2. The merchants' exception
3. Special circumstances

16-3a UCC §2-201(1)—The Basic Rule

A contract for the sale of goods of $500 or more is not enforceable unless there is some writing, signed by the defendant, indicating that the parties reached an agreement.

The key difference between the common law rule and the UCC rule is that the Code does *not* require *all* of the terms of the agreement to be in writing. The Code looks for something simpler: *an indication that the parties reached an agreement*. Only two things are required: the signature of the defendant and the quantity of goods being sold.

> The key difference between the common law rule and the UCC rule is that the Code does *not* require *all* of the terms of the agreement to be in writing.

Suppose a short memorandum between textile dealers indicates that Seller will sell to Buyer "grade AA 100 percent cotton, white athletic socks." If the writing does not state the price, the parties can testify at court about what the market price was at the time of the deal. If the writing says nothing about the delivery date, the court will assume a reasonable delivery date, say, 60 days. But how many socks were to be delivered? 100 pairs or 100,000? The court will have no objective evidence, and so, the quantity must be written.

---

[10]Stevens v. Publicis, S.A., 50 AD3d 253 (N.Y. Sup. Ct., 2008).

Writing	Result
"Confirming phone conversation today, I will send you 1,000 reams of paper for laser printing, usual quality & price. [Signed,] Seller."	This memorandum satisfies UCC §2-201(1), and the contract may be enforced against the seller. The buyer may testify as to the "usual" quality and price between the two parties, and both sides may rely on normal trade usage.
"Confirming phone conversation today, I will send you best quality paper for laser printing, $3.25 per ream, delivery date next Thursday. [Signed,] Seller."	This memorandum is not enforceable because it states no quantity.

The UCC's purpose is to make sales easier while still preventing fraud. Ultimately, courts seek to balance the formality of the writing requirement with their own common sense. They examine the situation as a whole to determine if there is enough evidence to show that the parties contracted. The following case involved an art auction, a wily buyer, and a precious Russian box worth, well, we do not know what it was worth, but definitely more than $500. The one thing lacking? A single document signed by the defendant.

William J. Jenack Estate Appraisers and Auctioneers, Inc. v. Rabizadeh

2013 NY Slip Op 08373
Court of Appeals of New York, 2013

Facts: William J. Jenack Estate Appraisers and Auctioneers, Inc., sold fine art and antiques at public auctions. Albert Rabizadeh wanted to buy a nineteenth-century Russian silver and enamel box, with an estimated value of $4,000, that was to be sold at one of Jenack's auctions. Rabizadeh could not attend the auction, so he submitted an "absentee bidder form," in accordance with Jenack's online and telephone bidder policy. Rabizadeh signed the form and listed his name, email address, telephone numbers, fax number, address, credit card number, and the items that he intended to bid on. Jenack assigned Rabizadeh bidder number 305.

The rare Russian box garnered much excitement from collectors who believed it was worth much more than its initially appraised value of $4,000. During the frenzied auction, Rabizadeh beat out many other bidders with a telephone bid of $400,000. (Yes, that is two zeros more than $4,000—it was quite a box.) Jenack recorded Rabizadeh's winning bid on an official "clerking sheet," along with the item, its description, and bidder number 305. When he received Jenack's invoice, Rabizadeh decided he did not want it anymore and refused to pay.

William J. Jenack Estate Appraisers & Auctioneers

This rare Russian box measured only $1\frac{1}{2}$ by $3\frac{5}{8}$ inches, but was worth a fortune.

Jenack sued Rabizadeh for breach of contract. Rabizadeh claimed that there was no contract because the sale was not in a signed writing, as required by the UCC for goods over $500. Jenack argued that the clerking sheet and related documents satisfied the writing requirement because they contained all the necessary terms. The trial court agreed with Jenack and awarded it $402,398. A New York appeals court reversed the decision. Jenack appealed to New York's highest court.

Issue: ***Did the clerking sheet and the absentee bidder form satisfy the Statute of Frauds?***

Excerpts from Judge Rivera's Decision: In general, a contract for the sale of goods at a price of $500 or more must comply with the signed writing requirement of the UCC. In the case of a public auction, a bid may satisfy the [UCC's] Statute of Frauds where there exists an appropriate writing "signed by the party against whom enforcement is sought to be charged" (*see* UCC §2-201). [New York law also permits] a memorandum specifying the nature and price of the item, the terms of sale, and the names of the parties.

It is well established that the writing need not be contained in one single document, but rather may be furnished by piecing together other, related writings. Therefore, a court may look to documents relevant to the bidding and the auction.

The clerking sheet, in isolation, does not satisfy the New York law because it requires the disclosure of the name of the buyer. We are unpersuaded by Jenack's arguments that this requirement can be satisfied by Jenack's insertion of numbers in place of those names. To allow for numbers, rather than names, would undermine the purpose of the Statute by increasing the possibility of fraud.

We must consider whether there are "related writings" that supply the required names, and which may be read, along with the clerking sheet, to provide the information necessary to constitute a memorandum. The absentee bidder form, along with the clerking sheet, provide the necessary information to establish the name of Rabizadeh as the buyer. This conclusion is inescapable given that each of the documents contained information pertaining to the terms of the sale. Both contain the item number, the bidder number, the auctioneer, and a detailed description of the item.

The Statute of Frauds was not enacted to afford persons a means of evading just obligations. [That] is precisely what Rabizadeh attempts to do here, but the law and the facts foreclose him from doing so. Rabizadeh took affirmative steps to participate in Jenack's auction, including executing an absentee bidder form with the required personal information. He then successfully won the bidding, closing out other interested bidders, with his $400,000 bid. He cannot seek to avoid the consequences of his actions by ignoring the existence of a documentary trail leading to him.

UCC §2-201(2)—The Merchants' Exception

When both parties are "merchants," that is, businesspeople who routinely deal in the goods being sold, the Code will accept an even more informal writing. **Within a reasonable time of making an oral contract, if a merchant sends a written confirmation to another, and if the confirmation is definite enough to bind the *sender herself*, then the merchant who receives the confirmation will *also* be bound by it unless he objects in writing within ten days.** This exception dramatically changes the rules from the common law, but it applies only between two merchants. The UCC's drafters assumed that experienced merchants are able to take care of themselves in fast-moving negotiations. The critical difference is this: A writing may create a binding contract *even when it is not signed by the defendant.*

Madge manufactures "beanies," that is, silly caps with plastic propellers on top. Rachel, a retailer, telephones her, and they discuss the price of the beanies, shipping time, and other details. Madge then faxes Rachel a memo: "This confirms your order for 2,500 beanies at $12.25 per beanie. Colors: blue, green, black, orange, red. Delivery date: 10 days. [Signed] Madge." Rachel receives the fax, reads it while negotiating with another manufacturer, and throws it in the wastebasket. Rachel buys her beanies elsewhere, and Madge sues. Rachel defends, claiming there is no written contract because she, Rachel, never signed anything. Madge wins under UCC §2-201(2). Both parties were merchants because they routinely dealt in these goods. Madge signed and sent a confirming memo that could have been used to hold her, Madge, to the deal. When Rachel read it, she was not free to disregard it. Obviously, the intelligent business practice would have been to promptly fax a reply saying, "I disagree. We do not have any deal for beanies." Since Rachel failed to respond within ten days, Madge has an enforceable contract.

UCC §2-201(3)—Special Circumstances

An oral contract *may* be enforceable, even without a written memorandum, if:

- **The seller is specially manufacturing the goods for the buyer,** ***or***
- **The defendant admits in court proceedings that there was a contract,** ***or***
- **The goods have been delivered or they have been paid for.**

Specially Manufactured Goods. If a seller, specially manufacturing goods for the buyer, begins work on them before the buyer cancels, and the goods cannot be sold elsewhere, the oral contract is binding. Bernice manufactures solar heating systems. She phones Jason and orders 75 special electrical converter units designed for her heating system, at $150 per unit. Jason begins manufacturing the units, but then Bernice phones again and says she no longer needs them. Bernice is bound by the contract. The goods are being manufactured for her and cannot be sold elsewhere. Jason had already begun work when she attempted to cancel. If the case goes to court, Jason will win.

Admissions in Court. When the defendant admits in court proceedings that the parties made an oral contract, the agreement is binding. Rex sues Sophie, alleging that she orally agreed to sell him five boa constrictors that have been trained to stand in a line and pass a full wineglass from one snake to the next. Sophie defends the lawsuit, but during a deposition, she says, "OK, we agreed verbally, but nothing was ever put in writing, and I knew I didn't have to go through with it. When I went home, the snakes made me feel really guilty, and I decided not to sell." Sophie's admission under oath dooms her defense.

Goods Delivered or Paid For. If the seller has delivered the goods, or the buyer has paid for them, the contract may be enforced even with nothing in writing. Malik orally agrees to sell 500 plastic chairs to a university for use in its cafeteria. Malik delivers 300 of the chairs, but then the university notifies him that it will not honor the deal. Malik is entitled to payment for the 300 chairs, although not for the other 200. Conversely, if the university had sent a check for one-half of the chairs, it would be entitled to 250 chairs.

EXAMStrategy

Question: Beasley is a commercial honey farmer. He orally agrees to sell 500,000 pounds of honey to Grizzly at $1 per pound. Grizzly immediately faxes Beasley a signed confirmation, summarizing the deal. Beasley receives the fax but ignores it, and he never responds to Grizzly. Five days later, Beasley sells his honey to Brown for $1.15 per pound. Grizzly sues Beasley for breach of contract. Beasley claims that he signed nothing and was free to sell his honey anywhere he wanted. Who will win?

Strategy: Honey is a movable thing, meaning that this contract is governed by the UCC. Under the Code, contracts for the sale of goods worth $500 or more must be in writing. However, the merchant exception changes things when both parties are merchants. Beasley and Grizzly are both merchants. Apply the merchant exception.

Result: Beasley breached the contract. Within a reasonable time after making the agreement, Grizzly sent a memo to Beasley confirming it. Beasley had ten days either to object in writing or to be held to the agreement. Beasley will lose this lawsuit because he ignored the faxed confirmation.

16-4 PAROL EVIDENCE

Tyrone agrees to buy Martha's house for $800,000. The contract obligates Tyrone to make a 10 percent down payment immediately and pay the remaining $720,000 in 45 days. As the two parties sign the deal, Tyrone discusses his need for financing. Unfortunately, at the end of 45 days, he has been unable to get a mortgage for the full amount. He claims that the parties orally agreed that he would get his deposit back if he could not obtain financing, but the written agreement says no such thing, and Martha disputes the claim. Who will win? Probably Martha, because of the parol evidence rule.

Parol evidence refers to anything (apart from the written contract itself) that was said, done, or written *before* the parties signed the agreement or *as they signed it*. Martha's conversation with Tyrone about financing the house was parol evidence because it occurred as they were signing the contract. Another important term is **integrated contract**, which means a writing that the parties intend as the final, complete expression of their agreement. Now for the rule.

Integrated contract
A writing that the parties intend as the final, complete expression of their agreement

The parol evidence rule: When two parties make an integrated contract, neither one may use parol evidence to contradict, vary, or add to its terms. Negotiations may last for hours, weeks, or even months. Almost no contract includes everything that the parties said. When parties consider their agreement integrated, any statements they made before or while signing are irrelevant. If a court determines that Martha and Tyrone intended their agreement to be integrated, it will prohibit testimony about Martha's oral promises. One way to avoid parol evidence disputes is to include an *integration clause*. That is a statement clearly proclaiming that this writing is the "full and final expression" of the parties' agreement, and that anything said before signing or while signing is irrelevant. In the following case, learned people learned about parol evidence the hard way.

You Be the Judge

Mayo v. North Carolina State University

168 N.C.App. 503
North Carolina Court of Appeals, 2005

Facts: Dr. Robert Mayo was a tenured engineering professor at North Carolina State University (NCSU). In July, he informed his department chair, Dr. Paul Turinsky, that he was leaving NCSU effective September 1. Turinsky accepted the resignation.

In October, after Mayo had departed, Phyllis Jennette, the university's payroll coordinator, informed Mayo that he had been overpaid. She explained that for employees who worked 9 months but were paid over 12 months, the salary checks for July and August were in fact prepayments for the period beginning that September. Because Mayo had not worked after September 1, the checks for July and August were overpayment. When he refused to refund the money, NCSU sued. The first step was a hearing before an administrative agency.

At the hearing, Turinsky and Brian Simet, the university's payroll director, explained that the "prepayment" rule was a basic part of every employee's contract. However, both acknowledged that the prepayment rule was not included in any of the documents that formed Mayo's contract, including his appointment letter, annual salary letter, and policies adopted by the university's trustees. The university officials used other evidence, outside the written documents, to establish the prepayment policy.

Based on the additional evidence, the agency ruled that NCSU was entitled to its money. However, Mayo appealed to court, and the trial judge declared that he owed nothing, ruling that the university was not permitted to rely on parol evidence to establish its policy. NCSU appealed.

You Be the Judge: *May NCSU rely on parol evidence to enforce its prepayment rule?*

Argument for Mayo: Your honors, what is the point of having a contract if a court can enforce random, additional terms from other policies? The terms of Dr. Mayo's employment are clearly stated in his appointment letter, his annual salary letter, and the written Faculty Policies. None of these documents detail this supposed prepayment rule. Parol evidence that changes, adds to, or contradicts written terms should not be introduced to explain the terms of an agreement that are otherwise crystal clear.

Argument for NCSU: Your honors, the parol evidence here is not *adding* new terms to Dr. Mayo's contract, it is simply *clarifying* the terms that are there. It is well known that summer salary payments are prepayments for the upcoming academic year. When a 9-month employee who is paid on a 12-month basis leaves before the fall semester, that person must return the amount of overpayment. This understanding formed part of the contract, regardless of whether it was in writing. Dr. Mayo took something that was not his and cannot rely on the silence of the written contract to justify his actions.

16-4a Exception: An Incomplete or Ambiguous Contract

If a court determines that a written contract is incomplete or ambiguous, it will permit parol evidence. Suppose that an employment contract states that the company will provide "full health coverage for Robert Watson and his family," but does not define *family*. Three years later, Watson divorces and remarries, acquiring three stepchildren, and a year later, his second wife has a baby. Watson now has two children by his first marriage and four by the second. The company refuses to insure Watson's first wife or his stepchildren. A court will probably find a key clause in his health care contract—"coverage for … *his family*"—is ambiguous. A judge cannot determine exactly what the clause means from the contract itself, so the parties will be permitted to introduce parol evidence to prove whether or not the company must insure Watson's extended family.[11]

16-4b Fraud, Misrepresentation, or Duress

A court will permit parol evidence of fraud, misrepresentation, or duress. To encourage Annette to buy his house, Will assures her that no floodwaters from the nearby river have ever come within 2 miles of the house. Annette signs a contract that is silent about flooding and includes an integration clause stating that neither party is relying on any oral statements made during negotiations. When Annette moves in, she discovers that the foundation is collapsing due to earlier flooding and that Will knew of the flooding and the damage. Despite the integration clause, a court will probably allow Annette to testify about Will's misrepresentations.[12]

CHAPTER CONCLUSION

Some contracts must be in writing to be enforceable, and the writing must be clear and unambiguous. Drafting the contract need not be arduous. The disputes illustrated in this chapter could all have been prevented with a few carefully crafted sentences. It is worth the time and effort to write them.

EXAM REVIEW

1. **THE STATUTE OF FRAUDS** Several types of contract are enforceable only if written:
   - **LAND** For the transfer of an interest in land.
   - **ONE YEAR** An agreement that *cannot* be performed within one year.

EXAMStrategy

CPA Question: Able hired Carr to restore Able's antique car for $800. The terms of their oral agreement provided that Carr had 18 months to complete the work. Actually, the work could be completed within one year. The agreement is:

(a) unenforceable because it covers services with a value in excess of $500.

(b) unenforceable because it covers a time period in excess of one year.

11See, for example, Eure v. Norfolk Shipbuilding & Drydock Corp., Inc., 561 S.E.2d 663 (2002).
12Lindberg v. Roseth, 137 Idaho 222 (2002).

(c) enforceable because personal service contracts are exempt from the Statute of Frauds.

(d) enforceable because the work could be completed within one year.

Strategy: This is a subtle question. Notice that the contract is for a sum greater than $500. But that is a red herring. Why? The contract also might take 18 months to perform. But it *could* be finished in less than a year. (See the "Result" at the end of this Exam Review section.)

- **DEBT OF ANOTHER** In which a party promises to pay the debt of another.

EXAMStrategy

Question: Donald Waide had a contracting business. He bought most of his supplies from Paul Bingham's supply center. Waide fell behind on his bills, and Bingham told Waide that he would extend no more credit to him. That same day, Donald's father, Elmer Waide, came to Bingham's store and said to Bingham that he would "stand good" for any sales to Donald made on credit. Based on Elmer's statement, Bingham again gave Donald credit, and Donald ran up $10,000 in goods before Bingham sued Donald and Elmer. What defense did Elmer make, and what was the outcome?

Strategy: This was an oral agreement, so the issue is whether the promise had to be in writing to be enforceable. Review the list of six contracts that must be in writing. Is this agreement there? (See the "Result" at the end of this Exam Review section.)

- **EXECUTORS** A promise made by an executor of an estate to pay a debt of the estate.
- **MARRIAGE** A promise made in consideration of marriage.
- **GOODS** The sale of goods of $500 or more.

EXAMStrategy

Question: James River-Norwalk, Inc., was a paper and textile company that needed a constant supply of wood. James River orally contracted with Gary Futch to supply wood for the company, and Futch did so for several years. The deal was worth many thousands of dollars, but nothing was put in writing. Futch actually purchased the wood for his own account and then resold it to James River. After a few years, James River refused to do more business with Futch. Did the parties have a binding contract?

Strategy: If this is a contract for services, it is enforceable without anything in writing. However, if it is one for the sale of goods, it must be in writing. Clearly what James River wanted was the wood, and it did not care where Futch found it. (See the "Result" at the end of this Exam Review section.)

---

2. **WRITING REQUIREMENT** The writing must be signed by the defendant and must state the name of all parties, the subject matter of the agreement, and all essential terms and promises. Electronic signatures are usually valid.

3. **UNIFORM COMMERCIAL CODE (UCC)** A contract or memorandum for the sale of goods may be less complete than those required by the common law.
   - The basic UCC rule requires only a memorandum signed by the defendant, indicating that the parties reached an agreement and specifying the quantity of goods.
   - Between merchants, even less is required. If one merchant sends written confirmation of a contract, the merchant who receives the document must object within ten days or be bound by the writing.
   - In the following special circumstances, no writing may be required: the goods are specially manufactured, one party admits in litigation that there was a contract, or one party pays for part of the goods or delivers some of the goods.

4. **PAROL EVIDENCE** When an integrated contract exists, neither party may generally use parol evidence to contradict, vary, or add to its terms. Parol evidence refers to anything (apart from the written contract itself) that was said, done, or written before the parties signed the agreement or as they signed it.

RESULTS

1. "One Year" Result: (d) A contract for the sale of goods worth $500 or more must be in writing—but this is a contract for *services*, not the sale of goods, so the $800 price is irrelevant. The contract *can* be completed within one year, and thus it falls outside the Statute of Frauds. This is an enforceable agreement.

1. "Debt of Another" Result: Elmer made a promise to pay the debt of another. He did so as a favor to his son. This is a collateral promise. Elmer never signed any such promise, and the agreement cannot be enforced against him.

1. "Goods" Result: James River was buying wood, and this is a contract for the sale of goods. With nothing in writing, signed by James River, Futch has no enforceable agreement.

MULTIPLE-CHOICE QUESTIONS

1. **CPA QUESTION** Two individuals signed a contract that was intended to be their entire agreement. The parol evidence rule will prevent the admission of evidence offered to:

   (a) explain the meaning of an ambiguity in the written contract.
   (b) establish that fraud had been committed in the formation of the contract.
   (c) prove the existence of a contemporaneous oral agreement modifying the contract.
   (d) prove the existence of a subsequent oral agreement modifying the contract.

2. Rafaella wants to plant a garden, and she agrees to buy a small piece of land for $300. Later, she agrees to buy a table for $300. Neither agreement is put in writing. The agreement to buy the land ______________ enforceable, and the agreement to buy the table ______________ enforceable.
   (a) is; is
   (b) is; is not
   (c) is not; is
   (d) is not; is not
3. The common law Statute of Frauds requires that to be "in writing," an agreement must be signed by:
   (a) the plaintiff.
   (b) the defendant.
   (c) both A and B.
   (d) none of these.
4. Mandy verbally tells a motorcycle dealer that she will make her son's motorcycle payments if he falls behind on them. Will Mandy be legally required to live up to this agreement?
   (a) Yes, absolutely.
   (b) Yes, if her son is under 18.
   (c) Yes, if Mandy will be the primary driver of the motorcycle.
   (d) Yes, if the motorcycle is worth less than $500.
   (e) No, absolutely not.
5. In December 2018, Eric hires a band to play at a huge graduation party he is planning to hold in May, 2020. The deal is never put into writing. In January 2020, if he wanted to cancel the job, Eric ____________ be able to do so. If he does not cancel, and if the band shows up and plays at the party in May 2020, Eric ____________ have to pay them.
   (a) will; will
   (b) will; will not
   (c) will not; will
   (d) will not; will not

CASE QUESTIONS

1. Richard Griffin and three other men owned a grain company, called Bearhouse, Inc., which needed to borrow money. First National Bank was willing to loan $490,000, but it insisted that the four men sign personal guarantees on the loan, committing themselves to repaying up to 25 percent of the loan each if Bearhouse defaulted. Bearhouse went bankrupt. The bank was able to collect some of its money from Bearhouse's assets, but it sued Griffin for the balance. At trial, Griffin wanted to testify that before he signed his guaranty, a bank officer assured him that he would only owe 25 percent of *whatever balance was unpaid*, not 25 percent of the total loan. How will the court decide whether Griffin is entitled to testify about the conversation?

2. Landlord owned a clothing store and agreed in writing to lease the store's basement to another retailer. The written lease, which both parties signed, (1) described the premises exactly, (2) identified the parties, and (3) stated the monthly rent clearly. But an appeals court held that the lease did not satisfy the Statute of Frauds. Why not?

3. ***YOU BE THE JUDGE* WRITING PROBLEM** Because of his success in a big case, a lawyer named Melbourne promised his assistant, Barbara, a large bonus. After the case settled, Melbourne met with Barbara to discuss when and how much he would pay her. In the conversation that she secretly recorded, Melbourne agreed to pay Barbara $1 million, plus $65,000 for a luxury automobile. Payments were to be made in monthly installments of $10,000, for ten years. Melbourne also agreed to sign a document confirming his promise. Barbara's lawyer drafted the writing, but Melbourne never signed it. He did pay nine monthly installments, along with an extra payment of $100,000. Did Melbourne and Barbara have a valid contract? **Argument for Barbara:** The Statute of Frauds exists to prevent fraud. The fear that a plaintiff would lie about a contract is not an issue here. We know what Melbourne agreed to do because we *heard* him. **Argument for Melbourne:** If there was an agreement, it could not have been performed in one year because it had ten years' worth of installment payments.

4. Robins, an art collector, sold a painting by artist Marlene Dumas named *Reinhardt's Daughter* to Zwirner, an art dealer. Since both men knew that Dumas would disapprove of the sale, Zwirner promised Robins that he would always keep the transaction confidential. Years later, Robins learned that Dumas would not sell to him anymore because Zwirner had told her about the sale. Will a court enforce Zwirner's oral promise? Why or why not?

5. When they were dating, Kris promised his wife Wendellyn that, if she moved to Wyoming and married him, he would take care of her for the rest of her life. Three years later, the couple filed for divorce and Wendellyn claimed that Kris's oral promise entitled her to care for life. Kris argued that his promise was unenforceable because it should have been in writing. Who is right?

DISCUSSION QUESTIONS

1. **ETHICS** Jacob Deutsch owned commercial property. He orally agreed to rent it for six years to Budget Rent A Car. Budget took possession, began paying monthly rent, and, over a period of several months, expended about $6,000 in upgrading the property. Deutsch was aware of the repairs. After a year, Deutsch attempted to evict Budget. Budget claimed it had a six-year oral lease, but Deutsch claimed that such a lease was worthless. Please rule. Is it ethical for Deutsch to use the Statute of Frauds in attempting to defeat the lease? Assume that, as landlord, you had orally agreed to rent premises to a tenant, but then for business reasons, you preferred not to carry out the deal. Would you evict a tenant if you thought the Statute of Frauds would enable you to do so? How should you analyze the problem? What values are most important to you?

2. Mast Industries and Bazak International were two textile firms. Mast verbally offered to sell certain textiles to Bazak for $103,000. Mast promised to send documents confirming the agreement, but it never did. Finally, Bazak sent a memorandum to Mast confirming the agreement, describing the goods, and specifying their quantity and the price. Bazak's officer signed the memo. Mast received the memo but never agreed to it in writing. When Mast failed to deliver the goods, Bazak sued. Who will win? Why?

3. A disc jockey named Z-Trip made a remix of a Beastie Boys song with the hip-hop group's permission. Monster Energy (ME), an energy drink company, wanted to use the remix as part of a video promotion. ME sent an email asking Z-Trip to approve the video. In an email, Z-Trip responded "Dope!" When the Beastie Boys sued ME for copyright infringement, ME claimed that Z-Trip's reply was a contract granting it approval to use the remix. Is there an enforceable contract between Z-Trip and ME?

4. Now that you know about *Browning v. Poirier* and the Statute of Frauds, will you change the way you enter into lottery pools?

5. Compare the common law Statute of Frauds to the UCC version. What are the specific differences? Which is more reasonable? Why?

CHAPTER 17

THIRD PARTIES

First, Ronald Schmalfeldt got his teeth knocked out . . . and then he got his wind knocked out by his dental bills. Here is what happened.

Schmalfeldt was at the Elite Bar playing a pick-up game of pool with another bar patron, whom he did not know. A heated argument ensued. Schmalfeldt tried to walk away but was struck in the face by the other player, who then fled—never to be heard from again. The brawl caused Schmalfeldt extensive dental damage, to the tune of $1,921. He asked the owner of the Elite Bar to pay his dental expenses, but the owner refused. Schmalfeldt was left with his teeth—and his dental bills—in his hands.

Schmalfeldt sought payment directly from North Pointe, which had issued a commercial liability insurance policy to the owner of the Elite Bar. He claimed that, as a pool-playing bar patron, he had a right to medical benefits under the policy. In its contract with Elite, North Pointe had agreed to pay up to $5,000 for medical expenses for a bodily injury caused by an accident occurring on Elite's premises, regardless of fault. When North Pointe refused to pay, Schmalfeldt sued. Could Schmalfeldt enforce the bar's contract rights, or did he have to put his money where his mouth was?[1]

Schmalfeldt was left with his teeth–and his dental bills–in his hands.

[1] Schmalfeldt v. North Pointe Ins. Co., 469 Mich. 422 (2003).

Chapters 13 through 16 examined the Contracts Checklist, so you now know all the elements that must be present for a valid contract to exist. In this chapter and Chapters 18 and 19, we turn our attention to other contract issues.

17-1 THIRD PARTY BENEFICIARY

The two parties who make a contract always intend to gain some benefit for themselves. Often, though, their bargain will also benefit *someone else*. **A third party beneficiary is someone who was not a party to the contract but stands to benefit from it.** Many contracts are clear in their intent to create third party beneficiaries—and some even mention these lucky people by name. Sometimes, however, unnamed third parties want to enforce others' contracts. In that case, courts must analyze the particulars of the deal to see who is entitled to recover. In the case from the opening scenario, the Michigan Supreme Court held that since the insurance contract was intended to benefit the insured (the bar) and made no mention of patrons, Schmalfeldt was not a third party beneficiary and, therefore, could not recover his damages.

As another example, suppose a major league baseball team contracts to purchase from Seller 20 acres of an abandoned industrial site to be used for a new stadium. The owner of a pizza parlor on the edge of Seller's land might benefit enormously, since 40,000 hungry fans in the neighborhood for 81 home games every season could turn her once-marginal operation into a gold mine of cheese and pepperoni.

But what if the contract falls apart? What if the team backs out of the land deal? Seller can certainly sue because it is a party to the contract. But what about the pizza parlor owner? Can she sue to enforce the deal and recover lost profits for unsold sausage and green pepper?

The outcome in cases like these depends upon the intentions of the two contracting parties. If they *intended* to benefit the third party, she will probably be permitted to enforce their contract. If they did not intend to benefit her, she probably has no power to enforce the agreement.

17-1a Intended Beneficiaries

Intended beneficiary Someone who may enforce a contract made between two other parties

Promisor Makes the promise that a third party seeks to enforce

Promisee The contract party *to whom* a promise is made

A person is an **intended beneficiary** and may enforce a contract if the parties intended her to benefit and if either (a) enforcing the promise will satisfy a *duty* of the promisee to the beneficiary or (b) the promisee intended to make a *gift* to the beneficiary. (The **promisor** is the one who makes the promise that the third party beneficiary is seeking to enforce. The **promisee** is the other party to the contract.)

In other words, a third party beneficiary must show two things in order to enforce a contract that two other people created. First, she must show that the two contracting parties were aware of her situation and knew that she would receive something of value from their deal. Second, she must show that the promisee wanted to benefit her for one of two reasons: either to satisfy some duty owed or to make her a gift.

If the promisee is fulfilling some duty, the third party beneficiary is called a **creditor beneficiary**. Most often, the duty that a promisee will be fulfilling is a debt already owed to the beneficiary. If the promisee is making a gift, the third party is a **donee beneficiary**.[2] As long as the third party is either a creditor or a donee beneficiary, she may enforce the contract. If she is only an incidental beneficiary, she may not.

John's father, Clarence, has an overgrown lawn. So, John enters into a contract with Billy Goat Landscapers for it to mow Clarence's lawn every week. Billy Goat is the promisor and John, the promisee. Although Clarence was not a party to the contract, he is the beneficiary—it is his lawn being cut. John did not owe his father a legal duty but simply intended to make

[2] "Donee" comes from the word *donate*.

him a gift, so, Clarence is an intended, donee beneficiary, and he can sue the landscaping company to enforce the contract himself.

By contrast, the pizza parlor owner will surely lose. A stadium is a multimillion-dollar investment, and it is most unlikely that the baseball team and the seller of the land were even aware of the owner's existence, let alone that they intended to benefit her. She probably cannot prove either the first element or the second element, and certainly not both.

In the following case, an unlikely plaintiff sues for breach of a state contract. Was the prison inmate an intended beneficiary or was his argument just smoke in mirrors? Who is entitled to sue?

Rathke v. Corrections Corporation of America, Inc.

153 P.3d 303
Alaska Supreme Court, 2007

Facts: The state of Alaska entered into a contract with Corrections Corporation of America (CCA), a private company, to house Alaska's inmates. The contract required CCA to abide by the terms of a settlement agreement between the state and its inmates known as the Cleary FSA. This agreement listed Alaska's duties to its prisoners and also provided a list of permissible disciplinary procedures.

Gus Rathke was an Alaska inmate at a CCA prison located in Arizona. A routine drug test revealed marijuana in his system. Rathke's level of marijuana was within the limit allowed by the Cleary FSA (50 ng/ml) but exceeded Arizona's limit (20 ng/ml). CCA applied the more stringent Arizona standard. As a result, Rathke spent 30 days in punitive segregation and lost his prison job.

Rathke sued CCA, seeking lost wages and an apology. He claimed that CCA breached its contract with Alaska when it punished him according to the stricter marijuana standard. Rathke argued that as an Alaska inmate, he was an intended third-party beneficiary of the contract between Alaska and CCA.

The trial court disagreed with Rathke. It held that, even though he was entitled to certain rights under the Cleary FSA, he was not a third-party beneficiary of the CCA/Alaska contract. It reasoned that the Clearly FSA duties were only between Alaska and the inmates, while the duties in the CCA/Alaska contract were only between CCA and the state. Rathke appealed to Alaska's Supreme Court.

Issue: ***Was Rathke an intended beneficiary of the contract between the state of Alaska and CCA?***

Excerpts from Justice Carpeneti's Decision: In determining whether a third party is an intended beneficiary of a contract, we refer to the Restatement (Second) of Contracts. According to §302, "a beneficiary of a promise is an intended beneficiary if the circumstances indicate that the promisee intends to give the beneficiary the benefit of the promised performance."

When applying these provisions, the motives of the parties in executing a contract—especially the promisee—are determinative. As a general rule, if the promised performance is rendered directly to the beneficiary, the intent to benefit the third party will be clearly manifested.

The state owes legal duties to all Alaska inmates, including those housed like Rathke at the CCA's Arizona facility. These duties are detailed in the Cleary FSA, which is an enforceable contract between Alaska inmates and the state.

We disagree with the [lower] court's analysis. First, the Cleary settlement is incorporated by reference into the state/CCA contract. Even more, many of its provisions are repeated virtually word for word in the contract. For example, portions of the discipline section of the state/CCA contract, allegedly breached in Rathke's case are virtually identical to the Cleary FSA.

Given this identity of provisions between the FSA and the state/CCA contract, we conclude that the prisoners are intended third-party beneficiaries of the portions of the contract which are taken directly from the FSA.

Accordingly, we hold that inmates have the right to sue CCA for violations of the Cleary FSA provisions contained in the CCA's contract with the state.

EXAMStrategy

Question: Mr. Inspector examines houses and gives its reports to potential buyers. Mr. Inspector contracts with Greenlawn, a real estate agent, to furnish reports on houses that Greenlawn is selling. The agreement allows the agent to give the reports to potential buyers. Greenlawn gives Molly one of Mr. Inspector's reports and, relying upon it, she buys a house. Although the report states that the house is structurally sound, it turns out that chronic roof leaks have caused water to seep into the walls. Molly sues Mr. Inspector. The inspector requests summary judgment, claiming that he had no contract with Molly.

Strategy: Mr. Inspector is right in saying he had no agreement with Molly. To prevail, Molly must demonstrate she is a third party beneficiary of the contract between the other two. A third party beneficiary may enforce a contract if the parties intended to benefit her and either (a) enforcing the promise will satisfy a duty of the promisee to the beneficiary or (b) the promisee intended to make a gift to the beneficiary.

Result: Greenlawn used the inspection summaries as sales tools. When Greenlawn assured a potential buyer that she could rely upon a report, the real estate agent took on a duty to deliver reliable information. Mr. Inspector understood that. The two parties intended to benefit Greenlawn's buyers. Molly may sue Mr. Inspector for breach of his contract with the agent. Mr. Inspector's motion for summary judgment is denied.

17-1b Incidental Beneficiaries

Incidental beneficiary
Someone who might have benefited from a contract between two others but has no right to enforce that agreement

A person who fails to qualify as a donee beneficiary or a creditor beneficiary is merely an **incidental beneficiary** and may not enforce the contract. The pizza parlor owner is an incidental beneficiary.

In an effort to persuade courts, many plaintiffs make creative arguments that they are intended beneficiaries with enforcement rights. Is every taxpayer an intended beneficiary of a government contract? Do labor unions have rights if a contract refers to them in general terms? Or are these plaintiffs incidental beneficiaries? The following case answers these questions.

Unite Here Local 30 v. California Department of Parks and Recreation

194 Cal. App. 4th 1200
Court of Appeals of California, 2011

Facts: The California Department of Parks and Recreation (DPR) and Delaware North Companies (DNC) entered into a contract giving DNC the right to operate a concession stand at a state park in San Diego for 10 years. Four years into the contract, DNC assigned its rights to operate the stand to another company.

DNC fired many of its employees, and the new operator did not rehire them. Some of these workers were members of the union Unite Here Local 30. Local 30 sued to block the assignment. It was joined in the suit by Bridgette Browning, who lived in the area and seemed to care who provided her hot dogs.

The trial court rejected the plaintiff's claims, and the plaintiffs appealed.

Issue: ***Were the plaintiffs incidental or donee beneficiaries?***

Excerpts from Judge Hull's Decision: Paragraph 37(a) of the contract limits assignments and reads: "No assignment shall be made unless first consented to in writing by State." Before State considers such assignment, the proposed assignment must comply with applicable law. DPR reviewed the evidence submitted by Delaware North and determined that the proposed assignment met the requirements under paragraph 37(a).

Plaintiffs contend a third party who is within the class of those for whose benefit a contract is made have standing to sue for breach of that contract. They further argue, Local

30 and the employees it represents are clearly intended beneficiaries of the original contract.

The test for determining whether a contract was made for the benefit of a third person is whether an intent to benefit a third person appears from the terms of the contract. Under the intent test, it is not enough that the third party would incidentally have benefited from performance. On the other hand, the third person need not be named or identified individually. A third party may enforce a contract where he shows that he is a member of a class of persons for whose benefit it was made.

Plaintiffs contend Bridgette Browning has a right to sue as a taxpayer of California. They point out that paragraph 37 procedures are intended to eliminate favoritism, fraud, corruption, and misuse of public funds. Thus, plaintiffs argue, can be said to have the intent to benefit the general public and the taxpayer. Of course, any contract entered into by the state would presumably be for the benefit of the state's residents and taxpayers, just as a contract entered into by a corporation would presumably be for the benefit of the corporation's shareholders. However, the fact that members of the public derive a benefit from the contract does not make them intended beneficiaries. A person is a donee beneficiary only if the promisee's contractual intent is to make a gift to him. Browning is no more than an incidental beneficiary who benefits merely because the state as a whole benefits.

Likewise, Local 30 is no more than an incidental beneficiary. Plaintiffs argue that because the Concession Contract contains a neutrality agreement regarding union organizing, Local 30 and the employees it represents are clearly intended beneficiaries of the original contract. The neutrality agreement states, in part, "Concessionaire shall not use the Premises to hold a meeting if the purpose is to promote or deter union organizing." This provision hardly reveals an intent to confer a benefit on Local 30, or any union for that matter. At best, it shows an intent not to provide either a benefit or a detriment to union organizing.

We conclude the trial court correctly determined plaintiffs are not third party beneficiaries and therefore lack standing to sue on that basis.

The judgment is affirmed.

17-2 ASSIGNMENT AND DELEGATION

After a contract is made, one or both parties may wish to substitute someone else for themselves. Six months before Maria's lease expires, an out-of-town company offers her a new job at a substantial increase in pay. After taking the job, she wants to sublease her apartment to her friend Sarah.

A contracting party may transfer his rights under the contract, which is called an **assignment** of rights. Or a party may transfer her obligations under the contract, which is a **delegation** of duties. Frequently, a party will make an assignment and delegation simultaneously, transferring both rights (such as the right to inhabit an apartment) and duties (like the obligation to pay monthly rent) to a third party.

Assignment
Transferring contract *rights*

Delegation
Transferring contract *duties*

17-2a Assignment

Lydia needs 500 bottles of champagne. Bruno agrees to sell them to her for $10,000, payable 30 days after delivery. He transports the wine to her.

Bruno owes Doug $8,000 from a previous deal. He says to Doug, "I don't have your money, but I'll give you my claim to Lydia's $10,000." Doug agrees. Bruno then *assigns* to Doug his rights to Lydia's money, and in exchange Doug gives up his claim against Bruno for $8,000. Bruno is the assignor, the one making an assignment, and Doug is the assignee, the one receiving an assignment.

Why would Bruno offer $10,000 when he owed Doug only $8,000? Because all he has is a *claim* to Lydia's money. Cash in hand is often more valuable. Doug, however, is willing to assume some risk for a potential $2,000 gain.

Bruno notifies Lydia of the assignment. Lydia, who owes the money, is called the **obligor**; that is, the one obligated to do something. At the end of 30 days, Doug arrives at Lydia's doorstep, asks for his money, and gets it, since Lydia is obligated to him. Bruno has no claim to any payment. See Exhibit 17.1.

Obligor
The party obligated to do something

EXHIBIT 17.1

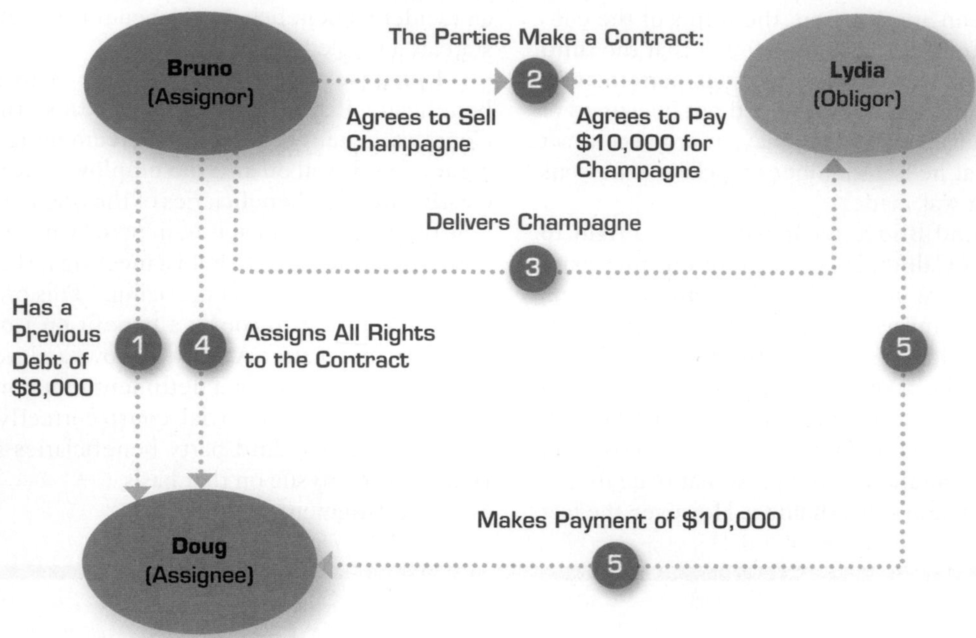

EXAMStrategy

Question: Hasannah, an art dealer, signs a contract with Jason. Hasannah will deliver a David Hockney painting to Jason's house. Jason may keep it for 30 days and then either return it or pay Hasannah $2 million. Hasannah delivers the painting. Hasannah finds a better building to house her gallery and agrees to buy it from Shannon. She and Shannon sign a contract allowing Shannon to receive Jason's payment if he keeps the picture. Hasannah then notifies Jason to pay Shannon the $2 million. Identify the obligor, the assignor, and the assignee.

Strategy: The obligor is the one obligated to do something. The assignor makes an assignment and the assignee receives it.

Result: Jason is obligated either to return the picture or pay $2 million for it. He is the obligor. Hasannah is entitled to the money, but she assigns her right to Shannon. Hasannah is the assignor and Shannon the assignee.

What Rights Are Assignable?

Most contract rights are assignable, but not all. Disputes sometimes arise between the two contracting parties about whether one of the parties could legally assign her rights to a third party. **Any contractual right may be assigned unless the assignment:**

- Would substantially change the obligor's rights or duties under the contract,
- Is forbidden by law or public policy, or
- Is validly precluded by the contract itself.[3]

[3]Restatement (Second) of Contracts §317(2). And note that UCC §2-210 is, for our purposes, nearly identical.

Substantial Change. An assignment is prohibited if it would substantially change the obligor's situation. For example, Bruno is permitted to assign to Doug his rights to payment from Lydia because it makes no difference to Lydia whether she writes a check to one person or another. But suppose that, before delivery, Lydia had wanted to assign her rights to the shipment of 500 bottles of champagne to a business in another country. In this example, Bruno would be the obligor, and his duties would substantially change. Shipping heavy items over long distances adds substantial costs, so Lydia would not be able to make the assignment.

Assignment is also prohibited when the obligor is agreeing to perform personal services. The close working relationship in such agreements makes it unfair to expect the obligor to work with a stranger. Warner, a candidate for public office, hires Mayer to be his campaign manager. Warner may not assign his right to Mayer's work to another candidate.

Public Policy. Some assignments are prohibited by public policy. For example, someone who has suffered a personal injury may not assign her claim to a third person. Vladimir is playing the piano on his roof deck when the instrument rolls over the balustrade and drops 35 stories before smashing Wanda's foot. Wanda has a valid tort claim against Vladimir, but she may not assign the claim to anyone else. As a matter of public policy, all states have decided that the sale of personal injury claims could create an unseemly and unethical marketplace.

Contract Prohibition. Finally, one of the contracting parties may try to prohibit assignment in the agreement itself. For example, most landlords include in the written lease a clause prohibiting the tenant from assigning the tenancy without the landlord's written permission.

Subleasing disputes between landlord and tenant are common. How much leeway does a landlord have in rejecting a proposed assignment? The following case provides the answer.

Tenet HealthSystem Surgical, L.L.C. v. Jefferson Parish Hospital Service District No. 1

426 F.3d 738
United States Court of Appeals for the Fifth Circuit, 2005

Facts: MSC, Inc., owned the Marrero Shopping Center and leased space to Tenet HealthSystem for use in outpatient surgery and general medical practice. The lease allowed Tenet to assign the lease with MSC's consent, and stated that consent would not be unreasonably withheld.

Two years later, MSC sold the shopping center to West Jefferson Medical Center, which owned an adjacent hospital and wanted the space for expansion. A few months after that, Tenet requested permission from West Jefferson to assign its lease to Pelican Medical, which intended to use the space for an occupational medical clinic. West Jefferson denied permission, stating that Pelican would be performing work not permitted under the original lease, and also because Pelican would compete with West Jefferson.

Tenet sued, claiming that West Jefferson was unreasonably withholding permission to assign. The trial court granted summary judgment for West Jefferson. Tenet appealed.

Issue: ***Did West Jefferson unreasonably withhold permission to assign the lease?***

Excerpts from Judge Davis's Decision: West Jefferson asserts that Pelican's contemplated uses of the facility exceed those permitted under the lease [and also argues] that its refusal was reasonable because the proposed use of the facility poses more competition to its adjacent hospital.

Tenet used the facility for an outpatient surgery center. Pelican planned to use the facility for an occupational medical clinic. The services offered by an occupational medicine practice are quite comprehensive, from physical examinations and drug screening to low acuity emergencies. The clinic can treat patients with depression, lacerations, broken bones [and] pneumonia, and provides related lab and x-ray services. Nothing in this description takes the proposed practice outside the limits of a "general medical and physician's offices, including related uses," a permitted use under the lease.

West Jefferson also opposes the lease assignment from Tenet to Pelican on the basis that Pelican's broadened scope of operations would include new areas of competition with its hospital. When determining the reasonableness of a landlord's refusal to consent to an assignment of a lease, the standard is that of a reasonable prudent man.

In determining whether a landlord's refusal to consent was reasonable in a commercial context, only factors that relate to the landlord's interest in preserving the leased property or in having the terms of prime lease performed should be considered. Among factors a landlord can consider are the financial responsibility of the proposed subtenant, the legality and suitability of proposed use and nature of the occupancy. A landlord's personal taste or convenience is not properly considered. Rather the landlord's objection must relate to ownership and operation of leased property, not lessor's general economic interest. Under this standard, West Jefferson's refusal to consent to the assignment of the Tenet lease because Pelican would be a new competitor relates not to the ownership and operation of the leased property, but to West Jefferson's general economic interest.

West Jefferson's reason for denying consent to the assignment to Pelican based on increased competition is wholly personal to West Jefferson and does not relate in any way to an objective evaluation of Pelican as a tenant. Further, allowing West Jefferson to deny consent on a basis personal to it, a successor owner who took subject to the existing lease, would expand West Jefferson's rights under the lease to the detriment of the lessee in a manner not bargained for in the lease itself. Accordingly, we conclude that West Jefferson's refusal of consent to the assignment of the lease on the basis of increased competition was unreasonable.

Reversed and remanded.

How Rights Are Assigned

Writing. In general, an assignment may be written or oral, and no particular formalities are required. However, when someone wants to assign rights governed by the Statute of Frauds, she must do it in writing. Suppose City contracts with Seller to buy Seller's land and then brings in Investor to complete the project. If City wants to assign to Investor its rights to the land, it must do so in writing.

Consideration. An assignment can be valid with or without consideration, but the lack of consideration may have consequences. Two examples should clarify this. Recall Bruno, who sells champagne to Lydia and then assigns to Doug his right to payment. In that case, there *is* consideration for the assignment. Bruno assigns his rights only because Doug cancels the old debt, and his agreement to do that is valid consideration. **An assignment for consideration is irrevocable.** Once the two men agree, Bruno may not telephone Doug and say, "I've changed my mind, I want Lydia to pay me after all." Lydia's $10,000 now belongs to Doug.

Gratuitous assignment
One made as a gift, for no consideration

But suppose that Bruno assigns his contract rights to his sister Brunhilde as a birthday present. This is a **gratuitous assignment**; that is, one made as a gift, for no consideration. **A gratuitous assignment is generally revocable if it is oral and generally irrevocable if it is written.** If Bruno verbally assigns his rights to Brunhilde, but then changes his mind, telephones Lydia, and says, "I want you to pay me after all," that revocation is effective and Brunhilde gets nothing. But if Bruno puts his assignment in writing and Brunhilde receives it, Bruno has given up his right to receive Lydia's payment.

If you assign your rights under a contract, inform the obligor immediately.

Notice to Obligor. The assignment is valid from the moment it is made, regardless of whether the assignor notifies the obligor. But an assignor with common sense will immediately inform the obligor of the assignment. Suppose that Maude has a contract with Nelson, who is obligated to deliver 700 live frogs to her shop. If Maude (assignor) assigns her rights to Obie (assignee), Maude should notify Nelson (obligor) the same day. If she fails to inform Nelson, he may deliver the frogs to Maude. Nelson will have no further obligations under the contract, and Maude will owe Obie 700 frogs.

Rights of the Parties after Assignment

Once the assignment is made and the obligor notified, the assignee may enforce her contractual rights against the obligor. If Lydia fails to pay Doug for the champagne she gets from Bruno, Doug may sue to enforce the agreement. The law will treat Doug as though he had entered into the contract with Lydia.

But if a lawsuit arises, the reverse is also true. **The obligor may generally raise all defenses against the assignee that she could have raised against the assignor.** Suppose that Lydia opens the first bottle of champagne—silently. "Where's the pop?" she wonders. There is no pop because all 500 bottles have gone flat. Bruno has failed to perform his part of the contract, and Lydia may use Bruno's nonperformance as a defense against Doug. If the champagne was indeed worthless, Lydia owes Doug nothing.

Assignor's Warranty. The law implies certain warranties, or assurances, on the part of the assignor. Unless the parties expressly agree to exclude them, the assignor warrants that (1) the rights he is assigning actually do exist and (2) there are no defenses to the rights other than those that would be obvious, such as nonperformance. But the assignor *does not* warrant that the obligor is solvent. Bruno is by implication warranting to Doug that Lydia has no defenses to the contract, but he is not guaranteeing Doug that she has the money to pay, or that she will pay.

Special Issue: The Uniform Commercial Code and Assignments of Security Interests

The provisions of the Uniform Commercial Code regarding assignments in contracts for the sale of goods are very similar to common law rules.[4] However, Article 9 of the UCC has special rules about the assignment of **security interests**, which are the legal rights in personal property that ensure payment. When an automobile dealer sells you a new car on credit, the dealer will keep a security interest in your car. If you do not make your monthly payments, the dealer retains a right to repossess the vehicle. That authority is called a *security interest*. (See Chapter 25 for a full discussion.)

Security interests
Rights in personal property that assure payment or the performance of some obligation

Companies that sell goods often prefer to assign their security interests to some other firm, such as a bank or finance company. The bank is the assignee. Just as we saw with the common law, the assignee of a security interest generally has all of the rights that the assignor had. And the obligor (the buyer) may also raise all of the defenses against the assignee that she could have raised against the assignor.

Under UCC §9-404, the obligor on a sales contract may generally assert any defenses against the assignee that arise from the contract, and any other defenses that arose before notice of assignment. The Code's reference to any defenses that arise from the contract means that if the assignor breached his part of the deal, the obligor may raise that as a defense. Suppose that a dealer sells you a new Porsche on credit, retaining a security interest. He assigns the security interest to the bank. The car is great for the first few weeks, but then the roof slides onto the street and both doors fall off. You refuse to make any more monthly payments. When the bank sues you, you may raise the automobile's defects as a defense, just as you could have raised them against the dealer itself. Where the Code talks about other defenses that arose before notice of assignment, it refers, for example, to fraud. Suppose that the dealer knew that before you bought the Porsche, it had been smashed up and rebuilt. If the dealer told you it was brand new, that was fraud, and you could raise the defense against the bank.

The car is great for the first few weeks, but then the roof slides onto the street and both doors fall off.

[4]UCC §2-210.

A contract may prohibit an obligor from raising certain defenses against an assignee. Sometimes a seller of goods will require the buyer to sign a contract that permits the seller to assign *and* prohibits the buyer from raising defenses against the assignee that he could have raised against the seller. University wants to buy a computer system on credit from Leland for $85,000. Leland agrees to the deal but insists that the contract permit him to assign his rights to anyone he chooses. He also wants this clause: "University agrees that it will not raise against an assignee any defenses that it may have had against Leland." This clause is sometimes called a *waiver clause* because the obligor is waiving (giving up) rights. Courts may also refer to it as an *exclusion clause* since the parties are excluding potential defenses. Leland wants a waiver clause because it makes his contract more valuable. As soon as University signs the agreement, Leland can take his contract to Krushem Collections, a finance company. Krushem might offer Leland $70,000 cash for the contract. Leland can argue, "You have to pay $85,000 for this. You are guaranteed payment by University since they cannot raise any defenses against you, even if the computer system collapses in the first half-hour." Leland gets cash and need not worry about collecting payments. Krushem receives the full value of the contract, with interest, spread out over several years.

Under UCC §9-403, an agreement by a buyer (or lessee) that he will not assert against an assignee any claim or defense that he may have against the seller (or lessor) is generally enforceable by the assignee if he took the assignment in good faith, for value, without notice of the potential defenses. In other words, Leland's waiver clause with University is enforceable. If Leland assigns the contract to Krushem Collections and the system proves worthless, Krushem is still entitled to its monthly payments from University. The school must seek its damages against Leland—a far more arduous step than simply withholding payment.

These waiver clauses are generally *not* valid in consumer contracts. If Leland sold a computer system to a consumer (an individual purchasing it for her personal use), the waiver would generally be unenforceable.

In the following case, one side pushes the waiver rule to its extreme. Can an assignee recover for money advanced . . . when the money was never advanced? You be the judge.

You Be the Judge

Wells Fargo Bank Minnesota v. BrooksAmerica Mortgage Corporation

419 F.3d 107
United States Court of Appeals for the Second Circuit, 2005

Facts: Michael Brooks desperately needed financing for his company, BrooksAmerica, so he agreed to a sale-leaseback agreement with Terminal Marketing Company. Terminal would pay BrooksAmerica $250,000, and in exchange it would obtain title to BrooksAmerica's computers and office equipment. BrooksAmerica would then lease the equipment for three years, for $353,000. The equipment would never leave BrooksAmerica's offices.

The contract included a "hell or high water clause" stating that BrooksAmerica's obligation to pay was "absolute and unconditional." Another clause permitted Terminal to assign its rights without notice to BrooksAmerica and stated that the assignee took its rights "free from all defenses, setoffs, or counterclaims."

Brooks also signed a "Delivery and Acceptance Certificate" stating that BrooksAmerica had received the $250,000 (even though no money had yet changed hands) and reaffirming BrooksAmerica's absolute obligation to pay an assignee, despite any defenses BrooksAmerica might have.

Terminal assigned its rights to Wells Fargo, which had taken about 2,000 other equipment leases from

Terminal. Terminal never paid any portion of the promised $250,000. Brooks refused to make the required payments (about $10,000 per month) and Wells Fargo sued. Brooks acknowledged that Wells Fargo paid Terminal for the assignment.

Both parties moved for summary judgment. The trial court ruled in favor of Wells Fargo, and Brooks appealed.

You Be the Judge: *Is Wells Fargo entitled to its monthly lease payments despite the fact that BrooksAmerica never received financing?*

Argument for BrooksAmerica: We acknowledge the general validity of UCC §9-403. However, in this case, Wells Fargo makes an absurd argument. Neither Terminal nor any assignee has a right to enforce a financing contract when Terminal failed to deliver the financing. There is no valid contract to enforce here because Terminal never paid the $250,000 owed to BrooksAmerica. "Good faith" required Wells Fargo to make sure that Terminal had performed. A simple inquiry would have informed Wells Fargo that Terminal was entitled to no money. This entire transaction is a sham, and §9-403 was never drafted to encourage financial swindles.

The trial court *penalized* BrooksAmerica for acting in good faith. Mr. Brooks signed the Delivery Certificate assuming that any reasonable company would promptly deliver the money it had promised. Unfortunately, Terminal does not operate at the same ethical level—a fact that Wells Fargo should know from its earlier assignments.

Argument for Wells Fargo: Under UCC §9-403, an assignee such as Wells Fargo may enforce a waiver of defenses clause if the assignment was taken in good faith, for value, and free of knowledge of any claims or defenses. Wells Fargo meets that test.

The "simple inquiry" argument has two flaws. First, §9-403 does not require one. The UCC requires good faith, not an investigation. Second, Wells Fargo *did* investigate by checking the contract and the Delivery Certificate. We have done more than required. We have taken thousands of equipment leases as assignees. In this case, we examined the contract and the Delivery Certificate, and assumed that BrooksAmerica had received its money. If Terminal had not paid, why did Mr. Brooks sign a certificate stating he had received his cash? We are entitled to payment. Any dispute between BrooksAmerica and Terminal is for those parties to resolve.

17-2b Delegation of Duties

Garret has always dreamed of racing stock cars. He borrows $250,000 from his sister, Maybelle, in order to buy a car and begin racing. He signs a promissory note, which is a document guaranteeing that he will repay Maybelle the full amount, plus interest, on a monthly basis over ten years. Regrettably, during his first race, Garret discovers that he has a speed phobia and quits the business. Garret transfers the car and all of his equipment to Brady, who agrees in writing to pay all money owed to Maybelle. Brady sends a check for a few months, but then the payments stop. Maybelle sues Garret, who defends based on the transfer to Brady. Will his defense work?

Garret has assigned his rights in the car and business to Brady, and that is entirely legal. But more important, he has *delegated his duties* to Brady. Garret was the delegator and Brady was the **delegatee**. In other words, the promissory note he signed was a contract, and the agreement imposed certain *duties* on Garret, primarily the obligation to pay Maybelle $250,000 plus interest. Garret had a right to delegate his duties to Brady, but delegating those duties did not relieve Garret of *his own* obligation to perform them. When Maybelle sues, she will win. Garret, like many debtors, would have preferred to wash his hands of his debt, but the law is not so obliging.

Most duties are delegable. But delegation does not by itself relieve the delegator of his own liability to perform the contract.

Garret's delegation to Brady was typical in that it included an assignment at the same time. If he had merely transferred ownership, that would have been only an assignment. If he had convinced Brady to pay off the loan without getting the car, that would have been merely a delegation. He did both at once. See Exhibit 17.2.

EXHIBIT 17.2

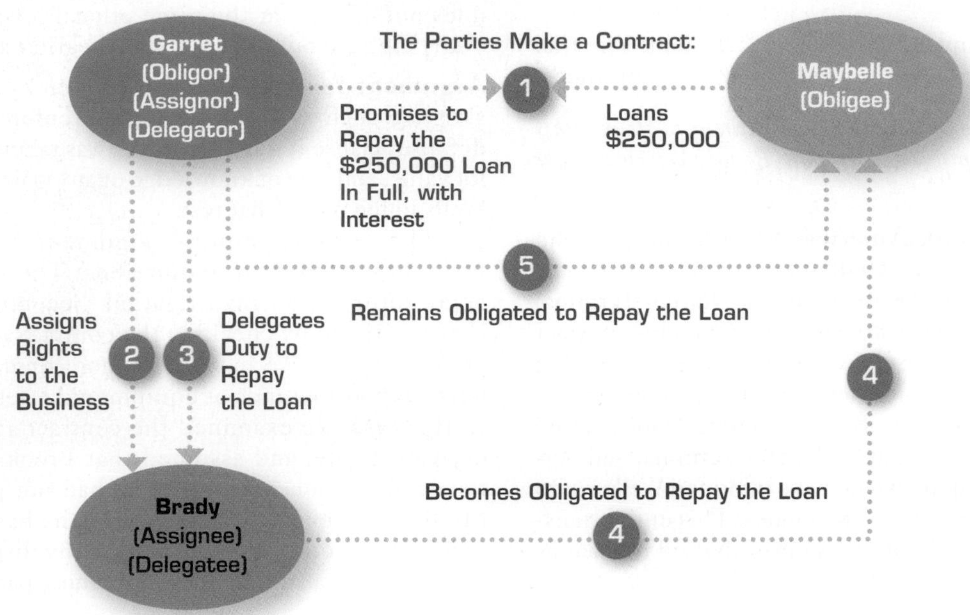

What Duties Are Delegable?

The rules concerning what duties may be delegated mirror those about the assignment of rights. And once again, the common law agrees with the UCC. An obligor may delegate his duties unless:

S. Meltzer/PhotoLink/Photodisc/Getty Images

One may delegate...

- Delegation would violate public policy, or
- The original contract prohibits delegation, or
- The obligee has a substantial interest in personal performance by the obligor.[5]

Public Policy. Delegation may violate public policy, such as in a public works contract. If City hires Builder to construct a subway system, state law may prohibit Builder from delegating his duties to Beginner. The theory is that a public agency should not have to work with parties that it never agreed to hire.

Contract Prohibition. It is very common for a contract to prohibit delegation. We saw in the "Assignment" section that courts may refuse to enforce a clause that

5Restatement (Second) of Contracts §318. And see UCC §2-210, establishing similar limits.

limits one party's ability to assign its contract rights. That does not hold true with delegation. The parties may forbid almost any delegation, and the courts will enforce the agreement. Hammer, a contractor, is building a house and hires Spot as his painter, including in his contract a clause prohibiting delegation. Just before the house is ready for painting, Spot gets a better job elsewhere and wants to delegate his duties to Brush. Hammer may refuse the delegation, even if Brush is equally qualified.

Dhannte/Shutterstock.com

. . .*and one may not.*

Substantial Interest in Personal Performance. Suppose Hammer had omitted the "nondelegation" clause from his contract with Spot. Could Hammer still refuse the delegation on the grounds that he has a substantial interest in having Spot do the work? No. Most duties are delegable, as long as they do not violate public policy or a clause in a contract. There is nothing so special about painting a house that one particular painter is required to do it. But some kinds of work do require personal performance, and obligors may not delegate these tasks. The services of lawyers, doctors, dentists, artists, and performers are considered too personal to be delegated. There is no single test that will perfectly define this group, but generally when the work will test the *character, skill, discretion, and good faith of the obligor,* she may *not* delegate her job.

EXAMStrategy

Question: Parker is a well-known actress. She agrees to act in Will's play for four weeks, for $30,000 per week. A week before rehearsals are to begin, Parker notifies Will that she cannot appear because a film producer has offered her over $1 million to start shooting immediately. She has arranged for Claire, another well-known actress, to appear in her place. Will objects. Parker claims, correctly, that their agreement does not prohibit her from making this substitution. Is Parker allowed to do this?

Strategy: Parker is attempting to delegate her duties. Under the Restatement, delegation is allowed unless (1) it would violate public policy, (2) it is prohibited by the contract, or (3) the obligee has a substantial interest in the obligor's personal performance.

Result: This is hardly a matter of public concern, and the contract does not speak to the issue. However, acting is a very personal kind of work. The actor must be right for the part, interact smoothly with other cast members, work well with the director, and help draw the audience. Will is entitled to have Parker perform the work, and she may not delegate her role.

Improper Delegation and Repudiation. Sometimes parties delegate duties they should not. Suppose Spot, having agreed not to delegate his painting job, is so tempted by the higher offer from another contractor that he delegates the work anyway. Hammer informs Spot he will not allow Brush on the job site. If Spot still refuses to work, he has repudiated the agreement; in other words, he has formally notified the other side that he will not perform his side of the contract. Hammer will probably sue him. On the other hand, if Hammer allows Brush up the ladder and Brush completes the job, Hammer has no claim against anybody.

Novation

Novation
A three-way agreement in which the obligor transfers all rights and duties to a third party

As we have seen, a delegator does not automatically get rid of his duties merely by delegating them. But there is one way a delegator *can* do so. A **novation** is a three-way agreement in which the obligor transfers all rights and duties to a third party. The obligee agrees to look only to that third party for performance.

Recall Garret, the forlorn race car driver. When he wanted to get out of his obligations to Maybelle, he should have proposed a novation. Were one created, he would assign all rights and delegate all duties to Brady, and Maybelle would agree that *only Brady* was obligated by the promissory note, releasing Garret from his responsibility to repay. Why would Maybelle do this? She might conclude that Brady was a better bet than Garret and that this was the best way to get her money. Maybelle would prefer to have both people liable. But Garret might refuse to bring Brady into the deal until Maybelle permits a novation. In the example given, Garret failed to obtain a novation, and hence he and Brady were *both* liable on the promissory note.

Since a novation has the critical effect of releasing the obligor from liability, you will not be surprised to learn that people sometimes fight over whether their revised agreement was a novation. Here is one such contest. RARE wanted to have its steak and eat it, too. But would a novation leave it stuck with the bill?

HDRE Business Partners Ltd. Group LLC v. RARE Hospitality Int'l, Inc.

2016 U.S. App. LEXIS 15269, 2016 WL 4427094
United States Court of Appeals for the Fifth Circuit, 2016

Facts: RARE Hospitality wanted to lease a property to open a LongHorn Steakhouse, but Stirling, the property owner, would only sell it. RARE convinced HDRE to buy the property and lease it to RARE. HDRE entered into an agreement to purchase the space from Stirling for $1.3 million, and, simultaneously, HDRE and RARE entered into a 15-year lease agreement. The lease contained fee-shifting provision, which provided that if RARE and HDRE ever had a dispute over the lease, the loser in court would pay both parties' attorneys' fees.

Before Stirling sold to HDRE, RARE decided that "the numbers would work better as a purchase," so RARE, HDRE, and Stirling renegotiated their deal. Under the revised contract (which the parties confusingly called the "Assignment"), HDRE assigned to RARE its rights and duties under the purchase agreement for a fee. Stirling consented. The Assignment gave RARE a one-week window to back out of the purchase if it could not obtain internal corporate approval. The Assignment was also notable in what it *did not* address: It said nothing about attorneys' fees and did not mention the lease between HDRE and RARE.

RARE executives did not approve the deal, so the company did not buy Stirling's property. HDRE then demanded that RARE comply with its original duty to lease the property. When RARE refused, HDRE sued for breach of contract. RARE argued that the "*Assignment*" was a really a *novation*, which released its duty to rent.

A jury agreed with RARE, finding that the parties intended a novation to replace the original deal and terminate the lease. But then the court ruled that HDRE had to pay RARE's attorneys' fees pursuant to the fee-shifting provision—to the tune of $750,000. HDRE appealed, arguing that the novation had also canceled the attorneys' fees clause.

Issue: ***Did the novation extinguish the attorneys' fees provision?***

Excerpts from Judge Walker Elrod's Decision: The availability of attorneys' fees in this case turns on the law of novation. Unless the parties express a clear intent to the contrary, a novation typically extinguishes a legal relationship in its entirety rather than surgically excising individual rights and duties. By definition, a novation extinguishes existing obligations.

Both RARE and HDRE clearly and unequivocally intended to substitute the Assignment for RARE's obligation under the Lease, so that RARE's obligation to lease was no longer enforceable. The implication of that finding is not that the Assignment had the narrow effect of excising RARE's duty to pay rent while leaving the remainder of the Lease intact. Rather, a novation means that the

Assignment extinguished the original lessor-lessee relationship in its entirety, including all of its rights and duties such as the right to prevailing party attorneys' fees.

Because novation turns on the parties' intent, parties can certainly limit the effects of a novation by expressly stating in their subsequent agreement that they wish to novate a prior agreement without wholly displacing it. In this case, however, the parties' subsequent agreement—the Assignment—did not address the issue of novating the lease agreement at all.

Because the Lease was extinguished in its entirety by novation, we REVERSE the district court's judgment awarding attorneys' fees to RARE under the Lease.

RARE v. HDRE tells us that novation effectively ends all previous rights and duties. It also teaches us about fee-shifting clauses, which are common in business contracts. Finally, the case is a cautionary tale against litigation: RARE could have bought more than half the property with the amount it spent in on attorney's fees. Both sides would have been better off with a settlement.

CHAPTER CONCLUSION

A moment's caution! It is important to remember that the parties to a contract may not have the right to substitute someone else into the contract. The parties to a contract always have legal rights themselves, but when outsiders enter the picture, subtle differences in key areas determine whether additional rights exist.

EXAM REVIEW

1. **THIRD PARTY BENEFICIARY** A third party beneficiary may enforce a contract if the parties intended her to benefit from the agreement and if either (1) enforcing the promise will satisfy a debt of the promisee to the beneficiary or (2) the promisee intended to make a gift to the beneficiary. The intended beneficiary described in (1) is a creditor beneficiary while (2) describes a donee beneficiary. Any beneficiary who meets neither description is an incidental beneficiary and has no right to enforce the contract.

2. **ASSIGNMENT AND DELEGATION** An assignment transfers the assignor's contract rights to the assignee. A delegation transfers the delegator's duties to the delegatee.

3. **RIGHTS ASSIGNABLE** A party generally may assign contract rights unless doing so would substantially change the obligor's rights or duties, is forbidden by law, or is validly precluded by the contract.

EXAMStrategy

Question: Angelo Zavarella and Yvette Rodrigues were injured in an automobile accident allegedly caused by a vehicle belonging to Truck Equipment of Boston. Travelers Insurance Co. paid insurance benefits to Zavarella and Rodrigues, who then assigned to Travelers their claims against Truck Equipment. Travelers sued Truck Equipment, which moved to dismiss. What is Truck Equipment's claim that the case should be dismissed, and how would you rule?

Strategy: Travelers is claiming to be the assignee of the plaintiffs' claims. Any contractual right may be assigned except in the three instances listed. Does one of those prohibitions apply? (See the "Result" at the end of this Exam Review section.)

4. **ENFORCEMENT** Once the assignment is made and the obligor notified, the assignee may enforce her contractual rights against the obligor. The obligor, in turn, may generally raise all defenses against the assignee that she could have raised against the assignor.

5. **THE UCC AND SECURITY INTERESTS** Article 9 of the UCC governs security interests, which are the legal rights to personal property that assure payment of a debt. Under Article 9, obligors may assert defenses against assignees that arise from contracts, and agreements not to enforce such defenses are generally valid.

6. **DUTIES DELEGABLE** Duties are delegable unless delegation would violate public policy, the contract prohibits delegation, or the obligee has a substantial interest in personal performance by the obligor.

EXAMStrategy

Question: Pizza of Gaithersburg, Maryland, owned five pizza shops. Pizza arranged with Virginia Coffee Service to install soft drink machines in each of its stores and maintain them. The contract made no mention of the rights of either party to delegate. Virginia Coffee delegated its duties to the Macke Co., leading to litigation between Pizza and Macke. Pizza claimed that Virginia Coffee was barred from delegating because Pizza had a close working relationship with the president of Virginia Coffee, who personally kept the machines in working order. Was the delegation legal?

Strategy: Any contractual duty may be delegated except in the three instances listed. Does one of those prohibitions apply? (See the "Result" at the end of this Exam Review section.)

7. **DISCHARGE** Unless the obligee agrees otherwise, delegation does not discharge the delegator's duty to perform.

8. **NOVATION** A novation is a three-way agreement in which the obligor delegates all duties to the delegatee and the obligee agrees to hold only the delegatee responsible.

EXAMStrategy

Question: Mardy, a general contractor, is building a house. He contracts with Plumbco to do all plumbing work for $120,000. Before Plumbco begins the work, it notifies Mardy in writing that Leo will be doing the work instead. Mardy does not respond. When Leo fails to perform, Mardy sues Plumbco. Plumbco is:

(a) liable.

(b) liable only if Plumbco agreed to remain responsible for the job.

(c) not liable because Mardy failed to repudiate the delegation.

(d) not liable because Plumbco validly delegated its duties.

(e) not liable because the parties entered into a novation.

Strategy: Delegation does not by itself relieve the delegator of his own liability to perform the contract. In a novation, the obligee agrees to look only to the third party for performance. Was this a delegation or a novation? (See the "Result" at the end of this Exam Review section.)

RESULTS

3. Result: Truck Equipment's winning argument was one sentence long: Claims for personal injury may not be assigned. Such assignments would transform accident claims into commercial commodities and encourage assignees to exaggerate the gravity of the harm.

6. Result: There is no public policy issue involved. The contract is silent as to delegation. And Pizza's only legitimate interest was in seeing that installation and maintenance were adequate. There is no reason to believe that Virginia Coffee would perform the work better than others. The duty was delegable, and Virginia Coffee wins.

8. Result: When Plumbco announced that Leo would do the work, Mardy did not respond. Mardy certainly did not agree to look exclusively to Leo for performance. There has not been a novation, and Plumbco remains liable on the contract. The correct answer is (a).

MULTIPLE-CHOICE QUESTIONS

1. **CPA QUESTION** Yost contracted with Egan for Yost to buy certain real property. If the contract is otherwise silent, Yost's rights under the contract are:
   (a) assignable only with Egan's consent.
   (b) nonassignable because they are personal to Yost.
   (c) nonassignable as a matter of law.
   (d) generally assignable.

2. **CPA QUESTION** One of the criteria for a valid assignment of a sales contract to a third party is that the assignment must:
   (a) not materially increase the other party's risk or duty.
   (b) not be revocable by the assignor.
   (c) be supported by adequate consideration from the assignee.
   (d) be in writing and signed by the assignor.

3. Amanda agrees to pay Jennifer $1,000 for a pair of tickets to see the Broadway show Hamilton. "Hamilton is my boyfriend Octavio's favorite play, and the tickets will be a great birthday present for him," she tells Jennifer. Amanda pays up and tells a delighted Octavio about the tickets, but Jennifer never delivers them. Octavio is a(n) __________ beneficiary of the agreement, and as such, he __________ have a right to enforce the contract himself.
   (a) donee; does
   (b) donee; does not
   (c) incidental; does
   (d) incidental; does not

4. A novation completely releases an ______________ from any further liability. To be effective, it ______________ require the agreement of both the obligor and obligee.
   (a) obligor; does
   (b) obligor; does not
   (c) obligee; does
   (d) obligee; does not

5. Will misses three straight payments on his SUV, and his bank repossesses it. The right to repossess ______________ a security interest. Security interests are governed by Article ______________ of the Uniform Commercial Code.
   (a) is; 2
   (b) is; 9
   (c) is not; 2
   (d) is not; 9

CASE QUESTIONS

1. Intercontinental Metals Corp. (IMC) contracted with the accounting firm of Cherry, Bekaert & Holland to perform an audit. Cherry issued its opinion about IMC, giving all copies of its report directly to the company. IMC later permitted Dun & Bradstreet to examine the statements, and Raritan River Steel Co. saw a report published by Dun & Bradstreet. Relying on the audit, Raritan sold IMC $2.2 million worth of steel on credit, but IMC promptly went bankrupt. Raritan sued Cherry, claiming that IMC was not as sound as Cherry had reported and that the accounting firm had breached its contract with IMC. Comment on Raritan's suit.

2. Woodson Walker and Associates leased computer equipment from Park Ryan Leasing. The lease said nothing about assignment. Park Ryan then assigned the lease to TCB as security for a loan. Park Ryan defaulted on its loan, and Walker failed to make several payments on the lease. TCB sued Walker for the lease payments. Was the assignment valid, given the fact that the original lease made no mention of it? If the assignment was valid, may Walker raise defenses against TCB that it could have raised against Park Ryan?

3. ***YOU BE THE JUDGE* WRITING PROBLEM** David Ricupero suspected his wife Polly of having an affair, so he taped her phone conversations and, based on what he heard, sued for divorce. David's lawyer, William Wuliger, had the recorded conversations transcribed for use at trial. The parties settled the divorce out of court and signed an agreement that included this clause:

   > Except as herein otherwise provided, each party hereto completely and forever releases the other and his attorneys from any and all rights each has or may have . . . to any property, privileges, or benefits accruing to either by virtue of their marriage, or conferred by the Statutory or Common Law of Ohio or the United States of America.

After the divorce was final, Polly sued William Wuliger for invasion of privacy and violation of federal wiretapping law. Wuliger moved to dismiss the case based on the clause quoted. Polly argued that Wuliger was not a party to the divorce settlement and had no right to enforce it. May Wuliger enforce the waiver clause from the Ricuperos' divorce settlement? **Argument for Wuliger:** The contract language demonstrates that the parties intended to release one another and their attorneys from any claims. That makes Wuliger an intended third party beneficiary, and he is entitled to enforce the agreement. If Polly did not want to release Wuliger from such claims, she was free not to sign the agreement. **Argument for Polly Ricupero:** A divorce agreement settles the affairs between the couple. That is all it is ever intended to do, and the parties here never intended to benefit a lawyer. Wuliger is only an incidental beneficiary and cannot use this contract to paper over his violation of federal wiretapping law.

4. The Rosenbergs sold their Dairy Queen franchise to Mary Pratt. The contract required Pratt to pay most of the purchase price over a 15-year period. Two years later, Pratt assigned her rights and delegated her duties under the sales contract to Son, Inc. The Rosenbergs agreed to the new arrangement. But the agreement made no mention of discharging Pratt from any further liability on the contract. When Son failed to pay, the Rosenbergs sued Mary Pratt. What result?

5. Raymond and Connie Loftus hired American Realty Co. to manage and sell their vacant home. ARC secured a buyer. Prior to closing, ARC hired Fitzpatrick to light the home's gas water heater. During the lighting, Fitzpatrick burned the house down. The Loftuses argued that ARC improperly delegated the duty to Fitzpatrick and that the realty company should be liable. What result?

DISCUSSION QUESTIONS

1. A century and a half ago, an English judge stated: "All painters do not paint portraits like Sir Joshua Reynolds, nor landscapes like Claude Lorraine, nor do all writers write dramas like Shakespeare or fiction like Dickens. Rare genius and extraordinary skill are not transferable." What legal doctrine is the judge describing? What is the ethical basis of this rule?

2. Nationwide Discount Furniture hired Rampart Security to install an alarm in its warehouse. A fire would set off an alarm in Rampart's office, and the security company was then supposed to notify Nationwide immediately. A fire did break out, but Rampart allegedly failed to notify Nationwide, causing the fire to spread next door and damage a building owned by Gasket Materials Corp. Gasket sued Rampart for breach of contract, and Rampart moved for summary judgment. Comment.

3. If a person promises to give you a gift, there is usually no consideration. The person can change his mind and decide not to give you the present, and there is nothing you can do about it. But if a person makes a contract with *someone else* and intends that you will receive a gift under the agreement, you are a donee beneficiary and you *do* have rights to enforce the deal. Are these rules unacceptably inconsistent? If so, which rule should change?

4. In response to the subprime mortgage crisis, the federal government created the Home Affordable Modification Program (HAMP) to help struggling homeowners refinance their mortgage debt, thereby reducing the foreclosure rate. HAMP facilitates contracts between the U.S. Treasury and mortgage lenders, who modify eligible homeowners' mortgage loans in return for incentive payments. The Mackenzies applied for a HAMP modification of their home. Although they were eligible, Flagstar bank foreclosed on their Massachusetts home. The Mackenzies sued Flagstar for breach of contract, claiming they were intended third party beneficiaries of the lender's contract with the government. Will the Mackenzies succeed on this theory?

5. In our society, a person can buy and sell almost anything. But as this chapter describes, you cannot sell personal injury claims. Should you be able to? Imagine that you are injured in a car wreck. You are told that you might win $100,000 in a lawsuit eventually, but that you might not receive payment for years, and you might also lose the case and recover nothing. If someone is willing to pay you $20,000 cash-on-the-barrelhead today for the rights to your claim, is it fair that public policy concerns prohibit you from taking the money?

CHAPTER

18

CONTRACT TERMINATION

Polly was elated. It was the grand opening of her new restaurant, Polly's Folly, and everything was bubbling. The waitstaff hustled, and Caesar, the chef, churned out succulent dishes. Polly had signed a contract promising him $1,500 per week for one year, "provided Polly is personally satisfied with his cooking." Polly was determined that her restaurant would be glorious. Her three-year lease would cost $6,000 per month, and she had signed an advertising deal with Billboard Bonanza for the same period. Polly had also promised Eddie, a publicity agent, a substantial monthly fee, to begin as soon as the restaurant was 80 percent booked for one month. Tonight, with candles flickering at packed tables, Polly beamed.

After a week, Polly's smiles were a bit forced. Some of Caesar's new dishes had been failures, including a grilled swordfish that was hard to pierce and shrimp jambalaya that was too spicy. The restaurant was only 60 percent full, and the publicity agent yelled at Caesar for costing him money. Later that month, Polly disliked a veal dish and gagged on one of Caesar's soups. She fired her chef.

Polly disliked a veal dish and gagged on one of Caesar's soups. She fired her chef.

Then troubles gushed forth—literally. A water main burst in front of Polly's restaurant, flooding the street. The city embarked on a two-month repair job that ultimately took four times that long. The street was closed to traffic, and no one could park within blocks of Polly's restaurant. Patronage dropped steadily as hungry customers refused to deal with the bad parking and construction noise. After several months, behind on the rent and in debt to everyone, Polly closed her doors for good.

Shortly, the court doors swung open, offering a full menu of litigation. Polly's landlord sued for three years' rent, and Billboard Bonanza demanded its money for the same period. Caesar claimed his year's pay. Eddie, the agent, insisted on some money for his hard work. Polly defended vigorously, seeking to be *discharged* from her various contracts.

18-1 PERFORMANCE

18-1a Discharge

Discharge
A party is discharged when she has no more duties under the contract.

If a party is **discharged**, she is "finished" and has no more duties under a contract. In each lawsuit, Polly asked a court to declare that her obligations were terminated and that she owed no money.

Most contracts are discharged by full performance. In other words, the parties generally do what they promise. Suppose, before the restaurant opened, Walter had promised to deliver 100 sets of cutlery to Polly and she had promised to pay $20 per set. Walter delivered the goods on time, and Polly paid $2,000 on delivery. The parties got what they expected, and that contract was fully discharged.

Rescind
To terminate a contract by mutual agreement

Sometimes the parties discharge a contract by agreement. For example, the parties may agree to **rescind** their contract, meaning that they terminate it by mutual agreement.[1] If Polly's landlord believed he could get more rent from a new tenant, he might agree to rescind her lease. But he was dubious about the rental market and refused to rescind.

At times, a court may discharge a party who has not performed. When things have gone amiss, a judge must interpret the contract and issues of public policy to determine who in fairness should suffer the loss. In the lawsuits brought by the landlord and Billboard Bonanza, Polly argued a defense called "commercial impracticability," claiming that she should not be forced to rent space that was useless to her or buy advertising for a restaurant that had closed. From Polly's point of view, the claim was understandable. But we can also respect the arguments made by the landlord and the advertiser, that they did not cause the burst water main. Claims of commercial impracticability are difficult to win, and Polly lost against both of these opponents. Though she was making no money at all from the restaurant, the court found her liable in full for the lease and the advertising contract.[2]

Polly's argument against Caesar raised another issue of discharge. Caesar claimed that his cooking was good professional work and that all chefs have occasional disasters, especially in a new restaurant. But Polly responded that they had a "personal satisfaction" contract. Under such contracts, "good" work may not suffice if it fails to please the promisee. Polly won this argument, and Caesar recovered nothing.

As to Eddie's suit, Polly raised a defense called "condition precedent," meaning that some event had to occur before she was obligated to pay. Polly claimed that she owed Eddie money only if and when the restaurant was 80 percent full for a month, and that had never happened. The court agreed and discharged Polly on Eddie's claim.

We will analyze each of these issues, and begin with a look at conditions.

18-1b Conditions

Condition
An event that must occur before a party becomes obligated under a contract

Parties often put conditions in a contract. A **condition** is an event that must occur before a party becomes obligated under a contract. "I'll agree to do something, but only if something else happens first." Polly agreed to pay Eddie, the agent, a percentage of her profits, but with an important condition: 80 percent of the tables had to be booked for a month. Unless and until those tables were occupied, Polly owed Eddie nothing. That never happened, or, in contract language, the *condition failed*, and so Polly was discharged.

---

[1]The parties could also decide that one party's duties will be performed by someone else, a modification called a novation. Alternatively, they could create an accord and satisfaction, in which they agree that one party will substitute a new kind of performance in place of his contract obligations. See Chapter 17 on third parties and Chapter 13 on consideration.

[2]Based on Luminous Neon v. Parscale, 17 Kan. App. 2d 241 (1992).

Conditions can take many forms. Alex would like to buy Kevin's empty lot and build a movie theater on it, but the city's zoning law will not permit that kind of business in that location. Alex signs a contract to buy Kevin's empty lot in 120 days, *provided that* within 100 days, the city rezones the area to permit a movie theater. If the city fails to rezone the area by day 100, Alex is discharged and need not complete the deal.

Another example: Friendly Insurance issues a policy covering Vivian's house, promising to pay for any loss due to fire, but only if Vivian furnishes proof of her losses within 60 days of the damage. If the house burns down, Friendly becomes liable to pay. But if Vivian arrives with her proof 70 days after the fire, she collects nothing. Friendly, though it briefly had a duty to pay, was discharged when Vivian failed to furnish the necessary information on time.

How Conditions Are Created

Express Conditions. The parties may expressly state a condition. Alex's contract with Kevin expressly discharged all obligations if the city failed to rezone within the stated period. Notice that **no special language is necessary to create the condition**. Phrases such as "provided that" frequently indicate a condition, but neither those nor any other specific words are essential. As long as the contract's language indicates that the parties *intended* to create a condition, a court will enforce it.

Because informal language can create a condition, the parties may dispute whether they intended one or not. Sand Creek Country Club, in Indiana, was eager to expand its clubhouse facilities and awarded the design work to CSO Architects. The club wanted the work done quickly but had not secured financing. The architects sent a letter confirming their agreement:

> It was our intent to allow Mr. Dan Moriarty of our office to start work on your project as early as possible in order to allow you to meet the goals that you have set for next fall. Also, it was the intent of CSO to begin work on your project and delay any billings to you until your financing is in place. As I explained to you earlier, we will continue on this course until we reach a point where we can no longer continue without receiving some payment.

The club gave CSO the go-ahead to begin design work, and the architects did their work and billed Sand Creek for $33,000. But the club, unable to obtain financing, refused to pay. Sand Creek claimed that CSO's letter created a *condition* in their agreement, namely, that the club would have to pay only if and when it obtained financing. The court was unpersuaded and ruled that the parties had never intended to create an express condition. The architects were merely delaying their billing as a convenience to the club. It would be absurd, said the court, to assume that CSO intended to perform $33,000 worth of work for free.[3]

Professional sports contracts are often full of conditions. Assume that the San Francisco Giants want to sign Tony Fleet to play center field. The club considers him a fine defensive player but a dubious offensive performer. The many conditional clauses in his contract reflect hard bargaining over an athlete who may or may not become a star. The Giants guarantee Fleet only $500,000, a very modest salary by Major League Baseball standards.

If the speedy outfielder appears in at least 120 games, his pay increases to $1 million. Winning a Gold Glove award is worth an extra $200,000 to him. The Giants insist on a team option to re-sign Fleet for the following season at a salary of $800,000, but if the center fielder plays in fewer than 100 games, the team loses that right, leaving Fleet free to negotiate for higher pay with other teams.

Implied Conditions. At other times, the parties say nothing about a condition, but it is clear from their agreement that they have implied one. Charlotte orally rents an apartment to Hakan for one year and promises to fix any problems in the unit. It is an implied condition

---

[3]Sand Creek Country Club, Ltd. v. CSO Architects, Inc., 582 N.E.2d 872 (Ind. Ct. App. 1991).

that Hakan will promptly notify Charlotte of anything needing repair. Although the parties have not said anything about notice, it is only common sense that Hakan must inform his landlord of defects since she will have no other way to learn of them.

Types of Conditions

Courts divide conditional clauses into three categories: (1) condition precedent, (2) condition subsequent, and (3) concurrent conditions.[4] But what they have in common is more important than any of their differences. The key to all conditional clauses is this: **If the condition does not occur, one party will probably be discharged without having to perform his obligations under a contract.**

Condition Precedent. In this kind of condition, an event must occur *before* a duty arises. Polly's contract with Eddie concerned a condition precedent. Polly had no obligation to pay Eddie anything *unless and until* the restaurant was 80 percent full for a month. Since that never happened, she was discharged. If the parties agreed to a condition precedent, the *plaintiff* has the burden to prove that the condition happened and that the defendant was obligated to perform.

Contracts for the sale of real estate often have conditions precedent. Buyers commonly make purchase offers contingent on events like obtaining a mortgage or an acceptable property inspection. In these cases, the buyer has no duty to pay until the conditions are met.

Condition Subsequent. This type of condition must occur *after* a particular duty arises. If the condition does not occur, the duty is discharged. Vivian's policy with Friendly Insurance contains a condition subsequent. As soon as the fire broke out, Friendly became obligated to pay for the damage. But if Vivian failed to produce her proof of loss on time, Friendly's obligation ended—it was discharged. Note that, with a condition subsequent, it is the *defendant* who must prove that the condition occurred, relieving him of any obligation.

Condition Precedent and Condition Subsequent Compared

	Condition Created	Does Condition Occur?	Duty Is Determined	Result
Condition Precedent	"Fee to be paid when restaurant is filled to 80 % capacity for one month."	Condition DOES occur: restaurant is packed.	Duty arises: Polly owes Eddie his fee.	Polly pays the fee.
		Condition DOES NOT occur: restaurant is empty.	Duty never arises: Polly is discharged.	Polly pays nothing.
	Condition Created	**Duty Is Determined**	**Does Condition Occur?**	**Result**
			Condition DOES occur: Vivian proves her losses within 60 days.	Friendly pays Vivian for her losses.
Condition Subsequent	"Vivian must give proof of loss within 60 days."	Fire damages property, and Friendly Insurance becomes obligated to pay Vivian.	Condition DOES NOT occur: Vivian fails to prove her losses within 60 days.	Friendly is discharged and owes nothing.

[4]The Restatement (Second) of Contracts has officially abandoned the terms *condition precedent* and *condition subsequent.* See Restatement §§224 et seq. But courts routinely use the terms, so it is difficult to avoid the old distinctions.

Concurrent Conditions. Here, both parties have a duty to perform *simultaneously*. Renee agrees to sell her condominium to Tim on July 5. Renee agrees to furnish a valid deed and clear title to the property on that date, and Tim promises to present a cashier's check for $200,000. The parties have agreed to concurrent conditions. Each performance is the condition for the other's performance. If Renee arrives at the Registry of Deeds and can say only, "Don't worry. I'm totally sure I own this property," Tim need not present his check. Similarly, if Tim arrives with only an "IOU" scribbled on the back of a candy wrapper, Renee has no duty to hand over a valid deed.

EXAMStrategy

Question: Roberto wants to buy Naomi's house for $350,000 and is willing to make a 20 percent down payment, which satisfies Naomi. However, he needs a $280,000 mortgage in order to complete the purchase, and he is not certain he can obtain one. Naomi is worried that Roberto might change his mind about buying the house and then use alleged financing problems to skip out of the deal. How can the two parties protect themselves?

Strategy: Both parties should use conditional clauses in the sales agreement. Naomi must force Roberto to do his best to obtain a mortgage. How? Roberto's clause should protect him if he cannot obtain a sufficient mortgage. How?

Result: Naomi should demand the 20 percent down payment. Further, her conditional clause should state that Roberto forfeits the down payment unless he demonstrates that, within two weeks, he has applied in good faith for a mortgage to at least three banks. Roberto should insist that if he promptly and fully applies to three banks but fails to obtain a mortgage, his down payment is refunded.

Public Policy. At times, a court will refuse to enforce an express condition on the grounds that it is unfair and harmful to the general public. In other words, a court might agree that the parties created a conditional clause but conclude that permitting its enforcement would hurt society. Did the insurance contract in the following case harm society? You be the judge.

You Be the Judge

Anderson v. Country Life Insurance Co.

180 Ariz. 625
Arizona Court of Appeals, 1994

Facts: On November 26, a Country Life Insurance agent went to the house of Donald and Anna Mae Anderson. He persuaded the Andersons to buy a life insurance policy and accepted a check for $1,600. He gave the Andersons a "conditional receipt for medical policy" dated that day. The form stated that the Andersons would have a valid life insurance policy with Country Life, effective November 26, but only when all conditions were met. The most important of these conditions was that the Country Life home office accepts the Andersons as medical risks. The Andersons were pleased with the new policy and glad that it was effective that same day.

It was not. Donald Anderson died of a heart attack a few weeks later. Country Life declined the Andersons as medical risks and refused to issue a policy. Anna Mae Anderson sued. Country Life pointed out that medical approval was a condition precedent. In other words, the company argued that the policy would be effective as of November 26, but only if it later decided to make the policy effective. Based on this argument, the trial court gave summary judgment for Country Life. Ms. Anderson appealed, claiming that the conditional clause was a violation of public policy.

You Be the Judge: *Did the conditional clause violate public policy?*

Argument for Ms. Anderson: Your honors, this policy is a scam. This so-called "conditional receipt for medical policy" is designed to trick customers and then steal their money. The company leads people to believe they are covered as of the day they write the check. But they aren't covered until *much later*, when the insurer gets around to deciding the applicant's medical status.

The company gets the customer's money right away and gives nothing in exchange. If the company, after taking its time, decides the applicant is not medically fit, it returns the money, having used it for weeks or even months to earn interest. If, on the other hand, the insurance company decides the applicant is a good bet, it then issues the policy effective for weeks or months *in the past, when coverage is of no use*. No one can die retroactively, your honors. The company is being paid for a period during which it had no risk. This is a fraud and a disgrace, and the company should pay the benefits it owes.

Argument for Country Life: Your honors, is Country Life supposed to issue life insurance policies without doing a medical check? That is the road to bankruptcy and would mean that no one could obtain this valuable coverage. Of course, we do a medical inquiry, as quickly as possible. It's in our interest to get the policy decided one way or the other.

The policy clearly stated that coverage was effective *only when approved by the home office*, after all inquiries were made. The Andersons knew that as well as the agent. If they were covered immediately, why would the company do a medical check? Country Life resents suggestions that this policy is a scam, when in reality it is Ms. Anderson who is trying to profit from a tragedy that the company had nothing to do with.

The facts of this case are unusual. Obviously, most insureds do not die between application and acceptance. It would be disastrous for society to rewrite every insurance policy in this state based on one very sad fact pattern. The contract was clear and it should be enforced as written.

18-1c Completion

Caitlin has an architect draw up plans for a monumental new house, and Daniel agrees to build it by September 1. Caitlin promises to pay $900,000 on that date. The house is ready on time, but Caitlin has some complaints. The living room was supposed to be 18 feet high, but it is only 17 feet; the pool was to be azure, yet it is aquamarine; the kids' rooms were not supposed to be wired for cable television, but they are. Caitlin refuses to pay anything for the house. Is she justified? Of course not, it would be absurd to give her a magnificent house for free when it has only tiny defects. But in this easy answer lurks a danger. Technically, Daniel did breach the contract, and yet the law allows him to recover the full contract price, or virtually all of it. Once that principle is established, how far will a court stretch it? Suppose the living room is only 14 feet high, or 12 feet, or 5 feet? What if the foundation has a small crack? A vast and dangerous split? What if Daniel finishes the house a month late? Six months late? Three years late? At some point, a court will conclude that Daniel has so thoroughly botched the job that he deserves little or no money. But where, exactly, is that point? This is a question that businesses—and judges—face often.

The more complex a contract, the more certain that at least one party will perform imperfectly. Nearly every house ever built has at least some small defects. A delivery of a thousand bushels of apples is sure to include a few rotten ones. A custom-designed computer system for a huge airline is likely to have some glitches. The cases raise several related doctrines, all concerning *how well* a party performed its contractual obligations.

Strict Performance and Substantial Performance

Strict performance
Requires one party to perform its obligations precisely, with no deviation from the contract terms

Strict Performance. When Daniel built Caitlin's house with three minor defects, she refused to pay, arguing that he had not *strictly performed* his obligations. Her assertion was correct, yet she lost anyway. Courts dislike strict performance because it enables one party to benefit without paying and sends the other one home empty-handed. A party is generally not required to render **strict performance** unless the contract expressly demands it *and* such a demand is reasonable. Caitlin's contract never suggested that Daniel would forfeit all payment if there were minor problems. Even if Caitlin had insisted on such a clause, few courts would have enforced it because the requirement would be unreasonable for a project as complicated as the construction of a $900,000 home.

There are some cases where strict performance does make sense. Marshall agrees to deliver 500 sweaters to Leo's store, and Leo promises to pay $20,000 cash on delivery. If Leo has only $19,000 cash and a promissory note for $1,000, he has failed to perform, and Marshall need not give him the sweaters. Leo's payment represents 95 percent of what he promised, but there is a big difference between getting the last $1,000 in cash and receiving a promissory note for that amount.

Substantial Performance. Daniel, the house builder, won his case against Caitlin because he fulfilled *most* of his obligations, even though he did an imperfect job. Courts often rely on the substantial performance doctrine, especially in cases involving services as opposed to those concerning the sale of goods or land. In a contract for services, a party that **substantially performs** its obligations will generally receive the full contract price, minus the value of any defects. Daniel receives $900,000, the contract price, minus the value of a ceiling that is 1 foot too low, a pool the wrong color, and so forth. It will be for the trial court to decide how much those defects are worth. If the court decides the low ceiling is a $10,000 defect, the pool color is worth $5,000, and the cable television wiring error is worth $500, then Daniel receives $884,500.

Substantial performance
Occurs when one party fulfills enough of its contract obligations to warrant payment

On the other hand, a **party that fails to perform substantially receives nothing on the contract itself and will recover only the value of the work, if any.** If the foundation cracks in Caitlin's house and the walls collapse, Daniel will not receive his $900,000. In such a case, he collects only the market value of the work he has done, which, since the house is a pile of rubble, is probably zero.

When is performance substantial? There is no perfect test, but courts look at these issues:

- How much benefit has the promisee received?
- If it is a construction contract, can the owner use the thing for its intended purpose?
- Can the promisee be compensated with money damages for any defects?
- Did the promisor act in good faith?

EXAMStrategy

Question: Jade owns a straight track used for drag racing. She hires Trevor to resurface it for $180,000, paying $90,000 down. When the project is completed, Jade refuses to pay the balance and sues Trevor for her down payment. He counterclaims for the $90,000 still due. At trial, Trevor proves that all of the required materials were applied by trained workers in an expert fashion, the dimensions were perfect, and his profit margin very modest. The head of the national drag racing association testifies that his group considers the strip unsafe. He noticed puddles in both asphalt lanes, found the concrete starting pads unsafe, and believed the racing surface needed to be ground off and reapplied. His organization refuses to sanction races at the track until repairs are made. Who wins the suit?

Strategy: When one party has performed imperfectly, we have an issue of substantial performance. To decide whether Trevor is entitled to his money, we apply four factors: (1) How much benefit did Jade receive? (2) Can she use the racing strip for its intended purpose? (3) Can Jade be compensated for defects? (4) Did Trevor act in good faith?

Result: Jade has received no benefit whatsoever. She cannot use her drag strip for racing. Compensation will not help Jade—she needs a new strip. Trevor's work must be ripped up and replaced. Trevor may have acted in good faith, but he failed to deliver what Jade bargained for. Jade wins all of the money she paid. (As we will see in Chapter 19, she may also win additional sums for her lost profits.)

Personal Satisfaction Contracts

Sujata, president of a public relations firm, hires Ben to design a huge multimedia project for her company, involving computer software, music, and live actors, all designed to sell frozen bologna sandwiches to supermarkets. His contract guarantees him two years' employment, provided all of his work "is acceptable in the sole judgment of Sujata." Ben's immediate supervisor is delighted with his work and his colleagues are impressed, but Sujata is not. Three months later, she fires him, claiming that his work is "uninspired." Does she have the right to do that?

Personal satisfaction contract
Permits the promisee to make subjective evaluations of the promisor's performance

This is a **personal satisfaction contract**, in which the promisee makes a personal, subjective evaluation of the promisor's performance. Employment contracts may require personal satisfaction of the employer; agreements for the sale of goods may demand that the buyer be personally satisfied with the product; and deals involving a credit analysis of one party may insist that his finances be satisfactory to the other party. In resolving disputes like Ben and Sujata's, judges must decide: When is it *fair* for the promisee to claim that she is not satisfied? May she make that decision for any reason at all, even on a whim?

A court applies a subjective standard only if assessing the work involves personal feelings, taste, or judgment and the contract explicitly demanded personal satisfaction. A "subjective standard" means that the promisee's personal views will greatly influence her judgment, even if her decision is foolish and unfair. Artistic or creative work, or highly specialized tasks designed for a particular employer, may involve subtle issues of quality and personal preference. Ben's work combines several media and revolves around his judgment. Accordingly, the law applies a subjective standard to Sujata's decision. Since she concludes that his work is uninspired, she may legally fire him, even if her decision is irrational.

AFP/Getty Images/Newscom

A woman offered to restore this mural for a church. The original mural is seen on the left. The mural before restoration is shown in the middle. The result of the restoration was the painting on the right. What would happen if the parties did not have a personal satisfaction clause?

Note that the promisee, Sujata, has to show two things: that assessing Ben's work involves her personal judgment *and* that their contract explicitly demands personal satisfaction. If the contract were vague on this point, Sujata would lose. Had the agreement merely said, "Ben will at all times make his best efforts," Sujata could not fire him.

In all other cases, a court applies an *objective* standard to the promisee's decision. In other words, the objective standard will be used if assessing the work does not involve personal judgment *or* if the contract failed to explicitly demand personal satisfaction. An objective standard means that the promisee's judgment of the work must be reasonable. Suppose Sujata hires Leila to install an alarm system for her company, and the contract requires that

Sujata be "personally satisfied." Leila's system passes all tests, but Sujata claims, "It just doesn't make me feel secure. I know that someday it's going to break down." May Sujata refuse to pay? No. Even though the contract used the phrase "personally satisfied," a mechanical alarm system does not involve personal judgment and taste. Either the system works or it does not. A reasonable person would find that Leila's system is just fine and, therefore, under the objective standard, Sujata must pay. The law strongly favors the objective standard because the subjective standard gives unlimited power to the promisee.

Either the system works or it does not.

Good Faith

The parties to a contract must carry out their obligations in good faith. The difficulty, of course, is applying this general rule to the wide variety of problems that may arise when people or companies do business. How far must one side go to meet its good faith burden? Marvin Shuster was a physician in Florida. Three patients sued him for alleged malpractice. Shuster denied any wrongdoing and asked his insurer to defend the claims. But the insurance company settled all three claims without defending and with a minimum of investigation. Shuster paid nothing out of his own pocket, but he sued the insurance company, claiming that it acted in bad faith. The doctor argued that the company's failure to defend him caused emotional suffering and meant that it would be impossible for him to obtain new malpractice insurance. The Florida Supreme Court found that the insurer acted in good faith. The contract clearly gave all control of malpractice cases to the company. It could settle or defend as it saw fit. Here, the company considered it more economical to settle quickly, and Shuster should have known, from the contract language, that the insurer might choose to do so.[5]

The following case involves a morality clause, a common provision in high-profile personal services contracts. Morality clauses allow one party to terminate the agreement if the other breaks the law, does something offensive, or otherwise behaves badly. Who behaved worse in this case?

Mendenhall v. Hanesbrands, Inc.

856 F.Supp.2d 717
United States District Court, Middle District, North Carolina, 2012

Facts: Rashard Mendenhall, an NFL football player, had a longstanding endorsement agreement with Hanesbrands (HBI), in which he promised to promote Champion athletic apparel. In Section 17(a), the agreement provided:

> If Mendenhall commits or is arrested for any crime or becomes involved in any situation or occurrence tending to bring Mendenhall into public disrepute, contempt, scandal, or ridicule, or tending to shock, insult or offend the majority of the consuming public or any protected class or group thereof, then we shall have the right to immediately terminate this Agreement.

Mendenhall was an avid Twitter user, often publicly expressing his controversial opinions on everything from Islam to parenting. HBI did not comment on Mendenhall's tweets, nor did it tell him to stop them or tone them down.

On May 1, 2011, President Obama announced the death of terrorist Osama bin Laden. In response, Mendenhall tweeted the following:

> What kind of person celebrates death? It's amazing how people can HATE a man they never even heard speak. We've only heard one side....
>
> For those of you who said we want to see Bin Laden burn in hell, I ask how would God feel about your heart?
>
> We'll never know what really happened. I just have a hard time believing a plane could take a skyscraper down demolition style.

[5]Shuster v. South Broward Hospital Dist. Physicians' Prof. Liability Ins. Trust, 591 So. 2d 174 (Fla. 1992).

Mendenhall's tweet got much attention, so he sent another message explaining that he was not in support of bin Laden, or against America, but rather wanted to make people think about the morality of celebrating *any* human death.

The next day HBI terminated Mendenhall's contract, pursuant to Section 17(a). At the same time, it issued a press statement suggesting that it only severed its relationship with the athlete because it disagreed with his legitimately held views.

Mendenhall sued for breach of the implied covenant of good faith and fair dealing. He argued that HBI acted unreasonably because the bin Laden tweets were not scandalous enough to warrant terminating the contract under 17(a). HBI filed a motion for judgment on the pleadings.

Issue: ***Did HBI violate the implied covenant of good faith and fair dealing when it terminated Mendenhall's contract?***

Excerpts from Judge Beaty's Decision: Implied in all contracts is a covenant of good faith and fair dealing in the course of contract performance, which requires parties not to act arbitrarily or irrationally. Courts have equated the covenant of good faith and fair dealing with an obligation to exercise discretion reasonably and with proper motive, not capriciously or in a manner inconsistent with the reasonable expectations of the parties. The duty of good faith and fair dealing, however, is not without limits, and no obligation can be implied that would be inconsistent with other terms of the contractual relationship.

In the present case, the agreement provides HBI with discretionary termination rights, which include an implied promise on HBI's part not to act arbitrarily, irrationally or unreasonably. HBI terminated the agreement pursuant to Section 17(a), while at the same time issuing a public statement indicating that HBI ended its business relationship with Mendenhall for another reason, that being because it strongly disagreed with Mendenhall's comments. Section 17(a) is applicable only to the extent that Mendenhall became involved in an act that tended to "bring him into public disrepute, contempt, scandal or ridicule," or tended "to shock, insult or offend the majority of the consuming public or any protected class or group thereof." Mere disagreement with Mendenhall's comments would not have triggered HBI's termination rights. Therefore, the Court can reasonably infer that Defendant's actions may have been unreasonable in light of the covenant of good faith and fair dealing.

Defendant contends that it had the right to terminate the contract as a result of the backlash caused by outrageous statements and that Plaintiff's statements caused an almost instantaneous public uproar. However, the Court notes that Plaintiff received supportive tweets from members of the public in response to his comments regarding the death of Osama bin Laden. Therefore, the Court finds that a dispute of fact exists between the parties as to the nature of the public's response to Plaintiff's tweets. At this early stage of the proceedings, Plaintiff has stated a plausible claim for breach of contract based on the implied covenant of good faith and fair dealing. The Court finds that a judgment on the pleadings would be premature at this time and is therefore denied.

EXAM Strategy

Question: Sun operates an upscale sandwich shop in New Jersey, in a storefront that she leases from Ricky for $18,000 per month. The lease, which expires soon, allows Sun to renew for five years at $22,000 per month. Ricky knows, but Sun does not, that in a year, high-end fashion designer Prada will open a store on the same block. The dramatic increase in pedestrian traffic will render Sun's space more valuable. Ricky says nothing about Prada, Sun declines to renew, and Ricky leases the space for $40,000 a month. Sun sues Ricky, claiming he breached his duty of good faith and fair dealing. How would a court rule?

Strategy: Ask yourself: How far must one side go to meet its good faith burden? Is it unreasonable or in bad faith for Ricky to omit the information about Prada? Your answer to these questions will help predict the ruling in Sun's suit.

Result: As one court said, "We do not expect a landlord or even an attorney to act as his brother's keeper in a commercial transaction." Sun's lease imposes no responsibility on Ricky to report on neighborhood changes or forecast profitability. Further, Sun made no requests to Ricky about the area's future (if he had, Ricky's omission would likely be fraud). Sun is asking Ricky to be "her brother's keeper," and neither this court nor any other will do that. She loses.

Time of the Essence Clauses

> Go, sir, gallop, and don't forget that the world was made in six days. You can ask me for anything you like, except time.
>
> –Napoleon, to an aide, 1803

Generals are not the only ones who place a premium on time. Ask Gene LaSalle. The Seabreeze Restaurant agreed to sell him all of its assets. The parties signed a contract stating the price and closing date. Seabreeze insisted on a clause saying, "Seabreeze considers that time is of the essence in consummating the proposed transaction." Such clauses are common in real estate transactions and in any other agreement where a delay would cause serious damage to one party. LaSalle was unable to close on the date specified and asked for an extension. Seabreeze refused and sold its assets elsewhere. A Florida court affirmed that Seabreeze acted legally.

A **time is of the essence clause** will generally make contract deadlines strictly enforceable. Seabreeze regarded a timely sale as important, and LaSalle agreed to the provision. There was nothing unreasonable about the clause, and LaSalle suffered the consequences of his delay.[6]

Time is of the essence clause
Generally makes contract dates strictly enforceable

Suppose that the contract had named a closing date but included no time of the essence clause. If LaSalle offered to close three days late, could Seabreeze sell elsewhere? No. **Merely including a date for performance does not make time of the essence.** Courts dislike time of the essence arguments because even a short delay may mean that one party forfeits everything it expected to gain from the bargain. If the parties do not *clearly* state that prompt performance is essential, then both are entitled to reasonable delays.

18-2 NON-PERFORMANCE

18-2a Breach

When one party breaches a contract, the other party is discharged. The discharged party has no obligation to perform and may sue for damages. Edwin promises that on July 1, he will deliver 20 tuxedos, tailored to fit male chimpanzees, to Bubba's circus for $300 per suit. After weeks of delay, Edwin concedes he hasn't a cummerbund to his name. Bubba is discharged and owes nothing. In addition, he may sue Edwin for damages.

Material Breach

As we know, parties frequently perform their contract duties imperfectly, which is why courts accept substantial performance rather than strict performance, particularly in contracts involving services. In a more general sense, **courts will discharge a contract only if a party committed a *material* breach.** A material breach is one that substantially harms the innocent party and for which it would be hard to compensate without discharging the contract. Suppose Edwin fails to show up with the tuxedos on June 1 but calls to say they will arrive under the big top the next day. He has breached the agreement. Is his breach material? No. This is a trivial breach, and Bubba is not discharged. When the tuxedos arrive, he must pay.

The following case raises the issue in the context of a major college sports program.

[6]Seabreeze Restaurant, Inc. v. Paumgardhen, 639 So.2d 69 (Fla. Dist. Ct. App. 1994).

O'Brien v. Ohio State University

2007-Ohio-4833
Court of Appeals of Ohio, 2007

Facts: Ohio State University (OSU), experiencing a drought in its men's basketball program, brought in Coach Jim O'Brien to turn things around. The plan was successful. In only his second year, he guided the team to its best record ever. The team advanced to the Final Four, and O'Brien was named national coach of the year. OSU's athletic director promptly offered the coach a new, multiyear contract worth about $800,000 per year.

Section 5.1 of the contract included termination provisions. The university could fire O'Brien *for cause* if (a) there was a material breach of the contract by the coach or (b) O'Brien's conduct subjected the school to NCAA sanctions. OSU could also terminate O'Brien *without cause,* but in that case, it had to pay him the full salary owed.

O'Brien began recruiting a talented 21-year-old Serbian player named Alex Radojevic. While getting to know the young man, O'Brien discovered two things. First, it appeared that Radojevic had been paid to play briefly for a Yugoslavian team, meaning that he was ineligible to play college basketball. Second, it was clear that Radojevic's family had suffered terribly during the strife in his homeland.

O'Brien concluded that Radojevic would never play for OSU or any major college. He also decided to loan Radojevic's mother some money. Any such loan would violate an NCAA rule if done to recruit a player, but O'Brien believed the loan was legal since Radojevic could not play in the NCAA anyway. Several years later, the university learned of the loan and realized that O'Brien had never reported it. Hoping to avoid trouble with the NCAA, OSU imposed sanctions on itself. The university also fired the coach, claiming he had lied, destroyed the possibility of post-season play, and harmed the school's reputation.

O'Brien sued, claiming he had not materially breached the contract. The trial court awarded the coach $2.5 million, and the university appealed.

Issue: ***Did O'Brien materially breach the contract?***

Excerpts from Judge Tyack's Decision: OSU argued that it was substantially injured by the self-imposed sanctions, which included a ban from post-season and NCAA tournament play [during the current season], and relinquishing two basketball scholarships from the [next] recruiting class. Contrary to OSU's argument, however, the trial court found these sanctions to be insubstantial. [Athletic Director] Geiger announced the one-year post-season ban in December, and it appears from the timing of that announcement that Geiger made the decision based on the fact that the team was unlikely to be invited to a post-season tournament in the first place.

The second alleged harm was harm to OSU's reputation. The trial court found that any reputational harm was similarly exaggerated, at least as it specifically related to the Radojevic matter. Radojevic never enrolled at OSU, and never played a single second for OSU's basketball team.

NCAA violations happen all the time. It's the nature of the beast. Also relevant to the issue of OSU's allegedly damaged reputation is the fact that almost immediately after firing O'Brien, OSU was able to lure one of the nation's top coaching prospects, [Thad Matta], to assume O'Brien's former position. Shortly thereafter, Matta successfully recruited possibly the best recruiting class ever. Based on this evidence, the trial court could reasonably find the Radojevic loan did not cause serious harm to OSU.

OSU argues that O'Brien acted in bad faith by covering up his misconduct for several years. In the words of OSU's counsel at oral argument: *"If lying to your employer for four years is not a material breach, it's hard to imagine what would be!"* Although the premise for counsel's argument is sound, it is unsound in application because it assumes facts not in evidence. Counsel for OSU assumes for the purposes of the argument that O'Brien systematically either denied allegations about the Radojevic loan, or took affirmative steps to conceal it from OSU. The evidence does not support such a conclusion. After Radojevic was drafted by the NBA, there is not a single inference that can be drawn from the record to suggest that O'Brien even thought about the loan. In O'Brien's own mind, he did not believe he had done anything wrong; thus, he would not have had a motive to conceal what he had done.

[There was no material breach.] Affirmed.

Anticipatory Breach

Sally will receive her bachelor's degree in May and already has a job lined up for September. She has signed a two-year contract to work as window display designer for Surebet Department Store. The morning of graduation, she reads in the paper that Surebet is going out of business that very day. Surebet has told Sally nothing about her status. Sally need not wait until September to learn her fate. Surebet has committed an **anticipatory breach by making it unmistakably clear that it will not honor the contract.** Sometimes a promisor will actually inform the promisee that it will not perform its duties. At other times, as here, the promisor takes some step that makes the breach evident. Sally is discharged and may immediately seek other work. She is also entitled to file suit for breach of contract. The court will treat Surebet's anticipatory breach just as though the store had actually refused to perform on September 1.

Statute of Limitations

A party injured by a breach of contract should act promptly. A **statute of limitations** begins to run at the time of injury and will limit the time within which the injured party may file suit. These laws set time limits for filing lawsuits. Statutes of limitations vary from state to state and from issue to issue within a state. Failure to file suit within the time limits discharges the party who breached the contract. Always consult a lawyer promptly in the case of a legal injury.

Statute of limitations
A statutory time limit within which an injured party must file suit

18-2b Impossibility

"Your honor, my client wanted to honor the contract. He just couldn't. *Honest.*" This plea often echoes around courtrooms as one party seeks discharge without fulfilling his contract obligations. Does the argument work? It depends. If performing a contract was truly impossible, a court will discharge the agreement. But if honoring the deal merely imposed a financial burden, the law will generally enforce the contract.

True Impossibility

These cases are easy and rare. **True impossibility means that something has happened making it literally impossible to do what the promisor said he would do.** Francoise owns a vineyard that produces Beaujolais Nouveau wine. She agrees to ship 1,000 cases of her wine to Tyrone, a New York importer, as soon as this year's vintage is ready. Tyrone will pay $50 per case. But a fungus wipes out her entire vineyard. Francoise is discharged. It is theoretically impossible for Francoise to deliver wine from her vineyard, and she owes Tyrone nothing.

Meanwhile, though, Tyrone has a contract with Jackson, a retailer, to sell 1,000 cases of Beaujolais Nouveau wine at $70 per case. Tyrone has no wine from Francoise, and the only other Beaujolais Nouveau available will cost him $85 per case. Instead of earning $20 per case, Tyrone will lose $15. Does this discharge Tyrone's contract with Jackson? No. It is possible for him to perform—it's just more expensive. He must fulfill his agreement.

True impossibility is generally limited to these three causes:

- **Destruction of the Subject Matter.** This is what happened with Francoise's vineyard.
- **Death of the Promisor in a Personal Services Contract.** When the promisor agrees personally to render a service that cannot be transferred to someone else, her death discharges the contract. Producer hires Josephine to write the lyrics for a new Broadway musical, but Josephine dies after writing only two words: "Act One." The contract was personal to Josephine and is now discharged. Neither Josephine's estate nor Producer has any obligation to the other. But notice that most contracts are not for personal services. Suppose that Tyrone, the wine importer, dies. His contract to sell wine to Jackson is not discharged because anyone can deliver the required wine. Tyrone's estate remains liable on the deal with Jackson.

- **Illegality.** Chet, a Silicon Valley entrepreneur, wants to capitalize on his computer expertise. He contracts with Construction Co. to build a factory in Iran that will manufacture computers for sale in that country. Construction Co. fails to build the factory on time, and Chet sues. Construction Co. defends by pointing out that the president of the United States has issued an executive order barring trade between the United States and Iran. Construction Co. wins; the executive order discharged the contract.

Commercial Impracticability and Frustration of Purpose

It is rare for contract performance to be truly impossible but very common for it to become a financial burden to one party. Suppose Bradshaw Steel in Pittsburgh agrees to deliver 1,000 tons of steel beams to Rice Construction in Saudi Arabia at a given price, but a week later, the cost of raw ore increases 30 percent. A contract once lucrative to the manufacturer is suddenly a major liability. Does that change discharge Bradshaw? Absolutely not. Rice signed the deal *precisely to protect itself against price increases.* As we have seen, the primary purpose of contracts is to enable the parties to control their future.

Yet there may be times when a change in circumstances is so extreme that it would be unfair to enforce a deal. What if a strike made it impossible for Bradshaw to ship the steel to Saudi Arabia, and the only way to deliver would be by air, at *five times* the sea cost? Must Bradshaw fulfill its deal? What if a new war meant that any ships or planes delivering the goods might be fired upon? Other changes could make the contract undesirable for *Rice.* Suppose the builder wanted steel for a major public building in Riyadh, but the Saudi government decided not to go forward with the construction. The steel would then be worthless to Rice. Must the company still accept it?

None of these hypotheticals involves true impossibility. It is physically possible for Bradshaw to deliver the goods and for Rice to receive. But in some cases, it may be so dangerous, costly, or pointless to enforce a bargain that a court will discharge it instead. Courts use the related doctrines of commercial impracticability and frustration of purpose to decide when a change in circumstances should permit one side to escape its duties.

Commercial impracticability means some event has occurred that neither party anticipated and *fulfilling the contract would now be extraordinarily difficult and unfair to one party.* If a shipping strike forces Bradshaw to ship by air, the company will argue that neither side expected the strike and that Bradshaw should not suffer a fivefold increase in shipping costs. Bradshaw will probably win the argument.

Frustration of purpose means some event has occurred that neither party anticipated and *the contract now has no value for one party.* If Rice's building project is canceled, Rice will argue that the steel now is useless to the company. Frustration cases are hard to predict. Some states would agree with Rice, but others would hold that it was Rice's obligation to protect itself with a government guarantee that the project would be completed. Courts consider the following factors in deciding impracticability and frustration claims:

- **Mere financial difficulties will never suffice to discharge a contract.** Barbara and Michael Luber divorced, and Michael agreed to pay alimony. He stopped making payments and claimed that it was impracticable for him to do so because he had hit hard times and simply did not have the money. The court dismissed his argument, noting that commercial impracticability requires some objective event that neither party anticipated, not merely the financial deterioration of one party.[7]

---

[7]Luber v. Luber, 418 Pa. Super. 542, 614 A.2d 771 (Pa. Super. Ct. 1992).

- **The event must have been truly unexpected.** Wayne Carpenter bought land from the state of Alaska, intending to farm it and agreeing to make monthly payments. The sales contract stated that Alaska did not guarantee the land for agriculture or any other purpose. Carpenter struggled to farm the land but failed; as soon as the ground thawed, the water table rose too high for crops. Carpenter abandoned the land and stopped making payments. Alaska sued and won. The high court rejected Carpenter's claim of impracticability since the "event"—bad soil—was not unexpected. Alaska had warned that the land might prove unworkable, and Carpenter had no claim for commercial impracticability.[8]
- **If the promisor must use a different means to accomplish her task, at a greatly increased cost, she probably does have a valid claim of impracticability.** If a shipping strike forces Bradshaw to use a different means of delivery—say, air—and this multiplies its costs several times, the company is probably discharged. But a mere increase in the cost of raw materials, such as a 30 percent rise in the price of ore, will almost never discharge the promisor.
- **A *force majeure* clause is significant but not necessarily dispositive.** To protect themselves from unexpected events, companies sometimes include a *force majeure* clause, allowing cancellation of the agreement in case of certain listed extraordinary and unexpected events. A typical clause might permit the seller of goods to delay or cancel delivery in the event of "acts of God, fire, labor disputes, accidents, or transportation difficulties." A court will always consider a *force majeure* clause, but it may not enforce it if one party is trying to escape from routine financial problems.

The following case involves risky business, complex financial instruments, and a lot of excuses. Does a global credit meltdown excuse a party's duty to pay?

Hoosier Energy Rural Electric Cooperative, Inc. v. John Hancock Life Insurance Co.

582 F.3d 721
United States Court of Appeals for the Seventh Circuit, 2009

Facts: John Hancock Life Insurance Co. receives lots of cash in premium payments, which it then invests so that it will have enough funds to pay claims from its policy holders. To this end, it entered into a leveraged lease with Hoosier Energy. This transaction was highly complex and only profitable because of convoluted provisions of the tax code. (You definitely do not want to try this at home.) In short, Hancock paid Hoosier $300 million to lease a power plant for 63 years, which Hoosier then leased back for 30 years.

But Hancock foresaw some risks: What if the power station became unprofitable? What if Hoosier stopped paying rent? (What would Hancock do if it was stuck with a power plant?) To mitigate these risks, it asked to Hoosier to secure a credit-default swap (CDS). A CDS is a financial contract that acts as insurance against a loan default and other contingencies. Ambac Assurance Corporation, the CDS provider, agreed to pay Hancock if certain events occurred. One of those triggering events was a decline in Ambac's own credit rating below a certain level. In that case, Hoosier had to find a replacement swap partner. If Hoosier was unsuccessful, Ambac would pay Hancock $120 million.

And then came 2008—and a global financial crisis. Ambac's credit rating plummeted, along with pretty much everyone else's. Hancock demanded that Hoosier find a replacement, but Hoosier stalled. If it replaced Ambac, it would have to pay big money—enough to send Hoosier into bankruptcy. So Hoosier sued, requesting an injunction to suspend its duty to find a swap partner. It claimed that the global financial crisis rendered its performance impossible—or at the very least, "temporarily impracticable" until the

[8]State v. Carpenter, 869 P.2d 1181 (Alaska 1994).

Dmitri Ma/Shutterstock.com

economy improved. The lower court sympathized with Hoosier and granted the injunction. Hancock appealed.

Issue: ***Did the global credit crisis render performance impossible?***

Excerpts from Judge Easterbrook's Decision: Like other states, New York recognizes the doctrine of impossibility—but even then only the kind of impossibility that the parties could not have anticipated. Here, the parties anticipated the possibility that Hoosier, Ambac, or both might get into financial distress and provided what was to happen.

Suppose that Hoosier had an in-the-money option to purchase the Indianapolis Colts, and that as a result of the reduced availability of credit it was unable to find a lender to finance the transaction. That would not make performance "impossible." The "impossibility" doctrine never justifies failure to make a payment, because financial distress differs from impossibility.

It is hard to see why Hoosier should be able to stiff John Hancock, just because the very risk specified in the contract has occurred. Hoosier did not expect an economic downturn. Downturns are types of things that happen, and against which contracts can be designed. When they do happen, the contractual risk allocation must be enforced rather than set aside.

The district court called the credit crunch of 2008 a "once-in-a-century" event. That's an overstatement (the Great Depression occurred within the last 100 years, and the 20th Century also saw financial crunches in 1973 and 1987), and also irrelevant. An insurer that sells hurricane or flood insurance against a "once in a century" catastrophe, or earthquake insurance in a city that rarely experiences tremblors, can't refuse to pay on the ground that, when a natural event devastates a city, its very improbability makes the contract unenforceable.

The defense works only if some unexpected event upsets all parties' expectations; it is not enough that the unexpected event puts one side in a bind. Financial distress could be and was foreseen; that's what the credit-default swap is all about.

CHAPTER CONCLUSION

Negotiate carefully. A casually written letter may imply a condition precedent that the author never intended. The term *personal satisfaction* should be defined so that both parties know whether one party may fire the other on a whim. Never assume that mere inconvenience, financial distress—or even a global recession—will discharge contractual duties.

EXAM REVIEW

1. **CONDITION** A condition is an event that must occur before a party becomes obligated. It may be stated expressly or implied, and no formal language is necessary to create one.

EXAMStrategy

Question: Stephen Krogness, a real estate broker, agreed to act as an agent for Best Buy Co., which wanted to sell several of its stores. The contract provided that Best Buy would pay Krogness a commission of 2 percent for "a sale to any prospect submitted directly to Best Buy by Krogness." Krogness introduced Corporate Realty Capital (CRC) to Best Buy, and the parties negotiated but could not reach agreement. CRC then introduced Best Buy to BB Properties (BB). Best Buy sold several properties to BB for $46 million. CRC acted as the broker. Krogness sought a commission of $528,000. Is he entitled to it?

Strategy: This contract contains a conditional clause. What is it? What must occur before Best Buy is obligated to pay Krogness? Did that event happen? (See the "Result" at the end of this Exam Review section.)

2. **SUBSTANTIAL PERFORMANCE** Strict performance, which requires one party to fulfill its duties perfectly, is unusual. In construction and service contracts, substantial performance is generally sufficient to entitle the promisor to the contract price, minus the cost of defects in the work.

3. **PERSONAL SATISFACTION** Personal satisfaction contracts are interpreted under an objective standard, requiring reasonable ground for dissatisfaction, unless the work involves personal judgment *and* the parties intended a subjective standard.

4. **GOOD FAITH** Good faith performance is required in all contracts.

5. **TIME OF THE ESSENCE** Time of the essence clauses result in strict enforcement of contract deadlines.

EXAMStrategy

Question: Colony Park Associates signed a contract to buy 44 acres of residential land from John Gall. The contract stated that closing would take place exactly one year later. The delay was to enable Colony Park to obtain building permits to develop condominiums. Colony Park worked diligently to obtain all permits, but delays in sewer permits forced Colony Park to notify Gall it could not close on the agreed date. Colony Park suggested a date exactly one month later. Gall refused the new date and declined to sell. Colony Park sued. Gall argued that since the parties specified a date, time was of the essence and Colony Park's failure to buy on time discharged Gall. Please rule.

Strategy: A time of the essence clause generally makes a contract date strictly enforceable. Was there one in this agreement? (See the "Result" at the end of this Exam Review section.)

6. **MATERIAL BREACH** A material breach is the only kind that will discharge a contract; a trivial breach will not.

7. **IMPOSSIBILITY** True impossibility means that some event has made it impossible to perform an agreement. It is typically caused by destruction of the subject matter, the death of an essential promisor, or intervening illegality.

EXAMStrategy

Question: Omega Concrete had a gravel pit and factory. Access was difficult, so Omega contracted with Union Pacific Railroad (UP) for the right to use a private road that crossed UP property and tracks. The contract stated that use of the road was solely for Omega employees and that Omega would be responsible for closing a gate that UP planned to build where the private road joined a public highway. In fact, UP never constructed the gate; Omega had no authority to construct the gate. Mathew Rogers, an Omega employee, was killed by a train while using the private road. Rogers's family sued Omega, claiming that Omega failed to keep the gate closed as the contract required. Is Omega liable?

Strategy: True impossibility means that the promisor cannot do what he promised to do. Is this such a case? (See the "Result" at the end of this Exam Review section.)

8. **COMMERCIAL IMPRACTICABILITY** Commercial impracticability means that some unexpected event has made it extraordinarily difficult and unfair for one party to perform its obligations.

9. **FRUSTRATION OF PURPOSE** Frustration of purpose may occur when an unexpected event renders a contract completely useless to one party.

RESULTS

1. Result: The conditional clause requires Best Buy to pay a commission for "a sale to any prospect submitted directly to Best Buy by Krogness." Krogness did not in fact introduce BB Properties to Best Buy. The condition has not occurred, and Best Buy is under no obligation to pay.

5. Result: Merely including a date for performance does not make time of the essence. A party that considers a date critical must make that clear. This contract did not indicate that the closing date was vital to either party, so a short delay was reasonable. Gail was ordered to convey the land to Colony Park.

7. Result: There was no gate, and Omega had no right to build one. This is a case of true impossibility. Omega was not liable.

MULTIPLE-CHOICE QUESTIONS

1. **CPA QUESTION** Nagel and Fields entered into a contract in which Nagel was obligated to deliver certain goods by September 10. On September 3, Nagel told Fields that he had no intention of delivering the goods. Prior to September 10, Fields may successfully sue Nagel under the doctrine of:
   (a) promissory estoppel.
   (b) accord and satisfaction.
   (c) anticipatory breach.
   (d) substantial performance.

2. Most contracts are discharged by:
   (a) agreement of the parties.
   (b) full performance.
   (c) failure of conditions.
   (d) commercial impracticability.
   (e) a material breach.

3. If a contract contains a condition precedent, the ______________ has the burden of proving that the condition actually happened. If a condition subsequent exists, the ______________ has the burden of showing that the condition occurred.
   (a) plaintiff; plaintiff
   (b) plaintiff; defendant
   (c) defendant; plaintiff
   (d) defendant; defendant

4. Big Co., a construction company, builds a grocery store. The contract calls for a final price of $5 million. Big Co. incurred $4.5 million in costs and stands to make a profit of $500,000. On a final inspection, the grocery store owner is upset. His blueprints called for 24 skylights, but the finished building has only 12. Installing the additional skylights would cost $100,000. Big Co. made no other errors. How much must the grocery store owner pay Big Co.?
   (a) $5,000,000
   (b) $4,900,000
   (c) $4,500,000
   (d) $0

5. Lenny makes K2, a synthetic form of marijuana, in his basement. He signs an agreement with the Super Smoke Shop to deliver 1,000 cans of K2 for $10,000. After the contract is signed, but before the delivery, Super Smoke Shop's state legislature makes the sale of K2 illegal. Lenny's contract will be discharged because of ______________.
   (a) true impossibility
   (b) commercial impracticability
   (c) frustration of purpose
   (d) none of these

CASE QUESTIONS

1. **ETHICS** Commercial Union Insurance Co. (CU) insured Redux, Ltd. The contract made CU liable for fire damage but stated that the insurer would not pay for harm caused by criminal acts of any Redux employees. Fire destroyed Redux's property. CU claimed that the "criminal acts" clause was a condition precedent, but Redux asserted it was a condition subsequent. What difference does it make, and who is legally right? Does the insurance company's position raise any ethical issues? Who drafted the contract? How clear were its terms?

2. Mustang Pipeline Co. hired Driver Pipeline Co. to lay 100 miles of pipeline in 98 days. On day 58, Driver had only completed 15 miles of pipe and gave up. Realizing that Driver was unlikely to make the deadline, Mustang terminated the contract. Under what principle did Mustang terminate? Was the termination justified?

3. Brunswick owned a tennis club on property that it leased from Route 18. Upon expiration of its 25-year lease, Brunswick had the option of either buying the property or purchasing a 99-year lease, both on very favorable terms. To exercise its option, Brunswick had to notify Route 18 no later than September 30 and had to pay the option price of $150,000. If Brunswick failed to exercise its options, the existing lease automatically renewed for 25 more years at more than triple the current rent. Over a year before the deadline, Brunswick informed Route 18 that it intended to exercise the option for a 99-year lease and asked to review the new lease. Route 18 responded with delays and did not provide a new lease, despite repeated pleas. After the September deadline passed, Route 18 notified Brunswick that it was too late to exercise the option because it did not pay the $150,000 on time. Brunswick sued, claiming that Route 18 had breached its duty of good faith and fair dealing. What result?

4. Loehmann's clothing stores, a nationwide chain with headquarters in New York, was the anchor tenant in the Lincoln View Plaza Shopping Center in Phoenix, Arizona, with a 20-year lease from the landlord, Foundation Development, beginning in 1978. Loehmann's was obligated to pay rent the first of every month and to pay common-area charges four times a year. The lease stated that if Loehmann's failed to pay on time, Foundation could send a notice of default, and that if the store failed to pay all money due within ten days, Foundation could evict. On February 23, 1987, Foundation sent Loehmann's the common-area charges for the quarter ending January 31, 1987. The balance due was $3,500. Loehmann's believed the bill was in error and sent an inquiry on March 18, 1987. On April 10, 1987, Foundation insisted on payment of the full amount within ten days. Foundation sent the letter to the Loehmann's store in Phoenix. On April 13, 1987, the Loehmann's store received the bill and, since it was not responsible for payments, forwarded it to the New York office. Because the company had moved offices in New York, a Loehmann's officer did not see the bill until April 20. Loehmann's issued a check for the full amount on April 24 and mailed it the following day. On April 28, Foundation sued to evict; on April 29, the company received Loehmann's check. Please rule.

5. ***YOU BE THE JUDGE* WRITING PROBLEM** Kuhn Farm Machinery, a European company, signed an agreement with Scottsdale Plaza Resort, of Arizona, to use the resort for its North American dealers' convention during March 1991. Kuhn agreed to rent 190 guest rooms and spend several thousand dollars on food and beverages. Kuhn invited its top 200 independent dealers from the United States and Canada and about 25 of its own employees from the United States, Europe, and Australia, although it never mentioned those plans to Scottsdale.

   On August 2, 1990, Iraq invaded Kuwait, and on January 16, 1991, the United States and allied forces were at war with Iraq. Saddam Hussein and other Iraqi leaders threatened terrorist acts against the United States and its allies. Kuhn became concerned about the safety of those traveling to Arizona, especially its European employees. By mid-February, 11 of the top 50 dealers with expense paid trips had either canceled their plans to attend or failed to sign up. Kuhn postponed the convention. The resort sued. The trial court discharged the contract under the doctrines of commercial impracticability and frustration of purpose. The resort appealed. Did commercial impracticability or frustration of purpose discharge the contract? **Argument for Scottsdale Plaza Resort:** The resort had no way of knowing that Kuhn anticipated bringing executives from Europe, and even less reason to expect that if anything interfered with their travel, the entire convention would become pointless. Most of the dealers could have attended the convention, and the resort stood ready to serve them. **Argument for Kuhn:** The parties never anticipated the threat of terrorism. Kuhn wanted this convention so that its European executives, among others, could meet top North American dealers. That is now impossible. No company would risk employee lives for a meeting. As a result, the contract has no value at all to Kuhn, and its obligations should be discharged by law.

DISCUSSION QUESTIONS

1. Evans built a house for Sandra Dyer, but the house had some problems. The garage ceiling was too low. Load-bearing beams in the "great room" cracked and appeared to be steadily weakening. The patio did not drain properly. Pipes froze. Evans wanted the money promised for the job, but Dyer refused to pay. Comment.

2. Krug International, an Ohio corporation, had a contract with Iraqi Airways to build aeromedical equipment for training pilots. Krug then contracted for Power Engineering, an Iowa corporation, to build the specialized gearbox to be used in the training equipment for $150,000. Power did not know that Krug planned to resell the gearbox to Iraqi Airways. When Power had almost completed the gearbox, the Gulf War broke out and the United Nations declared an embargo on all shipments to Iraq. Krug notified Power that it no longer wanted the gearbox. Power sued. Please rule.

3. Westinghouse sold uranium in long-term contracts at fixed prices, betting that market prices would be stable or fall (as they had been). But this was a bad bet: Uranium prices skyrocketed as a result of a cartel. Faced with large losses if it had to fulfill its contracts, Westinghouse argued that the unanticipated spike in uranium prices made its performance impossible. Should Westinghouse be freed of its contractual duties to sell uranium at a loss?

4. Jacobs Builders entered into a contract with Kent to build him a home. The agreement stated that Jacobs would use only certain brand-name materials. Upon completion of the home, Kent discovered that Jacobs had installed high-quality, but not brand-name, pipes throughout the house. This was an oversight, which even the architect failed to catch. Kent asked Jacobs to replace all the pipes, but this meant destroying all of the floors and walls in the house. Should Kent have to rebuild the house to get paid?

5. Franklin J. Moneypenny hires Angela to paint his portrait. She is to be paid $50,000 if the painting is acceptable "in Franklin's sole judgment." At the big unveiling, 99 of 100 attendees think that Angela has done a masterful job. Franklin disagrees. He thinks the painting makes him look like a toad. (He does in fact look like a toad, but he does not like to contemplate this fact.) Franklin refuses to pay, and, because he signed a personal satisfaction contract, Angela gets nothing. Is this fair? Should the law allow personal satisfaction contracts?

CHAPTER 19 REMEDIES

Margot had great expectations—the dating service, that is. She signed a contract in which she paid $3,790 to Great Expectations dating service. For this fee, the service promised to introduce her to at least 12 eligible bachelors who matched her requirements. Great Expectations would also provide high-quality photo shoots, dating advice, and invitations to members-only events. Representatives assured Margot that she would feel like "a kid in a candy store," with online access to over 175,000 Great Expectation members nationwide. They also told her that their location alone had had over 300 marriages in the last year.

As it turned out, Margot's experience was far from great. The company did not introduce her to anyone. (One man approached her after seeing her profile, but he was no prize.) Her photos were terrible, and the dating advice she received was useless because she had no dates. In fact, Great Expectations had greatly exaggerated their numbers of members and matches.[1]

Forlorn and angry, Margot sued the dating service. What did she *really* want? Margot did not want her money back: She wanted a date—many dates with many handsome, intelligent, and well-adjusted men of her age. She wanted them to swoon over her picture and tend to her every need. She wanted to get married. And she wanted to take back the three years she wasted with Great Expectations. But what could a court give her?

Margot sued the dating service. What did she *really* want? Margot did not want her money back: She wanted a date.

[1]Adapted from Doe v. Great Expectations, 10 Misc. 3d 618 (N.Y. City Civ. Ct. 2005) and various states' attorneys general complaints against the company.

19-1 IDENTIFYING THE "INTEREST" TO BE PROTECTED

Remedy
A court's compensation to the injured party

Interest
A legal right in something

Someone breaches a contract when he fails to perform a duty without a valid excuse. Great Expectations breached its contract with Margot when it failed to deliver 12 dates. But what can Margot do about this breach? In other words, what is her *remedy?* **A remedy is the method a court uses to compensate an injured party.**

The first step that a court takes in choosing a remedy is to decide what interest it is trying to protect. An **interest** is a legal right in something. Someone can have an interest in property, for example, by owning it, or renting it to a tenant, or lending money so someone else may buy it. He can have an interest in a *contract* if the agreement gives him some benefit. There are four principal contract interests that a court may seek to protect:

- **Expectation interest.** This interest is what the injured party reasonably thought she would get from the contract. The goal is to put her in the position she would have been in if both parties had fully performed their obligations. Margot's great expectation was to find a mate, but a court cannot require the defendant to produce a husband. Typically, an expectation interest is the profit the plaintiff would have earned under a contract.
- **Reliance interest.** Even if the injured party has not shown an expectation interest, he can still recover damages if he proves that he *spent money* in reliance on the agreement and that, in fairness, he should receive compensation. If Margot had spent money flying to another city to meet a date who, it turned out, was a serial killer just released after 30 years in prison, she might have a reliance interest.
- **Restitution interest.** The injured party may be unable to show an expectation interest or reliance. But perhaps she has conferred a benefit *on the other party*. Here, the objective is to restore to the injured party the benefit she has provided. Margot provided the service with a benefit—money. Her best argument is in restitution. A court will not get her a date, but it can return her money.
- **Equitable interest.** In some cases, money damages will not suffice to help the injured party. Something more is needed, such as an order for the breaching party to perform (specific performance) or an order forcing it to stop doing something (an injunction). If a party who has promised to sell land ultimately refuses to do so, a court may order specific performance or may enjoin the defendant from selling the property to someone else. As we will see, these actions are not always available to injured plaintiffs like Margot.

In this chapter, we study all four interests and the remedies that the law offers if they are violated.

Ethics

Although a court may have several alternative remedies available, it is important to note that most have one thing in common: The focus is on compensating the injured party rather than punishing the party in breach.

Some critics argue that someone who willfully breaches a contract should pay a penalty. Margot and other Great Expectations members were duped by its false promises and inflated numbers. Should a remedy reflect morality? In this chapter, we will see very few instances in which a court *punishes* unethical conduct. Is this right? Should contract law exact a price for bad behavior? Should it try to prevent the same thing from happening to others? What would Kant and Mill say?

19-2 EXPECTATION INTEREST

This is the most common remedy that the law provides for a party injured by a breach of contract. **The expectation interest is designed to put the injured party in the position she would have been in had both sides fully performed their obligations.** A court tries to give the injured party the money she would have made from the contract. If accurately calculated, this should take into account all the gains she reasonably expected and all the expenses and losses she would have incurred. The injured party should not end up better off than she would have been under the agreement, nor should she suffer a loss.

If you ever go to law school, you will almost certainly encounter the following case during your first weeks of classes. It has been used to introduce the concept of damages in contract lawsuits for generations. Enjoy the famous "case of the hairy hand."

Landmark Case

Hawkins v. McGee

84 N.H. 114
New Hampshire Supreme Court, 1929

Facts: Hawkins suffered a severe electrical burn on the palm of his right hand. After years of living with disfiguring scars, he went to visit Dr. McGee, who was well known for his early attempts at skin grafting surgery. The doctor told Hawkins "I will guarantee to make the hand a hundred percent perfect." Hawkins hired him to perform the operation.

McGee cut a patch of healthy skin from Hawkins's chest and grafted it over the scar tissue on Hawkins' palm. Unfortunately, the chest hair on the skin graft was very thick, and it continued to grow after the surgery. The operation resulted in a hairy palm for Hawkins. Feeling rather . . . embarrassed. . . . Hawkins sued Dr. McGee.

The trial court judge instructed the jury to calculate damages in this way: "If you find the plaintiff entitled to anything, he is entitled to recover for what pain and suffering he has been made to endure and what injury he has sustained over and above the injury that he had before."

The jury awarded Hawkins $3,000, but the court reduced the award to $500. Dissatisfied, Hawkins appealed.

Issue: ***How should Hawkins' damages be calculated?***

Excerpts from Justice Branch's Decision: The jury was permitted to consider two elements of damage, (1) pain and suffering due to the operation, and (2) positive ill effects of the operation upon the plaintiff's hand. [T]he foregoing instruction was erroneous.

By damages as that term is used in the law of contracts, is intended compensation to put the plaintiff in as good a position as he would have been in had the defendant kept his contract. The measure of recovery is what the defendant should have given the plaintiff, not what the plaintiff has given the defendant or otherwise expended.

We conclude that the true measure of the plaintiff's damage in the present case is the difference between the value to him of a perfect hand and the value of his hand in its present condition, including any incidental consequences fairly within the contemplation of the parties when they made their contract.

The extent of the plaintiff's suffering does not measure this difference in value. The pain necessarily incident to a serious surgical operation was a part of the contribution which the plaintiff was willing to make to his joint undertaking with the defendant to produce a good hand. It furnished no test of the difference between the value of the hand which the defendant promised and the one which resulted from the operation.

[Remanded for a] new trial.

Now let's consider a more modern example.

William Colby was a former director of the CIA. He wanted to write a book about his 15 years in Vietnam. He paid James McCarger $5,000 for help in writing an early draft and promised McCarger another $5,000 if the book was published. He then hired Alexander Burnham to co-write the book. Colby's agent secured a contract with Contemporary Books, which included a $100,000 advance. But Burnham was hopelessly late with the manuscript and Colby missed his publication date. Colby fired Burnham and finished the book without him. Contemporary published *Lost Victory* several years late, and the book flopped, earning no significant revenue. Because the book was so late, Contemporary paid Colby a total of only $17,000. Colby sued Burnham for his lost expectation interest. The court awarded him $23,000, calculated as follows:

	$100,000	Advance, the only money Colby was promised
	- 10,000	Agent's fee
	= 90,000	Fee for the two authors, combined
Divided by 2	= 45,000	Colby's fee (The other half went to the coauthor.)
	- 5,000	Owed to McCarger under the earlier agreement
	= 40,000	Colby's expectation interest
	- 17,000	Fee Colby eventually received from Contemporary
	= 23,000	Colby's **expectation damages**; that is, the additional amount he would have received had Burnham finished on time

Expectation damages
The money required to put one party in the position she would have been in had the other side performed the contract

The *Colby* case presented a relatively easy calculation of damages.[2] Other contracts are complex. Courts typically divide the expectation damages into three parts: (1) direct (or "compensatory") damages, which represent harm that flowed directly from the contract's breach; (2) consequential (or "special") damages, which represent harm caused by the injured party's unique situation; and (3) incidental damages, which are minor costs such as storing or returning defective goods, advertising for alternative goods, and so forth. The first two, direct and consequential, are the important ones.

Note that punitive damages are absent from our list. The golden rule in contracts cases is to give successful plaintiffs "the benefit of the bargain" and not to punish defendants. Punitive damages are occasionally awarded in lawsuits that involve both a contract *and* either an intentional tort (such as fraud) or a breach of fiduciary duty, but they are not available in "simple" cases involving only a breach of contract.

19-2a Direct Damages

Direct damages are those that flow directly from the contract. They are the most common monetary award for the expectation interest. These are the damages that inevitably result from the breach. Suppose that Ace Productions hires Reina to star in its new movie, *Inside Straight.* Ace promises Reina $3 million, providing she shows up June 1 and works until the film is finished. But in late May, Joker Entertainment offers Reina $6 million to star in its new feature, and, on June 1, Reina informs Ace that she will not appear. Reina has breached her contract, and Ace should recover direct damages.

What are the damages that flow directly from the contract? Ace has to replace Reina. If Ace hires Kayla as its star and pays her a fee of $4 million, Ace is entitled to the difference between what it expected to pay ($3 million) and what the breach forced it to pay ($4 million), or $1 million in direct damages.

---

2 Colby v. Burnham, 31 Conn. App. 707 (1993).

19-2b Consequential Damages

In addition to direct damages, the injured party may seek **consequential damages** or, as they are also known, "special damages." Consequential damages reimburse for harm that results from the *particular* circumstances of the plaintiff. These damages are only available if they are a *foreseeable consequence* of the breach. Suppose, for example, that Raould breaches two contracts—he is late picking both Sharon and Paul up for a taxi ride. His breach is the same for both parties, but the consequences are very different. Sharon misses her flight to San Francisco and incurs a substantial fee to rebook the flight. Paul is simply late for the barber, who manages to fit him in anyway. Thus, Raould's damages would be different for these two contracts. The rule concerning this remedy comes from a famous 1854 case, *Hadley v. Baxendale.* This is another case that all American law students read. Now it is your turn.

Consequential damages
Are those resulting from the unique circumstances of the injured party

Landmark Case

Hadley v. Baxendale

9 Ex. 341, 156 Eng. Rep. 145
Court of Exchequer, 1854

Facts: The Hadleys operated a flour mill in Gloucester. The crank-shaft broke, causing the mill to grind to a halt. The Hadleys employed Baxendale to cart the damaged part to a foundry in Greenwich, where a new one could be manufactured. Baxendale promised to make the delivery in one day, but he was late transporting the shaft, and, as a result, the Hadleys' mill was shut for five extra days. They sued, and the jury awarded damages based in part on their lost profits. Baxendale appealed.

Issue: ***Should the defendant be liable for profits lost because of his delay in delivering the shaft?***

Excerpts from Judge Alderson's Decision: Where two parties have made a contract which one of them has broken, the damages which the other party ought to receive in respect of such breach of contract should be such as may fairly and reasonably be considered either arising naturally, i.e. according to the usual course of things, from such breach of contract itself, or such as may reasonably be supposed to have been in the contemplation of both parties, at the time they made the contract, as the probable result of the breach of it. Now, if the special circumstances under which the contract was actually made were communicated by the plaintiffs to the defendants, and thus known to both parties, the damages resulting from the breach of such a contract, which they would reasonably contemplate, would be the amount of injury which would ordinarily follow from a breach of contract under these special circumstances so known and communicated. But, on the other hand, if these special circumstances were wholly unknown to the party breaking the contract, he, at the most, could only be supposed to have had in his contemplation the amount of injury which would arise generally, and in the great multitude of cases not affected by any special circumstances, from such a breach of contract.

Now, in the present case, if we are to apply the principles above laid down, we find that the only circumstances here communicated by the plaintiffs to the defendants at the time the contract was made, were that the article to be carried was the broken shaft of a mill, and that the plaintiffs were the millers of that mill. But how do these circumstances show reasonably that the profits of the mill must be stopped by an unreasonable delay in the delivery of the broken shaft by the carrier to the third person? Suppose the plaintiffs had another shaft in their possession put up or putting up at the time, and that they only wished to send back the broken shaft to the engineer who made it; it is clear that this would be quite consistent with the above circumstances, and yet the unreasonable delay in the delivery would have no effect upon the intermediate profits of the mill. It follows, therefore, that the loss of profits here cannot reasonably be considered such a consequence of the breach of contract as could have been fairly and reasonably contemplated by both the parties when they made this contract.

[The court ordered a new trial, in which the jury would *not* be allowed to consider the plaintiffs' lost profits.]

The rule from *Hadley v. Baxendale* has been unchanged ever since: **The injured party may recover consequential damages only if the *breaching party* should have *foreseen* them when the two sides formed the contract.**

Let us return briefly to *Inside Straight*. Suppose that, long before shooting began, Ace had sold the film's soundtrack rights to Spinem Sound for $2 million. Spinem believed it would make a profit only if Reina appeared in the film, so it demanded the right to discharge the agreement if Reina dropped out. When Reina quit, Spinem terminated the contract. Now, when Ace sues Reina, it will also seek $2 million in consequential damages for the lost music revenue.

The $2 million is not a direct damage. The contract between Reina and Ace has nothing directly to do with selling soundtrack rights. But the loss is nonetheless a consequence of Reina bailing out on the project. So, if Reina knew about Ace's contract with Spinem when she signed to do the film, the loss would be foreseeable to her, and she would be liable for $2 million. If she never realized she was an essential part of the music contract, and if a jury determines that she had no reason to expect the $2 million loss, she owes nothing for the lost soundtrack profits.

Injured plaintiffs often try to recover lost profits. Courts will generally award these damages if (1) the lost profits were foreseeable and (2) the plaintiff provides enough information so that the fact finder can reasonably estimate a fair amount. The calculation need not be done with mathematical precision. In the following case, the plaintiffs lost not only profits—but their entire business. Can they recover for harm that is so extensive? You decide.

You Be the Judge

Bi-Economy Market, Inc. v. Harleysville Ins. Co. of New York

2008 N.Y. Slip Op. 01418
New York Court of Appeals, 2008

Facts: Bi-Economy Market was a family-owned meat market in Rochester, New York. The company was insured by Harleysville Insurance. The "Deluxe Business Owner's" policy provided replacement cost for damage to buildings and inventory. Coverage also included "business interruption insurance" for one year, meaning the loss of pretax profit plus normal operating expenses, including payroll.

The company suffered a disastrous fire, which destroyed its building and all inventory. Bi-Economy immediately filed a claim with Harleysville, but the insurer responded slowly. Harleysville eventually offered a settlement of $163,000. A year later, an arbitrator awarded the Market $407,000. During that year, Harleysville paid for seven months of lost income but declined to pay more. The company never recovered or reopened.

Bi-Economy sued, claiming that Harleysville's slow, inadequate payments destroyed the company. The company also sought consequential damages for the permanent destruction of its business. Harleysville claimed that it was only responsible for damages specified in the contract: the building, inventory, and lost income. The trial court granted summary judgment for Harleysville. The appellate court affirmed, claiming that when they entered into the contract, the parties did not contemplate damages for termination of the business. Bi-Economy appealed to the state's highest court.

You Be the Judge: *Is Bi-Economy entitled to consequential damages for the destruction of its business?*

Argument for Bi-Economy: Bi-Economy is a small, family business. We paid for business interruption insurance for an obvious reason: In the event of a disaster, we lacked the resources to keep going while buildings were constructed and inventory purchased. We knew that in such a calamity, we would need prompt reimbursement—compensation covering the immediate damage and our ongoing lost income. Why else would we pay the premiums?

At the time we entered into the contract, Harleysville could easily foresee that if it responded slowly, with insufficient payments, we could not survive. They knew that is what we wanted to avoid—and it is just what happened. The insurer's bad faith offer of a low figure, and its payment of only seven months' lost income, ruined a fine family business. When the insurance company agreed to business interruption coverage, it was declaring that it would act fast and fairly to sustain a small firm in crisis. The insurer should now pay for the full harm it has wrought.

Argument for Harleysville: We contracted to insure the Market for three losses: its building, inventory, and lost income. After the fire, we performed a reasonable, careful evaluation and made an offer we considered fair. An arbitrator later awarded Bi-Market additional money, which we paid. However it is absurd to suggest that in addition to that, we are liable for an open-ended commitment for permanent destruction of the business.

Consequential damages are appropriate in cases where a plaintiff suffers a loss that was not covered in the contract. In this case, though, the parties bargained over exactly what Harleysville would pay in the event of a major fire. If the insurer has underpaid for lost income, let the court award a fair sum. However, the parties never contemplated an additional, enormous payment for cessation of the business. There is almost no limit as to what that obligation could be. If Bi-Market was concerned that a fire might put the company permanently out of business, it should have said so at the time of negotiating for insurance. The premium would have been dramatically higher.

Neither Bi-Market nor Harleysville ever imagined such an open-ended insurance obligation, and the insurer should not pay an extra cent.

19-2c Incidental Damages

Incidental damages are the relatively minor costs that the injured party suffers when responding to the breach. When Reina, the actress, breaches the film contract, the producers may have to leave the set and fly back to Los Angeles to hire a new actress. The travel cost is an incidental damage. In another setting, suppose Maud, a manufacturer, has produced 5,000 pairs of running shoes for Foot The Bill, a retail chain, but Foot The Bill breaches the agreement and refuses to accept the goods. Maud will have to store the shoes and advertise for alternate buyers. The storage and advertising costs are incidental expenses, and Maud will recover them.

Incidental damages
Relatively minor costs that the injured party suffers when responding to the breach

19-2d The UCC and Damages

Under the Uniform Commercial Code (UCC), remedies for breach of contract in the sale of goods are similar to the general rules discussed throughout this chapter. UCC §§2-703 through 2-715 govern the remedies available to buyers and sellers.

Seller's Remedies

If a buyer breaches a sale of goods contract, the seller generally has at least two remedies. She may resell the goods elsewhere. If she acts in good faith, she will be awarded **the difference between the original contract price and the price she was able to obtain in the open market.** Assume that Maud, the manufacturer, had a contract to sell her shoes to Foot The Bill for $55 per pair and Foot The Bill's breach forces her to sell them on the open market, where she gets only $48 per pair. Maud will win $7 per pair times 5,000 pairs, or $35,000, from Foot The Bill.

Alternatively, the buyer may choose not to resell and settle for the difference between the contract price and the market value of the goods. Maud, in other words, may choose to keep the shoes. If she can prove that their market value is $48 per pair, for example, by showing what other retailers would have paid her for them, she will still get her $7 each, representing the difference between what the contract promised her and what the market would support. In either case, the money represents direct damages. Maud is also entitled to incidental damages, such as the storage and advertising expenses described. But there is one significant difference under the UCC: **Most courts hold that the seller of goods is *not* entitled to consequential damages.** Suppose Maud hired two extra workers to inspect, pack, and ship the shoes for Foot The Bill. Those are consequential damages, but Maud will not recover them because she is the seller and the contract is for the sale of goods.

Buyer's Remedies

Cover
To make a good faith purchase of goods similar to those in the contract

The buyer's remedies in sale of goods contracts (which are, as always, governed by the UCC) are similar to those we have already considered. She typically has two options. First, the buyer can "cover" by purchasing substitute goods. To **cover** means to make a good faith purchase of goods similar to those in the contract. The buyer may then obtain **the difference between the original contract price and her cover price**. Alternatively, if the buyer chooses not to cover, she is entitled to the difference between the original contract price and the market value of the goods.

Suppose Mary has contracted to buy one thousand 6-foot Christmas trees at $25 per tree from Elmo. The market suddenly rises, and not feeling the spirit of the season, Elmo breaches his deal and sells the trees elsewhere. If Mary makes a good faith effort to cover but is forced to pay $40 per tree, she may recover the difference from Elmo, meaning $15 per tree times 1,000 trees, or $15,000. Similarly, if she chooses not to cover but can prove that $40 is now the market value of the trees, she is entitled to her $15 per tree.

Lori Sparkia/Shutterstock.com

What is the buyer entitled to if the seller does not deliver the trees as promised?

Under the UCC, the **buyer *is* entitled to consequential damages, provided that the seller could reasonably have foreseen them.** If Mary tells Elmo, when they sign their deal, that she has a dozen contracts to resell the trees for an average price of $50 per tree, she may recover $25 per tree, representing the difference between her contract price with Elmo and the value of the tree *to her*, based on her other contracts.[3] If she failed to inform Elmo of the other contracts, she would not receive any money based on them. The buyer is also entitled to whatever incidental damages may have accrued.

EXAMStrategy

Question: Chloe is a fashion designer. Her recent collection of silk-velvet evening gowns was gobbled up by high-end retailers, who now clamor for more. Chloe needs 300 yards of the same fabric by August 15. Mill House, which has supplied fabric to Chloe for many years, agrees to sell her 300 yards at $100 per yard, delivered on August 15. The market value of the fabric is $125, but Mill House gives Chloe a break because she is a major customer.

Chloe contracts with high-end retailers Barneys and Neiman Marcus to sell a total of 50 dresses, at an *additional* profit to Chloe of $800 per dress. On August 15, Mill House delivers defective fabric. Chloe cannot make her dresses in time, and the retailers cancel their orders. Chloe sues Mill House and wins—but what are her damages?

[3]As we discuss in the section on mitigation later in the chapter, Mary will get only her consequential damages if she attempts to cover.

Strategy: To determine damages, first ask whether the contract is governed by the common law or the UCC. This agreement concerns goods, so the Code applies. The UCC permits a buyer to recover damages for the difference between the contract price and the market value of the goods. The Code also allows consequential damages if the seller could have foreseen them. Apply those standards.

Result: Because Chloe's contract enabled her to save $25 per yard for 300 yards, she is entitled to $7,500. Chloe has also lost profits of $40,000. Mill House could easily have foreseen those losses because the supplier knew that Chloe was a designer who fabricated and sold dresses. Chloe is entitled to $47,500.

We turn now to cases where the injured party cannot prove expectation damages.

19-3 RELIANCE INTEREST

To win expectation damages, the injured party must prove the breach of contract caused damages that can be *quantified with reasonable certainty*. This rule sometimes presents plaintiffs with a problem.

George plans to manufacture and sell silk scarves during the holiday season. In the summer, he contracts with Cecily, the owner of a shopping mall, to rent a high-visibility stall for $100 per day. George then buys hundreds of yards of costly silk and gets to work cutting and sewing. But in September, Cecily refuses to honor the contract. George sues and proves Cecily breached a valid contract. But what is his remedy?

George cannot establish an expectation interest in his scarf business. He *hoped* to sell each scarf for a $40 gross profit. He *planned* on making $2,000 per day. But how much would he *actually* have earned? Enough to retire on? Enough to buy a salami sandwich for lunch? He has no way of proving his profits, and a court cannot give him his expectation interest.

Instead, George will ask for *reliance damages*. The **reliance interest** is designed to put an injured party in the position he would have been in had the parties never entered into a contract. This remedy focuses on the time and money the injured party spent performing his part of the agreement.

Reliance interest
Puts the injured party in the position he would have been in had the parties never entered into a contract

George should be able to recover reliance damages from Cecily. Assuming he is unable to sell the scarves to a retail store, which is probable since retailers will have made purchases long ago, George should be able to recover the cost of the silk fabric he bought and perhaps something for the hours of labor he spent cutting and sewing. But reliance damages can be difficult to win because *they are harder to quantify*. Courts prefer to compute damages using the numbers provided in a contract. If a contract states a price of $25 per Christmas tree and one party breaches, the arithmetic is easy. Judges can become uncomfortable when asked to base damages on vague calculations. How much was George's time worth in making the scarves? How good was his work? How likely were the scarves to sell? If George has a track record in the industry, he will be able to show a market price for his services. Without such a record, his reliance claim becomes a tough battle.

19-3a Promissory Estoppel

We have seen in earlier chapters that a plaintiff may sometimes recover damages based on promissory estoppel even when there is no valid contract. The plaintiff must show that the defendant made a promise knowing that the plaintiff would likely rely on it, that the plaintiff did rely, and that the only way to avoid injustice is to enforce the promise. **In promissory**

estoppel cases, a court will generally award *reliance damages*. It would be unfair to give expectation damages for the full benefit of the bargain when, legally speaking, there has been no bargain.

In the following case, the victorious plaintiff demonstrates how unreliable reliance damages are and how winning can be hard to distinguish from losing.

Toscano v. Greene Music

124 Ca. App. 4th 685
California Court of Appeals, 2004

Facts: Joseph Toscano was the general manager of Fields Pianos (Fields) in Santa Ana, California. He was unhappy with his job and decided to seek other employment. Toscano contacted Michael Greene, who owned similar stores. In July, Greene offered Toscano a sales management job starting September 1. Relying on that offer, Toscano resigned from Fields on August 1. However, in mid-August, Greene withdrew his employment offer. Toscano later found lower-paying jobs in other cities.

Toscano sued Greene for breach of contract and promissory estoppel. Greene argued that Toscano was not entitled to any expectation damages because his employment with Greene would have been at will, meaning he could lose the job at any time. Greene also urged that because Toscano was an at-will employee at Fields, he could recover, at most, one month's lost wage.

The trial court ruled that Toscano was entitled to reliance damages for all lost wages at Fields, starting from the day he resigned, going forward until his anticipated retirement in 2017. Toscano's expert accountant calculated his past losses (until the time of trial) at $119,061, and his future lost earnings at $417,772. The trial court awarded Toscano $536,833, and Greene appealed.

Issue: ***Was Toscano entitled to reliance damages?***

Excerpts from Judge O'Rourke's Decision: Given the equitable underpinnings of the promissory estoppel doctrine, we hold that a plaintiff such as Toscano, who relinquished his job in reliance on an unfulfilled promise of employment, may on an appropriate showing recover the lost wages he would have expected to earn from his former employer but for the defendant's promise. Such a damage measure is in keeping with the equitable nature of promissory estoppel. The object of equity is to do right and justice.

Our holding necessarily rejects the notion that the at-will nature of Toscano's former employment with Fields (undisputed by the parties here) is a strict impediment to recovery of future wages that Toscano would have earned at Fields had he not relied on Greene's promise.

[However,] we conclude that even drawing all inferences in Toscano's favor, the evidence was too speculative to lend support to the trial court's award of Toscano's lost future earnings from September 1 to his retirement.

Roberta Spoon, Toscano's damages expert, testified that in calculating Toscano's lost wages for the remainder of his career, "[a]ll I have done is arithmetic. I have simply analyzed the numbers." She testified she was not aware that Toscano's employment with Fields called for any specific tenure. Indeed, Spoon admitted Toscano could have quit or been fired from that job from the time he resigned to the present. She simply assumed Toscano would have continued employment with Fields or another employer at a comparable salary, observing that he had never in the past changed employers for anything other than a pay increase.

Spoon's testimony does not establish Toscano had a definite expectation of continued employment with Fields for any particular period of time. It is evident her supposition was based only on Toscano's history of remaining with his employers until offered new employment. However, *Toscano's* intentions or practices are not relevant to whether he could expect to remain with Fields until his retirement. Evidence of Toscano's intentions does not establish with any reasonable certainty that Fields, an at-will employer who had the right to terminate Toscano at any time for any reason, had some different understanding of the terms of Toscano's employment, or that it would have continued to employ him until the end of his career. Neither party presented testimony from Jerry Goldman, Toscano's boss at Fields. An expert's opinion must not be based upon speculative or conjectural data.

The award of future earnings calculated from [the day he quit] to the date of Toscano's retirement in 2017 is vacated and the matter remanded for a new trial on the issue of damages only. The judgment is otherwise affirmed.

Notice that the court never even mentions that Toscano acted in good faith, relying on Greene's promise, while the latter offered no excuse for suddenly withdrawing his offer. Is it fair to permit Greene to escape all liability? This court, like most, simply will not award significant damages where there is no contract permitting a clear calculation of losses.

The judges, though, have not entirely closed the door on Toscano. What is the purpose of the remand? What might Toscano demonstrate on remand? What practical difficulties will he encounter?

19-4 RESTITUTION INTEREST

Restitution means giving back. The **restitution interest** is designed to return to the injured party a benefit that he has conferred on the other party, which it would be unjust to leave with that person. In the opening scenario, Margot suffered many damages. Unfortunately for her, the only remedy a court will afford her is restitution. Great Expectations misrepresented its network of singles and breached the contract. But Margot cannot prove expectation damages (no matter how *Great*) or reliance damages, so she will have to settle for getting her money back.

Restitution interest
Designed to return to the injured party a benefit he has conferred on the other party

Restitution is awarded in three types of cases. First, the law allows restitution when a contract is breached or discharged. As you will recall, a contract is breached when one party fails to perform. A contract is said to be discharged when it is terminated by the nonoccurrence of a condition, impossibility, or another excuse. In such cases, a court may choose restitution because no other remedy is available or because no other remedy would be as fair. Second, judges allow restitution when the injured party to a voidable contract rescinds the agreement. Third, courts may award restitution in cases of quasi-contract, which we examined in Chapter 11. In quasi-contract cases, the parties never made a contract, but one side did benefit the other. We consider each kind of restitution interest in turn.

19-4a Restitution in Cases of Contract Breach or Discharge

When one party breaches a contract, the other may be entitled to recoup what he put in. Lillian and Harold Toews signed a contract to sell 1,500 acres of Idaho farmland to Elmer Funk. (No, not him—the Bugs Bunny character you are thinking of is Elmer Fudd.) He was to take possession immediately, but he would not receive the deed until he finished paying for the property, in ten years. This arrangement enabled him to enroll in a government program that would pay him "setasides" for *not* farming. Funk kept most aspects of his agreement. He did move onto the land and did receive $76,000 from the government for a year's worth of inactivity. (Nice work if you can get it.) The only part of the bargain Funk did not keep was his promise to pay. The Toews sued. Funk had clearly breached the deal. But what was the remedy?

The couple still owned the land, so they did not need to recover it. Funk had no money to pay for the farm, so they would never get their expectation interest. And they had expended almost no money complying with the deal, so they had no reliance interest. What they had done, though, was to *confer a benefit* on Funk. They had enabled him to obtain $76,000 in government money. The Toews wanted restitution. They argued that they had bestowed a $76,000 benefit on Funk and that it was unfair for him to keep it. The Idaho Court of Appeals agreed. It ruled that the couple had a restitution interest in the government setaside and ordered Funk to pay them the money.[4]

He did move onto the land and did receive $76,000 from the government for a year's worth of inactivity. (Nice work if you can get it.)

[4]Toews v. Funk, 129 Idaho 316 (Idaho Ct. App. 1994).

In the following case, both parties breached the contract. Could the famous football player get restitution even if he dropped the ball?

Taylor v. Kjaer

737 F.3d 854
United States Court of Appeals for the Third Circuit, 2013

Facts: Christian Kjaer and his relatives (Sellers) owned a small island off the coast of St. Thomas, U.S. Virgin Islands. Some investors, led by Miami Dolphins football player Jason Taylor agreed to buy it for $21 million.

Under the contract, Taylor paid a $1 million deposit and promised to close within 60 days. The contract allowed him to extend the closing date by paying an additional $500,000 nonrefundable deposit, which he did. The buyers' only other duty was to pay the remaining purchase price at closing. The Sellers committed to delivering clear title to the property, along with all of the island's permits.

According to the contract, if Taylor breached the contract, he would forfeit the deposits; if the Sellers breached, they would return the deposits. The contract did not say what would happen to the deposit if both parties breached.

On the closing date, the sale was not consummated; the Sellers delivered expired permits and did not convey clear title. Taylor and his partners did not pay. But the Sellers refused to return Taylor's deposit.

Taylor sued for restitution. The Sellers asserted they were entitled to the $1.5 million because Taylor breached the contract. Taylor argued that the Buyer's failure to deliver valid title discharged his obligation to close—and that allowing the Sellers to keep the money would unjustly enrich them. The district court found that since Taylor breached the valid contract, he could not recoup the deposit. Taylor challenged the lower court's call.

Issue: ***Was Taylor entitled to restitution?***

Excerpts from Judge Roth's Decision: Agreements concerning an exchange of promises require performance to be exchanged simultaneously whenever possible, unless the agreement indicates otherwise. This simultaneous exchange of performances creates concurrent conditions, under which performance by one party creates a condition precedent for performance by the other party.

Here, the Sellers were required to convey Clear and Marketable title and assignments of all permits, leases, and licenses necessary. Because the Contract of Sale did not indicate otherwise, the performance of each obligation was to occur simultaneously. Therefore, fulfillment of each obligation was a concurrent condition to the other.

With regard to awarding restitution in cases involving valid contracts, we look to the Restatement (Second) of Contracts:

> A party whose duty of performance does not arise or is discharged as a result of nonoccurrence of a condition is entitled to restitution for any benefit that he has conferred on the other party by way of part performance or reliance.[5]

For example, the Restatement illustrates: "A contracts to sell a tract of land to B for $100,000. After B has made a part payment of $20,000, A wrongfully refuses to transfer title. B can recover the $20,000 in restitution."

In applying the Restatement (Second) of Contracts, it is clear that restitution is in order. Taylor provided a deposit of $1.5 million to the Sellers with the intent to purchase the property. However, all of the parties failed to perform within the timeframe specified in the contracts, and their respective duties were discharged. Thus, as the Restatement instructs, Taylor is entitled to restitution for the benefit of the deposit that he conferred to the Sellers.

For the foregoing reasons, we will reverse the District Court and order the return of the deposit to Taylor.

---

[5]Restatement (Second) of Contracts §377 (1981).

19-4b Restitution in Cases of a Voidable Contract

Restitution is a common remedy in contracts involving fraud, misrepresentation, mistake, and duress. In these cases, restitution often goes hand in hand with **rescission**, which means to undo a contract and put the parties where they were before they made the agreement. Courtney sells her favorite sculpture to Adam for $95,000, both parties believing the work to be a valuable original by Barbara Hepworth. Two months later, Adam learns that the sculpture is a mere copy, worth very little. A court will permit Adam to rescind the contract on the ground of mutual mistake. At the same time, Adam is entitled to restitution of the purchase price. Courtney gets the worthless carving, and Adam receives his money back.

Rescission
To "undo" a contract and put the parties where they were before they made the agreement

19-4c Restitution in Cases of a Quasi-Contract

George Anderson owned a valuable 1936 Plymouth. He took it to Ronald Schwegel's repair shop, and the two orally agreed that Schwegel would restore the car for $6,000. Unfortunately, they never agreed on the meaning of the word *restore*. Anderson thought the term meant complete restoration, including body work and engine repairs, whereas Schwegel intended body work but no engine repairs. After doing some of the work, Schwegel told Anderson that the car needed substantial engine work, and he asked for Anderson's permission to allow an engine shop to do it. Anderson agreed, believing the cost was included in the original estimate. When the car was finished and running smoothly, Schwegel demanded $9,800. Anderson refused to pay more than the $6,000 agreed price, and Schwegel sued.

The court held that there was no valid contract between the parties. A contract requires a meeting of the minds. Here, said the court, there was no meeting of the minds on what *restore* included, and hence Schwegel could not recover either his expectation or his reliance interest since both require an enforceable agreement. Schwegel then argued that a quasi-contract existed. In other words, he claimed that even if there had been no valid agreement, he had performed a service for Anderson and that it would be unjust for Anderson to keep it without paying. **A court may award restitution, even in the absence of a contract, when one party has conferred a benefit on another and it would be unjust for the other party to retain the benefit.** The court ruled that Schwegel was entitled to the full $3,800 above and beyond the agreed price because that was the fair market value of the additional work. Anderson had asked for the repairs and now had an auto that was substantially improved. It would be unjust, ruled the court, to permit him to keep that benefit for free.[6]

Darren Brode/shutterstock.com

Who would keep the benefit of the restoration of this 1936 Plymouth?

19-5 EQUITABLE INTEREST AND REMEDIES

In contract lawsuits, plaintiffs are occasionally awarded the remedies of **specific performance**, injunction, and reformation.

Specific performance
Forces both parties to complete the deal

[6] Anderson v. Schwegel, 118 Idaho 362 (Idaho Ct. App. 1990).

19-5a Specific Performance

Leona Claussen owned Iowa farmland. She sold some of it to her sister-in-law, Evelyn Claussen, and, along with the land, granted Evelyn an option to buy additional property at $800 per acre. Evelyn could exercise her option anytime during Leona's lifetime or within six months of Leona's death. When Leona died, Evelyn informed the estate's executor that she was exercising her option. But other relatives wanted the property, and the executor refused to sell. Evelyn sued and asked for *specific performance*. She did not want an award of damages; she wanted *the land itself*. The remedy of specific performance forces the two parties to perform their contract.

A court will award specific performance, ordering the parties to perform the contract, only in cases involving the sale of land or some other asset that is considered "unique." Courts use this remedy when money damages would be inadequate to compensate an injured party. If the subject is unique and irreplaceable, money damages will not put the injured party in the same position she would have been in had the agreement been kept. So a court will order the seller to convey the rare object and the buyer to pay for it.

Historically, every parcel of land has been regarded as unique, and therefore **specific performance is always available in real estate contracts.** Family heirlooms and works of art are also often considered unique. Evelyn Claussen won specific performance. The Iowa Supreme Court ordered Leona's estate to convey the land to Evelyn for $800 per acre.[7] Generally, either the seller or the buyer may be granted specific performance. One limitation in land sales is that a buyer may obtain specific performance only if she was ready, willing, and able to purchase the property on time. If Evelyn had lacked the money to buy Leona's property for $800 per acre within the six-month time limit, the court would have declined to order the sale.

EXAMStrategy

Question: The Monroes, a retired couple who live in Illinois, want to move to Arizona to escape the northern winter. In May, the Monroes contract in writing to sell their house to the Temples for $450,000. Closing is to take place June 30. The Temples pay a deposit of $90,000. However, in early June, the Monroes travel through Arizona and discover it is too hot for them. They promptly notify the Temples they are no longer willing to sell, and return the $90,000, with interest. The Temples sue, seeking the house. In response, the Monroes offer evidence that the value of the house has dropped from about $450,000 to about $400,000. They claim that the Temples have suffered no loss. Who will win?

Strategy: Most contract lawsuits are for money damages, but not this one. The Temples want the house. Because they want the house itself, and not money damages, the drop in value is irrelevant. What legal remedy are the Temples seeking? They are suing for specific performance. When will a court grant specific performance? Should it do so here?

Result: In cases involving the sale of land or some other unique asset, a court will grant specific performance, ordering the parties to perform the agreement. All houses are regarded as unique. The court will force the Monroes to sell their house, provided the Temples have sufficient money to pay for it.

Other unique items, for which a court will order specific performance, include such things as secret formulas, patents, and shares in a closely held corporation. Money damages would be inadequate for all these things since the injured party, even if she got the cash, could not go out and buy a substitute item. By contrast, a contract for a new Cadillac Escalade is not enforceable by specific performance. If the seller breaches, the buyer is entitled to the

[7] In re Estate of Claussen, 482 N.W.2d 381 (Iowa 1992).

difference between the contract price and the market value of the car. The buyer can take his money elsewhere and purchase a virtually identical SUV.

19-5b Injunction

An **injunction** is a court order that requires someone to do or refrain from doing something.

Injunction
A court order that requires someone to do something or refrain from doing something

A **preliminary injunction** is an order issued early in a lawsuit prohibiting a party from doing something *during the course of the lawsuit.* The court attempts to protect the interests of the plaintiff immediately. If, after trial, it appears that the plaintiff has been injured and is entitled to an injunction, the trial court will make its order a **permanent injunction.** If it appears that the preliminary injunction should never have been issued, the court will terminate the order.

The following case involves sabotage on Wall Street. Were the financial advisor's wily ways enough to earn Morgan Stanley a preliminary injunction?

Morgan Stanley Smith Barney v. O'Brien

2013 U.S. Dist. LEXIS 159128, 2013 WL 5962103
United States District Court, Connecticut, 2013

Facts: To ensure fair competition and client privacy, many financial services firms signed an agreement known as the *Protocol for Broker Recruiting.* It outlined the procedures that all member firms, and their employees, had to follow when hiring financial advisors from any other signatory firm. The Protocol required departing advisors, acting in good faith, to give their old firm a list of their clients' basic contact information. Moreover, the advisor's new firm was required to limit the use of the listed information. The two firms in dispute in this case—Morgan Stanley and Raymond James—had both signed the Protocol.

Denis O'Brien was a financial advisor at Morgan Stanley. In his employment agreement, he promised not to solicit any of his Morgan Stanley customers for a year after his departure. Years later, O'Brien decided to work for Raymond James. The day before he resigned, O'Brien used the Morgan Stanley electronic database to print out a list of his clients and their contact information. Once he had the correct list, he went back into the database and altered 206 client telephone numbers. O'Brien gave Morgan Stanley his resignation along with a copy of the original, correct, printed list. After experiencing difficulty reaching O'Brien's clients, Morgan Stanley discovered that he had corrupted the database. During this delay, O'Brien lured 15 clients to Raymond James.

Morgan Stanley sued O'Brien, arguing that he acted in bad faith and breached his employment agreement by soliciting his former clients. The firm sought an injunction directing him to return the customer information and prohibiting him from soliciting Morgan Stanley customers.

Issue: ***Was Morgan Stanley entitled to an injunction?***

Excerpts from Judge Bryant's Decision: A preliminary injunction may be granted only upon a showing of (1) likely irreparable harm, and (2) either (a) a likelihood of success on the merits or (b) sufficiently serious questions going to the merits to make them a fair ground for litigation.

Morgan Stanley has shown a likelihood of success on the merits. O'Brien's deliberate use of the Morgan Stanley computer system and his calculated corruption to prevent Morgan Stanley from immediately contacting his portfolio of clients evidences bad faith and a contempt for his clients' right to freely choose whether to remain with Morgan Stanley. O'Brien undoubtedly intended and knew that his corruption of Morgan Stanley's database would create delay and confusion and would impede Morgan Stanley's ability to communicate with the clients. Leaving Morgan Stanley with a paper copy of his client list containing the correct telephone numbers was tantamount to a misrepresentation in furtherance of his sabotage.

O'Brien's calculated alteration of the customer telephone numbers has caused irreparable harm for which money damages may not adequately compensate. Because O'Brien was able to contact customers immediately upon his resignation, and because Morgan Stanley could not, some customers likely experienced a delay in receipt of a call from a Morgan Stanley financial analyst. These customers, in turn, may be apt to believe as a result of this delay that Morgan Stanley does not value their accounts and that they will receive lesser service than they would receive with O'Brien and Raymond James. This constitutes not only a potential loss of customers and the potential for future business brought in by these customers, but also a loss of Morgan Stanley's goodwill and reputation.

It is ORDERED that:

1. Defendant is directed to return to Morgan Stanley within 24 hours any and all customer information of any sort removed at any time from Morgan Stanley,
2. Defendant is enjoined from using or disclosing in any way any of the information to solicit Morgan Stanley customers, and
3. Defendant is enjoined from soliciting or attempting to solicit, directly or indirectly, any customer O'Brien served, or whose name became known to O'Brien, while in the employ of Morgan Stanley.

19-5c Reformation

Reformation
A court may partially rewrite a contract to fix a mistake or cure an unenforceable provision.

The final remedy, and perhaps the least common, is **reformation**, a process in which a court will partially rewrite a contract. Courts seldom do this because the whole point of a contract is to enable the parties to control their own futures. But a court may reform a contract if it believes a written agreement includes a simple mistake. Suppose that Roger orally agrees to sell 35 acres to Hannah for $600,000. The parties then draw up a written agreement, accidentally describing the land as including 50 additional acres that neither party considered part of the deal. Roger refuses to sell. Hannah sues for specific performance but asks the court to *reform* the written contract to reflect the true agreement. Most but not all courts would reform the agreement and enforce it.

A court may also reform a contract to save it. If Natasha sells her advertising business to Joseph and agrees not to open a competing agency in the same city anytime in the next ten years, a court may decide that it is unfair to force her to wait a decade. It could reform the agreement and permit Natasha to compete, say, three years after the sale. But some courts are reluctant to reform contracts and would throw out the entire noncompetition agreement rather than reform it. Parties should never settle for a contract that is sloppy or overbroad, assuming that a court will later reform errors. They may find themselves stuck with a bargain they dislike, or with no contract at all.

19-6 SPECIAL ISSUES

Finally, we consider some special issues of damages, beginning with a party's obligation to minimize its losses.

19-6a Mitigation of Damages

A party injured by a breach of contract may not recover for damages that he could have avoided with reasonable efforts. In other words, when one party perceives that the other has breached or will breach the contract, the injured party must try to prevent unnecessary loss. A party is expected to **mitigate** his damages; that is, to keep damages as low as he reasonably can.

Mitigate
To keep damages as low as reasonable

Malcolm agrees to rent space in his mall to Zena, for a major department store. As part of the lease, Malcolm agrees to redesign the interior to meet her specifications. After Malcolm has spent $20,000 in architect and design fees, Zena informs Malcolm that she is renting other space and will not occupy his mall. Malcolm nonetheless continues the renovation work, spending an additional $50,000 on materials and labor. Malcolm will recover the lost rental payments and the $20,000 expended in reliance on the deal. He will *not* recover the extra $50,000. He should have stopped work when he learned of Zena's breach.

19-6b Nominal Damages

Nominal damages are a token sum, such as one dollar, given to a plaintiff who demonstrates that the defendant breached the contract but cannot prove serious injury. A school board unfairly fires Gemma, a teacher. If she obtains a teaching job at a better school for identical pay the very next day, she probably can show no damages at all. Nonetheless, the school wrongfully terminated her, and a court may award nominal damages. Nominal damages provide plaintiff with a "moral victory."

Nominal damages
A token sum, such as one dollar, given to a plaintiff who demonstrates a breach but no serious injury

19-6c Liquidated Damages

It can be difficult or even impossible to prove how much damage the injured party has suffered. So lawyers and executives negotiating a deal may include in the contract a **liquidated damages clause**, a provision stating in advance how much a party must pay if it breaches. Assume that Laurie has hired Bruce to build a five-unit apartment building for $800,000. Bruce promises to complete construction by May 15. Laurie insists on a liquidated damages clause providing that if Bruce finishes late, Laurie's final price is reduced by $3,000 for each week of delay. Bruce finishes the apartment building June 30, and Laurie reduces her payment by $18,000. Is that fair?

Liquidated damages clause
A clause stating in advance how much a party must pay if it breaches

The answer depends on two factors: **A court will generally enforce a liquidated damages clause if (1) at the time of creating the contract, it was very difficult to estimate actual damages, and (2) the liquidated amount is reasonable.** In any other case, the liquidated damage will be considered a mere penalty and will prove unenforceable.

We will apply the two factors to Laurie's case. When the parties made their agreement, would it have been difficult to estimate actual damages caused by delay? Yes. Laurie could not prove that all five units would have been occupied or how much rent the tenants would have agreed to pay. Was the $3,000 per week reasonable? Probably. To finance an $800,000 building, Laurie will have to pay at least $6,000 interest per month. She must also pay taxes on the land and may have other expenses. Laurie does not have to prove that every penny of the liquidated damages clause is justified, but only that the figure is reasonable. A court will probably enforce her liquidated damages clause.

On the other hand, suppose Laurie's clause demanded $3,000 per day. There is no basis for such a figure, and a court will declare it a penalty clause and refuse to enforce it. Laurie will be back to square one, forced to prove in court any damages she claims to have suffered from Bruce's delay.

EXAMStrategy

Question: In March, James was accepted into the September ninth-grade class at the Brookstone Academy, a highly competitive private school. To reserve his spot, James's father, Rex, sent in a deposit of $2,000 and agreed in writing to pay the balance due, $19,000. If James withdrew in writing from the school by August 1, Rex owed nothing more to Brookstone. However, once that date passed, Rex was obliged to pay the full $19,000, whether or not James attended. On August 5, Rex hand-delivered to Brookstone a letter stating that James would not attend. Brookstone demanded the full tuition and, when Rex refused to pay, sued for $19,000. Analyze the case.

Strategy: When one party seeks contract damages that are specified in the agreement, it is relying on a liquidated damages clause. A court will generally enforce a liquidated damages clause provided the plaintiff can prove two things. What are those two things? Can this plaintiff meet that standard?

Result: Brookstone must prove that at the time of creating the contract it was difficult to estimate actual damages and that the liquidated amount is reasonable. Rex will probably argue that the liquidated amount is unreasonable, contending that a competitive school can quickly fill a vacancy with another eager applicant. Brookstone will counter that budgeting, which begins in January, is difficult and imprecise. Tuition money goes toward staff salaries, maintenance, utilities, and many other expenses. If the school cannot rely in January on a certain income, the calculation becomes impossible. Rex had four months to make up his mind, and by August 1, the school was firmly committed to its class size and budget. In a similar case, the court awarded the full tuition to the school, concluding that the sum was a reasonable estimate of the damages.

CHAPTER CONCLUSION

The powers of a court are broad and flexible and may suffice to give an injured party what it deserves. But problems of proof and the uncertainty of remedies demonstrate that the best solution is a carefully drafted contract and socially responsible behavior.

EXAM REVIEW

1. **BREACH** Someone breaches a contract when he fails to perform a duty without a valid excuse.

2. **REMEDY** A remedy is the method a court uses to compensate an injured party.

3. **INTEREST** An interest is a legal right in something, such as a contract. The first step that a court takes in choosing a remedy is to decide what interest it is protecting.

4. **EXPECTATION** The expectation interest puts the injured party in the position she would have been in had both sides fully performed. It has three components:
   a. Direct damages, which flow directly from the contract.
   b. Consequential damages, which result from the unique circumstances of the particular injured party. The injured party may recover consequential damages only if the breaching party should have foreseen them.
   c. Incidental damages, which are the minor costs an injured party incurs responding to a breach.

EXAMStrategy

Question: Mr. and Ms. Beard contracted for Builder to construct a house on property he owned and sell it to the Beards for $785,000. The house was to be completed by a certain date, and Builder knew that the Beards were selling their own home in reliance on the completion date. Builder was late with construction, forcing the Beards to spend $32,000 in rent. Ultimately, Builder never finished the house, and the Beards moved elsewhere. They sued. At trial, expert testimony indicated the market value of the house as promised would have been $885,000. How much money are the Beards entitled to, and why?

Strategy: Normally, in cases of property, an injured plaintiff may use specific performance to obtain the land or house. However, there is no house, so there will be no specific performance. The Beards will seek their expectation interest. Under the contract, what did they reasonably expect? They anticipated a finished house, on a particular date, worth $885,000. They did not expect to pay rent while waiting. Calculate their losses. (See the "Result" at the end of this Exam Review section.)

5. **RELIANCE** The reliance interest puts the injured party in the position he would have been in had the parties never entered into a contract. It focuses on the time and money that the injured party spent performing his part of the agreement. If there was no valid contract, a court might still award reliance damages under a theory of promissory estoppel.

EXAMStrategy

Question: Bingo is emerging as a rock star. His last five concerts have all sold out. Lucia signs a deal with Bingo to perform two concerts in one evening in Big City for a fee of $50,000 for both shows. Lucia then rents the Auditorium for that evening, guaranteeing to pay $50,000. Bingo promptly breaks the deal before any tickets are sold. Lucia sues, pointing out that the Auditorium seats 3,000 and she anticipated selling all tickets for an average of $40 each, for a total gross of $120,000. How much will Lucia recover, if anything?

Strategy: The parties created a valid contract, and Lucia relied on it. She claims two losses: the payment to rent the hall and her lost profits. A court may award reliance damages if the plaintiff can quantify them, provided the damages are not speculative. Can Lucia quantify either of those losses? Both of them? Were they speculative? (See the "Result" at the end of this Exam Review section.)

6. **RESTITUTION** The restitution interest returns to the injured party a benefit that she has conferred on the other party which would be unjust to leave with that person. Restitution can be awarded in the case of a contract created, for example, by fraud, or in a case of quasi-contract, where the parties never created a binding agreement.

7. **SPECIFIC PERFORMANCE** Specific performance, ordered only in cases of land or a unique asset, requires both parties to perform the contract.

8. **INJUNCTION** An injunction is a court order that requires someone to do something or refrain from doing something.

9. **REFORMATION** Reformation is the process by which a court will—occasionally—rewrite a contract to ensure that it accurately reflects the parties' agreement and/or to maintain the contract's viability.

10. **MITIGATION** The duty to mitigate means that a party injured by a breach of contract may not recover for damages that he could have avoided with reasonable efforts.

EXAMStrategy

Question: Ambrose hires Bierce for $25,000 to supervise the production of Ambrose's crop, but then breaks the contract by firing Bierce at the beginning of the season. A nearby grower offers Bierce $23,000 for the same growing season, but Bierce refuses to take such a pay cut. He stays home and sues Ambrose. How much money, if any, will Bierce recover from Ambrose, and why?

Strategy: Ambrose has certainly breached the contract. The injured party normally receives the difference between his expectation interest and what he actually received. Bierce expected $25,000 and received nothing. However, Bierce made no effort to minimize his losses. How much would Bierce have lost had he mitigated? (See the "Result" at the end of this Exam Review section.)

11. **NOMINAL DAMAGES** Nominal damages are a token sum, such as one dollar, given to an injured plaintiff who cannot prove damages.

12. **LIQUIDATED DAMAGES** A liquidated damages clause will be enforced if and only if, at the time of creating the contract, it was very difficult to estimate actual damages and the liquidated amount is reasonable.

RESULTS

4. Result: The Beards' direct damages represent the difference between the market value of the house and the contract price. They expected a house worth $100,000 more than their contract price, and they are entitled to that sum. They also suffered consequential damages. Builder knew they needed the house as of the contract date, and he could foresee that his breach would force them to pay rent. He is liable for a total of $132,000.

5. Result: Lucia can easily demonstrate that Bingo's breach cost her $50,000—the cost of the hall. However, it is uncertain how many tickets she would have sold. Unless Lucia has a strong track record selling tickets to concerts featuring Bingo, a court is likely to conclude that her anticipated profits were speculative. She will probably receive nothing for that claim.

10. Result: Even if he had mitigated, Bierce would have lost $2,000. He is entitled to that sum. However, he cannot recover the remaining $23,000. After Ambrose breached, Bierce had identical work available to him, but he failed to take it. His failure to mitigate is fatal.

MULTIPLE-CHOICE QUESTIONS

1. **CPA QUESTION** Master Mfg., Inc., contracted with Accur Computer Repair Corp. to maintain Master's computer system. Master's manufacturing process depends on its computer system operating properly at all times. A liquidated damages clause in the contract provided that Accur would pay $1,000 to Master for each day that Accur was late responding to a service request. On January 12, Accur was notified that Master's computer system had failed. Accur did not respond to Master's service request until January 15. If Master sues Accur under the liquidated damage provision of the contract, Master will:

   (a) win unless the liquidated damages provision is determined to be a penalty.

   (b) win because under all circumstances liquidated damage provisions are enforceable.

(c) lose because Accur's breach was not material.
(d) lose because liquidated damage provisions violate public policy.

2. **CPA QUESTION** Kaye contracted to sell Hodges a building for $310,000. The contract required Hodges to pay the entire amount at closing. Kaye refused to close the sale of the building. Hodges sued Kaye. To what relief is Hodges entitled?
(a) Punitive damages and direct damages
(b) Specific performance and direct damages
(c) Consequential damages or punitive damages
(d) Direct damages or specific performance

3. A manufacturer delivers a new tractor to Farmer Ted on the first day of the harvest season. But the tractor will not start. It takes two weeks for the right parts to be delivered and installed. The repair bill comes to $1,000. During the two weeks, some acres of Farmer Ted's crops die. He argues in court that his lost profit on those acres is $60,000. If a jury awards $1,000 for tractor repairs, it will be in the form of ______________ damages. If it awards $60,000 for the lost crops, it will be in the form of ______________ damages.
(a) direct; direct
(b) direct; consequential
(c) consequential; direct
(d) consequential; consequential
(e) direct; incidental

4. Julie signs a contract to buy Nick's 2015 Mustang GT for $20,000. Later, Nick changes his mind and refuses to sell his car. Julie soon buys a similar 2015 Mustang GT for $21,500. She then sues Nick and wins $1,500. The $1,500 represents her ______________.
(a) expectation interest
(b) reliance interest
(c) restitution interest
(d) none of these

5. Under the Uniform Commercial Code, a seller ______________ generally entitled to recover consequential damages, and a buyer ______________ generally entitled to recover consequential damages.
(a) is; is
(b) is; is not
(c) is not; is
(d) is not; is not

CASE QUESTIONS

1. Lewis signed a contract for the rights to all timber located on Nine-Mile Mine. He agreed to pay $70 per thousand board feet ($70/mbf). As he began work, Nine-Mile became convinced that Lewis lacked sufficient equipment to do the job well and forbade him to enter the land. Lewis sued. Nine-Mile moved for

summary judgment. The mine offered proof that the market value of the timber was exactly $70/mbf, and Lewis had no evidence to contradict Nine-Mile. The evidence about market value proved decisive. Why? Please rule on the summary judgment motion.

2. Parkinson was injured in an auto accident by a driver who had no insurance. Parkinson filed a claim with her insurer, Liberty Mutual, for $2,000 under her "uninsured motorist" coverage. Liberty Mutual told her that if she sought that money, her premiums would go "sky high," so Parkinson dropped the claim. Later, after she had spoken with an attorney, Parkinson sued. What additional claim was her attorney likely to make?

3. The Madariagas owned a restaurant where they served "Albert's Famous Mexican Hot Sauce." They entered into a contract to sell the restaurant and the formula for the secret sauce to Morris. Although Morris paid the agreed-upon price, the sellers refused to give him the recipe unless he also paid them lifetime royalties for the salsa. Which of these remedies should Morris seek: expectation, restitution, specific performance, or reformation? Why?

4. ***YOU BE THE JUDGE*** **WRITING PROBLEM** John and Susan Verba sold a Vermont lakeshore lot to Shane and Deborah Rancourt for $115,000. The Rancourts intended to build a house on the property, but after preparing the land for construction, they learned that a wetland protection law prevented building near the lake. They sued, seeking rescission of the contract. The trial court concluded that the parties had reached their agreement under a "mutual, but innocent, misunderstanding." The trial judge gave the Verbas a choice: they could rescind the contract and refund the purchase price, or they could give the Rancourts $55,000, the difference between the sales price and the actual market value of the land. The Rancourts appealed. Were the Rancourts entitled to rescission of the contract? **Argument for the Rancourts:** When the parties have made a mutual mistake about an important factual issue, either party is entitled to rescind the contract. The land is of no use to us and we want our money back. **Argument for the Verbas:** Both sides were acting in good faith and both sides made an honest mistake. We are willing to acknowledge that the land is worth somewhat less than we all thought, and we are willing to refund $55,000. The buyers shouldn't complain—they are getting the property at about half the original price, and the error was as much their fault as ours.

5. The Basketball Marketing Company (BMC) signed a long-term endorsement contract with a 16-year-old basketball player, Darko Milicic. Soon after his 18th birthday, Milicic successfully disaffirmed the contract. To prevent Milicic from entering into a contract with its competitors, BMC sent them letters claiming it had an enforceable contract with Milicic. Because of BMC's letter, Adidas ceased negotiating with Milicic. He sued BMC, seeking a preliminary injunction that would prohibit BMC from sending such letters to competitors. Should the court grant this injunction? Why or why not?

DISCUSSION QUESTIONS

1. **ETHICS** The National Football League owns the copyright to the broadcasts of its games. It licenses local television stations to telecast certain games and maintains a "blackout rule," which prohibits stations from broadcasting home games that are not sold out 72 hours before the game starts. Certain home games of the Cleveland Browns team were not sold out, and the NFL blocked local broadcast. But several bars in the Cleveland area were able to pick up the game's signal by using special antennas. The NFL wanted the bars to stop showing the games. What did it do? Was it unethical of the bars to broadcast the games that they were able to pick up? Apart from the NFL's legal rights, do you think it had the moral right to stop the bars from broadcasting the games?

2. Consequential damages can be many times higher than direct damages. Consider the "Farmer Ted" scenario raised in multiple-choice question 3, which is based on a real case.[8] Is it fair for consequential damages to be 60 times higher than direct damages? The Supreme Court is skeptical that *punitive* damages should be more than nine times compensatory damages in a tort case. Should a similar "soft limit" apply to consequential damages in contract cases?

3. PepsiCo entered into a contract to sell its corporate jet to Klein for $4.6 million. Before the deal closed, the plane was sent to pick up PepsiCo's chairman of the board, who was stranded at Dulles airport. The chairman then decided that the company should not part with the plane. Klein sued PepsiCo for specific performance, arguing that he could not find a similar jet on the market for that price. Should a court force PepsiCo to sell its plane?

4. Walgreens operated a pharmacy in the Sara Creek mall. As part of this long-term lease, Sara Creek agreed not to lease mall space to another pharmacy. During an economic recession, Sara Creek's largest tenant left and the landlord informed Walgreens that it intended to rent that space out to a "deep discount" store that would contain a pharmacy. It was the only way to remain profitable, according to Sara Creek. Walgreens sued for an injunction against Sara Creek until its contract expired in ten years. Should a court hold Sara Creek to its contract, even if this decision means bankrupting it?

5. Is it reasonable to require the mitigation of damages? If a person is wronged because the other side breached a contract, should she have any obligations at all? For example, suppose that a tenant breaches a lease by leaving early. Should the landlord have an obligation to try to find another tenant before the end of the lease?

---

[8]Prutch v. Ford, 574 P.2d 102 (Colo. 1977).

CHAPTER 20

PRACTICAL CONTRACTS

Two true stories:

One

Lawyer (on the phone with her client, Judd): Harry's lawyer just emailed me a letter that Harry says he got from you last year. I'm reading from the letter now: "Each year that you meet your revenue goals, you'll get a 1 percent equity interest." Is it possible you sent that letter?

Judd: I don't remember the exact wording, but probably something like that.

Lawyer: You told me, absolutely, positively, you had never promised Harry any stock. That he was making the whole thing up.

Judd: He was threatening to leave unless I gave him some equity, so I said what he wanted to hear. But that letter didn't *mean* anything. This is a family business, and no one but my children will ever get stock.

Two

Grace (on the phone with her lawyer): Providential has raised its price to $12 a pound. I can't afford to pay that! We had a deal that the price would never go higher than 10 bucks. I've talked to Buddy over there, but he is refusing to back down. We need to do something!

Lawyer: Let me look at the contract.

Grace (her voice rising): I don't know what the *contract* says—that's just the legal stuff. Our *business* deal was no more than $10 a pound!

I don't know what the *contract* says—that's just the legal stuff.

You have been studying the theory of contract law. This chapter is different: Its purpose is to demonstrate how that theory operates in *practice* and help you determine if the legal agreement reflects your business deal. We will look at the structure and content of a standard contract and answer questions such as: Do you need a written agreement? What provisions should be included? What do all these legal terms mean? By the end of the chapter, you will have a road map for understanding a written contract.[1] (Note that we do not repeat here what you have learned in prior chapters about the *substantive* law of contracts.) This chapter has another goal, too: We will look at the relationship between lawyers and their clients and their different roles in creating a contract.

Businesspeople, not surprisingly, tend to focus more on business than on the technicalities of contract law. However, *ignoring* the role of a written agreement can lead to serious trouble. Both of the clients in the opening scenario ended up in contracts they did not want.

To illustrate our discussion of contract provisions, we will use a real movie contract between an actor and a producer. For reasons of confidentiality, however, we have changed the names.

20-1 CREATING A CONTRACT

Before we begin our discussion of written contracts, it is important to ask: **Do you need a written agreement at all?** Some years ago, this author was with a group of lawyers, all of whom had done a major home renovation and *none of whom* had signed a contract with the builder. All of the projects had turned out well. The lawyers had not prepared a written contract because they trusted their builders, who all had good recommendations from prior clients. Also, a building project by its very nature requires regular negotiations because it is impossible to predict all the potential changes: How much would it cost to move that door? How much do we save if we use tile instead of granite?

These cases worked out well without a written contract, but **there are times when an agreement should *definitely* be in writing:**

1. The Statute of Frauds requires it.
2. The deal is crucial to your life or the life of your business.
3. The terms are complex.
4. You do not have an ongoing relationship of trust with the other party.

Once you decide you need a written contract, then what?

20-1a The Lawyer

The American Bar Association commissioned a study to find out what people think of lawyers. Survey participants responded with these words: greedy, corrupt, manipulative, snakes, and sharks.[2] Businesspeople sometimes refer to their lawyers as "the business prevention department." For this reason, they may be reluctant to ask an attorney to draft a contract for fear of the time and expense that lawyers can inject into the process. And they worry that the lawyers will interfere in the business deal itself, at best causing unnecessary hindrance, at worst killing the deal. Part of the problem is that lawyers and clients have different views of the future.

---

[1]For further reading on practical contracts, see Scott Burnham, *Drafting and Analyzing Contracts*, Lexis/Nexis, 2003; Charles M. Fox, *Working with Contracts*, Practical Law Institute, 2008; George W. Kuney, *The Elements of Contract Drafting*, Thomson/West, 2006.

[2]Robert Clifford, "Opening Statement: Now More Than Ever," 28 Litigation 1, Spring 2002.

Lawyers and Clients

Businesspeople are optimists—they believe that they have negotiated a great deal and everything is going to go well—sales will boom, the company will prosper. Lawyers have a different perspective—their primary goal is to protect their clients by avoiding litigation, now and in the future or, if litigation does occur, making sure their client wins. **For this reason, lawyers are trained to be pessimists—they try to foresee and protect against everything that can possibly go wrong.**

Businesspeople sometimes view this lawyering as a waste of time and a potential deal-killer. What if the two parties cannot agree about what to do in the event of a very unlikely circumstance? The deal might just collapse.

To take one example of this lawyerly perspective, a couple happily married for 40 years went to see a lawyer about changes in their will. The husband wanted to transfer assets to his wife. The lawyer advised against it—after all, the couple might divorce. They became angry and indignant because *they would never get divorced.* And they may very well be right. However, just that week, the lawyer had seen another couple who did divorce after 41 years of marriage. He thought it better to be on the safe side and consider the possibility that such events might happen.

Lawyers also prefer to negotiate touchy subjects at the beginning of a relationship, when everyone is on friendly terms and eager to make a deal, rather than waiting until trouble strikes. In the long run, nothing harms a relationship more than unpleasant surprises. The Artist in the movie contract featured in this chapter did not know in advance how tough conditions on the set would be, how grueling the shooting schedule, or how many friends and family would visit him. So his lawyer negotiated a deal in which the Producer agreed to provide a driver, a "first-class star trailer (which shall be a double pop-out)," a luxury hotel suite, and an adjacent room for visitors. In the end, because the role called for the Artist to live in the wilderness, he ultimately slept in a tent on the set to experience his part more fully, so he did not need the double pop-out trailer or the luxury suite. He also dispensed with the driver. But, under different circumstances, he might have wanted those luxuries, and his lawyer's goal was to protect his interests. It is a lot easier to forgo an expense than to add one to a movie budget.

One advantage of using lawyers to conduct these negotiations is that they can serve as the bad guys. Instead of the client raising tough issues, the lawyers do. Many a client has said, "but my lawyer insists. . . ." If the lawyer takes the blame, the client is able to maintain a better relationship with the other party. And hiring a lawyer communicates to the other parties that you are taking the deal seriously, and they will not be able to take advantage of you.

Of course, this lawyerly protection comes at a cost—legal fees, time spent bargaining, the hours used to read complex provisions, and the potential for goodwill to erode during negotiations.

Do you need a lawyer? The answer largely depends on the complexity and importance of the deal. Most people do not hire a lawyer to review an apartment lease—the language is standard, and the prospective tenant has little power to change the terms of the deal. But if a deal is significant—to you—do not proceed without a lawyer.

Hiring a Lawyer

If you do hire a lawyer, be aware of certain warning signs. Although the lawyer's goal is to protect you, a good attorney should be a dealmaker, not a deal-breaker. She should help you achieve your goals and, therefore, should never (or, at least, hardly ever) say, "You cannot do this." Instead, she should say, "Here are the risks to this approach" or "Here is another way to accomplish your objective."

Moreover, your lawyer's goal should not be to annihilate the other side. In the end, the contract will be more beneficial to everyone if the parties' relationship is harmonious. Trying to exact every last ounce of flesh, using whatever power you have to an abusive extreme, is not a sound long-term strategy. In the end, the best deals are those in which all the parties' incentives are aligned. Success for one means success for all—or at least, success for one party does not *prohibit* a positive outcome for the other side. If either side in the movie contract behaved unreasonably, word would quickly spread in the insular Hollywood world, damaging the troublemaker's ability to make other deals.

Now either you have a lawyer or you do not. The next step is to think about developing the contract.

20-1b Who Drafts the Contract?

Once businesspeople have agreed to the terms of the deal, it is time to prepare a draft of the contract. Generally, both sides would prefer to *control the pen* (i.e., to do the actual writing) because the drafter has the opportunity to choose a structure and wording that best represents his interests. (Maybe the people on the other side will not even bother to read all the provisions deep in the boilerplate weeds that are unfavorable to them.)

Typically, the party with the most bargaining power prepares the drafts. In the movie contract, Producer's lawyer was in charge of the first draft. The contract then went to Artist's lawyer, who added the provisions that mattered to his client.

20-1c How to Read a Contract

Reading a contract is not like cracking open a novel. Instead, it should be a focused, multi-step process:

- **Pre-reading.** Before you begin reading the first draft of a contract, spend some time thinking about the provisions that are important to you. If you skip this step, you may find that, as you read, your attention is so focused on the specific language of the contract that you lose sight of the larger picture and what you want.
- **The first read.** Read through once, just to get the basic idea of the contract—its structure and major provisions.
- **What-ifs.** This is the time to think about various outcomes, good and bad. Under the terms of the contract, what happens if all goes according to your plan? Also consider worst-case scenarios. In both situations, does the contract produce the result that you want? What happens if sales are higher than you expect, or if the product causes unexpected harm?
- **The second read.** Now read the contract to make sure that it handles the what-ifs in a manner that is satisfactory to you. Think about the relationship between various provisions—does it make sense?

Following this approach will help you avoid mistakes.

20-1d Mistakes

This author once worked with a lawyer who made a mistake in a contract. "No problem," he said. "I can win that one in court." Not a helpful attitude, given that one purpose of a contract is to *avoid* litigation. In this section, we look at the most common types of mistakes and how to avoid them.

Vagueness

Vagueness means that the parties to a contract *deliberately* include a provision that is unclear. Why would anyone do that? It may be that they are not sure what they can get from the other side, or in some cases, even what they really want. One party may be trying to get a commitment from the other party without obligating itself. Or one side may feel *almost* ready to

Vagueness
The parties to a contract deliberately include a provision that is unclear

commit and yet still have reservations. It wants the *other* party to make a commitment so that planning can go forward. So they create a contract that keeps their options open. They hope that they can decide later what the provision really meant. This approach is understandable but dangerous. As the following case illustrates: **Vagueness is your enemy.**

You Be the Judge

Quake Construction, Inc. v. American Airlines, Inc.

141 Ill. 2d 281
Supreme Court of Illinois, 1990

Facts: Jones Brothers Construction was the general contractor on a job to expand American Airlines' facilities at O'Hare International Airport. Jones verbally accepted Quake's bid to work on the project and promised that Quake would receive a written contract soon. Jones wanted the license numbers of the subcontractors that Quake would be using, but Quake could not furnish those numbers until it had assured its subcontractors that they had the job. Quake did not want to give that assurance until *it* was certain of its own work. So Jones sent a Letter Of Intent that stated, among other things:

> We have elected to award the contract for the subject project to your firm as we discussed on April 15. A contract agreement outlining the detailed terms and conditions is being prepared and will be available for your signature shortly.
>
> Your scope of work includes the complete installation of expanded lunchroom, restaurant, and locker facilities for American Airlines employees, as well as an expansion of American Airlines' existing Automotive Maintenance Shop. A sixty (60) calendar day period shall be allowed for the construction of the locker room, lunchroom, and restaurant area beginning the week of April 22. The entire project shall be completed by August 15.
>
> This notice of award authorizes the work set forth in the attached documents at a lump sum price of $1,060,568.00. Jones Brothers Construction Corporation reserves the right to cancel this letter of intent if the parties cannot agree on a fully executed subcontract agreement.

The parties never signed a more detailed written contract, and ultimately Jones hired another company. Quake sued, seeking to recover the money it spent in preparation and its loss of anticipated profit.

You Be the Judge: *Was the letter of intent a valid contract?*

Argument for Quake: This letter was a valid contract. It explicitly stated that Jones awarded the contract to Quake. It also said, "This notice of award authorizes the work." The letter included significant detail about the scope of the contract, including the specific facilities Quake would be working on. Furthermore, the work was to commence approximately 4 to 11 days after the letter was written. This short period of time indicates that the parties intended to be bound by the letter so that work could begin quickly. And, the letter contained a cancellation clause. If it was not a contract, why would anyone need to cancel it?

Argument for Jones: This letter was not a contract. It referred several times to the execution of a formal contract by the parties, thus indicating that they did not intend to be bound by the letter. Look at the cancellation clause carefully: It could also be interpreted to mean that the parties did not intend to be bound by any agreement until they entered into a formal contract.

Having to litigate the meaning of this letter of intent was a waste of time and money for both parties. If you were negotiating for Jones and wanted to clarify negotiations without committing your company, how could you do it? State in the letter that it is *not a contract*, and that *neither side is bound by it*. State that it is a memorandum summarizing negotiations thus far, but that neither party will be bound until a full written contract is signed.

But what if Quake cannot get a commitment from its subcontractors until they are certain that it has the job? Quake should take the initiative and present Jones with its own Letter Of Intent, stating that the parties *do* have a binding agreement for $1 million of work. Jones would then be forced to decide whether it was willing to make a binding commitment. If it was not willing to commit, let it say so openly. At least both parties would know where they stood.

The movie contract provides another example of vagueness. In these contracts, nudity is often a contentious issue. Producers believe that nudity sells movie tickets; actors are afraid that it will tarnish their reputation. Artist's lawyer wanted to include this provision:

> Artist may not be photographed and shall not be required to render any services nude below the waist or in simulated sex scenes without Artist's prior written consent.

(This clause also applied to any double depicting Artist.) However, the script called for a scene in which Artist was swimming nude and the director wanted the option of showing him below the waist from the back. Ultimately, the nudity clause read as follows:

> Producer has informed Artist that Artist's role in the Picture might require Artist to appear and be photographed (a) nude, which nudity may include only above-the-waist nudity and rear below-the-waist nudity, but shall exclude frontal below-the-waist nudity; and (b) in simulated sex scenes. Artist acknowledges and agrees that Artist has accepted such employment in the Picture with full knowledge of Artist's required participation in nude scenes and/or in simulated sex scenes and Artist's execution of the Agreement constitutes written consent by Artist to appear in the nude scenes and simulated sex scenes and to perform therein as reasonably required by Producer. A copy of the scenes from the screenplay requiring Artist's nudity and/or simulated sex are attached hereto. Artist shall have a right of meaningful prior consultation with the director of the Picture regarding the manner of photography of any scenes in which Artist appears nude or engaged in simulated sex acts.
>
> Artist may wear pants or other covering that does not interfere with the shooting of the nude scenes or simulated sex scenes. Artist's buttocks and/or genitalia shall not be shown, depicted, or otherwise visible without Artist's prior written consent. Artist shall have the absolute right to change his mind and not perform in any nude scene or simulated sex scene, notwithstanding that Artist had prior thereto agreed to perform in such scene.

What does this provision really mean? Artist has acknowledged that the script calls for nude scenes and he has agreed, in principle, to appear in them. However, since he had never worked with this director, he did not want to promise that he would definitely appear in nude scenes. So the contract states that Actor could refuse to shoot nude scenes altogether, or he could shoot them and then, after viewing them, decide not to allow them in the movie. Because of this clause, the director shot different versions of these scenes—some with nudity and some without—so that if Artist rejected a nude scene, the director still had options.

The true test of whether a vague clause belongs in a contract is this: Would you sign the contract if you knew that the other side's interpretation might win in court? In this example, each side was staking out its position, and deferring a final negotiation until there was an actual disagreement about a nude scene. If the other side's position is acceptable to you, the vague clause simply defers a fight that you can afford to lose. But if the point is really important, it may be wiser to resolve the issue before you sign the contract.

EXAMStrategy

Question: The nudity provision in the movie contract is vague. Rewrite it so that it accurately reflects the agreement between the parties.

Strategy: This is easy! Just say what the parties intended the deal to be.

Result: "The script for the Picture includes scenes showing Artist (a) with frontal nudity from the waist up and with rear below-the-waist nudity (but no frontal below-the-waist nudity); and (b) in simulated sex scenes. The Artist will give good faith consideration to appearing in these scenes, however, no scenes shall be shot in which Artist's buttocks and/or genitalia are shown, depicted, or otherwise visible without Artist's prior written consent. Artist shall have the absolute right not to perform in any nude scene or simulated sex scene. If shot, no nude or sex scenes may appear in the Picture without Artist's prior written consent."

Ambiguity

Ambiguity
When a provision in a contract is unclear by accident

Vagueness occurs when the parties do not want the contract to be clear. **Ambiguity** is different—it means that the provision is *accidentally* unclear. It occurs in contracts when the parties think only about what *they* want a provision to mean, without considering the literal meaning or the other side's perspective. When reading a contract, try to imagine all the different ways a clause can be interpreted. One case involved an employment contract that said, "Employee agrees not to work for a competitor for a period of three years from employment." The parties litigated whether this phrase meant three years from the date of hiring or the date of termination. That litigation could so easily have been avoided.

If a contract does contain an ambiguous provision, the courts interpret it against the drafter of the contract. That is, if both parties offer a reasonable interpretation of the disputed provision, the courts choose the one provided by the party that did *not* draft it. Although both sides need to be careful in reading a contract—litigation benefits no one—the side that prepares the documents bears a special burden. This rule is meant to:

1. Protect people from the dangers of form contracts that they have little power to change.
2. Protect people who are unlikely to be represented by a lawyer. Most people do not hire a lawyer to read form contracts such as leases or insurance policies. And without an experienced lawyer, it is highly unlikely that an individual would be aware of ambiguities.
3. Encourage those who prepare contracts to do so carefully.

Many ambiguity cases arise in the context of insurance contracts. The following case provides a good example of how complicated insurance policies can be. This complexity tends to erode judicial sympathy for the perpetrator.

Minkler v. Safeco Ins. Co. of America

49 Cal. 4th 315
Supreme Court of California, 2010

Facts: Scott Minkler alleged that when he was a child, his Little League baseball coach, David Schwartz, had molested him. During the period when these terrible events occurred, David was living at the home of his mother, Betty Schwartz, and some of the episodes had taken place at her house. Scott sued Betty, alleging that she had been negligent in supervising events in her own home.

Betty had a homeowners' policy with Safeco Insurance Company, which covered any harm caused by the *unintentional* acts of the home's residents, including David. Since David's acts were *intentional*, Safeco was not responsible for the claims against him. But Safeco also argued that it was not responsible for claims against Betty because the wrongdoing that had caused the harm (that is, David's acts) had been intentional.

In short, Betty's policy was ambiguous. Safeco said the policy did not provide coverage if *any* insured had engaged in intentional wrongdoing while Betty argued that it did cover her if her *own* actions had been unintentional.

Issue: ***How should the court interpret ambiguous provisions in a contract?***

Excerpts from Justice Saxe's Decision: Our goal in construing insurance contracts, as with contracts generally, is to give effect to the parties' mutual intentions. If contractual language is clear and explicit, it governs. If the terms are ambiguous i.e., susceptible of more than one reasonable interpretation, we interpret them to protect the objectively reasonable expectations of the insured.

Only if these rules do not resolve a claimed ambiguity do we resort to the rule that ambiguities are to be resolved against the insurer. The "tie-breaker" rule of construction against the insurer stems from the recognition that the insurer generally drafted the policy and received premiums to provide the agreed protection.

Safeco could easily have removed any uncertainty. Safeco's intent was not clearly expressed, and the ambiguity must be resolved in a way that preserves the objectively reasonable coverage expectations of the insured seeking coverage. Betty had no reason to expect that David's residence in her home, and his consequent status as an additional insured on her homeowners policies, would narrow her own coverage, and the protection of her separate assets, against claims arising from his intentional acts. Betty's coverage must be analyzed on the basis of whether she herself committed an act or acts that fell within the intentional act exclusion.

Typos

The bane of a lawyer's existence! This author worked on a securities offering in which the sales document almost went out with part of the company's name spelled *Pertoleum* instead of *Petroleum*. (And legend has it that a United Airlines securities offering once featured "Untied Airlines.") Although clients tend not to have a sense of humor about such errors, at least there would be no adverse legal result. That is not always the case with typos.

A group of condominium buyers ended up in litigation over a tiny typo in their purchase agreements: an "8" instead of a "9." What difference could that possibly make? A lot, it turns out. Extell Development Corporation built the Rushmore, a luxury condominium complex in Manhattan. When Extell began selling the units, it agreed to refund any buyer's down payment if the first closing did not occur by September 1, 2009. (The goal was to protect buyers who might not have any place to live if the building was not finished on time.) In the end, the first closing occurred in February 2009. No problem, right? No problem except that the purchase contract had a typo: It said September 1, *2008* rather than *2009*. In the meantime, the Great Recession had caused the Manhattan real estate market to slump, and many purchasers of Rushmore condominiums wanted to cancel their contracts and obtain a refund of their deposits.

Daisy Beatty

Because of a tiny typo, purchasers of condominiums in this building were able to back out of their deals.

Scrivener's error
A typo

What is the law of typos? First of all, the law has a fancier word than *typo*—it is **scrivener's error.** (A scrivener is a clerk who copies documents.) **In the case of a scrivener's error, a court will reform a contract if there is *clear and convincing* evidence that the alleged mistake does not actually reflect the true intent of the parties.** In the Rushmore case, an arbitrator refused to reform the contract, ruling that there was no clear and convincing evidence that the parties intended something other than the contract term as written.

In the following case, even more money was at stake.

You Be the Judge

Heritage Technologies, LLC v. Phibro-Tech, Inc.

2008 U.S. Dist. LEXIS 329, 2008 WL 45380
United States District Court for the Southern District of Indiana, 2008

Facts: Heritage wanted to buy tribasic copper chloride (TBCC) from Phibro, but because of uncertainty in the industry, the two companies could not agree on a price for future years. It turned out, though, that the price of TBCC tended to rise and fall with that of copper sulfate, so Heritage proposed that the amount it paid for TBCC would increase an additional $15 per ton for each $0.01 increase in the cost of copper sulfate over $0.38 per pound.

Two top officers of Heritage and Phibro met in the Delta Crown Room at LaGuardia Airport to negotiate the purchase contract. At the end of their meeting, the Phibro officer hand wrote a document stating the terms of their deal and agreeing to the Heritage pricing proposal.

Negotiations between the two companies continued, leading to some changes and additions to their Crown Room agreement. In a draft prepared by Phibro, the $.01 number was changed to $0.1—that is, from 1 cent to 10 cents. In other words, in the original draft, Heritage agreed to an increase in price if copper sulfate went above 39 cents per pound, an additional price rise at 40 cents, and so on. But in the Phibro draft, Heritage's first increase would not occur until the price of copper sulfate went above 48 cents a pound, with a second rise at 58 cents. The Phibro draft was much more favorable to Heritage than the Heritage proposal had been.

At some point during the negotiations, the lawyer for Heritage asked his client if the $0.1 figure was accurate. The Heritage officer said that the increase in this amount was meant to offset other provisions that favored Phibro. There is no evidence that this statement was true. The contract went through eight drafts and numerous changes, but after the Crown Room meeting, the two sides never again discussed the $0.1 figure.

After the execution of the agreement, Heritage discovered a different mistake. When Heritage brought the error to Phibro's attention, Phibro agreed to make the change even though it was to Phibro's disadvantage to do so.

All was peaceful until the price of copper sulfate went to $0.478 per pound. Phibro believed that because the price was above $0.38 per pound, it was entitled to an increased payment. Heritage responded that the increase would not occur until the price went above $0.48. Phibro then looked at the agreement and noticed the $0.1 term for the first time. Phibro contacted Heritage to say that the $0.1 term was a typo and not what the two parties had originally agreed in the Crown Room. Heritage refused to amend the agreement and Phibro filed suit.

You Be the Judge: *Should the court enforce the contract as written, or as the parties agreed in their Crown Room meeting? Which number is correct—$0.10 or $0.01?*

Argument for Phibro: In the Crown Room, the two negotiators agreed to a $15 per ton increase in the price of TBCC for each 1-cent increase in copper sulfate price. Then, by mistake, the contract said 10 cents. After the Crown Room meeting, the two parties never even discussed the 1-cent provision, much less agreed to change it. The court should revise this contract to be consistent with the parties' agreement, which was 1 cent.

Also, the 10-cent figure makes no economic sense. The point of the provision was that the price of TBCC would go up at the same rate as copper sulfate, and 1 cent for each ton is a much more accurate reflection of the relationship between these two commodities than 10 cents per ton.

Argument for Heritage: The Delta Crown Room agreement was nothing more than a draft. The parties then conducted negotiations by sending drafts back and forth rather than by talking on the phone. Each party was represented by a team of lawyers. Ultimately, the contract went through eight rounds of changes, and this pricing term was never altered again despite several other changes and additions. Moreover, the change in price was in return for other terms that benefited Phibro.

Certainly, there is no clear and convincing evidence that both parties were mistaken about what the document actually said. Ultimately, the parties agreed to 10 cents, and that is what the court should enforce.

Ethics

When Heritage found a different mistake in the contract, Phibro agreed to correct it, even though the correction was unfavorable to Phibro. But when a mistake occurred in Heritage's favor, it refused to honor the intended terms of the agreement. Is Heritage behaving ethically? Does Heritage have an obligation to treat Phibro as well as Phibro behaved toward Heritage? Is it right to take advantage of other people's mistakes? What Life Principle would you apply in this situation? Which philosopher would support Phibro's claim?

Preventing Mistakes

Here are ways to prevent mistakes in a contract.

Let your lawyer draft the contract. As a general rule, your lawyer is less likely to make mistakes than you are. Of all the players in the *Heritage* case, only one person noticed the error—Heritage's lawyer.

> **As a general rule, your lawyer is less likely to make mistakes than you are.**

Resist overlawyering. Yes, your lawyer should draft the contract, but that does not mean she should have free rein, no matter what. This author once worked with a real estate attorney who had developed his own standard mortgage contract, of which he was immensely proud. Whenever he saw a provision in another contract that was missing from his own, he immediately added it. His standard form contract soon topped 100 pages. That contract was painful to read and did no service to his clients.

Read the important terms carefully. Before signing a contract, check carefully and thoughtfully the names of the parties, the dates, dollar amounts, and interest rates. If all these elements are correct, you are unlikely to go too far wrong. And, of course, having read this chapter, you will never mistake $0.10 for $0.01.

When your lawyer presents you with a written contract, you should follow these rules:

1. Complain if your lawyer gives you a contract with provisions that are irrelevant to your situation.
2. If you do not know what a provision means, ask. If you still do not know (or if your lawyer does not know), ask him to take it out. Lawyers rarely draft from scratch; they tend to use other contracts as templates. Just because a provision was in another agreement does not mean that it is appropriate for you.
3. Remember that a contract is also a reference document. During the course of your relationship with the other party, you may need to refer to the contract regularly. That will be difficult if you do not understand portions of it, or if the contract is so disorganized you cannot find a provision when you need it.

Which brings us to our next topic—the structure of a contract. Once you understand the standard outline of a contract, it will be much easier to find your way through the thicket of provisions.

20-2 THE STRUCTURE OF A CONTRACT

20-2a Terms That Vary by Contract

In this section, we look at provisions that are unique to the specific facts of each agreement. The next section covers boilerplate—standard terms that change little from contract to contract.

Title

Contracts have a title, typically in capital letters, underlined, and centered at the top of the page. **The title should be as descriptive as possible**—a generic title such as AGREEMENT does not distinguish one contract from another. Much better to entitle it EMPLOYMENT AGREEMENT or CONFIDENTIALITY AGREEMENT. The title of our movie contract is MEMORANDUM OF AGREEMENT (not a particularly useful name), but in the upper-right corner, there is space for the date of the contract and the subject: "Dawn Rising/Clay Parker." It would have been even better if the title of the contract had been: AGREEMENT BETWEEN CLAY PARKER AND WINTERFIELD PRODUCTIONS FOR DAWN RISING.

Introductory Paragraph

The introductory paragraph includes the date, the names of the parties, and the nature of the contract. The names of the parties and the movie are defined terms, for example, Clay Parker ("Artist"). By defining the names, the actual names do not have to be repeated throughout the agreement. In this way, a standard form contract can be used in different deals without worrying about whether the names of the parties are correct throughout the document.

The introductory paragraph must also include specific language indicating that the parties entered into an agreement. Traditional contracts tended to use archaic words—*whereas* and *heretofore* were common. Modern contracts are more straightforward, without as many linguistic flourishes. Our movie contract takes the modern approach. Its opening paragraph states:

> This shall confirm the agreement ("Agreement") between WINTERFIELD PRODUCTIONS ("Producer") and CLAY PARKER ("Artist") regarding the acting services of Artist in connection with the theatrical motion picture tentatively entitled "DAWN RISING" (the "Picture"),[3] as follows:
>
> A more traditional movie contract might say:
>
> WHEREAS, Producer desires to retain the services of Artist for the purpose of making a theatrical motion picture; and
> WHEREAS, Artist desires to work for Producer on the terms and subject to the conditions set forth herein;

[3] These are not the parties' real names but are offered to illustrate the concepts.

NOW, THEREFORE, in consideration of the mutual covenants contained herein, and for other good and valuable consideration, the receipt and adequacy of which are hereby acknowledged, the parties agree as follows:

None of these flourishes are necessary, but some people prefer them.

Definitions

Most contracts have some definitions. As we have seen in the movie contract, *Artist, Producer,* and *Picture* were defined in the introductory paragraph. Sometimes, definitions are included in a separate section. Alternatively, they can appear throughout the contract. The movie contract does not have a definitions section, but many terms, such as *fixed compensation* and *teaser,* are defined in the body of the agreement.

Covenants

Now we get to the heart of the contract: What are the parties agreeing to do? Failure to perform these obligations constitutes a breach of the contract and will require the payment of damages. **Covenant** is a legal term that means a promise in a contract.

Covenant
A promise in a contract

At this stage, the relationship between lawyer and client is particularly important. They will obtain the best result if they work well together. And to achieve a successful outcome, both need to contribute. Clients should figure out what they need for the agreement to be successful. An hour or two of careful thought now could save months or even years of aggravation and expense later. It is at this point that clients have the most control over the deal, and they should exercise it. *It is a mistake to assume that everything will work itself out.* Lawyers can help in this negotiation and drafting process because they have worked on other similar deals and they know what can go wrong. Listen to them—they are on your side.

Imagine you are an actor about to sign a contract to make a movie. What provisions would you want? Begin by asking what your goals are for the project. Certainly, to make a movie that critics like and the public wants to see. So you will ask for as much control over the process and product as you can get—selection of the director and costars, for instance. Maybe influence on the editing process. But you also want to make sure that the movie does not hurt your career. What provisions would you need to achieve that goal? And shooting a movie can be grueling work, so you want to ensure that your physical and psychological needs are met, particularly when you are on location away from home. Try to think of all the different events that could happen and how they would affect you. The contract should make provisions for these occurrences.

Now take the other side and imagine what you would want if you were the producer. The producer's goal is to make money—which means creating a high-quality movie while spending as little as possible and maintaining control over the process and final product. As you can see, some of the goals conflict—both Artist and Producer want control over the final product. Who will win that battle?

Here are the terms of the contract that Actor and Producer ultimately signed. The Artist negotiated:

1. A fixed fee of $1,800,000, to be paid in equal installments at the end of each week of filming
2. Extra payment if the filming takes longer than ten weeks
3. 7.5 percent of the gross receipts of the movie
4. A royalty on any product merchandising, the rate to be negotiated in good faith
5. Approval over (but approval shall not be unreasonably withheld):
    i. The director, costars, hairdresser, makeup person, costume designer, stand-ins, and the look of his role (although he lists one director and costar whom he has preapproved);

ii. Any changes in the script that materially affect his role;
iii. All product placements, but he preapproves the placement of Snickers candy bars;
iv. Locations where the filming takes place;
v. All videos, photos, and interviews of him; and
vi. The translation of the script for French subtitles (he is fluent in French).

6. Approval (at his sole discretion) over the release of any blooper videos
7. His name to be listed first in the movie credits, on a separate card (i.e., alone on the screen)
8. That the producer not give any photographs from the set to tabloids (such as the *National Enquirer* or *Star*)
9. At least 12 hours off duty from the end of each day of filming to the start of the next day
10. First-class airplane tickets to any locations outside Los Angeles
11. Ten first-class airline tickets for his friends to visit him on location
12. A luxury hotel suite for himself and a room for his friends
13. A driver and four-wheel-drive SUV to transport him to the set
14. The right to keep some wardrobe items

The Producer negotiated:

1. All intellectual property rights to the movie
2. The right not to make the movie, although he would still have to pay Artist the fixed fee
3. Control over the final cut of the movie
4. That the Artist will show up on a certain date and work in good faith for:
   i. Two weeks in pre-production (wardrobe and rehearsals);
   ii. Ten weeks shooting the movie; and
   iii. Two free weeks after the shooting ends, in case the director wants to reshoot some scenes. The Artist must in good faith make himself available whenever the director needs him.
5. The right to fire Artist if his appearance or voice materially changes before or during the filming of the movie
6. That the Artist help promote the movie on dates subject to Artist's approval, which shall not be unreasonably withheld

Language of the Covenants. To clarify who exactly is doing what, covenants in a contract should use the active, not passive voice. In other words, a contract should say "Producer shall pay Artist $1.8 million," not "Artist shall be paid $1.8 million."

For important issues where disputes are likely to arise, the language should be precise, detailed, and complete. The movie contract uses 453 words to define the Artist's services just for shooting the movie, not including promotional efforts once the film is released. These acting services include "dubbing, retakes, reshoots, and added scenes."

Breach. What happens if one of the parties breaches a covenant in the contract? Throughout the life of a contract, there could be many small breaches. Say, Artist is late for filming one day or he gains five pounds. Maybe Producer deposits Artist's paycheck a few days late. Perhaps a pop-out trailer is not available. Although these events may technically be violations, a court would not impose sanctions over such minor issues. **To constitute a violation of the contract, the breach must be material.** A **material breach** is important enough to defeat an essential purpose of the contract. Although a court would probably not consider one missed day to be a material breach, if Artist repeatedly failed to show up, that would be material.

Material breach
A violation of a contract that defeats an essential purpose of the agreement

Given that one goal of a contract is to avoid litigation, it can be useful to define in the contract itself what a breach is. The movie contract uses this definition:

> "Artist fails or refuses to perform in accordance with Producer's instructions or is otherwise in material breach or material default hereof," and "Artist's use of drugs [other than prescribed by a medical doctor]."

The contract goes on, however, to give Artist one free pass:

> It being agreed that with regard to one instance of default only, Artist shall have 24 hours after receipt of notice during principal photography, or 48 hours at all other times, to cure any alleged breach or default hereof.

Sometimes, you will recall, contracts state the consequences of a breach, such as the amount of damages. (You remember from prior chapters that these are called *liquidated damages.*) A damages clause can specify a certain amount, a limitation on the total, or other variations. In other words, the contract could say, "If Artist breaches, Producer is entitled to $1 million in damages." Alternatively, a damage clause could say, "Damages will not exceed $1 million." But the vast majority of contracts have neither liquidated damages nor damage caps.

Good Faith. The covenants in the movie contract use three different standards of behavior: *reasonably, in good faith* or *sole discretion.* **Reasonably** means ordinary or usual under the circumstances. **Good faith** means an honest effort to meet both the spirit and letter of the contract. A party with **sole discretion** has the *absolute* right to make any decision on that issue. Sole discretion clauses are not entered into lightly.

Reasonably
Ordinary or usual under the circumstances

Good faith
An honest effort to meet both the spirit and letter of the contract

Sole discretion
The absolute right to make any decision on an issue

Reciprocal Promises and Conditions. If one party to a contract breaches it, the other parties want to make sure that they can walk away without any further obligation to keep performing their covenants. To ensure this result, the terms of the contract must be *conditional* not *reciprocal.* Suppose that a contract states:

1. Actor shall take part in the principal photography of Movie for ten weeks, commencing on March 1.
2. Producer shall pay Artist $180,000 per week.

In this case, even if Artist does not show up for shooting, Producer must still pay him. These provisions are **reciprocal promises**, which means that they are each enforceable independently. Producer must make payment and then sue Artist, hoping to recover damages in court.

Reciprocal promises
Promises that are each enforceable independently

The better approach is for the covenants to be **conditional**—a party agrees to perform them only if the other side also does what it promised. In the real movie contract, Producer promises to pay Artist "on the condition that Artist fully performs all of Artist's services and obligations and agreements hereunder and is not in material breach or otherwise in material default hereof."

Conditional promises
Promises that a party agrees to perform only if the other side also does what it promised

Representations and Warranties

Covenants are the promises the parties make about what they will do in the future. Representations and warranties are statements of fact about the past or present; they are true when the contract is signed (or at some other specific, designated time).[4] Representations

Representations and warranties
Statements of fact about the past or present

[4]Although, technically, there is a slight difference between a representation and a warranty, many lawyers confuse the two terms, and the distinction is not important. We will treat them as synonyms, as many lawyers do.

and warranties are important—without them, the other party might not have agreed to the contract. In the movie contract, Artist warrants that he is a member of the Screen Actors Guild. This provision is important because, if it was not true, Producer would either have to obtain a waiver or pay a substantial penalty.

In a contract between two companies, each side will generally represent and warrant facts such as: They legally exist, they have the authority to enter into the contract, their financial statements are accurate, they have revealed all material litigation, and they own all relevant assets. In a contract for the sale of goods, the contract will include warranties about the condition of the goods being sold.

EXAMStrategy

Question: Producer does not want Artist to pilot an airplane during the term of the contract. Would that provision be a representation and warranty or a covenant? How would you phrase it?

Strategy: Representations and warranties are about events in the past or present. A covenant is a promise for the future. If, for example, Producer wanted to know that Artist had never used drugs in the past, that provision would be a representation and warranty.

Result: A promise not to pilot an airplane is a covenant. The contract could say, "Until Artist completes all services required hereunder, he shall not pilot an airplane."

20-2b Boilerplate

These standard previsions are typically placed in a section entitled *Miscellaneous.* Many people think that *boilerplate* is a synonym for *boring and irrelevant,* but it is worth remembering that the term comes from the iron or steel that protects the hull of a ship—something that shipbuilders ignore to the passengers' peril. A contract without boilerplate is valid and enforceable, but these provisions do play an important protective role. In essence, boilerplate creates a private law that governs disputes between the parties. Courts can also play this role and, indeed, in the absence of boilerplate they will. But remember that an important goal of a contract is to avoid the courthouse.

Here are some standard, and important, boilerplate provisions.

Choice of Law and Forum

Choice of law provisions Determine which state's laws will be used to interpret the contract

Choice of forum provisions Determine the state in which any litigation would take place

Choice of law provisions determine which state's laws will be used to interpret the contract. **Choice of forum provisions** determine the state in which any litigation would take place. (One state's courts can apply another state's laws. And, indeed, as we saw in Chapter 3 on international law, one country can apply another country's laws.) Lawyers often view these two provisions as the most important boilerplate. Particular states might have dramatically different laws. Even the so-called uniform statutes, such as the Uniform Commercial Code, can vary widely from state to state. Variations are even more pronounced in other areas of the law, in particular in the common law, which is created by state courts.

As for forum, it is a lot more convenient and cheaper to litigate a case in one's home courts. The Supreme Court has ruled that trial courts must enforce these forum selection clauses even if the result is highly inconvenient for one of the parties.[5]

---

[5] Atl. Marine Constr. Co. v. United States Dist. Court, 134 S. Ct. 568 (2013).

When resolving a dispute, the choice of law and forum can strongly influence the outcome. For this reason, parties are sometimes reluctant to negotiate the provision and instead decide just to take their chances in the event of a lawsuit. Or they may choose a neutral, equally inconvenient forum such as Delaware. Without a choice of forum clause, the parties may well end up litigating where to litigate, or they may find themselves even worse off—with parallel cases filed by each party in its preferred forum.

The movie contract states: "This Agreement shall be deemed to have been made in the State of California and shall be construed and enforced in accordance with the law of the State of California." The contract did not, but should have, also specified the forum—that any litigation would be conducted in California.

The following case illustrates the importance of a forum selection clause. If the plaintiff had been forced to bring his lawsuit in Libya, which was then at war, he would not have been able to proceed. Note that the court uses the term "incorporate by reference." That phrase means that if, in a contract, you mention another document, you make that document part of the contract.

Kedkad v. Microsoft Corporation, Inc.

2013 U.S. Dist. LEXIS 126346
United States District Court for the Northern District of California, 2013

Facts: Microsoft Libya hired a Libyan citizen, Mahmoud Kedkad, to work as a Marketing Lead in Tripoli. Kedkad signed a one-year employment agreement (2010 Contract) providing that:

> This contract is subject to the prevailing labor law applicable in Libya. The Libyan courts shall have jurisdiction to decide any dispute that may arise in the future between the parties involved in this contract.

The next year, Kedkad signed another contract (2011 Contract) with the following Article 10:

> This Contract is subject to the provisions of Libyan Labor law No. 58 and its amendments and all other decisions, decrees, or regulations which have not been specifically mentioned in this contract.

During the term of the 2011 Contract, revolution erupted in Libya. Microsoft Libya shut down and evacuated all of its employees, including Kedkad, to the United States. Microsoft then reassigned Kedkad to Dubai, but he told the company he could not go because of the Post-Traumatic Stress Disorder (PTSD) he had acquired from his exposure to horrible violence in Libya. He asked either to be assigned to a job in the United States or to have his duties modified. Microsoft fired him.

Kedkad sued Microsoft in the United States alleging that it had violated his contract by firing him and also that it had refused to accommodate his PTSD disability as required by U.S. law. Microsoft filed a motion to dismiss on the grounds that the case should be heard in Libya and under Libyan law. It argued that such a requirement was implied in the 2011 Contract and, furthermore, No. 58 of the Libyan Labor Law required it. However, because No. 58 had been repealed and replaced by Libyan Labor Law No. 12, Microsoft argued that No. 12 also applied and that this statute would also have required the case to be heard in Libya.

Issue: ***Does Kedkad's contract require that his lawsuit be tried in Libya?***

Excerpts from Judge Henderson's Decision: Article 10 of the 2011 Contract does not, by its terms, contain a forum selection clause. This absence of forum selection language is particularly notable because the predecessor 2010 Contract contains both a choice of law provision *and* a forum selection provision:

> The *Libyan courts shall have jurisdiction to decide* any dispute that may arise in the future between the parties involved in this contract.

[As for Microsoft's second argument,] Article 10 does not reference Law No. 12 at all. By contrast, the 2010 Contract arguably used clear and unequivocal terms to alert Plaintiff that his claims were to be adjudicated in Libyan courts. Rather, Article 10 references Labor Law No.

58, which appears to have been repealed nearly one year before the parties executed the 2011 Contract. Reference to a repealed statute hardly provides clear and unequivocal reference.

Alternatively, [Microsoft argues] Article 10's catch-all provision could refer to Law No. 12: "This Contract is subject to . . . all other decisions, decrees or regulations which have not been specifically mentioned in this contract." [T]he Court finds that the incorporation by reference here to non-enumerated sections of amending legislation to a repealed statute is too attenuated. The Court finds Article 10 does not sufficiently call to Plaintiff's attention the statutory provisions that purportedly act as a forum selection clause contained in either Labor Law No. 58 or Law No. 12.

It is similarly unclear to the Court whether Labor Law 12 would have been known or easily available to Plaintiff. The Court finds that Article 10 is amorphous and would not have guided the reader to the purported forum selection clause in Law No. 12. Therefore, the Court declines to find Article 10 incorporates by reference a forum selection clause.

Accordingly, the Court DENIES Defendant's Motion To Dismiss.

Modification

Contracts should contain a provision governing modification. The movie contract states: "This Agreement may not be amended or modified except by an instrument in writing signed by the party to be charged with such amendment or modification."

"Charged with such amendment" means the party who is adversely affected by the change. If Producer agrees to pay Artist more, then Producer must sign the amendment. Without this provision, a conversation over beers between Producer and Artist about a change in pay might turn out to be an enforceable amendment.

The original version of the movie contract said that Artist would be photographed nude only above the waist. He ultimately agreed to rear-below-the-waist photography. That amendment (which the parties called a **rider**—another term for amendment or addition) took the form of a letter from Artist agreeing to the change. Producer then signed the letter, acknowledging receipt and acceptance. The amendment would have been valid even without Producer's signature because Artist was "charged with such Amendment."

Rider
An amendment or addition to a contract

If a contract has a provision requiring that amendments be in writing, there are three ways to amend it:

1. Signing an amendment (or rider).
2. Crossing out the wrong language and replacing it by hand with the correct terms. It is good practice for both parties to initial such changes. This method is typically used at the last minute, say if a mistake is first noticed at the closing.
3. Rewriting the entire contract to include the changed provisions. In this case, the contract is typically renamed: The Amended and Restated Agreement. This method is most appropriate if there are many complex alterations.

Most commercial contracts provide that any amendment or modification must be in writing. The failure to comply *precisely* with this provision can lead to unfortunate consequences. In one case, Plaintiff agreed to buy real estate from Defendant for $56 million, with a $5 million down payment. The contract stated that all amendments had to be in writing. However, many times the parties agreed orally to extend the closing date but then did not sign the written amendment until afterward. Ultimately, this casual approach backfired. They agreed to close at 12:00 noon on September 25 but Plaintiff did not arrive until 3:00 p.m. and, at that point, the two parties did not sign a modification.

Defendant then declared that, because Plaintiff had breached the agreement, Defendant could keep the $5 million deposit. Plaintiff sued, arguing that (a) it had complied with the contract by appearing at 3:00 p.m. and (b) the parties had orally agreed to postpone the closing (as they had done many times before). The court disagreed, ruling that Plaintiff had violated the contract by appearing three hours late, and that the oral modification was invalid because the contract provided that all amendments had to be in writing. Plaintiff learned a $5 million lesson (much, much more than the cost of this textbook).[6]

Also note that amending a contract may raise issues of consideration, a topic discussed in Chapter 13.

Assignment of Rights and Delegation of Duties

Assignment of rights
A transfer of benefits under a contract

Delegation of duties
A transfer of obligations under a contract

An **assignment of rights** is a transfer of the benefits under a contract to another person. Artist might, for example, want to assign his right to receive payment under the contract to his ex-wife. **Delegation of duties** is a transfer of the obligations under a contract. Suppose Artist received an offer to make another movie at the same time. He might want to assign his obligation to act in this movie to some other actor.

The movie contract treats the two parties differently on this issue. Producer has the right to assign the contract, but he must stay secondarily liable on it. In other words, Producer can transfer to someone else the right to receive the benefits of the contract (i.e., to make the movie with Artist), but he cannot transfer his obligations (to pay Artist). If the person who takes over the contract fails to pay Artist, then Producer is liable. Artist might be unhappy if another production company makes the movie, but he is still bound by the terms of the contract. At least he knows that Producer is ultimately liable for his paycheck.

However, the contract also provides:

> It is expressly understood and agreed that the services to be rendered by Artist hereunder are of the essence of this Agreement and that such services shall not be delegated to any other person or entity, nor shall Artist assign the right to receive compensation hereunder.

It matters to Producer which actor shows up to do the filming. Artist cannot say, "I'm too busy—here's my cousin Jack." And Producer also wants to make sure that no one else cashes the checks. He worries that if Artist assigns the right to receive payment, he will feel less motivated to do his job well.

Arbitration

Some contracts prohibit the parties from suing in court and require that disputes be settled by an arbitrator. Arbitration has its advantages—flexibility and savings of time and money—but it also has disadvantages. There is some evidence that arbitrators tend to favor businesses, who are likely to have many cases, over consumers who may only have one. Companies with multiple cases in front of an arbitrator are more than twice as likely to win than if they just have one case with the arbitrator. And many believe that employees receive a less favorable result when they arbitrate, rather than litigate, disputes with their employer.

Attorneys' Fees

As a general rule, if parties to a contract end up in litigation, they must pay their own legal fees, no matter who is in the wrong. But contracts may override this general rule and provide that the losing party in a dispute pays the attorneys' fees for both sides. Such a provision tends to discourage the poorer party from litigating with a rich opponent for fear of having to pay two sets of attorneys' fees. The movie contract provides:

> Artist hereby agrees to indemnify Producer from and against any and all losses, costs (including, without limitation, reasonable attorneys' fees), liabilities,

[6] Nassau Beekman, LLC v. Ann/Nassau Realty, LLC 960 N.Y.S.2d 70 (N.Y. App. Div. 2013).

> damages, and claims of any nature arising from or in connection with any breach by Artist of any agreement, representation, or warranty made by Artist under this Agreement.

There is no equivalent provision for breaches by Producer. What does that omission tell you about the relative bargaining power of the two parties?

Integration

During contract negotiations, the parties may discuss many ideas that are not ultimately included in the final version. The point of an integration clause is to prevent either side from later claiming that the two parties had agreed to additional provisions. The movie contract states:

> This Agreement, along with the exhibits attached hereto, shall constitute a binding contract between the parties hereto and shall supersede any and all prior negotiations and communications, whether written or oral, with respect hereto.

Without this clause, even a detailed written contract can be amended by an undocumented conversation—a dangerous situation since the existence and terms of the amendment will depend on what a court *thinks* was said and intended, which may or may not be what actually happened.

EXAMStrategy

Question: Daniel and Annie signed a contract providing that Daniel would lend \$50,000 to Annie's craft beer business at an interest rate of 8 percent. During negotiations, Daniel and Annie agreed that the interest rate would go down to 5 percent once she had sold 25,000 cases. This provision never made it into the contract. After the contract was signed, Daniel orally agreed to reduce the interest rate to 6 percent once volume exceeded 15,000 cases. The contract had an integration provision but no modification clause. Annie sold 30,000 cases. What interest rate must she pay?

Strategy: If a contract has an integration provision, then side agreements made during negotiations are unenforceable unless included in the written contract. Without a modification provision, oral agreements made after the contract was signed may be enforceable.

Result: A court would not enforce the side agreement that reduced the interest rate to 5 percent. However, it is possible that a court would enforce the 6 percent agreement.

Severability

If, for whatever reason, some part of the contract turns out to be unenforceable, **a severability provision asks the court simply to delete the offending clause and enforce the rest of the contract.** For example, courts will not enforce unreasonable non-compete clauses. (California courts will not enforce any non-competes, unless made in connection with the sale of a business.) In one case, a consultant signed an employment contract that prohibited him from engaging in his occupation "anyplace in the world." The court struck down this non-compete provision but ruled that the rest of the contract (which contained trade secret clauses) was valid.

The movie contract states:

> In the event that there is any conflict between any provision of this Agreement and any statute, law, or regulation, the latter shall prevail; provided, however, that in such event, the provision of this Agreement so affected shall be curtailed and limited only to the minimum extent necessary to permit compliance with the minimum requirement, and no other provision of this Agreement shall be affected thereby and all other provisions of this Agreement shall continue in full force and effect.

Force Majeure

A ***force majeure* event** is a disruptive, unexpected occurrence for which neither party is to blame and that prevents one or both parties from complying with the contract. *Force majeure* events typically include war, terrorist attack, fire, flood, or general acts of God. If a terrorist event halted air travel, Artist might not be able to appear on set as scheduled.

***Force majeure* event**
A disruptive, unexpected occurrence for which neither party is to blame that prevents one or both parties from complying with a contract

The movie contract defines *force majeure* events as:

> fire, war, governmental action or proceeding, third-party breach of contract, injunction, or other material interference with the production or distribution of motion pictures by Producer, or any other unexpected or disruptive event sufficient to excuse performance of this Agreement as a matter of law or other similar causes beyond Producer's control or by reason of the death, illness, or incapacity of the producer, director, or a member of the principal cast or other production personnel.

Notices

After a contract is signed, there may be times when the parties want to send each other official notices—of a breach, an objection, or an approval, for example. In this section, the parties list the addresses where these notices may be sent. For Producer, it is company headquarters. For Artist, there are three addresses: his agent, his manager, and his lawyer. The notice provision also typically specifies when the notice is effective: When sent, when it would normally be expected to arrive, or when it actually does arrive.

Closing

To indicate that the parties have agreed to the terms of the contract, they must sign it. A simple signature is sufficient, but contracts often contain flourishes. The movie contract states:

> IN WITNESS WHEREOF, the parties hereto have executed this Agreement as of the date first written above.

With clauses like this, it is important to make sure that there is an (accurate) date on the first page. If the parties' addresses are not otherwise provided in the "Notices" section, it is a good idea to include them here. The movie contract also listed Artist's social security number.

When a party to the contract is a corporation, the signature lines should read like this:

Winterfield Productions, Inc.
By: _______________
Name:
Title:

If an individual signs her own name without indicating that she is doing so in her role as an employee of Winterfield Productions, Inc., she would be personally liable.

In the end, both parties signed the contract and made the movie. According to Rotten Tomatoes, the online movie site, professional reviewers rated it 7.9 out of 10.

CHAPTER CONCLUSION

You will undoubtedly sign many contracts in your life. Their length and complexity can be daunting. (In the movie contract, one of the *paragraphs* was 1,000 words.) At least now you understand the structure and meaning of the most important provisions so that you can negotiate, read, and analyze contracts more effectively.

EXAM REVIEW

1. **VAGUENESS** When a provision in a contract is deliberately left unclear.

2. **AMBIGUITY** Any ambiguity in a contract is interpreted against the party who drafted the agreement.

3. **SCRIVENER'S ERROR** A scrivener's error is a typographical mistake. In the case of a scrivener's error, a court will reform a contract if there is clear and convincing evidence that the mistake does not reflect the true intent of the parties.

EXAMStrategy

Question: Martha intended to transfer one piece of land to Paul. By mistake, she signed a contract transferring two parcels of land. Each piece was accurately described in the contract. Will the court reform this contract and transfer one piece of land back to her?

Strategy: Begin by asking if this was a scrivener's error. Then consider whether the court will correct the mistake. (See the "Result" at the end of this Exam Review section.)

4. **BEFORE SIGNING A CONTRACT** Before signing a contract, check carefully and thoughtfully the names of the parties, the dates, dollar amounts, and interest rates.

5. **MATERIAL BREACH** A material breach is important enough to defeat an essential purpose of the contract.

EXAMStrategy

Question: Laurie's contract to sell her tortilla chip business to Hudson contained a provision that she had to continue to work at the business for five years. One year later, she quit. Hudson refused to pay her the amounts still owing under the contract. Laurie alleged that he was liable for the full amount because her breach was not material. Is Laurie correct?

Strategy: What was the essential purpose of the contract? Was Laurie's breach important enough to defeat it? (See the "Result" at the end of this Exam Review section.)

6. REASONABLY Reasonably means ordinary or usual under the circumstances.

7. GOOD FAITH Good faith means an honest effort to meet both the spirit and letter of the contract.

8. SOLE DISCRETION A party with sole discretion has the absolute right to make any decision on that issue.

EXAMStrategy

Question: A tenant rented space from a landlord for a seafood restaurant. Under the terms of the lease, the tenant could assign the lease only if the landlord gave her consent, which she had the right to withhold "for any reason whatsoever, at her sole discretion." The tenant grew too ill to run the restaurant and asked permission to assign the lease. The landlord refused. In court, the tenant argued that the landlord could not unreasonably withhold her consent. Is the tenant correct?

Strategy: A sole discretion clause grants the absolute right to make a decision. Are there any exceptions? (See the "Result" at the end of this Exam Review section.)

9. STRUCTURE OF A CONTRACT The structure of a contract looks like this:

1. Title
2. Introductory Paragraph
3. Definitions
4. Covenants
   i. Covenants are the promises the parties make about what they will do in the future.
5. Breach
6. Conditions
7. Representations and Warranties
   i. Representations and warranties are statements of fact about the present or past—they are true when the contract is signed (or at some other specific, designated time).
8. Boilerplate
   i. Choice of Law and Forum
   ii. Modification
   iii. Assignment of Rights and Delegation of Duties
   iv. Arbitration
   v. Attorney's Fees
   vi. Integration
   vii. Severability
   viii. *Force Majeure*
   ix. Notices
   x. Closing

RESULTS

3. Result: The court ruled that it was not a scrivener's error because it was not a typo or clerical error. Therefore, the court did not reform the contract and the land was not transferred back to Martha.

5. Result: The purpose of the contract was for Hudson to build up the business and make a profit. Laurie's departure interfered with that goal. The court ruled that the breach was material and Hudson did not have to pay the sums still owing under the contract.

8. Result: The court ruled for the landlord. She had the absolute right to make any decision so long as the decision was legal.

MULTIPLE-CHOICE QUESTIONS

1. Which of the following statements is true?

(a) Vagueness occurs when the parties do not want the contract to be clear.
(b) Ambiguity occurs when the parties do not want the contract to be clear.
(c) Vagueness in a contract is often appropriate as a way to clinch a deal.
(d) Ambiguity is an appropriate tactic, particularly by the party drafting the contract.

2. A contract provided, "On January 5, Purchaser shall provide Seller with a certified check in the amount of $100,000. Seller shall transfer a deed for the Property to Purchaser." What is wrong with this provision?

(a) It is not clear who Purchaser and Seller are.
(b) The number $100,000 should be written in words.
(c) The promises are reciprocal.
(d) The promises are conditional.

3. In the case of a scrivener's error, what happens?

(a) A court will not reform the contract. The parties must live with the document they signed.
(b) A court will reform the contract if there is clear and convincing evidence that the clause in question does not reflect the true intent of the parties.
(c) A court will reform the contract if a preponderance of the evidence indicates that that the clause in question does not reflect the true intent of the parties.
(d) A court will invalidate the contract in its entirety.

4. A contract states (1) that Buzz Co. legally exists and (2) will provide 2,000 pounds of wild salmon each week. Which of the following statements is true?

(a) Clause 1 is a covenant and Clause 2 is a representation.
(b) Clause 1 is a representation and Clause 2 is a covenant.
(c) Both clauses are representations.
(d) Both clauses are covenants.

5. Simon has signed a contract with Miley agreeing to provide her company with 1,000 frozen pizzas each week. The contract states: "This agreement can only be modified by a written instrument signed by the party to be charged with such amendment." But when Simon and Miley run into each other on the train, they agree that he will provide 750 pizzas instead. Which of the following statements is true?
   (a) As long as they both agree, they can amend the contract orally. They do not have to sign anything.
   (b) For the change to be valid, both parties must sign an amendment because both parties are affected by it.
   (c) Only Miley has to sign the amendment because she is the one to be charged by it.
   (d) Only Simon must sign the amendment because he is the one to be charged by it.

CASE QUESTIONS

1. Give an example of three types of contracts that should definitely be in writing, and one that probably does not need to be.

2. List three provisions in a contract that would be material, and three that would not be.

3. Blair Co.'s top officers asked an investment bank to find a buyer for the company. The bank sent an engagement letter to Blair with the following language: If, within 24 months after the termination of this agreement, Blair is bought by anyone with whom Bank has had substantial discussions about such a sale, Blair must pay Bank its full fee.

   Is there any problem with the drafting of this provision? What could be done to clarify the language?

4. Juan purchased an insurance policy on his house that did not protect against vandalism or burglary. An arsonist burned down the house. Did the insurance company have to pay?

5. Marc canceled his Comcast cable service. When the cable guy removed the Comcast equipment, he mistakenly left behind a modem worth $220. By some mix-up, this amount was sent to a collection agency. Upon discovering the error, Marc returned the modem to Comcast, which promised to correct his account. But the mistake remained on Marc's credit report. Because of the error, Marc had to pay an additional $26,000 when he refinanced his mortgage. Did Comcast violate its duty of good faith?

DISCUSSION QUESTIONS

1. In the movie contract, which side was the more successful negotiator? Can you think of any terms that either party left out? Are any of the provisions unreasonable?

2. What are the advantages and disadvantages of hiring a lawyer to draft or review a contract?

3. What are the penalties if Artist breaches the movie contract? Are these reasonable? Too heavy? Too light?

4. Upon graduation from business school, Zoe has been offered a job as a product manager at a start-up, Appsley Co. She would be Employee #18. But first she has to negotiate a contract with the CEO, Phil. He would like to pay her $75,000, which is half of what a product manager at a more established company would earn. However, Appsley has yet to earn a profit and Zoe might also be able to negotiate an equity interest in the company. Do a role-play with another student in your class in which one of you takes the role of Zoe and the other is Phil. What terms should each party consider? What does each side want? Draft the contract. Now compare your results with others in the class. Who has negotiated the best deal? Who has written the best contract?

5. **ETHICS** Sophia negotiated a contract with Pete under which she would buy his company for $10 million plus the amount of the company's outstanding debt (approximately $1 million). But when Pete sent a draft of the contract, it stated that the purchase price would be $10 million *less* the company's debt. What is Sophia's ethical obligation to Pete? Should she tell him about the mistake? What Life Principles would you apply in this situation? What would Kant say?

Sales

UNIT

4

CHAPTER 21

INTRODUCTION TO SALES

He Sued, She Sued. Noah and Nina made a great couple because both were compulsive entrepreneurs. One evening they sat on their penthouse roof deck, overlooking the twinkling Chicago skyline. Noah sipped a kale smoothie while negotiating, over Skype, with a real estate developer in San Antonio. Nina puffed an e-cigarette as she texted with a drone manufacturer in Cleveland. "I did it!" shrieked Nina, "I made an incredible deal for the kiddie drones—twenty bucks each!" "No, *I* did it!" trumpeted Noah, "I sold the 50 acres in Texas for $300,000 more than they're worth."

Nina sent a quick text: "Confirming our deal—100,000 Down-to-Earth Drones—you deliver Chicago—end of summer." She did not mention a price, or an exact delivery date, or when payment would be made. Noah took more time. He typed a thorough contract, describing precisely the land he was selling, the $2.3 million price, how and when each payment would be made and the deed conveyed. He printed out the contract, signed it and mailed it, along with a plot plan showing the surveyed land. Then the happy couple grabbed a bottle of champagne and placed a side bet on whose contract would prove more profitable. The loser would have to cook and serve dinner for six months.

Confirming our deal—100,000 Down-to-Earth Drones—you deliver Chicago—end of summer.

Neither Noah nor Nina ever heard again from the other parties. The drone manufacturer sold the Down-to-Earth Drones to another retailer at a higher price. Nina was forced to buy comparable machines elsewhere for $29 each. She sued. And the Texas property buyer changed his mind, deciding to develop an ecotourism lodge in Greenland instead and refusing to pay Noah for his land. He sued. Only one of the two plaintiffs succeeded. Which one?

The adventures of Noah and Nina illustrate the Uniform Commercial Code (UCC) in action. The Code is the single most important source of law for people engaged in commerce and controls the vast majority of contracts made every day in every state. The Code is ancient in origin, contemporary in usage, admirable in purpose, and flawed in application. "Yeah, yeah, that's fascinating," snaps Noah, "but who wins the bet?" Relax, Noah, we'll tell you in a minute.

21-1 DEVELOPMENT AND SCOPE OF THE UCC

In England in the 1500s, it was far more important to hold land than it was to have money. Large landowners—barons, earls, and dukes—stood in excellent positions. They had access to the king or queen, they were exempt from many kinds of arrest, and, if they did get into trouble, they generally were tried before other members of the nobility in special courts. It is not surprising that law was then centered squarely upon *real property*, which mainly consists of land and permanent structures. But society changes, and so do businesses. When this happens, the law may fall behind the times.

In the 1500s, merchants in England began to have problems using existing law to resolve commercial disputes. There were many laws about land, but few for contracts. English judges were only beginning to acknowledge that an exchange of mere promises, with no money or property changing hands, might lead to an enforceable agreement. But merchants dealt in the sale of goods, not real estate. Their livelihood depended upon promises, on the rapid movement of their wares, and on their ability to enforce bargains. Dissatisfied with the few remedies that courts offered, businessmen throughout England and the Continent began to treat their own customs as law and to settle disputes in trade organizations rather than civil courts. The body of rules they relied on became known as the *lex mercatoria*, or **law merchant**. The law merchant was thus a "custom made" law, created by the merchants who used it. The new doctrine focused on promises, the sale and exchange of goods, and payment.

In the middle of the twentieth century, contract law again required a reinvention. Two problems had become apparent in the United States. First, old contract law principles often did not reflect modern business practices. Second, contract law varied from state to state, creating unnecessary confusion. On many legal topics, contract law included, the national government has had little to say and has allowed the states to act individually. Illinois decides what kinds of agreements count as contracts in Illinois, and next door in Indiana, the rules may be very different. On many issues, states reached essentially similar conclusions, so contract law developed in the same direction. But sometimes, the states disagreed, and contract law took on the aspect of a patchwork quilt.

The UCC was created as an attempt to solve these two problems. It was a proposal written by legal scholars and not a law drafted by members of Congress or state legislatures. The scholars at the American Law Institute and the National Conference of Commissioners on Uniform State Laws had great ideas, but they had no legal authority to make anyone do anything.

Over time, lawmakers in all 50 states were persuaded to adopt many parts of the UCC. They responded to these persuasive arguments:

- Businesses will benefit if most commercial transactions are governed by the modern and efficient contract law principles that are outlined in the UCC.
- Businesses everywhere will be able to operate more efficiently, and transactions will be more convenient, if the law surrounding most of their transactions is the same in every state.

It is worth noting that the UCC is not a total replacement for older principles in contract law. Contract lawsuits not involving goods are still resolved using the older common law rules. The table below outlines the UCC and the types of contracts that it does govern.

The UCC is available online at www.law.cornell.edu/ucc.

Article	
Article 1:	
General Provisions	The purpose of the code, general guidance in applying it, and definitions.
Article 2:	
Sale of Goods	The sale of *goods*, such as a new car, 20,000 pairs of gloves, or 101 Dalmatians. This is one of the two most important articles in the UCC.
Article 2A:	
Leases	A temporary exchange of goods for money, such as renting a car.
Article 3:	
Negotiable Instruments	The use of checks, promissory notes, and other negotiable instruments.
Article 4:	
Bank Deposits and Collections	The rights and obligations of banks and their customers.
Article 4A:	
Funds Transfers	An instruction, given by a bank customer, to credit a sum of money to another's account.
Article 5:	
Letters of Credit	The use of credit, extended by two or more banks, to facilitate a contract between two parties who do not know each other and require guarantees by banks they trust.
Article 6:	
Bulk Transfers	The sale of a major part of a company's inventory or equipment. This article has been repealed in all but a few states.
Article 7:	
Warehouse Receipts, Bills of Lading, and Other Documents of Title	Documents proving ownership of goods that are being transported or stored. This article is being revised as we go to press.
Article 8:	
Investment Securities	Rights and liabilities concerning shares of stock or other ownership of an enterprise.
Article 9:	
Secured Transactions	A sale of goods in which the seller keeps a financial stake in the goods he has sold, such as a car dealer who may repossess the car if the buyer fails to make payments. This is one of the two most important articles in the Code.

21-1a Noah and Nina, Revisited

Noah and Nina each negotiated what they believed was an enforceable agreement, and both filed suit: Noah for the sale of his land, Nina for the purchase of drones. Only one prevailed. The difference in outcome demonstrates one of the changes that the UCC has wrought in the law of commercial contracts and illustrates why everyone in business needs a working knowledge of the Code. As we revisit the enterprising couple, Noah is clearing the dinner dishes while Nina lights an e-cig and compliments her partner on the pad Thai. Noah, scowling, wonders what went wrong.

Because his contract was for the sale of land, it was governed by the common law of contracts. The common law Statute of Frauds requires any agreement for the sale of land to be in writing and *signed by the party to be charged* (the defendant), in this case the buyer in Texas. Noah signed it, but the buyer never did, so Noah's meticulously detailed document was worthless.

Nina's text about the drones involved the sale of goods and was governed by Article 2 of the UCC. The Code requires less detail and formality in a writing. Because Nina and the seller were both merchants, her text could be enforced *even against the defendant,* who had never signed anything. The fact that Nina left out the price and other significant terms was not fatal to a contract under the UCC, although under the common law such omissions would have made the bargain unenforceable. We will look in greater detail at these UCC changes. For now it is enough to see that the Code has carved major changes into the common law of contracts, alterations that Noah is beginning to appreciate.

21-1b This Unit and This Chapter

This unit covers three principal subjects, all relating to commercial transactions that the Code governs. The first chapters concern the sale of goods and focus primarily on Article 2. In the present chapter, we emphasize how Code provisions work together to change the common law. In the following chapters, we examine title to goods and warranties (Chapter 22) and, finally, performance and remedies (Chapter 23).

Future chapters (Chapters 25 and 26) survey the law of negotiable instruments. Checks are the most common kind of negotiable instrument, but we will see that there are many other varieties and that each creates different rights and obligations. We include in the unit a chapter devoted to secured transactions (Chapter 24), that is, a sale of goods in which the seller keeps a financial stake in the goods he has sold, and later in the text is a chapter that analyzes bankruptcy law in Chapter 36.

This chapter will focus on Article 2 of the UCC, which applies to the sale of goods. Goods refer to all things that are movable except for money and securities (like stock certificates). A house is not a good, but the *stuff* in the house—the car in the garage, the computers, the furniture, and the paintings hanging on the wall—is. Article 2 applies to contracts that sell goods, as well as to contracts that sell a mix of goods and services if the *predominant purpose* of the deal is to sell goods. As you read the chapter, keep the following ideas in mind:

A house is not a good, but the *stuff* in the house—the car in the garage, the computers, the furniture, and the paintings hanging on the wall—is.

- **The UCC is pro-business.** The whole point of the UCC is to make business transactions more reliable, convenient, and predictable.

- **Tie goes to the contract.** In baseball, a tie goes to the runner. Under the UCC, the preference is to declare an agreement to be a contract if no clear reason exists to declare it invalid.

21-2 UCC BASICS

21-2a Code's Purpose

The Uniform Commercial Code proclaims its purposes clearly:

UCC §1-102(2): Underlying purposes and policies of this Act are:

a. To simplify, clarify and modernize the law governing commercial transactions;
b. To permit the continued expansion of commercial practices through custom, usage and agreement of the parties; and
c. To make uniform the law among the various jurisdictions.

This is not mere boilerplate. To "modernize," in (a), requires a focus on the needs of contemporary businesspeople, not on rules developed when judges rode horseback. Suppose a court must decide whether a writing is detailed enough to satisfy the Code's Statute of Frauds. The judge may rely on §1-102 to decide that because modern commerce is so fast, even the skimpiest of writings is good enough to demonstrate that the parties had reached a bargain. In doing so, the judge would deliberately be turning away from legal history to accommodate business practices in an electronic age.

Section 1-102 also states that "[t]his Act shall be liberally construed and applied to promote its underlying purposes," meaning that, when in doubt, courts should focus on the goals described. The Code emphasizes *getting the right results* rather than following rigid rules of contract law.

Goods
Are things that are movable, other than money and investment securities

21-2b Scope of Article 2

Because the UCC changes the common law, it is essential to know whether the Code applies in a given case. Negotiations may lead to an enforceable agreement when the UCC applies, even though the same bargaining would create no contract under the common law.

UCC §2-102: Article 2 applies to the sale of goods.[1] As mentioned, **goods** are things that are movable, other than money and investment securities. So an agreement for the delivery of 10,000 board feet of white pine is a contract for the sale of goods, and Article 2 governs it. But the article does not apply to a contract for the sale of an office building. Article 2 regulates sales, which means that one party transfers title to the other in exchange for money. If you sell your motorcycle to a friend, that is a sale of goods. If you lend the bike to your friend for the weekend, that is not a sale and Article 2 does not apply. Article 2 also does not apply to the leasing of goods, for example, when you rent a car. A sale involves a permanent change in ownership, whereas a lease concerns a temporary change in possession.

Kridsada Krataipet/Shutterstock.com

Article 2 of the UCC would apply to the sale of a good—such as a motorcycle—but would not apply to a lease or a loan.

[1]Officially, Article 2 tells us that it applies to *transactions* in goods, which is a slightly broader category than sale of goods. But most sections of Article 2, and most court decisions, focus exclusively on sales, and so shall we.

21-2c Mixed Contracts

To determine whether the UCC governs, we need to know what kind of an agreement the parties made. Was it one for the sale of goods (UCC) or one for services (common law)? In fact, the agreement combined both goods and services and was therefore a *mixed contract.* In a mixed contract, the UCC will govern if the *predominant purpose* is the sale of goods; the common law will control if the predominant purpose is providing services.

In the following case, the court had to determine whether something it could not touch was a good. Was software *untouchable* by the UCC?

Because some of the cases in this chapter involve more than one Code section, we will outline the relevant provisions at the outset.

Code Provisions Discussed in This Case

Issue	Relevant Code Section
1. What law governs?	UCC §2-102: Article 2 applies to the sale of goods.

Rottner v. AVG Technologies USA, Inc.

943 F. Supp. 2d 222
United States District Court, Massachusetts, 2013

Facts: Christopher Rottner's computer began malfunctioning—its performance decreased, and the internet speed was sluggish. Searching for a solution, Rottner found a free trial of PC TuneUp online. On the website, AVG, PC TuneUp's maker, claimed that the software would boost internet speed, eliminate freezing and crashing, optimize disk space and speeds, extend battery life, protect privacy, monitor hard drive health, and restore the PC to its peak performance. (It also made breakfast, but that was extra.)

Rottner was sold. The trial version of PC TuneUp reportedly diagnosed and fixed what it called "critical errors" on the computer. It advised him to perform weekly PC TuneUp scans of his computer. So Rottner purchased and installed the full version of the software. But it never worked.

When Rottner complained to AVG, he was told to download a PC TuneUp update. But this update caused Rottner's computer to completely freeze, forcing him to fully reformat his hard drive and lose valuable data.

A computer forensics expert found that the trial version of PC TuneUp was programed to consistently report multiple PC problems and exaggerate the number and severity of errors found. The cure was always the same: Purchase the full version of PC TuneUp.

Rottner sued AVG for breach of warranty under the UCC. AVG moved to dismiss, arguing that the UCC did not apply to software.

Issue: ***Did the UCC apply to software?***

Excerpts from Judge Stearns's Decision: Defendants contend that the claims for breach of express and implied warranties are inapplicable in this case because those claims are pled under Article 2 of the UCC, which covers sales of goods, whereas software—the subject of this dispute—is not, according to AVG, a "good" under Delaware law.

AVG relies on two cases for this proposition. In *Neilson*, the court held that a lease for computer hardware, software, and support services was predominantly a contract for goods, and thus came under the rubric of Article 2 of the UCC. However, the court left open the question of whether the sale of software alone would be considered a sale of a good under Article 2. In *Wharton*, the court found that the sale of customized software was a contract for services, and not goods, under the UCC.

Software is not clearly a good or a service in the abstract, and may qualify as either depending on the particular circumstances of the case. Delaware, like other jurisdictions that have adopted the UCC, applies a "predominance" test to determine whether a contract is for goods or services. The holding of *Neilson* turned on the fact that the contract involved the sale of tangible hardware along with software and services, and thus is readily distinguishable. That case involved a claim of copyright infringement, a dispute over intellectual property which is definitively not a "good" under the UCC. There is no suggestion that the purchase of PC TuneUp in this case involved any transfer of intellectual property.

However, PC TuneUp also bears no resemblance to the custom designed software in *Wharton*. In *Wharton*, the programmer had to prepare a study of the customer's existing operations, to design, develop, and install computer software which would meet his specific needs and objectives. In essence, it was the programmer's knowledge, skill and ability for which Wharton bargained. The means of transmission [was] not the object of the agreement.

In contrast, PC TuneUp is a generally available standardized software. Thus, the sale of PC TuneUp is more like the sale of a tangible good—it is movable at the time of identification to the contract for sale. Indeed, Rottner was able to download and install the full version of PC TuneUp after a one-stop payment over the Internet. Because the sale of PC TuneUp is predominantly like the sale of a good rather than the provision of services, the UCC warranty provisions apply.

21-2d Merchants

Merchant
Generally, someone who routinely deals in the particular goods involved

A **merchant** is someone who routinely deals in the particular goods involved *or* who appears to have special knowledge or skill in those goods *or* who uses agents with special knowledge or skill in those goods.[2] A used car dealer is a "merchant" when it comes to selling autos because he routinely deals in them. A man selling his own car to someone who responded to his classified ad is not acting as a merchant.

The UCC frequently holds a merchant to a higher standard of conduct than a non-merchant. For example, a merchant may be held to an oral contract if she received written confirmation of it, even though the merchant herself never signed the confirmation. That same confirmation memo, arriving at the house of a non-merchant, would *not* create a binding deal. We will see many instances of this dual level of responsibility, one for a merchant and the other for a non-merchant.

21-2e Good Faith and Unconscionability

The UCC imposes a duty of good faith in the performance of all contracts. For *non-merchants,* good faith means honesty in fact. For a *merchant,* good faith means honesty in fact *plus* the exercise of reasonable commercial standards of fair dealing.[3] Thus, when parties perform a contract, or in certain cases when they negotiate, neither side may lie or mislead. Further, a party who is a merchant must act as fairly as the business community routinely expects.

Unconscionable
A contract that is shockingly one-sided and fundamentally unfair

The UCC employs a second principle to encourage fair play and just results: the doctrine of unconscionability. A contract may be **unconscionable** if it is shockingly one-sided and fundamentally unfair.[4] If a court concludes that some part of a contract is unconscionable, it will refuse to enforce that provision. Courts seldom find a contract unconscionable if the two parties are businesses, but they are quicker to apply the doctrine when one party is a consumer.

The doctrine of good faith focuses on a party's behavior as it performs an agreement: Was it attempting to carry out its obligations in a reasonable manner and do what both sides expected when they made the deal? Unconscionability looks primarily at the contract itself, asking whether any terms are so grossly unfair that a court should reform or ignore them.

---

[2]UCC §2-104.
[3]UCC §§1-201(19), 1-203, and 2-103.
[4]UCC §2-302.

21-3 UCC CONTRACT FORMATION

The common law expected the parties to form a contract in a fairly predictable and traditional way: The offeror made a clear offer that included all important terms, and the offeree agreed to all terms. Nothing was left open and there was little flexibility. The drafters of the UCC recognized that businesspeople frequently do not think or work that way and that the law should reflect business reality.

21-3a Formation Basics: Section 2-204

UCC §2-204 provides three important rules that enable parties to make a contract quickly and informally:

1. **Any Manner That Shows Agreement.** The parties may make a contract in any manner sufficient to show that they reached an agreement. They have wide latitude. They may show the agreement with words, writings, or even their conduct. Lisa negotiates with Ed to buy 300 barbecue grills. The parties agree on a price, but other business prevents them from finishing the deal. Then six months later, Lisa writes, "Remember our deal for 300 grills? I still want to do it if you do." Ed does not respond, but a week later, a truck shows up at Lisa's store with the 300 grills and Lisa accepts them. The combination of their original discussion, Lisa's subsequent letter, Ed's delivery, and her acceptance all add up to show that they reached an agreement. The court will enforce their deal, and Lisa must pay the agreed upon price.
2. **Moment of Making Is Not Critical.** The UCC will enforce a deal even though it is difficult, in common law terms, to say exactly when it was formed. Was Lisa's deal formed when they orally agreed? When he delivered? She accepted? The Code's answer: It does not matter. The contract is enforceable.
3. **One or More Terms May Be Left Open.** The common law insisted that the parties clearly agree on all important terms. If they did not, there was no meeting of minds and no enforceable deal. The Code changes that. **Under the UCC, a court may enforce a bargain even though one or more terms were left open.** Lisa's letter never said when she required delivery of the barbecues or when she would pay. Under the UCC, the omission is not fatal. As long as there is some certain basis for giving damages to the injured party, the court will do just that. Suppose Lisa refused to pay, claiming that the agreement included no date for her payment. A court would rule that the parties assumed she would pay within a commercially reasonable time, such as 30 days.

The following Landmark Case shaped the way business is done on the internet today. Who knew that it would all come down to UCC §2-204?

Code Provisions Discussed in This Case

Issue	Relevant Code Section
1. What is required to form a contract?	UCC §2-204: Contract formation.

Landmark Case

ProCD, Inc. v. Zeidenberg

86 F3d 1447
United States Court of Appeals for the Seventh Circuit, 1996

Facts: ProCD sold SelectPhone, a database containing information from 3,000 telephone directories. It sold the software to consumers for $150; businesses paid a much higher price.

Every box containing the consumer version of SelectPhone was wrapped in plastic shrinkwrap and prominently featured text notifying buyers that an enclosed license restricted use of the software. After removing the cellophane cover and opening the box, buyers could access the printed license. Upon downloading the product, the consumer could not use the software without first accepting the license posted on the screen. This license prohibited the buyers from using the database commercially.

Graduate student Matthew Zeidenberg bought the consumer version of SelectPhone, but violated the license agreement by reselling the database's information on the internet.

ProCD sued Zeidenberg, who argued that the license did not apply to him because he never agreed to it. The district court ruled in his favor. It held that, under the UCC, the license did not bind Zeidenberg because it was on the inside of the shrinkwrapped box. Thus, he had not seen it until after he bought the product. ProCD appealed.

Issue: ***Did ProCD and Zeidenberg enter into a contract that included the terms of the license?***

Excerpts from Judge Easterbrook's Decision: The district court held that placing the package of software on the shelf is an "offer," which the customer "accepts" by paying the asking price and leaving the store with the goods. A contract includes only the terms on which the parties have agreed. One cannot agree to hidden terms. So far, so good—but one of the terms to which Zeidenberg agreed by purchasing the software is that the transaction was subject to a license.

Transactions in which the exchange of money precedes the communication of detailed terms are common. Consider the purchase of an airline ticket. The traveler is quoted a price, reserves a seat, pays, and gets a ticket, in that order. The ticket contains elaborate terms, which the traveler can reject by canceling the reservation. To use the ticket is to accept the terms, even terms that in retrospect are disadvantageous.

Consumer goods work the same way. Someone who wants to buy a radio visits a store, pays, and walks out with a box. Inside the box is a leaflet containing some terms, the most important of which usually is the warranty, read for the first time in the comfort of home. Drugs come with a list of ingredients on the outside and an elaborate package insert on the inside. The package insert describes drug interactions, contraindications, and other vital information—but, if Zeidenberg is right, the purchaser need not read the package insert, because it is not part of the contract.

What does the UCC have to say? We think that the place to start is § 2–204(1): "A contract for sale of goods may be made in any manner sufficient to show agreement, including conduct by both parties which recognizes the existence of such a contract." A vendor, as master of the offer, may invite acceptance by conduct, and may propose limitations on the kind of conduct that constitutes acceptance. A buyer may accept by performing the acts the vendor proposes to treat as acceptance.

And that is what happened. ProCD proposed a contract that a buyer would accept by *using* the software after having an opportunity to read the license at leisure. This Zeidenberg did. He had no choice because the software splashed the license on the screen and would not let him proceed without indicating acceptance. So although the district judge was right to say that a contract can be, and often is, formed simply by paying the price and walking out of the store, the UCC permits contracts to be formed in other ways. ProCD proposed such a different way, and without protest Zeidenberg agreed.

Ours is not a case in which a consumer opens a package to find an insert saying "you owe us an extra $10,000" and the seller files suit to collect. Any buyer finding such a demand can prevent formation of the contract by returning the package, as can any consumer who concludes that the terms of the license make the software worth less than the purchase price.

[The Seventh Circuit reversed the lower court and held for ProCD.]

If ProCD had lost its claim, we would live in a very different world because most online and e-commerce contracts would not be enforceable. Remember that next time you click to agree to a contract.[5]

21-3b Statute of Frauds

UCC §2-201 requires a writing for any sale of goods of $500 or more. However, under the UCC, the writing need not summarize the agreement completely, and it need not even be entirely accurate. Once again, the Code is modifying the common law rule, permitting parties to enforce deals with less formality. In some cases, the court grants an exception and enforces an agreement with no writing at all. Here are the rules.

Contracts for Goods of $500 or More

Section 2-201 demands a writing for any contract of goods over this limit, meaning that virtually every significant sale of goods has some writing requirement. Remember that a contract for goods costing less than $500 is still covered by the UCC, but it may be oral.

Writing Sufficient to Indicate a Contract

The Code only requires a writing *sufficient to indicate* that the parties made a contract. In other words, the writing need not *be* a contract. A simple memo is enough, or a letter or informal note mentioning that the two sides reached an agreement is enough. **In general, the writing must be signed by the defendant,** that is, whichever party is claiming there was no deal. Dick signs and sends to Shirley a letter saying, "This is to acknowledge your agreement to buy all 650 books in my rare book collection for $188,000." Shirley signs nothing. A day later, Louis offers Dick $250,000. Is Dick free to sell? No. He signed the memo, it indicates a contract, and Shirley can enforce it against him.

Now reverse the problem. Suppose that, after Shirley receives Dick's letter, she decides against rare books in favor of original scripts from *The Big Bang Theory* television show. Dick sues. Shirley wins because *she* signed nothing

Incorrect or Omitted Terms

If the writing demonstrates the two sides reached an agreement, it satisfies §2-201 even if it omits important terms or states them incorrectly. Suppose Dick writes "$1888,000," indicating almost $2 million, when he meant to write "$188,000." The letter still shows that the parties made a deal, and the court will enforce it, relying on oral testimony to determine the correct price.

Enforceable Only to the Quantity Stated

Since the writing only has to indicate that the parties agreed, it need not state every term of their deal. But one term is essential: quantity. **The Code will enforce the contract only up to the quantity of goods stated in the writing.** This is logical, since a court can surmise other terms, such as price, based on market conditions. Buyer agrees to purchase pencils from Seller. The market value of the pencils is easy to determine, but a court would have no way of knowing whether Buyer meant to purchase 1,000 pencils or 100,000; the quantity must be stated.

Exceptions

In the following three circumstances, the UCC Statute of Frauds is "turned off."

Merchants. This is a major change from the common law. **When two merchants make an oral contract, and one sends a confirming memo to the other within a reasonable time, and the**

[5]We explored the evolution of contract formation online post-ProCD in Chapter 12 on offers and acceptances.

memo is sufficiently definite that it could be enforced against the sender herself, then the memo is also valid against the merchant who receives it, unless he objects within ten days. Laura, a tire wholesaler, signs and sends a memo to Scott, a retailer, saying, "Confm yr order today—500 tires cat #886—cat price." Scott realizes he can get the tires cheaper elsewhere and ignores the memo. Big mistake. Both parties are merchants, and Laura's memo is sufficient to bind her. So it also satisfies the Statute of Frauds against Scott, unless he objects within ten days.

Specially Made Goods. If a buyer orders goods that are to be specially manufactured for the buyer and are not suitable for sale to others in the ordinary course of the seller's business, then a verbal agreement is enforceable even if it exceeds $500. Catherine and Rohit order 700 engraved invitations to their wedding on April 1. When they decide to elope instead, the UCC Statute of Frauds will not excuse them from paying the printer. Since no one else could use these customized invitations, it is only fair to enforce a verbal agreement for their sale.

Judicial Admission. If a defendant admits in his pleading, testimony, or otherwise in court that a contract for sale was made, then the contract he admitted to is enforceable against him.

The following case examines all three of these exceptions in the context of an agreement to buy carpet and tile. When the Supreme Court of Virginia issued its ruling, one company was floored.

Code Provisions Discussed in This Case

Issue	Relevant Code Section
1. Is there a confirmatory memo?	UCC §2-201(2)
2. Has the buyer ordered specialty goods?	UCC §2-201(3)(a)
3. Did the buyer admit in its testimony that an agreement existed?	UCC §2-201(3)(b)

Delta Star, Inc. v. Michael's Carpet World

276 Va. 524
Supreme Court of Virginia, 2008

Facts: Ivan Tepper, the CEO of Delta Star, met with the sales manager at Michael's, a flooring company. In a verbal agreement, he hired Michael's to install carpet in the entryway of his office suite, and tile in his personal office and the office of Nash, his assistant.

Michael's faxed Delta Star a purchase order which read, "Carpet for entrance to lobby, $832.22." Michael's installed the carpet and Delta Star paid the $832.22. But, Delta Star sought to cancel part of the remaining work installing tile, and Michael's sued.

At trial, Delta Star argued that, because the tiling was priced at more than $500, the UCC Statute of Frauds made the agreement unenforceable. The trial court disagreed, holding that the tile was specially manufactured, because Michael's had never ordered that type of tile for a customer before. The lower court also determined that Delta Star had admitted the existence of the contract in its testimony, and that the purchase order amounted to a writing in any event. Michael's was awarded $2,565 in damages, and Delta Star appealed.

Issue: ***Was the contract enforceable?***

Excerpts from Judge Stephenson's Decision: We first consider the trial court's finding that the flooring materials were specially manufactured goods or products for [Delta Star] and not readily suitable for sale [to] others in the ordinary course of [Michael's] business. The flooring materials chosen by Delta Star were selected from samples displayed, were not altered in any way to suit only Delta Star, and were suitable for sale to others in Michael's ordinary course of business. Therefore, the flooring materials were not "specifically manufactured" for Delta Star.

We next consider the trial court's finding that there exists a confirmatory writing establishing an enforceable contract. We do not agree that such a writing exists. At trial, Michael's contended that its invoice for the purchase and installation of flooring in Delta Star's entryway constituted confirmatory writings. [It] cannot serve as confirmation of a contract for the purchase and installation of flooring in Tepper's office. The invoice confirms only the parties' agreement with regard to the entryway flooring.

Finally, we consider the trial court's ruling that Delta Star admitted in its testimony the existence of a contract for the purchase and installation of flooring in Tepper's office. At trial, Michael's contended that Nash's testimony regarding her attempt to cancel that portion of the alleged contract dealing with Tepper's office constituted an admission that a contract existed because "you can't cancel something unless you're admitting that you got a contract and you want to cancel it." Delta Star contends that Nash did not admit that there existed a contract for the purchase and installation of flooring in Tepper's office.

We agree with Delta Star. A review of Nash's trial testimony reveals that she stated that Delta Star "didn't want to act on the estimate" [and] that Delta Star "hadn't agreed to ... order [the flooring for Tepper's office] yet." Therefore, Nash did not admit the existence of a contract for the purchase and installation of flooring in Tepper's office.

For the foregoing reasons, we hold that the trial court erred in overruling Delta Star's Statute of Frauds defense and in finding that an enforceable contract existed between Michael's and Delta Star for the purchase and installation of flooring in Tepper's office.

Reversed.

21-3c Added Terms: Section 2-207

Under the common law's mirror image rule, when one party makes an offer, the offeree must accept those exact terms. If the offeree adds or alters any terms, the acceptance is ineffective and the offeree's response becomes a counteroffer. In one of its most significant modifications of contract law, the UCC changes that result. **Under §2-207, an acceptance that adds or alters terms will often create a contract.** The Code has made this change in response to *battles of the form*. Every day, corporations buy and sell millions of dollars of goods using pre-printed forms. The vast majority of all contracts involve such documents. Typically, the buyer places an order using a pre-printed form, and the seller acknowledges with its own pre-printed acceptance form. Because each form contains language favorable to the party sending it, the two documents rarely agree. The Code's drafters concluded that the law must cope with real practices.

We discussed §2-207 in detail in Chapter 12 and summarize it here only to emphasize how it works with other UCC provisions. The section is confusing, and a diagram helps. **For a schematic look at UCC §2-207, see Exhibit 21.1.**

Intention

The parties must still *intend* to create a contract. Section 2-207 is full of exceptions, but there is no change in this basic requirement of contract law. If the differing forms indicate that the parties never reached an agreement, there is no contract.

Additional or Different Terms

An offeree may include a new term in his acceptance and still create a binding deal. Suppose Breeder writes to Pet Shop, offering to sell 100 guinea pigs at $2 each. Pet Shop emails saying, "We agree to buy 100 g.p. We get credit for any unhealthy pig." Pet Shop has added a new term, concerning unhealthy pigs, but the parties *have* created a binding contract because the writings show they intended an agreement. Now the court must decide what the terms of the contract are, since there is some discrepancy. The first step is to decide whether the new language is an *additional term* or a *different term*.

EXHIBIT 21.1

UCC §2-207

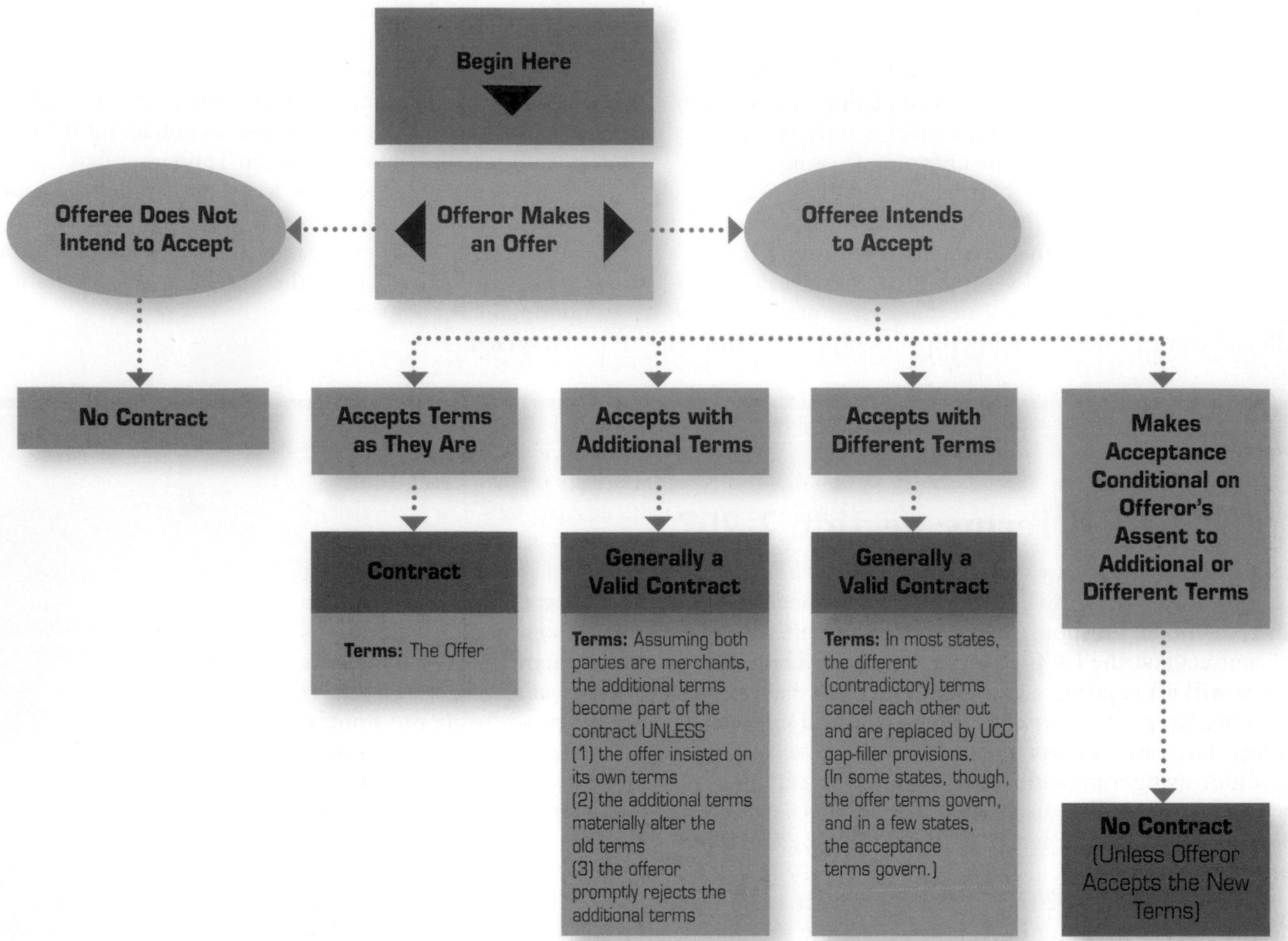

Additional terms
Proposed contract terms that raise issues not included in the offer

Additional Terms. **Additional terms** are those that raise issues not covered in the offer. The "unhealthy pig" issue is an additional term because the offer said nothing about it. **When both parties are *merchants*, additional terms generally become part of the bargain.** Pet Shop's insistence on credit for sick guinea pigs is binding on Breeder. In three circumstances, however, additional terms *do not* bind the parties:

1. If the original offer *insisted on its own terms*. If Breeder offered the pets for sale "on these and no other terms," Pet Shop's additional language would not become part of their deal.
2. If the additional terms *materially alter* the offer. Pet Shop's new language about credit for unhealthy animals is fairly uncontroversial. But suppose Pet Shop wrote

back, "Breeder is liable for any illness of any animal in Pet Shop within 90 days of shipment of guinea pigs." Breeder would potentially have to pay for a $500 iguana with pneumonia or a $6,000 parrot with gout. This is a material alteration of the bargain and is not part of the contract.

3. If the offeror *promptly objects* to the new terms. If Breeder received Pet Shop's email and immediately called up to say "No credit for unhealthy pigs," then Pet Shop's additional term is not part of their deal.

In all other circumstances, additional terms do become part of an agreement between merchants.

Different Terms. Different terms are terms that *contradict* those in the offer. Suppose Brilliant Corp. orders 1,500 cellular phones from Makem Co., for use by Brilliant's sales force. Brilliant places the order using a pre-printed form stating that the product is fully warranted for normal use and that seller is liable for compensatory *and consequential* damages. This means, for example, that Makem could be liable for lost profits if a salesman's phone fails during a lucrative sales pitch. Makem responds with its own memo stating that, in the event of defective phones, Makem is liable only to repair or replace, and *is not liable for consequential damages, lost profits, or any other damages.*

Makem's acceptance has included a *different* term because its language contradicts the offer. Almost all courts would agree that the parties intended to reach an agreement and therefore the contract is enforceable. The question is, what are its terms? Is the full warranty of the offer included, or the very limited warranty of the acceptance? The majority of states hold that different terms cancel each other out. Neither party's language goes into the contract. But what then *are* the terms of the deal?

If the evidence indicates that the parties had orally agreed on the issue disputed in the forms, then the courts will ignore the contradictory writings and enforce the oral contract. **If there is no clear oral agreement, the Code supplies its own terms, called gap-fillers,** which cover prices, delivery dates and places, warranties, and other subjects. In the cellular phone case, the contradicting warranty provisions cancel each other out. The parties had not orally agreed on a warranty, so a court would enforce the Code's gap-filler warranty, which does permit recovery of compensatory and consequential damages. Therefore, Makem *would* be liable for lost profits. We outline most of the gap-filler terms in Chapter 12. Warranty provisions are analyzed in greater detail in Chapter 22.

In the following case, the Rhode Island Supreme Court seeks the fairest method of sorting out conflicting terms.

Code Provisions Discussed in This Case

Issue	Relevant Code Section
1. Which are the terms of this agreement?	UCC §2-207: *Additional* terms generally but not always become part of the bargain. *Different* terms generally cancel each other out.
2. What is the Code's provision concerning delivery?	UCC §2-309: The time for shipment or delivery if not agreed upon is a reasonable time.
3. What is a "reasonable" delivery time?	UCC §1-204: A "reasonable" time depends on the nature, purpose, and circumstances of the action.

Superior Boiler Works, Inc. v. R. J. Sanders, Inc.

711 A2d 628
Rhode Island Supreme Court, 1998

Facts: R. J. Sanders, Inc., had a contract with the federal government to install the heating system at a federal prison camp. The company negotiated with Superior Boiler Works to purchase three large commercial units. On March 27, Superior sent a proposal to Sanders, offering to sell three boilers for a total of $156,000 and estimating time of delivery at four weeks. The parties exchanged further documents and held various discussions. Finally, on July 20, Sanders sent a "purchase order" for three boilers, agreeing to pay $145,827 and stating "Date required: 4 Weeks," that is, August 20. On August 6, Superior sent a "sales order," agreeing to sell the three boilers at that price, but providing a shipping date of October 1. This later delivery date forced Sanders to rent temporary boilers at a cost of $45,315. On October 1, Superior shipped the boilers, which arrived on October 5. Sanders sent a check in the amount of $100,000, claiming that Superior had delivered the boilers late and deducting the cost of its rental equipment. Superior sued for the additional $45,000 and moved for summary judgment, which the trial court granted. Sanders appealed, claiming that the contract had required Superior to deliver the boilers within four weeks.

Issue: ***Did Superior's October delivery breach the contract?***

Excerpts from Justice Flanders's Decision: Sanders' amended purchase order of July 20 and Superior's August 6 response agree exactly on the specifications and on the price of the boilers. The fact that these two documents disagree on one important term—the time for delivery—does not prevent the formation of a contract under the UCC because it is apparent from their subsequent conduct that both parties intended to be bound contractually. What becomes of the parties' conflicting positions on the shipment period (Sanders' specified four-week delivery versus Superior's stated October 1 shipping date) is a question that must be considered in light of section 2-207(2).

[The court mentioned that other states had responded in various ways to "different" terms, that is, those that conflict. Judge Flanders declared that Rhode Island would side with the majority and adopt the "knock-out" rule, meaning that conflicting terms knock each other out, leaving a hole in the contract that is filled by one of the Code's gap-filler provisions.] Here, the void relating to delivery time would be filled by Section 2-309, which reads, "The time for shipment or delivery ... if ... not agreed upon shall be a reasonable time."

Because of the UCC's gap-filling provisions, we recognize that this approach might result in the enforcement of a contract term that neither party agreed to and, in fact, in regard to which each party expressed an entirely different preference. We note in response to this concern that the offeror and the offeree both have the power to protect any term they deem critical by expressly making acceptance conditional on assent to that term. And as merchants, both parties should have been well aware that their dealings were subject to the UCC and to its various gap-filling provisions. In this case, because the two variant shipping-date terms cancel each other out, the amended purchase order and the August 6 sales order formed a contract that required the three boilers to be delivered within a reasonable period after August 6.

In the usual case the question of what constitutes a reasonable time under the UCC is one for the finder of fact to determine from the nature, the purpose, and the circumstances surrounding the transaction, including the parties' course of dealing, usages of trade in the pertinent industry, or the parties' course of performance. See [UCC §1-204(2). In this case, however, the only available evidence indicated that Superior's performance was reasonable, by industry standards.]

For the foregoing reasons the appeal is denied, and the Superior Court's judgment is affirmed.

EXAMStrategy

Question: Martin, a diamond wholesaler, writes Serge, a jewelry retailer, offering to sell 75 specified diamonds for $2 million. Martin's offer sheet specifies the price, quantity, date of delivery, and other key terms. The sheet also states, "Offer is made on these terms and no other." Serge sends Martin his own purchase order, naming the diamonds, price, and so forth, but adding a clause requiring any disputes to be settled by a diamond-industry arbitrator. In the diamond industry, arbitration by such a person is standard. Martin does not object to the arbitration clause. Martin delivers the gems but Serge refuses to pay the full price, claiming that many of the stones are of inferior quality. Martin sues for the balance due, but Serge insists that any dispute must be settled by arbitration. May Martin litigate, or must he arbitrate the case?

Strategy: Under the common law, there might not be a contract between these parties, because Serge added a new term. However, this agreement concerns the sale of goods, meaning that the UCC governs. Under UCC §2-207, when both parties are merchants (as they are here), additional terms become part of the contract except in three instances. Review those three instances, and apply them here.

Result: Additional terms become part of the agreement unless the original offeror insisted on its own terms, the new term materially alters the offer, or the offeror promptly rejects the new term. Martin's offer insisted on its own terms and Serge's arbitration clause does not become part of the agreement. Martin may litigate his dispute.

21-3d Open Terms: Sections 2-305 and 2-306

Open Prices

Under §2-305, the parties may conclude a contract even though they have not settled the price. Again, this is a change from the common law, which required certainty of such an important contract term. Under the Code, if the parties have not stated one, **the price is a reasonable price at the time of delivery.** A court will use market value and other comparable sales to determine what a reasonable price would have been. If the contract permits the buyer or seller to *determine* the price during contract performance, §2-305 requires that she do so in good faith.

EXAMStrategy

Question: Coffee Retailer sends a form to Cupper, ordering 100 cartons of specified coffee cups to be delivered the first of each month for six months. The order form says nothing about price. For three months, Cupper delivers on time and sends an invoice, which Retailer pays. On the fourth month, Cupper's invoice is 8 percent higher than before. Retailer refuses to pay the increase and informs Cupper that it will accept no more deliveries. Cupper sues. Retailer claims there was no enforceable contract. Cupper says there was a bargain and that it has the right to determine the price. Who is right?

Strategy: Retailer's offer included no price. Under the common law, the absence of such an essential term would mean there was no contract. However, these are goods, and, under the UCC, the parties can make an enforceable deal without specifying the price. This is a valid contract. The companies may, if they choose, permit one party to determine the price. Did they do so here? If so, is Cupper's conduct reasonable? If the parties did not allow one side to set the price, how would a court do so?

Result: This contract neither stated a price nor allowed one party to determine it. That means that the price is a reasonable one at the time of delivery. A court will use market value, and any comparable sales, to determine the price.

21-3e Output and Requirements Contracts

Under §2-306, an output contract obligates the seller to sell all of his output to the buyer, who agrees to accept it. Suppose Joel has a small plant in which he manufactures large plants; that is, handcrafted artificial flowers and trees, made of silk and other materials. Joel is not sure how many he can produce in a year, but he wants a guaranteed market. He makes an output contract with Yolanda, in which he promises to sell the entire output of his plant, and she agrees to buy it all.

A requirements contract is the reverse, obligating a buyer to purchase all his needed goods from the seller. Joel might sign a requirements contract with Worm Express, agreeing to buy from Worm all the silk he needs. Both output and requirements contracts are valid under the Code, although they create certain problems. By definition, the exact quantity of goods is not specified. But then how much may one party demand? Is there any upper or lower limit?

The UCC requires that the parties in an output or requirements contract make their demands in good faith. For example, in a requirements contract, a buyer may not suddenly increase her demand far beyond what the parties expected merely because there has been a market change. Suppose the price of silk skyrockets. Joel's requirements contract obligates Worm Express to sell him all the silk he needs. Could Joel demand ten times the silk he had anticipated, knowing he could resell it at a big profit to other manufacturers? No. That would be bad faith. Come on, Joel, play by the rules.

May the buyer *reduce* his demand far below what the parties anticipated? Yes, as long as he makes the reduction in good faith.

The following case involves several issues, including a claim that an output contract existed. Some contracts are meticulously written by veteran lawyers who use deliberate and precise legal terms in every part of the agreement. Of course, agreements are not always done so carefully. See what sense you can make of the "Weaner Pig Purchase Agreement."

Code Provisions Discussed in This Case

Issue	Relevant Code Section
1. Which law governs this agreement?	UCC §2-102
2. Is there a writing sufficient to indicate a contract?	UCC §2-201
3. Was an output contract formed?	UCC §2-306

You Be the Judge

Lohman v. Wagner

862 A2d 1042
Court of Special Appeals of Maryland, 2004

Facts: Legal research can take you in odd directions. Today, for example, we learn that a "weaner pig" is a very young pig that has just been weaned from its mother. You must raise and sell a lot of them to make a living. Farmers who raise pigs to full size need to sell fewer animals to get by.

Farmer Charles Lohman talked extensively with John Wagner about raising weaner pigs for a new "pork network" that Wagner, the owner of Swine Services, was thinking of putting together. Lohman eventually decided to join Wagner and convert his pig farm to one that specialized

Weaner pigs are usually about eight weeks old when they are sold.

in raising weaner pigs. He needed to borrow money to remodel his farm, and he needed to convince his bankers that, if they loaned him the necessary money, he would be in a reasonable position to repay them.

He told Wagner that he "would need something to show his banker." Wagner faxed over a document with several blanks entitled "Weaner Pig Purchase Agreement." It said, in part, "PRODUCER agrees to supply ______________ weaner pigs weekly." When he received the fax, Lohman wrote "300" in the blank. After showing the fax to his banker, Lohman was able to secure his loan. He never sent Wagner a copy of the document with the blank filled in.

For a while, everyone was happy. Lohman shipped weaner pigs to Wagner and was paid $28 each for them. But eventually, problems arose. The price Wagner offered for weaner pigs dropped to $18, and Wagner never assembled the promised pork network, which Lohman argued would have helped to boost prices. Lohman sued Wagner for breach of contract.

The trial court found that the agreement did not meet the UCC's requirement that a quantity term be included, that it was unenforceable, and that Lohman was entitled to nothing. Lohman appealed.

You Be the Judge: *Does Lohman have an enforceable agreement with Wagner?*

Argument for Lohman: Your honor, I won't "boar" you with a long story. Our arguments, briefly stated, are these.

First, the UCC's Statute of Frauds, and its requirement that a quantity term be included, should not apply. This agreement is essentially one for services, and not for goods. My client furnishes housing for weaner pigs, labors to raise them, and ships them to the defendant. His services are the largest part of this contract.

Even if this contract is deemed to be a sale of goods, there is a quantity term included in the Weaner Pig Purchase Agreement—300. The number was entered by my client as a good-faith estimate of the number of animals he could produce.

In any event, UCC 2-306 does not require a quantity term in this case. This agreement was an output contract. Lohman sold every weaner pig he produced to Wagner, and Wagner accepted and paid for them. Output contracts, by definition, do not include specific quantity terms; they merely obligate a seller to sell all of his output to the buyer.

This case amounts to nothing more or less than a greedy man trying to reap what he did not sow and to use legal technicalities to hog all the profits for himself.

Argument for Wagner: My counterpart has managed to make several nifty pig-related references in his argument, but nevertheless, no contract exists. The UCC does apply to this agreement, because pigs are clearly goods. Most products require some labor to assemble and bring to market. Someone "labored" to make my shoes, my necktie, and my pen. But all are goods.

In a UCC contract, a quantity must be written by the defendants, but here the "300" was written by the plaintiff. It was never communicated to my client. He never agreed to it, or even had a chance to review it. The same holds true for the claim that this is an output contract. My client never agreed to buy all the pigs that Lohman produced.

My opponent is grasping at straws. Which pigs eat. I think. Get it? Oh, forget it….

21-3f Modification

Another way in which the UCC is pro-contract and pro-business is in its treatment of contract modifications. If two sides have a contract and seek to make changes, are the changes enforceable?

Example 1. Being the best at almost anything pays well, and soccer is no exception. Cristiano Ronaldo's contract with the Real Madrid soccer club runs through 2021 and averages a whopping $50 million per season. Assume that this year he leads Real to the fabled treble—a La Liga championship, a victory in the Copa del Rey, and a win in the Champions League. Afterward, the club offers him a raise to $60 million per season through 2021, and Ronaldo accepts. If Spanish law is the same as American law, does the team have a legal obligation to pay the extra millions? No.

This is a services contract, and not a sale of goods. Therefore, common law principles would apply, and they require new consideration for contract modifications to stand. Since Ronaldo did not agree to play any additional seasons or give any other new value to the team, no consideration exists.

We hate to leave out fans of Spain's other big club, so, for the next example, we will pay our 85 euros for a ticket on the AVE train and settle in for a three-hour trip eastward to Barcelona.

Example 2. FC Barcelona is planning "Lionel Messi Bobblehead Day," and the team orders 10,000 units for the occasion. Unfortunately, the boat carrying the shipment from China is boarded by Somali pirates and the entire shipment is stolen.

The manufacturer calls the team and asks for a three-week extension on the original delivery deadline. The team is very understanding, agrees to the delay, and reschedules the promotion for a later game. Is this modification to extend the delivery date now a valid part of the contract? Yes.

In §2-209, the UCC does away with the consideration requirement for changes to contracts, so long as both sides agree to the modification. In this example, no consideration exists to support the extended deadline because the manufacturer gets all the benefit, and the team gets nothing. But, that does not create a problem in enforcing the new deal.

Parties make a contract attempting to control their futures. But one party's certainty can be undercut by the ease with which the other party may obtain a modification. Section 2-209 acknowledges this tension by enabling the parties to limit changes. The UCC allows the parties to modify some contracts orally, but **they may agree to prohibit oral modifications and insist that all modifications be in writing and signed. Between merchants, such a clause is valid. But if either party is *not* a merchant, such a clause is valid only if the non-merchant *separately* signs it.**

Once again the Code gives greater protection to non-merchants than to merchants. As part of their bargain, two merchants may agree that any future modifications will be valid only if written and signed. But this limitation on modifications is not valid against a non-merchant unless she separately signs the limiting clause itself. Suppose a furniture retailer orders 200 beds from a manufacturer. The retailer's order form requires any modifications to be in writing. The manufacturer initials the retailer's form at the bottom. The parties have a valid agreement and no oral modifications will be enforced. But suppose the retailer sells a bed to a customer. The sales form also bars oral modifications. That prohibition is void unless the customer separately signs it.

EXAMStrategy

Question: Dale turns 18. For his birthday, he gets $500 cash and his grandmother's ancient station wagon. And yes, it is the kind with wood paneling on the side. Dale cannot do much about how the car looks, but he decides that he can at least make it sound awesome. So, he immediately takes the car to Big Mike's Custom Stereo.

At Big Mike's, Dale makes a verbal agreement to buy an amplifier and two Rockford Fosgate speakers and to have them installed at a cost of $499. The amp and speakers come to $420, and the installation charge is $79. He decides to have them installed while he waits.

After an hour, a clerk finds him and says, "Hey, man, we're out of stock on those speakers. But I can get you some Alpines right now—same size, same price, just as loud." Dale is eager to drive out with a new system, and agrees to the speaker substitution.

Moments later, Dale finds the clerk and says, "Wait, I'm not sure about all of this. I don't think I want to buy any of it after all." Can Dale get his money back, or is he stuck with his purchases?

Strategy: Under UCC principles, a contract is considered to be for the sale of goods if the value of the items far exceeds the cost of the labor (installation), and the contract's predominant purpose is a sale of goods. The UCC Statute of Frauds does not apply to a transaction under $500. A contract can be modified without consideration.

Result: The UCC governs this contract because the speakers are much more expensive than the labor. The contract does not have to be in writing because it is for less than $500. The agreement to use Alpine speakers rather than Rockford Fosgates is enforceable, even without consideration for the change. Dale will have to live with the deal, including the Alpine speakers.[6]

The following table concludes this chapter with an illustration of the Code's impact on the common law.

Selected Code Provisions That Change the Common Law

Issue	Common Law Rule	UCC Sec.	UCC Rule	Example
Contract formation	Offer must be followed by acceptance that shows meeting of the minds on all important terms.	§2-204 and §2-305	Contract can be made in any manner sufficient to show agreement; moment of making not critical; one or more terms, including the price, may be left open.	Tilly writes Meg, "I need a new van for my delivery company." Meg delivers a van and Tilly starts to use it. Under the common law, there is no contract because no price was ever mentioned; under the UCC, the writing plus the conduct show an intention to contract (§2-204). The price is a *reasonable* one (§2-305).
Writing requirement	All essential terms must be in writing.	§2-201	Any writing is sufficient if it indicates a contract; terms may be omitted or misstated; "merchant" exception can create a contract enforceable against a party who receives the writing and does nothing within ten days.	Douglas, a car dealer, signs and sends to Michael, another dealer, a memo saying, "Confirming our deal for your blue Rolls." Michael reads it but ignores it; ten days later Douglas has satisfied the Statute of Frauds under the UCC's merchant exception.

[6]Bonus point from Chapter 15 material: Since this is Dale's 18th birthday, if he were even one day younger, he could back out of this deal on the grounds that he is a minor and has formed a voidable agreement.

Issue	Common Law Rule	UCC Sec.	UCC Rule	Example
Added terms in acceptance	An acceptance that adds or changes any term is a counteroffer.	§2-207	Additional or different terms are not necessarily counteroffers; their presence does not prevent a contract from being formed, and in some cases the new terms will become a part of the bargain.	Roberts sends a pre-printed form to Julia, offering to buy 25 laptops and stating a price; Julia responds with her own pre-printed form, accepting the offer but adding a term that balances unpaid after 30 days incur a finance charge. The additional term is not a counteroffer; there is a valid contract; and the finance charge is part of the bargain.
Modification	A modification is valid only if supported by new consideration.	§2-209	A modification needs no consideration to be binding.	Martin, a computer manufacturer, agrees to sell Steve, a retailer, 500 computers at a specified price, including delivery. The next day Martin learns that his delivery costs have gone up 20%; he calls Steve, who emails a note agreeing to pay 15% extra. Under the common law, the modification would be void; under the Code, it is enforceable.

CHAPTER CONCLUSION

The Uniform Commercial Code enables parties to create a contract quickly. While this can be helpful in a fast-paced business world, it also places responsibility on businesspeople. Informal conversations may cause at least one party to conclude that it has a binding agreement—and the law may agree.

EXAM REVIEW

1. **UNIFORM COMMERCIAL CODE** The Code is designed to modernize commercial law and make it uniform throughout the country.

2. **SALE OF GOODS** Article 2 applies to the sale of goods, which are movable things other than money and investment securities.

EXAMStrategy

Question: While shopping at his local mall, Fred buys an iPad for $399, a barbecue grill for $509, and then pays $25 to have his watchband cleaned. Which of Fred's transactions are governed by Article 2 of the UCC?

Strategy: To answer this question, you must identify the transactions that amount to a sale of goods. Land and buildings are not goods. Neither are money and securities, but other movable physical objects are. Also, be sure not to confuse the question "Does Article 2 apply?" with the question "Does this agreement need to be in writing?" (See the "Result" at the end of this Exam Review section.)

3. **LEASING** Article 2A governs the leasing of goods.

4. **MIXED CONTRACTS** In a mixed contract involving goods and services, the UCC applies if the predominant purpose is the sale of goods.

5. **MERCHANTS** A merchant is someone who routinely deals in the particular goods involved, or who appears to have special knowledge or skill in those goods, or who uses agents with special knowledge or skill. The UCC frequently holds a merchant to a higher standard of conduct than a non-merchant.

6. **GOOD FAITH** The UCC imposes a duty of good faith in the performance of all contracts.

7. **UNCONSCIONABILITY** A contract is unconscionable if it is shockingly one-sided and fundamentally unfair. A court is much likelier to use unconscionability to protect a consumer than a business.

EXAMStrategy

Question: Jim Dan, Inc., owned a golf course that had trouble with crabgrass. Jim Dan bought 20 bags of Scotts Pro Turf Goosegrass/Crabgrass Control for $835 and applied it to the greens. The Pro Turf caused over $36,000 in damage to the greens. Jim Dan sued Scotts. Scotts defended by claiming that it sold the Pro Turf with a clearly written, easy-to-read disclaimer that stated that in the event of damage, the buyer's only remedy would be a refund of the purchase price. Jim Dan, Inc., argued that the clause was unconscionable. Please rule.

Strategy: There are two steps to deciding an issue of unconscionability. First, does the contract involve a consumer, or is this an agreement between two businesses? Second, is the agreement shockingly one-sided? (See the "Result" at the end of this Exam Review section.)

8. **FORMATION** UCC §2-204 permits the parties to form a contract in any manner that shows agreement.

9. **WRITING** For the sale of goods worth $500 or more, UCC §2-201 requires some writing that indicates an agreement. Terms may be omitted or misstated, but the contract will be enforced only to the extent of the quantity stated.

10. **MERCHANT EXCEPTION** When two merchants make an oral contract, and one sends a confirming memo to the other within a reasonable time, and the memo is sufficiently definite that it could be enforced against the sender herself, then the merchant who receives it will also be bound unless he objects within ten days.

11. **ADDITIONAL TERMS** UCC §2-207 governs an acceptance that does not "mirror" the offer. *Additional terms* usually, but not always, become part of the contract. *Different terms* contradict a term in the offer. When that happens, most courts reject both parties' proposals and rely on gap-filler terms.

EXAMStrategy

Question: Cookie Co. offered to sell Distrib Markets 20,000 pounds of cookies at $1.00 per pound, subject to certain specified terms for delivery. Distrib replied in writing as follows: "We accept your offer for 20,000 pounds of cookies at $1.00 per pound, weighing scale to have valid city certificate." Under the UCC:

(a) A contract was formed between the parties.

(b) A contract will be formed only if Cookie agrees to the weighing scale requirement.

(c) No contract was formed because Distrib included the weighing scale requirement in its reply.

(d) No contract was formed because Distrib's reply was a counteroffer.

Strategy: Distrib's reply included a new term. That means it is governed by UCC §2-207. Is the new term an additional term or a different term? An additional term goes beyond what the offeror stated. Additional terms become a part of the contract except in three specified instances. A different term contradicts one made by the offeror. Different terms generally cancel each other out. (See the "Result" at the end of this Exam Review section.)

12. **PRICE** Under UCC §2-305 a contract is enforceable even if the price is not stated. In such cases, the price must be reasonable.

13. **MODIFICATION** UCC §2-209 permits contracts to be modified even if there is no consideration. The parties may prohibit oral modifications, but such a clause is ineffective against a non-merchant unless she signed it.

RESULTS

2. Result: The purchases of the iPad and the barbecue grill are covered by Article 2 of the UCC. Both agreements involve goods. $500 is a figure that is relevant to whether the Statute of Frauds applies to the agreements, but it is not material to the threshold question of whether Article 2 applies in the first place. All sales of goods, from pencils to Ferraris, fall under Article 2. The watch cleaning is a service, and not a sale of goods. It is not governed by Article 2.

7. Result: This is a bargain between two businesses, and courts rarely find clauses in such agreements unconscionable. The assumption is that sophisticated businesspeople understand what they are getting into and are able to protect themselves. If Jim Dan could run a golf course, the company was sophisticated enough to understand the simple disclaimer in this contract. Scotts wins.

11. Result: (a). The "valid city certificate" phrase raises a new issue; it does not contradict anything in Cookie's offer. That means it is an additional term and becomes part of the deal unless Cookie insisted on its own terms, the additional term materially alters the offer, or Cookie promptly rejects it. Cookie did not insist on its terms, this is a minor addition, and Cookie never rejected it. The new term is part of a valid contract.

MULTIPLE-CHOICE QUESTIONS

1. For a contract governed by the UCC sales article, which one of the following statements is correct?
   (a) Merchants and non-merchants are treated alike.
   (b) The contract may involve the sale of any type of personal property.
   (c) The obligations of the parties to the contract must be performed in good faith.
   (d) The contract must involve the sale of goods for a price of $500 or more.
2. Which of the following transactions is *not* governed by Article 2 of the UCC?
   (a) Purchasing an automobile for $35,000
   (b) Leasing an automobile worth $35,000
   (c) Purchasing a sound system worth $501
   (d) Purchasing a sound system worth $499
3. Fred assembles computers in his garage and sells them. He makes an agreement with Alpha Company under which Alpha will deliver 100 keyboards. The agreement does not specify when payment is due. Which of the following is true?
   (a) Fred has no obligation to pay, because there was no "meeting of the minds" and no contract was formed.
   (b) Fred must pay within ten days of making the agreement.
   (c) Fred must pay within ten days of accepting the keyboards.
   (d) Fred must pay within a commercially reasonable time.

4. Under the UCC Statute of Frauds, a contract must be signed by the ______________ to count as being "in writing." Also, the ______________ of the goods must be written.
   (a) plaintiff; price
   (b) plaintiff; quantity
   (c) defendant; price
   (d) defendant; quantity

5. Assume that a contract is modified. New consideration must be present for the modification to be binding if the deal is governed by which of the following?
   (a) The common law
   (b) The UCC
   (c) Both A and B
   (d) Neither A nor B

CASE QUESTIONS

1. The Massachusetts Bay Transit Authority (MBTA) awarded the Perini Corp. a large contract to rehabilitate a section of railroad tracks. The work involved undercutting the existing track, removing the ballast and foundation, rebuilding the track, and disposing of the old material. Perini solicited an offer from Atlantic Track & Turnout Co. for Atlantic to buy whatever salvageable material Perini removed. Perini estimated the quantity of salvageable material that would be available. Atlantic offered to purchase "all available" material over the course of Perini's deal with the MBTA, and Perini accepted. But three months into the project, the MBTA ran short of money and told Perini to stop the undercutting part of the project. That was the work that made Perini its profit, so Perini requested that the MBTA terminate the agreement, which the agency did. By that point, Perini had delivered to Atlantic only about 15 percent of the salvageable material that it had estimated. Atlantic sued. What kind of contract do the parties have? Who should win and why?

2. Lara owns a used car lot. She emails Seth, a used car wholesaler who has a huge lot of cars in the same city. The email reads, "Confirming our agrmt—I pick any 15 cars from your lot—30% below blue book value." Seth reads the email, laughs, and deletes it. Two weeks later, Lara arrives and demands to purchase 15 of Seth's cars beneath marked value. Is he obligated to sell?

3. The Brugger Corp. owned a farm operated by Jason Weimer, who acted as the company's business agent. Tri-Circle, Inc., was a farm equipment company. On behalf of Brugger, Weimer offered to buy from Tri-Circle certain equipment for use on the farm. Tri-Circle accepted the offer, using a pre-printed form. The form included a finance charge for late payment. Weimer's offer had said nothing about finance charges, but he made no objection to the new term. Tri-Circle supplied the farm equipment but later alleged that Brugger had refused to pay for $12,000 worth of the supplies. Tri-Circle sued. In deciding whether Tri-Circle was entitled to finance charges, the court first inquired whether Brugger, Weimer, and Tri-Circle were merchants. Why did it look into that issue? *Were* they merchants?

4. Ohio Fresh Eggs (OFE) operated an egg farm. OFE and LandTech entered into a contract in which OFE promised to sell its chicken manure to LandTech. As to quantity, the contract read: "all available tonnage per year of manure. Specific quantity to be determined by and mutually agreeable [sic] both parties." When OFE failed to perform, LandTech sued for breach, arguing the parties had an enforceable contract under the UCC. Please rule.

5. A.C. Furniture (ACF) manufactured custom furniture for national restaurant chains. A representative of Arby's Restaurant Group emailed ACF an order for 4,500 chairs at $44 per chair, with detailed specifications of seat pads, model numbers, and Arby's signature colors. A year later, Arby's emailed a request for 3,300 more of the same chairs. ACF custom made 7,800 chairs to Arby's specs, but Arby's only purchased 1,117. ACF sued Arby's, but the restaurant chain argued that the parties never had an enforceable contract and moved to dismiss. Who wins and why?

DISCUSSION QUESTIONS

Apply the following facts to the first two questions below.

The publication of the original UCC in 1952 sparked an expansion of the Statute of Frauds in the United States to cover sales of goods of $500 or more. At about the same time (in 1954), the British Parliament repealed its long-standing Statute of Frauds as applied to sales of goods. Some have argued that we should scrap UCC §2-201 on the grounds that it encourages misdealing as much as it prevents fraud. Consider the following two hypotheticals:

(In the United States) Johnny is looking at a used Chevy Tahoe. He knows that the $7,000 price is a good one, but he wants to go online and see if he can find an even better deal. In the 20 minutes he has been with the car's current owner, the owner has received three phone calls about the car. Johnny wants to make sure that no one else buys the car while he is thinking the deal over, so he makes a verbal agreement to buy the car and shakes the seller's hand. He knows that because of the Statute of Frauds and the fact that nothing is in writing, he does not yet have any enforceable obligation to buy the car.

(In the United Kingdom) Nigel sells used Peugeots in Liverpool. When he senses interest from customers, he aggressively badgers them until they verbally commit to buy. If the customers later get cold feet and try to back out of the deal, he holds them to the verbal contracts. Because there is no longer a UCC-style Statute of Frauds in Britain, the buyers are stuck.

1. Rate the degree to which you believe Johnny and Nigel acted wrongfully. Did one behave more wrongfully than the other? If so, which one, and why?

2. Do you think that the UCC Statute of Frauds as it currently exists is more likely to prevent fraud, or is it more likely to encourage misunderstandings and deception? Why? Overall, is it sensible to require that purchases of big-ticket items be in writing before they are final?

3. The UCC was written by a group of scholars and adopted by elected state legislators. But many contracts that do not involve a sale of goods are still governed by old common law principles that have been created by judges over a period of centuries. Who makes for better lawmakers—judges or legislators? Do you prefer the way in which common law principles or UCC rules were created?

4. Gene and Martha Jannusch owned a food truck business. They verbally agreed to sell it to Lindsey and Louann Naffziger for $150,000. The Naffzigers paid an initial $10,000 deposit and took possession of all the concession equipment, including the truck, trailer, and cooking equipment. The remaining balance was to be paid when the buyers secured a loan. When the Naffzigers backed out of the deal, the Jannuschs sued. The buyers argued that there was never a contract because (1) the UCC did not apply to the sale of a food truck business and (2) the contract was missing essential terms. Rule.

5. This chapter revisits the idea of unconscionability. Courts will sometimes refuse to enforce deals that are, as UCC §2-302 states it, "shocking and fundamentally unfair." Consider the following two cases. In each, an electronics store sells an HDTV with a fair market value of $600 for $1500.

   a. Sale #1 is made to Ann. She has a terrible credit score and is willing to pay $1500 because the store offers to finance the television, and she has no other available credit.

   b. Sale #2 is made to Franklin J. Moneypenny, a very wealthy investment banker, on Christmas Eve. He knows the price is much too high, but he is in a big hurry to finish his last-minute shopping.

   In both cases, the consumers paid 2.5 times the fair value of the television. In your opinion, is either transaction unconscionable? If so, why? If not, why not?

CHAPTER 22

OWNERSHIP, RISK, AND WARRANTIES

This is the story of the Seated Woman with a Bent Left Leg. Only she knows where she went and what she saw between 1938 and 1963. The problem? She is a piece of work—*artwork*, that is.

Franz Friedrich Grunbaum was a famous Austrian Jewish songwriter and cabaret performer. In March of 1938, when the Nazis stormed into Austria, they caught Grunbaum and his wife at the Czech border and immediately imprisoned him at Dachau concentration camp. The law required Jews to submit a statement listing all of their property, so Mrs. Grunbaum filed the document, which included 81 drawings by modernist Egon Schiele.

The problem? She is a piece of work—*artwork*, that is.

Grunbaum died in Dachau in January of 1941, after performing a New Year's show for his fellow prisoners. At that time, Mrs. Grunbaum, who was still free, filed a death certificate claiming he had no property and making no mention of the art. Mrs. Grunbaum was arrested by the Nazis on October 5, 1942, and died shortly thereafter in a Minsk concentration camp. Nothing else is known about the whereabouts of the drawings at that time.

Fast-forward 65 years: A drawing entitled "Seated Woman with Bent Left Leg" went up for auction at the famed Sotheby's auction house. Its alleged owner, David Bakalar, claimed to have purchased it in good faith for $4,300 from a reputable art dealer in 1963. But the winning bid of $675,000 was suddenly withdrawn when Milos Vavra and Leon Fischer, Grunbaum's heirs, sent a letter claiming that Bakalar was not the Seated Woman's rightful owner—because the Nazis had stolen it from their family. Would Bakalar have to take a backseat to the heirs' ownership claims?[1]

[1] Based on Bakalar v. Vavra, 500 Fed. Appx. 6 (2nd Cir. 2012).

Who owns the drawing? Grunbaum's heirs wanted it back. But 44 years earlier, Bakalar had paid good money for it, without knowledge of its tumultuous past. Both parties to this lawsuit are unhappy, but fortunately for us, they have illustrated the theme for our chapter: When two parties claim a conflicting legal interest in particular goods, *who wins?* Who obtains the law's protection? These are disputes over *conflicting interests in goods*.

An interest is a legal right in something. More than one party can have an interest in particular goods. Suppose you lease a new car from a dealer, agreeing to pay $400 per month for three years. Several parties will have legal interests in the car. The dealer still *owns* the car—interest number one. At the end of three years, the dealer gets it back. For three years, you have the *use* of the car—interest number two. You may use the car for all normal purposes, and you are obligated to make monthly payments. Your payments go to a finance agency, which has made an arrangement with the dealer to obtain the right to your $400 monthly payment. The finance agency has a *security interest* in the car—interest number three. If you fail to pay on time, the finance company has the right to repossess your car. If you take the car to a garage for maintenance, the garage has *temporary possession* of the car—interest number four. The garage has the right to keep the car locked up overnight, to work on it, and to test drive it. Sometimes legal interests clash, and it is those conflicts we look at here.

Often the parties will claim ownership, each arguing that his interest is stronger than the other's. But in this chapter, we also consider cases where each party argues that the *other* one owns the goods. Suppose a seller manufactures products for a buyer, but while the goods are being shipped, they are destroyed in a fire. The seller may argue that it no longer owned the goods, and the fire is the buyer's misfortune. But the buyer will claim it had not yet acquired the items.

In other cases, a *third party* will be involved. You pay $30,000 cash to buy a new car and expect to pick it up in three days. But the day before you arrive, the dealer's bank seizes all of the cars on the lot, claiming the dealer has defaulted on loans. Now the fight over legal interest is between you and the bank, with the dealer a relatively passive observer.

22-1 LEGAL INTEREST AND TITLE

Historically, courts settled disputes about legal interest by looking at one thing: title. But the drafters of the UCC concluded that "title" was too abstract an answer for the assorted practical questions that arose. It sometimes could be hard to prove exactly who did have title, and it made no sense to settle a wide variety of business problems with one legal idea. Today, title is only one of several issues that a court will use to resolve conflicting interests in goods. *Identification* and *insurable interest* have become more important, and title has diminished in significance. We can begin to understand all three doctrines if we examine how title passes from seller to buyer.

22-1a Existence and Identification

Title in goods can pass from one person to another only if the goods exist and have been identified to the contract.

Existence

Goods must exist before title can pass.[2] Although most goods do exist when people buy and sell them, some have not yet come into being, such as crops to be grown later or goods that have not yet been manufactured. A farmer may contract to sell corn even before it is planted, but title to the corn cannot pass until it actually exists.

---

[2]UCC §2-105 (2).

Identification

Goods must be identified to the contract before title can pass.[3] This means that the parties must have designated the specific goods being sold. Often, identification is obvious. If Dealer agrees to sell to Buyer a 60-foot yacht with identification number AKX472, the parties have identified the goods. But suppose Paintco agrees to sell Brushworks 1,000 gallons of white base paint at a specified price. Paintco has 25,000 gallons in its warehouse. Title cannot pass until Paintco identifies the specific gallons that will go to Brushworks.

The parties may agree in their contract how and when they will identify the goods.[4] They are free to identify them to the contract in any way they want. Paintco and Brushworks might agree, for example, that within one week of signing the sales agreement, Paintco will mark appropriate gallons. If the gallons are stored 50 to a crate, then Paintco will have a worker stick a "Brushworks" label on 20 crates. Once the label is on, the goods are identified to the contract.

If the parties do not specify any particular method, identification will occur according to these rules:

- Identification occurs when the parties enter into a contract if the agreement describes specific goods that already exist. If the Dealer agrees to sell a yacht and the parties include the ID number in their contract, the goods are identified (even though the parties never use the term *identify*).
- For unborn animals, identification generally takes place when they are conceived; for crops, identification normally happens when they are planted.
- For other goods, identification occurs when the seller marks, ships, or in some other way indicates the *exact* goods that are going to the buyer.[5]

Zeljko Radojko/Shutterstock.com

Identification for crops generally happens when they are planted. Thus, they are identified before they have grown and produced their yield.

EXAMStrategy

Question: Arielle, an artist, has 25 hand-painted room screens in her studio. She contracts to sell five of them to Retailer for $5,000 each. The contract allows Arielle to choose which five she will sell. Arielle moves five screens from her studio to a warehouse, but a week later, a fire destroys the building and its contents. Two insurance companies dispute whether title to the screens has passed to Retailer. The warehouse insurer claims the goods were identified and title passed; Retailer's insurer says the goods were not identified and title never passed. The contract says nothing about identification. Have the goods been identified?

Strategy: Title cannot pass until the goods have been identified to the contract. Identification can occur in three ways: The parties describe specific goods that already exist, animals are conceived or crops planted, or the seller marks, ships, or otherwise indicates which are going to the buyer. Did any of those things happen?

Result: The parties never described the goods. The goods are neither animals nor crops. However, when Arielle moved five of the screens to the warehouse, she "indicated which goods were going to the buyer." The goods were identified.

3UCC §2-401 (1).
4UCC §2-501 (1).
5UCC §2-501.

22-1b Passing of Title

Once goods exist and are identified to the contract, ownership can pass from one person to another. **Title may pass in any manner on which the parties agree (UCC §2-401).** Once again, the Code allows the parties to control their affairs with commonsense decisions. The parties can agree, for example, that title passes when the goods leave the manufacturer's factory or when they reach the shipper who will transport them or at any other time and place. If the parties do not agree on passing title, §2-401 decides. There are three possibilities:

1. *When the goods are being moved,* title passes to the buyer when the seller completes whatever transportation it is obligated to do. Suppose the Seller is in Milwaukee and the Buyer is in Honolulu. The contract requires the Seller to deliver the goods to a ship in San Francisco. Title passes when the Seller completes its last *contractually required* step. In this example, that happens when the goods reach the ship in San Francisco.
2. *When the goods are* not *being moved and a contract calls for delivery of ownership documents,* title passes when the seller delivers these documents to the buyer. Suppose Seller, located in Louisville, has manufactured 5,000 baseball bats, which are stored in a warehouse in San Diego. Under the terms of their contract, Buyer will take possession of the bats at the warehouse. When Seller gives Buyer ownership documents, title passes.
3. *When the goods are* not *being moved and the contract does* not *call for delivery of ownership documents,* title passes when the parties form the contract. For example, if the Buyer owns the warehouse where the bats are stored, Buyer needs no documents to take possession; title passes when the parties reach agreement.

22-1c Insurable Interest

Closely related to identification and title is the idea of insurable interest. Anyone buying or selling expensive goods should make certain that the goods are insured. There are some limits, though, on who may insure goods, and when. As we saw in Chapter 13, a party may insure something such as property or a human life only when she has a legitimate interest in it. If the person buying the policy lacks a real interest in the thing insured, the law regards the policy as a gambling agreement and considers it void.

When does someone have an insurable interest in goods? The UCC gives one answer for buyers and one for sellers. **A buyer obtains an insurable interest when the goods are identified to the contract (UCC §2-501).** Suppose that in January, Grain Broker contracts with Farmer to buy his entire wheat crop. Neither party mentions "identification." In January, the crop is not identified and Broker has no insurable interest. In May, after weeks of breaking the soil, Farmer plants his wheat crop. Once he has planted it, the goods are identified. The Broker now has an insurable interest and purchases insurance. In July, a drought destroys the crop, and the Broker never gets one grain of wheat. The Broker need not worry: His insurance policy will cover his losses.

The seller's insurable interest is different. **The seller retains an insurable interest in goods as long as she has either title to the goods or a security interest in them (UCC §2-501).** "Security interest" refers to cases in which the buyer still owes money for the goods and the seller can repossess the goods if payment is not made. Suppose Flyola Manufacturing sells a small aircraft to WingIt, a dealer, for $300,000. WingIt pays $30,000 cash and agrees to pay interest on the balance until it sells the plane. Flyola has an insurable interest even while the aircraft is in WingIt's showroom and may purchase insurance anytime until WingIt pays off the last dime.

And so, a seller and a buyer can have an insurable interest in the same goods simultaneously. Suppose the heavy-metal band Flulike Symptoms hires Inkem Corp., in Minneapolis, to make 25,000 T-shirts with the band's logo, for sale at rock concerts. The parties agree that the T-shirts are identified as soon as the logo is printed, and that title will pass when Inkem delivers the T-shirts to the office of the Symptoms' manager in Kansas City. Inkem obviously has an insurable interest while the company is making the T-shirts and continues to have an interest until it delivers the T-shirts in Kansas City. But the Flulike Symptoms' insurable interest arises the moment their logo is stamped on each shirt, so the Symptoms could insure the goods while they are still stored in Inkem's factory. Why would the Symptoms spend hard-earned cash to insure goods they do not have? They may be uncertain that Inkem has obtained proper insurance.

In the following case, a car accident leads several insurance companies to dispute who owned the damaged auto. Each company wants to claim that the car belonged to—someone *else*.

Code Provisions Discussed in This Case

Issue	Relevant Code Section
1. Which party had title to the car?	UCC §2-401: Title to goods may pass in any manner on which the parties agree.
2. Did the seller have an insurable interest in the car?	UCC §2-501: The seller retains an insurable interest in the goods as long as it holds title to or a security interest in them.

Valley Forge Insurance Co. v. Great American Insurance Co.

1995 Ohio App. LEXIS 3939; 1995 WL 540128
Ohio Court of Appeals, 1995

Facts: On a Friday afternoon, Karl and Linda Kennedy went to John Nolan Ford to buy a new Mustang. The parties signed all necessary documents, including a New Vehicle Buyer's Order, an Agreement to Provide Insurance, and credit applications. The Kennedys made a down payment, but they could not arrange financing before the dealership closed. John Nolan Ford determined that the Kennedys were creditworthy and allowed them to take the car home for the weekend. That evening, Karl Kennedy permitted his brother-in-law, Cella, to take the car for a drive, along with a passenger named Campbell. Cella wrecked the car, injuring his passenger. Campbell sued, and the question was which insurance company was liable: John Nolan Ford's insurer (Milwaukee Mutual), Cella's insurer (Valley Forge), or Kennedy's insurer (Great American). The trial court ruled that title had never passed to Kennedy and found Milwaukee Mutual liable. The insurance company appealed.

Issue: ***Had title passed to Kennedy at the time of the accident?***

Excerpts from the *Per Curiam* Decision: Milwaukee argues that the risk of loss and insurable interest had passed because the car had been delivered. Further, Milwaukee states that the Kennedys explicitly agreed to provide insurance. Great American counters that the parties had "otherwise explicitly agreed" in the New Vehicle Buyer's Order that any interest in the car would not pass until "either the full purchase price is paid in cash or a satisfactory deferred payment agreement is executed by the parties[.]" No financing had been arranged at the time of the accident.

Two terms of the New Vehicle Buyer's Order apply to the situation at bar. Under the "Agreement" provision, the contract states that "it is expressly agreed that the purchaser acquires no right, title or interest in or to the property which he agrees to purchase hereunder until such property is delivered to him and either the full purchase price is paid in cash or a satisfactory deferred payment agreement is executed by the parties hereto[.]"

Milwaukee also argues that the Kennedys explicitly agreed to provide insurance by signing the "Agreement to Provide Insurance." While the agreement does state that the Kennedys agreed to provide insurance, it is not clear when the Kennedys were to obtain the insurance. In fact, because the agreement refers to an "instalment [sic] contract," it is possible that the Kennedys were to provide insurance once a financing agreement was reached. In light of the fact that the agreement is ambiguous, we construe the contract strictly against the drafter and hold that any agreement to provide insurance was to take effect after financing was obtained.

We hold that because the parties had otherwise agreed that interest in the car, including insurable interest, would not pass until the financing was complete, John Nolan Ford still had the risk of loss and the insurable interest when the accident occurred. [Affirmed.]

22-1d Imperfect Title

Bona Fide Purchaser

Some people are sleazy, and sales law must accommodate that reality. Bad Guy Abe steals Marvin's BMW in the middle of the night and promptly sells it to Elaine for $35,000 cash. Two weeks later, the police locate the car. Abe skipped town, leaving a dispute between two innocent parties. Either the original owner (Marvin) or the buyer (Elaine) must bear the loss. Who loses?

The Question: Who Must Suffer the Loss?

Owner →	Bad Guy →	Buyer
Has valid title	Obtains goods from Owner and sells	Buys goods from Bad Guy

First, we need to know what kind of title Bad Guy obtains: Is it void or voidable? The key is this: Did Bad Guy *take* the item against the will of the owner, or did he fraudulently *trick* the owner into voluntarily handing the item to him?

When Abe stole it, he obtained void title, which is no title at all. When Bad Guy sells the goods to Buyer, she also gets *no title at all.* Elaine must return the car to Marvin and suffer the $35,000 loss for Abe's theft. This policy makes sense because Marvin has done nothing wrong. If the law permitted Elaine to get valid title, it would encourage theft.

In the chapter opener, Grunbaum's heirs argued that Bakalar had void title to the drawing because he had purchased artwork taken by the Nazis and a thief cannot pass good title. Unfortunately for their heirs, they were not able to prove that the drawing was indeed stolen: Bakalar introduced evidence that Mrs. Grunbaum's sister, Mathilde Lukacs, sold it to a Swiss dealer in 1956, a fact inconsistent with the heirs' Nazi loot theory. In the absence of evidence that the drawing was originally stolen, Grunbaum's heirs did not succeed in their claim.[6]

The outcome is different in the case of voidable title. If Bad Guy attempts to purchase the goods from Owner using fraud or deception, he obtains voidable title, meaning limited rights in the goods, inferior to those of the owner. The owner should be able to recover the goods from Bad Guy (if he can be found), but not from anyone else who ends up with them. Suppose the Swiss dealer had convinced Lukacs to part with the drawing through deceit. As a result, the devious dealer obtains only voidable title. If Lukacs learns of the fraud before the dealer sells the drawing to someone else, she will get her drawing back.

Now assume that before Lukacs caught on, the sneaky dealer sold it to Bakalar, who did not know of the Swiss swindle. Who keeps the drawing? Bakalar wins the artwork if he is a bona fide purchaser. **A person with voidable title has power to transfer valid title for value to a good faith purchaser, generally called a *bona fide purchaser* or *BFP*.**[7]

Voidable title
Limited rights in goods, inferior to those of the owner

The collector can prove that he is a bona fide purchaser by showing two things:

1. That he gave value for the goods *and*
2. That he acted in good faith.

---

[6] Bakalar v. Vavra, 500 Fed. Appx. 6 (2nd Cir. 2012).

[7] UCC §2-403(1).

It is generally easy for purchasers to show that they gave value. The real issue becomes whether the buyer acted in good faith. If Bakalar paid a reasonable purchase price and had no reason to suspect wrongdoing, he acted in good faith. Bakalar keeps the Seated Woman.

On the other hand, suppose Bakalar knew the drawing was worth much more than the dealer's $4,300 price. The Swiss dealer was in a frantic hurry to unload the drawing and would only meet in a dark alley in Zurich. The dealer would not produce any information about the provenance, or the origin, of the art. The dealer's conduct, together with the obvious discount, would make a reasonable person suspicious. In that case, the collector would not be acting in good faith and therefore is not a bona fide purchaser. The Grunbaum heirs would reclaim the drawing, and Bakalar would lose his $4,300.

Entrustment

Your old Steinway grand piano needs a complete rebuilding. You hire Fred Showpan, Inc., a company that repairs and sells instruments. Showpan hauls your piano away and promises to return it in perfect shape. Two months later, you are horrified to spot Showpan's showroom boarded up and pasted with bankruptcy notices. Worse still, you learn that Fred sold your beloved instrument to a customer, Frankie List. When you track down List, he claims he paid $18,000 for the piano and likes it just fine. Is he entitled to keep it?

Quite likely he is. Section 2-403(1), the BFP provision we just discussed, would not apply because Showpan did not *purchase* the piano from you. But §2-403(2) does apply. This is the "entrustment" section, and it covers cases in which the owner of goods voluntarily *leaves* them with a merchant, who then sells the goods without permission. According to **UCC §2-403(2), any entrusting to a merchant who deals in goods of that kind gives him power to transfer all rights of the entruster to a buyer in the ordinary course of business (BIOC).** There are several important ideas in this section:

Entrusting means delivering goods to a merchant or permitting the merchant to retain them.[8] In the piano example, you clearly entrusted goods to a merchant. If you buy a used car from Fast Eddie's and then leave it there for a week while you obtain insurance, you have entrusted it to Eddie.

Deals in Goods of That Kind. The purpose of the section is to protect innocent buyers who enter a store, see the goods they expect to find, and purchase something, having no idea that the storekeeper is illegally selling the property of others. Shoppers should not have to demand proof of title to everything in the store. Further, if someone has to bear the risk, let it be the person who has entrusted her goods; she is in the best position to investigate the merchant's integrity. But this protection does not extend to a buyer who arrives at a vacuum cleaner store and buys an $80,000 mobile home parked in the lot.

In the Ordinary Course of Business. **A buyer in the ordinary course of business (BIOC)** is one who acts in good faith, without knowing that the sale violates the owner's rights. If Frank List buys your piano assuming that Showpan owns it, he has acted in good faith. If Frank was your neighbor, recognized your instrument, and bought it anyway, he is not buying in the ordinary course of business and must hand over the piano.

Buyer in the ordinary course of business (BIOC)
One who acts in good faith, without knowing that the sale violates the owner's rights

Of course, a merchant who violates the owner's rights is liable to that owner. If Showpan were still in business when you discovered your loss, you could sue and recover the value of the piano. The problems arise when the merchant is bankrupt or otherwise unable to reimburse the owner.

[8]For a discussion of who is and who is not a merchant, see Chapter 21.

EXAMStrategy

Question: Pamela went to University Used Auto and asked if the company had a Lincoln Navigator. University had no such SUV, but a sales representative told Pamela that he would find her one. The representative contacted Royal auto dealership, which sold new and used cars. Royal agreed to supply University with a car, on the understanding that an interested buyer would pay *Royal*, which in turn would give a finder's fee to University. The companies had worked this way in the past. Royal delivered a Navigator as requested. But when the used car company sold the vehicle to Pamela, the company instructed her to pay University directly, which she did. Royal sued Pamela, seeking the car, and the court had to determine whether there had been an entrustment. Royal argued that it never entrusted the Navigator to University because the parties agreed to require payment to Royal.

Strategy: Entrustment means delivering goods to a merchant who routinely deals in such articles.

Result: Royal delivered a used car to a used car dealer. That is entrustment. It is true that both dealers understood that Pamela was to pay Royal—but she did not know that. Entrustment protects good faith buyers, and Pamela wins.

22-2 RISK OF LOSS

Many of the issues we have looked at thus far involve someone doing something wrong, often a scoundrel selling goods that he never owned. Now we turn to cases where there may be no wrongdoer.

Accidents hurt businesses. When goods are damaged, the law may again need to decide whether it is the seller or buyer who must suffer the loss. In the cases we have seen thus far, the parties were arguing, "It's mine!"—"Like heck it is, it's *mine!*" In risk of loss cases, the parties are generally shouting, "It was yours!"—"No way, dude, it was *yours!*"

Athena, a seafood wholesaler, is gearing up for the Super Bowl, which will bring 150,000 hungry visitors to her city for a week of eating and gabbing. Athena orders 25,000 lobsters from Poseidon's Fishfoods, 500 miles distant, and simultaneously contracts with a dozen local restaurants to resell them. Poseidon loads the lobsters, still kicking, into refrigerated railcars owned by Demeter Trucking. But halfway to the city, the train collides with a prison van. None of the convicts escape, but the lobsters do, hurtling into swamps from which they are never recaptured. Athena loses all of her profits and sues. As luck would have it, Demeter Trucking had foolishly let its insurance lapse. Poseidon claims the goods were out of its hands. Who loses?

The common law answered this problem by looking at which party had title to the goods at the time of loss. But the Uniform Commercial Code again rejects the old concept, striving once more for a practical solution. The UCC permits the parties to agree on who bears the risk of loss. **UCC §2-509(4) states that the parties may allocate the risk of loss any way they wish.**

Often the parties will do just that, avoiding arguments and litigation in the event of an accident. As part of her agreement with Poseidon, Athena should have included a one-sentence clause, such as "Seller bears all risk of loss until the lobsters are delivered to Athena's warehouse." As long as the parties make their risk allocation clear, the Code will enforce their terms.

22-2a Shipping Terms

The parties can quickly and easily allocate the risk of loss by using common shipping terms that the Code defines. FOB means free on board; FAS indicates free alongside a ship; and CIF stands for cost, insurance, and freight. By combining these designations with other terms, the parties can specify risk in a few words:

- **FOB place of shipment.** The seller is obligated to put the goods into the possession of the carrier at the place named. The seller bears the expense and risk until they are in the carrier's possession. From that moment onward, the buyer bears the risk.
- **FOB place of destination.** The seller must deliver the goods at the place named and bears the expense *and risk* of shipping.
- **CIF.** The price includes in a lump sum: the cost of the goods and the insurance and freight to the named destination.
- **C&F.** The price includes in a lump sum: the cost of the goods and freight, but *not* insurance.

Thus, if Athena had put a clause in her contract saying, "FOB Athena's warehouse," Poseidon would have had the risk of any loss up to the time the lobsters were unloaded in Athena's possession. Poseidon would then have known that it must insure the lobsters during transit.

22-2b When the Parties Fail to Allocate the Risk

If the parties fail to specify when the risk passes from seller to buyer, the Code provides the answer. When neither party breached the contract, §2-509 determines the risk; when a party has breached the contract, §2-510 governs. The full analysis of risk is somewhat intricate, so we first supply you with a short version: **When neither party has breached the contract, the risk of loss generally passes from seller to buyer when the seller has transported the goods as far as he is obligated to. When a party has breached, the risk of loss generally lies with that party.**

And now, for the courageous student, the full version of how the UCC allocates the risk of loss when the parties failed to specify it.

When Neither Party Breaches

In the example of Athena and Poseidon, both parties did what they were supposed to do, so there was no breach of contract. To settle these cases, we need to know whether the contract obligated the seller to ship the goods or whether the goods were handled in some other way. There are three possibilities: (1) the contract required the seller to ship the goods, or (2) the contract involved a bailment, or (3) other cases.

If the Seller Must Ship the Goods. Most contracts require the seller to arrange shipment of the goods. In a *shipment contract,* the seller must deliver the goods *to a carrier,* which will then transport the goods to the buyer. The carrier might be a trucking company, railroad, airline, or ship, and is generally located near the seller's place of business. **In a shipment contract, the risk passes to the buyer when the seller delivers the goods to the carrier.** Suppose Old Wood, in North Carolina, agrees to sell $100,000 worth of furniture to Pioneer Company, in Anchorage. The contract requires Old Wood to deliver the goods to Great Northern Railroad lines in Chicago. From North Carolina to Chicago, Old Wood bears the risk of loss. If the furniture is damaged, stolen, or destroyed, Old Wood is out of luck. But once the furniture is on board the train in Chicago, the risk of loss passes to Pioneer. If the train derails in Montana and every desk and chair is smashed to kindling, Pioneer must nevertheless pay the full $100,000 to Old Wood.

If the train travels 3,000 miles and then plunges off a bridge in Alaska, 45 feet from its destination, Old Wood picks up the tab.

In a *destination contract*, the seller is responsible for delivering the goods *to the buyer*, and risk passes to the buyer when the goods reach the destination. If the contract required Old Wood to deliver the furniture to Pioneer's warehouse in Anchorage, then Old Wood bears the loss for the entire trip. If the train travels 3,000 miles and then plunges off a bridge in Alaska, 45 feet from its destination, Old Wood picks up the tab.

If There Is a Bailment. Freezem Corp. produces 500 room air conditioners and stores them in Every-Ware's Warehouse. This is a **bailment, meaning that one person or company is legally holding goods for the benefit of another**. Freezem is the **bailor**, the one who owns the goods, and Every-Ware is the **bailee**, the one with temporary possession. Suppose Freezem agrees to sell 300 of its air conditioners to KeepKool Appliances. KeepKool does not need the machines in its store for six months, so it plans to keep them at Every-Ware's until then. But two weeks after Freezem and KeepKool make their deal, Every-Ware burns to the ground. Who bears the loss of the 300 air conditioners? **If the contract requires a bailee to hold the goods for the buyer, the risk passes when the buyer obtains documents entitling her to possession, or when the bailee acknowledges her right to the goods.** If fire broke out in Every-Ware's before KeepKool received any documents enabling it to take the air conditioners away, then the loss would fall on Freezem.

Bailor
The one who owns goods legally held by another

Bailee
The one with temporary possession of another's goods

Other Cases. The great majority of contracts involve either shipment by the seller or a bailment. In the remaining cases, if the seller is a *merchant*, risk passes to the buyer on receipt. This means that a merchant is only off the hook if the buyer actually accepts the goods. If the seller is *not a merchant*, risk passes when the seller tenders the goods, meaning that she makes them available to the buyer. The Code is giving more protection to buyers when they deal with a merchant.

When One Party Breaches

We now look at how the Code allocates risk when one of the parties *does* breach. Again there are three possibilities: (1) seller breaches and buyer rejects; (2) seller breaches, buyer accepts, but then revokes; or (3) buyer breaches.

Seller Breaches and Buyer Rejects. PlayStore, a sporting goods store, orders 75 canoes from Floataway. PlayStore specifies that the canoes must be 12 feet long, lightweight metal, and dark green. Floataway delivers 75 canoes to Truckit, a trucking company. When Truckit's trucks arrive, PlayStore finds that the canoes are the right material and color, but 18 feet long. PlayStore rejects the craft, and Truckit heads back to Floataway. But one of the trucks is hijacked and the 25 canoes it carries are never recovered. Floataway demands its money for the 25 lost canoes. Who loses?

Floataway had delivered **nonconforming goods**; that is, merchandise which differs from that specified in the contract. A buyer has a right to reject such goods. **When the buyer rejects nonconforming goods, the risk of loss remains with the seller until he cures the defect or the buyer decides to accept the goods.** In our example, Floataway must suffer the loss for the stolen canoes. If PlayStore had decided to accept the canoes, even though they were the wrong size, then the risk would have passed to the sports store.

Nonconforming goods
Merchandise that differs from what is specified in the contract

Seller Breaches, Buyer Accepts, but Then Revokes. PlayStore orders 200 tennis rackets from High Strung. When the rackets arrive, they seem fine, so the store accepts them. But then a salesperson notices that the grips are loose. Every racket has the same problem. PlayStore returns the rackets to High Strung, but they are destroyed when a blimp crashes into the delivery truck. **When a buyer accepts goods but then rightfully revokes acceptance, the risk remains with the seller to the extent that the buyer's insurance will not cover the loss.**

If PlayStore's insurance covers the damaged rackets, there is no problem. If PlayStore's insurance does not cover the loss of goods in transit, High Strung must pay.

Buyer Breaches. One last time. PlayStore orders 60 tents from ExploreMore. About the time the tents leave the factory, PlayStore decides to drop its line of camping goods and specialize in team sports. PlayStore notifies ExploreMore that it wants to explore less and will not pay. The tents are destroyed in a collision involving a prison van and a train carrying lobsters. This time, PlayStore is liable. **When a buyer breaches the contract before taking possession, it assumes the risk of loss to the extent that the seller's insurance is deficient.** Exhibit 22.1 should clarify.

In the following case, neither party breached, so §2-509 governs.

Harmon v. Dunn

1997 Tenn. App. LEXIS 217; 1997 WL 136462
Tennessee Court of Appeals, 1997

Facts: Bess Harmon owned a two-year-old Tennessee Walking Horse named Phantom Recall. Harmon, who lived in Tennessee, boarded her horse with Steve Dunn at his stables in Florence, Alabama. Dunn cared for Phantom Recall and showed him at equestrian events. Harmon instructed Dunn to sell the horse for $25,000, and Dunn arranged for his friend Scarbrough to buy the colt. On June 30, Dunn delivered Scarbrough's $25,000 check to Harmon, who handed over the horse's certificate of registration and a "transfer of ownership" document. That night at a horse show, Dunn told Scarbrough that he had delivered the check and had the ownership papers in his car. Dunn did not actually give the documents to his friend. Scarbrough knew that Phantom Recall was at Dunn's stable, where Scarbrough had boarded other horses. Sadly, the colt developed colitis and died suddenly, on July 4. Scarbrough stopped payment on his check, and Harmon sued for her money. The trial court found for Harmon, and Scarbrough appealed.

Issue: ***Which party bore the risk of Phantom Recall's death?***

Excerpts from Judge Farmer's Decision: [UCC §2-509 states:] Risk of loss in the absence of breach …

(2) Where the goods are held by a bailee to be delivered without being moved, the risk of loss passes to the buyer:

(a) on his receipt of a negotiable document of title covering the goods, or

(b) on acknowledgment by the bailee of the buyer's right to possession of the goods, or

(c) after his receipt of a non-negotiable document of title or other written direction to deliver …

Michael Wade/Icon SMI/Newscom

Phantom Recall died of colitis—but that was just the beginning of the drama.

We conclude that the facts before us clearly establish a bailor-bailee relationship between Harmon and Dunn. It is not disputed that the latter was the agent of the former. Here, it was agreed that Dunn would train and care for Phantom Recall at the Dunn Stables in Florence, Alabama. He was also responsible for transporting the horse to various shows. The record establishes that prior to the horse's death, he had been entered and shown by Dunn himself in three separate events.

Having established Dunn a bailee for purposes of [§2-509(2)] and in the absence of any prior arrangement with Dunn or Harmon that the horse be delivered elsewhere upon purchase from the latter, we find that the risk of loss passed to Scarbrough if and when the applicable provisions under subsection (2) occurred. Subsection (2)(a) and (b) provide that the risk of loss passes to the buyer "on his receipt of a negotiable document of title covering the goods; or on acknowledgment by the bailee of the buyer's right to possession of the goods."

We find that Scarbrough received the ability to control possession of the horse no later than July 1 irrespective of the fact that he did not actually receive physical possession of the ownership documents at that time. The documents which were necessary for transfer of ownership and taking possession of the horse were already in the hands of the bailee. We find an actual physical back and forth exchange between the two unnecessary under these facts where the bailee and the seller's agent are one and the same. Certainly Scarbrough had the ability to control possession of the horse no later than July 1 when he was made aware that Dunn had the transfer papers.

[Affirmed.]

22-3 WARRANTIES

Warranty
A contractual assurance that goods will meet certain standards

The *Harmon* case illustrates what happens when an accident destroys the goods sold and neither party is at fault. But what if Harmon had guaranteed Scarbrough a healthy horse and delivered a sick one? The UCC also addresses this issue in its warranty provisions. A **warranty** is a promise that goods will meet certain standards. Normally a manufacturer or a seller gives a warranty and a buyer relies on it. A warranty might be explicit and written: "The manufacturer warrants that the light bulbs in this package will illuminate for 2,000 hours." Or a warranty could be oral: "Don't worry, this machine can harvest any size of wheat crop ever planted in the state."

Sometimes a manufacturer offers a warranty as a means of attracting buyers: "We provide the finest bumper-to-bumper warranty in the automobile industry." Other times, *the law itself* imposes a warranty on goods, requiring the manufacturer to meet certain standards whether it wants to or not. We will begin with the first option—when the seller voluntarily provides a warranty.

22-3a Express Warranties

Express warranty
One that the seller creates with his words or actions

An **express warranty** is one that the seller creates with his words or actions.[9] Whenever a seller *clearly indicates* to a buyer that the goods being sold will meet certain standards, she has created an express warranty. For example, if the sales clerk for a paint store tells a professional house painter that "this exterior paint will not fade for three years, even in direct sunlight," that is an express warranty and the store is bound by it. Or, if the clerk gives the painter a brochure that makes the same promise, the store is again bound by its express warranty. On the other hand, if the salesperson merely says, "I know you're going to be happy with this product," there is no warranty because the promise is too vague.

[9]UCC §2-313.

EXHIBIT 22.1

Did the Parties Allocate the Risk in Their Contract?

If the parties have allocated the risk in their contract, that agreement will control and everything on this chart is gloriously irrelevant.

If the parties have *not* allocated the risk of loss, then §2-509 and §2-510 will determine who suffers the loss.

In using the two Code sections to determine the risk, the first question is whether either party has breached the contract.

No Breach (§2-509)
If neither party breaches, there are three possibilities:

1. Contract requires Seller to ship goods by carrier.
   - a. *Shipment Contract* requires Seller to deliver the goods to a carrier. → **Risk** passes to Buyer when Seller delivers goods to carrier.
   - b. *Destination Contract* requires Seller to deliver goods to a specified destination. → **Risk** passes to Buyer when carrier tenders goods at the destination.
2. Contract requires a bailee to hold goods for Buyer. → **Risk** passes to Buyer when she obtains documents entitling her to possession, or when Bailee acknowledges she is entitled to possession.
3. Other cases.
   - a. If Seller *is* a merchant → **Risk** passes to Buyer on receipt of goods.
   - b. If Seller *is not* a merchant → **Risk** passes to Buyer on tender of delivery.

Breach (§2-510)
If a party breaches, there are three possibilities:

1. Seller breaches. The goods are nonconforming and the Buyer rightfully rejects them. → **Risk** remains with the Seller until he cures the defects or the Buyer decides to accept the goods.
2. Seller breaches. The buyer accepts but then revokes his acceptance → **Risk** remains with the Seller to the extent that the Buyer's own insurance is deficient.
3. Buyer breaches. Buyer repudiates conforming goods or in some other way breaches the contract before he takes possession of the goods. → **Risk** passes to the Buyer to the extent that the Seller's insurance is deficient, for a commercially reasonable time.

The UCC establishes that the seller may create an express warranty in three ways: (1) with an affirmation of fact or a promise, (2) with a description of the goods, or (3) with a sample or model. In addition, the buyer must demonstrate that what the seller said or did was part of the *basis of the bargain*.

Affirmation of Fact or Promise

Any affirmation of fact—or any promise—can create an express warranty.[10] An affirmation of fact is simply a statement about the nature or quality of the goods, such as "this scaffolding is made from the highest grade of steel available at any price" or "this car will accelerate from 0 to 60 in 5.3 seconds." A promise can include phrases such as, "we guarantee you that this air conditioning system will cool your building to 72 degrees, regardless of the outdoor temperature."

A common problem in cases of express warranty is to separate true affirmations of fact from mere sales puffery or seller's opinion, which creates no express warranty. "You meet the nicest people when you ride a Honda motorcycle," is mere puffery. If you purchase a Honda and meet only deadbeats, the manufacturer owes you nothing.

A statement is more likely to be an affirmation of fact if:

- **It is specific and can be proven true or false.** Suppose the brochures of a home builder promise to meet "the strictest building codes." Since there is a code on file, the builder's work can be compared to it, and his promise is binding.
- **It is written.** An oral promise *can* create an express warranty. But promises in brochures are more likely to be taken seriously. Statements in a *written contract* are the likeliest of all to create a binding warranty.
- **Defects are not obvious.** If a used car salesman tells you that a car is rust-free when the driver's door is pockmarked with rust, you should not take the statement seriously—since a court will not, either.
- **Seller has greater expertise.** If the seller knows more than the buyer, his statements will be more influential with buyer and court alike. If your architect assures you that the new porch will be structurally sound, the law recognizes that you will naturally rely on her expertise.

Description of Goods

Any description of the goods can create an express warranty.[11] The statement can be oral or written. A description might be a label on a bag of seed, referring to the seed as a particular variety of tomato; it could be a tag on airplane parts, assuring the buyer that the goods have met safety tests. Wherever the words appear, if they describe the goods as having particular characteristics or qualities, the seller has probably created an express warranty.

Sample or Model

Any sample or model can create an express warranty.[12] A sample can be a very effective way of demonstrating the quality of goods to a customer. However, a seller who uses a sample is generally warranting that the merchandise sold will be just as good.

10UCC §2-313(1)(a).

11UCC §2-313(1)(b).

12UCC §2-313(1)(c).

Basis of Bargain

The seller's conduct must have been part of the basis of the bargain. To prove an express warranty, a buyer must demonstrate that the two parties *included the statements or acts in their bargain*. Some courts have interpreted this to mean that the buyer must have *relied* on the seller's statements. There is logic to this position. For example, suppose a sales brochure makes certain assurances about the quality of goods, but the buyer never sees the brochure until she files suit. Should the seller be held to an express warranty? Some courts would rule that the seller is not liable for breach of warranty.

Other courts, however, have ruled that a seller's statement can be part of the basis of the bargain even when the buyer has not clearly relied on it. These courts are declaring that a seller who chooses to make statements about his goods will be held to them *unless the seller can convince a court that he should not be liable*. This is a policy decision, taken by many courts, to give the buyer the benefit of the doubt since the seller is in the best position to control what he says.

Coffee junkies love their joe. Was Starbucks brewing trouble?

You Be the Judge

Strumlauf v. Starbucks Corp.

2016 U.S. Dist. LEXIS 87574; 2016 WL 3361842
United States District Court, N.D. California, 2016

Facts: A latte (which means "milk" in Italian) is a coffee drink made with milk and often topped with milk foam. According to the Starbucks menu, its Grande (which means "big" in Italian) lattes contained 16 fl. oz.

Sean Wandzilak/Shutterstock.com

Starbucks lovers argued that the Grandes were not as "grande" as promised.

A group of heated Grande-latte-drinkers sued Starbucks for breach of express warranty, alleging that the coffee company consistently underfilled its lattes by 25 percent. That is, they claimed, the Grande-sized lattes contained only 12 ounces of coffee topped with about an inch of foam, instead of the promised 16 ounces of liquid coffee.

The plaintiffs offered the following evidence: Starbucks provided baristas with pitchers that had "fill to" lines that were too low for the finished product to actually be 16 oz. Additionally, the latte recipe instructed baristas to "leave at least 1/4 inch of space below the rim of the serving cup." But the serving cup's capacity was exactly 16 oz., which meant that the Grande lattes could not possibly contain the promised amount.

Starbucks filed a motion to dismiss, arguing that the plaintiffs should just relax and get another cup of coffee.

You Be the Judge: *Did Starbucks breach an express warranty by underfilling its lattes?*

Argument for Plaintiffs: Your honors, the Starbucks menu clearly represented that its Grande lattes contained 16 fluid ounces. Any reasonable consumer would understand that statement as a promise to deliver 16 ounces of liquid coffee, not 12 ounces of coffee with a 4-ounce foamy filler on top. My clients would not have paid as much as they did for the latte if they had known it was only 12 ounces of actual coffee. Starbucks breached its express warranty and injured my clients, who received much less than what was promised. Moreover, Starbucks knew what it was doing because its company-wide policy instructed baristas to underfill latte cups. Starbucks needs to stand by its word.

Argument for the Defendant: Your honors, Starbucks did not expressly warrant that it would deliver 16 ounces of liquid coffee. Instead, it promised to deliver a 16 ounce latte—and that is exactly what it did. The definition of a latte is a milk-based coffee drink topped with milk foam. Any reasonable latte-drinker knows that the foam added to the top of the coffee is part of the drink and counts toward the total fluid ounce measurement. If a consumer does not want foam in her coffee, she is free to drink an Americano, a macchiato, or the drip coffee of the day.

22-3b Implied Warranties

Sean decides to plow driveways during the winter. Emily sells him a snowplow and installs it on his truck, but she makes no promises about its performance. When winter arrives, Sean has plenty of business, but he finds that the plow cannot be raised or lowered whenever the temperature falls below 40 degrees. He demands a refund from Emily, but she declines, saying, "I never said that thing would work in the winter. Tough luck." Is she off the hook? No. It is true she made no express warranties. But many sales are covered by implied warranties.

Implied warranties are those created by the UCC itself, not by any act or statement of the seller. The Code's drafters concluded that goods should generally meet certain standards of quality, regardless of what the seller did or did not say. So the UCC creates both an implied warranty of merchantability and an implied warranty of fitness.

Implied Warranty of Merchantability

This is the most important warranty in the UCC. Buyers, whether individual consumers or billion-dollar corporations, are more likely to rely on this than any other section. Sellers must understand it thoroughly when they market goods. **Unless excluded or modified, a warranty that the goods are merchantable is implied in a contract for their sale if the seller is a merchant with respect to goods of that kind. Merchantable** means that the goods are fit for the ordinary purposes for which they are used.[13] This rule contains several important principles:

Merchantable
The goods are fit for the ordinary purpose for which they are used.

- *Unless excluded or modified* means that the seller does have a chance to escape this warranty. We later discuss what steps a seller may take if she wants to sell goods that are *not* merchantable.
- *Merchantability* requires that goods be fit for their normal purposes. To be merchantable, a ladder must be able to rest securely against a building and support someone who is climbing it. The ladder need not be serviceable as a boat ramp.
- *Implied* means that the law itself imposes this liability on the seller even if it is not written down.
- *A merchant with respect to goods of that kind* means that the seller is someone who routinely deals in these goods or holds himself out as having special knowledge about such goods. When selling vehicles, a car dealer is acting as a merchant, but an accountant who sells his used car by listing it online is not.

Dacor Corp. manufactured and sold scuba diving equipment. It ordered air hoses from Sierra Precision, specifying the exact size and couplings so that the hose would fit tightly and safely into Dacor's oxygen units. Within about one year, customers returned a dozen Dacor units, complaining that the hose connections had cracked or sheared and were unusable. Dacor recalled 16,000 units and refit them with safe hoses, at a cost of more than $136,000. Dacor sued Sierra, claiming a breach of the implied warranty of merchantability. The Illinois court ruled that Sierra was a merchant with respect to scuba hoses because it routinely manufactured and sold them. Further, the court ruled that since use of the faulty hose assemblies under water would be life-threatening, they were clearly not fit for the purpose for which

[13] UCC §2-314(1).

they were sold—which was, after all, scuba diving! The court ordered Sierra to pay the cost of Dacor's recall.[14]

The scuba equipment was not merchantable because a properly made scuba hose should never crack under normal use. But what if the product being sold is food, and the food contains something that is harmful—yet quite normal?

Goodman v. Wenco Foods, Inc.

333 N.C. 1
North Carolina Supreme Court, 1992

Facts: Fred Goodman and a friend stopped for lunch at a Wendy's restaurant in Hillsborough, North Carolina. Goodman had eaten about half of his double hamburger when he bit down and felt immediate pain in his lower jaw. He took from his mouth a one-half-inch piece of cow bone, along with several pieces of his teeth. Goodman's pain was intense, and his dental repairs took months.

The restaurant purchased all of its meat from Greensboro Meat Supply Company (GMSC). Wendy's required its meat to be chopped and "free from bone or cartilage in excess of 1/8 inch in any dimension." GMSC beef was inspected continuously by state regulators and was certified by the United States Department of Agriculture (USDA). The USDA considered any bone fragment less than three-quarters of an inch long to be "insignificant."

Goodman sued, claiming a breach of the implied warranty of merchantability. The trial court dismissed the claim, ruling that the bone was natural to the food and that the hamburger was therefore fit for its ordinary purpose. The appeals court reversed this ruling, holding that a hamburger could be unfit even if the bone occurred naturally. Wendy's appealed to the state's highest court.

Issue: ***Was the hamburger unfit for its ordinary purpose?***

Excerpts from Justice Exum's Decision: We hold that when a substance in food causes injury to a consumer, it is not a bar to recovery against the seller that the substance was "natural" to the food, provided that the substance's presence should not reasonably have been anticipated by the consumer.

A one-half-inch, inflexible bone shaving is indubitably "inherent" in or "natural" to a cut of beef, but whether it is so "natural" to hamburger as to put a consumer on his guard—whether it "is to be reasonably expected by the consumer"—is, in most cases, a question for the jury. We are not requiring that the respondent's hamburgers be perfect, only that they be fit for their intended purpose. It is difficult to conceive of how a consumer might guard against the type of injury present here, short of removing the hamburger from its bun, breaking it apart and inspecting its small components.

Wendy's argues that the evidence supported its contention that its hamburger complied with [legal] standards. Wendy's reasons that [regulators permit] some bone fragments in meat and that its hamburgers are therefore merchantable as a matter of law. The court of appeals rejected this argument, noting that compliance "with all state and federal regulations is only some evidence which the jury may consider in determining whether the product was merchantable." We agree.

We thus conclude, as did the court of appeals majority, that a jury could reasonably determine the meat to be of such a nature and the bone in the meat of such a size that a consumer should not reasonably have anticipated the bone's presence. The court of appeals therefore properly reversed the directed verdict for Wendy's on plaintiff's implied warranty of merchantability claim.

Implied Warranty of Fitness for a Particular Purpose

The other warranty that the UCC imposes on sellers is the implied warranty of fitness for a particular purpose. This cumbersome name is often shortened and referred to as simply the *warranty of fitness*. **Where the seller at the time of contracting *knows* about a particular purpose**

[14]Dacor Corp. v. Sierra Precision, 19 F3d 21 (7th Cir. 1994).

for which the buyer wants the goods, and knows that the buyer is relying on the seller's skill or judgment, there is (unless excluded or modified) an implied warranty that the goods shall be fit for the purpose.[15] Here are the key points:

- **Particular purpose.** The seller must know about some *special* use that the buyer plans for the goods. For example, if a lumber salesman knows that a builder is purchasing lumber to construct houses in a swamp, the UCC implies a warranty that the lumber will withstand water.
- **Seller's skill.** The buyer must be depending upon the seller's skill or judgment in selecting the product, and the seller must know it. Suppose the builder says to the lumber salesman, "I need four-by-eights that I will be using to build a house in the swamp. What do you have that will do the job?" The builder's reliance is obvious, and the warranty is established. By contrast, suppose that an experienced Alaskan sled driver offers to buy your three huskies, telling you she plans to use them to pull sleds. She has the experience and you do not, and, if the dogs refuse to pull more than a 1-pound can of dog food, you have probably not breached the implied warranty of fitness.
- **Exclusion or modification.** Once again, the seller is allowed to modify or exclude any warranty of fitness.

Two Last Warranties: Title and Infringement

Strapped for cash, Maggie steals her boyfriend's rusty Chevy and sells it to Paul for $2,500. As we saw earlier in this chapter, Maggie gets no valid title by her theft, and therefore Paul receives no title either. When the boyfriend finds his car parked at a nightclub, he notifies the police and gets his wheels back. Poor Paul is out of pocket $2,500 and has no car to show for it. That clearly is unjust, and the UCC provides Paul with a remedy: **The seller of goods warrants that her title is valid and that the goods are free of any security interest that the buyer knows nothing about, unless the seller has clearly excluded or modified this warranty.**[16] Once again, the Code is imposing a warranty on any seller except those who explicitly exclude or modify it. When Maggie sells the car to Paul, she warrants her valid title to the car and simultaneously breaches that warranty since she obviously has no title. If he can find her, Paul will win a lawsuit against Maggie for $2,500.

The same Code section imposes what it calls an infringement warranty. This warranty means that, **unless otherwise agreed, a seller who is a merchant warrants that the goods are free of any rightful claim of copyright, patent, or trademark infringement.**[17]

Wesley sells to Komputer Corp. a device that automatically blasts purple smoke out of a computer screen anytime a student's paper is really dreadful. Unless Komputer Corp. agrees otherwise, Wesley is automatically giving the buyer a warranty that no one else invented the device or has any copyright, patent, or trademark in it.

22-3c Warranty Disclaimers

Disclaimer
A statement that a particular warranty does not apply

The Code permits a seller to *disclaim* some express or implied warranties. A **disclaimer** is a statement that a particular warranty *does not* apply.

---

15 UCC §2-315.
16 UCC §2-312(1).
17 UCC §2-313(3).

Oral Express Warranties

Under the Code, a seller may disclaim an oral express warranty. Suppose Traffic Co. wants to buy a helicopter from HeliCorp for use in reporting commuter traffic. HeliCorp's salesman tells Traffic Co., "Don't worry, you can fly this bird day and night for six months with nothing more than a fuel stop." HeliCorp's contract may disclaim the oral warranty. The contract could say, "HeliCorp's entire warranty is printed below. Any statements made by any agent or salesperson are disclaimed and form no part of this contract." That disclaimer is valid. If the helicopter requires routine servicing between flights, HeliCorp has not breached an oral warranty.

Written Express Warranties

This is the one type of warranty that is almost impossible to disclaim. **If a seller includes an express warranty in the *sales contract,* any disclaimer is definitely invalid.** Suppose HeliCorp sells an industrial helicopter for use in hauling building equipment. The sales contract describes the aircraft as "operable to 14,000 feet." Later, the warranty section of the contract specifically disclaims, "any other warranties or statements that appear in this document or in any other document." That disclaimer is invalid and does not cancel the assurance that the helicopter can operate to 14,000 feet. The Code will not permit a seller to take contradictory positions in a document. The goal is simply to be fair, and the UCC assumes that it is confusing and unjust for a seller to say one thing to help close a deal and the opposite to limit its losses.[18]

What if the express written statement is in a different document, such as a sales brochure? The disclaimer is void if it would *unfairly surprise* the buyer. Assume, again, that HeliCorp promises a helicopter that requires no routine maintenance for six months, but this time, the promise appears in a sales brochure that Traffic Co. reads and relies on. If HeliCorp attempts to disclaim the written warranty, it will probably fail. Most people take written information seriously, and courts usually find that consumers would be unfairly surprised if a company tried to go back on promises made in a sales brochure.

Implied Warranties

A seller may disclaim the implied warranty of merchantability provided he *actually mentions the word* merchantability *and makes the disclaimer conspicuous.* Courts demand to see the specific word *merchantability* in the disclaimer to be sure the buyer realized she was giving up this fundamental protection. If the word is there, and the disclaimer is conspicuous enough that the buyer should have seen it, she has forfeited the warranty. A seller may disclaim the implied warranty of fitness with any language that is clear and conspicuous.

To make life easier, the Code permits a seller to disclaim *all* implied warranties by conspicuously stating that the goods are sold "as is" or "with all faults." Notice the tension between this provision and the one just discussed. A seller who wants to disclaim *only* the warranty of merchantability must explicitly mention that term; but a seller wishing to exclude *all* implied warranties may do so with a short expression, such as "sold as is."

Many states, though, prohibit a seller from disclaiming implied warranties in the sale of consumer goods. In these states, if a home furnishings store sells a bunk bed to a consumer, and the top bunk tips out the window on the first night, the seller is liable. Even if the sales contract clearly stated "no warranties of merchantability," the court would reject the clause and find that the seller breached the implied warranty of merchantability.

---

[18]UCC §2-316(1).

EXAMStrategy

Question: Marcos's backyard pool, which measured 35 feet by 18 feet, needed a new filter. A sales brochure stated, "This filter will keep any normal backyard pool, up to 50 feet by 25, clean and healthy all summer for a minimum of 5 years." Marcos signed a sales contract, which included this disclaimer: "The filter will work to normal industry standards. This is the only warranty. No other statements, written or oral, apply. Pools vary widely, and the Seller cannot guarantee any specific level of performance or cleanliness. Buyer agrees to this disclaimer." The filter failed to keep Marcos's pool clean, and he sued for breach of warranty. Who should win?

Strategy: Sellers are often able to disclaim oral warranties, but usually not written ones. Here, the initial promise and the disclaimer were in different documents. Does that change the outcome? Finally, Marcos was a consumer. Courts treat consumers differently from corporate buyers.

Result: It is difficult or impossible for sellers to disclaim written warranties, even if the promise and disclaimer are in different documents. A disclaimer that would unfairly surprise the buyer is void. Marcos relied on the sales brochure—as the company intended—and the seller will probably lose. Furthermore, most states give extra protection to consumers, knowing that they are less sophisticated buyers. A court is likely to find in favor of Marcos based on the seller's express warranty, as well as the implied warranties of merchantability and fitness.

22-3d Remedy Limitations

The seller may also limit the buyer's *remedy*, which means that, even if there is a breach of warranty, the buyer still may have only a very limited chance to recover against the seller. Simon Aerials, Inc., manufactured boomlifts, the huge cranes used to construct multistoried buildings. Simon agreed to design and build eight unusually large machines for Logan Equipment Corp. Simon delivered the boomlifts late, and they functioned poorly. Logan requested dozens of repairs and modifications, which Simon attempted to accomplish over many months, but the equipment never worked well. Logan gave up and sued for $7.5 million, representing the profits it expected to make from renting the machines and the damage to its reputation. Logan clearly had suffered major losses, and it recovered—nothing. How could that be?

Limitation of remedy clause
Contract clause allowing parties to limit or exclude applicable UCC remedies

Simon had negotiated a **limitation of remedy clause**, by which the parties may limit or exclude the normal remedies permitted under the UCC.[19] These important rights are entirely distinct from disclaimers. A disclaimer limits the seller's warranties and thus affects whether the seller has breached her contract in the first place. A remedy limitation, by contrast, states that if a party *does* breach its warranty, the injured party will not get all of the damages the Code normally allows.

In its contract, Simon had agreed to repair or replace any defective boomlifts, but that was all. The agreement said that if a boomlift was defective, and Logan lost business, profits, and reputation, Simon was not liable. The court upheld the remedy limitation. Since Simon

[19]UCC §2-719. A few states prohibit remedy limitations, but most permit them.

had repeatedly attempted to repair and redesign the defective machines, it had done everything it promised to do. Logan got nothing.[20]

Consequential Damages

Simon's contract clause is typical: Many sellers exclude liability for consequential damages, which can be so vast and unpredictable. Recall that a party injured by breach of contract normally gets direct, or *compensatory* damages.[21] In the sale of goods, that means the difference between the value of the goods promised and those actually delivered. A seller can anticipate and probably tolerate such damages since the seller understands exactly how much it costs to repair or replace the goods it has sold.

Consequential damages, however, are different. They are losses stemming from the buyer's particular circumstances. The buyer might have entered into dozens of contracts in reliance on the goods it expects from the seller. The seller will have no way of knowing how great the consequential damages could be. Logan Equipment claimed that it would have earned profits in the millions, and it was just such a claim that Simon had determined to avoid.

Consequential damages
Contract damages resulting as an indirect consequence of the breach

Notice that there is one major restriction on limitation of remedy clauses: **An exclusion of consequential damages is void if it is unconscionable.** The word *unconscionable* means that a remedy restriction is shockingly one-sided and fundamentally unfair. If the buyer is a consumer, a court will be likelier to consider such an exclusion unfair since the typical consumer will not understand the terms and may never even notice them.

If the buyer is a consumer who suffers a *personal injury*, a court is nearly certain to reject an exclusion for consequential damages. It is unfair for a corporation to market defective goods and escape liability because an unsuspecting consumer failed to understand contract language. Suppose Byron buys a hot-air popcorn popper that comes with a label that attempts to limit remedies. Byron is seriously burned when the popper ignites. Virtually all courts will ignore the label and permit Byron to recover his full damages, which in his case might include such consequential items as lost wages or the cost of the nonrefundable airline ticket for the trip he cannot take as a result of the breach.

However, when the buyer is a corporation, courts assume it had adequate legal advice and an opportunity to reject unacceptable terms. When two companies agree to a remedy limitation, they are allocating the risk of loss as one part of their bargain. A court will seldom substitute its judgment for that of the contracting companies. In the *Logan Equipment* case, both parties were corporations, and sophisticated executives negotiated the boomlift sale. The court found nothing unconscionable in the bargain and enforced the limitation that the parties had agreed to.[22]

22-3e Privity

When two parties contract, they are *in privity*. If Lance buys a chainsaw from the local hardware store, he is in privity with the store. But Lance has no privity with Kwiksaw, the manufacturer of the chainsaw. Under traditional contract law, a plaintiff injured by a breach of contract could sue only a defendant with whom he had privity. So, many years ago, if Lance's chainsaw had been seriously defective, he could have sued only the store. Kwiksaw would have had no liability because it was not in privity with Lance. This rule hurt consumers because the local retailer often had fewer assets to compensate for serious injuries. Today,

[20] Logan Equipment Corp. v. Simon Aerials, Inc., 736 F. Supp. 1188 (D. Mass. 1990).

[21] Compensatory, consequential, and incidental damages are discussed in Chapter 19 on remedies.

[22] Logan Equipment, 736 F. Supp. at 1195.

privity is gradually disappearing as a defense. Various states are approaching the issue in different ways, so there is no single rule. We can, however, highlight the trends.

Personal Injury

Where a product causes a personal injury, most states permit a warranty lawsuit even without privity. If the chain on Lance's power saw flies off and slashes his arm, he has suffered a personal injury. Of course, he may sue the store, with which he has privity. But he will want to sue the manufacturer, which has more money. In the majority of states, he will be able to sue the manufacturer for breach of warranty even though he had no privity with it. (Note that Lance is sure to make other claims against the manufacturer, including negligence and strict liability, both discussed in Chapter 9.)

Economic Loss

If the buyer suffers only economic loss, privity may still be required to bring a suit for breach of warranty. **If the buyer is a business, the majority of states require privity.** Fab-Rik makes fabric for furniture and drapes, which it sells to various wholesalers. Siddown makes sofas. Siddown buys Fab-Rik fabric from a wholesaler and, after installing it on 200 sofas, finds the material defective. Siddown may sue the wholesaler but, in most states, will be unable to sue Fab-Rik for breach of any warranties. There was no privity.

By contrast, when the buyer is a *consumer*, more states will permit a suit against the manufacturer, even without privity. Lance, the consumer, buys his power saw to landscape his property. This time, the saw malfunctions without injuring him, but Lance must buy a replacement for considerably more money. Many states—but not all—will permit him to recover his losses from Kwiksaw, the manufacturer, on the theory that Kwiksaw intends its product to reach consumers and is in the best position to control losses.

In the following case, a jailhouse tragedy prompts a product liability suit.

Reed v. City of Chicago

263 F. Supp. 2d 1123
United States District Court for the Northern District of Illinois, 2003

Facts: J. C. Reed was arrested and brought to Chicago's Fifth District Police Station. Police were allegedly aware that he was suicidal, having seen him slash his wrists earlier. They removed his clothing and dressed him in a paper isolation gown. Sadly, Reed used the gown to hang himself.

Reed's mother, on his behalf, sued the police (for failing to monitor a suicidal inmate) and also Cypress Medical Products, the manufacturer of the isolation gown. The claim was that the gown should have been made of material that would tear if someone attempted to hang himself with it. Cypress moved to dismiss the suit, claiming that Reed had no privity with the company.

Issue: ***Could Reed maintain a lawsuit against Cypress despite lack of privity?***

Excerpts from Judge Moran's Decision: The single issue we must decide is whether plaintiff, as a nonpurchaser, can recover from the manufacturer and designer of the gown for breach of warranty. Historically, Illinois law has required privity. Lack of privity occurs when a user of the product, beside the purchaser, is injured. Section 2-318 of the Uniform Commercial Code (UCC), as adopted by the Illinois legislature, contains mandatory exceptions to the general requirement of privity:

> A seller's warranty whether express or implied extends to any natural person who is in the family or household of his buyer or who is a guest in his home if it is reasonable to expect that such person may use, consume or be affected by the goods and who is injured in person by breach of the warranty.

The Illinois Supreme Court has determined that privity is no longer an absolute requirement for breach of warranty actions. While section 2-318 lists specific exceptions to the privity requirement, Illinois courts have noted that this list is not necessarily exhaustive.

The vast majority of cases examining the limits of section 2-318 in Illinois have dealt with the employment context, expanding the class of potential breach of warranty plaintiffs to employees of the ultimate purchaser. In [a case called *Whitaker*,] plaintiff was injured while using a bandsaw that had been purchased by his employer. The court determined that the employee was essentially a third party beneficiary to the sale in that the employee's safety while using the bandsaw was "either explicitly or implicitly part of the basis of the bargain when the employer purchased the goods."

In cases examining the limits of section 2-318 in other contexts, courts have been reluctant to find additional exceptions to the privity requirement. In [a case called *Hemphill*,] the court refused to allow a breach of warranty claim by a university football player against the manufacturer of his helmet.

While no Illinois courts have expanded the plaintiff class for breach of warranty actions beyond employees, we believe that the law requires us to do so here. The beneficiary of any warranty made by the manufacturer and designer of the gown is necessarily a potentially suicidal detainee like Reed. If protection is not provided to plaintiffs like Reed, any warranty as to the safety of the gown would have little, if any, effect. In designing and manufacturing the gown, defendants contemplated that the users of the gown would be detainees. Moreover, the safety of these detainees was necessarily a part of the bargain, whether explicitly or implicitly, between the seller and buyer. For these reasons, a detainee of the City like Reed must be able to enforce the protections of any warranties made by the manufacturer and designer of the gown.

For the foregoing reasons, defendants' motion to dismiss is denied.

22-3f Buyer's Misuse

Misuse by the buyer will generally preclude a warranty claim. Common sense tells us that the seller only warrants its goods if they are properly used. Lord & Taylor warranted that its false eyelashes would function well and cause no harm. But when Ms. Caldwell applied them, they severely irritated one eye. She sued, but the store prevailed. Why? Caldwell applied the eyelashes improperly, getting the glue into one eye. On her other eye, she used the product correctly and suffered no harm. Her misuse proved painful to her eye—and fatal to her lawsuit.[23]

22-3g Statute of Limitations and Notice of Breach

It is right that a seller be responsible for the goods it places in the market. On the other hand, a seller should not face potential liability *forever*. A company cannot be a perpetual insurer for goods that it sold decades earlier. So, the UCC imposes two important time limits on a buyer's claim of breach.

The Code sets a four-year statute of limitations. This means that the buyer must bring any lawsuit for breach of a warranty no later than four years after the goods were delivered. The Code puts an additional burden on a buyer asserting a breach of warranty. **The UCC requires that a buyer notify the seller of defects within a reasonable time.**[24] The purpose here is to enable the seller to cure, by repairing or replacing, any problems with the goods. Ideally, a seller that receives notice of a potential breach will fix the problem and there will *be* no lawsuit.

The circumstances will determine what is a "reasonable" amount of time. An inexperienced consumer could reasonably take many months to figure out that a new laptop computer had a serious operating defect. Further, a delay of six or eight months would not harm a large computer manufacturer. On the other hand, a corporate buyer of perishable food products must act very quickly if it wishes to claim the goods are defective.

23Caldwell v. Lord & Taylor, Inc., 142 Ga. App. 137 (Ga. Ct. App. 1977).

24UCC §2-067.

CHAPTER CONCLUSION

Bad things happen. Deals fall through. Goods disappear. Products injure. Unfortunately, people often fail to consider these possibilities when making a contract. In that case, the UCC steps in with default rules that address critical issues in commercial transactions, such as when an insurable interest exists, the risk of loss shifts, and warranties are made. But these default rules will not always be in a party's best interest. Fortunately, the UCC gives buyers and sellers the freedom to change their default settings. Businesspeople who understand the UCC can tailor the rules to their own advantage. Armed with this chapter's information, they will know how and when to alter the UCC's rules to suit their business purposes and protect themselves if and when bad things *do* happen.

EXAM REVIEW

1. **INTEREST AND TITLE** An *interest* is a legal right in something. *Title* means the normal rights of ownership.
2. **IDENTIFICATION** Goods must *exist* and be *identified* to the contract before title can pass. The parties may agree in their contract how and when they will identify goods; if they do not specify, the Code stipulates when it happens. The parties may also state when title passes, and once again, if they do not, the Code provides rules.

EXAMStrategy

Question: On September 10, Bell Corp. entered into a contract to purchase 50 lamps from Glow Manufacturing. Bell prepaid 40 percent of the purchase price. Glow became insolvent on September 19 before segregating, in its inventory, the lamps to be delivered to Bell. Bell will not be able to recover the lamps because:

(a) Bell is regarded as a merchant.

(b) The lamps were not identified to the contract.

(c) Glow became insolvent fewer than ten days after receipt of Bell's prepayment.

(d) Bell did not pay the full price at the time of purchase.

Strategy: In analyzing issues about ownership, remember that title can never change hands until the goods have been identified to the contract. Identification can occur in three ways: the parties describe specific goods that already exist; animals are conceived or crops planted; or the seller marks, ships, or otherwise indicates which are going to the buyer. (See the "Result" at the end of this Exam Review section.)

3. **INSURABLE INTEREST** A buyer obtains an *insurable interest* when the goods are identified to the contract. A seller retains an insurable interest in goods as long as she has either title or a security interest in them.

4. **VOID AND VOIDABLE TITLE** *Void title* is no title at all. *Voidable title* means limited rights in the goods, inferior to those of the owner. A person with voidable title has power to transfer good title to a *bona fide purchaser (BFP);* that is, someone who purchases in good faith, for value.
5. **ENTRUSTING** Any *entrusting* of goods to a merchant who deals in goods of that kind gives him the power to transfer all rights of the entruster to a buyer in the ordinary course of business.
6. **BIOC** A buyer in the ordinary course of business generally takes goods free and clear of any security interest.

EXAMStrategy

Question: Fay Witcher owned a Ford Bronco. Steve Risher operated a used car lot. Witcher delivered his automobile to Risher, asking him to resell it if he could. Witcher specified that he wanted all cash for his car, not cash plus a trade-in. Risher sold the car to Richard Parker for $12,800, but he took a trade-in as part payment. Risher promised to deliver the Bronco's certificate of title to Parker within a few days but never did. He was also obligated to deliver proceeds of the sale to Witcher, and, of course, he failed to do that. Parker claimed that the car was rightfully his. Witcher argued that Parker owned nothing because he never got the title and because Witcher never got his money. Who loses?

Strategy: Any entrusting of goods to a merchant who deals in goods of that kind gives him the power to transfer all rights of the entruster to a buyer in the ordinary course of business. A buyer in the ordinary course of business generally takes goods free and clear of any security interest. Did Witcher entrust the auto? Was Parker a BIOC? Why or why not? (See the "Result" at the end of this Exam Review section.)

7. **RISK OF LOSS** In their contract, the parties may allocate the *risk of loss* any way they wish. If they fail to do so, the Code provides several steps to determine who pays for any damage. When neither party has breached, the risk of loss generally passes from seller to buyer when the seller has transported the goods as far as he is obligated to. When a party has breached, the risk of loss generally lies with the party that has breached.

EXAMStrategy

Question: Bradkeyne International, Ltd., an English company, bought a large quantity of batteries from Duracell, Inc. The contract specified delivery "FOB cargo ship, Jacksonville, Florida." Duracell supervised the loading of the batteries onto a ship in Jacksonville in early July, and they arrived in England in August. When loaded onto the ship, the batteries were conforming goods that could be used for normal purposes. But on board the ship, excessive heat damaged them. By the time they reached England, they were worth only a fraction of the original price. Bradkeyne sued Duracell. Who loses?

Strategy: The advantage of standard shipping terms is that they make business predictable and exam questions easy. If you know what "FOB cargo ship, Jacksonville, Florida" means, you know the answer. (See the "Result" at the end of this Exam Review section.)

8. **EXPRESS WARRANTY** Seller can create an express warranty with any affirmation description of the goods, or sample or model, provided the promise part of the basis of the bargain.
9. **IMPLIED WARRANTY OF MERCHANTABILITY** With certain exceptions, the Code implies a warranty that the goods will be fit for their ordinary purpose.
10. **IMPLIED WARRANTY OF FITNESS FOR A PARTICULAR PURPOSE** With some exceptions, the Code implies a warranty that the goods are fit for the buyer's special purpose, provided that the seller knows of that purpose when the contract is made and knows of the buyer's reliance.

RESULTS

2. Result: The contract was silent about which goods were involved, neither animals nor plants were involved, and Glow never segregated the lamps. The lamps were never identified to the contract, and the correct answer is (b).

6. Result: Risher was a merchant dealing in automobiles, meaning that Witcher did entrust the car to him. Parker was a BIOC: He acted in good faith, without knowing that the sale violated the agreement between Witcher and Risher. Parker wins, and he keeps the car.

7. Result: "FOB cargo ship, Jacksonville, Florida" means that the seller bears all risks until the goods are placed in the carrier's possession. From that moment onward, the buyer bears the risk. The batteries were fine when delivered, so Duracell was off the hook once they were on board. Bradkeyne bears the loss.

MULTIPLE-CHOICE QUESTIONS

1. **CPA QUESTION** On Monday, Wolfe paid Aston Co., a furniture retailer, $500 for a table. On Thursday, Aston notified Wolfe that the table was ready to be picked up. On Saturday, while Aston was still in possession of the table, it was destroyed in a fire. Who bears the loss of the table?
   (a) Wolfe because Wolfe had title to the table at the time of loss
   (b) Aston unless Wolfe is a merchant
   (c) Wolfe unless Aston breached the contract
   (d) Aston because Wolfe had not yet taken possession of the table
2. Sheri signs a contract with Farmer Charlie on February 1. Under the deal, she will pay $25,000 for Charlie's entire pumpkin crop on October 1. Charlie plants pumpkin seeds on March 1, and they begin to sprout on April 1. When are the pumpkins identified?
   (a) February 1
   (b) March 1
   (c) April 1
   (d) October 1

3. Sam obtains a Patek Philippe watch from Greg by fraud. It has a retail price of $10,000. He sells it to Melissa for $9,000. She believes he owns the watch. Melissa _______________ a bona fide purchaser. Sam disappears. If Greg discovers that she has the watch and demands that it be returned, Melissa _______________ have to give the watch to Greg.
   (a) is; will
   (b) is; will not
   (c) is not; will
   (d) is not; will not
4. **CPA QUESTION** Vick bought a used boat from Ocean Marina that disclaimed "any and all warranties." Ocean was unaware that the boat had been stolen from Kidd. Vick surrendered it to Kidd when confronted with proof of the theft. Vick sued Ocean. Who prevails?
   (a) Vick because the implied warranty of title has been breached
   (b) Vick because a merchant cannot disclaim implied warranties
   (c) Ocean because of the disclaimer of warranties
   (d) Ocean because Vick surrendered the boat to Kidd
5. **CPA QUESTION** Which of the following conditions must be met for an implied warranty of fitness for a particular purpose to arise?
   I. The warranty must be in writing.
   II. The seller must know that the buyer was relying on the seller in selecting the goods.
   (a) I only
   (b) II only
   (c) Both I and II
   (d) Neither I nor II
6. **CPA QUESTION** Under the UCC sales article, an action for breach of the implied warranty of merchantability by a party who sustains personal injuries may be successful against the seller of the product only when:
   (a) the seller is a merchant of the product involved.
   (b) an action based on negligence can also be successfully maintained.
   (c) the injured party is in privity of contract with the seller.
   (d) an action based on strict liability in tort can also be successfully maintained.

CASE QUESTIONS

1. Franklin Miller operated Miller Seed Co. in Pea Ridge, Arkansas. He bought, processed, and sold fescue seed, which is used for growing pasture and fodder grass. Farmers brought seed to Miller, who would normally clean, bag, and store it. In some cases, the farmers authorized Miller to sell the seed, in some cases not. Miller mixed together the seed that was for sale with the seed in storage so that a customer could not see any difference between them. Miller defaulted on a $380,000 loan from the First State Bank of Purdy. First State attempted to seize all

of the seed in the store. Tony Havelka, a farmer, protested that his 490,000 pounds of seed was merely in storage and not subject to First State's claim. Who is entitled to the seed?

2. John C. Clark, using an alias, rented a Lexus from Alamo Rent-A-Car in San Diego, California. Clark never returned the car to Alamo and obtained a California "quick title" using forged signatures. He then advertised in the *Las Vegas Review Journal* newspaper and sold the car to Terry and Yvonne Mendenhall for $34,000 in cash. The Mendenhalls made improvements to the car and had it insured, smog- and safety-tested, registered, licensed, and titled in the state of Utah. When Alamo reported the car stolen, the Nevada Department of Motor Vehicles seized the auto and returned it to Alamo. The Mendenhalls sued Alamo. The trial court concluded that the Mendenhalls had purchased the car for value and without notice that it was stolen, and so they were bona fide purchasers entitled to the Lexus. Alamo appealed. Please rule.

3. Universal Consolidated Cos. contracted with China Metallurgical Import and Export Corp. (CMIEC) to provide CMIEC with new and used equipment for a cold rolling steel mill. Universal then contracted with Pittsburgh Industrial Furnace Co. (Pifcom) to engineer and build much of the equipment. The contract required Pifcom to deliver the finished equipment to a trucking company, which would then transport it to Universal. Pifcom delivered the goods to the trucking company as scheduled. But before all of the goods reached Universal, CMIEC notified Universal it was canceling the deal. Universal, in turn, notified Pifcom to stop work, but all goods had been delivered to the shipper and ultimately reached Universal. Pifcom claimed that it retained title to the goods, but Universal claimed that title had passed to it. Who is right?

4. ***YOU BE THE JUDGE* WRITING PROBLEM** Construction Helicopters paid Heli-Dyne Systems $315,000 for three helicopters that were in Argentina. Two were ready to fly, and one was disassembled for routine maintenance. The contract said nothing about risk of loss (the parties could have saved a lot of money by reading this chapter). Heli-Dyne arranged for an Argentine company to oversee their loading on board the freight ship *Lynx*. The 2 helicopters and 25 crates containing the disassembled craft were properly loaded, but when the ship arrived in Miami, only 7 of the crates appeared. Heli-Dyne refused to supply more parts, and Construction sued. Who bears the loss? **Argument for Construction:** Construction had no control over the goods until they reached Miami. Although we do not know exactly what happened to the crates, we know the one party that had *nothing* to do with the loss: Construction. The company should not pay for damage it never caused. **Argument for Heli-Dyne:** Because the contract failed to specify risk of loss, it is a shipment contract. In such an agreement, risk of loss passes to the buyer when the seller delivers the goods to a carrier. Heli-Dyne delivered the goods and has no further responsibility.

5. When Sony released its PlayStation 3 (PS3), it represented that the gaming system: (1) connected to the PlayStation Network, (2) had the ability to run other operating systems, and (3) was expected to last for over ten years. But the product's terms of service provided that future updates might disable some functions. Four years later, Sony's software update forced users to choose between features (1) and (2) listed above. Disgruntled gamers sued, claiming that Sony made an express warranty that the PS3 would work as promised for ten years, but took away a fundamental product feature after only four years. Was Sony's representation an enforceable express warranty?

DISCUSSION QUESTIONS

1. **ETHICS** Myrna and James Brown ordered a $35,000 motor home from R.V. Kingdom, Inc. The manufacturer delivered the vehicle to R.V. Kingdom, with title in the dealer's name. The Browns agreed to accept the motor home, but they soon regretted spending the money and asked R.V. Kingdom to resell it. The motor home stayed on R.V. Kingdom's lot for quite a few months, but when the Browns decided to come get it, they learned that R.V. Kingdom had illegally used the vehicle as collateral for a loan and that a bank had repossessed it. The Browns filed a claim with their insurance company, State Farm. The insurer agreed that the vehicle had been stolen and agreed that the Browns' policy covered newly acquired vehicles. But the company refused to pay, claiming that the Browns had not taken title or possession to the goods and therefore had no insurable interest. The Browns sued. Please rule on their case.

   Let's also look at the ethics of the case by creating a contrasting hypothetical. Suppose that among the insurance company's thousands of customers was Arvee, a recreational vehicle dealership similar to the one in the real case. Imagine that Arvee had taken in an automobile for resale from a customer named Parker and kept the vehicle on its lot. If Parker's auto were stolen, what argument would the insurance company be making? How would the company define insurable interest in *that* case?

2. Imagine that your laptop gets a virus, and you take it to a local computer repair shop. The shop sells your computer to Heidi. Under the entrustment rules in the UCC, Heidi is a buyer in the ordinary course of business. And so, even if you find Heidi and demand that she return your laptop, *she gets to keep it*. Is this fair? Does the law give too much protection to purchasers in this situation, and not enough to victims?

3. Greg manufactures and sells T-shirts. As a seller, would he be better off if his contracts indicated "FOB (place of shipment)" or "FOB (place of destination)"? Explain your answer.

4. A seller can disclaim all implied warranties by stating that goods are sold "as is" (or by using other, more specific language). Is this fair? The UCC's implied warranties seem reasonable—that goods are fit for their normal purposes, for example. Should it be so easy for sellers to escape their obligations?

5. After learning more about implied warranties and disclaimers, would you ever buy an item sold "as is?" Imagine a car salesman who offers you a car for $8,000, but who also says that he can knock the price down to $6,500 if you will buy the car "as is." If you live in a state that does not give consumers special protections, which deal would be more appealing?

23

CHAPTER

PERFORMANCE AND REMEDIES

Was it a 1930s roadster? A drag racing car from the 1950s? Both. When the Plymouth Prowler first hit the road, with its motorcycle-styled front fenders and low-slung hot rod body, it was nearly impossible to get your hands on one. Dealers were swamped with orders, but they did not know if they would receive a single car from the manufacturer.

Donald Hessler wanted a Prowler—and he was a determined man. Hessler went to Crystal Lake Chrysler-Plymouth, met with its owner, Gary Rosenberg, and signed an agreement to buy a Prowler anytime during the next year for $5,000 over the manufacturer's list price. Three months later, Rosenberg revealed that the list price would be $39,000. However, the car dealer also entered into a contract to sell a Prowler to another customer for $50,000.

The next time they spoke, Rosenberg told Hessler that Crystal Lake would not be allotted any Prowlers. The eager buyer, though, responded that a Chrysler representative had told him Crystal Lake would receive at least one car. Rosenberg was furious with a customer, who had "gone behind his back" to contact Chrysler, and said he would not sell Hessler a car, even if he did receive one.

Hessler telephoned 38 Chrysler dealers, but none would promise him a car. One month later, at a promotional event for the car, he saw a new Prowler—with Crystal Lake's name on it! He located Rosenberg, offered to buy the car on the spot—and was again rebuffed. Frustrated and angry, but still determined, Hessler somehow found a Prowler later the same day from another dealer, and bought it—for $77,706.

Ecstatic with his new car, Hessler drove straight to court, where he sued Crystal Lake.

> **Donald Hessler wanted a Prowler—and he was a determined man.**

Was Rosenberg within his rights, refusing to sell a car to Hessler? Was the customer entitled to compensation for spending so much more on the coveted auto? These are typical issues of contract performance under the Uniform Commercial Code. We look at the issue in this chapter, along with principles of *remedy*. When Hessler bought a car elsewhere, he was *covering*. Did he act reasonably in spending almost $40,000 above list price? You will have to wait a few pages to find out, but we promise to give you the answer before anyone else gets it.

23-1 RIGHTS AND OBLIGATIONS OF CONTRACTING PARTIES

23-1a Obligation on All Parties: Good Faith

Surely it is a good idea to begin this final chapter on sale of goods issues in good faith.

The R. G. Ray Corp. needed T-bolts to use in automobile parts it was manufacturing for the Garrett Co. Ray contracted for Maynard Manufacturing to deliver 57,000 T-bolts and provided Maynard with detailed specifications. The contract stated that Ray would be the "final judge" of whether the T-bolts conformed to its specifications and that Ray had the right to return any or all non-conforming bolts. **Conforming goods satisfy the contract terms. Non-conforming goods do not.**[1]

Unfortunately, Ray rejected the 57,000 bolts and sued, demanding every penny it had paid as well as additional damages for its lost business with Garrett. Ray moved for summary judgment, pointing out that the contract explicitly allowed it to judge the bolts, to reject any it found unsatisfactory, and to cancel the contract. The court acknowledged that the contract did give Ray these one-sided powers, yet it denied summary judgment. There was still an issue of *good faith*.

The UCC requires *good faith* in the performance and enforcement of every contract. Good faith means honesty in fact. Between merchants, it also means the use of reasonable commercial standards of fair dealing.[2] So Ray's right to reject the T-bolts was not absolute. There was some evidence that Ray had lost its contract with Garrett for reasons having nothing to do with Maynard's T-bolts. If that was true, and Ray had rejected the T-bolts simply because it no longer needed them, then Ray acted in bad faith and would be fully liable on the contract. The court ruled that Maynard should have its day in court to prove bad faith.[3]

Good faith
The UCC requires that contracting parties perform and enforce their deals honestly.

In the following case, the contract was clear, but one party's behavior was opaque. Was it bad faith? You be the judge.

You Be the Judge

The Burton Corp. v. ViQuest Precision Industries Co.

2010 U.S. Dist. LEXIS 78392; 2010 WL 3024319
United States District Court for the Southern District of New York, 2010

Facts: Burton is a Vermont-based designer, manufacturer, and seller of snowboards. ViQuest is a manufacturer of injection-molded products. Burton and ViQuest contracted for ViQuest to manufacture Burton's snowboard bindings.

The agreement also contained the following provisions:

- The agreement's initial term was one year, with automatic successive one-year renewals.
- Burton could terminate the Agreement at any time if it determined that "ViQuest's financial position posed a risk to Burton's business."
- Any dispute between the parties would go to arbitration.

The agreement automatically renewed for a second one-year period. Things appeared to be going well until

[1] UCC §2-106(2).

[2] UCC §§1-203, 2-103(1)(b).

[3] R. G. Ray Corp. v. Maynard Manufacturing Co., 1993 U.S. Dist. LEXIS 15754, 1993 WL 462841 (N.D. Ill. 1993).

two months later when Burton unexpectedly terminated the agreement claiming that "ViQuest's financial position" was too risky. However, the opposite seemed to be true: Burton owed ViQuest approximately $1.8 million in unpaid purchase orders, which it refused to pay.

An arbitration panel ruled for ViQuest after it determined that Burton's reasons for terminating the contract lacked any basis in fact and were in bad faith. Burton asked that the court vacate the award, claiming the arbitrators misconstrued the contract by imposing an additional duty to prove that ViQuest was indeed risky. A court reviewed the panel's decision.

You Be the Judge: *Did Burton's terminate the contract in bad faith?*

Argument for Burton: Business is business. Contracts are contracts. And the contract language is clear: Burton had the right to terminate at any time if it determined that "ViQuest's financial position posed a risk." Burton had no duty to prove how it reached this conclusion or whether it was reasonable. It was simply a business decision—an area where courts and arbitrators should not meddle. The arbitrators exceeded their authority by reading into the contract a requirement to prove that ViQuest was financially challenged. This decision was based on what the arbitrators thought the contract should have said, not on the actual terms of the deal. Stick to the contract.

Argument for ViQuest: The UCC imposes a covenant of good faith and fair dealing in the performance and enforcement of every contract—including this one. This duty is implicit. Burton argues that the contract allowed it to terminate if it unilaterally determined ViQuest's financial position was risky—a determination it reached based on ... nothing. In effect, Burton is saying that it could, at its whim, terminate the contract at any time just by saying so, without producing any reason or evidence. But that is not what the contract said. And it should not be interpreted that way. Burton terminated the contract in bad faith and, as such, is sledding on very thin ice.

23-1b Seller's Rights and Obligations

The seller's primary obligation is to deliver conforming goods to the buyer.[4] But because a buyer might not be willing or able to accept delivery, the UCC demands only that the seller make a reasonable *attempt* at delivery. **The seller must *tender* the goods, which means to make conforming goods available to the buyer.**[5] Normally, the contract will state where and when the seller is obligated to tender delivery. For example, the parties may agree that Manufacturer is to tender 1,000 printers at a certain warehouse on July 3. If Manufacturer makes the printers available on that date, Buyer is obligated to pick them up then and there and is in breach if it fails to do so.

Although a seller must always tender delivery, that does not mean a seller always transports the goods. Sometimes the contract will require the buyer to collect the goods. Regardless of where delivery is being made, however, the seller must (1) make the goods available at a reasonable time, (2) keep the goods available for a reasonable period, and (3) deliver to the buyer any documents that it needs to take possession. And as we have said, the seller is expected to deliver *conforming* goods, which brings us to the next rule.

Perfect Tender Rule

Perfect Tender Rule
Under the UCC, tendered goods must be exactly as described in the contract.

Under the Perfect Tender Rule, the buyer may reject the goods if they fail in any respect to conform to the contract.[6]

Stanley and Joan Jakowski agreed to buy a new Camaro automobile from Carole Chevrolet. The contract stated that Carole would apply a polymer undercoating. The Jakowskis paid in full for the car, but the next day, they informed Carole that the car lacked the undercoating.

[4]UCC §2-301.
[5]UCC §2-503.
[6]UCC §2-601.

Carole acknowledged the defect and promised to apply the undercoating, but, before it could do so, a thief stole the car. The Jakowskis demanded their money back, but Carole refused, saying that the risk of loss had passed to the Jakowskis when Carole tendered delivery. The Jakowskis sued claiming that they had rejected the Camaro as non-conforming. Carole responded that this was absurd: The car was perfect in every respect except for the very minor undercoating, which Carole had promised to fix promptly. Carole Chevrolet lost the case because of the Perfect Tender Rule.

The New Jersey court found that the defect was minor but said that "despite seller's assertion to the contrary, the degree of their non-conformity is irrelevant in assessing the buyer's right to reject them…. [N]o particular quantum of non-conformity is required." The Jakowskis had lawfully rejected non-conforming goods, and Carole Chevrolet was forced to pay them the full value of the missing car.[7]

Restrictions on the Perfect Tender Rule

The UCC includes sections that limit the Perfect Tender Rule's effect. Indeed, courts often apply the limitations more enthusiastically than the rule itself, and so while perfect tender is the law, it must be understood in the context of other provisions. We will look at the most common ways that the law undercuts the Perfect Tender Rule. In doing so, we will see the typically flexible approach that the Code takes to a business transaction.

Usage of Trade, Course of Dealing, and Course of Performance. The Uniform Commercial Code takes the commonsense view that a contract for the sale of goods does not exist in a vacuum. It requires courts to consider three things when they apply the Perfect Tender Rule.

Usage of trade
A practice or way of dealing that is expected in an industry

"Usage of trade" means any practice that members of an industry *expect* to be part of their dealings.[8] The Perfect Tender Rule may not permit a buyer to reject goods with minor flaws. For example, the textile industry interprets the phrase "first-quality fabric" to permit a limited number of flaws in most materials. If a seller delivers 1,000 bolts of fabric and 5 of them have minor defects, the seller has *not* violated the Perfect Tender Rule.

Course of dealing
The conduct between the parties during previous transactions

The course of dealing between the two parties may also limit the rule. **The term *course of dealing* refers to previous commercial transactions between the *same parties*.**[9] The UCC requires that a current contract be interpreted in the light of any past dealings that have created reasonable expectations. Suppose a buyer orders 20,000 board feet of "highest-grade pine" from a lumber company, just as it has in each of the three previous years. In the earlier deliveries, the buyer accepted the lumber even though 1 or 2 percent was not the highest grade. That course of dealing will probably control the present contract, and the buyer will not be permitted suddenly to reject an entire shipment because 1 percent is a lower grade of pine. Such a tender is not "perfect," but it would be good enough.

Course of performance
The conduct between the parties to a particular transaction

The course of performance has the same effect on contract interpretation. **The term *course of performance* refers to the history of dealings between the parties *in a single contract*, and thus assumes that it is the kind of contract demanding an ongoing relationship.**[10]

Suppose a newspaper company signs a deal to purchase 5 tons of newsprint from a paper company every week for a year, and the contract also specifies the grade of paper to be delivered. If, during the first three months, the newspaper company routinely accepts paper containing a small number of flaws, that course of performance will control the contract. During the final month, the newspaper may not suddenly reject the type of paper it had earlier accepted.

---

[7] Jakowski v. Carole Chevrolet, Inc., 180 N.J. Super. 122 (N.J. Super. Ct. 1981).

[8] UCC §1-205(2).

[9] UCC §1-205(1).

[10] UCC §2-208(1).

Parties' Agreement. The parties may also choose to limit the effect of the Perfect Tender Rule *themselves* by drafting a contract that *permits* imperfection in the goods. In some industries, this practice is routine. For example, contracts requiring the seller to design or engineer goods especially for the buyer will generally state a level of performance that the equipment must meet. If the goods meet the level described, the buyer has no right to reject, even if the product has some flaws.

Right to cure

The UCC gives the seller the opportunity to fix the problem of non-conforming goods.

Cure. A basic goal of the UCC is a fully performed contract that leaves both parties satisfied. The seller's right to *cure* helps achieve this goal. **When the buyer rejects non-conforming goods, the seller has the right to cure by delivering conforming goods before the contract deadline.**[11] LightCo is obligated to deliver 10,000 specially manufactured bulbs to Burnout Corp. by September 15. LightCo delivers the bulbs on August 20, and on August 25 Burnout notifies the seller that the bulbs do not meet contract specifications. If LightCo promptly notifies Burnout that it intends to cure and then delivers conforming light bulbs on September 15, it has fulfilled its contract obligations and Burnout must accept the goods. The seller may even cure *after the contract deadline* if the seller (1) reasonably believed the original goods were acceptable and (2) promptly notified the buyer of his intent to cure within a reasonable time. This gives the seller a second chance to replace defective goods. Suppose Chip Co. delivers 25,000 computer chips to Assembler one day before the contract deadline, and two days later, Assembler notifies Chip that the goods are defective. If Chip had tested the chips thoroughly before they left its factory and reasonably believed they met contract specifications, then Chip may cure by promptly notifying Assembler that it will supply conforming goods within a *reasonable* period. Thus, even if the conforming chips arrive two weeks after the contract deadline, Chip will have cured unless Assembler can show that the delay caused it serious harm.

What if a shipment of goods has several non-conformities and the seller offers to fix *some* of the problems? The following case addresses the issue.

Zion Temple First Pentecostal Church of Cincinnati, Ohio, Inc. v. Brighter Day Bookstore & Gifts

2004 Ohio 5499
Ohio Court of Appeals, 2004

Facts: Zion Temple First Pentecostal Church ordered new choir robes from Brighter Day Bookstore, a retailer that sold robes manufactured by Murphy Cap & Gown.

When Brighter Day delivered the robes to the Zion Temple, the church members found many faults. They did not like the color or material, which they considered very different from a sample they had reviewed at Brighter Day. The sleeves had been attached facing the wrong way, and on the overlays the Velcro and tags were visible.

Zion complained to Murphy. The manufacturer offered to repair the sleeves, but Zion declined the offer because of the other problems. Zion returned the robes and, when it failed to get its money back, filed suit.

The trial court gave summary judgment for the defendants, and Zion Temple appealed.

Issue: ***Did Zion Temple afford Murphy a chance to cure?***

Excerpts from Judge Doan's Decision: The record shows that the choir members actually inspected the robes when Brighter Day delivered them and Zion found what it deemed to be non-conformities. This inspection was reasonable and was made within a reasonable time. Thus, Zion never accepted the robes but instead rejected them as not conforming to the contract. Since Zion rejected the goods, Murphy had a right to cure.

Murphy offered to cure any problem with the sleeves. Where the buyer rejects a non-conforming

[11] UCC §2-508.

tender which the seller had reasonable ground to believe would be acceptable with or without money allowance, the seller may, if he seasonably notifies the buyer, have a further reasonable time to substitute a conforming tender. Murphy manufactured the sleeves on the robes according to its design specifications. Because of an error in the catalog that Zion had consulted before placing its order, the sleeves as properly manufactured appeared different from the sleeves as depicted in the catalog. Murphy clearly had the right to cure this non-conformity and indicated its intention to do so within a reasonable time.

Zion had other reasons for contending that the robes did not conform to the contract. It claimed that Velcro was visible on the reversible overlays and that the tags on the overlays could be seen when the overlays were reversed. Murphy never indicated its intention to cure these alleged non-conformities. Consequently, the trial court erred in granting Murphy's motion for summary judgment.

We reverse the entry of summary judgment for Murphy and remand this case for trial or further proceedings consistent with this court's opinion.

EXAMStrategy

Question: Xuberant Inc. orders 2,000 wristwatches from Timely Co. The watches, with Xuberant's logo on the face, are to be delivered by September 15 so that Xuberant can give them away at its September 25 sales convention. Timely tests the watches and is satisfied they work. But when Xuberant receives them, on September 15, the company rejects them because its name is misspelled. Timely offers to correct the error and deliver the new watches by September 22, but Xuberant refuses and sues. Likely outcome?

Strategy: Timely has delivered non-conforming goods, and Xuberant is entitled to reject them. However, the seller has the right to cure by delivering conforming goods before the contract deadline. Timely is offering to deliver shortly after the deadline. Is it entitled to do so?

Result: If the seller reasonably believed the goods were conforming, it may cure within a reasonable time after the deadline. If the court believes that Timely's spelling error was unreasonable, the company has no right to cure. However, a basic goal of the Code is a fully performed contract. A court is likely to declare that the error was excusable and the new delivery date adequate for Xuberant's purpose. Timely will probably win.

Substantial Impairment. Sometimes the Code holds buyers to a higher standard and makes it more difficult to refuse goods. Perfect tender is the usual rule, but, in two circumstances, a buyer who claims goods are non-conforming must show that the defects *substantially impair* their value. This standard applies (1) if the buyer is revoking acceptance of goods or (2) if the buyer is rejecting an installment.

For example, a buyer who initially *accepts* a dozen cement mixers but *later* discovers problems with their engines may revoke his acceptance only by showing that the defects have caused him serious problems. Similarly, if a contract requires a buyer to accept one shipment of diesel fuel each month for two years, the buyer may reject one monthly installment only if the problem with the fuel substantially lowers its value.

Destruction of the Goods. A farmer contracts to sell 250,000 pounds of sunflower seeds to a broker. The contract describes the 125 acres that the farmer will plant to grow the sunflowers. He plants his crop on time, but a drought destroys most of the plants

If a valuable crop is destroyed, who suffers the loss?

and he is able to deliver only 75,000 pounds. Is the farmer liable for the seeds he could not deliver? No. **Is the broker required to accept the smaller crop? No. If identified goods are *totally* destroyed before risk passes to the buyer, the contract is void. If identified goods are *partially* destroyed, the buyer may choose whether to accept the goods at a reduced price or void the contract.**[12]

The crop of sunflowers was identified to the contract when the farmer planted it. When a drought destroyed most of the crop, the contract became voidable. The buyer had the right to accept the smaller crop, at a reduced price, or to reject the crop entirely. The farmer is not liable for the shortfall because the destruction was not his fault.[13]

Commercial impracticability
The UCC may excuse contract performance when an unforeseen, external event disrupts the contract relationship.

Commercial Impracticability. **Commercial impracticability means that a supervening event excuses performance of a contract, if the event was *not* within the parties' contemplation when they made the agreement.**[14] An event is "supervening" if it interrupts the normal course of business and dominates performance of the contract. But a supervening event will excuse performance only if neither party had thought there was a serious chance it would happen.

Harris RF Systems was an American company that manufactured radio equipment. Svenska, a Swedish corporation, bought Harris radio systems and sold them in many countries, including Iran. One contract required Harris to ship a large quantity of spare radio parts, which Svenska would pay $600,000 for and then resell in Iran. Harris attempted to ship the parts to Svenska, but U.S. Customs seized the goods, and the U.S. Department of Defense notified Harris that it believed the parts would be of military value to Iran.

The Defense Department acknowledged that technically, Harris was licensed to ship the goods, but it made two things clear: First, that it would litigate rather than permit the goods to reach Iran; and second, that if Harris attempted to complete the sale in Iran, the department would place all of Harris's future radio shipments on a Munitions List, making it difficult to ship them anywhere in the world. Svenska, on the other hand, pointed out that it had binding contracts to deliver the radio parts to various customers in Iran. If the parts were not forthcoming, Svenska would hold Harris liable for all of its losses. Harris attempted to reach a satisfactory compromise with all parties but failed and eventually agreed not to ship the parts overseas.

Svenska sued. Harris defended, relying on commercial impracticability. Harris persuaded the court that neither party had foreseen the government's intervention and that both parties realized it would be virtually impossible to export goods the Defense Department was determined to block. The court dismissed Svenska's suit.[15]

The accompanying chart outlines the seller's obligations.

---

12 UCC §2-613. Identification of goods is discussed in Chapter 22.

13 Based on Red River Commodities, Inc. v. Eidsness, 459 N.W.2d 805 (N.D. 1990).

14 UCC §2-615.

15 Harriscom Svenska AB v. Harris Corp., 947 F2d 627 (2nd Cir. 1991).

Basic Obligation: The seller's basic obligation is to deliver conforming goods. **The Perfect Tender Rule permits the buyer to reject the goods if they are in any way non-conforming.** But many Code provisions limit the harshness of the Perfect Tender Rule.

Limitation on Seller's Obligation	Code Provision	Effect on Seller's Obligations
Good faith	§1-201(19) and §2-103(1)(b)	Prohibits the buyer from using the Perfect Tender Rule as a way out of a contract that has become unprofitable.
Course of dealing, usage of trade, and course of performance	§1-205(1), §1-205(2), and §2-208	If applicable, will limit the buyer's right to reject for relatively routine defects.
The parties' agreement	§2-106	May describe tolerances for imperfections in the goods.
Cure	§2-508	Allows the seller to replace defective goods with conforming goods, if time permits.
Revocation of acceptance	§2-608	A buyer who has accepted goods may later revoke them only if she can show that the defects *substantially impair* its value.
Installment contracts	§2-612	A buyer may reject an installment only if the defects *substantially impair* its value.
Destruction of goods	§2-613	If goods identified in the contract are destroyed, the contract is void.
Commercial impracticability	§2-615	A supervening event excuses performance of a contract, if the event was not within the parties' contemplation when they made the agreement.

23-1c Buyer's Rights and Obligations

The buyer's primary obligation is to accept conforming goods and pay for them.[16] The buyer must also **provide adequate facilities to receive the goods.**[17] For example, if the contract requires the seller to deliver to the buyer's warehouse, and the parties anticipate that delivery will be by rail, then the buyer must have facilities for unloading railcars at its warehouse.

Inspection and Acceptance

The buyer generally has the right to inspect the goods before paying or accepting.[18] If the contract is silent on this issue, the buyer may inspect. Typically, a buyer will insist on this right, but contracts can be created which do *not* give the parties a right to inspect—for example, a contract allowing shipment C.O.D., which means "cash on delivery." In that case, the buyer must pay upon receipt and do her inspecting later.

16UCC §2-301.
17UCC §2-503(1)(b).
18UCC §2-513.

Along with the right of inspection comes the obligation to do it within a reasonable time and to notify the seller promptly if the buyer intends to reject the goods. **The buyer accepts goods** if (1) after a reasonable opportunity to inspect, she indicates to the seller that the goods are conforming or that she will accept them in spite of non-conformity; or (2) she has had a reasonable opportunity to inspect the goods and has *not rejected them*; or (3) she performs some act indicating that she now owns the goods, such as altering or reselling them.[19]

Partial Acceptance. A buyer has the right to accept some goods while rejecting others if the goods can be divided into *commercial units*. Such a unit is any grouping of goods that the industry normally treats as a whole. For example, one truckload of gravel would be a commercial unit. If the contract called for 100 truckloads of gravel, a buyer could accept 10 that conformed to contract specifications while rejecting 90 that did not.

Revocation. As we mentioned earlier, a buyer has a limited right to revoke acceptance of goods. **A buyer may revoke acceptance but only if the non-conformity *substantially impairs* the value of the goods and only if she had a legitimate reason for the initial acceptance.**[20] This means the Perfect Tender Rule does *not* apply: A buyer in this situation may not revoke because of minor defects. Further, the buyer must show that she had a good reason for accepting the goods originally. Acceptable reasons would include defects that were not visible on inspection or defects that the seller promised but failed to cure.

Rejection. **The buyer may reject non-conforming goods by notifying the seller within a reasonable time.**[21] Huntsville Hospital purchased electrocardiogram equipment from Mortara Instrument for $155,000. The equipment failed to work properly, and the hospital notified Mortara within a reasonable time that it was rejecting it. The hospital asked Mortara to pick up the equipment and refund the full purchase price, but Mortara did neither. When the hospital sued, Mortara claimed that the hospital should have returned the equipment to Mortara and that its failure left it liable for the full cost. The court of appeals was unpersuaded and gave judgment for the hospital, declaring that the hospital's only obligation was to notify the seller of a rejection and hold the goods for the seller to collect.[22]

Installment contract
Agreement in which performance is to be made in a series of separate payments or deliveries

The rule is different in the case of an installment contract. An **installment contract** is one that *requires* goods to be delivered in *separate lots*. If Bus Co. contracts for Oil Co. to deliver 5,000 gallons of gasoline every week for one year, that is an installment contract. **A buyer may reject a non-conforming installment but only if it *substantially impairs* the value of that installment and cannot be cured.**[23] The Perfect Tender Rule does not apply. Bus Co. has no right to reject an installment containing 4,900 gallons of gasoline because the minor shortfall does not impair the shipment's substantial value. On the other hand, if Oil Co. delivered gasoline with lead in it, Bus Co. could reject it since Bus Co. would be legally prohibited from using the gas. (Remember, though, that Oil Co., like all sellers, has the right to cure.)

The following case deals with rejection and revocation. Have a peek inside the trailer, but mind the slippery puddles.

19UCC §2-606.

20UCC §§2-607, 608.

21UCC §§2-601, 602.

22Huntsville Hospital v. Mortara Instrument, 57 F3d 1043 (11th Cir. 1995).

23UCC §2-612.

Lile v. Kiesel

871 N.E. 2d 995
Indiana Court of Appeals, 2007

Facts: Edward and Kelly Kiesel bought a new pullbehind trailer from James Lile, the owner of Lile's Trailer Sales. That same day, the couple took their new trailer on its first camping trip. It rained all night, and, in the morning, the Kiesels noticed water inside the trailer. The next time it rained, Edward noticed more water pooling in various parts of the trailer. A week later, Edward brought the trailer in for repairs.

Lile repaired the roof, using new silicone. However, a week later the trailer again leaked, and Kelly reported this to Lile, demanding a full refund. Lile refused a refund but offered to seal any leaks, replace interior walls, and sand and paint the exterior. The Kiesels instead took the trailer to a different auto body shop where the owner said that extensive interior rust indicated the trailer had leaked longer than the Kiesels owned it. The Kiesels sued. Lile claimed that the Kiesels had accepted the vehicle and unfairly refused repairs. The trial court awarded the Kiesels the full price of the trailer, and Lile appealed.

Issue: ***Were the Kiesels entitled to the trailer's purchase price?***

Excerpts from Judge Riley's Decision[24]**:** Lile's asserts that the Kiesels accepted the trailer and consequently could not reject the goods. We agree that in purchasing the trailer, using it on more than one occasion, as well as licensing and titling it in their names, the Kiesels accepted the trailer and lost any right to reject the sale of the trailer. However, even though acceptance precludes the rejection of goods, it does not impair a buyer's ability to revoke acceptance and seek a remedy for the non-conformity of goods. Specifically, [UCC §2-608] provides for the revocation of acceptance of goods in whole or in part, stating:

> The buyer may revoke his acceptance of a lot or commercial unit whose non-conformity substantially impairs its value to him if he has accepted it … without discovery of such non-conformity if his acceptance was reasonably induced either by the difficulty of discovery before acceptance or by the seller's assurances.

In our view, there is no question that leaking and rust damage substantially impairs the value of a trailer. In addition, leaks due to rain would have been difficult to discover prior to the trailer's purchase. Furthermore, in reporting the problem to Lile's within less than a week of purchasing the trailer, the Kiesels undoubtedly notified Lile's within a reasonable time after they discovered the leaks. As a result, we conclude the Kiesels met the requisite elements under [§2-608] for revocation of acceptance of the trailer.

Lile's also asks this court to hold that the Kiesels did not act in good faith following their acceptance of the trailer when they refused to allow Lile's to make repairs on the trailer. Lile's relies on [§2-508] to argue that the Kiesels had to give Lile's an opportunity to cure the trailer's defects. We disagree. First, we note that [§2-508] pertains to a buyer's *rejection* of non-conforming goods upon delivery. Lile's has already asked us and we have already concluded that the Kiesels accepted the trailer; consequently, as previously determined, the Kiesels can only *revoke* their acceptance at this point. Additionally, there is no evidence in the record to suggest that the Kiesels did not act in good faith in dealing with Lile's. In fact, although they were not obligated to do so, the record clearly shows that the Kiesels gave Lile's an opportunity to cure the leaks when they brought the trailer into Lile's for replacement of silicone on parts of the trailer's roof.

The trial court properly ordered Lile's to reimburse the Kiesels for the purchase price of the trailer. Affirmed.

23-2 REMEDIES OF CONTRACTING PARTIES

23-2a Seller's Remedies

When a buyer breaches a contract, the UCC provides the seller with a variety of potential remedies. Exactly which ones are available depends upon who has the goods (buyer or seller)

24Once again, the authors of this text have substituted the parties' names for the court's "appellant" and "appellee."

and what steps the seller took after the buyer breached. The seller can always **cancel the contract**. She may also be able to:

- Stop delivery of the goods,
- Identify goods to the contract,
- Resell and recover damages,
- Obtain damages for non-acceptance, or
- Obtain the contract price.

Stop Delivery

Sometimes a buyer breaches before the seller has delivered the goods (for example, by failing to make a payment due under the contract or perhaps by repudiating the contract). A party **repudiates** when it indicates that it will not perform, which it can do either by its conduct or by failing to answer a written demand for assurances that it intends to perform.

If a buyer breaches, **the seller may refuse to deliver the goods.**[25] If, when the buyer breaches, the seller has already placed the goods in the hands of a carrier (such as UPS), the seller may instruct the carrier not to deliver the goods, provided the shipment is at least a carload or larger.

Identify Goods to the Contract

If the seller has not yet identified goods to the contract when the buyer breaches, he may do so as soon as he learns of the breach.[26] Suppose an electronics manufacturer, with 5,000 Blu-ray players in its warehouse, learns that a retailer refuses to pay for the 800 units it contracted to buy. The manufacturer may now attach a label to 800 units in its warehouse, identifying them to the contract. This will help it recover damages when it resells the identified goods or uses one of the other remedies described in the next section.

Resale

A seller may resell goods that the buyer has refused to accept, provided she does it reasonably. **If the resale is commercially reasonable, the seller may recover the difference between the resale price and contract price, plus incidental damages, minus expenses saved.**[27]

Incidental damages are expenses the seller incurs in holding the goods and reselling them—costs such as storage, shipping, and advertising for resale. The seller must deduct expenses saved by the breach. For example, if the contract required the seller to ship heavy machinery from Detroit to San Diego, and the buyer's breach enables the seller to sell its goods in Detroit, the seller must deduct from its claimed losses the transportation costs that it saved.

A seller who acts in a commercially reasonable manner is entitled to the following damages:	
	Contract price (the price Seller expected from the original contract)
–	the resale price (the money Seller got at resale)
+	incidental damages (storage, advertising, etc.)
–	expenses saved
=	Seller's damages

25UCC §2-705.
26UCC §2-704.
27UCC §2-706.

A seller is also permitted to resell goods privately; that is, by simply negotiating a deal with another party. But if the seller does so, she must first give the buyer reasonable notice of the private resale.

EXAMStrategy

Question: Fork manufactures forklift trucks. Fork agrees to sell ten trucks, for $30,000 each, to McKnife. Fork will store the trucks in a warehouse near McKnife for three months, when the buyer will collect them. Storage will cost Fork $2,000 per month. A week after signing the deal, before Fork has moved the trucks to the warehouse, McKnife notifies Fork it cannot pay for the trucks. Fork spends $2,000 advertising the machines and sells them for $25,000 each in a commercially reasonable manner. Fork then sues McKnife. Fork will win—but how much?

Strategy: Apply the formula outlined in the previous section.

Result: Fork is entitled to:

	The contract price	$300,000
–	the resale price	250,000
+	incidental damages	2,000
–	expenses saved	6,000
=	Fork's damages	$ 46,000

Damages for Non-Acceptance

A seller who does not resell, or who resells unreasonably, may recover the difference between the original contract price and the market value of the goods at the time of delivery.[28] Oilko agrees to sell Refinery 100,000 barrels of oil for $100 per barrel, to be delivered on November 1. Oilko tenders the oil on November 1. but Refinery refuses to accept it. Three months later, on February 20, Oilko resells the oil to another purchaser for $92 per barrel and sues Refinery for $800,000 (the difference between its contract price and what it finally obtained), plus the cost of storage. Will Oilko win? No. Oilko's resale was unreasonable. Because there is a ready market for oil, Oilko should have resold immediately. Because Oilko acted unreasonably, it will not obtain damages under the Code's resale provision. Oilko will be forced to base its damages on market value.

Often this remedy will be less valuable to the seller than resale damages. Suppose that on November 1, the market value of Oilko's oil was $99 per barrel. Oilko's contract with Refinery was actually worth only $1 per barrel to Oilko—the amount by which its contract price exceeded the market value. That is all that Oilko will get in court.[29] A seller with a reasonable chance to resell should be certain to do it.

The following chart compares resale and non-acceptance damages:

28UCC §2-708.

29Based on Baii Banking Corp. v. Atlantic Richfield Co., 28 F3d 103 (2nd Cir. 1994).

Resale Damages §2-706		Non-Acceptance Damages §2-708	
Contract price	$10,000,000	Contract price	$10,000,000
Resale price	-9,200,000	Market value of goods	-9,900,000
	$ 800,000		$ 100,000

Action for the Price

The seller may recover the contract price if (1) the buyer has already accepted the goods *or* (2) the seller's goods are conforming and the seller is unable to resell after a reasonable effort.[30] Royal Jones was a company that constructed rendering plants—factories that use sophisticated equipment to extract valuable minerals from otherwise useless material. Royal Jones contracted for First Thermal to construct three rendering tanks, at a cost of $64,350. First Thermal built the tanks to Royal Jones's specifications, but Royal Jones never accepted or paid for them, and First Thermal sued. Royal Jones argued that First Thermal deserved no money because it had not attempted to resell the goods, but the court awarded the full contract price, stating:

> First Thermal proved that any effort at resale would have been unavailing because these were the only rendering tanks First Thermal ever made, the tanks were manufactured according to Royal Jones's specifications, First Thermal had no other customers to which it could resell the tanks, and it was unaware how the tanks could have been marketed for resale.[31]

Resale is normally the safest route for an injured seller to recover the maximum amount, but when it is unrealistic, as in the *First Thermal* case, a lawsuit for the full price is appropriate.

All of the seller's remedies are summarized in the review at the end of the chapter. We now move on to the buyer's remedies.

23-2b Buyer's Remedies

Direct damages
Are the natural result of the breach

The buyer, too, has a variety of potential remedies. If a seller fails to deliver goods, repudiates, or if the buyer rightfully rejects the goods, the buyer is entitled to **cancel the contract**. The buyer may **recover money paid** to the seller, assuming he has not received the goods. These are known as **direct damages**. Direct damages are those that necessarily result from the breach. In addition, he may be entitled to:

- Incidental and consequential damages,
- Specific performance,
- Cover,
- Damages for non-delivery,
- Accept the non-conforming goods and seek damages, or
- Liquidated damages.

Incidental and Consequential Damages

An injured buyer is generally entitled to incidental *and* consequential damages. Incidental damages for buyers include such costs as advertising for replacements, sending buyers to obtain new goods, and shipping the replacement goods. Consequential damages, or losses that are indirectly caused by a breach, can be much more extensive and may include lost profits caused by the seller's failure to deliver.

---

30 UCC §2-709.

31 Royal Jones & Associates, Inc. v. First Thermal Systems, Inc., 566 So. 2d 853 (Fla. Ct. App. 1990).

A buyer, however, only gets consequential damages for harm that was *unavoidable*. Suppose Wholesaler has a contract to sell 10,000 rosebushes at $10 per bush to FloraMora. Wholesaler contracts to buy 10,000 rosebushes from Growem at $6 per bush, but Growem fails to deliver. Wholesaler in fact could obtain comparable roses at $8 per bush but fails to do so and loses the chance to sell to FloraMora. Wholesaler sues Growem, seeking the $4-per-bush profit it would have made on the FloraMora deal. The company will receive only $2 per bush, representing the difference between its contract price and the market value of the plants. Wholesaler will be denied the additional $2 per bush.

An ancient Chinese proverb advises, "If your enemy wrongs you, buy each of his children a drum." In the following case, a Chinese company *sold* drums, and made an enemy in the process. The outcome was as annoying as children with drums—and the plaintiff took a beating. But which damages would apply?

Armadillo Distribution Enterprises, Inc. v. Hai Yun Musical Instruments Manufacture Co. Ltd.

142 F. Supp. 3d 1245
United States District Court, M.D. Florida, 2015

Facts: For years, Hai Yun, a Chinese instrument manufacturer, made high-quality drums for Armadillo, which was a major distributor of musical instruments in the United States.

Armadillo put great time and effort into developing a new line of drum kits called "Diablo." Hai Yun provided samples of possible Diablo kits. After Armadillo approved both the design and quality of an appropriate drum kit, it placed an order with Hai Yun for 1,000 Diablos.

Hai Yun delivered the kits in five shipping containers (of 200 units each) to Armadillo's Florida headquarters. Because Armadillo trusted Hai Yun, it immediately sent the first container of 200 to its retail stores, without checking them first.

Almost immediately, Armadillo was overwhelmed with complaints: The drums looked nothing like the approved samples and the wood was warped and cracked beyond repair. Upon inspection, Armadillo confirmed that all the other drum kits were also catastrophically defective. Armadillo tried to fix them, but they could not be salvaged or sold.

Hai Yun did not respond to complaints and failed to take any steps to cure the defective goods. Because the Diablo brand was damaged beyond repair, Armadillo had to cease distribution and discontinue the line.

Armadillo sued Hai Yun for breach of contract seeking direct, incidental, and circumstantial damages. Because the parties had agreed that Florida law would govern their agreement, the UCC applied to this international contract. Continuing its trend of unresponsiveness, Hai Yun did not answer the complaint and the court issued a default judgment. The main issues for determination were the categories and amount of damages.

Issue: ***Was Armadillo entitled to direct, incidental, and consequential damages?***

Excerpts from Judge Honeywell's Order: Where the buyer rightfully revokes acceptance of non-conforming goods, the buyer is entitled to the return of the purchase price that has been paid and recovery of incidental and consequential damages.

A. Direct Damages

First, Armadillo alleges that it is entitled to direct damages, which was the amount paid for defective, non-conforming drum kits. The purchaser of non-conforming goods retains the option to claim either the difference in value or to cancel the deal and get his money back. This principle is based on the common sense idea that the purchaser is entitled to receive what he wanted to buy and pay for and that the seller is not free to supply any non-conforming item she wishes just so long as the deviant goods are worth just as much.

Armadillo alleges that the drum kits, as delivered, were worth $0—therefore making the damages the full price paid for the drum kits.

B. Incidental damages

Incidental damages resulting from the seller's breach include expenses reasonably incurred in inspection, receipt, transportation and care and custody of goods rightfully rejected, any commercially reasonable charges, expenses or commissions in connection with effecting cover and any other reasonable expense incident to the delay or other breach. Armadillo alleges that it is entitled to the following incidental damages:

- Incoming freight charges for five containers of defective drum kits
- Import duty
- 14.3% incoming freight and duty charges relating to the return of defective drum kits by retail customers
- Freight costs and packing materials related to the return of the drum kits by retail customers
- Off-site storage and trucking for defective drum kits
- Labor costs related to inspections and moving the product; and
- Disposal costs

A buyer's expenses incurred before discovering a defect are recoverable as incidental damages. The shipments were all defective. However, none of these defects could have been discovered prior to receipt of the shipments. The incoming freight charges are supported by invoices. Armadillo has also provided invoices to support the import duty. Thus, the incoming freight and duty charges are recoverable.

The remaining costs fall within the statutory definition of incidental damages. However, Armadillo has not provided documentation to support all of these alleged costs. Therefore, only off-site storage costs and disposal costs can be awarded.

C. Consequential damages
Finally, consequential damages are those damages resulting from general or particular needs of the purchaser.

Armadillo seeks the following consequential damages:

- Lost profits

In awarding such damages, the court must consider whether (1) the seller's breach naturally caused (2) the buyer to suffer damages arising from the buyer's general or particular needs that (3) the seller had reason to know of at the time of contracting, and (4) those damages can be proven to a reasonable certainty, but (5) the buyer could not have prevented them by cover or otherwise."

The alleged lost profits represent the difference between the price point at which Armadillo sold the 'Diablo' drum kits and the price that Armadillo paid Hai Yun for the defective, non-conforming drum kits. However, this statement is the only evidence supporting the lost profits claim. This is entirely insufficient to support an award for lost profits. Accordingly, if Armadillo wishes to pursue a claim for lost profits it must do so at trial.

Armadillo's business suffered a nightmare: It ended up with angry clients, a worthless brand, and a thousand defective drums. The case also demonstrates the importance of *proof* in establishing damages. Note that the court only awarded the damages that were supported by documentation. Remember that the next time you throw away a receipt.

Specific Performance

Specific performance
A court order requiring the seller to perform as promised

If the contract goods are rare or unique, the buyer may be allowed *specific performance*, which means a court order requiring the seller to deliver those particular goods.[32] This remedy is most common when the goods are one of a kind. Suppose Gallery agreed to sell to Trisha an original Corot painting for $120,000 but then refused to perform (because another buyer offered more money). Trisha can obtain specific performance because the painting cannot be replaced: The court will order Gallery to deliver the work. By contrast, a car rental company stymied by a dealer's refusal to sell 500 new Ford Mustangs will not obtain specific performance since the rental company can simply buy the same cars from another dealer and sue for the difference.

Cover

If the seller breaches, the buyer may "cover" by reasonably obtaining substitute goods; it may then obtain the difference between the contract price and its cover price, plus incidental and consequential damages, minus expenses saved.[33] Casein, a protein derived from milk, is used to make cheese and

---

[32]UCC §2-716.
[33]UCC §2-712.

to process many other foods. Erie Casein Co. contracted with Anric Corp. to supply several hundred thousand pounds of casein for about $1 per pound. Half was to be delivered in March of the first year and the other half in March of the second year. By May of the first year, Anric had not finished its first delivery because it was having difficulty obtaining the casein, but Erie told Anric to keep trying. Anric delivered some of the casein later the same year, but by March of the second year was forced to admit it could not meet the second delivery. Anric suggested that it might be able to obtain more casein in the autumn of that second year.

An injured buyer does not have to do a perfect job of covering, only a reasonable job.

Erie waited until August of the second year, but it finally obtained its casein elsewhere at a price of $1.45 per pound. Erie sued Anric for the extra money it had paid, about $66,000. Anric argued that Erie had no right to the difference because Erie had waited until the price of casein was sky-high before obtaining substitute goods.

The court found for Erie. Even though the company might have covered a year earlier, when the price was much lower, it was reasonable for the buyer to wait because Anric indicated it might be able to supply the goods later. Erie had acted in good faith, and when it ultimately covered, it did so at the best price it could find. An injured buyer does not have to do a perfect job of covering, only a reasonable job, and Erie got its full $66,000.[34]

Note that an injured buyer may also be awarded consequential damages, which we discuss in the next section. Finally, if covering saves expense, the savings are deducted from any damages.

We hope that you recall Donald Hessler, whom we met in the chapter opener. We last saw him circling the courthouse in his Plymouth Prowler, anxiously awaiting the outcome of his suit against the dealership that promised him the same car for a lot less money. It has been a long wait; you and Donald deserve an answer.

Q-Images/Alamy Stock Photo

Hessler was on the prowl for a Prowler.

Hessler v. Crystal Lake Chrysler-Plymouth, Inc.

338 Ill. App. 3d 1010
Illinois Court of Appeals, 2003

Facts: The facts are provided in the chapter opening. The trial court awarded Hessler $29,853, representing the difference between his contract with Crystal Lake and the sum he ultimately spent purchasing a new Prowler. Crystal Lake appealed, arguing that Hessler covered unreasonably.

Issue: ***Did Hessler cover reasonably?***

Excerpts from Judge Callum's Decision: We conclude that the trial court did not err in finding that defendant's foregoing actions reasonably indicated to plaintiff that defendant would not deliver to him a Prowler under the Agreement. As we determined above, defendant contracted to deliver a Prowler to plaintiff as soon as possible. It was not against the manifest weight of the evidence for the trial court to find that defendant [breached] the Agreement when it repeatedly informed plaintiff that it would not deliver to him the first Prowler it received. Such actions made it sufficiently clear to plaintiff that defendant would not perform under the Agreement.

[34]Erie Casein Co. v. Anric Corp., 217 Ill. App. 3d 602 (Ill. App. Ct. 1991).

Defendant's final argument is that the trial court erred in calculating the damages award because plaintiff effected an inappropriate cover. Defendant contends that plaintiff did not recontact the 38 dealers he had called in September to inquire if they would sell him a Prowler. Instead, on the same day that Rosenberg refused to sell him a car, plaintiff visited another dealership and purchased a Prowler for about $40,000 over the list price.

Comment 2 to section 2-712 of the UCC provides, in relevant part:

> The test of proper cover is whether at the time and place the buyer acted in good faith and in a reasonable manner, and it is immaterial that hindsight may later prove that the method of cover used was not the cheapest and most effective.

Plaintiff testified that he called Rosenberg on September 22 to inform him that defendant was on a tentative list to receive a Prowler and that Rosenberg responded that he would not sell to plaintiff a car and that plaintiff was not the first person with whom he had contracted. Rosenberg testified that he informed plaintiff on this date that the Prowler was "already committed." The trial court also heard plaintiff's testimony that, following his September 22 conversation with Rosenberg, he had "serious doubts" that defendant would sell to him a Prowler and he contacted about 38 dealerships to inquire about purchasing a vehicle, but was unable to obtain a car.

Following Rosenberg's refusal to sell a car to plaintiff on October 25, plaintiff visited another dealership on that day and purchased a Prowler for about $30,000 over what he would have paid defendant for the same car. The trial court concluded that the price plaintiff ultimately paid for a Prowler was the "best price" he could receive after defendant refused to sell a car to him. We agree. The trial court heard testimony from both parties about the Prowler's limited supply. It also heard plaintiff's testimony about his efforts to obtain a car one month before his purchase date. We conclude that the court's determination that plaintiff effected a proper cover was not against the manifest weight of the evidence.

For the foregoing reasons, the judgment of the circuit court is affirmed.

Non-Delivery

In some cases, the buyer does not cover, or fails to cover *reasonably*, leaving it with damages for non-delivery. **The measure of damages for non-delivery is the difference between the market price at the time the buyer learns of the breach and the contract price, plus incidental and consequential damages, minus expenses saved.**[35] Suppose that in the case described earlier, Erie had not covered but simply filed suit against Anric. Instead of its $66,000, Erie would have obtained the difference between its contract price with Anric and the market value on the date of breach. That market price was probably only a few pennies higher than the contract price, and Erie would have obtained less than $10,000.

Acceptance of Non-Conforming Goods

A buyer will sometimes accept non-conforming goods from the seller, either because no alternative is available or because the buyer expects to obtain some compensation for the defects. **Where the buyer has accepted goods but notified the seller that they are non-conforming, he may recover damages for the difference between the goods as promised and as delivered, plus incidental and consequential damages.**[36]

Liquidated Damages

Liquidated damages are those that the parties agree, at the time of contracting, will compensate the injured party. **They are enforceable, but only in an amount that is reasonable in light of the harm, the difficulties of proving actual loss, and the absence of other remedies.**[37] A clause that establishes unreasonably large or unreasonably small liquidated damages is void. Courts only enforce a liquidated damages clause if it would have been difficult to estimate actual damages when the parties reached the agreement.

---

[35] UCC §2-713.
[36] UCC §2-714.
[37] UCC §2-718.

Cessna Aircraft agreed to build a "Citation V" business jet and sell it to Aero Consulting for $3,995,000. Cessna's contract required Aero to pay an initial deposit of $125,000, a second deposit of $300,000 six months prior to delivery, and the balance upon delivery. The contract also stated that if Aero failed to pay the balance due, Cessna would keep all deposited monies by way of liquidated damages.

Aero made both deposits, and Cessna built the plane and tendered it to Aero, but Aero refused to pay the full balance due. Cessna notified Aero that it would keep the $425,000 deposited. When Aero sued, seeking a return of the deposits, the issue was whether this liquidated damage was fair. The court concluded that it was. At the time Cessna entered into the deal, it was difficult to estimate actual damages in the event of Aero's breach. The long period required to build a jet aircraft and the uncertainties about supply and demand in the marketplace meant that neither party could say for sure how much Cessna would lose should Aero breach. Further, the liquidated damage here was about 10 percent of the total cost, not an unreasonably high figure. Cessna kept the money (and the plane).[38]

EXAMStrategy

Question: You have a red wine problem. Your California vineyard has strong sales throughout the United States, and it is time to expand into Europe. To penetrate foreign markets, you offer your product at steep discounts to a Swiss importer. Your intent is that the importer will sell your wine inexpensively to retailers, so that low prices will entice consumers. The danger, though, is that the importer will return the wine to the United States and undersell your own product in an established market, taking advantage of your advertising and infuriating established dealers. Such a resale could occur before your wine ever left the country. What can you do to keep this problem from fermenting?

Strategy: A liquidated damages clause can put teeth into your plan to sell the wine to overseas consumers. You might specify substantial compensation if any of your exported wine finds its way back home. However, an overly aggressive clause will be declared a penalty—and void. How can you avoid such a disaster?

Result: Liquidated damages are enforceable in an amount that is reasonable in light of the harm and the difficulties of proving actual loss. Your clause may certainly compensate you for lost goodwill among domestic retailers and for harm to your efforts at establishing the brand in Europe. Make *good faith* estimates of those losses—if the clause gives you too much compensation, a court may void it altogether. Lost profits per case sold in the United States are probably easy to calculate and should *not* be part of the liquidated damages clause.

CHAPTER CONCLUSION

The drafters of the UCC intended the law to reflect contemporary commercial practices but also to require a satisfactory level of sensible, ethical behavior. For example, the Code allows numerous exceptions to the Perfect Tender Rule so that a buyer may not pounce on minor defects in goods to avoid a contract that has become financially burdensome. Similarly, a seller forced to resell his goods must do so in a commercially reasonable manner. Good faith and common sense are the hallmarks of contract performance and remedies.

38 Aero Consulting Corp. v. Cessna Aircraft Co., 867 F. Supp. 1480 (D. Kan. 1994).

EXAM REVIEW

1. **GOOD FAITH** The Code requires good faith in the performance and enforcement of every contract.

2. **CONFORMING GOODS** Conforming goods are those that satisfy the contract terms; non-conforming goods fail to do so.

3. **TENDER** The seller must tender the goods, which means make conforming goods available to the buyer. The Perfect Tender Rule permits a buyer to reject goods that are non-conforming in any respect, although there are numerous exceptions.

4. **USAGE OF TRADE** Usage of trade, course of dealing, and course of performance may enable a seller to satisfy the Perfect Tender Rule even though there are some defects in the goods.

5. **CURE** When the buyer rejects non-conforming goods, the seller has the right to cure by delivering conforming goods before the contract deadline.

EXAMStrategy

Question: Allied Semi-Conductors International agreed to buy 50,000 computer chips from Pulsar, for a total price of $365,750. Pulsar delivered the chips, which Allied then sold to Apple Computer. But at least 35,000 of the chips proved defective, so Apple returned them to Allied, which sent them back to Pulsar. Pulsar agreed to replace any defective chips, but only after Allied, at its expense, tested each chip and established the defect. Allied rejected this procedure and sued. Who wins?

Strategy: The chips were non-conforming goods, and Allied was entitled to reject them. Pulsar, in turn, had a right to cure the defects; that is, to solve the problem that it created. Did Pulsar offer to cure? (See the "Result" at the end of this Exam Review section.)

6. **DESTRUCTION OF THE GOODS** If identified goods are destroyed before risk passes to the buyer, the contract is void.

EXAMStrategy

CPA Question: Under a sales contract governed by the UCC, which of the following statements is correct?

(a) Unless both the seller and the buyer are merchants, neither party is obligated to perform the contract in good faith.

(b) The contract will not be enforceable if it fails to expressly specify a time and a place for delivery of the goods.

(c) The seller may be excused from performance if the goods are accidentally destroyed before the risk of loss passes to the buyer.

(d) If the price of the goods is less than $500, the goods need not be identified to the contract for title to pass to the buyer.

Strategy: (a) Sounds unlikely. Remind yourself which contracts must be performed in good faith. (b) As we learned in Chapter 21, the Code permits open terms. What are they? (c) Review the rules on destruction of the goods. (d) Goods must be identified to the contract before title can pass. Is there an exception for goods under $500? (See the "Result" at the end of this Exam Review section.)

---

7. **COMMERCIAL IMPRACTICABILITY** Under commercial impracticability, a supervening event excuses performance if it was not within the parties' contemplation when they made the contract.

8. **INSPECTION** The buyer generally has the right to inspect goods before paying or accepting. If the buyer does not reject goods within a reasonable time after inspecting them, she may be deemed to have accepted them.

EXAMStrategy

CPA Question: Smith contracted in writing to sell Peters a used laptop for $600. The contract did not specifically address the time for payment, place of delivery, or Peters' right to inspect the computer. Which of the following statements is correct?

(a) Smith is obligated to deliver the computer to Peters' home.

(b) Peters is entitled to inspect the computer before paying for it.

(c) Peters may not pay for the computer using a personal check unless Smith agrees.

(d) Smith is not entitled to payment until 30 days after Peters receives the computer.

Strategy: This question should be no problem. Three of the four possible answers offer rules that appear *nowhere* in the Code. (a) There is no reference in the Code to "home delivery" of goods. (b) The buyer has the right to inspect goods before paying or accepting, unless the contract specifies otherwise. (c) Nowhere does the UCC prohibit payment by check. (d) You have never read in the Code any presumption of a 30-day delay in payment—so do not imagine one. (See the "Result" at the end of this Exam Review section.)

---

9. **REVOCATION** A buyer may revoke his acceptance of non-conforming goods, but only if the defects substantially impair the value of the goods.

10. **REJECTION** A buyer may reject non-conforming goods by notifying the seller within a reasonable time.

The following chart summarizes the contrasting remedies available to the two parties.

Seller's Remedies	Issue	Buyer's Remedies
§2-705: The seller generally may stop delivery, whether it was to be done by the seller herself or a carrier.	Delivery	§2-716: Specific performance: Buyer may obtain specific performance only if the goods are unique.
§2-706: Resale: If the resale is made in good faith and a commercially reasonable manner, the seller may recover the difference between the resale price and the contract price, plus incidental costs, minus savings.	When the injured party makes an alternate contract	§2-712: Cover: The buyer may purchase alternate goods and obtain the difference in price, plus incidental and consequential damages, minus expenses saved.
§2-708: Non-acceptance: The measure of damages for non-acceptance is the time and place of tender and the contract price (plus incidental damages minus expenses saved).	When the goods have not changed hands	§2-713: Non-delivery: If the seller fails to deliver, the buyer's damages are the difference between the market price at the time he learned of the breach and the contract price (plus incidental and consequential damages, minus expenses saved).
§2-709: The seller may sue for the price.	When the buyer has accepted the goods	§2-714: A buyer who has accepted nonconforming goods and notified the seller may recover damages for resulting losses.
§§2-706, 2-708, 2-709, 2-710: The seller is entitled to incidental damages but not consequential damages.	Incidental and consequential damages	§2-715: The buyer is entitled to incidental and consequential damages.
LIQUIDATED DAMAGES §2-718: Either party may obtain liquidated damages but only in an amount that is reasonable at the time of the contract.		

RESULTS

5. Result: Pulsar never offered a true cure. When the seller delivers defective goods and wishes to cure, it must take all steps—at its expense—to fix the problem. Pulsar could cure only by delivering, at its expense and in a timely manner, 50,000 conforming chips. Pulsar failed to cure, and Allied recovers the entire purchase price.

6. Result: (c) is the correct answer. Answer (a) is wrong because all contracts must be performed in good faith. Answer (b) is wrong because a contract with open terms is enforceable. Answer (c) is right because it correctly states the rule on destruction of goods. Answer (d) is wrong because title never passes unless the goods were identified to the contract.

8. Result: Answer (b) is correct. Peters is entitled to inspect the computer unless the contract states otherwise, which it did not.

MULTIPLE-CHOICE QUESTIONS

1. **CPA QUESTION** Cara Fabricating Co. and Taso Corp. agreed orally that Taso would custom-manufacture a compressor for Cara at a price of $120,000. After Taso completed the work at a cost of $90,000, Cara notified Taso that the compressor was no longer needed. Taso is holding the compressor and has requested payment

from Cara. Taso has been unable to resell the compressor for any price. Taso incurred storage fees of $2,000. If Cara refuses to pay Taso and Taso sues Cara, the most Taso will be entitled to recover is:

(a) $92,000.
(b) $105,000.
(c) $120,000.
(d) $122,000.

2. **CPA QUESTION** On February 15, Mazur Corp. contracted to sell 1,000 bushels of wheat to Good Bread, Inc. at $6 per bushel with delivery to be made on June 23. On June 1, Good advised Mazur that it would not accept or pay for the wheat. On June 2, Mazur sold the wheat to another customer at the market price of $5 per bushel. Mazur had advised Good that it intended to resell the wheat. Which of the following statements is correct?

(a) Mazur can successfully sue Good for the difference between the resale price and the contract price.
(b) Mazur can resell the wheat only after June 23.
(c) Good can retract its anticipatory breach at any time before June 23.
(d) Good can successfully sue Mazur for specific performance.

3. Under the UCC, to tender delivery, a seller must ______________.

(a) make the goods available at a reasonable time
(b) keep the goods available for a reasonable period
(c) deliver to the buyer any documents that it needs to take possession
(d) all of these
(e) none of these

4. Blackburn FC orders 10,000 soccer jerseys from Alpha Co. to sell in its stadium store. They are to be delivered on July 10. When they arrive early on July 2, Blackburn is disappointed because the collars, which are supposed to be white, are blue. Blackburn notifies Alpha of the error. Alpha says that it wants a chance to "make it right." If Alpha delivers another shipment of 10,000 conforming jerseys on July 10, Blackburn ______________.

(a) absolutely must accept the new shipment
(b) must accept the new shipment if Alpha offers a reasonable discount
(c) must accept the new shipment if it has suffered no measurable losses
(d) may accept the new shipment, but has the option to reject it

5. Assume that a year has passed, and Blackburn FC once again orders 10,000 soccer jerseys from Alpha, to be delivered on July 10. This time, non-conforming jerseys are delivered on July 10. Alpha thoroughly inspected the shirts before shipping and had no reason to spot the error. When Blackburn notifies Alpha of the problem, Alpha says that it intends to cure the defect. If Blackburn cannot show that it will suffer any serious harm, does the UCC require Blackburn to give Alpha a chance to cure this time?

(a) No because the contract's deadline has passed.
(b) Yes, it must give Alpha until July 17 to cure.
(c) Yes, it must give Alpha until July 20 to cure.
(d) Yes, it must give Alpha a reasonable amount of time to cure.

CASE QUESTIONS

1. Mastercraft Boat manufactured boats and often used instrument panels and electrical systems assembled or manufactured by Ace Industries. Typically, Ace would order electrical instruments and other parts and assemble them to specifications that Mastercraft provided. Mastercraft decided to work with a different assembler, M & G Electronics, so it terminated its relationship with Ace. Mastercraft then requested that Ace deliver all of the remaining instruments and other parts that it had purchased for use in Mastercraft boats. Ace delivered the inventory to Mastercraft, which inspected it and kept some of the items, but returned others to Ace, stating that the shipment had been unauthorized. Later, Mastercraft requested that Ace deliver the remaining parts (which Mastercraft had sent back to Ace) to M & G, which Ace did. Mastercraft then refused to pay for these parts, claiming that they were non-conforming. Is Ace entitled to its money for the parts?

2. The AM/PM Franchise association was a group of 150 owners of ARCO Mini-Market franchises in Pennsylvania and New York. Each owner had an agreement to operate a gas station and mini-market, obtaining all gasoline, food, and other products from ARCO. The association sued, claiming that ARCO had experimented with its formula for unleaded gasoline, using oxinol, and that the poor-quality gas had caused serious engine problems and a steep drop in customers. The association demanded (1) lost profits for gasoline sales, (2) lost profits for food and other items, and (3) loss of goodwill. The trial court dismissed the case, ruling that the plaintiff's claims were too speculative, and the association appealed. Please rule.

3. ***YOU BE THE JUDGE* WRITING PROBLEM** Clark Oil agreed to sell Amerada Hess several hundred thousand barrels of oil at $24 each by January 31, with the sulfur content not to exceed 1 percent. On January 26, Clark tendered oil from various ships. Most of the oil met specifications, but a small amount contained excess sulfur. Hess rejected all of the oil. Clark recirculated the oil, meaning that it blended the high-sulfur oil with the rest, and it notified Amerada that it could deliver 100 percent of the oil, as specified, by January 31. Hess did not respond. On January 30, Clark offered to replace the oil with an entirely new shipment, due to arrive February 1. Hess rejected the offer. On February 6, Clark retendered the original oil, all of which met contract terms, and Hess rejected it. Clark sold the oil elsewhere for $17.75 per barrel and filed suit. Is Clark entitled to damages? **Argument for Clark:** A seller is entitled to cure any defects. Clark did so in good faith and offered all of the oil by the contract deadline. Clark went even further, offering an entirely new shipment of oil. Hess acted in bad faith, seeking to obtain cheaper oil. Clark is entitled to the difference between the contract price and its resale price. **Argument for Hess:** Hess was entitled to conforming goods, and Clark failed to deliver. Under the Perfect Tender Rule, that is the end of the discussion. Hess had the right to reject non-conforming goods, and it promptly did so. Hess chose not to deal further with Clark because it had lost confidence in Clark's ability to perform.

4. Under the terms of a long-term supply contract, Linde supplied United Aluminum Corporation (UAC) with nitrogen at $0.23 per unit. Upon expiration, that contract gave UAC the sole option to renew the agreement for five additional years at the same price. When UAC exercised the option, Linde refused, arguing that the

price of nitrogen had risen by 38 percent over the life of the contract. UAC sued, seeking to enforce the $0.23 price. Linde claimed commercial impracticability. Will a court force Linde to abide by the terms of the original deal?

5. Having heard that it was a profitable new business, Smith decided to breed emus. They are flightless birds that reproduce rapidly and provide high-quality meat. For $4,000, Penbridge Farms sold Smith a "proven breeder pair," guaranteeing that the lovebirds had already bred together. When the birds failed to mate, Smith discovered that they were both male. Penbridge refused to return Smith's money. Smith sued, asking the court for direct, as well as incidental and consequential damages. The evidence suggested that Smith stood to make $100,000 from one season's chicks. To what kind of damages is Smith entitled? Will he recover lost profits?

DISCUSSION QUESTIONS

1. Laura and Bruce Trethewey hired Basement Waterproofing Nationwide, Inc. (BWNI) to waterproof the walls in their basement for a fee of $2,500. BWNI's contract stated: "BWNI will service any seepage in the areas waterproofed at no additional cost to the customer. All labor and materials will be at the company's expense. Liability for any damage shall be limited to the total price paid for this contract." The material that BWNI used to waterproof the Tretheweys' walls swelled and caused large cracks to open in the walls. Water poured into the basement, and the Tretheweys ultimately spent $38,000 to repair the damage. They sued, claiming negligence and breach of warranty, but BWNI claimed its liability was limited to $2,500. Please rule.

2. **ETHICS** Based on the facts in question 1, comment on BWNI's ethics. BWNI wanted to protect itself against unlimited damage claims. Is this a legitimate way to do it? If you think BWNI *did* behave ethically, what advice would you have for consumers who hire home improvement companies? If you believe the company did *not* behave ethically, imagine that you are a BWNI executive charged with drafting a standard contract for customers. How would you protect your company's interests while still acting in a way you consider moral?

3. Consider the UCC's exceptions to the Perfect Tender Rule: usage of trade, course of dealing, and course of performance. Do these all seem reasonable, or are they too lenient on sellers who deliver non-conforming goods?

4. Are the UCC's rules related to cure sensible? If a seller ships goods that are not what you ordered, should you (in many circumstances) be *required* to give them a chance to make it right?

5. European consumer laws are much more protective than the UCC. In the European Union, buyers have an unqualified 14-day right of return for all goods—no questions asked. If a seller fails to inform the buyer of this right, the return window is extended for one year. Some commentators have suggested that the EU system is too consumer-friendly and the American system is too merchant-friendly. Which one do you prefer? Is there a happy medium? If so, what would it look like?

Additional CPA Topics

UNIT

5

24

CHAPTER

SECURED TRANSACTIONS

James is a secret agent. His mission? To capture the targets. His tactics? Fast and sneaky. His equipment? State-of-the-art digital technology. His victims? Both shaken and stirred.

But James is not working for the government—he is employed by a bank. James is a modern repo man, paid to recover vehicles from delinquent borrowers. Equipped with a digital camera, he drives up and down highways and city streets capturing images of every passing license plate. Instantaneously, his on-board computer matches these numbers to a database of "wanted" vehicles.

And a match means the chase is on. Armed with digital maps, he follows the target car. Once it is parked, he swoops in and takes it away. Does this sound wrong? Everything James does is legal. The moral of the story? He knows who you are and where you live. Pay your car loan on time.[1]

He knows who you are and where you live. Pay your car loan on time.

[1]Based on Ken Belson, "The Wired Repo Man: He's Not 'As Seen on TV,'" *The New York Times*, February 26, 2010.

24-1 ARTICLE 9: TERMS AND SCOPE

We can sympathize with the delinquent borrowers that James stalks, but as we will see in this chapter, the bank is entitled to its money. The car buyers and their banks entered into secured transactions, meaning that one party gave credit to another, demanding in return an assurance of repayment. Whether a used-car lot sells a car on credit for $18,000 or a bank takes collateral for a $600 million corporate loan, the parties have created a secured transaction.

Article 9 of the Uniform Commercial Code (UCC) governs secured transactions in personal property. It is essential to understand the basics of this law because we live and work in a world economy based on credit. Gravity may cause the earth to spin, but it is secured transactions that keep the commercial world going 'round. The quantity of disputes tells us how important this law is: About *one-half* of all UCC lawsuits involve Article 9.

This part of the Code employs terms not used elsewhere, so we must lead off with some definitions.

24-1a Article 9 Vocabulary

- **Fixtures** are goods that have become attached to real estate. For example, elevators are *goods* when a company manufactures them and also when it sells them to a retailer. But when a contractor installs an elevator in a new building, it becomes a *fixture*.
- **Security interest** means an interest in personal property or fixtures that secures the performance of some obligation. If an automobile dealer sells you a new car on credit and retains a security interest in the car, it means it is keeping legal rights in your car, including the right to drive it away if you fall behind in your payments. Usually, your obligation is to pay money, such as the money due on the new car. Occasionally, the obligation is to perform some other action, but, in this chapter, we concentrate on the payment of money because that is what security interests are generally designed to ensure.
- **Secured party** is the person or company that holds the security interest. The automobile dealer who sells you a car on credit is the *secured party*.
- **Collateral** is the property subject to a security interest. When a dealer sells you a new car and keeps a security interest, the vehicle is the *collateral*.
- **Debtor and obligor.** For our purposes, **debtor** refers to a person who has some original ownership interest in the collateral. Having a security interest in the collateral does not make one a debtor. If Alice borrows money from a bank and uses her Mercedes as collateral, she is the debtor because she owns the car. **Obligor** means a person who must repay money, or perform some other task.

Throughout this chapter, the obligor and debtor will generally be the same person, but not always. When Alice borrows money from a bank and uses her Mercedes as collateral, she is the obligor because she must repay the loan; as we know, Alice is also the debtor. However, suppose that Toby borrows money from a bank and provides no collateral; Jake co-signs the loan as a favor to Toby, using his Steinway piano as collateral. Jake is the only debtor because he owns the piano. Both parties are obligors because both have agreed to repay the loan.

- **Security agreement** is the contract in which the debtor gives a security interest to the secured party. This agreement protects the secured party's rights in the collateral.
- **Default** occurs when the debtor fails to pay money that is due, for example, on a loan or for a purchase made on credit. *Default* also includes other failures by the debtor, such as failing to keep the collateral insured.
- **Repossession** occurs when the secured party takes back collateral because the debtor has defaulted. Typically, the secured party will demand that the debtor deliver the collateral; if the debtor fails to do so, the secured party may find the collateral and take it, as James did in the chapter opener.
- **Perfection** is a series of steps the secured party must take to protect its rights in the collateral against people other than the debtor. This is important because if the debtor cannot pay his debts, several creditors may attempt to seize the collateral, but only one may actually obtain it. To perfect its rights in the collateral, the secured party will typically file specific papers with a state agency.
- **Financing statement** is a document that the secured party files to give the general public notice that it has a secured interest in the collateral.
- **Record** refers to information written on paper or stored in an electronic or other medium.
- **Authenticate** means to sign a document or to use any symbol or encryption method that identifies the person and clearly indicates she is adopting the record as her own. You authenticate a security agreement when you sign papers at an auto dealership, for example. A corporation electronically authenticates a loan agreement by using the internet to transmit an encrypted signature.

An Example

Here is an example using the terms just discussed. A medical equipment company manufactures a CAT scan machine and sells it to a clinic for $2 million, taking $500,000 cash and the clinic's promise to pay the rest over five years. The clinic simultaneously authenticates a security agreement, giving the manufacturer a security interest in the CAT scan. If the clinic fails to make its payments, the manufacturer can repossess the machine. The manufacturer then electronically files a financing statement with an appropriate state agency. This *perfects* the manufacturer's rights, meaning that its security interest in the CAT scanner is now valid against all the world. If the clinic goes bankrupt and many creditors try to seize its assets, the manufacturer has first claim to the CAT scan machine. Exhibit 24.1 illustrates this transaction.

The clinic's bankruptcy is of great importance. When a debtor has money to pay all of its debts, there are no concerns about security interests. But what if there is not enough money to go around? A creditor insists on a security interest to protect itself in the event the debtor cannot pay all of its debts. **The secured party intends (1) to give itself a legal interest in specific property of the debtor and (2) to establish a priority claim in that property, ahead of other creditors.** In this chapter, we look at a variety of issues that arise in secured transactions.

24-1b Scope of Article 9

Article 9 applies to any transaction intended to create a security interest in personal property or fixtures.

EXHIBIT 24.1

A simple security agreement:

(1) The manufacturer sells a CAT scan machine to a clinic, taking $500,000 and the clinic's promise to pay the balance over five years.

(2) The clinic simultaneously authenticates a security agreement.

(3) The manufacturer perfects by electronically filing a financing statement.

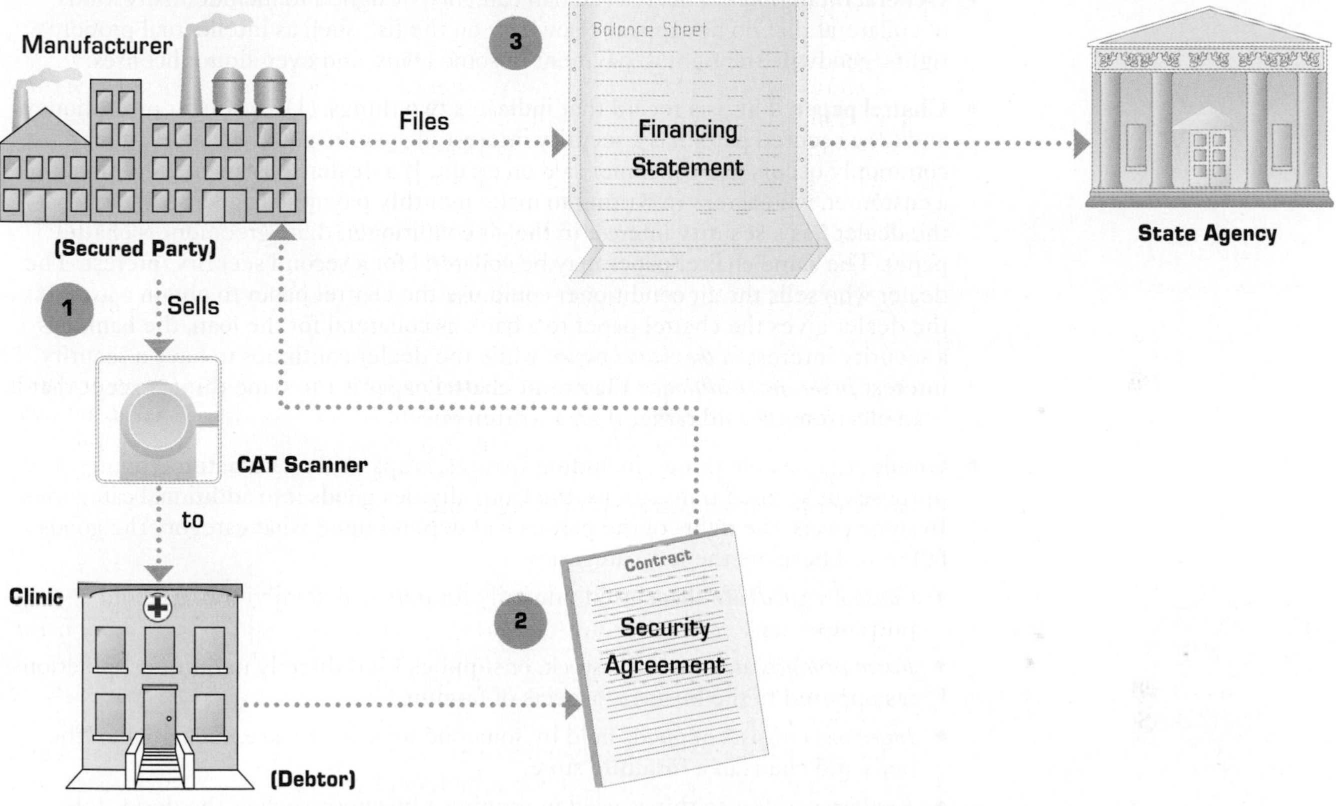

Types of Collateral

The personal property used as collateral may be goods, such as cars or jewelry, but it may also be a variety of other things:

- **Instruments.** Drafts, checks, certificates of deposit, and notes may all be used as collateral, as may stocks, bonds, and other securities.
- **Investment property,** which refers primarily to securities and related rights.
- **Documents of title.** These are papers used by an owner of goods who ships or stores them. The documents are the owner's proof that he owns goods no longer in his possession. For example, an owner sending goods by truck will obtain a *bill of lading,* a receipt indicating where the goods will be shipped and who gets them when they arrive. Similarly, a *warehouse receipt* is the owner's receipt for goods stored at a warehouse. The owner may use these and other similar documents of title as collateral.

- **Account** means a right to receive payment for goods sold or leased. This includes, for example, accounts receivable, indicating various buyers owe a merchant money for goods they have already received. The category now includes health-insurance receivables.
- **Deposit accounts.** Article 9 also covers security interests in money held in bank accounts.
- **Commercial tort claims.** An organization that has filed a tort suit may use its claim as collateral. Personal injuries to *individuals* are not covered by this article.
- **General intangibles.** This is a catchall category, designed to include many kinds of collateral that do not appear elsewhere on the list, such as intellectual property rights, goodwill, the right to payment of some loans, and even liquor licenses.[2]
- **Chattel paper.** This is a record that indicates two things: (1) an obligor owes money and (2) a secured party has a security interest in specific goods. Chattel paper most commonly occurs in a consumer sale on credit. If a dealer sells an air conditioner to a customer, who agrees in writing to make monthly payments and also agrees that the dealer has a security interest in the air conditioner, that agreement is chattel paper. The same chattel paper may be collateral for a second security interest. The dealer who sells the air conditioner could use the chattel paper to obtain a loan. If the dealer gives the chattel paper to a bank as collateral for the loan, the bank has a security interest *in the chattel paper*, while the dealer continues to have a security interest *in the air conditioner*. **Electronic chattel paper** is the same thing, except that it is an electronic record rather than a written one.
- **Goods** are movable things, including fixtures, crops, and manufactured homes. For purposes of secured transactions, the Code divides goods into additional categories. In some cases, the rights of the parties will depend upon what category the goods fall into. These are the key categories:
  - *Consumer goods* are those used primarily for personal, family, or household purposes.
  - *Farm products* are crops, livestock, or supplies used directly in farming operations (as opposed to the business aspects of farming).
  - *Inventory* consists of goods held by someone for sale or lease, such as all of the beds and chairs in a furniture store.
  - *Equipment* refers to things used in running a business, such as the desks, telephones, and computers needed to operate a retail store.
- **Software** is distinguished from goods in Article 9. This distinction becomes important when competing creditors are fighting over both a computer system and the software inside it. A program embedded in a product counts as goods in two ways: (1) *if* it is customarily considered part of those goods, such as a toy robot, *or* (2) if, by purchasing the goods, the owner acquires the right to use the program, such as the operating system included in a personal computer purchase. A program that does *not* meet those criteria is termed *software,* and will be treated differently for some purposes.

---

[2]Gibson v. Alaska Alcoholic Beverage Control Board, 377 F. Supp. 151 (D. Alaska 1974).

Article 9 applies anytime the parties intended to create a security interest in any of the items just listed. But note that the nature of the item itself is not the only factor used in determining the type of collateral. Collateral may change classification depending on how it is used and by whom. The same laptop is inventory in the hands of a vendor, equipment in the hands of an entrepreneur using it for business, and a consumer good when a student uses it in daily life. Since different rules apply to each category, creditors must foresee the item's future uses to ensure that the financing statements reflect their intended collateral.

Melody Smart/Shutterstock.com

Article 9 determines when software is goods.

24-2 ATTACHMENT OF A SECURITY INTEREST

Attachment is a vital step in a secured transaction. This means that the secured party has taken all of the following steps to create an enforceable security interest:

Attachment
A three-step process that creates an enforceable security interest

- The two parties made a security agreement, and either the debtor has authenticated a security agreement describing the collateral *or* the secured party has obtained *possession* or *control*;
- The secured party has given value to obtain the security agreement; and
- The debtor has rights in the collateral.[3]

24-2a Agreement

Without an agreement, there can be no security interest. Generally, the agreement will be in writing and signed by the debtor or electronically recorded and authenticated by the debtor. The agreement must reasonably identify the collateral. A description of collateral by *type* is often acceptable. For example, a security agreement may properly describe the collateral as "all equipment in the store at 123 Periwinkle Street."[4] In a security agreement for consumer goods, however, a description by type is *not* sufficient, and more specificity is required.

A security agreement at a minimum might:

- State that Happy Homes, Inc., and Martha agree that Martha is buying an Arctic Co. refrigerator and identify the exact unit by its serial number;
- Give the price, the down payment, the monthly payments, and interest rate;
- State that because Happy Homes is selling Martha the refrigerator on credit, it has a security interest in the refrigerator; and
- Provide that if Martha defaults on her payments, Happy Homes is entitled to repossess the refrigerator.

---

[3]UCC §9-203.

[4]A security agreement may not use a super-generic term such as "all of Smith's personal property." We will see later that, by contrast, such a super-generic description is legally adequate in a *financing statement*.

An actual security agreement will add many details, such as Martha's obligation to keep the refrigerator in good condition and to deliver it to the store if she defaults; a precise definition of "default"; and how Happy Homes may go about repossessing if Martha defaults and fails to return the refrigerator.

24-2b Control and Possession

In many cases, the security agreement need not be in writing if the parties have an oral agreement and the secured party has either **control** or **possession**. For many kinds of collateral, it is safer for the secured party actually to take the item than to rely upon a security agreement. The rules follow.

Control

For deposit accounts, electronic chattel paper, and certain other collateral, the security interest attaches if the secured party has control. The UCC specifies exactly what the secured party must do to obtain control for each type of collateral. In a general sense, control means that the secured party has certain exclusive rights to dispose of the collateral.

- **Deposit account (in a bank).** The secured party has control if it is itself the bank holding the deposit or if the debtor has authorized the bank to dispose of funds according to the secured party's instructions.
- **Electronic chattel paper.** A secured party has control of electronic chattel paper when it possesses the only authoritative copy of it, and the record(s) designate the secured party as the assignee. This means that the parties have agreed on an electronic method to verify the uniqueness of the record, so that any copies of the electronic original are clearly recognizable as reproductions.
- **Investment property and letter-of-credit rights.** The Code specifies analogous methods of controlling investment properties and letter-of-credit rights.[5]

Possession

For most other forms of collateral, including goods, securities, and most other items, a security interest attaches if the secured party has *possession*. For example, if you loan your neighbor $175,000 and he gives you a Winslow Homer watercolor as collateral, you have an attached security interest in thc painting once it is in your possession. It would still be wise to put the agreement in writing, to be certain both parties understand all terms and can prove them if necessary, but the writing is not legally required.

EXAMStrategy

Question: Hector needs money to keep his business afloat. He asks his uncle for a $1 million loan. The uncle agrees, but he insists that his nephew grant him a security interest in Hector's splendid gold clarinet, worth over $2 million. Hector agrees. The uncle prepares a handwritten document summarizing the agreement and asks his nephew to sign it. Hector hands the clarinet to his uncle and receives his money, but he forgets to sign the document. Has a security agreement attached?

---

[5] *Control* is described in the following sections: 9-104 (deposit accounts), 9-105 (electronic chattel paper), 9-106 (investment property), and 9-107 (letter-of-credit rights).

Strategy: Attachment occurs if the parties made a security agreement and there was authentication or possession, the secured party has given value, and the debtor had rights in the collateral.

Result: Hector agreed to give his uncle a security interest in the instrument. He never authenticated (signed) the agreement, but the uncle did take possession of the clarinet. The uncle gave Hector $1 million, and Hector owned the instrument. Yes, the security interest attached.

24-2c Value

For the security interest to attach, the secured party must give value. Usually, the value will be apparent. If a bank loans $400 million to an airline, that money is the value, and the bank, therefore, may obtain a security interest in the planes that the airline is buying. If a store sells a living room set to a customer for a small down payment and two years of monthly payments, the value given is the furniture.

Future Value

The parties may also agree that some of the value will be given in the future. For example, a finance company might extend a $5 million line of credit to a retail store, even though the store initially takes only $1 million of the money. The remaining credit is available whenever the store needs it to purchase inventory. The UCC considers the entire $5 million line of credit to be the value.[6]

24-2d Debtor Rights in the Collateral

The debtor can grant a security interest in goods only if he has some legal right to those goods himself. Typically, the debtor owns the goods. But a debtor may also give a security interest if he is leasing the goods or even if he is a bailee, meaning that he is lawfully holding them for someone else. Suppose Importer receives a shipment of scallops on behalf of Seafood Wholesaler. Wholesaler asks Importer to hold the scallops for three days as a favor, and to keep a customer happy, Importer agrees. Importer then arranges a $150,000 loan from a bank, using the scallops as collateral. Although Importer has acted unethically, it does have *some right* in the collateral—the right to hold them for three days. That is enough to satisfy this rule.

By contrast, suppose Railroad is transporting ten carloads of cattle on behalf of Walter, the owner. A devious Meat Dealer uses forged documents to trick Railroad into believing that Meat Dealer is entitled to the animals. Meat Dealer trucks the cattle away and uses them to obtain a bank loan, giving the bank a security interest in the animals. That "security interest" has never attached and is invalid because Dealer had *no* legal interest in the cattle. When Walter, the rightful owner, locates his cattle, he may take them back. The bank can only hope to find the deceitful Dealer, who in fact has probably disappeared.

Once the security interest has attached to the collateral, the secured party is protected against the debtor. If the debtor fails to pay, the secured party may repossess the collateral.

24-2e Attachment to Future Property

The security agreement may specify that the security interest attaches to personal property that the debtor does not yet possess but might obtain in the future.

6UCC §9-204(c).

After-Acquired Property

After-acquired property
Items that the debtor obtains after the parties have made their security agreement

After-acquired property refers to items that the debtor obtains after the parties have made their security agreement. **The parties may agree that the security interest attaches to after-acquired property.**[7] Basil is starting a catering business, but owns only a beat-up car. He borrows $55,000 from the Pesto Bank, which takes a security interest in the car. But Pesto also insists on an after-acquired clause. When Basil purchases a commercial stove, cooking equipment, and freezer, Pesto's security interest attaches to each item as Basil acquires it.

Proceeds

Proceeds are whatever is obtained by a debtor who sells the collateral or otherwise disposes of it. **The secured party *automatically* obtains a security interest in the *proceeds* of the collateral, unless the security agreement states otherwise.**[8] Suppose the Pesto Bank obtains a security interest in Basil's $4,000 freezer. Basil then decides he needs a larger model and sells the original freezer to his neighbor for $3,000. The $3,000 cash is proceeds, in which Pesto automatically obtains a security interest.

24-3 PERFECTION

Once the security interest has attached to the collateral, the secured party is protected against *the debtor*; but it may not be protected against *anyone else*. Pesto Bank loaned money to Basil and has a security interest in all of his property. If Basil defaults on his loan, Pesto may insist he deliver the goods to the bank. If he fails to do that, the bank can seize the collateral. But Pesto's security interest is valid only against Basil; if a third person claims some interest in the goods, the bank may never get them. For example, Basil might have taken out *another* loan, from his friend Olive, and used the same property as collateral.

Olive knew nothing about the bank's original loan. To protect itself against Olive, and all other parties, the bank must *perfect* its interest.

There are several kinds of perfection:

- Perfection by filing,
- Perfection by possession,
- Perfection of consumer goods, and
- Perfection of movable collateral and fixtures.

In some cases, the secured party will have a choice of which method to use; in other cases, only one method works.

24-3a Perfection by Filing

Financing statement
A statement that gives the names of all parties, describes the collateral, and outlines the security interest

The most common way to perfect an interest is by filing a financing statement with one or more state agencies. A **financing statement** gives the names of all parties, describes the collateral, and outlines the security interest, enabling any interested person to learn about it. Suppose the Pesto Bank obtains a security interest in Basil's catering equipment and then perfects by filing with the secretary of state. When Basil asks his friend Olive for a loan, she has the opportunity to check the records to see if anyone already has a security interest in the catering equipment. If Olive's search uncovers Basil's previous security agreement,

---

[7]UCC §9-204(a).
[8]UCC §9-203(f).

EXHIBIT 24.2

The Pesto Bank:

(1) Loans money to Basil and
(2) Takes a security interest in his equipment.

Later, when Olive:

(3) Considers loaning Basil money, she will
(4) Check to see if any other creditors already have a security interest in his goods.

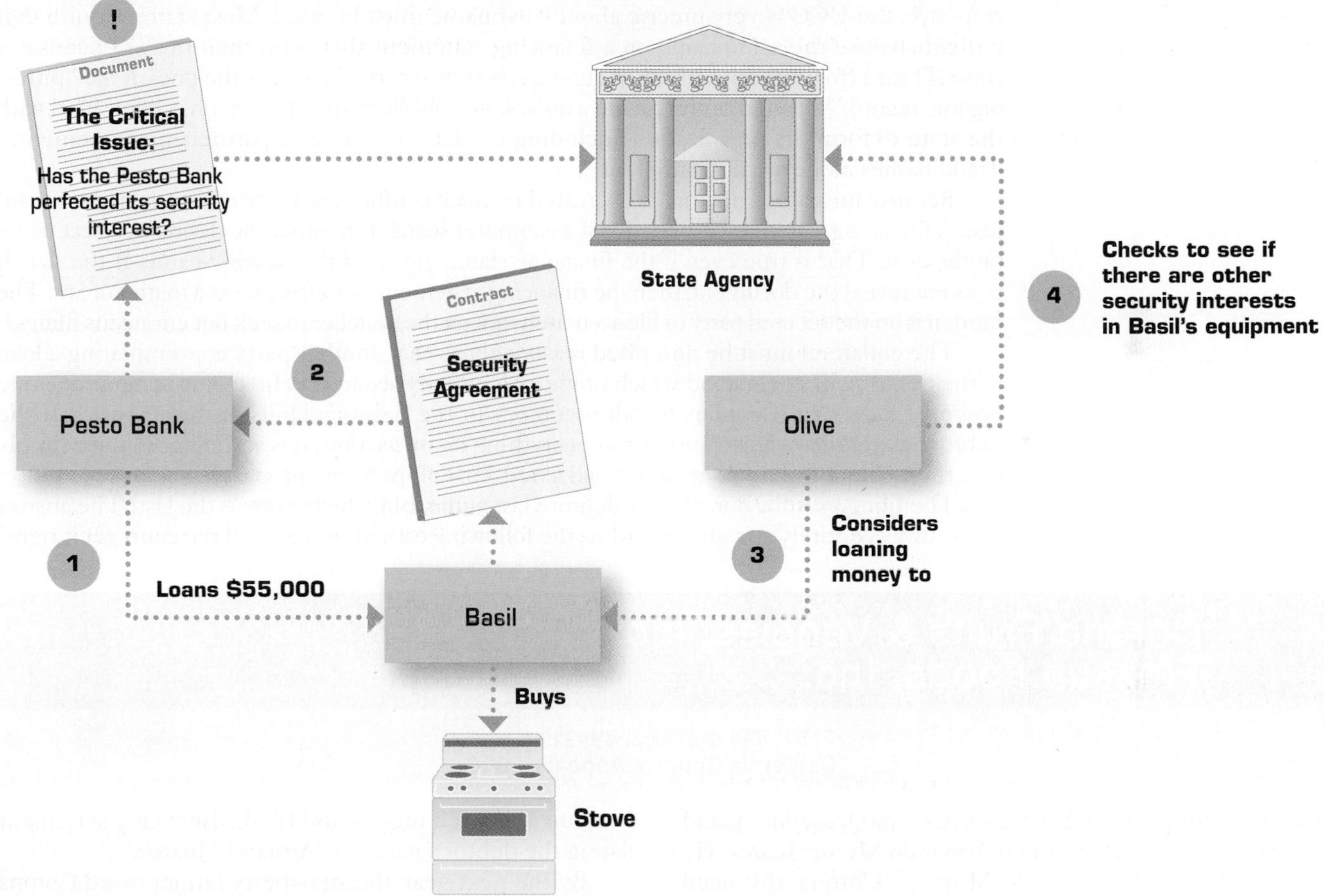

she will realize it would be unwise to make the loan. If Basil were to default, the collateral would go straight to Pesto Bank, leaving Olive empty-handed. See Exhibit 24.2.

Article 9 prescribes one form to be used nationwide for financing statements.[9] Commonly called UCC-1, the financing form is available online. Remember that the filing may be done on paper or electronically.

If the collateral is either *accounts* or *general intangibles,* filing is the *only* way to perfect. Suppose Nestor uses his copyright in a screenplay as collateral for a loan. The bank that gives him the loan may perfect *only* by filing.

---

[9]UCC §9-521.

The most common problems that arise in filing cases are (1) whether the financing statement contained enough information to put other people on notice of the security interest and (2) whether the secured party filed the papers in the right place.

Contents of the Financing Statement

A financing statement is sufficient if it provides the name of the debtor, the name of the secured party, and an indication of the collateral.[10]

The name of the debtor is critical because that is what an interested person will use to search among the millions of other financing statements on file. Faulty descriptions of the debtor's name have led to thousands of disputes and untold years of litigation, as subsequent creditors have failed to locate any record of an earlier claim on the debtor's property. In response, the UCC is very precise about what name must be used. Most states require that individuals use the same name on a financing statement that is on their driver's license or state ID card (for non-drivers).[11] For organizations, the correct name is the one on the "public organic record," defined as any record available for public inspection that has been filed with the state to form the organization, including its charter or limited partnership agreement.[12] Trade names alone are not sufficient.

Because misnamed debtors have created so much conflict, the Code offers a straightforward test: A financing statement is effective if a computer search run under the debtor's correct name produces it. That is true even if the financing statement used the *incorrect* name. If the search does not reveal the document, then the financing statement is ineffective as a matter of law. The burden is on the secured party to file accurately, not on the searcher to seek out erroneous filings.[13]

The collateral must be described reasonably so that another party contemplating a loan to the debtor will understand which property is already secured. A financing statement could properly state that it applies to "all inventory in the debtor's Houston warehouse." If the debtor has given a security interest in everything he owns, then it is sufficient to state simply that the financing statement covers "all assets" or "all personal property."

The filing must be done by the debtor's last name. But which name is the last? The answer is not always entirely straightforward, as the following case indicates. Did the court get it right?

Corona Fruits & Veggies, Inc. v. Frozsun Foods, Inc.

143 Cal. App. 4th 319
California Court of Appeals, 2006

Facts: Corona Fruits & Veggies (Corona) leased farmland to a strawberry farmer named Armando Munoz Juarez. He signed the lease "Armando Munoz." Corona advanced money for payroll and farm production expenses. The company filed a UCC-1 financing statement, claiming a security interest in the strawberry crop. The financing statement listed the debtor's name as "Armando Munoz." Six months later, Armando Munoz Juarez contracted with Frozsun Foods, Inc., to sell processed strawberries. Frozsun advanced money and filed a financing statement listing the debtor's name as "Armando Juarez."

By the next year, the strawberry farmer owed Corona $230,000 and Frozsun $19,600. When he was unable to make payments on Corona's loan, the company repossessed the farmland. And, while it may sound a bit . . . odd . . . it also repossessed the strawberries.

Both Corona and Frozsun claimed the proceeds of the crop. The trial court awarded the money to Frozsun,

10 UCC §9-502(a).

11 UCC §9-503. If a person has neither kind of state ID card, then her surname and first personal name will be required to perfect by filing.

12 UCC §9-102(a)(68).

13 UCC §9-506(c).

finding that Corona had filed its financing statement under the wrong last name and therefore had failed to perfect its security interest in the strawberry crop. Corona appealed.

Issue: ***Did Corona correctly file its financing statement?***

Excerpts from Judge Yegan's Decision: Shakespeare asked, "What's in a name?" We supply an answer only for the Uniform Commercial Code lien priority statutes: Everything when the last name is true and nothing when the last name is false. When a creditor files a UCC-1 financing statement, the debtor's true last name is crucial because the financing statements are indexed by last names. A subsequent creditor who loans money to a debtor with the same name is put on notice that its lien is secondary.

Substantial evidence supports the finding that debtor's true last name was "Juarez" and not "Munoz." The pleadings state that debtor's last name is "Juarez," as do many of appellants' business records. Debtor provided appellants with a photo I.D. and Green Card bearing the name "Armando Munoz Juarez." The name appears on the sublease and other documents including the Farmer Agreement, a Crop Exhibit, a second sublease agreement (identifying debtor as "Juarez Farms, Armando Munoz Juarez"), a crop assignment, appellants' accounting records, receipts for advances, appellants' letters to debtor, and checks issued by appellants.

As a general rule, minor errors in a UCC financing statement do not affect the effectiveness of the financing statement unless the errors render the document seriously misleading to other creditors. If a search of the filing office's records under the debtor's correct name, using the filing office's standard search logic, would nevertheless disclose that financing statement, the name provided does not make the financing statement seriously misleading.

The record indicates that Frozsun's agent conducted a "Juarez" debtor name search and did not discover appellants' UCC-1 financing statement. No evidence was presented that the financing statement would have been discovered under debtor's true legal name, using the filing office's standard search logic. Absent such a showing, the trial court reasonably concluded that the "Armando Munoz" debtor name in appellants' financing statement was seriously misleading. The secured party, not the debtor or uninvolved third parties, has the duty of insuring proper filing and indexing of the notice.

Appellants contend that the debtor name requirement is governed by the naming convention of Latin American countries because debtor is from Mexico. We reject the argument because the strawberries were planted in and the debt obligation arose in Santa Barbara County, not Mexico. In most Latin American countries, the surname is formed by listing first the father's name then the mother's name. This is exactly opposite Anglo-American tradition. Debtor's last name did not change when he crossed the border into the United States. The "naming convention" is legally irrelevant for UCC-1 purposes and, if accepted, would seriously undermine the concept of lien perfection.

Appellants knew that debtor's legal name was "Armando Juarez" or "Armando Munoz Juarez." Elodia Corona, appellants' account manager, prepared the UCC Financing Statements and testified: "I don't know why I didn't put his last name on the financing statement. I could have made a mistake." Ms. Corona was asked: "So the last name on all the Agreements is Juarez, but on the U.C.C. 1 Forms, you filed them as Munoz?" Ms. Corona answered, "Yes."

Appellants are [defeated by their own] pleadings, the contracts, business records, the checks for the cash advances, debtor's identification papers and tax papers, and the testimony of appellants' account manager. Appellants could have protected themselves by using both names on their financing statements. The trial court did not err in finding that the UCC-1 financing statement filed by Frozsun Foods perfected a security interest superior to appellants' liens.

The judgment is affirmed.

Notice one important item that is *not* required on a financing statement: the debtor's signature. Does this allow a secured party to create any financing statement it wishes? No. The debtor must have entered into a valid security agreement before the secured party is entitled to file any financing statement. Of course, there is the possibility of a fraudulent filing, but the drafters of the UCC reasoned that the efficiency of facilitating electronic filing far outweighs the danger of occasional fraud.

Place of Filing

The United States is a big country, and potential creditors do not want to stagger from one end of it to the other to learn whether particular collateral is already secured elsewhere. Article 9 specifies *where* a secured party must file. These provisions may vary from state to state, so it is essential to check local law because a misfiled record accomplishes nothing. The general rules are as follows.

A secured party must file in the state of the debtor's location. An individual is located at his principal residence. If Luigi, the debtor, lives in Maryland, works in Virginia, and has a vacation home in Florida, a secured party must file in Maryland. An organization that has only one place of business is located in that state. If the organization has more than one place of business, it is considered to be located at its chief executive office.[14]

Article 9 prescribes central filing within the state for most types of collateral. For goods, the central location will typically be the secretary of state's office, although a state may designate some other office if it wishes. For fixtures, the secured party generally has a choice between filing in the same central office that is used for goods (which, again, is usually the secretary of state's office), or filing in the local county office that would be used to file real estate mortgages.[15]

Duration of Filing

Once a financing statement has been filed, it is effective for five years.[16] After five years, the statement will expire and leave the secured party unprotected, unless she files a continuation statement within six months prior to expiration. The continuation statement is valid for an additional five years, and if necessary, a secured party may continue to file one periodically, forever.[17]

24-3b Perfection by Possession or Control

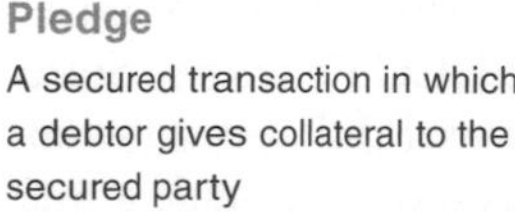
Pledge
A secured transaction in which a debtor gives collateral to the secured party

For most types of collateral, in addition to filing, a secured party generally may perfect by possession or control. So if the collateral is a diamond brooch or 1,000 shares of stock, a bank may perfect its security interest by holding the items until the loan is paid off. When the debtor gives collateral to the secured party, it is often called a **pledge**: The debtor pledges her goods to secure her performance, and the secured party (sometimes called the **pledgee**) takes the goods to perfect its interest.

iStockphoto.com/PhilipCacka

A bank may wish to perfect its security interest by holding this valuable ring in its vault.

Possession

When may a party use possession? Whenever the collateral is goods, negotiable documents, instruments, money, chattel paper that is tangible (as opposed to electronic), or most securities.[18]

Perfection by possession has some advantages. First, notice to other parties is very effective. No reasonable finance company assumes that it can obtain a security interest in a Super Bowl championship ring when another creditor already holds the ring. Second, possession enables the creditor to ensure that the collateral will not be damaged during the life of the security interest. A bank that loans money based on a rare painting may worry about the painting's condition, but it knows the painting is safe if it is locked up in the bank's vault. Third, if the debtor defaults, a secured party has no difficulties repossessing goods that it already holds.

Of course, for some collateral, possession is impractical. If a consumer buys a new yacht on credit, the seller can hardly expect to perfect its security interest by possession. The buyer would become edgy sailing the boat around the dealer's parking lot. In such a case, the secured party must perfect by filing.

---

14 UCC §9-307.

15 UCC §9-501.

16 The exception to this is for a manufactured home, where it lasts 30 years.

17 UCC §9-515.

18 UCC §9-313.

Mandatory Possession

A party *must* perfect a security interest in *money* by taking possession.[19] Money is easy to transfer, and one $100 bill is the same as another, so only possession will do. Suppose Ed's Real Estate claims that Jennifer, a former employee, has opened her own realty business in violation of their non-compete agreement. Jennifer promises to move her business to another city within 90 days, and Ed agrees not to sue. To secure Jennifer's promise to move, Ed takes a security interest in $50,000 cash. If she fails to move on time, he is entitled to the money. To perfect that interest, Ed must take possession of the money and hold it until Jennifer is out of town.

Control

A security interest in investment property, deposit accounts, letter-of-credit rights, and electronic chattel paper may be perfected by control.[20] We described control in the section on attachment. **In general, control means that the secured party has certain exclusive rights to dispose of the collateral.** Recall, for example, that a secured party which is a bank has control of any deposit account located in that bank.

Mandatory Control. Security interests in deposit accounts and letter-of-credit rights may be perfected *only* by control.[21] Once again, filing would be ineffectual with forms of collateral so easily moved, and the UCC will grant perfection only to a secured party that has control.

Care of the Collateral

Possession and control give several advantages to the secured party, but also one important duty: **A secured party must use reasonable care in the custody and preservation of collateral in her possession or control.**[22] If the collateral is something tangible, such as a painting, the secured party must take reasonable steps to ensure that it is safe from harm.

24-3c Perfection of Consumer Goods

The UCC gives special treatment to security interests in most consumer goods. Merchants sell a vast amount of consumer goods on credit. They cannot file a financing statement for every bed, refrigerator, and home theater system for which a consumer owes money. Yet perfecting by possession is also impossible since the consumer expects to take the goods home. To understand the UCC's treatment of these transactions, we need to know two terms. The first is *consumer goods*, which as we saw earlier means goods used primarily for personal, family, or household purposes. The second term is *purchase money security interest*.

A **purchase money security interest (PMSI)** is one taken by the person who sells the collateral or by the person who advances money so the debtor can buy the collateral.[23] Assume the Gobroke Home Center sells Marion a $5,000 stereo system. The sales document requires a payment of $500 down and $50 per month for the next three centuries, and gives Gobroke a security interest in the system. Because the security interest was "taken by the seller," the document is a PMSI. It would also be a PMSI if a bank had loaned Marion the money to buy the system and the document gave the bank a security interest.

Purchase money security interest (PMSI)
An interest taken by the person who sells the collateral or advances money so the debtor can buy it

But aren't all security interests PMSIs? No, many are not. Suppose a bank loans a retail company $800,000 and takes a security interest in the store's present inventory. That is not a PMSI since the store did not use the $800,000 to purchase the collateral.

19 UCC §9-312(b)(3).
20 UCC §9-314(a).
21 UCC §9-312(b)(1).
22 UCC §9-207.
23 UCC §9-103.

What must Gobroke Home Center do to perfect its security interest? Nothing. **A PMSI in *consumer goods* perfects *automatically*, without filing.**[24] Marion's new stereo is clearly consumer goods because she will use it only in her home. Gobroke's security interest is a PMSI, so the interest has perfected automatically. (See Exhibit 24.3.)

EXHIBIT 24.3

A purchase money security interest can arise in either of two ways. In the first example, a store sells a stereo system to a consumer on credit; the consumer in turn signs a PMSI, giving the *store* a security interest in the stereo. In the second example, the consumer buys the stereo with money loaned from a bank; the consumer signs a PMSI giving the *bank* a security interest in the stereo system.

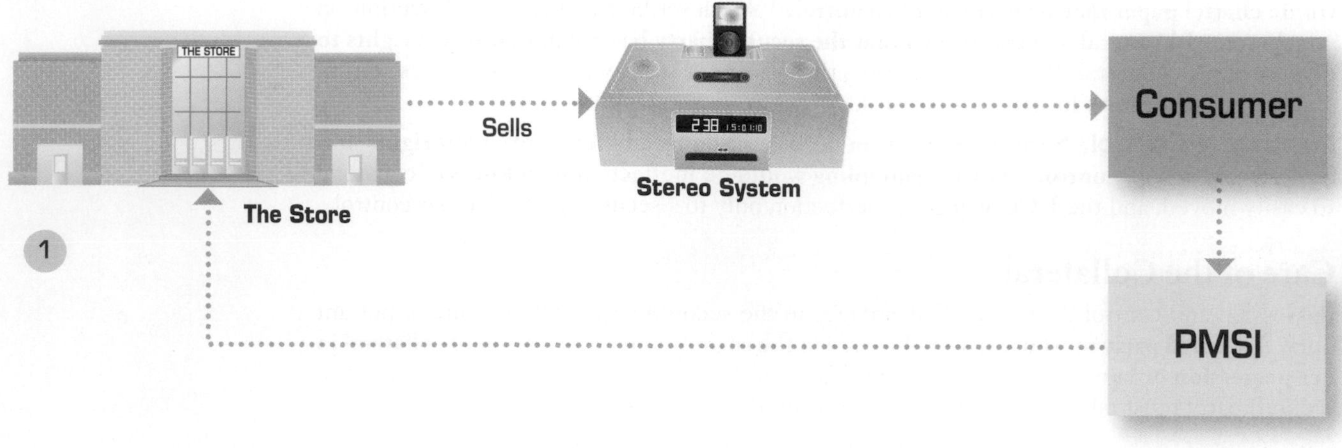

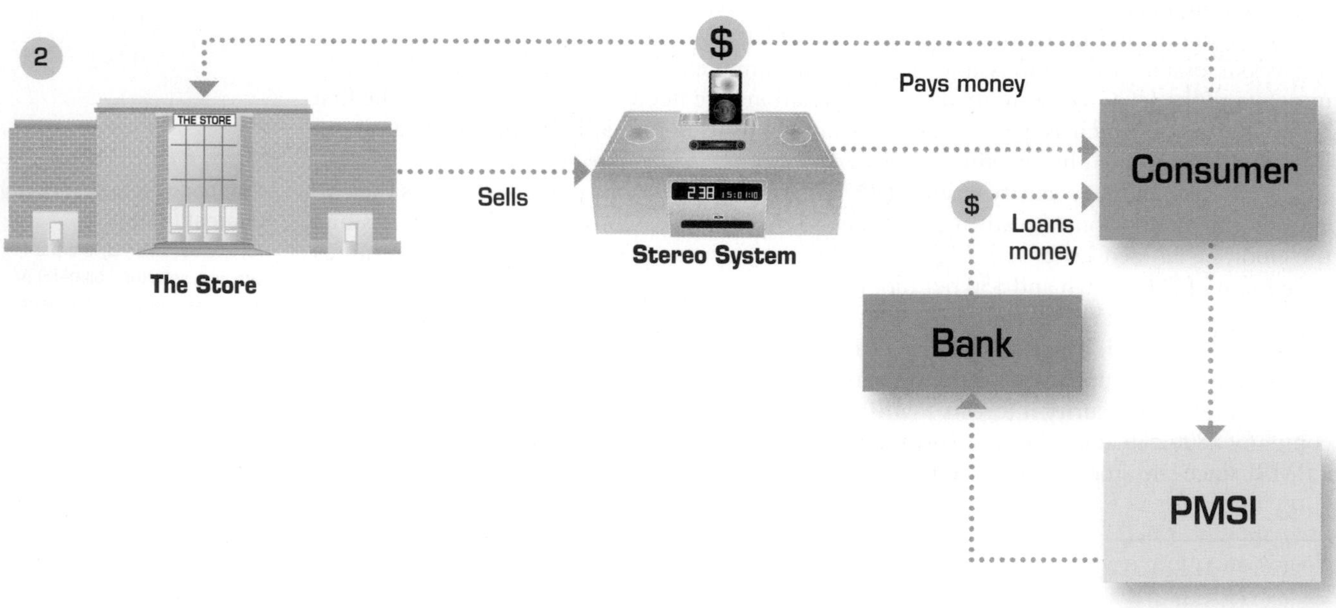

24UCC §9-309(1).

EXAMStrategy

Question: Winona owns a tropical fish store. To buy a spectacular new aquarium, she borrows $25,000 from her sister, Pauline, and signs an agreement giving Pauline a security interest in the tank. Pauline never files the security agreement.

Winona's business goes belly up, and both Pauline and other creditors angle to repossess the tank. Does Pauline have a perfected interest in the tank?

Strategy: Generally, a creditor obtains a perfected security interest by filing or possession. However, a PMSI in consumer goods perfects automatically, without filing. Was Pauline's security agreement a PMSI? Was the fish tank a consumer good?

Result: A PMSI is one taken by the person who sells the collateral or advances money for its purchase. Pauline advanced the money for Winona to buy the tank, so Pauline does have a PMSI, but she has a problem because PMSIs perfect automatically only for *consumer goods*. Consumer goods are those used primarily for personal, family, or household purposes, and so this was not a consumer purchase. Pauline failed to perfect and is unprotected against other creditors.

24-3d Perfection of Movable Collateral and Fixtures

The rules for perfection are slightly different for security interests in movable goods, such as cars and boats, and in fixtures. We look briefly at each.

Movable Goods Generally

Goods that are easily moved create problems for creditors. Suppose a bank in Colorado loans Dorothy money, takes a security interest in her Degas sculpture, and perfects its interest in the proper state offices in Colorado. But then Dorothy moves to Ohio and uses the same collateral for another loan. A lender in Ohio will never discover the security interest perfected in Colorado. If Dorothy defaults, who gets the sculpture?

For most collateral, when the debtor moves to a new state, a security interest from the old state remains perfected for four months; when the collateral is transferred to a new state, the security interest remains perfected for one year.[25] If the secured party re-perfects in the new state within the time limits mentioned, the security interest remains valid until it would normally expire. If the secured party fails to re-perfect in the new state, the security interest lapses. Suppose Dorothy takes her Degas into Ohio on February 10 and on March 5 uses it as collateral for a new loan. The original Colorado bank still has a valid security interest in the sculpture and may seize the art if Dorothy defaults. But if Dorothy applies for her new loan on October 10, and the Colorado bank has failed to re-perfect, the Colorado bank has lost its protection.

Motor Vehicles and the Like

The UCC's provisions about perfecting generally do not apply to motor vehicles, trailers, mobile homes, boats, or farm tractors.[26] Because all of these are so numerous and so mobile, filing may be ineffective and possession is impossible. As a result, almost all states have created special laws to deal with this problem. Anyone offering or taking a security interest in any of these goods must consult local law.

---

[25]UCC §9-316(a).

[26]UCC §9-311(a)(2).

State title laws generally require that a security interest in an automobile be noted directly on the vehicle's certificate of title. A driver needs a certificate of title to obtain registration plates, so the law presumes that the certificate will stay with the car. By requiring that the security interest be noted on the certificate, the law gives the best possible notice to anyone thinking of buying the car or accepting it as collateral. Generally, if a buyer or lender examines the certificate and finds no security interest, he may accept the vehicle for sale, or as collateral, and take it free of any interest. In most states, the same requirement applies to boats.

Fixtures

Fixtures, you recall, are goods that have become attached to real estate. A security interest may be created in goods that *are* fixtures and may continue in goods that *become* fixtures; however, the UCC does not permit a security interest in ordinary building materials, such as lumber and concrete, once they become part of a construction project.

The primary disputes in these cases are between a creditor holding a security interest in a fixture, such as a furnace, and another creditor with rights in the real estate, such as a bank holding a mortgage on the house. The issues are complex, involving local real property law, and we cannot undertake here a thorough explanation of them. However, we can highlight the issues that arise so that you can anticipate the potential problems. Common disputes concern:

- The status of the personal property when the security interest was created (Was it still goods, or had it already been attached to real estate and become a fixture?);
- The status of the real estate (Does the debtor *also* have a legal interest in the *real property?*);
- The type of perfection (Which was recorded first, the security interest in the fixture or the real estate? Does the secured party hold a PMSI?); and
- The physical status of the fixture (Can it be removed without damaging the real estate?).[27]

Any creditor who considers accepting collateral that might become a fixture must anticipate these problems and clarify with the debtor exactly what she plans to do with the goods. Armed with that information, the creditor should consult local law on fixtures and make an appropriate security agreement (or just refuse to accept the fixture as collateral).

24-4 PROTECTION OF BUYERS

Generally, once a security interest is perfected, it remains effective regardless of whether the collateral is sold, exchanged, or transferred in some other way. Bubba's Bus Co. needs money to meet its payroll, so it borrows $150,000 from Francine's Finance Co., which takes a security interest in Bubba's 180 buses and perfects its interest. Bubba, still short of cash, sells 30 of his buses to Antelope Transit. But even that money is not enough to keep Bubba solvent: He defaults on his loan to Francine and goes into bankruptcy. Francine pounces on Bubba's buses. May she repossess the 30 that Antelope now operates? Yes. The security interest continued in the buses even after Antelope purchased them, and Francine can whisk them away. (Antelope has a valid claim against Bubba for the value of the buses, but the claim may prove fruitless, since Bubba is now bankrupt.)

---

[27]UCC §9-334.

There are some exceptions to this rule. The Code gives a few kinds of buyer's special protection.

24-4a Buyers in Ordinary Course of Business

Buyer in ordinary course of business (BIOC) Someone who buys goods in good faith from a seller who routinely deals in such goods

As we saw in Chapter 22, a **buyer in ordinary course of business (BIOC)** is someone who buys goods in good faith from a seller who routinely deals in such goods.[28] For example, Plato's Garden Supply purchases 500 hemlocks from Socrates' Farm, a grower. Plato is a BIOC: He is buying in good faith, and Socrates routinely deals in hemlocks. This is an important status because a BIOC is generally *not affected* by security interests in the goods. However, if Plato *actually realized* that the sale violated another party's rights in the goods, there would be no good faith. If Plato knew that Socrates was bankrupt and had agreed with a creditor not to sell any of his inventory, Plato would not achieve BIOC status.

A buyer in ordinary course of business takes the goods free of a security interest created by its seller even though the security interest is perfected.[29] Suppose that, a month before Plato made his purchase, Socrates borrowed $200,000 from the Athenian Bank. Athenian took a security interest in all of Socrates' trees and perfected by filing. Then Plato purchased his 500 hemlocks. If Socrates defaults on the loan, Athenian will have *no right* to repossess the 500 trees that are now at the Garden Supply. Plato took them free and clear. (Of course, Athenian can still attempt to repossess other trees from Socrates.)

The BIOC exception is designed to encourage ordinary commerce. A buyer making routine purchases should not be forced to perform a financing check before buying. But the rule, efficient though it may be, creates its own problems. A creditor may extend a large sum of money to a merchant based on collateral, such as inventory, only to discover that by the time the merchant defaults the collateral has been sold to BIOCs.

EXAMStrategy

Question: Troy owns an art gallery specializing in Greek artifacts. To modernize the gallery, Troy borrows $150,000 from the Sparta Bank, which takes a security interest in all of his inventory. Sparta promptly perfects. A month later, Troy sells Helen an Athenian warrior's helmet for $675,000. Helen does not bother to perform a financing check, and she is unaware of Sparta's security interest. Troy soon goes bankrupt, and Sparta attempts to seize all of the inventory, including the helmet. Sparta proves that a routine financing check would have revealed its interest. Who wins the helmet?

Strategy: A creditor perfects a security interest to ensure that it is protected against all the world. However, exceptions leave the secured party unprotected in certain cases, including those of consumers. Analyze this case using that exception.

Result: A BIOC takes the goods free of a security interest created by his seller. Helen acted in good faith, buying from a dealer who routinely dealt in such goods. And it was Troy, Helen's seller, who created the security interest. Helen takes the helmet free of the bank's security interest, despite the fact that it was perfected.

28UCC §1-201(9).

29UCC §9-320(a). In fact, the buyer takes free of the security interest *even if the buyer knew of it.* Yet a BIOC, by definition, must be acting in good faith. Is this a contradiction? No. Plato might know that a third party has a security interest in Socrates' crops yet not realize that his purchase violates the third party's rights. Generally, for example, a security interest will permit a retailer to sell consumer goods, the presumption being that part of the proceeds will go to the secured party. A BIOC cannot be expected to determine what a retailer plans to do with the money he is paid.

Because the BIOC exception undercuts the basic protection given to a secured party, the courts interpret it narrowly. BIOC status is available only if the *seller* created the security interest. Oftentimes, a buyer will purchase goods that have a security interest created by someone other than the seller. If that happens, the buyer is not a BIOC. However, should that rule be strictly enforced even when the results are harsh? You make the call.

You Be the Judge

Conseco Finance Servicing Corp. v. Lee

2004 WL 1243417; 2004 Tex. App. LEXIS 5035
Texas Court of Appeals, 2004

Facts: Lila Williams purchased a new Roadtrek 200 motor home from New World R.V., Inc. She paid about $14,000 down and financed $63,000, giving a security interest to New World. The RV company assigned its security interest to Conseco Finance, which perfected. Two years later, Williams returned the vehicle to New World (the record does not indicate why), and New World sold the RV to Robert and Ann Lee for $42,800. A year later, Williams defaulted on her payments to Conseco.

The Lees sued Conseco, claiming to be BIOCs and asking for a court declaration that they had sole title to the Roadtrek. Conseco counterclaimed, seeking title based on its perfected security interest. The trial court ruled that the Lees were BIOCs, with full rights to the vehicle. Conseco appealed.

You Be the Judge: *Were the Lees BIOCs?*

Argument for Conseco: Under UCC §9-319, a BIOC takes free of a security interest created by the buyer's seller. The buyers were the Lees. The seller was New World. New World did not create the security interest—Lila Williams did. There is no security interest created by New World. The security interest held by Conseco was created by someone else (Williams) and is not affected by the Lees's status as BIOC. The law is clear and Conseco is entitled to the Roadtrek.

Argument for the Lees: Conseco weaves a clever argument, but let's look at what they are really saying. Two honest buyers, acting in perfect good faith, can walk into an RV dealership, spend $42,000 for a used vehicle, and end up with—nothing. Conseco claims it is entitled to an RV that the Lees paid for because someone that the Lees have never dealt with, never even heard of, gave to this RV seller a security interest which the seller, years earlier, passed on to a finance company. Conseco's argument defies common sense and the goals of Article 9.

Rebuttal from Conseco: The best part of the Lees' argument is the emotional appeal; the worst part is that it does not reflect the law. Yes, $42,000 is a lot of money. That is why a reasonable buyer is careful to do business with conscientious, ethical sellers. New World, which knew that Williams financed the RV and knew who held the security interest, never bothered to check on the status of the payments. If the Lees have suffered wrongdoing, it is at the hands of an irresponsible seller—the company with which they chose to work, the company from which they must seek relief.

Rebuttal from the Lees: The purpose of the UCC is to make dealing fair and commerce work; one of its methods is to get away from obscure, technical arguments. Conseco's suggestion would demolish the used-car industry. What buyers will ever pay serious money—*any* money—for a used vehicle, knowing that thousands of dollars later, the car might be towed out of their driveway by a finance company they never heard of?

24-4b Buyers of Consumer Goods

Another exception exists to protect buyers of consumer goods who do not realize that the item they are buying has a security interest in it. This exception tends to apply to relatively casual purchases, such as those between friends. Typically, the pattern is that one purchaser buys consumer goods on credit and then resells. The original purchaser is considered a debtor-seller since she still owes money but is now selling to a second buyer. **In the case of consumer goods purchased from a debtor-seller, a buyer takes free of a security interest if he is not aware of the security interest, he pays value for the goods, he is buying for his own family or household use, and the second party has not yet filed a financing statement.**[30]

Here is how this exception works. Charles Lau used a Sears credit card to buy a 46-inch television, a sleeper sofa, loveseat, entertainment center, diamond ring, gold chain, and microwave. He had the items delivered to the house of his girlfriend Teresa Rierman because he did not want his father to know he had been using the credit card (we can't imagine why). Lau later sold the items to Rierman's family and then (wait for it) defaulted on his payments to Sears and declared bankruptcy. Sears attempted to repossess its merchandise, but the Riermans claimed they were innocent buyers. The court ruled that if the Riermans could show that they knew nothing about Sears's security interest in the goods, they could keep the goods.[31]

This rule may be confusing because earlier, we discussed the automatic perfection of a security interest in consumer goods. When Sears sold the merchandise to Lau, it took a purchase money security interest in consumer goods. That interest perfected automatically (without filing) and was valid against *almost* everyone. Suppose Lau had used the furniture as collateral to obtain a bank loan. Sears would have retained its perfected security interest in the goods, and when Lau defaulted, Sears could have repossessed everything, leaving the bank with no collateral and no money.

The one person that Sears's perfect security interest could not defeat, however, was a buyer purchasing for personal use without knowledge of the security interest—in other words, the Riermans. Assuming the Riermans knew nothing of the security interest, they win. If Sears considers this type of loss important, it must, in the future, protect itself by filing a financing statement. Taking this extra step will leave Sears protected against everyone. Then, if a buyer defaults, Sears can pull the sofa out from under any purchaser.

24-4c Buyers of Chattel Paper, Instruments, and Documents

We have seen that debtors often use chattel paper, instruments, or documents as collateral. Because each of these is so easily transferred, Article 9 gives buyers special protection. **A buyer who purchases chattel paper or an instrument in the ordinary course of her business and then takes possession generally takes free of any security interest.**[32]

Suppose Tele-Maker sells 500 smart televisions to Retailer on credit, keeping a security interest in the televisions and the proceeds. The proceeds are any money or paper that Retailer earns from selling the sets. Retailer sells 300 of the units to customers, most of whom pay on credit. The customers sign chattel paper, promising to pay for the smart televisions over time (and giving Retailer a security interest in the sets). All of this chattel paper is proceeds, so Tele-Maker has a perfected security interest in it. The chattel paper is worth about $150,000 if all of the customers pay in full. But Retailer wants money now, so Retailer sells its chattel paper to Financer, who pays $120,000 cash for it. Next, Retailer defaults on its obligation to pay Tele-Maker for the sets. Tele-Maker cannot repossess the televisions because

30 UCC §9-320.

31 In re Lau, 140 B.R. 172 (N.D. Ohio 1992).

32 UCC §9-330(a)(b)(d).

each customer was a BIOC (buyer in ordinary course of business) and took the goods free of any security interest. So Tele-Maker attempts to repossess the chattel paper. Will it succeed? No. The buyer of chattel paper takes it free of a perfected security interest. See Exhibit 24.4.

EXHIBIT 24.4

The buyer of chattel paper takes it free of a perfected security interest. In this case, Tele-Maker (1) sells 500 units to Retailer on credit, keeping (2) a security interest in the televisions and the proceeds. Retailer (3) sells the sets to customers who (4) sign chattel paper. Retailer (5) sells the chattel paper to Financer and then defaults on its obligations to Tele-Maker.

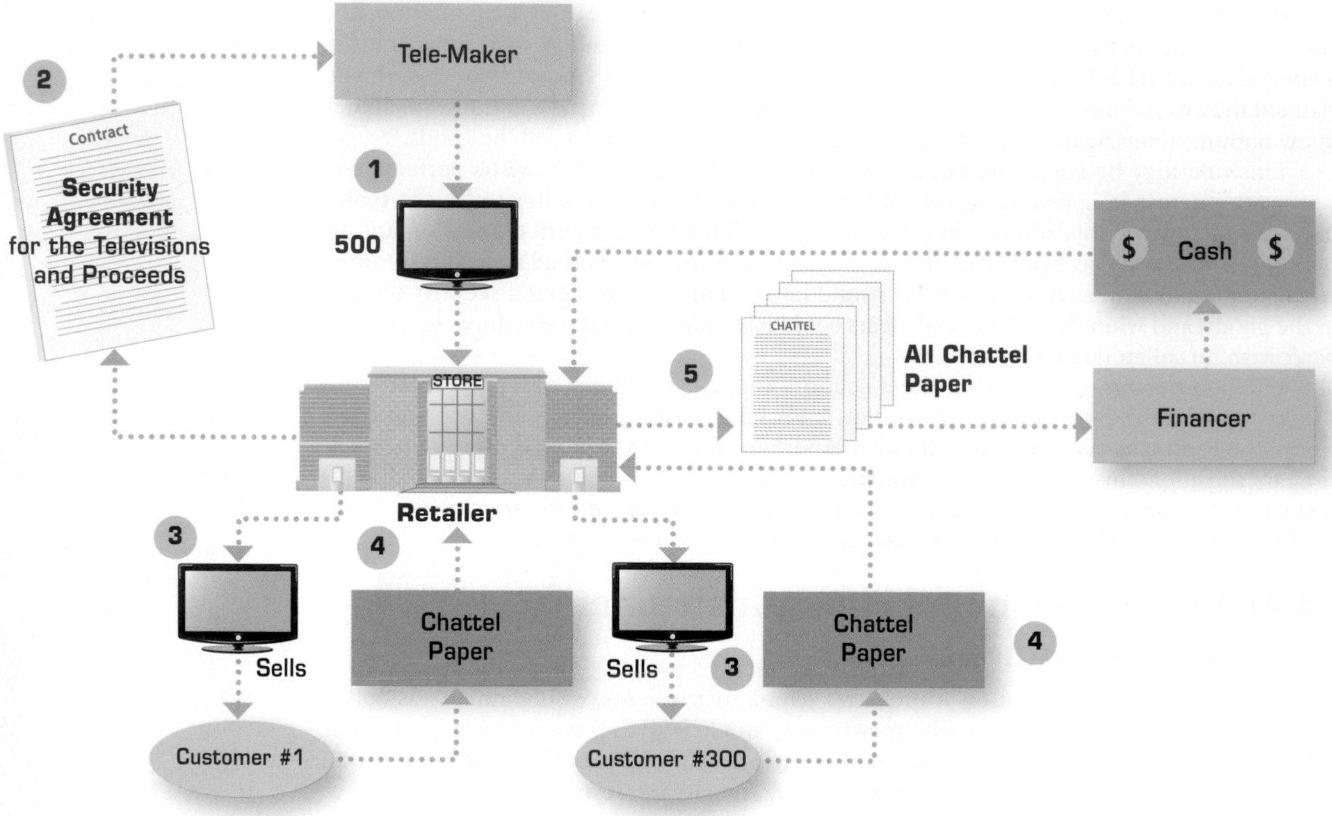

Other Paper

Similar rules apply for holders in due course of instruments and for purchasers of securities and documents of title. Those parties obtain special rights, described in Articles 3, 7, and 8 of the UCC. The details of those rules are beyond the scope of this chapter, but once again, the lesson for any lender is simple: A security interest is safest when the collateral is in your vault. If you do not take possession of the paper, you may lose it to an innocent buyer.[33]

33 UCC §9-331.

24-4d Liens

Law student Paul King got a costly lesson when his $28.09 check for an oil change bounced and the repo man snatched his prized Corvette. The bill for the car's return: $644. King was a third-year law student working part time in a private firm in Houston. He had just walked in from lunch when coworkers told him his car was being towed.

"I thought they were joking," King said. They weren't. King saw a tow truck backing up to his car and hurried out to speak with the workers. They advised him that Texas law authorized them to pick up his car to satisfy a lien for work done to the car. King hurried inside to telephone the company that had performed the oil change. Unable to make a deal on the phone, he ran back outside and found—no car.

> **Unable to make a deal on the phone, he ran back outside and found—no car.**

King phoned Harris County Repossession to see about getting his car back. That's easy, they told him. But you owe some fees: $28.09 for the oil change, $20 for the returned check, $25 for the legal notice in the newspapers, $21.24 per day for storage—plus, of course, the $550 repossession fee.[34]

Is that legal? Probably. The service station had a **lien** on the car. A lien is a security interest created by law (rather than by agreement). State and federal law both allow parties to assert a lien against a debtor under prescribed conditions. For example, a state may claim a lien based on unpaid taxes; the state is giving notice to the world that it may seize the debtor's property and sell it. A company may claim a lien based on work performed by the debtor.

Lien
A security interest created by law, rather than by agreement

To understand the difference between a lien and a security interest, assume that when Paul King bought his Corvette, he made a down payment and signed a security agreement to ensure future payments. His agreement gave the dealer a security interest in the sports car. Later, when he paid for an oil change, his check bounced. State law gave the service station a lien on the auto, meaning the right to hold the car if it is in the garage and to seize the auto if it is elsewhere.

Because automobile repossessions provide such a graphic view of secured transactions, we will return to the subject later in the chapter. In this case, the oil company had an **artisan's lien**, meaning a security interest in personal property created when a worker makes some improvement to the property. A car mechanic, a computer repair technician, and a furniture restorer all create artisan's liens. A **mechanic's lien** is similar and is created when a worker improves real property. A carpenter who puts an addition on a kitchen and a painter who paints the kitchen's interior both have a mechanic's lien on the house. The owner of an apartment may obtain a landlord's lien in a tenant's personal property if the tenant fails to pay the rent. These security interests vary from state to state, so an affected person must consult local law.

Artisan's lien
A security interest in personal property

Mechanic's lien
A security created when a worker improves real property

Because liens are the creation of statutes rather than agreements, Article 9 generally does not apply to them. The one aspect of liens that Article 9 does govern is priority between lienholders and other secured parties, which we examine in the following section. In Paul King's case, the repair shop certainly had a valid lien on his car, even though the amount in question was small. The company's method of collecting on its lien is more debatable. King admitted that the company had telephoned him and given him a chance to pay for the bounced check. Some courts would hold that the repair shop had done all it was required to do, but others might rule that it should have shown more patience and avoided running up the bill.

24-5 PRIORITIES AMONG CREDITORS

What happens when two creditors have a security interest in the same collateral? The party who has **priority** in the collateral gets it. Typically, the debtor lacks assets to pay everyone, so all creditors struggle to be the first in line. After the first creditor has repossessed the

[34] Rad Sallee and James T. Campbell, "Repo Men Hitch Up Big Fee to Car," *Houston Chronicle*, October 15, 1991, Section A, p. 21.

collateral, sold it, and taken enough of the proceeds to pay off his debt, there may be nothing left for anyone else. Who gets priority? There are three principal rules.

The first rule is easy: **A party with a perfected security interest takes priority over a party with an unperfected interest.**[35] This, of course, is the whole point of perfecting: to ensure that your security interest gets priority over everyone else's. On August 15, Meredith's Market, an antique store, borrows $100,000 from Happy Bank, which takes a security interest in all of Meredith's inventory. Happy Bank does not perfect. On September 15, Meredith uses the same collateral to borrow $50,000 from Suspicion Bank, which files a financing statement the same day. On October 15, as if on cue, Meredith files for bankruptcy and stops paying both creditors. Suspicion wins because it holds a perfected interest, whereas Happy Bank holds merely an unperfected interest.

The second rule: **If neither secured party has perfected, the first interest to attach gets priority.**[36] Suppose that Suspicion Bank and Happy Bank had both failed to perfect. In that case, Happy Bank would have the first claim to Meredith's inventory since Happy's interest attached first.

And the third rule follows logically: **Between perfected security interests, the first to file or perfect wins.**[37] Diminishing Perspective, a railroad, borrows $75 million from First Bank, which takes a security interest in Diminishing's railroad cars and immediately perfects by filing. Two months later, Diminishing borrows $100 million from Second Bank, which takes a security interest in the same collateral and also files. When Diminishing arrives, on schedule, in bankruptcy court, both banks will race to seize the rolling stock. First Bank gets the railcars because it perfected first.

March 1:	April 2:	May 3:	The Winner:
First Bank lends money and perfects its security interest by filing a financing statement.	Second Bank lends money and perfects its security interest by filing a financing statement.	Diminishing goes bankrupt, and both banks attempt to take the rolling stock.	First Bank, because it perfected first.

The general rules of priority are quite straightforward; however, you will not be surprised to learn that there are some exceptions.

24-5a Filing versus Control or Possession

Recall that a secured party may use either filing or control to perfect its security interest in deposit accounts, investment property, and letter-of-credit rights. Which method *should* the secured party use? Control. **For these three types of collateral, a secured party who has control wins over a party who merely filed.**[38] Early Bank obtains a security interest in Lionel's investment property and perfects by filing. Nine months later, Late Bank obtains a security interest in the same property and perfects by taking control. Late Bank wins.

Similarly, a secured party may perfect its interest in an instrument either by filing or possession. Once again, possession is the better idea: **Between competing secured parties, the one who possesses wins, even over one who filed earlier.**[39]

---

[35]UCC §9-322(a)(2).

[36]UCC §9-322(a)(3).

[37]UCC §9-322(a)(1).

[38]UCC §§9-327, 9-328, 9-329. If more than one creditor has control of the same collateral, the security interests rank according to the time of obtaining control.

[39]UCC §9-330(d).

24-5b Priority Involving a Purchase Money Security Interest

You may recall that a purchase money security interest (PMSI) is a security interest taken by the seller of the collateral or by a lender whose loan enables the debtor to buy the collateral. A PMSI can be created only in goods, fixtures, and software. On November 1, Manufacturer sells a specially built lathe, a machine for shaping wood, to Tool Shop for $80,000 and takes a security interest in the lathe. The parties have created a PMSI. Parties holding a PMSI often take priority over other perfected security interests in the same goods, even if the other security interest was perfected first. How can the conflict arise? Suppose that on February 1, Tool Shop had borrowed $100,000 from the Gargoyle Bank, giving Gargoyle a security interest in after-acquired property. When the lathe arrives at the Tool Shop on November 1, Gargoyle's security interest attaches to it. But Manufacturer has a PMSI in the lathe, hence the conflict.

We need to examine PMSIs involving inventory and those involving noninventory. **Inventory** means goods that the seller is holding for sale or lease in the ordinary course of its business. The furniture in a furniture store is inventory; the store's computer, telephones, and filing cabinets are not.

Inventory
Goods that a seller is holding for sale or lease in the ordinary course of its business

PMSI in Inventory

A PMSI in inventory takes priority over a conflicting perfected security interest (even one perfected earlier), if two conditions are met:

- Before filing its PMSI, the secured party must check for earlier security interests and, if there are any, must notify the holder of that interest concerning the new PMSI; and
- The secured party must then perfect its PMSI (normally by filing) *before* the debtor receives the inventory.[40]

If the holder of the PMSI has met both of these conditions, its PMSI takes priority over any security interests filed earlier, as illustrated in the following chart.

1. February 1:	2. March 2:	3. March 3:	4. March 4:
Coltrane Bank loans Monk's Jazz Store $90,000, taking a security interest in all after-acquired property, including inventory.	Monk offers to buy ten saxophones from Webster's Supply for $3,000 each.	Webster checks the financing records and learns that Coltrane Bank has a security interest in all of Monk's after-acquired property.	Webster notifies Coltrane Bank that he is selling ten saxophones to Monk for $30,000 and is taking a PMSI in the instruments, which Webster carefully describes.
5. March 4:	**6. March 5:**	**7. September:**	**8. The Winner:**
Webster files a financing statement indicating a PMSI in the ten saxophones.	Webster sells the ten saxophones to Monk.	Monk goes bankrupt.	Webster. His PMSI in inventory takes priority over Coltrane's earlier interest.

[40]UCC §9-324(b)(c).

PMSI in Noninventory Collateral

PMSIs are often given for noninventory goods. When Tool Shop bought the lathe, in the example discussed, the company gave a PMSI to the seller. The bank simultaneously obtained a security interest in the same lathe, based on its after-acquired property interest. Who wins?

A PMSI in collateral other than inventory takes priority over a conflicting security interest if the PMSI is perfected at the time the debtor receives the collateral or within 20 days after he receives it.[41] As long as Computer Co. perfects (by filing) within 20 days of delivering the computer, its PMSI takes priority over the bank's earlier security interest. Manufacturer may repossess the machine, and the bank may never get a dime back.

Again, we must note that the PMSI exception undercuts the ability of a creditor to rely on its perfected security interest. As a result, courts insist that a party asserting the PMSI exception demonstrate that it has complied with every requirement. In the following case, the creditor just got in under the wire.

In re Roser

613 F3d 1240
United States Court of Appeals for the Tenth Circuit, 2010

Facts: Robert Roser obtained a loan from Sovereign Bank, which he promptly used to buy a car. Nineteen days later, Sovereign filed a lien with the state of Colorado. The bank expected that with a perfected interest, it would have priority over everyone else.

Unknown to Sovereign Bank, Roser had declared bankruptcy only 12 days after he purchased the car. Later, the bankruptcy trustee argued that he had priority over Sovereign because the bankruptcy filing happened before Sovereign perfected its security interest. When the court found for the trustee, Sovereign Bank appealed.

Issue: ***Did Sovereign Bank, a PMSI holder, obtain priority over the bankruptcy trustee?***

Excerpts from Judge Hartz's Decision: The Bankruptcy Code gives the bankruptcy trustee the rights and powers of a person who acquired a judicial lien on the debtor's property at the time that the bankruptcy petition was filed. In general, the trustee can avoid liens that are unperfected when the petition for bankruptcy is filed. But in some circumstances, a lien that is perfected after the bankruptcy filing may nevertheless have priority.

The Bank presents a straightforward argument why its lien would have priority under Colorado law over a lien of a judgment creditor who obtained judgment at the time Roser filed for bankruptcy. Under the UCC:

> If a person [1] files a financing statement [2] with respect to a purchase-money security interest [3] before or within twenty days after the debtor receives delivery of the collateral, the security interest takes priority over the rights of a buyer, lessee, or lien creditor which arise between the time the security interest attaches and the time of filing.

There is no doubt that the Bank satisfied the requirements of this section. The filing of a lien constitutes the filing of a financing statement. Nor is there any dispute that the Bank held a purchase-money security interest in Roser's vehicle. Thus, because the Bank filed its lien within 20 days of Roser's obtaining the vehicle, it contends that [the] UCC gives its lien a priority over any rights in the vehicle—including the Trustee's interest.

The Trustee's arguments to the contrary are not persuasive. The Trustee cannot avoid the Bank's lien. We reverse the judgment of the district court and remand for further proceedings consistent with this opinion.

24-6 DEFAULT AND TERMINATION

We have reached the end of the line. Either the debtor has defaulted or it has performed its obligations and may terminate the security agreement.

41 UCC §9-324(a).

24-6a Default

The parties define "default" in their security agreement. **Generally, a debtor defaults when he fails to make payments due or enters bankruptcy proceedings.** The parties can agree that other acts will constitute default, such as the debtor's failure to maintain insurance on the collateral. When a debtor defaults, the secured party has two principal options: (1) It may take possession of the collateral or (2) it may file suit against the debtor for the money owed. The secured party does not have to choose between these two remedies; it may try one remedy, such as repossession, and if that fails, attempt the other.[42]

Taking Possession of the Collateral

When the debtor defaults, the secured party may take possession of the collateral.[43] How does the secured party do so? In either of two ways: The secured party can file suit against the debtor to obtain a court order requiring the debtor to deliver the collateral. Otherwise, the secured party may act on its own, without any court order, and simply take the collateral, provided this can be done without a breach of the peace. A **breach of the peace** occurs when the repossession disturbs public tranquility, such as through violent, threatening, or harassing acts.

Breach of the peace
Any action that disturbs public tranquility and order

Secured parties often repossess automobiles without the debtor's cooperation. Typically, the security agreement will state that, in the event of default, the secured party has a right to take possession of the car and drive it away. As we saw earlier, the secured party could be the seller or it could be a mechanic with an artisan's lien on the car.

The following case discusses a repossession in which everything went wrong. It was a disaster, but was it a breach of the peace?

Chapa v. Traciers & Associates, Inc.

267 S.W.3d 386
Texas Court of Appeals, 2008

Facts: Marissa Chapa defaulted on her car loan, so Ford Motor Credit Corp. hired Traciers & Associates to repossess her white Ford Expedition. Traciers assigned its field manager, Paul Chambers, to the task and gave him the vehicle's tag number and address. Chambers staked out the house, waiting for a chance to make his move.

One fateful morning, Chambers observed a woman drive the car out into the street and leave it running while she ran back into the house. Chambers seized the moment. It only took him 30 seconds to hook up his tow truck to the Ford and drive away. Chambers may have been quick but he was mistaken about two things. First, he took the wrong car: This white Expedition belonged to Marissa's brother Carlos and his wife Maria. It was not in default. Second, their two children were in the backseat of the towed vehicle.

When Maria emerged from the house and saw that the Expedition, with her children, was gone, she naturally panicked and hysterically called 911. Meanwhile, on an adjacent street, Chambers noticed that the Expedition's wheels were turning. When he stopped the tow truck to investigate, he discovered the two Chapa children. Within minutes, Chambers returned the kids and the car to a hysterical Maria.

Carlos and Maria Chapa sued Traciers, Chambers, and FMCC for breach of the peace. The trial court dismissed the case and the Chapas appealed.

Issue: ***Did Chambers commit a breach of the peace in repossessing the car?***

Excerpts from Justice Guzman's Decision: After default, a secured party may take possession of the collateral without judicial process, if it proceeds without breach of the peace. The Chapas argue that the act of taking children from the possession of their mother which leaves her in a hysterical crying state, is clearly a breach of peace.

[42] UCC §9-601(a)(b)(c).
[43] UCC §9-609.

The expression "breach of the peace" as used in the Uniform Commercial Code connotes conduct that incites or is likely to incite immediate public turbulence, or that leads to or is likely to lead to an immediate loss of public order and tranquility. [The] secured creditor, in exercising its privilege to enter upon premises of another to repossess collateral, may not perpetrate any action manifesting force or violence, or naturally calculated to provide a breach of peace. Although actual violence is not required to find breach of the peace, disturbance or violence must be reasonably likely, and not merely a remote possibility. In addition, breach of the peace refers to conduct at, near, or incident to seizure of property. Even in attempted repossession of a chattel off a street, parking lot, or unenclosed space, if repossession is contested at actual time of and in immediate vicinity of attempted repossession, the secured party must desist and pursue his remedy in court.

Here, there is no evidence that Chambers proceeded with the attempted repossession over an objection communicated to him at, near, or incident to the seizure of the property. To the contrary, Chambers immediately desisted repossession efforts and peaceably returned the vehicle and the children when he learned of their presence. Moreover, Chambers actively avoided confrontation. By removing an apparently unoccupied vehicle from a public street when the driver was not present, he reduced the likelihood of violence or other public disturbance.

In sum, Chambers's conduct did not violate a duty imposed by section 9.609 of the Texas Business and Commerce Code.

Disposition of the Collateral

Once the secured party has obtained possession of the collateral, it has two choices. The secured party may (1) dispose of the collateral or (2) retain the collateral as full satisfaction of the debt.

Disposal of the Collateral. **A secured party may sell, lease, or otherwise dispose of the collateral in any commercially reasonable manner.**[44] Typically, the secured party will sell the collateral in either a private or a public sale. First, however, the debtor must receive reasonable notice of the time and place of the sale so that she may bid on the collateral. The higher the price that the secured party gets for the collateral, the lower the balance still owed by the debtor. Giving the debtor notice of the sale and a chance to bid ensures that the collateral will not be sold for an unreasonably low price.

Suppose Bank loans $65,000 to Farmer to purchase a tractor. While still owing $40,000, Farmer defaults. Bank takes possession of the tractor and then notifies Farmer that it intends to sell the tractor at an auction. Farmer has the right to attend and bid on the tractor.

When the secured party has sold the collateral, it applies the proceeds of the sale: first, to its expenses in repossessing and selling the collateral, and second, to the debt.[45] Assume Bank sold the tractor for $35,000 and that the process of repossessing and selling the tractor cost $5,000. Bank applies the remaining $30,000 to the debt.

Deficiency
Having insufficient funds to pay off a debt

Surplus
A sum of money greater than the debt incurred

Deficiency or Surplus. The sale of the tractor yielded $30,000 to be applied to the debt, which was $40,000. The disposition has left a **deficiency**; that is, insufficient funds to pay off the debt. **The debtor is liable for any deficiency.** So the bank will sue the farmer for the remaining $10,000. On the other hand, sometimes the sale of the collateral yields a **surplus**; that is, a sum greater than the debt. In that case, the secured party must pay the surplus to the debtor.[46]

When a secured party disposes of collateral in a commercially unreasonable manner, then a deficiency or surplus claim may be adjusted based on the sum that should have been obtained.[47] Suppose that Seller, who is owed $300,000, repossesses 500 bedroom sets from a hotel and,

44UCC §9-610.
45UCC §9-615(a).
46UCC §9-615(d).
47UCC §9-626(a)(3).

without giving proper notice, quickly sells them for a net amount of $200,000. Seller sues for the $100,000 deficiency. If a court determines that a properly announced sale would have netted $250,000, Seller is only entitled to a deficiency judgment of $50,000. Similarly, if the collateral is sold to the secured party or someone related, and the price obtained is significantly below what would be expected, then any deficiency or surplus must be calculated on what the sale would normally have brought. This protects the debtor from a sale in which the secured party has followed all formalities but ended up owning the goods for a suspiciously low price.[48]

Acceptance of Collateral. In many cases, the secured party has the option to satisfy the debt simply by keeping the collateral. **Acceptance** refers to a secured party's retention of the collateral as full or partial satisfaction of the debt. **Partial satisfaction** means that the debtor will still owe some deficiency to the secured party. This is how the system works.[49]

Acceptance
Retention of the collateral by a secured party as full or partial satisfaction of a debt

A secured party who wishes to accept the collateral must notify the debtor. If the debtor agrees in an authenticated record, then the secured party may keep the collateral as full *or* partial satisfaction of the debt. If the debtor does not respond within 20 days, the secured party may still accept the collateral as full satisfaction, but not as partial satisfaction. In other words, the debtor's silence does not give the secured party the right to keep the goods and still sue for more money.

Suppose the buyer of a $13 million yacht, Icarus, has defaulted, and the retailer has repossessed the boat. The firm may decide the boat is worth more than the debt, so it notifies the buyer that it plans to keep Icarus. If the buyer does not object, the retailer automatically owns the boat after 20 days.

If the buyer promptly objects to acceptance, the retailer must then dispose of Icarus as described earlier, typically by sale. Why would a debtor object? Because she believes the boat is worth more than the debt. The debtor anticipates that a sale will create a surplus.

Consumers receive additional protection. A secured party may not accept collateral that is consumer goods if the debtor has possession of the goods *or* if the debtor has paid 60 percent of the purchase price. If Maud has defaulted on an oven that is in her kitchen, the Gobroke retail store may be entitled to repossess the oven, but the company must then dispose of the goods (sell the oven) and apply the proceeds to Maud's debt. Similarly, if Ernest is paying for his $10,000 television set in a "layaway" plan, with Gobroke warehousing the goods until the full price is paid, the store may not accept the television once Ernest has paid $6,000. Finally, a secured party is never permitted to accept consumer goods in partial satisfaction.[50]

Right of Redemption. Up to the time the secured party disposes of the collateral, the debtor has the right to **redeem** it, that is, to pay the full value of the debt. If the debtor redeems, she obtains the collateral back. Sylvia borrows $25,000 from the bank and pledges a ruby necklace as collateral. She defaults, still owing $9,000, and the bank notifies her that it will sell the necklace. If Sylvia pays the full $9,000 before the sale occurs, plus any expenses the bank has incurred in arranging the sale, she receives her necklace back.[51]

Redeem
To pay the full value of a debt to get the collateral back

Proceeding to Judgment

Occasionally, the secured party will prefer to ignore its rights in the collateral and simply sue the debtor. **A secured party may sue the debtor for the full debt.**[52] Why would a creditor, having gone to so much effort to perfect its security interest, ignore that interest and simply file a lawsuit? The collateral may have decreased in value and be insufficient to cover the debt.

48UCC §§9-615(f), 9-626(a)(5).
49UCC §9-620.
50UCC §9-620(a)(3), (e), (g).
51UCC §9-623.
52UCC §9-601(a).

Suppose a bank loaned $500,000 to a debtor to buy a rare baseball cap worn by Babe Ruth in a World Series game. The debtor defaults, owing $390,000. The bank discovers that the cap was damaged and is now worth only $230,000. It is true that the bank could sell the cap and sue for the deficiency. But the sale will take time, and the outcome is uncertain. Suppose the bank knows that the debtor has recently paid cash for a $2 million house. The bank may promptly file suit for the full $230,000. The bank will ask the court to freeze the debtor's bank account and legally hold the house until the suit is resolved. The bank expects to prove the debt quickly—the loan documents are clear, and the amount of debt is easily calculated. It will obtain its $230,000 without ever donning the cap. Of course, the bank has the option of doing both things simultaneously: It may slap on the cap and a lawsuit all at once.

24-6b Termination

Termination statement
A document indicating that a secured party no longer claims a security interest in the collateral

When the debtor pays the full debt, the secured party must complete a **termination statement**, a document indicating that it no longer claims a security interest in the collateral.[53] These forms are commonly called UCC-3 statements.

For a consumer debt, the secured party must file the termination statement in every place that it filed a financing statement. The secured party must do this within one month from the date the debt is fully paid, or within 20 days of a demand from the consumer, whichever comes first. For other transactions, the secured party must, within 20 days, either file the termination statement or send it to the secured party so that he may file it himself. In both cases, the goal is the same: to notify all interested parties that the debt is extinguished.

One important takeaway is that the law of secured transactions can be unforgiving. As we saw in *Corona Fruits v. Frozsun*, an inconsistency on a UCC filing can be fatal to a creditor's claim. The following case ends the chapter with some drama. A lawyer made a $1.5 billion mistake—and no one was sympathetic.

In re Motors Liquidation Co.

2015 U.S. App 859
United States Court of Appeals for the Second Circuit, 2015

Facts: General Motors was the debtor on two unrelated secured transactions. The first was a $300 million loan (known as the "Synthetic Lease"); the second was a $1.5 billion term loan (the "Term Loan"). JPMorgan Chase Bank was the secured party on both transactions.

When GM decided to pay off the Synthetic Lease, it instructed its lawyers at the firm of Mayer Brown to prepare the necessary termination statements for that loan. A partner at the firm assigned an associate, who then instructed a paralegal to perform a search for all the financing statements against GM recorded in Delaware. The search yielded both the Synthetic Lease and the Term Loan. Unaware that the Term Loan was unrelated to the Synthetic Loan, Mayer Brown prepared the documentation to terminate them both and circulated it for GM, JPMorgan, and JPMorgan's lawyers (at another law firm named Simpson Thacher) to review. All the parties approved the documents, which were promptly filed with Delaware's secretary of state. No one realized that terminating security for the Term Loan was a mistake.

When General Motors filed for bankruptcy the following year, JPMorgan discovered the error. GM's unsecured creditors argued that, because of the faulty termination statement, the Term Loan was now unsecured. If true, the loan was much less likely to be repaid. In bankruptcy court, JPMorgan argued that there was no termination of the security agreement because it had not intended or authorized it.

On appeal, the Second Circuit posed two questions: (1) Did Delaware law require the secured party to intend the consequences of its filings? and (2) Did JPMorgan's actions authorize the filing? Since the first question involved state law, the federal appeals court asked the Delaware Supreme Court to address it. That court held that, for a filing to be

[53] UCC §9-513.

effective under Delaware law, it is not necessary for the secured lender to intend its effects. JPMorgan then argued that it only authorized termination of security for the Synthetic Loan, not the Term Loan. The Second Circuit revisited the case to address the second question.

Issue: ***Did JPMorgan authorize the filing of the termination statement that mistakenly listed the Term Loan?***

Excerpts from the Per Curiam Decision: In JPMorgan's view, it never instructed anyone to file the UCC-3 in question, and the termination statement was therefore ineffective. What JPMorgan intended to accomplish, however, is a distinct question from what actions it authorized to be taken on its behalf.

The draft termination statements were sent for review to JPMorgan and to JPMorgan's counsel. Neither directly nor through its counsel did JPMorgan express any concerns about the draft UCC-3 termination statements. A Simpson Thacher attorney responded simply as follows: "Nice job on the documents."

After preparing the closing documents and circulating them for review, Mayer Brown drafted an Escrow Agreement that specified that the parties would deliver to the escrow agent the set of three termination statements (identified by number). When Mayer Brown emailed a draft to JPMorgan's counsel for review, the same Simpson Thacher attorney responded that "it was fine" and signed the agreement.

From these facts it is clear that although JPMorgan never intended to terminate the Term Loan, it authorized the filing of a termination statement that had that effect. Actual authority is created by a principal's manifestation to an agent that, as reasonably understood by the agent, expresses the principal's assent that the agent take action on the principal's behalf.

JPMorgan and Simpson Thacher's repeated manifestations to Mayer Brown show that JPMorgan and its counsel knew that, upon the closing of the Synthetic Lease transaction, Mayer Brown was going to file the termination statement that identified the Term Loan for termination and that JPMorgan reviewed and assented to the filing of that statement. Nothing more is needed.

Although everyone agreed that including the Term Loan on the UCC-3 was a mistake, it could not be undone. UCC filings are the backbone of the law of secured transactions—and much depends on their integrity. To protect the reliability of the system, the law will not excuse parties from the consequences of their mistaken filings, no matter how severe.

CHAPTER CONCLUSION

Secured transactions are essential to modern commerce. Billions of dollars' worth of goods are sold on credit annually, and creditors normally demand an assurance of payment. A secured party that understands Article 9 and follows its provisions to the letter should be well protected. A company that operates in ignorance of Article 9 invites disaster because others may obtain superior rights in the goods, leaving the "secured" party with no money, no security—and no sympathy from the courts.

EXAM REVIEW

1. **ARTICLE 9** Article 9 applies to any transaction intended to create a security interest in personal property or fixtures.

2. **ATTACHMENT** Attachment means that (1) the two parties made a security agreement *and* either the debtor has *authenticated a security agreement* describing the collateral *or* the secured party has obtained *possession* or *control;* (2) the secured party gave value in order to get the security agreement; and (3) the debtor has rights in the collateral.

3. **AFTER-ACQUIRED PROPERTY** A security interest may attach to after-acquired property.

4. **PERFECTION** Attachment protects against the debtor. Perfection of a security interest protects the secured party against parties other than the debtor.

5. **FILING** Filing is the most common way to perfect. For many forms of collateral, the secured party may also perfect by obtaining either possession or control.

6. **PMSI** A purchase money security interest (PMSI) is one taken by the person who sells the collateral or advances money so the debtor can buy the collateral.

7. **PMSI PERFECTION** A PMSI in consumer goods perfects automatically, without filing.

EXAMStrategy

Question: John and Clara Lockovich bought a 22-foot Chaparrel Villian II boat from Greene County Yacht Club for $32,500. They paid $6,000 cash and borrowed the rest of the purchase price from Gallatin National Bank, which took a security interest in the boat. Gallatin filed a financing statement in Greene County, Pennsylvania, where the bank was located. But Pennsylvania law requires financing statements to be filed in the county of the debtor's residence, and the Lockoviches lived in Allegheny County. The Lockoviches soon washed up in bankruptcy court. Other creditors demanded that the boat be sold, claiming that Gallatin's security interest had been filed in the wrong place. Who wins?

Strategy: Gallatin National Bank obtained a special kind of security interest in the boat. Identify that type of interest. What special rights does this give to the bank? (See the "Result" at the end of this Exam Review section.)

8. **BIOC** A buyer in ordinary course of business (BIOC) takes the goods free of a security interest created by his seller even though the security interest is perfected.

9. **CHATTEL PAPER** A buyer who purchases chattel paper or an instrument in good faith in the ordinary course of his business and then obtains possession or control generally takes free of any security interest.

10. **PRIORITY** Priority among secured parties is generally as follows:
    (1) A party with a perfected security interest takes priority over a party with an unperfected interest.
    (2) If neither secured party has perfected, the first interest to attach gets priority.
    (3) Between perfected security interests, the first to file or perfect wins.

EXAMStrategy

Question: Barwell, Inc., sold McMann Golf Ball Co. a "preformer," a machine that makes golf balls, for $55,000. Barwell delivered the machine on February 20. McMann paid $3,000 down, the remainder to be paid over several years, and signed an agreement giving Barwell a security interest in the preformer. Barwell did not perfect its interest. On March 1, McMann borrowed $350,000 from First of America Bank, giving the bank a security interest in McMann's present and after-acquired property. First of America perfected by filing on March 2. McMann, of course, became insolvent, and both Barwell and the bank attempted to repossess the preformer. Who gets it?

Strategy: Two parties have a valid security interest in this machine. When that happens, there is a three-step process to determine which party gets priority. Apply it. (See the "Result" at the end of this Exam Review section.)

11. **PMSI AND PRIORITY** A PMSI may take priority over a conflicting perfected security interest (even one perfected earlier) if the holder of the PMSI meets certain conditions.

12. **CONTROL OR POSSESSION** For deposit accounts, investment property, letter-of-credit rights, and instruments, a secured party who obtains control or possession takes priority over one who merely filed.

13. **DEFAULT** When the debtor defaults, the secured party may take possession of the collateral on its own, without a court order, if it can do so without a breach of the peace.

14. **DISPOSAL OF COLLATERAL** A secured party may sell, lease, or otherwise dispose of the collateral in any commercially reasonable way; in many cases, it may accept the collateral in full or partial satisfaction of the debt. The secured party may also ignore the collateral and sue the debtor for the full debt.

EXAMStrategy

Question: Jerry Payne owed the First State Bank of Pflugerville $342,000. The loan was secured by a 9.25-carat diamond ring. The bank claimed a default on the loan and, without notifying Payne, sold the ring. But the proceeds did not pay off the full debt, and the bank sued Payne for the deficiency. Is Payne liable for the deficiency?

Strategy: A secured party may dispose of the collateral in any commercially reasonable way. What must the secured party do to ensure commercial reasonableness? (See the "Result" at the end of this Exam Review section.)

15. **TERMINATION** When the debtor pays the full debt, the secured party must complete a termination statement, notifying the public that it no longer claims a security interest in the collateral.

RESULTS

7. Result: Gallatin advanced the money that the Lockoviches used to buy the boat, meaning the bank obtained a PMSI. A PMSI in consumer goods perfects automatically, without filing. The boat was a consumer good. Gallatin's security interest perfected without any filing at all, and so the bank wins.

10. Result: This question is resolved by the first of those three steps. A party with a perfected security interest takes priority over a party with an unperfected interest. The bank wins because its perfected security interest takes priority over Barwell's unperfected interest.

14. Result: The secured party must give the debtor notice of the time and place of the sale. This ensures that the debtor may bid on the collateral, preventing an unreasonably low sales price. The bank failed to give such notice, and so it lost its right to the deficiency.

MULTIPLE-CHOICE QUESTIONS

1. **CPA QUESTION** Under the UCC Article 9, which of the following actions will best perfect a security interest in a negotiable instrument against any other party?
   (a) Filing a security agreement
   (b) Taking possession of the instrument
   (c) Perfecting by attachment
   (d) Obtaining a duly executed financing statement
2. Jim's birth certificate lists him as "James Brown Smith"; his driver's license identifies him as "Jim Smith"; his business card reads "J.B. Smith"; and his friends call him Jimbo. How should the financing statement list this debtor's name?
   (a) James Smith
   (b) J.B. Smith
   (c) Jim Smith
   (d) James Brown Smith
3. **CPA QUESTION** Under the UCC Article 9, perfection of a security interest by a creditor provides added protection against other parties in the event the debtor does not pay its debts. Which of the following parties is not affected by perfection of a security interest?
   (a) Other prospective creditors of the debtor
   (b) The trustee in a bankruptcy case
   (c) A buyer in ordinary course of business
   (d) A subsequent personal injury judgment creditor
4. **CPA QUESTION** Mars, Inc., manufactures and sells VCRs on credit directly to wholesalers, retailers, and consumers. Mars can perfect its security interest in the VCRs it sells without having to file a financing statement or take possession of the VCRs if the sale is made to which of the following?
   (a) Retailers
   (b) Wholesalers that sell to distributors for resale
   (c) Consumers
   (d) Wholesalers that sell to buyers in ordinary course of business

5. Alpha perfects its security interest by properly filing a financing statement on January 1, 2016. Alpha files a continuation statement on September 1, 2020. It files another continuation statement on September 1, 2024. When will Alpha's financing statement expire?
   (a) January 1, 2021
   (b) September 1, 2025
   (c) September 1, 2029
   (d) Never

CASE QUESTIONS

1. Eugene Ables ran an excavation company. He borrowed $500,000 from the Highland Park State Bank. Ables signed a note promising to repay the money and an agreement giving Highland a security interest in all of his equipment, including after-acquired equipment. Several years later, Ables agreed with Patricia Myers to purchase a Bantam Backhoe from her for $16,000, which he would repay at the rate of $100 per month, while he used the machine. Ables later defaulted on his note to Highland, and the bank attempted to take the backhoe. Myers and Ables contended that the bank had no right to take the backhoe. Was the backhoe covered by Highland's security interest? Did Ables have sufficient rights in the backhoe for the bank's security interest to attach?

2. A boat manufacturer incorporated under the name "Glasco, Inc.," but operated its business solely under the name "Elite Boats, Division of Glasco, Inc." When Citizens Bank agreed to finance Glasco's marine engines, it filed a UCC-1 financing statement listing the debtor as "Elite Boats, Division of Glasco, Inc." Glasco later filed for bankruptcy. Since the financing statement only listed Glasco's trade name, it did not come up on the bankruptcy trustee's search. The trustee sold the engines to a third party. The bank sued the trustee for the proceeds of the sale, arguing the financing statement was adequate. What result?

3. Sears sold a lawn tractor to Cosmo Fiscante for $1,481. Fiscante paid with his personal credit card. Sears kept a valid security interest in the lawnmower but did not perfect. Fiscante had the machine delivered to his business, Trackers Raceway Park, the only place he ever used the machine. When Fiscante was unable to meet his obligations, various creditors attempted to seize the lawnmower. Sears argued that because it had a purchase money security interest (PMSI) in the lawnmower, its interest had perfected automatically. Is Sears correct?

4. The state of Kentucky filed a tax lien against Panbowl Energy, claiming unpaid taxes. Six months later, Panbowl bought a powerful drill from Whayne Supply, making a down payment of $11,500 and signing a security agreement for the remaining debt of $220,000. Whayne perfected the next day. Panbowl defaulted. Whayne sold the drill for $58,000, leaving a deficiency of just over $100,000. The state filed suit, seeking the $58,000 proceeds. The trial court gave summary judgment to the state, and Whayne appealed. Who gets the $58,000?

5. Cooke borrowed money from Haddon and gave as collateral four cases of champagne and a promissory note. When Cooke failed to pay the debt, Haddon obtained a judgment for the outstanding balance. Cooke promptly paid and demanded return of the collateral. But Haddon had consumed part of the champagne. Cooke sued Haddon for the value of the champagne. Who wins and why?

DISCUSSION QUESTIONS

1. Collateral may change categories depending on its holder and how it is being used at the time of default. Classify a refrigerator in the following circumstances:
   (a) When sold by an appliance store
   (b) When used by a restaurateur in his business
   (c) When installed in a homeowner's kitchen

2. **ETHICS** The Dannemans bought a Kodak copier worth over $40,000. Kodak arranged financing by GECC and assigned its rights to that company. Although the Dannemans thought they had purchased the copier on credit, the papers described the deal as a lease. The Dannemans had constant problems with the machine and stopped making payments. GECC repossessed the machine and, without notifying the Dannemans, sold it back to Kodak for $12,500, leaving a deficiency of $39,927. GECC sued the Dannemans for that amount. The Dannemans argued that the deal was not a lease, but a sale on credit. Why does it matter whether the parties had a sale or a lease? Is GECC entitled to its money? Finally, comment on the ethics. Why did the Dannemans not understand the papers they had signed? Who is responsible for that? Are you satisfied with the ethical conduct of the Dannemans? Kodak? GECC?

3. After a federal judge refused to dismiss criminal charges against him, Michael Reed took revenge by electronically filing a UCC financing statement listing the judge as the debtor on a $3.4 million loan. Reed himself was listed as the secured party. The lien became part of the public record. Reed was prosecuted for violating a statute prohibiting harassment of public officials. Reed argued that he was innocent because the financing statement did not list collateral—and would never have succeeded in perfecting a claim. Is this a good argument?

4. After reading this chapter, will your behavior as a consumer change? Are there any types of transactions that you might be more inclined to avoid?

5. After reading this chapter, will your future behavior as a businessperson change? What specific steps will you be most careful to take to protect your interests?

CHAPTER 25

CREATING A NEGOTIABLE INSTRUMENT

The figure lay on the couch by the fireplace. No signs of violence were visible, and a casual observer would have thought the man was napping. But Detective Waterston's trained eye immediately recognized the unnatural stiffness and pallor of a corpse. Walking behind the body, she saw matted blood against black hair and a heavy brass fireplace iron on the floor. She also noticed the crumpled document clutched in the victim's hand.

As the coroner was removing the body, Waterston slipped the crumpled paper out of the corpse's grasp. Sergeant Malloy asked whether she was ready to interview witnesses. "No," she said thoughtfully, looking at the document, "I believe I have everything I need right here." An hour later, the police arrested Tony Jenkins, the dead man's business partner. Jenkins immediately confessed.

"How did you know?" Malloy demanded.

"Simple," Waterston responded, "The answer is right here on this promissory note." She spread the crumpled page on the table. "On the front, it's a straightforward note for $1 million, payable by Tony Jenkins, the accused, to Letitia Lamour on August 1. You remember—she was recently arrested for selling fraudulent securities. Jenkins must have invested in one of her enterprises.

In his rage and frustration, Jenkins picked up the first thing that came to hand and struck Haverstock with the brass iron.

"It gets even more interesting on the back, though," she said, turning the paper over. "Lamour held on to the note for some time. But you see, on August 15th, she wrote on the back 'Pay to the order of Sebastian Haverstock.'"

"The dead man," Malloy whistled through his teeth.

"Precisely. Haverstock and Jenkins were planning to take their internet company public in a month or two. The sale would have made them both wealthy men.

But Haverstock called Jenkins to demand payment on the note. Jenkins did not have a million dollars; he had lost everything in a series of unfortunate investments. Haverstock demanded that Jenkins turn over his shares in the company as payment for the note. In his rage and frustration, Jenkins picked up the first thing that came to hand and struck Haverstock with the brass iron. An antique instrument and very heavy.

"It's a shame, really," Detective Waterston continued. "If Jenkins had understood Article 3 of the Uniform Commercial Code, he would not have been tempted to murder. In fact, he owed Haverstock nothing. You see, the note was overdue—it should have been paid on August 1st, but today is the 31st. You can't be a holder in due course on an overdue note. Since Haverstock was not a holder in due course, Jenkins could have used the fraud claim he had against Lamour as a defense to Haverstock's demand for payment. In any event, Haverstock was well aware that Lamour had committed fraud—he was the one who set her up in business in the first place. Jenkins could have used Haverstock's knowledge of the fraud as another weapon against any demands for payment. That legal weapon would have been a better choice than a fireplace iron," Waterston concluded wryly.

25-1 NEGOTIABLE INSTRUMENTS

This chapter is about negotiable instruments, which are a type of commercial paper.

25-1a Commercial Paper

Commercial paper plays an important role in your life if you write checks or borrow money. Historically speaking, however, commercial paper is a relatively new development. In early human history, people lived on whatever they could hunt, grow, or make for themselves. Imagine what your life would be like if you had to subsist only on what you could make yourself. Over time, people improved their standard of living by bartering for goods and services that other people could provide more efficiently. But traders needed a method for keeping account of who owed how much to whom. That was the role of currency. Many items have been used for currency over the years, including silver, gold, copper, and cowrie shells. Even cigarettes were used briefly in Greece at the end of World War II after Hitler's troops left. These currencies have two disadvantages—they are easy to steal and difficult to carry.

Sweden had traditionally used copper as currency. These ingots were very large and heavy (heavier even than gold), so it was not surprising when, in 1661, Sweden became the first country in Europe to issue paper currency. But paper bills created new problems—they were even easier to steal than hard currency like gold. As a result, money had to be kept in a safe place, and banks developed to meet that need. However, money in a vault is not very useful unless it can be readily spent. Society needed a system for transferring paper funds easily. Commercial paper is that system. When successful, it acts as a substitute for currency.

Commercial paper is a contract to pay money. It is used as:

- **A Substitute for Money.** When Krystal stops at Drive-In-Convenience to buy food for dinner, she has only 32¢ in her wallet. Not a problem, she can pay by check. Krystal's check is a promise that she has money in the bank. It is also an order to the bank to transfer funds to Drive-In-Convenience. Krystal is going to eat immediately (in the car on the way home), and the store would also like to be paid quickly. For commercial paper to be a substitute for money, it must be payable on demand.
- **A Loan of Money.** This type of commercial paper is a contract to pay what is owed sometime in the future. Krystal cannot afford the tuition at Fabulous University, so she borrows money from the federal government. To obtain the loan, she must sign a **promissory note** stating that she will repay the money after she leaves college.

Promissory note
A written promise to pay money

This chapter and the following one focus on Article 3 of the UCC, which regulates commercial paper. When the United States Treasury issues currency, it is consistent—all dollar bills look alike. But when practically every person in the United States issues commercial paper, creativity takes over and consistency disappears. The purpose of Article 3 is to transform these pieces of paper into something almost as easily transferable and reliable as currency.

CHECKLIST
- ☐ Negotiable
- ☐ Negotiated
- ☐ Holder in Due Course
- ☐ No Valid Defenses

The fundamental "rule" of commercial paper can be stated this way:

The possessor of a piece of commercial paper has an unconditional right to be paid, so long as (1) the paper is *negotiable*, (2) it has been *negotiated* to the possessor, (3) the possessor is a *holder in due course*, and (4) the issuer cannot claim any of a limited number of "*real*" *defenses*.

This rule is the backbone of the chapter, so you will want to keep it in mind as you read on.

25-1b Types of Negotiable Instruments

There are two kinds of commercial paper: negotiable and non-negotiable instruments. Note that *negotiable* instruments are more valuable than *non*-negotiable ones because the worth of a *non*-negotiable instrument depends on the validity of the original contract that created it. A negotiable instrument is valid on its face, without reference to the original contract.

Maker
The issuer of a promissory note

Payee
Someone who is owed money under the terms of an instrument

Payable on demand
The maker must pay whenever he is asked.

Article 3 of the Code covers only negotiable instruments; non-negotiable instruments are governed by ordinary contract law. There are also two categories of negotiable instruments: notes and drafts. The essential difference between the two is that a note is a *promise* to do something while a draft is an *order* to someone else to do it. That is an overview; now for the details.

A note (also called a promissory note) is your promise that you will pay money. A promissory note is used in virtually every loan transaction, whether the borrower is paying for a multimillion dollar company, a television, or college tuition. For example, when Krystal borrows money from the government to pay tuition, she signs a note stating, "I promise to pay to the Department of Education all loan amounts disbursed under the terms of this Promissory Note, plus interest and other charges and fees that may become due as provided in this Promissory Note." She is the **maker** because she is the one who has made the promise. The Department of Education is called the **payee** because it expects to be paid. Remember that only *two* parties are involved in a note: the maker and the payee. Some notes are due on a date in the future. Others are **payable on demand**, which means that the maker must pay whenever he is asked. Krystal does not have to repay her student loan until she leaves college.

Danny E Hooks/Shutterstock.com

To obtain a student loan, this college student had to sign a promissory note.

Certificate of deposit
A note that is made by a bank (also known as a CD)

If the note is made by a bank, it is called a **certificate of deposit** (also known as a CD). When investors loan money to a bank, the bank gives them a note promising to repay the loan at a specific date in the future. The bank is the maker and the investor is the payee. The bank pays a higher rate of interest on CDs than it does on regular savings accounts because the investor cannot demand payment on the CD until its due date. In return for the lower rate on a savings account, the depositor can withdraw that money anytime.

Draft
The drawer of this instrument orders someone else to pay money.

Check
The most common form of a draft, it is an order telling a bank to pay money.

Drawer
The person who issues a draft

Drawee
The one ordered by the drawer to pay money to the payee

Issuer
The maker of a promissory note or the drawer of a draft

A **draft** is an order directing someone else to pay money for you. A **check** is the most common form of a draft—it is an order telling a bank to pay money. In a draft, three people are involved: the **drawer** orders the **drawee** to pay money to the payee. Now before you slam the book shut in despair, let us sort out the players. Suppose that Madison Keys wins a tennis tournament. The Women's Tennis Association (WTA) Tour writes her a check for $1 million. This check is an order by the WTA Tour (the drawer) to its bank (the drawee) to pay money to Keys (the payee). The terms make sense if you remember that, when you take money out of your account, you *draw* it out. Therefore, when you write a check, you are the drawer and the bank is the drawee. The person to whom you make out the check is being paid, so he is called the payee.

The following table illustrates the difference between notes and drafts. Even courts sometimes confuse the terms *drawer* (the person who signs a check) and *maker* (someone who signs a promissory note). But the UCC is a very precise set of rules, so it is important to get the details right. **Issuer** is an all-purpose term that means both maker and drawer.

	Who Pays	Who Plays
Note	You make a promise that you will pay.	Two people are involved: maker and payee.
Draft	You order someone else to pay.	Three people are involved: drawer, drawee, and payee.

Cashier's check
A check that is drawn by a bank on itself

Keys presumably feels confident that the WTA Tour has enough money in its account to cover the check. When Stewart goes to the MegaLoud store to buy a $10,000 sound system, MegaLoud has no way of knowing if his check is good. Even if MegaLoud calls the bank to confirm Stewart's balance, he could withdraw it all by the time MegaLoud deposits the check that evening. To protect itself, MegaLoud insists upon a cashier's check. A **cashier's check** is drawn by a bank on itself. When Stewart asks for a cashier's check, the bank takes the money out of his account on the spot and then issues a check itself, payable out of its own funds. When MegaLoud gets the cashier's check from Stewart, it knows that the check is good as long as the bank itself is solvent.

Accept
To sign a draft

All checks are drafts, but not all drafts are checks. A draft is a check only if it is drawn on a bank. Sometimes drafts are drawn on individuals or companies. Suppose that, in September, Sasha's Saddlery sells 16 saddles to the Circle S Stable. The stable expects that, in December, it will receive its first deposits from tourists making reservations for the following summer. The stable promises to pay Sasha $8,000 in January. Sasha is happy to make the sale, but she needs the funds now. So she prepares a draft ordering Circle S to pay $8,000 to Citizen's Bank in January. After Circle S signs (**accepts**) the draft, Sasha takes it to Citizen's, which investigates Circle S's credit reputation. Satisfied, Citizen's agrees to buy the draft for $7,000. (It pays less than the full amount because it has to wait for the money and because there is always a chance Circle S will not pay.) Sasha is the drawer, Circle S the drawee, and Citizen's Bank the payee. So Sasha's Saddlery receives $7,000 from Citizen's in September. In January, Circle S pays Citizen's the full $8,000.

Trade acceptance
A draft drawn by a seller of goods on the buyer and payable to the seller or some third party

The draft on Circle S is a **trade acceptance**, which is a draft drawn by a seller of goods on the buyer and payable to the seller or some third party. In our case, Sasha is the seller, Circle S the buyer, and Citizen's the third party that will be paid. To be valid, the draft must be accepted (i.e., signed) by the buyer. A **sight draft** is payable on demand; a **time draft** is payable in the future. Circle S's draft is a time draft because it is not payable until January.

Sight draft
Payable on demand

Time draft
Payable in the future

25-1c Negotiability

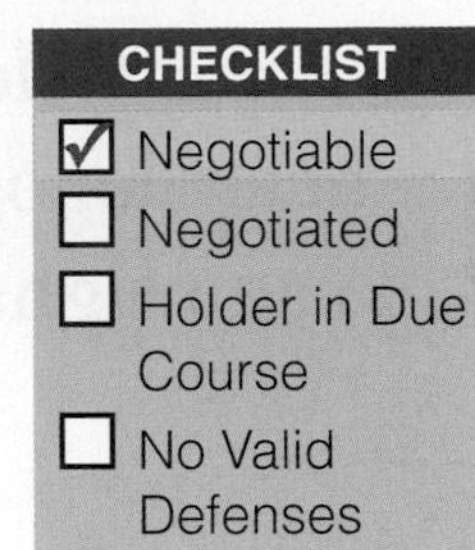

To work as a substitute for currency, commercial paper must be freely transferable in the marketplace. In other words, it must be *negotiable*. Suppose that Krystal buys a used car from the Trustie Car Lot so that she can drive to school. She cannot afford to pay the full $15,000 right now, but she is willing to sign a note promising to pay later. As long as Trustie keeps the note, Krystal's obligation to pay is contingent upon the validity of the underlying contract. If, for instance, the car is defective, then Krystal might not be liable to Trustie for the full amount of the note. Trustie, however, does not want to keep the note. He needs the cash *now* so that he can buy more cars to sell to other customers. Reggie's Finance Co. is happy to buy Krystal's promissory note from Trustie, but the price Reggie is willing to pay depends upon whether her note is negotiable.

The possessor of *non*-negotiable commercial paper has the same rights—no more, no less—as the person who made the original contract. With non-negotiable commercial paper, the transferee's rights are *conditional* because they depend upon the rights of the original party to the contract. If, for some reason, the original party loses his right to be paid, so does the transferee. The value of non-negotiable commercial paper is greatly reduced because the transferee cannot be absolutely sure what his rights are or whether he will be paid at all.

If Krystal's promissory note is non-negotiable, Reggie gets exactly the same rights that Trustie had. As the saying goes, he steps into Trustie's shoes. Other people's shoes may not be a good fit. Suppose that Trustie tampered with the odometer and, as a result, Krystal's car is worth only $12,000 instead of the $15,000 she paid for it. If, under contract law, she owes Trustie only $12,000, then that is all she has to pay Reggie, even though the note *says* $15,000.

The possessor of *negotiable* commercial paper has *more* rights than the person who made the original contract. With negotiable commercial paper, the transferee's rights are *unconditional* and generally do not depend upon the rights of the original party to the contract. If Krystal's promissory note is a negotiable instrument, she must pay the full amount to whoever has possession of it, no matter what complaints she might have against Trustie. Even if the car explodes within the month, Krystal must still pay Reggie the full $15,000.

Exhibit 25.1 illustrates the difference between negotiable and non-negotiable commercial paper.

EXHIBIT 25.1

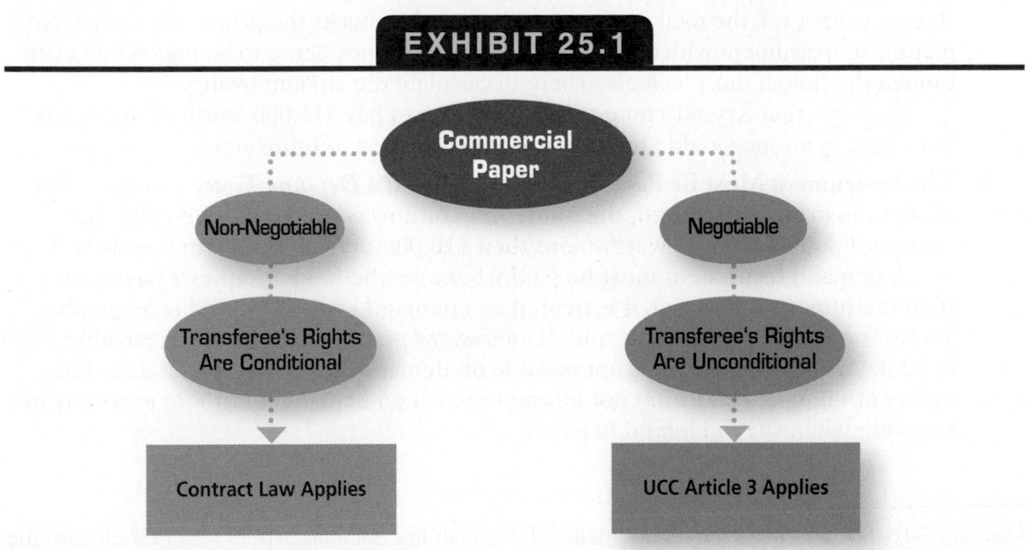

Requirements for Negotiability

Because negotiable instruments are more valuable than non-negotiable ones, it is important for buyers and sellers to be able to tell, easily and accurately, if an instrument is indeed negotiable. **An instrument is negotiable if it meets the following six standards**[1]: .

An interlocking heart logo counts as a signature.

1. **The Instrument Must Be in *Writing*.** Trustie cannot negotiate Krystal's *oral* promise to pay $15,000. However, the writing need not be on any official form or even on paper. To protest a speeding ticket, Barry Lee Brown of Missoula, Montana, wrote a check for the $35 fine on a pair of old (but clean!) underpants. The bank was able to cash it.
2. **The Instrument Must Be *Signed* by the Maker or Drawer.** Any signature counts—initials, an "X," a stamp—as long as the issuer intends to indicate her signature. If Krystal normally signs her documents with an interlocking heart logo, that symbol counts as a signature.
3. **The Instrument Must Contain an *Unconditional Promise* or *Order* to Pay.** The whole point of a negotiable instrument is that the holder can sleep soundly at night confident that he will be paid *without conditions.* If Krystal's promissory note says, "I will pay $15,000 as long as the car is still in working order," it is not negotiable. If, however, the note says, "I will pay $15,000 for the yellow car," it is negotiable because this statement is not a *condition*; it is simply describing the transaction.

   The instrument must also contain a promise or order to pay. It is not enough simply to say, "Krystal owes Trustie $15,000." She has to indicate that she owes the money and also that she intends to pay it. "Krystal promises to pay Trustie $15,000" would work.
4. **The Instrument Must State a *Definite Amount* of Money.** It is not easy to sell an instrument if the buyer cannot tell how much it is worth; to be negotiable, therefore, the document must clearly state "within its four corners" how much money is owed. For example, a note is not negotiable if it says, "Payment as required by Section 3 of the Agreement," because you would have to look at some other document to determine how much is owed.

   There is one modest exception to this rule. If the document is a note, with interest due, the holder may not be able to tell how much interest is owing simply by looking at the note. Suppose a note says, "with interest at 1 percent above prime rate." Reggie cannot tell the total amount owed unless he checks the prime rate online. No matter, an instrument with a variable interest rate is considered to be negotiable even though the holder must look elsewhere to calculate the amount owing.

   Suppose that Krystal's note says, "I promise to pay $15,000 worth of diamonds." This note is not negotiable because it does not state a definite amount of *money.*
5. **The Instrument Must Be Payable on *Demand* or at a *Definite Time*.** To determine what an instrument is worth, the holder must know when he will be paid. Ten thousand dollars today is worth more than $10,000 the day the earth stands still

   A demand instrument must be paid whenever the holder requests payment. If an instrument is undated, it is treated as a demand instrument and is negotiable. There is one exception to this rule. If an *undated* promissory note says, "payable in 90 days," the instrument is not payable on demand and is non-negotiable. The maker of the note clearly did not intend to pay it on demand, but there is no way of knowing when she did intend to pay it.

[1]Section 3-104(a) sets out all the requirements of negotiability. Sections 3-105 to 3-119 then describe the requirements in more detail.

An instrument can be negotiable even if it will not be paid until sometime in the future, provided that the payment date can be determined *when the document is made*. A prep school graduate wrote a generous check to his alma mater, but for payment date he put, "The day the headmaster is fired." This check is not negotiable because it is neither payable on demand nor at a definite time. When the check was written, no one knew when (or whether) the headmaster would be fired. If the headmaster is finally fired, the check does not suddenly become negotiable.

Suppose that Krystal simply signs her note without specifying the due date. Reggie can demand payment anytime. By contrast, if the due date on the note is Easter Sunday 2021, Reggie may have to check his calendar to figure out when that is (since the date of Easter changes every year), but the note is nonetheless negotiable. If, however, the due date on the note is "three months after Krystal receives her MBA degree," the note is non-negotiable because the date of Krystal's graduation is uncertain.

6. **The Instrument Must Be Payable to *Order* or to *Bearer*.** To be negotiable, an instrument must be either order paper or bearer paper. **Order paper** must include the words "Pay to the order of" Trustie (or an equivalent, such as "Pay to Trustie, or order"). "Pay to the order of Trustie" means that the money will be paid to Trustie *or to anyone Trustie designates*. By including the word *order*, the maker is indicating that the instrument is not limited to only one person. If the note simply says "Pay to Trustie," it is not negotiable.

Order paper
An instrument that includes the words "pay to the order of" or their equivalent

An instrument is **bearer paper** if it is made out to "bearer" or it is not made out to any specific person. It can be redeemed by any holder in due course (a term we will define shortly). The good news is that bearer paper is easily and freely transferable, but the bad news is that it may be too easily redeemed. Suppose that Krystal's note is payable to bearer, and Reggie mails it to his sweetheart Sue as a birthday present. If dastardly Dan steals the note from Sue's mailbox and sells it to unknowing Neal, Krystal will have to pay Neal when he presents the note.

Bearer paper
An instrument is bearer paper if it is made out to "bearer" or it is not made out to any specific person. It can be redeemed by any holder in due course.

If Krystal's note says, "Pay to the order of cash," or "Pay to the order of Happy Birthday," it is bearer paper. If Krystal signs a note but leaves blank the space after "Pay to the order of," that note is also bearer paper.

The rules for checks are different from other negotiable instruments. **If filled out properly, checks are negotiable. And sometimes they are negotiable even if not filled out correctly.** Most checks are pre-printed with the words, "Pay to the order of," but sometimes people inadvertently cross out "order of." Even so, the check is still negotiable. Checks are frequently received by consumers who, sadly, have not completed a course on business law. The drafters of the UCC did not think it fair to penalize them when the drawer of the check was the one who made the mistake. If a check is made out to "Reggie *and* Sue," both payees must sign it before it can be transferred. If the check is made out to "Reggie *or* Sue," the signature of either is sufficient.

EXAMStrategy

Question: Sam had a checking account at Piggy Bank. Piggy sent him special checks that he could use to draw down a line of credit. When he used these checks, Piggy did not take money out of his account; instead, it treated the checks as loans and charged him interest. The interest rate was not apparent from the face of the check. When Sam wrote checks, Piggy sold them to Wolfe. Were the checks negotiable instruments?

Strategy: When faced with a question about negotiability, begin by looking at the list of six requirements. In this case, there is no reason to doubt that the checks are in writing, signed by the issuer, with an unconditional promise to pay to order at a definite time.

But do the checks state a definite amount of money? Can the holder "look at the four corners of the check" and determine how much Sam owes?

Result: Sam was required to pay Piggy the face amount of the check *plus* interest. Wolfe does not know the amount of the interest unless he reads the loan agreement. Therefore, the checks are not negotiable.

Interpretation of Ambiguities

Perhaps you have noticed that people sometimes make mistakes. Although the UCC establishes simple and precise rules for creating negotiable instruments, people do not always follow these rules to the letter. It might be tempting simply to invalidate defective documents (after all, money is at stake here). But, instead, the UCC favors negotiability and has rules to resolve uncertainty and supply missing terms.

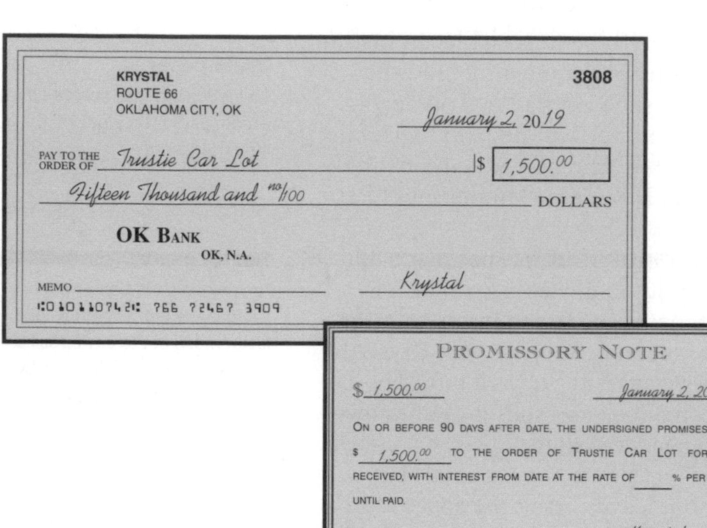

KRYSTAL
ROUTE 66
OKLAHOMA CITY, OK
3808
January 2, 2019
PAY TO THE ORDER OF Trustie Car Lot $ 1,500.00
Fifteen Thousand and no/100 DOLLARS
OK BANK
OK, N.A.
MEMO
Krystal
⑆0101107424⑆ 766 72467 3909

PROMISSORY NOTE
$ 1,500.00 January 2, 2019
ON OR BEFORE 90 DAYS AFTER DATE, THE UNDERSIGNED PROMISES TO PAY $ 1,500.00 TO THE ORDER OF TRUSTIE CAR LOT FOR VALUE RECEIVED, WITH INTEREST FROM DATE AT THE RATE OF ___ % PER ANNUM, UNTIL PAID.
Krystal

Notice anything odd about the check pictured here? Is it for $1,500 or $15,000? **When the terms in a negotiable instrument contradict each other, three rules apply:**

- Words beat numbers.
- Handwritten terms prevail over typed and printed terms.
- Typed terms win over printed terms.

According to these rules, Krystal's check is for $15,000 because, in a conflict between words and numbers, words win.

What is wrong with the promissory note here? The interest rate is left blank. When this happens, the UCC directs that the judgment rate applies. The **judgment rate** is simply the rate that courts use on court-ordered judgments.

Judgment rate
The interest rate that courts use on court-ordered judgments

In the following case, the amount of the check was not completely clear. Was it a negotiable instrument?

You Be the Judge

Blasco v. Money Services Center

352 B.R. 888
United States Bankruptcy Court for the Northern District of Alabama, 2006

Facts: Christina Blasco borrowed $500 from the Money Services Center (MSC). To repay the loan, she gave MSC a check for $587.50, which it promised not to cash for two weeks. This kind of transaction is called a "payday loan" because it is made to someone who needs money to tide him over until the next paycheck. (Note that in this case, Blasco was paying 17.5 percent interest for a two-week loan, which is an annual compounded interest rate of 6,500 percent. This is the dark side of payday loans—interest rates are often exorbitant.)

Before MSC could cash the check, Blasco filed for bankruptcy protection. Although MSC knew about Blasco's filing, it deposited the check. It is illegal for creditors to collect debts after a bankruptcy filing, except that creditors *are* entitled to payment on negotiable instruments.[2]

Ordinarily, checks are negotiable instruments, but only if they are for a definite amount. This check had a wrinkle: The numerical amount of the check was $587.50 but the amount in words was written as "five eighty-seven and 50/100 dollars." Did the words mean "five *hundred* eighty-seven" or "five *thousand* eighty-seven" or perhaps "five *million* eighty-seven"? Was the check negotiable despite this ambiguity?

You Be the Judge: *Was this check for a definite amount? Was it a negotiable instrument?*

Argument for Blasco: For a check to be negotiable, two rules apply:

1. The check must state a definite amount of money, which is clear within its four corners.
2. If there is a contradiction between the words and numbers, words take precedence over numbers.

Words prevail over numbers, which means that the check is for "five eighty-seven and 50/100 dollars." This amount is not definite. A holder cannot be sure of the precise amount of the check simply by looking within its four corners. Therefore, the check is not a negotiable instrument and MSC had no right to submit it for payment.

Argument for MSC: Blasco is right about the two rules. However, she is wrong in their interpretation. If there is a *contradiction* between the words and numbers, words take precedence over numbers. In this case, there was no contradiction. The words were ambiguous but they did not contradict the numbers. If the words had said "five *thousand* eighty-seven," that would have been a contradiction. Instead, the numbers simply clarified the words. Even someone who was a stranger to this transaction could figure out the amount of the check. Therefore, it is negotiable.

25-1d Negotiation

CHECKLIST

- ☐ Negotiable
- ☑ Negotiated
- ☐ Holder in Due Course
- ☐ No Valid Defenses

Remember the fundamental rule that underlies this chapter: **The possessor of a piece of commercial paper has an unconditional right to be paid, as long as (1) the paper is negotiable, (2) it has been negotiated to the possessor, (3) the possessor is a holder in due course, and (4) the issuer cannot claim any of a limited number of *real* defenses.**

***Negotiated* means that an instrument has been transferred to the holder by someone *other than the issuer*.** If the issuer has transferred the instrument to the holder, then it has not been negotiated and the issuer can refuse to pay the holder if there was some flaw in the underlying contract. Thus, if Jake gives Emerson a promissory note for $800 in payment for a new tablet computer, but the tablet crashes and burns the first week, Jake has the right to refuse to pay the note. Jake was the issuer, and the note was not negotiated. But if, before the tablet self-destructs, Emerson transfers the note to Kayla, then Jake is liable to Kayla for the full amount of the note, regardless of his claims against Emerson.

Negotiated
An instrument has been transferred to the holder by someone other than the issuer.

To be negotiable, an instrument must be order paper (payable to the order of someone) or bearer paper (payable to anyone in possession). (Note that a check made out to "cash" is bearer paper.) These two types of instruments have different rules for negotiation: **To be negotiated, order paper must first be *indorsed and then delivered* to the transferee. Bearer paper must simply be *delivered* to the transferee; no indorsement is required.**[3]

In its simplest form, an **indorsement** is the signature of the payee. Tess writes a rent check for $600 to her landlord, Larnell. He would like to use this money to pay Patty for painting the building. If Larnell signs the back of the check and delivers it to Patty, he has

Indorsement
The signature of a payee

[2] Under §3-305 of the UCC, once the debt is *discharged* by a bankruptcy court, the creditor cannot collect on a negotiable instrument. In this case, Blasco had filed for bankruptcy protection but her debts had not yet been discharged.

[3] Section 3-201. The UCC spells the word "indorsed." Outside the UCC, the word is more commonly spelled "endorsed."

met the two requirements for negotiating order paper: indorsement and delivery. (Note that, for indorsements, a signature is sufficient. Larnell need not write "pay to" or "pay to the order of.") If Larnell delivers the check to Patty but forgets to sign it, the check has not been indorsed and therefore cannot be negotiated—it has no value to Patty. Similarly, the check is no use to Patty if Larnell signs it but never gives it to her. If someone forges Larnell's name, the indorsement is invalid and no subsequent transfer counts as a negotiation.

There are three different types of indorsements:

- **Blank Indorsement.** A blank indorsement occurs when Larnell simply signs the check on the back without designating any particular payee. A blank indorsement turns the check into bearer paper. Larnell can give the check to Patty the painter or Ellen the electrician. In either case, he has properly negotiated the check.
- **Special Indorsement.** A special indorsement limits an instrument to one particular *person*. If Larnell writes on the back of the check, "Pay Ellen Wilson" or "Pay to the order of Ellen Wilson," then only Ellen can cash the check.
- **Restrictive Indorsement.** A restrictive indorsement limits the check to one particular *use*. When Ellen receives the check from Larnell, she writes on the back, "For deposit only," and then signs her name. The check can only be deposited in Ellen's account. If Conrad finds the check, he cannot cash it or deposit it in his own account. This type of indorsement is the safest.

EXAMStrategy

Question: Tess makes a check out to cash and delivers it to Larnell. He writes on the back, "Pay to the order of Patty." She signs her name. Is this check bearer paper or order paper? Has it been negotiated?

Strategy: Whenever a negotiable instrument is transferred, it is important to ask if the instrument has been properly negotiated. To be negotiated, order paper must be indorsed and delivered; bearer paper need only be delivered, but in both cases by someone other than the issuer.

Result: This check changes back and forth between order and bearer paper, depending on what the indorsement says. When Tess makes out a check to cash, it is bearer paper. When she gives it to Larnell, it is not negotiated because she is the issuer. When he writes on the back "Pay to the order of Patty," it becomes order paper. When he gives it to Patty, it is properly negotiated because he is not the issuer and he has both indorsed the check and transferred it to Patty. When she signs it, the check becomes bearer paper. And so on it could go forever.[4]

25-2 HOLDER IN DUE COURSE

The fundamental rule of this chapter tells us that a holder in due course has an automatic right to receive payment for a negotiable instrument (unless the issuer can claim a limited number of *real* defenses). If the possessor of an instrument is not a holder in due course, then his right to payment depends upon the relationship between the issuer and payee. He inherits whatever

[4]Even when all the space on the back of the check is filled, the holder can attach a separate paper for indorsements, called an *allonge.*

claims and defenses arise out of that contract. Clearly, then, holder in due course status dramatically increases the value of an instrument because it enhances the probability of being paid. Thus, it is very important to understand what it takes to be a holder in due course.

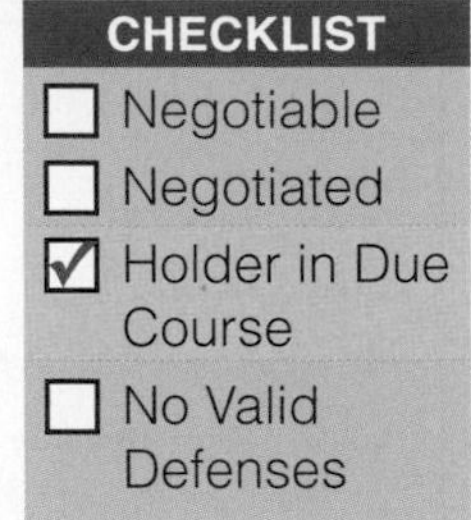

25-2a Requirements for Being a Holder in Due Course

A holder in due course is a *holder* who has *given value* for the instrument, in *good faith*, *without notice* of outstanding claims or other defects.[5] Let's define these terms.

Holder

A holder in due course must, first of all, be a holder. For order paper, a **holder** is anyone in possession of the instrument if it is payable to or indorsed to her. For bearer paper, a **holder** is anyone in possession. When Felix borrows money from his mother, she insists that he sign a promissory note for the loan. He promptly writes, "I hereby promise to pay to the order of Imogene $5,000." He signs his name and gives the note to her. She is a holder because she has possession of the instrument and it is payable to her. She would like to give the note to her lawyer, Lance, to pay the legal bill she incurred when Felix smashed up a nightclub. If she simply hands the note to Lance, he is not a holder because the note is not payable to him. If she writes on the back of the note, "Pay to the order of Lance," but does not give it to him, he is not a holder either.

Holder in due course
Someone who has given value for an instrument, in good faith, without notice of outstanding claims or other defenses

Holder
For order paper, the holder is anyone in possession of the instrument if it is payable to or indorsed to her. For bearer paper, the holder is anyone in possession.

Value
The holder has already done something in exchange for the instrument.

Value

A holder in due course must give value for an instrument. Value means that the holder has *already* done something in exchange for the instrument. Lance has already represented Felix, so he has given value. Once Imogene indorses and delivers the note to Lance, he is a holder in due course.

Although a promise to do something in the future is *consideration* under contract law, such a promise does not count as *value* for a negotiable instrument. If the holder receives an instrument in return for a promise, he does not deserve to be paid unless he performs the promise. But if he was a holder in due course, he would be entitled to payment whether he performed or not. Suppose that Imogene gave Lance the promissory note in exchange for his promise to represent Felix in an upcoming arson trial. Lance would not be a holder in due course because he had not yet performed the service. It would be unfair for him to be a holder in due course, with an unconditional right to be paid, if he does not, in the end, represent Felix.

Someone who receives a negotiable instrument as a gift is not a holder in due course because he has not given value. If Imogene gives Felix's note to her daughter, Joy, as a birthday present, Joy is not a holder in due course.

Good Faith

There are two tests to determine if a holder acquired an instrument in good faith. **The holder must meet both of these tests:**

- **Subjective Test.** Did the holder *believe* the transaction was honest in fact?
- **Objective Test.** Did the transaction *appear* to be commercially reasonable?

Felix persuades his neighbor, Hope, that he has invented a fabulous beauty cream guaranteed to remove wrinkles. She gives him a $10,000 promissory note, payable

Does Hope have to pay Dick for samples Felix didn't deliver?

[5]Section 3-302.

PROMISSORY NOTE

$500.00 September 5, 1950

On or before 60 days after date, I promise to pay $500 to the order of Soames for value received.

Irene

The holder of this note should realize that there may be a problem.

in 90 days, in return for exclusive sales rights in Pittsburgh. Felix sells the note to his old friend Dick for $2,000. Felix never delivers the sales samples to Hope. When Dick presents the note to Hope, she refuses to pay on the grounds that Dick is not a holder in due course. She contends that he did not buy the note in good faith.

Dick fails both tests. Any friend of Felix knows he is not trustworthy, especially when presenting a promissory note signed by a neighbor. Dick did not believe the transaction was honest in fact. Also, $10,000 notes are not usually discounted to $2,000; $9,500 would be more normal. This transaction is not commercially reasonable, and Dick should have realized immediately that Felix was up to no good.

Notice of Outstanding Claims or Other Defects

In the following circumstances, a holder is on notice that an instrument has an outstanding claim or other defect.

1. **The Instrument Is Overdue.** An instrument is overdue the day after its due date. At that point, the recipient is on notice that it may have a defect. He ought to wonder why no one has bothered to collect the money owed. However, an instrument is not overdue simply because the interest is unpaid. If, on July 25, Dick buys Harriet's note that was due on July 24, Dick is not a holder in due course because the note is overdue. But if he buys the note on July 23, knowing that Harriet has not paid all the interest owing, he can still be a holder in due course.

   A check is overdue 90 days after its date. Any other *demand* instrument is overdue (1) the day after a request for payment is made or (2) a reasonable time after the instrument was issued. Suppose that Felix tries to sell Tom a demand note from Hope. If Felix happens to mention, "I asked the old lady for the money yesterday, but so far, no luck," then Tom is not a holder in due course because he knows the note is overdue.

2. **The Instrument Is Dishonored.** To dishonor an instrument is to refuse to pay it. If Tom knows that Hope has refused to pay her note, then Tom cannot be a holder in due course. Likewise, once a check has been stamped "Insufficient Funds" by the bank, it has been dishonored, and no one who obtains it afterward can be a holder in due course.

3. **The Instrument Is Altered, Forged, or Incomplete.** Anyone who knows that an instrument has been altered or forged cannot be a holder in due course. Suppose Joe wrote a check to Tony for $200. While showing the check to Liza, Tony cackles to himself and says, "Can you believe what that goof did? Look, he left the line blank after the words 'two hundred.'" Taking his pen out with a flourish, Tony changes the zeroes to nines and adds the words, "ninety-nine." He then indorses the check over to Liza, who is definitely not a holder in due course. However, if, instead of giving the check to Liza, Tony sells it to Kate, she is a holder in due course because she had no idea the check had been altered.

   Likewise, if Joe filled out the check, but failed to sign it, Liza cannot be a holder in due course after she watches Tony fill in Joe's signature. And even if Liza did not see the forgery, she might be on notice if Tony has misspelled Joe's name as "Jo."

   Sometimes people (foolishly) sign blank promissory notes or checks. These issuers are liable for any amount subsequently filled in. However, anyone who is aware that a material term was added later is not a holder in due course. Suppose that Joe gives Tony a signed, blank check. If Tony fills in the amount in front of Liza, then naturally she is not a holder in due course. But if Tony fills in the check *before* he gives it to Liza, she is a holder in due course.

4. **The Holder Has Notice of Certain Claims or Disputes.** No one can qualify as a holder in due course if she is on notice that (1) someone else has a claim to the instrument or (2) there is a dispute between the original parties to the instrument. Matt hires Sheila to put aluminum siding on his house. In payment, he gives her a $15,000 promissory note with the due date left blank. They agree that the note will not be due until 60 days after completion of the work. Despite the agreement, Sheila fills in the date immediately and sells the note to Rupert at American Finance Corp., who has bought many similar notes from Sheila. Rupert knows that the note is not supposed to be due until after the work is finished. Usually, before he buys a note from her, he demands a signed document from the homeowner certifying that the work is complete. Also, he lives near Matt and can see that Matt's house is only half finished. Rupert is not a holder in due course because he has reason to suspect there is a dispute between Sheila and Matt.

Holder in due course status is determined *when the holder receives the instrument.* If, at the very moment when he takes possession, the holder has no notice of outstanding claims or other defects, then he is a holder in due course, no matter what else happens afterward. If Rupert knows nothing of Sheila's sneaky ways when he buys Matt's note, then he is a holder in due course even if Matt calls him ten minutes later to report that Sheila has violated their contract.

In the following case, the holder of the notes had reason to know that all was not well between the parties to the original contract. But did the dentists' claim have teeth?

In re Brican Am. LLC Equip. Lease Litig.

2015 U.S. Dist. LEXIS 5923; 2015 WL 235409
United States District Court for the Southern District of Florida, 2015

Facts: Brican LLC was running a scam. The victims were dentists who wanted to lease multimedia systems (called "Exhibeos") for use in their waiting rooms. Each Exhibeo consisted of a computer and a television which could, say, demonstrate proper flossing technique and show ads for expensive cosmetic procedures.

The sales process worked this way: Brican would sell an Exhibeo to NCMIC Finance Corporation, which would then lease the equipment to a dentist. Brican promised all the dentists that another company, Viso Lasik, would buy enough advertising on the Exhibeos to cover the monthly lease payments. Further, if Viso ever stopped its advertising, Brican would buy the Exhibeos back from the dentists and they could cancel their contracts. In short, Brican lured the dentists with the promise that the Exhibeos were effectively free.

This plan not only sounded too good to be true, it was. Brican sold each Exhibeo to NCMIC for $24,000. But Brican was also paying Viso for the ads it placed with the dentists, which amounted to $29,000 over five years. In short, Brican was losing money on every Exhibeo it sold but would pocket the $24,000 from NCMIC *upfront* and then worry *later* about the $29,000 it owed in Viso ads. The only way this system could work, in the short run, was if Brican kept selling more and more machines. In the long run—well, there was no chance of a long run.

NCMIC was attracted to the deal because dentists typically have a good credit rating and were agreeing to pay a high interest rate. It is possible that, at the beginning, NCMIC was unaware of Brican's scam. However, once NCMIC discovered the truth, it responded by sharply *increasing* its lending to a rate of ten times more than it had been the year before.

Eventually, the inevitable happened. Brican sales declined, it ran out of cash and then stopped paying for Viso ads on the Exhibeos. The dentists quit making their lease payments and NCMIC sued them. Because the leases were legally the same as a promissory note, the dentists alleged that NCMIC could not enforce the agreement because it was not a holder in due course—it had not acted in good faith because it was aware of Brican's fraud.

Issue: ***Was NCMIC a holder in due course?***

Excerpts from Judge Seitz's Decision: [T]he elements at issue are "good faith" and "without notice of a defense or claim." Good faith requires "honesty in fact and the observance of reasonable commercial standards of fair dealing." Therefore, an assignee cannot ignore suspicious circumstances that cry out for investigation and then claim to have taken the assignment in good faith.

NCMIC received notice on numerous occasions that Brican promised customers that the Exhibeo would be effectively "free" because the advertising fees would offset the lease payments and that they could cancel their lease obligation if the payments ceased. In response to these disturbing circumstances that called for investigation, NCMIC took no action constituting the observance of reasonable commercial standards of fair dealing. Although NCMIC had established procedures for investigating fraud, it did not use them.

NCMIC blithely continued increasing its lending while ignoring suspicious circumstances. NCMIC never inquired into Viso's ability to meet its commitment to buy advertising, such as by asking for Viso's financial records.

Based on the evidence, NCMIC failed to satisfy its burden to prove that it took assignment of the Agreements "in good faith" and "without notice" of Brican's fraud. Therefore, it is not a holder in due course.

25-2b Shelter Rule

Under the shelter rule, the transferor of an instrument passes on all of his rights. When a holder in due course transfers an instrument, the recipient acquires all the same rights *even if he is not a holder in due course himself*.[6]

Cigna Insurance Company sent James Mills a check for $484.12 in payment for his insurance claim. Dishonest fellow that he was, Mills told Cigna that the check never arrived. Cigna stopped payment and issued a new check. Mills took the *old* check to Sun's Market and used it to buy goods there. At this point, Sun was a holder in due course and was entitled to payment from Cigna. When Sun deposited the check at its bank, the bank refused to pay and stamped the check "Stop Payment." Instead of presenting the check to Cigna and having a fight over whether or not the insurance company was liable on the instrument, Sun sold the check to Robert Triffin, who was in the business of buying dishonored instruments. Triffin then sued Cigna for payment. Triffin acknowledged that he was not a holder in due course because he knew the check had been dishonored. However, under the shelter rule, he acquired Sun's rights as a holder in due course, and he was entitled to payment.[7]

The point of the shelter rule is not to benefit Mills or Triffin; it is to protect Sun. It would not do Sun much good to be a holder in due course if it was unable to sell the instrument to anyone.

There is one small exception to the shelter rule. If a holder in due course transfers the instrument back to a prior holder who was a party to fraud involving the instrument, that prior holder does not acquire the rights of a holder in due course. Thus, if Triffin transferred the check back to Mills, then Mills would not be entitled to payment from Cigna (even if he had the nerve to ask).

25-2c Defenses against a Holder in Due Course

Negotiable instruments are meant to be a close substitute for currency, and, as a general rule, holders expect to be paid. However, an issuer may legitimately refuse to pay an instrument under certain circumstances. The UCC lists so-called *real* defenses that an issuer may legitimately use even against a holder in due course.[8] If the holder is not in due course but is simply a plain ordinary holder, the issuer may use both real defenses and *personal* defenses. **Real and personal defenses are valid against an ordinary holder; only real defenses can be used against a holder in due course.**

---

6 Section 3-203(b).

7 Triffin v. Cigna, 297 N.J. Super. 199 (N.J., App. Div. 1997).

8 Section 3-305.

CHECKLIST

- ☐ Negotiable
- ☐ Negotiated
- ☐ Holder in Due Course
- ☑ No Valid Defenses

Real Defenses

The following real defenses are valid against both a holder and a holder in due course:

Forgery. If Sharon forges Jared's name to a promissory note and sells it to Jennifer, Jared does not have to pay Jennifer, even if she is a holder in due course.

Bankruptcy. If Jared signs a promissory note and then his debts are discharged in a bankruptcy proceeding, he does not have to pay the note, even to a holder in due course.

Being Underage. If someone who is underage (typically under 18) has the right to void a contract under state law, then he also has the right not to pay a negotiable instrument, even to a holder in due course.

Alteration. If the amount of an instrument is wrongfully changed, the holder in due course can collect only the original (correct) amount. But, if the instrument was incomplete, the holder in due course can collect the full face amount, even if the instrument was incorrectly filled in. Suppose that Jared gives a $2,000 promissory note to Rose. As soon as he leaves, she whips out her pen and adds a zero to the note. She then takes it to the auto showroom to pay for her new car. If the showroom is a holder in due course, it is entitled to be paid the original amount of the note ($2,000), not the altered amount ($20,000). But, if Jared had accidentally forgotten to fill out the amount of the note, and Rose wrote in $20,000, the showroom could recover the full $20,000. Although the two notes *look* the same, they have a different result. In the case where Rose changed the amount, Jared was not to blame; but he *was* at fault for signing a blank note.

Duress, Mental Incapacity, or Illegality. These are customary contract defenses that you remember well from your study of contracts. They are a defense against a holder in due course if they are severe enough to make the underlying transaction void (not simply voidable) under state law. An instrument is not valid even in the hands of a holder in due course if, for example, Rose holds a gun to Jared's head to force him to sign it, or Jared has been declared mentally incompetent at the time he signs it, or Jared is using the instrument to pay for something illegal (cocaine, say).

Fraud in the Execution. In cases of fraud in the execution, the issuer has been tricked into signing without knowing what the instrument is and without any reasonable way to find out. In such instances, even a holder in due course cannot recover. Jared cannot read English. Helen, his boss, orders him to sign a document required by the company's health insurance plan. In fact, the document is a promissory note, payable to Helen. Jared does not have to pay the note, even to a holder in due course, because of fraud in the execution.

Personal Defenses

Personal defenses are valid against a holder, but *not* against a holder in due course. Typically, personal defenses have some connection to the initial transaction in which the instrument was issued.

Breach of Contract. Ross signs a contract to sell a new airplane to Paige in return for a $1 million promissory note. If Paige discovers that the plane is defective and that Ross has breached the contract, she can refuse to pay him because he is a mere holder. If, however, Ross sells the note to Helga, a holder in due course, Paige must pay her.

Lack of Consideration. Ross gives his mother, Gertrude, a $1,000 check for her birthday. Then they have a disagreement, so Ross stops payment on Gertrude's check. Gertrude has no right to the $1,000 because she is a mere holder who did not give value for the check. But if Gertrude has already cashed the check at her bank, Ross must pay the bank because it is a holder in due course. Even though the check was a gift, and therefore lacking in value, the bank is a holder in due course because it has given value for the check, even if Gertrude has not.

Prior Payment. Two years before, Gertrude had loaned Ross money to start his business. When he paid off the note to Gertrude, he forgot to retrieve the original from her. Angry at him over the check, she sells the note to Carla. Of course, Ross would not have to pay Gertrude *again,* but he cannot refuse to pay Carla, who is a holder in due course. The moral is: When you pay off a note, be sure to retrieve it or mark it canceled.

Unauthorized Completion. Ross writes a check to Carla to pay the note. He forgets to fill in the amount of the check, but Carla very helpfully does, for $5,000 more than he actually owes. If she uses that check to pay her debt at the bank, the bank is a holder in due course, and Ross must honor the check. Remember, however, that if the bank knew Carla had filled in the amount, it would not be a holder in due course and could not recover on the check.

Fraud in the Inducement. Carla uses a promissory note to pay for stock in Sean's company. It turns out that the company is a fraud. Carla would not have to pay Sean (a holder), but, if Sean transfers the note to Peter, a holder in due course, Carla must pay Peter even though the underlying contract was fraudulent. Note that *fraud in the execution* (real defense) has a different result from *fraud in the inducement* (personal defense).

Non-Delivery. The note that Carla issued to Sean was bearer paper. When Oliver steals it and sells it to a holder in due course, Carla must pay the note even though neither she nor Sean had ever delivered it to the holder. Carla would not have to pay Oliver because he is a mere holder and she did not deliver it to him.

The following table lists, for quick reference, real and personal defenses.

Real Defenses	Personal Defenses
Forgery	Breach of contract
Bankruptcy	Lack of consideration
Being underage	Prior payment
Alteration	Unauthorized completion
Duress	Fraud in the inducement
Mental incapacity	Non-delivery
Illegality	
Fraud in the execution	

The following case illustrates the value of being a holder in due course. Remember that, to be a holder, you must be in possession of thc instrument.

Creative Ventures, LLC v. Jim Ward & Associates

195 Cal. App. 4th 1430
California Court of Appeals, 2011

Facts: When Creative Ventures, LLC borrowed $3 million from defendant Jim Ward & Associates (JWA), it signed promissory notes, payable to JWA. Thereafter, JWA sold this loan to 54 individual investors (Investors) but kept possession of the notes. When Creative made payments under the loan to JWA, it paid the Investors their share.

Under California law, the interest rate on a loan cannot be greater than 8 percent, except in certain circumstances.

Those circumstances include loans by a licensed real estate broker. JWA claimed that it was such a broker, but it was not. When Creative discovered this lie, it sued JWA and the Investors to obtain a refund of all interest it had paid under the loan, as is permitted by California law. The Investors argued that they were entitled to keep the interest because, as holders in due course, they had taken the note free of the claim against JWA.

The trial court found for the Investors and Creative appealed.

Issues: *Were the Investors holders in due course? Were they entitled to keep the interest that Creative had paid on the illegal loan?*

Excerpts from Justice Premo's Decision: Under the California Uniform Commercial Code, a holder in due course takes his or her interest free of many defenses, including the defense of usury. [I]n order to be a holder in due course, one must be a holder of the instrument. The holder is the person in possession of a negotiable instrument that is payable either to bearer or to the person in possession. The promissory notes in this case are payable to JWA, which is also in possession of the notes. Accordingly, JWA is the holder.

Investors might have become holders had JWA negotiated the notes by indorsing and transferring possession to Investors. It follows that, since there is no evidence that JWA negotiated the promissory notes by indorsement and delivery, Investors cannot be holders in due course. [A]bsent negotiation, the transferee's rights are gleaned not from the instrument but are derivative of the rights held by the transferor. [Investors are not entitled to keep the interest Creative paid.] The trial court erred in finding otherwise.

Claims in Recoupment

A **claim in recoupment** is not the same as a defense, but it has a similar impact. It means that the issuer subtracts (i.e., "sets off") any *other* claims he has against the initial payee from the amount he owes on the instrument. The distinction is subtle, but a *claim in recoupment* means, "I'm not going to pay the full amount of the instrument because she owes me money for something else," whereas a *defense* means, "I'm not going to pay the full amount of the instrument because there is some problem with *this* instrument or the underlying deal on which *this* instrument is based."

Claim in recoupment
The issuer subtracts (i.e., "sets off") any other claims he has against the initial payee from the amount he owes on the instrument.

A claim in recoupment is valid against a holder but not against a holder in due course. Carla gives Sean a promissory note to pay for stock that turns out to be fraudulent. Therefore, Carla has a defense against Sean when he requests that she pay her note. Suppose, however, that the stock is perfectly legitimate, but Sean has never paid Carla $18,000 for the used car he bought from her. When Sean presents the note on the stock deal for payment, Carla makes a claim for recoupment and subtracts $18,000 from the amount owing on the note. If, however, Sean had already sold the note to Olaf, a holder in due course, Carla would have to pay the full amount of the note and then sue Sean for the $18,000.

EXAMStrategy

Question: Jack agreed to loan Tim money. Although Tim gave Jack a promissory note, Jack never actually paid Tim the money. Jack sold the note to Leslie. Can Leslie collect from Tim? Would it matter if Leslie knew that Tim never received the money?

Strategy: Whenever a question asks if someone will be paid on a negotiable instrument, the first step is to determine if she is a holder in due course. The second step is to ask if there are any applicable defenses.

Result: If Leslie *knew* that Jack had never paid Tim, then she is a mere holder, not a holder in due course. Tim can use any personal defenses (such as lack of consideration) against a holder. In that case, Tim does not have to pay Leslie. But, if Leslie did not know of the dispute, she is a holder in due course and can collect from Tim, despite the fact that Tim never received payment from Jack.

25-2d Consumer Exception

The most common use for negotiable instruments is in consumer transactions. A consumer pays for a refrigerator by giving the store a promissory note. The store promptly sells the note to a finance company. Even if the refrigerator is defective, UCC Article 3 would require the consumer to pay full value on the note because the finance company is a holder in due course. To solve this problem, some states require promissory notes given by a consumer to carry the words *consumer paper*. Notes with these words are non-negotiable and no one is a holder in due course.

Consumer credit contract
A contract in which a consumer borrows money from a lender to purchase goods and services from a seller who is affiliated with the lender

Meanwhile, the Federal Trade Commission (FTC) has special rules for consumer credit contracts. A **consumer credit contract** is one in which a consumer borrows money from a lender to purchase goods and services *from a seller who is affiliated with the lender*. If Sears loans money to Gerald to buy a 3-D television at Sears, that is a consumer credit contract. It is not a consumer credit contract if Gerald borrows money from his cousin Vinnie to buy the television from Sears. **The FTC requires all promissory notes in consumer credit contracts to contain the following language:**

NOTICE

ANY HOLDER OF THIS CONSUMER CREDIT CONTRACT IS SUBJECT TO ALL CLAIMS AND DEFENSES WHICH THE DEBTOR COULD ASSERT AGAINST THE SELLER OF GOODS OR SERVICES OBTAINED WITH THE PROCEEDS HEREOF.

Under the UCC, no one can be a holder in due course of an instrument with this language.[9] If the language is omitted from a consumer note, it is possible to be a holder in due course, but the seller is subject to a fine.[10]

In the following case, consumers found that a home improvement contract, far from improving their home, almost caused them to lose it.

Antuna v. Nescor, Inc.

2002 Conn. Super. LEXIS 1003
Superior Court of Connecticut, 2002

Facts: Steven Vlohotis was a salesman for NESCOR, a home improvement company. He convinced the Antunas to sign a consumer credit contract with NESCOR to install vinyl siding and windows. The contract provided that the Antunas would pay for the improvements in installments. It was secured by the Antunas' home. NESCOR assigned the contract to First Consumer Credit, LLC, which reassigned it to The Money Store (TMS). In keeping with FTC requirements, the contract contained the following language: "Any holder of this consumer credit contract is subject to all claims and defenses which the debtor could assert against the Seller of the goods or services pursuant hereto or with the proceeds hereof."

A Connecticut statute (the Act) provides that, "No home improvement contract shall be valid or enforceable against an owner unless it is entered into by a registered salesman or a registered contractor." The NESCOR salesman, Vlohotis, was not registered.

Unhappy with NESCOR's work, the Antunas stopped making payments under the contract. TMS filed suit, seeking to foreclose on their house. The Antunas moved for summary judgment, arguing that TMS could not enforce the contract because it was not a holder in due course.

Issue: ***Does TMS have the right to foreclose on the Antunas' home?***

---

9 Section 3-106(d).

10 In 2002, the Uniform Law Commissioners approved a revision of Article 3 which provides that, even if this language is omitted from a consumer note, the instrument will be treated as if it had been included. Thus, no one can be a holder in due course on a promissory note issued in connection with a consumer credit contract. However, at this writing, only about 20 percent of the states have passed this new version of Article 3.

Excerpts from Judge Shortall's Decision: In employing Vlohotis to call on the plaintiffs as its salesman, NESCOR was performing an illegal act, one explicitly prohibited. Accordingly, the court finds that NESCOR's material non-compliance with [the Act] renders the home improvement contract invalid and unenforceable and precludes it from enforcing the consumer credit contract against the plaintiffs.

It is only by giving consumers like the plaintiffs a shield against enforcement of these consumer credit contracts that the Act's declaration that a contract is invalid and unenforceable has any meaning. The language appearing in the consumer credit contract held by TMS, viz., that the contract is "subject to all claims and defenses which" the plaintiffs could assert against NESCOR is mandated in all such contracts by the FTC to prevent the seller of goods from cutting off the consumer's right to assert claims and defenses against the seller's assignee. So, in this case, where the Act, itself, gives the plaintiffs the right to defend against enforcement of the home improvement contract, the language in the consumer credit contract held by TMS gives them the same right as against TMS.

Accordingly, because the TMS is subject to those same claims and defenses under the very language of its contract with the plaintiffs. TMS may not enforce the consumer credit contract it holds by foreclosing on the plaintiffs' property for nonpayment.

The plaintiffs' motion for summary judgment is granted.

CHAPTER CONCLUSION

Whenever someone acquires commercial paper, the first question he ought to ask is "How certain am I to be paid the face value of this document?" Article 3 of the UCC contains the answer to this question: If a negotiable instrument is negotiated to a holder in due course, then that holder knows he has an unconditional right (subject only to a few real defenses) to be paid the value of the note. In some ways, Article 3 is like a marine drill instructor: rigid, but predictable if you follow the rules.

EXAM REVIEW

1. **COMMERCIAL PAPER** Commercial paper is a contract to pay money. It can be used either as a substitute for money or as a loan of money.

2. **THE FUNDAMENTAL RULE OF COMMERCIAL PAPER** The possessor of a piece of commercial paper has an unconditional right to be paid, so long as:
   - The paper is negotiable,
   - It has been negotiated to the possessor,
   - The possessor is a holder in due course, and
   - The issuer cannot claim any of the few "real" defenses.

3. **NEGOTIABILITY** The possessor of non-negotiable commercial paper has the same rights—no more, no less—as the person who made the original contract. The possessor of negotiable commercial paper has more rights than the person who made the original contract.

4. **REQUIREMENTS FOR NEGOTIABILITY** To be negotiable, an instrument must:
   - Be in writing,
   - Be signed by the maker or drawer,
   - Contain an unconditional promise or order to pay,
   - State a definite amount of money,
   - Be payable on demand or at a definite time, and
   - Be payable to order or to bearer.

5. **AMBIGUITY** When the terms in a negotiable instrument contradict each other, three rules apply:
   - Words take precedence over numbers.
   - Handwritten terms prevail over typed and printed terms.
   - Typed terms win over printed terms.

6. **NEGOTIATION** To be negotiated, order paper must first be indorsed and then delivered to the transferee. Bearer paper must simply be delivered to the transferee; no indorsement is required.

7. **HOLDER IN DUE COURSE** A holder in due course is a holder who has given value for the instrument, in good faith, without notice of outstanding claims or other defects.

EXAMStrategy

Question: After Irene fell behind on her mortgage payments, she answered an advertisement from Best Financial Consultants offering attractive refinancing opportunities. During a meeting at a McDonald's restaurant, a Best representative told her that the company would arrange for a complete refinancing of her home, pay off two of her creditors, and give her an additional $5,000 in spending money. Irene would only have to pay Best $4,000. Irene signed a blank promissory note that Best representatives later filled in for $14,986.61. Best did not fulfill its promises to Irene, but within two weeks, it sold the note to Robin for just under $14,000. Irene refused to pay the note, alleging that Robin was not a holder in due course. Is Irene liable to Robin?

Strategy: Whenever a question asks if someone is a holder in due course, ask: Is this person a *holder* who has given *value* for the instrument, in *good faith, without notice* of outstanding claims or other defects? (See the "Result" at the end of this Exam Review section.)

8. **REAL DEFENSES** These real defenses are valid against both a holder and a holder in due course:
   - Forgery
   - Discharge in a bankruptcy proceeding
   - Being underage
   - Alteration
   - Duress, mental incapacity, or illegality
   - Fraud in the execution

9. **PERSONAL DEFENSES** These personal defenses are valid against any holder except a holder in due course:
   - Breach of contract
   - Lack of consideration
   - Prior payment
   - Unauthorized completion
   - Fraud in the inducement
   - Non-delivery

EXAMStrategy

Question: Gary, a farmer in Missouri, was having financial problems. He agreed to let Nasib assume control of his farm's finances. After a few months, Gary begged Nasib for money. One week later, Rexford State Bank wired Gary $30,000. Gary thought that Nasib would be responsible for repaying this sum. A man who worked for Nasib stopped Gary on the street and asked him to sign a receipt for the $30,000. Gary signed without intending to commit himself to repaying the money. In fact, the document Gary signed was a blank promissory note, payable to Rexford. Someone later filled in the blanks, putting in $50,000 instead of $30,000. Nasib had received $50,000 before transferring $30,000 to Gary. When Rexford sued Gary to enforce the note, Gary asserted the defense of fraud. Is Gary liable on the note?

Strategy: Whenever someone alleges a defense, the first step is to determine if the defense is real or personal. Personal defenses are not valid against a holder in due course. (See the "Result" at the end of this Exam Review section.)

10. **A CLAIM IN RECOUPMENT** A claim in recoupment means the issuer can set off any other claims he has against the initial payee from the amount he owes on the instrument. A claim in recoupment cannot be used against a holder in due course.

11. **CONSUMER CREDIT CONTRACTS** The FTC requires all promissory notes in consumer credit contracts to contain language preventing any subsequent holder from being a holder in due course.

EXAMStrategy

Question: Gina purchased a Chrysler car with a 70,000-mile warranty. She signed a loan contract with the dealer to pay for the car in monthly installments. The dealer sold the contract to the Chrysler Credit Corp. Soon, the car developed a tendency to accelerate abruptly without warning. Two Chrysler dealers were unable to correct the problem. Gina filed suit against Chrysler Credit Corp., but the company refused to rescind the loan contract. The company argued that, as a holder in due course on the note, it was entitled to be paid regardless of any defects in the car. How would you decide this case if you were the judge?

Strategy: Whenever consumers are involved, consider the possibility that there is a consumer credit contract. The plaintiff in this case is a consumer who borrowed money from a lender to purchase goods from a seller who is affiliated with the lender (both seller and lender are owned by Chrysler). Thus, the contract is a consumer credit contract. (See the "Result" at the end of this Exam Review section.)

RESULTS

7. Result: In this case, Robin is a holder who has given value. Did she act in good faith? We do not know if she actually *believed* the transaction was honest, but the court held that the transaction did not *appear* to be commercially reasonable because Robin's profit was so high. Thus, Robin was not a holder in due course, and Irene was not liable to her.

9. Result: Fraud in the execution is a real defense; fraud in the inducement is personal. In this case, there was no fraud in the execution. Gary could have read the note he signed, but he did not bother. Nasib committed fraud in the inducement, but that is not a valid defense because the Bank is a holder in due course.

11. Result: Chrysler Credit was not a holder in due course. Therefore, it is subject to any defenses that Gina might have against the dealer, including that the car was defective.

MULTIPLE-CHOICE QUESTIONS

1. Which of the following statements are true?
   (a) A draft is always a check.
   (b) A check is always a draft.
   (c) A note must involve at least three people.
   (d) All of these are true.
2. Which of the following standards are *required* for negotiability?
   (a) The instrument must be signed by the payee.
   (b) The instrument must be payable on demand.
   (c) The instrument must contain a promise or order to pay.
   (d) The instrument must be dated.

3. Marla is not a holder in due course if she takes an instrument ____________.
   (a) believing that the underlying contract was honest, although it turned out to be dishonest
   (b) that is a consumer credit contract
   (c) that appeared commercially reasonable when made but it turned out to be dishonest
   (d) All of these

4. **CPA QUESTION** In order to negotiate bearer paper, one must ______________.
   (a) indorse the paper
   (b) indorse and deliver the paper with consideration
   (c) deliver the paper
   (d) deliver and indorse the paper

5. **CPA QUESTION** Bond fraudulently induced Teal to make a note payable to Wilk, to whom Bond was indebted. Bond delivered the note to Wilk. Wilk negotiated the instrument to Monk, who purchased it with knowledge of the fraud and after it was overdue. If Wilk qualifies as a holder in due course, which of the following statements is correct?
   (a) Monk has the standing of a holder in due course through Wilk.
   (b) Teal can successfully assert the defense of fraud in the inducement against Monk.
   (c) Monk personally qualifies as a holder in due course.
   (d) Teal can successfully assert the defense of fraud in the inducement against Wilk.

CASE QUESTIONS

1. Kay signed a promissory note for $220,000 that was payable to Investments, Inc. The company then indorsed the note over to its lawyers to pay past and future legal fees. Were the lawyers holders in due course?

2. Shelby wrote this check to Dana. When is it payable and for how much?

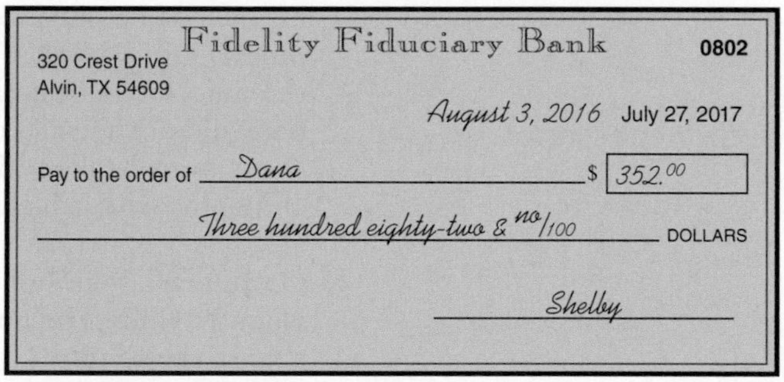

Fidelity Fiduciary Bank 0802
320 Crest Drive
Alvin, TX 54609

August 3, 2016 July 27, 2017

Pay to the order of *Dana* $ *352.00*

Three hundred eighty-two & no/100 DOLLARS

Shelby

3. Ian was CEO of a company. He stole money from the company by writing a series of checks made out to "Cash," which he deposited in his own personal account at Bank. (Please do not try this at home.) Of course, he then spent the money. The company sued the Bank to get the money back. Was the Bank a holder in due course?

4. Able was a partner in the law firm of Able, Baker & Charley. He wrote nine checks on the firm's checking account payable to "Bank of the United States." The law firm was not a customer of the Bank, but Able was. He deposited these checks into his personal account at the Bank and, of course, spent the money. The law firm sued the Bank to get its money back. Was the Bank liable to the law firm? Was it a holder in due course of the checks?

5. Roofing Company wrote a check to Dan for his work on a house. Dan cashed the check at Check Cashing, which deposited the check into its account at Bank. Roofing Company then discovered that Dan had not actually completed the work on the house so it placed a stop payment on the check it had issued to Dan. Because of the stop payment order, Bank refused to pay Check Cashing, which then sued Roofing Company for the amount of the check. Was Check Cashing a holder in due course? Was it entitled to be paid?

DISCUSSION QUESTIONS

1. Catherine suffered serious physical injuries in an automobile accident and became acutely depressed as a result. One morning, she received a check for $17,400 in settlement of her claims arising out of the accident. She indorsed the check and placed it on the kitchen table. She then called Robert, her longtime roommate, to tell him the check had arrived. That afternoon, she jumped from the roof of her apartment building, killing herself. The police found the check and a note from her, stating that she was giving it to Robert. Had Catherine negotiated the check to Robert?

2. **ETHICS** In desperate financial trouble and fearful of losing his house, Abbott asked his friend Taylor for help. Taylor had been an officer of the Bank, so she put Abbott in touch with some of her former colleagues there. When a $300,000 loan was ready for closing, Taylor informed Abbott that she expected a commission of $15,000. Taylor threatened to block the loan if her demands were not met. Abbott was desperate, so he agreed to give Taylor $4,000 in cash and a promissory note for $11,000. On what grounds might Abbott claim that the note is invalid? Would this be a valid defense? Even if Taylor was in the right legally, was she in the right ethically?

3. Kendall raised hogs. The Grain Company would provide him with hogs and grain and, in return, he would sign a promissory note in an amount equal to the value of these items. Once the pigs were grown, Kendall would sell them and repay the loan. One time, an officer of the Grain Company asked Kendall to sign not only his own name but also his wife's name to the promissory note. Kendall did so, but put his initials, KH, after her name to indicate that he was the one who had signed the note. Grain Company sold this note to Bank. It turned out that the Grain Company did not actually own the hogs it had given Kendall and the true owner took them away. Bank sued Kendall for payment on the promissory note. Are Kendall and/or his wife liable on the note?

4. On June 30, John signed a demand promissory note for $2,000 to the Camelot Country Club. The note stated that it was being given in payment for a membership in the country club, but, in fact, the club was insolvent, its memberships had no value, and John was already a member. He was also the club's golf pro. John signed the note at the request of the club's manager to enable the club to borrow money from the National Bank. The Bank of Dallas purchased the note on July 14 and immediately made demand. John alleged the note was overdue, and therefore the bank could not be a holder in due course. Do you agree? What is the moral of this story?

5. On October 12, James Camp agreed to provide services to Shawn Sheth by October 15. In payment, Sheth gave Camp a check for $1,300 that was postdated October 15. On October 13, Camp sold the check to Buckeye Check Cashing for $1,261.31. On October 14, fearing that Camp would violate the contract, Sheth stopped payment on the check. Also, on October 14, Buckeye deposited the check with its bank, believing that the check would reach Sheth's bank on October 15. Buckeye was unaware of the stop payment order. Sheth's bank refused to pay the check. Buckeye filed suit against Sheth. Was Buckeye a holder in due course? Must Sheth pay Buckeye?

26

CHAPTER

LIABILITY FOR NEGOTIABLE INSTRUMENTS

In the old Wild West, cattle rustling was a common crime. But that was hard, dusty work. Now, in the new West, there are easier ways to steal. This is a story about *check* rustling. Friese Co., a company near Bellingham, Washington, was in the business of buying, processing, and shipping cow hides to leather factories in Asia. The company mailed a check for $37,000 to West Coast Reduction, a supplier in *Canada*. Twelve days later, 19-year-old Christopher Mulligan went to a bank in *Brooklyn*, New York, opened a checking account in the name of West Coast, and deposited the check. His business plans were, however, temporarily disrupted when he was arrested for marijuana possession and sale. After spending a month in a New York jail, Mulligan returned to the bank to withdraw the money.

His business plans were, however, temporarily disrupted when he was arrested for marijuana possession and sale.

Of course, inquiring minds want to know how the check got into Mulligan's hands, but that is an unsolved mystery. The more important legal question is this: Once Mulligan withdraws these funds, who loses out—Friese (who sent the check), West Coast (who never received it), or the bank?

Without reading this chapter, you can guess that West Coast is not the loser because it never had possession. (And, indeed, it has no right to recover from either the thief or the bank. Friese will have to issue West Coast another check.) Obviously, the thief is liable—he has committed *conversion*, the legal term for stealing an instrument (such as a check). But recovering from any thief is unlikely, especially a teenaged, marijuana-selling, jailbird thief. Luckily, however, for Friese, if the bank pays out the money to anyone other than West Coast, the bank is liable for conversion. Although it did not intentionally do wrong, the bank must refund the stolen money to Friese.

As it turns out, though, this story has a happier ending. The bank's fraud department was suspicious of teenagers who, out of the blue, deposit large checks. When Mulligan showed up to withdraw the funds, the bank called 911 and Mulligan was captured. It seems that he might be making a return trip to jail, but this time for longer than a month.[1]

26-1 INTRODUCTION

In Chapter 25, you learned that the issuer of a negotiable instrument is liable to a holder in due course, unless the issuer can assert one of a limited number of real defenses.[2] Against a mere holder, an issuer can assert both personal and real defenses. The life of a negotiable instrument, however, is more complicated than these simple statements indicate. Not everyone who signs a negotiable instrument is an issuer, and not everyone who presents an instrument for payment is a holder in due course or even a holder. This chapter focuses on the liability of these extra players: non-issuers who sign an instrument and non-holders who receive payment.

26-1a The Contract versus the Instrument

People generally do not hand out promissory notes or checks to random strangers. Negotiable instruments are issued to fulfill a contract. The instruments create a *second* contract to pay the debt created by the *first* agreement. When Beverly agrees to buy a house from John, Contract No. 1 is formed. Giving him a promissory note in payment is Contract No. 2. When Jodie buys lunch with a Visa card, her promise to repay Visa by check at the end of the month is Contract No. 1. The check she mails to Visa is Contract No. 2.

Once an instrument has been accepted in payment for a debt, the debt is *suspended* until the instrument is paid or dishonored. Suppose that when Beverly buys a house from John, she pays with a promissory note that is not due for five years. Until she defaults on the note, he cannot sue her for payment even if, after a year, he decides he wants all the money right

[1]These facts are based on an article in *The New York Times*: Michael Wilson, "Cattle Hides Out West, and Suspected Check Rustling Back East," September 20, 2013.

[2]In Chapter 25, you also learned that *issuer* means the *drawer* of a check or the *maker* of a note.

away. When Visa receives Jodie's check, her debt is suspended until the company tries to cash the check. If the check is returned for insufficient funds, the obligation is revived and Visa can pursue Jodie until she pays it for real.

26-1b Enforcing an Instrument

Under the Uniform Commercial Code (UCC), the following participants have the right to enforce payment of an instrument[3]:

- A holder of the instrument;
- Anyone to whom the shelter rule applies (i.e., any non-holder with the rights of a holder; if this explanation makes no sense to you, review the shelter rule discussion in Chapter 25); and
- A holder who has lost the instrument.[4]

Recall that a holder is someone in possession of an instrument that has been validly negotiated.[5] Keep in mind, however, that the real and personal defenses discussed in Chapter 25 can be used against a holder. Therefore, in practice, the answer to the question "Who has the right to demand payment on an instrument?" is "A holder against whom no defenses can be used." Exhibit 26.1 illustrates this concept.

26-1c Primary versus Secondary Liability

A number of different people may be liable on the same negotiable instrument, but some are *primarily* liable; others are only *secondarily* liable. Someone with **primary liability** is unconditionally liable—he must pay unless he has a valid defense. Those with **secondary liability** pay only if the person with primary liability does not. **The holder of an instrument must first ask for payment from those who are primarily liable before making demand against anyone who is only secondarily liable.**

EXHIBIT 26.1

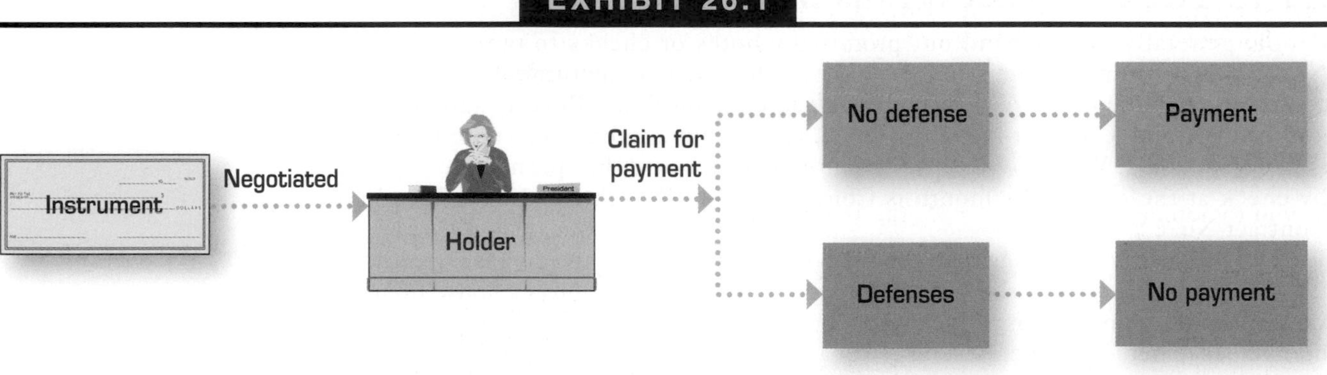

[3]UCC §3-301.

[4]Although technically some non-holders (such as a holder who has lost the instrument) can demand payment, in this chapter, we use "holder" as shorthand to include anyone entitled to enforce an instrument.

[5]Negotiation is discussed in Chapter 25.

26-1d The Payment Process

The payment process comprises as many as three steps:

- **Presentment.** Presentment means that the holder of the instrument demands payment from someone who is obligated to pay it (such as the maker or drawee).[6] To present, the holder must (1) exhibit the instrument, (2) show identification, and (3) surrender the instrument (if paid in full) or give a receipt (if only partially paid).
- **Dishonor.** The instrument is due, but the maker (of a note) or the drawer (of a draft) refuses to pay.[7]
- **Notice of Dishonor.** The holder of the instrument notifies those who are secondarily liable that the instrument has been dishonored.[8] This notice can be given by any reasonable means, including oral, written, or electronic communication. It must, however, be given within 30 days of the dishonor (except in the case of banks, which must give notice by midnight of the next banking day). The notice must simply identify the instrument and indicate that it has been dishonored. Anyone who has ever bounced a check has received a notice of dishonor—a check stamped "Insufficient Funds."

Presentment
A holder of an instrument demands payment from someone who is obligated to pay it.

Dishonor
An obligor refuses to pay an instrument that is due.

This check has been dishonored.

26-2 SIGNATURE LIABILITY

Virtually everyone who signs an instrument is potentially liable for it, which is called **signature liability**. However, the liability depends upon the capacity in which the instrument was signed. The maker of a note, for example, has different liability from an indorser. Capacity can sometimes be difficult to determine if the signature is not labeled—"maker," "indorser," "guarantor," "acceptor," and so forth. (All of these terms will be defined in the next sections.) In the absence of a label, courts generally look at the location of the signature. Someone who signs a check or a note in the lower-right corner is presumed to be an issuer. If a drawee bank signs on the face of a check, it is an acceptor. Someone who signs on the back of an instrument is considered to be an indorser.

Signature liability
The liability of someone who signs an instrument

26-2a Maker

As you remember from Chapter 25, the issuer of a note is called the **maker**. **The maker is *primarily* liable.**[9] He has promised to pay, and he must pay, unless he has a valid defense.[10] If two makers sign a note, they are both *jointly and severally* liable. The holder can demand full payment from either or partial payment from both (but never more than the full amount of the note). Suppose that Marilyn agrees to sell her bookstore to Shane in return for a $20,000 promissory note. Because Shane has no assets, Marilyn insists that his supplier, Alexis, also sign the note as co-maker. Once Alexis signs the note, Marilyn

Maker
The issuer of a note

6UCC §3-501.
7UCC §3-502.
8UCC §3-503.
9UCC §3-412.
10For example, if the maker's debts are discharged in bankruptcy, he does not have to pay the note because discharge is a defense even against a holder in due course.

has the right to demand full payment from either her or Shane. Of course, if Alexis pays the note, she can demand that Shane reimburse her. If Shane refuses, it is Alexis's problem, not Marilyn's.

26-2b Drawer

Drawer
The issuer of a draft

Draft
An instrument ordering someone else to pay money

The **drawer** is the person who writes a check (or other **draft**). Checks are the most common form of a draft so we use them as an example throughout this chapter, but these same rules apply to all drafts.

The drawer of a check has *secondary* liability. He is not liable until he has received notice that the bank has dishonored the check.[11] Although the bank pays the check with the drawer's funds, the drawer is secondarily liable in the sense that he does not have to write a new check or give cash to the holder unless the bank dishonors the original check. Suppose that Shane writes a $10,000 check to pay Casey for the new inventory. Casey is nervous and, before he can get to the bank to deposit the check, he calls Shane seven times to ask whether the check is good. He even asks Shane for payment in cash instead of by check. Shane finally snarls at Casey, "Just go cash the check and get off my back, will you?" At this point, Casey has no recourse against Shane because Shane is only secondarily liable.

Anne Elliot
Kellynch, N.Y.
0912
August 27, 2019
PAY TO THE ORDER OF Frederick Wentworth $ 15,000.00
Fifteen Thousand and no/100 DOLLARS
TSN Savings Bank
MEMO real estate
Anne Elliot
010110562 766 72467 3967

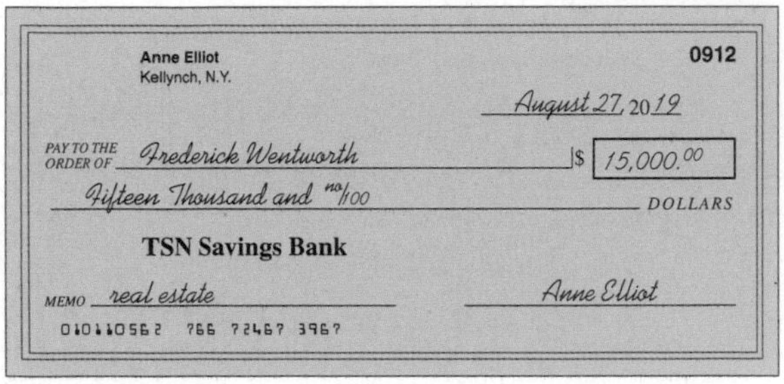

Anne Elliot is only secondarily liable, but no one is primarily liable until the bank accepts the check.

Sadly, however, Casey's fears are realized. When he presents the check to the bank teller, she informs him that Shane's account is overdrawn. Casey snatches the check off the counter and hurries over to Shane's shop. It makes no difference that Casey forgot to let the teller stamp "Insufficient Funds" on the check—notice of dishonor can be made orally. Once the bank has refused to pay, the check has been dishonored. Casey has informed Shane, who must now pay the $10,000.

26-2c Drawee

Drawee
The bank on which a check is drawn

The **drawee** is the bank on which a check is drawn. Since the draw*er* of a check is only secondarily liable, logically you might expect the drawee bank to be primarily liable. That is not the case, however. When a drawer signs a check, the instrument enters a kind of limbo. **The bank is not liable to the holder and owes no damages to the holder for refusing to pay the check.**[12] The bank may be liable to the *drawer* for violating their checking account agreement, but this contract does not extend to the holder of the check.

When a holder presents a check, the bank can do one of two things:

- Pay the check. In this case, the holder has no complaints.
- Dishonor the check. In this case, the holder must pursue remedies against the drawer.

Certified check
A check that the issuer's bank has signed, indicating its acceptance of the check

Cashier's check
A check drawn on the bank itself. It is a promise that the bank will pay out of its own funds.

Even if Shane has enough money in his account when he gives the check to Casey, it may be gone by the time Casey deposits the check. To protect himself, Casey can insist that Shane give him a certified check or a cashier's check. A **certified check** is one that the issuer's bank has signed, indicating its acceptance of the check. The bank then becomes primarily liable. A **cashier's check** is drawn on the bank itself and is a promise that the bank will pay out of its own funds. In either case, Casey is sure to be paid as long as the bank stays solvent.[13] To protect itself once it issues either check, Shane's bank will immediately remove that money from his account.

In the following case, the real estate lawyer relied on written and oral promises, instead of a certified check. As the court pointed out, he was "bamboozled."

---

[11] UCC §3-414.
[12] UCC §3-408.
[13] UCC §3-104.

Harrington v. MacNab

163 F. Supp. 2d 583
United States District Court for the District of Maryland, 2001

Facts: Richard Harrington's client sold property to the MacNabs. Although Harrington was an experienced attorney, he made a rookie mistake. The MacNabs came to the closing with a personal check drawn on their Merrill Lynch cash management account for $150,128.70. The check had not been certified. Harrington should have delayed the closing, but instead called Merrill Lynch and spoke with a Ms. Ruark. She told him there were sufficient funds in the MacNabs' account to cover the check and that she would put a hold on the account in the amount of the check. When asked to confirm this promise in writing, Ruark sent the following fax to Harrington: "This letter is to verify that the funds are available in the Merrill Lynch account. There is a pend on the funds for the check that was given you."

In fact, the MacNabs' account did not contain sufficient *cleared* funds to cover the check, which bounced. The MacNabs repeatedly promised to make the check good, but never did. Harrington paid his clients the amount owing and then sought recovery from Merrill Lynch.

Issue: ***Is Merrill Lynch liable to Harrington?***

Excerpts from Judge Smalkin's Decision: [T]he Court of Appeals of Maryland has been careful, in cases of negligent misrepresentation resulting in economic loss, to confine the tort claim to situations where the giver and the recipient of the negligently made misrepresentation or promise have an "intimate nexus," such as contractual privity or its equivalent. Here, there is simply no contractual privity or its equivalent between Mr. Harrington and Merrill Lynch, which was in a position equivalent to that of the drawee on the MacNabs' check.

That is, to hold that an "intimate nexus" relationship existed in this case would lead to the result that any payee on a check who makes inquiry is in the equivalent of contractual privity with the drawee, a proposition that would place substantial and potentially unlimited liability on drawees for uncertified checks, in contravention of the basic policies underlying the checking system in the United States as codified in the Uniform Commercial Code.

[A] drawee has no contract liability on a check to a payee unless and until it has accepted the check, *viz.*, certified it. Acceptance requires, as it has since Lord Mansfield's day,[14] the formality of the drawee's signature on the check. To recognize a cause of action under the circumstances of this case essentially would create a tort remedy allowing suit to be brought for oral certification of checks, in clear violation of the policies of the Commercial Code and hundreds of years of commercial law.

Accordingly, an Order will be entered granting Merrill Lynch's motion for summary judgment.

26-2d Indorser

An **indorser** is anyone, other than an issuer or acceptor, who signs an instrument. Shane gives Hannah a check to pay her for installing new shelves in his bookstore. On the back of Shane's check, Hannah writes, "Pay to Christian," signs her name, and then gives the check to Christian in payment for back rent. Underneath Hannah's name, Christian signs his own name and gives the check to Trustie Car Lot as a deposit on his new Prius. Hannah and Christian are both indorsers. This is the chain of ownership:

Indorser
Anyone, other than an issuer or acceptor, who signs an instrument

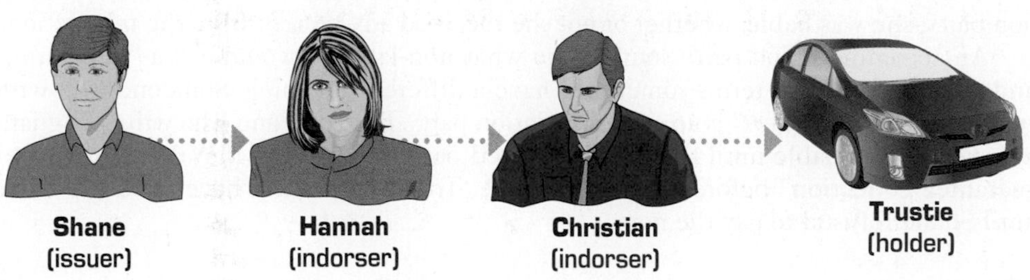

[14] 1705–1793.

Indorsers are *secondarily* liable; they must pay, but only if the issuer does not. But indorsers are liable only to those who come *after* them in the chain of ownership, not to those who held the instrument beforehand.[15] If Shane refuses to pay Trustie, the auto dealership can demand payment from Christian or Hannah. If Christian pays Trustie, Christian can then demand payment from Hannah. If, however, Hannah pays Trustie, she has no right to go after Christian because he is not liable to a previous indorser.

There are some exceptions to this rule. **Indorsers are not liable if:**

- They write the words "without recourse" next to their signature on the instrument,
- A bank certifies the check,
- The check is presented for payment more than 30 days after the indorsement, or
- The check is dishonored and the indorser is not notified within 30 days.[16]

Christian has doubts about the creditworthiness of Hannah and Shane, so he writes the words "without recourse" when he indorses the check to Trustie. This sounds like a good idea, and perhaps every indorser should try it. However, if the manager of Trustie Car Lot is familiar with the UCC, he will not accept an instrument that has been indorsed without recourse because he wants to make sure that Christian is also liable, not just Shane and Hannah. After all, Christian is the person he knows and who best knows Hannah.

26-2e Accommodation Party

Accommodation party
Someone other than an issuer, acceptor, or indorser who adds her signature to an instrument for the purpose of being liable on it

Accommodated party
Someone who receives a benefit from an accommodation party

An **accommodation party** is anyone—other than an issuer, acceptor, or indorser—who adds her signature to an instrument for the purpose of being liable on it.[17] The accommodation party typically receives no direct benefit from the instrument but is acting for the benefit of the **accommodated party**. Shane wants to buy a truck from the Trustie Car Lot. Trustie, however, will not accept a promissory note from Shane unless his father, Walter, also signs it. Shane has no assets, but Walter is wealthy. When Walter signs, he becomes an accommodation party to Shane, who is the accommodated party. The accommodation party can sign for an issuer, acceptor, or indorser. Anyone who signs an instrument is deemed to be an accommodation party unless it is clear that he is an issuer, acceptor, or indorser.

An accommodation party has the same liability to the holder as the person for whom he signed. The holder can make a claim directly against the accommodation party without first demanding payment from the accommodated party. Walter is liable to Trustie, whether or not Trustie first demands payment from Shane. If forced to pay Trustie, Walter can try to recover from Shane.

Sometimes the UCC leads to results that may seem hard and unfair. But to the drafters of the UCC, following the rules is fair. Therefore, it is crucial to understand what the rules are. Take this example: Kathy Couchot and her mother-in-law, Jean Couchot, borrowed $6,000 from a bank to pay the funeral expenses of Kathy's husband. Jean signed the note to the bank as maker, while Kathy signed as an accommodation party. Jean spent the money but did not repay the loan. When the bank sued Kathy, she argued that she was liable only for the amount of money that had directly benefited her. Predictably, the court ruled that, as an accommodation party, she was liable, whether or not she received any benefit from the transaction.[18]

An accommodation party sounds like what non-lawyers would call a "guarantor," but under the UCC these terms sometimes have a different meaning. Someone who writes "I guarantee this *instrument*" is an accommodation party. But someone who writes "I guarantee *collection*" is not liable until the accommodated party fails to pay. If Walter had written "to guarantee collection" before signing his name, Trustie could not have collected from him until Shane refused to pay the note.

---

[15] UCC §3-415.
[16] UCC §3-415.
[17] UCC §3-419.
[18] In re Couchot, 169 B.R. 40 (Bankr. S.D. Ohio 1994).

In an earlier example, Shane's supplier, Alexis, had signed a note as co-maker. What is the difference between a co-maker and an accommodation party? **The co-maker is liable both to the holder and to the other co-maker. The accommodation party is liable only to the holder, not to the maker.** If Shane pays the note on which Alexis is co-maker, then Alexis is liable to him for half the payment. But if Shane pays the note on which Walter is the accommodation party, Walter has no liability to Shane.

26-2f Agent

Many business transactions are conducted by agents acting on behalf of a principal. A corporation, for example, cannot sign an instrument itself; all of its transactions must be conducted by company employees. When signing for a principal, the agent should be careful to ensure that only the principal is liable.

To avoid personal liability when signing an instrument, an agent must (1) indicate that she is signing as an agent and (2) give the name of the principal.[19] An agent who fails to follow these two simple steps will be *personally* liable on the instrument to any holder in due course who did not know that the agent was acting for someone else. The agent will not be liable to holders who are not in due course if she can prove that the original parties did not intend for her to be liable. An agent who signs her name, "Harley Calhoun, as agent for Slippery Corp." is safe; she is not liable on the instrument. But if Harley simply signs the note, "Harley Calhoun, Agent," then she will be personally liable to Ralph, a holder in due course, unless she can prove that Ralph knew she was acting for someone else when he acquired the note. (That is a great deal of trouble easily avoided by simply including the name of the principal.) Even if Ralph is not a holder in due course, Harley will be liable unless she can prove that the original parties never intended her to be.

The principal is liable if the agent signs correctly, the agent signs just her own name, or the agent signs only the name of the principal. Thus, if Harley signs the note, "Harley Calhoun" or "Slippery Corp.," the corporation is liable to Ralph (and so is Harley). He can sue either. If Ralph recovers from Harley, she can try to recover from Slippery; but if the company goes out of business, Harley will find herself in a sticky situation. Exhibit 26.2 illustrates the liability of agents and principals.

Checks are an exception to this general rule on agent liability. If an agent is authorized to sign a check on the principal's bank account, the agent is not personally liable even if she forgets to indicate that she is simply an agent. Because the check is probably printed with the principal's name anyway, no one is likely to think that the check is coming out of the agent's personal funds.

EXAMStrategy

Question: Harold wants to buy a power catamaran for the low, low price of $175,000. He offers to give the dealer a promissory note, but the dealer will not make the sale unless Harold's partner, Maude, also signs the note. She writes her name across the top front. When and to whom is Maude liable?

Strategy: Whenever a case involves the liability of someone who has signed an instrument, you must start by reviewing the rules on signature liability. Ask first what kind of signer Maude is. Then determine the liability for someone who signs in that capacity.

Result: If Maude had signed the note in the lower-right corner, she would be a co-maker. An indorser signs on the back. An acceptor is a drawee bank. Maude is none of these things. We know, however, that anyone who signs an instrument, but is not a co-maker, acceptor, or indorser, is deemed to be an accommodation party. So that is what Maude is. The dealer can seek payment from her without first demanding payment from Harold, although if she has to pay, Harold would be liable to her. However, if Harold pays the note, she is not liable to him.

19UCC §3-402.

EXHIBIT 26.2

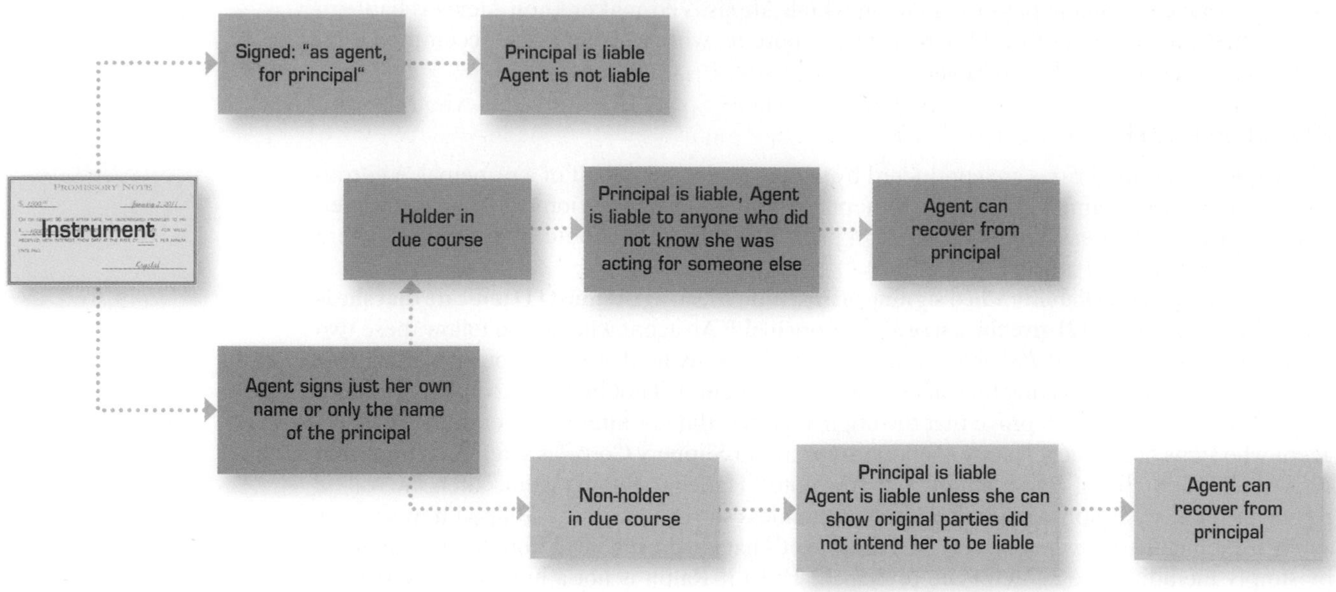

26-3 WARRANTY LIABILITY

Warranty liability
The liability of someone who receives payment on an instrument

The liability of someone who receives payment on an instrument is called **warranty liability**. These rules apply when an instrument is invalid because it has been forged, altered, or stolen.

26-3a Basic Rules of Warranty Liability

1. **The wrongdoer is always liable.** If a forger signs someone else's name to an instrument, that signature counts as the forger's, not as that of the person whose name she signed. The forger is liable for the value of the instrument plus any other expenses or lost interest that subsequent parties may experience because of the forgery. If Hope signs David's name on one of his checks, Hope is liable, but not David. Although this is a sensible rule, the problem is that forgers are difficult to catch and, even when found, often do not have the money to pay what they owe.

2. **The drawee bank is liable if it pays a check on which the *drawer's* name is forged. The bank can recover from the payee only if the payee had reason to suspect the forgery.**[20] If a bank cashes David's forged check, it must reimburse him whether or not it ever recovers from Hope. Suppose that Hope forged the check to pay for a new tattoo. If Gus, the owner of the tattoo parlor, deposits the check and the bank

20UCC §3-418.

pays it, the bank can recover from Gus only if he had reason to suspect the forgery. Perhaps Gus did suspect because "David" was the name on the check and Hope does not look much like a David.

Why hold the bank liable for something that is not its fault? In theory, the bank has David's signature on file and can determine that Hope's version does not match. As the saying goes, the drawee bank must know the drawer's signature as a mother knows her own child. Such a rule may have been appropriate in an era when people went to their neighborhood bank to cash checks and a teller would indeed recognize dear Miss Plotkin's signature. In this day and age, most checks—especially those for small amounts—are handled by machine, so perhaps this rule makes less sense. Nonetheless, the rule stands, for good reason or bad.

3. **In any other case of wrongdoing, a person who first acquires an instrument from a wrongdoer is ultimately liable to anyone else who pays value for it.** These rules are based on the provisions in Article 3 of the UCC that establish transfer and presentment warranties.

26-3b Transfer Warranties

When someone transfers an instrument, she warrants all of the following:

- She is a holder of the instrument—in other words, she is a legitimate owner,
- All signatures are authentic and authorized,
- The instrument has not been altered,
- No defense can be asserted against her, and
- As far as she knows, the issuer is solvent.[21]

When someone transfers an instrument, she promises that it is valid. The wrongdoer—the person who created the defective instrument in the first place—is always liable, but if he does not pay what he owes, the person who took it from him is liable in his place. She may not be that much at fault, but she is more at fault than any of the other innocent people who paid good value for the instrument.

Suppose that Annie writes a check for $100 to pay for a fancy dinner at Barbara's Bistro. Cecelia steals the check from Barbara's cash register, indorses Barbara's name, and uses the check to buy a leather jacket from Deirdre. In her turn, Deirdre takes the check home and indorses it over to her condominium association to pay her monthly service fee. Barbara notices the check is gone and asks Annie to stop payment on it. Once payment is stopped, the condominium association cannot cash the check. Who is liable to whom? The chain of ownership looks like this:

21UCC §3-416.

Cecelia is the wrongdoer and, of course, she is liable. Unfortunately, she is currently studying at the University of the Azores and refuses to return to the United States. The condominium association makes a claim against Deirdre. When she transferred the check, she warranted that all the signatures were authentic and authorized, but that was not true because Barbara's signature was forged. (Deirdre should have asked Cecelia for identification.) Deirdre cannot make a claim against Annie or Barbara because neither of them violated their transfer warranties—all the signatures at that point were authentic and authorized.

There are a few additional wrinkles to the transfer warranty rules:

- When someone violates the transfer warranties, **she is liable for the value of the instrument, plus expenses and interest**. If the condominium association is charged a fee by the bank for the returned check, Deirdre must pay it.
- **Transfer warranties flow to all subsequent holders in good faith who have indorsed the instrument.** If the condominium association indorses the check over to its maintenance company, Deirdre is liable when the maintenance company makes a claim.
- **If the instrument is *bearer* paper, the transfer warranties extend only to the first transferee.** If Annie had made her check out to cash, it would have been bearer paper, and her transfer warranties would have extended only to Barbara. If Barbara transfers the check to Hannah, Barbara's transfer warranties extend to Hannah; Annie's do not.
- **If a warranty claim is not made within 30 days of discovering the breach, damages are reduced by the amount of harm that the delay caused.** Suppose that the condominium association waits two months to tell Deirdre the check is invalid. Cecelia has been into Deirdre's store several times to try on matching leather pants. By the time Deirdre finds out the check is bad, Cecelia has again left town. Deirdre may not be liable on the check at all because the delay has prevented her from making a claim against Cecelia.
- **Transfer warranties apply only if the instrument has been transferred for consideration.** Suppose Deirdre gives the check to an employee, Emily, as a birthday present. When the check turns out to be worthless, Emily has no claim against Deirdre.

The following sad case illustrates how important transfer warranties are and how easy it is to be conned, even if you are a careful person. Is there anything more Quimby could have done to protect himself?

You Be the Judge

Quimby v. Bank of America

2009 U.S. Dist. LEXIS 98575; 2009 WL 3517984
United States District Court for the District of Oregon, 2009

Facts: Steve Szabo, a Venezuelan resident, had a checking account with the Bank of America in Palm Beach Gardens, Florida. Someone with an internet address in Nigeria hacked into Szabo's account online, called the bank's customer service department to change the telephone number listed on the account, and ordered blank checks.

Someone then wrote a check on Szabo's account for $120,000 to pay for an investment in Freddie Quimby's gold mine. On February 20, Quimby presented the check for payment at the Bank of America's branch in Osburn, Idaho. At Quimby's request, the branch manager verified through Bank of America's records that Szabo's account had sufficient funds to cover the check. The branch manager also called the telephone number in Szabo's account records and spoke to someone claiming to be Szabo, who confirmed that the check was valid.

Quimby indorsed the check to the bank and received in return a cashier's check for $120,000, which he deposited to his account at Bank of America in Baker City, Oregon. (You remember that a cashier's check is a check drawn on the bank itself.) "Szabo" then contacted Quimby, stating that he had changed his mind about the gold mine investment and asking Quimby to return the funds. On February 22, Quimby wired $111,000.00 from his account with Bank of America to an account in Hong Kong. Those funds disappeared, and Bank of America was unable to reclaim them.

On March 3, the real Szabo reported to the bank that his signature on the Quimby check was a forgery. The bank repaid Szabo and then filed suit against Quimby, seeking repayment on the cashier's check it had issued to him, with interest. The bank argued that Quimby had violated his transfer warranties when he indorsed the forged check to it.

You Be the Judge: *Did Quimby violate his transfer warranties? Is he liable to the Bank of America?*

Argument for the Bank: When Quimby indorsed the check to the bank, he warranted that all signatures were authentic and authorized. That was not true—the signature was a forgery and the check was invalid. Moreover, he waited only two days before wiring the funds. If he had waited longer, the fraud might have been discovered in time.

The bank had to refund $120,000 to Szabo. Quimby must repay the bank.

Argument for Quimby: This whole problem is the bank's fault. Let us count the ways: The bank (1) permitted a thief to hack into Szabo's account, (2) issued blank checks to the thief, (3) assured Quimby that there were good funds to pay the check, (4) issued a cashier's check to Quimby, and (5) wired funds to Hong Kong that it cannot trace.

In short, the bank was repeatedly negligent and now it seeks to recover from Quimby, who did all he could to ensure that the check was valid. That is unfair and preposterous.

26-3c Comparison of Signature Liability and Transfer Warranties

Transfer warranties fill in holes left by the signature liability rules:

- A forged signature is invalid and therefore creates no signature liability on the part of the person whose name was signed. However, someone who receives a forged instrument may recover under transfer warranty rules, which provide that anyone who transfers a forged instrument is liable for it.
- The signature liability rules do not apply to the transfer of bearer paper. Bearer paper can be negotiated simply by delivery; no indorsement is required. No signature means no signature liability (for anyone other than the issuer—who is the only person actually signing the instrument). Transfer warranties apply to each transfer of bearer paper (although the transferor of bearer paper is liable only to the person to whom he gives the instrument, not to any transferees further down the line).
- Under the signature liability rules, the holder of an instrument cannot make a claim until the indorser or drawer has been notified that the instrument was presented and dishonored.[22] Under the transfer warranty rules, the holder need not wait for presentment or dishonor before making a claim against the transferor.

26-3d Presentment Warranties

Transfer warranties impose liability on anyone who sells a negotiable instrument, such as Deirdre. **Presentment warranties** apply to someone who demands payment for an instrument from the maker, drawee, or anyone else liable on it. Thus, if the condominium association cashes Annie's check, it is subject to presentment warranties because it is demanding payment from her bank, the drawee. In a sense, transfer warranties apply to all transfers *away* from the issuer; presentment warranties apply when the instrument *returns* to the maker or drawee for payment. As a general rule, payment on an instrument is final, and the payer has

22 UCC §3-503(a).

no right to a refund, unless the presentment warranties are violated. **Anyone who presents a *check* for payment warrants all of the following:**

- She is a holder,
- The check has not been altered, and
- She has no reason to believe the drawer's signature is forged.[23]

If any of these promises is untrue, the bank has a right to demand a refund from the presenter. Suppose that Adam writes a $500 check to pay Bruce for repairing his motorcycle. Bruce changes the amount of the check to $1,500 and indorses it over to Chip as payment for an oil bill. When Chip deposits the check, the bank credits his account for $1,500 and deducts the same amount from Adam's account. When Adam discovers the alteration, the bank credits his account for $1,000. Chip violated his *presentment* warranties when he deposited an altered check (even though he did not *know* it was altered). Although Chip was not at fault, he must still reimburse the bank for $1,000. But Chip is not without recourse—Bruce violated his *transfer* warranties to Chip (by transferring an altered check). Bruce must repay the $1,000. Chip loses out only if he cannot make Bruce pay.

The presentment warranty rules for a promissory note are different from those for a check. **Anyone who presents a *promissory note* for payment makes only one warranty—that he is a holder of the instrument.** Someone presenting a note does not need to warrant that the note is unaltered or the maker's signature is authentic because a note is presented for payment to the issuer himself. The issuer presumably remembers the amount of the note and whether he signed it. Suppose Adam gives a promissory note to Bruce to pay for a new motorcycle. If Bruce increases the note from $5,000 to $10,000 before he presents it for payment in six months' time, Adam will almost certainly realize the note has been changed and refuse to pay it.

The presenter of a note warrants that he is a holder. A forged signature prevents subsequent owners from being a holder, so anyone who presents a note with a forged signature is violating the presentment warranties. Suppose that Bruce is totally honest and does not alter the note, but Chip steals it and forges Bruce's indorsement before passing the note on to Donald, who presents it to Adam for payment. Donald has violated his *presentment* warranties because he is not a holder. Adam can refuse to pay him. For his part, Donald can claim repayment from Chip, who violated his *transfer* warranties by passing on a note with a forged signature.

EXAMStrategy

Question: Hillary owed Evan $500. She gave Evan's roommate John a check made out to Evan. John indorsed the check to Mike by signing Evan's name. Mike deposited the check in his account at the Amstel Bank. Amstel removed $500 from Hillary's account. Are John and Mike liable on this check?

Strategy: Whenever an instrument goes astray, begin by asking which warranties have been violated and by whom.

Result: Transfer warranties apply to all transfers *away* from the issuer; presentment warranties apply when the instrument *returns* to the maker or drawee for payment. John violated transfer warranties because Evan's signature is neither authentic nor authorized. When Mike deposited the check, he violated presentment warranties because he is not a holder. Remember from Chapter 25 that a holder is anyone in possession of an instrument if it is payable to or indorsed to him. This check was not properly indorsed to Mike because Evan has not signed it. John and Mike are liable. In the next section, we will see that Amstel is also liable because it paid a forged check.

23UCC §3-417.

26-4 OTHER LIABILITY RULES

This section contains other UCC rules that establish liability for wrongdoing on instruments.

26-4a Conversion Liability

Conversion means that (1) someone has stolen an instrument or (2) a bank has paid a check that has a forged indorsement.[24] The rightful owner of the instrument can recover from either the thief or the bank.

Conversion
(1) Someone has stolen an instrument or (2) a bank has paid a check that has a forged indorsement.

For example, Glenn Altman was a lawyer representing Barbara Kirchoff. He settled her case for $12,000, but when he received the check, he forged her indorsement and deposited the check in his own account without telling her. He gave her the money four months later, but by then she had discovered his dishonesty. What claims do the various parties have?

Kirchoff has a claim against the bank because it paid a check with a forged indorsement. If the bank pays Kirchoff, then it can recover from Altman because he violated his presentment warranties. Note, however, that Kirchoff could not sue Altman for violating presentment warranties because he had not presented the check to her for payment. Nor could she sue him for violating transfer warranties because he had not transferred the check *to* her. To the contrary, he had transferred the check *away* from her.

Kirchoff does have a claim against Altman for conversion because he stole the check from her.[25] What about the issuer of the check—can it also sue Altman for conversion? No, an action for conversion cannot be brought by an issuer because the check technically belongs to the payee (Kirchoff). The issuer can bring a claim only against the bank that pays the forged check.

... he forged her indorsement and deposited the check in his own account without telling her.

26-4b Impostor Rule

If someone issues an instrument to an impostor, then any indorsement in the name of the imposter payee is valid as long as the person (a bank, say) who pays the instrument does not know of the fraud.[26] A teenager knocks on your door and tells you he is selling magazine subscriptions to pay for a school trip to Washington, D.C. After signing up for *Career* and *Popular Accounting*, you make out a check to "Family Magazine Subscriptions." Unfortunately, the boy does not represent Family Magazine at all. He does cash the check, however, by forging an indorsement for the magazine company. Is the bank liable for cashing the fraudulent check?

No. The teenager was an impostor—he said he represented the magazine company, but he did not. If anyone indorses the check in the name of the payee (Family Magazine Subscriptions), you must pay the check and the bank is not liable. Does this rule seem harsh? Maybe, but you were in the best position to determine if the teenager really worked for the magazine company. You were more at fault than the bank, and you must pay. Of course, the teenager would be liable to you, if you could ever find him.

Note that the Imposter Rule does not apply to this chapter's opening scenario because Friese did not issue the instrument to Mulligan. The check was somehow stolen, through no fault of Friese's.

---

24 UCC §3-420.

25 A payee (i.e., Kirchoff) cannot bring a claim for conversion unless she first receives the check. In this case, Altman was Kirchoff's agent and he received the check for her, so she could bring a conversion action against him.

26 UCC §3-404(a).

26-4c Fictitious Payee Rule

If someone issues an instrument to a person who does not exist, then any indorsement in the name of the payee is valid as long as the person (a bank, say) who pays the instrument does not know of the fraud.[27] The *Impostor* Rule applies if you give a check with a real name to the wrong person. The *Fictitious Payee* Rule applies if you write a check to someone who does not exist. This type of fraud can be very difficult to prevent. Even a large law firm was stung. Dennis Masellis, the manager of payroll for Baker & McKenzie's New York office, stole more than $7 million from the firm by creating fictitious employees and then depositing their salaries in his own account.

26-4d Employee Indorsement Rule

If an employee with responsibility for issuing instruments forges a check or other instrument, then any indorsement in the name of the payee, or a similar name, is valid as long as the person (a bank, say) who pays the instrument does not know of the fraud.[28] A dishonest employee, especially one with the authority to issue checks, has the opportunity to steal a great deal of money. The employer cannot shift blame (and liability) onto the bank that unknowingly cashes the forged checks because the employer was more to blame—it not only hired the thief, it failed to supervise him carefully.

Dennis M. Hartotunian had a major gambling problem—he owed nearly $10 million. Unfortunately, he was also the controller and accountant for the Aesar Group, a precious metals company. Over the course of three years, he wrote himself 154 checks worth $9.24 million. Any check for more than $500 required the signature of Aesar's general manager, but Hartotunian forged it. After an internal audit revealed that millions were missing, company officers asked to talk with Hartotunian. When he heard they were coming, he walked out and never came back.

It is always a bad sign when the company controller disappears. If an employee is generally authorized to prepare or sign checks, then the bank is not liable on checks that the employee forges. Hartotunian was clearly covered by this rule because he was the company controller. If he had been a mailroom employee without authority to sign checks, the bank would have been liable. The employee indorsement rule applies to both single and double forgeries. In a **single forgery**, the employee writes a check to himself, signs his employer's name, and cashes the check. In a **double forgery**, the employee writes a check to someone else, forges his employer's name, and also forges the name of the payee.

iStockphoto.com/pepifoto

Does this teenager look authorized to cash a business check?

26-4e Negligence

Regardless of the Impostor Rule, the Fictitious Payee Rule, and the Employee Indorsement Rule (the "three Rules"), **anyone who behaves negligently in creating or paying an unauthorized instrument is liable to an innocent third party**. If two people are negligent, they share the loss according to their negligence. Here are two examples:

- **Anyone who is careless in paying an unauthorized instrument is liable, despite the three Rules.**[29] Suppose that the boy selling bogus magazine subscriptions goes into the bank and indorses the check: "Family Magazine Subscriptions, by Butch McGraw." The teller peers over her counter and sees a 13-year-old boy standing there with torn jeans and a baseball cap. She may be negligent if she cashes the check without asking for further identification. And, in that case, the bank would be liable.
- **Anyone who is careless in allowing a forged or altered instrument to be created is also liable, whether or not he has violated one of the three Rules.** W. Foutch bought a cow from B. Foutch. W. signed a blank check and then watched B. fill in the amount of

27UCC §3-404(b).

28UCC §3-405.

29UCC §§3-404(d), 3-405(b).

$18. However, as he did so, B. left space in front of both the numbers and the words on the check. Later, he added the number "4" in front of "18" and the words "four hundred" in front of "eighteen." On the memo line, he added the words "& note" after "cow." Because B. had filled out the check, all the writing was the same.

When B. cashed the check at the bank, it paid him $418. W. sued the bank for $400 on the grounds that it had paid an altered check. However, the court ruled that, because W. had been so negligent in allowing B. to fill out the check with blank spaces, the bank was not liable.[30]

In the following case, a luxury department store allowed a customer to pay her bills with checks from someone else's account. Was the store liable to the victim?

Burns v. Neiman Marcus Group, Inc.

173 Cal. App. 4th 479
California Court of Appeals, 2009

Facts: During the time that Carol Young worked as an assistant to Brian P. Burns, her salary never exceeded $75,000 a year. But during this period, she opened several credit card accounts with Neiman Marcus on which she charged more than $1 million in luxury goods. Although Neiman knew Young's salary, it assigned her a personal shopper to encourage more buying.

Young was paying for all these purchases by forging checks from Burns's personal bank account and then taking them to the Customer Service Center in Neiman Marcus's San Francisco store—sometimes several days in a row. When Young received Burns's bank statements, she systematically destroyed her forged Neiman Marcus checks and altered Burns's account records to make it appear the checks had been to other third parties. This behavior went on for 12 years.

When Burns finally realized what was going on, he could no longer sue the bank because that statute of limitations had expired. Instead, Burns sued Neiman Marcus, alleging that the company was liable because of its negligence in accepting Burns's checks to pay Young's bills. Burns argued that, when Neiman Marcus saw these massive checks drawn on his personal account, it should have contacted him, especially since the company knew that Young could not possibly afford such large expenditures.

The trial court found for Neiman Marcus and Burns appealed.

Issue: ***Is Neiman Marcus liable for the checks that Young forged?***

Excerpts from Judge Mahoney's Decision: Regardless of the internal policies that a merchant might have in place to verify third party checks, there are practical problems with imposing a duty of inquiry on a retail merchant before he can accept a person's payment for goods and services. Because the retail merchant could not rely upon anything told to him by the person tendering the third party check, the retail merchant would have to stop his business every time he received such a check in order to make an *independent* inquiry of the drawer.

Assuming the retail merchant could readily locate the drawer of the check, he would then have to ascertain what would constitute a reasonable inquiry so as to avoid liability. Would one or two attempts to reach the drawer by telephone be sufficient; or would a letter have to be written? The scope of this proposed—yet ill-defined—duty of inquiry is boundless, and would impose a significant and unwarranted burden on retail merchants to ascertain the veracity of a third party check any time the instrument is proffered in payment for goods and services, which would far outweigh any resulting benefit in detecting the isolated instance of embezzlement.

There is no allegation that Neiman Marcus actively participated in Young's alleged embezzlement of funds from plaintiff. Plaintiff's failure to detect Young's alleged embezzlement within the statute of limitations timeframe should not be the impetus for imposing liability on other persons in the chain of custody of the checks. As among the parties to this dispute, plaintiff—whose misplaced trust or inattention enabled Young to misappropriate funds, undetected, for years—was plainly the party best able to prevent the losses and to protect himself by insurance. Had plaintiff properly reviewed his bank statements over the 12 years, he would, of course, have realized that his checks were being diverted.

Accordingly, we reject plaintiff's invitation to impose a duty upon Neiman Marcus.

30 Foutch v. Alexandria Bank & Trust Co., 177 Tenn. 348 (1941).

EXAMStrategy

Question: Jonathan is the head of payroll at Yearbook, Inc. He issues checks to his sister, Elizabeth, who happens *not* to work for Yearbook. She does, however, deposit the checks into her bank account. A teller at the bank knows that Elizabeth does not work for Yearbook, but he deposits the checks for her without raising any questions. Is the bank liable for the fraudulent checks?

Strategy: Whenever fraudulent checks are signed by an authorized employee, you will naturally think first of the Employee Indorsement Rule. However, it is important to remember that the bank's negligence overrides this rule.

Result: If the bank was not negligent, then under the Employee Indorsement Rule, it would not be liable because Jonathan was authorized to sign checks. However, because the bank was negligent in paying the checks, it must share the loss with Yearbook. The amount each would have to pay depends upon their share of the blame.

26-4f Crimes

It is beyond the scope of this chapter to catalog all of the crimes that can be committed with negotiable instruments, but students should be aware of these.

Bouncing a Check

It is illegal to write a check on an account that has insufficient funds. Generally, no serious penalties are imposed if sufficient funds are immediately deposited. (This is a good thing, considering that hundreds of *millions* of checks bounce each year.) However, both banks and merchants impose substantial fees for their trouble. People who make a career of bouncing checks may find they have plenty of time to read up on UCC Article 3 in the prison library.

Check Kiting

Check kiting
Moving funds between bank accounts to take advantage of the float

Check kiting means moving funds between bank accounts to take advantage of the float.[31] It is possible because banks start paying interest before deposits clear. But it is illegal. Saquib Khan owned a wholesale cigarette and grocery business on Staten Island, New York. Then Hurricane Sandy destroyed many of the businesses to which he sold goods. Desperate to pay his bills, Khan began large-scale check kiting. He wrote checks to himself which he deposited in one bank, and then, before those funds had cleared, wrote checks on (or wired funds from) that account to deposit in a different bank. In the end, he wrote wrongful checks totaling $82 million, on which he received millions of dollars in interest.[32] He ultimately pleaded guilty to bank fraud and faced up to six years in prison and deportation to Pakistan.[33]

Forgery

Utter
To pass on an instrument that one knows to be forged

It is illegal to forge an instrument or to pass on (**utter**) an instrument that one knows to be forged. In the United States, billions of dollars of checks are forged each year.

31"Float" is the period after an account holder writes a check but before the check clears and that money is deducted from his account.

32Sam Dolnick, "$82 Million Fraud Was Staged With Bad Checks, U.S. Asserts," *The New York Times*, February 21, 2013.

33Mosi Secret, "Staten Island Wholesale King Pleads Guilty to Bank Fraud," *The New York Times*, May 21, 2013.

26-5 DISCHARGE

26-5a Discharge of the Obligor

Discharge
Liability on an instrument terminates

Discharge means that liability on an instrument terminates. Article 3 establishes five different ways to discharge an instrument[34]:

- **By Payment.** Payment discharges an instrument, as long as the payment is *from* someone obliged to pay and goes *to* the holder. If you mail a check to the wrong bank when paying off a promissory note, you obviously have not discharged the note. Or if you ask an employee to take money to the bank to pay off the note, but she goes to Hawaii instead, no discharge has occurred. Similarly, payment does not discharge an instrument if the payor knows that the instrument is stolen.
- **Agreement.** The parties to the instrument can agree to a discharge, even if the instrument is not paid. The discharge, however, must be in writing; it cannot be oral. You give a promissory note to your company to pay for company stock. The company president tells you that the company will forgive the loan and discharge the note as a reward for your fabulous performance. A few months later, the president is ousted. Your agreement was not in writing and you are liable on the note. (You may have a contract claim against the company, but the note itself is still valid.)

One way to cancel an instrument.

John Foxx/Stockbyte/Getty Images

- **Cancellation.** Cancellation means the intentional, voluntary surrender, destruction, or disfigurement of an instrument. If Ted accidentally forgets to take a check out of his pocket before throwing his shirt in the wash, he has not canceled the check (even though it was destroyed) because the destruction was unintentional. If, while arguing with his business partner, he takes her promissory note and tears it into a thousand pieces while screaming, "This is what I think of you and your business skills," he has canceled the note. He could achieve the same result less dramatically by simply writing "canceled" on it or by giving it back to her.
- **Certification.** When a bank certifies or accepts a check, the drawer and all indorsers of the check are discharged, and only the bank is liable.
- **Alteration.** An instrument is discharged if its terms are intentionally changed. Laura gives Todd a promissory note. Thinking he is being very clever, Todd changes the amount of her note from $200 to $2,000. He has actually done Laura a favor because he has discharged the note.

Keep in mind, however, that no discharge is effective against a holder in due course who acquires the instrument without knowledge of the discharge. If Todd sells Laura's note to Max, who does not know of the discharge, Max can enforce the instrument against Laura, but only for the original amount of $200.

The following case involves a mystery: A canceled note arrives in the mail. No one knows who sent it or why. Was the cancellation valid?

34UCC Article 3, Part 6.

Manley v. Wachovia Small Bus. Capital

349 S.W.3d 233
Texas Court of Appeals, 2011

Facts: File this case under: What parents will do for their children (whether or not they should). Wachovia Bank loaned Daniel Manley $420,000 in return for a promissory note in that amount. His father, Thomas, guaranteed payment of the note. Seven years later, Daniel stopped making payments, so Wachovia sent him a default notice. When he did not resume payments, the bank filed suit to collect the money owed.

At trial, Thomas testified that, shortly after Daniel received his first default notice, he, Thomas, had taken $375,000 in $100 bills to Wachovia as a payment on the note. Thomas further testified that he had asked for a receipt from the bank employee to whom he had given the cash but the employee had told him that a receipt would be mailed to him after the cash was counted. Thomas never got a receipt but, three months later, Daniel received the original note in the mail. It was in a Wachovia envelope and had been stamped "Paid."

Wachovia employees testified they had no record of a $375,000 cash payment and that the note had never been paid. Nor could they find the original note. They had no idea who had marked the note paid, or how Daniel had possession of it.

Daniel and Thomas argued that, by marking the note "paid," Wachovia had discharged it and they were no longer liable.

Issues: ***Was the note discharged? Were the Manley men liable on it?***

Excerpts from Justice Moseley's Decision[35]: The Manleys rely on [Section 3.604 of the UCC], which provides that the person entitled to enforce the instrument may discharge the obligation by an intentional voluntary act. The Manleys contend Wachovia's acts of stamping the original note "paid" and sending it to Daniel were intentional and voluntary and are conclusive evidence that Wachovia discharged the note. [T]hey assert that only the act (stamping and returning the note) must be intentional and voluntary, not the result (discharge of the obligation). We disagree.

Discharge requires the intent to render the instrument ineffective as a legal obligation. This intent requirement has led courts to conclude that mistakenly marking a note "paid" (or the equivalent) will not discharge the debt.

There is evidence that although the note was stamped paid, it had not, in fact, been paid and amounts remained due and owing at the time of trial. There is also evidence Wachovia's normal procedures following the payment of a note were not followed in this case, and [an employee] testified that it was a mistake for Daniel to receive the note. This, along with other evidence in the record, is some evidence that the surrender of the note and stamping it paid were the result of a mistake and not intentional or voluntary.

[W]e conclude the mere fact Daniel received the original note in a Wachovia envelope with "paid" stamped on it does not conclusively prove that Wachovia, by an intentional voluntary act, discharged Daniel's obligation on the note.

26-5b Discharge of an Indorser or Accommodation Party

Article 3 provides that virtually any change in an instrument that harms an indorser or accommodation party also discharges them unless they consent to the change. These fatal changes include an extension of the due date on the instrument, a material modification of the instrument, or any impairment of the collateral that secures the instrument. When Chelsea borrows money from Jordan, she issues a promissory note due on December 24. Helena signs the note as an accommodation party. Chelsea cannot pay, but Jordan does not have the nerve to declare Chelsea in default on Christmas Eve. He generously extends the due date for another week. Helena is no longer liable, even secondarily, because Jordan has granted an extension of the due date.

35For ease of reading the opinion, we have substituted "the Manleys" for "Appellants."

CHAPTER CONCLUSION

It is never wise to play an important game without understanding the rules. As you can see from the cases in this chapter, real harm can come to those who do not know the rules of negotiable instruments.

EXAM REVIEW

1. **PRIMARY V. SECONDARY LIABILITY** Someone who is primarily liable on a negotiable instrument must pay unless he has a valid defense. Those with secondary liability only pay if the person with primary liability does not.

2. **PAYMENT PROCESS** The payment process for a negotiable instrument comprises as many as three steps:
   - Presentment. The holder makes a demand for payment to the issuer.
   - Dishonor. The instrument is due, but the issuer does not pay.
   - Notice of Dishonor. The holder of the instrument notifies those who are secondarily liable that the instrument has been dishonored.

3. **PRIMARY SIGNATURE LIABILITY** The maker of a note is primarily liable.

4. **SECONDARY SIGNATURE LIABILITY**
   - The drawer of a check has secondary liability: he is not liable until he has received notice that the bank has dishonored the check.
   - Indorsers are secondarily liable; they must pay if the issuer does not. But an indorser is only liable to those who come after him in the chain of ownership, not to those who held the instrument before he did.

EXAMStrategy

Question: Sidney entered into a contract for $35,000 with MacDonald Roofing Co., Inc., to reroof his building. Sidney made his initial payment by writing a check for $17,500 payable to "MacDonald Roofing Company, Inc., and Friendly Supply Company." MacDonald took the check to Friendly and requested an indorsement, which Friendly provided. When MacDonald failed to complete the roofing work, Sidney filed suit for damages against Friendly. Sidney argued that Friendly was liable as an indorser. Do you agree?

Strategy: Whenever you are faced with an issue of indorser liability, remember that indorsers are liable only to those who come after them in the chain of ownership. (See the "Result" at the end of this Exam Review section.)

5. **SIGNATURE LIABILITY FOR AN ACCOMMODATION PARTY** The accommodation party signs an instrument to benefit the accommodated party. By signing the instrument, an accommodation party agrees to be liable on it, whether or not she directly benefits from it. She has the same liability as the person for whom she signed.

6. **SIGNATURE LIABILITY OF AN AGENT** To avoid personal liability when signing an instrument, an agent must indicate that he is signing as an agent and must give the name of the principal.

7. **WARRANTY LIABILITY** The basic rules of warranty liability are as follows:
   - The wrongdoer is always liable.
   - The drawee bank is responsible if it pays a check on which the drawer's name is forged.
   - In any other case of wrongdoing, a person who initially acquires an instrument from a wrongdoer is ultimately liable to anyone else who pays value for it.

8. **TRANSFER WARRANTIES** When someone transfers an instrument, she warrants all of the following:
   - She is a holder of the instrument.
   - All signatures are authentic and authorized.
   - The instrument has not been altered.
   - No defense can be asserted against her.
   - As far as she knows, the issuer is solvent.

9. **PRESENTMENT WARRANTIES FOR A CHECK** Anyone who presents a check for payment warrants all of the following:
   - She is a holder.
   - The check has not been altered.
   - She has no reason to believe the drawer's signature is forged.

10. **PRESENTMENT WARRANTIES FOR A NOTE** The presenter of a note only warrants that he is a holder.

11. **CONVERSION** Conversion means that (1) someone has stolen an instrument or (2) a bank has paid a check that has a forged indorsement. The rightful owner of the instrument can recover from either the wrongdoer or the bank.

EXAMStrategy

Question: Marie hired an attorney, James, to collect money she was owed. When James received the check payable to Marie for $26,676.16, he forged her indorsement and deposited the check in his own account at the bank. He later withdrew the entire amount. Is the bank liable to Marie?

Strategy: Checks go astray in two ways: Either someone transfers the check on purpose (to the wrong person or for the wrong reason, but nonetheless, on purpose) or someone steals the check. Whenever the check is stolen, it is conversion. In the case of conversion, the rightful owner can recover from either the thief or the bank that pays the check. (See the "Result" at the end of this Exam Review section.)

12. **IMPOSTOR RULE** If someone issues an instrument to an impostor, then any indorsement in the name of the payee is valid as long as the person who pays the instrument is ignorant of the fraud.

13. **FICTITIOUS PAYEE RULE** If someone issues an instrument to a person who does not exist, then any indorsement in the name of the payee is valid as long as the person who pays the instrument does not know of the fraud.

14. **EMPLOYEE INDORSEMENT RULE** If an employee with responsibility for issuing instruments forges a check or other instrument, then any indorsement in the name of the payee is valid as long as the person who pays the instrument is ignorant of the fraud.

15. **LIABILITY FOR NEGLIGENCE** Anyone who behaves negligently in creating or paying an unauthorized instrument is liable to an innocent third party. If two people are negligent, they share the loss according to their relative negligence.

16. **DISCHARGE** Discharge means that liability on an instrument terminates. An instrument may be discharged by payment, agreement, cancellation, certification, or alteration.

EXAMStrategy

CPA Question: Vex Corp. executed a negotiable promissory note payable to Tamp, Inc. The note was collaterized by some of Vex's business assets. Tamp negotiated the note to Miller for value. Miller indorsed the note in blank and negotiated it to Bilco for value. Before the note became due, Bilco agreed to release Vex's collateral. Vex refused to pay Bilco when the note became due. Bilco promptly notified Miller and Tamp of Vex's default. Which of the following statements is correct?

(a) Bilco will be unable to collect from Miller because Miller's indorsement was in blank.

(b) Bilco will be able to collect from either Tamp or Miller because Bilco was a holder in due course.

(c) Bilco will be unable to collect from either Tamp or Miller because of Bilco's release of the collateral.

(d) Bilco will be able to collect from Tamp because Tamp was the original payee.

Strategy: For this question, you can save time by quickly identifying the one right answer and not agonizing over each possibility. You know that if an indorser is in any way harmed by the acts of a subsequent holder, the indorser is discharged. (See the "Result" at the end of this Exam Review section.)

RESULTS

4. Result: In this case, Sidney issued the check and came before Friendly in the chain of ownership. Friendly is not liable.

11. Result: Marie can recover from the bank.

16. Result: In this case, Bilco has released Vex's collateral, thereby harming the two indorsers because now there are fewer assets that can be used to pay the note. The correct answer is (c).

MULTIPLE-CHOICE QUESTIONS

1. **CPA QUESTION** A check has the following indorsements on the back:

   Paul Frank
   Without recourse
   George Hopkins
   Payment guaranteed
   Ann Quarry
   Collection guaranteed
   Rachel Ott

   Which of the following conditions occurring subsequent to the indorsements would discharge all of the indorsers?
   (a) Lack of notice of dishonor
   (b) Late presentment
   (c) Insolvency of the maker
   (d) Certification of the check

2. **CPA QUESTION** Which of the following actions does not discharge a prior party to a commercial instrument?
   (a) Good-faith payment or satisfaction of the instrument
   (b) Cancellation of that prior party's indorsement
   (c) The holder's oral renunciation of that prior party's liability
   (d) The holder's intentional destruction of the instrument

3. What is the difference between a co-maker and an accommodation party?
   (a) A co-maker is liable both to the holder and the other co-maker, while an accommodation party is liable only to the holder.
   (b) A co-maker is liable to subsequent indorsers, while an accommodation party is not.
   (c) A co-maker is liable only to the other co-maker, while the accommodation party is liable to the holder.
   (d) A co-maker is not liable once a bank certifies a check, while an accommodation party is still liable even after certification.

4. Karim writes a check to Lew but Karim's bank accidently refuses to pay the check, despite the fact that Karim's account has sufficient funds. As a result, Lew bounces

many checks from his own account and has to pay substantial fees to his bank. Which of the following statements is true?

(a) Lew can recover damages from both Karim and Karim's bank.
(b) Lew can recover damages only from Karim.
(c) Lew can recover damages only from Karim's bank.
(d) Lew cannot recover any damages.

5. Nan forges Mina's name on a check to buy a television set from Costmart. The store deposits that check into its account at Bank, but Bank does not credit Costmart's account for the amount of the check. From whom can Costmart recover?

(a) Nan
(b) Mina
(c) Bank
(d) All of these

CASE QUESTIONS

1. One of Doris's job responsibilities at Winkie, Inc., was preparing company checks for the president, Willie, to sign. Using Winkie's check-signing machine, Doris forged $150,000 of checks on her employer's account. Willie did not (1) look at the sequence of check numbers, (2) examine the monthly account statements, or (3) reconcile company records with bank statements. Winkie's bank, as a matter of policy, did not check indorsements on checks with a face value of less than $1,000. By accident, it paid a forged check that had not even been indorsed. Is the bank liable to Winkie, Inc., for the forged checks?

2. Before Parris's lawsuit against Railroad had settled, he left town and closed out his account with Bank. Railroad then issued a check to him which somehow came to be in Eddy's possession. Eddy indorsed the check "Railroad Eddy" and deposited it in his own account at Bank. Parris sued Bank, alleging that it was liable to him for having paid the check over an unauthorized indorsement. Is Bank liable to Parris? On what theory?

3. Merlyn borrowed money from Finance Co. to buy equipment for his farm. He promised Finance that he would accept payment for his crops only with checks that named him and Finance as co-payees. This way, Merlyn could not cash the checks without Finance's indorsement. Merlyn sold corn to Farmer's Co-op, which paid by check made out to "Merlyn, Finance Co." When Merlyn deposited this check, the comma between Merlyn and Finance appeared as "or." Only Merlyn had indorsed the check. When Finance sued Bank for having paid this check, Bank in turn filed suit against Merlyn, demanding indemnification for Finance's claims. What claim did Bank make against Merlyn?

4. David had five bank accounts spread over four banks. Each morning, he directed his assistant, Maureen, to call all of the banks and obtain balance information. He would then direct her to write checks transferring funds in each account to another account. Is there any problem with this practice?

5. Regions Bank refused to lend money to ZLM, Inc., unless its owner, Stewart, signed the note as an accommodation party. He did, and, sadly, ZLM did not repay the loan. But because the note was due on February 16, which that year happened to be Mardi Gras Day (a major festival in Louisiana), the bank waited until the next day to declare the note in default. Stewart alleged that he was not liable on the note because the extension had discharged his liability. Do you agree?

DISCUSSION QUESTIONS

1. Recall the *Quimby* case. This type of fraud is increasingly common. What could Quimby have done to avoid this problem?

2. Mary wrote a check on her account at First Bank for $23,000.00 payable to the order of Eagle Construction Company. Sylvia, who was an Eagle employee, deposited Mary's check in her personal account at Second Bank, without first having someone indorse it. When the check was presented for payment, First Bank paid. Only later did it realize that the check had no indorsement. Meanwhile, Sylvia has stolen the funds and disappeared. Who is liable for the missing funds—First Bank or Second Bank?

3. **ETHICS** When Steven was killed in an automobile accident, he left his wife, Debra, a life insurance policy for $60,000. She decided to move from Bunkie to Sulphur, Louisiana. Debra executed a document authorizing her mother-in-law, Helen, to sign checks on Debra's account at the bank. Debra also signed several blank checks and gave them to Helen with instructions to use them to pay off the remaining debt on Debra's trailer. When Helen received the life insurance checks, she deposited them in Debra's account. So far, so good. But then she immediately withdrew $50,000 from the account by using one of the blank checks Debra had left her. She did not use these funds to pay off the trailer debt. When Debra discovered the theft, she sued the bank for having paid an unauthorized check. How would you rule in this case? Debra has suffered a grievous loss—her husband died tragically in an automobile accident. She trusted her mother-in-law and counted on her help. Should the bank show compassion? If the bank made good on the forged checks, how great would be the injury to the bank's shareholders, compared with the harm to Debra if she loses this entire sum? What would Kant and Mill say?

4. Banks are liable for forged checks except in the case of the three rules (Impostor Rule, Fictitious Payee Rule, and the Employee Indorsement Rule). Do you think this is the proper allocation of liability? Why, in this era of automated check machines, should banks be liable for forged checks? Alternatively, could you argue that the three rules provide too much protection to banks?

5. Many accommodation parties and guarantors do not understand their liability when they sign an instrument. (As the saying goes, "Nothing is more dangerous than a fool with a pen.") Should the UCC require that some sort of disclosure be made to an accommodation party or guarantor before they sign, or that their obligations be clearly spelled out? What language would you require for an accommodation or guaranty to be valid?

CHAPTER 27

ACCOUNTANTS' LIABILITY

The accounting firm Arthur Andersen prided itself on its ethics. Old-timers would tell new recruits the legend of the firm's founder: How, in 1914, the young Arthur Andersen had refused a client's request to certify a dubious earnings report. Although Andersen knew his firm would be fired, and he might not be able to meet payroll, he nonetheless stood on principle. He was vindicated a few months later when the client went bankrupt. This emphasis on ethics continued—the firm later established a program to train business school faculty to teach ethics. This was a company that walked the talk. Or so everyone thought.

The firm collapsed in disgrace, the first major accounting firm ever to be convicted of a crime.

The firm that began its life as the exemplar of ethical behavior, the firm whose audits were considered the gold standard in the industry, died ignominiously—convicted of obstructing a government investigation into the infamous Enron case.[1] How did this once noble firm go so wrong? And what lessons does this sad fable teach about the accounting profession?

For its first 35 years, Andersen was primarily in the business of auditing public companies. Although its partners did not become rich, they made a good living. In the 1960s, a typical Andersen partner made the equivalent of $215,000 a year in today's dollars. Then, one of the partners had a breakthrough, which at the time seemed marvelous but ultimately started the firm down a dangerous and slippery slope. This fellow figured out how to take one of those newfangled devices—a computer—out of the science lab and into the bookkeeping department. Soon, Andersen was earning huge profits advising companies on how to automate their bookkeeping.

The technology consultants in the firm began generating much greater profits—and earning much higher salaries—than the auditors. Competition in the auditing field was driving income down anyway. Audits were fast becoming loss leaders to attract consulting business. Lower revenues led to lower quality as Andersen (and other auditors) felt they could not afford to invest as many hours in their audits. And the audits were becoming less

[1]Although the Supreme Court overturned Andersen's conviction, the damage was already done. It was too late to resurrect the firm.

effective because partners were increasingly afraid to deliver bad news for fear of losing both audit and consulting fees.[2]

Across the industry, major accounting firms earned only about one-quarter of their revenues from auditing; the rest came from consulting. Like its competitors, Andersen drove its auditors to bring in revenues from other sources such as tax advising or technology consulting. The firm began offering internal bookkeeping services to its audit clients—thereby creating a situation in which it was auditing itself. Audit partners who could not bring in enough revenue from other sources faced termination. The Andersen website described its mission as "Convergence: We help you navigate the forces of change." There was no mention of "We carefully audit your books."

To save money, the firm began to force partners to retire at 56. These actions drove salaries up, but reduced the general level of experience and expertise. At the same time, accounting was becoming more complicated.

Predictably, mistakes happened, lawsuits were filed, and settlements were made. Andersen's pristine name was soiled by its role in financial disasters at Boston Market, Sunbeam, Waste Management, Global Crossing, and WorldCom. And then there was Enron. Andersen opened an office in Enron's headquarters staffed with more than 150 Andersen employees, who dressed like, acted like, and partied with Enron employees. In some cases, Enron failed to fix problems in its accounts, but Andersen certified them anyway. The company paid Andersen $23 million a year for auditing services and $29 million for its consulting advice.

When the federal government began investigating Enron's bankruptcy, panicked Andersen employees shredded documents, leading the government to file a criminal charge of obstructing justice. And so, the firm that began as a model of ethics in the accounting profession collapsed in disgrace, the first major accounting firm ever to be convicted of a crime.[3]

Worse was to come. As more accounting irregularities came to light involving other companies and other auditors, and as scores of major companies restated (i.e., lowered reports of) their earnings, investors doubted they could rely on public financial statements. In the month following the Andersen verdict in June 2002, the stock market went into a tailspin, losing 20 percent of its value.

---

[2]Later in this chapter, the Winstar case provides a good example of this point.

[3]Based in part on information in Ken Brown and Ianthe Jeanne Dugan, "Andersen's Fall from Grace Is a Tale of Greed and Miscues," *The Wall Street Journal*, June 7, 2002.

27-1 INTRODUCTION

After the stock market tumbled, Congress acted to restore investor confidence by passing the Sarbanes-Oxley Act of 2002 (SOX). The major provisions of SOX as it relates to auditors are as follows.

27-1a The Sarbanes-Oxley Act of 2002 (SOX)

The Public Company Accounting Oversight Board

Congress established the **Public Company Accounting Oversight Board (PCAOB)** to ensure that investors receive accurate and complete financial information. The board has the authority to regulate public accounting firms, establishing everything from audit rules to ethics guidelines. All accounting firms that audit public companies must register with the board, and the board must inspect them regularly. The PCAOB has the authority to revoke an accounting firm's registration or prohibit it from auditing public companies. The PCAOB has reported that it found flaws in over one-third of the audits performed by Big Four accounting firms, a percentage that is increasing over time.[4]

Public Company Accounting Oversight Board (PCAOB)
The PCAOB regulates public accounting firms.

Reports to Audit Committee

Traditionally, auditors reported to the senior management of a client. This reporting relationship created obvious conflicts of interest—the auditors were reporting concerns to the very people who could be causing, and benefiting from, these problems. **Under SOX, auditors must report to the audit committee of the client's board of directors, not to senior management.** The accountants must inform the audit committee of any: (1) significant flaws they find in the company's internal controls, (2) alternative options that the firm considered in preparing the financial statements, and (3) accounting disagreements with management.

Consulting Services

As we saw in the chapter opening, Enron paid Arthur Andersen more for its consulting services than for its auditing efforts. SOX prohibits accounting firms that audit public companies from providing consulting services to those clients on topics such as bookkeeping, financial information systems, human resources, and legal issues (unrelated to the audit). Any consulting agreements must be approved by a client's audit committee. Auditing firms cannot base their employees' compensation on sales of consulting services to clients.

Some observers argue that these conflict of interest rules are too lenient—that auditors should do nothing but audit. They argue that even providing advice on taxes or internal control systems, as SOX permits, could warp an accountant's objectivity about auditing issues. In the United States, the largest accounting firms earn 39 percent of their total revenues from consulting work (usually to nonaudit clients). Also, SOX rules on these issues apply only in the United States. Globally, the Big Four earn 57 percent of their income from consulting.

It seems that consulting income will continue to be important to accounting firms because the audit market is mature while the consulting industry has significant growth potential. Indeed, consulting revenue at the Big Four has been growing at twice the rate of auditing income.

Conflicts of Interest

An accounting firm cannot audit a company if one of the client's top officers has worked for that accounting firm within the prior year and was involved in the company's audit. In short, a client cannot hire one of its auditors to ensure a friendly attitude.

---

[4]The Big Four are: Deloitte LLP, EY LLP, KPMG LLP, and PwC LLP.

Term Limits on Audit Partners

After five years with a client, the lead audit partner must rotate off the account for at least five years. Other partners must rotate off an account every seven years for at least two years.

27-1b Consolidation in the Accounting Profession

The top of the accounting industry has become very concentrated. Before the existing Big Four accounting firms, there used to be eight. These four remaining firms audit 98 percent of all companies in the United States with revenues over $1 billion. In such a concentrated industry, you would expect audit fees to rise. But instead, the audit fees that companies pay per dollar of revenue earned have declined even as SOX has required auditors to do more work. Industry observers have asked: Are auditors in fact doing all the work they are supposed to? Or are auditors taking risks because they believe that regulators are afraid to kill a Big Four firm? Should the Big Four be broken into smaller firms to enhance competition?

Ethics

Deloitte partner Christopher Anderson made serious auditing mistakes, which caused the PCAOB to ban him for one year. He resigned his Deloitte partnership, but stayed on at the firm in the prestigious job of providing advice on complicated auditing issues. Oddly enough, during the time that he was providing this advice, Deloitte failed to correct serious ongoing problems with these complicated issues. The fox may not have been in the henhouse but he allowed other foxes in.

What should Deloitte have done in response to Anderson's punishment? What ethics traps did the firm face? What would Kant and Mill say?

27-1c Audits

Audits are a major source of potential liability for accountants, so it is important to understand what an auditor does. Traditionally, auditors were primarily a watchdog for management, charged with detecting and anticipating financial problems. As the public ownership of stocks increased, however, investors began to need reliable financial information for evaluating their investments. Whereas the accountant had traditionally been a watchdog *for* management, investors needed a watchdog to keep an eye *on* management. Now, one of the accountant's most important roles is to serve as an independent evaluator of the financial statements issued by management to investors and creditors. The audit report of a CPA firm, particularly one of the Big Four, is practically required as an admission ticket to the capital markets—investors will not put up their money without it. In a very real sense, accountants serve two masters—company management and the investing public. It is sometimes difficult for auditing firms to forget, however, that of the two masters, management pays the fees.

When conducting an audit, accountants verify information provided by management. Since it is impossible to check each and every transaction, they verify a sample of various types of transactions. If these are accurate, they assume all are. To verify transactions, accountants use two mirror image processes—vouching and tracing. In **vouching**, they choose a transaction listed in the company's books and check backward to make sure that there are original data to support it. They might, for example, find in accounts payable a bill for the purchase of 1,000 reams of photocopy paper. They would check to ensure that all the paper

Vouching
An auditor chooses a transaction listed in a company's books and checks backward for original data to support it.

had actually arrived and that the receiving department had properly signed and dated the invoice. The auditors would also check the original purchase order to ensure the acquisition had been properly authorized.

In **tracing**, the accountant begins with an item of original data and traces it forward to ensure that it has been properly recorded throughout the bookkeeping process. For example, the sales ledger might report that 30 aircraft engines were sold. The accountant checks the information in the sales ledger against the original invoice to ensure that the date, price, quantity, and customer's name all match. The auditor then verifies each step along the paper trail until the engines leave the warehouse.

Tracing
An auditor takes an item of original data and tracks it forward to ensure that it has been properly recorded throughout the bookkeeping process.

Since accountants do not check every transaction, the process of selecting those items to verify requires skill and experience. Auditors must continually modify their original plan to reflect discoveries they make during the audit. If they find that one aspect of the company's accounting system seems weak, they need to check those results more carefully.

In performing their duties, accountants must follow two sets of rules: (1) generally accepted accounting principles (**GAAP**) and (2) generally accepted auditing standards (**GAAS**). GAAP are the rules for preparing financial statements, and GAAS are the rules for conducting audits. These two sets of standards include broadly phrased general principles as well as specific guidelines and illustrations. The application and interpretation of these rules require acute professional skill.

GAAP
"Generally accepted accounting principles," the rules for preparing financial statements

GAAS
"Generally accepted auditing standards," the rules for conducting audits

International Standards

In 2007, the Securities and Exchange Commission (SEC) began allowing foreign companies to use **international financial reporting standards (IFRS)** instead of GAAP.[5] The SEC is considering a proposal that would allow U.S. companies to supplement their GAAP filings with IFRS information.

IFRS
"International financial reporting standards," an international alternative to GAAP

Opinions

After an audit is complete, the accountant issues an opinion that indicates how accurately the financial statements reflect the company's true financial condition. The auditor has four choices:

- **Unqualified opinion.** Also known as a **clean opinion**, this is the most favorable report an auditor can give. It indicates that the company's financial statements fairly present its financial condition in accordance with GAAP. A less-than-clean opinion is a warning to potential investors and creditors that something may be wrong.

Clean opinion
An unqualified opinion, the most favorable report an auditor can give

- **Qualified opinion.** This opinion indicates that, although the financial statements are generally accurate, there is nonetheless an outstanding, unresolved issue. This may be a violation of GAAP or perhaps some important issue whose ultimate impact is uncertain. For example, the company may face potential liability from environmental law violations but the liability cannot yet be accurately estimated. Depending upon the reason for the qualification, this type of opinion does not necessarily prevent a company from borrowing money or selling stock.

5IFRS are established by the International Accounting Standards Board, a privately funded organization located in London.

- **Adverse opinion.** This opinion is definitely bad news. In the auditor's view, the company's financial statements do not accurately reflect its financial position. In other words, the company is lying about its finances (or to put it more politely, is "materially misstating certain items on its financial statements"). A company with an adverse opinion is generally unable to sell stock or borrow money.
- **Disclaimer of opinion.** Although not as damning as an adverse opinion, a disclaimer is still not good news. It is issued when the auditor does not have enough information to form an opinion. If the auditor knows that the statements are inaccurate, she cannot hide behind a disclaimer of opinion; she must issue an adverse opinion.

27-2 LIABILITY TO CLIENTS

When financial matters go wrong, as they sometimes do, clients are tempted to sue their accountants, who often have deep pockets. While some lawsuits filed against large firms are frivolous, this section discusses the bases for legitimate litigation.

27-2a Contract

Engagement letter
A written contract by which a client hires an accountant

Contracts between accountants and their clients are either written or oral. A written contract is often called an **engagement letter**. The contract has both express and implied terms. The accountant *expressly* promises to perform a particular project by a given date. The accountant also *implies* that he will work as carefully as an ordinarily prudent accountant would under the circumstances. When an accountant enters into a contract to prepare, say, tax returns, she is making two promises—to complete the returns on time and to prepare them accurately. If she fails to do either, she has breached her contract and may be liable for any damages that result.

27-2b Negligence

An accountant is liable for negligence to a client who can prove *both* of the following elements:

- **The accountant breached his duty to his client by failing to exercise the degree of skill and competence that an ordinarily prudent accountant would under the circumstances.** For example, if the accountant fails to follow GAAP or GAAS, she has almost certainly breached her duty. But the reverse is not true—compliance with GAAP and GAAS does not necessarily protect an accountant from liability.
- **The accountant's violation of duty caused foreseeable harm to the client.** To recover damages, the client must be able to show that the accountant's misdeeds injured him.

In the following case, the accounting firm was clearly negligent. But had its wrongdoing actually caused harm to the client?

Oregon Steel Mills, Inc. v. Coopers & Lybrand, LLP

336 Ore. 329
Oregon Supreme Court, 2004

Facts: Oregon Steel Mills, Inc., was a publicly traded company whose financial statements were audited by Coopers & Lybrand, LLP, for many years. When Oregon sold the stock in one of its subsidiaries, Coopers advised Oregon that the transaction should be reported as a $12.3 million gain. This advice was wrong, and Coopers was negligent in giving it.

Two years later, Oregon began a public offering of additional shares of stock. Shortly before Oregon intended to file the stock offering with the SEC, Coopers told the company that the sale of its subsidiary had been misreported and that it would have to revise its financial statements. As a result, the offering was delayed from May 2 to June 13. During this period of delay, the price of the stock fell from $16 to $13.50.

Oregon filed suit against Coopers, seeking as damages the difference between what Oregon actually received for its stock and what it would have received if the offering had occurred on May 2, an amount equal to approximately $35 million.

The trial court granted Coopers motion for summary judgment, but the court of appeals reversed it. Coopers appealed.

Issue: ***Did Coopers' negligence cause the loss to Oregon?***

Excerpts from Justice Balmer's Decision:[6] [T]he critical issue is whether Oregon's market losses were a reasonably foreseeable result of Coopers' wrongful conduct. [N]o one could foresee, at the time of Coopers' accounting errors, the risk that Oregon would suffer a loss because its securities would be sold at market-determined prices on June 13, rather than on May 2.

Oregon argues that it is foreseeable that stock prices will fluctuate, and that is certainly true. It also is foreseeable that negligent conduct by an accounting firm may harm a client by impairing its ability to raise capital. Coopers' conduct caused the delay in the offering that led to an unintended adverse result. However, the intervening action of market forces on the price of Oregon's stock was the harm-producing force, and Coopers' actions did not cause the decline in the stock price so as to support liability for that decline. As a matter of law, the risk of a decline in Oregon's stock price in June was not a reasonably foreseeable consequence of Coopers' negligent acts.

Oregon argues that the losses in this case were foreseeable because Coopers knew that Oregon intended to enter the market and sell its securities at a specific and favorable time. However, the record does not support Oregon's assertion. First, Oregon's complaint does not allege that the securities offering was scheduled to occur at a specific, advantageous time. Although Coopers knew that Oregon contemplated a public offering at some point, the timing of that offering was known only in the most general sense at the time of Coopers' wrongful conduct. Nor does the record contain any other suggestion by Oregon that it expected that market conditions would be favorable at the time the offering was originally planned, why those conditions were favorable, or why conditions would be any less favorable six weeks later. On the contrary, the uncontroverted evidence in the record shows that the increase and then decrease in steel company stock prices, including Oregon's, between April and June were due to market forces unrelated to Oregon's financial condition or to Coopers' conduct.

For the reasons discussed above, we conclude that, although Coopers breached its duty to Oregon by failing to provide competent accounting services, Coopers had no duty to protect Oregon against market fluctuations in Oregon's stock price. The trial court correctly granted Coopers' motion for summary judgment.

Was Coopers liable when Oregon Steel Mills got burned in the stock market?

[6]For readability, we have changed "defendant" and "plaintiff" to "Coopers" and "Oregon."

27-2c Common Law Fraud

Accountants are liable to their clients for fraud if (1) they make a false statement of a material fact, (2) they either know it is not true or recklessly disregards the truth, (3) the client justifiably relies on the statement, and (4) the reliance results in damages. William deliberately inflated numbers in the financial statements he prepared for Tess so that she would not discover that he had made some disastrous investments for her. Because of these distortions, Tess did not realize her true financial position for some years. William committed fraud.

A fraud claim is an important weapon because it permits the client to ask for punitive damages. In negligence or contract cases, a client is typically entitled only to compensatory damages. Punitive damages can be several times higher than a compensatory claim.

27-2d Breach of Trust

Accountants occupy a position of enormous trust because financial information is often sensitive and confidential. Clients may put as much trust in their accountants as they do in their lawyers, clergy, or psychiatrists. **Accountants have a legal obligation to (1) keep all client information confidential and (2) use client information only for the benefit of the client.** Alexander Grant & Co. did accounting work for Consolidata Services, Inc. (CDS), a company that provided payroll services. The two firms had a number of clients in common. When Alexander Grant discovered discrepancies in CDS's client funds accounts, it notified those companies that were clients of both firms. Not surprisingly, these mutual clients fired CDS, which then went out of business. The court held that Alexander Grant had violated its duty of trust to CDS.[7]

Clients may put as much trust in their accountants as they do in their lawyers, clergy, or psychiatrists.

27-2e Fiduciary Duty

Fiduciary relationship
One party has an obligation (1) to act in a trustworthy fashion for the benefit of the other person and (2) to put that person's interests first.

In a **fiduciary relationship**, one party has an obligation (1) to act in a trustworthy fashion for the benefit of the other person and (2) to put that person's interests first. As a general rule, accountants do *not* have a fiduciary duty to their clients. However, clients often do put great faith in their accountants, and sometimes accountants take on responsibilities that extend beyond the typical scope of an accountant–client relationship. As the following case illustrates, in such situations, accountants may be deemed a fiduciary and held to a higher standard of accountability.

Leber v. Konigsberg

2010 U.S. Dist. Lexis 128910; 2010 WL 5067549
United States District Court for the Southern District of Florida, 2010

Facts: Steven Leber (Leber) was the trustee of the Steven E. Leber Charitable Remainder Unitrust (Trust), which, at its peak, had assets of $4 million. The defendant, Paul Konigsberg (Konigsberg), was a certified public accountant and the named partner of Konigsberg Wolf & Co., P.C. (the firm).

[7]Wagenheim v. Alexander Grant & Co., 19 Ohio App. 3d 7 (App. Ct. Oh. 1983).

Leber invested all of the Trust's assets with Bernard Madoff (Madoff), who, it turns out, was running a $65 billion Ponzi scheme.[8] Ultimately, Madoff's sons revealed the fraud, and investors around the world learned that all of their investments were gone. [A trustee has since recovered some of the stolen assets.]

Leber alleges that he made this disastrous investment on the advice of Konigsberg, who not only recommended Madoff but promised that he would personally supervise, monitor, and provide due diligence for the Trust's account with Madoff.

Leber filed suit against Konigsberg and the firm on the grounds that they breached their fiduciary duty to him and the Trust. He sought payment of $4 million. Defendants filed a motion for summary judgment, alleging that accountants do not owe their clients a fiduciary duty.

Issue: ***Do accountants owe a fiduciary duty to their clients?***

Excerpts from Judge Marra's Decision: Defendants assert that under New York law, accountants do not owe fiduciary duties to their clients. Defendants' contention is generally true ("general rule").

A fiduciary relationship arises when one has reposed trust or confidence in the integrity or fidelity of another who thereby gains a resulting superiority of influence over the first, or when one assumes control and responsibility over another.

Leber avers [that] Konigsberg talked about how he and his firm provided financial advisory services and helped place clients in certain investments. Konigsberg advised that he thought that as a result of his role as a financial advisor to the [Trust,] that it was expected that the [Trust] would retain Konigsberg Wolf as its tax accountants as well. Konigsberg indicated that [Leber] must hire Konigsberg Wolf in order to get the proper analysis of the Madoff account of the [Trust] and that if this was done, [their] relationship could continue. It was clear that if [Leber] didn't hire Konigsberg Wolf, that Konigsberg would no longer be the [Trust's] financial advisor and that the [Trust's] account at Madoff would be jeopardized. [Konigsberg's bills indicated] that he was charging not only for "tax analysis" but also for analysis of the monthly reports of Madoff for the [Trust].

Under circumstances such as those listed above, a breach of fiduciary duty claim against an accountant pursuant to New York law may proceed. [An accountant] may be found to have assumed additional duties of care when acting as a financial advisor. [In a prior case,] the plaintiff sufficiently stated a cause of action for breach of fiduciary duty where it was alleged that plaintiff had placed total trust and reliance upon an accountant's investment advice, and that the accountant concealed pertinent information about those investments, such as the nature of the risk involved.

As a result, summary judgment on Leber's claims against Defendants for breach of fiduciary duty cannot be granted.

EXAMStrategy

Question: Zapper, Inc., hired the accounting firm PriceTouche to determine if constructing an apartment building was financially feasible. After PriceTouche determined that the building would be profitable, Zapper started construction.

Before the structure was complete, it burned to the ground. Although Zapper rebuilt it, the apartment building turned out not to be profitable, at least in part because of the delay in construction. Is PriceTouche liable to Zapper?

Strategy: There are four potential bases for liability—contract, negligence, breach of trust, and violation of a fiduciary duty. Which apply here?

Result: If PriceTouche did not perform as carefully as an ordinarily prudent accountant would under the circumstances, then it has violated its contract with Zapper and would be liable under contract law. It would also be negligent. But it would be liable only if its negligence caused the harm. It might be that the apartment building was not profitable because

[8]In a Ponzi scheme, the fraudster uses money from new investors to pay large returns to prior victims. The scheme can be very profitable for all involved until the fraudster runs out of new "investors." Indeed, investors often attract new victims for the fraudster by bragging about their incredible returns (which are, indeed, incredible). For years, Madoff had been well known in the investment community as someone who earned implausibly steady returns, no matter the market conditions.

it burned down during construction. If this is the case, PriceTouche would not be liable for negligence. There is no breach of trust because it has not violated client confidentiality. It has not violated a fiduciary duty because there was no evidence that PriceTouche gave bad advice or that Zapper had placed particular trust in PriceTouche's advice.

27-3 LIABILITY TO THIRD PARTIES

Suppose that a professional basketball team signs a star college player to a three-year contract. A leading cardiologist examines the player and pronounces him "in perfect health." Relying on this assertion, you purchase stock in the team. Unfortunately, the cardiologist is wrong, and the player collapses in his first pro game. His career is over, and the team's future is bleak. The value of your stock plummets. Although you feel the doctor has single-handedly wiped out your investment, you cannot recover from him because he owes you no duty.

Suppose, on the other hand, that you had purchased stock in the team because you were impressed with its financial prospects as revealed in its audited financial statements. Unfortunately, the auditors had failed to detect that the company had overstated its income. The value of the stock dives when the mistake comes to light. You may be able to recover from the auditors. Why are accountants different from doctors or other professionals?

No issue in the accounting field is more controversial than liability to third parties. Plaintiffs argue that auditors owe a duty to a trusting public (such as creditors and investors) that physicians and other professionals do not. The job of the auditor, they say, is to provide an independent, professional source of assurance that a company's audited financial statements are accurate. If the auditors do their job properly, they have nothing to fear.

The accounting profession rebuts that, if everyone who has ever been harmed even remotely by a faulty audit can recover damages, there will soon be no auditors left. In return for a limited fee on the upside, auditors face potentially unlimited liability when things go wrong. Big Four firms spend between 10 and 20 percent of their revenues on litigation (including settlements and insurance).

One observation before beginning: Accountants are generally not liable to third parties in *contract* because there is no contract between the accountant and the third parties (i.e., there is no "privity of contract").[9] Most third parties are incidental beneficiaries who are not entitled to enforce a contract. (We discussed third party beneficiaries in Chapter 17.)

27-3a Negligence

Accountants' liability for negligence to third parties is determined by state law. Most states follow one of the following rules: the Ultramares doctrine, the foreseeable doctrine, or the Restatement doctrine.

Ultramares Doctrine

Fred Stern & Co. asked the Ultramares Corp. for a loan to finance its rubber imports. As a condition of any loans, Ultramares insisted upon an audited balance sheet. The auditors, Touche, Niven & Co., were never told exactly who would see the financial statements, but they knew a number of potential creditors might. On the basis of a balance sheet listing a net worth of $1 million, Ultramares loaned money to Stern. In reality, however, management had falsified the books and the company was insolvent. The auditors failed to follow paper

[9]Two parties are in "privity of contract" if they have entered into a contract with each other. If two parties enter into a contract that affects a third party, that third party is not in privity.

trails leading to off-the-books transactions that, if properly analyzed, would have revealed the company's insolvency. When Stern failed to repay the loans, Ultramares sued Touche for negligence. The jury awarded Ultramares $187,576.32. (The case was decided in 1931, at the height of the Great Depression. That is the equivalent of $2.8 million today.)

In an opinion written by the influential judge Benjamin Cardozo, the New York Court of Appeals (the highest court of that state) overturned the negligence verdict. If third parties were able to recover for negligence against an accounting firm, then "thoughtless slip or blunder, the failure to detect a theft or forgery beneath the cover of deceptive entries, may expose accountants to a liability in an indeterminate amount for an indeterminate time to an indeterminate class." Cardozo thought this hazard too extreme. **Under the Ultramares doctrine, accountants who fail to exercise due care are liable to a third party only if they know that the third party (1) will see their work product and (2) will rely on the work product for a particular, known purpose. To be liable, the accountants must know the *identity* of the third party.**[10]

In a later case, a court did find an accountant liable under the Ultramares doctrine: A limited partner sued an accountant who failed to disclose in an audit report that the general partners were withdrawing funds in violation of the partnership agreement. The limited partnership agreement contained an express provision requiring an annual audit by a CPA, and the auditor had also prepared the partnership's tax returns on which the limited partners relied in preparing their personal returns. The accountant knew that his work product would be shown to the limited partners, and he knew their identity.[11]

Foreseeable Doctrine

The courts in a limited number of states have held that accountants are liable to any *foreseeable* users who suffer harm as a result of their carelessness. Harry and Barry (we are not making this up) Rosenblum sold their business to Giant Stores Corp. in return for Giant common stock. In assessing the value of this stock, the two men relied on an audit by Touche Ross & Co. (coincidentally, the same accounting firm in the *Ultramares* case). You will not be surprised to learn that Giant's financial statements turned out to be fraudulent and the stock worthless. Giant had manipulated its books by falsely recording assets that it did not own and omitting substantial amounts of accounts payable. **The court held that an accountant who fails to exercise due care is liable to a third party if (1) it was foreseeable that the third party would receive financial statements from the accountant's client, and (2) the third party relied on these statements.**[12] This standard creates greater liability for accountants than the Ultramares doctrine.

Restatement Doctrine

The majority of state courts have rejected the Ultramares doctrine as too narrow and the foreseeable doctrine as too broad. They prefer, instead, a middle ground that was adopted by the Restatement (Second) of Torts.[13] **According to the Restatement doctrine, accountants who fail to exercise due care are liable to (1) anyone they knew would rely on the information and (2) anyone else in the same class.** Adrienne knows she is preparing financial statements for the BeachBall Corp. to use in obtaining a bank loan from the First National Bank of Tucson. If Adrienne is careless in preparing the statements and BeachBall collapses, she will be liable to First Bank *under all three tests:* the Ultramares doctrine, the foreseeable doctrine, and the Restatement doctrine.

---

[10] Ultramares Corp. v. Touche, 255 N.Y. 170 (App Ct NY 1931). Cardozo later served on the U.S. Supreme Court.

[11] White v. Guarente, 43 N.Y.2d 356 (App Ct NY 1977).

[12] H. Rosenblum, Inc. v. Adler, 93 N.J. 324 (S. Ct. NJ 1983).

[13] The American Law Institute, an organization of legal scholars, prepares the Restatement of Torts (and other restatements). It is not a statute, but a summary of the common law that courts often rely on.

Suppose, however, that the company takes its financial statements to the Last National Bank of Tucson instead. Under the Ultramares doctrine, Adrienne would not be liable because she did not prepare the documents for the Last Bank. She would be liable under the foreseeable doctrine because it was foreseeable that the Last Bank would receive the financial statements from the client and rely on them. She would also be liable under the Restatement doctrine because the Last Bank is in the *same class* as the First Bank. Once Adrienne knows that *a* bank will rely on the statements she has prepared, the identity of the particular bank should not make any difference to her when doing her work.

Suppose that BeachBall uses the financial statements to persuade a landlord to rent it a manufacturing facility. In this case, Adrienne would be liable under the foreseeable doctrine because this was a foreseeable use of the financial statements. She would not be liable under the Restatement doctrine, however, because the landlord is not in the same class as the First Bank, for whom Adrienne knew she was preparing the documents. Finally, if a major shareholder of BeachBall uses the financial statements to convince her boyfriend to marry her, Adrienne is not liable under any doctrine.

The following table summarizes the three doctrines:

Under this doctrine:	**Accountants who fail to exercise due care are liable to a third party if:**
Ultramares Doctrine	They know the identity of the third party who: • Will see their work product and • Will rely on the work product for a particular, known purpose.
Foreseeable Doctrine	• It is foreseeable that the third party will receive financial statements from the accountant's client and • The third party relies on these statements.
Restatement Doctrine	• The accountants knew the third party would rely on the information or • The third party was in the same class as someone who the accountant knew would rely on the information.

In the following case, a potential employee relied on audited financial statements that proved to be faulty. Was the accounting firm liable under the Restatement doctrine? You be the judge.

You Be the Judge

Ellis v. Grant Thornton

530 F.3d 280
United States Court of Appeals for the Fourth Circuit, 2008

Facts: The First National Bank of Keystone could do nothing right. For five years, it issued many risky mortgage loans on which the borrowers defaulted. Then Keystone management turned bad into worse by lying about the value of the loans. When the Office of the Comptroller of the Currency (OCC) first began to smell trouble, it required Keystone to hire a nationally recognized independent accounting firm to audit its books. The bank hired Grant Thornton (GT), who assigned Stan Quay as the lead partner on the account.

As Quay was finishing his audit, the board began talking with Gary Ellis about becoming president of the bank. Ellis already had a perfectly good job, so he was understandably reluctant to move to a bank that the OCC was investigating. To reassure him, the Keystone board suggested he talk with Quay and look at the bank's financials. Quay told Ellis that Keystone would receive a clean, unqualified opinion. Ellis then attended a shareholders' meeting at which Quay announced that his opinion would be unqualified.

Quay did ultimately issue a clean opinion reporting shareholders' equity of $184 million when, in fact, the bank was insolvent to the tune of hundreds of millions of dollars. The first page of the report stated: "This report is intended for the information and use of the Board of Directors and Management of The First National Bank of Keystone and its regulatory agencies and should not be used by third parties for any other purpose." A week later, the Board voted to hire Ellis, who then quit his job elsewhere to join Keystone.

Five months later, the OCC declared Keystone insolvent and shut it down. Ellis was out of work. He filed suit against GT, seeking compensation for his lost wages. The district court ruled in favor of Ellis and granted him $2.5 million in damages. GT appealed.

You Be the Judge: *Was GT liable to Ellis for its negligence in preparing Keystone's financial statements?*

Arguments for Ellis: Stan Quay was negligent in preparing Keystone's financial statements. He reassured Ellis that the statements were accurate. Ellis reasonably relied on both Quay's written financial statements and oral assurances. As a result, Ellis suffered grave harm. It is only reasonable to hold GT liable to Ellis for a harm that was completely foreseeable.

Arguments for Grant Thornton: Under the Restatement doctrine, accountants who fail to exercise due care are liable to (1) anyone they knew would rely on the information and (2) anyone else in the same class. Keystone's financial statements very clearly stated that they were designed for the benefit of Keystone's board of directors, management and regulatory agencies. Ellis was not in any of these classes when he got the audit report. Therefore, he cannot recover from GT for any harm he may have suffered.

Moreover, Keystone did not pay GT to discuss the financial statements with existing or potential employees. Indeed, GT was unaware that Ellis might be hired until *after* it had reached a decision to give a clean opinion. It is unreasonable to hold GT liable for a risk of which it was unaware.

EXAMStrategy

Question: Tara bought stock in Flying Feet. In doing so, she relied on financial statements prepared for the company by YoungPrice. The accounting firm was negligent and Flying Feet crashed into bankruptcy. Can Tara recover from Young?

Strategy: The answer depends on which standard the court applies.

Result: Young would not be liable under the Ultramares doctrine because Young did not know Tara. It could certainly foresee that investors would rely on the financial statements, so it would be liable under the foreseeable doctrine. Young would not be liable to Tara under the Restatement doctrine because it did not know that Tara would rely and she was not in the same class as someone who Young knew would rely. The statements were prepared for the company, not for Tara.

27-3b Fraud

Under common law, courts consider fraud to be much worse than negligence because it is intentional. Therefore, the penalty is heavier. **An accountant who commits fraud is liable to any *foreseeable* user of the work product who justifiably relied on it.** This rule applies in all jurisdictions, even those that have adopted the Ultramares doctrine. TechDisk manufactured computer components. When customers placed more orders than the company could fill, executives feared that, if investors found out, the stock price would fall. So they boosted their sales numbers by shipping out bricks wrapped up to look like components.

Nigel Paul Monckton/Shutterstock.com

Hard to confuse these with computer parts

Company accountants deliberately altered the financial statements to pretend that the bricks were indeed computer parts. These accountants would be liable to any foreseeable users—including investors, creditors, and customers.

27-3c Liability for Qualified Opinions

Auditors can, under some circumstances, protect themselves from liability by issuing a less than clean opinion; that is, a qualified, adverse, or disclaimer of opinion. **To avoid liability, the less than clean opinion must be issued for the right reasons.** If the auditor indicates that it has issued a qualified opinion because of uncertainty about environmental litigation, then it is not liable when that lawsuit bankrupts the company. But if the company runs into financial trouble because of inventory thefts that the auditors should have caught, the auditors would be liable.

27-3d Securities Act of 1933

Third parties who have been injured by an accountant's error often file suit under the securities laws. Chapter 37 on securities regulation provides a general overview of the liability provisions for both the Securities Act of 1933 (1933 Act) and the Securities Exchange Act of 1934 (1934 Act). This chapter offers a summary of these liability provisions as they affect accountants.

The 1933 Act requires an issuer to register securities before offering them for sale to the public. To do this, the issuer files a registration statement with the SEC. This registration statement must include audited financial statements. **Under §11 of the 1933 Act, auditors are liable for any material misstatement or omission in the financial statements that they prepare for a registration statement.**

To prevail under §11, the plaintiff must prove only that (1) the registration statement contained a material misstatement or omission and (2) she lost money. Ernst & Young served as the auditor for FP Investments, Inc., a company that sold interests in tax shelter partnerships. These partnerships were formed to cultivate tropical plants in Hawaii. The prospectus for this investment neglected to mention that the partnerships did not have enough cash on hand to grow the plants. A jury found that Ernst & Young violated §11 and awarded damages of $18.9 million to the investors.[14]

Due diligence
A reasonable investigation of a registration statement

However, auditors can avoid liability under §11 by showing that they made a reasonable investigation of the financial statements and had reasonable grounds to believe the statements did not contain material omissions or misstatements. This investigation is called **due diligence**. Typically, auditors will not be liable if they can show that they complied with GAAP and GAAS.

27-3e Securities Exchange Act of 1934

A company that is subject to the 1934 Act must file with the SEC an annual report containing audited financial statements and quarterly reports with unaudited financials.

Liability for Inaccurate Disclosure in a Required Filing

Under §18 of the 1934 Act, an auditor who makes a false or misleading statement in a required filing is liable to any buyer or seller of the stock who has acted in reliance on the statement. The auditors can avoid liability by showing that they acted in *good faith* and did not know the information was misleading.

---

[14]Hayes v. Haushalter, 1994 U.S. App. LEXIS 23608 (9th Cir. 1994).

Fraud

Primary Liability. Most securities litigation against accountants is brought under §10(b) and Rule 10b-5 of the 1934 Act because it is easier for investors to win under these provisions than under §18. Under §18, the plaintiff must show that he actually relied on the misrepresentation when purchasing the stock. This burden is hard to meet. Under §10(b), the courts are willing to assume reliance if the misstatement was material or it affected the price of the stock.

Under §10(b), an auditor is liable for making (1) a misstatement or omission of a material fact (2) knowingly or recklessly with the intent to deceive, manipulate, or defraud (3) that the plaintiff relies on in purchasing or selling a security. This is called primary liability because the accountants are liable for statements that they make themselves. Note that accountants are liable only if they have acted knowingly or recklessly with an intent to deceive, manipulate, or defraud. This requirement is called **scienter**.

Scienter
An action is done knowingly or recklessly with an intent to deceive, manipulate, or defraud.

Because this concept is so important, we present two cases—one in which there was scienter and another one in which there was not. As you read the following case, you might ask yourself why Grant Thornton accountants were willing to do what they did.

Gould v. Winstar Communs., Inc.

692 F.3d 148
United States Court of Appeals for the Second Circuit, 2011

Facts: Grant Thornton (GT) audited Winstar, a broadband communications company that provided businesses with wireless internet connectivity. Winstar was one of GT's largest and most important clients, but only 12 percent of the company's fees came from auditing, the rest were for consulting projects. Winstar asked that the partner in charge of its audit be replaced and also threatened to fire GT. In response, Winstar assigned two auditors who had no experience with telecommunications companies.

When Winstar's real revenues fell, it began to report fake ones. For example, at the end of the fiscal year, it reported that a large percentage of its revenue was from equipment sales to Lucent Technologies, a strategic partner. Equipment sales were not part of Winstar's core business and there was little documentation that these sales had taken place. Winstar also reported revenue for a feasibility study for Lucent, which had not yet been performed and promotional credits purchased by Lucent for services not yet rendered. Rather than spreading out the revenue over the life of various leases, it reported most revenue when the document was signed. It also engaged in round-trip transactions in which it overpaid other companies for goods and services and, in return, those companies bought unneeded equipment from Winstar. These transactions were material to Winstar's results.

These practices violated GAAP and SEC rules. At first, GT warned that the transactions were red flags and warranted further examination. But GT ultimately allowed the revenues and issued an unqualified audit opinion. A year later, Winstar filed for bankruptcy protection.

Companies that had purchased stock in Winstar after GT issued its clean opinion filed suit against the accounting firm alleging securities fraud under §10(b). GT filed a motion for summary judgment, which the trial court granted on the grounds that the firm had not acted with scienter. Plaintiffs appealed.

Issues: ***Did GT violate §10(b)? Did it act with scienter?***

Excerpts from Judge Lohier's Decision: Plaintiffs may satisfy the scienter requirement by producing evidence of conscious misbehavior or recklessness. Scienter based on conscious misbehavior, in turn, requires a showing of deliberate illegal behavior, a standard met when it is clear that a scheme, viewed broadly, is necessarily going to injure. Scienter based on recklessness may be demonstrated where a defendant has engaged in conduct that was highly unreasonable, representing an extreme departure from the standards of ordinary care to the extent that the danger was either known to the defendant or so obvious that the defendant must have been aware of it. Recklessness may be established where a defendant failed to review or check information that it had a duty to monitor, or ignored obvious signs of fraud.

Some evidence supports the Plaintiffs' contention that GT consciously ignored Winstar's fraud when it approved Winstar's recognition of revenue for the suspicious transactions. This evidence goes beyond a mere failure to uncover the accounting fraud. There is also evidence that GT failed to confirm Winstar's representations regarding these transactions or to retain and review documents evidencing each transaction.

Broadly speaking, there was admissible evidence that in the course of its audit GT learned of and advised against the use of indisputably deceptive accounting schemes, but eventually acquiesced in the schemes by issuing an unqualified audit opinion. At this stage, the Plaintiffs have proffered enough facts constituting evidence of conscious misbehavior or recklessness to survive summary judgment.

We note that in granting summary judgment in GT's favor, the District Court placed particular emphasis on the magnitude of GT's audit work, both in time spent and documents reviewed. The number of hours spent on an audit cannot, standing alone, immunize an accountant from charges that it has violated the securities laws.

[A] jury reasonably could determine that the audit was so deficient as to be an extreme departure from the standards of ordinary care to the extent that the danger was either known to GT or so obvious that GT must have been aware of it.

For the foregoing reasons, we VACATE the District Court's grant of summary judgment, and we REMAND for further proceedings.

In the following case, auditors issued a clean opinion to a fraudulent company, but were not liable because there was no scienter. The same judge wrote the opinion in both of these scienter cases.

Advanced Battery Techs., Inc. v. Bagell

781 F.3d 638
United States Court of Appeals for the Second Circuit, 2015

Facts: ABAT was a Delaware corporation operating in China that designed and manufactured lithium batteries for use in consumer products. Because its stock was listed on a U.S. stock exchange, ABAT was required to file financial statements with both the U.S. Securities and Exchange Commission (SEC) and China's State Administration of Industry and Commerce (AIC).

For four years, ABAT's SEC filings reported increased revenues and profits while, at the same time, its AIC filings showed significant losses. For example, at the same time that ABAT told the SEC that it had revenues of $31.9 million and a profit of $10.2 million, it reported to AIC revenues of $145,000 and a loss of $1 million. (Differences between U.S. and Chinese reporting requirements could not explain the discrepancies: If anything, Chinese accounting rules permit more generous revenue recognition than GAAP in the United States.)

When financial websites reported these discrepancies, the price of ABAT shares plunged by almost half. Ruble Sanderson and other ABAT shareholders sued the company's auditors, Bagell, Josephs, Levine & Co., because the firm had issued clean audit opinions under GAAP. The trial court granted Bagell's motion to dismiss Sanderson's complaint because it did not allege conduct that was reckless or intentional enough to constitute scienter. Sanderson appealed.

Issues: ***Did Bagell commit securities fraud? Did it act with scienter?***

Excerpts from Judge Lohier's Decision: In determining whether the facts alleged in the Complaint establish the requisite strong inference of scienter, a court must consider plausible, nonculpable explanations for the defendant's conduct. In other words, the inference of scienter must be at least as compelling as any opposing inference one could draw from the facts alleged.

Sanderson argues that the Complaint adequately alleges facts that constitute strong circumstantial evidence of conscious recklessness. In the securities fraud context, recklessness must be conduct that is highly unreasonable, representing an extreme departure from the standards of ordinary care. And for an independent auditor, the conduct must, in fact, approximate an actual intent to aid in the fraud being perpetrated by the audited company, for example, when a defendant conducts an audit so deficient as to amount to no audit at all, or disregards signs of fraud so obvious that the defendant must have been aware of them. Mere allegations of GAAP violations or accounting irregularities, or even a lack of due diligence, will not state a securities fraud claim absent evidence of corresponding fraudulent intent.

Sanderson argues that the Complaint [is sufficient because] it alleges that when Bagell audited ABAT's SEC filings, it had access to ABAT's conflicting AIC filings and financial information, and no reasonable auditor would have failed to obtain ABAT's AIC filings.

We agree with the District Court that these allegations fail to constitute strong circumstantial evidence of recklessness. As Sanderson conceded at oral argument, none of the accounting standards on which he relies—the Generally Accepted Auditing Standards or GAAP—specifically requires an auditor to inquire about or review a company's foreign regulatory filings.

Sanderson alternatively argues that the Auditor Defendants had a duty to review ABAT's AIC filings in view of ABAT's unusually high profit margins reported in its SEC filings. [I]n our view, ABAT's report of high profit margins in its SEC filings triggered, at most, a duty to perform a more rigorous audit of those filings. They did not obligate Bagell to review ABAT's AIC filings. And the fact that Bagell did not automatically equate record profits with misconduct cannot be said to be reckless.

Nor are we persuaded to infer recklessness from the allegations that Bagell had access to and presumably relied on the raw financial data underlying ABAT's AIC filings in China but failed to see that the data contradicted ABAT's SEC filings. Sanderson urges that the only non-speculative inference to be drawn from these allegations is that Bagell's failure to spot the discrepancies was reckless. We disagree: a somewhat more compelling inference is that ABAT maintained two sets of data for its Chinese regulators and another for its regulators in the United States—and fed Bagell false data to complete its audits.

For these reasons we agree that Bagell's failure to detect ABAT's fraudulent reporting is not conduct approximating an actual intent to aid in the fraud being perpetrated by the audited company.

We AFFIRM the judgment of the District Court.

Aiding and Abetting. For a *primary* violation of §10(b), the defendant must have made a knowing or reckless omission or misstatement. It is clear that **the *SEC* also has the right to sue anyone who aids and abets others in making untrue statements in connection with the purchase or sale of a security.**[15] Historically, it was unclear whether injured *private parties* could recover from aiders and abettors. The *Stoneridge* case, discussed in Chapter 37, involved two suppliers, not accountants, but it indicates the Supreme Court's general hostility toward aiding and abetting cases brought by private parties.[16] As a result, accountants will likely lose less sleep over this type of liability.

Whistleblowing

Under §10A of the 1934 Act, auditors who suspect that a client has committed an illegal act must ensure that the client's board of directors is notified. **If the board fails to take appropriate action, the auditors must issue an official report to the board. If the board receives such a report from its auditors, it must notify the SEC within one business day and send a copy of this notice to the auditors. If the auditors do not receive this copy, they must notify the SEC themselves.**

The scope of §10A is broad, covering insider trading, price fixing, and any other violations of state and federal law. While doing an audit of the Cronos Group, Arthur Andersen questioned a $1.5 million "disbursement." When the shipping company refused either to provide an explanation or to investigate this mysterious payment, the accounting firm filed an official report with the board of directors and resigned as Cronos's auditor. Cronos then filed the Andersen report with the SEC, which investigated the incident. Not surprisingly, many auditors are unenthusiastic about this statute. It is not a pretty choice—the wrath of the SEC if they fail to cooperate or the anger of their clients if they do comply.

[15]Private Securities Litigation Reform Act, Pub. L. No. 104-67, 109 Stat. 737 (1995).

[16]Stoneridge Investment Partners, LLC v. Scientific-Atlanta, Inc., 552 U.S. 148 (S. Ct. 2008).

Joint and Several Liability

Joint and several All members of a group are liable. They can be sued as a group, or any of them can be sued individually for the full amount owing. But the plaintiff may not recover more than 100 percent of her damages.

Traditionally, liability under the 1934 Act was **joint and several**. When several different participants were potentially liable, a plaintiff could sue any one defendant or any group of defendants for the full amount of the damages. If a company committed fraud and then went bankrupt, its accounting firm might well be the only defendant with assets. Even if the accountants had caused only, say, 5 percent of the damages, they could be liable for the full amount.

Congress has amended the 1934 Act to provide that accountants are liable jointly and severally only if they knowingly violate the law. Otherwise, the defendants are proportionately liable, meaning that they are liable only for the share of the damages that they themselves caused.

27-4 CRIMINAL LIABILITY

Thus far, this chapter has focused on civil liability. The penalty for a civil offense is the payment of monetary damages. However, **some offenses are criminal acts for which the punishment is a fine and imprisonment:**

- The Justice Department has the right to prosecute willful violations under either the 1933 Act or the 1934 Act.
- The Internal Revenue Code imposes various criminal penalties on accountants for wrongdoing in the preparation of tax returns.
- Many states prosecute violations of their securities laws.

EXAMStrategy

Question: When Benjamin hired Howard to prepare financial statements for American Equities, he gave Howard a handwritten sheet of paper entitled "Pro Forma Balance Sheet." It contained a list of real estate holdings and the balance sheets of two corporations that Benjamin claimed were owned by American Equities. From this one piece of paper, and without any examination of books and records, Howard prepared an Auditor's Report for the company. Benjamin used the Auditor's Report to sell stock in American Equities. Has Howard committed a criminal offense?

Strategy: Willful violations of the securities laws are criminal offenses.

Result: A court held that Howard's actions were willful. He was found guilty of a criminal violation.

27-5 OTHER ACCOUNTANT–CLIENT ISSUES

27-5a The Accountant–Client Relationship

SEC rules require accountants to maintain independence from the companies they audit. The accountant must be "capable of exercising objective and impartial judgment on all issues...."[17] To this general guideline, the SEC has also added specific rules. **An auditor**

[17] CFR §210.2-01(b).

or her family must not, for example, maintain a financial or business relationship with a client.

SEC rules on independence specifically prohibit accountants or their families from owning stock in a company that their firm audits. To take one woeful example, the SEC discovered that most of PricewaterhouseCoopers' partners were in violation of this rule, including half of the partners who were charged with enforcing it. All told, firm employees had committed more than *8,000* violations. Although the firm had been caught violating the same rule only a few years before, it nonetheless had a trifecta in place: Many partners pleaded ignorance of the rule, the firm made little effort to enforce it, and, as a result, violations were widespread. In response to this second infraction, the firm fired ten employees, including five partners. The SEC notified 52 of the firm's clients that there were potential concerns about the integrity of their financial statements and even requested that some of the companies select a new auditor.

The SEC may ban any accountant who engages in "unethical or improper professional conduct" from auditing any publicly traded company for some period of time.

27-5b Accountant–Client Privilege

Traditionally, an accountant–client privilege did not exist under federal law. Accountants were under no obligation to keep confidential any information they received from their clients. In one notorious case, the IRS suspected that the owner of a chain of pizza parlors was underreporting his income. The agency persuaded the owner's CPA, James Checksfield, to spy on him for eight years. (The IRS agreed to drop charges against Checksfield, who had not paid his own taxes.) Thanks to the information that Checksfield passed to the IRS, his client was indicted on criminal charges of evading taxes.

Then Congress passed the Internal Revenue Service Restructuring and Reform Act which provides limited protection for confidential communications between accountants and clients. That is the good news. The bad news is the word "limited." This privilege applies only in civil cases involving the IRS or the U.S. government. It does not apply to criminal cases, civil cases not involving the U.S. government, or cases with other federal agencies such as the SEC. Nor does it apply to the preparation of tax returns. Thus, this new accountant–client privilege would not have protected Checksfield's client because he was charged with a criminal offense.

Some states do recognize an accountant–client privilege, but a state privilege applies only to issues of state law and provides no protection against federal charges. The *Checksfield* case took place in Missouri, which does have an accountant–client privilege. However, because the IRS filed suit, federal law applied and Checksfield's information could be used in court. In the end, however, the IRS dropped the tax evasion charges out of concern that a jury would not believe Checksfield's testimony. Ironically, Checksfield suffered worse punishment than his client—the Missouri state board of accountancy revoked his CPA license for violating state law.

Working Papers

When working for a client, accountants use the client's own documents and also prepare working papers of their own—notes, memoranda, and research. In theory, each party owns whatever it has prepared itself. Thus, accountants own the working papers they have created. In practice, however, the client controls even the accountant's working papers. The accountant (1) cannot show the working papers to anyone without the client's permission (or a valid court order) and (2) must allow the client access to the working papers. Under SOX, accountants for public companies must keep all audit work papers for at least seven years.

CHAPTER CONCLUSION

Accountants serve many masters and, therefore, face numerous potential conflicts. Clients, third parties, and the government all rely on their work. Privy to clients' most intimate financial secrets, accountants must decide which of these secrets to reveal and which to keep confidential. The wrong decision may destroy the client, impoverish its shareholders, and subject its auditors to substantial penalties.

EXAM REVIEW

1. **THE PUBLIC COMPANY ACCOUNTING OVERSIGHT BOARD (PCAOB)** The PCAOB regulates public accounting firms.

2. **THE SARBANES-OXLEY ACT (SOX):**
   - Requires an accounting firm to make regular and complete reports to the audit committees of its clients.
   - Prohibits accounting firms that audit public companies from providing consulting services to those companies on certain topics, such as bookkeeping, financial information systems, human resources, and legal issues (unrelated to the audit).
   - Prohibits an accounting firm from auditing a company if one of the company's top officers has worked for the firm within the last year and was involved in the company's audit.
   - Provides that a lead audit partner cannot work for a client in any auditing role for a period of more than five years.

3. **OPINIONS** After an audit is complete, the accountant issues an opinion that indicates how accurately the financial statements reflect the company's true financial condition. The auditor has four choices:
   - Unqualified opinion
   - Qualified opinion
   - Adverse opinion
   - Disclaimer of opinion

4. **LIABILITY TO CLIENTS FOR NEGLIGENCE** Accountants are liable to their clients for negligence if:
   - They breach their duty to their clients by failing to exercise the degree of skill and competence that an ordinarily prudent accountant would under the circumstances and
   - The violation of this duty causes harm to the client.

5. **LIABILITY TO CLIENTS FOR FRAUD** Accountants are liable to their clients for fraud if:
   - They make a false statement of a material fact,

- They know it is not true or recklessly disregard the truth,
- The client justifiably relies on the statement, and
- The reliance results in damages.

6. **CLIENT INFORMATION** Accountants have a legal obligation to:
   - Keep all client information confidential and
   - Use client information only for the benefit of the client.

7. **FIDUCIARY DUTY** As a general rule, accountants do *not* have a fiduciary duty to their clients. However, accountants sometimes take on responsibilities that extend beyond the typical scope of an accountant–client relationship, such as when they serve as a financial advisor. In these situations, they may have a fiduciary duty.

8. **LIABILITY TO THIRD PARTIES FOR NEGLIGENCE** State law determines an accountant's liability for negligence to third parties. Most states follow one of the following three rules:
   - Ultramares doctrine. Accountants who fail to exercise due care are liable to a third party only if they know the identity of the third party who:
     - Will see their work product and
     - Will rely on the work product for a particular, known purpose.
   - Foreseeable doctrine. Accountants who fail to exercise due care are liable to a third party if:
     - It is foreseeable that the third party will receive financial statements from the client and
     - The third party relies on these statements.
   - Restatement doctrine. Accountants who fail to exercise due care are liable to:
     - Anyone they knew would rely on the information and
     - Anyone else in the same class.

EXAMStrategy

Question: Krouse made errors in its audit of Summit Power. Toro Co. relied on Krouse's faulty financial statements when making loans to Summit. Krouse did not know that Toro would rely on these reports. These events took place in a state that adheres to the Ultramares doctrine. Is Krouse liable to Toro?

Strategy: Whenever there is an issue of liability to a third party, it is important to apply the correct rule because the outcome is very different under the various rules. (See the "Result" at the end of this Exam Review section.)

9. **LIABILITY TO THIRD PARTIES FOR FRAUD** An accountant who commits fraud is liable to any foreseeable user of the work product who justifiably relies on it.

EXAMStrategy

Question: When Jeff said that he did not want to invest in Edge Energies, the general partner suggested he call Jackson, the partnerships' accountant. Jackson told Jeff that Edge partnerships were a "good deal," that they were "good money makers," and "they were expecting something like a two-year payoff." In fact, Jackson knew that the operators were mismanaging these ventures and that the partnerships were bad investments. Jeff relied on Jackson's recommendation and invested in Edge. He subsequently lost his entire investment. Is Jackson liable to Jeff? Does it matter which negligence doctrine applies?

Strategy: Whenever there is intentional wrongdoing, think fraud. (See the "Result" at the end of this Exam Review section.)

10. **SECURITIES ACT OF 1933** Under §11 of the 1933 Act, auditors are liable for any material misstatement or omission in the financial statements that they provide for a registration statement if investors lose money.

EXAMStrategy

Question: To be successful in a civil action under §11 of the Securities Act of 1933 concerning liability for a misleading registration statement, the plaintiff must prove:

Defendant's Intent to Deceive	Plaintiff's Reliance on the Registration Statement
(a) No	Yes
(b) No	No
(c) Yes	No
(d) Yes	Yes

Strategy: Section 11 of the 1933 Act has a lower liability standard than the 1934 Act. In other words, a successful plaintiff has to show less wrongdoing on the part of the accountant. (See the "Result" at the end of this Exam Review section.)

11. **SECURITIES EXCHANGE ACT OF 1934**
    - Under §10(b), an auditor is liable for making (1) a misstatement or omission of a material fact (2) knowingly or recklessly with the intent to deceive, manipulate, or defraud (3) that the plaintiff relies on in purchasing or selling a security. This requirement of intent is called scienter.
    - The SEC can sue those who aid and abet others in making untrue statements in connection with the purchase or sale of a security.
    - Under §10A of the 1934 Act, auditors who suspect that a client has committed an illegal act must ensure that the client's board of directors is notified.
    - Accountants are liable jointly and severally only if they knowingly violate the law. Otherwise, they are proportionately liable.

12. **CRIMINAL LIABILITY**
    - The Justice Department has the right to prosecute willful violations under the 1933 Act and the 1934 Act.
    - The Internal Revenue Code imposes various criminal penalties on accountants for wrongdoing in the preparation of tax returns.
    - Many states prosecute violations of their securities laws.
13. **CONFLICT OF INTEREST** An auditor or her family must not maintain a financial or business relationship with a client.
14. **ACCOUNTANT–CLIENT PRIVILEGE** A *limited* accountant–client privilege exists under federal law for confidential communications between accountants and clients. Some states also recognize this privilege and apply it in matters involving state law.

RESULTS

8. Result: Krouse was not liable because he did not know that Toro would rely on the reports.

9. Result: Fraud is different from negligence, so it does not matter which negligence doctrine applies. Jackson was liable to Jeff for fraud because Jeff was a foreseeable user of the information and justifiably relied on it.

10. Result: (b) is the correct answer.

MULTIPLE-CHOICE QUESTIONS

1. **CPA QUESTION** A CPA's duty of due care to a client most likely will be breached when a CPA:
   (a) gives a client an oral instead of a written report.
   (b) gives a client incorrect advice based on an honest error of judgment.
   (c) fails to give tax advice that saves the client money.
   (d) fails to follow GAAS.
2. **CPA QUESTION** One of the elements necessary to hold a CPA liable to a client for conducting an audit negligently is that the CPA:
   (a) acted with *scienter* or guilty knowledge.
   (b) was a fiduciary of the client.
   (c) failed to exercise due care.
   (d) executed an engagement letter.
3. One of the elements necessary to hold a CPA liable under §10(b) is that the CPA:
   (a) acted with *scienter* or guilty knowledge.
   (b) was a fiduciary of the client.
   (c) failed to exercise due care.
   (d) executed an engagement letter.

4. An accountant has a fiduciary duty:
   (a) to a client when conducting an audit.
   (b) to an investor who buys stock in a company the accountant has audited.
   (c) to any third party that the accountant knows will be relying on an audit.
   (d) only for services that go beyond routine accounting work.

5. Accountants who commit fraud in the preparation of financial statements are liable to any third party who uses those statements if:
   (a) that person is a foreseeable user.
   (b) the accountant knows that person's identity.
   (c) it is foreseeable that that person will receive the financial statements.
   (d) that person is in the same class as someone who the accountant knew would rely on the statements.

CASE QUESTIONS

1. After reviewing Color-Dyne's audited financial statements, the plaintiffs provided materials to the company on credit. These financial statements showed that Color-Dyne owned $2 million in inventory. The audit failed to reveal, however, that various banks held secured interests in this inventory. The accountant did not know that the company intended to give the financial statements to plaintiffs or any other creditors. Color-Dyne went bankrupt. Is the accountant liable to plaintiffs under the Restatement doctrine?

2. The British Broadcasting Corp. (BBC) broadcast a television program alleging that Terry Venables, a former professional soccer coach, had fraudulently obtained a £1 million loan by misrepresenting the value of his company. Venables had been a sportscaster for the BBC but had switched to a competing network. The source of the BBC's story was "confidential working papers" from Venables's accountant. According to the accountant, the papers had been stolen. Who owns these working papers? Does the accountant have the right to disclose the content of working papers?

3. A partnership of doctors in Billings, Montana, sought to build a large office building. When it decided to finance this project using industrial revenue bonds under a complex provision of the Internal Revenue Code, it hired Peat Marwick to do the required financial work. The deal was all set to close when it was discovered that the accountants had made an error in structuring the deal. As a result, the partnership was forced to pay a significantly higher rate of interest. When the partnership sued Peat for breach of contract, the accounting firm asked the court to dismiss the claim on the grounds that the client could only sue for the tort of negligence, not for breach of contract. Peat argued that it had performed its duties under the contract. The statute of limitations had expired for a tort case, but not for a contract case. Should the doctors' case be dismissed?

4. James T. Adams was a partner at Deloitte—a partner with a gambling issue. He ended up borrowing tens of thousands of dollars from a casino—a casino that he was in charge of auditing. Does he face any penalties? If so, what?

5. An accounting team's worst nightmare might be to wake up one morning and discover that a company for which it had repeatedly issued clean opinions did not really exist. In fact, the company had been stolen a few years earlier—its operations and related revenues all transferred away. Shareholders sued the auditors under §10(b) but the court granted the accountants' request for summary judgment. Why?

DISCUSSION QUESTIONS

1. Are the SOX rules on consulting services sufficiently strict? Should auditing firms be prohibited from performing any consulting services for companies that they audit?

2. Which of the three negligence doctrines—Ultramares, Foreseeable, or Restatement—is the most reasonable and appropriate?

3. Accountants do not have a fiduciary duty to their clients when performing accounting services. Why not?

4. Under the 1934 Act, accountants are only liable if they act with scienter. Make an argument that they should be liable for negligence. What do you think is the right standard?

5. **ETHICS** Wayne and Arlene Selden invested in Competition Aircraft, a fraudulent company that pretended to sell airplanes. Accountant William Burnett had recommended the investment to several of his clients, who told the Seldens. They were not clients of his. After the company went bankrupt, the Seldens sought to recover from Burnett. The court adopted the Restatement doctrine. Is Burnett liable? Whether or not Burnett faces legal liability, was it a good idea for him to recommend investments to his clients? Does it create any potential conflicts of interest?

Agency and Employment Law

UNIT 6

28

AGENCY LAW

Lauren Brenner had a great idea for a new kind of fitness studio in New York. Called Pure Power Boot Camp, Brenner's gym was modeled on a U.S. Marine training facility, with an indoor obstacle course, camouflage colors, and a rubber floor designed to look like dirt. Brenner's special insight was that people would be more likely to stick to an exercise regime if they worked out together in a small group. So she limited classes to 16 people (called "recruits") who went through the training program together (a "tour of duty"). Brenner also hired retired Marines as "drill instructors."

Ruben Belliard, a retired Marine, was Pure Power's head drill instructor. On his recommendation, Brenner also hired Alexander Fell. But, as Brenner began plans to franchise her concept, the two men went to war against her. They decided to start their own copycat gym, which was to be called Warrior Fitness Boot Camp.

The two men went to war against her.

While still employed by Brenner, Belliard and Fell rented a gym space nearby. Belliard stole copies of Pure Power's confidential customer list, business plan, and operations manuals. The two men sent marketing emails about Warrior to Pure Power's clients and even invited them to a cocktail party to announce Warrior Fitness's launch.

Then one day at Pure Power, Fell openly defied Brenner's instructions, screaming at her that he dared her to fire him. She had little choice but to do so. Belliard then convinced her to fire another drill inspector. Two weeks later, Belliard quit without giving notice, intentionally leaving Brenner with only one drill instructor. Two months later, Fell and Belliard opened Warrior Fitness.

Thus far, this book has primarily dealt with issues of *individual* responsibility: What happens if *you* knock someone down or *you* sign an agreement? But most businesses need more than one worker. Certainly Lauren Brenner could not operate her business by herself.

That is where agency law comes in. It is concerned with your responsibility for the actions of others and their obligations to you. What happens if your agent assaults someone or signs a contract in your name? Or tries to leave with all of your clients?

Hiring other people presents a significant trade-off: If you do everything yourself, you have control over the result. But the size and scope of your business (and your life) will be severely limited. Once you bring in other people, both your risks and your rewards can increase immensely.

The *Pure Power* case highlights a common agency issue: If your employees decide to leave, what obligation do they owe you in that period before they actually walk out the door? The court's opinion is later in the chapter.

28-1 THE AGENCY RELATIONSHIP

Principals have substantial liability for the actions of their agents.[1] Therefore, disputes about whether an agency relationship exists are not mere legal quibbles but important issues with potentially profound financial consequences.

28-1a Creating an Agency Relationship

Let's begin with two important definitions:

- **Principal:** A person who has someone else acting for him
- **Agent:** A person who acts for someone else

Principal
In an agency relationship, the person for whom an agent is acting

Agent
In an agency relationship, the person who is acting on behalf of a principal

In an agency relationship, someone (the agent) agrees to perform a task for, and under the control of, someone else (the principal). **To create an agency relationship, there must be:**

- A **principal** and
- An **agent,**
- Who mutually **consent** that the agent will act on behalf of the principal and
- Be subject to the principal's **control**
- Thereby creating a **fiduciary relationship**.

Consent

To establish consent, the principal must ask the agent to do something, and the agent must agree. In the most straightforward example, you ask a neighbor to walk your dog, and she agrees. Matters were more complicated one night when Steven James sped down a highway and crashed into a car that had stalled on the roadway, thereby killing the driver. In a misguided attempt to help his client, James's lawyer took him to the local hospital for a blood test. Unfortunately, the test confirmed that James had indeed been drunk at the time of the accident.

[1] The word *principal* is always used when referring to a person. It is not to be confused with the word *principle*, which refers to a fundamental idea.

The attorney knew that if this evidence was admitted at trial, his client would soon be receiving free room and board from the Massachusetts Department of Corrections. So at trial, the lawyer argued that the blood test was protected by the client-attorney privilege because the hospital had been his agent and therefore a member of the defense team. The court disagreed, however, holding that the hospital employees were not agents for the lawyer because they had not consented to act in that role.

The court upheld James's conviction of murder in the first degree by reason of extreme atrocity or cruelty.[2]

Control

Principals are liable for an agent's acts because they exercise control over that person. If principals direct their agents to commit an act, it seems fair to hold the principal liable when that act causes harm. How would you apply that rule to the following situation?

William Stanford was an employee of the Agency for International Development. While on his way home to Pakistan to spend the holidays with his family, his plane was hijacked and taken to Iran, where he was killed. Stanford had originally purchased a ticket on Northwest Airlines but had traded it for a seat on Kuwait Airways (KA). The airlines had an agreement permitting passengers to exchange tickets from one to the other. Stanford's widow sued Northwest on the theory that KA was Northwest's agent. The court found, however, that no agency relationship existed because Northwest had no control over KA.[3] Northwest did not tell KA how to fly planes or handle terrorists; therefore, it should not be liable when KA made fatal errors. Not only must an agent and principal consent to an agency relationship, but the principal also must have control over the agent.

Fiduciary Relationship

Fiduciary relationship
The trustee must act in the best interests of the beneficiary.

A **fiduciary relationship** is one of trust: The beneficiary places special confidence in the fiduciary who, in turn, is obligated to act in good faith and candor, doing what is best for the beneficiary, rather than acting in his own best interest. **Agents have a fiduciary duty to their principals.**

All three elements—consent, control, and a fiduciary duty—are necessary to create an agency relationship. In some relationships, for example, there might be a *fiduciary duty* but no *control*. A trustee of a trust must act for the benefit of the beneficiaries, but the beneficiaries have no right to control the trustee. Therefore, that trustee is not an agent of the beneficiaries. *Consent* is present in every contractual relationship, but that does not necessarily mean that the two parties are agent and principal. If Horace sells his car to Lily, they both expect to benefit under the contract, but neither has a *fiduciary duty* to the other and neither *controls* the other, so there is no agency relationship.

Elements Not Required for an Agency Relationship

Consent, control, and a fiduciary relationship are necessary to establish an agency relationship. **The following elements are *not* required for an agency relationship:**

Equal dignities rule
If an agent is empowered to enter into a contract that must be in writing, then the appointment of the agent must also be written.

- **Written agreement.** In most cases, an agency agreement does not have to be in writing. An oral understanding is valid, except in one circumstance—the **equal dignities rule**. According to this rule, if an agent is empowered to enter into a contract that must be in writing, then the appointment of the agent must also be written. For example, under the Statute of Frauds, a contract for the sale of land is unenforceable unless in writing, so the agency agreement to sell land must also be in writing.

---

[2]Commonwealth v. James, 427 Mass. 312 (S.J.C. MA 1998).

[3]Stanford v. Kuwait Airways Corp., 648 F. Supp. 1158 (S.D.N.Y. 1986).

- **Formal agreement.** The principal and agent need not agree formally that they have an agency relationship. They do not even have to utter the word *agent.* So long as they act like an agent and a principal, the law will treat them as such.
- **Compensation.** An agency relationship need not meet all the standards of contract law. For example, a contract is not valid without consideration, but an agency agreement is valid *even if the agent is not paid.*

28-1b Duties of Agents to Principals

As we have seen, agents owe a fiduciary duty to their principals. There are four elements to this duty.

Duty of Loyalty

An agent has a fiduciary duty to act loyally for the principal's benefit in all matters connected with the agency relationship.[4] The agent has an obligation to put the principal first, to strive to accomplish the principal's goals.

The following case reveals the outcome of the opening scenario.

Pure Power Boot Camp, Inc. v. Warrior Fitness Boot Camp, LLC

813 F. Supp. 2d 489
United States District Court for the Southern District of New York, 2011

Facts: Based on the facts in the opening scenario, Brenner filed suit against Belliard and Fell, alleging that they had violated their duty of loyalty to her company.

Issue: ***Did Belliard and Fell violate their duty of loyalty to Pure Power?***

Excerpts from Judge Katz's Decision: An agent is obligated under New York law to be loyal to his employer and is prohibited from acting in any manner inconsistent with his agency or trust and is at all times bound to exercise the utmost good faith and loyalty in the performance of his duties. This duty is not dependent upon an express contractual relationship, but exists even where the employment relationship is at-will.

When an employee uses an employer's proprietary or confidential information when establishing a competing business, the employee breaches his or her fiduciary duty to the employer. Although an employee may, of course, make preparations to compete with his employer while still working for the employer, he or she may not do so at the employer's expense, and may not use the employer's resources, time, facilities, or confidential information; specifically, whether or not the employee has signed an agreement not-to-compete, the employee, while still employed by the employer, may not solicit clients of his employer, may not copy his employer's business records for his own use, may not charge expenses to his employer, which were incurred while acting on behalf of his own interest, and may not actively divert the employer's business for his own personal benefit or the benefit of others. In addition, even in the absence of trade secret protection, employees are not permitted to copy their employer's client list, and such acts have been deemed to be an egregious breach of trust and confidence.

This ongoing and deliberate conduct, transpiring over the course of several months, constitutes a clear breach of the duty of loyalty owed by employees, Belliard and Fell, to their employer, Pure Power. [Belliard and Fell must pay Brenner $245,000.]

[4]Restatement (Third) of Agency §8.01.

The various components of the duty of loyalty follow.

Outside Benefits. **An agent may not receive profits unless the principal knows and approves.** Suppose that Emma is an employee of the agency Big Egos and Talents, Inc. (BEAT). She has been representing Zac Efron in his latest movie negotiations.[5] Efron often drives her to meetings in his new Aston Martin. He is so thrilled that she has arranged for him to star in the movie *Little Men* that he buys her an Aston Martin. Can Emma keep this generous gift? Only with BEAT's permission. She must tell BEAT about the gift; the company may then take the vehicle itself or allow her to keep it.

Confidential Information. The ability to keep secrets is important in any relationship, but especially a fiduciary relationship. **Agents can neither disclose nor use for their own benefit any confidential information they acquire during their agency.** As the following case shows, this duty continues even after the agency relationship ends.

Abkco Music, Inc. v. Harrisongs Music, Ltd.

722 F2d 988
United States Court of Appeals for the Second Circuit, 1983

Facts: Bright Tunes Music Corp. (Bright Tunes) owned the copyright to the song "He's So Fine," a hit for the Chiffons. The company sued Beatle George Harrison alleging that his composition "My Sweet Lord" copied "He's So Fine." At the time the suit was filed, Allen B. Klein handled the business affairs of the Beatles.

Klein (representing Harrison) met with the president of Bright Tunes to discuss possible settlement of the copyright lawsuit. Klein suggested that Harrison might be interested in purchasing the copyright to "He's So Fine." Shortly thereafter, Klein's management contract with the Beatles expired. Without telling Harrison, Klein began negotiating with Bright Tunes to purchase the copyright to "He's So Fine" for himself. To advance these negotiations, Klein gave Bright Tunes information about royalty income for "My Sweet Lord"—information that he had gained as Harrison's agent.

The trial judge in the copyright case ultimately found that Harrison had infringed the copyright on "He's So Fine" and assessed damages of $1.6 million. After the trial, Klein purchased the "He's So Fine" copyright from Bright Tunes and with it, the right to recover from Harrison for his breach of copyright.

Issue: ***Did Klein violate his fiduciary duty to Harrison by using confidential information after the agency relationship terminated?***

George Harrison, a few months after writing "My Sweet Lord"

Excerpts from Judge Pierce's Decision: There is no doubt that the relationship between Harrison and [Klein] prior to the termination of the management agreement was that of principal and agent, and that the relationship was fiduciary in nature. [A]n agent has a duty not to use confidential knowledge acquired in his employment in competition with his principal. This duty exists as well after the employment is terminated as during its continuance.

[5]Do not be confused by the fact that Emma works as an agent for movie stars. As an employee of BEAT, her duty is to the company. She is an agent of BEAT, and BEAT works for the celebrities.

On the other hand, use of information based on general business knowledge or gleaned from general business experience is not covered by the rule, and the former agent is permitted to compete with his former principal in reliance on such general publicly available information. The evidence presented herein is not at all convincing that the information imparted to Bright Tunes by Klein was publicly available.

While the initial attempt to purchase [the copyright to "He's So Fine"] was several years removed from the eventual purchase on [Klein]'s own account, we are not of the view that such a fact rendered [Klein] unfettered in the later negotiations. Taking all of these circumstances together, we agree that [Klein's] conduct did not meet the standard required of him as a former fiduciary.

Ethics

Both this case and Pure Power provide examples of agents who competed against their principal. You may well be in this situation at some point in your own life. As we saw in the Ethics chapter, rationalization is a common, and dangerous, trap. Imagine how Klein, Belliard, and Fell might have rationalized their wrong-doing. What steps can you take to ensure that you do not fall prey to this same ethics trap?

Competition with the Principal. Agents are not allowed to compete with their principal in any matter within the scope of the agency business. If Allen Klein had purchased the "He's So Fine" copyright while he was George Harrison's agent, he would have committed an additional sin against the agency relationship. Owning song rights was clearly part of the agency business, so Klein could not make any such purchases without Harrison's consent. Once the agency relationship ends, however, so does the rule against competition. Klein was entitled to buy the "He's So Fine" copyright after the agency relationship ended; he was just not allowed to use confidential information.

Conflict of Interest between Two Principals. Unless otherwise agreed, an agent may not act for two principals whose interests conflict. Suppose Travis represents both director Steven Spielberg and actor Jennifer Lawrence. Spielberg is casting the title role in his new movie, *Nancy Drew: Girl Detective*, a role that Lawrence covets. Travis cannot represent these two clients when they are negotiating with each other unless they both agree to let her. The following Exam Strategy illustrates the dangers of acting for two principals at once.

EXAMStrategy

Question: The Sisters of Charity was an order of nuns in New Jersey. Faced with growing healthcare and retirement costs, they decided to sell off a piece of property. The nuns soon found, however, that the world is not always a charitable place. They agreed to sell the land to Linpro for nearly $10 million. But before the deal closed, Linpro signed a contract to resell the property to Sammis for $34 million. So, you say, the sisters made a bad deal. There is no law against that. But it turned out that the nuns' law firm also represented Linpro. Their lawyer at the firm, Peter Berkley, never told the sisters about the deal between Linpro and Sammis. Was that the charitable—or legal—thing to do?

Strategy: Always begin by asking if there is an agency relationship. Was there consent, control, and a fiduciary relationship? *Consent:* Berkley had agreed to work for the nuns. *Control:* they told him what he was to do—sell the land. The purpose of a *fiduciary relationship* is for one person to benefit another. The point of the nuns' relationship with Berkley was for him to help them. Once you know there is an agency relationship, then ask if the agent has violated his duty of loyalty.

Result: You know that an agent is not permitted to act for two principals whose interests conflict. Here, Berkley was working for the nuns, who wanted the highest possible price for their land, and Linpro, who wanted the lowest price. Berkley has violated his duty of loyalty.

Secretly Dealing with the Principal. If a principal hires an agent to arrange a transaction, the agent may not become a party to the transaction without the principal's permission. Suppose Spielberg hires Trang to read new scripts for him. Unbeknownst to Spielberg, Trang has written her own script, which she thinks would be ideal for him. But she may not sell it to him without revealing that she wrote it herself. Spielberg may be perfectly happy to buy Trang's script, but he has the right, as her principal, to know that she is the person with whom he is dealing.

Appropriate Behavior. An agent may not engage in inappropriate behavior that reflects badly on the principal. This rule applies even to *off-duty* conduct. While off-duty (but still in uniform), a coed trio of flight attendants went wild at a hotel bar in London. They kissed and caressed each other, showed off their underwear, and poured alcohol down their trousers. The airline fired two of the employees and gave a warning letter to the third.

Other Duties of an Agent

Before Taylor left for a five-week trip to Antarctica, he hired Angie to rent out his vacation house for a year. Angie neither listed his house on the Multiple Listing Service used by all the area brokers, nor posted it online, but when the Fords contacted her looking for rental housing, she did show them Taylor's place. They offered to rent it for $2,000 per month.

Angie emailed Taylor in Antarctica to tell him. He responded that he would not accept less than $3,000 a month, which Angie thought the Fords would be willing to pay. He told Angie to email him back if there was any problem. The Fords decided that they would go no higher than $2,500 a month. Although Taylor had told Angie that he had no cell phone service in Antarctica, she texted him the Fords's counteroffer. Taylor never received it, so he failed to respond. When the Fords pressed Angie for an answer, she said she could not get in touch with Taylor. Not until Taylor returned home did he learn that the Fords had rented another house. Did Angie violate any of the duties that agents owe to their principals?

Duty to Obey Instructions. An agent must obey her principal's instructions unless the principal directs her to behave illegally or unethically. Taylor instructed Angie to email him if the Fords rejected the offer. When Angie failed to do so, she violated her duty to obey instructions. If, however, Taylor had asked her to say that the house's basement was dry when in fact a river flowed through it every spring, Angie would be under no obligation to follow those illegal instructions.

Duty of Care. An agent has a duty to act with reasonable care. In other words, an agent must act as a reasonable person would, under the circumstances. A reasonable person would not have texted Taylor while he was in Antarctica.

Under some circumstances, an agent is held to a higher—or lower—standard than usual. **An agent with special skills is held to a higher standard because she is expected to use those skills.** A trained real estate agent should know enough to post all listings online.

But suppose Taylor had asked his neighbor, Jed, to help him sell the house. Jed is not a trained real estate agent, and he is not being paid, which makes him a **gratuitous agent**. A gratuitous agent is held to a lower standard because he is doing his principal a favor and, as the old saying goes, you get what you pay for—up to a point. **Gratuitous agents are liable if they commit *gross* negligence, but not *ordinary* negligence.** If Jed, as a gratuitous agent, texted Taylor an important message because he forgot that Taylor could not receive these messages in Antarctica, he would not be liable for that ordinary negligence. But if Taylor had, just that day, sent Jed an email complaining that he could not get any text messages, Jed would be liable for gross negligence and a violation of his duty.

Gratuitous agent
Someone not paid for performing duties

Duty to Provide Information. **An agent has a duty to provide the principal with all information in her possession that she has reason to believe the principal wants to know. She also has a duty to provide accurate information.** Angie knew that the Fords had counteroffered for $2,500 a month. She had a duty to pass this information on to Taylor.

Principal's Remedies When the Agent Breaches a Duty

A principal has three potential remedies when an agent breaches her duty:

- **Damages.** The principal can recover from the agent any damages the breach has caused. Thus, if Taylor can rent his house for only $2,000 a month instead of the $2,500 the Fords offered, Angie would be liable for $6,000—$500 a month for one year.
- **Profits.** If an agent breaches the duty of loyalty, he must turn over to the principal any profits he has earned as a result of his wrongdoing. Thus, after Klein violated his duty of loyalty to Harrison, he forfeited profits he would have earned from the copyright of "He's So Fine." Some states also allow punitive damages against disloyal employees.
- **Rescission.** If the agent has violated her duty of loyalty, the principal may rescind the transaction. When Trang sold a script to her principal, Spielberg, without telling him that she was the author, she violated her duty of loyalty. Spielberg could rescind the contract to buy the script.[6]

28-1c Duties of Principals to Agents

Because an agent's job can be so varied, the law needs to define that person's duties carefully. The role of the principal, on the other hand, is typically less complicated—often little more than paying the agent as required by the agreement. Thus, the law enumerates fewer duties for the principal. Primarily, the principal must indemnify (i.e., reimburse) the agent for reasonable expenses and cooperate with the agent in performing agency tasks. The respective duties of agents and principals can be summarized as follows:

Duties of Agents to Principals	Duty of Principals to Agents
Duty of loyalty	Duty to compensate as provided by the agreement
Duty to obey instructions	Duty to indemnify for reasonable expenses
Duty of care	Duty to cooperate with the agent
Duty to provide information	

[6] A principal can rescind his contract with an agent who has violated her duty but, as we shall see later in the chapter, the principal might not be able to rescind a contract that the agent has made with a third party.

Duty to Indemnify

As a general rule, the principal must indemnify the agent for any expenses she has reasonably incurred. These reimbursable expenses fall into three categories:

- **A principal must indemnify an agent for any expenses or damages reasonably incurred in carrying out his agency responsibilities.** Peace Baptist Church of Birmingham, Alabama, asked its pastor to buy land for a new church. He paid part of the purchase price out of his own pocket, but the church refused to reimburse him. Although the pastor lost in church, he won in court.[7]
- **A principal must indemnify an agent for tort claims brought by a third party if the principal authorized the agent's behavior and the agent did not realize he was committing a tort.** Marisa owns all the apartment buildings on Elm Street, except one. She hires Rajiv to manage the units and tells him that, under the terms of the leases, she has the right to ask guests to leave if a party becomes too rowdy. But she forgets to tell Rajiv that she does not own one of the buildings, which happens to house a college sorority. One night, when the sorority is having a raucous party, Rajiv hustles over and starts ejecting the noisy guests. The sorority is furious and sues Rajiv for trespass. If the sorority wins its suit against Rajiv, Marisa would have to pay the judgment, plus Rajiv's attorney's fees, because she had told him to quell noisy parties and he did not realize he was trespassing.
- **The principal must indemnify the agent for any liability to third parties that the agent incurs as a result of entering into a contract on the principal's behalf, including attorney's fees and reasonable settlements.** An agent signed a contract to buy cucumbers for Vlasic Food Products Co. to use in making pickles. When the first shipment of cucumbers arrived, Vlasic inspectors found them unsuitable and directed the agent to refuse the shipment. The agent found himself in a pickle when the cucumber farmer sued. The agent notified Vlasic, but the company refused to defend him. He settled the claim himself and, in turn, sued Vlasic. The court ordered Vlasic to reimburse the agent because he had notified them of the suit and had acted reasonably and in good faith.[8]

Duty to Cooperate

Principals have a duty to cooperate with their agent:

- **The principal must furnish the agent with the opportunity to work.** If Lewis agrees to serve as Ida's real estate agent in selling her house, Ida must allow Lewis access to the house. It is unlikely that Lewis will be able to sell the house without taking anyone inside.
- **The principal cannot unreasonably interfere with the agent's ability to accomplish his task.** Ida allows Lewis to show the house, but she refuses to clean it and then makes disparaging comments to prospective purchasers. "I really get tired of living in such a dark, dreary house," she says. "And the neighborhood children are vicious thugs." This behavior would constitute unreasonable interference with an agent.
- **The principal must perform her part of the contract.** Once the agent has successfully completed the task, the principal must pay him, even if the principal has changed her mind and no longer wants the agent to perform. Ida is a 78-year-old widow who has lived alone for many years in a house that she loves. Her asking price is outrageously

---

7 Lauderdale v. Peace Baptist Church of Birmingham, 246 Ala. 178 (S. Ct. AL 1944).

8 Long v. Vlasic Food Products Co., 439 F2d 229 (4th Cir. 1971).

high because she does not really want to sell. She put her house on the market so that she could show it to all the nice young families who move to town. When Lewis actually finds a couple willing to pay Ida's price, she rejects the offer. But the contract had provided that Lewis would find a willing buyer at the asking price. Because he has done so, Ida must pay his real estate commission even if she refuses to sell her house.

28-1d Terminating an Agency Relationship

Either the agent or the principal has the right to terminate the agency relationship at any time (although there may be financial consequences). In addition, the relationship sometimes terminates automatically.

Termination by Agent and/or Principal

The two parties—principal and agent—have these choices in terminating their relationship:

- **Term agreement.** If the principal and agent agree in advance how long their relationship will last, they have a term agreement. For example:
  - **Time.** Alexandra hires Boris to help her add to her collection of guitars previously owned by rock stars. If they agree that the relationship will last two years, they have a term agreement.
  - **Achieving a purpose.** The principal and agent can agree that the agency relationship will terminate when the principal's goals have been achieved. Alexandra and Boris might agree that their relationship will end when Alexandra has purchased ten guitars.
  - **Mutual agreement.** No matter what the principal and agent agree at the start, they can always change their minds later on, so long as the change is mutual. If Boris and Alexandra originally agree to a two-year term, but Boris decides he wants to go to business school and Alexandra runs out of money after only one year, they can decide together to terminate the agency.
- **Agency at will.** If they make no agreement in advance about the term of the agreement, either principal or agent can terminate at any time.
- **Wrongful termination.** A principal and agent have a personal relationship. Hiring an agent is not like buying a book. You might not care which copy of the book you buy, but you do care which agent you hire. If an agency relationship is not working out, the courts will not force the agent and principal to stay together.

Either party always has the *power* to terminate. They may not, however, have the *right*. If one party's departure from the agency relationship violates the agreement and causes harm to the other party, the wrongful party must pay damages. Nonetheless, he will be permitted to leave. If Boris has agreed to work for Alexandra for two years but he wants to leave after one, he can leave, provided he pays Alexandra the cost of hiring and training a replacement.

If the agent is a gratuitous agent (i.e., is not being paid), he has both the power and the right to quit any time he wants, regardless of the agency agreement. If Boris is doing this job for Alexandra as a favor, he will not owe her damages when he stops work.

Principal or Agent Can No Longer Perform Required Duties

If the principal or the agent is unable to perform the duties required under the agency agreement, the agreement terminates:

- **Either the agent or the principal fails to obtain (or keep) a required license.** Caleb hires Allegra to represent him in a lawsuit. If she is disbarred, their agency agreement terminates because the agent is no longer allowed in court. Alternatively, if

Emil hires Bess to work in his gun shop, their agency relationship terminates when he loses his license to sell firearms.

- **The bankruptcy of the agent or the principal affects their ability to perform required duties.** Bankruptcy rarely interferes with an agent's responsibilities. After all, there is generally no reason why an agent cannot continue to act for the principal whether the agent is rich or poor. If Lewis, the real estate agent, becomes bankrupt, he can continue to represent Ida or anyone else who wants to sell a house. The bankruptcy of a principal is different, however, because after filing for bankruptcy, the principal loses control of his assets. A bankrupt principal may be unable to pay the agent or honor contracts that the agent enters into on his behalf. Therefore, the bankruptcy of a principal is more likely to terminate an agency relationship.
- **Either the principal or the agent dies or becomes incapacitated.** Agency is a personal relationship that requires action. If either party is unable to act, whether through death or incapacity, the relationship ends.[9]
- **The agent violates her duty of loyalty.** Agents are appointed to represent the principal's interest; if they fail to do so, there is no point to the relationship. Thus, in the *Pure Power* case, Belliard's and Fell's agency relationship with Brenner automatically ended once they engaged in disloyal activities. She had the right to fire them on the spot, whether or not they had employment contracts.

Change in Circumstances

After the agency agreement is negotiated, circumstances may change. **If these changes are significant enough to undermine the purpose of the agreement, the relationship ends automatically.** For example:

- **War.** Andrew hired Melissa to open a branch of his clothing store in Syria. But after civil war broke out, Melissa could no longer reasonably believe that Andrew wished to have a branch there. Her authority terminated automatically.
- **Change of law.** Oscar hired Marta to ship him succulent avocados from California's Imperial Valley. Before she sent the shipment, Mediterranean fruit flies were discovered, and all fruits and vegetables in California were quarantined. The agency agreement terminated because it had become illegal to ship the California avocados.
- **Loss or destruction of subject matter.** Sam hired Damian to sell his New Orleans home, but before Damian could even measure the living room, Hurricane Katrina destroyed it. The agency agreement automatically terminated.

Effect of Termination

Once an agency relationship ends, the agent no longer has the authority to act for the principal. If she continues to act, she is liable to the principal for any damages he incurs as a result. The Mediterranean fruit fly quarantine ended Marta's agency. If she sends Oscar the avocados anyway and he is fined for possession of a fruit fly, Marta must pay the fine.

The agent loses her authority to act, but **some of the duties of both the principal and agent continue even after the relationship ends:**

---

[9]Restatement (Third) of Agency §§3.05, 3.06, 3.07, 3.08.

- **Principal's duty to indemnify agent.** Oscar must reimburse Marta for expenses she incurred before the agency ended. If Marta accumulated mileage on her car during her search for the perfect avocado, Oscar must pay her for gasoline and depreciation. But he owes her nothing for her expenses after the agency relationship ends.
- **Confidential information.** An agent is not entitled to use confidential information even after the agency relationship terminates. In the George Harrison case earlier in the chapter, the former agent was wrong to use confidential information to negotiate on his own behalf the purchase of the "He's So Fine" copyright.

28-2 LIABILITY TO THIRD PARTIES

Thus far, this chapter has dealt with the relationship between principals and agents. Although an agent can dramatically increase his principal's ability to accomplish her goals, an agency relationship also dramatically increases the risk of legal liability to third parties. A principal may be liable in tort for any harm the agent causes and also liable in contract for agreements that the agent signs. Indeed, once a principal hires an agent, she may be liable to third parties for the agent's acts, even if he *disobeys* instructions. Agents may also find themselves liable to third parties.

28-2a Principal's Liability for Contracts

Many agents are hired for the primary purpose of entering into contracts on behalf of their principals. Salespeople, for example. Most of the time, the principal is pleased to be liable on these contracts. But even if the principal is unhappy (because, say, the agent has disobeyed orders), the principal generally cannot rescind contracts entered into by the agent. After all, if someone is going to suffer, it should be the principal who hired the disobedient agent, not the innocent third party.

The principal is liable for the acts and statements of his agent if (1) the agent had authority or (2) the principal ratified the acts of the agent. In other words, the principal is as responsible as if he had performed those acts himself. Thus, when a lawyer lied on an application for malpractice insurance, the insurance company was allowed to void the policy for the entire law firm. It was as if the firm had lied. In addition, the principal is deemed to know any information that the agent knows or should know.

Authority

A principal is bound by the acts of an agent if the agent had authority. There are three types of authority: express, implied, and apparent. Express and implied authority are categories of actual authority because the agent is truly authorized to act for the principal. In apparent authority, the principal is liable for the agent's actions even though the agent was *not* authorized.

Express Authority. The principal grants express authority by words or conduct that, reasonably interpreted, cause the agent to believe the principal desires her to act on the principal's account.[10] In other words, the principal asks the agent to do something and the agent does it. Craig calls his stockbroker, Alice, and asks her to buy 100 shares of Banshee Corp. for his account. She has *express authority* to carry out this transaction.

10Restatement (Third) of Agency §2.01.

Implied Authority. Unless otherwise agreed, authority to conduct a transaction includes authority to do acts that are reasonably necessary to accomplish it.[11] The principal does not have to micromanage the agent. After David inherits a house from his grandmother, he hires Nell to auction off its contents. She advertises the event, rents a tent, and generally does everything necessary to conduct a successful auction. After withholding her expenses, she sends the balance to David. Totally outraged, he calls her phone, "How dare you buy ads and rent a tent? I never gave you permission! I absolutely *refuse* to pay these expenses!"

David is wrong. A principal almost never gives an agent absolutely complete instructions. Unless some authority is implied, David would have had to say, "Open the car door, get in, put the key in the ignition, drive to the store, buy stickers, mark an auction number on each sticker, ..." and so forth. To solve this problem, the law assumes that the agent has authority to do anything that is reasonably necessary to accomplish her task.

Apparent Authority. A principal can be liable for the acts of an agent who is not, in fact, acting with authority if the *principal's* conduct causes a third party reasonably to believe that the agent is authorized.[12] In the case of *express* and *implied* authority, the principal has authorized the agent to act. Apparent authority is different: The principal has *not* authorized the agent, but has done something to make an innocent third party *believe* the agent is authorized. As a result, the principal is every bit as liable to the third party as if the agent had had authority.

Zbigniew Lambo and Scott Kennedy were brokers at Paulson Investment Co., a stock brokerage firm in Oregon. The two men violated securities laws by selling unregistered stock, which ultimately proved to be worthless. Kennedy and Lambo were liable, but they were unable to repay the money. Either Paulson or its customers would have to bear the loss. What is the fair result? The law takes the view that the principal is liable, not the third party, if the principal, by word or deed, allowed the third party to believe that the agent was acting on the principal's behalf. In that case, the principal could have prevented the third party from losing money.

Although the two brokers did not have *express* or *implied* authority to sell the stock (Paulson had not authorized them to break the law), the company was nonetheless liable on the grounds that the brokers had *apparent* authority. Paulson had sent letters to its customers notifying them when it hired Kennedy. The two brokers made sales presentations at Paulson's offices. The company had never told customers that the two men were not authorized to sell this worthless stock.[13] Thus the agents *appeared* to have authority, even though they did not. Of course, Paulson had the right to recover from Kennedy and Lambo, if they still had assets.

Remember that the issue in apparent authority is always what the *principal* has done to make the *third party* believe that the *agent* has authority. Suppose that Kennedy and Lambo never worked for Paulson but, on their own, printed up Paulson stationery. The company would not be liable for the stock the two men sold because it had never done or said anything that would reasonably make a third party believe that the men were its agents.

Ratification

If a person accepts the benefit of an unauthorized transaction or fails to repudiate it, then he is as bound by the act as if he had originally authorized it. He has *ratified* the act.[14]

11 Restatement (Third) of Agency §2.02.

12 Restatement (Third) of Agency §2.03.

13 Badger v. Paulson Investment Co., 311 Ore. 14 (S. Ct. OR 1991).

14 Restatement (Third) of Agency §4.01.

Many of the cases in agency law involve instances in which one person acts *without* authority for another. But sometimes, after the fact, the principal decides that he approves of what the agent has done even though it was not authorized at the time. The law would be perverse if it did not permit the principal, under those circumstances, to agree to the deal the agent has made. The law is not perverse, but it is careful. **Even if an agent acts without authority, the principal can decide later to be bound by her actions as long as these requirements are met:**

- The "agent" indicates to the third party that she is acting for a principal.
- The "principal" knows all the material facts of the transaction.
- The "principal" accepts the benefit of the whole transaction, not just part.
- The third party does not withdraw from the contract before ratification.

A night clerk at the St. Regis Hotel in Detroit was brutally murdered in the course of a robbery. A few days later, the *Detroit News* reported that the St. Regis management had offered a $1,000 reward for any information leading to the arrest and conviction of the killer. Two days after the article appeared, Robert Jackson turned in the man who was subsequently convicted of the crime. But then it was Jackson's turn to be robbed—the hotel refused to pay the reward on the grounds that the manager who had made the offer had no authority.

Jackson still had one weapon left: He convinced the court that the hotel had ratified the offer. One of the hotel's owners admitted he read the *Detroit News*. The court concluded that if someone reads a newspaper, he is sure to read any articles about a business he owns; therefore, the owner must have been aware of the offer. He accepted the benefit of the offer by failing to revoke it publicly by, say, announcing to the press that the reward was invalid. This failure to revoke constituted a ratification, and the hotel was liable.[15]

Subagents

Many of the examples in this chapter involve a single agent acting for a principal. Real life is often more complex. Daniel, the owner of a restaurant, hires Michaela to manage it. She in turn hires chefs, waiters, and dishwashers. Michaela is called an **intermediary agent**—someone who hires **subagents** for the principal. Daniel has never even met the restaurant help, yet they are his subagents.

As a general rule, an agent has no authority to delegate her tasks to another unless the principal authorizes her to do so. **But when an agent is authorized to hire a subagent, the principal is as liable for the acts of the subagent as he is for the acts of a regular agent.** After Daniel authorizes Michaela to hire a restaurant staff, she hires Lydia to serve as produce buyer. When Lydia buys food for the restaurant, Daniel must pay the bill.

FRANCES M. ROBERTS/Newscom

If these subagents serve rotten tomatoes, the owner of the restaurant is liable.

Intermediary agent
Someone who hires subagents for the principal

Subagent
Someone appointed by an agent to perform the agent's duties

28-2b Agent's Liability for Contracts

The agent's liability on a contract depends upon how much the third party knows about the principal. Disclosure is the agent's best protection against liability.

15Jackson v. Goodman, 69 Mich. App. 225 (1976).

Fully Disclosed Principal

An agent is not liable for any contracts she makes on behalf of a *fully* disclosed principal. A principal is fully disclosed if the third party knows of his *existence* and his *identity*. Augusta acts as an agent for Parker when he buys Tracey's prize-winning show horse. Augusta and Tracey both grew up in posh Grosse Pointe, Michigan, where they attended the same elite schools. Tracey does not know Parker, but she figures any friend of Augusta's must be OK. She figures wrong—Parker is a charming deadbeat. He injures Tracey's horse, fails to pay the full contract price, and promptly disappears. Tracey angrily demands that Augusta make good on Parker's debt. Unfortunately for Tracey, Parker was a fully disclosed principal—Tracey knew of his *existence* and his *identity*. Although Tracey partly relied on Augusta's good character when contracting with Parker, Augusta is not liable because Tracey knew who the principal was and could have (should have) investigated him. Augusta did not promise anything herself, and Tracey's only recourse is against the principal, Parker (wherever he may be).

To avoid liability when signing a contract on behalf of a principal, an agent must clearly state that she is an agent and also must identify the principal. Augusta should sign a contract on behalf of her principal, Parker, as follows: "Augusta, as agent for Parker" or "Parker, by Augusta, Agent."

Unidentified Principal

In the case of an *unidentified* principal, the third party can recover from either the agent or the principal. (An unidentified principal is also sometimes called a "partially disclosed principal.") A principal is unidentified if the third party knew of his *existence* but not his *identity*. Suppose that, when approaching Tracey about the horse, Augusta simply says, "I have a friend who is interested in buying your champion." Any friend of Augusta's is a friend of Tracey's—or so Tracey thinks. Parker is an unidentified principal because Tracey knows only that he exists, not who he is. She cannot investigate his creditworthiness because she does not know his name. Tracey relies solely on what she is able to learn from the agent, Augusta. Parker and Augusta are **jointly and severally liable** to Tracey. Thus, Tracey can recover from either or both of them. However, she cannot recover more than the total she is owed.

Jointly and severally liable
All members of a group are liable. They can be sued as a group, or any one of them can be sued individually for the full amount owed. But the plaintiff cannot recover more than the total she is owed.

Undisclosed Principal

In the case of an *undisclosed* principal, the third party can recover from either the agent or the principal. A principal is undisclosed if the third party did not know of his existence. Suppose that Augusta simply asks to buy the horse herself, without mentioning that she is purchasing it for Parker. In this case, Parker is an undisclosed principal because Tracey does not know that Augusta is acting for someone else. Both Parker and Augusta are jointly and severally liable. As Exhibit 28.1 illustrates, **the principal is *always* liable, but the agent is *only* liable when the principal's identity is unknown.**

In some ways, the concept of an undisclosed principal violates principles of contract law. If Tracey does not even know that Parker exists, how can they have an agreement or a meeting of the minds? Is such an arrangement fair to Tracey? The following incident illustrates why this type of contract is permitted.

William Zeckendorf was a man with a plan. For years, he had been eyeing a six-block tract of land along New York's East River. It was a wasteland of slums and slaughterhouses, but he could see its potential. The meat packers had always refused to sell to him but, finally, he got the phone call he had been waiting for. The companies were willing to sell—at more than three times the market price of surrounding land. Undeterred, Zeckendorf immediately put down a deposit. But to make his investment worthwhile, he needed to buy the neighboring property—once the slaughterhouses were gone, the other land would be much more valuable.

Zeckendorf was well known as a wealthy developer. If sellers realized that he was involved in the deal, prices would skyrocket, and the project would become too costly. So he hired agents to purchase the land for him. To conceal his involvement further, he went

EXHIBIT 28.1

The principal is *always* liable on a contract but the agent is *only* liable when the principal's identity is unknown.

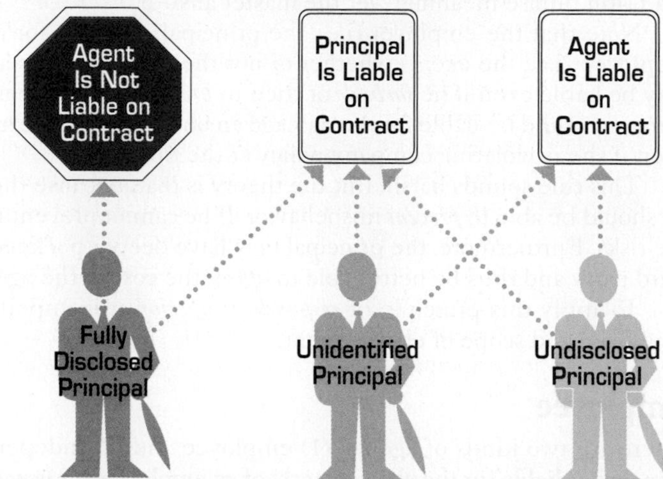

to South America for a month. When he returned, his agents had completed 75 different purchases, and he owned 18 acres of Manhattan land.

Shortly afterward, the United Nations (UN) began seeking a site for its headquarters. President Truman favored Boston, Philadelphia, or a location in the Midwest. The UN committee suggested Greenwich or Stamford, Connecticut. But John D. Rockefeller settled the question once and for all. He purchased Zeckendorf's land and donated it to the UN (netting Zeckendorf a 25 percent profit). Without the cooperation of agency law, the UN headquarters would not be in New York today.

Without the cooperation of agency law, the UN headquarters would not be in New York today.

Because of concerns about fair play, there are some exceptions to the rule on undisclosed principals. **A third party is not bound to the contract with an undisclosed principal if (1) the contract specifically provides that the third party is not bound to anyone other than the agent or (2) the agent lies about the principal because she knows the third party would refuse to contract with him.** Suppose that a large university is buying up land in an impoverished area near its campus. An owner of a house there wants to make sure that if he sells to the university, he gets a higher price than if he sells to an individual with more limited resources. A cagey property owner, when approached by one of the university's agents, could ask for a clause in the contract providing that the agent was not representing someone else. If the agent told the truth, the owner could demand a higher price. If the agent lied, then the owner could rescind the contract when the truth emerged.

Unauthorized Agent

Thus far in this section, we have been discussing an agent's liability to a third party for a transaction that was authorized by the principal. Sometimes, however, agents act without the authority of a principal. **If the agent has no authority (express, implied, or apparent), the principal is not liable to the third party, and the agent is.** Suppose that Augusta agrees to sell Parker's horse to Tracey. Unfortunately, Parker has never met Augusta and has certainly not authorized this transaction. Augusta is hoping that she can persuade him to sell, but Parker refuses. Augusta, but not Parker, is liable to Tracey for breach of contract.

28-2c Principal's Liability for Negligent Physical Torts

Respondeat superior
A principal is liable for certain torts committed by an agent.

An employer is liable for *physical* torts negligently committed by an employee acting within the scope of employment.[16] This rule is based on the principle of ***respondeat superior***, which is a Latin phrase meaning: "let the master answer."

Note that the employer (i.e., the principal) is liable for negligent misbehavior by the employee (i.e., the agent) whether or not the employer was at fault. Indeed, the employer may be liable even if he *forbade* or tried to *prevent* the employee from misbehaving. Thus, a company could be liable for the damage an on-duty worker causes if speeding while driving, even if she is violating company policy at the time.

This rule sounds harsh. But the theory is that, because the principal controls the agent, he should be able to *prevent* misbehavior. If he cannot prevent it, at least he can *insure* against the risks. Furthermore, the principal may have deeper pockets than the agent or the injured third party and thus be better able to *afford* the cost of the agent's misbehavior.

To apply this principle of *respondeat superior*, it is important to understand the terms: employee and scope of employment.

Employee

There are two kinds of agents: (1) employee and (2) independent contractor. **Generally, a principal *is* liable for the physical torts of an employee but is *not* liable for the physical torts of an independent contractor.** Because of this rule, the distinction between an employee and an independent contractor is important.

Employee or Independent Contractor? Unfortunately, however, the line between employee and independent contractor is fuzzy. Essentially, the more control the principal has over an agent, the more likely that the agent will be considered an employee. However, the courts evaluate each set of facts on a case-by-case basis. **When determining if agents are employees or independent contractors, courts consider whether:**

- The principal supervises details of the work.
- The principal supplies the tools and place of work.
- The agents work full time for the principal.
- The agents receive a salary or hourly wages, not a fixed price for the job.
- The work is part of the regular business of the principal.
- The principal and agents believe they have an employer–employee relationship.
- The principal is in business.[17]

Suppose that Mutt and Jeff work 40 hours a week at Swansong Media preparing food for the company's onsite dining room. They earn a weekly salary. Swansong provides food, utensils, and a kitchen. This year, however, Swansong decides to go all out for its holiday party, so it hires FiFi LaBelle to cater the event. She buys the food, prepares it in her own kitchen, and delivers it to the company in time for the party. She is an independent contractor, while Mutt and Jeff are employees.

Although this example is clear-cut, the following case illustrates how difficult these situations can be. These musicians and their employer were not dancing to the same tune.

16Restatement (Third) of Agency §7.07.

17Restatement (Third) of Agency §7.07.

You Be the Judge

Lancaster Symphony Orchestra v. NLRB

822 F3d 563
United States Court of Appeals for the District of Columbia Circuit, 2016

Facts: The orchestra in Lancaster, Pennsylvania hired musicians to play about four classical music concerts each year. These musicians could choose to play in however many concerts they wished. They then signed a Musician Agreement, which stated that they were independent contractors.

The musicians sought to unionize, but only employees, not independent contractors, have the right to join a union. The National Labor Relations Board ruled that the musicians were employees. The symphony disagreed and appealed the decision.

You Be the Judge: *Are the musicians employees or independent contractors?*

Argument for the Orchestra: The musicians are independent contractors because:

- They are highly skilled and receive little supervision. They are responsible for rehearsing on their own.
- The musicians provide their own tools—their instruments.
- They do not work full time for the Orchestra but have other jobs as well.
- They are paid by the job—for each concert.
- The musicians do not believe they are employees—they signed a contract stating that they are independent contractors.

Argument for the Musicians: The musicians are employees because:

- The Orchestra regulates virtually all aspects of the musicians' performance, including their dress and posture:
  - They are not permitted to cross their legs.
  - When the conductor signals for the orchestra to acknowledge applause, the musician handbook states that they must stand immediately, turn to face the audience, and smile.
  - During rehearsals, musicians are not permitted to talk about anything other than the rehearsal. They may not talk at all when the conductor is on the podium.
  - The conductor determines the musicians' volume and pitch, and the technique they use (such as the way they bow or use vibrato).
- Although the musicians supply their own instruments, the Orchestra supplies other crucial tools: music, stands, chairs, and concert hall.
- Musicians are in effect paid by the hour because they receive additional pay for each 15 minutes that a rehearsal or concert exceeds two and a half hours.
- Their work is part of the regular business of the employer.
- Just because the Orchestra says the musicians are independent contractors does not mean the musicians believe that to be true.
- The principal is in business.

The Gig Economy. In four years, Uber went from zero drivers to 400,000. Its drivers could work full time, or just a few hours a week, during the day or only at night. They logged onto an app rather than punching a clock.

The gig economy is based on companies that, instead of hiring full-time employees, use mobile apps to facilitate peer-to-peer transactions that pay per job. This employment practice is increasingly common. Almost one-third of the American workforce does some gig work. And it is not just ride-sharing; it is chores, cleaning, delivery, repairs, and shipping. You name the job, there is an app for that. The good news for workers? Flexibility (work for any company any time) and low barriers to entry (a clean car and you are in business). The downside? No benefits, no job security, no right to join a union, often low wages.

EXHIBIT 28.2

The Difference in Liability between an Employee and an Independent Contractor

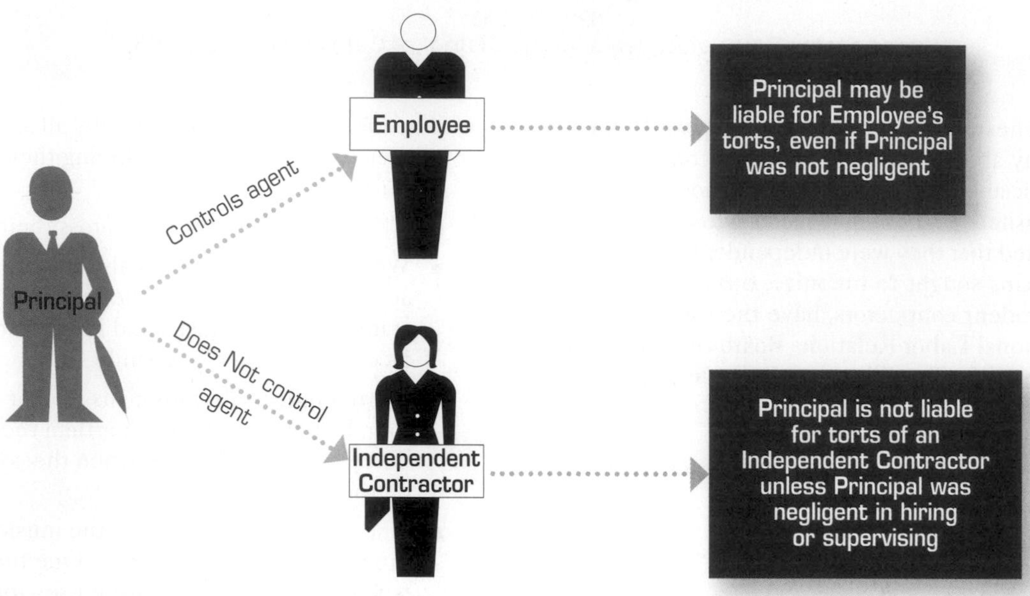

Inevitably the issue arises: Are these freelance workers independent contractors or employees? The companies themselves have an incentive to classify their workers as independent contractors because then they not only avoid tort liability, but also have no obligation to pay the minimum wage or overtime, provide health care or pay taxes such as unemployment, Social Security, and Medicare. Uber drivers have filed lawsuits in multiple states contending that they are more like employees and should, therefore, receive employee benefits. Although some states have ruled that some Uber drivers are employees under some state programs, the jury is still out....

Negligent Hiring. Although, as we have seen, principals are generally not liable for the physical torts of an independent contractor, there is one exception to this rule: **A principal is liable for both the negligent and intentional physical torts of an independent contractor *if* the principal has been negligent in hiring or supervising her.** Remember that the principal is liable *without fault* for the torts of *employees*. The case of independent contractors is different: The principal is liable only if he was *at fault* by being careless in his hiring or supervising.

Exhibit 28.2 illustrates the difference in liability between an employee and an independent contractor.

Scope of Employment

You remember: An employer is liable for a negligent physical tort committed by an employee acting within the scope of employment. **An employee is acting within the scope of employment if the act:**

- Is one that employees are generally responsible for,
- Takes place during hours that the employee is generally employed,

- Is part of the principal's business,
- Is similar to the one the principal authorized,
- Is one for which the principal supplied the tools, and
- Is not seriously criminal.

If an employee leaves a pool of water on the floor of a store and a customer slips and falls, the employer is liable. But if the same employee leaves water on his own kitchen floor and a friend falls, the employer is not liable because the employee is not acting within the scope of employment.

Scope of employment cases raise two major issues: authorization and abandonment.

Authorization. In authorization cases, the agent is clearly working for the principal but commits an act that the principal has not authorized. Although Jane has often told the driver of her delivery van not to speed, Hank ignores her instructions and plows into Bernadette. At the time of the accident, he is working for Jane, delivering flowers for her shop, but his act is not authorized. **An act is within the scope of employment, even if expressly forbidden, if it is of the same general nature as that authorized or if it is incidental to the conduct authorized.** Hank was authorized to drive the van, but not to speed. However, his speeding was of the same general nature as the authorized act, so Jane is liable to Bernadette.

EXAMStrategy

Question: While on a business trip, Trevor went sightseeing on his day off. Although company policy forbade talking on a cell phone while driving, Trevor did answer his phone while in his car. Distracted, he crashed into Olivia's house, causing substantial damage. Was his employer liable for the damage?

Strategy: Whenever a case involves a company's liability for the acts of an employee, begin by asking if *respondeat superior* applies. Was he acting within the scope of employment? Does it matter that it was his day off and he was violating company policy?

Result: In a similar case, the court ruled that the employer was liable because it is foreseeable that traveling employees will go sightseeing and, therefore, companies should include this potential liability as a cost of doing business.[18] The fact that the employer's policy prohibits talking on a cell phone while driving does not protect the company from liability if an employee violates that policy. The employer should not have hired such a disobedient worker.

Abandonment. This EXAM Strategy also illustrates the second major issue in a scope of employment case: abandonment. **The principal is liable for the actions of the employee that occur while the employee is at work, but not for actions that occur after the employee has abandoned the principal's business.** In other words, the employer is liable if the employee is simply on a *detour* from company business, but the employer is not liable if the employee is off on a *frolic of his own*. Suppose that Hank, the delivery van driver, is in an accident during his afternoon commute home. An employee is generally not acting within the scope of his employment when he commutes to and from work, so his principal, Jane, is not liable. On the other hand, if Hank stops at the Burger Box drive-in window en route to making a delivery, Jane is liable when he crashes into Anna on the way out of the parking lot because this time, he is simply making a detour.

---

[18] Potter v. Shaw, 60 Mass. App. Ct. 1112 (Mass. App. Ct. 2004).

Was the employee in the following case acting within the scope of his employment while driving to work? You be the judge.

You Be the Judge

Zankel v. United States of America

2008 U.S. Dist. LEXIS 23655; 2008 WL 828032
United States District Court for the Western District of Pennsylvania, 2008

Facts: Staff Sergeant William E. Dreyer was a recruiter for the United States Marine Corps, which provided Dreyer a car to drive while on government business. He was not permitted to use this car while commuting to and from home unless he had specific authorization from his boss, Major Michael Sherman, but Sherman was lenient in giving authorization and even permitted his soldiers to obtain permission simply by leaving a message on his voicemail. He had denied only about a dozen of such requests over a three-year period.

Each month, Dreyer was expected to meet specific quotas for the number of contracts signed and recruits shipped to basic training. However, despite working 16 to 18 hours every day of the week, Dreyer had not met his recruiting quotas for months. Sherman had formally reprimanded him and increased his target for the following month.

On the day before the accident, Dreyer left home at 6:30 a.m., driving his own car. At the office, he switched to a government car and worked until 10:45 p.m. He then discovered that his personal car would not start. He did not want to call Sherman that late, so he drove his government car home without permission. He believed that, had he called, Sherman would have approved. Dreyer arrived home at midnight. He was under orders to attend an early morning training session the next day. So he awoke early and left home at 6:35 a.m. At 6:40 a.m., his car struck and killed 12-year-old Justin Zankel.

The child's parents sued the U.S. government, claiming that it was liable for Dreyer's actions because he had been acting within the scope of his employment at the time of the accident.

You Be the Judge: *Was Dreyer within the scope of employment when he killed Zankel? Is the government liable?*

Argument for the Zankels: At the time of the accident, Dreyer was driving a government vehicle. Although he had not requested permission to drive the car, if he had done so, permission certainly would have been granted.

Moreover, even if Dreyer was not authorized to drive the Marine Corps car, the government is still liable because his activity was of the same general nature as that authorized and it was incidental to the conduct authorized. Driving the car was part of Dreyer's work. Indeed, he could not perform his job without it. In addition, Dreyer was on the road early so that he could attend a required training session. He was exhausted from trying to reach impossible goals. The Marine Corps must bear responsibility for this tragic accident.

Argument for the United States: The government had a clear policy stating that recruiters were not authorized to drive a government car without first requesting permission. Dreyer had not done so. Therefore, he was not authorized to drive the government car at the time of the accident.

Moreover, it is well established that an employee commuting to and from work is not within the scope of employment. If Dreyer had been driving from one recruiting effort to another, that would be a different story. But in this case, he had not yet started work for the Marine Corps, and therefore the government is not liable.

28-2d Principal's Liability for Intentional Physical Torts

A principal is *not* liable for the *intentional* physical torts of an employee unless (1) the employee intended to serve some purpose of the employer or (2) the employer was negligent in hiring or supervising this employee. Thieves have stolen a number of computers and purses from the desks of Compania employees. When Aubrey sees a stranger walking down the hallway carrying a computer, she tackles him from behind, breaking his nose. It turns out that he was an authorized computer repair person. Compania is liable for Aubrey's actions because she was motivated, at least in part, by a desire to help her employer. But if Aubrey attacks someone in the company lunch room because he took the last cupcake, Compania is *not* liable. Aubrey was acting out of personal frustration, not a desire to help her employer.

This liability issue has been litigated many times in cases involving Catholic priests who molested children. To take one example, Father Albert Liberatore taught at a college for young men studying to be priests. After he engaged in illicit sexual relationships with some of his students, his Bishop assigned him to work at a church. During Liberatore's time at this church, everyone from the cleaning staff to other priests told the Bishop that Liberatore was engaging in inappropriate sexual behavior with a young boy. The boy himself told another priest that he was being sexually abused. No one did anything to protect that boy or other children until after Father Liberatore pleaded guilty to multiple counts of sexual abuse.

Although Liberatore's intentional acts were clearly not intended to serve some purpose of his employer, the Church was liable for its negligence in supervising the priest.[19]

28-2e Principal's Liability for Nonphysical Torts

Nonphysical tort
One that harms only reputation, feelings, or wallet

So far, we have seen the rules on *physical* torts. A **nonphysical tort** is one that harms only reputation, feelings, or wallet. **Nonphysical torts (whether intentional or unintentional) are treated like a contract claim: The principal is liable only if the employee acted with express, implied, or apparent authority.**[20] Suppose that Dwayne buys a house insurance policy from Andy, who is an agent of the Balls of Fire Insurance Company. Andy throws away Dwayne's policy and pockets his premiums. When Dwayne's house burns down, Balls of Firc is liable because Andy was acting with apparent authority.

EXAMStrategy

Question: Daisy was the founder of an internet start-up company. Jay was her driver. One day, after driving Daisy to a board meeting, he went to the car wash. There, he told a woman that he worked for a money management firm. She gave him money to invest. On the way out of the car wash, he was so excited that he hit another customer's expensive car. Who is liable for Jay's misdeeds?

Strategy: In determining a principal's liability, begin by figuring out whether the agent has committed a physical or nonphysical tort. Remember that the principal is liable for negligent physical torts that occur within the scope of employment, but for nonphysical torts, she is liable only if the employee acted with authority.

Result: In this case, Daisy is liable for the damage to the car because that was a negligent physical tort within the scope of employment. But she is not liable for the investment money because Jay did not have authority (express, implied, or apparent) to take those funds.

---

[19] Doe v. Liberatore, 478 F. Supp. 2d 742 (M.D. Pa. 2007).

[20] Restatement (Third) of Agency §7.08.

28-2f Agent's Liability for Torts

The focus of the prior section was on the *principal's* liability for the agent's torts. But it is important to remember that **agents are always liable for their own torts**. Agents who commit torts are personally responsible, whether or not their principal is also liable. Even if the tort was committed to benefit the principal, the agent is still liable. So the sailor who got into a fistfight while rousing a shipmate from bed is liable even though he thought he was acting for the benefit of his principal.

This rule makes obvious sense. If the agent was not liable, he would have little incentive to be careful. Imagine Hank driving his delivery van for Jane. If he was not personally liable for his own torts, he might think, "If I drive fast enough, I can make it through that light even though it just turned red. And if I don't, what the heck, it'll be Jane's problem, not mine." Agents, as a rule, may have fewer assets than their principal, but it is important that their personal assets be at risk in the event of their negligent behavior.

If the agent and principal are *both* liable, which one does the injured third party sue? The principal and the agent are *jointly and severally liable*, which means, as we have seen, that the injured third party can sue either one or both, as she chooses. If she recovers from the principal, he can sue the agent.

CHAPTER CONCLUSION

When students enroll in a business law course, they fully expect to learn about torts and contracts, corporations, and antitrust. They probably do not think much about agency law; many of them have not even heard the term before. Yet it is an area of the law that affects us all because each of us has been and will continue to be both an agent and a principal many times in our lives.

EXAM REVIEW

1. **CREATING AN AGENCY RELATIONSHIP** A principal and an agent mutually consent that the agent will act on behalf of the principal and be subject to the principal's control, thereby creating a fiduciary relationship.

2. **ELEMENTS NOT REQUIRED** An agency relationship can exist without either a written agreement, a formal agreement, or compensation.

3. **AN AGENT'S DUTIES TO THE PRINCIPAL** An agent owes these duties to the principal: duty of loyalty, duty to obey instructions, duty of care, and duty to provide information.

4. **THE PRINCIPAL'S REMEDIES IN THE EVENT OF A BREACH** The principal has three potential remedies when the agent breaches her duty: recovery of damages the breach has caused, recovery of any profits earned by the agent from the breach, and rescission of any transaction with the agent.

EXAMStrategy

Question: Jonah tells his friend Derek that he would like to go parasailing. Derek suggests that they try an outfit called Wind Beneath Your Wings because he has heard good things about it. Derek offers to arrange everything. He makes a reservation, puts the $600 fee on his credit card, and picks Jonah up to drive him to the Wings location. What a friend! But the day does not turn out as Jonah had hoped. While he is soaring up in the air over the Pacific Ocean, his sail springs a leak, he goes plummeting into the sea and breaks both legs. During his recuperation in the hospital, he learns that Wings is unlicensed. He also sees an ad for Wings offering parasailing for only $350. And Derek is listed in the ad as one of the company's owners. Was Derek Jonah's agent? Has he violated his fiduciary responsibility?

Strategy: There are three issues to consider in answering this question: (1) Was there an agency relationship? This requires consent, control, and a fiduciary relationship. (2) Is anything missing—does it matter if the agent is unpaid or the contract is not in writing? (3) Has the agent fulfilled his duties? (See the "Result" at the end of this Exam Review section.)

5. **THE PRINCIPAL'S DUTIES TO THE AGENT** The principal has three duties to the agent: to compensate as provided by the agreement, to indemnify for reasonable expenses, and to cooperate with the agent.

6. **POWER AND RIGHT TO TERMINATE** Both the agent and the principal have the power to terminate an agency relationship, but they may not have the right. If the termination violates the agency agreement and causes harm to the other party, the wrongful party must pay damages.

7. **AUTOMATIC TERMINATION** An agency relationship automatically terminates if the principal or agent no longer can perform the required duties or if a change in circumstances renders the agency relationship pointless.

8. **A PRINCIPAL'S LIABILITY FOR CONTRACTS** A principal is liable for the contracts of the agent if the agent has express, implied, or apparent authority.

9. **EXPRESS AUTHORITY** The principal grants express authority by words or conduct that, reasonably interpreted, cause the agent to believe that the principal desires her to act on the principal's account.

10. **IMPLIED AUTHORITY** Implied authority includes authority to do acts that are incidental to a transaction, usually accompany it, or are reasonably necessary to accomplish it.

11. **APPARENT AUTHORITY** Apparent authority means that a principal is liable for the acts of an agent who is not, in fact, acting with authority if the principal's conduct causes a third party reasonably to believe that the agent is authorized.

EXAMStrategy

Question: Dr. James Leonard wrote Dr. Edward Jacobson to offer him the position of chief of audiology at Jefferson Medical College in Philadelphia. In the letter, Leonard stated that this appointment would have to be approved by the promotion and appointment committee. Jacobson believed that the appointment committee acted only as a rubber stamp, affirming whatever recommendation Leonard made. Jacobson accepted Leonard's offer and proceeded to sell his house and quit his job in Colorado. You can guess what happened next. Two weeks later, Leonard sent Jacobson another letter, rescinding his offer because of opposition from the appointment committee. Did Leonard have apparent authority?

Strategy: In cases of apparent authority, begin by asking what the principal did to make the third party believe that the agent was authorized. What did the Medical College do? (See the "Result" at the end of this Exam Review section.)

12. **AN AGENT'S LIABILITY FOR A CONTRACT** If an agent makes a contract on behalf of a fully disclosed principal, the agent is not liable on the contract, but the principal is. In the case of an unidentified or undisclosed principal, both the agent and the principal are liable on the contract.

13. **NEGLIGENT PHYSICAL TORTS OF AN EMPLOYEE** An employer is liable for a physical tort negligently committed by an employee acting within the scope of employment.

EXAMStrategy

Question: While drunk, the driver of a subway car plows into the back of the car ahead of him, killing a passenger. It was against the rules for the driver to be drunk. Is the subway authority liable for the negligence of its employee?

Strategy: With a tort case, always determine first if the agents are employees or independent contractors. This worker was an employee. Then ask if the employee was acting within the scope of employment. Yes, he was driving a subway car, which is what he was hired to do. Does it matter that he had violated subway rules? No, his violation of the rules does not eliminate his principal's liability because his actions are of the same general nature as those that are authorized. (See the "Result" at the end of this Exam Review section.)

14. **INDEPENDENT CONTRACTOR** The principal is liable for both the intentional and negligent physical torts of an independent contractor only if the principal has been negligent in hiring or supervising him.

15. **INTENTIONAL PHYSICAL TORTS** A principal is not liable for the intentional physical torts of an employee unless (1) the employee intended to serve some purpose of the employer or (2) the employer was negligent in hiring or supervising this employee.

16. **NONPHYSICAL TORTS** A principal is liable for nonphysical torts of an employee (whether intentional or unintentional) only if the employee was acting with express, implied, or apparent authority.

17. **AGENT'S LIABILITY FOR TORTS** Agents are always liable for their own torts.

RESULTS

4. Result: There is an agency relationship: Derek had agreed to help Jonah; it was Jonah who set the goal for the relationship (parasailing); the purpose of this relationship was for one person to benefit another. It does not matter if Derek was not paid or the agreement not written. Derek has violated his duty to exercise due care. He should not have taken Jonah to an unlicensed company. He has also violated his duty to provide information: He should have told Jonah the true cost for the lessons and also revealed that he was a principal of the company. And he violated his duty of loyalty when he worked for two principals whose interests were in conflict.

11. Result: No. Leonard had told Jacobson that he did not have authority. If Jacobson chose to believe otherwise, that was his problem.

13. Result: The subway authority is liable.

MULTIPLE-CHOICE QUESTIONS

1. At Business University, semester enrollment begins at midnight on April 1. Jasper asked his roommate, Alonso, to register him for an important required course as a favor. Alonso agreed to do so but then overslept. As a result, Jasper could not enroll in the required course he needed to graduate and had to stay in school for an additional semester. Is Alonso liable to Jasper?
   (a) No because an agency agreement is invalid unless the agent receives payment.
   (b) No because Alonso was not grossly negligent.
   (c) No because the agreement was not in writing.
   (d) Yes because Alonso was negligent.

2. Finn learns that, despite his stellar record, he is being paid less than other salespeople at Barry Co., so he decides to start his own company. During his last month on the Barry payroll, he tells all of his clients about his new business. He also tells them that Barry is a great company, but his fees will be lower. After he opens the doors of his new business, most of his former clients move with him. Is Finn liable to Barry?
   (a) No because he has not been disloyal to Barry—he praised the company.
   (b) No because Barry was underpaying him.
   (c) No because his clients have the right to hire whichever company they choose.
   (d) Yes, Finn has violated his duty of loyalty to Barry.

3. Kurt asked his car mechanic, Quinn, for help in buying a used car. Quinn recommends a Ford Focus that she has been taking care of its whole life. Quinn was working for the seller. Which of the following statements is true?
   (a) Quinn must pay Kurt the amount of money she received from the Ford's prior owner.
   (b) After buying the car, Kurt finds out that it needs $1,000 in repairs. He can recover that amount from Quinn, but only if Quinn knew about the needed repairs before Kurt bought the car.
   (c) Kurt cannot recover anything because Quinn had no obligation to reveal her relationship with the car's seller.
   (d) Kurt cannot recover anything because he had not paid Quinn for her help.

4. Figgins is the dean of a college. He appointed Sue as acting dean while he was out of the country and posted an announcement on the college website announcing that she was authorized to act in his place. He also told Sue privately that she did not have the right to make admissions decisions. While Figgins was gone, Sue overruled the admissions committee to admit the child of a wealthy alumnus. Does the child have the right to attend this college?
   (a) No because Sue was not authorized to admit him.
   (b) No because Figgins did not ratify Sue's decision.
   (c) Yes because Figgins was a fully disclosed principal.
   (d) Yes because Sue had apparent authority.

5. **CPA QUESTION** A principal will not be liable to a third party for a tort committed by an agent:
   (a) unless the principal instructed the agent to commit the tort.
   (b) unless the tort was committed within the scope of the agency relationship.
   (c) if the agency agreement limits the principal's liability for the agent's tort.
   (d) if the tort is also regarded as a criminal act.

6. **CPA QUESTION** Cox engaged Datz as her agent. It was mutually agreed that Datz would not disclose that he was acting as Cox's agent. Instead, he was to deal with prospective customers as if he were a principal acting on his own behalf. This he did and made several contracts for Cox. Assuming Cox, Datz, or the customer seeks to avoid liability on one of the contracts involved, which of the following statements is correct?
   (a) Cox must ratify the Datz contracts to be held liable.
   (b) Datz has no liability once he discloses that Cox was the real principal.
   (c) The third party can avoid liability because he believed he was dealing with Datz as a principal.
   (d) The third party may choose to hold either Datz or Cox liable.

CASE QUESTIONS

1. An elementary school custodian hit a child who wrote graffiti on the wall. Is the school district liable for this intentional tort by its employee?

2. What if the custodian hit one of the schoolchildren for calling him a name? Is the school district liable?

3. One afternoon while visiting friends, tennis star Vitas Gerulaitis fell asleep in their pool house. A mechanic had improperly installed the swimming pool heater, which leaked carbon monoxide fumes into the house where he slept, killing him. His mother filed suit against the owners of the estate. On what theory would they be liable?

4. Fernando worked for Affinity, which made furniture deliveries for Sears. Fernando signed a contract stating that he was an independent contractor. He was paid $23 per delivery. He typically worked five to seven days a week, but Affinity would call him each day to tell him whether or not he would be working the following day. Fernando was not required to, but he did, lease his truck from Affinity. The company handled upkeep on the truck. Affinity required all drivers to buy their mobile telephones and their uniforms from the company. It also established personal grooming requirements. Was Fernando an employee or independent contractor?

5. Betsy has a two-year contract as a producer at Jackson Movie Studios. She produces a remake of the movie *Footloose.* Unfortunately, it bombs, and Jackson is so furious that he fires her on the weekend the movie opens. Does he have the power to do this?

DISCUSSION QUESTIONS

1. **ETHICS** Mercedes has just begun work at Photobook.com. What a great place to work! Although the salary is not high, the company has fabulous perks. The dining room provides great food from 7 a.m. to midnight, five days a week. There is also a free laundry and dry-cleaning service. Mercedes's social life has never been better. She invites her friends over for Photobook meals and has their laundry done for free. And because her job requires her to be online all the time, she has plenty of opportunity to stay in touch with her friends by messaging, tweeting, and checking Facebook updates. She is, however, shocked that one of her colleagues takes paper from the office for his children to use at home. Are these employees behaving ethically? Are they meeting their obligations as agents?

2. Kevin was the manager of a radio station, WABC. A competing station hired him away. In his last month on the job at WABC, he notified two key on-air personalities that if they were to leave the station, he would not hold them to their non-compete agreements. What can WABC do?

3. Jesse worked as a buyer for the Vegetable Co. Rachel offered to sell Jesse 10 tons of tomatoes for the account of Vegetable. Jesse accepted the offer. Later, Jesse discovered that Rachel was an agent for Sylvester Co. Who is liable on this contract?

4. The Pharmaceutical Association holds an annual convention. At the convention, Brittany, who was president of the association, told Luke that Research Corp. had a promising new cancer vaccine. Luke was so excited that he chartered a plane to fly to Research's headquarters. On the way, the plane crashed and Luke was killed. Is the Pharmaceutical Association liable for Luke's death?

5. A year ago, Hot Air Systems installed a new heating system in Dolly's house. A month ago, Chuck called Dolly and told her he worked for Hot Air and it was time to perform the yearly inspection. After his inspection, Chuck said it was lucky he had called because her system needed urgent repairs. He then charged her $500 for the repairs. Later, Dolly discovered there had been nothing wrong with her system and Chuck had never worked for Hot Air. Is the company liable for Chuck's wrongdoing?

29 EMPLOYMENT AND LABOR LAW

Before there were laws to protect employees, working conditions could be horrific. In the nineteenth century, many laborers worked a minimum of 12 to 16 hours a day, 6 days a week—and made about $4 a week. Sometimes child workers received room and board instead of any payment. Employers might impose arbitrary fines that consumed most of a worker's pay. Men earned twice as much as women and children, but that just meant factories would not hire them. In some factories, half of the workers were under the age of 12.

Factories were so dirty that workers became sick and even died from illnesses such as pneumonia and tuberculosis. They were deafened by machine noise and suffered horrible accidents—commonly being mutilated and even crushed by the machines.[1]

Conditions were particularly bad for children. Employers beat them with leather straps, nailed their ears to tables, and threw buckets of water on them to keep them awake.

Children as young as four worked in mines, sitting in the dark all day, opening the door for coal trucks. At six, they carried coal; at nine, it was heavy boxes on their heads.[2]

Conditions were particularly bad for children.

[1]For some particularly graphic examples, see http://spartacus-educational.com/IRaccidents.htm.

[2]Adapted from Barbara M. Tucker, "Liberty Is Exploitation: The Force of Tradition in Early Manufacturing," *OAH Magazine of History*, Vol. 19, No. 3, Market Revolution (May, 2005), pp. 21–24 and www.bbc.co.uk/schools/gcsebitesize/history/shp/britishsociety/livingworkingconditionsrev1.shtml.

How did society arrive at a place where workers (*children*, no less) were treated this way? Why were these abuses allowed?

29-1 EMPLOYMENT AT WILL

For most of history, the concept of career planning was unknown. By and large, people were born into their jobs. Whatever their parents had been—landowner, soldier, farmer, servant, merchant, or beggar—they became, too. People not only knew their place, they also understood the rights and obligations inherent in each position. The landowner had the right to receive labor from his tenants, but he also cared for them if they fell ill. Certainly, there were abuses, but at a time when people held religious convictions about their position in life and workers had few expectations that their lives would be better than their parents', the role of law was limited.

The primary English law of employment simply established that, in the absence of a contract, an employee was hired for a year at a time. This rule was designed to prevent injustice in a farming society. If an employee worked through harvest time, the landowner could not fire him in the unproductive winter. Conversely, a worker could not stay the winter and then leave for greener pastures in the spring.

In the eighteenth and nineteenth centuries, the Industrial Revolution profoundly altered the employment relationship. Many workers left the farms and villages for large factories in the city. Bosses no longer knew their workers personally, so they felt little responsibility toward them. The old laws that had suited an agrarian economy with stable relationships did not fit the new employment conditions. Instead of duties and responsibilities, courts emphasized the freedom to contract. Since employees could quit their factory jobs whenever they wanted, it seemed only fair for employers to have the same freedom to fire a worker. That was indeed the rule adopted by the courts: Unless workers had an explicit employment contract, they were employees at will. **An *employee at will* could be fired for a good reason, a bad reason, or no reason at all.** For nearly a century, this was the basic common law rule of employment. A court explained the rule this way:

> Precisely as may the employee cease labor at his whim or pleasure, and, whatever be his reason, good, bad, or indifferent, leave no one a legal right to complain; so, upon the other hand, may the employer discharge, and, whatever be his reason, good, bad, or indifferent, no one has suffered a legal wrong.[3]

However evenhanded this common law rule of employment may have sounded in theory, in practice, it could lead to harsh results. As the opening scenario illustrates, the lives of many workers were grim. It was not as if they could simply pack up and leave; conditions were no better elsewhere. Courts and legislatures gradually began to recognize that individual workers were generally unable to negotiate fair contracts with powerful employers. Since the beginning of the twentieth century, employment law has changed dramatically. Now, the employment relationship is more strictly regulated by statutes and by the common law.

Note well, though: Unless you have a contract that specifies a particular term, or the company in some other way limits its rights by, for example, stating in the handbook that employees will only be fired for good cause, then you are an employee at will. **In the absence of a *specific legal exception*, the rule in the United States is *still* that an employee at will can be fired for any reason.**

Those *specific legal exceptions* to the employment-at-will doctrine are the topic of this chapter and the next. Many employment statutes were passed by Congress and therefore apply *nationally*. The common law, however, comes from state courts and only applies *locally*. We will look at a sampling of cases that illustrates trends, even though the law varies from state to state.

---

[3]Union Labor Hospital Association v. Vance Redwood Lumber Company, 158 Cal. 551, 554 (Cal. 1910).

This chapter covers five topics in employment law: (1) employment security, (2) workplace freedom, (3) workplace safety, (4) financial protection, and (5) labor unions. Chapter 30 covers employment discrimination.

29-2 EMPLOYMENT SECURITY

29-2a Common Law Protections

The employment-at-will doctrine was created by the courts. Because that rule sometimes led to grossly unfair results, the courts created a major exception: **wrongful discharge.**

Wrongful discharge
An employer may not fire a worker for a reason that violates basic social rights, duties, or responsibilities.

Wrongful Discharge: Violating Public Policy

Olga Monge was a schoolteacher in her native Costa Rica. After moving to New Hampshire, she attended college in the evenings to earn U.S. teaching credentials. At night, she worked at the Beebe Rubber Co. During the day, she cared for her husband and three children. When she applied for a better job at her plant, the foreman offered to promote her if she would go out on a date with him. When she refused, he assigned her to a lower-wage job, took away her overtime, made her clean the washrooms, and generally ridiculed her. Finally, she collapsed at work, and he fired her.[4]

Imagine that you are one of the judges who decided this case. Olga Monge was an employee at will and therefore could be fired for any reason. But how can you let the foreman get away with this despicable behavior? The New Hampshire Supreme Court decided that even an employee at will has some rights:

> We hold that a termination by the employer of a contract of employment at will which is motivated by bad faith or malice or based on retaliation is not in the best interest of the economic system or the public good and constitutes a breach of the employment contract.[5]

The *Monge* case illustrates the concept of **wrongful discharge, which prohibits an employer from firing a worker for certain particularly *bad reasons.*** A bad reason is one that violates public policy. Unfortunately, this public policy rule is easier to name than it is to define because its definition and application vary from state to state. **In essence, the public policy rule prohibits an employer from firing a worker for a reason that violates fundamental social rights, duties, or responsibilities.**

Almost every employee who has ever been fired feels that a horrible injustice has been done. The difficulty, from the courts' perspective, is to distinguish those cases of dismissal that are offensive enough to harm the community at large from those that injure only the employee. The courts have primarily applied the public policy rule when an employee refuses to violate the law, exercises a legal right, or supports fundamental societal values.

Refusing to Violate the Law. **As a general rule, employees may not be discharged for refusing to break the law.** Courts have protected employees who refused to participate in an illegal price-fixing scheme, falsify pollution control records required by state law, pollute navigable waters in violation of federal law, or assist a supervisor in stealing from customers.[6]

4Monge v. Beebe, 114 N.H. 130 (NH 1974).

5Monge v. Beebe, 114 N.H. 133 (NH 1974).

6Tameny v. Atlantic Richfield Co., 27 Cal. 3d 167 (Cal. 1980); Trombetta v. Detroit, T. & I. R., 81 Mich. App. 489 (Mich. Ct. App. 1978); Sabine Pilot Service, Inc. v. Hauck, 28 Tex. Sup. J. 339 (Tex. 1985); Vermillion v. AAA Pro Moving & Storage, 146 Ariz. 215 (Ariz. Ct. App. 1985).

Not surprisingly, courts are particularly protective of the judicial process. For example, employers are generally not allowed to fire workers for testifying truthfully in court. A patient at the Duke Hospital suffered brain damage after a doctor administered the wrong anesthetic. When nurse Marie Sides was called to testify in the patient's case against the hospital, a number of Duke doctors told her that she would be "in trouble" if she testified. She did testify, and after three months of harassment, she was fired. When she sued Duke University, the court held:

> It would be obnoxious to the interests of the state and contrary to public policy and sound morality to allow an employer to discharge any employee on the ground that the employee declined to commit perjury, an act specifically enjoined by statute.[7]

Judges have also consistently held that an employee may not be fired for serving on a jury.

Exercising a Legal Right. **As a general rule, an employer may not discharge a worker for exercising a legal right if that right supports public policy.** Dorothy Frampton was injured while working at the Central Indiana Gas Co. After she filed a claim under the state's workers' compensation plan, the company fired her. When she sued, the court held that the gas company had violated public policy. If workers fear that making a claim for workers' comp will get them fired, then no one will file and the whole point of the statute will be undermined.[8]

Supporting Societal Values. **Courts are sometimes willing to protect employees who do the right thing, even if they violate the boss's orders.** A company fired an armored truck driver because he disobeyed company policy by leaving his vehicle to help two women who were being attacked by a bank robber. A court ruled for the driver on the grounds that, although he had no affirmative legal duty to intervene in such a situation, society values those who aid people in danger.[9] This issue is, however, one on which the courts are divided. Not all judges would have made the same decision.

In the following case, an employee was fired for exercising her legal right to use medical marijuana. Did her employer violate public policy?

You Be the Judge

Roe v. TeleTech Customer Care Mgmt. (Colo.) LLC

171 Wn.2d 736
Washington Supreme Court, 2011

Facts: The voters of Washington state passed the Medical Use of Marijuana Act (MUMA), which stated:

> Humanitarian compassion necessitates that the decision to authorize the medical use of marijuana by patients with terminal or debilitating illnesses is a personal, individual decision, based upon their physician's professional medical judgment and discretion.
>
> Qualifying patients and medical practitioners shall not be found guilty of a crime under state law for their possession and limited use of marijuana. Any person meeting the requirements appropriate to his or her status under this chapter shall not be penalized in any manner, or denied any right or privilege, for such actions.
>
> Nothing in this chapter requires any accommodation of any on-site medical use of marijuana in any place of employment.

Jane Roe suffered from debilitating migraine headaches that caused chronic pain, nausea, and blurred vision. On a medical questionnaire, she described her average pain as

---

[7]Sides v. Duke University, 74 N.C. App. 331 (N.C. Ct. App. 1985).

[8]Frampton v. Central Indiana Gas Co., 260 Ind. 249 (Ind. 1973).

[9]Gardner v. Loomis Armored, Inc., 128 Wn.2d 931 (Wash. 1996).

an 8 on a scale of 1 to 10 where 10 represented "pain as bad as you can imagine." Because other medications were not effective, she obtained a prescription for medical marijuana. It alleviated her symptoms without side effects and allowed Roe to work and care for her children. She ingested marijuana only in her home.

TeleTech Customer Care Mgmt. offered Roe a position as a customer service representative but required that she first pass a drug test. She told the company about her medical marijuana use. On the day she started work, TeleTech received notice that Roe had failed the drug test. A week later, it fired her.

Roe sued TeleTech for wrongful discharge, alleging that her termination had violated public policy. (She filed suit under a pseudonym because medical marijuana use is illegal under federal law.) The trial court granted TeleTech's motion for summary judgment. The appeals court confirmed. The Washington Supreme Court agreed to hear the case.

You Be the Judge: *Did TeleTech violate public policy when it fired Roe? Was this discharge wrongful?*

Argument for Roe: Roe is exactly the sort of person this statute is intended to protect. Medical marijuana changed her life—now she can hold a job and care for her family. But, of course, she cannot hold a job if employers fire her for using this legal medication. TeleTech is undermining the whole point of the statute and jeopardizing its clear policies. A ruling in favor of TeleTech would inhibit other people from using medication that citizens voted to make available.

Furthermore, the statute specifically states that, "No person ... shall be penalized in any manner, or denied any right or privilege, for such actions." Being fired is a substantial penalty.

No one is asking TeleTech to tolerate drug-impaired workers. Marijuana should be treated like any other medication—it cannot be used if it hurts job performance. But there is no evidence that it did so.

Argument for TeleTech: Just because medical marijuana is legal in Washington does not mean that it is an important social right. Indeed, employers can fire workers for many *legal* behaviors, such as smoking, or being disagreeable.

The purpose of MUMA is to protect doctors and patients from criminal liability, not to create an unlimited right to use medical marijuana. The statute does not explicitly prevent employers from banning its use. And how can marijuana use be an important public policy when it is still illegal under federal law?

Contract Law

Traditionally, many employers (and employees) thought that only a formal, signed document qualified as an employment contract. Increasingly, however, courts have been willing to enforce an employer's more casual promises, whether written or oral. Sometimes courts have also been willing to *imply* contract terms in the absence of an *express* agreement.

Promises Made During the Hiring Process. Promises made to job applicants are generally enforceable, even if not approved by the company's top executives. When the Tanana Valley Medical-Surgical Group, Inc., hired James Eales as a physician's assistant, it promised him that, as long as he did his job, he could stay there until retirement age. Six years later, the company fired him without cause. The Alaska Supreme Court held that the clinic's promise was enforceable.[10]

Employee Handbooks. The employee handbook at Blue Cross & Blue Shield stated that employees could be fired only for just cause and then only after warnings, notice, a hearing, and other procedures. Charles Toussaint was fired summarily five years after he joined the company. Although this decision was ultimately reviewed by the personnel department, company president, and chairman of the board of trustees, Toussaint was not given the benefit of all of the procedures in the handbook. The court held that **an employee handbook creates a contract.**[11]

---

10 Eales v. Tanana Valley Medical-Surgical Group, Inc., 663 P.2d 958 (Alaska 1983).

11 Toussaint v. Blue Cross & Blue Shield, 408 Mich. 579 (Mich. 1980).

Some employers have responded to cases like this by including provisions in their handbooks stating that it is not a contract and can be modified at any time. Generally, these provisions have been enforced.[12] However, employers cannot have it both ways. If a handbook states that it is not a contract, then employers cannot enforce provisions favorable to them, such as required arbitration clauses.[13]

Covenant of Good Faith and Fair Dealing. About half the states imply a covenant of good faith and fair dealing in contracts. This covenant requires both parties to behave reasonably, making an honest effort to meet both the spirit and letter of the contract.

In the employment context, these cases mostly arise in situations in which an employer fires a worker to avoid paying promised income or benefits. When Forrest Fleming went to work for Parametric Technology Corp., the company promised him valuable stock options if he met his sales goals. He would not be able to *exercise* the options (i.e., purchase the stock), however, until several years after they were granted, and then only if he was still employed by the company. When the value of his options reached almost $1 million, the company fired him. Although Parametric had not violated the explicit terms of the option agreement, the jury believed it had violated the covenant of good faith and fair dealing by firing Fleming to prevent him from exercising his options. It awarded him $1.6 million in damages.[14]

Tort Law

Workers have successfully sued their employers under the following tort theories.

Defamation. Employers may be liable for defamation when they give false references about an employee. In his job as a bartender at the Capitol Grille restaurant, Christopher Kane often flirted with customers. After he was fired from his job, his ex-boss claimed that Kane had been "fired from every job he ever had for sexual misconduct." In fact, Kane had never been fired before. He recovered $300,000 in damages for this defamation.

Qualified privilege
Employers who give references are liable only for false statements that they know to be false or that are primarily motivated by ill will.

More than half of the states recognize a qualified privilege for employers who give references about former employees. A **qualified privilege** means that employers are liable only for false statements that they know to be false or that are primarily motivated by ill will. After Becky Chambers left her job at American Trans Air, Inc., she discovered that her former boss was telling anyone who called for a reference that Chambers "does not work good with other people," is a "troublemaker," and "would not be a good person to rehire." Chambers was unable, however, to present compelling evidence that her boss had been primarily motivated by ill will. Neither Trans Air nor the boss was held liable for these statements because they were protected by a qualified privilege.[15]

To reduce the likelihood of defamation suits, many companies refuse to provide references for former employees. They instruct their managers to reveal only a person's salary and dates of employment and not to offer an opinion on job performance.

What about risky workers? Do employers have any obligation to warn about them? **Generally, courts have held that employers do *not* have a legal obligation to disclose information about former employees. But, in the case of violence, courts are divided.** While Jeffrey St. Clair worked as a maintenance man at the St. Joseph Nursing Home, he was disciplined 24 times for actions ranging from extreme violence to drug and alcohol use. When he applied for a job with another firm, St. Joseph refused to give any information other than St. Clair's dates of employment. After he savagely murdered a

---

[12] See, for example, Federal Express Corp. v. Dutschmann, 36 Tex. Sup. J. 530 (Tex. 1993).

[13] See, for example, Sparks v. Vista Del Mar Child & Family Services, 207 Cal. App. 4th 1511 (Cal. App. 2d Dist. 2012).

[14] Fleming v. Parametric Tech. Corp., 1999 U.S. App. LEXIS 14864 (9th Cir. 1999).

[15] Chambers v. American Trans Air, Inc., 577 N.E.2d 612 (Ind. Ct. App. 1991).

security guard at his new job, the guard's family sued, but a Michigan court dismissed the case.[16]

A California court, however, reached the opposite decision in a school case. Officials from two junior high schools gave Robert Gadams glowing letters of recommendation without mentioning that he had been fired for inappropriate sexual conduct with students. While an assistant principal at a new school, he molested a 13-year-old. The court held that the writer of a letter of recommendation owes to third parties (in this case, the student) "a duty not to misrepresent the facts in describing the qualifications and character of a former employee, if making these misrepresentations would present a substantial, foreseeable risk of physical injury to the third persons."[17]

To assist employers in giving references, Lehigh economist Robert Thornton has written *The Lexicon of Intentional Ambiguous Recommendations* (LIAR). For a candidate with interpersonal problems, he suggests saying, "I am pleased to say that this person is a former colleague of mine." Or, for a candidate with drug or alcohol problems: "We remember the hours she spent working with us as happy hours."

Workplace Bullying. About 25 percent of employees have been bullied at work. California law requires employers to conduct training on how to prevent abusive conduct. So far, however, courts and legislatures have generally been reluctant to consider bullying a violation of public policy.[18] Although, if the behavior is particularly extreme and outrageous, employers may face liability under the tort of **intentional infliction of emotional distress** (discussed in Chapter 8 on intentional torts).

Intentional infliction of emotional distress
An intentional tort in which the harm results from extreme and outrageous conduct that causes serious emotional harm

Morris Shields, a supervisor at GTE, was continuously in a rage. He would yell and scream profanity at the top of his voice while pounding his fists. He would charge at employees, stopping uncomfortably close to their faces while screaming and yelling. He regularly threatened to fire the clerks he supervised. At least once a day, he would call one of the clerks into his office and have her stand in front of him, sometimes for as long as 30 minutes, while he stared at her, read papers, or talked on the phone. Once, when Shields discovered a spot on the carpet, he made a clerk get on her hands and knees to clean it while he stood over her yelling. The Supreme Court of Texas upheld a jury award of $100,000 for the workers.[19]

29-2b Family and Medical Leave Act

The United States is the only industrialized nation that does not require employers to offer *paid* sick leave. It is the only country in the world, besides Papua New Guinea, that requires maternity leave, but permits it to be unpaid.

The Family and Medical Leave Act (FMLA) guarantees both men and women up to 12 weeks of *unpaid* leave each year for childbirth, adoption, or a serious health condition of their own or in their immediate family.[20] This statute defines an immediate family member as a spouse, child, or parent—but not a sibling, grandchild, or in-law. An employee who takes a leave must be allowed to return to the same or an equivalent job with the same pay and benefits. The FMLA applies only to companies with at least 50 workers and to employees who have been with the company full time for at least a year, which means that only about 60 percent of workers are covered by this statute.

---

16 Moore v. St. Joseph Nursing Home, Inc., 184 Mich. App. 766 (Mich. Ct. App. 1990).

17 Randi W. v. Muroc Joint Unified School District, 14 Cal. 4th 1066 (1997), modified, 14 Cal. 4th 1282c, 97 Cal. Daily Op. Service 1439.

18 See, for example, Jaber v. FirstMerit Corp., 2017 Ohio App. LEXIS 276 (Ct. App. Ohio, 2017).

19 GTE Southwest v. Bruce, 42 Tex. Sup. J. 907 (Tex. 1999).

20 Some states, such as Oregon, require employers to offer paid sick leave. Other states, such as Massachusetts, have sick leave requirements that also apply to companies with fewer than 50 employees. Federal contractors must offer employees seven paid sick days a year.

Here are some examples of what counts as a "serious health condition" under the FMLA:

- Any health issue that requires hospitalization
- A condition that requires more than one visit to a healthcare provider; the visits may be spread out over as long as a year
- A condition that requires only one visit to a healthcare provider but also requires a course of treatment such as physical therapy or prescription medication

Thus, the FMLA would apply in the case of a heart attack, ongoing kidney dialysis, and an ear infection requiring antibiotics. It would generally not cover food poisoning that did not require hospitalization, the common cold, or a sprained ankle.

In many FMLA lawsuits, a worker claims that he or she was fired in retaliation for taking leave, while the employer argues that the termination was for some other reason. The following case illustrates this dynamic.

Peterson v. Exide Technologies

477 Fed. Appx. 474
United States Court of Appeals for the Tenth Circuit, 2012

Facts: Over time, Exide Technologies had issued repeated warnings to Robert Peterson for driving forklifts too fast and violating other safety rules. After he was injured in a forklift crash, Peterson took FMLA leave for ten days while he recovered.

During the leave period, Exide fired him for "flagrant violations of safety rules." Peterson sued, claiming that the company terminated him in retaliation for exercising his right to take FMLA leave. The lower court granted summary judgment to Exide, and Peterson appealed.

Issue: ***Was Peterson fired in retaliation for claiming FMLA leave?***

Excerpts from Judge Baldock's Decision: The FMLA makes it unlawful for any employer to interfere with, restrain, or deny the exercise of the rights provided by the FMLA, or to discriminate against any individual for opposing any practice prohibited by the FMLA.

[I]f Plaintiff makes out a prima facie retaliation case, the burden shifts to Defendant to demonstrate a legitimate, nonretaliatory reason for its termination decision. If Defendant meets this burden, the burden shifts back to Plaintiff to show that there is a genuine dispute of material fact as to whether Defendant's explanations are pretextual.

Defendant asserts it dismissed Plaintiff for the legitimate reason that he violated company safety policies. According to Defendant's Plant Manager:

> Based on my own review of the photographs and the damage they depicted, Plaintiff was driving too fast at the time of the crash and was not operating his forklift in a safe manner. Such conduct on Plaintiff's part was a flagrant violation of company health and safety policy and posed a threat to the safety of Plaintiff and other Exide employees.

The Plant Manager also based his decision to fire Plaintiff on the "history of careless and unsafe conduct" reflected in Plaintiff s personnel file. Defendant has adequately demonstrated a nonretaliatory reason for Plaintiff's termination: his repeated safety violations. Thus, the burden shifts back to Plaintiff to show pretext.

Plaintiff argues Defendant's asserted justification is pretextual because the forklift accident was a "minor incident." Whether the accident was "minor" is questionable. But even if it was, we see nothing that prevents Defendant from firing employees for minor safety violations. Particularly where, as here, the employee has a record of unsafe work performance, even a minor infraction could be the last straw.

Plaintiff has produced no evidence to undermine Defendant's nonretaliatory explanation for the termination. Aside from the fact Plaintiff was on FMLA leave when he was fired, no evidence suggests a causal connection between Plaintiff's firing and his exercise of FMLA rights. Therefore, the district court properly granted summary judgment.

AFFIRMED.

29-2c Whistleblowing

No one likes to be accused of wrongdoing even if (or, perhaps, especially if) the accusations are true. This is exactly what **whistleblowers** do: They are employees who disclose illegal behavior on the part of their employer. Not surprisingly, some companies, when faced with such an accusation, prefer to shoot the messenger. Rather than fixing the reported problem, they retaliate against the informer.

Whistleblower
Someone who discloses wrongdoing

For eight years, medical device maker C.R. Bard paid kickbacks to doctors and hospitals to get them to buy its radioactive seeds for treating prostate cancer. To cover the cost of the kickbacks, the company inflated its bills to Medicare. Bard paid the government $48 million to settle this case. Of this amount, $10 million went to Julie Darity, a former Bard employee who was fired after she blew the whistle on the company's wrongdoing.

The law on whistleblowers varies across the country. As a general rule, however, whistleblowers are protected in the following situations:

- **The False Claims Act.** Darity recovered under the federal False Claims Act, a statute that permits lawsuits against anyone who defrauds the government. The recovery is shared between the government and the whistleblower. This act prohibits employers from retaliating against workers who file suit under the statute. Over half the states have also passed their own false claims acts.
- **Sarbanes-Oxley Act of 2002.** This act protects employees of publicly traded companies who provide evidence of fraud to investigators (whether in or outside the company). A successful plaintiff is entitled to reinstatement, back pay, and attorney's fees.
- **The Dodd-Frank Wall Street Reform and Consumer Protection Act.** Anyone who provides information to the government about violations of securities or commodities laws is entitled to a payout of from 10 to 30 percent of whatever award the government receives, provided that the award tops $1 million. (The courts are split as to whether the Dodd-Frank whistleblowing provisions apply to people who report wrongdoing to their employer instead of to the government.[21]) If a company retaliates against tipsters, they are entitled to reinstatement, double back pay, and attorney's fees.
- **Constitutional protection for government employees.** Employees of federal, state, and local governments have a right to free speech under the U.S. Constitution. Therefore, the government cannot retaliate against public employees who blow the whistle if the employee is speaking out on a matter of *public concern*. A New York City social worker complained on television that the city child welfare agency was not adequately protecting children from horrible abuse. When the city suspended her, she sued. The court ruled that the government has the right to prohibit some employee speech, but if the employee speaks on matters of public concern, the government bears the burden of justifying any retaliation. In this case, the court held for the social worker.[22]
- **Statutory protection for federal employees.** The Civil Service Reform Act and the Whistleblower Protection Act prevent retaliation against federal employees who report wrongdoing. They also permit the award of back pay and attorney's fees to the whistleblower. This statute was used to prevent the National Park Service from disciplining two managers who wrote a report expressing concern over development in Yellowstone National Park.

---

[21] See Berman v. Neo@Ogilvy LLC, 801 F.3d 145 (2d Cir. 2015) and Asadi v. G.E. Energy (USA), L.L.C., 20 F.3d 620 (5th Cir. 2013).

[22] Harman v. City of New York, 140 F.3d 111 (2d Cir. 1998).

- **State laws.** The good news is that all 50 states have laws that protect whistleblowers from retaliation by their employers. The bad news is that the scope of this protection varies greatly from state to state. Most courts, however, prohibit the discharge of employees who report illegal activity. A Connecticut court held a company liable when it fired a quality control director who reported to his boss that some products had failed quality tests, in violation of state law.[23]

EXAMStrategy

Question: When Shiloh interviewed for a sales job at a medical supply company, the interviewer promised that she would only have to sell medical devices, not medications. Once she began work (as an employee at will), Shiloh discovered that the sales force was organized around regions, not products, so she had to sell both devices and drugs. When she complained to her boss over lunch in the employee cafeteria, he said in a loud voice, "You're a big girl now—it's time you learned that you don't always get what you want." He then fired her on the spot. Does she have a valid claim against the company?

Strategy: Shiloh is an employee at will. She has had two key interactions with the company—being hired and being fired. What protections does the law provide?

Result: The employer's promises made during the hiring process are enforceable. Here, the company is liable because the interviewer clearly made a promise that the company did not keep. What about the way in which Shiloh was fired? She might allege that she is entitled to damages for the intentional infliction of emotional distress. But Shiloh is unlikely to win on that claim—the behavior was not extreme and outrageous enough.

29-3 WORKPLACE FREEDOM

The line between home and workplace often blurs. Employees respond to work emails 24/7, while their behavior at home (say, drug use) can have an impact on their employer. This section deals with worker freedom: the right to personal lifestyle choices and to the public expression of opinions about the workplace.

> Employers *do* have the right to fire workers for off-duty conduct.

29-3a Off-Duty Activities

In the absence of a specific law to the contrary, employers *do* have the right to fire workers for off-duty conduct. Employees have been fired or disciplined for such extracurricular activities as taking part in dangerous sports (such as skydiving), dating coworkers, smoking, or even having high cholesterol.

Lifestyle Laws

A few states, such as California, have passed lifestyle laws that protect the right of employees to engage in *any* lawful activity or use any lawful product when off duty. Thus, if California residents skydive while smoking a cigarette, they may lose their lives, but not their jobs. Some laws also protect *particular* off-duty conduct.

---

[23] Sheets v. Teddy's Frosted Foods, Inc., 179 Conn. 471 (Conn. 1980).

Smoking

Smokers tend to take more sick days and have higher healthcare expenses than other employees. Research estimates that it costs an extra $5,800 a year to employ a worker who smokes. As a result, several thousand employers, including Union Pacific and Alaska Airlines, simply refuse to hire those who light up. **In roughly 60 percent of the states, however, employers cannot prohibit workers from smoking.**

Some workers have also claimed that nicotine addiction is a disability under the Americans with Disabilities Act (ADA; see Chapter 30 for more information about this statute), but, so far, courts have been skeptical that Congress intended ADA coverage for the roughly 36.5 million Americans who smoke.[24]

Alcohol and Drug Use

Private Employers. **Under *federal* law, *private* employers are permitted to test job applicants and workers for alcohol and *illegal* drugs.** They may sanction workers who fail the test, even if the drug or alcohol use was off duty. *State* laws on drug testing vary widely.

Although employers were traditionally most concerned about illegal drugs, they now also worry about *legal* use of prescription drugs such as Xanax and oxycodone because these medications may cause impairment. In one study, workers drug-tested after accidents in the workplace were four times more likely to have opiates in their system than job applicants.

However, **the Equal Employment Opportunity Commission (EEOC), the federal agency charged with enforcing federal employment laws, prohibits testing for prescription drugs unless a worker seems impaired.** The EEOC filed suit against a company that randomly tested for legal use of prescription drugs, and a jury awarded substantial damages to the employees.[25]

Government Employers. Governments are somtimes allowed to conduct drug and alcohol tests of their employees. Public safety workers, such as police and firefighters, can be randomly tested for illegal drugs, and they may also be required to report legal drug use that could compromise their ability to perform their jobs. If their drug use (legal or not) is a threat to public safety, they may be suspended or fired from their jobs. Other government employees, whose work does not involve public safety, can be tested only if they show signs of impairment.

29-3b The Right to Free Speech

The National Labor Relations Act

The National Labor Relations Act (NLRA) is well known as legislation that protects employees' right to unionize. However, many people do not realize that **the NLRA protects *all employees* (1) who engage in collective activity (2) relating to work conditions and (3) who are not supervisors.** The National Labor Relations Board (NLRB), which enforces this statute, has long held that **even non-unionized workers cannot be fired for complaining about their jobs, so long as these complaints are shared with other employees and are not inappropriately hostile or violent.** In the following case, a teacher in the theater department got dramatic. Could the school fire him?

---

24 See Brashear v. Simms, 138 F.Supp.2d 693 (D.Md. 2001).

25 Bates v. Dura Auto Sys Inc., 2011 U.S. Dist. LEXIS 97469 (M.D. Tenn 2011).

Dalton School, Inc. and David Brune

2015 NLRB LEXIS 399
National Labor Relations Board, 2015

Facts: For 12 years, David Brune taught theater and drama at the Dalton School, an elite private school in New York City. Like other Dalton faculty, he worked on a renewable one-year contract.

The school chose *Thoroughly Modern Millie* as the middle school's annual play and made Brune the production manager. However, a month before the premiere, the school halted the production because some parents were offended by the play's stereotypical depiction of Asians. But then students were upset about not being able to perform. The school ultimately opted to allow a rewritten, sanitized version of the play to go forward. All these changes required significant time and effort from Brune and other members of the theater department, who had to produce the new version in only three days.

Brune and his colleagues were frustrated with the school administration. They felt that the leadership had ignored their concerns, put additional burdens on them without recognizing the extra effort required, and mishandled communication throughout the school community. To communicate their distress, Robert Sloan, the chair of the theater department, circulated to his faculty a draft letter that he proposed sending to Ellen Stein, the Head of School. Brune replied with a lengthy, ranting email to the group, proposing that the administration should be told:

> We have been grievously wronged and we would like an apology. You lied. Apologize for lying, for not being honest, forthright, upstanding, moral, considerate, much less intelligent or wise.

Without Brune's knowledge, Sloan gave a copy of this email to Stein, and she summoned Brune to a meeting. He denied having called her dishonest or immoral. Five weeks later, Stein met with Brune again. This time, she showed him a copy of his email and he admitted he had written it. She then fired him, effective at the end of the school year. A month later, she told him he had been fired for lying.

Issue: ***Did Stein violate the NLRA by firing Brune?***

Excerpts from the NLRB's Decision[26]**:** [The NLRA] provides that, "employees shall have the right to engage in concerted activities for the purpose of collective bargaining or other mutual aid or protection." [T]he activities of a single employee in enlisting the support of fellow employees in mutual aid and protection is concerted activity.

Brune's discharge would not be rendered lawful even if he lied to Stein. The "lie" was elicited by Stein during an investigation that was motivated by Stein's animus towards Brune's protected email. Brune was under no obligation to respond truthfully.

The discussion amongst employees in the theater department as to how to address their concerns regarding the manner in which *Thoroughly Modern Millie* was handled was clearly protected concerted activity. Brune's email was clearly intended to induce group action.

The issue in this case is whether the statements made in this email are of such a nature that they forfeit the protection of the Act. His protected activity was not a face-to-face outburst to management. Moreover, his email was accessible only to fellow employees, not students, parents or the general public. In fact, the email was not intended to be seen by management and was not directly accessible to management. [In a prior case], the Board held that an employee engaged in protected activity did not lose the protection of the Act by calling his supervisor a "f-g liar." Otherwise protected activity remains protected unless found to be so violent or of such serious character as to render the employee unfit for further service.

Brune did not forfeit the protection of the Act. He did not make any malicious and/or untrue statements of fact. Brune did not use any obscenities. He did not threaten management; he merely demanded an apology.

[Dalton], having discriminatorily discharged an employee, must offer him reinstatement and make him whole for any loss of earnings and other benefits.[27]

---

26 For ease of reading, we have replaced "Respondent" with "Stein."

27 This decision was upheld at 2016 NLRB LEXIS 408.

Social Media Policies

Many companies now have social media policies that limit employee commentary. As the *Dalton* case suggests, however, these **policies violate the NLRA if they unreasonably limit employee speech about work conditions.** On a Saturday night, Lydia texted her co-worker Marianna, warning her that she intended to tell their boss that other employees were slackers. Marianna posted a Facebook message complaining about Lydia and asking other employees how they felt. Four of them posted negative comments about Lydia. All of the complainers were fired on the grounds that they had violated the company's anti-bullying policy. But the court ruled that the NLRA protected their speech because it was concerted activity dealing with working conditions.[28]

Note, however, that to be protected, the employee speech must be "concerted." The *Arizona Daily Star* fired a reporter for tweeting a series of comments, including:

> You stay homicidal, Tucson. What?!?!? No overnight homicide? WTF? You're slacking Tucson.

The NLRB ruled that these tweets were not protected activity because the reporter had been acting alone, not in concert with other workers.[29]

Employers are generally allowed to discipline employees who post or tweet content that reflects badly on the employer and does not involve a discussion of working conditions. An employee of a BMW dealership was fired after he posted comments on his Facebook page complaining about the cheap food the dealership had served at a customer event. He also posted both a photo of a car that a 13-year-old had accidentally driven into a pond, and snide comments about the incident. The NLRB ruled that the comments about the food related to working conditions. Although the employee had posted them alone, he and other employees had already discussed the bad food and his Facebook comments were, therefore, held to be concerted activity. However, the photo of car in the pond, had nothing to do with working conditions and, therefore, was not protected.[30]

Privacy on Social Media

As we saw in Chapter 10 on cyberlaw and privacy, the Stored Communications Act (SCA) prohibits unauthorized access to electronic communications, which includes email, voice mail, and social media. However, an employer has the right to monitor workers' electronic communications if (1) the employee consents; (2) the monitoring occurs in the ordinary course of business; or (3) in the case of email, if the employer provides the computer system. This monitoring may include an employee's social media activities.

It is one thing to monitor what an employee posts, but what if the social media account is work related and the employee leaves? Who controls it then? In one case, an employee used her personal Twitter account to promote her employer. She also created the company's Facebook page through her personal Facebook account and managed its login information and posts. After she took an unexpected medical leave, the company found her passwords and used them to access and post on the accounts. When the employee sued, the court held that, if she had not authorized the company to access her accounts, then it had violated the SCA.[31]

---

28 Hispanics United of Buffalo, Inc., 359 NLRB No. 37 (N.L.R.B. 2012).

29 NLRB Case No. 28-CA-23267.

30 Karl Knauz Motors, 358 NLRB No.164 (2012).

31 Maremont v. Susan Fredman Design Group, Ltd., 2014 U.S. Dist. LEXIS 26557 (N.D. Ill. 2014).

29-3c Polygraph Tests

A polygraph exam is a type of lie detector test. **Under the Employee Polygraph Protection Act of 1988, employers may not require, or even *suggest*, that an employee or job candidate submit to a polygraph test *except* in the following cases:**

- An employee who is part of an "ongoing investigation" into crimes that have already occurred;
- An applicant applying for a government job; or
- An applicant for a job in public transport, security services, banking, or at pharmaceutical firms that deal with controlled substances.

If an employer requires a polygraph test, it must give advance written notice of when the test will be given and advise workers that they are entitled to legal counsel. A private employer may not fire or discriminate against an employee who fails a polygraph exam unless it also finds supporting evidence that the worker has done something wrong.

EXAMStrategy

Question: To ensure that its employees did not use illegal drugs in or outside the workplace, Marvel Grocery Store required all employees to take a polygraph exam. Moreover, managers began to check employees' Facebook pages for reference to drug use. Jagger was fired for refusing to take the polygraph test. Pete was dismissed after revealing on his Facebook page that he was using marijuana (illegally). Has the company acted in accordance with the law?

Strategy: First: As employees at will, are Jagger and Pete protected by a statute? The Employee Polygraph Protection Act permits employers to require a polygraph test as part of ongoing investigations into crimes that have occurred.

Second: What about Pete's marijuana use? No statutes protect a worker for *illegal* off-duty conduct. Can the company punish Pete for what he wrote on his Facebook page? Not if it relates to work conditions and involves concerted activity.

Result: Here, Marvel has no reason to believe that a crime occurred, so it cannot require a polygraph test. Pete's Facebook postings have nothing to do with work conditions and illegal activity is not protected. So the company is liable to Jagger for requiring him to take the polygraph exam, but not to Pete for firing him over illegal drug use.

29-4 WORKPLACE SAFETY

29-4a OSHA

In 1970, Congress passed the Occupational Safety and Health Act (OSHA) to ensure safe working conditions. **Under OSHA:**

- Employers must comply with specific health and safety standards. For example, healthcare personnel who work with blood are not permitted to eat or drink in areas where the blood is kept. Protective clothing—gloves, gowns, and laboratory coats—must be impermeable to blood.

- Employers are under a general obligation to keep their workplace "free from recognized hazards that are causing or are likely to cause death or serious physical harm" to employees.
- Employers must keep records of all workplace injuries and accidents.
- The Occupational Safety and Health Administration (which is also known as OSHA) may inspect workplaces to ensure that they are safe. OSHA may assess fines for violations and order employers to correct unsafe conditions.

29-4b Employee Data

Employers necessarily obtain personal data from their workers: date of birth, Social Security number, and banking information. Are employers liable when hackers steal this valuable data? In a recent case, hackers accessed employee information at the University of Pittsburgh Medical Center, used it to file fake tax returns, and then stole the tax refunds. However, a court found the hospital was not liable to the affected workers because it is reasonable for employers to store sensitive employee data electronically, even knowing that some of it will inevitably be stolen.[32]

29-4c Guns

Employers have the right to prohibit guns in the workplace but, in almost half the states, Bring Your Gun to Work Laws prevent companies from banning firearms in their parking lot. Some states also prohibit employers from asking workers if they have a firearm in their car, or searching their vehicles for guns. Some states further prevent employers from discriminating against workers who own firearms.

Gun advocates argue that workers have the right to protect themselves during their commutes and that, ultimately, such laws improve employee safety. However, research indicates that workplaces with guns are five times as likely to suffer a homicide as one in which they are banned.[33] Nonetheless, courts have held that, in states that permit guns in parking lots, employers may not rely on OSHA to ban these firearms.[34]

Some executives worry about the dangers of disciplining workers in states with Bring Your Gun to Work laws. An employment lawyer reported that he had attended termination meetings in which executives wore bulletproof vests or brought armed guards. In one case, a company held a termination meeting in an airport conference room so that participants would have to pass through security first.[35]

29-5 FINANCIAL PROTECTION

Congress and the states have enacted laws designed to provide employees with a measure of financial security. All of the laws in this section were created by statute, not by the courts.

---

32 Dittman v. UPMC, 2017 Pa. Super. LEXIS 13 (Pa. Super. Ct. 2017).

33 Dana Loomis, Stephen W. Marshall, and Myduc L. Ta, "Employer Policies Toward Guns and the Risk of Homicides in the Workplace," *Am J Public Health*. May 2005, 95(5): 830–832.

34 Ramsey Winch, Inc. v. Henry, 555 F.3d 1199 (10th Cir. 2009).

35 Sara Murray, "Guns in the Parking Lot: A Delicate Workplace Issue," *The Wall Street Journal*, October 15, 2013.

29-5a Fair Labor Standards Act: Minimum Wage, Overtime, and Child Labor

Passed in 1938, the Fair Labor Standards Act (FLSA) regulates wages and limits child labor nationally. It provides that hourly workers must be paid a minimum wage of $7.25 per hour, plus time and a half for any hours over 40 in one week. These wage provisions do not apply to salaried workers, such as managerial, administrative, or professional staff. More than half the states and even some cities set a higher minimum wage, so it is important to check local guidelines as well.

One significant issue that employers face under the FLSA is: What counts as work, and how do you keep track of it? What if an hourly worker answers email during lunch or takes a phone call on the train ride home? If these activities count as work, how can the employer keep track of them? Carla Bird, an assistant at Oprah Winfrey's production company, submitted timesheets showing 800 hours of overtime in 17 weeks. She said she had worked 12 or 13 hours a day, seven days a week, for four months. The company paid her $32,000 in overtime.[36]

Another issue facing employers: Are unpaid internships covered by the FLSA? Eric Glatt and Alexander Footman were unpaid interns at Fox Searchlight Pictures, Inc., where they worked on the movie *Black Swan*. When they sued for compensation, the appellate court ruled that interns have the right to be paid only if the employer is the primary beneficiary of the relationship. The court then remanded the case to the trial court to determine who had benefited most from the internship—the workers or the employer.[37]

The FLSA also prohibits "oppressive child labor," which means that children under 14 may work only in agriculture, entertainment, a family business, babysitting, or newspaper delivery. Fourteen- and fifteen-year-olds are permitted to work *limited* hours after school in nonhazardous jobs, such as retail. Sixteen- and seventeen-year-olds may work *unlimited* hours in nonhazardous jobs.

29-5b Workers' Compensation

Workers' compensation statutes ensure that employees receive payment for injuries incurred at work. Before workers' comp, injured employees could recover damages only if they sued their employer. It was the brave worker who was willing to risk a suit against his boss. Lawsuits not only poisoned the atmosphere at work, but employers frequently won anyway by claiming that (1) the injured worker was contributorily negligent, (2) a fellow employee had caused the accident, or (3) the injured worker had assumed the risk of injury. As a result, seriously injured workers (or their families) often had no recourse against the employer.

Workers' comp statutes provide a fixed, certain recovery to the injured employee, no matter who was at fault for the accident. In return, employees are not permitted to sue their employers for negligence. The amounts allowed (for medical expenses and lost wages) under workers' comp statutes are often less than a worker might recover in court, but the injured employee trades the certainty of some recovery for the higher risk of rolling the dice at trial. Payments are approved by an administrative board that conducts an informal hearing into each claim.

36Lisa Belkin, "O.T. Isn't as Simple as Telling Time," *The New York Times*, September 20, 2007.

37Glatt v. Fox Searchlight Pictures, Inc., 811 F.3d 528 (2d Cir. 2015).

29-5c Health Insurance

Under the Consolidated Omnibus Budget Reconciliation Act (COBRA), **former employees must be allowed to continue their health coverage for 18 months after leaving their job.** But they must pay the cost themselves, plus as much as an additional 2 percent to cover administrative expenses. COBRA applies to any company with 20 or more workers.

Fox Photos/Hulton Archive/Getty Images

Before Social Security, breadlines were often the only safety net available to the unemployed.

29-5d Social Security

The federal Social Security system began in 1935, during the depths of the Great Depression, to provide a basic safety net for the elderly, ill, and unemployed. **The Social Security system pays benefits to workers who are retired, disabled, or temporarily unemployed, and to the spouses and children of disabled or deceased workers.** The Social Security program is financed through a tax on wages that is paid by employers, employees, and the self-employed.

The Federal Unemployment Tax Act (FUTA) is the part of the Social Security system that provides support to the unemployed. FUTA establishes some national standards, but states are free to set their own benefit levels and payment schedules. **A worker who quits voluntarily or is fired for just cause is ineligible for unemployment benefits.** While receiving payments, she must make a good-faith effort to look for other employment.

29-5e Pension Benefits

In 1974, Congress passed the Employee Retirement Income Security Act (ERISA) to protect workers covered by private pension plans. Under ERISA, employers are not required to establish pension plans, but if they do, they must follow these federal rules. The law was aimed, in particular, at protecting benefits of retired workers if their companies subsequently go bankrupt. The statute also prohibits risky investments by pension plans. In addition, the statute sets rules on the vesting of benefits. (An employer cannot cancel *vested* benefits; *nonvested* benefits are forfeited when the employee leaves.) Before ERISA, retirement benefits at some companies did not vest until the employee retired—if he quit or was fired before retirement, even after years of service, he lost his pension. Under current law, employee benefits normally must vest within five years of employment.

29-6 LABOR UNIONS

The opening scenario of this chapter provides a graphic example of how painful (literally) working conditions could be in the past. In a desire for better pay and improved working conditions, workers in the nineteenth and early twentieth centuries sought strength through collective bargaining. They began to join together in unions.

But American courts treated any coordinated effort by workers as a criminal conspiracy. They convicted workers merely for the act of joining together, even if no strike took place. A company could usually obtain an immediate injunction merely by alleging that a strike *might* cause harm. Courts were so quick to issue injunctions that most companies became immune to union efforts.

But with the economic collapse of 1929 and the vast suffering of the Great Depression, public sympathy shifted to the workers. Congress responded with two landmark statutes.

29-6a Key Pro-Union Statutes

The Norris-LaGuardia Act prohibits federal court injunctions in nonviolent labor disputes. No longer could management stop a strike merely by saying the word *strike*. By taking away the injunction remedy, Congress was declaring that workers should be permitted to organize unions and to use their collective power to achieve legitimate economic ends. This statute led to explosive growth in union membership.

The National Labor Relations Act (NLRA or Wagner Act) ensures the right of workers to form unions and encourages management and unions to bargain collectively and productively. With the enactment of the NLRA, Congress put an end to any notion that unions were inherently illegal.

Section 7 of the NLRA guarantees employees the right to:

- **Organize and join unions,**
- **Bargain collectively through representatives of their own choosing, and**
- **Engage in other concerted activities.**

Supervisor
Anyone with the authority to make independent decisions on hiring, firing, disciplining, or promoting other workers

Note, however, that for the purposes of this statute, **"supervisors" are not employees and do not have the right to join a union.** A **supervisor** is anyone with the authority to make independent decisions on hiring, firing, disciplining, or promoting other workers.[38] For example, the Supreme Court ruled that university faculty were supervisors and, therefore, were not covered by the NLRA.[39]

Section 8 prohibits employers from engaging in the following unfair labor practices (ULPs):

- Interfering with union organizing efforts,
- Dominating or interfering with any union,
- Discriminating against a union member, and
- Refusing to bargain collectively with a union.

Section 8 prohibits unions from engaging in these ULPs:

- Interfering with employees who are exercising their labor rights,
- Causing an employer to discriminate against workers as a means to strengthen the union, and
- Charging excessive dues.

When a union tried to organize Starbucks workers, the company prohibited employees from discussing the union or their working conditions and posting union material on employee bulletin boards. It also punished pro-union employees with unfavorable work assignments. All of these actions were ULPs.[40]

The NLRA also established the National Labor Relations Board (NLRB) to administer and interpret the statute and to adjudicate labor cases. For example, when a union charges that an employer has committed a ULP—say, by refusing to bargain—the claim goes first to the NLRB.

---

38 29 U.S.C. §152(11).

39 NLRB v. Yeshiva Univ., 444 U.S. 672 (U.S. 1980).

40 NLRB v. Starbucks Corp., 679 F.3d 70 (2d Cir. 2012).

29-6b Labor Unions Today

Organized labor is in flux in the United States. In the 1950s, about 25 percent of workers belonged to a union. Today, only about 11 percent do. That is the lowest level since 1916. Even more remarkable, membership in private sector unions has declined from 30 percent in the 1950s to 6.6 percent now. The major reasons for this decline are:

- More states have passed right-to-work laws that permit employees in unionized workplaces to opt out of joining the union or paying dues.
- Some large employers (such as Boeing) have relocated to states with little union presence.
- The number of manufacturing workers has declined.
- Employment is increasing in industries, such as services, that have not traditionally been unionized.

Note that public employees (such as teachers and police officers) are much more likely to be unionized, but they are generally not covered by the NLRA. Instead, state labor laws apply, which tend to provide less protection than federal statutes.

This decline in strength reduces union bargaining power. Thus, the auto unions agreed to a two-tiered structure that pays new workers little more than half the wages of long-term employees. Furthermore, when union wages fall in a state, so does the compensation for non-unionized hourly workers. Some argue that all of these factors have contributed to stagnation in pay for the bottom half of wage earners, even as their productivity has increased dramatically.

29-6c Organizing a Union

Exclusivity

Under §9 of the NLRA, a validly recognized union is the *exclusive* representative of the employees. This means that the union represents all of the designated employees, even if a particular worker does not want to be included, has not joined the union, or has not paid dues. The company may not bargain directly with any employee in the group, nor with any other organization representing the designated employees.

However, a union may not exercise power however it likes: Along with a union's exclusive bargaining power goes a duty of fair representation, which requires that it treat all members fairly, impartially, and in good faith. A union may not favor some members over others, nor may a union discriminate against a member based on characteristics such as race or gender.

The Organizing Process

A union organizing effort generally involves the following pattern:

Campaign. Union organizers talk with employees and try to persuade them to form a union. The organizers may be employees of the company, who simply chat with fellow workers about unsatisfactory conditions; or a union may send nonemployees of the company to hand out union leaflets to workers as they arrive and depart from work. The employer generally may not limit the content of any leaflets that are somewhat related to union activity.

An employer cannot prohibit workers from using their already existing company email accounts to talk about union issues during nonworking time.[41] However, an employer may restrict organizing discussions if they interfere with business. A worker on a moving assembly line has no right to walk away from his task to talk with other employees about organizing a

[41] Purple Communs., Inc., 361 NLRB No. 126 (N.L.R.B. 2014).

union; these discussions must be left until lunch or some other break time.[42] Likewise, management may prohibit union discussions in the presence of customers.

The employer may also vigorously present anti-union views to its employees but may not use either threats or rewards to defeat a union drive.[43] A company may not fire a worker who favors a union; nor may it suddenly grant a significant pay raise in the midst of a union campaign. Walmart broke the law when one of its managers told employees that workers who went on strike would be looking for a new job and also that "If it were up to me, I'd shoot the union."

Authorization Cards. Union organizers ask workers to sign authorization cards, which state that the particular worker requests the specified union to act as her sole bargaining representative.

If a union obtains authorization cards from a sizable percentage of workers, it seeks recognition as the exclusive representative for the bargaining unit. The union may ask the employer to recognize it as the bargaining representative, but, most of the time, employers refuse to recognize the union voluntarily.

Petition. Assuming that the employer does not voluntarily recognize a union, the union generally petitions the NLRB for an election. It must submit to the NLRB regional office authorization cards signed by at least 30 percent of the workers. The regional office verifies whether there are enough valid cards to warrant an election and looks closely at the proposed bargaining unit to make sure that it is appropriate. A bargaining unit is a "group of employees with a clear and identifiable community of interests."

If the regional office determines that the union has identified an appropriate bargaining unit and has enough valid cards, it orders an election.

Election. The NLRB closely supervises the election to ensure fairness. All members of the proposed bargaining unit vote on whether they want the union to represent them. If more than 50 percent of the workers vote for the union, the NLRB designates that union as the exclusive representative of all members of the bargaining unit. When unions hold representation elections, they win about 60 percent of the time.

EXAMStrategy

Question: The Teamsters Union is attempting to organize the drivers at We Haul trucking company. Workers who favor a union have been using the lunchroom to hand out petitions and urge other drivers to sign authorization cards. The company posts a notice in the lunchroom: "Many employees do not want unions discussed in the lunchroom. Out of respect for them, we are prohibiting further union efforts in this lunchroom." Is this sign legal?

Strategy: The NLRA guarantees employees the right to talk among themselves about forming a union and to hand out literature. Management has the right to present anti-union views.

Result: We Haul has violated the NLRA. The company has the right to urge employees not to join the union. However, it may not prevent the union from talking with employees. Even assuming the company is correct that some employees do not want unions discussed, it has no right to prohibit such activities.

42NLRB v. Babcock & Wilcox Co., 351 U.S. 105 (S. Ct. 1956).

43NLRB v. Gissel Packing Co., 395 U.S. 575 (S. Ct. 1969).

29-6d Collective Bargaining

Once a union is formed, a company must then bargain with it toward the goal of creating a new contract, which is called a **collective bargaining agreement (CBA).**

Collective bargaining agreement (CBA)
A contract between a union and a company

The NLRA *permits* the parties to bargain almost any subject they wish, but **it *requires* them to bargain wages, hours, and other terms and conditions of employment.** An employer may not *unilaterally* make changes in these areas without first bargaining with the union. Conditions of employment include: benefits, order of layoffs and recalls, production quotas, work rules (such as safety practices), retirement benefits, and on-site food service and prices.

The union and the employer are *not* obligated to reach an agreement, but they are required to bargain in good faith. In other words, the two sides must meet with open minds and make a reasonable effort to reach a contract. In the following Landmark Case, a company violated this rule.

Landmark Case

NLRB v. Truitt Manufacturing Co.

351 U.S. 149
United States Supreme Court, 1956

Facts: Truitt Manufacturing Company refused to agree to the raise that the union requested, arguing that the increase would bankrupt the company. The union demanded to examine Truitt's books, and, when the company refused, the union complained to the NLRB.

The NLRB determined that the company had committed a ULP by failing to bargain in good faith and ordered it to allow union representatives to examine its finances. A court of appeals found no ULP and refused to enforce the Board's order. The Supreme Court granted *certiorari*.

Issue: ***Did the company refuse to bargain in good faith?***

Excerpts from Justice Black's Decision: While Congress did not compel agreement between employers and bargaining representatives, it did require collective bargaining in the hope that agreements would result. [T]he Act admonishes both employers and employees to exert every reasonable effort to make and maintain agreements.

In their effort to reach an agreement here, both the union and the company treated the company's ability to pay increased wages as highly relevant. Claims for increased wages have sometimes been abandoned because of an employer's unsatisfactory business condition; employees have even voted to accept wage decreases because of such conditions.

Good-faith bargaining necessarily requires that claims made by either bargainer should be honest claims. This is true about an asserted inability to pay an increase in wages. If such an argument is important enough to present in the give and take of bargaining, it is important enough to require some sort of proof of its accuracy.

The Board concluded that under the facts and circumstances of this case, the respondent was guilty of an unfair labor practice in failing to bargain in good faith. We see no reason to disturb the findings of the Board.

Reversed.

29-6e Concerted Action

Concerted action refers to any tactics that union members take in unison to gain some bargaining advantage. It is this power that gives a union strength. **The NLRA guarantees the right of employees to engage in concerted action for mutual aid or protection.**[44] The most common forms of concerted action are strikes and picketing.

Concerted action
Tactics taken by union members to gain bargaining advantage

[44] NLRA §7.

Strikes

The NLRA guarantees employees the right to strike, but with some limitations.[45] A union has a guaranteed right to call a strike if the parties are unable to reach a CBA. A union may also call a strike to protest a ULP, or to preserve work that the employer is considering sending elsewhere. Note that the union can bargain away the right to strike. Indeed, management will generally insist that the CBA include a **no-strike clause**, which prohibits the union from striking while the CBA is in force. A strike is illegal in several other situations as well; here, we mention the most important.

No-strike clause
A clause in a CBA that prohibits the union from striking while the CBA is in force

Cooling-Off Period. **Before striking to terminate or modify a CBA, a union must give management 60 days' notice.** This cooling-off period is designed to give both sides a chance to reassess negotiations and to decide whether some additional compromise would be wiser than enduring a strike.

Statutory Prohibition. **Many states have outlawed strikes by public employees.** The purpose of these statutes is to ensure that unions do not use public health or welfare as a weapon to secure an unfair bargaining advantage.

Sit-down strike
Members stop working but remain at their job posts, blocking replacement workers

Sit-Down Strikes. In a **sit-down strike**, members stop working but remain at their job posts, physically blocking replacement workers from taking their places. This type of strike is illegal.

Partial Strikes. A partial strike occurs when employees strike intermittently, stopping and starting repeatedly. This tactic is particularly disruptive because management cannot bring in replacement workers. **A union may either walk off the job or stay on it, but it may not alternate.**

Replacement Workers

When employees go on strike, management has the right to use replacement workers to keep the business operating. What about after the strike ends? May the employer offer the replacement workers *permanent* jobs, or must the company give union members their jobs back? It depends on the type of strike.

An **economic strike** is one intended to gain wages or benefits. **During an economic strike, an employer may hire permanent replacement workers.** When the strike is over, the company has no obligation to lay off the replacement workers to make room for the strikers. However, if and when the company does hire more workers, it may not discriminate against the strikers.

After an unfair labor practices (ULP) strike, union members are entitled to their jobs back, even if that means the employer must lay off replacement workers. In the *Truitt* case, the Supreme Court ruled that the company had committed a ULP. If the union had gone out on strike, the company would have had to hire back all the union members once the strike was over, regardless of how many replacement workers it had hired.

a katz/Shutterstock.com

Picketing is legal as long as no physical force is used to prevent people from crossing the line.

Economic strike
One intended to gain wages or benefits

Picketing

The goal of picketing is to discourage employees, replacement workers, and customers from doing business with the company. **Picketing the employer's workplace in support of a strike is generally lawful.** However, the picketers are not permitted to use physical force to prevent someone from crossing the line. The company may terminate violent picketers and permanently replace them, regardless of the nature of the strike.

---

[45] NLRA §13.

Secondary boycotts are generally illegal. A **secondary boycott** is a picket line established not at the employer's premises but at a different workplace. If Union is on strike against Truck Co., it may picket Truck Co.'s office and terminal. But Union may not pressure Truck Co. by setting up a picket line at a supermarket where Truck Co. delivers food, in an effort to persuade shoppers and other workers to boycott the store.

Secondary boycott A picket line established not at the employer's premises but at a different workplace

Lockouts

The workers have bargained with management for weeks, and discussions have turned belligerent. It is 6:00 a.m., the start of another day at the factory. But as 150 employees arrive for work, they are surprised to find the company's gate locked and armed guards standing on the other side. This is a **lockout**: Management is prohibiting workers from entering the premises and earning their paychecks. By withholding work and wages, the company hopes to pressure the union to bargain less aggressively. **Most lockouts are legal.**

Lockout Management prohibits workers from entering the premises.

CHAPTER CONCLUSION

Since the first time one person worked for another, there has been tension in the workplace. The law attempts to balance the right of a boss to run a business with the right of a worker to fair treatment. Different countries balance these rights differently. American bosses have great freedom to manage their employees. The United States guarantees its workers fewer rights than virtually any other industrialized nation. Alternatively, in Canada, France, Germany, Great Britain, and Japan, employers must show just cause before terminating workers. Which system is best? On the one hand, being mistreated at work can be a terrible, life-altering experience, but on the other, companies that cannot lay off unproductive employees are less likely to add to their workforce, which may be one reason that Europe tends to have a higher unemployment rate than the United States.

EXAM REVIEW

1. **TRADITIONAL COMMON LAW RULE** The traditional common law rule of employment provided that an employee at will could be fired for a good reason, a bad reason, or no reason at all. But modern law has created exceptions to this rule that prohibit firing an employee at will for a *bad* reason.

2. **WRONGFUL DISCHARGE AND PUBLIC POLICY** Generally, an employee may not be fired for refusing to violate the law, exercising a legal right, or supporting fundamental societal values.

EXAMStrategy

Question: When Theodore Staats went to his company's "Council of Honor Convention," he was accompanied by a woman who was not his wife, although he told everyone she was. The company fired him. Staats alleged that his termination violated public policy because it infringed upon his freedom of association. He also alleged that he had been fired because he was too successful—his commissions were so high, he out-earned even the highest-paid officer of the company. Has Staats's employer violated public policy?

Strategy: Is Staats protected by a statute? No. Is he being asked to break the law? No. Is he being denied a legal right? Is he supporting fundamental societal values? (See the "Result" at the end of this Exam Review section.)

3. **PROMISES MADE DURING THE HIRING PROCESS** Promises made during the hiring process are generally enforceable, even if not approved by the company's top executives. An employee handbook also creates a contract.

EXAMStrategy

Question: When Phil McConkey interviewed for a job as an insurance agent with Alexander & Alexander, the company did not tell him that it was engaged in secret negotiations to merge with Aon. When the merger went through soon thereafter, Aon fired McConkey. Was Alexander liable for not telling McConkey about the possible merger?

Strategy: Was McConkey protected by a statute? No. Did the company make any promises to him during the hiring process? (See the "Result" at the end of this Exam Review section.)

4. **HANDBOOKS** An employee handbook may create a contract.
5. **COVENANT OF GOOD FAITH AND FAIR DEALING** About half the states imply a covenant of good faith and fair dealing in contracts. This covenant requires both parties to behave reasonably, making an honest effort to meet both the spirit and letter of the contract.
6. **DEFAMATION** Employers may be liable for defamation when they give false references about an employee. More than half of the states, however, recognize a qualified privilege for employers who give references about former employees.
7. **INTENTIONAL INFLICTION OF EMOTIONAL DISTRESS** Employers may face liability under the tort of intentional infliction of emotional distress if they permit extreme and outrageous conduct in the workplace.
8. **FMLA** The Family and Medical Leave Act guarantees workers up to 12 weeks of unpaid leave each year for childbirth, adoption, or a serious health condition of their own or in their immediate family.
9. **WHISTLEBLOWERS** Employees who disclose illegal behavior in the workplace receive some protection under both federal and state laws.
10. **OFF-DUTY ACTIVITIES** In the absence of a specific law to the contrary, employers have the right to fire workers for off-duty conduct.
11. **ALCOHOL AND DRUG USE** Under federal law, private employers are permitted to test job applicants and workers for alcohol and illegal drugs. The Equal Employment Opportunity Commission prohibits testing for prescription drugs unless a worker seems impaired.

12. **FREE SPEECH** Under the NLRA, non-unionized workers cannot be fired for complaining about their jobs, so long as these complaints are shared with other employees and are not inappropriately hostile or violent. This rule does not protect supervisors.

13. **STORED COMMUNICATIONS ACT (SCA)** Under the SCA, an employer has the right to monitor workers' electronic communications if (1) the employee consents; (2) the monitoring occurs in the ordinary course of business; or (3) in the case of email, if the employer provides the computer system. This monitoring may include an employee's social media activities.

14. **OSHA** The goal of the Occupational Safety and Health Act is to ensure safe conditions in the workplace.

15. **GUNS** Employers have the right to ban guns from the workplace, but, in almost half the states, laws prevent companies from banning firearms in their workplace parking lot.

16. **THE FAIR LABOR STANDARDS ACT (FLSA)** The Fair Labor Standards Act regulates minimum and overtime wages. It also limits child labor.

17. **WORKERS' COMPENSATION** Workers' compensation statutes ensure that employees receive payment for injuries incurred at work.

18. **HEALTH INSURANCE** Former employees must be allowed to continue their health insurance for 18 months after being terminated from their job, but they must pay for it themselves.

19. **SOCIAL SECURITY** The Social Security system pays benefits to workers who are retired, disabled, or temporarily unemployed and to the spouses and children of disabled or deceased workers.

20. **UNEMPLOYMENT COMPENSATION** Workers are eligible for unemployment compensation unless they have quit their job voluntarily or were fired for just cause.

21. **ERISA** The Employee Retirement Income Security Act regulates private pension plans.

22. **RIGHT TO ORGANIZE** Section 7 of the NLRA guarantees employees the right to organize and join unions, bargain collectively, and engage in other concerted activities. Section 8 of the NLRA makes it a ULP for an employer to interfere with union organizing, discriminate against a union member, or refuse to bargain collectively. During a union organizing campaign, an employer may vigorously present anti-union views to its employees, but it may not use threats or rewards to defeat the union effort.

23. **EXCLUSIVITY** Under §9 of the NLRA, a validly recognized union is the exclusive representative of the employees.

EXAMStrategy

Question: Power, Inc., which operated a coal mine, suffered financial losses and had to lay off employees. The United Mine Workers of America (UMWA) began an organizing drive. Power's general manager warned miners that if the company was unionized, it would be shut down. An office manager told one of the miners that the company would get rid of union supporters. Shortly before the election was to take place, Power laid off 13 employees, all of whom had signed union cards. A low-seniority employee who had not signed a union card was not laid off. The union claimed that Power had committed ULPs. Comment.

Strategy: The NLRA guarantees employees the right to organize. An employer may vigorously advocate against a union organizing campaign. However, it is a ULP to interfere with union organizing or discriminate against a union member. (See the "Result" at the end of this Exam Review section.)

24. **BARGAINING** The employer and the union *must* bargain over wages, hours, and other terms and conditions of employment. They *may* bargain over other subjects, but neither side may insist on doing so. The union and the employer must bargain in good faith, but they are not obligated to reach an agreement.

25. **STRIKES** The NLRA guarantees employees the right to strike, with some limitations. After an *economic* strike, an employer is not obligated to lay off replacement workers to give strikers their jobs back, but it may not discriminate against strikers when filling job openings. After a ULP strike, the striking workers must get their jobs back.

26. **PICKETING** Picketing the employer's workplace in support of a strike is generally lawful. Secondary boycotts are generally illegal.

27. **LOCKOUTS** Most lockouts are legal.

RESULTS

2. Result: The court held that freedom of association is an important social right and should be protected. However, being fired for bringing a lover to an employer's convention is not a threat to public policy. Nor is discharge for being too successful.

3. Result: The court held that when Alexander hired him, it was making an implied promise that he would not be fired immediately. The company was liable for not having revealed the merger negotiations.

23. Result: Each of the acts described was a ULP. Threatening layoffs or company closure are classic examples of ULPs. Laying off those who had signed union cards, but not those who refused, was clear discrimination.

MULTIPLE-CHOICE QUESTIONS

1. When Brook went to work at an advertising agency, his employment contract stated that he was "at will and could be terminated at any time." After 28 months with the company, he was fired without explanation. Which of the following statements is true?
   (a) The company must give him an explanation for his termination.
   (b) Because he had a contract, he was not an employee at will.
   (c) He could only be fired for a good reason.
   (d) He could be fired for any reason.
   (e) He could be fired for any reason except a bad reason.

2. **CPA QUESTION** An unemployed CPA generally would receive unemployment compensation benefits if the CPA _______________.
   (a) was fired as a result of the employer's business reversals
   (b) refused to accept a job as an accountant while receiving extended benefits
   (c) was fired for embezzling from a client
   (d) left work voluntarily without good cause

3. During a job interview with Venetia, Jack reveals that he and his wife are expecting twins. Venetia asks him if he is planning to take a leave once the babies are born. When Jack admits that he would like to take a month off work, he can see her face fall. She ultimately decides not to hire him because of the twins. Which of the following statements are true?
   (a) Venetia has violated the FMLA.
   (b) Venetia has violated COBRA.
   (c) Both A and B are true.
   (d) None of these are true.

4. Which of the following statements is true?
   (a) In about half the states, employees have the right to bring guns into their workplace.
   (b) In about half the states, employees have the right to bring guns into their workplace parking lot.
   (c) Both A and B are true.
   (d) None of these are true.

5. Alpha Company's workers go on strike. The company hires replacement workers so that it can continue to operate its business. When the strike ends, Alpha must rehire the original workers if the strike was over _______________.
   (a) wages
   (b) a ULP
   (c) Both A and B
   (d) None of these are true.

CASE QUESTIONS

1. ***YOU BE THE JUDGE* WRITING PROBLEM** Apex gave Marcie an employment handbook stating that (1) she was an at-will employee, (2) the handbook did not create any contractual rights, and (3) employees who were fired had the right to a termination hearing. The company fired Marcie, claiming that she had falsified delivery records. She said that Apex was retaliating against her because she had complained of sexual harassment. Apex refused her request for a termination hearing. Did the employee handbook create a contract guaranteeing Marcie a hearing? **Argument for Apex:** The handbook could not have been clearer—it did not create a contract. Marcie is an employee at will and is not entitled to a hearing. **Argument for Marcie:** Apex intended that employees would rely on the handbook. The company used promises of a hearing to attract and retain good employees. Marcie was entitled to a hearing.

2. Triec, Inc., is a small electrical contracting company in Springfield, Ohio, owned by its executives, Yeazell, Jones, and Heaton. Employees contacted the International Brotherhood of Electrical Workers, which began an organizing drive, and 6 of the 11 employees in the bargaining unit signed authorization cards. The company declined to recognize the union, which petitioned the NLRB to schedule an election. The company then granted several new benefits for all workers, including higher wages, paid vacations, and other measures. When the election was held, only 2 of the 11 bargaining unit members voted for the union. Did the company violate the NLRA?

3. Sally is sent home from school with the chicken pox. Her father takes her to a pediatrician who says that she will be fine in about a week and in the meantime just needs bed rest and plenty of fluids. Is Sally's father entitled to leave under the FMLA to care for Sally?

4. Catherine Wagenseller was a nurse at Scottsdale Memorial Hospital and an employee at will. While on a camping trip with other nurses, Wagenseller refused to join in a parody of the song "Moon River," which concluded with members of the group "mooning" the audience. Her supervisor seemed upset by her refusal. Prior to the trip, Wagenseller had received consistently favorable performance evaluations. Six months after the outing, Wagenseller was fired. She contends it was because she had not mooned. Is it legal for the hospital to fire Wagenseller for this reason?

5. Noelle was the principal of a charter school and an employee at will. The head administrator imposed a rule requiring cafeteria workers to stamp the hands of children who did not have sufficient funds in their lunch accounts. Some of these children were entitled to free lunches, others needed to ask their parents to replenish their accounts. Noelle directed the cafeteria workers to stop this humiliating practice. The administrator fired her. Does Noelle have a valid claim for wrongful termination?

DISCUSSION QUESTIONS

1. Debra Agis worked as a waitress in a Ground Round restaurant. The manager informed the waitresses that "there was some stealing going on." Until he found out who was doing it, he intended to fire all the waitresses in alphabetical order, starting with the letter "A." Dionne then fired Agis. Does she have a valid claim against her employer?

2. **ETHICS** Should employers be allowed to fire smokers? Nicotine is highly addictive and many smokers begin as teenagers, when they may not fully understand the consequences of their decisions. As Mark Twain, who began smoking at 12, famously said, "Giving up smoking is the easiest thing in the world. I know because I've done it thousands of times."

3. Walmart employees were not unionized. A group of outside organizers called "Our Walmart" created an app that Walmart employees could use to communicate with one another and obtain legal and other workplace advice. Walmart told its managers to warn workers that the app was not made by Walmart and might be used to steal their personal information. Would that behavior on the part of managers be legal?

4. **ETHICS** As the manager of BigBox Store, you are afraid that, if your workers unionize, you will not be able to compete against stores with a non-union workforce. You would very much like to fire Geraldo, the employee who is leading the unionization effort. Of course, you know this action would be a violation of the NLRA. But you also know that, if you were found to have violated the law (after years of litigation), you would simply be required to reinstate Geraldo, pay him some back wages, and post a notice promising never to do it again.[46] (After all that time, Geraldo probably would not even want his BigBox job back.) In the meantime, all the other employees would be so scared, they would not support the union. This strategy is the most cost effective, but is it the right thing to do? What would Mill and Kant say?

5. Despite its detailed dress code for employees, Starbucks stores permitted workers to wear multiple pins and buttons, some of which, but not all, were related to its employee-reward and product-promotion programs. When a union tried to organize employees, management prohibited workers from wearing more than one pro-union pin at a time. (One employee had tried to wear eight union buttons.) Is this rule a ULP?

6. ***YOU BE THE JUDGE* WRITING PROBLEM** Nationwide Insurance Co. circulated a memorandum asking all employees to lobby in favor of a bill that had been introduced in the Pennsylvania House of Representatives. By limiting the damages that an injured motorist could recover from a person who caused an accident, this bill promised to save Nationwide significant money. Not only did John Novosel refuse to lobby, but he privately criticized the bill for harming consumers. Nationwide was definitely not on his side—it fired him. Novosel filed suit,

[46]House Report 110-023 Employee Free Choice Act of 2007.

alleging that his discharge had violated public policy by infringing his right to free speech. Did Nationwide violate public policy by firing Novosel? **Argument for Novosel:** The U.S. Constitution and the Pennsylvania Constitution both guarantee the right to free speech. Nationwide has violated an important public policy by firing Novosel for expressing his opinions. **Argument for Nationwide:** For all the high-flown talk about the Constitution, what we have here is an employee who refused to carry out company policy. If the employee wins in this case, where will it all end? What if an employee for a tobacco company refuses to market cigarettes because he does not approve of smoking? How can businesses operate without loyalty from their employees?

7. **ETHICS** Edward Snowden was a contractor at the National Security Agency (NSA) who publicly released a huge number of highly classified documents. From these files, the world learned for the first time that the NSA had been collecting vast amounts of information about the email, mail, and telephone usage of millions of people, many of them American citizens. In releasing this data, Snowden had embarrassed U.S. officials and possibly damaged spy operations. However, the NSA's own auditor found that the NSA had exceeded its authority. Two federal judges ruled that the NSA had violated the Constitution. Because Snowden broke the law, he was not protected by whistleblower statutes. He sought asylum overseas because, if he returned to the United States, he faced life in prison. Does he deserve life in prison? Should he be offered amnesty? A reduced sentence? How important is it to encourage whistleblowing?

CHAPTER

30 EMPLOYMENT DISCRIMINATION

Imagine that you are on the hiring committee of a top San Francisco law firm. You come across a résumé from a candidate who grew up on an isolated ranch in Arizona. Raised in a house without electricity or running water, he had worked alongside the ranch hands his entire childhood. At the age of 16, he left home for Stanford University, and from there had gone on to Stanford Law School, where he finished third in his class. You think to yourself, "This sounds like a real American success story. A great combination of grit and intelligence." But without hesitation, you toss the résumé into the wastebasket.

You think, "This sounds like a real American success story." But you toss the résumé into the wastebasket.

This is a true story. Indeed, there was a candidate with these credentials who was unable to find a job as a lawyer in any San Francisco law firm. The only jobs on offer were as a secretary, because the year was 1952 and this candidate was a woman—Sandra Day O'Connor, who went on to become one of the most influential lawyers of her era and the first woman justice on the Supreme Court of the United States.

Before 1964, you might never see a female or African-American doctor, engineer, police officer, or corporate executive. If women or minorities did get jobs, it was legal to treat them differently from white men. Women, for example, could be paid less for the same job and could be fired if they got married or pregnant.

30-1 EMPLOYMENT OPPORTUNITY BEFORE 1964

The United States has traveled a long and bumpy road toward equality of opportunity in the workplace. This story begins after the Civil War, when a torn and bleeding country sought to protect the rights of freed slaves and undo the terrible harm of a century of slavery. The country began by ratifying three Constitutional amendments: The Thirteenth prohibits slavery, the Fourteenth guarantees due process of law and equal protection under the law, and the Fifteenth prohibits restrictions on the right to vote because of race or color. In addition, Congress passed the Civil Rights Act of 1866, which provided that all people born in the United States (except Native Americans) were citizens of the United States and had the same rights as white citizens.[1]

However, in response to these laws, many states passed (and the Supreme Court upheld) statutes that undermined these protections. The most notorious case was *Plessy v. Ferguson*, in which the Supreme Court upheld the constitutionality of a Louisiana law that prohibited blacks from riding in railroad cars reserved for whites. Blacks were provided with "separate but equal" cars.[2]

Not until 1954, almost a century after the Civil War, did the Supreme Court reverse its *Plessy* decision. In the landmark case *Brown v. Board of Education*, the high court ruled that "separate but equal" policies were unconstitutional.[3] In particular, it prohibited segregated public schools. However, many school districts were slow to comply with the case, and even ten years later, segregated public schools still existed in many parts of the country. Nonetheless, *Brown* inspired a generation of civil rights leaders, such as Martin Luther King, Jr. and Rosa Parks, who led protests, boycotts, and voter registration drives.

These actions influenced Congress to pass the Civil Rights Act of 1964. Title VII of this Act prohibits certain types of employment discrimination, which is the focus of this chapter. However, the statute was even more far-reaching because it prohibited a broad range of discrimination, including in education, voting, and public accommodations (such as hotels, restaurants, and movie theaters).

We begin now with a review of constitutional provisions that prohibit discrimination in the workplace and follow with a discussion of the major federal anti-discrimination statutes: the Civil Rights Act of 1866, the Equal Pay Act of 1963, Title VII of the Civil Rights Act of

---

[1] 42 USC 21 §1981.

[2] 163 U.S. 537 (S. Ct. 1896).

[3] 347 U.S. 483 (S. Ct. 1954).

1964, the Pregnancy Discrimination Act, the Age Discrimination in Employment Act, the Rehabilitation Act of 1973, the Americans with Disabilities Act, and the Genetic Information Nondiscrimination Act.

30-1a The United States Constitution

The Fifth Amendment to the Constitution prohibits the *federal government* from depriving individuals of "life, liberty, or property" without due process of law. The Fourteenth Amendment prohibits *state governments* from violating an individual's right to due process and equal protection. **The courts have interpreted these provisions to prohibit employment discrimination by federal, state, and local governments.**

30-1b Civil Rights Act of 1866

As we have seen, the Civil Rights Act of 1866 was meant to provide freed slaves with the same rights as white citizens. **It has been interpreted to prohibit *racial* discrimination in both private and public employment (except it does not apply to the federal government).** As we will see later in the Enforcement section of this chapter, it offers plaintiffs some significant advantages over Title VII.

30-1c Equal Pay Act of 1963

Under the Equal Pay Act, a worker may not be paid at a lesser rate than employees of the opposite sex for equal work. "Equal work" means tasks that require equal skill, effort, and responsibility under similar working conditions. Citicorp rewarded Heidi Wilson's good work with a promotion to manager, but neglected to include a raise or even a bonus. She protested that the man she replaced had earned 75 percent more, but Citicorp argued that salaries were based not just on position but also on seniority and experience. Also, the economy was suffering through a recession. So Wilson requested a market analysis, but Citicorp refused. She also discovered that Citicorp had rewarded other employees with *bonuses* that were higher than Wilson's *salary*. An arbitrator awarded Wilson $340,000 in back pay.[4]

30-2 THE CIVIL RIGHTS ACT OF 1964

Under Title VII of the Civil Rights Act of 1964, it is illegal for employers with 15 or more employees to discriminate on the basis of race, color, religion, sex, or national origin. Discrimination under Title VII applies to every aspect of the employment process, from job ads to postemployment references, and includes hiring, firing, promoting, placement, wages, benefits, and working conditions of anyone who is in one or more of the so-called **protected categories** under the statute.

Protected categories
Race, color, religion, sex, or national origin

30-2a Prohibited Activities

There are four types of illegal activities under this statute: disparate treatment, disparate impact, hostile environment, and retaliation. All of these activities are illegal if used against anyone in a protected category.

[4]Elizabeth Behrman, "Tampa Woman Wins Lawsuit against Citicorp for Pay Discrimination," *The Tampa Bay Times*, April 16, 2012.

Disparate Treatment

To prove a disparate treatment case, the plaintiff must show that she was *treated* less favorably than others because of her sex, race, color, religion, or national origin.

The required steps in a disparate treatment case are:

1. **The plaintiff presents evidence that:**
   - She belongs to a protected category under Title VII,
   - She suffered adverse employment action, and
   - This action occurred under conditions giving rise to an inference of discrimination.

   Prima facie
   From the Latin, meaning "from its first appearance," something that appears to be true upon a first look

   If the plaintiff can show these facts, she has made a ***prima facie*** case, that is, a case that appears to be true upon first look. The plaintiff is not required to *prove* discrimination; she need only create a *presumption* that discrimination occurred.

   Sandra Guzman was an editor at *The New York Post*.[5] She was also black, Hispanic, Puerto Rican, and female. The company fired her, while keeping a white editor. Although an editor's position was open, the company did not offer her that job. This evidence alone is not *proof* of discrimination because the *Post* may have had a perfectly good, nondiscriminatory explanation. However, its behavior *could have been* motivated by discrimination.

2. **The defendant must present evidence that its decision was based on legitimate, nondiscriminatory reasons**. The *Post* said that it had fired Guzman because the section she edited, Tempo, was unprofitable. The white editor had been kept on because she had an employment contract; Guzman did not. The company had not offered Guzman the open position because the pay was substantially less. The *Post* moved for summary judgment.

3. **To win, the plaintiff must now prove that the employer intentionally discriminated, although this motive can be *inferred* from differences in treatment**. The burden of proof is on the plaintiff. She may prove her case by showing either that (1) the reasons the employer offered were simply a *pretext* or (2) that a discriminatory intent is more likely than not. Guzman offered evidence that Tempo was not closed until after she was fired and that it had been more successful than the rest of the *Post*. She testified that she would have taken the open job, even at a lower salary. She also alleged that many *Post* employees had made racist and sexist remarks. Furthermore, the *Post* had run a cartoon, which was widely viewed as a racist insult to then President Barack Obama, because it seemingly compared him to a monkey.[6] If Guzman can prove these facts to be true, she will win because she has offered evidence of both pretext and intent. Thus, the court denied the *Post*'s request for summary judgment.

EXAMStrategy

Question: The appearance policy at Starwood Hotels prohibited employees from wearing hairstyles that showed excessive scalp. When Carmelita Vazquez repeatedly came to work with her hair in cornrows, Starwood fired her for violating its policy. Vazquez was African-American and Hispanic. White women were allowed to wear their hair in braids. Vazquez filed a disparate treatment claim under Title VII.

---

[5]Guzman v. News Corp., 2013 U.S. Dist. LEXIS 155026, 2013 WL 580705 (S.D.N.Y. 2013).

[6]To see this cartoon, google "Obama chimp cartoon NY Post."

Strategy: The steps of a disparate treatment case are:

1. Vazquez has presented a *prima facie* case—she is in a protected category and was treated differently from similar people who are not protected under Title VII, giving rise to an inference of discrimination.
2. Starwood presented evidence that its decision was based on legitimate reasons—Vazquez had violated its appearance policy.
3. To win, Vazquez must show that Starwood's decision was a pretext or had a discriminatory intent.

Result: The court found for Vazquez, believing that Starwood did have a discriminatory intent.[7]

Disparate Impact

We have already studied the *Griggs v. Duke Power* case in Chapter 4, but it is a landmark case in employment law, so worth reviewing again.[8] Duke Power required all applicants to its most desirable departments to have a high school education or satisfactory scores on two tests that measured intelligence and mechanical ability. Neither test gauged the ability to perform a particular job. The pass rate for whites was much higher than for blacks, and whites were also more likely than blacks to have a high school diploma. Although Duke Power was not, on its face, discriminating against blacks, the upshot of these employment rules was that more whites got the good jobs.

The Supreme Court ruled that Duke Power was violating Title VII because its rules had a disparate impact on a protected category. The court stated:

> Nothing in [Title VII] precludes the use of testing or measuring procedures; obviously they are useful. What Congress has commanded is that any tests used must measure the person for the job and not the person in the abstract.

Disparate impact applies if the employer has a rule that, *on its face*, is not discriminatory, but *in practice* excludes too many people in a protected category.

The required steps in a disparate impact case are:

1. **The plaintiff must present a *prima facie* case.** The plaintiff is not required to prove discrimination; he need only show a disparate impact—that the employment practice in question excludes a disproportionate number of people in a protected group (women and minorities, for instance). In the *Griggs* case, a far higher percentage of whites than blacks passed the tests required for one of the good jobs. The Equal Employment Opportunity Commission (EEOC) defines a disparate impact as one in which the pass rate for a protected category is less than 80 percent of that for others. (As we will see, the EEOC is the federal agency charged with enforcing most discrimination statutes.)
2. **The defendant must offer some evidence that the employment practice was a job-related business necessity.** Duke Power would have to show that the tests predicted job performance.
3. **To win, the plaintiff must now prove either that the employer's reason is a pretext or that other, less discriminatory, rules would achieve the same results.** Note that, unlike disparate treatment, the plaintiff in a disparate impact case, does not have

[7] Vazquez v. Caesar's Paradise Stream Resort, 2013 U.S. Dist. LEXIS 170178, 2013 WL 6244568 (M.D. Pa. 2013).

[8] 401 U.S. 424 (S. Ct. 1971).

to prove *intentional* discrimination. The plaintiffs in *Griggs* showed that the tests were not a job-related business necessity—workers who had been hired before the tests were introduced performed the jobs well. Duke Power could no longer use them as a hiring screen. If the power company wanted to use tests, it would have to find some that measured an employee's ability to perform particular jobs.

Griggs was decided almost a half century ago. Yet, as the following case illustrates, hiring tests remain a frequent subject of litigation.

Gulino v. Bd. of Educ. of the City Sch. Dist. of N.Y.

907 F. Supp. 2d 492
United States District Court for the Southern District of New York, 2012

Facts: A New York State task force on teacher qualifications decided that all teachers needed a basic understanding of liberal arts and sciences. National Evaluation Systems (NES), a professional test development company, was hired to develop the Liberal Arts and Sciences Test (LAST) to measure this knowledge.

NES began by establishing two committees of teachers and professors (Committees) to ensure that the LAST was both relevant to the job of a New York public school teacher and free from bias. The Committees reviewed a draft framework, a list of exam subtopics, and sample questions. NES then sent its draft framework and subtopics for review to 1,200 New York public school teachers and education professors. It also tested some sample questions on students at various state education colleges.

To determine what a passing score should be, the Committees estimated what percentage of test-takers would answer each question correctly. They recommended a passing score of between 38 and 48. The New York State Education Commissioner ultimately established 43 as the required score.

Teachers could not be licensed to teach in New York City unless they passed the LAST. Whites succeeded at a higher rate than African-Americans and Latinos. A group of minority teachers filed suit against the Board of Education for the City of New York (Board) alleging that the LAST violated Title VII.

Issue: ***Did the LAST violate Title VII?***

Excerpts from Judge Wood's Decision: Under Title VII, an exam is job related if it has been properly validated. The essence of validation is in the requirement that the content of the test be related to the content of the job.

There are several flaws in the way that NES developed [the LAST] that prevent the Court from finding that the company conducted a suitable job analysis. First, NES never created a list of the tasks teachers perform, nor determined whether the subtopics identify knowledge needed to perform those tasks.

Second, NES representatives testified that the company collected materials from schools and colleges throughout the state, interviewed deans and administrators of liberal arts programs at colleges and universities in New York, and consulted with education experts. The representatives, however, could not describe how the information collected was used or how it supported the choice of subtopics. It also appears that NES actually drafted the subtopics prior to collecting materials and conducting interviews.

The third requirement is that the content of the exam must be directly related to the content of the job. The fact that the LAST is related generally to the liberal arts and sciences does not prove that the exam is job related; indeed, the liberal arts and sciences is an extremely broad field that encompasses far more than the basic knowledge all teachers need in order to be competent. Rather, to be job related, the LAST must test for the minimum level of knowledge about the liberal arts and sciences that is necessary to ensure that all teachers are competent to teach. There is no evidence in the record establishing the minimum level of knowledge about the liberal arts and sciences needed by all teachers. Consequently, the Court finds that the Board has failed to establish that the LAST is directly related to teachers' jobs.

[A court must also] determine whether the exam is scored in a way that usefully selects those applicants who can better perform the job. There is no evidence that the committees were given any guidance as to the definition of "minimally-competent." At the same time, there was no evidence that higher scores on the LAST correlated with better teacher or student performance in the classroom.

In conclusion, the Court finds that the LAST is not job related, and the Board violated Title VII by requiring Plaintiffs to pass the exam in order to receive a teaching license.

In response to this case, the Board of Education adopted a different licensing exam, which whites still passed at higher rates than African-Americans and Latinos. But the judge upheld its use because she found it to be job related.[9] Ultimately, however, New York State eliminated this second test because it was contributing to a shortage of minority teachers.

Hostile Work Environment

Employers violate Title VII if they permit a work environment that is so hostile toward people in a protected category that it affects their ability to work. This rule applies whether the hostility is based on race, color, religion, sex, or national origin. (As we will see, this rule also applies to those treated badly because of pregnancy, age, or disability.) This concept of hostile environment first arose in the context of sexual harassment.

Sexual Harassment. When Professor Anita Hill accused Supreme Court nominee Clarence Thomas of sexually harassing her, people across the country were glued to their televisions, watching the Senate hearings on her charges. Thomas was ultimately confirmed to the Supreme Court, but "sexual harassment" became a household phrase. The number of cases—and the size of the damage awards—skyrocketed.

Sexual harassment became a household phrase.

Sexual harassment involves unwelcome sexual advances, requests for sexual favors, and other verbal or physical conduct of a sexual nature which are so severe and pervasive that they interfere with an employee's ability to work. **There are two categories of sexual harassment**:

- ***Quid pro quo***. From a Latin phrase that means "one thing in return for another," *quid pro quo* harassment occurs if any aspect of a job is made contingent upon sexual activity. In the Guzman case, the plaintiff alleged that a male editor had offered a permanent reporter job to a young female copy assistant in exchange for sexual performance.
- **Hostile work environment**. An employee has a valid claim of sexual harassment if sexual talk and activity are so pervasive that they interfere with her (or his) ability to work. Courts have found that offensive jokes, intrusive comments about clothes or body parts, and public displays of pornographic pictures can create a hostile environment. Guzman claimed that a male editor had shown her a photo of a naked man while telling stories about another editor's "voracious sexual appetite."

The following case lays out the elements of a hostile work environment claim. It also illustrates the dangers of fishing off the company pier.

Gatter v. IKA-Works, Inc.

2016 U.S. Dist. LEXIS 174816
United States District Court for the Eastern District of Pennsylvania, 2016

Facts: Courtney Gatter was a sales representative for IKA. The company was owned by the Stiegelmann family, which included René (who worked for the company), and his son, Marcel (who did not). Gatter reported to Refika Bilgic, who was both managing director and René's romantic partner. Gatter was aware of rumors linking René romantically with various female employees.

The company took all of its employees (and Marcel) on a sailing trip in the Mediterranean. Gatter had never met Marcel before the trip. On the first day, while Gatter was reclining on deck, René snapped a photograph "up her shorts."

9 Gulino v. Bd. of Educ., 122 F. Supp. 3d 115 (S.D.N.Y. 2015).

Marcel, who did not have an assigned bedroom, had been sleeping on deck. On the third night, he complained that this arrangement was uncomfortable and asked Gatter if he could sleep in her room. Once in her room, they kissed and he suggested sexual intercourse, but Gatter rejected his advance. Because Gatter knew that René had liaisons with female employees, she felt "damned if she did, and damned if she didn't" accept Marcel's advances. Ultimately, Gatter gave in. Although René was upset when he learned that his son and his employee were in a sexual relationship, the affair continued during the trip.

As the ship sailed on, Gatter grew more and more uncomfortable with the sexualized environment. On two occasions, she saw René naked: once while he was exiting the shower into a common area on the boat and, on another day, as a towel blew up while he changed into his bathing suit on the beach.

On the final day of the trip, Gatter apologized to Bilgic and René for her affair with Marcel. René then berated her, asking her, "How can you spread your legs after the second day?" He gave Gatter an ultimatum: quit working for IKA or break up with Marcel. Gatter agreed to end the relationship. Although Marcel and Gatter never met again, they did continue to text. When Bilgic found out, she fired Gatter.

Gatter filed suit against IKA alleging sexual harassment. IKA filed a motion for summary judgment.

Issue: ***Was Gatter sexually harassed?***

Excerpts from Judge Beetlestone's Decision[10]: To prevail, Gatter must show that: 1) she suffered intentional discrimination; 2) the discrimination was severe or pervasive; 3) the discrimination detrimentally affected Gatter; 4) the discrimination would detrimentally affect a reasonable person in like circumstances; and 5) the [employer's] liability.

[T]he "intent" element of a hostile work environment claim refers only to whether the behavior was intentionally based on a protected status, not on whether the alleged harasser intended hostility or abuse. The incident which occurred when Gatter saw René toweling himself off after a shower was undisputedly unintentional. The second incident—which occurred when René changed into a bathing suit on a public beach guarded only by a towel—also falls short of intentional discrimination. While changing clothes on a public beach during a company-sponsored trip may exhibit poor judgment, there is no evidence that René intended to expose himself.

[Whether the photograph] can be perceived as intentional discrimination is a close call. [T]he fact that the photo provides a view "up Gatter's shorts" could allow a reasonable jury to conclude that the photograph was an intentional act based on Gatter's sex.

Marcel's proposition of sexual activity to Gatter easily satisfies the "intentional discrimination" element. While the sexual relationship between Gatter and Marcel was eventually consensual, it is undisputed that Gatter rejected Marcel's initial sexual advances and a jury could reasonably conclude that a sexual proposition from a part-owner of IKA constitutes intentional sex discrimination.

[T]he ultimate inquiry is whether the harassment was sufficiently severe or pervasive as to alter the conditions of Gatter's employment and create an abusive working environment. [A] claim can arise from isolated incidents when those incidents are "extremely serious." [A] jury could reasonably conclude that Gatter was subjected to sexual harassment sufficiently severe to alter her conditions of employment.

Within the first days of that trip, Gatter was propositioned for sex by a part-owner of the company (who she had never previously met), and the trip concluded with her being berated for accepting that proposition by his father who was the president of the company. This scenario represents an intermingling of sex-based discrimination and employment conditions. Indeed, Gatter testified that she felt that she was "damned if I do, damned if I don't" in relation to Marcel's initial proposition for sex, particularly in light of René's history of engaging in relationships with female employees, including Bilgic. The fact that a consensual relationship eventually emerged between Marcel and Gatter does not mitigate the severity of the initial proposition as an instance of sexual harassment. [A] jury could reasonably conclude that this environment, though brief, was sufficiently severe as to constitute a change in the conditions of Gatter's employment. For the same reasons a jury could find that the conduct would detrimentally affect a reasonable similarly situated employee.

When a hostile work environment claim is based on alleged harassment by a supervisor, an employer's liability is established if the harassment culminates in a tangible employment action. [L]iability for harassment by René can be imputed to IKA because he was the President and part-owner, and undisputedly had authority over all IKA matters. With respect to Marcel, even if he was not acting as a supervisor, a jury could reasonably find that IKA was negligent given that the entire sailing trip happened in the immediate presence of Gatter's direct supervisor and that Marcel, René, and Bilgic were in close communication throughout the trip.

IKA's motion for summary judgment shall be denied.

10We have replaced "Plaintiff" with "Gatter" and "IKA" with "Defendant."

Same-Sex Harassment. Suppose that one man makes unwelcome sexual overtures to another man in the workplace. The Supreme Court ruled that same-sex harassment is also a violation of Title VII.[11]

Corning Consumer Products Co. provides a set of practical guidelines for eliminating sexual harassment. It asks employees to apply four tests in determining whether their behavior violates Title VII:

- Would you say or do this in front of your spouse or parents?
- What about in front of a colleague of the opposite sex?
- Would you like your behavior reported in your local newspaper?
- Does it need to be said or done at all?

Hostile Environment Based on Race. Reginald Jones was an African-American man who drove a truck for UPS. He began finding bananas and banana peels on his truck in the terminal. Some employees wore Confederate shirts and hats. After he reported these incidents to a supervisor, two other drivers came up to him one night in the parking lot holding a crowbar. They asked him if he had reported them to the supervisor. He again reported this event and again found banana peels on his truck. When Jones sued UPS, alleging a racially hostile work environment, the trial court granted UPS's motion for summary judgment. But the appellate court overturned this decision, ruling that the case should go to a jury because these events could, indeed, have created a hostile work environment.[12]

Hostile Environment Based on Color. Title VII prohibits discrimination based on both race and color. Although many people assume that they are essentially the same, that is not necessarily the case. Dwight Burch alleged that his coworkers at an Applebee's restaurant created a hostile work environment when they called him hateful names because of his dark skin color. These colleagues were also African-American but had lighter skin. While denying any wrongdoing, Applebee's settled the case by paying Burch $40,000 and agreeing to conduct anti-discrimination training.

Hostile Environment Based on National Origin. Title VII also prohibits a hostile environment based on national origin. While working at Steel Technologies, Inc., Tony Cerros was promoted several times. So what was the problem? Coworkers and supervisors called him names like "brown boy," "spic," and "wetback." They also told him that "if it ain't white, it ain't right," and wrote "Go Back to Mexico" on the bathroom wall. Although the company removed the bathroom graffiti, it did not investigate Cerros's complaints until he filed suit. At that point, it determined that Cerros had not faced discrimination. The trial court agreed because Cerros had, after all, been promoted. However, the appeals court overturned the decision, finding for Cerros on the grounds that he had suffered a hostile work environment, which is in itself a violation of Title VII, even if there is no evidence of adverse employment actions.[13]

Employer Liability for Harassment. Employees who engage in illegal harassment are liable for their own misdeeds. But is their company also liable? The Supreme Court has held:

- The company is liable if it knew or should have known about the conduct and failed to stop it.
- Even if the company was unaware of the misbehavior, it is nonetheless liable if the victimized employee suffered a "tangible employment action" such as firing, demotion, or reassignment.

---

[11]Oncale v. Sundowner Offshore Services, Inc., 523 U.S. 75 (S. Ct. 1998).

[12]Jones v. UPS Ground Freight, 683 F.3d 1283 (11th Cir. 2012).

[13]Cerros v. Steel Techs, Inc., 288 F.3d 1040 (7th Cir. 2002).

- If the company was unaware of the behavior and the victimized employee did not suffer a tangible employment action, the company is still liable unless it can prove that (1) it used reasonable care to prevent and correct harassing behavior, and (2) the employee unreasonably failed to take advantage of the complaint procedure or other preventive opportunities provided by the company.[14]

In the *Gatter* case, the court held that her employer was liable because she suffered a "tangible employment action," that is, she was fired.

Retaliation

Title VII also prohibits employers from retaliating against workers who oppose discrimination, bring a claim under the statute, or take part in an investigation or hearing. Retaliation means that the employer has done something that would deter a reasonable worker from complaining about discrimination. Research indicates that retaliation occurs in as many as 60 percent of discrimination cases.

However, a defendant can defeat a retaliation claim by showing that there were other, nondiscriminatory reasons for his action. In basic discrimination cases, a plaintiff can win by showing that discrimination was a motivating factor, although other factors were also involved. But the standard of proof is higher for retaliation claims where the plaintiff must demonstrate that, but for the defendant's desire to retaliate, he would never have taken the harmful action. (This standard is called **but-for causation**.)

But-for causation
The retaliatory action would not have occurred but for the defendant's discriminatory intent.

Dr. Naiel Nassar taught at the University of Texas Southwestern Medical Center (University). He alleged that Dr. Beth Levine, who was one of his supervisors, was biased against him because he was Muslim and of Middle Eastern heritage. Among other claims, she allegedly said, "Middle Easterners are lazy." When Nassar left his job at the University, he sent a letter to Levine's boss, Dr. Gregory Fitz, and others, blaming her harassment for his departure. Because Fitz was worried that these letters harmed Levine's reputation, he persuaded a hospital to withdraw its job offer to Nassar. Fitz defended his actions by claiming that the University and the hospital had an exclusivity agreement, under which the hospital could only hire University faculty as staff physicians. The Supreme Court ruled that, to prevail in his lawsuit, Nassar would have to show that Fitz would not have interfered *but for* his discriminatory intent.[15] This standard is a high one to meet. Even if Fitz did retaliate, Nassar would still lose so long as Fitz could show that he had other nondiscriminatory reasons, such as the exclusivity agreement.

Title VII prohibits disparate treatment, disparate impact, hostile environment, and retaliation when used against any of the categories protected by Title VII—race, color, religion, sex, and national origin. Now we look at particular rules that apply to only some of these categories.

30-2b Religion

Religion is a particularly important employment issue as more than two-thirds of the people in this country consider themselves to be at least "moderately" religious. **Employers cannot discriminate against a worker because of his religious beliefs. In addition, employers must make reasonable accommodation for a worker's religious practices unless the request would cause undue hardship for the business.** A common issue involves employees who cannot work on their Sabbath. This refusal might be an "undue hardship" if there are no other employees who could perform that work on those days. What would you do in the following cases if you were the boss?

---

[14]Burlington Industries, Inc. v. Ellerth, 524 U.S. 742 (S. Ct. 1998); Faragher v. Boca Raton, 524 U.S. 775 (S. Ct. 1998). Although these cases involve sexual harassment, the EEOC has ruled that the same principles apply to other forms of illegal harassment.

[15]Univ. of Tex. Southwestern Med. Ctr. v. Nassar, 133 S. Ct. 2517 (S. Ct. 2013).

1. A Christian says he cannot work at Walmart on Sundays—his Sabbath. It also happens to be one of the store's busiest days.
2. A Jewish police officer wants to wear a beard and yarmulke as part of his religious observance. The police department bans all facial hair and any indoor headgear.
3. Muslim workers at a meat-packing plant want to pray at sundown, but specific break times were specified in the labor contract and sundown changes from day to day. The workers begin to take bathroom breaks at sundown, stopping work on the production line.
4. A Jehovah's Witness needs to miss one of his scheduled shifts at UPS so that he can attend the Memorial, one of that religion's most important events.

Disputes such as these are on the rise and are not easy to handle fairly. In the end, Walmart fired the Christian, but when he sued on the grounds of religious discrimination, the company settled the case. A judge ruled that the police officer could keep his beard because the force allowed other employees with medical conditions to wear facial hair, but the head covering had to go. The boss at the meat-packing plant fired the Muslim employees who left their posts to pray. UPS paid $70,000 to settle the Jehovah's Witness suit.

30-2c Sex

What does discrimination on the basis of sex mean? In a landmark case that defined this provision of Title VII, the Supreme Court ruled that **"gender must be irrelevant to employment decisions."**[16] In this case, the accounting firm Price Waterhouse had refused to promote Ann Hopkins to partner. Of the 88 people who came up for partner that year, she was the only woman. She was not only a high performer, she was also the most successful in bringing in business. The problem? She was "sometimes overly aggressive, unduly harsh, difficult to work with, and impatient with staff." Partners commented that she was macho, overcompensated for being a woman, and needed to take a course at charm school. They were opposed to her use of profanity because it was a "lady using foul language." A partner explicitly told her that she should "walk more femininely, talk more femininely, dress more femininely, wear makeup, have her hair styled, and wear jewelry."

Cynthia Johnsor/The LIFE Images Collection/Getty Images

Price Waterhouse decided that Ann Hopkins was not feminine enough to be a partner. But the Supreme Court disagreed.

In ruling in her favor, the Supreme Court held that **Title VII forbids sexual stereotyping**. The opinion said, "An employer who objects to aggressiveness in women but whose positions require this trait places women in an intolerable and impermissible catch-22: out of a job if they behave aggressively and out of a job if they do not. Title VII lifts women out of this bind."

30-2d Attractiveness

Attractive men and women have advantages in life: Voters, jurors, teachers, college admissions staffs, and bosses treat them better. Studies have shown that investors are willing to pay more for the stock of companies with attractive CEOs.[17]

---

[16] Price Waterhouse v. Hopkins, 490 U.S. 228 (S. Ct. 1989).

[17] Halford, Joseph Taylor and Hsu, Scott H. C., Beauty Is Wealth: CEO Appearance and Shareholder Value (November 20, 2013). Available at SSRN: http://ssrn.com/abstract=2357756.

Peter Kramer/NBC/NBC NewsWire/Getty Images

When she was CEO of Yahoo, Marissa Mayer was ranked among the top 5 percent of executives for attractiveness. Did her looks increase the value of Yahoo stock?

Is it legal for employers to discriminate on the basis of attractiveness, to hire the best looking? In 1966, Eastern Airlines placed the following ad for flight attendants in *The New York Times*:

> A high school graduate, single (widows and divorcees with no children considered), 20 years of age (girls 19½ may apply for future consideration). 5'2" but no more than 5'9," weight 105 to 135 in proportion to height and have at least 20/40 vision without glasses.

Airlines hoped that young, attractive, thin, single, female flight attendants would be a lure for the mostly male passengers.

Unattractiveness is not a protected category under Title VII, so any discrimination claim would have to fit into one of the existing categories. (However, several jurisdictions—Washington, D.C., and San Francisco, for example—do have regulations prohibiting attractiveness discrimination.) Ultimately, flight attendants (with the help of the EEOC) were able to make the case that most of these requirements were sex discrimination, largely because they did not also apply to men. Imagine an airline refusing to hire married pilots. Although airlines still set weight limits, now they are related to safety—helping passengers evacuate planes—not attractiveness. In a more recent case, Abercrombie & Fitch paid $50 million to settle a case alleging that it only hired young, white, physically fit salespeople because that was part of the Abercrombie "look."

What about the opposite problem—when an employee is *too* attractive? Melissa Nelson worked as a dental assistant for James Knight. When his wife found out that he was attracted to Nelson, she insisted that he fire her, which he did. The Iowa Supreme Court ruled that her termination did not constitute sex discrimination, partly because she was replaced by another (presumably unattractive) woman.[18]

In the following case, a casino fired a female bartender for refusing to wear makeup. Did the casino violate Title VII? You be the judge.

You Be the Judge

Jespersen v. Harrah's

444 F.3d 1104

United States Court of Appeals for the Ninth Circuit, 2006

Facts: Darlene Jespersen was a bartender at the sports bar in Harrah's Casino in Reno, Nevada. She was an outstanding employee, frequently praised by both her supervisors and customers.

After Jespersen had been at Harrah's for almost 20 years, the casino implemented a program that required bartenders to be "well groomed, appealing to the eye." Men had to have short hair and could not wear nail polish or makeup. Women had to have their hair "teased, curled, or styled and were also required to wear makeup, which included: foundation/concealer and/or face powder, as well as blush, mascara, and lip color. An expert was brought in to show the employees (both male and female) how to dress. The workers were then photographed and told that they must look like the photographs every day at work.

[18] Nelson v. James H. Knight DDS, P.C., 834 N.W.2d 64 (Iowa 2013).

Jespersen tried wearing makeup for a short period of time but then refused to do so. She did not like the feel of it and also believed that this new appearance interfered with her ability to deal with unruly, intoxicated guests because it "took away [her] credibility as an individual and as a person."

After Harrah's fired Jespersen, she sued under Title VII. The district court granted Harrah's motion for summary judgment. Jespersen appealed.

You Be the Judge: *Did Harrah's requirement that women wear makeup violate Title VII?*

Argument for Jespersen: Jespersen refused to wear makeup to work because the cost—in time, money, and personal dignity—was too high.

Employers are free to adopt different appearance standards for each sex, but these standards may not impose a greater burden on one sex than the other. Men were not required to wear makeup, but women were. That difference meant a savings for men of hundreds of dollars and hours of time.[19] Harrah's did not have the right to fire Jespersen for violating a rule that applies only to women, with no equivalent for men.

Argument for Harrah's: Employers are permitted to impose different appearance rules on women than on men as long as the overall burden on employees is the same. For example, it is not discriminatory to require men to wear their hair short. On balance, Harrah's rules did not impose a heavier burden on women than on men.

30-2e Family Responsibility Discrimination

Suppose that you are in charge of hiring at your company. You receive applications from four people: a mother, a father, a childless woman, and a childless man. All have equivalent qualifications. Which one would you hire? In studies, participants repeatedly rank mothers as less qualified than other employees and fathers as most desirable, even when their credentials are exactly the same. Partly as a result, unmarried childless women earn 96 percent of what men do while married mothers earn 76 percent.

Family responsibility discrimination is a violation of Title VII if it involves men and women being treated differently—say, mothers being offered less appealing assignments than fathers or fathers being denied benefits that are available to mothers. After Dawn Gallina, an associate at a big law firm, revealed to her boss that she had a young child, he began to treat her differently from her male colleagues and spoke to her "about the commitment differential between men and women." A court ruled that her belief of illegal discrimination was reasonable.[20]

The EEOC has issued guidelines indicating that stereotypes are not a legitimate basis for personnel decisions and may violate Title VII. In addition, some state and local laws prohibit either parenthood discrimination or family responsibility discrimination.

30-2f Sexual Orientation

As a manager at Scott Medical Health Center, Robert McClendon frequently called one of his gay reports derogatory and offensive names, including "fag" and "queer." McClendon also asked intrusive and insulting questions about his employee's sex activity.

The specific language of Title VII does not include sexual orientation as a protected category, but some courts now interpret the statute to include it as one. In the Scott Medical case, the court stated:

> That someone can be subjected to a barrage of insults, humiliation, hostility and/or changes to the terms and conditions of their employment, based upon nothing

---

[19]See for example, Michael Kinsley, "Making Up Is Hard to Do," *The Washington Post*, March 26, 2008.
[20]Gallina v. Mintz, Levin, 123 Fed. Appx. 558 (4th Cir. 2005).

more than the aggressor's view of what it means to be a man or a woman, is exactly the evil Title VII was designed to eradicate.[21]

In addition, by executive order the federal government prohibits discrimination on the basis of sexual orientation among its own employees and also among government contractors. Also, almost half the states and hundreds of cities have statutes that prohibit discrimination based on sexual orientation.

The Supreme Court has ruled that it is unconstitutional to withhold federal benefits from same-sex married couples.[22]

30-2g Gender Identity and Expression

David Schroer was in the Army for 25 years, including a stint tracking terrorists. The Library of Congress offered him a job as a specialist in terrorism. However, when he revealed that he was in the process of becoming *Diane* Schroer, the Library of Congress withdrew the offer. As you can guess, he sued under Title VII.

Traditionally, courts took the view that sex under Title VII applied only to how people were born, not what they "chose" to become. Courts assumed that gender non-conformity was a personal choice, rather than a characteristic. Employers could and did fire workers for changing gender. About half of transgender people reported in a survey that they had experienced an adverse employment action because of gender non-conformity.[23] However, a federal court found the Library of Congress in violation of Title VII for withdrawing Schroer's offer.[24] And some other courts have reached a similar result, In addition, **the EEOC ruled that discriminating against someone for being transgender is a violation of Title VII** and about one-third of the states and hundreds of cities prohibit gender identity and expression discrimination. Also, the federal government prohibits discrimination on gender identity among its employees and among government contractors.

30-2h Background and Credit Checks

When a new contractor took over a BMW plant, it required existing employees to undergo criminal background checks. As a result of these checks, it fired 88 workers, some of whom had been at the plant for more than ten years. Although only 55 percent of the plant's employees were black, 80 percent of the terminated workers were. The EEOC accused BMW of violating Title VII because its policy had a disparate impact on black employees.

Nearly one-third of working-age adults in America have a criminal record. About the same percentage of the population has a degree from a four-year college. **EEOC regulations prohibit companies from using criminal history information in a way that has an adverse impact on employees in a protected category if the background information is irrelevant in**

21United States EEOC v. Scott Med. Health Ctr., P.C., 2016 U.S. Dist. LEXIS 153744 (W.D. Pa. 2016). One federal appeals court recently ruled that discrimination on the basis of sexual orientation is a violation of Title VII while another ruled that it is not. (Hively v. Ivy Tech Cmty. College of Ind., 853 F.3d 339, 341 [7th Cir. 2017] and Evans v. Ga. Reg'l Hosp., 850 F.3d 1248 [11th Cir. 2017]).

22United States v. Windsor, 133 S. Ct. 2675 (S. Ct. 2013).

23Jaime M. Grant, Lisa A. Mottet, Justin Tanis, Jack Harrison, Jody L. Herman, and Mara Keisling, Nat'l Ctr. for Transgender Equal. and Nat'l Gay and Lesbian Task Force, Injustice at Every Turn: A Report of the National Transgender Discrimination Survey 2 (2011) reported in Jason Lee, "Symposium: Lost in Transition: The Challenges of Remedying Transgender Employment Discrimination under Title VII," 35 Harv. J. L. & Gender 423.

24Schroer v. Billington, 577 F. Supp. 2d 293 (U.S. Dt. Ct. 2008).

determining whether the employee is appropriate for the job. In the BMW case, the EEOC argued that old data should not be used to terminate long-term workers with an unblemished employment record.

Job applications often include a box that applicants must check if they have a criminal record. However, this practice is changing. At least 24 states and more than 150 localities have passed so-called "ban the box" legislation, which prohibits employers from asking about the applicant's criminal record until after an interview is conducted or an offer is made.

Employers may not consider arrest records because that is not evidence of wrongdoing. **The EEOC also discourages the use of credit checks because minorities tend to have worse credit ratings than whites.**

30-2i Immigration

Under Title VII, it is illegal for employers to discriminate against noncitizens because "national origin" is a protected category. Therefore, employers should not ask about a job applicant's country of origin, but they are permitted to inquire if the person is authorized to work in the United States. If the applicant says, "Yes," the interviewer cannot ask for evidence until the person is hired. At that point, the employer must complete an I-9 form—Employment Eligibility Verification—within three days. This form lists the acceptable documents that can be used for verification. Employees have the right to present whichever documents they want from the list of acceptable items. The employer may not ask for some other document. The I-9 form must be kept for three years after the worker is hired or one year after termination.

30-2j Reverse Discrimination

George Dulin was a white man who had worked as a lawyer at Greenwood Leflore Hospital for 24 years. The local newspaper reported that, during a meeting with members of a local voters' league, the hospital board was urged to replace Dulin with someone black. What could possibly go wrong with (publicly) firing a white male *lawyer* and replacing him with a black woman? A jury held that the board had illegally discriminated against Dulin and ordered it to pay damages.[25]

Reverse discrimination means making an employment decision that harms a non-Hispanic white person or a man because of his gender, color, or race. As a general rule, it is just as illegal as discriminating against a minority or a woman.

Reverse discrimination
Making an employment decision that harms a white person or a man because of his gender, color, or race

However, there is one exception to this rule: **affirmative action**. The goal of these programs is to remedy the effects of past discrimination. An employer who has refused to hire people of color in the past might be required to hire a certain percentage for a limited period in the future. How people feel about affirmative action tends to be a function of how they define the term. Most people are opposed to quotas, but at the same time, they support outreach and recruitment efforts aimed at women and disadvantaged minorities.

Affirmative action programs
These programs remedy the effects of past discrimination.

Affirmative action is not required by Title VII, nor is it prohibited. Affirmative action programs have three different sources.

Litigation. Courts have the power under Title VII to order affirmative action to remedy the effects of past discrimination.

---

[25]Dulin v. Bd. of Comm'rs of the Greenwood Leflore Hosp., 586 Fed. Appx. 643 (5th Cir. 2014). This case was brought under the Civil Rights Act of 1866 which, you remember, prohibits racial discrimination. The court applied Title VII standards in this case.

Voluntary Action. Employers can *voluntarily* introduce an affirmative action plan to remedy the effects of past practices or to achieve (but not to maintain) equitable representation of minorities and women, provided that the plan is not too unfair to majority members.[26] For example, in the university and community college system in Nevada, only 1 percent of the faculty were black (and roughly 25 percent were female). In response, the university instituted a policy that permitted any department that hired a minority candidate to also hire an additional candidate of any race. Although Yvette Farmer was one of three finalists for a job in the sociology department, it hired a black African male without even granting her an interview. The Court ruled that the university's affirmative action plan was legal.[27]

Government Contracts. The government may use affirmative action programs when awarding contracts only if (1) it can show that the programs are needed to overcome specific past discrimination, (2) they have time limits, and (3) nondiscriminatory alternatives are not available.

30-2k Defenses to Charges of Discrimination

Under Title VII, the defendant has four possible defenses.

Merit

A defendant is not liable if he shows that the person he favored was the most qualified. Test results, education, or productivity can all be used to demonstrate merit, provided they relate to the job in question. Harry can show that he hired Bruce for a coaching job instead of Louisa because Bruce has a master's degree in physical education and seven years of coaching experience. On the other hand, the fact that Bruce scored higher on the National Latin Exam in the eighth grade is not a legitimate reason to hire him over Louisa.

Seniority

Many companies use seniority as an important factor in determining everything from compensation to layoffs. While such systems offer many advantages—they encourage a commitment to the company, an incentive to learn job-specific skills, and a willingness to train other workers without fear of losing one's job—they also tend to perpetrate prior discriminatory practices. If historic trends result in black employees having less seniority, they will also be paid less and laid off more. However, a seniority system is legal under Title VII unless it was designed with the *intention* to discriminate. **A legitimate seniority system is legal even if it perpetuates past discrimination.**

Bona Fide Occupational Qualification (BFOQ)

Bona fide occupational qualification (BFOQ)
An employer is permitted to establish discriminatory job requirements if they are *essential* to the position in question.

An employer is permitted to establish discriminatory job requirements if they are *essential* to the position in question. The business must show that it cannot fulfill its primary function unless it discriminates. Such a requirement is called a **bona fide occupational qualification (BFOQ)**. (Note that only religion, sex, or national origin can be a BFOQ—never race or color.)

Catholic schools may, if they choose, refuse to hire non-Catholic teachers; clothing companies may refuse to hire men to model women's attire. Generally, however, courts are not sympathetic to claims of BFOQ. They have almost always rejected BFOQ claims that are based on customer preference. For example, an employer violated the law when it refused to appoint a woman to a position as vice president of international operations because of its fear that men in other countries might not want to work with her.[28]

---

26 United Steelworkers of America v. Weber, 443 U.S. 193 (S. Ct. 1979).
27 University and Community College System of Nevada v. Farmer, 113 Nev. 90 (S. Ct. Nev. 1997).
28 Fernandez v. Wynn Oil Co., 653 F.2d 1273 (9th Cir. 1981).

However, the courts recognize three situations in which employers may consider customer preference:

- **Safety.** The Supreme Court ruled that a maximum security men's prison could refuse to hire women correctional officers. If a woman wanted to risk her life, that was her choice, but the court feared that an attack on her would threaten the safety of both male guards and inmates.[29]
- **Privacy.** An employer may refuse to hire women to work in a men's bathroom, and vice versa.
- **Authenticity.** An employer may refuse to hire a man for a woman's role in a movie. In addition, a court ruled that Disney could fire an Asian man from the Norwegian exhibit at its Epcot international theme park, not because he was Asian, but because he was not culturally authentic. He did not have firsthand knowledge of Norwegian culture and did not speak Norwegian.[30]

30-3 PREGNANCY DISCRIMINATION ACT

When Peggy Young became pregnant, she was working as a driver for UPS. Her doctor advised her not to lift more than 20 pounds but the company required its drivers to be able to lift up to 70 pounds. Although UPS had made accommodations for other employees, including drivers who had lost their license because of motor vehicle accidents, it would not do so for her. When she sued, the Supreme Court held that she had the right to be treated the same as people who had a similar inability to work.[31]

Under the Pregnancy Discrimination Act, an employer may not fire, refuse to hire, or fail to promote a woman because she is pregnant. An employer also violates this statute if the work environment is so hostile toward a pregnant woman that it affects her ability to do her job. And an employer must treat pregnancy and childbirth as any other temporary disability. If, for example, employees are allowed time off from work for other medical disabilities, women must also be allowed a maternity leave.

The Pregnancy Discrimination Act also protects a woman's right to terminate a pregnancy. An employer cannot fire a woman for having an abortion.[32]

30-4 AGE DISCRIMINATION IN EMPLOYMENT ACT

Under the Age Discrimination in Employment Act (ADEA), an employer with 20 or more workers may not fire, refuse to hire, fail to promote, or otherwise reduce a person's employment opportunities because he is 40 or older. Nor may an employer require workers to retire at a certain age. (This retirement rule does not apply in some jobs, such as police officer, airline

[29]Dothard v. Rawlinson, 433 U.S. 321 (S. Ct. 1977).
[30]Gupta v. Walt Disney World Co, 256 Fed. Appx. 279 (11th Cir. 2007).
[31]Young v. UPS, 135 S. Ct. 1338 (S. Ct. 2015).
[32]Doe v. C.A.R.S Protection Plus, Inc., 527 F.3d 358 (3rd Cir. 2008).

pilot, and top-level corporate executive.) The goal of the statute is to counteract stereotypes about the abilities of older workers. A plaintiff in an age discrimination case can show discrimination in three ways: disparate treatment, disparate impact, and hostile work environment.

30-4a Disparate Treatment

In a disparate treatment claim, the plaintiff must show that the employer intentionally discriminated against him because of his age, or enacted a policy that intentionally treated employees differently because of their age. Proof of intent involves obvious statements and behavior or more subtle circumstantial evidence.

Under the ADEA, a disparate treatment case requires three steps:

1. The plaintiff must show that:
   - He is 40 or older,
   - He suffered an adverse employment action,
   - He was qualified for the job for which he was fired or not hired, and
   - He was replaced by a younger person.
2. The employer must present evidence that its decision was based on legitimate, nondiscriminatory reasons.
3. The plaintiff must show that:
   - The employer's reasons are a pretext;
   - In fact, the employer intentionally discriminated; and
   - But for the plaintiff's age, the employer would not have taken the action it did.

Note that the standard of proof is tougher in an age discrimination case than in Title VII litigation because, under the ADEA, the plaintiff must show that age was not just one factor, it was the deciding factor. When Jack Gross was 54 years old, his employer transferred most of his responsibilities to a younger woman and demoted him. Age may well have been one factor in his employer's decision, but there were other reasons as well. The Supreme Court ruled for the employer, on the grounds that Gross had not shown that age was the deciding reason.[33] This case made the road much steeper for ADEA plaintiffs.

In passing the ADEA, Congress was particularly concerned about employers who relied on unfavorable stereotypes rather than job performance. The following case provides further support for the adage: "Loose lips sink ships."

Reid v. Google, Inc.

50 Cal. 4th 512
Supreme Court of California, 2010

Facts: Google's vice-president of engineering, Wayne Rosing (aged 55), hired Brian Reid (52) as director of operations and director of engineering. Reid had a Ph.D. in computer science and had been a professor of electrical engineering at Stanford University. At the time, the top executives at Google were CEO Eric Schmidt (47), Vice-President of Engineering Operations Urs Hölzle (38), and founders Sergey Brin (28), and Larry Page (29).

During his two years at Google, Reid's only written performance review stated that he had consistently met expectations. The comments indicated that Reid was very intelligent and creative and was a terrific problem solver

33 Gross v. FBL Fin. Servs., 557 U.S. 167 (S. Ct. 2009).

with an excellent aptitude and attitude. He also dealt confidently with fast-changing situations. However, the review also commented that "Adapting to Google culture is the primary task. Right or wrong, Google is simply different: younger contributors, inexperienced first-line managers, and the super-fast pace are just a few examples of the environment."

According to Reid, even as he received a positive review, Hölzle and other employees made derogatory age-related remarks such as his ideas were "obsolete," "ancient," and "too old to matter," that he was "slow," "fuzzy," "sluggish," and "lethargic," an "old man," an "old guy," and an "old fuddy-duddy," and that he did not "display a sense of urgency" and "lacked energy."

Nineteen months after Reid joined Google, he was fired. Google says it was because of his poor performance. Reid alleges he was told it was based on a lack of "cultural fit."

Reid sued Google for age discrimination. The trial court granted Google's motion for summary judgment on the grounds that Reid did not have enough evidence of discrimination. The Court of Appeal overruled the trial court. The Supreme Court of California agreed to hear the case.

Issue: ***Did Reid have enough evidence of age discrimination to warrant a trial?***

Excerpts from Justice Chin's Decision: Google contends that the Court of Appeal should have applied the stray remarks doctrine, i.e., should have categorized the alleged statements by Hölzle and Rosing as irrelevant stray remarks and disregarded them in reviewing the merits of the summary judgment motion. [S]trict application of the stray remarks doctrine, as urged by Google, would result in a court's categorical exclusion of evidence even if the evidence was relevant. An age-based remark not made directly in the context of an employment decision or uttered by a non-decision-maker may be relevant, circumstantial evidence of discrimination. [T]he United States Supreme Court indicates that even if age-related comments can be considered stray remarks because they were not made in the direct context of the decisional process, a court should not categorically discount the evidence if relevant; it should be left to the factfinder to assess its probative value.

[T]he stray remarks cases merely demonstrate the common-sense proposition that a slur, in and of itself, does not prove actionable discrimination. A stray remark alone may not create a triable issue of age discrimination. But when combined with other evidence, an otherwise stray remark may create an ensemble [that] is sufficient to defeat summary judgment.

For the reasons stated above, we affirm the judgment of the Court of Appeal.

30-4b Disparate Impact

Disparate impact claims arise when an employer's actions do not explicitly discriminate, but nonetheless have an adverse impact on people aged 40 or over. Here, too, the standards are different under the ADEA than under Title VII. **Under the ADEA a disparate impact case requires only two steps:**

1. The plaintiffs must present a *prima facie* case that the employment practice in question excludes a disproportionate number of people 40 and older.
2. The employer wins if it can show that the discriminatory decision was based on a *reasonable factor other than age*.

One reasonable factor other than age is cost. Sometimes companies fire older workers because they are paid more, receive higher pension benefits, or generally cost more (e.g., higher healthcare expenses). Courts have supported these decisions, holding that an employer is entitled to prefer *lower-paid* workers even if that preference results in the company also choosing *younger* workers. As the court put it in one case, "An action based on price differentials represents the very quintessence of a legitimate business decision."[34] Thus, Circuit City Stores fired 8 percent of its employees because they could be replaced with people who would work for less. The fired workers were more experienced—and older. This action was legal under the ADEA.

[34] Marks v. Loral Corp., 57 Cal. App. 4th 30 (Cal. Ct. App. 1997).

30-4c Hostile Work Environment

Diane Kassner (age 79) and Marsha Reiffe (61) worked for 2nd Avenue Delicatessen. They filed suit under the ADEA, alleging that their boss and coworkers made comments to them about their age, such as "Drop dead," "Retire early," "Take off all of that makeup," and "Take off your wig." In addition, their boss pressured the two women to retire and pointed to the front of the restaurant and said, "There's the door." But the two women were never fired.

The court ruled that the ADEA prohibits a hostile work environment based on age. A workplace is considered hostile if a reasonable person would find that intimidation, ridicule, and insult based on age are pervasive.[35] In short, this case, combined with the *Google* case, indicate that it is wise to avoid any comments about an employee's age.

30-4d Bona Fide Occupational Qualification

As is the case under Title VII, age is rarely a BFOQ. **To set a maximum age, the employer must show that**:

- The age limit is reasonably necessary to the essence of the business and either
- Virtually everyone that age is unqualified for the job or
- Age is the only way an employer can determine who is qualified.

Although some courts have held that age can be a BFOQ in cases where public safety is at issue, such as for pilots and bus drivers, the EEOC is not always in agreement. In short, the BFOQ defense is very limited in ADEA cases.

EXAMStrategy

Question: Solapere ran a job ad on Monster.com, which said that the company would only consider hiring people who either had a job or had been unemployed for less than six months. The average length of unemployment in the United States at that time was nine months, which meant that such a policy eliminated millions of job applicants. Did this ad violate federal law?

Strategy: Solapere was not intentionally discriminating against anyone, thus no disparate treatment claim. What about a disparate impact claim? Did this policy exclude too many people in a protected category? The unemployed are not a protected category under Title VII, but this policy might have had an impact on groups that are protected.

Result: Older people and members of some minority groups have higher unemployment rates than other workers. Therefore, this practice could violate both Title VII and the ADEA unless Solapere could show that it was a job-related business necessity. Could it be a job-related business necessity?

35Kassner v. 2nd Ave. Delicatessen, Inc., 496 F.3d 229 (2nd Cir. 2007).

30-5 DISCRIMINATION ON THE BASIS OF DISABILITY

30-5a The Rehabilitation Act of 1973

The Rehabilitation Act of 1973 prohibits discrimination on the basis of disability by the executive branch of the federal government, federal contractors, and entities that receive federal funds. It also requires these organizations to develop affirmative action plans for the hiring, placement, and promotion of the disabled. The same legal standards apply to both this statute and the Americans with Disabilities Act, discussed next. Cases interpreting one statute also apply to the other.

30-5b Americans with Disabilities Act

The Americans with Disabilities Act (ADA) prohibits employers with 15 or more workers from discriminating on the basis of disability.

Disability

A disabled person is someone with a physical or mental impairment that substantially limits a major life activity or the operation of a major bodily function or someone who is regarded as having such an impairment. Major life activities include the following tasks: caring for oneself, performing manual tasks, seeing, hearing, eating, sleeping, walking, standing, lifting, bending, speaking, breathing, learning, reading, concentrating, thinking, communicating, and working. Major bodily functions include functions of the immune system, normal cell growth, and digestive, bowel, bladder, neurological, brain, respiratory, circulatory, endocrine, and reproductive functions. The ADA applies to *recovered* drug addicts but not to the *current* use of drugs, sexual disorders, pyromania, exhibitionism, or compulsive gambling. Although the ADA protects alcoholics who can meet the definition of disabled, employers can nonetheless fire alcoholics if their drinking adversely affects job performance.

Suppose an employee has a disabling illness, but one that can be successfully treated. The employee is still considered to be disabled, even if the illness is well controlled. Thus, someone with diabetes is disabled, even if the illness is managed so well that it does not interfere with major life activities.

Accommodating the Disabled Worker

Once it is established that a worker is disabled, employers may not discriminate on the basis of disability as long as the worker can, with *reasonable accommodation*, perform the *essential functions* of the job. An accommodation is unreasonable if it would create *undue hardship* for the employer. Let's look at those terms more closely.

Reasonable Accommodation. To meet this standard, employers are expected to:

- Make facilities accessible,
- Permit part-time schedules,
- Acquire or modify equipment, and
- Assign a disabled person to an open position that he can perform. (Note that the employer is not required to create a new job or find a perfect position, just a reasonable one.)

Willoughby v. Conn. Container Corp.

2013 U.S. Dist. LEXIS 168457; 2013 WL 6198210
United States District Court for the District of Connecticut, 2013

Facts: Anthony Willoughby worked for Connecticut Container Corp. (CCC). When Willoughby was diagnosed with diabetes, he submitted a doctor's form to CCC's Human Resources department. Despite treatment, Willoughby experienced side effects that included swelling, dizziness, blurred vision, and frequent bathroom use. Heat caused the symptoms to worsen.

For two weeks, Willoughby was assigned to particularly strenuous activity in the heat. One night, his ankles swelled and his vision deteriorated. When he told his supervisor, Darlene Bailey, she said "do the work or go home." Willoughby also informed the shift supervisor, who ignored him.

Later that night, after Willoughby did not respond to pages, Bailey found him in a chair. Willoughby says he had passed out; Bailey states that he was sleeping. He presented HR with a note from a physician verifying that he had passed out due to low blood sugar. Willoughby was fired for sleeping on the job.

Willoughby filed suit, alleging that CCC had violated the ADA because it had failed to provide reasonable accommodation for his disability. CCC filed a motion for summary judgment.

Issues: ***Was Willoughby disabled? If so, did CCC provide reasonable accommodation?***

Excerpts from Judge Haight's Decision[36]: The Court finds that Willoughby could easily be found by a jury to be an individual who has a physical impairment that substantially limits one or more major life activities of such individual and, accordingly, has a disability under the ADA. As EEOC regulations themselves note, diabetes substantially limits endocrine function, and therefore it should easily be concluded that diabetes will, at a minimum, substantially limit what amounts to a major life activity.

CCC avers that Willoughby's claim under the ADA that CCC failed to provide [him] with an accommodation is baseless in view of the fact that Willoughby himself testified he never asked for an accommodation. [W]hile generally, it is the responsibility of the individual with a disability to inform the employer that an accommodation is needed, it is, in fact, an employer's duty reasonably to accommodate an employee's disability if the disability is obvious—which is to say, if the employer knew or reasonably should have known that the employee was disabled. [T]he ADA contemplates that employers will engage in 'an interactive process' with their employees and in that way work together to assess whether an employee's disability can be reasonably accommodated.

Given that CCC did in fact have notice of Willoughby's disability, and given that CCC did not, prior to Willoughby's termination, engage with Willoughby in any sort of interactive process by which the parties worked together to assess whether Willoughby's disability could be reasonably accommodated, the Court finds that a jury could permissibly find that Willoughby is able to meet this claim that CCC failed to provide reasonable accommodation under the ADA.

Essential Functions of the Job. A juvenile corrections officer was hit by a baseball that fractured her wrist. Nine months after returning to her job, she was assigned to the night shift, where the only other officer was a newcomer. Concerned that her wrist was not strong enough for her to restrain some of the inmates on her own, she asked to be paired with an experienced officer. Her employer fired her on the grounds that she could not perform the essential functions of the job. But the court ruled that, since she had been working successfully as an officer during the day, clearly she could perform the essential functions.[37]

Undue Hardship. What constitutes undue hardship is the subject of much litigation. Many courts hold that employers may use cost–benefit analysis—they are not required to make an expensive accommodation that provides little benefit. Nor are they required to provide identical working conditions for all employees. A woman who was wheelchair-bound asked that

36For ease of reading, we have substituted the parties' names for Plaintiff and Defendant.

37Leuzinger v. County of Lake, 2007 U.S. Dist. LEXIS 35955 (N.D. CA 2007).

her employer lower the sink in the kitchenettes that were being built in her building. Otherwise, she would have to use the bathroom sink which, she felt, segregated and stigmatized her. The cost to lower the kitchen sinks ranged from as much as $2,000 (to do all the sinks in the building) to as little as $150 (for just the sink on her floor). The court ruled that the employer had no obligation to provide identical conditions and that it had already made a reasonable accommodation by lowering the sink in the bathroom. Although the employer could, in theory, afford this request, it did not have an obligation to spend so much money for so little benefit.[38]

Medical Exams

Employers interact with workers at three key stages: applying, entering (after hiring but before the job starts), and working. The ADA sets different standards for medical exams at these three stages:

- **Applicants.** An employer generally may not require a medical exam or ask about disabilities, except that the interviewer may ask:
    - Whether an applicant can perform the work (provided that the same question is asked of all applicants),
    - For the applicant to demonstrate how he would perform the job, and
    - (In the event that a disability is obvious) what accommodation the applicant would need.
- **Entering employees.** The company may require a medical test and make it a condition of employment, but the test must be:
    - Required of all employees in similar jobs, whether or not they are disabled, and
    - Treated as a confidential medical record (except for managers who need to know).
- **Existing employees.** An employer may require medical exams or discuss any suspected disability, but only to determine if a worker is still able to perform the existing functions of her job.

Relationship with a Disabled Person

An employer may not discriminate against someone because of his *relationship* with a disabled person.

Obesity

According to the EEOC, just being overweight is not a disability unless it has some underlying physiological cause, such as a thyroid disorder. **However, being morbidly obese (defined as having double the normal body weight) is a disability, no matter what the cause.**

Lisa Harrison weighed 527 pounds when Family House fired her. The normal weight for someone her height—5 feet, 2 inches tall—was between 102 and 130 pounds. The EEOC filed suit, claiming that Family House had fired her for a perceived disability and had failed to make reasonable accommodation. Family House filed a motion for summary judgment alleging that it had fired Harrison because her obesity impaired her job performance. In denying this motion, the court ruled that her severe obesity was a disability under the ADA.[39]

---

[38]Vande Zande v. Wisconsin Department of Administration, 44 F.3d 538 (7th Cir. 1995).

[39]EEOC v. Res. for Human Dev., Inc., 827 F. Supp. 2nd 688 (E.D. La. 2011).

Mental Disabilities

Under EEOC rules, physical and mental disabilities are to be treated the same. Physical ailments such as diabetes and deafness may sometimes be easier to diagnose, but psychological disabilities are also covered by the ADA. Among other accommodations, the EEOC rules indicate that employers should be willing to put up barriers to isolate people who have difficulty concentrating, offer flexible hours to allow for therapy, or provide detailed day-to-day feedback to those who need greater structure in performing their jobs.

Disparate Treatment and Disparate Impact

Both disparate treatment and disparate impact claims are valid under the ADA. The steps in a disparate *treatment* case are:

1. The plaintiff must offer *prima facie* evidence that the employer discriminated because of his disability.
2. The employer must then offer a legitimate, nondiscriminatory reason for its action.
3. To win, the plaintiff must now prove that the employer intentionally discriminated. She may do so either by showing that (1) the reasons offered were simply a *pretext* or (2) that a discriminatory intent is more likely than not.

To win a disparate *impact* case, the plaintiff must show that a policy that *looks* neutral falls more harshly on a protected group and cannot be justified by business necessity.

The following Exam Strategy illustrates how disparate treatment and disparate impact are applied in an ADA case and also demonstrates the importance of choosing the correct theory.

EXAMStrategy

Question: Hughes Missile Systems fired Joel Hernandez because he tested positive for cocaine, which, not surprisingly, was a violation of workplace rules. He, however, had no hard feelings, and two years later, he reapplied for a job at Hughes. At the time, he provided evidence that he was clean. However, the company rejected his application because it had a policy against hiring anyone who had been fired for cause. Did the company violate the ADA?

Strategy: Under the ADA, it is legal to discriminate against a drug user, but not against a recovered drug addict. To win a disparate *treatment* case, Hernandez had to show that Hughes's excuse for not rehiring him was just a pretext and its decision was really motivated by an intent to discriminate based on his disability. To win a disparate *impact* claim, Hernandez had to show that the no-rehire policy affected disabled people more than others and that it was not justified by business necessity. Could he prove either of these claims?

Result: The Supreme Court ruled that Hernandez could not prove his disparate treatment claim because its no-rehire rule was legitimate and not just a pretext for discrimination. And because Hernandez had not raised the issue of disparate impact in the lower courts, the Supreme Court refused to consider it. So he lost his case.[40]

40Raytheon Co. v. Hernandez, 540 U.S. 44 (S. Ct. 2003).

Hostile Work Environment

An employee is entitled to recovery under the ADA if she is subjected to a hostile work environment because of her disability. Sandra Flowers's boss fired her eight months after finding out that she was HIV-positive. During that eight months, Flowers's entire work environment changed. Before, Flowers and her boss had been friends who went out together for lunch, drinks, and the movies. Afterward, the socializing stopped, the boss began monitoring Flowers's phone calls, and then subjected her to four "random" drug tests in one week. A jury found that Flowers's termination was not based on her disability, but that her boss had nonetheless created a hostile work environment by unreasonably interfering with Flowers's ability to work.[41]

While lauding the ADA's objectives, many managers have been apprehensive about its impact on the workplace. Most acknowledge, however, that society is better off if every member has the opportunity to work. And as advocates for the disabled point out, we are all, at best, only temporarily able-bodied. Even with the ADA, only 35 percent of the disabled population who are of working age are employed, whereas 78 percent of able-bodied people have jobs.

30-6 GENETIC INFORMATION NONDISCRIMINATION ACT

Suppose you want to promote someone to CFO, but you know that her mother and sister both died young of breast cancer. Is it legal to consider that information in making a decision? Not since Congress passed the Genetic Information Nondiscrimination Act (GINA). **Under GINA, employers with 15 or more workers may not require genetic testing, or use information about genetic makeup or family medical history as a factor in hiring, firing, or promoting employees.** Nor may health insurers use such information to decide coverage or premiums. Thus, even an employer Wellness Program cannot *require* participants to answer questions about their family medical history.

Note, however, that insurance companies may seek the results of genetic testing before issuing disability, life, or long-term care policies. Only a few states prohibit the use of such information for these types of policies.

30-7 HIRING PRACTICES

The hiring process is an easy place for employers to go wrong. Here are pitfalls to avoid.

30-7a Interviews

It used to be that interviewers would ask all sorts of inappropriate questions about topics such as marital status and plans to have children. The following list provides guidelines to help interviewers comply with the laws in this chapter.

[41] Flowers v. S. Reg'l Physician Servs, 247 F.3d 229 (5th Cir. 2001).

Don't Even Consider Asking	Go Ahead and Ask (if job related)
How many days were you sick last year?	Have you ever received a performance warning due to your attendance?
What medications are you currently taking?	Are you currently using drugs illegally?
Where were you born? Are you a U.S. citizen?	Are you authorized to work in the United States?
How old are you?	What work experience have you had?
How tall are you? How much do you weigh?	Could you carry a 100-pound weight, as required by this job?
When did you graduate from college?	Where did you go to college?
How did you learn this language?	What languages do you speak and write fluently?
Have you ever been arrested?	Have you ever been convicted of a crime that would affect the performance of this job?
Do you plan to have children? How old are your children? What method of birth control do you use?	Can you work weekends? Travel extensively? Would you be willing to relocate?
Are you a man or a woman? Are you single or married? What does your spouse do? What will happen if your spouse is transferred? What clubs, societies, or lodges do you belong to?	Talk about the job instead!

30-7b Social Media

Almost all employers now rely on social media as a part of their hiring process.[42] They may look at LinkedIn to find potential candidates or check Facebook for evidence of unprofessional behavior. These searches sometimes reveal information that is illegal for employers to act on, such as age, religion, pregnancy, or illness. Yet, sometimes employers do. In one experiment, researchers replied to job postings with identical (fake) résumés that were linked to a Facebook page identifying the applicant's religion as either Christian or Muslim. Christians were more likely to obtain an interview.

Such misuse of social media has consequences. A university decided not to hire an applicant after it learned from his website that, because of his religion, he doubted the theory of evolution. The university argued that these religious views would impede the performance of his job, which required him to raise funds in the science community and work with university scientists.[43] A federal judge denied the university's request for summary judgment, so the university settled the case for $125,000.

To help prevent this type of liability, some employers keep the role of hiring separate from that of "cyber-vetting" and even hire outside consultants to do the checking.

30-8 ENFORCEMENT

30-8a Constitutional Claims

People bringing a claim under the Constitution must file suit on their own.

[42]One study reported that 94% of employers "now use or expect to use social media."
[43]Gaskell v. Univ. of Ky., 2010 U.S. Dist. LEXIS 124572 (E.D. Ky. 2010).

30-8b The Civil Rights Act of 1866

For plaintiffs alleging racial discrimination, the Civil Rights Act of 1866 offers substantial advantages over Title VII:

- A four-year statute of limitations (versus less than a year under Title VII)
- Unlimited compensatory and punitive damages (which, in one case, amounted to $7 million)[44]
- Applicability to all employers, not just those with 15 or more employees

However, this statute is not enforced by the EEOC, which means that the plaintiff is on his own when it comes to negotiating with or filing suit against an employer.

30-8c The Rehabilitation Act of 1973

This statute is enforced by the EEOC (for claims against the executive branch of the federal government), the Department of Labor (for claims against federal contractors), and the Department of Justice (for claims against entities that receive federal funds).

30-8d Other Statutory Claims

The EEOC is the federal agency responsible for enforcing Title VII, the Equal Pay Act, the Pregnancy Discrimination Act, the ADEA, the ADA, and GINA.

Before a plaintiff can bring suit under any of these statutes (except the Equal Pay Act), she must first file a charge with the EEOC. Generally, the plaintiff must file within 180 days of the wrongdoing.[45] But if the plaintiff is alleging that she was paid less than she should have been, each paycheck she receives starts the statute of limitations all over again. After it receives a filing, the EEOC conducts an investigation and also attempts to mediate the dispute. If it determines that discrimination has occurred, it will typically file suit on behalf of the plaintiff. This arrangement is favorable for the plaintiff because the government pays the legal bill. If the EEOC decides *not* to bring the case, or does not make a decision within six months, it issues a right to sue letter, and the plaintiff may proceed on her own in court within 90 days. Under the ADEA, a plaintiff may bring suit 60 days after filing a charge with the EEOC. Many states also have their own version of the EEOC.

Remedies available to the successful plaintiff include hiring, reinstatement, retroactive seniority, back pay, front pay (to compensate for future lost wages), and reasonable attorney's fees. Under Title VII and the ADA, plaintiffs are also entitled to compensatory and punitive damages up to $300,000, but only in certain disparate treatment cases, not disparate impact suits. Compensatory damages include future monetary losses, mental anguish, loss of enjoyment of life, and damage to reputation. Punitive damages are available if the defendant acted with malice or reckless indifference to the plaintiff's rights. Under the ADEA, plaintiffs can recover compensatory damages but are eligible for punitive damages only in the case of "willful" violations; that is, knowing or reckless disregard of the law. In the case of willful violations, the damage award is typically doubled.

Two trends, however, have reduced employees' chances of taking home substantial damages. Concerned about a rise in discrimination lawsuits, employers now often require new hires to agree in advance to arbitrate, not litigate, any future employment claims. The Supreme Court has upheld the enforceability of mandatory arbitration provisions.[46]

---

44 Edwards v. MBTA (June 8, 2001). After the verdict, the case settled.

45 This is the case unless he resides in a state with an appropriate state agency, in which case he has 300 days.

46 Gilmer v. Interstate/Johnson Lane Corp., 500 U.S. 20 (S. Ct. 1991).

Employees sometimes receive worse results in the arbitrator's office than in the courtroom because arbitrators tend to favor repeat customers (such as management) over one-time users (such as employees). In addition, discovery is more limited in arbitration than in court, which means that the plaintiff may not be able to make the strongest case. Also, arbitration awards are usually not disclosed publicly, so employers have less incentive to avoid misbehavior.

But even if a case does go to trial, plaintiffs in job discrimination cases have a much worse track record than other types of plaintiffs—they win less often at trial, and they lose more often on appeal. As a result, the number of discrimination cases in the federal courts has declined.[47]

CHAPTER CONCLUSION

This chapter began with an example from the country's past, when discrimination was legal and many people were foreclosed from the American dream of opportunity and advancement. Anti-discrimination laws have had an enormous impact on the American workplace—half of all workers are now women. In 1960, about 5 percent of doctors and lawyers were women or minorities; now about one-third are. It is a sign of how much the world has changed that, after finishing this chapter, the authors realized that female or minority judges wrote the opinions in four of the five cases. Economists estimate that about a quarter of the enormous increase in this country's GDP over the last 50 years came from admitting women and blacks more fully into the workforce.[48] And research indicates that companies with more women in high positions perform better.[49]

But discrimination has not disappeared. As we saw earlier in the chapter, at least one experiment showed that Muslims are less likely to be hired than Christians. In another study, almost one-third of recruiters reported that they would "react negatively" to "overly religious" posts on social media.[50] After being laid off, older workers take longer to find work and that new job is likely to pay less. Women and minorities remain underrepresented at the top of the employment ladder, as CEOs, partners in law and consulting firms, department heads in hospitals, or chaired professors in universities.

On average, women working full time earn less than their male coworkers, even after accounting for occupation, industry, race, marital status, and job tenure. Although there are undoubtedly many reasons for this inequality, such as women taking time out of work to care for children, gender discrimination also seems to play a role. For example, male CFOs in public companies earn 16 percent ($215,000) more per year than female CFOs, even after controlling for age, time in the job, company size, and market capitalization.[51] It is also true that women tend not to negotiate their salaries as aggressively as men do. The problem is that women (but not men) who negotiate for higher pay are viewed as less likeable.[52] Indeed, the CEO of Microsoft (a man) advised women that they should not ask for a raise, but instead should have faith in the system.

As adults, we spend more time working than in any other single activity. A job that we love can permeate our lives with satisfaction and even joy. Work that bores or bedevils us may shorten our lives. We have devoted two chapters to employment law precisely because work *is* so important in our lives. Now you know both your rights as a worker and your obligations as an employer. We hope that when you have other people's lives in your hands, you will treat them as you would wish to be treated.

---

47 Kevin M. Clermont and Stewart J. Schwab, "Employment Discrimination Plaintiffs in Federal Court: From Bad to Worse?" *3 Harv. l. & Pol'y Rev.* 103 (2009).

48 Data from David Wessel, "The Positive Economics of Leaning In," *The Wall Street Journal*," April 3, 2013.

49 "Closing the Gap," *The Economist*, November 26, 2011.

50 Jobvite's 6th Annual Social Recruiting Survey.

51 www3.cfo.com/article/2012/4/compensation_gmi-gender-gap-gofoernance-metrics

52 https://hbr.org/2014/06/why-women-dont-negotiate-their-job-offers

EXAM REVIEW

1. **CONSTITUTION** The U.S. Constitution prohibits employment discrimination by federal, state, and local governments.

2. **THE CIVIL RIGHTS ACT OF 1866** The Civil Rights Act of 1866 prohibits racial discrimination in both private and public employment (except it does not apply to the federal government).

3. **EQUAL PAY ACT OF 1963** Under the Equal Pay Act, a worker may not be paid at a lesser rate than employees of the opposite sex for equal work.

4. **TITLE VII** Under Title VII of the Civil Rights Act of 1964, it is illegal for employers with 15 or more workers to discriminate on the basis of race, color, religion, sex, or national origin.

5. **TYPES OF DISCRIMINATION** There are four types of prohibited activities under Title VII: disparate treatment, disparate impact, hostile environment, and retaliation.

6. **DISPARATE TREATMENT** To prove a disparate treatment case, the plaintiff must show that she was *treated* less favorably than others because of her sex, race, color, religion, or national origin.

7. **DISPARATE IMPACT** Disparate impact applies if the employer has a rule that *on its face* is not discriminatory, but *in practice* excludes too many people in a protected group and the rule is not a job-related business necessity.

8. **HOSTILE WORK ENVIRONMENT** Employers violate Title VII if they permit a work environment that is so hostile toward people in a protected category that it affects their ability to work.

9. **SEXUAL HARASSMENT** Sexual harassment involves unwelcome sexual advances, requests for sexual favors, or other verbal or physical conduct of a sexual nature that are so severe and pervasive that they interfere with an employee's ability to work.

10. **RETALIATION** Title VII also prohibits employers from retaliating against workers who oppose discrimination, bring a claim under the statute, or take part in an investigation or hearing.

11. **RELIGION** Employers cannot discriminate against a worker because of his religious beliefs. In addition, employers must make reasonable accommodation for a worker's religious practices unless the request would cause undue hardship for the business.

12. **SEX** Title VII forbids sex stereotyping.

13. **ATTRACTIVENESS** Unattractiveness is not itself a protected category under Title VII, so any discrimination claim would have to fit into one of the existing categories.

14. **FAMILY RESPONSIBILITY DISCRIMINATION** Men and women may not be treated differently because of their family responsibilities.

15. **SEXUAL ORIENTATION** The specific language of Title VII does not include sexual orientation as a protected category but at least some courts now interpret the statute to include it as one. Almost half the states and hundreds of cities do have statutes that prohibit such discrimination. Also, the federal government prohibits discrimination based on sexual orientation among its own employees and also among government contractors.

16. **GENDER IDENTITY AND EXPRESSION** Traditionally, courts ruled that employees were not protected from discrimination based on gender identity. But some federal courts, the EEOC, about one-third of the states, and hundreds of cities prohibit gender identity and expression discrimination. Also, the federal government prohibits discrimination on the basis of gender identity among its employees and among government contractors.

17. **BACKGROUND AND CREDIT CHECKS** EEOC regulations prohibit companies from using criminal history information in a way that has an adverse impact on employees in a protected category if the background information is irrelevant in determining whether the employee is appropriate for the job. Some states and localities have passed "ban the box" legislation, which prohibits employers from asking about the applicant's criminal record until after an interview is conducted or an offer is made. The EEOC also discourages the use of credit checks.

18. **IMMIGRATION** Under Title VII, it is illegal to discriminate against noncitizens because "national origin" is a protected category.

19. **DEFENSES** Under Title VII, the defendant has four possible defenses: merit, seniority, bona fide occupational qualification, and affirmative action.

20. **BONA FIDE OCCUPATIONAL QUALIFICATION** Under the BFOQ standard, an employer is permitted to establish discriminatory job requirements if they are essential to the position in question.

EXAMStrategy

Question: When Southwest Airlines first started, it refused to hire male flight attendants because its strategy was to court its (mostly male) customers by promoting an image of "feminine spirit, fun, and sex appeal." Its ads featured women in provocative uniforms serving "love bites" (almonds) and "love potions" (cocktails). Its ticketing system featured a "quickie machine" to provide "instant gratification." Is this refusal to hire men a violation of Title VII?

Strategy: Southwest argued that its "Love" campaign was an essential marketing tool. Was being a woman a BFOQ? Remember that the courts have almost always rejected BFOQ claims that are based on customer preference. (See the "Result" at the end of this Exam Review section.)

21. **REVERSE DISCRIMINATION** Reverse discrimination means making an employment decision that harms a non-Hispanic white person or a man because of his gender, color, or race. As a general rule, it is just as illegal as discriminating against a minority or a woman.

22. **PREGNANCY DISCRIMINATION ACT** Under the Pregnancy Discrimination Act, an employer may not fire, refuse to hire, or fail to promote a woman because she is pregnant or because she has had an abortion. An employer must also treat pregnancy as it would any other temporary disability.

23. **AGE DISCRIMINATION IN EMPLOYMENT ACT** Under the ADEA, an employer with 20 or more workers may not fire, refuse to hire, fail to promote, or otherwise reduce a person's employment opportunities because he is 40 or older.

EXAMStrategy

Question: Kathy was over 40 when SFI refused to hire her as an insurance agent; it said because she had no sales experience. But the job ad had not specified that sales experience was required. It turned out that when SFI hired agents from outside the company, it was much more likely to hire people under 40. But when promoting from within, it was much more likely to promote people over 40. Did SFI violate the ADEA when it refused to hire Kathy?

Strategy: An ADEA case involves a three-step analysis:

1. Kathy must show that she is older than 40, suffered an adverse employment action, was qualified for the job, and a younger person actually got the job.
2. SFI has to show that its decision was based on a legitimate reason. No sales experience is a good reason.
3. Kathy must prove that her age was the deciding factor. (See the "Result" at the end of this Exam Review section.)

24. **REHABILITATION ACT** The Rehabilitation Act of 1973 prohibits discrimination on the basis of disability by the federal government, federal contractors, and all entities that receive federal funds.

25. **AMERICANS WITH DISABILITIES ACT** The ADA prohibits employers with 15 or more workers from discriminating on the basis of disability.

26. **DISABILITY** A disabled person is someone with a physical or mental impairment that substantially limits a major life activity or the operation of a major bodily function or someone who is regarded as having such an impairment.

27. **TREATMENT OF DISABLED WORKERS** Once it is established that a worker is disabled, employers may not discriminate on the basis of disability so long as she can, with reasonable accommodation, perform the essential functions of the job. An accommodation is not reasonable if it would create undue hardship for the employer.

EXAMStrategy

Question: When Thomas Lussier filled out a Postal Service employment application, he did not admit that he had twice pleaded guilty to charges of disorderly conduct. Lussier suffered from Post Traumatic Stress Disorder (PTSD) acquired during military service. Because of this disorder, he sometimes had panic attacks that required him to leave meetings. He was also a recovered alcoholic and drug user. During his stint with the Postal Service, he had some personality conflicts with other employees. Once, another employee hit him. He also had one episode of "erratic emotional behavior and verbal outburst." In the meantime, a postal employee in Ridgewood, New Jersey, killed four colleagues. The postmaster general encouraged all supervisors to identify workers who had dangerous propensities. Lussier's boss discovered that he had lied on his employment application about the disorderly conduct charges and fired him. Is the Postal Service in violation of the law?

Strategy: Was Lussier disabled under the ADA? He had a mental impairment (PTSD) that substantially limited a major life activity. Could Lussier, with reasonable accommodation, perform his job? Yes. Was his firing illegal? (See the "Result" at the end of this Exam Review section.)

28. **GENETIC INFORMATION NONDISCRIMINATION ACT** Under GINA, employers with 15 or more workers may not require genetic testing, or use information about genetic makeup or family medical history as a factor in hiring, firing, or promoting employees.

29. **EEOC** The EEOC is the federal agency responsible for enforcing Title VII, the Equal Pay Act, the Pregnancy Discrimination Act, the ADEA, the ADA, and GINA.

    Before a plaintiff can bring suit under any of these statutes (except the Equal Pay Act), she must first file a charge with the EEOC.

RESULTS

20. Result: Safety, privacy, and authenticity are three situations in which customer preference can be a BFOQ. None of these issues was a factor in this case. The court ruled against Southwest on the grounds that it was "not a business where vicarious sex entertainment is the primary service provided."[53]

23. Result: In the absence of specific comments about age, it is very difficult to show that age is the deciding factor. Kathy is likely to lose her case.

27. Result: The court held that the Postal Service was in violation of the law because Lussier had been dismissed solely as a result of his disability. Clearly, he could perform his job with reasonable accommodation.

---

53 Wilson v. Southwest Airlines, 517 F. Supp 292 (N.D. Tex 1981).

MULTIPLE-CHOICE QUESTIONS

1. Gregg Young, the CEO of BJY Inc., insisted on calling Mamdouh El-Hakem "Manny" or "Hank" even when El-Hakem asked him not to. El-Hakem was of Arab heritage. Young argued that a "Western" name would increase El-Hakem's chances for success and would be more acceptable to BJY's clientele. Does this behavior violate the law?
   (a) Yes, Young violated Title VII by discriminating against El-Hakem on the basis of his national origin.
   (b) Yes, Young was creating a hostile work environment.
   (c) Both A and B
   (d) No, Manny is just a nickname. No harm was intended and, indeed, no harm resulted.
   (e) No because customers did prefer a Western name.

2. The CEO of BankTwo realized that not one single officer of the bank was female or a member of a minority group. He announced that henceforth, the bank would only hire people in these two groups until they comprised at least 30 percent of the officers. Is this plan legal?
   (a) Yes, voluntary affirmative action plans are always legal.
   (b) Yes because fewer than 20 percent of the officers are female or minority.
   (c) No, to be legal, the goal of an affirmative action plan cannot be greater than 20 percent female or minority.
   (d) No, the plan is too unfair to white men, who have no chance of being hired for a long time.

3. When Allain University was looking for a diversity officer, it decided it would only hire a person of color. Is this decision legal?
   (a) Yes, color is a BFOQ for this position.
   (b) No, color is never a BFOQ, but race could be.
   (c) No, neither race nor color can be a BFOQ.
   (d) No, race and color can be a BFOQ, but are not in this situation. A person does not have to be a member of a minority group to promote diversity.

4. For 30 years, Ralph has built architectural models at Snowdrop Architects. The firm replaces him with Charlotte, who is 24 and willing to work for much less than Ralph. The firm never offered to let him stay for less pay. When he left, one of the partners told him, "Frankly, it's not a bad thing to have a cute young person working with the clients." Which of the following statements is true?
   (a) Snowdrop is liable because it had an obligation to offer Ralph the lower salary.
   (b) Snowdrop violated the law by replacing an older worker with a younger one just to save money.
   (c) Snowdrop is liable because age was a factor in Ralph's firing.
   (d) Snowdrop is not liable because age was not the deciding factor in Ralph's firing.

5. During chemotherapy for bone cancer, Pete, a delivery man, is exhausted, nauseated, and weak. He has asked permission to come in later, work a shorter day, and limit his lifting to 10 pounds. Delivery people typically carry packages of up to 70 pounds. Does Pete's employer, Vulcan, have the right to fire him?
   (a) No, Vulcan must create a new position so that the employee can do something else.
   (b) No, Vulcan must transfer the employee to another position, but only if one is vacant and he is able to perform it.
   (c) Yes, Vulcan can fire Pete because none of his major life activities has been affected.
   (d) Yes, Vulcan can fire Pete because he cannot perform the essential functions of his job.
   (e) Yes, Vulcan can fire Pete because he is not disabled—once the chemotherapy treatments end, he will feel fine again.

CASE QUESTIONS

1. An employer placed a job advertisement for security guards, specifying that applicants had to be U.S. citizens. It also required applicants to present a Social Security card. Was this ad legal?

2. In the 2008 recession, Roger (age 52) lost his job as a comptroller. Desperate for work after a year of unemployment, he began to apply for any accounting job at any company. But no one would hire him because he was "overqualified and overexperienced." He repeatedly explained that he was eager to fill the job that was available. Have these companies that refused to hire Roger violated the ADEA?

3. FedEx refused to promote José Rodriguez to a supervisor's position because of his foreign accent and "how he speaks." Is FedEx in violation of the law?

4. Pam Huber worked at Walmart filling grocery orders and earning $13 an hour. While on the job, she suffered a permanent injury to her right arm and hand. Both she and Walmart agreed that she was disabled under the ADA. As a reasonable accommodation, she asked for a job as a router, which was then vacant. Although she was qualified for that job, she was not the most qualified. Walmart filled the job with the most qualified person. It offered Huber a position as a janitor at $6.20 per hour. Did Walmart violate the ADA?

5. After the terrorist attacks of 9/11, the United States tightened its visa requirements. In the process, baseball teams discovered that 300 foreign-born professional players had lied about their age. (A talented 16-year-old is much more valuable than a 23-year-old with the same skills.) In some cases, the players had used birth certificates that belonged to other (younger) people. To prevent this fraud, baseball teams began asking prospects for DNA tests on them and their families to make sure they were not lying about their identity. Is this testing legal?

6. Ryan could not stay awake at work—and was unable to remember and keep track of key parts of his job. When questioned, he told his boss that he had sleep apnea, a sleep disorder that causes a person to stop breathing during sleep. His report from his doctor said that it was possible Ryan did have sleep apnea, but there was no definitive diagnosis because Ryan refused to take the necessary tests. The report also said that Ryan's sleepiness could be caused by bad habits, like irregular sleep times, a poor diet, and heavy caffeine consumption. What legal obligations does his employer have to Ryan? Can Ryan be fired?

7. Atlas operated warehouses that stored food for grocery stores. Imagine the upset when a mystery employee began leaving his feces in a warehouse. To solve the mystery of the devious defecator, Atlas required cheek swabs from two of its workers so that it could compare their DNA with that of the feces. Was Atlas liable to the workers?

DISCUSSION QUESTIONS

1. You are the hiring manager for a bus company. One of the applicants for a job as a bus driver seems perfectly qualified and he is a minority. You would like to hire him, but a background check reveals that he was convicted of second degree murder 40 years before, when he was 15. Should you hire him?

2. Generally, the BFOQ defense does not apply to customer preference. But recently, some clients have been pressuring their law firms to staff their cases with female and minority lawyers. If a firm does so, would the BFOQ defense be valid? Should it be?

3. A high-end boutique in Phoenix would hire only women to work in sales because fittings and alterations took place in the dressing room or immediately outside. The customers were buying expensive clothes and demanded a male-free dressing area. Has the store violated Title VII? What would its defense be?

4. Lisa T. Jackson, who was white, worked at Uncle Bubba's Seafood and Oyster House. She filed suit under Title VII, alleging that the restaurant discriminated against black employees. They had to enter through the restaurant's rear entrance and could not use the customer bathrooms. Neither of these prohibitions applied to white staff. Jackson's boss also repeatedly told racist jokes. Jackson stated that this behavior caused her great difficulty in managing the staff and also immense emotional distress because she had biracial nieces. In addition, one of her bosses asked her how she "looked so white," given that her father was of Sicilian descent. Can Jackson recover under Title VII?

5. Peter Oiler was a truck driver who delivered groceries to Winn-Dixie stores. He revealed to his boss that in his free time he liked to dress as a woman, even though he was happily married to a woman. Oiler had been diagnosed with transvestic fetishism with gender dysphoria and a gender identity disorder. Winn-Dixie fired him for fear that, if customers found out, they would go elsewhere to buy their groceries. Does Oiler have a claim against Winn-Dixie?

Business Organizations

UNIT

7

31

CHAPTER

STARTING A BUSINESS: LLCs AND OTHER OPTIONS

Poor Jeffrey Horning. If only he had understood business law. Horning owned a thriving construction company which operated as a corporation—Horning Construction Company, Inc. To lighten his crushing workload, he decided to bring in two partners to handle more day-to-day responsibility. It seemed a good idea at the time.

Horning transferred the business to Horning Construction LLC, and then gave one-third ownership each to two trusted employees, Klimowski and Holdsworth. But Horning did not pay enough attention to the legal formalities—the new LLC had no operating agreement.

Nothing worked out as he had planned. The two men did not take on extra work. Horning's relationship with them went from bad to worse, with the parties bickering over every petty detail and each man trying to sabotage the others. It got to the point that Klimowski sent Horning a letter full of insults and expletives. At his wit's end, Horning proposed that the LLC buy out his share of the business. Klimowski and Holdsworth refused. Totally frustrated, Horning asked a court to dissolve the business on the grounds that Klimowski despised him, Holdsworth resented him, and neither of them trusted him. In his view, it was their goal to "make my remaining time with Horning, LLC so unbearable that I will relent and give them for a pittance the remainder of the company for which they have paid nothing to date."

Jeffrey Horning was stuck in purgatory, with two business partners he loathed and no way out.

Although the court was sympathetic, it refused to help. Because Horning Construction LLC did not have an operating agreement that provided for a buyout, it had to depend upon the New York LLC statute, which only permitted dissolution "whenever it is not reasonably practicable to carry on the business." But Horning Construction LLC was very successful, grossing over $25 million annually. Jeffrey Horning was stuck in purgatory, with two business partners he loathed and no way out.[1]

Every business, no matter how large, was at one point little more than a gleam in an entrepreneur's eye. The goal of the law is to balance the rights, duties, and liabilities of entrepreneurs, managers, investors, and other stakeholders. Time and again in these next chapters, we will see that legal issues can have as profound an impact on the success of a company as any business decision. The law affects virtually every aspect of business. Wise (and successful) entrepreneurs know how to use the law to their advantage. Think of the grief Jeffrey Horning could have saved himself if he had understood the implications of the LLC statute.

To begin, entrepreneurs must select a form of organization. The correct choice can reduce taxes, liability, and conflict while facilitating outside investment. If entrepreneurs do not make a choice for themselves, the law will automatically select a (potentially undesirable) default option.

31-1 SOLE PROPRIETORSHIPS

Sole proprietorships are the most common form of business, so we begin there. A **sole proprietorship** is an unincorporated business owned by one person. Linda owns ExSciTe (which stands for Excellence in Science Teaching), a sole proprietorship that helps teachers prepare hands-on science experiments in the classroom using such basic items as vinegar, lemon juice, and red cabbage.

Sole proprietorship
An unincorporated business owned by one person

The advantages of a sole proprietorship are:

- **Ease of formation.** No formal steps are necessary to create a sole proprietorship. Once Linda starts a business, she automatically has a sole proprietorship. Generally, there is no need to hire a lawyer or register with the state, so costs are low. Although a very few states, and some cities and towns, do require sole proprietors to obtain a business license. And states generally require sole proprietors to register their business name if it is different from their own. Linda, for example, would file a "d/b/a" or "doing business as" certificate for ExSciTe.
- **Taxes.** A sole proprietorship is a **flow-through tax entity**, which means that the business itself does not pay taxes and does not even file a separate tax return. Instead, Linda pays *personal* income tax on all business profits.

Flow-through tax entity
An organization that does not pay income tax on its profits but instead passes them through to its owners who pay personal income tax on all business profits

Sole proprietorships also have some serious disadvantages:

- **Liability.** As the owner of the business, Linda is responsible for all of its debts. If ExSciTe cannot pay its suppliers or a student is injured by an exploding cabbage, Linda is *personally* liable. She may have to sell her house to pay the debt.
- **Limited capital.** The owner of a sole proprietorship has limited options for financing her business. Debt is generally her only source of working capital because she has no stock or memberships to sell. For this reason, sole proprietorships work best for businesses without large capital needs.

[1] Matter of Jeffrey M. Horning v. Horning Constr. LLC, 12 Misc. 3d 402 (N.Y. Sup. Ct. 2006).

31-2 CORPORATIONS

Corporations are the dominant form of organization for a simple reason—they have been around for a long time and, as a result, they are numerous and the law that regulates them is well developed. They also, of course, offer some significant advantages to their owners.

The concept of a corporation is very old indeed—it began with the Greeks and spread from them through the Romans into English law. At the beginning, however, corporations were viewed with deep suspicion. A British jurist commented that they had "neither bodies to be punished nor souls to be condemned."[2] And what were shareholders doing that required limited liability? Why did they have to cower behind a corporate shield?

For this reason, shareholders originally had to obtain special permission to form a corporation. In England, corporations could be created only by special charter from the monarch or, later, from Parliament. But with the advent of the Industrial Revolution, large-scale manufacturing enterprises needed huge amounts of capital from investors who were not involved in management and did not want to be personally liable for the debts of an organization that they were not managing. In 1811, New York became the first jurisdiction in the United States to permit routine incorporation.[3]

Despite the initial suspicion with which corporations were viewed, economists now suggest that this form of organization, combined with technological advances such as double-entry bookkeeping and stock markets, provided the Western hemisphere with an enormous economic advantage. In particular, the corporate form permitted the creation of large, enduring businesses because corporations could attract outside investors and were more likely than partnerships to survive the death of their founders.

31-2a Corporations in General

As is the case for all forms of organization, corporations have their advantages and disadvantages.

Advantages of a Corporation

Limited Liability. If a business flops, its shareholders lose their investment in the company but not their other assets. Likewise, if Emily Employee injures another motorist while driving a company van, the business is liable for any harm, but its shareholders are not personally liable.

Be aware, however, that limited liability does not protect against all debts. Individuals are always responsible for their *own* acts. If Emily was careless, then she would be liable even though she was a company shareholder because being a shareholder does not protect her from liability for her own wrongdoing. If the company did not pay the judgment, Emily would have to, from her personal assets. **A corporation shields managers and investors from personal liability for the debts of the corporation and the actions of others, but not against liability for their own torts and crimes.**

Transferability of Interests. Corporations provide flexibility for enterprises small (with one owner) and large (with thousands of shareholders). As we will see, partnership interests are not transferable without the permission of the other partners, whereas corporate stock can be bought and sold easily.

Duration. When a sole proprietor dies, legally, so does the business. But corporations have perpetual existence: They can continue without their founders.

[2]Edward, Baron Thurlow, during the trial of Warren Hastings.

[3]An Act Relative to Incorporation for Manufacturing Purpose, 1811 N.Y. Laws, ch. 67, §111.

Disadvantages of a Corporation

But the corporate form is not perfect. Here are some disadvantages:

Logistics. Corporations require substantial expense and effort to create and operate. The cost of establishing a corporation includes legal and filing fees, not to mention the expense of annual filings and taxes. Corporations must also hold meetings for both shareholders and directors. Minutes of these meetings must be kept indefinitely in the company minute book. Failure to comply with these requirements may even destroy the limited liability of the organization.

Taxes. As we have seen, a sole proprietorship is a flow-through entity that does not pay taxes itself; all taxes are paid directly by the owner. Shortly, we will look at other flow-through entities, such as partnerships and limited liability companies (LLCs) where, again, all taxes are paid directly by the owners, and none by the business itself. In contrast, a corporation is a taxable entity, which means it must pay income taxes on its profits and also file a tax return. Shareholders must then pay tax on any dividends from the corporation. Thus, with a flow-through organization, a dollar is taxed only once before it ends up in the owner's bank account, but with a taxable entity, that dollar is taxed twice before it is deposited by a shareholder.

Exhibit 31.1 compares the single taxation of an LLC (a flow-through entity) with the double taxation of corporations. Suppose, as shown in the exhibit, that a corporation and an LLC each receive $10,000 in additional income. The corporation pays tax at a top rate of

EXHIBIT 31.1

Members of an LLC pay lower taxes than shareholders.

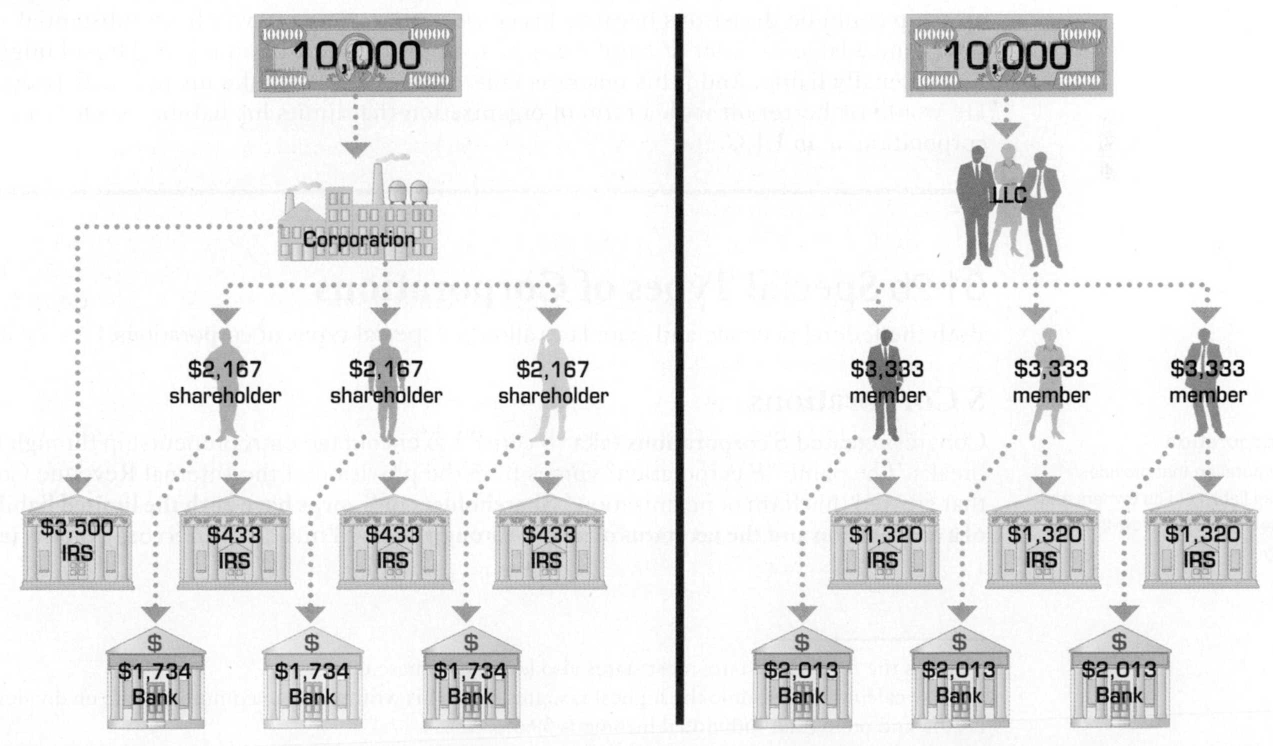

35 percent.[4] Thus, the corporation pays $3,500 of the $10,000 in tax. The corporation pays out the remaining $6,500 as a dividend of $2,167 to each of its three shareholders. Then the shareholders are taxed at the special dividend rate of 20 percent, which means they each pay a tax of $433. They are each left with $1,734. Of the initial $10,000, almost 48 percent ($4,799) has gone to the Internal Revenue Service (IRS).[5]

Compare the corporation to an LLC. The LLC itself pays no taxes, so it can pass on $3,333 to each of its owners (who are called "members"). Assuming a 39.6 percent individual rate, each member pays an income tax of $1,320. As members, they pocket $2,013, which is $279 more than they could keep as shareholders. Of the LLC's initial $10,000, 39.6 percent ($3,960) has gone to the IRS, compared with the corporation's 48 percent.

EXAMStrategy

Question: Consider these two entrepreneurs: Judith formed a corporation to write a blog which is unlikely to generate substantial revenues. Drexel operated his construction business as a sole proprietorship. Were these forms of organization right for these businesses?

Strategy: Prepare a list of the advantages and disadvantages of each form of organization. Sole proprietorships are best for businesses without substantial capital needs. Corporations can raise capital but are expensive to operate.

Result: Judith would be better off with a sole proprietorship—her revenues will not support the expenses of a corporation. Also, her debts are likely to be small, so she will not need the limited liability of a corporation. And no matter what her form of organization, she would be personally liable for any negligent acts she commits, so a corporation would not provide any additional protection. But for Drexel, a sole proprietorship could be disastrous because his construction company will have substantial debts and a large number of employees. If an employee causes an injury, Drexel might be personally liable. And if his business fails, the court would take his personal assets. He would be better off with a form of organization that limits his liability, such as a corporation or an LLC.

31-2b Special Types of Corporations

Both the federal tax code and state laws allow for special types of corporations.

S Corporations

S corporation
A corporation that provides limited liability to its owners and the tax status of a flow-through entity

Congress created **S corporations** (aka "S corps") to encourage entrepreneurship through tax breaks. The name "S corporation" comes from the provision of the Internal Revenue Code that created this form of organization.[6] **Shareholders of S corps have both the limited liability of a corporation and the tax status of a flow-through entity**. Thus, all of an S corp's profits (and

[4]This is the federal tax rate; most states also levy a corporate tax.

[5]These calculations assume the highest tax rates. As of this writing, the maximum tax rate on dividends is 20% and on regular individual income is 39.6%.

[6]26 U.S.C. §1361.

losses) pass through to the shareholders, who pay tax at their individual rates. It avoids the double taxation of a regular corporation (sometimes called a "**C corporation**").[7] If, as is often the case with start-ups, the business loses money, investors can deduct these losses against their other income. Later, should circumstances change, it is easy to terminate S corp status and become a C corporation.

C corporation
A corporation that provides limited liability to its owners, but is a taxable entity

S corps do face some major restrictions:

- There can be only one class of stock.
- There can be no more than 100 shareholders.
- Shareholders must be individuals, estates, charities, pension funds, or trusts, not partnerships or corporations.
- Shareholders must be citizens or residents of the United States, not nonresident aliens.
- All shareholders must agree that the company should be an S corporation.

Close Corporations

As with S corps, a goal of close corporation statutes is to encourage entrepreneurship. But close corporations are created by state law and, therefore, these entities are not entitled to special treatment under the federal tax code unless they also register with the IRS. Likewise, a corporation that qualifies for S corp status with the IRS, will not necessarily be treated as a close corporation under state law unless it complies with those particular requirements.

A typical **close corporation** has a small number of shareholders (usually fewer than 50), stock that is not publicly traded, and shareholders who play an active role in the management of the enterprise. In some states, close corporations are created by statute; in others they are devised by courts under the common law. Although the rules of close corporations may vary from state to state, generally these organizations share certain features:

Close corporation
A corporation with a small number of shareholders whose stock is not publicly traded and whose shareholders play an active role in management. It is entitled to special treatment under some state laws.

- **Protection of minority shareholders.** As there is no public market for the stock of a close corporation, a minority shareholder who is being mistreated by the majority cannot simply sell his shares and depart. Therefore, close corporation laws typically protect minority shareholders by providing that majority shareholders owe them a fiduciary duty. In addition, the charter of a close corporation may require a unanimous vote of all shareholders to choose officers, set salaries, or pay dividends. It could also grant each shareholder veto power over all important corporate decisions.
- **Transfer restrictions.** The shareholders of a close corporation often need to work closely together in the management of the company. Therefore, the charter may require that a shareholder first offer shares to the other owners before selling them to an outsider. In that way, the remaining shareholders have some control over who their new co-owners will be.
- **Flexibility.** Close corporations can typically operate without a board of directors, a formal set of bylaws, or annual shareholder meetings.
- **Dispute resolution.** The shareholders are allowed to agree in advance that any one of them can dissolve the corporation if some particular event occurs or, if they choose, for any reason at all. Even without such an agreement, a shareholder can ask a court to dissolve a close corporation if the other owners behave "oppressively" or "unfairly."

[7]Although *most* states follow the federal lead on S corporations, a small number require these companies to pay state corporate tax.

EXAMStrategy

Question: While working as a plant superintendent at Rodd, Joseph bought stock in the company, which was a close corporation. On his death, he owned 20 percent, while the founder's children owned the rest. Later, Joseph's widow, Euphemia, found out that Rodd had bought back all of the children's stock, while refusing to buy any of hers. What can Euphemia do?

Strategy: Remember that majority shareholders in a close corporation owe a fiduciary duty to minority shareholders.

Result: Euphemia was a minority shareholder. The court ruled that, because the majority shareholders had violated their fiduciary duty to her, the company had to buy her stock, too.[8] Otherwise, her shares would have been worthless.

31-3 LIMITED LIABILITY COMPANIES

An LLC offers the limited liability of a corporation and the tax status of a flow-through entity. As such, it is an extremely useful form of organization often favored by entrepreneurs because it offers the best of both worlds—limited liability and lower taxes. It is not, however, as simple as it perhaps should be.

To begin with, it is a relatively new form of organization so the law is not as established as with, say, corporations. Wyoming passed the first LLC statute in 1977, but most states did not follow suit until after 1991. Also, owing to a complex history that involves painful interaction between IRS regulations and state laws (the details of which we will spare you), the specific provisions of state laws vary greatly. An effort to remedy this confusion—the Uniform Limited Liability Company Act (ULLCA)—has only been adopted by half the states. So we will not limit our discussion to the ULLCA but, instead, will review general trends in LLC law.

Limited liability is one of the most important features of an LLC. Are the members in the following case protected? You decide.

You Be the Judge

Ridgaway v. Silk

2004 Conn. Super. LEXIS 548; 2004 WL 574526
Superior Court of Connecticut, 2004

Facts: Norman Costello and Robert Giordano were members of Silk, LLC, which owned a bar and night club in Groton, Connecticut, called Silk Stockings. Anthony Sulls went drinking there one night—and drinking heavily. Although he was obviously drunk, employees at Silk Stockings continued to serve him. Costello and Giordano were working there that night. They both greeted customers (who numbered in the hundreds), supervised employees, and performed "other PR work." When Sulls left the nightclub at 1:45 a.m. with two friends, he drove off the highway at high speed, killing himself and one of his passengers, William Ridgaway, Jr.

Ridgaway's estate sued Costello and Giordano personally. The defendants filed a motion for summary judgment seeking dismissal of the complaint.

---

[8] Donahue v. Rodd Electrotype Co., 367 Mass. 578 (Mass. 1975).

You Be the Judge: *Are Costello and Giordano personally liable to Ridgaway's estate?*

Argument for Costello and Giordano: The defendants did not own Silk Stockings; they were simply members of an LLC that owned the nightclub. The whole point of an LLC is to protect members against personal liability. The assets of Silk, LLC, are at risk, but not the personal assets of Costello and Giordano.

Argument for Ridgaway's Estate: The defendants are not liable for being members of Silk, LLC, they are liable for their own misdeeds as employees of the LLC. They were both present at Silk Stockings on the night in question, meeting and greeting customers and supervising employees. It is possible that they might actually have served drinks to Sulls, but in any event, they did not adequately supervise and train their employees to prevent them from serving alcohol to someone who was clearly drunk. We do not want to live in a world where employees are free to be as careless as they wish, knowing that they are not liable because they are members of an LLC.

In deciding whether an LLC is right for your business, there are other features besides liability and tax status that you should consider.

31-3a Formation

It is easy to form an LLC; the only required document is a certificate of organization (also called a charter). The certificate of organization is short, containing basic information such as name and address. It must be filed with the secretary of state in the jurisdiction in which the LLC is being formed.

In addition, an LLC should have an operating agreement that sets out the rights and obligations of the members. This document is not required, but can be exceedingly helpful, as Jeffrey Horning learned in the opening scenario. If an LLC does not have an operating agreement, then the default provisions of the state's LLC statute govern the organization.

When members of an LLC do choose to have an operating agreement, the law respects their freedom to contract and gives them wide latitude in drafting the agreement, particularly as regards the relationship among themselves. This approach sounds like a good idea, but the freedom to contract is also the freedom to make mistakes. If members make careless choices in drafting an operating agreement, courts will not interfere to protect them from the consequences. Thus, it is absolutely crucial that an operating agreement be carefully crafted and that members understand its provisions.

On this issue, corporations have an advantage over LLCs. Corporations are so familiar that the standard documents (such as a charter, bylaws, and shareholder agreement) are well established and widely available. Lawyers can form a corporation easily, and the internet offers a host of free forms. Also, the law of corporations is more established and predictable.

The problem in the *Horning* case was that the LLC had no operating agreement. But a bad operating agreement is every bit as dangerous. The agreement for Satellite, LLC provided that the company could only be dissolved by a unanimous vote of its members. Although the two members were in total conflict, one of them refused to vote for dissolution. If there had been no operating agreement, state law would have permitted a court to dissolve the LLC. Instead, the unhappy member had no way to get out.[9] He learned the hard way about the dangers of the freedom to contract.

[9]Huatuco v. Satellite Healthcare, 2013 Del. Ch. LEXIS 298; 2013 WL 6460898 (Del. Ch. 2013).

The following case illustrates yet another way that LLCs can go bad.

Ferret v. Courtney

32 Mass. L. Rep. 592
Superior Court of Massachusetts, 2015

Facts: Eric Ferret and Stephen Courtney founded Sci.X Science Studio, LLC, a Delaware LLC. Sci.X's operating agreement required that all disagreements be decided by arbitration rather than litigation. But neither member ever signed the agreement. Five years later, after a series of conflicts, Ferret sued Courtney. In response, Courtney filed a motion to dismiss, arguing that the operating agreement required Ferret's claim to be arbitrated.

Issues: ***Is the unsigned Sci.X operating agreement enforceable? Does Ferret have to arbitrate his claim?***

Excerpts from Judge Curran's Decision: Ferret argues that the operating agreement is unenforceable because it is not signed by any of the members of Sci.X.

The operating agreement clearly states that it is to be governed by Delaware law. However, curiously, under Delaware law, an LLC operating agreement need not be signed in order to be enforceable. In fact, the Delaware limited liability statute expressly allows oral operating agreements. Thus, the fact that the written operating agreement was unsigned does not render it unenforceable.

Nevertheless, unsigned LLC operating agreements still remain subject to the statute of frauds. If an LLC agreement contains a provision or multiple provisions which cannot possibly be performed within one year, such provision or provisions are unenforceable. However, Mr. Ferret failed to argue as to why the statute of frauds would preclude enforcement of the operating agreement in this case. Whether or not a statute of frauds defense exists is not for this court to interject, as it can only consider the claims and defenses before it.

Ferret's only argument is that the operating agreement is incomplete, unsigned, and undated. As noted above, this argument is meritless.

Both Delaware law and the ULLCA permit oral operating agreements, which adds a whole new level of complication. How can you tell (without litigating) whether an unsigned operating agreement is enforceable or, indeed, whether any other discussions could be interpreted to be an enforceable agreement? And then you have to determine whether the Statute of Frauds requires a writing. In short, be careful.

31-3b Flexibility

Unlike S corporations, LLCs can have members that are corporations, partnerships, or nonresident aliens. LLCs can also have different classes of members. Unlike corporations, LLCs are not required to hold annual meetings or maintain a minute book.

31-3c Transferability of Interests

As a general rule, unless the operating agreement provides otherwise, existing members of an LLC cannot transfer their ownership rights, nor can the LLC admit a new member, without the unanimous permission of the other members. However, members can transfer their economic interests in an LLC—that is, their right to share in the profits of the enterprise. In other words, members can transfer their right to receive a check from the LLC, but not their right to participate in decision-making.

31-3d Duration

Some state laws provide that LLCs automatically dissolve upon the withdrawal of a member (owing to, for example, death, resignation, or bankruptcy). However, most state laws and the ULLCA provide that an LLC has perpetual existence and, thus, continues in operation even after a member withdraws. Unless, that is, the operating agreement provides otherwise.

31-3e Going Public

Once an LLC goes public, it loses its favorable tax status and is taxed as a corporation, not as a partnership.[10] Thus, there is no advantage to using the LLC form of organization for a publicly traded company. And there are some disadvantages: Unlike corporations, publicly traded LLCs do not enjoy a well-established set of statutory and case law that is relatively consistent across the many states. For this reason, privately held companies that begin as LLCs often change to corporations when they go public.

31-3f Changing Forms

Some companies that are now corporations might prefer to be LLCs. However, the IRS would consider this change to be a sale of the corporate assets and would levy a tax on the value of these assets. For this reason, few corporations have made the change. However, switching from a partnership to an LLC or from an LLC to a corporation is not considered a sale and does not have the same adverse tax impact.

31-3g Piercing the Company Veil

Limited liability is one of the great advantages of an LLC. However, if members abuse their rights, a court may remove their limited liability. This process is called **piercing the company veil**. **A court may pierce an LLC's veil in four circumstances:**

Piercing the company veil
A court holds members of an LLC personally liable for the debts of the organization.

1. **Failure to observe formalities.** Members must treat the LLC like a separate organization. Thus, if an LLC enters into an agreement (particularly with a member), a legitimate contract needs to be signed.
2. **Commingling assets.** This trap is the most dangerous. An LLC and its members must keep their assets separate. If courts cannot tell who owns what, they are likely to grant creditors access to the assets of both the organization and its members.
3. **Inadequate capitalization.** In extreme cases, if an LLC is established without enough capital to run its business, then a court may look to the members' assets. An LLC had capital of only about $20,000 but proceeded to borrow millions of dollars from one of the members. That ratio looked wrong.
4. **Fraud.** Courts are unwilling to protect fraudsters who try to use an LLC as a shield against liability.

In the following case, the defendant seemed not to have bad intent but was simply careless. Nonetheless, he was liable.

---

[10] 26 U.S.C. §7704. There are some exceptions to this rule for companies in energy, natural resources, real estate, and some in finance.

BLD Products, LTC v. Technical Plastics of Oregon, LLC

2006 U.S. Dist. LEXIS 89874; 2006 WL 3628062
United States District Court for the District of Oregon, 2006

Facts: Mark Hardie was the sole member of Technical Plastics of Oregon, LLC (TPO). He operated the business out of an office in his home. Hardie regularly used TPO's accounts to pay such expenses as landscaping and housecleaning. TPO also paid some of Hardie's personal credit card bills, loan payments on his Ford truck, the expense of constructing a deck on his house, his stepson's college bills, and the cost of family vacations, as well as miscellaneous bills from Wrestler's World, K-Mart, and Mattress World. At the same time, Hardie deposited cash advances from his personal credit cards into the TPO checking account. Hardie did not draw a salary from TPO. When the company filed for bankruptcy, it owed BLD Products approximately $120,000 for goods that it had purchased.

BLD filed suit asking the court to pierce TPO's company veil and hold Hardie personally liable for the organization's debts.

Issues: ***Should the court pierce TPO's company veil? Should Hardie be personally liable for TPO's debts?***

Excerpts from Judge King's Decision: We have characterized that formulation [for piercing a company veil] as a three-part test:

1. The defendant controlled the debtor [company],
2. The defendant engaged in improper conduct, and
3. As a result of that improper conduct plaintiff was unable to collect on a debt against the insolvent [company].

There is no issue that Hardie, as the sole member and manager of TPO, controlled the company. Turning to the second prong of the test, there is substantial evidence of improper conduct, particularly in the nature of commingling of assets and a general disregard of TPO's LLC form and status as a separate legal entity. Hardie frequently and in significant amounts paid his personal expenses from the TPO business account. The amounts are well beyond small dips into petty cash. There is inadequate documentation about how funds flowed between Hardie, as an individual, and TPO. I realize that Hardie elected to be paid in a manner other than by a regular salary but that does not excuse the lack of documentation. Hardie treated TPO and its assets as his personal funds.

That leaves the third prong of the test, whether Hardie's improper conduct resulted in BLD being unable to collect on its approximately $120,000 debt. I cannot determine as a matter of law that the inability to pay the entire $120,000 debt was due to Hardie's improper conduct over the years. Consequently, I grant partial summary judgment that BLD is entitled to pierce the [company] veil, making Hardie personally liable, but that the amount for which Hardie is personally liable will have to be determined by the jury.

31-3h Legal Uncertainty

As we have observed, LLCs are a relatively new form of organization. This newness inevitably causes legal uncertainty. As if to emphasize this point, a Delaware court recently decided that a court can, if necessary to avoid an unfair result, overrule both the state LLC statute and any operating agreement.[11] Members of an LLC may find themselves in the unhappy position of litigating issues of law which, although well established for corporations, are not yet clear for LLCs.

---

[11]In re Carlisle Etcetera LLC, 114 A.3d 592 (Del. Ch. 2015).

31-3i Choices: LLC versus Corporation

When starting a business, which form makes the most sense—LLC or corporation? The tax status of an LLC is a major advantage over a corporation. Although an S corporation has the same tax status as an LLC, it also has all the annoying rules about classes of stock and number of shareholders. Once an LLC is established, it is simpler to operate—it does not, for example, have to make annual filings or hold annual meetings. However, the LLC is not right for everyone. If done properly, an LLC is more expensive to set up than a corporation because it needs to have a thoughtfully crafted operating agreement. Also, venture capitalists sometimes prefer to invest in C corporations for three reasons: (1) LLCs involve arcane tax issues; (2) C corporations are easier to merge, sell, or take public; and (3) the law of LLCs is uncertain.

EXAMStrategy

Question: Hortense and Gus are each starting a business. Hortense's business is an internet start-up. Gus will be opening a yarn store. Hortense needs millions of dollars in venture capital and expects to go public soon. Gus has borrowed $10,000 from his girlfriend, which he hopes to pay back soon. Should either of these businesses organize as an LLC?

Strategy: Sole proprietorships may be best for businesses without substantial capital needs and without significant liability issues. Corporations are best for businesses that will need substantial outside capital and expect to go public quickly.

Result: An LLC is not the best choice for either of these businesses. Venture capitalists will insist that Hortense's business be a corporation, especially if it is going public soon. A yarn store has few liability issues, and Gus can always buy insurance. Furthermore, he does not expect to have any outside investors. Hence, a sole proprietorship would be more appropriate for Gus's business.

31-4 SOCIAL ENTERPRISES

Well more than half the states now offer charters for some type of socially conscious organization, collectively referred to as **social enterprises**. The most common forms of these organizations are benefit corporations and low-profit limited liability companies (L3Cs). **Social enterprises pledge to behave in a socially responsible manner, even as they pursue profits. (Thus, they are *not* nonprofits.) Their focus is on the triple bottom line: "people, planet, and profits."** In other words, they must create value for some combination of their stakeholders (employees, suppliers, customers, creditors), their community, the environment, and their investors. Such a company is not required to maximize shareholder returns but may instead trade off some profitability in the interests of social responsibility.

Social enterprises
These organizations pledge to behave in a socially responsible manner even as they pursue profits.

To comply with the Model Benefit Corporation Act, an organization must:

- State in its charter that it is a benefit corporation,
- Obtain approval of its charter from two-thirds of its shareholders,

Ed Endicott/Alamy Stock Photo

What kind of tough decisions might a social enterprise, such as Patagonia, face that another company might not?

- Measure its social benefit using a standard set by an objective third party, and
- Prepare an annual benefit report assessing its performance in creating a public benefit.

Businesses that have taken advantage of these new laws include Etsy, Method Products, Patagonia, and Warby Parker. Internationally, there are over 1,000 social benefit organizations in 33 countries. However, most of these organizations are relatively small, with fewer than 50 employees.

31-5 GENERAL PARTNERSHIPS

Partnership
An unincorporated association of two or more co-owners who operate a business for profit

General partner
One of the owners of a general partnership

A **partnership** is an unincorporated association of two or more co-owners who operate a business for profit.[12] Each co-owner is called a **general partner**.

31-5a Tax Status

Partnerships are flow-through entities: The partnership itself does not pay income tax; instead the profits pass through to the partners, who report it on their personal returns.

12Uniform Partnership Act (UPA) §6(1).

31-5b Liability

Each partner is personally liable for the debts of the enterprise whether or not he caused them. Thus, a partner is liable for any injury that another partner or an employee causes while on partnership business as well as for any contract signed on behalf of the partnership.

31-5c Formation

Given the liability disadvantage, why does anyone do business as a general partnership? The short answer is that very few businesses deliberately choose to be a general partnership. They are more likely to drift into it unknowingly, because **a partnership is easy to form.** Ideally, a partnership should have a written agreement, but it is perfectly legal without one. In fact, nothing is required in the way of forms or filings or agreements. If two or more people do business together, sharing management, profits, and losses, they have a partnership, whether they know it or not, and are subject to all the rules of partnership law. A partnership is the default option for people who do not know better. Luckily, now you do.

A partnership is the default option for people who do not know better.

31-5d Management

In the absence of a partnership agreement that provides otherwise, all partners in a firm have an equal right to share in management. For this reason, smaller partnerships make more sense than larger ones. When two sisters-in-law form a small accounting firm, they can easily discuss business issues—from hiring a new associate to choosing a printer. But if a partnership had 1,000 accountants speaking four different languages on three continents, consultation and agreement would be difficult.

31-5e Raising Capital

Financing a partnership may be difficult because the firm cannot sell shares as a corporation does. **The capital needs of the partnership must be provided by contributions from partners or by borrowing.**

31-5f Transfer of Ownership

A partner cannot sell his share of the organization without the permission of the other partners. He can only transfer the *value* of his partnership interest, not the interest itself. He cannot, for example, transfer the right to participate in firm management or vote on firm matters. Evan's mother is a partner in the McBain Consulting firm. After her death, he goes to her office to take over her job and her partnership. But her partners tell him that although he can inherit the *value* of her partnership, he has no right to be a partner. He is out on the sidewalk within the hour. The partners have promised him a check in the mail.

31-5g Dissociation

When a partner leaves (whether voluntarily or by expulsion, death, or bankruptcy), that event is called a **dissociation**. A dissociation is a fork in the road: The partnership can either buy out the departing partner(s) and continue in business or wind up the business and terminate the partnership.

Dissociation
When a partner leaves a partnership

31-6 LIMITED LIABILITY PARTNERSHIPS

A limited liability partnership (LLP) offers the limited liability of a corporation and the tax status of a flow-through organization. Partners are not liable for the debts of the partnership but, naturally, they are liable for their own misdeeds.[13] (Note that an LLP has no general partners, only limited ones.[14])

To form an LLP, the partners must file a statement of qualification with state officials. LLPs must also file annual reports. It is absolutely crucial to comply with all the technicalities of the statute. Otherwise, partners lose protection against personal liability. Note the sad result for Michael Gaus and John West, who formed a Texas LLP. Unfortunately, they did not renew the LLP registration each year, as the statute required. After the registration had expired, the partnership entered into a lease. When the partners ultimately stopped paying rent and abandoned the premises, they both were held personally liable for the rent. As the court pointed out, the statute does not contain a "substantial compliance" section, nor does it contain a grace period for filing a renewal application.[15] "Close" only counts in horseshoes and hand grenades, not in LLPs.

Why would a business elect to be an LLP rather than an LLC? In some states, professionals such as lawyers and accountants are not permitted to operate as an LLC; the LLP form is their only option other than a general partnership. And sometimes lawyers just like to maintain the tradition of operating as a partnership, even if in a more modern version.

31-7 PROFESSIONAL CORPORATIONS

Professional corporations (PCs) are mostly a legacy form of organization—few businesses would now elect to be a PC. But there are still many PCs in existence because, in the past, PCs were the only option available to professionals (such as lawyers and doctors) other than a general partnership.

PCs offer the limited liability of a regular corporation. If a member of a PC commits malpractice, the corporation's assets are at risk, but not the personal assets of the innocent members. If Drs. Sharp, Payne, and Graves form a *partnership*, all the partners will be personally liable when Dr. Payne accidentally leaves her scalpel inside a patient. If the three doctors have formed a *PC* instead, Dr. Payne's Aspen condo and the assets of the PC will be at risk, but not the personal assets of the two other doctors.

PCs have some limitations:

- **All shareholders of the corporation must be members of the same profession.** For Sharp, Payne, & Graves, PC, that means all shareholders must be licensed physicians. Other valued employees cannot own stock.
- Like other corporations, **the required legal technicalities for forming and maintaining a PC are expensive and time consuming.**
- **Tax issues are much more complicated** than for an LLC or LLP.

---

13 UPA §306(c).

14 Do not be confused with limited partnerships, which we do not cover in this book because they are generally only used to hold sophisticated investments. In a limited partnership, the limited partners have little control and no personal liability. There is at least one general partner who controls the organization and is personally liable.

15 Apcar Inv. Partners VI, Ltd. v. Gaus, 161 S.W.3d 137 (Tex. App. 2005).

31-8 JOINT VENTURES

A **joint venture** is a partnership for a limited purpose. **It is not a legal entity, so all tax liability is shared among the participants in the venture. Similarly, these participants also share any liability that arises out of the joint venture's activities.** Imax Corp. decided to form a joint venture with cinema operators—it supplied its big screens in return for a share of the box office revenue. IMAX and the cinema operators did not merge; they simply worked together. Each organization retained its own identity. IMAX would be liable if the electrician who installed the IMAX screen was not paid, but it would not be liable to the cinema's popcorn supplier because providing food was not part of the joint venture.

Joint venture
A partnership for a limited purpose

31-9 FRANCHISES

This chapter has presented an overview of the various forms of organization. Franchises are not, strictly speaking, a separate form of organization. They are included here because they represent an important option for entrepreneurs. The United States has more than three-quarters of a million franchised establishments, which employ more than 9 million people. Well-known franchises include Subway, McDonald's, and The UPS Store. Most franchisors and franchisees are corporations or LLCs, although some franchisees are sole proprietorships.

31-9a Advantages of a Franchise

Owning a Business

In theory, buying a franchise combines the best of all worlds—a franchisee gets to be his own boss *and* he acquires an established business with all the kinks worked out. As the International Franchise Association puts it, "Owning a franchise allows you to go into business for yourself, but not by yourself." Subject to franchisor approval, franchisees are free to choose which franchise to buy, where to locate it, and how to staff it.

Support

The franchisor helps get the business up and running quickly, offers ongoing training and support, and invests money in keeping the brand relevant and successful. The McDonald's operations manual explains everything from how to set the temperature controls on the stove, to the number of seconds that fries must cook, to the length of time they can be held in the rack before being discarded. An established name like McDonald's or Subway brings customers through the door. And landlords may be more willing to rent to the owner of a franchise.

Franchisees can also help one another. By acting collectively, they can obtain better prices on everything from ingredients to insurance.

31-9b The Drawbacks of a Franchise

Control

Franchisees sometimes complain that franchisor control is too tight—tips on cooking fries might be appreciated, but rules on how often to sweep the floor are not. Sometimes franchisors, in their zeal to maintain standards, prohibit innovation that appeals to regional tastes. Just because spicy biscuits are not popular in New England does not mean they should be off the menu in the South. Still, innovation is possible: one McDonald's franchisee famously invented the Big Mac, which subsequently spread worldwide.

Franchisors may, however, need to rethink their level of control if they want to avoid liability for the acts of franchisees. The National Labor Relations Board (NLRB) has alleged that because McDonald's exercised substantial control over its franchisees, it was a "joint employer" and therefore liable for its franchisees' violations of the National Labor Relations Act (NLRA).[16] (The NLRA, which is covered in Chapter 29, protects employees' right to organize and unionize.) New York's Attorney General has made similar allegations against Domino's Pizza. Also, a federal court in California ruled that McDonald's might be liable to workers if they reasonably *believed* that the fast-food chain was their employer.[17] McDonald's paid $3.75 million to settle this case. This recent legal trend has forced franchisors to act: Many have reduced their control to avoid liability and some have persuaded their state legislatures to pass laws limiting this type of liability.

Cost

Franchisees face various expenses:

- **Initial purchase.** A franchise can be very costly to acquire, anywhere from several thousand dollars to many millions. That fee is usually payable up front, whether or not a McMuffin is ever sold.
- **Royalty fee.** On top of the upfront fee, franchisees also typically pay a royalty fee that is a percentage of gross sales revenues, not profit. Sometimes the fee seems to eat up all the profits.
- **Supplies.** Franchisees are often required to buy supplies from headquarters or an approved supplier. In theory, the franchisors can purchase hamburger meat and paper plates more cheaply in bulk and also maintain quality controls. On the other hand, the franchisees are a captive audience, and they sometimes allege that headquarters has little incentive to keep prices low. Indeed, some franchisors make most of their profit from the products they sell to their store owners. Often, the franchise agreement permits the company to change the terms of the agreement at any time by raising fees or expenses.
- **Joint advertising.** Franchisees may be required to contribute to expensive "co-op advertising" that benefits all the outlets nationally or in a particular region.
- **System standards.** To keep the brand image fresh and uniform, franchisees are periodically required to renovate their storefronts and update their computer and payment systems. At their own expense, of course.

The sandwich franchise Quiznos spent $95 million to settle litigation with potential franchisees who claimed that the company took their fees without finding a store location for them. Some existing store owners complained that the company forced them to buy everything (including soap in the bathrooms and the piped-in music) from the company at inflated prices. Of course, many franchised businesses operate smoothly and have provided their owners with substantial income and even wealth.

31-9c Legal Requirements

Franchise Disclosure Document (FDD)
A disclosure document that a franchisor must deliver to a potential purchaser

All franchisors must comply with the Federal Trade Commission's (FTC) Franchise Rule. In addition, some states also impose their own requirements. Under FTC rules, a franchisor must deliver to a potential purchaser a **Franchise Disclosure Document (FDD)** at least 14 calendar days before any contract is signed or money is paid. **The FDD must provide information on:**

- The history of the franchisor and its key executives
- Litigation with franchisees

---

[16] McDonald's USA, LLC, 2016 NLRB LEXIS 209 (N.L.R.B. Mar. 17, 2016).
[17] Ochoa v. McDonald's Corp., 133 F. Supp. 3d 1228 (N.D. Cal. 2015).

- Bankruptcy filings by the company and its officers and directors
- Costs to buy and operate a franchise
- Restrictions, if any, on suppliers, products, and customers
- Territory—any limitations (in either the real or virtual worlds) on where the franchisee can sell or any restrictions on other franchisees selling in the same territory
- Business continuity—under what circumstances the franchisor can terminate the franchisee and the franchisee's rights to renew or sell the franchise
- Franchisor's training program
- Required advertising expenses
- A list of current franchisees and those that have left in the prior three years (A significant number of departures may be a bad sign.)
- A report on prior owners of stores that the franchisor has reacquired
- Earnings information is not required; but if disclosed, the franchisor must reveal the basis for this information
- Audited financials for the franchisor
- A sample set of the contracts that a franchisee is expected to sign

The purpose of the FDD is to ensure that the franchisor discloses all material facts. It is not a guarantee of quality because the FTC does not investigate to make sure that the information is accurate or the business idea sound. After the fact, if the FTC discovers the franchisor has violated the rules, it may sue on the franchisee's behalf.

The franchisee does not have the right to bring suit personally against someone who violates FTC franchise rules, but it may be able to sue under state law. Many state regulators can also bring enforcement actions against those who violate state franchise laws.

Suppose you obtain an FDD for "Shrinking Cats," a franchise that offers psychiatric services for neurotic felines. The company has lost money on all the outlets it operates itself; it has sold only three franchises, two of which have gone out of business; and all the required contracts are ridiculously favorable to the franchisor. Nevertheless, the FTC will still permit sales as long as the franchisor discloses all the information required in the FDD.

Many states have laws governing the franchisor-franchisee relationship after the purchase. These laws vary by state, but are typically on the side of franchisees. They might, for example, limit the circumstances under which a franchisee can be terminated. California has recently amended its law to prohibit termination unless the franchisee is in substantial violation of the franchise agreement. A single minor infraction is not sufficient.

John Lund/Photolibrary/Getty Images

Sometimes my human refuses to scratch my ears.

A number of states are considering legislation that would grant franchisees more power. Some of these statutes would allow franchisees to set their own prices on the products they sell and renew their franchise contracts without a fee increase. However, none of these bills has passed into law and their success is uncertain.

As the following case illustrates, under current law, the franchisor has much of the power in a franchise relationship.

National Franchisee Association v. Burger King Corporation

2010 U.S. Dist. LEXIS 123065; 2010 WL 4811912
United States District Court for the Southern District of Florida, 2010

Facts: The Burger King Corporation would not allow franchisees to have it their way. Instead, Burger King forced them to sell the double-cheeseburger (DCB) and, later, the Buck Double (the DCB minus one slice of cheese) for no more than $1.00. Franchisees alleged that, because this price was below their cost, they were losing money on every DCB they sold. The National Franchisee Association (NFA), to which 75 percent of Burger King's individual franchisees belonged, filed suit alleging that (1) Burger King did not have the right to set maximum prices and (2) that even if Burger King had such a right, it had violated its obligation under the franchise agreement to act in good faith.

The court dismissed the first claim because the franchise agreement unambiguously permitted Burger King to set whatever prices it wanted. But the court allowed the NFA to proceed with the second claim. Burger King filed a motion to dismiss.

Issue: ***Was Burger King acting in bad faith when it forced franchisees to sell items below cost?***

Excerpts from Judge Moore's Decision: [B]ad faith involves a subterfuge or evasion of contractual duties. [T]here are at least two ways a plaintiff can go about raising a claim of bad faith. Plaintiffs can allege facts identifying defendant's improper ulterior motive(s). For example, if a franchisee had evidence that a franchisor had a secret agenda to take over the franchise and operate it as a company-owned business, and was deliberately setting prices to weaken the targeted franchisee, such a plaintiff could raise a claim of bad faith by alleging the existence of that plan.

It is more likely, however, that plaintiffs will lack direct evidence of dishonesty. In these cases, plaintiffs must allege some facts tending to show that no reasonable person could have thought that the steps taken by the defendant were a reasonable means of carrying out the contract's defined purposes. If no reasonable person would have exercised discretion as defendant had, the natural inference is that defendant must have had some hidden improper motive.

[T]he magnitude of the injury claimed by plaintiff is of central importance. [A]n inference of bad faith may arise when the defendant exercises discretion in such a manner as to effectively destroy whatever benefits the plaintiff could have reasonably expected under the contract. The logic is that the measure with such severe results could not have been within the contemplation of the parties.

[N]one of the facts alleged by plaintiffs are sufficient to support a claim of bad faith. Plaintiffs rely principally on their allegation that franchisees could not produce and sell DCB or Buck Doubles at a cost less than $1.00, and therefore that franchisees suffer a loss on each of these items sold. There are a variety of legitimate reasons why a firm selling multiple products may choose to set the price of a single product below cost. Among other things, such a strategy might help build goodwill and customer loyalty, hold or shift customer traffic away from competitors, or serve as loss leaders to generate increased sales on other higher margin products.

The issue is not whether such a strategy was wise or ultimately successful or mistaken. In the absence of some other evidence of improper motive, the question is whether it was so irrational and capricious that no reasonable person would have made such a decision. There is nothing about the pricing decision that suggests Burger King was doing anything other than seeking to promote the performance of its franchisees. Nothing about this action suggests bad faith.

For the foregoing reasons, it is ORDERED AND ADJUDGED that Defendant's Motion to Dismiss is GRANTED.

CHAPTER CONCLUSION

The process of starting a business is immensely time consuming. Eighteen-hour days are the norm. Not surprisingly, entrepreneurs are sometimes reluctant to spend their valuable time on legal issues that, after all, do not contribute directly to the bottom line. No customer buys more tacos because the franchise is a limited liability company instead of a corporation. Wise entrepreneurs know, however, that careful attention to legal issues is an essential component of success. The form of organization affects everything from taxes to liability to management control. The idea for the business may come first, but legal considerations should occupy a close second place.

EXAM REVIEW

	Separate Taxable Entity	Personal Liability for Owners	Ease of Formation	Transferable Interests (Easily Bought and Sold)	Perpetual Existence	Other Features
Sole Proprietorship	No	Yes	Very easy	No, can only sell entire business	No	
Corporation	Yes	No	Difficult	Yes	Yes	
Close Corporation	Yes, for C corp; No, for S corp	No	Difficult	Transfer restrictions	Yes	Protection of minority shareholders. No board of directors is required.
S Corporation	No	No	Difficult	Transfer restrictions	Yes	Only 100 shareholders. Only one class of stock. All shareholders must agree to S status and must be citizens or residents of the United States. Partnerships and corporations cannot be shareholders.
Limited Liability Company	No	No	Charter is easy, but should have thoughtful operating agreement.	Yes, if the operating agreement permits	Varies by state, but generally, yes	Becomes taxable entity if it goes public
General Partnership	No	Yes	Easy	No	Depends on the remaining partners	
Limited Liability Partnership	No	No	Difficult	No	Depends on the partnership agreement	

(continued)

	Separate Taxable Entity	Personal Liability for Owners	Ease of Formation	Transferable Interests (Easily Bought and Sold)	Perpetual Existence	Other Features
Professional Corporation	Yes	No	Difficult	Shareholders must all be members of same profession.	Yes, as long as it has shareholders	Complex tax issues
Joint Venture	No	Yes	Easy	No	No	Partnership for a limited purpose
Franchise	All these issues depend on the form of organization chosen by participants.					Established business. Name recognition. Management assistance. Loss of control. Fees may be high.

MULTIPLE-CHOICE QUESTIONS

1. A sole proprietorship _______________.
   (a) must file a tax return
   (b) requires no formal steps for its creation
   (c) must register with the secretary of state
   (d) may sell stock
   (e) provides limited liability to the owner

EXAMStrategy

2. **CPA QUESTION** Assuming all other requirements are met, a corporation may elect to be treated as an S corporation under the Internal Revenue Code if it has _______________.
   (a) both common and preferred stockholders
   (b) a partnership as a stockholder
   (c) 100 or fewer stockholders
   (d) the consent of a majority of the stockholders

   Strategy: Review the list of requirements for an S corporation. (See the "Result" at the end of this Multiple-Choice Questions section.)

3. A limited liability company _______________.
   (a) is regulated by a well-established body of law
   (b) pays taxes on its income
   (c) cannot have members that are corporations
   (d) is a form of organization favored by venture capitalists
   (e) can have an oral operating agreement

4. **CPA QUESTION** A joint venture is a(n) ____________.
   (a) association limited to no more than two persons in business for profit
   (b) enterprise of numerous co-owners in a nonprofit undertaking
   (c) corporate enterprise for a single undertaking of limited duration
   (d) association of persons engaged as co-owners in a single undertaking for profit
5. A limited liability partnership ____________.
   (a) protects partners from liability for their own misdeeds
   (b) protects the partners from liability for the debts of the partnership
   (c) must pay taxes on its income
   (d) both A and B
   (e) A, B, and C are all correct.

RESULT

2. Result: An S corporation can have only one class of stock. A partnership cannot be a stockholder, and all the shareholders must consent to S corporation status. (c) is the correct answer.

CASE QUESTIONS

EXAMStrategy

1. **Question:** Alan Dershowitz, a law professor famous for his prominent clients, joined with other lawyers to open a kosher delicatessen, Maven's Court. Dershowitz met with greater success at the bar than in the kitchen—the deli failed after barely a year in business. One supplier sued for unpaid bills. What form of organization would have been the best choice for Maven's Court?

   Strategy: A sole proprietorship would not have worked because there was more than one owner. A partnership would have been a disaster because of unlimited liability. They could have met all the requirements of an S corporation or an LLC. (See the "Result" at the end of this Case Questions section.)

2. Ned and Sarah formed an LLC to buy and renovate apartment buildings. They did not sign an operating agreement but they orally agreed that they would dissolve the LLC if they could not get along. The two owners argued repeatedly and Ned refused to meet with Sarah, although he was willing to take her phone calls. Ned continued to work on the renovation that was then underway. Sarah asked a court to dissolve the LLC. Under state law, an LLC without an operating agreement could only be dissolved if (1) the management of the entity is unwilling to reasonably promote the stated purpose of the entity or (2) continuing the entity is financially unfeasible. What result in Sarah's lawsuit? What is the moral of this story?

3. According to the company's website, "d.light is a global leader in delivering affordable solar-powered solutions designed for the two billion people in the developing world without access to reliable energy." It is a for-profit enterprise. What form of organization makes the most sense for this business. Why?

EXAMStrategy

4. **Question:** Huma and Zuma want to start Spring High, a business that would take high school students on safe, educational trips during spring break. Eventually, they hope to seek venture capital money and expand the business nationally. After reading up on the legal issues online, Huma thinks Spring High should be a close corporation, while Zuma proposes that it be a S corporation. Neither thinks they should choose an LLC. Who is right?

   Strategy: At the moment, they could qualify as a close corporation because they only have two shareholders. As long as neither of them is a nonresident alien, Spring High could also be an S corporation. Although Spring High could be an LLC, it is not a form favored by venture capitalists. (See the "Result" at the end of this Case Questions section.)

5. If you were to look online for a description of a professional corporation, you might find websites stressing that, in a PC, shareholders are still responsible for their own wrongdoing. For example: "In some states, these professionals can form a corporation, but with the distinction that each professional is still liable for his or her own wrongful professional actions." Why is this statement at best unnecessary and at worst misleading?

RESULTS

1. Result: In this situation, most entrepreneurs would choose an LLC because it would be easier than forming an S corp and registering with the IRS. However, they really should have a good operating agreement.

4. Result: They are both right. Spring High should not be an LLC because that would discourage venture capital investment. The enterprise should probably be both a close corporation and an S corp. In some states, they would qualify for close corporation status without having to elect it. In any event, there is little downside to such an election. An S corporation is also a reasonable choice because, for now, it makes sense to limit their tax liability. Should they expand to the point that they no longer meet all the S corp requirements, it would be easy to become a C corporation.

DISCUSSION QUESTIONS

1. Leonard, an attorney, was negligent when he represented Anthony. In settlement of Anthony's malpractice claim, Leonard signed a promissory note for $10,400 on behalf of his law firm, an LLC. When the law firm did not pay, Anthony filed suit against Leonard personally for payment of the note. Is a member personally liable for the debt of an LLC that was caused by his own negligence?

2. Think of a business concept that would be appropriate for each of the following: a sole proprietorship, a corporation, and an LLC.

3. As you will see in Chapter 33, Facebook began life as a corporation, not an LLC. Why did the founder, Mark Zuckerberg, make that decision?

4. Corporations developed to encourage investors to contribute the capital needed to create large-scale manufacturing enterprises. But LLCs are often start-ups or other small businesses. Why do their members deserve limited liability? Is it fair that LLCs do not pay income taxes?

5. **ETHICS** Frank Brown, who is African-American, tried to buy lunch at a McDonald's at the Dadeland Mall in Florida. The manager, Omar Zaveri, not only refused to serve Brown but verbally abused him, used racial slurs, and told all the other employees that he would fire them if they served Brown. This McDonald's was owned by a franchisee. Is McDonald's liable to Brown? Whether or not McDonald's is technically liable, should it pay Brown anyway?

CHAPTER 32

PARTNERSHIPS

You would think that lawyers would know better, but even they can fall into the partnership trap.

After graduating from law school, Raymond Nadel went to work for attorney Morris Starkman. At the beginning, Nadel was clearly an associate, not a partner, but after some years working together, the two men signed an agreement that changed their relationship—although *to what* is not clear. The agreement clarified many important issues (such as Nadel's vacation time), but it failed to resolve the most crucial question: Was Nadel now a partner?

The agreement offered some hints to answering this question, but unfortunately the clues pointed in different directions. On one hand, the contract stated that the firm had "heretofore" been owned solely by Starkman, but now Nadel would have an interest and a right to receive a percentage of its net income. On the other hand, the agreement declared that the firm would continue to be owned and managed solely by Starkman. It characterized Nadel as an independent contractor, but agreed to pay for his benefits.

While Nadel was on vacation, Starkman sent him a letter firing him.

To further complicate the picture, Nadel's name appeared prominently on the firm's signage, letterhead, and advertisements, but not on its checks. In fact, he had no authority to sign checks.

Later, Starkman decided that the firm should become a limited liability company (LLC). The agreement he prepared stated that he would own 99 percent to Nadel's 1 percent—and that Nadel was an employee. Nadel refused to sign the agreement.

The agreement referred to the two men's "excellent relationship"; well, that did not last. While Nadel was on vacation, Starkman sent him a letter firing him and then formed a partnership with another lawyer.

Nadel filed suit, asking the court to determine the reasonable value of his partnership interest.[1] At trial, witnesses testified that Starkman had told them Nadel was his partner and was owed a substantial buyout. The trial judge believed Nadel, while finding Starkman evasive and dishonest. She ruled that the two men had formed a partnership and Nadel was entitled to a payout. Starkman appealed. Had the men been partners?

---

[1]Nadel v. Starkman, 2010 N.J. Super. Unpub. LEXIS 2542 (App.Div. 2010).

As you remember from Chapter 31, a partnership is a flow-through tax entity that does not provide its members with limited liability. Each partner is personally liable for the debts of the partnership and the wrongdoing of any other partner. Because of this liability issue, few people would now actively choose to operate a business as a partnership; better options are available (such as an LLC, LLP, or S corp).

That was not always the case. It used to be that partnerships were important (and, as a result, were featured on the CPA exam) because that was the only form of organization available to some professionals, such as accountants, lawyers, and doctors. But now, such restrictions no longer apply.

Partnership law is, however, relevant because partnerships are still common, largely because they are so easy to form. It can be done by accident. If two or more people own a business for profit, *presto!*, they are partners, unless they actively elect one of the other forms of organization and comply with those other technicalities. A partnership is the default option.

You will see in this chapter that many partnerships involve friends and family working together. This combination makes the disputes that much more bitter and complex. It is bad enough if your business is falling apart, worse when that dispute also taints your personal life. **The moral of this chapter is: Beware of unintentional partnerships. Protect yourself by understanding partnership law.**

What happened to Starkman and Nadel? After six years of litigation, the court ruled that there was no partnership because (1) the agreement stated that Nadel was an independent contractor, (2) it did not grant him the right to make management decisions, (3) he did not share in the firm's losses, and (4) the firm did not file a partnership tax return. Sometimes even lawyers have to learn about the law the hard way.

This chapter focuses on general partnerships (not to be confused with limited liability partnerships). Traditionally, general partnerships were regulated by common law, but a lack of consistency among the states became troublesome as interstate commerce grew. To solve this problem, the National Conference of Commissioners on Uniform State Laws drafted the Uniform Partnership Act (UPA). Most states have now passed the latest revision, so we base our discussion on that version of the act.

Although the UPA has made life easier, common law still plays an important role in regulating partnerships. To some degree, that is always true with statutes because courts are called upon to interpret their provisions. In addition, the UPA directs courts to apply the common law to resolve any issue that it does not cover. Finally, many of the rules in the UPA are so-called **default rules**, meaning that they apply unless the partners reach a different agreement. When partners write their own rules, they sometimes need judicial help to interpret ambiguous provisions.

Default rules
Rules that govern a partnership unless the partners agree otherwise

32-1 CREATING A PARTNERSHIP

Some legal relationships are carefully delineated. By and large, people know whether or not they are married. Similarly, people usually know if they have formed a corporation. Partnerships are trickier, more like living together than getting married. It can be difficult to tell if a live-in relationship—or a partnership—really exists. **The UPA does not *require* partnerships to make a formal filing or prepare a written agreement.** However, the UPA does *permit* a partnership to file a statement with the local secretary of state that contains basic information about the partnership.[2]

[2] UPA §105.

32-1a Is This a Partnership?

How can you tell if you have a partnership? According to the UPA, **the association of two or more persons to carry on as co-owners of a business for profit forms a partnership, whether or not they intend to form a partnership.**[3]

Because human beings (who have never had a business law course) are involved, the circumstances surrounding a disputed partnership are often messy. Then the courts have to do the best they can to sort out the reality of a complicated relationship. **In determining if a partnership exists, the courts consider these factors:**

- **Profit.** To qualify as a partnership, the organization must intend to make a profit. Because charitable businesses do not technically make profits, they cannot be a partnership. When Aaron and Elijah agree to run the annual jamboree at their children's school, they expect to clear $35,000 after expenses, but they are not partners because their fund-raising has a charitable purpose.
- **Sharing profits.** No matter what their arrangement, if two people do not share the profits of their business, they are not partners. *Period.* However, just because they do share in the profits does not necessarily make them partners. In other words, sharing profits is a necessary but not sufficient condition for being partners.
- **Sharing losses.** Although landlords, employees, and even creditors may share in business profits, usually no one other than a partner is willing to share the losses. Sharing losses is strong evidence of a partnership.
- **Management of the business.** If participants are not involved in management, the courts will generally not consider them to be partners.
- **Oral or written agreement.** In a partnership, actions speak louder than words. If the people act like partners, then the law will treat them as such. If they do not act like partners, then nothing they say, orally or in writing, is enough, on its own, to create a partnership. Note, however, that in a close case, referring to themselves as partners may help sway a court, but it is not enough *by itself* to create a partnership.

Now let's apply these rules to a real example. When Nancy Green borrowed money from Joseph DiFebo to make a down payment on four houses, they agreed that they were partners. Although Green bought the properties in her name alone, the two signed this document:

> Nancy R. Green and Joseph A. DiFebo are equal partners in the following Wilmington, Delaware, properties: 807 Pine Street, 427 East 3rd St., 611 East 7th Street, 613 East 7th Street.
>
> On the death of Nancy R. Green, her half-interest is left to her daughters, Kelly R. Green and Stacy R. Green. On the death of Joseph A. DiFebo, his half-interest is left to his daughters, Amy DiFebo and Beth Durham.
>
> If Nancy R. Green survives Joseph A. DiFebo, she makes all decisions on the above properties.

DiFebo did some repair work on the buildings but never asked Green for a share of the rentals. When the city condemned one of the properties, Green refused to give DiFebo half the proceeds. DiFebo testified that, in his mind, the money he transferred to Green established a partnership between them. Green testified that at no time did she consider their arrangement to be a partnership.

The court was less concerned about what the *agreement said* than how the *parties acted.* Although they had called themselves "equal partners," they did not share profits. DiFebo said he had not taken his share of the profits because he did not want his wife to find out

---

[3]UPA §202(a).

about his arrangements (financial and otherwise) with Green. Ruling that their contract was a will, not a partnership agreement, the court denied DiFebo's claim.[4]

In the following case, two men made many mistakes, not the least of which was failing to return an important phone call. Were they partners? You be the judge.

You Be the Judge

Herman v. Pickell & Kaleidoscope Books

2016 Mich. App. LEXIS 700; 2016 WL 1445385
Michigan Court of Appeals, 2016

Facts: Jeffrey Pickell was the sole proprietor of Kaleidoscope Books in Ann Arbor, Michigan. While Martin Herman's daughter was a student at the University of Michigan, he became a customer of the store. At some point, the two men agreed that Herman would give Pickell $50,000.

That seems to be the last time they agreed on anything. Herman believed that the $50,000 was the purchase price for a 10 percent share of the business, while Pickell claimed that the money was a loan, and, furthermore, even if he and Herman had been in a partnership, they had subsequently dissolved it. Correspondence from their early relationship tells a story:

Letter No. 1: When Herman made the investment, Pickell wrote to Herman stating that Herman was now a 10 percent silent partner in the business. This meant he was entitled to 10 percent of the net earnings, and, upon any sale of the business, would receive 10 percent of the value of the assets. Furthermore, although Herman was not responsible for any business decisions, Pickell would seek his advice because of his business experience.

Letter No. 2: Four months later, Pickell reiterated that Herman owned 10 percent of the business until the $50,000 loan was completely repaid. Upon repayment, the two would dissolve the partnership.

Letter No. 3: In another five months, Herman wrote to Pickell referring to the $50,000 as both an "investment" and a "loan." He mentioned that he would hold his "10% interest in Kaleidoscope until full payment was received."

Pickell ultimately repaid Herman about $20,000, but he never paid Herman a share of the profits, claiming there were none. (In fact, the business showed a profit of about $15,000 a year.) Pickell did allow Herman to take his choice of merchandise from the store. Herman characterized these items as small gifts with a total value of less than $100, but Pickell claimed that Herman loaded "box after box" of merchandise into a minivan over an eight-hour period.

Then, for 12 years, the parties had no contact. When Herman finally sought repayment, Pickell did not return his phone call. Herman then sued Pickell for his share of the partnership and its profits, alleging that he was a 10 percent owner.

You Be the Judge: *Did Pickell and Herman have a partnership? Was Herman entitled to a share of the profits?*

Argument for Herman: As stated in Letter No. 1, Herman paid $50,000 for a 10 percent interest in the partnership, with a right to a share of the profits. That letter also said that he would contribute his business expertise, that is, he would be involved in management of the business.

Letters No. 2 and 3 provided that Pickell could repurchase Herman's partnership interest by repaying the full $50,000. But Pickell never repaid the total amount. Even if Herman did actually take a minivan full of merchandise (which he denies), that did not constitute repayment of the $30,000 he was owed. If Pickell had intended the merchandise to be repayment of the loan, he should have obtained a written receipt.

Argument for Pickell: To be a partnership, both parties have to be involved in the management of the business. Letter No. 1 explicitly states that Herman was not responsible for business decisions. Furthermore, the two men did not speak for 12 years. How could Herman be a partner if he had no involvement for more than a decade?

Yes, Herman loaned Pickell money but Pickell repaid the amount, partly in cash and partly by allowing Herman to take a whole minivan full of merchandise. Why else would Pickell have allowed Herman to take all these items?

4Green v. Schagrin, 1989 Del. Super. LEXIS 295, 1989 WL 89576 (Del. Super. Ct. 1989).

32-1b Partnership by Estoppel

Partnership by estoppel
Two parties incur the liability of a partnership without actually being partners.

In the *Herman* case and the opening scenario, the plaintiffs wanted to be partners so that they could share in the profits of the enterprise. **Partnership by estoppel** is concerned with the opposite situation—a person does not want to be considered a partner because he wishes to avoid the *liability* of the partnership. The twist is that **partnership by estoppel applies in situations where the participants are *not*, in fact, partners but are held to be liable as if they were. Partnership by estoppel applies if:**

- **Participants tell other people that they are partners (even though they are not)**, or they allow other people to say, without contradiction, that they are partners;
- **A third party relies on this assertion**; and
- **The third party suffers harm.**

Dr. William Martin was held liable under a theory of partnership by estoppel because he told a patient that he and Dr. John Maceluch were partners (although they were not), the patient relied on this statement and made appointments to see Dr. Maceluch, and she was harmed by Dr. Maceluch's malpractice. He refused to come to the hospital when she was in labor, and as a result, her child was born with brain damage. Although Dr. Martin was out of the country at the time, he was also liable.[5]

Dr. Martin could have avoided this problem by being very careful *not* to refer to Dr. Maceluch as his partner. Presumably, he used the word "partner" to reassure the patient. Instead of "partner," he could have said "colleague," "associate," or "assistant." Dr. Martin should also have been careful to correct anyone who referred to Dr. Maceluch as his partner.

Note that, even though the court in the opening scenario determined that Nadel and Starkman were *not* partners, Nadel could still be liable to a third party who had been harmed by the firm if Starkman had told that person that Nadel was a partner. In short, Nadel could end up with all of the downside but none of the upside of being a partner.

32-2 THE PARTNERSHIP AND OUTSIDERS

Under the UPA, **the rules governing the liability of the partnership to outsiders are mandatory.** Partners may not change them. **In contrast, many of the rules governing the relationship *among* partners are *default* provisions**, meaning that the partners can change these rules if they desire.[6]

In the relationship between the partnership and outsiders, two questions arise: When is the partnership liable to outsiders? If the partnership is liable, who must pay the debt?

32-2a Liability of the Partnership to Outsiders

Authority

Partnership liability is based on the rules of agency law, discussed in Chapter 28. **Every partner is an agent for the partnership. Therefore, the partnership is liable if a partner acts with one of these three types of authority:**

[5] Haught v. Maceluch, 681 F2d 290 (5th Cir. 1982).
[6] The exceptions are listed in UPA §103.

- **Actual authority**. A partnership is liable for any act of a partner that it authorized. Suppose Tamika and Daniel have formed the TD partnership to buy and sell rare books. They decide that they would be willing to pay up to $100,000 for a first edition of *The Adventures of Tom Sawyer* by Mark Twain. When Daniel agrees to pay $90,000 to a seller who offers such a book, the partnership is liable.
- **Implied authority**. A partnership is liable for any act of a partner that is reasonably necessary to carry out an authorized transaction. If Daniel spends $20 to take a taxi to meet a potential book seller, the partnership must reimburse him.
- **Apparent authority**. A partnership is liable for an *unauthorized* act of a partner if the partner *appears* to be conducting the business of the partnership or even business of the same type. Without Daniel's knowledge, Tamika promises to pay a large sum for Jane's classic record collection. Jane is a regular customer of the TD partnership and simply assumes that Tamika has authority to act. The TD partnership is liable because buying used LPs is the same kind of business as buying used books.

This issue frequently arises when a partnership breaks up but fails to notify customers. If Tamika and Daniel terminate their partnership but do not tell Jane, both of the former partners are liable on any deal Tamika enters into with Jane, as long as the transaction reasonably relates to the TD business.

Ratification

As with every agency relationship, partners can ratify unauthorized acts. **If the partnership accepts the benefit of the unauthorized transaction or fails to repudiate it, the partnership has ratified it**. Once ratified, these actions are as valid as if they had been authorized from the beginning. Thus, Daniel exceeds his authority when he offers Matthew $10,000 for any Stephen King first edition. Tamika is outraged, but she never tells Matthew that the deal is no good. After scouring the city, Matthew finds a first edition of *Misery*. The partnership must pay for the book, no matter how miserable it makes Tamika.

Information

As agent, a partner has a duty to pass on all relevant information to the partnership. Whether or not a partner actually fulfills this obligation, the partnership is treated as if it had been notified. Under the UPA, **whatever one partner knows, the partnership is deemed to know**. TD's storefront lease requires the landlord to give 90 days' notice if he does not want to renew. The landlord does give notice to Tamika, but she forgets to tell Daniel. The notice is nonetheless valid, and the landlord has every right to evict the partnership. If someone is going to suffer harm because of Tamika's mistake, in all fairness, it should be the partnership, which had the bad judgment to take on an unreliable partner.

Tort Liability

A partnership is responsible for the intentional and negligent torts of a partner that occur in the ordinary course of the partnership's business or with the actual authority of the partners. When Daniel tells a customer that a book is a valuable first edition when he knows that it is worthless, the partnership is liable for this intentional misrepresentation because it occurred in the ordinary course of the partnership's business. But if Daniel gets in a fight in a bar on Saturday night, the partnership is not liable because that had nothing to do with the partnership's business.

32-2b Paying the Debts of the Partnership

The basic rule of partnership liability is simply stated: **All partners are personally liable for all debts of the partnership.** All of a partner's assets are at risk. This rule applies whether or not the individual partner was in any way responsible for the debts. Thus, when the accounting firm Laventhol & Horwath went bankrupt, the partners were personally liable, and some had to sell their houses to pay the partnership's debts.

Joint and Several Liability

Joint and several liability
The partnership and the partners are all individually liable for the full amount of the debt, but the creditor cannot collect more than the total amount he is owed.

Partners have joint and several liability for partnership obligations. Joint and several liability means that a creditor can sue the partnership and the partners together, or in separate lawsuits, or in any combination. The partnership and the partners are all individually liable for the full amount of the debt, but the creditor cannot keep collecting after he has already received the total amount owed. **Also note that creditors cannot go after an individual partner's assets until all the partnership's assets are exhausted.**[7]

Letitia, one of the world's wealthiest people, enters into a partnership with penniless Harry to drill for oil on her land. While driving on partnership business, Harry crashes into Gus, seriously injuring him. Gus can sue any combination of the partnership, Letitia, and Harry for the full amount, even though Letitia was 2,000 miles away on her Caribbean island when the accident occurred and she had many times cautioned Harry to drive carefully. However, if Gus obtains a judgment against Letitia, he cannot recover against her while the partnership still has assets. So, for all practical purposes, he must try to collect first against the partnership. If the partnership is bankrupt and he manages to collect the full amount from Letitia, he cannot then try to recover against Harry. (As we will see in a minute, Letitia could, in theory, recover from Harry some portion of what she paid Gus, but Harry is penniless, so good luck.)

Letitia was not wild about Harry's behavior, so she had insisted that he agree in writing to share all liabilities of the partnership 50/50. Unfortunately for Letitia, the liability rule for outsiders is *mandatory*, not a default provision, so her agreement with Harry has absolutely no impact on the rights of Gus or any other creditor. He can still recover from Letitia for all debts of the partnership and she can always try to recover from Harry.

Liability of Incoming Partners

A partner is personally liable only for obligations the partnership incurred while he was a partner. His liability for debts incurred before he became partner is limited to his investment in the partnership.[8] Does this rule make sense? Why should an incoming partner be liable in any way for debts the partnership incurred before he became a partner?

These issues haunted the investment bank Goldman Sachs when Englishman Robert Maxwell drowned. Long known as an international wheeler-dealer, Maxwell stole money from his companies' pension plans to pay for the purchase of newspapers and publishing houses around the world. He drowned after falling—or jumping—over the side of his yacht late one evening. After his death, investigators discovered that more than $1 billion was missing from his various enterprises. The looted pension plans sued Goldman, which settled the lawsuits for $250 million.

He drowned after falling—or jumping—over the side of his yacht late one evening.

That was the simple part. The more complicated issue was how to divide this liability among the Goldman partners. Current partners argued that the liability should be borne by those who were Goldman partners when the Maxwell transactions occurred. But the ex-partners balked at having to pay as much as $4 million apiece for a settlement they had not agreed to or even had a chance to vote on.

---

[7]UPA §307.
[8]UPA §306.

In the end, Goldman's ex-partners were personally liable for debts incurred while they were members of the firm. However, current partners were also liable, up to the amount of their investment in the partnership, for debts incurred even before they joined.

EXAMStrategy

Question: Mark and Shania are students who also have a business on the side selling baskets of fruit and vegetables that are cut to look like flowers. They advertise that all ingredients are organic. One day, Mark is in a hurry, and instead of driving across town to the organic food co-op, he purchases ingredients from the closest grocery store, Unsafeway. Hannibal has a chemical allergy, so when he eats fruit from Mark's basket, he becomes ill. He sues Mark and Shania and is awarded $10,000 in damages. Is Shania personally liable?

Strategy: First decide if Mark and Shania have a partnership. If so, is the partnership liable for Mark's actions? Is Shania liable for the debts of the partnership that were incurred by Mark?

Result: Although Mark and Shania are students, they also run a business for profit and, therefore, are partners for purposes of that business. The partnership is liable for Mark's actions because he was acting in the ordinary course of the partnership business. Hannibal must first try to recover the judgment from the partnership. Only if the partnership has no assets can he recover from Mark or Shania individually. At that point, Hannibal has the right to recover from Shania, even though she personally did nothing wrong.

32-3 THE RELATIONSHIP AMONG PARTNERS

As we have seen, the rules governing the relationship between partners and outsiders are mandatory; the partners cannot change them. In contrast, the rules regulating the relationship among partners are more flexible—the partners can alter many of them by agreement. If these rules can be changed, why are they in the UPA at all? Because partnerships are often formed casually, without attention to legal technicalities; sometimes the partners themselves do not even realize they have a partnership. In situations such as these, the default rules are useful. Also, some partnerships may not want to undertake the effort and expense of preparing their own agreement. For them, the off-the-rack rules work well enough, and they do not need a custom-tailored version.

32-3a Financial Rights

Sharing Profits

Partners share profits equally unless they agree otherwise. This basic rule applies no matter how much money, time, or effort an individual partner contributes to the partnership. After graduation, Dawn convinces her friends, Niels and Sonya, to return with her to Jackson, Mississippi, to open a coffee bar. Niels and Sonya each contribute $15,000. Dawn has nothing to contribute financially. But she does know Jackson. When Dawn's Coffee Bar

kgelati/Shutterstock.com

Dawn does not pour the coffee, but she is entitled to an equal share of the profits.

opens for business, she attracts sellout crowds. Meanwhile, Niels and Sonya are working 20-hour days, first renovating the building and then serving customers. Dawn rarely sees the dawn, or even noon. Niels and Sonya have contributed more time and money and may have done more for the bar's success, but they must share profits equally with Dawn unless the three agreed otherwise.

Sharing Losses

Partners share losses according to their share of profits unless they agree otherwise. If Dawn's Coffee Bar fizzles after the first few months of success, then Dawn is responsible for one-third of the losses because she received one-third of the profits. It is too late for her to argue that it was not her fault the business failed.

Payment for Work Done

Partners are not entitled to any payment beyond their share of profits unless they agree otherwise. Niels and Sonya have no right to a greater share of the profits in return for their extra work. It is simply too difficult for the courts to evaluate each partner's contribution. ("Sonya didn't get to work until 9:15." "That's not true, I was there at 8:45, but you didn't see me because I was out back washing your dirty dishes....") This rule may seem arbitrary, but at least it is easy to enforce. The only exception, which we will see later, is that partners are entitled to remuneration for services performed in winding up the partnership.

In the following case, family members made mistakes. The father died without a will and his sons operated a business without a written partnership agreement or an understanding of partnership law. The result was the last thing any family wants: all-out war over a pair of sunglasses.

Banker v. Estate of Banker

911 N.Y.S.2d 691
Supreme Court of New York, 2010

Facts: Banker owned Peaceful Valley Campground (PV), which should more accurately have been called Angry Family Battleground. When Banker died without a will, each of his four sons inherited 10 percent, while his widow got the rest. One son, Arnold, bought out his mother's share, so he owned over two-thirds.

Because the four brothers did not choose any other form of organization, PV operated as a partnership. Arnold was the only brother who worked in the business. He lived year-round in a house on the campground, where he was on call 24 hours a day during the seven-month camping season. He dealt with routine camp business (including reservations and maintenance), as well as emergencies. Off-season, he made repairs and did office work. His live-in girlfriend, Linda Romero, did office work and cleaning.

PV paid a salary of $25,000 a year to Arnold and $10,000 a year to Romero. The partnership also paid some of Arnold's expenses. The other brothers had not agreed to these payments. When they found out about them, they insisted that Arnold return everything he and Romero had received because, as a partner, he had no right to payment for work performed on behalf of the partnership.

Issue: ***Was either Arnold or Romero entitled to the payments they received from the partnership?***

Excerpts from Justice Peckham's Decision: The personal expenses of Arnold alleged to have been paid from the partnership include meals and lodging, a truck, furniture and fixtures, and sunglasses. The meals and lodging were trips related to campground business.

The furniture and fixtures were actually two additional cabins for the campground. The truck was purchased for use at the campground hauling materials and supplies and also canoes the camp rents out. The sunglasses were for Arnold's use working around the camp. [T]he objection to these expenses is denied.

There is no written partnership agreement and no proof was introduced that the partners ever agreed to Arnold's salary. [W]hen there is no written partnership agreement, the New York Partnership Law effectively becomes the partnership agreement. Under the Partnership Law of New York, consent by all the partners was needed [for a partner to receive] compensation for services rendered to the partnership. No such consent was given by the three minority partners in the Peaceful Valley partnership. No consent having been given, the payment of a salary violated the partnership agreement and the law and must be refunded.

The work Ms. Romeo performed is the same type of work done by Arnold and could have been done by him. The other partners did not agree to hire Ms. Romeo, nor to the payments made to her. [Arnold must repay these amounts.]

Partnership Property

All partnership property belongs to the partnership as a whole, not to the individual partners. A partner has no right to use or sell property except for the benefit of the partnership. Suppose that the partnership owns the building that houses Dawn's Coffee Bar. Upstairs, above the bar, are three apartments. "Wow! This is great," says Niels, "I get the front unit." Does Niels have the right to live in one of the three apartments? After all, Dawn and Sonya can have the other two. Although the arrangement sounds fair, in fact, Niels has no right to live there unless the other partners agree.

Right to Transfer a Partnership Interest

A partnership is a personal relationship built on trust. Therefore, a partner can no more sell his partnership share to a stranger than a spouse can come home one night and announce, "I'm leaving the marriage but, don't worry, I've found a substitute." **Without the approval of the other partners, a partner cannot sell her share; she can only transfer her right to receive profits and losses.** A new partner can only be admitted to a partnership by unanimous consent of the other partners.[9]

It would be unfair to force partners to work with, or face unlimited liability for, someone they do not consider trustworthy. Sonya gets in serious debt to a fellow gambler, Nathan Detroit. Fearful that Nathan will ruin her manicure if she does not pay her debt, she agrees to give him her only asset, which is her share of the partnership. He knows a lot about coffee, and she is sure he will do fine as a partner. Although Niels and Dawn feel sorry for Sonya's predicament, they refuse to admit Nathan as a partner. Without their permission, Sonya has no right to transfer ownership rights or management authority to Nathan. Niels and Dawn cannot be forced to work with someone they do not want to touch with a 10-foot pole. However, Sonya can transfer to Nathan the right to receive her share of the partnership's profits.

What if Sonya refuses to assign to Nathan her right to receive profits from the partnership? **Creditors can attach partnership profits through a charging order.** A **charging order** is simply a court order granting a third party the right to receive a share of partnership profits.

Charging order
A court order granting a third party the right to receive a share of partnership profits

Similar rules apply when a partner dies. A partner's heirs have no right to specific partnership property; they do not become partners themselves, nor do they have any say in partnership management. They do have a right to receive the value of a partnership share. It is generally useful, therefore, if a partnership agreement prevents any argument by establishing in advance how to calculate the value of a partnership interest.

9UPA §401(i).

32-3b Management Rights

Right to Manage

Each and every partner has equal rights in the management and conduct of the business unless the partners agree otherwise. It can be difficult for many managers to run an organization, so when large law or accounting firms operated as partnerships, they were typically run by one or a few partners who were designated as *managing partners* or *members of the executive committee.*

Right to Bind the Partnership

If a partner acts on behalf of the partnership with actual, implied, or apparent authority, the partnership is liable to third parties for the partner's actions.

If the actions are not authorized by the partnership, the partner still has the *power* to bind the partnership, but not the *right*. In other words, if the partner acts with apparent authority, the partnership is liable to the third party, and the partner is liable to the partnership.

If the partner acts with actual or implied authority, then he has both the *power* and the *right*, which means that he is not personally liable to the partnership no matter how harmful his actions. A partner has actual or implied authority to bind the partnership for any transaction within the ordinary course of its business unless the partner knows that the other partners would disapprove. Dawn decides she would rather buy coffee from Hadley than from the regular supplier in New York. She has the authority to switch suppliers unless she knows some reason that Sonya and Niels would object. If she acts with authority, the partnership is liable to Hadley, but Dawn is not liable to the partnership. But if Dawn signs a contract with Hadley, knowing that her partners disapprove because Hadley's coffee is not free trade, the partnership is liable to Hadley, while Dawn is liable to the partnership.

Right to Vote

Unless the partners agree otherwise, all partners have an equal vote, regardless of their contributions to the partnership. For ordinary partnership affairs, the majority has the right to make a decision. To amend the partnership agreement or to make decisions outside the ordinary course of business, the vote must be unanimous. What happens when Dawn wants to introduce flavored teas, over Niels's dead body? The partners vote. Since this is an ordinary partnership matter, the majority rules. If Dawn can get Sonya on her side, she will win approval for the new teas. It makes no difference that Dawn never contributed any cash to the partnership; she has the right to vote.

Right to Know

The UPA requires that all partners have the right to ample information:

- Each partner has the right to inspect and copy the partnership's books and records. This right is unconditional and does not depend upon the partner's purpose or motive.
- All partners and the partnership:
  - Must *volunteer* any information that might reasonably be necessary for other partners to exercise their rights and
  - Have a duty to supply any other information that a partner reasonably requests.

These rules are mandatory; the partners may not change them by agreement among themselves.

32-3c Management Duties

Partners have the right to manage the partnership. In addition, they also have duties to the partnership and the other partners. These duties are mandatory; the partners may not waive them.

Duty of Care

Partners are liable to the partnership for gross negligence, reckless conduct, intentional misconduct, or a knowing violation of the law. Partners are not liable for ordinary negligence.[10] As you remember from earlier in this chapter, a partnership is liable to outsiders for the intentional and negligent torts of a partner that occur in the ordinary course of business. But, as you have just learned, the partner is not liable to the partnership for ordinary negligence. These two rules intersect in the following case in which the court does not allow a partnership to recover damages from a partner for an injury that she negligently caused to a third party (who happened to be her son).

Moren v. Jax Restaurant

679 N.W.2d 165
Minnesota Court of Appeals, 2004

Facts: Jax was a pizza restaurant in Foley, Minnesota, owned by two sisters: Nicole Moren and Amy Benedetti. They operated it as a partnership. One afternoon, Moren ended her regular shift at 4:00 p.m. and left to pick up her two-year-old son, Remington, from day care. When her sister called her to say that one of the cooks had not come to work, Moren returned to the restaurant with Remington. Moren's husband promised he would pick the child up in 20 minutes.

Because Moren did not want Remington running around the restaurant, she brought him into the kitchen with her, sat him on top of the counter, and began rolling out pizza dough using the dough-pressing machine. As she was making pizzas, Remington reached his hand into the dough press, which crushed his hand, causing permanent injuries. His father brought suit on Remington's behalf against the partnership for negligence. The partnership, in its turn, sued Moren, arguing that she had to personally reimburse it for any liability. The district court granted summary judgment to Moren. The restaurant appealed.

Issue: ***Is Moren liable to the partnership for her own negligence?***

Excerpts from Judge Crippen's Decision: The partnership [argues] that its obligation to compensate Remington is diminished in proportion to the predominating negligence of Moren as a mother, although it is responsible for her conduct as a business owner. Under Minnesota's Uniform Partnership Act of 1994 (UPA), a partnership is liable for loss or injury caused to a person as a result of a wrongful act or omission, or other actionable conduct, of a partner acting in the ordinary course of business of the partnership or with authority of the partnership. [Moreover], a partnership [must] indemnify a partner for liabilities incurred by the partner in the ordinary course of the business of the partnership. Thus, under the plain language of the UPA, a partner has a right to indemnity from the partnership, but the partnership's claim of indemnity from a partner is not authorized or required.

The district court correctly concluded that Nicole Moren's conduct was in the ordinary course of business of the partnership and, as a result, indemnity by the partner to the partnership was inappropriate. It is undisputed that one of the cooks scheduled to work that evening did not come in, and that Moren's partner asked her to help in the kitchen. It also is undisputed that Moren was making pizzas for the partnership when her son was injured. Because her conduct at the time of the injury was in the ordinary course of business of the partnership, under the UPA, her conduct bound the partnership and it owes indemnity to her for her negligence.

[The restaurant] also claims that because Nicole Moren's action of bringing Remington into the kitchen was partly motivated by personal reasons, her conduct was outside the ordinary course of business. Even if the predominant motive of the partner was to benefit himself or third persons, such does not prevent the concurrent business purpose from being within the scope of the partnership. [W]e conclude that the conduct of Nicole Moren was no less in the ordinary course of business because it also served personal purposes. It is undisputed that Moren was acting for the benefit of the partnership by making pizzas when her son was injured, and even though she was simultaneously acting in her role as a mother, her conduct remained in the ordinary course of the partnership business.

Affirmed.

---

10 UPA §404.

Duty of Loyalty

Partners have a limited fiduciary duty to their partnership.

Competing with the Partnership. **Each partner must turn over to the partnership all earnings from any activity that is related to the partnership's business.** Cara, Max, and Brooke are partners in a Beverly Hills law firm. While Cara is vacationing near Santa Fe, a guest in the hacienda next door is arrested in the middle of the night for drunk driving. Cara goes down to the police station and persuades the police officer to release the guest. Her new client gratefully insists on paying her $5,000 for her efforts. Cara figures the fee will go a long way toward paying the cost of her vacation. Cara figures wrong. She must turn the fee over to the partnership because she earned it doing the kind of work that the partnership does. It is irrelevant that she was on vacation.

Taking a Business Opportunity. **A partner may not take an opportunity away from the partnership unless the other partners consent.** Suppose that Beverly Hills needs a lawyer to serve as city counsel and offers the post to Max. He cannot take the job himself without the firm's permission. If he violates this duty, the partnership is entitled to the value of the opportunity he has taken.

Using Partnership Property. **A partner must turn over to the partnership any profit he earns from use of partnership property without the consent of the partners.** The partnership's office is in a beautifully restored historic building. Max runs a party planning service on the side—MAXimum Fun. He occasionally holds parties on the weekends in the partnership's elegant foyer without telling Brooke and Cara. When they find out, they are maximum angry, and for good reason—Max has violated his duty to the partnership.

Conflict of Interest. **A partner has a conflict of interest whenever the partnership does business with him, a member of his family, or a business partly or fully owned by him.** In that case, the partner must turn all profits over to the partnership unless he first obtained consent. Thus, when Max secretly hires MAXimum Fun to put on the firm's tenth-anniversary celebration, he must turn over to the partnership any profits he earns from the party.

In the following case, one partner bought partnership property at a public auction. Is that a conflict of interest?

Marsh v. Gentry

642 S.W.2d 574
Kentucky Supreme Court, 1982

Facts: Tom Gentry and John Marsh were partners in a business that bought and sold racehorses. The partnership paid $155,000 for Champagne Woman, who subsequently had a foal named Excitable Lady. The partners decided to sell Champagne Woman at Keeneland, the world's premier thoroughbred horse auction. At the auction, Gentry bid on the horse personally, without telling Marsh. He bought Champagne Woman for $135,000.

Later, Gentry told Marsh that someone from California had approached him about buying Excitable Lady. Marsh agreed to the sale. Although he repeatedly asked Gentry the name of the purchaser, Gentry refused to tell him. Not until 11 months later did Marsh learn that Gentry had been the purchaser of both horses. Marsh became the Excitable Man.

Issue: ***Did Gentry violate his fiduciary duty when he bought partnership property without telling his partner?***

Excerpts from Justice O'Hara's Decision: Admittedly, at an auction sale, the specific identity of a purchaser cannot be ascertained before the sale, but [Kentucky partnership law] required a full disclosure by Gentry to Marsh that he would be a prospective purchaser.

As to the private sale of Excitable Lady, Marsh consented to a sale from the partnership, at a specified price, to the prospective purchaser in California. Even though Marsh obtained the stipulated purchase price, a partner has an absolute right to know when his partner is the purchaser. Partners scrutinize buyouts by their partners in an entirely different light than an ordinary third-party sale. This distinction is vividly made without contradiction when Marsh later indicated that he would not have consented to either sale had he known that Gentry was the purchaser.

[P]artners, in their relations with other partners, [must] maintain a higher degree of good faith due to the partnership agreement. The requirement of full disclosure among partners as to partnership business cannot be escaped. Had Gentry made a full disclosure to his partner of his intentions to purchase the partnership property, Marsh would not later be heard to complain of the transaction.

Finally, Gentry maintains that it is an accepted practice at auction sales of thoroughbreds for one partner to secretly bid on partnership stock to accomplish a buyout. We would emphatically state, however, for the benefit of those engaged in such practices, that where an "accepted business practice" conflicts with existing law, the law, whether statutory or court ordered, is controlling. To hold otherwise would be chaotic.

Daniel Dempster Photography/Alamy Stock Photo

In the Marsh case, the horses won, but one of the partners lost.

Good Faith and Fair Dealing

Partners have an obligation of good faith and fair dealing to each other and to the partnership. They must deal with each other *fairly* and *without coercion*. Behavior that would be acceptable in an arm's-length transaction may be unacceptable between partners.

Hartz Mountain Industries, Inc., was the managing partner of a real estate business in northern New Jersey. Eugene Heller was Hartz's partner. According to the partnership agreement, when Heller left the partnership, Hartz would have the properties appraised and buy Heller's share. Hartz had the right to choose the appraiser. Over Heller's objection, Hartz chose Robert DiFalco. Hartz's own internal appraisals valued the properties at more than $214 million, but DiFalco produced an appraisal of $133 million—a slight discrepancy of about $80 million.

The court found that, while Hartz had technically complied with the partnership agreement, it had breached its obligation of good faith and fair dealing. When both parties have agreed in advance to the appraisal process, courts generally accept the resulting appraisals. But the court did not accept the result in this case because Hartz had violated its duty to Heller by choosing such an unreliable appraiser.[11]

---

[11] Heller v. Hartz Mountain Industries, Inc., 270 N.J. Super. 143 (N.J. Super. Ct. 1993).

EXAMStrategy

Question: Tom and Penelope start a test prep business. The partnership agreement specifies that Penelope is entitled to 30 percent of the profits, but that Tom is the managing partner with the right to run the day-to-day affairs of the business. Because students love Penelope's gentle demeanor, the business flourishes. A large university offers the partnership a contract to provide test prep services to all of its students. Tom decides to take that business himself without telling Penelope.

He also decides to reduce her payments from the partnership. She asks for data on the partnership's profitability, but Tom refuses to give it to her. He then moves the business into a shabbier, cheaper building that Penelope hates. What rights does Penelope have?

Strategy: The partnership agreement determines most of the rights between partners, but some rights are mandatory and cannot be changed by the partners.

Result: Tom does have the right to move the partnership into a different building, but he cannot take the opportunity to provide services to the university without telling Penelope. She is entitled to see the books and records of the partnership.

32-4 TERMINATING A PARTNERSHIP

Partnership at will
A partnership with no fixed duration. Any of the partners may leave at any time, for any reason.

Term partnership
A partnership in which the partners agree in advance how long it will last

The rules on termination depend, in part, on the type of partnership. If the partners have not agreed how long their partnership will last, they have a **partnership at will**, and any of them may leave at any time, for any reason. Taylor, Jay, and Gabriela are partners in the Donut Partnership, which owns a racehorse by the name of Speedy Donut. They see their business as a lark, to last as long as they are having fun, so they make no decision about its duration. When Taylor decamps after only two months, leaving Jay and Gabriela holding the feedbag, they have no legal right to complain.

In a **term partnership**, the partners agree in advance how long it will last. At the end of the specified term, the partnership automatically ends. If Taylor, Jay, and Gabriela agree that they will end their business relationship and sell Speedy Donut in five years, or if they agree the partnership will end after Speedy Donut runs five races, they have a term partnership.

32-4a Dissociation

Dissociation
When a partner leaves the partnership

A partnership begins with an association of two or more people. Appropriately, the end of a partnership begins with a **dissociation**. A dissociation occurs when a partner leaves. However, a dissociation does not inevitably cause the termination of the partnership business. A dissociation is a fork in the road: **When one or more partners dissociate, the partnership can either buy out the departing partner(s) and continue in business or wind up the business and terminate the partnership.** Exhibit 32.1 illustrates the dissociation process under the UPA.

Rightful versus Wrongful Dissociation

A partnership is a personal relationship built on trust. As we have seen, all partners are agents for the partnership, and each partner is personally liable for its debts. The actions of one partner can profoundly affect the financial health of every other partner. Under these

EXHIBIT 32.1

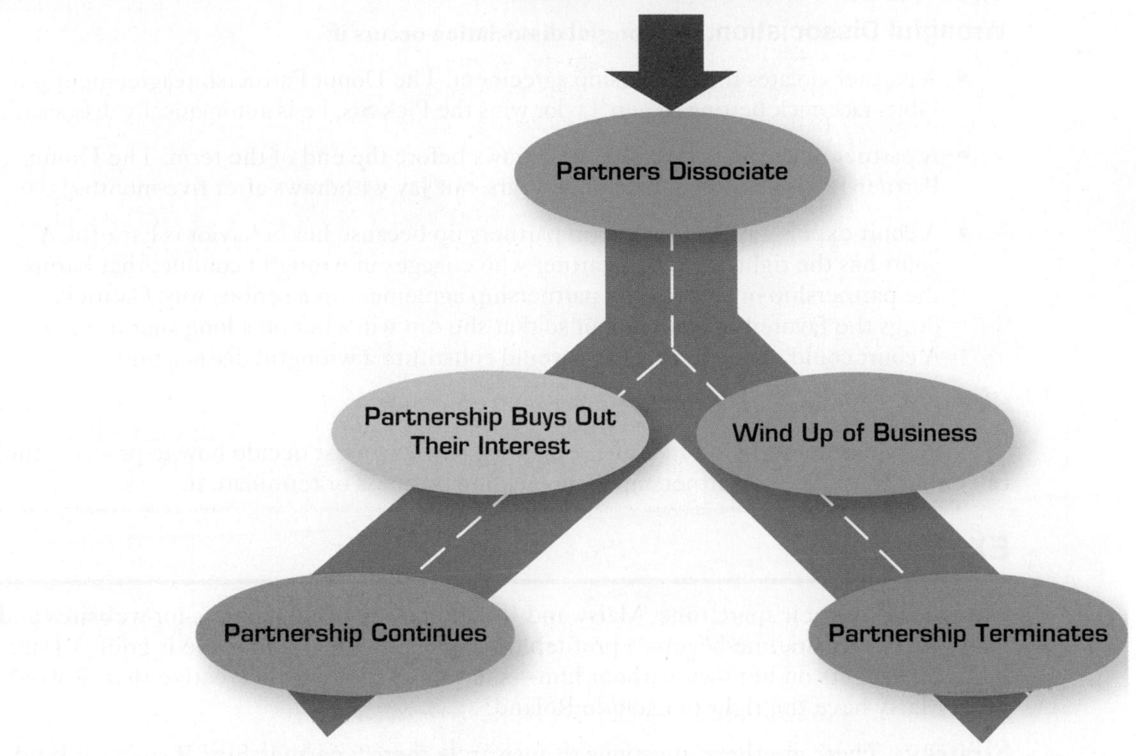

circumstances, courts will not force someone to remain in a partnership, no matter what the partnership agreement says, any more than they will force a couple to stay married because of their vows at the altar. Partners can always dissociate, but like any divorcing spouse, they may have to pay damages for the harm that their departure causes. In other words, **a partner always has the power to leave a partnership but may not have the right.**

Rightful Dissociation. A rightful dissociation occurs if:

- A partner in a partnership at will serves notice that he intends to withdraw.
- The partners agree in advance on an event that causes dissociation. Jay plans to attend business school in three years, so the partnership agreement provides that he will be automatically dissociated from the partnership at that point.
- A partner dies or becomes incompetent.
- A partner is expelled by the other partners. Partnership agreements can establish a process for expelling a partner. Often, under such agreements, the partnership does not even have to give a reason for expulsion. If a certain percentage of the partners (say, 75 percent) vote against someone, she is out. However, in the absence of such a provision in the partnership agreement, the UPA permits the expulsion of a partner only if (1) it is illegal to carry on the business with her or (2) she has transferred her partnership interest.

As we have seen, even lawyers sometimes forget partnership law. The prestigious law firm of Cadwalader, Wickersham, & Taft fired a partner, despite the fact that the partnership agreement said nothing about expulsion. A court upheld the firing but awarded the former partner $3 million in damages. In short, the law firm had the power, but not the right, to expel a partner.

Wrongful Dissociation. A wrongful dissociation occurs if:

- A partner violates the partnership agreement. The Donut Partnership agreement prohibits racetrack betting. When Taylor wins the Pick Six, he is automatically dissociated.
- A partner in a term partnership withdraws before the end of the term. The Donut Partnership is supposed to last five years, but Jay withdraws after five months.
- A court expels a partner in a term partnership because her behavior is harmful. A court has the right to expel a partner who engages in wrongful conduct that harms the partnership or violates the partnership agreement in a serious way. Gabriela drugs the favored Speedy Donut so that she can win a bet on a long shot in the race. A court could expel her, and that would constitute a wrongful dissociation.
- A partner in a term partnership becomes bankrupt.

Once a partner is dissociated, the remaining partners must decide how to proceed; they can either continue the partnership as an ongoing business or terminate it.

EXAMStrategy

Question: In their spare time, Maisy and Roland like to build widgets for websites and blogs. After this sideline becomes profitable, Maisy tells Roland that she is going to start building widgets on her own without him—she thinks she is more creative than Roland. Does Maisy have the right to exclude Roland?

Strategy: There are three questions to answer: Is there a partnership? If so, what kind of partnership? Does Maisy have the right to withdraw from it?

Result: Maisy and Roland do have a partnership—they are carrying on as co-owners of a business for profit. It does not matter that the word "partnership" has never passed their lips. Because there is no partnership agreement, they have a partnership at will. With this form of partnership, Maisy can withdraw at any time for any reason.

32-4b Continuation of the Partnership Business

If a partner is dissociated from the partnership, the partners have to vote on whether to continue the business. The ex-partner can vote on this decision if her dissociation was rightful; otherwise, she has no vote.

Financial Settlement

If the partnership decides to continue, it must pay the ex-partner the value of her share of the business. This value is equal to her share of the proceeds if (1) the partnership was sold as an ongoing business or (2) the partnership's assets were liquidated, whichever calculation is greater. If Gabriela is adjudged incompetent by a court, she is automatically dissociated from the Donut Partnership. At that point, Speedy Donut is worth $500,000 and the partnership has debts of $50,000, for a total value of $450,000. Gabriela is entitled to at least a one-third share—$150,000. If, however, the partnership is worth $600,000 as an ongoing business, Gabriela is entitled to $200,000.

Now the plot thickens. If Gabriela's dissociation was *wrongful*, the partnership can subtract any damages she caused from the amount it owes her. A court expels Gabriela from the partnership because she drugged Speedy Donut. His recovery is slow and he is unable to race for months, costing the partnership $100,000. Taylor and Jay could subtract that $100,000 from the $200,000 they owe her, so she ultimately receives a check for only $100,000. If her bad acts caused more than $200,000 in damage, she owes them money.

Liability of the Dissociated Partner to Outsiders for Debts Incurred *before* Dissociation

A dissociated partner is liable to outsiders for debts incurred during her term as a partner, but the partnership must indemnify her for these debts. After Gabriela departs, a bank sues the partnership for failure to repay its loan. Although Gabriela is no longer a partner, she was one when the partnership borrowed the money. As we have seen, the bank may be able to recover from her. If it does, however, the partnership must indemnify her; that is, the partnership must reimburse her for any amounts she pays the bank. This outcome is only fair because, when the partnership purchased her share, it reduced the payment to reflect liabilities such as this.

Liability of the Dissociated Partner to Outsiders for Debts Incurred *after* Dissociation

A dissociated partner is liable to outsiders for the debts of the partnership incurred within two years after she leaves, but only if the creditor reasonably believes she is still a partner. The partnership must indemnify her for these debts. If Taylor and Jay buy an expensive saddle on credit from their regular supplier, Gabriela is also liable unless the saddler knows she is dissociated. The partnership would have to reimburse her (if it has enough funds). To protect herself, however, Gabriela can file a statement of dissociation with the secretary of state. Although the saddler rarely spends his free afternoons perusing the public records, he is deemed to have notice of this filing 90 days after Gabriela makes it.

Liability of the Dissociated Partner to the Partnership

If the ex-partner harms the partnership after she leaves, she is liable for the damage she causes. If Gabriela lets a feed supplier believe that she is still a partner and then buys feed on credit, the partnership may be liable for her charges. If so, she must reimburse the partnership.

32-4c Termination of the Partnership Business

When a partner is dissociated, the partnership may choose to terminate the business rather than continue it. **Ending a partnership business involves three steps: dissolution, winding up, and termination.**

Dissolution

Unless the partners agree otherwise, a partnership dissolves under the following circumstances:

- In a partnership at will, when a partner notifies the partnership that he intends to withdraw and the remaining partners cannot agree unanimously to continue the business.
- If, for a period of 90 days, the partnership has only one partner.[12]

---

[12]UPA, §801(6).

- In a term partnership, when:
  - A partner is dissociated before the end of the term and half of the remaining partners vote to wind up the partnership business. When Jay dies, he is dissociated from the partnership. If Gabriela votes to wind up the business, the partnership is dissolved.
  - All the partners agree to dissolve. Although the Donut Partnership is supposed to last five years, Taylor, Jay, and Gabriela can agree among themselves to wind up the business whenever they want. If Speedy Donut is a cream puff on the racetrack, they can decide to dissolve their partnership and sell him.
  - The term expires or the partnership achieves its goal. If Speedy Donut runs five races, the Donut Partnership automatically dissolves, because that is what the partners had originally decided.
- In any partnership, when:
  - An event occurs which the partners had agreed would cause dissolution. The Donut Partnership agreement provided that the partnership would dissolve if Speedy Donut failed to win a race in any 12-month period. When Speedy Donut goes winless, the partnership dissolves.
  - The partnership business becomes illegal. If horse racing is banned, the Donut Partnership automatically dissolves.
  - A court determines that the partnership is unlikely to succeed. If the partners simply cannot get along or they cannot make a profit, any partner has the right to ask a court to dissolve the partnership. If Taylor and Jay hate each other and are unable to reach agreement on anything, a court is likely to agree to dissolve the partnership.

Note that, even if one of these events occurs, partners can always decide (by unanimous vote) to continue a partnership. Indeed, even after the winding-up process begins, the partners can change their minds and continue the business.

Winding Up

During the winding-up process, all debts of the partnership are paid, and the remaining proceeds are distributed to the partners.

Who Does It? Unless the partnership agreement provides otherwise, any partner who has not wrongfully dissociated has the right to oversee the winding up.

Are They Paid? As we have seen, partners are not entitled to be paid for work they do during the life of the partnership, but that rule does not apply during the winding-up process. Partners are entitled to reasonable compensation for their work in winding up the partnership.

What Do They Do? The winding-up process can be complex and take as long as several years to complete. The partners in charge can either sell the entire business as a whole, sell the individual assets of the business, distribute specific assets to the partners, or some combination of these options. They have the right to complete unfinished transactions and do whatever is necessary to wind up the business, but they may not take on new business.

If Taylor is winding up the Donut Partnership, he can sell Speedy Donut outright, pay the horse's expenses until the sale, sue to recover any winnings that have not been paid, and settle partnership debts. But can he enter the horse in additional races? In a similar case, a court permitted the partner in charge of winding up a racing business to pay entrance fees for races even though the horses would, in all likelihood, be sold before the races. The court assumed that buyers would pay more for horses that were eligible to race in upcoming events.[13]

13Central Trust & S. Deposit Co. v. Respass, 112 Ky. 606, 66 S.W. 421 (1902).

The partnership is bound by the acts of the partners in charge of winding up. As the following case illustrates, this rule can sometimes lead to unhappy results.

Jefferson Insurance Co. v. Curle

771 S.W.2d 424
Tennessee Court of Appeals, 1989

Facts: Michael Curle and Steven Shelley were partners doing business under the name C & S Roofing. When the partnership dissolved, Curle agreed to complete one unfinished project (the Bishop house) and left Shelley to wind up the other partnership business. Shelley canceled the partnership's general liability insurance policy without telling Curle. While painting the Bishop house, Dennis Whitsett fell through a hole in the roof that was covered only with tar paper. When Whitsett sought to recover from the partnership for his serious injuries, Curle and Shelley asked the insurance company to pay the claim.

The trial court found the policy canceled as to Steven Shelley, individually, but in full force and effect as to the partnership and Michael Curle, individually. The insurance company appealed.

Issue: ***Was the partnership bound by Shelley's decision during the winding-up process to cancel the policy, even though he had not told Curle?***

Excerpts from Judge McLemore's Decision: [The Tennessee Partnership Act] clearly states: "After dissolution a partner can bind the partnership … by any act appropriate for winding up partnership affairs or completing transactions unfinished at dissolution." The liquidating partner owes a continuing fiduciary duty to the other partners and has an obligation to act equitably toward them. However, these obligations run between partners and do not absolve any partner from being bound by the liquidating partner's actions in winding up partnership affairs. In the present case, we hold Shelley's cancellation of the partnership insurance policy and collection of unused premiums to be within his authority in winding up the partnership's affairs.

For the foregoing reasons, the judgment of the trial court holding the policy canceled as to Steven Shelley, individually, is affirmed, but that portion of the judgment holding that the policy is in full force and effect as to C & S Roofing, a partnership, and Michael Curle, individually, is reversed; and we hold that the policy is canceled as to all insureds and, thus, provides no coverage to any of the defendants for the accident alleged by Dennis Whitsett.

Who Is Liable If a Partner Takes on New Business? During the winding-up process, the partners continue to be liable for the debts of the partnership that were incurred before dissolution. But what if a partner oversteps her bounds during the winding-up process and takes on new business? All of the other partners are liable unless they have filed a statement of dissolution with the secretary of state. This statement is effective 90 days after it is filed.

How Are Partnership Proceeds Distributed? During the winding-up process, the assets of the partnership are paid out in the following order:

- First, to creditors of the partnership, including creditors who are partners. Suppose that the Donut Partnership has assets of $30,000. It owes $20,000 each to the feed supplier, the stables, and Jay, for a total of $60,000. It will pay $10,000 to each of the three creditors—Jay is treated exactly like the outsiders.
- Second, any leftover funds (or obligations) are distributed to the partners. Unless the partnership agreement provides otherwise, partners share equally in profits—and losses. In this example, the Donut Partnership had only enough assets to pay half its $60,000 debt. Each partner would then contribute $10,000 to pay the amount still owing. Jay's payment would be a wash—he owes $10,000, but he is also entitled to be paid $10,000.

Termination

Termination happens automatically once the winding up is finished. The partnership is not required to do anything official; it can go out of the world even more quietly and simply than it came in.

CHAPTER CONCLUSION

A partnership is an old-fashioned form of organization. From the late 1770s until the mid-nineteenth century, virtually all businesses were partnerships. Then corporations gained in popularity, followed by new forms such as LLCs and LLPs, which have many of the advantages of a partnership without the disadvantage of unlimited liability.

It is no surprise that, to protect their partners from personal liability, most accounting firms, law firms, brokerage houses, advertising agencies, and investment banks that were originally partnerships have changed their form of organization to one of the newer options. But, whatever their form of organization, many of these businesses continue to act like partnerships, with operating agreements that track partnership law.

Partnership law is also important because, as we have seen in this chapter, partnerships are often formed inadvertently by people who do not realize they are in such a relationship until a dispute arises. It is useful to know in advance the kind of behavior that will create a partnership and understand the consequences.

EXAM REVIEW

1. **PARTNERSHIP** A partnership is an association of two or more persons to carry on as co-owners a business for profit.

2. **FORMING A PARTNERSHIP** In determining whether a partnership exists, a court will consider whether the parties:
   - Intend to make a profit,
   - Share the profits of the business,
   - Share the losses of the business,
   - Share management of the business, and
   - Have an oral or written partnership agreement.

EXAMStrategy

Question: When Chase, Bailey, and Zack started working together to build a house, they signed a document stating, "The undersigned expressly agree that they are not partners." If they continued to work together, sharing the profits and the management, would they be partners?

Strategy: Remember that, in the case of partnerships, actions speak louder than words. (See the "Result" at the end of this Exam Review section.)

3. **PARTNERSHIP BY ESTOPPEL** If someone is not a member of a partnership, she will nonetheless be considered a partner by estoppel if (1) she tells other people she is a partner or allows other people to say, without contradiction, that she is a partner; (2) a third party relies on this assertion; and (3) the third party suffers harm.

EXAMStrategy

Question: Bryan was giving flying lessons to Edward. With both men standing on the ground, Edward cranked up the engine of the airplane. The throttle was set too far open, so the plane began to move. Edward chased the plane on foot, grabbed its left wing, and swung the airplane in a semicircle, crashing it into Helen's new car, which was in the parking lot. Bryan operated his flying business under the name Bryan-Carl Air Service. Bryan and Carl were not partners, but Helen sued them both on a theory of partnership by estoppel. She argued that they had used a name for their business that sounded like a partnership. She had never heard of their business until the collision. Is Carl liable to Helen as a partner by estoppel?

Strategy: These elements are required for partnership by estoppel: The participants must have held themselves out as partners even though they are not; a third party must have relied on that representation and suffered harm. (See the "Result" at the end of this Exam Review section.)

4. **PARTNERS AS AGENTS** Every partner is an agent of the partnership for the purpose of its business. A partnership is liable if a partner acts with actual, implied, or apparent authority.

5. **TORT LIABILITY** A partnership is responsible for the intentional and negligent torts of a partner that occur in the ordinary course of the partnership's business or with the actual authority of the partners.

EXAMStrategy

Question: While Warren was representing Betty in divorce proceedings, she inherited $60,000. Warren suggested Betty invest her money in a corporation of which he was president. Although he promised her a substantial return, the company went bankrupt shortly thereafter. Warren was a partner in a law firm. The firm was not in the business of giving investment advice, it did not know that Warren was giving such advice, nor did it receive any fee from Betty for the "investment service." Is the law firm liable for Betty's loss?

Strategy: Was Warren acting within the ordinary course of the partnership's business? Was he acting with actual, implied, or apparent authority? (See the "Result" at the end of this Exam Review section.)

6. **A PARTNER'S LIABILITY FOR THE DEBTS OF THE PARTNERSHIP** All partners are personally liable for all debts of the partnership incurred while they were members of the partnership. Partners have joint and several liability

for partnership obligations. However, creditors cannot go after an individual partner's assets until all the partnership's assets are exhausted. A partner's liability for debts incurred before she became a partner is limited to her investment in the partnership.

7. **DEFAULT RULES AMONG PARTNERS** Unless they agree otherwise, partners:
    - Share profits equally;
    - Share losses according to their share of profits;
    - Are not entitled to any payment beyond their share of profits, even if they perform work for the partnership;
    - Have no right to use or sell specific partnership property except for the benefit of the partnership;
    - Each have an equal vote, regardless of their contributions to the partnership; and
    - Each have an equal right to manage the business.

8. **TRANSFERRING A PARTNERSHIP SHARE** Without the approval of the other partners, a partner cannot sell her share. She can only transfer the right to receive profits and losses. A new partner can be admitted to a partnership only by unanimous consent of the other partners.

9. **CREDITORS' RIGHTS** Creditors can attach partnership profits through a charging order.

10. **A PARTNER'S LIABILITY TO THE PARTNERSHIP** Partners are liable to the partnership for any damages resulting from their gross negligence, reckless conduct, intentional misconduct, or a knowing violation of the law. Partners are not liable to the partnership for ordinary negligence.

11. **OUTSIDE EARNINGS** Each partner must turn over to the partnership all earnings from any activity that is related to the partnership's business.

12. **PARTNERSHIP OPPORTUNITY** A partner may not take an opportunity away from the partnership unless the other partners consent.

13. **CONFLICT OF INTEREST** A partner has a conflict of interest whenever the partnership does business with him, a member of his family, or a business partly or fully owned by him. Unless the other partners consent in advance, the conflicted partner must turn all profits over to the partnership.

14. **A PARTNER'S OBLIGATION TO THE PARTNERSHIP** Partners have an obligation of good faith and fair dealing to each other and to the partnership.

15. **DISSOCIATION** A dissociation occurs when a partner leaves the partnership.

16. **AFTER DISSOCIATION** When one or more partners dissociate, the partnership can either buy out the departing partner(s) and continue in business or wind up the business and terminate the partnership.

17. **THE RIGHT TO WITHDRAW** A partner always has the power to leave a partnership but may not have the right.

18. **PARTNERSHIP AT WILL** If partners do not have an agreement about the duration of their partnership, they are in a partnership at will, and any of them can leave at any time for any reason.

19. **TERM PARTNERSHIP** With a term partnership, the partners have agreed in advance how long the partnership will last.

20. **DISSOCIATED PARTNER** A dissociated partner is liable to outsiders for debts incurred during his term as a partner, but the partnership must indemnify him for these debts. A dissociated partner is liable for the debts of the partnership incurred within two years after she leaves, but only if the creditor reasonably believes she is still a partner. The partnership must indemnify her for these debts.

21. **ENDING A PARTNERSHIP** If the partners decide to end the partnership business, they must take three steps: dissolution, winding up, and termination.

22. **THE WINDING-UP PROCESS** During the winding-up process, the partners have the right to complete unfinished transactions and do whatever is necessary to terminate the business. They do not have the right to take on new business. The assets of the partnership are paid out:
    - First, to creditors of the partnership, including creditors who are partners, and
    - Second, to partners.

RESULTS

2. Result: The document would have had no impact. So long as they act like partners, they are partners.

3. Result: Two of the three elements are there—Brian and Carl held themselves out as partners and Helen suffered harm. But Carl was not a partner by estoppel because, before the accident, Helen did not know that Carl had held himself out as Bryan's partner. She had not *relied on* their representation.

5. Result: The firm was not in the investment advisory business, so Warren was not acting within the ordinary course of business. He did not have actual authority, but he might have had apparent authority, in which case the firm would be liable.

MULTIPLE-CHOICE QUESTIONS

1. **CPA QUESTION** Which of the following is not necessary to create a partnership?
   (a) Execution of a written partnership agreement
   (b) Agreement to share ownership of the partnership
   (c) Intention of conducting a business for profit
   (d) Intention of creating a relationship recognized as a partnership

2. If a partner dissociates, he is entitled to ______________.
   (a) force the termination of the partnership
   (b) receive indemnification from liability for present partnership debt
   (c) receive indemnification from damages he caused the partnership
   (d) receive his share of the value of the partnership assets
3. **CPA QUESTION** Cobb, Inc., a partner in TLC Partnership, assigns its partnership interest to Bean, who is not made a partner. After the assignment, Bean asserts the right to (1) participate in the management of TLC and (2) Cobb's share of TLC's partnership profits. Bean is correct as to which of these rights?
   (a) 1 only
   (b) 2 only
   (c) 1 and 2
   (d) Neither 1 nor 2
4. **CPA QUESTION** Ted Fein, a partner in the ABC Partnership, wishes to withdraw from the partnership and sell his interest to Gold. All of the other partners in ABC have agreed to admit Gold as a partner and to hold Fein harmless for the past, present, and future liabilities of ABC. A provision in the original partnership agreement states that the partnership will continue upon the death or withdrawal of one or more of the partners. As a result of Fein's withdrawal and Gold's admission to the partnership, Gold______________.
   (a) is personally liable for partnership liabilities arising before and after his admission as a partner
   (b) has the right to participate in the management of ABC
   (c) acquired only the right to receive Fein's share of the profits of ABC
   (d) must contribute cash or property to ABC in order to be admitted with the same rights as the other partners
5. Blackriver Partnership is in the process of winding up. It has three partners: Jason, Kiera, and Lancelot. The partnership has assets of $90,000, but debts of $60,000, including $30,000 it owes to Jason. Who gets what?
   (a) Each partner receives $10,000.
   (b) Each partner receives $30,000.
   (c) Jason receives $30,000 and the other two get $10,000 each.
   (d) Jason receives $40,000 and the other two get $10,000 each.

CASE QUESTIONS

1. **ETHICS** Arthur, John, and George formed a partnership to drill and maintain cesspools for two years. After less than two months, John and George sent a letter to Arthur, informing him that they were dissolving the partnership. Arthur sued the two other men, asking the court to declare that the partnership still existed and he had the right to continue in the business. Do John and George have the power to dissolve a term partnership before the end of the term? Aside from the legal issue, is it fair to Arthur for the court to allow his two partners to walk away from their partnership? He had counted on a two-year commitment; they gave only two months.

2. ***YOU BE THE JUDGE* WRITING PROBLEM** Herbert, an artist, entered into an agreement with Randy for the reproduction and distribution of his paintings. Herbert was to receive 50 percent of the gross sales revenues. Randy was responsible for all losses and for management of the business. Before leaving on a trip to Israel, where he feared he might be in some danger, Randy signed a partnership agreement with Herbert stating that they jointly owned the business. Shortly after Randy returned from the trip, the two men terminated their business relationship, and Herbert revoked his authorization for the sale of prints. When Randy continued selling the prints, Herbert filed suit. Randy argued that the two had formed a partnership and that he was authorized to sell assets of the partnership. Were Herbert and Randy partners? **Argument for Herbert:** A partnership agreement does not create a partnership. Randy alone managed the business. Herbert shared only revenues, not profits or losses. **Argument for Randy:** Herbert and Randy both provided services to the business: Randy paid for the printing, and Herbert did the artwork. These two men signed a partnership agreement, and they obviously intended to be partners.

3. When Michael Eagan married James Gory's daughter Jennifer, the two men started a business flipping houses. Eagan found the houses and supervised their renovation. Gory provided the funds, purchased the houses in his name, and made all major decisions. He gave Eagan 50 percent of the net profits, but did not make Eagan responsible for any losses. After Eagan and Jennifer divorced, Gory sold two houses that he had purchased with Eagan's help, but he did not share any of the profits. Eagan sued, claiming they had a partnership and he was entitled to 50 percent of the profit. Did the two men have a partnership?

4. Pedro and Juan have a business selling ties with fraternity insignia. Pedro finds out that an online shirt business is for sale. It sounds like a great idea—customers send in their measurements and get back a custom-made shirt at a price no higher than an off-the-rack shirt at the local department store. Does Pedro have to let Juan in on the great opportunity?

5. Four friends pooled their money to buy a small airplane because they enjoyed flying. Sometimes they flew separately, other times they went on vacation trips together. Abbi, who was one of the owners, heard that a boat was missing out on the Gulf of Mexico. She took a neighbor's son Sam along with her in the plane to help search for the boat. After Abbi carelessly took off in bad weather, the plane crashed and both Abbi and Sam were killed. Sam's father sued the other three owners, alleging that they were partners who were liable for Abbi's negligence. Is there a partnership? If there was a partnership, were the partners liable?

DISCUSSION QUESTIONS

1. Mike Love and Brian Wilson were members of the Beach Boys. In the 1960s, they wrote songs together. The copyrights for these songs were later sold to Rondor, which paid the two men royalties when the songs were played. In 2004, Wilson re-recorded some of these songs on a CD called *Good Vibrations*. This CD was distributed in the United Kingdom by the newspaper *The Mail on Sunday*. Love sued Wilson, arguing that the two men had a partnership and Wilson had violated the partnership agreement by re-recording the songs without Love's permission. Did Mike Love and Brian Wilson have a partnership?

2. Dutch, Bill, and Heidi were equal partners in a lawn-care business. Bill and Heidi wanted to borrow money from the bank to buy more trucks and expand the business. Dutch was dead set against the idea. When the matter came to a vote, Bill and Heidi voted in favor, Dutch against. Dutch was so annoyed that he told the bank not to lend the money and, further, that he would not be responsible for repaying the loan. The bank loaned the money, the business failed, and the bank sued all three partners. Is Dutch liable on the loan?

3. Carrie and Laura started a business together to sell bridesmaid dresses online. Carrie spent months preparing the financials and meeting with potential investors while Laura designed dresses and found suppliers. Once Carrie was finished with the financials and had identified some potential investors, Laura announced that she preferred to work with Scott, and Carrie was out of the business. What rights does Carrie have?

4. Lucan and Alison agreed to practice law together. Their stationery said, "The Lucan and Alison Partnership" and they told everyone they were partners. They signed a partnership agreement providing that Lucan would receive a "guaranteed annual draw of $100,000." The rest of the profits went to Alison. Are they partners?

5. Is there any good reason to be in a partnership? If so, for what sort of business would it make sense?

CHAPTER 33

LIFE AND DEATH OF A CORPORATION

On July 26, 2004, Mark Zuckerberg signed a certificate of incorporation for his company, which he called TheFacebook, Inc. At 11:34 a.m. on July 29, 2004, that certificate was filed with the secretary of state for Delaware, and what is now known as Facebook began its life as a corporation. Zuckerberg had started this social networking internet site the previous February in his dorm room at Harvard. Today, Facebook is valued at $400 billion. As Zuckerberg built his company, what did he need to know about the law?

Zuckerberg started Facebook in his dorm room at Harvard. Today, it is worth $400 billion.

Many of the country's businesses, both large and small, are corporations. In this chapter, you will learn how to form a corporation and also how to avoid traps that await the unwary entrepreneur before and after a business is formed.

33-1 BEFORE THE CORPORATION IS FORMED

Facebook operated for five months before it was incorporated. During this period, Zuckerberg needed to be careful to avoid liability as a promoter.

33-1a Promoter's Liability

The promoter is the person who creates the corporation. It is his idea; he raises the capital, hires the lawyers, calls the shots. Mark Zuckerberg was Facebook's promoter. Sometimes, promoters are so eager to get their business going that they sign contracts on behalf of the corporation before it is legally formed. Zuckerberg moved company headquarters to Palo Alto, California, before the certificate of incorporation was filed. Suppose that he found the perfect location for his headquarters and was eager to sign the lease but Facebook did not legally exist yet because it was not incorporated. What would happen if he signed the lease anyway?

AP Images/Paul Sakuma

Within a few years, MarkZuckerberg went from college student to Silicon Valley billionaire.

- **A *promoter* is personally liable on any contract signed before the corporation is formed.** If Zuckerberg signed the lease before Facebook, Inc., legally existed, he would be personally liable for the rent due.
- **The *corporation* is not liable on any contracts signed *before* incorporation unless it adopts the contract *after* incorporation.** What does **adoption** mean? Either the board of directors takes a formal vote saying, "We hereby adopt this contract," or they act as if they had adopted it. If Facebook used the space Zuckerberg rented, it would have adopted the contract. But Zuckerberg would still be on the hook.

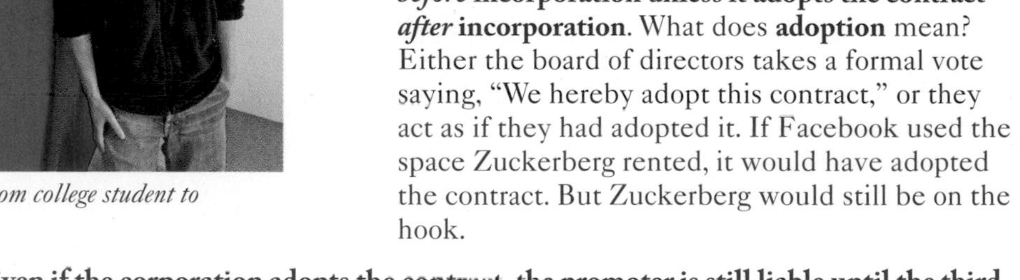

- **Even if the corporation adopts the contract, the promoter is still liable until the third party (in this case, the landlord) agrees to a *novation*.** A **novation** creates a *new* contract. Even if Facebook adopted the contract, Zuckerberg would still be personally liable to the landlord until the landlord signed a new contract with him and Facebook explicitly stating that only the corporation was liable, not Zuckerberg.

Adoption
When a corporation accepts legal responsibility for a contract

Novation
A new contract

Like many rules, this one has an exception:

- **If it is clear that the parties did not intend the promoter to be liable, then he is released from liability once the corporation adopts the contract.** To protect himself, Zuckerberg would have wanted the lease to state that Facebook was not yet formed but would be liable when it was formed, and that he would not be personally liable once Facebook adopted the contract.

EXAMStrategy

Question: Dr. Warfield hired Wolfe, a young carpenter, to build his house. A week or so after they signed the contract, Wolfe incorporated Wolfe Construction, Inc. Warfield made payments to the corporation. Unfortunately, the work on the house was shoddy. The architect said he did not know whether to blow up the house or try to salvage what was there. Warfield sued Wolfe and Wolfe Construction, Inc., for damages. Wolfe argued that if he was liable as a promoter, then the corporation must be absolved and that, conversely, if the corporation was held liable, he, as an individual, must not be. Who is liable to Warfield? Does it matter if Wolfe signed the contract in his own name or in the name of the corporation?

Strategy: Wolfe's argument is wrong. Warfield does not have to choose between suing him individually or suing the corporation. He can certainly sue both.

Result: Wolfe is personally liable on any contract signed before incorporation, no matter whose name is on the contract. The corporation is liable only if it adopts the contract. Did it do so here? The fact that the corporation cashed checks that were made out to it means that the corporation is also liable. So Warfield can sue both Wolfe and the corporation.

33-1b Defective Incorporation

A promoter is liable on contracts signed before the corporation exists. What happens, though, if the promoter makes some reasonable effort to incorporate but does not succeed? In these situations, the law can be reasonably tolerant. (Remember, however, that litigation is extremely painful and it is far, far better just to comply with all the rules.)

De Jure Corporation

De jure is Latin for "by law." A ***de jure* corporation** means that the promoter has substantially complied with the requirements for incorporation but has made some minor error. He has perhaps misspelled the name of the corporation's registered agent (more about the registered agent later). **In the case of a *de jure* corporation, no one, not even the state, can challenge its validity.**

De jure
A Latin phrase meaning "by law"

***De jure* corporation**
A promoter has substantially complied with the requirements for incorporation but has made some minor error.

De Facto Corporation

De facto is Latin for "in fact." A ***de facto* corporation** means that the promoter has made a good faith effort to incorporate and has actually used the corporation to conduct business. **In the case of a *de facto* corporation, the state can challenge the validity of the corporation, but a third party cannot.** Suppose that Mark Zuckerberg filled out the incorporation form and filed it, but the secretary of state did not stamp it for weeks. In the meantime, Zuckerberg signed a lease for Facebook. In many states, no stamp means no corporation. Nonetheless, Zuckerberg would have had a *de facto* corporation because he had made a reasonable effort to incorporate and had used the corporation to conduct business. The landlord could not challenge the validity of the corporation and claim that Zuckerberg was personally liable on the lease. Only the corporation would have been liable.

De facto
A Latin phrase meaning "in fact"

***De facto* corporation**
The promoter has made a good-faith effort to incorporate and has actually used the corporation to conduct business.

Corporation by Estoppel

Corporation by estoppel
If a party enters into a contract believing in good faith that the corporation exists, that party cannot later take advantage of the fact that it does not.

A **corporation by estoppel** means that, if a party enters into a contract *believing* in good faith that the corporation exists, that party cannot later take advantage of the fact that it does not. Suppose that Zuckerberg's attorney told him that Facebook, Inc., had been formed, but in fact she had never filed the necessary documents. In the meantime, Zuckerberg bought many Apple computers in Facebook's name. Under the theory of corporation by estoppel, Zuckerberg would *not* be personally liable even though the corporation did not exist. Both he and Apple thought he was buying on behalf of the corporation. Why should Apple benefit, and Zuckerberg suffer, simply because his lawyer had made a mistake?

In the following case, a contract is so unclear, the courts have to step in. What is the proper legal result? What is fair?

You Be the Judge

GS Petroleum, Inc. v. R and S Fuel, Inc.

2009 Del. Super. LEXIS 200; 2009 WL 1554680
Superior Court of Delaware, 2009

Facts: On March 13, GS Petroleum (GS) signed an agreement to sell a Shell gas station to R and S Fuel, Inc. (Fuel). On April 2, Fuel opened a corporate bank account and began writing checks on it. On April 15, Fuel took possession of the Shell station. Later, it took out insurance in the company's name. Unfortunately, what Fuel did not do was pay the money it owed under the contract.

So far, this looks like just a breach of contract case. But there is one more fact that greatly complicates this simple picture: Fuel did not actually come into existence until March 27, two weeks after the contract was signed. The introduction to the contract stated that it was "entered by and between R and S Fuel, Inc., and GS Petroleum, Inc." The signature lines at the end looked like this:

> *Richard Simpson*
> R and S Fuel, Inc.
> Buyer
> Susan Stamm and Richard Simpson

In other words, although the names of both Stamm and Simpson are printed on the signature page, only Simpson actually signed the document.

GS filed suit for $124,000 against the corporation but also personally against Richard Simpson and Susan Stamm. The two individuals filed a motion for summary judgment.

You Be the Judge: *Were Simpson and Stamm personally liable for the debts of Fuel?*

Argument for GS: Simpson and Stamm were the promoters of the corporation, which did not yet exist when the contract was signed. Promoters are liable for any contracts signed before the business is incorporated. Their names appear on the contract, and Simpson actually signed it. No corporate title is attached to his name on the signature line, which indicates he was signing as an individual, not a corporate officer. And when Simpson signed the contract, he was acting as Stamm's agent. So she is liable, too.

The business was not a *de facto* corporation, because they did not make a good faith effort to comply with corporate law. They had not even bothered to file the forms with the secretary of state.

Even if Fuel adopted the contract, Simpson and Stamm are still liable until the parties sign a novation. That did not happen here. And no provision of the contract explicitly or impliedly released the two defendants.

To find Simpson and Stamm liable is the only fair result. Someone is going to be out a lot of money. It should not be the innocent party who sold a perfectly good business.

Argument for Simpson and Stamm: It is true that Simpson's signature line did not list a corporate title, but that was simply an oversight. He was clearly signing for the corporation. As for Stamm, she cannot be liable for an agreement she did not sign.

If it is clear that the parties did not intend the promoters to be liable, then they are released from liability once the corporation adopts the contract. GS effectively adopted the contract by signing it. Note that the document states it is an agreement with just Fuel; not Fuel, Simpson, and Stamm. If GS wanted the two individuals to be liable, the document should have said so. Even before the corporate documents were filed, Simpson and Stamm ran the business as a corporation. They opened a bank account in the company's name, they used only business checks, and they bought insurance in the corporate name.

Also, R and S Fuel was a *de facto* corporation at the time the agreement was signed. Simpson and Stamm were in the process of organizing it, they were making a good faith effort, and they were using the corporation to conduct business. In the case of a *de facto* corporation, third parties such as GS have no right to challenge its validity.

33-2 INCORPORATION PROCESS

Because there is no federal corporation code, a company can incorporate only under state law. No matter where a company actually does business, it may incorporate in any state. This decision is important because the organization must live by the laws of whichever state it chooses for incorporation.

To encourage similarity among state corporation statutes, the American Bar Association drafted the Model Business Corporation Act (the Model Act) as an example. Many states use the Model Act as a guide, although Delaware does not. This chapter provides examples from both the Model Act and Delaware. Why Delaware? Despite its small size, it has a disproportionate influence on corporate law. Over half of all public companies are incorporated there, including about two-thirds of Fortune 500 companies. About 85 percent of initial public offerings (IPOs) involve Delaware companies.

33-2a Where to Incorporate?

A corporation has to pay filing fees and franchise taxes in its state of incorporation, as well as in any state in which it does ongoing business. To avoid this double set of fees, a business that will be operating primarily in one state typically selects that state for incorporation. But if a company is going to do business in several states, it might consider choosing Delaware.

Delaware has not always been a popular choice for corporations. In the early 1900s, New Jersey held the position that Delaware does today. When Woodrow Wilson became governor (on his way to the White House), he toughened New Jersey's laws. Looking for a state with a more hospitable environment, companies found one across the Delaware River. What is good for business is good for Delaware, too. Almost one-quarter of Delaware's revenues come from its incorporation business, provided by companies that, for the most part, conduct little business in the state.

Delaware offers corporations several advantages:

- **Flexible laws that favor management.** If shareholders or directors want to take a vote in writing instead of holding a meeting, many other states require the vote to be unanimous; Delaware requires only a majority to agree. However, this advantage is diminishing as other states copy Delaware's laws.
- **An efficient court system.** Delaware has a special court (called "Chancery Court") that hears nothing but business cases and has judges who are experts in corporate law. In other states, judges who practiced in fields such as criminal law or divorce also hear corporate cases.[1] In an emergency involving, say, a hostile takeover,

[1]When Pennzoil sued Texaco in Texas over a breach of contract, the judge who tried the case was experienced in hearing divorce cases. Many lawyers felt that his ignorance of corporate matters contributed to the jury's Texas-sized verdict—$11 *billion*.

Delaware judges will hear cases and reach decisions on short notice. This preferential treatment is typically not available elsewhere, although, some other states have recently copied Delaware by establishing a business court.

- **An established body of law.** Because so many businesses incorporate in the state, its courts hear a vast number of corporate cases, creating a large body of precedent. Thus, lawyers feel they can more easily predict the outcome of a case in Delaware than in a state where few corporate disputes are tried.
- **A neutral arena.** Because very few businesses are actually based in Delaware, it is a neutral location to do battle. Better to try a case against Amazon or Microsoft in Delaware than Washington State.

The financial bonanza that Delaware realizes from its incorporation business has not gone unnoticed by other states. Nevada has modified its laws to attract companies and it is now the second most popular locale after Delaware. Other states, such as New York, Ohio, Pennsylvania, Massachusetts, and, ironically, New Jersey have also modified their corporate laws to improve the business environment in their state.

Once a company has decided *where* to incorporate, the next step is to prepare and file the charter (which may also be called the Articles of Incorporation or the Articles of Organization). The charter must always be filed with the secretary of state; some jurisdictions also require that it be filed in a county office. Some states supply a form to be completed. Delaware and the Model Act require that certain information be included, but the incorporators can list it any way they want. The incorporators may also include some optional provisions.

33-2b Charter's Required Provisions

Name

The Model Act imposes two requirements in selecting a name. First, **all corporations must use one of the following words in their name: Corporation, Incorporated, Company, or Limited. Delaware also accepts some additional terms, such as Association or Institute.** Both the Model Act and Delaware permit abbreviations (such as Inc. or Corp.) or equivalent terms in another language (such as S.A., which is the French abbreviation for corporation).

Second, under both the Model Act and Delaware law, **a new corporate name must be different from that of any corporation that already exists in that state**. If your name is Freddy du Pont, you cannot name your corporation "Freddy du Pont, Inc.," because Delaware already has a company named "E. I. du Pont de Nemours and Company." It does not matter that Freddy du Pont is your real name or that the existing company is a large chemical business while you want to open a frozen yogurt shop. The names are too similar. In addition, some states ban improper names. For example, Pennsylvania refused to accept "I Choose Hell Productions" because its statute prohibits names that "constitute blasphemy, profane cursing or swearing, or that profane the Lord's name." The state did accept ICH Productions. Zuckerberg chose "TheFacebook" because that was what Harvard students called their freshman directory.

What if you wake from a deep sleep late one night with the perfect corporate name in your head, but the charter is not quite ready for filing? In Delaware, you can reserve a name for 120 days for a fee of $75. That takes care of Delaware, but you know your corporation will soon be going national. How can you protect your name in other states? The Model Act also permits the advance registration of a corporate name. Alternatively, you can form a "nameholder" organization: A corporation that incurs minimum annual fees because it is inactive but does reserve its name.

All this bother and expense discourage most start-ups from reserving their names nationwide. If they later expand into another state where someone else is already using their name, they either buy the name back or use a different name in that jurisdiction. The problem multiplies if they want to register their name overseas as well. When Steven Spielberg, Jeffrey Katzenberg, and David Geffen launched their Hollywood studio, DreamWorks SKG, they spent nearly $500,000 to clear rights to the name in 108 countries around the world. (Of course, that was a small drop in the $2 billion bucket they raised from investors.)

Address and Registered Agent

A company must have an official address in the state in which it is incorporated so that the secretary of state knows where to contact it and so that anyone who wants to sue the corporation can serve the complaint in the state. Since most companies incorporated in Delaware do not actually have an office there, they hire a registered agent to serve as their official presence in the state.

Incorporators

The **incorporator** signs the charter and files it with the secretary of state. The incorporator is not required to buy stock, nor does he necessarily have any future relationship with the company. Often, the lawyer who prepares the charter serves as incorporator. If no lawyer is involved, typically the promoter is also the incorporator. That is what happened with Facebook—Mark Zuckerberg served as the incorporator. The incorporator incurs liability only if he knows that something in the charter is not true when he signs it.

Incorporator
The person who signs the charter and files it with the secretary of state

Ethics

Mark Zuckerberg was happy to have anyone and everyone know that he was behind Facebook because he was operating a legal business. Other, scarier types—terrorists, drug dealers, kleptocrats, and tax evaders—use so-called "shell corporations" to hide illegal money. The incorporation documents are submitted by lawyers or other professionals who do not actually own the organization, without revealing the names of the true owners.

In one case, a Nevada corporation received thousands of suspicious wire transfers totaling millions of dollars, but the authorities could not identify who was involved because there was no way to determine the actual ownership of the company. Shell corporations are listed as the buyer of almost half of the homes in America that sell for over $5 million.[2]

The U.S. Treasury issued new regulations requiring banks and mutual funds to verify the owners of any corporation or LLC that opens an account. And the Treasury has a program to identify the real buyers behind purchases of luxury real estate. What about states? Should they require corporations to disclose more information? Should they assume the role of corporate police and risk a decline in revenue from businesses that want to be secret? What is the right thing to do? What would Kant and Mill say?

bartuchna@yahoo.pl/Shutterstock.com

How much information should purchasers of these luxury apartments be required to disclose?

[2]See, for example, John A. Cassara, "Delaware, Den of Thieves," *The New York Times*, November 1, 2013. Louise Story, "U.S. Will Track Secret Buyers of Luxury Real Estate," *The New York Times*, January 13, 2016.

Purpose

The corporation is required to give its purpose for existence. In the nineteenth century, when corporations were a new concept, states thought it important to keep tight control over them. Under the ***ultra vires* doctrine**, a corporation cannot undertake any transaction unless its charter permits it. Corporate officers understandably chafed at this restriction. To avoid problems of *ultra vires*, most companies now use a very broad purpose clause such as Facebook's:

***Ultra vires* doctrine**
A corporation cannot undertake any transaction unless its charter permits it.

> The purpose of the Corporation is to engage in any lawful act or activity for which corporations may be organized under the General Corporation Law of Delaware.

Essentially, the only way to violate this purpose clause is to commit an illegal act.

Stock

The charter must provide three items of information about the company's stock.

Par Value. The concept of par value was designed to protect investors. Originally, par value was supposed to be close to market price. A company could not issue stock at a price less than par, which meant that it could not sell to insiders at a sweetheart price well below market value. (Once the stock was *issued*, it could be *traded* at any price.) In modern times, par value does not relate to market value; it is usually some nominal figure such as 1¢ or $1 per share. Companies can dispense with the concept altogether and issue stock that has no par value. When making this decision, the company should check the state's filing fees because they may be based on the par value of the company's stock. Facebook stock has a par value of $0.0001 (one-hundredth of one cent) per share.

Number of Shares. Before stock can be sold, it must first be authorized in the charter. The corporation can authorize as many shares as the incorporators choose, but the more shares, the higher the filing fee. After incorporation, a company can add authorized shares by simply amending its charter and paying the additional fee. The Facebook charter authorized the creation of ten million shares.

Stock that has been authorized but not yet sold is called **authorized and unissued**. Stock that has been sold is termed **authorized and issued** or **outstanding**. Stock that the company has sold but later bought back is **treasury stock**.

Authorized and unissued
Stock that has been authorized, but not yet sold

Authorized and issued or outstanding
Stock that has been authorized and sold

Treasury stock
Stock that a company has sold, but later bought back

Classes and series
Categories of stock with different rights

Classes and Series. Different shareholders often make different contributions to a company. Some may be involved in management, while others may simply contribute financially. Early investors may feel that they are entitled to more control than those who come along later (and who perhaps take less risk).

Corporate structure can be infinitely flexible in defining the rights of these various shareholders. Stock can be divided into categories called **classes**, and these classes can be further divided into subcategories called **series**. All stock in a series has the same rights, and all series in a class are fundamentally the same, except for minor distinctions. For example, in a *class* of preferred stock, all shareholders may be entitled to a dividend, but the amount of the dividend may vary by *series*. Different classes of stock, however, may have very different rights—a class of preferred stock is different from a class of common stock. Exhibit 33.1 illustrates the concept of class and series. Defining the rights of a class or series of stock is like baking a cake—**stock can contain virtually any combination of the following ingredients** (although the result may not be to everyone's taste):

- **Dividend rights.** The charter establishes whether the shareholder is entitled to dividends and may also specify the amount and timing of payment. No matter what the

EXHIBIT 33.1

Classes and Series of Stock

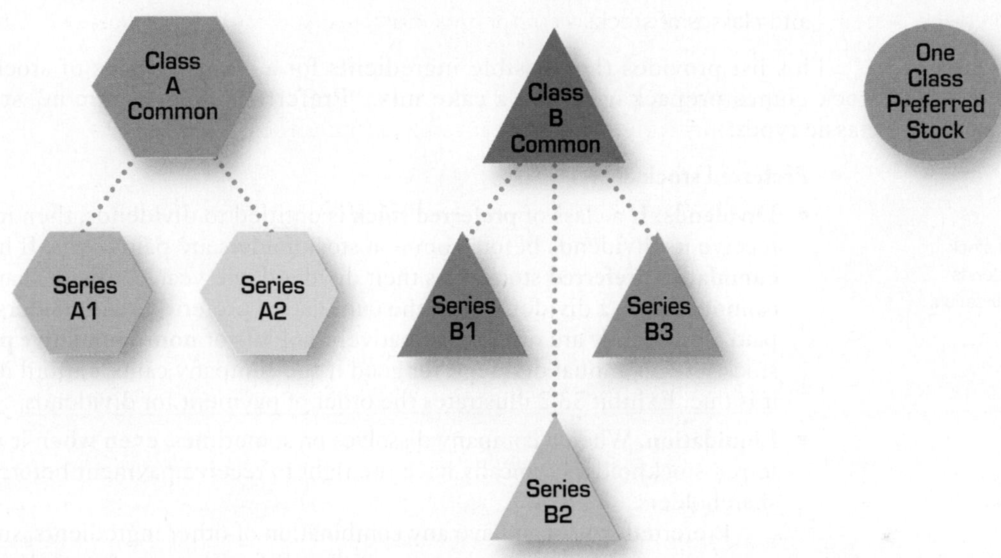

charter says, the corporation may not pay dividends unless it is solvent, that is, unless it has enough assets to pay its debts.

- **Liquidation rights.** The charter specifies the order in which classes of stockholders will be paid upon dissolution of the company. This provision is important if there are not enough assets to pay everyone.
- **Conversion rights.** Some classes of stock may have the right to convert into shares of a different class. Many companies issue preferred shares to early investors that can convert into common stock.
- **Redemption rights.** Similarly, the shareholders of some classes of stock may have the right to force a company to buy their stock back if, for example, the company does not meet its financial goals.
- **Preemptive rights.** If a corporation later issues additional shares of its stock, the original shareholders will own a smaller percentage of the company. For example, if a company has ten shareholders, each owning one share, and it later issues another ten shares to others, each of the old shareholders will then own 5 percent of the company instead of 10 percent. Preemptive rights give the old shareholders the right to purchase enough new stock to prevent their share of the company from being diminished. In our example, the old shareholders would be entitled to buy enough new shares to keep their ownership at 10 percent. Of course, they are not required to buy this stock.
- **Anti-dilution rights.** If the holders of one class of stock (say, convertible preferred) have the right to convert their shares into common stock, anti-dilution rights adjust

that conversion ratio. Thus, when the company issues more shares of common stock, each share of convertible preferred will be able to convert into more shares of common.

- **Voting rights.** Shareholders are usually entitled to elect directors and vote on charter amendments, among other issues, but these rights can vary among different series and classes of stock.

This list provides the possible ingredients for a class or series of stock. But some stock comes prepackaged like a cake mix. "Preferred" and "common" stock are two classic types:

Preferred stock
The owners of preferred stock have preference on dividends and also, typically, in liquidation.

- **Preferred stock.**
  - **Dividends.** If a class of **preferred stock** is entitled to dividends, then it must receive its dividends before common stockholders are paid theirs. If holders of **cumulative preferred** stock miss their dividend one year, common shareholders cannot receive a dividend until the cumulative preferred shareholders have been paid all that they are owed. Alternatively, holders of **non-cumulative preferred** stock lose an annual dividend for good if the company cannot afford it in the year it is due. Exhibit 33.2 illustrates the order of payment for dividends.
  - **Liquidation.** When a company dissolves or, sometimes, even when it is sold, preferred stockholders typically have the right to receive payment before common shareholders.

    Preferred stock can have any combination of other ingredients, such as preemptive, anti-dilution, or conversion rights. Sometimes preferred shareholders have voting rights, but usually they do not.
- **Common stock.** Common shareholders have a right to share in the profits of the company and typically have most of the voting rights.
- **Participating preferred stock.** Venture capitalists (professional investors who are in the business of financing companies) often choose this type of stock, which permits them to have their cake and eat it, too. Upon liquidation of the company, these shareholders are paid first, receiving whatever they paid for the stock plus accrued dividends. Then they are treated as if they had converted their preferred shares into common stock, so they share the rest of the proceeds with common shareholders.

EXHIBIT 33.2

The Order of Payment for Dividends to Preferred and Common Stockholders

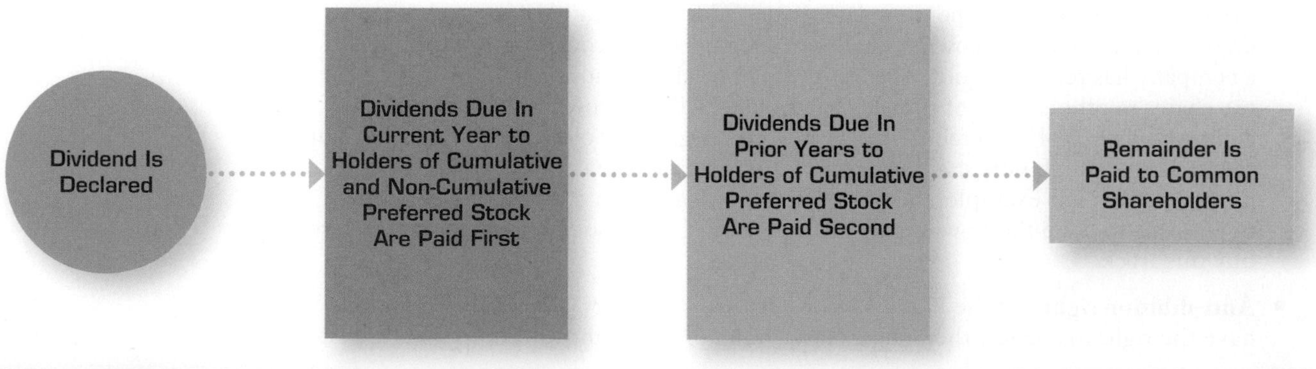

Ethics

Entrepreneurs and venture capitalists are increasingly sophisticated at protecting their rights, which sometimes means that employees and investors in public offerings are very much second-class owners.

When venture capitalists buy into a company, they typically obtain preferred shares with anti-dilution and liquidation rights that are not available to, say, regular employees or common shareholders. Then, if the company is sold for a per-share price lower than the amount preferred shareholders paid, or less than their liquidation rights, the common shareholders get nothing. Thus, when BlackBerry bought Good Technology (which was not so good), venture capitalists with preferred shares received $125 million, while many of the employees with common stock were left with nothing.

Common shareholders who buy in an initial public offering (IPO) may also receive second-class treatment. Some companies—including Google, GoPro, Groupon, Facebook, Under Armour, and Zynga, have gone public with a multi-class structure under which outside investors have few voting rights. In a typical case, the founders or insiders own Class A stock that has ten times the voting power of the Class B share that is sold to the public (although in Zynga's case, it was 70 times). In this way, insiders can still control the company, even as they sell off their stock.

Now, some of these companies have decided that a ten to one ratio is no longer sufficient. Google, Zillow, and Under Armour have authorized for future issuance a class of stock with no voting rights at all. In its IPO, the hot tech company Snap only sold stock that had no right to vote. As a result, Snap's founders owned 40 percent of the company but controlled 70 percent of the voting rights. (Although if their ownership falls below 30 percent, their shares convert into regular common stock.)

The founders of these companies justify their decision by arguing that they are visionaries with a long-term perspective who need protection from short-term shareholders. But under this class structure, any dissent to any decision is impossible. Many of these young founders could be in control for decades. Is CEO-For-Life a good idea? Is it reasonable to bet that they will be at the top of their game for so long? Or that they will always do the right thing for the company?

Overall, these tightly controlled companies have lower shareholder returns and return on equity but CEO pay that is 40 percent higher than in noncontrolled firms.[3] Recently, a group of CEOs and money managers issued a "Commonsense Principles of Corporate Governance" that advised against these multi-class voting rights.[4]

What ethical obligation do these founders and venture capitalists have? Is all fair in love, war, and start-ups? What would Kant and Mill say? What Life Principles are operating?

33-2c Charter's Optional Provisions

Many corporations add optional provisions to their charters. Bear in mind, however, that once a provision is in the charter, it can be changed only by a vote of the shareholders and the filing of an amendment with the secretary of state. This process can be cumbersome and expensive. Therefore, when in doubt, it is usually a good idea not to include extra provisions in the charter. Nonetheless, some provisions are so important that they belong there, despite the effort and expense required to change them.

---

[3]Edward Kamonjoh, "Controlled Companies in the Standard & Poor's 1500," Investor Responsibility Research Center Institute, March 2016.

[4]The CEOs included Mary Barra (GM), Warren Buffett (Berkshire Hathaway), James Dimon (J.P. Morgan), and Jeffrey Immelt (GE).

Director Liability

Although incorporation protects shareholders against personal liability for the debts of the company, anyone involved in the management of the business can be personally liable for his own wrongdoing. For example, shareholders may sue directors for making an unprofitable decision. The potential liability in such a lawsuit is enormous. Even if the director is found not liable, the legal fees can be devastating.

Exculpatory clause
A provision that protects directors from personal liability to the corporation and its shareholders

Under most state statutes, a corporation may include in its charter a provision that protects directors from personal liability to the corporation and its shareholders for anything other than egregious misbehavior involving, for example, bad faith or intentional misconduct.[5] These provisions are called **exculpatory clauses**. The Facebook charter has an exculpatory clause stating:

> To the fullest extent permitted by the Delaware General Corporation Law . . . a director of the Corporation shall not be personally liable to the Corporation or its stockholders for monetary damages for breach of fiduciary duty as a director.

Indemnification provision
A company pays the legal fees of directors who are sued for actions taken on behalf of the company.

Corporations also typically add an **indemnification provision** to their charter that requires the company to pay the legal fees of directors who are sued for actions taken on behalf of the company. Without these protective provisions, companies would find it difficult to hire directors.

The following case illustrates the power of an exculpatory clause: The directors would not be liable—even for acts of gross negligence.

Rodriguez v. Loudeye Corporation

144 Wn. App. 709
Washington Court of Appeals, 2008

Facts: Loudeye Corporation provided digital music for cell phones and other consumer electronics. It was headquartered in Seattle, Washington, but incorporated in Delaware (where it did not have any offices). As permitted under Delaware law, Loudeye's charter had an exculpatory clause protecting directors from liability. Such provisions were unenforceable under Washington law.

When Loudeye's directors decided to sell the company, Nokia offered a price that was three times market value. After extensive negotiations with Nokia and an unsuccessful search for other buyers, Loudeye's board accepted Nokia's bid.

A Loudeye shareholder named Eli Rodriguez filed suit against five members of the board of directors, alleging that they had breached their fiduciary duties by failing to obtain the best price. He thought the board should have conducted a formal auction. He also alleged that the board had conflicts of interest and had approved the sale because they would receive special financial benefits (such as severance payments and stock options).

The Loudeye directors filed a motion to dismiss, alleging that the exculpatory clause in the company's charter protected them from liability. Rodriguez argued that Washington law applied and, therefore, the clause was invalid. He also argued that, even if the exculpatory clause was valid, it did not protect the directors in this case. The trial court granted the motion to dismiss and Rodriguez appealed.

Issues: ***Which state law applies to a company that is headquartered in Washington but incorporated in Delaware? Are the directors liable?***

Excerpts from Judge Agid's Decision: Shareholder claims involving a corporation's internal affairs are governed by the law of the state in which the corporation was

[5] See, for example, 8 Del. C. §102b(7).

incorporated. Thus, because Loudeye is a Delaware corporation, Delaware law applies here.

[T]o the extent these allegations describe gross negligence in the sale of the corporation, their conduct is not actionable. [O]nly if there are allegations establishing that the director's conduct is motivated by an actual intent to do harm, or occurs when directors consciously and intentionally disregard their responsibilities, and is conduct so far beyond the bounds of reasonable judgment that it seems essentially inexplicable on any ground other than bad faith [are the directors liable].

[A]s the directors point out, [that] situation typically is when the directors in the acquired corporation also have interests in the acquiring corporation or when directors seek to entrench themselves in their positions of control. But neither situation is present here. The complaint therefore fails to state a claim.

We affirm the trial court's dismissal of the complaint.

Cumulative Voting

For sheer drama, few corporate battles have exceeded the fight between the elephant, Gulf Oil, and the flea, Mesa Petroleum. When T. Boone Pickens, the CEO of Mesa, announced that Gulf Oil was badly managed, he was picking on the sixth-largest oil company in America. Pickens nominated himself to be Gulf's savior. His plan was to buy enough of the company's shares so that he could elect himself to the board of directors. Pickens's goal was possible only because Gulf was incorporated in Pennsylvania, a state that then required cumulative voting.

At the time, Gulf Oil had 15 directors, all elected annually. Under a *regular* voting system, the 15 people who receive the most votes are awarded the seats. If Pickens owned one share, he could vote for as many as 15 *different* candidates, but he could not aggregate his votes; that is, he could not cast multiple votes for any one candidate. Thus, he could only vote for himself to be director once. To be sure of getting elected to the board, he would have to buy half of Gulf's shares, plus one. Gulf had 165 million shares outstanding, so Pickens would have to buy 82,500,001 shares. Once he had bought that many shares, he could elect *all* the directors because he would own a majority of the company's stock. As Gulf's stock was trading at around $40 per share, Pickens would have had to invest more than $3 billion ($3,300,000,040) to achieve his goal.

For sheer drama, few corporate battles have exceeded the fight between the elephant, Gulf Oil, and the flea, Mesa Petroleum.

Under a cumulative voting system, however, Pickens could aggregate his shares and vote them all for the same person (in this case, himself). How many shares would Pickens have to own to elect himself to the board? This is the formula:

$$\text{Number of shares needed to elect one director} = \frac{\text{Number of shares outstanding}}{\text{Number of directors being elected} + 1} + 1$$

This is how the formula worked in Pickens's case, where x stands for the number of shares he needed to elect one director:

$$x = \frac{165{,}000{,}000}{15 + 1} + 1$$

$$x = 10{,}312{,}501$$

Ten million shares is a lot less than the 82 million he needed under a regular voting system. At a price per share of $40, Pickens would have had to invest roughly $400 million ($412,500,040) under a cumulative voting system, compared with $3 billion under a regular system.

In a desperate effort to prevent Pickens from being elected to its board of directors, Gulf called a special meeting of shareholders to change its state of incorporation from Pennsylvania to Delaware and eliminate cumulative voting. (Delaware and the Model Act both permit, but do not require it.) For months, both sides ran full-page advertisements in newspapers across the country to persuade shareholders. Gulf spent $9 million and Mesa $8 million on the fight alone, not counting money spent buying Gulf shares. In the end, Gulf won the battle but lost the war. It won the shareholder vote by a small margin, but the company was so weakened by this fight that it sold out to Chevron Oil shortly thereafter. The fight so frightened other companies that many changed their state of organization to Delaware. Pennsylvania then changed its statute to be like Delaware's.

33-3 AFTER INCORPORATION

Once the charter has been filed (and the filing fee paid), the corporation legally exists, but work is not done yet. A few additional tasks remain.

33-3a Directors and Officers

Once the corporation is organized, **the incorporators elect the first set of directors. Thereafter, shareholders elect directors.** Under the Model Act, a corporation is required to have at least one director unless (1) *all* the shareholders sign an agreement that eliminates the board or (2) the corporation has 50 or fewer shareholders. To elect directors, the shareholders may hold a meeting, or, in the more typical case for a small company, they elect directors by **written consent**. (Under the Model Act, all the shareholders must sign but, as you remember, a majority is sufficient in Delaware.) A typical written consent looks like this:

Written consent
A signed document that takes the place of a shareholders' or directors' meeting

---

Classic American Novels, Inc.
Written Consent

The undersigned shareholders of Classic American Novels, Inc., a corporation organized and existing under the General Corporation Law of the State of Wherever, hereby agree that the following action shall be taken with full force and effect as if voted at a validly called and held meeting of the shareholders of the corporation:

Agreed: That the following people are elected to serve as directors for one year, or until their successors have been duly elected and qualified:

Herman Melville
Louisa May Alcott
Mark Twain

Dated:_______________ Signed:_______________
Willa Cather

Dated:_______________ Signed:_______________
Nathaniel Hawthorne

Dated:_______________ Signed:_______________
Harriet Beecher Stowe

Once the incorporators or shareholders have chosen the directors, **the directors must elect the officers of the corporation**. They can use a consent form, if they wish. Delaware law and the Model Act simply require a corporation to have whatever officers are described in the bylaws. The same person can hold more than one office. Exhibit 33.3 illustrates the election process in corporations.

EXHIBIT 33.3

The Election Process in Corporations

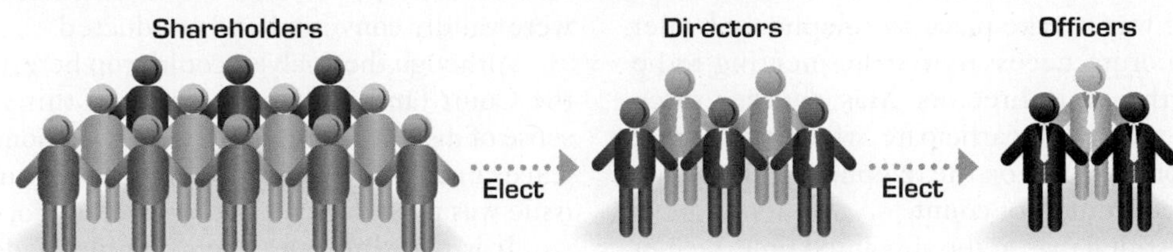

The written consents and any records of actual meetings are kept in a **minute book**, which is a record of the corporation's official actions. Entrepreneurs sometimes feel they are too busy to bother with all these details, but if a corporation is ever sold, the lawyers for the buyers will insist on a well-organized and complete minute book. In one case, a company that was seeking a bank loan could not find all of its minutes. Many of its early shareholders and directors were not available to reauthorize prior deeds. In the end, the company had to merge itself into a newly created corporation so it could start fresh with a new set of corporate records. The company spent 10 percent of the loan principal just on this task. Be warned!

Minute book
A book that contains a record of a corporation's official actions

33-3b Bylaws

The **bylaws** list the organizational rules for the corporation. For example, bylaws set the date of the annual shareholders' meeting, define what a **quorum** is (e.g., how many people or shares must be present for a meeting to count), indicate the required number of directors, give titles to officers, fix the procedure for calling a special meeting of the shareholders or directors, and establish the fiscal (i.e., tax) year of the corporation. When there is a choice, it is usually better to place provisions in the bylaws rather than the charter, because the bylaws are easier to change.

Bylaws
A document that specifies the organizational rules of a corporation or other organization, such as the date of the annual meeting and the required number of directors

Under Delaware law, shareholders have the right to amend the bylaws, but the charter can also permit the directors to do so. The shareholders can always override the directors, but they rarely do. The Facebook charter provides that "... the Board of Directors of the Corporation is expressly authorized to make, amend, or repeal Bylaws of the Corporation."

Quorum
How many people or shares must be present for a meeting to count

In the following case, the directors' ignorance of their own bylaws led to disaster.

In re Bigmar

2002 Del. Ch. LEXIS 45; 2002 WL 550469
Court of Chancery, Delaware, 2002

Facts: Bigmar was a Delaware corporation that manufactured and marketed pharmaceuticals in Europe. While trying to raise additional capital, the company's founder, John Tramontana, met Cynthia May. She lied to him about her education, wealth, and connections. Unfortunately, he believed her. The upshot was that May became Bigmar's president and a director of the company. She soon took control of the company's financial records and refused to give Tramontana any information (always a bad sign).[6] When Bigmar ran out of money, Tramontana sent May an email asking for her resignation. She did not respond. (Also a bad sign.)

6She did, however, send him this email: I wish for GOd's sake that you would GROW [UP] just a little . . . you've F the banking up here in Sweden so I can't get the money that I made [arrangements] for . . . damn idiot . . . take a shower and clean your ears out . . . you can't follow a straight line without having your ego and little hissy fits . . . Get off the playground . . . before the big boys beat you up. . ..

The company was in desperate financial shape, but Tramontana managed to find a bank willing to buy $1 million of Bigmar stock. He called a special meeting of the board of directors to approve the sale of shares and to fire May. The meeting was to take place by telephone. Under the bylaws, the quorum necessary for the meeting to be valid was five of the nine directors. May and her three allies on the board refused to participate, which meant that every other director had to be on the telephone at the same time or the meeting would not count.

Tramontana testified that, at the appointed time, he met with two directors in his office. They used a speaker feature on a cell phone that Tramontana borrowed from Danilo Graticola to call two other directors, one of whom was in Heathrow Airport in London. The five directors unanimously voted to sell the stock to the bank. The meeting then adjourned so that they could consult counsel. It was reconvened the next day, at which time they voted to fire May.

The following day, Tramontana instructed the company's transfer agent to send stock certificates to the bank, but May contradicted his order. Tramontana and May went to court to determine if the directors' meeting was valid and the bank entitled to the shares.

Issue: ***Was the meeting of the Bigmar board of directors valid?***

Excerpts from Judge Jacobs's Decision: Ms. May attacks the validity of the meeting(s) [claiming that] no meeting at which a quorum of directors was present ever took place.

There is evidence that the meeting(s) did occur. Minutes of the meetings were prepared, and all but one of the Tramontana directors gave sworn testimony that the meeting(s) took place exactly as the minutes recite. Ordinarily that would be sufficient, but this is not an ordinary case, for several reasons.

First, the minutes were prepared by counsel, who was not present at the meetings and who simply reduced to writing what Mr. Tramontana told him had occurred. Second, there is no independent documentation or testimony of any third-party witness that corroborates the directors' testimony. Moreover, any notes taken at the meeting(s) were destroyed. Further, many of the telephone records whose production was requested were not produced, and the records that were produced either fail to corroborate the Tramontana directors' testimony,[7] or those documents are inconsistent with that testimony.[8] Accordingly, the Court is unable to determine that those directors' meetings were validly convened and conducted.

Although the analysis could stop here, that would leave the Court (and perhaps a reader of this Opinion) with a sense of dissatisfaction because Mr. Tramontana's testimony leaves unanswered questions. In purely human terms, this issue was most difficult and perplexing for the Court.

It is plausible, and the available evidence does indicate, that Mr. Tramontana attempted to assemble all of his colleagues for a telephonic meeting. [But one director] was unavailable, as he was en route from London to Ireland at that time. Because a quorum required the attendance of five directors, [this director's] unavailability meant that the telephonic meeting failed for lack of a quorum. Mr. Tramontana believed, nonetheless, that the problem could be solved by obtaining from himself and his colleagues' individual written consent resolutions taking the actions recited in the minutes. Unfortunately (and unbeknownst to Mr. Tramontana), Bigmar's by-laws required that any director action by written consent must be unanimous. [When] Mr. Tramontana learned of that unanimity requirement, [he] decided to [say] that a quorum of five directors was present and that a board meeting was held.

I am persuaded that [Mr. Tramontana and his colleagues acted] in the good-faith belief that unless the issuance of the shares to the Bank was upheld, the Company would fall into the hands of Ms. May, who was incapable of saving the Company. I think it plausible that they believed that at worst, they failed to observe a highly technical legal requirement that, on balance, was too insignificant to justify the ruination of the Company.

The principles of corporate governance, such as those violated here, exist precisely because those procedures enable courts and parties to distinguish between acts that lawfully bind the corporation and its constituents, from those that do not. The directors may have believed in good faith that they had no alternative but to testify as they did, but good faith is not sufficient to validate a procedurally invalid proceeding.

---

[7][The] cell phone bills for the [director who is supposed to have received a call in the London airport] do not show any incoming calls to him at Heathrow Airport at 3:00 p.m., London time, which is when the meeting is said to have started. Since [his] cell phone provider was located in Ireland where he lived, [this director] would have incurred a roaming charge for any calls received outside of Ireland, and the roaming charge would have been reflected on his cell phone bill.

[8]For example, Mr. Tramontana's telephone records show that he made an 11-minute telephone call to Mr. Graticola's cell phone number at 7:12 p.m.—a time that Mr. Tramontana claimed to have had Mr. Graticola's cell phone in his possession.

33-3c Shareholder Agreements

The shareholders of a start-up company often work together intensively. If a shareholder sells her stock to someone who does not share the same vision, conflict is inevitable. To avoid this situation, **shareholders of start-ups often sign a shareholder agreement that establishes a process for selling their stock, should the need arise.** A typical agreement establishes a formula by which a fair price can be calculated for insider sales and also provides for a right of first refusal if a shareholder wants to sell to an outsider. In the case of an outside sale, a shareholder is usually required to first offer the stock to the company at the same price that the outsider is willing to pay. If, after 30 days, the company has not agreed to buy the stock, she must then offer it to the other shareholders. Only if they also refuse to buy it within 30 days can she then sell it to an outsider at the same price that she offered to the company and shareholders. Similarly, if a shareholder dies, his estate may be required to offer the stock to the company or other shareholders at an agreed-upon formula. Later in this chapter, you will read the *Shawe* case—litigation that could have been avoided with the right shareholder agreement.

33-3d Foreign Corporations

A company is called a **domestic corporation** in the state in which it was incorporated and a **foreign corporation** everywhere else. **A corporation must *qualify to do business* in any state in which it is doing business but was not incorporated.** "Doing business" means opening an office or establishing any other ongoing presence in the state. To obtain the required certificate of authority, the company must register, list a registered agent, and pay annual fees and taxes on income generated in that jurisdiction.

Domestic corporation
A corporation operating in the state in which it was incorporated

Foreign corporation
A corporation operating in a state in which it was not incorporated

Qualify to do business
Registering as a foreign corporation in any state in which a business operates but was not incorporated

As a general rule, of course, companies would prefer not to qualify to do business. Some states fine any companies they catch doing business without registering. Under the Model Act, a company that is doing business without qualifying cannot bring a lawsuit in that state until it registers (and pays back fees, taxes, and penalties). But note that, if a corporation is not actually doing business, then it may file suit without qualifying first. And whether or not a corporation has qualified, it can always *defend* against a lawsuit.

Ned has sworn that he will never again suffer through a bitter Chicago winter. No, he is not relocating; he has invented a new fabric that looks like fur. It is better than real fur, though, because it is waterproof and washable. He knows that his business will soon be a national success.

Ned, like many entrepreneurs before him, incorporates Fabulous Fake Furs, Inc. (FFF), in Delaware. Company headquarters are in Chicago, the main manufacturing facility in Texas, with warehouses in Minnesota and New York. A sales staff calls on all the major department stores and online merchants across the country.

Ned has obligations to the state of Delaware because he incorporated there—he must pay taxes and annual fees. But what about the other states where he is doing business? Someone had to pay to build the roads and educate the workforce in these states. Must he contribute, too? The states certainly think so. Clearly, FFF must register in Illinois, Texas, Minnesota, and New York because it has a permanent presence in these states.

Typically, the following activities do *not* count as doing business: holding meetings, opening a bank account, soliciting sales orders, or any isolated transaction. If FFF's directors hold a meeting in Alaska, Ned attends a trade show in Wisconsin, or a sales rep takes an order at a store in California, those activities do not constitute doing business, and FFF does not have to register in those states.

EXAMStrategy

Question: You are about to form a corporation. What do you have to do before filling out the form? Which provisions are boilerplate and, therefore, do not require special effort on your part?

Strategy: Review the description of required and optional charter provisions.

Result: Before filling out the form, you need to choose a name and check to make sure it is available. If you are incorporating someplace where you do not have an office, you will also have to hire a registered agent. You do not have to decide the purpose of the corporation; standard boilerplate works here. Unless you will have outside investors from the beginning, you do not have to think a lot about your capital structure—that is, the number and par value of your shares. Just authorize as many shares as you can for the base filing fee, and choose a nominal par value. It makes sense to add an exculpatory clause to protect your directors from liability, especially if you are going to be one. There is no need for cumulative voting at this stage.

33-4 DEATH OF THE CORPORATION

Sometimes, a corporation fails—either the business is unsuccessful, or the shareholders cannot work together. This death can be voluntary (the shareholders elect to terminate the corporation) or forced (by a decision of the secretary of state or by court order).

33-4a Voluntary Termination by the Shareholders

To terminate a corporation, the shareholders undertake a three-step process:

1. **Vote.** The directors recommend to the shareholders that the corporation be dissolved, and a majority of the shareholders agree.
2. **Filing.** The corporation files Articles of Dissolution with the secretary of state.
3. **Winding up.** The officers of the corporation pay its debts and distribute the remaining property to shareholders. When the winding up is completed, the corporation ceases to exist.

33-4b Termination by the State

The secretary of state may dissolve a corporation that fails to comply with state requirements such as paying the required annual fees. Indeed, many corporations, particularly small ones, do not bother with the formal dissolution process. They simply walk away and let the secretary of state act.

A court may also dissolve a corporation or order that it be sold, if it is insolvent or if its directors and shareholders cannot resolve conflict over how the corporation should be managed. The court will then appoint a custodian to oversee the process.

You might remember that Chapter 31 on starting a business began with a case involving Horning LLC. The three members despised each other but, under the LLC statute, the court could not intervene because the business was successful.[9] The three members of the LLC were left to fight it out.

The following case is a similar situation: The business idea was great—the corporation had revenues of almost half a billion dollars—but the two shareholders were at each other's throats. Under Delaware corporation law a court can intervene, even if the business is successful.

[9]The NY statute in that case provided that the court could only order dissolution of an LLC "whenever it is not reasonably practicable to carry on the business." The Delaware LLC statute has the same language.

Shawe v. Elting

2017 Del. LEXIS 62
Delaware Supreme Court, 2017

Facts: Elizabeth Elting and Philip Shawe had been both business and romantic partners. Operating from their dorm room at the New York University business school, they founded TransPerfect Global, Inc., (TPG or the Company) in 1992. They both owned half of TPG's stock, were co-chief executive officers, and were the only directors. By the time of this litigation, the company was providing translation, website localization, and litigation support services at 92 offices in 86 cities worldwide, operating in 170 different languages.[10]

In 1997, when Elting broke off the couple's plan to marry, Shawe promised to "create constant pain" for her (which certainly confirmed the wisdom of her decision). His systematic harassment campaign included:

- Intercepting Elting's mail, monitoring her phone calls, and breaking into her email accounts.
- Circulating an email to company employees wrongly accusing her of financial misdeeds.
- Hiring numerous employees without her knowledge by creating "off book" arrangements and fabricating documents.
- Interfering with TPG's audit process.
- Telling the police that she had assaulted him during a disagreement in the office. When he filed the police report, he deliberately referred to her as his "ex-fiancée" (17 years after their break up) knowing that, in domestic violence cases, the police had to arrest the assaulting party.
- Taking a flight to Paris just so he could surprise her by sitting across the aisle and then bragging that she changed seats to get away from him.

Shawe and Elting also engaged in "mutual hostaging." For example, Elting would not allow Shawe to hire employees or pay a lawyer's bill unless he agreed to the profit distribution she wanted. Senior officers who took sides were threatened with firing, huge fines, or the withholding of compensation and promotions.

As a result of this turmoil, major clients became reluctant to renew contracts. TPG executives called the feud the "biggest business issue" facing the Company. Shawe himself acknowledged the conflict's "potential for grievously harming" the Company.

Elting filed suit asking the Delaware Court of Chancery to order the sale of TPG. After mediation efforts failed, the court appointed a custodian to sell the Company. Shawe appealed.

Issue: ***Should the court have ordered the sale of a highly profitable business?***

Excerpts from Justice Seitz's Decision: [Delaware law] provides that a custodian may be appointed when "the business of the corporation is suffering or is threatened with irreparable injury because the directors are so divided respecting the management of the affairs of the corporation." "[I]rreparable injury" takes into account factors like harm to a corporation's reputation, goodwill, customer relationships, and employee morale.

[T]he Court of Chancery accepted the fact that the Company was profitable, but also recognized the extremely dysfunctional relationship between the founders and its effect on all of the Company's operations. If allowed to persist, the Company was likely to continue on the path of plummeting employee morale, key employee departures, customer uncertainty, damage to the Company's public reputation and goodwill, and a fundamental inability to grow the Company through acquisitions. The trial record amply supports the Court of Chancery's finding that the deadlock and dysfunction between the founders is causing irreparable injury to the Company.

We agree with Shawe that a sale is a remedy to be employed reluctantly and cautiously, after a consideration of other options. [T]he court attempted other less intrusive measures by appointing a mediator. Further, the court considered whether to appoint a custodian to serve as a third director or some form of tie-breaking mechanism in the governance of the Company. But the court rejected this option because it would enmesh an outsider, and, by extension, the Court into matters of internal corporate governance for an extensive period of time. Shawe and Elting are both relatively young. [T]heir tenure as directors and co-CEOs of the Company could continue for decades. It is not sensible for the Court to exercise essentially perpetual oversight over the internal affairs of the Company.

By preserving the Company as a whole, the Chancellor's remedy also was well designed to protect the other constituencies of the Company—notably its employees—by positioning the company to succeed and thus to secure the jobs of its workforce.

The Court of Chancery's orders are affirmed.

---

[10] Website localization is the process of adapting a website from one country into the language and culture of another.

A court also has the right to take a step that is much more damaging to shareholders than simply selling or dissolving the corporation—it can remove the shareholders' limited liability.

33-4c Piercing the Corporate Veil

Pierce the corporate veil
A court holds shareholders personally liable for the debts of the corporation.

One of the major purposes of a corporation is to protect its owners—the shareholders—from personal liability for the debts of the organization. However, as was the case with LLCs, courts have the right to **pierce the corporate veil**, that is, to hold shareholders personally liable for the debts of the corporation. As you remember from Chapter 31 on starting a business, **courts generally pierce a corporate veil in four circumstances:**

- **Failure to observe formalities.** If an organization does not act like a corporation, it will not be treated like one. It must, for example, hold required shareholders' and directors' meetings (or ensure that consents are signed), keep a minute book as a record of these meetings, and make all the required state filings. Even a corporation with only one shareholder must comply with these formalities. Sole shareholders usually just sign a written consent in lieu of a meeting.

  In addition, as we saw in the *GS Petroleum* case, officers must be careful to sign all corporate documents with a corporate title, not as an individual. Otherwise, creditors may well be in doubt about whether they were dealing with an individual or a corporation and the officer may be personally liable. An officer should sign like this:

  Classic American Novels, Inc.
  By: Stephen Crane

  Stephen Crane, President

- **Commingling assets.** Nothing makes a court more willing to pierce a corporate veil than evidence that shareholders used corporate assets to pay their personal debts or mixed their assets with those of the corporation. If shareholders commingle assets, it is genuinely difficult for creditors to determine which assets belong to whom. This confusion is generally resolved in favor of the creditors—*all* assets are deemed to belong to the corporation.

- **Inadequate capitalization.** If the founders of a corporation do not raise enough capital (either through debt or equity) to give the business a fighting chance of paying its debts, courts may require shareholders to pay corporate obligations. Therefore, if the corporation does not have sufficient capital, it needs to buy insurance, particularly to protect against tort liability. Judges are likely to hold shareholders liable if the alternative is to send an injured tort victim away empty-handed. Oriental Fireworks Co. had hundreds of thousands of dollars in annual sales but only $13,000 in assets. The company did not bother to obtain any liability insurance, keep a minute book, or defend lawsuits. There was no need because the company had no money. But then a court pierced the corporate veil and found the owner of the company personally liable.[11]

- **Fraud.** Corporations cannot be used to shelter fraud. If a con artist uses a corporation to steal money, the victims can go after his personal assets, even though the fraud was committed in the name of a corporation.

[11] Rice v. Oriental Fireworks Co., 75 Or. App. 627 (Or. Ct. App. 1985).

EXAMStrategy

Question: Jose was an employee and shareholder of Birdsong, a company that sold farm equipment. Jose showed Marta how to use the hay baler she had just bought from the company. He also gave her an instructional pamphlet that Birdsong had prepared. Unfortunately, Jose's advice was wrong, and so was the pamphlet's. Marta was injured while using the baler. It turned out that Birdsong's charter had been revoked for failure to make the required annual filings with the Arkansas secretary of state. In all other ways, Birdsong operated as a corporation. Were Birdsong and Jose liable to Marta?

Strategy: Jose could be liable as a shareholder (1) because the charter of the corporation had been revoked or (2) if the corporate veil was pierced. In addition, he could have been personally liable for his own wrongdoing.

Result: Birdsong was held liable for its carelessness in preparing the pamphlet. Although Birdsong was not technically a corporation, it had operated as one. Therefore, under the theory of corporation by estoppel, Jose was not liable for that corporate wrongdoing. Nor had Birdsong done anything to warrant its veil being pierced. Jose was, however, liable for his own negligence. Therefore, he was liable for the bad advice he gave Marta.

CHAPTER CONCLUSION

Virtually every businessperson will, at some point, work for a corporation or own shares in one. Indeed, corporations are so important that wc devote three chapters to them. Although they are an exceedingly useful form of organization, they are also exceedingly formal. State corporation codes contain precise rules that must bc followed to the letter. To do otherwise is to court disaster.

EXAM REVIEW

1. **PROMOTERS** Promoters are personally liable for contracts they sign before the corporation is formed unless the corporation adopts the contract and the third party agrees to a novation or it is clear that the parties to the contract did not intend the promoter to be liable.

EXAMStrategy

Question: Ajouelo signed an employment contract with Wilkerson. The contract stated: "Whatever company, partnership, or corporation that Wilkerson may form for the purpose of manufacturing shall succeed Wilkerson and exercise the rights and assume all of Wilkerson's obligations as fixed by this contract." Two months later, Wilkerson formed Auto-Soler Co. Ajouelo entered into a new contract with Auto-Soler that provided that the company was liable for Wilkerson's obligations under the old contract. Neither Wilkerson nor the company ever paid Ajouelo. He sued Wilkerson personally. Does Wilkerson have any obligations to Ajouelo?

Strategy: A promoter is not liable for a contract he signed on behalf of a yet-to-be formed corporation if the third party (in this case, Wilkerson) agrees to a novation. (See the "Result" at the end of this Exam Review section.)

---

2. **STATE OF INCORPORATION** A company may incorporate in any state. A business that will be operating primarily in one state typically selects that state for incorporation. However, if it intends to operate in several states, it may choose to incorporate in a jurisdiction known for its favorable corporate laws, such as Delaware or Nevada.
3. **THE CHARTER: REQUIRED PROVISIONS** A corporate charter must include the company's name, address, registered agent, purpose, and a description of its stock, and it must be signed by the incorporator.
4. **THE CHARTER: OPTIONAL PROVISIONS** A company's charter may include a number of optional provisions, such as cumulative voting and indemnification for directors.

EXAMStrategy

Question: Does par value matter? Did it ever?

Strategy: Par value does not matter much, except that choosing the wrong one could cost the company more money. (See the "Result" at the end of this Exam Review section.)

Question: Suppose that Internet Start-up, Inc., has 2.8 million shares outstanding and eight directors. Without cumulative voting, how many shares would you have to purchase to be sure of electing yourself to the board? If the company's charter required cumulative voting, how many shares would you have to buy to achieve this goal?

Strategy: The formula for cumulative voting is:

$$\begin{array}{c}\text{Number of shares needed}\\ \text{to elect one director}\end{array} = \frac{\text{Number of shares outstanding}}{\text{Number of directors being elected} + 1} + 1$$

(See the "Result" at the end of this Exam Review section.)

---

5. **ELECTION OF OFFICERS AND DIRECTORS** Shareholders elect the directors of a corporation. The directors elect the officers.
6. **FOREIGN CORPORATION** A corporation must qualify to do business in any state in which it is doing business but was not incorporated.

7. **TERMINATION** To terminate a corporation, the shareholders undertake a three-step process: a shareholder vote, the filing of Articles of Dissolution, and the winding up of the enterprise's business. The secretary of state may also dissolve a corporation that violates state law by, for example, failing to pay the required annual fees. And a court may dissolve a corporation or order that it be sold if it is insolvent or if its directors and shareholders cannot resolve conflict over how the corporation should be managed.

8. **PIERCING THE CORPORATE VEIL** A court may hold a corporation's shareholders personally liable if they fail to observe legal formalities, commingle assets, inadequately capitalize the organization or use it to commit fraud.

RESULTS

1. Result: Wilkerson may have had an ethical obligation to Ajouelo but not a legal one. The court held that the second contract was a novation, which ended Wilkerson's obligations under the first contract.

4. Result: First question: The original purpose of par value was to protect shareholders from unscrupulous managers who wanted to issue stock at below market value. Now, it has no purpose other than as the basis for state filing fees. The only issue for modern entrepreneurs is to set it low enough that it does not trigger a higher-than-necessary filing fee. Second question: Without cumulative voting, you would have to buy 1 share more than 1.4 million shares. With cumulative voting, you would have to buy 311,112 shares.

MULTIPLE-CHOICE QUESTIONS

1. **CPA QUESTION** Generally, a corporation's articles of incorporation must include all of the following except the:
   (a) name of the corporation's registered agent.
   (b) name of each incorporator.
   (c) number of authorized shares.
   (d) quorum requirements.

2. **CPA QUESTION** Destiny Manufacturing, Inc., is incorporated under the laws of Nevada. Its principal place of business is in California, and it has permanent sales offices in several other states. Under the circumstances, which of the following is correct?
   (a) California may validly demand that Destiny incorporate under the laws of the state of California.
   (b) Destiny must obtain a certificate of authority to transact business in California and the other states in which it does business.
   (c) Destiny is a foreign corporation in California, but *not* in the other states.
   (d) California may prevent Destiny from operating as a corporation if the laws of California differ regarding organization and conduct of the corporation's internal affairs.

3. **CPA QUESTION** A corporate stockholder is entitled to which of the following rights?
   (a) Elect officers
   (b) Receive annual dividends
   (c) Approve dissolution
   (d) Prevent corporate borrowing

4. Participating preferred stockholders:
   (a) only receive payment after other preferred shareholders have been paid.
   (b) only receive payment after common shareholders have been paid.
   (c) are treated like both a preferred shareholder and a common shareholder.
   (d) receive all their payments before all other shareholders.

5. Which of the following statements is/are true?
   (a) Shareholders can amend the bylaws.
   (b) Directors can amend the bylaws.
   (c) Both shareholders and directors must approve any amendment to the bylaws.
   (d) Both A and B.

CASE QUESTIONS

1. Michael incorporated Erin Homes, Inc., to manufacture mobile homes. He issued himself a stock certificate for 100 shares for which he made no payment. He and his wife served as officers and directors of the organization, but during the eight years of its existence, the corporation held only one meeting. Erin always had its own checking account, and all proceeds from the sales of mobile homes were deposited there. It filed federal income tax returns each year using its own federal identification number. John and Thelma purchased a mobile home from Erin, but the company never delivered it to them. John and Thelma sued Erin Homes and Michael, individually. Should the court pierce the corporate veil and hold Michael personally liable?

2. Waste Management, Inc., the country's largest waste hauler, changed its name to WMX Technologies, Inc. Similarly, U.S. Steel changed its name to USX Corp., and American Airlines became AMR Corp. What legal steps would be necessary for these companies to protect their new corporate names?

3. Dickens, Inc., is a bookstore incorporated in Nevada. From its warehouse in Montana, it ships books to all 50 states. The company's owner lives in New York, and its web designer lives in California. Where is Dickens a domestic corporation? Where must it qualify to do business?

4. Suppose that a bank loaned money to Facebook at a time when both the bank and Mark Zuckerberg believed that the business had been incorporated, but they were wrong. It had not been. Could Zuckerberg refuse to pay back the loan on the grounds that it was invalid because it had been made to an entity that did not exist?

5. Auto sold used luxury vehicles. Steven owned 90 percent of Auto while his son, Joshua, was a 10 percent owner. Steven controlled Auto's finances. While Steven generally maintained appropriate, separate corporate records, the address listed on Auto's bank account was his personal address, not Auto's place of business. Steven initially capitalized Auto with a few thousand dollars, but afterward was not sure of the exact amount because he contributed funds as needed. He also claimed to have loaned $900,000 to Auto, but there was no documentation. He deposited and withdrew money from Auto's bank account at his sole discretion. Joshua worked one year at Auto, for a salary of $474,850, at a time when the company had many debts. A group of customers who never received the cars they had paid for, filed suit against Auto, Steven, and Joshua. Who is liable?

6. As *Shawe v. Elting* teaches us, a good shareholder agreement can prevent years of turmoil and litigation. If you were going to start a business, what provisions would you include in a shareholder agreement to avoid the type of all-out war that engulfed them?

DISCUSSION QUESTIONS

1. Facebook's charter has an exculpatory clause, which protects directors from liability unless they act in bad faith or they intentionally engage in wrongdoing. Is that a reasonable standard?

2. Some companies have created multiple classes of common stock that enable the founders to control their company long after it goes public. Should corporate laws permit this? If the founders want to control a company, why shouldn't they own enough regular stock to do so?

3. When Facebook went public, its disclosure document read:

   > As a board member and officer, Mr. Zuckerberg owes a fiduciary duty to our stockholders and must act in good faith in a manner he reasonably believes to be in the best interests of our stockholders. As a stockholder, even a controlling stockholder, Mr. Zuckerberg is entitled to vote his shares in his own interests, which may not always be in the interests of our stockholders.

   Should corporate laws permit Zuckerberg to control the company without imposing a duty to act in the best interests of the other shareholders?

4. **ETHICS** In the *Bigmar* case, the court clearly believed that the directors had lied on the witness stand. Should the directors have been charged with perjury? Did they do the right thing when they lied on the stand to protect their company from the evil Ms. May? What would Mill and Kant have said?

5. Some commentators have proposed tenure voting as an alternative to multi-class voting systems. With tenure voting, the longer a shareholder owns the stock, the more votes it is worth. Thus, shares held for three years might be entitled to three votes each. The theory is that such a system would encourage long-term ownership and also serve as a counterweight to insiders who have multiple votes per share. Does such a system make sense? What are the pros and cons?

34 CHAPTER

MANAGEMENT DUTIES

Dole Food Co. was one of the world's largest producers of fresh fruit and vegetables. David Murdock originally owned all of Dole but, after encountering financial difficulties, he sold 60 percent of the company to the public in an initial public offering (IPO). After the sale, he was a controlling shareholder, chairman, CEO, and comptroller. Murdock was also bully-in-chief: punishing those who disagreed with him, forcing out a board member who challenged him, and referring to himself as "the boss." "The boss does what he wants to do," he would boast. Murdock's assistant scoundrel was Michael Carter, who served as president, COO, and general counsel. (Yes, sadly, the lawyer was a bad guy.)

Yes, sadly, the lawyer was a bad guy.

Almost immediately after the IPO, Murdock began plotting to regain control of Dole. He wanted to buy out the public shareholders—as cheaply as possible. Four years after the public offering, Murdock offered to purchase the public shares for $12.00 each (a 50¢ discount from the IPO price). Under Delaware law, a purchase offer from a controlling shareholder had to be approved by a committee of the independent members of the company's board (the Committee) and also by the other shareholders.

This plan sounds perfectly reasonable, except that Murdock and Carter immediately began undermining the Committee and the shareholder vote. Their plan was to make Murdock's offer look good by driving down Dole's share price with negative information about the company. To the public, Carter announced substantially worse cost estimates than the two men truly expected. To the Committee, he presented low-ball, five-year financial projections (the July Projections) that he had manipulated to look worse than they were. The very next day he disclosed more positive (and accurate) information to Murdock's bankers in a secret meeting and in violation of the Committee's rules. The false predictions did, indeed, cause Dole's stock price to fall.

Because the Committee and its investment bank, Lazard Frères, did not believe the July Projections, they took heroic steps to prepare their own financial forecasts. But, because the information they obtained from the Dole management was wrong, so were their projections.

At the same time, other companies were interested in buying Dole stock. But Murdock refused to consider outside offers, regardless of what was best for the other shareholders. He did, however, raise his offer to $13.50.

The Committee approved Murdock's offer and so did the board. Ultimately 50.9 percent of the other shareholders voted in favor of the sale. Should this deal go through?

As you will see later in this chapter when you read the opinion in this case, Murdock and Carter violated the fundamental obligations that managers owe to shareholders. Those obligations are the subject of this chapter.

34-1 CONFLICT

Before the Industrial Revolution in the eighteenth and nineteenth centuries, a business owner typically supplied both capital and management. However, the cash needs of the great manufacturing enterprises spawned by the Industrial Revolution were larger than any small group of individuals could supply. To find capital, firms sought outside investors, who often had neither the knowledge nor the desire to manage the enterprise. Investors without management skills complemented managers without capital.

Corporations have two sets of managers: directors and officers.[1] The Model Business Corporation Act describes the directors' role thus:

> All corporate powers shall be exercised by or under the authority of, and the business and affairs of the corporation managed by or under the direction of, its board of directors ....[2]

Shareholders elect directors who set policy and then the directors appoint officers to implement these corporate goals.

34-1a What the Parties Want

Although, in theory, managers and shareholders have the same goals—the success of the business—the reality is that their interests often conflict. Legislators at both the federal and state level have tried to balance the power inside corporations, providing managers the freedom to run a business while ensuring that they act in the best interests of their shareholders.

Managers now also have the right to consider the interests of **stakeholders**: those who are affected by the activities of a corporation, such as employees, customers, creditors, suppliers, shareholders, and the communities in which they operate.

Stakeholder
Anyone who is affected by the activities of a corporation, such as employees, customers, creditors, suppliers, shareholders, and the communities in which they operate

To illustrate the differing interests of these corporate constituencies, we begin with the example of Michael Dell, who started a business selling computers out of his dorm room at the University of Texas. For many years, Dell, Inc., was a highly successful, publicly traded company. But then the company faltered as consumers replaced their desktops and laptops with tablet computers. As CEO, Michael feared the company might fail altogether unless it reinvented itself as a provider of enterprise software. But to make such a dramatic change, he thought the company needed to go private. So he offered to buy the stock of the public shareholders. But Carl Icahn, a billionaire activist investor, bought $1 billion in Dell stock

[1] Throughout these corporation chapters, the term *manager* includes both directors and officers.

[2] A committee of the American Bar Association drafted the Model Business Corporation Act to serve as a guideline for states to use when enacting a corporate code. The corporate statutes of Delaware also serve as a model for other states.

and threatened years of litigation to scuttle the deal if Michael did not raise the price. Icahn called the board of directors a dictatorship. For months, the two men fought and maneuvered. In the end, Michael was forced to raise the offer price, but the deal went through.

Managers, shareholders, and stakeholders have a conflict of interest because they each have different goals:

- Managers want three things: to maximize their income, keep their jobs, and build an institution that will survive them. Michael's goal was to keep his job, his business, and his legacy alive.
- Shareholders want a high stock price, *right now*, not five years from now. Icahn buys large blocks of stock in companies and then pressures their board to make changes. Once the price rises, he sells his stock.
- Stakeholders want the business to survive in their community and continue to provide jobs and customers. Dell, Inc., was the third largest employer in Austin, Texas.

Hostile takeover
An attempt by an outsider to acquire a company in the face of opposition from the target corporation's board of directors

The fact that we are even discussing stakeholders is a relatively new legal development. Traditionally, the law required the officers and directors of a company to focus solely on the interests of the corporation and its shareholders. But, in the 1980s, there came a wave of **hostile takeovers** and communities began to realize that, when a company was acquired, they were hurt too. A plant might be shuttered or headquarters moved. It was not just laid-off employees who suffered; real estate prices, tax receipts, charitable giving—everything did. The names used by managers and stakeholders to describe these outside investors demonstrate their unpopularity: black knight, corporate raider, predator, shark, speculator. (A more benign name is "activist.")

The Delaware Supreme Court responded. In the following Landmark Case, Delaware's Supreme Court explicitly permits the board to consider the interests of stakeholders over those of some shareholders. Commentators have described this case as "the most innovative and promising case in our recent corporation law."[3]

Landmark Case

Unocal Corp. v. Mesa Petroleum Co.

493 A.2d 946
Delaware Supreme Court, 1985

Facts: Mesa Petroleum Co. offered to purchase some of Unocal's stock at a cash price of $54 per share. Upon merger of the two companies, Mesa planned to exchange the remaining Unocal shares for "junk bonds" that Mesa (but no one else, including the court) valued at $54 per share. Unocal's investment bankers advised the board of directors that the Mesa proposal was wholly inadequate and that an offer of over $60 per share would have been reasonable. The board rejected the Mesa proposal and then made its own competing offer of $72 per share to all shareholders except Mesa. (This type of offer is called a "selective exchange offer.") The board's offer effectively preempted Mesa because no shareholder would accept the $54 Mesa offer when the $72 Unocal offer was also available.

The Delaware court issued a preliminary injunction against Unocal's offer unless it included Mesa.

Issues: ***Could Unocal make an offer to buy stock from all shareholders except Mesa? In making this offer, did Unocal have the right to consider the interests of other stakeholders?***

Excerpts from Justice Moore's Decision: In the board's exercise of corporate power to forestall a takeover bid, our analysis begins with the basic principle that corporate directors have a fiduciary duty to act in the best interests of the corporation's stockholders. The restriction placed upon a selective stock repurchase is that the directors may not have acted solely or primarily out of a desire to perpetuate

[3]City Capital Associates Ltd. Partnership v. Interco Inc. 551 A.2d 787 (Del.Ch. 1988).

themselves in office. This entails an analysis by the directors of the nature of the takeover bid and its effect on the corporate enterprise. Examples of such concerns may include inadequacy of the price offered, nature and timing of the offer, questions of illegality, the impact on "constituencies" other than shareholders (i.e., creditors, customers, employees, and perhaps even the community generally), the risk of nonconsummation, and the quality of securities being offered in the exchange. While not a controlling factor, it also seems to us that a board may reasonably consider the basic stockholder interests at stake, including those of short term speculators, whose actions may have fuelled the coercive aspect of the offer at the expense of the long-term investor.

In adopting the selective exchange offer, the board stated that its objective was either to defeat the inadequate Mesa offer or, should the offer still succeed, provide its stockholders with $72 a share. We find that both purposes are valid. However, such efforts would have been thwarted by Mesa's participation in the exchange offer. First, if Mesa could tender its shares, Unocal would effectively be subsidizing the former's continuing effort to buy Unocal stock at $54 per share. Second, Mesa could not, by definition, fit within the class of shareholders being protected from its own coercive and inadequate tender offer. Thus, we are satisfied that the selective exchange offer is reasonably related to the threats posed.

Some states have adopted statutes that codify the *Unocal* decision. These statutes permit directors, when making a decision, to consider, for example, "both the short-term and long-term best interests of the corporation, taking into account, and weighing as the directors deem appropriate, the effects thereof on the corporation's shareholders and the other corporate constituent groups…."[4]

34-1b The Business Judgment Rule

The Unocal case and equivalent state statutes *permit* managers to consider the interests of stakeholders. But the relationship with shareholders is different: **Managers have an affirmative duty to protect the interests of shareholders and the corporation.**

The officers and directors of a corporation owe a fiduciary duty to both the corporation and its shareholders.[5] As we have seen, a fiduciary relationship is one of trust. It means that the officers and directors must act in the best interest of the corporation and the shareholders.[6]

This fiduciary duty rule is easy to say but more difficult to enforce. The problem is that even well-intentioned people make mistakes. It is unreasonable to hold managers liable if they mean well but still make an unprofitable decision. And who would want to manage a corporation if they knew they could be liable for every mistake? ("How was I to know not to sell all the product merchandising rights for Star Wars to George Lucas for only $20,000?")

Over time, the business judgment rule developed to protect officers and directors who make good-faith decisions, even those that turn out badly. This rule is a common law concept that has achieved national acceptance. It is a fundamental principle of corporate law. **The business judgment rule accomplishes three goals:**

1. **It permits directors to do their job.** Business is risky. No one can guarantee perfect decision making all the time. If directors were afraid they would be liable for every decision that led to a loss, they would never make a decision, or at least not a risky one.

4Indiana Code §23-1-35-1.

5See, for example, Malone v. Brincat, 722 A.2d 5 (Del. 1998) and Gantler v. Stephens, 965 A.2d 695 (Del. 2009).

6As we have seen, a corporation can include in its charter a provision that protects directors from liability unless they act intentionally or with bad faith. No such provision is available to protect officers.

2. **It keeps judges out of corporate management.** Shareholders would generally prefer that their investments be overseen by experienced corporate managers, not judges. Without the business judgment rule, judges would be tempted, if not required, to second-guess managers' decisions.

3. **It encourages directors to serve.** No one in his right mind would serve as a director if he knew that every decision was open to attack in the courtroom. Even if the company pays the legal bills, who wants to spend years in litigation?

Under the business judgment rule, managers are not liable for decisions they make:

Duty of Loyalty	• In good faith • For a lawful purpose • Without a conflict of interest • To advance the best interests of the corporation
Duty of Care	• With the care that an ordinarily prudent person would take in a similar situation

Even if a manager violates the business judgment rule, he is still protected from liability (and his decision is upheld) under any of the following circumstances:

Special committee
Independent board members form a committee to review a transaction that violates the business judgment rule.

- **The disinterested members of the board of directors form a *special committee* that approves the decision.** Disinterested directors are those who do not themselves benefit from the transaction. The approval process must be independent and thorough.
- **The disinterested shareholders approve it.** The decision is valid if the shareholders who do not benefit from it are willing to approve it. The disclosure to the shareholders must be accurate and complete.
- **Neither board members nor shareholders approve the decision, but the court determines it was entirely fair to the corporation.** In determining fairness, the courts will consider the impact of the decision on the corporation and whether the price was reasonable.

Exhibit 34.1 illustrates the business judgment rule. Two important notes:

1. If a controlling shareholder of the company violates the business judgment rule, the court will always examine the entire fairness of the transaction, no matter how the special committee votes.[7] The controlling shareholder will be liable unless the transaction was entirely fair.
2. Even if the corporation has an indemnification provision in its charter protecting the manager from liability for wrongdoing, she will still be personally liable for any violations of the duty of loyalty, but not the duty of care.

[7]The theory behind this exception is that the independent directors will fear retaliation by the controlling shareholder if they rule against him.

EXHIBIT 34.1

The Business Judgment Rule

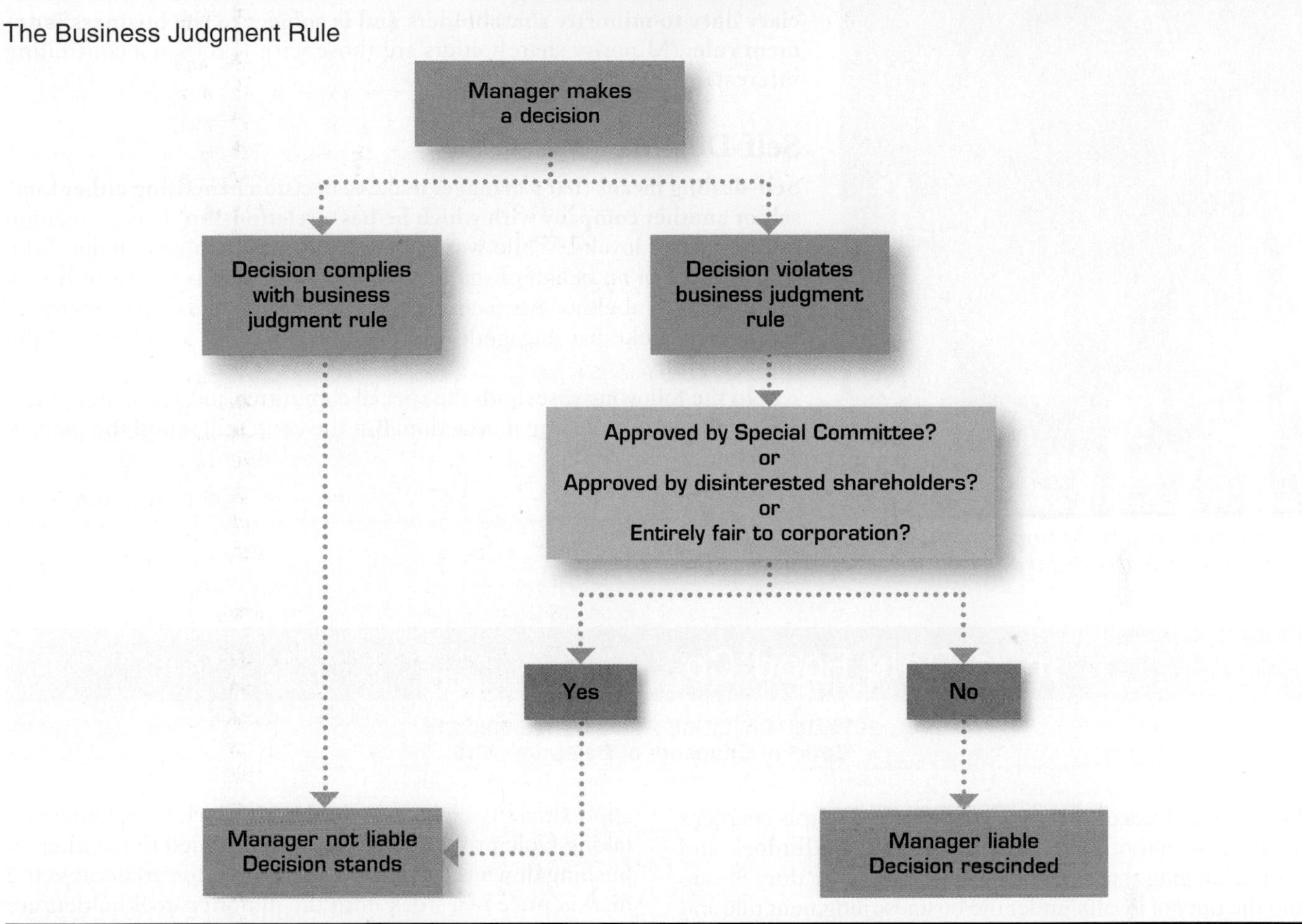

34-1c Applications of the Business Judgment Rule

Legality

An illegal activity automatically violates the business judgment rule, even if it actually helps the company and is entirely fair. The managing director of an amusement park in New York used corporate funds to purchase the silence of people who threatened to complain that the park was illegally operating on Sunday. The court ordered the director to repay the money he had spent on bribes, even though the company had earned large profits on Sundays.[8]

[8] Roth v. Robertson, 64 Misc. 343 (N.Y. Sup. Ct. 1909).

Frank Cezus/Photographer's Choice/Getty Images

The manager was liable for paying bribes to keep this profitable ride operating on Sundays.

Liability of Controlling Shareholders

Anyone who owns enough stock to control a corporation has a fiduciary duty to minority shareholders and is subject to the business judgment rule. (Minority shareholders are those with less than a controlling interest).

Self-Dealing

Self-dealing means that a manager makes a decision benefiting either himself or another company with which he has a relationship. It is a violation of the duty of loyalty. While working at the Blue Moon restaurant, Zeke signs a contract on behalf of the restaurant to purchase bread from Rising Sun Bakery. Unbeknownst to anyone at Blue Moon, he is a part owner of Rising Sun. Zeke has engaged in self-dealing, which is a violation of the duty of loyalty.

In the following case, both the special committee and the shareholders approved the self-dealing transaction. But the court still found the managers liable.

In re Dole Food Co.

2015 Del. Ch. LEXIS 223; 2015 WL 5052214
Court of Chancery of Delaware, 2015

Facts: The facts of this case are described in this chapter's opening scenario. Dole shareholders sued Murdock and Carter, alleging that they had violated both the duty of care and the duty of loyalty under the business judgment rule and were, therefore, personally liable for the difference between the price Murdock paid for Dole stock and a "fair" price.

Murdock and Carter argued that they were not liable because the price was fair and also because Dole's charter had an exculpatory clause providing that "no director of the Corporation shall be personally liable to the Corporation or its stockholders for monetary damages for breach of fiduciary duty as a director."

Issues: ***Did Murdock pay a fair price for the Dole stock? Were Murdock and Carter liable under the business judgment rule?***

Excerpts from Judge Laster's Decision: When a transaction involving self-dealing by a controlling shareholder is challenged, the applicable standard of judicial review is entire fairness, with the defendants having the burden of persuasion. The concept of fairness has two basic aspects: fair dealing and fair price.

The evidence at trial established that the [sale] was not a product of fair dealing. Carter engaged in fraud. For approximately eighteen months, Murdock had planned on taking Dole private. But Carter first primed the market by pushing down the stock. A calculated effort to depress the market price of a stock until the minority stockholders are eliminated constitutes unfair dealing.

Carter told the markets that Dole's "current expectation" was that it would only achieve cost savings in the $20 million range. [T]he evidence at trial forced me to conclude that Carter's estimate was false. Other analyses suggested the total cost savings could be higher. Carter intentionally [gave] the market a subterranean estimate of Dole's anticipated cost savings.

The projections Carter provided were knowingly false. Carter intentionally tried to mislead the Committee for Murdock's benefit. By providing the Committee with false information, Carter ensured that the process could not be fair. Through his actions, Carter rendered the Committee ineffective as a bargaining agent for the minority stockholders, notwithstanding the Committee's valiant efforts.

Carter's fraud tainted the approval of the [sale] by the Committee, as well as the stockholder vote. Perhaps, with the benefit of full information, the Committee would have approved the [sale] anyway. Whether they would have approved the transaction is inherently unknowable because there is no way to learn what the Committee would have done in the absence of the fiduciaries' disloyal conduct.

The second aspect of the entire fairness inquiry is fair price. Modifying Lazard's analysis to take into account the information that Carter misrepresented or withheld suggests that with the benefit of full information about Dole's value, including its plans for cost savings, the [sale] price was not fair. Assuming for the sake of argument that the $13.50 price fell within a range of fairness, the plaintiffs are entitled under the circumstances to a "fairer" price. This is because by engaging in fraud, Carter deprived the Committee of its ability to obtain a better result on behalf of the stockholders, prevented the Committee from having the knowledge it needed to potentially say "no," and foreclosed the ability of the stockholders to protect themselves by voting down the deal.

The effect of a provision like the Exculpatory Clause is to eliminate director liability only for 'duty of care' violations [not for duty of loyalty claims]. [A] provision like the Exculpatory Clause does not apply to a defendant in his capacity as a controlling stockholder. As Dole's controlling stockholder, Murdock breached his duty of loyalty to the plaintiff shareholder class. For that breach of duty Murdock is liable.

Murdock is also liable in his capacity as a director. He breached his duty of loyalty by orchestrating an unfair, self-interested transaction. In addition, as the buyer, he derived an improper personal benefit from the transaction.

Carter is personally liable for damages resulting from the [sale]. He is liable both as a director and as an officer. Carter is not entitled to exculpation in his capacity as a director because he breached his duty of loyalty to the corporation and its stockholders and his acts and omissions were not in good faith. The duty of loyalty includes a requirement to act in good faith. At a minimum, good faith requires that the decision-maker act honestly and without pretext. A corporate fiduciary thus acts in bad faith when motivated by a purpose other than that of advancing the best interests of the corporation and its stockholders. Carter demonstrated that his primary loyalty was to Murdock, not to Dole or to its stockholders. As an officer, Carter owed the same duties that he owed as a director, but the Exculpatory Clause does not protect him when acting in those capacities.

Murdock and Carter are liable for breaches of their duty of loyalty in the amount of $148,190,590.18.

With interest, the total amount owed was about $170 million. However, Murdock settled the case by agreeing to pay $74 million. He then sued Dole's insurers, alleging that they should pay this sum.

Corporate Opportunity

The self-dealing rules prevent managers from *forcing* their companies into unfair deals. The corporate opportunity doctrine is the reverse—it prohibits officers, directors, and controlling shareholders from *excluding* their company from favorable deals. **Managers are in violation of the corporate opportunity doctrine if they compete against the corporation without its consent.** To avoid liability, a manager must first offer an opportunity to disinterested directors and shareholders, and only if they turn it down does the manager have the right to take advantage of the opportunity himself. (Note, however, that Delaware now permits its corporations to opt out of the corporate opportunity doctrine.[9])

Long ago, Charles Guth was president of Loft, Inc., which operated a chain of candy stores that sold Coca-Cola. Guth purchased the Pepsi-Cola Company personally, without offering the opportunity to Loft. A Delaware court found that Guth had violated the corporate opportunity doctrine and ordered him to transfer all his shares in PepsiCo to Loft.[10] That was in 1939 and Pepsi-Cola was bankrupt; today, PepsiCo, Inc., is worth more than $150 billion.

Sometimes, however, either through oversight or ignorance, managers do not seek permission in advance. **The manager can still avoid liability by showing that the company would have been unable to benefit from the opportunity.** Cellular Information Systems, Inc., had just

[9]Del. Code Ann. tit. 8, §122(17).

[10]Guth v. Loft, 5 A.2d 503 (Del. 1939).

emerged from bankruptcy proceedings when one of its directors learned that a cell phone license covering part of Michigan was for sale. The director purchased the license himself, and the company sued. The court found the director not liable because the company could not have afforded to purchase the license itself.[11]

A manager will often find it difficult to prove that the company could not have used an opportunity itself. However, these disputes are easy to avoid—the manager must simply ask permission first. Certainly, if a manager suspects that company officers would be displeased to learn about his new sideline, that is an indication that he is skating on thin ice.

If a manager suspects that company officers would be displeased to learn about his new sideline, that is an indication that he is skating on thin ice.

In the following case, the manager felt that he had a good reason for taking a corporate opportunity. But the court disagreed.

Anderson v. Bellino

265 Neb. 577
Nebraska Supreme Court, 2003

Facts: Richard Bellino and Robert Anderson formed LaVista Lottery, Inc. (Lottery), to operate a restaurant, lounge, and keno game in LaVista, Nevada.[12] They each owned 50 percent of the stock of Lottery, and both were officers and directors. During the next nine years, Lottery grossed more than $100 million. Bellino and Anderson each received over $4 million in salary and dividends. Although Bellino and Anderson were both involved in Lottery, Bellino spent more time there, in part because of his personal relationship with Lottery's lounge manager. During this period, Bellino did not complain to Anderson about his lack of involvement in Lottery, and Anderson never refused to do anything that Bellino asked him to do.

Resentful of Anderson's work ethic, Bellino convinced LaVista's city council to put the keno contract up for competitive bid. Bellino incorporated LaVista Keno, Inc. (Keno), to bid on the contract.

Bellino wrote to Anderson complaining that, because he (Bellino) was doing too much work for Lottery at too little pay, he intended to resign from Lottery and bid on the city contract himself. (Evidently, $4 million is not as much as it used to be.) Anderson offered to do more work or whatever Bellino wanted, but Bellino refused any effort at reconciliation. He then submitted a bid on behalf of Keno. At the time he submitted the bid, he was still an officer of Lottery, as well as a director and a 50 percent shareholder. Anderson also bid on the contract on behalf of Lottery. The city awarded the new contract to Keno.

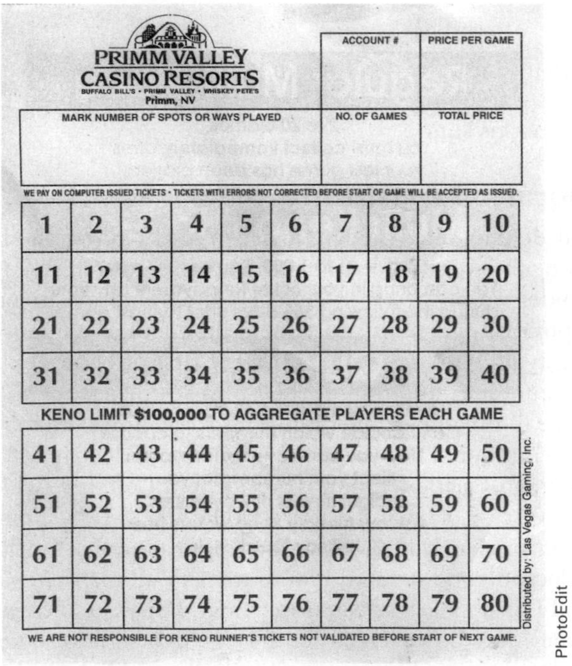

PhotoEdit

A keno card.

[11]Broz v. Cellular Information Systems, Inc., 673 A.2d 148 (Del. 1996).

[12]Keno is a game of chance similar to bingo except that in keno the players choose the numbers on their ticket.

Anderson and Lottery filed suit against Bellino and Keno, alleging that they had usurped a corporate opportunity. The lower court found for Anderson and Lottery. It ordered Bellino to pay $645,000 but provided that Bellino could receive a credit of $172,000 against the judgment, if Bellino transferred the stock of Keno to Lottery and persuaded the city to relicense the keno contract from Keno to Lottery.

Issues: ***Did Bellino usurp a corporate opportunity? Is he liable to Lottery?***

Excerpts from Justice Miller-Lerman's Decision: Bellino and Keno claim that if a corporate opportunity existed, it was limited to the opportunity to bid for the keno contract, that Bellino did nothing to impede Lottery from bidding for the keno contract by merely submitting a competing bid, and that, therefore, Bellino did not usurp a corporate opportunity.

Contrary to the arguments asserted by Bellino and Keno, the corporate opportunity was not the right to bid; the bidding process was merely the preliminary step by which Lottery sought to acquire the opportunity embodied in the award of the keno contract. The facts thus establish that the keno contract was a corporate opportunity for Lottery.

Although an officer or a director of a corporation is not necessarily precluded from entering into a separate business because it is in competition with the corporation, his fiduciary relationship to the corporation and its stockholders is such that if he does so he must prove that he did so in good faith and did not act in such a manner as to cause or contribute to the injury or damage of the corporation, or deprive it of business; if he fails in this proof, there has been a breach of that fiduciary trust or relationship.

The evidence is uncontroverted that Bellino's successful bid for the LaVista keno contract deprived Lottery of its only source of business. Bellino, through Keno, should not have competed with Lottery for the LaVista keno contract.

We affirm the district court's order.

EXAMStrategy

Question: Otto and his nephew Nick formed a corporation to operate a furniture store in Washington, D.C. Otto owned 51 percent and Nick 49 percent of the company's stock. Otto then entered into an agreement between himself and the furniture store to lease a storefront that he owned. Otto also purchased a warehouse which he then leased to the corporation. Nick sued, alleging that the two leases were invalid. Were they?

Strategy: Otto violated the business judgment rule twice.

Result: The lease between him and the corporation for the storefront was self-dealing—it directly benefited him. When he purchased the warehouse, he took a corporate opportunity that he should have offered first to the company. He is personally liable for any damages to the corporation. The company also has the right to cancel both leases and to purchase the warehouse from him.

Rational Business Purpose

Courts agree in principle that **any decision that has no rational business purpose automatically violates the business judgment rule.** In practice, however, these same courts have been extremely supportive of managerial decisions, looking hard to find some justification. For years, the Chicago Cubs baseball team was the only major American professional sports team to play in a stadium without lights. A shareholder sued on the grounds that the Cubs' revenues were peanuts and Cracker Jack compared with those generated by teams that played at night. In their defense, the Cubs argued that a large night crowd would cause the neighborhood to deteriorate, depressing the value of Wrigley Field (which the Cubs did not own). The court rooted for the home team and found that the Cubs' excuse was a "rational purpose" and a legitimate exercise of the business judgment rule.[13]

[13]Shlensky v. Wrigley, 95 Ill. App.2d 173 (Ill. App. Ct. 1968).

Informed Decision

The duty of care requires managers to make an *informed* decision—that is, with the care that an ordinarily prudent person would take in a similar situation. As long as the managers are careful, courts are not concerned about the *result* of the decision—whether it ultimately harms the company—they focus instead on the *process*. However, if the process is careless, then the managers will be liable unless the decision was entirely fair to the shareholders.

The board of Technicolor, Inc., agreed to sell the film-processing company, knowing little about the terms of the deal and without seeking other bidders. The directors simply knew that the sales price was higher than the appraised value of the company. Five years later, the buyer sold the company for a $750 million profit. The former shareholders sued, alleging that the directors had made an uninformed decision. The state supreme court held that because the directors had been so careless, they had to prove that the price and the process by which it had been determined were both fair.[14]

In the following case, the board of directors failed to hold meetings. Were their decisions informed?

RSL Communications v. Bildirici

2006 U.S. Dist. LEXIS 67548; 2006 WL 2689869
United States District Court for the Southern District of New York, 2006

Facts: Ronald S. Lauder founded RSL Ltd., a multinational telecommunications corporation. RSL PLC was a subsidiary of RSL Ltd. The subsidiary began by issuing $1.4 billion of bonds. A few years later, in July, Lauder provided the subsidiary with a $100 million line of credit, although its board of directors never held a meeting to approve the loan. In August, RSL PLC drew down $25 million from that loan. The following March, the company's directors held their first board meeting in a year. Five days later, RSL PLC filed for bankruptcy.

The bankruptcy trustees of RSL PLC sued the members of its board of directors alleging that they breached their duty of care to the company by failing to hold board meetings at a time when the company was in a precarious financial position.

Issue: ***Did the directors of RCL PLC violate their duty of care to the corporation?***

Excerpts from Judge Karas's Decision: Under New York law, a director shall perform his duties as a director, in good faith and with that degree of care which an ordinarily prudent person in a like position would use under similar circumstances. It is well settled that the duty of due care requires that a director's decision be made on the basis of reasonable diligence in gathering and considering material information.

When faced with allegations of misconduct, a defendant director may raise the business judgment rule as an absolute defense. [U]nder Delaware law the business judgment rule applies even where conclusions were

---

14The state supreme court sent the case back to the lower court to determine whether the deal had been fair to the shareholders. Cede & Co., Inc. v. Technicolor, Inc., 634 A.2d 345 (Del. 1993). The lower court ultimately decided that the transaction had indeed been fair. Cinerama, Inc. v. Technicolor, Inc., 663 A.2d 1134 (Del. Ch. 1994). The state supreme court, however, disagreeing with the valuation method used by the trial court, reversed that decision and remanded it once again to the trial court for further proceedings. Cede & Co. v. Technicolor, 684 A.2d 289 (Del. 1996). Yet again, in 2000, the Delaware Supreme Court (somewhat apologetically) overruled the trial court and returned the case for another trial. Cede & Co. v. Technicolor, Inc., 758 A.2d 485 (Del. 2000). The results from this trial were again appealed. Finally, in 2005, the Delaware Supreme Court upheld most of the trial court rulings and remanded with simple instructions to change the interest rate it used to calculate damages. Cede & Co. v. Technicolor, Inc., 875 A.2d 602 (Del. 2005). The original sale of stock took place in 1983. This was the longest case in the 200-year history of the Delaware Court of Chancery.

stupid or irrational, as long as the process employed was either rational or employed in a *good faith* effort to advance corporate interests.

Although the standard of review for business judgments is deferential, to receive the protection of the business judgment rule, a director must show an exercise of judgment, not simply the existence of a business decision. Directors' fiduciary duties require them to do more than passively rubber-stamp the decisions of the active managers. Thus, where the directors' methodologies and procedures are so restricted in scope, so shallow in execution, or otherwise so *pro forma* or half-hearted as to constitute a pretext or a sham, inquiry into their acts is not shielded by the business judgment rule. The Directors may not seek the protection of the business judgment rule on the ground that they made no decisions and took no actions.

It is undisputed that the Defendants did not hold board meetings on behalf of RSL PLC during the time period relevant to this action. Despite this, RSL PLC still operated and took actions such as drawing down $25 million from the Lauder loan, apparently at the direction of RSL Ltd. However, no independent board discussions regarding the propriety of this and other business decisions were held on behalf of RSL PLC by its board of directors.

Indeed, the law does not tolerate inaction of the sort Defendants are alleged to have engaged in, as Defendants allegedly failed to consider any information they had regarding the company's financial health and allegedly failed to make a business judgment as a board regarding any financial decision on behalf of RSL PLC.

Defendants point to cases which hold that small, closely held corporations with directors frequently in close contact with one another may dispense with formalities such as board meetings when making business decisions. However, RSL PLC is not a small corporation, as it accrued more than $1.4 billion in debt. Further, while it is clear that some of RSL PLC'S board members had some contact during the period in question, [there were no] behind-the-scenes meetings where the business of RSL PLC was discussed by these members, let alone an agreement not to have a board meeting.

Defendants argue that they were fully informed regarding RSL PLC'S financial matters because some Defendants were also board members of RSL Ltd., and that in that capacity, they exercised judgment on behalf of RSL Ltd, the parent of RSL PLC. This argument is unpersuasive. [I]ndividuals who act in a dual capacity as directors of two corporations, one of whom is parent and the other subsidiary, owe the same duty of good management to both corporations.

EXAMStrategy

Question: You are the CEO of an app company. You will only allow your engineers to create apps for iPads, not for Android or Microsoft tablets because you think iPads are cooler. Some of your shareholders disagree with this policy. Is your decision protected by the business judgment rule?

Strategy: Remember that, under the business judgment rule, you must have a rational business purpose for your decision.

Result: The courts are very generous in defining a rational business purpose. They would probably uphold your decision as long as it was not in some way personally benefiting you, for example, as long as you are not a major shareholder of Apple.

34-2 MORE CONFLICT: TAKEOVERS

For more than 30 years, hostile takeovers have been a feature of American corporate life. As a result, a body of both common law (applying the business judgment rule) and statutes has developed to govern these conflicts. Let's begin with a review of takeovers.

34-2a Takeovers: The Basics

There are three ways to acquire control of a company:

- **Buy the company's assets.** Such a sale must be approved by both the shareholders and the board of directors of the acquired company.
- **Merge with the company.** In a merger, one company absorbs another. The acquired company ceases to exist. A merger must be approved by the shareholders and the board of directors of the target.
- **Buy stock from the shareholders.** This method is called a **tender offer** because the acquirer asks shareholders to "tender," or offer their stock for sale. As long as shareholders tender enough stock, the acquirer gains control. Typically, the bidder makes an offer (at a price above market value). This offer is usually contingent—that is, if a certain percentage of the shareholders do not tender, the offer terminates automatically. Although an acquisition can proceed without the approval of the board of the target company, resistance from the board can hinder, and even defeat, the deal.

Tender offer
A public offer to buy a block of stock directly from shareholders

Three scenarios are common in hostile takeovers:

- The target has assets that the bidder genuinely wants.
- The bidder seeks to profit either by improving the target's operations, or by dismembering the company and selling off its parts.
- The bidder expects that the target company will buy its own stock back at a premium price.

34-2b Takeover Defenses

Antitakeover devices or shark repellents
Defensive measures to protect against a hostile takeover

To protect themselves from hostile takeovers, companies adopt defensive measures known as **antitakeover devices** or **shark repellents. Common shark repellents include the following:**

- **Poison pill** (aka shareholder rights plan). These plans interfere with an outsider's ability to buy company stock. In one instance, a Delaware court allowed Sotheby's (the auction house) to adopt a poison pill that limited the number of shares that an activist investor could buy.[15] Alternatively, these plans may allow an activist to buy shares, but once he hits a certain threshold, the value of those shares is diluted. About 5 percent of S&P 1500 companies have poison pills.

  Casablanca, Inc., is a successful film production company that Turner wants to acquire. The company issues a special share of preferred stock to each current shareholder. If a shark purchases more than 15 percent of Casablanca's stock and subsequently merges with Casablanca, this preferred stock can be converted into 10 shares of the acquiring company. Thus, for each share of Casablanca that Turner buys, he also has to give away 10 of his own shares, making the takeover much more expensive for him. No wonder this tactic is called a "poison pill"; it could certainly prove fatal to a shark.[16]

---

[15] Third Point LLC v. Ruprecht, 2014 Del. Ch. LEXIS 64 (Del. Ch. 2014).

[16] Interestingly, research indicates that poison pills *increase* the probability that a company will be taken over. The theory is that these pills create a road map for the bidder, who knows that if he overcomes the poison pill, he wins. Matthew D. Cain, Stephen B. McKeon, and Steven Davidoff Solomon, "Do Takeover Laws Matter? Evidence from Five Decades of Hostile Takeovers," (July 12, 2016). *Journal of Financial Economics (JFE)*, Forthcoming. Available at SSRN: https://ssrn.com/abstract=2517513.

- **Blank check preferred stock.** In theory, before Casablanca issued poison pill shares, the shareholders would have to approve the new class of stock. But many companies have blank check preferred stock in their charters. When this stock is authorized, its rights and other characteristics are left blank, to be filled in by the board of directors upon issuance. It is like an unloaded gun that can be armed by the board whenever a shark threatens.
- **Asset lockup** (aka "scorched earth strategy"). The target sells off the assets that the shark most wants. Turner is after Casablanca because he covets its library of old films. Casablanca tries to pass the bait to someone else, either by selling the film library or by giving someone else the option to buy it.
- **Greenmail.** The target buys back the shark's stock at a premium price. Turner is not really interested in owning Casablanca stock; he simply wants to turn a quick profit. So the company offers to buy back his stock at a price 30 percent higher than he paid for it.
- **Staggered board of directors.** With a typical board of directors, all directors run for election each year, with the result that the entire board can be voted out at the same time. But about one-third of large U.S. companies have a staggered board, which means that only a portion of the directors are elected each year. Thus, replacing the entire board takes some years to accomplish. Casablanca has a staggered board, in which each director serves a three-year term and only four of the twelve directors are elected each year. If Turner takes over the company, he will not gain control of the board for two years, and it will be three before he can replace all the directors.
- **Supermajority voting.** Ordinarily, shareholders can approve charter amendments by a majority vote, but some companies require a higher percentage to approve important changes. If Casablanca wants to make a takeover more difficult, the board can ask shareholders to amend its charter to require a supermajority vote of, say, 80 percent to approve a merger. In that way, Turner would not be able to merge his company with Casablanca unless he bought 80 percent of its shares.
- **Disqualifying directors.** Some companies have amended their bylaws to provide that anyone who receives payment from an activist is disqualified from serving as a director. (Typically these potential directors receive payment either for their time before they join the board or as incentive compensation if the company does well.)

Note that management typically cannot use poison pills, blank check preferred stock, staggered boards of directors, and supermajority voting without shareholder approval. (Although management could issue stock under a poison pill plan, the stock would first have to be authorized by the shareholders.) Shareholder approval is not required to implement the other shark repellents.

34-2c Takeovers: The Business Judgment Rule

As we have seen, under the business judgment rule, courts allow boards of directors great latitude in making decisions, which includes a decision to fight off a takeover. However, the courts will not completely ignore the rights of shareholders. In short, they try to balance the rights of managers, shareholders, and, sometimes, stakeholders. They want to allow the board of a target company enough time to communicate with shareholders, search for alternatives, and force a higher price from the bidder, while at the same time allowing shareholders enough power to sell the company if they desire. Perhaps for this reason, legal rules on antitakeover devices are complex and sometimes seem to depend on the specific details of a particular case. **But these are the general guidelines:**

- **When establishing takeover defenses, shareholder welfare must be the board's primary concern.** The directors may institute shark repellents, but they must do so to ensure that bids are high, not to protect their own jobs. A poison pill is acceptable if it gives management enough bargaining power to negotiate a high price for shareholders, but not if it makes a takeover impossible.
- **If it is clear that the company will ultimately be sold, the board must auction the company to the highest bidder; it cannot give preferential treatment to a lower bidder.** The board cannot sell the company at a lower price simply because it dislikes the shark.

In the following case, a bidder tried a new approach to winning a hostile takeover. Should the court permit this action? You be the judge.

You Be the Judge

Airgas, Inc. v. Air Products and Chemicals, Inc.

8 A.3d 1182
Delaware Supreme Court, 2010

Facts: Air Products and Chemicals, Inc. (Air Products), launched a tender offer to acquire 100 percent of the shares of Airgas, Inc. (Airgas). The Airgas board of directors rejected these bids because they were lower than the market price. Airgas's charter provided for a staggered board of nine directors—at each annual meeting, three would run for election.

At Airgas's annual meeting in September, shareholders elected three of Air Products's nominees to the board. Air Products also proposed a bylaw (the January Bylaw) that switched Airgas's annual meeting to January rather than September. This change would mean that the next annual meeting would be in only four months. Air Products's plan was to vote out three more directors in January, which would have the effect of reducing their terms by eight months. Shareholders approved this amendment with a 51 percent vote in favor. Because not all shareholders voted, the favorable vote actually constituted only 45.8 percent of the outstanding shares. To amend the Airgas charter and eliminate the staggered board would have taken a 67 percent vote of the shareholders who cast ballots.

Airgas filed suit, alleging that the January Bylaw was invalid because it was a back-door method of eliminating the staggered board without a 67 percent vote of the shareholders, as required by the charter. (A bylaw is invalid if it conflicts with the charter.) The lower court upheld the January Bylaw, and Airgas appealed.

You Be the Judge: *Was the January Bylaw valid?*

Argument for Air Products: Airgas's charter provides that directors serve terms that expire at "the annual meeting of stockholders held in the third year following the year of their election." The January Bylaw complies with this charter provision as written because the January meeting will take place "in the third year after the directors' election." Nowhere does the charter say that directors have to serve three full years. If Airgas wins this case, corporations in Delaware will have to calculate the dates of their annual meetings with mathematical precision to make sure that they are at least one year apart.

Moreover, 51 percent of the shares at the annual meeting voted in favor of the January Bylaw. If it was unfair or against the best interests of shareholders, they could have voted against it. Why should the court thwart the shareholders' intent?

Argument for Airgas: In 25 years, Airgas has never held its annual meeting earlier than July 28. We are not arguing that Airgas has to wait exactly 365 days to schedule its next annual meeting, but it should delay at least 11 months. Moreover, the company's fiscal year ends on March 31, so if the meeting were to be held in January, Airgas would not have new financial results to report to its shareholders.

The charter term is ambiguous—does it mean that directors have to serve into the start of the third year, or do they have to serve three full years? Regardless of what the actual language says, the *intent* is clear—directors are meant to serve three years. Air Products has found a loophole that violates the spirit of the charter provision and frustrates the purpose of staggered boards, which is to provide stability. The court should not allow Air Products to avoid the clear intent of the charter so that it can acquire a company at less than market value.

It is true that that 51 percent of the shares *at the meeting* voted in favor of the January Bylaw, but this was only 45.8 percent of the shares outstanding. That is not even a majority, never mind the 67 percent vote required to amend the charter. Moreover, if the January Bylaw is upheld, effectively three of the board members will be removed without cause. Under the charter, removal without cause also requires a 67 percent vote.

EXAMStrategy

Question: You are the CEO of Bubble Gum, Inc., a publicly traded company. Pink Co. has just made an offer to buy Bubble. Pink is particularly interested in Bubble's farmland, on which grows the corn for the sweetener used in the gum. You despise the CEO of Pink and know if Pink takes over the company, you will be fired. Your friend at ChewCo says his company would be interested in buying Bubble, but at a lower price than Pink is willing to pay. You are convinced that the company is better off long-term with ChewCo. What can you do immediately to protect Bubble (and yourself) from Pink?

Strategy: Shark repellents that require shareholder approval will not work because you do not have time to call a shareholders' meeting. Remember that your primary duty is to your shareholders.

Result: You cannot simply agree to a sale to ChewCo—once it is clear that the company will be sold, you must auction it to the highest bidder. You could try an asset lockup—selling off the company's farmland. Perhaps that would discourage Pink from making the purchase.

34-2d Takeover Legislation

In the beginning, federal and state governments barely regulated takeovers. Over time, targets began to ask Congress and their state legislatures for help in warding off these unwelcome attacks. Both the federal government and almost all states have intervened, primarily on the side of the target rather than the bidder.

A Federal Statute: The Williams Act

The Williams Act regulates tender offers. It applies only if the target company's stock is publicly traded. **Under the Williams Act:**

- Any individual or group who together acquire more than 5 percent of a company's stock must file, within 10 days, a public disclosure document (called a "Schedule 13D") with the Securities and Exchange Commission (SEC);
- Under Schedule 13D, the filer must disclose any plans it has to acquire the target company;
- On the day a tender offer begins, a bidder who intends to acquire more than 5 percent of the target must file a disclosure statement with the SEC;
- Within 10 days of the commencement of a tender offer, the target company must state its position on the offer;

- A bidder must keep a tender offer open for at least 20 business days initially and for at least 10 business days after any substantial change in the terms of the offer;
- Any shareholder may withdraw acceptance of the tender offer at any time while the offer is still open;
- If the bidder raises the price offered, all selling shareholders must be paid the higher price, regardless of when they tendered; and
- If the stockholders tender more shares than the bidder wants to buy, it must purchase shares *pro rata* (in other words, it must buy the same proportion from everyone, *not* first come, first served).

Observe that the Williams Act largely regulates the behavior of the *bidder*, not that of the *target company*. After Congress passed the Act, the number of tender offers declined and the average premium over market price increased. But target companies did not rely merely on the Williams Act to protect against the threat of takeovers. They also sought help in state legislatures.

Takeovers: State Statutes

In fighting takeover battles, companies have found support in state governments because legislators fear the impact on the local economy if a major employer leaves. When the Belzberg family threatened a hostile takeover of auto parts manufacturer Arvin Industries, the Indiana legislature quickly passed a tough antitakeover bill that had been drafted by Arvin's own lawyers. As a result, the Belzbergs failed in their attempt. Arvin was not only the second-largest employer in Columbus, Indiana, it was also an all-purpose fairy godmother. Among its charitable activities, it built two new schools, subsidized the salary of the school superintendent, and opened a summer camp. Columbus residents were delighted that Arvin survived the takeover attempt, but company shareholders might have preferred a bidding war for their stock. After all, shareholders do not necessarily care if the children of Columbus spend their summers at leafy Camp Grenada or sleazy Mall City. The interests of these two corporate constituencies clashed.

Most states have now passed laws to deter hostile takeovers. Among the common varieties are the following:

- **Statutes that automatically impede hostile takeovers.** These statutes, for instance, might ban hostile mergers for five years after the acquirer buys 10 percent of a company. Or investors who acquire as much as 20 percent of a company lose their voting rights unless the other shareholders move to reinstate the rights (not likely!). These provisions do not apply to bids that have been approved by the board of directors of the target company. In many states, such as Delaware, the board can opt out of the takeover provisions altogether and refuse to accept their protection.
- **Statutes that authorize companies to fight off hostile takeovers.** As we have seen, some states have followed the lead of the *Unocal* case and passed statutes that permit management, when responding to a hostile takeover, to consider the welfare of company stakeholders, such as the community, customers, suppliers, and employees, or even the regional or national economy. Since takeovers are almost always harmful to these other constituencies, company management has a ready excuse for fighting the takeover.

Most of these statutes do not totally eliminate hostile takeovers. A determined, well-financed bidder can still be successful.

Ethics

Supporters of these state statutes argue that large, publicly traded corporations owe a duty to all of their stakeholders. The loss of a large corporate presence can be immensely disruptive to a community. Perhaps a state should have the right to prevent economic upheaval within its borders.

Opponents contend that shareholders own the company and their interests ought to come first. Antitakeover legislation entrenches management and prevents shareholders from obtaining the premium that accompanies a takeover. Opponents also argue that, if other stakeholders are so concerned with the well-being of the company, let them put their money where their mouths are and buy stock. And if current managers cannot offer shareholders as high a stock price as an activist investor, they ought to be replaced.

Delaware companies can choose not to accept the protection of the antitakeover statute. What is the ethical choice for directors?

CHAPTER CONCLUSION

Managers run a corporation on behalf of its shareholders. But sometimes managers, shareholders, and stakeholders have different goals and interests. The law, whether federal or state, common or statutory, tries to balance these interests. In this chapter, we have studied a manager's duties. In the next chapter, we look at a shareholder's rights.

EXAM REVIEW

1. **STAKEHOLDERS** The *Unocal* case and equivalent state statutes permit managers to consider the interests of stakeholders.

2. **FIDUCIARY DUTY** The officers and directors of a corporation owe a fiduciary duty to both the corporation and its shareholders.

3. **BUSINESS JUDGMENT RULE** The business judgment rule provides that managers are not liable for decisions they make:
   - In good faith
   - For a lawful purpose
   - Without a conflict of interest
   - To advance the best interests of the corporation
   - With the care that an ordinarily prudent person would take in a similar situation

4. **MANAGER'S PROTECTION FROM LIABILITY** Even if a manager violates the business judgment rule, he is still protected from liability (and his decision is upheld) under any of the following circumstances:
   - The disinterested members of the board of directors form a special committee that approves the decision.

- The disinterested shareholders approve it.
- A court determines it was entirely fair to the corporation.

5. **ILLEGAL ACTIVITY** An illegal activity automatically violates the business judgment rule, even if it actually helps the company and is entirely fair.

EXAMStrategy

Question: Employees of Exxon Corp. paid some $59 million in corporate funds as bribes to Italian political parties to secure special favors and other illegal commitments. The board of directors decided not to sue the employees who had committed the illegal acts. Were these decisions protected by the business judgment rule?

Strategy: Two decisions are at issue here: illegal payments and the decision not to sue. (See the "Result" at the end of this Exam Review section.)

---

6. **CONTROLLING SHAREHOLDER** Anyone who owns enough stock to control a corporation has a fiduciary duty to minority shareholders and is subject to the business judgment rule.

7. **SELF-DEALING** Self-dealing means that a manager makes a decision benefiting either himself or another company with which he has a relationship. It is a violation of the duty of loyalty.

8. **CORPORATE OPPORTUNITY** Under the duty of loyalty, a manager must first offer an opportunity to disinterested directors and shareholders and, only if they turn it down, does the manager have the right to take advantage of the opportunity himself.

EXAMStrategy

Question: Vern owned 32 percent of Coast Oyster Co. and served as president and director. Coast was struggling to pay its debts, so Vern suggested that the company sell some of its oyster beds to Keypoint Co. After the sale, officers at Coast discovered that Vern owned 50 percent of Keypoint. They demanded that he give the Keypoint stock to Coast. Did Vern violate the business judgment rule?

Strategy: Here, Vern has violated the business judgment rule not once, but twice. (See the "Result" at the end of this Exam Review section.)

---

9. **RATIONAL BUSINESS PURPOSE** Any decision that has no rational business purpose violates the business judgment rule.

10. **INFORMED DECISION** Under the duty of care, managers must make an informed decision, that is, with the care that an ordinarily prudent person would take in a similar situation.

11. TAKEOVER DEFENSES Under common law, shareholder welfare must be the board's primary concern when establishing takeover defenses. If it is clear that the company will ultimately be sold, the board must auction the company to the highest bidder; it cannot give preferential treatment to a lower bidder.

EXAMStrategy

Question: The board of Harmony, Inc., is concerned that the company may be the target of a hostile takeover. It has decided to adopt antitakeover devices. Which one of the following statements is *false*?

(a) Harmony may divest one of its divisions, as long as it does so at fair market value.

(b) Harmony may adopt a poison pill, but only if the board's primary concern is enhancing shareholder welfare, not protecting their own jobs.

(c) If it becomes clear that Harmony is going to be sold, the directors have an obligation to auction the company off to the highest bidder, even if they think that another company would be a better fit.

(d) If Harmony offers to buy back any of its stock, it must treat its shareholders equally.

Strategy: Apply the principle established in the *Unocal* case earlier in the chapter. (See the "Result" at the end of this Exam Review section.)

12. WILLIAMS ACT The Williams Act is a federal statute that regulates tender offers for stock in a publicly traded corporation.

13. STATE STATUTES Most states have passed laws to deter hostile takeovers.

RESULTS

5. Result: The business judgment rule would not protect the underlying illegal payments, but it did protect the decision not to sue. In other words, anyone who *made* an illegal payment had violated the business judgment rule, but the people who decided not to pursue the violators had not themselves breached the business judgment rule because they had not violated the duty of care or the duty of loyalty.

8. Result: If the shareholders and directors did not know of Vern's interest in Keypoint, they could not evaluate the contract properly. Vern should have told them before he engaged in self-dealing. Also, by purchasing stock in Keypoint, Vern took a corporate opportunity. He had to turn over any profits he had earned on the transaction, as well as his stock in Keypoint.

11. Result: In the *Unocal* case, the court permitted the company to exclude one shareholder from its buyback offer. (d) is the correct answer.

MULTIPLE-CHOICE QUESTIONS

1. If a manager engages in self-dealing, which of the following answers will *not* protect him from a finding that he violated the business judgment rule?
   (a) A special committee of the disinterested members of the board approved the transaction.
   (b) The transaction was of minor importance to the company.
   (c) The disinterested shareholders approved the transaction.
   (d) The transaction was entirely fair to the corporation.

2. The duty of care ______________.
   (a) is not a requirement of the business judgment rule
   (b) protects directors who make an uninformed decision if it was entirely fair to the company
   (c) protects a decision that has a rational business purpose, even if the activity was illegal
   (d) will not protect directors who make a decision that harms the company

3. Under the Williams Act, ______________.
   (a) if shareholders offer more stock than the bidder wants, it must purchase shares *pro rata*
   (b) target companies must reveal the names of any shareholders who acquire more than 5 percent of its stock
   (c) a bidder must file a disclosure statement at least 24 hours before the tender offer begins
   (d) once a shareholder has accepted a tender offer, she cannot withdraw it

4. When Attack made an offer to acquire the stock of Target, the Target board welcomed the offer. Not so when Francis Co. also indicated an interest in Target. In its negotiations with Francis, the Target board of directors failed to reveal that Microsoft had offered to pay $450 million for Target's patent portfolio. Francis made an offer that was slightly lower than Attack's. Which of the following statements is true?
   (a) The Target board has the right to sell the company to whomever it wants.
   (b) The Target board must appoint a special committee of disinterested directors to assess both offers.
   (c) The Target board has no obligation to Francis because its offer was lower than Attack's.
   (d) The Target board had an obligation to tell Francis about the Microsoft offer because, if Francis had known, it might have made a higher offer.

5. Oil Co. was a controlling shareholder of Pogo, a company that drilled for oil and gas in the Gulf of Mexico. When some additional leases became available, Oil Co. purchased all of them for itself. Which of the following statements is true?
   (a) To avoid liability, Oil Co. had to offer the leases to Pogo's board of directors.
   (b) To avoid liability, Oil Co. had to offer the leases to Pogo's other shareholders.
   (c) Oil Co. could avoid liability by proving that Pogo could not afford to pay for the additional leases.
   (d) Both A and B.
   (e) All of these

CASE QUESTIONS

1. ***YOU BE THE JUDGE* WRITING PROBLEM** Asher and Stephen owned and worked for a corporation named "Ampersand" that produced plays. Stephen decided to write *Philly's Beat*, focusing on the history of rock and roll in Philadelphia. As the play went into production, however, the two men quarreled. Stephen resigned from Ampersand and formed another corporation to produce the play. Did the opportunity to produce *Philly's Beat* belong to Ampersand? **Argument for Stephen**: Ampersand was formed for the purpose of producing plays, not writing them. When Stephen wrote *Philly's Beat*, he was not competing against Ampersand. Furthermore, Ampersand could not afford to produce the play even if it had had the opportunity. **Argument for Asher**: Ampersand was in the business of producing plays, and it wanted *Philly's Beat*. Ampersand was perfectly able to afford the cost of production—until Stephen resigned.

2. Rodney Platt was the vice chairman of the board of Mylan. He was also one of the owners of an office park that Mylan leased, making him Mylan's landlord. How could Mylan comply with the business judgment rule in connection with this transaction?

3. Congressional Airlines was highly profitable operating flights between Washington, D.C., and New York City. The directors approved a plan to offer flights from Washington to Boston. This decision turned out to be a major mistake, and the airline ultimately went bankrupt. Under what circumstances would shareholders be successful in bringing suit against the directors?

4. Careless Inc. ran HIV/AIDS treatment clinics. Some of its employees violated federal law by paying kickbacks to doctors who referred patients to Careless facilities. But the Careless employee in charge of preventing this kind of behavior was careless: He did not see some obvious problems. The board had never asked about the company's monitoring process. Was the board of directors liable for this employee's wrongdoing?

5. Wallace, Inc. adopted a poison pill. Five years later, Moore Corp. offered to buy all Wallace's stock for $56 a share, which was 27 percent over the existing market price. However, the offer was contingent upon the Wallace board eliminating the poison pill. Wallace consulted with its investment banker, which advised the company that the offer was inadequate but did not indicate what the shares were really worth. Moore then raised its offer price to $60 per share, and again the bankers opined that the offer was inadequate. Both the board and its banker believed that Wallace's recently adopted corporate strategy would lead to an increased stock price. Indeed, the company's recent financial results had been better than expected. Despite these improved results, more than 73 percent of Wallace shareholders offered their shares to Moore. When Wallace refused to remove the poison pill, Moore filed suit. Was the board's refusal to remove the poison pill a violation of the business judgment rule?

DISCUSSION QUESTIONS

1. Some companies adopt a staggered board of directors as an antitakeover defense. How does a staggered board affect cumulative voting?

2. The United States is the only developed country that allows boards to adopt poison pills. Are they a good idea? Do they protect shareholders? Or do they entrench management? Why shouldn't any investor be allowed to purchase the stock of any willing seller without having to jump through the poison pill hoop?

3. Under Delaware law, corporations have the right to decide that the corporate opportunity doctrine does not apply to its managers. Thousands of companies have done so. Why would a company do that? Should it? Does such a decision help or hurt shareholders?

4. **ETHICS** Ronald O. Perelman, chairman of the board and CEO of Pantry Pride, met with his counterpart at Revlon, Michel C. Bergerac, to discuss a friendly acquisition of Revlon by Pantry Pride. Revlon rebuffed Pantry Pride's overtures, perhaps in part because Bergerac did not like Perelman. The Revlon board of directors agreed to sell the company to Forstmann Little & Co. at a price of \$56 per share. Pantry Pride announced that it would engage in fractional bidding to top any Forstmann offer by a slightly higher one. To discourage Pantry Pride, the Revlon board granted Forstmann the right to purchase Revlon's Vision Care and National Health Laboratories divisions at a price some \$100–\$175 million below their value. Was the board within its rights in selling off these two divisions? Do the shareholders of Revlon have the right to prevent a sale of the company to Forstmann at a price lower than Pantry Pride offered? Is it ethical for a board to base a takeover decision on personal animosity? What are a board's ethical obligations to shareholders?

5. An appraiser valued a subsidiary of Signal Co. at between \$230 million and \$260 million. Six months later, Burmah Oil offered to buy the subsidiary at \$480 million, giving Signal only three days to respond. The board of directors accepted the offer without obtaining an updated valuation of the subsidiary or determining if other companies would offer a higher price. Members of the board were sophisticated, with a great deal of experience in the oil industry. A Signal Co. shareholder sued the board for having violated the duty of care. Is the Signal board protected by the business judgment rule?

6. James owned Despatch Industries. When his son, Wade, and son-in-law, Alan, started working for the company, they both signed identical employment contracts, which provided for a severance payment if they left the company. After Wade and James had a falling-out, Wade resigned. The Despatch board agreed to make severance payments of \$1.3 million to both Wade and Alan, although Alan continued to work for the company and receive a salary. There were no disinterested directors or shareholders. Did the company have the right to make these payments?

CHAPTER 35
SHAREHOLDER RIGHTS

Trouble arrived at Hewlett-Packard Company when CEO Carleton Fiorina laid off 10 percent of the company's employees and forced through the acquisition of Compaq Computer Corporation, which was bitterly opposed by members of the Hewlett family. But trouble took up permanent residence four years later, when a member of the dysfunctional board of directors leaked confidential information to *The Wall Street Journal*. The company hired private investigators, who then illegally obtained the phone records of board members and journalists. The chair of the board was indicted for this wrongdoing. Although the charges were ultimately dropped, she resigned from a board that was in turmoil. Fiorina also left the company, with a $21 million severance package.

I didn't know there was such a thing as corporate suicide, but now we know that there is.

The board then hired Mark Hurd as CEO. In his five years at the helm, company revenues and stock price soared. But he achieved these results by dramatically cutting product development, marketing, and jobs. Thus, the company never developed a product that could compete with the iPad, an industry game changer. It seemed that the only person profiting from HP's success was Hurd himself: He took home $35 million a year, and found room in the marketing budget for HP to sponsor tennis tournaments (his favorite sport). Worse yet was his derisive treatment of employees. Almost two-thirds of HP employees reportedly wanted to quit. As one long-time HP employee put it, "He was wrecking our image, personally demeaning us, and chopping our future."[1]

---

[1]This report is based in part on: Joe Nocera, "Real Reason for Ousting H.P.'s Chief," *The New York Times*, August 13, 2010; Ashlee Vance, "Despite H.P.'s Efforts, Spectacle of a Chief Goes On," *The New York Times*, August 16, 2010; and James Bandler with Doris Burke, "How Hewlett Packard Lost Its Way," *CNN Money*, May 8, 2012.

But that behavior was not enough to oust Hurd. Oh, no. That took a sex scandal. Even as Hurd was slashing budgets, he authorized more than $75,000 in compensation and first-class travel for soft porn actor Jodie Fisher. Her assignment was to introduce him to customers at marketing events. And dine with him in his hotel room. Their relationship became public when she accused him of sexual harassment. Although HP investigators found no evidence for that charge, the board fired Hurd for having lied on his expense accounts to hide the relationship. On his way out, the board handed him a $12 million severance package.

To replace Hurd, the board hired Léo Apotheker as CEO. His qualifications? He had been fired after just seven months from his prior job running a company that had one-eighth of HP's revenues. His reputation? Nasty and unwilling to learn. The board's hiring process? It was so drained from all the in-fighting, they did not bother even to interview him. Famed venture capitalist Thomas Perkins said about HP: "I didn't know there was such a thing as corporate suicide, but now we know that there is."[2] He described that HP board as "the worst board in the history of business."[3]

The new CEO quickly made two big decisions: To sell off HP's computer division and acquire Autonomy, an English software company for $11 billion. Neither Apotheker nor anyone else on the board read the due diligence report before agreeing to this critical deal. If they had even glanced at the Executive Summary, they would have learned of serious issues. After only 11 months on the job, Apotheker was shown the door. His severance pay for a job badly done was $23 million.

This time, the board chose Meg Whitman as CEO. She had been eBay's successful CEO and a board member of HP. As a director, she had voted for the Autonomy purchase, which many inside and outside the company thought to be a terrible deal when made and ultimately turned out to be a candidate for one of the worst corporate deals ever. HP ended up taking an $8.8 billion write-down on it. The next year, the company wrote off another $18 billion in mistakes. As a director, Whitman had also voted to sell the PC division; two months later, as CEO, she decided to keep it after all.

And how did shareholders fare during all this turmoil? During the three years after Apotheker's arrival at HP, the company's stock fell by 50 percent; during the same period, the S&P 500 increased by 50 percent.[4]

---

[2]James B. Stewart, "For Seamless Transitions, Don't Look to Hewlett," *The New York Times*, August 26, 2011.

[3]James B. Stewart, "Voting to Hire a Chief Without Meeting Him," *The New York Times*, August 26, 2011.

[4]The S&P 500 is an index based on the 500 largest companies listed on the NYSE and NASDAQ.

35-1 INTRODUCTION

What could Hewlett-Packard shareholders have done about the "worst board in the history of business?" This chapter will answer that question.

35-1a Who Are the Shareholders?

At one time, corporate stock was primarily owned by individuals. But now, institutional investors—pension plans, mutual funds, asset-management firms, hedge funds, insurance companies, banks, foundations, and university endowments—are the most important shareholders of public companies. Not only do they own about two-thirds of all publicly traded companies, but they also are much more likely to vote their shares than individual shareholders are.

Because they have such vast amounts to invest, if they are unhappy with management, it is difficult for them to do the "Wall Street walk"—that is, sell their shares—because a sale of their large stock holdings would depress the market price. And where would they invest the proceeds? Institutional investors cannot all profit simply by trading shares among themselves. For better or worse, the fate of institutional investors hangs on the success of these large companies.

35-1b The Relationship between Shareholders and Managers

The relationship between corporations and their shareholders has long been contentious. In this century, we have already experienced two financial meltdowns that starkly revealed the different incentives faced by shareholders and managers. Too often, managers earned exorbitant compensation from highly risky, short-term decisions that in the long run left shareholders holding an empty bag. If CEOs made a risky decision that paid off, they profited enormously. If the decision failed, they might be fired, but they would have received compensation that left them wealthy beyond most people's dreams. In the two years before investment banks Bear Stearns and Lehman Brothers failed, their top five executives took home $1.4 billion and $1 billion respectively, even as their shareholders were left with nothing.

Even worse, investigations after the financial crises revealed that too many managers had gamed compensation plans, stacked the boards of their companies with their friends, and ignored shareholder interests. Compliant boards had been little more than rubber stamps, approving whatever the officers wanted. In anger and frustration, shareholders, Congress, the Securities and Exchange Commission (SEC), and stock exchanges undertook an unprecedented effort to rebalance corporate power.

Shareholders are flexing their new muscles. In the last chapter, we saw that companies have adopted shark repellents to fend off hostile takeovers. But today, companies tend to be less afraid of a hostile takeover than they are of an activist investor telling them how to run their company (and demanding seats on the board of directors). An **activist investor** is a shareholder with a large block of stock whose goal is to influence management decisions and strategic direction. Carl Icahn, who in Chapter 34 was battling Michael Dell, also tried to persuade Apple to use its $140 billion in cash to buy back its stock and increase its dividends.

Activist investor
A shareholder with a large block of stock whose goal is to influence management decisions and strategic direction

Research indicates that activists tend to target underperforming companies and that these targeted firms do improve their results for at least the following five years.[5] Perhaps because of this evidence, traditional institutional investors are now more likely to support

[5] Lucian A. Bebchuk, Alon Brav, and Wei Jiang, "The Long-Term Effects of Hedge Fund Activism," *Columbia Law Review*, Vol. 115, No. 5 (June 2015), pp. 1085–1155.

Proxy advisory firms
Companies that advise shareholders on how to vote in corporate elections

activists. In one recent year, these shareholders won 73 percent of the battles they waged for board seats. **Proxy advisory firms** are also playing a larger role. They are firms that advise shareholders on how to vote in corporate elections. And communication among shareholders is easier—the press and social media provide a convenient platform for communication, even among small shareholders.

All these factors have increased shareholder influence on management. The question you will want to ask yourself at the end of the chapter: Have shareholders and managers achieved the appropriate balance of power?

35-2 RIGHTS OF SHAREHOLDERS

If you own a car, you expect to be able to drive it whenever you want. If you own it with four of your friends, you may not be able to use it every Saturday night, but you will get to drive it sometimes, even if only on Sunday afternoons. Of course, you will also be responsible for changing the oil sometimes too. Owning stock in a corporation is different. As an owner, you have no right to use any specific asset of the corporation. If you own stock in Starbucks Corp., your share of stock plus $4.95 entitles you to a Grande Pumpkin Spice Latte, the same as everyone else. By the same token, if the pipes freeze and the local Starbucks store floods, the manager has no right to call you, as a shareholder, to help clean up the mess. **As a shareholder, you have neither the right nor the obligation to manage the day-to-day business of the enterprise.** So what rights do you have?

35-2a Right to Information

A company's obligation to provide shareholders with information depends on whether it is publicly or privately held. The disclosure rules for privately held companies are set by state law and are quite limited, while publicly traded enterprises must comply with the much more extensive requirements of the SEC and any stock exchange on which their securities are listed.

Even if a corporation is not *required* to volunteer information, shareholders have the *right* to obtain certain data upon request. **Under the Model Business Corporation Act (Model Act), shareholders acting *in good faith* and *with a proper purpose* have the right to inspect and copy the corporation's minute book, accounting records, and shareholder lists.**[6]

Proper purpose
One that aids a shareholder in managing and protecting her investment

A **proper purpose** is one that aids the shareholder in managing and protecting her investment. If Celeste receives an offer to sell her shares in a bakery called Devil Desserts, Inc., she may want to look carefully at the company's accounting records to determine the value of her stock. Or, if she is convinced the directors are mismanaging the company, she might demand a list of shareholders so that she can ask them to join her in a lawsuit. This purpose is proper—though the company may not like it—and the company is required to give her the list. If, however, Celeste wants to use the shareholder list as a potential source for her new business selling exercise equipment, the company could legitimately turn her down.

The following case is typical: The court must decide if the shareholder is acting in his role as owner or competitor.

[6]A committee of the American Bar Association drafted the Model Business Corporation Act to serve as a guideline for states to use when enacting a corporate code. The corporate statutes of Delaware also serve as a model for some states.

You Be the Judge

Chopra v. Helio Solutions, Inc.

2007 Cal. App. Unpub. LEXIS 5909; 2007 WL 2070387
Court of Appeal of California, 2007

Facts: Paul Chopra was a minority shareholder and former director of Helio Solutions, Inc. Both he and Helio were in the business of reselling Sun Microsystems products. Chopra suspected that (1) some of Helio's majority shareholders had purchased a building and leased it to Helio at an excessive rent, (2) the company had broken a lease so that it could rent this building, (3) some shareholders had used assets of the corporation to secure a personal loan, (4) Helio had permitted ex-employees to take away substantial business, and (5) the company had not collected a $1 million debt it was owed. In addition, he wanted to know if Helio was planning to issue stock and thereby dilute his ownership. Finally, he felt that his dividend of $1,952.55 was unreasonably low, given that Helio had $88 million in revenue.

Chopra hired a forensic accountant to help him investigate Helio's finances. At the accountant's request, Chopra asked Helio for these documents:

1. Articles of incorporation
2. Minutes of meetings of the board of directors and shareholders
3. All financial statements
4. All tax returns
5. The general ledger with accompanying journals
6. Income and balance sheets
7. Schedule of accounts payable and received and inventory
8. Depreciation schedule for fixed assets
9. Supporting documents, including bank loans, lines of credit, accrued payroll liabilities, sales tax liabilities, other receivables, loans to officers and owners, significant prepayments or deposits, and equipment lease agreements
10. Monthly bank statements
11. Company credit card statements
12. Compensation records
13. The following contracts: life insurance policies for officers and/or stockholders, pension plan and profit-sharing plans, stock purchase plans, equipment and building leases, employment and bonus agreements for owners or key employees, covenants not to compete, loan agreements and credit information, documents connected with the company's real property, option grants, and each owner's curriculum vitae
14. A list of patents held by the company
15. Budget projections for the current year
16. Company brochures and/or marketing information
17. A list of key management personnel with job titles
18. An overview of the objectives for each department manager
19. Information regarding contingencies and lawsuits

Helio Solutions gave Chopra items 1–6 but refused to turn over the other material. He filed suit.

You Be the Judge: *Which of these documents must a company provide to its shareholders?*

Argument for Chopra: All these documents are necessary for assessing the value of Chopra's investment in the company and determining whether his interests as a minority shareholder are being protected. For example, without employee agreements and compensation information, a shareholder cannot assess the current corporate financial situation, value the company, determine if the business is being properly managed, or discover whether the majority shareholders or directors are improperly diverting corporate funds for their own benefit. Chopra also needs the contracts and agreements related to equipment and building leases to determine whether the majority shareholders had purchased a building and leased it to Helio at an excessive rate.

Argument for Helio: Chopra is simply on a fishing expedition to find information that would help him compete against Helio. He wants to use Helio's budget projections and managerial objectives so that he can beat them to the punch on some of their new initiatives. Many of the requests relate to specific shareholders rather than to the company. Moreover, it would take weeks of work to find and scan these documents. Shareholders have some rights to corporate information, but they are not entitled to unlimited access to corporate secrets.

35-2b Corporate Changes

Right to Approve Changes

A corporation must seek shareholder approval in the following circumstances:

- **Dissolution.** A corporation cannot *voluntarily* dissolve without shareholder approval. However, as discussed in Chapter 33, the state or a court can *involuntarily* dissolve a corporation regardless of shareholder views.
- **Amendments to the charter.** Directors propose amendments to the charter, but these amendments are not valid until approved by shareholders.
- **Amendments to the bylaws.** Both directors and shareholders have the right to amend the bylaws, but shareholders can override the directors' changes.
- **Mergers.** As a general rule, one corporation cannot merge with another unless a majority of both sets of shareholders approve. This rule is always true for shareholders of the *acquired* company because they are always affected by the merger. But when an elephant acquires a peanut, it makes little sense for the elephant to vote. So, shareholders of the *acquiring* company vote only if the merger will have a major impact on their company.
- **Sale of assets.** Shareholders do not have to approve routine sales of assets—say, each printer that HP sells. But a company cannot sell "all or substantially all" of its assets without shareholder approval.

Appraisal Rights

Appraisal rights
If a corporation decides to undertake a fundamental change, the company must buy back at fair value the stock of any shareholders who object.

If a corporation undertakes a fundamental change (such as a merger or sale of assets), the Model Act and **many state laws require the company to buy back at fair value the stock of any shareholders who object to this decision.** To take advantage of these so-called **appraisal rights**, the shareholders must vote against the proposed change and then ask a court to determine the fair value of their stock.

You remember the *Dole* case from the prior chapter. There, corporate officers Murdock and Carter violated the business judgment rule by deliberately depressing Dole's stock so that Murdock would get a better deal when he bought it. The court ordered the men to pay substantial damages to the injured shareholders. In addition, however, *before* the stock purchase took place, some dissenting shareholders (who were hedge funds) brought an appraisal lawsuit asking a court to determine the fair value of their Dole stock. Ultimately, this suit was settled.

35-2c Protection of Minority Shareholders

Fiduciary Duty

As we saw in the prior chapter, **anyone who owns enough stock to control a corporation has a fiduciary duty to minority shareholders** (those with less than a controlling interest). The courts have long recognized that minority shareholders are entitled to extra protection because it is easy (perhaps even natural) for controlling shareholders to take advantage of them. In the following case, craigslist adopted a rights plan (which, as you may remember from the prior chapter, is also called a poison pill). But the pill was too bitter for eBay to swallow.

eBay Domestic Holdings, Inc. v. Newmark

16 A.3d 1
Court of Chancery of Delaware, 2010

Facts: eBay, Inc., was a publicly traded company that operated online auction sites worldwide and employed over 16,000 people. Its primary goal was to maximize profit and market share. eBay bought 28 percent of craigslist, which operated a popular website for classified ads. craigslist had just two shareholders—Craig Newmark and Jim Buckmaster—and only 34 employees. Its goal was to enhance its user community.

In the purchase documents, Craig and Jim had agreed that eBay could compete with craigslist. But when eBay launched a rival website, the pair were furious. (As other people have discovered, agreeing in theory to an open marriage is very different from actually experiencing it.) Jim and Craig asked out of the deal, but eBay refused to sell its stock.

Agreeing in theory to an open marriage is very different from actually experiencing it.

In their role as directors, Craig and Jim adopted a rights plan that prevented eBay from buying more shares of craigslist, selling its existing shares to third parties, or choosing a board member. They maintained that this plan would protect craigslist's unique culture and promote shareholder value. eBay filed suit, alleging that Craig and Jim had violated craigslist's fiduciary duty to eBay as a minority shareholder.

Issue: ***Did Craig, Jim, and craigslist violate their fiduciary duty to the minority shareholder?***

Excerpts from Chancellor Chandler's Decision: [C]ontrolling stockholders are fiduciaries of their corporations' minority stockholders.

[T] he two main issues I confront are: First, did Jim and Craig properly and reasonably perceive a threat to craigslist's corporate policy and effectiveness? Second, if they did, is the Rights Plan a proportional response to that threat?

Jim and Craig contend that they identified a threat to craigslist and its corporate policies that will materialize after they both die and their craigslist shares are distributed to their heirs. To prevent this unwanted potential future reality, Jim and Craig have adopted the Rights Plan *now* so that their vision of craigslist's culture can bind *future* fiduciaries and stockholders from beyond the grave. Jim and Craig ask this Court to validate their attempt to use a pill to shape the future of the space-time continuum.

Ultimately, defendants failed to prove that craigslist possesses a palpable, distinctive, and advantageous culture that sufficiently promotes stockholder value to support the indefinite implementation of a poison pill. It may be that offering free classifieds is an essential component of a successful online classifieds venture. Giving away services to attract business is a sales tactic, however, not a corporate culture. [These] business measures reflect the American capitalist culture, not something unique to craigslist.

The defendants also failed to prove at trial that when adopting the Rights Plan, they concluded in good faith that there was a sufficient connection between the craigslist "culture" (however amorphous and intangible it might be) and the promotion of stockholder value. Jim and Craig simply disliked the possibility that the Grim Reaper someday will catch up with them and that a company like eBay might, in the future, purchase a controlling interest in craigslist. They considered this possible future state unpalatable, not because of how it affects the value of the entity for its stockholders, but rather because of their own personal preferences. Jim and Craig therefore failed to prove at trial that they acted in the good faith pursuit of a proper *corporate* purpose when they deployed the Rights Plan.

The corporate form in which craigslist operates is not an appropriate vehicle for purely philanthropic ends, at least not when there are other stockholders interested in realizing a return on their investment. If Jim and Craig were the only stockholders affected by their decisions, then there would be no one to object. eBay, however, holds a significant stake in craigslist, and Jim and Craig's actions affect others besides themselves.

As long as Jim and Craig have control, they can maintain the craigslist "culture" regardless of whether eBay sells some or all of its shares. The Rights Plan therefore does not have a reasonable connection to Jim and Craig's professed goal. It therefore falls outside the range of reasonableness.

I rescind the Rights Plan in its entirety.

Ordinary Business Transactions

Minority shareholders have the right to overturn an ordinary business transaction between the corporation and a controlling shareholder unless the corporation can show that the transaction is fair to the minority shareholders. The Sinclair Oil Co. owned 97 percent of Sinclair Venezuelan Oil Co. (Sinven). Sinven's minority shareholders complained that Sinclair:

- Forced Sinven to pay dividends so large that the subsidiary faced bankruptcy;
- Hired other, wholly owned, subsidiaries but not Sinven; and
- Refused to force its other subsidiaries to abide by their contracts with Sinven, for instance, a Sinclair subsidiary signed a contract with Sinven to buy crude oil but failed to purchase the required amount.[7]

The court ruled that the dividend policy was fair to the minority shareholders because they received the dividends too. Sinclair was not under any obligation to hire Sinven. But Sinclair did have to ensure that other subsidiaries complied with their Sinven contracts.

Protection from Being Expelled

Many states prohibit a company from expelling shareholders unless the firm pays a fair price for the minority stock and the expulsion has a legitimate business purpose. Delaware has an even higher standard—the transaction must be "entirely fair." This standard requires that both the price and the process of approval be fair. Theodore Lerner owned 70 shares in the family real estate company, Lawrence Lerner, only 25. When Lawrence sued Theodore for mismanagement, Theodore amended the charter to reclassify each share of stock into 1/35 of a share and to buy out any fractional shares. Lawrence ended up with 5/7 of a share, which the company purchased. The court, however, halted the squeeze-out because it had no legitimate business purpose.[8]

> **The court halted the squeeze-out because it had no legitimate purpose.**

EXAMStrategy

Question: The five Brown children were all owners of the Roundup Ranch, Inc., in Montana. Peter owned 51 percent of the corporation; the rest was evenly divided among his four siblings. Because coal companies were encroaching on Roundup, Peter traded the Montana ranch for equivalent land in New Mexico. His siblings were unhappy because they had a sentimental attachment to their family homestead. What could they do?

Strategy: Because Peter owned a majority of the shares, he had the right to sell the ranch. But because he is undertaking a fundamental change, his siblings do have some rights.

Result: The siblings have appraisal rights—that is, the right to require the company to buy back their stock, which is what the unhappy siblings required the unhappier Peter to do.

---

[7]Sinclair Oil Corp. v. Levien, 280 A.2d 717 (Del. 1971).
[8]Lerner v. Lerner, 306 Md. 771 (Md. App. 1986).

35-2d Right to Vote

A corporation must have at least one class of stock with voting rights. Typically, common shareholders have the right to vote and preferred shareholders do not, but there are many exceptions to this rule.

Shareholder Meetings

A corporation must hold some version of an annual shareholders meeting to conduct such matters as electing directors. Small, private companies often meet this requirement by signing unanimous written consents. (Written consents are discussed in Chapter 33.) Under the Model Act, the board of directors and shareholders owning at least 10 percent of the company's stock each have the right to call a special meeting at any time.

Record date
Everyone who owns stock on this date is entitled to vote at the shareholders meeting.

Quorum
A certain percentage of the company's shares are represented, either in person or by proxy, at a meeting.

Both the New York Stock Exchange (NYSE) and NASDAQ require listed companies to hold an annual meeting. Everyone who owns stock on the **record date** is entitled to vote at the shareholders meeting, whether it is an annual or a special meeting. The record date can be any day that is no more than 70 days before the meeting. The votes taken at a shareholder meeting are not valid unless a **quorum** is present, meaning that a certain percentage of the outstanding shares are represented, either in person or by proxy.

About half the states (including Delaware) permit corporations to hold shareholder meetings online rather than in person. More than 150 companies now hold virtual-only annual meetings. In this way, they save the cost of renting space, avoid disruptive protesters (think SeaWorld and animal rights protesters), and expand access beyond the shareholders who can travel to a meeting. But they also avoid interaction with their shareholders.

Lennart Preiss/Getty Images

A live shareholder meeting looks like this. Is a virtual meeting a reasonable substitute?

Symantec Corporation was the first Fortune 500 company to hold a virtual-only version. It broadcast only in audio, not video, which meant that participants had no opportunity to read body language or even know that three directors were absent. In the question-and-answer period, management read and answered only two questions from shareholders, without providing an opportunity for follow-up questions. Nor did management reveal who had asked the questions or what questions they had chosen not to answer.

An annual meeting is often shareholders' only chance to meet with management (during, but also before and after the meeting) and it may be directors' only opportunity to hear directly from the company's owners. For this reason, a number of shareholder groups oppose all-virtual meetings.

Proxies

Shareholders have the right to appoint someone else to vote for them at a meeting of the corporation. Both this person and the card the shareholder signs to appoint the substitute voter are called a **proxy**.

Proxy
The person whom a shareholder appoints to vote for her at a meeting of the corporation; also, the document a shareholder signs appointing this substitute voter

Proxy statement
Information a company provides to shareholders in preparation for the annual meeting

Annual report
A document containing detailed financial information that public companies provide to their shareholders

All public companies solicit proxies because that is the only practical way to obtain a quorum. Along with the proxy card, the SEC requires companies to give shareholders a **proxy statement** and an **annual report** to aid them in voting their stock. The proxy statement provides information such as management compensation and a list of directors who miss too many meetings. The annual report contains detailed financial data. A public company is required to post its annual report on its website, distribute it to shareholders, and file it with the SEC.

Under the Model Act, a proxy is valid for only 11 months unless the form provides for a longer period. For public corporations, however, SEC rules specify that a proxy is valid only for the next meeting. After that, it automatically expires. Under both state and federal law, the shareholder can generally revoke a proxy at any time.

Election of Directors

At the annual meeting, shareholders have the right to elect directors. But "corporate democracy" in America bears little resemblance to a political democracy.

Plurality versus Majority Voting. The election process begins when the nominating committee of the board of directors produces a slate of directors, with one name per opening. Once a slate of nominees is selected, it is placed in the proxy statement and sent to shareholders, whose only choice is to vote in favor of a nominee or to withhold their vote (i.e., not vote at all).

Traditionally, a successful candidate did not have to receive a majority of all votes cast; he simply needed more than any opponent. Since there were no opponents, one vote was sufficient (and that vote could be his own). This method is called **plurality voting**. Even if a large number of shareholders withheld their votes, the nominee might be embarrassed, but as long as he received that one vote, he was elected.

Plurality voting
To be elected, a candidate only needs to receive more votes than his opponent, not a majority of the votes cast.

Majority voting
Directors must resign if more than half the shares that vote in an uncontested election withhold their vote from them.

Zombie directors
Directors who serve on a board with less than majority support from shareholders

However, because of pressure from shareholder activists, 90 percent of large companies now require **majority voting**, that is, directors must resign if more than half the shares that vote in an uncontested election withhold their vote from them. Among smaller companies—those in the Russell 3000 Index—70 percent still permit plurality voting, where one vote is often sufficient to insure election.[9]

But even if directors are rejected by shareholders, the other board members can refuse to accept their resignation. This phenomenon is so common that these directors who serve on a board with less than majority support from shareholders have a name: **zombie directors**. In one recent year, 40 of the 44 directors at Russell 3000 companies who failed to get a majority vote, stayed on the board. When one company's shareholders voted against all of its directors, the ousted group offered to resign. But not for long; the board met and the directors decided not to accept their own resignations. However, at some companies, including HP, a number of directors have resigned after receiving a vote that was just barely a majority.

After all the troubles at HP, proxy advisory firms recommended that shareholders withhold their vote from two of the company's directors. Nonetheless, a majority of shareholders still voted in favor of all 11 directors. Why would they do that?

By and large shareholders do not withhold their votes from directors. In one recent year, only 0.2 percent of directors failed to get majority support. Many large shareholders are mutual funds and asset managers who may hesitate to offend the management of a company that has billions of dollars in retirement plans to invest. HP's retirement plan has more than $14 billion in assets and its two largest shareholders are, you guessed it, a mutual fund and an asset management firm, both of whom voted for the HP slate of directors.[10]

Proxy Access. Suppose that shareholders want to do more than just withhold their vote—they want to nominate their own candidates to the board. Typically they would have to prepare and distribute a proxy statement to other shareholders and then communicate why their slate is superior, all the while fighting against the company's almost unlimited financial resources. This process is complex, expensive, and disruptive to any company. Not surprisingly, only a few shareholder groups undertake this effort each year. Research does indicate, however, that companies with a director elected through proxy contests outperform their peers in both the short and long run.[11]

---

9 The Russell 3000 is made up of the largest 3,000 companies in the United States, representing 98 percent of the investable U.S. equity market.

10 James B. Stewart, "Bad Directors and Why They Aren't Thrown Out," *The New York Times*, March 29, 2013.

11 The Investor Responsibility Research Center Institute. See www.irrcinstitute.org/pdf/PR_5_25_09.pdf. Also, Vyacheslav Fos, "The Disciplinary Effects of Proxy Contests," *Management Science*, 201763:3, 655–671.

Under new SEC rules, **a company must adopt proxy access if a majority of shareholders vote in favor.** A proxy access bylaw typically provides that anyone who has owned 3 percent of the company's stock for three years can nominate candidates to the board. These nominees are then included in the *company's* proxy material, saving substantial expense and effort. These outsider nominees compete directly against directors nominated by the board. But the number of directors elected via proxy access is typically limited to the greater of two directors or 20 percent of board seats. In other words, proxy access cannot be used to gain control of a company.

About 58 percent of S&P 500 companies and about 14 percent of S&P 1500 companies have proxy access. Hewlett-Packard is one of them. Indeed, it voluntarily asked shareholders to approve a proxy access bylaw. According to research by the SEC, the returns for companies with proxy access were 0.5 percent higher than similar companies without such a system.[12]

Independent Directors. **Independent directors** are members of the board who are not employed by the company and do not have close ties to the CEO. **For publicly traded companies, independent directors must comprise:**

Independent directors
Members of the board of directors who are not employees of the company and do not have close ties to the CEO; also known as outside directors

- A majority of the board;
- The entire audit committee (and at least three members must be financially literate); and
- The entire compensation, corporate governance, and nominating committees.

In addition, independent directors must meet regularly on their own without **inside directors**; that is, without members of the board who are also employees of the corporation.

Inside directors
Members of the board of directors who are also employees of the corporation

But what counts as independent? The president of Stanford University served on the board of Google even as the company financed $25 million worth of university activities. Linda Marvin, a board member at Allegiant Travel was the company's former CFO and had worked for the current Allegiant CEO at two other companies. She counted as an independent director as she voted to approve self-dealing transactions by the CEO. Although CEOs cannot serve on the nominating committee of the board, they often influence the selection process for new directors. Biogen-Idec hired a search firm to look for a new independent board member. It then selected a candidate whose children attended the same private school as the CEO's. Was he truly independent?

One study found that 45 percent of directors who are technically independent have friendship ties to the CEO. And even if directors start out independent, the longer they serve on the board the more likely they are to become the CEO's friend. In S&P 500 firms, one-third of all board seats have been held for at least 10 years. At Costco, eight of the ten directors have averaged 19 years on the board.

Research also suggests that board members with friendship ties are more likely to (1) make decisions that benefit the CEO over the company and (2) allow self-interested behavior on the part of the CEO.[13] Not surprisingly, boards with independent directors who really are, well, independent achieve better financial results.[14]

---

[12]Emily Chasan, "Ammunition for Shaking up a Board," *The Wall Street Journal*, August 14, 2015.

[13]Jacob M. Rose, Anna M. Rose, Carolyn Strand Norman, and Cheri R. Mazza, "Will Disclosure of Friendship Ties between Directors and CEOs Yield Perverse Effects?" *The Accounting Review*, July 2014, Vol. 89, No. 4, pp. 1545–1563. B. Hwang, S. Kim, "It Pays to Have Friends," *Journal of Financial Economics* 93:138–158.

[14]Kathy Fogel, Liping Ma, and Randall Morck, "Powerful Independent Directors," (September 2, 2015). European Corporate Governance Institute (ECGI), Finance Working Paper No. 404/2014. Available at SSRN: https://ssrn.com/abstract=2377106.

Executive Compensation

Pay for Performance. In 1978, average (inflation-adjusted) compensation for CEOs in the top 350 firms was $1.5 million. By 2014, it had increased about ten times to $16.3 million. That was double the rate of stock market growth during this same period, which was about five times. At the same time, the pay for private sector, nonsupervisory workers (82 percent of the workforce) hardly went up at all—just one-tenth. Exhibit 35.1 illustrates these growth rates.

But, you say, executives are paid for performance—they only do well when their shareholders also profit. Not exactly. First of all, as we have seen, CEO pay went up at twice the rate of the stock market, which means that the average CEO did much better than the average investor. Second, research consistently shows that the correlation between CEO pay and performance is somewhere between slightly positive (up to 12 percent) and significantly negative—that is, the higher the pay, the worse the performance.[15] **Whatever explains CEO pay increases it is not, by and large, improved performance.** Luck is a much bigger determiner than skill.[16] And, also, it turns out is good press. When CEOs get favorable mention in the news media, their salaries go up, but, unfortunately, not the performance of their companies.[17]

Let's look at some examples. HP's Mark Hurd earned $85 million in three years, and he was fired. So was Léo Apotheker, and his rate of pay was even better: $25 million for one disastrous year. Or take oil companies, when the price of crude oil goes up, so do their profits and therefore the salaries of oil company CEOs.[18]

Total shareholder return
The percentage increase in stock price appreciation and dividends

Net returns on invested capital
The company's return on its capital investments, such as plants and equipment, less the opportunity cost of those investments

A truly shameful example of the compensation game occurred after the 9/11 terrorist attacks. The stock market was closed for four days and, when it reopened, stocks took their biggest plunge since the Nazis invaded France at the beginning of World War II. Taking advantage of these low prices, more than double the usual number of companies granted stock options to executives, which meant their executives profited from this national tragedy.[19]

In measuring performance, many companies use **total shareholder return** (i.e., the percentage increase in stock price appreciation and dividends). If a board of directors truly wanted executive compensation to mirror performance, **net returns on invested capital**

---

15 "The Alignment Gap Between Creating Value, Performance Measurement, and Long-Term Incentive Design," IRRC Institute,2014. Adam Davidson, "C.E.O.'s Don't Need to Earn Less. They Need to Sweat More," *The New York Times*, May 29, 2013. "Executive Pay and Performance," The Economist, February 7, 2012. Robert Daines, Vinay B. Nair, and Lewis A. Kornhauser, "The Good, the Bad and the Lucky: CEO Pay and Skill," (August 2005). University of Pennsylvania, Institute for Law and Economics Research Paper 05-07; New York University, Law and Economics Research Paper No. 04-035. Available at SSRN: http://ssrn.com/abstract=622223. Ric Marshall and Linda-Eling Lee, "Are CEOs Paid for Performance?" MSCI, July 2016. Gretchen Morgenson, "Pay for Performance? It Depends on the Measuring Stick," *The New York Times*, April 12, 2015. Gretchen Morgenson, "When the Stock Price Hides Trouble," The New York Times," October 12, 2013.

16 Moshe Levy, "90 Cents of Every 'Pay-For-Performance' Dollar Are Paid for Luck (September 11, 2016). Available at SSRN: https://ssrn.com/abstract=2837504. Marianne Bertrand and Sendhil Mullainathan, "Are CEOs Rewarded for Luck? The Ones Without Principals Are," *The Quarterly Journal of Economics*, August 2001.

17 Ulrike Malmendier and Geoffrey Tate, "Superstar CEOs," *The Quarterly Journal of Economics*, 2009, 124 (4): 1593-1638.

18 Marianne Bertrand and Sendhil Mullainathan, "Are CEOs Rewarded for Luck? The Ones Without Principals Are," *The Quarterly Journal of Economics*, August 2001.

19 Charles Forelle, James Bandler, and Mark Maremont, "Executive Pay: The 9/11 Factor," *The Wall Street Journal*, July 15, 2006, p. A1.

EXHIBIT 35.1

The Relative Increase in CEO Compensation

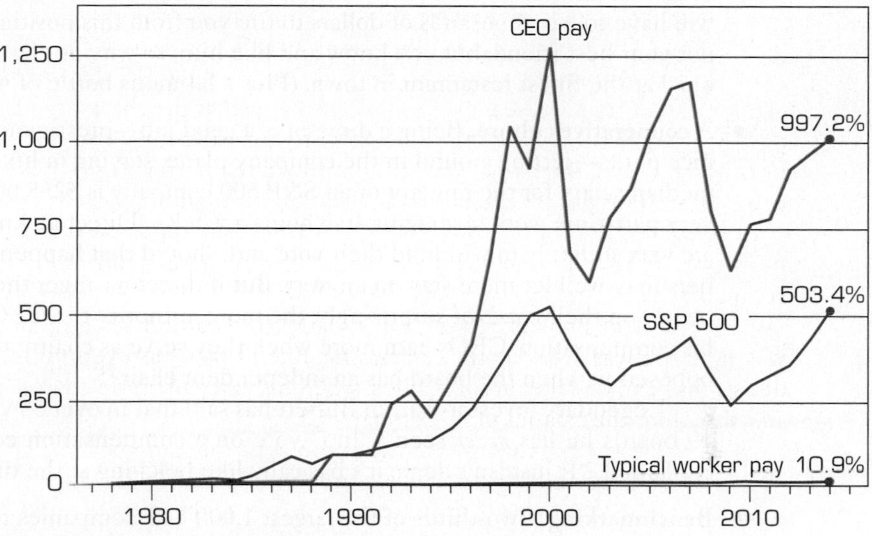

Sources: Economic Policy Institute analysis of data from Compustat's ExecuComp database, Federal Reserve Economic Data (FRED) from the Federal Reserve Bank of St. Louis, the Current Employment Statistics program, and the Bureau of Economic Analysis NIPA tables, as seen in ***Top CEOs Make 300 Times More than Typical Workers.***

Economic Policy Institute

would be a better measure of real economic value (i.e., the company's return on its capital investments, such as plants and equipment, less the opportunity cost of those investments). Only about 17 percent of companies use this measure in any way to determine CEO compensation and thus there is little correlation between pay and this crucial measure of performance.[20]

Executive compensation that is unrelated to performance not only wastes shareholder money, it has other effects as well:

- Companies whose CEOs have generous stock options experience more product recalls.[21]

- There is a negative correlation between CEO pay and approval ratings by the company's workers.[22]

20Gary Lutin, Mark Van Clieaf, and Stephen F. O'Byrne, "Executive Pay Analysis for the New York Times" (June 16, 2016).

21A. J. Wowak, M. J. Mannor, and K. D. Wowak, "Throwing Caution to the Wind: The Effect of CEO Stock Option Pay on the Incidence of Product Safety Problems," (2015), *Strategic Management Journal*, 36: 1082–1092.

22What Makes a Great CEO?" Glassdoor Research Report, August 2016.

- Materialistic CEOs (i.e., those who own particularly expensive cars, boats, and real estate) spend less on corporate social responsibility.[23]

Why don't directors use more accurate measures of performance? Several reasons:

- **Other people's money.** It is always easy to spend other people's money. Imagine that you have the right to decide how much your next-door neighbor can spend on dinner tonight. No matter what you decide, faceless, nameless residents ten blocks away will have to pay for the meal and, if they object to the amount you choose, they will have to pay thousands of dollars to fire you from this position. Your neighbor is not your best friend, but you know and like him, so why not let him have a gourmet meal at the finest restaurant in town. (Plus a fabulous bottle of wine!)

- **A cooperative culture.** Being a director is a good job—prestigious, well paid, with nice perks—jetting around in the company plane, staying in luxury hotels. The median salary for the director of an S&P 500 company is $255,000 a year for what is very part-time work (averaging five hours a week). Directors know that shareholders are very unlikely to withhold their vote and, should that happen, fellow board members may well let them stay on anyway. But if directors anger the CEO, they may be out on their ear. Not surprisingly, the more authority the CEO has, the higher his compensation: CEOs earn more when they serve as chairman of the board, as opposed to when the board has an independent chair.[24]

  Legendary investor Warren Buffett has said that in over 55 years he has served on 19 boards he has *never* seen a "no" vote on a compensation committee report. He explained, "It just isn't done, it's basically like belching at the dinner table."

- **Benchmarking.** Two-thirds of the largest 1,000 U.S. companies reported that they performed better than their peers.[25] They obtain those results, in part, by manipulating their comparative points of reference, or benchmarks. Campbell Soup used one set of benchmark companies to determine executive compensation but another group to evaluate its total shareholder return.

  Mylan executives had the second highest compensation of any drug or biotech company in the United States. Yet during this period, its stock price gains were average. The company justified this pay by benchmarking against much larger companies. It also made the news by dramatically raising the price of life-saving EpiPens, which helped its executives meet their performance goals.[26]

  Compensation consultants do a lot of the benchmarking. When a company hires a compensation consultant, the CEO's raise is on average 7.5 percent higher than comparable companies, unless the CEO chose the consultant himself, in which case his raise is 13 percent greater.[27] A consultant is much more likely to be fired for recommending too little than too much.

---

23 Robert H. Davidson, Aiyesha Dey, and Abbie J. Smith, "CEO Materialism and Corporate Social Responsibility" (March 23, 2016). Chicago Booth Research Paper No. 16-11; Fama-Miller Working Paper Forthcoming. Available at SSRN: https://ssrn.com/abstract=2794099.

24 Institutional Shareholder Services, Inc. "Board Leadership Structure; Impact on CEO Pay, U.S." (2016).

25 Kevin J. Murphy, "Politics, Economics and Executive Compensation," 63 University of Cincinnati Law Review 713, 1995.

26 Mark Maremont, "EpiPen Maker Dispenses Outsize Pay," *The Wall Street Journal*," September 13, 2016.

27 Jenny Chu, Jonathan Faasse, and P. Raghavendra Rau, "Do Compensation Consultants Enable Higher CEO Pay?" (February 12, 2017). Available at SSRN: https://ssrn.com/abstract=2500054.

- **Belief in a competitive market.** Managers argue that their pay is set by the market. Is there really a competitive market for executive talent? If CEOs are underpaid, will they be bid away by another company? The data do not reveal significant inter-company bidding for CEO talent: Fewer than 2 percent of CEOs have held that same post at another company.[28] And there is evidence that insider CEOs perform better than outside candidates anyway.

- **It is hard to see the harm.** If a company has a trillion dollar balance sheet, what harm is done if the CEO gets $10 million or $25 million or $100 million? Two things: One, economic theory teaches us that organizations should be profit maximizing. If that principle does not apply at the top, it sets a bad example throughout the organization. Two, CEOs who earn mind-boggling amounts of money become insulated from reality. If they have so much money that five generations of their family will never have to work, why would they care what other people, such as shareholders, think? They live in a different world.

- **Rationalization.** You need look no further than the *Raul* case later in this chapter for some fine examples of rationalization. If a company's stock price is doing well, then, by all means, the executives must be rewarded to keep them from jumping ship. But, if the company is performing poorly, the officers also need to be rewarded—you guessed it—to keep them from jumping ship. Indeed, the data indicate that CEOs benefit greatly from good corporate results, but suffer no pay penalty for poor outcomes.[29]

- **Ownership by institutional investors.** As we have seen, about two-thirds of the stock of publicly-traded companies is owned by institutional investors. These shareholders vote in favor of pay packages 96 percent of the time. Because these investors are so large, they often own stock of companies that compete against each other. BlackRock, for example, is the largest shareholder of four of the five biggest banks in the United States. Therefore, it is not in BlackRock's best interest for banks to compete against each other in a way that might harm their competitors by, say, waging a price war. It wants all the large banks to do well. Institutional investors do tend to reward managers when the overall industry does well rather than individual companies.[30]

Government Regulation. The federal government has tried to change the landscape of corporate governance and executive compensation in the following ways:

- **Lead director.** The independent members of the board are required to meet regularly on their own, without management. About 60 percent of S&P 500 companies have appointed a so-called lead director to run these meetings and serve as a counterweight to the CEO chair.

- **Clawbacks.** The SEC has the right to clawback some CEO and CFO compensation if misconduct on the part of *any employee* causes the company to restate its financials.[31] In addition, a public company must establish a clawback policy, whereby it can

---

[28] Charles M. Elson and Craig K. Ferrere, "Executive Superstars, Peer Groups and Overcompensation: Cause, Effect and Solution" (August 7, 2012). Available at SSRN: http://ssrn.com/abstract=2125979.

[29] Lucian A. Taylor, "CEO Wage Dynamics: Estimates from a Learning Model," *Journal of Financial Economics*, 2013, 108(1): 79–98.

[30] Miguel Anton, Florian Ederer, Mireia Gine, and Martin C. Schmalz, "Common Ownership, Competition, and Top Management Incentives" (August 15, 2016). Ross School of Business Paper No. 1328. Available at SSRN: https://ssrn.com/abstract=2802332.

[31] United States SEC v. Jensen, 835 F.3d 1100 (9th Cir. 2016).

require the CEO and CFO to reimburse the company for any bonus or profits they receive from selling company stock within a year of the release of flawed financials.

So far, however, few companies have sought reimbursement for executive wrongdoing. Wells Fargo employees engaged in massive fraud, setting up millions of accounts that customers had not requested, just to generate fees and meet sales goals. Years after the press first broke this scandal, Congressional committees finally called CEO John Stumpf to testify about the fraud. Only under pressure from Congress did the board clawback $69 million of the $286 million Stumpf had earned during his tenure at the bank.

- **Disclosure.** The SEC has adopted rules requiring companies to disclose the ratio between the CEO's total pay and the median total compensation for all other company employees. However, the commission has not implemented these rules.
- **Say-on-pay.** At least once every three years, companies must take a *nonbinding* shareholder vote on the compensation of the five highest-paid executives. Recently, however, only 1.5 percent of the say-on-pay votes have been negative. And when firms are faced with a vote, they tend to reduce CEO salaries and golden parachutes but increase stock awards and pensions. On net, total pay is higher.[32]

The following case shows that a board of directors has the absolute right to ignore say-on-pay votes.

Raul v. Rynd

929 F. Supp. 2d 333
United States District Court for the District of Delaware, 2013

Facts: Hercules Offshore, Inc., provided drilling services to the oil and natural gas industry. After a year in which its financial results and stock price had declined substantially, the Hercules board unanimously approved a compensation plan that *raised* executive pay by between 40 percent and 190 percent. In its proxy statement to shareholders, Hercules stated:

> Our compensation committee will continue to design compensation arrangements with the objectives of emphasizing pay for performance and aligning the financial interests of our executives with the interests of long-term stockholders.

When, as required by say-on-pay rules, the company presented this compensation plan to shareholders at the annual meeting, 59 percent of Hercules's shares voted against it. The board ignored the shareholder vote and continued with the plan anyway.

A Hercules shareholder brought suit, alleging that the board had breached its fiduciary duty by approving the compensation plan in the face of a negative shareholder vote. He also alleged that the compensation plan violated the company's pay-for-performance philosophy as outlined in the proxy statement.

Hercules filed a motion to dismiss.

Issue: ***Did the Hercules board violate its fiduciary duty when it approved the compensation plan?***

Excerpts from Judge Stark's Decision: Plaintiff relies heavily on the fact that the Hercules shareholders voted against the executive compensation plan yet the Board thereafter did nothing to rescind or modify that plan in response. However, [the Dodd-Frank statute] explicitly states that say-on-pay votes "shall not be binding" on a company or its board of directors. Dodd-Frank also explicitly states that the results of say-on-pay votes may not be

[32]Mathias Kronlund and Shastri Sandy, "Does Shareholder Scrutiny Affect Executive Compensation?" (November 18, 2016). Available at SSRN: https://ssrn.com/abstract=2358696.

construed in any of the following ways: (1) as overruling a decision by a company or its board of directors; [or] (2) to create or imply any change to the fiduciary duties of a company or its board of directors. Plaintiff's allegations and arguments fail to recognize these realities of Dodd-Frank.

Plaintiff also relies heavily on his view that Hercules has adopted a strict pay-for-performance policy. It is true that Hercules's Proxy Statement explains that pay for performance is part of the philosophy and objectives of the Company's compensation programs. However, the same statement also identifies other goals. One of these goals merits particular discussion in light of Plaintiff's allegations. This is the Company's goal of retaining its executive officers, a goal that may have taken on increased importance precisely because of the difficult financial circumstances in which the Company found itself. As the Proxy Statement explains:

> The Board of Directors and its Compensation Committee remain committed to retaining the existing management team, and as a result, have offered cash retention incentives to recover some of the shortfall in long-term incentive compensation levels. The committee believes that the implementation of this plan has been critical in deflecting efforts by competitors that can offer attractive compensation opportunities, and in keeping the management team focused on executing the current business strategy for future shareholder value creation.

The goal of retaining an executive could, under certain circumstances, lead to increased executive compensation even if the Company is experiencing poor financial performance.

In addition, Plaintiff's allegations incorrectly presume that executive compensation is solely awarded retrospectively. As is common practice in executive compensation, the Proxy Statement makes clear that much of the Company's executive compensation is prospective. Hence, Plaintiff's characterization of the Hercules executive compensation policy as essentially mandating a strong correlation between certain financial aspects of the Company's performance and the compensation of the Company's executives is incorrect.

The Hercules Motion to Dismiss is GRANTED.

Shareholder Proposals

Shareholders have the right to make proposals for company action, which are then subject to vote at the annual meeting. Recently, the most common topic has been proxy access, but others have included: (1) corporate governance issues, such as majority voting or an independent chair of the board; (2) politics—how much the company spent on donations and lobbying; (3) the environment—reporting on the production of greenhouse gases and the company's exposure to the risk of climate change; and (4) social policy—asking for a report on a firm's gender pay gap and for the inclusion of sexual orientation and gender identity in its nondiscrimination policy. Wells Fargo shareholders asked the company to prepare a report (1) analyzing why so many employees set up fraudulent accounts and (2) steps the bank could take to prevent future wrongdoing.

There are, however, limitations on shareholders' rights to make proposals:

- **To place a proposal in the proxy statement, the shareholder must have continuously owned for one year at least 1 percent of the company or $2,000 worth of stock.**
- **The proposal cannot relate to the ordinary business operations of the corporation.** So HP shareholders could not have proposed that the company sell its PC division.
- **Many proposals are not binding on the company.** Resolutions are binding on a company only if they are within the narrow realm of shareholder power. Because shareholders have the right to amend company bylaws, these proposals (such as for proxy access) are binding. But a shareholder vote that requires the board to take action is not binding because the board, not the shareholders, has the right to manage the company. Thus, even though the SEC requires companies to allow a vote on proposals about succession planning, the board still does not *have* to develop a succession plan, even if a majority of shareholders vote in favor. Companies implement fewer than half of the proposals that their shareholders approve.

Prior to 1985, only *two* proposals had been approved—*ever*. In recent years, shareholders approved about 17 percent of the proposals put to them.[33] Most successful proposals were about governance issues.

EXAMStrategy

Question: Shareholders of Beazer Homes USA asked for a proposal requiring disclosure about the construction company's risks in the mortgage market. This was a time when many companies were struggling with bad loans to home buyers. Beazer asked the SEC for permission to exclude this proposal from its proxy statement. What did the SEC rule?

Strategy: The SEC allows companies to exclude proposals that relate to the ordinary business operations of the company.

Result: The SEC ruled that Beazer Homes was required to include the mortgage proposal because these risks directly affected the value of the company in a time of extraordinary challenges in this industry. Shortly thereafter, Beazer announced that it would stop originating mortgages.

35-3 ENFORCING SHAREHOLDER RIGHTS

Shareholders in serious conflict with management have two different mechanisms for enforcing their rights: a direct lawsuit or derivative litigation.

35-3a Direct Lawsuits

Shareholders are permitted to sue the corporation directly only if their *own* rights have been harmed. If, for example, the corporation denies shareholders the right to inspect its books and records or to hold a shareholder meeting, they may sue in their own name and keep any damages awarded. The corporation is not required to pay the shareholders' legal fees.

A shareholder sued HP to obtain a copy of a letter that the lawyer for the soft porn actor sent to the HP board about her relationship with Mark Hurd. The Delaware court ruled that the letter was part of the books and records of the company and the shareholder was entitled to a copy of it.[34]

35-3b Derivative Lawsuits

A derivative lawsuit is brought by shareholders to remedy a wrong to the corporation. Any damage to the shareholders themselves is indirect, through their ownership of the organization. For example, shareholders sued HP's directors, charging that they had breached their fiduciary duty to the *corporation* by granting an excessive severance payment to Hurd. Shareholders were harmed by that payment only indirectly, through its negative impact on HP. Thus, they could not bring a direct lawsuit; instead, they had to file derivative litigation.

---

33 Calculated from Sullivan & Cromwell LLP, "2016 Proxy Season Review."

34 Espinoza v. Hewlett-Packard Co., 2011 Del. Ch. LEXIS 45, 2011 WL 941464 (Del. Ch. 2011).

But, because it is the corporation that was harmed, the lawsuit must be brought on behalf of the corporation. The same rule applies whether the harm was caused by an insider, such as a director, or an outsider. If HP decided not to sue a customer that refused to pay its bill, the shareholders could file suit themselves, but only in a derivative action, that is, only on behalf of the corporation.

Because the suit is brought in the name of the corporation, all proceeds of the litigation go to the corporation. Individual shareholders benefit only to the extent that the settlement causes their stock to rise in value. Litigation is tremendously expensive. How can shareholders afford to sue if they are not entitled to damages? A corporation that loses a derivative suit must pay the legal fees of the victorious shareholders. So most derivative lawsuits are initiated by lawyers eager to earn these fees.[35] Without this incentive, few shareholders would bring derivative suits and much corporate wrongdoing would go unchallenged. However, some derivative lawsuits have little merit and seem to be filed for the purpose of generating a settlement offer that includes substantial legal fees. In one recent year in Delaware, shareholders filed suit in 97.5 percent of all takeovers with a value of more than $100 million.[36]

A derivative lawsuit is brought on behalf of the corporation. Who has the authority to make decisions for the corporation? The directors. In the HP case, and most derivative actions, it is the directors who are accused of wrongdoing. Why would they authorize litigation against themselves? The answer is that they would not. There is a procedure whereby shareholders can do an end run around an uncooperative board, but it is not easy.

Making Demand. **Shareholders must begin the litigation process by asking the board of directors to bring suit.** This act is called **making demand**. In other words, shareholders must notify the board that the corporation has been wronged and ask the board to bring suit on the corporation's behalf.

Making demand
When shareholders ask the board of directors to authorize litigation on behalf of the corporation

Once shareholders have made demand, the board has three choices:

1. **Agree with the shareholders and file suit on behalf of the corporation.** If the board sues, the shareholders cannot bring their own derivative action. Although, technically, the board is required to put the interests of the corporation first, boards do not file suit against themselves.
2. **Reject the demand (or fail to respond).** To proceed with their suit once the board has rejected demand, shareholders must convince a court that this rejection was a violation of the business judgment rule. Again, this is a low-probability event. (The business judgment rule was discussed in Chapter 34.)
3. **Appoint a special litigation committee (SLC).** An SLC is typically composed of at least two independent directors (usually those elected after the disputed activity occurred). If the SLC determines that the lawsuit is without merit, shareholders are not able to bring suit themselves unless they can convince a court that the rejection was uninformed or not in good faith. There does not appear to be a single case in which an SLC recommended that litigation continue or a court overturned the decision of an SLC.

Is Demand Futile? Shareholders know that making demand is a waste of time and money because the directors will appoint an SLC, which will then kill the suit. Therefore, shareholders typically file suit without making demand. If they can show that a majority of the directors cannot make a proper decision on behalf of the corporation because they have a conflict of interest, they lack the independence to act in the best interests of the corporation, or they

[35]Losing shareholders are not required to pay the corporation's legal fees, except that, under the Private Securities Litigation Reform Act, class action plaintiffs in suits brought under the securities laws must pay the corporation's legal expenses if the court determines that the suit was frivolous or abusive. 104 Pub. L. No. 67, 109 Stat. 737.

[36]Matthew D. Cain and Steven Davidoff Solomon, "Takeover Litigation in 2013," (January 9, 2014). Ohio State Public Law Working Paper No. 236. Available at SSRN: https://ssrn.com/abstract=2377001.

EXHIBIT 35.2

A Derivative Lawsuit

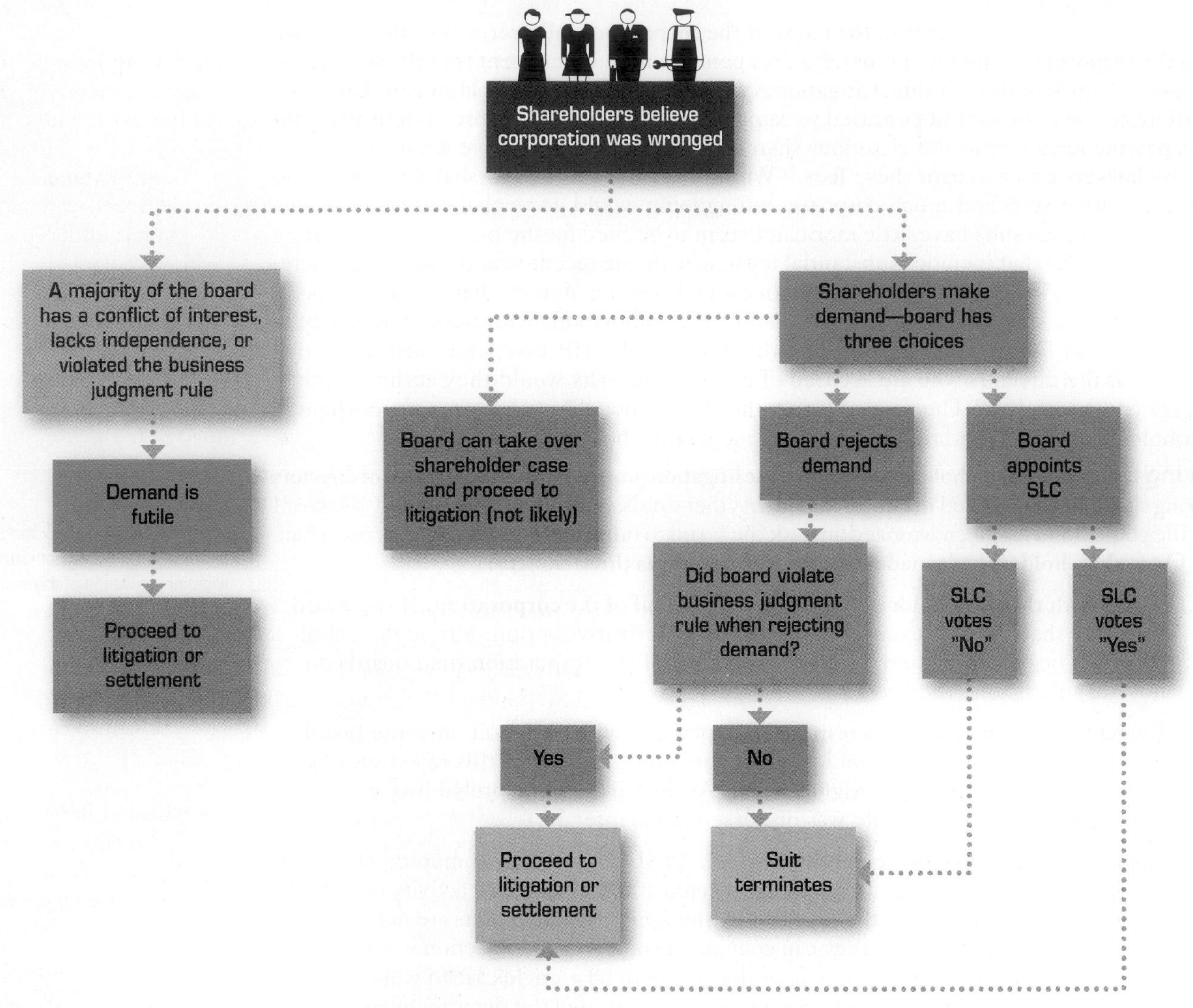

have violated the business judgment rule, then the court will decide that shareholders have the right to bring the lawsuit in the name of the corporation without the directors' approval. **In other words, the court will rule that "demand is futile."**

Once a court rules that demand is futile, the shareholders have won and the case almost always settles. But if the court instead requires demand, the shareholders know they have lost and typically withdraw the case. Exhibit 35.2 illustrates the course of derivative litigation.

Most derivative suits are brought in Delaware, so this discussion is based on Delaware law. The Model Act deviates from Delaware law by proposing that demand be required in *all* derivative cases. This approach essentially ignores the possibility that demand might be futile.

In the following case, the judge felt that the plaintiff should been more thorough in researching the facts before filing suit. Indeed, the judge chides the plaintiff for not having searched on "the tool provided by the company whose name has become a verb." Nonetheless, the court still determined that demand was futile.

Sandys v. Pincus

152 A.3d 124
Delaware Supreme Court, 2016

Facts: Zynga, the online and mobile gaming company that created Farmville, had a rule that its insiders could not trade their Zynga stock until three days after an earnings announcement. The plaintiff alleged, however, that Zynga had allowed some insiders, including Mark Pincus (its chairman, controlling stockholder, and former CEO) and Reid Hoffman (board member), to trade in violation of this rule. These insiders sold 20.3 million shares of stock while knowing that unfavorable earnings announcements were pending. Afterwards, the stock price fell from $12.00 to $3.18.

The plaintiff filed suit, alleging that these sales constituted a violation of the business judgment rule. When the plaintiff failed to make demand, the defendants moved to dismiss the case. Plaintiff argued that demand was futile.

The Zynga board had nine directors, including: Pincus, Hoffman, William Gordon, John Doerr, Ellen Siminoff, and Don Mattrick. The Court of Chancery ruled for Zynga, holding that the plaintiff was required to make demand because five of the nine directors did not have a conflict of interest and therefore could make a fair decision in the case. The plaintiff appealed.

Issues: ***Did a majority of the board have a conflict of interest? Was demand futile?***

Excerpts from Chief Justice Strine's Decision: The Court of Chancery properly determined that directors Pincus and Hoffman were interested in the transaction. Furthermore, Mattrick is Zynga's CEO. Zynga's controlling stockholder, Pincus, is interested in the transaction under attack, and therefore, Mattrick cannot be considered independent.

Thus, the question for us is whether the plaintiff pled facts that create a reasonable doubt about the independence of two of the remaining six Zynga directors. [A] lack of independence turns on whether the director's ability to act impartially on a matter important to the interested party can be doubted because that director may feel either subject to the interested party's dominion or beholden to that interested party.

The Court of Chancery found that Siminoff was independent even though she and her husband co-own a private airplane with Pincus. Co-ownership of a private plane involves a partnership in a personal asset that is not only very expensive, but that also requires close cooperation in use, which is suggestive of detailed planning indicative of a continuing, close personal friendship. In fact, it is suggestive of the type of very close personal relationship that, like family ties, one would expect to heavily influence a human's ability to exercise impartial judgment. Here, the facts support an inference that Siminoff would not be able to act impartially when deciding whether to move forward with a suit implicating a very close friend with whom she and her husband co-own a private plane.

[T]he following facts pertain to Gordon and Doerr: both are partners at Kleiner Perkins Caufield & Byers, which controls approximately 9.2% of Zynga's equity; and, Kleiner Perkins is also invested in One Kings Lane, a company that Pincus's wife co-founded. Not only that, defendant Reid Hoffman and Kleiner Perkins both have investments in Shopkick, Inc., and Hoffman serves on that company's board along with yet another partner at Kleiner Perkins. These relationships, suggest the plaintiff, indicate that Gordon and Doerr have a mutually beneficial network of ongoing business relations with Pincus and Hoffman that they are not likely to risk by causing Zynga to sue them.

Amplifying this argument, is the voice of Gordon's and Doerr's fellow Zynga directors who did not consider them to be independent directors. According to its own public disclosures, the Zynga board determined that Gordon and Doerr do not qualify as independent directors under NASDAQ Rules. [U]nder the NASDAQ rules a director is not independent if she has a "relationship which, in the opinion of the Company's board of directors, would interfere with the exercise of independent judgment in carrying out the responsibilities of a director."

Of course, the defendants argue that the relationships among these directors flowed all in one direction and that it is Pincus who is likely beholden to Gordon, Doerr, and Kleiner Perkins for financing. But, the reality is that firms

Mikhail Starodubov/Shutterstock.com

Was Ellen Siminoff independent of Mark Pincus even though they owned a private plane together?

like Kleiner Perkins compete with others to finance talented entrepreneurs like Pincus, and networks arise of repeat players who cut each other into beneficial roles in various situations. There is, of course, nothing at all wrong with that. In fact, it is crucial to commerce and most human relations. But, precisely because of the importance of a mutually beneficial ongoing business relationship, it is reasonable to expect that sort of relationship might have a material effect on the parties' ability to act adversely toward each other.

Causing a lawsuit to be brought against another person is no small matter, and is the sort of thing that might plausibly endanger a relationship. When, as here, facts suggest such a relationship exists and the company's own board has determined that the directors whose ability to consider a demand impartially is in question cannot be considered independent, a reasonable doubt exists.

[W]e reverse the Court of Chancery's dismissal.

EXAMStrategy

Question: What outcome would you predict for the cases in which HP shareholders sued the board of directors over Mark Hurd's severance payments? What process would they have to follow to get their day in court?

Strategy: Shareholders can bring suit directly only if they have been personally harmed. If the harm is to the corporation, then shareholders must bring a derivative action in the name of the company.

Result: In these cases, the harm was to the corporation. The shareholders were harmed only indirectly, when the price of their stock went down. A derivative action was their only option. They would have to (1) show that demand was futile because the directors had a conflict of interest, they lacked the independence to act in the best interests of the corporation, or they violated the business judgment rule or (2) make demand. HP shareholders have not been successful because they were unable to demonstrate that demand was futile.[37]

The following table displays some of the important distinguishing features of derivative suits and direct actions:

Features	Derivative Action	Direct Action
Enforces the Rights of:	The corporation	The shareholder(s)
Damages Are Paid to:	The corporation	The shareholder(s)
Procedural Requirements	• Plaintiffs make demand on the board unless clearly futile. • If demand is futile, plaintiffs proceed with the case. • If demand is made, either the board or the SLC can terminate the case.	The same as regular litigation

[37]In re HP Derivative Litigation, 2012 U.S. Dist. LEXIS 137640 (N.D. Cal. 2012).

CHAPTER CONCLUSION

We began this chapter by asking what HP shareholders could have done about "the worst board in the history of business." Of course, the term *shareholders* really means the large institutions that own the bulk of HP's stock. Here are their options:

- **Vote out the directors.** Right after the Apotheker debacle, the two largest HP shareholders voted in favor of all 11 directors. But the next year, Vanguard, the world's largest mutual fund company, withheld its vote from two HP directors. Although these two directors still received slightly more than 50 percent of the vote, they both resigned.
- **Nominate their own candidates.** Because HP now has proxy access, large shareholders could nominate candidates to the board, at least for 20 percent of the seats. That number would not be enough to control the company, but it would ensure they were heard.
- **Separating CEO from chair.** The institutional investors could propose amending the company's bylaws so that the CEO is not also the chair of the board.
- **Say-on-pay.** Shareholders could threaten a negative say-on-pay vote unless HP developed a compensation plan based on net returns on invested capital and eliminated generous severance packages for failure.

In short, determined, proactive institutional investors might have the tools to increase their monitoring of the board of directors and inhibit the type of bad behavior featured in the chapter opener.

Corporate governance has changed over the last decade. Most large companies have majority voting. More directors are at least technically independent and more boards have lead directors. But profound, systematic issues in corporate governance remain. Many shareholders are still reluctant to challenge directors. They voted in favor of every member of "the worst board in the history of business," even as HP's stock price plummeted. CEO compensation soars with little evidence that it correlates with performance. Activist investors often focus on their own welfare, not that of other shareholders.

Corporate governance is so simple in theory: The shareholders who own the organization elect directors to oversee their investment. The directors then appoint officers to implement corporate goals. Yet in practice corporate governance is intensely complicated with few boards who consistently act in the best interests of shareholders. Managers argue that shareholders interfere too much. But, as Lord Acton said, "Absolute power corrupts absolutely."

EXAM REVIEW

1. **SHAREHOLDER RIGHTS** Shareholders have neither the right nor the obligation to manage the day-to-day business of the enterprise. Shareholders do have:
   - The right to inspect and copy the corporation's records (for a proper purpose);
   - The right to approve fundamental corporate changes, such as a merger or a sale of most assets;
   - Appraisal rights after a fundamental change;
   - The right to protection from a controlling shareholder;
   - The right to attend shareholder meetings; and
   - The right to elect directors.

EXAMStrategy

Question: The board of directors of Finalco Group, Inc., decided to sell most of the company's assets to Western Savings. Shortly after the proposed sale was announced, Finalco's largest shareholder said he opposed the transaction. Does Finalco need his approval for the sale?

Strategy: Shareholders have the right to approve fundamental corporate changes. Was this a fundamental change? (See the "Result" at the end of this Exam Review section.)

2. **MINORITY SHAREHOLDERS** Minority shareholders:
   (a) Are owed a fiduciary duty by controlling shareholders,
   (b) Have the right to overturn an ordinary business transaction between the corporation and a controlling shareholder unless the corporation can show that the transaction is fair to the minority shareholders, and
   (c) Are protected from being expelled unless the firm pays a fair price for the minority stock and the expulsion has a legitimate business purpose.

3. **PROXY** A proxy authorizes someone else to vote in place of the shareholder.

4. **PROXY ACCESS** Proxy access bylaws require companies to include in their proxy material the names of board nominees selected by large shareholders and to allow all shareholders to vote for these nominees.

5. **INDEPENDENT DIRECTORS** For publicly traded companies, independent directors must comprise a majority of the board and only independent directors can serve on audit, compensation, corporate governance, and nominating committees.

6. **EXECUTIVE COMPENSATION** Since 1978, CEO pay has increased by twice the rate of stock market growth. Research consistently shows little correlation between CEO pay and firm performance.

7. **CLAWBACKS** The SEC has the right to clawback some CEO and CFO compensation if misconduct on the part of *any employee* causes the company to restate its financials. Companies must establish clawback policies, whereby they can require the CEO and CFO to reimburse the company for any bonus or profits they received from selling company stock within a year of the release of flawed financials.

8. **SAY-ON-PAY** At least once every three years, companies must take a *nonbinding* shareholder vote on the compensation of the five highest-paid executives.

9. **SHAREHOLDER PROPOSALS** Shareholders have the right to make proposals for company action, which are then subject to vote at the annual meeting.

EXAMStrategy

Question: An institutional investor wanted A&P, a grocery store chain, to permit large shareholders to comment on the company's financial performance in its proxy statement. Which would be a better strategy for achieving this goal: a shareholder proposal or an amendment to the company's bylaws?

Strategy: Shareholder proposals are treated differently from bylaw amendments. Which one is more likely to affect the behavior of the company? (See the "Result" at the end of this Exam Review section.)

10. **DIRECT LAWSUITS** Shareholders are permitted to sue the corporation directly only if their own rights have been harmed.

11. **DERIVATIVE LAWSUITS** A derivative lawsuit is brought by shareholders to remedy a wrong to the corporation. The suit is brought in the name of the corporation, and all proceeds of the litigation go to the corporation.

EXAMStrategy

Question: Daniel Cowin was a minority shareholder of Bresler & Reiner, Inc., a public company that developed real estate in Washington, D.C. He alleged numerous instances of corporate mismanagement, fraud, self-dealing, and breach of fiduciary duty by the board of directors. He sought damages for the diminished value of his stock. Could Cowin bring this suit as a direct action or must it be a derivative suit?

Strategy: If the wrong was to the corporation, then Cowin must bring a derivative lawsuit. He can bring a direct action only if the harm was to him personally. (See the "Result" at the end of this Exam Review section.)

RESULTS

1. Result: Yes, it was a sale of most of the company's assets. The board could not proceed without the approval of the owners of a majority of shares.

9. Result: A shareholder proposal is not binding on the company. Even if the shareholders approved a proposal, A&P would be under no obligation to carry it out. A bylaw amendment, on the other hand, would be binding on the company.

11. Result: The court ruled that the injury had fallen equally on all the shareholders, and therefore, a derivative suit was appropriate.

MULTIPLE-CHOICE QUESTIONS

1. A majority of shareholders at Weed, Inc., wanted to reinstate the former CEO of the company and sell off an unprofitable division. Do shareholders have the right to make these two decisions?
   (a) Yes to both.
   (b) No to both.
   (c) The shareholders have the right to sell off an unprofitable division, but not to reinstate the president.
   (d) The shareholders have the right to reinstate the president but not to sell off an unprofitable division.

2. Companies are required to ______________.
   I. disclose the relationship between financial performance and executive compensation
   II. appoint a lead director to run the meetings of the independent directors
   III. establish a clawback policy
   IV. have an independent chair of the board
   (a) All of these
   (b) II and III
   (c) I, II, and III
   (d) Just III

3. A company is allowed to hold its annual meeting online ______________.
   (a) if a majority of its shareholders approve
   (b) if it also holds a live meeting for shareholders who want to attend in person
   (c) if it simulcasts a video of the meeting
   (d) without shareholder approval

4. By law, a candidate for the board of a publicly traded company must receive a ______________.
   (a) majority of the votes cast
   (b) majority vote of the shares outstanding
   (c) plurality of the votes cast
   (d) plurality of the shares outstanding

5. If directors and officers cause harm to their company, ______________.
   (a) shareholders have the right to file suit against them and recover damages
   (b) shareholders have the right to file suit against them and recover damages only if the board permits the suit
   (c) shareholders have the right to file suit against them and recover damages only if the board permits the suit or a court deems the demand futile
   (d) shareholders do not have the right to file suit against them

CASE QUESTIONS

1. Pfizer Inc., paid $2.3 billion to settle civil and criminal charges alleging that it had illegally marketed 13 of its most important drugs. This settlement made history, but not in a good way. It was both the largest criminal fine and the largest settlement of civil healthcare fraud charges *ever* paid. Shareholders filed a derivative suit against the Pfizer board and top executives. Defendants responded with a motion to dismiss on the grounds that shareholders had not made demand on the board. Was demand necessary?

2. William H. Sullivan, Jr., purchased all the voting shares of the New England Patriots Football Club, Inc. (the Old Patriots). He organized a new corporation called the New Patriots Football Club, Inc. The boards of directors of the two companies agreed to merge. After the merger, the nonvoting stock in the Old Patriots was to

be exchanged for cash. Do minority shareholders of the Old Patriots have the right to prevent the merger? If so, under what theory?

3. DeVry Inc. runs for-profit schools. Its shareholders submitted a proposal that would require the company to "annually report to shareholders on the expected ability of students at Company-owned institutions to repay their student loans." Must DeVry include this proposal in its proxy material for its annual meeting?

4. ***YOU BE THE JUDGE* WRITING PROBLEM** Two shareholders of Bruce Co., Harry and Yolanda Gilbert, were fighting management for control of the company. They asked for permission to inspect Bruce's stockholder list so that they could either solicit support for their slate of directors at the upcoming stockholder meeting, attempt to buy additional stock from other stockholders, or both. Bruce's board refused to allow the Gilberts to see the shareholder list on the grounds that the Gilberts owned another corporation that competed with Bruce. Do the Gilberts have the right to see Bruce's shareholder list? **Argument for the Gilberts:** If shareholders of a company have a proper purpose, they are entitled to inspect shareholder lists. Soliciting votes and buying stock are both proper purposes. **Argument for Bruce:** The Gilberts are simply offering a pretext. They could use this information to compete against the company. No shareholder has the right to cause harm.

5. **ETHICS** After a recent annual meeting, Cisco Systems reported the results of the votes on both management and shareholder proposals. The company reported the results of its own proposals as a simple ratio of those in favor divided by the total number of votes cast. But for shareholder proposals, it reported the percentage as a ratio of those in favor divided by all outstanding shares. As a result, it reported the favorable vote for one shareholder proposal as 19 percent when, in fact, 34 percent of the votes cast supported this proposal. Is Cisco behaving ethically? What would Kant and Mill say? What ethics traps might the company face?

6. When Comcast decided to hold a virtual annual shareholders meeting, an investor submitted a proposal that would have required the company to hold a hybrid meeting—that is, both in person and online. Must Comcast allow a vote on this proposal at its annual meeting?

DISCUSSION QUESTIONS

1. Corporate executives are not the only people to earn fabulous salaries. Some athletes earn even more than CEOs. What is the difference between athletes and executives (besides a hook shot)?

2. For several years, CSK Auto, Inc., fraudulently reported inflated earnings. During this period, Maynard Jenkins was CEO. He was not involved in the fraud, however, and was never charged with a crime. Nonetheless, the SEC sought to clawback some of his earnings during this period. Is Jenkins financially responsible for fraud that occurred on his watch, even though he did not participate? Should he be liable?

3. Shareholders at Citigroup have offered a shareholder proposal that would require the bank to hold back a substantial percentage of its top executives' pay for ten years. This sum could then be used to pay any fines or other liability arising out of illegal activities that take place on the executives' watch. They would forfeit their pay even if they did not personally engage in any wrongdoing. Under SEC rules, is Citigroup required to include this proposal in its proxy material? If it is passed by shareholders, is it binding? Is the proposal a good idea?

4. In a recent year, three individuals accounted for 70 percent of all shareholder proposals at Fortune 250 companies. Fewer than 10 percent of those proposals passed. These individuals typically own only a few hundred shares of each company. If, as firms estimate, the cost of including each proposal is $87,000, then the total expense, just from these three people, is over $6 million. In some cases, the shareholders submit the same proposals year after year. Should the rule on shareholder proposals be amended? If so, how?

5. Would the following initiatives improve corporate governance? Can you think of others that would?
   (a) Require the board of directors to implement shareholder proposals that receive a majority vote
   (b) Require proxy access
   (c) Prohibit boards of directors from seating directors who fail to receive a majority vote of shares cast
   (d) Base compensation on net returns on invested capital
   (e) Make say-on-pay votes binding

CHAPTER 36 BANKRUPTCY

Three bankruptcy stories:

1. Tim's account: "First, there was Christmas. Was I really going to deny my eight-year-old the virtual reality gaming console he'd been begging for? Then my daughter's basketball team qualified for the nationals at Disney World. She's a talented player, and if she sticks with it, maybe she'll get a college scholarship. The kids had never been to Disney World. How could we say no? Then my car died. And I didn't get a bonus this year. Next thing you know, we had $27,000 in credit card debt. Then we had some uninsured medical bills. We were seriously underwater. There was just no way we could pay all that money back."

The kids had never gone to Disney World. How could we say no?

2. Kristen was a talented gardener and had always loved flowers. Sometimes she did the flowers for friends' weddings. When the guy who owned the local flower shop wanted to retire, it seemed a great opportunity to buy the business. She had lots of good ideas for improving it. First, she renovated the space so that people could hold parties there. She hired staff to keep the shop open longer hours. Everything went really well. Then the recession hit, and people cut back on nonessentials like flowers. How could she pay her loans?

3. General Motors (GM), once a symbol of American business, filed for bankruptcy in 2009. At the time, its liabilities were $90 billion more than its assets. It also had 325,000 employees and even more stakeholders: Retired employees, car owners, suppliers, investors, and communities in which it operated and in which its employees lived and paid taxes. GM emerged from bankruptcy 40 days later with fewer brands, factories, and workers, but ready to do business. The next year, the company was profitable.

Bankruptcy law always has been and always will be controversial. Typically, in other countries, the goal of bankruptcy law is to protect creditors and punish debtors, even sending debtors to prison. Indeed, many of America's first settlers fled England to escape debtors' prison. As if to compensate for Europe's harsh regimes, American bankruptcy laws were traditionally more lenient toward debtors.[1]

The General Motors example illustrates the good news about American bankruptcy. It is efficient (40 days!) and effective at reviving ailing companies. Everyone—investors, employees, the country—benefited from GM's survival. And although Kristen's flower shop did not survive, bankruptcy laws will protect her so that she is not afraid to try entrepreneurship again.[2] New businesses fail more often than not, but they are nonetheless important engines of growth for our country. We all benefit from the jobs they create and the taxes they pay. Tech entrepreneurs in Silicon Valley like to say, "Fail fast, fail often." Europe, where bankruptcy is more likely to be viewed as disgraceful, has fewer start-up businesses.

Tim represents the bad news in bankruptcy laws. Unfortunately, he is often the type of person who first comes to mind when people think about bankrupts. And people do not like Tim very much. They think: Why should he be rewarded for his irresponsibility, when I get stuck paying all my bills? But a more difficult bankruptcy process will probably not discourage Tim. He is the kind of guy who cares a lot about current pleasures and little about future pain. No matter what bankruptcy laws we have, he will not say no to Disney World. Should the laws become too onerous, businesses will fail, entrepreneurs will be discouraged, and the Tims of the world will continue to spend more than they should.

But maybe America has too much of a good thing. This nation has the highest bankruptcy rate in the world. In one recent year, there was one bankruptcy filing for every 200 Americans.[3] Clearly, bankruptcy laws play a vital role in our economy. They have the potential to resuscitate failing companies while encouraging entrepreneurship. At the same time, it is important not to enable irresponsible spendthrifts. Do American bankruptcy laws reach the right balance?

36-1 OVERVIEW OF THE BANKRUPTCY CODE

The federal Bankruptcy Code (the Code) is divided into eight chapters. All chapters except one have odd numbers. Chapters 1, 3, and 5 are administrative rules that generally apply to all types of bankruptcy proceedings. These chapters, for example, define terms and establish the rules of the bankruptcy court. Chapters 7, 9, 11, 12, and 13 are substantive rules for different types of bankruptcies. All of these substantive chapters have one of two objectives—rehabilitation or liquidation.

The objective of Chapters 11 and 13 is to rehabilitate the debtor. Many debtors can return to financial health provided they have the time and breathing space to work out their problems. These chapters hold creditors at bay while the debtor develops a payment plan.

---

1 Bankruptcy law was so important to the drafters of the Constitution that they specifically listed it as one of the subjects that Congress had the right to regulate (Article 1, Section 8).

2 See, for example, Seung-Hyun Lee, Yasuhiro Yamakawa, Mike W. Peng, and Jay B. Barney, "How do bankruptcy laws affect entrepreneurship development around the world?" *Journal of Business Venturing*, 2011, vol. 26, issue 5, pp. 505–520.

3 Some of these filings are by businesses, although that percentage is small. In the last 15 years, more than 95% of all bankruptcy filings have been by consumers.

In return for retaining some of their assets, debtors typically promise to pay creditors a portion of their future earnings.

When debtors are unable to develop a feasible plan for rehabilitation under Chapter 11 or 13, **Chapter 7 provides for liquidation** (also known as a **straight bankruptcy**). Most of the debtor's assets are distributed to creditors, but the debtor has no obligation to share future earnings.

Straight bankruptcy
Also known as liquidation, this form of bankruptcy mandates that the bankrupt's assets be distributed to creditors, but the debtor has no obligation to share future earnings.

36-1a Chapter Description

The following options are available under the Bankruptcy Code:

Number	Topic	Description
Chapter 7	Liquidation	The bankrupt's assets are sold to pay creditors. If the debtor owns a business, it terminates. The creditors have no right to the debtor's future earnings.
Chapter 11	Reorganization	This chapter is designed for businesses and wealthy individuals. Businesses continue in operation, and creditors receive a portion of the debtor's current assets and future earnings.
Chapter 13	Consumer reorganization	Chapter 13 offers reorganization for the typical individual. Creditors usually receive a portion of the individual's current assets and future earnings.

Debtors are sometimes eligible to file under more than one chapter. No choice is irrevocable because both debtors and creditors have the right to ask the court to convert a case from one chapter to another at any time during the proceedings. For example, if creditors have asked for liquidation under Chapter 7, a bankrupt consumer may request rehabilitation under Chapter 13.

36-1b Goals

The Bankruptcy Code has three primary goals:

1. **To preserve as much of the debtor's property as possible.** In keeping with this goal, the Code requires debtors to disclose all of their assets and prohibits them from transferring assets immediately before a bankruptcy filing.

2. **To divide the debtor's assets fairly between the debtor and creditors.** On the one hand, creditors are entitled to payment. On the other hand, debtors are often so deeply in debt that full payment is virtually impossible in any reasonable period of time. The Code tries to balance the creditors' right to be paid with the bankrupts' desire to get on with their lives, unburdened by prior debts.

3. **To divide the creditors' share of the assets fairly among them.** Creditors rarely receive all they are owed, but at least they are treated fairly, according to established rules. Creditors do not benefit from simply being the first to file or from any other gamesmanship.

36-2 CHAPTER 7 LIQUIDATION

All bankruptcy cases proceed in a roughly similar pattern, regardless of chapter. We use Chapter 7 as a template to illustrate common features of all bankruptcy cases. Later on, the discussions of the other chapters will indicate how they differ from Chapter 7.

36-2a Filing a Petition

Bankrupt
Someone who cannot pay his debts and files for protection under the Bankruptcy Code

Debtor
Another term for bankrupt

Voluntary petition
Filed by a debtor to initiate a bankruptcy case

Involuntary petition
Filed by creditors to initiate a bankruptcy case

Any individual, partnership, corporation, or other business organization that lives, conducts business, or owns property in the United States can file under the Code. (Chapter 13, however, is available only to individuals.) The traditional term for someone who could not pay his debts was **bankrupt**, but the Code uses the term **debtor** instead. We use both terms interchangeably.

A case begins with the filing of a bankruptcy petition in federal district court. The district court typically refers bankruptcy cases to a specialized bankruptcy judge. Either party can appeal decisions of the bankruptcy judge back to the district court and, from there, to the federal appeals court.

Debtors may go willingly into the bankruptcy process by filing a **voluntary petition**, or they may be dragged into court by creditors who file an **involuntary petition**. Originally, when the goal of bankruptcy laws was to protect creditors, voluntary petitions did not exist; all petitions were involuntary. Because the bankruptcy process is now viewed as being favorable to debtors, the vast majority of bankruptcy filings in this country are voluntary petitions.

Voluntary Petition

Any debtor (whether a business or an individual) has the right to file for bankruptcy. It is not necessary that the debtor's liabilities exceed assets. Debtors sometimes file a bankruptcy petition because cash flow is so tight they cannot pay their debts, even though they are not technically insolvent. **However, *individuals* must meet two requirements before filing:**

1. Within 180 days before the filing, an individual debtor must undergo credit counseling with an approved agency.
2. Individual debtors may only file under Chapter 7 if they earn less than the median income in their state *or* they cannot afford to pay back at least $7,700 over five years.[4] Generally, all other debtors must file under Chapter 11 or Chapter 13. (These chapters require the bankrupt to repay some debt.)

The voluntary petition must include the following documents:

Document	Description
Petition	Begins the case. Easy to fill out, it requires checking a few boxes and typing in little more than name, address, and Social Security number.
List of Creditors	The names and addresses of all creditors
Schedule of Assets and Liabilities	A list of the debtor's assets and debts
Claim of Exemptions	A list of all assets that the debtor is entitled to keep
Schedule of Income and Expenditures	The debtor's job, income, and expenses
Statement of Financial Affairs	A summary of the debtor's financial history and current financial condition. In particular, the debtor must list any recent payments to creditors and any other property held by someone else for the debtor.

[4]In some circumstances, debtors with income higher than these amounts may still be eligible to file under Chapter 7, but the formula is highly complex and more than most readers want to know. The formula is available at 11 USC Section 707(b)(2)(A). Also, you can google "bapcpa means test" and then click on the Department of Justice website. The dollar amounts are updated every three years. You can find them by googling "federal register bankruptcy revision of dollar amounts."

Involuntary Petition

Creditors may force a debtor into bankruptcy by filing an involuntary petition. The creditors' goal is to preserve as much of the debtor's assets as possible and to ensure that all creditors receive a fair share. Naturally, the Code sets strict limits—debtors cannot be forced into bankruptcy every time they miss a credit card payment. In the event that a debtor objects to an involuntary petition, the bankruptcy court must hold a trial to determine whether the creditors have met the Code's requirements.

An involuntary petition must meet all of the following requirements:

- The debtor must owe at least $15,775 in unsecured claims to the creditors who file.[5]
- If the debtor has at least 12 creditors, 3 or more must sign the petition. If the debtor has fewer than 12 creditors, any one of them may file a petition.
- The creditors must allege either that a custodian for the debtor's property has been appointed in the prior 120 days or that the debtor has generally not been paying debts that are due.

What does "a custodian for the debtor's property" mean? *State* laws sometimes permit the appointment of a custodian to protect a debtor's assets. The Code allows creditors to pull a case out from under state law and into federal bankruptcy court by filing an involuntary petition.

Once a voluntary petition is filed or an involuntary petition approved, the bankruptcy court issues an **order for relief**. This order is an official acknowledgment that the debtor is under the jurisdiction of the court, and it is, in a sense, the start of the whole bankruptcy process. An involuntary debtor must now make all the filings that accompany a voluntary petition.

Order for relief
An official acknowledgment that a debtor is under the jurisdiction of the bankruptcy court

36-2b Trustee

The trustee is responsible for gathering the bankrupt's assets and dividing them among creditors. This is a critical role in a bankruptcy case. Trustees are typically lawyers or CPAs, but any generally competent person can serve. Creditors have the right to elect the trustee, but often they do not bother. If the creditors do not elect a trustee, then the **U.S. Trustee** makes the selection. The U.S. Attorney General appoints a U.S. Trustee for each region of the country to administer bankruptcy law.

U.S. Trustee
Oversees the administration of bankruptcy law in a region

36-2c Creditors

After the court issues an order for relief, the U.S. Trustee calls a meeting of all of the creditors. At the meeting, the bankrupt must answer (under oath) any question the creditors pose about his financial situation. If the creditors want to elect a trustee, they do so at this meeting.

After the meeting of creditors, unsecured creditors must submit a **proof of claim**. This document is a simple form stating the name of the creditor and the amount of the claim. The trustee and the debtor also have the right to file on behalf of a creditor. But if a claim is not filed, the creditor loses any right to be paid. The trustee, debtor, or any creditor can object to a claim on the grounds that the debtor does not really owe that money. The court then holds a hearing to determine the validity of the claim.

Proof of claim
A form stating the name of an unsecured creditor and the amount of the claim against the debtor

---

[5]In Chapter 24 on secured transactions, we discuss the difference between secured and unsecured claims at some length. A secured claim is one in which the creditor has the right to foreclose on a specific piece of the debtor's property (known as "collateral") if the debtor fails to pay the debt when due. If Lee borrows money from GMAC Finance to buy a car, the company has the right to repossess the car if Lee fails to repay the loan. GMAC's loan is "secured." An "unsecured" loan has no collateral. If the debtor fails to repay, the creditor can make a general claim against the debtor but has no right to foreclose on a particular item of the debtor's property.

Secured creditors do not file proofs of claim unless the claim exceeds the value of their collateral. In this case, they are unsecured creditors for the excess amount and must file a proof of claim for it. Suppose that Deborah borrows $750,000 from Morton in return for a mortgage on her house. If she does not repay the debt, he can foreclose. Unfortunately, property values plummet, and, by the time Deborah files a voluntary petition in bankruptcy, the house is worth only $500,000. Morton is a secured creditor for $500,000 and need file no proof of claim for that amount. But he is an unsecured creditor for $250,000 and will lose his right to this excess amount unless he files a proof of claim for it.

36-2d Automatic Stay

A fox chased by hounds has no time to make rational long-term decisions. What that fox needs is a safe burrow. Similarly, it is difficult for debtors to make sound financial decisions when hounded night and day by creditors shouting, "Pay me! Pay me!" The Code is designed to give debtors enough breathing space to sort out their affairs sensibly. An automatic stay is a safe burrow for the bankrupt. It goes into effect as soon as the petition is filed. An **automatic stay** prohibits creditors from collecting debts that the bankrupt incurred before the petition was filed. **Creditors may not sue a bankrupt to obtain payment, nor may they take other steps, outside of court, to pressure the debtor for payment.** The following case illustrates how persistent creditors can be.

Automatic stay
Prohibits creditors from collecting debts that the bankrupt incurred before the petition was filed

Jackson v. Holiday Furniture

309 B.R. 33
United States Bankruptcy Court for the Western District of Missouri, 2004

Facts: In April, Cora and Frank Jackson purchased a recliner chair on credit from Dan Holiday Furniture. They made payments until November. That month, they filed for protection under the Bankruptcy Code. Dan Holiday received a notice of the bankruptcy. This notice stated that the store must stop all efforts to collect on the Jacksons' debt.

Despite this notice, a Dan Holiday collector telephoned the Jacksons' house ten times between November 15 and December 1 and left a card at their door threatening repossession of the chair. On December 1, Frank—without Cora's knowledge—went to Dan Holiday to pay the $230 owed for November and December. He told the store owner about the bankruptcy filing but allegedly added that he and his wife wanted to continue making payments directly to Dan Holiday. Frank died shortly thereafter.

In the following two months, Dan Holiday collectors telephoned the widow 26 times, even though the company knew Frank had died. The store owner's sister left the following message on Cora's voice mail:

> Hello. This is Judy over at Dan Holiday Furniture. And this is the last time I am going to call you. If you do not call me, I will be at your house. And I expect you to call me today. If there is a problem, I need to speak to you about it. You need to call me. We need to get this thing going. You are a January and February payment behind. And if you think you are going to get away with it, you've got another thing coming.

When Cora returned home on February 18, she found seven bright yellow slips of paper in her doorjamb stating that a Dan Holiday truck had stopped by to repossess her furniture. She also received a letter from the store stating, "Repossession Will Be Made and Legal Action Will Be Taken." These threats were merely a ruse to frighten Cora. Dan Holiday did not really want the recliner back; the owner just wanted to negotiate a payment plan with her.

That same day, Cora's bankruptcy attorney contacted Dan Holiday. Thereafter, all collection activity ceased.

Issues: ***Did Dan Holiday violate the automatic stay provisions of the Bankruptcy Code? What is the penalty for a violation?***

Excerpts from Judge Venters's Decision:[6] The automatic stay prohibits the commencement or continuation of any action against the debtor that arose before the commencement of the bankruptcy case and forbids any act by a pre-petition creditor to obtain possession of property of the bankruptcy estate. An individual injured by a creditor's violation of the automatic stay shall recover actual damages, including costs and attorneys' fees, and, in appropriate circumstances, may recover punitive damages.

In this case, there is no question that Dan Holiday repeatedly violated the automatic stay. [T]he Court finds that the Jacksons suffered financial damages in the amount of $230.00, which represents the coerced payments that Dan Holiday received from Frank Jackson on December 1.

The Court finds that punitive damages are warranted in this case based on Dan Holiday's egregious, intentional violations of the automatic stay. Dan Holiday's conduct was remarkably bad in that, after it had actual knowledge of the Jacksons' bankruptcy, and after coercing payments from the Jacksons covering the months of November and December, it made no less than twenty-six telephone calls to the Jacksons' household in January and February. Dan Holiday's continued collection efforts were in flagrant violation of the protections Congress afforded to debtors under the automatic stay.

In this matter, the Court is somewhat hampered in assessing punitive damages by the lack of evidence concerning the ability of Dan Holiday to pay. [An owner] testified that Dan Holiday was a family-owned business that has been in existence for 52 years, and the Court assumes that it is a relatively small business. Under the circumstances of this case, the Court believes that an appropriate penalty would be $100.00 for each illegal contact with the Jacksons after December 1, when it is crystal clear that Dan Holiday had actual knowledge of the Jacksons' bankruptcy filing, for a total of $2,800.00.[7] The Court believes that this penalty will be sufficient to sting the pocketbook of Dan Holiday and impress upon Dan Holiday and its owners and employees the importance of debtor protections under the Bankruptcy Code, as well as to deter further transgressions.

The Court also will award the Jacksons their attorneys' fees and costs in the amount of $1,142.42, an amount the Court considers eminently fair and reasonable under the circumstances of this case.

36-2e Bankruptcy Estate

The filing of the bankruptcy petition creates a new legal entity separate from the debtor—the **bankruptcy estate.** All of the bankrupt's assets pass to the estate except exempt property and new property that the debtor acquires after the petition is filed.

Bankruptcy estate
The new legal entity created when a bankruptcy petition is filed. The debtor's existing assets pass into the estate.

Exempt Property

Unpaid creditors may be angry, but generally they do not want the debtor to starve to death. **The Code permits *individual* debtors (but not organizations) to keep some property for themselves.** This exempt property saves the debtor from destitution during the bankruptcy process and provides the foundation for a new life once the process is over.

In this one area of bankruptcy law, the Code defers to state law. Although the Code lists various types of exempt property, it permits states to opt out of the federal system and define a different set of exemptions. A majority of states have indeed opted out of the Code, and for their residents, the Code exemptions are irrelevant. Alternatively, some states allow the debtor to choose between state or federal exemptions.

Under the *federal* Code, a debtor is allowed to exempt only $23,675 of the value of her home. If the house is worth more than that, the trustee sells it and returns $23,675 of the proceeds to the debtor. Most *states* exempt items such as the debtor's home, household goods, cars, work tools, disability and pension benefits, alimony, and health aids. Some states set no limit on the value of exempt property. Both Florida and Texas, for example, permit debtors

[6]For readability's sake, we refer to the plaintiffs as "the Jacksons," not "debtors," as the court did.

[7]The court stated that Holiday has made illegal contact at least 26 times, and then assessed punitive damages of $100 for each episode, for a total of $2,800. It is not clear what the other two episodes were.

to keep homes of unlimited value and a certain amount of land. (Texas also allows debtors to preserve two firearms; athletic and sporting equipment; 12 head of cattle, two horses, mules or donkeys and a saddle, blanket, and bridle for each; up to a total value of $60,000 per family.) Not surprisingly, these generous exemptions sometimes lead to abuses. Therefore, the Code provides that debtors can take advantage of state exemptions only if they have lived in that state for two years prior to the bankruptcy. And they can exempt only $160,375 of any house that was acquired during the 40 months before the bankruptcy.

Voidable Preferences

Preferences
When a debtor unfairly pays creditors immediately before filing a bankruptcy petition

A major goal of the bankruptcy system is to divide the debtor's assets fairly among creditors. It would not be fair, or in keeping with this goal, if debtors were permitted to pay off some of their creditors immediately before filing a bankruptcy petition. These transfers are called **preferences** because they give unfair preferential treatment to some creditors. The trustee has the right to void such preferences.

Preferences can take two forms: payments and liens. A *payment* simply means that the debtor gives a creditor cash that would otherwise end up in the bankruptcy estate. A *lien* means a security interest in the debtor's property. In bankruptcy proceedings, secured creditors are more likely to be paid than unsecured creditors. If the debtor grants a security interest in specific property, he vaults that creditor out of the great unwashed mass of unsecured creditors and into the elite company of secured creditors. If it happens immediately before the petition is filed, it is unfair to other unsecured creditors.

Insider
Family members of an individual debtor, officers and directors of a corporation, or partners of a partnership that has filed for bankruptcy

Fraudulent transfer
A transfer is fraudulent if it is made within the year before a petition is filed and its purpose is to hinder, delay, or defraud creditors.

The trustee can void any transfer (whether payment or lien) that meets all of the following requirements:

- The transfer was to a creditor of the bankrupt.
- It was to pay an existing debt.
- The creditor received more from the transfer than she would have received during the bankruptcy process.
- The debtor's liabilities exceeded assets at the time of the transfer.
- The transfer took place in the 90-day period before the filing of the petition.

In addition, the trustee can void a transfer to an insider that occurs in the *year* preceding the filing of the petition. **Insiders** are family members of an individual, officers and directors of a corporation, or partners of a partnership that has filed for bankruptcy.

Don Farrall/Photodisc/Getty Images

The debtor who hides assets from the approaching storm of bankruptcy is making a fraudulent transfer.

Fraudulent Transfers

Suppose that a debtor sees bankruptcy approaching across the horizon like a tornado. He knows that, once the storm hits and he files a petition, everything he owns except a few items of exempt property will become part of the bankruptcy estate. Before that happens, he may be tempted to give some of his property to friends or family to shelter it from the tornado. If he succumbs to temptation, however, he is committing a **fraudulent transfer**.

A transfer is fraudulent if it is made within the year before a petition is filed and its purpose is to hinder, delay, or defraud creditors. The trustee can void any fraudulent transfer. The debtor has committed a crime and may be prosecuted.

Not all payments by a debtor prior to filing are considered voidable preferences or fraudulent transfers. **A trustee cannot void pre-petition payments made in the ordinary course.** In a business context, that means a trustee cannot void payments from, say, a grocery store to its regular fruit supplier. For consumers, the trustee cannot void payments below $675 or other routine payments, say, to the electric or water company. In these situations, the bankrupt is clearly not trying to cheat creditors. Even the insolvent are allowed to shower with the lights on.

Even the insolvent are allowed to shower with the lights on.

EXAMStrategy

Question: Eddie and Lola appeared to be happily married. But then Eddie's business failed, and he owed millions. Suddenly, Lola announced that she wanted a divorce. In what had to be the friendliest divorce settlement of all time, Eddie quickly agreed to transfer all of the couple's remaining assets to her. Are you suspicious? Is there a problem?

Strategy: Was this a voidable preference or a fraudulent transfer? What difference does it make?

Result: In a voidable preference, the debtor makes an unfair transfer to a creditor. In a fraudulent transfer, the bankrupt's goal is to hold on to assets himself. In a case similar to this one, the court ruled that the transfer was fraudulent because Eddie intended to shield his assets from all creditors.

36-2f Payment of Claims

Imagine a crowded delicatessen on a Saturday evening. People are pushing and shoving because they know there is not enough food for everyone; some customers will go home hungry. The delicatessen could simply serve whoever pushes to the front of the line, or it could establish a number system to ensure that the most deserving customers are served first—longtime patrons or those who called ahead. The Code has, in essence, adopted a number system to prevent a free-for-all fight over the bankrupt's assets. Indeed, one of the Code's primary goals is to ensure that creditors are paid in the proper order, not according to who pushes to the front of the line.

All claims are placed in one of three classes: (1) secured claims, (2) priority claims, and (3) unsecured claims. The second class—priority claims—has seven subcategories; the third class—unsecured claims—has three. **The trustee pays the bankruptcy estate to the various classes of claims in order of rank.** A higher class is paid in full before the next class receives any payment at all. Exhibit 36.1 illustrates the payment order.

Secured Claims

Creditors whose loans are secured by specific collateral are paid first. Secured claims are fundamentally different from all other claims because they are paid by selling a specific asset, not out of the general funds of the estate. Sometimes, however, collateral is not valuable enough to pay off the entire secured debt. In this case, the creditor must wait in line with the unsecured creditors for the balance. Deborah (whom we met earlier in the section entitled "Creditors") borrowed $750,000 from Morton, secured by a mortgage on her house. By the time she files a voluntary petition, the house is worth only $500,000. Morton is a secured creditor for $500,000 and is paid that amount as soon as the trustee sells the house.

EXHIBIT 36.1

The Order in Which Claims Are Paid

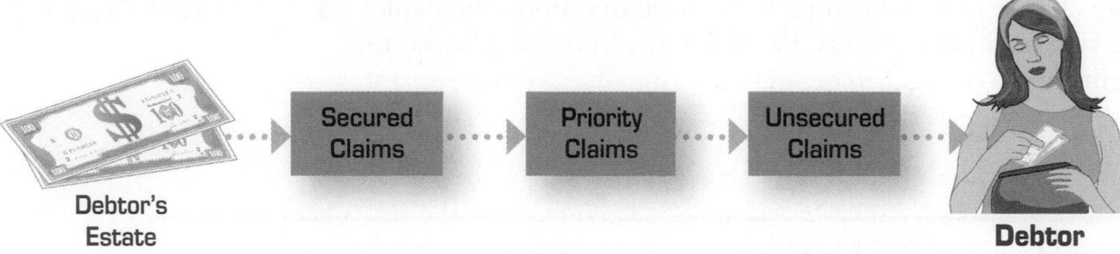

But Morton is an unsecured creditor for $250,000 and will only receive this amount if the estate has enough funds to pay the unsecured creditors.

Priority Claims

There are seven subcategories of priority claims. Each category is paid in order, with the first group receiving full payment before the next group receives anything. If there are not enough funds to pay an entire subcategory, all claimants in that group receive a *pro rata* share.

- **Alimony and child support.** The trustee must first pay any claims for alimony and child support. However, if the trustee is administering assets that could pay these support claims, then the trustee's fees are paid first.
- **Administrative expenses.** These include fees to the trustee, lawyers, and accountants.
- **Gap expenses.** If creditors file an involuntary petition, the debtor will continue to operate her business until the order for relief. Any expenses she incurs in the ordinary course of her business during this so-called **gap period** are paid now.

Gap period
The period between the time that a creditor files an involuntary petition and the court issues the order for relief

- **Payments to employees.** The trustee now pays back wages to the debtor's employees for work performed during the 180 days prior to the date of the petition. The trustee, however, can pay no more than $12,850 to each employee. Any other wages become unsecured claims.
- **Employee benefit plans.** The trustee pays what the debtor owes to employee pension, health, or life insurance plans for work performed during the 180 days prior to the date of the petition. The total payment for wages and benefits under this and the prior paragraph cannot exceed $12,850 times the number of employees.
- **Consumer deposits.** Any individual who has put down a deposit with the bankrupt for consumer goods is entitled to a refund of up to $2,850. If Stewart puts down a $4,000 deposit on a Miata sports car, he is entitled to a refund of $2,850 when the Trustie Car Lot goes bankrupt.
- **Taxes.** The trustee pays the debtor's income taxes for the three years prior to filing and property taxes for one prior year.
- **DUI injuries.** The trustee next pays the claims of anyone injured by a bankrupt who was driving a vehicle under the influence of drugs or alcohol.

Unsecured Claims

Last, and frequently very much least, the trustee pays unsecured claims. All *unsecured* claims are treated the same, and, if there are not enough funds to pay the *entire* class, everyone in the class shares *pro rata*. If, for example, there is only enough money to pay 10 percent of the claims owing to unsecured creditors, then each creditor receives 10 percent of her claim. In bankruptcy parlance, this is referred to as "getting 10 cents on the dollar."

- **Secured claims that exceed the value of the available collateral.** If funds permit, the trustee pays Morton the $250,000 that his collateral did not cover.
- **Priority claims that exceed the priority limits.** The trustee now pays employees, Stewart, and the tax authorities who were not paid in full the first time around because their claims exceeded the priority limits.
- **All other unsecured claims.** Unsecured creditors have now reached the delicatessen counter. They can only hope that some food remains.

The debtor is entitled to any funds remaining after all claims have been paid.

36-2g Discharge

Filing a bankruptcy petition is embarrassing, time-consuming, and disruptive. It can affect the debtor's credit rating for years, making the simplest car loan a challenge. To encourage debtors to file for bankruptcy despite the pain involved, the Code offers a powerful incentive: a **fresh start**. Once a bankruptcy estate has been distributed to creditors, they cannot make a claim against the debtor for money owed before the filing, *whether or not they actually received any payment*. These pre-petition debts are **discharged**. All is forgiven, if not forgotten.

Fresh start
After the termination of a bankruptcy case, creditors cannot make a claim against the debtor for money owed before the initial bankruptcy petition was filed.

Discharged
The debtor no longer has an obligation to pay a debt.

Discharge is an essential part of bankruptcy law. Without it, debtors would have little incentive to take part. To avoid abuses, however, the Code limits both the type of debts that can be discharged and the circumstances under which discharge can take place. In addition, a debtor must complete an approved course on financial management before receiving a discharge.

Debts That Cannot Be Discharged

The following debts are *never* discharged, and the debtor remains liable in full until they are paid:

- Income taxes for the three years prior to filing and property taxes for the prior year
- Money obtained fraudulently. Kenneth Smith ran a home repair business that fleeced senior citizens by making unnecessary repairs. Three months after he was found liable for fraud, he filed a voluntary petition in bankruptcy. The court held that his liability on the fraud claim could not be discharged.[8]
- Any loan of more than $675 that a consumer uses to purchase luxury goods within 90 days before the order for relief is granted
- Cash advances on a credit card totaling more than $950, that an individual debtor takes out within 70 days before the order for relief
- Debts omitted from the Schedule of Assets and Liabilities that the debtor filed with the petition, if the creditor did not know about the bankruptcy and therefore did not file a proof of claim

[8]In re Smith, 848 F.2d 813 (7th Cir. 1988).

- Money that the debtor stole or obtained through a violation of his fiduciary duty
- Money owed for alimony or child support
- Debts stemming from intentional and malicious injury
- Fines and penalties owed to the government
- Liability for injuries caused by the debtor while operating a vehicle under the influence of drugs or alcohol. (Yet another reason why friends don't let friends drive drunk.)
- Liability for breach of duty to a bank
- Debts stemming from a violation of securities laws
- Student loans. This topic requires more explanation.

Prior to 2010, most student loans were *made* by for-profit lenders and then *guaranteed* by the federal government. In these private student loans, both the amount of the principal and the interest rate were unregulated, and, as a result, the amount owed could easily grow to be overwhelming. Since 2010, the government has made student loans directly, with Congress setting the interest rate. However, because there are limits on how much students may borrow in federal funds, students sometimes seek loans from private lenders. Private loans are more expensive and offer fewer protections than government loans.

Beginning in 2009, Congress introduced a so-called income-based repayment (IBR) plan for government loans that are not in default. (And, recently the Department of Education has been offering rehabilitation programs that allow borrowers to get out of default upon payment of as little as $5 per month.[9]) If debtors are accepted into an IBR plan (because they have a "partial financial hardship"), their monthly payments are based on their income, not the size of their debt. After 20 years (for undergrad loans) or 25 years (for graduate students), any outstanding balance is canceled. Many eligible debtors do not apply for this program because they are unaware of it or are confused by the complex process.[10] Also, these IBR plans are only available for *government*, not *private*, loans.

Jim West/ImageBROKER RM/Glow Images

What happens if these graduating students cannot pay their student loans?

Recently, students who attended for-profit schools have sought to take advantage of a so-called "defense to repayment" statute that permits the Department of Education to forgive amounts that students borrowed to attend a school that engaged in wrongdoing under state law; such as institutions that misrepresented the employment rates and income of its graduates. But the wording of the statute is vague and it has never before been used in this way.[11] In short, the likely success of this approach is uncertain.

Debtors who are not eligible for an IBR may seek to discharge their debts through bankruptcy. But the discharge of student loan debt cannot be done as a regular part of the bankruptcy process. Instead, the debtor must bring a separate suit against the creditor, asking the court to discharge the loan.[12] Unfortunately, this requirement imposes an additional expense on people who have little disposable income.

---

[9]See, for example, goo.gl/ITCM67.

[10]The following article offers advice on repaying student loans: goo.gl/ajHXoD. The Consumer Financial Protection Bureau also offers advice, here: goo.gl/nyrKTo.

[11]20 USC 1087e(h).

[12]FED. R. BANKR. P. 7001(6).

Furthermore, student loans cannot be discharged in bankruptcy unless repayment would cause undue hardship. The standard for what constitutes "undue hardship" is called the Brunner Test.[13] **Under the Brunner Test, a student loan will be discharged if:**

- The debtor cannot maintain, based on current income and expenses, a minimal standard of living for himself and his dependents if forced to repay the loans;
- This state of affairs is likely to persist for a significant portion of the repayment period of the student loans; and
- The debtor has made good-faith efforts to repay the loans.

The second prong of the Brunner Test has been particularly controversial. It is referred to as the "hopelessness test" because it essentially asks the court to decide if there is any hope this debtor will ever have a better life. Courts do not like to be in the prediction business and debtors do not like to think their life is hopeless.

In the reported cases, plaintiffs who have been successful in obtaining discharge tend to be in dire circumstances, with serious illnesses. Carol Todd was 63 years old and autistic. She had been unemployed for a decade and was living on Social Security disability income payments. The court discharged her $340,000 in debt.[14] Janet Roth suffered numerous medical issues, including: diabetes, depression, limited vision, and reduced mobility. After losing her job decorating cakes at Walmart, she applied for 280 different jobs, all without success. Despite this record, the bankruptcy court ruled that she did not meet the Brunner Test because she had not made a good-faith effort to pay her loans. The appellate court, however, overruled this decision and discharged her debts.[15]

In the following case, the debtors were not successful in obtaining discharge.

Kelly v. Mich. Fin. Auth. (In re Kelly)

496 B.R. 230
United States Bankruptcy Court for the Middle District of Florida, 2013

Facts: Lisa Kelly had a master's in Special Education and worked at an elementary school in Florida. Her husband, Adam, had a B.A. in Fine Arts with a concentration in Digital Cinema. He worked remotely from their home so that he could provide care for one of their sons. Noah, who was 18 months old, had been born with spina bifida, in which the backbone and spinal canal do not close before birth. He also had hydrocephalus, a build-up of fluid inside the skull that leads to brain swelling. Noah had already undergone two surgeries and faced large ongoing medical expenses. Under their health insurance plan, the family had to pay 20 percent of the cost of their medical care.

The Kellys' annual income was $70,000; but their combined educational loans exceeded $160,000. When the Kellys filed for bankruptcy, they asked the court to discharge these student loans.

Issue: ***Would repayment of their student loans cause the Kellys undue hardship?***

Excerpts from Judge Jennemann's Decision:[16] Unless a debtor is able to meet all three prongs of the Brunner Test, a debtor's student loan debt is not dischargeable. A finding of undue hardship is an incredibly high hurdle to overcome. Debtors must prove more than just a garden variety of hardship.

Although the Kellys are not required to live in poverty, they have failed to adjust their lifestyle sufficiently to demonstrate undue hardship. By the Kellys' own

---

13 It was established in a case by that name: Brunner v. New York State Higher Educ. Servs. Corp., 831 F.2d 395 (2d Cir. 1987).

14 Todd v. Access Group, Inc. (In re Todd), 473 B.R. 676 (Bankr. D. Md. 2012).

15 Roth v. Educ. Credit Mgmt. Corp. (In re Roth), 490 B.R. 908 (B.A.P. 9th Cir. 2013).

16 For readability, we have substituted the parties' names for "plaintiff."

estimates, [they] would need to reduce their expenses by only $374.88 per month to pay their student loans in full. The Kellys' discretionary spending is subject to reduction by at least $400 per month.

Here, the Kellys have recently traveled to Michigan over the holidays, to Miami twice in February, and to Clearwater in March to visit with family. Reducing these types of trips would help minimize their gas expenses and other travel-related costs. Given that Mr. Kelly works at home and that much of the Kellys' gas costs are associated with these trips, the Court finds gas costs of $200 per month is reasonable, as opposed to the $400 per month estimated by the Kellys.

The Kellys currently maintain two newer vehicles. If the Debtors truly need two vehicles, perhaps they can lease a less expensive model or buy an older car to further reduce payments. The Court specifically finds the Kellys could significantly reduce their vehicle expenses by at least $300 per month while still maintaining a minimal standard of living.

The Court also finds that the Kellys' $800 monthly food expense is high. The United States Department of Agriculture lists the average monthly cost of a thrifty meal plan for a family of four as approximately $550.65. One step up from the thrifty plan is the low-cost plan, which is commonly used by bankruptcy courts to determine a debtor's necessary food expenses. The average monthly cost of a low cost meal plan for a family of four is approximately $700. Both plans assume that all meals are purchased at grocery stores and prepared at home. The Kellys' reasonable food expenses should fall somewhere between those listed under the thrifty meal plan and those listed under the low cost meal plan. The Court estimates $625 per month (as opposed to $800 per month) for food costs, which allows for an extra $175 per month that can be used to pay their student loans.

After deducting [these sums], the Kellys have net disposable income enough to make their monthly student loan payment. Consequently, the Kellys have failed the first prong of the Brunner Test.

[The] second prong of the Brunner Test requires them to prove that their current financial situation is likely to persist for a significant portion of the repayment period of their student loans. The evidence shows that the Kellys' incomes are trending upward. Both of the Kellys are healthy, educated, and employed. Both Kellys have maintained employment within their chosen fields since obtaining their degrees.

Although the Court is cognizant of the financial uncertainty that necessarily stems from Noah's medical condition and is very sympathetic to the family's situation, courts do not discharge student loans because a debtor might have a precarious financial situation. The Kellys have failed to show their current financial problems would persist for the majority of repayment period.

[The] Kellys' student loans are not dischargeable.

Although this case did not end well for the Kellys, research shows that more people could benefit from seeking discharge. Only 0.1 percent of debtors who file for bankruptcy ask for a discharge of their student loans.[17] Yet studies have shown that somewhere between one-third and almost two-thirds of student-loan debtors who ask for discharge receive at least some partial relief from their debts. And those who do receive a discharge are typically no worse off beforehand than those who never even apply.

EXAMStrategy

Question: Someone stole a truck full of cigarettes. Zeke found the vehicle abandoned at a truck stop. Not being a thoughtful fellow, he took the truck and sold it with its cargo. Although Tobacco Company never found out who stole the truck originally, it did discover Zeke's role. A court ordered Zeke to pay Tobacco $50,000. He also owed his wife

17 Iuliano, Jason, "An Empirical Assessment of Student Loan Discharges and the Undue Hardship Standard," 86 Am. Bankr. L.J. 495 (2012).

$25,000 in child support. Unfortunately, he only had $20,000 in assets. After he files for bankruptcy, who will get paid what?

Strategy: There are two issues: The order in which the debts are paid and whether they will be discharged.

Result: Child support is a priority claim, so that will be paid first. And it cannot be discharged. In a similar case, the court also refused to discharge the claim over the theft of the truck, ruling that it was an intentional and malicious injury. So Zeke will still owe both debts, but the child support must be paid first.

Circumstances That Prevent Debts from Being Discharged

Apart from identifying the *kinds* of debts that cannot be discharged, **the Code also prohibits the discharge of debts under the following *circumstances*:**

- **Business organizations.** Under Chapter 7 (but *not* the other chapters), only the debts of individuals can be discharged, not those of business organizations. Once its assets have been distributed, the organization must cease operation. If it continues in business, it is responsible for all pre-petition debts. Shortly after E. G. Sprinkler Corp. entered into an agreement with its union employees, it filed for bankruptcy under Chapter 7. Its debts were discharged, and the company began operation again. A court ordered it to pay its obligations to the employees because, once the company resumed business, it was responsible for all of its pre-filing debts.[18]
- **Revocation.** A court can revoke a discharge within one year if it discovers the debtor engaged in fraud or concealment.
- **Dishonesty or bad faith behavior.** The court may deny discharge altogether if the debtor has, for example, made fraudulent transfers, hidden assets, falsified records, disobeyed court orders, refused to testify, lied under oath, committed actual fraud, or otherwise acted in bad faith. For instance, a court denied discharge under Chapter 7 to a couple who failed to list 15 pounds of marijuana on their Schedule of Assets and Liabilities. The court was unsympathetic to their arguments that a listing of this asset might have caused larger problems than merely being in debt.[19]
- **Repeated filings for bankruptcy.** Congress feared that some debtors, attracted by the lure of a fresh start, would make a habit of bankruptcy. Therefore, a debtor who has received a discharge under Chapter 7 or 11 cannot receive another discharge under Chapter 7 for at least eight years after the prior filing. And a debtor who has received a prior discharge under Chapter 13 cannot, in most cases, receive one under Chapter 7 for at least six years.

In the following case, the Supreme Court clarifies the definition of "actual fraud" under the statute.

[18] In re Goodman, 873 F.2d 598 (2d Cir. 1989).

[19] In re Tripp, 224 B.R. 95 (1998). Possession of marijuana is legal in some states under some circumstances, but not under federal law.

Husky Int'l Elecs., Inc. v. Ritz

136 S. Ct. 1581
United States Supreme Court, 2016

Facts: Daniel Lee Ritz, Jr., was a controlling shareholder and director of Chrysalis Manufacturing Corp. He also used Chrysalis as his personal ATM: systematically transferring large sums from that company to other entities he controlled.

Far from turning into a butterfly, Chrysalis was unable to pay its debts, including those to Husky International Electronics. When Husky sued Ritz, seeking to hold him personally liable for the Chrysalis debt, he filed for Chapter 7 bankruptcy. Husky asked the bankruptcy court not to discharge Ritz's debts on the grounds that he had committed actual fraud.

The trial court held that Ritz had not committed actual fraud and therefore his debts could be discharged in bankruptcy. The Fifth Circuit Court of Appeals affirmed. The Supreme Court granted *certiorari*.

Issues: ***Did Ritz commit actual fraud? Can his debts be discharged in bankruptcy?***

Excerpts from Justice Sotomayor's Decision: The Fifth Circuit [held] that a necessary element of "actual fraud" is a misrepresentation from the debtor to the creditor, as when a person applying for credit adds an extra zero to her income or falsifies her employment history. In transferring Chrysalis' assets, Ritz may have hindered Husky's ability to recover its debt, but the Fifth Circuit found that he did not make any false representations to Husky regarding those assets or the transfers and therefore did not commit "actual fraud."

"Actual fraud" has two parts: actual and fraud. The word "actual" has a simple meaning in the context of common-law fraud: It denotes any fraud that "involves moral turpitude or intentional wrong." [F]rom the beginning of English bankruptcy practice, courts and legislatures have used the term "fraud" to describe a debtor's transfer of assets that, like Ritz' scheme, impairs a creditor's ability to collect the debt.

[T]he common law also indicates that fraudulent conveyances, although a "fraud," do not require a misrepresentation from a debtor to a creditor. Fraudulent conveyances typically involve a transfer to a close relative, a secret transfer, a transfer of title without transfer of possession, or grossly inadequate consideration. In such cases, the fraudulent conduct is not in dishonestly inducing a creditor to extend a debt. It is in the acts of concealment and hindrance. In the fraudulent-conveyance context, therefore, the opportunities for a false representation from the debtor to the creditor are limited. The debtor may have the opportunity to put forward a false representation if the creditor inquires into the whereabouts of the debtor's assets, but that could hardly be considered a defining feature of this kind of fraud.

Relatedly, under [English law], both the debtor and the recipient of the conveyed assets were liable for fraud even though the recipient of a fraudulent conveyance of course made no representation, true or false, to the debtor's creditor. That principle also underscores the point that a false representation has never been a required element of "actual fraud," and we decline to adopt it as one today.

We therefore reverse the judgment of the Fifth Circuit and remand the case for further proceedings consistent with this opinion.

So ordered.

Ethics

Banks and credit card companies lobbied Congress hard for the prohibition against repeated bankruptcy filings. They argued that irresponsible consumers run up debt and then blithely walk away. You might think that, if this were true, lenders would avoid customers with a history of bankruptcy. Research indicates, though, that lenders actually target those consumers, repeatedly sending them offers to borrow money. The reason is simple: These consumers are much more likely to take cash advances, which carry very high interest rates. And they must repay their loans for the simple reason that they cannot declare bankruptcy again.[20] Is this strategy ethical?

[20]See Katherine M. Porter, "Bankrupt Profits: The Credit Industry's Business Model for Postbankruptcy Lending," 93 Iowa L. Rev. 1369 (2008).

Reaffirmation

Sometimes debtors are willing to **reaffirm** a debt, meaning they promise to pay even after discharge. They may want to reaffirm a secured debt to avoid losing the collateral. For example, a debtor who has taken out a loan secured by a car may reaffirm that debt so that the finance company will not repossess it. Sometimes debtors reaffirm because they feel guilty or want to maintain a good relationship with the creditor. They may have borrowed from a family member or an important supplier. Because discharge is a fundamental pillar of the bankruptcy process, creditors are not permitted to unfairly pressure the bankrupt. **To be valid, the reaffirmation must:**

Reaffirm
To promise to pay a debt even after it is discharged

- Not violate common law standards for fraud, duress, or unconscionability. If creditors force a bankrupt into reaffirming a debt, the reaffirmation is invalid.
- Have been filed in court before the discharge is granted.
- Include the detailed disclosure statement required by the statute (§524).
- Be approved by the court if the debtor is not represented by an attorney or if, as a result of the reaffirmed debt, the bankrupt's expenses exceed his income.

In the following case, the debtor sought to reaffirm the loan on his truck. He may have been afraid that if he did not, the lender would repossess it, leaving him stranded. It is hard to get around Dallas without a car. Should the court permit the reaffirmation?

In re Grisham

436 B.R. 896
United States Bankruptcy Court for the Northern District of Texas, 2010

Facts: When he filed for bankruptcy, William Grisham owed $17,500 on the Dodge truck he had purchased two months before, but it was worth only $16,000. The annual interest rate was 17.5 percent, the monthly payments were $400, and the payment schedule was almost 6 years. In addition, Grisham owed:

$29,000 to the IRS
$75,000 in alimony
$100,000 in student loans
<u>$70,000</u> in unsecured debt
$274,000 total, in addition to the truck

Should the court allow him to reaffirm the truck loan?

Issue: ***Would reaffirmation of this debt create an undue hardship for the debtor?***

Excerpts from Judge Jernigan's Decision: [F]rom the outset, this court was concerned that the Debtor wished to reaffirm debt on personal property in which there is no equity. [T]he Debtor describes himself as "retired/unemployed." The Debtor's only source of income is $1,928 per month of social security income and $1,698 per month of unemployment benefits—the latter of which will soon expire. The Debtor owns no real property and testified that he currently resides rent-free at a relative's home. The Debtor's monthly net income, after deducting his living expenses, is a negative $1,091.

While the monthly payments on the vehicle are not eye-popping, for this Debtor, in his current situation, it is unduly burdensome. In particular, this Debtor is burdened with several obligations that will likely survive his discharge in bankruptcy (large IRS debt; large alimony; and large student loan debt). Finally, the court heard no compelling testimony to justify why the Debtor purchased his vehicle right before filing bankruptcy (sometimes this may be defensible and sometimes not). In summary, the court will not stamp its seal of approval on the Debtor's reaffirmation of the debt. To do so would create a hardship on this Debtor and does not otherwise seem justified.

Bankruptcy is about "fresh starts" and new beginnings. It is about belt-tightening and shedding past bad habits. Too often, a reaffirmation agreement will reveal that someone just does not comprehend this and wants to go forward in a manner that will impair his fresh start and perpetuate bad habits from the past.

The court realizes that this is sometimes complicated. [T]here are probably situations in which a vehicle-lender will repossess the debtor's vehicle post-discharge, even when the debtor is making regular and timely contractual payments for the car post-discharge—for the simple reason that the debtor did not "reaffirm." Moreover, perhaps the debtor genuinely needs a car and worries that, absent an attempt at a reaffirmation agreement, he will surely lose the car post-discharge and may not be able to purchase (*i.e.*, obtain financing) for another vehicle in the near future.

Many reaffirmation agreements presented to the court are the farthest thing from a "fresh start" that one could ever imagine. Many times it is time to say "good riddance" to the car. And many times—maybe, just maybe—a car lender will see the wisdom of renegotiating a car loan if reaffirmation is denied.

Accordingly,

IT IS ORDERED that the Reaffirmation Agreement is disapproved.

36-3 CHAPTER 11 REORGANIZATION

For a business, the goal of a Chapter 7 bankruptcy is euthanasia—putting it out of its misery by shutting it down and distributing its assets to creditors. Chapter 11 has a much more complicated and ambitious goal—resuscitating a business so that it can ultimately emerge as a viable economic concern, as General Motors did. Keeping a business in operation benefits virtually all company stakeholders: employees, customers, creditors, shareholders, and the community.

Both individuals and businesses can use Chapter 11. Businesses usually prefer Chapter 11 over Chapter 7 because Chapter 11 does not require them to dissolve at the end, as Chapter 7 does. The threat of death creates a powerful incentive to try rehabilitation under Chapter 11. Individuals usually file under Chapter 7 if they can meet the income requirements because then they emerge from bankruptcy debt free (except for debts that are not dischargeable). Chapter 13 is specifically designed for individuals, but is only available to those whose debt does not exceed certain limits. For consumers with even modest income and high debt, Chapter 11 is the only option.

A Chapter 11 proceeding follows many of the same steps as Chapter 7: a petition (either voluntary or involuntary), order for relief, meeting of creditors, proofs of claim, and an automatic stay. There are, however, some significant differences.

36-3a Debtor in Possession

Debtor in possession
The debtor acts as trustee in a Chapter 11 bankruptcy.

Chapter 11 does not require a trustee. The bankrupt is called the **debtor in possession** and, in essence, serves as trustee. The debtor in possession has two jobs: to operate the business and to develop a plan of reorganization. A trustee is chosen only if the debtor is incompetent or uncooperative. In that case, the creditors can elect the trustee, but if they do not choose to do so, the U.S. Trustee appoints one.

36-3b Creditors' Committee

In a Chapter 11 case, the creditors' committee is important because typically, there is no neutral trustee to watch over their interests. Besides protecting the interests of all creditors, the committee may play a role in developing the plan of reorganization. The U.S. Trustee typically appoints the seven largest *un*secured creditors to the committee. However, the court may require the U.S. Trustee to appoint some small-business creditors as well. Secured creditors do not serve because their interests require less protection.

If the debtor is a corporation, the U.S. Trustee may also appoint a committee of shareholders. The Code refers to the *claims* of creditors and the *interests* of shareholders.

36-3c Plan of Reorganization

Once the bankruptcy petition is filed, an automatic stay goes into effect to provide the debtor with temporary relief from creditors. The next stage is to develop a plan of reorganization that provides for the payment of debts and the continuation of the business. For the first 120 days (which the court can extend up to 18 months), the debtor has the exclusive right to propose a plan. If the debtor fails to file a plan, or if the court rejects it, then creditors and shareholders can develop their own plan.

36-3d Confirmation of the Plan

Anyone who proposes a plan of reorganization must also prepare a **disclosure statement** to be distributed with the plan. The purpose of this statement is to provide creditors and shareholders with enough information to make an informed judgment. The statement describes the company's business, explains the plan, calculates the company's liquidation value, and assesses the likelihood that the debtor can be rehabilitated. The court must approve a disclosure statement before it is sent to creditors and shareholders.

Disclosure statement
Provides creditors and shareholders with enough information to make an informed judgment about a proposed plan of reorganization

All the creditors and shareholders have the right to vote on the plan of reorganization. In preparation for the vote, each creditor and shareholder is assigned to a class. Everyone in a class has similar claims or interests. Chapter 11 classifies claims in the same way as Chapter 7: (1) secured claims, (2) priority claims, and (3) unsecured claims. Each secured claim is usually in its own class because each one is secured by different collateral. Shareholders are also divided into classes depending upon their interests. For example, holders of preferred stock are in a different class from common shareholders.

After the vote, the bankruptcy court holds a confirmation hearing to determine whether it should accept the plan. **The court will approve a plan if a majority of the debtors *in each class* votes in favor of it *and* if the "yes" votes hold at least two-thirds of the total debt in that class.**

As long as at least one class votes in favor of the plan, the court can confirm it over the opposition of other classes in what is called a **cramdown** (as in "the plan is crammed down the creditors' throats"). The court imposes a cramdown if, in its view, the plan is feasible, fair, and in the best interests of the creditors. If the court rejects the plan of reorganization, the creditors must develop a new one.

Cramdown
When a court approves a plan of reorganization over the opposition of some creditors

36-3e Discharge

A confirmed plan of reorganization is binding on the debtor, creditors, and shareholders. **The debtor now owns the assets in the bankruptcy estate, free of all obligations except those listed in the plan.** Under a typical plan of reorganization, the debtor gives some current assets to creditors and also promises to pay them a portion of future earnings. In contrast, the Chapter 7 debtor typically relinquishes all assets (except exempt property) to creditors but then has no obligation to turn over future income (except for nondischargeable debts). Exhibit 36.2 illustrates the steps in a Chapter 11 bankruptcy.

EXHIBIT 36.2

The Steps in a Chapter 11 Bankruptcy

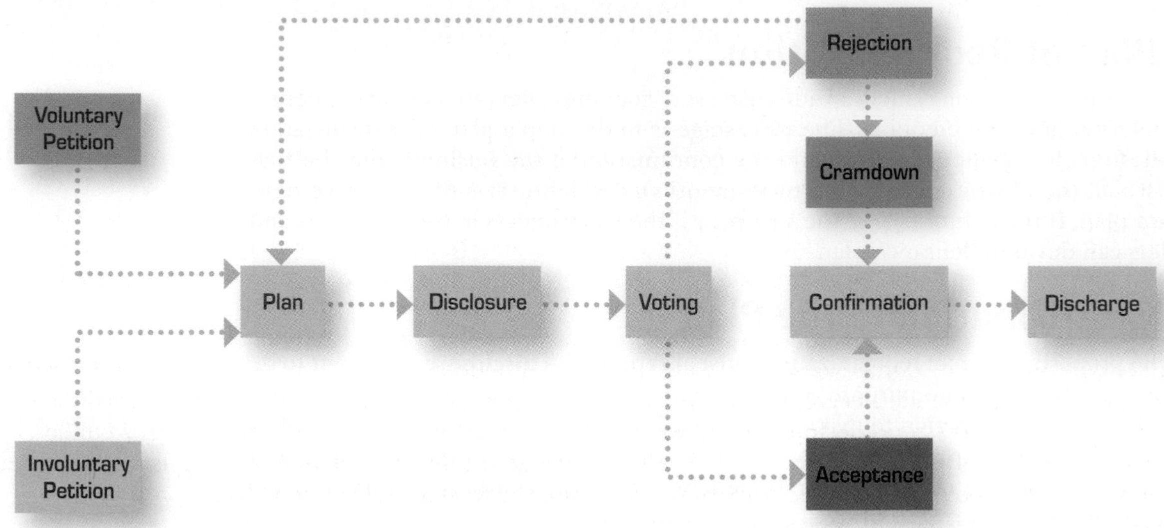

36-3f Small-Business Bankruptcy

To aid the creditors of small businesses, Congress added provisions that speed up the bankruptcy process for entities with less than $2,566,050 million in debt. After the order for relief, the bankrupt has the exclusive right to file a plan for 180 days. Both a plan and a disclosure statement must be filed within 300 days. The court must confirm or reject the plan within 45 days after its filing. If these deadlines are not met, the case can be converted to Chapter 7 or dismissed.

36-4 CHAPTER 13 CONSUMER REORGANIZATIONS

The purpose of Chapter 13 is to rehabilitate an individual debtor. It is only available to individuals with less than $394,725 in unsecured debts and $1,184,200 in secured debts. Under Chapter 13, the bankrupt consumer typically keeps most of her assets in exchange for a promise to repay some of her debts using future income. Therefore, to be eligible, the debtor must have a regular source of income. Individuals who do not qualify for Chapter 7 usually choose this chapter because it is easier and cheaper than Chapter 11. Consequently, more money is retained for both creditors and debtor.

As you read at the beginning of the chapter, debtors can convert from one chapter to another as they wish. In the following case, the trustees objected to a conversion. The case went all the way to the Supreme Court, which split 5-4. How would you have voted?

You Be the Judge

Marrama v. Citizens Bank of Massachusetts

549 U.S. 365
United States Supreme Court, 2007

Facts: When Robert Marrama filed a voluntary petition under Chapter 7, he lied. Although he disclosed that he was the sole beneficiary of a trust that owned a house in Maine, he listed its value as zero. Marrama also denied that he had transferred any property during the prior year. Neither statement was true: The Maine property was valuable (how many houses are worth zero?), and he had given it for free to the trust seven months prior to filing for bankruptcy protection. Marrama also lied when he claimed that he was not entitled to a tax refund. In fact, he knew that a check for $8,700 from the Internal Revenue Service was in the mail.

Once Marrama found out that the bankruptcy trustees were going after the Maine property, he filed a notice to convert his Chapter 7 bankruptcy to Chapter 13. The trustee and creditors objected. They contended that because Marrama had acted in bad faith when he tried to conceal the Maine property from his creditors, he should not be permitted to convert. The bankruptcy court and the appeals court agreed. The Supreme Court granted *certiorari*.

You Be the Judge: *Can a bankruptcy court refuse to allow a debtor to convert from Chapter 7 to Chapter 13?*

Argument for Marrama: Under the Bankruptcy Code, a Chapter 7 debtor may convert a case, with only two restrictions. First, the bankrupt can convert only once. Second, the debtor must meet the conditions that would have been required for him to file under the new chapter in the first place. Nothing in the Code suggests that a bankruptcy judge has the right to prohibit a conversion because of the debtor's bad faith.

If a debtor acts in bad faith, the court has other remedies: It can convert the case back to a Chapter 7 liquidation, it can refuse to approve the plan of payment, or it can charge the debtor with perjury. That is the law, whether or not the trustee and creditors like it.

Argument for the Bankruptcy Trustee: A bankruptcy court has the unquestioned right to dismiss a Chapter 13 petition if the debtor demonstrates bad faith. There seems no logical reason why a court would have the right to dismiss a case for bad faith but not the right to prohibit a filing under Chapter 13 to begin with. In both cases, the court is simply saying that the individual does not qualify as a debtor under Chapter 13. That individual is not a member of the class of honest but unfortunate debtors whom the bankruptcy laws were enacted to protect.

EXAMStrategy

Question: Why did Marrama first file under Chapter 7 and then try to switch to Chapter 13 after he was caught lying?

Strategy: This question is a good test of your understanding of the advantages and disadvantages of the different chapters. For help in answering this question, you might want to look at the chart at the end of the chapter. Remember that Chapter 7 is a liquidation provision—it takes more of the bankrupt's money upfront but then discharges his debts and gives him a fresh start for the future. Chapter 13 does not take as many assets during the bankruptcy process but may attach all the debtor's disposable income for the next five years.

Result: Marrama filed under Chapter 7 in the hope that he could hold on to his house while all his debts were discharged. Once that plan failed, he tried to switch to Chapter 13 hoping that he could keep the house and give up his disposable income instead. This case illustrates the different emphases of Chapters 7 and 13.

A bankruptcy under Chapter 13 generally follows the same course as Chapter 11: The debtor files a petition, creditors submit proofs of claim, the court imposes an automatic stay, the debtor files a plan, and the court confirms the plan. But there are some differences.

36-4a Beginning a Chapter 13 Case

To initiate a Chapter 13 case, the debtor must file a voluntary petition. **Creditors cannot use an involuntary petition to force a debtor into Chapter 13.** In all Chapter 13 cases, the U.S. Trustee appoints a trustee to supervise the debtor, although the debtor remains in possession of the bankruptcy estate. The trustee also serves as a central clearinghouse for the debtor's payments to creditors. The debtor pays the trustee who, in turn, transmits these funds to creditors. For this service, the trustee is allowed up to 10 percent of the payments.

36-4b Plan of Payment

The debtor must file a plan of payment within 15 days after filing the voluntary petition. Only the debtor can file a plan; the creditors have no right to file their own version. **Under the plan, the debtor must (1) commit some future earnings to pay off debts, (2) promise to pay all secured and priority claims in full, and (3) treat all remaining classes equally.** If the plan does not provide for the debtor to pay off creditors in full, then all of the debtor's disposable income for the next five years must go to creditors.

Within 30 days after filing the plan of payment, the debtor must begin making payments to the trustee under the plan. The trustee holds these payments until the plan is confirmed and then transmits them to creditors. The debtor continues to make payments to the trustee until the plan has been fully implemented. If the plan is rejected, the trustee returns the payments to the debtor.

Only the bankruptcy court has the authority to confirm or reject a plan of payment. Creditors have no right to vote on it. However, **to confirm a plan, the court must ensure that:**

- The creditors have the opportunity to voice their objections at a hearing,
- All of the unsecured creditors receive at least as much as they would have if the bankruptcy estate had been liquidated under Chapter 7,
- The plan is feasible and the bankrupt will be able to make the promised payments,
- The plan does not extend beyond three years without good reason and in no event lasts longer than five years, and
- The debtor is acting in good faith, making a reasonable effort to pay obligations.

36-4c Discharge

Once confirmed, a plan is binding on all creditors whether they like it or not. **The debtor is washed clean of all pre-petition debts except those provided for in the plan but, unlike Chapter 7, the debts are not *permanently* discharged.** If the debtor violates the plan, all of the debts are revived, and the court may either dismiss the case or convert it to a liquidation proceeding under Chapter 7. The debts become permanently discharged only when the bankrupt fully complies with the plan.

Note, however, that any debtor who has received a discharge under Chapter 7 or 11 within the prior four years, or under Chapter 13 within the prior two years, is not eligible for another discharge under Chapter 13.

If the debtor's circumstances change, the debtor, the trustee, or unsecured creditors can ask the court to modify the plan. Most such requests come from debtors whose income has declined. However, if the debtor's income rises, the creditors or the trustee can ask that payments increase, too.

CHAPTER CONCLUSION

Whenever an individual or organization incurs more debts than it can pay in a timely fashion, everyone loses. The debtor loses control of his assets and the creditors lose money. Bankruptcy laws cannot create assets where there are none (or not enough), but they can ensure that the debtor's assets, however limited, are fairly divided between the debtor and creditors. Any bankruptcy system that accomplishes this goal must be deemed a success. Is the U.S. Bankruptcy Code fair?

EXAM REVIEW

This chart sets out the important elements of each bankruptcy chapter.

	Chapter 7	Chapter 11	Chapter 13
Objective	Liquidation	Reorganization	Consumer reorganization
Who May Use It	Individual or organization	Individual or organization	Individual
Type of Petition	Voluntary or involuntary	Voluntary or involuntary	Only voluntary
Administration of Bankruptcy Estate	Trustee	Debtor in possession (trustee selected only if debtor is unable to serve)	Trustee
Selection of Trustee	Creditors have right to elect trustee; otherwise, U.S. Trustee makes appointment.	Usually no trustee	Appointed by U.S. Trustee
Participation in Formulation of Plan	No plan is filed.	Both creditors and debtor can propose plans.	Only debtor can propose a plan.
Creditor Approval of Plan	Creditors do not vote on plan because there is no plan.	Creditors vote on the plan, but court may approve plan without the creditors' support.	Creditors do not vote on plan.
Impact on Debtor's Post-petition Income	Not affected; debtor keeps all future earnings.	Must contribute toward payment of pre-petition debts.	Must contribute toward payment of pre-petition debts.

The following table sets out the waiting times before debtors can file a new bankruptcy petition:

Prior case	To file under Chapter 7, must wait:	To file under Chapter 13, must wait:
Chapter 7	8 years	4 years
Chapter 11	8 years	4 years
Chapter 13	6 years	2 years

EXAMStrategy

1. Question: Mark Milbank repeatedly borrowed money from his wife and her father to fund his furniture business. He promised that the loans would enable him to spend more time with his family. Instead, he spent more time in bed with his next-door neighbor. After the divorce, his ex-wife and her father demanded repayment of the loans. Milbank filed for protection under Chapter 13. What could his ex-wife and her father do to help their chances of being repaid?

Strategy: First ask yourself what kind of creditor they are: secured or unsecured. Then think about what creditors can do to get special treatment. (See the "Result" at the end of this Exam Review section.)

EXAMStrategy

2. Question: After a jury ordered actor Kim Basinger to pay $8 million for breaching a movie contract, she filed for bankruptcy protection, claiming $5 million in assets and $11 million in liabilities. Under which chapter should she file? Why?

Strategy: Look at the requirements for each chapter. Was Basinger eligible for Chapter 13? What would be the advantages and disadvantages of Chapters 7 and 11? (See the "Result" at the end of this Exam Review section.)

EXAMStrategy

3. Question: Midland Fumigant filed a voluntary petition under Chapter 11 of the Bankruptcy Code. It owed money to United Phosphorus, which also happened to be a competitor. United refused to approve Midland's plan of reorganization. What recourse did Midland have?

Strategy: What was United's likely motive in voting against the plan? What is the approval process for a plan of organization under Chapter 11? (See the "Result" at the end of this Exam Review section.)

RESULTS

1. Result: The father and the ex-wife were unsecured creditors who, as a class, come last on the priority list. However, the court granted their request that their loans not be discharged, on the grounds that Milbank had acted in bad faith.

2. Result: Basinger was not eligible to file under Chapter 13 because she had debts of $11 million. She first filed under Chapter 11 in an effort to retain some of her assets, but then her creditors would not approve her plan of reorganization, so she converted to liquidation under Chapter 7.

3. Result: United was a competing business, so it preferred that Midland not reorganize but instead be liquidated under Chapter 7. The court imposed a cramdown of the plan over United's objection.

MULTIPLE-CHOICE QUESTIONS

1. **CPA QUESTION** A voluntary petition filed under the liquidation provisions of Chapter 7 of the federal Bankruptcy Code ________.
   (a) is not available to a corporation unless it has previously filed a petition under the reorganization provisions of Chapter 11 of the Code
   (b) automatically stays collection actions against the debtor except by secured creditors
   (c) will be dismissed unless the debtor has 12 or more unsecured creditors whose claims total at least $5,000
   (d) does not require the debtor to show that the debtor's liabilities exceed the fair market value of assets

2. **CPA QUESTION** Decal Corp. incurred substantial operating losses for the past three years. Unable to meet its current obligations, Decal filed a petition of reorganization under Chapter 11 of the federal Bankruptcy Code. Which of the following statements is correct?
   (a) A creditors' committee, if appointed, will consist of unsecured creditors.
   (b) The court must appoint a trustee to manage Decal's affairs.
   (c) Decal may continue in business only with the approval of a trustee.
   (d) The creditors' committee must select a trustee to manage Decal's affairs.

3. **CPA QUESTION** Unger owes a total of $50,000 to eight unsecured creditors and one fully secured creditor. Quincy is one of the unsecured creditors and is owed $6,000. Quincy has filed a petition against Unger under the liquidation provisions of Chapter 7 of the federal Bankruptcy Code. Unger has been unable to pay debts as they become due. Unger's liabilities exceed Unger's assets. Unger has filed papers opposing the bankruptcy petition. Which of the following statements regarding Quincy's petition is correct?
   (a) It will be dismissed because the secured creditor failed to join in the filing of the petition.
   (b) It will be dismissed because three unsecured creditors must join in the filing of the petition.
   (c) It will be granted because Unger's liabilities exceed Unger's assets.
   (d) It will be granted because Unger is unable to pay Unger's debts as they become due.

4. Dale is in bankruptcy proceedings under Chapter 13. Which of the following statements is true?
   (a) His debtors must have filed an involuntary petition.
   (b) His unsecured creditors will be worse off than if he had filed under Chapter 7.
   (c) All of his debts are discharged as soon as the court approves his plan.
   (d) His creditors have an opportunity to voice objections to his plan.

5. Grass Co. is in bankruptcy proceedings under Chapter 11. ________ serves as trustee. In the case of ________ the court can approve a plan of reorganization over the objections of the creditors.
   (a) The debtor in possession, a cramdown
   (b) A person appointed by the U.S. Trustee, fraud
   (c) The head of the creditors' committee, reaffirmation
   (d) The U.S. Trustee, a voidable preference

CASE QUESTIONS

1. Mary Price went for a consultation about a surgical procedure to remove abdominal fat. When Robert Britton met with her, he wore a name tag that identified him as a doctor, and was addressed as "doctor" by the nurse. Britton then examined Price, touching her stomach and showing her where the incision would be made. Britton was not a doctor; he was the office manager. Although a doctor actually performed the surgery on Price, Britton was present. The doctor left a tube in Price's body at the site of the incision. The area became infected, requiring corrective surgery. A jury awarded Price $275,000 in damages in a suit against Britton. He subsequently filed a Chapter 7 bankruptcy petition. Is this judgment dischargeable in bankruptcy court?

2. ***YOU BE THE JUDGE* WRITING PROBLEM** To finance her education at DeVry Institute of Technology, Lydia borrowed $20,000 from a private lender. After graduation, she could not find a job in her field, so she went to work as a clerk at an annual salary of $12,500. Lydia and her daughter lived with her parents free of charge. After setting aside $50 a month in savings and paying bills that included $233 for a new car and $50 for jewelry, her disposable income was $125 per month. Lydia asked the bankruptcy court to discharge her debt. Would paying this debt impose an undue hardship on her? **Argument for Lydia:** Although she saves money by living with her parents, she would still have to spend every single penny of her disposable income for nearly 15 years to pay back her $20,000 debt. That would be an undue hardship. **Argument for the Creditor:** Paying back this debt would not constitute undue hardship because Lydia could easily reduce her expenses. She should not be buying new cars and jewelry. Nor does she have the right to save money when she has outstanding debt.

3. Dr. Ibrahim Khan caused an automobile accident in which a fellow physician, Dolly Yusufji, became a quadriplegic. Khan signed a contract to support her for life. When he refused to make payments under the contract, she sued him and obtained a judgment for $1,205,400. Khan filed a Chapter 11 petition. At the time of the bankruptcy hearing, five years after the accident, Khan had not paid Yusufji anything. She was dependent on a motorized wheelchair; he drove a Rolls-Royce. Is Khan's debt dischargeable under Chapter 11?

4. After filing for bankruptcy, Yvonne Brown sought permission of the court to reaffirm a $6,000 debt to her credit union. The debt was unsecured, and she was under no obligation to pay it. The credit union had published the following notice in its newsletter:

   > If you are thinking about filing bankruptcy, THINK about the long-term implications. This action, filing bankruptcy, closes the door on TOMORROW. Having no credit means no ability to purchase cars, houses, credit cards. Look into the future—no loans for the education of your children.

   Should the court approve Brown's reaffirmation?

5. **ETHICS** On November 5, Hawes, Inc., a small subcontractor, opened an account with Basic Corp., a supplier of construction materials. Hawes promised to pay its bills within 30 days of purchase. Although Hawes purchased a substantial quantity of goods on credit from Basic, it made few payments on the accounts until the following March, when it paid Basic over $21,000. On May 14, Hawes filed a voluntary petition under Chapter 7. Why did Hawes pay Basic in March? Does the bankruptcy trustee have a right to recover this payment? Is it fair to Hawes's other creditors if Basic is allowed to keep the $21,000 payment?

6. Terry and Kerry filed for divorce. Terry then filed for bankruptcy. What impact would the bankruptcy filing have on the divorce?

DISCUSSION QUESTIONS

1. Look on the internet for your state's rules on exempt property. Compared with other states and the federal government, is your state generous or stingy with exemptions? In considering a new bankruptcy statute, Congress struggled mightily over whether or not to permit state exemptions at all. Is it fair for exemptions to vary by state? Why should someone in one state fare better than his neighbor across the state line? How much should the exemption be?

2. Some states permit debtors an unlimited exemption on their homes. Is it fair for bankrupts to be allowed to keep multimillion dollar homes while their creditors remain unpaid? But other states allow as little as $5,000. Should bankrupts be thrown out on the street? What amount is fair?

3. What about the rules regarding repeated bankruptcy filings? (See the chart in Exam Review.) Are these rules too onerous, too lenient, or just right?

4. A bankrupt who owns a house has the option of either paying the mortgage or losing his home. The court cannot reduce the amount owed; its choice is to discharge the entire debt or leave it whole. Congress considered a bill that would permit a bankruptcy judge to adjust the terms of mortgages to aid debtors in holding onto their houses. Proponents argued that this change in the law would reduce foreclosures and stabilize the national housing market. Opponents said that it was not fair to reward homeowners for being irresponsible. How would you have voted on this bill?

5. In the *Grisham* case, the debtor had virtually no income but owed about $200,000 in debts that could not be discharged. What kind of fresh start is that? Should limits be placed on the total debt that cannot be discharged? Is the list of nondischargeable debts appropriate?

Government Regulation

UNIT
8

37

CHAPTER

SECURITIES REGULATION

In 1926, America was gripped by a fever of stock market speculation. "Playing the market" became a national mania. The most engrossing news on any day's front page was the market. Up and up it soared. The cause of this psychological virus is uncertain, but the focus of the infection was the New York Stock Exchange (NYSE). Between 1926 and 1929, annual volume more than doubled.

Much of this feverish trading was done on margin. Customers put down only 10 or 20 percent of a stock's purchase price and then borrowed the rest from their broker. This easy-payment plan excited the gambling instinct of unwary amateurs and professional speculators alike. By September 1929, the volume of these margin loans was equal to about half the entire public debt of the United States.

Soon there was a mad scramble of selling as prices plunged in wild disorder.

On September 4, 1929, stock prices began to soften, and, for the next month, they slid gently. Over the weekend of October 19, brokers sent out thousands of margin calls, asking customers to pay down loans that now exceeded the value of their stock. If customers failed to pay, brokers dumped their stock on the market, causing prices to fall further and brokers to make more margin calls.

Soon there was a mad scramble of selling as prices plunged in wild disorder. On Tuesday, October 29, 1929, the stock market completely collapsed. Tens of thousands of investors across the country were wiped out.

This market crash spawned the Great Depression—the most pervasive, persistent, and destructive economic crisis the nation has ever faced. In 1933, more businesses failed than in any other year in history. Surviving businesses responded to the crisis by cutting dividends, reducing inventories, laying off workers, slashing wages, and canceling capital investments.

Unemployment statistics were the most poignant of all. In 1932, one in every five people in the labor force was out of a job, more than twice the highest level reached in the most recent U.S. recession. And this was at a time before widespread unemployment benefits. Distress cut across all economic and social classes. Bankers, architects, and lawyers joined the throng of unemployed. Articles such as the following were common in newspapers across the land:

> *New York, Jan. 6, 1933 (AP)*—After vainly trying to get a stay of dispossession from his apartment in Brooklyn, yesterday, Peter J. Cornell, 48 years old, a former roofing contractor out of work and penniless, fell dead in the arms of his wife. A doctor gave the cause of his death as heart disease, and the police said it had at least partly been caused by the bitter disappointment of a long day's fruitless attempt to prevent himself and his family being put out on the streets.[1]

37-1 FEDERAL SECURITIES LAWS

At the time of the great stock market crash, only state, not federal, law regulated securities (such as stocks and bonds). Congress recognized that the country needed a national securities system if it was to avoid another such catastrophe. In 1933, Congress passed the **Securities Act of 1933** to regulate the issuance of new securities. The next year, it passed the **Securities Exchange Act of 1934** to regulate companies with publicly traded securities. The 1934 Act also established the Securities and Exchange Commission (SEC).

Securities Act of 1933
Also referred to as the 1933 Act, this statute regulates the issuance of new securities.

Securities Exchange Act of 1934
Also referred to as the 1934 Act, this statute regulates companies with publicly traded securities.

37-1a The Securities and Exchange Commission

The SEC is the federal agency that enforces securities laws. It can bring cease and desist orders against those who violate the law, and it can also levy fines or confiscate profits from illegal transactions. Those accused of wrongdoing can appeal these sanctions to the courts. The SEC does not have the authority to bring a criminal action; it refers criminal cases to the Justice Department.

37-1b What Is a Security?

Both the 1933 and the 1934 Acts regulate securities. The statutory definition of a security includes stock, bonds, treasury stock, notes, debentures, evidence of indebtedness, certificates of interest or participation in any profit-sharing agreement, and 17 other equivalents. **The courts have defined a security to be any transaction in which the buyer (1) invests money in a common enterprise and (2) expects to earn a profit predominantly from the efforts of others.**

Security
Any transaction in which the buyer invests money in a common enterprise and expects to earn a profit predominantly from the efforts of others

This definition includes investments that are not necessarily *called* securities. They may be called orange trees. W. J. Howey Co. owned large citrus groves in Florida. It sold these trees to investors, most of whom were from out of state and knew nothing about farming. Purchasers were expected to hire someone to take care of their trees—someone like Howey-in-the-Hills, Inc., a related company that just happened to be in the service business. Customers were free to hire any service company, but most of the acreage was covered by service contracts with Howey-in-the-Hills. The court held that Howey was selling a security (no matter how orange or tart) because the purchaser was investing in a common enterprise (the orange grove) expecting to earn a profit from Howey's farm work.

---

[1]The material in this section is adapted from Cabell Phillips, *From the Crash to the Blitz* (Toronto: Macmillan, 1969).

Luis Leyva/Southcreek/ZUMAPRESS.com/Alamy Stock Photo

This football player can be a security.

Other courts have interpreted the term *security* to include animal breeding arrangements (chinchillas, silver foxes, or beavers, take your pick), condominium purchases in which the developer promises the owner a certain level of income from rentals, and even athletes. In these deals, investors make a lump sum payment now, in return for a share of the athlete's future earnings.

37-2 SECURITIES ACT OF 1933

The 1933 Act requires that before offering or selling securities, the issuer must register them with the SEC unless they qualify for an exemption. An **issuer** is a company that sells its own stock.

Issuer
A company that sells its own stock

The guiding principle of the federal securities laws is that investors can make a reasoned decision on whether to buy or sell securities if they have full and accurate information about a company and the security it is selling. The responsibility is on the buyer to evaluate quality. **The SEC does not, itself, evaluate or investigate the *quality* of any offering; it simply ascertains that, on the surface, the company has *disclosed* all required information about itself and the security it is selling.** Permission from the SEC to sell securities does not mean that the company has a good product or will be successful.

When the Green Bay Packers football team sold an offering of stock to finance stadium improvements, the prospectus admitted:

> IT IS VIRTUALLY IMPOSSIBLE that any investor will ever make a profit on the stock purchase. The company will pay no dividends, and the shares cannot be sold.

This does not sound like a stock you want in your retirement fund; on the other hand, the SEC will not prevent Green Bay from selling it, or you from buying it, as long as you understand what the risks are.

Registering securities with the SEC in a public offering is a major undertaking, but the 1933 Act exempts some securities and also some particular types of securities transactions from the full-blown registration requirements of a public offering.

There is an important distinction between exempt *securities* and exempt *transactions*. **Exempt *securities* are always exempt, throughout their lives, no matter how many times they are sold. Stock sold in an exempt *transaction* is exempt only that one time, not necessarily in any subsequent sale.** County Bank is never required to register stock that it sells to the public, no matter how many times it changes hands. But suppose that Tumbleweed, Inc., a quilt maker, sells $5 million worth of stock in a private offering that is exempt from registration. Shamika buys 100 shares of this stock. Seven years later, the company decides to sell securities in a public offering that must be registered. As part of this public offering, Shamika sells her 100 shares. This time, her stock must be registered because it is being sold in a public offering.

37-2a Exempt Securities

The 1933 Act exempts some types of securities from registration because they (1) are inherently low risk, (2) are regulated by other statutes, or (3) are not really investments. **The following securities are exempt from registration:**

- **Government securities**, which include any security issued or guaranteed by federal or state government
- **Bank securities**, which include any security issued or guaranteed by a bank

- **Short-term notes**, which are high-quality negotiable notes or drafts that are due within nine months of issuance and are not sold to the general public
- **Nonprofit issues**, which include any security issued by a nonprofit religious, educational, or charitable organization
- **Insurance policies and annuity contracts**, which are governed by insurance regulations

37-2b Exempt Transactions

The 1933 Act permits **private offerings**, i.e., a sale of securities in which the issuer provides less disclosure in return for selling less stock, to fewer (often wealthier) investors, than in a public offering. For example, in some private offerings, the issuer does not have to provide audited financial statements. The theory is that the investors in a private offering do not need as much disclosure because they have enough experience to make good decisions or are so wealthy that they can afford a loss. Or, the amount at stake is too small to justify the heavy expense of a public offering.

Private offering
A sale of securities in which the issuer provides less disclosure in return for selling less stock to fewer investors than in a public offering

Now, let's look at the different types of private offerings.

Intrastate Offering Exemption

Under SEC Rule 147A, an issuer is not required to register securities that are sold only to residents of one state if that state is the issuer's principal place of business. This exemption was designed to provide local financing for local businesses. Neither the issuer nor any purchaser can sell the securities outside the state for six months after the offering.

Regulation D

Regulation D is far and away the most popular route for private offerings. Tens of thousands of these offerings take place each year. To understand Regulation D (often referred to as Reg D), there are several important definitions you need to know:

- **Accredited investors** are institutions (such as banks and insurance companies) or financially qualified individuals. To qualify, individuals must have a net worth (not counting their home) of more than $1 million or an annual income of more than $200,000.
- **Sophisticated investors** are people who can assess the risks of an offering themselves.
- **Purchaser representatives** have enough knowledge and experience to evaluate the merits and risks of a stock purchase. Reg D requires unsophisticated, unaccredited investors to consult a purchaser representative.
- **Restricted stock** means the securities must be purchased for investment purposes. As a general rule, the buyer cannot resell it, either publicly or privately, for one year.

Accredited investors
Institutions (such as banks and insurance companies) or financially qualified individuals

Sophisticated investors
People who can assess the risks of an offering

Purchaser representatives
Have enough knowledge and experience to evaluate stock purchases

Restricted stock
Securities purchased for investment purposes

Reg D is a series of rules that control:

- How much stock can be sold,
- How many and what type of purchaser can buy the stock,
- How the issuer can advertise,
- What the issuer must disclose, and
- When the securities can be resold.

These rules are highly complex. The following table summarizes the menu of choices under Reg D:

	Maximum Value of Securities Sold in a 12-Month Period	Maximum Number of Investors	Disclosure Required	Is Public Advertising Permitted?	Are Securities Restricted?
Rule 504 Option 1:	$5 million	Unlimited	Nothing specific	No	Yes
Option 2:	$5 million	Unlimited	Disclosure under state law	Yes	No
Option 3:	$5 million, provided offering is exempt under state law	Unlimited accredited investors	Nothing specific	Yes	No
Rule 506	No limit	No limit on accredited investors; no more than 35 unaccredited investors, who must either be sophisticated or have a purchaser representative	Only for unaccredited investors	No, if sold to unaccredited investors; yes, if sales are limited to accredited investors	Yes

Regulation A

Although an offering under Regulation A (Reg A) is called a private offering, it really is a small public offering. **Reg A offerings have the following features:**

- Issuers may advertise.
- The stock is an unrestricted security.
- Issuers must make certain disclosures to investors.

There are two types of Reg A offerings:

- **Tier 1.** An issuer may sell publicly up to $20 million of securities in any 12-month period, with no limit on the maximum amount an investor may buy.
- **Tier 2.** An issuer may sell publicly up to $50 million of securities in any 12-month period. Unaccredited investors may not buy stock that costs more than the greater of 10 percent of their annual income or net worth. The disclosure requirements are complex.

Crowdfunding

Regulation Crowdfunding permits privately held companies to sell up to $1 million in securities in any 12-month period provided that they do all of the following:[2]

- Sell the securities through only one online platform that must be operated by a broker-dealer or a funding portal (e.g., a website) that:
  - Registers with the SEC,
  - Takes steps to prevent fraud,

[2]These amounts will be inflation-adjusted at least once every five years.

    - Does not offer investment advice or solicit purchases,
    - Provides disclosure, and
    - Offers a channel for discussions of its securities offerings.
- File an offering statement with the SEC, and make it available to investors and the online platform.
- File annual reports with the SEC and post them on the company website.
- Limit investments by individuals to either 5 or 10 percent of their income or net worth (depending on their wealth).
- Limit any outside advertising to a simple notice that offering information is available on the online platform.
- Do not pay anyone (other than the online platform) to sell their securities.
- Prohibit resale of the stock for one year (except to the company, accredited investors, family members, or as part of a registered offering).

New businesses are risky, with about half of them failing within the first five years. The SEC delayed implementation of Regulation Crowdfunding because these investments are risky, and the statute provides for little oversight. The SEC does not review these companies to ensure that they are complying with the statute, which means that any oversight is left to the crowdfunding websites, some of which do not meet their regulatory responsibilities. One review found that half the offering companies did not provide required financial statements.

As we remember from our discussion of the business judgment rule in Chapter 34, managers will have wide latitude in how they spend the funds they raise. Investors will have little recourse for off-plan expenditures. Since few of these companies will ever go public, investors will have limited opportunities to sell their stock or realize any return on their investment.

Direct Public Offerings

In a **direct public offering (DPO)**, a company sells stock to the public without using an investment bank. It is, if you will, a do-it-yourself initial public offering (IPO). The issuer commonly uses Rule 147A, Reg D, or Reg A and primarily sells shares to its stakeholders: customers, employees, suppliers, or the community, often on the internet. Ben & Jerry's used a DPO under Reg A to sell its stock publicly for the first time.

Direct public offering (DPO)
A method by which a company sells stock to the public itself, without an investment bank

Selling stock without the help of an investment bank can be challenging. Thanksgiving Coffee Co. used both modern technology and old-fashioned methods. It advertised on its website but also placed ads on bags of coffee beans, in its catalogs, and in notices to suppliers. The company raised $1.25 million.

The advantages of a DPO are:

- It is cheaper and faster than using an underwriter.
- It is an effective marketing tool—shareholders become even more loyal customers.

The downsides of a DPO are:

- There is a limit to how much a company can raise in this way.
- Company officers typically do not have as much expertise in selling stock as securities lawyers, investment bankers, and other professionals.
- Each investor must receive written information about the company. The cost of this disclosure can be prohibitive when dealing with many small investors. Providing a

$10 disclosure document to hundreds of investors who only want to buy $50 worth of stock each may not be an efficient means of raising money.

- Although shareholders are warned that they should view their purchases as long-term investments, some will inevitably want to sell their shares. Setting up a system to permit these trades can be tricky and time consuming.

EXAMStrategy

Question: Sandy is about to graduate from Excellent University with an MBA ... and piles of debt. But he has a brilliant idea: He will sell shares in his career. For only $1,000, an investor can obtain a small percentage of his future earnings. Is Sandy's plan legal?

Strategy: Sandy is selling a security. Buyers would be investing in him, hoping that they can earn a profit from his efforts. So he must comply with securities laws.

Result: Sandy has a number of options. He will not want to do a public offering through an investment bank—that route would be too expensive and no bank would do it. But Sandy can do an offering himself. He might consider Rule 147A, if he is only selling to friends and family who all live in his state, or Regulation D if he wants to sell stock in more than one state. Crowdfunding is a possibility if a funding portal will allow him to list himself.

37-2c Public Offerings

When a company wishes to raise significant amounts of capital from a large number of people, it must do a public offering. Preparing for an IPO is neither fast nor cheap. A typical IPO can cost $10 million; an exceptional one as much as $40 million. Because companies are now more successful in raising money privately, the number of IPOs has declined from an annual average of around 500 in the 1990s to less than half that recently. Any public sale of securities by an issuer after an IPO is called a **secondary offering**.

Secondary offering
Any public sale of securities by an issuer after the initial public offering

This is the process an issuer follows for either an IPO or a secondary offering:

1. **Underwriting.** For a public offering, companies hire an investment bank to serve as underwriter. In a **firm commitment underwriting**, the underwriter buys the stock from the issuer and resells it to the public. The underwriter bears the risk that the stock may sell at a lower price than expected. In a **best efforts underwriting**, the underwriter does not buy the stock but instead acts as the company's agent in selling it. If the stock sells at a low price, the company, not the underwriter, is the loser.

Firm commitment underwriting
The underwriter buys stock from the issuer and resells it to the public.

Best efforts underwriting
The underwriter does not buy the stock from the issuer but instead acts as the issuer's agent in selling the securities.

2. **Registration statement.** The **registration statement** has two purposes: to notify the SEC that a sale of securities is pending and to disclose information to prospective purchasers. The registration statement must include detailed information about the issuer and its business, a description of the stock, the proposed use of the proceeds from the offering, and three years of audited financial statements.

Registration statement
The document that an issuer files with the SEC to initiate a public offering of securities

3. **Prospectus.** All investors must receive a copy of the **prospectus** before purchasing the stock. (It is included in the registration statement that is sent to the SEC.) The prospectus includes important disclosures about the company and the security that is to be sold. The registration statement includes additional information that is of interest to the SEC but not to the typical investor, such as the names and addresses of the lawyers for the issuer and underwriter.

Prospectus
A document that provides potential investors with information about a security

4. **Sales effort.** Even before the final registration statement and prospectus are completed, the investment bank begins its sales effort. As part of this effort, company executives and the investment bankers conduct a **road show**; that is, they travel around the country making presentations to potential investors. The investment bank cannot actually make sales during this period, but it can solicit offers. The SEC closely regulates an issuer's sales effort to make sure that no one is unduly hyping the stock. The SEC delayed an offering of stock by Google after *Playboy* magazine published an interview with its founders.

Road show
As part of the sales process, company executives and investment bankers make presentations to potential investors.

5. **Going effective.** Once its review of the preliminary registration statement is complete, the SEC sends the issuer a **comment letter**, listing changes that must be made to the registration statement. An issuer almost always amends the registration statement at least once, and sometimes more. Remember that the SEC does not assess the value of the stock or the merit of the investment. Its role is to ensure that the company has disclosed enough to enable investors to make an informed decision. Immediately after the SEC has approved a final registration statement (which includes, of course, the final prospectus), the issuer and underwriter agree on a price for the stock and the date to **go effective**; that is, to begin the sale.

Comment letter
A letter from the SEC to an issuer with a list of changes that must be made to the registration statement

Go effective
The SEC authorizes a company to begin the public sale of its stock.

The following table compares a public offering, Reg A, Reg D, and crowdfunding:

	Initial Public Offering	Regulation A	Regulation D	Crowdfunding
Maximum Value of Securities Sold	No limit	\$20 million or \$50 million	\$5 million, or no limit, depending on the rule	\$1 million
Public Solicitation of Purchasers	Permitted	Permitted	Permitted under some rules	Permitted, with limitations
Suitability Requirements for Purchasers	No requirements	No requirements for Tier 1. For Tier 2, limits on purchases by unaccredited investors.	Must determine if investors are accredited or sophisticated	Limited to a certain percentage of investor's annual income or net worth
Disclosure Requirements	Elaborate registration statement, audited financials	Limited disclosure but tougher requirements for Tier 2 than for Tier 1	Limited disclosure	Limited disclosure
Resale of Securities	Permitted	Permitted	Prohibited for one year	Prohibited within one year except to the company, accredited investors, or family members

Ethics

When going public, companies rely on their investment bankers to guide them and represent their interests. Their trust may sometimes be misplaced because investment banks have a conflict of interest. Companies want the banks to pay the highest possible price for their shares; the banks prefer to pay a low price so that they can be sure to sell the stock quickly and profitably.

When Goldman Sachs took eToys public, it agreed to purchase the shares at a price of \$18.65, for resale to the public at \$20. But on the first day, the stock closed at \$77. As the saying goes, eToys left a lot of money on the table. Money it could very much have used—the company ultimately ran out of cash and went bankrupt.

eToys' creditors sued Goldman, alleging that it had made side deals with other clients, allowing them to purchase shares in eToys' offering in exchange for kickbacks to Goldman of a portion of their profits on the stock. Such an arrangement would virtually guarantee that Goldman underpriced the stock. During discovery, eToys found damning evidence to support their claims. There was even evidence that the Goldman executive in charge of the deal bet her colleagues that the eToys price would reach $80 on the first day.[3] Goldman ultimately settled the case by paying $7.5 million, a small percentage of the more than $400 million that eToys would have received had the IPO been properly priced.

How might the Goldman people have rationalized this behavior? What other ethics traps did they face?

37-2d Sales of Restricted Securities

The SEC wants to ensure that the public sale of stock takes place in an orderly manner. Therefore, it imposes some restrictions on the sale of stock even after a company has gone public. **Rule 144 limits the resale of two types of securities issued by public companies: *control securities* and *restricted securities*.**

Restricted security
Stock purchased in a private offering

Any stock purchased from the issuer in a private offering (such as Reg D) is a **restricted security**. If the issuer is private (i.e., not subject to the reporting requirements of the 1934 Act), these restricted securities cannot be sold for one year. But, once the company goes public, the holding period on restricted securities shrinks to six months from the date of purchase. After six months, these restricted securities can be sold freely unless they are also control securities, in which case certain restrictions still apply.

Control security
Stock held by any shareholder who owns more than 10 percent of a class of stock or by any officer or director of the company

A **control security** is stock held by any shareholder who owns more than 10 percent of a class of stock or by any officer or director of the company. In any three-month period, such an insider can sell only an amount of stock equal to the average weekly trading volume for the prior four weeks or 1 percent of the number of shares outstanding, whichever is greater. The purpose of this rule is to protect other investors from precipitous declines in stock price. If company insiders sold all of their stock in one day, the price would plunge, causing losses to the other shareholders.

37-2e Liability under the 1933 Act

Criminal Liability

Under §24 of the 1933 Act, the Justice Department can prosecute anyone who willfully violates the Act.

Selling Unregistered Securities

Section 12(a)(1) of the 1933 Act imposes liability on anyone who sells a security that is neither registered nor exempt. The purchaser of the security can demand rescission—a return of his money (plus interest) in exchange for the stock—or, if he no longer owns the stock, he can ask for damages.

Fraud

Under §12(a)(2) of the 1933 Act, the seller of a security is liable for making any material misstatement or omission, either oral or written, in connection with the offer or sale of

[3]Joe Nocera, "Rigging the I.P.O. Game," *The New York Times*, March 9, 2013.

a security. Material means important enough to affect an investor's decision. This provision applies to offerings that are *public* or *private* and *registered* or *unregistered* if there is some use of interstate commerce, such as mail, telephone (even for an *intra*state call), or check (that clears). It is difficult to imagine a securities transaction that does not involve interstate commerce. Both the SEC and any purchasers of the stock can sue the issuer.

Material
Important enough to affect an investor's decision

Errors in the Registration Statement

Section 11 of the 1933 Act establishes the penalties for any errors in a registration statement. **If a final registration statement contains a material misstatement or omission, the purchaser of the security can recover from everyone who signed the registration statement.** This list of signatories includes the issuer, its directors, and chief officers; experts (such as auditors, engineers, or lawyers); and the underwriters. Everyone who signed the registration statement is jointly and severally liable for any error, except the experts, who are liable only for misstatements in the part of the registration statement for which they were responsible.[4] Thus, an auditor is liable for misstatements in the financials but not, say, for omissions about the CEO's criminal past.

Damages. To prevail under §11, the plaintiff need only prove that there was a material misstatement or omission and that she lost money. The plaintiff does not have to prove that she relied on (or even *read*) the registration statement, that she bought the stock from the issuer, or that the defendant was negligent. The plaintiff can recover the difference between what she paid for the stock and its value on the date of the lawsuit.

Due Diligence. All is not hopeless, however, for those who have signed the registration statement. If the statement contains a material misstatement or omission, the company is liable and has no defense. **But everyone else who signed the registration statement can avoid liability by showing that he investigated the registration statement as thoroughly as a "prudent person in the management of his own property."**

This investigation is called **due diligence**. Its importance cannot be overstated. The SEC does not conduct its own investigation to ensure that the registration statement is accurate. It can only ensure that, on the surface, the issuer has supplied all relevant information. If an issuer chooses to lie, the SEC has no way of knowing. It is the job of the underwriters to check the accuracy of the filing. Thus, underwriters typically spend weeks visiting the company, reading all its corporate documents (including minutes back to the beginning), and calling its bankers, customers, suppliers, and competitors to ensure that the registration statement is accurate and no skeletons have been overlooked.

Due diligence
An investigation of the registration statement by someone who signs it

When §11 was first passed, investment bankers were outraged. Some predicted that this liability provision would cause capital in America to dry up, that grass would grow on Wall Street. In fact, the first case under §11 arose 35 years and 27,000 registration statements later. In that case—*Escott v. BarChris Construction Corp.*—the registration statement was profoundly flawed.[5] The underwriter failed to read the minutes of the executive committee meetings that revealed the company to be in serious financial trouble. Much of the company's alleged backlog of orders was from nonexistent corporations. Proceeds of the offering were earmarked to pay off debt, not to buy a new plant and equipment as the registration statement had indicated. The company's directors, underwriters, and underwriters' counsel were held liable.

---

[4]Joint and several liability means that all members of a group are liable. The plaintiff can sue them as a group or anyone of them individually for the full amount owing. The plaintiff cannot recover more than the total amount of the damages owing, however.

[5]283 F. Supp. 643 (S.D.N.Y 1968).

37-3 SECURITIES EXCHANGE ACT OF 1934

Most buyers do not purchase new securities from the issuer in an initial public offering. Rather they buy stock that is publicly traded in the open market. This stock is, in a sense, *secondhand* because others, perhaps many others, have already owned it. The purpose of the 1934 Act is to maintain the integrity of this secondary market.

37-3a Registration Requirements

As we have seen, the 1933 Act requires an issuer to register securities before selling them. That is a one-time effort for the company. The 1933 Act does not require the issuer to provide shareholders with any additional information in later years. Suppose that an automobile company registered and sold securities for the first time in 1946. Purchasers of those securities knew a lot about the firm—in 1946. But how can current investors assess the company? The 1934 Act plugs this hole. It requires issuers with publicly traded stock to continue to make information available to the public so that current—and potential— shareholders can evaluate the company. It is said that the 1933 Act registers securities and the 1934 Act registers companies.

Under the 1934 Act, an issuer must register with the SEC if:

- It completes a public offering under the 1933 Act or
- Its securities are traded on a national exchange (such as the NYSE) or
- It has at least 2,000 shareholders (or 500 who are unaccredited investors) *and* total assets that exceed $10 million.

Shareholders who acquire stock through an employee compensation plan or through the crowdfunding exemption do not count toward these limits.

A company can *de*register if its number of shareholders falls below 300 or if it has fewer than 500 shareholders and assets of less than $10 million. Although the shares are still publicly traded, the company does not have to file financial statements with the SEC. This process is called **going dark** because shareholders are now in the dark.

Going dark
When a company deregisters under the 1934 Act

37-3b Disclosure Requirements

The 1934 Act requires *ongoing*, regular disclosure for any company with a class of stock that is publicly traded. Companies that register under the 1934 Act are called **reporting companies**.

Reporting companies
Companies registered under the 1934 Act

Section 13 requires reporting companies to file the following documents:

- An initial, detailed information statement when the company first registers (similar to the filing required under the 1933 Act);
- Annual reports on Form 10-K, containing audited financial statements, a detailed analysis of the company's performance, and information about officers and directors;
- Quarterly reports on Form 10-Q, which are less detailed than 10-Ks and contain unaudited financials; and
- Form 8-K to report any significant developments, such as bankruptcy, a change in control, a purchase or sale of significant assets, the resignation of a director as a result of a policy dispute, a change in fiscal year, or a change in auditing firms.

A company's CEO and CFO must certify that:

- The information in the quarterly and annual reports is true,
- The company has effective internal controls, and
- The officers have informed the company's audit committee and its auditors of any concerns that they have about the internal control system.

A reporting company must send its annual report to shareholders. All annual reports and other 1934 Act filings are available on the SEC website.

37-3c Liability under the 1934 Act

Liability for Filings

Under §18, anyone who makes a false or misleading statement in any filing under the 1934 Act is liable to buyers or sellers who (1) acted in reliance on the statement and (2) can prove that the price at which they bought or sold was affected by the false filing. A court ruled that plaintiffs could bring suit against the directors and officers of a pharmaceutical company that manufactured a contraceptive device called the Dalkon Shield. In its annual report filed with the SEC, the company emphasized the safety, reliability, and efficiency of the Dalkon Shield, but failed to reveal evidence that the device was less effective and more harmful than it had disclosed. The company did not, for example, reveal that seven women had died from using the Dalkon Shield, and many others were rendered infertile.[6]

Fraud

Section 10(b) prohibits fraud in connection with the purchase and sale of any security, whether or not the security is registered under the 1934 Act. The SEC adopted Rule 10b-5 to clarify §10(b). **Rule 10b-5 prohibits any person, in connection with a purchase or sale of any security, from employing any device, scheme, or artifice to defraud.** In one case, a corporate officer was liable because he bought up shares of his company's stock even as he made pessimistic public statements about the company. In another case, a company violated the statute when it repeatedly and falsely denied that it was involved in merger negotiations.[7]

The courts have interpreted Rule 10b-5 as follows:

- **Misstatement or omission of a material fact.** Anyone who fails to disclose material information, or makes incomplete or inaccurate disclosure, is liable.
- **Scienter.** This is a legal term meaning that someone has acted with the intent to deceive or with deliberate recklessness as to the possibility of misleading investors. Negligence is not enough to create liability. A group of shareholders sued auditing firm Ernst & Ernst because it failed to discover that a company's chief executive was stealing funds. The shareholders believed that, if the auditors had realized that the executive refused to allow anyone else to open his mail, they would have known that he was engaged in wrongdoing. But the court found Ernst & Ernst not liable. Although its employees may have been negligent, they had not acted with intent or deliberate recklessness.[8]

Scienter
Acting with the intent to deceive or with deliberate recklessness

- **Purchase or sale.** Rule 10b-5 covers both buyers and sellers. It does not include, however, someone who failed to purchase stock because of a material misstatement. In the case of the corporate officer who spread negative rumors about his company while he bought stock, those who sold because of his false rumors could sue under Rule 10b-5, but not those who simply failed to buy.

6Ross v. A. H. Robins Co., 607 F.2d 545 (2d Cir 1979).
7Basic v. Levinson, 485 U.S. 224 (S. Ct. 1988).
8Ernst & Ernst v. Hochfelder, 425 U.S. 185 (S. Ct. 1976).

- **Reliance.** A plaintiff must show that she relied on the misstatement or omission. In the case of open-market trades, reliance is difficult to prove, so the courts are willing to assume it, unless the defendant can show that reliance was lacking.
- **Economic loss.** The plaintiffs must suffer a loss in the value of their investment. A couple sold their pharmaceutical business to another company in exchange for stock of the purchaser. Sometime later, they discovered that the purchaser had lied about its financial condition. However, the court held that the couple could not recover because, by the time they sold their stock in the purchaser, it was worth substantially more than when they acquired it. Thus, they had not suffered an economic loss.
- **Loss causation.** The economic loss must have been caused by the misstatement of a material fact. A group of investors alleged that, when they bought stock in Dura Pharmaceuticals, they had relied on statements by company executives that (1) its drug sales would be profitable and (2) the Food and Drug Administration (FDA) would approve its new asthma spray device. Neither of these statements turned out to be true, and the company's stock price fell. Plaintiffs argued that, if it had not been for the misrepresentations, the price would have been lower when they purchased their stock and then would not have fallen as far (or at all) when the truth came out. The Supreme Court ruled, however, that the plaintiffs could not recover because there was no proof that the misstatements had *caused* the decline in stock price. The price drop could have been the result of other factors, such as changes in the industry or in the economy as a whole.[9]

EXAMStrategy

Question: Events occurred in the following order:

1. Halliburton made a series of statements about its potential liabilities and expected revenue.
2. Erica purchased Halliburton stock on the open market.
3. The company corrected its prior disclosures.
4. Its stock price fell, causing Erica to lose money.
5. Erica filed suit against Halliburton, alleging that the company's initial statements had violated Rule 10b-5.

Will Erica win?

Strategy: Under Rule 10b-5, Erica must show reliance. Can she do so with these facts? Who carries the burden of proof?

Result: In cases involving open-market trades, the court assumes that the plaintiff did rely on the false statements, unless the defendant proves otherwise. Here, the court ruled that Erica had relied.[10]

Much securities litigation involves the interpretation of §10(b). For that reason, this chapter presents three cases that interpret this statute.

Material is an important term, not just for Rule 10b-5, but for other securities laws as well. In the following case, a unanimous Supreme Court provided guidance on what *material* means.

9Dura Pharmaceuticals, Inc. v. Broudo, 544 U.S. 336 (S. Ct. 2005).

10Halliburton Co. v. Erica P. John Fund, Inc., 134 S. Ct. 2398 (S. Ct. 2014).

Matrixx Initiatives, Inc. v. Siracusano

563 U.S. 27
United States Supreme Court, 2011

Facts: Zicam Cold Remedy was a nasal spray (or gel) that accounted for 70 percent of Matrixx's sales revenue. Its active ingredient was zinc gluconate. Matrixx began receiving reports that some Zicam users had developed anosmia (that is, they had lost their sense of smell). For three years, the company did nothing. Then it learned for the first time that some studies had linked the use of zinc sulfate to the loss of smell.

A year later, Matrixx found out that two doctors were planning to make a presentation at a conference about patients who had developed anosmia after Zicam use. Matrixx sent them a letter warning them that they did not have permission to use the name Matrixx or its products. The doctors deleted references to Zicam.

Nine people filed suit against Matrixx, alleging that Zicam had damaged their sense of smell. Matrixx issued statements that Zicam was poised for growth and that revenues would increase by more than 80 percent. In its 10-Q filing with the SEC, Matrixx warned of the potential "material adverse effect" that could result from product liability claims, "whether or not proven to be valid." It did not disclose, however, that Matrixx had already been sued.

After the FDA announced that it was investigating Zicam, Matrixx's stock price fell. Matrixx issued a press release stating:

> Matrixx believes statements alleging that Zicam products caused anosmia are completely unfounded and misleading. In no clinical trial of zinc gluconate gel products has there been a single report of lost or diminished olfactory function. A multitude of environmental and biologic influences are known to affect the sense of smell. Chief among them is the common cold. As a result, the population most likely to use cold remedy products is already at increased risk of developing anosmia.

The day after this press release, Matrixx stock price bounced back. Shortly thereafter, however, the TV show *Good Morning America* reported that more than a dozen patients had suffered from anosmia after using Zicam and that some had filed lawsuits against Matrixx. The company's stock price plummeted.

A group of shareholders filed suit, alleging that Matrixx had violated §10(b) and Rule 10b-5. The trial court granted Matrixx's motion to dismiss on the grounds that, without a statistical correlation between the use of Zicam and anosmia, the reported incidents were not material. The Court of Appeals reversed. The Supreme Court granted *certiorari*.

Issue: ***Were Matrixx's misleading statements about material facts?***

Excerpts from Justice Sotomayor's Decision: To prevail on a §10(b) claim, a plaintiff must show that the defendant made a statement that was *misleading* as to a *material* fact. [T]his materiality requirement is satisfied when there is a substantial likelihood that the disclosure of the omitted fact would have been viewed by the reasonable investor as having significantly altered the "total mix" of information made available.

[M]edical researchers consider multiple factors in assessing causation. A lack of statistically significant data does not mean that medical experts have no reliable basis for inferring a causal link between a drug and adverse events. Not only does the FDA rely on a wide range of evidence of causation, it sometimes acts on the basis of evidence that suggests, but does not prove, causation. For example, the FDA requires manufacturers of over-the-counter drugs to revise their labeling to include a warning as soon as there is reasonable evidence of an association of a serious hazard with a drug; a causal relationship need not have been proved. Given that medical professionals and regulators act on the basis of evidence of causation that is not statistically significant, it stands to reason that in certain cases, reasonable investors would as well.

Application of [the] "total mix" standard does not mean that pharmaceutical manufacturers must disclose all reports of adverse events. The fact that a user of a drug has suffered an adverse event, standing alone, does not mean that the drug caused that event. Something more is needed, but that something more is not limited to statistical significance.

[W]e conclude that respondents have adequately pleaded materiality. Matrixx received information that plausibly indicated a reliable causal link between Zicam and anosmia. Importantly, Zicam Cold Remedy accounted for 70 percent of Matrixx's sales. It is substantially likely that a reasonable investor would have viewed this information as having significantly altered the "total mix" of information made available. Matrixx told the market that revenues were going to rise 80 percent. [H]owever, Matrixx had information indicating a significant risk to its leading revenue-generating product.

For the reasons stated, the judgment of the Court of Appeals for the Ninth Circuit is Affirmed.

Ethics

Matrixx learned that its products were potentially causing a loss of smell, which is no minor matter. People with anosmia cannot properly taste food, so they often lose interest in eating, which can lead to malnutrition and depression. Did the company have an ethical obligation to alert the public to this issue? What ethics traps did these executives face?

In the following case, Hewlett-Packard (HP) and its executives made many inaccurate statements. But did they have scienter? You be the judge.

You Be the Judge

In re HP Secs. Litig.

2013 U.S. Dist. LEXIS 168292; 2013 WL 6185529
United States District Court for the Northern District of California, 2013

Facts: Shortly after Léo Apotheker became CEO of HP, he decided to acquire Autonomy Corporation at a cost of over $11 billion. His decision met with strong resistance from HP executives, including CFO Catherine Lesjak. But he persisted. The day after HP announced the acquisition, its stock price dropped 20 percent.

A week before the Autonomy deal was to close, the board of directors replaced Apotheker as CEO with Meg Whitman. She sought to terminate the Autonomy acquisition but was told that the United Kingdom's takeover rules made that impossible. Here is the timeline of events thereafter:

1. October: The Autonomy acquisition closed. Over the next few months, HP learned that Autonomy's earnings and growth numbers were inaccurate.
2. February of the following year: In a conference call with investors, Lesjak attributed HP's weak revenue numbers to "acquisition-related integration costs and accounting adjustments."
3. May 23:
   a. Whitman learned that a senior executive at Autonomy (referred to as "Whistleblower No. 4") was warning of serious accounting improprieties. HP hired PricewaterhouseCoopers to investigate.
   b. Lesjak told analysts that HP's "second-quarter operating profit for software was unfavorably impacted by acquisition-related integration costs." She was not asked about, nor did she choose to comment on, Autonomy's performance.
   c. On the same call, Whitman said, "When Autonomy turned in disappointing results, HP actually did a fairly deep dive to understand what had happened here. And in my view, Autonomy is a terrific product. There is an enormous demand for Autonomy."
4. June 5: During a press interview, Whitman stated about Autonomy:

   > In my view, this is the classic case of scaling a business from startup to grownup. Going through that barrier of a billion dollars in sales is not easy because you can't run the organization at $1.5 billion the same way you did at $500 million. You just can't. And for many entrepreneurs, processes and discipline are dirty words, and you have to have those things, especially within the context of HP. I know exactly how this world works. I have every confidence that Autonomy will be a very big and very profitable business.

5. August 22: On a conference call, Whitman said, "Autonomy still requires a great deal of attention and we've been aggressively working on that business."
6. September 10: HP's Form 10-Q reported that "At the time of the Autonomy acquisition

in October 2011, the fair value of Autonomy approximated the carrying value."

7. Fifteen months later, on November 20: The PricewaterhouseCoopers investigation was complete. HP announced that Autonomy had been a fraud. It wrote down the investment by $8.8 billion. HP's stock dropped another 12 percent.

Shareholders filed suit alleging that Whitman, Lesjak, and HP had committed fraud under §10(b). The defendants filed a motion to dismiss, arguing that they did not have scienter.

You Be the Judge: *Did the defendants have scienter? Did they act either intentionally or with deliberate recklessness?*

Argument for the Shareholders: Even before the deal closed, executives at HP knew that it was a mistake. Lesjak argued against it; Whitman tried to back out; yet still, it went forward. Then HP discovered that Autonomy's numbers were inaccurate. Later, Whistleblower No. 4 came forward. (It is always a bad sign when there are so many whistleblowers, they have to take a number.)

Yet, for eight months, HP executives made filings with the SEC and statements to investors that gave no hint of trouble. Whitman even made up a whole story about how Autonomy was just going through growing pains. She stated that "Autonomy is a terrific product"—an odd description for a fraudulent deal. She could have honestly answered any questions about Autonomy by saying she did not know why it had underperformed but was actively investigating.

HP said in a filing that, at the time of the Autonomy acquisition in October, its fair value approximated the carrying value. The senior executives could not possibly have believed that statement to be true. In short, they deliberately duped and defrauded investors.

Argument for the Company and Its Executives: Yes, there were rumors and allegations about Autonomy, but not until November 20, when the Pricewaterhouse investigation finished, did the defendants know for sure that the deal had been a fraud. As soon as the company knew, it made a public announcement. Taking time to investigate a situation before making disclosures to the investing public is not fraudulent, it is prudent and reasonable.

Moreover, many of defendants' statements were nothing more than puffery. Whitman said that "Autonomy is a terrific product. There is an enormous demand for Autonomy." This sort of optimistic language does not create liability.

Even if some of their statements were untrue, HP executives are not liable if they acted carelessly, or even recklessly. Under the scienter requirement, shareholders must show that the defendants acted with intent or deliberate recklessness. Autonomy was a bad deal, but no one intentionally engaged in wrongdoing. HP was the one who was duped.

Aiding and Abetting

In the case of large frauds, the company at the heart of the wrongdoing is often bankrupt, so plaintiffs scramble to find other deep pockets from which to recover their losses. One approach is, instead of going after those who committed the fraud themselves, suing those who aided and abetted the wrongdoing. Section 10(b) is often their weapon of choice. As the following case demonstrates, however, the Supreme Court is unsympathetic to this tactic.

Stoneridge Investment Partners, LLC v. Scientific-Atlanta, Inc.

28 S. Ct. 761
United States Supreme Court, 2008

Facts: Charter Communications, Inc., was a cable operator that engaged in a variety of fraudulent practices to pump up its financial statements. When it still failed to meet Wall Street expectations, Charter approached two of its suppliers—Scientific-Atlanta and Motorola—for help in furthering the fraud. These two companies sold Charter the set-top boxes that Charter furnished its customers. Charter arranged to overpay the suppliers $20 for each set-top box it purchased, with the understanding that they would return the overpayment by purchasing advertising from Charter. These transactions had no economic purpose other than inflating Charter's revenue and operating cash flow numbers. They also violated generally accepted accounting principles. The plan was successful—Charter did manage to fool its auditors.

The inflated numbers were included in financial statements filed with the SEC and reported to the public. Purchasers of Charter stock sued the two suppliers, alleging that they had violated §10(b). The District Court granted defendants' motion to dismiss. The U.S. Court of Appeals for the Eighth Circuit affirmed. The Supreme Court granted *certiorari.*

Issue: ***Is someone who aids and abets a violation of §10(b) liable under the statute?***

Excerpts from Justice Kennedy's Decision: Reliance by the plaintiff upon the defendant's deceptive acts is an essential element of the §10(b) cause of action. [In this case, no] member of the investing public had knowledge, either actual or presumed, of [defendants'] deceptive acts during the relevant times. Petitioner, as a result, cannot show reliance upon any of [defendants'] actions except in an indirect chain that we find too remote for liability.

It is true that a dynamic, free economy presupposes a high degree of integrity in all of its parts. Were the implied cause of action to be extended to the practices described here, however, there would be a risk that the federal power would be used to invite litigation beyond the immediate sphere of securities litigation and in areas already governed by functioning and effective state-law guarantees. Section 10(b) does not incorporate common-law fraud into federal law.

[E]xtensive discovery and the potential for uncertainty and disruption in a lawsuit allow plaintiffs with weak claims to extort settlements from innocent companies. Adoption of petitioner's approach would expose a new class of defendants to these risks. [C]ontracting parties might find it necessary to protect against these threats, raising the costs of doing business. Overseas firms with no other exposure to our securities laws could be deterred from doing business here. This, in turn, may raise the cost of being a publicly traded company under our law and shift securities offerings away from domestic capital markets.

Here respondents were acting in concert with Charter in the ordinary course as suppliers, not in the investment sphere. Charter was free to do as it chose in preparing its books, conferring with its auditor, and preparing and then issuing its financial statements. In these circumstances, the investors cannot be said to have relied upon any of [defendants'] deceptive acts in the decision to purchase or sell securities; and as the requisite reliance cannot be shown, [the defendants] have no liability to [plaintiffs]. The judgment of the Court of Appeals is affirmed.

37-3d Insider Trading: §§16 and 10(b)

Why is insider trading a crime? Who is harmed? After all, if you buy or sell stock, presumably you are reasonably content with the price or you would not have traded. **Insider trading is illegal because:**

- It undermines the integrity of stock markets. Investors will not be willing to buy in the market unless they believe in its fundamental honesty.
- It offends our fundamental sense of fairness. No one wants to play in a rigged game.
- Investment banks typically "make a market" in stocks, meaning that they hold extra shares so that orders can be filled smoothly. If an insider buys stock because she knows the company is about to sign an important contract, she earns the profit on that information at the expense of the market maker who sold her the stock. These market makers expect to earn a certain profit. If they do not earn it from normal stock appreciation, they simply raise the commission they charge for being a market maker. As a result, everyone who buys and sells stock pays a slightly higher price because insider trading skims off some of the profits.

Everyone who buys and sells stock pays a slightly higher price because insider trading skims off some of the profits.

The 1934 Act bans three types of insider trading: short-swing trading, classic insider trading, and misappropriation.

Section 16: Short-Swing Trading

Insiders know more about their company than outsiders do. During congressional hearings after the 1929 stock market crash, witnesses testified that insiders had used this special knowledge to manipulate the stock market. They would, for example, buy a large block of stock, announce a substantial dividend, and then divest before the dividend was reduced. Section 16 was designed to prevent corporate insiders from taking unfair advantage of privileged information to manipulate the market.

Section 16 applies to officers, directors, and controlling shareholders who own more than 10 percent of the company. The statute imposes two requirements on insiders:

1. **Report.** Anyone who becomes an insider must report this status to the SEC. They then must report any trades in company stock within two business days. This report must also reveal their total stock holdings in the company. The filings must be made to the SEC electronically, and both the SEC and the company are required to post them on their respective websites within one business day after the report is made.
2. **Disgorge.** Insiders must *turn over to the corporation* any profits they make from the purchase and sale or sale and purchase of company securities in a six-month period.

Section 16 is a strict liability provision. It applies even if the insider did not actually take advantage of secret information or try to manipulate the market; if she bought and sold or sold and bought stock in a six-month period, she is liable.

Manuela buys 20,000 shares of her company's stock in June at $10 a share. In September, her (uninsured) winter house in Florida is destroyed by a hurricane. To raise money for rebuilding, she sells the stock at $12 per share, making a profit of $40,000. She has violated §16 and must turn over the profit to her company.

Section 10(b): Classic Insider Trading

The SEC has dramatically increased not only its number of classic insider trading prosecutions but also the size of the prison terms and fines it seeks. However, despite its efforts, this crime is pervasive. Recent research indicates that insider trading takes place in about 25 percent of public mergers and acquisitions. The SEC only litigates about 8 percent of these cases.[11] Although this percentage sounds low, is an 8 percent chance of years in prison and huge fines worth it?

The main elements of this crime are as follows.

Insiders. A corporate insider is guilty of insider trading under §10(b), if he:

- **Has material, nonpublic information and**
- **Breaches a fiduciary duty *to his company***
- **By trading on the information**
- **Whether or not he makes a profit.**

Corporate insiders who have a fiduciary duty include board members, major shareholders, employees, and so-called temporary insiders, such as lawyers and investment bankers who are doing deals for the company. Examples:

---

[11] Patrick Augustin, Menachem Brenner, and Marti G. Subrahmanyam, "Informed Options Trading Prior to M&A Announcements: Insider Trading?" August 16, 2016, available at SSRN: https://ssrn.com/abstract=2441606 or http://dx.doi.org/10.2139/ssrn.2441606.

- If the director of research for MediSearch, Inc., buys stock in the company at a time when she knows that its scientists have found a vaccination for Zika but before that information is public, she has violated Rule 10b-5. So has a lawyer who finds out about this breakthrough because he works at the firm that is patenting MediSearch's new discovery and then buys stock before the information is public.
- Suppose, however, that while looking in a dumpster, Harry finds correspondence that reveals MediSearch's new vaccination. He then buys MediSearch stock that promptly quadruples in value. Harry will be dining at the Ritz, not in federal prison, because he has no fiduciary duty to MediSearch.

Tippers. Sometimes insiders do not trade themselves, but instead pass on information to others (such as friends and family) with the expectation that they will somehow personally benefit.

Insiders are liable as tippers if:

- **They reveal material, nonpublic information about their company in violation of their fiduciary duty;**
- **They know the information is confidential; and**
- **They benefit (or expect to benefit) directly or indirectly.**

A gift to a friend or family member counts as personal gain. Example:

- W. Paul Thayer was a corporate director, deputy secretary of defense, and former fighter pilot who gave stock tips, based on information he had learned as a director, to his girlfriend in lieu of paying her rent. That counted as personal gain, and he spent a year and a half in prison.

Tippees. Those who receive inside information, or tips, may also be liable, even if they do not have a fiduciary relationship to the company or the tipper. Tippees are liable when:

- They trade on the information,
- They know it is confidential,
- They know that it came from an insider who was violating his fiduciary duty, and
- The insider benefited (or expected to benefit) directly or indirectly.

Example:

- Barry Switzer, then head football coach at the University of Oklahoma, went to a track meet to see his son compete. While sunbathing on the bleachers, he overheard an insider talking about a company that was going to be acquired. Switzer bought the stock but was acquitted of insider trading charges because the insider had not breached his fiduciary duty. He had not tipped anyone on purpose—he had simply been careless. Also, the insider had not benefited in any way.[12]

Lane Oatey/blue jean images/Jupiterimages

If he carelessly reveals confidential information during a casual conversation, is he guilty of insider trading?

In the following case, two brothers started down a slippery slope of tipping that ended with a family member going to prison.

---

12 SEC v. Switzer, 590 F. Supp. 756 (W.D. Okla. 1984).

Salman v. United States

137 S. Ct. 420
United States Supreme Court, 2016

Facts: Maher Kara was an investment banker specializing in the healthcare industry at Citigroup. To understand scientific aspects of his job, Maher sought help from his older brother Michael, who was a chemist. Later, when their father was ill, Maher told his brother about companies that were secretly developing innovative treatments. Eventually Maher realized that Michael was trading on this secret information.

Maher implored Michael to stop, even offering him money. But Michael just wanted information. Although he disapproved of Michael's trades, Maher continued to feed him tips, knowing that he would trade on it.

When Maher started dating (and ultimately married) Bassam Salman's sister, Michael and Salman became friends. Without telling Maher, Michael began sharing Maher's tips with Salman, who made over $1.5 million in profits. Salman knew the information was coming from Maher.

All three men were charged with insider trading. Michael and Maher pleaded guilty and testified against Salman at his trial. (Talk about awkward family dynamics.) Salman was convicted of insider trading, sentenced to 36 months imprisonment, and ordered to pay over $730,000 in restitution. He appealed, arguing that he was not guilty of insider trading because the tipper (Maher) had not received a benefit. The Ninth Circuit affirmed his conviction. The Supreme Court granted *certiorari.*

Issues: ***Did the tipper receive a benefit? Did Salman engage in illegal insider trading?***

Excerpts from Justice Alito's Decision: Section 10(b) of the Securities Exchange Act of 1934 and the Securities and Exchange Commission's Rule 10b-5 prohibit undisclosed trading on inside corporate information by individuals who are under a duty of trust and confidence that prohibits them from secretly using such information for their personal advantage.

The tippee acquires the tipper's duty to disclose or abstain from trading if the tippee knows the information was disclosed in breach of the tipper's duty. A tipper breaches such a fiduciary duty when the tipper discloses the inside information for a personal benefit. In determining whether a tipper derived a personal benefit, we instruct courts to focus on objective criteria, i.e., whether the insider receives a direct or indirect personal benefit from the disclosure, such as a pecuniary gain or a reputational benefit that will translate into future earnings. This personal benefit can often be inferred from objective facts and circumstances, such as a relationship between the insider and the recipient that suggests a quid pro quo from the latter, or an intention to benefit the particular recipient.

[A violation also occurs] when an insider makes a gift of confidential information to a trading relative or friend. Maher, the tipper, provided inside information to his brother Michael. Maher would have breached his duty had he personally traded on the information here himself then given the proceeds as a gift to his brother. It is obvious that Maher would personally benefit in that situation. But Maher effectively achieved the same result by disclosing the information to Michael, and allowing him to trade on it.

Here, by disclosing confidential information as a gift to his brother with the expectation that he would trade on it, Maher breached his duty of trust and confidence to Citigroup and its clients—a duty Salman acquired, and breached himself, by trading on the information with full knowledge that it had been improperly disclosed.

EXAMStrategy

Question: Paul was an investment banker who sometimes bragged about deals he was working on. One night he told a bartender, Ryanne, about an upcoming deal, without revealing his connection to it. Ryanne bought stock in the company Paul had mentioned. Both were prosecuted for insider trading. Ryanne was acquitted but Paul was convicted, even though Ryanne was the one who made money. How is that possible?

Strategy: Note that there are different standards for tippers and tippees.

Result: Paul is liable if he knew the information was confidential and he benefited directly or indirectly. A gift counts as personal gain. Ryanne was not liable because she did not know the information was confidential and that it came from an insider who was violating his fiduciary duty.

Misappropriation

Misappropriation is a violation of §10(b). It is illegal for anyone:

- **With material, nonpublic information**
- **To breach a fiduciary duty to the *source of the information***
- **By revealing or trading on the information.**

Anyone who trades on material, secret information obtained through the workplace is guilty of misappropriation. In addition, someone who trades on information obtained through a *personal* relationship is also guilty of misappropriation if the two people have a fiduciary relationship. The courts have determined that a personal fiduciary relationship exists if:

- The recipient has promised to keep the information secret;
- The communicator has a reasonable expectation that the recipient will not tell because of their relationship of trust; or
- The recipient has obtained the information from her spouse, parent, child, or sibling.

Examples:

- In the workplace: James O'Hagan was a lawyer in a firm that represented a company attempting to take over Pillsbury Co. Although O'Hagan did not work on the case, he heard about it and then bought stock in Pillsbury. After the takeover attempt was publicly announced, O'Hagan sold his stock in Pillsbury at a profit of more than $4.3 million.[13] The Supreme Court ruled that O'Hagan had violated insider trading laws. While it was true that he had no fiduciary duty to Pillsbury, he did owe one to his law firm, which was the source of the information. According to the court, what he had done was the same thing as embezzlement.[14]
- Personal relationship: Amy Goodson had just found out that her employer, VeriFone, was about to be acquired by Hewlett-Packard. She confided in her husband, Floyd, that she was worried she might lose her job. But, according to the government, Floyd found a way to profit even from this bad news—by phoning his father, who promptly bought stock in VeriFone. And promptly made a $62,000 profit. What Floyd was alleged to have done was misappropriation because he had violated his fiduciary duty to his wife.[15]

Tippees are also guilty of misappropriation. Floyd's father would also be guilty because he obtained information from the person who carried out the misappropriation.

Takeovers

Rule 14e-3 prohibits trading on inside information during a tender offer if the trader knows the information was obtained from either the bidder or the target company. The trader or tipper need not have violated a fiduciary duty. Example:

[13] O'Hagan used the profits that he gained through this trading to conceal his previous embezzlement of client funds. There is a moral here.

[14] United States v. O'Hagan, 521 U.S. 642 (S. Ct. 1997).

[15] United States SEC v. Goodson, 2001 U.S. Dist. LEXIS 26493, 2001 WL 819431 (N.D. Ga. 2001).

- Patrick tells Jane that he can't play golf with her this weekend because he is having to respond to a potential takeover offer against his company. If Jane buys stock in Patrick's company, he is not liable under Rule 10b-5 because he did not expect any personal gain. But Jane has violated Rule 14e-3 because the information was acquired from the target company during a tender offer.

Advanced Planning

Under Rule 10b5-1, an insider can avoid insider trading charges if she commits in advance to a plan to sell securities. Thus, if an insider knows that she will want to sell stock to pay a child's college tuition, she can establish such a sales plan in advance. She will then not be liable for the sales, no matter what inside information she knows. But, she *must* sell according to the plan, despite any change in circumstances.

Although this rule sounds like a good idea, it is easy to abuse. Because executives do not have to disclose their plans or file them with the SEC, it is hard for anyone outside the company to monitor sales or even know if there is a plan. Also, executives are free to cancel or modify any plan at any time. One study found that when plans required the sale of stock, half of all cancellations occurred shortly before the company released good news, while only 11 percent occurred shortly before bad news.[16] Research has also found that some CEOs time the release of corporate information to increase their returns under 10b5-1 plans.[17]

37-4 BLUE SKY LAWS

In 1911, Kansas became the first state to regulate the sale of securities. It was concerned that some securities, "had no more substance than so many cubic feet of Kansas blue sky."[18] Hence, state securities statutes are called **blue sky laws**. Currently, all states and the District of Columbia have blue sky laws.

Blue sky laws
State securities statutes

37-4a Exemption from State Regulation

To make life easier for issuers of stock, Congress passed the **National Securities Markets Improvement Act (NSMIA) of 1996. Essentially, states may no longer regulate offerings of securities that are:**

- Traded on a national exchange,
- Exempt under Regulation D Rule 506,
- Sold only to qualified purchasers (usually defined as accredited investors), or
- Issued as a Tier 2 offering under Regulation A.

16Susan Pulliam and Rob Barry, "Executives' Good Luck in Trading Own Stock," *The Wall Street Journal*, November 27, 2012.
17Eliezer M. Fich, Robert Parrino, and Anh L. Tran, "Timing Stock Trades for Personal Gain: Private Information and Sales of Shares by CEOs," July 10, 2015. SSRN: https://ssrn.com/abstract=2579047 or http://dx.doi.org/10.2139/ssrn.2579047.
18*The Economist*, "Suspiciously Quiet," September 1, 2012.

37-4b State Regulation

Any securities offerings not covered by the NSMIA must comply with state securities laws, which can be complex. Among other things, some state statutes focus on the quality of the investment and require a so-called *merit review*, in contrast with the 1933 Act which is primarily concerned with disclosure. In 1981, the Massachusetts securities commissioner refused to allow Apple Computer Co. to sell its initial public offering in Massachusetts because he believed the stock, selling at 92 times earnings, was too risky. He "protected" Massachusetts residents from this investment.

States generally offer several programs to facilitate the sales of securities. They include:

- Coordinated Review-Equity (CR-Equity), which is designed for use during an IPO. Under this program, the issuer only has to deal with two jurisdictions: one for disclosure concerns and another for merit issues.
- Coordinated Review-Small Company Offering Registration (CR-SCOR), which allows the use of a simplified disclosure form for small offerings. It also permits issuers to file in one or more of four regions, rather than separately for each state.

CHAPTER CONCLUSION

The 1929 stock market crash and the Great Depression that followed were an economic catastrophe for the United States. The Securities Act of 1933 and the Securities Exchange Act of 1934 were designed to prevent such disasters from ever occurring again. Whether or not they achieve that goal, they undoubtedly enhance the reliability and stability of the securities markets.

EXAM REVIEW

1. **SECURITY** A security is any transaction in which the buyer invests money in a common enterprise and expects to earn a profit predominantly from the efforts of others.

EXAMStrategy

Question: Jonah bought 12 paintings from Theo's Art Gallery at a total cost of $1 million. Theo told Jonah that the paintings were a safe investment that could only go up in value. (If anyone ever tells you that, run!) The gallery permitted purchasers to trade in a painting in return for any other artwork the gallery owned. In the trade-in, the purchaser would get credit for the amount of the original painting and then pay the difference if the new painting was worth more. When Jonah's paintings did not increase in value, he sued Theo for a violation of the securities laws. Were these paintings securities?

Strategy: Are all the elements of a security present here? (See the "Result" at the end of this Exam Review section.)

2. **REGISTRATION** Before any offer or sale, an issuer must register securities with the SEC unless the securities qualify for an exemption.

3. **EXEMPTIONS** These securities are exempt from the registration requirement: government securities, bank securities, short-term notes, nonprofit issues, insurance policies, and annuity contracts.

4. **SECURITIES OFFERINGS** The following table compares the different types of securities offerings under the 1933 Act:

	Public Offering	Intrastate Offering Rule 147A	Regulation A: Tier 1	Regulation A: Tier 2	Regulation D: Rule 504	Regulation D: Rule 506	Crowdfunding
Maximum Value of Securities Sold	Unlimited	Unlimited	$20 million	$50 million	$5 million	Unlimited	$1 million
Public Solicitation of Purchasers	Permitted	Permitted	Permitted	Permitted	Sometimes permitted	Yes, if sales are limited to accredited investors, otherwise, not permitted	Permitted with limitations
Suitability Require-ments for Purchasers	No requirements	Must reside in issuer's state	No requirements	Unaccredited investors may not buy stock that costs more than 10% of their annual income or net worth, whichever is greater.	May be limited to accredited investors	No limit on accredited investors; no more than 35 unaccredited investors who, if unso-phisticated, must have a purchaser representative	Investors can only buy stock worth up to a certain per-centage of their annual income or net worth.
Resale of Securities	Permitted	Permitted, but may not be made out of state for six months	Permitted	Permitted	Sometimes permitted	Not permitted for one year	Prohibited within one year except to the company, accredited investors, or family members

EXAMStrategy

CPA Question: Hamilton Corp. makes a $4.5 million securities offering under Rule 506 of Regulation D of the Securities Act of 1933. Under this regulation, Hamilton is:

(a) required to provide full financial information to accredited investors only.

(b) allowed to make the offering through a general solicitation to both accredited and unaccredited investors.

(c) limited to selling to no more than 35 accredited investors.

(d) allowed to sell an unlimited amount of stock.

Strategy: The answer is not (a) because accredited investors are never entitled to *more* disclosure than other investors. The answer is not (b) because Rule 506 does not permit a general solicitation to unaccredited investors. The answer is not (c) because Rule 506 is limited to only 35 *un*accredited investors. (See the "Result" at the end of this Exam Review section.)

---

5. **RULE 144** This rule limits the resale of two types of securities issued by public companies: control securities and restricted securities.

6. **LIABILITY UNDER THE 1933 ACT** The 1933 Act imposes liability on anyone who sells a security that is neither registered nor exempt. A seller of a security is liable for making any material misstatement or omission, either oral or written, in connection with the offer or sale of a security.

7. **THE 1934 ACT** The 1934 Act requires public companies to make regular filings with the SEC.

8. **LIABILITY UNDER THE 1934 ACT** Anyone who makes a false or misleading statement in a filing under the 1934 Act is liable to buyers or sellers who (1) acted in reliance on the statement and (2) can prove that the price at which they bought or sold was affected by the false filing. Section 10(b) prohibits fraud in connection with the purchase and sale of any security, whether or not the security is registered under the 1934 Act.

9. **SECTION 16** Under §16, insiders must disclose any trades they make in company stock. Furthermore, if they buy and sell or sell and buy company stock within a six-month period, they must turn over to the corporation any profits from the trades.

EXAMStrategy

Question: You are the president of Turbocharge, Inc., a publicly traded company. You have been buying stock recently because you think the company's product—a more efficient hybrid engine—is very promising. One day, you show up at work and find your desk in the hallway. The CEO has fired you. In a huff, you sell all your company stock. The only silver lining to your cloud is that you make a large profit. Or is this a silver lining?

Strategy: You can be in violation of §16 even if you did not have any inside information when you traded. (See the "Result" at the end of this Exam Review section.)

---

10. **CLASSIC INSIDER TRADING** Any corporate insider (1) with material, nonpublic information (2) who breaches a fiduciary duty *to his company* (3) by trading on the information is guilty of insider trading in violation of §10(b). Tippers and tippees may also be liable.

11. **MISAPPROPRIATION** Anyone with material, nonpublic information who breaches a fiduciary duty to the source of the information by trading on this information is guilty of insider trading in violation of §10(b).

12. **TAKEOVERS** Rule 14e-3 prohibits trading on inside information during a tender offer if the trader knows the information was obtained from either the bidder or the target company.

13. **THE NSMIA** The National Securities Markets Improvement Act prohibits states from regulating securities offerings that are:
    - Traded on a national exchange,
    - Exempt under Regulation D Rule 506,
    - Sold only to qualified purchasers (usually defined as accredited investors), or
    - Issued as a Tier 2 offering under Reg A.

14. **BLUE SKY LAWS** Any securities offerings not covered by the NSMIA must comply with state securities laws, which are varied and complex.

RESULTS

1. Result: The paintings were not securities because there was no "common enterprise." The investors did not pool funds or share profits with other investors.

4. Result: The answer is (d) because there is no limit on the amount of stock sold under Rule 506.

9. Result: You are in violation of §16. Even though you acted without any bad intent, you must turn over all your profits to the company.

MULTIPLE-CHOICE QUESTIONS

1. **CPA QUESTION** When a common stock offering requires registration under the Securities Act of 1933, _______________.
   (a) the registration statement is automatically effective when filed with the SEC
   (b) the issuer would act unlawfully if it were to sell the common stock without providing the investor with a prospectus
   (c) the SEC will determine the investment value of the common stock before approving the offering
   (d) the issuer may make sales ten days after filing the registration statement

2. **CPA QUESTION** Pace Corp. previously issued 300,000 shares of its common stock. The shares are now actively traded on a national securities exchange. The original offering was exempt from registration under the Securities Act of 1933. Pace has $2.5 million in assets and 425 unaccredited shareholders. With regard to the Securities Exchange Act of 1934, Pace is _______________.
   (a) required to file a registration statement because its assets exceed $2 million in value
   (b) required to file a registration statement even though it has fewer than 500 unaccredited shareholders

(c) not required to file a registration statement because the original offering of its stock was exempt from registration

(d) not required to file a registration statement unless insiders own at least 5 percent of its outstanding shares of stock

3. Lily would like to raise money for her video game start-up by selling shares. If she decides to raise money through crowdfunding, she ______________.

(a) can only sell to accredited investors

(b) can sell up to $5 million in stock during each 12-month period

(c) can sell through any website

(d) must file an offering statement with the SEC

(e) can advertise all the terms of the offering

4. If a publicly traded company wishes to issue more public stock, it will undertake a(n)______________. If the underwriter buys the stock and resells it to the public, that is a______________ underwriting. Before buying the stock, investors must receive a copy of the______________.

(a) IPO; best efforts; registration statement

(b) IPO; firm commitment; registration statement

(c) secondary offering; best efforts; prospectus

(d) secondary offering; firm commitment; prospectus

5. Three months ago, Noah bought stock under Rule 506 in TreesNFlowers, Inc. He has lost interest in the company and would like to sell the stock. Which of the following statements is true?

(a) He can sell the stock now, so long as he sells it to an accredited investor.

(b) He can sell the stock now, so long as the company grants permission.

(c) He must hold on to the stock for at least nine more months.

(d) He could sell the stock in three months, but only if the company goes public in the meantime.

CASE QUESTIONS

1. Fluor, an engineering and construction company, was awarded a $1 billion project to build a coal gasification plant in South Africa. Fluor signed an agreement with a South African client that prohibited them both from announcing the agreement until March 10. Accordingly, Fluor denied all rumors that a major transaction was pending. Between March 3 and March 6, the State Teachers Retirement Board pension fund sold 288,257 shares of Fluor stock. After the contract was announced, the stock price went up. Did Fluor violate Rule 10b-5?

2. Do you love ice cream? Here is an opportunity for you! For only $800, you can buy a cow from Berkshire Ice Cream. The company gets milk from the cow, and you get to share in the profits from the sale of ice cream. Just last month, Berkshire mailed $32,000 worth of checks to investors, who are expecting a 20 percent annual rate of return. Are there any problems with this plan?

3. **ETHICS** Suppose that, while waiting in line at the grocery store, you overhear a stranger saying that the FDA is going to approve a new drug tomorrow—one that will be a huge success for Alpha Pharmaceuticals. Is it legal for you to buy stock in Alpha? Is it ethical? What would Kant and Mill say?

4. **ETHICS** David Sokol worked at Berkshire Hathaway for legendary investor Warren Buffett, who is renowned not only for his investment skills but also for his ethics. Bankers suggested to both Sokol and the CEO of Lubrizol that the company might be a good buy for Berkshire. Sokol then found out that the CEO of Lubrizol planned to approach Berkshire about a possible acquisition. Sokol purchased $10 million worth of Lubrizol stock before recommending Lubrizol to Buffett. Sokol mentioned to Buffett "in passing" that he owned shares of Lubrizol. Buffett did not ask any questions about the timing or amount of Sokol's purchases. Sokol made a $3 million profit when Berkshire acquired Lubrizol. Did Sokol violate insider trading laws? Did he behave ethically? What are Buffett's ethical obligations?

5. At an Alcoholics Anonymous meeting, a man told his mentor, Timothy McGee, that he had started drinking again because he was so stressed out about his company being acquired. McGee bought stock in that company. Has McGee done anything wrong legally? Ethically?

DISCUSSION QUESTIONS

1. Omnicare was a company that sold medication to nursing homes. When it made these sales, it often received rebates from drug companies. In its registration statement under the 1933 Act, the company stated that the rebates were legal. Ultimately, however, some states sued drug companies for making these payments, alleging that they were really illegal bribes. The drug companies then stopped making the payments. Investors sued Omnicare on the grounds that its statement in the registration statement was false and material. Was Omnicare liable under §11 of the 1933 Act?

2. Federal security laws are based on the assumption that, as long as the issuer provides adequate disclosure, investors are knowledgeable enough to assess the quality of a stock. Many states take a different approach—they refuse to permit the sale of securities that they deem to be of poor quality. Should securities laws protect investors in this way?

3. Securities laws are a balancing act between companies' desire to raise money and investors' need for protection. Congress recently changed Rule 506 to permit public advertising to accredited investors. Just because accredited investors are financially secure, does that mean they have investment savvy? (Think doctors and lawyers.) Should Congress have made this change? Furthermore, the income and net worth limits for accredited investors were established in 1982. Should they be increased?

4. The SEC believes that anyone in possession of material, nonpublic information about a company should be required to disclose it before trading on the stock of that enterprise. Instead, the courts have developed a more complex set of rules. Do you agree with the SEC or the courts on this issue?

5. Is Regulation Crowdfunding a good idea? Does it provide enough protection to investors?

CHAPTER 38

ANTITRUST

On his way into Sleepy Time to buy a mattress, Sean noticed that Girl Scout Troop 1474 was selling cookies. There was nothing he liked more than Thin Mint cookies crushed into vanilla ice cream, and $3 a box seemed like a reasonable price. But he decided to buy the mattress first. After much lying down on pocketed coils, pillowtops, and memory foam, he ultimately decided on a Tempur-Pedic made out of visco elastic, temperature-sensitive material. Wouldn't that be bliss?

If they found out I'd reduced the price, they'd yank those mattresses out of my store so fast, even the dust mites couldn't keep up.

But Sean was no fool. He knew that the economy was weak and retail stores were eager for customers. He figured he could negotiate a handsome discount from the list price of $2,399. But when he asked Gavin, the sales guy, what his best price was, Gavin just shrugged, a hangdog expression on his face. "I'm on commission and would love to sell you a mattress, but Tempur-Pedic won't let us offer any discounts. If they found out I'd reduced the price, they'd yank those mattresses out of my store so fast, even the dust mites couldn't keep up. The price is $2,399 or nothing." He lowered his voice. "In the old days, manufacturers couldn't do that, but our company lawyer made this big deal about how the Supreme Court has changed antitrust law and made this kind of price-fixing legal. They call it 'resale price maintenance' or something like that. Anyway, our hands are tied."

That was a stiff price for a soft mattress, so Sean decided he would shop around. By now he was hungry and eager for some Girl Scout cookies. But Troop 1474 had gone home. It seemed as if this was just not his day.

His mood lifted, though, when he stopped to pick up Chinese takeout and saw a different Girl Scout troop selling cookies. That was until he noticed the price was $4 a box. "Why the price gouging?" he demanded grouchily. One of the girls spoke up reluctantly, "When I was studying for my Law and Order badge, I found out it's a violation of antitrust law for Girl Scout councils to get together and agree on the prices their troops will charge. Each council has to decide its own price. We hear that Cambridge is charging $3, but in Winchester, it's $4."

Gavin the sales guy says that manufacturers can set the price for mattresses, but the Girl Scouts claim their councils are not permitted to agree on the cost of a box of cookies. Who is right? Are there different laws for cookies and mattresses?

Both the Girl Scouts and Gavin are correct in their interpretation of the law. They are each talking about a different type of price-fixing. The sale of the mattresses involves vertical price-fixing, so called because the manufacturer and the store are at different stages of the production process. Thus, they do not compete against each other, and that type of price-fixing is generally legal. No matter how hard Sean looks, he is not likely to find a cheaper price on the mattress he wants. But horizontal price-fixing—which involves agreements among competitors—is automatically illegal. The Girl Scout councils are competitors, so they are prohibited from agreeing among themselves what price they all will charge. If the consumer wants to save $1 a box on cookies, all he has to do is drive from Winchester to Cambridge.

Competition is an essential element of the American economic system. Antitrust laws are the rules that govern that competition. As we will see in this chapter, these laws affect many aspects of our lives—both as consumers and as businesspeople.

38-1 OVERVIEW OF ANTITRUST LAWS

38-1a History

Throughout much of the nineteenth century, competition in America was largely a local affair. The country was so big and transportation so poor that companies primarily competed in small local markets. State laws, rather than national statutes, regulated competition.

By the second half of the nineteenth century, four railroad lines crossed the continent from coast to coast. For the first time, national markets were a real possibility. John D. Rockefeller saw the potential. In 1859, Edwin L. Drake, a retired railroad conductor, drilled the first commercially successful oil well in the United States. Three years later, when the 23-year-old Rockefeller entered the scene, the oil industry was full of producers too small to benefit from economies of scale. Production was inefficient, and prices varied dramatically in different parts of the country.

Rockefeller set out to reorganize the industry. He began by buying refineries, first in Cleveland and then in other cities. He and his partners spread into all segments of the oil industry—buying oil fields, building pipelines, and establishing an efficient marketing system. To unify the management of these companies, they transferred their stock to the Standard Oil Trust. By 1870, Rockefeller had achieved his goal—the Standard Oil Trust controlled virtually all the oil in the country, from producer to consumer. At age 31, Rockefeller was the wealthiest person in the *world*.

Some of Rockefeller's tactics were controversial. When a competitor tried to build an oil pipeline, Rockefeller used every weapon short of violence to stop it. He planted stories in the press suggesting the pipes would leak and ruin nearby fields. He flooded local builders with orders for tank cars so no workers would be available to build the pipeline. When the pipeline was finished, he refused to allow his oil to flow through it. These tactics were frightening, especially in an industry as important as oil. What if Rockefeller decided to raise prices unfairly? Or cut off oil altogether? Newspapers began to attack him ferociously.

Big Is Bad

Legislators worried that large companies might be able to control other industries as well. **To prevent extreme concentrations of economic power, Congress passed the Sherman Act in 1890**. It was one of the first national laws designed to regulate competition. Because this statute was aimed at the Standard Oil Trust and other similar organizations, it was termed antitrust legislation. In 1892, the Ohio Supreme Court dissolved the Standard Oil Trust, which was replaced by the Standard Oil Co. But the government was not satisfied until a spring day in 1911, when U.S. Supreme Court Chief Justice Edward White quietly read aloud from the bench his dramatic 20,000-word opinion ordering the breakup of Standard Oil.[1] The 33 companies that made up Standard Oil were forced to compete as separate businesses. Today, descendants of Standard Oil include Atlantic Richfield, Chevron, Exxon-Mobil, Pennzoil, Sunoco, and parts of British Petroleum (BP). Imagine what kind of giant they would be if still united.

For the first 70 or so years after the passage of the Sherman Act, most scholars and judges took the view that large concentrations of economic power were suspect, even if they had no obvious impact on competition itself. **Big was bad—it meant too much economic and political power.** As Senator John Sherman, sponsor of the Sherman Act, put it, a nation that "would not submit to an emperor should not submit to an autocrat of trade." Fragmented, competitive markets were desirable in and of themselves. Standard Oil should not control the oil markets even if the company was very efficient and had gained control by completely acceptable methods.

Protecting Competition

Beginning in the 1960s and 1970s, however, **a group of influential economists and lawyers at the University of Chicago began to argue that the goal of antitrust enforcement should be efficiency.** Let a company grow as large as it likes, provided that this growth is based on a superior product or lower costs, not ruthless tactics. Insist on a clean fight, but do not handicap large successful companies to help weaker competitors. Some companies will thrive, others will die, but in either case, the consumer will come out ahead. Adherents of the **Chicago School** argued further that the *market* should decide the most efficient size for each industry. In some cases, such as automobiles or aircrafts, the most efficient size might be very large indeed. **Under traditional antitrust analysis, courts often asked, "Has a competitor been harmed?" The Chicago School suggests that courts should ask instead, "Has *competition* been harmed?"**

Chicago School
A group of economists and lawyers at the University of Chicago who argued that the goal of antitrust enforcement should be efficiency

At the turn of the twentieth century, President Theodore Roosevelt personally plotted the breakup of Standard Oil. (As one of Rockefeller's compatriots said of Roosevelt, "We bought the son of a bitch, and then he didn't stay bought.") At the turn of the twenty-first century, two descendants of Standard Oil—Exxon and Mobil—announced their intention to merge. This time, not one politician grabbed a microphone to object to the recombination. Where once size alone was cause for concern, now regulators believe that a certain bulk may be necessary if American companies are to compete in the intense global economy.

Protecting Consumers

Antitrust policy, however, has continued to evolve. Adherents of the so-called **Post Chicago School** believe that competition alone may not be enough to protect consumers. For example, an industry with a large number of competitors may foster collusion, not competition. Or, activities that appear consumer-friendly, such as giving away a product for free, may in the long run harm consumers. (Microsoft's decision to give away its internet browser for free seemed to benefit consumers, but the Department of Justice (DOJ) alleged that this giveaway caused harm over the long run by driving competitors out of business.) **Now, when deciding whether to take action, federal trustbusters often focus directly on consumers, asking two questions:**

1. Will this action cause consumers to pay higher prices?
2. Are the higher prices sustainable in the face of existing competition?

[1]Standard Oil Company of New Jersey v. United States, 221 U.S. 1 (S. Ct. 1911).

As you read the cases in this chapter, think about which factors the court considers important: size, competition, or the impact on consumers.

38-1b Provisions of the Antitrust Laws

The major provisions of the antitrust laws are:

- Section 1 of the Sherman Act prohibits all agreements "in restraint of trade."
- Section 2 of the Sherman Act bans "monopolization"—the wrongful acquisition or maintenance of a monopoly.
- The Clayton Act prohibits anticompetitive mergers, tying arrangements, and exclusive dealing agreements.
- The Robinson-Patman Act bans price discrimination that reduces competition.

All agreements restrain trade: If I agree to sell my land to you, I cannot then also sell it to Theo. **Antitrust laws prohibit only *unreasonable* restraints of trade.**

Violations of the antitrust laws are divided into two categories: *per se* and rule of reason. As the name implies, ***per se* violations** are automatic. Defendants charged with this type of violation cannot defend themselves by saying, "But the impact wasn't so bad" or "No one was hurt." The court will not listen to excuses, and the defendants are subject to both criminal and civil penalties.

***Per se* violation**
An automatic breach of antitrust laws

Rule of reason violation
An action that breaches antitrust laws only if it has an anticompetitive impact

Rule of reason violations, on the other hand, are illegal only if they have an anticompetitive impact. A group of consumers sued television networks, alleging that they had violated antitrust laws by refusing to allow consumers to buy just a few channels (cheaply) rather than an expensive package of many channels. The consumers argued that this practice was illegal tying under the Clayton Act. However, the court dismissed their claim because the consumers had shown only that they were harmed, not that competition had been hurt.[2]

Although rule of reason violators may be subject to civil penalties or private lawsuits, traditionally the DOJ has not sought criminal penalties against them.[3]

Both the DOJ and the Federal Trade Commission (FTC) have authority to enforce the antitrust laws. However, only the DOJ can bring criminal proceedings; the FTC is limited to civil injunctions and other administrative remedies. **In addition to the government, anyone injured by an antitrust violation has the right to sue for treble (i.e., triple) damages.** The United States is unusual in this regard—in most other countries, only the government is able to sue antitrust violators.

Another important point before we begin our discussion of particular antitrust provisions: **Any conduct *overseas* that has an anticompetitive impact in the United States is a violation of U.S. law** provided that (1) the foreign actor intended to affect the U.S. market and (2) the foreign conduct has a direct and substantial effect on the U.S. market. A Japanese businessman and nine Japanese companies pleaded guilty to fixing the price of auto parts sold in the United States.

In developing a competitive strategy, managers typically consider two different approaches:

1. Cooperative strategies that allow companies to work together to their mutual advantage or
2. Aggressive strategies designed to create an advantage over competitors.

We look now at the legality of these strategies under antitrust law.

---

[2]Brantley v. NBC Universal, Inc., 675 F.3d 1192 (9th Cir. 2012).

[3]For a criminal conviction under the antitrust laws, the government must prove intent, which is difficult to do in a rule of reason violation. United States v. United States Gypsum Co., 438 U.S. 422 (S. Ct. 1978).

38-2 COOPERATIVE STRATEGIES

Three types of cooperative strategies are potentially illegal:

1. **Horizontal agreements** among competitors. An agreement among the Girl Scout councils in the opening scenario would be horizontal.
2. **Vertical agreements** among participants at different stages of the production process. The agreement in the opening scenario between a mattress manufacturer and Sleepy Time is vertical.
3. **Mergers and joint ventures** among competitors. Here, companies go beyond simple agreements to combine forces more permanently.

Horizontal agreement
An agreement among competitors

Vertical agreement
An agreement among participants operating at different stages of the production process

The following table lists the cooperative strategies that will be discussed in this chapter:

Horizontal Strategies	Vertical Strategies	Mergers
Market division	Reciprocal dealing	Horizontal mergers
Price-fixing	Price discrimination	Vertical mergers
Bid-rigging		Joint ventures
Refusal to deal		

38-2a Horizontal Cooperative Strategies

Although the term "cooperative strategies" *sounds* benign, these tactics can be harmful to competition. Indeed, many horizontal cooperative strategies are *per se* violations of the law and can lead to prison terms, heavy fines, and expensive lawsuits with customers and competitors.

Market Division

Any effort by a group of competitors to divide its market is a *per se* violation of §1 of the Sherman Act. Illegal arrangements include agreements to allocate customers, territory, or products. For example, these business schools would be in violation if:

- Georgetown agreed to accept only men and, in return, George Washington would take only women;[4]
- Stanford agreed to accept only students from west of the Mississippi, leaving the east to Yale; or
- Northwestern agreed not to provide courses in entrepreneurship, while the University of Chicago eliminated its international offerings.

Price-Fixing and Bid-Rigging

When competitors agree on the prices at which they will buy or sell products or services, their price-fixing is a *per se* violation of §1 of the Sherman Act. Also a *per se* violation are bid-rigging and any other agreements about the terms of sale, such as the interest rate that buyers are

[4]This, of course, does not mean that all single-sex schools are violating the antitrust laws. They are in violation only if their admissions policy results from an agreement with competitors.

charged. In bid-rigging, competitors eliminate price competition by agreeing on who will submit the lowest bid.

But what if competitors set a *reasonable* price? The Supreme Court rejected this justification, observing that "the reasonable price fixed today may through economic and business changes become the unreasonable price of tomorrow."[5]

The Supreme Court has referred to this type of collusion as "the supreme evil of antitrust," and it has been illegal for the better part of a century.[6] But it never seems to go away. Here are some examples:

- MasterCard, Visa, JPMorgan Chase, and Bank of America paid a $6 billion fine for having fixed the prices they charged merchants for processing credit and debit card payments.
- Using a computer to analyze the bids that schools received on their milk contracts, the Florida attorney general uncovered a pervasive price-fixing scheme. Forty-three companies were convicted or pleaded guilty; two dozen individuals went to prison. Companies paid fines in excess of $90 million.
- Colleges were concerned about the cost of their athletic programs. In particular, the cost of the coaching staffs seemed out of control. In response, NCAA schools (i.e., members of the National Collegiate Athletic Association) agreed to cap the salaries of assistant coaches. But a court blew the whistle, finding that the NCAA had engaged in illegal price-fixing. A jury awarded the coaches $66 million.
- Two Chinese companies paid a fine of $162 million for fixing the price of Vitamin C. The U.S. court did not accept the defense that their government made them do it.

CORBIS/AGE Fotostock

Schools pay more for milk if their suppliers fix prices.

People who engage in price-fixing sometimes do so as a way of fighting back against a powerful buyer. But no matter how price fixers rationalize what they have done, it is still illegal.

United States v. Apple Inc.

791 F.3d 290
United States Court of Appeals for the Second Circuit, 2015

Facts: Amazon's ebook reader, the Kindle, not only changed how people bought and read books, it lowered prices dramatically.[7] Amazon charged $9.99 for every ebook, no matter how much its print version cost. On many of the books it sold, Amazon lost money because it paid the publisher more than it charged customers. It did so to create a market for the Kindle.

But publishers were unhappy because the $9.99 ebook price made it harder to sell print books. Why would anyone pay $30 for a hardcover? Also, publishers worried (with reason) that cheap ebooks threatened the viability of the brick-and-mortar stores in which books were displayed and sold. But Amazon had such market power, it was able to ignore the individual publisher's pleas to raise prices.

---

5 United States v. Trenton Potteries Co., 273 U.S. 392 (S.Ct. 1927).

6 Verizon Communs., Inc. v. Trinko, LLP, 540 U.S. 398 (S. Ct. 2004).

7 This case involves trade books, which are novels and general interest nonfiction, not texts or reference books.

On to this unhappy scene came Apple, about to launch its first iPad. To ensure the iPad's success, Apple needed to be able to offer books in its iBookstore. Apple was not, however, willing to sell books below cost as Amazon did. But why would anyone buy from iBookstore if its books cost more than Amazon's?

To solve this problem, Apple approached the six major U.S. publishers with a proposal: They would all agree on a higher ebook price for the iBookstore, but also insist that Amazon charge the same higher price.[8] Apple would benefit by obtaining titles for its iBookstore, while also ensuring that competition with Amazon was based on technology (iPad versus Kindle), which Apple thought it could win, rather than on price, where Amazon had the advantage.

All of the publishers except Random House agreed to Apple's plan.[9] They met, emailed, and spoke on the phone with Apple and each other hundreds of times to negotiate the precise terms of the deal—in particular, the prices that would be charged for each category of books. All these discussions were hardly secret—*The Wall Street Journal* reported on them. Finally, a deal was reached.

The publishers then each individually informed Amazon of the new pricing structure. Amazon at first resisted but ultimately agreed to the prices that the publishers and Apple had negotiated. It then sent a letter of complaint to the FTC. As a result of the Apple agreement, prices of ebooks and hardcover books rose substantially while the number of ebooks sold and the amount publishers received per ebook both decreased.

The FTC and some states filed suit against Apple and the five publishers (Publisher Defendants), alleging illegal price-fixing in violation of §1 of the Sherman Act. The five publishers admitted guilt and settled their cases, but Apple went to trial. The trial court found that Apple had violated §1 of the Sherman Act. Apple appealed.

Issue: ***Did Apple engage in illegal price-fixing?***

Excerpts from Judge Livingston's Decision: Apple's basic argument is that its Contracts with the Publisher Defendants provide only ambiguous evidence of a §1 conspiracy.

We disagree. Apple's benign portrayal of its Contracts with the Publisher Defendants is not persuasive—not because those Contracts were independently unlawful, but because, in context, they provide strong evidence that Apple consciously orchestrated a conspiracy among the Publisher Defendants. Apple understood that its proposed Contracts were attractive to the Publisher Defendants *only* if they collectively shifted their relationships with Amazon—which Apple knew would result in higher consumer-facing ebook prices.

In addition to these Contracts, ample additional evidence established both that the Publisher Defendants' [negotiation] with Amazon was the result of express collusion among them and that Apple consciously played a key role in organizing that collusion. Apple was more than an innocent bystander. Apple offered each Big Six publisher a proposed Contract that would be attractive only if the publishers acted collectively.

That the Publisher Defendants were in constant communication regarding their negotiations with both Apple and Amazon can hardly be disputed. Indeed, Apple never seriously argues that the Publisher Defendants were not acting in concert.

From the outset, [Apple] told the publishers that [it] would launch its iBookstore only if a sufficient number of them agreed to participate and that each publisher would receive identical terms. Later on, [Apple] kept the publishers updated about how many of their peers signed Apple's Contracts, and reminded them that it was offering the best chance for publishers to challenge the $9.99 price point before it became cemented in consumer expectations. When time ran short, Apple coordinated phone calls between the publishers who had agreed and those who remained on the fence.

Apple's conspiracy continued even past the signing of its agreements. Apple stayed abreast of the Publisher Defendants' progress as they set coordinated deadlines with Amazon and shared information with one another during negotiations.

The question is whether the vertical organizer of a horizontal conspiracy designed to raise prices has agreed to a restraint that is any less anticompetitive than its co-conspirators, and can therefore escape *per se* liability. We think not. In other words, the Publisher Defendants took by collusion what they could not win by competition. A coordinated effort to raise prices across the relevant market was present in every chapter of this story.

Because we conclude that Apple violated §1 of the Sherman Act by orchestrating a horizontal conspiracy among the Publisher Defendants to raise ebook prices, the judgment of the district court is AFFIRMED.

---

[8]The publishers were Hachette, HarperCollins, Macmillan, Penguin Group, Random House, and Simon & Schuster.

[9]Ultimately, Random House also joined the agreement when Apple refused to allow it to sell its own app.

In this case, the DOJ found hard evidence of an illegal agreement. But what if there is only *circumstantial* evidence? Suppose competitors just happen to charge the same prices. You may have noticed that airlines tend to charge the same fares over the same routes. If competitors act in concert but without an explicit agreement, their behavior is called **conscious parallelism. This behavior is legal unless there is additional evidence of wrongdoing**, such as a high level of communication among firms. In general, it is a bad idea for competitors to communicate with each other, especially about terms of sale.

Conscious parallelism
When competitors who do not have an explicit agreement nonetheless all make the same competitive decisions

Refusals to Deal

Every company generally has the right to decide with whom it will or will not do business. **However, a refusal to deal is a rule of reason violation of the Sherman Act, and illegal if it harms competition.** In a refusal to deal, a group of competitors boycotts a buyer, supplier, or even another competitor. A group of clothing manufacturers agreed that they would not sell apparel to retailers who also bought from style pirates—companies that copied the manufacturers' designs. The Supreme Court held that this was an illegal refusal to deal because it was harming competition.[10]

EXAMStrategy

Question: Lawyers who were paid by the government to represent poor clients in Washington, D.C., agreed among themselves not to accept any new cases until their fees were raised to the level they had agreed upon. Have the lawyers violated the Sherman Act? If so, what kind of violation is it?

Strategy: This is a trick question because the lawyers committed not one, but two violations of the Sherman Act. Remember, too, that there are two types of Sherman Act violations—rule of reason and *per se*.

Result: First, the attorneys were fixing prices—they agreed together on their fees. Price-fixing is a *per se* violation and therefore automatically illegal. In addition, they engaged in a refusal to deal. This is a rule of reason violation, which is illegal only if it harms competition.

38-2b Vertical Cooperative Strategies

Vertical cooperative strategies are agreements among participants at different stages of the production process.

Reciprocal Dealing Agreements

Under a reciprocal dealing agreement, a buyer refuses to purchase goods from a supplier unless the supplier also purchases items from the buyer. Imagine that you are in the business of processing beets into sugar. During this process, it is easy to separate the seeds, which can then be used to grow more beets. Why not suggest to your beet suppliers that they buy their seeds from you? Why not further suggest that if they refuse, you will switch suppliers?[11]

---

[10] Fashion Originators' Guild of America, Inc. v. Federal Trade Commission, 312 U.S. 457 (S. Ct. 1941).
[11] See Betaseed, Inc. v. U & I, Inc., 681 F.2d 1203 (9th Cir. 1982).

You are proposing a reciprocal dealing agreement. In the past, such arrangements were common. Many major corporations even kept records of purchases, sales, and "balance of trade" with other companies. Although these arrangements might have made business sense, the government took the view that they were also rule of reason violations of the Sherman Act; that is, they were illegal if they had an anticompetitive effect. The government brought suit against several companies, including a beet processor. It also halted a number of mergers that might have resulted in internal reciprocal arrangements. In recent years, however, the government has brought few of these cases. **Reciprocal dealing agreements today are likely to be a problem only if they foreclose a significant share of the market and if the participants agree not to buy from others.**

Price Discrimination

Under the Robinson-Patman Act (RPA), it is illegal to charge different prices to different purchasers if:

- The items are the same and
- The price discrimination lessens competition.

However, it is legal to charge a lower price to a particular buyer if:

- The costs of serving this buyer are lower or
- The seller is simply meeting competition.

Congress passed the RPA in 1936 to prevent large chains from driving small, local stores out of business. Owners of these mom and pop stores complained that the large chains could sell goods cheaper because suppliers charged them less. As a result of the RPA, managers who would otherwise like to develop different pricing strategies for specific customers or regions may hesitate to do so for fear of violating this statute. In reality, however, they have little to fear.

Under the RPA, a plaintiff must prove that price discrimination occurred and that it lessened competition. It is perfectly permissible, for example, for a supplier to sell at a different price to its Texas and California distributors, or to its healthcare and educational distributors, as long as the distributors are not in competition with one another.

The RPA also expressly permits price variations that are based on differences in cost. Thus, Kosmo's Kitchen would be perfectly within its legal rights to sell its frozen enchiladas to Giant at a lower price than to Corner Grocery if Kosmo's costs are lower to do so. Giant often buys shipments the size of railroad containers that cost less to deliver than smaller boxes.

The courts have offered little encouragement to RPA cases. The Supreme Court has, for example, set a high bar for obtaining damages. Chrysler Motors charged some dealerships in Birmingham, Alabama more for cars than others. Unable to compete, the Payne dealership went out of business. But, the Supreme Court held that, to recover damages, Payne had to show that competitors (1) were able to buy at a lower cost; (2) these competitors passed their savings on to customers; and, (3) as a result, Payne lost profits.[12] These are difficult facts to prove. In a recent five-year period, fewer than 5 percent of private plaintiffs won their RPA cases.[13]

In the following case, everyone agreed that the manufacturers were charging different prices to various competitors. But were they violating the RPA?

---

12 J. Truett Payne Co., Inc. v. Chrysler Motors Corp., 451 U.S. 557 (S. Ct. 1981).

13 Ryan Luchs, Tansev Geylani, Anthony Dukes, and Kannan Srinivasan, "The End of the Robinson-Patman Act? Evidence from Legal Case Data," *Management Science*, Vol. 56, No. 12, December 2010, pp. 2123–2133.

Coalition for a Level Playing Field, L.L.C. v. Autozone, Inc.

737 F. Supp. 2d 194
United States District Court for the Southern District of New York, 2010

Facts: Auto parts manufacturers used two distribution channels: (1) a two-step process in which they sold to big box stores, such as Walmart, Sam's Club, and AutoZone, who then sold the parts to end users, and (2) a three-step process in which they sold to warehouse distributors (WDs), who then sold to mom and pop auto parts stores (also called jobbers), who sold to end users.

The WDs and jobbers alleged that the manufacturers and big box stores were violating the Robinson-Patman Act because the manufacturers charged the WDs the official list price, while granting all sorts of discounts to the big box stores, such as volume discounts and allowances for obsolete merchandise. AutoZone only paid for a part once the item sold, while plaintiffs were required to pay within 30 days of receipt. According to the plaintiffs, manufacturers sold to the defendants below their cost of production—at a price 40 to 50 percent less than they charged plaintiffs.

The defendants filed a motion to dismiss.

Issue: ***Did the manufacturers and big box stores violate the Robinson-Patman Act?***

Excerpts from Judge Holwell's Decision: Congress enacted the Robinson-Patman Act because of its concern that large chain stores were exercising economic power to obtain anticompetitive discounts on large purchases of goods. However, with the RPA, Congress did not intend to outlaw price differences that result from or further the forces of competition. Despite its seemingly broad coverage, it would be a mistake to assume that [the RPA] regulates all transactions that somehow involve a price differential.

First, courts have held that a seller may charge a buyer reduced prices if the reduced prices reflect a bona fide functional discount—in essence, a set-off for the value of services the purchaser performs for the seller. Second, courts have held that a seller is not obligated to charge the same prices for a commodity if its sales contracts with different buyers contain materially different terms. Thus, courts have long held that a seller may charge different prices for goods sold under long-term contracts than for those sold on the spot market, for the same reason a seat on the 6:00 a.m. flight from Chicago to New York is not the same as a seat on the 5:00 p.m. flight.

The nub of the complaint in this action is that the retailer defendants take a number of discounts pursuant to their vendor agreements with the parts manufacturers, and that these discounts in fact are a subterfuge for illegal price discrimination. In support of this theory, the complaint cites a large amount of pricing data, including examples of parts where the retailer defendants' retail prices are lower than plaintiffs' wholesale prices. But while the complaint plausibly alleges differentials, it contains virtually no allegations as to whether those differentials are justified.

It is common ground that compared to WDs and jobbers, the retailer defendants pay lower wholesale prices, operate in a different distribution chain, and provide a different mix of distribution, warehousing, marketing, and promotional services to the parts manufacturers. A plausible inference to draw from these differences is that manufacturers and buyers engage in hard negotiation over all aspects of their commercial relationship, and the retailer defendants offer the manufacturers a mix of services that is more valuable than that offered by traditional WDs and jobbers.

[T]he complaint here alleges conduct (price differentials) which becomes illegal only if (i) discounts are given for services that are not being performed at all, or (ii) the amount of discounts greatly exceeds the value of the services provided by the retailer defendants. There are no factual allegations, however, tending to show that either of these conditions is satisfied.

Defendants' motion to dismiss for failure to state a claim is granted.

38-2c Mergers and Joint Ventures

The Clayton Act prohibits mergers that are anticompetitive. Under the Hart-Scott-Rodino amendment to the Clayton Act, companies with substantial assets must notify the FTC *before* consummating a merger. This notification gives the government an opportunity to prevent a merger ahead of time rather than trying to untangle one after the fact.

Horizontal versus Vertical Mergers

Traditionally the government has been more aggressive at challenging horizontal than vertical mergers because horizontal combinations are more likely to reduce competition and raise prices. Thus, the government prevented AT&T from acquiring another cellular company, T-Mobile, because of concerns that such a merger would cause cell phone rates to rise.

Vertical mergers can also be anticompetitive, especially if they reduce entry into a market by locking up an important supplier or a top distributor. But often the participants are better able to show some advantage to consumers. The government allowed cable company Comcast to acquire content provider NBC Universal, on the condition that Comcast allowed other competitors to buy content from NBC. Comcast made the case that this merger would enable it to provide consumers with more programming choices.

It used to be that, in evaluating a horizontal merger, the government operated on the theory that a large market share was bad, of and in itself. As the following Landmark Case shows, however, the government and the courts now base their decision on how the merger will affect competition, consumers, and prices. If barriers to entry are low and competition is keen, the size of the market share is not as important because new competitors can enter the market and prevent prices from rising.

Landmark Case

United States v. Waste Management, Inc.

743 F.2d 976
United States Court of Appeals for the Second Circuit, 1984

Facts: Waste Management, Inc., (WMI) acquired Texas Industrial Disposal, Inc. (TIDI). Both companies were in the trash collection business. In Dallas, their combined market share was 48.8 percent. The trial court held that the merger was illegal and ordered WMI to divest itself of TIDI.

Issue: ***Did WMI violate the Clayton Act by acquiring TIDI?***

Excerpts from Judge Winter's Decision: A post-merger market share of 48.8 percent is sufficient to establish *prima facie* illegality under *United States v. Philadelphia National Bank* and its progeny. That decision held that large market shares are a convenient proxy for appraising the danger of monopoly power resulting from a horizontal merger. Under its rationale, a merger resulting in a large market share is presumptively illegal, rebuttable only by a demonstration that the merger will not have anticompetitive effects.

[In the present case, the *Philadelphia National Bank*] presumption is rebutted by the fact that competitors can enter the Dallas waste hauling market with such ease. WMI argues that it is unable to raise prices over the competitive level because new firms would quickly enter the market and undercut them. A person wanting to start in the trash collection business can acquire a truck, a few containers, drive the truck himself, and operate out of his home. A great deal depends on the individual's personal initiative, and whether he has the desire and energy to perform a high quality of service. If he measures up well by these standards, he can compete successfully with any other company for a portion of the trade, even though a small portion. Over the last 10 years or so, a number of companies have started in the commercial trash collection business.

We conclude that the 48.8 percent market share attributed to WMI does not accurately reflect future market power. Since that power is in fact insubstantial, the merger does not, therefore, substantially lessen competition in the relevant market and does not violate the [Clayton Act].

Here are other examples of mergers that the government has reviewed:

- Office supplies:
  - First, the FTC blocked the horizontal merger of office supply giants Staples, Inc., and Office Depot although the two companies controlled only 4 percent of the national market for office supplies. But rather than national market share, the FTC focused instead on the companies' ability to control prices *locally*. The agency found that when both stores operated in the same market, prices were significantly lower than when only one store was present. In the FTC's view, if the two stores combined, they would have had enough power in local markets to raise prices and harm consumers.
  - Fifteen years later, the FTC permitted a horizontal merger between Office Depot and OfficeMax because the office supply industry was facing significant competition from big box stores like Walmart and online businesses like Amazon. The FTC no longer feared that a merger between dedicated office supply stores would harm consumers or raise prices.
  - Then, two years after that, the FTC blocked a merger between Staples and Office Depot, on the grounds that it would hurt large buyers who are unlikely to order office supplies from Amazon.
- Healthcare:
  - The FTC allowed a horizontal merger of two of the three largest online pharmacies: Express Scripts and Medco. This combination had a 40 percent market share. But the government decided that these online pharmacies faced substantial competition from health insurance plans that provided their own in-house pharmacies.
  - In a three-week period, two different courts blocked mergers of health insurance companies—one between Anthem and Cigna, another between Aetna and Humana. These two mergers would have reduced the number of national health insurance companies from five to three. The courts were concerned that these mergers would lead to higher prices to consumers and other anticompetitive effects.[14]

Joint Ventures

A joint venture is a partnership for a limited purpose—the companies do not combine permanently, they simply work together on a specific project. The government will usually permit a joint venture, even between competitors with significant market power. The FTC approved, over strenuous objections from competitors, a joint venture between General Motors and Toyota to produce cars.

38-3 AGGRESSIVE STRATEGIES

The goal of an aggressive strategy is to gain an advantage over competitors.

38-3a Monopolization

Aggressive competition is beneficial for consumers—up until the moment a company develops enough power to control a market. **Under §2 of the Sherman Act, it is illegal to monopolize or attempt to monopolize a market**. To monopolize means to acquire or maintain

[14]United States v. Aetna Inc., 2017 U.S. Dist. LEXIS 8490 (D.D.C. 2017) and United States v. Anthem, Inc., 2017 U.S. Dist. LEXIS 20707 (D.D.C. 2017).

a monopoly in the wrong way. *Having* a monopoly is legal unless it is *gained* or *maintained* through improper conduct.

To determine if a defendant has illegally monopolized, we must ask three questions:

1. **What is the market?** Without knowing the market, it is impossible to determine if someone is controlling it.
2. **Does the company control the market?** Without control, there is no monopoly.
3. **How did the company acquire or maintain its control?** Monopolization is illegal only if gained or maintained in the wrong way.

What Is the Market?

This question is not as easy to answer as it sounds. **The short answer is that if buyers view two products as close substitutes, then the items are in the same market.** The longer answer is that every product actually has two markets. The **product market** consists of other items that a purchaser could buy; the **geographic market** is other areas where a purchase could be made.

Product market
Items that compete against one another for purchase

Geographic market
Areas where the same purchase can be made

Imagine that your company sells soft drinks in Smallville. These drinks have unusual food flavors—steak and cheese, among others. You are the only company in that area that sells food-flavored soft drinks, so, by definition, you control 100 percent of the market. But is that the *relevant* market? Perhaps the relevant market is flavored drinks or soft drinks or all beverages. **To determine the relevant product market, economists ask: How high can your prices rise before your buyers will switch to a different product?** (This concept is called **cross-elasticity of demand**.) If a price increase causes many of your customers to buy Coke instead, it is clear you are part of a larger market. Moreover, if changes in the prices of other drinks affect *your* sales, your products and theirs are probably close competitors. However, if you could triple your price and still hold on to many of your customers, then you might well be in your own market. **Likewise, the relevant geographic market is the area where buyers will go to buy your drink.** Thus, if you raise your prices in Smallville and then many of your customers begin buying your drinks at a lower price in Metropolis, both cities are in the same geographic market.

Cross-elasticity of demand
How high can prices rise before buyers switch to a different product?

EXAMStrategy

Question: Ticketmaster sells tickets online to sports and entertainment events. RMG sued Ticketmaster, alleging that it was engaged in an illegal effort to monopolize national ticket sales. What was the relevant market?

Strategy: RMG had to define both a product market and a geographic market.

Result: If Ticketmaster raises the prices for NFL tickets in Miami, customers will probably not choose instead to buy seats to a Taylor Swift concert in Oakland, CA. Therefore, national ticket sales are not the relevant market. Rather, the markets are small and focused. The court dismissed RMG's monopolization claim because the company had defined the wrong market.[15]

[15] Ticketmaster L.L.C. v. RMG Techs., Inc., 536 F. Supp. 2d 1191 (C.D. Cal. 2008).

Does the Company Control the Market?

Typically, courts will find that a company does not control a market unless it has:

- At least a 50 percent market share and
- The long-term ability to exclude competitors or raise prices.

A court ruled that a movie theater chain with a 93 percent share of the box office in Las Vegas did not have a monopoly because its market share had decreased to 75 percent within three years. This decline indicated that the company did not control the market.[16] Alternatively, a court found that Microsoft did have a monopoly in the market for PC operating systems because it could substantially raise its prices without losing business.[17]

How Did the Company Acquire or Maintain Its Control?

Possessing a monopoly is not necessarily illegal; using improper conduct to acquire or maintain one is. If the law prohibited the mere possession of a monopoly, it might discourage companies from producing excellent products or offering low prices. Anyone who can produce a better product cheaper is entitled to a monopoly. In your case, you have very cleverly developed a secret method for adding flavors to carbonated water. You also have an efficient factory and highly trained workers, so you can sell your drinks for 50¢ a bottle less than your competitors. If, in fact, you do have a monopoly, it is for all the right reasons. You have demonstrated exactly the kind of innovative, efficient behavior that benefits consumers. If you were sued for a violation of the antitrust laws, you would win.

Some companies use ruthless tactics to acquire or maintain a monopoly. **It is these "bad acts" that render a monopoly illegal**. One of Microsoft's bad acts was to include Internet Explorer in its Windows operating system while making it technically difficult for users to choose a non-Microsoft browser.

In the following case, a drug company took steps to extend its monopoly. Were these actions wrongful?

New York v. Actavis PLC

787 F.3d 638
United States Court of Appeals for the Second Circuit, 2015

Facts: Namenda IR is a drug used to treat Alzheimer's disease (a devastating form of dementia). "IR" stands for "instant release," meaning the drug has to be taken twice a day. Because Actavis had the patent on Namenda, it had the exclusive right to sell the drug for 20 years. As the end of the patent term neared, other companies developed generic alternatives. Actavis expected that, once these generics entered the market, it would keep only 30 percent of its annual $1.5 billion in sales. To protect its market, Actavis introduced a more convenient once-a-day pill, called Namenda XR ("extended release").

Once XR became available, the company adopted a "soft switch" strategy to convert patients to the newer pill: While cutting all advertising for IR, it marketed XR extensively, and charged a lower price for XR than IR.

But, determined to maintain its market share, Actavis moved to a "hard switch" strategy. A year before the generic IR became available, Actavis completely withdrew Namenda IR from the market, thereby forcing Alzheimer's patients to switch to XR. The nature of Alzheimer's disease makes patients especially vulnerable to changes in routine, which means that doctors and caregivers are reluctant to

[16] United States v. Syufy Enterprises, 903 F.2d 659 (9th Cir. 1990).
[17] United States v. Microsoft Corp., 84 F. Supp. 2d 9, 12 (D.D.C. 1999).

Did Actavis violate antitrust law when it implemented a strategy that harmed elderly, demented patients?

change a patient's medication. As a result, many patients would never switch back to IR even after the generic version became available.

Under most state laws, a pharmacist can substitute a generic pill for a name brand, if the two are exactly the same. But pharmacists would not have the right to supply the generic pill in place of XR because IR and XR were different. Actavis estimated that the hard switch would enable it to keep 80 to 100 percent of the drug market.

The state of New York filed suit seeking an injunction against Actavis, for violating §§1 and 2 of the Sherman Act. The trial court granted an injunction and Actavis appealed.

Issue: ***Did Actavis violate the Sherman Act?***

Excerpts from Judge Walker's Decision: To establish monopolization in violation of §2, a plaintiff must prove not only that the defendant possessed monopoly power in the relevant market, but that it willfully acquired or maintained that power as distinguished from growth or development as a consequence of a superior product, business acumen, or historic accident. To safeguard the incentive to innovate, the possession of monopoly power will not be found unlawful unless it is accompanied by an element of anticompetitive conduct.

Defendants' patents on Namenda IR indisputably grant them a legal monopoly in the U.S. market. [T]his case turns on whether Defendants willfully sought to maintain or attempted to maintain that monopoly in violation of §2. As a general rule, courts are properly very skeptical about claims that competition has been harmed by a dominant firm's product design changes. Product innovation generally benefits consumers and inflicts harm on competitors.

In this case, Defendants argue that withdrawing a product is not anticompetitive or exclusionary conduct, especially when the new product is superior to the old product. Certainly, neither product withdrawal nor product improvement alone is anticompetitive. But when a monopolist combines product withdrawal with some other conduct, the overall effect of which is to coerce consumers rather than persuade them on the merits, and to impede competition, actions are anticompetitive under the Sherman Act.

Defendants' hard switch crosses the line from persuasion to coercion and is anticompetitive. Had Defendants allowed Namenda IR to remain available until generic entry, doctors and Alzheimer's patients could have decided whether the benefits of switching to once-daily Namenda XR would outweigh the benefits of adhering to twice-daily therapy using less-expensive generic IR (or perhaps lower-priced Namenda IR). By removing Namenda IR from the market prior to generic IR entry, Defendants sought to deprive consumers of that choice. In this way, Defendants could avoid competing against lower-cost generics based on the merits of their redesigned drug by forcing Alzheimer's patients to take XR, with the knowledge that the [switch back] by patients from XR to generic IR [was] highly unlikely.

Because Defendants' forced switch through something other than competition on the merits has the effect of significantly reducing usage of rivals' products and hence protecting its own monopoly, it is anticompetitive.

[W]e AFFIRM the District Court's order.

Once the predator has the market to itself, it raises prices to make up lost profits—and more besides.

38-3b Predatory Pricing

Predatory pricing occurs when a company lowers its prices below cost to drive competitors out of business. Once the predator has the market to itself, it raises prices to make up lost profits—and more besides.

Recall that, under §2 of the Sherman Act, it is illegal "to monopolize" and also to "attempt to monopolize." Typically, the goal of a predatory pricing scheme is either to win control of a market or to maintain it. **To win a predatory pricing case, the plaintiff must prove three elements:**

1. The defendant is selling its products *below cost.*
2. The defendant *intends* that the plaintiff go out of business.
3. If the plaintiff does go out of business, the defendant will be able to earn sufficient profits to *recoup* its prior losses.

The classic example of predatory pricing is a large grocery store that comes into a small town offering exceptionally low prices subsidized by profits from its other branches. Once all the mom and pop corner groceries go out of business, MegaGrocery raises its prices to much higher levels.

The term "predatory pricing" *sounds* bad but, despite its name, courts generally are not as concerned about it now as they used to be. For one thing, consumers benefit from price wars, at least in the short run. **For another, the cases are hard to prove. Here is why:**

- **The defendant is selling its products below cost.** This rule sounds sensible, but what does "cost" mean? As you know from your economics courses, there are many different kinds of costs—total, average variable, marginal, to name a few. Under current law, any price below *average variable cost* is generally presumed to be predatory.[18] The rule may be easy to state, but, in real life, average variable cost is difficult to calculate. First, plaintiffs must obtain most of the data from the defendant. Even if a defendant has a good idea of what its average variable costs are, it will not willingly tell all in court. Moreover, many of the economic decisions about what items fit into which cost category are subjective. It is difficult for the plaintiff to prove that its subjective view is closer to the truth than the defendant's.
- **The defendant intends that the plaintiff go out of business.** Even if Mom and Pop can calculate MegaGrocery's average variable cost to the satisfaction of a court, they will not necessarily win their case. They must prove that MegaGrocery intended to put them out of business. That is a pretty tall order, short of finding some smoking gun like a strategic plan that explicitly says MegaGrocery wants Mom and Pop gone.
- **If the plaintiff does go out of business, the defendant will be able to earn sufficient profits to recoup its prior losses.** Until Mom and Pop go out of business, MegaGrocery will lose money—after all, it is selling food below cost. To win their case, Mom and Pop must show that MegaGrocery will be able to make up all its lost profits once the corner grocery is out of the way. They need to prove, for example, that no other grocery chain will come to town. It is difficult to prove a negative proposition like that, especially in the grocery business where barriers to entry are low.

---

[18]To calculate average variable cost, add all the firm's costs except its fixed costs and then divide by the total quantity of output.

To take one example, Liggett began selling generic cigarettes 30 percent below the price of branded cigarettes. Brown & Williamson retaliated by introducing its own generics at an even lower price. Liggett sued, claiming that Brown's prices were below cost. The Supreme Court agreed that Brown not only was selling below cost but also intended to harm Liggett. Brown still won the case, however, because there was no evidence that it would be able to recover its losses from the below-cost pricing. If Brown raised its prices, other competitors would come back into the market.[19]

38-3c Tying Arrangements

A **tying arrangement** is an agreement to sell a product on the condition that the buyer also purchases a different (or tied) product. **A tying arrangement is a rule of reason violation under §3 of the Clayton Act and §1 of the Sherman Act. It is illegal if:**

Tying arrangement
An agreement to sell a product on the condition that a buyer also purchases another, usually less desirable, product

- Two products are clearly separate,
- The seller requires the buyer to purchase the two products together,
- The seller has significant power in the market for the tying product, and
- The seller is shutting out a significant part of the market for the tied product.

Six movie distributors refused to sell individual films to television stations. Instead, they insisted that a station buy an entire package of movies. To obtain classics such as *Treasure of the Sierra Madre* and *Casablanca* (the **tying product**), the station also had to purchase such forgettable films as *Nancy Drew Troubleshooter*, *Gorilla Man*, and *Tugboat Annie Sails Again* (the **tied product**).[20] The distributors were engaging in an illegal tying arrangement. **These are the questions that the court asked:**

Tying product
In a tying arrangement, the product offered for sale on the condition that another product be purchased as well

Tied product
In a tying arrangement, the product that a buyer must purchase as the condition for being allowed to buy another product

- **Are the two products clearly separate?** A left and a right shoe are not separate products, and a seller can legally require that they be purchased together. *Gorilla Man*, on the other hand, is a separate product from *Casablanca*.
- **Is the seller requiring the buyer to purchase the two products together?** Yes, that is the whole point of these "package deals."
- **Does the seller have significant power in the market for the tying product?** In this case, the tying products are the classic movies. Since they are copyrighted, no one else can show them without the distributor's permission. The six distributors controlled a great many classic movies. So, yes, they do have significant market power.
- **Is the seller shutting out a significant part of the market for the tied product?** In this case, the tied products are the undesirable films like *Tugboat Annie Sails Again*. Television stations forced to take the unwanted films did not buy "B" movies from other distributors. These other distributors were effectively foreclosed from a substantial part of the market.

EXAMStrategy

Question: A group of cemeteries required everyone who purchased a burial plot to also buy the gravestone from the cemetery. Is this an illegal tying arrangement?

Strategy: To answer this question, you need to determine if the seller has significant power in the market for the tying product. To do that, you must first know what the relevant market is.

---

19 Brooke Group Ltd. v. Brown & Williamson Tobacco Corp., 509 U.S. 209 (S. Ct. 1993).
20 United States v. Loew's Inc., 371 U.S. 38 (S. Ct. 1962).

Result: The plaintiffs in this case argued that each cemetery was its own market and, therefore, controlled the market. But if you look at the preceding section called "What Is the Market?" you will see that the relevant question is: If a cemetery raises its prices, what will consumers do? The answer is that they will choose another cemetery nearby, of which there were plenty. Thus, the market was all the cemeteries within reasonable driving distance. Therefore, the tying arrangement was not illegal because no one cemetery had significant market power.[21]

38-3d Controlling Distributors and Retailers

Controlling distributors and retailers is one strategy for excluding competitors. It is difficult to compete in a market if you are foreclosed from the best distribution channels.

Allocating Customers and Territory

As we saw earlier in this chapter, a *horizontal* agreement by *competitors* to allocate customers and territories is a *per se* violation of §1 of the Sherman Act. **However, a vertical allocation of customers or territory is illegal only if it adversely affects competition in the market as a whole.** It is a rule of reason, not a *per se*, violation.

Suppose that Hot Sound, Inc., produces expensive, high-quality speakers. It grants its distributors the exclusive right to sell in a particular territory or the exclusive right over a particular type of customer (consumers, corporate, automobiles). In return for these exclusive rights, Hot Sound requires the distributors to stock a wide range of inventory, hire highly trained (expensive) sales help, and advertise widely. Such requirements not only increase sales but also enhance distributor loyalty. The distributors have such a large investment in Hot Sound's products that they are reluctant to switch to another manufacturer. A change would mean unloading a large inventory, developing new advertisements, and retraining or laying off some of the sales force.

Hot Sound clearly has good business reasons for adopting such a plan. It is reducing intrabrand competition (among its dealers) but enhancing interbrand competition (between brands). With its committed dealer network, Hot Sound can compete more fiercely against other brands. Vertical allocation is a rule of reason violation, which means that the law will intervene only if Hot Sound's activities have an anticompetitive impact on the market as a whole. But because Hot Sound's plan increases interbrand competition, it is unlikely to have an anticompetitive impact.

Exclusive Dealing Agreements

Exclusive dealing contract
A contract in which a distributor or retailer agrees with a supplier not to carry the products of any other supplier

An **exclusive dealing contract** is one in which a distributor or retailer agrees with a supplier not to carry the products of any other supplier. **Under §1 of the Sherman Act and §3 of the Clayton Act, exclusive dealing contracts are subject to a rule of reason and are illegal only if they have an anticompetitive effect.**

The FTC alleged that Intel secretly paid Dell, IBM, Hewlett-Packard, and other companies not to use any chips manufactured by AMD (which were better quality). A number of antitrust enforcement authorities, in the United States and abroad, levied fines on the companies.

21 Mich. Div.—Monument Builders of N. Am. v. Mich. Cemetery Ass'n, 524 F.3d 726 (6th Cir. 2008).

Four pharmaceutical companies paid a fine of $100 million because they had entered into exclusive dealing contracts covering some ingredients required in two best-selling anti-anxiety medications. These contracts meant that competitors had higher costs, which led to increased prices to consumers.[22]

38-3e Vertical Price-Fixing

You remember, from earlier in this chapter, that all *horizontal* price-fixing is a *per se* violation. But vertical price restraints fall under the rule of reason. There are two types of vertical price-fixing: minimum and maximum.

Resale Price Maintenance

Resale price maintenance (RPM) means a manufacturer sets *minimum* prices that retailers may charge. The goal is to prevent the retailer from discounting. Why does the manufacturer care? After all, once the retailer purchases the item, the manufacturer has made its profit. The only way the manufacturer makes more money is to raise its *wholesale* price, not the *retail* price. RPM guarantees a profit margin for the *retailer*.

Resale price maintenance (RPM)
A manufacturer sets minimum prices that retailers may charge.

Manufacturers care about retail prices because pricing affects the product's image with consumers. Nike's high-end sneakers sell for around $250. What conclusion do you draw about the quality of those shoes? Would your opinion change if you saw them being sold at heavily discounted prices? You can understand why Nike might want to prohibit retailers from lowering the prices on its goods. Consumer advocates contend, however, that manufacturers such as Nike are simply protecting dealers from competition. Discounting may or may not harm products, but, they insist, RPM certainly hurts consumers. As you saw in the opening scenario, Tempur-Pedic's RPM prevented Sean from negotiating a lower price for his mattress.

In the following case, the Supreme Court held that **RPM is a rule of reason not a *per se* violation.**

Leegin Creative Leather Products, Inc. v. PSKS, Inc.

127 S. Ct. 2705
United States Supreme Court, 2007

Facts: Leegin manufactured belts and other women's accessories under the brand name "Brighton." It sold these products only to small boutiques and specialty stores. Sales of the Brighton brand accounted for about half the profits at Kay's Kloset, a boutique in Lewisville, Texas.

Leegin decided it would no longer sell to retailers who discounted the prices on Brighton products. It wanted to ensure that stores could afford to offer excellent service. It was also concerned that discounting harmed Brighton's image. Despite warnings from Leegin, Kay's Kloset persisted in marking down Brighton products, so Leegin cut the store off.

Kay's sued Leegin, alleging that RPM was a *per se* violation of the law. The trial court found for Kay's and entered judgment against Leegin for almost $4 million. The Court of Appeals affirmed. The Supreme Court granted *certiorari*. On appeal, Leegin did not dispute that it had entered into RPM agreements with retailers. Rather, it contended that the rule of reason should apply to those agreements.

---

[22] FTC v. Mylan Labs., Inc., 62 F. Supp. 2d 25 (D.D.C. 1999).

Issue: ***Is resale price maintenance a* per se *or rule of reason violation of the Sherman Act?***

Excerpts from Justice Kennedy's Decision:[23] To justify a *per se* prohibition, a restraint must have manifestly anticompetitive effects and lack any redeeming virtue. The few recent studies documenting the competitive effects of resale price maintenance cast doubt on the conclusion that the practice meets the criteria for a *per se* rule.

Minimum resale price maintenance can stimulate interbrand competition—the competition among manufacturers selling different brands of the same type of product—by reducing intrabrand competition—the competition among retailers selling the same brand. A single manufacturer's use of vertical price restraints tends to eliminate intrabrand price competition; this in turn encourages retailers to invest in tangible or intangible services or promotional efforts that aid the manufacturer's position as against rival manufacturers. Resale price maintenance also has the potential to give consumers more options so that they can choose among low-price, low-service brands; high-price, high-service brands; and brands that fall in between.

Absent vertical price restraints, the retail services that enhance interbrand competition might be under-provided. This is because discounting retailers can free-ride on retailers who furnish services and then capture some of the increased demand those services generate. Consumers might learn, for example, about the benefits of a manufacturer's product from a retailer that invests in fine showrooms, offers product demonstrations, or hires and trains knowledgeable employees. Or consumers might decide to buy the product because they see it in a retail establishment that has a reputation for selling high-quality merchandise. If the consumer can then buy the product from a retailer that discounts because it has not spent capital providing services or developing a quality reputation, the high-service retailer will lose sales to the discounter, forcing it to cut back its services to a level lower than consumers would otherwise prefer.

While vertical agreements setting minimum resale prices can have procompetitive justifications, they may have anticompetitive effects in other cases. A manufacturer with market power might use resale price maintenance to give retailers an incentive not to sell the products of smaller rivals or new entrants. If the rule of reason were to apply to vertical price restraints, courts would have to be diligent in eliminating their anticompetitive uses from the market.

Vertical price restraints are to be judged according to the rule of reason.

Vertical Maximum Price-Fixing

In the case of resale price maintenance, the manufacturer sets the *minimum* prices its distributors can charge. **Vertical maximum price-fixing (when a manufacturer sets maximum prices) is also a rule of reason violation of the Sherman Act.** The defendant is liable only if the price-fixing harms competition.

When State Oil Co. leased a gas station to Barkat Khan, it set a maximum price that Khan could charge for gas. Khan sued State Oil, but the Supreme Court ruled in favor of the oil company on the grounds that cutting prices to increase business is the very essence of competition and, furthermore, low prices benefit consumers.[24]

CHAPTER CONCLUSION

The purpose of the antitrust laws in the United States is to promote free and fair competition and, ultimately, to protect consumers. Although managers sometimes resent the constraints imposed on them by antitrust laws, they are what ensure the fair and open competition necessary for a healthy economy.

---

23 As an indication of how controversial this issue is, the court split 5-4.

24 State Oil Co. v. Khan, 522 U.S. 3 (S. Ct. 1997).

EXAM REVIEW

1. ***PER SE* VERSUS RULE OF REASON** *Per se* violations are automatic; courts do not consider mitigating circumstances. Rule of reason violations, on the other hand, are illegal only if they have an anticompetitive effect.

2. **MARKET DIVISION** Any effort by a group of competitors to divide their market is a *per se* violation of the Sherman Act. Illegal arrangements include agreements to allocate customers, territory, or products.

EXAMStrategy

Question: Harcourt Brace Jovanovich (HBJ) granted BRG an exclusive license to market HBJ's bar review program, which was study materials to prepare law students for Georgia's state licensing exam. HBJ agreed not to compete with BRG in Georgia, and BRG agreed not to compete with HBJ outside the state. HBJ was entitled to receive $100 per student enrolled by BRG and 40 percent of revenues over $350 per student. Did this agreement violate the antitrust laws?

Strategy: These two competitors have agreed to allocate territory. (See the "Result" at the end of this Exam Review section.)

3. **HORIZONTAL PRICE-FIXING AND BID-RIGGING** Horizontal price-fixing and bid-rigging are *per se* violations of the Sherman Act.

4. **REFUSALS TO DEAL** Any agreement by competitors to exclude a particular supplier, buyer, or even another competitor, is a rule of reason violation of the Sherman Act—illegal if the agreement would have an anticompetitive effect.

5. **RECIPROCAL DEALING AGREEMENT** Under a reciprocal dealing agreement, a buyer refuses to purchase goods from a supplier unless the supplier also purchases items from the buyer. Reciprocal dealing agreements are likely to be a problem only if they foreclose a significant share of the market and if the participants agree not to buy from others.

6. **ROBINSON-PATMAN ACT** The Robinson-Patman Act prohibits companies from selling the same item at different prices if the sale lessens competition. However, a seller may charge different prices if these prices reflect different costs or the seller is simply meeting competition.

7. **MERGERS AND JOINT VENTURES** Under the Clayton Act, the federal government has the authority to prohibit anticompetitive mergers and joint ventures.

8. **MONOPOLIZATION** Possessing a monopoly is illegal only if it is acquired or maintained through improper conduct. To determine if a company is guilty of monopolization, ask three questions:
   (a) What is the market?
   (b) Does the company control the market?
   (c) How did the company acquire or maintain its control?

EXAMStrategy

Question: Another example of a bar review company behaving badly. This industry is highly competitive because the product—test preparation materials—is relatively undistinguishable. BAR/BRI was the largest bar review company in the country, with branches in 45 states. Barpassers was a much smaller company located only in Arizona and California. BAR/BRI distributed pamphlets on campuses falsely suggesting that Barpassers was near bankruptcy. Enrollments in Barpassers' courses dropped, and the company was forced to postpone plans for expansion. Did Barpassers have an antitrust claim against BAR/BRI?

Strategy: It is illegal to use improper conduct to acquire or maintain a monopoly. Was this conduct improper? (See the "Result" at the end of this Exam Review section.)

9. **PREDATORY PRICING** To win a predatory pricing case, a plaintiff must prove three elements:
   (a) The defendant is selling its products below cost.
   (b) The defendant intends that the plaintiff go out of business.
   (c) If the plaintiff does go out of business, the defendant will be able to earn sufficient profit to recoup its prior losses.

10. **TYING ARRANGEMENT** A tying arrangement is illegal if:
   - The two products are clearly separate,
   - The seller requires that the buyer purchase the two products together,
   - The seller has significant power in the market for the tying product, and
   - The seller is shutting out a significant part of the market for the tied product.

EXAMStrategy

Question: Two medical supply companies in the San Francisco area provided oxygen to patients at home. The companies were owned by the doctors who prescribed the oxygen. These doctors made up 60 percent of the lung specialists in the area. Did this arrangement create an antitrust problem?

Strategy: Did the seller have significant power in the market for the tying product (lung patients)? Was it shutting out a significant part of the market for the tied product (oxygen)? (See the "Result" at the end of this Exam Review section.)

11. **CONTROLLING DISTRIBUTION** Efforts by a manufacturer to allocate customers or territory among its distributors are subject to a rule of reason. These allocations are illegal only if they have an anticompetitive effect.

12. **EXCLUSIVE DEALING** An exclusive dealing contract is one in which a distributor or retailer agrees with a supplier not to carry the products of any other supplier. These contracts are subject to a rule of reason and are illegal only if they have an anticompetitive effect.

13. **RESALE PRICE MAINTENANCE** If a manufacturer enters into an agreement with distributors or retailers to fix minimum prices, this arrangement is subject to the rule of reason standard—illegal only if it has an anticompetitive effect.

14. **VERTICAL MAXIMUM PRICE-FIXING** An arrangement whereby a manufacturer sets maximum prices is subject to the rule of reason standard—illegal only if it has an anticompetitive effect.

RESULTS

2. Result: Agreements between competitors to allocate territories are illegal under §1 of the Sherman Act.

8. Result: A jury found that BAR/BRI had violated §2 of the Sherman Act by attempting to create an illegal monopoly. The jury ordered BAR/BRI to pay Barpassers more than $3 million plus attorneys' fees.

10. Result: The FTC accused the doctors of an illegal tying arrangement. Because the doctors effectively controlled such a high percentage of the patients needing the service, other oxygen companies could not enter the market. The doctors settled the case.

MULTIPLE-CHOICE QUESTIONS

1. Are horizontal price-fixing and vertical price-fixing *per se* violations of the Sherman Act?
   (a) Yes; Yes
   (b) Yes; No
   (c) No; Yes
   (d) No; No

2. If Sterling Steel (SS) refused to buy concrete from Carat Concrete (CC) unless CC bought steel from SS, would that arrangement be a violation of antitrust laws?
   (a) Yes, a *per se* violation.
   (b) It used to be a violation but is no longer.
   (c) Yes, if it has an anticompetitive impact.
   (d) Yes, if SS has a monopoly.

3. Reserve Supply Corp., a cooperative of 379 lumber dealers, charged that Owens-Corning Fiberglass Corp. violated the Robinson-Patman Act by selling at lower prices to Reserve's competitors. It presented proof that these prices had harmed

competition. Owens-Corning admitted that it had granted lower prices to a number of Reserve's competitors to meet, but not beat, the prices of other insulation manufacturers. Is Owens-Corning in violation of the RPA?

(a) Yes because the RPA requires that manufacturers charge all competitors the same price.
(b) Yes because any difference in price is a *per se* violation of the RPA.
(c) Yes because these price variations harmed competition.
(d) No because a manufacturer is not liable under the RPA if it charges lower prices to meet competition.

4. All the first-run movie theaters in Houston, Texas, charge the same prices for tickets. If one cinema raises its prices, so do the others. What is this type of activity called, and is it a violation of the antitrust laws?

(a) Refusal to deal; it is a rule of reason violation.
(b) Conscious parallelism; it is not a violation in itself.
(c) Price-fixing; it is a *per se* violation.
(d) Resale price maintenance; it is a rule of reason violation.

5. A horizontal merger is automatically illegal if ______________.

(a) the resulting company controls at least 90 percent of the market
(b) the resulting company controls at least 50 percent of the market
(c) the resulting company has the ability to exclude competitors
(d) all of these

CASE QUESTIONS

1. After acquiring the Schick brand name and electric shaver assets, North American Phillips controlled 55 percent of the electric shaver industry in the United States. Remington, a competitor, claimed that the acquisition of such a large market share was a violation of the law because the increased competition from Phillips would decrease Remington's profits. Does Remington have a valid claim?

2. It used to be that disposable contact lenses cost $169 a year. But then each of the five major manufacturers independently told retailers to charge at least $270 a year. Is this legal?

3. Businesses in Silicon Valley often struggle to recruit enough engineers and, as a result, salaries are highly competitive. Adobe, Apple, Google, Intel, Intuit, Pixar, Lucasfilm, and eBay entered into various agreements with each other not to recruit the other's employees. Is this legal?

4. ***YOU BE THE JUDGE* WRITING PROBLEM** American Academic Suppliers (AAS) and Beckley-Cardy (B-C) both sold educational supplies to schools. When B-C's sales began to plummet, it responded by reducing its catalog prices. It also offered an additional discount in states in which AAS was making substantial gains. What claim might AAS make against B-C? Is it likely to prevail in court? **Argument for AAS:** B-C has committed predatory pricing. The company is selling below cost for the purpose of driving us out of business. **Argument for B-C**: Even if we were to drive AAS out of business, we do not have enough market power to recoup our losses.

5. In Boston, 50 restaurants threatened to stop accepting the American Express credit card if the company refused to reduce the commission it charged on each purchase. Visa International, one of American Express's rivals, offered to pay the group's legal expenses. American Express then lowered its commission for all restaurants except for those with a volume lower than $1 million a year. Have either the restaurants, Visa, or American Express potentially violated the antitrust laws?

DISCUSSION QUESTIONS

1. **ETHICS** To conceive a child, some infertile couples need an egg from a fertile woman. In this market, eggs from smart, pretty women are the most valuable. However, the American Society for Reproductive Medicine recommended that clinics cap any payments to donors at $10,000 per cycle. It was concerned that high prices might coerce women into donating, despite some risks to their health, or lead donors to conceal health issues that would make them ineligible to donate. Are these price limits legal? Ethical?

2. Pricegrabber.com is a website that helps online shoppers find the lowest-priced goods on the internet. But it cannot always find the cheapest items because some online sellers are unwilling to list their prices. If you go to Amazon.com, for example, you will see some items for which there is no price, just the note, "To see our price, add this item to your cart." Amazon does that for fear that, after the *Leegin* case, manufacturers will refuse to supply items that it sells below the established retail price. Manufacturers worry that if they do not set some floor to their prices, other retailers will drop the products altogether. eBay and Amazon argue that the consumer is best served by a free market that permits them to set whatever prices they want. What is your view on RPM?

3. **ETHICS** Clarice, a young woman with a mental disability, brought a malpractice suit against a doctor at the Medical Center. As a result, the Medical Center refused to treat her on a nonemergency basis. Clarice then went to another local clinic, which was later acquired by the Medical Center. Because the new clinic also refused to treat her, Clarice had to seek medical treatment in another town 40 miles away. Has the Medical Center violated the antitrust laws? Was it ethical to deny treatment to a patient? What Life Principles are at issue here?

4. Proponents of the Post Chicago School argue that federal antitrust regulators should undertake enforcement actions that will lead to lower consumer prices. Look at the five cases in this chapter. Are the courts' decisions likely to cause consumer prices to go up or down? Do you agree with the courts' decisions?

5. Is it appropriate for U.S. antitrust laws to apply overseas? Should businesspeople who never set foot in the United States be liable for activities they conducted in their own countries?

39

CHAPTER

CONSUMER PROTECTION

The following online review was written by JA2009 on the consumer website my3cents.com:

In yesterday's Sunday newspaper insert, I saw that Staples was featuring an Acer laptop for $449. This laptop typically retails for $599. I immediately drove over to the nearest Staples store, and arrived 5 minutes after it opened.

Upon my arrival, I found an associate who informed me that the laptops were in stock. However, before he would get me one, he proceeded to try to sell me his "protection plan." Now, for a number of reasons, including my own knowledge of computers as well as ready access to free computer repair services, I declined this. The sales associate walked away to, I assumed, get my computer. He returned with the store's general manager who again proceeded to aggressively push the protection plan onto me. He was EXTREMELY rude, implying that I was "cheap" for not adding the plan. He walked away when I finally maintained I did not want it. Moments later, the sales associate informed me that the laptop was not in stock after all. Just to summarize the timeline ... it was available ... I declined the approximately $150 protection plan that would have boosted the price of the laptop to the regular sale price ... then suddenly it was unavailable.

He was EXTREMELY rude, implying that I was "cheap" for not adding the plan.

I then called a 2nd Staples store and was told the store had multiple laptops and they should definitely be there when I arrived. I arrived exactly 8 minutes later at the location. The store was virtually empty. I found the exact person who I had spoken to and asked him if they were indeed in stock, and he indicated that they were. And then, before he goes back to get one, he asks me if I want the service plan. I responded, "No thanks." He said "fine" and walked away. 2–3 minutes later ... he walks back and, just like the last store, the inventory suddenly has vanished. Half smirking (obviously knowing that what he was saying had no truth to it), he implied that all of them had been sold in the last 8 minutes.

Why would these salespeople refuse to sell the advertised computer? Because they knew that if they did not sell $200 in extras, they would be in serious trouble and might even be fired.[1] This practice is classic bait-and-switch and, as we will see, it is illegal.

This chapter provides many examples of businesses that are determined to separate consumers from their money, no matter what it takes. But, luckily, both Congress and the states have passed statutes to protect consumers from these bad actors and Congress has empowered two federal agencies to enforce consumer laws:

- **Federal Trade Commission (FTC).** You might remember the FTC from Chapter 38 because it enforces antitrust law. The FTC also regulates a wide range of business activities that affect consumers. The FTC can impose a fine or file suit in federal court asking for damages on behalf of an injured consumer.
- **Consumer Financial Protection Bureau (CFPB).** After the most recent financial crisis, Congress created the CFPB to regulate consumer financial products and services, including mortgages, credit cards, and checking accounts.

  Consumers can file complaints about financial services companies with the CFPB. It then sends the complaints to the companies, which have 15 days to respond and 60 days to resolve the issues. The CFPB also publishes these complaints online in its Consumer Response Database.

39-1 SALES

Section 5 of the Federal Trade Commission Act (FTC Act) prohibits unfair and deceptive acts or practices.

39-1a Deceptive Acts or Practices

Many deceptive acts or practices involve advertisements. **Under the FTC Act, an advertisement is deceptive if it contains an important misrepresentation or omission that is likely to mislead a reasonable consumer.** The most common deceptive claims involve—you guessed it—weight loss. Please do not believe that you can have the body of a supermodel simply by sprinkling a powder on your food. Or that L'Occitane's Almond Beautiful Shape body cream will magically burn away fat, resulting in a "noticeably slimmer, trimmer you." *You* may not believe these ads, but many people bought the products before the FTC intervened.

Dirima/Shutterstock.com

It takes more than a little powder or body cream to look like this.

The FTC ad rules also apply to apps and social media. AcneApp falsely claimed that applying its blue and red lights to skin would reduce acne. The FTC required these developers to withdraw the app and pay a fine.

Moreover, as mentioned in Chapter 10 on cyberlaw and privacy, blogs and social media ads must clearly and conspicuously indicate if the endorser has received anything of value. "#Ad" or "#sponsored" is sufficient but "#sp" or "#spon" or a "thank you" to the brand is not.

In the following case, the court discussed the type of evidence necessary to support health claims in advertisements.

[1]As reported in David Segal, "Selling It with Extras, or Not at All," *The New York Times*, September 8, 2012.

POM Wonderful, LLC v. FTC

777 F.3d 478
United States Court of Appeals for the District of Columbia Circuit, 2015

Facts: Stewart and Lynda Resnick, who owned thousands of acres of pomegranate orchards, formed POM Wonderful, LLC, to make and sell pomegranate juice. POM spent more than $35 million on medical research, sponsoring at least 100 studies on the impact of pomegranate juice on heart disease, prostate cancer, and erectile dysfunction.

POM might be wonderful, but, unfortunately, the results of the medical studies were not. Any health benefit was at best slight and obtained only in studies that were scientifically invalid. Despite the absence of scientific support, POM conducted national advertising campaigns trumpeting the benefits of pomegranate juice, such as: "POM Wonderful Pomegranate Juice can help prevent premature aging, heart disease, stroke, Alzheimer's, even cancer."

The Federal Trade Commission charged the Resnicks and POM under the FTC Act for making false, misleading, and unsubstantiated statements. It ordered them to stop making health claims without scientific evidence. POM and the Resnicks appealed.

Issue: ***Did the Resnicks and POM violate the FTC Act?***[2]

Excerpts from Judge Srinivasan's Decision: [The POM] ads repeatedly claimed the benefits of POM's products in the treatment or prevention of heart disease, prostate cancer, or erectile dysfunction, and consistently touted medical studies ostensibly supporting those claimed benefits. Moreover, they invoked medical symbols, referenced publication in medical journals, and described the substantial funds spent on medical research, fortifying the overall sense that the referenced clinical studies establish the claimed benefits. When an ad represents that tens of millions of dollars have been spent on medical research, it tends to reinforce the impression that the research supporting product claims is established.

Consider, for instance, the advertisement for POM appearing in Playboy magazine. According to that ad, POM is "backed by $34 million in medical research at the world's leading universities." The ad next asserts that "an initial UCLA study on our juice found hopeful results for prostate health." Finally, the ad states that "a preliminary study on our juice showed promising results for heart health."

[A]t least a significant minority of reasonable consumers would construe the ad to claim that drinking POM juice can treat, prevent, or reduce the risk of prostate cancer and heart disease. The ad's references to the described studies as "promising," "initial" or "preliminary" do not neutralize the claims made when the specific results are otherwise described in unequivocally positive terms. [A]n effective disclaimer [would be] a statement that the "evidence in support of this claim is inconclusive."

[E]xperts in the relevant fields would require one or more properly randomized and controlled human clinical trials—"RCTs"—in order to establish a causal relationship between a food and the treatment, prevention, or reduction of risk of heart disease, prostate cancer, or erectile dysfunction. Without at least one such RCT, POM's efficacy claims were inadequately substantiated.

Petitioners contend that it is too onerous to require RCTs to substantiate disease-related claims about food products because of practical, ethical, and economic constraints on RCT testing in that context. The Commission was unpersuaded by that argument, so are we. [Indeed,] several juice studies they sponsored were double-blinded and placebo-controlled.

An advertiser may assert a health-related claim backed by medical evidence falling short of an RCT if it includes an effective disclaimer disclosing the limitations of the supporting research. Petitioners did not do so.

39-1b Unfair Practices

The FTC Act also prohibits unfair acts or practices. Google paid consumers $19 million to settle the FTC's complaint that it had unfairly billed parents for charges that their children made through apps downloaded from the Google Play app store. (Google employees actually referred to these charges as "friendly fraud" and "family fraud." Perhaps that should have been a red flag.) Google promised to obtain informed consent from parents before allowing children to incur charges.

[2]"Petitioners" refers to the Resnicks and POM.

The Commission considers a practice to be *unfair* if it meets all of the following three tests:

1. **It causes a substantial consumer injury.** Qchex.com set up an online system that permitted any person to draw checks on any bank account, as long as the user knew the name, account number, and routing number. Qchex did not verify if users were authorized to withdraw funds from that account. Using this system, fraudsters stole more than $400 million. Even the FTC was a victim. (Helpful hint: If you are going to run a fraud, make sure not to cheat the FTC.) The court ruled that this injury was substantial.
2. **The harm of the injury outweighs any countervailing benefit.** Qchex's product was of limited use to an ordinary consumer because all large banks offer the same services at a cheaper price and with greater security. So do other third parties in the marketplace, like PayPal or Square. There was little benefit and great injury.
3. **The consumer could not reasonably avoid the injury.** Consumers were unable to avoid the injury because they did not even know it was happening. Afterward, they could get their money back from their bank, but only after a substantial investment of time and energy. Some consumers never noticed the unauthorized withdrawals. The court injoined Qchex from continuing its business and ordered it to turn over its profits.[3]

In addition, the FTC may decide that a practice is unfair simply because it violates public policy, even if it does not meet these three tests. Many consumers, who cannot afford to pay up front for big-ticket items such as televisions, sofas, and washing machines, instead buy them through "rent-to-own" plans. But buyers do not actually own the goods until the last payment is made. The FTC determined that sellers in rent-to-own deals were violating public policy if they did not disclose on the item's label: the total cost of purchase, the weekly or monthly payment amount, the number of payments required to obtain ownership, and whether the merchandise was new or used.

39-1c Abusive Acts

The CFPB has the authority to take action against anyone committing "abusive acts." It defines abusive acts as taking "unreasonable advantage of … a lack of understanding on the part of the consumer of the material risks, costs, or conditions of the product or service." PayPal paid $25 million to settle a charge by the CFPB that it had behaved abusively when it signed up consumers for its online product, PayPal Credit. It had acted without customers' permission, deceptively advertised promotional benefits, and then mishandled billing disputes.

39-1d Additional Sales Rules

Bait-and-Switch

FTC rules prohibit bait-and-switch advertisements: A merchant may not advertise a product and then disparage it (or otherwise make it unavailable) to consumers in an effort to sell a different (more expensive) item. In addition, merchants must have enough stock on hand to meet reasonable demand for any advertised product.

The opening scenario describes a classic bait-and-switch. The Acer computer at $449 was the **bait**—an alluring offer that sounds almost too good to be true. Of course, it is. Once a customer asks to buy it, the company tries to sell an upgraded product at a much higher price. That is the **switch**. The real purpose of the advertisement was simply to lure interested customers into a trap to buy a more expensive item.

Bait-and-switch
A practice whereby sellers advertise products that are not generally available but are being used to draw interested parties in so that they will buy other products

[3]FTC v. Neovi, Inc., 604 F.3d 1150 (9th Cir. 2010).

Merchandise Bought by Mail, by Telephone, or Online

Many Americans buy everything, from clothing to medicine to furnishings and food, by mail, by telephone, or online. **The FTC has established the following rules for these types of sales:**

- Sellers must ship an item within the time stated or, if no time is given, within 30 days after receipt of the order.
- If a company cannot ship the product when promised, it must send the customer a notice with the new shipping date and an opportunity to cancel. If the new shipping date is within 30 days of the original one and the customer does not cancel, the order is still valid.
- If the company cannot ship by the second shipment date, it must send the customer another notice. This time, however, the company must cancel the order unless the customer returns the notice, indicating that he still wants the item.

Staples, Inc., violated these FTC rules when it told customers that they were viewing "real-time" inventory and that products would be delivered in one day, even on weekends. In fact, the website was not updated in real time, one-day delivery only applied to customers who lived within 20 miles of a Staples store, and it never happened on weekends. The company paid a fine of $850,000 to settle these charges.

Telemarketing

The telephone rings: "Could I speak with Alexander Johanson? This is Denise from Master Chimney Sweeps." It is 7:30 p.m.; you have just straggled in from work and are looking forward to a tranquil dinner of takeout cuisine. You are known as Sandy, your last name is pronounced "Yohanson," and you do not have a chimney. A telemarketer has struck again! What can you do to protect your peace and quiet?

The FTC prohibits telemarketers from calling or texting any telephone number listed on its do-not-call registry.[4] You can register your home and cell phone numbers with the FTC online at www.donotcall.gov or by telephone at (888) 382-1222. FTC rules also prohibit telemarketers from blocking their names and telephone numbers on Caller ID systems. If you receive telemarketing calls after your telephone number has been in the registry for 31 days, you can file a complaint at donotcall.gov or at the toll free number above. To do so, you need to know the date of the call and the company's name or phone number. A telemarketer may be fined up to $40,000 for each call.

What is even more annoying than telemarketing calls from a live person? Robocalls—autodialed and prerecorded commercial telemarketing calls. **The Telephone Consumer Protection Act (TCPA) prohibits telemarketers from making autodialed and/or prerecorded calls or texts to cell phones and prerecorded calls to residential land lines unless the consumer unambiguously consents in writing.** Furthermore, any prerecorded telemarketing calls must provide an opt-out option at the beginning so that the caller can avoid receiving any future calls from that source. If you receive any of these prohibited contacts, you can file a complaint at www.fcc.gov/complaints. Or you can sue and recover from $500 to $1,500 per call. Informational calls, political messages, charitable outreach, and healthcare messages are exempted from this ban.

The Telemarketing Sales Rule specifies that once telemarketers do talk with a consumer, they must tell the truth clearly and completely before the customer pays.

---

[4]Although the statute was passed in 1991, before text messaging was invented, a court has ruled that it does cover texting. Satterfield v. Simon & Schuster, Inc., 569 F.3d 946 (9th Cir. 2009).

Unordered Merchandise

Under §5 of the FTC Act, anyone who receives unordered merchandise in the mail may treat it as a gift. She may use it, throw it away, or do whatever else she wants with it.

There you are, watching an infomercial for Anushka products, guaranteed to fight that scourge of modern life—cellulite! Rushing to your phone, you place an order. The Anushka cosmetics arrive, but for some odd reason, the cellulite remains. A month later, another bottle arrives, like magic, in the mail. The magic spell is broken, however, when you get your credit card bill and see that, without your authorization, the company has charged you for the new supply of Anushka. Is this a hot new marketing technique? Not exactly. The FTC ordered the company to cease and desist this unfair and deceptive practice. This company was in violation of FTC rules because it charged consumers without permission and did not notify them that they could treat the unauthorized products as a gift, to use or throw out as they wished.

Door-to-Door Sales

Consumers at home need special protection from unscrupulous salespeople. In a store, customers can simply walk out, but at home, they may feel trapped. Also, it is difficult at home to compare products or prices offered by competitors. **Under the FTC door-to-door rules, a salesperson is required to notify the buyer that she has the right to cancel the transaction at any time before midnight of the third business day thereafter.** This notice must be given both orally and in writing; the actual cancellation must be in writing. The seller must return the buyer's money within ten days.

EXAMStrategy

Question: To sell its products, Midland Industries would call a random employee at a target company and say, falsely, that it had done business with the target and just needed to confirm a shipping address. Midland would then send the target unordered, overpriced staples such as lightbulbs and cleaning products. The person who processed the invoices often did not know that no one had ordered the merchandise. Midland would then send further unordered merchandise on a regular basis. Also, when anyone questioned an invoice, the company would lie that it had audio recordings confirming the order. Is this practice legal?

Strategy: Review the various sales regulations—more than one is involved in this case.

Result: This sales plan was a trifecta: Midland violated §5 of the FTC Act by engaging in a deceptive practice, the Telemarketing Sales Rule by failing to make full and truthful disclosure, and the rules on unordered merchandise by billing for these products.

39-2 CONSUMER CREDIT

Historically, the practice of charging interest on loans was banned by most countries and by three of the most prominent religions—Christianity, Islam, and Judaism. As the European economy developed, however, moneylending became essential. To compromise, governments began to permit interest charges but limited the maximum rate to 6 percent.

Even in modern times, many states limit the maximum interest rate a lender may charge consumers. (Although, usury laws typically do not apply to credit card debt, mortgages, consumer leases, or commercial loans.) The penalty for violating usury statutes varies among the states. Depending upon the jurisdiction, the lender may forfeit the illegal interest, all interest, or, in some states, the entire loan.

Jonathan Weiss/Shutterstock.com

Wells Fargo cheated its customers for years and then tried to prevent them from bringing their cases to court.

This section discusses the most important rules on consumer lending. Consumers have sometimes struggled to enforce their rights because many lenders require that all disputes be arbitrated. Historically, arbitrators have tended to favor the repeat customer (lenders) over the one-time litigant (consumers). Arbitration clauses prohibit class actions, which means that many consumers who suffer small injuries cannot band together to bring a large lawsuit. Also, arbitrations are secret.

Wells Fargo illustrates the problem with forced arbitration clauses. Under pressure to meet sales goals, Wells Fargo employees set up millions of accounts that their customers had not requested. The bank continued its wrongdoing years after it was first caught because no one outside the organization, other than the individual consumers, knew about the arbitrations. Even after the scandal became public and the head of Wells Fargo was called to testify before Congress, the bank tried to keep injured consumers out of court. It argued that, although the customers had not agreed to the fake accounts set up in their name, they had consented to arbitrate any disputes over these bogus accounts.

The CFPB has proposed a rule that would prohibit consumer lenders such as banks, credit card issuers, and auto and payday lenders from using arbitration clauses to block class action lawsuits. This rule would apply only to new accounts.

39-2a Payday Loans

A woman borrows $2,600 and then makes payments on the loan for over a year, totaling $4,000. But still she owes $2,500, almost as much as she borrowed. How is that possible? Because the interest rate was so high. She borrowed from CashCall, which charged annual interest rates of between 90 percent and 350 percent. Over the four-year term of her loan, she would have repaid almost $14,000. Is that legal? In some states, but not in North Carolina, where this woman lived. The CFPB accused CashCall of unfair, deceptive, and abusive practices and asked the court to order CashCall to return all the funds it obtained from borrowers.

Payday loan
Small loans with high interest rates made to people who need money to make it to the next paycheck

Loans by CashCall and similar companies are called **payday loans** because they are made to desperate people who need money to make it to the next paycheck. A payday loan can be a lifesaver for borrowers who pay back their loans within a week or two, but only 15 percent of payday borrowers do. The rest are stuck with loans that carry exorbitant interest rates and fees, with the result that most borrowers never dig out from under their debt. They may even pay *fees* that actually exceed the amount they borrowed. You might remember the *Blasco* case in Chapter 25, in which a woman was paying an annual compounded interest rate of 6,500 percent on a payday loan.

Although **these loans violate the usury laws in some states**, the internet allows unscrupulous lenders to reach desperate borrowers everywhere. It is a cat-and-mouse game with the FTC, CFPB, and state regulators trying to catch those who violate the law. Now Google will not run ads by payday lenders. The CFPB has proposed new payday lending rules, although many commentators view them as too lenient.

39-2b Truth in Lending Act—General Provisions

Before Congress passed the Truth in Lending Act (TILA), lenders found many creative methods to disguise the real interest rate from the authorities who enforced usury laws. In this process, they also hid it from borrowers. Indeed, before TILA, many consumers had no idea what interest rate they were really paying. Congress passed this statute to ensure that consumers were adequately informed about credit terms before entering into a loan and could compare the cost of credit. **Note, however, TILA does not regulate interest rates or the terms of a loan; these rules are set by state law. TILA simply requires lenders to *disclose* the terms of a loan in an understandable and complete manner.**

Applicability

TILA applies to a transaction only if all of the following tests are met:

- It is a consumer loan. That means a loan to an individual for personal, family, or household purposes, not a loan to a business.
- The loan has a finance charge or will be repaid in more than four installments.
- The loan is for less than $54,600, is secured by a mortgage on real estate, or is a private education loan.[5]
- The loan is made by someone in the business of offering credit.

Disclosure

In all loans covered by TILA, the lender must:

- **Disclose all information clearly.** A TILA disclosure statement should not be a scavenger hunt. A finance company violated TILA when it loaned money to Dorothy Allen. The copany made all the required disclosures but scattered them throughout the loan document and intermixed them with confusing terms that were not required by TILA.[6]
- **Disclose the following facts:**
    - **The amount financed.** That is, the amount the consumer has borrowed.
    - **The total of payments.** The amount the consumer will have paid by the end of the loan.
    - **The finance charge.** The finance charge is the amount, in dollars, the consumer will pay in interest and fees over the life of the loan. It is important for consumers to know this amount because otherwise, they may not understand the real cost of the loan. Of course, the longer the loan, the higher the finance charge. Someone who borrows $5,000 for ten years at 10 percent annual interest will pay $500 each year for ten years, for a total finance charge of $5,000—equal to the principal borrowed. In 30-year mortgages, the finance charge will typically exceed the amount of the principal.
    - **The annual percentage rate (APR).** This number is the actual rate of interest the consumer pays on an annual basis. Without this disclosure, it would be easy in a short-term loan to disguise a very high APR because the finance charge is low. Boris borrows $5 for lunch from his employer's credit union. Under the terms of the loan, he must repay $6 the following week. His finance charge is only $1, but his APR is astronomical—20 percent per week—which is over 1,000 percent for a year.

39-2c Home Loans

Mortgage Loans

In the first decade of this century, the United States suffered through a bubble in housing prices, followed by a dramatic crash. Like all bubbles, this one began when prices rose and people began to believe that they could not lose money. They thought they could always

[5]This amount adjusts every December 31, to reflect inflation. To find out the latest figure, google "Regulation z exemption threshold."

[6]Allen v. Beneficial Fin. Co. of Gary, 531 F.2d 797 (7th Cir. 1976).

sell a house for more than they had paid for it.[7] Lenders fueled this mania by giving out mortgages without first verifying the borrower's income or assets; indeed, in some cases, lenders encouraged loans that any reasonable observer would know the borrower could not repay. When the inevitable occurred and many homeowners were unable to pay back their loans, banks began huge numbers of foreclosures, which caused prices to fall further. Bleak tracts of abandoned houses stood across America. Congress amended TILA hoping to prevent another such crash.

TILA prohibits unfair, abusive, or deceptive home mortgage lending practices. (Some of the following rules seem little more than common sense, but that was an attribute sorely missing during the bubble.) **Under TILA, lenders:**

- Must make a good faith, reasonable effort to determine whether a borrower can afford to repay the loan, considering data such as income, assets, debt, and credit history;
- May not coerce or bribe an appraiser into misstating a home's value; and
- Cannot charge prepayment penalties on adjustable rate mortgages.

Qualified mortgage (QM)
A mortgage that, according to the CFPB, complies with TILA

To help lenders comply with these requirements, the CFPB established criteria for what it calls **qualified mortgages (QMs)**. If lenders give a QM, they are deemed to have complied with TILA because it is likely that the borrower can afford to repay the loan. **QMs:**

- Limit all of a borrower's debt (not just her mortgage) to 43 percent of her income,
- Limit up-front points and fees to 3 percent, and
- Prohibit harmful features such as:
  - Interest-only periods—when the borrower is not paying down the principal of the loan,
  - Balloon payments (very large payments at the end), and
  - Negative amortization—when the principal of the loan continues to grow instead of being paid down.

In a further effort to solve some of the problems that contributed to the housing crash, **the CFPB also sets requirements for the companies that collect mortgage payments. These mortgage servicers must:**

- Provide a clear monthly statement,
- Fix errors quickly,
- Credit payments on the day they are received,
- Provide early notice if the interest rate is about to change,
- Contact borrowers who are 36 days late in making a payment,
- Wait 120 days after nonpayment to begin foreclosure, and
- Help delinquent borrowers understand their options.

Home Equity Loans

There are, of course, many legitimate lenders in the home equity business, but scam artists sometimes prey upon the elderly, who are vulnerable to pressure, and upon the poor, who may not have access to conventional financing. Swindlers offer home equity loans, secured by a second mortgage, to finance fraudulent repairs.

[7] But as the group Blood, Sweat & Tears once observed, "What goes up, must come down."

In response to such scams, Congress amended TILA to provide additional consumer safeguards for home equity installment loans. **If a home equity installment loan:**

- Has an APR (interest rate) that is more than 10 percentage points higher than Treasury securities, or
- The consumer must pay fees and points at closing that are higher than 8 percent of the total loan amount, then,
- At least three business days before the loan closing, the lender must notify the consumer that (1) he does not have to go through with the loan (even if he has signed the loan agreement) and (2) he could lose his house if he fails to make payments, and
- Loans that are for less than five years may not contain balloon payments (i.e., a payment at the end that is more than twice the regular monthly payment).

Rescission

If a lender violates TILA, **consumers have the right to rescind a mortgage for up to three business days after the signing (including Saturdays). However, if the lender does not comply with the *disclosure* provisions of TILA, the consumer can rescind for up to three *years* from the date of the mortgage.** Understand, though, that rescission does not mean that the borrower gets to keep the money. The borrower must repay the principal of the loan in return for the lender giving back all interest and closing costs. This right of rescission does not apply to a first mortgage used to finance a house purchase or to any refinancing with the consumer's existing lender.

39-2d Plastic: Credit, Debit, and ATM Cards

Credit, debit, and ATM cards are extremely important to most consumers, so Congress and the regulatory agencies have built in substantial protection.

Credit Cards: Fees

In the absence of regulation, credit card companies used to be highly creative at finding ways to impose fees on their customers. Among other tricks, they would change the due date from month to month, set the deadline in the middle of the day, or charge inactivity fees for failure to use a card. During the economic crisis that began in 2008, many consumers struggled to pay their credit card bills. In response, Congress passed the CARD Act to prohibit unfair fees and to provide transparency so that consumers can compare the costs of different cards.

These are the major provisions of the CARD Act:

- **Due dates:**
  - Due dates must be disclosed.
  - Due dates must be set for the same time each month and occur at the end of a business day.
  - The bill must be mailed at least 21 days ahead of time.
- **Rates and fees:**
  - During the first year, fees must be less than 25 percent of a card's credit limit.
  - Increases in rates and fees:
    - Are not allowed on any charges already incurred (until a cardholder has missed two consecutive payments).
    - Are only permitted for future purchases and only if the credit card company provides 45 days' notice to the consumer and permits cancellation of the card.

- **Late payment fees** are limited to $25 for the first event and $35 thereafter.
- **Payment must be applied to whichever debt on the card has the highest interest rate** (say, a cash advance rather than a new purchase).
- **Consumers have the right to set a fixed credit limit.** Consumers cannot be charged a fee if the company accepts charges above that limit unless the consumer has agreed to the fee. Only one overlimit fee per statement is permitted.
- **People under 21 cannot obtain a credit card unless they have income or a co-signer.**

Research indicates that this statute reduced overall borrowing costs to consumers by $11.9 billion per year. The largest benefit was for consumers with the worst credit ratings.[8]

Ethics

Each of the rules in the previous section was aimed at eliminating existing abuses. Should Congress really have to tell credit card companies that they cannot raise rates on charges already incurred? Or set a due date on a Sunday and then charge a late fee if payment arrives on Monday? What Life Principles might the executives of credit card companies use when setting policies?

Debit and ATM Cards: Fees

Check cards
Another name for debit cards

Debit cards are used to make purchases (they are also called **check cards**). ATM cards withdraw cash from a bank account. Although they look and feel like credit cards, legally they are a different plastic altogether. When you use a credit card, the funds do not leave your account until you pay the bill. But with both debit and ATM cards, funds are deducted immediately.

> Although debit and ATM cards look and feel like credit cards, legally they are a different plastic altogether.

Many people prefer to use debit and ATM cards because their expenditures are limited by the size of their bank accounts, and they can avoid the interest fees and late charges levied on credit card overspending.

In the case of ATM and debit cards, banks cannot overdraw an account and charge an overdraft fee unless the consumer signs up for an overdraft plan. Of course, this rule means that consumers who do not "opt in" to the overdraft plan will not be able to overdraw their account, no matter how desperate they are. Be wary, however, because more than half of consumers who paid overdraft fees do not remember having opted in. Either they were not paying attention, or they have been improperly charged.

Also note that if you do opt in to an overdraft plan, banks can charge a flat fee (typically $35) *each time* cardholders overdraw their bank account, no matter how small the overdraft. A customer can, say, be charged $150 in overdraft fees on $50 worth of overdrafts. Suppose that someone makes a $20 overdraft that he repays in two weeks, but in the meantime, he incurs a $27 fee. In that case, he has paid an interest rate of 3,520 percent. In one recent year, banks charged $6 billion in debit card penalties.

---

[8]Sumit Agarwal, Souphala Chomsisengphet, Neale Mahoney, and Johannes Stroebel, "Regulating Consumer Financial Products: Evidence from Credit Cards," *Quarterly Journal of Economics* (2015) 130 (1): 111–164.

Prepaid Debit Cards: Fees

Prepaid debit cards sound like they are a variation of a debit card, but they are, in fact, completely different. Unlike debit cards, they are not linked to your bank account. Instead, you pay in advance to load funds onto the card and you can only spend what is there. Many low-income workers use these cards instead of bank accounts, to the tune of more than $100 billion a year.

Traditionally, this type of card had minimal regulation, so issuers were highly creative in assessing fees and charges. **To address this problem, the CFPB issued rules to protect prepaid card users:**

- Before consumers buy a card, issuers must clearly disclose key account information, such as all fees.
- Issuers must make account information available for free by telephone, online, and in writing upon request.
- If the card allows consumers to overdraw their accounts, they are entitled to the same protections as credit card holders under the CARD Act.

Liability

Your wallet is missing, and with it your cash, your driver's license, a photo of your dog, a Groupon, and—oh, no!—all your plastic! What is your liability if the thief spends up a storm on your stolen cards? The answer depends on the type of card.

- **Credit cards:**
  - **You are liable only for the first $50 in charges the thief makes before you notify the credit card company.** If you call the company before any charges are made, you have no liability at all. Of course, if you carry a wallet full of cards, $50 for each one can add up to a sizable total.
  - If the thief steals just your credit card number, but not the card itself, you are not liable for any unauthorized charges.
- **Debit and ATM cards:**
  - **If you report the loss before anyone uses your card, you are not liable for any unauthorized withdrawals.**
  - If you report the theft within two days of discovering it, the bank will reimburse you for all losses above $50.
  - If you wait until after two days, your bank will only replace stolen funds above $500.
  - If you wait more than 60 days after receipt of your bank statement, the bank is not responsible for any losses.
  - If an unauthorized transfer takes place using just your number, not your card, then you are not liable at all as long as you report the loss within 60 days of receiving the bank statement showing the loss. After 60 days, however, you are liable for the full amount.
- **Prepaid debit cards:**
  - If you report the theft within two days of discovering it, the bank will reimburse you for all losses above $50.
  - If you wait until after two days, the bank will only replace stolen funds above $500.

A helpful hint: If your cards are stolen, immediately call the issuer but also follow up with a letter or email (to the address provided for billing errors), documenting the date the card was stolen and when you reported it. Be sure to report immediately any unauthorized transactions on the card. Also file a police report as further documentation of the theft.

Disputes with Merchants

You use your credit card to buy a new tablet computer at ShadyComputers, but when you take it out of the box, it will not even turn on. You have a major $600 problem. But all is not lost. **In the event of a dispute between a customer and a merchant, the credit card company cannot bill the customer if (1) she makes a good faith effort to resolve the dispute, (2) the dispute is for more than $50, and (3) the merchant is in the same state where she lives, or within 100 miles of her house.**

What happens if the merchant and the consumer cannot resolve their dispute or if the merchant is not in the same state as the consumer? Clearly, credit card companies do not want to be caught in the middle between consumer and merchant. In practice, they now require all merchants to sign a contract specifying that, in the event of a dispute between the merchant and a customer, the credit card company has the right to charge back the merchant's account, regardless of where the consumer lives. If a customer seems to have a reasonable claim against a merchant, the credit card company will typically transfer the credit it has given the merchant back to the customer's account. Of course, the merchant can try to sue the customer for any money owed.

Disputes with Credit Card Companies

A dispute between a consumer and a credit card company used to consist of little more than an avalanche of threatening form letters from the company while it ignored any response from the hapless cardholder. Then, in 1975, Congress passed the Fair Credit Billing Act (FCBA), which provides protection for credit card holders (and for holders of so-called *revolving charge accounts*—such as those from stores).

The FCBA provides that if a consumer has a complaint about a bill and writes to the credit card company within 60 days of receipt of the bill, the company must acknowledge receipt of the complaint within 30 days and, then, within two billing cycles (but no more than 90 days) investigate the complaint and respond.

39-2e Electronic Fund Transfers

The Electronic Fund Transfer Act (EFTA) protects consumers who make electronic payments using a telephone, computer, or wire transfers.

Preauthorized Transfers

Preauthorized transfer
An electronic fund transfer authorized in advance to recur at regular intervals

Consumers may ask banks to wire funds on a regular basis to pay, say, their monthly health club fee or their mortgage. An electronic fund transfer authorized in advance to recur at regular intervals is called a **preauthorized transfer. For preauthorized transactions, the bank must follow two rules:**

1. It may not make preauthorized transfers without written instructions from the consumer.
2. It must allow the consumer to stop payment of the transfer by oral or written notice up to three business days before the scheduled date.

Here is a good example of the EFTA at work: Suk Jae Chang saw a great offer online for the free poster of his choice. He just had to pay a 99¢ shipping fee. He entered his debit card data to pay the shipping cost. He also checked a box agreeing to the terms and conditions, which of course he did not read. Next thing he knew, $29.99 a month was being deducted from his bank account to pay for his membership in a poster club. The website had said nothing about the club—including how to cancel his membership. Nor did the terms and conditions. After irate consumers filed suit under the EFTA, the poster company agreed to pay back all the funds it had received. Not such a good business plan after all.

In the following case, a customer sued her bank for making a preauthorized transfer that she thought she had stopped. Perhaps most impressive, she represented herself in court.

Broxton-King v. Lasalle Bank, N.A.

2001 U.S. Dist. LEXIS 14653
United States District Court for the Northern District of Illinois, 2001

Facts: Eunice Broxton-King paid $28 a month to belong to the YMCA. On the first day of each month, this sum was transferred automatically from her account at the LaSalle Bank to the YMCA. On August 31, Broxton-King went to the bank, paid an overdraft on her account, and then closed it. However, on September 1, the bank transferred $28 to the YMCA. Because there was no money in her account, the bank charged an overdraft fee of $22 and a service charge of $3. The overdraft totaled $53. On September 7, the bank sent Broxton-King a notice of this overdraft. She told the bank that her account had been closed on August 31, that the debit to the YMCA should be stopped, and the fees refunded. But on October 1, the bank again debited plaintiff's checking account for the $28 YMCA fee and added an additional $27 in overdraft and service fees.

Alleging that the bank had violated the EFTA, Broxton-King filed a *pro se* lawsuit.[9] The bank filed a motion to dismiss.

Issue: ***Did the bank violate the EFTA?***

Excerpts from Judge Gottschall's Decision: [T]he EFTA provides that "a consumer may stop payment of a preauthorized electronic fund transfer by notifying the financial institution orally or in writing at any time up to three business days preceding the scheduled date of such transfer." Defendant contends that if plaintiff had wished to prevent the first transfer of funds in question (the one that occurred on September 1), plaintiff should have, pursuant to the EFTA, requested a stop to the funds transfer three days prior to the transfer date. Instead, defendant notes, plaintiff alleges that she closed her account and ended all transactions with her account on August 31: the day before the transfer date.

As for the October 1 transfer of funds, defendant argues, it had properly allowed the funds transfer because plaintiff had failed to pay off the overdraft resulting from the first transfer of funds. Therefore, the account remained open during the time of the funds transfer.

Defendant's motion to dismiss is granted as to plaintiff's EFTA claim regarding the September 1 transfer. Because the request happened less than three days prior to September 1, defendant is correct that plaintiff cannot sue under the EFTA for the transfer that occurred on September 1.

It appears, however, that under the EFTA, the fact that plaintiff's account was open is immaterial to whether plaintiff could stop a funds transfer from her account. Nowhere in [its] language does the Act require that plaintiff have made the request to stop a funds transfer at a time when the account was closed, as defendant appears to argue. Defendant's motion to dismiss is denied as to plaintiff's EFTA claim regarding the October 1 transfer.

Errors in Electronic Fund Transfers

If an unauthorized withdrawal is made from your account:

- **Your liability:**
  - You are not liable for any transactions that occur up until the date of your bank statement.

[9]*Pro se* is a Latin phrase meaning "on one's own behalf." A *pro se* lawsuit is one in which the party represents herself instead of hiring a lawyer.

- If you report the transaction (either orally or in writing) within 60 days of the date of the bank statement, you are not liable for any transactions after the date of the statement.
- But, if you do not notify the bank within 60 days, you are fully liable for all transactions between 60 days and the date when you provide notification.

- **Once you notify the bank:**
  - It has ten business days to investigate and three days to report the results to you.
  - If the bank is unable to complete its investigation in this time frame, it has to credit your account for the full amount less $50.
  - It then must complete its investigation in 45 calendar days.
  - It must correct any mistakes within one day of discovering that it had made a mistake.
  - If it concludes that the transaction was legitimate, it has to provide you with a written notice within three business days, before removing any funds that it had credited to your account.

If a bank violates these provisions, it must pay the consumer treble damages (three times the amount in dispute).

39-2f Credit Reports

Accuracy of Credit Reports

Gossip and rumor can cause great harm. Bad enough when whispered behind one's back, worse yet when placed in files and distributed to potential creditors. A sullied credit report makes life immensely more difficult because most adults rely on credit—to acquire a house, credit cards, overdraft privileges at the bank, or to rent an apartment. About half of businesses use credit checks as part of the hiring process, although some states now prohibit this practice.

Consumer reporting agencies
Businesses that collect and sell personal information on consumers to third parties

Consumer report
Any communication about a consumer's creditworthiness, character, general reputation, or lifestyle that is considered as a factor in establishing credit

Investigative reports
Discuss character, reputation, or lifestyle. They become obsolete in three months.

Consumer reporting agencies are businesses that collect and sell personal information on consumers to third parties. A **consumer report** is any communication about a consumer's creditworthiness, character, general reputation, or lifestyle that is considered as a factor in establishing credit, obtaining insurance, securing a job, or acquiring a government license.

Under the Fair Credit Reporting Act (FCRA):

- **A consumer report can be used only for a legitimate business need.**
- **A consumer reporting agency cannot report obsolete information.**
  - Ordinary credit information is obsolete after seven years, bankruptcies after ten years.
  - **Investigative reports** that discuss character, reputation, or lifestyle become obsolete in three months. An investigative report cannot be ordered without first informing the consumer.
- **A consumer reporting agency cannot report medical information without the consumer's permission.**
- **An employer cannot request a consumer report on any current or potential employee without the employee's permission.** An employer cannot take action because of information in the consumer report without first giving the current or potential employee a copy of the report and a description of the employee's rights under this statute.
- **Anyone who makes an adverse decision against a consumer because of a credit report must reveal the name and address of the reporting agency that supplied the information.** An "adverse decision" includes denying credit or charging higher rates.

- **Upon request from a consumer, a reporting agency must disclose all information in his file**, the source of the information (except for investigative reports), the name of anyone to whom a report has been sent in the prior year (two years for employment purposes), and the name of anyone who has requested a report in the prior year.
- **If a consumer tells an agency that some of the information in his file is incorrect, the agency must both investigate and forward the data to the information provider.** The information provider must investigate and report the results to the agency. If the data are inaccurate, the information provider must so notify all national credit agencies.

According to the CFPB, the major reporting agencies—Equifax, Experian, and TransUnion—were the three most complained-about financial companies in the country last year, and the rate of complaints increased by double digits over the prior year.[10] Twenty-six percent of consumers had errors in their credit report at one of these agencies. In tests, investigative reporters have found it virtually impossible to get their mistakes corrected.[11] In one case, a jury ordered Equifax to pay $18 million to a woman in Portland, Oregon, who, despite two years of heroic effort, had been unsuccessful in convincing an agency to fix errors. Because of the mistakes, she could not co-sign a car loan for her disabled brother.[12] A number of state officials brought charges against the big three reporting agencies and, ultimately, the companies entered into a national agreement with the New York Attorney General to improve the accuracy of their reports and the process by which disputes are resolved.

EXAMStrategy

Question: Clyde goes into a Tesla dealership to investigate buying a car. He does not look as if he can afford a Tesla, so the sales staff orders a credit report on him before assisting him. After all, no point in wasting their time. Do they have the right to order a report on Clyde? Which consumer statute applies?

Strategy: The FCRA regulates the issuance of consumer reports. These reports can be used only for a legitimate business need.

Result: A car dealership cannot obtain a consumer report on someone who simply asks general questions about prices and financing or who wants to test-drive a car; nor can the dealer order a report to use in negotiations. However, a dealer has the right to a report to arrange financing requested by the consumer or to verify a buyer's creditworthiness when he pays for a vehicle with a personal check.

Access to Credit Reports and Credit Scores

Under the Fair and Accurate Credit Transactions Act (FACTA), consumers are entitled by law to one free credit report every year from each of the three major reporting agencies. You can order these reports at https://www.annualcreditreport.com. (Note, though, that many websites with similar names *pretend* to offer a free credit report but instead enroll customers in paid programs to monitor their credit reports. Be sure to go to the right website.)

10The next four most complained about were banks: Bank of America, Wells Fargo, JPMorgan Chase, and Citibank.

11Todd Ruger, "FTC Report Finds Widespread Errors in Consumer Credit Reports," *The National Law Journal*, February 11, 2013.

12Tara Siegel Bernard, "An $18 Million Lesson in Handling Credit Report Errors," *The New York Times*, August 2, 2013.

Consumer advocates recommend that you check your credit reports every year to make sure they are accurate and that no one else has been obtaining credit in your name. If you find any errors, notify the agency in writing and warn it that failing to make corrections is a violation of the law.

Credit score
A number that is supposed to predict your ability to pay your bills

Although your credit report is valuable information, you do not know how creditors will evaluate it. For that, you need to know your **credit score** (usually called a FICO score).[13] This number (which ranges between 300 and 850) is based on your credit report and is supposed to predict your ability to pay your bills. Currently, it is not automatically included as part of your credit report, although the CFPB has urged reporting agencies to provide it for free. Anyone who penalizes you because of your score is required to give it to you for free, as well as information about how your score compares with others.

39-2g Debt Collection

Have you ever fallen behind on your car payments? That is hardly a crime—but debt collectors might *treat* you as a criminal. Their creativity knows no bounds. They might use text messages and emails threatening to arrest you. Or they might change the password on your cell phone account and obtain your cell phone records so that they could pose as a police officer and call your friends, relatives, and past employers to tell them there was an arrest warrant out for you, even if this was not true. Meanwhile, they may not give you enough information to know if the debt is valid.

Although these actions are illegal, they do happen. A CFPB survey found that three-quarters of collectors violate the law on contacting debtors, half of the people contacted by collectors did not actually owe anything, and one-quarter of those contacted said the collector had threatened them.[14] It is important to know your rights.

Under the Fair Debt Collection Practices Act (FDCPA):

- A collector must, within five days of contacting a debtor, send the debtor a written notice containing the amount of the debt, the name of the creditor to whom the debt is owed, and a statement that if the debtor disputes the debt (in writing), the collector will cease all collection efforts until it has sent evidence of the debt.
- Collectors may not:
  - Call or write a debtor who has notified the collector in writing that he wishes no further contact;
  - Call or write a debtor who is represented by an attorney;
  - Call a debtor before 8:00 a.m. or after 9:00 p.m.;
  - Threaten a debtor or use obscene or abusive language;
  - Call or visit the debtor at work if the consumer's employer prohibits such contact;
  - Imply that they are attorneys or government representatives when they are not or use a false name;
  - Make any false, deceptive, or misleading statement;
  - Contact acquaintances of the debtor for any reason other than to locate the debtor (and then only once);
  - Tell acquaintances that the consumer is in debt; or
  - Collect charges in addition to the debt unless permitted by state law or any contract the debtor has signed.

---

[13] It is called a FICO score because it was developed by the Fair Isaac Corporation.

[14] Consumer Experiences with Debt Collection, the Consumer Financial Protection Bureau, January 2017.

The CFPB is considering rules that would require debt collectors to verify debts before collecting them, supply information about the debt and how it can be disputed, and limit contact with a consumer to six times per week. Oh, and they could not contact a dead debtor's family until 30 days after his death. Note that none of these rules prevents a collector from filing suit against the debtor.

Once contacted by a debt collector, debtors should keep a file of all letters, emails, or texts received or sent as well as notes about date, time, and content of any phone calls. In the event of a violation of the FDCPA, the debtor should contact the FTC or the CFPB. Debtors also have the right to sue collectors who violate the statute and, if successful in court, are entitled to damages, court costs, and attorney's fees.

It is bad enough to be hassled over a debt that one does, in fact, owe, but many times, consumers are threatened and harangued for debts that are not legitimate. Typically, companies sell their consumer debts for pennies on the dollar to collection agencies that do not spend a lot of time and energy ascertaining whether the debt is real. Some debt collectors buy spreadsheets with nothing more than a list of names, addresses, Social Security numbers, and amounts allegedly owed. The collectors do not know if the debts are valid or if the same spreadsheet has been sold to others who have already collected the debts. Some scammers sell fake portfolios listing real consumers' Social Security numbers with false debts.

In the following case, the CFPB accused a law firm of violating the Fair Debt Collection Act.

Consumer Fin. Prot. Bureau v. Frederick J. Hanna & Assocs., P.C.

114 F. Supp. 3d 1342
United States District Court for the Northern District of Georgia, 2015

Facts: Frederick J. Hanna & Associates, P.C. (the Firm), was a law firm that represented credit-card issuers and debt buyers, that is, companies that purchase portfolios of defaulted loans. Over a four-year period, the Firm filed more than 350,000 (yes, 350,000) debt collection lawsuits. Yet the firm only had about a dozen lawyers.

The Consumer Financial Protection Bureau (the Bureau) alleged that the Firm's lawyers were not actually doing the legal work. How could they be? One attorney signed about 138,000 lawsuits in a two-year period. Assuming this one lawyer did nothing but review collection suits for eight hours a day, five days a week, every week of the year without vacation, he would literally have spent less than a minute on each suit.

Instead of lawyers, the Firm used an automated system and support staff to decide which cases to file and then to draft the pleadings. The Firm also routinely filed affidavits asserting that the debts were valid. But these sworn statements were made by people with no knowledge of or connection to the cases.

The Bureau filed suit alleging that the Firm had violated the Fair Debt Collection Practices Act (FDCPA). The Firm filed a motion to dismiss the complaint.

Issues: ***Did the Firm violate the FDCPA? Should the motion to dismiss be granted?***

Excerpts from Judge Totenberg's Decision: [C]ourts have routinely held that a communication that is literally from an attorney (in the sense that it may be signed by an attorney or comes from her office) may violate [the FDCPA] if the attorney was not meaningfully involved in drafting the communication.

In [a prior case, the court] held that a lawyer violated the [the FDCPA] when he authorized the sending of debt collection letters bearing his name and a facsimile of his signature without first reviewing the collection letters or the files of the persons to whom the letters were sent. An unsophisticated consumer, getting a letter from an 'attorney,' knows the price of poker has just gone up. And that clearly is the reason why the dunning campaign escalates from the collection agency, which might not strike fear in the heart of the consumer, to the attorney, who is better positioned to get the debtor's knees knocking.

The same is equally if not more true for consumers who are served with an actual debt collection lawsuit. [I]f an attorney wants to take advantage of the fear that serving a complaint would inspire in a debtor, the lawyer should at the very least ensure that he has become professionally involved in the decision to file the lawsuit. In other words, a reasonable inference to draw is that a consumer faced with a debt collection lawsuit filed by the Firm would view the complaint as a legally valid statement of the consumer's obligation because the complaint was purportedly prepared by counsel. It is thus plausible that such consumers would therefore effectively be coerced into paying a debt that they may or may not actually owe or doing the same through default.

[A] reasonable inference one can draw is that the Firm files lawsuits on a massive scale, not based on any legal determination that each lawsuit is warranted, but instead as an extension or replacement of dunning letters, to scare debtors into paying up.

For the foregoing reasons, the Court **DENIES** Defendants' Motion to Dismiss.

39-2h Equal Credit Opportunity Act

The Equal Credit Opportunity Act (ECOA) prohibits any creditor from discriminating against a borrower because of race, color, religion, national origin, sex, marital status, age (as long as the borrower is old enough to enter into a legal contract), or because the borrower is receiving welfare. A lender must respond to a credit application within 30 days. If a lender rejects an application, it must either tell the applicant why or notify him that he has the right to a written explanation of the reasons for this adverse action. Ally Financial and Ally Bank (formerly known as GMAC, Inc.) agreed to pay nearly $100 million to settle charges that they violated this statute by charging higher interest rates on car loans to African-Americans, Hispanics, and Asians.

Speaking of car loans, the dealer in the following case was sleazy, but did it violate the ECOA?

You Be the Judge

Treadway v. Gateway Chevrolet Oldsmobile, Inc.

362 F.3d 971
United States Court of Appeals for the Seventh Circuit, 2004

Facts: Gateway Chevrolet Oldsmobile, a car dealership, sent an unsolicited letter to Tonja Treadway notifying her that she was "preapproved" for the financing to purchase a car. Gateway did not provide financing itself; instead, it arranged loans through banks or finance companies.

Treadway called the dealer to say that she was interested in purchasing a used car. With her permission, Gateway obtained her credit report. Based on this report, the dealer determined that Treadway was not eligible for financing. This was not surprising, given that Gateway had purchased Treadway's name from a list of people who had recently filed for bankruptcy.

Instead of applying for a loan on behalf of Treadway, Gateway called her and invited her to come to the dealership. There, she was told that Gateway had found a bank that would finance her transaction, but only if she purchased a new car and provided a co-signer. Treadway agreed to purchase a new car and came up with Pearlie Smith, her godmother, to serve as a co-signer.

Concerned as it was with customer service, Gateway had an agent deliver papers directly to Smith's house to be signed immediately. If Smith had read the papers before she signed them, she might have realized that she had committed herself to be the sole purchaser and owner of the car. But she had no idea that she was the owner until she began receiving bills on the car loan. After Treadway made the first payment on behalf of Smith, both women refused to pay more—Smith because she did not want a new car; Treadway because the car was not hers. The car was repossessed, but the financing company continued to demand payment.

On closer inspection, it appears that Gateway was running a scam. It would lure desperate prospects off the bankruptcy rolls and into the showroom with promises of financing for a used car, and then sell a new car to their "co-signer" (who was, in fact, the sole signer). Instead of selling a used car to Tonja Treadway, Gateway sold a new car to Pearlie Smith.

Treadway filed suit against Gateway, alleging that it had violated the ECOA by not notifying her that it had taken an adverse action against her. The district court granted Gateway's motion for summary judgment on the grounds that Gateway had not committed an adverse action under the ECOA. An appeal followed.

You Be the Judge: *Did Gateway violate the ECOA?*

Argument for Treadway: One goal of the ECOA is to provide notice to credit applicants about why they have been denied credit. By failing to send Treadway's application to *any* lender, Gateway effectively denied credit to Treadway. The result is the same whether the dealership or a lender makes the decision—Treadway does not get a loan. There is no logical reason why a denial of credit is an "adverse action" when done by a lender but not by a dealership. The statute required Gateway to tell Treadway that it had failed to submit her application and why.

Another goal of the statute is to prevent credit discrimination. If the dealership does not have to reveal to Treadway that it failed to send her credit application to a lender, she will never even know if she was the victim of discrimination. Under that interpretation of the statute, car dealers would be free to discriminate—they could throw the credit report of every minority applicant in the "circular file" and none would be the wiser.

Argument for Gateway: The ECOA applies to "any creditor." Its goal is to prevent discrimination in granting credit. Gateway is not a creditor; it is a car dealership. It did not deny Treadway credit for the simple reason that it is not in the credit business; it simply failed to send the application to a lender. Treadway could have applied for credit on her own, but elected not to.

Gateway did Treadway a favor when it offered her another option for obtaining a vehicle—having her godmother sign the documents. Smith could have refused but, instead, signed without having even bothered to read the documents. No statute should protect her against her own negligence.

39-3 MAGNUSON-MOSS WARRANTY ACT

Imagine that you have bought a glossy grand piano with beautiful sound. You love that piano. All is well, until the piano tuner tells you that the sound board is cracked. No worries, you think, because it is still under warranty. But then you discover that the warranty requires you to return the piano to the factory on the other side of the country. You are now singing the blues.

This is the way the world used to be before the Magnuson-Moss Warranty Act. Sellers offered warranties that sounded good but were meaningless. The goal of the Act was to provide more protection to consumers. Note, however, that the Act does *not* require manufacturers or sellers to provide a warranty on their products. **Instead, the goal of the Act is to:**

- Ensure that consumers understand the terms of a warranty before they buy a product,
- Enable consumers to compare warranty options before buying,
- Encourage sellers to compete on the basis of the warranties they provide (which has happened in the auto industry), and
- Ensure that sellers abide by the terms of any warranties they offer.

The Act only applies to written warranties on consumer products (not services). **It requires the seller to disclose:**

- The terms of any written warranty in simple, understandable language.
- Whether the warranty is full or limited. Under a full warranty, the seller must promise to fix a defective product for a reasonable time without charge. If, after a reasonable number of efforts to fix the defective product, it still does not work, the consumer must have the right to a refund or a replacement without charge.

- The name and address of the person the consumer should contact to obtain warranty service.
- The parts that are covered and those that are not.
- What services the warrantor will provide, at whose expense, and for what period of time.
- A statement of what the consumer must do and what expenses he must pay.

Now, at least, you can be sure not to buy a piano whose warranty requires you to ship it to the factory.

39-4 CONSUMER PRODUCT SAFETY

In 1969, the federal government estimated that consumer products caused 30,000 deaths, 110,000 disabling injuries, and 20 million trips to the doctor. Toys were among the worst offenders, injuring 700,000 children a year.

Although injured consumers had the right to seek damages under tort law, the goal of the Consumer Product Safety Act of 1972 (CPSA) was to prevent injuries in the first place. This act created the Consumer Product Safety Commission (CPSC) to evaluate consumer products and develop safety standards. **Under the CPSA:**

- Manufacturers must report all potentially hazardous product defects within 24 hours of discovery;
- The Commission can impose civil and criminal penalties on those who violate its standards; and
- Individuals have the right to sue for damages, including attorney's fees, from anyone who knowingly violates a consumer product safety rule.

You can find out about product recalls or file a report on an unsafe product at the Commission's website (www.cpsc.gov) or at saferproducts.gov.

Ethics

Imagine that you are Robert Eckert, CEO of Mattel, Inc. Your company has sold millions of Jeep Wrangler Power Wheels. These toys are designed for children as young as two years old. You have just been notified that 150 of the cars have caught on fire, while thousands of others have overheated. In some cases, these toys have burned so fiercely that they have caught their garage on fire, endangering all of the home's occupants. You know that under CPSC rules, you are required to report toy defects within 24 hours. You also know that making the required report could have a significant impact on Mattel's profitability. What would you do?

Mattel decided to figure out what the problem was before reporting anything to the CPSC. In the end, it delayed months. Eckert was quoted as saying that the law was unreasonable and the company would not follow it.[15]

Is Mattel's stance ethical? What would Kant and Mill say? What Life Principle is he applying? Under what circumstances is it ethical to violate this law?

---

[15]Based on an article by Nicholas Casey and Andy Pasztor, "Safety Agency, Mattel Clash over Disclosures," *The Wall Street Journal*, September 4, 2007, p. A1.

CHAPTER CONCLUSION

Virtually no one will go through life without seeing advertisements, ordering online, borrowing money, acquiring a credit report, or using a consumer product. It is important to know your rights.

EXAM REVIEW

1. **UNFAIR PRACTICES** The Federal Trade Commission (FTC) prohibits "unfair and deceptive acts or practices." A practice is unfair if it violates public policy or if it meets all of the following three tests:
   (a) It causes a substantial consumer injury.
   (b) The harm of the injury outweighs any countervailing benefit.
   (c) The consumer could not reasonably avoid the injury.

2. **DECEPTIVE ADVERTISEMENTS** The FTC considers an advertisement to be deceptive if it contains an important misrepresentation or omission that is likely to mislead a reasonable consumer.

3. **CONSUMER FINANCIAL PROTECTION BUREAU (CFPB)** The CFPB is charged with regulating consumer financial products and services, including mortgages, credit cards, and checking accounts. The CFPB has the authority to take action against those committing "abusive acts" against consumers.

4. **BAIT-AND-SWITCH** FTC rules prohibit bait-and-switch advertisements. A merchant may not advertise a product and then disparage it (or make it unavailable) to consumers in an effort to sell a different item.

5. **MERCHANDISE BOUGHT BY MAIL, BY TELEPHONE, OR ONLINE** Under FTC rules for this type of merchandise, sellers must ship an item within the time stated or, if no time is given, within 30 days after receipt of the order.

6. **DO-NOT-CALL REGISTRY** The FTC prohibits telemarketers from calling or texting any telephone numbers listed on its do-not-call registry.

7. **TELEMARKETING** The Telephone Consumer Protection Act (TCPA) prohibits telemarketers from making autodialed and/or prerecorded calls or texts to cell phones and prerecorded calls to residential land lines unless the consumer unambiguously consents in writing.

8. **UNORDERED MERCHANDISE** Consumers may keep as a gift any unordered merchandise that they receive in the mail.

9. **DOOR-TO-DOOR RULES** Under the FTC door-to-door rules, a salesperson is required to notify the buyer that she has the right to cancel the transaction prior to midnight of the third business day thereafter.

10. **PAYDAY LOANS** These high-interest-rate loans violate the usury laws in some states.

11. **TRUTH IN LENDING ACT (TILA)** In all loans regulated by TILA, the disclosure must be clear and in meaningful sequence. The lender must disclose the amount financed, the total of payments, the finance charge, and the annual percentage rate.

12. **MORTGAGES** Lenders must make a good faith effort to determine whether a borrower can afford to repay the loan. They may not coerce or bribe an appraiser into misstating a home's value. Nor may they charge prepayment penalties on adjustable rate mortgages.

13. **QUALIFIED MORTGAGES** If lenders give a qualified mortgage, they are deemed to have complied with TILA.

14. **HOME EQUITY LOANS** In the case of a high-rate home equity loan, the lender must notify the consumer at least three business days before the closing that (1) he does not have to go through with the loan (even if he has signed the loan agreement) and (2) he could lose his house if he fails to make payments. If the duration of a high-rate home equity loan is less than five years, it may not contain balloon payments.

15. **RESCINDING A MORTGAGE** If a lender violates TILA, consumers have the right to rescind a mortgage (other than a first mortgage) for three business days after the signing if the lender is not the same as for the first mortgage. If this lender does not comply with the disclosure provisions of TILA, the consumer may rescind for up to three years from the date of the mortgage.

EXAMStrategy

Question: In August, Ethel went to First American Mortgage and Loan Association of Virginia (the Bank) to sign a second mortgage on her home. Her first mortgage was with a different bank. She left the closing without a copy of the required TILA disclosure forms. Ethel defaulted on her loan payments, and, the following May, the Bank began foreclosure proceedings on her house. In June, she notified the Bank that she wished to rescind the loan. Does Ethel have a right to rescind the loan ten months after it was made?

Strategy: In questions about mortgages, it is important to notice if the question involves a first or subsequent mortgage because the rules are different. Also, it matters whether the bank is the same for both mortgages. (See the "Result" at the end of this Exam Review section.)

16. **CREDIT CARD FEES** Credit card companies are not allowed to increase fees and interest rates on any charges already incurred (until a cardholder has missed two consecutive payments). Such increases are only permitted for future purchases and only if the company gives the consumer 45 days' notice and permits cancellation of the card.

17. **DEBIT AND ATM CARD FEES** Banks may not overdraw an account and charge an overdraft fee unless the consumer signs up for an overdraft plan.

18. **PREPAID DEBIT CARD FEES** Issuers must disclose all fees before a consumer buys a card. If the card allows consumers to overdraw their accounts, they are entitled to the same protections as credit card holders.

19. **LIABILITY FOR CREDIT CARDS** A credit card holder is liable only for the first $50 in unauthorized charges made before the credit card company is notified that the card was stolen.

20. **LIABILITY FOR DEBIT AND ATM CARDS** If the consumer reports the theft of a debit or ATM card within two days of discovering it, the bank must make good on all losses above $50. If the consumer waits more than two days, the bank will only replace stolen funds above $500. If the consumer waits more than 60 days after receipt of the bank statement, the bank is not responsible for any losses.

21. **PREPAID DEBIT CARDS** If the consumer reports the theft of a prepaid debit card within two days of discovering it, the bank will reimburse him for all losses above $50. If he waits until after two days, the bank will only replace stolen funds above $500.

22. **CREDIT CARD DISPUTES WITH A MERCHANT** In the event of a dispute between a customer and a merchant, the credit card company cannot bill the customer if:

    - She makes a good faith effort to resolve the dispute,
    - The dispute is for more than $50, and
    - The merchant is in the same state where she lives or is within 100 miles of her house.

    In practice, credit card companies typically ignore the requirement that the merchant be in the same state or within 100 miles of the consumer's home.

23. **DISPUTES WITH A CREDIT CARD COMPANY** Under the Fair Credit Billing Act (FCBA), a credit card company must promptly investigate and respond to any consumer complaints about a credit card bill.

24. **ELECTRONIC FUNDS** A consumer can stop payment on a transfer by oral or written notice up to three business days before the scheduled date.

25. **ERRORS IN ELECTRONIC FUND TRANSFERS** If a consumer reports an unauthorized electronic funds withdrawal within 60 days of the date of the bank statement, she is not liable.

26. **CONSUMER REPORTS** Under the Fair Credit Reporting Act (FCRA):

    - A consumer report can be used only for a legitimate business need,
    - A consumer reporting agency cannot report obsolete information,
    - An employer cannot request a consumer report on any current or potential employee without the employee's permission, and
    - Anyone who makes an adverse decision against a consumer because of a credit report must reveal the name and address of the reporting agency that supplied the negative information.

EXAMStrategy

Question: When Edo applied for insurance with Geico, the company reviewed his credit history and financial circumstances. It did not offer him the best possible premium, but this was because of his current finances, not his credit history. Was this an "adverse decision" under the FCRA, and was Geico required to notify him?

Strategy: Review the requirements of the FCRA. An adverse decision means that Edo was worse off because of a bad credit report. (See the "Result" at the end of this Exam Review section.)

27. **OBTAINING CREDIT REPORTS** Under the Fair and Accurate Credit Transactions Act (FACTA), consumers have the right to obtain one free credit report every year from each of the three major reporting agencies. Also, anyone who penalizes a consumer because of her credit score must give it to her at no charge.

28. **DEBT COLLECTORS** Under the Fair Debt Collection Practices Act (FDCPA), a debt collector may not harass or abuse debtors.

29. **CREDIT DISCRIMINATION** The Equal Credit Opportunity Act (ECOA) prohibits any creditor from discriminating against a borrower on the basis of race, color, religion, national origin, sex, marital status, age, or because the borrower is receiving welfare.

EXAMStrategy

Question: Kathleen, a single woman, applied for an Exxon credit card. Exxon rejected her application without giving any specific reason and without providing the name of the credit bureau it had used. When Kathleen asked for a reason for the rejection, she was told that the credit bureau did not have enough information about her to establish creditworthiness. In fact, Exxon had denied her credit application because she did not have a major credit card or a savings account, she had been employed for only one year, and she had no dependents. Did Exxon violate the law?

Strategy: Exxon violated two laws. Review the statutes in the "Consumer Credit" section of the chapter. (See the "Result" at the end of this Exam Review section.)

30. **WARRANTIES** The Magnuson-Moss Warranty Act requires any seller that offers a written warranty on a consumer product to disclose the terms of the warranty in simple and readily understandable language.

31. **CONSUMER PRODUCT SAFETY** The Consumer Product Safety Commission evaluates consumer products and develops safety standards. Under the Consumer Product Safety Act (CPSA), manufacturers must report all potentially hazardous product defects within 24 hours of discovery.

RESULTS

15. Result: Ethel entered into a second mortgage that was not from the same bank as her first mortgage. Because the bank violated TILA, Ethel had an automatic right to rescind for three business days. However, because the lender did not give the required forms to her at the closing, she could rescind for up to three years.

26. Result: Edo's premium was based on his *current* situation, not his credit history. Therefore, Geico did not have to notify Edo of an adverse decision because his premium would have been the same even if his credit report had been neutral.

29. Result: The court held that Exxon violated both the Fair Credit Reporting Act (FCRA) and the Equal Credit Opportunity Act (ECOA). The FCRA requires Exxon to tell Kathleen the name of the credit bureau that it used. Under the ECOA, Exxon was required to tell Kathleen the real reasons for the credit denial.

MULTIPLE-CHOICE QUESTIONS

1. Dell sold computers online with a particular software. In fact, the software was not available for several months. Instead, Dell sent customers a coupon for the software "when available." What did Dell do wrong?

I. Failed to offer buyers the opportunity to cancel their orders
II. Did not automatically cancel the orders
III. Did not ship the software within 30 days

(a) I and II
(b) I, II, and III
(c) I and III
(d) II and III

2. If you receive a product in the mail that you did not order, ______________.

(a) you must pay for it or return it
(b) you must pay for it only if you use it
(c) you must throw it away
(d) it is a gift to you
(e) you must return it, but the company must reimburse you for postage

3. Zach sells Cutco Knives door to door. Which of the following statements is *false*?

(a) The buyer has three days to cancel the order.
(b) Zach must tell the buyer of her rights.
(c) Zach must give the buyer a written notice of her rights.
(d) The seller can cancel orally or in writing.
(e) If the seller cancels, Zach must return her money within ten days.

4. Depending on state law, if a lender violates the usury laws, the borrower could possibly be allowed to keep ______________.

I. the interest that exceeds the usury limit

II. all the interest

III. all of the loan and the interest

(a) All of these
(b) Only I
(c) Only II
(d) Only III
(e) None of these

5. Companies must obtain permission from a consumer before charging for overdrafts on ______________.

(a) debit cards
(b) credit cards
(c) neither
(d) both

6. On the first of every month, your rent is automatically deducted from your bank account. You are moving out and want to make sure the payments stop. What should you do?

(a) You must call the bank at least three days before the first of the month.
(b) You must write the bank at least three days before the first of the month.
(c) Either A or B.
(d) You must have the landlord sign a form, which you then mail or deliver to the bank at least three days before the first of the month.

CASE QUESTIONS

1. A company offered credit cards to consumers with low credit scores. These cards had a $300 limit, a $75 sign-up fee, a $6 per month participation fee, and a $5 monthly fee for paper billing. Despite the fees, 98,000 people signed up. Is there anything wrong with that?

2. Synchrony (formerly known as GE Capital) offered a special deal providing that if credit card holders paid part of what they owed, it would write off the rest and the customer would never have to pay it. The company did not offer this deal to people who lived in Puerto Rico or were native Spanish-speakers. Is there anything wrong with that?

3. This post appeared on Instagram:

> khloekardashian Ever since I started taking two @sugarbearhair a day, my hair has been fuller and stronger than ever!! Even with all the heat and bleaching I do to it! 🐻 #sugarbearhair

Is there anything wrong with that?

4. There you are on FindMeLove.com. You joined for free, but you have to upgrade to a paid version if you want to see full-size photos or send personalized messages. So far, you are fine with the free version. But then, a really attractive guy messages you and wants to chat. To respond, you have to upgrade. Once you do, you never hear from him again. Only later do you realize that his profile had a little "VC" in the upper corner. That meant he was a "virtual cupid," that is, not a real person. Is there anything wrong with that?

5. **ETHICS** After TNT Motor Express hired Joseph Bruce Drury as a truck driver, it ordered a background check from Robert Arden & Associates. TNT provided Drury's Social Security number and date of birth, but not his middle name. Arden discovered that a Joseph *Thomas* Drury, who coincidentally had the same birth date as Joseph *Bruce* Drury, had served a prison sentence for drunk driving. Not knowing that it had the wrong Drury, Arden reported this information to TNT, which promptly fired Drury. When he asked why, the TNT executive refused to tell him. Did TNT violate the law? Whether or not TNT was in violation, did its executives behave ethically? Who would have been harmed or helped if TNT managers had informed Drury of the Arden report?

DISCUSSION QUESTIONS

1. Many people need a car to get to work, take care of their families, live their lives. But obtaining an auto loan can be difficult for those with a bad credit rating. Some finance companies are now willing to extend credit to people who are poor risks, on one condition: the company can install on the car tracking software that has the ability to disable the ignition if the debtor misses a payment. This procedure has left drivers stranded on highways and in dangerous neighborhoods. Is this practice unfair? Do the benefits of obtaining a loan outweigh the harm caused by this violation of privacy and loss of control?

2. ***YOU BE THE JUDGE* WRITING PROBLEM** Process cheese food slices must contain at least 51 percent natural cheese. Imitation cheese slices, by contrast, contain little or no natural cheese and consist primarily of water, vegetable oil, flavoring, and "fortifying agents." Kraft, Inc., makes Kraft Singles, which are individually wrapped process cheese food slices. When Kraft began losing market share to imitation slices that were advertised as both less expensive and equally nutritious as Singles, Kraft responded with a series of advertisements informing consumers that Kraft Singles cost more than imitation slices because they are made from 5 ounces of milk. Kraft does use 5 ounces of milk in making each Kraft Single, but imitation slices contain the same amount of calcium as Kraft Singles. Are the Kraft advertisements deceptive? **Argument for Kraft:** This statement is completely true—Kraft does use 5 ounces of milk in each Kraft Single. The FTC is assuming that the only value of milk is the calcium. In fact, people might prefer having milk rather than vegetable oil, regardless of the calcium. **Argument for the FTC:** It is deceptive to advertise more milk if the calcium is the same after all the processing.

3. **ETHICS** Should employers check an applicant's credit report as part of the hiring process? Each year retailers lose $30 *billion* a year from employee theft and $55 million because of workplace violence. Those who commit fraud are often living above their means, but there is no evidence that workers with poor credit reports

are more likely to steal from their employers, be violent, or quit their jobs. And refusing to hire someone with a low credit score creates a sad catch-22: People have poor credit records because they are unemployed and because they have poor credit records they continue to be unemployed. What is the right thing for an employer to do?

4. **ETHICS** Go to youtube.com and watch the advertisements for freecreditreport.com. Although the characters repeat the word *free* over and over, in fact the reports are not free unless the consumer signs up for the paid credit monitoring service. At the end of the ad, a voice quickly says, "Offer applies with enrollment in Triple Advantage." Are these ads deceptive under FTC rules? Are they ethical according to your Life Principles?

5. Advertisements for Listerine mouthwash claimed that it was as effective as flossing in preventing tooth plaque and gum disease. This statement was true, but only if the flossing was done incorrectly. In fact, many consumers do floss incorrectly. However, if flossing is done right, it is more effective against plaque and gum disease than Listerine. Is this advertisement deceptive?

CHAPTER

40 ENVIRONMENTAL LAW

"When my mother was left a widow almost 50 years ago, she taught school to support her family. A few years after my father's death, she took her savings and bought a small commercial building on a downtown lot in our little town in Oregon. The building, she said, would offer what my father couldn't—a source of support in her old age. In one half of the building was a children's clothing store; in the other, a dry cleaner. The two stores served Main Street shoppers for years.

The building that once represented security has produced a menace with the potential to bankrupt my mother.

Now the building that once represented security has produced a menace with the potential to bankrupt my mother. The discovery of contamination in city park well water triggered groundwater tests in the area. Waste products discarded by dry cleaners were identified as a likely source of contamination. Although a dry cleaner hasn't operated for 20 years on my mother's property, chemicals remain in the soil. Mother knew nothing of this hazard until a letter came from the Oregon Department of Environmental Quality (DEQ). It said she should decide if she would oversee further testing and cleanup herself or if she would let the government handle it. In either case, my mother would pay the costs.

The building is worth just under $70,000. Cleanup costs will be at least $200,000. At 84, my mother has enough savings to preserve her independence. She does not have enough money to bear the enormous costs of new community standards. The dry cleaner that operated in my mother's building disposed of chemicals the same way other dry cleaners did. None of these businesses was operated in a negligent fashion. They followed standards accepted by the community at the time. Now we are learning that we must live more carefully if we are to survive in a world that is safe and clean. My question is: Who will pay? Who will be responsible for cleaning up environmental messes made before we knew better?"[1]

[1]Excerpt from Carolyn Scott Kortge, "Taken to the Cleaners," *Newsweek*, October 23, 1995, p. 16. Reprinted with permission of the author.

Ultimately, the DEQ accepted that this elderly woman could not pay the cost of the cleanup. It allowed her to continue to manage the building and collect rent. When she died 12 years later at age 96, the DEQ took the building, and with it the estimated $600,000 cost of cleaning up the pollutants.

40-1 INTRODUCTION

40-1a Environmental Awareness

The environmental movement in the United States began in 1962 with the publication of Rachel Carson's book *Silent Spring*. She was the first to expose the deadly—and lingering—impact of DDT and other pesticides. These chemicals spread a wide web, poisoning not only the targeted insects, but the entire food chain—fish, birds, and humans. Since Carson first sounded the alarm, environmental issues have appeared regularly in the news—everything from acute disasters such as the 2014 chemical spill in West Virginia and the 2010 explosion of BP's Deepwater Horizon drilling platform in the Gulf of Mexico to chronic concerns such as polluted air and toxic materials in consumer goods.

40-1b The Cost–Benefit Trade-Off

The environmental movement began with the fervor of a moral crusade. How could anyone be against a clean environment? It has become clear, however, that the issue is more complex. It is not enough simply to say, "We are against pollution." As the opening scenario reveals, the question is: Who will pay? Who will pay for past damage inflicted before anyone understood the harm that pollutants cause? Who will pay for current changes necessary to prevent damage now and in the future? Will consumers insulate their homes or buy more energy-efficient appliances? Cities upgrade their public transportation systems? Developers protect wetlands? Car buyers accept the higher cost of greener technology?

The first President George Bush, a Republican, said, "Beyond all the studies, the figures, and the debates, the environment is a moral issue." But Newt Gingrich, a Republican Speaker of the House of Representatives, called the Environmental Protection Agency "the biggest job-killing agency in inner-city America."[2]

Externality
When people do not bear the full cost of their decisions

The cost–benefit trade-off is particularly complex in environmental issues because those who pay the cost often do not receive the benefit. If a company dumps toxic wastes into a stream, its shareholders benefit by avoiding the expense of safe disposal. Those who fish or drink the waters pay the real cost without receiving any of the benefit. Economists use the term **externality** to describe the situation in which people do not bear the full cost of their decisions. Externalities prevent the market system from achieving a clean environment on its own. Most commonly, government involvement is required to realign costs and benefits. The theme of this chapter—and of environmental law in general—can best be summarized as: **How should the law balance the costs and benefits of environmental decisions?** As we will see, this question is one of law, economics, ethics, and very hot politics.

---

[2]Both men are quoted in Robert V. Percival, Alan S. Miller, Christopher H. Schroeder, and James P. Leape, *Environmental Regulation* (Boston: Little, Brown & Co., 1992), p. 1, and 1995 supp. p. 2.

40-1c Environmental Protection Agency

In 1970, Congress created the Environmental Protection Agency (EPA) to consolidate environmental regulation under one roof. Prior to that time, environmental abuses had been (ineffectively) governed by tort law and a smattering of local ordinances. Now, environmental law is a mammoth structure of federal and state regulation.

Those who violate environmental laws are liable for civil damages. In addition, some statutes, such as the Clean Water Act, the Resource Conservation and Recovery Act, and the Endangered Species Act, provide for *criminal* penalties, including imprisonment. The EPA has the right to seek criminal prosecution of those who knowingly violate these statutes and of those corporate officers with responsibility and control who fail to prevent criminal negligence by their employees.

40-2 AIR POLLUTION

Airborne pollution causes a variety of harms:

- **Human health:** Air pollution can cause or increase the severity of serious disorders such as asthma, bronchitis, cancer, dementia, emphysema, heart disease, obesity, pneumonia, and strokes. The EPA estimates that it causes 5 percent of the deaths in America. Even pollution that is less than one-third of EPA standards increases the death rate. Air pollution also damages cognitive function. Exposure to dirty air before birth is linked to lower birth weight, brain function, and IQ scores as well as an increased risk of behavioral problems. And dirty air causes adult brains to age prematurely.
- **The physical environment:** Crops, forests, lakes, rivers, buildings, monuments, and vehicles are damaged.
- **Animals:** On land and in water, animals are injured and killed. The rate of extinction rises. The food chain is threatened.
- **Climate change:** During the last 100 years, the average temperature worldwide has increased between 0.5 degree and 1.1 degree Fahrenheit. During the next 100 years, the world's average temperature is likely to rise another 2–6 degree Fahrenheit, producing the warmest climate in the history of humankind. (By comparison, the planet is only 5–9 degree Fahrenheit warmer than during the last Ice Age.) This global warming is causing climate change.

The major sources of air pollution are power plants, refineries, factories, and motor vehicles. Residential furnaces, farm operations, forest fires, vapors from building materials, and dust from mines and construction sites also contribute.

Air pollution is both a national and global issue, with particularly acute externalities. Within the United States, prevailing west-to-east winds blow air pollution—and the harm it causes—across country. States in the Midwest and South produce pollution that travels to the Mid-Atlantic and Northeast.

Internationally, the issues are even more problematic because so many more regulatory bodies are involved. Meanwhile, the burning of fossil fuels in the United States causes worldwide global warming. Air pollution from China creates smog in the United States.

40-2a Clean Air Act

In the United States, air pollution is regulated by the Clean Air Act of 1963 (CAA).

Major Provisions

Under the CAA, the EPA has the authority to regulate both the total amount of existing air pollution and its ongoing production. Any individual state may impose *stricter* rules than the EPA.

The CAA's major provisions are as follows:

NAAQS
National ambient air quality standards

- **Primary standards.** Congress directed the EPA to establish national ambient air quality standards (**NAAQS**) for primary pollution, that is, pollution that harms the public health. The EPA's mandate was to set standards that protected public health and provided an adequate margin of safety *without regard to cost.*[3]
- **Secondary standards.** Congress also directed the EPA to establish NAAQS for pollution that may not be a threat to health but has other unpleasant effects, such as obstructing visibility and harming plants or materials.
- **State implementation plans (SIPs).** The CAA envisioned a partnership between the EPA and the states. After the EPA sets primary and secondary standards, states produce SIPs to meet these standards. If a state fails to produce an acceptable SIP, the EPA develops its own plan for that state.

Stationary source
Any building or facility that emits a certain level of pollution

BACT
Best available control technology

- **Regulation of stationary sources.** A **stationary source** is any building or facility that emits a certain level of pollution. The EPA sets limits on the amount of pollution these facilities produce and requires that they obtain permits for construction, operation, or renovation. They must use the best available control technology (**BACT**) for every pollutant.
- **Prevention of significant deterioration (PSD) program.** One purpose of the CAA is to "protect and enhance" air quality. Therefore, the EPA does not permit states to let air quality decline, even if the new higher levels of pollution would still meet the EPA's existing national standards. Any applicant for a permit must demonstrate that its emissions will not cause an overall decline in air quality, *regardless of health impact.* In essence, national policy values a clean environment for its own sake, apart from any health benefits.

NESHAPS
National Emission Standards for Hazardous Air Pollutants

MACT
Maximum achievable control technology

- **Toxics.** The CAA directed the EPA to set so-called National Emission Standards for Hazardous Air Pollutants (**NESHAPS**), which are safety standards for each of 189 toxics plus any other toxics the EPA chose to include. These standards are based on the maximum achievable control technology (**MACT**), which is the lowest feasible level given existing technology. Although these standards do not eliminate health risks, courts have upheld them.
- **Citizen suits.** The CAA (and many other environmental statutes) permits anyone who is or might be adversely affected by any violation to file suit against a polluter or against the EPA for failing to enforce the statute. Citizens have often been more assertive than the EPA in enforcing environmental statutes.

As we have seen, an important theme of this chapter is how to balance the costs and benefits of protecting the environment. Under the CAA, the EPA must set primary air quality standards without considering cost. The following two cases consider cost–benefit analysis

---

[3] Whitman v. Am. Trucking Ass'ns, 531 U.S. 457 (S. Ct. 2001).

under other provisions of the CAA. The first case is about a provision of the statute that directs the EPA to regulate power plant emissions, if "appropriate and necessary." Should the EPA consider costs when making that decision?

Michigan v. EPA

135 S. Ct. 2699
United States Supreme Court, 2015

Facts: In the Clean Air Act (CAA), Congress directed the EPA to study the impact of power plant emissions on public health and then to regulate power plants if the study indicated that regulation was "appropriate and necessary."

After conducting a study, the EPA found regulation "appropriate" because (1) power plants' emissions posed risks to human health and the environment and (2) controls were available to reduce these emissions. It found regulation "necessary" because the CAA's other provisions did not eliminate these risks.

The EPA's cost-benefit analysis estimated that the regulations would cost power plants $9.6 billion per year. Although the EPA could not fully quantify the benefits of reducing power plants' emissions, its best estimate was a benefit of $4 to $6 million per year. The costs to power plants were thus between 1,600 and 2,400 times as great as the quantifiable benefits. However, when the EPA considered other benefits of the regulations, which were not covered by this provision of the CAA, such as the impact on global warming and a reduction of fine particulate matter, their benefit estimate increased to $37 to $90 billion per year. In any event, although it had conducted a cost-benefit analysis, the EPA decided that, under the statute, it should issue regulations without regard to costs.

Twenty-three states and the National Mining Association challenged the EPA's decision to ignore costs when issuing these regulations. The Court of Appeals upheld the EPA's decision. The Supreme Court granted *certiorari*.

Issue: ***Should the EPA have considered cost when issuing power plant regulations?***

Excerpts from Justice Scalia's Decision: EPA's disregard of cost rested on its interpretation of [the statute] which directs the Agency to regulate power plants if it "finds such regulation is appropriate and necessary." The Agency accepts that it *could* have interpreted this provision to mean that cost is relevant to the decision to add power plants to the program. But it chose to read the statute to mean that cost makes no difference to the initial decision to regulate.

One does not need to open up a dictionary in order to realize the capaciousness of this phrase. In particular, "appropriate" is the classic broad and all-encompassing term that naturally and traditionally includes consideration of all the relevant factors. Although this term leaves agencies with flexibility, an agency may not entirely fail to consider an important aspect of the problem when deciding whether regulation is appropriate. Read naturally in the present context, the phrase "appropriate and necessary" requires at least some attention to cost. One would not say that it is even rational, never mind "appropriate," to impose billions of dollars in economic costs in return for a few dollars in health or environmental benefits.

In addition, "cost" includes more than the expense of complying with regulations; any disadvantage could be termed a cost. EPA's interpretation precludes the Agency from considering *any* type of cost—including, for instance, harms that regulation might do to human health or the environment. The Government concedes that if the Agency were to find that emissions from power plants do damage to human health, but that the technologies needed to eliminate these emissions do even more damage to human health, it would *still* deem regulation appropriate. No regulation is "appropriate" if it does significantly more harm than good.

Consideration of cost reflects the understanding that reasonable regulation ordinarily requires paying attention to the advantages *and* the disadvantages of agency decisions. It also reflects the reality that too much wasteful expenditure devoted to one problem may well mean considerably fewer resources available to deal effectively with other (perhaps more serious) problems. [I]t is unreasonable to read an instruction to an administrative agency to determine whether "regulation is appropriate and necessary" as an invitation to ignore cost.

We need not and do not hold that the law unambiguously required the Agency, when making this preliminary estimate, to conduct a formal cost-benefit analysis in which each advantage and disadvantage is assigned a monetary value. It will be up to the Agency to decide (as always, within the limits of reasonable interpretation) how to account for cost.

We hold that EPA interpreted [the statute] unreasonably when it deemed cost irrelevant to the decision to regulate power plants.

And in yet another cost–benefit case, a power plant argued that the EPA had imposed a solution whose cost far outweighed its benefit. There is only one Grand Canyon. Should its visibility be preserved at any cost?

You Be the Judge

Central Arizona Water Conservation District v. EPA

990 F.2d 1531
United States Court of Appeals for the Ninth Circuit, 1993

Facts: In the Clean Air Act, Congress directed the EPA to issue regulations that would protect visibility at national landmarks. The Navaho Generating Station (NGS) was a power plant 12 miles from the Grand Canyon. In response to a citizen suit filed by the Environmental Defense Fund under the Clean Air Act, the EPA ordered NGS to reduce its sulfur dioxide emissions by 90 percent. To do so would cost NGS $430 million initially in capital expenditures and then $89.6 million annually. Average winter visibility in the Grand Canyon would be improved by, at most, 7 percent, but perhaps less. NGS sued to overturn the EPA's order. A court may nullify an EPA order if it determines that the agency action was arbitrary and capricious.

You Be the Judge: *Did the EPA act arbitrarily and capriciously in requiring NGS to spend half a billion dollars to improve winter visibility at the Grand Canyon by, at most, 7 percent?*

Argument for NGS: This case is a perfect example of environmentalism run amok. Half a billion dollars for the *chance* of increasing winter visibility at the Grand Canyon by 7 percent? No rational person would choose to spend his own money that way, but the EPA is happy to spend NGS's. Winter visitors to the Grand Canyon would undoubtedly prefer that NGS provide them with a free lunch rather than a 7 percent improvement in visibility. The EPA order is simply a waste of money.

Argument for the EPA: Under the Clean Air Act, Congress instructed the EPA to protect visibility at national landmarks such as the Grand Canyon. How can NGS, or anyone else, measure the benefit of protecting a national treasure like the Grand Canyon? Even people who never have and never will visit it during the winter sleep better at night knowing that the canyon is protected. NGS has been causing harm to the Grand Canyon, and now it should remedy the damage.

Courts generally defer to federal agencies, whose experts deal with similar problems all the time. The EPA has greater expertise in these matters than either NGS or this court.

You Touch Pix of EuToch/Shutterstock.com

Is improving winter visibility at the Grand Canyon by 7 percent worth half a billion dollars?

Implementation: Cap and Trade

Cap and Trade
A market-based system for reducing emissions

The Cap and Trade program is a method for limiting air pollutants in an economically efficient manner. First, an overall limit on emissions is set for a particular area. Then, each year, pollution sources receive an emissions allowance, meaning that they are allowed to emit a certain amount of pollutants. If an enterprise does not need its entire allowance because it uses cleaner fuels or more effective pollution control devices, it can sell the leftover allowance to other companies or stockpile it for future use. Facilities with high levels of pollution either buy more allowances or reduce their own emissions, depending on which alternative is cheaper. In effect, the government establishes the maximum amount of pollution, and then the market sets the price for meeting the standard.

The cap and trade approach is particularly successful in regulating power plant pollution that crosses state lines. The EPA sets a limit on pollution from upwind states, which can then use a cap and trade program to meet their pollution budget.[4] A federal appeals court twice struck down these EPA rules, but ultimately, the Supreme Court upheld them.[5]

40-2b Climate Change

Scientific evidence underlying the theory of climate change has been debated for a long time, but today, scientists accept that the burning of fossil fuels produces gases—carbon dioxide, methane, and nitrous oxide (**greenhouse gases** or **GHGs**)—that trap heat in the Earth's atmosphere. **This global warming leads to significant climate change.**

Greenhouse gases or GHGs
Gases that trap heat in the Earth's atmosphere, thereby causing global warming

The United Nations Intergovernmental Panel on Climate Change issued a report concluding that if governments fail to limit GHGs by 2030, profound global warming will be impossible to prevent using the technologies currently available. The report further warns that climate change will cause extreme storms, flooding, drought, landslides, air pollution, water and food shortages, the extinction of plants and animals, and an increase in refugees and poverty worldwide. Some of these effects will be seen this century. In just the next 30 years, climate change could lead to the displacement of as many as 200 million people. Sea levels are now rising at a faster rate than any time in the last 28 centuries.[6]

A bipartisan committee of American business leaders, politicians, and academics issued a report detailing the impact of climate change on the United States. It predicts constant flooding along the coasts, and the destruction of important industries in the south, such as tourism and agriculture, as summers become too hot to grow crops—or even to be outside.[7]

Meanwhile, businesses are seeing the effects of global warming. Coke has found that its supply of ingredients—beets, sugar, and citrus—is sometimes disrupted. And it was denied an operating license in India because of a water shortage. Floods shut down a Nike factory and droughts have damaged the cotton production that it needs for its clothing.[8]

Preventing climate change is a highly complex problem because any solution requires international political cooperation coupled with major behavioral changes. Finding a solution is even more challenging because, as the following ethics discussion illustrates, some powerful players have refused to accept its reality.

4This program is called the Clean Air Interstate Rule (CAIR).

5North Carolina v. EPA, 531 F.3d 896 (D.C. Cir. 2008); North Carolina v. EPA, 550 F.3d 1176 (D.C. Cir. 2008); EME Homer City Generation, L.P. v. EPA, 696 F.3d 7 (D.C. Cir. 2012); EPA v. EME Homer City Generation, L.P., 134 S. Ct. 1584 (S. Ct. 2014).

6The National Oceanic and Atmospheric Administration has developed a web tool showing the impact of rising sea levels. Google "NOAA rising sea level viewer."

7Risky Business: The Economic Risks of Climate Change in the United States. Available at riskybusiness.org.

8Coral Davenport, "Industry Awakens to Threat of Climate Change," *The New York Times*, January 23, 2014.

Ethics

In the 1970s, Exxon scientists reported to the company's Board of Directors that fossil fuels were causing serious damage to the planet. The Board reacted by mounting a disinformation campaign to undermine the evidence that its own scientists believed to be true. Not until 2007 did the company admit that climate change was a serious problem. It then stopped funding organizations that deny climate change. Why did the Exxon Board make these choices? What ethics traps did it fall into? How did it rationalize its decisions? How could a board of directors improve its decision-making process?

Paris Accord

Paris Accord An international agreement to prevent climate change by reducing GHGs

In 2015, 195 countries entered into the **Paris Accord**, an agreement to prevent climate change by reducing GHGs.[9] **The Accord does not set specific standards. Instead, each country establishes its own goals and there are no penalties for countries that set low goals or who fail to achieve their set targets.** However, all countries have pledged to meet every five years to report the results of their emissions programs and to issue more aggressive plans. The hope is that peer pressure will lead countries to set ambitious goals. In any event, under the Paris Accord the world has started working together to solve this global problem.

Historically, the United States has produced more total GHGs than any other country. In 2015, in response to the Paris Accord, the United States committed to cutting its GHG emissions by between 26 and 28 percent by 2025 and issued CAA regulations that would have achieved at least part of this goal. However, these regulations were politically contentious because they imposed high current costs in return for future benefits. In 2017, the Trump Administration overturned the regulations and withdrew from the Paris Accord. However, more than 1,200 mayors, governors, and business leaders in the United States have promised to continue efforts to meet the Paris Accord standards.

Domestic Regulation

The Supreme Court ruled that if GHGs endanger health or welfare, the EPA must regulate them.[10] The Obama administration issued a Clean Power Plan to reduce GHG emissions. However, as with most environmental decisions, large externalities were at play: Costs and benefits were not born equally by everyone. Those who felt the costs were too high, such as power plants, sued to stop enforcement of the rules. The Trump administration then directed the EPA to revoke the Clean Power Plan.

In addition, **states are able to set their own standards for air pollution, so long as they are stricter than federal rules.** California and ten eastern states, including New York and those in New England, have adopted a cap and trade plan for GHGs produced by electric utilities.[11] In addition, more than half the states have established plans to increase renewable sources for electricity generation. In any event, whether these limited plans can affect an international problem is uncertain.

9Most of these countries have also ratified the agreement.

10Massachusetts v. Environmental Protection Agency, 549 U.S. 497 (S. Ct. 2007). In Util. Air Regulatory Group v. EPA, 134 S. Ct. 2427 (S. Ct. 2014), the Supreme Court upheld the EPA's regulatory program for GHGs.

11California won a court challenge to its plan, but the case is on appeal as of this writing.

Ethics

Devastating typhoons and tsunamis have hit South Asia. Africa suffers under severe droughts. Small island nations fear being submerged by rising sea levels. Representatives of these nations call for "Climate Justice." They argue that countries that contribute least to climate change suffer the most from its effects. They ask that richer nations make financial contributions to cover the "loss and damage" that poorer countries have suffered from environmental causes. What obligation do rich countries with high energy consumption have to poorer nations with lower energy use but greater damage?

40-2c Automobile Pollution

Motor vehicles create more than 50 percent of the hazardous pollutants in the air. They also produce about a third of America's GHGs. The good news: New cars run 97 percent cleaner than 1970 models. The bad news: Americans are driving more—and bigger—cars on longer trips.

The EPA sets standards for the pollution control devices in motor vehicles and also the composition of fuel. The Obama administration had imposed fuel economy rules that were forcing the automobile industry to build more fuel-efficient cars, including hybrid and electric models. However, after car manufacturers complained to the Trump administration that the cost of complying with these rules was too high, it withdrew the Obama rules and began work on new ones.

Generally, states are not permitted to adopt their own vehicle emission standards because automobile makers would struggle to meet 50 different sets of rules. But because California regulated automobile pollution before the CAA was passed, the Act grants it special permission to set even stricter pollution standards, as long as it obtains a waiver from the EPA. Other states then have the right to adopt California standards instead of federal rules. California has set tougher standards that, among other features, would require one in seven cars sold in the state by 2025 to be low or no emission, such as those powered by battery or hydrogen fuels. Typically, about one-third of the states follow California's lead. However, under the Trump administration, the EPA is trying to revoke the existing California waiver.

Ethics

Since Tim Cook became CEO of Apple in 2011, more than three-quarters of the company's buildings worldwide have been adapted to run on sustainable energy—sun, wind, water, or geothermal. Cook hired a former head of the EPA to manage the company's sustainability program. But, at an annual meeting, a large shareholder asked Cook to limit Apple's environmental activities to those that also enhanced company profits. Cook responded that many environmental policies do make economic sense. But then he added, "We do a lot of things for reasons besides profit motive. We want to leave the world better than we found it." His advice to the objecting shareholder: "Get out of the stock."

Should Cook be spending shareholder money on activities that do not enhance the bottom line? If so, how should the company evaluate unprofitable activities? What metrics should it use? What are Cook's Life Principles?[12]

---

[12]Chris Taylor, "Tim Cook to Climate Change Deniers: Get Out of Apple Stock," *Mashable*, March 1, 2014.

EXAMStrategy

Question: Suppose that the legislature of the state of Kentucky was unhappy with the national automobile emissions standards set by the EPA. Under the Clean Air Act, could it pass a statute setting a different standard? What if it wanted its standards for air toxics to be different from those set by the EPA?

Strategy: There are different rules for automobile emissions and other air pollutants. Why is that?

Result: Kentucky does not have the right to create its own standards for auto pollution, but it does have the right to adopt California's rules. States can set tighter, but not looser, standards for other air pollutants. It is important to have national standards for auto emissions because car manufacturers cannot produce different vehicles for each state. For the other pollutants, uniformity does not matter.

40-3 WATER POLLUTION

Water pollution is harmful to:

- **Human health:** Pathogens can cause a number of loathsome diseases, such as typhus, dysentery, and hepatitis. Chemicals are poisonous and can cause serious diseases such as cancer.
- **Animals:** Fish, shellfish, dolphins, whales, and birds die or reproduce more slowly. The food chain is disrupted.
- **The physical environment:** Damaged water systems are unable to support biodiversity in plants and animals. They are no longer attractive or useful for recreational purposes.

Sources of water pollution include:

Point source
Discharges from a single producer

Nonpoint source
Pollutants that have no single source, such as water runoff from city streets

- **Point sources**: Discharges from a single producer, such as a pipe from waste treatment plants, factories, and refineries
- **Nonpoint sources**: Pollutants that have no single source but result from events such as storm-water runoff. As it flows over the ground, it brings along chemicals, pesticides, fertilizer, motor oil, heavy metals, animal waste, and dirt. Rain is also a nonpoint source. It carries pollutants from the air into the water. About half of the water pollution in the United States comes from nonpoint sources.
- **Accidents:** Such as an oil spill in the Gulf of Mexico and a chemical spill in West Virginia
- **Heat:** When industrial plants use water as a coolant, they return it to the waterways at a high temperature that damages the ecosystem.

40-3a Clean Water Act

In 1972, Congress passed a statute, now called the Clean Water Act (CWA), with two ambitious goals: (1) to make all navigable water suitable for swimming and fishing by 1983 and (2) to eliminate the discharge of pollutants into navigable water by 1985. Like the CAA, the CWA also permits citizen suits. The CWA's goals have not, so far, been met.

Under the CWA:

- **Navigable waters.** The CWA governs only "navigable" waters. Traditionally, the courts had interpreted the term "navigable water" very broadly to include wetlands, intermittent streams (those that do not flow all the time), and ponds that might affect other bodies of water. This definition gave the EPA the right to regulate vast areas. **But the Supreme Court changed the interpretation of navigable water to *exclude* (1) intermittent streams or wetlands, (2) ponds or lakes that are not connected to open bodies of water, and (3) waterways that are all within one state, even though pollutants can leak from them into drinking water.**[13]

  The EPA under the Obama administration then issued a new rule, called the Waters of the United States (WOTUS), to clarify its authority under the CWA. Farmers, golf course owners, pesticide makers, and others challenged the rule because they felt its limits on pesticide use were too stringent. The Trump administration is trying to withdraw the rule.
- **Point sources.** Any discharge into navigable water from a point source is illegal without a permit (from the EPA or a state).
- **Pollution limits.** The EPA sets limits, by industry, on the amount of each type of pollution any point source can discharge and the technology that must be used to treat it. These standards are based on best available technology (BAT). The EPA faces a gargantuan task in determining the best available technology that each industry can use to reduce pollution. Furthermore, standards become obsolete quickly as technology changes.
- **National water quality standards.** The EPA must set national standards for water quality generally. Standards vary depending upon use: higher for drinking, fishing, or recreation than for irrigation or industry.
- **State plans.** Each state must develop plans to achieve these EPA standards.
  - **Water use.** States must identify how each body of water is used. The EPA evaluates the uses and criteria developed by the states, and either approves them or else proposes and promulgates its own set of standards. No matter what the water's designated use, standards may not be set at a level lower than its current condition.
  - **TMDLs.** For each body of water that does not meet water quality standards, the state is required to establish a set of total maximum daily loads (**TMDLs**) sufficient to bring the body into compliance with water quality standards. Each TMDL establishes the maximum amount of each pollutant that may be added to the water body daily from all sources (runoff, point sources, etc.). About 44,000 water bodies require TMDLs.

TMDLs
Total maximum daily loads of permitted pollution

  - **Nonpoint sources.** States, not the EPA, must develop a plan for nonpoint source pollution. Congress left nonpoint source pollution to the states because it is so difficult to regulate. This regulation also involves complex issues such as land use planning that are, in theory, better handled at the local level than by national fiat. However optimistic Congress may have been, to date the states have not successfully implemented this section of the CWA. They appear to lack both the political will and the technical know-how, for which they are not totally to blame. Determining the impact of individual pollutants on the overall quality of a body of water used for many different purposes is a complex problem. Land use planning requires a delicate and volatile mix of consensus and control.

---

[13]Solid Waste Agency v. United States Army Corps of Eng'rs, 531 U.S. 159 (S. Ct. 2001); Rapanos v. United States, 547 U.S. 715 (S. Ct. 2006).

- **Wetlands.** Wetlands are the transition areas between land and open water. They may look like swamps, they may even *be* swamps, but their unattractive appearance should not disguise their vital role in the aquatic world. They are natural habitats for many fish and wildlife. They also serve as a filter for neighboring bodies of water, trapping chemicals and sediments. Moreover, they are an important aid in flood control because they can absorb a high level of water and then release it slowly after the emergency is past.

  The CWA prohibits any discharge of dredge and fill material into wetlands without a permit. Originally, under the CWA, many other activities that harm wetlands, such as draining them, did not require a permit. (However, many states require permits for draining wetlands.) After some particularly egregious abuses, the EPA issued regulations to limit the destruction of wetlands. These new regulations were, however, successfully challenged in the courts.[14] The EPA then rewrote the regulations. Although, in theory, the government's official policy is no net loss of wetlands, in reality about 60,000 acres of wetlands are lost each year.
- **Wastewater.** Sewer lines feed into publicly owned wastewater treatment plants, also known as municipal sewage plants. A municipality must obtain a permit for any discharge from a wastewater treatment plant. To obtain a permit, the municipality must first treat the waste to reduce its toxicity. However, taxpayers have resisted the large increases in taxes or fees necessary to fund required treatments. Since the fines imposed by the EPA are almost always less than the cost of treatment, some cities have been slow to comply.

  A significant percentage of the sewage systems in this country have admitted to violating the law by dumping incompletely treated human waste and harmful chemicals into waterways. Fewer than 20 percent of those were penalized. There have, however, been some notable successes. For instance, the Charles River in Boston, which was the inspiration for the pop song, "Dirty Water," recently received a grade of B+ by the EPA—an impressive improvement over the D it received in 1995. The river is now almost always safe for boating and swimming in the summer, although the bottom still contains heavy metals and other toxics. A tetanus shot is no longer required—unless a swimmer touches bottom.

The following case demonstrates how complicated environmental issues can be. The EPA found a more efficient method for setting pollution standards. But should the court allow it? You be the judge.

You Be the Judge

Va. Dot v. United States EPA

2013 U.S. Dist. LEXIS 981; 2013 WL 53741
United States District Court for the Eastern District of Virginia, 2013

Facts: The Accotink Creek is a 25-mile long tributary of the Potomac River. After the Commonwealth of Virginia violated the CWA by failing to set TMDLs that would enable the Creek to meet water quality standards, the EPA established its own set of TMDLs.

The Creek was unhealthy because it had too much sediment from storm-water runoff. Sediment is a pollutant and, therefore, regulated by the CWA. However, it is difficult for scientists to measure and set daily pollution standards for *sediment* because its content varies and it is

14 National Mining Ass'n v. U.S. Army Corps of Engineers, 145 F.3d 1399 (D.C. Cir. 1998).

not always clear which components cause what problems and how the various ingredients react with each other. *Storm-water runoff* is easy to assess and measure but it is not technically classified as a pollutant.

The EPA established TMDLs for the flow rate of storm water into the Creek, but Virginia sued, alleging that the EPA had no right to regulate storm water because it is not a pollutant.

You Be the Judge: *Does the EPA have the right to limit storm-water runoff (which is not a pollutant) because it carries pollutants?*

Argument for Virginia: The statute is very clear: The EPA has the right to regulate pollutants. Storm water is not a pollutant. Therefore, the EPA cannot regulate it. Beginning and end of story.

Argument for the EPA: Here is what we know: (1) how to measure and handle storm-water runoff, because civil engineers deal with it all the time; (2) how much storm water will carry enough sediment to harm the Accotink Creek; (3) that to repair the Creek, Virginia has to limit storm-water runoff because that is how the sediment enters the water.

What we do not know is how much of each pollutant will, on a daily basis, damage the Creek. Why spend huge amounts of time and money assessing each individual component of the sediment just to end up at the same result—limiting runoff?

Remember that the goal of the CWA is to eliminate the discharge of pollutants into navigable water. We have come up with a reasonable methodology that is very much in keeping with the goals of the CWA.

40-3b Other Water Pollution Statutes

The Safe Drinking Water Act of 1974:

- Requires the EPA to set national standards for substances if:
  - They are potentially harmful to human health,
  - They are likely to be found in drinking water at a dangerous level and frequency,
  - Their regulation would reduce health risks,
  - It is feasible for water systems to remove them, and
  - The benefits of regulation exceeds its costs.
- Assigns enforcement responsibility to the states but permits the EPA to take enforcement action against states that do not adhere to the standards,
- Prohibits the use of lead in any pipes through which drinking water flows, and
- Requires community water systems to send every customer an annual consumer confidence report disclosing the level of contaminants in the drinking water.

We can only hope that consumers will remain confident after receiving the report because violations of the Safe Drinking Water Act have occurred in every state. Even more worrisome, the EPA only regulates in drinking water about 100 chemicals out of the 85,000 currently sold in the United States (although states can monitor additional chemicals). The EPA regulates so few chemicals because the statute is complex and every decision contentious, even as Congress cuts the EPA's budget. In the last 20 years, the EPA has added only one chemical (perchlorate) to its regulation list. Just the process of adding this substance took ten years, and five years later, the final rule is still not complete. Moreover, despite the EPA's ban on lead pipes, millions of older pipes with lead are still in use, leaching this dangerous contaminant into tap water.

The **Ocean Dumping Act of 1972** prohibits the dumping of wastes in ocean water without a permit from the EPA.

Congress passed the **Oil Pollution Act of 1990** in response to the mammoth 1989 *Exxon Valdez* tanker oil spill in Prince William Sound, Alaska. To prevent defective boats from leaking oil, this statute sets design standards for ships operating in U.S. waters. It also requires ship owners to pay for damage caused by oil discharged from their ships.

EXAMStrategy

Question: Edward lives on a ranch near Wind River. He uses water from the river for irrigation. To divert more water to his ranch, he builds a dam in the river using scrap metal, cottonwood trees, car bodies, and a washing machine. This material does not harm downstream water. Has Edward violated the CWA?

Strategy: The CWA prohibits the discharge of pollution without a permit. Was this pollution?

Result: Yes, the court ruled that the material Edward placed in the water was pollution. It was irrelevant that the material did not flow downstream.

40-4 WASTE DISPOSAL

The time is 1978. The place is 96th Street in Niagara Falls, New York. Six women are afflicted with breast cancer, one man has bladder cancer, another suffers from throat cancer. A seven-year-old boy suddenly goes into convulsions and dies of kidney failure. Other residents have chromosomal abnormalities, epilepsy, respiratory problems, and skin diseases. This street is three blocks away from Love Canal.

In 1945, Hooker Chemical Co. disposed of 21,800 tons of 82 different chemicals by dumping them into Love Canal or burying them nearby, although the company knew that children swam in the canal. An internal memorandum warned that this decision would lead to "potential future hazard" and be a "potential source of lawsuits." Despite knowledge of the danger, Hooker sold the dumpsite to a local school board to build an elementary school (but only after inserting a clause in the deed to eliminate the company's liability).

Schoolchildren tripped over drums of chemicals that worked their way up to the surface.

Schoolchildren tripped over drums of chemicals that worked their way up to the surface. They were burned playing with hot balls of chemical residue—what they called "fire stones"—that popped up through the ground. Homeowners noticed foul odors in their basements after heavy rains. Finally, a national health emergency was declared at Love Canal, and a joint federal-state program relocated 800 families. Occidental Chemical Corp. (which had since bought Hooker) agreed to pay hundreds of millions of dollars to the state of New York and the EPA.[15] In the end, the cleanup took 21 years to complete.

In the past, it was common for companies to discard waste in waterways, landfills, or open dumps. Out of sight was out of mind. Waste disposal continues to be a major problem in the United States. It has been estimated that the cost of cleaning up *existing* waste products will exceed $1 trillion. At the same time, the country continues to produce billions of tons of agricultural, commercial, industrial, and domestic waste each year.

40-4a Resource Conservation and Recovery Act

The Resource Conservation and Recovery Act (RCRA) focuses on *preventing* future Love Canals by regulating the production, transportation, and disposal of solid wastes, both hazardous material and ordinary garbage. It also regulates spills at RCRA-regulated facilities.

[15]William Glaberson, "Love Canal: Suit Focuses on Records from 1940s," *The New York Times*, October 22, 1990. Copyright © 1990 by The New York Times Co.

Ordinary Garbage

Before 1895, the City of New York did not collect garbage. Residents simply piled it up in the streets, causing the streets to rise 5 feet in height over the century. At present, each American generates 4.3 pounds of solid waste a *day,* an increase of 60 percent since 1960. Of this amount, we recycle or compost 1.5 pounds a day.

The disposal of nonhazardous solid waste has generally been left to the states, but they must follow guidelines set by the RCRA. The RCRA:

- Bans new open dumps,
- Requires that garbage be sent to sanitary landfills,
- Sets minimum standards for landfills,
- Requires landfills to monitor nearby groundwater,
- Requires states to develop a permit program for landfills, and
- Provides some financial assistance to aid states in waste management.

Underground Storage Tanks

Concerned that underground gasoline storage tanks were leaking into water supplies, Congress required the EPA to issue regulations for detecting and correcting leaks in existing tanks and establishing specifications for new receptacles. **Anyone who owns property with an underground storage tank must notify the EPA and comply with regulations that require installation of leak detectors, periodic testing, and, in some cases, removal of old tanks.**

Hazardous Wastes

Identification. The EPA must establish criteria for determining what is, and is not, hazardous waste. It must then prepare a list of wastes that qualify as hazardous.

Disposal. Walmart paid $82 million to settle claims that it had illegally disposed of hazardous wastes. Its workers had thrown toxic products such as bleach and fertilizer into the local sewer system. It was also sending hazardous items that consumers had returned, such as pesticides, to an unlicensed facility.[16]

Hazardous wastes must be (1) tracked from creation to final disposal and (2) disposed of at a certified facility. In addition:

- Anyone who creates, transports, stores, treats, or disposes of more than a certain quantity of hazardous wastes must apply for an EPA permit.
- Anyone who generates more than a certain amount of hazardous waste in any month:
  - Must obtain an identification number for its wastes.
  - When shipping this waste to a disposal facility, must send along a manifest that identifies the waste, the transporter, and the destination.
  - Must notify the EPA if it does not receive a receipt from the disposal site indicating that the waste has been received.

16Stephanie Clifford, "Wal-Mart Is Fined $82 Million over Mishandling of Hazardous Wastes," *The New York Times*, May 28, 2013.

40-4b Superfund

In this chapter's opening scenario, an elderly woman faced financial ruin from the cost of cleaning up pollutants that her dry cleaner tenants had left. She was liable under the **Comprehensive Environmental Response, Compensation, and Liability Act (CERCLA),** more commonly known as **Superfund. The goal of Superfund is cleaning up hazardous wastes that were illegally dumped in the past.**

Superfund
Another name for the Comprehensive Environmental Response, Compensation, and Liability Act (CERCLA)

The philosophy of Superfund is "the polluter pays." **Therefore, under Superfund, anyone who has *ever owned or operated* a site on which hazardous wastes are found, or who has *transported* wastes to the site, or who has *arranged* for the disposal of wastes that were released at the site, is liable for:**

- The cost of cleaning up the site,
- Any damage done to natural resources, and
- Any required health assessments.

All polluters at a site are jointly and severally liable unless they can show that they were only responsible for a portion of the damages. In practical terms, this means that the EPA seeks full recovery from whichever polluters are financially sound. These defendants then seek to reduce their liability by showing that they were only responsible for part of the damage at the site.

In a "shovels first, lawyers later" approach, Congress established a revolving trust fund for the EPA to use in cleaning up sites even before obtaining reimbursement from those responsible for the damage or if the polluters cannot be found. The trust fund was initially financed by a tax on the oil and chemical industries, which produce the bulk of hazardous waste. In 1995, however, the taxes expired, and Congress refused to renew them. Since then, the EPA has had to rely on reimbursements from polluters and congressional appropriations.

Property owners have complained, and litigated, bitterly because:

- Current and former owners are liable even though they did nothing illegal at the time, and indeed even if they did nothing more than own property where someone else had previously dumped hazardous wastes. This liability has been called **toxic succession** because anyone who ever owns the property is liable, no matter how innocent. In addition, officers or controlling shareholders in closely held corporations can be personally liable for operations of the company.
- Joint and several liability means that a small amount of pollution can lead to a very large damage claim.
- The expense of a Superfund cleanup can be devastating—higher than $100 million on some sites—and much more than the value of the land. Property owners have often viewed litigation as a better investment.

Toxic succession
Anyone who has ever owned a polluted property is liable for its clean-up.

EXAMStrategy

Question: Leo was an auto mechanic who owned his own business. One morning, after a heavy rainstorm, he noticed the edge of what turned out to be an underground storage tank sticking out of the ground. He dug it up and, without looking to see what was inside it, sent the tank to an auto salvage site. Has Leo violated the law?

Strategy: Review the requirements on waste disposal. Leo has violated the law three times.

Result: To start, he should have notified the EPA of the underground tank. Second, he needed to determine if the tank contained any hazardous wastes. If it did, then he had to obtain an EPA permit to dispose of the waste. Third, he should have sent the tank to a certified facility, not to an auto salvage site.

40-5 CHEMICALS

More than 85,000 chemicals are used in food, drugs, cosmetics, pesticides, and other products. Up to 3,000 new chemicals are introduced each year. Although consumers may think that these products have been safety tested, that is not true for many of them.

Chemicals are so common in consumer products (such as shampoo, clothing, furniture, and even cash register receipts) that babies are now born with hundreds of chemicals in their blood. Some of these chemicals are linked to, among other harm, cancer, birth defects, infertility, obesity, diabetes, endocrine disruption, and neurological damage.[17]

Several federal agencies share responsibility for regulating chemicals. The Food and Drug Administration (FDA) has control over foods, drugs, and cosmetics. The Occupational Safety and Health Administration (OSHA) is responsible for protecting workers from exposure to toxic chemicals. The Nuclear Regulatory Commission (NRC) regulates radioactive substances. The EPA regulates pesticides and other toxic chemicals. Some states do their own testing of chemicals.

40-5a Toxic Substances Control Act

The Toxic Substances Control Act (TSCA) regulates chemicals other than pesticides, foods, drugs, and cosmetics. **The major provisions of the TSCA:**

- **New chemicals.** Prior to 2016, chemicals could be used without any testing, but an amendment to the TSCA **now prohibits the use of new chemicals (or old chemicals in a new way) until the EPA has determined that they are safe.**
- **Existing chemicals.** Prior to 2016, 64,000 chemicals were being used without any testing. **The 2016 amendment:**
  - Requires the EPA to (1) test at least 20 of these chemicals at a time, (2) spend no more than seven years testing any of them, (3) issue regulations within two (or, if necessary, four) years, and then (4) begin a ban or phase-out (where necessary) as quickly as possible but within no more than five years.
  - Permits the EPA to ban chemicals if they pose an "unreasonable risk."
  - Requires the EPA to begin testing the riskiest chemicals and to evaluate their impact on the most vulnerable people, such as pregnant women, children, and industrial workers.
  - Requires the EPA to consider only the health and environmental benefits, not compliance costs.
  - Prohibits states from regulating chemicals that the EPA either has reviewed or is in the process of evaluating.

[17]The National Institute of Health defines endocrine disruptors as "chemicals that may interfere with the body's endocrine system and produce adverse developmental, reproductive, neurological, and immune effects in both humans and wildlife."

- Requires the chemical industry to pay user fees of as much as $25 million a year to support the testing process (although, since this statute, Congress has cut the EPA's budget dramatically).
- Requires manufacturers to notify the EPA if they obtain evidence that a particular chemical is dangerous.

40-5b Pesticides

Under the Federal Insecticide, Fungicide, and Rodenticide Act (FIFRA) and other related statutes:

- **Registration.** Manufacturers must register all pesticides with the EPA. Before registering a pesticide, the EPA must ensure that it will not cause unreasonable adverse effects; in other words, that benefits exceed its (then-known) risks.
- **Tolerance levels.** The EPA sets tolerance levels: How much exposure is safe, over a human lifetime, with a special focus on exposure in children? To make this calculation, the agency must consider exposure via all food and drinking water. If the data for children are unclear, the EPA must reduce levels to one-tenth the amount then permitted in food.

  These provisions are highly controversial. The pesticide industry argues that the EPA could effectively ban many valuable chemicals for years while carefully researching their impact on children. Environmental advocates, on the other hand, are dismayed that the EPA has not demanded more thorough research before setting standards for some pesticides.
- **Residue.** The EPA then sets maximum levels for pesticide residue in raw or processed food so as to ensure that the tolerance levels will not be exceeded. The FDA can confiscate food with pesticide levels that exceed the EPA standards.
- **Re-registration.** Many of the 50,000 pesticides that are currently registered were approved at a time when little was known about their risks. The EPA is now in the process of re-registering any that were initially registered before 1984. This process has been very slow. Before the EPA cancels a registration, the manufacturer is entitled to a formal hearing, which may take several years. In the event of an emergency, the EPA may order an immediate suspension; otherwise, the chemical stays on the market until the hearing. If a pesticide is banned, the EPA must reimburse end users of the chemicals for their useless inventory.

40-6 NATURAL RESOURCES

Thus far, this chapter has focused on the regulation of pollution. Congress has also passed statutes whose purpose is to preserve the country's natural resources.

40-6a National Environmental Policy Act

The National Environmental Policy Act of 1969 (NEPA) requires all federal agencies to prepare an environmental impact statement (EIS) for every major federal action significantly affecting the quality of the human environment. An agency need not prepare an EIS for a particular proposal if it finds, on the basis of a shorter environmental assessment (EA), that the action will not have a significant impact on the environment.

An EIS is a major undertaking—often hundreds, if not thousands, of pages long. It must discuss (1) environmental consequences of the proposed action; (2) available alternatives; (3) direct and indirect effects; (4) energy requirements; (5) impact on urban quality and historic and cultural resources; and (6) the means to mitigate adverse environmental impacts. Once a draft report is ready, the federal agency must hold a hearing to allow for outside comments.

The EIS requirement applies not only to actions *undertaken* by the federal government, but also to activities *regulated* or *approved* by the government. For instance, the following projects required an EIS:

- Installing a work of art by Christo and Jeanne-Claude, which consisted of 5.9 miles of fabric panels suspended above the Arkansas River
- Expanding the Snowmass ski area in Aspen, Colorado, because approval was required by the Forest Service
- Killing a herd of wild goats that was causing damage at the Olympic National Park (outside Seattle)
- Creating a golf course outside Los Angeles because the project required a government permit to build in wetlands

The EIS process is controversial. If a project is likely to have an important impact, environmentalists almost always litigate the adequacy of the EIS. Industry advocates argue that environmentalists are simply using the EIS process to delay—or halt—any projects they oppose. In 1976, seven years after NEPA was passed, a dam on the Teton River in Idaho burst, killing 17 people and causing $1 billion in property damage. The Department of the Interior had built the dam in the face of allegations that its EIS was incomplete; it did not, for example, confirm that a large, earth-filled dam resting on a riverbed was safe. To environmentalists, this tragedy graphically illustrated the need for a thorough EIS.

Researchers have found that the EIS process generally has a beneficial impact on the environment. The mere prospect of preparing an EIS tends to eliminate the worst projects. Litigation over the EIS eliminates the next weakest group. If an agency does a good faith EIS, honestly looking at the available alternatives, projects tend to be kinder to the environment, at little extra cost.

40-6b Endangered Species Act

Worldwide, 25 percent of mammals, 13 percent of birds, 33 percent of reptiles, and 70 percent of plants are threatened with extinction. This threat is largely caused by humans. **The Endangered Species Act (ESA):**

- **Requires the Department of the Interior's Fish and Wildlife Service (FWS) to:**
  - Prepare a list of species that are in danger of becoming extinct or likely to become endangered and
  - Develop plans to revive these species.
- **Requires all federal agencies to:**
  - Ensure that their actions will not jeopardize an endangered species and
  - Avoid damage to habitat that is critical to the survival of endangered species.

Sandrinka/Shutterstock.com

The rusty patched bumble bee is the first species of bee to be added to the endangered species list.

- **Prohibits:**
  - Any sale or transport of these species,
  - Any taking of an endangered animal species (taking is defined as harassing, harming, killing, or capturing any endangered species or modifying its habitat in such a way that its population is likely to decline), and
  - The taking of any endangered plant species on federal property.

No environmental statute has been more controversial than the ESA. In theory, everyone is in favor of saving endangered species. To quote the House of Representatives Report on the ESA:

> As we homogenize the habitats in which these plants and animals evolved ... we threaten their—and our own—genetic heritage.... Who knows, or can say, what potential cures for cancer or other scourges, present or future, may lie locked up in the structures of plants which may yet be undiscovered, much less analyzed?

In practice, however, the cost of saving a species can be astronomical. One of the earliest ESA battles involved the snail darter—a 3-inch fish that lived in the Little Tennessee River. The Supreme Court upheld a decision under the ESA to halt work on a dam that would have blocked the river, flooding 16,500 acres of farmland and destroying the snail darter's habitat. To the dam's supporters, this decision was ludicrous: Stopping a dam (on which $100 million in taxpayer money had already been spent) to save a little fish that no one had ever even thought of before the dam (or damn) controversy. The real agenda, they argued, was simply to halt development. Environmental advocates argued, however, that the wanton destruction of whole species will ultimately and inevitably lead to disaster for humankind. In the end, Congress overruled the Supreme Court and authorized completion of the dam. It turned out that the snail darter survived in other rivers.

The snail darter was the first in a long line of ESA controversies that have included charismatic animals such as bald eagles, grizzly bears, bighorn sheep, and rockhopper penguins, but also more obscure fauna such as the Banbury Springs limpet and the triple-ribbed milkvetch. In 2007, a federal court moved to protect the delta smelt by ordering officials to shut down from time to time pumps that supplied as much as one-third of Southern California's water.[18] (That case was in litigation for seven years, but was ultimately upheld by the appeals court.[19]) And despite all these efforts, drought in California has led to a substantial decline in the numbers of delta smelts anyway. Opponents of the ESA argue that too much time and money have been spent to save too few species of too little importance.

Those issues involve some of the 1,500 species in the United States that have already been listed. Deciding which species make the list is also controversial. Nearly 100 species had become extinct while on the list or waiting to be listed. After being sued by environmental groups, the FWS agreed to make a decision on all the backlogged species by 2018.

The following case discusses the advantages of protecting endangered species.

Gibbs v. Babbitt

214 F.3d 483
United States Court of Appeals for the Fourth Circuit, 2000

Facts: The red wolf used to roam throughout the southeastern United States but, owing to development and hunting, its numbers had declined and it was placed on the endangered species list. The FWS trapped the remaining red wolves, placed them in a captive breeding program, and then reintroduced them into the wild. Ultimately, the

[18] Natural Resources Defense Council v. Kempthorne, 2007 U.S. Dist. LEXIS 91968 (E.D. Cal. 2007).
[19] San Luis & Delta-Mendota Water Auth. v. Jewell, 2014 U.S. App. LEXIS 4781 (9th Cir. 2014).

FWS reintroduced 75 wolves into wildlife refuges in North Carolina and Tennessee.

About 40 red wolves wandered from their refuge onto private property. Richard Mann shot a red wolf that he feared might attack his cattle. Mann pled guilty to taking an endangered species without a permit.

Two individuals and two counties in North Carolina filed suit against the federal government, alleging that the anti-taking provision of the ESA as applied to the red wolves on private land exceeded Congress's power under the Interstate Commerce Clause of the U.S. Constitution.

Issue: ***Is the anti-taking provision of the ESA constitutional?***

Excerpts from Justice Wilkinson's Decision: Congress' commerce authority includes the power to regulate those activities having a substantial relation to interstate commerce. Although the connection to economic or commercial activity plays a central role in whether a regulation will be upheld under the Commerce Clause, economic activity must be understood in broad terms.

The red wolves are part of a $29.2 billion national wildlife-related recreational industry that involves tourism and interstate travel. Many tourists travel to North Carolina from throughout the country for "howling events"—evenings of listening to wolf howls accompanied by educational programs. According to a study conducted by Dr. William E. Rosen of Cornell University, the recovery of the red wolf and increased visitor activities could result in a significant regional economic impact. Rosen estimates that northeastern North Carolina could see an increase of between $39.61 and $183.65 million per year in tourism-related activities, and that the Great Smoky Mountains National Park could see an increase of between $132.09 and $354.50 million per year. This is hardly a trivial impact on interstate commerce.

The regulation of red wolf takings is also closely connected to a second interstate market—scientific research. Scientific research generates jobs. It also deepens our knowledge of the world in which we live. The red wolf reintroduction program has already generated numerous scientific studies. Scientific research can also reveal other uses for animals—for instance, approximately 50 percent of all modern medicines are derived from wild plants or animals.

The anti-taking regulation is also connected to a third market—the possibility of a renewed trade in fur pelts. Wolves have historically been hunted for their pelts. In such a case, businessmen may profit from the trading and marketing of that species for an indefinite number of years, where otherwise it would have been completely eliminated from commercial channels. In 1975, the American alligator was nearing extinction and listed as endangered, but by 1987 conservation efforts restored the species. Now there is a vigorous trade in alligator hides.

Finally, the taking of red wolves is connected to interstate markets for agricultural products and livestock. For instance, landowners find red wolves a menace because they threaten livestock and other animals of economic and commercial value. This effect on commerce, however, still qualifies as a legitimate subject for regulation.

It is well settled under Commerce Clause cases that a regulation can involve the promotion or the restriction of commercial enterprises and development.

It is anything but clear that red wolves harm farming enterprises. They may in fact help them, and in so doing confer additional benefits on commerce. For instance, red wolves prey on animals like raccoons, deer, and rabbits—helping farmers by killing the animals that destroy their crops.

[I]t is reasonable for Congress to decide that conservation of species will one day produce a substantial commercial benefit to this country and that failure to preserve a species will result in permanent, though unascertainable, commercial loss. If a species becomes extinct, we are left to speculate forever on what we might have learned or what we may have realized. If we conserve the species, it will be available for the study and benefit of future generations. We therefore hold that the anti-taking provision at issue here involves regulable economic and commercial activity as understood by current Commerce Clause jurisprudence.

CHAPTER CONCLUSION

Environmental laws have a pervasive impact on our lives. Their cost has been great, causing higher prices for everything from cars and electricity to sewage. Some argue that cost is irrelevant—that a clean environment has incalculable value for its own sake. Others insist on a more pragmatic approach and wonder if the future benefits outweigh the current costs. They worry that environmental regulations hurt employment and business.

What benefits has the country gained from environmental regulation? The EPA estimates that the CAA has saved trillions of dollars by preventing lost work and school days, illness, and premature deaths. As for the CWA, although many bodies of water fail to meet national standards and wetland acreage continues to decline at a rapid rate, the number of Americans whose sewage goes to wastewater treatment facilities has more than doubled. Sixty percent of the nation's waters are safe for fishing and swimming, up from only 30 percent when the Clean Water Act was passed.

Despite this progress, as a nation we still face many intractable problems. We have not developed consensus on climate change. We have done little to assess and regulate the thousands of chemicals that pervade our lives. The EPA is overwhelmed by its obligations, sometimes taking decades to issue regulations, even as Congress cuts its budget.

Although many people, including many politicians, readily acknowledge the importance of the environment to both present and future generations, when the time comes to allocate funds, change lifestyles, and make tough choices, the consensus too often breaks down, with the result that resources are spent on litigation instead of the environment.

EXAM REVIEW

1. **ENVIRONMENTAL STATUTES** The following table provides a list of environmental statutes:

Air Pollution	Water Pollution	Waste Disposal	Chemicals	Natural Resources
Clean Air Act	Clean Water Act	Resource Conservation and Recovery Act	Toxic Substances Control Act	National Environmental Policy Act
	Safe Drinking Water Act	Comprehensive Environmental Response, Compensation, and Liability Act (Superfund)	Federal Insecticide, Fungicide, and Rodenticide Act	Endangered Species Act
	Ocean Dumping Act			
	Oil Pollution Act			

2. **AIR** Under the Clean Air Act (CAA), the EPA has the authority to regulate both the total amount of existing air pollution and its ongoing production. The EPA must establish national ambient air quality standards for both primary and secondary pollution. States then produce implementation plans to meet the EPA standards. The EPA must also regulate greenhouse gases.

3. **CAP AND TRADE** The Cap and Trade program is a method for limiting air pollutants in an economically efficient manner. It allows for the purchase and sale of emissions allowances.

4. **CLIMATE CHANGE** The Paris Accord is an international agreement to prevent climate change by reducing GHGs. Each country establishes its own goals and there are no penalties for countries that set low goals or who fail to achieve their set targets. However, all countries have pledged to meet every five years to report the results of their emissions programs and to issue more aggressive plans. The United States has withdrawn from the Paris Accord.

5. **WATER** Under the Clean Water Act (CWA), any discharge into navigable water from a point source is illegal without a permit (from the EPA or a state). The EPA must set national standards for water quality generally and then each state has to develop plans to achieve these standards. States must also develop a plan for non-point source pollution.

EXAMStrategy

Question: Astro Circuit Corp. in Lowell, Massachusetts, produced twice as much wastewater as its treatment facility could handle. Astro's production supervisor, David Boldt, directed that the surplus be dumped into the city sewer. Has he violated the law? If so, what penalties might he face?

Strategy: Whenever water is involved, look at the provisions of the CWA. (See the "Result" at the end of this Exam Review section.)

6. **WETLANDS** The CWA prohibits any discharge of dredge and fill material into wetlands without a permit.

7. **DRINKING WATER** The Safe Drinking Water Act requires the EPA to set national standards for every contaminant potentially harmful to human health that is found in drinking water.

8. **OCEANS** The Ocean Dumping Act prohibits the dumping of wastes in ocean water without a permit from the EPA.

9. **SHIPS** The Oil Pollution Act of 1990 sets design standards for ships operating in U.S. waters and requires ship owners to pay for damage caused by oil discharged from their ships.

10. **WASTE DISPOSAL** The Resource Conservation and Recovery Act (RCRA) establishes rules for treating both hazardous and nonhazardous forms of solid waste.

11. **HAZARDOUS WASTE** Under the Comprehensive Environmental Response, Compensation, and Liability Act (CERCLA or Superfund), anyone who has ever owned or operated a site on which hazardous wastes are found, who has transported wastes to the site, or who has arranged for the disposal of wastes that were released at the site is liable for (1) the cost of cleaning up the site, (2) any damage done to natural resources, and (3) any required health assessments.

EXAMStrategy

Question: In 1963, FMC Corp. purchased a manufacturing plant in Virginia from American Viscose Corp., the owner of the plant since 1937. During World War II, the government's War Production Board had commissioned American Viscose to make rayon for airplanes and truck tires. In 1982, inspections revealed a chemical used to manufacture this rayon, in groundwater near the plant. American Viscose was out of business. Who is responsible for cleaning up the chemical? Under what statute?

Strategy: Look at the statutes that govern waste disposal. (See the "Result" at the end of this Exam Review section.)

12. **CHEMICALS** The Toxic Substances Control Act (TSCA) prohibits the use of new chemicals (or old chemicals in a new way) until the EPA has determined that they are safe. It also requires the EPA to test chemicals that are now on the market without having been tested.

13. **PESTICIDES** Under the Federal Insecticide, Fungicide, and Rodenticide Act (FIFRA) and related statutes, manufacturers are required to register all pesticides with the EPA. The EPA must set tolerance levels for lifetime exposure to pesticides and then use those levels to set maximum levels for pesticide residue in raw or processed food.

14. **ENVIRONMENTAL IMPACT** The National Environmental Policy Act (NEPA) requires all federal agencies to prepare an environmental impact statement (EIS) for every major federal action significantly affecting the quality of the environment.

EXAMStrategy

Question: The U.S. Forest Service planned to build a road in the Nez Perce National Forest in Idaho to provide access to loggers. Is the Forest Service governed by any environmental statutes? Must it seek permission before building the road?

Strategy: Does a road significantly affect the quality of the environment? Is an EIS required? (See the "Result" at the end of this Exam Review section.)

15. **ENDANGERED SPECIES** The Endangered Species Act (ESA) requires the Fish and Wildlife Service (FWS) to list endangered species and then prohibits activities that harm them.

RESULTS

5. Result: Although Boldt was in an unfortunate situation—he could have lost his job if he had not been willing to dump the industrial waste—he was found guilty of a criminal violation of the CWA. There are worse things than being fired—such as being fired *and* sent to prison.

11. Result: Both FMC and the U.S. government were liable for cleanup under CERCLA.

14. Result: As an agency of the federal government, the Forest Service must prepare an EIS (under the National Environmental Policy Act) for every action that significantly affects the quality of the environment. Although the road itself may not have been significant enough to require an impact statement, its purpose was to provide access for logging, which did require an EIS.

MULTIPLE-CHOICE QUESTIONS

1. Suppose that you are the manager of a General Motors plant that is about to start producing Hummers. The Hummer requires special protective paint that, as it turns out, reacts with other chemicals during the application process to create a pollutant. What does the CAA require of you?

   (a) Reduce other emissions from the plant so that the total quantity of pollutants is the same

(b) Provide an analysis showing that the benefits outweigh the costs

(c) Provide the EPA with evidence that your plant meets the national ambient air quality standards

(d) Obtain a PSD certificate from the EPA

2. The EPA ______________ have authority to regulate greenhouse gases. The states ______________ impose their own standards for these gases.

(a) does; can

(b) does; cannot

(c) does not; cannot

(d) does not; can

3. For purposes of the Clean Water Act, Farmer Brown's fields ______________ a point source. A canal that collects rainwater and discharges it into the Everglades ______________ a point source.

(a) are; is

(b) are; is not

(c) are not; is

(d) are not; is not

4. You own property on which hazardous wastes are found. You know the identity of three former owners. You are ______________.

(a) liable for all the costs of the cleanup because you are the current owner

(b) liable for one-quarter of the costs of the cleanup

(c) liable for the percentage of the harm that you are able to show that you actually caused

(d) not liable for any of the costs of the cleanup because the damage occurred before you bought the land

5. The Toxic Substances Control Act ______________.

(a) requires manufacturers to test new chemicals, or old chemicals being used in a new way, for safety before they can be used in products

(b) requires the EPA to test new chemicals, or old chemicals being used in a new way, before they can be used in products

(c) does not allow any chemicals to be used in products before the EPA certifies that they are safe

(d) requires the EPA, within seven years, to test all chemicals that are currently being used in products

(e) permits the EPA to require testing of a chemical only if there is evidence that it is dangerous

CASE QUESTIONS

1. Tariq Ahmad decided to dispose of some of his laboratory's hazardous chemicals by shipping them to his home in Pakistan. He sent the chemicals to Castelazo (a company in the United States) to prepare the materials for shipment. Ahmad did not tell the driver who picked up the chemicals that they were hazardous, nor did

he give the driver any written documentation. What law has Ahmad violated? What does this law require? What penalties might he face?

2. ***YOU BE THE JUDGE* WRITING PROBLEM** The Lordship Point Gun Club operated a trap and skeet shooting club in Stratford, Connecticut, for 70 years. During this time, customers deposited millions of pounds of lead shot on land around the club and in the Long Island Sound. Forty-five percent of sediment samples taken from the Sound exceeded the established limits for lead. Was the Gun Club in violation of the RCRA? **Argument for the Gun Club:** The Gun Club does not *dispose* of hazardous wastes, within the meaning of the RCRA. Congress meant the statute to apply only to companies in the business of manufacturing articles that produce hazardous waste. If the Gun Club happens to produce wastes, that is only *incidental* to the normal use of a product. **Argument for the Plaintiff:** Under the RCRA, lead shot is hazardous waste. The law applies to anyone who produces hazardous waste, no matter how.

3. Before the Department of Agriculture issued regulations on genetically modified beets, what steps did it need to take under the environmental statutes?

4. Rundy Custom Homes was building a subdivision of new houses next to a stream. During the building process, pipes on the property discharged storm water with sediment into the stream. Is this legal? What statute applies? Who would be liable? What if the EPA fails to act?

5. The Navy wanted to conduct training exercises off the coast of California for sonar submarines. Scientists were concerned that the sounds emitted by the sonar would harm marine mammals, such as whales, dolphins, and sea lions. Environmental groups filed suit, asking that the Navy prepare an EIS. The Navy argued that it should not have to do so because the submarine exercises were important for national security. Should the courts permit the Navy to proceed without an EIS?

DISCUSSION QUESTIONS

1. Life is about choices—and never more so than with the environment. Being completely honest, which of the following are you willing to do? Why?
   - Drive a smaller, lighter, more fuel-efficient car
   - Take public transportation or ride your bike to work
   - Vote for political candidates who are willing to impose higher taxes on polluters and pollutants
   - Insulate your home
   - Unplug appliances when not in use
   - Recycle your wastes
   - Pay higher taxes to clean up Superfund sites

2. The Commonwealth of Virginia refused to prepare TMDLs for polluted Accotink Creek. When the EPA prepared its own set of TMDLs, Virginia sued to avoid compliance. Should Virginia be allowed to determine how much pollution to permit in its own waters? Alternatively, is it ethical for Virginia to refuse to comply with the law and to prolong the dispute with litigation?

3. **ETHICS** Externalities pose an enormous problem for the environment. Often, the people making decisions do not bear the full cost of their choices. And businesses tend to fight efforts to make them pay these externalities. For example, CropLife America lobbied against a bill that would support research on the effects of chemicals on children. On the other hand, Nike resigned its seat on the board of the U.S. Chamber of Commerce in response to the Chamber's active lobbying against legislation that would regulate greenhouse gases. But Nike decided to remain a member of the group. What ethical obligation do American companies have to support environmental legislation that may impose higher costs? Do they have an obligation to look out for the greater good, or should they focus on maximizing their shareholder returns? What Life Principles would you apply? What would Kant and Mill say?

4. The Supreme Court ruled that, under the CAA, the EPA may not consider cost when setting air quality standards to protect the public health.[20] A bipartisan group of 42 of the country's most respected economists filed a brief arguing that, from an economic perspective, it is wrong *not* to consider costs. Should the EPA consider costs in all of its decisions? Or are some decisions priceless?

5. Is cost–benefit analysis an effective tool in environmental disputes? How do we measure the costs and benefits? How do we know what benefits we might gain from saving endangered species, or improving visibility at the Grand Canyon? Should you survey people to ask them how much it is worth? Or just think in terms of lives saved or sick days avoided?

---

[20]The *Michigan* case, in which the Supreme Court ruled that the EPA did have to consider costs, involved power plant emissions, not air quality standards.

Property

UNIT

9

41

CHAPTER

INTELLECTUAL PROPERTY

Stephanie Lenz and her young children were jamming after dinner in her rural Pennsylvania home. Prince's song "Let's Go Crazy" was playing in the background as her pajama-clad toddler ran laps around the kitchen with a push toy. "What do you think of the music?" the mom said, as she encouraged her son to dance. The smiling toddler bounced to the rhythm of the music as Prince belted, "*C'mon baby, let's get nuts.*"

Lenz uploaded the 29-second video of her dancing child to YouTube for friends and family to enjoy.[1] Although the song was barely audible in the background, its copyright owner objected to Lenz's unauthorized posting. So YouTube took down the video. Lenz then challenged YouTube's decision, battling it in the courts for seven years. (See below for the outcome.) Clearly, someone had gone nuts. Was Lenz an infringer? Was YouTube wrong? Or had copyright *gone crazy?*

Lenz uploaded the 29-second video of her dancing child to YouTube for friends and family to enjoy.

[1]To watch Stephanie's video, search the internet for "Lenz v. Universal Music dancing baby video."

For much of history, land was the most valuable form of property. It was the primary source of wealth and social status. Today, intellectual property is a major source of wealth. New ideas—for manufacturing processes, computer programs, medicines, and books—bring both affluence and influence.

Although both can be valuable assets, land and intellectual property are fundamentally different. The value of land lies in the owner's right to exclude, to prevent others from entering it. Intellectual property, however, has little economic value unless others use it. This ability to share intellectual property is both good news and bad. On the one hand, the owner can produce and sell unlimited copies of, say, a song, but on the other hand, the owner has no easy way to determine if someone is using the song for free. The high cost of developing intellectual property, combined with the low cost of reproducing it, makes it particularly vulnerable to theft. The role of intellectual property law is to balance the rights of those who create intellectual property and those who would enjoy—or need—it. On the one hand, strong intellectual property laws establish incentives for creation and innovation. They also protect against copyists looking to unfairly profit from another's work. On the other hand, intellectual property laws limit the public's access to important creations. For example, patents increase the price of medicines that could save more lives if only they were cheaper and, therefore, more readily available.

In this chapter, we examine four types of intellectual property: patents, copyrights, trademarks, and trade secrets.

41-1 PATENTS

Patents give inventors the right to prevent others from making, using, or selling their inventions for a limited time. During this period, no one may make, use, or sell the invention without permission. In return, the inventor publicly discloses information about the invention that anyone can use upon expiration of the patent. The Patent and Trademark Office (PTO) issues patents after a long application process known as a prosecution, but courts can invalidate patents that the PTO has granted improperly. In the last 20 years, the number of patent applications has increased dramatically: from around 600 to 1,725 a day. Also, the typical patent application is longer and more complicated. As a result, more than 1.2 million applications are now pending. Approval of a patent can take anywhere from three to six years from the date of filing.

Patent
Patents give inventors the right to prevent others from making, using, or selling their inventions for a limited time.

41-1a Types of Patents

There are three types of patents: design patents, plant patents, and utility patents.

Design Patents

A design patent protects the appearance, not the function, of an item. These types of patents protect the design of products ranging from Star Wars action figures to Coca-Cola bottles, and Nike shoes to Ferrari chassis.

Design patents are granted to anyone who invents a new, original, and ornamental design for an article. They last 14 years from the date of issuance. Design patents are particularly valuable for preventing knock-offs that copy the look and feel of a product. Samsung paid Apple $548 million after a jury determined that it had copied, among other things, the iPad and iPhone's distinctive home button and rounded-corner design, which are protected by design patents in various countries. But this case was just one of about 50 patent infringement cases in progress between the smartphone giants all over the world—which could lead to billions of dollars in judgments. Suffice to say, design patents are an important asset.

Plant Patents

Anyone who creates a new type of plant can patent it, provided that the inventor is able to reproduce it asexually—through grafting, for instance, rather than by planting its seeds. For example, one company patented a unique rose whose color combination did not exist in nature. This type of patent lasts for 20 years from the date of application.

Plant patents are not without controversy. Monsanto, a multinational biotechnology company, patented a genetically modified canola seed designed to resist certain herbicides. When the wind blew some of those patented seeds into an unsuspecting farmer's field and these grew into herbicide-resistant plants, the farmer decided to save some seeds for future plantings. Monsanto sued the farmer and won because the farmer had infringed Monsanto's plant patent by using the stored seeds without permission.

LUke1138/Getty Images

Apple has a design patent that protects the iPhone's distinctive look from being copied.

Utility Patents

Whenever people use the word *patent* by itself, they are referring to a utility patent. In fact, about 94 percent of all patents are utility patents. For this reason, we will focus the rest of our patent discussion on them.

While design patents protect the way inventions look, utility patents protect how they work. **Utility patents are valid for 20 years from the date of *filing* the application.** Utility patents are available to those who invent (or significantly improve) any of the following:

Type of Invention	Example
Mechanical invention	A hydraulic jack used to lift heavy aircraft
Electrical invention	A prewired, portable wall panel for use in large, open-plan offices
Chemical invention	The chemical 2-chloroethylphosphonic acid used as a plant growth regulator
Process	A method for applying a chemical compound to an established plant such as rice in order to inhibit the growth of weeds selectively; the application can be patented separately from the actual chemical
Machine	A device that enables a helicopter pilot to control all flight functions (pitch, roll, and heave) with one hand
Composition of matter	A sludge used as an explosive at construction sites; the patent specifies the water content, the density, and the types of solids contained in the mixture

41-1b Requirements for a Utility Patent

Thomas Jefferson wrote of the "difficulty of drawing a line between the things which are worth to the public the embarrassment of an exclusive patent, and those which are not."[2] Here is how the U.S. patent system draws that line.

[2]Letter from Thomas Jefferson to Isaac McPherson, August 13, 1813.

To receive a patent, an invention must be:

- **Novel**. An invention is not patentable if it has already been (1) patented, (2) described in a printed publication, (3) in public use, (4) on sale, or (5) otherwise available to the public anyplace in the world. For example, an inventor discovered a new use for existing chemical compounds but was not permitted to patent it because the compounds had already been described in prior publications, though the new uses had not.[3] Note, however, that a disclosure does not count under this provision if it was made by the inventor in the one year prior to filing the application.
- **Nonobvious**. An invention is not patentable if it is obvious to a person with ordinary skill in that particular area. To determine if an invention is obvious, the PTO and courts look at the difference between it and existing technologies to see if that difference would be unexpected to someone skilled in the field (at the time of patenting). For example, if a four-legged stool with a square seat already exists, the patent application for a four-legged stool with a circular seat would be denied because it is, duh, obvious. Changing the shape of the seat may be new and useful, but it is not unexpected enough to earn a patent. On this basis, a court declared that the patent for an online shopping cart was invalid because that technology would not have been a surprise to technologists of the day.[4]
- **Utility**. To be patented, an invention must be useful. It need not necessarily be commercially valuable, but generally, it must *do* something. This requirement is the least restrictive: An invention will only be denied a patent if it has absolutely no practical utility. For example, the PTO has granted patents for disposable diapers with camouflage patterns, a comb in the shape of a bacon strip, and a thumb-shaped lollipop. To the PTO, useful does not mean *socially beneficial*; it simply means capable of some use.
- **Patentable subject matter**. Not every innovation is patentable. A patent is not available solely for an idea, but only for its tangible application. Thus, laws of nature, scientific principles, mathematical algorithms, mental processes, intellectual concepts, or formulas (such as $a^2 + b^2 = c^2$) are not patentable.

The Limits of Patentable Subject Matter: Living Organisms and Business Methods

Technology and business are constantly challenging patent law and the limits of what is patentable, especially when it comes to living things and innovative ways of doing business. Under what conditions are life forms and business practices patentable?

Living Organisms. In 1980, the Supreme Court ruled that living organisms could be patented.[5] The case of *Diamond v. Chakrabarty* involved genetically engineered bacteria that were to treat oil spills. Those challenging the patent argued that living things could not be patented. The Court held that the bacteria—and other living organisms—could be patented if they are different from anything found in nature, and a product of human ingenuity; that is, if they were made or significantly modified by humans. *Diamond v. Chakrabarty* made famous the phrase that patentable subject matter included "anything under the sun that is made by man." But, seriously, *anything*?

[3] In re Schoenwald, 964 F.2d 1122 (Fed. Cir. 1992).

[4] Soverain Software LLC v. Newegg, Inc., No. 2011-1009 (Fed. Cir. 2013).

[5] Diamond v. Chakrabarty, 447 U.S. 303 (1980).

As a result of this ruling, the PTO began issuing patents on human genetic material. A total of 20 percent of all genes were patented, and the companies that owned these patents were valued at billions of dollars. But it was just a matter of time before patents on human genes were challenged in court. And that is exactly what occurred in the following groundbreaking Supreme Court case.

Association for Molecular Pathology v. Myriad Genetics, Inc.

133 S.Ct 2107
United States Supreme Court, 2013

Facts: Mutations in two genes known as BRCA1 and BRCA2 can dramatically increase the risk of breast and ovarian cancer. Myriad Genetics, Inc. (Myriad) obtained a number of patents on these genes. One patent gave Myriad the exclusive right to isolate an individual's naturally occurring BRCA1 and BRCA2 genes. Another patent granted Myriad the exclusive right to synthetically create variants of BRCA1 and BRCA2 in the laboratory (cDNA).

A group of researchers filed a lawsuit seeking a declaration that Myriad's patents were invalid. The district court struck down the patents on the grounds that they covered products of nature. The appeals court reversed, holding that both DNA and cDNA were patentable. The Supreme Court granted *certiorari.*

Issues: ***Is naturally occurring DNA patentable? Is man-made cDNA patentable?***

Excerpts from Justice Thomas's Decision: Section 101 of the Patent Act provides:

> Whoever invents or discovers any new and useful … composition of matter, or any new and useful improvement thereof, may obtain a patent therefor, subject to the conditions and requirements of this title.

We have long held that this provision contains an important implicit exception: Laws of nature, natural phenomena, and abstract ideas are not patentable. Rather, they are the basic tools of scientific and technological work that lie beyond the domain of patent protection. As the Court has explained, without this exception, there would be considerable danger that the grant of patents would "tie up" the use of such tools and thereby inhibit future innovation premised upon them. This would be at odds with the very point of patents, which exist to promote creation.

In this case, Myriad did not create anything. To be sure, it found an important and useful gene, but separating that gene from its surrounding genetic material is not an act of invention. Groundbreaking, innovative, or even brilliant discovery does not by itself satisfy the §101 inquiry. Myriad found the location of the BRCA1 and BRCA2 genes, but that discovery, by itself, does not render the BRCA genes "new … composition[s] of matter," that are patent eligible.

cDNA does not present the same obstacles to patentability as naturally occurring, isolated DNA segments. Creation of a cDNA sequence results in a molecule that is not naturally occurring. The lab technician unquestionably creates something new when cDNA is made. cDNA retains the naturally occurring exons of DNA, but it is distinct from the DNA from which it was derived. As a result, cDNA is not a "product of nature" and is patent eligible under §101.

For the foregoing reasons, the judgment of the Federal Circuit is affirmed in part and reversed in part.[6]

---

[6]As a result of this decision, other companies now offer tests that gauge the risk of breast and ovarian cancer. Although cheaper than the Myriad version, they may not be as accurate or as comprehensive. And, in any event, Myriad has sued to prevent the use of these competing tests.

Ethics

Association for Molecular Pathology v. Myriad Genetics tells us that it is legal for companies to patent the human genes they have modified, cDNA. Inevitably, the PTO will face the question of whether a human being whose genes are all created in a lab should be patentable. Does this sound like futuristic science fiction? Not so fast.

The PTO has already issued patents on modified human genes, as well as on stem cells, and animals with human genes. In 1984, the PTO granted a chimera patent for a "geep," a combination of a goat and a sheep created in a lab. (A chimera is a combination of two different animals' cells that creates a third animal with a genetic blend of the two.) In 1988, Harvard University obtained a patent on a genetically manipulated mouse with human genes that made it susceptible to cancer. New breeds and combinations of human beings are certainly within scientific sight.

For a long time, there was no law prohibiting human patents, but by policy, the PTO refused to issue such a patent. In 2011, the America Invents Act both clarified and added to the confusion. The law states that "no patent may issue on a claim directed to or encompassing a human organism."[7] But the law does not define "human organism." Clearly it prohibits human cloning, because that process creates a human being, but how about other engineered animals containing human DNA? How about human-animal chimeras made in a lab (maybe called a "heep")? At what point is an invention *too human* to patent?

Business Method Patents. Historically, patent law did not protect methods of doing business. But after the advent of computers, the PTO began issuing patents on ways of doing business with software, computers, and the internet. Amazon.com patented its 1-Click method of instant ordering. Another company patented the online shopping cart. Facebook was granted a patent on a process that "provides a news feed about a user of a social network." These patents are particularly controversial because they allow one company to block others from using relatively common technologies. Many of them have been challenged.

The Supreme Court has held that business methods are *generally* patentable, but has not precisely explained *them*. In *Alice Corporation v. CLS Bank International*, the Supreme Court invalidated a patent on an electronic escrow service. (An escrow is a traditional business arrangement in which a third party holds money for the transacting parties until the deal is completed.) The Court held that the mere computerization of an abstract idea (in this case, an escrow) does not make it patentable.[8] Patentable business methods must involve an inventive step above and beyond an abstract idea.

Since *Alice*, e-commerce patents have declined by 95 percent and many existing patents have been invalidated. One court rejected a patent for playing bingo on a computer. Because it is unclear how the law of business methods patents will evolve, businesses continue to file for them, all the while wondering if they are valid.

EXAMStrategy

Question: In 1572, during the reign of Queen Elizabeth I of England, a patent application was filed for a knife with a bone handle rather than a wooden one. Would this patent be granted under current U.S. law?

Strategy: Was a bone handle novel, nonobvious, and useful?

7Leahy-Smith America Invents Act §33.
8134 S. Ct. 2347 (2014).

Result: It was useful—no splinters from a bone handle. It was novel—no one had ever done it before. But the patent was denied because it was obvious.

41-1c Patent Application and Issuance

To obtain a patent, the inventor must file a complex application with the Patent and Trademark Office. If a patent examiner determines that the application meets all legal requirements, the PTO will issue the patent. If an examiner denies a patent application for any reason, the inventor can appeal that decision to the Patent Trial and Appeal Board in the PTO and from there to the Court of Appeals for the Federal Circuit in Washington, D.C.[9]

During the patent application process, third parties have the right to submit evidence that the invention is not novel. For the nine months after a patent has been granted, third parties have a broad right to challenge its validity in the PTO (without having to go to court). Thereafter, a patent may still be challenged but the grounds are limited to evidence of a prior patent or publication.

Priority between Two Inventors

When two people invent the same product, who is entitled to a patent—the first to invent or the first to file an application? For most of American history, the person who invented and first put the invention into practice had priority over the first filer. But in 2013, the America Invents Act (AIA) changed the law so that the first person to *file* a patent application has priority. The AIA brought the United States into conformity with most of the rest of the world's patent laws, which generally have first-to-file regimes.

Prior Sale

An inventor must apply for a patent within one year of selling the product commercially anywhere in the world. The purpose of this rule is to encourage prompt disclosure of inventions. It prevents someone from inventing a product, selling it for years, and then obtaining a 20-year monopoly with a patent.

41-1d Patent Infringement

A patent holder has the exclusive right to make, use, or sell the patented invention during the term of the patent. A holder can prohibit others from using any product that is substantially the same, license the product to others for a fee, and recover damages from anyone who uses the product without permission. But note that patents, like other areas of intellectual property, are territorial, meaning that the holder of a U.S. patent can only enforce those rights in the United States. A U.S. patent does not give its holder the right to sue a counterfeiter who makes, uses, or sells the invention outside this country.

41-1e International Patent Treaties

Because patents are territorial, an inventor must apply for a patent in each country where patent protection is sought. This is no easy feat. Nevertheless, about half of all patent applications are filed in more than one country. This process used to be a logistical nightmare because almost every country had its own unique filing procedures and standards. Companies were reluctant to develop products based on technology that they were not sure they actually owned.

---

[9]Recall from Chapter 3 that the Court of Appeals for the Federal Circuit is the 13th United States Court of Appeals. It hears appeals from specialized trial courts.

Several treaties of the World Intellectual Property Organization now facilitate this process, although it is still not the one-stop (or one-click) effort that inventors desire. **The Paris Convention for the Protection of Industrial Property** (Paris Convention) requires each member country to accept and recognize all patent and trademark applications filed with it by anyone who lives in any member country. For example, the French patent office cannot refuse to accept an application from an American, as long as the American has complied with French law. Under this treaty, inventors who file in one country have up to one year to file elsewhere and still maintain patent protection.

Under the **Patent Cooperation Treaty** (PCT), applicants are offered a single filing and streamlined review process. Upon filing an international patent application, inventors receive patent pending protection for 30 months in the 151 PCT member countries, so that they have time to pursue their application. Once a PCT application is filed, one of the major patent offices prepares an "international search report" and issues an opinion on whether the invention is patentable. This report, while nonbinding, helps applicants assess the patentability of their inventions and provides persuasive evidence to national patent offices. Inventors who wish to proceed internationally must then have the report translated and filed with applications and fees in whichever countries they want a patent.

In addition to these treaties, any country that joins the World Trade Organization (WTO) must agree to trade-related aspects of intellectual property rights (TRIPS). This agreement does not create an international patent system, but it does require all participants to meet minimum standards for the protection of intellectual property. How individual countries achieve that goal is left to them.

41-2 COPYRIGHTS

A copyright gives its creator the exclusive right to reproduce, distribute, and perform his original work for a limited time. But copyright protects the way that ideas are presented, not the ideas themselves. In other words, a copyright holder has rights to the way she expressed an idea, not a monopoly on the underlying idea or process. Abner Doubleday could have copyrighted a book setting out his particular version of the rules of baseball, but he could not have copyrighted the rules themselves, nor could he have required players to pay him a royalty. Similarly, the inventor of double-entry bookkeeping could copyright a pamphlet explaining his system, but not the system itself.

In the following case, a celebrity yogi was incensed. Could copyright cool him down?

Bikram's Yoga College of India, L.P. v. Evolation Yoga, LLC

803 F.3d 1032
United States Court of Appeals for the Ninth Circuit, 2015

Facts: Derived from ancient Hindu scriptures, the Indian practice and philosophy of yoga date back thousands of years. It involves a combination of meditation, breathing exercises, and physical poses (called *asanas*).

Bikram Choudhury was a lifelong student of a type of yoga known as Hatha. In the early 1970s, he developed a method of practicing yoga, which he called Bikram. It consisted of a sequence of 26 Hatha yoga *asanas*, arranged in an order designed to work the muscles optimally (the Sequence). Choudhury's other innovation was to teach the Sequence in a room heated to 105 degrees. Choudhury published and copyrighted a book that included descriptions, photographs, and drawings of the Sequence.

Many years later, Mark Drost and Zefea Samson, Choudhury's former students, opened Evolation Yoga, a studio offering "hot yoga" classes. Evolation instructors taught the Sequence in a heated room in a manner and order identical to Bikram Yoga.

Choudhury sued Evolation Yoga for copyright infringement. He claimed that he deserved the exclusive right to perform the Sequence because he developed it over years of research and had copyrighted the book describing it. The district court granted summary judgment to Evolation, reasoning that the Sequence was an idea that could not be protected under copyright law.

Issue: ***Was the Sequence copyrightable?***

Excerpts from Judge Wardlaw's Decision: The Copyright Act of 1976 excludes protection for any idea, procedure, process, system, method of operation, concept, principle, or discovery. Section 102(b) codifies the "idea/expression dichotomy," under which "every idea, theory, and fact in a copyrighted work becomes instantly available for public exploitation at the moment of publication."

The idea/expression dichotomy has two constitutional foundations: the Copyright Clause and the First Amendment. Under the Copyright Clause, the primary objective of copyright is not to reward the labor of authors, but to promote the Progress of Science and useful Arts. Copyright assures authors the right to their original expression, but encourages others to build freely upon the ideas and information conveyed by a work.

Courts have routinely held that the copyright for a work describing how to perform a process does not extend to the process itself. Recipes contained in a copyrighted cookbook are not entitled to copyright protection, for they merely describe a procedure by which the reader may produce many dishes, and there can be no monopoly in the copyright sense in the ideas for producing certain foodstuffs.

Does Choudhury's copyright protection for his book extend to the Sequence itself? Under the fundamental tenets of copyright law, the answer is no. The Sequence is a "system." An essential element of this "system" is the order in which the yoga poses are arranged. Simply put, this attempt is precluded by copyright's idea/expression dichotomy.

The copyright for a book describing how to perform a complicated surgery does not give the holder the exclusive right to perform the surgery. Like the series of movements a surgeon makes, the Sequence is, as Choudhury tells readers, a method designed to alleviate physical injuries and illness. Monopoly protection for such a method can only be secured, if it can be secured at all, by patent.

The object of the book is explanation: it tells readers how to perform the Sequence and encourages them to try it. Consumers would have little reason to buy Choudhury's book if Choudhury held a monopoly on the practice of the very activity he sought to popularize. Rather than stimulating creativity for the general public good, copyright protection for the Sequence would prevent the public from engaging with Choudhury's idea and building upon it.

Although there is no cause to dispute the many health, fitness, spiritual, and aesthetic benefits of Bikram Yoga, they do not bring the Sequence into the realm of copyright protection.

Unlike patents, the ideas underlying copyrighted material need not be novel. For example, two 2011 movies—*No Strings Attached* and *Friends with Benefits*—are about friends who engage in a casual physical relationship and end up falling in love. The movies have the same plot, but there is no copyright violation because their *expressions* of the basic idea are different.

The first U.S. copyright law in 1790 protected only maps, charts, and books. Today, the Copyright Act protects literature, music, drama, choreography, photography, sculpture, movies, recordings, architectural works, computer programs, and even tattoos. Unlike patent, copyright does not protect useful creations. For example, fashion designs are not copyrightable because clothes are functional items. Despite the fashion industry's efforts to change the law, only the nonfunctional elements of clothing, such as prints and patterns, are protectable.

A work is copyrighted *automatically* once it is in tangible form. For example, once a songwriter puts notes on paper, the work is copyrighted without further ado. But if she whistles a happy tune without writing it down, the song is not copyrighted, and anyone else can use it without permission. Registration with the Copyright Office of the Library of Congress is necessary only if the holder wishes to bring suit to enforce the copyright. Although authors still routinely place the copyright symbol (©) on their works, such a precaution is not necessary in the United States. However, some lawyers still recommend using the copyright symbol because other countries recognize it. It also puts potential infringers on notice: The penalties for intentional copyright infringement are heavier than for unintentional violations, and the presence of the © is evidence that the infringer's actions were intentional.

41-2a Copyright Term

More than 300 years ago, on April 10, 1710, Queen Anne of England approved the first copyright statute. Called the Statute of Anne, it provided copyright protection for 14 years, which could be extended by another 14 years if the copyright owner was still alive when the first term expired. Many credit the Statute of Anne with greatly expanding the burst of intellectual activity that we now refer to as the Enlightenment.

American law adopted the idea of time limits. The Constitution's Copyright Clause provides for a system that promotes "the Progress of Science and useful Arts, by securing for *limited Times* to Authors and Inventors the exclusive Right to their respective Writings and Discoveries." Since then, legislators have revised copyright law many times to address new technologies and lengthen its term. **Today, a copyright is valid until 70 years after the death of the author, or, in the case of works owned by a corporation, for 95 years from publication or 120 years from creation, whichever is shorter**. Once a copyright expires, the work is said to be in the "public domain," meaning that anyone may use the material. Mark Twain died in 1910, so anyone may now publish *Tom Sawyer* without permission and without paying a copyright fee.

41-2b Copyright Infringement

Anyone who uses copyrighted material without permission is violating the Copyright Act. **To prove a violation, the plaintiff must present evidence that the work was original** and that either:

- The infringer actually copied the work or
- The infringer had access to the original and the two works are substantially similar.

A court may (1) prohibit the infringer from committing further violations; (2) order destruction of the infringing material; and (3) require the infringer to pay damages, profits earned, and attorney's fees. Damages can be substantial. One jury ordered software multinational SAP to pay Oracle $1.3 *billion* for copyright infringement of Oracle's software.

41-2c Defenses to Copyright Infringement

In some circumstances, copying or selling a protected work is justified by public policy. This section examines two doctrines that excuse what would otherwise be copyright infringement: first sale and fair use.

First Sale Doctrine

Suppose you buy a textbook that, in the end, you never read. (Unlikely, we know.) Under the ***first sale doctrine***, you have the legal right to sell that textbook. **The first sale doctrine permits a person who owns a lawfully made copy of a copyrighted work to sell or otherwise dispose of the copy**. This exception to copyright is essential to commerce. If there were no first sale doctrine, people would not be able to rent movies or sell their used cars (or anything else). eBay might not exist. And museums and libraries would certainly be out of business because any display or distribution of a copyrighted work would constitute infringement.

Note, however, that the first sale doctrine does not permit the owner to *make a copy and sell it*. If you read the textbook and then decide to sell it, that is legal. But it is not legal to scan the textbook onto your iPad and then sell the original or any copy of it. In the following case, an entrepreneurial college student developed a business that tested the limits of the first sale doctrine. This case reflects the ongoing tension between copyright holders who want to control all aspects of their material and consumers who seek the lowest possible price. Part of the problem is that consumers focus on the marginal cost of creating copyrighted material (which is often quite low), while producers care most about the much higher average cost.

Kirtsaeng v. John Wiley & Sons, Inc.

133 U.S. 1351
United States Supreme Court, 2013

Facts: John Wiley & Sons, Inc. ("Wiley"), published English language textbooks. It sold some of these books abroad through its subsidiary, Wiley Asia, at much lower prices than in the United States. These overseas books included a notice on their inside cover that they were not to be taken into the United States without Wiley's permission.

In 1997, Supap Kirtsaeng moved from Thailand to the United States to attend Cornell University as an undergraduate. He asked friends and family back home to buy foreign editions of Wiley's English-language textbooks and mail them to him in the United States. He then sold the books online, reimbursed his family and friends, and kept the profit.

Wiley filed suit against Kirtsaeng, claiming that his unauthorized importation and resale of its books was copyright infringement. Furthermore, Wiley argued that the first sale doctrine did not apply because it was limited geographically to products "lawfully made" in the United States. Kirtsaeng responded that the first sale doctrine permitted his actions because his books were "lawfully made" according to the Copyright Act (that is, made with the copyright owner's permission) and that the first sale doctrine was not limited by geography. The District Court held for Wiley, concluding that the doctrine did not apply to goods manufactured abroad. On appeal, the Second Circuit affirmed. The Supreme Court granted *certiorari*.

Issue: ***Did the first sale doctrine apply to copyrighted works purchased abroad?***

Excerpts from Justice Breyer's Decision: We must decide whether the words "lawfully made under this title" restrict the scope of §109(a)'s "first sale" doctrine geographically.

In our view, §109(a)'s language, its context, and the common-law history of the "first sale" doctrine, taken together, favor a nongeographical interpretation. The language of §109(a) read literally favors Kirtsaeng's nongeographical interpretation, namely, that "lawfully made under this title" means made "in accordance with" or "in compliance with" the Copyright Act. The language of §109(a) says nothing about geography.

Both historical and contemporary statutory context indicate that Congress, when writing the present version of §109(a), did not have geography in mind. The "first sale" doctrine is a common-law doctrine with an impeccable historic pedigree. In the early 17th century, Lord Coke explained the importance of leaving buyers of goods free to compete with each other when reselling or otherwise disposing of those goods. American law too has generally thought that competition, including freedom to resell, can work to the advantage of the consumer.

The "first sale" doctrine also frees courts from the administrative burden of trying to enforce restrictions upon difficult-to-trace, readily movable goods. And it avoids the selective enforcement inherent in any such effort. Thus, it is not surprising that for at least a century the "first sale" doctrine has played an important role in American copyright law.

We also doubt that Congress would have intended to create the practical copyright-related harms with which a geographical interpretation would threaten ordinary scholarly, artistic, commercial, and consumer activities. The American Library Association tells us that library collections contain at least 200 million books published abroad. How are the libraries to obtain permission to distribute these millions of books? Used-book dealers tell us that, from the time when Benjamin Franklin and Thomas Jefferson built commercial and personal libraries of foreign books, American readers have bought used books published and printed abroad. But under a geographical interpretation a contemporary tourist who buys, say, at Shakespeare and Co. (in Paris), a dozen copies of a foreign book for American friends might find that she had violated the copyright law.

We consequently conclude that Kirtsaeng's nongeographical reading is the better reading of the Act.

The judgment of the Court of Appeals is reversed.

Kirtsaeng reminds us that copyright law must constantly adapt to the new challenges presented by business, globalization, and technology.

Ethics

This textbook used to be sold in developing countries at a much lower price than you will have paid (if you bought this book new). The publisher earned little or no profit on overseas sales but its goal was to facilitate the spread of knowledge worldwide. However, because so many U.S. students were ordering this book from overseas websites, the publisher instituted so-called "one world pricing" and now charges the same price everywhere. The authors receive pleading emails from professors overseas who would like to use the book, but whose students cannot afford it at first world prices. Is it right for U.S. students to evade the publisher's overseas pricing plan?

Fair Use

Because the period of copyright protection is so long, it has become even more important to uphold the exceptions to the law. Bear in mind that the point of copyright laws is to encourage creative work. Writers and artists who can control, and profit from, their work will be inclined to produce more. If enforced oppressively, however, the copyright laws could stifle creativity by denying access to copyrighted work. For example, Patricia Caulfield published a photograph of hibiscus flowers in *Modern Photography*. Andy Warhol cropped, flattened, and distorted that image to create a very different picture that he meant as commentary on the consumerism of the 1960s.[10]

The **fair use doctrine** is important because it permits limited use of copyrighted material without permission of the author. However, determining whether something is a fair use is often challenging because the analysis is based on a complex set of issues and the boundaries are not always obvious. As a result, fair use has been abused by those who use it as an excuse to avoid paying legitimate copyright fees, while at the same time it has sometimes inhibited perfectly legal use of copyrighted material by people who fear violating the law. For this reason, it is important to understand the following four factors, which determine whether a use is a fair one.

Fair use doctrine
Permits limited use of copyrighted material without permission of the author for purposes such as criticism, comment, news reporting, scholarship, or research

1. **The purpose and character of the use**. When copyrighted material is used for purposes such as criticism, parody, comment, news reporting, scholarship, research, or education, it is more likely to be a fair use. Political, educational, and social commentary have long been granted special respect in our society. For example, the Supreme Court permitted the rap group 2 Live Crew to make fun of the Roy Orbison's original hit song "Oh, Pretty Woman," holding that even a commercial parody—that is, one intended for profit-making purposes—could be a fair use of copyrighted material.[11]

   When the resulting work transforms the original in a significant way, it is also more likely to be fair use. After Google scanned tens of millions of books to create

10Caulfield learned of Warhol's work when she saw it in a poster. She then sued him for copyright infringement. Warhol had a strong fair use case because of his transformation of the original image and his social commentary. Regardless, Caulfield felt strongly that it was a moral issue because using an image without acknowledgment or permission "denigrates the original talent." Warhol and Caulfield settled out of court. Martha Buskirk, *The Contingent Object of Contemporary Art* (MIT Press, 2003). To see this image, search the internet for "Warhol hibiscus Guggenheim collection."

11Campbell v. Acuff-Rose Music, Inc., 510 U.S. 569 (1994).

the world's largest searchable digital library, a group of authors accused the company of copyright infringement, but a federal court held that Google's actions were protected by fair use. Even though Google had a profit-making goal, its copying served a public purpose and was transformative.

2. **The nature of the copyrighted work**. Facts receive less protection than fiction. If we were not permitted to use, say, the facts described in a textbook, education would be stifled. But J. K. Rowling, the author of the *Harry Potter* series of books, was able to prevent the publication of the *Harry Potter Lexicon*, an unauthorized reference guide that contained direct quotations, paraphrases, and plot summaries. The court ruled that although such a guide can be fair use, this one was not because the author had copied too much of Rowling's distinctive original language.[12]

3. **The amount and proportion of the work that is used**. Digitally sampled songs use a riff from a classic song.[13] Faculty members show a short clip of a Hollywood film in class. A reviewer quotes a passage from a book without the author's permission. How do we know if these are acceptable uses? Less is more. Or, in the copyright context, less is more likely to be fair use.

   However, when the use, even if minimal, involves the "heart" of the work—or its most important part—it is more likely to be an infringement. Right before President Gerald Ford published his biography, a magazine excerpted the part of it that people were most curious about: his description of his decision to pardon President Richard Nixon. Even though the magazine only published 300–400 words of a 500-page book, the Supreme Court held that it was not fair use because the "heart" of the work had been taken. A spoiler is not fair use.

   Similarly, some faculty had been in the habit of routinely preparing lengthy course packets of copyrighted material without permission of the authors. In *Basic Books, Inc. v. Kinkos Graphic Corp.*, a federal court held that this practice violated the copyright laws because the material was more than one short passage and because it was sold to students.[14]

4. **The effect of the use upon the potential market**. Courts generally do not permit a use that will deprive the copyright owner of income or decrease revenues from the original work by, say, competing with it. For example, when users conduct an internet search for a picture, search engines bring up indexed thumbnail-sized images from various sites. A commercial photographer sued a search engine, claiming that its search results showing his photos violated his copyright in the images.[15] The court held that the search results were a fair use because the thumbnails did not harm the market or value of the original photographs. Instead, they were attracting potential buyers to the original work. Again, this case balances the rights of those who create material with others who want to use it for their own purposes.

One of the major challenges for legal institutions in regulating copyrights is simply that modern intellectual property is so easy to copy.

41-2d Digital Music and Movies

One of the major challenges for legal institutions in regulating copyrights is simply that modern intellectual property is so easy to copy. Many consumers are in the habit of

---

[12] Warner Bros. Entertainment, Inc. v. RDR Books, 575 F. Supp. 2d 513 (S.D.N.Y. 2008).

[13] Sampling is the act of using small portions of other sound recordings (a beat, a rhythm break, spoken or sung words) in constructing a new song.

[14] 758 F.Supp. 1522 (S.D.N.Y. 1991).

[15] Kelly v. Arriba Soft Corporation, 336 F.3d 811 (9th Cir. 2003).

violating the law by downloading copyrighted material—music, movies, and books—for free. They seem to believe that if it is accessible, then taking it is somehow acceptable. In one survey of adolescents, 75 percent agreed with the statement, "file-sharing is so easy to do, it's unrealistic to expect people not to do it."[16]

But who is liable for this mass infringement? The Recording Industry Association of America (RIAA) developed a strategy of aggressively suing those who download music illegally, but it could only get so far by suing college students. Then a coalition of the largest entertainment businesses led by MGM sued two companies (Grokster and StreamCast) that distributed the file-sharing software used by many consumers to violate copyright law. Nearly 90 percent of the files available for download through Grokster or StreamCast were, in fact, copyrighted. The companies even marketed themselves as copyright renegades. The chief technology officer of StreamCast said that "the goal is to get in trouble with the law and get sued. It's the best way to get in the news." Bad enough to develop this business strategy, worse yet to admit it publicly.

The entertainment industry coalition argued that Grokster and StreamCast were liable because they knew about and encouraged the copyright infringement. Ultimately, the Supreme Court agreed. In *MGM v. Grokster, Ltd.*, the Court held that anyone who distributes a device whose main purpose is to violate copyright is liable for the resulting infringement. Soon after the opinion, the following announcement appeared on Grokster's defunct website:

> The United States Supreme Court unanimously confirmed that using this service to trade copyrighted material is illegal. Copying copyrighted motion picture and music files using unauthorized peer-to-peer services is illegal and is prosecuted by copyright owners. There are legal services for downloading music and movies. This service is not one of them. YOUR IP ADDRESS IS XXX.XXX.XXX.XXX. AND HAS BEEN LOGGED. Don't think you can't get caught. You are not anonymous.

And so ended the saga of Grokster, but not copyright's battle to keep up with ever-changing technologies.

41-2e The Digital Millennium Copyright Act

To bring copyright law into the internet age, Congress passed the **Digital Millennium Copyright Act** (DMCA), which provides that:

- **It is illegal to delete copyright information, such as the name of the author or the title of the article**. It is also illegal to distribute false copyright information.
- **It is illegal to circumvent encryption or scrambling technologies that protect copyrighted works**. For example, some software programs are designed so that they can only be copied once. Anyone who overrides this protective device to make another copy is violating the law. (The statute does permit purchasers of copyrighted software to make one backup copy.) If you buy a Disney DVD that prevents you from fast-forwarding through commercials, you are violating the DMCA if you figure out how to do it anyway.
- **It is illegal to distribute tools and technologies used to circumvent encryption devices**. If you tell others how to fast-forward through the Disney commercials, you have violated the statute.
- **Internet service providers are not liable for posting copyrighted material as long as they are unaware that the material is illegal and they remove it promptly after**

[16] http://pewinternet.org/Reports/2009/9-The-State-of-Music-Online-Ten-Years-After-Napster/The-State-of-Music-Online-Ten-Years-After-Napster.aspx?view=all#footnote25 or search the internet for "pew 10 years after napster."

receiving a "takedown" notice that it violates copyright law. This type of provision is called a safe harbor and is the reason YouTube is still in business. For many years, copyright holders sent sweeping takedown requests and websites blindly took down any and all material that was alleged to be illegal. In our chapter opener, we met Stephanie Lenz, the Pennsylvania mom who recorded her child dancing to "Let's Go Crazy." Universal Music, the copyright holder of Prince's famous song, sent YouTube a DMCA takedown notice and the website promptly took the video down. Lenz sued Universal, claiming that her video was protected by fair use and that the music company's takedown abused the DMCA process. A federal appeals court agreed with Lenz, prompting companies to think twice—and consider fair use—before sending takedown requests.[17]

EXAMStrategy

Question: Many of the videos posted on YouTube are copyrighted material, including thousands of hours of shows owned by Viacom, such as *The Colbert Report* and *The Daily Show*. Viacom sued YouTube for violating its copyrights. Among the evidence Viacom presented was an email from one YouTube founder to another, saying, "... please stop putting stolen videos on the site. We're going to have a tough time defending the fact that we're not liable for the copyrighted material on the site because we didn't put it up when one of the cofounders is blatantly stealing content from other sites and trying to get everyone to see it."[18]

YouTube presented evidence that it had responded within one day to Viacom's "takedown notice." Is YouTube liable?

Strategy: Viacom argued that YouTube was well aware that much of its content was illegal. YouTube responded that it met the requirements of the Safe Harbor provision.

Result: The court found for YouTube. General awareness that many postings infringed copyrights did not impose a duty for YouTube to monitor its videos. Its only requirement was to respond when notified of infringement. YouTube did just that in this case.[19]

41-2f International Copyright Treaties

Like patents, copyright laws vary by country. In the absence of international treaties, artists and authors would be required to register their works on a country-by-country basis. But treaties such as **the Berne Convention for the Protection of Literary and Artistic Works require all 172 member countries to provide automatic copyright protection to any works created in other member countries**. The protection does not expire until 50 years after the death of the author.[20] The WIPO (World Intellectual Property Organization) Copyright Treaty and the WIPO Performances and Phonograms Treaty add computer programs, movies, and music to the list of copyrightable materials.

17Lenz v. Universal Music Corp., 801 F.3d 1126 (9th Cir., 2015), The Electronic Frontier Foundation provided a lawyer for Lenz, for free.

18Quoted in "Federal Judge Hands Google Victory in Viacom's $1 Billion Suit over YouTube Content" by Michael Liedtke on Law.com, June 24, 2010.

19Viacom Int'l, Inc. v. YouTube, Inc., 676 F.3d 19(2nd Cir., 2012).

20Under U.S. law, copyrights last the life of the author plus 70 years. The United States must grant works created in other signatory countries a copyright that lasts either 50 years or the length of time granted in that country, whichever is longer, but in no case longer than life plus 70 years.

41-3 TRADEMARKS

A trademark is any combination of words and symbols that a business uses to identify its products or services and distinguish them from others. Trademarks are important to both consumers and businesses. Consumers use trademarks to distinguish between competing products. People who feel that Nike shoes fit their feet best can rely on the Nike trademark to know they are buying the shoe they want. A business with a high-quality product can use a trademark to develop a loyal base of customers who are able to distinguish its product from another.

Trademark
Any combination of words and symbols that a business uses to identify its products or services and distinguish them from others

Federal trademarks are governed by the Lanham Act. A trademark is valid for ten years, but the owner can renew it for an unlimited number of ten-year terms as long as the mark is still in use.

41-3a Types of Marks

There are four different types of marks:

1. **Trademarks** are affixed to *goods*.
2. **Service marks** are used to identify *services*, not products. Holiday Inn, Burger King, and Weight Watchers are service marks. In this chapter, the terms *trademark* and *mark* are used to refer to both trademarks and service marks.
3. **Certification marks** are words or symbols used by a person or organization to attest that products and services produced by others meet certain standards. The Good Housekeeping Seal of Approval means that the Good Housekeeping organization has determined that a product meets its standards.
4. **Collective marks** are used to identify members of an organization. The Lions Club, the Girl Scouts of America, and the Masons are examples of collective marks.

41-3b Trademark Registration

Under common law, the first person to use a mark in trade owns it. Registration with the federal government is not necessary. However, under the federal Lanham Act, the owner of a mark may register it on the Lanham Act Principal Register. A trademark owner may use the symbol ™ at any time, even before registering it, but not until the mark is registered can the symbol ® be placed next to it. Registration has several advantages:

- Even if a mark has been used in only one or two states, registration makes it valid nationally.
- Registration notifies the public that a mark is in use because anyone who applies for registration first searches the Public Register to ensure that no one else has rights to the mark.
- Five years after registration, a mark becomes virtually incontestable because most challenges are barred.
- The damages available under the Lanham Act are higher than under common law.
- The holder of a registered trademark generally has the right to use it as an internet domain name.

Under the Lanham Act, the owner files an application with the PTO. The PTO will accept an application only if the owner has already used the mark attached to a product in interstate commerce or promises to use the mark within six months after the filing. In addition, the applicant must be the *first* to use the mark in interstate commerce.

41-3c Valid Trademarks

Words (Amazon), symbols (Microsoft's flying window logo), phrases and slogans (Nike's "Just do it"), shapes (teardrop of a Hershey's kiss), sounds (Macintosh's startup chime), colors (jeweler Tiffany's blue), and even scents (bubble-gum scented flip-flops) can be trademarked. **To be valid, a trademark must be distinctive**—that is, the mark must clearly distinguish one product from another and identify the product's source. Courts lay out three categories of marks that can be trademarked, from strongest (most distinctive) to weakest:

1. Fanciful marks and arbitrary marks are immediately protectable as trademarks. **Fanciful marks** are made-up words such as Exxon or Saucony. **Arbitrary marks** use existing words that do *not* describe the product—"Starbucks" for coffee, for example. Starbuck was a whaler in *Moby Dick*—and the novel said nothing about the character drinking a latte.
2. **Suggestive marks** *indirectly* describe the product's function, qualities, or characteristics. "Microsoft" suggests software for microcomputers, and "Coppertone" suggests what customers will look like after applying the product. These marks are also protectable.
3. **Descriptive marks** *directly* describe the product in some way. A calendar named "365-Day Calendar" is one example. These marks cannot, by themselves, be trademarked unless they have acquired **secondary meaning**, that is, they have been used for so long that they are now associated with the product in the public's mind. "Holiday Inn" (motel) and "Windows" are two examples of descriptive marks that have attained secondary meaning.

The following categories *cannot* be trademarked:

- **Generic trademarks.** No one is permitted to trademark an item's ordinary name—*shoe* or *book*, for example. Sometimes, however, a word begins as a trademark and later becomes a generic name. Zipper, escalator, aspirin, linoleum, thermos, yo-yo, band-aid, ping-pong, and nylon all started out as trademarks but became generic. Once a name is generic, the owner loses the trademark because the name can no longer be used to distinguish one product from another—all products are called the same thing. That is why Xerox Corp. encourages people to say, "I'll photocopy this document," rather than "I'll xerox it." Jeep, Rollerblade, and TiVo are names that began as trademarks and may now be generic. What about "app store"? Microsoft has sued Apple, disputing its right to trademark this term. Meanwhile, Facebook has trademarked, "face," "book," "like," "wall," and "poke." The goal is not to prevent consumers from using these terms but rather to warn off other companies.
- **Personal names.** The PTO generally will not grant a trademark in a surname unless it has acquired secondary meaning due to an association with a specific business or product. Companies like Dell, Ford, and Heinz have trademarks because, more than just surnames, they achieved recognition as brands in themselves.
- **Geographical terms.** Similarly, geographical names that describe the product's place of origin, such as Maine lobster or Idaho potatoes cannot be trademarked because they are generic. However, geographical terms that are used arbitrarily, can be protected, such as: Boston Market, California Pizza Kitchen, and Nantucket Nectars.
- **Deceptive marks.** The PTO will not register a mark that is deceptive. It refused to register a trademark with the words "National Collection and Credit Control" and an eagle superimposed on a map of the United States because this trademark gave the false impression that the organization was an official government agency.

- **Similar to an existing mark.** To avoid confusion, the PTO will not grant a trademark that is similar to one already in existence on a similar product. Once the PTO had granted a trademark for "Pledge" furniture polish, it refused to trademark "Promise" for the same product. Houghton-Mifflin Co. successfully sued to prevent a punk rock band from calling itself Furious George because the name is too similar to Curious George, the star of a series of children's books.

Ethics

For 70 years, the PTO refused to register marks that were considered offensive or disparaging.

In 2014, the Trademark Trial and Appeal Board, the judicial arm of the PTO, canceled the trademark for the Washington Redskins football team upon finding that the name offended some members of the Native American community. An Asian-American rock group called the "Slants" challenged this law by insisting that they should be able to trademark the name even though some might find it insulting. When the PTO refused to grant the band a trademark, the members appealed to the Supreme Court. In a case named *Matal v. Tam,*[21] the Court held that the rule prohibiting insulting trademarks was unconstitutional: the First Amendment prohibits the government from silencing offensive words and messages—no matter how hurtful. As a result, the Slants were able to register their name and the Redskins will likely recover theirs. Do you agree with this outcome?

41-3d Infringement and Dilution

To win a trademark infringement suit, the original trademark owner must show that the alleged infringer's trademark is likely to confuse customers about who has made the goods or provided the services.

The following Landmark Case established the factors that determine trademark infringement.

Landmark Case

AMF Inc. v. Sleekcraft Boats

599 F.2d 341
United States Court of Appeals for the Ninth Circuit, 1979

Facts: AMF sold recreational boats named "Slickcraft." Unaware of this product, Bruce Nescher named his company's boats "Sleekcraft." When AMF notified Nescher of the alleged trademark infringement, Nescher added "Boats by Nescher" to its logo to distinguish his product.

Both Slickcraft and Sleekcraft made sporty, fiberglass boats of a similar size and price. However, Slickcraft boats were made and marketed for family recreation, such as fishing, while Sleekcraft boats were aimed at high speed racing enthusiasts. These uses did somewhat overlap. Both companies sold their boats nationally, advertised in magazines, and exhibited their product lines at the same boat shows.

AMF sued Sleekcraft Boats for trademark infringement, arguing that its similar name was likely to confuse consumers. But the lower court decided that confusion was unlikely because the boats had different markets. AMF appealed.

---

[21] 582 U.S. ___ (2017).

Issue: ***Was the use of Sleekcraft versus Slickcraft likely to confuse consumers?***

Excerpts from Judge Anderson's Decision: In determining whether confusion between related goods is likely, the following factors are relevant:

1. Strength of the mark

A strong mark is inherently distinctive, for example, an arbitrary or fanciful mark; it will be afforded the widest ambit of protection from infringing uses. A descriptive mark tells something about the product; it will be protected only when secondary meaning is shown. In between lie suggestive marks which subtly connote something about the products.

Although the distinction between descriptive and suggestive marks may be inarticulable, several criteria offer guidance. The primary criterion is "the imaginativeness involved in the suggestion,": that is, how immediate and direct is the thought process from the mark to the particular product. From the word Slickcraft one might readily conjure up the image of appellant's boats, yet a number of other images might also follow. A secondary criterion is whether granting the trademark owner a limited monopoly will in fact inhibit legitimate use of the mark by other sellers. There is no evidence here that others have used or desire to use Slickcraft in describing their goods. Another criterion is whether the mark is actually viewed by the public as an indication of the product's origin. We think buyers probably will understand that Slickcraft is a trademark, particularly since it is generally used in conjunction with the mark AMF.

We hold that Slickcraft is a suggestive mark when applied to boats. Although appellant's mark is protectible, it is a weak mark entitled to a restricted range of protection. Thus, only if the marks are quite similar, and the goods closely related, will infringement be found.

2. Proximity of the goods

For related goods, the danger presented is that the public will mistakenly assume there is an association between the producers of the related goods, though no such association exists. Although these product lines are non-competing, they are extremely close in use and function.

3. Similarity of the marks

Similarity of the marks is tested on three levels: sight, sound, and meaning. Standing alone the words Sleekcraft and Slickcraft are the same except for two inconspicuous letters in the middle of the first syllable. To the eye, the words are similar. Sound is also important because reputation is often conveyed word-of-mouth. We recognize that the two sounds can be distinguished, but the difference is only in a small part of one syllable. The final criterion reinforces our conclusion. Closeness in meaning can itself substantiate a claim of similarity of trademarks. The words are virtual synonyms.

4. Evidence of actual confusion

Evidence that use of the two marks has already led to confusion is persuasive proof that future confusion is likely. AMF introduced evidence that confusion had occurred both in the trade and in the mind of the buying public.

5. Marketing channels

Convergent marketing channels increase the likelihood of confusion. The normal marketing channels used by both AMF and Nescher are parallel. Although different submarkets are involved, the general class of boat purchasers exposed to the products overlap.

6. Type of goods and purchaser care

Both parties produce high quality, expensive goods. Boats are purchased only after thoughtful, careful evaluation of the product and the performance the purchaser expects. When the goods are expensive, the buyer can be expected to exercise greater care in his purchases; again, though, confusion may still be likely.

7. Intent

Nescher was unaware of the Slickcraft mark when he adopted the Sleekcraft name. When the alleged infringer knowingly adopts a mark similar to another's, reviewing courts presume that the defendant can accomplish his purpose: that is, that the public will be deceived.

8. Likelihood of expansion

A "strong possibility" that either party may expand his business to compete with the other will weigh in favor of finding that the present use is infringing. The evidence shows that both parties are diversifying their model lines.

We hold that Nescher has infringed the Slickcraft mark. Since Nescher's use is continuing, an injunction should have been entered.

In the event of infringement, the rightful owner may be entitled to an injunction prohibiting further violations. In the *AMF* case, the court prohibited Nescher from using the name "Sleekcraft" ever again—a costly punishment for any business. Other infringement remedies include (1) destruction of the infringing material, (2) up to three times actual damages, (3) any profits the infringer earned on the product, and (4) attorney's fees.

Trademark holders can also object to the use of their mark in a way that dilutes its value. **Trademark dilution occurs in two important ways: blurring and tarnishment. Blurring, or the lessening of a mark's capacity to identify**, can occur when a famous mark is identified with unrelated products or services, like Microsoft lipstick or Tesla bicycles. **Tarnishment is an association with unwholesome goods or services.** Barbie's Playhouse was an adult website with the look and feel of Mattel's trademarked Barbie doll. The website also featured images of dolls that looked like Barbies. The court found that Barbie's Playhouse had tarnished Mattel's trademark.[22]

Remember fair use in copyright? This important concept can also excuse trademark dilution. When a dog toy maker named a chew toy "Chewy Vuitton," the famous French luxury goods company Louis (pronounced "Lewy") Vuitton sued for dilution. The court held that Chewy successfully parodied Louis and that the toy did not blur or diminish the value of the famous mark.[23]

41-3e International Trademark Treaties

Under the **Paris Convention**, if someone registers a trademark in one country, then he has a grace period of six months, during which he can file in any other country using the same original filing date. Under the **Madrid Agreement**, any trademark registered with the international registry is valid in all signatory countries. (The United States is a signatory.) The **Trademark Law Treaty** simplifies and harmonizes the process of applying for trademarks around the world. Now, a U.S. firm seeking international trademark protection need only file one application, in English, with the PTO, which sends the application to the WIPO, which transmits it to each country in which the applicant would like trademark protection.

EXAMStrategy

Question: Jerry Falwell was a nationally known Baptist minister whose website was falwell.com. One of his most outspoken critics registered the website fallwell.com—note the misspelling—to criticize the minister's views on homosexuality. This site has a disclaimer indicating that it was not affiliated with Reverend Falwell. The minister sued fallwell.com, alleging a violation of trademark law. Was there a violation?

Strategy: To win a trademark claim, the reverend had to show a likelihood of consumer confusion between the two sites.

Result: The reverend lost. The court ruled that there was no confusion—fallwell.com had a clear disclaimer. Also, there was no indication of bad faith. The court was reluctant to censor political commentary.

41-4 TRADE SECRETS

What do the formulas for Coca-Cola and motor oil have in common with computer circuitry, a machine for making adhesive tape, and a procedure for applying hair dye? They are all trade secrets. **A trade secret is a formula, device, process, method, or compilation of information that, when used in business, gives the owner an advantage over competitors who do not know it.** In determining if information is a trade secret, courts consider:

Trade secret
A formula, device, process, method, or compilation of information that, when used in business, gives the owner an advantage over competitors

- How difficult (and expensive) was the information to obtain? Was it readily available from other sources?

22 Mattel, Inc. v. Jcom, Inc., 97 Civ. 7191 (S.D.N.Y., 1998).
23 Louis Vuitton Malletier S.A. v. Haute Diggity Dog, 507 F.3d 252 (4th Cir. 2007).

- Does the information create an important competitive advantage?
- Did the company make a reasonable effort to protect it?

It has been estimated that the theft of trade secrets costs U.S. businesses over $300 billion a year. In response, most states have adopted the **Uniform Trade Secrets Act (UTSA)**. Anyone who misappropriates a trade secret is liable to the owner for (1) actual damages, (2) unjust enrichment, or (3) a reasonable royalty. If the misappropriation was willful or malicious, the court may award attorney's fees and double damages. A jury awarded Avery Dennison Corp. $40 million in damages from a competitor that had misappropriated secret information about the adhesives used in self-stick stamps.

Some companies opt for trade secret protection because their creations cannot be patented. Recipes, customer lists, business plans, and marketing strategies are some examples. But sometimes, even if a patent is available, trade secret protection may make more business sense. Patent registration requires that the formula be disclosed publicly, which may be a boon for competitors and copyists alike. In addition, a patent expires after 20 years, but takes years and thousands of dollars to acquire. For these reasons (and as the following case shows), trade secrets are common in rapidly changing industries involving design and technology.

We all know the value of friends, followers, and contacts on social media. But could these be trade secrets? You be the judge.

You Be the Judge

CDM Media USA, Inc. v. Simms

2015 U.S. Dist. LEXIS 37458; 2015 WL 1399050 N.D. Ill., 2015

Facts: Robert Simms worked for CDM Media USA, a marketing company focused on the technology industry. As CDM's point person for social media, Simms created, controlled, and managed various social media groups and profiles to promote his employer.

LinkedIn is a leading social media site for professional and business networking. The site's user agreement informs its members that "your account belongs to you." Through his personal LinkedIn account and on behalf of CDM, Simms launched a LinkedIn group called the CIO Speaker Bureau. This private online community sought to bring together technology executives interested in CDM's services. Simms adopted LinkedIn's strictest privacy setting, so the names of Bureau members and their communications were not available to the public at large. Over time, the group grew to 679 members and became a valuable source of clients for CDM.

Four years later, Simms left to work for a technology company called Box, which was one of CDM's largest clients. Upon departure, Simms refused to relinquish control of the LinkedIn group or to provide CDM with the group's membership list. CDM sued Simms for misappropriation, arguing that the LinkedIn members were a company trade secret.

You Be the Judge: *Is the list of members in a LinkedIn group a trade secret?*

Argument for Plaintiff: Trade secret law prevents departing employees from taking valuable information. CDM spent significant time and money over four years to develop the Bureau. It was an exclusive group, with access limited by strict privacy settings and containing information extremely valuable to any CDM competitor. Although Simms used his personal LinkedIn account to create the group, he gathered this information as part of his job at CDM. He cannot take CDM's secret client list to a new employer.

Argument for Defendant: Membership of a LinkedIn group cannot be a trade secret for the simple reason that it is not secret. Although membership is not widely known, neither the existence of the group nor its composition is a secret. CDM announced the creation of the group through a press release. Members know each other and there is nothing confidential about their identities or interaction (which, after all, is the point of social networking!). Also, LinkedIn's terms are clear: The account belongs to the individual user who created it, which in this case is Simms. If CDM was so interested in its client list, it should have taken other steps to protect it.

Only civil penalties are available under the Uniform Trade Secrets Act. To safeguard national security and maintain the nation's industrial and economic edge, Congress passed the **Economic Espionage Act of 1996, which makes it a *criminal* offense to steal (or attempt to steal) trade secrets for the benefit of someone other than the owner, including for the benefit of any foreign government.** Xiaodong Sheldon Meng was convicted of violating this statute after he was caught stealing computer code used in military weapons. He had committed the theft on behalf of the government of China. Meng was sentenced to 24 months in prison. Analyst Sameth Agrawal spent three years in prison for giving his employer's high-frequency trading algorithms to a New York-based hedge fund.

CHAPTER CONCLUSION

Intellectual property takes many different forms. It can be an internet domain name, a software program, a cartoon character, a recipe for fried chicken, or a process for making drugs. Yet, for many individuals and companies, intellectual property is the most valuable asset they will ever own. As its economic value increases, so does the need to understand the rules of intellectual property law.

EXAM REVIEW

	Patent	Copyright	Trademark	Trade Secrets
Protects:	Mechanical, electrical, chemical inventions; processes; machines; composition of matter; designs; plants	The tangible expression of an idea, but not the idea itself	Words and symbols that a business uses to identify its products or services	A formula, device, process, method, or compilation of information that, when used in business, gives the owner an advantage over competitors who do not know it
Requirements for Legal Protection:	Application approved by PTO	An item is automatically copyrighted once it is in tangible form	Use is the only requirement; registration is not necessary but does offer some benefits	Must be kept confidential
Duration:	20 years after the application is filed (14 years from date of issuance for a design patent)	70 years after the death of the work's only or last living author or, for a corporation, 95 years from publication or 120 years from creation	Valid for 10 years but the owner can renew for an unlimited number of terms as long as the mark is still being used	As long as it is kept confidential

EXAMStrategy

1. Question: DatagraphiX manufactured and sold computer graphics equipment that allowed users to transfer large volumes of information directly from computers to microfilm. Customers were required to keep maintenance documentation onsite for the DatagraphiX service personnel. The service manual carried this legend: "No other use, direct or indirect, of this document or of any information derived there from is authorized. No copies of any part of this document shall be made without written approval by DatagraphiX." In addition, on every page of the maintenance manual, the company placed warnings that the information was proprietary and not to be duplicated. Frederick J. Lennen left DatagraphiX to start his own company that serviced DatagraphiX equipment. Can DatagraphiX prevent Lennen from using its manuals?

Strategy: With trade secrets, the key is that the owner has made a reasonable effort to protect them. (See the "Result" at the end of this Exam Review section.)

EXAMStrategy

2. Question: "Hey, Paula," a pop hit that spent months on the music charts, was back on the radio 30 years later, but in a form the song's author never intended. Talk-show host Rush Limbaugh played a version with the same music as the original but with lyrics that poked fun at President Bill Clinton's alleged sexual misconduct with Paula Jones. Has Limbaugh violated the author's copyright?

Strategy: Although this example may look like a copyright violation, it falls under an exception. (See the "Result" at the end of this Exam Review section.)

EXAMStrategy

3. Question: Research Corp. applied for a patent for a so-called halftoning technique that uses a mathematical formula to enable monitors and printers with limited color options to simulate a wider range of colors. Is this technique patentable?

Strategy: Are these inventors attempting to patent a mathematical algorithm or formula? (See the "Result" at the end of this Exam Review section.)

RESULTS

1. Result: The court held that these manuals were DatagraphiX's trade secrets.

2. Result: Parody (especially about politics!) is a fair use of copyrighted material so long as use of the original is not excessive.

3. Result: The trial court ruled that this patent application was invalid because it was too abstract. But the appellate court overruled, holding that, although the patent used mathematical algorithms, the inventors were patenting the process not the algorithms. It upheld the patent.[24]

[24] Research Corporation Technologies, Inc. v. Microsoft Corporation, 627 F.3d 859 (Fed. Cir. 2010).

MULTIPLE-CHOICE QUESTIONS

1. Taylor Swift wanted to trademark her song lyrics: "And I'll write your name." She ________________.
   (a) can trademark it because it is a short phrase associated with her entertainment services
   (b) can trademark it only if it is in a tangible form
   (c) cannot trademark it because it is generic
   (d) none of these because short phrases cannot be trademarked
2. Thomas's English Muffins wanted to protect the method by which it makes muffins with air pockets—what it calls "nooks and crannies." What would be the best way to achieve this goal?
   (a) Patent
   (b) Copyright
   (c) Trademark
   (d) Trade secret
   (e) This method cannot be protected.
3. VitaminWater has become such a success that other companies are also now selling similar (but not identical) flavored colored water. Some competitors bottle their drinks in a similar bell-shaped bottle with a two-toned label that has a horizontal color band. What is the best infringement claim for VitaminWater to make against these competitors?
   (a) Patent
   (b) Copyright
   (c) Trademark
   (d) Trade secret
   (e) There is no good claim.
4. Faber-Castell began manufacturing pencils in 1761. Although pencils and erasers had both existed for some time, the company did not begin putting erasers on the ends of its pencils until the 1870s. The company was sued by an inventor who had previously patented this idea. The case went to the Supreme Court. Who won the case?
   (a) The patent holder because no one had ever put an eraser on a pencil before
   (b) The patent holder because the PTO had approved his patent
   (c) Faber-Castell because the pencil with an eraser was not novel
   (d) Faber-Castell because the pencil with an eraser was not useful
5. If you buy a DVD, you have the legal right to ______________.
   (a) watch it as many times as you want and then give it away
   (b) copy it to your computer and then give it to a friend
   (c) copy it to your computer and sell it on eBay
   (d) all of these
   (e) A and B only

6. A couple thought of a clever name for an automobile. They wanted to protect this name so that they could ultimately sell it to a car manufacturer. What would be the best method to attain this goal?
   (a) Patent
   (b) Copyright
   (c) Trademark
   (d) Trade secret
   (e) This name cannot be protected.

CASE QUESTIONS

1. While in college, David invented a new and useful machine to make macaroni and cheese (he called it the "Mac 'n' Cheeser"). It was like nothing on the market, but David did not apply for a patent. At that time, he offered to sell his invention to several kitchen products companies. His offers were all rejected and he never sold the invention. Years later, he decided to apply for a utility patent. Is David entitled to a utility patent?

2. Alice Randall wrote a novel entitled *The Wind Done Gone*, which retells the Civil War novel *Gone with the Wind* from the perspective of Scarlett O'Hara's (imagined) black half-sister and slave. The novel does not use any of the names of the original, but clearly references the same characters, places, and plot lines. Randall was sued, but alleged fair use. Should she win?

3. Rebecca Reyher wrote (and copyrighted) a children's book entitled *My Mother Is the Most Beautiful Woman in the World*. The story was based on a Russian folk tale told to her by her own mother. Years later, the children's television show *Sesame Street* televised a skit entitled "The Most Beautiful Woman in the World." The *Sesame Street* version took place in a different locale and had fewer frills, but the sequence of events in both stories was identical. Has *Sesame Street* infringed Reyher's copyright?

4. Hair Corp. sells shampoo in the United States and internationally. Its international prices are 30 percent less than its domestic prices. Big Seller, Inc., is in the business of buying products internationally in bulk and reselling them in the United States Big Seller buys Hair Corp's shampoos in Peru and imports them to the United States to be sold at international rates. Can Hair Corp successfully sue Big Seller for copyright infringement?

5. Victoria's Secret, a well-known lingerie company, found out that a man named Victor Moseley was running a small store in Kentucky named "Victor's Little Secret." Moseley's shop sold clocks, patches, temporary tattoos, stuffed animals, coffee mugs, leather biker wallets, Zippo lighters, diet formula, jigsaw puzzles, jewelry, candles, and adult novelties. Women's lingerie represented about 5 percent of its sales. Does Victoria's Secret have a valid intellectual property claim?

6. Sequenom developed a noninvasive prenatal diagnostic test to assess the risk of Down syndrome or other chromosomal abnormalities in fetuses. The test analyzes DNA from the fetus that is found in the mother's blood. Prior to this test, women had to undergo invasive tests that carried a slight risk of miscarriage. The PTO awarded Sequenom a patent on the test, but other diagnostic testing companies sued to invalidate the patent. Is Sequenom's patent valid?

DISCUSSION QUESTIONS

1. **ETHICS** Virtually any television show, movie, or song can be downloaded for free on the internet. Most of this material is copyrighted and was very expensive to produce. Most of it is also available for a fee through such legitimate sites as iTunes. What is your ethical obligation? Should you pay $1.99 to download an episode of *The Big Bang Theory* from iTunes or take it for free from an illegal site? What is your Life Principle?

2. For much of history, the copyright term was limited to 28 years. Now, because the term is based on the life of the creator, the average copyright lasts about 150 years. What is a fair copyright term? Some commentators argue that because so much intellectual property is stolen, owners need longer protection. Do you agree with this argument?

3. The America Invents Act allows inventors to expedite review of their inventions by paying a fee. This clearly favors those applicants with money. Do you agree with this practice? Why or why not?

4. Should Amazon be able to patent the One-Click method of ordering? What about Facebook's patent on a process that "dynamically provides a news feed about a user of a social network"? Were these inventions really novel and nonobvious? What should the standard be for business method patents?

5. In New Orleans, Mardi Gras "Indians" are carnival revelers who dress up for Mardi Gras in costumes influenced by Native American ceremonial attire. "Indians" often spend the entire year and thousands of dollars crafting their intricate designs with feathers, beads, and other decorations. As cultural icons in New Orleans, their images are often captured by photographers, who profit from the sale of these pictures. The Indians' creations are not copyrightable because the law views costumes as functional, not aesthetic works. What are the Indians' best arguments to change the law? Should cultural works be owned?

6. Music stars Beyoncé and Jay-Z named their newborn daughter Blue Ivy and then rushed to trademark the name, because they planned to use it in commerce. Their application was denied because a wedding planner in Massachusetts was already using "Blue Ivy" as the name of her business. Is this the correct outcome? Should people have priority in protecting personal names? Should a small business have priority over what would surely have been a much larger, more profitable use of this name?

42

CHAPTER

REAL PROPERTY AND LANDLORD–TENANT LAW

Some men have staked claims to land for its oil, others for its gold. But Paul Termarco and Gene Murdoch are staking their claim to an island using ... hot dogs. For years, the two friends sold chili dogs, cheese dogs, and the ever traditional hot dogs from a stand on a tiny island on a lake. Locals knew it as "Hot Dog Island" and visited frequently on jet skis.

Paul Termarco and Gene Murdoch are staking their claim to an island using ... hot dogs.

But the pair's entrepreneurial vision did not end with hot dogs. Property records showed that the state owned the lake and lake floor, but nobody owned the island. An attorney told them about the law of adverse possession. If Murdoch and Termarco could show that they used the island openly for a continuous period, it would be eventually be theirs.

As crazy as the scheme sounded, they figured it was worth trying. After all, not everyone can say they own an island.[1]

[1] Leslie Haggin, "Pair Stake Their Claim to Hot Dog Island," *The Record* (Bergen, NJ), September 5, 1994, p. A12.

Can two friends acquire an island simply by *pretending* they own it? Yes. As we will see, the law of adverse possession permits people to obtain title to land by openly using it, if they meet certain stringent criteria. We examine the rules later in the chapter and determine the likelihood of success for the hot dog duo. For now, the lesson is that real property law can provide surprises—and profit.

42-1 NATURE OF REAL PROPERTY

Property falls into three categories: real, personal, and intellectual. Real property, which is the focus of this chapter, consists of the following:

- **Land.** Land is the most common and important form of real property. In England, land was historically the greatest source of wealth and social status, far more important than industrial or commercial enterprises. As a result, the law of real property has been of paramount importance for nearly 1,000 years, developing very gradually to reflect changing conditions.

  Real property usually also includes anything underground (subsurface right) and some amount of airspace above land (air rights).
- **Buildings.** Buildings are real property. Houses, office buildings, apartments, and factories all fall in this category.
- **Plant life.** Plant life growing on land is real property whether the plants are naturally occurring, such as trees, or cultivated crops. When a landowner sells his property, plant life is automatically included in the sale unless the parties agree otherwise.

  A landowner may also sell the plant life separately if he wishes. A sale of the plant life alone, without the land, is a sale of goods. (Goods, as you may recall, are movable things.) If Douglas chops down all of his land's fir trees to sell to Frasier, this sale of goods will be governed by the Uniform Commercial Code (UCC).
- **Fixtures.** Fixtures are goods that have become attached to real property. A house (which is real property) contains many fixtures. The chandelier and the faucets were goods when they were manufactured and when they were sold to the builder because they were movable. But when the builder attached them to the house, the items became fixtures. By contrast, neither the refrigerator nor the grand piano is a fixture.

When an owner sells real property, the buyer normally obtains the fixtures unless the parties specify otherwise. Sometimes it is difficult to determine whether something is a fixture. The general rule is this: **An object is a fixture if (1) it is attached to property in such a way that removing it would damage the property, (2) it was especially made or adapted to the particular property (such as custom-made bookshelves fitted in a library), or (3) the owner of the property clearly intends the item to remain permanently.**

The judge in the following case applied these factors to determine whether a cattle scale was a fixture.

Freeman v. Barrs

237 S.W.3d 285
Missouri Court of Appeals, 2007

Facts: Mary Ann Barrs paid $3.5 million to Francis Freeman for 4,000 acres of ranch land, including a covered "pole-barn," which had open sides, a large cattle scale, and an enclosed veterinarian's office. The parties used a form contract, which stated that all fixtures were included with the sale. The document offered space for the parties to specify items that were included or excluded with the sale, but neither party listed the cattle scale as either in or out of the deal. After the agreement went through, Barrs and Freeman got into a beef over who owned the scale. The trial judge grilled numerous witnesses and ultimately weighed in on the side of Barrs, declaring the scale a fixture that belonged to the real estate. Broiling, Freeman appealed.

Issue: ***Was the cattle scale a fixture?***

Excerpts from Judge Parrish's Decision: Steve McFadden, the president of Sooner Scale, Inc., the maker of the scale, testified that he had designed the present scale. The scale was designed to be portable, and 70 percent of the scales he sold were installed in the present manner. He further stated that he could move the present scales by cutting away a welded metal fence and lifting the scale with heavy machinery, [a] process he often performs. McFadden further stated that the removal of the fence would take approximately one hour with use of a cutting torch, and thereafter the scale could be moved within fifteen minutes.

Characterization of an item as a fixture depends upon the finding of three elements: annexation to the realty, adaptation to the use to which the realty is devoted, and intent of the annexor that the object become a permanent accession to the freehold. The latter two elements, adaptation and intent, are more important in determining whether a chattel became a fixture than the method by which the chattel is affixed to a freehold.

Annexation. The scale was purchased by plaintiff to "start selling cattle from the ranch and not sending them to the sale barn to keep the price up a little." The scale weighs approximately 6,500 pounds. A fence and gates within the structure had to be cut off in order to install the scale. A concrete slab was poured in the structure for placement of the scale. The scale was placed on pipes on the ground and pushed with a tractor across the pipes onto the slab. Concrete ramps were installed on two sides of the scale and fencing was constructed to direct cattle onto the scale. The metal posts for the fence were set in the concrete. The scale has remained in place since its installation.

Adaptation. Ray Stone had been ranch manager for plaintiff. At the time of trial he had an agreement with defendant that permitted him to run cattle on the property. He "just kind of saw after the place" for her. He told the court that the scale was integral to a cattle-working facility. The scale was used to weigh cattle for sale and to determine required dosages of medicine administered to cattle.

Intent. The manufacturer sold peripheral items that permitted the scale to be moved. This included a trailer and an inverter. Plaintiff did not buy that equipment. Ray Stone told the court that the scale was purchased "to be stationary whether it was portable or not."

This court concludes that the scale was a fixture; that, therefore, the sale of the real estate on which it was situated included the sale of the scale. A 6,500-pound scale placed on a specially sized concrete pad and surrounded by metal pole fencing set in the concrete is annexed to the real estate on which the concrete pad is poured. The permanency of the installation is emphasized by the fact the facility is covered and has a veterinary office in which the printer for the scale may be operated. The scale was put in place to facilitate the cattle operation on the premises. It had been used for that purpose since its purchase. Its adaptation for that purpose enhanced the operation of the cattle ranch.

Affirmed.

42-2 INTERESTS IN REAL PROPERTY

Fee simple absolute
Full ownership privileges in a property

Use and ownership of real estate can take many different legal forms. A person may own property outright, having the unrestricted use of the land and an unlimited right to sell it. Such a person owns a **fee simple absolute**. However, it is also possible to own a lesser interest in real property. The different rights that someone can hold in real property are known as **estates** or **interests**.[2] Both terms simply indicate specified rights in property.

Estates and interests
Types of rights in land

42-2a Concurrent Estates

When two or more people own real property at the same time, they have **concurrent estates**. The most common forms of concurrent estates are tenancy in common, joint tenancy, and tenancy by the entirety.

Concurrent estates
Two or more people owning property at the same time

Tenancy in Common

The most common form of concurrent estate is **tenancy in common**. Suppose Patricia owns a house, which she agrees to sell to Quincy and Rebecca. When she *conveys* the deed—i.e., transfers the deed—"to Quincy and Rebecca," those two now have a tenancy in common. This kind of estate can also be created in a will. If Patricia had died still owning the house and left it in her will to "Sam and Tracy," then Sam and Tracy would have a tenancy in common. Tenancy in common is the "default setting" when multiple people acquire property. Co-owners are automatically considered tenants in common unless another type of interest (joint tenancy, tenancy by the entirety) is specified.

Tenancy in common
Two or more people holding equal interest in a property, but with no right of survivorship

A tenancy in common might have 2 owners, or 22, or any number. The tenants in common do not own a particular section of the property; they own an equal interest in the entire property. Quincy and Rebecca each own a 50 percent interest in the entire house.

Any co-tenant may convey her interest in the property to another person. Thus, if Rebecca moves 1,000 miles away, she may sell her 50 percent interest in the house to Sidney. Further, when a co-tenant dies, her interest in the property passes to her heirs, along with all of her other assets.

Partition by kind
A form of partition in which a property is divided among co-owners

Partition. Since any tenant in common has the power to convey her interest, some people may find themselves sharing ownership with others they do not know or, worse, dislike. What to do? Partition, or division of the property among the co-tenants. Any co-tenant is entitled to demand partition of the property. If the various co-tenants cannot agree on a fair division, a co-tenant may request a court to do it. **All co-tenants have an absolute right to partition.**

Joint tenancy
Two or more people holding equal interest in a property, with the right of survivorship

A court will normally attempt a **partition by kind**, meaning that it actually divides the land equally among the co-tenants. If three co-tenants own a 300-acre farm and the court can divide the land so that the three sections are of roughly equal value, it will perform a partition in kind, even if one or two of the co-tenants oppose partition. If partition by kind is impossible because there is no fair way to divide the property, the court will order the real estate sold and the proceeds divided equally.

Image Source/Jupiterimages

Partition by kind might be the best way to divide a piece of property like this vineyard.

Joint Tenancy

Joint tenancy is similar to tenancy in common but is used less frequently. The parties, called joint tenants, again own a percentage of the entire property and also have the absolute right of partition. The primary difference is that a **joint tenancy** includes the right of survivorship. This means that when one joint tenant dies, his interest

[2]The authors use estates and interests interchangeably to mean types of rights in land.

in the property passes to *the surviving joint tenants*. Recall that a tenant in common, by contrast, has the power to leave his interest in the real estate to his heirs. Because a joint tenant cannot leave the property to his heirs, courts do not favor this form of ownership. The law presumes that a concurrent estate is a tenancy in common; a court will interpret an estate as a joint tenancy only if the parties creating it clearly intended that result.

Joint tenancy has one other curious feature. Although joint tenants may not convey their interest by will, they may do so during their lifetime. If Frank and George own vacation property as joint tenants, Frank has the power to sell his interest to Harry. But as soon as he does so, the joint tenancy is **severed**: that is, broken. Harry and George are now tenants in common, and the right of survivorship is destroyed.

But when does a severance officially take place? The answer was of critical importance in the following case.

Jackson v. Estate of Green

771 N.W.2d 675
Michigan Supreme Court, 2009

Facts: Green and Jackson owned land as joint tenants. Green filed a petition asking a court to partition the parcels, but he died while the partition was still pending.

The lower courts found that because the partition was not complete at the time of Green's death, the land reverted to Jackson.

Green's estate appealed.

Issue: ***Does filing for the partition of a joint tenancy terminate survivorship rights?***

Excerpts from Justice Corrigan's Decision: We agree with the Court of Appeals that defendant's interest in the parcel of land automatically reverted to plaintiff when defendant died. Thus, defendant's estate has no interest in the property, and even if defendant's partition action survived his death under Michigan's survival statute, nothing remains to partition.

The principal characteristic of the joint tenancy is the right of survivorship. Upon the death of one joint tenant, the surviving tenant or tenants take the whole estate. An ordinary joint tenancy may be severed, and the right of survivorship thereby destroyed, by an act of the parties, conveyance by either party, or levy and sale on an execution against one of the parties.

A party can sever a joint tenancy by compelling a partition. Until an order of partition has been entered, however, a partition has not been compelled and, thus, the joint tenancy has not been severed. It is not the filing of the partition action which terminates the joint tenancy, but only the judgment in such action which has that effect.

This rule is based on two related concepts: First, the theory of survivorship—that at the moment of death, ownership vests exclusively in the surviving joint tenant or tenants—and, second, the doctrine that severance of the joint tenancy does not occur until the partition suit reaches final judgment.

Accordingly, we would hold that the filing of the partition action did not sever the joint tenancy because an order effectuating a partition had not entered at the time of defendant's death. Therefore, regardless whether defendant's partition action survived his death under the survival statute, his interest in the parcel of land did not.

Affirmed.

Exhibit 42.1 illustrates tenancy in common and joint tenancy.

EXAMStrategy

Question: Thomas, aged 80, has spent a lifetime accumulating unspoiled land in Oregon. He owns 16,000 acres, which he plans to leave to his five children. He is not so crazy about his grandchildren. Thomas cringes at the problems the grandchildren would

EXHIBIT 42.1

Tenancy in Common and Joint Tenancy, Compared

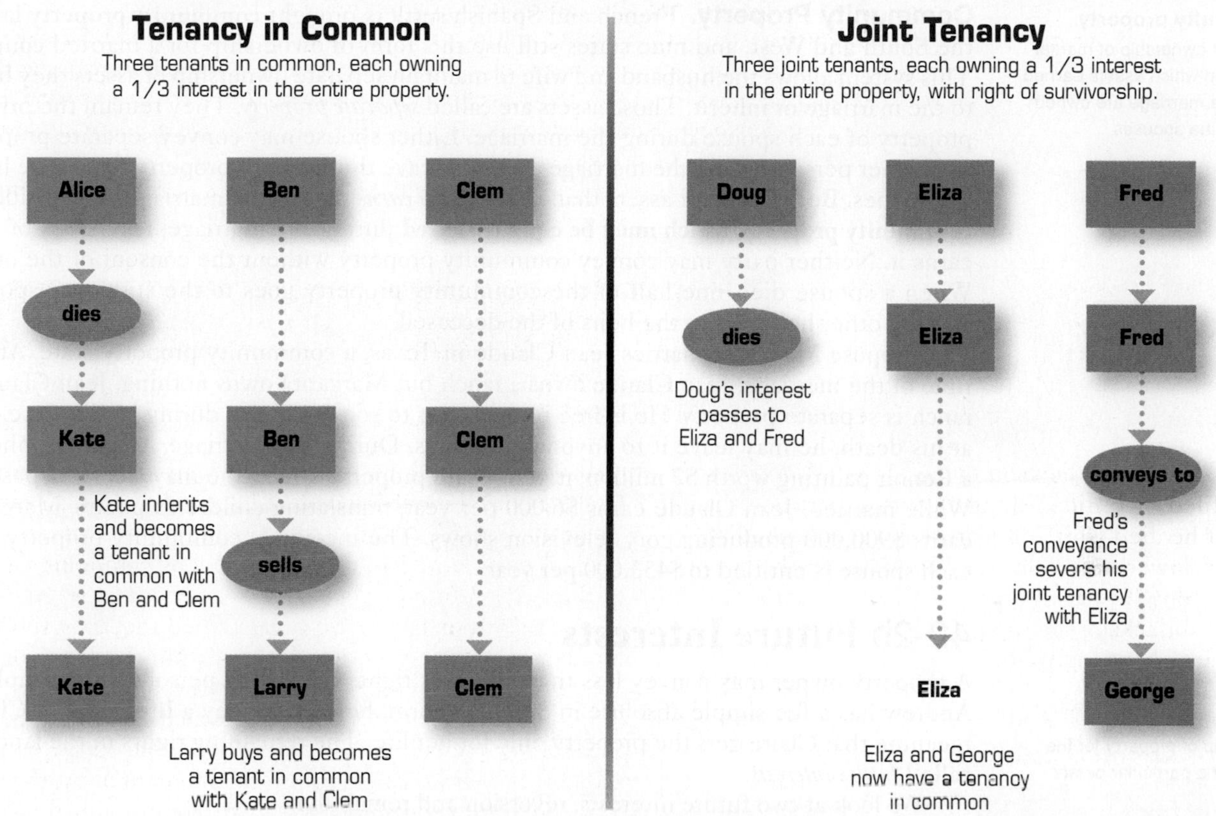

cause if some of them inherited an interest in the land and became part-owners along with Thomas's own children. Should Thomas leave his land to his children as tenants in common or joint tenants?

Strategy: When a co-tenant dies, her interest in property passes to her heirs. When a joint tenant dies, his interest in the property passes to the surviving joint tenants.

Result: Thomas is better off leaving the land to his children as joint tenants. That way, when one of his children dies, that child's interest in the land will go to Thomas's surviving children, not to his grandchildren. (There are other approaches Thomas could take, such as creation of a trust, and they are discussed in Chapter 44 on planning for the future.)

Tenancy by the Entirety. This form of ownership exists in about half of the states. The husband and wife each own the entire property, and they both have a right of survivorship. So when the husband dies, his one-half interest in the property automatically passes to his wife. Neither party has a right to convey his or her interest. If the parties wish to sell their

Tenancy by the entirety
A system of ownership of marital property in which each spouse owns the entire estate

interests, they must do so together. An advantage of this is that no creditor may seize the property based on a debt incurred by only one spouse. If a husband goes bankrupt, creditors may not take his house if he and his wife own it as tenants by the entirety. Divorce terminates a tenancy by the entirety and leaves the two parties as tenants in common.

Community property
System of ownership of marital property in which assets earned during the marriage are owned jointly by the spouses

Community Property. French and Spanish settlers brought **community property** law to the South and West, and nine states still use this form of ownership for a married couple.[3] This system allows the husband and wife to maintain separate ownership of assets they bring to the marriage or inherit. Those assets are called *separate property*. They remain the private property of each spouse during the marriage. Either spouse may convey separate property to another person during the marriage and may leave the separate property to anyone he or she wishes. But income or assets that either party *earns* during the marriage are considered **community property, which must be equally shared** during the marriage, regardless of who earns it. Neither party may convey community property without the consent of the other. When a spouse dies, one-half of the community property goes to the surviving spouse, and the other half goes to the heirs of the deceased.

Suppose Margarita marries Jean Claude in Texas, a community property state. At the time of the marriage, Jean Claude owns a ranch but Margarita owns nothing. Jean Claude's ranch is separate property. He is free to convey it to someone else during his lifetime, and at his death, he may leave it to anyone he wishes. During the marriage, Margarita inherits a Renoir painting worth $3 million; it is separate property, which she may freely dispose of. While married, Jean Claude earns $6,000 per year, translating children's poetry. Margarita earns $900,000 producing gory television shows. The income is community property, and each spouse is entitled to $453,000 per year.

42-2b Future Interests

Life estate
Ownership of property for the lifetime of a particular person

A property owner may convey less than all of his rights to another person. For example, if Andrew has a fee simple absolute in Serenity Farm, he may convey a **life estate** to Claire, meaning that Claire gets the property only for her life. The remaining rights in the land are called *future interests*.

We look at two future interests: reversion and remainder.

Reversion

Reversion
The right of an owner (or her heirs) to property upon the death of a life tenant

If Andrew conveys Serenity Farm "to Claire for her life," Claire has a life estate in the property. Andrew has a **reversion**, meaning that upon Claire's death, the property automatically returns to him or to his heirs. The significance of a future interest is this: Even though Claire may live for 50 more years, Andrew may convey his reversion at any time. The right to own Serenity Farm upon Claire's death is a valuable right, and Andrew may sell the reversion. Once a sale is made, however, the buyer has to bide his time until Claire's death, but when she dies, the land is his.

Remainder

Remainder
The right of a third person to property upon the death of a life tenant

Suppose Andrew conveys Tranquility Farm "to Douglas for life, and then to Ernie." Douglas has a life estate and Ernie has a **remainder**. A remainder has exactly the same value as a reversion. The difference is that when the life tenant dies, the property goes to a named third person, not to the original owner.

[3]Arizona, California, Idaho, Louisiana, Nevada, New Mexico, Texas, and Washington all have a community property law, while Wisconsin's system is a variation of the same principle.

Example: Andrew owns a fee simple absolute in property and ...	What was conveyed?	What future interest remains?
Conveys the property "to Betty."	Sale of the entire estate	None
Conveys the property "to Claire for her life."	Life estate	Andrew has a reversion. The property reverts to him or his heirs upon Claire's death.
Conveys the property "to Douglas for his life and then to Ernie."	Life estate	Ernie has a remainder and Andrew has nothing.

42-2c Nonpossessory Interests

All of the estates and interests that we have examined thus far focused on one thing: possession of the land. Now we look at interests that *never* involve possession. These interests may be very valuable, even though the holder never lives on the land.

Easements

The Alabama Power Co. drove a flatbed truck over land owned by Thomas Burgess, damaging the property. The power company did this to reach its power lines and wooden transmission poles. Burgess had never given Alabama Power permission to enter his land, and he sued for the damage that the heavy trucks caused. He recovered—nothing. Alabama Power had an *easement* to use Burgess's land.

An **easement** gives one person the right to enter land belonging to another and make a limited use of it, without taking anything away. Burgess had bought his land from a man named Denton, who years earlier had sold an easement to Alabama Power. The easement gave the power company the right to construct several transmission poles on one section of Denton's land and to use reasonable means to reach the poles. Alabama Power owned that easement forever, and when Burgess bought the land, he took it subject to the easement. Alabama Power drove its trucks across a section of land where the power company had never gone before, and the easement did not explicitly give the company this right. But the court found that the company had no other way to reach its poles, and therefore, the easement allowed this use. Burgess is stuck with his uninvited guest as long as he owns the land.[4]

Easement
The right to cross or use someone else's land for a particular purpose

Creation of Easements

Easements can be created by property owners or implied by law.

Grant or Reservation. Property owners normally create easements in one of two ways. A **grant** occurs when a landowner expressly intends to convey an easement to someone else. This is how Alabama Power acquired its easement. The company offered to buy the right to use the land, and Denton agreed to sell. The parties signed an agreement and *recorded* the easement, meaning they placed it on file in the land registry, so that interested parties were on notice. When Burgess bought the land from Denton, he knew (or should have known) about the easement.

Easement by grant
Occurs when one party expressly transfers an easement to another party

A **reservation** occurs when an owner sells land but keeps some right to enter the property. A farmer might sell 40 acres to a developer but reserve an easement giving him the right to drive his equipment across a specified strip of the land.

Easement by reservation
Occurs when a party reserves the right to retain an easement in a transferred property

[4]Burgess v. Alabama Power Co., 658 So. 2d 435 (Ala. 1995).

Easement by implication
Results from surrounding circumstances that indicate that the parties must have intended an easement

Implication or Necessity. An **easement by implication** arises when an owner subdivides land in a way that *clearly implies* the creation of an easement in favor of the new parcels. Suppose Jason owns lakefront property with a boat ramp. He subdivides his land and sells several parcels that do not reach the lake, promising all purchasers use of the boat ramp. This subdivision clearly implies the right to cross Jason's land to use the boat ramp since there is no other access. The new owners have an easement by implication.

An **easement by necessity** arises when the dominant tenement *absolutely must* make use of other property. Yolanda leases a ninth-floor apartment to Darrin. Darrin has an easement by necessity to use the stairs and elevators since he has no other method of reaching his apartment, short of skydiving.

Profit

Profit
The right to enter land belonging to another and take something from it

A **profit** gives one person the right to enter land belonging to another and take something away. You own 100 acres of vacation property, and suddenly a mining company informs you that the land contains valuable nickel deposits. You may choose to sell a profit to the mining company, allowing it to enter your land and take away the nickel. You receive cash up front, and the company earns money from the sale of the mineral. The rules about creating and transferring easements apply to profits as well.

License

License
The right to temporarily enter land belonging to another

A **license** gives the holder temporary permission to enter another's property. Unlike an easement or profit, a license is a *temporary* right. When you attend a basketball game by buying a ticket, the basketball team that sells you the ticket is the licensor and you are the licensee. You are entitled to enter the licensor's premises, namely the basketball arena, and to remain during the game, though the club can revoke the license if you behave unacceptably.

Mortgage

Mortgage
A security interest in real property

Mortgagor
An owner who gives a security interest in property in order to obtain a loan

Mortgagee
The party acquiring a security interest in property

Lien
An encumbrance on a property to secure a debt

Generally, in order to buy a house, a prospective owner must borrow money. The bank or other lender will require security before it hands over its money, and the most common form of security for a real estate loan is a mortgage. A **mortgage** is a security interest in real property. The homeowner who borrows money is the **mortgagor** because she is *giving* the mortgage to the lender. The lender, in turn, is the **mortgagee**, the party acquiring a security interest. The mortgagee in most cases obtains a **lien** on the house, meaning the right to foreclose on the property if the mortgagor fails to pay back the money borrowed. A mortgagee forecloses by taking legal possession of the property, auctioning it to the highest bidder, and using the proceeds to pay off the loan.

42-3 ADVERSE POSSESSION

You may recall the entrepreneurs who hoped to acquire Hot Dog Island by simply setting up shop on it. They were relying on the doctrine of adverse possession. This rule allows someone to take title to land if he meets certain tests.

In most states, to gain ownership of land by adverse possession, the user must prove:

- Entry and exclusive possession;
- Open and notorious possession;
- A claim adverse, or hostile, to the owner; and
- Continuous possession for a statutory period.

42-3a Entry and Exclusive Possession

The user must take physical possession of the land and must be the only one to do so. If the owner is still occupying the land, or if other members of the public share its use, there can be no adverse possession.

42-3b Open and Notorious Possession

The user's presence must be visible and generally known in the area, so that the owner is on notice that his title is contested. This ensures that the owner can protect his property by ejecting the user. Someone making secret use of the land gives the owner no opportunity to do this, and hence acquires no rights in the land.

42-3c A Claim Adverse or Hostile to the Owner

The user must clearly assert that the land is his. He does not need to register a deed or take other legal steps, but he must act as though he is the sole owner. If the user occupies the land with the owner's permission, there is no adverse claim and the user acquires no rights in the property. To succeed, the user must protect his possession of the land against all others the way any normal landowner would. This may mean erecting a home if the area is residential, or fencing property that is used to graze cattle, or posting "No Trespassing" signs in a wilderness area.

Must the user *believe* he has a title, or only act as though he does? The states are divided on this question. Many states focus only on the adverse *acts* of the user: It is sufficient if his conduct indicates he is the sole owner, regardless of what he thinks. This is the modern trend. But other states require a mistaken *belief* that the user has title to the land. For example, some states require that the user demonstrate "color of title," meaning that he has some document that *he believed* gave him good title to the land, although in reality it never did.

42-3d Continuous Possession for the Statutory Period

State statutes on adverse possession prescribe a period of years for continuous use of the land. Originally, most states required about 20 years to gain adverse possession, but the trend has been to shorten this period. Many states now demand ten years, and a few require only five years' use.

Regardless of the length of time required, the use must be continuous. In a residential area, the user would have to occupy the land year round for the prescribed period. In a wilderness area generally used only in the summer, a user could gain ownership by seasonal use.

A user may be able to meet the statutory period by **tacking**, which permits her to add on to her years of occupancy any years certain predecessors were in possession. The predecessors must have been in *privity* with the current user, meaning there was some legal relationship. Suppose that for 12 years, Martha adversely possesses land owned by Jake. Martha then moves, selling her interest in the land to Nancy, who occupies the land for nine years. The total of 21 years is sufficient for adverse possession in any state, and Nancy now owns the land.

Sailing back to Hot Dog Island, how did Murdoch and Termarco fare? They certainly entered on the land and established themselves as the exclusive occupants. Their use has been open and notorious, allowing anyone who claimed ownership to take steps to eject them from the property. Their actions have been adverse to anyone else's claim. If the two have grilled those dogs for the full statutory period, they should take title to the island.[5]

The poet Robert Frost observed, "Good fences make good neighbors."[6] In the following case, the opposite was true: A fence unleashed a neighbor's fury, and a claim of adverse possession.

---

5 Unfortunately, there are no press accounts to inform us of the island's current status.

6 See Frost's poem entitled "Mending Wall" (1914).

Medford v. Cruz

2016 WL 4439992
Court of Special Appeals of Maryland, 2016

Facts: Lots A and B were adjacent properties in a residential community near the Chesapeake Bay. Their only access to the beach was through a vacant tract of land—the Disputed Area—which was not part of either lot. Because the Disputed Area was a coastal buffer zone, state law prohibited its development.

Beginning in 1983, Marlene Andrus, the owner of Lot A, regularly maintained the Disputed Area. She mowed it, removed debris, and asked trespassers to leave. When she sold her house to Dean Carter, he continued to care for the Disputed Area and treat it as his own.

In 1999, Carter built a permitted pier on the waterfront beyond the Disputed Area with Rob Williams, the owner of the undeveloped Lot B. The friendly neighbors agreed that their properties would co-own and share the pier.

In 2002, Brigitte Cruz purchased Lot B from Williams with the understanding that she would share ownership of the pier. Soon after, Carter put a fence around his property (Lot A) and the Disputed Area. The fence obstructed Cruz's access to the pier, but Carter refused to remove it. Instead, he orally agreed to allow Cruz to reach the pier through a gate that opened to the Disputed Area.

After Carter died, Vicky Medford purchased his home on Lot A. By that time, Cruz had built a house on Lot B and moved in. When Cruz attempted to enter through the gate to the Disputed Area, Medford kicked her out and accused her of trespassing. Medford then placed "No Trespassing" signs along the fence, but Cruz climbed it anyway.

The neighbors sued each other to determine if Medford owned the Disputed Area by adverse possession. The trial court held that she did not, and Medford appealed.

Issue: ***Did Medford acquire title to the Disputed Area by adverse possession?***

Excerpts from Judge Kehoe's Decision: To establish title by adverse possession, the claimant must show possession of the claimed property for the statutory period of 20 years. Such possession must be (1) actual, open, notorious, exclusive, (2) continuous or uninterrupted, and (3) hostile, under claim of title or ownership.

Possession must be actual, open and notorious, and exclusive. The degree of occupancy required is dependent on the character of the land involved. The Disputed Area lies within the buffer for the Chesapeake Bay. State regulations significantly restrict a property owner's ability to develop, and even to engage in such routine maintenance

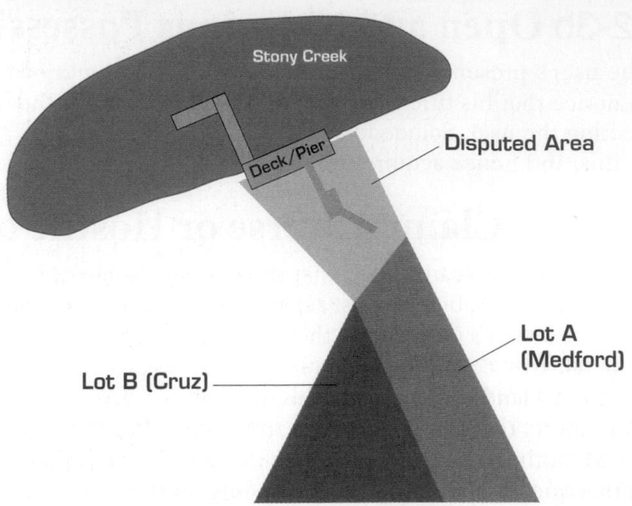

activities as clearing trees and shrubs within the area is limited. In light of this, engaging in conduct such as mowing, removing debris, and cutting down dead foliage is sufficient evidence of occupancy of the Disputed Area. These activities constitute the type of "ordinary management" that one would expect of an actual owner considering the status of the area.

The second element of adverse possession is continuity; in the present case the key question is whether each successive lot owner's possession of the Disputed Area tacked onto the prior owner's possession. Two possessions will be tacked if it appears that the adverse possessor actually turned over possession of that part as well as of that portion of the land expressly included in his deed.

The record supports the conclusion that Andrus and Carter intended to convey the Disputed Area when they transferred the deed to the property. Andrus believed the Disputed Area was part of her property; this stated belief, coupled with the fact that Carter continued to maintain the area, indicates that Carter believed he obtained the Disputed Area as part of his deed. The same is true of Medford. Medford specifically stated that, when she was considering buying the house, she relied on the fact that she was obtaining the Disputed Area—even though the pier was jointly owned. These facts are sufficient to create a privity of estate for tacking—thus the possession was continuous for the twenty-year period.

The final necessary element is hostility of possession. Once a claimant has made a satisfactory showing as to open, continuous use for the statutory period, the burden then shifts to the landowner to show that the use was permissive. Cruz failed to meet this burden. All that Cruz's evidence shows is that Carter was providing Cruz with reasonable access to the pier that they jointly owned.

In light of the evidence, we conclude that Medford has established that she has title to the Disputed Area through adverse possession. Medford's ownership of the Disputed Area is subject to Cruz's right to have reasonable access to the parties' jointly-owned pier.

In the end, both neighbors won: Medford obtained ownership of the Disputed Area and Cruz earned an easement to the pier—without having to jump the fence. Only time would tell whether they would push each other off the pier.

42-4 LAND USE REGULATION

42-4a Nuisance Law

A **nuisance** is an unprivileged interference with a person's use and enjoyment of her property. Offensive noise, odors, or smoke often give rise to nuisance claims. Courts typically balance the utility of the act that is causing the problem against the harm done to neighboring property owners. If a suburban homeowner begins to raise pigs in her backyard, the neighbors may find the bouquet offensive; a court will probably issue an **abatement**; that is, an order requiring the homeowner to eliminate the nuisance.

Community members can use the old doctrine of nuisance for more serious problems than pigs. Neighbors were successful in using the law of nuisance to sue a landlord in Berkeley, California, who allowed an apartment building to operate as a drug house. Because of this building, their neighborhood swarmed with drug dealers and prostitutes. Shootings and police chases became part of their everyday life. The landlord was ordered to pay substantial damages.[7]

42-4b Zoning

Zoning statutes are state laws that permit local communities to regulate building and land use. The local communities, whether cities, towns, or counties, then pass zoning ordinances that control many aspects of land development. For example, a town's zoning ordinance may divide the community into an industrial zone where factories may be built, a commercial zone in which stores of a certain size are allowed, and several residential zones in which only houses may be constructed. Within the residential zones, there may be further divisions, for example, permitting two-family houses in certain areas and requiring larger lots in others.

An owner prohibited by an ordinance from erecting a certain kind of building, or adding on to his present building, may seek a **variance** from the zoning board, meaning an exception granted for special reasons unique to the property. Whether a board will grant a variance generally depends upon the type of the proposed building, the nature of the community, the reason the owner claims he is harmed by the ordinance, and the reaction of neighbors.

Variance
A variation from the applicable zoning law

Ethics

Many people abhor "adult" businesses, such as strip clubs and pornography shops. Urban experts agree that the presence of these businesses in a neighborhood often causes crime to increase and property values to drop. Nonetheless, many people patronize such businesses, which can earn a good profit. Should a city have the right to restrict adult businesses? New York City

7Lew v. Superior Court, 20 Cal. App. 4th 866 (Cal. Ct. App. 1993).

officials determined that the number of sex shops had grown steadily for two decades and that their presence harmed various neighborhoods. With the support of community groups, the city passed a zoning ordinance that prohibited adult businesses from all residential neighborhoods, from some commercial districts, *and* from being within 500 feet of schools, houses of worship, day-care centers, or other sex shops (to avoid clustering). Owners and patrons of these shops protested, claiming that the city was unfairly denying the public access to a form of entertainment that it obviously desired. Is the New York City zoning ordinance reasonable?

42-4c Eminent Domain

Eminent domain
The government's right to take private property for public use upon just compensation to the owner

Eminent domain is the power of the government to take private property for public use. A government may need land to construct a highway, airport, university, or public housing. All levels of government—federal, state, and local—have this power. But the Fifth Amendment of the U.S. Constitution states: "... nor shall private property be taken for public use, without just compensation." The Supreme Court has held that this clause, the Takings Clause, applies not only to the federal government but also to state and local governments. So, although all levels of government have the power to take property, they must pay the owner a fair price.

Condemnation
Occurs when the government seizes private property and compensates the owner

A "fair price" generally means the reasonable market value of the land. Generally, if the property owner refuses the government's offer, the government will file suit seeking **condemnation** of the land; that is, a court order specifying what compensation is just and awarding title to the government.

Recall our discussion of *Kelo v. City of New London* in Chapter 5 on constitutional law. That case, which was the most controversial eminent domain case of our time, upheld the right of a local government to condemn private land for a private developer's use. The Supreme Court held that encouraging economic growth and private redevelopment was a permissible "public use."

42-5 LANDLORD–TENANT LAW

The relationship between landlords and tenants involves three types of law: property, contract, and tort law.

Freehold estate
The right to possess land for an undefined length of time

Leasehold interest
One party has the right to occupy the property for a given length of time

Reversionary interest
The landlord's right to occupy the property at the end of the lease

Property Law. What we think of as "owning" land is in fact a **freehold estate**, that is, the right to possess real property and use it in any lawful manner for an indefinite time. **When an owner of a freehold estate allows another person temporary, exclusive possession of the property, the parties have created a *landlord–tenant relationship*.** The freehold owner is the landlord, and the person allowed to possess the property is the tenant. The landlord has conveyed a **leasehold interest** to the tenant, meaning the right to temporary possession. The landlord is also keeping a **reversionary interest** in the property, meaning the right to possess the property when the lease ends. Courts sometimes use the word tenancy to describe the tenant's right to possession.

Lease
An agreement in which an owner gives a tenant the right to use property

Contract Law. The basic agreement between the landlord and tenant is a contract, called a **lease.**

The Statute of Frauds generally requires that a long-term lease be in writing. A long-term lease is one year or more; anything shorter is usually enforceable without a writing. But even when an oral lease is permitted, it is wiser for the parties to put their agreement in writing because a written lease avoids many misunderstandings. At a minimum, a lease must state the names of the parties, the premises being leased, the duration of the agreement, and the rent. But a well-drafted lease generally includes many provisions, called *covenants* and *conditions*.

Covenant
A promise or undertaking contained in a lease whose breach does not result in eviction

A **covenant** is simply a promise by either the landlord or the tenant to do something or refrain from doing something. Most leases include covenants concerning the tenant's security deposit, use of the premises, and maintenance of the property. Generally, tenants may be fined, but not evicted, for violating lease covenants. A **condition** is similar to a covenant, but it allows for a landlord to evict a tenant if there is a violation. The rise of home-sharing websites like Airbnb and VRBO highlights the important difference between a covenant and a condition. Many leases contain prohibitions against subletting, or short-term leasing. However, this practice has become both lucrative and popular, as consumers seek cheaper alternatives to hotels. The subletting tenant who is bound by a covenant is home free; the one whose lease contains a condition may find himself out on the street.

Condition
A promise or undertaking contained in a lease whose breach may result in eviction

Tort Law. Negligence law may determine the liability of the **landlord** and **tenant** when a person is injured or property is damaged.

Landlord
The owner of a freehold estate who allows another person temporarily to live on his property

Tenant
A person given temporary possession of the landlord's property

42-5a Types of Tenancy

There are four types of tenancy: a tenancy for years, a periodic tenancy, a tenancy at will, and a tenancy at sufferance. The most important feature distinguishing one from the other is how each tenancy terminates. In some cases, a tenancy terminates automatically, while in others, one party must take certain steps to end the agreement.

Tenancy for Years

Any lease for a stated, fixed period is a **tenancy for years**. If a landlord rents a summer apartment for the months of June, July, and August of next year, that is a tenancy for years. A company that rents retail space in a mall beginning January 1, 2018, and ending December 31, 2021, also has a tenancy for years. A tenancy for years terminates automatically when the agreed period ends.

Tenancy for years
A lease for a stated, fixed period

Periodic Tenancy

A **periodic tenancy** is created for a fixed period and then automatically continues for additional periods until either party notifies the other of termination. This is probably the most common variety of tenancy, and the parties may create one in either of two ways. Suppose a landlord agrees to rent you an apartment "from month to month, rent payable on the first." That is a periodic tenancy. The tenancy automatically renews itself every month unless either party gives adequate notice to the other that she wishes to terminate. A periodic tenancy could also be for one-year periods—in which case it automatically renews for an additional year if neither party terminates—or for any other period.

Periodic tenancy
A lease for a fixed period, automatically renewable unless terminated

The parties also create a periodic tenancy if, when a *tenancy for years* expires, the tenant continues to pay rent and the landlord accepts it. Ariadne agrees to rent property called Naxos for three years, with rent payable once per month. When the three years are up, the tenancy for years expires automatically. Ariadne continues to pay the monthly rent, however, and the landlord accepts her checks. The parties have created a periodic tenancy.

What is the period? If the tenant is renting *commercial property*, the new periodic tenancy is for the same period as the old tenancy for years, up to a maximum of one year. In other words, if Naxos is an office building, Ariadne's new periodic tenancy is for one year (since her original lease was for more than a year). Once the landlord accepts a single monthly rental check, both he and Ariadne are bound for the full year. In many states, if the property is *residential*, the new periodic tenancy is month to month. If Naxos is a vacation house, either party can end the lease with 30 days' notice. A landlord's notice terminating a tenancy is often called a **notice to quit**.

Notice to quit
A landlord's notice terminating a tenancy

Tenancy at Will

A **tenancy at will** has no fixed duration and may be terminated by either party at any time. Tenancies at will are unusual tenancies. Typically, the agreement is vague, with no specified rental period and with payment, perhaps, to be made in kind. The parties might agree, for example, that a tenant farmer could use a portion of his crop as rent. Since either party can end the agreement at any time, it provides no security for either landlord or tenant.

Tenancy at will
A tenancy with no fixed duration, which may be terminated by either party at any time

Tenancy at Sufferance

Tenancy at sufferance
A tenancy that exists without the permission of the landlord, after the expiration of a true tenancy

A **tenancy at sufferance** occurs when a tenant remains on the premises, against the wishes of the landlord, after the expiration of a true tenancy. Thus, a tenancy at sufferance is not a true tenancy because the tenant is staying without the landlord's agreement. The landlord has the option of seeking to evict the tenant or of forcing the tenant to pay a *use and occupancy fee* for as long as she stays. These distinctions are technical but important.

In the following case, all parties acknowledged that the tenant refused to pay rent. But it was the landlord's failure to understand different types of tenancy that proved more important and led to a surprising result.

Elwell v. Minor

2006 WL 1920562; 2006 Conn. Super. LEXIS 1933
Connecticut Superior Court, 2006

Facts: Winfield Elwell orally agreed to rent an apartment in Vernon, Connecticut, to Lucille Minor on a month-to-month basis. The rent was $575. Four years later, Elwell increased the rent to $625, and the next year to $650, taking effect that September. Minor tendered $625 and included a letter explaining that she did not want to pay the increased rent for September or October but that she would pay the increase in later months. Elwell rejected the payment. Minor then tendered the check a second time, and Elwell again returned it.

Elwell told Minor to pay $650 or vacate. She did neither, so Elwell began eviction proceedings (called "summary process") by serving on Minor a Notice to Quit for non-payment of rent. After additional negotiations failed, Elwell served a second Notice to Quit. At trial, Minor argued that non-payment of *rent* was an improper grounds for evicting a tenant at sufferance. She asked the court to dismiss the case.

Issue: ***May a landlord evict a tenant at sufferance for non-payment of rent?***

Excerpts from Judge White's Decision: During the month of September, Minor and Elwell corresponded extensively. In her letters, Minor refused to pay the increased rental amount which Elwell demanded. She gave reasons why she did not want to pay $650 instead of $625 and even attempted to negotiate postponing the rent increase until later months. Elwell rejected Minor's efforts by returning the checks that she tendered and continuing to insist on a $650 rental amount. These communications reveal a definite dispute between the parties which precludes the formation of a new one-month lease.

Because Minor remained in possession of the premises without a new monthly contract, she should be treated as a holdover occupying the apartment without the legal right to do so [in other words, as a tenant at sufferance]. In this case, the defendant was not a tenant at will, because such a tenancy exists only when the occupation of the property is with the landlord's consent, continuing during the tenancy. Elwell also served Minor with the first notice to quit for non-payment of rent expressing his intention to terminate the lease. Once the lease terminated, Minor became a tenant at sufferance.

Non-payment of rent is not a proper ground for the eviction of a tenant at sufferance because a tenant at sufferance is not required to pay rent, but only use and occupancy. When two parties enter into a month-to-month lease, they do not ordinarily designate a definite date when the lease, by its own terms, will expire. Instead the parties establish a tenancy at will which the tenant may terminate by moving out and the landlord may terminate by serving a notice to quit. Such a lease could never expire by lapse of time because there is no term defining the temporal existence of the lease. So, the law treats a month-to-month lease as a series of individual leases which expire at the end of the month and are ordinarily renewed each month by implication. Once the agreement expires by operation of law, the tenant's obligation to pay rent transforms into an obligation to pay a reasonable sum for the use and occupancy of the premises. Without an obligation to pay rent there can be no summary process for non-payment of rent.

The proper statutory basis for pursuing summary process against a tenant who failed to pay a reasonable sum for use and occupancy would be that the tenant originally had the right or privilege to occupy the premises but such right or privilege has terminated. Elwell's second notice to quit cites improper grounds for the eviction of a tenant at sufferance. The notice to quit is defective and deprives this court of subject matter jurisdiction in this summary process action. This action is dismissed.

42-5b Landlord's Duties

Duty to Deliver Possession

The landlord's first important duty is to deliver possession of the premises at the beginning of the tenancy; that is, to make the rented space available to the tenant. In most cases, this presents no problems and the new tenant moves in. But what happens if the previous tenant has refused to leave when the new tenancy begins?

The "**English rule**" obligates the landlord to remove the previous tenant in time for the new tenant to take possession. The majority of American states enforce this rule. If the old tenant is still in possession when the new tenant arrives, the landlord has breached the lease. The new tenant has two alternative remedies. She may terminate the lease and sue the landlord for costs she incurs obtaining other accommodations. Or she may affirm the lease, refuse to pay rent for the period in which she cannot take possession, sue for the cost of other accommodations, and then take possession when the old tenant is finally evicted.

The "**American rule**" is more favorable to the landlord. (Although called the American rule, this is in fact the minority rule in this country—anything to keep you off balance.) This rule holds that the landlord has no duty to deliver actual possession of the premises. If the previous tenant remains in possession, the landlord has not breached the lease. Under this rule, the new tenant generally has the power to act as a landlord toward the old tenant. The new tenant may evict the old tenant and recover damages caused by her delay in leaving. Alternatively, the new tenant may treat the holdover as a tenant at will for a new rental period and may charge the normal rent for that period.

Quiet Enjoyment

All tenants are entitled to quiet enjoyment of the premises, meaning the right to use the property without the interference of the landlord. Most leases expressly state this covenant of quiet enjoyment. And if a lease includes no such covenant, the law implies the right of quiet enjoyment anyway, so all tenants are protected. If a landlord interferes with the tenant's quiet enjoyment, he has breached the lease, entitling the tenant to damages.

The most common interference with quiet enjoyment is an **eviction**, meaning some act that forces the tenant to abandon the premises. Of course, some evictions are legal, as when a tenant fails to pay the rent. But some evictions are illegal. There are two types of eviction: actual and constructive.

Eviction
An act that forces a tenant to abandon the property

Actual Eviction. If a landlord prevents the tenant from possessing the premises, he has actually evicted her. Suppose a landlord decides that a group of students are "troublemakers." Without going through lawful eviction procedures in court, the landlord simply waits until the students are out of the apartment and changes all the locks. By denying the students access to the premises, the landlord has actually evicted them and has breached their right of quiet enjoyment. He is liable for all expenses they suffer, such as retrieving their possessions, the cost of alternate housing, and moving expenses. In some states, he may be liable for punitive damages for failing to go through proper eviction procedures.

Even a partial eviction is an interference with quiet enjoyment. Suppose Louise rents an apartment with a storage room. If the landlord places his own goods in the storage room, he has partially evicted Louise because a tenant is entitled to the *exclusive* possession of the premises. In all states, Louise would be allowed to deduct from her rent the value of the storage space, and in many states, she would not be obligated to pay any rent for the apartment as long as the landlord continued the partial eviction.

Constructive Eviction. If a landlord substantially interferes with the tenant's use and enjoyment of the premises, he has constructively evicted her. Courts construe certain behavior as the equivalent of an eviction. In these cases, the landlord has not actually prevented the tenant from *possessing* the premises but has instead interfered so greatly with her *use and*

Frances Roberts/Alamy Stock Photo

Landlords have the duty to keep their properties in habitable conditions.

enjoyment that the law regards the landlord's actions as equivalent to an eviction. Suppose the heating system in an apartment house in Juneau, Alaska, fails during January. The landlord, an avid sled dog racer, tells the tenants he is too busy to fix the problem. If the tenants move out, the landlord has constructively evicted them and is liable for all expenses they suffer.

To claim a constructive eviction, the tenant must vacate the premises. The tenant must also prove that the interference was sufficiently serious and lasted long enough that she was forced to move out. A lack of hot water for two days is not fatal, but lack of any water for two weeks creates a constructive eviction.

Other Interference. A landlord's conduct may interfere with quiet enjoyment even when it is not so harmful as to force a constructive eviction. Suppose a landlord, living in the ground-floor unit, gives trumpet lessons in his apartment six nights a week until 1:00 a.m., producing such a cacophony that a group of students living upstairs can neither study nor sleep. If the students continue to live in the apartment because they cannot afford a better place, there has been no constructive eviction. But the landlord's conduct interferes with the tenants' quiet enjoyment, and the students are entitled to damages.

Duty to Maintain Premises

Historically, the common law placed no burden on the landlord to repair and maintain the premises. This made sense because rental property had traditionally been farmland. Buildings, such as a house or barn, were far less important than the land itself, and no one expected the landlord to fix a leaking roof. Today, the vast majority of rental property is used for housing or business purposes. Space in a building is frequently all that a tenant is renting, and the condition of the building is of paramount importance. Most states have changed the common law rule and placed various obligations on the landlord to maintain the property.

In most states, a landlord has a duty to deliver the premises in a habitable condition and a continuing duty to maintain the habitable condition. This duty overlaps with the quiet enjoyment obligation, but it is not identical. The tenant's right to quiet enjoyment focuses primarily on the tenant's *ability to use* the rented property. The landlord's duty to maintain the property focuses on whether the property *meets a particular legal standard*. The required standard may be stated in the lease, created by a state statute, or implied by law.

Lease. The lease itself generally obligates the landlord to maintain the exterior of any buildings and the common areas. If a lease does not do so, state law may imply the obligation.

Building Codes. Many state and local governments have passed building codes, which mandate minimum standards for commercial and/or residential property. The codes are likely to be stricter for residential property and may demand such things as minimum room size, sufficient hot water, secure locks, proper working kitchens and bathrooms, absence of insects and rodents, and other basics of decent housing. Generally, all rental property must comply with the building code, whether the lease mentions the code or not.

Implied Warranty of Habitability. Three college students rented a house from Les and Martha Vanlandingham. The monthly rent was $900. But the roommates failed to pay any rent for the final five months of the tenancy. After they moved out, the Vanlandinghams sued. How much did the landlords recover? Nothing. The landlords had breached the implied warranty of habitability.

The implied warranty of habitability requires that a landlord meet all standards set by the local building code, or that the premises be fit for human habitation. Most states, though not all, *imply* this warranty of habitability, meaning that the landlord must meet this standard whether the lease includes it or not. In some states, the implied warranty means that the premises must at least satisfy the local building code. Other states require property that is "fit for human habitation," which means that a landlord might comply with the building code, yet still fail the implied warranty of habitability if the rental property is unfit to live in.

The Vanlandinghams breached the implied warranty. The students had complained repeatedly about a variety of problems. The washer and dryer, which were included in the lease, frequently failed. A severe roof leak caused water damage in one of the bedrooms. Defective pipes flooded the bathroom. The refrigerator frequently malfunctioned, and the roommates repaired it several times. The basement often flooded, and when it was dry, rats and opossums lived in it. The heat sometimes failed.

The basement often flooded, and when it was dry, rats and opossums lived in it.

In warranty of habitability cases, a court normally considers the severity of the problems and their duration. If the defective conditions seriously interfere with the tenancy, the court declares the implied warranty breached and orders a **rent abatement**; that is, a reduction in the rent owed. The longer the defects continued and the greater their severity, the more the rent is abated. In the case of the students, the court abated the rent 50 percent. They had already paid more than the abated rent to the landlord, so they owed nothing for the last five months.[8]

Rent abatement
A reduction in the rent owed

Duty to Return Security Deposit. Most landlords require tenants to pay a security deposit, in case the tenant damages the premises. In many states, a landlord must either return the security deposit soon after the tenant has moved out or notify the tenant of the damage and the cost of the repairs. In addition, landlords are often obligated to credit tenants with interest earned on the deposit. Many states have statutes requiring a landlord who fails to return the deposit in a timely fashion to pay double or even triple damages to the tenant.

In a commercial lease, the tenant may have less statutory protection but more bargaining power. A financially sound company might negotiate a lease with no security deposit or perhaps offer a letter of credit for security instead of cash. The interest saved over several years could be substantial.

42-5c Tenant's Duties

Duty to Pay Rent

Rent is the compensation the tenant pays the landlord for use of the premises, and paying the rent is the tenant's foremost obligation. The lease normally specifies the amount of rent and when it must be paid. Typically, the landlord requires that rent be paid at the beginning of each rental period, whether that is monthly, annually, or otherwise.

Rent
Compensation paid by a tenant to a landlord

Both parties must be certain they understand whether the rent includes utilities such as heat and hot water. Some states mandate that the landlord pay certain utilities, such as water. Many leases include an **escalator clause**, permitting the landlord to raise the rent during the course of the lease if his expenses increase for specified reasons. For example, a tax escalator clause allows the landlord to raise the rent if his real estate taxes go up. Any escalator clause should state the percentage of the increase that the landlord may pass on to the tenant.

Escalator clause
A lease clause allowing the landlord to raise the rent for specified reasons

Landlord's Remedies for Non-payment of Rent. If the tenant fails to pay rent on time, the landlord has several remedies. She is entitled to apply the security deposit to the unpaid rent. She may also sue the tenant for non-payment of rent, demanding the unpaid sums, cost of collection, and interest. Finally, the landlord may evict a tenant who has failed to pay rent.

---

[8]Vanlandingham v. Ivanow, 246 Ill. App. 3d 348 (Ill. Ct. App. 1993).

State statutes prescribe the steps a landlord must take to evict a tenant for non-payment. Typically, the landlord must serve a termination notice on the tenant and wait for a court hearing. At the hearing, the landlord must prove that the tenant has failed to pay rent on time. If the tenant has no excuse for the non-payment, the court grants an order evicting him. The order authorizes a sheriff to remove the tenant's goods and place them in storage, at the tenant's expense. However, if the tenant was withholding rent because of unlivable conditions, the court may refuse to evict.

EXAMStrategy

Question: Leo rents an apartment from Donna for $900 per month, both parties signing a lease. After six months, Leo complains about defects, including bugs, inadequate heat, and window leaks. He asks Donna to fix the problems, but she responds that the heat is fine and that Leo caused the insects and leaks. Leo begins to send in only $700 for the monthly rent. Donna repeatedly phones Leo, asking for the remaining rent. When he refuses to pay, she waits until he leaves for the day, then has a moving company place his belongings in storage. She changes the locks, making it impossible for him to re-enter. Leo sues. What is the likely outcome?

Strategy: A landlord is entitled to begin proper eviction proceedings against a tenant who has not paid rent. However, the landlord must follow specified steps, including a termination notice and a court hearing. Review the consequences for actual eviction, described in the "Quiet Enjoyment" section.

Result: Donna has ignored the legal procedures for evicting a tenant. Instead, she engaged in *actual eviction*, which is quick, and in the short term, effective. However, by breaking the law, Donna has ensured that Leo will win his lawsuit. He is entitled to possession of the apartment, as well as damages for rent he may have been forced to pay elsewhere, injury to his possessions, and the cost of retrieving them. He may receive punitive damages as well. Bad strategy, Donna.

Duty to Mitigate. Pickwick & Perkins, Ltd., was a store in the Burlington Square Mall in Burlington, Vermont. Pickwick had a five-year lease but abandoned the space almost two years early and ceased paying rent. The landlord waited approximately eight months before renting the space to a new tenant and then sued, seeking the unpaid rent. Pickwick defended on the grounds that Burlington had failed to **mitigate damages**; that is, to keep its losses to a minimum by promptly seeking another tenant. Burlington argued that it had no legal obligation to mitigate. Burlington's position accurately reflected the common law rule, which permitted the landlord to let the property lie vacant and allow the damages to add up. But the common law evolves over time, and this time, the Vermont Supreme Court changed the rule. The judges pointed out that, historically, a lease was a conveyance of an estate, and property law had never required mitigation. However, the court asserted, a lease is now regarded as both a contract and a conveyance. Under contract law, the nonbreaching party must make a reasonable effort to minimize losses, and that same rule applies, said the court, to a landlord. Burlington lost.

Duty to Use Premises for Proper Purpose

A lease normally lists what a tenant may do in the premises and prohibits other activities. For example, a residential lease allows the tenant to use the property for normal living purposes, but not for any retail, commercial, or industrial purpose. A commercial lease might allow a tenant to operate a retail clothing store but not a restaurant. A landlord may evict a tenant who violates the lease by using the premises for prohibited purposes.

A tenant may not use the premises for any illegal activity, such as gambling or selling drugs. The law itself implies this condition in every lease, so a tenant who engages in illegal acts on the leased property is subject to eviction, regardless of whether the lease mentions such conduct.

Duty Not to Damage Premises

A tenant is liable to the landlord for any significant damage he causes to the property. The tenant is not liable for normal wear and tear. If, however, he knocks a hole in a wall or damages the plumbing, the landlord may collect the cost of repairs, either by using the security deposit or by suing, if necessary. A landlord may also seek to evict a tenant for serious damage to the property.

A tenant is permitted to make reasonable changes in the leased property so that he can use it as intended. Someone leasing an apartment is permitted to hang pictures on the wall. But a tenant leasing commercial space should make certain that the lease specifies the alterations he can make and whether he is obligated to return the premises to their original condition at the end of the lease.

Duty Not to Disturb Other Tenants

Most leases, commercial and residential, include a covenant that the tenant will not disturb other tenants in the building. A landlord may evict a tenant who unreasonably disturbs others. The test is *reasonableness*. A landlord does not have the right to evict a residential tenant for giving one loud party but may evict a tenant who repeatedly plays loud music late at night and disturbs the quiet enjoyment of other tenants.

42-5d Liability of Landlords and Tenants

You invite a friend to dinner in your rented home, but after the meal, she slips and falls, seriously injuring her back. Are you liable? Is the landlord?

Tenant's Liability

A tenant is generally liable for injuries occurring within the premises she is leasing, whether that is an apartment, a store, or otherwise. If a tenant permits grease to accumulate on a kitchen floor and a guest slips and falls, the tenant is liable. If a merchant negligently installs display shelving that tips onto a customer, the merchant pays for the harm. Generally, a tenant is not liable for injuries occurring in common areas over which she has no control, such as exterior walkways. If a tenant's dinner guest falls because the building's common stairway has loose steps, the landlord is probably liable.

Landlord's Liability

Common Law Rules. Historically, the common law held a landlord responsible for injuries on the premises only in a limited number of circumstances, which we will describe. In reading these common law rules, be aware that many states have changed them, dramatically increasing the landlord's liability.

Latent Defects. If the landlord knows of a dangerous condition on the property and realizes the tenant will not notice it, the landlord is liable for any injuries. For example, if a landlord knows that a porch railing is weak and fails to inform the tenant, the landlord is responsible if the tenant plunges off the porch. But notice that, under the common law, if the landlord notifies the tenant of the latent defect, he is no longer liable.

Common Areas. The landlord is usually responsible for maintaining the common areas, and along with this obligation may go liability for torts. As we saw earlier, if your guest falls downstairs in a common hallway because the stairs were defective, the landlord is probably liable.

Negligent Repairs. Even in areas where the landlord has no duty to make repairs, if he volunteers to do so and does the work badly, he is responsible for resulting harm.

Public Use. If the premises are to be used for a public purpose, such as a store or office, the landlord is generally obligated to repair any dangerous defects, although the tenant is probably liable as well. The purpose of this stricter rule is to ensure that the general public can safely visit commercial establishments. If a landlord realizes that the plate glass in a store's door is loose, he must promptly repair it or suffer liability for any injuries.

Modern Trend. Increasingly, state legislatures and courts are discarding the common law classifications previously described and holding landlords liable under the normal rules of negligence law. **In many states, a landlord must use reasonable care to maintain safe premises and is liable for foreseeable harm.** For example, the common law rule merely required a landlord to notify a tenant of a latent defect, such as a defective porch railing. Most states now have building codes that require a landlord to maintain structural elements such as railings in safe condition. States further imply a warranty of habitability, which mandates reasonably safe living conditions. So, in many states, a landlord is no longer saved from negligence suits merely by giving notice of defects—he has to fix them.

In the following case, the court held that a landlord was required to take reasonable steps to protect a tenant.

Lindsay P. v. Towne Properties Asset Management Co., Ltd.

2013-Ohio-4124
Ohio Court of Appeals, 2013

Facts: Lindsay[9] and her young daughter lived above Rhonda Schmidt in an apartment complex operated by Towne Properties (TP). Schmidt's boyfriend, Courtney Haynes, often stayed in Schmidt's apartment but was not on her lease. The couple blared rap music and fought loudly, often waking Lindsay's child.

Lindsay frequently complained to TP about the noise coming from Schmidt's apartment. In retaliation, Haynes banged on Lindsay's door with a fire extinguisher and confronted her menacingly. When Lindsay reported this intimidating behavior, TP representatives suggested she call the police. One TP agent even offered to sit with a terrified Lindsay so she would not be alone in her apartment.

Late one night, Haynes sent Lindsay a series of Facebook messages. He anonymously wrote, "leave all your worries and concerns and troubles behind and have fun with me, let things go beyond and experience excitement together like never before. . . . You will really like having a friend so close that can satisfy you in so many great ways." Haynes also included a link to a pornographic website. Lindsay knew it was Haynes.

Lindsay immediately reported the Facebook incident to TP managers. Fearing for her safety, she begged TP to let her out of her lease. TP refused, and offered instead to move her to an available first-floor unit. Although Lindsay was wary of living on the first floor, TP assured her it would be safe.

Meanwhile, TP advised Schmidt that since Haynes was not on the lease, he would have to leave. In response, Schmidt insisted on adding him to the lease and TP agreed to go forward with the paperwork. In the process, TP divulged that Lindsay was moving to another unit.

A few days later, Haynes broke into Lindsay's new apartment and raped her in her daughter's presence. He was ultimately sentenced to nine years in prison. Lindsay sued TP, alleging that it was negligent. The trial court found that TP had no duty to protect its tenant from the criminal acts of third parties and dismissed the case. Lindsay appealed.

Issue: ***Was the landlord liable for the tenant's injuries?***

Excerpts from Judge Piper's Decision: Generally, landlords do not have a duty to protect their tenants from the criminal acts of third parties. However, such a duty exists when the landlord should have reasonably foreseen the

[9]The court refers to Lindsay by her first name alone to protect her privacy.

criminal activity and failed to take reasonable precautions to prevent such activity.

This court is cognizant that the criminal acts of third parties are very difficult to predict. However, there are issues of fact regarding whether TP should have reasonably foreseen Haynes' criminal activity. The record demonstrates that TP was aware of how Haynes was acting toward Lindsay. The record also demonstrates that TP was aware of Haynes' dangerous propensities, as it knew that Lindsay felt threatened by Haynes to the point that an employee offered to sit with Lindsay even after business hours so that she would not be alone.

TP was also made aware of Haynes' Facebook communication with Lindsay and that he propositioned her sexually. TP told Lindsay that it was "taking care of it," and asked Lindsay to contact police so that such police records would allow TP "the means we need to take action on the matter." TP also told Lindsay that it would "keep an eye on" the relations between Haynes and Lindsay.

In addition to not letting Lindsay break her lease, expressly informing Haynes that Lindsay was moving, and then placing Lindsay in a first-floor apartment even though she expressed concern for her safety, TP also began the process of adding Haynes to Schmidt's lease. When various facts are put into context with one another, it creates a question of fact as to whether TP took reasonable steps to protect Lindsay.

Summary judgment is not proper in this case. Accordingly, we remand to the trial court for further proceedings.

Exculpatory Clauses. You have found an apartment you can afford, in the right neighborhood, and the landlord presents you with a lease to sign. You notice an **exculpatory clause**, which states that the landlord is *not* liable for any injuries that occur on the rented premises, whether to you or your guests, regardless of the cause. You feel uncomfortable about the clause because it seems to suggest that the landlord can ignore serious defects and still escape liability. Should you sign the lease?

Exculpatory clause
A lease clause that relieves a landlord of liability for injuries

Today, **exculpatory clauses are generally void in residential leases.** Courts dislike such clauses because the parties typically have unequal bargaining power, and the goal of the law is to encourage safe housing managed by responsible landlords. So courts in many states simply ignore exculpatory clauses and apply normal rules of negligence to determine whether or not a landlord is liable for an injury. However, this is not universally the case; in some states, a court may still enforce an exculpatory clause in a residential lease. A concerned tenant should learn the local law before signing such a lease.

CHAPTER CONCLUSION

Real property law is ancient but forceful. Although real property today is not the dominant source of wealth that it was in medieval England, it is still the greatest asset that most people will ever possess—and is worth understanding.

When property is rented, a special relationship exists between landlord and tenant. Each has numerous obligations to the other. The current trend is clearly for expanded landlord liability, but how far that will continue is impossible to divine.

EXAM REVIEW

1. **REAL PROPERTY; FIXTURES** Real property includes land, buildings, air and subsurface rights, plant life, and fixtures. A fixture is any good that has become attached to other real property, such as land.

EXAMStrategy

Question: Paul and Shelly Higgins had two wood stoves in their home. Each rested on, but was not attached to, a built-in brick platform. The downstairs wood stove was connected to the chimney flue and was used as part of the main heating system for the house. The upstairs stove, in the master bedroom, was purely decorative. It had no stovepipe connecting it to the chimney. The Higginses sold their house to Jack Everitt, and neither party said anything about the two stoves. Is Everitt entitled to either stove? Both stoves?

Strategy: An object is a fixture if a reasonable person would consider the item to be a permanent part of the property, taking into account attachment, adaptation, and other objective manifestations of permanence. (See the "Result" at the end of this Exam Review section.)

2. **CONCURRENT ESTATES** When two or more people own real property at the same time, they have a concurrent estate. In both a tenancy in common and a joint tenancy, all owners have a share in the entire property. The primary difference is that joint tenants have the right of survivorship, meaning that when a joint tenant dies, his interest passes to the other joint tenants. A tenant in common has the power to leave her estate to her heirs.

EXAMStrategy

Question: Howard Geib, Walker McKinney, and John D. McKinney owned two vacation properties as joint tenants with right of survivorship. The parties were not getting along well, and Geib petitioned the court to partition the properties. The trial court ruled that the fairest way to do this was to sell both properties and divide the proceeds. The two McKinneys appealed, claiming that a partition by sale was improper because it would destroy their right of survivorship. Comment.

Strategy: Do joint tenants have a right to partition? Are there any limits on that right? (See the "Result" at the end of this Exam Review section.)

3. **FUTURE INTERESTS** Future interests are presently existing nonpossessory rights that may or may not develop later.

4. **ADVERSE POSSESSION** Adverse possession permits the user of land to gain title if he can prove entry and exclusive possession, open and notorious possession, a claim adverse to the owner, and continuous possession for the required statutory period.

5. **GOVERNMENT REGULATION** Nuisance law, zoning ordinances, and eminent domain all permit a government to regulate property and in some cases to take it for public use.

6. **LANDLORD–TENANT** When an owner of a freehold estate allows another person temporary, exclusive possession of the property, the parties have created a landlord–tenant relationship.

7. **TENANCIES** Any lease for a stated, fixed period is a tenancy for years. A periodic tenancy is created for a fixed period and then automatically continues for additional periods until either party notifies the other of termination. A tenancy at will has no fixed duration and may be terminated by either party at any time. A tenancy at sufferance occurs when a tenant remains, against the wishes of the landlord, after the expiration of a true tenancy.

8. **QUIET ENJOYMENT** All tenants are entitled to the quiet enjoyment of the premises, without the interference of the landlord.

9. **SECURITY DEPOSITS** Landlords may require tenants to post a deposit that can be used to pay for repairs if a tenant damages the property. But many landlords fail to promptly return security deposits to tenants who leave no damage behind. In those cases, tenants are often able to sue for as much as three times their security deposit.

10. **RENT** The tenant is obligated to pay the rent, and the landlord may evict the tenant for non-payment. The modern trend is to require a landlord to mitigate damages caused by a tenant who abandons the premises before the lease expires.

EXAMStrategy

Question: Loren Andreo leased retail space in his shopping plaza to Tropical Isle Pet Shop for five years at a monthly rent of $2,100. Tropical Isle vacated the premises 18 months early, turned in the key to Andreo, and acknowledged liability for the unpaid rent. Andreo placed a "for rent" sign in the store window and spoke to a commercial real estate broker about the space. But, for nine months, he did not enter into a formal listing agreement with the broker, or take any other steps to rent the space. With approximately nine months remaining on the unused part of Tropical's lease, Andreo did finally hire a commercial broker. He also sued Tropical for 18 months' rent. Comment.

Strategy: When a tenant abandons leased property early, the landlord is obligated to mitigate damages. Did Andreo? (See the "Result" at the end of this Exam Review section.)

11. **DAMAGE** A tenant is liable to the landlord for any significant damage he causes to the property.

12. **DISTURBANCES** A tenant must not disturb other tenants.

EXAMStrategy

Question: Doris Rowley rented space from the city of Mobile, Alabama, to run the Back Porch Restaurant. Her lease prohibited assignment or subletting without the landlord's permission. Rowley's business became unprofitable, and she asked the city's real estate officer for permission to assign her lease. She told the officer that she had "someone who would accept if the lease was assigned." Rowley provided no other information about the assignee. The city refused permission. Rowley repeated her requests several times without success, and finally she sued. Rowley alleged that the city had unreasonably withheld permission to assign and had caused her serious financial losses as a result. Comment.

Strategy: A landlord may not unreasonably refuse permission to assign a lease. Was the city's refusal unreasonable? (See the "Result" at the end of this Exam Review section.)

13. **PERSONAL INJURY** At common law, a landlord had very limited liability for injuries on the premises, but today many courts require a landlord to use reasonable care and hold her liable for foreseeable harm.

RESULTS

1. Result: A buyer normally takes all fixtures. The downstairs stove was permanently attached to the house and used as part of the heating system. The owner who installed it intended that it remain, and it was a fixture; Everitt got it. The upstairs stove was not permanently attached and was not a fixture; the sellers could take it with them.

2. Result: The McKinneys lost. Any co-tenant (including a joint tenant) has an absolute right to partition. Difficulties in partitioning are irrelevant.

10. Result: For about nine months, Andreo made no serious effort to lease the store. The court rejected his rent claim for that period, permitting him to recover unpaid money only for the period he made a genuine effort to lease the space.

12. Result: A landlord is allowed to evaluate a prospective assignee, including its financial stability and intended use of the property. Mobile could not do that because Rowley provided no information about the proposed assignee. Mobile wins.

MULTIPLE-CHOICE QUESTIONS

1. Quick, Onyx, and Nash were deeded a piece of land as tenants in common. The deed provided that Quick owned one-half the property and Onyx and Nash owned one-quarter each. If Nash dies, the property will be owned as follows:
   (a) Quick 1/2, Onyx 1/2
   (b) Quick 5/8, Onyx 3/8
   (c) Quick 1/3, Onyx 1/3, Nash's heirs 1/3
   (d) Quick 1/2, Onyx 1/4, Nash's heirs 1/4

2. Which of the following forms of tenancy will be created if a tenant stays in possession of leased premises without the landlord's consent, after the tenant's one-year written lease expires?
   (a) Tenancy at will
   (b) Tenancy for years
   (c) Periodic tendency
   (d) Tenancy at sufferance

3. To be enforceable, a long-term residential real estate lease must ________.
(a) require the tenant to obtain liability insurance
(b) define the tenant's duty to mitigate
(c) be in writing
(d) specify a due date for rent
(e) all of these

4. A tenant renting an apartment under a three-year written lease that does not contain any specific restrictions may be evicted for ________.
(a) counterfeiting money in the apartment
(b) keeping a dog in the apartment
(c) failing to maintain a liability insurance policy on the apartment
(d) making structural repairs to the apartment

5. A tenant's personal property will become a fixture and belong to the landlord if its removal would ________.
(a) increase the value of the personal property
(b) cause a material change to the personal property
(c) result in substantial harm to the landlord's property
(d) change the use of the landlord's property back to its prior use

CASE QUESTIONS

1. In 1944, W. E. Collins conveyed land to the Church of God of Prophecy. The deed said: "This deed is made with the full understanding that should the property fail to be used for the Church of God, it is to be null and void and property to revert to W. E. Collins or heirs." In the late 1980s, the church wished to move to another property and sought a judicial ruling that it had the right to sell the land. The trial court ruled that the church owned a fee simple absolute and had the right to sell the property. Comment.

2. In 1966, Arketex Ceramic Corp. sold land in rural Indiana to Malcolm Aukerman. The deed described the southern boundary as the section line between sections 11 and 14 of the land. Farther south than this section line stood a dilapidated fence running east to west. Aukerman and Arketex both believed that this fence was the actual southern boundary of his new land, though in fact it lay on Arketex's property. Aukerman installed a new electrified fence, cleared the land on "his" side of the new fence, and began to graze cattle there. In 1974, Harold Clark bought the land that bordered Aukerman's fence, assuming that the fence was the correct boundary. In 1989, Clark had his land surveyed and discovered that the true property line lay north of the electric fence. Aukerman filed suit, seeking a court order that he had acquired the disputed land by adverse possession. The statutory period in Indiana is 20 years. Who wins and why?

3. ***YOU BE THE JUDGE* WRITING PROBLEM** Frank Deluca and his son David owned the Sportsman's Pub on Fountain Street in Providence, Rhode Island. The Delucas applied to the city for a license to employ topless dancers in the pub. Did the city have the power to deny the Delucas' request? **Argument for the Delucas:** Our pub is perfectly legal. Further, no law in Rhode Island prohibits topless dancing. We are morally and legally entitled to present this entertainment. The city should not use some phony moralizing to deny customers what they want. **Argument for Providence:** This section of Providence is zoned to prohibit topless dancing, just as it is zoned to bar manufacturing. There are other parts of town where the Delucas can open one of their sleazy clubs if they want to, but we are entitled to deny a permit in this area.

4. Lisa Preece rented an apartment from Turman Realty, paying a $300 security deposit. Georgia law states: "Any landlord who fails to return any part of a security deposit which is required to be returned to a tenant pursuant to this article shall be liable to the tenant in the amount of three times the sum improperly withheld plus reasonable attorney's fees." When Preece moved out, Turman did not return her security deposit, and she sued for triple damages plus attorney's fees, totaling $1,800. Turman offered evidence that its failure to return the deposit was inadvertent and that it had procedures reasonably designed to avoid such errors. Is Preece entitled to triple damages? Attorney's fees?

5. Angel and Linda Mendez bought a home next door to Rancho Valencia, a fancy hotel on 45 acres of land. The house was about 600 feet from the site where the hotel held outdoor wedding receptions and parties. Even though the Rancho Valencia had installed noise-abating equipment, the Mendezes could still hear music and announcements from its sound system for about 8 hours a month, mostly during the evenings. These noise levels complied with the applicable county noise ordinances. On what theory could the Mendezes sue Rancho Valencia? Will they succeed?

DISCUSSION QUESTIONS

1. The Estates is a suburb outside of Los Angeles. Local zoning ordinances require that lots be "at least 1 acre in size." Al owns a 1-acre lot in The Estates which has never been developed. He needs cash and wants to sell the property. Al finds a potential buyer who offers him $100,000 for the acre. But he also finds a pair of interested buyers who each offer him $75,000 for half of his acre. Al is furious that he cannot divide his acre and sell it to two buyers. "I need that extra $50,000," he rants. "It's my land, and I should be able to do what I want with it!" Do you sympathize with Al, or do you think the zoning restriction is reasonable?

2. Donny Delt and Sammy Sigma are students and roommates. They lease a house in a neighborhood near campus. Few students live on the block. The students do not have large parties, but they often have friends over at night. The friends sometimes play high-volume music in their cars and sometimes speak loudly when going to and from their cars. Also, departing late-night guests often leave beer cans and fast-food wrappers in the street. Neighbors complain about being awakened in the wee hours of the morning. They are considering filing a nuisance lawsuit against Donny and Sammy. Would such an action be reasonable? Do you think Donny and Sammy are creating a nuisance? If so, why? If not, where is the line—what amount of late-night noise does amount to a nuisance?

3. **ETHICS** During the Great Recession, home foreclosures hit an all-time high. In many instances, banks ended up as landlords and property managers, a job for which they were ill-prepared. As a result, many homes were abandoned for long periods. Some people who knew a little bit about adverse possession decided to take advantage of this ancient common law doctrine: They shamelessly occupied vacant homes, claiming them as their own, changing locks, and purchasing electricity. The new residents argued that they were not hurting anyone and acting within the bounds of the law. In response, some states lengthened the time period necessary for adverse possession. Examine the squatters' ethics. What do you think of their behavior? Does your opinion vary if the squatters were the home's former owners? What if the banks were ignoring the home? What would Kant and Mill say?

4. Imagine that you sign a lease and that you are to move into your new apartment on August 15. When you arrive, the previous tenant has not moved out. In fact, he has no intention of moving out. Compare the English and the American rules. Should the landlord be in charge of getting rid of the old tenant, or should you have the obligation to evict him?

5. When landlords wrongfully withhold security deposits, they can often be sued for three times the amount of the security deposit. Is this reasonable? Should a landlord have to pay $3,000 for a $1,000 debt? What if you fail to pay a rent on time? Should you have to pay three times the amount of your normal rent? If your answers to these two questions are different, why?

43

CHAPTER

PERSONAL PROPERTY AND BAILMENT

Ferris Bueller was not really sick. Neither were his sidekicks, Cameron and Sloane. But the trio concocted an elaborate plan for the perfect "day off" from the doldrums of their senior year of high school. And no day off would be complete without a joyride. So Ferris persuaded the stiff Cameron to take his father's prized 1961 Ferrari 250 GT California for a field trip into downtown Chicago. (A similar Ferrari sold at auction for $18 million.) "It is his love, it is his passion," Cameron argued. "It is his *fault* for not locking the garage," Ferris responded.

As one would, the teenagers decided to deposit the vehicle with a parking valet service. (Parking in downtown Chicago is tough.) But Cameron was nervous. "No, not here," he uttered. *Why?* "It could get wrecked, stolen, scratched, it could get breathed on wrong," he fretted. Ferris consoled him by generously "dropping" the parking attendant a five-dollar bill.

And no day off would be complete without a joyride.

"Relax. You guys got nothin' to worry about. I'm a professional," said the wily attendant with a glimmer in his eye.

After a long day full of adventures, the friends returned to collect the car, only to discover that its mileage has gone from 124.5 to 329. The attendants enjoyed a better joyride than they did. Cameron would have a lot of explaining to do.[1]

[1]Adapted from the classic 1986 John Hughes film *Ferris Bueller's Day Off*.

This chapter is about a lot of stuff, things, and possessions—in other words, personal property—and the duties incurred in giving it, finding it, and loaning it.

Personal property means all tangible property other than real property. In Chapter 42, we saw that real property is land and things firmly attached to it, such as buildings, crops, and minerals. All other physical objects are personal property—a toothbrush, a share of stock, a 1961 Ferrari 250 GT California.

Personal property
All tangible property other than real property

In this chapter, we look at three ways to acquire personal property: by gift, by finding it, and by accession. We will then turn to bailments, which occur when the owner of personal property permits another to possess it.

43-1 ACQUIRING PERSONAL PROPERTY

43-1a Gifts

A **gift** is a voluntary transfer of property from one person to another without any consideration. Recall from Chapter 13 that, for consideration to exist, parties must make an exchange. But a gift is a one-way transaction, without anything given in return. The person who gives property away is the **donor**, and the one who receives it is the **donee**.

Gift
A voluntary transfer of property from one person to another, without consideration

Donor
A person who gives property away

Donee
A person who receives a gift of property

A gift involves three elements:

1. The donor *intends to transfer* ownership of the property to the donee immediately.
2. The donor *delivers* the property to the donee.
3. The donee *accepts* the property.

If all three elements are met, the donee becomes the legal owner of the property. If the donor later says, "I've changed my mind, give that back!" the donee is free to refuse.

Intention to Transfer Ownership

The donor must intend to transfer ownership to the property right away, immediately giving up all control of the item. Notice the two important parts of this element. First, the donor's intention must be to *transfer ownership*; that is, to give title to the donee. Merely proving that the owner handed you property does not guarantee that you have received a gift; if the owner only intended that you use the item, there is no gift, and she can demand it back.

Second, the donor must also intend the property to transfer *immediately*. A promise to make a gift in the future is unenforceable. Promises about future behavior are governed by contract law, and a contract is unenforceable without consideration. If Sarah hands Lenny the keys to a $600,000 yacht and says, "Lenny, it's yours," then it *is* his, since Sarah intends to transfer ownership right away. But if Sarah says to Max, "Next week, I'm going to give you my yacht," Max has not received a gift because Sarah did not intend an immediate transfer. Nor does Max have an enforceable contract since there is no consideration for Sarah's promise.

Rudolph Greene sent his son Stuart an envelope, but asked him not to open it until after his death. Stuart dutifully waited until after Rudolph died, and then opened the letter to find out Rudolph wanted Stuart to have two valuable federal bonds. Stuart's stepmother challenged the gift as invalid and a court agreed with her: A letter to be opened in the future is not a *present* transfer of ownership.[2]

---

[2]Greene v. Greene, 92 A.D.3d 838 (S. Ct. N.Y. 2012).

A *revocable gift* is governed by a special rule, and it is actually not a gift at all. Suppose Harold tells his daughter Faith, "The mule is yours from now on, but if you start acting silly again, I'm taking her back." Harold has retained some control over the animal, which means he has not intended to transfer ownership. There is no gift, and no transfer of ownership. Harold still owns the mule.

When Dominic Tenaglia's automobile broke down, his brother Nick generously offered to give him a replacement car. Nick delivered a Chevrolet to Dominic, and both brothers understood that the car was a gift. Nick wrote "gift" on the car's certificate of title, but he did not immediately give the certificate to Dominic. A week later, while Dominic was driving the Chevrolet, he was involved in an accident. Both brothers had insurance, through different insurers, for cars they owned. The two companies disputed which one was liable for Dominic's accident. The court determined that Nick's company was still liable for any damage caused by the Chevrolet. Nick had presented the car to Dominic but had not relinquished *all* control over it. Ownership of a car is unlike ownership of a computer or a sweater because it requires possession of the certificate of title. Because Nick still had the certificate at the time of the accident, he had the power to take back the Chevrolet whenever he wanted. He had not made a valid gift of the automobile, and Dominic's insurer won the case.[3]

Delivery

Physical Delivery. **The donor must deliver the property to the donee.** Generally, this involves physical delivery—a handoff, if you will. If Anna hands Eddie a Rembrandt drawing, saying "I want you to have this forever," she has satisfied the delivery requirement. But such a dramatic statement is not necessary.

Constructive Delivery. Physical delivery is the most common and the surest way to make a gift, but it is not always required. **A donor makes constructive delivery by transferring ownership without a physical delivery.** Most courts permit constructive delivery only when physical delivery is impossible or extremely inconvenient. Suppose Anna wants to give her niece Jen a blimp, which is parked in a hangar at the airport. The blimp will not fit through the doorway of Jen's dorm. Instead of flying the aircraft to the university, Anna may simply deliver to Jen the certificate of title and the keys to the blimp. When she has done that, Jen owns the aircraft.

Delivery to an Agent. A donor might deliver the property to an agent, either someone working for him or for the donee. Assume that Randolph says to Mortimer, "Old boy, I should like for you to have my Rolls Royce." If Randolph gives the keys and the title to his own butler, there is no gift. By definition, the agent works for the donor, and thus the donor still has control and ownership of the property. But if the donor delivers the property to the donee's agent, the gift is made. So, if Randolph delivers the car to Mortimer's butler, then Mortimer owns the car.

Property Already in Donee's Possession. Sometimes a donor decides to give property to a donee who already has possession of it. In that case, no delivery is required, and the donee need only demonstrate that the donor intended to transfer present *ownership*. Larry lends a grand piano to Leslie for the summer. At the end of the summer, Larry announces that she can keep the instrument. As long as Larry clearly intends that Leslie gets ownership of the piano, the gift is completed.

---

[3]Motorists Mutual Insurance Co. v. State Farm Mutual Automobile Insurance Co., 1990 Ohio App. LEXIS 3027, 1990 WL 103746 (Ohio Ct. App. 1990).

Inter Vivos Gifts and Gifts *Causa Mortis*

A gift can be either *inter vivos* or *causa mortis*. An ***inter vivos* gift** means a gift made "during life," that is, when the donor is not under any fear of impending death. The vast majority of gifts are *inter vivos*, involving a healthy donor and donee. Shirley, age 30 and in good health, gives Terry an eraser for his birthday. This is an *inter vivos* gift, which is absolute. The gift becomes final upon delivery, and the donor may *not* revoke it. If Shirley and Terry have a fight the next day, Shirley has no power to erase her eraser gift.

***Inter vivos* gift**
A gift made during the donor's life, with no fear of impending death

A **gift *causa mortis*** is one made in contemplation of approaching death. The gift is valid if the donor dies as expected, but it is revoked if he recovers. Suppose Lenny's doctors have told him he will probably die of a liver ailment within a month. Lenny calls Jane to his bedside and hands her a fistful of cash, saying, "I'm dying, this money is yours." Jane sheds a tear, then sprints to the bank. If Lenny dies of the liver ailment within a few weeks, Jane gets to keep the money. The law permits the gift *causa mortis* to act as a kind of substitute for a will since the donor's delivery of the property clearly indicates his intentions. But note that this kind of gift is revocable. Since a gift *causa mortis* is conditional (upon the donor's death), the donor has the right to revoke it at any time before he dies. If Lenny telephones Jane the next day and says that he has changed his mind, he gets the money back. Further, if the donor recovers and does not die as expected, the gift is automatically revoked.

Gift *causa mortis*
A gift made in contemplation of approaching death

Acceptance

The donee must accept the gift. This rarely leads to disputes, but if a donee should refuse a gift and then change her mind, she is out of luck. Her repudiation of the donor's offer means there is no gift, and she has no rights in the property.

EXAMStrategy

Question: Julie does good deeds for countless people, and many are deeply grateful. On Monday, Wilson tells Julie, "You are a wonderful person, and I have a present for you. I am giving you this baseball, which was the 500th home run hit by one of the great players of all time." He hands her the ball, which is worth nearly half a million dollars.

Julie's good fortune continues on Tuesday, when another friend, Cassandra, tells Julie, "I only have a few weeks to live. I want you to have this signed first edition of *Ulysses*. It is priceless, and it is yours." The book is worth about $200,000. On Wednesday, Wilson and Cassandra decide they have been foolhardy, and both demand that Julie return the items. Must she do so?

Strategy: Both of these donors are attempting to revoke their gifts. An *inter vivos* gift cannot be revoked, but a gift *causa mortis* can be. To answer the question, you must know what kind of gifts these were.

Result: A gift *causa mortis* is one made in fear of approaching death, and this rule applies to Cassandra. Such a gift is revocable any time before the donor dies, so Cassandra gets her book back. A gift *inter vivos* is one made without any such fear of death. Most gifts fall in this category, and they are irrevocable. Wilson was not anticipating his demise, so his was a gift *inter vivos*. Julie keeps the baseball.

The following table distinguishes between a contract and a gift:

A Contract and a Gift Distinguished

A Contract:	
Lou: I will pay you $2,000 to paint the house if you promise to finish by July 3.	Abby: I agree to paint the house by July 3 for $2,000.
Lou and Abby have a contract. Each promise is consideration in support of the other promise. Lou and Abby can each enforce the other's promise.	
A Gift:	
Lou hands Phil two opera tickets saying, "I want you to have these two tickets to *Rigoletto*."	Phil says, "Hey, thanks."
This is a valid *inter vivos* gift. Lou intended to transfer ownership immediately and delivered the property to Phil, who now owns the tickets.	
Neither Contract nor Gift:	
Lou: You're a great guy. Next week, I'm going to give you two tickets to *Rigoletto*.	Jason: Hey, thanks.
There is no gift because Lou did not intend to transfer ownership immediately, and he did not deliver the tickets. There is no contract because Jason has given no consideration to support Lou's promise.	

The following case involves the age-old question: Who keeps the engagement ring when a relationship sours?

Estate of Lowman v. Martino

2016 R.I. Super. LEXIS 4; 2016 WL 197267
Superior Court of Rhode Island, Providence, 2016

Facts: David Lowman and Sarah Martino had a tumultuous 14-year romance in which they intermittently lived together. When Lowman was diagnosed with a serious heart condition, Martino cared for him and put him on her health insurance plan. Their relationship was at its peak when Lowman proposed to Martino with a $15,000 engagement ring on Valentine's Day.

But five years later, the relationship was on the rocks—and Lowman was dying. Martino told Lowman that she would not marry him, rarely visited him, and threatened to revoke his health insurance. Lowman tried contacting her 10 to 15 times, but she refused to return his calls, much less the ring.

Lowman sued Martino for the return of the engagement ring. When he died, his estate took over as plaintiff. It argued that the ring was a gift conditioned upon a marriage, which never happened.

Issue: ***Was Martino entitled to keep the engagement ring?***

Excerpts of Judge Procaccini's Decision: *"Love looks not with the eyes but with the mind, and therefore is winged Cupid painted blind."*[4] The Court is reminded of the sage observation of William Shakespeare, as it commences its examination of the relationship between Lowman and Martino.

Rhode Island precedent is silent as to who owns an engagement ring when a marriage does not ensue. Under these circumstances, the majority trend in the United States is to classify the ring as a conditional gift, and return the ring to the donor if no marriage results. The Supreme

[4] William Shakespeare, *A Midsummer Night's Dream*, Act I, Scene I.

Court of Pennsylvania noted that their case law "clearly recognized the giving of an engagement gift as having an implied condition that the marriage must occur in order to vest title in the donee; mere acceptance of the marriage proposal is not the implied condition for the gift." The court further commented that this no fault approach was the emerging modern trend, which correlated with states also adopting no-fault divorces.

Following the majority trend, this Court agrees with the reasoning that an engagement ring is a gift conditioned on marriage. In the present case, Ms. Martino testified that she believed the engagement was still on until Mr. Lowman died. Ms. Martino denied that they ever broke up, that she did not want to marry him, or that he requested the ring back.

However, the Court finds the circumstances tell a different story. [T]he original Complaint included allegations that Ms. Martino threatened to take Mr. Lowman off of her health insurance plan. Then Mr. Lowman was deposed and asked about the engagement ring. Mr. Lowman explained that Ms. Martino declined to marry him because he could not afford the house she wanted. Mr. Lowman asked for the ring back. Surprisingly, the evidence at trial also establishes that Ms. Martino visited Mr. Lowman only a few times while he was [dying]. After reviewing all the evidence presented on this issue, this Court does not find Ms. Martino's testimony that the ring on her finger still symbolized the love and commitment associated with the engagement.

This Court finds Mr. Lowman's testimony supports the conclusion that Ms. Martino broke off their engagement prior to his death. Because the ring is considered a conditional gift, the donor is entitled to have the gift returned. Ms. Martino may return the ring to Mr. Lowman's estate or reimburse the estate for the full value of the ring, $15,000.

As the court suggests, many states have adopted the rule that an engagement ring is a conditional gift that must be returned to the giver if no marriage ensues.[5] Other states agree that the ring is a conditional gift, but nonetheless allow the recipient to keep the ring if the giver is to blame for the split.[6] However, when an engagement occurs on a holiday, like Christmas, Valentine's Day, or a birthday, courts in every state are more likely to view the ring as an irrevocable gift. Finally, at least one state always views the ring as a pre-marriage gift, provided that the three elements of a gift are satisfied.[7]

43-1b Found Property

The law of found property has bewitched the courts of this country for nearly two centuries. Judges have made valiant attempts to base their rulings on principles of sound public policy, but the results have been confusing and contradictory. **The primary goal of the common law has been to get found property back to its proper owner, if possible.** The finder must make a good faith effort to locate the owner of the property and return the goods to him. In some states, the finder is obligated to notify the police of what she has found and entrust the property to them until the owner can be located or until a stated period has passed. **A second policy has been to reward the finder if no owner can be located.** But courts are loath to encourage trespassing, so finders who discover personal property on someone else's land generally cannot keep it. Those basic policies yield various outcomes, depending on the nature of the property. In the end, the law recognizes four kinds of found property:

1. **Abandoned property** is something that the owner has knowingly discarded because she no longer wants it. A vase thrown into a garbage can is abandoned. Generally, a finder is permitted to keep abandoned property. But because the owner loses all rights in abandoned property, a court never *presumes* abandonment. The finder must prove that the owner intended to relinquish all rights.

---

[5]These states include Iowa, Kansas, New Jersey, New Mexico, New York, Pennsylvania, Tennessee, and Wisconsin.

[6]States adopting fault considerations include California, Texas, and Washington.

[7]Montana is one example.

2. **Lost property** is something accidentally given up. A ring that falls off a finger into the street is lost property. Usually, the finder of lost property has rights superior to all the world except the true owner. If the true owner comes forward, he gets his property back; otherwise, the finder may keep it. However, if the finder has discovered the item on land belonging to another, the landowner is probably entitled to keep it.
3. **Mislaid property** is something the owner has intentionally placed somewhere and then forgotten. A book deliberately placed on a bus seat by an owner who forgets to take it with her is mislaid property. Generally, the finder gets no rights in property that has simply been mislaid. If the true owner cannot be located, the mislaid item belongs to the owner of the premises where the item was found.
4. **Treasure trove** is coins or currency concealed by an owner so long ago that it is likely the owner has died. A sackful of gold coins minted in 1860, found under the roots of a 150-year-old tree, is treasure trove. The finder can generally keep treasure trove.

Finding statutes
Laws that govern found property, also known as estray statutes

Many states have enacted laws, called **finding statutes** or **estray statutes**, governing found property. In some cases, the legislation incorporates the common law principles just outlined, but in other states, the new law modifies the old rules. A New York statute, for example, has removed the distinction between lost and mislaid property and now generally permits the finder to keep what he has discovered, regardless of where he found it. The finder is, however, required to turn over the property either to the police or the owner of the premises where the item was found. If the true owner is not located during a stated period, the finder is then entitled to whatever he found.

The following case has contributed significantly to modern legal ideas on found property. It may seem to come from a Charles Dickens novel, but it actually happened. A villainous goldsmith sought to take advantage of a poor boy. Would he get away with it? Read on.

Landmark Case

Armorie v. Delamirie

93 ER 664 Middlesex, 1722

Facts: Before Parliament banned the practice in 1840, many English chimney sweeps forced young children to climb the narrow flues and do the cleaning. Armorie was one such boy. But fortune smiled on him, and he found a jeweled ring. To discover its value, he carried the ring to a local goldsmith.

Armorie handed the ring to the goldsmith's apprentice, who removed the jewels from the ring and pretended to weigh it. He called out to the goldsmith that the ring was worth three halfpence. The goldsmith then offered that amount to Armorie.

Not being a fool, Armorie refused the offer and demanded that the ring be returned. The apprentice gave him the ring, but without the jewels.

Issue: ***Did the chimney sweep have a legal right to retain possession of the found jewels?***

Excerpts from Justice Pratt's Decision: The finder of a jewel, though he does not by such finding acquire an absolute property or ownership, has such a property as will enable him to keep it against all but the rightful owner. As to the value of the jewel, the Chief Justice directed the jury that unless the defendant did produce the jewel, and shew it not to be of the finest water, they should presume the strongest against him, and make the value of the best jewels the measure of their damages: which they accordingly did.

43-1c Accession

Accession occurs when one person uses labor, materials, or both to add value to personal property belonging to another. This generally occurs by agreement. Suppose Leasing Corp. agrees to lease a truck to Delivery Co. for use in its business. The contract may permit Delivery to modify the truck's storage space to meet its special needs. If so, the agreement should also state whether Delivery has to return the truck to its original condition at the end of the lease and whether Delivery is entitled to any payment for improvements made.

Accession
Occurs when one person uses labor, materials, or both to add value to personal property belonging to another person

Sometimes one party makes accessions without agreement. If the improvements can be "undone" without damage to the property, then the improver must do that. For example, if Delivery Co. simply bolts a few shelves into the truck, it should remove them before returning the truck. Problems arise when the improvements cannot be removed without damaging the property. Assuming the property has become more valuable, must the owner pay the improver for the work done? It normally depends upon whether the improver acted wrongfully, or merely made a mistake.

Wrongful Accessions

If the improver knows he is making accessions without authority, the owner may generally take the improved property without paying for the work done. Suppose the lease between Leasing Corp. and Delivery Co. states that Delivery may not modify the truck without written permission. Delivery goes ahead anyway and reconfigures the truck to meet its needs. Even if the work substantially increases the truck's value, Leasing Corp. probably owes nothing for the accessions.

Mistaken Accessions

If the improver mistakenly believes he is entitled to add accessions, the owner probably has to pay for the increased value. Suppose that, based on its previous leases with Leasing Corp., Delivery Co. believes it has the right to modify its new truck, though in fact it has no such permission. If the modifications increase the value of the vehicle, Leasing probably has to pay for the accessions.

43-2 BAILMENT

A **bailment** is the rightful possession of goods by someone who is not the owner. The one who delivers the goods is the **bailor** and the one in possession is the **bailee**. In the chapter opener, Cameron is the reluctant bailor and the joyriding valet is the bailee. Such bailments are common. Suppose you are going out of town for the weekend and lend your motorcycle to Stan. You are the bailor, and your friend is the bailee. When you check your suitcase with the airline, you are again the bailor and the airline is the bailee. If you rent a car at your destination, you become the bailee, while the rental agency is the bailor. In each case, someone other than the true owner has rightful, temporary possession of personal property.

Bailment
The rightful possession of goods by one who is not the owner, usually by mutual agreement between the bailor and bailee

Parties generally create a bailment by agreement. In each of the preceding examples, the parties consented to the bailment. In two cases, the agreement included payment, which is common but not essential. When you buy your airline ticket, you pay for your ticket, and the price may include the airline's agreement, as bailee, to transport your suitcase. When you rent a car, you pay the bailor for the privilege of using it. By lending your motorcycle, you engage in a bailment without either party paying compensation.

A bailment without any agreement is called a **constructive, or involuntary, bailment**. Suppose you find a wristwatch in your house that you know belongs to a friend. As we saw in the

Involuntary bailment
A bailment that occurs without an agreement between the bailor and bailee

Stringer Italy/Reuters

Would you entrust this vehicle to a valet?

earlier section, you are obligated to return the watch to the true owner, and until you do so, you are the bailee, liable for harm to the property. This exchange is called a constructive bailment because, with no agreement between the parties, the law is *construing* a bailment.

43-2a Control

To create a bailment, the bailee must assume physical control of an item with intent to possess. A bailee may be liable for loss or damage to the property, and so it is not fair to hold him liable unless he has taken physical control of the goods, intending to possess them.

Disputes about whether someone has taken control often arise in parking lot cases. When a car is damaged or stolen, the lot's owner may try to avoid liability by claiming it lacked control of the parked auto and therefore was not a bailee. If the lot is a "park and lock" facility, where the car's owner retains the key and the lot owner exercises *no control at all,* there is probably no bailment and no liability for damage.

By contrast, when a driver leaves her keys with a parking attendant, the lot clearly is exercising control of the auto, and the parties have created a bailment. The lot is probably liable for loss or damage in that case.

The following case examines whether a bailment was created during one of history's greatest tragedies. It was not quite a parking or car rental agreement, but was it a bailment?

de Csepel v. Hungary

714 F.3d 591
United States District Court for the District of Columbia, 2013

Facts: Baron Mór Lipót Herzog was a passionate Hungarian-Jewish art collector who, in the first half of the twentieth century, assembled more than two thousand paintings, sculptures, and other artworks. Known as the "Herzog Collection," this body of artwork was one of Europe's great private collections, and included paintings by renowned artists such as El Greco, Velázquez, Renoir, and Monet.

Then, during World War II, Adolf Hitler sent German troops into Hungary. The country enacted anti-Semitic laws and deported Hungarian Jews to concentration camps. The government required all Hungarian Jews to register their artwork and valuables. It then confiscated the most prized pieces.

The Herzogs attempted to save the collection by hiding it in the cellar of one of the family's factories. But the Hungarian government and its Nazi collaborators discovered the hiding place. They took the artwork directly to SS Commander Adolf Eichmann, who personally selected the best pieces for transfer to Germany. The remainder was handed over to Hungarian museums for safekeeping. The Herzog family was forced to flee Hungary or face extermination.

At the end of World War II, the Herzog heirs were dispersed all over the world—from the United States to Argentina. They claim that, at the time, they arranged for the Hungarian government to retain possession of most of the collection so that the works could continue to be displayed in Hungary. But when the Herzogs requested the collection's return, Hungary refused and thus began a seven-decade struggle over the artwork.

Finally, in 2010, the Herzog family sued the Republic of Hungary over the art, asserting a claim for bailment. They alleged that the family's postwar arrangement with Hungary formed a bailment agreement, whereby Hungary assumed a duty of care to protect the property and to return it to the family on demand. Hungary moved to dismiss, arguing that no such bailment was created. The district court denied the motion and Hungary appealed.

Issue: ***Did the parties create a valid bailment agreement?***

Excerpts from Judge Tatel's Decision: The Herzog family seeks to recover not for the original expropriation of the Collection, but rather for the subsequent breaches of bailment agreements they say they entered into with Hungary. Specifically, the complaint alleges that Hungary's possession or repossession of any portion of the Herzog Collection following World War II constituted an express or implied-in-fact bailment contract under which Hungary assumed a duty of care to protect the property and to return it to the Herzog family, and which Hungary breached by refusing to return the Collection. The family's claims, they reiterate, are nothing more than straightforward bailment claims.

Hungary argues that the complaint fails to state a claim for bailment because it nowhere alleges the necessary element of "mutual consent of the parties." But the complaint contains allegations that the parties directly agreed to a bailment relationship, with Hungary arranging with representatives of the Herzog Heirs to retain possession of most of the Herzog Collection and the Herzog family agreeing to allow the artworks to be 'returned' to the Museums or the University for safekeeping.

According to Hungary, however, any showing of consent is negated by the allegations that the Herzog family had no choice but to agree to allow most of the works belonging to the Herzog Collection to remain in Hungary's physical possession because they were harassed and threatened by Hungarian government officials. We disagree. Even if the family's consent was induced by duress—a conclusion we would be reluctant to draw at the motion to dismiss stage—that would mean only that the family could disclaim the agreement, not that the agreement was invalid.[8] Thus, for purposes of a motion to dismiss, the family has adequately pleaded the element of consent.

EXAMStrategy

Question: Jack arrives at Airport Hotel's valet parking area in a Ferrari, just as Kim drives up in her Smart Car. A valet drives Kim's car away, but the supervisor asks Jack to park the Ferrari himself, in the hotel's lot across the street. Jack parks as instructed, locking the Ferrari and keeping the keys. During the night, both vehicles are stolen. The owners sue for the value of their vehicles—about $10,000 for Kim's Smart Car and $350,000 for Jack's Ferrari. Each owner will win if there was a bailment but lose if there was not. Can either or both prove a bailment?

Strategy: To create a bailment, the bailee must assume physical control with intent to possess.

Result: When the valet drove Kim's car away, the hotel assumed control with intent to possess. The parties created a bailment, and the hotel is liable. But Jack loses. The hotel never had physical control of the Ferrari. Employees did not park the vehicle, and Jack kept the keys. Jack's was a "park and lock" case, with no bailment.

43-2b Rights of the Bailee

The bailee's primary right is possession of the property. **Anyone who interferes with the bailee's rightful possession is liable to her.** Suppose that, after you lend your motorcycle to Stan, Mel sees Stan park the bike, realizes Stan is not the owner, rides the motorcycle away, and locks it up until you return. Mel is liable to Stan for any damages Stan suffered while deprived of transportation.

Even a bailor is liable if he wrongfully takes back property from a bailee. If a car agency rents Francine a car for a three-day weekend but then repossesses it for use elsewhere, it is liable to her for any damages, even though it owns the car. The bailor must abide by the agreement.

[8] In other words, if the Herzogs entered into the contract under duress, it was voidable by them, but not by Hungary.

The valet in the chapter opener had no right to red-line the vehicle all over Chicago.

The bailee is typically, though not always, permitted to use the property. Obviously, a customer is permitted to drive a car rented from an agency. When a farmer loans his tractor to a neighbor, the bailee is entitled to use the machine for normal farm purposes. But some bailees have no authority to use the goods. The valet in the chapter opener had no right to red-line the vehicle all over Chicago. If you store your furniture in a warehouse, the storage company is your bailee, but it has no right to curl up in your bed. The bailee may be entitled to compensation. This depends upon the agreement. If Owner leaves a power boat at the boatyard for repairs, the boatyard, a bailee, is entitled to payment for the work it does. As with any contract, the exact compensation should be clearly agreed upon before any work begins. If there is no agreement, the boatyard will probably receive the reasonable value of its services.

43-2c Duties of the Bailee

The bailee is strictly liable to redeliver the goods on time to the bailor, or to whomever the bailor designates. Strict liability means there are virtually no exceptions. Rudy stores his $6,000 drum set with Melissa's Warehouse while he is on vacation. Blake arrives at the warehouse and shows a forged letter, supposedly from Rudy, granting Blake permission to remove the drums. If Melissa permits Blake to take the drums, she will owe Rudy $6,000, even if the forgery was a high-quality job.

Due Care

The bailee is obligated to exercise due care. **The level of care required depends upon who receives the benefit of the bailment.** There are three possibilities:

1. **Sole benefit of bailee.** If the bailment is for the sole benefit of the bailee, the bailee is required to use **extraordinary care** with the property. Generally, in these cases, the bailor loans something for free to the bailee. Since the bailee is paying nothing for the use of the goods, most courts consider her the only one to benefit from the bailment. If your neighbor loans you a power lawn mower, the bailment is probably for your sole benefit. You are liable if you are even slightly inattentive in handling the lawn mower and can expect to pay for virtually any harm done.

2. **Mutual benefit.** Most bailments benefit both parties. When Ferris and his friends parked the Ferrari with the valet, they benefited from the convenience, and the parking service profited from the fee paid. When the bailment is for the mutual benefit of bailor and bailee, the bailee must use **ordinary care** with the property. Ordinary care is what a reasonably prudent person would use under the circumstances. It is certainly *not* what the valet attendant exercised in the opening scenario.

3. **Sole benefit of bailor.** When the bailment benefits only the bailor, the bailee must use only **slight care**. This kind of bailment is called a **gratuitous bailment**, and the bailee is liable only for **gross negligence**. Michelle enters a pie-eating contest and asks you to hold her $29,000 diamond engagement ring while she competes. You put the ring in your pocket. Michelle wins the $20 first prize, but the ring has disappeared. This was a gratuitous bailment, and you are not liable to Michelle unless she can prove gross negligence on your part. If the ring dropped from your pocket or was stolen, you are not liable. If you used the ring to play catch with friends, you are liable.

Burden of Proof

In an ordinary negligence case, the plaintiff has the burden of proof to demonstrate that the defendant was negligent and caused the harm alleged. In bailment cases, the burden of proof is reversed. **Once the bailor has proven the existence of a bailment and loss or harm to the goods, a presumption of negligence arises, and the burden shifts to the bailee to prove adequate care.** This is a major change from ordinary negligence cases. Georgina's car is struck by another auto. If Georgina sues for negligence, it is her burden to prove that the defendant was driving unreasonably and caused the harm. By comparison, assume that Georgina rents Chance her sailboat for a month. At the end of the month, Chance announces that the boat is at the bottom of Lake Michigan. If Georgina sues Chance, she only needs to demonstrate that the parties had a bailment and that Chance failed to return the boat. The burden then shifts to Chance to prove that the boat was lost through no fault of his own. If Chance cannot meet that burden, Georgina recovers the full value of the boat.

43-2d Exculpatory Clauses

Bailees often use exculpatory clauses in an effort to limit their liability. Recall that an **exculpatory clause** is any part of a contract that attempts to relieve one of the parties of future liability. Exculpatory clauses are commonly employed in parking garages, coat check locations in restaurants, warehouses, suitcase lockers, and so forth. A parking service's exculpatory clause might state that it is not responsible for any loss or damage to the automobile, for example. Are such clauses valid? That depends upon several factors.

Exculpatory clause
A contract clause that attempts to relieve one of the parties from future liability

An exculpatory clause is generally unenforceable if it attempts to exclude an intentional tort or reckless behavior. In the event of a lawsuit over the Ferrari's diminished value, an exculpatory clause will not help the parking attendant in the opening scenario because his actions were both intentional and reckless.

Courts often look to the parties' relative bargaining power in deciding whether to enforce an exculpatory clause. If the bailor is a corporation and it has bargaining power roughly equal to the bailee's, a court will probably enforce an exculpatory clause. If a manufacturer agrees to park five of its aircraft in a hangar owned by Hannah Corp., and Hannah's storage contract states that it is not responsible for any losses caused by fire, flood, or hurricane, then Hannah is probably protected when fire destroys the manufacturer's planes. Both parties are businesses, and the law assumes they should live with whatever agreement they bargained for.

When the bailor is a consumer, the exculpatory clause stands on shaky ground because judges generally presume the parties have unequal bargaining power. Courts look to see whether the clause was clearly written and easily visible.

EXAMStrategy

Question: A producer shot a low-budget horror movie and then delivered ten reels of negative film to Filmprocess Corp. for processing. Filmprocess lost the reels. The producer sued for $5 million, the cost of production. Filmprocess based its defense on an exculpatory clause in the parties' contract, which stated that the producer accepted the full risk of loss for any film delivered to Filmprocess and that the producer would insure against such loss. Who will win the lawsuit?

Strategy: The producer delivered its film to Filmprocess. What relationship did that create? A bailment is the rightful possession of goods by one who is not the owner. The parties have created a bailment. Are exculpatory clauses enforced in bailments? If the bailor is a corporation and it has bargaining power roughly equal to the bailee's, a court will probably enforce a bailment exculpatory clause, except in cases of intentional tort or gross negligence.

Result: The producer will lose its claim for $5 million. Both parties were corporations, with roughly equal bargaining power, and the exculpatory clause is valid. There was no intentional tort or gross negligence, so the clause will be enforced.

The following case arises in a familiar setting and indicates the wide reach of bailment principles.

Tannenbaum v. New York Dry Cleaning, Inc.

2001 N.Y. Slip Op. 40076 (U)
Civil Court of the City of New York, 2001

Facts: When Rob Tannenbaum picked up his $160 shirt at the dry cleaners, he found it badly torn. He sued, claiming negligence. New York Cleaners denied causing the tearing. In addition, the cleaner claimed that even if the company damaged the shirt, an exculpatory clause on the back of the ticket limited its liability to 10 times the cleaning fee of $2, or $20.

Issues: ***Was the cleaner negligent? If so, did the exculpatory clause limit the company's liability?***

Excerpts from Judge Samuels' Decision: To the customer, it doesn't seem reasonable that he should be able to recover only $20 for the destruction of the $160 shirt he took to the dry cleaner to be laundered.

The Limitation Clause reads as follows:

> In laundering, we cannot guarantee against color loss, and shrinkage; or against damage to weak and tender fabrics. The company's liability with respect to any lost article shall not exceed 10 times our charge for processing it.

The foregoing is printed in gray type, against a light yellow background, and is significantly more difficult for a person with good eyesight to read than the text on the front of the claim ticket.

This case is clearly one of bailment for hire. When a bailee is unable to return the bailed item, or (as here) returns it in damaged condition, a rebuttable presumption arises that the loss of, or damage to, the item is attributable to the bailee's negligence.

At trial, Defendant denied that the Shirt had been damaged while in its care, but did not offer, in the alternative, any explanation negating the presumption of negligence. Accordingly, Defendant is liable for negligence, unless its disclaimer is effective.

New York law has long disfavored exculpatory clauses that relieve a party to a contract from liability for the consequences of its own negligence. The law's disfavor has been expressed in strict requirements that the disclaimer of liability for negligence be made explicit and be communicated in such a way as to ensure that the party who is to be bound by the disclaimer has knowingly accepted such disclaimer.

It appears that Defendant sought to enjoy the protections of a disclaimer without alarming its customers by causing them actually to contemplate the Limitation Clause. Defendant offered no evidence that it had taken any steps to call Claimant's attention to its terms beyond giving him the Claim Ticket. [T]he Court finds that Claimant was not aware of, and did not assent to be bound by, the Limitation Clause.

Claimant is awarded judgment in the amount of $160, plus interest and costs.

43-2e Rights and Duties of the Bailor

The bailor's rights and duties are the reverse of the bailee's. The bailor is entitled to the return of his property on the agreed-upon date. He is also entitled to receive the property in good condition and to recover damages for harm to the property if the bailee failed to use adequate care.

43-2f Liability for Defects

Depending upon the type of bailment, the bailor is potentially liable for known or even unknown defects in the property. **If the bailment is for the sole benefit of the bailee, the bailor must notify the bailee of any known defects.** Suppose Megan lends her stepladder to Dave. The top rung is loose and Megan knows it, but she forgets to tell Dave. The top rung crumbles, and Dave falls onto his girlfriend's iguana. Megan is liable to Dave and the girlfriend unless the defect in the ladder was obvious. Notice that Megan's liability is not only to the bailee, but also to any others injured by the defects. Megan would not be liable if she had notified Dave of the defective rung.

In a mutual-benefit bailment, the bailor is liable not only for known defects but also for unknown defects that the bailor could have discovered with reasonable diligence. Suppose RentaLot rents a power sander to Dan. RentaLot does not realize that the sander has faulty wiring, but a reasonable inspection would have revealed the problem. When Dan suffers a serious shock from the defect, RentaLot is liable to him, even though it was unaware of the problem.

If the bailor is in the business of renting property, the bailment is probably subject to implied warranties. As we saw in Chapter 22 on warranties, the Uniform Commercial Code creates various implied warranties for goods sold or leased by a merchant. Recall that a merchant is someone in the business of selling or leasing that type of goods. A car rental company is a merchant with respect to its cars, so it rents the autos subject to implied warranties that they are fit for their normal purposes. Because these warranties are implied by law, they normally exist whether the parties say anything about them or not. Bailors may attempt to limit these implied warranties by provisions in the bailment agreement, but courts disfavor such limitations, especially when the bailee is a consumer.

43-2g Common Carriers and Contract Carriers

A carrier is a company that transports goods for others. It is a bailee of every shipment entrusted to it. There are two kinds of carriers: common carriers and contract carriers. The distinction is important because each type of company has a different level of liability.

A **common carrier** makes its services available on a regular basis to the general public. For example, a trucking company located in St. Louis that is willing to haul freight for anyone, to any destination in the country, is a common carrier. **Generally, a common carrier is strictly liable for harm to the bailor's goods.** Common carriers are governed by a statute known as the Carmack Amendment.[9] Under this law, a bailor needs only to establish that it delivered property to the carrier in good condition and that the cargo arrived damaged. The carrier is then liable unless it can show that it was not negligent *and* that the loss was caused by an act of God (such as a hurricane), an act of a public enemy (a nation at war with the United States), an act of the bailor itself (e.g., by packaging the goods improperly), an act of a public authority (e.g., a state inspector forcing a delay), or the inherent nature of the goods (such as fruit that spoiled naturally). These defenses are difficult to prove, and in most cases, a common carrier is liable for harm to the property.

A common carrier is, however, allowed to limit its liability by contract. For example, a common carrier might offer the bailor the choice of two shipping rates: a low rate,

Common carrier

A company that transports goods and makes its services regularly available to the general public

Fort Worth Star-Telegram/McClatchy-Tribune/Getty Images

A trucking company is an example of a common carrier.

[9]49 U.S.C. §11707.

with a maximum liability, say, of $10,000, or a higher shipping rate, with full liability for any harm to the goods. In that case, if the bailor chooses the lower rate, the limitation on liability is enforceable. Even if the bailor proves a loss of $300,000, the carrier owes merely $10,000.

A **contract carrier** does not make its services available to the general public but engages in continuing agreements with particular customers. Assume that Steel Curtain Shipping is a trucking company in Pittsburgh that hauls cargo to California for two or three steel producers and carries manufactured goods from California to Pennsylvania and New York for a few West Coast companies. Steel Curtain is a contract carrier. **A contract carrier does not incur strict liability.** The normal bailment rules apply, and a contract carrier can escape liability by demonstrating that it exercised due care of the property.

Contract carrier
A company that transports goods for particular customers

43-2h Innkeepers

Hotels, motels, and inns frequently act as bailees of their guests' property. Most states have special innkeeper statutes that regulate liability.

Hotel patrons often assume that anything they bring to a hotel is safe. But some state innkeeper statutes impose an absolute limit on a hotel's liability. Other statutes require guests to leave valuables in the inn's safe deposit box. And even that may not be enough to protect them fully. For example, a state statute might require the guest to register the nature and value of the goods with the hotel. These statutes are designed to limit risk—but of course, some people *like* risk. In the following case, a high-stakes gambler placed a large bet … on his hotel dresser.

Gnoc Corp. v. Powers

2006 WL 560687; 2006 N.J. Super. Unpub. LEXIS 699
N.J. Superior Court, Appellate Division, 2006

Facts: David Powers liked to wager. He and a friend arrived at the Hilton Casino in Atlantic City for a two-day stay. It was Powers's fourth visit to the hotel. They checked in at the front desk and received electronic room keys. Clearly visible signs, posted there and in each room, notified guests that the hotel was not responsible "for valuables or other property left in room," and that the hotel had a safe for valuables.

Powers won $76,000, which he converted into $25,000 cash, ten gray chips worth $5,000 each, and one white $1,000 chip. He and his friend retired to their rooms. During the night, both Powers and his friend had various room service deliveries. Sometime before he went to bed, Powers placed his cash, chips, and a money clip on the dresser. At 4:19 a.m., the front desk issued a second key to Powers's room to an unknown person. Powers awoke to discover that his cash, chips, and clip were gone.

Powers ended up $25,000 in debt to the casino, and when he refused to pay, the hotel sued. Powers claimed that the Hilton owed him $76,000 for the stolen merchandise. The trial judge ruled in favor of the Hilton based on New Jersey's innkeeper statute, which states:

> If the proprietor of any hotel shall provide a safe or other depository in the hotel's office or in another convenient place, for the safekeeping of *any valuables belonging to guests* of the hotel, and shall place, in a conspicuous position in the room or rooms occupied by each guest, a notice stating the fact that a safe is provided in which valuables may be deposited, and any guest shall neglect to deliver valuables to the person in charge of the safe, the proprietor shall not be liable in any sum for the loss of valuables sustained by that guest, by theft or otherwise…. "Valuables" *includes* money, bank notes, bonds, precious stones, jewelry, ornaments [etc] and *any other articles of similar value.*

Powers appealed.

Issue: ***Did the innkeeper statute protect the hotel?***

Excerpts from the *Per Curiam* Decision: It is defendant's contention that because casino chips are not specifically enumerated in [the innkeeper statute] and are not items of value as they are merely an accounting mechanism to evidence a debt owed by the casino, [the statute] does not apply to them. Further, he asserts that the chips do not "belong to guests," pointing to [a related statute] which provides:

> Each gaming chip and plaque is solely evidence of a debt that the issuing casino licensee owes to

the person legally in possession of the gaming chip or plaque, and *shall remain in the property of the issuing casino licensee.*

To be sure, casino chips are not specifically listed as one of the enumerated items in the definition of "valuables." But the list is not exhaustive, as it is preceded by the word "includes" and followed by the words "any other articles of similar value." Included under the statutory definition of valuables are "money, bank notes, bonds, securities, checks, business papers, documents." As the motion judge observed: "While the statute may not say casino chips, it does have in there the things that have, like chips, no intrinsic value of their own [but] are evidence of either value or debt." And too, although the hotel owns the chips, while they are in the possession of the guest they belong to that guest until redeemed for cash.

So too, defendant's reliance upon [an earlier case called *Heinz*] is misplaced. *Heinz* concerned strict compliance with the statutorily required notice. Here, defendant concedes that the Hilton complied with the statutory notice requirements. Where, as here, a hotel is in strict compliance with the notice requirements, the Act operates as a bar to plaintiff's recovery.

Affirmed.

CHAPTER CONCLUSION

Personal property law plays an almost daily role in all of our lives. The valet parker, the finder of lost property, and a bank officer who rents safe deposit boxes must all realize that they could incur substantial liability for personal property, whether they intend to accept that obligation or not. Understanding personal property law can be worth a lot of chips—but do not leave them lying around your hotel room.

EXAM REVIEW

1. **GIFTS** A gift is a voluntary transfer of property from one person to another without consideration. The elements of a gift are intention to transfer ownership immediately, delivery, and acceptance.

2. **FOUND PROPERTY** The finder of property must attempt to locate the true owner unless the property was abandoned. State estray statutes have made some changes in the common law, but the following principles generally govern:
   - Abandoned property—the finder may keep it.
   - Lost property—the finder generally has rights superior to everyone but the true owner, except that if she found it on land belonging to another, the property owner generally is entitled to it.
   - Mislaid property—generally, the finder has no rights in the property.
   - Treasure trove—generally, the finder may keep it.

EXAMStrategy

Question: The government accused Carlo Francia and another person of stealing a purse belonging to Frances Bainlardi. A policeman saw Francia sorting through the contents of the purse, which included a photo identification of Bainlardi. Francia kept some items, such as cash, while discarding others. At trial, Francia claimed that he had thought the purse was lost or abandoned. Besides the fact that Francia's accomplice was holding burglary tools, what is the weakness in Francia's defense?

Strategy: The finder of property must attempt to locate the true owner unless the property was abandoned. Is there any likelihood that the purse was abandoned? If it was not abandoned, did Francia attempt to locate the owner? (See the "Result" at the end of this Exam Review section.)

3. **ACCESSION** Accession occurs when one person uses labor, materials, or both to add value to personal property belonging to another. If the improver knows he is making accessions without authority, the owner may generally take the improved property without compensating for the work done. If the improver mistakenly believes that he is entitled to add accessions, the owner probably has to pay for the increased value.

4. **BAILMENT** A bailment is the rightful possession of goods by one who is not the owner. The one who delivers the goods is the bailor, and the one in possession is the bailee. To create a bailment, the bailee must assume physical control with intent to possess.

5. **BAILEE'S RIGHTS** The bailee is always entitled to possess the property, is frequently allowed to use it, and may be entitled to compensation.

6. **REDELIVERY** The bailee is strictly liable to redeliver the goods to the bailor.

EXAMStrategy

Question: Shannon borrows Marty's car, but when she returns the auto, she hands the keys to Scott, who claims he is Marty's brother. Scott offers a driver's license and passport to reassure Shannon. Scott is actually a con artist. Marty sues Shannon. Outcome?

(a) Marty will win.

(b) Marty will win only if a reasonable person would have spotted the fraud.

(c) Marty will win only if he in fact has no brother named Scott.

(d) Marty will lose because Scott offered reasonable identification.

Strategy: Make sure you know the standard a bailee must meet for redelivering goods. (See the "Result" at the end of this Exam Review section.)

7. **BAILEE'S DUTY OF CARE** The bailee is obligated to exercise due care. The level of care required depends upon who receives the benefit of the bailment: if the bailee is the sole beneficiary, she must use extraordinary care; if the parties mutually benefit, the bailee must use ordinary care; and if the bailor is the sole beneficiary of the bailment, the bailee must use only slight care.

8. **PRESUMPTION OF NEGLIGENCE** Once the bailor has proven the existence of a bailment and loss, a presumption of negligence arises, and the burden shifts to the bailee to prove adequate care.

EXAMStrategy

Question: Lonny Joe owned two rare 1955 Ford Thunderbird automobiles, one red and one green, both in mint condition. He stored the cars in his garage. His friend Stephanie wanted to use the red car in a music video, so Lonny Joe rented it to her for two days, for $300 per day. When she returned the red car, Lonny Joe discovered a long scratch along one side. That same day, he noticed a long scratch along the side of the green car. He sued Stephanie for harm to the red car. Lonny Joe sued an electrician for damage to the green car, claiming that the scratch occurred while the electrician was fixing a heater in the garage. Explain the different burdens of proof in the two cases.

Strategy: In an ordinary negligence case, the plaintiff must prove all elements by a preponderance of the evidence. However, in a bailment, a *presumption* of negligence arises. To answer this question, you need to know whether Lonny Joe established a bailment with either or both defendants. (See the "Result" at the end of this Exam Review section.)

9. **EXCULPATORY CLAUSES** Exculpatory clauses, seeking to relieve a bailee of liability for damage to the goods, may be enforced between two corporations of equal bargaining power but are seldom enforced against a consumer.

10. **DEFECTS** The bailor must keep the property in suitable repair, free of any hidden defects. If the bailor is in the business of renting property, the bailment is probably subject to implied warranties.

11. **COMMON CARRIERS** Generally, a common carrier is strictly liable for harm to the bailor's goods. A contract carrier incurs only normal bailment liability.

12. **INNKEEPERS** The liability of an innkeeper is regulated by state statute. A guest intending to store valuables with an innkeeper must follow the statute to the letter.

RESULTS

2. Result: Abandoned property is something that the owner has knowingly discarded because she no longer wants it. The burden is on the finder to prove that the property was abandoned, which will be impossible in this case since no one would throw away cash and credit cards. Because the purse contained photo identification, Francia could easily have located its owner. He made no attempt to do so, and his defense is unpersuasive.

6. Result: The bailee is strictly liable to redeliver the goods to the bailor. There are no excuses. The "reasonable person" standard does not apply. The correct answer is (a).

8. Result: Lonny Joe had no bailment with the electrician because the electrician never assumed control of the car. To win that case, Lonny Joe must prove that the electrician behaved unreasonably and caused the scratch. However, when Lonny Joe rented Stephanie the red car, the parties created a bailment, and the law presumes Stephanie caused the damage unless she can prove otherwise. That is a hard burden, and Stephanie will likely lose.

MULTIPLE-CHOICE QUESTIONS

1. Which of the following requirements must be met to create a bailment?

I. Delivery of personal property to the intended bailee

II. Possession by the intended bailee

(a) I only

(b) II only

(c) Both I and II

(d) None of these

2. Consider the following:

I. A house (value: $250,000)

II. The giant high-definition smart television in the house (value: $2,999)

III. The land that the house sits upon (value: $30,000)

IV. An old car in the house's garage (value: $5,001)

How many of these items are personal property?

(a) All four of them

(b) Three of them

(c) Two of them

(d) One of them

(e) None of them

3. Holding out an envelope, Alan says, "Ben, I'm giving you these opera tickets." Without taking the envelope, Ben replies, "Why would I want opera tickets? Loser." Alan leaves, crestfallen. Later that day, a girl whom Ben has liked for some time says, "I sure wish I were going to the opera tonight." Ben scrambles, calls Alan, and says, "Alan, old buddy, I accept your gift of the opera tickets. I'm on my way over to pick them up." Does Ben have a legal right to the tickets?

(a) Yes because Alan intended to transfer ownership.

(b) Yes because offers to give gifts cannot be revoked.

(c) No because no consideration was given.

(d) No because Ben did not accept the gift when offered.

4. Gina has season tickets to Cardinals games. One Monday, she promises to give her tickets to Friday's game to Ed, a friend who works across town. On Tuesday, Gina hands the tickets to Al, an administrative assistant. An hour later, when Al still has the tickets and has not given them to Ed, Gina returns. "Sorry," she says, "but my cousins are coming to town this weekend. I'll need those tickets back." Gina is entitled to get the tickets back if Al works for ______________.

(a) Gina

(b) Ed

(c) Both A and B

(d) None of these

5. Craig finds a rare 1955 doubled-die penny, worth $1,500, on a city sidewalk outside a coin collectors' convention. The penny is ______________ property. If the true owner cannot be found, then the penny will belong to ______________.

(a) lost; Craig
(b) lost; the city
(c) abandoned; Craig
(d) abandoned; the city
(e) mislaid; Craig

CASE QUESTIONS

1. During her second year at the Juilliard School of Music in New York City, Ann Rylands had a chance to borrow for one month a rare Guadagnini violin made in 1768. She returned the violin to the owner in Philadelphia, but then she telephoned her father to ask if he would buy it for her. He borrowed money from his pension fund and paid the owner. Ann traveled to Philadelphia to pick up the violin. She had exclusive possession of the violin for the next 20 years, using it in her professional career. Unfortunately, she became an alcoholic, and during one period when she was in a treatment center, she entrusted the violin to her mother for safekeeping. At about that time, her father died. When Ann was released from the center, she requested return of the violin, but her mother refused. Who owns the violin?

2. During the Great Depression of the 1930s, the federal government's Works Progress Administration hired artists to create public works of art. The goal was to provide employment and beautify the nation. The artist James Daugherty painted six murals on the walls of the public high school in Stamford, Connecticut. During the 1970s, the city began to restore its high school. The architect and school officials agreed that the Daugherty murals should be preserved. They arranged for the construction workers to remove the murals to prevent harm. By accident, the workers rolled them up and placed them near the trash dumpsters for disposal. A student found the murals and took them home, and later notified the federal government's General Services Administration (GSA) of his find. The GSA arranged to transport the murals to an art restorer named Hiram Hoelzer for storage and eventual restoration, when funds could be arranged. Over *19 years* went by before anyone notified the Stamford School system where the murals were. In the meantime, neither the GSA nor anyone else paid Hoelzer for the storage or restoration. By 1989, the murals were valued at $1.25 million by Sotheby's, an art auction house. Hoelzer filed suit, seeking a declaration that the murals had been abandoned. Were they abandoned? What difference would that make when determining ownership?

3. ***YOU BE THE JUDGE* WRITING PROBLEM** Eileen Murphy often cared for her elderly neighbor, Thomas Kenney. He paid her $25 per day for her help and once gave her a bank certificate of deposit worth $25,000. She spent the money. Murphy alleged that shortly before his death, Kenney gave her a large block of shares in three corporations. He called his broker, intending to instruct him to transfer the shares to Murphy's name, but the broker was ill and unavailable. So Kenney told Murphy to write her name on the shares and keep them, which she did. Two weeks later, Kenney died. When Murphy presented the shares to Kenney's broker to transfer ownership to her, the broker refused because Kenney had never endorsed the shares as the law requires—that is, signed them over to Murphy. Was Murphy entitled to the $25,000? To the shares? **Argument for Murphy:** The purpose of the law is to do what a donor intended, and it is obvious that Kenney intended Murphy

to have the $25,000 and the shares. Why else would he have given them to her? A greedy estate should not be allowed to interfere with the deceased's intentions. **Argument for the Estate:** Murphy is not entitled to the $25,000 because we have no way of knowing what Kenney's intentions were when he gave her the money. She is not entitled to the shares of stock because Kenney's failure to endorse them over to her meant he never *delivered* them, and that is an essential element of a gift.

4. **ETHICS** Famous artists Georgia O'Keefe and Alfred Stieglitz donated 101 artworks to Fisk University in the 1940s. But the gift had two conditions: The pieces could not be sold and they had to be displayed as one collection. Over 50 years later, Fisk could not pay to maintain the collection and decided to sell two of the pieces. Proceeds of the sale would go to restore its endowment and build a new science building. The Georgia O'Keefe Foundation sued to stop the sale, arguing that the artists would have opposed it. Should the law permit this sale? Do you agree with Fisk's actions? What duties do gift recipients have to donors? What would Kant and Mill say?

5. The Louisiana Civil Code limits an innkeeper's liability for stolen property to $500 and only covers cash, jewelry, rare art items, furs, cameras, and negotiable instruments. While staying at the New Orleans Hilton, Allen Chase was drugged by a woman he met at the hotel bar. He woke up the next morning to find that his gold watch, wallet, credit cards, passport, business papers, and camera were gone. As a result of the drug, Chase suffered health problems, which seriously affected his business. Believing that the hotel bartender had helped the woman who drugged him, Chase sued Hilton for negligence in the amount of $575,000. Who wins and why?

DISCUSSION QUESTIONS

1. "Finders keepers, losers weepers" is a common children's rhyme. Does the law mirror its sentiment?

2. Is it sensible to distinguish between *inter vivos* gifts and gifts *causa mortis*? Should someone "on his deathbed" be able to change his mind so easily?

3. Historically, the law has viewed animals as personal property. As a result, when a pet is wrongfully killed, its owner can only recover the cost of replacing the animal. Some groups have challenged this view, arguing that animals are fundamentally different from other forms of personal property. Do you agree? How should the law address the ownership of animals?

4. Common carriers are usually liable when property is damaged, but they are not liable for "acts of God"—floods, hurricanes, and the like. Is this fair? If you send a friend an important item via UPS and the UPS truck is hit by a tornado, who should pay for the lost item? Isn't UPS in a better financial position to pay for the loss? (In the end, the company might well offer to pay for the loss even though the law does not require it.)

5. If there has been no account activity for an extended period of time, state laws require banks to turn the customers' property over to the state. State treasurers or comptrollers are responsible for holding the abandoned or lost property, which often includes money, watches, jewelry, and coins from abandoned safe deposit boxes. What rules should govern this property? How long should citizens have to claim it? What should the government do with unclaimed property?

CHAPTER

44

PLANNING FOR THE FUTURE: WILLS, TRUSTS, AND INSURANCE

Emily and Nick had been friends since childhood. In high school, they were teammates on the cross-country squad; in college, they often commiserated over tough courses and difficult romances. After college, Emily went to business school, and from there to a hedge fund. Nick followed his lifelong dream of becoming a high school teacher. But they were still members of the same running club. They even purchased houses near each other. When an old estate went on the market, Emily bought the manor house, Nick the gatekeeper's cottage.

By age 45, Nick was married with two children. Although his salary was modest, he saved carefully, purchased enough life insurance to replace his income if he died prematurely, and signed a will that would pass on his assets in an orderly way. To pay the premiums on his life insurance, his family gave up resort vacations and new cars.

To pay the premiums on his life insurance, his family gave up resort vacations.

"Boring!" Emily scolded Nick. "I can't believe you spend so much on life insurance. You can't afford it." For her part, Emily was making a fortune each and every year. She had been divorced once, was currently separated from her second husband, had one child from each marriage, and was involved in a passionate affair with her personal trainer. Her husband was living in the house with their child, while Emily resided with her boyfriend in a fancy condo she owned downtown. She took lavish vacations, traveled first class, bought expensive jewelry and artwork, and kept intending to write a will. She earned so much money, she figured she did not need life insurance.

One bright fall day, Emily and Nick were driving in Emily's new sports car. She was so busy showing Nick all the bells and whistles that she did not notice when the truck in front of them stopped suddenly. Her car plowed into the truck, killing them both instantly.

Nick's widow was devastated. But because of their careful planning, she was able to keep her house and maintain the family's lifestyle. Emily's extended family did not fare so well. The ex-spouse, estranged spouse, children, and boyfriend spent years and hundreds of thousands of dollars litigating over the right to her assets. Her hedge fund went out of business and was unable to pay her pension. Because her first and second husbands were no longer receiving support from her, they had to sell their houses and move. For children who had just lost their mother, this was an added emotional blow.

Bad things happen. This chapter is about mitigating risks by planning for the future. Most people should have a will, and absolutely everyone should make careful, considered decisions about how much and what kinds of insurance coverage they need.

44-1 INTRODUCTION TO ESTATE PLANNING

There is one immutable law of the universe: "You can't take it with you." Eventually, you and your material goods will part. But you *can* control where your assets go after your death. Or you can decide not to bother with an estate plan and leave all in chaos behind you.

44-1a Definitions

Estate planning has special terminology:

- **Estate planning.** The process of giving away property after (or in anticipation of) death.
- **Estate.** The legal entity that holds title to assets after the owner dies and before the property is distributed.
- **Decedent.** The person who has died.
- **Testator** or **testatrix**. Someone who has signed a valid will. **Testatrix** is the female version (from the Latin).
- **Intestate.** To die without a will.
- **Heir.** Technically, the term *heir* refers to someone who inherits from a decedent who died intestate. **Devisee** means someone who inherits under a will. However, most people and many courts use *heir* to refer to anyone who inherits property, and we follow that usage in this chapter.
- **Issue.** A person's direct descendants, such as children and grandchildren.

- **Probate.** The process of carrying out the terms of a will.
- **Executor** or **executrix.** A personal representative *chosen by the decedent* to carry out the terms of the will. An **executrix** is a female executor.
- **Administrator** or **administratrix.** A personal representative appointed *by the probate court* to oversee the probate process for someone who has died intestate (or without appointing an executor). As you can guess, an **administratrix** is a female administrator.
- **Grantor** or **settlor.** Someone who creates a trust.
- **Donor.** Someone who makes a gift or creates a trust.

Throughout this chapter, we use the masculine and feminine versions of *testator, executor,* and *administrator* interchangeably. These are dated terms that reflect an era when men and women had different legal rights. It would be more progressive to bury these words in the same graveyard as *authoress* and *poetess*, but courts and lawyers still use them, and so must we.

44-1b Purpose

Estate planning has two primary goals: to ensure that property is distributed as the owner desires and to minimize estate taxes. Although tax issues are beyond the scope of this chapter, they are an important element of estate planning, often affecting not only how people transfer their property but, in some cases, to whom. For instance, wealthy people may set up trusts as a means of passing on money tax-free. Or they may give money to charity, at least in part, to minimize the taxes on the rest of their estate.

44-1c Probate Law

The federal government and many states levy estate taxes (although traditionally, state taxes have been much lower). But only the states, and not the federal government, have probate codes to regulate the creation and implementation of wills and trusts. These codes vary from state to state. This chapter, therefore, speaks only of general trends among the states. Certainly, anyone who is preparing a will must consult the laws of the relevant state.

To make probate law more consistent, the National Conference of Commissioners on Uniform State Laws drafted a Uniform Probate Code (UPC). Although we refer to it in this chapter, fewer than half of the states have adopted it.

44-2 WILLS

A will is a legal document that disposes of the testator's property after death. It can, in most instances, be revoked or altered at any time until death. By having a will, testators can:

Will
A legal document that disposes of the testator's property after death

- Ensure that their assets are distributed in accordance with their wishes.
- Provide guardians for minor children. If parents do not appoint a guardian before they die, a court will. Presumably, the parents are best able to make this choice.
- Select a personal representative to oversee the estate. If the decedent does not name an executor in a will, the court will appoint an administrator. Generally, people prefer to have someone they know, rather than a court, in charge of their property.
- Save money. Those who die intestate often leave behind issues for lawyers to resolve. A properly drafted will can also reduce the estate tax bill.

The following examples suggest another purpose for a will: to say what you really think.[1]

> I give to the Lieutenant-General Cromwell one of my words … which he must want, seeing that he hath never kept any of his own.
>
> —Philip, fifth Earl of Pembroke, seventeenth century

> Seeing that I had the misfortune to be married to the aforesaid Elizabeth, who, ever since our union, has tormented me in every possible way; that not content with making game of all my remonstrances, she has done all she could to render my life miserable; that Heaven seems to have sent her into the world solely to drive me out of it; that the strength of Samson, the genius of Homer, the prudence of Augustus, the skill of Pyrrhus, the patience of Job, the philosophy of Socrates, the subtlety of Hannibal, the vigilance of Hermogenes, would not suffice to subdue the perversity of her character … weighing seriously all these considerations … I bequeath, to my said wife Elizabeth, the sum of one shilling.
>
> —John George, 1791

> I leave Parson Chavasse (Maggy's husband) the snuff box I got from the Sarnia Militia, as a small token of gratitude for the service he has done my family in taking a sister that no man of taste would have taken.
>
> —William Dunlop, 1842

> Before anything else is to be done, 50 cents is to be paid to my son-in-law to enable him to buy for himself a good stout rope with which to hang himself, and thus rid mankind of one of the most infamous scoundrels that ever roamed this broad land or dwelt outside of a penitentiary.
>
> —Garvey B. White, 1908

44-2a Requirements for a Valid Will

Generally speaking, a person may leave his assets to whomever he wants. However, the testatrix must be:

- **Of legal age** (which is 18).
- **Of sound mind.** That is, she must be able to understand what a will is, more or less what she owns, who her relatives are, and how she is disposing of her property.
- **Acting of her own free will, without undue influence.** Undue influence means that one person has enough influence over another to persuade her to do something against her free will.

In the following case, an elderly man disowned his children. Was he acting under undue influence? You be the judge.

You Be the Judge

Cresto v. Cresto

302 Kan. 820
Kansas Supreme Court, 2015

Facts: Francis Cresto was married three times over a 50-year period. He had three biological children with his first wife; a stepdaughter, Lauri, with his second wife; and seven stepchildren with his third wife, Kathleen. At the time of his death, Francis and Kathleen lived in Kansas and the numerous family seemed to get along well.

[1] Jeff Stryker, "They Couldn't Resist: Oh, One Last Thing …," *The New York Times*, May 21, 2000, p. 7.

Francis owned a large stock portfolio, part of a family farm, and valuable family heirlooms. Prior to meeting Kathleen, he executed an estate plan (both a will and a trust) prepared by his long-time lawyer, Edward White. This plan gave the family farm and heirlooms to his children, while dividing the stock portfolio among his three children and his stepdaughter, Lauri. A few years later, Francis tweaked this estate plan, but the primary result was the same—everything went to his three children and Lauri.

Shortly after marrying Kathleen, Francis asked White to re-draft his estate plan to give Kathleen the income from his assets during her lifetime. At her death, everything went to his three children and Lauri.

Four years later, Francis called Patricia Hackett, an Indiana lawyer, to ask for her help in revising his estate plan. Hackett was in a romantic relationship with Kathleen's daughter Rita. Hackett agreed, but told Francis he would need a Kansas lawyer to review the plan to ensure that it was valid in that state. Although White was available, Hackett suggested another Kansas lawyer, James Logan, who had been a federal judge.

The estate plan that Hackett drafted left everything to Kathleen. But if she died before Francis, her children would receive all of his personal property (including the family heirlooms), plus $25,000 each, and the rest would go to several charities. Hackett sent the documents to Logan for review, but did not disclose her relationship with Kathleen's daughter.

When Francis went to Logan's office to execute the documents, they spent 30 minutes discussing his assets and his reasons for the changes in his estate plan. Logan testified that, although Kathleen was present, Francis was competent and in charge. Francis had said that his children were successful business people and did not need the money. He wanted to take care of Kathleen.

Eighteen months later, Francis was diagnosed with dementia. He died the following year. His children sued to overturn his estate plan, alleging that Kathleen had exercised undue influence over him.

You Be the Judge: *Did Kathleen exercise undue influence? Was Francis's estate plan valid?*

Argument for Francis's Children: Before meeting Kathleen, Francis had always used Edward White, a lawyer who knew the family well. With White's help, Francis had made three estate plans that left all of his assets to his children and Lauri. Even after he married Kathleen, the plan drafted by White provided for her in her lifetime, but then gave everything to his children and Lauri.

Then Francis fired White and went to Hackett, who was out of state and the romantic partner of one of Kathleen's children. Hackett clearly had a conflict of interest, which she did not disclose to Logan before he helped Francis execute the documents. Undue influence cases often begin with the firing of a long-time, trusted legal adviser. Also, Kathleen was in the room when Francis signed the documents. Suddenly he left everything to her, including family heirlooms and farm. Even if he outlived Kathleen, his assets would go to charity rather than his children. This act, this sudden change of heart, does not reflect Francis's free will.

Moreover, eighteen months after making this plan, Francis was diagnosed with dementia. He could well have had diminished capacity when he signed his final estate plan.

Argument for Kathleen: Francis and Kathleen had a happy marriage. But he was not that close to his children. Moreover, his children were all well-off, she was not. It made sense for him to take care of his wife.

Francis switched to Hackett because he liked her, she knew the family well, and was likely to outlive him. Logan, an impartial lawyer, interviewed Francis extensively before he signed the documents. This was an experienced, objective lawyer who had no prior relationship with either Hackett or Francis. He took his fiduciary obligations seriously and would not have participated in a scheme that looked to him like undue influence.

A testator must comply with the legal requirements for executing a will:

- It must be in writing.
- The testator must sign it or direct someone else to sign it for him, if he is too weak.
- Generally, two witnesses must also sign the will. Under the UPC, a notarized will does not require any witnesses, but only a few states have passed this provision.
- No one named in a will should also serve as a witness because, in many states, a witness may not inherit under a will.

The importance of abiding by the legal technicalities cannot be overstated. No matter what the testator's intent, courts generally do not enforce a will unless each requirement of the law has been fully met. Close only counts in horseshoes and hand grenades.

Holographic Will

Holographic will
A will that is handwritten and signed by the testator, but not witnessed

Some states recognize a **holographic will**, which is a will that is handwritten and signed by the testatrix, but not witnessed. **A holographic will *must* be in a testator's own handwriting—it cannot be typed or written by someone else.**

Suppose Rowena is on a plane that suffers engine trouble. For 15 minutes, the pilot struggles to control the plane. Despite his efforts, it crashes, killing everyone aboard. During those 15 minutes, Rowena writes on a Post-it note, "This is my last will and testament. I leave all my assets to the National Gallery of Art in Washington, D.C.," and then signs her name. This note is found in the wreckage of the plane. Her previous will, signed and witnessed in a lawyer's office, left everything to her significant other, Ivan. If Rowena resides in one of the majority of states that accepts a holographic will, then Ivan is out of luck and the National Gallery will inherit all. One court has, indeed, accepted as a will a handwritten Post-it note that had not been witnessed.

Nuncupative Will

Noncupative will
An oral will

A few states will also accept a **nuncupative will** for personal property but not for real estate.[2] This is the formal term for an oral will. **For a nuncupative will to be valid:**

- The testatrix must know she is dying,
- There must be two witnesses, and
- These witnesses must know that they are listening to her will.

Suppose that Rowena survives the airplane crash for a few hours. Instead of writing a will on the plane, she whispers to a nurse in the hospital, "I'd like all my property to go to the Angell Memorial Cat Hospital." This oral will is valid if there are two witnesses and Rowena also says the equivalent of, "I'm dying. Please witness my oral will." The cat hospital, however, is only entitled to her personal property. Ivan would inherit her farm under the written will she executed in her lawyer's office.

44-2b Spouse's Share

In community property states, a spouse can override the will and claim one-half of all marital property acquired during the marriage, except property that the testator inherited or received as a gift.[3] Although this rule sounds easy and fair, implementation can be troublesome. If a couple has been married for many years and has substantial assets, it can be very difficult to sort out what is and is not community property. Suppose that the testatrix inherited a million dollars 20 years before her death. She and her husband both earned sizable incomes during their careers. How can a court tell what money bought which asset? Anyone in such a situation should keep detailed records.

In most non-community property states, a spouse can override the will and claim some percentage of the decedent's estate (which varies by state). The UPC provides a complex formula that depends on how long the couple was married and what percentage of marital assets each owned.

---

[2]For a good summary of state laws on nuncupative and holographic wills, google "find law state laws wills."

[3]Arizona, California, Idaho, Louisiana, Nevada, New Mexico, Texas, and Washington all have a community property law; Wisconsin's system is a variation of the same principle.

The percentage of a decedent's estate that a spouse is entitled to claim is called a **forced share** or **statutory share**. A spouse can always waive his right to a forced share by written contract.

Forced share or statutory share
The percentage of a decedent's estate that a spouse is entitled to claim, regardless of the will's content

44-2c Children's Share

Parents are not required to leave assets to their children. They may disinherit their children for any reason.[4] In most states, this is true even if the children are minors whom the testator was obligated to support while alive.

However, the law presumes that a **pretermitted child** (i.e., a child left nothing under the parent's will) was omitted by accident unless the parent clearly indicates in the will that he has omitted the child on purpose. To do so, he must either leave her some nominal amount, such as $1, or specifically write in the will that the omission was intentional: "I am making no bequest to my daughter because she has chosen a religion of which I disapprove."

Pretermitted child
A child who is left nothing under the parent's will

If a pretermitted child is left out by accident, she is generally entitled to the same share she would have received if her parent had died intestate; that is, without a will. Does this rule make sense? How likely is it that a parent with sufficient mental capacity to make a valid will would *forget* a child? Do you think the father in the following case simply forgot?

In re Estate of Josiah James Treloar, Jr.

151 N.H. 460
New Hampshire Supreme Court, 2004

Facts: Josiah James Treloar, Jr.'s, first will left his estate to his wife unless she died before he did, in which case one piece of land was to go to his daughter Evelyn, another to his son, Rodney, and the rest of his estate was to be divided equally among Evelyn, Rodney, and another daughter, Beverly.

After his daughter Evelyn died, Josiah executed a new will. To help his lawyer in preparing this document, Josiah gave him a copy of the old will with handwritten changes, including Evelyn's name crossed out. The new will left the estate to Rodney and Beverly equally. Evelyn's children and her husband, Leon, got nothing, although Leon was named as executor. Josiah referred to Leon as "my son-in-law."

Under New Hampshire law, all issue (including children and grandchildren) can qualify as pretermitted heirs. The law assumes that if the testator does not leave anything to his issue or does not refer to them in his will, it is because he has forgotten them. They are therefore entitled to a share of his estate. If Josiah had mentioned Evelyn, then the assumption would be that he had not forgotten her or her children. Evelyn's children argued that they were entitled to a share of Josiah's estate because he had not left her or them out on purpose. Josiah's attorney was serving as executor (not Leon). When he refused to pay the children, they sued.

Issue: ***Are Evelyn's children entitled to a share of Josiah's estate?***

Excerpts from Justice Galway's Decision[5]**:** The purpose of the statute [on pretermitted heirs] is to prevent a mistake or unintended failure by the testator to remember the natural object of his or her bounty. This rule of law is conclusive unless there is evidence in the will itself that the omission was intentional. To be a pretermitted heir, the child must not be named in the will, referred to in the will, or be a devisee or legatee under the will.

The executor asserts that, although the will names neither Evelyn nor her children, there are sufficient

[4]The only exception to this rule is Louisiana, whose laws are based on the French model.
[5]For readability, we use the term "Evelyn's children" instead of "respondents" and "executor" instead of "petitioner."

indirect references to Evelyn to satisfy the statute. The executor first argues that the reference in the will to revoking "all prior wills and testamentary instruments" coupled with evidence of the prior will, which specifically named Evelyn, and the testator's handwritten changes to it, demonstrate that he had Evelyn in mind when he prepared the will.

The court's task is not to investigate the circumstances to divine the intent of the testator; rather, it is to review the language contained within the four corners of the will for a determination of whether the testator named or referred to Evelyn's children. We disagree with the executor that we must read the wills together. [The new] will stands on its own.

The executor next argues that the reference to Leon as the testator's "son-in-law" showed that he had Evelyn in mind when he drafted the [new] will. [T]he testator did not use his daughter's name. Nor did he use the phrase "son-in-law" in a bequest. Rather, he used the phrase "son-in-law" to identify the individual he wished to appoint as his executor.

Even if the will indirectly referred to Evelyn, these indirect references would not satisfy the statute for the purposes of disinheriting Evelyn's children. [T]he naming of one person, however closely related to another, without more, is no reference to that other. It is well established that there must be a reference in the will to the child himself. It is not sufficient to infer that the child was not forgotten because a sibling or other relative was remembered in the will.

For all of the above reasons, we conclude that Evelyn's children are pretermitted heirs.

As we have observed before, the laws regarding wills are very precise. It seems highly unlikely that Josiah had forgotten Evelyn. No matter—the will did not meet the requirements of the statute, so her children were in luck.

In drafting a will, lawyers use the term *issue* instead of children. ***Issue*** means all direct descendants, such as children, grandchildren, great-grandchildren, and so on. If the will leaves property to "my children" and one child dies before the testator, the child's children would not inherit their parent's share. But if the will says "to my issue" and one child dies first, her children will inherit her share.

Per stirpes
Each branch of the family receives an equal share

Per capita
Each heir receives the same amount

The will must also indicate whether issue are to inherit *per stirpes* or *per capita*. **Per stirpes** means that each *branch* of the family receives an equal share. Thus, each child of the decedent receives the same amount, and, if a child has already died, her heirs inherit her share. **Per capita** means that each *heir* receives the same amount. If the children have died, then each grandchild inherits the same amount.

Suppose that Gwendolyn has two children, Lance and Arthur. Lance has one child; Arthur has four. Both sons predecease their mother. If Gwendolyn's will says"per stirpes," Lance's child will inherit her father's entire share, which is half of Gwendolyn's estate. Arthur's four children will share their father's portion, so each will receive one-eighth (¼ × ½). If Gwendolyn's will says, "per capita," each of her grandchildren will inherit one-fifth of her estate. Although it might sound fairer to give all grandchildren the same inheritance, most people choose a per stirpes distribution on the theory that they are treating their *children* equally. The chart on the next page illustrates the difference between per stirpes and per capita.

44-2d Digital Assets

Many people own digital assets with substantial value, both sentimental and financial, such as photos, music, movies, books, websites, blogs, social media accounts, email, software, client lists, bitcoins, and gaming accounts. If the owner dies, some of this content (such as family photos) should be shared with loved ones, but other items (use your imagination) are best kept private.

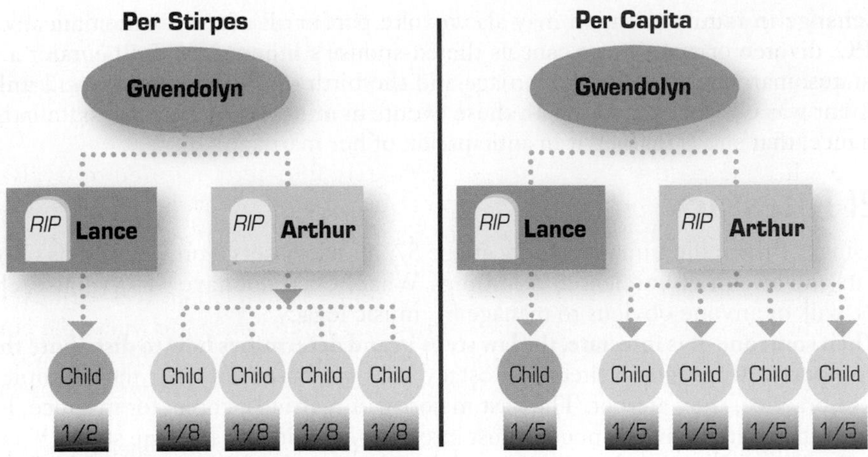

The rules on the inheritance of digital assets are based on:

- **Service provider policies.** Some of those terms and conditions (which we all agree to without reading), specify what happens after death (although many do not). For example:
  - Google has set up an Inactive Account Management system ("Inactive" is Googlese for "dead"). You can tell Google what to do when you become inactive: Either it can delete your whole account or you can specify who will have access to what.
  - Facebook now takes a similar approach. After 15-year-old Eric Rash committed suicide, his family hoped to find some explanation in his Facebook account, but the company would not grant them access. Then Facebook changed its policy to permit users to choose a "legacy contact" to manage their account after death. The legacy contact has the right to download an archive of posts, but is not allowed to see private messages. Users can also specify that Facebook delete their account. If the user makes neither choice, Facebook will, at the request of a family member and upon proof of death, either convert a user's timeline to a "memorial page" or deactivate it altogether. It will not reveal passwords.
- **Statutes.** Almost half the states have adopted the Uniform Fiduciary Access to Digital Assets Act. This statute permits a decedent to specify in his will who will inherit his digital assets. If he does not do so, his executor or administrator can access them and then either distribute them or dispose of them.

44-2e Amending a Will

A testator can generally revoke or alter a will at any time prior to death. In most states, he can revoke a will by destroying it, putting an *X* through it, writing "revoked" (or some synonym) on it, or signing a new will. He can also execute an amendment—called a **codicil**—to change specific terms of the will while keeping the rest of it intact. A codicil must meet all the requirements of a will, such as two witnesses. Suppose that Uncle Herman, who has a long and elaborate will, now wants his sterling silver Swiss Army knife to go to Cousin Larry rather than Niece Shannon. Instead of redoing his whole will, he can ask his lawyer to draw up a codicil changing only that one provision.

Codicil
An amendment to a will

A change in family situation may also revoke part or all of a will automatically. Under the UPC, divorce or annulment cancels the ex-spouse's inheritance rights under a will. In some states, marriage, divorce, or marriage and the birth of a child revoke a will unless the instrument was clearly executed with those events in mind. A testatrix can state in the will, for instance, that she is making it in anticipation of her marriage.

44-2f Intestacy

When singer Prince died unexpectedly at age 57, he had assets worth hundreds of millions of dollars and a vault of unreleased recordings. What he did not have was a spouse, children, parents, will, or anyone obvious to manage his music legacy.

When someone dies intestate, the law steps in and determines how to distribute the decedent's property. Although, in theory, intestacy laws are based on what most people would prefer, in practice, they are not. The vast majority of married people, for instance, leave all their assets to their surviving spouse. Most intestacy laws do not. In some states, if a married person dies intestate, some portion of her property (one-half or two-thirds) goes to her spouse, and the remainder to her issue (including grandchildren). Few people would actually want grandchildren to take a share of their estate in preference to their spouse. In other states, the decedent's estate is shared among her issue, her spouse, and her parents. If she has no issue, her spouse shares the estate with her parents. The moral of the story? As the late great law professor A. James Casner used to say, "Only a fool would die without a will."

44-2g Power of Attorney

A **power of attorney** is a document that permits the **attorney-in-fact** to act for the principal. (An attorney-in-fact need not be a lawyer.) Typically, a power of attorney expires if the principal revokes it, becomes incapacitated, or dies. But a **durable power** is valid even if the principal can no longer make decisions for herself. An **immediate power** becomes effective when signed; a **springing power** is effective at some time in the future, typically when the principal becomes incompetent and is no longer able to manage his affairs.

Lawyers generally recommend that their clients execute a durable power of attorney, particularly if they are elderly or in poor health. The power of attorney permits the client not only to choose an attorney-in-fact, but also to give advance instructions, such as "loan money to my son, Billy, if ever he needs it." If a client becomes incompetent and has no power of attorney, a court will appoint a conservator (to manage assets) and/or a guardian (to manage the person's daily life). As a general rule, it is better to make choices yourself rather than leave them to a court.

Kevin Mazur/Wirelmage/Getty Images

When he died, Prince had assets worth hundreds of millions of dollars but no will.

44-2h Probate

The testatrix cannot implement the terms of the will from beyond the grave, so she appoints an executor for this task. Typically, the executor is a family member, lawyer, or close friend. If the decedent does not select an executor, the probate court appoints an administrator to fulfill the same functions. The executor (or the administrator) has important responsibilities and, in a large estate, may spend a significant amount of time carrying out his functions. He has a fiduciary duty to the estate and is potentially liable to the heirs for any mistakes—from bad investment choices to errors in property valuation. Both the executor and the administrator are entitled to reasonable compensation—typically between 1 and 5 percent of the estate's value, although family members and friends often waive the fee.

44-2i Property Not Transferred by Will

A will does not control the distribution of retirement benefits, life insurance, or most joint property. As explained in Chapter 42, most property that is held in a joint tenancy automatically passes to the surviving owner, regardless of provisions in the decedent's will. This form of ownership is often used by family members—spouses or parents and children—as a simple method of transferring ownership without a will. Pension plans, other retirement benefits, and life insurance pass to whomever is named as beneficiary in the plans or policies themselves.

Life insurance
Provides for payments to a beneficiary upon the death of the insured

44-2j Anatomical Gifts

The demand for transplants of organs, such as hearts, corneas, kidneys, livers, pituitary glands, and even skin, is much greater than the supply. **You can register to be an organ donor:**

- Under the Uniform Anatomical Gift Act (UAGA), by putting a provision in your will or by signing an organ donation card in the presence of two witnesses;
- By using a smartphone app such as the Donate Life section of the iPhone Health app; or
- In some states, by signing up when you apply for or renew a driver's license.

The UAGA also provides that unless a decedent has affirmatively indicated her desire not to be a donor, family members have the right to make a gift of her organs after death.

44-2k End of Life Health Issues

Living Wills

Experts estimate that more than 75 percent of the population will not be capable of making their own medical decisions at the end of their lives. **Living wills (also called advance directives) allow people to:**

- Appoint a **healthcare proxy** to make decisions for them in the event that they become incompetent.
- Refuse, in advance, medical treatment that would, in their view, unreasonably prolong their lives, such as artificial feeding, cardiac resuscitation, or mechanical respiration. The Center for Ethics in Health Care offers POLST (Physician Orders for Life-Sustaining Treatment), which gives medical providers detailed instructions on specific interventions.
- Resolve disputes among family members. Terri Schiavo was only 26 years old when her heart stopped beating one evening, causing brain damage that put her in a persistent vegetative state. Her husband said she would not have wanted to live that way and asked to have her feeding tube removed; her parents disagreed and fought him through the courts. Even Congress intervened to try to keep the tube in place.

  Her husband ultimately prevailed and the tube was removed, but only after 15 years of litigation and public uproar. If Schiavo had had a living will, her family would have had more privacy, fewer legal bills, and, perhaps, greater peace.

Healthcare proxy
Someone who is appointed to make healthcare decisions on behalf of a person who is not competent to do so

If Schiavo had had a living will, her family would have had more privacy, fewer legal bills, and, perhaps, greater peace.

Physician-Assisted Death

Doctors are legally permitted to shorten a patient's life by withholding treatment. A handful of states—California, Colorado, Montana, Oregon, Vermont, and Washington—also allow doctors to prescribe a lethal dose of medication at the request of a terminal patient who is suffering intolerably. This process is called **physician-assisted death** or **assisted suicide**.

Physician-assisted death or assisted suicide
When a doctor prescribes a lethal dose of medication at the request of a terminal patient who is suffering intolerably

EXAMStrategy

Question: Tim's will leaves all his money to his cat, Princess Ida. After he dies, his widow and children claim that they are entitled to a share of his estate. Is this true? Will Princess Ida be living like royalty?

Strategy: The answer is different for his wife and children.

Result: Tim's wife is entitled to some percentage of his assets (which varies by state). His children have no automatic right to a share of his estate so long as he indicated in his will that they had been left out on purpose.

44-3 TRUSTS

Trusts are an increasingly popular method for managing assets, both during life and after death. A **trust** is an entity that separates legal and beneficial ownership. It involves three people: the **grantor** (also called the settlor or donor), who creates and funds it; the **trustee**, who manages the assets; and the **beneficiary**, who receives the financial proceeds. Although the trustee technically owns the property, she must use it for the good of the beneficiary. In other words, the trustee holds *legal* title, while the beneficiary holds *equitable* title. A grantor can create a trust during her lifetime or after her death through her will. **There are four requirements for establishing a trust:**

Trust
An entity that separates the legal and beneficial ownership of assets

Grantor
Someone who creates and funds a trust, also called a *settlor* or *donor*

Trustee
Someone who manages the assets of a trust

Beneficiary
Someone who receives the financial proceeds of a trust

1. **Legal capacity.** As with any contract, the grantor must be of legal age and sound mind.
2. **Trustee.** The grantor must appoint at least one trustee (who may be the grantor himself). The trust does not end if the appointed trustee dies or resigns. Either the trust instrument provides for successor trustees or a court can appoint one.
3. **Beneficiary.** A trust must have specific beneficiaries, although it need not list them by name. It can instead list a class, such as "living children of the grantors."
4. **Trust property.** The grantor must transfer specific assets to the trust, although these assets can be nominal. A grantor might, for instance, establish a trust with $10 and then add other assets later.

The Uniform Trust Code (UTC) establishes consistent laws on the creation and administration of trusts. More than half the states have passed some version of this code.

44-3a Advantages and Disadvantages

The advantages of a trust include:

- **Control.** The grantor can control her assets after her death. She can decide who gets how much when.

Suppose the grantor has a husband and children. She wants to provide her husband with adequate income after her death, but she does not want him to spend so lavishly that nothing is left for the children. Nor does she want him to spend all her money on his second wife. The grantor could create a trust in her will that allows her husband to spend the income and, upon his death, gives the principal to their children.

Real estate tycoon Leona Helmsley set up a trust providing that her grandchildren would only receive payments if they visited their father's grave. She also left a trust for her dog, Trouble.[6]

- **Caring for children.** Minor children cannot legally manage property on their own, so parents or grandparents often establish trusts to take care of assets until the children are of age.
- **Tax savings.** Although tax issues are beyond the scope of this chapter, it is worth noting that trusts can reduce estate taxes. For example, many married couples use a *marital trust* and parents or grandparents can establish *generation-skipping trusts* to reduce their estate tax bill.
- **Privacy.** A will is filed in probate court and becomes a matter of public record. Anyone can obtain a copy of it. Some companies are even in the business of providing copies to celebrity hounds. Jacqueline Kennedy Onassis's will is particularly popular. Trusts, however, are private documents and are not available to the public.
- **Probate.** Because a will must go through the often lengthy probate process, the heirs may not receive assets for some time. Assets that are put into a trust *before the grantor dies* do not go through probate; the beneficiaries have immediate access to them.
- **Protecting against creditors.** About a third of the states permit so-called **domestic asset protection trusts (DAPTs)**. Creditors have no right to reach any assets that a donor has placed in a DAPT, but the donor can spend the assets, as long as he has the trustees' permission. Hartwell has an unfortunate alcohol and drug problem, but he is no fool. When he inherited millions on his twenty-first birthday, he placed them all in an asset protection trust. Later, he married, had children, and got divorced. He also was in a car accident that caused the death of a young investment banker. Both his ex-wife and the banker's husband sued him, looking for financial support. But they are both out of luck. His assets are protected from all creditors. The downside: He can only spend trust assets with the trustee's permission, and they may not always agree on what constitutes reasonable payouts to him.

Domestic asset protection trusts (DAPTs)
Creditors cannot reach the assets that a donor has placed in a DAPT.

The major *disadvantage* of a trust is expense. Although it is always possible for the grantor to establish a trust himself with the aid of online tools, trusts are complex instruments with many potential pitfalls. In addition to the legal fees required to establish a trust, the trustees may have to be paid. Also, trust income taxes can be higher than if the assets are held by an individual.

44-3b Types of Trusts

Depending upon the goal in establishing a trust, a grantor has two choices.

6 Laura Saunders, "How to Control Your Heirs from the Grave," *The Wall Street Journal*, August 10, 2012.

Living Trust

Inter vivos trust or living trust
Established while the grantor is alive

Revocable
A trust that can be terminated or changed at any time

Also known as an **inter vivos trust**, a **living trust** is established while the grantor is still alive. In the typical living trust, the grantor serves as trustee during his lifetime. He maintains total control over the assets and avoids a trustee's fee. If the grantor becomes disabled or dies, the successor trustee, who is named in the trust instrument, takes over automatically. All of the assets stay in the trust and avoid probate. Most (but not all) living trusts are **revocable**, meaning that the grantor can terminate or change the trust at any time.

Testamentary Trust

Testamentary trust
A trust that goes into effect when a grantor dies

A **testamentary trust** is created by a will. It goes into effect when the grantor dies. Naturally, it is irrevocable because the grantor is dead. The grantor's property must first go through probate on its way to the trust. Many wealthy people use a testamentary trust to control their assets after death.

44-3c Trust Administration

The primary obligation of trustees is to carry out the terms of the trust. They may exercise any powers expressly granted to them in the trust instrument and any implied powers reasonably necessary to implement the terms of the trust, unless that power has been specifically prohibited. **In carrying out the terms of the trust, the trustees have a fiduciary duty to the beneficiary. This fiduciary duty includes:**

- **A duty of loyalty.** In managing the trust, the trustees must put the interests of the beneficiaries first and disclose any relevant information to them. Trustees may not commingle their own assets with those of the trust, do business with the trust (unless expressly permitted by the terms of the trust), or favor one beneficiary over another (unless permitted by the trust documents).
- **A duty of care.** The trustee must act as a reasonable person would when managing the assets of *another*. (This is a higher standard than requiring a trustee to act as a reasonable person would when managing his *own* affairs.) The trustee must make careful investments, keep accurate records, and collect debts owed the trust.

44-3d A Trust's Term

There are three possible outcomes for a trust: decanting, termination, or perpetual life.

Decanting

Decanting means pouring the assets out of one trust into another. This process can be used for two purposes: changing the terms of the original trust or distributing all of the trust assets to the beneficiaries. About half the states permit decanting, so long as the trustee has the power to make unlimited distributions to the beneficiaries but only a few states have passed the new Uniform Trust Decanting Act.

Trustees might want to decant a trust so that they can move the assets to a state with more favorable laws. Or so that they can change the payment schedule to beneficiaries—either to delay distributions if need be (the beneficiary is still in that cult) or hasten payments if appropriate (in time to start tuition payments). Typically, the trustee does not need approval from the beneficiaries. Suppose that an executive placed stock of his start-up company in a trust for his children. After the company's IPO, the trust is worth tens of millions of dollars. He does not want his offspring to have access to such a large sum at a young age, so he persuades the trustee to decant the funds into another trust with a later payout schedule.[7]

[7] Adapted from Liz Moyer, "When to 'Decant' a Trust," *The Wall Street Journal*, January 3, 2014.

Termination

A trust ends upon the occurrence of any of these events:

- On the date indicated by the grantor.
- If the trust is revocable, when revoked by the grantor. Even if the trust is irrevocable, the grantor and all the beneficiaries can agree to revoke it.
- When the purpose of the trust has been fulfilled. If the grantor established the trust to pay college tuition for his grandchildren, the trust ends when the last grandchild graduates.

Perpetual Trusts

The **Rule against Perpetuities** provides that a trust must end within 21 years of the death of some named person who was alive when the trust was created. This rule has been the law in England and the United States since the seventeenth century. Its goal is to ensure that trusts do not last forever.

Rule against Perpetuities
A trust must end within 21 years of the death of some named person who was alive when the trust was created.

However, more than half the states now permit so-called **perpetual** or **dynasty trusts**—trusts that last for hundreds of years, or sometimes forever. These trusts avoid estate taxes and generally allow donors to control their money. Whether eternal control is a good idea is best left to psychology texts.

Perpetual or dynasty trusts
Trusts that last forever

EXAMStrategy

Question: Maddie set up a trust for her children, with Field as trustee. Field decided to sell a piece of trust real estate to his wife, without obtaining an appraisal, attempting to market the property, or consulting a real estate agent. Maddie was furious and ordered him not to make the sale. Can she stop him? Would she have to go to court?

Strategy: The answer depends upon the type of trust she has established.

Result: If the trust is revocable, Maddie can simply terminate it and take the property back. If it is irrevocable, she could still prevent the sale by going to court because Field has violated the duties he owes to the beneficiaries. He has violated the duty of loyalty by selling trust property to his wife. He has violated the duty of care by failing to act as a reasonable person would in managing the assets of another.

44-4 INTRODUCTION TO INSURANCE

We are all at risk for injury, illness, fires, early death, and other catastrophes. It is no wonder that, from earliest times, people have sought insurance against these unpredictable dangers.

Insurance has its own terminology:

- **Person.** An individual, corporation, partnership, or any other legal entity
- **Insurance.** A contract in which one person, in return for a fee, agrees to guarantee another against loss caused by a specific type of danger
- **Insurer.** The person who issues the insurance policy and serves as guarantor
- **Insured.** The person whose loss is the subject of the insurance policy

- **Owner.** The person who enters into the insurance contract and pays the premiums
- **Premium.** The consideration that the owner pays under the policy
- **Beneficiary.** The person who receives the proceeds from the insurance policy

The beneficiary, the insured, and the owner can be, but are not necessarily, the same person. If a homeowner buys fire insurance for her house, she is the insured, the owner, and the beneficiary because she bought the policy and receives the proceeds if her house burns down. If a mother buys a life insurance policy on her son that is payable to his children in the event of his death, then the mother is the owner, the son is the insured, and the grandchildren are the beneficiaries.

Before beginning a study of insurance law, it is important to understand the economics of the insurance industry. Suppose that you have recently purchased a $500,000 house. The probability your house will burn down in the next year is 1 in 1,000. That is a low risk, but the consequences would be devastating, especially since you could not afford to rebuild. Instead of bearing that risk yourself, you take out a fire insurance policy. You pay an insurance company $1,200 in return for a promise that, if your house burns down in the next 12 months, the company will pay you $500,000. The insurance company sells the same policy to 1,000 similar homeowners, expecting that on average one of these houses will burn down. If all 1,000 policyholders pay $1,200, the insurance company takes in $1.2 million each year, but expects to pay out only $500,000. It will put some money aside in case two houses burn down, or even worse, a major forest fire guts a whole tract of houses. It must also pay overhead expenses, such as marketing and administration. And, of course, shareholders expect profits.

44-5 INSURANCE CONTRACT

An insurance policy must meet all the common law requirements for a contract. There must be an offer, acceptance, and consideration. The owner must have legal capacity; that is, he must be an adult of sound mind. Fraud, duress, and undue influence invalidate a policy. In theory, insurance contracts need not be in writing because the Statute of Frauds does not apply to any contract that can be performed within one year, and it is possible that the house may burn down or the car may crash within a year. Some states, however, specifically require insurance contracts to be in writing.

44-5a Offer and Acceptance

The purchaser of a policy makes an offer by delivering an application and a premium to the insurer. The insurance company then has the option of either accepting or rejecting the offer. **It can accept by oral notice, by written notice, or by delivery of the policy. It also has a fourth option—a written binder.** A **binder** is a short document acknowledging receipt of the application and premium. It indicates that a policy is *temporarily* in effect, but it does not constitute *final* acceptance. The insurer still has the right to reject the offer once it has examined the application carefully.

Binder
A short document acknowledging receipt of an application and premium for an insurance policy. It indicates that a policy is temporarily in effect.

Kyle buys a house on April 1 and wants insurance right away. The insurance company issues a binder to him the same day. If Kyle's house burns down on April 2, the insurer must pay, even though it has not yet issued the final policy. If, however, there is no fire, but on April 2, the company decides Kyle is a bad risk, it has the right to reject his application at that time.

44-5b Limiting Claims by the Insured

Insurance policies can sometimes look like a quick way to make easy money. More than one person suffering from overwhelming financial pressure has insured a building to the hilt and then burned it down for the insurance money. Unbelievably, more than one parent has killed a child to collect the proceeds of a life insurance policy. Therefore, the law has created a number of rules to protect insurance companies from fraud and bad faith on the part of insureds.

Insurable Interest

An insurance contract is not valid unless the owner has an insurable interest in the subject matter of the policy. Here is a tragic example of why an insurable interest is important. When Deana Wild, James Coates and his mother, Virginia Rearden, went for a walk along the edge of a cliff at Big Sur, Wild slipped and fell to her death. The day before this deadly walk, Rearden had taken out a $35,000 life insurance policy on Wild, naming Coates and Rearden as beneficiaries. But the policy was invalid because neither Reardon nor Coates had an insurable interest in the dead woman. Although Coates and Wild were supposedly engaged, Coates was actually married to someone else and, therefore, could not be Wild's fiancé. Ultimately, a jury determined that Rearden had pushed Wild over the cliff to collect on the policy and it convicted her of first degree murder.

These are the rules on insurable interest:

- **Definition.** A person has an insurable interest if she would be harmed by the danger that she has insured against. If Jessica takes out a fire insurance policy on her own barn, she will presumably be reluctant to burn it down. However, if she buys a policy on Nathan's barn, she will not mind—she could be delighted—when fire sweeps through the building. She may even burn the barn down herself.
- **Amount of loss.** The insurable interest can be no greater than the actual amount of loss suffered. If her barn is worth $50,000, but Jessica insures it (and pays premiums) for $100,000, she will recover only $50,000 when it burns down. The goal is to make sure that Jessica does not profit from the policy.
- **Life insurance.** A person always has an insurable interest in his own life and the life of his spouse or fiancée. Parents and minor children also have an insurable interest in each other. Creditors have a legitimate interest in someone who owes them money. For some states, the standard is that you have an insurable interest in someone if that person is worth more to you alive than dead.
- **Work relationships.** Business partners, employers, and employees have an insurable interest in each other if they would suffer some financial harm from the death of the insured. Companies sometimes buy **key person life insurance** on their officers to help the business recover if they were to die.

Ron Kacmarcik/Shutterstock.com

Virginia Rearden pushed Deanna Wild to her death from a Big Sur cliff. If the insurance company had known that Rearden did not have an insurable interest in Wild, the company would have refused to issue the policy, and Wild might not have died.

Key person life insurance
Companies buy insurance on their officers to help the companies recover if they were to die.

In the following case, one family entity owned some properties—and a different family company managed them. No one considered the issue of insurable interest when they purchased insurance. That was a mistake.

Banta Props. v. Arch Specialty Ins. Co.

553 Fed. Appx. 908
United States Court of Appeals for the Eleventh Circuit, 2014

Facts: The Banta family controlled a complex network of companies. One family company, Banta Family, owned three apartment complexes in Florida. A different family business, Banta Properties, managed these complexes in return for 4 percent of the gross income. Banta Properties bought $11 million in property insurance on the three complexes from Arch Specialty Insurance. Two months later, Hurricane Wilma badly damaged all three.

As a result of the hurricane damage, the apartments lost approximately $39,000 in rents. Banta Properties's share of those rents was about $1,600. It filed an insurance claim for $6.1 million, which was the cost to repair the damage that Wilma had caused to the apartments. Arch refused to pay, claiming that Banta Properties had no insurable interest in the complexes because it did not own them. At trial, the jury disagreed, valuing Banta Properties's insurable interest at $5 million.

Arch appealed.

Issue: ***Did Banta Properties have an insurable interest in the three apartment complexes?***

Excerpts from the Per Curiam Decision[8]: An insured does not need to own property to have an insurable interest. Instead, Florida law defines an insurable interest as a "substantial economic interest" in keeping the property "free from loss, destruction, or pecuniary damage or impairment." In sum, the measure of an insurable interest is the loss the insured might suffer from damage to the property.

Banta Properties actually had no property rights in the apartment complexes whatsoever. The only right Banta Properties had at the time of loss was the contractual right to receive 4 percent of gross income in exchange for its service as property manager. The sole injury Banta Properties could have suffered from the impairment or destruction of the apartment complexes was the loss of revenue from that contractual right. We conclude that Florida law thus limits the extent of Banta Properties's insurable interest to the potential loss of that revenue.

The Banta Family created numerous business entities to manage its business ventures. Consequently, they are bound to both the benefit and burden of the limited liability of the entities. The only plaintiff in this suit is Banta Properties, a company that obtained insurance for buildings it never owned, only managed. The sole injury Banta Properties suffered to its insurable interest due to Hurricane Wilma was $1,600, its 4 percent share of $39,000 in business interruption.

The judgment of the district court is reversed, and the case is remanded for entry of a judgment in favor of Arch.

Misrepresentation

Insurers have the right to void a policy if, during the application process, the insured makes a material misstatement or conceals a material fact. The policy is voidable whether the misstatement was oral or in writing, and in many states, whether it was intentional or unintentional. **Material** means that the misstatement or omission affected the insurer's decision to issue the policy or set a premium amount. Note that a lie can void a policy even if it does not relate to the actual loss.

Material
Important to the insurer's decision to issue a policy or set a premium amount

John Cummings tested positive for cocaine during a visit to a hospital for treatment of a gunshot wound to his chest. When he applied for life insurance six months later, he said on the application that, in the prior five years, he had not used any controlled drugs without a prescription by a physician. He also specifically denied using cocaine. A year later, Cummings died of a gunshot wound to his head. (He truly should have upgraded his social circle.) In investigating his death, the insurance company obtained medical records from the hospital which revealed the cocaine use. When the insurance company refused

[8] *Per curiam* is a Latin phrase that literally means "by the court." In other words, the decision was unanimous and no individual judge signed the opinion.

to pay, his beneficiary sued, but the court ruled that a misrepresentation can be material even if it is not related to the actual cause of death. Although the cocaine did not directly kill him, it certainly made him a riskier bet. If the company had known about his drug use, it would not have issued the policy or it would have demanded a higher premium. Cummings's policy was void.[9]

44-5c Bad Faith by the Insurer

Insurance policies often contain a *covenant of good faith and fair dealing.* Even if the policy itself does not *explicitly* include such a provision, an increasing number of courts (but not all) *imply* this covenant. **An insurance company can violate the covenant of good faith and fair dealing by:**

- Fraudulently inducing someone to buy a policy,
- Refusing to pay a valid claim, or
- Refusing to accept a reasonable settlement offer that has been made to an insured.

When an insurance company violates the covenant of good faith and fair dealing, it becomes liable for both compensatory and punitive damages.

Fraud

In recent years, some insurance companies have paid serious damages to settle fraud charges involving the sale of life insurance. The companies trained their salespeople to tell elderly customers that a new policy was better when, in fact, it was much worse. State Farm Insurance agreed to pay its customers $200 million to settle such a suit. Officials in Florida ordered Prudential Insurance Company of America to pay as much as $2 billion in damages after they determined that, for more than a decade, the company had deliberately cheated its customers.

Ethics

Presumably, the agents knew that defrauding elderly people was wrong. Why did they do it? What ethics traps did they face? How could you protect yourself from being in that situation?

Refusing to Pay a Valid Claim

Consumers complain that insurance companies too often act in bad faith by: refusing to pay legitimate claims; offering unreasonably low sums in settlement; or setting claims quotas that limit how much their adjusters can pay out each year, regardless of the merits of each individual claim. Perhaps because juries feel sympathy for those who must deal with an immovable bureaucracy, damage awards in these cases are often sizable, as the following case illustrates.

---

9 Cummings v. American General Life Insurance Co., 2008 U.S. Dist. LEXIS 37157, 2008 WL 1971323 (Fed. Dist. Ct. 2008).

Berg v. Nationwide Mut. Ins. Co.

2014 Pa. Dist. & Cnty. Dec. LEXIS 543
Common Pleas Court of Berks County, Pennsylvania, 2014

Facts: Sheryl Berg was in a serious accident while driving her Jeep Grand Cherokee. Luckily, she was not injured; unluckily, she had to deal with her insurance company, Nationwide Mutual.

A Nationwide appraiser determined that the Jeep was damaged beyond repair and recommended that the company pay her the value of the car, which was $25,000. In response, Nationwide brought in a second appraiser who decided the car should be repaired, which would cost only $12,500.

Although the car was in the shop for four months, Nationwide only provided a replacement car for the first month. After that, the Berg family had to travel in Mr. Berg's panel truck, with their son sitting on the floor in the back.

Even after four months, the car was not safe to drive: The frame was crooked and neither the headlights nor the airbags worked. Berg repeatedly returned the car to the repair shop, but it was never fixed. Despite her many requests for help, Nationwide did nothing until Berg's lease expired two years later. It then paid $18,000 to buy the car from the bank that had held her lease. Nationwide had the Jeep destroyed because it was worried about its liability if the bank sold the defective car to someone who was then injured. In short, Nationwide could have fairly settled with Berg for $25,000 but opted instead to pay over $30,500 ($12,500 for bad repairs, $18,000 to the bank, plus disposal fees) and risk Berg driving a dangerous car for two years.

In the past, it had been Nationwide's written policy to fight lawsuits at all cost. Even in cases where it made economic sense to settle, the company's goal was to be so unreasonable as to discourage other wronged customers from suing. A court in a prior case had ordered the company to end this policy.

The Bergs sued Nationwide for damages. During this litigation, Nationwide repeatedly hid evidence and violated discovery orders by refusing to turn over documents. It dragged out the litigation for 16 years, in the process spending more than $3 million in legal fees. (And also lying to the court about the amount of these fees.)

Berg then filed this suit alleging that Nationwide had acted in bad faith. She also sought punitive damages.

Issues: ***Did Nationwide act in bad faith? Should it pay punitive damages?***

Excerpts from Judge Sprecher's Decision: Defendant was reckless in handling this claim because it allowed an unsafe vehicle to be placed on the highway. Defendant was motivated [by] the 50% savings to Defendant to repair rather than replace the Jeep. The savings of approximately $12,500 when considered throughout the country for hundreds of other repair claims results in hundreds of thousands of dollars being saved by Defendant for each year that this strategy is in place.

Plaintiffs' attorneys undertook this case on a contingency fee basis. The high risk of losing the case was compounded by Defendant's concealment of evidence and its iron fisted litigation strategy. Plaintiffs' attorneys have not yet been paid anything for their effort and have funded this lawsuit for more than sixteen years at astonishing cost, risk, and exposure. [I]n the interest of fundamental fairness this court is reluctant to award counsel fees to the Plaintiffs in any amount less than Defendant paid its own attorneys who were paid timely and without risk.

In a bad faith case, the insured must prove that the insurer did not have a reasonable basis for denying benefits under the policy and that the insurer knew of or recklessly disregarded its lack of reasonable basis in denying the claim. To constitute bad faith it is not necessary that the refusal to pay be fraudulent; however, mere negligence or bad judgment is not bad faith. The insured must also show that the insurer breached the duty of good faith and fair dealing, through a motive of self-interest or ill will. [T]he insured Plaintiff must prove the insurers' bad faith by clear and convincing evidence, a higher burden than by preponderance of the evidence.

We live in a civilized society in which we solve disputes in a civilized manner through our courts of law. In our case, Nationwide strong armed its own policyholder rather than negotiating in good faith to compensate Plaintiff for the loss suffered in the automobile collision. Defendant applied extensive examples of bad faith in failing and refusing to disclose vital information to its policyholder and violated the rules of civil procedure by the same conduct with regard to discoverable documents and things relevant to the litigation.

What Defendant managed to do was send the ultimate message to Plaintiffs, their attorney, and [other lawyers]: 1) do not mess with us if you know what is good for you, 2) you cannot run with the big dogs, 3) there is no level playing field to be had in your case, 4) you cannot afford it, 5) we can get away with anything we want to, and 6) you cannot stop us.

Sadly, Defendant did wear down the Plaintiffs. Berg will never receive her due justice. After years of fighting for her life against the ravenous disease of cancer, she died just last month.

AND NOW, this court awards the following damages:

a. Interest on the amount of the claim from the date the claim was made in an amount equal to the prime rate of interest plus 3%.
b. Punitive damages in the amount of $18 million.
c. Court costs and attorney fees of $3 million.

Refusing to Accept a Settlement Offer

An insurer also violates the covenant of good faith and fair dealing when it wrongfully refuses to settle a claim. Suppose that Dmitri has a $100,000 automobile insurance policy. After he injures Tanya in a car accident, she sues him for $5 million. As provided in the policy, Dmitri's insurance company defends him against Tanya's claim. She offers to settle for $100,000, but the insurance company refuses because it only has $100,000 at risk anyway. It may get lucky with the jury. Instead, a jury comes in with a $2 million verdict. The insurance company is only liable for $100,000, but Dmitri must pay $1.9 million. A court might well find that the insurance company had violated its covenant of good faith and fair dealing and require it to pay the full amount.

EXAMStrategy

Question: Geoff takes out renters' insurance with Fastball Insurance Co. On the application where it asks if he has any pets, he fills in "poodle." Although he does not know it, his "poodle" is really a Portuguese water dog. The two breeds look a lot alike. A month later, his apartment is robbed. Fastball investigates and discovers that Geoff does not have a poodle after all. It denies his claim. Geoff files suit. What result?

Strategy: There are two issues here: Was Geoff's answer on the application a *material* misstatement? Was Fastball's denial in bad faith?

Result: Geoff's misrepresentation was not material—the difference between these two breeds of dog would not have affected liability on the renter's policy. If he had said he had an attack dog such as a Doberman, perhaps the premium would have been lower because the dog would scare off intruders (or higher because the dog would also attack friends and neighbors), but poodles and Portuguese water dogs are equally friendly. Fastball could be liable for refusing to pay this legitimate claim.

44-6 TYPES OF INSURANCE

Insurance is available for virtually any risk. Bruce Springsteen insured his voice and Rihanna her legs. When Kerry Wallace shaved her head to promote the *Star Trek* films, she bought insurance in case her hair failed to grow back. Afraid of alien abduction? There is insurance for that, too. Most people, however, get by with six different types of insurance: property, life, health, disability, liability, and automobile.

Rihanna insured her legs for $1 million.

44-6a Property Insurance

Property insurance (also known as *casualty insurance*) covers physical damage to real estate, personal property (boats, furnishings), or inventory from causes such as fire, smoke, lightning, wind, riot, vandalism, or theft.

44-6b Life Insurance

Life insurance is really death insurance—it provides for payments to a beneficiary upon the death of the insured. The purpose is to replace at least some of the insured's income to protect his family or his employer.

Term Insurance

Term insurance is the simplest, cheapest life insurance option. It is purchased for a specific period, such as 1, 5, or 20 years. If the insured dies during the period of the policy, the insurance company pays the policy amount to the beneficiary. If the owner stops paying premiums, the policy terminates and the beneficiary receives nothing. The premiums do not rise during the term of the policy, but they may each time it is renewed. A $200,000 10-year term policy on a 25-year-old nonsmoking woman in good health costs as little as $110 annually; at age 60, the same policy costs about $480. Term insurance is the best choice for someone who simply wants to protect his family by replacing his income if he dies before retirement.

Whole Life Insurance

Whole life (also called *straight life*) insurance is designed to cover the insured for his entire life. A portion of the premiums pays for insurance, and the remainder goes into savings. This savings portion is called the cash value of the policy. The company pays dividends on this cash value and typically, after some years, the dividends are large enough to cover the premium so that the owner does not have to pay any more. The cash value accrues without being taxed until the policy is cashed in. The owner can borrow against the cash value, in many cases at a below-market rate. In addition, if the owner cancels the policy, the insurance company will pay her the policy's cash value. When the owner purchases the policy, the company typically sets a premium that stays constant over the life of the policy. A healthy 25-year-old nonsmoking woman pays annual premiums of roughly $2,000 per year on a $200,000 policy.

The advantage of a whole life policy is that it forces people to save. It also has some significant disadvantages:

- The investment returns from the savings portion of whole life insurance have traditionally been mediocre. Mutual funds may offer better investment opportunities.
- A significant portion of the premium for the first year goes to pay overhead and commissions. Insurance agents have a great incentive to sell whole life policies, rather than term, because their commissions are much higher.
- Unless the customer holds a policy for about 20 years, it will typically generate little cash value. Half of all whole life policyholders drop their policies in the first seven or eight years. At that point, the policy has generated little more than commissions for the agent.

- Whole life insurance provides the same amount of insurance throughout the insured's life. Most people need more insurance when they have young children and less as they approach retirement age.

Universal Life

Universal life insurance is a flexible combination of whole life and term. The owner can adjust the premiums over the life of the policy and also adjust the allocation of the premiums between insurance and savings. The options are sometimes so complex that customers have difficulty understanding them.

Annuities

As life expectancy has increased, people have begun to worry as much about supporting themselves in their old age as they do about dying young. **Annuities** are the reverse of life insurance—they make payments *until* death, whereas life insurance pays *after* death. In the basic annuity contract, the owner makes a lump-sum payment to an insurance company in return for a fixed annual income for the rest of her life, no matter how long she lives. If she dies tomorrow, the insurance company makes a huge profit. If she lives to be 95, the company loses money. But whatever happens, she knows she will have income until the day she dies.

Annuity
Provides payment to a beneficiary during his lifetime

In a **deferred annuity contract**, the owner makes a lump-sum payment now but receives no income until some later date, say, in 10 or 20 years when he retires. From that date forward, he will receive payments for the rest of his life.

Deferred annuity contract
The owner makes a lump-sum payment now but receives no income until a later date

44-6c Health Insurance

Traditional health insurance plans are *pay for service*. The insurer pays for virtually any treatment that any doctor orders. The good news under this system is that policyholders have the largest possible choice of doctor and treatment. The bad news is that doctors and patients have an incentive to overspend on health care because the insurance company picks up the tab. Complexity and quantity are rewarded, not outcomes. It has been estimated that as many as one-third of the medical procedures performed in pay for service plans have little medical justification, which in the end is not good for the patient. As a surgeon once said, "There is no condition so bad I can't make it worse by operating."

Pay for service plans
The insurer pays for whatever treatments a doctor orders

Instead of, or in addition to, pay for service plans, many insurers offer *managed care plans*. There are many variations on this theme, but they all work to limit treatment choices. In some plans, the patient has a primary care physician who must approve all visits to specialists. In ***health maintenance organizations***, known as ***HMOs***, the patient can be treated only by doctors in the organization unless there is some extraordinary need for an outside specialist. Patients are sometimes resentful of these constraints.

Managed care plans
Health insurance plans that limit treatment choices to reduce costs

Health maintenance organization (HMO)
Generally, patients can only be treated by doctors who are employees of the organization.

Currently, the federal government is encouraging a third option, so-called *value-based care*. The idea is that medical providers, operating in *accountable care organizations*, are paid based on patient outcomes, not quantity and complexity of services performed. Thus, doctors could receive a bonus for reducing avoidable hospital readmissions. Conversely, hospitals may not be paid to treat preventable conditions, such as bedsores. Finding the right level of medical care and choice is a complex problem.

Value-based care
Payment to medical providers is based on patient outcomes, not quantity and complexity of services performed.

44-6d Disability Insurance

Disability insurance replaces the insured's income if he becomes unable to work because of illness or injury. Perhaps you are thinking, "That will never happen to me." In fact, the average person is seven times more likely to be disabled for at least 90 days than

Disability insurance
Replaces the insured's income if he becomes unable to work because of illness or injury

he is to die before age 65. A significant percentage of all mortgage foreclosures are caused by an owner's disability. Everyone should have disability insurance to replace between 60 and 75 percent of their income. (There is no need for 100 percent replacement because expenses while unemployed are lower.) Many employers provide disability protection.

44-6e Liability Insurance

Liability insurance
Reimburses the insured for any liability she incurs by accidentally harming someone else

Most insurance—property, life, health, disability—is designed to reimburse the insured (or his family) for any harm he suffers. **Liability insurance** is different. **Its purpose is to reimburse the insured for any liability he incurs by (accidentally) harming someone else. Personal liability insurance covers tort claims by:**

- Those injured on property owned by the insured—the mail carrier who slips and falls on the front sidewalk or the parents of the child who drowns in the pool,
- Those injured by the insured away from home or business—the jogger knocked down by an insured who loses control of his skateboard, and
- Those whose property is damaged by the insured—the owner whose stone wall is pulverized by the insured's swerving car.

These are the types of claims covered in a *personal* liability policy. ***Business*** **liability policies may also protect against other sorts of claims:**

- Professional malpractice protects accountants, architects, doctors, engineers, or lawyers against claims of wrongdoing.
- Product liability covers any injuries caused by the company's products.
- Employment practices liability insurance protects employers against claims of sexual harassment, discrimination, and wrongful termination on the part of an employee. Note that this insurance typically does not protect the person who actually commits the wrongdoing—the sexual harasser, for instance—but it does protect the innocent insureds, such as the company itself.

44-6f Automobile Insurance

An automobile insurance policy is a combination of several different types of coverage that, depending on state law, are either mandatory or optional. **These are the basic types of coverage:**

- **Collision** covers the cost of repairing or replacing a car that is damaged in an accident.
- **Comprehensive** covers fire, theft, and vandalism—but not collision.
- **Liability** covers harm that the owner causes to other people or their property—such as their bodies, cars, or fences. Most states require drivers to carry liability insurance.
- **Personal injury protection** pays the medical expenses and lost wages of the owner, his passengers, and anyone living in his house or authorized to drive the car.
- **Uninsured motorist** covers the owner and anyone else in the car who is injured by a driver without insurance.

CHAPTER CONCLUSION

Life is a risky business. Cars crash, houses burn, people die. So what can we do? Sign a will, buy insurance, and get on with our lives, knowing that we have prepared as best we can.

EXAM REVIEW

1. **WILL** A legal document that disposes of the testator's property after death.
2. **HOLOGRAPHIC WILL** A will that is handwritten and signed by the testatrix but not witnessed.
3. **NUNCUPATIVE WILL** The formal term for an oral will.

EXAMStrategy

Question: If you were in an emergency situation and desperately wanted to prepare a new will, under what circumstances would a holographic will be preferable to the nuncupative option?

Strategy: The two types of wills have different requirements for witnesses. (See the "Result" at the end of this Exam Review section.)

4. **SURVIVING SPOUSE AND CHILDREN** A spouse is entitled to a certain share of the decedent's estate. Children have no automatic right to share in a parent's estate as long as the parent indicates in his will that the pretermitted children have been left out on purpose.

EXAMStrategy

Question: Josh was a grouchy fellow, often at odds with his family. In his will, he left his son an autographed copy of his book, *A Guide to Federal Prisons*. He completely omitted his daughter, instead leaving the rest of his substantial estate to the Society for the Assistance of Convicted Felons. Which child fared better?

Strategy: Pretermitted children fare differently from those named in the will. (See the "Result" at the end of this Exam Review section.)

5. **PER STIRPES V. PER CAPITA** In a will, a per stirpes distribution means that each *branch* of the family receives an equal share. Per capita means that each *heir* receives the same amount.

6. **REVOCATION OF A WILL** A testator may generally revoke or alter a will at any time prior to death.

7. **INTESTACY** Dying without a will. In this event, the law determines how the decedent's property will be distributed.

8. **PROPERTY NOT COVERED BY A WILL** A will does not control the distribution of retirement benefits, life insurance, or most joint property.

9. **LIVING WILL** A living will allows people to appoint a healthcare proxy and/or refuse medical treatment that would prolong life.

10. **PHYSICIAN-ASSISTED DEATH** Physician-assisted death occurs when a doctor prescribes a lethal dose of medication at the request of a terminal patient who is suffering intolerably.

11. **TRUST** A trust is an entity that separates legal and beneficial ownership.

12. **TRUSTEE'S DUTY** In carrying out the terms of a trust, the trustee has a fiduciary duty to the beneficiary.

13. **TRUST'S TERM** There are three possible outcomes for a trust: decanting, termination, or perpetual life.

14. **INSURANCE CONTRACT** An insurance policy must meet all the common law requirements for a contract—offer, acceptance, consideration, and legal capacity.

15. **INSURABLE INTEREST** A person has an insurable interest if she would be harmed by the danger that she has insured against.

16. **MATERIAL MISREPRESENTATION** Insurers have the right to void a policy if the insured makes a material misstatement or conceals a material fact.

EXAMStrategy

Question: When Mark applied for life insurance with Farmstead, he indicated on the application that he had not received any traffic tickets in the preceding five years. In fact, he had received several such citations for driving while intoxicated. Two years later, Mark was shot to death. When Farmstead discovered the traffic tickets, it denied coverage to his beneficiary. Was Farmstead in the right?

Strategy: A misrepresentation is material if it affects the insurer's decision to issue a policy or set a premium amount. (See the "Result" at the end of this Exam Review section.)

17. **BAD FAITH BY INSURER** Many courts have held that insurance policies contain a covenant of good faith and fair dealing and have found insurance companies liable for compensatory and punitive damages if they commit fraud, refuse to pay legitimate claims in a timely manner, or wrongfully refuse to settle a claim.

18. **PROPERTY INSURANCE** Property insurance covers physical damage to real estate, personal property (boats, furnishings), or inventory from causes such as fire, smoke, lightning, wind, riot, vandalism, or theft.

19. **ANNUITIES** Annuities are the reverse of life insurance policies; they make payments *until* death.

20. **HEALTH INSURANCE** Health insurance is available in pay for service plans, managed care plans, or HMOs. Some doctors and hospitals are now experimenting with value-based care.

21. **DISABILITY INSURANCE** Disability insurance replaces the insured's income if he becomes unable to work because of illness or injury.

22. **LIABILITY INSURANCE** Liability insurance reimburses the insured for any liability that she incurs by accidentally harming someone else.

23. **AUTOMOBILE INSURANCE** Basic automobile insurance includes collision, comprehensive, liability, personal injury protection, and uninsured motorist.

RESULTS

3. Result: A holographic will does not require witnesses; a nuncupative will requires two.

4. Result: Because the son was not totally omitted from the will, he is entitled to nothing more than the book, while the daughter who received nothing under the will gets more than her brother—she receives whatever share she would be entitled to if Josh had died intestate.

16. Result: If Mark had told the truth, Farmstead still would have issued the policy, but the premium would have been higher. It can refuse to pay the claim, even though the issue that he lied about was not a factor in his death.

MULTIPLE-CHOICE QUESTIONS

1. **CPA QUESTION** A decedent's will provided that the estate was to be divided among the decedent's issue per capita and not per stirpes. If there are two surviving children and three grandchildren who are children of a predeceased child at the time the will is probated, how will the estate be divided?
   (a) 1/2 to each surviving child
   (b) 1/3 to each surviving child and 1/9 to each grandchild
   (c) 1/4 to each surviving child and 1/6 to each grandchild
   (d) 1/5 to each surviving child and grandchild

2. Hallie is telling her cousin Anne about the will she has just executed. "Because of my broken arm, I couldn't sign my name, so I just told Bertrand, the lawyer, to sign it for me. Bertrand was also the witness to the will." Anne said, "You made a big mistake:

   I. "You should have made at least some sort of mark on the paper."

   II. "The lawyer is not permitted to witness the will."

   III. "You did not have enough witnesses."

   Which of Anne's statements is true?

   (a) I, II, and III
   (b) Neither I, II, nor III
   (c) Just I
   (d) Just II
   (e) Just III

3. Blake tells his client that there are five good reasons to set up a trust. Which of the following is *not* a good reason?

   (a) To pay his grandchildren's college tuition if they go to the same college he attended
   (b) To save money, since setting up a trust is cheaper than a will
   (c) To make sure the money is properly invested
   (d) To avoid probate
   (e) To safeguard his privacy

4. A(n) _______________power of attorney becomes effective when signed. A(n) _______________ power of attorney becomes effective at a later date. A(n) _______________ power of attorney is valid even if the principal becomes incapacitated.

   (a) durable; springing; immediate
   (b) springing; durable; durable
   (c) immediate; springing; durable
   (d) immediate; durable; durable

5. If Chip buys an insurance policy covering his daughter Sarah's apartment, then _______________is the insured, _______________ is the beneficiary, and _______________ is the owner.

   (a) Sarah; Sarah; Sarah
   (b) Chip; Chip; Chip
   (c) Sarah; Chip; Chip
   (d) Sarah; Sarah; Chip

CASE QUESTIONS

1. If your grandparents were to die leaving a large estate, and all of their children were also dead, would you have a larger inheritance under a per stirpes or a per capita distribution?

2. ***YOU BE THE JUDGE* WRITING PROBLEM** Linda and Eddie had two children before they were divorced. Under the terms of their divorce, Eddie became the owner of their house. When he died suddenly, their children inherited the property. Linda moved into the house with the children and began paying the mortgage that was in Eddie's name. She also took out fire insurance. When the house burned down, the insurance company refused to pay the policy because she did not have an insurable interest. Do you agree? **Argument for the Insurance Company:** Linda did not own the house; therefore, she had no insurable interest. **Argument for Linda:** She was harmed when the house burned down because she and her children had no place to live. She was paying the mortgage, so she also had a financial interest.

3. Dannie Harvey sued her employer, O. R. Whitaker, for sexual harassment, discrimination, and defamation. Whitaker counterclaimed for libel and slander, requesting $1 million in punitive damages. Both Whitaker and Harvey were insured by Allstate under identical homeowner's policies. This policy explicitly promised to defend Harvey against the exact claim Whitaker had made against her. Harvey's Allstate agent, however, told her that she was not covered. Because the agent kept all copies of Harvey's insurance policies in his office, she took him at his word. She had no choice but to defend against the claim on her own. Whitaker mounted an exceedingly hostile litigation attack, taking 80 depositions. After a year, Allstate agreed to defend Harvey. However, instead of hiring the lawyer who had been representing her, it chose another lawyer who had no expertise in this type of case and was a close friend of Whitaker's attorney. Harvey's new lawyer refused to meet her or to attend any depositions. Harvey and Whitaker finally settled. Whitaker had spent $1 million in legal fees, Harvey $169,000, and Allstate $2,513. Does Harvey have a claim against Allstate?

4. When Gregg died, his will left his money equally to his two children, Max and Alison, whom he explicitly named. Max had died a few years earlier, leaving behind a widow and four children. Who will get Gregg's money?

5. Suzy Tomlinson, 74, met a tragic end—she drowned, fully clothed, in her bathtub after a night out partying with 36-year-old J.B. Carlson. He had taken her home at 1:00 a.m. and was the last person to see her alive. The two were not only party buddies; Suzy was on the board of directors of a company J.B. had started. Her family was stunned to find out that she had a $15 million life insurance policy, with the proceeds payable to a company J.B. controlled. He said it was a key person policy. He wanted to protect the company if she died because she had frequently introduced him to potential investors. Is the life insurance policy valid?

DISCUSSION QUESTIONS

1. **ETHICS** Donna and Carl Nichols each bought term life insurance from Prudential Insurance Company of America. These policies contained a provision stating that if the insured became disabled, the premiums did not have to be paid and the policy would still stay in effect. This term is called a *waiver of premium*. Carl became totally disabled, and his premiums were waived. Some years later, two Prudential

sales managers convinced the Nicholses to convert their term life insurance policies into whole life policies. They promised that, once Carl made the conversion, he would only have to pay premiums on the new policy for a six-month waiting period. They even wrote "WP to be included in this policy" on the application form. "WP" stood for waiver of premium benefit. Only after the new policy was issued did the Nicholses learn that Prudential would not waive the premium. The Nicholses had exchanged a policy on which they owed nothing further for a policy on which they now had to pay premiums that they could not afford. Do the Nicholses have a claim against Prudential? Regardless of the legal outcome, did Prudential have an ethical obligation to the Nicholses?

2. Should you have a will? Do you have one?

3. **ETHICS** Is an asset protection trust ethical? Should wealthy people be able to avoid paying legitimate creditors? What about perpetual trusts that avoid estate taxes forever? Legislators pass laws that permit such trusts to attract trust business from out of state. Trusts generate billions of dollars in fees each year. If you were a state legislator, how would you vote when this legislation came up for approval? If you had substantial assets, would you put them in such a trust? What Life Principles apply here?

4. Billionaire Warren Buffett said that children should inherit enough money so that they can do anything, but not so much that they can do nothing. Is it good for people to inherit money? How much? At what age? How much would you like to leave your children?

5. **ETHICS** Life insurance policies place the burden on beneficiaries to notify the insurance company when an insured dies. The company itself has no obligation to hunt down the heirs of dead customers. But sometimes beneficiaries do not know that their relative had a policy. Some state authorities are now requiring insurance companies to run a list of their policy owners through a database of people who have died. But the insurance companies are objecting because, they say, they priced the policies originally on the assumption that a certain percentage of them would never be paid. What is the ethical choice for insurers? What would Kant or Mill say?

APPENDIX A

THE CONSTITUTION OF THE UNITED STATES

Preamble We the People of the United States, in Order to form a more perfect Union, establish Justice, insure domestic Tranquility, provide for the common defense, promote the general Welfare, and secure the Blessings of Liberty to ourselves and our Posterity, do ordain and establish this Constitution for the United States of America.

ARTICLE I

Section 1. All legislative Powers herein granted shall be vested in a Congress of the United States, which shall consist of a Senate and House of Representatives.

Section 2. The House of Representatives shall be composed of Members chosen every second Year by the People of the several States, and the Electors in each State shall have the Qualifications requisite for Electors of the most numerous Branch of the State Legislature.

No Person shall be a Representative who shall not have attained to the Age of twenty five Years, and been seven Years a Citizen of the United States, and who shall not, when elected, be an Inhabitant of that State in which he shall be chosen.

Representatives and direct Taxes shall be apportioned among the several States which may be included within this Union, according to their respective Numbers, which shall be determined by adding to the whole Number of free Persons, including those bound to Service for a Term of Years, and excluding Indians not taxed, three fifths of all other Persons. The actual Enumeration shall be made within three Years after the first Meeting of the Congress of the United States, and within every subsequent Term of ten Years, in such Manner as they shall by Law direct. The number of Representatives shall not exceed one for every thirty Thousand, but each State shall have at Least one Representative; and until such enumeration shall be made, the State of New Hampshire shall be entitled to chuse three, Massachusetts eight, Rhode Island and Providence Plantations one, Connecticut five, New-York six, New Jersey four, Pennsylvania eight, Delaware one, Maryland six, Virginia ten, North Carolina five, South Carolina five, and Georgia three.

When vacancies happen in the Representation from any State, the Executive Authority thereof shall issue Writs of Election to fill such vacancies.

The House of Representatives shall chuse their Speaker and other Officers; and shall have the sole Power of Impeachment.

Section 3.

The Senate of the United States shall be composed of two Senators from each State, chosen by the Legislature thereof, for six Years; and each Senator shall have one Vote.

Immediately after they shall be assembled in Consequence of the first Election, they shall be divided as equally as may be into three Classes. The Seats of the Senators of the first Class shall be vacated at the Expiration of the second Year, of the second Class at the Expiration of the fourth Year, and of the third Class at the Expiration of the sixth Year, so that one third may be chosen every second Year; and if Vacancies happen by Resignation or otherwise, during the Recess of the Legislature of any State, the Executive thereof may make temporary Appointments until the next Meeting of the Legislature, which shall then fill such Vacancies.

No Person shall be a Senator who shall not have attained to the Age of thirty Years, and been nine Years a Citizen of the United States, and who shall not, when elected, be an Inhabitant of that State for which he shall be chosen.

The Vice President of the United States shall be President of the Senate, but shall have no Vote, unless they be equally divided.

The Senate shall chuse their other Officers, and also a President pro tempore, in the Absence of the Vice President, or when he shall exercise the Office of President of the United States.

The Senate shall have the sole power to try all Impeachments. When sitting for that Purpose, they shall be an Oath or Affirmation. When the President of the United States is tried, the Chief Justice shall preside: And no Person shall be convicted without the Concurrence of two thirds of the Members present.

Judgment in Cases of Impeachment shall not extend further than to removal from Office, and disqualification to hold and enjoy any Office of honor, Trust or Profit under the United States: but the Party convicted shall nevertheless be liable and subject to Indictment, Trial, Judgment and Punishment, according to Law.

Section 4.

The Times, Places and Manner of holding Elections for Senators and Representatives, shall be prescribed in each State by the Legislature thereof: but the Congress may at any time by Law make or alter such Regulations, except as to the Places of chusing Senators.

The Congress shall assemble at least once in every Year, and such Meeting shall be on the first Monday in December, unless they shall by Law appoint a different Day.

Section 5.

Each House shall be the Judge of the Elections, Returns and Qualifications of its own Members, and a Majority of each shall constitute a Quorum to do Business; but a smaller Number may adjourn from day to day, and may be authorized to compel the Attendance of absent Members, in such Manner, and under such Penalties as each House may provide.

Each House may determine the Rules of its Proceedings, punish its Members for disorderly Behaviour, and, with the Concurrence of two thirds, expel a Member.

Each House shall keep a Journal of its Proceedings, and from time to time publish the same, excepting such Parts as may in their Judgment require Secrecy; and the Yeas and Nays of the Members of either House on any question shall, at the Desire of one fifth of those Present, be entered on the Journal.

Neither House, during the Session of Congress, shall, without the Consent of the other, adjourn for more than three days, nor to any other Place than that in which the two Houses shall be sitting.

Section 6. The Senators and Representatives shall receive a Compensation for their Services, to be ascertained by Law, and paid out of the Treasury of the United States. They shall in all Cases, except Treason, Felony and Breach of the Peace, be privileged from Arrest during their Attendance at the Session of their respective Houses, and in going to and returning from the same; and for any Speech or Debate in either House, they shall not be questioned in any other Place.

No Senator or Representative shall, during the Time for which he was elected, be appointed to any civil Office under the Authority of the United States, which shall have been created, or the Emoluments whereof shall have been encreased during such time; and no Person holding any Office under the United States, shall be a Member of either House during his Continuance in Office.

Section 7. All Bills for raising Revenue shall originate in the House of Representatives; but the Senate may propose or concur with Amendments as on other Bills.

Every Bill which shall have passed the House of Representatives and the Senate, shall, before it become a Law, be presented to the President of the United States; If he approve he shall sign it, but if not he shall return it, with his Objections to that House in which it shall have originated, who shall enter the Objections at large on their Journal, and proceed to reconsider it. If after such Reconsideration two thirds of that House shall agree to pass the Bill, it shall be sent, together with the Objections, to the other House, by which it shall likewise be reconsidered, and if approved by two thirds of that House, it shall become a Law. But in all such Cases the Votes of both Houses shall be determined by Yeas and Nays, and the Names of the Persons voting for and against the Bill shall be entered on the Journal of each House respectively. If any Bill shall not be returned by the President within ten Days (Sundays excepted) after it shall have been presented to him, the Same shall be a Law, in like Manner as if he had signed it, unless the Congress by their Adjournment prevent its Return, in which Case it shall not be a Law.

Every Order, Resolution, or Vote to which the Concurrence of the Senate and House of Representatives may be necessary (except on a question of Adjournment) shall be presented to the President of the United States; and before the Same shall take Effect, shall be approved by him, or being disapproved by him, shall be repassed by two thirds of the Senate and House of Representatives, according to the Rules and Limitations prescribed in the Case of a Bill.

Section 8. The Congress shall have Power to lay and collect Taxes, Duties, Imposts and Excises, to pay the Debts and provide for the common Defence and general Welfare of the United States; but all Duties, Imposts and Excises shall be uniform throughout the United States;

To borrow Money on the credit of the United States;

To regulate Commerce with foreign Nations, and among the several States, and with the Indian Tribes;

To establish an uniform Rule of Naturalization, and uniform Laws on the subject of Bankruptcies throughout the United States;

To coin Money, regulate the Value thereof, and of foreign Coin, and fix the Standard of Weights and Measures;

To provide for the Punishment of counterfeiting the Securities and current Coin of the United States;

To establish Post Offices and post Roads;

To promote the Progress of Science and useful Arts, by securing for limited Times to Authors and Inventors the exclusive Right to their respective Writings and Discoveries;

To constitute Tribunals inferior to the Supreme Court;

To define and punish Piracies and Felonies committed on the high Seas, and Offenses against the Law of Nations;

To declare War, grant Letters of Marque and Reprisal, and make Rules concerning Captures on Land and Water;

To raise and support Armies, but no Appropriation of Money to that Use shall be for a longer Term than two Years;

To provide and maintain a Navy;

To make Rules for the Government and Regulation of the land and naval Forces;

To provide for calling forth the Militia to execute the Laws of the Union, suppress Insurrections and repel Invasions;

To provide for organizing, arming, and disciplining, the Militia, and for governing such Part of them as may be employed in the Service of the United States, reserving to the States respectively, the Appointment of the Officers, and the Authority of training the Militia according to the discipline described by Congress;

To exercise exclusive Legislation in all Cases whatsoever, over such District (not exceeding ten Miles square) as may, by Cession of particular States, and the Acceptance of Congress, become the Seat of the Government of the United States, and to exercise like Authority over all Places purchased by the Consent of the Legislature of the State in which the Same shall be, for the Erection of Forts, Magazines, Arsenals, dock-Yards, and other needful Buildings;—And To make all Laws which shall be necessary and proper for carrying into Execution the foregoing Powers, and all other Powers vested by this Constitution in the Government of the United States, or in any Department or Officer thereof.

Section 9.

The Migration or Importation of such Persons as any of the States now existing shall think proper to admit, shall not be prohibited by the Congress prior to the Year one thousand eight hundred and eight, but a Tax or Duty may be imposed on such Importation, not exceeding ten dollars for each Person.

The Privilege of the Writ of Habeas Corpus shall not be suspended, unless when in Cases of Rebellion or Invasion the public Safety may require it.

No Bill of Attainder or ex post facto Law shall be passed.

No Capitation, or other direct, Tax shall be laid, unless in Proportion to the Census or Enumeration herein before directed to be taken.

No Tax or Duty shall be laid on Articles exported from any State.

No Preference shall be given by any Regulation of Commerce or Revenue to the Ports of one State over those of another; nor shall Vessels bound to, or from, one State, be obliged to enter, clear, or pay Duties in another.

No Money shall be drawn from the Treasury, but in Consequence of Appropriations made by Laws; and a regular Statement and Account of the Receipts and Expenditures of all public Money shall be published from time to time.

No Title of Nobility shall be granted by the United States: And no Person holding any Office of Profit or Trust under them, shall, without the Consent of the Congress, accept of any present, Emolument, Office, or Title, of any kind whatever, from any King, Prince, or foreign State.

Section 10.

No State shall enter into any Treaty, Alliance, or Confederation; grant Letters of Marque and Reprisal; coin Money; emit Bills of Credit; make any Thing but gold and silver Coin a Tender in Payment of Debts; pass any Bill of Attainder, ex post facto Law, or Law impairing the Obligation of Contracts, or grant any Title of Nobility.

No State shall, without the Consent of the Congress, lay any Imposts or Duties on Imports or Exports, except what may be absolutely necessary for executing its inspection Laws: and the net Produce of all Duties and Imposts, laid by any State on Imports or Exports, shall be for the Use of the Treasury of the United States; and all such Laws shall be subject to the Revision and Controul of the Congress.

No State shall, without the Consent of Congress, lay any Duty of Tonnage, keep Troops, or Ships of War in time of Peace, enter into any Agreement or Compact with another State, or with a foreign Power, or engage in War, unless actually invaded, or in such imminent Danger as will not admit of delay.

ARTICLE II

Section 1.

The executive Power shall be vested in a President of the United States of America. He shall hold his Office during the Term of four Years, and, together with the Vice President, chosen for the same Term, be elected, as follows:

Each State shall appoint, in such Manner as the Legislature thereof may direct, a Number of Electors, equal to the whole Number of Senators and Representatives to which the State may be entitled in the Congress: but no Senator or Representative, or Person holding an Office of Trust or Profit under the United States, shall be appointed an Elector.

The Electors shall meet in their respective States, and vote by Ballot for two Persons, of whom one at least shall not be an Inhabitant of the same State with themselves. And they shall make a list of all the Persons voted for, and of the Number of Votes for each; which List they shall sign and certify, and transmit sealed to the Seat of the Government of the United States, directed to the President of the Senate. The President of the Senate shall, in the presence of the Senate and House of Representatives, open all the Certificates, and the Votes shall be counted. The Person having the greatest Number of Votes shall be the President, if such Number be a Majority of the whole Number of Electors appointed; and if there be more than one who have such Majority, and have an equal Number of Votes, then the House of Representatives shall immediately chuse by Ballot one of them for President; and if no Person have a Majority, then from the five highest on the List the said House shall in like Manner chuse the President. But in chusing the President, the Votes shall be taken by States, the Representation from each State having one Vote; A quorum for this Purpose shall consist of a Member or Members from two thirds of the States, and a Majority of all the States shall be necessary to a Choice. In every Case, after the Choice of the President, the Person having the greatest Number of Votes of the Electors shall be the Vice President. But if there should remain two or more who have equal Votes, the Senate shall chuse from them by Ballot the Vice President.

The Congress may determine the Time of Chusing the Electors, and the Day on which they shall give their Votes; which Day shall be the same throughout the United States.

No Person except a natural born Citizen, or a Citizen of the United States, at the time of the Adoption of this Constitution, shall be eligible to the Office of President; neither shall any Person be eligible to that Office who shall not have attained to the Age of thirty five Years, and been fourteen Years a Resident within the United States.

In Case of the Removal of the President from Office, or of his Death, Resignation, or Inability to discharge the Powers and Duties of the said Office, the Same shall devolve on the Vice President, and the Congress may by Law provide for the Case of Removal, Death, Resignation or Inability, both of the President and Vice President, declaring what Officer shall then act as President, and such Officer shall act accordingly, until the Disability be removed, or a President shall be elected.

The President shall, at stated Times, receive for his Services, a Compensation, which shall neither be encreased nor diminished during the Period for which he shall have been elected, and he shall not receive within that Period any other Emolument from the United States, or any of them.

Before he enter on the Execution of his Office, he shall take the following Oath or Affirmation:—"I do solemnly swear (or affirm) that I will faithfully execute the Office of President of the United States, and will to the best of my Ability, preserve, protect and defend the Constitution of the United States."

Section 2.

The President shall be Commander in Chief of the Army and Navy of the United States, and of the Militia of the several States, when called into the actual Service of the United States; he may require the Opinion, in writing, of the principal Officer in each of the executive Departments, upon any Subject relating to the Duties of their respective Offices, and he shall have Power to grant Reprieves and Pardons for Offenses against the United States, except in Cases of Impeachment.

He shall have Power, by and with the Advice and Consent of the Senate, to make Treaties, providing two thirds of the Senators present concur; and he shall nominate, and by and with the Advice and Consent of the Senate, shall appoint Ambassadors, other public Ministers and Consuls, Judges of the supreme Court, and all other Officers of the United States, whose Appointments are not herein otherwise provided for, and which shall be established by Law: but the Congress may by Law vest the Appointment of such inferior Officers, as they think proper, in the President alone, in the Courts of Law, or in the Heads of Departments.

The President shall have Power to fill up all Vacancies that may happen during the Recess of the Senate, by granting Commissions which shall expire at the End of their next Session.

Section 3.

He shall from time to time give to the Congress Information of the State of the Union, and recommend to their Consideration such Measures as he shall judge necessary and expedient; he may, on extraordinary Occasions, convene both Houses, or either of them, and in Case of Disagreement between them, with Respect to the Time of Adjournment, he may adjourn them to such Time as he shall think proper, he shall receive Ambassadors and other public Ministers; he shall take Care that the Laws be faithfully executed, and shall Commission all the Offices of the United States.

Section 4.

The President, Vice President and all civil Officers of the United States, shall be removed from Office on Impeachment for, and Conviction of, Treason, Bribery, or other high Crimes and Misdemeanors.

ARTICLE III

Section 1.

The judicial Power of the United States, shall be vested in one supreme Court, and in such inferior Courts as the Congress may from time to time ordain and establish. The Judges, both of the supreme and inferior Courts, shall hold their Offices during good Behaviour, and shall, at Times, receive for their Services, a Compensation, which shall not be diminished during their Continuance in Office.

Section 2.

The judicial Power shall extend to all Cases, in Law and Equity, arising under this Constitution, the Laws of the United States, and Treaties made, or which shall be made, under their Authority;—to all Cases affecting Ambassadors, other public Ministers and Consuls;—to all Cases of admiralty and maritime Jurisdiction;—to Controversies to which the United States shall be a Party;—to controversies between two or more States;—between a State and Citizens of another State;—between Citizens of different States;—between Citizens of the same State claiming Lands under Grants of different States; and between a State, or the Citizens thereof, and foreign States, Citizens or Subjects.

In all Cases affecting Ambassadors, other public Ministers and Consuls, and those in which a State shall be Party, the supreme Court shall have original Jurisdiction. In all the other Cases before mentioned, the supreme Court shall have appellate Jurisdiction, both as to Law and Fact, with such Exceptions, and under such Regulations as the Congress shall make.

The Trial of all Crimes, except in Cases of Impeachment, shall be by Jury; and such Trial shall be held in the State where the said Crimes shall have been committed; but when not committed within any State, the Trial shall be at such Place or Places as the Congress may by Law have directed.

Section 3.

Treason against the United States, shall consist only in levying War against them, or in adhering to their Enemies, giving them Aid and Comfort. No Person shall be convicted of Treason unless on the Testimony of two Witnesses to the same overt Act, or on Confession in open Court.

The Congress shall have Power to declare the Punishment of Treason, but no Attainder of Treason shall work Corruption of Blood, or Forfeiture except during the Life of the Person attainted.

ARTICLE IV

Section 1.

Full Faith and Credit shall be given in each State to the public Acts, Records, and judicial Proceedings of every other State. And the Congress may by general Laws prescribe the Manner in which such Acts, Records and Proceedings shall be proved, and the Effect thereof.

Section 2.

The Citizens of each State shall be entitled to all Privileges and Immunities of Citizens in the several States.

A Person charged in any State with Treason, Felony, or other Crime, who shall flee from Justice, and be found in another State, shall on Demand of the executive Authority of the State from which he fled, be delivered up, to be removed to the State having Jurisdiction of the Crime.

No Person held to Service or Labour in one State, under the Laws thereof, escaping into another, shall, in Consequence of any Law or Regulation therein, be discharged from such Service or Labour, but shall be delivered up on Claim of the Party to whom such Service or Labour may be due.

Section 3.

New States may be admitted by the Congress into this Union; but no new State shall be formed or erected within the Jurisdiction of any other State; nor any State be formed by the Junction of two or more States, or Parts of States, without the Consent of the Legislatures of the States concerned as well as the Congress.

The Congress shall have Power to dispose of and make all needful Rules and Regulations respecting the Territory or other Property belonging to the United States; and nothing in this Constitution shall be so construed as to Prejudice any Claims of the United States, or of any particular State.

Section 4.

The United States shall guarantee to every State in this Union a Republican Form of Government, and shall protect each of them against Invasion; and on Application of the Legislature, or of the Executive (when the Legislature cannot be convened) against domestic Violence.

ARTICLE V

The Congress, whenever two thirds of both Houses shall deem it necessary, shall propose Amendments to this Constitution, or, on the Application of the Legislatures of two thirds of the several States, shall call a Convention for proposing Amendments, which, in either Case, shall be valid to all Intents and Purposes, as Part of this Constitution, when ratified by the Legislatures of three fourths of the several States, or by Conventions in three fourths thereof, as the one or the other Mode of Ratification may be proposed by the Congress; Provided that no Amendment which may be made prior to the Year One thousand eight hundred and eight shall in any Manner affect the first and fourth Clauses in the Ninth Section of the first Article; and that no State, without its Consent, shall be deprived of its equal Suffrage in the Senate.

ARTICLE VI

All Debts contracted and Engagements entered into, before the Adoption of this Constitution, shall be as valid against the United States under this Constitution, as under the Confederation.

This Constitution, and the Laws of the United States which shall be made in Pursuance thereof; and all Treaties made, or which shall be made, under the Authority of the United States, shall be the supreme Law of the Land; and the Judges in every State shall be bound thereby, any Thing in the Constitution or Laws of any State to the Contrary notwithstanding.

The Senators and Representatives before mentioned, and the Members of the several State Legislatures, and all executive and judicial Officers, both of the United States and of the Several States, shall be bound by Oath or Affirmation, to support this Constitution; but no religious Test shall ever be required as a Qualification to any Office or public Trust under the United States.

ARTICLE VII

The Ratification of the Conventions of nine States, shall be sufficient for the Establishment of this Constitution between the States so ratifying the Same.

Amendment I [1791].

Congress shall make no law respecting an establishment of religion, or prohibiting the free exercise thereof; or abridging the freedom of speech, or the press; or the right of the people peaceably to assemble, and to petition the Government for a redress of grievances.

Amendment II [1791].

A well regulated Militia, being necessary to the security for a free State, the right of the people to keep and bear Arms, shall not be infringed.

Amendment III [1791].

No Soldier shall, in time of peace be quartered in any house, without the consent of the Owner, nor in time of war, but in a manner to be prescribed by law.

Amendment IV [1791].

The right of the people to be secure in their persons, houses, papers, and effects, against unreasonable searches and seizures, shall not be violated, and no Warrants shall issue, but upon probable cause, supported by Oath or Affirmation, and particularly describing the place to be searched, and the persons or things to be seized.

Amendment V [1791].

No person shall be held to answer for a capital, or otherwise infamous crime, unless on a presentment or indictment of a Grand Jury, except in cases arising in the land or naval forces, or in the Militia, when in actual service in time of War or public danger; nor shall any person be subject for the same offense to be twice put in jeopardy of life or limb; nor shall be compelled in any criminal case to be a witness against himself, nor be deprived of life, liberty, or property, without due process of law; nor shall private property be taken for public use, without just compensation.

Amendment VI [1791].

In all criminal prosecutions, the accused shall enjoy the right to a speedy and public trial, by an impartial jury of the State and district wherein the crime shall have been committed, which district shall have been previously ascertained by law, and to be informed of the nature and cause of the accusation; to be confronted with the Witnesses against him; to have compulsory process for obtaining witnesses in his favor, and to have the Assistance of counsel for his defence.

Amendment VII [1791].

In suits at common law, where the value in controversy shall exceed twenty dollars, the right of trial by jury shall be preserved, and no fact tried by a jury, shall be otherwise re-examined in any Court of the United States, than according to the rules of the common law.

Amendment VIII [1791].

Excessive bail shall not be required, no excessive fines imposed, nor cruel and unusual punishments inflicted.

Amendment IX [1791].

The enumeration in the Constitution, of certain rights, shall not be construed to deny or disparage others retained by the people.

Amendment X [1791].

The powers not delegated to the United States by the Constitution, nor prohibited by it to the States, are reserved to the States respectively, or to the people.

Amendment XI [1798].

The judicial power of the United States shall not be construed to extend to any suit in law or equity, commenced or prosecuted against one of the United States by Citizens of another State, or by Citizens or Subjects of any Foreign State.

Amendment XII [1804].

The Electors shall meet in their respective states and vote by ballot for President and Vice-President, one of whom, at least, shall not be an inhabitant of the same state with themselves; they shall name in their ballots the person voted for as President, and in distinct ballots the person voted for as Vice-President, and they shall make distinct lists of all persons voted for as President, and of all persons voted for as Vice-President, and of the number of votes for each, which lists they shall sign and certify, and transmit sealed to the seat of the government of the United States, directed to the President of the Senate;—The President of the Senate shall, in the presence of the Senate and House of Representatives, open all the certificates and the votes shall then be counted;—The person having the greatest number of votes for President, shall be the President, if such number be a majority of the whole number of Electors appointed; and if no person have such majority, then from the persons having the highest numbers not exceeding three on the list of those voted for as President, the House of Representatives shall choose immediately, by ballot, the President. But in choosing the President, the votes shall be taken by states, the representation from each state having one vote; a quorum for this purpose shall consist of a member or members from two-thirds of the states, and a majority of all the states shall be necessary to a choice. And if the House of Representatives shall not choose a President whenever the right of choice shall devolve upon them, before the fourth day of March next following, then the Vice-President shall act as President, as in the case of the death or other constitutional disability of the President. The person having the greatest number of votes as Vice-President, shall be the Vice-President, if such number be a majority of the whole number of Electors appointed, and if no person have a majority, then from the two highest numbers on the list, the Senate shall choose the Vice-President; a quorum for the purpose shall consist of two-thirds of the whole number of Senators, and a majority of the whole number shall be necessary to a choice. But no person constitutionally ineligible to the office of President shall be eligible to that of the Vice-President of the United States.

Amendment XIII [1865].

Section 1. Neither slavery nor involuntary servitude, except as a punishment for crime whereof the party shall have been duly convicted, shall exist within the United States, or any place subject to their jurisdiction.

Section 2. Congress shall have power to enforce this article by appropriate legislation.

Amendment XIV [1868].

Section 1. All persons born or naturalized in the United States, and subject to the jurisdiction thereof, are citizens of the United States and of the State wherein they reside. No State shall make or enforce any law which shall abridge the privileges or immunities of citizens of the United States; nor shall any State deprive any person of life, liberty, or property, without due process of law; nor deny to any person within its jurisdiction the equal protection of the laws.

Section 2. Representatives shall be appointed among the several States according to their respective numbers, counting the whole number of persons in each State, excluding Indians not taxed. But when the right to vote at any election for the choice of electors for President and Vice President of the United States, Representatives in Congress, the Executive and Judicial officers of a State, or the members of the Legislature thereof, is denied to any of the male inhabitants of such State, being twenty-one years of age, and citizens of the United States, or in any way abridged, except for participation in rebellion, or other crime, the basis of representation therein shall be reduced in the proportion which the number of such male citizens shall bear the whole number of male citizens twenty-one years of age in such State.

Section 3. No person shall be a Senator or Representative in Congress, or elector of President and Vice President, or hold any office, civil or military, under the United States, or under any State, who, having previously taken an oath, as a member of Congress, or as an officer of the United States, or as a member of any State legislature, or as an executive or judicial officer of any State, to support the Constitution of the United States, shall have engaged in insurrection or rebellion against the same, or given aid or comfort to the enemies thereof. But Congress may by a vote of two-thirds of each House, remove such disability.

Section 4. The validity of the public debt of the United States, authorized by law, including debts incurred for payment of pensions and bounties for services in suppressing insurrection or rebellion, shall not be questioned. But neither the United States nor any State shall assume or pay any debt or obligation incurred in aid of insurrection of rebellion against the United States, or any claim for the loss or emancipation of any slave; but all such debts, obligations and claims shall be held illegal and void.

Section 5. The Congress shall have power to enforce, by appropriate legislation, the provisions of this article.

Amendment XV [1870].

Section 1. The right of citizens of the United States to vote shall not be denied or abridged by the United States or by any State on account of race, color, or previous condition of servitude.

Section 2. The Congress shall have power to enforce this article by appropriate legislation.

Amendment XVI [1913].

The Congress shall have power to lay and collect taxes on incomes, from whatever source derived, without apportionment among the several States, and without regard to any census or enumeration.

Amendment XVII [1913].

The Senate of the United States shall be composed of two Senators from each State, elected by the people thereof, for six years; and each Senator shall have one vote. The electors in each State shall have the qualifications requisite for electors of the most numerous branch of the State legislatures.

When vacancies happen in the representation of any State in the Senate, the executive authority of each State shall issue writs of election to fill such vacancies; *Provided*, That the legislature of any State may empower the executive thereof to make temporary appointments until the people fill the vacancies by election as the legislature may direct.

This amendment shall not be construed as to affect the election or term of any Senator chosen before it becomes valid as part of the Constitution.

Amendment XVIII [1919].

Section 1. After one year from the ratification of this article the manufacture, sale, or transportation of intoxicating liquors within, the importation thereof into, or the exportation thereof from the United States and all territory subject to the jurisdiction thereof for beverage purposes is hereby prohibited.

Section 2. The Congress and the several States shall have concurrent power to enforce this article by appropriate legislation.

Section 3. This article shall be inoperative unless it shall have been ratified as an amendment to the Constitution by the legislatures of the several States, as provided in the Constitution, within seven years from the date of the submission hereof to the States by the Congress.

Amendment XIX [1920].

The right of citizens of the United States to vote shall not be denied or abridged by the United States or by any State on account of sex.

Congress shall have power to enforce this article by appropriate legislation.

Amendment XX [1933].

Section 1. The terms of the President and Vice President shall end at noon on the 20th day of January, and the terms of Senators and Representatives at noon on the 3d day of January, of the years in which such terms would have ended if this article had not been ratified; and the terms of their successors shall then begin.

Section 2. The Congress shall assemble at least once in every year, and such meeting shall begin at noon on the 3d day of January, unless they shall by law appoint a different day.

Section 3. If, at the time fixed for the beginning of the term of the President, the President elect shall have died, the Vice President elect shall become President. If a President shall not have been chosen before the time fixed for the beginning of his term, or if the President elect shall have failed to qualify, then the Vice President elect shall act as President until a President shall have qualified; and the Congress may by law provide for the case wherein neither a President elect nor a Vice President elect shall have qualified, declaring who shall then act as President, or the manner in which one who is to act shall be selected, and such person shall act accordingly until a President or Vice President shall have qualified.

Section 4. The Congress may by law provide for the case of the death of any of the persons from whom the House of Representatives may choose a President whenever the right of choice shall have devolved upon them, and for the case of the death of any of the persons from whom the Senate may choose a Vice President whenever the right of choice shall have devolved upon them.

Section 5. Sections 1 and 2 shall take effect on the 15th day of October following the ratification of this article.

Section 6. This article shall be inoperative unless it shall have been ratified as an amendment to the Constitution by the legislatures of three-fourths of the several States within seven years from the date of its submission.

Amendment XXI [1933].

Section 1. The eighteenth article of amendment to the Constitution of the United States is hereby repealed.

Section 2. The transportation or importation into any State, Territory, or possession of the United States for delivery or use therein of intoxicating liquors, in violation of the laws thereof, is hereby prohibited.

Section 3. This article shall be inoperative unless it shall have been ratified as an amendment to the Constitution by conventions in the several States, as provided in the Constitution, within seven years from the date of the submission hereof to the States by the Congress.

Amendment XXII [1951].

Section 1. No person shall be elected to the office of the President more than twice, and no person who has held the office of President, or acted as President, for more than two years of a term to which some other person was elected President shall be elected to the office of the President more than once. But this Article shall not apply to any person holding the office of President when this Article was proposed by the Congress, and shall not prevent any person who may be holding the office of President, or acting as President, during the term within which this Article becomes operative from holding the office of President, or acting as President during the remainder of such term.

Section 2. This article shall be inoperative unless it shall have been ratified as an amendment to the Constitution by the legislatures of three-fourths of the several States within seven years from the date of its submission to the States by the Congress.

Amendment XXIII [1961].

Section 1. The District constituting the seat of Government of the United States shall appoint in such manner as the Congress may direct:

A number of electors of President and Vice President equal to the whole number of Senators and Representatives in Congress to which the District would be entitled if it were a State, but in no event more than the least populous State; they shall be in addition to those appointed by the States, but they shall be considered, for the purposes of the election of President and Vice President, to be electors appointed by a State; and they shall meet in the District and perform such duties as provided by the twelfth article of amendment.

Section 2. The Congress shall have power to enforce this article by appropriate legislation.

Amendment XXIV [1964].

Section 1. The right of citizens of the United States to vote in any primary or other election for President or Vice President, for electors for President or Vice President, or for Senator or Representative in Congress, shall not be denied or abridged by the United States or any State by reason of failure to pay any poll tax or other tax.

Section 2. The Congress shall have power to enforce this article by appropriate legislation.

Amendment XXV [1967].

Section 1. In case of the removal of the President from office or of his death or resignation, the Vice President shall become President.

Section 2. Whenever there is a vacancy in the office of the Vice President, the President shall nominate a Vice President who shall take office upon confirmation by a majority vote of both Houses of Congress.

Section 3. Whenever the President transmits to the President pro tempore of the Senate and the Speaker of the House of Representatives his written declaration that he is unable to discharge the powers and duties of his office, and until he transmits to them a written declaration to the contrary, such powers and duties shall be discharged by the Vice President as Acting President.

Section 4. Whenever the Vice President and a majority of either the principal officers of the executive departments or of such other body as Congress may by law provide, transmit to the President pro tempore of the Senate and the Speaker of the House of Representatives their written declaration that the President is unable to discharge the powers and duties of his office, the Vice President shall immediately assume the powers and duties of the office as Acting President.

Thereafter, when the President transmits to the President pro tempore of the Senate and the Speaker of the House of Representatives his written declaration that no inability exists, he shall resume the powers and duties of his office unless the Vice President and a majority of either the principal officers of the executive department or of such other body as Congress may by law provide, transmit within four days to the President pro tempore of the Senate and the Speaker of the House of Representatives their written declaration that the President is unable to discharge the powers and duties of his office. Thereupon Congress shall decide the issue, assembling within forty-eight hours for that purpose if not in session. If the Congress, within twenty-one days after receipt of the latter written declaration, or, if Congress is not in session, within twenty-one days after Congress is required to assemble, determines by two-thirds vote of both Houses that the President is unable to discharge the powers and duties of his office, the Vice President shall continue to discharge the same as Acting President; otherwise, the President shall resume the powers and duties of his office.

Amendment XXVI [1971].

Section 1. The right of citizens of the United States, who are eighteen years of age or older, to vote shall not be denied or abridged by the United States or by any State on account of age.

Section 2. The Congress shall have power to enforce this article by appropriate legislation.

Amendment XXVII [1992].

No law, varying the compensation for the services of the Senators and Representatives, shall take effect, until an election of Representatives shall have intervened.

APPENDIX B

UNIFORM COMMERCIAL CODE (SELECTED PROVISIONS)

The code consists of the following articles:

Art.

1. General provisions
2. Sales

2A. Leases

3. Negotiable instruments
4. Bank deposits and collections

4A. Fund transfers

5. Letters of credit
6. Repealer of Article 6—Bulk Transfers and [Revised] Article 6—Bulk sales
7. Warehouse Receipts, Bills of Lading and Other Documents of Title
8. Investment Securities
9. Secured Transactions
10. Effective Date and Repealer
11. Effective Date and Transmission provisions

ARTICLE I GENERAL PROVISIONS

PART 1 Short Title, Construction, Application and Subject Matter of the Act

§ 1–101. Short Title.

This Act shall be known and may be cited as Uniform Commercial Code.

§ 1–102. Purposes; Rules of Construction; Variation by Agreement.

(1) This Act shall be liberally construed and applied to promote its underlying purposes and policies.

(2) Underlying purposes and policies of this Act are

(a) to simplify, clarify and modernize the law governing commercial transactions;

(b) to permit the continued expansion of commercial practices through custom, usage and agreement of the parties;

(c) to make uniform the law among the various jurisdictions.

(3) The effect of provisions of this Act may be varied by agreement, except as otherwise provided in this Act and except that the obligations of good faith, diligence, reasonableness and care prescribed by this Act may not be disclaimed by agreement but the parties may by agreement determine the standards by which the performance of such obligations is to be measured if such standards are not manifestly unreasonable.

(4) The presence in certain provisions of this Act of the words "unless otherwise agreed" or words of similar import does not imply that the effect of other provisions may not be varied by agreement under subsection (3).

(5) In this Act unless the context otherwise requires

(a) words in the singular number include the plural, and in the plural include the singular;

(b) words of the masculine gender include the feminine and the neuter, and when the sense so indicates words of the neuter gender may refer to any gender.

§ 1–103. Supplementary General Principles of Law Applicable.

Unless displaced by the particular provisions of this Act, the principles of law and equity, including the law merchant and the law relative to capacity to contract, principal and agent, estoppel, fraud, misrepresentation, duress, coercion, mistake, bankruptcy, or other validating or invalidating cause shall supplement its provisions.

§ 1–104. Construction Against Implicit Repeal.

This Act being a general act intended as a unified coverage of its subject matter, no part of it shall be deemed to be impliedly repealed by subsequent legislation if such construction can reasonably be avoided.

§ 1–105. Territorial Application of the Act; Parties' Power to Choose Applicable Law.

(1) Except as provided hereafter in this section, when a transaction bears a reasonable relation to this state and also to another state or nation the parties may agree that the law either of this state or of such other state or nation shall govern their rights and duties. Failing such agreement this Act applies to transactions bearing an appropriate relation to this state.

(2) Where one of the following provisions of this Act specifies the applicable law, that provision governs and a contrary agreement is effective only to the extent permitted by the law (including the conflict of laws rules) so specified:

Rights of creditors against sold goods. Section 2–402. Applicability of the Article on Leases. Sections 2A–105 and 2A–106.

Applicability of the Article on Bank Deposits and Collections. Section 4–102.

Governing law in the Article on Funds Transfers. Section 4A-507.

Letters of Credit. Section 5–116.

Bulk sales subject to the Article on Bulk Sales. Section 6–103.

Applicability of the Article on Investment Securities.

Section 8–106.

Law governing perfection, the effect of perfection or non-perfection, and the priority of security interests and agricultural liens. Sections 9–301 through 9–307.

As amended in 1972, 1987, 1988, 1989, 1994, 1995, and 1999.

§ 1–106. Remedies to Be Liberally Administered.

(1) The remedies provided by this Act shall be liberally administered to the end that the aggrieved party may be put in as good a position as if the other party had fully performed but neither consequential or special nor penal damages may be had except as specifically provided in this Act or by other rule of law.

(2) Any right or obligation declared by this Act is enforceable by action unless the provision declaring it specifies a different and limited effect.

§ 1–107. Waiver or Renunciation of Claim or Right After Breach.

Any claim or right arising out of an alleged breach can be discharged in whole or in part without consideration by a written waiver or renunciation signed and delivered by the aggrieved party.

§ 1–108. Severability.

If any provision or clause of this Act or application thereof to any person or circumstances is held invalid, such invalidity shall not affect other provisions or applications of the Act which can be given effect without the invalid provision or application, and to this end the provisions of this Act are declared to be severable.

§ 1–109. Section Captions.

Section captions are parts of this Act.

PART 2 General Definitions and Principles of Interpretation

§ 1–201. General Definitions.

Subject to additional definitions contained in the subsequent Articles of this Act which are applicable to specific Articles or Parts thereof, and unless the context otherwise requires, in this Act:

(1) "Action" in the sense of a judicial proceeding includes recoupment, counterclaim, set-off, suit in equity and any other proceedings in which rights are determined.

(2) "Aggrieved party" means a party entitled to resort to a remedy.

(3) "Agreement" means the bargain of the parties in fact as found in their language or by implication from other circumstances including course of dealing or usage of trade or course of performance as provided in this Act (Sections 1–205 and 2–208). Whether an agreement has legal consequences is determined by the provisions of this Act, if applicable; otherwise by the law of contracts (Section 1–103). (Compare "Contract".)

(4) "Bank" means any person engaged in the business of banking.

(5) "Bearer" means the person in possession of an instrument, document of title, or certificated security payable to bearer or indorsed in blank.

(6) "Bill of lading" means a document evidencing the receipt of goods for shipment issued by a person engaged in the business of transporting or forwarding goods, and includes an airbill. "Airbill" means a document serving for air transportation as a bill of lading does for marine or rail transportation, and includes an air consignment note or air waybill.

(7) "Branch" includes a separately incorporated foreign branch of a bank.

(8) "Burden of establishing" a fact means the burden of persuading the triers of fact that the existence of the fact is more probable than its non-existence.

(9) "Buyer in ordinary course of business" means a person that buys goods in good faith, without knowledge that the sale violates the rights of another person in the goods, and in the ordinary course from a person, other than a pawnbroker, in the business of selling goods of that kind. A person buys goods in the ordinary course if the sale to the person comports with the usual or customary practices in the kind of business in which the seller is engaged or with the seller's own usual or customary practices. A person that sells oil, gas, or other minerals at the wellhead or minehead is a person in the business of selling goods of that kind. A buyer in ordinary course of business may buy for cash, by exchange of other property, or on secured or unsecured credit,

and may acquire goods or documents of title under a pre-existing contract for sale. Only a buyer that takes possession of the goods or has a right to recover the goods from the seller under Article 2 may be a buyer in ordinary course of business. A person that acquires goods in a transfer in bulk or as security for or in total or partial satisfaction of a money debt is not a buyer in ordinary course of business.

(10) "Conspicuous": A term or clause is conspicuous when it is so written that a reasonable person against whom it is to operate ought to have noticed it. A printed heading in capitals (as: NON-NEGOTIABLE BILL OF LADING) is conspicuous. Language in the body of a form is "conspicuous" if it is in larger or other contrasting type or color. But in a telegram any stated term is "conspicuous". Whether a term or clause is "conspicuous" or not is for decision by the court.

(11) "Contract" means the total legal obligation which results from the parties' agreement as affected by this Act and any other applicable rules of law. (Compare "Agreement".)

(12) "Creditor" includes a general creditor, a secured creditor, a lien creditor and any representative of creditors, including an assignee for the benefit of creditors, a trustee in bankruptcy, a receiver in equity and an executor or administrator of an insolvent debtor's or assignor's estate.

(13) "Defendant" includes a person in the position of defendant in a cross-action or counterclaim.

(14) "Delivery" with respect to instruments, documents of title, chattel paper, or certificated securities means voluntary transfer of possession.

(15) "Document of title" includes bill of lading, dock warrant, dock receipt, warehouse receipt or order for the delivery of goods, and also any other document which in the regular course of business or financing is treated as adequately evidencing that the person in possession of it is entitled to receive, hold and dispose of the document and the goods it covers. To be a document of title a document must purport to be issued by or addressed to a bailee and purport to cover goods in the bailee's possession which are either identified or are fungible portions of an identified mass.

(16) "Fault" means wrongful act, omission or breach.

(17) "Fungible" with respect to goods or securities means goods or securities of which any unit is, by nature or usage of trade, the equivalent of any other like unit. Goods which are not fungible shall be deemed fungible for the purposes of this Act to the extent that under a particular agreement or document unlike units are treated as equivalents.

(18) "Genuine" means free of forgery or counterfeiting.

(19) "Good faith" means honesty in fact in the conduct or transaction concerned.

(20) "Holder" with respect to a negotiable instrument, means the person in possession if the instrument is payable to bearer or, in the cases of an instrument payable to an identified person, if the identified person is in possession. "Holder" with respect to a document of title means the person in possession if the goods are deliverable to bearer or to the order of the person in possession.

(21) To "honor" is to pay or to accept and pay, or where a credit so engages to purchase or discount a draft complying with the terms of the credit.

(22) "Insolvency proceedings" includes any assignment for the benefit of creditors or other proceedings intended to liquidate or rehabilitate the estate of the person involved.

(23) A person is "insolvent" who either has ceased to pay his debts in the ordinary course of business or cannot pay his debts as they become due or is insolvent within the meaning of the federal bankruptcy law.

(24) "Money" means a medium of exchange authorized or adopted by a domestic or foreign government and includes a monetary unit of account established by an intergovernmental organization or by agreement between two or more nations.

(25) A person has "notice" of a fact when

(a) he has actual knowledge of it; or

(b) he has received a notice or notification of it; or

(c) from all the facts and circumstances known to him at the time in question he has reason to know that it exists.

A person "knows" or has "knowledge" of a fact when he has actual knowledge of it. "Discover" or "learn" or a word or phrase of similar import refers to knowledge rather than to reason to know. The time and circumstances under which a notice or notification may cease to be effective are not determined by this Act.

(26) A person "notifies" or "gives" a notice or notification to another by taking such steps as may be reasonably required to inform the other in ordinary course whether or not such other actually comes to know of it. A person "receives" a notice or notification when

(a) it comes to his attention; or

(b) it is duly delivered at the place of business through which the contract was made or at any other place held out by him as the place for receipt of such communications.

(27) Notice, knowledge or a notice or notification received by an organization is effective for a particular transaction from the time when it is brought to the attention of the individual conducting that transaction, and in any event from the time when it would have been brought to his attention if the organization had exercised due diligence. An organization exercises due diligence if it maintains reasonable routines for communicating significant information to the person conducting the transaction and there is reasonable compliance with the routines. Due diligence does not require an individual acting for the organization to communicate information unless such communication is part of his regular duties or unless he has reason to know of the transaction and that the transaction would be materially affected by the information.

(28) "Organization" includes a corporation, government or governmental subdivision or agency, business trust, estate, trust, partnership or association, two or more persons having a joint or common interest, or any other legal or commercial entity.

(29) "Party", as distinct from "third party", means a person who has engaged in a transaction or made an agreement within this Act.

(30) "Person" includes an individual or an organization (see Section 1–102).

(31) "Presumption" or "presumed" means that the trier of fact must find the existence of the fact presumed unless and until evidence is introduced which would support a finding of its non-existence.

(32) "Purchase" includes taking by sale, discount, negotiation, mortgage, pledge, lien, issue or re-issue, gift or any other voluntary transaction creating an interest in property.

(33) "Purchaser" means a person who takes by purchase.

(34) "Remedy" means any remedial right to which an aggrieved party is entitled with or without resort to a tribunal.

(35) "Representative" includes an agent, an officer of a corporation or association, and a trustee, executor or administrator of an estate, or any other person empowered to act for another.

(36) "Rights" includes remedies.

(37) "Security interest" means an interest in personal property or fixtures which secures payment or performance of an obligation. The term also includes any interest of a consignor and a buyer of accounts, chattel paper, a payment intangible, or a promissory note in a transaction that is subject to Article 9. The special property interest of a buyer of goods on identification of those goods to a contract for sale under Section 2–401 is not a "security interest", but a buyer may also acquire a "security interest" by complying with Article 9. Except as otherwise provided in Section 2–505, the right of a seller or lessor of goods under Article 2 or 2A to retain or acquire possession of the goods is not a "security interest", but a seller or lessor may also acquire a "security interest" by complying with Article 9. The retention or reservation of title by a seller of goods notwithstanding shipment or delivery to the buyer (Section 2–401) is limited in effect to a reservation of a "security interest".

Whether a transaction creates a lease or security interest is determined by the facts of each case; however, a transaction creates a security interest if the consideration the lessee is to pay the lessor for the right to possession and use of the goods is an obligation for the term of the lease not subject to termination by the lessee, and

(a) the original term of the lease is equal to or greater than the remaining economic life of the goods,

(b) the lessee is bound to renew the lease for the remaining economic life of the goods or is bound to become the owner of the goods,

(c) the lessee has an option to renew the lease for the remaining economic life of the goods for no additional consideration or nominal additional consideration upon compliance with the lease agreement, or

(d) the lessee has an option to become the owner of the goods for no additional consideration or nominal additional consideration upon compliance with the lease agreement.

A transaction does not create a security interest merely because it provides that

(a) the present value of the consideration the lessee is obligated to pay the lessor for the right to possession and use of the goods is substantially equal to or is greater than the fair market value of the goods at the time the lease is entered into,

(b) the lessee assumes risk of loss of the goods, or agrees to pay taxes, insurance, filing, recording, or registration fees, or service or maintenance costs with respect to the goods,

(c) the lessee has an option to renew the lease or to become the owner of the goods,

(d) the lessee has an option to renew the lease for a fixed rent that is equal to or greater than the reasonably predictable fair market rent for the use of the goods for the term of the renewal at the time the option is to be performed, or

(e) the lessee has an option to become the owner of the goods for a fixed price that is equal to or greater than the reasonably predictable fair market value of the goods at the time the option is to be performed.

For purposes of this subsection (37):

(x) Additional consideration is not nominal if (i) when the option to renew the lease is granted to the lessee the rent is stated to be the fair market rent for the use of the goods for the term of the renewal determined at the time the option is to be performed, or (ii) when the option to become the owner of the goods is granted to the lessee the price is stated to be the fair market value of the goods determined at the time the option is to be performed. Additional consideration is nominal if it is less than the lessee's reasonably predictable cost of performing under the lease agreement if the option is not exercised;

(y) "Reasonably predictable" and "remaining economic life of the goods" are to be determined with reference to the facts and circumstances at the time the transaction is entered into; and

(z) "Present value" means the amount as of a date certain of one or more sums payable in the future, discounted to the date certain. The discount is determined by the interest rate specified by the parties if the rate is not manifestly unreasonable at the time the transaction is entered into; otherwise, the discount is determined by a commercially reasonable rate that takes into account the facts and circumstances of each case at the time the transaction was entered into.

(38) "Send" in connection with any writing or notice means to deposit in the mail or deliver for transmission by any other usual means of communication with postage or cost of transmission provided for and properly addressed and in the case of an instrument to an address specified thereon or otherwise agreed, or if there be none to any address reasonable under the circumstances. The receipt of any writing or notice within the time at which it would have arrived if properly sent has the effect of a proper sending.

(39) "Signed" includes any symbol executed or adopted by a party with present intention to authenticate a writing.

(40) "Surety" includes guarantor.

(41) "Telegram" includes a message transmitted by radio, teletype, cable, any mechanical method of transmission, or the like.

(42) "Term" means that portion of an agreement which relates to a particular matter.

(43) "Unauthorized" signature means one made without actual, implied or apparent authority and includes a forgery.

(44) "Value". Except as otherwise provided with respect to negotiable instruments and bank collections (Sections 3–303, 4–210 and 4–211) a person gives "value" for rights if he acquires them

(a) in return for a binding commitment to extend credit or for the extension of immediately available credit whether or not drawn upon and whether or not a chargeback is provided for in the event of difficulties in collection; or

(b) as security for or in total or partial satisfaction of a pre-existing claim; or

(c) by accepting delivery pursuant to a preexisting contract for purchase; or

(d) generally, in return for any consideration sufficient to support a simple contract.

(45) "Warehouse receipt" means a receipt issued by a person engaged in the business of storing goods for hire.

(46) "Written" or "writing" includes printing, typewriting or any other intentional reduction to tangible form.

§ 1–202. Prima Facie Evidence by Third Party Documents.

A document in due form purporting to be a bill of lading, policy or certificate of insurance, official weigher's or inspector's certificate, consular invoice, or any other document authorized or required by the contract to be issued by a third party shall be prima facie evidence of its own authenticity and genuineness and of the facts stated in the document by the third party.

§ 1–203. Obligation of Good Faith.

Every contract or duty within this Act imposes an obligation of good faith in its performance or enforcement.

§ 1–204. Time; Reasonable Time; "Seasonably".

(1) Whenever this Act requires any action to be taken within a reasonable time, any time which is not manifestly unreasonable may be fixed by agreement.

(2) What is a reasonable time for taking any action depends on the nature, purpose and circumstances of such action.

(3) An action is taken "seasonably" when it is taken at or within the time agreed or if no time is agreed at or within a reasonable time.

§ 1–205. Course of Dealing and Usage of Trade.

(1) A course of dealing is a sequence of previous conduct between the parties to a particular transaction which is fairly to be regarded as establishing a common basis of understanding for interpreting their expressions and other conduct.

(2) A usage of trade is any practice or method of dealing having such regularity of observance in a place, vocation or trade as to justify an expectation that it will be observed with respect to the transaction in question. The existence and scope of such a usage are to be proved as facts. If it is established that such a usage is embodied in a written trade code or similar writing the interpretation of the writing is for the court.

(3) A course of dealing between parties and any usage of trade in the vocation or trade in which they are engaged or of which they are or should be aware give particular meaning to and supplement or qualify terms of an agreement.

(4) The express terms of an agreement and an applicable course of dealing or usage of trade shall be construed wherever reasonable as consistent with each other; but when such construction is unreasonable express terms control both course of dealing and usage of trade and course of dealing controls usage trade.

(5) An applicable usage of trade in the place where any part of performance is to occur shall be used in interpreting the agreement as to that part of the performance.

(6) Evidence of a relevant usage of trade offered by one party is not admissible unless and until he has given the other party such notice as the court finds sufficient to prevent unfair surprise to the latter.

§ 1–206. Statute of Frauds for Kinds of Personal Property Not Otherwise Covered.

(1) Except in the cases described in subsection (2) of this section a contract for the sale of personal property is not enforceable by way of action or defense beyond five thousand dollars in amount or value of remedy unless there is some writing which indicates that a contract for sale has been made between the parties at a defined or stated price, reasonably identifies the subject matter, and is signed by the party against whom enforcement is sought or by his authorized agent.

(2) Subsection (1) of this section does not apply to contracts for the sale of goods (Section 2–201) nor of securities (Section 8–113) nor to security agreements (Section 9–203).

As amended in 1994.

§ 1–207. Performance or Acceptance Under Reservation of Rights.

(1) A party who with explicit reservation of rights performs or promises performance or assents to performance in a manner demanded or offered by the other party does not thereby prejudice the rights reserved. Such words as "without prejudice", "under protest" or the like are sufficient.

(2) Subsection (1) does not apply to an accord and satisfaction.

As amended in 1990.

§ 1–208. Option to Accelerate at Will.

A term providing that one party or his successor in interest may accelerate payment or performance or require collateral or additional collateral "at will" or "when he deems himself insecure" or in words of similar import shall be construed to mean that he shall have power to do so only if he in good faith believes that the prospect of payment or performance is impaired. The burden of establishing lack of good faith is on the party against whom the power has been exercised.

§ 1–209. Subordinated Obligations.

An obligation may be issued as subordinated to payment of another obligation of the person obligated, or a creditor may subordinate his right to payment of an obligation by agreement with either the person obligated or another creditor of the person obligated. Such a subordination does not create a security interest as against either the common debtor or a subordinated creditor. This section shall be construed as declaring the law as it existed prior to the enactment of this section and not as modifying it. Added in 1966.

Note: *This new section is proposed as an optional provision to make it clear that a subordination agreement does not create a security interest unless so intended.*

ARTICLE II SALES

PART 1 Short Title, General Construction and Subject Matter

§ 2–101. Short Title.

This Article shall be known and may be cited as Uniform Commercial Code—Sales.

§ 2–102. Scope; Certain Security and Other Transactions Excluded from This Article.

Unless the context otherwise requires, this Article applies to transactions in goods; it does not apply to any transaction which although in the form of an unconditional contract to sell or present sale is intended to operate only as a security transaction nor docs this Article impair or repeal any statute regulating sales to consumers, farmers or other specified classes of buyers.

§ 2–103. Definitions and Index of Definitions.

(1) In this Article unless the context otherwise requires

(a) "Buyer" means a person who buys or contracts to buy goods.

(b) "Good faith" in the case of a merchant means honesty in fact and the observance of reasonable commercial standards of fair dealing in the trade.

(c) "Receipt" of goods means taking physical possession of them.

(d) "Seller" means a person who sells or contracts to sell goods.

(2) Other definitions applying to this Article or to specified Parts thereof, and the sections in which they appear are:

"Acceptance". Section 2-606.

"Banker's credit". Section 2-325.

"Between merchants". Section 2–104.

"Cancellation". Section 2–106(4).

"Commercial unit". Section 2–105.

"Confirmed credit". Section 2–325.

"Conforming to contract". Section 2–106.

"Contract for sale". Section 2–106.

"Cover". Section 2–712.

"Entrusting". Section 2–403.

"Financing agency". Section 2–104.

"Future goods". Section 2–105.

"Goods". Section 2–105.

"Identification". Section 2–501.

"Installment contract". Section 2–612.

"Letter of Credit". Section 2–325.

"Lot". Section 2–105

"Merchant". Section 2–104.

"Overseas". Section 2–323.

"Person in position of seller". Section 2–707.

"Present sale". Section 2–106.

"Sale". Section 2–106.

"Sale on approval". Section 2–326.

"Sale or return". Section 2–326.

"Termination". Section 2–106.

(3) The following definitions in other Articles apply to this Article:

"Check". Section 3–104.

"Consignee". Section 7–102.

"Consignor". Section 7–102.

"Consumer goods". Section 9–109.

"Dishonor". Section 3–507.

"Draft". Section 3–104.

(4) In addition Article 1 contains general definitions and principles of construction and interpretation applicable throughout this Article.

As amended in 1994 and 1999.

§ 2–104. Definitions: "Merchant"; "Between Merchants"; "Financing Agency".

(1) "Merchant" means a person who deals in goods of the kind or otherwise by his occupation holds himself out as having knowledge or skill peculiar to the practices or goods involved in the transaction or to whom such knowledge or skill may be attributed by his employment of an agent or broker or other intermediary who by his occupation holds himself out as having such knowledge or skill.

(2) "Financing agency" means a bank, finance company or other person who in the ordinary course of business makes advances against

goods or documents of title or who by arrangement with either the seller or the buyer intervenes in ordinary course to make or collect payment due or claimed under the contract for sale, as by purchasing or paying the seller's draft or making advances against it or by merely taking it for collection whether or not documents of title accompany the draft. "Financing agency" includes also a bank or other person who similarly intervenes between persons who are in the position of seller and buyer in respect to the goods (Section 2–707).

(3) "Between merchants" means in any transaction with respect to which both parties are chargeable with the knowledge or skill of merchants.

§ 2–105. Definitions: Transferability; "Goods"; "Future" Goods; "Lot"; "Commercial Unit".

(1) "Goods" means all things (including specially manufactured goods) which are movable at the time of identification to the contract for sale other than the money in which the price is to be paid, investment securities (Article 8) and things in action. "Goods" also includes the unborn young of animals and growing crops and other identified things attached to realty as described in the section on goods to be severed from realty (Section 2–107).

(2) Goods must be both existing and identified before any interest in them can pass. Goods which are not both existing and identified are "future" goods. A purported present sale of future goods or of any interest therein operates as a contract to sell.

(3) There may be a sale of a part interest in existing identified goods.

(4) An undivided share in an identified bulk of fungible goods is sufficiently identified to be sold although the quantity of the bulk is not determined. Any agreed proportion of such a bulk or any quantity thereof agreed upon by number, weight or other measure may to the extent of the seller's interest in the bulk be sold to the buyer who then becomes an owner in common.

(5) "Lot" means a parcel or a single article which is the subject matter of a separate sale or delivery, whether or not it is sufficient to perform the contract.

(6) "Commercial unit" means such a unit of goods as by commercial usage is a single whole for purposes of sale and division of which materially impairs its character or value on the market or in use. A commercial unit may be a single article (as a machine) or a set of articles (as a suite of furniture or an assortment of sizes) or a quantity (as a bale, gross, or carload) or any other unit treated in use or in the relevant market as a single whole.

§ 2–106. Definitions: "Contract"; "Agreement"; "Contract for Sale"; "Sale"; "Present Sale"; "Conforming" to Contract; "Termination"; "Cancellation".

(1) In this Article unless the context otherwise requires "contract" and "agreement" are limited to those relating to the present or future sale of goods. "Contract for sale" includes both a present sale of goods and a contract to sell goods at a future time. A "sale" consists in the passing of title from the seller to the buyer for a price (Section 2–401). A "present sale" means a sale which is accomplished by the making of the contract.

(2) Goods or conduct including any part of a performance are "conforming" or conform to the contract when they are in accordance with the obligations under the contract.

(3) "Termination" occurs when either party pursuant to a power created by agreement or law puts an end to the contract otherwise than for its breach. On "termination" all obligations which are still executory on both sides are discharged but any right based on prior breach or performance survives.

(4) "Cancellation" occurs when either party puts an end to the contract for breach by the other and its effect is the same as that of "termination" except that the cancelling party also retains any remedy for breach of the whole contract or any unperformed balance.

§ 2–107. Goods to Be Severed from Realty: Recording.

(1) A contract for the sale of minerals or the like (including oil and gas) or a structure or its materials to be removed from realty is a contract for the sale of goods within this Article if they are to be severed by the seller but until severance a purported present sale thereof which is not effective as a transfer of an interest in land is effective only as a contract to sell.

(2) A contract for the sale apart from the land of growing crops or other things attached to realty and capable of severance without material harm thereto but not described in subsection (1) or of timber to be cut is a contract for the sale of goods within this Article whether the subject matter is to be severed by the buyer or by the seller even though it forms part of the realty at the time of contracting, and the parties can by identification effect a present sale before severance.

(3) The provisions of this section are subject to any third party rights provided by the law relating to realty records, and the contract for sale may be executed and recorded as a document transferring an interest in land and shall then constitute notice to third parties of the buyer's rights under the contract for sale.

As amended in 1972.

PART 2 Form, Formation and Readjustment of Contract

§ 2–201. Formal Requirements; Statute of Frauds.

(1) Except as otherwise provided in this section a contract for the sale of goods for the price of $500 or more is not enforceable by way of action or defense unless there is some writing sufficient to indicate that a contract for sale has been made between the parties and signed by the party against whom enforcement is sought or by his authorized agent or broker. A writing is not insufficient because it omits or incorrectly states a term agreed upon

but the contract is not enforceable under this paragraph beyond the quantity of goods shown in such writing.

(2) Between merchants if within a reasonable time a writing in confirmation of the contract and sufficient against the sender is received and the party receiving it has reason to know its contents, it satisfies the requirements of subsection (1) against such party unless written notice of objection to its contents is given within ten days after it is received.

(3) A contract which does not satisfy the requirements of subsection (1) but which is valid in other respects is enforceable

(a) if the goods are to be specially manufactured for the buyer and are not suitable for sale to others in the ordinary course of the seller's business and the seller, before notice of repudiation is received and under circumstances which reasonably indicate that the goods are for the buyer, has made either a substantial beginning of their manufacture or commitments for their procurement; or

(b) if the party against whom enforcement is sought admits in his pleading, testimony or otherwise in court that a contract for sale was made, but the contract is not enforceable under this provision beyond the quantity of goods admitted; or

(c) with respect to goods for which payment has been made and accepted or which have been received and accepted (Section 2–606).

§ 2–202. Final Written Expression: Parol or Extrinsic Evidence.

Terms with respect to which the confirmatory memoranda of the parties agree or which are otherwise set forth in a writing intended by the parties as a final expression of their agreement with respect to such terms as are included therein may not be contradicted by evidence of any prior agreement or of a contemporaneous oral agreement but may be explained or supplemented

(a) by course of dealing or usage of trade (Section 1–205) or by course of performance (Section 2–208); and

(b) by evidence of consistent additional terms unless the court finds the writing to have been intended also as a complete and exclusive statement of the terms of the agreement.

§ 2–203. Seals Inoperative.

The affixing of a seal to a writing evidencing a contract for sale or an offer to buy or sell goods does not constitute the writing a sealed instrument and the law with respect to sealed instruments does not apply to such a contract or offer.

§ 2–204. Formation in General.

(1) A contract for sale of goods may be made in any manner sufficient to show agreement, including conduct by both parties which recognizes the existence of such a contract.

(2) An agreement sufficient to constitute a contract for sale may be found even though the moment of its making is undetermined.

(3) Even though one or more terms are left open a contract for sale does not fail for indefiniteness if the parties have intended to make a contract and there is a reasonably certain basis for giving an appropriate remedy.

§ 2–205. Firm Offers.

An offer by a merchant to buy or sell goods in a signed writing which by its terms gives assurance that it will be held open is not revocable, for lack of consideration, during the time stated or if no time is stated for a reasonable time, but in no event may such period of irrevocability exceed three months; but any such term of assurance on a form supplied by the offeree must be separately signed by the offeror.

§ 2–206. Offer and Acceptance in Formation of Contract.

(1) Unless other unambiguously indicated by the language or circumstances

(a) an offer to make a contract shall be construed as inviting acceptance in any manner and by any medium reasonable in the circumstances;

(b) an order or other offer to buy goods for prompt or current shipment shall be construed as inviting acceptance either by a prompt promise to ship or by the prompt or current shipment of conforming or nonconforming goods, but such a shipment of nonconforming goods does not constitute an acceptance if the seller seasonably notifies the buyer that the shipment is offered only as an accommodation to the buyer.

(2) Where the beginning of a requested performance is a reasonable mode of acceptance an offeror who is not notified of acceptance within a reasonable time may treat the offer as having lapsed before acceptance.

§ 2–207. Additional Terms in Acceptance or Confirmation.

(1) A definite and seasonable expression of acceptance or a written confirmation which is sent within a reasonable time operates as an acceptance even though it states terms additional to or different from those offered or agreed upon, unless acceptance is expressly made conditional on assent to the additional or different terms.

(2) The additional terms are to be construed as proposals for addition to the contract. Between merchants such terms become part of the contract unless:

(a) the offer expressly limits acceptance to the terms of the offer;

(b) they materially alter it; or

(c) notification of objection to them has already been given or is given within a reasonable time after notice of them is received.

(3) Conduct by both parties which recognizes the existence of a contract is sufficient to establish a contract for sale although the writings of the parties do not otherwise establish a contract.

In such case the terms of the particular contract consist of those terms on which the writings of the parties agree, together with any supplementary terms incorporated under any other provisions of this Act.

§ 2–208. Course of Performance or Practical Construction.

(1) Where the contract for sale involves repeated occasions for performance by either party with knowledge of the nature of the performance and opportunity for objection to it by the other, any course of performance accepted or acquiesced in without objection shall be relevant to determine the meaning of the agreement.

(2) The express terms of the agreement and any such course of performance, as well as any course of dealing and usage of trade, shall be construed whenever reasonable as consistent with each other; but when such construction is unreasonable, express terms shall control course of performance and course of performance shall control both course of dealing and usage of trade (Section 1–205).

(3) Subject to the provisions of the next section on modification and waiver, such course of performance shall be relevant to show a waiver or modification of any term inconsistent with such course of performance.

§ 2–209. Modification, Rescission and Waiver.

(1) An agreement modifying a contract within this Article needs no consideration to be binding.

(2) A signed agreement which excludes modification or rescission except by a signed writing cannot be otherwise modified or rescinded, but except as between merchants such a requirement on a form supplied by the merchant must be separately signed by the other party.

(3) The requirements of the statute of frauds section of this Article (Section 2–201) must be satisfied if the contract as modified is within its provisions.

(4) Although an attempt at modification or rescission does not satisfy the requirements of subsection (2) or (3) it can operate as a waiver.

(5) A party who has made a waiver affecting an executory portion of the contract may retract the waiver by reasonable notification received by the other party that strict performance will be required of any term waived, unless the retraction would be unjust in view of a material change of position in reliance on the waiver.

§ 2–210. Delegation of Performance; Assignment of Rights.

(1) A party may perform his duty through a delegate unless otherwise agreed or unless the other party has a substantial interest in having his original promisor perform or control the acts required by the contract. No delegation of performance relieves the party delegating of any duty to perform or any liability for breach.

(2) Except as otherwise provided in Section 9–406, unless otherwise agreed, all rights of either seller or buyer can be assigned except where the assignment would materially change the duty of the other party, or increase materially the burden or risk imposed on him by his contract, or impair materially his chance of obtaining return performance.

A right to damages for breach of the whole contract or a right arising out of the assignor's due performance of his entire obligation can be assigned despite agreement otherwise.

(3) The creation, attachment, perfection, or enforcement of a security interest in the seller's interest under a contract is not a transfer that materially changes the duty of or increases materially the burden or risk imposed on the buyer or impairs materially the buyer's chance of obtaining return performance within the purview of subsection (2) unless, and then only to the extent that, enforcement actually results in a delegation of material performance of the seller. Even in that event, the creation, attachment, perfection, and enforcement of the security interest remain effective, but (i) the seller is liable to the buyer for damages caused by the delegation to the extent that the damages could not reasonably be prevented by the buyer, and (ii) a court having jurisdiction may grant other appropriate relief, including cancellation of the contract for sale or an injunction against enforcement of the security interest or consummation of the enforcement.

(4) Unless the circumstances indicate the contrary a prohibition of assignment of "the contract" is to be construed as barring only the delegation to the assignee of the assignor's performance.

(5) An assignment of "the contract" or of "all my rights under the contract" or an assignment in similar general terms is an assignment of rights and unless the language or the circumstances (as in an assignment for security) indicate the contrary, it is a delegation of performance of the duties of the assignor and its acceptance by the assignee constitutes a promise by him to perform those duties. This promise is enforceable by either the assignor or the other party to the original contract.

(6) The other party may treat any assignment which delegates performance as creating reasonable grounds for insecurity and may without prejudice to his rights against the assignor demand assurances from the assignee (Section 2–609).

As amended in 1999.

PART 3 General Obligation and Construction of Contract

§ 2–301. General Obligations of Parties.

The obligation of the seller is to transfer and deliver and that of the buyer is to accept and pay in accordance with the contract.

§ 2–302. Unconscionable Contract or Clause.

(1) If the court as a matter of law finds the contract or any clause of the contract to have been unconscionable at the time it was made the court may refuse to enforce the contract, or it may enforce the remainder of the contract without the unconscionable clause, or it may so limit the application of any unconscionable clause as to avoid any unconscionable result.

(2) When it is claimed or appears to the court that the contract or any clause thereof may be unconscionable the parties shall be afforded a reasonable opportunity to present evidence as to its commercial setting, purpose and effect to aid the court in making the determination.

§ 2–303. Allocations or Division of Risks.

Where this Article allocates a risk or a burden as between the parties "unless otherwise agreed", the agreement may not only shift the allocation but may also divide the risk or burden.

§ 2–304. Price Payable in Money, Goods, Realty, or Otherwise.

(1) The price can be made payable in money or otherwise. If it is payable in whole or in part in goods each party is a seller of the goods which he is to transfer.

(2) Even though all or part of the price is payable in an interest in realty the transfer of the goods and the seller's obligations with reference to them are subject to this Article, but not the transfer of the interest in realty or the transferor's obligations in connection therewith.

§ 2–305. Open Price Term.

(1) The parties if they so intend can conclude a contract for sale even though the price is not settled. In such a case the price is a reasonable price at the time for delivery if

(a) nothing is said as to price; or

(b) the price is left to be agreed by the parties and they fail to agree; or

(c) the price is to be fixed in terms of some agreed market or other standard as set or recorded by a third person or agency and it is not so set or recorded.

(2) A price to be fixed by the seller or by the buyer means a price for him to fix in good faith.

(3) When a price left to be fixed otherwise than by agreement of the parties fails to be fixed through fault of one party the other may at his option treat the contract as cancelled or himself fix a reasonable price.

(4) Where, however, the parties intend not to be bound unless the price be fixed or agreed and it is not fixed or agreed there is no contract. In such a case the buyer must return any goods already received or if unable so to do must pay their reasonable value at the time of delivery and the seller must return any portion of the price paid on account.

§ 2–306. Output, Requirements and Exclusive Dealings.

(1) A term which measures the quantity by the output of the seller or the requirements of the buyer means such actual output or requirements as may occur in good faith, except that no quantity unreasonably disproportionate to any stated estimate or in the absence of a stated estimate to any normal or otherwise comparable prior output or requirements may be tendered or demanded.

(2) A lawful agreement by either the seller or the buyer for exclusive dealing in the kind of goods concerned imposes unless otherwise agreed an obligation by the seller to use best efforts to supply the goods and by the buyer to use best efforts to promote their sale.

§ 2–307. Delivery in Single Lot or Several Lots.

Unless otherwise agreed all goods called for by a contract for sale must be tendered in a single delivery and payment is due only on such tender but where the circumstances give either party the right to make or demand delivery in lots the price if it can be apportioned may be demanded for each lot.

§ 2–308. Absence of Specified Place for Delivery.

Unless otherwise agreed

(a) the place for delivery of goods is the seller's place of business or if he has none his residence; but

(b) in a contract for sale of identified goods which to the knowledge of the parties at the time of contracting are in some other place, that place is the place for their delivery; and

(c) documents of title may be delivered through customary banking channels.

§ 2–309. Absence of Specific Time Provisions; Notice of Termination.

(1) The time for shipment or delivery or any other action under a contract if not provided in this Article or agreed upon shall be a reasonable time.

(2) Where the contract provides for successive performances but is indefinite in duration it is valid for a reasonable time but unless otherwise agreed may be terminated at any time by either party.

(3) Termination of a contract by one party except on the happening of an agreed event requires that reasonable notification be received by the other party and an agreement dispensing with notification is invalid if its operation would be unconscionable.

§ 2–310. Open Time for Payment or Running of Credit; Authority to Ship Under Reservation.

Unless otherwise agreed

(a) payment is due at the time and place at which the buyer is to receive the goods even though the place of shipment is the place of delivery; and

(b) if the seller is authorized to send the goods he may ship them under reservation, and may tender the documents of title, but the buyer may inspect the goods after their arrival before payment is due unless such inspection is inconsistent with the terms of the contract (Section 2–513); and

(c) if delivery is authorized and made by way of documents of title otherwise than by subsection (b) then payment is due at the time and place at which the buyer is to receive the documents regardless of where the goods are to be received; and

(d) where the seller is required or authorized to ship the goods on credit the credit period runs from the time of shipment but post-dating the invoice or delaying its dispatch will correspondingly delay the starting of the credit period.

§ 2–311. Options and Cooperation Respecting Performance.

(1) An agreement for sale which is otherwise sufficiently definite (subsection (3) of Section 2–204) to be a contract is not made invalid by the fact that it leaves particulars of performance to be specified by one of the parties. Any such specification must be made in good faith and within limits set by commercial reasonableness.

(2) Unless otherwise agreed specifications relating to assortment of the goods are at the buyer's option and except as otherwise provided in subsections (1)(c) and (3) of Section 2–319 specifications or arrangements relating to shipment are at the seller's option.

(3) Where such specification would materially affect the other party's performance but is not seasonably made or where one party's cooperation is necessary to the agreed performance of the other but is not seasonably forthcoming, the other party in addition to all other remedies

(a) is excused for any resulting delay in his own performance; and

(b) may also either proceed to perform in any reasonable manner or after the time for a material part of his own performance treat the failure to specify or to cooperate as a breach by failure to deliver or accept the goods.

§ 2–312. Warranty of Title and Against Infringement; Buyer's Obligation Against Infringement.

(1) Subject to subsection (2) there is in a contract for sale a warranty by the seller that

(a) the title conveyed shall be good, and its transfer rightful; and

(b) the goods shall be delivered free from any security interest or other lien or encumbrance of which the buyer at the time of contracting has no knowledge.

(2) A warranty under subsection (1) will be excluded or modified only by specific language or by circumstances which give the buyer reason to know that the person selling does not claim title in himself or that he is purporting to sell only such right or title as he or a third person may have.

(3) Unless otherwise agreed a seller who is a merchant regularly dealing in goods of the kind warrants that the goods shall be delivered free of the rightful claim of any third person by way of infringement or the like but a buyer who furnishes specifications to the seller must hold the seller harmless against any such claim which arises out of compliance with the specifications.

§ 2–313. Express Warranties by Affirmation, Promise, Description, Sample.

(1) Express warranties by the seller are created as follows:

(a) Any affirmation of fact or promise made by the seller to the buyer which relates to the goods and becomes part of the basis of the bargain creates an express warranty that the goods shall conform to the affirmation or promise.

(b) Any description of the goods which is made part of the basis of the bargain creates an express warranty that the goods shall conform to the description.

(c) Any sample or model which is made part of the basis of the bargain creates an express warranty that the whole of the goods shall conform to the sample or model.

(2) It is not necessary to the creation of an express warranty that the seller use formal words such as "warrant" or "guarantee" or that he have a specific intention to make a warranty, but an affirmation merely of the value of the goods or a statement purporting to be merely the seller's opinion or commendation of the goods does not create a warranty.

§ 2–314. Implied Warranty: Merchantability; Usage of Trade.

(1) Unless excluded or modified (Section 2–316), a warranty that the goods shall be merchantable is implied in a contract for their sale if the seller is a merchant with respect to goods of that kind. Under this section the serving for value of food or drink to be consumed either on the premises or elsewhere is a sale.

(2) Goods to be merchantable must be at least such as

(a) pass without objection in the trade under the contract description; and

(b) in the case of fungible goods, are of fair average quality within the description; and

(c) are fit for the ordinary purposes for which such goods are used; and

(d) run, within the variations permitted by the agreement, of even kind, quality and quantity within each unit and among all units involved; and

(e) are adequately contained, packaged, and labeled as the agreement may require; and

(f) conform to the promises or affirmations of fact made on the container or label if any.

(3) Unless excluded or modified (Section 2–316) other implied warranties may arise from course of dealing or usage of trade.

§ 2–315. Implied Warranty: Fitness for Particular Purpose.

Where the seller at the time of contracting has reason to know any particular purpose for which the goods are required and that the buyer is relying on the seller's skill or judgment to select or furnish suitable goods, there is unless excluded or modified under the next section an implied warranty that the goods shall be fit for such purpose.

§ 2–316. Exclusion or Modification of Warranties.

(1) Words or conduct relevant to the creation of an express warranty and words or conduct tending to negate or limit warranty shall be construed wherever reasonable as consistent with each other; but subject to the provisions of this Article on parol or extrinsic evidence (Section 2–202) negation or limitation is inoperative to the extent that such construction is unreasonable.

(2) Subject to subsection (3), to exclude or modify the implied warranty of merchantability or any part of it the language must mention merchantability and in case of a writing must be conspicuous, and to exclude or modify any implied warranty of fitness the exclusion must be by a writing and conspicuous. Language to exclude all implied warranties of fitness is sufficient if it states, for example, that "There are no warranties which extend beyond the description on the face hereof."

(3) Notwithstanding subsection (2)

(a) unless the circumstances indicate otherwise, all implied warranties are excluded by expressions like "as is", "with all faults" or other language which in common understanding calls the buyer's attention to the exclusion of warranties and makes plain that there is no implied warranty; and

(b) when the buyer before entering into the contract has examined the goods or the sample or model as fully as he desired or has refused to examine the goods there is no implied warranty with regard to defects which an examination ought in the circumstances to have revealed to him; and

(c) an implied warranty can also be excluded or modified by course of dealing or course of performance or usage of trade.

(4) Remedies for breach of warranty can be limited in accordance with the provisions of this Article on liquidation or limitation of damages and on contractual modification of remedy (Sections 2–718 and 2–719).

§ 2–317. Cumulation and Conflict of Warranties Express or Implied.

Warranties whether express or implied shall be construed as consistent with each other and as cumulative, but if such construction is unreasonable the intention of the parties shall determine which warranty is dominant. In ascertaining that intention the following rules apply:

(a) Exact or technical specifications displace an inconsistent sample or model or general language of description.

(b) A sample from an existing bulk displaces inconsistent general language of description.

(c) Express warranties displace inconsistent implied warranties other than an implied warranty of fitness for a particular purpose.

§ 2–318. Third Party Beneficiaries of Warranties Express or Implied.

Note: If this Act is introduced in the Congress of the United States this section should be omitted. (States to select one alternative.)

Alternative A A seller's warranty whether express or implied extends to any natural person who is in the family or household of his buyer or who is a guest in his home if it is reasonable to expect that such person may use, consume or be affected by the goods and who is injured in person by breach of the warranty. A seller may not exclude or limit the operation of this section.

Alternative B A seller's warranty whether express or implied extends to any natural person who may reasonably be expected to use, consume or be affected by the goods and who is injured in person by breach of the warranty. A seller may not exclude or limit the operation of this section.

Alternative C A seller's warranty whether express or implied extends to any person who may reasonably be expected to use, consume or be affected by the goods and who is injured by breach of the warranty. A seller may not exclude or limit the operation of this section with respect to injury to the person of an individual to whom the warranty extends.

As amended in 1966.

§ 2–319. F.O.B. and F.A.S. Terms.

(1) Unless otherwise agreed the term F.O.B. (which means "free on board") at a named place, even though used only in connection with the stated price, is a delivery term under which

(a) when the term is F.O.B. the place of shipment, the seller must at that place ship the goods in the manner provided in this Article (Section 2–504) and bear the expense and risk of putting them into the possession of the carrier; or

(b) when the term is F.O.B. the place of destination, the seller must at his own expense and risk transport the goods to that place and there tender delivery of them in the manner provided in this Article (Section 2–503);

(c) when under either (a) or (b) the term is also F.O.B. vessel, car or other vehicle, the seller must in addition at his own expense and risk load the goods on board. If the term is F.O.B. vessel the buyer must name the vessel and in an appropriate case the seller must comply with the provisions of this Article on the form of bill of lading (Section 2–323).

(2) Unless otherwise agreed the term F.A.S. vessel (which means "free alongside") at a named port, even though used only in connection with the stated price, is a delivery term under which the seller must

(a) at his own expense and risk deliver the goods alongside the vessel in the manner usual in that port or on a dock designated and provided by the buyer; and

(b) obtain and tender a receipt for the goods in exchange for which the carrier is under a duty to issue a bill of lading.

(3) Unless otherwise agreed in any case falling within subsection (1)(a) or (c) or subsection (2) the buyer must seasonably give any needed instructions for making delivery, including when the term is F.A.S. or F.O.B. the loading berth of the vessel and in an appropriate case its name and sailing date. The seller may treat the failure of needed instructions as a failure of cooperation under this Article (Section 2–311). He may also at his option move the goods in any reasonable manner preparatory to delivery or shipment.

(4) Under the term F.O.B. vessel or F.A.S. unless otherwise agreed the buyer must make payment against tender of the required documents and the seller may not tender nor the buyer demand delivery of the goods in substitution for the documents.

§ 2–320. C.I.F. and C. & F. Terms.

(1) The term C.I.F. means that the price includes in a lump sum the cost of the goods and the insurance and freight to the named destination. The term C. & F. or C.F. means that the price so includes cost and freight to the named destination.

(2) Unless otherwise agreed and even though used only in connection with the stated price and destination, the term C.I.F. destination or its equivalent requires the seller at his own expense and risk to

(a) put the goods into the possession of a carrier at the port for shipment and obtain a negotiable bill or bills of lading covering the entire transportation to the named destination; and

(b) load the goods and obtain a receipt from the carrier (which may be contained in the bill of lading) showing that the freight has been paid or provided for; and

(c) obtain a policy or certificate of insurance, including any war risk insurance, of a kind and on terms then current at the port of shipment in the usual amount, in the currency of the contract, shown to cover the same goods covered by the bill of lading and providing for payment of loss to the order of the buyer or for the account of whom it may concern; but the seller may add to the price the amount of the premium for any such war risk insurance; and

(d) prepare an invoice of the goods and procure any other documents required to effect shipment or to comply with the contract; and

(e) forward and tender with commercial promptness all the documents in due form and with any indorsement necessary to perfect the buyer's rights.

(3) Unless otherwise agreed the term C. & F. or its equivalent has the same effect and imposes upon the seller the same obligations and risks as a C.I.F. term except the obligation as to insurance.

(4) Under the term C.I.F. or C. & F. unless otherwise agreed the buyer must make payment against tender of the required documents and the seller may not tender nor the buyer demand delivery of the goods in substitution for the documents.

§ 2–321. C.I.F. or C. & F.: "Net Landed Weights"; "Payment on Arrival"; Warranty of Condition on Arrival.

Under a contract containing a term C.I.F. or C. & F.

(1) Where the price is based on or is to be adjusted according to "net landed weights", "delivered weights", "out turn" quantity or quality or the like, unless otherwise agreed the seller must reasonably estimate the price. The payment due on tender of the documents called for by the contract is the amount so estimated, but after final adjustment of the price a settlement must be made with commercial promptness.

(2) An agreement described in subsection (1) or any warranty of quality or condition of the goods on arrival places upon the seller the risk of ordinary deterioration, shrinkage and the like in transportation but has no effect on the place or time of identification to the contract for sale or delivery or on the passing of the risk of loss.

(3) Unless otherwise agreed where the contract provides for payment on or after arrival of the goods the seller must before payment allow such preliminary inspection as is feasible; but if the goods are lost delivery of the documents and payment are due when the goods should have arrived.

§ 2–322. Delivery "Ex-Ship".

(1) Unless otherwise agreed a term for delivery of goods "ex-ship" (which means from the carrying vessel) or in equivalent language is not restricted to a particular ship and requires delivery from a ship which has reached a place at the named port of destination where goods of the kind are usually discharged.

(2) Under such a term unless otherwise agreed

(a) the seller must discharge all liens arising out of the carriage and furnish the buyer with a direction which puts the carrier under a duty to deliver the goods; and

(b) the risk of loss does not pass to the buyer until the goods leave the ship's tackle or are otherwise properly unloaded.

§ 2–323. Form of Bill of Lading Required in Overseas Shipment; "Overseas".

(1) Where the contract contemplates overseas shipment and contains a term C.I.F. or C. & F. or F.O.B. vessel, the seller unless otherwise agreed must obtain a negotiable bill of lading stating that the goods have been loaded on board or, in the case of a term C.I.F. or C. & F., received for shipment.

(2) Where in a case within subsection (1) a bill of lading has been issued in a set of parts, unless otherwise agreed if the documents are not to be sent from abroad the buyer may demand tender of the full set; otherwise only one part of the bill of lading need be tendered. Even if the agreement expressly requires a full set

(a) due tender of a single part is acceptable within the provisions of this Article on cure of improper delivery (subsection (1) of Section 2–508); and

(b) even though the full set is demanded, if the documents are sent from abroad the person tendering an incomplete set may nevertheless require payment upon furnishing an indemnity which the buyer in good faith deems adequate.

(3) A shipment by water or by air or a contract contemplating such shipment is "overseas" insofar as by usage of trade or agreement it is subject to the commercial, financing or shipping practices characteristic of international deep water commerce.

§ 2–324. "No Arrival, No Sale" Term.

Under a term "no arrival, no sale" or terms of like meaning, unless otherwise agreed,

(a) the seller must properly ship conforming goods and if they arrive by any means he must tender them on arrival but he assumes no obligation that the goods will arrive unless he has caused the non-arrival; and

(b) where without fault of the seller the goods are in part lost or have so deteriorated as no longer to conform to the contract or arrive after the contract time, the buyer may proceed as if there had been casualty to identified goods (Section 2–613).

§ 2–325. "Letter of Credit" Term; "Confirmed Credit".

(1) Failure of the buyer seasonably to furnish an agreed letter of credit is a breach of the contract for sale.

(2) The delivery to seller of a proper letter of credit suspends the buyer's obligation to pay. If the letter of credit is dishonored, the seller may on seasonable notification to the buyer require payment directly from him.

(3) Unless otherwise agreed the term "letter of credit" or "banker's credit" in a contract for sale means an irrevocable credit issued by a financing agency of good repute and, where the shipment is overseas, of good international repute. The term "confirmed credit" means that the credit must also carry the direct obligation of such an agency which does business in the seller's financial market.

§ 2–326. Sale on Approval and Sale or Return; Rights of Creditors.

(1) Unless otherwise agreed, if delivered goods may be returned by the buyer even though they conform to the contract, the transaction is

(a) a "sale on approval" if the goods are delivered primarily for use, and

(b) a "sale or return" if the goods are delivered primarily for resale.

(2) Goods held on approval are not subject to the claims of the buyer's creditors until acceptance; goods held on sale or return are subject to such claims while in the buyer's possession.

(3) Any "or return" term of a contract for sale is to be treated as a separate contract for sale within the statute of frauds section of this Article (Section 2–201) and as contradicting the sale aspect of the contract within the provisions of this Article or on parol or extrinsic evidence (Section 2–202).

As amended in 1999.

§ 2–327. Special Incidents of Sale on Approval and Sale or Return.

(1) Under a sale on approval unless otherwise agreed

(a) although the goods are identified to the contract the risk of loss and the title do not pass to the buyer until acceptance; and

(b) use of the goods consistent with the purpose of trial is not acceptance but failure seasonably to notify the seller of election to return the goods is acceptance, and if the goods conform to the contract acceptance of any part is acceptance of the whole; and

(c) after due notification of election to return, the return is at the seller's risk and expense but a merchant buyer must follow any reasonable instructions.

(2) Under a sale or return unless otherwise agreed

(a) the option to return extends to the whole or any commercial unit of the goods while in substantially their original condition, but must be exercised seasonably; and

(b) the return is at the buyer's risk and expense.

§ 2–328. Sale by Auction.

(1) In a sale by auction if goods are put up in lots each lot is the subject of a separate sale.

(2) A sale by auction is complete when the auctioneer so announces by the fall of the hammer or in other customary manner. Where a bid is made while the hammer is falling in acceptance of a prior bid the auctioneer may in his discretion reopen the bidding or declare the goods sold under the bid on which the hammer was falling.

(3) Such a sale is with reserve unless the goods are in explicit terms put up without reserve. In an auction with reserve the auctioneer may withdraw the goods at any time until he announces completion of the sale. In an auction without reserve, after the auctioneer calls for bids on an article or lot, that article or lot cannot be withdrawn unless no bid is made within a reasonable time. In either case a bidder may retract his bid until the auctioneer's announcement of completion of the sale, but a bidder's retraction does not revive any previous bid.

(4) If the auctioneer knowingly receives a bid on the seller's behalf or the seller makes or procures such as bid, and notice has not been given that liberty for such bidding is reserved, the buyer may at his option avoid the sale or take the goods at the price of the last good faith bid prior to the completion of the sale. This subsection shall not apply to any bid at a forced sale.

PART 4 Title, Creditors and Good Faith Purchasers

§ 2–401. Passing of Title; Reservation for Security; Limited Application of This Section.

Each provision of this Article with regard to the rights, obligations and remedies of the seller, the buyer, purchasers or other third parties applies irrespective of title to the goods except where the provision refers to such title. Insofar as situations are not covered by the other provisions of this Article and matters concerning title became material the following rules apply:

(1) Title to goods cannot pass under a contract for sale prior to their identification to the contract (Section 2–501), and unless otherwise explicitly agreed the buyer acquires by their identification a special property as limited by this Act. Any retention or reservation by the seller of the title (property) in goods shipped or delivered to the buyer is limited in effect to a reservation of a

security interest. Subject to these provisions and to the provisions of the Article on Secured Transactions (Article 9), title to goods passes from the seller to the buyer in any manner and on any conditions explicitly agreed on by the parties.

(2) Unless otherwise explicitly agreed title passes to the buyer at the time and place at which the seller completes his performance with reference to the physical delivery of the goods, despite any reservation of a security interest and even though a document of title is to be delivered at a different time or place; and in particular and despite any reservation of a security interest by the bill of lading

(a) if the contract requires or authorizes the seller to send the goods to the buyer but does not require him to deliver them at destination, title passes to the buyer at the time and place of shipment; but

(b) if the contract requires delivery at destination, title passes on tender there.

(3) Unless otherwise explicitly agreed where delivery is to be made without moving the goods,

(a) if the seller is to deliver a document of title, title passes at the time when and the place where he delivers such documents; or

(b) if the goods are at the time of contracting already identified and no documents are to be delivered, title passes at the time and place of contracting.

(4) A rejection or other refusal by the buyer to receive or retain the goods, whether or not justified, or a justified revocation of acceptance revests title to the goods in the seller. Such revesting occurs by operation of law and is not a "sale".

§ 2–402. Rights of Seller's Creditors Against Sold Goods.

(1) Except as provided in subsections (2) and (3), rights of unsecured creditors of the seller with respect to goods which have been identified to a contract for sale are subject to the buyer's rights to recover the goods under this Article (Sections 2–502 and 2–716).

(2) A creditor of the seller may treat a sale or an identification of goods to a contract for sale as void if as against him a retention of possession by the seller is fraudulent under any rule of law of the state where the goods are situated, except that retention of possession in good faith and current course of trade by a merchant-seller for a commercially reasonable time after a sale or identification is not fraudulent.

(3) Nothing in this Article shall be deemed to impair the rights of creditors of the seller

(a) under the provisions of the Article on Secured Transactions (Article 9); or

(b) where identification to the contract or delivery is made not in current course of trade but in satisfaction of or as security for a pre-existing claim for money, security or the like and is made under circumstances which under any rule of law of the state where the goods are situated would apart from this Article constitute the transaction a fraudulent transfer or voidable preference.

§ 2–403. Power to Transfer; Good Faith Purchase of Goods; "Entrusting".

(1) A purchaser of goods acquires all title which his transferor had or had power to transfer except that a purchaser of a limited interest acquires rights only to the extent of the interest purchased. A person with voidable title has power to transfer a good title to a good faith purchaser for value. When goods have been delivered under a transaction of purchase the purchaser has such power even though

(a) the transferor was deceived as to the identity of the purchaser, or

(b) the delivery was in exchange for a check which is later dishonored, or

(c) it was agreed that the transaction was to be a "cash sale", or

(d) the delivery was procured through fraud punishable as larcenous under the criminal law.

(2) Any entrusting of possession of goods to a merchant who deals in goods of that kind gives him power to transfer all rights of the entruster to a buyer in ordinary course of business.

(3) "Entrusting" includes any delivery and any acquiescence in retention of possession regardless of any condition expressed between the parties to the delivery or acquiescence and regardless of whether the procurement of the entrusting or the possessor's disposition of the goods have been such as to be larcenous under the criminal law.

(4) The rights of other purchasers of goods and of lien creditors are governed by the Articles on Secured Transactions (Article 9), Bulk Transfers (Article 6) and Documents of Title (Article 7).

As amended in 1988.

PART 5 Performance

§ 2–501. Insurable Interest in Goods; Manner of Identification of Goods.

(1) The buyer obtains a special property and an insurable interest in goods by identification of existing goods as goods to which the contract refers even though the goods so identified are nonconforming and he has an option to return or reject them. Such identification can be made at any time and in any manner explicitly agreed to by the parties. In the absence of explicit agreement identification occurs

(a) when the contract is made if it is for the sale of goods already existing and identified;

(b) if the contract is for the sale of future goods other than those described in paragraph (c), when goods are shipped, marked or otherwise designated by the seller as goods to which the contract refers;

(c) when the crops are planted or otherwise become growing crops or the young are conceived if the contract is for the sale of unborn young to be born within twelve months after contracting or for the sale of crops to be harvested within twelve months or the next normal harvest season after contracting whichever is longer.

(2) The seller retains an insurable interest in goods so long as title to or any security interest in the goods remains in him and where the identification is by the seller alone he may until default or insolvency or notification to the buyer that the identification is final substitute other goods for those identified.

(3) Nothing in this section impairs any insurable interest recognized under any other statute or rule of law.

§ 2–502. Buyer's Right to Goods on Seller's Insolvency.

(1) Subject to subsections (2) and (3) and even though the goods have not been shipped a buyer who has paid a part or all of the price of goods in which he has a special property under the provisions of the immediately preceding section may on making and keeping good a tender of any unpaid portion of their price recover them from the seller if:

(a) in the case of goods bought for personal, family, or household purposes, the seller repudiates or fails to deliver as required by the contract; or

(b) in all cases, the seller becomes insolvent within ten days after receipt of the first installment on their price.

(2) The buyer's right to recover the goods under subsection (1)(a) vests upon acquisition of a special property, even if the seller had not then repudiated or failed to deliver.

(3) If the identification creating his special property has been made by the buyer he acquires the right to recover the goods only if they conform to the contract for sale.

As amended in 1999.

§ 2–503. Manner of Seller's Tender of Delivery.

(1) Tender of delivery requires that the seller put and hold conforming goods at the buyer's disposition and give the buyer any notification reasonably necessary to enable him to take delivery. The manner, time and place for tender are determined by the agreement and this Article, and in particular

(a) tender must be at a reasonable hour, and if it is of goods they must be kept available for the period reasonably necessary to enable the buyer to take possession; but

(b) unless otherwise agreed the buyer must furnish facilities reasonably suited to the receipt of the goods.

(2) Where the case is within the next section respecting shipment tender requires that the seller comply with its provisions.

(3) Where the seller is required to deliver at a particular destination tender requires that he comply with subsection (1) and also in any appropriate case tender documents as described in subsections (4) and (5) of this section.

(4) Where goods are in the possession of a bailee and are to be delivered without being moved

(a) tender requires that the seller either tender a negotiable document of title covering such goods or procure acknowledgment by the bailee of the buyer's right to possession of the goods; but

(b) tender to the buyer of a non-negotiable document of title or of a written direction to the bailee to deliver is sufficient tender unless the buyer seasonably objects, and receipt by the bailee of notification of the buyer's rights fixes those rights as against the bailee and all third persons; but risk of loss of the goods and of any failure by the bailee to honor the non-negotiable document of title or to obey the direction remains on the seller until the buyer has had a reasonable time to present the document or direction, and a refusal by the bailee to honor the document or to obey the direction defeats the tender.

(5) Where the contract requires the seller to deliver documents

(a) he must tender all such documents in correct form, except as provided in this Article with respect to bills of lading in a set (subsection (2) of Section 2–323); and

(b) tender through customary banking channels is sufficient and dishonor of a draft accompanying the documents constitutes non-acceptance or rejection.

§ 2–504. Shipment by Seller.

Where the seller is required or authorized to send the goods to the buyer and the contract does not require him to deliver them at a particular destination, then unless otherwise agreed he must

(a) put the goods in the possession of such a carrier and make such a contract for their transportation as may be reasonable having regard to the nature of the goods and other circumstances of the case; and

(b) obtain and promptly deliver or tender in due form any document necessary to enable the buyer to obtain possession of the goods or otherwise required by the agreement or by usage of trade; and

(c) promptly notify the buyer of the shipment.

Failure to notify the buyer under paragraph (c) or to make a proper contract under paragraph (a) is a ground for rejection only if material delay or loss ensues.

§ 2–505. Seller's Shipment under Reservation.

(1) Where the seller has identified goods to the contract by or before shipment:

(a) his procurement of a negotiable bill of lading to his own order or otherwise reserves in him a security interest in the goods. His procurement of the bill to the order of a financing agency or of the buyer indicates in addition only the seller's expectation of transferring that interest to the person named.

(b) a non-negotiable bill of lading to himself or his nominee reserves possession of the goods as security but except in a case of conditional delivery (subsection (2) of Section 2–507) a non-negotiable bill of lading naming the buyer as consignee reserves no security interest even though the seller retains possession of the bill of lading.

(2) When shipment by the seller with reservation of a security interest is in violation of the contract for sale it constitutes an improper contract for transportation within the preceding section but impairs neither the rights given to the buyer by shipment and identification of the goods to the contract nor the seller's powers as a holder of a negotiable document.

§ 2–506. Rights of Financing Agency.

(1) A financing agency by paying or purchasing for value a draft which relates to a shipment of goods acquires to the extent of the payment or purchase and in addition to its own rights under the draft and any document of title securing it any rights of the shipper in the goods including the right to stop delivery and the shipper's right to have the draft honored by the buyer.

(2) The right to reimbursement of a financing agency which has in good faith honored or purchased the draft under commitment to or authority from the buyer is not impaired by subsequent discovery of defects with reference to any relevant document which was apparently regular on its face.

§ 2–507. Effect of Seller's Tender; Delivery on Condition.

(1) Tender of delivery is a condition to the buyer's duty to accept the goods and, unless otherwise agreed, to his duty to pay for them. Tender entitles the seller to acceptance of the goods and to payment according to the contract.

(2) Where payment is due and demanded on the delivery to the buyer of goods or documents of title, his right as against the seller to retain or dispose of them is conditional upon his making the payment due.

§ 2–508. Cure by Seller of Improper Tender or Delivery; Replacement.

(1) Where any tender or delivery by the seller is rejected because non-conforming and the time for performance has not yet expired, the seller may seasonably notify the buyer of his intention to cure and may then within the contract time make a conforming delivery.

(2) Where the buyer rejects a non-conforming tender which the seller had reasonable grounds to believe would be acceptable with or without money allowance the seller may if he seasonably notifies the buyer have a further reasonable time to substitute a conforming tender.

§ 2–509. Risk of Loss in the Absence of Breach.

(1) Where the contract requires or authorizes the seller to ship the goods by carrier

(a) if it does not require him to deliver them at a particular destination, the risk of loss passes to the buyer when the goods are duly delivered to the carrier even though the shipment is under reservation (Section 2–505); but

(b) if it does require him to deliver them at a particular destination and the goods are there duly tendered while in the possession of the carrier, the risk of loss passes to the buyer when the goods are there duly so tendered as to enable the buyer to take delivery.

(2) Where the goods are held by a bailee to be delivered without being moved, the risk of loss passes to the buyer

(a) on his receipt of a negotiable document of title covering the goods; or

(b) on acknowledgment by the bailee of the buyer's right to possession of the goods; or

(c) after his receipt of a non-negotiable document of title or other written direction to deliver, as provided in subsection (4)(b) of Section 2–503.

(3) In any case not within subsection (1) or (2), the risk of loss passes to the buyer on his receipt of the goods if the seller is a merchant; otherwise the risk passes to the buyer on tender of delivery.

(4) The provisions of this section are subject to contrary agreement of the parties and to the provisions of this Article on sale on approval (Section 2–327) and on effect of breach on risk of loss (Section 2–510).

§ 2–510. Effect of Breach on Risk of Loss.

(1) Where a tender or delivery of goods so fails to conform to the contract as to give a right of rejection the risk of their loss remains on the seller until cure or acceptance.

(2) Where the buyer rightfully revokes acceptance he may to the extent of any deficiency in his effective insurance coverage treat the risk of loss as having rested on the seller from the beginning.

(3) Where the buyer as to conforming goods already identified to the contract for sale repudiates or is otherwise in breach before risk of their loss has passed to him, the seller may to the extent of any deficiency in his effective insurance coverage treat the risk of loss as resting on the buyer for a commercially reasonable time.

§ 2–511. Tender of Payment by Buyer; Payment by Check.

(1) Unless otherwise agreed tender of payment is a condition to the seller's duty to tender and complete any delivery.

(2) Tender of payment is sufficient when made by any means or in any manner current in the ordinary course of business unless the seller demands payment in legal tender and gives any extension of time reasonably necessary to procure it.

(3) Subject to the provisions of this Act on the effect of an instrument on an obligation (Section 3–310), payment by check is conditional and is defeated as between the parties by dishonor of the check on due presentment.

As amended in 1994.

§ 2–512. Payment by Buyer Before Inspection.

(1) Where the contract requires payment before inspection non-conformity of the goods does not excuse the buyer from so making payment unless

(a) the non-conformity appears without inspection; or

(b) despite tender of the required documents the circumstances would justify injunction against honor under this Act (Section 5–109(b)).

(2) Payment pursuant to subsection (1) does not constitute an acceptance of goods or impair the buyer's right to inspect or any of his remedies.

As amended in 1995.

§ 2–513. Buyer's Right to Inspection of Goods.

(1) Unless otherwise agreed and subject to subsection (3), where goods are tendered or delivered or identified to the contract for sale, the buyer has a right before payment or acceptance to inspect them at any reasonable place and time and in any reasonable manner. When the seller is required or authorized to send the goods to the buyer, the inspection may be after their arrival.

(2) Expenses of inspection must be borne by the buyer but may be recovered from the seller if the goods do not conform and are rejected.

(3) Unless otherwise agreed and subject to the provisions of this Article on C.I.F. contracts (subsection (3) of Section 2–321), the buyer is not entitled to inspect the goods before payment of the price when the contract provides

(a) for delivery "C.O.D." or on other like terms; or

(b) for payment against documents of title, except where such payment is due only after the goods are to become available for inspection.

(4) A place or method of inspection fixed by the parties is presumed to be exclusive but unless otherwise expressly agreed it does not postpone identification or shift the place for delivery or for passing the risk of loss. If compliance becomes impossible, inspection shall be as provided in this section unless the place or method fixed was clearly intended as an indispensable condition failure of which avoids the contract.

§ 2–514. When Documents Deliverable on Acceptance; When on Payment.

Unless otherwise agreed documents against which a draft is drawn are to be delivered to the drawee on acceptance of the draft if it is payable more than three days after presentment; otherwise, only on payment.

§ 2–515. Preserving Evidence of Goods in Dispute.

In furtherance of the adjustment of any claim or dispute

(a) either party on reasonable notification to the other and for the purpose of ascertaining the facts and preserving evidence has the right to inspect, test and sample the goods including such of them as may be in the possession or control of the other; and

(b) the parties may agree to a third party inspection or survey to determine the conformity or condition of the goods and may agree that the findings shall be binding upon them in any subsequent litigation or adjustment.

PART 6 Breach, Repudiation and Excuse

§ 2–601. Buyer's Rights on Improper Delivery.

Subject to the provisions of this Article on breach in installment contracts (Section 2–612) and unless otherwise agreed under the sections on contractual limitations of remedy (Sections 2–718 and 2–719), if the goods or the tender of delivery fail in any respect to conform to the contract, the buyer may

(a) reject the whole; or

(b) accept the whole; or

(c) accept any commercial unit or units and reject the rest.

§ 2–602. Manner and Effect of Rightful Rejection.

(1) Rejection of goods must be within a reasonable time after their delivery or tender. It is ineffective unless the buyer seasonably notifies the seller.

(2) Subject to the provisions of the two following sections on rejected goods (Sections 2–603 and 2–604),

(a) after rejection any exercise of ownership by the buyer with respect to any commercial unit is wrongful as against the seller; and

(b) if the buyer has before rejection taken physical possession of goods in which he does not have a security interest under the provisions of this Article (subsection (3) of Section 2–711), he is under a duty after rejection to hold them with reasonable care at the seller's disposition for a time sufficient to permit the seller to remove them; but

(c) the buyer has no further obligations with regard to goods rightfully rejected.

(3) The seller's rights with respect to goods wrongfully rejected are governed by the provisions of this Article on Seller's remedies in general (Section 2–703).

§ 2–603. Merchant Buyer's Duties as to Rightfully Rejected Goods.

(1) Subject to any security interest in the buyer (subsection (3) of Section 2–711), when the seller has no agent or place of business at the market of rejection a merchant buyer is under a duty after rejection of goods in his possession or control to follow any reasonable instructions received from the seller with respect to the

goods and in the absence of such instructions to make reasonable efforts to sell them for the seller's account if they are perishable or threaten to decline in value speedily. Instructions are not reasonable if on demand indemnity for expenses is not forthcoming.

(2) When the buyer sells goods under subsection (1), he is entitled to reimbursement from the seller or out of the proceeds for reasonable expenses of caring for and selling them, and if the expenses include no selling commission then to such commission as is usual in the trade or if there is none to a reasonable sum not exceeding ten percent on the gross proceeds.

(3) In complying with this section the buyer is held only to good faith and good faith conduct hereunder is neither acceptance nor conversion nor the basis of an action for damages.

§ 2–604. Buyer's Options as to Salvage of Rightfully Rejected Goods.

Subject to the provisions of the immediately preceding section on perishables if the seller gives no instructions within a reasonable time after notification of rejection the buyer may store the rejected goods for the seller's account or reship them to him or resell them for the seller's account with reimbursement as provided in the preceding section. Such action is not acceptance or conversion.

§ 2–605. Waiver of Buyer's Objections by Failure to Particularize.

(1) The buyer's failure to state in connection with rejection a particular defect which is ascertainable by reasonable inspection precludes him from relying on the unstated defect to justify rejection or to establish breach

(a) where the seller could have cured it if stated seasonably; or

(b) between merchants when the seller has after rejection made a request in writing for a full and final written statement of all defects on which the buyer proposes to rely.

(2) Payment against documents made without reservation of rights precludes recovery of the payment for defects apparent on the face of the documents.

§ 2–606. What Constitutes Acceptance of Goods.

(1) Acceptance of goods occurs when the buyer

(a) after a reasonable opportunity to inspect the goods signifies to the seller that the goods are conforming or that he will take or retain them in spite of their nonconformity; or

(b) fails to make an effective rejection (subsection (1) of Section 2–602), but such acceptance does not occur until the buyer has had a reasonable opportunity to inspect them; or

(c) does any act inconsistent with the seller's ownership; but if such act is wrongful as against the seller it is an acceptance only if ratified by him.

(2) Acceptance of a part of any commercial unit is acceptance of that entire unit.

§ 2–607. Effect of Acceptance; Notice of Breach; Burden of Establishing Breach After Acceptance; Notice of Claim or Litigation to Person Answerable Over.

(1) The buyer must pay at the contract rate for any goods accepted.

(2) Acceptance of goods by the buyer precludes rejection of the goods accepted and if made with knowledge of a non-conformity cannot be revoked because of it unless the acceptance was on the reasonable assumption that the non-conformity would be seasonably cured but acceptance does not of itself impair any other remedy provided by this Article for non-conformity.

(3) Where a tender has been accepted

(a) the buyer must within a reasonable time after he discovers or should have discovered any breach notify the seller of breach or be barred from any remedy; and

(b) if the claim is one for infringement or the like (subsection (3) of Section 2–312) and the buyer is sued as a result of such a breach he must so notify the seller within a reasonable time after he receives notice of the litigation or be barred from any remedy over for liability established by the litigation.

(4) The burden is on the buyer to establish any breach with respect to the goods accepted.

(5) Where the buyer is sued for breach of a warranty or other obligation for which his seller is answerable over

(a) he may give his seller written notice of the litigation. If the notice states that the seller may come in and defend and that if the seller does not do so he will be bound in any action against him by his buyer by any determination of fact common to the two litigations, then unless the seller after seasonable receipt of the notice does come in and defend he is so bound.

(b) if the claim is one for infringement or the like (subsection (3) of Section 2–312) the original seller may demand in writing that his buyer turn over to him control of the litigation including settlement or else be barred from any remedy over and if he also agrees to bear all expense and to satisfy any adverse judgment, then unless the buyer after seasonable receipt of the demand does turn over control the buyer is so barred.

(6) The provisions of subsections (3), (4) and (5) apply to any obligation of a buyer to hold the seller harmless against infringement or the like (subsection (3) of Section 2–312).

§ 2–608. Revocation of Acceptance in Whole or in Part.

(1) The buyer may revoke his acceptance of a lot or commercial unit whose nonconformity substantially impairs its value to him if he has accepted it

(a) on the reasonable assumption that its nonconformity would be cured and it has not been seasonably cured; or

(b) without discovery of such non-conformity if his acceptance was reasonably induced either by the difficulty of discovery before acceptance or by the seller's assurances.

(2) Revocation of acceptance must occur within a reasonable time after the buyer discovers or should have discovered the ground for it and before any substantial change in condition of the goods which is not caused by their own defects. It is not effective until the buyer notifies the seller of it.

(3) A buyer who so revokes has the same rights and duties with regard to the goods involved as if he had rejected them.

§ 2–609. Right to Adequate Assurance of Performance.

(1) A contract for sale imposes an obligation on each party that the other's expectation of receiving due performance will not be impaired. When reasonable grounds for insecurity arise with respect to the performance of either party the other may in writing demand adequate assurance of due performance and until he receives such assurance may if commercially reasonable suspend any performance for which he has not already received the agreed return.

(2) Between merchants the reasonableness of grounds for insecurity and the adequacy of any assurance offered shall be determined according to commercial standards.

(3) Acceptance of any improper delivery or payment does not prejudice the party's right to demand adequate assurance of future performance.

(4) After receipt of a justified demand failure to provide within a reasonable time not exceeding thirty days such assurance of due performance as is adequate under the circumstances of the particular case is a repudiation of the contract.

§ 2–610. Anticipatory Repudiation.

When either party repudiates the contract with respect to a performance not yet due the loss of which will substantially impair the value of the contract to the other, the aggrieved party may

(a) for a commercially reasonable time await performance by the repudiating party; or

(b) resort to any remedy for breach (Section 2–703 or Section 2–711), even though he has notified the repudiating party that he would await the latter's performance and has urged retraction; and

(c) in either case suspend his own performance or proceed in accordance with the provisions of this Article on the seller's right to identify goods to the contract notwithstanding breach or to salvage unfinished goods (Section 2–704).

§ 2–611. Retraction of Anticipatory Repudiation.

(1) Until the repudiating party's next performance is due he can retract his repudiation unless the aggrieved party has since the repudiation cancelled or materially changed his position or otherwise indicated that he considers the repudiation final.

(2) Retraction may be by any method which clearly indicates to the aggrieved party that the repudiating party intends to perform, but must include any assurance justifiably demanded under the provisions of this Article (Section 2–609).

(3) Retraction reinstates the repudiating party's rights under the contract with due excuse and allowance to the aggrieved party for any delay occasioned by the repudiation.

§ 2–612. "Installment Contract"; Breach.

(1) An "installment contract" is one which requires or authorizes the delivery of goods in separate lots to be separately accepted, even though the contract contains a clause "each delivery is a separate contract" or its equivalent.

(2) The buyer may reject any installment which is non-conforming if the non-conformity substantially impairs the value of that installment and cannot be cured or if the non-conformity is a defect in the required documents; but if the non-conformity does not fall within subsection (3) and the seller gives adequate assurance of its cure the buyer must accept that installment.

(3) Whenever non-conformity or default with respect to one or more installments substantially impairs the value of the whole contract there is a breach of the whole. But the aggrieved party reinstates the contract if he accepts a non-conforming installment without seasonably notifying of cancellation or if he brings an action with respect only to past installments or demands performance as to future installments.

§ 2–613. Casualty to Identified Goods.

Where the contract requires for its performance goods identified when the contract is made, and the goods suffer casualty without fault of either party before the risk of loss passes to the buyer, or in a proper case under a "no arrival, no sale" term (Section 2–324) then

(a) if the loss is total the contract is avoided; and

(b) if the loss is partial or the goods have so deteriorated as no longer to conform to the contract the buyer may nevertheless demand inspection and at his option either treat the contract as voided or accept the goods with due allowance from the contract price for the deterioration or the deficiency in quantity but without further right against the seller.

§ 2–614. Substituted Performance.

(1) Where without fault of either party the agreed berthing, loading, or unloading facilities fail or an agreed type of carrier becomes unavailable or the agreed manner of delivery otherwise becomes commercially impracticable but a commercially reasonable substitute is available, such substitute performance must be tendered and accepted.

(2) If the agreed means or manner of payment fails because of domestic or foreign governmental regulation, the seller may withhold or stop delivery unless the buyer provides a means or manner of payment which is commercially a substantial equivalent. If delivery has already been taken, payment by the means or in the manner provided by the regulation discharges the buyer's obligation unless the regulation is discriminatory, oppressive or predatory.

§ 2–615. Excuse by Failure of Presupposed Conditions.

Except so far as a seller may have assumed a greater obligation and subject to the preceding section on substituted performance:

(a) Delay in delivery or non-delivery in whole or in part by a seller who complies with paragraphs (b) and (c) is not a breach of his duty under a contract for sale if performance as agreed has been made impracticable by the occurrence of a contingency the nonoccurrence of which was a basic assumption on which the contract was made or by compliance in good faith with any applicable foreign or domestic governmental regulation or order whether or not it later proves to be invalid.

(b) Where the causes mentioned in paragraph (a) affect only a part of the seller's capacity to perform, he must allocate production and deliveries among his customers but may at his option include regular customers not then under contract as well as his own requirements for further manufacture. He may so allocate in any manner which is fair and reasonable.

(c) The seller must notify the buyer seasonably that there will be delay or non-delivery and, when allocation is required under paragraph (b), of the estimated quota thus made available for the buyer.

§ 2–616. Procedure on Notice Claiming Excuse.

(1) Where the buyer receives notification of a material or indefinite delay or an allocation justified under the preceding section he may by written notification to the seller as to any delivery concerned, and where the prospective deficiency substantially impairs the value of the whole contract under the provisions of this Article relating to breach of installment contracts (Section 2–612), then also as to the whole,

(a) terminate and thereby discharge any unexecuted portion of the contract; or

(b) modify the contract by agreeing to take his available quota in substitution.

(2) If after receipt of such notification from the seller the buyer fails so to modify the contract within a reasonable time not exceeding thirty days the contract lapses with respect to any deliveries affected.

(3) The provisions of this section may not be negated by agreement except in so far as the seller has assumed a greater obligation under the preceding section.

PART 7 Remedies

§ 2–701. Remedies for Breach of Collateral Contracts Not Impaired.

Remedies for breach of any obligation or promise collateral or ancillary to a contract for sale are not impaired by the provisions of this Article.

§ 2–702. Seller's Remedies on Discovery of Buyer's Insolvency.

(1) Where the seller discovers the buyer to be insolvent he may refuse delivery except for cash including payment for all goods theretofore delivered under the contract, and stop delivery under this Article (Section 2–705).

(2) Where the seller discovers that the buyer has received goods on credit while insolvent he may reclaim the goods upon demand made within ten days after the receipt, but if misrepresentation of solvency has been made to the particular seller in writing within three months before delivery the ten day limitation does not apply. Except as provided in this subsection the seller may not base a right to reclaim goods on the buyer's fraudulent or innocent misrepresentation of solvency or of intent to pay.

(3) The seller's right to reclaim under subsection (2) is subject to the rights of a buyer in ordinary course or other good faith purchaser under this Article (Section 2–403). Successful reclamation of goods excludes all other remedies with respect to them.

§ 2–703. Seller's Remedies in General.

Where the buyer wrongfully rejects or revokes acceptance of goods or fails to make a payment due on or before delivery or repudiates with respect to a part or the whole, then with respect to any goods directly affected and, if the breach is of the whole contract (Section 2–612), then also with respect to the whole undelivered balance, the aggrieved seller may

(a) withhold delivery of such goods;

(b) stop delivery by any bailee as hereafter provided (Section 2–705);

(c) proceed under the next section respecting goods still unidentified to the contract;

(d) resell and recover damages as hereafter provided (Section 2–706);

(e) recover damages for non-acceptance (Section 2–708) or in a proper case the price (Section 2–709);

(f) cancel.

§ 2–704. Seller's Right to Identify Goods to the Contract Notwithstanding Breach or to Salvage Unfinished Goods.

(1) An aggrieved seller under the preceding section may

(a) identify to the contract conforming goods not already identified if at the time he learned of the breach they are in his possession or control;

(b) treat as the subject of resale goods which have demonstrably been intended for the particular contract even though those goods are unfinished.

(2) Where the goods are unfinished an aggrieved seller may in the exercise of reasonable commercial judgment for the purposes of avoiding loss and of effective realization either complete the

manufacture and wholly identify the goods to the contract or cease manufacture and resell for scrap or salvage value or proceed in any other reasonable manner.

§ 2–705. Seller's Stoppage of Delivery in Transit or Otherwise.

(1) The seller may stop delivery of goods in the possession of a carrier or other bailee when he discovers the buyer to be insolvent (Section 2–702) and may stop delivery of carload, truckload, planeload or larger shipments of express or freight when the buyer repudiates or fails to make a payment due before delivery or if for any other reason the seller has a right to withhold or reclaim the goods.

(2) As against such buyer the seller may stop delivery until

(a) receipt of the goods by the buyer; or

(b) acknowledgment to the buyer by any bailee of the goods except a carrier that the bailee holds the goods for the buyer; or

(c) such acknowledgment to the buyer by a carrier by reshipment or as warehouseman; or

(d) negotiation to the buyer of any negotiable document of title covering the goods.

(3) (a) To stop delivery the seller must so notify as to enable the bailee by reasonable diligence to prevent delivery of the goods.

(b) After such notification the bailee must hold and deliver the goods according to the directions of the seller but the seller is liable to the bailee for any ensuing charges or damages.

(c) If a negotiable document of title has been issued for goods the bailee is not obliged to obey a notification to stop until surrender of the document.

(d) A carrier who has issued a non-negotiable bill of lading is not obliged to obey a notification to stop received from a person other than the consignor.

§ 2–706. Seller's Resale Including Contract for Resale.

(1) Under the conditions stated in Section 2–703 on seller's remedies, the seller may resell the goods concerned or the undelivered balance thereof. Where the resale is made in good faith and in a commercially reasonable manner the seller may recover the difference between the resale price and the contract price together with any incidental damages allowed under the provisions of this Article (Section 2–710), but less expenses saved in consequence of the buyer's breach.

(2) Except as otherwise provided in subsection (3) or unless otherwise agreed resale may be at public or private sale including sale by way of one or more contracts to sell or of identification to an existing contract of the seller. Sale may be as a unit or in parcels and at any time and place and on any terms but every aspect of the sale including the method, manner, time, place and terms must be commercially reasonable. The resale must be reasonably identified as referring to the broken contract, but it is not necessary that the goods be in existence or that any or all of them have been identified to the contract before the breach.

(3) Where the resale is at private sale the seller must give the buyer reasonable notification of his intention to resell.

(4) Where the resale is at public sale

(a) only identified goods can be sold except where there is a recognized market for a public sale of futures in goods of the kind; and

(b) it must be made at a usual place or market for public sale if one is reasonably available and except in the case of goods which are perishable or threaten to decline in value speedily the seller must give the buyer reasonable notice of the time and place of the resale; and

(c) if the goods are not to be within the view of those attending the sale the notification of sale must state the place where the goods are located and provide for their reasonable inspection by prospective bidders; and

(d) the seller may buy.

(5) A purchaser who buys in good faith at a resale takes the goods free of any rights of the original buyer even though the seller fails to comply with one or more of the requirements of this section.

(6) The seller is not accountable to the buyer for any profit made on any resale. A person in the position of a seller (Section 2–707) or a buyer who has rightfully rejected or justifiably revoked acceptance must account for any excess over the amount of his security interest, as hereinafter defined (subsection (3) of Section 2–711).

§ 2–707. "Person in the Position of a Seller".

(1) A "person in the position of a seller" includes as against a principal an agent who has paid or become responsible for the price of goods on behalf of his principal or anyone who otherwise holds a security interest or other right in goods similar to that of a seller.

(2) A person in the position of a seller may as provided in this Article withhold or stop delivery (Section 2–705) and resell (Section 2–706) and recover incidental damages (Section 2–710).

§ 2–708. Seller's Damages for Non-Acceptance or Repudiation.

(1) Subject to subsection (2) and to the provisions of this Article with respect to proof of market price (Section 2–723), the measure of damages for non-acceptance or repudiation by the buyer is the difference between the market price at the time and place for tender and the unpaid contract price together with any incidental damages provided in this Article (Section 2–710), but less expenses saved in consequence of the buyer's breach.

(2) If the measure of damages provided in subsection (1) is inadequate to put the seller in as good a position as performance would have done then the measure of damages is the profit (including reasonable overhead) which the seller would have made from full performance by the buyer, together with any

incidental damages provided in this Article (Section 2–710), due allowance for costs reasonably incurred and due credit for payments or proceeds of resale.

§ 2–709. Action for the Price.

(1) When the buyer fails to pay the price as it becomes due the seller may recover, together with any incidental damages under the next section, the price

(a) of goods accepted or of conforming goods lost or damaged within a commercially reasonable time after risk of their loss has passed to the buyer; and

(b) of goods identified to the contract if the seller is unable after reasonable effort to resell them at a reasonable price or the circumstances reasonably indicate that such effort will be unavailing.

(2) Where the seller sues for the price he must hold for the buyer any goods which have been identified to the contract and are still in his control except that if resale becomes possible he may resell them at any time prior to the collection of the judgment. The net proceeds of any such resale must be credited to the buyer and payment of the judgment entitles him to any goods not resold.

(3) After the buyer has wrongfully rejected or revoked acceptance of the goods or has failed to make a payment due or has repudiated (Section 2–610), a seller who is held not entitled to the price under this section shall nevertheless be awarded damages for non-acceptance under the preceding section.

§ 2–710. Seller's Incidental Damages.

Incidental damages to an aggrieved seller include any commercially reasonable charges, expenses or commissions incurred in stopping delivery, in the transportation, care and custody of goods after the buyer's breach, in connection with return or resale of the goods or otherwise resulting from the breach.

§ 2–711. Buyer's Remedies in General; Buyer's Security Interest in Rejected Goods.

(1) Where the seller fails to make delivery or repudiates or the buyer rightfully rejects or justifiably revokes acceptance then with respect to any goods involved, and with respect to the whole if the breach goes to the whole contract (Section 2–612), the buyer may cancel and whether or not he has done so may in addition to recovering so much of the price as has been paid

(a) "cover" and have damages under the next section as to all the goods affected whether or not they have been identified to the contract; or

(b) recover damages for non-delivery as provided in this Article (Section 2–713).

(2) Where the seller fails to deliver or repudiates the buyer may also

(a) if the goods have been identified recover them as provided in this Article (Section 2–502); or

(b) in a proper case obtain specific performance or replevy the goods as provided in this Article (Section 2–716).

(3) On rightful rejection or justifiable revocation of acceptance a buyer has a security interest in goods in his possession or control for any payments made on their price and any expenses reasonably incurred in their inspection, receipt, transportation, care and custody and may hold such goods and resell them in like manner as an aggrieved seller (Section 2–706).

§ 2–712. "Cover"; Buyer's Procurement of Substitute Goods.

(1) After a breach within the preceding section the buyer may "cover" by making in good faith and without unreasonable delay any reasonable purchase of or contract to purchase goods in substitution for those due from the seller.

(2) The buyer may recover from the seller as damages the difference between the cost of cover and the contract price together with any incidental or consequential damages as hereinafter defined (Section 2–715), but less expenses saved in consequence of the seller's breach.

(3) Failure of the buyer to effect cover within this section does not bar him from any other remedy.

§ 2–713. Buyer's Damages for Non-Delivery or Repudiation.

(1) Subject to the provisions of this Article with respect to proof of market price (Section 2–723), the measure of damages for non delivery or repudiation by the seller is the difference between the market price at the time when the buyer learned of the breach and the contract price together with any incidental and consequential damages provided in this Article (Section 2–715), but less expenses saved in consequence of the seller's breach.

(2) Market price is to be determined as of the place for tender or, in cases of rejection after arrival or revocation of acceptance, as of the place of arrival.

§ 2–714. Buyer's Damages for Breach in Regard to Accepted Goods.

(1) Where the buyer has accepted goods and given notification (subsection (3) of Section 2–607) he may recover as damages for any non-conformity of tender the loss resulting in the ordinary course of events from the seller's breach as determined in any manner which is reasonable.

(2) The measure of damages for breach of warranty is the difference at the time and place of acceptance between the value of the goods accepted and the value they would have had if they had been as warranted, unless special circumstances show proximate damages of a different amount.

(3) In a proper case any incidental and consequential damages under the next section may also be recovered.

§ 2–715. Buyer's Incidental and Consequential Damages.

(1) Incidental damages resulting from the seller's breach include expenses reasonably incurred in inspection, receipt, transportation and care and custody of goods rightfully rejected, any commercially reasonable charges, expenses or commissions in connection with effecting cover and any other reasonable expense incident to the delay or other breach.

(2) Consequential damages resulting from the seller's breach include

(a) any loss resulting from general or particular requirements and needs of which the seller at the time of contracting had reason to know and which could not reasonably be prevented by cover or otherwise; and

(b) injury to person or property proximately resulting from any breach of warranty.

§ 2–716. Buyer's Right to Specific Performance or Replevin.

(1) Specific performance may be decreed where the goods are unique or in other proper circumstances.

(2) The decree for specific performance may include such terms and conditions as to payment of the price, damages, or other relief as the court may deem just.

(3) The buyer has a right of replevin for goods identified to the contract if after reasonable effort he is unable to effect cover for such goods or the circumstances reasonably indicate that such effort will be unavailing or if the goods have been shipped under reservation and satisfaction of the security interest in them has been made or tendered. In the case of goods bought for personal, family, or household purposes, the buyer's right of replevin vests upon acquisition of a special property, even if the seller had not then repudiated or failed to deliver.

As amended in 1999.

§ 2–717. Deduction of Damages from the Price.

The buyer on notifying the seller of his intention to do so may deduct all or any part of the damages resulting from any breach of the contract from any part of the price still due under the same contract.

§ 2–718. Liquidation or Limitation of Damages; Deposits.

(1) Damages for breach by either party may be liquidated in the agreement but only at an amount which is reasonable in the light of the anticipated or actual harm caused by the breach, the difficulties of proof of loss, and the inconvenience or nonfeasibility of otherwise obtaining an adequate remedy. A term fixing unreasonably large liquidated damages is void as a penalty.

(2) Where the seller justifiably withholds delivery of goods because of the buyer's breach, the buyer is entitled to restitution of any amount by which the sum of his payments exceeds

(a) the amount to which the seller is entitled by virtue of terms liquidating the seller's damages in accordance with subsection (1), or

(b) in the absence of such terms, twenty percent of the value of the total performance for which the buyer is obligated under the contract or $500, whichever is smaller.

(3) The buyer's right to restitution under subsection (2) is subject to offset to the extent that the seller establishes

(a) a right to recover damages under the provisions of this Article other than subsection (1), and

(b) the amount or value of any benefits received by the buyer directly or indirectly by reason of the contract.

(4) Where a seller has received payment in goods their reasonable value or the proceeds of their resale shall be treated as payments for the purposes of subsection (2); but if the seller has notice of the buyer's breach before reselling goods received in part performance, his resale is subject to the conditions laid down in this Article on resale by an aggrieved seller (Section 2–706).

§ 2–719. Contractual Modification or Limitation of Remedy.

(1) Subject to the provisions of subsections (2) and (3) of this section and of the preceding section on liquidation and limitation of damages,

(a) the agreement may provide for remedies in addition to or in substitution for those provided in this Article and may limit or alter the measure of damages recoverable under this Article, as by limiting the buyer's remedies to return of the goods and repayment of the price or to repair and replacement of nonconforming goods or parts; and

(b) resort to a remedy as provided is optional unless the remedy is expressly agreed to be exclusive, in which case it is the sole remedy.

(2) Where circumstances cause an exclusive or limited remedy to fail of its essential purpose, remedy may be had as provided in this Act.

(3) Consequential damages may be limited or excluded unless the limitation or exclusion is unconscionable. Limitation of consequential damages for injury to the person in the case of consumer goods is prima facie unconscionable but limitation of damages where the loss is commercial is not.

§ 2–720. Effect of "Cancellation" or "Rescission" on Claims for Antecedent Breach.

Unless the contrary intention clearly appears, expressions of "cancellation" or "rescission" of the contract or the like shall not be construed as a renunciation or discharge of any claim in damages for an antecedent breach.

§ 2–721. Remedies for Fraud.

Remedies for material misrepresentation or fraud include all remedies available under this Article for non-fraudulent breach. Neither rescission or a claim for rescission of the contract for sale nor rejection or return of the goods shall bar or be deemed inconsistent with a claim for damages or other remedy.

§ 2–722. Who Can Sue Third Parties for Injury to Goods.

Where a third party so deals with goods which have been identified to a contract for sale as to cause actionable injury to a party to that contract

(a) a right of action against the third party is in either party to the contract for sale who has title to or a security interest or a special property or an insurable interest in the goods; and if the goods have been destroyed or converted a right of action is also in the party who either bore the risk of loss under the contract for sale or has since the injury assumed that risk as against the other;

(b) if at the time of the injury the party plaintiff did not bear the risk of loss as against the other party to the contract for sale and there is no arrangement between them for disposition of the recovery, his suit or settlement is, subject to his own interest, as a fiduciary for the other party to the contract;

(c) either party may with the consent of the other sue for the benefit of whom it may concern.

§ 2–723. Proof of Market Price: Time and Place.

(1) If an action based on anticipatory repudiation comes to trial before the time for performance with respect to some or all of the goods, any damages based on market price (Section 2–708 or Section 2–713) shall be determined according to the price of such goods prevailing at the time when the aggrieved party learned of the repudiation.

(2) If evidence of a price prevailing at the times or places described in this Article is not readily available the price prevailing within any reasonable time before or after the time described or at any other place which in commercial judgment or under usage of trade would serve as a reasonable substitute for the one described may be used, making any proper allowance for the cost of transporting the goods to or from such other place.

(3) Evidence of a relevant price prevailing at a time or place other than the one described in this Article offered by one party is not admissible unless and until he has given the other party such notice as the court finds sufficient to prevent unfair surprise.

§ 2–724. Admissibility of Market Quotations.

Whenever the prevailing price or value of any goods regularly bought and sold in any established commodity market is in issue, reports in official publications or trade journals or in newspapers or periodicals of general circulation published as the reports of such market shall be admissible in evidence. The circumstances of the preparation of such a report may be shown to affect its weight but not its admissibility.

§ 2–725. Statute of Limitations in Contracts for Sale.

(1) An action for breach of any contract for sale must be commenced within four years after the cause of action has accrued. By the original agreement the parties may reduce the period of limitation to not less than one year but may not extend it.

(2) A cause of action accrues when the breach occurs, regardless of the aggrieved party's lack of knowledge of the breach. A breach of warranty occurs when tender of delivery is made, except that where a warranty explicitly extends to future performance of the goods and discovery of the breach must await the time of such performance the cause of action accrues when the breach is or should have been discovered.

(3) Where an action commenced within the time limited by subsection (1) is so terminated as to leave available a remedy by another action for the same breach such other action may be commenced after the expiration of the time limited and within six months after the termination of the first action unless the termination resulted from voluntary discontinuance or from dismissal for failure or neglect to prosecute.

(4) This section does not alter the law on tolling of the statute of limitations nor does it apply to causes of action which have accrued before this Act becomes effective.

ARTICLE II AMENDMENTS (EXCERPTS)[1]

PART 1 Short Title, General Construction and Subject Matter

§ 2–103. Definitions and Index of Definitions.

* * * *

(1) In this article unless the context otherwise requires

* * * *

(b) "Conspicuous", with reference to a term, means so written, displayed, or presented that a reasonable person against which it is to operate ought to have noticed it. A term in an electronic record intended to evoke a response by an electronic agent is conspicuous if it is presented in a form that would enable a reasonably configured electronic agent to take it into account or react to it without review of the record by an individual. Whether a term is "conspicuous" or not is a decision for the court. Conspicuous terms include the following:

(i) for a person:

(A) a heading in capitals equal to or greater in size than the surrounding text, or in contrasting type, font, or color to the surrounding text of the same or lesser size;

(B) language in the body of a record or display in larger type than the surrounding text, or in contrasting type, font, or color to the surrounding text of the same size, or set off from surrounding text of the same size by symbols or other marks that call attention to the language; and

(ii) for a person or an electronic agent, a term that is so placed in a record or display that the person or electronic agent cannot proceed without taking action with respect to the particular term.

(c) "Consumer" means an individual who buys or contracts to buy goods that, at the time of contracting, are intended by the individual to be used primarily for personal, family, or household purposes.

(d) "Consumer contract" means a contract between a merchant seller and a consumer.

* * * *

(j) "Good faith" means honesty in fact and the observance of reasonable commercial standards of fair dealing.

(k) "Goods" means all things that are movable at the time of identification to a contract for sale. The term includes future goods, specially manufactured goods, the unborn young of animals, growing crops, and other identified things attached to realty as described in Section 2–107. The term does not include information, the money in which the price is to be paid, investment securities under Article 8, the subject matter of foreign exchange transactions, and choses in action.

* * * *

(m) "Record" means information that is inscribed on a tangible medium or that is stored in an electronic or other medium and is retrievable in perceivable form.

(n) "Remedial promise" means a promise by the seller to repair or replace the goods or to refund all or part of the price upon the happening of a specified event.

* * * *

(p) "Sign" means, with present intent to authenticate or adopt a record,

(i) to execute or adopt a tangible symbol; or

(ii) to attach to or logically associate with the record an electronic sound, symbol, or process.

* * * *

PART 2 Form, Formation, Terms and Readjustment of Contract; Electronic Contracting

§ 2–201. Formal Requirements; Statute of Frauds.

(1) A contract for the sale of goods for the price of $5,000 or more is not enforceable by way of action or defense unless there is some record sufficient to indicate that a contract for sale has been made between the parties and signed by the party against whom which enforcement is sought or by the party's authorized agent or broker. A record is not insufficient because it omits or incorrectly states a term agreed upon but the contract is not enforceable under this subsection beyond the quantity of goods shown in the record.

(2) Between merchants if within a reasonable time a record in confirmation of the contract and sufficient against the sender is received and the party receiving it has reason to know its contents, it satisfies the requirements of subsection (1) against such party the recipient unless notice of objection to its contents is given in a record within 10 days after it is received.

(3) A contract which does not satisfy the requirements of subsection (1) but which is valid in other respects is enforceable

(a) if the goods are to be specially manufactured for the buyer and are not suitable for sale to others in the ordinary course of the seller's business and the seller, before notice of repudiation is received and under circumstances which reasonably indicate that the goods are for the buyer, has made either a substantial beginning of their manufacture or commitments for their procurement; or

(b) if the party against whom which enforcement is sought admits in the party's pleading, or in the party's testimony or otherwise under oath that a contract for sale was made, but the contract is not enforceable under this paragraph beyond the quantity of goods admitted; or

(c) with respect to goods for which payment has been made and accepted or which have been received and accepted (Section 2–606).

(4) A contract that is enforceable under this section is not rendered unenforceable merely because it is not capable of being performed within one year or any other applicable period after its making.

* * * *

§ 2–207. Terms of Contract; Effect of Confirmation.

If (i) conduct by both parties recognizes the existence of a contract although their records do not otherwise establish a contract, (ii) a contract is formed by an offer and acceptance, or (iii) a contract formed in any manner is confirmed by a record that contains terms additional to or different from those in the contract being confirmed, the terms of the contract, subject to Section 2–202, are:

(a) terms that appear in the records of both parties;

(b) terms, whether in a record or not, to which both parties agree; and

(c) terms supplied or incorporated under any provision of this Act.

* * * *

PART 3 General Obligation and Construction of Contract

* * * *

§ 2–312. Warranty of Title and Against Infringement; Buyer's Obligation Against Infringement.

(1) Subject to subsection (2) there is in a contract for sale a warranty by the seller that

(a) the title conveyed shall be good, good and its transfer rightful and shall not, because of any colorable claim to or interest in the goods, unreasonably expose the buyer to litigation; and

(b) the goods shall be delivered free from any security interest or other lien or encumbrance of which the buyer at the time of contracting has no knowledge.

(2) Unless otherwise agreed a seller that is a merchant regularly dealing in goods of the kind warrants that the goods shall be delivered free of the rightful claim of any third person by way of infringement or the like but a buyer that furnishes specifications to the seller must hold the seller harmless against any such claim that arises out of compliance with the specifications.

(3) A warranty under this section may be disclaimed or modified only by specific language or by circumstances that give the buyer reason to know that the seller does not claim title, that the seller is purporting to sell only the right or title as the seller or a third person may have, or that the seller is selling subject to any claims of infringement or the like.

§ 2–313. Express Warranties by Affirmation, Promise, Description, Sample; Remedial Promise.

(1) In this section, "immediate buyer" means a buyer that enters into a contract with the seller.

* * * *

(4) Any remedial promise made by the seller to the immediate buyer creates an obligation that the promise will be performed upon the happening of the specified event.

§ 2–313A. Obligation to Remote Purchaser Created by Record Packaged with or Accompanying Goods.

(1) This section applies only to new goods and goods sold or leased as new goods in a transaction of purchase in the normal chain of distribution. In this section:

(a) "Immediate buyer" means a buyer that enters into a contract with the seller.

(b) "Remote purchaser" means a person that buys or leases goods from an immediate buyer or other person in the normal chain of distribution.

(2) If a seller in a record packaged with or accompanying the goods makes an affirmation of fact or promise that relates to the goods, provides a description that relates to the goods, or makes a remedial promise, and the seller reasonably expects the record to be, and the record is, furnished to the remote purchaser, the seller has an obligation to the remote purchaser that:

(a) the goods will conform to the affirmation of fact, promise or description unless a reasonable person in the position of the remote purchaser would not believe that the affirmation of fact, promise or description created an obligation; and

(b) the seller will perform the remedial promise.

(3) It is not necessary to the creation of an obligation under this section that the seller use formal words such as "warrant" or "guarantee" or that the seller have a specific intention to undertake an obligation, but an affirmation merely of the value of the goods or a statement purporting to be merely the seller's opinion or commendation of the goods does not create an obligation.

(4) The following rules apply to the remedies for breach of an obligation created under this section:

(a) The seller may modify or limit the remedies available to the remote purchaser if the modification or limitation is furnished to the remote purchaser no later than the time of purchase or if the modification or limitation is contained in the record that contains the affirmation of fact, promise or description.

(b) Subject to a modification or limitation of remedy, a seller in breach is liable for incidental or consequential damages under Section 2–715, but the seller is not liable for lost profits.

(c) The remote purchaser may recover as damages for breach of a seller's obligation arising under subsection (2) the loss resulting in the ordinary course of events as determined in any manner that is reasonable.

(5) An obligation that is not a remedial promise is breached if the goods did not conform to the affirmation of fact, promise or description creating the obligation when the goods left the seller's control.

§ 2–313B. Obligation to Remote Purchaser Created by Communication to the Public.

(1) This section applies only to new goods and goods sold or leased as new goods in a transaction of purchase in the normal chain of distribution. In this section:

(a) "Immediate buyer" means a buyer that enters into a contract with the seller.

(b) "Remote purchaser" means a person that buys or leases goods from an immediate buyer or other person in the normal chain of distribution.

(2) If a seller in advertising or a similar communication to the public makes an affirmation of fact or promise that relates to the goods, provides a description that relates to the goods, or makes a remedial promise, and the remote purchaser enters into a transaction of purchase with knowledge of and with the expectation that the goods will conform to the affirmation of fact, promise, or description, or that the seller will perform the remedial promise, the seller has an obligation to the remote purchaser that:

(a) the goods will conform to the affirmation of fact, promise or description unless a reasonable person in the position of the remote purchaser would not believe that the affirmation of fact, promise or description created an obligation; and

(b) the seller will perform the remedial promise.

(3) It is not necessary to the creation of an obligation under this section that the seller use formal words such as "warrant" or "guarantee" or that the seller have a specific intention to

undertake an obligation, but an affirmation merely of the value of the goods or a statement purporting to be merely the seller's opinion or commendation of the goods does not create an obligation.

(4) The following rules apply to the remedies for breach of an obligation created under this section:

(a) The seller may modify or limit the remedies available to the remote purchaser if the modification or limitation is furnished to the remote purchaser no later than the time of purchase. The modification or limitation may be furnished as part of the communication that contains the affirmation of fact, promise or description.

(b) Subject to a modification or limitation of remedy, a seller in breach is liable for incidental or consequential damages under Section 2–715, but the seller is not liable for lost profits.

(c) The remote purchaser may recover as damages for breach of a seller's obligation arising under subsection (2) the loss resulting in the ordinary course of events as determined in any manner that is reasonable.

(5) An obligation that is not a remedial promise is breached if the goods did not conform to the affirmation of fact, promise or description creating the obligation when the goods left the seller's control.

* * * *

§ 2–316. Exclusion or Modification of Warranties.

* * * *

(2) Subject to subsection (3), to exclude or modify the implied warranty of merchantability or any part of it in a consumer contract the language must be in a record, be conspicuous and state "The seller undertakes no responsibility for the quality of the goods except as otherwise provided in this contract," and in any other contract the language must mention merchantability and in case of a record must be conspicuous. Subject to subsection (3), to exclude or modify the implied warranty of fitness the exclusion must be in a record and be conspicuous. Language to exclude all implied warranties of fitness in a consumer contract must state "The seller assumes no responsibility that the goods will be fit for any particular purpose for which you may be buying these goods, except as otherwise provided in the contract," and in any other contract the language is sufficient if it states, for example, that "There are no warranties which extend beyond the description on the face hereof." Language that satisfies the requirements of this subsection for the exclusion and modification of a warranty in a consumer contract also satisfies the requirements for any other contract.

(3) Notwithstanding subsection (2):

(a) unless the circumstances indicate otherwise, all implied warranties are excluded by expressions like "as is", "with all faults" or other language which in common understanding calls the buyer's attention to the exclusion of warranties, makes plain that there is no implied warranty, and in a consumer contract evidenced by a record is set forth conspicuously in the record; and

(b) when the buyer before entering into the contract has examined the goods or the sample or model as fully as desired or has refused to examine the goods after a demand by the seller there is no implied warranty with regard to defects which an examination ought in the circumstances to have revealed to the buyer; and

(c) an implied warranty can also be excluded or modified by course of dealing or course of performance or usage of trade.

* * * *

§ 2–318. Third Party Beneficiaries of Warranties Express or Implied.

(1) In this section:

(a) "Immediate buyer" means a buyer that enters into a contract with the seller.

(b) "Remote purchaser" means a person that buys or leases goods from an immediate buyer or other person in the normal chain of distribution.

Alternative A to subsection (2) (2) A seller's warranty whether express or implied to an immediate buyer, a seller's remedial promise to an immediate buyer, or a seller's obligation to a remote purchaser under Section 2–313A or 2–313B extends to any natural person who is in the family or household of the immediate buyer or the remote purchaser or who is a guest in the home of either if it is reasonable to expect that the person may use, consume or be affected by the goods and who is injured in person by breach of the warranty, remedial promise or obligation. A seller may not exclude or limit the operation of this section.

Alternative B to subsection (2) (2) A seller's warranty whether express or implied to an immediate buyer, a seller's remedial promise to an immediate buyer, or a seller's obligation to a remote purchaser under Section 2–313A or 2–313B extends to any natural person who may reasonably be expected to use, consume or be affected by the goods and who is injured in person by breach of the warranty, remedial promise or obligation. A seller may not exclude or limit the operation of this section.

Alternative C to subsection (2) (2) A seller's warranty whether express or implied to an immediate buyer, a seller's remedial promise to an immediate buyer, or a seller's obligation to a remote purchaser under Section 2–313A or 2–313B extends to any person that may reasonably be expected to use, consume or be affected by the goods and that is injured by breach of the warranty, remedial promise or obligation. A seller may not exclude or limit the operation of this section with respect to injury to the person of an individual to whom the warranty, remedial promise or obligation extends.

* * * *

PART 5 Performance

* * * *

§ 2–502. Buyer's Right to Goods on Seller's Insolvency.

(1) Subject to subsections (2) and (3) and even though the goods have not been shipped a buyer who that has paid a part or all

of the price of goods in which the buyer has a special property under the provisions of the immediately preceding section may on making and keeping good a tender of any unpaid portion of their price recover them from the seller if:

(a) in the case of goods bought by a consumer, the seller repudiates or fails to deliver as required by the contract; or

(b) in all cases, the seller becomes insolvent within ten days after receipt of the first installment on their price.

(2) The buyer's right to recover the goods under subsection (1) vests upon acquisition of a special property, even if the seller had not then repudiated or failed to deliver.

(3) If the identification creating the special property has been made by the buyer, the buyer acquires the right to recover the goods only if they conform to the contract for sale.

* * * *

§ 2–508. Cure by Seller of Improper Tender or Delivery; Replacement.

(1) Where the buyer rejects goods or a tender of delivery under Section 2–601 or 2–612 or except in a consumer contract justifiably revokes acceptance under Section 2–608 (1)(b) and the agreed time for performance has not expired, a seller that has performed in good faith, upon seasonable notice to the buyer and at the seller's own expense, may cure the breach of contract by making a conforming tender of delivery within the agreed time. The seller shall compensate the buyer for all of the buyer's reasonable expenses caused by the seller's breach of contract and subsequent cure.

(2) Where the buyer rejects goods or a tender of delivery under Section 2–601 or 2–612 or except in a consumer contract justifiably revokes acceptance under Section 2–608 (1)(b) and the agreed time for performance has expired, a seller that has performed in good faith, upon seasonable notice to the buyer and at the seller's own expense, may cure the breach of contract, if the cure is appropriate and timely under the circumstances, by making a tender of conforming goods. The seller shall compensate the buyer for all of the buyer's reasonable expenses caused by the seller's breach of contract and subsequent cure.

§ 2–509. Risk of Loss in the Absence of Breach.

(1) Where the contract requires or authorizes the seller to ship the goods by carrier

(a) if it does not require the seller to deliver them at a particular destination, the risk of loss passes to the buyer when the goods are delivered to the carrier even though the shipment is under reservation (Section 2–505); but

(b) if it does require the seller to deliver them at a particular destination and the goods are there tendered while in the possession of the carrier, the risk of loss passes to the buyer when the goods are there so tendered as to enable the buyer to take delivery.

(2) Where the goods are held by a bailee to be delivered without being moved, the risk of loss passes to the buyer

(a) on the buyer's receipt of a negotiable document of title covering the goods; or

(b) on acknowledgment by the bailee to the buyer of the buyer's right to possession of the goods; or

(c) after the buyer's receipt of a non-negotiable document of title or other direction to deliver in a record, as provided in subsection (4)(b) of Section 2–503.

(3) In any case not within subsection (1) or (2), the risk of loss passes to the buyer on the buyer's receipt of the goods.

* * * *

§ 2–513. Buyer's Right to Inspection of Goods.

* * * *

(3) Unless otherwise agreed, the buyer is not entitled to inspect the goods before payment of the price when the contract provides

(a) for delivery on terms that under applicable course of performance, course of dealing, or usage of trade are interpreted to preclude inspection before payment; or

(b) for payment against documents of title, except where such payment is due only after the goods are to become available for inspection.

* * * *

PART 6 Breach, Repudiation and Excuse

* * * *

§ 2–605. Waiver of Buyer's Objections by Failure to Particularize.

(1) The buyer's failure to state in connection with rejection a particular defect or in connection with revocation of acceptance a defect that justifies revocation precludes the buyer from relying on the unstated defect to justify rejection or revocation of acceptance if the defect is ascertainable by reasonable inspection

(a) where the seller had a right to cure the defect and could have cured it if stated seasonably; or

(b) between merchants when the seller has after rejection made a request in a record for a full and final statement in record form of all defects on which the buyer proposes to rely.

(2) A buyer's payment against documents tendered to the buyer made without reservation of rights precludes recovery of the payment for defects apparent on the face of the documents.

* * * *

§ 2–607. Effect of Acceptance; Notice of Breach; Burden of Establishing Breach After Acceptance; Notice of Claim or Litigation to Person Answerable Over.

* * * *

(3) Where a tender has been accepted

(a) the buyer must within a reasonable time after the buyer discovers or should have discovered any breach notify the seller;

however, failure to give timely notice bars the buyer from a remedy only to the extent that the seller is prejudiced by the failure and

(b) if the claim is one for infringement or the like (subsection (3) of Section 2–312) and the buyer is sued as a result of such a breach the buyer must so notify the seller within a reasonable time after the buyer receives notice of the litigation or be barred from any remedy over for liability established by the litigation.

* * * *

§ 2–608. Revocation of Acceptance in Whole or in Part.

* * * *

(4) If a buyer uses the goods after a rightful rejection or justifiable revocation of acceptance, the following rules apply:

(a) Any use by the buyer that is unreasonable under the circumstances is wrongful as against the seller and is an acceptance only if ratified by the seller.

(b) Any use of the goods that is reasonable under the circumstances is not wrongful as against the seller and is not an acceptance, but in an appropriate case the buyer shall be obligated to the seller for the value of the use to the buyer.

* * * *

§ 2–612. "Installment Contract"; Breach.

* * * *

(2) The buyer may reject any installment which is non-conforming if the non-conformity substantially impairs the value of that installment to the buyer or if the non-conformity is a defect in the required documents; but if the non-conformity does not fall within subsection (3) and the seller gives adequate assurance of its cure the buyer must accept that installment.

(3) Whenever non-conformity or default with respect to one or more installments substantially impairs the value of the whole contract there is a breach of the whole. But the aggrieved party reinstates the contract if the party accepts a non-conforming installment without seasonably notifying of cancellation or if the party brings an action with respect only to past installments or demands performance as to future installments.

* * * *

PART 7 Remedies

§ 2–702. Seller's Remedies on Discovery of Buyer's Insolvency.

* * * *

(2) Where the seller discovers that the buyer has received goods on credit while insolvent the seller may reclaim the goods upon demand made within a reasonable time after the buyer's receipt of the goods. Except as provided in this subsection the seller may not base a right to reclaim goods on the buyer's fraudulent or innocent misrepresentation of solvency or of intent to pay.

* * * *

§ 2–705. Seller's Stoppage of Delivery in Transit or Otherwise.

(1) The seller may stop delivery of goods in the possession of a carrier or other bailee when the seller discovers the buyer to be insolvent (Section 2–702) or when the buyer repudiates or fails to make a payment due before delivery or if for any other reason the seller has a right to withhold or reclaim the goods.

* * * *

§ 2–706. Seller's Resale Including Contract for Resale.

(1) In an appropriate case involving breach by the buyer, the seller may resell the goods concerned or the undelivered balance thereof. Where the resale is made in good faith and in a commercially reasonable manner the seller may recover the difference between the contract price and the resale price together with any incidental or consequential damages allowed under the provisions of this Article (Section 2–710), but less expenses saved in consequence of the buyer's breach.

* * * *

§ 2–708. Seller's Damages for Non-Acceptance or Repudiation.

(1) Subject to subsection (2) and to the provisions of this Article with respect to proof of market price (Section 2–723)

(a) the measure of damages for non-acceptance by the buyer is the difference between the contract price and the market price at the time and place for tender together with any incidental or consequential damages provided in this Article (Section 2–710), but less expenses saved in consequence of the buyer's breach; and

(b) the measure of damages for repudiation by the buyer is the difference between the contract price and the market price at the place for tender at the expiration of a commercially reasonable time after the seller learned of the repudiation, but no later than the time stated in paragraph (a), together with any incidental or consequential damages provided in this Article (Section 2–710), but less expenses saved in consequence of the buyer's breach.

(2) If the measure of damages provided in subsection (1) or in Section 2–706 is inadequate to put the seller in as good a position as performance would have done then the measure of damages is the profit (including reasonable overhead) which the seller would have made from full performance by the buyer, together with any incidental or consequential damages provided in this Article (Section 2–710).

§ 2–709. Action for the Price.

(1) When the buyer fails to pay the price as it becomes due the seller may recover, together with any incidental or consequential damages under the next section, the price

(a) of goods accepted or of conforming goods lost or damaged within a commercially reasonable time after risk of their loss has passed to the buyer; and

(b) of goods identified to the contract if the seller is unable after reasonable effort to resell them at a reasonable price or the circumstances reasonably indicate that such effort will be unavailing.

* * * *

* * * *

* * * *

§ 2–710. Seller's Incidental and Consequential Damages.

(1) Incidental damages to an aggrieved seller include any commercially reasonable charges, expenses or commissions incurred in stopping delivery, in the transportation, care and custody of goods after the buyer's breach, in connection with return or resale of the goods or otherwise resulting from the breach.

(2) Consequential damages resulting from the buyer's breach include any loss resulting from general or particular requirements and needs of which the buyer at the time of contracting had reason to know and which could not reasonably be prevented by resale or otherwise.

(3) In a consumer contract, a seller may not recover consequential damages from a consumer.

* * * *

§ 2–713. Buyer's Damages for Non-Delivery or Repudiation.

(1) Subject to the provisions of this Article with respect to proof of market price (Section 2–723), if the seller wrongfully fails to deliver or repudiates or the buyer rightfully rejects or justifiably revokes acceptance

(a) the measure of damages in the case of wrongful failure to deliver by the seller or rightful rejection or justifiable revocation of acceptance by the buyer is the difference between the market price at the time for tender under the contract and the contract price together with any incidental or consequential damages provided in this Article (Section 2–715), but less expenses saved in consequence of the seller's breach; and

(b) the measure of damages for repudiation by the seller is the difference between the market price at the expiration of a commercially reasonable time after the buyer learned of the repudiation, but no later than the time stated in paragraph (a), and the contract price together with any incidental or consequential damages provided in this Article (Section 2–715), but less expenses saved in consequence of the seller's breach.

* * * *

§ 2–725. Statute of Limitations in Contracts for Sale.

(1) Except as otherwise provided in this section, an action for breach of any contract for sale must be commenced within the later of four years after the right of action has accrued under subsection (2) or (3) or one year after the breach was or should have been discovered, but no longer than five years after the right of action accrued. By the original agreement the parties may reduce the period of limitation to not less than one year but may not extend it; however, in a consumer contract, the period of limitation may not be reduced.

(2) Except as otherwise provided in subsection (3), the following rules apply:

(a) Except as otherwise provided in this subsection, a right of action for breach of a contract accrues when the breach occurs, even if the aggrieved party did not have knowledge of the breach.

(b) For breach of a contract by repudiation, a right of action accrues at the earlier of when the aggrieved party elects to treat the repudiation as a breach or when a commercially reasonable time for awaiting performance has expired.

(c) For breach of a remedial promise, a right of action accrues when the remedial promise is not performed when due.

(d) In an action by a buyer against a person that is answerable over to the buyer for a claim asserted against the buyer, the buyer's right of action against the person answerable over accrues at the time the claim was originally asserted against the buyer.

(3) If a breach of a warranty arising under Section 2–312, 2–313(2), 2–314, or 2–315, or a breach of an obligation other than a remedial promise arising under Section 2–313A or 2–313B, is claimed the following rules apply:

(a) Except as otherwise provided in paragraph (c), a right of action for breach of a warranty arising under Section 2–313 (2), 2–314 or 2–315 accrues when the seller has tendered delivery to the immediate buyer, as defined in Section 2–313, and has completed performance of any agreed installation or assembly of the goods.

(b) Except as otherwise provided in paragraph (c), a right of action for breach of an obligation other than a remedial promise arising under Section 2–313A or 2–313B accrues when the remote purchaser, as defined in Sections 2–313A and 2–313B, receives the goods.

(c) Where a warranty arising under Section 2–313(2) or an obligation other than a remedial promise arising under Section 2–313A or 2–313B explicitly extends to future performance of the goods and discovery of the breach must await the time for performance the right of action accrues when the immediate buyer as defined in Section 2–313 or the remote purchaser as defined in Sections 2–313A and 2–313B discovers or should have discovered the breach.

(d) A right of action for breach of warranty arising under Section 2–312 accrues when the aggrieved party discovers or should have discovered the breach. However, an action for breach of the warranty of non-infringement may not be commenced more than six years after tender of delivery of the goods to the aggrieved party.

* * * *

ARTICLE IIA LEASES

PART 1 General Provisions § 2A–101. Short Title.

This Article shall be known and may be cited as the Uniform Commercial Code—Leases.

§ 2A–102. Scope.

This Article applies to any transaction, regardless of form, that creates a lease.

§ 2A–103. Definitions and Index of Definitions.

(1) In this Article unless the context otherwise requires:

(a) "Buyer in ordinary course of business" means a person who in good faith and without knowledge that the sale to him [or her] is in violation of the ownership rights or security interest or leasehold interest of a third party in the goods buys in ordinary course from a person in the business of selling goods of that kind but does not include a pawnbroker. "Buying" may be for cash or by exchange of other property or on secured or unsecured credit and includes receiving goods or documents of title under a pre-existing contract for sale but does not include a transfer in bulk or as security for or in total or partial satisfaction of a money debt.

(b) "Cancellation" occurs when either party puts an end to the lease contract for default by the other party.

(c) "Commercial unit" means such a unit of goods as by commercial usage is a single whole for purposes of lease and division of which materially impairs its character or value on the market or in use. A commercial unit may be a single article, as a machine, or a set of articles, as a suite of furniture or a line of machinery, or a quantity, as a gross or carload, or any other unit treated in use or in the relevant market as a single whole.

(d) "Conforming" goods or performance under a lease contract means goods or performance that are in accordance with the obligations under the lease contract.

(e) "Consumer lease" means a lease that a lessor regularly engaged in the business of leasing or selling makes to a lessee who is an individual and who takes under the lease primarily for a personal, family, or household purpose [if the total payments to be made under the lease contract, excluding payments for options to renew or buy, do not exceed $____].

(f) "Fault" means wrongful act, omission, breach, or default.

(g) "Finance lease" means a lease with respect to which:

(i) the lessor does not select, manufacture or supply the goods;

(ii) the lessor acquires the goods or the right to possession and use of the goods in connection with the lease; and

(iii) one of the following occurs:

(A) the lessee receives a copy of the contract by which the lessor acquired the goods or the right to possession and use of the goods before signing the lease contract;

(B) the lessee's approval of the contract by which the lessor acquired the goods or the right to possession and use of the goods is a condition to effectiveness of the lease contract;

(C) the lessee, before signing the lease contract, receives an accurate and complete statement designating the promises and warranties, and any disclaimers of warranties, limitations or modifications of remedies, or liquidated damages, including those of a third party, such as the manufacturer of the goods, provided to the lessor by the person supplying the goods in connection with or as part of the contract by which the lessor acquired the goods or the right to possession and use of the goods; or

(D) if the lease is not a consumer lease, the lessor, before the lessee signs the lease contract, informs the lessee in writing (a) of the identity of the person supplying the goods to the lessor, unless the lessee has selected that person and directed the lessor to acquire the goods or the right to possession and use of the goods from that person, (b) that the lessee is entitled under this Article to any promises and warranties, including those of any third party, provided to the lessor by the person supplying the goods in connection with or as part of the contract by which the lessor acquired the goods or the right to possession and use of the goods, and (c) that the lessee may communicate with the person supplying the goods to the lessor and receive an accurate and complete statement of those promises and warranties, including any disclaimers and limitations of them or of remedies.

(h) "Goods" means all things that are movable at the time of identification to the lease contract, or are fixtures (Section 2A–309), but the term does not include money, documents, instruments, accounts, chattel paper, general intangibles, or minerals or the like, including oil and gas, before extraction. The term also includes the unborn young of animals.

(i) "Installment lease contract" means a lease contract that authorizes or requires the delivery of goods in separate lots to be separately accepted, even though the lease contract contains a clause "each delivery is a separate lease" or its equivalent.

(j) "Lease" means a transfer of the right to possession and use of goods for a term in return for consideration, but a sale, including a sale on approval or a sale or return, or retention or creation of a security interest is not a lease. Unless the context clearly indicates otherwise, the term includes a sublease.

(k) "Lease agreement" means the bargain, with respect to the lease, of the lessor and the lessee in fact as found in their language or by implication from other circumstances including course of dealing or usage of trade or course of performance as provided in this Article. Unless the context clearly indicates otherwise, the term includes a sublease agreement.

(l) "Lease contract" means the total legal obligation that results from the lease agreement as affected by this Article and any other applicable rules of law. Unless the context clearly indicates otherwise, the term includes a sublease contract.

(m) "Leasehold interest" means the interest of the lessor or the lessee under a lease contract.

(n) "Lessee" means a person who acquires the right to possession and use of goods under a lease. Unless the context clearly indicates otherwise, the term includes a sublessee.

(o) "Lessee in ordinary course of business" means a person who in good faith and without knowledge that the lease to him [or her] is in violation of the ownership rights or security interest or leasehold interest of a third party in the goods, leases in ordinary course from a person in the business of selling or leasing goods of that kind but does not include a pawnbroker. "Leasing" may be for cash or by exchange of other property or on secured or unsecured credit and includes receiving goods or documents of title under a pre-existing lease contract but does not include a transfer in bulk or as security for or in total or partial satisfaction of a money debt.

(p) "Lessor" means a person who transfers the right to possession and use of goods under a lease. Unless the context clearly indicates otherwise, the term includes a sublessor.

(q) "Lessor's residual interest" means the lessor's interest in the goods after expiration, termination, or cancellation of the lease contract.

(r) "Lien" means a charge against or interest in goods to secure payment of a debt or performance of an obligation, but the term does not include a security interest.

(s) "Lot" means a parcel or a single article that is the subject matter of a separate lease or delivery, whether or not it is sufficient to perform the lease contract.

(t) "Merchant lessee" means a lessee that is a merchant with respect to goods of the kind subject to the lease.

(u) "Present value" means the amount as of a date certain of one or more sums payable in the future, discounted to the date certain. The discount is determined by the interest rate specified by the parties if the rate was not manifestly unreasonable at the time the transaction was entered into; otherwise, the discount is determined by a commercially reasonable rate that takes into account the facts and circumstances of each case at the time the transaction was entered into.

(v) "Purchase" includes taking by sale, lease, mortgage, security interest, pledge, gift, or any other voluntary transaction creating an interest in goods.

(w) "Sublease" means a lease of goods the right to possession and use of which was acquired by the lessor as a lessee under an existing lease.

(x) "Supplier" means a person from whom a lessor buys or leases goods to be leased under a finance lease.

(y) "Supply contract" means a contract under which a lessor buys or leases goods to be leased.

(z) "Termination" occurs when either party pursuant to a power created by agreement or law puts an end to the lease contract otherwise than for default.

(2) Other definitions applying to this Article and the sections in which they appear are:

"Accessions". Section 2A–310(1).

"Construction mortgage". Section 2A–309(1)(d).

"Encumbrance". Section 2A–309(1)(e).

"Fixtures". Section 2A–309(1)(a).

"Fixture filing". Section 2A–309(1)(b).

"Purchase money lease". Section 2A–309(1)(c).

(3) The following definitions in other Articles apply to this Article:

"Accounts". Section 9–106.

"Between merchants". Section 2–104(3).

"Buyer". Section 2–103(1)(a).

"Chattel paper". Section 9–105(1)(b).

"Consumer goods". Section 9–109(1).

"Document". Section 9–105(1)(f).

"Entrusting". Section 2–403(3).

"General intangibles". Section 9–106.

"Good faith". Section 2–103(1)(b).

"Instrument". Section 9–105(1)(i).

"Merchant". Section 2–104(1).

"Mortgage". Section 9–105(1)(j).

"Pursuant to commitment". Section 9–105(1)(k).

"Receipt". Section 2–103(1)(c).

"Sale". Section 2–106(1).

"Sale on approval". Section 2–326.

"Sale or return". Section 2–326.

"Seller". Section 2–103(1)(d).

(4) In addition Article 1 contains general definitions and principles of construction and interpretation applicable throughout this Article. As amended in 1990 and 1999.

§ 2A–104. Leases Subject to Other Law.

(1) A lease, although subject to this Article, is also subject to any applicable:

(a) certificate of title statute of this State: (list any certificate of title statutes covering automobiles, trailers, mobile homes, boats, farm tractors, and the like);

(b) certificate of title statute of another jurisdiction (Section 2A–105); or

(c) consumer protection statute of this State, or final consumer protection decision of a court of this State existing on the effective date of this Article.

(2) In case of conflict between this Article, other than Sections 2A–105, 2A–304(3), and 2A–305(3), and a statute or decision referred to in subsection (1), the statute or decision controls.

(3) Failure to comply with an applicable law has only the effect specified therein.

As amended in 1990.

§ 2A–105. Territorial Application of Article to Goods Covered by Certificate of Title.

Subject to the provisions of Sections 2A–304(3) and 2A–305(3), with respect to goods covered by a certificate of title issued under a statute of this State or of another jurisdiction, compliance and the effect of compliance or noncompliance with a certificate of title statute are governed by the law (including the conflict of laws rules) of the jurisdiction issuing the certificate until the earlier of (a) surrender of the certificate, or (b) four months after the goods are removed from that jurisdiction and thereafter until a new certificate of title is issued by another jurisdiction.

§ 2A–106. Limitation on Power of Parties to Consumer Lease to Choose Applicable Law and Judicial Forum.

(1) If the law chosen by the parties to a consumer lease is that of a jurisdiction other than a jurisdiction in which the lessee resides at the time the lease agreement becomes enforceable or within 30 days thereafter or in which the goods are to be used, the choice is not enforceable.

(2) If the judicial forum chosen by the parties to a consumer lease is a forum that would not otherwise have jurisdiction over the lessee, the choice is not enforceable.

§ 2A–107. Waiver or Renunciation of Claim or Right After Default.

Any claim or right arising out of an alleged default or breach of warranty may be discharged in whole or in part without consideration by a written waiver or renunciation signed and delivered by the aggrieved party.

§ 2A–108. Unconscionability.

(1) If the court as a matter of law finds a lease contract or any clause of a lease contract to have been unconscionable at the time it was made the court may refuse to enforce the lease contract, or it may enforce the remainder of the lease contract without the unconscionable clause, or it may so limit the application of any unconscionable clause as to avoid any unconscionable result.

(2) With respect to a consumer lease, if the court as a matter of law finds that a lease contract or any clause of a lease contract has been induced by unconscionable conduct or that unconscionable conduct has occurred in the collection of a claim arising from a lease contract, the court may grant appropriate relief.

(3) Before making a finding of unconscionability under subsection (1) or (2), the court, on its own motion or that of a party, shall afford the parties a reasonable opportunity to present evidence as to the setting, purpose, and effect of the lease contract or clause thereof, or of the conduct.

(4) In an action in which the lessee claims unconscionability with respect to a consumer lease:

(a) If the court finds unconscionability under subsection (1) or (2), the court shall award reasonable attorney's fees to the lessee.

(b) If the court does not find unconscionability and the lessee claiming unconscionability has brought or maintained an action he [or she] knew to be groundless, the court shall award reasonable attorney's fees to the party against whom the claim is made.

(c) In determining attorney's fees, the amount of the recovery on behalf of the claimant under subsections (1) and (2) is not controlling.

§ 2A–109. Option to Accelerate at Will.

(1) A term providing that one party or his [or her] successor in interest may accelerate payment or performance or require collateral or additional collateral "at will" or "when he [or she] deems himself [or herself] insecure" or in words of similar import must be construed to mean that he [or she] has power to do so only if he [or she] in good faith believes that the prospect of payment or performance is impaired.

(2) With respect to a consumer lease, the burden of establishing good faith under subsection (1) is on the party who exercised the power; otherwise the burden of establishing lack of good faith is on the party against whom the power has been exercised.

PART 2 Formation and Construction of Lease Contract

§ 2A–201. Statute of Frauds

(1) A lease contract is not enforceable by way of action or defense unless:

(a) the total payments to be made under the lease contract, excluding payments for options to renew or buy, are less than $1,000; or

(b) there is a writing, signed by the party against whom enforcement is sought or by that party's authorized agent, sufficient to indicate that a lease contract has been made between the parties and to describe the goods leased and the lease term.

(2) Any description of leased goods or of the lease term is sufficient and satisfies subsection (1)(b), whether or not it is specific, if it reasonably identifies what is described.

(3) A writing is not insufficient because it omits or incorrectly states a term agreed upon, but the lease contract is not enforceable under subsection (1)(b) beyond the lease term and the quantity of goods shown in the writing.

(4) A lease contract that does not satisfy the requirements of subsection (1), but which is valid in other respects, is enforceable:

(a) if the goods are to be specially manufactured or obtained for the lessee and are not suitable for lease or sale to others in the ordinary course of the lessor's business, and the lessor, before notice of repudiation is received and under circumstances that reasonably indicate that the goods are for the lessee, has made either a substantial beginning of their manufacture or commitments for their procurement;

(b) if the party against whom enforcement is sought admits in that party's pleading, testimony or otherwise in court that a lease contract was made, but the lease contract is not enforceable under this provision beyond the quantity of goods admitted; or

(c) with respect to goods that have been received and accepted by the lessee.

(5) The lease term under a lease contract referred to in subsection (4) is:

(a) if there is a writing signed by the party against whom enforcement is sought or by that party's authorized agent specifying the lease term, the term so specified;

(b) if the party against whom enforcement is sought admits in that party's pleading, testimony, or otherwise in court a lease term, the term so admitted; or

(c) a reasonable lease term.

§ 2A–202. Final Written Expression: Parol or Extrinsic Evidence.

Terms with respect to which the confirmatory memoranda of the parties agree or which are otherwise set forth in a writing intended by the parties as a final expression of their agreement with respect to such terms as are included therein may not be contradicted by evidence of any prior agreement or of a contemporaneous oral agreement but may be explained or supplemented:

(a) by course of dealing or usage of trade or by course of performance; and

(b) by evidence of consistent additional terms unless the court finds the writing to have been intended also as a complete and exclusive statement of the terms of the agreement.

§ 2A–203. Seals Inoperative.

The affixing of a seal to a writing evidencing a lease contract or an offer to enter into a lease contract does not render the writing a sealed instrument and the law with respect to sealed instruments does not apply to the lease contract or offer.

§ 2A–204. Formation in General.

(1) A lease contract may be made in any manner sufficient to show agreement, including conduct by both parties which recognizes the existence of a lease contract.

(2) An agreement sufficient to constitute a lease contract may be found although the moment of its making is undetermined.

(3) Although one or more terms are left open, a lease contract does not fail for indefiniteness if the parties have intended to make a lease contract and there is a reasonably certain basis for giving an appropriate remedy.

§ 2A–205. Firm Offers.

An offer by a merchant to lease goods to or from another person in a signed writing that by its terms gives assurance it will be held open is not revocable, for lack of consideration, during the time stated or, if no time is stated, for a reasonable time, but in no event may the period of irrevocability exceed 3 months. Any such term of assurance on a form supplied by the offeree must be separately signed by the offeror.

§ 2A–206. Offer and Acceptance in Formation of Lease Contract.

(1) Unless otherwise unambiguously indicated by the language or circumstances, an offer to make a lease contract must be construed as inviting acceptance in any manner and by any medium reasonable in the circumstances.

(2) If the beginning of a requested performance is a reasonable mode of acceptance, an offeror who is not notified of acceptance within a reasonable time may treat the offer as having lapsed before acceptance.

§ 2A–207. Course of Performance or Practical Construction.

(1) If a lease contract involves repeated occasions for performance by either party with knowledge of the nature of the performance and opportunity for objection to it by the other, any course of performance accepted or acquiesced in without objection is relevant to determine the meaning of the lease agreement.

(2) The express terms of a lease agreement and any course of performance, as well as any course of dealing and usage of trade, must be construed whenever reasonable as consistent with each other; but if that construction is unreasonable, express terms control course of performance, course of performance controls both course of dealing and usage of trade, and course of dealing controls usage of trade.

(3) Subject to the provisions of Section 2A–208 on modification and waiver, course of performance is relevant to show a waiver or modification of any term inconsistent with the course of performance.

§ 2A–208. Modification, Rescission and Waiver.

(1) An agreement modifying a lease contract needs no consideration to be binding.

(2) A signed lease agreement that excludes modification or rescission except by a signed writing may not be otherwise modified or rescinded, but, except as between merchants, such a requirement on a form supplied by a merchant must be separately signed by the other party.

(3) Although an attempt at modification or rescission does not satisfy the requirements of subsection (2), it may operate as a waiver.

(4) A party who has made a waiver affecting an executory portion of a lease contract may retract the waiver by reasonable notification received by the other party that strict performance will be required of any term waived, unless the retraction would be

unjust in view of a material change of position in reliance on the waiver.

§ 2A–209. Lessee Under Finance Lease as Beneficiary of Supply Contract.

(1) The benefit of the supplier's promises to the lessor under the supply contract and of all warranties, whether express or implied, including those of any third party provided in connection with or as part of the supply contract, extends to the lessee to the extent of the lessee's leasehold interest under a finance lease related to the supply contract, but is subject to the terms warranty and of the supply contract and all defenses or claims arising therefrom.

(2) The extension of the benefit of supplier's promises and of warranties to the lessee (Section 2A–209(1)) does not: (i) modify the rights and obligations of the parties to the supply contract, whether arising therefrom or otherwise, or (ii) impose any duty or liability under the supply contract on the lessee.

(3) Any modification or rescission of the supply contract by the supplier and the lessor is effective between the supplier and the lessee unless, before the modification or rescission, the supplier has received notice that the lessee has entered into a finance lease related to the supply contract. If the modification or rescission is effective between the supplier and the lessee, the lessor is deemed to have assumed, in addition to the obligations of the lessor to the lessee under the lease contract, promises of the supplier to the lessor and warranties that were so modified or rescinded as they existed and were available to the lessee before modification or rescission.

(4) In addition to the extension of the benefit of the supplier's promises and of warranties to the lessee under subsection (1), the lessee retains all rights that the lessee may have against the supplier which arise from an agreement between the lessee and the supplier or under other law.

As amended in 1990.

§ 2A–210. Express Warranties.

(1) Express warranties by the lessor are created as follows:

(a) Any affirmation of fact or promise made by the lessor to the lessee which relates to the goods and becomes part of the basis of the bargain creates an express warranty that the goods will conform to the affirmation or promise.

(b) Any description of the goods which is made part of the basis of the bargain creates an express warranty that the goods will conform to the description.

(c) Any sample or model that is made part of the basis of the bargain creates an express warranty that the whole of the goods will conform to the sample or model.

(2) It is not necessary to the creation of an express warranty that the lessor use formal words, such as "warrant" or "guarantee," or that the lessor have a specific intention to make a warranty, but an affirmation merely of the value of the goods or a statement purporting to be merely the lessor's opinion or commendation of the goods does not create a warranty.

§ 2A–211. Warranties Against Interference and Against Infringement; Lessee's Obligation Against Infringement.

(1) There is in a lease contract a warranty that for the lease term no person holds a claim to or interest in the goods that arose from an act or omission of the lessor, other than a claim by way of infringement or the like, which will interfere with the lessee's enjoyment of its leasehold interest.

(2) Except in a finance lease there is in a lease contract by a lessor who is a merchant regularly dealing in goods of the kind a warranty that the goods are delivered free of the rightful claim of any person by way of infringement or the like.

(3) A lessee who furnishes specifications to a lessor or a supplier shall hold the lessor and the supplier harmless against any claim by way of infringement or the like that arises out of compliance with the specifications.

§ 2A–212. Implied Warranty of Merchantability.

(1) Except in a finance lease, a warranty that the goods will be merchantable is implied in a lease contract if the lessor is a merchant with respect to goods of that kind.

(2) Goods to be merchantable must be at least such as

(a) pass without objection in the trade under the description in the lease agreement;

(b) in the case of fungible goods, are of fair average quality within the description;

(c) are fit for the ordinary purposes for which goods of that type are used;

(d) run, within the variation permitted by the lease agreement, of even kind, quality, and quantity within each unit and among all units involved;

(e) are adequately contained, packaged, and labeled as the lease agreement may require; and

(f) conform to any promises or affirmations of fact made on the container or label.

(3) Other implied warranties may arise from course of dealing or usage of trade.

§ 2A–213. Implied Warranty of Fitness for Particular Purpose.

Except in a finance of lease, if the lessor at the time the lease contract is made has reason to know of any particular purpose for which the goods are required and that the lessee is relying on the lessor's skill or judgment to select or furnish suitable goods, there is in the lease contract an implied warranty that the goods will be fit for that purpose.

§ 2A–214. Exclusion or Modification of Warranties.

(1) Words or conduct relevant to the creation of an express warranty and words or conduct tending to negate or limit a warranty must be construed wherever reasonable as consistent with each other; but, subject to the provisions of Section 2A–202 on parol or extrinsic evidence, negation or limitation is inoperative to the extent that the construction is unreasonable.

(2) Subject to subsection (3), to exclude or modify the implied warranty of merchantability or any part of it the language must mention "merchantability", be by a writing, and be conspicuous. Subject to subsection (3), to exclude or modify any implied warranty of fitness the exclusion must be by a writing and be conspicuous. Language to exclude all implied warranties of fitness is sufficient if it is in writing, is conspicuous and states, for example, "There is no warranty that the goods will be fit for a particular purpose".

(3) Notwithstanding subsection (2), but subject to subsection (4),

(a) unless the circumstances indicate otherwise, all implied warranties are excluded by expressions like "as is" or "with all faults" or by other language that in common understanding calls the lessee's attention to the exclusion of warranties and makes plain that there is no implied warranty, if in writing and conspicuous;

(b) if the lessee before entering into the lease contract has examined the goods or the sample or model as fully as desired or has refused to examine the goods, there is no implied warranty with regard to defects that an examination ought in the circumstances to have revealed; and

(c) an implied warranty may also be excluded or modified by course of dealing, course of performance, or usage of trade.

(4) To exclude or modify a warranty against interference or against infringement (Section 2A–211) or any part of it, the language must be specific, be by a writing, and be conspicuous, unless the circumstances, including course of performance, course of dealing, or usage of trade, give the lessee reason to know that the goods are being leased subject to a claim or interest of any person.

§ 2A–215. Cumulation and Conflict of Warranties Express or Implied.

Warranties, whether express or implied, must be construed as consistent with each other and as cumulative, but if that construction is unreasonable, the intention of the parties determines which warranty is dominant. In ascertaining that intention the following rules apply:

(a) Exact or technical specifications displace an inconsistent sample or model or general language of description.

(b) A sample from an existing bulk displaces inconsistent general language of description.

(c) Express warranties displace inconsistent implied warranties other than an implied warranty of fitness for a particular purpose.

§ 2A–216. Third-Party Beneficiaries of Express and Implied Warranties.

Alternative A A warranty to or for the benefit of a lessee under this Article, whether express or implied, extends to any natural person who is in the family or household of the lessee or who is a guest in the lessee's home if it is reasonable to expect that such person may use, consume, or be affected by the goods and who is injured in person by breach of the warranty. This section does not displace principles of law and equity that extend a warranty to or for the benefit of a lessee to other persons. The operation of this section may not be excluded, modified, or limited, but an exclusion, modification, or limitation of the warranty, including any with respect to rights and remedies, effective against the lessee is also effective against any beneficiary designated under this section.

Alternative B A warranty to or for the benefit of a lessee under this Article, whether express or implied, extends to any natural person who may reasonably be expected to use, consume, or be affected by the goods and who is injured in person by breach of the warranty. This section does not displace principles of law and equity that extend a warranty to or for the benefit of a lessee to other persons. The operation of this section may not be excluded, modified, or limited, but an exclusion, modification, or limitation of the warranty, including any with respect to rights and remedies, effective against the lessee is also effective against the beneficiary designated under this section.

Alternative C A warranty to or for the benefit of a lessee under this Article, whether express or implied, extends to any person who may reasonably be expected to use, consume, or be affected by the goods and who is injured by breach of the warranty. The operation of this section may not be excluded, modified, or limited with respect to injury to the person of an individual to whom the warranty extends, but an exclusion, modification, or limitation of the warranty, including any with respect to rights and remedies, effective against the lessee is also effective against the beneficiary designated under this section.

§ 2A–217. Identification.

Identification of goods as goods to which a lease contract refers may be made at any time and in any manner explicitly agreed to by the parties. In the absence of explicit agreement, identification occurs:

(a) when the lease contract is made if the lease contract is for a lease of goods that are existing and identified;

(b) when the goods are shipped, marked, or otherwise designated by the lessor as goods to which the lease contract refers, if the lease contract is for a lease of goods that are not existing and identified; or

(c) when the young are conceived, if the lease contract is for a lease of unborn young of animals.

§ 2A–218. Insurance and Proceeds.

(1) A lessee obtains an insurable interest when existing goods are identified to the lease contract even though the goods identified are nonconforming and the lessee has an option to reject them.

(2) If a lessee has an insurable interest only by reason of the lessor's identification of the goods, the lessor, until default or insolvency or notification to the lessee that identification is final, may substitute other goods for those identified.

(3) Notwithstanding a lessee's insurable interest under subsections (1) and (2), the lessor retains an insurable interest until an option to buy has been exercised by the lessee and risk of loss has passed to the lessee.

(4) Nothing in this section impairs any insurable interest recognized under any other statute or rule of law.

(5) The parties by agreement may determine that one or more parties have an obligation to obtain and pay for insurance covering the goods and by agreement may determine the beneficiary of the proceeds of the insurance.

§ 2A–219. Risk of Loss.

(1) Except in the case of a finance lease, risk of loss is retained by the lessor and does not pass to the lessee. In the case of a finance lease, risk of loss passes to the lessee.

(2) Subject to the provisions of this Article on the effect of default on risk of loss (Section 2A–220), if risk of loss is to pass to the lessee and the time of passage is not stated, the following rules apply:

(a) If the lease contract requires or authorizes the goods to be shipped by carrier

(i) and it does not require delivery at a particular destination, the risk of loss passes to the lessee when the goods are duly delivered to the carrier; but

(ii) if it does require delivery at a particular destination and the goods are there duly tendered while in the possession of the carrier, the risk of loss passes to the lessee when the goods are there duly so tendered as to enable the lessee to take delivery.

(b) If the goods are held by a bailee to be delivered without being moved, the risk of loss passes to the lessee on acknowledgment by the bailee of the lessee's right to possession of the goods.

(c) In any case not within subsection (a) or (b), the risk of loss passes to the lessee on the lessee's receipt of the goods if the lessor, or, in the case of a finance lease, the supplier, is a merchant; otherwise the risk passes to the lessee on tender of delivery.

§ 2A–220. Effect of Default on Risk of Loss.

(1) Where risk of loss is to pass to the lessee and the time of passage is not stated:

(a) If a tender or delivery of goods so fails to conform to the lease contract as to give a right of rejection, the risk of their loss remains with the lessor, or, in the case of a finance lease, the supplier, until cure or acceptance.

(b) If the lessee rightfully revokes acceptance, he [or she], to the extent of any deficiency in his [or her] effective insurance coverage, may treat the risk of loss as having remained with the lessor from the beginning.

(2) Whether or not risk of loss is to pass to the lessee, if the lessee as to conforming goods already identified to a lease contract repudiates or is otherwise in default under the lease contract, the lessor, or, in the case of a finance lease, the supplier, to the extent of any deficiency in his [or her] effective insurance coverage may treat the risk of loss as resting on the lessee for a commercially reasonable time.

§ 2A–221. Casualty to Identified Goods.

If a lease contract requires goods identified when the lease contract is made, and the goods suffer casualty without fault of the lessee, the lessor or the supplier before delivery, or the goods suffer casualty before risk of loss passes to the lessee pursuant to the lease agreement or Section 2A–219, then:

(a) if the loss is total, the lease contract is avoided; and

(b) if the loss is partial or the goods have so deteriorated as to no longer conform to the lease contract, the lessee may nevertheless demand inspection and at his [or her] option either treat the lease contract as avoided or, except in a finance lease that is not a consumer lease, accept the goods with due allowance from the rent payable for the balance of the lease term for the deterioration or the deficiency in quantity but without further right against the lessor.

PART 3 Effect of Lease Contract

§ 2A–301. Enforceability of Lease Contract.

Except as otherwise provided in this Article, a lease contract is effective and enforceable according to its terms between the parties, against purchasers of the goods and against creditors of the parties.

§ 2A–302. Title to and Possession of Goods.

Except as otherwise provided in this Article, each provision of this Article applies whether the lessor or a third party has title to the goods, and whether the lessor, the lessee, or a third party has possession of the goods, notwithstanding any statute or rule of law that possession or the absence of possession is fraudulent.

§ 2A–303. Alienability of Party's Interest Under Lease Contract or of Lessor's Residual Interest in Goods; Delegation of Performance; Transfer of Rights.

(1) As used in this section, "creation of a security interest" includes the sale of a lease contract that is subject to Article 9, Secured Transactions, by reason of Section 9–109(a)(3).

(2) Except as provided in subsections (3) and Section 9–407, a provision in a lease agreement which (i) prohibits the voluntary or involuntary transfer, including a transfer by sale, sublease, creation or enforcement of a security interest, or attachment, levy, or other judicial process, of an interest of a party under

the lease contract or of the lessor's residual interest in the goods, or (ii) makes such a transfer an event of default, gives rise to the rights and remedies provided in subsection (4), but a transfer that is prohibited or is an event of default under the lease agreement is otherwise effective.

(3) A provision in a lease agreement which (i) prohibits a transfer of a right to damages for default with respect to the whole lease contract or of a right to payment arising out of the transferor's due performance of the transferor's entire obligation, or (ii) makes such a transfer an event of default, is not enforceable, and such a transfer is not a transfer that materially impairs the prospect of obtaining return performance by, materially changes the duty of, or materially increases the burden or risk imposed on, the other party to the lease contract within the purview of subsection (4).

(4) Subject to subsection (3) and Section 9–407:

(a) if a transfer is made which is made an event of default under a lease agreement, the party to the lease contract not making the transfer, unless that party waives the default or otherwise agrees, has the rights and remedies described in Section 2A–501(2);

(b) if paragraph (a) is not applicable and if a transfer is made that (i) is prohibited under a lease agreement or (ii) materially impairs the prospect of obtaining return performance by, materially changes the duty of, or materially increases the burden or risk imposed on, the other party to the lease contract, unless the party not making the transfer agrees at any time to the transfer in the lease contract or otherwise, then, except as limited by contract, (i) the transferor is liable to the party not making the transfer for damages caused by the transfer to the extent that the damages could not reasonably be prevented by the party not making the transfer and (ii) a court having jurisdiction may grant other appropriate relief, including cancellation of the lease contract or an injunction against the transfer.

(5) A transfer of "the lease" or of "all my rights under the lease", or a transfer in similar general terms, is a transfer of rights and, unless the language or the circumstances, as in a transfer for security, indicate the contrary, the transfer is a delegation of duties by the transferor to the transferee. Acceptance by the transferee constitutes a promise by the transferee to perform those duties. The promise is enforceable by either the transferor or the other party to the lease contract.

(6) Unless otherwise agreed by the lessor and the lessee, a delegation of performance does not relieve the transferor as against the other party of any duty to perform or of any liability for default.

(7) In a consumer lease, to prohibit the transfer of an interest of a party under the lease contract or to make a transfer an event of default, the language must be specific, by a writing, and conspicuous.

As amended in 1990 and 1999.

§ 2A–304. Subsequent Lease of Goods by Lessor.

(1) Subject to Section 2A–303, a subsequent lessee from a lessor of goods under an existing lease contract obtains, to the extent of the leasehold interest transferred, the leasehold interest in the goods that the lessor had or had power to transfer, and except as provided in subsection (2) and Section 2A–527(4), takes subject to the existing lease contract. A lessor with voidable title has power to transfer a good leasehold interest to a good faith subsequent lessee for value, but only to the extent set forth in the preceding sentence. If goods have been delivered under a transaction of purchase the lessor has that power even though:

(a) the lessor was deceived as to the identity of the lessee;

(b) the delivery was in exchange for a check which is later dishonored; or

(c) the delivery was procured through fraud punishable as larcenous under the criminal law.

(2) A subsequent lessee in the ordinary course of business from a lessor who is a merchant dealing in goods of that kind to whom the goods were entrusted by the existing lessee of that lessor before the interest of the subsequent lessee became enforceable against that lessor obtains, to the extent of the leasehold interest transferred, all of that lessor's and the existing lessee's rights to the goods, and takes free of the existing lease contract.

(3) A subsequent lessee from the lessor of goods that are subject to an existing lease contract and are covered by a certificate of title issued under a statute of this State or of another jurisdiction takes no greater rights than those provided both by this section and by the certificate of title statute.

As amended in 1990.

§ 2A–305. Sale or Sublease of Goods by Lessee.

(1) Subject to the provisions of Section 2A–303, a buyer or sublessee from the lessee of goods under an existing lease contract obtains, to the extent of the interest transferred, the leasehold interest in the goods that the lessee had or had power to transfer, and except as provided in subsection (2) and Section 2A–511(4), takes subject to the existing lease contract. A lessee with a voidable leasehold interest has power to transfer a good leasehold interest to a good faith buyer for value or a good faith sublessee for value, but only to the extent set forth in the preceding sentence. When goods have been delivered under a transaction of lease the lessee has that power even though:

(a) the lessor's transferor was deceived as to the identity of the lessor;

(b) the delivery was in exchange for a check which is later dishonored;

(c) it was agreed that the transaction was to be a "cash sale"; or

(d) the delivery was procured through fraud punishable as larcenous under the criminal law.

(2) A buyer in the ordinary course of business or a sublessee in the ordinary course of business from a lessee who is a merchant dealing in goods of that kind to whom the goods were entrusted by the lessor obtains, to the extent of the interest transferred, all of the lessor's and lessee's rights to the goods, and takes free of the existing lease contract.

(3) A buyer or sublessee from the lessee of goods that are subject to an existing lease contract and are covered by a certificate of title issued under a statute of this State or of another jurisdiction takes no greater rights than those provided both by this section and by the certificate of title statute.

§ 2A–306. Priority of Certain Liens Arising by Operation of Law.

If a person in the ordinary course of his [or her] business furnishes services or materials with respect to goods subject to a lease contract, a lien upon those goods in the possession of that person given by statute or rule of law for those materials or services takes priority over any interest of the lessor or lessee under the lease contract or this Article unless the lien is created by statute and the statute provides otherwise or unless the lien is created by rule of law and the rule of law provides otherwise.

§ 2A–307. Priority of Liens Arising by Attachment or Levy on, Security Interests in, and Other Claims to Goods.

(1) Except as otherwise provided in Section 2A–306, a creditor of a lessee takes subject to the lease contract.

(2) Except as otherwise provided in subsection (3) and in Sections 2A–306 and 2A–308, a creditor of a lessor takes subject to the lease contract unless the creditor holds a lien that attached to the goods before the lease contract became enforceable.

(3) Except as otherwise provided in Sections 9–317, 9–321, and 9–323, a lessee takes a leasehold interest subject to a security interest held by a creditor of the lessor.

As amended in 1990 and 1999.

§ 2A–308. Special Rights of Creditors.

(1) A creditor of a lessor in possession of goods subject to a lease contract may treat the lease contract as void if as against the creditor retention of possession by the lessor is fraudulent under any statute or rule of law, but retention of possession in good faith and current course of trade by the lessor for a commercially reasonable time after the lease contract becomes enforceable is not fraudulent.

(2) Nothing in this Article impairs the rights of creditors of a lessor if the lease contract (a) becomes enforceable, not in current course of trade but in satisfaction of or as security for a pre-existing claim for money, security, or the like, and (b) is made under circumstances which under any statute or rule of law apart from this Article would constitute the transaction a fraudulent transfer or voidable preference.

(3) A creditor of a seller may treat a sale or an identification of goods to a contract for sale as void if as against the creditor retention of possession by the seller is fraudulent under any statute or rule of law, but retention of possession of the goods pursuant to a lease contract entered into by the seller as lessee and the buyer as lessor in connection with the sale or identification of the goods is not fraudulent if the buyer bought for value and in good faith.

§ 2A–309. Lessor's and Lessee's Rights When Goods Become Fixtures.

(1) In this section:

(a) goods are "fixtures" when they become so related to particular real estate that an interest in them arises under real estate law;

(b) a "fixture filing" is the filing, in the office where a mortgage on the real estate would be filed or recorded, of a financing statement covering goods that are or are to become fixtures and conforming to the requirements of Section 9–502 (a) and (b);

(c) a lease is a "purchase money lease" unless the lessee has possession or use of the goods or the right to possession or use of the goods before the lease agreement is enforceable;

(d) a mortgage is a "construction mortgage" to the extent it secures an obligation incurred for the construction of an improvement on land including the acquisition cost of the land, if the recorded writing so indicates; and

(e) "encumbrance" includes real estate mortgages and other liens on real estate and all other rights in real estate that are not ownership interests.

(2) Under this Article a lease may be of goods that are fixtures or may continue in goods that become fixtures, but no lease exists under this Article of ordinary building materials incorporated into an improvement on land.

(3) This Article does not prevent creation of a lease of fixtures pursuant to real estate law.

(4) The perfected interest of a lessor of fixtures has priority over a conflicting interest of an encumbrancer or owner of the real estate if:

(a) the lease is a purchase money lease, the conflicting interest of the encumbrancer or owner arises before the goods become fixtures, the interest of the lessor is perfected by a fixture filing before the goods become fixtures or within ten days thereafter, and the lessee has an interest of record in the real estate or is in possession of the real estate; or

(b) the interest of the lessor is perfected by a fixture filing before the interest of the encumbrancer or owner is of record, the lessor's interest has priority over any conflicting interest of a predecessor in title of the encumbrancer or owner, and the lessee has an interest of record in the real estate or is in possession of the real estate.

(5) The interest of a lessor of fixtures, whether or not perfected, has priority over the conflicting interest of an encumbrancer or owner of the real estate if:

(a) the fixtures are readily removable factory or office machines, readily removable equipment that is not primarily used or leased for use in the operation of the real estate, or readily removable replacements of domestic appliances that are goods subject to a consumer lease, and before the goods become fixtures the lease contract is enforceable; or

(b) the conflicting interest is a lien on the real estate obtained by legal or equitable proceedings after the lease contract is enforceable; or

(c) the encumbrancer or owner has consented in writing to the lease or has disclaimed an interest in the goods as fixtures; or

(d) the lessee has a right to remove the goods as against the encumbrancer or owner. If the lessee's right to remove terminates, the priority of the interest of the lessor continues for a reasonable time.

(6) Notwithstanding paragraph (4)(a) but otherwise subject to subsections (4) and (5), the interest of a lessor of fixtures, including the lessor's residual interest, is subordinate to the conflicting interest of an encumbrancer of the real estate under a construction mortgage recorded before the goods become fixtures if the goods become fixtures before the completion of the construction. To the extent given to refinance a construction mortgage, the conflicting interest of an encumbrancer of the real estate under a mortgage has this priority to the same extent as the encumbrancer of the real estate under the construction mortgage.

(7) In cases not within the preceding subsections, priority between the interest of a lessor of fixtures, including the lessor's residual interest, and the conflicting interest of an encumbrancer or owner of the real estate who is not the lessee is determined by the priority rules governing conflicting interests in real estate.

(8) If the interest of a lessor of fixtures, including the lessor's residual interest, has priority over all conflicting interests of all owners and encumbrancers of the real estate, the lessor or the lessee may (i) on default, expiration, termination, or cancellation of the lease agreement but subject to the agreement and this Article, or (ii) if necessary to enforce other rights and remedies of the lessor or lessee under this Article, remove the goods from the real estate, free and clear of all conflicting interests of all owners and encumbrancers of the real estate, but the lessor or lessee must reimburse any encumbrancer or owner of the real estate who is not the lessee and who has not otherwise agreed for the cost of repair of any physical injury, but not for any diminution in value of the real estate caused by the absence of the goods removed or by any necessity of replacing them. A person entitled to reimbursement may refuse permission to remove until the party seeking removal gives adequate security for the performance of this obligation.

(9) Even though the lease agreement does not create a security interest, the interest of a lessor of fixtures, including the lessor's residual interest, is perfected by filing a financing statement as a fixture filing for leased goods that are or are to become fixtures in accordance with the relevant provisions of the Article on Secured Transactions (Article 9).

As amended in 1990 and 1999.

§ 2A–310. Lessor's and Lessee's Rights When Goods Become Accessions.

(1) Goods are "accessions" when they are installed in or affixed to other goods.

(2) The interest of a lessor or a lessee under a lease contract entered into before the goods became accessions is superior to all interests in the whole except as stated in subsection (4).

(3) The interest of a lessor or a lessee under a lease contract entered into at the time or after the goods became accessions is superior to all subsequently acquired interests in the whole except as stated in subsection (4) but is subordinate to interests in the whole existing at the time the lease contract was made unless the holders of such interests in the whole have in writing consented to the lease or disclaimed an interest in the goods as part of the whole.

(4) The interest of a lessor or a lessee under a lease contract described in subsection (2) or (3) is subordinate to the interest of

(a) a buyer in the ordinary course of business or a lessee in the ordinary course of business of any interest in the whole acquired after the goods became accessions; or

(b) a creditor with a security interest in the whole perfected before the lease contract was made to the extent that the creditor makes subsequent advances without knowledge of the lease contract.

(5) When under subsections (2) or (3) and (4) a lessor or a lessee of accessions holds an interest that is superior to all interests in the whole, the lessor or the lessee may (a) on default, expiration, termination, or cancellation of the lease contract by the other party but subject to the provisions of the lease contract and this Article, or (b) if necessary to enforce his [or her] other rights and remedies under this Article, remove the goods from the whole, free and clear of all interests in the whole, but he [or she] must reimburse any holder of an interest in the whole who is not the lessee and who has not otherwise agreed for the cost of repair of any physical injury but not for any diminution in value of the whole caused by the absence of the goods removed or by any necessity for replacing them. A person entitled to reimbursement may refuse permission to remove until the party seeking removal gives adequate security for the performance of this obligation.

§ 2A–311. Priority Subject to Subordination.

Nothing in this Article prevents subordination by agreement by any person entitled to priority.

As added in 1990.

PART 4 Performance of Lease Contract: Repudiated, Substituted and Excused

§ 2A–401. Insecurity: Adequate Assurance of Performance.

(1) A lease contract imposes an obligation on each party that the other's expectation of receiving due performance will not be impaired.

(2) If reasonable grounds for insecurity arise with respect to the performance of either party, the insecure party may demand in writing adequate assurance of due performance. Until the insecure party receives that assurance, if commercially reasonable the insecure party may suspend any performance for which he [or she] has not already received the agreed return.

(3) A repudiation of the lease contract occurs if assurance of due performance adequate under the circumstances of the particular case is not provided to the insecure party within a reasonable time, not to exceed 30 days after receipt of a demand by the other party.

(4) Between merchants, the reasonableness of grounds for insecurity and the adequacy of any assurance offered must be determined according to commercial standards.

(5) Acceptance of any nonconforming delivery or payment does not prejudice the aggrieved party's right to demand adequate assurance of future performance.

§ 2A–402. Anticipatory Repudiation.

If either party repudiates a lease contract with respect to a performance not yet due under the lease contract, the loss of which performance will substantially impair the value of the lease contract to the other, the aggrieved party may:

(a) for a commercially reasonable time, await retraction of repudiation and performance by the repudiating party;

(b) make demand pursuant to Section 2A–401 and await assurance of future performance adequate under the circumstances of the particular case; or

(c) resort to any right or remedy upon default under the lease contract or this Article, even though the aggrieved party has notified the repudiating party that the aggrieved party would await the repudiating party's performance and assurance and has urged retraction. In addition, whether or not the aggrieved party is pursuing one of the foregoing remedies, the aggrieved party may suspend performance or, if the aggrieved party is the lessor, proceed in accordance with the provisions of this Article on the lessor's right to identify goods to the lease contract notwithstanding default or to salvage unfinished goods (Section 2A–524).

§ 2A–403. Retraction of Anticipatory Repudiation.

(1) Until the repudiating party's next performance is due, the repudiating party can retract the repudiation unless, since the repudiation, the aggrieved party has cancelled the lease contract or materially changed the aggrieved party's position or otherwise indicated that the aggrieved party considers the repudiation final.

(2) Retraction may be by any method that clearly indicates to the aggrieved party that the repudiating party intends to perform under the lease contract and includes any assurance demanded under Section 2A–401.

(3) Retraction reinstates a repudiating party's rights under a lease contract with due excuse and allowance to the aggrieved party for any delay occasioned by the repudiation.

§ 2A–404. Substituted Performance.

(1) If without fault of the lessee, the lessor and the supplier, the agreed berthing, loading, or unloading facilities fail or the agreed type of carrier becomes unavailable or the agreed manner of delivery otherwise becomes commercially impracticable, but a commercially reasonable substitute is available, the substitute performance must be tendered and accepted.

(2) If the agreed means or manner of payment fails because of domestic or foreign governmental regulation:

(a) the lessor may withhold or stop delivery or cause the supplier to withhold or stop delivery unless the lessee provides a means or manner of payment that is commercially a substantial equivalent; and

(b) if delivery has already been taken, payment by the means or in the manner provided by the regulation discharges the lessee's obligation unless the regulation is discriminatory, oppressive, or predatory.

§ 2A–405. Excused Performance.

Subject to Section 2A–404 on substituted performance, the following rules apply:

(a) Delay in delivery or nondelivery in whole or in part by a lessor or a supplier who complies with paragraphs (b) and (c) is not a default under the lease contract if performance as agreed has been made impracticable by the occurrence of a contingency the nonoccurrence of which was a basic assumption on which the lease contract was made or by compliance in good faith with any applicable foreign or domestic governmental regulation or order, whether or not the regulation or order later proves to be invalid.

(b) If the causes mentioned in paragraph (a) affect only part of the lessor's or the supplier's capacity to perform, he [or she] shall allocate production and deliveries among his [or her] customers but at his [or her] option may include regular customers not then under contract for sale or lease as well as his [or her] own requirements for further manufacture. He [or she] may so allocate in any manner that is fair and reasonable.

(c) The lessor seasonably shall notify the lessee and in the case of a finance lease the supplier seasonably shall notify the lessor and the lessee, if known, that there will be delay or nondelivery and, if allocation is required under paragraph (b), of the estimated quota thus made available for the lessee.

§ 2A–406. Procedure on Excused Performance.

(1) If the lessee receives notification of a material or indefinite delay or an allocation justified under Section 2A–405, the lessee may by written notification to the lessor as to any goods involved, and with respect to all of the goods if under an installment lease contract the value of the whole lease contract is substantially impaired (Section 2A–510):

(a) terminate the lease contract (Section 2A–505(2)); or

(b) except in a finance lease that is not a consumer lease, modify the lease contract by accepting the available quota in substitution, with due allowance from the rent payable for the balance of the lease term for the deficiency but without further right against the lessor.

(2) If, after receipt of a notification from the lessor under Section 2A–405, the lessee fails so to modify the lease agreement within a reasonable time not exceeding 30 days, the lease contract lapses with respect to any deliveries affected.

§ 2A–407. Irrevocable Promises: Finance Leases.

(1) In the case of a finance lease that is not a consumer lease the lessee's promises under the lease contract become irrevocable and independent upon the lessee's acceptance of the goods.

(2) A promise that has become irrevocable and independent under subsection (1):

(a) is effective and enforceable between the parties, and by or against third parties including assignees of the parties, and

(b) is not subject to cancellation, termination, modification, repudiation, excuse, or substitution without the consent of the party to whom the promise runs.

(3) This section does not affect the validity under any other law of a covenant in any lease contract making the lessee's promises irrevocable and independent upon the lessee's acceptance of the goods.

As amended in 1990.

PART 5 Default

A. In General

§ 2A–501. Default: Procedure.

(1) Whether the lessor or the lessee is in default under a lease contract is determined by the lease agreement and this Article.

(2) If the lessor or the lessee is in default under the lease contract, the party seeking enforcement has rights and remedies as provided in this Article and, except as limited by this Article, as provided in the lease agreement.

(3) If the lessor or the lessee is in default under the lease contract, the party seeking enforcement may reduce the party's claim to judgment, or otherwise enforce the lease contract by self-help or any available judicial procedure or nonjudicial procedure, including administrative proceeding, arbitration, or the like, in accordance with this Article.

(4) Except as otherwise provided in Section 1–106(1) or this Article or the lease agreement, the rights and remedies referred to in subsections (2) and (3) are cumulative.

(5) If the lease agreement covers both real property and goods, the party seeking enforcement may proceed under this Part as to the goods, or under other applicable law as to both the real property and the goods in accordance with that party's rights and remedies in respect of the real property, in which case this Part does not apply.

As amended in 1990.

§ 2A–502. Notice After Default.

Except as otherwise provided in this Article or the lease agreement, the lessor or lessee in default under the lease contract is not entitled to notice of default or notice of enforcement from the other party to the lease agreement.

§ 2A–503. Modification or Impairment of Rights and Remedies.

(1) Except as otherwise provided in this Article, the lease agreement may include rights and remedies for default in addition to or in substitution for those provided in this Article and may limit or alter the measure of damages recoverable under this Article.

(2) Resort to a remedy provided under this Article or in the lease agreement is optional unless the remedy is expressly agreed to be exclusive. If circumstances cause an exclusive or limited remedy to fail of its essential purpose, or provision for an exclusive remedy is unconscionable, remedy may be had as provided in this Article.

(3) Consequential damages may be liquidated under Section 2A–504, or may otherwise be limited, altered, or excluded unless the limitation, alteration, or exclusion is unconscionable. Limitation, alteration, or exclusion of consequential damages for injury to the person in the case of consumer goods is prima facie unconscionable but limitation, alteration, or exclusion of damages where the loss is commercial is not prima facie unconscionable.

(4) Rights and remedies on default by the lessor or the lessee with respect to any obligation or promise collateral or ancillary to the lease contract are not impaired by this Article.

As amended in 1990.

§ 2A–504. Liquidation of Damages.

(1) Damages payable by either party for default, or any other act or omission, including indemnity for loss or diminution of anticipated tax benefits or loss or damage to lessor's residual interest, may be liquidated in the lease agreement but only at an amount or by a formula that is reasonable in light of the then anticipated harm caused by the default or other act or omission.

(2) If the lease agreement provides for liquidation of damages, and such provision does not comply with subsection (1), or such provision is an exclusive or limited remedy that circumstances cause to fail of its essential purpose, remedy may be had as provided in this Article.

(3) If the lessor justifiably withholds or stops delivery of goods because of the lessee's default or insolvency (Section 2A–525 or 2A–526), the lessee is entitled to restitution of any amount by which the sum of his [or her] payments exceeds:

(a) the amount to which the lessor is entitled by virtue of terms liquidating the lessor's damages in accordance with subsection (1); or

(b) in the absence of those terms, 20 percent of the then present value of the total rent the lessee was obligated to pay for the balance of the lease term, or, in the case of a consumer lease, the lesser of such amount or $500.

(4) A lessee's right to restitution under subsection (3) is subject to offset to the extent the lessor establishes:

(a) a right to recover damages under the provisions of this Article other than subsection (1); and

(b) the amount or value of any benefits received by the lessee directly or indirectly by reason of the lease contract.

§ 2A–505. Cancellation and Termination and Effect of Cancellation, Termination, Rescission, or Fraud on Rights and Remedies.

(1) On cancellation of the lease contract, all obligations that are still executory on both sides are discharged, but any right based on prior default or performance survives, and the cancelling party also retains any remedy for default of the whole lease contract or any unperformed balance.

(2) On termination of the lease contract, all obligations that are still executory on both sides are discharged but any right based on prior default or performance survives.

(3) Unless the contrary intention clearly appears, expressions of "cancellation," "rescission," or the like of the lease contract may not be construed as a renunciation or discharge of any claim in damages for an antecedent default.

(4) Rights and remedies for material misrepresentation or fraud include all rights and remedies available under this Article for default.

(5) Neither rescission nor a claim for rescission of the lease contract nor rejection or return of the goods may bar or be deemed inconsistent with a claim for damages or other right or remedy.

§ 2A–506. Statute of Limitations.

(1) An action for default under a lease contract, including breach of warranty or indemnity, must be commenced within 4 years after the cause of action accrued. By the original lease contract the parties may reduce the period of limitation to not less than one year.

(2) A cause of action for default accrues when the act or omission on which the default or breach of warranty is based is or should have been discovered by the aggrieved party, or when the default occurs, whichever is later. A cause of action for indemnity accrues when the act or omission on which the claim for indemnity is based is or should have been discovered by the indemnified party, whichever is later.

(3) If an action commenced within the time limited by subsection (1) is so terminated as to leave available a remedy by another action for the same default or breach of warranty or indemnity, the other action may be commenced after the expiration of the time limited and within 6 months after the termination of the first action unless the termination resulted from voluntary discontinuance or from dismissal for failure or neglect to prosecute.

(4) This section does not alter the law on tolling of the statute of limitations nor does it apply to causes of action that have accrued before this Article becomes effective.

§ 2A–507. Proof of Market Rent: Time and Place.

(1) Damages based on market rent (Section 2A–519 or 2A–528) are determined according to the rent for the use of the goods concerned for a lease term identical to the remaining lease term of the original lease agreement and prevailing at the times specified in Sections 2A–519 and 2A–528.

(2) If evidence of rent for the use of the goods concerned for a lease term identical to the remaining lease term of the original lease agreement and prevailing at the times or places described in this Article is not readily available, the rent prevailing within any reasonable time before or after the time described or at any other place or for a different lease term which in commercial judgment or under usage of trade would serve as a reasonable substitute for the one described may be used, making any proper allowance for the difference, including the cost of transporting the goods to or from the other place.

(3) Evidence of a relevant rent prevailing at a time or place or for a lease term other than the one described in this Article offered by one party is not admissible unless and until he [or she] has given the other party notice the court finds sufficient to prevent unfair surprise.

(4) If the prevailing rent or value of any goods regularly leased in any established market is in issue, reports in official publications or trade journals or in newspapers or periodicals of general circulation published as the reports of that market are admissible in evidence. The circumstances of the preparation of the report may be shown to affect its weight but not its admissibility.

As amended in 1990.

B. Default by Lessor

§ 2A–508. Lessee's Remedies.

(1) If a lessor fails to deliver the goods in conformity to the lease contract (Section 2A–509) or repudiates the lease contract (Section 2A–402), or a lessee rightfully rejects the goods (Section 2A–509) or justifiably revokes acceptance of the goods (Section 2A–517), then with respect to any goods involved, and with respect to all of the goods if under an installment lease contract the value of the whole lease contract is substantially impaired (Section 2A–510), the lessor is in default under the lease contract and the lessee may:

(a) cancel the lease contract (Section 2A–505(1));

(b) recover so much of the rent and security as has been paid and is just under the circumstances;

(c) cover and recover damages as to all goods affected whether or not they have been identified to the lease contract (Sections 2A–518 and 2A–520), or recover damages for nondelivery (Sections 2A–519 and 2A–520);

(d) exercise any other rights or pursue any other remedies provided in the lease contract.

(2) If a lessor fails to deliver the goods in conformity to the lease contract or repudiates the lease contract, the lessee may also:

(a) if the goods have been identified, recover them (Section 2A–522); or

(b) in a proper case, obtain specific performance or replevy the goods (Section 2A–521).

(3) If a lessor is otherwise in default under a lease contract, the lessee may exercise the rights and pursue the remedies provided in the lease contract, which may include a right to cancel the lease, and in Section 2A–519(3).

(4) If a lessor has breached a warranty, whether express or implied, the lessee may recover damages (Section 2A–519(4)).

(5) On rightful rejection or justifiable revocation of acceptance, a lessee has a security interest in goods in the lessee's possession or control for any rent and security that has been paid and any expenses reasonably incurred in their inspection, receipt, transportation, and care and custody and may hold those goods and dispose of them in good faith and in a commercially reasonable manner, subject to Section 2A–527(5).

(6) Subject to the provisions of Section 2A–407, a lessee, on notifying the lessor of the lessee's intention to do so, may deduct all or any part of the damages resulting from any default under the lease contract from any part of the rent still due under the same lease contract.

As amended in 1990.

§ 2A–509. Lessee's Rights on Improper Delivery; Rightful Rejection.

(1) Subject to the provisions of Section 2A–510 on default in installment lease contracts, if the goods or the tender or delivery fail in any respect to conform to the lease contract, the lessee may reject or accept the goods or accept any commercial unit or units and reject the rest of the goods.

(2) Rejection of goods is ineffective unless it is within a reasonable time after tender or delivery of the goods and the lessee seasonably notifies the lessor.

§ 2A–510. Installment Lease Contracts: Rejection and Default.

(1) Under an installment lease contract a lessee may reject any delivery that is nonconforming if the nonconformity substantially impairs the value of that delivery and cannot be cured or the nonconformity is a defect in the required documents; but if the nonconformity does not fall within subsection (2) and the lessor or the supplier gives adequate assurance of its cure, the lessee must accept that delivery.

(2) Whenever nonconformity or default with respect to one or more deliveries substantially impairs the value of the installment lease contract as a whole there is a default with respect to the whole. But, the aggrieved party reinstates the installment lease contract as a whole if the aggrieved party accepts a nonconforming delivery without seasonably notifying of cancellation or brings an action with respect only to past deliveries or demands performance as to future deliveries.

§ 2A–511. Merchant Lessee's Duties as to Rightfully Rejected Goods.

(1) Subject to any security interest of a lessee (Section 2A–508 (5)), if a lessor or a supplier has no agent or place of business at the market of rejection, a merchant lessee, after rejection of goods in his [or her] possession or control, shall follow any reasonable instructions received from the lessor or the supplier with respect to the goods. In the absence of those instructions, a merchant lessee shall make reasonable efforts to sell, lease, or otherwise dispose of the goods for the lessor's account if they threaten to decline in value speedily. Instructions are not reasonable if on demand indemnity for expenses is not forthcoming.

(2) If a merchant lessee (subsection (1)) or any other lessee (Section 2A–512) disposes of goods, he [or she] is entitled to reimbursement either from the lessor or the supplier or out of the proceeds for reasonable expenses of caring for and disposing of the goods and, if the expenses include no disposition commission, to such commission as is usual in the trade, or if there is none, to a reasonable sum not exceeding 10 percent of the gross proceeds.

(3) In complying with this section or Section 2A–512, the lessee is held only to good faith. Good faith conduct hereunder is neither acceptance or conversion nor the basis of an action for damages.

(4) A purchaser who purchases in good faith from a lessee pursuant to this section or Section 2A–512 takes the goods free of any rights of the lessor and the supplier even though the lessee fails to comply with one or more of the requirements of this Article.

§ 2A–512. Lessee's Duties as to Rightfully Rejected Goods.

(1) Except as otherwise provided with respect to goods that threaten to decline in value speedily (Section 2A–511) and subject to any security interest of a lessee (Section 2A–508(5)):

(a) the lessee, after rejection of goods in the lessee's possession, shall hold them with reasonable care at the lessor's or the supplier's disposition for a reasonable time after the lessee's seasonable notification of rejection;

(b) if the lessor or the supplier gives no instructions within a reasonable time after notification of rejection, the lessee may store the rejected goods for the lessor's or the supplier's account or ship them to the lessor or the supplier or dispose of them for the lessor's or the supplier's account with reimbursement in the manner provided in Section 2A–511; but

(c) the lessee has no further obligations with regard to goods rightfully rejected.

(2) Action by the lessee pursuant to subsection (1) is not acceptance or conversion.

§ 2A–513. Cure by Lessor of Improper Tender or Delivery; Replacement.

(1) If any tender or delivery by the lessor or the supplier is rejected because nonconforming and the time for performance has not yet expired, the lessor or the supplier may seasonably notify the lessee of the lessor's or the supplier's intention to cure and may then make a conforming delivery within the time provided in the lease contract.

(2) If the lessee rejects a nonconforming tender that the lessor or the supplier had reasonable grounds to believe would be acceptable with or without money allowance, the lessor or the supplier may have a further reasonable time to substitute a conforming tender if he [or she] seasonably notifies the lessee.

§ 2A–514. Waiver of Lessee's Objections.

(1) In rejecting goods, a lessee's failure to state a particular defect that is ascertainable by reasonable inspection precludes the lessee from relying on the defect to justify rejection or to establish default:

(a) if, stated seasonably, the lessor or the supplier could have cured it (Section 2A–513); or

(b) between merchants if the lessor or the supplier after rejection has made a request in writing for a full and final written statement of all defects on which the lessee proposes to rely.

(2) A lessee's failure to reserve rights when paying rent or other consideration against documents precludes recovery of the payment for defects apparent on the face of the documents.

§ 2A–515. Acceptance of Goods.

(1) Acceptance of goods occurs after the lessee has had a reasonable opportunity to inspect the goods and

(a) the lessee signifies or acts with respect to the goods in a manner that signifies to the lessor or the supplier that the goods are conforming or that the lessee will take or retain them in spite of their nonconformity; or

(b) the lessee fails to make an effective rejection of the goods (Section 2A–509(2)).

(2) Acceptance of a part of any commercial unit is acceptance of that entire unit.

§ 2A–516. Effect of Acceptance of Goods; Notice of Default; Burden of Establishing Default After Acceptance; Notice of Claim or Litigation to Person Answerable Over.

(1) A lessee must pay rent for any goods accepted in accordance with the lease contract, with due allowance for goods rightfully rejected or not delivered.

(2) A lessee's acceptance of goods precludes rejection of the goods accepted. In the case of a finance lease, if made with knowledge of a nonconformity, acceptance cannot be revoked because of it. In any other case, if made with knowledge of a nonconformity, acceptance cannot be revoked because of it unless the acceptance was on the reasonable assumption that the nonconformity would be seasonably cured. Acceptance does not of itself impair any other remedy provided by this Article or the lease agreement for nonconformity.

(3) If a tender has been accepted:

(a) within a reasonable time after the lessee discovers or should have discovered any default, the lessee shall notify the lessor and the supplier, if any, or be barred from any remedy against the party notified;

(b) except in the case of a consumer lease, within a reasonable time after the lessee receives notice of litigation for infringement or the like (Section 2A–211) the lessee shall notify the lessor or be barred from any remedy over for liability established by the litigation; and

(c) the burden is on the lessee to establish any default.

(4) If a lessee is sued for breach of a warranty or other obligation for which a lessor or a supplier is answerable over the following apply:

(a) The lessee may give the lessor or the supplier, or both, written notice of the litigation. If the notice states that the person notified may come in and defend and that if the person notified does not do so that person will be bound in any action against that person by the lessee by any determination of fact common to the two litigations, then unless the person notified after seasonable receipt of the notice does come in and defend that person is so bound.

(b) The lessor or the supplier may demand in writing that the lessee turn over control of the litigation including settlement if the claim is one for infringement or the like (Section 2A–211) or else be barred from any remedy over. If the demand states that the lessor or the supplier agrees to bear all expense and to satisfy any adverse judgment, then unless the lessee after seasonable receipt of the demand does turn over control the lessee is so barred.

(5) Subsections (3) and (4) apply to any obligation of a lessee to hold the lessor or the supplier harmless against infringement or the like (Section 2A–211).

As amended in 1990.

§ 2A–517. Revocation of Acceptance of Goods.

(1) A lessee may revoke acceptance of a lot or commercial unit whose nonconformity substantially impairs its value to the lessee if the lessee has accepted it:

(a) except in the case of a finance lease, on the reasonable assumption that its nonconformity would be cured and it has not been seasonably cured; or

(b) without discovery of the nonconformity if the lessee's acceptance was reasonably induced either by the lessor's assurances or, except in the case of a finance lease, by the difficulty of discovery before acceptance.

(2) Except in the case of a finance lease that is not a consumer lease, a lessee may revoke acceptance of a lot or commercial unit if the lessor defaults under the lease contract and the default substantially impairs the value of that lot or commercial unit to the lessee.

(3) If the lease agreement so provides, the lessee may revoke acceptance of a lot or commercial unit because of other defaults by the lessor.

(4) Revocation of acceptance must occur within a reasonable time after the lessee discovers or should have discovered the ground for it and before any substantial change in condition of the goods which is not caused by the nonconformity. Revocation is not effective until the lessee notifies the lessor.

(5) A lessee who so revokes has the same rights and duties with regard to the goods involved as if the lessee had rejected them.

As amended in 1990.

§ 2A–518. Cover; Substitute Goods.

(1) After a default by a lessor under the lease contract of the type described in Section 2A–508(1), or, if agreed, after other default

by the lessor, the lessee may cover by making any purchase or lease of or contract to purchase or lease goods in substitution for those due from the lessor.

(2) Except as otherwise provided with respect to damages liquidated in the lease agreement (Section 2A–504) or otherwise determined pursuant to agreement of the parties (Sections 1–102(3) and 2A–503), if a lessee's cover is by lease agreement substantially similar to the original lease agreement and the new lease agreement is made in good faith and in a commercially reasonable manner, the lessee may recover from the lessor as damages (i) the present value, as of the date of the commencement of the term of the new lease agreement, of the rent under the new lease agreement applicable to that period of the new lease term which is comparable to the then remaining term of the original lease agreement minus the present value as of the same date of the total rent for the then remaining lease term of the original lease agreement, and (ii) any incidental or consequential damages, less expenses saved in consequence of the lessor's default.

(3) If a lessee's cover is by lease agreement that for any reason does not qualify for treatment under subsection (2), or is by purchase or otherwise, the lessee may recover from the lessor as if the lessee had elected not to cover and Section 2A–519 governs.

As amended in 1990.

§ 2A–519. Lessee's Damages for Non-Delivery, Repudiation, Default, and Breach of Warranty in Regard to Accepted Goods.

(1) Except as otherwise provided with respect to damages liquidated in the lease agreement (Section 2A–504) or otherwise determined pursuant to agreement of the parties (Sections 1–102(3) and 2A–503), if a lessee elects not to cover or a lessee elects to cover and the cover is by lease agreement that for any reason does not qualify for treatment under Section 2A–518(2), or is by purchase or otherwise, the measure of damages for non-delivery or repudiation by the lessor or for rejection or revocation of acceptance by the lessee is the present value, as of the date of the default, of the then market rent minus the present value as of the same date of the original rent, computed for the remaining lease term of the original lease agreement, together with incidental and consequential damages, less expenses saved in consequence of the lessor's default.

(2) Market rent is to be determined as of the place for tender or, in cases of rejection after arrival or revocation of acceptance, as of the place of arrival.

(3) Except as otherwise agreed, if the lessee has accepted goods and given notification (Section 2A–516(3)), the measure of damages for non-conforming tender or delivery or other default by a lessor is the loss resulting in the ordinary course of events from the lessor's default as determined in any manner that is reasonable together with incidental and consequential damages, less expenses saved in consequence of the lessor's default.

(4) Except as otherwise agreed, the measure of damages for breach of warranty is the present value at the time and place of acceptance of the difference between the value of the use of the goods accepted and the value if they had been as warranted for the lease term, unless special circumstances show proximate damages of a different amount, together with incidental and consequential damages, less expenses saved in consequence of the lessor's default or breach of warranty.

As amended in 1990.

§ 2A–520. Lessee's Incidental and Consequential Damages.

(1) Incidental damages resulting from a lessor's default include expenses reasonably incurred in inspection, receipt, transportation, and care and custody of goods rightfully rejected or goods the acceptance of which is justifiably revoked, any commercially reasonable charges, expenses or commissions in connection with effecting cover, and any other reasonable expense incident to the default.

(2) Consequential damages resulting from a lessor's default include:

(a) any loss resulting from general or particular requirements and needs of which the lessor at the time of contracting had reason to know and which could not reasonably be prevented by cover or otherwise; and

(b) injury to person or property proximately resulting from any breach of warranty.

§ 2A–521. Lessee's Right to Specific Performance or Replevin.

(1) Specific performance may be decreed if the goods are unique or in other proper circumstances.

(2) A decree for specific performance may include any terms and conditions as to payment of the rent, damages, or other relief that the court deems just.

(3) A lessee has a right of replevin, detinue, sequestration, claim and delivery, or the like for goods identified to the lease contract if after reasonable effort the lessee is unable to effect cover for those goods or the circumstances reasonably indicate that the effort will be unavailing.

§ 2A–522. Lessee's Right to Goods on Lessor's Insolvency.

(1) Subject to subsection (2) and even though the goods have not been shipped, a lessee who has paid a part or all of the rent and security for goods identified to a lease contract (Section 2A–217) on making and keeping good a tender of any unpaid portion of the rent and security due under the lease contract may recover the goods identified from the lessor if the lessor becomes insolvent within 10 days after receipt of the first installment of rent and security.

(2) A lessee acquires the right to recover goods identified to a lease contract only if they conform to the lease contract.

C. Default by Lessee

§ 2A–523. Lessor's Remedies.

(1) If a lessee wrongfully rejects or revokes acceptance of goods or fails to make a payment when due or repudiates with respect to a part or the whole, then, with respect to any goods involved, and with respect to all of the goods if under an installment lease contract the value of the whole lease contract is substantially impaired (Section 2A–510), the lessee is in default under the lease contract and the lessor may:

(a) cancel the lease contract (Section 2A–505(1));

(b) proceed respecting goods not identified to the lease contract (Section 2A–524);

(c) withhold delivery of the goods and take possession of goods previously delivered (Section 2A–525);

(d) stop delivery of the goods by any bailee (Section 2A–526);

(e) dispose of the goods and recover damages (Section 2A–527), or retain the goods and recover damages (Section 2A–528), or in a proper case recover rent (Section 2A–529);

(f) exercise any other rights or pursue any other remedies provided in the lease contract.

(2) If a lessor does not fully exercise a right or obtain a remedy to which the lessor is entitled under subsection (1), the lessor may recover the loss resulting in the ordinary course of events from the lessee's default as determined in any reasonable manner, together with incidental damages, less expenses saved in consequence of the lessee's default.

(3) If a lessee is otherwise in default under a lease contract, the lessor may exercise the rights and pursue the remedies provided in the lease contract, which may include a right to cancel the lease. In addition, unless otherwise provided in the lease contract:

(a) if the default substantially impairs the value of the lease contract to the lessor, the lessor may exercise the rights and pursue the remedies provided in subsections (1) or (2); or

(b) if the default does not substantially impair the value of the lease contract to the lessor, the lessor may recover as provided in subsection (2).

As amended in 1990.

§ 2A–524. Lessor's Right to Identify Goods to Lease Contract.

(1) After default by the lessee under the lease contract of the type described in Section 2A–523(1) or 2A–523(3)(a) or, if agreed, after other default by the lessee, the lessor may:

(a) identify to the lease contract conforming goods not already identified if at the time the lessor learned of the default they were in the lessor's or the supplier's possession or control; and

(b) dispose of goods (Section 2A–527(1)) that demonstrably have been intended for the particular lease contract even though those goods are unfinished.

(2) If the goods are unfinished, in the exercise of reasonable commercial judgment for the purposes of avoiding loss and of effective realization, an aggrieved lessor or the supplier may either complete manufacture and wholly identify the goods to the lease contract or cease manufacture and lease, sell, or otherwise dispose of the goods for scrap or salvage value or proceed in any other reasonable manner.

As amended in 1990.

§ 2A–525. Lessor's Right to Possession of Goods.

(1) If a lessor discovers the lessee to be insolvent, the lessor may refuse to deliver the goods.

(2) After a default by the lessee under the lease contract of the type described in Section 2A–523(1) or 2A–523(3)(a) or, if agreed, after other default by the lessee, the lessor has the right to take possession of the goods. If the lease contract so provides, the lessor may require the lessee to assemble the goods and make them available to the lessor at a place to be designated by the lessor which is reasonably convenient to both parties. Without removal, the lessor may render unusable any goods employed in trade or business, and may dispose of goods on the lessee's premises (Section 2A–527).

(3) The lessor may proceed under subsection (2) without judicial process if that can be done without breach of the peace or the lessor may proceed by action.

As amended in 1990.

§ 2A–526. Lessor's Stoppage of Delivery in Transit or Otherwise.

(1) A lessor may stop delivery of goods in the possession of a carrier or other bailee if the lessor discovers the lessee to be insolvent and may stop delivery of carload, truckload, planeload, or larger shipments of express or freight if the lessee repudiates or fails to make a payment due before delivery, whether for rent, security or otherwise under the lease contract, or for any other reason the lessor has a right to withhold or take possession of the goods.

(2) In pursuing its remedies under subsection (1), the lessor may stop delivery until

(a) receipt of the goods by the lessee;

(b) acknowledgment to the lessee by any bailee of the goods, except a carrier, that the bailee holds the goods for the lessee; or

(c) such an acknowledgment to the lessee by a carrier via reshipment or as warehouseman.

(3) (a) To stop delivery, a lessor shall so notify as to enable the bailee by reasonable diligence to prevent delivery of the goods.

(b) After notification, the bailee shall hold and deliver the goods according to the directions of the lessor, but the lessor is liable to the bailee for any ensuing charges or damages.

(c) A carrier who has issued a nonnegotiable bill of lading is not obliged to obey a notification to stop received from a person other than the consignor.

§ 2A–527. Lessor's Rights to Dispose of Goods.

(1) After a default by a lessee under the lease contract of the type described in Section 2A–523(1) or 2A–523(3)(a) or after the lessor refuses to deliver or takes possession of goods (Section 2A–525 or 2A–526), or, if agreed, after other default by a lessee, the lessor may dispose of the goods concerned or the undelivered balance thereof by lease, sale, or otherwise.

(2) Except as otherwise provided with respect to damages liquidated in the lease agreement (Section 2A–504) or otherwise determined pursuant to agreement of the parties (Sections 1–102(3) and 2A–503), if the disposition is by lease agreement substantially similar to the original lease agreement and the new lease agreement is made in good faith and in a commercially reasonable manner, the lessor may recover from the lessee as damages (i) accrued and unpaid rent as of the date of the commencement of the term of the new lease agreement, (ii) the present value, as of the same date, of the total rent for the then remaining lease term of the original lease agreement minus the present value, as of the same date, of the rent under the new lease agreement applicable to that period of the new lease term which is comparable to the then remaining term of the original lease agreement, and (iii) any incidental damages allowed under Section 2A–530, less expenses saved in consequence of the lessee's default.

(3) If the lessor's disposition is by lease agreement that for any reason does not qualify for treatment under subsection (2), or is by sale or otherwise, the lessor may recover from the lessee as if the lessor had elected not to dispose of the goods and Section 2A–528 governs.

(4) A subsequent buyer or lessee who buys or leases from the lessor in good faith for value as a result of a disposition under this section takes the goods free of the original lease contract and any rights of the original lessee even though the lessor fails to comply with one or more of the requirements of this Article.

(5) The lessor is not accountable to the lessee for any profit made on any disposition. A lessee who has rightfully rejected or justifiably revoked acceptance shall account to the lessor for any excess over the amount of the lessee's security interest (Section 2A–508(5)).

As amended in 1990.

§ 2A–528. Lessor's Damages for Non-acceptance, Failure to Pay, Repudiation, or Other Default.

(1) Except as otherwise provided with respect to damages liquidated in the lease agreement (Section 2A–504) or otherwise determined pursuant to agreement of the parties (Section 1–102(3) and 2A–503), if a lessor elects to retain the goods or a lessor elects to dispose of the goods and the disposition is by lease agreement that for any reason does not qualify for treatment under Section 2A–527(2), or is by sale or otherwise, the lessor may recover from the lessee as damages for a default of the type described in Section 2A–523(1) or 2A–523(3)(a), or if agreed, for other default of the lessee, (i) accrued and unpaid rent as of the date of the default if the lessee has never taken possession of the goods, or, if the lessee has taken possession of the goods, as of the date the lessor repossesses the goods or an earlier date on which the lessee makes a tender of the goods to the lessor, (ii) the present value as of the date determined under clause (i) of the total rent for the then remaining lease term of the original lease agreement minus the present value as of the same date of the market rent as the place where the goods are located computed for the same lease term, and (iii) any incidental damages allowed under Section 2A–530, less expenses saved in consequence of the lessee's default.

(2) If the measure of damages provided in subsection (1) is inadequate to put a lessor in as good a position as performance would have, the measure of damages is the present value of the profit, including reasonable overhead, the lessor would have made from full performance by the lessee, together with any incidental damages allowed under Section 2A–530, due allowance for costs reasonably incurred and due credit for payments or proceeds of disposition.

As amended in 1990.

§ 2A–529. Lessor's Action for the Rent.

(1) After default by the lessee under the lease contract of the type described in Section 2A–523(1) or 2A–523(3)(a) or, if agreed, after other default by the lessee, if the lessor complies with subsection (2), the lessor may recover from the lessee as damages:

(a) for goods accepted by the lessee and not repossessed by or tendered to the lessor, and for conforming goods lost or damaged within a commercially reasonable time after risk of loss passes to the lessee (Section 2A–219), (i) accrued and unpaid rent as of the date of entry of judgment in favor of the lessor (ii) the present value as of the same date of the rent for the then remaining lease term of the lease agreement, and (iii) any incidental damages allowed under Section 2A–530, less expenses saved in consequence of the lessee's default; and

(b) for goods identified to the lease contract if the lessor is unable after reasonable effort to dispose of them at a reasonable price or the circumstances reasonably indicate that effort will be unavailing, (i) accrued and unpaid rent as of the date of entry of judgment in favor of the lessor, (ii) the present value as of the same date of the rent for the then remaining lease term of the lease agreement, and (iii) any incidental damages allowed under Section 2A–530, less expenses saved in consequence of the lessee's default.

(2) Except as provided in subsection (3), the lessor shall hold for the lessee for the remaining lease term of the lease agreement any goods that have been identified to the lease contract and are in the lessor's control.

(3) The lessor may dispose of the goods at any time before collection of the judgment for damages obtained pursuant to subsection (1). If the disposition is before the end of the remaining lease term of the lease agreement, the lessor's recovery against the lessee for damages is governed by Section 2A–527 or Section 2A–528, and the lessor will cause an appropriate credit to be provided against a judgment for damages to the extent that the amount of the judgment exceeds the recovery available pursuant to Section 2A–527 or 2A–528.

(4) Payment of the judgment for damages obtained pursuant to subsection (1) entitles the lessee to the use and possession of the goods not then disposed of for the remaining lease term of and in accordance with the lease agreement.

(5) After default by the lessee under the lease contract of the type described in Section 2A–523(1) or Section 2A–523 (3)(a) or,

if agreed, after other default by the lessee, a lessor who is held not entitled to rent under this section must nevertheless be awarded damages for non-acceptance under Sections 2A–527 and 2A–528.

As amended in 1990.

§ 2A–530. Lessor's Incidental Damages.

Incidental damages to an aggrieved lessor include any commercially reasonable charges, expenses, or commissions incurred in stopping delivery, in the transportation, care and custody of goods after the lessee's default, in connection with return or disposition of the goods, or otherwise resulting from the default.

§ 2A–531. Standing to Sue Third Parties for Injury to Goods.

(1) If a third party so deals with goods that have been identified to a lease contract as to cause actionable injury to a party to the lease contract (a) the lessor has a right of action against the third party, and (b) the lessee also has a right of action against the third party if the lessee:

(i) has a security interest in the goods;

(ii) has an insurable interest in the goods; or

(iii) bears the risk of loss under the lease contract or has since the injury assumed that risk as against the lessor and the goods have been converted or destroyed.

(2) If at the time of the injury the party plaintiff did not bear the risk of loss as against the other party to the lease contract and there is no arrangement between them for disposition of the recovery, his [or her] suit or settlement, subject to his [or her] own interest, is as a fiduciary for the other party to the lease contract.

(3) Either party with the consent of the other may sue for the benefit of whom it may concern.

§ 2A–532. Lessor's Rights to Residual Interest.

In addition to any other recovery permitted by this Article or other law, the lessor may recover from the lessee an amount that will fully compensate the lessor for any loss of or damage to the lessor's residual interest in the goods caused by the default of the lessee. As added in 1990.

REVISED ARTICLE III NEGOTIABLE INSTRUMENTS

PART 1 General Provisions and Definitions

§ 3–101. Short Title.

This Article may be cited as Uniform Commercial Code- Negotiable Instruments.

§ 3–102. Subject Matter.

(a) This Article applies to negotiable instruments. It does not apply to money, to payment orders governed by Article 4A, or to securities governed by Article 8.

(b) If there is conflict between this Article and Article 4 or 9, Articles 4 and 9 govern.

(c) Regulations of the Board of Governors of the Federal Reserve System and operating circulars of the Federal Reserve Banks supersede any inconsistent provision of this Article to the extent of the inconsistency.

§ 3–103. Definitions.

(a) In this Article:

(1) "Acceptor" means a drawee who has accepted a draft.

(2) "Drawee" means a person ordered in a draft to make payment.

(3) "Drawer" means a person who signs or is identified in a draft as a person ordering payment.

(4) "Good faith" means honesty in fact and the observance of reasonable commercial standards of fair dealing.

(5) "Maker" means a person who signs or is identified in a note as a person undertaking to pay.

(6) "Order" means a written instruction to pay money signed by the person giving the instruction. The instruction may be addressed to any person, including the person giving the instruction, or to one or more persons jointly or in the alternative but not in succession. An authorization to pay is not an order unless the person authorized to pay is also instructed to pay.

(7) "Ordinary care" in the case of a person engaged in business means observance of reasonable commercial standards, prevailing in the area in which the person is located, with respect to the business in which the person is engaged. In the case of a bank that takes an instrument for processing for collection or payment by automated means, reasonable commercial standards do not require the bank to examine the instrument if the failure to examine does not violate the bank's prescribed procedures and the bank's procedures do not vary unreasonably from general banking usage not disapproved by this Article or Article 4.

(8) "Party" means a party to an instrument.

(9) "Promise" means a written undertaking to pay money signed by the person undertaking to pay. An acknowledgment of an obligation by the obligor is not a promise unless the obligor also undertakes to pay the obligation.

(10) "Prove" with respect to a fact means to meet the burden of establishing the fact (Section 1–201(8)).

(11) "Remitter" means a person who purchases an instrument from its issuer if the instrument is payable to an identified person other than the purchaser.

(b) [Other definitions' section references deleted.]

(c) [Other definitions' section references deleted.]

(d) In addition, Article 1 contains general definitions and principles of construction and interpretation applicable throughout this Article.

§ 3–104. Negotiable Instrument.

(a) Except as provided in subsections (c) and (d), "negotiable instrument" means an unconditional promise or order to pay a fixed amount of money, with or without interest or other charges described in the promise or order, if it:

(1) is payable to bearer or to order at the time it is issued or first comes into possession of a holder;

(2) is payable on demand or at a definite time; and

(3) does not state any other undertaking or instruction by the person promising or ordering payment to do any act in addition to the payment of money, but the promise or order may contain (i) an undertaking or power to give, maintain, or protect collateral to secure payment, (ii) an authorization or power to the holder to confess judgment or realize on or dispose of collateral, or (iii) a waiver of the benefit of any law intended for the advantage or protection of an obligor.

(b) "Instrument" means a negotiable instrument.

(c) An order that meets all of the requirements of subsection (a), except paragraph (1), and otherwise falls within the definition of "check" in subsection (f) is a negotiable instrument and a check.

(d) A promise or order other than a check is not an instrument if, at the time it is issued or first comes into possession of a holder, it contains a conspicuous statement, however expressed, to the effect that the promise or order is not negotiable or is not an instrument governed by this Article.

(e) An instrument is a "note" if it is a promise and is a "draft" if it is an order. If an instrument falls within the definition of both "note" and "draft," a person entitled to enforce the instrument may treat it as either.

(f) "Check" means (i) a draft, other than a documentary draft, payable on demand and drawn on a bank or (ii) a cashier's check or teller's check. An instrument may be a check even though it is described on its face by another term, such as "money order."

(g) "Cashier's check" means a draft with respect to which the drawer and drawee are the same bank or branches of the same bank.

(h) "Teller's check" means a draft drawn by a bank (i) on another bank, or (ii) payable at or through a bank.

(i) "Traveler's check" means an instrument that (i) is payable on demand, (ii) is drawn on or payable at or through a bank, (iii) is designated by the term "traveler's check" or by a substantially similar term, and (iv) requires, as a condition to payment, a countersignature by a person whose specimen signature appears on the instrument.

(j) "Certificate of deposit" means an instrument containing an acknowledgment by a bank that a sum of money has been received by the bank and a promise by the bank to repay the sum of money. A certificate of deposit is a note of the bank.

§ 3–105. Issue of Instrument.

(a) "Issue" means the first delivery of an instrument by the maker or drawer, whether to a holder or nonholder, for the purpose of giving rights on the instrument to any person.

(b) An unissued instrument, or an unissued incomplete instrument that is completed, is binding on the maker or drawer, but nonissuance is a defense. An instrument that is conditionally issued or is issued for a special purpose is binding on the maker or drawer, but failure of the condition or special purpose to be fulfilled is a defense.

(c) "Issuer" applies to issued and unissued instruments and means a maker or drawer of an instrument.

§ 3–106. Unconditional Promise or Order.

(a) Except as provided in this section, for the purposes of Section 3–104(a), a promise or order is unconditional unless it states (i) an express condition to payment, (ii) that the promise or order is subject to or governed by another writing, or (iii) that rights or obligations with respect to the promise or order are stated in another writing. A reference to another writing does not of itself make the promise or order conditional.

(b) A promise or order is not made conditional (i) by a reference to another writing for a statement of rights with respect to collateral, prepayment, or acceleration, or (ii) because payment is limited to resort to a particular fund or source.

(c) If a promise or order requires, as a condition to payment, a countersignature by a person whose specimen signature appears on the promise or order, the condition does not make the promise or order conditional for the purposes of Section 3–104(a). If the person whose specimen signature appears on an instrument fails to countersign the instrument, the failure to countersign is a defense to the obligation of the issuer, but the failure does not prevent a transferee of the instrument from becoming a holder of the instrument.

(d) If a promise or order at the time it is issued or first comes into possession of a holder contains a statement, required by applicable statutory or administrative law, to the effect that the rights of a holder or transferee are subject to claims or defenses that the issuer could assert against the original payee, the promise or order is not thereby made conditional for the purposes of Section 3–104(a); but if the promise or order is an instrument, there cannot be a holder in due course of the instrument.

§ 3–107. Instrument Payable in Foreign Money.

Unless the instrument otherwise provides, an instrument that states the amount payable in foreign money may be paid in the foreign money or in an equivalent amount in dollars calculated by using the current bank-offered spot rate at the place of payment for the purchase of dollars on the day on which the instrument is paid.

§ 3–108. Payable on Demand or at Definite Time.

(a) A promise or order is "payable on demand" if it (i) states that it is payable on demand or at sight, or otherwise indicates that it is payable at the will of the holder, or (ii) does not state any time of payment.

(b) A promise or order is "payable at a definite time" if it is payable on elapse of a definite period of time after sight or acceptance or at a fixed date or dates or at a time or times readily ascertainable at the time the promise or order is issued, subject to rights of (i) prepayment, (ii) acceleration, (iii) extension at the option of the holder, or (iv) extension to a further definite time at the option of the maker or acceptor or automatically upon or after a specified act or event.

(c) If an instrument, payable at a fixed date, is also payable upon demand made before the fixed date, the instrument is payable on demand until the fixed date and, if demand for payment is not made before that date, becomes payable at a definite time on the fixed date.

§ 3–109. Payable to Bearer or to Order.

(a) A promise or order is payable to bearer if it:

(1) states that it is payable to bearer or to the order of bearer or otherwise indicates that the person in possession of the promise or order is entitled to payment;

(2) does not state a payee; or

(3) states that it is payable to or to the order of cash or otherwise indicates that it is not payable to an identified person.

(b) A promise or order that is not payable to bearer is payable to order if it is payable (i) to the order of an identified person or (ii) to an identified person or order. A promise or order that is payable to order is payable to the identified person.

(c) An instrument payable to bearer may become payable to an identified person if it is specially indorsed pursuant to Section 3–205(a). An instrument payable to an identified person may become payable to bearer if it is indorsed in blank pursuant to Section 3–205(b).

§ 3–110. Identification of Person to Whom Instrument Is Payable.

(a) The person to whom an instrument is initially payable is determined by the intent of the person, whether or not authorized, signing as, or in the name or behalf of, the issuer of the instrument. The instrument is payable to the person intended by the signer even if that person is identified in the instrument by a name or other identification that is not that of the intended person. If more than one person signs in the name or behalf of the issuer of an instrument and all the signers do not intend the same person as payee, the instrument is payable to any person intended by one or more of the signers.

(b) If the signature of the issuer of an instrument is made by automated means, such as a check-writing machine, the payee of the instrument is determined by the intent of the person who supplied the name or identification of the payee, whether or not authorized to do so.

(c) A person to whom an instrument is payable may be identified in any way, including by name, identifying number, office, or account number. For the purpose of determining the holder of an instrument, the following rules apply:

(1) If an instrument is payable to an account and the account is identified only by number, the instrument is payable to the person to whom the account is payable. If an instrument is payable to an account identified by number and by the name of a person, the instrument is payable to the named person, whether or not that person is the owner of the account identified by number.

(2) If an instrument is payable to:

(i) a trust, an estate, or a person described as trustee or representative of a trust or estate, the instrument is payable to the trustee, the representative, or a successor of either, whether or not the beneficiary or estate is also named;

(ii) a person described as agent or similar representative of a named or identified person, the instrument is payable to the represented person, the representative, or a successor of the representative;

(iii) a fund or organization that is not a legal entity, the instrument is payable to a representative of the members of the fund or organization; or

(iv) an office or to a person described as holding an office, the instrument is payable to the named person, the incumbent of the office, or a successor to the incumbent.

(d) If an instrument is payable to two or more persons alternatively, it is payable to any of them and may be negotiated, discharged, or enforced by any or all of them in possession of the instrument. If an instrument is payable to two or more persons not alternatively, it is payable to all of them and may be negotiated, discharged, or enforced only by all of them. If an instrument payable to two or more persons is ambiguous as to whether it is payable to the persons alternatively, the instrument is payable to the persons alternatively.

§ 3–111. Place of Payment.

Except as otherwise provided for items in Article 4, an instrument is payable at the place of payment stated in the instrument. If no place of payment is stated, an instrument is payable at the address of the drawee or maker stated in the instrument. If no address is stated, the place of payment is the place of business of the drawee or maker. If a drawee or maker has more than one place of business, the place of payment is any place of business of the drawee or maker chosen by the person entitled to enforce the instrument. If the drawee or maker has no place of business, the place of payment is the residence of the drawee or maker.

§ 3–112. Interest.

(a) Unless otherwise provided in the instrument, (i) an instrument is not payable with interest, and (ii) interest on an interest-bearing instrument is payable from the date of the instrument.

(b) Interest may be stated in an instrument as a fixed or variable amount of money or it may be expressed as a fixed or variable rate or rates. The amount or rate of interest may be stated or described in the instrument in any manner and may require reference to information not contained in the instrument. If an instrument provides for interest, but the amount of interest payable cannot be ascertained from the description, interest is payable at the judgment rate in effect at the place of payment of the instrument and at the time interest first accrues.

§ 3–113. Date of Instrument.

(a) An instrument may be antedated or postdated. The date stated determines the time of payment if the instrument is payable at a fixed period after date. Except as provided in Section 4–401(c), an instrument payable on demand is not payable before the date of the instrument.

(b) If an instrument is undated, its date is the date of its issue or, in the case of an unissued instrument, the date it first comes into possession of a holder.

§ 3–114. Contradictory Terms of Instrument.

If an instrument contains contradictory terms, typewritten terms prevail over printed terms, handwritten terms prevail over both, and words prevail over numbers.

§ 3–115. Incomplete Instrument.

(a) "Incomplete instrument" means a signed writing, whether or not issued by the signer, the contents of which show at the time of signing that it is incomplete but that the signer intended it to be completed by the addition of words or numbers.

(b) Subject to subsection (c), if an incomplete instrument is an instrument under Section 3–104, it may be enforced according to its terms if it is not completed, or according to its terms as augmented by completion. If an incomplete instrument is not an instrument under Section 3–104, but, after completion, the requirements of Section 3–104 are met, the instrument may be enforced according to its terms as augmented by completion.

(c) If words or numbers are added to an incomplete instrument without authority of the signer, there is an alteration of the incomplete instrument under Section 3–407.

(d) The burden of establishing that words or numbers were added to an incomplete instrument without authority of the signer is on the person asserting the lack of authority.

§ 3–116. Joint and Several Liability; Contribution.

(a) Except as otherwise provided in the instrument, two or more persons who have the same liability on an instrument as makers, drawers, acceptors, indorsers who indorse as joint payees, or anomalous indorsers are jointly and severally liable in the capacity in which they sign.

(b) Except as provided in Section 3–419(e) or by agreement of the affected parties, a party having joint and several liability who pays the instrument is entitled to receive from any party having the same joint and several liability contribution in accordance with applicable law.

(c) Discharge of one party having joint and several liability by a person entitled to enforce the instrument does not affect the right under subsection (b) of a party having the same joint and several liability to receive contribution from the party discharged.

§ 3–117. Other Agreements Affecting Instrument.

Subject to applicable law regarding exclusion of proof of contemporaneous or previous agreements, the obligation of a party to an instrument to pay the instrument may be modified, supplemented, or nullified by a separate agreement of the obligor and a person entitled to enforce the instrument, if the instrument is issued or the obligation is incurred in reliance on the agreement or as part of the same transaction giving rise to the agreement. To the extent an obligation is modified, supplemented, or nullified by an agreement under this section, the agreement is a defense to the obligation.

§ 3–118. Statute of Limitations.

(a) Except as provided in subsection (e), an action to enforce the obligation of a party to pay a note payable at a definite time must be commenced within six years after the due date or dates stated in the note or, if a due date is accelerated, within six years after the accelerated due date.

(b) Except as provided in subsection (d) or (e), if demand for payment is made to the maker of a note payable on demand, an action to enforce the obligation of a party to pay the note must be commenced within six years after the demand. If no demand for payment is made to the maker, an action to enforce the note is barred if neither principal nor interest on the note has been paid for a continuous period of 10 years.

(c) Except as provided in subsection (d), an action to enforce the obligation of a party to an unaccepted draft to pay the draft must be commenced within three years after dishonor of the draft or 10 years after the date of the draft, whichever period expires first.

(d) An action to enforce the obligation of the acceptor of a certified check or the issuer of a teller's check, cashier's check, or traveler's check must be commenced within three years after demand for payment is made to the acceptor or issuer, as the case may be.

(e) An action to enforce the obligation of a party to a certificate of deposit to pay the instrument must be commenced within six years after demand for payment is made to the maker, but if the instrument states a due date and the maker is not required to pay before that date, the six-year period begins when a demand for payment is in effect and the due date has passed.

(f) An action to enforce the obligation of a party to pay an accepted draft, other than a certified check, must be commenced (i) within six years after the due date or dates stated in the draft or acceptance if the obligation of the acceptor is payable at a definite time, or (ii) within six years after the date of the acceptance if the obligation of the acceptor is payable on demand.

(g) Unless governed by other law regarding claims for indemnity or contribution, an action (i) for conversion of an instrument, for money had and received, or like action based on conversion, (ii) for breach of warranty, or (iii) to enforce an obligation, duty, or right arising under this Article and not governed by this section must be commenced within three years after the [cause of action] accrues.

§ 3–119. Notice of Right to Defend Action.

In an action for breach of an obligation for which a third person is answerable over pursuant to this Article or Article 4, the defendant may give the third person written notice of the litigation, and the person notified may then give similar notice to any other person who is answerable over. If the notice states (i) that the person notified may come in and defend and (ii) that failure to do so will bind the person notified in an action later brought by the person giving the notice as to any determination of fact common to the two litigations, the person notified is so bound unless after seasonable receipt of the notice the person notified does come in and defend.

PART 2 Negotiation, Transfer, and Indorsement

§ 3–201. Negotiation.

(a) "Negotiation" means a transfer of possession, whether voluntary or involuntary, of an instrument by a person other than the issuer to a person who thereby becomes its holder.

(b) Except for negotiation by a remitter, if an instrument is payable to an identified person, negotiation requires transfer of possession of the instrument and its indorsement by the holder. If an instrument is payable to bearer, it may be negotiated by transfer of possession alone.

§ 3–202. Negotiation Subject to Rescission.

(a) Negotiation is effective even if obtained (i) from an infant, a corporation exceeding its powers, or a person without capacity, (ii) by fraud, duress, or mistake, or (iii) in breach of duty or as part of an illegal transaction.

(b) To the extent permitted by other law, negotiation may be rescinded or may be subject to other remedies, but those remedies may not be asserted against a subsequent holder in due course or a person paying the instrument in good faith and without knowledge of facts that are a basis for rescission or other remedy.

§ 3–203. Transfer of Instrument; Rights Acquired by Transfer.

(a) An instrument is transferred when it is delivered by a person other than its issuer for the purpose of giving to the person receiving delivery the right to enforce the instrument.

(b) Transfer of an instrument, whether or not the transfer is a negotiation, vests in the transferee any right of the transferor to enforce the instrument, including any right as a holder in due course, but the transferee cannot acquire rights of a holder in due course by a transfer, directly or indirectly, from a holder in due course if the transferee engaged in fraud or illegality affecting the instrument.

(c) Unless otherwise agreed, if an instrument is transferred for value and the transferee does not become a holder because of lack of indorsement by the transferor, the transferee has a specifically enforceable right to the unqualified indorsement of the transferor, but negotiation of the instrument does not occur until the indorsement is made.

(d) If a transferor purports to transfer less than the entire instrument, negotiation of the instrument does not occur. The transferee obtains no rights under this Article and has only the rights of a partial assignee.

§ 3–204. Indorsement.

(a) "Indorsement" means a signature, other than that of a signer as maker, drawer, or acceptor, that alone or accompanied by other words is made on an instrument for the purpose of (i) negotiating the instrument, (ii) restricting payment of the instrument, or (iii) incurring indorser's liability on the instrument, but regardless of the intent of the signer, a signature and its accompanying words is an indorsement unless the accompanying words, terms of the instrument, place of the signature, or other circumstances unambiguously indicate that the signature was made for a purpose other than indorsement. For the purpose of determining whether a signature is made on an instrument, a paper affixed to the instrument is a part of the instrument.

(b) "Indorser" means a person who makes an indorsement.

(c) For the purpose of determining whether the transferee of an instrument is a holder, an indorsement that transfers a security interest in the instrument is effective as an unqualified indorsement of the instrument.

(d) If an instrument is payable to a holder under a name that is not the name of the holder, indorsement may be made by the holder in the name stated in the instrument or in the holder's name or both, but signature in both names may be required by a person paying or taking the instrument for value or collection.

§ 3–205. Special Indorsement; Blank Indorsement; Anomalous Indorsement.

(a) If an indorsement is made by the holder of an instrument, whether payable to an identified person or payable to bearer, and the indorsement identifies a person to whom it makes the instrument payable, it is a "special indorsement." When specially indorsed, an instrument becomes payable to the identified person and may be negotiated only by the indorsement of that person. The principles stated in Section 3–110 apply to special indorsements.

(b) If an indorsement is made by the holder of an instrument and it is not a special indorsement, it is a "blank indorsement." When indorsed in blank, an instrument becomes payable to bearer and may be negotiated by transfer of possession alone until specially indorsed.

(c) The holder may convert a blank indorsement that consists only of a signature into a special indorsement by writing, above the signature of the indorser, words identifying the person to whom the instrument is made payable.

(d) "Anomalous indorsement" means an indorsement made by a person who is not the holder of the instrument. An anomalous indorsement does not affect the manner in which the instrument may be negotiated.

§ 3–206. Restrictive Indorsement.

(a) An indorsement limiting payment to a particular person or otherwise prohibiting further transfer or negotiation of the instrument is not effective to prevent further transfer or negotiation of the instrument.

(b) An indorsement stating a condition to the right of the indorsee to receive payment does not affect the right of the indorsee to enforce the instrument. A person paying the instrument or taking it for value or collection may disregard the condition, and the rights and liabilities of that person are not affected by whether the condition has been fulfilled.

(c) If an instrument bears an indorsement (i) described in Section 4–201(b), or (ii) in blank or to a particular bank using the words "for deposit," "for collection," or other words indicating a purpose of having the instrument collected by a bank for the indorser or for a particular account, the following rules apply:

(1) A person, other than a bank, who purchases the instrument when so indorsed converts the instrument unless the amount paid for the instrument is received by the indorser or applied consistently with the indorsement.

(2) A depositary bank that purchases the instrument or takes it for collection when so indorsed converts the instrument unless the amount paid by the bank with respect to the instrument is received by the indorser or applied consistently with the indorsement.

(3) A payor bank that is also the depositary bank or that takes the instrument for immediate payment over the counter from a person other than a collecting bank converts the instrument unless the proceeds of the instrument are received by the indorser or applied consistently with the indorsement.

(4) Except as otherwise provided in paragraph (3), a payor bank or intermediary bank may disregard the indorsement and is not liable if the proceeds of the instrument are not received by the indorser or applied consistently with the indorsement.

(d) Except for an indorsement covered by subsection (c), if an instrument bears an indorsement using words to the effect that payment is to be made to the indorsee as agent, trustee, or other fiduciary for the benefit of the indorser or another person, the following rules apply:

(1) Unless there is notice of breach of fiduciary duty as provided in Section 3–307, a person who purchases the instrument from the indorsee or takes the instrument from the indorsee for collection or payment may pay the proceeds of payment or the value given for the instrument to the indorsee without regard to whether the indorsee violates a fiduciary duty to the indorser.

(2) A subsequent transferee of the instrument or person who pays the instrument is neither given notice nor otherwise affected by the restriction in the indorsement unless the transferee or payor knows that the fiduciary dealt with the instrument or its proceeds in breach of fiduciary duty.

(e) The presence on an instrument of an indorsement to which this section applies does not prevent a purchaser of the instrument from becoming a holder in due course of the instrument unless the purchaser is a converter under subsection (c) or has notice or knowledge of breach of fiduciary duty as stated in subsection (d).

(f) In an action to enforce the obligation of a party to pay the instrument, the obligor has a defense if payment would violate an indorsement to which this section applies and the payment is not permitted by this section.

§ 3–207. Reacquisition.

Reacquisition of an instrument occurs if it is transferred to a former holder, by negotiation or otherwise. A former holder who reacquires the instrument may cancel indorsements made after the reacquirer first became a holder of the instrument. If the cancellation causes the instrument to be payable to the reacquirer or to bearer, the reacquirer may negotiate the instrument. An indorser whose indorsement is canceled is discharged, and the discharge is effective against any subsequent holder.

PART 3 Enforcement of Instruments

§ 3–301. Person Entitled to Enforce Instrument.

"Person entitled to enforce" an instrument means (i) the holder of the instrument, (ii) a nonholder in possession of the instrument who has the rights of a holder, or (iii) a person not in possession of the instrument who is entitled to enforce the instrument pursuant to Section 3–309 or 3–418(d). A person may be a person entitled to enforce the instrument even though the person is not the owner of the instrument or is in wrongful possession of the instrument.

§ 3–302. Holder in Due Course.

(a) Subject to subsection (c) and Section 3–106(d), "holder in due course" means the holder of an instrument if:

(1) the instrument when issued or negotiated to the holder does not bear such apparent evidence of forgery or alteration or is not otherwise so irregular or incomplete as to call into question its authenticity; and

(2) the holder took the instrument (i) for value, (ii) in good faith, (iii) without notice that the instrument is overdue or has been dishonored or that there is an uncured default with respect to payment of another instrument issued as part of the same series, (iv) without notice that the instrument contains an unauthorized signature or has been altered, (v) without notice of any claim to the instrument described in Section 3–306, and (vi) without

notice that any party has a defense or claim in recoupment described in Section 3–305(a).

(b) Notice of discharge of a party, other than discharge in an insolvency proceeding, is not notice of a defense under subsection (a), but discharge is effective against a person who became a holder in due course with notice of the discharge. Public filing or recording of a document does not of itself constitute notice of a defense, claim in recoupment, or claim to the instrument.

(c) Except to the extent a transferor or predecessor in interest has rights as a holder in due course, a person does not acquire rights of a holder in due course of an instrument taken (i) by legal process or by purchase in an execution, bankruptcy, or creditor's sale or similar proceeding, (ii) by purchase as part of a bulk transaction not in ordinary course of business of the transferor, or (iii) as the successor in interest to an estate or other organization.

(d) If, under Section 3–303(a)(1), the promise of performance that is the consideration for an instrument has been partially performed, the holder may assert rights as a holder in due course of the instrument only to the fraction of the amount payable under the instrument equal to the value of the partial performance divided by the value of the promised performance.

(e) If (i) the person entitled to enforce an instrument has only a security interest in the instrument and (ii) the person obliged to pay the instrument has a defense, claim in recoupment, or claim to the instrument that may be asserted against the person who granted the security interest, the person entitled to enforce the instrument may assert rights as a holder in due course only to an amount payable under the instrument which, at the time of enforcement of the instrument, does not exceed the amount of the unpaid obligation secured.

(f) To be effective, notice must be received at a time and in a manner that gives a reasonable opportunity to act on it.

(g) This section is subject to any law limiting status as a holder in due course in particular classes of transactions.

§ 3–303. Value and Consideration.

(a) An instrument is issued or transferred for value if:

(1) the instrument is issued or transferred for a promise of performance, to the extent the promise has been performed;

(2) the transferee acquires a security interest or other lien in the instrument other than a lien obtained by judicial proceeding;

(3) the instrument is issued or transferred as payment of, or as security for, an antecedent claim against any person, whether or not the claim is due;

(4) the instrument is issued or transferred in exchange for a negotiable instrument; or

(5) the instrument is issued or transferred in exchange for the incurring of an irrevocable obligation to a third party by the person taking the instrument.

(b) "Consideration" means any consideration sufficient to support a simple contract. The drawer or maker of an instrument has a defense if the instrument is issued without consideration. If an instrument is issued for a promise of performance, the issuer has a defense to the extent performance of the promise is due and the promise has not been performed. If an instrument is issued for value as stated in subsection (a), the instrument is also issued for consideration.

§ 3–304. Overdue Instrument.

(a) An instrument payable on demand becomes overdue at the earliest of the following times:

(1) on the day after the day demand for payment is duly made;

(2) if the instrument is a check, 90 days after its date; or

(3) if the instrument is not a check, when the instrument has been outstanding for a period of time after its date which is unreasonably long under the circumstances of the particular case in light of the nature of the instrument and usage of the trade.

(b) With respect to an instrument payable at a definite time the following rules apply:

(1) If the principal is payable in installments and a due date has not been accelerated, the instrument becomes overdue upon default under the instrument for nonpayment of an installment, and the instrument remains overdue until the default is cured.

(2) If the principal is not payable in installments and the due date has not been accelerated, the instrument becomes overdue on the day after the due date.

(3) If a due date with respect to principal has been accelerated, the instrument becomes overdue on the day after the accelerated due date.

(c) Unless the due date of principal has been accelerated, an instrument does not become overdue if there is default in payment of interest but no default in payment of principal.

§ 3–305. Defenses and Claims in Recoupment.

(a) Except as stated in subsection (b), the right to enforce the obligation of a party to pay an instrument is subject to the following:

(1) a defense of the obligor based on (i) infancy of the obligor to the extent it is a defense to a simple contract, (ii) duress, lack of legal capacity, or illegality of the transaction which, under other law, nullifies the obligation of the obligor, (iii) fraud that induced the obligor to sign the instrument with neither knowledge nor reasonable opportunity to learn of its character or its essential terms, or (iv) discharge of the obligor in insolvency proceedings;

(2) a defense of the obligor stated in another section of this Article or a defense of the obligor that would be available if the person entitled to enforce the instrument were enforcing a right to payment under a simple contract; and

(3) a claim in recoupment of the obligor against the original payee of the instrument if the claim arose from the transaction that gave rise to the instrument; but the claim of the obligor may be asserted against a transferee of the instrument only to reduce the amount owing on the instrument at the time the action is brought.

(b) The right of a holder in due course to enforce the obligation of a party to pay the instrument is subject to defenses of the obligor stated in subsection (a)(1), but is not subject to defenses of the obligor stated in subsection (a)(2) or claims in recoupment stated in subsection (a)(3) against a person other than the holder.

(c) Except as stated in subsection (d), in an action to enforce the obligation of a party to pay the instrument, the obligor may not assert against the person entitled to enforce the instrument a defense, claim in recoupment, or claim to the instrument (Section 3–306) of another person, but the other person's claim to the instrument may be asserted by the obligor if the other person is joined in the action and personally asserts the claim against the person entitled to enforce the instrument. An obligor is not obliged to pay the instrument if the person seeking enforcement of the instrument does not have rights of a holder in due course and the obligor proves that the instrument is a lost or stolen instrument.

(d) In an action to enforce the obligation of an accommodation party to pay an instrument, the accommodation party may assert against the person entitled to enforce the instrument any defense or claim in recoupment under subsection (a) that the accommodated party could assert against the person entitled to enforce the instrument, except the defenses of discharge in insolvency proceedings, infancy, and lack of legal capacity.

§ 3–306. Claims to an Instrument.

A person taking an instrument, other than a person having rights of a holder in due course, is subject to a claim of a property or possessory right in the instrument or its proceeds, including a claim to rescind a negotiation and to recover the instrument or its proceeds. A person having rights of a holder in due course takes free of the claim to the instrument.

§ 3–307. Notice of Breach of Fiduciary Duty.

(a) In this section:

(1) "Fiduciary" means an agent, trustee, partner, corporate officer or director, or other representative owing a fiduciary duty with respect to an instrument.

(2) "Represented person" means the principal, beneficiary, partnership, corporation, or other person to whom the duty stated in paragraph (1) is owed.

(b) If (i) an instrument is taken from a fiduciary for payment or collection or for value, (ii) the taker has knowledge of the fiduciary status of the fiduciary, and (iii) the represented person makes a claim to the instrument or its proceeds on the basis that the transaction of the fiduciary is a breach of fiduciary duty, the following rules apply:

(1) Notice of breach of fiduciary duty by the fiduciary is notice of the claim of the represented person.

(2) In the case of an instrument payable to the represented person or the fiduciary as such, the taker has notice of the breach of fiduciary duty if the instrument is (i) taken in payment of or as security for a debt known by the taker to be the personal debt of the fiduciary, (ii) taken in a transaction known by the taker to be for the personal benefit of the fiduciary, or (iii) deposited to an account other than an account of the fiduciary, as such, or an account of the represented person.

(3) If an instrument is issued by the represented person or the fiduciary as such, and made payable to the fiduciary personally, the taker does not have notice of the breach of fiduciary duty unless the taker knows of the breach of fiduciary duty.

(4) If an instrument is issued by the represented person or the fiduciary as such, to the taker as payee, the taker has notice of the breach of fiduciary duty if the instrument is (i) taken in payment of or as security for a debt known by the taker to be the personal debt of the fiduciary, (ii) taken in a transaction known by the taker to be for the personal benefit of the fiduciary, or (iii) deposited to an account other than an account of the fiduciary, as such, or an account of the represented person.

§ 3–308. Proof of Signatures and Status as Holder in Due Course.

(a) In an action with respect to an instrument, the authenticity of, and authority to make, each signature on the instrument is admitted unless specifically denied in the pleadings. If the validity of a signature is denied in the pleadings, the burden of establishing validity is on the person claiming validity, but the signature is presumed to be authentic and authorized unless the action is to enforce the liability of the purported signer and the signer is dead or incompetent at the time of trial of the issue of validity of the signature. If an action to enforce the instrument is brought against a person as the undisclosed principal of a person who signed the instrument as a party to the instrument, the plaintiff has the burden of establishing that the defendant is liable on the instrument as a represented person under Section 3–402(a).

(b) If the validity of signatures is admitted or proved and there is compliance with subsection (a), a plaintiff producing the instrument is entitled to payment if the plaintiff proves entitlement to enforce the instrument under Section 3–301, unless the defendant proves a defense or claim in recoupment. If a defense or claim in recoupment is proved, the right to payment of the plaintiff is subject to the defense or claim, except to the extent the plaintiff proves that the plaintiff has rights of a holder in due course which are not subject to the defense or claim.

§ 3–309. Enforcement of Lost, Destroyed, or Stolen Instrument.

(a) A person not in possession of an instrument is entitled to enforce the instrument if (i) the person was in possession of the instrument and entitled to enforce it when loss of possession occurred, (ii) the loss of possession was not the result of a transfer by the person or a lawful seizure, and (iii) the person cannot reasonably obtain possession of the instrument because the instrument was destroyed, its whereabouts cannot be determined, or it is in the wrongful possession of an unknown person or a person that cannot be found or is not amenable to service of process.

(b) A person seeking enforcement of an instrument under subsection (a) must prove the terms of the instrument and the person's right to enforce the instrument. If that proof is made,

Section 3–308 applies to the case as if the person seeking enforcement had produced the instrument. The court may not enter judgment in favor of the person seeking enforcement unless it finds that the person required to pay the instrument is adequately protected against loss that might occur by reason of a claim by another person to enforce the instrument. Adequate protection may be provided by any reasonable means.

§ 3–310. Effect of Instrument on Obligation for Which Taken.

(a) Unless otherwise agreed, if a certified check, cashier's check, or teller's check is taken for an obligation, the obligation is discharged to the same extent discharge would result if an amount of money equal to the amount of the instrument were taken in payment of the obligation. Discharge of the obligation does not affect any liability that the obligor may have as an indorser of the instrument.

(b) Unless otherwise agreed and except as provided in subsection (a), if a note or an uncertified check is taken for an obligation, the obligation is suspended to the same extent the obligation would be discharged if an amount of money equal to the amount of the instrument were taken, and the following rules apply:

(1) In the case of an uncertified check, suspension of the obligation continues until dishonor of the check or until it is paid or certified. Payment or certification of the check results in discharge of the obligation to the extent of the amount of the check.

(2) In the case of a note, suspension of the obligation continues until dishonor of the note or until it is paid. Payment of the note results in discharge of the obligation to the extent of the payment.

(3) Except as provided in paragraph (4), if the check or note is dishonored and the obligee of the obligation for which the instrument was taken is the person entitled to enforce the instrument, the obligee may enforce either the instrument or the obligation. In the case of an instrument of a third person which is negotiated to the obligee by the obligor, discharge of the obligor on the instrument also discharges the obligation.

(4) If the person entitled to enforce the instrument taken for an obligation is a person other than the obligee, the obligee may not enforce the obligation to the extent the obligation is suspended. If the obligee is the person entitled to enforce the instrument but no longer has possession of it because it was lost, stolen, or destroyed, the obligation may not be enforced to the extent of the amount payable on the instrument, and to that extent the obligee's rights against the obligor are limited to enforcement of the instrument.

(c) If an instrument other than one described in subsection (a) or (b) is taken for an obligation, the effect is (i) that stated in subsection (a) if the instrument is one on which a bank is liable as maker or acceptor, or (ii) that stated in subsection (b) in any other case.

§ 3–311. Accord and Satisfaction by Use of Instrument.

(a) If a person against whom a claim is asserted proves that (i) that person in good faith tendered an instrument to the claimant as full satisfaction of the claim, (ii) the amount of the claim was unliquidated or subject to a bona fide dispute, and (iii) the claimant obtained payment of the instrument, the following subsections apply.

(b) Unless subsection (c) applies, the claim is discharged if the person against whom the claim is asserted proves that the instrument or an accompanying written communication contained a conspicuous statement to the effect that the instrument was tendered as full satisfaction of the claim.

(c) Subject to subsection (d), a claim is not discharged under subsection (b) if either of the following applies:

(1) The claimant, if an organization, proves that (i) within a reasonable time before the tender, the claimant sent a conspicuous statement to the person against whom the claim is asserted that communications concerning disputed debts, including an instrument tendered as full satisfaction of a debt, are to be sent to a designated person, office, or place, and (ii) the instrument or accompanying communication was not received by that designated person, office, or place.

(2) The claimant, whether or not an organization, proves that within 90 days after payment of the instrument, the claimant tendered repayment of the amount of the instrument to the person against whom the claim is asserted. This paragraph does not apply if the claimant is an organization that sent a statement complying with paragraph (1)(i).

(d) A claim is discharged if the person against whom the claim is asserted proves that within a reasonable time before collection of the instrument was initiated, the claimant, or an agent of the claimant having direct responsibility with respect to the disputed obligation, knew that the instrument was tendered in full satisfaction of the claim.

§ 3–312. Lost, Destroyed, or Stolen Cashier's Check, Teller's Check, or Certified Check.*

(a) In this section:

(1) "Check" means a cashier's check, teller's check, or certified check.

(2) "Claimant" means a person who claims the right to receive the amount of a cashier's check, teller's check, or certified check that was lost, destroyed, or stolen.

(3) "Declaration of loss" means a written statement, made under penalty of perjury, to the effect that (i) the declarer lost possession of a check, (ii) the declarer is the drawer or payee of the check, in the case of a certified check, or the remitter or payee of the check, in the case of a cashier's check or teller's check, (iii) the loss of possession was not the result of a transfer by the declarer or a lawful seizure, and (iv) the declarer cannot reasonably obtain possession of the check because the check was destroyed, its whereabouts cannot be determined, or it is in the wrongful possession of an unknown person or a person that cannot be found or is not amenable to service of process.

(4) "Obligated bank" means the issuer of a cashier's check or teller's check or the acceptor of a certified check.

(b) A claimant may assert a claim to the amount of a check by a communication to the obligated bank describing the check with reasonable certainty and requesting payment of the amount of the check, if (i) the claimant is the drawer or payee of a certified check or the remitter or payee of a cashier's check or teller's check, (ii) the communication contains or is accompanied by a declaration of loss of the claimant with respect to the check, (iii) the communication is received at a time and in a manner affording the bank a reasonable time to act on it before the check is paid, and (iv) the claimant provides reasonable identification if requested by the obligated bank. Delivery of a declaration of loss is a warranty of the truth of the statements made in the declaration. If a claim is asserted in compliance with this subsection, the following rules apply:

(1) The claim becomes enforceable at the later of (i) the time the claim is asserted, or (ii) the 90th day following the date of the check, in the case of a cashier's check or teller's check, or the 90th day following the date of the acceptance, in the case of a certified check.

(2) Until the claim becomes enforceable, it has no legal effect and the obligated bank may pay the check or, in the case of a teller's check, may permit the drawee to pay the check. Payment to a person entitled to enforce the check discharges all liability of the obligated bank with respect to the check.

(3) If the claim becomes enforceable before the check is presented for payment, the obligated bank is not obliged to pay the check.

(4) When the claim becomes enforceable, the obligated bank becomes obliged to pay the amount of the check to the claimant if payment of the check has not been made to a person entitled to enforce the check. Subject to Section 4–302(a)(1), payment to the claimant discharges all liability of the obligated bank with respect to the check.

(c) If the obligated bank pays the amount of a check to a claimant under subsection (b)(4) and the check is presented for payment by a person having rights of a holder in due course, the claimant is obliged to (i) refund the payment to the obligated bank if the check is paid, or (ii) pay the amount of the check to the person having rights of a holder in due course if the check is dishonored.

(d) If a claimant has the right to assert a claim under subsection (b) and is also a person entitled to enforce a cashier's check, teller's check, or certified check which is lost, destroyed, or stolen, the claimant may assert rights with respect to the check either under this section or Section 3–309.

Added in 1991.

PART 4 Liability of Parties

§ 3–401. Signature.

(a) A person is not liable on an instrument unless (i) the person signed the instrument, or (ii) the person is represented by an agent or representative who signed the instrument and the signature is binding on the represented person under Section 3–402.

(b) A signature may be made (i) manually or by means of a device or machine, and (ii) by the use of any name, including a trade or assumed name, or by a word, mark, or symbol executed or adopted by a person with present intention to authenticate a writing.

§ 3–402. Signature by Representative.

(a) If a person acting, or purporting to act, as a representative signs an instrument by signing either the name of the represented person or the name of the signer, the represented person is bound by the signature to the same extent the represented person would be bound if the signature were on a simple contract. If the represented person is bound, the signature of the representative is the "authorized signature of the represented person" and the represented person is liable on the instrument, whether or not identified in the instrument.

(b) If a representative signs the name of the representative to an instrument and the signature is an authorized signature of the represented person, the following rules apply:

(1) If the form of the signature shows unambiguously that the signature is made on behalf of the represented person who is identified in the instrument, the representative is not liable on the instrument.

(2) Subject to subsection (c), if (i) the form of the signature does not show unambiguously that the signature is made in a representative capacity or (ii) the represented person is not identified in the instrument, the representative is liable on the instrument to a holder in due course that took the instrument without notice that the representative was not intended to be liable on the instrument. With respect to any other person, the representative is liable on the instrument unless the representative proves that the original parties did not intend the representative to be liable on the instrument.

(c) If a representative signs the name of the representative as drawer of a check without indication of the representative status and the check is payable from an account of the represented person who is identified on the check, the signer is not liable on the check if the signature is an authorized signature of the represented person.

§ 3–403. Unauthorized Signature.

(a) Unless otherwise provided in this Article or Article 4, an unauthorized signature is ineffective except as the signature of the unauthorized signer in favor of a person who in good faith pays the instrument or takes it for value. An unauthorized signature may be ratified for all purposes of this Article.

(b) If the signature of more than one person is required to constitute the authorized signature of an organization, the signature of the organization is unauthorized if one of the required signatures is lacking.

(c) The civil or criminal liability of a person who makes an unauthorized signature is not affected by any provision of this Article which makes the unauthorized signature effective for the purposes of this Article.

§ 3–404. Impostors; Fictitious Payees.

(a) If an impostor, by use of the mails or otherwise, induces the issuer of an instrument to issue the instrument to the impostor, or to a person acting in concert with the impostor, by impersonating the payee of the instrument or a person authorized to act for the payee, an indorsement of the instrument by any person in the name of the payee is effective as the indorsement of the payee in favor of a person who, in good faith, pays the instrument or takes it for value or for collection.

(b) If (i) a person whose intent determines to whom an instrument is payable (Section 3–110(a) or (b)) does not intend the person identified as payee to have any interest in the instrument, or (ii) the person identified as payee of an instrument is a fictitious person, the following rules apply until the instrument is negotiated by special indorsement:

(1) Any person in possession of the instrument is its holder.

(2) An indorsement by any person in the name of the payee stated in the instrument is effective as the indorsement of the payee in favor of a person who, in good faith, pays the instrument or takes it for value or for collection.

(c) Under subsection (a) or (b), an indorsement is made in the name of a payee if (i) it is made in a name substantially similar to that of the payee or (ii) the instrument, whether or not indorsed, is deposited in a depositary bank to an account in a name substantially similar to that of the payee.

(d) With respect to an instrument to which subsection (a) or (b) applies, if a person paying the instrument or taking it for value or for collection fails to exercise ordinary care in paying or taking the instrument and that failure substantially contributes to loss resulting from payment of the instrument, the person bearing the loss may recover from the person failing to exercise ordinary care to the extent the failure to exercise ordinary care contributed to the loss.

§ 3–405. Employer's Responsibility for Fraudulent Indorsement by Employee.

(a) In this section:

(1) "Employee" includes an independent contractor and employee of an independent contractor retained by the employer.

(2) "Fraudulent indorsement" means (i) in the case of an instrument payable to the employer, a forged indorsement purporting to be that of the employer, or (ii) in the case of an instrument with respect to which the employer is the issuer, a forged indorsement purporting to be that of the person identified as payee.

(3) "Responsibility" with respect to instruments means authority (i) to sign or indorse instruments on behalf of the employer, (ii) to process instruments received by the employer for bookkeeping purposes, for deposit to an account, or for other disposition, (iii) to prepare or process instruments for issue in the name of the employer, (iv) to supply information determining the names or addresses of payees of instruments to be issued in the name of the employer, (v) to control the disposition of instruments to be issued in the name of the employer, or (vi) to act otherwise with respect to instruments in a responsible capacity. "Responsibility" does not include authority that merely allows an employee to have access to instruments or blank or incomplete instrument forms that are being stored or transported or are part of incoming or outgoing mail, or similar access.

(b) For the purpose of determining the rights and liabilities of a person who, in good faith, pays an instrument or takes it for value or for collection, if an employer entrusted an employee with responsibility with respect to the instrument and the employee or a person acting in concert with the employee makes a fraudulent indorsement of the instrument, the indorsement is effective as the indorsement of the person to whom the instrument is payable if it is made in the name of that person. If the person paying the instrument or taking it for value or for collection fails to exercise ordinary care in paying or taking the instrument and that failure substantially contributes to loss resulting from the fraud, the person bearing the loss may recover from the person failing to exercise ordinary care to the extent the failure to exercise ordinary care contributed to the loss.

(c) Under subsection (b), an indorsement is made in the name of the person to whom an instrument is payable if (i) it is made in a name substantially similar to the name of that person or (ii) the instrument, whether or not indorsed, is deposited in a depositary bank to an account in a name substantially similar to the name of that person.

§ 3–406. Negligence Contributing to Forged Signature or Alteration of Instrument.

(a) A person whose failure to exercise ordinary care substantially contributes to an alteration of an instrument or to the making of a forged signature on an instrument is precluded from asserting the alteration or the forgery against a person who, in good faith, pays the instrument or takes it for value or for collection.

(b) Under subsection (a), if the person asserting the preclusion fails to exercise ordinary care in paying or taking the instrument and that failure substantially contributes to loss, the loss is allocated between the person precluded and the person asserting the preclusion according to the extent to which the failure of each to exercise ordinary care contributed to the loss.

(c) Under subsection (a), the burden of proving failure to exercise ordinary care is on the person asserting the preclusion. Under subsection (b), the burden of proving failure to exercise ordinary care is on the person precluded.

§ 3–407. Alteration.

(a) "Alteration" means (i) an unauthorized change in an instrument that purports to modify in any respect the obligation of a party, or (ii) an unauthorized addition of words or numbers or other change to an incomplete instrument relating to the obligation of a party.

(b) Except as provided in subsection (c), an alteration fraudulently made discharges a party whose obligation is affected by the alteration unless that party assents or is precluded from asserting the alteration. No other alteration discharges a party, and the instrument may be enforced according to its original terms.

(c) A payor bank or drawee paying a fraudulently altered instrument or a person taking it for value, in good faith and without notice of the alteration, may enforce rights with respect to the instrument (i) according to its original terms, or (ii) in the case of an incomplete instrument altered by unauthorized completion, according to its terms as completed.

§ 3–408. Drawee Not Liable on Unaccepted Draft.

A check or other draft does not of itself operate as an assignment of funds in the hands of the drawee available for its payment, and the drawee is not liable on the instrument until the drawee accepts it.

§ 3–409. Acceptance of Draft; Certified Check.

(a) "Acceptance" means the drawee's signed agreement to pay a draft as presented. It must be written on the draft and may consist of the drawee's signature alone. Acceptance may be made at any time and becomes effective when notification pursuant to instructions is given or the accepted draft is delivered for the purpose of giving rights on the acceptance to any person.

(b) A draft may be accepted although it has not been signed by the drawer, is otherwise incomplete, is overdue, or has been dishonored.

(c) If a draft is payable at a fixed period after sight and the acceptor fails to date the acceptance, the holder may complete the acceptance by supplying a date in good faith.

(d) "Certified check" means a check accepted by the bank on which it is drawn. Acceptance may be made as stated in subsection (a) or by a writing on the check which indicates that the check is certified. The drawee of a check has no obligation to certify the check, and refusal to certify is not dishonor of the check.

§ 3–410. Acceptance Varying Draft.

(a) If the terms of a drawee's acceptance vary from the terms of the draft as presented, the holder may refuse the acceptance and treat the draft as dishonored. In that case, the drawee may cancel the acceptance.

(b) The terms of a draft are not varied by an acceptance to pay at a particular bank or place in the United States, unless the acceptance states that the draft is to be paid only at that bank or place.

(c) If the holder assents to an acceptance varying the terms of a draft, the obligation of each drawer and indorser that does not expressly assent to the acceptance is discharged.

§ 3–411. Refusal to Pay Cashier's Checks, Teller's Checks, and Certified Checks.

(a) In this section, "obligated bank" means the acceptor of a certified check or the issuer of a cashier's check or teller's check bought from the issuer.

(b) If the obligated bank wrongfully (i) refuses to pay a cashier's check or certified check, (ii) stops payment of a teller's check, or (iii) refuses to pay a dishonored teller's check, the person asserting the right to enforce the check is entitled to compensation for expenses and loss of interest resulting from the nonpayment and may recover consequential damages if the obligated bank refuses to pay after receiving notice of particular circumstances giving rise to the damages.

(c) Expenses or consequential damages under subsection (b) are not recoverable if the refusal of the obligated bank to pay occurs because (i) the bank suspends payments, (ii) the obligated bank asserts a claim or defense of the bank that it has reasonable grounds to believe is available against the person entitled to enforce the instrument, (iii) the obligated bank has a reasonable doubt whether the person demanding payment is the person entitled to enforce the instrument, or (iv) payment is prohibited by law.

§ 3–412. Obligation of Issuer of Note or Cashier's Check.

The issuer of a note or cashier's check or other draft drawn on the drawer is obliged to pay the instrument (i) according to its terms at the time it was issued or, if not issued, at the time it first came into possession of a holder, or (ii) if the issuer signed an incomplete instrument, according to its terms when completed, to the extent stated in Sections 3–115 and 3–407. The obligation is owed to a person entitled to enforce the instrument or to an indorser who paid the instrument under Section 3–415.

§ 3–413. Obligation of Acceptor.

(a) The acceptor of a draft is obliged to pay the draft (i) according to its terms at the time it was accepted, even though the acceptance states that the draft is payable "as originally drawn" or equivalent terms, (ii) if the acceptance varies the terms of the draft, according to the terms of the draft as varied, or (iii) if the acceptance is of a draft that is an incomplete instrument, according to its terms when completed, to the extent stated in Sections 3–115 and 3–407. The obligation is owed to a person entitled to enforce the draft or to the drawer or an indorser who paid the draft under Section 3–414 or 3–415.

(b) If the certification of a check or other acceptance of a draft states the amount certified or accepted, the obligation of the acceptor is that amount. If (i) the certification or acceptance does not state an amount, (ii) the amount of the instrument is subsequently raised, and (iii) the instrument is then negotiated to a holder in due course, the obligation of the acceptor is the amount of the instrument at the time it was taken by the holder in due course.

§ 3–414. Obligation of Drawer.

(a) This section does not apply to cashier's checks or other drafts drawn on the drawer.

(b) If an unaccepted draft is dishonored, the drawer is obliged to pay the draft (i) according to its terms at the time it was issued or, if not issued, at the time it first came into possession of a holder, or (ii) if the drawer signed an incomplete instrument, according to its terms when completed, to the extent stated in Sections 3–115 and 3–407. The obligation is owed to a person entitled to enforce the draft or to an indorser who paid the draft under Section 3–415.

(c) If a draft is accepted by a bank, the drawer is discharged, regardless of when or by whom acceptance was obtained.

(d) If a draft is accepted and the acceptor is not a bank, the obligation of the drawer to pay the draft if the draft is dishonored by the acceptor is the same as the obligation of an indorser under Section 3–415(a) and (c).

(e) If a draft states that it is drawn "without recourse" or otherwise disclaims liability of the drawer to pay the draft, the drawer is not liable under subsection (b) to pay the draft if the draft is not a check. A disclaimer of the liability stated in subsection (b) is not effective if the draft is a check.

(f) If (i) a check is not presented for payment or given to a depositary bank for collection within 30 days after its date, (ii) the drawee suspends payments after expiration of the 30–day period without paying the check, and (iii) because of the suspension of payments, the drawer is deprived of funds maintained with the drawee to cover payment of the check, the drawer to the extent deprived of funds may discharge its obligation to pay the check by assigning to the person entitled to enforce the check the rights of the drawer against the drawee with respect to the funds.

§ 3–415. Obligation of Indorser.

(a) Subject to subsections (b), (c), and (d) and to Section 3–419(d), if an instrument is dishonored, an indorser is obliged to pay the amount due on the instrument (i) according to the terms of the instrument at the time it was indorsed, or (ii) if the indorser indorsed an incomplete instrument, according to its terms when completed, to the extent stated in Sections 3–115 and 3–407. The obligation of the indorser is owed to a person entitled to enforce the instrument or to a subsequent indorser who paid the instrument under this section.

(b) If an indorsement states that it is made "without recourse" or otherwise disclaims liability of the indorser, the indorser is not liable under subsection (a) to pay the instrument.

(c) If notice of dishonor of an instrument is required by Section 3–503 and notice of dishonor complying with that section is not given to an indorser, the liability of the indorser under subsection (a) is discharged.

(d) If a draft is accepted by a bank after an indorsement is made, the liability of the indorser under subsection (a) is discharged.

(e) If an indorser of a check is liable under subsection (a) and the check is not presented for payment, or given to a depositary bank for collection, within 30 days after the day the indorsement was made, the liability of the indorser under subsection (a) is discharged.

As amended in 1993.

§ 3–416. Transfer Warranties.

(a) A person who transfers an instrument for consideration warrants to the transferee and, if the transfer is by indorsement, to any subsequent transferee that:

(1) the warrantor is a person entitled to enforce the instrument;

(2) all signatures on the instrument are authentic and authorized;

(3) the instrument has not been altered;

(4) the instrument is not subject to a defense or claim in recoupment of any party which can be asserted against the warrantor; and

(5) the warrantor has no knowledge of any insolvency proceeding commenced with respect to the maker or acceptor or, in the case of an unaccepted draft, the drawer.

(b) A person to whom the warranties under subsection (a) are made and who took the instrument in good faith may recover from the warrantor as damages for breach of warranty an amount equal to the loss suffered as a result of the breach, but not more than the amount of the instrument plus expenses and loss of interest incurred as a result of the breach.

(c) The warranties stated in subsection (a) cannot be disclaimed with respect to checks. Unless notice of a claim for breach of warranty is given to the warrantor within 30 days after the claimant has reason to know of the breach and the identity of the warrantor, the liability of the warrantor under subsection (b) is discharged to the extent of any loss caused by the delay in giving notice of the claim.

(d) A [cause of action] for breach of warranty under this section accrues when the claimant has reason to know of the breach.

§ 3–417. Presentment Warranties.

(a) If an unaccepted draft is presented to the drawee for payment or acceptance and the drawee pays or accepts the draft, (i) the person obtaining payment or acceptance, at the time of presentment, and (ii) a previous transferor of the draft, at the time of transfer, warrant to the drawee making payment or accepting the draft in good faith that:

(1) the warrantor is, or was, at the time the warrantor transferred the draft, a person entitled to enforce the draft or authorized to obtain payment or acceptance of the draft on behalf of a person entitled to enforce the draft;

(2) the draft has not been altered; and

(3) the warrantor has no knowledge that the signature of the drawer of the draft is unauthorized.

(b) A drawee making payment may recover from any warrantor damages for breach of warranty equal to the amount paid by the drawee less the amount the drawee received or is entitled to receive from the drawer because of the payment. In addition, the drawee is entitled to compensation for expenses and loss of interest resulting from the breach. The right of the drawee to recover damages under this subsection is not affected by any failure of the drawee to exercise ordinary care in making payment. If the drawee accepts the draft, breach of warranty is a defense to the obligation of the acceptor. If the acceptor makes payment with respect to the draft, the acceptor is entitled to recover from any warrantor for breach of warranty the amounts stated in this subsection.

(c) If a drawee asserts a claim for breach of warranty under subsection (a) based on an unauthorized indorsement of the draft or an alteration of the draft, the warrantor may defend by proving that the indorsement is effective under Section 3–404 or 3–405 or the drawer is precluded under Section 3–406 or 4–406 from asserting against the drawee the unauthorized indorsement or alteration.

(d) If (i) a dishonored draft is presented for payment to the drawer or an indorser or (ii) any other instrument is presented for payment to a party obliged to pay the instrument, and (iii) payment is received, the following rules apply:

(1) The person obtaining payment and a prior transferor of the instrument warrant to the person making payment in good faith that the warrantor is, or was, at the time the warrantor transferred the instrument, a person entitled to enforce the instrument or authorized to obtain payment on behalf of a person entitled to enforce the instrument.

(2) The person making payment may recover from any warrantor for breach of warranty an amount equal to the amount paid plus expenses and loss of interest resulting from the breach.

(e) The warranties stated in subsections (a) and (d) cannot be disclaimed with respect to checks. Unless notice of a claim for breach of warranty is given to the warrantor within 30 days after the claimant has reason to know of the breach and the identity of the warrantor, the liability of the warrantor under subsection (b) or (d) is discharged to the extent of any loss caused by the delay in giving notice of the claim.

(f) A [cause of action] for breach of warranty under this section accrues when the claimant has reason to know of the breach.

§ 3–418. Payment or Acceptance by Mistake.

(a) Except as provided in subsection (c), if the drawee of a draft pays or accepts the draft and the drawee acted on the mistaken belief that (i) payment of the draft had not been stopped pursuant to Section 4–403 or (ii) the signature of the drawer of the draft was authorized, the drawee may recover the amount of the draft from the person to whom or for whose benefit payment was made or, in the case of acceptance, may revoke the acceptance. Rights of the drawee under this subsection are not affected by failure of the drawee to exercise ordinary care in paying or accepting the draft.

(b) Except as provided in subsection (c), if an instrument has been paid or accepted by mistake and the case is not covered by subsection (a), the person paying or accepting may, to the extent permitted by the law governing mistake and restitution, (i) recover the payment from the person to whom or for whose benefit payment was made or (ii) in the case of acceptance, may revoke the acceptance.

(c) The remedies provided by subsection (a) or (b) may not be asserted against a person who took the instrument in good faith and for value or who in good faith changed position in reliance on the payment or acceptance. This subsection does not limit remedies provided by Section 3–417 or 4–407.

(d) Notwithstanding Section 4–215, if an instrument is paid or accepted by mistake and the payor or acceptor recovers payment or revokes acceptance under subsection (a) or (b), the instrument is deemed not to have been paid or accepted and is treated as dishonored, and the person from whom payment is recovered has rights as a person entitled to enforce the dishonored instrument.

§ 3–419. Instruments Signed for Accommodation.

(a) If an instrument is issued for value given for the benefit of a party to the instrument ("accommodated party") and another party to the instrument ("accommodation party") signs the instrument for the purpose of incurring liability on the instrument without being a direct beneficiary of the value given for the instrument, the instrument is signed by the accommodation party "for accommodation."

(b) An accommodation party may sign the instrument as maker, drawer, acceptor, or indorser and, subject to subsection (d), is obliged to pay the instrument in the capacity in which the accommodation party signs. The obligation of an accommodation party may be enforced notwithstanding any statute of frauds and whether or not the accommodation party receives consideration for the accommodation.

(c) A person signing an instrument is presumed to be an accommodation party and there is notice that the instrument is signed for accommodation if the signature is an anomalous indorsement or is accompanied by words indicating that the signer is acting as surety or guarantor with respect to the obligation of another party to the instrument. Except as provided in Section 3–605, the obligation of an accommodation party to pay the instrument is not affected by the fact that the person enforcing the obligation had notice when the instrument was taken by that person that the accommodation party signed the instrument for accommodation.

(d) If the signature of a party to an instrument is accompanied by words indicating unambiguously that the party is guaranteeing collection rather than payment of the obligation of another party to the instrument, the signer is obliged to pay the amount due on the instrument to a person entitled to enforce the instrument only if (i) execution of judgment against the other party has been returned unsatisfied, (ii) the other party is insolvent or in an insolvency proceeding, (iii) the other party cannot be served with process, or (iv) it is otherwise apparent that payment cannot be obtained from the other party.

(e) An accommodation party who pays the instrument is entitled to reimbursement from the accommodated party and is entitled to enforce the instrument against the accommodated party. An accommodated party who pays the instrument has no right of recourse against, and is not entitled to contribution from, an accommodation party.

§ 3–420. Conversion of Instrument.

(a) The law applicable to conversion of personal property applies to instruments. An instrument is also converted if it is taken by transfer, other than a negotiation, from a person not entitled to enforce the instrument or a bank makes or obtains payment with respect to the instrument for a person not entitled to enforce the instrument or receive payment. An action for conversion of an instrument may not be brought by (i) the issuer or acceptor of the instrument or (ii) a payee or indorsee who did not receive delivery of the instrument either directly or through delivery to an agent or a co-payee.

(b) In an action under subsection (a), the measure of liability is presumed to be the amount payable on the instrument, but recovery may not exceed the amount of the plaintiff's interest in the instrument.

(c) A representative, other than a depositary bank, who has in good faith dealt with an instrument or its proceeds on behalf of one who was not the person entitled to enforce the instrument is not liable in conversion to that person beyond the amount of any proceeds that it has not paid out.

PART 5 Dishonor

§ 3–501. Presentment.

(a) "Presentment" means a demand made by or on behalf of a person entitled to enforce an instrument (i) to pay the instrument made to the drawee or a party obliged to pay the instrument or, in the case of a note or accepted draft payable at a bank, to the bank, or (ii) to accept a draft made to the drawee.

(b) The following rules are subject to Article 4, agreement of the parties, and clearing-house rules and the like:

(1) Presentment may be made at the place of payment of the instrument and must be made at the place of payment if the instrument is payable at a bank in the United States; may be made by any commercially reasonable means, including an oral, written, or electronic communication; is effective when the demand for payment or acceptance is received by the person to whom presentment is made; and is effective if made to any one of two or more makers, acceptors, drawees, or other payors.

(2) Upon demand of the person to whom presentment is made, the person making presentment must (i) exhibit the instrument, (ii) give reasonable identification and, if presentment is made on behalf of another person, reasonable evidence of authority to do so, and (...) sign a receipt on the instrument for any payment made or surrender the instrument if full payment is made.

(3) Without dishonoring the instrument, the party to whom presentment is made may (i) return the instrument for lack of a necessary indorsement, or (ii) refuse payment or acceptance for failure of the presentment to comply with the terms of the instrument, an agreement of the parties, or other applicable law or rule.

(4) The party to whom presentment is made may treat presentment as occurring on the next business day after the day of presentment if the party to whom presentment is made has established a cut-off hour not earlier than 2 P.M. for the receipt and processing of instruments presented for payment or acceptance and presentment is made after the cut-off hour.

§ 3–502. Dishonor.

(a) Dishonor of a note is governed by the following rules:

(1) If the note is payable on demand, the note is dishonored if presentment is duly made to the maker and the note is not paid on the day of presentment.

(2) If the note is not payable on demand and is payable at or through a bank or the terms of the note require presentment, the note is dishonored if presentment is duly made and the note is not paid on the day it becomes payable or the day of presentment, whichever is later.

(3) If the note is not payable on demand and paragraph (2) does not apply, the note is dishonored if it is not paid on the day it becomes payable.

(b) Dishonor of an unaccepted draft other than a documentary draft is governed by the following rules:

(1) If a check is duly presented for payment to the payor bank otherwise than for immediate payment over the counter, the check is dishonored if the payor bank makes timely return of the check or sends timely notice of dishonor or nonpayment under Section 4–301 or 4–302, or becomes accountable for the amount of the check under Section 4–302.

(2) If a draft is payable on demand and paragraph (1) does not apply, the draft is dishonored if presentment for payment is duly made to the drawee and the draft is not paid on the day of presentment.

(3) If a draft is payable on a date stated in the draft, the draft is dishonored if (i) presentment for payment is duly made to the drawee and payment is not made on the day the draft becomes payable or the day of presentment, whichever is later, or (ii) presentment for acceptance is duly made before the day the draft becomes payable and the draft is not accepted on the day of presentment.

(4) If a draft is payable on elapse of a period of time after sight or acceptance, the draft is dishonored if presentment for acceptance is duly made and the draft is not accepted on the day of presentment.

(c) Dishonor of an unaccepted documentary draft occurs according to the rules stated in subsection (b)(2), (3), and (4), except that payment or acceptance may be delayed without dishonor until no later than the close of the third business day of the drawee following the day on which payment or acceptance is required by those paragraphs.

(d) Dishonor of an accepted draft is governed by the following rules:

(1) If the draft is payable on demand, the draft is dishonored if presentment for payment is duly made to the acceptor and the draft is not paid on the day of presentment.

(2) If the draft is not payable on demand, the draft is dishonored if presentment for payment is duly made to the acceptor and payment is not made on the day it becomes payable or the day of presentment, whichever is later.

(e) In any case in which presentment is otherwise required for dishonor under this section and presentment is excused under Section 3–504, dishonor occurs without presentment if the instrument is not duly accepted or paid.

(f) If a draft is dishonored because timely acceptance of the draft was not made and the person entitled to demand acceptance consents to a late acceptance, from the time of acceptance the draft is treated as never having been dishonored.

§ 3–503. Notice of Dishonor.

(a) The obligation of an indorser stated in Section 3–415 (a) and the obligation of a drawer stated in Section 3–414(d) may not be enforced unless (i) the indorser or drawer is given notice of dishonor of the instrument complying with this section or (ii) notice of dishonor is excused under Section 3–504(b).

(b) Notice of dishonor may be given by any person; may be given by any commercially reasonable means, including an oral, written, or electronic communication; and is sufficient if it reasonably identifies the instrument and indicates that the instrument has been dishonored or has not been paid or accepted. Return of an instrument given to a bank for collection is sufficient notice of dishonor.

(c) Subject to Section 3–504(c), with respect to an instrument taken for collection by a collecting bank, notice of dishonor must be given (i) by the bank before midnight of the next banking day following the banking day on which the bank receives notice of dishonor of the instrument, or (ii) by any other person within 30 days following the day on which the person receives notice of dishonor. With respect to any other instrument, notice of dishonor must be given within 30 days following the day on which dishonor occurs.

§ 3–504. Excused Presentment and Notice of Dishonor.

(a) Presentment for payment or acceptance of an instrument is excused if (i) the person entitled to present the instrument cannot with reasonable diligence make presentment, (ii) the maker or acceptor has repudiated an obligation to pay the instrument or is dead or in insolvency proceedings, (iii) by the terms of the instrument presentment is not necessary to enforce the obligation of indorsers or the drawer, (iv) the drawer or indorser whose obligation is being enforced has waived presentment or otherwise has no reason to expect or right to require that the instrument be paid or accepted, or (v) the drawer instructed the drawee not to pay or accept the draft or the drawee was not obligated to the drawer to pay the draft.

(b) Notice of dishonor is excused if (i) by the terms of the instrument notice of dishonor is not necessary to enforce the obligation of a party to pay the instrument, or (ii) the party whose obligation is being enforced waived notice of dishonor. A waiver of presentment is also a waiver of notice of dishonor.

(c) Delay in giving notice of dishonor is excused if the delay was caused by circumstances beyond the control of the person giving the notice and the person giving the notice exercised reasonable diligence after the cause of the delay ceased to operate.

§ 3–505. Evidence of Dishonor.

(a) The following are admissible as evidence and create a presumption of dishonor and of any notice of dishonor stated:

(1) a document regular in form as provided in subsection (b) which purports to be a protest;

(2) a purported stamp or writing of the drawee, payor bank, or presenting bank on or accompanying the instrument stating that acceptance or payment has been refused unless reasons for the refusal are stated and the reasons are not consistent with dishonor;

(3) a book or record of the drawee, payor bank, or collecting bank, kept in the usual course of business which shows dishonor, even if there is no evidence of who made the entry.

(b) A protest is a certificate of dishonor made by a United States consul or vice consul, or a notary public or other person authorized to administer oaths by the law of the place where dishonor occurs. It may be made upon information satisfactory to that person. The protest must identify the instrument and certify either that presentment has been made or, if not made, the reason why it was not made, and that the instrument has been dishonored by nonacceptance or nonpayment. The protest may also certify that notice of dishonor has been given to some or all parties.

PART 6 Discharge and Payment

§ 3–601. Discharge and Effect of Discharge.

(a) The obligation of a party to pay the instrument is discharged as stated in this Article or by an act or agreement with the party which would discharge an obligation to pay money under a simple contract.

(b) Discharge of the obligation of a party is not effective against a person acquiring rights of a holder in due course of the instrument without notice of the discharge.

§ 3–602. Payment.

(a) Subject to subsection (b), an instrument is paid to the extent payment is made (i) by or on behalf of a party obliged to pay the instrument, and (ii) to a person entitled to enforce the instrument. To the extent of the payment, the obligation of the party obliged to pay the instrument is discharged even though payment is made with knowledge of a claim to the instrument under Section 3–306 by another person.

(b) The obligation of a party to pay the instrument is not discharged under subsection (a) if:

(1) a claim to the instrument under Section 3–306 is enforceable against the party receiving payment and (i) payment is made with

knowledge by the payor that payment is prohibited by injunction or similar process of a court of competent jurisdiction, or (ii) in the case of an instrument other than a cashier's check, teller's check, or certified check, the party making payment accepted, from the person having a claim to the instrument, indemnity against loss resulting from refusal to pay the person entitled to enforce the instrument; or

(2) the person making payment knows that the instrument is a stolen instrument and pays a person it knows is in wrongful possession of the instrument.

§ 3–603. Tender of Payment.

(a) If tender of payment of an obligation to pay an instrument is made to a person entitled to enforce the instrument, the effect of tender is governed by principles of law applicable to tender of payment under a simple contract.

(b) If tender of payment of an obligation to pay an instrument is made to a person entitled to enforce the instrument and the tender is refused, there is discharge, to the extent of the amount of the tender, of the obligation of an indorser or accommodation party having a right of recourse with respect to the obligation to which the tender relates.

(c) If tender of payment of an amount due on an instrument is made to a person entitled to enforce the instrument, the obligation of the obligor to pay interest after the due date on the amount tendered is discharged. If presentment is required with respect to an instrument and the obligor is able and ready to pay on the due date at every place of payment stated in the instrument, the obligor is deemed to have made tender of payment on the due date to the person entitled to enforce the instrument.

§ 3–604. Discharge by Cancellation or Renunciation.

(a) A person entitled to enforce an instrument, with or without consideration, may discharge the obligation of a party to pay the instrument (i) by an intentional voluntary act, such as surrender of the instrument to the party, destruction, mutilation, or cancellation of the instrument, cancellation or striking out of the party's signature, or the addition of words to the instrument indicating discharge, or (ii) by agreeing not to sue or otherwise renouncing rights against the party by a signed writing.

(b) Cancellation or striking out of an indorsement pursuant to subsection (a) does not affect the status and rights of a party derived from the indorsement.

§ 3–605. Discharge of Indorsers and Accommodation Parties.

(a) In this section, the term "indorser" includes a drawer having the obligation described in Section 3–414(d).

(b) Discharge, under Section 3–604, of the obligation of a party to pay an instrument does not discharge the obligation of an indorser or accommodation party having a right of recourse against the discharged party.

(c) If a person entitled to enforce an instrument agrees, with or without consideration, to an extension of the due date of the obligation of a party to pay the instrument, the extension discharges an indorser or accommodation party having a right of recourse against the party whose obligation is extended to the extent the indorser or accommodation party proves that the extension caused loss to the indorser or accommodation party with respect to the right of recourse.

(d) If a person entitled to enforce an instrument agrees, with or without consideration, to a material modification of the obligation of a party other than an extension of the due date, the modification discharges the obligation of an indorser or accommodation party having a right of recourse against the person whose obligation is modified to the extent the modification causes loss to the indorser or accommodation party with respect to the right of recourse. The loss suffered by the indorser or accommodation party as a result of the modification is equal to the amount of the right of recourse unless the person enforcing the instrument proves that no loss was caused by the modification or that the loss caused by the modification was an amount less than the amount of the right of recourse.

(e) If the obligation of a party to pay an instrument is secured by an interest in collateral and a person entitled to enforce the instrument impairs the value of the interest in collateral, the obligation of an indorser or accommodation party having a right of recourse against the obligor is discharged to the extent of the impairment. The value of an interest in collateral is impaired to the extent (i) the value of the interest is reduced to an amount less than the amount of the right of recourse of the party asserting discharge, or (ii) the reduction in value of the interest causes an increase in the amount by which the amount of the right of recourse exceeds the value of the interest. The burden of proving impairment is on the party asserting discharge.

(f) If the obligation of a party is secured by an interest in collateral not provided by an accommodation party and a person entitled to enforce the instrument impairs the value of the interest in collateral, the obligation of any party who is jointly and severally liable with respect to the secured obligation is discharged to the extent the impairment causes the party asserting discharge to pay more than that party would have been obliged to pay, taking into account rights of contribution, if impairment had not occurred. If the party asserting discharge is an accommodation party not entitled to discharge under subsection (e), the party is deemed to have a right to contribution based on joint and several liability rather than a right to reimbursement. The burden of proving impairment is on the party asserting discharge.

(g) Under subsection (e) or (f), impairing value of an interest in collateral includes (i) failure to obtain or maintain perfection or recordation of the interest in collateral, (ii) release of collateral without substitution of collateral of equal value, (iii) failure to perform a duty to preserve the value of collateral owed, under Article 9 or other law, to a debtor or surety or other person secondarily liable, or (iv) failure to comply with applicable law in disposing of collateral.

(h) An accommodation party is not discharged under subsection (c), (d), or (e) unless the person entitled to enforce the instrument knows of the accommodation or has notice under Section 3–419(c) that the instrument was signed for accommodation.

(i) A party is not discharged under this section if (i) the party asserting discharge consents to the event or conduct that is the basis of the discharge, or (ii) the instrument or a separate agreement of the party provides for waiver of discharge under this section either specifically or by general language indicating that parties waive defenses based on suretyship or impairment of collateral.

ADDENDUM TO REVISED ARTICLE III

Notes to Legislative Counsel

1. If revised Article 3 is adopted in your state, the reference in Section 2–511 to Section 3–802 should be changed to Section 3–310.

2. If revised Article 3 is adopted in your state and the Uniform Fiduciaries Act is also in effect in your state, you may want to consider amending Uniform Fiduciaries Act § 9 to conform to Section 3–307(b)(2)(iii) and (4)(iii). See Official Comment 3 to Section 3–307.

APPENDIX C

ANSWERS TO SELECTED END-OF-CHAPTER QUESTIONS

MULTIPLE-CHOICE QUESTIONS

Presented are the answers for the ODD-numbered multiple-choice questions in the end-of-chapter material.

CHAPTER 1
1. C
3. D
5. D

CHAPTER 2
1. A
3. C
5. B

CHAPTER 3
1. A
3. B
5. C

CHAPTER 4
1. C
3. E
5. A

CHAPTER 5
1. B
3. C
5. A

CHAPTER 6
1. B
3. A
5. C

CHAPTER 7
1. B
3. C
5. B

CHAPTER 8
1. C
3. B
5. A

CHAPTER 9
1. A
3. C
5. B

CHAPTER 10
1. C
3. A
5. B

CHAPTER 11
1. D
3. B
5. C

CHAPTER 12
1. E
3. B
5. D

CHAPTER 13
1. A
3. C
5. B

CHAPTER 14
1. D
3. C
5. B

CHAPTER 15
1. D
3. E
5. B

CHAPTER 16
1. C
3. B
5. A

CHAPTER 17
1. D
3. A
5. B

CHAPTER 18
1. C
3. B
5. A

CHAPTER 19

1. A
3. B
5. C

CHAPTER 20

1. D
3. B
5. D

CHAPTER 21

1. C
3. D
5. A

CHAPTER 22

1. D
3. B
5. A

CHAPTER 23

1. D
3. D
5. D

CHAPTER 24

1. B
3. C
5. B

CHAPTER 25

1. B
3. B
5. A

CHAPTER 26

1. D
3. A
5. A

CHAPTER 27

1. D
3. A
5. A

CHAPTER 28

1. B
3. A
5. B

CHAPTER 29

1. E
3. D
5. B

CHAPTER 30

1. C
3. C
5. B

CHAPTER 31

1. B
3. E
5. B

CHAPTER 32

1. A
3. B
5. D

CHAPTER 33

1. D
3. C
5. D

CHAPTER 34

1. B
3. A
5. C

CHAPTER 35

1. B
3. D
5. C

CHAPTER 36

1. D
3. D
5. A

CHAPTER 37

1. B
3. B
5. D

CHAPTER 38

1. B
3. D
5. C

CHAPTER 39

1. B
3. D
5. B

CHAPTER 40

1. C
3. C
5. B

CHAPTER 41

1. A
3. C
5. A

CHAPTER 42

1. D
3. C
5. C

CHAPTER 43

1. C
3. D
5. A

CHAPTER 44

1. D
3. B
5. D

CASE QUESTIONS

Presented are the answers for the ODD-numbered case questions in the end-of-chapter material.

CHAPTER 1

1. Answer: The civil case will be brought by the victim (the entity or person from whom Lance stole the credit card numbers), and the outcome of a successful case against Lance would be some type of monetary award such as restitution. The criminal case will be brought by state prosecutors, and the outcome would be imprisonment for Lance.

3. Answer: For most of the "You Be the Judge" writing problems, we provide the case citation and holding. For this question, of course, there is no definitive answer.

5. Answer: This is a civil lawsuit.

CHAPTER 2

1. Answer: (A) Money, rationalization, conformity, following orders, lost in a crowd (B) Loyalty, exit, voice.

3. Answer: Kant would say it was wrong. Mill would say the study helped save the eyesight and lives of lots of other children.

5. Answer: Money, competition, conformity, following orders, short-term perspective, optimism bias.

CHAPTER 3

1. Answer: Based on *Saudi Arabia v. Nelson* (U.S. S. Ct. 1993). The Supreme Court found that FSIA applied to immunize Saudi Arabia from the suit. While employing someone is a commercial activity, the Court reasoned that the injury stemmed from his arrest. Since a private citizen cannot jail someone, this is purely a governmental activity.

3. Answer: The United States challenged this practice, and WTO ruled that GM food had to be allowed into the EU. The WTO held that no scientific evidence supported the EU's fears and, therefore, the regulation unduly burdened trade.

5. Answer: *Chateau de Charmes Wine v. Sabate USA*, 328 F.3d 528 (9th Cir. 2003). The court held that the CISG applied, and it did not require a writing. The forum selection clause was not part of the original contract and was therefore void.

CHAPTER 4

1. Answer: The groups should, and did, file an "FOIA request"—that is, a request for documents pursuant to the Freedom of Information Act. Most agency information must be made available to the public. But certain information may be exempt. The FOIA exempts matters pertaining to national security. In addition, the Aviation Security Improvement Act of 1990 added additional documents that can be exempt—namely, those pertaining to airport security.

3. Answer: The members of Congress could introduce a bill overruling the Supreme Court's interpretation of federal antitrust statutes. The bill would specify that baseball is part of trade and commerce and that Congress intends that it be subject to the antitrust laws, the same as any other nationwide industry.

5. Answer: The tobacco companies can sue the agency like Fox did in *Fox Television v. FCC*.

DC Circuit initially held for R. J. Reynolds, reasoning that the FDA could not provide evidence that general warnings on packaging reduced smoking rates, therefore, there was no "substantial government interest" in compelling tobacco companies' speech. *R. J. Reynolds Tobacco Co. v. Food and Drug Administration*, 696 F.3d 1205 (2012). However, this case was subsequently overruled by the DC Circuit in *American Meat Institute v. USDA*, 760 F.3d 18 (2014). This case held that government interests in correcting prior deception could justify a mandate for disclosure of information in a commercial context.

CHAPTER 5

1. Answer: The right of privacy is stated nowhere in the Constitution, and its enforcement is an example of the Court applying substantive due process. Justice Black thought the law was terrible, but he thought it was even worse for the Court to invent constitutional doctrine simply because it disliked a particular law. He would have preferred to practice judicial restraint—that is, to leave it up to the voters and the state legislature to decide the matter. Clearly, a court should not go so far with judicial activism that it becomes a superlegislature. The Constitution makes it clear that courts should have a more limited role. Yet, since *Marbury v. Madison*, federal courts have taken it upon themselves to say what the law is, and that frequently means overturning state and federal statutes. An activist court presents society with the danger of unelected judges, with lifetime tenure, foisting their own social agenda on an unwilling populace—but it also offers the potential for powerful officials, who do not have to worry about polls or reelections, to protect the people and the rights that are most vulnerable.

3. Answer: Based on *Passions Video v. Nixon*, 458 F.3d 837 (8th cir., 2006). The court of appeals found that the restriction was an unconstitutional infringement on commercial speech.

5. Answer: Based on *Salib v. City of Mesa*, 133 p.3d 756 (Arizona Court of Appeals, 2006). The court concluded that the Sign Code directly advances a substantial governmental interest and is narrowly tailored to directly advance the goal of improved aesthetics.

CHAPTER 6

1. Answer: Yes. Try blending ADR mechanisms. Have the ADR clause state that, in the event of a dispute, the parties will negotiate it in good faith and will take no further steps for 30 days. If negotiation fails, an additional 30-day cooling-off period follows. The next step could be a mini-trial in front of three people, two of whom represent the parties and the third who acts as a neutral mediator. Finally, if the mini-trial fails to produce a settlement, the parties will hire an arbitrator. You might require that the arbitrator be a national of neither Turkey nor the United States. You must specify the law to be applied and where the arbitration will take place. List any claims that are not arbitrable, such as antitrust or securities claims. This should preserve a working relationship while ensuring that disputes will be settled rapidly.

3. Answer: Discovery is more efficient in Britain, since the solicitors are honor-bound to notify of relevant documents. The fighting over discovery motions that drains time and money in the United States is uncommon there. However, the absence of depositions means that the parties go into court with less information about the opponent's case, making trials more open to surprise.

5. Answer: Kelly will win because the agreement gives Giant the sole right to choose the arbitrators. An arbitration clause under those conditions is invalid.

CHAPTER 7

1. Answer: Friedman argued entrapment, claiming that there was no evidence of his predisposition to traffic in drugs. The Alabama Supreme Court ruled against him. The court noted that Friedman admitted to occasional use of marijuana, that he had been able quickly to locate marijuana to resell to the agent, and that he showed a sophisticated knowledge of the drug when bargaining over the price of three pounds. The court held that there was no evidence of entrapment. *Friedman v. State*, 654 So.2d 50, 1994 Ala. Crim. App. LEXIS 179 (1994).

3. Answer: The appeals court affirmed the sentence on the grounds that it did not violate standards of decency. *United States v. Gementera*, 379 F.3d 596 (2004).

5. Answer: No. So long as police reasonably believed the search was valid, the search is legal.

CHAPTER 8

1. Answer: These are difficult problems which a manager must think through carefully. Negative statements can lead to a defamation lawsuit. If you have irrefutable proof that Gates did steal, you are probably on safe ground. But if you doubt your ability to prove his theft, you must be very careful. If you state to the personnel officer precisely what you know about the theft, and nothing more, you are probably on safe ground. Even if you are incorrect, most courts will hold that you have qualified privilege to speak to someone who needs to know the truth. As long as you display no malice, you are not committing slander. Some managers, though, are extra careful and simply refuse to say anything in such a situation. As for posting the notices, you should not do it. The other employees have no need to know your allegations about Gates, and thus you have no qualified privilege to inform them. If you are wrong, it is libel, and juries are often very sympathetic to injured employees.

3. Answer: The U.S. District Court gave summary judgment for United, and the Court of Appeals affirmed. *Pacific Express, Inc. v. United Airlines, Inc.*, 959 F.2d 814, 1992 U.S. App. LEXIS 5139 (9th Cir. 1992). The primary issue was whether United was genuinely trying to compete, which it had the right to do, or was simply out to destroy Pacific, which would be interference with a prospective advantage (as well as an antitrust violation). United officials testified that the expanded routes would generate new connecting traffic for other San Francisco flights. That is a competitive purpose, which is legitimate, and enough to defeat Pacific's claim.

5. Answer: *Greene v. Paramount Pictures, et al.*, 138 F. Supp. 3d 226 (2015). To prove defamation, a plaintiff must prove a defamatory statement that was false and communicated to others. He must also prove that the statement caused injury. District Judge denied Paramount's motion to dismiss the lawsuit as to defamation. Even though the movie did not use Greene's name or image, the court found that making the connection to the plaintiff was reasonable and the likeness "unmistakable." Greene would have to prove the elements above.

CHAPTER 9

1. Answer: The case was reversed and remanded for trial. *Powers v. Ryder Truck*, 625 So. 2d 979, 1993 Fla. App. LEXIS 10729 (Fla. Dist. Ct. App. 1993). Whether an event is a superseding cause is a jury question, unless it is so bizarre as to be entirely unforeseeable by the defendant. Here, even if Powers was negligent in attaching a nylon rope, that negligence was not so bizarre as to be unforeseeable by Ryder.

3. Answer: The standard is whether the defendant acted as a "reasonable person" would have. The appeals court reversed, holding that the plaintiffs had made out a valid negligence claim and were entitled to take their evidence to a jury. Plaintiffs could argue, for example, that Texaco should have provided warnings of the danger, should have discouraged distributors from selling to retailers who illegally packaged the goods in used milk containers, and should have refused to sell to distributors who didn't cooperate. *Hunnings v. Texaco, Inc.*, 29 F.3d 1480, 1994 U.S. LEXIS 21833 (11th Cir. 1994).

5. Answer: *McGarry v. Sax*, Cal.Rptr.3d. The Court of Appeal held that McGarry could not state a cause of action for negligence because he was a willing participant in the competition for the skateboard deck and he assumed the risk of being injured.

CHAPTER 10

1. Answer: The FTC found that this system was unfair and deceptive under Section 5 of the FTC Act. Chitika entered into a consent order under which opt-out provision would last five years.

3. Answer: The court ruled *no*; Barrow did not have a reasonable expectation of privacy. *United States v. Barrows*, 481 F.3d 1246 (10th Cir. 2007).

5. Answer: *Simpson v Simpson, 5th Cir,* 1974. The court held that the statute did not extend to spouses in the marital home. Students should assess whether the wife had a reasonable expectation of privacy.

CHAPTER 11

1. Answer: Foley is arguing that he has an implied contract with Interactive based on the informal discussions concerning his future and the employee handbook. His argument convinced the California Supreme Court. *Foley v. Interactive Data Corp.*, 47 Cal. 3d 654, 765 P.2d 373, 1988 Cal. LEXIS 269 (1988). Foley had no express contract for any period, and thus he started work as an employee at will. But the company's repeated assurances, plus the handbook, created an implied contract.

3. Answer: *Bailey v. West,* 249 A.2d 414 (1969). A volunteer may not recover for a benefit conferred under quasi-contract. Bailey acted as a volunteer at his own risk that he might not be compensated. There was no implied-in-fact contract because there was no evidence that the parties ever actually intended to contract. If performance is rendered by one party without request by another, that person will generally not owe a duty to compensate the performing party.

5. Answer: *Jennifer Trehar v. Brightway Center, Inc.*, 2015-Ohio-4144 (2015). The court reversed the lower court's grant of summary judgment to Brightway. Reasonable people could conclude that Trehar's boss and the president of the company induced Trehar to believe that no adverse employment action would result from her move.

CHAPTER 12

1. Answer: No contract, no sale. An auction is with reserve unless stated otherwise. The ad was silent on the subject, so this auction was with reserve. That means that all of the bids, including the highest, are merely offers. The auctioneer, in this case the town, has the right to reject all of the offers, and the Chevaliers have no right to the lot. *Chevalier v. Town of Sanford,* 475 A.2d 1148 (Me. 1984).

3. Answer: Excerpt from Judge's decision: Plaintiff's motion to enforce "the settlement" has generated considerable debate between the parties. Plaintiff asserts that the defendant is bound to a settlement. Plaintiff's problem is that there was no "agreement" to speak of. To be sure, there was an offer from the defendant. During the above-quoted colloquy, clearly there were also words of acceptance from plaintiff. But when the words, "my client will take the settlement" were uttered, it was too late for them to be effective. By that time, defense counsel had made it clear that if the jury had already come to a verdict, the offer was off the table. That condition could not be ignored, as the verdict that would mean all bets were off had already been reached. For the foregoing reasons, plaintiff's motion is denied.

5. Answer: Based on *Norman v. Miller,* 326 S.E.2d 11 (1985). Miller rejected Norman's offer by submitting a counteroffer. Because the counteroffer operated as a rejection of Norman's original offer, the terms of Norman's original offer were not transferred to the counteroffer. Norman did not have a contract to purchase the property from Miller because Norman failed to accept the counteroffer before it was revoked.

CHAPTER 13

1. Answer: Empire won over $3.2 million dollars, and the appeals court affirmed. *Empire Gas Corp. v. American Bakeries Co.*, 840 F.2d 1333, 1988 U.S. App. LEXIS 2482 (7th Cir. 1988). Since this was a requirements contract for the sale of goods (the conversion units and the propane gas were the goods), it was governed by UCC §2-306. American Bakeries did have the right to reduce the number of conversions from the estimated 3,000. It could potentially reduce them even to zero, but any reduction had to be done *in good faith*, meaning that changed circumstances made a reduction important. Here, American Bakeries never offered any reason at all, and the jury verdict was reasonable.

3. Answer: Gintzler should, and did. The consideration to support Melnick's promise of repairs was Gintzler's acceptance of the defective foundation. He was under no obligation to accept a house in that condition. *Gintzler v. Melnick,* 116 N.H. 566,364 A.2d 637 (1976).

5. Answer: *Slattery v. Wells Fargo Armored Service Corp.*, 366 So.2d 157 (1979). Slattery is not entitled to the reward because the performance of a preexisting duty does not amount to the consideration necessary to form a contract.

CHAPTER 14

1. Answer: No. The non-compete clause is unenforceable here because the two companies are not really in competition and Guyan, therefore, has no confidential information or customer lists to protect. *Voorhees v. Guyan Machinery Co.*, 191 W. Va. 450, 446 S.E.2d 672, 1994 W.Va. LEXIS 27 (1994).

3. Answer: Based on *Basulto v Hialeah Automotive. Roberto Basulto, et al. v. Hialeah Automotive, etc., et al.*, No. SC09-2358, 2014 WL 1057334 (March 20, 2014). The Florida Supreme Court held that the transaction was laden with both procedural and substantive unconscionablity and on that basis invalidated the arbitration agreement.

5. Answer: Oasis Waterpark won, and Hydrotech's case was dismissed. The court was not persuaded that many owners would seek out unlicensed builders and then trick them into working, with the intention of denying payment. The judges believed that awarding damages would encourage unlicensed builders to ignore the statute's requirement. In the long run, homeowners and others who rely on licensed workers would suffer. *Hydrotech Systems, Ltd. v. Oasis Waterpark*, 52 Cal.3d 988, 803 P.2d 370, 1991 Cal. LEXIS 139, (Sup.Ct. Cal. 1991).

CHAPTER 15

1. Answer: No. The statements are all puffery. *Mason v. Chrysler Corp.*, 1995 Ala. LEXIS 30 (Ala. 1995).

3. Answer: Yes. There was no fraud or misrepresentation because Conley knew nothing of the tanks. But there is mutual mistake: The parties were both in error about an important factual assumption—namely, the ground's condition. Morell was permitted to rescind. *Morell v. Conley Detective and Security Guard Agency, Inc.*, Michigan Lawyers Weekly No. 18079, Nov. 28, 1994 (Mich. Ct. App. 1994).

5. Answer: Answers will vary.

CHAPTER 16

1. Answer: Under the parol evidence rule, if the parties intended the guaranty to be integrated, which they almost certainly did, Griffin may testify only if the writing is ambiguous or incomplete. The state supreme court ruled that the document was complete and unambiguous, and Griffin owed the entire remaining balance. *First National Bank v. Griffin*, 310 Ark. 164, 832 S.W.2d 816, 1992 Ark. LEXIS 439 (1992).

3. Answer: At trial, jurors heard the tape recording, which confirmed the oral agreement. The jury concluded that the parties had reached a binding agreement and awarded Barbara $900,000. However, the court granted a judgment notwithstanding the verdict for Melbourne because the agreement was barred by the Statute of Frauds. Barbara appealed. Does the Statute of Frauds prevent enforcement of Melbourne's promise? **Argument for Barbara**: The Statute of Frauds exists to prevent fraud. The fear of a plaintiff making up a false contract is legitimate, but obviously it does not apply in this case. We know that Melbourne agreed to pay a million dollars because we heard him. His own words verify the exact terms of the agreement and his promise to sign his name to it. What more evidence do you need? **Argument for Melbourne**: This is a simple case. If there was an agreement, it could not have been performed in one year because it had ten years' worth of installment payments. Under the Statute of Frauds, an agreement that cannot be performed within one year is unenforceable unless written and signed.

5. Answer: *Wendellyn Kay Dane v. Kris Alan Dane*, 2016 WY 38; 368 P.3d 914; 2016 Wyo. LEXIS 40. Court held for the husband. The husband's alleged promises relating to support should have been in writing. It was a promise in consideration of marriage.

CHAPTER 17

1. Answer: Raritan was hoping to be a third party beneficiary of the contract between IMC and Cherry, Bekaert, & Holland. But the court was unpersuaded. It found that the accountants had no intention of benefiting anyone other than IMC, they had no knowledge at all of Raritan, and Raritan had never even seen the original audit but merely a report of the audit. The court declared that Raritan was an incidental beneficiary and hence a loser. *Raritan River Steel Co. v. Cherry, Bekaert, & Holland*, 329 N.C. 646, 407 S.E.2d 178, 1991 N.C. LEXIS 519 (1991).

3. Answer: Wuliger wins. David intended that Wuliger benefit from Polly's promised release. The contract expressly included the attorneys in the release. Further, Polly's divorce attorney indicated in deposition that David Ricupero would not have signed the decree if the release did not include the attorneys. The lawyers are the intended beneficiaries of the release, and they may enforce it. *Ricupero v. Wuliger*, 1994 U.S. Dist. LEXIS 12538, U.S. Dist. Ct., No. Dist. Ohio (1994).

5. Answer: Based on *Loftus v. American Realty Co.*, 334 NW2d 366 (1983). The Court of Appeals of Iowa held that, under the contract, the realty company was to assume the responsibility for performing any tasks necessary for the closing of the transaction, including turning on utilities. It held that ARC could properly delegate the duty to light the water heater, but this delegation did not excuse it from liability for the faulty performance of the subcontractor.

CHAPTER 18

1. Answer: The type of condition determines who must prove the source of the fire. CU claimed that the clause was a condition precedent, meaning that Redux had the burden of proving the fire was not arson. Redux argued that the clause was a condition subsequent, meaning that CU became liable to pay benefits as soon as the fire started and could escape its duty only if the insurer proved Redux had committed arson. The court agreed with Redux, held that the clause was a condition subsequent, and placed the burden on CU to prove arson. *Redux, Ltd. v. Commercial Union Ins. Co.*, 1995 U.S. Dist. LEXIS 2545 (D. Kan. 1995). The most obvious ethical issues arise around the language of the contract and the sale of the policy. The contract says that the insurer is not liable for harm caused by criminal acts of employees. However, the contract says nothing about who must prove whether the harm was caused by such crimes. Further, it is very unlikely that the insurance agent explained, when selling the policy, that in the event of fire the insured company would have to prove the harm was not caused by employee arson. Some would say, as this court did, that the company is attempting to sneak one by its policyholders, using ambiguous language to help sell the policy then sandbagging the insured once a loss occurs, claiming a contract interpretation that it had never before mentioned. Many would argue that the company that drafts a contract has an ethical obligation to make its terms clear. It is hard to believe that the insurance company would desire to be treated this way—for example, by reinsurers upon whom it depends.

3. Answer: Based on *Brunswick Hills Racquet Club Inc. v. Route 18 Shopping Center Associates*, 182 N.J. 210. Supreme Court of New Jersey (2005). The court held that Route 18 breached its duty of good faith and fair dealing.

5. Answer: Reversed. Summary judgment granted for Scottsdale Plaza, with the case remanded to the trial court to assess damages. Kuhn has no legitimate claim for impossibility or impracticability. Kuhn does not and cannot allege that it was impossible for it to perform, but rather that the *resort's* performance had been rendered worthless. That is a claim of frustration of purpose. To win on such a claim, Kuhn must show that the principal purpose in entering the contract was a convention at which the European employees would appear. That was not a principal purpose of the contract. Further, the majority of dealers were still prepared to attend. There has been no frustration of purpose. *7200 Scottsdale Road v. Kuhn Farm Machinery, Inc.*, 909 P.2d 408, 1995 Ariz. App. LEXIS 108 (Ariz. Ct. App. 1995).

CHAPTER 19

1. Answer: Motion granted. Nine Mile may have breached the agreement, but there is no evidence that Lewis lost money. To win, he must demonstrate a difference between the contract price and the market value of the timber. There was no difference, and he recovers nothing. *Lewis v. Nine Mile Mines, Inc.*, 886 P.2d 912, 1994 Mont. LEXIS 283 (Mont. 1994).

3. Answer: Based on *Madariaga v. Morris*, 639 S.W.2d 709 (1982). The court granted specific performance on the sale of the hot sauce recipe. "Morris does not have an adequate remedy at law and cannot be adequately compensated in damages. This is apparent from the subject matter of the sale. The business, including the hot sauce formula and goodwill, has a special, peculiar, unique value or character; it consists of property which Morris needs and could not be obtained elsewhere."

5. Answer: *Milicic v. Basketball Marketing Company, Inc.*, 2004 Pa.A Super. 333 Superior Court of Pennsylvania (2004). The court granted the preliminary injunction to prevent continuing irreparable harm to Milicic.

CHAPTER 20

1. Answer: Should be in writing:

- The sale of stock
- A merger agreement
- The sale of land
- Anything that falls under the Statute of Frauds

Need not be in writing:

- An agreement with friends in which not much money is involved—to chip in to buy a present
- With someone with whom you have an ongoing relationship, who has proved to be trustworthy in the past, and to whom you can afford the loss—a routine supplier
- You do not have time to do a proper written contract, and you would prefer to bear the risk of loss over the risk of not getting the deal done

3. Answer: Answers will vary. This case ended up in litigation over the definition of the word "substantial." Litigation is never a happy result.

5. Answer: The court ruled that although Comcast had made a series of mistakes, it had not violated its duty to act in good faith.

CHAPTER 21

1. Answer: The parties have an output contract because Perini has promised to deliver to Atlantic 100 percent of its output of certain material and Atlantic has agreed to buy it all. Under UCC §2-306, such contracts are valid, even though the quantity of goods is, by definition, not stated. The parties must act in good faith. Here, Perini's reason for stopping delivery is entirely legitimate: the original contract with MBTA has been terminated for business reasons. In an output contract, the buyer assumes the risk that the seller may have a legitimate reason for greatly reducing, or even halting, its supply of goods. Judgment for Perini. *Atlantic Track & Turnout Co. v. Perini Corporation*, 989 F.2d 541, 1993 U.S. App. LEXIS 6248 (1st Cir. 1993).

3. Answer: Tri-Circle has added an additional term to Weimer's offer. Under UCC §2-207, in a contract between merchants, an additional term becomes part of the contract unless (1) the offer insisted on its own terms, (2) the additional term materially alters the offer, or (3) the offeror promptly objects to the added term. None of those things occurred, so the additional term was part of the sales agreement if all three parties were merchants. They routinely dealt in farm goods, so they were merchants, and thus the finance charge was binding. *Tri-Circle, Inc. v. Brugger Corporation*, 121 Idaho 950, 829 P.2d 540, 1992 Idaho App. LEXIS 29 (1992).

5. Answer: *AC Furniture v. Arby's Restaurant Group*, 2014 WL 4961055 US Dist Ct, WD Virginia (2014). The judge denied Arby's Restaurant's motion to dismiss because there was a signed writing ordering the chairs with ample detail. This proved that there was a meeting of the minds. It did not have to be in writing because the specially manufactured goods exception to the Statute of Frauds applies.

CHAPTER 22

1. Answer: First State gets it. UCC §2-326(3) creates a presumption in favor of creditors. When goods are delivered *to be sold*, the goods are subject to the creditors' claims unless the owner (Havelka) takes one of the statutory steps to protect himself, such as posting a sign indicating that he owns the merchandise. He did not do that here. The only issue is whether Havelka delivered the seed *to sell.* The court held that because Havelka and other farmers had used Miller to sell seed in the past, which the bank knew, and because the stored seed was indistinguishable from the seed for sale, the purpose of §2-326 would be accomplished by protecting the creditor. The bank had no way of knowing that some of the goods that Miller appeared to own really belonged to others. *First State Bank of Purdy v. Miller*, 119 Bankr. 660, 1990 U.S. Dist. LEXIS 12407 (W.D. Ark. 1990).

3. Answer: Universal is right. UCC §2401 provides that when goods are being moved, title passes to the buyer when the seller completes whatever transportation it is obligated to do. Pifcom completed its work by delivering to the trucking company, at which time title passed. *Pittsburgh Industrial Furnace Co. v. Universal Consolidated Companies, Inc.*, 789 F. Supp. 184, 1991 U.S. Dist. LEXIS 19936 (W.D. Pa. 1991).

5. Answer: *In re Sony PS3 "Other OS" Litigation*, 2014 U.S. App. LEXIS 187, 2014 WL 31217 (2014). The court, on appeal, reversed the dismissal of claims under the Consumer Legal Remedies Act. Plaintiffs sufficiently allege that Sony's representations mischaracterized the dual functionality of the PS3 and suffered damages in the form of lost "premium" payments. Sony eventually settled. Gamers who used the "other OS" function received $55, and gamers who chose to continue using their PS3 for the Play Station Network features were entitled to $9 if they could prove that they bought their PS3 during the relevant time frame.

CHAPTER 23

1. Answer: Yes, Ace is entitled to its money because inspection sometimes creates acceptance. Mastercraft inspected the goods, kept some, and returned others, without stating that they were non-conforming. Mastercraft later ordered Ace to forward the goods to M & G. An inspection without a reasonably prompt rejection is generally an acceptance. Mastercraft's instruction to ship the goods to M & G also establishes acceptance, since such a request indicates that Mastercraft owns them. *Ace Industries, Inc. v. Mastercraft Boat Co.*, 1995 Tenn. App. LEXIS 286 (Tenn. Ct. App. 1995).

3. Answer: The court granted Clark's motion for summary judgment. Clark's statement that it would reblend the oil was a legally sufficient offer to cure. Hess responded by offering to pay less, which was a counteroffer, that is, a rejection of the offer to cure. That entitled Clark to summary judgment under UCC §2-508(1). The company is also entitled to summary judgment under §2-508(2) because a seller is allowed a reasonable time to cure following expiration of the contract if it reasonably believed that the original goods conformed. Clark's belief that the goods conformed was reasonable because its tests indicated as much. *Clark Oil Trading Co. v. Amerada Hess Trading Co.*, 1993 U.S. Dist. LEXIS 10801, U.S. Dist. Ct., So. Dist. N.Y. (1993).

5. Answer: *Smith v. Penbridge Associates, Inc.*, 440 Pa. Super. 410 Superior Court of Pennsylvania (1995). The court held for Smith. The Uniform Commercial Code provides the following circumstances for the recovery of consequential damages resulting from the breach of the seller: any loss resulting from general or particular requirements and needs of which the seller at the time of contracting had reason to know and which could not reasonably be prevented by "cover" or otherwise. [UCC §2-715(2).] There was enough evidence to suggest that Smith's lost profits were not speculative.

CHAPTER 24

1. Answer: Yes to both questions. The bank had a valid security interest in all of Ables's equipment, including after-acquired equipment. After-acquired clauses are valid. The only question is whether the bank's security interest could attach to the backhoe. Attachment requires that the debtor has rights in the collateral. But this does not mean that the debtor must own the goods. Here, Ables had the lawful use and possession of the backhoe, based on his purchase agreement with Myers. Thus, he had rights in the backhoe, and, as soon as he took possession of it, the bank's security interest attached. The bank gets the backhoe. *United States v. Allies*, 739 F. Supp. 1439, 1990 U.S. Dist. LEWIS 7064 (D. Kan. 1990).

3. Answer: No. A PMSI in consumer goods perfects automatically. A consumer good is one that is used primarily for personal, family, or household purposes. Many lawnmowers are consumer goods, but this one was not, and

Sears's security interest was not perfected. *In re Cosmo Nick Fiscante*, 141 Bankr. 303, 1992 Bankr. LEXIS 907 (W.D. Pa. 1992).

5. Answer: *Cooke v. Haddon*, 176 Eng. Rep. 103 (1862). Judgment for Cooke. A pledgee has a duty to preserve collateral in his possession.

CHAPTER 25

1. Answer: The lawyers could not be holders in due course unless they had given value for the note. The appeals court asked the trial court to determine the value of the legal services the lawyers had performed for the corporation at the time the note was given to them. *Fernandez v. Cunningham*, 268 So.2d 166 (Ct. App. Fla. 1972).

3. Answer: The court ruled that the Bank was a holder in due course because it did not know of Ian's wrongdoing. *McConnico v. Third Nat'l Bank*, 499 S.W.2d 874 (Tenn. 1973).

5. Answer: The court found that the Check Cashing was a holder in due course because it took the check for value, in good faith, and without any notice that it was overdue or had been dishonored. Check Cashing was entitled to be paid. *Hurst Enters., LLC v. Crawford*, 40 Kan. App. 2d 1018 (Kan. Ct. App. 2008).

CHAPTER 26

1. Answer: The court found for the bank on the grounds that the owner of the company had been negligent in not reviewing his bank statements. If he had done so, he would have discovered forgeries early in the game and limited his losses. *Winkie, Inc. v. Heritage Bank of Whitefish Bay*, 299 N.W.2d 829 (S.Ct. Wis. 1981).

3. Answer: The court held that Merlyn was liable to the bank because he had violated his presentment warranties when he altered and then deposited the check.

5. Answer: Answers will vary.

CHAPTER 27

1. Answer: The accountant was not liable. 356 S.E.2d 198 (Ga. 1987).

3. Answer: The doctors could file suit either in tort or in contract. It was implied in the contract that Peat would act like a reasonably careful accountant under the circumstances. When Peat was negligent, it violated the contract. *Billings Clinic v. Peat Marwick Alain & Co.*, 797 P.2d 899, 1990 Mont. LEXIS 241 (Mont. 1990).

5. Answer: The court held there was no scienter because the plaintiffs had not alleged that the auditors had actual knowledge of the fraud, but rather that they conducted an inadequate audit and missed red flags. That was not sufficient to establish scienter. *In re Puda Coal Secs., Inc.*, 30 F. Supp. 3d 230 (S.D.N.Y. 2014).

CHAPTER 28

1. Answer: Yes, because the custodian thought he was serving the purpose of his employer.

3. Answer: Principals are liable for the torts of their independent contractors only if they have been negligent in hiring the contractors. Presumably, Gerulaitis's mother will try to prove that the owners were negligent in hiring the mechanic who installed the heater.

5. Answer: Yes, he has the power. He does not, however, have the right because she has a two-year contract. Therefore, although he can prevent her from working at the Studio, he must pay her damages.

CHAPTER 29

1. Answer: The Supreme Court of Texas ruled that there was no implied contract. Marcie was not entitled to a hearing.

3. Answer: No, because treatment for Sally's illness only needed one visit to a healthcare provider, without any course of treatment or prescription medication.

5. Answer: Is Noelle refusing to violate the law, performing a legal duty, exercising a legal right, or supporting basic societal values? Is it a violation of public policy to fire her? This case has not yet been resolved.

CHAPTER 30

1. Answer: No. Title VII prohibits discrimination based on national origin. Also, the I-9 form lists the acceptable documents that can be used for verification. Employees have the right to present whatever documents they want from this list.

3. Answer: The Sixth Circuit Court of Appeals ruled that this behavior could be illegal discrimination based on national origin because "accent and national origin are inextricably intertwined." The employer would have to show that the accent and speech characteristics would prevent the employee from performing the job.

5. Answer: There have not been any cases yet, but commentators speculate that the testing would violate the Genetic Information Nondiscrimination Act. It seems clear the teams would be in violation if they used the information to predict whether a player is susceptible to disease.

7. Answer: A court held that Atlas had violated GINA, which prohibits employers from requesting genetic information from its workers. It doesn't matter that the DNA did not match. *Lowe v. Atlas Logistics Group Retail Servs. Atlanta*, LLC, 102 F. Supp. 3d 1360 (N.D. Ga. 2015).

CHAPTER 31

1. Answer: A sole proprietorship would not have worked because there was more than one owner. A partnership would have been a disaster because of unlimited liability. An LLP was a possibility, as long as the owners did not anticipate selling their shares. A limited liability partnership would have worked too. An S corporation would have been possible because the owners could have deducted their losses on this investment from their (substantial) other income and still enjoyed limited liability. The owners would probably not have been troubled by the restraints of an S corporation—only one class of stock, for example—but the technicalities involved in forming and maintaining an S corporation can be vexing. Like many start-ups today, Maven's Court probably would have been an LLC.

3. Answer: d.light is a benefit corporation. It is for profit but uses its profits to provide light to people in the developing world.

5. Answer: In every organization, the professional is responsible for his or her own wrongful acts.

CHAPTER 32

1. Answer: The court refused to re-create the partnership. It held that the defendants could terminate the partnership any time they wanted, even in violation of the partnership agreement, but they would be ordered to pay damages for breaching the agreement. *Engelbrecht v. McCullough*, 80 Ariz. 77, 292 P.2d 845 (1956).

3. Answer: The court ruled that there was no partnership because:

- The obligation to share losses is one of the most important indications of a partnership and that was missing here.
- Eagan had no right to make decisions.
- Not every business arrangement involving profit-sharing is a partnership—profit-sharing is but one relevant factor.

Eagan v. Gory, 374 Fed. Appx. 335 * (3d Cir. N.J. 2010).

5. Answer: In a similar case, the court ruled that there was no partnership because ownership of the plane was not a profit-making enterprise. If there was a partnership, the partners would be liable if the trip was in the ordinary course of the partnership's business.

CHAPTER 33

1. Answer: The appeals court pierced the corporate veil and held the shareholder liable because the corporation had grossly inadequate capitalization, had disregarded corporate formalities, and the shareholder was also actively participating in the operation of the business. *Laya v. Erin Homes, Inc.*, 177 W. Va. 343, 352 S.E.2d 93 (1986).

3. Answer: It is a domestic corporation in Nevada. It must qualify to do business in Montana because it has a permanent presence there. If the web designer in California is a full-time employee, it would also have to register there.

5. Answer: Auto was liable. The court pierced the corporate veil and held Steven liable too because he treated Auto's assets as his own. He freely deposited and withdrew Auto's funds. He ignored corporate formalities by having the bank statements sent to his house and by not documenting the loan. Joshua was not liable because he did not ignore corporate formalities nor did he commingle his assets with those of the corporation. Based on *Azte Inc. v Auto Collection, Inc.*, 36 Misc. 3d 1238(A) (N.Y. Sup. Ct. 2012).

CHAPTER 34

1. Answer: Producing ***Philly's Beat*** was clearly within the scope of Ampersand's business. Although it was not clear if Ampersand could have raised enough money to produce the play, any doubt should be resolved in favor of Ampersand. Stahl was ordered to disgorge any profits from the play. *Ampersand Productions, Inc. v. Stahl*, (Feb. 20, 1986), No. 85-435 (Dt. Ct., E.D. Pa.).

3. Answer: Even if the plan was bad, it met the standard of having a "rational business purpose." Only if there had been self-dealing on the part of the board or if they had made an uninformed decision, would shareholders have a chance of being successful in their suit.

5. Answer: The court ruled for Wallace on the grounds that the board had a good faith belief that the offer was inadequate. The board was in a better position to assess the offer than shareholders. In the end, though, the shareholders were right. Eight years later, Wallace agreed to merge with Moore at a price that was $5 per share less than originally offered. In the interim, the stock market had gone up by 20 percent.

CHAPTER 35

1. Answer: The court excused demand because the Complaint alleged "misconduct of such pervasiveness and magnitude, undertaken in the face of the board's own express formal undertakings to directly monitor and prevent such misconduct, that the inference of deliberate disregard by each and every member of the board [was] entirely reasonable." In short, the board was so careless in exercising its responsibilities that demand would be futile.

3. Answer: The SEC ruled that DeVry could exclude this proposal because it relates to the company's ordinary business operations. In particular, the proposal relates to the quality of its educational products and proposals that concern product quality are generally excludable.

5. Answer: Answers will vary.

CHAPTER 36

1. Answer: Under Chapter 7, fraud claims are not dischargeable. *In re Britton*, 950 F.2d 602, 1991 U.S. App. LEXIS 28487 (9th Cir. 1991).

3. Answer: The court would not permit this debt to be discharged because Dr. Khan was not acting in good faith. *In re M. Ibrahim Khan*, P.S.C., 34 Bankr. 574 (Bankr. W.D. Ky. 1983).

5. Answer: The bankruptcy court ruled that this payment was a voidable preference. It was not made in the ordinary course. Although Hawes was supposed to pay its bills within 30 days, it had in fact made no payments for four months and then promptly made a large one just before it filed for bankruptcy. *In re Fred Hawes Org., Inc.*, 957 F.2d 239, 1992 U.S. App. LEXIS 2300 (6th Cir. 1990).

CHAPTER 37

1. Answer: Fluor was not in violation because the company lacked scienter. Fluor had no intent to defraud investors; it was simply making a good faith effort to comply with the terms of its contract. *State Teachers Retirement Board v. Fluor Corp.*, 654 F.2d 843 (2d Cir. 1981).

3. Answer: Answers will vary.

5. Answer: He was guilty of misappropriation under §10(b). *United States v. McGee*, 763 F.3d 304 (3d Cir. 2014).

CHAPTER 38

1. Answer: The court held that a 55 percent market share creates a presumption of antitrust illegality. It reasoned, however, that a decrease in Remington's profits did not constitute an antitrust injury. The law seeks to prevent injury from reduced competition, not from increased competition. As long as the market is highly competitive, the court was unwilling to intervene. It dismissed Remington's claim. This decision uses classic Chicago School analysis. Note the emphasis on protecting competition not competitors. *Remington Products, Inc. v. North American Phillips Corp.*, 755 F. Supp. 52, 1991 U.S. Dist. LEXIS 494 (D. Conn. 1991).

3. Answer: The Justice Department charged them with violating Section 1 of the Sherman Act—for entering into agreements that unreasonably restrained trade.

5. Answer: Answers will vary.

CHAPTER 39

1. Answer: During the first year, credit card fees must be less than 25 percent of a card's credit limit.

3. Answer: Ads on Instagram must clearly indicate that they are ads. Two weeks later, "#ad" was added at the beginning of this post.

5. Answer: The Fair Credit Reporting Act required TNT to ask Drury's permission before requesting a consumer report. Then, before firing him, TNT was required to give him a copy of the report and a description of his rights under this statute. *Drury v. TNT Holland Motor Express, Inc.*, 885 F. Supp. 161, 1994 U.S. Dist. LEXIS 11583 (D.Ct. 1994).

CHAPTER 40

1. Answer: Ahmad was convicted of transporting hazardous waste in violation of the Resource Conservation and Recovery Act. He was subject to criminal penalties under the Act. *United States v. Ahmad*, 1995 U.S. App. LEXIS 28350 (9th Cir. 1995).

3. Answer: The Department had to conduct an EA (environmental assessment) to determine if an EIS (environmental impact statement) was necessary.

5. Answer: The court ruled that the Navy did not have to file an EIS. The president—the commander in chief—determined that training with sonar was essential to national security. The courts do not have enough information to overrule him on national security issues. *Winter v. Natural Resources Defense Council, Inc.*, 555 U.S. 7(S.Ct. 2008).

CHAPTER 41

1. Answer: No, while the Mac n' Cheeser was new, useful, and nonobvious at the time it was invented, David's disclosure to the kitchen products companies years before renders it not novel now. Inventors have a grace period of one year once disclosure is made to apply for a patent. That time lapsed. Patent rejected.

3. Answer: The court held that *Sesame Street* had not infringed Reyher's copyright because Reyher could not copyright the plot of a story, only her expression of the plot. *Reyher v. Children's Television Workshop*, 533 F.2d 87, 190 U.S.P.Q. (BNA) 387 (2d Cir. 1976).

5. Answer: Yes, it won a claim under the Trademark Dilution Act.

CHAPTER 42

1. Answer: The trial court was wrong. The church held a fee simple defeasible. The moment the church ceased to use the property as a church, the land reverted automatically to Collins and his heirs. *Collins v. Church of God of Prophecy*, 304 Ark. 37, 800 S.W.2d 418, 1990 Ark. LEXIS 566 (1990).

3. Answer: Yes, the city could use its zoning powers to deny the license. Earlier zoning ordinances had allowed topless dancing in the section of the city where the pub was located, but the current ordinance prohibited such dancing in that section. The city had no obligation to grant a variance for the Delucas and denied the request. Jonathan Saltzman, "License Is Denied for Topless Dancing at Downtown Pub," *Providence Journal-Bulletin*, July 11, 1995, p. 2C.

5. Answer: *Mendez v. Rancho Valencia Resort Partners*, 3 Cal.App.5th 248 (2016). The couple sued for nuisance. The trial court entered a judgment for the hotel and the couple appealed. The judgment of the lower court was upheld. As the trial court noted, "[t]his is one of those situations, so common in discussions of legal philosophy, where reasonable minds can differ. It is not unreasonable for someone . . . to retire for the evening before 10:00 p.m. It is similarly not unreasonable for people . . . to value their solitude and to prefer the sounds of nature to those associated with human habitation. . . . Others find music and laughter, in moderation and at a reasonable hour, pleasant, or at least not disturbing." **558 Given all of the evidence, the trial court reasonably determined that it "cannot conclude that noise levels from the Resort that otherwise comply with the General Sound Level Limits of the County Noise Ordinance are nonetheless 'disturbing, excessive or offensive' within the meaning of section 36.414."

CHAPTER 43

1. Answer: Ann does. Ann's father made a valid *inter vivos* gift of the violin while Ann was still a student. He intended to transfer ownership to her immediately and made delivery by permitting her to pick up the violin. From that point on, Ann owned it. *Rylands v. Rylands*, 1993 Conn. Super. LEXIS 823 (Conn. Super. Ct. 1993).

3. Answer: Murphy gets the $25,000. There was delivery, acceptance, and adequate evidence that Kenney intended the items as gifts. Murphy is not entitled to the shares, though, because without the endorsement there is no delivery, an essential element. Kenney lived for two weeks after instructing Murphy to write her name on the shares, and during that time he should have endorsed them to her or caused a broker to do so. *In re Estate of Kenney*, 1993 Ohio App. LEXIS 2481 (Ohio Ct. of App., 1993).

5. Answer: Based on *Allen Chase v. Hilton Hotels*, 682 F. Supp. 316 (1988). The court limited Chase's recovery to $500 per the statute.

CHAPTER 44

1. Answer: Answers will vary. It depends on the number of siblings you have in relation to the number of children in each of the other branches of the family. For example, if the decedents had two children, under per stirpes distribution, they would each inherit half the estate. If the children were dead, their children (the grandchildren of the decedents) would split the parents' portions. So, if you were an only child, you would get half the estate. If you had three siblings, you would get 1/4 of half, or 1/8 of the estate. In the same example, but under per capita, each grandchild would get 1/5 of the estate. So, per stirpes is better if you have few siblings; per capita is better if your sibling group is larger than the average sibling group in the extended family.

3. Answer: Harvey sued Allstate for a violation of the covenant of good faith and fair dealing. A jury awarded her $94,000 plus attorney's fees. *Harvey v. Allstate Insurance Co.*, 1993 U.S. app. LEXIS 33865 (10th Cir. 1993).

5. Answer: Did Carlson have an insurable interest? The court denied the insurance company's motion for summary judgment in its suit seeking a declaration that Carlson did not have an insurable interest. That was in 2010 and there have been no further proceedings, which indicates the case may have settled. There was lots of suspicious evidence, however. Tomlinson's children say that she never took baths. When she applied for insurance, she claimed assets of $47 million. In fact, she had virtually no assets. Carlson had taken out a loan at 17 percent interest to pay the premiums, and the loan was about to come due. *Am. Gen. Life Ins. Co. v. Germaine Tomlinson Ins. Trust*, 2010 U.S. Dist. LEXIS 103730 (S.D. Ind. Sept. 30, 2010).

GLOSSARY

A

Absolute privilege A witness testifying in a court or legislature may never be sued for defamation.

Acceptance Retention of the collateral by a secured party as full or partial satisfaction of a debt.

Accept To sign a draft.

Accession Occurs when one person uses labor, materials, or both to add value to personal property belonging to another person.

Accommodated party Someone who receives a benefit from an accommodation party.

Accommodation party Someone other than an issuer, acceptor, or indorser who adds her signature to an instrument for the purpose of being liable on it.

Accord and satisfaction A completed agreement to settle a debt for less than the sum claimed.

Accredited investors Institutions (such as banks and insurance companies) or financially qualified individuals.

Act Any action that a party was not legally required to take in the first place.

Activist investor A shareholder with a large block of stock whose goal is to influence management decisions and strategic direction.

Additional terms Proposed contract terms that raise issues not included in the offer.

Adhesion contracts Standard form contracts prepared by one party and presented to the other on a "take it or leave it" basis.

Adjudicate To hold a formal hearing about an issue and then decide it.

Administrative law judge (ALJ) An agency employee who acts as an impartial decision maker.

Adoption When a corporation accepts legal responsibility for a contract.

Affirm To allow the decision to stand.

Affirmative action programs These programs remedy the effects of past discrimination.

Affirmed Permitted to stand.

After-acquired property Items that the debtor obtains after the parties have made their security agreement.

Agent In an agency relationship, the person who is acting on behalf of a principal.

Agreement on Trade Related Aspects of Intellectual Property (TRIPs) A treaty on intellectual property.

Alternative dispute resolution Any other formal or informal process used to settle disputes without resorting to a trial.

Ambiguity When a provision in a contract is unclear by accident.

Annual report A document containing detailed financial information that public companies provide to their shareholders.

Annuity Provides payment to a beneficiary during his lifetime.

Antitakeover devices or shark repellents Defensive measures to protect against a hostile takeover.

Appeals courts Higher courts that review the trial record to see if the court made errors of law.

Appellant The party filing the appeal.

Appellee The party opposing the appeal.

Appraisal rights If a corporation decides to undertake a fundamental change, the company must buy back at fair value the stock of any shareholders who object.

Arbitration A binding process of resolving legal disputes by submitting them to a neutral third party.

Arson The malicious use of fire or explosives to damage or destroy real estate or personal property.

Artisan's lien A security interest in personal property.

Assault An act that makes a person reasonably fear an imminent battery.

Assignment Transferring contract *rights*.

Assignment of rights A transfer of benefits under a contract.

Assisted suicide or physician-assisted death When a doctor prescribes a lethal dose of medication for use by a terminal patient who is suffering intolerably.

Attachment A three-step process that creates an enforceable security interest.

Authorized and issued Stock has been authorized and sold; another word for it is *outstanding*.

Authorized and unissued Stock that has been authorized, but not yet sold.

Automatic stay Prohibits creditors from collecting debts that the bankrupt incurred before the petition was filed.

B

BACT Best available control technology.

Bailee A person who rightfully possesses goods belonging to another.

Bailee The one with temporary possession of another's goods.

Bailment Giving possession and control of personal property to another person.

Bailment The rightful possession of goods by one who is not the owner, usually by mutual agreement between the bailor and bailee.

Bailor One who creates a bailment by delivering goods to another.

Bailor The one who owns goods legally held by another.

Bait-and-switch A practice whereby sellers advertise products that are not generally available but are being used to draw interested parties in so that they will buy other products.

Bankrupt Someone who cannot pay his debts and files for protection under the Bankruptcy Code.

Bankruptcy estate The new legal entity created when a bankruptcy petition is filed. The debtor's existing assets pass into the estate.

Bargained for When something is sought by the promisor and given by the promise in exchange for their promises.

Battery An intentional touching of another person in a way that is harmful or offensive.

Bearer paper An instrument is bearer paper if it is made out to "bearer" or it is not made out to any specific person. It can be redeemed by any holder in due course.

Bench trial There is no jury; the judge reaches a verdict.

Beneficiary Someone who receives the financial proceeds of a trust.

Best efforts underwriting The underwriter does not buy the stock from the issuer but instead acts as the issuer's agent in selling the securities.

Beyond a reasonable doubt The government's burden of proof in a criminal prosecution.

Beyond a reasonable doubt The very high burden of proof in a criminal trial, demanding much more certainty than required in a civil trial.

Bilateral contract A promise made in exchange for another promise.

Bill A proposed statute, submitted to Congress or a state legislature.

Binder A short document acknowledging receipt of an application and premium for an insurance policy. It indicates that a policy is temporarily in effect.

Blue sky laws State securities statutes.

Bona fide occupational qualification (BFOQ) An employer is permitted to establish discriminatory job requirements if they are *essential* to the position in question.

Breach of the peace Any action that disturbs public tranquility and order.

Briefs Written arguments on the case.

But-for causation The retaliatory action would not have occurred but for the defendant's discriminatory intent.

Buyer in the ordinary course of business (BIOC) One who acts in good faith, without knowing that the sale violates the owner's rights.

Buyer in ordinary course of business (BIOC) Someone who buys goods in good faith from a seller who routinely deals in such goods.

Bylaws A document that specifies the organizational rules of a corporation or other organization, such as the date of the annual meeting and the required number of directors.

C

C corporation A corporation that provides limited liability to its owners, but is a taxable entity.

Cap and Trade A market-based system for reducing emissions.

Cashier's check A check drawn on the bank itself. It is a promise that the bank will pay out of its own funds.

Certificate of deposit A note that is made by a bank (also known as a CD).

Certified check A check that the issuer's bank has signed, indicating its acceptance of the check.

Challenges for cause A claim that a juror has demonstrated probable bias.

Charging order A court order granting a third party the right to receive a share of partnership profits.

Check The most common form of a draft, it is an order telling a bank to pay money.

Check cards Another name for debit cards.

Check kiting Moving funds between bank accounts to take advantage of the float.

Chicago School A group of economists and lawyers at the University of Chicago who argued that the goal of antitrust enforcement should be efficiency.

Children's Online Privacy Protection Act of 1998 (COPPA) Federal statute enforced by the FTC regulating children's privacy online.

Choice of forum provisions Determine the state in which any litigation would take place.

Choice of law provisions Determine which state's laws will be used to interpret the contract.

Civil law Civil law regulates the rights and duties between parties.

Claim in recoupment The issuer subtracts (i.e., "sets off") any other claims he has against the initial payee from the amount he owes on the instrument.

Class action One plaintiff represents the entire group of plaintiffs, including those who are unaware of the lawsuit or even unaware they were harmed.

Classes and series Categories of stock with different rights.

Clean opinion An unqualified opinion, the most favorable report an auditor can give.

Close corporation A corporation with a small number of shareholders whose stock is not publicly traded and whose shareholders play an active role in management. It is entitled to special treatment under some state laws.

Codicil An amendment to a will.

Collective bargaining agreement (CBA) A contract between a union and a company.

Comment letter A letter from the SEC to an issuer with a list of changes that must be made to the registration statement.

Commerce Clause The part of Article I, section 8, that gives Congress the power to regulate commerce with foreign nations and among states.

Commercial impracticability The UCC may excuse contract performance when an unforeseen, external event disrupts the contract relationship.

Commercial speech Communication, such as advertisements, that has the dominant theme of proposing a business transaction.

Common carrier A company that transports goods and makes its services regularly available to the general public.

Common law Judge-made law.

Communications Decency Act of 1996 (CDA) Provides ISPs immunity from liability when information was provided by an end user.

Community property System of ownership of marital property in which assets earned during the marriage are owned jointly by the spouses.

Compensatory damages Money intended to restore a plaintiff to the position he was in before the injury.

Complaint A short, plain statement of the facts alleged and the legal claims made.

Compliance program A plan to prevent and detect improper conduct at all levels of the company.

Concerted action Tactics taken by union members to gain bargaining advantage.

Concurrent estates Two or more people owning property at the same time.

Condemnation Occurs when the government seizes private property and compensates the owner.

Condition A promise or undertaking contained in a lease whose breach may result in eviction.

Condition An event that must occur before a party becomes obligated under a contract.

Conditional promises Promises that a party agrees to perform only if the other side also does what it promised.

Conscious parallelism When competitors who do not have an explicit agreement nonetheless all make the same competitive decisions.

Consequential damages Are those resulting from the unique circumstances of the injured party.

Consequential damages Contract damages resulting as an indirect consequence of the breach.

Consideration The inducement, price, or promise that causes a person to enter into a contract and forms the basis for the parties' exchange.

Consumer credit contract A contract in which a consumer borrows money from a lender to purchase goods and services from a seller who is affiliated with the lender.

Consumer protection statute Laws protecting consumers from fraud.

Consumer report Any communication about a consumer's creditworthiness, character, general reputation, or lifestyle that is considered as a factor in establishing credit.

Consumer reporting agencies Businesses that collect and sell personal information on consumers to third parties.

Contract A legally enforceable agreement.

Contract carrier A company that transports goods for particular customers.

Control security Stock held by any shareholder who owns more than 10 percent of a class of stock or by any officer or director of the company.

Conversion (1) Someone has stolen an instrument or (2) a bank has paid a check that has a forged indorsement.

Conversion Taking or using someone's personal property without consent.

Corporate social responsibility An organization's obligation to contribute positively to the world around it.

Corporation by estoppel If a party enters into a contract believing in good faith that the corporation exists, that party cannot later take advantage of the fact that it does not.

Counterclaim A second lawsuit by the defendant against the plaintiff.

Counteroffer A different proposal made in response to an original offer.

Course of dealing The conduct between the parties during previous transactions.

Course of performance The conduct between the parties to a particular transaction.

Covenant A promise in a contract.

Covenant A promise or undertaking contained in a lease whose breach does not result in eviction.

Cover To make a good faith purchase of goods similar to those in the contract.

Cramdown When a court approves a plan of reorganization over the opposition of some creditors.

Credit score A number that is supposed to predict your ability to pay your bills.

Criminal law Criminal law prohibits certain behavior for the benefit of society.

Criminal law Prohibits and punishes conduct that threatens public safety and welfare.

Criminal procedure The process by which criminals are investigated, accused, tried, and sentenced.

Cross-elasticity of demand How high can your prices rise before buyers switch to a different product?

Cross-examine To ask questions of an opposing witness.

Customary international law International rules that have become binding through a pattern of consistent, longstanding behavior.

D

De facto A Latin phrase meaning "in fact."

***De facto* corporation** The promoter has made a good faith effort to incorporate and has actually used the corporation to conduct business.

De jure A Latin phrase meaning "by law."

***De jure* corporation** A promoter has substantially complied with the requirements for incorporation but has made some minor error.

Debtor Another term for bankrupt.

Debtor in possession The debtor acts as trustee in a Chapter 11 bankruptcy.

Default judgment A decision that the plaintiff wins without trial because the defendant failed to answer in time.

Default rules Rules that govern a partnership unless the partners agree otherwise.

Defendant The party being sued.

Deferred annuity contract The owner makes a lump-sum payment now but receives no income until a later date.

Deficiency Having insufficient funds to pay off a debt.

Delegation Transferring contract *duties*.

Delegation of duties A transfer of obligations under a contract.

Deontological From the Greek word for *obligation*; the duty to do the right thing, regardless of the result.

Deponent The person being questioned in a deposition.

Difference principle Rawls's suggestion that society should reward behavior that provides the most benefit to the community as a whole.

Direct damages Are the natural result of the breach.

Direct public offering (DPO) A method by which a company sells stock to the public itself, without an investment bank.

Directed verdict A ruling that the plaintiff has entirely failed to prove some aspect of her case.

Disability insurance Replaces the insured's income if he becomes unable to work because of illness or injury.

Disaffirm To give notice of refusal to be bound by an agreement.

Discharge A party is discharged when she has no more duties under the contract.

Discharge Liability on an instrument terminates.

Discharged The debtor no longer has an obligation to pay a debt.

Disclaimer A statement that a particular warranty does not apply.

Disclosure statement Provides creditors and shareholders with enough information to make an informed judgment about a proposed plan of reorganization.

Dishonor An obligor refuses to pay an instrument that is due.

Dissociation When a partner leaves the partnership.

Diversity jurisdiction Applies when (1) the plaintiff and defendant are citizens of different states and (2) the amount in dispute exceeds $75,000.

Domestic asset protection trusts (DAPTs) Creditors cannot reach the assets that a donor has placed in a DAPT.

Domestic corporation A corporation operating in the state in which it was incorporated.

Donee A person who receives a gift of property.

Donor A person who gives property away.

Double jeopardy A criminal defendant may be prosecuted only once for a particular criminal offense.

Draft An instrument ordering someone else to pay money.

Draft The drawer of this instrument orders someone else to pay money.

Drawee The bank on which a check is drawn.

Drawee The one ordered by the drawer to pay money to the payee.

Drawer The issuer of a draft.

Drawer The person who issues a draft.

Due diligence A reasonable investigation of a registration statement.

Due diligence An investigation of the registration statement by someone who signs it.

Due process Requires fundamental fairness at all stages of the case.

Duress An improper threat made to force another party to enter into a contract.

Dynasty or perpetual trusts Trusts that last forever.

E

Easement The right to cross or use someone else's land for a particular purpose.

Easement by grant Occurs when one party expressly transfers an easement to another party.

Easement by implication Results from surrounding circumstances that indicate that the parties must have intended an easement.

Easement by reservation Occurs when a party reserves the right to retain an easement in a transferred property.

Economic strike One intended to gain wages or benefits.

Electronic Communications Privacy Act of 1986 (ECPA) A federal statute prohibiting unauthorized interception of, access to, or disclosure of wire and electronic communications.

Embezzlement The fraudulent conversion of property already in the defendant's possession.

Eminent domain The power of the government to take private property for public use.

Eminent domain The government's right to take private property for public use upon just compensation to the owner.

Engagement letter A written contract by which a client hires an accountant.

Equal dignities rule If an agent is empowered to enter into a contract that must be in writing, then the appointment of the agent must also be written.

Equal Protection Clause A clause in the Fourteenth Amendment that generally requires the government to treat people equally.

Error of law Because of this, the appeals court may require a new trial.

Escalator clause A lease clause allowing the landlord to raise the rent for specified reasons.

Estates and interests Types of rights in land.

Ethics How people should behave.

Ethics decision Any choice about how a person should behave that is based on a sense of right and wrong.

EU General Data Protection Regulation (GDPR) Sets out the data privacy rights of all Europeans.

Eviction An act that forces a tenant to abandon the property.

Exclusionary rule Evidence obtained illegally may not be used at trial.

Exclusive dealing contract A contract in which a distributor or retailer agrees with a supplier not to carry the products of any other supplier.

Exculpatory clause A contract provision that attempts to release one party from liability in the event the other is injured.

Exculpatory clause A contract clause that attempts to relieve one of the parties from future liability.

Exculpatory clause A lease clause that relieves a landlord of liability for injuries.

Exculpatory clause A provision that protects directors from personal liability to the corporation and its shareholders.

Executed contract An agreement in which all parties have fulfilled their obligations.

Executory contract An agreement in which one or more parties has not yet fulfilled its obligations.

Expectation damages The money required to put one party in the position she would have been in had the other side performed the contract.

Express contract An agreement with all the important terms explicitly stated.

Express warranty One that the seller creates with his words or actions.

Externality When people do not bear the full cost of their decisions.

Extraterritoriality The power of one country's laws to reach activities outside of its borders.

F

Fair use doctrine Permits limited use of copyrighted material without permission of the author for purposes such as criticism, comment, news reporting, scholarship, or research.

False imprisonment The intentional restraint of another person without reasonable cause and without consent.

Federal question A case in which the claim is based on the U.S. Constitution, a federal statute, or a federal treaty.

Federal Sentencing Guidelines The detailed rules that judges must follow when sentencing defendants convicted of crimes in federal court.

Fee simple absolute Full ownership privileges in a property.

Felony A serious crime, for which a defendant can be sentenced to one year or more in prison.

Fiduciary relationship One party has an obligation (1) to act in a trustworthy fashion for the benefit of the other person and (2) to put that person's interests first.

Fiduciary relationship The trustee must act in the best interests of the beneficiary.

Financing statement A statement that gives the names of all parties, describes the collateral, and outlines the security interest.

Finding statutes Laws that govern found property, also known as estray statutes.

Firm commitment underwriting The underwriter buys stock from the issuer and resells it to the public.

Flow-through tax entity An organization that does not pay income tax on its profits but instead passes them through to its owners who pay personal income tax on all business profits.

Forbearance Refraining from doing something that one has a legal right to do.

***Force majeure* event** A disruptive, unexpected occurrence for which neither party is to blame that prevents one or both parties from complying with a contract.

Forced share or statutory share The percentage of a decedent's estate that a spouse is entitled to claim, regardless of the will's content.

Foreign corporation A corporation operating in a state in which it was not incorporated.

Foreign enforcement Means that the court system of a country will assist in enforcing or collecting on the verdict awarded by a foreign court.

Foreign Intelligence Surveillance Act (FISA) Federal statute governing the government's collection of foreign intelligence in the United States.

Foreign recognition Means that a foreign judgment has legal validity in another country.

Foreign Sovereign Immunities Act (FSIA) A U.S. statute that provides that American courts generally cannot entertain suits against foreign governments.

Franchise Disclosure Document (FDD) A disclosure document that a franchisor must deliver to a potential purchaser.

Fraud Deception for the purpose of obtaining money or property.

Fraud Injuring another person by deliberate deception.

Fraudulent transfer A transfer is fraudulent if it is made within the year before a petition is filed and its purpose is to hinder, delay, or defraud creditors.

Freehold estate The right to possess land for an undefined length of time.

Fresh start After the termination of a bankruptcy case, creditors cannot make a claim against the debtor for money owed before the initial bankruptcy petition was filed.

Fundamental rights Rights so basic that any governmental interference with them is suspect and likely to be unconstitutional.

G

GAAP "Generally accepted accounting principles," the rules for preparing financial statements.

GAAS "Generally accepted auditing standards," the rules for conducting audits.

Gap period The period between the time that a creditor files an involuntary petition and the court issues the order for relief.

Gap-filler provisions UCC rules for supplying missing terms.

General Agreement on Trade in Services (GATS) A treaty on transnational services.

General partner One of the owners of a general partnership.

Geographic market Areas where the same purchase can be made.

Gharar The Islamic prohibition on risk and deception.

Gift A voluntary transfer of property from one person to another, without consideration.

Gift *causa mortis* A gift made in contemplation of approaching death.

Go effective The SEC authorizes a company to begin the public sale of its stock.

Going dark When a company deregisters under the 1934 Act.

Good faith An honest effort to meet both the spirit and letter of the contract.

Good faith The UCC requires that contracting parties perform and enforce their deals honestly.

Goods Are things that are movable, other than money and investment securities.

Grand jury A group of ordinary citizens that decides whether there is probable cause the defendant committed the crime with which she is charged.

Grantor Someone who creates and funds a trust, also called a *settlor* or *donor*.

Gratuitous agent Someone not paid for performing duties.

Gratuitous assignment One made as a gift, for no consideration.

Greenhouse gases or GHGs Gases that trap heat in the Earth's atmosphere, thereby causing global warming.

Guilty A judge or jury's finding that a defendant has committed a crime.

H

Hacking Gaining unauthorized access to a computer system.

Harmless error A mistake by the trial judge that was too minor to affect the outcome.

Healthcare proxy Someone who is appointed to make healthcare decisions on behalf of a person who is not competent to do so.

Health maintenance organization (HMO) Generally, patients can only be treated by doctors who are employees of the organization.

Holder For order paper, the holder is anyone in possession of the instrument if it is payable to or indorsed to her. For bearer paper, the holder is anyone in possession.

Holder in due course Someone who has given value for an instrument, in good faith, without notice of outstanding claims or other defenses.

Holographic will A will that is handwritten and signed by the testator, but not witnessed.

Horizontal agreement An agreement among competitors.

Hostile takeovers An attempt by an outsider to acquire a company in the face of opposition from the target corporation's board of directors.

I

IFRS "International financial reporting standards," an international alternative to GAAP.

Incidental beneficiary Someone who might have benefited from a contract between two others but has no right to enforce that agreement.

Incidental damages Relatively minor costs that the injured party suffers when responding to the breach.

Incorporator The person who signs the charter and files it with the secretary of state.

Incoterms rules A series of three-letter codes used in international contracts for the sale of goods.

Indemnification provision A company pays the legal fees of directors who are sued for actions taken on behalf of the company.

Independent directors Members of the board of directors who are not employees of the company and do not have close ties to the CEO. Also known as outside directors.

Indictment The government's formal charge that the defendant has committed a crime and must stand trial.

Indorsement The signature of a payee.

Indorser Anyone, other than an issuer or acceptor, who signs an instrument.

Injunction A court order that requires someone to do something or refrain from doing something.

Inside directors Members of the board of directors who are also employees of the corporation.

Insiders Family members of an individual debtor, officers and directors of a corporation, or partners of a partnership that has filed for bankruptcy.

Installment contract Agreement in which performance is to be made in a series of separate payments or deliveries.

Integrated contract A writing that the parties intend as the final, complete expression of their agreement.

Intended beneficiary Someone who may enforce a contract made between two other parties.

Intentional infliction of emotional distress An intentional tort in which the harm results from extreme and outrageous conduct that causes serious emotional harm.

Intentional torts Harm caused by a deliberate action.

***Inter vivos* gift** A gift made during the donor's life, with no fear of impending death.

Inter vivos trust or living trust Established while the grantor is alive.

Interest A legal right in something.

Intermediary agent Someone who hires subagents for the principal.

International Court of Arbitration (ICA) A forum for international dispute resolution, run by the ICC.

International Court of Justice (ICJ) The judicial branch of the United Nations.

Internet service providers (ISPs) Companies that connect users to the internet.

Inventory Goods that a seller is holding for sale or lease in the ordinary course of its business.

Investigative reports Discuss character, reputation, or lifestyle. They become obsolete in three months.

Invitee A person who has a right to enter another's property because it is a public place or a business open to the public.

Involuntary bailment A bailment that occurs without an agreement between the bailor and bailee.

Involuntary petition Filed by creditors to initiate a bankruptcy case.

Issuer A company that sells its own stock.

Issuer The maker of a promissory note or the drawer of a draft.

J

Joint and several All members of a group are liable. They can be sued as a group, or any of them can be sued individually for the full amount owing. But the plaintiff may not recover more than 100 percent of her damages.

Joint and several liability The partnership and the partners are all individually liable for the full amount of the debt, but the creditor cannot collect more than the total amount he is owed.

Joint tenancy Two or more people holding equal interest in a property, with the right of survivorship.

Joint venture A partnership for a limited purpose.

Jointly and severally liable All members of a group are liable. They can be sued as a group, or any one of them can be sued individually for the full amount owed. But the plaintiff cannot recover more than the total she is owed.

Judgment *non obstante veredicto* (JNOV) A judgment notwithstanding the jury's verdict.

Judgment rate The interest rate that courts use on court-ordered judgments.

Judicial activism A court's willingness to decide issues on constitutional grounds.

Judicial restraint A court's attitude that it should leave lawmaking to legislators.

Jurisdiction A court's power to hear a case.

Jurisprudence The philosophy of law.

Jus cogens When rule of customary international law becomes a fundamental legal principle across all nations, it cannot be changed by custom or practice.

K

Kant's categorical imperative An act is only ethical if it would be acceptable for everyone to do the same thing.

Kantian Evasion or palter A truthful statement that is nonetheless misleading.

Key person life insurance Companies buy insurance on their officers to help the company to recover if they were to die.

L

Landlord The owner of a freehold estate who allows another person temporarily to live on his property.

Larceny The trespassory taking of personal property with the intent to steal it.

Lease An agreement in which an owner gives a tenant the right to use property.

Leasehold interest One party has the right to occupy the property for a given length of time.

Letter of intent A letter that summarizes negotiating progress.

Liability insurance Reimburses the insured for any liability she incurs by accidentally harming someone else.

Libel Written defamation.

Libel per se When written statements relate to criminal or sexual conduct, contagious diseases, or professional abilities, they are assumed to be harmful to the subject's reputation.

License The right to temporarily enter land belonging to another.

Licensee A person on another's land for her own purposes but with the owner's permission.

Lien An encumbrance on a property to secure a debt.

Lien A security interest created by law, rather than by agreement.

Life estate Ownership of property for the lifetime of a particular person.

Life insurance Provides for payments to a beneficiary upon the death of the insured.

Life Principles The rules by which you live your life.

Life prospects The circumstances into which we are born.

Limitation of remedy clause Contract clause allowing parties to limit or exclude applicable UCC remedies.

Liquidated damages clause A clause stating in advance how much a party must pay if it breaches.

Liquidated debt A debt in which there is no dispute about the amount owed.

Litigation The process of filing claims in court and ultimately going to trial.

Lockout Management prohibits workers from entering the premises.

Long-arm statute A statute that gives a court jurisdiction over someone who commits a tort, signs a contract, or conducts "regular business activities" in the state.

M

MACT Maximum achievable control technology.

Mailbox rule Acceptance is generally effective upon dispatch. Terminations are effective when received.

Majority voting Directors must resign if more than half of the shares that vote in an uncontested election withhold their vote from them.

Maker The issuer of a note.

Maker The issuer of a promissory note.

Making demand When shareholders ask the board of directors to authorize litigation on behalf of the corporation.

Managed care plans Health insurance plans that limit treatment choices to reduce costs.

Material Important enough to affect an investor's decision.

Material Important to the insurer's decision to issue a policy or set a premium amount.

Material breach A violation of a contract that defeats an essential purpose of the agreement.

Mechanic's lien A security created when a worker improves real property.

Merchant Generally, someone who routinely deals in the particular goods involved.

Merchantable The goods are fit for the ordinary purpose for which they are used.

Minute book A book that contains a record of a corporation's official actions.

Mirror image rule Requires that acceptance be on precisely the same terms as the offer.

Misdemeanor A less serious crime, often punishable by less than a year in a county jail.

Mitigate To keep damages as low as reasonable.

Modify To affirm the outcome but with changes.

Money laundering Using the proceeds of criminal acts either to promote crime or conceal the source of the money.

Moral licensing After doing something ethical, many people then have a tendency to act unethically.

Moral relativism A belief that a decision may be right even if it is not in keeping with one's own ethics standards.

Moral universalism A belief that some acts are always right or always wrong.

Mortgage A security interest in real property.

Mortgagee The party acquiring a security interest in property.

Mortgagor An owner who gives a security interest in property in order to obtain a loan.

Most favored nation WTO/GATT requires that favors offered to one country must be given to all member nations.

Motion A formal request to the court that it take some step or issue some order.

Motion for a protective order Request that the court limit discovery.

Motion to dismiss A request that the court terminate a case because the law does not offer a legal remedy for the plaintiff's problem.

N

NAAQS National ambient air quality standards.

National treatment The principle of nondiscrimination between foreigners and locals.

Negotiated An instrument has been transferred to the holder by someone other than the issuer.

NESHAPS National Emission Standards for Hazardous Air Pollutants.

Net neutrality The principle that all information flows on the internet must receive equal treatment.

Net returns on invested capital The company's return on its capital investments, such as plants and equipment, less the opportunity cost of those investments.

New York Convention Widely accepted treaty on the court enforcement of arbitral awards.

Nominal damages A token sum, such as one dollar, given to a plaintiff who demonstrates a breach but no serious injury.

Noncompetition agreement A contract in which one party agrees not to compete with another.

Nonconforming goods Merchandise that differs from what is specified in the contract.

Nonphysical tort One that harms only reputation, feelings, or wallet.

Nonpoint source Pollutants that have no single source, such as water runoff from city streets.

North American Free Trade Agreement (NAFTA) A treaty that reduced trade barriers among Canada, the United States, and Mexico.

No-strike clause A clause in a CBA that prohibits the union from striking while the CBA is in force.

Notice to quit A landlord's notice terminating a tenancy.

Novation A new contract.

Novation A three-way agreement in which the obligor transfers all rights and duties to a third party.

Nuncupative will An oral will.

O

Obligor The party obligated to do something.

Offer An act or statement that proposes definite terms and permits the other party to create a contract by accepting those terms.

Offeree The person to whom an offer is made.

Offeror The person who makes an offer.

Optimism bias A belief that the outcome of an event will be more positive than the evidence warrants.

Order for relief An official acknowledgment that a debtor is under the jurisdiction of the bankruptcy court.

Order paper An instrument that includes the words "pay to the order of" or their equivalent.

Output contract Obligates the seller to sell all of his output to the buyer, who agrees to accept it.

Output contract Contract in which the seller guarantees to sell all of its output to one buyer, and the buyer agrees to accept the entire quantity.

P

Paris Accord An agreement to prevent climate change by reducing GHGs.

Partition by kind A form of partition in which a property is divided among co-owners.

Partnership An unincorporated association of two or more co-owners who operate a business for profit.

Partnership at will A partnership with no fixed duration. Any of the partners may leave at any time, for any reason.

Partnership by estoppel Two parties incur the liability of a partnership without actually being partners.

Patent A patent gives inventors the right to prevent others from making, using, or selling their invention for a limited time.

Payable on demand The maker must pay whenever he is asked.

Payday loans Small loans with high interest rates made to people who need money to make it to the next paycheck.

Payee Someone who is owed money under the terms of an instrument.

Pay for service plans The insurer pays for whatever treatments a doctor orders.

Per capita Each heir receives the same amount.

***Per se* violation** An automatic breach of antitrust laws.

Per stirpes Each branch of the family receives an equal share.

Peremptory challenges The right to excuse a juror for virtually any reason.

Perfect Tender Rule Under the UCC, tendered goods must be exactly as described in the contract.

Periodic tenancy A lease for a fixed period, automatically renewable unless terminated.

Perpetual or dynasty trusts Trusts that last forever.

Personal jurisdiction A court's authority to bind the defendant to its decisions.

Personal property All tangible property other than real property.

Personal satisfaction contract Permits the promisee to make subjective evaluations of the promisor's performance.

Phishing A fraudster sends a message directing the recipient to enter personal information on a website that is an illegal imitation of a legitimate site.

Physician-assisted death or assisted suicide When a doctor prescribes a lethal dose of medication for use by a terminal patient who is suffering intolerably.

Pierce the corporate veil A court holds shareholders personally liable for the debts of the corporation.

Piercing the company veil A court holds members of an LLC personally liable for the debts of the organization.

Plaintiff The party who is suing.

Plea bargain An agreement in which the defendant pleads guilty to a reduced charge, and the prosecution recommends to the judge a relatively lenient sentence.

Pleadings The documents that begin a lawsuit, consisting of the complaint, the answer, and sometimes a reply.

Pledge A secured transaction in which a debtor gives collateral to the secured party.

Plurality voting To be elected, a candidate only needs to receive more votes than his opponent, not a majority of the votes cast.

Point source Discharges from a single producer.

Preauthorized transfer An electronic fund transfer authorized in advance to recur at regular intervals.

Precedent An earlier case that decided the issue.

Precedent Earlier decisions by the state appellate courts on similar or identical issues.

Precedent The tendency to decide current cases based on previous rulings.

Preferences When a debtor unfairly pays creditors immediately before filing a bankruptcy petition.

Preferred stock The owners of preferred stock have preference on dividends and also, typically, in liquidation.

Preponderance of the evidence The plaintiff's burden of proof in a civil lawsuit.

Presentment A holder of an instrument demands payment from someone who is obligated to pay it.

Pretermitted child A child who is left nothing under the parent's will.

Prima facie From the Latin, meaning "from its first appearance," something that appears to be true upon a first look.

Principal In an agency relationship, the person for whom an agent is acting.

Private international law International rules and standards applying to cross-border commerce.

Private offering A sale of securities in which the issuer provides less disclosure in return for selling less stock to fewer investors than in a public offering.

Probable cause It is likely that evidence of a crime will be found in the place to be searched.

Procedural due process The doctrine that ensures that before the government takes liberty or property, the affected person has a fair chance to oppose the action.

Procedural unconscionability One party uses its superior power to force a contract on the weaker party.

Product market Items that compete against each other for purchase.

Profit The right to enter land belonging to another and take something from it.

Promisee The contract party *to whom* a promise is made.

Promisor Makes the promise that a third party seeks to enforce.

Promissory estoppel A *possible* remedy for an injured plaintiff in a case with no valid contract, when the plaintiff can show a promise, reasonable reliance, and injustice.

Promissory note A written promise to pay money.

Proof of claim A form stating the name of an unsecured creditor and the amount of the claim against the debtor.

Proper purpose One that aids a shareholder in managing and protecting her investment.

Prospectus A document that provides potential investors with information about a security.

Protected categories Race, color, religion, sex, or national origin.

Proxy The person whom a shareholder appoints to vote for her at a meeting of the corporation; also, the document a shareholder signs appointing this substitute voter.

Proxy advisory firms Companies that advise shareholders on how to vote in corporate elections.

Proxy statement Information a company provides to shareholders in preparation for the annual meeting.

Public Company Accounting Oversight Board (PCAOB) The PCAOB regulates public accounting firms.

Public disclosure of private facts A tort providing redress to victims of unauthorized and embarrassing disclosures.

Public international law Rules and norms governing relationships among states and international organizations.

Punitive damages Damages that are intended to punish the defendant for conduct that is extreme and outrageous.

Purchase money security interest (PMSI) An interest taken by the person who sells the collateral or advances money so the debtor can buy it.

Purchaser representative Has enough knowledge and experience to evaluate stock purchases.

Q

Qualified mortgage (QM) A mortgage that, according to the CFPB, complies with TILA.

Qualified privilege Employers who give references are liable only for false statements that they know to be false or that are primarily motivated by ill will.

Qualify to do business Registering as a foreign corporation in any state in which a business operates but was not incorporated.

Quantum meruit "As much as he deserves"—the damages awarded in a quasi-contract case.

Quasi-contract A *possible* remedy for an injured plaintiff in a case with no valid contract, when the plaintiff can show benefit to the defendant, reasonable expectation of payment, and unjust enrichment.

Quorum A certain percentage of the company's shares are represented, either in person or by proxy, at a meeting.

Quorum How many people or shares must be present for a meeting to count.

R

Racketeer Influenced and Corrupt Organizations Act (RICO) A powerful federal statute, originally aimed at organized crime, now used against many ordinary businesses.

Racketeering acts Any of a long list of specified crimes, such as embezzlement, arson, mail fraud, wire fraud, and so forth.

Ratification Words or actions indicating an intention to be bound by a contract.

Reaffirm To promise to pay a debt even after it is discharged.

Reasonable expectation of privacy The test to analyze whether privacy should be protected.

Reasonably Ordinary or usual under the circumstances.

Reciprocal promises Promises that are each enforceable independently.

Record date Everyone who owns stock on this date is entitled to vote at the shareholders meeting.

Redeem To pay the full value of a debt to get the collateral back.

Reformation A court may partially rewrite a contract to fix a mistake or cure an unenforceable provision.

Regional trade agreements (RTAs) Treaties that reduce trade restrictions and promote common policies among member nations.

Registration statement The document that an issuer files with the SEC to initiate a public offering of securities.

Reliance interest Puts the injured party in the position he would have been in had the parties never entered into a contract.

Remainder The right of a third person to property upon the death of a life tenant.

Remedy A court's compensation to the injured party.

Rent Compensation paid by a tenant to a landlord.

Rent abatement A reduction in the rent owed.

Reply An answer to a counterclaim.

Reporting companies Companies registered under the 1934 Act.

Representations and warranties Statements of fact about the past or present.

Requirements contract Contract in which a buyer agrees to purchase all of her goods from one seller.

Requirements contract Obligates a buyer to obtain all of his needed goods from the seller.

Res ipsa loquitur The facts *imply* that the defendant's negligence caused the accident.

Resale price maintenance (RPM) A manufacturer sets minimum prices that retailers may charge.

Rescind To cancel.

Rescind To cancel a contract.

Rescind To terminate a contract by mutual agreement.

Rescission To "undo" a contract and put the parties where they were before they made the agreement.

Respondeat superior A principal is liable for certain torts committed by an agent.

Restitution A court order that a guilty defendant reimburse the victim for the harm suffered.

Restitution Restoring an injured party to its original position.

Restitution interest Designed to return to the injured party a benefit he has conferred on the other party.

Restricted security Stock purchased in a private offering.

Restricted stock Securities purchased strictly for investment purposes.

Reverse and remand To nullify the lower decision and return the case for reconsideration or retrial.

Reverse discrimination Making an employment decision that harms a white person or a man because of his gender, color, or race.

Reversed Nullified.

Reversion The right of an owner (or her heirs) to property upon the death of a life tenant.

Reversionary interest The landlord's right to occupy the property at the end of the lease.

Revocable A trust that can be terminated or changed at any time.

Rider An amendment or addition to a contract.

Right to cure The UCC gives the seller the opportunity to fix the problem of non-conforming goods.

Road show As part of the sales process, company executives and investment bankers make presentations to potential investors.

Rule against perpetuities A trust must end within 21 years of the death of some named person who was alive when the trust was created.

Rule of reason violation An action that breaches antitrust laws only if it has an anticompetitive impact.

S

S corporation A corporation that provides limited liability to its owners and the tax status of a flow-through entity.

Scienter Acting with the intent to deceive or with deliberate recklessness.

Scienter An action is done knowingly or recklessly with an intent to deceive, manipulate, or defraud.

Scrivener's error A typo.

Secondary boycott A picket line established not at the employer's premises but at a different workplace.

Secondary offering Any public sale of securities by an issuer after the initial public offering.

Securities Act of 1933 Also referred to as the 1933 Act, this statute regulates the issuance of new securities.

Securities Exchange Act of 1934 Also referred to as the 1934 Act, this statute regulates companies with publicly traded securities.

Security Any transaction in which the buyer invests money in a common enterprise and expects to earn a profit predominantly from the efforts of others.

Security interests Rights in personal property that assure payment or the performance of some obligation.

Sight draft Payable on demand.

Signature liability The liability of someone who signs an instrument.

Single recovery principle Requires a court to settle the matter once and for all by awarding a lump sum for past and future expenses.

Sit-down strike Members stop working but remain at their job posts, blocking replacement workers.

Slander Oral defamation.

Slander per se When oral statements relate to criminal or sexual conduct, contagious diseases, or professional abilities, they are assumed to be harmful to the subject's reputation.

SLAPP A SLAPP, or strategic lawsuit against public participation, is a defamation lawsuit whose main objective is to silence speech through intimidation, rather than win a defamation case on the merits.

Social enterprises These organizations pledge to behave in a socially responsible manner even as they pursue profits.

Sole discretion The absolute right to make any decision on an issue.

Sole proprietorship An unincorporated business owned by one person.

Sophisticated investors People who can assess the risks of an offering.

Sovereign The recognized political power, whom citizens obey.

Spam Unsolicited commercial email.

Spear phishing Involves personalized messages that look as if they have been sent by someone the victim knows.

Special committee Independent board members form a committee to review a transaction that violates the business judgment rule.

Specific performance A court order requiring the seller to perform as promised.

Specific performance Forces both parties to complete the deal.

Stakeholder Anyone who is affected by the activities of a corporation, such as employees, customers, creditors, suppliers, shareholders, and the communities in which they operate.

Stare decisis "Let the decision stand," that is, the ruling from a previous case.

Stare decisis The principle that legal conclusions must be reached after an analysis of past judgments.

Stationary source Any building or facility that emits a certain level of pollution.

Statute A law created by a legislature.

Statute of limitations A statutory time limit within which an injured party must file suit.

Stored Communications Act The section of the ECPA that prohibits the unlawful access to stored communications, such as email.

Straight bankruptcy Also known as liquidation, this form of bankruptcy mandates that the bankrupt's assets be distributed to creditors, but the debtor has no obligation to share future earnings.

Strict liability A branch of tort law that imposes a much higher level of liability when harm results from ultrahazardous acts or defective products.

Strict performance Requires one party to perform its obligations precisely, with no deviation from the contract terms.

Subagent Someone appointed by an agent to perform the agent's duties.

Subject matter jurisdiction A court's authority to hear a particular type of case.

Subpoena An order to appear at a particular place and time. A subpoena *duces tecum* requires the person to produce certain documents or things.

Substantial performance Occurs when one party fulfills enough of its contract obligations to warrant payment.

Substantive due process A form of due process that holds that certain rights are so fundamental that the government may not eliminate them.

Substantive unconscionability A contract with extremely one-sided and unfair terms.

Summary judgment A ruling by the court that no trial is necessary because there are no essential facts in dispute.

Summons The court's written notice that a lawsuit has been filed against the defendant.

Superfund Another name for the Comprehensive Environmental Response, Compensation, and Liability Act (CERCLA).

Supervisor Anyone with the authority to make independent decisions on hiring, firing, disciplining, or promoting other workers.

The Supremacy Clause Makes the Constitution, and federal statutes and treaties, the supreme law of the land.

Surplus A sum of money greater than the debt incurred.

T

Takings Clause A clause in the Fifth Amendment that ensures that when any governmental unit takes private property for public use, it must compensate the owner.

Tenancy at sufferance A tenancy that exists without the permission of the landlord, after the expiration of a true tenancy.

Tenancy at will A tenancy with no fixed duration, which may be terminated by either party at any time.

Tenancy by the entirety A system of ownership of marital property in which each spouse owns the entire estate.

Tenancy for years A lease for a stated, fixed period.

Tenancy in common Two or more people holding equal interest in a property, but with no right of survivorship.

Tenant A person given temporary possession of the landlord's property.

Tender offer A public offer to buy a block of stock directly from shareholders.

Term partnership A partnership in which the partners agree in advance how long it will last.

Termination statement A document indicating that a secured party no longer claims a security interest in the collateral.

Testamentary trust A trust that goes into effect when a grantor dies.

Tied product In a tying arrangement, the product that a buyer must purchase as the condition for being allowed to buy another product.

Time draft Payable in the future.

Time is of the essence clause Generally make contract dates strictly enforceable.

TMDLs Total maximum daily loads of permitted pollution.

Tort A violation of a duty imposed by the civil law.

Tortious interference with a contract An intentional tort in which the defendant improperly induced a third party to breach a contract with the plaintiff.

Tortious interference with a prospective advantage Malicious interference with a developing economic relationship.

Total shareholder return The percentage increase in stock price appreciation and dividends.

Toxic succession Anyone who has ever owned a polluted property is liable for its clean-up.

Tracing An auditor takes an item of original data and tracks it forward to ensure that it has been properly recorded throughout the bookkeeping process.

Trade acceptance A draft drawn by a seller of goods on the buyer and payable to the seller or some third party.

Trade secret A formula, device, process, method, or compilation of information that, when used in business, gives the owner an advantage over competitors.

Trademark Any combination of words and symbols that a business uses to identify its products or services and distinguish them from others.

Treasury stock Stock that a company has sold, but later bought back.

Treaty An agreement between two or more states that is governed by international law.

Trespass Intentionally entering land that belongs to someone else or remaining on the land after being asked to leave.

Trespasser A person on another's property without consent.

Trial courts Determine the facts of a particular dispute and apply to those facts the law given by earlier appellate court decisions.

Trust An entity that separates the legal and beneficial ownership of assets.

Trustee Someone who manages the assets of a trust.

Tying arrangement An agreement to sell a product on the condition that a buyer also purchases another, usually less desirable, product.

Tying product In a tying arrangement, the product offered for sale on the condition that another product be purchased as well.

U

U.S. Trustee Oversees the administration of bankruptcy law in a region.

***Ultra vires* doctrine** A corporation cannot undertake any transaction unless its charter permits it.

Unconscionable A contract that is shockingly one-sided and fundamentally unfair.

Unilateral mistake Occurs when only one party enters a contract under a mistaken assumption.

Unliquidated A debt that is disputed because the parties disagree over its existence or amount.

Usage of trade A practice or way of dealing that is expected in an industry.

User-generated content Any content created and made publicly available by end users.

Utter To pass on an instrument that one knows to be forged.

V

Vagueness The parties to a contract deliberately include a provision that is unclear.

Value The holder has already done something in exchange for the instrument.

Value-based care Payment to medical providers is based on patient outcomes, not quantity and complexity of services performed.

Variance A variation from the applicable zoning law.

Veil of ignorance The rules for society that we would propose if we did not know how lucky we would be in life's lottery.

Vertical agreement An agreement among participants operating at different stages of the production process.

Veto The power of the president to reject legislation passed by Congress.

Void agreement A contract that neither party can enforce, because the bargain is illegal or one of the parties had no legal authority to make it.

Voidable contract An agreement that may be terminated by one of the parties.

Voidable contract When a contract is voidable, the injured party may choose to terminate it.

Voidable title Limited rights in goods, inferior to those of the owner.

Voir dire The process of selecting a jury.

Voluntary petition Filed by a debtor to initiate a bankruptcy case.

Vouching An auditor chooses a transaction listed in a company's books and checks backward for original data to support it.

W

Warrant Written permission from a neutral officer to conduct a search.

Warranty A contractual assurance that goods will meet certain standards.

Warranty liability The liability of someone who receives payment on an instrument.

Whistleblower Someone who discloses wrongdoing.

Will A legal document that disposes of the testator's property after death.

Wiretap Act The section of the ECPA that prohibits the interception of face-to-face oral communications and telephone calls.

World Trade Organization (WTO) An international organization whose mandate is to lower trade barriers.

Writ of *Certiorari* A petition asking the Supreme Court to hear a case.

Written consent A signed document that takes the place of a shareholders' or directors' meeting.

Wrongful discharge An employer may not fire a worker for a reason that violates basic social rights, duties, or responsibilities.

Z

Zombie directors Directors who serve on a board with less than majority support from shareholders.

TABLE OF CASES

A

B

G

H

I

J

K

L

P

Q

R

S

T

U

INDEX

A

B

C

F

G

H

I

J

M

Q

R

T

V

W

X

Y

Z